WORLDMARK ENCYCLOPEDIA OF THE NATIONS

Volume 4

WORLDMARK
ENCYCLOPEDIA OF THE NATIONS

ASIA & OCEANIA

Formerly published by Worldmark Press, Ltd.

An International Thomson Publishing Company

I(T)P

NEW YORK • LONDON • BONN • BOSTON • DETROIT • MADRID
MELBOURNE • MEXICO CITY • PARIS • SINGAPORE • TOKYO
TORONTO • WASHINGTON • ALBANY NY • BELMONT CA • CINCINNATI OH

Gale Research Inc. Staff

Jane Hoehner, *Developmental Editor*
Allison McNeill, Rebecca Nelson, and Kelle S. Sisung, *Contributing Developmental Editors*
Marie Ellavich, Jolen Gedridge, and Camille Killens, *Associate Developmental Editors*
Lawrence W. Baker, *Senior Developmental Editor*

Mary Beth Trimper, *Production Director*
Evi Seoud, *Assistant Production Manager*
Mary Kelley, *Production Associate*

Cynthia Baldwin, *Product Design Manager*
Barbara J. Yarrow, *Graphic Services Supervisor*
Todd Nessell, *Macintosh Artist*

Library of Congress Cataloging-in-Publication Data

Worldmark encyclopedia of the nations. — 8th ed.
   5 v.
   Includes bibliographical references and index.
   Contents: v. 1. United Nations — v. 2. Africa — v. 3. Americas —
v. 4. Asia & Oceania — v. 5. Europe.
   ISBN 0-8103-9878-8 (set). — ISBN 0-8103-9893-1 (v. 1). — ISBN
0-8103-9880-x (v. 2)
   1. Geography—Encyclopedias. 2. History—Encyclopedias.
3. Economics—Encyclopedias. 4. Political science—Encyclopedias.
5. United Nations—Encyclopedias.
G63.W67 1995
903—dc20   94–38556
                                        CIP

This book is printed on acid-free paper that meets the minimum requirements of American National Standard for Information Sciences—Permanence Paper for Printed Library Materials, ANSI Z39.48-1984. ∞™

ISBN 0-8103-9882-6

Printed in the United States of America by Gale Research Inc.
Published simultaneously in the United Kingdom
by Gale Research International Limited
(An affiliated company of Gale Research Inc.)

10 9 8 7 6 5 4 3 2 1

The trademark **ITP** is used under license.

CONTENTS

For Conversion Tables, Abbreviations and Acronyms, Glossaries, World Tables, Notes to the Eighth Edition, and other supplementary materials, see Volume 1.

GUIDE TO COUNTRY ARTICLES

All information contained within a country article is uniformly keyed by means of small superior numerals to the left of the subject headings. A heading such as "Population," for example, carries the same key numeral (6) in every article. Thus, to find information about the population of Albania, consult the table of contents for the page number where the Albania article begins and look for section 6 thereunder. Introductory matter for each nation includes coat of arms, capital, flag (descriptions given from hoist to fly or from top to bottom), anthem, monetary unit, weights and measures, holidays, and time zone.

FLAG COLOR SYMBOLS

| Yellow | Red | Green | Blue | Orange | Brown | White | Black |

SECTION HEADINGS IN NUMERICAL ORDER

1 Location, size, and extent	27 Energy and power
2 Topography	28 Industry
3 Climate	29 Science and technology
4 Flora and fauna	30 Domestic trade
5 Environment	31 Foreign trade
6 Population	32 Balance of payments
7 Migration	33 Banking and securities
8 Ethnic groups	34 Insurance
9 Languages	35 Public finance
10 Religions	36 Taxation
11 Transportation	37 Customs and duties
12 History	38 Foreign investment
13 Government	39 Economic development
14 Political parties	40 Social development
15 Local government	41 Health
16 Judicial system	42 Housing
17 Armed forces	43 Education
18 International cooperation	44 Libraries and museums
19 Economy	45 Media
20 Income	46 Organizations
21 Labor	47 Tourism, travel, and recreation
22 Agriculture	48 Famous persons
23 Animal husbandry	49 Dependencies
24 Fishing	50 Bibliography
25 Forestry	
26 Mining	

SECTION HEADINGS IN ALPHABETICAL ORDER

Agriculture	22	Income	20
Animal husbandry	23	Industry	28
Armed forces	17	Insurance	34
Balance of payments	32	International cooperation	18
Banking and securities	33	Judical system	16
Bibliography	50	Labor	21
Climate	3	Languages	9
Customs and duties	37	Libraries and museums	44
Dependencies	49	Local government	15
Domestic trade	30	Location, size, and extent	1
Economic development	39	Media	45
Economy	19	Migration	7
Education	43	Mining	26
Energy and power	27	Organizations	46
Environment	5	Political parties	14
Ethnic groups	8	Population	6
Famous persons	48	Public finance	35
Fishing	24	Religions	10
Flora and fauna	4	Science and technology	29
Foreign investment	38	Social development	40
Foreign trade	31	Taxation	36
Forestry	25	Topography	2
Government	13	Tourism, travel, and recreation	47
Health	41	Transportation	11
History	12		
Housing	42		

FREQUENTLY USED ABBREVIATIONS AND ACRONYMS

ad—Anno Domini
am—before noon
b.—born
bc—Before Christ
c—Celsius
c.—circa (about)
cm—centimeter(s)
Co.—company
Corp.—corporation
cu ft—cubic foot, feet
cu m—cubic meter(s)
d.—died
e—east
e—evening
e.g.—exempli gratia (for example)
ed.—edition, editor
est.—estimated
et al.—et alii (and others)

etc.—et cetera (and so on)
f—Fahrenheit
fl.—flourished
FRG—Federal Republic of Germany
ft—foot, feet
ft³—cubic foot, feet
GATT—General Agreement on Tariffs and Trade
GDP—gross domestic products
gm—gram
GMT—Greenwich Mean Time
GNP—gross national product
GRT—gross registered tons
ha—hectares
i.e.—id est (that is)
in—inch(es)
kg—kilogram(s)
km—kilometer(s)

kw—kilowatt(s)
kwh—kilowatt-hour(s)
lb—pound(s)
m—meter(s); morning
m³—cubic meter(s)
mi—mile(s)
Mt.—mount
Mw—megawatt(s)
n—north
n.d.—no date
NA—not available
oz—ounce(s)

pm—after noon
r.—reigned
rev. ed.—revised edition
s—south
sq—square
St.—saint
UK—United Kingdom
UN—United Nations
US—United States
USSR—Union of Soviet Socialist Republics
w—west

A fiscal split year is indicated by a stroke (e.g. 1987/88).
For acronyms of UN agencies and ther intergovernmental organizations, as well as other abbreviations used in text, see the United Nations volume.
A dollar sign ($) stands for US$ unless otherwise indicated.
Note that 1 billion = 1,000 million = 10^9.

AFGHANISTAN

Islamic State of Afghanistan
Jamhurriyati Afghanistan

CAPITAL: Kabul.

FLAG: The national flag has three equal horizontal stripes of green, white, and black. In the center is the national coat of arms.

ANTHEM: *Esllahte Ardi (Land Reform),* beginning "So long as there is the earth and the heavens."

MONETARY UNIT: The afghani (Af) is a paper currency of 100 puls. There are coins of 25 and 50 puls and 1, 2, and 5 afghanis, and notes of 10, 20, 50, 100, 500, and 1,000 afghanis. Af1 = $0.0198 (or $1 = Af50.60).

WEIGHTS AND MEASURES: The metric system is the legal standard, although some local units are still in use.

HOLIDAYS: Now Rooz (New Year's Day), 21 March; Anniversary of the Saur Revolution, 27 April; May Day, 1 May; Independence Day, 18 August. Movable religious holidays include First Day of Ramadan, 'Id al-Fitr, 'Id al-'Adha', 'Ashura, and Milad an-Nabi. The Afghan calendar year begins on 21 March; the Afghan year 1366 began on 21 March 1987.

TIME: 4:30 PM = noon GMT.

¹LOCATION, SIZE, AND EXTENT

Afghanistan is a landlocked country in South Asia with a long, narrow strip in the northeast (the Vakhan corridor). Afghanistan is slightly smaller than the state of Texas, with a total area of 647,500 sq km (250,001 sq mi), extending 1,240 km (770 mi) NE–SW and 560 km (350 mi) SE–NW. Afghanistan is bounded on the N by Turkenistan, Uzbekistan, and Tajikistan, on the extreme NE by China, on the E and S by Pakistan, and on the W by Iran, with a total boundary length of 5,529 km (3,436 mi). Afghanistan's capital city, Kabul, is located in the east central part of the country.

²TOPOGRAPHY

Although the average altitude of Afghanistan is about 1,200 m (4,000 ft), the Hindu Kush mountain range rises to more than 6,100 m (20,000 ft) in the northern corner of the Vakhan panhandle in the northeast and continues in a southwesterly direction for about 970 km (600 mi), dividing the northern provinces from the rest of the country. Central Afghanistan, a plateau with an average elevation of 1,800 m (6,000 ft), contains many small fertile valleys and provides excellent grazing for sheep, goats, and camels. To the north of the Hindu Kush and the central mountain range, the altitude drops to about 460 m (1,500 ft), permitting the growth of cotton, fruits, grains, ground nuts, and other crops. Southwestern Afghanistan is a desert, hot in summer and cold in winter. The four major river systems are the Amu Darya (Oxus) in the north, flowing into the Aral Sea; the Harirud and Morghab in the west; the Helmand in the southwest; and the Kabul in the east, flowing into the Indus. There are few lakes.

³CLIMATE

The ranges in altitude produce a climate with both temperate and semitropical characteristics, and the seasons are clearly marked throughout the country. Wide temperature variations are usual from season to season and from day to night. Summer temperatures in Kabul may range from 16°C (61°F) at sunrise to 38°C (100°F) by noon. The mean January temperature in Kabul is 0°C (32°F); the maximum summer temperature in Jalalabad is about 46°C (115°F). There is much sunshine, and the air is usually clear and dry. Rainfall averages about 25 to 30 cm (10 to 12 in); precipitation occurs in winter and spring, most of it in the form of snow. Wind velocity is high, especially in the west.

⁴FLORA AND FAUNA

There are over 3,000 plant species, including hundreds of varieties of trees, shrubs, vines, flowers, and fungi. The country is particularly rich in such medicinal plants as rue, wormwood, and asafetida; fruit and nut trees are found in many areas. Native fauna include the fox, lynx, wild dog, bear, mongoose, shrew, hedgehog, hyena, jerboa, hare, and wild varieties of cats, asses, mountain goats, and mountain sheep. Trout is the most common fish. There are more than 100 species of wildfowl and birds.

⁵ENVIRONMENT

Afghanistan's most significant ecological problems are deforestation and the effects of the war and displaced population. Neglect, scorched earth tactics, and the damage caused by extensive bombardments have destroyed previously productive agricultural areas; tons of unexploded ordnance make it dangerous for farmers and herdsman. A major earthquake and flash floods in 1991 added to the devastation of the environment. Afghanistan responded to its fuel needs for a growing population by cutting down many of its already sparse forests. Consequently, as of 1994, less than 3% of Afghanistan's total land mass contained forest land.

Although its effectiveness, like that of all Kabul agencies, is limited because its writ runs barely beyond the capital, the Environmental Protection Agency of the Ministry of Agriculture has primary responsibility for environmental monitoring and protection. By 1994, 13 species of mammals, 13 species of birds, and 4 plant species of were endangered. Endangered species in Afghanistan include the snow leopard, Bactrian red deer, Kabul markhor, Central Asian cobra, Siberian white crane and the hyena.

⁶POPULATION

The effects of 15 years of warfare since 1979 make Afghanistan's population—never certain in any case—even more difficult to assess. As many as three million afghans are estimated to have died, and an additional five million sought refuge in Pakistan, Iran and elsewhere in the world during the worst of the fighting when thousands of Soviet troops were present. As of 1991, population estimates ranged from 12 to 19 million, with the official government estimate—no better than a guess—of 16,433,000 (excluding the 15% who are nomads). The estimated annual growth of population in 1985–90 was 2.63%. The UN projected a population of 26,767,000 for 2000, based on a crude birth rate of 48.7 per 1,000 population in 1995–2000, a crude death rate of 20.1, and a net natural increase of 28.6. However, experts question the reliability of the estimates of population during the last decade, as well as the projections for population.

Afghanistan's estimated population density (excluding nomads) was 25 per sq km (65 per sq mi) in 1991. Kabul, the capital, had an estimated population of 1,424,400 in 1988. Other cities, with their 1988 estimated populations, were Qandahār, 225,500; Herāt, 177,300; and Mazār-e Sharif, 130,600. Only about 20% of the population lived in urban areas in 1995.

⁷MIGRATION

Following the Soviet intervention in Afghanistan in December 1979, a massive emigration of Afghans took place. According to the UNHCR, there were 3,098,000 Afghan refugees (18.8% of the estimated population) across the Pakistani border by the end of 1991, living in more than 300 tent villages in Pakistan's North-West Frontier Province and Baluchistan; some had moved to Karachi, Lahore, and other cities in search of work. The number in Iran was 3,186,600. By March 1993 about 2 million refugees had returned—1.8 million from Pakistan and 200,000 from Iran. But 2,900,700 remained in Iran and 1,627,000 in Pakistan at the end of 1992. Afghanistan was harboring about 90,000 refugees from Tajikstan in 1993.

⁸ETHNIC GROUPS

About the middle of the second millennium BC, Indo-Aryans began to move into and through the present area of Afghanistan. Much later came other tribal groups from Central Asia—Pactyes (from whom the present-day name "Pashtoons" derives), Sakas, Kushans, Hephthalites, and others—and a procession of Iranians and Greeks. In the 7th century AD, Arabs arrived from the south, spreading the new faith of Islam. In the same century, Turks moved in from the north, followed in the 13th century by Mongols, and, finally, in the 15th century by Turko-Mongols. This multiplicity of movements made Afghanistan a loose conglomeration of racial and linguistic groups.

All citizens are called Afghans, but the Pashtoons (the name may also be written as "Pushtun" or "Pukhtun," and in Pakistan as "Pathan") are often referred to as the "true Afghans." Numbering about 43% of the population in 1980, they are known to have centered in the Sulaiman range to the east; it is only in recent centuries that they moved into eastern and southern Afghanistan, where they now predominate. They have long been divided into two major divisions, the Durranis and the Ghilzais, each with its own tribes and subtribes.

The Tajiks, of Iranian stock, comprise nearly 25% of the population and are mainly concentrated in the north and northeast. In the central ranges are found the Hazaras (about 5%), who are said to have descended from the Mongols. To the north of the Hindu Kush, Turkic and Turko-Mongol groups were in the majority until 1940. Each of these groups is related to groups north of the Amu Darya and within the former USSR; among them are the Uzbeks, who number about 6% of the population. Other groups include the Aimaks, Farsiwans (Persians) and Bra-

hiu. In the northeast are the Kafirs, or infidels. After their conversion to Islam at the end of the 19th century, they were given the name of Nuristanis, or "people of the light."

⁹LANGUAGES

Both Pashtu (or Pushtu) and Dari (Afghan Persian) are the official languages of the country. Although Pashtu has a literature of its own, Dari is the principal language of cultural expression, of the government, and of business. Baluchi belongs to the same linguistic group, as do several languages spoken in the high Pamirs. The Hazaras speak their own dialect of Dari. The Turkic languages include Uzbek, Turkoman, and Kirghiz, and the Nuristanis speak some seven different dialects belonging to the Dardic linguistic group.

¹⁰RELIGIONS

Almost all Afghans are Muslims. More than 75% are Sunnis; the rest are Shi'is, including some Isma'ilis. The Pashtuns, most of the Tajiks, the Uzbeks, and the Turkomans are Sunnis, while the Hazaras are Shi'is. Before the 1978 Communist coup, Islam was the official religion of Afghanistan; in an effort to win over religious leaders, the Marxist regime set up a Department of Islamic Affairs in 1981 and began providing funds for new mosques and for the maintenance of old ones. As a result of civil war from 1988 to 1992, an Islamic State was again proclaimer under control of the mujahidin, and Islam again became the official religion.

¹¹TRANSPORTATION

Many roads had been built in the years prior to 1979 to connect the principal cities and to open up formerly isolated areas. Afghanistan has an estimated 21,000 km (13,000 mi) of roads, of which 2,800 km (1,700 mi) are paved. Roads connect Kabul with the provincial capitals and with Peshawar in Pakistan through the Khyber Pass. The road from Herat to Mashhad in Iran was completed in 1971. The Salang Tunnel through the Hindu Kush, completed with Soviet assistance in 1964, considerably shortened the distance between Kabul and northern Afghanistan. The tunnel was modernized in the mid-1980s. The Qandahar-Torghundi highway was completed in 1965. In 1992 there were 40,000 passenger cars and 35,000 trucks and buses in use.

The Khyber Pass in Pakistanis the best known of the passes providing land access to Afghanistan. Transit arrangements with Iran provide an alternative route for its commercial traffic. However, the great bulk of the country's trade moves through the former USSR. The only railways in the country in 1991 were a 9.6-km (6-mi) spur from Kushka, Turkmenistan to Towraghondi, a 15 km (9.3 mi) line from Termez, Uzbekistan to the Kheyrabad transshipment point on the South bank of the Amu Darya, and a short span into Spin Baldak in the southeast. There are no navigable rivers except for the Amu Darya, on Turkmenistan's border, which can carry steamers up to about 500 tons. During 1986, Afghanistan's domestic and international airlines were merged to form Bakhtar Afghan Airlines. Kabul and Qandahar have airports capable of receiving international flights.

¹²HISTORY

Afghanistan has existed as a distinct polity for less than three centuries. Previously, the area was made up of various principalities, usually hostile to each other and occasionally ruled by one or another conqueror from Persia and the area to the west or from central Asia to the north, usually on his way to India. These included the Persian Darius I in the 6th century BC, and 300 years later, Alexander the Great. As the power of his Seleucid successors waned, an independent Greek kingdom of Bactria arose with its capital at Balkh, but after about a century it fell to invading tribes (notably the Sakas, who gave their name to Sakastan, or Sistan). Toward the middle of the 3rd century BC, Buddhism

LOCATION: 29°28′ to 38°30′ N; 60°30′ to 74°53′ E. **BOUNDARY LENGTHS:** China, 76 km (47 mi); Iran, 936 km (582 mi); Pakistan, 2,430 km (1,511 mi); Tajikistan, 1,206 km (750 mi); Turkmenistan, 744 km (463 mi); Uzbekistan, 137 km (85mi).

spread to Afghanistan from India, and for centuries prior to the beginning of the 9th century AD, at least half the population of eastern Afghanistan was Buddhist.

Beginning in the 7th century, Muslim invaders brought Islam to the region, and it eventually became the dominant cultural influence. For almost 200 years, Ghazni was the capital of a powerful Islamic kingdom, the greatest of whose rulers, Mahmud of Ghazni (r.997–1030), conquered most of the area from the Caspian to the Ganges. The Ghaznavids were displaced by the Seljuk Turks, who mastered Persia and Anatolia (eastern Turkey), and by the Ghorids, who, rising from Ghor, southeast of Herat, established an empire stretching from Herat to Ajmir in India. They were displaced in turn by the Turko-Persian rulers of the Khiva oasis in Transoxiana, who, by 1217, had created a state that included the whole of Afghanistan until it disintegrated under attack by Genghis Khan in 1219. His grandson Timur, also called "Timur the Lame" or Tamerlane, occupied all of what is now

Afghanistan from 1365 to 1384, establishing a court of intellectual and artistic brilliance at Herat. The Timurids came under challenge from the Uzbeks, who finally drove the them out of Herat in 1507. The great Babur, one of the Uzbek princes, occupied Kabul in 1504 and Delhi in 1526, establishing the Mughal Empire in which eastern Afghanistan was ruled from Delhi, Agra, Lahore, or Srinagar, while Herat and Sistan were governed as provinces of Persia.

In the 18th century, Persians under Nadir Shah conquered the area, and after his death in 1747, one of his military commanders, Ahmad Shah Abdali, was elected emir of Afghanistan. The formation of a unified Afghanistan under his emirate marks Afghanistan's beginning as a political entity. Among his descendants was Dost Muhammad who established himself in Kabul in 1826 and gained the emirate in 1835. Although the British defeated Dost in the first Afghan War (1838–42), they restored him to power, but his attempts and those of his successors to play off Czarist Russian interests against the British concerns about the security of their Indian Empire led to more conflict. In the second Afghan War (1877–79), the forces of Sher Ali, Dost's son, were defeated by the British, and his entire party, ousted. Abdur Rahman Khan, recognized as emir by the British in 1880, established a central administration, and supported the British interest in a neutral Afghanistan as a buffer against the expansion of Russian influence.

Intermittent fighting between the British and Pushtun-speaking tribes from eastern Afghanistan continued even after the establishment, in 1893, of a boundary (the Durand line) between Afghanistan and British India. An Anglo-Russian agreement concluded in 1907 guaranteed the independence of Afghanistan (and Tibet) under British influence, and Afghanistan remained neutral in both World Wars. Afghan forces under Amanullah Khan, who had become emir in 1901, briefly intruded across the Durand Line in 1919. At the end of brief fighting—the third Afghan War—the Treaty of Rawalpindi (1919) accorded the government of Afghanistan the freedom to conduct its own foreign affairs.

Internally, Amanullah's Westernization program was strongly opposed, forcing him to abdicate in 1929. After a brief civil war, a tribal assembly chose Muhammad Nadir Shah as king. In his brief four years in power, he restored peace while continuing Amanullah's modernization efforts at a more moderate pace. Assassinated in 1933, he was succeeded by his son, Muhammad Zahir Shah, who continued his modernization efforts, governing for 40 years, even though sharing effective power with his uncles and a first cousin, who served as his prime ministers.

In the 1960s, there was considerable tension between Pakistan and Afghanistan as a result of Afghanistan's effort to assert influence among, and ultimately responsibility for, Pushtu-speaking Pathan tribes living on both sides of the Durand Line under a policy calling for the establishment of an entity to be called "Pushtunistan." The border was closed several times during the following years, and relations with Pakistan remained generally poor until 1977.

In 1964, a new constitution was introduced, converting Afghanistan into a constitutional monarchy, and a year later the country's first general election was held. In July 1973, Muhammad Daoud Khan, the king's first cousin and brother-in-law, who had served as prime minister from 1953 until early 1963, seized power in a near-bloodless coup, establishing a republic and appointing himself president, and prime minister of the Republic of Afghanistan. He exiled Zahir Shah and his immediate family, abolished the monarchy, dissolved the legislature, and suspended the constitution. Daoud ruled as a dictator until 1977, when a republican constitution calling for a one-party state was adopted by the newly convened Loya Jirga (Grand National Assembly), which then elected Daoud president for a six-year term.

Afghanistan Under PDPA Rule

On 27 April 1978, Daoud was deposed and executed in a bloody coup (the "Saur Revolution" because it took place during the Afghan month of Saur), and the Democratic Republic of Afghanistan emerged. Heading the new Revolutionary Council was Nur Muhammad Taraki, secretary-general of the communist People's Democratic Party of Afghanistan (PDPA), assisted by Babrak Karmal and Hafizullah Amin, both named deputy prime ministers. The former Soviet Union immediately established ties with the new regime, and in December 1978, the two nations concluded a treaty of friendship and cooperation. Soon after the coup, rural Afghan groups took up arms against the regime, which increasingly relied on Soviet arms for support against what came to be known as the mujahidin guerrillas.

Meanwhile, the Khalq (masses) and Parcham (flag) factions of the PDPA, which had united for the April takeover, became embroiled in a bitter power struggle within the PDPA and the government. In September 1979, Taraki was ousted and executed by Amin, who had beat out Karmal to become prime minister the previous March and who now assumed Taraki's posts as president and party leader. Amin was himself replaced on 27 December by Karmal, the Parcham faction leader. This last change was announced not by Radio Kabul but by Radio Moscow and was preceded by the airlift of 4,000 to 5,000 Soviet troops into Kabul on 25–26 December, purportedly at the request of an Afghan government whose president, Hafizullah Amin, was killed during the takeover.

The Soviet presence increased to about 85,000 troops in late January 1980, and by spring, the first clashes between Soviet troops and the mujahidin had occurred. Throughout the early and mid-1980s, the mujahidin resistance continue to build, aided by Afghan army deserters and arms from the United States, Pakistan, and the nations of the Islamic Conference Organization (ICO). Much of the countryside remained under mujahidin control as the insurgency waged on year by year, while in Kabul, Soviet advisers assumed control of most Afghan government agencies.

By late 1987, more than a million Afghans had lost their lives in the struggle, while the United Nations High Commission for Refugees (UNHCR) estimated that some 5 million others had sought refuge in Pakistan, Iran, and elsewhere. Soviet sources at the time acknowledged Soviet losses of between 12,000 and 30,000 dead and 76,000 wounded. Soviet troop strength in Afghanistan at the end of 1987 was about 120,000, while according to Western sources, Afghan resistance forces numbered nearly 130,000.

In early 1987, Babrak Karmal fled to Moscow after being replaced as the head of the PDPA in May 1986 by Najibullah, former head of the Afghan secret police. Najibullah offered the mujahidin a ceasefire and introduced a much publicized national reconciliation policy; he also released some political prisoners, offered to deal with the resistance leaders, and promised new land reform. The mujahidin rejected these overtures, declining to negotiate for anything short of Soviet withdrawal and Najibullah's removal.

International efforts to bring about a political solution to the war—including nearly unanimous General Assembly condemnations of the Soviet presence in Afghanistan—were pursued within the UN framework from 1982 onward. Among these efforts were "proximity talks" between Afghanistan and Pakistan conducted by a Special Representative of the UN Secretary General. After a desultory beginning, these talks began to look promising in late 1987 and early 1988 when Soviet policymakers repeatedly stated, in a major policy shift, that the removal of Soviet troops from Afghanistan was not contingent on the creation of a transitional regime acceptable to the former USSR. On 14 April 1988, documents were signed and exchanged in which the USSR agreed to pull its troops out of Afghanistan within nine months, the US reserved the right to continue military aid to Afghan guerrillas as long as the USSR continued to aid the government in Kabul, and Pakistan and Afghanistan pledged not to interfere in each other's internal affairs.

The Russians completed the evacuation of their forces on schedule 15 February 1989, but in spite of continuing pressure by the well-armed mujahidin, the Najibullah government remained in power until April 1992, when Najibullah fled Kabul as mujahidin forces closed in on the city. With the fall of the Najibullah government, the Seven Party Alliance (SPA) of the Islamic groups based in Pakistan moved to consolidate its "victory" by announcing plans to set up an Interim Afghan Government (AIG) charged with preparing the way for elections. Meanwhile, they moved to assert their control of Afghanistan, but their efforts to establish the AIG in Kabul failed when within ten days of Najibullah's departure, well-armed forces of the Hizbi-Islami and Jamiat-i-Islami clashed in fighting for the control of the capital. In July, Jamiat leader Burhanuddin Rabbani replaced Sibgatullah Mojaddedi as president of the AIG, as previously agreed by all the SPA parties but the Hizbi-Islami.

Continued fighting between Jamiat and Hizbi-Islami militias halted further progress, and Rabbani's forces, under Commander Masood, dug in to block those under the control of interim "Prime Minister" Gulbuddin Hekmatyar's Hizbi-Islami and his ally, General Rashid Dostum, from taking control of Kabul. In a 24-hour rocket exchange in August 1992 in Kabul, an estimated 3000 Afghans died, and before the end of the year, upwards of 700,000 Afghans had fled the city. Since then, deep differences among the SPA/AIG leadership, embittered by decades of bad blood, ethnic distrust, and personal enmity, have prevented any further progress toward creating a genuine interim government capable of honoring the 1992 SPA pledge to write a constitution, organize elections, and create a new Afghan polity from the wreckage of 15 years of insurgency and anarchy.

[13]GOVERNMENT

Between 1964 and 1973, Afghanistan was a constitutional monarchy, for the first time in its history. The head of government was the prime minister, appointed by the king and responsible to the bicameral legislature. This system gave way to a more traditional authoritarian system on 17 July 1973, when Afghanistan became a republic, headed by Muhammad Daoud Khan, who became both president and prime minister. A new constitution in 1977 created a one-party state with a strong executive and a weak bicameral legislature. The communist PDPA abrogated this constitution after they seized power in April 1978.

Between 1978 and 1980, a communist-style 167-member Revolutionary Council exercised legislative powers. The chief of state (president) headed the presidium of that council, to which the 20-member cabinet was formally responsible. A provisional constitution, introduced in April 1980, guaranteed respect for Islam and national traditions, condemned colonialism, imperialism, Zionism, and fascism, and proclaimed the PDPA as "the guiding and mobilizing force of society and state." Seven years later, a new constitution providing for a very strong presidency was introduced as part of the PDPA's propaganda campaign of "national reconciliation." Najibullah remained as president.

That constitution has no legal standing at present, and the situation is anarchic. No new constitution has been drafted since the end of the Najibullah government, and while an Afghan Interim Government (AIG) headed by Burhanuddin Rabbani is nominally in control, in fact multiple sovereignties exist in Kabul and elsewhere in the country, and there is no central authority.

[14]POLITICAL PARTIES

Political parties have usually been illegal in Afghanistan, forcing most political activity—typically along ideological, linguistic, and ethnic lines—to operate underground or from abroad (or both). The 1964 constitution provided for the formation of political parties, but since the framers of the constitution decided that political parties should be permitted only after the first elections, all candidates for the parliamentary elections of August and September 1965 stood as independents; subsequently, the framers recanted on their intention to allow political parties. Under the 1977 constitution, only the National Revolutionary Party (NRP), the ruler's chosen instrument, was allowed.

The 1978 coup was engineered by the illegal People's Democratic Party of Afghanistan (PDPA) which had been founded in 1965. During its brief history, this Marxist party had been riven by a bloody struggle between its pro-Soviet Parcham (flag) faction and its larger but less influential Khalq (masses) faction, with Maoist leanings. Babrak Karmal was the leader of the Parcham group, while the Khalq faction was headed until 1979 by Muhammad Taraki and Hafizullah Amin. The factional struggle continued after the 1978 coup, prompting the Soviet intervention of 1979. Factional bloodletting continued thereafter also, with repeated purges and assassinations of Khalq adherents as well as bitter infighting within Parcham, this last leading to Babrak Karmal's replacement as PDPA secretary-general May 1986 by Najibullah.

The Islamic resistance forces opposing the PDPA government and its Soviet backers in Afghanistan represent conservative, ethnically-based Islamic groups which themselves have had a long history of partisan infighting (and repression by successive Kabul governments). They came together in the early 1980s to fight the common enemy, the communist PDPA and the Soviet invaders and, in 1985, under pressure from Pakistan and the United States, they were loosely united into a Seven Party Alliance (SPA), headquartered in Peshawar, Pakistan. By 1987, commando groups affiliated with one or more of these seven parties controlled more than 80% of the land area of Afghanistan.

With arms flowing in from the outside—they were not halted until the end of 1991—the fighting continued, but with the final withdrawal of Soviet troops in February 1989, the SPA stepped up its military and political pressure on the communist PDPA government. However, President Najibullah proved to have more staying power than previously estimated, using Soviet arms supplies, which continued until the end of 1991 to buttress his position, while playing upon divisions among the resistance, embracing nationalism and renouncing communism, and even changing the name of the PDPA to the Wattan (Homeland) Party. It was only in April 1992, with the Soviet Union now history, his army defecting from beneath him, and the mujahidin closing on Kabul that he fled the country, leaving Kabul in the hands of the rival ethnic and regional mujahidin militias that continue to battle for its loyalty and control.

Current parties active in the struggle for power in Afghanistan include: (1) the Jamiat-i-Islami (JI) of Burhanuddin Rabbani and Ahmad Masood; (2) the Hizbi-Islami of Gulbuddin Hekmatyar; (3) a Hizbi-Islami offshoot, of Yunis Khalis; (4) the Ittihad-i-Islami Barai Azadi Afghanistan, of Abdul Rasul Sayyaf; (5) the Harakat-Inqilab-i-Islami, of Mohammad Nabi Mohammadi; (6) Jabha-i-Najat-i-Milli, of Sibghatullah Mojaddedi; (7) the Mahaz-i-Milli-i-Islami, of Sayad Ahmad Gailani; (8) the Hizbi Wahdat, of Abdul Ali Mazari; (9) the Haraakat-i-Islami, of Mohammed Asif Mohseni; and, (10) the Jonbesh-i-Milli, of Rashid Dostum, a former Afghan army general, now a regional "warlord" who heads a northern Uzbek organization allied with Hizbi-Islami. In addition to these Islamic parties, remnants of the Khalq and Parchem factions of the former PDPA/Wattan Party, although discredited and fragmented, reportedly have made common cause, largely on ethnic grounds, with various of the Islamic parties and factions, as well as with independent local authorities. As of late 1994, the situation remained anarchic and confused.

[15]LOCAL GOVERNMENT

Afghanistan has traditionally been divided into 28 provinces governed by centrally appointed governors with considerable autonomy in local affairs. During the Soviet occupation and the development of country-wide resistance, local areas came increasingly under the control of mujahidin groups that achieved independence from any central authority; local commanders, in some instances, asserted a measure of independence also from the mujahidin leadership in Pakistan, establishing their own systems of local government, collecting revenues, running educational and other facilities, and even engaging in local negotiations.

With the absence of an effective central authority, Afghanistan is "a disfigured state," in the words of one scholar. The country remains divided into areas controlled more or less by the various mujahidin alliance groups, much as it existed during and after the Soviet withdrawal. In non-Pushtun areas, the administration remains mostly in place but under the authority of regional Uzbek and Tajik figures. Stability, based on reported Sunni-Shi'a cooperation, appears to have returned to the Herat area on the west. In Pushtun areas of the east and southeast, Hizbi-Islami forces are in control, while in the northeast, Jamiat-i-Islami (and other) militias appear to be control. With little agreement among the main parties on the shape of the future polity, these various regions reportedly have produced an array of regional security bodies whose operations as of late 1994 remain independent of both the remnant of a central administration and of central party authorities.

[16]JUDICIAL SYSTEM

The Supreme Court, abolished after the 1973 coup, was reestablished in 1978. According to the 1980 provisional constitution, the Supreme Court, functioning as an organ of the Revolutionary Council, supervises provincial, city, and district courts and military tribunals. All judges are appointed by the council presidium.

The ongoing civil war has disrupted government functions to such an extent that there is no functioning central legal system. Some local and provincial courts continue to operate. These courts apply procedural and substantive law based on the Shari'a (Islamic law) and traditional tribal law.

[17]ARMED FORCES

The regular armed forces may have had 45,000 men in 1993 following the collapse of the Soviet supported Najibullah regime. As a result of defections after the Soviet intervention in December 1979, Afghan armed strength declined in number to about 50,000 in 1985 (45,000 army and 5,000 air force). By 1986, the government had lowered the minimum conscription age from 20 to 15 and increased the maximum age from 35 to 55. The Afghan forces were under the control of the Soviet high command in Afghanistan until the Russian withdrawal in 1989. The victorious mujahidin factions, which may exceed ten in number, maintain their own armies, armed with Russian vehicles and weapons. These factional forces number at least 40,000. There is no reliable estimate on military expenditures. Total arms imports are estimated at over $1 billion a year, largely financed by a flourishing drug trade.

[18]INTERNATIONAL COOPERATION

Afghanistan has been a member of the UN since 19 November 1946 and is a member of ESCAP and all the nonregional specialized agencies except IMO and WIPO. Afghanistan also belongs to the Asian Development Bank and G-77.

[19]ECONOMY

Afghanistan's economy has been devastated by over 15 years of war. Though economic indicators are fragmentary at best, those available suggest that by 1991 wheat output—the mainstay of the agricultural economy—had withered to less than 65% of total production in 1980, and less than half of prewar levels. Recorded exports had dwindled to about a third of those documented ten years earlier. Concerted UN-backed efforts are currently underway to reconstruct the ravaged economy, although continuing civil strife in many parts of the country are severely constraining aid operations.

Hampered by an unintegrated economy until relatively late in the post-World War II period, only in the 1950s did the building of new roads begin to link the country's commercial centers with the wool and fruit-producing areas. Largely agricultural and pastoral, Afghanistan depends on the cultivation of fruits and cotton, the production of wool and karakul skins, and traditional handicrafts like carpet weaving. Modern industry consisted of cotton and wool textiles, sugar refining, cement, fertilizers, and food processing. The country has valuable mineral resources, including large reserves of iron ore at Hajigak discovered before the war, but only coal, salt, lapis lazuli, barite, and chrome are being exploited. The discovery of large quantities of natural gas in the

north, for which a pipeline to the former USSR was completed in 1967, increased the country's fuel resources and export earnings, at least until escalation of civil strife in the late 1970s and 1980s.

Since the outbreak of war in the late 1970s, economic data have been contradictory and of doubtful reliability. According to a government report, GDP grew 3.5% a year during 1981–85, though the latest indicators suggest steeply negative real growth in the GDP since 1987, bringing the 1985–91 average to -3.5%. Journalists and other Westerners who have traveled inside Afghanistan have reported a steady erosion in the country's economic infrastructure overall, particularly in rural areas. In September 1987, the Afghan foreign minister stated that 350 bridges and 258 factories had been destroyed since the fighting began in 1979. By the early 1990s, two-thirds of all paved roads were unusable, and the countryside appeared severely depopulated, with more than than 25% of the population—twice the prewar average—residing in urban areas that until recently offered relatively more secure protection. Successive UN Action Plans initiated in strife-free areas of the country in 1988 emphasized restoration of agricultural productivity as the top reconstruction priority. However, with the escalation of open conflict between rival mujahidin factions, what little is left of the country's infrastructure is rapidly being destroyed. Within this vacuum, three separate economic systems are emerging in the west, east and northern parts of the country, sustained mainly by clandestine support for local leaders from Iran, Pakistan and the Central Asian republics respectively. In mid-1992, all UN agency personnel were pulled out of the country due to escalating warfare in Kabul and other urban centers, and as many as 700,000 people fled Kabul.

[20]INCOME

In 1990 the GDP was reported to be $2.27 billion. The per capita national product was estimated to be $200 in 1989. The UN has estimated that agriculture, hunting, forestry, and fishing contributed 52% to GDP; mining and quarrying, manufacturing, electricity, gas, and water, 26%; construction, 7%; wholesale and retail trade, 9%; transport, storage, and communication, 4%; and other sources 2%. However, most experts agree that none of these estimates is reliable.

[21]LABOR

Afghanistan's labor force was variously estimated at 5.6 million in 1976, 4 million in 1979, and 5 million in 1980, with about two-thirds engaged in agriculture and animal husbandry. More recent estimates are not available. There are some 2.5 million nomads. The textile industry is the largest employer of industrial labor; weaving of cloth and carpets is the most important home industry. In 1978, the government established the Central Council of Afghanistan Trade Unions in order to develop the trade union movement. In the mid-1980s, the council had some 285,000 members. As of 1992, no labor rallies or strikes were reported; the government does not currently appear to have the means to enforce worker rights, as there is no functioning constitution or legal framework which defines them.

[22]AGRICULTURE

About 12% of the land is arable. Normally, Afghanistan grew about 95% of its needs in wheat and rye, and more than met its needs in rice, potatoes, pulses, nuts, and seeds; it depended on imports only for some wheat, sugar, and edible fats and oils. Fruit, both fresh and preserved (with bread), is a staple food for many Afghans. Agricultural production, however, is a fraction of its potential. Of the country's total land area, about 12% (8,054,000 hectares/19,900,000 acres) was under cultivation with temporary or permanent crops in 1991. Agriculture and animal husbandry engage 11% of the labor force.

The variety of the country's crops corresponds to its topography. The areas around Qandahar, Herat, and the broad Kabul plain yield fruits of many kinds. The northern regions from Takhar to Badghis and Herat and Helmand provinces produce cotton. Corn is grown extensively in Paktia and Nangarhar provinces, and rice mainly in Qonduz, Baghlan, and Laghman provinces. Wheat is common to several regions. Estimated crop production in 1992 (in tons) included wheat, 1,650,000; fruits, 614,000; corn, 300,000; vegetables, 490,000; rice, 300,000; barley, 150,000; and seed cotton, 42,000.

Pistachios and almonds are widely grown, and substantial quantities are exported. Agricultural products accounted for about 36% of Afghanistan's exports in 1992, of which fruits and nuts were a large portion. In some regions, agricultural production had all but ceased due to destruction caused by the war and the migration of Afghans out of those areas. A law of May 1987 relaxed the restrictions on private landowning set in 1978: the limit of permitted individual holding was raised from 6 to 18 hectares (from 15 to 45 acres). Opium and cannabis are also widely grown for the drug trade.

23ANIMAL HUSBANDRY
The availability of land suitable for grazing has made animal husbandry an important part of the economy. Natural pastures cover some 3 million hectares (7.4 million acres) but are being overgrazed. The northern regions around Mazar-e Sharif and Meymaneh are the home range for about 6 million karakul sheep. In 1992 there were an estimated 13.5 million sheep, and 2.1 million goats.

The output of livestock products in 1992, as projected by the FAO, included 340,000 tons of cows' milk, 200,000 tons of sheep's milk, 40,000 tons of goats' milk, 14,200 tons of eggs, 16,500 tons of wool (greasy basis), and 21,409 tons of sheep- and goatskins. Much of Afghanistan's livestock was removed from the country by early waves of refugees who fled to Pakistan and Iran. Indications are that, despite some replenishing, livestock products since the mid-1980s no longer approach prewar totals.

24FISHING
Some fishing takes place in the lakes and rivers, but fish does not constitute a significant part of the Afghan diet. The average annual catch is about 1,500 tons.

25FORESTRY
The formerly abundant forests have been greatly depleted, and in the mid-1980s, only about 3% of the land area was forested, mainly in the east. Significant stands of trees have been destroyed by the ravages of the war. Exploitation has been hampered by lack of power and access roads. In 1991, about 6.7 million cu m of roundwood were produced.

26MINING
Afghanistan has valuable deposits of barite, beryl, chrome, coal, copper, iron, lapis lazuli, lead, mica, natural gas, petroleum, salt, silver, sulfur, and zinc. Reserves of high-grade iron ore are estimated to total 2 billion tons.

On average, some 114,000 tons of coal were mined each year during 1978–84. Production in 1991 amounted to 170,000 tons. In 1991, Afghanistan produced 12,000 tons of salt, 3,000 tons of gypsum, 5,000 tons of copper, 2,000 tons of barite, and 112,000 tons of cement. Deposits of lapis lazuli in Badakhshan are mined in small quantities. Like other aspects of Afghanistan's economy, exploitation of natural resources has been disrupted by the war.

27ENERGY AND POWER
In 1991, production of electricity totaled 1,015 million kwh; total installed capacity was 494,000 kw. Three hydroelectric plants were opened between 1965 and 1970, at Jalalabad, Naghlu, and Mahi Par, near Kabul; another, at Kajaki, in the upper Helmand River Valley, was opened in the mid-1970s. Additional hydroelectric plants are at Sarobi, west of Kabul; Pol-e Khomri; and Qandahar.

Natural gas reserves are estimated to total 120 billion cu m. As of 1991, a new gas field had been discovered in Chekhcha, Jowzjan Province, which added 10 billion cu m to the reserves. Production started in 1967 with 342 million cu m but has risen to an annual average of 2.6 billion cu m during 1987–91. A pipeline carries gas to Turkmenistan. Gas exports to the former USSR were reported at 300 million cu m during the winter of 1990–91. At the end of 1991, 31 natural gas wells were uncapped in the Sibirgan fields to resume supplying the former Soviet republics, initially on an in-kind basis. As of 1992, Afghanistan had to pay for imports with either hard currency or natural gas.

Two power facilities, financed with the help of Bulgaria, have recently been completed to help ease power supply problems: a 400 kv substation in the Chaman-e Huzori area of Kabul (at a cost of $3 million), and an 800 kw power station in Kabul which cost $1.4 million. Two more power stations, with a combined capacity of 600 kw, are planned to be built in Samandarah village, Charikar City. As of 1991, a new 72-collector solar installation was completed in Kabul at a cost of $364 million. The installation heats 40,000 l (10,500 gal) of water to an average temperature of 60°c (140°F) around the clock.

28INDUSTRY
Still in a primary stage of growth before the outbreak of war, industry's development has been stunted since; those few industries that continued production through the 1980s remained limited to processing of local materials. The principal modern industry is cotton textile production, with factories at Pol e Khomri, Golbahar, Begram, Balkh, and Jabal os Saraj, just north of Charikar. There are also small woolen and rayon textile industries; the former produced 167,200 meters of woolen fabric in 1989/1990. Other industries are wheat flour processing (186,000 tons in 1989/90); cement (69,300 tons in 1989/90 as compared with 107,800 tons in 1982/83), raisin cleaning and fruit preservation (32,800 tons in 1989/90), leather tanning, preparation of casings, sugar refining and vegetable oil extraction. A large urea plant at Mazar-e Sharif, financed on credit from the former USSR, started production in 1975 and until recently managed to remain operative despite the war, producing 105,500 tons in 1989/90.

Carpet making is the most important handicraft industry, but it has suffered with the flight of rug makers. Production has fluctuated widely from year to year, increasing somewhat during the early 1990s with the establishment of selected "zones of tranquility" targeted for UN reconstruction assistance. Other handicrafts include feltmaking and the weaving of cotton, woolen, and silk cloth. As with other sectors of the economy, Afghanistan's already beleaguered industries have been devastated by escalating civil strife that left most of the countries factories and even much of the cottage industry sector inoperative by 1992.

29SCIENCE AND TECHNOLOGY
The Afghanistan Academy of Sciences, founded in 1979, is the principal scientific institution. Its Science Research Centre has 40 researchers and maintains a computer center, a botanical garden, plants museum, and institutes of botany, zoology, geology and chemistry, and seismology.

The Department of Geology and Mineral Survey within the Ministry of Mines and Industries conducts geological and mineralogical research, mapping, prospecting and exploration.

The Institute of Public Health, founded in 1962, conducts public health training and research and study of indigenous diseases, has a Government reference laboratory, and compiles statistical data.

Kabul University, founded in 1932, has faculties of Science, Pharmacy, Veterinary Medicine, and Geo-Sciences. Bayazid Roshan University of Nangarhar, founded in 1962, has faculties of Medicine and Engineering. The Institute of Agriculture, founded in 1924, offers courses in veterinary medicine. Kabul Polytechnic College, founded in 1951, offers post-graduate engineering courses.

30DOMESTIC TRADE

Kabul, Qandahār, Mazār-e Sharif, and Herāt are the principal commercial cities of eastern, southern, northern, and western Afghanistan, respectively. The first two are the main distribution centers for imports arriving from the direction of Pakistan; the latter two, for materials arriving from Iran and the former USSR. Hours of business vary. The destruction of paved roads has severely constrained normal domestic trade in most rural parts of the country. Heavy fighting in Kabul in 1992 closed an estimated 40% of the city's shops and traders.

31FOREIGN TRADE

In the late 1970s, Afghanistan became increasingly integrated into the CMEA trade bloc. Between 1977/78 and 1980/81, Afghan exports to CMEA countries grew from 38.8% to 62.8% of the total, and imports from these countries increased their share from 40% to 65.5%. The former USSR was Afghanistan's leading trade partner up until the dissolution of the Soviet block; USSR-Afghanistan trade was based on the exchange of natural gas for petroleum products, machinery, and consumer goods. Increased exportation of natural gas to the USSR after 1982 helped to keep export statistics from declining during much of the 1980s. However, natural gas production and export was disrupted by increased inter-factional conflict and disintegrating central government control after Soviet troop withdrawal in 1988; overall exports declined by 22.9% in 1987/88, dropping another 40.3% in 1988/89.

As reconstruction efforts proceeded in many of the country's provinces, trade flows appeared to recover somewhat by the late 1980s. Exports for 1990/91 were up by 3.4% from the year before, though still totaling only $243 million as compared with $557 million in 1985/86.

Imports totaled $737 million in 1990/91 (as compared with $1,194 million for 1985/86), much of this comprised of fuel and food, leaving a deficit of $494 million. In 1989/90, Afghanistan's main export markets included Germany, the United Kingdom, India, Pakistan and the United States. Major suppliers included Japan, Singapore, Germany, the UK and the US. In the early 1990s, undocumented and largely smuggled trade with the Central Asian republics and border regions of Pakistan is reported to have expanded considerably. Over the last two years, various mujahideen groups and warlords have set up customs and tax collection posts on the main supply routes from Central Asia and Pakistan. In wake of the country's economic and political disintegration, heroin has become its major export item.

32BALANCE OF PAYMENTS

Between 1951 and 1973, Afghanistan's year-end international reserves were never lower than $38 million or higher than $65 million. Development of the natural gas industry and favorable prices for some of the country's agricultural exports led to increases in international reserves, to $67.5 million in 1974 and to $115.4 million as of 31 December 1975. Exploitation of natural gas also freed Afghanistan from extreme dependence on petroleum imports and from the rapid increases in import costs that most countries experienced in 1973 and 1974. Increased trade with the former USSR and Eastern Europe in the late 1970s and 1980s resulted in a reduction of foreign exchange earnings, since trade surpluses are counted as a credit against future imports.

Foreign exchange reserves declined from $411.1 million at the close of 1979 to $262 million as of 30 May 1987. The public foreign debt in early 1982 stood at $1,105 million. Reliable statistics are not available for the ensuing years.

33BANKING AND SECURITIES

The government central bank, the Bank of Afghanistan, founded in 1939 and with 65 branches throughout the country in 1993, issues bank notes, administers government loans, grants loans to municipalities and to other banks, and provides short-term loans. The money supply, as measured by M2, totaled Af421 billion in 1993, reportedly.

All banks in Afghanistan were nationalized in 1975. In the early 1980s there were seven banks in the country, including the Agricultural Development Bank, the Export Promotion Bank, the Industrial Development Bank, and the Mortgage and Construction Bank. Foreign banks are not permitted in Afghanistan. Afghans may not own foreign securities. There is no organized domestic securities market.

34INSURANCE

The fate of the Afghan National Insurance Co., which covered fire, transport, and accident insurance, is unknown as of late 1994.

35PUBLIC FINANCE

The fiscal year ends 21 September. Budget breakdowns have not been available since 1979/80, when revenues totaled Af15,788 million and expenditures Af16,782 million. As of 1993, there was no central authority recognized; governmental functions were sparse and split up between the contending political factions. No federal system of collecting and disbursing public finances is currently in place.

36TAXATION

In the early 1980s, direct taxes accounted for about 15% of government revenues. The share provided by indirect taxes declined from 42% to 30%, as revenues from natural gas and state enterprises played an increasing role in government finance. Tax collection, never an effective source of revenue in rural areas, has been essentially disabled by the disruption caused by fighting and mass flight.

37CUSTOMS AND DUTIES

Before the turmoil of the late 1970s, customs duties, levied as a source of revenue rather than as a protective measure, constituted more than one-fourth of total government revenue. As of 1993, both specific and ad valorem duties of 20–35% were levied on imports. Other costs included service and Red Crescent charges; monopoly and luxury taxes; authorization and privilege charges, and a commission-type duty.

38FOREIGN INVESTMENT

A 1967 law encouraged investment of private foreign capital in Afghanistan, but under the PDPA government, Western investment virtually ceased. Between 1979 and 1987, the former USSR provided technical and financial assistance on more than 200 projects, including various industrial plants, irrigation dams, agricultural stations, and a new terminal at the Kabul airport. Since 1990, reconstruction investments from Russia, Japan, and the US have been channeled through the United Nations.

39ECONOMIC DEVELOPMENT

Between 1956 and 1972, Afghanistan completed three five-year plans (1956–61, 1962–66, and 1967–72). The first two plans aimed primarily at establishing basic socioeconomic infrastructure and developing the nation's mineral resources. The third plan marked the country's entry into a new phase of development, during which it undertook such quick-payoff projects as irrigation and chemical fertilizer and food-processing plants. Development outlays for the first plan were $350 million, for the second $696 million, and for the third an estimated $856 million. The implementation of the first plan was impeded by a severe shortage of technical and administrative skills. The second plan was also only partially realized; only five-sixths of the target amount of $807 million was actually utilized. On the other hand, although the increase in agricultural output merely kept pace with population growth, the country did acquire the transportation, communications, and power facilities needed to spur further progress. The third plan aimed to increase agricultural production so as to yield an exportable surplus in raw materials; to increase and diversify industrial output; to encourage private investment, which had been markedly sluggish; and to train technical and administrative personnel. The fourth plan was aborted by the 1973 coup. Afghanistan's economic policy was thereafter switched to a seven-year cycle. However, this new plan, scheduled to extend from 1976 to 1983, was interrupted by the 1978 coup.

Another five-year plan, prepared for the years 1979–84, envisaged an investment of $2.2 billion, mainly for industry. About one-third of the plan's funding was to come from domestic sources, and the rest from external assistance, mainly from the former USSR. At the second congress of the PDPA, held in March 1982, President Babrak Karmal repeatedly emphasized that Afghanistan had to develop a mixed economy. In the latest economic plan (1986–91), AF115,000 million was to be spent, with emphasis on improving the economic infrastructure and increasing investment in industry.

Economic development in Afghanistan was supported through large foreign loans and grants. Between 1950 and 1979, Afghanistan received about $1.6 billion in foreign assistance, most of it from the former USSR. Following the Soviet military intervention in December 1979, most Western countries suspended foreign aid to Afghanistan. Only the UNDP continued to contribute, donating $16.2 million during 1980–85. According to an official Afghan report, nonmilitary assistance from the former Soviet Union during 1981–85 amounted to Af26.7 billion and represented three-quarters of all external aid. Total loans received from the Soviet Union by 1990 equalled $2.1 billion.

Large-scale development assistance to Afghanistan from the former USSR and the OECD countries resumed with the initiation of the UN reconstruction effort in 1988, targeting about 14 provinces. The 1990/91 Action Plan prioritized bridge and road repair, mine removal, repatriation of refugees, provision of basic medical care, construction of food storage facilities, and disbursement of seeds, agricultural inputs, as well as building materials particularly for the repair of local irrigation systems. Total committments pledged by early 1991 equalled $1,029 billion. However very little of this amount has actually been disbursed, given renewed warfare in the country and the acute economic difficulties being experienced by Russia, originally one of the Plan's largest financial backers.

[40]SOCIAL DEVELOPMENT

Social welfare in Afghanistan has traditionally relied on family and tribal organization. In the villages and small towns, a tax is levied on each man to benefit the poor. Disabled people are cared for in social welfare centers in the provincial capitals. Most other welfare activities are still unorganized and in private hands.

The Afghan Family Guidance Association is affiliated with the International Planned Parenthood Federation. In 1989, 137,400 persons received family planning advice. The fertility rate during 1985–90 was 6.9. Abortion is legal only if the mother's life is in danger. In the 1980s, the Communist regime sanctioned a wider role for women than the traditional one, limiting them largely to the home and the fields, but the victory of the Mujahidin has largely reversed this trend.

[41]HEALTH

Even before the war disrupted medical services, health conditions in Afghanistan were inadequate by western standards. There are modern pharmacies in Kabul and in provincial centers. A national medical school was established in 1931 and, in the following year, the first tuberculosis hospital was built. In 1990, for every 100,000 people, 278 were stricken with tuberculosis. Since 1980, efforts to take medical services to war-ravaged areas of Afghanistan and to areas left without public health programs due to the termination of services have been waged by volunteer medical programs from France, Sweden, the US, and other countries. In 1991, there were 2,233 doctors, 510 pharmacists, 267 dentists, 1,451 nurses, and 338 midwives. In 1992 only 29% of the population had access to health services.

In 1992, estimated life expectancy was 43 years—one of the lowest in the world—and infant mortality was estimated at 165 per 1,000 live births. The death rate in 1993 was 22 per 1,000 people. From 1978 to 1991, there were over 1,500,000 war-related deaths.

[42]HOUSING

Houses in farming communities are largely of mud brick and frequently grouped within a fortified enclosure, to provide protection from marauders. The roofs are flat, with a coating of mixed straw and mud rolled hard above a ceiling of horizontal poles, although in areas where timber is scarce, separate mud brick domes crown each room. Every town has at least one wide thoroughfare, but other streets are narrow lanes between houses of mud brick, taller than those in the villages and featuring decorative wooden balconies. The war has severely damaged or destroyed countless houses. According to an official report, there were 200,000 dwellings in Kabul in the mid-1980s. The latest available figures for 1980–88 show a total housing stock of 3,500,000 with 4.4 people per dwelling.

[43]EDUCATION

Adult literacy in 1990 was estimated at 45.1% for men and 14.9% for women. Education is free at all levels, and primary education is theoretically compulsory and lasts for eight years, while secondary education lasts for a further four years. Children are taught in their mother tongue, Dari (Persian) or Pashtu (Pashto), during the first three grades; the second official language is introduced in the fourth grade. Children are also taught Arabic so that they may be able to read the Koran (Qur'an). The school year extends from early March to early December. According to a 1989 official report, an estimated 726,287 pupils were enrolled in primary schools. UNESCO reports that in 1990 24% of the children in this age group (boys 32% and girls 17%) attended school while an estimated 9% of children in the secondary level were enrolled (boys 12% and girls 6%).

The University of Kabul, which is now coeducational, was founded in 1932. In 1962, a faculty of medicine was established at Jalalabad in Nangarhar Province; this faculty subsequently became the University of Nangarhar. By 1988 a total of 5 universities were established in Afghanistan apart from 8 vocational colleges and 15 technical colleges. Teacher-training institutes have been established in the provinces of Balkh and Qandahar.

By mid-1980s, education of Afghan children in the former USSR and Eastern bloc countries was gaining popularity and even after the collapse of communism in 1992 and the dissolution of the USSR, Afghan students were permitted by their government to continue their studies in Russia, Uzbekistan, Tajikistan, and Kazakhstan, under the terms of earlier agreements with the former Soviet Union.

[44]LIBRARIES AND MUSEUMS

For centuries, manuscript collections were in the hands of the rulers, local feudal lords, and renowned religious families. Printing came fairly late to Afghanistan, but with the shift from the handwritten manuscript to the printed book, various collections were formed. Kabul has a public library with 60,000 volumes, and the library of the University of Kabul has 500,000 volumes.

The Kabul Museum possesses an unrivaled collection of stone heads, bas-reliefs, ivory plaques and statuettes, bronzes, mural paintings, and Buddhist material from excavations at Hadda, Bamian, Begram, and other sites. It also contains an extensive collection of coins and a unique collection of Islamic bronzes, marble reliefs, Kusham art, and ceramics from Ghazni. There are provincial museums at Ghazni, Herat, Mazar-e Sharif, and Qandahar. Major religious shrines have collections of valuable objects.

[45]MEDIA

Principal cities and some smaller towns and villages are served by the government-operated telegraph and telephone system; there are some 31,700 telephones in use. Radio and television broadcasting originates in Kabul; the first television broadcasting began in 1978. In 1991, there were 1,890,000 radios and 147,000 television sets in the country. An agreement was signed with the former USSR in 1981 to develop communications.

The only Afghan newspapers and magazines permitted are operated by the government. In 1991 there were 14 daily newspapers and 3 regular periodicals. The major newspapers, all headquartered in Kabul, (with estimated 1991 circulations) were *Anis* (3,700), published in Dari and Pashto; *Hiwad* (4,600), in Dari and Pashto; *Sarbaz* (5,000); and *Kabul New Times* (1,500), in English.

[46]ORGANIZATIONS

Organizations to advance public aims and goals are of recent origin, and most are sponsored and directed by the government. The National Fatherland Front, consisting of tribal and political groups that support the government, was founded in June 1981.

The Pashto Tolanah promotes knowledge of Pashto literature, and the Historical Society (Anjumani Tarikh) amasses information on Afghan history. The Women's Welfare Society carries on educational enterprises, provides training in handicrafts, and dispenses charitable aid, while the Maristun, a social service center, looks after children, men, and women and teaches them crafts and trades. The Red Crescent, the equivalent of the Red Cross, is active in every province. The Afghan Carpet Exporters' Guild, founded in 1987, promotes foreign trade of Afghan carpets and works for the improvement of the carpet industry.

[47]TOURISM, TRAVEL, AND RECREATION

The tourist industry, developed with government help in the early 1970s, has been negligible since 1979 due to internal political instability. A passport and visa are required for entrance into Afghanistan.

[48]FAMOUS AFGHANS

The most renowned ruler of medieval Afghanistan, Mahmud of Ghazni (971?–1030), was the Turkish creator of an empire stretching from Ray and Isfahan in Iran to Lahore in India (now in Pakistan) and from the Amu Darya (Oxus) River to the Arabian Sea. Zahir ud-Din Babur (1483–1530), a Timurid prince of Ferghana (now in the former USSR), established his base at Kabul and from there waged campaigns leading to the expulsion of an Afghan ruling dynasty, the Lodis, from Delhi and the foundation of the Mughal Empire in India.

Many eminent figures of Arab and Persian intellectual history were born or spent their careers in what is now Afghanistan. Al-Biruni (973–1048), the great Arab encyclopedist, was born in Khiva but settled in Ghazni, where he died. Abdul Majid Majdud

Sana'i (1070–1140), the first major Persian poet to employ verse for mystical and philosophical expression, was a native of Ghazni. Jalal ud-Din Rumi (1207–73), who stands at the summit of Persian poetry, was born in Balkh but migrated to Konya (Iconium) in Turkey. The last of the celebrated Persian classical poets, Abdur Rahman Jami (1414–92), was born in Khorasan but spent most of his life in Herat. So did Behzad (1450?–1520), the greatest master of Persian painting.

The founder of the state of Afghanistan was Ahmad Shah Abdali (1724–73), who changed his dynastic name to Durrani. He conquered Kashmir and Delhi and, with his capital at Qandahar, ruled over an empire that also stretched from the Amu Darya to the Arabian Sea. Dost Muhammad (1789–1863) was the founder of the Muhammadzai (Barakzai) dynasty. In a turbulent career, he both fought and made peace with the British in India, and unified the country. His grandson, Abdur Rahman Khan (1844–1901), established order after protracted civil strife. Amanullah Khan (1892–1960), who reigned from 1919 to 1929, tried social reforms aimed at Westernizing the country but was forced to abdicate. Muhammad Nadir Shah (d.1933), who was elected king by a tribal assembly in 1929, continued Amanullah's Westernization program. His son, Muhammad Zahir Shah (b.1914), was king until he was deposed by a coup in July 1973. Lieut. Gen. Sardar Muhammad Daoud Khan (1909–78), cousin and brother-in-law of King Zahir, was the leader of the coup and the founder and first president of the Republic of Afghanistan. Leaders in the violent years since the 1978 "Saur Revolution" have been Nur Muhammad Taraki (1917–79), founder of the PDPA; Hafizullah Amin (1929–79), Taraki's successor as president of the Revolutionary Council and secretary-general of the PDPA; Babrak Karmal (b.1929), leader of the pro-Soviet Parcham group of the PDPA and chief of state from December 1979 until May 1986; and Dr. Najibullah (b.1947), former head of the Afghan secret police.

[49]DEPENDENCIES

Afghanistan has no territories or colonies.

[50]BIBLIOGRAPHY

Adamec, Ludwig W. *Historical Dictionary of Afghanistan.* Metuchen, N.J.: Scarecrow Press, 1991.

Afghanistan: A Country Study, 5th ed. Washington, D.C.: Government Printing Office, 1986.

Afghanistan—In Pictures. Minneapolis: Lerner Publications, 1989.

Allchin, F. R., and N. Hammond (eds.). *The Archaeology of Afghanistan: From Earliest Times to the Timurid Period.* New York: Academic Press, 1978.

Arnold, Anthony. *Afghanistan: The Soviet Invasion in Perspective.* Stanford, Calif.: Hoover Institution Press, 1985.

Bonner, Arthur. *Among the Afghans.* Durham, N.C.: Duke University Press, 1987.

Bradsher, Henry S. *Afghanistan and the Soviet Union.* Durham, N.C.: Duke University Press, 1985.

Clifford, Mary Louise. *The Land and People of Afghanistan.* New York: Lippincott, 1989.

Emadi, Hafizullah. *State, Revolution, and Superpowers in Afghanistan.* New York: Praeger, 1990.

Griffiths, John Charles. *Afghanistan: Key to a Continent.* Boulder, Colo.: Westview Press, 1981.

Jones, Schuyler. *Afghanistan.* Oxford, England; Santa Barbara, Calif.: Clio Press, 1992.

Newell, Nancy P. and Richard S. *The Struggle for Afghanistan.* Ithaca, N.Y.: Cornell University Press, 1981.

Roy, Oliver. *Islam and Resistance in Afghanistan.* New York: Cambridge University Press, 1990.

Urban, Mark. *War in Afghanistan, 2nd ed.* New York: St. Martin's Press, 1990.

AUSTRALIA

Commonwealth of Australia

CAPITAL: Canberra.

FLAG: The flag has three main features: the red, white, and blue Union Jack in the upper left quarter, indicating Australia's membership in the Commonwealth of Nations; the white five-star Southern Cross in the right half; and the white seven-pointed federal star below the Union Jack. The flag has a blue ground. Of the five stars of the Southern Cross, four have seven points and one has five points.

ANTHEM: *God Save the Queen* is reserved for regal and state occasions and whenever singing is appropriate; the national tune is *Advance Australia Fair*.

MONETARY UNIT: The Australian dollar (A$) is a paper currency of 100 cents. There are coins of 5, 10, 20, and 50 cents and 1 and 2 dollars, and notes of 5, 10, 20, 50 and 100 dollars. A$1 = US$0.7008 (US$1 = A$1.4269).

WEIGHTS AND MEASURES: Metric weights and measures are used. The Australian proof gallon equals 1.37 US proof gallons.

HOLIDAYS: New Year's Day, 1 January; Australia Day, last Monday in January; Anzac Day, 25 April; Queen's Birthday, 2d Monday in June; Christmas, 25 December; Boxing Day, 26 December. Numerous state holidays are also observed. Movable religious holidays include Good Friday, Easter Saturday, and Easter Monday.

TIME: Western Australia, 8 PM = noon GMT; South Australia and Northern Territory, 9:30 PM; Victoria, New South Wales, Queensland, and Tasmania, 10 PM. Summer time is 1 hour later in all states except Western Australia, Queensland, and the Northern Territory.

¹LOCATION, SIZE, AND EXTENT

Lying southeast of Asia, between the Pacific and Indian oceans, Australia, the world's smallest continent, is almost completely surrounded by ocean expanses. Australia is slightly smaller than the United States, with a total area of 7,686,850 sq km (2,967,909 sq mi). The five mainland states are New South Wales, 801,600 sq km (309,500 sq mi); Queensland, 1,727,200 sq km (666,900 sq mi); South Australia, 984,000 sq km (379,900 sq mi); Victoria, 227,600 sq km (87,900 sq mi); and Western Australia, 2,525,500 sq km (975,100 sq mi). The island state of Tasmania has an area of 67,800 sq km (26,200 sq mi); the Northern Territory, 1,346,200 sq km (519,800 sq mi); and the Australian Capital Territory, 2,400 sq km (900 sq mi). The country, including Tasmania, extends about 4,000 km (2,500 mi) E–W and 3,180 km (1,980 mi) N–S. Australia is bounded on the N by the Timor and Arafura seas, on the NE by the Coral Sea, on the E by the Pacific Ocean, on the SE by the Tasman Sea, and on the S and W by the Indian Ocean, with a total coastline of 25,760 km (16,007 mi). Neighboring areas include Irian Jaya (part of Indonesia) and Papua New Guinea to the north, New Zealand to the southeast, and Indonesia to the northwest.

Australia's capital city, Canberra, is located in the southeastern part of the country.

²TOPOGRAPHY

The continent of Australia is divided into four general topographic regions: (1) a low, sandy eastern coastal plain; (2) the eastern highlands, ranging from 300 to more than 2,100 m (1,000–7,000 ft) in altitude and extending from Cape York Peninsula in northern Queensland southward to Tasmania; (3) the central plains, consisting largely of a north-south series of drainage basins, including the Great Artesian Basin, which underlies about 1,751,480 sq km (676,250 sq mi) of territory and is the most extensive area of internal drainage in the world; and (4) the western plateau, covered with great deserts and "bigger plains" (regularly spaced sand ridges and rocky wastes), rising 300 to 600 m (1,000–2,000 ft) high and constituting most of the western half of the continent. Australian mountains have eroded over recent geological periods, and only about 5% of the continent is above 600 m (2,000 ft); the average elevation is less than 300 m (1,000 ft). The highest point is Mt. Kosciusko, 2,228 m (7,310 ft), in the Australian Alps of the southeastern corner of New South Wales; the lowest point is Lake Eyre in South Australia, 12 m (39 ft) below sea level. In 1983, grains of rock from Western Australia were dated at 4.1–4.2 billion years old, making them the oldest ever found on earth.

The most important river system, and the only one with a permanent, year-round flow, is formed by the Murray, Darling, and Murrumbidgee rivers in the southeast. The Murray River, Australia's largest, rises in the Australian Alps of New South Wales and flows some 2,600 km (1,600 mi) west and southwest to empty into the sea below Adelaide, South Australia. Several other rivers are important, but for the most part they carry great amounts of water in the wet season and are dry for the rest of the year. The largest lakes have no outlet and are usually dry. The coastline is smooth, with few bays or capes. The two largest sea inlets are the Gulf of Carpentaria in the north, between Arnhem Land and the Cape York Peninsula, and the Great Australian Bight in the south. The Great Barrier Reef, the longest coral reef in the world, extends for about 2,010 km (1,250 mi) off the east coast of Queensland.

11

[3]CLIMATE

Although it has a wide diversity of climatic conditions, Australia is generally warm and dry, with no extreme cold and little frost, its temperatures ranging from comfortably mild in the south to hot in the central interior and north. July mean temperatures average 9°C (48°F) in Melbourne in the southeast and 25°C (77°F) in Darwin in the north. January mean temperatures average 20°C (68°F) in Melbourne and 30°C (86°F) in Darwin. Summer readings often reach 38°C (100°F) or more in almost any area of the continent and may exceed 46°C (115°F) in interior regions. Winds are light to moderate, except along the coasts, where cyclones have occurred.

The continent is subject to great variations in rainfall, but except for a few areas rainfall is insufficient, and the rate of evaporation is high. Mean annual rainfall is 42 cm (17 in), much less than the world mean of 66 cm (26 in). About 40% of the continent is desert, and 40% is subhumid. Only about 20% has more than 76 cm (30 in) of rain annually, but these areas suffer from a long dry season, while others have too much rain. Only Tasmania, Victoria, and parts of New South Wales have enough rainfall all year round. Droughts and floods occur irregularly but frequently over large areas. On 25 December 1974, a cyclone and flood devastated most of Darwin; at least 49 people were killed, and some 20,000 were left homeless. Drought conditions became very severe in the early 1980s, leading to dust storms, fires, and multibillion-dollar crop losses.

[4]FLORA AND FAUNA

Many distinctive forms of plant and animal life are found, especially in the coastal and tropical areas. There are some 500 species of eucalyptus and 600 species of acacia (wattle). Other outstanding trees are the baobab, blackwood, red cedar, coachwood, jarrah, Queensland maple, silky oak, and walnut. Native trees shed bark instead of leaves. Numerous types of wild flowers grow in the bush country, including boronia, Christmas bush, desert pea, flanner flower, Geraldton wax plant, kangaroo paw, pomaderris, and waratah. There are 470 varieties of orchids. About 400 kinds of mammals, 200 kinds of lizards, and 700 kinds of birds are indigenous. Apart from marsupials (bandicoots, kangaroos, koalas, opossums, Tasmanian devils, tree kangaroos, and wallabies), the most unusual animals are the dingo, echidna, flying fox (fruit bat), platypus, and wombat. Birds include the anhinga, bellbird, bowerbird, cassowary, emu, galah, kookaburra (laughing jackass), lyrebird, fairy penguin, rosella, and many types of cockatoos, parrots, hawks, and eagles.

Many species of trees, plants, and domestic animals have been imported, often thriving at the expense of indigenous types. Herds of wild buffalo, camels, donkeys, horses, and pigs, descendants of stock that strayed from herds imported by pioneers, roam the sparsely settled areas. The proliferation of rabbits resulted in a menace to sheep, and in 1907, a thousand-mile-long fence was built to keep rabbits out of Western Australia. Subsequently, a similar fence was erected in the east to prevent the incursion of dingos.

[5]ENVIRONMENT

The principal government institutions having responsibility for environmental matters are the Department of Home Affairs and Environment, the Australian Environment Council, and the Council of Nature Conservation Ministers. A national conservation strategy, developed by the states, the Northern Territory, and the federal government, in cooperation with the International Union for the Conservation of Nature and Natural Resources, the World Wildlife Fund, and the UNEP, became national policy in 1980.

The Environment Protection (Impact of Proposals) Act of 1974 establishes procedures for ensuring that environmental impact is considered in governmental decision making. The Whale Protection Act of 1981 prohibits killing, capturing, injuring, or interfering with a whale, dolphin, or porpoise within Australia's 200-mi economic zone or, beyond the zone, by Australian vessels and aircraft and their crews. The Environment Protection (Nuclear Codes) Act of 1978 mandates the development of uniform safety standards for uranium mining and milling and for the transport of radioactive materials. The Protection of the Sea (Discharge of Oil from Ships) Act of 1981 and the Protection of the Sea (Prevention of Pollution from Ships) Act of 1983 prevent or limit pollution from oil or noxious substances.

Water being a scarce resource in Australia, problems of water quality and availability are a constant concern. As of 1994, the country had only 82.3 cu mi of water supply. Attention focused in the 1980s on increased salinity in the Murray Valley, caused by diverting water inland from the coast for irrigation, and on the rise in saline water tables in Western Australia, due to excessive land clearing for dry-land farming. Another significant environmental problem is inland damage due to soil erosion. The quality of the soil is also affected by salinization. Gas emissions from the burning of fossil fuel affect the ozone layer and constitute a health hazard as well. As of 1994, Australians contributed 1.1% of the total global greenhouse gas emissions. Australia ranks seventh in the world as a producer of carbon dioxide emissions from industry.

Of the 102 mammals in southern Australia, 28% are extinct and 40% are endangered. As of 1993, 38 species of mammals, 39 species of birds, and 2,133 species of plants were threatened. As of 1987, endangered species in Australia included the banded anteater, greater rabbit-eared bandicoot, Leadbeater's opossum, northern hairy-nosed wombat, woylie, bridled nail-tail wallaby, five species of turtle (western swamp, green sea, hawksbill, leatherback, and olive ridley), Tasmanian freshwater limpet, granulated Tasmanian snail, African wild ass, western ground parrot, paradise parakeet, helmeted honey eater, noisy scrub-bird, western rufous bristlebird, Lord Howe wood rail, Lord Howe currawong, small hemiphlebia damselfly, Otway stonefly, giant torrent midge, and Tasmanian torrent midge.

[6]POPULATION

The estimated population in mid-1992 was 17,528,982. The populations of the six states and two mainland territories in 1992 were estimated as follows: New South Wales, 5,974,146; Victoria, 4,458,895; Queensland, 3,037,405; South Australia, 1,459,622; Western Australia, 1,662,777; Tasmania, 471,118; Australian Capital Territory, 296,376; and Northern Territory, 168,643. Population growth between 1950 and 1986 averaged 1.45% annually; between 1987 and 1992, it was 1.51%. A population of 19,595,000 was projected by the UN for the year 2000, assuming a crude birthrate of 15.1 per 1,000 population, a death rate of 7.7, and a net natural increase of 7.4 during 1995–2000.

Density in 1992 was 2.3 persons per sq km (5.9 per sq mi). The population is unevenly distributed. One-third of Australia is virtually uninhabited; another third is sparsely populated. Most of the people live in the southeast section and in other coastal areas. Less than 15% of the population is rural. In 1991, the metropolitan-area populations of the six state capitals were estimated as follows: Sydney, New South Wales, 3,698,500; Melbourne, Victoria, 3,153,500; Brisbane, Queensland, 1,327,000; Perth, Western Australia, 1,143,265; Adelaide, South Australia, 1,023,617; and Hobart, Tasmania, 183,838. The national capital is Canberra (278,894 in 1991) in the Australian Capital Territory, a specially designated area within New South Wales. Three other large cities (with 1991 populations) are Newcastle, New South Wales, 432,600; Gold Coast, Queensland, 274,200; Wollongong, New South Wales, 239,900; and Geelong, Victoria, 152,800.

AUSTRALIA

0   200   400   600 Miles

0   200   400   600 Kilometers

LOCATION: (including Tasmania): 113°09′ to 153°39′E; 10°41′ to 43°39′s. **TERRITORIAL SEA LIMIT:** 3 mi.

[7]MIGRATION

Since World War II, the government has promoted immigration of the maximum number of persons Australia can absorb without economic disequilibrium. In 1979, however, with the unemployment rate rising, the government tightened immigration requirements so that Australians would not lose jobs to the newcomers. Under the new system, assessments of applications are based on such factors as age, skills, and family ties, with priority given to reunion of families sponsored by Australian residents. In 1991,

21.7% of the population was born overseas.

Most of the 4.2 million immigrants to Australia between 1945 and 1985 were of working age, but although the government encouraged rural settlement, many immigrants had skills in short supply and preferred to work in the cities. The main countries of origin of such workers were the UK, Italy, and Greece. The number of permanent settlers arriving in 1991 was 116,650, up from a postwar low of 52,748 in 1975/76. The record high for new settlers was 185,099, in 1969/70. From World War II to 1991, over

460,000 refugees settled in Australia. These included more than 130,000 Indochinese.

Interstate migration favors Queensland, which gained 282,300 more people from the rest of Australia than it lost between 1982–92. Victoria lost a net of 125,300 people through interstate migration in this period.

8 ETHNIC GROUPS

Most Australians are of British or Irish ancestry. In 1991, nearly four-fifths were Australian-born. Persons born in the UK and Ireland formed another 7% of the population. European-born persons declined from 16.7% of the population in 1976 to 13.9% in 1991, while the Asian-born population grew from 0.3% in 1947 to 4.1% in 1991.

After the coming of the Europeans, the aboriginal population declined drastically, from about 300,000–1,000,000 to some 60,000 by the early 1920s. By the 1950s, however, the decline was reversed. In the 1991 census 265,492 people identified themselves as being of aboriginal or Torres Strait Islander origin, or 1.5% of the population. (Of these, the latter numbered 26,902.) Many of them live in tribal conditions on government reservations in the north and northwest; some 39,918 were in the Northern Territory in the 1991 census and 41,792 in Western Australia. Queensland had 70,130, and New South Wales, 70,020. Their social organization is among the most complex known to anthropologists. They do not cultivate the soil but are nomadic hunters and food gatherers, without settled communities. Anthropologists believe the aboriginals, also known as Australoids, are relatively homogeneous, although they display a wide range of physical types. Their serological, or blood-group, pattern is unique, except for a faint affinity with the Paniyan of southern India and the Veddas of Sri Lanka. The aboriginals probably originated from a small isolated group subject to chance mutation but not to hybridization. There seems to be a sprinkling of Australoid groups in India, Sri Lanka, Sumatra, Timor, and New Guinea. In 1963, aboriginals were given full citizenship rights, although as a group they continued to suffer from discrimination and a lower living standard than European Australians generally.

Beginning in the 1960s, the government abandoned its previous policy of "assimilation" of the aboriginals, recognizing the uniqueness of aboriginal culture and the right of the aboriginals to determine their own patterns of development. From the passage of the Aboriginal Land Rights (Northern Territory) Act in 1976 to mid 1990, aboriginals in the Northern Territory were given ownership of about 34% of territorial lands (461,486 sq km or 178,180 sq mi). The South Australia state government and its aboriginals also signed a land-rights agreement, and similar legislation was developed in other states during the 1980s. In all, aboriginals held 647,772 sq km (250,104 sq mi) of land under freehold in mid-1989 and another 1871,801 sq km (70,193 sq mi) under leasehold. A reservation in Western Australia consisted of 202,223 sq km (78,078 sq mi). By 1991, however, two-thirds of the aboriginals had left rural lands to settle in urban areas.

9 LANGUAGES

More than 99% of the population speaks English. There are no class variations of speech, and few if any local dialects.

Many languages or dialects are spoken by the aboriginal tribes, but phonetically they are markedly uniform. There is no written aboriginal language, but the markings on "letter sticks," sometimes carried by messengers from one tribe to another, are readily understood by tribal headmen. Aboriginal languages are in use in certain schools in the Northern Territories and, to a lesser extent, in schools of other states.

In rural areas, 42% of the aboriginal and Torres Strait Islander people aged 5 years or more spoke an aboriginal language at home in 1986. In urban areas the figure was only 6%.

10 RELIGIONS

Constitutionally, there can be no state religion or state aid to any religion; the exercise of any religion cannot be prohibited, and a religious test as qualification for public office is forbidden. As of 1992, 25.9% of Australians were Anglicans, 24.3% other Protestants, 27.5% Roman Catholics, and 2.7% Eastern Orthodox. About 12.7% of Australians indicated in 1992 that they had no religion. As of 1992 there were an estimated 88,000 Jews.

11 TRANSPORTATION

As of 1991, government-operated railways totaled about 40,478 km (25,153 mi). There are also some private railways, mainly for the iron ore industry in Western Australia. Australian railway systems do not interconnect well, and rail travel between principal cities involves changing trains. Modern equipment is gradually replacing older stock. As of August 1991, all interstate freight movements by rail were brought under the control of the National Rail Corporation (NRC).

Highways provide access to many districts not served by railroads. As of 1991 there were 837,872 km (520,674 mi) of roads, about 30% of which were paved. Motor vehicles in 1992 totaled about 9,954,000, including 7,913,000 passenger cars, and 2,041,000 commercial trucks, buses, and taxis.

Inland water transport is negligible, but ocean shipping is important for domestic and overseas transport. Most overseas trade is carried in non-Australian ships, while most coastwise vessels are of Australian registry. Although the fine natural harbors of Sydney and Hobart can readily accommodate ships of 11-m (36-ft) draft, many other harbors have been artificially developed. Other international shipping ports include Adelaide, Brisbane, Cairns, Darwin, Devonport, Fremantle, Geelong, Launceston, Mackay, Melbourne, and Townsville. All main ports have ample wharfage, modern cargo-handling equipment, and storage facilities. In 1991 there were some 70 commercially significant ports. The nation's merchant marine in 1991 included 76 vessels, with a combined GRT of 2.2 million.

Domestic air services are operated primarily by the privately owned Ansett Airlines. As of 1991, there were 37 commuter airlines with about 210 aircraft carrying 1.6 million passengers annually. The Australian overseas airline, Qantas, is owned and operated by the Commonwealth government. Qantas carries more than 3 million passengers per year to and from Australia, nearly 40% of the total carried by all airlines serving Australia. There are international airports at Adelaide, Brisbane, Cairns, Darwin, Hobart, Melbourne, Perth, Sydney, and Townsville, and 747 airfields in the country, of which 270 have permanent surface runways. In 1992 there were 8,984 registered civil aircraft; some 30.9 million passengers were carried on domestic and overseas flights via the major airports.

12 HISTORY

Stone objects found in 1978 but still only tentatively dated suggest that human beings may have inhabited what is now Australia as long as 100,000 years ago. The aboriginals migrated to Australia from Southeast Asia at least 40,000 years before the first Europeans arrived on the island continent. A cremated skeleton of a woman found at Lake Mungo in Western Australia, carbon-dated at 26,000 years, is the earliest evidence so far of aboriginal cremation practices; the boomerang dates back at least 10,000 years. Living as hunters and gatherers, roaming in separate family groups or bands, the aboriginals developed a rich, complex culture and numbered about 300,000 by the 18th century. However, with the onset of European settlement, conflict and disease reduced their numbers.

Although maps of the 16th century indicate European awareness of the location of Australia, the first recorded explorations of the continent by Europeans took place early in the 17th century, when Dutch, Portuguese, and Spanish explorers sailed along the coast and discovered what is now Tasmania. None took formal possession of the land, and not until 1770, when Capt. James Cook charted the east coast and claimed possession in the name of Great Britain, was any major exploration undertaken. Up to the early 19th century, the area was known as New Holland, New South Wales, or Botany Bay.

The first settlement—a British penal colony at Port Jackson (now Sydney) in 1788—was soon enlarged by additional shipments of prisoners, and (until the system was abolished during 1840–68) about 161,000 of the settlers were transported convicts. With the increase of free settlers, the country developed, the interior was penetrated, and six colonies were created: New South Wales in 1786, Van Diemen's Land in 1825 (renamed Tasmania in 1856), Western Australia in 1829, South Australia in 1834, Victoria in 1851, and Queensland in 1859.

Sheep raising and wheat growing were introduced and soon became the backbone of the economy. The wool industry made rapid progress during the period of squatting migration, which began on a large scale about 1820. The graziers followed in the wake of explorers, reaching new pastures, or "runs," where they squatted and built their homes. Exports of wool increased from 111 kg (245 lb) in 1807 to 1.1 million kg (2.4 million lb) in 1831. The increased flow of immigrants following the Ripon Land Regulations of 1831, as well as natural increase, raised the population from about 34,000 in 1820 to some 405,000 in 1850. The discovery of gold in Victoria (1851) attracted thousands, and in a few years the population had quadrupled. Under the stimulus of gold production, the first railway line—Melbourne to Port Melbourne—was completed in 1854. Representative government spread throughout the continent, and the colonies acquired their own parliaments.

Until the end of the 19th century, Australia's six self-governing colonies remained separate. However, the obvious advantages of common defense and irrigation, and many other joint functions, led to the federation of the states into the Commonwealth of Australia in 1901. (A constitution had been approved by the British Parliament in the previous year.) The Northern Territory, which belonged to South Australia, became a separate part of the Commonwealth in 1911. In the same year, territory was acquired from New South Wales for a new capital at Canberra, and in 1927, the Australian Parliament began meeting there. Liberal legislation provided for free and compulsory education, industrial conciliation and arbitration, the secret ballot, female suffrage, old age pensions, invalid pensions, and maternity allowances (all before World War I). Child subsidies and unemployment and disability benefits were introduced during World War II.

Australian forces fought along with the British in Europe during World War I. In World War II, the Australian forces supported the UK in the Middle East between 1940 and 1942 and, after the Japanese attack on Pearl Harbor, played a major role in the Pacific theater. After the war, a period of intense immigration began. The Labour government was voted out of office in 1949, beginning 23 years of continuous rule by a Liberal Country Party (later National Country Party and now National Party) coalition. During that period, Australian foreign policy stressed collective security and support for the US presence in Asia. Australian troops served in Viet-Nam between 1965 and 1971. When Labour returned to power in December 1972, it began the process of dissociating Australia from US and UK policies and strengthening ties with non-Communist Asian nations; in addition, diplomatic relations with the People's Republic of China were established. After a constitutional crisis late in 1975, when the opposition in the Senate successfully blocked the Labour Party's budgetary measures and thereby threatened the government with bankruptcy, the governor-general dismissed the Labour

prime minister, Gough Whitlam, and new elections were called for December. The Liberal National Party coalition won majorities in both the House and Senate and swept back into power. The Australian Labour Party (ALP) returned to power in 1983, following a campaign in which such economic issues as unemployment and inflation predominated. In 1984, Labour won a majority in the House but not in the Senate. The same results occurred in 1987. In March 1990 the ALP, led by Bob Hawke, gained a fourth consecutive federal election victory.

[13]GOVERNMENT

The Commonwealth of Australia, an independent, self-governing nation within the Commonwealth of Nations, has a federal parliamentary government. The federation was formed on 1 January 1901 from six former British colonies, which thereupon became states. The constitution combines the traditions of British parliamentary practice with important elements of the US federal system. Powers of the federal government are enumerated and limited.

The government consists of the British sovereign, represented by a governor-general, and the Australian Parliament. Bill Hayden became the new Governor-General in February 1989, succeeding Sir Ninian Stephen, who had held the post since 1982. Nominally, executive power is vested in the governor-general and an executive council, which gives legal form to cabinet decisions; in practice, however, it is normally exercised by a cabinet chosen and presided over by a prime minister, representing the political party or coalition with a majority in the House of Representatives. The number of cabinet ministers is variable.

Legislative power is vested in the Parliament, which is composed of a 76-member Senate, representing the states and territories, and a 148-member House of Representatives, representing electoral districts. Members must be Australian citizens of full age, possess electoral qualification, and have resided for three years in Australia. Twelve senators are elected by proportional representation from each state voting as a single electorate and two senators each from the Northern Territory and Capital Territory; they are elected for six years, with half the members retiring at the end of every third year. House membership is not quite double that of the Senate, with a minimum of five representatives for each state. House members are elected according to population by preferential voting in specific electoral districts; they serve for three years, unless the House is dissolved sooner. There are two members from the Australian Capital Territory and one from the Northern Territory; they have been able to vote on all questions since 1968. Parliament must meet at least once a year. Taxation and appropriation measures must be introduced in the lower house; the Senate has the power to propose amendments, except to money bills, and to defeat any measure it may choose.

The parties in the House elect their leaders in caucus. The party or coalition with a majority of seats forms the government. The leader of the majority party becomes prime minister and selects his cabinet from members of his party who are members of Parliament, while the leader of the principal minority party becomes leader of the official opposition. The party in power holds office as long as it retains its majority or until the governor-general decides that new elections are necessary; he exercised this inherent constitutional power during the 1975 crisis.

The Labour Government, especially under Paul Keating, has proposed a referendum to change Australia to a republican form of government. Keating formed a Republic Advisory Committee in April 1993. Sydney merchant banker, Malcolm Turnbull, headed the committee.

Suffrage is universal for all persons 18 years of age and older, subject to citizenship and certain residence requirements. Voting is compulsory in national and state parliamentary elections.

[14]POLITICAL PARTIES

Since most Australians have been shaped by the same language and by a similar cultural and religious heritage, their internal differences are largely based on economic issues. Attachments to the UK are compounded of sentiment, tradition, and economic advantage. Australian nationalism has been associated more closely with the Australian Labour Party (ALP) than with its rivals, who tend to regard Australian interests as almost identical with those of the UK. Because of Australia's geographical position as a "European people on an Asian limb," the economic element in its nationalism has been mixed with the fear of external conquest or domination.

Except in 1929–31, when a Labour government was in office, interwar governments were dominated by non-Labour groupings. When war seemed certain in 1939, the government was resolutely imperial, considering Australia to be at war automatically when the UK went to war. This view was challenged by the Labourites, who, though not opposing a declaration of war on Germany, wanted the step to be taken so as to show Australia's independence.

Labour was in office from 1941 to 1949. The Liberal and Country Parties were in office as a coalition for a long period afterward, from 1949 to 1972, and again beginning in December 1975 (by that time, the Country Party had become the National Country Party, and it later became the National Party). A direct descendant of the governments of the 1920s and 1930s, the coalition is principally linked with business (Liberal) and farming (National) and is officially anti socialist. In economic and foreign affairs, its outlook is still involved with the Commonwealth of Nations, but it supports the UN, as well as the alliance with the US in the ANZUS pact. It is sympathetic toward the new Asian countries and values the link with these countries afforded by the Colombo Plan. The Labour Party is a trade-union party, officially socialist in policy and outlook. It initially maintained an isolationist posture, but since the early 1940s, its policy has been a mixture of nationalism and internationalism. Smaller parties include the Democratic Labour Party, the Communist Party, the Australian Democrats Party, and the Green Party.

In the general elections of 13 December 1975, a caretaker government, formed the preceding month by the Liberal-National Country Party coalition after the dismissal of the Labour government of Prime Minister Gough Whitlam, obtained large majorities in both houses of the legislature. Although its majorities were eroded in the elections of December 1977 and October 1980, the coalition remained in power until 5 March 1983, when Labour won 75 out of 147 seats in the House of Representatives. Robert Hawke, leader of the Labour Party, took office as prime minister; he was reelected in 1984, 1987, and 1990. Paul Keating replaced Hawke as Labour's leader, and as Prime Minister, in December 1991. This was the first time an Australian prime minister had been ousted by his own party. Keating led the ALP to an unprecedented fifth consecutive election victory in the general election on 13 March 1993, increasing both its percentage share of the vote and its number of seats in the legislature. Labour won 80 seats, the Liberal-National coalition won 65, and independents gained 2 seats. In the Senate the Liberal-Nationalists won 36 seats, Labour 30, the Australian Democrats 7, the Greens 2, and independents 1.

[15]LOCAL GOVERNMENT

Powers not specifically granted to the federal government in the constitution are reserved to the states, although some powers (such as health, Labour, and social services) are held concurrently. Each state has an appointed governor who serves as the representative of the sovereign. Except for Queensland, which has a unicameral legislature, the parliament in each state is composed of two houses. The lower houses—the dominant legislative bodies—are popularly elected; the upper houses are elected by franchise limited to property holders and to those with certain academic or professional qualifications. The state prime minister achieves office and selects his cabinet in the same fashion as does the Commonwealth prime minister. The Northern Territory, which became self-governing in 1978, has a unicameral legislature.

Local communities (variously designated as boroughs, cities, district councils, municipalities, road districts, shires, and towns) have limited powers of government; but they are responsible for some health, sanitation, light, gas, and highway undertakings. Even the largest cities do not provide their own police protection, nor do they conduct or support education; these are state functions. Local aldermen or councilors ordinarily are elected on a property franchise, and mayors are elected annually or biennially by the aldermen from among their own number or by taxpayers. State departments of local government regulate the organization of local government. Some large interior areas are directly controlled by state governments.

[16]JUDICIAL SYSTEM

The Constitution vests federal jurisdiction in a High Court of Australia which consists of a Chief Justice and six Associate Justices appointed by the General Governor. The High Court has the authority to conduct constitutional review of state and federal legislation and is the supreme authority on constitutional interpretation. The High Court also has original jurisdiction over interstate and international matters.

Until 1985, in certain cases involving state law, appeals from courts below the High Court could be taken to the Privy Council in the UK, the final court of the Commonwealth of Nations. Special cases may be referred to a 25-member federal court which deals with commercial law, copyright law, taxation, and trade practices. There is also a family court.

States and territories have their own court systems. Cases in the first instance are tried in local or circuit courts of general and petty sessions, magistrates' courts, children's courts, or higher state courts. Capital crimes are tried before state supreme courts.

The state and federal courts are fully independent. The High Court has recently ruled that indigent defendants have a right to counsel at state expense. Criminal defendants are presumed innocent, and a plethora of due process rights include the right to confront witnesses and the right to appeal.

[17]ARMED FORCES

The all-volunteer Australian armed forces numbered 67,900 in 1993. The army had an official strength of 30,300; the navy, 15,300; the air force, 22,300; and reserve forces, 29,200, for all three services. The active forces include 8,500 women. Military weapons systems included 103 Leopard 1A3 main battle tanks, 5 submarines, 3 destroyers, 8 frigates, 157 airforce combat aircraft, and 15 navy armed helicopters. One company (reinforced) serves in Malaysia, another small (100) task force in Papua New Guinea, and around 500 personnel on UN missions.

Australia's defense expenditure in 1992 was $7.5 billion, 2.4% of GDP. Australia imported $210 million in arms in 1991 and exported $5 million. Imported arms come from the United States and Western Europe.

[18]INTERNATIONAL COOPERATION

Australia is a charter member of the UN, to which it gained admission on 1 November 1945. It belongs to ESCAP and all the nonregional specialized agencies and is a signatory to GATT and the Law of the Sea. Australia also participates in the Commonwealth of Nations and ANZUS, as well as the Asian Development Bank, Colombo Plan, OECD, South Pacific Commission, South Pacific Forum, and other intergovernmental organizations.

[19]ECONOMY

Wool, food, and minerals provide raw materials for home processing industries and around two-thirds of foreign earnings. Australia grows all needed basic foodstuffs and has large surpluses for export. Australia is the world's largest wool-producing country, as well as one of the world's great wheat exporters, and also exports large quantities of meat and dairy products. The country is also a major world supplier of iron ore, bauxite, lead, zinc, and copper; coal, beach sand minerals, and nickel have become major industries as well. Since the 1960s manufactured goods have provided an ever-increasing share of the country's exports. Heavy-industry expansion has taken place at a rapid pace, with steel output more than quadrupling from 1960 to 1970; by the 1980s, however, Australian steel was facing stiff competition from abroad, and production was stagnating.

Australia's economy began to recover from the 1990 recession in mid-1991. Economic growth, supported by rising consumption and higher export demand, reached 4% in the fourth quarter of 1993. However, the unemployment rate of about 11% was near a post-war record.

[20]INCOME

In 1992, Australia's GNP was $299,323 million at current prices, or $17,070 per capita. For the period 1985–92 the average inflation rate was 5.2%, resulting in a real growth rate in per capita GNP of 0.7%.

The US CIA estimates that in 1992 the GDP was $293.5 billion in current US dollars. It is estimated that in 1991 agriculture, hunting, forestry, and fishing contributed 3% to GDP; mining and quarrying, 4%; manufacturing, 15%; electricity, gas, and water, 3%; construction, 7%; wholesale and retail trade, 18%; transport, storage, and communication, 7%; finance, insurance, real estate, and business services, 22%; community, social, and personal services, 17%; and other sources 2%.

[21]LABOR

As of December 1991, the Australian work force was 8,700,000 of whom 5 million were men. From 1966/67 to 1985/86, the work force grew faster than the population, primarily because of increasing participation by women and immigrants. During this period, the proportion of women in the labor force to the total adult female population increased from 31% to 46%. From 1989 to 1993, however, the population grew on average by 1.3% per year, while the labor force expanded by only 1.1% annually. In 1991, women made up 41.6% of the economically active population. Unemployment averaged 7.5% during 1990 and rose to 10.6% by December 1991. The 1991 occupational pattern was as follows: wholesale and retail trade, 20%; social, personal, and community services, 29.7%; manufacturing, 14.6%; financial services, 11%; construction, 7%; agriculture, fishing, and forestry, 5.1%; and other sectors, 12.6%.

Australia is highly unionized; about 40% of all wage and salary earners are trade unionists. In 1991, 275 trade unions (down from 329 in 1985) had a membership of 2,660,000. The central trade union organization is the Australian Council of Trade Unions, which has been encouraging union amalgamation in order to eventually pare the numbers down to 17–20 major unions.

Awards by federal and state industrial tribunals contain minimum or award rates of pay, extended to women in 1974. Management and labor can negotiate pay rates above the award rates, and overaward pay varies with the employment situation. Overaward payments are commonly provided when market conditions warrant. The standard workweek is under 40 hours, generally from Monday through Friday. Nearly all Australian workers receive four weeks of annual vacation, many at rates of pay 17.5% above regular pay.

[22]AGRICULTURE

Australia is an important producer and exporter of agricultural products and a major world supplier of cereals, sugar, and fruit. Its rural holdings in 1990 comprised about 467 million ha (1,154 million acres), representing about 60.7% of total land area. However, approximately 90% of the utilized land area is in its natural state or capable of only limited improvement and is used largely for rough grazing. Droughts, fires, and floods are common hazards. The area actively cultivated for crops is less than 3.6% of all utilized land. Lack of water is the principal limiting factor, but unsuitable soil and topography are also important determinants. As of 1991, some 1,831,000 ha (4,524,400 acres) of land were irrigated. Agriculture has declined from 20% of GDP in the 1950s to 4.1% in 1992. Agricultural exports, which accounted for 60% of Australia's exports in the 1960s, now account for 22.5%. Total crop value in 1989/90 was at A$9,876 million, a rise of about 29% from 1987/88.

Grain crops have been cultivated since the first year of European settlement. In November 1790, plantings around Sydney of wheat, barley, and corn totaled 34 ha (84 acres). Today, winter cereals are cultivated in all states. Three cereals are often grown on one farm for grain, green fodder, and hay for livestock. Most wheat and barley and about half the oats are grown for grain. The estimated wheat area sown for grain decreased from 11,135,000 ha (27,515,000 acres) in 1986/87 to 9,236,000 ha (22,822,000 acres) in 1990/91. Production of wheat for grain in 1990/91 was an estimated 13,053,000 tons, down 19% from 16,119,000 tons in 1986/87. Western Australia and New South Wales are the chief wheat-producing states. In 1990/91, Australia produced 4,054,000 tons of barley, 1,501,000 tons of oats, and 1,061,000 tons of legumes for grain. In 1992, 210,000 tons of corn and 1,133,000 tons of potatoes were produced.

Sugarcane is grown along a 2,000-km (1,200-mi) stretch of coastal land in New South Wales and Queensland. About 95% of sugar production comes from Queensland. A normal crushing season is from June to December. The estimated 1992 harvest from 348,000 ha (860,000 acres), yielded about 29.3 million tons of sugar cane. The industry faces problems of excessive supply and price elasticity; sugar is sold primarily to Japan, the US, Canada, South Korea, Malaysia, China, and Singapore. In 1990/91, sugar exports were estimated to have amounted to A$1 billion. Although tobacco growing is a relatively small industry, it is important in some areas. In 1992, some 5,000 ha (12,400 acres) were planted with tobacco, and about 13,000 tons were produced.

Cotton has been grown in the coastal river valleys of Queensland for more than a century but on a limited scale, and it has provided only a small percentage of Australia's lint requirements. In the 1980s, however, successful development of cotton-growing areas in New South Wales and Western Australia has resulted in spectacular production increases. In 1985/86, 685,000 tons of cotton were produced (almost triple the amount in 1979/80), but in 1992, production only amounted to 431,000 tons.

Australia's wide climate differences permit the cultivation of a range of fruits, from pineapples in the tropical zone to berry fruits in the cooler areas of temperate zones. In 1990/91, over 18.2 million ha (45 million acres) were under orchard fruit (apples, oranges, pears, peaches) cultivation, and 17.5 million ha (43.1 million acres) were cultivated for tropical (bananas and pineapples) and other fruit. Australia's wine industry is also growing; viticulture engaged 59,241 ha (146,385 acres) and produced 825,792 tons of grapes for winemaking, drying, and other uses.

[23]ANIMAL HUSBANDRY

More than 54% of Australia's land is used in stock raising. Animal husbandry is concentrated in the eastern highlands, but it spreads across the wide interior spaces and even to low-rainfall areas, in which up to 12 ha (30 acres) are required to support one sheep and from which cattle must be taken overland hundreds of miles to coastal meat-packing plants. In 1985/86, the total estimated gross value of livestock slaughters was A\$4,067 million.

Sheep raising has been a mainstay of the economy since the 1820s, when mechanization of the British textile industry created a huge demand for wool. In 1850 there were 17.5 million sheep in Australia; by 1894, some 100 million; and in 1970, a record high of some 180 million. Australia's flocks, some 146.8 million in 1992, now constitute approximately 13% of the world's sheep but produce about 28% of the world's wool supply. Wool production, the largest in the world, was an estimated 1,305,346 tons in 1992. About 95% is exported; nevertheless, wool, which represented 50% of Australia's merchandise exports (by value) in 1957/58, constituted only 6.2% in 1992. Australia produces about one-third of the world's wool, and accounts for 75% of the world's exports of wool apparel. During periods of great drought, such as the early 1980s, the number of sheep has diminished by 40 million or more. In the better lands, however, animal husbandry ranks high on a world scale. Large, scientifically managed stations have produced some of the world's finest stock. Sheep of the Merino breed, noted for its heavy wool yield, make up about three-quarters of Australian flocks.

In 1992 there were an estimated 2.7 million hogs and 23.6 million head of cattle. In the same year, meat production totaled an estimated 3,269,000 tons. Of these, beef and veal constituted 1,791,000 tons; mutton and lamb, 666,000 tons; and ham, pork, and bacon, 336,000 tons. Total poultry production in 1992 was 444,000 tons (dressed weight). Butter production in 1992 (in factories) amounted to an estimated 110,680 tons; whole milk was estimated 6,200 million liters; and cheese (factory production) was about 197,445 tons. Egg production is around 200 million dozen per year, predominantly for domestic consumption. Australia produces some 25,000 to 30,000 tons of honey per year, half of which is exported. With a value of over \$2.1 billion, Australia led the world in beef exports in 1992, which accounted for 5% of total exports. Nearly 60% of total beef production is exported annually, most of it going to the US, South Korea, and Taiwan.

24FISHING

Fishing is relatively unimportant. Even with a low per capita fish consumption, Australia must import about half its normal requirements. Pearl and other shell fishing are relatively significant. The 1991 catch of fish, crustaceans, and mollusks totaled 227,300 tons, 98% from marine waters. Exports of fishery products in 1991 were valued at \$577,592,000.

25FORESTRY

In 1991, native forestland covered 106 million ha (261.9 million acres), or about 13.9% of the total area; most timberland is neither exploited nor potentially exploitable. Native forests consist principally of hardwood and other fine cabinet and veneer timbers; eucalyptus dominates about 35 million ha (86.5 million acres). Limited softwood resources had become seriously depleted, but new plantations were established in the 1980s at a rate of 33,000 ha (81,500 acres) annually. Softwood plantations supply more than half the timber harvested annually. Roundwood production in 1991 totaled about 19.3 million cu m. Timber and other forest products valued at about \$471.5 million were exported in 1991, an increase of nearly 50% from the 1988 total, while imports were worth A\$1,215.6 million, a decrease of 2% over the same period. Australia's leading forest products are softwood logs and chips. Whereas all of the softwood log production is consumed at home, all commercial woodchip production is exported. National parks and wildlife preserves occupy about 3.8 million ha (9.4 million acres), or 9% of the total forestlands. Extensive reforestation—62,000 ha (153,000 acres) annually during the 1980s—was been undertaken to combat soil erosion. Since hardwoods grow slowly, Australia will probably have to import a great deal of lumber in future years to meet its timber needs.

26MINING

More than 60 varieties of minerals and metals have been commercially produced in Australia, and successful exploration in the late 1960s led to a long-term mineral boom and a sharp increase in exports. The country is now the world's leading producer of alumina, bauxite, diamonds, ilmenite, mined lead, monazite, opal, rutile, sapphire, and zircon, and the second-largest producer of mined zinc. In addition, Australia is the third leading producer of mined gold and iron ore; fourth in aluminum; fifth in manganese; and among the top 10 in the production of mined antimony, coal, mined tin, salt, and mined silver. Australia is the world's leading exporter of alumina, coal, ilmenite, refined lead, monazite, rutile, zircon, and iron ore (reclaiming the lead from Brazil for the first time since 1985).

As of 1991, Australia was estimated to possess about 474,000 tons of recoverable uranium. Bauxite deposits in northern Queensland are among the world's largest, and bauxite deposits in the Northern Territory are also in production. The Argyle diamond mine, near the shores of Lake Argyle in Western Australia, began production in 1984; the largest diamond mine in the world, it can supply some 35 million carats a year; in 1991, about 5% of production was of gem quality, including a small number of very rare pink diamonds. Production of iron ore was 117.1 million tons in 1991. In the same year, production of alumina was 11.7 million tons; zinc, 1,048,000 tons; lead, 571,000 tons; copper, 311,000 tons; and nickel, 69,000 tons. Among mineral sands, 1991 production of ilmenite concentrates was 1,363,000 tons; zircon concentrates, 292,000 tons; and rutile concentrates, 201,000 tons. Exports of mineral resources (including fuels) accounted for 42% of total exports in 1990/91, rising in value by 14% over the previous year to a record A\$27.5 billion. The major nonfuel mineral exports to gain value in 1991 were gold, worth A\$3.7 billion (up 31% from 1990) and iron ore, valued at A\$2.5 billion (up 16% from 1990).

27ENERGY AND POWER

Because of its relatively small hydroelectric resources and only recently discovered oil, Australia has had to rely on coal-burning steam plants for about three-quarters of its public power requirements. The remainder has been supplied by hydroelectricity, gas turbines, and internal combustion generators. Net installed electrical capacity in 1991 was 35.4 million kw; power generation in 1991 totaled 156,883 million kwh, of which less than 8% was privately produced.

Major electric power undertakings, originally privately owned and operated, were by 1952 under the control of state organizations. Manufacturing has been developed most extensively in or near coal areas, and distribution of electricity to principal users is therefore relatively simple. All major cities except Perth use 240-volt, 50-cycle, three-phase alternating current; Perth has 250-volt, 40-cycle, single-phase alternating current.

The Snowy Mountains hydroelectric scheme in southeast New South Wales, Australia's most ambitious public works project, comprises seven power stations, a pumping station, 16 large and many smaller dams, and 145 km (90 mi) of tunnels and 80 km (50 mi) of aqueducts. The project took 25 years to complete and has a generating capacity of 3,740 Mw. The Snowy Mountains scheme and other large power projects in New South Wales, Victoria, and Tasmania have greatly increased the nation's aggregate installed capacity. The only state with water resources sufficient for continuous operation of large hydroelectric power stations is Tasmania, which possesses about 50% of Australia's hydroelectric energy potential. Production and use of such power is on the increase throughout the country, however.

In early 1983, Alcoa Australia signed a contract with the Western Australian State Energy Commission, at an estimated cost of A$11.2 billion, for supplying natural gas from the Northwest Shelf. In 1985, eight Japanese companies agreed to buy 5.84 million tons of liquefied natural gas a year from 1989 to 2009. Another phase involves the construction of an additional offshore platform and onshore facilities for additional shipments to begin in 1995. In early 1992, petroleum exploration began in the Timor Sea; the area had been off limits for over a decade in order to establish a zone of cooperation with Indonesia. Total gas reserves amounted to 18,200 billion cu m in 1992; commercial production in 1991 was 21,687 million cu m. Oil production, which began in 1964, totaled 198,821,000 barrels in 1991; reserves in 1991 were estimated at 1.66 billion barrels. As of 1991, commercially exploitable uranium reserves were 474,000 tons; production totaled about 3,776 tons in the same year. In 1991, fuels and energy accounted for only 5.7% of total imports.

28INDUSTRY

In proportion to its total population, Australia is one of the world's most highly industrialized countries. The manufacturing sector has undergone significant expansion in recent years and turns out goods ranging from automobiles to chemicals and textiles. The leading industries are food processing, beverages, motor vehicles, metalworking, and paper and paper products. In 1991, manufacturing accounted for 14.5% of GDP and provided an equal percentage of Australia's jobs.

Australia is self-sufficient in beverages, most foods, building materials, many common chemicals, some domestic electrical appliances, radios, plastics, textiles, and clothing; in addition, most of its needed communications equipment, farm machinery (except tractors), furniture, leather goods, and metal manufactures are domestically produced. Recent years have seen the rapid growth of high-tech industries including aircraft, communications and other electronic equipment, electrical appliances and machinery, pharmaceuticals, and scientific equipment, and the government has supported the growth of these new sectors. Many manufacturing companies are closely connected—financially and technically—with manufacturers in the UK, the US, or Japan.

29SCIENCE AND TECHNOLOGY

Two organizations support most of Australian government R&D. The Commonwealth Scientific and Industrial Research Organization (CSIRO) is an independent government agency which is also the largest government research agency. It supports R&D in industrial technologies, information science, minerals, energy, and other areas. The role of the Defense Science and Technology Organization (DSTO) is to support military R&D by providing scientific and technological assistance to the Australian Defense Force and Department of Defense.

Several issues dominate current Australian science and technology policy: the concentration of R&D in national research centers; tensions among and between university researchers over allocation of R&D funding resources; effective communication between industry, government, and university researchers; the growing role which industry is playing in support of national R&D; and the role which Australia is playing in international science and technology collaboration.

In 1991, total R&D funding was A$3 billion (or US$2 billion). The Australian government funds 47% of all R&D, industry 40%, and State governments, 12%. There are more than 200 scientifically-oriented professional associations and societies, the foremost of which is the Australian Academy of Science, founded in 1954 by royal charter. The Australian Academy of Technological Sciences was founded in 1976. The Australian Science and Technology Council (ASTEC) provides an independent source of

counsel for the Australian Prime Minister; its role was augmented in 1986 by the creation of a post for a Minister Assisting the Prime Minister with portfolio for science and technology.

30DOMESTIC TRADE

There are many small specialty shops, but in the larger cities department stores sell all kinds of items. Supermarkets have been widely established, and telephone shopping and delivery services are becoming popular. Installment selling, called hire purchase, is used in the sale of many products. Reliable commercial credit agencies cover all the main cities and many smaller towns. Retail turnover in November 1992 (seasonally adjusted) was A$8,098 million, up from A$7,692 million for the same period in the previous year.

The usual business hours are from 9 AM to 5 PM, Monday–Friday, and from 9 AM to noon on Saturday.

Most advertising is done through the press, radio, and television. Principal advertising agencies are in Sydney and Melbourne.

31FOREIGN TRADE

Measured by foreign trade volume per capita, Australia is one of the great trading nations, and it continues to show a steady rise in trade volume. Throughout the 1970s, exports regularly exceeded imports. In the early 1980s, however, there was a deficit. In 1984/85, the value of Australian exports amounted to roughly A$30.6 billion and the value of imports amounted to A$30 billion, leaving a slightly favorable balance of about A$600 million. In 1988/89, total exports were valued at A$43,462 million, and imports at A$47,064 million.

Australia is mainly an exporter of primary products and an importer of manufactured and semifinished goods. Transport or reexport trade is negligible. Mineral fuels, minerals, wheat, textile fibers, and meat are the principal exports. Machinery is the major import item.

Principal exports in 1990/91 (in millions of Australian dollars) were as follows:

Food and live animals	6,499
Beverages and tobacco	194
Crude materials, inedible, except fuels	7,251
Mineral fuels, lubricants and related materials	7,319
Animal and vegetable oils, fats and waxes	26
Chemicals and related products	972
Manufactured goods classified by material	4,598
Machinery and transport equipment	2,757
Miscellaneous manufactured articles	856
Commodities and transactions not classified according to kind	6,983
TOTAL	37,455

Principal imports in 1990/91 (in millions of Australian dollars) were as follows:

Food and live animals	1,528
Beverages and tobacco	302
Crude materials, inedible, except fuels	903
Mineral fuels, lubricants and related materials	2,302
Animal and vegetable oils, fats and waxes	108
Chemicals and related products, n.e.s.	3,516
Manufactured goods classified by material	5,846
Machinery and transport equipment	6,697
Miscellaneous manufactured articles	5,560
Commodities and transactions not classified according to kind	1,144
TOTAL	27,906

Japan is Australia's chief trading partner, accounting for roughly 25% of its exports. In recent years, Australia's foreign trade has tended to shift from European markets to developing Asian nations, which now account for nearly 35% of Australia's exports, compared with about 10% 20 years ago. Principal trade partners in 1988/89 (in thousands of Australian dollars) were as follows:

	EXPORTS	IMPORTS
Japan	11,840,476	9,766,472
Total EC	6,002,623	10,775,865
United States	4,422,388	10,129,362
Total ASEAN	3,868,367	2,813,211
New Zealand	2,219,170	1,970,469
Korea, Republic of	2,182,749	1,262,000
Hong Kong	1,888,518	891,539
Taiwan	1,566,501	1,919,905
China	1,209,390	1,026,650
Canada	709,104	1,066,693

32BALANCE OF PAYMENTS

Australia registered massive deficits on current accounts in the 1980s, partly because of lagging exports and partly because the outflow of invisibles remained at its usual high level. On the capital accounts, however, overseas borrowing by private and public enterprises helped to make up for the shortfall. Despite the 1990 recession, robust export activity produced a merchandise trade surplus of more than A$3 billion in 1990/91 and A$4 billion in 1991/92. As a result, the current account deficit fell from A$16.2 billion in 1990/91 to A$12.4 billion in 1991/92. As the economy expands and imports rise, however, the current account deficit is expected to grow again.

In 1992 merchandise exports totaled $42,392 million and imports $40,819 million. The merchandise trade balance was $1,572 million. The following table summarizes Australia's balance of payments for 1991 and 1992 (in millions of US dollars):

	1991	1992
CURRENT ACCOUNT		
Goods, services, and income	−12,055	−11,884
Unrequited transfers	1,869	1,206
TOTALS	−10,185	−10,677
CAPITAL ACCOUNT		
Direct investment	2,719	5,295
Portfolio investment	4,244	−420
Other long-term capital	5,291	5,266
Other short-term capital	1,149	20
Other liabilities	−8	11
Reserves	324	4,753
TOTALS	13,720	14,926
Errors and omissions	−3,535	−4,249
Total change in reserves	−270	5,326

33BANKING AND SECURITIES

The Reserve Bank of Australia, the central bank, reconstituted in 1960, functions as a banker's bank and financial agent of the federal and some state governments, issuing notes, controlling interest and discount rates, mobilizing Australia's international reserves, and administering exchange controls and government loans. It is connected through a common governor and board with the Commonwealth Trading Bank—a general bank—the Commonwealth Savings Bank, and the Commonwealth Development Bank. Its departments provide special services, such as rural credits, mortgage banking, and industrial financing. As of 1993 the Reserve Bank had A$21,415 million in foreign assets and A$14,337 million in claims on the government.

Trading banks—4 major ones and 5 others as of 1993—conduct commercial banking in Australia. In 1993 there were 18 foreign banks with offices in Australia. There are 3 savings banks, as well as various agricultural or rural banks, finance companies,

trust companies, building societies, and life insurance companies.

In 1993, depositors' balances in all banks amounted to A$53,720 million. In 1993, the money supply as measured by M2, was A$251,953 million.

Stock and bond markets are active in new issues, especially equities, and are important sources of funds for businesses and mineral exploration. The six major stock exchanges, one in each state capital, are united under a central authority, the Australian Associated Stock Exchanges, which has 14 directors.

34INSURANCE

Life insurance firms, through premiums on policies and interest earned on accumulated funds, account for substantial annual savings. The companies invest in government securities, in company securities (including shares and fixed-interest obligations), and in mortgage loans and loans against policies in force. Most loans (to individuals and building societies) are for housing. In 1989, there were 226 insurance companies in Australia, including composite and reinsurance companies. General insurance premiums in 1990–91 totaled $A7.56 billion, and claims for the same period totaled $A5.45 billion. In 1992, life insurance in force was $A529.5 million.

35PUBLIC FINANCE

The fiscal year begins 1 July and ends 30 June. After World War II, the Commonwealth government assumed greater responsibility for maintaining full employment and a balanced economy, as well as for providing a wide range of social services. Social security and welfare payments are the largest category of government expenditure. The central government has financed almost all its defense and capital works programs from revenue and has made available to the states money raised by public loans for public works programs. Deficits are common. In the latter half of the 1980s, however, five consecutive years of significant surpluses occurred as a result of expenditure restraints. The actual deficit in 1991/92 amounted to A$9.34 billion, or 2.4% of GDP. The deficit grew to the equivalent of 3.3% of GDP in 1992/93. New training and wage subsidies and other employment schemes (which were allocated A$742 million in 1992/93 in order to reduce unemployment by 1%) could burden the Treasury as long as unemployment remains high. The government nevertheless has ambitions of reducing the deficit to 1% of GDP by 1996/97.

The following table shows actual revenues and expenditures for 1990 and 1991 in millions of Australian dollars.

	1990	1991
REVENUES		
Tax revenue	90,684	92,597
Non-tax revenue	8,999	10,146
Capital revenue	245	170
TOTAL	99,928	102,913
EXPENDITURES & LENDING MINUS REPAYMENTS		
General public service	8,253	8,907
Defense	7,904	8,738
Public order and safety	856	907
Education	6,336	7,182
Health	11,865	12,967
Social security and welfare	26,262	30,526
Housing and community amenities	1,663	1,386
Recreation, cultural, and religious affairs	1,032	1,026
Economic affairs and services	6,623	8,423
Other expenditures	22,330	22,058
Lending minus repayments	−1,332	−1,615
TOTAL	91,793	100,513
Deficit/surplus	8,135	2,400

In 1990 Australia's total public debt stood at A$49,479 million, of which A$6,953 million was financed abroad.

36TAXATION

The main taxes (personal and corporate income, payroll, and sales taxes) are levied by the Commonwealth, but the states and municipalities impose other levies. Federal rates are determined in legislation that is foreshadowed in the budget, presented each August; rates apply to the fiscal year beginning in July, except for company tax rates, which apply to the previous year's income.

The 1992/93 corporate tax rate was 39% for both public and private firms. Undistributed profits of private firms are taxed at a higher rate. Nonresident companies pay an additional tax of 5%. Wholesalers pay a federal sales tax of 20%, levied on almost all products, generally on the last transaction, in which goods are sold to a retailer. However, many goods are subject to special rates. Both the Commonwealth and states can levy land taxes, and states levy both stamp duties on various documents and payroll taxes. Excise taxes are levied on alcoholic beverages, tobacco products, coal, kerosene, liquefied petroleum gas, and indigenous crude oil.

Personal taxation is levied by the Commonwealth on a sharply progressive basis. The pay-as-you-earn system (called PAYE) is used. As of 30 June 1993, taxes (on income, after deductions) ranged from zero on income up to A$5,400 to 29% on income of up to A$20,700, with a marginal rate of 47% on amounts over A$50,000. Social security taxes are included as part of income taxes. Deductions are allowed for dependents, donations, medical expenses, and children's educational expenses, and for payment of life insurance or pension premiums. There is also a pensioner rebate that varies depending on income.

37CUSTOMS AND DUTIES

Federal policy is to use the tariff to protect local industries (especially the automobile industry), and tariff debates are nonparty affairs. Intermediate and most-favored-nation rates, established for many products, apply to most foreign countries. Developing and preferential countries receive rates 5 percentage points below the general rate. As a contracting party to GATT, Australia has consented to a number of other tariff reductions since 1947. There is also a preference scheme for developing nations, under which they pay 10–15% less than the general rate. Under the South Pacific Regional Trade and Economic Cooperation Agreement (SPARTECA), which went into effect on 1 January 1981, Australia and New Zealand offer the other South Pacific Forum members duty-free or concessional access to their markets. Tariffs on industrial machinery and plant equipment ordinarily are low where they do not compete with Australian enterprise, and machinery and equipment required by new industries may be imported duty-free or at concessional rates. The only free-trade zone is the Northern Territory Trade Development Zone.

Besides the duties levied under the customs tariff, revenue duties are imposed on a wide range of goods.

38FOREIGN INVESTMENT

According to preliminary figures, foreign investment in Australia in 1985/86 reached a peak of A$19,850 million. The US was the leading investor (A$4,811 million), followed by Japan (A$2,195 million), and the UK (A$1,475 million). In 1985/86, a total of A$5,892 million in overseas payments was made by companies in Australia. The most recent focus of foreign investment has been the booming tourist industry, and commercial and residential property development. Hotels and resorts on the north New South Wales and Queensland coasts are attracting capital from abroad, as are large office block and hotel projects in the capital cities.

Australia prefers the inflow of long-term development capital to that of short-term speculative capital. It also welcomes the technical competence usually accompanying foreign investment. Investment incentives include tariff protection, bounties for the manufacture of certain products, and tax incentives. Total foreign ownership is permitted, but ownership in certain sectors is subject to restrictions.

39ECONOMIC DEVELOPMENT

Commonwealth and state governments have devoted special attention to the production and marketing of main primary products, and since 1920, legislation has provided subsidies or other marketing aids to certain commodities. Direct subsidies, however, are not common, and butter, cheese, and cotton are among the few export commodities subsidized. Federal and state aid is given to industries established in approved fields of manufacture. The Export Market Development Grant Acts of 1974 provided government assistance in the development of export markets through June 1983. In 1975, the government set up the Export Finance and Insurance Corp. (replacing the Export Payments Insurance Corp.) to provide Australian exporters with insurance and other financial services not readily available commercially.

The government endeavors to prevent undue fluctuation in the economy. Price controls were in effect during World War II and part of the postwar period and are now imposed on a few essential household items. As an alternative to price controls, the Commonwealth government, in mid-1975, introduced a policy of wage indexation, allowing wages to rise as fast as, but no faster than, consumer prices; major labor unions, however, opposed this restraint, which was ended in 1981.

The need for foreign capital is recognized by the major political parties, and conventions for the avoidance of double taxation have been entered into with the UK, the US, and a number of other countries. In an attempt to stem large capital outflows, the government has devalued the Australian dollar. The government has also promoted the exportation of manufactured goods to offset the trade deficit.

Monetary policy has supported recovery while resulting in low inflation. After August 1993, the focus of fiscal policy was expected to shift towards deficit reduction.

40SOCIAL DEVELOPMENT

The Commonwealth Social Services Act of 1947, as amended, provides for invalid and old age pensions and a variety of other benefits. Invalid pensions are payable to persons 16 years of age and older who have lived at least 5 years in Australia and have become totally incapacitated or permanently blind. Old age pensions are payable to men 65 years of age and over, and to women 60 years of age and over, who have lived in Australia continuously for at least 10 years at some stage in their lives. The continuous-residence requirement may be waived for those who have been residents for numerous shorter periods.

The Commonwealth Maternity Allowance Act of 1912, as amended, provides for allowances for every child born, and the Commonwealth Child Endowment Act of 1941 provides for weekly payments to children under 16 years of age. Widows' pensions are also provided. The Commonwealth Unemployment and Sickness Benefits Act of 1945 provides weekly payments to persons between the ages of 16 and 65 (60 for females) who are not qualified to receive old age, invalid, widows', or service pensions.

In 1986 there were 114,832 marriages, for a crude rate of 7.1 per 1,000 population, and 39,417 divorces, or 2.4 per 1,000 (down from a peak of 4.6 in 1976). The fertility rate declined to an average of 1.9 children per woman of childbearing age in 1985–90 from 2.51 in 1971–75. Meanwhile, the median age of mothers at first birth was steadily rising, reaching 26.3 in 1985. Surveys during 1985 showed that of all married women aged 15–44, 67% were using contraception. The Sex Discrimination Act of 1984 bars discrimination on the basis of sex, marital status or pregnancy, and in 1992 the Parliament passed amendments that strengthened it significantly.

[41]HEALTH

Australia, with its 17.8 million people (1993), is one of the most healthiest countries in the world. The common cold and other respiratory infections are the most prevalent forms of illness; arteriosclerosis is the most common cause of death. Water in most cities is good and safe for household purposes, and garbage and trash are collected in cities and towns.

All levels of government are concerned with public health, with the municipalities functioning largely as agents for the administration of state policies. State health departments are responsible for infant welfare, school medical and dental services (provided free of charge), treatment and eradication of infectious and contagious diseases and tuberculosis, industrial hygiene programs, maintenance of food and drug standards, public and mental hospitals, and the regulation of private hospitals. The Commonwealth government makes grants for medical research, coordinates state health programs, and maintains specialist medical research institutions and laboratories.

Public sector funding accounts for over two-thirds of health care expenditure in Australia; of this, some is allocated via the central government and some via local authorities. Since the introduction of Medicare (the national health insurance program) in 1984, the share of funding provided by the federal government has risen. Under the Medicare system, all Australians have access to free care at public hospitals. The plan also meets three-fourths of the bill for private hospital treatment, while patients pay the remainder (and can take out private health insurance to cover this, although comprehensive private medical insurance was abolished in the 1984 act).

Since 1950, certain drugs have been provided free of charge when prescribed by a medical practitioner. All patients other than pensioners must pay A\$2 for every prescription supplied under the scheme; the remainder is met by the government. For those not eligible for free public health care and who have basic medical insurance, the government pays 30% of the scheduled benefit fee for each medical service. Such insurance, including the government contribution, covers 85% of scheduled fees. The federal government provides grants to the states and aboriginal organizations for the development of special health services for aboriginals, who are often reluctant to use general community health services. As of 1992, aboriginals and Torres Strait Islanders had unacceptably low levels of health. They have access to the same health care system as any other Australian, but don't take full advantage of it. Unemployed persons, recent immigrants and refugees, and certain low-income persons are entitled to health care cards that entitle the bearer and dependents to free medical and hospital treatment.

Health services are efficient. Hospitals are generally modern and well equipped, but space often is at a premium. In 1992, there were more than 1,000 hospitals, excluding psychiatric hospitals and nursing homes. While most hospitals are public, there are approximately 350 private hospitals. In 1992, there were 6 hospital beds per 1,000 people. Most private hospitals tend to be fairly small, and there are a large number of private hospitals run by religious groups. Hospital facilities are concentrated in the states of New South Wales and Queensland, which together account for 55% of hospitals and 57% of hospital beds.

From 1988 to 1992, there were 2.29 doctors per 1,000 inhabitants, and in 1992, there were more than 30,000 physicians, more than 6,000 dentists, and about 140,000 professionally registered nurses. Competent general physicians and specialists are available in most cities, and the Royal Flying Doctor Service provides medical care and treatment to people living in remote areas.

In 1993, the death rate was 7.7 per 1,000 population, and between 1985 and 1990, mortality per 100,000 people was due to the following: (1) communicable diseases, maternal/perinatal causes—31; (2) noncommunicable diseases—424; and (3) injuries—48. Infant mortality was 7 per 1,000 live births. There were 265,000 births in 1992, with 67% of married women (ages 15-49) using contraception between 1980 and 1993. The 1993 birth rate was 15.1 per 1,000 inhabitants. The estimated life expectancy in 1992 was 77 years (80 years for females and 74 for males). Between 1990 and 1992, one-year-old children were immunized as follows: diphtheria, pertussis, and tetanus (95%); polio (72%); and measles (86%). In 1990, only 6 out of 100,000 people were diagnosed with tuberculosis.

[42]HOUSING

In 1992, there were 6,339,000 dwellings in Australia. A total of 132,000 new houses and apartments were completed the same year, down from 134,000 in 1991. Central heating, formerly available only in the most modern and expensive homes and apartments, is now generally available in the coldest areas of the country. Most apartments and houses are equipped with hot-water service, refrigeration, and indoor bath and toilet facilities.

[43]EDUCATION

Illiteracy is virtually nonexistent except among the aboriginals. Education is compulsory for children from the age of 6 to 15 (16 in Tasmania). Free education is provided in municipal kindergartens and in state primary, secondary, and technical schools. There are also state-regulated private schools. Correspondence courses and educational broadcasts are given for children living in the remote "outback" areas and unable to attend school because of distance or physical handicap. One-teacher schools and correspondence schools also satisfy these needs. Although each state controls its own system, education is fairly uniform throughout Australia. The government expenditure on education in the 1989–1990 financial year was 13.2% of the total government spending. Education is the joint responsibility of the federal government and each state government and territory. The federal government directly controls schools in the Northern Territory and in the Australian Capital Territory. Primary education generally begins at six years of age and lasts for six years. Secondary usually lasts for another five years. In Australia, more than 70% of students attend government schools. In 1992, nearly 2.2 million children attended government schools and 864,000 attended private institutions. As a major educational reform, in 1988 a unified national system was introduced. Although most aboriginal and Torres Strait Islander students use the regular school system, there are special programs to help them continue on to higher education.

Australia has 39 higher education institutions with 339,000 full-time students and 220,000 part-time and external students enrolled in 1992. There is a state university in each capital city and each provincial area; a national post-graduate research institute in Carberra and a university of technology in Sydney with a branch at Newcastle. There are also a number of privately funded higher-education institutions including theological and teacher training colleges. Adult education includes both vocational and non-vocational courses. Most universities offer education programs for interested persons.

[44]LIBRARIES AND MUSEUMS

The National Library of Australia traces its origins back to 1902, but it was not until 1960 that it was legislatively separated from the Commonwealth Parliamentary Library and made a distinct entity. The National Library is now housed in modern facilities in

Canberra and has over 4.7 million volumes. Three other libraries in Australia of comparable size are the library of the University of Sydney (over 4.3 million volumes), founded in 1852; the State Library of New South Wales (over 3 million), founded in 1826; and the State Library of Victoria (over 1.5 million), founded in 1854. The state capital cities have large noncirculating reference libraries, as well as municipal public circulating libraries. The university libraries in Brisbane, Adelaide, Canberra, and Melbourne all have sizable collections. Recent years have seen programs with increased cooperation between libraries, which has resulted in increased service.

A national art collection has been assembled in the Australian National Gallery at Canberra, which was opened to the public in October 1982. The National Museum of Australia (founded 1980) in Canberra, exhibits Australian history and social history. There are eight other major museums, two each in Sydney and Melbourne and one in each of the other state capitals. Some of the smaller cities also have museums. The National Gallery of Victoria in Melbourne has a fine collection of paintings and other art works, and the South Australian Museum in Adelaide has excellent collections relating to Australian entomology, zoology, and ethnology. Botanical gardens are found in every capital city.

[45]MEDIA

On 1 July 1975, responsibility for the nation's postal service was vested in the Australian Postal Commission, and for telecommunications in the Australian Telecommunications Commission; previously these functions had been administered by the Department of the Postmaster General. Local and long-distance telephone services are rated highly. As of 1991 there were 8,727,163 telephones, about 1 for every 1.9 Australians. Nearly 99% of the total service is automatic.

The government administers and supervises broadcasting through the Australian Broadcasting Commission, which operates a nationwide noncommercial radio and television service; the Australian Broadcasting Tribunal, which licenses and regulates commercial broadcasters; and the Special Broadcasting Service, which prepares and broadcasts multilingual radio and television programs. Federal government stations are financed from budget revenues, and the private commercial stations derive their income from business advertising. In 1992 there were 258 AM stations and 67 FM stations. Commercial and government-owned networks broadcast over 134 television stations. In 1991, an estimated 22,000,000 radios and 8,330,000 television sets were in use.

In 1991 there were 68 newspapers. In general, news is presented straightforwardly, and political criticism is fair and responsible. The *Australian,* one of only two national newspapers, was established in 1964 and is published in all state capitals. It is independent and had an estimated daily circulation in 1991 of 147,200. The other national daily, the *Australian Financial Review,* had a Monday–Friday average circulation of 77,500 in the same year.

Other leading dailies and their estimated 1991 circulation figures are listed in the following table:

	ORIENTATION	CIRCULATION
Herald-Sun (Melbourne, m)	Conservative	612,500
Daily Telegraph-Mirror (NSW, m)	NA	480,000
Morning Herald (Sydney, m)	Conservative	365,900

Major Sunday newspapers include the *Sun-Herald* (562,600) and the *Sunday Telegraph* (562,215) in Sydney, and the *Sunday Mail* in Brisbane (340,600).

The major news agency is the Australian Associated Press, founded in 1935; it has been associated with Reuters since 1946. Many international news services have bureaus in Sydney.

[46]ORGANIZATIONS

Chambers of commerce and chambers of manufacture are active throughout Australia, especially in the state capital cities; the Australian Chamber of Commerce (1091) coordinates their activities. The Australia Council (founded in 1943) encourages amateur activities in the arts and sponsors traveling exhibitions of ballet, music, and drama. There are associations or scholarly societies in the fields of architecture, art, international affairs, economics, political and social science, engineering, geography, history, law, literature, medicine, philosophy, and the natural sciences. Many publish scholarly journals. Theatrical, musical, and dance groups perform in the larger cities and towns. Skiing and tobogganing clubs function in the mountainous areas. Sydney, Melbourne, Hobart, and several other cities have large yacht clubs, and every state capital city has swimming and surfing clubs.

[47]TOURISM, TRAVEL, AND RECREATION

Among Australia's natural tourist attractions are the Great Barrier Reef, a mecca for scuba divers; the varied and unusual flora and fauna; and the sparsely habited outback regions, which in some areas may be toured by camel. Other attractions include Ballarat and other historic gold-rush towns near Melbourne; wineries, particularly in the Barossa Valley, 55 km (34 mi) northeast of Adelaide; Old Sydney Town, north of Sydney, a recreation of the Sydney Cove Settlement as it was in the early 19th century; and the arts festivals held in Perth every year and in Adelaide every two years, featuring foreign as well as Australian artists.

Among the sports that lure tourists are surfing, sailing, fishing, golf, tennis, cricket, and rugby. Melbourne is famous for its horse racing (Australia's most celebrated race is the Melbourne Cup) and for its 120,000-capacity cricket ground, reputedly the biggest in the world. In 1983, *Australia II* captured the America's Cup, emblematic of world yachting supremacy, in a series of races against *Liberty,* the US entrant, at Newport, R.I. In 1987, however, *Stars & Stripes* regained the cup for the US by defeating *Kookaburra III* in races held off the coast of southwestern Australia. In 1985, the first Australia Games were held in Melbourne. There were over 1,600 participants, including 804 foreign athletes from 30 countries.

In 1988, Australia had a year-long bicentennial celebration, commemorating the 200th anniversary of the founding of the colony of Port Jackson. The national government provided funds to state, territorial, and local governments for projects that would stress "living together," a theme reflecting Australia's diverse heritage and culture. Other countries participating in the celebration were Germany, France, Japan, the Netherlands, New Zealand, and the US. Among the events planned were the Australian Bicentennial Exhibition, a traveling show expected to visit about 50 cities and towns throughout the country; a race of tall ships from Hobart to Sydney, in which 30 foreign countries had been invited to participate; and the construction of a Bicentennial Science Centre in Canberra.

Except for nationals of New Zealand and certain other Commonwealth countries, visitors must have valid passports issued by an Australian or British consul or passport officer. They must also be in possession of sufficient funds to maintain themselves while in Australia and hold tickets for travel to a destination outside Australia. Health examinations are made at all Australian ports of entry. Immunizations are required only of tourists coming from an infected area.

In 1991, Australia attracted 2,370,400 foreign visitors, of whom 22% were Europeans, 20% came from New Zealand, and 14% were North American residents; tourist expenditures totaled us$4.18 billion. The government actively promotes tourism., and hopes to increase the number of foreign visitors to 5.8 million by the year 2000 and raise the number of hotel rooms above its 1991 level of 161,913.

48FAMOUS AUSTRALIANS

The most highly regarded contemporary Australian writer is Patrick White (b.1912), author of *The Eye of the Storm* and other works of fiction and winner of the 1973 Nobel Prize for literature. Other well-known novelists are Henry Handel Richardson (Henrietta Richardson Robertson, 1870–1946), Miles Franklin (1879–1954), Christina Stead (b.1902), and Thomas Michael Keneally (b.1935). Henry Lawson (1867–1922) was a leading short-story writer and creator of popular ballads. Germaine Greer (b.1939) is a writer on feminism. A prominent Australian-born publisher of newspapers and magazines, in the UK and the US as well as Australia, is Keith Rupert Murdoch (b.1931).

Three renowned scholars of Australian origin are Sir Gilbert Murray, O.M. (1866–1957), classicist and translator of ancient Greek plays; Samuel Alexander, O.M. (1859–1938), influential scientific philosopher; and Eric Partridge (1894–1979), authority on English slang. An outstanding bacteriologist was Sir Frank Macfarlane Burnet, O.M. (1899–1985), director of the Melbourne Hospital and cowinner of the 1960 Nobel Prize for medicine. Elizabeth Kenny (1886–1952) made important contributions to the care and treatment of infantile paralysis victims. Sir John Carew Eccles (b.1903) shared the 1963 Nobel Prize for medicine for his work on ionic mechanisms of the nerve cell membrane. John Warcup Cornforth (b.1917) shared the 1975 Nobel Prize for chemistry for his work on organic molecules.

Among Australia's most prominent film directors are Fred Schepisi (b.1939), Bruce Beresford (b.1940), George Miller (b.1943), Peter Weir (b.1944), and Gillian Armstrong (b.1950); film stars have included Australian-born Errol Flynn (1909–50), Paul Hogan (b.1940), and US-born Mel Gibson (b.1956). Leading Australian-born figures of the theater include the actors Dame Judith Anderson (b.1898) and Cyril Ritchard (1898–1977) and the ballet dancer, choreographer, and stage actor and director Sir Robert Murray Helpmann (1909–86). Musicians of Australian birth include the operatic singers Dame Nellie Melba (1861–1931), John Brownlee (1901–69), Marjorie Lawrence (1907–79), and Dame Joan Sutherland (b.1926) and the composers Percy Grainger (1882–1961), Arthur Benjamin (1893–1960), Peggy Glanville-Hicks (b.1912), and Peter Joshua Sculthorpe (b.1929). Popular singers include Helen Reddy (b.1941) and Olivia Newton-John (b.UK, 1948). Alfred Hill (1870–1960) is regarded as the founder of the art of musical composition in Australia. Albert Namatjira (1902–59), an Aranda aboriginal, achieved renown as a painter, as has Sir Sidney Robert Nolan (b.1917). The aviator Sir Charles Edward Kingsford-Smith (1897–1935) pioneered flights across the Pacific Ocean. A popular figure of folklore was the outlaw Ned (Edward) Kelly (1855?–80).

In recent decades, the tennis world was dominated by such Australian players as Frank Sedgman (b.1927), Lewis Hoad (b.1934), Kenneth Rosewall (b.1934), Rod (George) Laver (b.1938), John David Newcombe (b.1944), and Evonne Goolagong Cawley (b.1951). Sir Donald George Bradman (b.1908) was one of the outstanding cricket players of modern times. Record-breaking long-distance runners include John Landy (b.1930) and Herb Elliott (b.1938). Jon Konrads (b.1942) and his sister Ilsa (b.1944) have held many world swimming records, as did Dawn Fraser (b.1937), the first woman to swim 100 meters in less than a minute, and Murray Rose (b.1939).

The principal modern Australian statesman is Sir Robert Gordon Menzies (1894–1978), who served as prime minister from 1939 to 1941 and again from 1949 to 1966. Subsequent prime ministers have included Edward Gough Whitlam (b.1916), who held office from 1972 to 1975; John Malcolm Fraser (b.1930), who succeeded Whitlam late in 1975; and Robert James Lee Hawke (b.1929), who came to power in 1983.

49DEPENDENCIES

Since 1936, Australia has claimed all territory in Antarctica (other than Adélie Land) situated south of 60°S and between 45° and 160°E, an area of some 6.1 million sq km (2.4 million sq mi), or nearly 40% of the continent. Three scientific and exploratory bases are now in operation: Mawson (established February 1954), Davis (established January 1957), and Casey (established February 1969).

Ashmore and Cartier Islands

The uninhabited, reef-surrounded Ashmore Islands, three in number, and Cartier Island, situated in the Indian Ocean about 480 km (300 mi) north of Broome, Western Australia, have been under Australian authority since May 1934. In July 1938, they were annexed as part of the Northern Territory.

Christmas Island

Situated at 10°30′S and 105°40′E in the Indian Ocean, directly south of the western tip of Java, Christmas Island is 2,623 km (1,630 mi) northwest of Perth and has an area of about 135 sq km (52 sq mi). Until its annexation by the UK in 1888, following the discovery of phosphate rock, the island was uninhabited. The total population in 1992 was 1,685, of whom roughly two-thirds were Chinese and one-sixth Malay. The only industry was phosphate extraction. The governments of Australia and New Zealand decided to close the mine in December 1987. Christmas Island was transferred from the UK to Australia on 1 October 1958. Abbott's booby is an endangered species on the island.

Cocos (Keeling) Islands

The Territory of Cocos (Keeling) Islands is a group of coral atolls consisting of 27 islands with a total land area of 14 sq km (5 sq mi) in the Indian Ocean, at 12°5′S and 96°53′E, about 2,770 km (1,720 mi) northwest of Perth. The population of the two inhabited islands was 597 in 1992. A British possession since 1857, the islands were transferred to Australia in 1955 and are administered by the minister for territories. In 1978, the Australian government bought out the remaining interests (except for personal residences) of the Clunies-Ross heirs on the islands. The climate is pleasant, with moderate rainfall. Principal crops are copra, coconut oil, and coconuts. The airport is a link in a fortnightly service between Australia and South Africa.

Coral Sea Islands

The Coral Sea Islands were declared a territory of Australia in legislation enacted during 1969 and amended slightly in 1973. Spread over a wide ocean area between 10° and 23°30′S and 154° and 158°E, the tiny islands are administered by the minister for the Capital Territory and have no permanent inhabitants.

Territory of Heard and McDonald Islands

Heard Island, at 53°6′S and 72°31′E, about 480 km (300 mi) southeast of the Kerguelen Islands and about 4,000 km (2,500 mi) southwest of Perth, is about 910 sq km (350 sq mi) in size. Bleak and mountainous, it is dominated by a dormant volcano, Big Ben, about 2,740 m (8,990 ft) high. There was a station at Atlas Cove from 1947 to 1955, but the island is now uninhabited and is visited occasionally by scientists. Just north is Shag Island, and 42 km (26 mi) to the west are the small, rocky McDonald Islands. The largest island of the group was visited for the first time, it is believed, on 27 January 1971, by members of the Australian National Antarctic Expedition. The territory was transferred from the UK to Australia at the end of 1947.

Macquarie Island

Macquarie Island, at 54°30's and 158°40'E, is about 1,600 km (1,000 mi) southeast of Hobart. The rocky, glacial island, 34 km (21 mi) long and about 3 to 5 km (2 to 3 mi) wide, is uninhabited except for a base maintained at the northern end since February 1948. Macquarie Island has been a dependency of Tasmania since the early 19th century. At the most southerly point, the island has what is believed to be the biggest penguin rookery in the world. Two small island groupings are off Macquarie Island: Bishop and Clerk, and Judge and Clerk.

Norfolk Island

Norfolk Island, with an area of 36 sq km (14 sq mi), is situated at 29°3's and 167°57'E, 1,676 km (1,041 mi) east-northeast of Sydney. Discovered in 1774 by Capt. James Cook, it was the site of a British penal colony during 1788–1814 and 1825–55. In 1856, it was settled by descendants of the *Bounty* mutineers. As of 1993, the permanent population was 2,665. Transport is almost exclusively by motor vehicle. The soil is fertile and the climate conducive to the growing of fruits and bean seed. There is a small whaling industry, and tourism is important. As of 1987, endangered species on Norfolk Island included the gray-headed blackbird, Norfolk Island parakeet, and white-breasted silver-eye.

[50]BIBLIOGRAPHY

Albinski, Henry S. *The Australian-American Security Relationship.* St. Lucia: University of Queensland Press, 1982.

Altman, J. C., and J. P. Nieuwenhuysen. *The Economic Status of Australian Aborigines.* New York: Cambridge University Press, 1979.

Atkinson, Alan. *The Muddle-headed Republic.* New York: Oxford University Press, 1993.

Atlas of Australian Resources. Canberra: Department of National Development, 1953–date.

Australia in Pictures Publications Company. Minneapolis, Minn.: Lerner, 1993, 1990.

Baker, Sidney John. *The Australian Language.* Sydney: Angus & Robertson, 1945.

Bassett, Jan. *The Oxford Illustrated Dictionary of Australian History.* New York: Oxford University Press, 1993.

Bell, Philip. *Implicated: the United States in Australia Bell.* Melbourne; New York: Oxford University Press, 1993.

Bell, Stephen. *Australian Manufacturing and the State: the Politics of Industry Policy in the Post-war Era.* New York: Cambridge University Press, 1993.

Blainey, Geoffrey. *The Tyranny of Distance: How Distance Shaped Australia's History.* Melbourne: Macmillan, 1968.

Bleakley, J. W. *The Aborigines of Australia.* Brisbane: Jacaranda, 1959.

Bolton, Geoffrey (gen. ed.) *The Oxford History of Australia.* New York: Oxford University Press, 1986–90.

Bottomley, Gill, and Marie M. de Lepervanche (eds.). *Ethnicity, Class, and Gender in Australia.* Sydney: Allen & Unwin, 1984.

Brugger, Bill, and Dean Jaensch. *Australian Politics: Theory and Practice.* Sydney: Allen & Unwin, 1985.

Cameron, Roderick. *Australia.* New York: Columbia University Press, 1971.

Castles, Francis G. *Australia Compared: People, Policies and Politics.* North Sydney, Australia: Allen & Unwin Pty Ltd, 1991.

Clark, C. M. H. *A Short History of Australia.* Rev. ed. Sydney: Mead & Beckett, 1983.

Coleman, Peter. *Australian Civilisation.* Sydney: Angus & Robertson, 1962.

Cranston, Ross. *Law, Government and Public Policy.* New York: Oxford University Press, 1987.

David, Sir Tannatt William Edgewater. *Geology of the Commonwealth of Australia.* 3 vols. London: Arnold, 1950.

Docherty, J. C. *Historical Dictionary of Australia.* Metuchen, N.J.: Scarecrow Press, 1992.

Dyster, B. *Australia in the International Economy: in the Twentieth Century.* New York: Cambridge University Press, 1990.

Fitzpatrick, Brian Charles. *The Australian People, 1788–1945.* Melbourne: Melbourne University Press, 1946.

Gibson, Ross. *South of the West: Postcolonialism and the Narrative Construction of Australia.* Bloomington: Indiana University Press, 1992.

Gillett, Keith, and Frank McNeill. *The Great Barrier Reef and Adjacent Isles.* Sydney: Coral Press, 1960.

Goldberg, S.L. and F.B. Smith (eds.) *Australian Cultural History.* New York: Cambridge University Press, 1988.

Greenwood, Gordon (ed.). *Australia: A Social and Political History.* Sydney: Angus & Robertson, 1966.

Gunther, John. *John Gunther's Inside Australia.* New York: Harper & Row, 1972.

Hancick, Keith (ed.) *Australian Society.* New York: Cambridge University Press, 1989.

Hefford, Ron, *et al. An Introduction to the Australian Economy.* Brisbane: University of Queensland Press, 1980.

Howitt, Alfred William. *The Native Tribes of South-East Australia.* London: Macmillan, 1904.

Jaensch, Dean. *The Australian Party System.* Sydney: Allen & Unwin, 1983.

Jones, Michael A. *The Australian Welfare State: Growth, Crisis, and Change.* Rev. ed. Sydney: Allen & Unwin, 1979.

Kasper, Wolfgang, et al. *Australia at the Crossroads.* New York Law & Business, Inc., 1980.

Kemp, David Alistair. *Foundations for Australian Political Analysis: Politics and Authority.* New York: Oxford University Press, 1988, 1989.

Kramer, Leonie, *et al.* (eds.). *The Oxford History of Australian Literature.* Melbourne: Oxford University Press, 1981.

Kurian, George Thomas. *Facts on File National Profiles. Australia and New Zealand.* New York: Facts on File Publications, 1990.

Lane, P. H. *The Australian Federal System.* 2d ed. Sydney: Law Book Co. of Australasia, 1979.

London, H. I. *Non-White Immigration and the "White Australia" Policy.* New York: New York University Press, 1970.

Maddock, Rodney and Ian W. McLean (eds.) *The Australian Economy in the Long Run.* New York: Cambridge University Press, 1987.

Massola, Aldo. *The Aborigines of Southeastern Australia.* New York: Scribner, 1974.

McGregor, C. *The Australian People.* Sydney: Hodder & Stoughton, 1980.

Official Year Book of the Commonwealth of Australia. Canberra: Commonwealth Government Printer, 1908–to date.

Osborne, Charles (ed.). *Australia, New Zealand and the South Pacific: A Handbook.* New York: Praeger, 1970.

Parliamentary Handbook and Record of Elections. Canberra: Commonwealth Government Printer, 1915–to date.

Robinson, K. W. *Australia, New Zealand and the Southwest Pacific.* London: University of London Press, 1960.

Sawer, Geoffrey. *Australian Government To-day.* Rev. ed. Melbourne: Melbourne University Press, 1978.

Shaw, John (ed.) *The Concise encyclopedia of Australia, Rev.* 2nd ed. Queensland: D. Bateman, 1989.

Sherington, Geoffrey. *Australia's Immigrants.* London: Allen & Unwin, 1981.

Solomon, D. H. *Australia's Government and Parliament.* 6th ed. Melbourne: Nelson, 1984.

Spencer, Sir Baldwin, and Francis James Gillen. *The Arunta: A Study of a Stone Age People.* London: Macmillan, 1927.

Spencer, Sir Baldwin. *Wanderings in Wild Australia.* London: Macmillan, 1928.

Taylor, Thomas Griffith. *Australia: A Study of Warm Environments and Their Effect on British Settlement.* London: Methuen, 1955.

The Australian Environment. Melbourne: Melbourne University Press, 1960.

Wannan, Bill. *The Australian: Yarns, Ballads, Legends and Traditions of the Australian People.* Melbourne: Australasian Book Society, 1954.

Ward, R. B. *The Australian Legend.* 2d ed. Melbourne: Oxford University Press, 1977.

Ward, R. B. *Concise History of Australia Drawings.* St Lucia, Qld.: University of Queensland Press, 1992.

Whitaker, Donald P. *Area Handbook for Australia.* Washington, D.C.: US Govt. Print. Off., 1974.

Who's Who in Australia. Melbourne: Colorgravure Publications, 1906–to date.

Wynes, William Anstey. *Legislative, Executive and Judicial Powers in Australia.* Sydney: Law Book Co. of Australasia, 1956.

AZERBAIJAN

Azerbaijani Republic
Azarbaijchan Respublikasy

CAPITAL: Baku.

FLAG: Three equal horizontal bands of blue (top), red, and green; a crescent and eight-pointed star in white are centered in the red band.

ANTHEM: *Azerbaijan National Anthem,* composed by Uzeyir Hajibayov.

MONETARY UNIT: Manat, introduced in 1992, remains tied to the Russian ruble; exchange rates are widely fluctuating as of 1994.

WEIGHTS AND MEASURES: The metric system is in force.

HOLIDAYS: Day of Sorrow (commemorating 1990 Soviet invasion of Baku), 20 January; Novrus (Holiday of Spring), 1 March; Independence Day (1918), 28 May; Day of Solidarity of Azerbaijanis, 31 December.

TIME: 4 PM = noon GMT.

¹LOCATION, SIZE, AND EXTENT

Azerbaijan is located in southeastern Europe, between Armenia and the Caspian Sea. Comparatively, Azerbaijan is slightly larger than the state of Maine with a total area of 86,600 sq km (33,436 sq mi). This area includes the Nakhichevan Autonomous Republic and the Nagorno-Karabakh Autonomous Oblast. Azerbaijan shares boundaries with Russia on the N, the Caspian Sea on the E, Iran on the S, Armenia on the W, and Georgia on the NW. Azerbaijan's boundary length totals 2,013 km (1,251 mi). Azerbaijan's capital city, Baku, is located on the Apsheron Peninsula that juts into the Caspian Sea.

²TOPOGRAPHY

The topography of Azerbaijan features the large, flat Kura-Aras Lowland (much of it below sea level) with the Great Caucasus Mountains to the north. The Karabakh Upland lies in the west. Eighteen percent of Azerbaijan's land is arable with approximately 16% under irrigation.

³CLIMATE

The country's climate is subtropical in the eastern and central parts. In the mountains regions the climate is alpine-like. The southeastern section of the country has a humid subtropical climate. The mean temperature in the capital, Baku, in July is 27.2°C (81°F). In January the mean temperature is 1.1°C (34°F). Rainfall varies according to the nine climate zones in the country.

⁴FLORA AND FAUNA

The country's flora and fauna is rich and varied. There are 16 nature reserves and more than 28 forest reserves and hunting farms.

⁵ENVIRONMENT

Azerbaijan's current environmental problems are in part the result of its association with the economic priorities and practices of the former Soviet Union. General mismanagement of the country's resources has resulted in a serious threat to several areas of the environment. UN agencies report severe air and water pollution in Azerbaijan. The combination of industrial, agricultural, and oil-drilling pollution has created an environmental crisis in the Caspian Sea. These sources of pollution have contaminated 100% of the coastal waters in some areas and 45.3% of Azerbaijan's rivers. The pollution of the land through the indiscriminate use of agricultural chemicals such as the pesticide DDT is also a serious problem. Azerbaijan's war with Armenia has hampered the government's ability to improve the situation. Due to the severity of pollution on all levels, the country's wildlife and vegetation are also seriously affected. As of 1994, 14 species of mammals, 36 species of birds, 5 species of fish, 13 reptiles, and 40 species of insects are threatened with extinction.

⁶POPULATION

The population of Azerbaijan was 7,037,867 in 1989. It was estimated at 7,450,787 in mid-1992. A population of 7,987,000 was projected for 2000, based on a crude birth rate of 17.4 per 1,000 population, a crude death rate of 5.9, and a natural increase of 11.5 for 1995–2000.

The population density was estimated at 86 per sq km (223 per sq km) in 1992. Baku, the capital, had an estimated population of 1,149,000 at the beginning of 1990. Gyanja (formerly Kirovabad) had a population of about 287,000 people, and Sumgait about 235,000.

⁷MIGRATION

According to the government, in early 1994 more than a million people in Azerbaijan were refugees uprooted by the war with Armenia.

⁸ETHNIC GROUPS

In 1989, 83% of the population consisted of Azerbaijanis, about 5.6% were Russians, and another 5.6%, Armenians. Lezghins, a Caucasian people, came to 2.4%.

⁹LANGUAGES

Azerbaijani (or Azari) is a language related to Turkish and is also spoken in northwestern Iran. It is traditionally written in Arabic script. In 1939, the Soviets introduced a Cyrillic alphabet, with eight special characters.

¹⁰RELIGIONS

For most of the 20th century, from 1920 to 1991, the Azerbaijan Soviet Socialist Republic observed the restrictions in religious belief and practice common throughout the former Soviet Union. Statistics available after the declaration of independence of 30 August 1991 87% of the population was Moslem, 70% of whom are Shi'is and the remainder Sunnis. Russian (5.6%) and Armenian (5.6%), and Jewish religion are present as well, with a population of 21,000 Jews identified in 1990.

¹¹TRANSPORTATION

Railroads in Azerbaijan extend some 1,200 km (750), with Baku as the hub. Suburban trains carry 150,000 passengers each day. In 1990, the highway system totaled 36,700 km (22,800 mi), of which 31,800 km (19,800 mi) were hard-surfaced. Ships from the Caspian fleet have called at some 125 ports in over 30 countries. There are flights from Baku's Bina Airport to more than 70 cities of the former Soviet Union.

¹²HISTORY

The territory of present-day Azerbaijan has been continuously inhabited since the Paleolithic era. The first evidence of tribal alliances date to the first millenium BC, when such peoples as the Mannaians, the Medes, the Cadusiis, the Albanoi, and the Caspians appeared. In the 7th century BC, the state of Media appeared in what now is southern Azerbaijan, growing to cover large portions of the Near East. The Medians were displaced by the Persian dynasty of Achaemenids, who in turn were defeated by Alexander the Great. In the 4th century BC, another state arose which Greek sources called Atropatena, or "Land of the Fire Keepers"; it is this name, reflecting the predominance of Zoroastrianism, which give the present state its name. Around the beginning of the common era Atropatena was succeeded by a state called Albania, which the Romans attempted to conquer.

In the 3rd and 4th centuries AD, Azerbaijan existed with fluid boundaries between the Sassanid state in Persia and the Romans, whose battles inflicted great damage, leaving Azerbaijan open to raids by Turkic nomadic tribes from the north, including Khazars and Huns. Outside influence reappeared in the 7th and 8th centuries, when Arabs conquered much of Transcaucasia. As their influence receded, a number of small local states were established, the best known of which was the Shirvanshahs.

In the 11th century Azerbaijan was invaded by Oguz Turks, of the Seljuk dynasty. By the 13th century the gradual displacement of pre-Turkic local languages was complete, although many traces of non-Turkic predecessors remain in the Azerbaijani language. Persian, however, remained the language of art, science, and education.

In the 1230s Azerbaijan was conquered by Genghiz Khan, whose power remained in the Il-Khanid state, which at the end of the 14th century was displaced by the armies of Tamerlaine. In the 16th century, the Safawid state emerged, coming to control most of the land between the Syr Darya and the Euphrates, and re-establishing agriculture and commerce destroyed under the Mongols. In the 17th century, the Safawids became Persianized, which made present-day Azerbaijan decline in importance.

In the 18th century Azerbaijan became the intersection of the Turkish, Persian, and Russian empires, as well as the focus of British and French attempts to block Russian expansion. The northern part of the territory was incorporated into Russia in the first third of the 19th century, but the area did not become important until the 1880s, when the area's abundant oil gained commercial importance. The southern portion of what was originally Azerbaijan has remained in Iran, save for the period 1941–46, when it was occupied by Soviet troops.

When the 1917 revolution came, Turkey attempted to reclaim the territory, and for a time British forces controlled the capital, Baku, supporting the local Musavat, or nationalist, government. That government was overthrown by the Bolsheviks in 1920, and Azerbaijan was declared a Soviet state. In 1922 it was made part of the Transcaucasian Federated Socialist Republic, along with Georgia and Armenia. That was dissolved in 1936, when the three states were each made into separate Soviet Socialist Republics.

In 1988, attempts by ethnic Armenians living in Azerbaijan's Karabakh district to be incorporated into the Armenian republic led to a civil war which continued into 1994. This predominantly Armenian area had been unsuccesfully claimed by the Armenians in the 1920s, at the time of the creation of Soviet Azerbaijan. Inability to solve the Nagorno-Karabakh conflict was one of the problems which ultimately brought down Mikhail Gorbachev and broke apart the USSR. In January 1990, Soviet armed forces shelled Baku, which set off demonstrations which forced Moscow to replace Vezirov with Mutalibov as republic head. The legislature elected Mutalibov president in May 1990. Independence was declared on 30 August 1991, and Mutalibov was reaffirmed as president in a popular, uncontested election in September 1991.

In December 1991, the Armenians of Nagorno-Karabakh voted to secede from Azerbaijan, and with the help of irregulars from the neighboring republic, set about physically joining the two territories. Mutalibov was held responsible for not having prevented a massacre of Azeris in late February 1992, and was forced to resign. His replacement, Parliament Chairman Mamedov, was also forced to resign in May 1992, when Armenian irregulars made large gains against the Azeri army. Mutalibov was then reinstated, but had to flee two days later, when insurrectionists called the Azeri Popular Front seized power. A former dissident and strong Azeri nationalist, Elchibey, was elected president in June 1992.

The nationalist government attempted to sever contacts with Russia, refusing to participate as a member of the Commonwealth of Independent States and trying to align more with Turkey. However, the war with Armenia continued to deteriorate, and Azerbaijan's growing independence in exploiting its oil wealth was not popular in Russia. In 1993, Heydar Aliev, who had been leader of the republic from 1971–85 (under Leonid Brezhnev) but then was disgraced and dismissed by Mikhail Gorbachev, began to press for Elchibey's dismissal. Aliyev was elected chairman of the parliament in June. At about this time, army commander Guseinov turned on Elchibey, and began to lead his troops toward the capital. Another commander, Gumbatov, who is an ethnic Talysh, became head of a secessionist Talysh-Mungan republic in the south. This pressure on Elchibey finally forced him to flee, leaving the way open for Aliev to take control of the government. In August 1993, Aliev was formally elected president.

¹³GOVERNMENT

The 450-member Soviet-era Supreme Soviet was put in abeyance in mid-1992, following massive popular demonstrations. Its was replaced by a 50-member National Council which had been created the previous November as a continuously sitting "small parliament". When Aliev returned as president, the parliament was reconvened, now called the Majlis. The nation has been operating on the constitution of 1978, as modified by Presidential and parliamentary decree. Efforts had begun under the Elchibey government to produce a new Constitution, but that effort appears now to be stalled. Effective governmental authority appears to reside in the president and in the ministers whom he appoints, as enforced by the state security apparatus. Aliev's powers were strengthened in November 1993 by the Majlis's adoption of a War Powers Act. However, Elchibey has set up residence in the Nakichevan Autonomous region, which is physically discontinous with the rest of Azerbaijan, and continues to claim to be the legitimate president, as does Mutalipov, who now lives in Moscow.

¹⁴POLITICAL PARTIES

In March 1994, there were 28 political parties registered in Azerbaijan. The most important is probably the New Azerbaijan Party, which Aliev created in his return to power. The party that brought Elchibey to power was the Azerbaijan Popular Front, which became an opposition party with the ascendancy of Aliev. Two other opposition parties are the Milli Istiglal, or National Independence Party (Mamedov, chair), founded in 1992, and the Musavat (Kambarov, former Speaker of Parliament, chair), which sees itself as the descendant of the party of the same name which was founded in 1911, and which headed Azerbaijan's short-lived independent government of 1918–20. In March 1994, the APF, Musavat, and three other opposition parties created the Democratic Congress Bloc. There are also separatist parties or groups advocating independence for three ethnic groups: the Armenians in Nagorno-Karabakh, the Talysh in the south, and the Lezghins in the north.

¹⁵LOCAL GOVERNMENT

Soviet-era Azerbaijan was subdivided administratively into one autonomous republic, Nakhichevan, a physically discontinuous area which had its own parliament of 110 members; an autonomous oblast, Nagorno-Karabakh; six cities which were administratively responsible directly to the central government; and 51 raions, or regions. Although the major administrative divisions appear to have been retained since independence, their functions have been modified by the continued political instability. Nagorno-Karabakh has claimed an independent existence since December 1991, and many of the regions around it have been captured by Armenian irregulars. Nakhichevan seems to have become at least in part home to Elchibey's alternative government, while other areas of the nation seem to be under the control of Guseinov.

¹⁶JUDICIAL SYSTEM

The old Soviet system continues to be utilized. The court system includes district courts and municipal courts of first instance and a Supreme Court which performs the function of appellate review. Criminal defendants have the right to an attorney and to appointed counsel, the right to be present at trial, to confront witnesses, and to a public trial.

Civil unrest and fighting have led to human rights abuses, which remain largely unchecked. The judiciary is not independent in practice. In July 1993, the government fired the Supreme Court chief justice because of alleged political loyalties to the opposition.

¹⁷ARMED FORCES

A successor state from the former Soviet Union, Azerbaijan is still garrisoned by 62,000 Russian troops, but has formed its own National Defense Army of 5,000, with perhaps 30,000 serving in paramilitary units. These forces face 30,000–50,000 rebels in Nagorno–Karabakh. Azerbaijan has a conscription law. Its defense expenditures may be the equivalent of $1.7 billion or more than 10% of GDP.

¹⁸INTERNATIONAL COOPERATION

Azerbaijan was admitted to the UN on 2 March 1992. The country is also a member of the Black Sea Cooperation Group, CSCE, EBRD, Economic Cooperation Organization (Turkey, Iran, Pakistan, Russian Federation, Central Asian States, and Afghanistan), IMF, Organization of the Islamic States, and UNCTAD. The country is also a member of the CIS. Several nations have recog-

LOCATION: 40°30′N; 47°0′E **BOUNDARY LENGTHS:** Total boundary lengths, 2,013 km (1,251 mi); Armenia (west), 566 km (352 mi); Armenia (south), 221 km (137 mi); Georgia, 322 km (200 mi); Iran (south), 432 km (268 mi); Iran (southeast), 179 km (111 mi).

nized Azerbaijan's independence from the former Soviet Union and have established diplomatic ties. Foreign relations with Azerbaijan are dictated by the country's continued sovereignty over Nagorno-Karabakh, which would like to become part of Armenia. The US recognized Azerbaijan's sovereignty on 25 December 1991, but has not established diplomatic relations because of the situation with Nagorno-Karabakh.

¹⁹ECONOMY

Azerbaijan is one of the oldest oil-producing regions of the world. As a constituent republic of the USSR it was a leading supplier to the rest of the Union until the focus of Soviet oil development efforts shifted to the Ural mountains and western Siberia during the 1970s and 1980s. Remaining oil reserves are estimated to be about 1 billion tons, and gas reserves about 6 trillion cu ft. In addition, the country is endowed with ample deposits of iron, aluminum, zinc, copper, arsenic, molybdenum, marble, and fire clay. Azerbaijan boasts a diversified industrial sector that accounted for approximately 37% of NMP and 16% of employment (excluding construction). Agriculture, which employed about 33% of the labor force and accounted for 41% of NMP (including forestry), also rests on a relatively diversified base, producing cotton, tobacco, grapes, and a variety of foodstuffs. The transport sector is well developed, integrating the country's various regions and facilitating both domestic and external trade. Estimated at R2,056 million in 1990, per capita GDP is somewhat lower than average for the former USSR republics although its social indicators compare favorably with those of middle-income countries.

Already experiencing a decline in the size of its NMP by 1989, like other post-Soviet republics, the Azeri economy has been severely affected by the disruption of traditional trading arrangements within the former USSR, a steep drop in consumer buying power, and the decline in military-related industrial activity; the instability caused by conflicts over the provinces of Nagorno-Karabakh and Nakhichevan has also exacerbated these economic difficulties. By 1993, the country's estimated GDP was only 60% that of 1988 in real terms.

Following price liberalization in 1992, inflation reached 1,500% in 1992; real wages declined by 35% during the year. In June 1991, the Law on the Fundamentals of Economic Independence was passed by the government, initiating the process of economic restructuring toward a market economy. Despite declining economic activity since independence, in comparison with many other post-Soviet republics, Azerbaijan has been more successful at controlling its fiscal deficit and at expanding trade with countries beyond the former Soviet Union. Along with the country's relatively well-educated labor force, these indicators suggest a good potential for economic recovery should political stability be quickly established. To stabilize a growing currency shortage, Azerbaijan introduced its own currency, the manat, in August 1992. Both the manat and the ruble currently exist as legal tender in the economy, although an official switch to the sole use of the former is expected.

20INCOME
In 1992, Azerbijan's GNP was $6,290 million at current prices, or $870 per capita. For the period 1985–92 the average inflation rate was 38.8%. In 1992, the GDP was $5,432 million in current US dollars.

21LABOR
There are nearly 2.8 million people in the Azerbaijani labor force. In 1991, agriculture accounted for 34% of employment; industry, 16%; education and culture, 12%; and other sectors, 38%.

As of 1992, labor unions still operated under the Soviet system. Strikes are legally permitted and increasing in frequency. Unions are free to form federations and participate in international bodies. Collective bargaining is at a rudimentary level; wages are still set by government ministries for organizations within the budget.

There is a nationwide minimum wage, which was raised several times in 1992. Although the minimum wage alone does not provide a decent standard of living for a worker and family, the reliance on outside income sources and the structure of extended families generally ensure a decent living. The legal workweek is 41 hours.

22AGRICULTURE
Some 17.4% of Azerbaijan's area was cultivated or considered arable preceding the breakup of the USSR. There are currently 59 agricultural regions in 10 geographic zones; the principal crops are grapes, cotton, and tobacco.

During the Soviet period, some 1,200 state and cooperative farms existed. Since independence, former state-owned farms have become more productive, and private fruit and vegetable farming is increasing. Of the total crop production of 1991,

grapes accounted for 23%; cotton, 19%; tobacco, 13%; fruits and vegetables, 30%; grains, 7%; and other crops, 8%.

More than 1.3 million tons of grapes are produced annually, which provides for an expanding wine-producing industry; Azerbaijani wines have frequently won awards at international exhibitions.

23ANIMAL HUSBANDRY
Azerbaijan has some 2.2 million ha (5.4 million acres) of permanent pasture. The livestock population in 1992 included 27,000,000 chickens, 5,000,000 sheep, 1,800,000 cattle, 212,000 goats, 100,000 pigs, and 35,000 horses. Meat production in 1992 amounted to 145,000 tons, almost three-fourths of which was beef and mutton. In 1992, about 800,000 tons of cow's milk, 49,400 tons of eggs, 14,400 tons of greasy wool, and 2,500 tons of butter were produced.

24FISHING
The Caspian Sea is Azerbaijan's principal fishing resource. Commercial fishing centers on caviar and sturgeon.

25FORESTRY
About 11% of the land area consists of forests and woodlands. Soviet-era policies gave priority to high production and rapid growth at the expense of the environment. The State Committee for Ecology and Use of Natural Resources has recently introduced new regulations to protect forest resources.

26MINING
Besides its mineral fuel reserves of petroluem and natural gas along the Caspian Sea, Azerbaijan also has iron ore reserves near the disputed Nagorno–Karabakh region, as well as lead, zinc, and copper–molybdenum deposits in the Nakhichivan area. Other mineral commodities in Azerbaijan include alunite and bromine–iodine.

27ENERGY AND POWER
At the turn of this century, Azerbaijan accounted for half of the world's oil production. Oil wells have been operating in Baku since the 1840s. Almost all production now comes from offshore in the Caspian Sea. Azerbaijan was one of only four former Soviet republics (along with Russian, Kazakhstan and Turkmenistan) to be self-sufficient in petroleum. Proven oil reserves at the end of 1992 totaled 1.3 billion barrels (200 million tons), or about 0.1% of the world's reserves. Production in 1992 totaled 220,000 barrels per day; less than one-quarter comes from onshore fields.

The State Oil Company of Azerbaijan (SOCAR) has planned for joint development of the offshore fields (which are now largely untapped) and has entered into several agreements to build oil pipelines. For instance, a project with the Caspian Pipeline Consortium would carry oil from the Caspian Sea to the Russian Black Sea port of Novorossiysk. Another deal with Turkey will involve the construction of a pipeline to carry crude oil via Iran (bypassing Armenia) and connecting with the Iraq-Turkey pipeline which runs to the Mediterranean. Ukraine and Iran also are interested in running a natural gas pipeline through Azerbaijan en route to Eastern Europe.

Natural gas production has become more important in recent years, especially in Baku, where some of the oil wells have been exhausted. Estimated reserves amount to 11 trillion cu ft (310 billion cu m). Production of natural gas in 1992 totaled 280 billion cu ft (7.8 billion cu m).

Electricity production in 1992 totaled 19.8 billion kwh. The main power plants (both thermal) were near Ali-Bayramly (1100 Mw) and Mingechaur (2100 Mw). Consumption of electricity in 1992 was 19.6 billion kwh.

Petroleum and natural gas resources are the basis for an extensive system of refineries which produce gasoline, herbicides, fertilizers, kerosene, synthetic rubber, and plastics.

28INDUSTRY

The oil and gas industry has traditionally been pivotal to the wider industrial sector in Azerbaijan; in 1991 fuel production accounted for 12% of total industrial output. Oil refining is concentrated in the Aznefteyag and New Baku Oil refineries, both located on the outskirts of Baku, with a total capacity of 300,000 barrels per day or 20 million tons per year. Petroleum production is now controlled by the state oil company, Azerinfeft, and its two subsidiaries, Azneft and Kasmorenftgaz. Specific outputs from the country's refineries include fuel oil, diesel oil, gasoline, kerosene, and other products. Failure to replace worn and outdated technology as well as falling demand from the rest of the former USSR has resulted in a steady decline in the production of oil products since the early 1980s; total output averaged 291,000 barrels per day in 1991, as compared with 416,000 barrels per day in 1986. Output of diesel fuel was only 3,211 thousand tons in 1992, as compared with a high of 5,159 thousand in 1987; production of gasoline dropped from 2,121 thousand tons in 1987 to 1,035 thousand tons in 1992.

In line with the historic importance of the oil sector for the Azeri economy, the fabrication of equipment related to petroleum production is one of the country's major industries, comprising 4% of total manufacturing output. As a source of 65% of the former Soviet Union's oilfield equipment, it also holds great importance for other oil-producing post-Soviet republics who will continue to depend on Azerbaijan as a source of affordable equipment for some time to come. Azerbaijan's petroleum equipment manufacturing industry comprises the second largest concentration of such industries in the world (behind that of the US). Like most other of the country's economic sectors, however, the industry is plagued by plant obsolescence; a significant portion of its own equipment needs is currently being supplied by Turkey in exchange for crude oil on a barter basis. In 1992, the production of oil drilling, geological research, and related equipment yielded a value of R6,900 million rubles (current prices), down from R8,486 million in 1990.

Other important industrial sectors in the Azeri economy include agro-based industry, light industry, finished metal goods, machine tools, chemicals and petrochemicals, and some electronics. As with fuel and oilfield equipment production, however, output in almost all of these sectors declined or stagnated in the early 1990s. The production of milk products declined from 203,000 tons in 1990 to 81,000 in 1992; grape wine production dropped from 9,362 thousand bottles to 5,416 thousand; cotton fiber production from 167,000 tons in 1990 to 148,000 tons in 1992. In the light industry sector, fabric yields (cotton, wool, and silk) declined from 146 million m in 1990 to 105 million cu m in 1992. The manufacture of steel tubes shrank from 493,000 tons in 1990 to about 260,000 tons in 1992, while the production of alumina remained the same at about 240,000 tons. Only 95,000 AC electric engines were produced in 1992, as compared with 266,000 in 1990; similarly, power transformer production dropped from 1,996 thousand to 657 thousand kilowatt hour equivalency. The assembly of home air conditioners—fostered during the Soviet regime—yielded only 268,000 units in 1992, down from 309,000 in 1990. In the chemicals sector, mineral fertilizer output sank to 81,000 tons from 212,000 between 1990 and 1992; sulfureous acid production to 269,000 tons from 603,000 tons; and caustic soda to 92,000 tons from 160,000.

In aggregate terms, the real value of total industrial production in Azerbaijan dropped 31% in 1992, following already steep declines of 17% in 1990 and 8% in 1991. In the course of this decline, the structure of the industrial sector has changed as well, with the fuel industry as well as metal processing and machinery replacing agro-based industry and light industry as the main sources of total industrial output in value terms (despite declining yields in volume terms in all sectors). This shift has resulted mainly from the higher prices now garnered for upstream products like fuel and processed metals, which are characterized by brighter prospects on the international market than most light and processed food industry goods in wake of price liberalization.

29SCIENCE AND TECHNOLOGY

The Azerbaijan Academy of Sciences has departments of mathematical, chemical, earth, and biological sciences with 34 institutes.

Azerbaijan also has 20 institutes conducting research in agriculture, energy, engineering, and medicine. The Azerbaijan Engineering and Technical University, founded in 1950, has 13,242 students. Baku State University, founded in 1919, has faculties of mathematics, physics, chemistry, biology, geology, and geography. Azerbaijan also has five higher institutes offering courses in agriculture, medicine, petroleum engineering, and engineering.

30DOMESTIC TRADE

With privatization still in a preliminary phase in Azerbaijan, legal domestic retail trade continues to take place largely through state-owned outlets. However, the underground economy is estimated to be growing rapidly in wake of the country's political and economic instability, claiming a sizeable share of domestic trade. Prices were liberalized for 80% of consumer goods in 1992, with controls remaining on a variety of staples including oil and gas.

31FOREIGN TRADE

Like other post-Soviet economies, Azerbaijan is highly trade-dependent; however, it is endowed with a more diversified export structure than many other former USSR countries, especially in neighboring Central Asia. While the centrally planned state ordering system is steadily losing its place as the basis for inter-republic trade in the former Soviet Union, the Azeri Ministry of Foreign Economic Relations still controls the export of all products considered to be of strategic importance to the national economy. Total exports in 1992 amounted to R207,756 million in current domestic prices, as compared with R12,199 million in 1991; the value of imports jumped from R11,010 million in 1991 to R131,580 million in 1992. Athough partly due to inconsistencies in the collection and reporting of trade data, the steep rise in the nominal value of total trade between 1991 and 1992 also resulted from the effect of higher prices following price decontrol. The sudden rise in the country's trade surplus reflected in part the improved terms of trade resulting from rising oil prices.

Despite inconsistencies in recent statistical data, existing indicators do suggest a significant expansion in exports to non-former Soviet Union countries, from an estimated $375 million in 1990 to about $754 million in 1992. The real value of trade with the post-Soviet countries, by contrast, is estimated to have contracted sharply due to the general destabilization of trading arrangements within the former USSR. Exports dropped from about R6,105 million in 1990 to about R2,583 million in 1992 (in constant 1990 rubles) while imports declined from R4,247 million in 1990 to R2,105 million in 1992. Processed foods, petroleum, and machinery and metal works together accounted for about 85% of inter-republic exports in 1992 (in current domestic prices); inter-republic imports were dominated by ferrous metallurgy, machinery and processed metals, and chemicals and petroleum, which accounted for 67% of the total. Major inter-republic trading partners are Russia, which absorbed 48% of total inter-republic exports and supplied 41% of imports in 1992; Ukraine, which accounted for 19% of all inter-republic exports and 35% of imports; as well as Turkmenistan, Kazakhstan, and Georgia, which each claimed about 5–8% of exports and 3–7% of imports. Trade with other post-Soviet countries is largely based on a series of bilateral trade agreements.

Major trading partners beyond the former Soviet Union in 1992 included Iran (30% of exports and 17% of imports); Turkey (17% of exports and 26% of imports); and the UK (19% of total extra-republic exports and 13% of imports). Seventy-six percent of extra-republic exports in 1992 were made up of oil and petroleum. Leading imports from beyond the former USSR were grains, flour, other foodstuffs, and machinery, the combined value of which equaled about 70% of total extra-republic imports.

32BALANCE OF PAYMENTS

The war in and around Nagorno–Karabakh has facilitated Azerbaijan's trade deterioration, which is further exacerbated by the collapse of the local currency. Reviving ruble-related trade links with Russia was a key reason for Azerbaijan's entry into the Commonwealth of Independent States in September 1992.

33BANKING AND SECURITIES

The National Bank of Azerbaijan is the central bank of Azerbaijan. The central bank is charged with regulating the money supply, circulating currency, and regulating the commercial banks of the country. The dual currency units are the manat and the ruble, although the government is shifting official currency to the manat. Commercial banks in Azerbaijan include the Agricultural Bank (1988), with 68 branches; the Bank for Industry and Construction (1899); and the International Bank (1992). There is a state-owned national bank in Azerbaijan that has 1,400 branches and offices.

34INSURANCE

No recent information is available.

35PUBLIC FINANCE

The external debt was estimated at $1.3 billion in 1991.

36TAXATION

Personal income is taxed at rates ranging from 12–55%, and the corporate tax rate varies from 10–70%. Also levied are a 42% employer payroll tax, a 20% value-added tax, and a 10–90% excise tax.

37CUSTOMS AND DUTIES

Tariffs ranging from 30–1,300% are imposed on foreign imports. In 1992, Azerbaijan signed trade agreements with all the republics of the former USSR except Armenia and Russia. Azerbaijan is a member of the Economic Cooperation Organization, whose foreign ministers agreed in February 1992 to cut tariffs on listed goods by 10%.

38FOREIGN INVESTMENT

Although still insignificant at present, in the coming decade foreign investment is expected to play a major role in financing the development of much of Azerbaijan's industrial sector, especially the oil and gas-related industries. However, while the new Law on Foreign Investment provides many basic guarantees to foreign investors, it remains ambiguous on a number of points including questions of nondiscriminatory treatment, the repatriation of profits, guarantees against expropriation, and dispute settlement. Only about 100 joint venture projects were registered by mid-1992; these are dominated by Turkish firms and involve primarily

trade and textiles. In the oil sector, preliminary agreements have been signed with US, Scottish, British, and other foreign companies for the exploration and development of several major oil fields in the Caspian Sea. In 1992, Azerbaijan joined a consortium with Oman, Kazakhstan, and Russia aimed at constructing a pipeline through either Armenia, Iran and Turkey, or Georgia. Thus far, however, little action has been taken on these agreements, due to heightened political tensions. Should existing oil-related agreements be realized pending the achievement of greater political stability, it is expected that total foreign investment inflows will equal $250 to $300 million in 1994, increasing to an annual average of $1.2 billion in 1996 and 1997.

39ECONOMIC DEVELOPMENT

Rapid development of the Azeri economy in the former USSR was based on the expansion of both its industrial sector, led by oil-related industries, and its agricultural sector, led by grape, tobacco, and cotton production. With grape and wine production weakened by the effects of Gorbachev's anti-alcoholism campaign in the 1980s, and much of the country's industrial sector afflicted by technological obsolescence, overall economic growth in the republic had already begun to decline by 1989, when NMP dropped 6%. Key strategies of the Azeri government to bring about economic revitalization have included both an economic restructuring program as well as efforts to expand its economic ties to countries beyond the former Soviet Union. To the latter end, Azerbaijan joined the Economic Cooperation Organization set up by Iran, Pakistan, and Turkey to promote trade among Muslim countries. It was also the first of the former Soviet republics to become a member of the Islamic Development Bank, which provides potential access to financing for programs related to agriculture, construction, training, and food aid.

The restructuring program in Azerbaijan has been similar to those of other countries in the former USSR. Its main points include stabilization measures (price liberalization, introduction of national currency, and establishment of an exchange rate stabilization fund); introduction of new legislation regarding privatization, foreign investment, and employment; fiscal and monetary reform (including introduction of a value-added tax and controls on government expenditures); civil service reform; and development of the banking sector. Four committees on antitrust, support for enterprises, state property, and land reform have been established to oversee the implementation of reform legislation. Privatization of the state enterprise sector is in the very early stages of implementation, with further enabling legislation required to begin the actual transfer process. Particular attention is being directed at modernizing those strategic sectors of the economy with the greatest potential for export growth, particularly the oil industry and, to a lesser extent, textile production; the role of foreign investment is seen as pivotal in these areas. The pursuit of development plans, however, remains hampered by ongoing political conflict in the country. Defense and internal security commanded the second-largest share of government expenditures in 1992, or 20% while allocations to the national economy (capital investments and transfers to the enterprise sector) claimed only 11%. Expenditures on education and health amounted to 38% of the budget. Agreement between Russia and Azerbaijan has been reached, transferring the latter's share of total former USSR debt (1.6%) in exchange for relinquishing all claims on Russian assets.

40SOCIAL DEVELOPMENT

The disintegration of the Soviet economy has led to economic decline, with falling living standards and rising unemployment (28% in 1992). The minimum wage was raised several times in 1992 as the ruble collapsed, but it still does not provide adequately for a worker and family. A decent living can only be assured by the "safety net" of the extended family structure. Health and safety standards are often ignored in the workplace.

Women nominally enjoy the same legal status as men. Heydar Aliev appointed several women to senior government positions. Women receive extensive opportunities for education, work, and political activity. However, social traditions of the Caucasus tend to keep them in a subordinate positions. The divorce rate was 4.6 per 1,000 women in 1989, and the 1990 fertility rate was 2.8.

[41]HEALTH

As part of the former Soviet Union, Azerbaijan has had to develop and maintain its own health care system and standards. In 1992, there were 3.93 doctors and 10.2 hospital beds per 1,000 people. Total health expenditures for 1990 reached $785 million.

Azerbaijan's infant mortality rate for 1992 was 37 per 1,000 live births. Between 1990 and 1992, the country immunized one-year-old children against the following diseases: tuberculosis (53%); diphtheria, pertussis, and tetanus (69%); polio (70%); and measles (50%).

The overall death rate in 1993 was 7 per 1,000 inhabitants. Mortality from 1985 to 1990 was broken down as follows: communicable diseases, maternal/perinatal causes, 110 per 100,000 people; noncommunicable diseases, 595 per 100,000; and injuries, 46 per 100,00. In 1990, there were 47 cases of tuberculosis per 100,000 people. In addition, thousands of lives were lost between 1989 and 1992 when the country was at war with Armenia.

[42]HOUSING

In 1990, Azerbaijan had 12.5 sq m of housing space per capita. As of 1 January 1991, 138,000 households (or 15.6%) were on waiting lists for housing in urban areas. In 1989, 31.5% of all privately owned urban housing had running water, 6.7% had sewer lines, 5.7% had bathtubs, and 96.8% had gas.

[43]EDUCATION

The educational system is extensive and illiteracy is practically unknown. In 1990, adult literacy rate was estimated at 97.3% (males: 98.9% and females: 95.9%). The usual language of instructions is Azerbaijani, although Russian, Armenian, and Georgian are also offered by some schools.

Russian is more commonly used at higher level institutions but this is slowly changing with a growing demand for the use of Azerbaijani. Education is free.

There are two universities: the Azerbaijan Polytechnic Institute, located in Baku, has seven departments and an enrollment of 12,000 students; the State University, also located at Baku was founded in 1919 and has an enrollment of over 15,000 students in 11 departments. Another 100,000 students are enrolled in more than 15 other institutions of higher learning.

Baku is sometimes referred to as an "oil academy" because of its ongoing research in the areas of turbine drilling, cementation of oil wells, and the development of synthetic rubber from natural gas.

[44]LIBRARIES AND MUSEUMS

The Ichari Shahar, or Old Town, in Baku has the Shirvanshah Palace, an architectural monument from the 15th and 16th centureis which has been restored and is now a museum. Other museums are the Museum of History of Azerbaijan, which exhibits archeological, ethnographic, and other relics; The Rustam Mustfayev Azerbaijan State Arts Museum, displaying works of Azerbaijani, Russian and West European artists from the 15th–19th centuries along with the works of modern Azerbaijani artists; The State Museum of Azerbaijani Carpets and Folk and Applied Art; and

The Nizami State Museum of Azerbaijani Literature, depicting the stages of literary development. The Gobustan Museum features prehistoric dwellings and cave paintings over 10,000 years old. In all, there are 4,605 libraries in Azerbaijan, 125 museums, and 20 theaters. Baku remains an important cultural and intellectual center in Transcaucasia.

[45]MEDIA

Azerbaijan is connected to other former Soviet republics by land-line or microwave, and to other countries through Moscow. There are several radio stations in the capital broadcasting in a variety of languages, as well as Baku Television, established in 1956.

In 1989 there were over 150 newspapers, 133 published in Azerbaijani. Those with the greatest circulation were *Khalg Gazeti*, published six days a week, *Gadzhlyar* (three days a week), and *Azadlyg* (weekly). Over 100 periodicals are published, more than half in Azerbaijani.

[46]ORGANIZATIONS

Important political associations in the Republic of Azerbaijan include the Helsinki Group, a human rights group, the National Democratic Movement, and Musavat (Equality). The Chamber of Commerce and Industry of the Republic of Azerbaijan promotes the country's goods and services in world markets.

[47]TOURISM, TRAVEL, AND RECREATION

The capital city of Baku is one of the prime tourist destinations of the Caucasus region. Its Old Town, with the Shirvanshah palace dating back to the 15–16th centuries, is especially popular with sightseers. Other attractions include the Museum of History and the State Arts Museum, as well as museums of folk art and literature. Elsewhere in Azerbaijan, the Gobustan Museum displays prehistoric dwellings and cave paintings, and the village of Surakhani attracts visitors to the Atashgah Fire-Worshipper's Temple. Visitors are also welcome at the carpet-weaving factory in the village of Nardaran, the Wine-making State Farm in the Shamakhi area, the Fruit And Vegetable State Farm around the town of Guba, and the Mashtagha Subtropical Fruit State Farm.

[48]FAMOUS AZERBAIJANIS

Peter the Great conquered what is now Azerbaijan in 1723. Heydar Aliyev has been acting president since June 1993. The poet Nizami Ganjavi (1141?–1209?) is celebrated for his *Khamsa*, a collection of five epic poems. Muhammed Fizuli (1438–1556) based his poems on traditional folktales, and his poetic versions provide the bases for many 20th centure plays and operas. Abul Hasan Bakhmanyar, an 11th century scientist, wrote respected books on mathematics and philosophy. Hasan Shirvani wrote a book on astronomy.The composer Uzeyis Hajibayov wrote the first Azerbaijani opera, and also founded the Azerbaijani Symphonic Orchestra and composed Azerbaijan's National Anthem.

[49]DEPENDENCIES

Azerbaijan has no territories or colonies.

[50]BIBLIOGRAPHY

Aganbegyan, Abel. *Perestrokda Revolution*. New York: Harper & Row, 1990.

Altstadt, Audrey L. *The Azerbaijani Turks: Power and Identity Under Russian Rule*. Stanford, Calif.: Hoover Institution Press, Stanford University, 1992.

Atabaki, Touraj. *Azerbaijan: Ethnicity and Autonomy in Twentieth-century Iran*. New York: British Academy Press, 1993.

Edwards-Jones, Imogen. *The Taming of Eagles: Exploring the New Russia*. London: Weidenfeld & Nicolson, 1993.

Fawcett, Louise L'Estrange. *Iran and the Cold War: the Azerbaijan Crisis of 1946*. Cambridge, and New York: Cambridge University Press, 1992.

Rost, Yuri. *Armenian Tragedy*. New York: St. Martin's, 1990.

Shoemaker, M. Wesley. *Russia, Eurasian States and Eastern Europe 1993*. Washington, D.C.: Stryker-Post, 1993.

Ulam, Adam B. *Expansion and Coexistence*. New York: Praeger, 1968.

Wolfe, Bertram. *Three Who Made a Revolution*. New York: Dial Press, 1948.

BAHRAIN

State of Bahrain
Dawlat al-Bahrayn

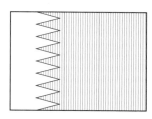

CAPITAL: Manama (Al-Manamah).

FLAG: Red with a white vertical stripe on the hoist, the edge between them being serrated.

ANTHEM: Music without words.

MONETARY UNIT: The Bahrain dinar (BD) is divided into 1,000 fils. There are coins of 5, 10, 25, 50, and 100 fils and notes of 500 fils and 1, 5, 10, and 20 dinars. BD1 = $2.6596 (or $1 = BD0.3760).

WEIGHTS AND MEASURES: The metric system is used; local measures are also used.

HOLIDAYS: New Year's Day, 1 January; National Day, 16 December. Movable Muslim religious holidays include Hijra (Muslim New Year), 'Ashura, Prophet's Birthday, 'Id al-Fitr, and 'Id al-'Adha'.

TIME: 3 PM = noon GMT.

¹LOCATION, SIZE, AND EXTENT

Situated in the western Persian Gulf, 29 km (18 mi) NW of Qatar, the State of Bahrain consists of a group of 33 islands (6 inhabited) with a total area of 620 sq km (239 sq mi), extending 48 km (30 mi) N–S and 19 km (12 mi) E–W. Comparatively, Bahrain occupies slightly less than 3.5 times the area of Washington, D.C. Bahrain, the main island, is linked by causeways and bridges to Muharraq and Sitra islands and to Sa'udi Arabia; other islands include the Hawar group, Nabih Salih, Umm an-Nasan, and Jidda. The total coastline is 161 km (100 mi). Bahrain's capital city, Manama, is located on the northeastern coast.

²TOPOGRAPHY

A narrow strip of land along the north coast of Bahrain is irrigated by natural springs and artesian wells. South of the cultivable area, the land is barren. The landscape consists of low rolling hills with numerous rocky cliffs and wadis. From the shoreline the surface rises gradually toward the center, where it drops into a basin surrounded by steep cliffs. Toward the center of the basin is Jabal ad-Dukhan, a rocky, steep-sided hill that rises 76 m (250 ft) above the surrounding plain and 137 m (450 ft) above sea level. Most of the lesser islands are flat and sandy, while Nabih Salih is covered with date groves.

³CLIMATE

Summers in Bahrain are hot and humid, and winters are relatively cool. Daily average temperatures in July range from a minimum of 29°C (84°F) to a maximum of 37°C (99°F); the January minimum is 14°C (57°F), the maximum 20°C (68°F). Rainfall averages less than 10 cm (4 in) annually and occurs mostly from December to March. Prevailing southeast winds occasionally raise dust storms.

⁴FLORA AND FAUNA

Outside the cultivated areas, numerous wild desert flowers appear, most noticeably after rain. Desert shrubs, grasses, and wild date palms are also found. Mammalian life is limited to the jerboa (desert rat), gazelle, mongoose, and hare; some 14 species of lizard and 4 types of land snake are also found. Bird life is especially varied. Larks, song thrushes, swallows, and terns are frequent visitors, and residents include the bulbul, hoopoe, parakeet, and warbler.

⁵ENVIRONMENT

Bahrain's principal environmental problems are scarcity of fresh water, desertification, and pollution from oil production. Population growth and industrial development have reduced the amount of agricultural land and lowered the water table, leaving aquifers vulnerable to saline contamination. In recent years, the government has attempted to limit extraction of groundwater (in part by expansion of seawater desalinization facilities) and to protect vegetation from further erosion. In 1994, 100% of Bahrain's urban dwellers and 57% of the rural population had pure water. Bahrain has developed its oil resources at the expense of its agricultural lands. As a result, lands that might otherwise be productive are gradually claimed by the expansion of the desert. Pollution from oil production was accelerated by the Persian Gulf War and the damage to oil-producing facilities in the Gulf area. It threatens the purity of both coastal and ground water.

A wildlife sanctuary established in 1980 is a home for threatened Gulf species, including the Arabian oryx, gazelle, zebra, giraffe, Defassa waterbuck, addax, and lesser kudu. Bahrain has also established captive breeding centers for falcons and for the rare Houbara bustard. As of 1987, the goitered gazelle and the green sea turtle were considered endangered species.

⁶POPULATION

In 1991, the population was 508,037, an increase of 44.8% over the 1981 census figure of 350,789. The population projection for the year 2000 is 653,000, assuming a crude birthrate of 23.2 per 1,000 population, a crude death rate of 3.6, and a net natural increase of 19.6 during 1995–2000. Population density was 738 per sq km (1,910 per sq mi) in 1991, when 83% of the total population was urban and 17% rural. Manama, the capital, had a 1990 estimated population of 133,784; it is connected by causeway with the other major city, Al-Muharraq (75,906).

⁷MIGRATION

The proportion of aliens increased from 20% of the total population in 1975 to an estimated 33% (171,872) in 1990. Most of them are temporary workers from other Arab countries, Iran, Pakistan, India, and the Republic of Korea. Many skilled workers are Europeans.

[8] ETHNIC GROUPS

In 1990, 67% of the population consisted of indigenous Bahrainis (336,165), the vast majority of whom are of northern Arab (Adnani) stock, infused with black racial traits. Iranians form the largest nonindigenous group (perhaps 20% of the total), followed by other Arabs (principally Omanis), Pakistanis, and Indians.

[9] LANGUAGES

Arabic is the universal language; the Gulf dialect is spoken. English is widely understood, Farsi and Urdu less so.

[10] RELIGIONS

In 1993, an estimated 70% of indigenous Bahrainis were Shi'ite Muslim and about 30% Sunni Muslim, the latter mostly in rural areas. Religious minorities comprised mostly of foreign workers, who make up 30% of the total population, included Christians and small numbers of Hindus and Baha'is. Islam is the official religion.

[11] TRANSPORTATION

The outline of the present road network was traced in the early 1930s, soon after the discovery of oil. The four main islands and all the towns and villages are linked by excellent roads. In 1991 there were 200 km (124 mi) of bituminous surfaced highways. A four-lane, 2.8-km (1.7-mi) causeway and bridge connect Manama with Al-Muharraq, and another bridge joins Sitra to the main island. A four-lane highway atop a 24-km (15-mi) causeway, linking Bahrain with the Sa'udi Arabian mainland via Umm an-Nasan, was completed in December 1986 and financed by Sa'udi Arabia. In 1991 there were 132,180 motor vehicles.

Bahrain's port of Mina Sulman can accommodate 16 oceangoing vessels drawing up to 11 m (36 ft). In 1991, Bahrain had a merchant fleet of 9 ships with 188,000 GRT. The international airport near Al-Muharraq can handle large jet aircraft and serves more than two dozen international airlines. Gulf Air, headquartered in Bahrain and owned equally by the governments of Bahrain, Oman, Qatar, and the United Arab Emirates (UAE), flies to other Gulf countries, India, and Europe.

[12] HISTORY

The history of Bahrain has been traced back 5,000 years to Sumerian times. Known as Dilmun, Bahrain was a thriving trade center around 2000 BC; the islands were visited by the ships of Alexander the Great in the 3d century BC. Bahrain accepted Islam in the 7th century AD, after which it was ruled alternately by its own princes and by the caliphs' governors. The Portuguese occupied Bahrain from 1522 to 1602. The present ruling family, the Khalifa, who are related to the Sabah family of Kuwait and the Sa'udi royal family, captured Bahrain in 1782. Following an initial contact in 1805, the ruler of Bahrain signed the first treaty with Britain in 1820. A binding treaty of protection, similar to those with other Persian Gulf principalities, was concluded in 1861 and revised in 1892 and 1951. After World War II, Britain maintained at Bahrain its headquarters for treaty affairs in the lower Gulf. Claims to Bahrain pressed by Iran were abandoned in 1971 after a UN mission ascertained that the Bahrainis wished to remain independent of that nation.

Between 1968 and 1971, Bahrain participated in discussions aimed at forming a federation of the nine sheikhdoms of the southern Gulf. On 14 August 1971, Sheikh 'Isa bin Salman al-Khalifa declared that, in view of the failure of the larger federation to materialize, Bahrain would declare its independence. Its treaties with the UK were replaced by a treaty of friendship and cooperation, and on 15 August, the country became the sovereign State of Bahrain. Bahrain promulgated its first constitution in 1973, which occasioned the convening of an elective National Assembly; the legislature was dissolved in August 1975 amid charges of Communist influence. The emir has continued to set state policy, and his brother, Crown Prince Hamad bin 'Isa al-Khalifa, has directed government administration.

Owing to its small size, Bahrain generally takes its lead in foreign affairs from its Arab neighbors on the Gulf. A founding member of the Gulf Cooperation Council, it shares with the other five members a concern with pressures from Iran and Iraq. During the Iran-Iraq War, Bahrain joined most other Arab states in supporting Iraq. Subsequently, it has carefully tried to foster better relations with Iran through trade. When Iraq invaded Kuwait, Bahrain stood with the allies, contributing military support and facilities to the defeat of Iraq.

Bahrain has long assisted the American naval presence in the Persian Gulf. In 1977, a formal agreement for home-porting US naval ships was replaced by arrangements to continue ship visits and other security cooperation. Since the Gulf War, this cooperation has expanded with arms sales, plans for joint exercises and US pre-positioning of military material for future contingencies. In 1991, the US signed an agreement giving the Department of Defense access to facilities on the island.

[13] GOVERNMENT

Under the constitution ratified in June 1973, Bahrain is a constitutional monarchy headed by an emir. A council of ministers, appointed by the emir, is presided over by the prime minister, who since 1973 has been Sheikh Khalifa bin Salman al-Khalifa, a brother of the emir. Members of the ruling family hold most of the important government posts, including the ministries of foreign affairs, defense, justice and interior. Although the constitution provides for a National Assembly composed of 30 elected members and 14 cabinet ministers, no National Assembly has been allowed to exist since 1975. The council of ministers exercises the legislative function.

[14] POLITICAL PARTIES

Political parties are illegal under the emirate. Several underground groups, including branches of Hizbollah and other pro-Iranian militant Islamic groups, have been active and are vigorously pursued by government security services. Anti-regime dissidents are frequently jailed or exiled.

[15] LOCAL GOVERNMENT

Bahrain's six major towns are administered by a single municipal council, whose members are appointed by the emir. In the five rural communities, administration continues to be conducted along traditional lines by village headmen (mukhtars).

[16] JUDICIAL SYSTEM

The law of Bahrain represents a mixture of Islamic religious law (Shari'a) and government decrees dealing with criminal and commercial matters. The Al Khalifa family dominates the government and the judiciary. Professional judges serve on civil and criminal courts and on courts of appeal. In ordinary civil and criminal courts there are open trials, a right to counsel (including legal aid when determined to be necessary) and a right to appeal.

There are separate courts for members of the Sunni and Shiite sects. Religious courts handle divorces. While both women and men may initiate a divorce, religious courts have the discretion to refuse a woman's request. Military courts handle cases involving military personnel accused of violating the military code of justice. The Supreme Court of Appeals may sit as a security court. When so operating it conducts secret proceedings and is exempt form the usual procedures guaranteed by the penal code. Detentions without trial are permissible under the 1974 Security Law.

17ARMED FORCES

After an attempted coup in 1981, a bilateral defense agreement was signed with Sa'udi Arabia. Bahrain is a member of the Gulf Cooperation Council (GCC), which provided it and Oman $1.8 billion (1984–94) for defense modernization. The Bahrain army in 1993 had 5,000 officers and men in one combined arms brigade with US and UK weapons. The naval force had 500 men; and the air force which numbers 650, flies 24 US F–5 or F–16 aircraft and 12 armed helicopters. The armed forces have doubled since the emergence of Iraq and Iran as threats, and Bahrain sent troops to Sa'udi Arabia in 1990–91. Defense expenditures in 1990 were $194 million or 6% of gross domestic product. Bahrain spent $50 million abroad in 1991 for arms. The state police numbered 9,000.

18INTERNATIONAL COOPERATION

Bahrain joined the UN on 21 September 1971 and is a member of ESCWA, all major regional organizations, and all the nonregional specialized agencies except IAEA, IDA, IFAD, IFC, UNIDO, and WIPO. It also belongs to the League of Arab States and G-77, and is a de facto adherent of GATT and a signatory of the Law of the Sea. Bahrain was a founding member of the Gulf Cooperation Council, inaugurated in 1981.

19ECONOMY

For centuries, Bahrain depended almost exclusively on trade, pearl diving, and agriculture. The discovery of oil on 1 June 1932 came at a providential time, when the pearl trade was being drastically undercut by the development of cultured pearls. Although its economy has been based on oil for the last five decades, Bahrain's development has been tempered by relatively limited reserves. With present oil supplies limited to one diminishing oil field, expected to be exhausted in the late 1990s, the government has developed auxiliary sectors, such as petroleum refining and aluminum production, and increased natural gas production to some 20 million cu m per day. Proven gas reserves are currently estimated at some 209,000 million cu m and should last approximately 30 years.

Significant progress has been made in enhancing Bahrain as an entrepôt and as a service and commercial center for the Gulf region. Bahrain provides ample warehousing for goods in transit and drydock facilities for marine engine and ship repairs. Bahrain also acts as a major banking, telecommunications, and air transportation center.

20INCOME

In 1992, Bahrain's GNP was $3,690 million at current prices. For the period 1985–92 the average inflation rate was 0.2%, resulting in a real growth rate in per capita GNP of –1.7%.

It is estimated that in 1990 agriculture, hunting, forestry, and fishing contributed 1% to GDP; mining and quarrying, 22%; manufacturing, 17%; electricity, gas, and water, 2%; construction, 6%; wholesale and retail trade, 10%; transport, storage, and communication, 10%; finance, insurance, real estate, and business services, 13%; community, social, and personal services, 5%; and other sources 14%.

21LABOR

The employed private sector population in 1991 totaled 103,488, of whom nearly 60% were non-Bahrainis; the majority of workers were employed in community, social, and personal services. Bahrain boasts a high proportion of skilled workers, among both its foreign residents and the indigenous population, many of whom have benefited from local technical and vocational training programs.

Although the constitution permits workers to organize, there are no trade unions and the government openly discourages

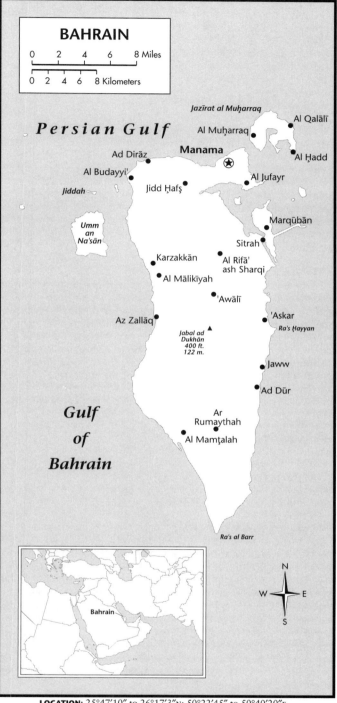

LOCATION: 25°47'10" to 26°17'3"N; 50°22'45" to 50°40'20"E.
TOTAL COASTLINE: 161 km (100 mi). **TERRITORIAL SEA LIMIT:** 3 mi.

unionization. With this absence of legitimate trade unions, no collective bargaining enties or collective agreements exist.

Bahrain enacted a comprehensive labor law in 1958; it provides for an 8-hour day, 48-hour week, minimum wage plus overtime and severance pay, paid vacations, and sick and maternity leave. All foreign workers must be sponsored by Bahrainis or Bahrain-based companies, which can revoke the residence permit of anyone under their sponsorship. Migrant workers from developing countries are often unwilling to report health and safety abuses for fear of forced repatriation.

22AGRICULTURE

Agriculture accounts for only about 1% of the GDP. Ninety farms and small holdings produce fruit and vegetables, as well as alfalfa for fodder. The date palm industry has declined sharply in recent years due to heavy demands on the limited water supply, and dates have become a luxury item. In 1992, 10,000 tons of vegetables and 23,000 tons of fruit crops were produced. The government's goal is for output to meet 16% of demand, compared with the current 6%.

23ANIMAL HUSBANDRY

Most domestic meat consumption is supplied through imports of live cattle, goats, and sheep. A few thousand cattle and goats are kept for milk and meat production. A thriving poultry industry met 88% of the local demand for eggs in 1992 and 22% of the poultry demands. In 1992, Bahrain produced 2,950 tons of eggs. Dairy farming has recently been expanded, and a national dairy pasteurization plant has been established in order to centralize all milk processing and distribution. In 1984, an abattoir opened to slaughter imported sheep and cattle.

24FISHING

Although the more than 300 species of fish found in Bahraini waters constitute an important food source for much of the population, local fishing and pearl diving have declined because of industrial pollution. The catch totaled 7,553 tons in 1991. The government operates a fleet of seven trawlers. By encouraging traditional angling, giving incentives to fishermen, improving fishing and freezing equipment, and establishing cooperatives, the government is attempting to increase the annual catch. There is a modern fishing harbor at Al-Muharraq which provides docking and landing facilities, storage areas, an ice plant, and a water supply.

25FORESTRY

There are no forests in Bahrain.

26MINING

The mining industry consists almost entirely of oil and natural gas production. Some cement is also produced.

27ENERGY AND POWER

The Arabian Peninsula's first oil well was drilled in Bahrain in 1932, and production began in 1934. From the 1930s to the mid-1970s, oil development was a monopoly of the Bahrain Petroleum Co. (BAPCO), which in 1936 came under the ownership of Caltex, a corporation registered in Canada and jointly owned by Texaco and Standard Oil of California. In 1975, the Bahrain government acquired a 60% holding in BAPCO, and it later formed the Bahrain National Oil Co. (BANOCO) to take over full ownership. In 1980, BANOCO announced its acquisition of a 60% interest in Bahrain's main refinery, which had been wholly owned by Caltex. In 1993, an estimated 70% ($2.4 billion) of export revenues came from petroleum exports.

Total daily crude petroleum production, after reaching a peak of 77,000 barrels in 1970, declined gradually; in 1992, it was 40,000 barrels. Total recoverable oil reserves in the Bahrain field were estimated at 69.6 million barrels in 1993. For 20 years, Bahrain had been getting a 70,000-barrel-per-day share of the revenues from Bahrain's 50% share in the Abu Sa'fa field; this small offshore field lies halfway within Sa'udi Arabian territorial waters, but its daily production is split between Bahrain and Sa'udi Arabia under an arrangement reached in 1972. In 1992, Saudi Arabia agreed to increase Bahrain's share to 100,000 barrels per day until 1994.

Bahrain's natural gas resources were estimated at 5.8 trillion cu ft (200 billion cu m) in 1992, sufficient to last more than 22 years at 1992 extraction levels. Production of gas totaled 290 billion cu ft (8.2 billion cu m) in 1992, of which about 20% was associated with oil drilling and 80% was produced directly from gas reserves.

In 1991, Bahrain had a net installed power capacity of 1,040 Mw and total output of 3,495 million kwh, principally derived from a municipal power station at Jufair, from the Sitra power and water station, from two gas turbines at Al-Muharraq, and from the power station at East Rifaa, which was completed in 1985 and is the largest and most modern.

In 1994, the dispute between Bahrain and Qatar over the sovereignty of the possibly oil-rich Hawar Islands will be heard by the International Court of Justice at The Hague. The dispute nearly caused the two countries to go to war in April 1986.

28INDUSTRY

Petroleum refining, begun modestly in 1942, was Bahrain's first modern industrial enterprise. By 1976, the oil refinery at Sitra had a daily output of 250,000 barrels, but its capacity has far outstripped the local supply of crude oil, and about 84% of the oil is pumped from Sa'udi Arabia by sea and land lines. Although modernization was delayed by the Gulf conflict, work began in 1992 to expand refining capacity to some 360,000 barrels per day. A total of 67,618 million barrels of petroleum products were produced in 1985 and 89,543 million barrels in 1986. A new gas liquefaction plant was opened by the Bahrain National Gas Co. (BANAGAS) in 1979.

A government-controlled aluminum industry, Aluminum Bahrain BSC (ALBA), was launched in 1971 with a smelter capacity of 120,000 tons annually; 174,825 tons were produced in 1985. The successful completion of a 1985 expansion project increased production capacity to 460,000 tons; 212,500 tons were produced in 1990 and 450,000 tons in 1993. The Arab Shipbuilding and Repair Yard, a pan-Arab industrial venture undertaken by OAPEC, became operational in 1977. Another pan-Arab venture, the Arab Iron and Steel Co., began producing steel pellets for export in 1984. The plant can produce 4 million tons of iron oxide pellets a year, but output was only 680,000 tons in 1985 because of low demand. The plant has been lying idle since mid-1986 because of supply and marketing difficulties. In August 1987, shareholders voted to liquidate the company, clearing the way for a takeover by Kuwait Petroleum Corporation.

29SCIENCE AND TECHNOLOGY

The economy depends heavily on advanced petrochemical technologies, and many Bahrainis have had or are receiving technical training. The University of Bahrain, at 'Isa Town, has a college of engineering. The Arabian Gulf University, founded in 1980, has colleges of medicine and applied sciences. The Bahrain Society of Engineers, in Manama, is a leading professional group. The College of Health Sciences, founded in 1976, has 1,086 students. The Bahrain Centre for Studies and Research, founded in 1981, conducts research in technology and energy.

30DOMESTIC TRADE

Bahraini shops have become increasingly modernized and specialized. Business hours for most shops are from 8 AM to 12 noon and from 3:30 to 6 PM, Saturday through Thursday; government offices, banks, and some large companies are open in the mornings only. Of all the Gulf states, Bahrain offers the most scope for consumer advertising through its publications, cinemas, direct mail facilities, and radio and television stations.

31FOREIGN TRADE

Refined oil products are the principal exports, accounting for over 80% of the island's exports which were valued at $3.76 billion in 1990. Refined aluminum, frozen shrimp, paper goods, air-conditioning units, and flour are other export earners. Imports in 1990 totaled $3.34 billion, with crude oil the principal commodity, followed by machinery, manufactured goods, food, and live animals. The principal markets for Bahrain's exports in 1989 were Sa'udi Arabia, which took 18.2% of total export value; US, 7.3%; and the UAE, 6.9%; and Japan, 5.9%. The major suppliers were the UK, which provided 16.3% of 1989 import value, and the US and Japan, which accounted for 12.4% and 10.5%, respectively.

32BALANCE OF PAYMENTS

Traditionally, Bahrain relied on a substantial influx of funds from Sa'udi Arabia, Kuwait, Abu Dhabi, and Iran to finance capital outlays. In recent years, however, surpluses in the petroleum trade, as well as increased income from tourism and financial services, have placed Bahrain in a favorable payments position.

In 1992 merchandise exports totaled $3,417.3 million and imports $3,730.3 million. The merchandise trade balance was $-313.0 million. The following table summarizes Bahrain's balance of payments for 1991 and 1992 (in millions of us dollars):

	1991	1992
CURRENT ACCOUNT		
Goods, services, and income	−594.4	−822.6
Unrequited transfers	−201.6	−170.7
TOTALS	−796.0	−993.4
CAPITAL ACCOUNT		
Direct investment	−6.9	−8.5
Portfolio investment	−34.6	—
Other long-term capital	−16.8	−5.3
Other short-term capital	−288.8	380.1
Reserves	−281.6	81.9
TOTALS	−628.7	448.1
Errors and omissions	1,424.7	545.3
Total change in reserves	−279.8	116.2

33BANKING AND SECURITIES

The Bahrain Monetary Agency, the central banking authority, issues and redeems bank notes, regulates the value of the Bahrain dinar, supervises interest rates, and licenses and monitors the activities of money changers. Currency in circulation amounted to BD1,231.5 million in 1993. Bahrain has become a major regional center for commercial and financial operations in the Gulf. In 1993 there were 79 commercial banks, including 48 foreign banks operating in Bahrain's offshore banking zone. Foreign assets of commercial banks were BD1,140.9 million at the end of 1993. There is no stock exchange; share trading is through the banks

34INSURANCE

In 1985, 5 domestic and 13 foreign insurance firms were conducting business in Bahrain; 16 firms are registered as exempt companies and mainly do offshore business. Nearly 40 underwriters, brokers, and agents were operating in 1985. The Arab Insurance Group had authorized capital of $3 billion in 1986.

35PUBLIC FINANCE

The budget is presented biennially and regularly updated, and represents a large section of economic activity. In 1989 revenues totaled us$1.2 billion, of which 60% was derived from petroleum production and processing. Estimated expenditures for 1989 were us$1.32 billion.

36TAXATION

The only taxes in Bahrain are an income tax on oil production

and a municipal tax of 10% on residential rents; the rate is 7.5% on furnished rentals, office, and commercial rents. As an offshore tax haven, Bahrain allows foreign firms to remit accumulated profits and capital without taxation.

37CUSTOMS AND DUTIES

Import licenses are not required for most commodities. Principal prohibited items are arms, ammunition, liquor (except by authorized importers), and cultured pearls. Customs duties are 5% on foodstuffs, essential goods, and plant and equipment for use in local industry; 10% on non-essential goods; 30% on tobacco; and 100% on authorized imports of liquor.

38FOREIGN INVESTMENT

While continuing to encourage foreign investment, the government has acquired majority holdings in most of the country's principal enterprises that were formerly foreign held. Businesses with capital equivalent to more than BD20,000 can be incorporated for up to 25 years. The government offers substantial incentives for companies wishing to establish plants in Bahrain. With the exception of petroluem royalties, Bahrain does not tax either corporate or individual earnings.

39ECONOMIC DEVELOPMENT

Since the late 1960s, the government has concentrated on policies and projects that will provide sufficient diversification in industrial, commercial, and financial activities to sustain growth in income, employment, and exports into the post-oil era. Despite diversification efforts, the oil and gas sectors remain the cornerstone of the economy.

40SOCIAL DEVELOPMENT

Impoverished families receive subsistence allowances from the Ministry of Labor and Social Affairs. Free child guidance clinics—the first in the Gulf—and expanded benefit and pension provisions for government employees were introduced in 1975. Since 1976, a social security fund has provided old age, disability, survivor, and accident insurance. Contributions are 5% of earnings by the worker and 7% by the employer. For accident insurance, the insured pays nothing and the employer contributes 3% of payroll.

Islamic law, either Shi'a or Sunni, dictates the legal rights of Bahraini women. Women may initiate divorce proceedings, own and inherit property, and represent themselves in legal matters. Women make up over 20% of the labor force, and their employment is encouraged by the government, itself a leading employer of women. Bahrain's labor law does not recognize the concept of equal pay for equal work.

41HEALTH

In 1960, Bahrain inaugurated a free national health service, available to both foreign and indigenous segments of the population through a system of primary care health centers and modern hospital facilities. Bahraini patients who require sophisticated surgery or treatment are sent abroad at government expense.

In 1990, there were 4 government-operated hospitals (including a psychiatric hospital and a geriatric hospital), 5 maternity hospitals, 19 health centers, 6 environment health centers, and 16 maternity and child welfare centers. Hospital and health center expansion had been underway, and the number of hospital beds was expected to increase to 2,131 by the end of 1993. In 1991, Bahrain had 668 physicians, 123 pharmacists, and 66 dentists.

Infant mortality was 13 per 1,000 live births in 1992, with 14,000 births that year. The 1993 birth rate was 26.1 per 1,000 people, and the general mortality rate was 3.9 per 1,000 people. Between 1991 and 1992, 87% of the country's 1-year-old children were vaccinated aginst measles. In 1990, 100% of the population had access to health care services, and 93% had access to safe drinking water. Life expectancy in 1992 was 71 years.

[42]HOUSING
There were 50,798 households at the 1981 census. Roughly 45% of all housing units were traditional dwellings with interior courtyards, 22% were flats, 17% were modern detached houses, 8% were villas, and 3% were collective compounds. Owners occupied 48% of all dwellings, 33% were rented, 9% were occupied rent free, and 7% were furnished by employers. About 69% were made of brick, 16% were stone, 8% were concrete, and 5% were prefabricated. 'Isa Town, the first low-cost government housing scheme, which was initiated in 1963 in barren desert between Manama and West Rifaa, had a population of 35,000 in 1984. Mamad Town was completed in 1984; in 1987, it had 12,000 residential units. A major program for low- and middle-income housing, costing $195 million, also was inaugurated with Sa'udi aid.

[43]EDUCATION
Bahrain introduced a free public education system to the Gulf region in 1919. The government aims to provide free educational opportunities for all children.

In 1990, the literacy rate was estimated by UNESCO at 77.4% (82.7% males and 69.3% females). The official language is Arabic but English is widely spoken. School education is in three stages: primary lasts for six years, intermediate for three years, and secondary—general, industrial, or commercial—for three years.

There are two universities. The University of Bahrain (established in 1986) has five colleges, including an English language center; colleges of arts, sciences, engineering, education, and business administration. The Arabian Gulf University (founded in 1980) has faculties in science, engineering and medicine and is in fact a joint venture project among the six Gulf Cooperation Council members and Iraq. Each nation is allocated 10% of the seats (total 70%) and the remaining 30% are given to other countries.

There are also 67 adult education centers in Bahrain, which have helped to reduce the illiteracy rate of the country.

For promoting technical education, a "10,000 Training Plan" was launched in 1980. Nearly 6,500 students have participated in this program since its inception and scholarships are given to students to pursue higher studies at Bahrain or abroad. For improving the quality of instruction in schools, a teacher training program was launched in 1986.

[44]LIBRARIES AND MUSEUMS
The Ministry of Education maintained 10 public libraries with a total of 218,000 volumes in 1989 including the Central Public Library in Isa Town which has 123,500 volumes. The Bahrain Museum, with archaeological and historical exhibits, is located in Manama.

[45]MEDIA
Modern telephone, cable, and telex systems are available; telephones numbered 141,245 in 1991. The government operates a radio station and a color television station. Radio Bahrain transmits AM and FM broadcasts on two channels. In 1991 there were 278,000 radios and 215,000 television sets in use. Bahrain's first daily newspaper in Arabic, *Akhbar al-Khalij* (circulation 25,000 in 1991), began publication in 1976, and the first English daily, the *Gulf Daily News* (12,000), in 1991.

[46]ORGANIZATIONS
In addition to the Chamber of Commerce and Industry, there are numerous Bahraini and multinational groups, including the Bahrain Red Crescent Society, the Children's and Mothers' Welfare Society, and the Boy Scouts.

[47]TOURISM, TRAVEL, AND RECREATION
The opening of the Saudi-Bahrain causeway in 1986 and active efforts by the government have boosted tourism. In 1990, Bahrain had 3,222 hotel rooms and 4,572 beds with a 55.9 percent occupancy rate. In 1991 there were 1.67 million tourist arrivals, mostly from Sa'udi Arabia and other Arab countries, and tourism receipts totaled US$162 million. Tourist attractions include archeological sites, notably Qal-at Al-Bahrain (The Portuguese Fort), the National Museum, and the Heritage Center. Most visitors need a visa and valid passport. Holders of UK passports and citizens of neighboring Arab states are exempt from the visa requirement.

[48]FAMOUS BAHRAINIS
Since 1961, the emir has been Sheikh 'Isa bin Salman al-Khalifa (b. 1933).

[49]DEPENDENCIES
Bahrain has no territories or colonies.

[50]BIBLIOGRAPHY
Al-Tajir, Mahdi Abdalla. *Bahrain, 1920–1945: Britain, the Shaikh, and the Administration.* London and New York: Croom Helm, 1987.
American University. *Area Handbook for the Persian Gulf States.* Washington, D.C.: Government Printing Office, 1984.
Fakhro, Munira A. (Munira Ahmed). *Women at Work in the Gulf: A Case Study of Bahrain Fakhro.* London and New York: Kegan Paul International, 1990.
Jenner, Michael. *Bahrain, Gulf Heritage in Transition.* New York: Longman, 1984.
Lawson, Fred Haley. *Bahrain: the Modernization of Autocracy.* Boulder, Colo.: Westview Press, 1989.
Nugent, Jeffrey B., and Theodore Thomas (eds.). *Bahrain and the Gulf: Past Perspectives and Alternate Futures.* New York: St. Martin's, 1985.

BANGLADESH

People's Republic of Bangladesh
Gana-Prajatantri Bangladesh

CAPITAL: Dhaka (formerly Dacca).

FLAG: The national flag is a red circle against a dark-green background.

ANTHEM: *Amar Sonar Bangla (My Golden Bengal).*

MONETARY UNIT: The taka (T) of 100 poisha is a paper currency set on a par with the Indian rupee. There are coins of 1, 2, 5, 10, 25, and 50 poisha, and notes of 1, 5, 10, 20, 50, and 100 taka. T1 = $0.0248 (or $1 = T40.250).

WEIGHTS AND MEASURES: Bangladesh adopted the metric system as of 1 July 1982. Customary numerical units include the lakh (equal to 100,000) and the crore (equal to 10 million).

HOLIDAYS: New Year's Day, 1 January; National Mourning Day (Shaheel Day), 21 February; Independence Day, 26 March; May Day, 1 May; Victory Day, 16 December; Christmas, 25 December; Boxing Day, 26 December. Movable religious holidays include Good Friday, Jamat Wida, Shab-i-Bharat, 'Id al-Fitr, 'Id al-'Adha', and Durga Puja.

TIME: 6 PM = noon GMT.

¹LOCATION, SIZE, AND EXTENT

Situated in the northeastern corner of the South Asian subcontinent, Bangladesh, before it became an independent state, was the eastern province of Pakistan, known as East Bengal and, later, as East Pakistan. Bangladesh is slightly smaller than the state of Wisconsin with a total area of 144,000 sq km (55,599 sq mi), extending 767 km (477 mi) SSE–NNW and 429 km (267 mi) ENE–WSW. Bangladesh is bordered in the N, E, and W by India, on the SE by Burma, and on the S by the Bay of Bengal, with a total boundary length of 4,826 km (2,999 mi). A border demarcation agreement was signed with Burma in May 1979. Demarcation of the marine boundary with India remains unresolved. Bangladesh's capital city, Dhaka, is located near the center of the country.

²TOPOGRAPHY

Bangladesh is a tropical country, situated mainly on the deltas of large rivers flowing from the Himalayas. The Brahmaputra River, known locally as the Jamuna, unites with part of the Ganges to form the Padma, which, after its juncture with a third large river, the Meghna, flows into the Bay of Bengal. Offshoots of the Ganges-Padma, including the Burishwar, Garai, Kobadak, and Madhumati, also flow south to the Bay of Bengal. No part of the delta area is more than 150 m (500 ft) above sea level, and most of it is but a meter or two (a few feet) above sea level. Its soil consists mostly of fertile alluvium, which is intensively farmed; mineral deposits are negligible. During the rainy season floodwater covers most of the land surface, damaging crops and injuring the economy. The northwestern section of the country, drained by the Tista (Teesta) River, is somewhat higher and less flat, but the only really hilly regions are in the east, notably in the Chittagong Hill Tracts to the southeast and the Sylhet District to the northeast. Near the Burmese border, in the extreme southeast, is the Keokradang, which at 1,230 m (4,034 ft) is the highest peak in Bangladesh.

³CLIMATE

Bangladesh has a tropical monsoon climate. Annual rainfall is high, averaging from about 119 cm (47 in) up to 145 cm (57 in).

There are three distinct seasons. The winter, which lasts from November through February, is cool and dry. The average January temperature for most of the country is about 7°C (45°F); total winter rainfall averages about 18 cm (7 in) in the east and less than 8 cm (3 in) in the northwest. Temperatures rise rapidly in early March, and during the summer season—March through May—average about 32°C (90°F). Rainfall also increases during this period. However, nearly 80% of the annual rainfall falls from June to October, when moisture-laden winds blow from the south and southeast. Temperatures drop somewhat, seldom exceeding 31°C (88°F), but humidity remains high. In April and May and from September through November, tropical cyclones, accompanied by high seas and heavy flooding, are common. There were severe cyclones in May 1963, May and December 1965, October 1966, and most notably during the night of 12/13 November 1970, when a storm and resultant flooding killed more than 200,000 persons. A cyclone on 30 April 1991 left over 131,000 people dead and 9 million homeless. Monsoon floods in 1974, 1980, and 1983 also devastated the country and caused many deaths, and a cyclonic storm on 24/25 May 1985 took more than 11,000 lives. The monsoon in August and September 1988 left three-fourths of the country flooded, 1,300 persons dead, and over three million people homeless, with damage to the country's infrastructure estimated at $1 billion.

⁴FLORA AND FAUNA

Bangladesh has the plant and animal life typical of a tropical and riverine swamp. The landscape, which for most of the year is lush green, is dotted with palms and flowering trees. The large forest area of the Sunderbans in the southwest is the home of the endangered Bengal tiger; there are also cheetahs, leopards, crocodiles, elephants, spotted deer, monkeys, boars, bears, pheasants, and many varieties of birds and waterfowl.

⁵ENVIRONMENT

Overpopulation has severely strained Bangladesh's limited natural resources. Nearly all arable land is already cultivated, and forestland has been greatly reduced by agricultural expansion and by timber and firewood cutting. Bangladesh's environmental problems have been complicated by natural disasters that add to the strain on an agricultural system which supports one of the world's most populous countries. Water supply is also a major problem because of population size, lack of purification procedures, and the spread of untreated contaminants into the usable water supply by flood waters. To ease these problems, the government has established drainage, irrigation, and flood protection systems, and has drilled thousands of tube wells to supply safe drinking water in villages. In 1994, safe water was available to only about 70% of the urban and 81% of the rural population.

Despite passage of the Wildlife Preservation Act of 1973, wildlife continues to suffer from human encroachment. In 1994, there were 15 species of mammals, 27 species of birds and 33 plant species that are considered to be endangered, including the Asian elephant, Bengal tiger, estuarine crocodile, gavial, and river terrapin. The Assam rabbit, Sumatran rhinoceros, Javan rhinoceros, and pygmy hog have become extinct.

6POPULATION

Bangladesh is one of the world's most densely populated nations, and controlling population growth is a major government priority. The census population in 1991 was 104,766,143; with adjustment for undercount, the total was put at 109,876,977. This represented an increase of 22.2% from the 1981 figure. A population of 144,265,000 is projected for 2000. The annual population growth declined from 3.4% in 1975 to 2.2% in 1991. As of 1991, the crude birthrate was at 31.6 per 1,000 population, the crude death rate at 11, and the net natural increase at 21.6. The estimated population density was 763 per sq km (1,976 per sq mi), making Bangladesh one of the most densely populated countries on earth. The distribution is uneven, with extremely heavy concentrations in the districts of Dhaka and Comilla.

The population is heavily rural, with the great majority living in more than 85,000 villages. The country's urban population was only about 19.5% in 1991. The largest cities, with 1991 populations, were Dhaka, 3,637,892; Chittagong, 1,566,070; Khulna, 601,051; and Rajshahi, 324,532. Other major cities were Barisal, Rangpur, and Jessore.

7MIGRATION

Since 1947 there has been a regular interchange of population between India and what is now Bangladesh, with Hindus migrating to India and Muslims emigrating from India. There was also substantial migration between Bangladesh (then East Pakistan) and West Pakistan until the 1971 war. Before and during the war, an estimated 8 to 10 million Bengalis fled to India; most of these refugees returned after the independence of Bangladesh was firmly established. Although more than 100,000 Biharis who had sided with Pakistan during the war later migrated to Pakistan, an estimated 238,000 Biharis were still living in 66 refugee camps in Bangladesh at the end of 1993, despite a repatriation agreement signed in 1992.

In 1993, repatriation began of an estimated 56,000 Chakma refugees from the Indian state of Tripura to the Chittagong Hill Tracts of Bangladesh. They had fled unrest in this area. In 1991–92 about 265,000 Rohingyas—Muslims from Myanmar—fled to Bangladesh to escape repression. They were housed at 19 camps, where about 200,000 remained at the end of 1993, while the rest returned.

8ETHNIC GROUPS

Some 98% of the people are Bengalis (or Banglas). About 12 tribes inhabiting the Chittagong Hill Tracts (with population of 897,828 in 1991, less than 1% of the population) are ethnically distinct from the Bengalis; their facial features and language are closer to the Burmese. The government's policy of resettling Bengalis in the region, which is much less densely populated than Bangladesh as a whole, led to racial and religious disturbances and a small-scale tribal insurgency in the early 1980s. About 600,000 of the national population consists of Biharis, non-Bengali Muslims who migrated from India to what was then East Pakistan after the partition of the subcontinent in 1947. In the coastal areas of Bangladesh, Arab, Portuguese, and Dutch settlers have gradually come to adopt the Bengali life-style.

9LANGUAGES

Bengali (Bangla), part of the Indo-European language family, is the official language of Bangladesh and is spoken by about 98% of the population. The successful move to make Bengali coequal with Urdu as an official language was a hallmark of Bengali nationalism in the early 1950s. Non-Bengali migrants from India still speak Urdu (and Hindi)today, and this language is widely understood in urban areas. A few tribal groups, notably the tribal peoples of the Chittagong Hill Tracts, also speak distinct Tibeto-Burmese languages, akin to Burmese and Assamese. Among those speaking Bangla there are differences of dialect according to region. The people of Chittagong, Noakhali, and Sylhet are known for their distinctive dialects. Although today Bangla is the official language, English is also used for official and legal purposes and widely used in business.

10RELIGIONS

The 1981 census listed a total of 86.6% of the people are believers in Islam, making Bangladesh the world's third-largest Muslim country after Indonesia and Pakistan. Most of these are Sunni. From 12% to 16% of the population today is Hindu, 0.6% Buddhist, and 0.3% Christian, the later evenly divided between Roman Catholics and Protestants. Although Islam was established as the state religion in 1988, freedom of worship continues to be guaranteed under its constitution.

11TRANSPORTATION

The large number of rivers and the annual flooding hazard make it difficult to build and maintain adequate transportation facilities in Bangladesh. Railways and waterways are the chief means of transportation. The railways are managed by the government and reach most districts of the country. The Bangladesh Railway, which operated 2,892 km (1,797 mi) of track in 1984/85, carried 90.3 million passengers and 3 million tons of freight. The quality of service has declined because of the expense of importing new equipment. Enlarging and improving the railway system is also costly, partly because of the number of bridges needed.

The country has two deepwater ports: Chittagong, serving the eastern sector, and Chalna, serving the west. There are five main river ports—Dhaka, Nārāyanganj, Chandpur, Barisal, and Khulna—and more than 1,500 smaller ports. The inland water system in 1991 had an estimated 5,150–8,046 km (3,200–5,000 mi) of navigable waterways, including 2,575–3,058 km (1,600–1,900 mi) of main cargo routes. The oceangoing merchant fleet in 1991 consisted of 47 ships with a combined capacity of 342 GRT.

Road connections are inadequate, but conditions have improved significantly in recent years. There were 3,840 km (2,386 mi) of paved roads in 1985. A large part of the highway system becomes submerged in the rainy season; bridges, ferries, embankments, and dikes are therefore necessary to the inland transportation system. Because of the difficulties of land travel, the number of motor vehicles remains relatively small. In 1992 there were an estimated 130,000 motorized vehicles, including 67,000 passenger automobiles, and 63,000 commercial taxis, trucks, and buses.

Bangladesh Biman is the national airline. It has an extended network connecting major cities and operates international flights from Dhaka airport. In 1992, the airline carried 1,051,500 domestic and international passengers.

12HISTORY

In ancient times, the area now known as Bangladesh was the eastern portion of a huge river delta region called Bang, where the Ganges and Brahmaputra River systems empty into the Bay of Bengal and the Indian Ocean. The region became known as Bengal in more modern times, but recorded history of the region can be traced to the 4th century BC when it was home to an apparently flourishing riverain civilization. The oldest surviving remains of this civilization are the ruins of the city of Mahasthan, the ancient Pundranagar, which continued to flourish for more than 1500 years, even though the region was conquered by the Hindu Maurya empire that reached its height under Emperor Asoka around 207 BC. From this time onward, the history of Bengal was part of the wider historical experience of the Indian subcontinent, and during most of India's classical Hindu period—AD 320 to AD 1000—Bengal was a loosely incorporated outpost of empires centered in the Gangetic plain.

Islam came to South Asia in the years following AD 800 but did not reach Bengal until Muslim invaders from the west secured a foothold there around AD 1200. In the 13th and 14th centuries, after successive waves of Turkish, Persian, and Afghan invaders, Islam began to take a firm hold in the area now Bangladesh. The region was annexed by the Mughal Empire in 1576 under the Muslim Akbar and ruled by his successors into the 17th century. The fealty lesser Nawabs (or Nabobs) of the Bengal area paid to the Mughals ensured the political stability and economic prosperity of the region, which became known for its industries based on the weaving of silk and cotton cloth.

The arrival of the French and British East India Companies in the early 18th century coincided with Mughal decline, the death of Emperor Auranzeb, and an intense period of competition and conflict between Britain and France. By the middle of the 18th century, the British emerged supreme in what they created as the Bengal Presidency, establishing themselves in Calcutta and expanding with alacrity into all of what is now Bangladesh, as well as the Indian states of West Bengal, Bihar, Assam and Orissa. From Calcutta, British traders and administrators successfully played off rivalries among the satraps of the late Mughal empire to gain control of most of the subcontinent in the years between the Battle of Plassey in 1756 and the assumption of the company's domain by the British Crown in 1859. Calcutta remained the seat of British power in the subcontinent and the center of British control over the Indian Empire until 1931 when the capital was moved to the new city of New Delhi, adjacent to the traditional seat of Mughal power in old Delhi.

In general, Hindus in Bengal prospered under the British, apparently taking more easily to British ways and British law than the numerically dominant Muslims. The Muslim aristocracy of eastern Bengal—feudal barons under the Mughals—resisted British rule. By the turn of the 20th century, both communities had begun to develop a political-cum cultural consciousness of their own in reaction to the western culture brought by the British. They took offense at British efforts to impose western educational systems on local universities, reducing their independence. Hindus were further enraged by the British decision in 1905, in an effort to improve administration and to placate Muslims, to divide the overly large Bengal Presidency in two, with the Muslim-dominant part of eastern Bengal and Assam to be a separate province. The 1905 partition was the first acknowledgment of a sense of separateness among Muslims by the British and foreshadowed events of 42 years later when Bengal was divided between Muslim-majority and Hindu-majority districts to create East Pakistan.

LOCATION: 20°34′ to 26°38′N; 88°1′ to 92°41′E. BOUNDARY LENGTHS: India, 2,583 km (1,605 mi); Myanmar, 197 km (122 mi); Bay of Bengal coastline, 574 km (357 mi). TERRITORIAL SEA LIMIT: 12 mi.

The 1905 action was strongly opposed by Bengali Hindus and resulted in increasing acts of violence until it was un-done 6 years later in favor of reuniting Bengal and instead separating out what would become the provinces of Orissa and Bihar. But the agitation provoked by the 1905 partition and the Hindu-Muslim enmities it left behind continued to support terrorist actions against British rule until headed off by the evolution of non-violence as a mode of political struggle, as later enunciated in the cause of Indian self-rule by Mohandas (Mahatma) Gandhi of the Indian National Congress.

British reforms in 1909 and 1919 expanded local self-rule in their Indian domains, but the pace fell short of the pace of demands put forth by the rising tide of nationalist espoused by the Indian National Congress, which—in 1929—committed itself to the goal of complete independence. And as the struggle gained momentum, the majority Hindu and minority Muslim communities in India as a whole began to divide on the eventual "end game." While the majority Hindu community saw a single Indian polity, committed to secularism and diversity, as the goal of the independence movement, Muslims came to fear that their community would be a permanent electoral minority in such single successor state, an anxiety they saw borne out in the 1937 elections held under British auspices. To look after their unique cultural interests, they formed the All-India Muslim League, and under the Muslim League leadership, Muslim sentiment began to coalesce around the "two nation" theory propounded earlier by the poet Iqbal, a belief that South Asian Muslims and Hindus were and should be two separate nations, i.e. that Muslims required the creation of an independent nation of their own—Pakistan—in which they would predominate. In 1940, the Muslim League adopted this as its goal, under the leadership of Mohammad Ali Jinnah, a Bombay attorney who resisted all efforts at compromise through all the difficult days leading up to the grant of independence in 1947.

The new state of Pakistan, made up of Muslim-majority districts in both eastern and western reaches of formerly British India, was at best an unwieldy creation. It cut across long-established lines of trade and communication, divided families, provoked a mass movement of millions of refugees caught on the "wrong" side of the partition markers, and forced the creation of a new but divided polity. Pakistan consisted of two distinct territories, separated 1600 km. (1000 miles) of secular but predominantly Hindu India. West Pakistan, with a population of 34 million, consisted mainly of the former provinces of Baluchistan, Sindh, the Northwest Frontier, and (partially) Punjab (which, like Bengal, was also partitioned). East Pakistan, its 42 million people including nearly nine million Hindus, encompassed the eastern half of Bengal province as shaped in 1912, plus the Sylhet District of Assam.

In language, culture, ethnic background, population density, political experience, and economic potential, East and West Pakistan were totally disparate—the main bonds being Islam and a fear of potential Indian (Hindu) revanchism. Pakistan's early years as a nation were dominated by unsuccessful attempts—punctuated by bouts of authoritarian rule—to create a national polity that would somehow bridge these differences. Larger in population and in economic importance than the west wing, the Bengali east wing chafed under national policies effectively dominated by the leadership residing in the west wing. When its influence was further reduced under repeated bouts of martial law and by the reconstruction of West Pakistan as a single province so as to balance out the political ability of the eastern province to make its weight felt on population and economic terms, demands for autonomy in the east began to mount. This insistent demand for autonomy in East Pakistan proved more than the fragile sense of Islamic nationhood could sustain.

Nationhood

After yet another round of martial law in Pakistan in the 1969, national elections were scheduled for 1970. But when the popular verdict in those elections—even in the national assembly—supported greater autonomy for East Pakistan than the West Pakistan-dominated national leadership was prepared to accord, the results were set aside.

Subsequent civil unrest escalated quickly to civil war in East Pakistan. Swamped with a million refugees from the fighting, India intervened militarily in December 1971, tipping the scales in favor of the rebels and facilitating the creation of Bangladesh in 1972. Sheikh Mujibur (Mujib) Rahman, leader of the Awami League and of the fight for autonomy, was released from prison in West Pakistan (which became the Islamic Republic of Pakistan)

and became Prime Minister of the new nation of Bangladesh.

The 1971 civil war was a disaster for Bangladesh, undoing much of the limited progress East Pakistan had made in recovering from the socio-economic disruption of the 1947 partition. The charismatic Mujib faced a task for which his administrative and political experience was lacking. He fought and won a massive victory at the polls in 1973, but two years later, he suspended the political process and took power into his own hands—as president. Bangla opinion turned against Mujib, coalescing two main opposition groups that otherwise shared little in common besides their opposition to Mujib and to Indian influence: they were the ultra conservative Islamic groups, led by the Jamaat-i-Islami, and the radical left, led by Maoists, who opposed both Indian and Soviet influence.

On 15 August 1975, a group of young military officers seized power, killing Mujib and many of his family members and imposing martial law. A counter-coup three months later produced a new military government with Gen. Zia-ur Rahman at its head. Elections scheduled for February 1977 were postponed, and Zia became president himself in April 1977. A year later, with limited political activity permitted, he was elected President and lifted martial law. And in February 1979, he restored parliamentary government after elections gave his new party, the Bangladesh National Party (BNP) a two-thirds majority in the National Assembly.

Zia's assassination during an abortive military coup in May 1981 set back the progress he had made. He was succeeded in power by his vice president, Abdus Sattar, an elderly civilian who was elected to the office in his own right at elections that November. Respected but weak, Sattar was deposed the following March by his army chief, Gen. Hussain Mohammad Ershad, who declared martial law, became Chief Martial Law Administrator (CMLA), suspended the 1972 constitution, and banned political parties.

Ershad gained support by cracking down on corruption and opening up the economy to foreign collaboration, although his plans to introduce "Islamize" the legal system—as his counterpart in Pakistan sought to do—caused considerable unrest among the country's still substantial Hindu minority. In 1983, he assumed the presidency, and by January 1986, he had restored full political activity in which his own party, the Jatiyo (People's) Party took a prominent part. He retired from the army and was elected president without opposition in October 1986, but in July 1987, mounting opposition to his often dictatorial rule among the united opposition parties led him again to declare a state of emergency, dissolve the assembly, and schedule new elections for March 1988. His Jatiyo Party triumphed in those elections, due mainly to the refusal of the opposition parties to participate. At the end of 1990, in the face of widespread demonstrations and some Hindu-Muslim violence, his opposition had grown so strong that Ershad was forced to resign the presidency, turning the government over to Supreme Court Chief Justice Shahabuddin Ahmed, the unanimous choice of the opposition parties.

An interim government scheduled elections for February 1991, and the result—in what has been described as the fairest polling ever held in the country—was the election of an assembly in which the BNP, now headed by Begum Khaleda Zia-ur Rahman, Zia's widow, held a plurality. With the support of independents and non-elected members of the assembly, the BNP formed the government that continues to govern to the present.

13GOVERNMENT

Bangladesh inherited the provincial government under which first the Dominion, then Republic, of Pakistan was governed, a parliamentary system based on the Westminster model, with a unicameral legislature. Following this model, the constitution of December 1972 established a unitary, democratic republic, with an indirectly-elected president as nominal head of state and a prime minister as head of government and chief executive. The prime minister and his government are responsible to a unicameral legislature—the National Assembly—elected no less frequently than every five years and composed of 330 members, including 30 in appointive seats reserved for women. The constitution incorporated four basic principles of state policy: nationalism, secularism, socialism, and democracy. With considerable controversy, because of its impact on the nearly 17% of the population which is non-Muslim, Islam replaced secularism as a state principle by constitutional amendment in 1977.

The constitution was amended in 1975, at the initiative of Prime Minister Mujibur Rahman, to abrogate most guarantees of civil liberties, to establish a one-party polity, and to make the presidency, rather than the prime ministership, the chief executive of the government. Mujib's assassination later that year, and the countercoup that occurred three months later resulted in a four-year suspension of the constitution by Bangladesh's martial law ruler, Gen. Zia-ur Rahman. The constitutional democracy that was restored in 1979 lasted only until March 1982 when Gen. Ershad seized power and imposed martial law. Parliamentary and presidential elections were held in 1986, under a mild relaxation of martial law provisions and with widespread accusations of electoral fraud and rigging. In November—after the elections—the government lifted martial law but left in place many restrictions on assembly and political activity under emergency provisions of the constitution.

Ershad's resignation at the end of 1990, in the face of a rising crescendo of anti-government rallies, strikes, and violence, led the interim government that followed to schedule and hold what most observers regard as the most free and fair elections ever held in Bangladesh, in 1991.

Among her first acts as prime minister, Begum Khaleda Zia-ur Rahman ended the Ershad-imposed state of emergency. And, in September 1991 she reversed her former position in favor of retaining a strong presidential system to lead the campaign, with strong AL support, that resulted in overwhelming parliamentary approval of a constitutional amendment to restore the parliamentary system of 1972 and to return to the prime ministership the powers removed by Mujib in 1975. The president, elected by the national assembly on 8 October 1991, is former Speaker Abdur Rahman Biswas, elected in open polling. The next elections for the assembly and the president must be held by February 1996.

14POLITICAL PARTIES

From 1947 through the end of 1971, East Pakistan—now Bangladesh—was governed as a single province, one of the two wings of Pakistan. In all, there were more than 30 political parties operating in the east wing, most of the them small, fractious, and with few elected members. The major parties at that time operated on the all-Pakistan level as well, and they included the moderate Pakistan Muslim League (PML), a national movement-become the party of independence and at the outset the ruling party of Pakistan; the moderate socialist Awami (Freedom) League (AL), a spin-off from the Muslim League and the advocate of Bengali autonomy, with the bulk of its support in the east wing; the ultra-conservative Islamic Jamaat-i-Islami (JI), grounded in Sunni Islamic orthodoxy (in Pakistan as in India) and initially opposed to the 1947 partition; and the leftist peasants and workers party, the Krishak Sramik Party (KSP) of Fazlul Haq. The Communist Party of Pakistan (CPP) was banned in 1952 and remained illegal until its east wing component became the Bangladesh Communist Party (BCP) after 1971.

The PML governed East Pakistan from 1947, but in elections in 1954, the Awami League and the Krishak Sramik, supported in a United Front by the Jamaat, ousted the Muslim League from office. Four years of political instability ensued, as the United

Front government of the AL and KSP fell to squabbling immediately and was displaced by the central government under "Governor's Rule," an the emergency provisions of the 1935 Government of India Act, then Pakistan's constitution. When the East Pakistan government was restored in August 1955, the KSP ruled in its own right until displaced by an AL government headed by Maulana Bhashani in 1956. Loss of Hindu support in 1958 cost the AL its majority in 1958, but "Governor's Rule" was again imposed, the provision having been carried over into the 1956 Pakistan Constitution (as it was also, as "President's Rule," in the Indian Constitution of 1950). Martial law was imposed in Pakistan in 1965 and in elections held thereafter, under a limited political franchise, the Muslim League, now a shadow of its former self and the vehicle for General Ayub Khan's entry into elective politics, came to power briefly. Imposition of martial law in 1969 suspended political activity again until the scheduling of elections in 1970 restored political activity.

By 1970, the moderate-to-left. populist Pakistan People's Party (PPP) of Zulfikar Bhutto and the Awami League of Sheikh Mujibur Rahman, now advocating far-reaching autonomy for East Bengal, had become the dominant political forces, respectively, in West and East Pakistan. Elections confirmed this position, with the AL winning 167 of East Pakistan's 169 seats in the National Assembly and absolute control in East Pakistan. The AL was the only constituent in the Bangla Government-in-Exile in 1971, with leftist parties in support and Islamic parties in opposition. After independence, the Islamic party leaders were jailed, their parties having been banned, and in 1973, Mujib's Awami League elected 293 members of the 300-elective seats in the Assembly.

In January 1975, with his power slipping, President Mujib amended the constitution to create a one-party state, renaming his party the Bangladesh Krishak Sramik Awami League (BKSAL). After the coup later in 1975, the BKSAL was disbanded and disappeared. When Zia-ur Rahman lifted the ban on political parties in 1978, his presidential bid was supported a newly formed Nationalist Front, dominated by his Bangladesh National Party (BNP), which won 207 of the assembly's 300 elective seats. All political activity was banned anew in March 1982 when Gen. Ershad seized power, but as he settled into power, Ershad supported the formation of the Jatiyo (People's) Party, which became his vehicle for ending martial law and transforming his regime into a parliamentary government. In elections marked by violence and discredited by extensive fraud, Ershad's Jatiyo Party won more than 200 of the 300 elective seats at stake. The Awami League, now under the leadership of Mujib's daughter, Sheikh Hasina Wajid, took 76 seats as the leading opposition party. The JI held but 10 seats, and the rest were spread widely among independents and splinter parties. Begum Khaleda Zia's BNP, heading an alliance of seven parties, boycotted the elections and gained considerable respect by this action. The BNP, the AL, and all other parties boycotted Ershad's 1988 election as well, discrediting the result that gave the Jatiyo a 2/3 majority and fueling the fires of discontent that led to Ershad's resignation on 4 December 1990. Ershad was arrested on corruption charges 8 days later by the interim government, convicted, and imprisoned on corruption charges.

A BNP plurality in the elections on 27 February 1991 enabled Begum Khaleda Zia to form a government with the support of 28 of the appointive members of the assembly and of the JI, which won 18 seats. The leader of the opposition is Sheikh Hasina Wajid of the Awami League (AL), which won 88 seats to claim the second ranking position in the assembly. Other parties in the assembly include the badly fractionalized Jatiyo Party (JP) of the now jailed Ershad, with 35 seats, the Bangladesh Communist Party (BCP), with 5, and six splinter parties with one seat each. National elections must be held in Bangladesh by February 1996 when the five-year term of this government is completed.

15LOCAL GOVERNMENT

As a unity state, the key administrative unit in Bangladesh is the region (also referred to popularly as the district), of which there are 21 in all. For administrative convenience, regions are grouped into (and report through) four divisions, under a senior civil servant with the title of division commander (formerly commissioner).

Regions or districts are under the charge of a senior civil servant with the title of deputy commissioner; they are appointed by the national government and are vested with broad powers to collect revenues and taxes, assist in development activities, and maintain law and order. As of 1985, regions or districts are subdivided into zilas; in urban areas, these are further broken down into municipalities, wards, mohallas, and thanas, while in rural areas, the breakdown is into upazilas, unions, mouzas, and villages.

The principal organs of local self-government are municipal councils (pourashavas) and rural councils (union parishads); upazila (sub-district) councils were abolished in November 1991. The national police, under the authority of the deputy commissioner in each region, is backed up by rural police forces which also participate in rural development and family planning programs.

16JUDICIAL SYSTEM

The judicial system, modeled after the British system, is similar to that of neighboring countries. Besides the 1972 constitution, the fundamental law of the land, there are codes of civil and criminal laws. The civil law incorporates certain Islamic and Hindu religious principles relating to marriage, inheritance, and other social matters.

The constitution provides for an impartial and independent judiciary. After the 1982 coup, the constitution was suspended, martial law courts were established throughout the country, and Lieut.Gen Ershad assumed the power to appoint judges. The constitution was reinstated in November 1986.

The judicial system consists of a Low Court and a Supreme Courts both of which hear civil and criminal cases. The Low Court consist of administrative courts (magistrate courts) and session judges. The Supreme Court also has two divisions, a High Court which hears original cases and reviews decisions of the Low Court and an Appellate Court which hears appeals from the High Court. The upper level of courts have exercised quite independent judgment, recently ruling against the government on a number of occasions in criminal, civil and even political trials.

17ARMED FORCES

In 1993, Bangladesh had an army of 93,000 men, a navy of 7,500, and an air force of 6,500. Paramilitary forces of border guards, armed police, and security guards totaled 55,000. The military budget in 1992 was $339 million or 1.5% of gross domestic product.

About 15,000 Bengali soldiers in the Pakistan army in 1971 defected to the liberation forces (Mukhti Bahini), and they formed the core of the Bangladesh army after independence. This force, armed mainly with Chinese weapons, is organized into 1 armored and 14 infantry brigades. The Navy mans 4 Chinese frigates and 35 patrol and coastal craft. The air force flies 85 Chinese fighter-bombers of limited capability.

18INTERNATIONAL COOPERATION

Bangladesh joined the UN on 17 September 1974; it belongs to ESCAP and all the nonregional specialized agencies. A member of the Asian Development Bank, the Commonwealth of Nations, and G-77, Bangladesh participates in the nonaligned movement and in international Muslim organizations and conferences. The nation is a signatory to GATT and the Law of the Sea. In 1985,

Bangladesh became one of seven constituent members of the new SAARC. In 1977, Bangladesh signed an agreement with India on sharing water from the Ganges River.

Soon after independence, Bangladesh signed a friendship treaty with India, but the new leaders after the 1975 coup instituted a policy of equal cooperation with other neighboring countries. Pakistan recognized Bangladesh in February 1974, and the two have developed close relations, their past differences notwithstanding. Generally, Bangladesh follows a nonaligned foreign policy and in recent years has sought closer relations with other Islamic states, ASEAN, and China.

19ECONOMY

Bangladesh is a poor country endowed with few natural resources and an economy dominated by subsistence agriculture. About 63% of the country's total land area is currently cropped, while almost 68% of the economically active population derive their livelihood from farming. The incidence of poverty is very high, with roughly one-half of the total population estimated to be earning less than enough to afford a daily diet considered minimally adequate by international standards. Nevertheless, signs of modest improvement in the economy have been evident during the past decade, despite difficult weather and international market conditions. Agriculture still accounts for 35% of the GDP, although this proportion has dropped significantly from 50% in 1979/80, as industry's share has increased from 15.9% to 16.6% and that of services from 34.4% to 48.3%. GDP growth reached 3.4% in 1990/91 and 4.2% in 1991/92.

Over the last several decades, Bangladesh has endured the ravages of the 1971 war with Pakistan, a severe famine in 1971, and a succession of weather-related disasters, the most recent of which included a devastating cyclone in April 1991. After the mid-1970s, financial stabilization measures, encouragement of private investment, and generally good weather contributed to an agricultural growth rate that exceeded the rate of population growth. However, real economic growth under the five-year plan that ended in mid-1985 averaged only slightly over 3% a year, well below the original target of 7.2%. The government responded with a tightened monetary policy and efforts to restrain expenditure and increase revenues.

The new 1985–90 five-year plan continued to emphasize agricultural production and envisaged a growth rate of 5.4% a year. Stabilization, export promotion, and flexible exchange rate management policies strengthened during the mid-1980s helped to decrease fiscal and external deficits, boost non-traditional exports, especially of garments, and reduce inflation to below double-digit figures by the end of the decade. Economic growth was, however, hampered by heavy flooding that occurred in 1987 and 1988, which resulted in negative to no real change in agricultural output for those years. Industrial growth, on the other hand, remained relatively strong, helping to sustain an average GDP growth of 3.7% for the 1985–90 period overall.

In 1990/91, the combined effects of the Gulf war, domestic political disturbances, and a devastating cyclone resulted in a drop in GDP growth rate from 6.6% in 1989/90 to only 3.4%. Pursuit of further stabilization and structural adjustment measures by the newly elected government in 1991 allowed Bangladesh to weather these crises, strengthen its revenue base, bring inflation to a record low of 1.4% in 1993, and maintain a good balance of payments position. Though promising, these indicators have also been accompanied by sluggish development investments, limited growth in manufacturing value added, and persistent bureaucratic inefficiency in aid disbursement and project realization. Thus, while general macroeconomic indicators are relatively strong, it is not yet clear whether much real progress is being achieved in reducing extreme poverty in the country.

20INCOME

In 1992, Bangladesh's GNP was $24,672 million at current prices, or $220 per capita. For the period 1985–92 the average inflation rate was 7.8%, resulting in a real growth rate in per capita GNP of 1.7%.

In 1992 the GDP was $23,783 million in current US dollars. It is estimated that agriculture, hunting, forestry, and fishing contributed 35% to GDP; manufacturing, 9%; electricity, gas, and water, 2%; construction, 6%; wholesale and retail trade, 8%; transport, storage, and communication, 11%; finance, insurance, real estate, and business services, 11%; community, social, and personal services, 13%; and other sources 5%.

21LABOR

The civilian labor force in 1991/92 was estimated at approximately 50 million, of whom slightly over 6% were employed in the industrial sector. Average daily wages in 1991/92 averaged less than $2.00 per day, and per capita annual income, at about $200, is among the lowest in the world.

Most industrial workers are unionized, yet union membership only represents 3.4% of the total civilian labor force. There are industrial tribunals to settle labor disputes. The government can impose labor settlements through arbitration, as well as by declaring a strike illegal. Unemployment (7.3%) and underemployment (43.4%) continue to be high, and agricultural workers are not protected by disability compensation. In 1991, 147,131 workers took jobs abroad, mainly in Arab lands. Over 700,000 Bangladeshis work outside the country.

22AGRICULTURE

Agriculture accounts for 35% of GDP and 75% of employment. Most of the farmers own no more than a few acres of land, and their holdings are badly fragmented. The land is fertile, but yields are low because of a lack of capital for input.

Rice dominates the production of about 80% of all cropped land in Bangladesh. Of the varieties grown, *aman* rice, which can be raised in inundated land and saline soil, occupies nearly 60% of the total land under rice. *Aus* rice, which cannot be grown in flooded fields, is raised mostly in higher areas of Bangladesh. *Boro* rice is grown in the winter, mainly in the swamps and marshy areas, but government-supported irrigation projects have encouraged its extension to other areas. To meet the challenge of the food shortages, the government of Bangladesh and international aid programs introduced a high-yielding variety of rice called IRRI with considerable success. Total rice production in 1992 was 27,400,000 tons. Before November 1992, the government artificially inflated rice prices by buying over 1 million tons per harvest. With subsidies gone, the subsequent fall in rice prices reflected an adjustment of the market after 20 years of prices propped up by government sales and purchases, and helped keep inflation down in 1992/93.

Jute is the main cash crop of Bangladesh, which produces about one-quarter of the total jute supply of the world. Grown in most parts of the country, jute is harvested from July to September. Its strong fibers are used to produce carpets, burlap bags, mats, upholstery, and other products. Jute is also used to manufacture textiles for clothes. The government took several steps toward privatization of the jute industry in 1992/93, but exports of jute were 14% below anticipated levels during July 1992–April 1993, in part the result of a drop in the worldwide use of jute for packing. In 1992, 898,000 tons of jute were produced.

Although tea is the second most important agricultural export, it accounted for only 2.5% of export earnings. Most tea plantations are in the Sylhet Region and the Chittagong Hill Tracts. Much of the tea is consumed domestically; total production in 1992 was 45,000 tons.

The agricultural economy, though disrupted by the 1971 war, largely recovered and by the late 1980s was growing at a rate of about 1.5% a year, reflecting efforts to diversify crops, expand acreage, and improve yields. Frequent monsoons and cyclones keep the economy vulnerable. In 1990 the agricultural sector grew by 10%, due to a bumper harvest of rice. However, growth in the agricultural sector in 1991 and 1992 was down to 1.6% and 2.0%, respectively. Crop output (in tons) included sugarcane, 7,446,000; wheat, 1,065,000; potatoes, 1,379,000; bananas, 630,000; sweet potatoes, 470,000; pulses, 506,000; mangoes, 183,000; pineapples, 160,000; coconuts, 82,000; tobacco, 36,000; and barley, 10,000.

23ANIMAL HUSBANDRY

The country continues to rely on buffalo and bullocks for draft power. Buffalo milk is an important item of consumption, especially in the form of clarified butterfat. Livestock quality is not high. Bangladeshi cows produce only 25% of the meat and 10% of the milk produced by their counterparts in developed countries. There were about 23.7 million head of cattle, 820,000 buffaloes, 18,000,000 goats, 700,000 sheep and poultry in 1992.

As of 1993, much of the cattle stock was smuggled from India because of the reduced local availability of cows and bulls, especially during the mid-year Muslim holiday of *Eid Ul Azha*, when cattle are sacrificed throughout the country. The scarcity of cattle in recent years is the result of lack of vaccines and fodder, natural disasters, and an absence of farmer incentives. In order to boost livestock production, the government plans to train 40,000 men and women in livestock management. In 1992, exports of animal hides totaled $144 million, or 7% of total exports.

24FISHING

Fish is a staple food of Bangladesh and the main source of protein. There are hundreds of varieties, including carp, salmon, pomfret, shrimp, catfish, and many local varieties. Dried fish is considered a delicacy in many parts of the country. About 892,700 tons of fish (71% from inland waters) were produced in 1991. While much of the fish is consumed domestically, Bangladesh exports a sizable quantity of freshwater fish to India and other neighboring countries, and freshwater shrimp and lobster are exported to a number of countries. It is also a major source of frogs' legs, which are "farmed" commercially. Fishermen's cooperatives foster the use of modern fishcatching trawlers in the Bay of Bengal, and the government has established a fisheries corporation to stimulate production of freshwater fish for export. Fish prices soared in 1992 because of sudden fish scarcity; an abnormally low amount of rainfall and/or industrial pollution and river damage are believed to be possible causes.

25FORESTRY

Bangladesh has 1,891,000 hectares (4,673,000 acres) of forest, covering some 15% of land area. In recent years, the pressure of population has led to enormous deforestation. The government-controlled Forest Industries Development Corp. supervises the development and exploitation of forest resources. About 97% of timber cut is used for firewood.

The main forest zone is the Sunderbans area in the southwest, consisting mostly of mangrove forests. Two principal species dominate the Sunderban forests: sundari trees, which grow about 15–18 m (50–60 ft) high and are of tough timber, and gewa trees, a softer wood used for making newsprint. Teak and bamboo are grown in the central forests.

26MINING

Aside from natural gas, Bangladesh has few mineral resources. The Bay of Bengal area is being explored for oil, and in some offshore areas, drilling is being conducted by international companies. Bangladesh has reserves of good quality coal in the northern districts, but extraction has been difficult since many deposits are located at a depth of more than 900 m (3,000 ft). However, as of 1991, Chinese consultants confirmed the presence of 300 million tons of good quality coal at depths above 150m (500 ft) at the Boropukuria coalfield in the norther Diajpur District. Production estimates of mineral commodoties in Bangladesh in 1991 included cement, 274,551 tons; marine salt, 300,000 tons; and limestone (mined in the Sylhet and Chittagong regions), 42,484 tons.

27ENERGY AND POWER

A substantial portion of Bangladesh's electrical supply is met by the country's only hydroelectric plant, at Kaptai, which has a capacity of 130 Mw; the rest of the country's power is produced by burning coal, gas, and oil. Except for a few private installations on the tea plantations and a few other industries, the power and energy sector is controlled by a government-managed corporation. Total power production was 8,930 million kwh in 1991, of which about 9% was hydroelectric. Installed capacity totaled 2,690,000 kw (9% hydroelectric).

Reserves of 700 billion cu m of natural gas in 13 fields have been found; production totaled 4,893 million cu m in 1991. Natural gas is used for fertilizers as well as for electricity generation; the government controls the gas industry. The UAE-based Scimitar Exploration Co. drilled an exploratory natural gas well in 1991. About $508 million was scheduled to be invested in the oil and natural gas sector from 1992 to 1994, financed by the World Bank and Asian Development Bank. Chinese consultants confirmed the existence of 300 million tons of good quality coal at the Boropukuria coal field in northern Diajpur District during 1991.

28INDUSTRY

Although private investment has been encouraged since the mid-1980s, until recently it remained closely regulated, and state-owned firms dominated production in many sectors, including the centrally important jute industry. Lack of growth in manufacturing's share of total GDP during the 1980s suggested the constraints of this policy regime. In 1991, the government announced a new Industrial Policy, planning investment liberalization, the interim restructuring of several large parastatals, as well as the gradual privatization of public enterprises in all but the airways, railways, and minting sectors. To promote development of export-oriented industries, two export processing zones have been developed, one in the port city of Chittagong (established 1983) and one in Savar (inaugurated in 1993, 30 km from Dhaka). Another EPZ is scheduled to be developed at Khulna, about 150 west of Chittagong, within the next two years

Transitional difficulties in the restructuring of important state enterprises resulted in some output decline in a few industries in the early 1990s. Total output from principal industries for 1991/92 as compared with 1990/91 (in parentheses) included: jute textiles, 416,400 tons (433,900 tons); garments, 17,674 dozen pieces; cotton yarn, 60,516,000 kg (56,000,000 kg); cotton cloth, 58,865,000 meters (60,025,000 m); fertilizer, 1,989,000 tons (1,367,000 tons); cement, 272,500 tons (274,600 tons); steel ingots, 36,800 tons (57,500 tons), paper and newsprint, 88,300 tons (90,100 tons); tea, 45,500 kg (44,400 kg); sugar 195,400 tons (246,100 tons).

29SCIENCE AND TECHNOLOGY

Bangladesh lacks the trained personnel necessary for intensive technological development. The Bangladesh University of Engineering and Technology (founded in 1961) does train some technicians, however, and the Bangladesh Council for Scientific and Industrial Research and the Bangladesh Academy of Sciences conduct basic research. Bangladesh has five other institutes conducting research in agriculture, medicine, and atomic energy, and eight other colleges and universities offering scientific training.

30DOMESTIC TRADE

Except for jute, tea, paper, garments, frozen shrimp, and a few other items, most of the commodities produced in Bangladesh are consumed inside the country. Normally, the farmers or fishermen sell to the wholesalers, and they in turn sell to distributors and retailers. Industrial commodities for domestic consumption are distributed through the same procedure. The middlemen in the distribution process have often benefited from excessive profits, creating hardships for farmers and consumers. To meet this situation, the government has introduced mechanisms by means of which farmers can sell directly to cooperative agencies acting on behalf of buyers. The government has also set up fair-price shops for consumers. Much domestic trade in rural areas is conducted in the marketplaces, where farmers sell directly to consumers.

Foreign products are imported by large commercial concerns located in the capital city of Dhaka or in the ports, and are then distributed through wholesalers and retailers. Normal business hours are between 9 AM and 5 PM, but most retail stores are open until 8 PM. Most establishments close on Fridays and on Thursday afternoons and evenings. Limited advertising is done through the newspapers, movie houses, handbills, and television.

31FOREIGN TRADE

Since independence, Bangladesh has had a strongly negative trade balance. Imports steadily ran more than double the value of exports between 1971 and 1990/91. With a surge in export growth since 1990/91, the trade deficit has finally narrowed significantly; imports exceeded exports by about 92% in 1990/91, and by only 67% in 1992/93, as opposed to more than 120% in 1989/90. As a result of successful export promotion measures undertaken by the government during the 1980s, exports of ready-made-garments are now Bangladesh's leading earner of foreign exchange, trailed by once-dominant jute and jute manufactures. Leather goods and frozen seafood have also become important exports, in addition to tea and more traditional dried fish. Major imports are manufactured goods, foodgrains, and petroleum. Average current tariffs on imports have been reduced to about 50% with a ceiling of 100% specified by the government.

In 1990/91, Bangladesh's principal export purchasers were the US the Federal Republic of Germany, and the UK. Exports to and imports from the main trading partners were as follows (in millions of taka):

	EXPORTS	IMPORTS	BALANCE
USA	17,407	7,776	9,631
Japan	2,056	11,736	−9,680
FRG	5,778	3,944	1,834
Singapore	2,276	7,321	−5,045
Hong Kong	680	7,633	−6,953
UK	4,647	3,273	1,374
China	1,222	6,491	−5,269
India	195	6,981	−6,786
Other countries	26,010	60,350	−34,340
TOTAL	60,271	115,505	−55,234

32BALANCE OF PAYMENTS

The continuing trade deficit has been offset in small part by private transfers, mainly from earnings of workers in the Middle East, but large amounts of foreign aid and heavy short-term borrowing are needed to handle the balance-of-payments problem. In 1991/92, the infusion of $1.59 billion in foreign and transfers helped lessen a negative balance of payments. In 1992 merchandise exports totaled $2,097.9 million and imports $3,351.2 million. The merchandise trade balance was $−1,253.4 million.

³³BANKING AND SECURITIES

Central banking is conducted by the Bangladesh Bank, which has its head office in Dhaka. It is responsible for the circulation of money, supervision of commercial banks, and control of credit and foreign exchange. Total bank deposits of commercial banks came to T48,294 million as of 1993, and currency in circulation, as measured by M2, amounted to T329,301 million.

As of 1993 there were 22 commercial banks in Bangladesh, of which 4 were nationalized. As of 30 June, time deposits of the commercial banks totaled T236,020 million; demand deposits amounted to T48,294 million. The Dhaka stock exchange as of 1993 listed the securities of 120 companies.

³⁴INSURANCE

The insurance business was nationalized in 1972, creating a government-controlled insurance corporation. Premiums are mainly in commercial or industrial fields. Life insurance is still limited to city dwellers and middle-class professionals; as of 1985 there were 280,272 ordinary life insurance policies in force.

³⁵PUBLIC FINANCE

The fiscal year runs from June to July. In 1990/91, monetary growth was at a record low of 12.5%, and the fiscal deficit fell within the parameters of IMF, World Bank, and Asian Development Bank donors. The budget deficit in 1990/91 amounted to 9.27% of GDP, up from 9.04% in 1989/90. Foreign aid infusions typically account for 7–8% of GDP. Large pay increases given to civil servants in 1991/92 have recently cast some doubt over the government's commitment to fiscal responsibility. Bangladesh's national debt was $11.09 billion in 1991, up 8% from the June 1990 debt of $10.26 billion.

³⁶TAXATION

The principal direct taxes are personal income taxes and corporate income taxes (40–45%), and a sales tax levied on all important consumer goods. Essential agricultural implements and irrigation pumps are excluded from certain taxes.

³⁷CUSTOMS AND DUTIES

Bangladesh gets a major portion of its current revenue from import duties and excise taxes. In 1993 tariffs averaged 50%, with a ceiling of 100%. Automobiles and other items are heavily taxed, as are tobacco and alcohol.

³⁸FOREIGN INVESTMENT

Bangladesh nationalized most industries in 1972 and set up nine corporations to oversee them. Subsequently, the Bangladesh government relaxed its policy toward foreign investment and announced a program granting tax holidays to new foreign investors. In 1989 the Directorate of Industries was renamed the Board of Industries and delegated the task of providing various forms of assistance to new investors. More recently, the 1991 Industrial Policy has liberalized conditions for foreign investment much further—100% foreign equity is now allowed on investments anywhere in the country, not simply in export processing zones, and many regulations discriminating between foreign and domestic investors have been abolished. Reflecting the more favorable policy environment, foreign direct investment first flowed into the country in significant amounts, albeit still haltingly, in the late 1980s. As of 1992, the value of all US investments in the country totaled $40 million. Expanding the flow of foreign investment to the country is likely to hinge upon further proof of government commitment to facilitating private business activity.

³⁹ECONOMIC DEVELOPMENT

The major objectives of planned development have been increased national income, rural development, self-sufficiency in food, and increased industrial production. However, progress in achieving development goals has been slow. Bangladesh's first five-year plan (1973–78) aimed to increase economic growth by 5.5% annually, but actual growth averaged only 4% per year. A special two-year plan (1978–80), stressing rural development, also fell short of its projected growth target, as did the second five-year plan (1980–85), which targeted 7.2% annual growth. The third five-year plan (1985–90) had a 5.4% annual growth target though only 3.7% was actually achieved.

After several years of escalating political unrest, in 1991 the newly elected government embarked upon a three-year "Enhanced Structural Adjustment Facility" (ESAF) program following the original SAF program initiated in 1987. Important components of the renewed adjustment efforts have included financial sector reform and liberalization measures to encourage investment, government revenue improvement efforts (realized largely through implementation of a value-added-tax), tight monetary policy, and the restructuring and privatization of most public enterprises. Income transfer measures, Food-for-Work, and other programs are being implemented to help protect the poorest segments of the population from the transitional effects of structural reform. Given sustained reform efforts, substantial improvements in the current investment rate and government project performance are expected to occur, along with further reductions in fiscal and current account deficits, continued export growth of over 8% annually, and a GDP growth rate of 5.5% by 1995.

⁴⁰SOCIAL DEVELOPMENT

Promotion of social welfare was a declared objective of public policy under the constitution of December 1972, and a major government department—the Ministry of Social Welfare and Women's Affairs—is devoted to social welfare tasks. However, funding has been limited. There are also several hundred voluntary welfare organizations operating throughout the country.

The gravest threat to Bangladesh is uncontrolled population growth. In 1976, the National Population Council was formed to develop a coherent population control program, and the Ministry of Health assumed responsibility for family planning, providing information on contraceptive use and delivering free contraceptives to women. The third five-year plan (1985–90) set goals of sterilization of 3,400,000 people and an increase of couples practicing family planning to 10,500,000, from 4,500,000 in 1984. By 1991, the contraceptive prevalence rate had risen to 30% from 3% in 1970, and the total fertility rate had fallen from almost 7 births per woman to 4.8 in two decades.

While women have and exercise full voting rights, they receive unequal treatment in many areas, including education, employment, and family matters such as divorce and inheritance.

⁴¹HEALTH

Malaria, tuberculosis, and other serious diseases remain endemic, and public health problems are aggravated by widespread malnutrition and periodic natural disasters. In 1990, the prevalence of malnutrition in children under five years old was 60%, and there were 220 cases of tuberculosis per 100,000 people. Because the lack of Vitamin A plays a role in blindness and malnutrition, in 1993 the government of Bangladesh used a national system to distribute Vitamin A capsules to children (with about 25% having been served at that time).

In 1990, there were 8,566 doctors (15 per 1,000 people), 2,630 pharmacists, 523 dentists, and 5,074 nurses. In 1992, only 45% of the population had access to health services. In 1992 there were 0.3 hospitals beds per 1,000 people.

Average life expectancy at birth in 1992 was 53 years, with a death rate of 13.6 per 1,000 people in 1993. The infant mortality rate was 97 per 1,000 live births in 1992. It is estimated that 31% of married women (ages 15–49) use contraception.

42HOUSING

Housing has long been a vital concern in Bangladesh. The government maintains an urban housing program but does not have any housing development program for villages. The House Building Finance Corp. lends money for private as well as public housing. Dhaka and Chittagong urban development is conducted under the guidance of town planning authorities, which develop land and allocate it for private dwelling and commercial purposes. As of 1981, 63% of all housing units were straw or bamboo, 20% were mud or unburnt brick, 12% were cement or wood roofed with iron sheets, and 5% were cement or brick.

43EDUCATION

In 1990, 35.3% of the adult population of Bangladesh was literate (males: 47.1% and females: 22%). The government, as a matter of policy, is attempting to broaden the educational base to eradicate mass illiteracy. Most educational institutions are supported by the government either fully or partially. The language of instruction is Bangla.

Bangladesh has five years of compulsory education. In 1990, the number of primary schools was 45,917 with 189,508 teachers and 11,939,949 students. At the secondary level, there were 130,949 teachers and 3,592,995 students. There are 7 universities, 10 medical colleges, and 10 teacher-training colleges. Research institutions include the Bangla Academy (which sponsors translations of scientific and literary works into Bangla), the Asiatic Society, and the National Institute of Public Administration's Institute of Law and International Affairs. In 1990, there were 22,447 teachers and 434,309 students in all higher level institutions.

44LIBRARIES AND MUSEUMS

The largest library in Bangladesh is the National library with 1.0 million volumes. The largest academic library is Dhaka University Library (with 541,000 volumes). It houses the university's collection and that of the former Public Library of East Pakistan. Dhaka's Central Public Library has 100,000 volumes. The Bangla Academy maintains an excellent research collection.

The Dhaka Museum contains a variety of sculptures and paintings from the Buddhist, Hindu, and Muslim periods. Both it and the Balda Museum have outstanding collections of Bengali art and ancient artifacts. A museum at Comilla houses 7th-century archaeological finds, and the museum of Rajshahi contains many artifacts from the ruins of an 8th-century Buddhist monastery excavated nearby. There is a gallery of contemporary paintings as well as an ethnological museum in Chittagong.

45MEDIA

There were 241,250 telephones in 1992. The major Bangla daily newspapers (with 1991 circulations), all in Dhaka, are *Ittefaq* (200,000), *Banglar Bani* (125,000), *Sangbad* (75,000), and *Dainik Bangla* (40,000); the largest English dailies, also in Dhaka, are the *Bangladesh Observer* (65,000) and *Bangladesh Times* (35,600). In all, there are 72 dailies, with a total 1991 circulation of 1,016,000.

In 1991, Bangladesh had 26 radio broadcasting stations and 11 television stations, which were accessible to about 90% of the population; color television was introduced in 1980. As of the same year, there were 4,990,000 radios and 540,000 television sets. All postal and telecommunications services are controlled by the government.

46ORGANIZATIONS

Various associations for the Muslim, Hindu, Christian, and Buddhist communities have long been active in organizing religious festivals and social activities. Every town also has several cultural groups. The Bangladesh Women's Association, the Boy Scouts, and the Girl Guides are active in social life. There are also many philanthropic organizations and workers' associations, along with several national athletic organizations.

47TOURISM, TRAVEL, AND RECREATION

At the end of the 1980s tourism declined due to political unrest. In 1991, 113,242 foreign visitors arrived, 44,890 from South Asia and 18,206 from Eastern Asia. There were 3,063 hotel rooms with 6,267 beds and a 48.6%occupancy rate. Tourism revenues totaled $9 million. The main tourist attractions include the old Mughal capital at Dhaka, nearby Sonargaon with its ancient architecture, the Buddhist cultural center of Mainamati, and the beach resort of Cox's Bazar.

48FAMOUS BANGLADESHIS

Many Bengalis distinguished themselves in political life before the creation of Bangladesh. A. K. Fazlul Huq (d.1962), the former premier of Bengal Province, moved the Lahore Resolution of 1940, calling for an independent Pakistan, and dominated Bengali politics for half a century. H. S. Suhrawardy (1895–1964), another former premier of Bengal, served for a time as premier of Pakistan and was a mentor to the next generation of Bengali leaders. Sheikh Mujibur Rahman (1920–75), a leader of the Awami League, led the successful fight for the independence of East Pakistan and was the first premier of Bangladesh (1972–75). Maj. Gen. Zia-ur Rahman (1936–81) was military ruler of the country from 1976 until his assassination. As of 1994, the two leading Bangla politicians are women: prime minister Khalida Zia and opposition leader Skeikh Hasina Wajid.

49DEPENDENCIES

Bangladesh has no territories or colonies.

50BIBLIOGRAPHY

Baxter, Craig. *Historical Dictionary of Bangladesh Rahman.* Metuchen, N.J.: Scarecrow Press, 1989.

Chakrabarti, Dilip K. *Ancient Bangladesh, a Study of the Archaeological Sources.* Delhi; New York: Oxford University Press, 1992.

Heitzman, James and Robert L. Worden, eds. *Bangladesh, a Country Study,* 2d ed. Washington, D.C.: Library of Congress, U.S. Government Printing Office, 1989.

Johnson, B. L. *Bangladesh,* 2d ed., rev. Totowa, N.J.: Barnes & Noble, 1982.

Khan, Azizur Rahman. *The Strategy of Development in Bangladesh and Mahabub Hossain.* New York: St. Martin's Press, 1990.

Sisson, Richard. *War and Secession: Pakistan, India, and the Creation of Bangladesh.* Berkeley: University of California Press, 1990.

Zaheer, Hasan. *The Separation of East Pakistan: the Rise and Realization of Bengali Muslim Nationalism.* Karachi; New York: Oxford University Press, 1994.

Ziring, Lawrence. *Bangladesh: from Mujib to Ershad: an Interpretive Study.* Karachi; New York: Oxford University Press, 1992.

BHUTAN

Kingdom of Bhutan
Druk-Yul

CAPITAL: Thimphu (Tashi Chho Dzong).

FLAG: The flag is divided diagonally into an orange-yellow field above and a crimson field below. In the center is a wingless white Chinese dragon.

ANTHEM: *Gyelpo Tenjur,* beginning "In the Thunder Dragon Kingdom, adorned with sandalwood."

MONETARY UNIT: The ngultrum (N) is a paper currency of 100 chetrum. There are coins of 5, 10, 25, and 50 chetrum and 1 ngultrum, and notes of 1, 5, 10, and 100 ngultrum. The ngultrum is at par with the Indian rupee (R), which also circulates freely. N1 = $0.0319 (or $1 = N31.370).

WEIGHTS AND MEASURES: The metric system is the legal standard, but some traditional units are still in common use.

HOLIDAYS: King's Birthday, 11–13 November; National Day, 17 December. Movable Buddhist holidays and festivals are observed.

TIME: 5:30 PM = noon GMT.

¹LOCATION, SIZE, AND EXTENT

Bhutan, a landlocked country in the Himalaya mountain range, has an area of 47,000 sq km (18,147 sq mi), extending 306 km (190 mi) E–W and 145 km (90 mi) N–S. Comparatively, the area occupied by Bhutan is slightly more than half the size of the state of Indiana. It is bordered on the E, S, and W by India and on the N and NW by China, with a total boundary length of 1,075 km (668 mi). The capital city of Bhutan, Thimphu, is located in the west central part of the country.

²TOPOGRAPHY

Bhutan is a mountainous country of extremely high altitudes and irregular, often precipitous terrain, which may vary in elevation by several thousand feet within a short distance. Elevation generally increases from south to north. The mountains are a series of parallel north-south ranges. The loftiest peaks, found in the Himalayan chain that stretches along the northern border, include Kula Kangri (7,554 m/24,783 ft) and Chomo Lhari (7,314 m/ 23,997 ft). Great spurs extend south from the main chain along the eastern and western borders. In the rest of the country are mainly ranges of steep hills separated by narrow valleys. Bhutan is drained by many rivers flowing south between these ranges and for the most part ultimately emptying into the Brahmaputra River in India. The Amo River drains the Chumbi Valley. The Wong, with its tributaries, drains the valleys of Paro Dzong and Thimphu; the Mo drains Punakha Valley. Several rivers of eastern Nepal flow into the Manas.

³CLIMATE

Because of the irregular terrain, the climate varies greatly from place to place. In the outer foothills adjoining the Indian plains, rainfall ranges from about 150 cm to 300 cm (60–120 in) a year; the jungles and forests are hot and steaming in the rainy season, while the higher hills are cold, wet, and misty. Violent Himalayan thunderstorms gave rise to Bhutan's Dzongkha name, Druk-Yul, which translates as "Land of the Thunder Dragon." Rainfall is moderate in the central belt of flat valleys

(1,100–3,000 m/3,500–10,000 ft). The uplands and high valleys (above 3,700 m/12,000 ft) are relatively dry. There is less rainfall in eastern Bhutan. In general, the mountainous areas are cold most of the year. Temperatures average 4°C (39°F) in January and 17°C (63°F) in July.

⁴FLORA AND FAUNA

Dense jungle growth is characteristic at altitudes below 1,500 m (5,000 ft). Above that height the mountain slopes are covered with forest, including beech, ash, birch, maple, cypress, and yew. At 2,400–2,700 m (8,000–9,000 ft) are forests of oak and rhododendron. Above this level, firs and pines grow to the timber line. Primulas, poppies (including the rare blue variety), magnolias, and orchids abound.

The relative abundance of wild animals is attributed to the Buddhist reluctance to take life. In the lower parts of southern Bhutan, mammals include the cheetah, goral, sambar, bear, and rhinoceros; in the higher regions are snow deer, musk deer, and barking deer. Game birds include pheasants, partridges, pigeons, and quail.

⁵ENVIRONMENT

In 1994, the most significant environmental problems in Bhutan were soil erosion and water pollution. The erosion of the soil occurs because 50% of the land in Bhutan is situated on mountainous slopes which are subject to landslides during the monsoon season. Other contributing factors are overcutting of timber, road construction, and the building of irrigation channels. The nation has 22.8 cubic miles of water supply, but 40% of all city dwellers and 70% of people in rural areas do not have pure water.

The Manas Game Sanctuary is located along the banks of the Manas River in southeastern Bhutan. By 1994, there were 15 species of endangered mammals including the tiger, snow leopard, Asian elephant, and wild yak, and 10 bird species were threatened with extinction, as well as 15 threatened species of plants and one endangered reptile.

⁶POPULATION

The population of Bhutan was estimated by the UN at 1,612,000 in 1992. According to UN estimates, the annual growth rate was 2.2% in 1985–90, and the projected population for the year 2000 was 1,942,000, assuming a crude birthrate of 37.6 per 1,000 population, a crude death rate of 14.4, and a net natural increase of 23.2 during 1995–2000. Population density was 34.6 per sq km (89.6 per sq mi) in 1992. Some 93.6% of the population was rural in 1995. The laboring population is not gathered into towns but lives in the countryside in the vicinity of fortresses called dzongs. A dzong, the official center of a region or district, often houses substantial numbers of Buddhist monks. Many place names incorporate the word dzong, which means "castle-monastery." The capital, Thimphu, had an estimated population of 27,000 in 1990. Phuntsholing had more than 10,000 people.

⁷MIGRATION

Bhutan opposes immigration and forbids the entry of new settlers from Nepal. Since 1959, when about 4,000 Tibetan refugees entered Bhutan, the border with Tibet has been closed to immigration. By 1980, most of the refugees had become citizens of Bhutan; the rest migrated to India. The border between Bhutan and India is open, and citizens of Bhutan are free to live and work in India.

⁸ETHNIC GROUPS

Bhutanese are mainly of Tibetan stock, and are also known as Buotias. The Ngalop (also called Bhobe) are people of Tibetan origin who live in northern and western Bhutan; the Sharchop inhabit the eastern regions and also have ethnic affinities with the people of China's Tibetan region. Aboriginal or indigenous tribal peoples live in villages scattered throughout Bhutan. The remaining peoples are Nepalese settlers (about 28–40% of the population), living mostly in the south. Some 85,000 were expelled to Nepal in 1992–93, and about 5,000–15,000 more moved to India.

⁹LANGUAGES

Four main languages are spoken in Bhutan. The official language is Dzongkha, a Tibetan dialect spoken mainly by Ngalop in the northern and western parts of the country. Bumthangkha, an aboriginal language, is spoken in central Bhutan, while Sharchop-kha is spoken in eastern Bhutan. Both of these are used in primary schools in areas where their speakers predominate. The Nepalese largely retain their own language, Nepali.

¹⁰RELIGIONS

About 70% of the Bhutanese are Buddhists, and about 25% are Hindus, Mahayana Buddhism being the state religion. The Drukpa (people of the dragon) subsect of the Kagyupa sect of Buddhism, introduced from Tibet in the 12th century, dominates the collective life of the Bhutanese through a large clerical body estimated at more than 6,000 lamas or monks, centered in 8 major monasteries (dzongs) and 200 smaller shrines (gompas) scattered throughout the land. This sect incorporates both the ideology of the classical Buddhist scriptures and the indigenous pre-Buddhist animistic beliefs called Bon. Muslims make up most of the remaining 5% of the population.

¹¹TRANSPORTATION

Traditionally, Bhutan's communications have been mostly with Tibet, through several strategic mountain passes. Most travelers continue to journey on foot or mounted on hardy ponies bred to withstand great altitudes and steep slopes. Goods are transported by porters or on pack animals. Many of the rivers are still crossed by native cantilever bridges of excellent construction.

Prior to the 1961–66 development plan there were no surfaced roads in Bhutan. Since then, a network of roads and suspension bridges has been built by India. In 1991 there were about 1,304 km (810 mi) of roads, including about 418 km (260 mi) of surfaced roads. Of the 186 suspension bridges projected in the 1981–87 economic plan, 102 were completed by 1985. There is bus service linking Paro Dzong and Tashi Gang Dzong with Indian border towns. The national air carrier, Druk Airlines, began operations in 1983 with regular flights between Calcutta and Paro Dzong, the site of Bhutan's main airfield.

¹²HISTORY

Little is known of the history of Bhutan before the 17th century. Buddhism was originally introduced from India in the 8th century, although the Buddhism of today's Bhutan is very much Tibetan in character. The forebears of the Bhotes (or Bhotias) came from Tibet, probably in the 9th century, when Tibetans invaded the area and met little resistance from the indigenous Tephu tribe. In the middle of the fifteenth century, Shabdung Ngawang Nangyal, a Tibetan lama exercising temporal as well as spiritual power, united the country and built most of the fortified villages (dzongs). His successors in power established a dual system, separating the temporal ruler (Desi or deb raja) and the spiritual ruler (Je Khempo or dharma raja).

The first recorded contact with the West occurred in 1772, when the British East India Company repelled a Bhutanese invasion of the princely state of Cooch Behar in India; they concluded a peace treaty two years later. During the 18th century and most of the 19th, British efforts to open trade with Bhutan proved futile, with the Bhutanese frequently attacking the relatively level areas of Assam and Bengal along their southern border. In 1865, the British finally defeated the Bhutanese, and Bhutan formally accepted a British subsidy of R50,000 a year, which was dependent upon their keeping the peace.

With British approval, Ugyen Dorji Wangchuk became the first hereditary king in 1907, replacing the temporal ruler. In 1910, the Punakha Treaty was concluded between the British Indian Government and Bhutan, under which British India agreed explicitly not to interfere in Bhutanese internal affairs, while Bhutan accepted British "guidance" in handling external matters—a role independent India assumed after 1947. A formal Indo-Bhutanese accord concluded in 1949 reaffirmed and amplified the earlier Punakha Treaty. Besides increasing Bhutan's annual subsidy to R500,000 and returning to Bhutan 83 square kilometers (32 square miles) of territory around Dewangiri (wrested by the British in 1865), it made India responsible for Bhutan's defense and strategic communications, committing India to avoid interfering in Bhutan's affairs and affirming Bhutan's agreement to be "guided by the advice of" India in foreign affairs.

In 1959, China published maps of the Himalayan frontier with South Asia that showed as Chinese part of the territory claimed by Bhutan; Chinese representatives also asserted that Bhutan belonged to a greater Tibet. In response, Indian prime minister Jawaharlal Nehru warned that an attack on Bhutan would be deemed an act of war against India. Fighting between India and China in neighboring border regions in the fall of 1962 did not violate Bhutan's borders, although survivors from Indian army units decimated east of Bhutan straggled back to India through Bhutan.

In April 1964, the long-time prime minister, Jigme Dorji, was assassinated, revealing fissures among the ruling elite. The plotters who were caught were executed, including the deputy commander of the army; others fled to Nepal. In the 1960s, Bhutan's advance toward modernization and the end of its insularity were accelerated by economic plans prepared and underwritten by India.

Relations with Nepal have grown difficult in recent years, the result of violence and cross-border attacks in southern Bhutan from which thousands of ethnic Nepalese—both illegal immigrants and Bhutanese citizens—have migrated (or been forced to flee) in recent years. The king has used a mixture of firmness and conciliation in dealing with increasing violence by ethnic Nepalese who operate from Indian soil but with the tacit support of the Nepalese authorities, urging Bhutanese of Nepalese origin to remain in Bhutan. Meanwhile, his government has sought the cooperation of the governments of Nepal and India in dealing with this activity. Talks were held in 1992 and 1993 with the Nepalese prime minister and home minister, respectively, and an agreement reached during the Nepal home minister's visit to Bhutan in July 1993 resulted in the establishment of a Joint Committee which met later in Kāthmāndu and, according to a Nepal Government announcement in October 1993, will seek to identify and divide the estimated 85,000 refugees into four categories (1) bonafide Bhutanese; (2) Bhutanese emigres; (3) non-Bhutanese; and (4) Bhutanese who have committed crimes in Bhutan. Further meetings of the Joint Committee will discuss verification procedures. This process has the support of the Indian prime minister, who—during his visit to Bhutan in 1993—expressed confidence that Bhutan and Nepal could solve the ethnic question.

13GOVERNMENT

Bhutan has functioned as a limited monarchy since 1969. The king, who is chief of state and head of government, is appointed from the royal hereditary line by the National Assembly and may be removed at any time by a two-thirds vote of that body. The king appoints 2 of the 10 members (as of 1986) of the Royal Advisory Council, the country's chief administrative body, most of whose members are civil servants; some represent the Buddhist hierarchy. There is also a 7-member Council of Ministers with administrative functions.

The unicameral National Assembly, known as the Tsongdu, consists of 151 members. Of these, 33 are appointed by the king; 106 are elected to three-year terms by groups of village headmen, who are, in turn, elected by a one-family, one-vote system; and the remaining 12 are chosen by the lamas acting in concert. The Tsongdu meets twice a year at Thimphu, the capital (previously known as Punakha). Since 1969, it has become a more active, independent influence on government policy through its power to overrule bills proposed by the king or the Advisory Council.

During the 1960s, King Jigme Dorji Wangchuk (r.1952–72) was a prime mover behind social and political reforms that included emancipation of some 5,000 slaves, acceptance of limits on landholdings, and administrative changes that took the country in the direction of constitutional monarchy. Crown Prince Jigme Singye Wangchuk, assumed the throne upon his father's death in July 1972 and was crowned in June 1974. He continued his father's policy of sharing authority with the Council of Ministers and the National Assembly. As part of its modernization program, Bhutan conducted its most comprehensive census ever in 1991 and is attempting to adjust its laws and its governmental institutions to cope with changing social and political needs. To encourage greater responsibility for decision-making by government officials and to allow himself more time to address political affairs, the king gave up chairmanship of the Planning Commission, a post he had held for 19 years, in 1991.

The Government of Bhutan reported a major scandal in 1991 with the discovery that more than 350 southern Bhutanese civil servants—including some senior officials—had fled the country just one step ahead of an audit suggesting large-scale theft and malfeasance. Many were granted asylum in Nepal, and this was the subject of discussions between the two governments in December 1991.

14POLITICAL PARTIES

Political parties are illegal in Bhutan. An opposition group known as the Bhutan State Congress (BSC) composed mainly of ethnic Nepalese has long maintained its headquarters in nearby India;

LOCATION: 26°42′ to 28°21′N; 88°45′ to 92°8′E. BOUNDARY LENGTHS: India, 607 km (377 mi); China, 412 km (256 mi).

other such groups, all very small and headquartered in either India or in Nepal, include the People's Forum for Democratic Rights and the Students' Union of Bhutan. A new, militant opposition group, operating under the banner of the Bhutan People's Party (BPP) and affiliated with the Bhutan National Democratic Party (BNDP) in Nepal, was founded in 1990 in Siliguri, India. It claims to represent the interests of thousands of ethnic Nepalese—both illegal immigrants and Bhutanese citizens—who have migrated (or been forced to flee) from farming areas of southern Bhutan in recent years. Allegedly supported by the Communist Parties of India (CPI) and Nepal (CPN), the BPP was responsible for demonstrations in September 1990 in Bhutan; it has charged the Bhutan government with human rights violations and "ethnic cleansing" in the area.

BPP tactics in 1991 and 1992 included hit-and-run terrorist raids into Bhutan, burning schools, census and land records, and health facilities and attacking ethnic Bhutanese (as well as loyal Nepalese) in national dress; BPP activists also organized camps for the tens of thousands of "refugees" said to be in southern Nepal. In 1992, Bhutan government policy toward the terrorist attacks stiffened, with arrests and long prison sentences meted out to captured BPP activists. While seeking the cooperation of the governments of India and Nepal to bring this problem under control in 1993, the Bhutan government also sought the help of state authorities in the Indian states of Assam and West Bengal in staunching cross-border violence.

15LOCAL GOVERNMENT

The country is divided into four regions—East, Central, West, and South—each administered by a governor appointed by the king. As of 1985 there were 18 districts (dzongkhas) under the supervision of district commissioners (dzongdas), who are appointed by the Royal Civil Service Commission and are responsible for law and order. Districts are further subdivided into blocks (gewog), of which there are 192 in the country. As part of the king's efforts to encourage decentralization in decision-making, the government began a program to establish Block Development Committees in the 192 Blocks in the country.

16JUDICIAL SYSTEM

The legal system is based on English common law and Indian law. Local headmen and magistrates (thrimpon) hear cases in the first instance. Appeals may be made to an eight-member High Court, established in 1968. From the High Court, a final appeal may be made to the King who in turn delegates decisionmaking authority to the Royal Advisory Council. Judges are appointed for life by the King. There is no written constitution. Criminal matters and most civil matters are resolved by application of the 17th century legal code as revised in 1959. Questions of family law are governed by traditional Buddhist or Hindu law. Minor offenses are adjudicated by village headmen. Criminal defendants have no right to court appointment of an attorney and no right to a jury trial.

17ARMED FORCES

The army consists of about 4,000 lightly armed soldiers, trained by Indian officers, in the army and palace guard. India is responsible for Bhutan's defense.

18INTERNATIONAL COOPERATION

Bhutan joined the Colombo Plan organization in 1962 and became a UN member on 21 September 1971; it participates in ESCAP, FAO, IBRD, IDA, IFAD, IMF, IMO, UNESCO, UNIDO, UPU, and WHO. Bhutan also belongs to the Asian Development Bank and G-77 and is a signatory to the Law of the Sea. In addition, Bhutan is a member of the nonaligned movement and was a founding member of the South Asian Association for Regional Cooperation (SAARC). In 1978, its office in New Delhi was accorded the status of an embassy. Bhutan maintains full diplomatic relations with all of the South Asia countries, as well as several countries in the Middle East and Europe.

19ECONOMY

Isolated Bhutan has one of the smallest economies in the world, with a GDP of about $250 million and estimated per capita income of $180 in 1991. Much of the population functions outside the cash economy; 91% of the labor force lives by subsistence farming or herding. Agriculture and forestry together make up 43% of the country's GDP. Although the government relaxed its emphasis on maintaining food self-sufficiency during the 1980s, the country supplies most of its food needs through the production of grains, fruits, some meat, and yak butter. Services, with tourist-related business comprising a major share, account for a further 29%. By the mid-1970s, tourism had surpassed the sale of postage stamps as the chief source of Bhutan's limited foreign exchange revenue.

A series of five-year plans, initiated in 1961 and financed primarily by India, have begun to improve transportation, modernize agriculture, and develop hydroelectric power. Realization of several hydroelectric and industrial projects during the 1980s helped to increase industry's share of the GDP from 12.2% in 1980 to 27.5% in 1991, and inflated overall GDP growth rates to 7.3% annually during 1985–90. A slowdown in government project investment in the early 1990s, GDP growth stabilized at an average of 3.2% between 1990–92. Bhutan's extensive forests, mineral resources, and swift-running rivers offer great potential for future development, although preservation of the country's environment continues to rank high among the government's priorities.

20INCOME

Bhutan's GDP was estimated to be about $250 million in 1991. The estimated per capita income was $180. The inflation rate of consumer prices was estimated at 10% in 1991.

21LABOR

About 95% of the economically active population consists of farmers and herdsmen. There is a severe shortage of skilled labor, no legislated minimum wage, no standard workweek, and no health and safety standards. The salaried labor market is predominantly in the government service. Most of the industrial sector consists of home-based handicrafts and some 60 privately-owned small or medium-scale factories producing consumer goods.

22AGRICULTURE

Only about 2.8% of the land area, comprising 132,000 hectares (326,000 acres), was used for seasonal and permanent crop production in 1991. In 1991, agriculture contributed 43.4% to GDP, and engaged 90% of the population. Nonetheless, Bhutan's near self-sufficiency in food permitted quantities of some crops to be exported to India, in exchange for cereals. Since there is little level space available for cultivation, fields are generally terraced. Stone aqueducts carry irrigation water. The low-lying areas raise a surplus of rice; in 1992, output of paddy was estimated at 43,000 tons. Other crops include wheat, maize, millet, buckwheat, barley, potatoes, sugarcane, cardamom, walnuts, and oranges. Part of the crop yield is used in making beer and chong, a potent liquor distilled from rice, barley, and millet. Paper is made from the daphne plant, which grows wild. Walnuts, citrus fruits, apples, and apricots are grown in government orchards.

Agricultural holdings are restricted to 12 hectares (30 acres) per family; almost all farm families own their own land. Since the mid-1960s, the government has established demonstration farms, distributed fruit plants, and implemented irrigation schemes. High-yielding varieties of rice, wheat, and corn seeds have been introduced. Under the 1987–92 economic plan, farming cooperatives were introduced and apiculture was promoted.

23ANIMAL HUSBANDRY

Yaks, cattle, and some sheep graze in the lowland forests and, during the summer, in the uplands and high valleys. In 1992 there were an estimated 422,000 head of cattle, 74,000 hogs, 52,000 sheep, and 40,000 goats. Wool has been in short supply since its importation from Tibet was stopped by the government in 1960; sheep breeding is therefore encouraged. In 1992, 49 tons of greasy and 25 tons of scoured wool were produced.

24FISHING

The government has established a hatchery and started a program of stocking Bhutan's rivers and lakes with brown trout. Freshwater fish are found in most waterways. The total catch averages 1,000 tons annually.

25FORESTRY

About 54% of Bhutan is covered with forests. Although lack of transportation facilities has hampered forest development, timber has become a major export. Roundwood production in 1991 totaled 1,560,000 cu m, about 82% of which was used for fuel.

26MINING

For centuries, silver and iron have been mined in Bhutan for handicrafts. Deposits of copper, gypsum, mica, lead, zinc, limestone, and pyrites have also been found. Dolomite has constituted an important export to India since 1960. In 1991, production amounted to 50,000 tons. A graphite-processing plant has been established at Paro Dzong. Slate is also quarried for use as a dimensional stone.

27ENERGY AND POWER

About 85% of Bhutan's energy requirement is derived from firewood. Of commercial energy sources, petroleum accounts for 60% and coal for 30%, with electricity contributing only 10%. Electric power was introduced in Bhutan in 1962; by the mid-1980s, six hydroelectric and six diesel power stations were in operation. The 336-Mw Chukha hydroelectric project, in southwestern Bhutan, was completed in early 1987; the project was funded by India, which is to receive all the electrical output not used by Bhutan. Bhutan may have difficulty in using its own share because it lacks a national power grid. In 1991, Bhutan's net installed capacity was 360,000 kw; production totaled 1,580 million kwh, of which 99% was hydroelectric. In 1991, only about 12% of the electricity generated was domestically consumed; the rest was exported to India.

28INDUSTRY

Craft manufacture is the predominant industrial occupation, and homespun textiles—woven and embroidered cottons, wools, and silks—are the most important products. Other Bhutanese handicrafts include daphne paper; swords; wooden bowls; leather objects; copper, iron, brass, bronze, and silver work; wood carvings; and split-cane basketry. During the last decade, completion of the 336-Mw Chukha hydroelectric power plant has allowed the development of several modern industries as well. The country's first cement plant was completed by India in Penden, a border town, in 1982; the bulk of its output is exported to India. A second plant in Nanglam was established by the late 1980s, along with several manufacturing plants producing carbide, particle board and other products destined for the Indian market. Industrial estates have been set up at Phuntsholing and Geylegphug, as well as a sawmill with a furniture-making unit at Thimphu. A large number of small, privately owned sawmills operate throughout the country. Two major new industrial projects—another cement plant as well as a ferrosilicon production facility—are expected to be on line by 1994. In 1988, the Bhutan Development Finance Corporation was established to promote small- and medium-scale industries in various sectors of the economy. It is likely that liberalized trade policies recently adopted by the government will stimulate growth among small as well as larger scale producers in the export-oriented sector in the coming decade.

29SCIENCE AND TECHNOLOGY

Royal Bhutan Polytechnic College, founded in 1974, offers courses in civil, mechanical and electrical engineering. Sherubtse Degree College, founded in 1983, offers science courses.

30DOMESTIC TRADE

Retail sales are carried out mainly in small, local bazaars. Bartering is common at the local level, with grains, butter, and cloth being the principal commodities of exchange, although Indian and Bhutanese currencies are increasingly being employed. Indian traders sell imported articles and buy a number of handicraft items for export to India.

31FOREIGN TRADE

After the 1960 government ban on trade with Tibet, Bhutan's external sector became almost exclusively oriented towards trade with India. Over the last several years, however, exports to other countries have grown rapidly; third country trade now accounts for about 20% of the Bhutan's total. Major factors behind trade diversification include the recent depreciation of the Indian rupee to which the Bhutanese currency is closely linked as well as a 30% subsidy on third country exports introduced by the government in 1988 but now being phased out.

Bhutan's principal exports to India include vegetables, dolomite, timber, coal, oranges, cardamom, some preserved food, handicraft items, yak tails for fly whisks, and yak hair. In addition, 90% of the power generated by the Chukha hydroelectric plant is purchased by India, with electricity currently comprising the largest single source of export earnings (N374.4 million in 1989/90). The chief imports from India are petroleum products (mainly kerosene), motor vehicles, cereals, and cotton textiles. In 1989/90, total exports were estimated at N1,387.6 million and imports at N1,243.9 million.

32BALANCE OF PAYMENTS

The principal sources of foreign exchange are tourism and sales of electricity Bhutanese stamps. Exports of apples and oranges give Bhutan a trade surplus in agricultural produce. Trade deficits are largely made up through grants and loans from the Indian government.

33BANKING AND SECURITIES

Bhutan's central bank is the Royal Monetary Authority, established in 1982 to manage currency and foreign exchange. Its agent, the Bank of Bhutan, founded in 1968, has its main office at Phuntsholing and 25 branches (as of 1993) throughout the country. Bank reserves in 1992 were $192.7 million. Securities are not traded.

34INSURANCE

The Royal Bhutan Insurance Corp., half state-owned, covers all classes of insurance. The use of insurance, however, is limited.

35PUBLIC FINANCE

The largest category of annual current expenditure is public works, which presumably includes the maintenance of monasteries. Most of the annual budget deficit is covered by grants from India and from the UN and other international agencies. Increased foreign aid and domestic revenues allowed the government to increase public expenditures from 1981 to 1990 by a factor of five.

36TAXATION

The principal sources of domestic funds are excise taxes, taxes on real estate income, and taxes on profits from public companies.

37CUSTOMS AND DUTIES

Under the Indo-Bhutanese Treaty of 1949, goods pass from one country to another without payment of customs duties.

38FOREIGN INVESTMENT

Foreign investment comes primarily from India.

39ECONOMIC DEVELOPMENT

Under Bhutan's first four development plans, considerable improvements were made in agriculture and irrigation, road transportation, forestry, and electric power generation. The plans were underwritten by India, which contributed more than $197 million over the 20-year period.

Under the fifth economic plan (1981–87), total investments were projected at N4,338.1 million, with almost 31% of the outlays financed by India and with some 30% provided by the UN and other foreign sources. This plan aimed to increase the GNP by 6–8% annually, with priority given to agriculture and animal husbandry (14% of the outlays) and public works (13%).

The sixth plan (1987–92), with a projected outlay of N8,200 million, included among its goals encouragement of the private sector, revision of the tax system, greater decentralization to the district (dzongkha) level, and improvement of education and personnel training. The GDP was expected to grow by 6.9% annually, and priority was given to industry, trade, and commerce (20% of the outlays) and power (13%).

For 1992–97, the seventh plan (1992–97) reaffirms basic goals of economic self-sufficiency, preserving national identity, and human resource development. In addition, the plan strengthens the government's emphasis on development of the private sector as well as its commitment to environmental preservation. Privatization of public sector manufacturing firms and other measures are planned to expand the role of private manufacturing and services firms, especially within export-oriented manufacturing and mining industries as well as the tourist sector. Specific environmental objectives include the promotion of sustainable agriculture through soil erosion control as well as the setting aside of 20% of the country's land area as nature reserves and other areas protected from commercial timber extraction. Ambitious targets have been set for meeting all recurrent expenditures from domestic revenues by the end of the plan period. Successful achievement of this goal would end Bhutan's over-dependence on Indian financing for balancing its current fiscal debt. The expenditures required to meet other targets in the plan, however, make it unlikely that much progress will be achieved in this area in the near future.

[40]SOCIAL DEVELOPMENT

There is no national social welfare system, although the government implemented a modest maternal and child welfare program in the early 1980s, including family planning. The fertility rate in 1990 was 5.9. The sick, indigent, and aged are cared for within the traditional family structure.

Bhutan's culture does not isolate or disenfranchise women. Dowry is not practiced, and land is divided equally between sons and daughters. Girls receive nearly equal educational opportunities, and, while accorded a lower status than boys, they are cherished because they are the ones who care for parents in old age. The National Women's Association of Bhutan was created by the National Assembly in 1981 to help improve the socioeconomic status of women. It is now an independent organization.

[41]HEALTH

Bhutan suffers from a shortage of medical personnel with only 65% of the population having access to any form of medical care. In 1990, there were 141 doctors (113,110 people per physician), 5 pharmacists, 9 dentists, 233 nurses, and 70 midwives.

The average life expectancy in 1993 was only 48 years (49 years for females and 47 years for males), and the overall death rate was 16.7 per 1,000 people. The infant mortality rate was 131 per 1,000 live births. In 1993, it was estimated that 2% of married women (15–49 years) were using contraception.

Immunization rates between 1990 and 1992 for children up to one year old were: tuberculosis, 81%; diphtheria, pertussis, and tetanus, 79%; polio, 77%; and measles, 82%. Although smallpox has been wiped out, malaria, tuberculosis, and venereal disease remain widespread.

[42]HOUSING

Traditional houses are built of stone set in clay mixed with small stones and made into blocks or layers. Roofs are gently inclined and formed of pine shingles kept in place by heavy stones. As of 1990, 60% of urban and 30% of rural dwellers had access to a public water supply, while 80% of urban and 7% of rural dwellers had access to sanitation services.

[43]EDUCATION

Bhutan's estimated rate of adult literacy in 1990 was 38.4% (males: 51.3% and females: 24.6%). The official language is Dzongkha (written in the Tibetan script). However, English is widely used. Education is not compulsory. The educational system consists of six years of primary schooling followed by four years of secondary and two years of high school. In 1988, primary schools numbered 150 with 1,513 teachers and 55,340 pupils. General secondary schools had 695 teachers and 3,456 students. In 1991, Bhutan had 209 schools altogether, including 22 monastic schools; schools for Tibetan refugees; and 6 technical schools. There was at the highest level one junior college, two teacher training colleges and one degree college which was affiliated to the university at Delhi in India. Many teachers from India are employed in Bhutan.

[44]LIBRARIES AND MUSEUMS

A national museum opened to the public in 1968 at Paro Dzong in a seven story 17th-century fortress. Some monasteries have valuable collections of Buddhist manuscripts and art objects.

The National Library in Thimphu was established in 1969 and moved into a new building in 1984. A small public library, also in Thimphu, was established in 1980.

[45]MEDIA

International postal service was inaugurated in 1963; there are direct postal, telex, and microwave links to India. In 1988, Bhutan had only 1,990 telephones. There were 39 radio stations for internal government communications, as well as shortwave programming by the Bhutan Broadcasting Service. Bhutan did not have its own television station as of 1992 but received broadcasts from India and Bangladesh. In 1991, the country had an estimated 25,000 radios. A weekly government newspaper, *Kuensel*, is published in Dzongkha, English, and Nepali, with a circulation of about 12,500 as of 1991.

[46]ORGANIZATIONS

There are no commercial, scholarly, or professional organizations in the Western sense.

[47]TOURISM, TRAVEL, AND RECREATION

In 1974, Bhutan opened its door to tourists, but strict entry regulations, the remoteness of the country, and relatively limited transportation facilities have restricted the number of visitors. Income from tourism totaled approximately $2 million in 1990. In 1991, there were 2,106 foreign visitors. Under the 1987–92 plan, the target figure was 5,000 visitors a year. Tourists require a passport and visa and must either be invited guests or members of tour groups. The beautiful Thimphu, Paro, and Punakha valleys, with their many monasteries, are accessible to tourists. Archery is the national sport.

[48]FAMOUS BHUTANESE

Jigme Dorji Wangchuk (1928–72) instituted numerous social reforms during his reign as king of Bhutan. He was succeeded by his son Jigme Singye Wangchuk (b.1955).

[49]DEPENDENCIES

Bhutan has no territories or colonies.

[50]BIBLIOGRAPHY

Dogra, R. C. *Bhutan*. Oxford, England; Santa Barbara, Calif.: Clio Press, 1990.

Gibbons, Robert, and Bob Ashford. *Himalayan Kingdoms: Nepal, Sikkim, and Bhutan*. New York: Hippocrene, 1983.

Nepal and Bhutan: Country Studies Savada, 3rd ed. Washington, D.C.: Government Printing Office, 1993.

Pommaret-Imaeda, Françoise, and Yoshiro Imaeda. *Bhutan: A Kingdom in the Eastern Himalayas*. Translated by Ian Nobel. Boston: Shambhala, 1985.

Rose, Leo E. *The Politics of Bhutan*. Ithaca, N.Y.: Cornell University Press, 1977.

Singh, Amar Kaur Jasbir. *Himalayan Triangle: a Historical Survey of British India's Relations with Tibet, Sikkim and Bhutan 1765–1950*. London: British Library, 1988.

BRUNEI DARUSSALAM

Nation of Brunei, Abode of Peace
Negara Brunei Darussalam

CAPITAL: Bandar Seri Begawan.

FLAG: On a yellow field extend two diagonal stripes of white and black, with the state emblem centered in red.

ANTHEM: National Anthem, beginning *Ya Allah lanjutkan usia* ("God bless His Highness with a long life").

MONETARY UNIT: The Brunei dollar (B$, or ringgit) of 100 cents is valued at par with, and is interchangeable with, the Singapore dollar. There are coins of 1, 5, 10, 20, and 50 cents, and notes of 1, 5, 10, 50, 100, 500, 1,000, and 10,000 Brunei dollars. B$1 = US$0.4941; (or US$1 = B$2.024).

WEIGHTS AND MEASURES: Imperial weights and measures are in common use, as are certain local units, but a change to the metric system is slowly proceeding.

HOLIDAYS: New Year's Day, 1 January; National Day, 23 February; Anniversary of the Royal Brunei Armed Forces, 31 May; Sultan's Birthday, 15 July; Christmas Day, 25 December. Movable holidays include the Chinese New Year and various Muslim holy days.

TIME: 8 PM = noon GMT.

¹LOCATION, SIZE, AND EXTENT

Brunei occupies 5,770 sq km (2,228 sq mi) on the northwestern coast of the island of Borneo. Comparatively, the area occupied by Brunei is slightly larger than the state of Delaware. It comprises two small enclaves separated by the Limbang River Valley, a salient of the Malaysian State of Sarawak, which surrounds Brunei on the E, S, and W. Brunei's total boundary length is 542 km (337 mi).

Brunei's capital city, Bandar Seri Begawan, is located in the northern part of the country.

²TOPOGRAPHY

Brunei's western enclave contains most of the country's population, as well as the capital; the thinly populated eastern zone is mainly jungle. The land generally consists of primary and secondary tropical rain forest, with a narrow coastal strip on the western enclave. The eastern enclave is more hilly, rising to 1,850 m (6,070 ft) in the peak of Mt. Pagon in the extreme south.

³CLIMATE

The country has a tropical climate, with uniform temperatures ranging from 23° to 32°C (73–89°F). Humidity is high—about 80% all year round—and annual rainfall varies from about 275 cm (110 in) along the coast to more than 500 cm (200 in) in the interior. Rainfall is heaviest during the northeast monsoon season (landas), especially in November and December.

⁴FLORA AND FAUNA

The country is largely covered by mangrove and peat swamp, heath, montane vegetation, and dipterocarpaceous forest. The rain forest and swampland are inhabited by a plethora of small mammals, tropical birds, reptiles, and amphibians. Mammals include both wild and domesticated buffalo, honey bear, deer, and monkeys. Insects are abundant and sometimes harmful, in particular the malarial mosquito and biting midge.

⁵ENVIRONMENT

The nation has an extensive oil industry with reserves that are estimated to last 20 years. The forests are strictly protected by the government. Endangered species in 1987 included the estuarine crocodile.

⁶POPULATION

The estimated population in 1991 was 260,482, with a density of 45 persons per sq km (117 per sq mi). More than half the total population is urban; as of 1991, 46,229 Bruneians lived in the capital, Bandar Seri Begawan (formerly Brunei Town). Other important towns are Seria, Kuala Belait, and Tutong.

⁷MIGRATION

There is little emigration except among the Chinese minority. The government is battling considerable illegal immigration, especially from Indonesia and Sarawak.

⁸ETHNIC GROUPS

Malays formed 67% of the population in 1991. Minorities included an estimated 40,621 Chinese, 15,665 inhabitants of indigenous descent—mainly Dusans, Kedayans, and Maruts—and 29,871 others. There is a small Caucasian minority, chiefly of English, Dutch, American, and Australian stock.

⁹LANGUAGES

Malay and English are the official languages. The principal Chinese dialect is Hokkien, with Hakka, Cantonese, and Mandarin dialects also in use. Many native dialects are spoken as well.

¹⁰RELIGIONS

Islam, the official religion, dominates everyday life. Religious practice is controlled by the influential Religious Affairs Department. According to unofficial estimates, 63% of the population is Muslim. Another 9% of the people are Christians; the remaining 28% includes Buddhists (14%) and Chinese and tribal folk-religionists.

11TRANSPORTATION

Two seaports, at Muara and Kuala Belait, offer direct shipping services to Hong Kong, Singapore, and several other Asian ports. But wharf facilities at the deepwater port of Muara, though expanded to about 550 m (1,800 ft) in the mid-1980s, remain inadequate. There are only about 1,090 km (677 mi) of main roads. Links between the capital and the other western towns are good. Road connections between Brunei and Sarawak are being built. Buses are inexpensive but unreliable; river taxis and cars are for hire. In 1991, the sultanate had 115,495 passenger cars and 13,019 commercial vehicles registered.

The Brunei River, which flows by the capital, is a major thoroughfare. A 13-km (8-mi) railway is operated by the Brunei Shell Petroleum Co. The national carrier, Royal Brunei Airlines, operates regular flights to Singapore, Hong Kong, Manila, Bangkok, Jakarta, Kuala Lumpur, and other cities. Some foreign airlines serve Brunei International Airport at Barakas, outside the capital.

12HISTORY

From the 14th to the 16th century, Brunei was the center of a powerful native sultanate occupying what is now Sabah and Sarawak and extending northward through the Philippines almost to Manila. By the 19th century, much of this empire had been whittled away by war, piracy, and the colonial expansion of European nations. In 1847, the sultan concluded a treaty with Great Britain for the suppression of piracy and furtherance of commercial relations. In 1888, Brunei became a British protectorate, and in 1906 a resident British commissioner was established. By a 1959 agreement (amended in 1971), Brunei was recognized as fully self-governing, with Britain retaining responsibility for defense and foreign affairs. Brunei's first elections, held in 1962, resulted in a victory for the Brunei People's Party, militant nationalists who denounced Brunei's entry into a proposed federation with Malaysia, which had attained independence in 1957. Prevented from taking office, the nationalists, with Indonesian backing, revolted against Sultan Omar Ali Saifuddin in December 1962; the revolt was quickly put down with British assistance, but the sultan decided against federation in any case. From that time on, the sultanate has ruled by decree under a national state of emergency. In 1967, Sultan Omar abdicated in favor of his son, Muda Hassanal Bolkiah. Sultan Omar, who after his abdication remained as defense minister and assumed the royal title of Seri Begawan, died in 1986.

During the 1970s, Brunei emerged as the richest state in Southeast Asia, profiting from its oil wealth and the steep increases in international oil prices. Much of this vast oil income has been expended by the state on modernization and social services. Brunei renegotiated its treaty with the UK in mid-1978 and, on 7 January 1979, concluded a new treaty providing for independence within five years.

On 1 January 1984, the country attained full independence and was also proclaimed a member of the British Commonwealth. On 7 January 1984 Brunei joined the Association of South-East Asian Nations (ASEAN) and joined the United Nations in the same year. Brunei is also a member of the Organization of Islamic Conference.

In 1985 a new political party was formed, the Brunei National Democratic Party (BNDP), comprised predominantly of businessmen loyal to the Sultan. However, government employees were forbidden by the Sultan to join . The Chinese community was also excluded from membership. In 1986 an offshoot of the BNDP was formed, the Brunei National United Party (BNUP), which emphasized greater cooperation with the government. The BNUP's membership was open to Muslims and non-Muslims, but

still excluded Chinese. In 1986, Brunei was solicited by the US government to aid the Nicaraguan Contras, but the $10 million donation was credited to the wrong bank account and never reached its intended destination. The donation was eventually traced and returned to Brunei with interest.

In 1988 the top two leaders of the BNDP, President Haji Abdul latif bin Abdul Hamid, and Secretary-General, Haji Abdul Latif bin Chuchu, were arrested as they were about to fly to Australia. They were held under the Internal Security Act, which allows detention for up to two years without charges being filed, and were detained until 1990. In May of that year, Haji Abdul latif bin Abdul Hamid died. In 1990 the government released six other political prisoners who had been detained since 1962. Increasing emphasis on *Melayu Islam Beraja* (MIB) as a state ideology resulted in the affirmation of traditional values. In 1991 the import of alcohol and the public celebration of Christmas were banned. It is conjectured that the Sultan's emphasis on traditional values, rather than the liberalization he spoke of in 1989, is due to increasing concern about an affluent and worldly younger generation. His Majesty Sultan Haji Hassanal Bolkiah Mu'izzaddin Waddaulah celebrated 25 years on the throne in October 1992. As of 1993 *Fortune* magazine's estimate of the Sultan's personal wealth, US$37 billion, indicates that he may be the richest man in the world. Brunei, along with the People's Republic of China, Viet Nam, Malaysia, Taiwan, and the Philippines, is engaged in a regional dispute over claims to the Spratly Islands, situated in the South China Seas, which are strategically important and may have large oil reserves.

13GOVERNMENT

Brunei is an independent Islamic sultanate. The 1959 constitution (parts of which were suspended in 1962) confers supreme executive authority upon the sultan and provides for four Constitutional Councils: a Privy Council, Council of Ministers, Legislative Council, Religious Council, and Council of Succession to assist him. The members of these bodies are appointed by the sultan. The chief minister (mentri besar) is also appointed by the sultan and is responsible to him for the exercise of executive authority.

In a 1989 interview the Sultan said that he intends to proceed, with prudence, to establish more liberal institutions in the country, and that he will reintroduce elections and a legislature "when I see evidence of a genuine interest in politics on the part of a responsible majority of Bruneians." Instead, at his 1992 Silver Jubilee celebration the Sultan emphasized his commitment to preserving Brunei's political system based on the concept of *Melayu Islam Beraja* (MIB), or Malay Islam Monarchy, as the state ideology. MIB combines Islamic values and Malay culture within a monarchical political framework with the monarchy as defender of the faith.

14POLITICAL PARTIES

Parties were organized shortly after self-government was achieved in 1959. However, when the Brunei People's Party won 98% of the legislative seats in the country's only election, held in 1962, the sultan barred its candidates from office and outlawed all political parties under a continuing state of emergency. In 1988 political parties were banned and many of their leaders were arrested. At that time, the political parties were: the Brunei National Democratic Party (BNDP), founded in 1985, and the Brunei National United Party (BNUP), founded in 1986 by an offshoot of the BNDP. The President of the Brunei National Democratic Party (BNDP) was Haji Abdul latif bin Abdul Hamid and the secretary-general was Haji Abdul Latif bin Chuchu, and the party had an initial membership of around 200. About 150 quit in October 1985, led by party vice-president Mohammad Hatta bin Haji Zainal Abidin, who claimed that the BNDP refused to call a party congress to decide future leadership. The chairman of the new party, Brunei National Solidarity Party (BNSP) (aka Brunei National Democratic Party) was Haji Jumat bin Haji Idris, and the secretary-general was Mohammad Hatta bin Haji Zainal Abidin, and it had an initial membership of 21. In contrast to the BNDP, membership was open not to Brunei Malays only, but to other indigenous people, whether Muslim or not. The Chinese were left with the option of forming their own party. (Under Brunei's restrictive naturalization policies only 6000 Chinese had been granted citizenship.) Haji Jumat resigned as chair in April 1988; the party had only attracted about 60 members.

15 LOCAL GOVERNMENT

There are four administrative districts: Brunei-Muara, Kuala Belait, and Tutong in the western enclave, and Temburong in the east. Government is centrally controlled, but allowance is made for local tribal customs. District officers responsible to the ministers of home affairs administer each district. As part of the MIB ideology, village consultative councils are being introduced, making direct elections unnecessary. Instead, popularly elected headmen would function as mediators between the people and the central government. In June 1993 the Sultan stated "Brunei will strictly adhere to the MIB concept without resorting to fruitless political culture."

16 JUDICIAL SYSTEM

There are five levels of courts with final recourse available through the Privy Council in London. Beginning with the courts of first instance, there are courts of Kathis which handle family matters such as marriage and divorce by applying Islamic law (Shari'a). Lower courts called sultan's courts, presided over by magistrates, hear other ordinary cases involving minor disputes. Such cases may be appealed to the High Court, a court of unlimited original jurisdiction in both civil and criminal matters. The High Court is presided over by a Chief Justice and justices from Hong Kong appointed by the Sultan. Decisions of the High Court can be taken to the Court of Appeal, presided over by the President and two commissioner appointed by the Sultan. The Supreme Court consists of the High Court and the Court of Appeal.

17 ARMED FORCES

The Royal Brunei Armed Forces in 1993 consisted of an army of 3,600 men and women, a navy of 550, and an air force of 300 for counterinsurgency air operations. Great Britain provides an active Gurkha infantry battalion with helicopter support, and Singapore a force of 500 instructors and advisers. Paramilitary forces include a Gurkha reserve unit of 900 men and 1,750 members of the Brunei Royal Police. Brunei spent $233.1 million for defense in 1988 or 7.1% of gross domestic product.

18 INTERNATIONAL COOPERATION

Brunei was admitted to UN membership on 21 September 1984, and is a member of ICAO, IMO, ITU, and WMO. It is also a member of the Commonwealth of Nations, ASEAN, and the Organization of the Islamic Conference.

19 ECONOMY

Discovery of extensive petroleum and natural gas fields in the 1920s brought economic stability and modernization to Brunei. Today, the economy continues to depend almost entirely on oil and gas resources. This sector generates around half of GDP. Brunei's per capita GPD is one of the highest in Asia. Brunei's oil production peaked in 1979 at an estimated 240,000 to 261,000 barrels per day, but was deliberately cut back since then to preserve the country's oil reserves, which are conservatively esti-

LOCATION: 4°2′ to 5°3′N; 114° to 115°22′E. **BOUNDARY LENGTHS:** Malaysia, 418 km (260 mi); South China Sea and Brunei Bay coastlines, 161 km (100 mi). **TERRITORIAL SEA LIMIT:** 12 mi.

mated to last another 20–25 years. In 1992 average production was about 179,000 barrels a day. A 20-year contract to supply Japan with liquified natural gas (LNG) was renewed for another 20 years by the newly established Brunei Oil and Gas Authority in April 1993. Meanwhile, attempts to diversify the economy were being made under the national development plans.

20 INCOME

In 1992 the GDP was $3.5 billion in current US dollars. It is estimated that in agriculture, hunting, forestry, and fishing contributed 3% to GDP; mining and quarrying, 39%; manufacturing, 8%; electricity, gas, and water, 1%; construction, 4%; wholesale and retail trade, 13%; transport, storage, and communication, 4%; finance, insurance, real estate, and business services, 7%; and community, social, and personal services, 24%.

21 LABOR

Most of the Ibans and Dusans have forsaken hunting and gathering for government housing and paddy fields, while the majority of Malays, in turn, have deserted farming for more lucrative jobs in government and the oil industry. Brunei's acute labor shortage has drawn temporary workers, many of them illegal immigrants, from neighboring countries. In 1991 there were about 85,000 persons in the labor force, of whom 6,000 were in the oil and gas industry. Some 40% of all workers are employed by the government; only about 3% of all workers are farmers or fishermen. The Trade Unions Act of 1962 permits the formation of trade unions in the sultanate, but prohibits affiliation with labor organizations outside Brunei. There are four registered trade unions, all in the oil sector, with a total membership amounting to less than 5% of the work force.

22 AGRICULTURE

Temporary and permanent crops are actively cultivated on an estimated 7,000 hectares (17,300 acres), which represent 1.3% of total land area. Agriculture accounts for 2.6% of GDP and employs some 2% of the work force. Rice production is low, and Brunei imports more than 80% of its requirements. Urban migration and more profitable jobs in the oil industry have led to a shortage in farm labor. An agricultural training center, sponsored by Brunei Shell and the Department of Agriculture, was established in 1978 to encourage young people to return to the land. Crops for home consumption include bananas, sweet potatoes, cassava, coconuts, pineapples, and vegetables.

23 ANIMAL HUSBANDRY

Cattle, buffalo, hogs, goats, and fowl are raised. In 1978, McFarm (a Mitsubishi subsidiary) set up a cattle-breeding station in order to reduce meat imports. The government owns a cattle station in Australia that is larger in area than Brunei itself. As of 1991, the government was also encouraging livestock production through the Mitsubishi Cattle Breeding Project.

24 FISHING

Traditional fishing has declined in recent years, with only 60% of home consumption provided by local fishermen. The Fisheries Department has supplied a small trawling fleet, and continuing efforts are being made to develop both freshwater and saltwater aquaculture. Fish hatcheries are in operation on a 6-hectare (15-acre) site near Muara. The annual fish harvest in 1991 totaled 1,652 tons.

25 FORESTRY

Forest reserves constitute about 41% of the land area. Exports of timber are restricted. There is a small sawmill and logging industry for local needs. From 1988 to 1990, Brunei produced about 294,000 cu m of roundwood annually.

26 MINING

Brunei's mining industry was engaged only in the production and processing of crude oil and natural gas in 1991. Brunei's principal nonfuel mineral resource is its known reserves of silica sand of glassmaking quality.

27 ENERGY AND POWER

Commercial oil production, which began in 1929, dominates the economy. Production of crude oil in 1992 amounted to 9 million tons; output of natural gas was 10 billion cu m. In 1991, Brunei was the fourth largest producer of liquefied natural gas (LNG) in the world, and the third largest oil producer in Southeast Asia. In 1991, Brunei's export earnings were estimated at $2.1 billion, of which about 47% was derived from LNG exports, 42% from exports of crude petroleum, and 6% from exports of refined petroleum products. Exploratory drilling for new reserves continues, and capital expenditure on petroleum development remains high. As of the end of 1992, proven reserves of oil totaled 200 million tons (1.3 billion barrels); at the current rate of extraction, known oil reserves will have been depleted by 2013. In 1988, a self-imposed conservation quota of 150,000 barrels of oil per day was set; in 1992, production amounted to 185,000 barrels per day. Electric power and natural gas supplies are readily available at low cost. Net installed capacity in 1991 was 382,000 kw, all of it in conventional thermal plants; production of electricity totaled 1,242 million kwh.

28 INDUSTRY

Industry is almost entirely dependent on oil and natural gas production. Brunei ranks 32nd in the world in oil production, but is the third-largest oil producer in Southeast Asia, after Indonesia and Malaysia. Revenues from the petroleum sector account for around 50% of GDP. At Lumut, Brunei has one of the world's largest liquefied natural gas plants, which is owned by Brunei Shell Petroleum (BSP), a joint venture owned in equal shares by the government and the Royal Dutch/Shell Group of companies. After the government, BSP and four sister companies constitute the largest employer in Brunei.

Production of industrial goods in 1991 included 162,000 barrels of oil per day, 9,208.0 million cu m of gas, and 1,516.6 million kh of electricity. Figures for 1989 indicate 141,000 metric tons of gasoline, 88,000 metric tons of distillate fuel oils, and 12,000 metric tons of kerosene were produced. The small manufacturing sector includes production for the construction sector, sawmills and brick and tile factories. Government support of small-scale projects in food and beverage processing, textiles, furniture making and specialist optics has had limited results. Small commercial enterprise is still carried on mainly by Chinese entrepreneurs. In 1976, the government set up the Economic Development Board to assist new industries by granting tax and import exemptions, and recent efforts are aimed at increasing the employment of the local Malay population in the private sector.

29 SCIENCE AND TECHNOLOGY

Advanced science and technology have been imported in connection with development of the oil industry. Foreign technical expertise is employed in communications and other infrastructural programs. The Ministry of Industry and Primary Resources conducts agricultural research. The University of Brunei Darussalam has a faculty of science. The Technological Institute of Brunei and the Jefri Bolkiah College of Engineering offer engineering courses. In 1984, total expenditures for research and development amounted to $10.9 million; 116 technicians and 20 scientists and engineers were engaged in research and development.

30 DOMESTIC TRADE

Retail trade is largely in the hands of Chinese merchants. Since 1974, local cooperative societies have developed. As the result of heavy food subsidies and the increased availability of imported goods, Brunei has become a consumer society. Shops are generally open from 7:30 AM to 8 PM (some to 10 PM), seven days a week. Banking hours are 9 AM to 3 PM on weekdays, and 9 to 11 AM on Saturdays. Newspapers and television are the principal advertising media. The mainly English-language *Borneo Bulletin* is the only national newspaper that accepts advertising.

31 FOREIGN TRADE

Crude oil, petroleum products, and natural gas constitute more than 99% of Brunei's estimated 1991 export value of US$2.54 billion. Liquefied natural gas exports were valued at about B$1.9 billion; crude oil exports were valued at more than B$2.0 billion. Principal imports are machinery and transport equipment, manufactured goods, foodstuffs and chemicals. In 1991, estimated exports totaled B$4.1 million. In 1989 imports totaled about B$1.7 million. Brunei's imports increased in value from US$1.72 billion in 1990, to US$1.78 billion in 1991 and US$2.28 billion in 1992. Most of Brunei's beef is supplied by a government-owned cattle ranch in Australia which is larger than Brunei itself. In

1991 Brunei's major trading partner was Japan, which accounted for nearly 65% of total receipts, including the value of LNG exported. The second-largest customer was Thailand which received 8.7% of total export value. Other significant trading partners in 1991 were Singapore, absorbing 5.9% of export value, the Philippines, 4.0%, and South Korea, taking 10.6% of crude oil and petroleum exports. In 1989 Singapore was the largest import supplier in value terms, with 24.4% of the total. Other major suppliers in 1989 were Japan, 14.7%, the US, 12.7%, and Malaysia, 9.1%.

[32]BALANCE OF PAYMENTS

Brunei's huge trade surpluses have enabled it to maintain an enviable payments position. Foreign exchange reserves stood at about US$20 billion in 1986, or more than US$87,000 per capita.

[33]BANKING AND SECURITIES

The banking industry is controlled by the Association of Banks, in liaison with the government. In 1993 there were 7 banks with 33 branches operating in Brunei. Of these, 1 was locally incorporated and 6 were foreign, among them the Hongkong and Shanghai Banking Corp. and Citibank. The International Bank of Brunei, in which the sultan has a 51% stake, is the larger of the local banks. The other, the National Bank of Brunei, was seized in 1986 by the government, which charged the majority shareholders with irregularities, and later closed in the early 1990s.

[34]INSURANCE

British, Australian, and Hong Kong insurance firms have branch offices in Brunei.

[35]PUBLIC FINANCE

Brunei continues to maintain large surpluses in its annual budgets. The largest single items of expenditure were defense, education, and public works; taxes and royalties from the oil industry are by far the leading sources of government income. The 1991–96 National Development Plan allocates some B$5.5 billion for economic diversification.

[36]TAXATION

Taxation on petroleum income is subject to special legal provisions, dating from 1963. Individual income is not subject to tax. Companies pay a 30% tax on earnings. There is a double-taxation agreement between Brunei and the UK. Exemption from taxes can be granted by the sultan in council to industries deemed essential for the country's development.

[37]CUSTOMS AND DUTIES

Brunei levies tariffs ranging from zero to 20% and has a simple-column tariff structure. The country joined ASEAN in 1984 and is cooperating in current measures to reduce trade barriers between member nations.

[38]FOREIGN INVESTMENT

In July 1983, the sultanate withdrew its investment portfolio of more than B$3 billion (about half of total investment) from agents of the British crown, who traditionally had handled investment banking for Brunei. The Brunei Investment Agency, established in 1983, manages a substantial portfolio of assets invested around the world in long-term securities. Reportedly the interest earned on these investments is greater than the hydrocarbon revenues.

[39]ECONOMIC DEVELOPMENT

The development plan for 1986–90 envisioned expenditures of B$16.2 billion, of which B$2.6 billion was slated for new projects. The plan's main objective was to diversify the economy in order to prepare for the time when oil and gas reserves will run out. Thus, it emphasized development of the agricultural sector to lessen the country's reliance on imported foods. Industrial development projects focused on light industries, but also included plants for the production of cement and precast concrete. Service industries were encouraged, especially banking and finance, in the hope of developing Brunei into an international financial center. The establishment of a development bank also ranked high on the government's agenda. The Sixth National Development Plan (1991–95) was allocated a budget of B$5.5 billion to stimulate growth of the private sector, and to promote human resources and industrial development. The largest budget allocation was for social services (29.3%), with equal percentages for public utilities and transport and communications (20% each), 10 % allocated to trade and industry, and about 7% to security forces. The two main traditional employers are the government, which absorbs about half the work force, and Brunei Shell Petroleum. Development efforts for a non-oil, non-state sector and the potential for increasing foreign investment are limited by the small domestic market, a shortage of skilled manpower, and relatively high labor and transport costs.

[40]SOCIAL DEVELOPMENT

Typical of the problems of managing the transition from traditional tribal life to a modern life-style is that of Kampong Ayer, a "water village" along the Brunei River in the center of the capital. The village survives despite the government's efforts to induce the residents to move ashore, in part because the villagers' homes are already equipped with television sets and other modern comforts. Citizens enjoy extensive state welfare services, including free education and health care, wedding and burial allowances, and subsidized food and housing. The state provides pensions for the old and disabled, and financial aid for the destitute. An underlying social change in recent years has been the increasing influence of Islam as a way of life; converts include Bruneians of all ethnic backgrounds, including an increasing number of Chinese. Based on Islamic concepts, women are denied equal status with men in areas including divorce, inheritance, and child custody, and citizenship is passed on through males only.

In the mid-1980s, there were 7.4 marriages a year per 1,000 inhabitants and 0.7 divorces, and the average age of the bride was 24.

[41]HEALTH

The state provides free medical care, and remote regions are served by mobile clinics and a flying doctor service; there is also a school health service. As of 1986, there were 5 hospitals with about 850 beds; medical personnel in 1991 included 197 physicians, and, in 1989, 8 pharmacists and 30 dentists. The death rate declined from 4.2 per 1,000 population in 1974 to 4.4 per 1,000 in 1993. In 1992, the infant mortality rate was 8 per 1,000 live births, with 6,500 births that same year. Life expectancy in 1992 was estimated at 74 years. In 1990, 96% of the population had access to health care services, and 90% had access to safe drinking water. Between 1991 and 1992, 99% of the country's children were immunized against measles. Malaria has been eradicated from Brunei (although it remains a problem in adjacent Sarawak), and cholera is close to nonexistent. There is, however, still some risk of filariasis and tuberculosis.

[42]HOUSING

As of 1980, 36% of all houses had no electricity. Development plan for 1986–90 included a public housing program; government allocations for housing development totaled an estimated B$94 million in 1985. Most people who wish to leave their traditional homes have been able to find accommodations in housing units provided either by the government or by the oil companies.

43 EDUCATION

The state provides free education from kindergarten up, including university training abroad. In 1991 there were 149 primary schools, with 38,933 pupils and 2,543 teachers. Secondary schools had 25,699 students and 2,172 teachers. An estimated 95% of children and 71% of adults were literate. While education is compulsory for only nine years, a total of six years of primary and seven years of secondary education are available. Foreigners generally attend private mission schools, the International School, and the Chinese School. Brunei Shell also funds several schools, and there are numerous religious academies. There are two teacher-training colleges and five vocational technical schools, including an agricultural training center. Brunei also has a university, established in 1985, and institutes of education and technology. The official policy is to promote bilingual education, Malay and English, in all government-supported schools. The University of Brunei Darussalam (founded in 1985) has faculties for education, arts and social sciences, science, and management and administration. Many students, however, continue their education in foreign universities at government expense.

44 LIBRARIES AND MUSEUMS

The Language and Liturature Bureau Library (founded in 1961) serves as a reference and lending library in Bandar Seri Begawan. The library has a central facility, 4 branches, and 5 mobile units providing library services in remote areas. The Churchill Memorial Museum (founded 1971) illustrates the life of the famous statesman. Adjacent to the museum is the Sultan Hassanal Bolkiah Aquarium, one of the finest in Asia. Also notable are the Malay Technology Museum (founded 1988) and the Brunei Museum (founded 1965), the latter with archaeological and natural history collections.

45 MEDIA

The only commercial daily newspaper serving Brunei is the English *Borneo Bulletin*, with a circulation of 32,000 in 1991. The government publishes the Malay weekly *Peilta Brunei* (1991 circulation 45,000) and a monthly English newsletter, *Brunei Darussalam* (14,000). The *Straits Times* of Singapore circulates widely in Brunei, as do Chinese papers from Sarawak.

In 1991, there were 49,036 telephones in use. Radio Television Brunei broadcasts radio programs in English, Malay, and Chinese, and television programs in Malay and English. In 1991 there were an estimated 71,000 radios and 62,000 television sets.

46 ORGANIZATIONS

The powerful Religious Affairs Department permeates daily life; its activities include sponsoring Islamic pilgrimages and establishing village mosque committees. Sports facilities tend to be privately maintained. There are four chambers of commerce in the country.

47 TOURISM, TRAVEL, AND RECREATION

Brunei attracts few tourists (6,418 in 1985) because of a lack of facilities; as of 1986 there were four hotels in the capital, to which two new ones were added after the 1992 Silver Jubilee. However, tens of thousands of foreigners come to Brunei on business each year. Among Brunei's newest and most remarkable sights is the sultan's 1,788-room palace, built at a reported cost of us$300 million and topped by two golf-leaf domes. Native longhouses are also a tourist attraction but are hard to reach, and trips up the Brunei and Tutong rivers are interesting but not yet well organized. Tourism revenue in 1989 was an estimated us$32 million. Every visitor must have a valid passport; visas are normally required, but there are exemptions based on nationality, and purpose and length of visit.

48 FAMOUS BRUNEIANS

Omar Ali Saifuddin (1916–86) was sultan from 1950 to 1967 and minister of defense from 1984 to 1986. His son, Muda Hassanal Bolkiah (Bolkiah Mu'izuddin Waddaulah, b.1946), one of the wealthiest men in the world, has been sultan since 1967.

49 DEPENDENCIES

Brunei has no territories or colonies.

50 BIBLIOGRAPHY

Chalfont, Arthur Gwynne Jones, Baron. *By God's Will: a Portrait of the Sultan of Brunei*. 1st American ed. New York: Weidenfeld & Nicolson, 1989.

Crowther, Geoff, and Tony Wheeler. *Malaysia, Singapore, and Brunei*. 2d ed. New York: Hippocrene, 1986.

Krausse, Sylvia C. Engelen. *Brunei*. Oxford; Santa Barbara, CA.: Clio, 1988.

Major, John S. *The Land and People of Malaysia and Brunei*. New York, NY: HarperCollins, 1991.

Ranjit Singh. *Brunei, 1839–1983: the Problems of Political Survival*. New York: Oxford University Press, 1984.

Turnbull, C. Mary. *A Short History of Malaysia, Singapore and Brunei*. Singapore: Three Continents, 1981.

CAMBODIA

Cambodia

CAPITAL: Phnom Penh

NOTE: Cambodia (formerly known as Kampuchea and the Khmer Republic) was known as Cambodia until 1976 and again since 1989. As of 1994, there are two rival claimants for legitimate government authority. One of these, the People's Republic of Kampuchea (PRK), was established in January 1979 in the wake of a Vietnamese invasion; it maintained de facto control of the capital by means of an occupation force of Vietnamese troops. The other, Democratic Kampuchea (DK; Kampuchea Pracheathipateyy), is represented by a coalition government-in-exile, but with considerable following in the Cambodian countryside; it continues to hold Cambodia's seat in the UN.

FLAG: The flag has a red center field with a white silhouette of the temple complex at Angkor Wat. The center field is bordered top and bottom by blue bands.

MONETARY UNIT: Money was officially abolished in 1975, and for nearly five years the domestic economy operated almost exclusively on a system of barter and government rationing. In March 1980, the PRK reintroduced the riel (R) of 100 sen, equal in value to 1 kg (2.2 lb) of rice and with an approximate exchange value of R1 = $0.0004 (or $1 = R2,500).

WEIGHTS AND MEASURES: Both the metric system and traditional weights and measures are in general use.

HOLIDAYS: National Day, 9 January; New Year, April; Victory over American Imperialism Day, 17 April; Labor Day, 1 May; Day of Hatred, 20 May; Feast of the Ancestors, 22 September.

TIME: 7 PM = noon GMT.

¹LOCATION, SIZE, AND EXTENT

Situated in the southeast corner of Indochina, Cambodia has an area of 181,040 sq km (69,900 sq mi), extending 730 km (454 mi) NE-SW and 512 km (318 mi) SE-NW. It is bounded on the NE by Laos, on the E and SE by Viet-Nam, on the SW by the Gulf of Thailand, and on the W, NW, and N by Thailand, with a total boundary length of 3,015 km (1,873 mi). Comparatively, the area occupied by Cambodia is slightly smaller than the state of Oklahoma. In 1982, the PRK signed an agreement with Vietnam on their mutual maritime frontier. A treaty delineating the land border was signed in December 1985.

Cambodia's capital city, Phnom Penh, is located in the south-central part of the country.

²TOPOGRAPHY

Cambodia is a country of forested mountains and well-watered plains. The central part of the country forms a gigantic basin for the Tonle Sap, or Great Lake, and the Mekong River, which flows down from Laos to the southern border with Viet-Nam. Between the Tonle Sap and the Gulf of Thailand lie the Cardamom Mountains and the Elephant Range, which rise abruptly from the sea and from the eastern plains. In the north, the Dangrek Mountains, 320 km (200 mi) long and 300 to 750 m (1,000–2,500 ft) high, mark the Thailand frontier. The short coastline has an important natural harbor, Kompong Som Bay, where the port of Kompong Som (formerly Sihanoukville) is located.

The Mekong and the Tonle Sap dominate the life and economy of Cambodia. The Mekong overflows during the rainy season, deposits vast quantities of alluvial soil, and, backing toward the Tonle Sap, causes that lake to increase in size from about 260 sq km (100 sq mi) to almost 2,100 sq km (800 sq mi).

³CLIMATE

The climate is tropical, with a wet season from June through November and a dry season from December to June. Temperatures range from 20° to 36°C (68–97°F), and humidity is consistently high. The lowlands, which are inundated during the rainy season, receive about 200 cm (80 in) of rainfall annually, but there is less precipitation in the western and northern portions of the country.

⁴FLORA AND FAUNA

Cambodia, covered in its mountainous areas with dense virgin forests, has a wide variety of plant and animal life. There are palm, rubber, coconut, kapok, mango, banana, and orange trees, as well as the high sharp grass of the savannas. Birds, including cranes, pheasants, and wild ducks, and mammals such as elephants, wild oxen, panthers, and bears abound throughout the country. Fish, snakes, and insects also are present in abundance.

⁵ENVIRONMENT

Deforestation is a significant environmental problem in Cambodia. By 1985, the clearing of the land for agricultural purposes and the damage from the Viet Nam war resulted in the destruction of 116 square miles of forest land. The nation has 21.1 cubic miles of water with 94% used for farming activity and 1% used for industrial purposes. Cambodia's cities produce 0.2 million tons of solid waste per year. Three-fourths of Cambodia's wildlife areas have been lost through the destruction of its forests. As of 1994, 21 of Cambodia's mammal species and 13 of its bird species were endangered and 11 of its plant species were also threatened. As of 1987, endangered species in Cambodia included 3 species of gibbon (pileated, crowned, and caped), several species of wild dog and wild cat, leopard, tiger, Asian elephant, Sumatran rhinoceros, Thailand brow-antlered deer, kouprey, giant catfish, Indian python, Siamese crocodile, and estuarine crocodile.

6POPULATION

Estimates of Cambodia's population vary with the assessment of the impact of the 1970–75 war and its tumultuous aftermath. According to the official estimate, the population was 9,054,000 in 1992, but the US Bureau of the Census estimated a population of only 7,612,332 in 1994. On the basis of the official estimate, Cambodia had an overall population density of 50 per sq km (130 per sq mi). A population of 10,580,000 was forecast by the UN for the year 2000, assuming a crude birthrate of 35 per 1,000 population, a crude death rate of 12.3, and a net natural increase of 22.7 during 1995–2000.

A great majority of the people live in rural areas, with 90% of the population living in the plains of the central third of the country. The urban population was estimated at 13% in 1995. At the war's end, in April 1975, the population of the capital, Phnom Penh, had swollen to nearly 3 million because of a mass influx of refugees. The new government immediately embarked on a forced evacuation of all urban areas, and by March 1976, only 100,000–200,000 were thought to remain in Phnom Penh. After the installation of the PRK in 1979, the population of Phnom Penh began to increase, and by 1991 was estimated at 900,000. Other cities include Batdambang, Kampong Cham, Kampot, Siemreab, Kampong Saom, and Kracheh.

7MIGRATION

The first migration of persons in independent Cambodia took place during the 1950s and 1960s, when ethnic Chinese were permitted to settle in the mountainous and wasteland areas and cultivate land that otherwise would have remained useless. After 1970, about 200,000 Vietnamese living in Cambodia were repatriated to the RVN, ostensibly as a security measure. With the insurgent victory in April 1975, most of the country's remaining Vietnamese were reported to have emigrated to Viet Nam. In addition, thousands of refugees, including many former officials and military personnel, fled across the Thai border or were evacuated by US aircraft.

The new government launched a sweeping nationwide resettlement program under which some 2.5–3 million persons were moved from Phnom Penh and other cities into the countryside, where they were organized into work brigades. The food shortage in rural areas was only slightly less critical than in the cities, and widespread starvation led to the deaths of probably over one million people during the transition. After the installation of the PRK in January 1979, continued fighting and political instability resulted in a new exodus of refugees. About 630,000 Cambodians left the country between 1979 and 1981, of which about 208,000 were able to resettle in other countries, including 136,000 in the US. Most of the rest remained in camps on the border with Thailand, but they were repatriated to Cambodia in May 1993.

Between 1979 and 1987 there was a new migration of ethnic Vietnamese into Cambodia. Official sources insisted that the total number was under 60,000, and was comprised, for the most part, of residents who had left in the early 1970s, but opposition groups contended that the number totaled over 500,000 and was intended to consolidate Vietnamese control over the country.

8ETHNIC GROUPS

Over 90% of the entire population in 1994 were ethnic Khmers, descendants of the original population in the area. The largest minority groups were Chinese (about 61,000 in 1984) and the Vietnamese (officially estimated at 56,000 in 1984). National minorities are the Cham and a number of small tribal groups.

9LANGUAGES

Khmer, the national language, is spoken by most inhabitants. Unlike Thai or Vietnamese, Khmer is a nontonal language; most words are monosyllabic. French, the second language, is often used in commercial and official circles. The Vietnamese and the Chinese use their own languages, as do other minorities.

10RELIGIONS

Although Theravada Buddhism is the religion of some 90% of the inhabitants (1992), and has been the state religion since 1989, animism is adhered to by most persons as well. The Chinese and most Vietnamese in Cambodia practice a traditional mixture of Mahayana Buddhism, Taoism, Confucianism, ancestor worship, and animism. Before 1975 there were some 100,000 Muslims (mostly Cham-Malays), 50,000 Roman Catholics (Europeans and Vietnamese), and a few Protestants. The mountain tribes are animists; in the post-World War II years, Christian missionaries made some converts among them.

The government that took power in 1975 virtually abolished Buddhism, defrocking some 70,000 monks and turning pagodas into warehouses. Islamic spokesmen have claimed that 90% of Cambodia Muslims were massacred after 1975. Of some 6,000 Roman Catholics left in Cambodia at the time of the revolution, only a few survived. All mosques and Catholic churches were razed. The PRK regime that came to power in 1979 permitted the return of religious practice, and hundreds of pagodas were reopened. In insurgent areas controlled by the Khmer Rouge, Buddhism was allowed after 1979, and in non-Communist resistance camps there reportedly was full freedom of religion.

11TRANSPORTATION

Land transport facilities suffered wholesale destruction during the 1970–75 war. Cambodia's first railway, a 385-km (239-mi) single track from Phnom Penh to Paoy Pet, was badly damaged in the fighting; moreover, a just-completed 262-km (163-mi) line from Phnom Penh to Kampong Sam was also disabled. The line to Kampong Sam was restored in November 1979, and a Phnom Penh–Battambang railway was reopened in February 1980. Rail service has been periodically disrupted by guerrilla operations.

All major cities and towns are connected with Phnom Penh by highway, and from there roads connect to Viet-Nam, Laos, and Thailand. The US-built 214-km (133-mi) Khmer-America Friendship Highway links Phnom Penh with Kampong Sam. As of 1991, Cambodia had an estimated 13,351 km (8,234 mi) of main roads, of which 20% were bituminized; most are in poor condition.

The Mekong is the most important inland waterway. Total length of navigable waterways is 3,700 km (2,300 mi) to craft drawing 0.6 meters, but only 282 km (175 mi) for craft with a draft of 1.8 meters. Phnom Penh, on the Mekong, had a storage capacity of 14,000 tons in 1982. Until 1975, Saigon was the major transshipment point for outgoing and incoming Cambodian goods; the opening of the deepwater port of Kompong Som made Cambodia largely independent of Viet-Nam for oceangoing shipping.

Cambodia's main airport is at Phnom Penh; there are regular flights between Phnom Penh, Hanoi, Vientiane, and Ho Chi Minh City.

12HISTORY

The Cambodians are descendants of the Khmers, who in the 6th century established the Indian-influenced Angkor Empire, and for the next 900 years ruled the area of present-day Cambodia. According to legend, the founder of the Khmer dynasty was Kampu Svayambhuva, from whose name "Kampuchea" derives. From the 10th to the 14th century, after years of military expansion, the Khmers reached their apogee. Their empire extended over most of Southeast Asia (from central Viet Nam south-west

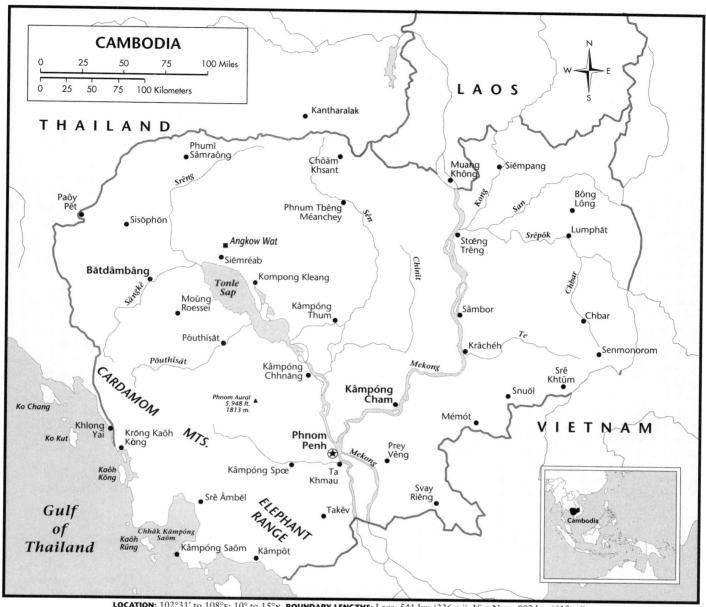

CAMBODIA

0 25 50 75 100 Miles

0 25 50 75 100 Kilometers

LOCATION: 102°31′ to 108°E; 10° to 15°N. **BOUNDARY LENGTHS:** Laos, 541 km (336 mi); Viet-Nam, 982 km (610 mi); Gulf of Thailand, 389 km (242 mi); Thailand, 803 km (499 mi). **TERRITORIAL SEA LIMIT:** 12 mi.

into the Malay Peninsula, and from Thailand north to the border of Burma, now known as Myanmar). Angkor, the capital city, was a flourishing complex of great temples, palaces, and shrines. In the subsequent centuries, however, continuing attacks by the Thai (who captured Angkor in 1431) and the Vietnamese weakened the empire, and by the end of the 18th century much of Cambodia had become a Thai and Vietnamese condominium. In 1863, the king of Cambodia placed the country under French protection. The French, joining Cambodia to Laos and Viet Nam to form French Indochina, ruled the protectorate until the end of World War II. Cambodian nationalism received its greatest impetus during the World War II period, while Japan controlled Indochina. King Norodom Sihanouk, who had ascended the throne in 1941 and had been held a virtual prisoner under the Japanese occupation, proclaimed Cambodia independent in 1945, but yielded before a temporary resumption of the French protectorate, enforced by Allied troops, which occupied Phnom Penh. Cambodia became a constitutional monarchy on 6 May

1947, and was granted nominal independence within the French Union on 9 November 1949. King Sihanouk, meanwhile, had assumed leadership of Cambodia's growing nationalist movement. On 17 October 1953, during the height of the Franco-Indochinese war, he was granted full military control of his country by France. Sihanouk, a skilled politician, abdicated in March 1955 in favor of his father and mother, King Suramarit and Queen Kossamak, and then emerged as prime minister with the unanimous support of the national legislature. King Suramarit died on 31 April 1960, but Prince Sihanouk, although retaining the title of chief of state, did not return to the throne. During the Franco-Indochinese war, Communist-controlled Viet-Minh troops from Viet Nam operated in Cambodia (1954), and gave support to a small Khmer Communist movement.

The Geneva agreements of July 1954, which ended the Franco-Indochinese war, secured the withdrawal of French and Viet-Minh troops from Cambodia and the surrender of most of the Khmer rebels. During the next 15 years, Sihanouk sought to keep

Cambodia neutral in the deepening Viet Nam conflict. This proved increasingly difficult, however, as the National Liberation Front (also known as the Viet-Cong) used Cambodian border areas as bases from which to launch attacks on the Republic of Vietnam (RVN, or South Vietnam), and as the US in 1969 launched an undeclared air war against the guerrilla sanctuaries. On 18 March 1970, Marshal Lon Nol, prime minister and army chief, overthrew the chief of state, Prince Sihanouk, while the prince was on a visit to the USSR; the right-wing coup ended 1,168 years of rule by Khmer monarchs. Sihanouk thereupon took up residence in Beijing, where, on 5 May, he announced formation of the Royal Government of National Union of Kampuchea (GRUNK) under the political auspices of the National United Front of Kampuchea. In the interim, on 30 April, US President Richard M. Nixon announced an "incursion" into Cambodia of 30,000 US and 40,000 RVN troops, with the object of destroying their opponents' strongholds along the Viet Nam border. The operation was terminated on 30 June with its military objectives apparently unfulfilled, and bombing of the region continued, to devastating effect on Cambodia's economy.

Formal diplomatic relations with the US, severed by Sihanouk in 1965, were resumed on 2 July 1970, and Sihanouk was condemned to death (in absentia) three days later. On 9 October, the Lon Nol government in Phnom Penh abolished the monarchy and changed Cambodia's name to the Khmer Republic. In elections held during June 1972, Lon Nol was elected president of the republic. Pressures from GRUNK insurgents continued to mount, especially following the conclusion of a cease-fire in Viet Nam in January 1973 and the withdrawal of the last US troops from that country in March. US aid to the Lon Nol government had been substantial, totaling $1.18 billion in military supplies and $503 million in economic assistance for the whole of the 1970–75 period, but with most of the aid concentrated in the early years of direct involvement. With the reversal of US policy in Viet Nam, however, support for the Khmer Republic began to taper off, and by the start of 1975, the Lon Nol government was plunged into a struggle for survival. In January, GRUNK military forces, generally referred to as the Khmer Rouge, launched a major offensive aimed at gaining control of the Mekong River and isolating Phnom Penh. Fierce and costly fighting ensued over the next three months, with the US undertaking a massive airlift to Phnom Penh in February to fend off starvation and military collapse. On 1 April, the strategic Mekong ferry crossing at Neak Luong fell to the insurgents, clearing the way to a direct, final assault on the capital. On that day, Lon Nol fled the country, to be followed by much of the ruling hierarchy. On 17 April, the Khmer Republic government officially capitulated to GRUNK forces, commanded by Khieu Samphan.

The GRUNK government reported in March 1976 that the war had resulted in 1 million casualties, including 800,000 killed. On 5 January 1976, the country was officially renamed Democratic Kampuchea (DK). On 20 March, the first general elections were held for a new 250-member People's Assembly. The Assembly on 14 April named Khieu Samphan chairman of the State Presidium, replacing Prince Sihanouk, who had returned to the country in September 1975, as head of state. Pol Pot was named prime minister. Even before these political reforms were undertaken, the GRUNK government had undertaken a massive—and perhaps unprecedented—reorganization of the country's economic and social life. As an initial step, the new government ordered the near-total evacuation of Phnom Penh, where food, shelter, and medical resources had been stretched to the limit by the press of some 2.5 million refugees. The country was thereupon plunged into almost complete isolation, even from its neighbors in Vientiane and Hanoi. Firsthand accounts are few, but it is known that currency was abolished, social relations completely overhauled, religion almost eradicated, education suspended, and

families divided. From 2 million to 3 million people may have died from starvation, exhaustion, disease, or massacre under the Pol Pot (Cambodian Communist leader Saloth Sar) regime.

Meanwhile, tensions with Viet Nam (traditional enemy of Cambodia until 1976 and again after 1989) were growing, and there were border clashes during 1977 and 1978. In December 1978, Viet Nam invaded Cambodia with a force of more than 100,000 troops; by January 1979, they had installed a pro-Vietnamese government, the People's Republic of Kampuchea (PRK), headed by Heng Samrin, a former division commander in the GRUNK army. The PRK had to contend with resistance from the very beginning, and the Khmer Rouge rebels, who had fled to the jungles in the west and south, continued to harass the government despite Vietnamese counteroffensives. In order to improve its international standing, the Khmer Rouge began in 1981 to pursue a united-front strategy; Pol Pot, branded with the 1975–79 atrocities, reportedly withdrew into the background, and Khieu Samphan, supposedly the most moderate of the Khmer Rouge leaders, emerged as chief spokesman. In 1982, the Khmer Rouge formed the Coalition Government of Democratic Kampuchea (CGDK), with two non-communist factions led by Prince Sihanouk and a former politician, Son Sann. The fighting during 1982–83 reflected a pattern of PRK and Vietnamese dry-season offensives alternating with an upsurge of guerrilla operations during the wet season. Militarily, the PRK and Viet Nam appeared firmly in control at the end of 1987; diplomatically, however, the PRK had won recognition only from Viet Nam, the former USSR, and their allies, with most nations joining the US and China in giving qualified support to the CGDK. In March 1986, an eight-point plan to settle the Cambodian conflict was issued by the leaders of the coalition. Although supported by China and ASEAN, the plan was rejected by Viet Nam and the PRK. In December 1987, Prince Sihanouk met with PRK Prime Minister Hun Sen in France in an effort to find a political solution to Cambodia's civil war; further talks were scheduled for 1988.

Progress towards a peaceful settlement had an uneven course in 1988. Prince Sihanouk resigned, retracted his resignation, and resigned again as president of the Democratic Kampuchean Government-in-exile. Informal meetings in Indonesia, one in July shunned by Prince Sihanouk and the other in October ignored by the Khmer Rouge, made no progress on peace plans. However, a subsequent announcement supported the creation of an international peacekeeping force. A conciliatory statement made in August of 1988 indicated the Khmer Rouge was ready to reduce its armed forces to the level of the other Cambodian factions. Viet Nam announced the repatriation of 50,000 troops from Cambodia in 1988 and the complete withdrawal of troops by late 1989, or early 1990. In January of 1989 Heng Samrin pledged that, if a political settlement could be achieved, all Vietnamese troops would be repatriated by September. Further encouraging gestures were made by Viet-Nam, China and Thailand: Thai and Vietnamese officials met in Hanoi; Vietnamese and Chinese ministers met in Beijing; and, Thailand abandoned its policy of isolating the Heng Samrin government and invited talks with them. In 1989 Prince Sihanouk resumed leadership of the Democratic Kampuchean Government-in-exile, later resigning from leadership of the National Front for an Independent, Neutral, Peaceful and Cooperative Cambodia (FUNCINPEC). In protest of Thailand's contact with the Heng Samrin government, Sihanouk refused to attend a second "informal meeting" in Jakarta. This meeting still failed to resolve two outstanding major issues: the make-up of an international force to oversee troop withdrawals and the composition of an interim government before elections. As a further sign of its commitment to change, in April 1989 an extraordinary session of Cambodia's National Assembly ratified amendments to the Constitution: the name of the country was changed to the State of Cambodia (SOC), a new national flag, emblem and anthem were introduced; Buddhism was reinstated as the state religion; and the death penalty abolished. At a May meeting in Jakarta with Prince Sihanouk, Hun Sen proposed to form a quadripartite supreme council to prepare for general elections; Sihanouk rejected this proposal as he wanted a quadripartite government to prepare for the election. Hun Sen also met in Bangkok with the Thai Prime Minister who appealed for a cease-fire among the four Cambodian factions [The government of the Kampuchean People's Revolutionary Party (KPRP) installed by the Vietnamese (the Heng Samrin government), abd threee anti-government gropus that comprise the umbrella organization, the national Government of Cambodia (NGC): FUNCINPEC, the Khmer Rouge, and the Khmer Peopl's National Liberation Front (KPNLF).] ; the Khmer Rouge rejected this suggestion. In July 1989 Hun Sen and Prince Sihanouk met in Paris prior to the Paris International Conference on Cambodia (PICC). A major accomplishment of the conference was agreement to send a UN reconnaissance party to Cambodia to assess prospects for a cease-fire and the installation of a peace-keeping force. In September 1989 Viet-Nam completed the timely withdrawal of its forces from Cambodia. Throughout 1988 and 1989 the Khmer Rouge forces continued to make military gains in Cambodia. In November pressure mounted in the UN to vacate the Cambodian seat pending the general election. The UN adopted a resolution supporting the formation of an interim government which included the Khmer Rouge, although past atrocities of the Khmer Rouge were alluded to indirectly.

In January 1990 the UN Security Council approved an Australian peace initiative—UN monitored cease-fire, the temporary assumption of executive powers by the UN secretary-general, formation of a national supreme council, and the holding of internationally supervised elections. Prince Sihanouk resigned as Supreme Commander of the High Council of National Defense and leader of the resistance coalition, but retained his position as President of Democratic Kampuchea. In February 1990 the Government-in-exile of Democratic Kampuchea was formally renamed by Sihanouk as the National Government of Cambodia and restored the traditional flag and anthem. This change distanced the coalition from association with the Khmer Rouge's former regime, Democratic Kampuchea (DK). (The DK had been named the Khmer Rouge by Sihanouk.) Hun Sen and Prince Sihanouk signed a joint communique in February 1990 stressing the need for UN participation in restoring peace. In a third meeting held in Jakarta in February the four Cambodian factions as well as representatives of Viet Nam, Laos, ASEAN, France, and Australia met and agreed to the main principles of the UN plan. During March and April the Phnom Penh regime reclaimed territory previously held by resistance forces. Also in April, Prince Sihanouk announced that the Sihanouk National Army (ANS), military forces loyal to him as the armed wing of FUNCINPEC, henceforth would be known as the National Army of Independent Cambodia. In May 1990 arbitration by Thailand resulted in the four Cambodian factions informally accepting plans for a future cease-fire. Prince Sihanouk resumed the presidency of the resistance coalition in May and in June he and Hun Sen signed a conditional cease-fire in Bangkok. In June a meeting in Tokyo was attended by representatives of all four Cambodian factions including Hun Sen and Prince Sihanouk. The Khmer Rouge, however, refused to sign a cease-fire agreement and proposed that each faction should have equal representation on a supreme national council. Prince Sihanouk offered support for the Khmer Rouge proposal, despite his previous agreement with Hun Sen; the discussions collapsed. In June and July reformist political allies of Hun Sen were dismissed or arrested for alleged attempts to establish a new party. Supporters of conservative Chea Sim, Chairman of the National Assembly, replaced them. Also in July the US withdrew its support for the National Government of

Cambodia's occupation of Cambodia's seat at the UN and indicated willingness to provide humanitarian assistance for the Phnom Penh regime. The UN Security Council in late August endorsed a plan for a comprehensive settlement in Cambodia: UN supervision of an interim government, military arrangements for the transitional period, free elections, and guarantees for the future neutrality of Cambodia. In addition, a special representative of the UN secretary-general would oversee the proposed United Nations Transitional Authority in Cambodia (UNTAC). The UN would also assume control of government ministries. Both China and the former USSR subsequently pledged to cease providing supplies of military equipment to their respective allies, the Khmer Rouge and the Phnom Penh regime. In reversals of previous policy the US announced it would hold talks with the Phnom Penh regime, and the USSR declared that it would hold talks with Prince Sihanouk. The four Cambodian factions accepted the UN proposals at an "informal meeting" in Jakarta in September 1990. In addition, they agreed to the formation of the Supreme National Council (SNC), with six representatives each from the National Government of Cambodia and Phnom Penh regime. The SNC was to occupy the Cambodian seat at the UN General Assembly. At its first meeting in September the SNC failed to elect a chairman. The Khmer Rouge heightened military action in the northern provinces. Even as the final draft of the peace plan was prepared by the UN Security Council the Phnom Penh regime continued to oppose the principal provisions of the plan. In December all 12 members of the SNC attended another meeting of the PICC and all factions endorsed most components of the UN plan.

The SOC replaced three of its six SNC members in February 1991. In early 1991 outside pressures for change in Cambodia were brought to bear: the US and Japan attempted to influence the Phnom Penh regime to compromise, and China indicated its intention to resume supplying arms to the Khmer Rouge. In May a temporary cease-fire was agreed upon by the four factions in order to facilitate discussions. In June the Khmer Rouge refused to discuss SNC leadership issues, requiring the Phnom Penh regime's prior acceptance of the full terms of the UN peace plan, and the Khmer Rouge refused to comply with a proposed extension of the temporary cease-fire. Prince Sihanouk became an ordinary member of the SNC chairing a meeting in Thailand where all four factions resolved several issues: implementation of an indefinite cease-fire, pledged not to receive further foreign military aid, approved a flag and anthem for the SNC, and established Phnom Penh as the headquarters for the SNC. Prince Sihanouk was elected to the chairmanship of the SNC and resigned as leader of the resistance coalition and as President of the National Government of Cambodia. His replacement in both positions was Son Sann. From August through October the SNC worked out the details of the armed forces reduction and election procedures. Elections would be held to establish a constituent assembly comprised of 120 seats, which would subsequently become a legislative assembly. The electoral system would be proportional representation based on the 21 provinces. The constituent assembly would be empowered to adopt a new constitution. In October the SOC released hundreds of political prisoners including the associates of Hun Sen arrested in 1990 for starting a political party. The Kampuchean (or Khmer) People's Revolutionary Party (KPRP), the communist party aligned with the Vietnamese communist movement, changed its name to the Cambodian People's Party (CPP), removed the hammer and sickle from the party emblem, and replaced Heng Samrin as Chairman of the Central Committee with the conservative Chea Sim. Reformist Hun Sen was elected Vice-Chairman of the CPP.

On 23 October 1991 an end to thirteen years of war in Cambodia was achieved with the signing of the Comprehensive Political Settlement for Cambodia by the four Cambodian factions and

19 participating countries. The agreement called for the creation of a United Nations Transitional Authority in Cambodia (UNTAC) to carry out the peacekeeping operations which included the demobilization of 70% of each faction's army and enforcement of a ceasefire; verifying the withdrawal of foreign forces; administering the country until an election in 1993 by taking over certain portfolios; assuring that human rights were maintained; and the repatriation of 600,000 refugees and internally displaced people. In November a threat to the tenuous peace process occurred when a mob attacked Khmer Rouge leaders Khieu Samphan and Son Sen in a Phnom Penh villa. The SNC government's response was slow, and it was alleged that Hun Sen sanctioned this incident and that Vietnamese officials were involved in it. In December violent student demonstrations protesting against high level corruption and in support of human rights were suppressed by the armed forces and in later demonstrations several protestors were killed. Several high level government officials were dismissed based on the corruption charges.

In January 1992 the four factions approved the formation of political associations and the promotion of freedom of expression. However, on 22 January Tea Bun Long, minister for religious affairs and an outspoken critique of corruption was killed, and on 28 January Oung Phan, organizer of a new political party emphasizing anti-corruption was shot, but survived. These and other arrests, threats, and disappearances were viewed as intimidation by the secret police geared at undermining the peace process and free elections, and served to intimidate government critics. Yasushi Akashi, the Japanese UN Under Secretary-General for Disarmament Affairs, was appointed as the UN Special Representative to Cambodia in charge of UNTAC. The UN Security Council authorized mine clearing operations, the dispatch of a 22,000 member peace keeping force to establish UNTAC, at an estimated cost of $2 billion.

In September 1991 approximately 5% of the Cambodian population was in refugee camps along the Thai-Cambodian border, 340,000 refugees in border area camps, and another 190,000 refugees within Cambodia. The refugees were in need of food, health care and tools. The plan was to move refugees to transit camps in Thailand, then on to six reception centers in Cambodia, and finally to villages. Refugees were eager to return home and claim plots of land before the mass exodus. It was estimated that 100,000 of the 340,000 refugees in border camps were families of fighters in the three resistance factions. It would be a problem if the Khmer Rouge refugees returned home first. In October the Khmer Rouge began to forcibly repatriate tens of thousands of civilians in UN refugee camps to areas under its control in Cambodia. International reaction prevented the Khmer Rouge from forcibly repatriating inhabitants of the Khmer Rouge controlled camp, Site 8, just one of the eight refugee camps. The UNTAC refugee repatriation program began in March, in spite of ceasefire violations between the Khmer Rouge and the State of Cambodia forces. The anticipated completion of this phase of the plan was the end of 1992, prior to the planned registration of voters. Throughout 1992 the Khmer Rouge denied free access to the zones it controlled, refused to comply with the disarmament phase, violated the cease-fire agreement, played upon long-standing racial/ethnic tensions by contending that Vietnamese soldiers were concealed in Cambodia, complained that the UN peacekeepers were not impartial to them, failed to attend meetings, and demanded the dismantling of the Phnom Penh regime as a precondition for the implementation of the peace accords, amongst other demands.

In May 1992 the Khmer People's National Liberation Front (KPNLF), the political and military party formed by Son Sann for the purpose of resisting the Vietnamese, was transformed into a political party called the Buddhist Liberal Democracy Party (BLDP) and still headed by Son Sann. FUNCINPEC also became a party, headed by Prince Ranariddh. At a Ministerial Conference on the Rehabilitation and Reconstruction of Cambodia held in Tokyo in June, the application of economic sanctions against the Khmer Rouge was considered and 33 donor nations and 12 non-governmental organizations attending the conference pledged $880 million to finance the peace-keeping operation. In August Akashi, the head of UNTAC, approved elections, and the registration of parties began. He also affirmed that the elections would proceed without the participation of the Khmer Rouge if it continued to refuse to co-operate. The demands of the Khmer Rouge were impossible to meet and were viewed as efforts to gain territory in order to increase its representation in the proposed national assembly, perhaps with as much as 35% of the population (a tactic laid down by Pol Pot in a 1988 speech). Differences of opinion between the UN French and Australian field commanders arose over strategies to deal with the Khmer Rouge. The French commander wanted to push the Khmer Rouge to comply, even with a show of force, if necessary, and the Australian commander wanted to give the Khmer Rouge an opportunity to switch from a military to a political agenda. In September the Khmer Rouge made two new demands, the resignation of Akashi and for a redrawn border between Cambodian and Viet Nam. This latter demand referred to territory allegedly annexed by Viet Nam which would make the elections incomplete if not returned to Cambodia. The Khmer Rouge protested an electoral law drafted by UNTAC which enfranchised citizens aged more than 18 years whose parents or grandparents were born in Cambodia, effectively permitting Vietnamese immigrants to take part in the election.

October 1992 UNTAC began voter registration. The Khmer Rouge boycotted voter registration and escalated destruction of bridges and roads, effectively cutting off its territory in the northeast from the rest of the country. The UN Security Council set a November deadline for the Khmer Rouge's compliance with the terms of the peace accord, but eventually extended the deadline to 31 January 1993 as the Khmer Rouge's last chance to participate in the elections. The Security Council also approved an embargo on supplies of petroleum products to the Khmer Rouge and a ban on timber exports (a principal source of income for the Khmer Rouge). The Khmer Rouge announced the formation of the Cambodian National Unity Party to contest the elections on the day the UN resolution was adopted. Ethnic and racial tensions were increasing as the Khmer Rouge incited and escalated actions against the Vietnamese based on deeprooted Cambodian sentiments towards the Vietnamese. In December the KPNLF joined the Khmer Rouge in the ethnic cleansing of the Vietnamese germs. Six members of the UN peace-keeping forces were seized and held for a few days by the Khmer Rouge in December 1992.

In January Prince Sihanouk ceased cooperation with UNTAC and suggested that a presidential election be held prior to the legislative election, but in February he reversed his position. Voter registration was completed in February; registered voters numbered 4.5 million and 20 political parties were registered. The election was set for May 23–25, 1993. The CPP intimidated its political rivals with attacks and stopped the gradual expansion of the Khmer Rouge into Phnom Penh government territory. In a dryseason offensive the SOC attacked 3 of 4 of the Khmer Rouge's most important zones. Thailand complied with the logging ban, but appealed that the door remain open for the Khmer Rouge to join the political process.

However, by February 1993 the Khmer Rouge refused to disarm and attacked UN offices, cars, helicopters, and personnel. In addition to the Khmer Rouge's accusations of collusion between UNTAC and the SOC, the presence of the UN forces was a source of growing tension and dissatisfaction in Cambodia. Inflation, official corruption, and crime were increasing and UNTAC's presence and policies were blamed. The Khmer Rouge issued their own currency, thus emphasizing steps toward further partition. In a secret speech a year earlier, (6 February 1992), Pol Pot had set out an incremental approach by which the Khmer Rouge could gain popular strength which he considered more important than land: develop local autonomy; set up a money economy with their own banks which would hold the surplus earnings of farmers (projected to be 30% of earnings); distribute land, sell land in order to support the army, and continue to fight the "yuon" (savage), or., Vietnamese. As the Khmer Rouge again refused to disarm and take part in the elections, it appeared to follow this program as it also increased attacks on Vietnamese fishermen and their families, killing 34 and injuring 29 in March at the floating village of Chong Kneas. Furthermore, citing its allegations that UNTAC colluded with the Vietnamese aggressors and rubber stamped the Vietnamese occupation, the Khmer Rouge refused to cooperate with the peace process. The UN goal was to have all refugees back in Cambodia by mid-April for elections. By 19 March 330,000 refugees were repatriated. A cash inducement had been added as incentive ($50/adults and $25 for children), and this rapidly accelerated the process. Roughly 87% had taken the cash option, nearly one–third going to Phnom Penh; 80-85% of the returnees chose areas under Phom Penh government (Hun Sen) control, (about 85% of the country's) territory; 10% chose areas controlled by the Khmer People's National Liberation Front; 2% chose zones controlled by forces loyal to Prince Sihanouk; and 1% chose Khmer Rouge areas. Many thousands of refugees had traveled to the Khmer Rouge without being taken their there by the UN High Commission on Refugees. In April the Khmer Rouge closed its office in Phnom Penh and slipped out of the city; it pledged to prevent the planned elections as a plot by Western powers to get rid of the guerilla nation. A Japanese UN worker was killed and eventually 30 of the 460 volunteers for the election work resigned. In May the Khmer Rouge mounted its boldest offensives yet with targets defined for maximum political impact including major cities; they took briefly the Siem Reap airport. Under these pressures UNTAC abandoned 400 of its 1800 polling places.

The election took place May 23–28, 1993; four million Cambodians or 85% of those registered voted. FUNCINPEC won the election with 45% of the vote, or 58 of 120 seats in the constituent assembly; the CPP took 38% of the votes, or 51 seats in the assembly; the BLDP had over 3% of the votes, which gave them 10 seats; and, MOULINAKA (Movement for the Liberation of Kampuchea, a pro-Sihanouk group formed in 1979 by Kong Sileah, considered an offshoot of FUNCINPEC) took one seat. The constituent assembly had three months within which to draft a constitution and form a new government. To the CPP its political defeat was an unacceptable surprise and it demanded a revote and threatened riots; the Khmer Rouge denounced the CPP for contesting the election. On June 3 Prince Sihanouk surprised everyone by announcing that he was forming a government and assuming executive powers, a plan that collapsed within a day. On June 10 Prince Norodom Chakrapong, deputy prime minister of the CPP government (a son of Sihanouk who was bitterly feuding with his half-brother Ranariddh), Sin Song, head of National Security, and Bou Thonof the CPP, threatened the secession of six eastern provinces bordering Viet Nam, or, 40% of Cambodia's territory. The secession movement collapsed on June 15 and Chakrapong fled to Viet Nam. The CPP's 51 assemblymen were technocrats and education officials (people who never wielded power within the party); this supported the belief that the CPP paid only lip service to constitutional arrangements as it maintained its grip on power. The CPP's two leaders, hardliner Chea Sim and reformer Hun Sen, were foci of this internal struggle. In a move towards cooperation the control of the major ministries was divided, with FUNCINPEC getting the finance and foreign affairs portfolios while the CPP retained the Information Minis-

try; FUNCINPEC leader Prince Norodom Ranariddh and CPP Primer Minister Hun Sen served as co-chairmen of the government. The CPP had 200,000 armed forces and 40,000 national police; FUNCINPEC's armed forces numbered 5,000. In August for the first time the three government factions, royalist FUNCINPEC, former Phnom Penh ruling regime CPP, and the BLDP, agreed to joint military operations. The Khmer Rouge would not be allowed to enter the political mainstream until it agreed to unconditionally join the unified armed forces and open up areas under its control, estimated to be 20% of Cambodia.

Cambodia's new constitution was adopted on 21 September 1993. Prince Norodom Sihanouk was crowned king, resuming the title first bestowed on him in 1941. With the support of the UN and the US the new government tackled long-standing territorial disputes with Thailand and Viet Nam, claims that both had taken Cambodian territory, and cited the tensions created by Thailand's continued support of the Khmer Rouge. Malaysia's support of Prince Chakrapong was also censured. On 29 October the new parliament endorsed a new 18-member cabinet and political program to guide the country for next five years. In an attempt to restore central control of the economy to the government on December 28 the National Assembly passed a national budget and financial laws. These new laws strip individuals of the power to collect taxes independently and by law all revenue is channeled to the national treasury. Minister of Economics and Finance Sam Rainsy set about to root out official corruption and centralize Cambodia's budget. The entrenched businesses protested, but Rainsy received the backing of Sihanouk and international lending institutions. The two co-prime ministers, First Premier Norodom Ranariddh and Second Premier Hun Sen, asked King Sihanouk for sanction to fire Rainsy, but instead received a statement praising Rainsy, who was becoming a popular hero. King Sihanouk also urged the government to grant total freedom to the domestic and foreign press.

In early 1994 while the new government sought to consolidate and to gain control of the economy, military activity continued between government forces and the Khmer Rouge. Cambodian currency, the riel, was stabilized and tax revenues increased. International donors pledged an extra $773 million in aid. Corruption and a free press were major issues. King Sihanouk was seriously ill with cancer. The government captured Pailin, official headquarters of the Khmer Rouge on 19 March, but the Khmer Rouge retook it one month later. The dry-season campaign by the government against the Khmer Rouge was a failure. Both sides were scheduled to resume peace negotiations on May 2–7. The Khmer Rouge looked to its military successes as leverage for a powersharing compromise with the government; Sihanouk sought to make powersharing deals that gave the Khmer Rouge some key posts in return for laying down its arms and opening areas under its control. Sihanouk maintained his hope of striking a deal with guerillas, but in May, as the Khmer Rouge defeated government forces, more than 60,000 villagers fled. Cambodia' political culture has no history of power sharing. One year after the elections major problems were security, corruption, and the economy. Security issues included demobilized unpaid soldiers turning to banditry, new mines being laid, Westerners were kidnapped, UN vehicles stolen, villagers fleeing the fighting, closed schools. It was unsafe to farm. Corruption included national assembly members keeping their seats while serving in other branches of government; parties swelling the number of senior officers and civil servants as they vied to match each other in number and in rank; and the National Assembly voting themselves a raise equal to 100 times that of a typical soldier. The economy was dermined by continuing military activity, and privatization was stalled by lack of capital and skilled workers, and political instability. The Khmer Rouge was seriously weakened, the government army was also weak, and politicians wanted to pass a bill to outlaw the Khmer Rouge. However, the king's policy of compromise with the Khmer Rouge seriously underminded military operations.

Within the SOC there was a further difference of opinion on how to deal with the Khmer Rouge. Prime Minister Prince Norodom Ranariddh counted on diplomacy to isolate the Khmer Rouge while using development aid and investment for job creation, and poverty reduction, infrastructure improvement, and the creation of vocational education programs. Coupled with this economic approach, both an infusion of arms and international support were necessary to isolate the Khmer Rouge. On the other hand, many of his counterparts in the CPP sought a military solution to the Khmer Rouge problem. There was consensus, however, that Cambodia should look to Malaysia's experience with the Malayan Communist Party, which consisted of marginalizing the Malaysian communists. UNTAC's failure not to disarm the Khmer Rouge was a burden for the new government. The Khmer Rouge was emerging with its prestige enhanced, territory expanded, and weaponry intact. Cambodia had been critical of the role Thailand played in supporting the Khmer Rouge, and renewed its appeals to Thai neutrality. The Khmer Rouge presence benefited Thailand by aiding in securing its border, and with lucrative trade in gems, timber, and armaments. The Khmer Rouge radio station was located inside Thai territory. The Thai government reiterated that it was the policy of Thailand not to support the Khmer Rouge, but that the Thai military controlled the border region and maintained close ties with the Khmer Rouge.

In June King Sihanouk was treated for cancer in Beijing. He emphasized that he was not now taking power, but would take power if the situation became desperate, proposing a government which included the Khmer Rouge. After two rounds of peace talks ended in failure, the government expelled the Khmer Rouge officials from the government compound in Phnom Penh. The Khmer Rouge response was to ask for the elected government to be dissolved and a new one formed in which they would have a share of the power. King Sihanouk said that if chaos broke out he might have to take over executive power. A comment which prompted Hun Sen to write to the King expressing his disapproval.

On 3 July 1994 there was a coup attempt. Less than 300 troops were involved and it was directed against FUNCINPEC, and possibly Hun Sen, by hard line figures at the highest levels of the CPP attempting to take over the government. Government troops proceeded immediately from putting down the rebels to storming the homes of Chakrapong and Sin Song. Sin Song was placed under house arrest and Chakrapong was allowed to leave the country for exile in Malaysia. A third CPP member, Sin Sen was also arrested along with 14 Thai citizens. Suspicion was placed on Deputy Prime Minister Sar Kheng's participation, but he categorically denied his involvement. Sources claim that the plan was to take over the national assembly, maintain an appearance of democracy, and install a new prime minister. After the coup attempt the National Assembly voted to outlaw the Khmer Rouge and seize its assets, a move that was partly directed at Thailand. The Khmer Rouge's response was to announce the formation of parallel government, with its headquarters in northern Cambodia and Khieu Samphan as president.

In July of 1994, it was estimated that 55,000 Cambodians were again fleeing Khmer Rouge attacks in the western provinces. For the first time since the 1970s, the US provided military aid to Cambodia. Starting in July 1994 the Defense Department sent 44 officers and enlisted men as trainers along with surplus equipment to build roads and find mines. King Sihanouk warned that without military aid Cambodia might again fall to the Khmer Rouge. The war in Cambodia has been called "The Coward's War," a name given by the human rights group Asia Watch.

Mines may have inflicted more wounds than any other weapon, and Cambodia has the world's highest percentage of physically disabled persons. Cambodia's constitution fails to guarantee human rights for racial groups other than ethnic Cambodians. The definition of Cambodians includes ethnic Chams and Chinese, but excludes ethnic Vietnamese.

[13]GOVERNMENT

Cambodia was a constitutional monarchy from 6 May 1947 until 9 October 1970, when Marshal Lon Nol formally established the Khmer Republic. On 30 April 1972, a new constitution was passed by a national referendum. It provided for a directly elected president and a bicameral legislature consisting of an elective 126-member National Assembly and 40-member Senate. Upon the surrender of the Lon Nol government to insurgent forces on 17 April 1975, rule by the Royal Government of National Union of Kampuchea (Gouvernement Royal de l'Union Nationale de Kampuchea—GRUNK) was installed in Phnom Penh, with Prince Norodom Sihanouk as titular head of state. A new constitution, effective 5 January 1976, provided for a unicameral, 250-member People's Assembly, elected for a five-year term by universal suffrage of citizens over age 18. The PRK government, installed in January 1979, enacted a new constitution in June 1981. Under this constitution, an elected National Assembly is the supreme organ of state power; it is headed by a 7-member Council of State, which the Assembly elects from among its own members. The president of the Council of State as 1988 began was Heng Samrin. Members of the legislature (117 in 1981) are elected to five-year terms by universal suffrage at age 18. There is a cabinet, the Council of Ministers, consisting of 17 ministers and 18 vice-ministers. In early 1988, the chairman of the Council was Hun Sen. The CGDK, which held Cambodia's seat at the UN, consisted of a president, Prince Sihanouk; a vice-president, Khmer Rouge leader Khieu Samphan; a prime minister, Son Sann, representing another antigovernment group, the Khmer People's National Liberation Front (KPNLF); and four coordinating committees, dealing with defense, finance and economy, education and culture, and health and social affairs.

In 1990 no single authority controlled the entire country. The National Government of Cambodia (NGC), formerly the Coalition Government of Democratic Kampuchea (CGDK), and the Vietnamese-installed authorities in Phnom Penh vied for authority in the newly named State of Cambodia. In August 1990 the United Nations Security Council endorsed a plan for a comprehensive settlement providing for UN supervision of an interim government, military arrangements for the transition, and free elections. The United Nations Transitional Authority in Cambodia (UNTAC) would oversee the transition. The four Cambodian factions accepted this proposal in September 1990. [The factions are the government of the Kampuchean People's Revolutionary Party (KPRP) installed by the Vietnamese (also known as the Heng Samrin government) and three antigovernment groups under the umbrella organization, NGC: FUNCINPEC, the Khmer Rouge, and the Khmer People's National Liberation Front (KPNLF).] A Supreme National Council (SNC) was formed with six representatives each from the Phnom Penh regime and from the National Government of Cambodia, but they failed to elect a chairman. The SNC occupied the Cambodia seat at the UN General Assembly. In completing the 1991 UN peace agreement the type of electoral system for the coming national election was the final sticking point. At issue were two proposed voting systems. The resistance factions and the five permanent members of the United Nations Security Council preferred proportional representation on a national basis. Hun Sen of the KPRP, Communist Party installed by Vietnam in 1979, wanted a constituency-balloting, "first-past-the-post" system. The compromise electoral system was a proportional representation system based on the 20 provinces as constituencies. This solution would allow the Khmer Rouge faction representation in the new legislature, but not as much as they might have gained based on nationwide proportional representation. On 23 October 1991 the UN peace accord was signed by Cambodia's four factions.

From May 23–28, 1993 a six day election, the first multiparty election in more than 20 years, was held to determine the 120 members of the national assembly. FUNCINPEC took 45.5% of the votes amounting to 58 seats in the assembly; the Cambodian People's Party (CPP), formerly the Kampuchean People's Revolutionary Party (KPRP), received 38.2% of the votes equaling 51 assembly seats; and Buddhist Liberal Democratic Party (BLDP) had 3% of the votes giving them 10 seats; and Moulinaka (Movement for the Liberation of Kampuchea, a pro-Sihanouk group formed in 1979 by Kong Sileah, considered an offshoot of FUNCINPEC) took one seat. This newly elected National Assembly was authorized to draft a constitution. In June 1993 FUNCINPEC and the Cambodian People's Party agreed to joint control of the defense and interior ministries, while FUNCINPEC controlled the foreign and finance ministries; Hun Sen and Prince Ranariddh served as co-chairmen of the interim government. The National Assembly ratified a new constitution on 21 September 1993. The monarchy, was re-established and commitments to liberal democracy, the rule of law, and women's rights were inluded. Prince Norodom Sihanouk ratified the constitution and again became King of Cambodia. The government of the State of Cambodia has maintained itself as a fragile coalition since the elections. A secessionist action in June 1993 and a coup 3 July 1994 occurred and Prince Chakrapong was involved in both events, highlighting the internal power struggle within the CPP between hardliners like Chea Sim, and reformers, like Hun Sen. The Khmer Rouge which opted out of the 1991 peace pact and boycotted the elections, controlled about 20% of Cambodia's territory. On 11 June 1994 the Khmer Rouge announced that it had formed a parallel government headquartered in northern Cambodia with Khieu Samphan as president. The National Assembly voted to outlaw the Khmer Rouge in early July 1994.

¹⁴POLITICAL PARTIES

Under Sihanouk, the People's Social Community Party (Sang Kam) was the most important political group. In the 1955, 1958, 1962, and 1966 elections, with a platform of nonalignment, economic aid, and development, it captured all seats in the National Assembly. Exiled in Beijing following his overthrow by Lon Nol in March 1970, Sihanouk allied himself with Cambodia's leftist insurgents under a group called the National United Front of Kampuchea (Front National Uni de Kampuchea—FNUK). Under the Khmer Republic government headed by Lon Nol, five political groups came to the fore. The Socio-Democratic Party (SDP), Lon Nol's own group, was quickly established as the most powerful political organization. Centrist opposition groups included the Republican Party and the Democratic Party. Smaller groups included the Women's Party and the Pracheachon Party, representing a Marxist faction. In the presidential elections held in June 1972, Lon Nol, the SDP's candidate, won by a relatively narrow margin of 55%. With the victory of their forces in April 1975, leaders of the pro-communist FNUK became the dominant political power in Kampuchea. The leading element in FNUK was the Khmer Communist Party (KCP), founded in 1951 and now dominated by radicals Pol Pot (previously known as Saloth Sar) and Khieu Samphan. Khieu Samphan was named prime minister of the new regime, while Pol Pot remained party head. During the next few years the Pol Pot faction systematically purged all suspected pro-Vietnamese members of the party organization. In late 1978, opposition elements, headed by Heng Samrin, formed the Kampuchean National United Front for National Salvation (KNUFNS) in an effort to overthrow the Pol Pot regime. Follow-

ing a Vietnamese invasion in December, Heng Samrin became the head of the pro-Vietnamese PRK government installed in January 1979. In 1981, the KNUFNS was renamed the Kampuchean United Front for National Construction and Defense, the primary mass organization in the PRK. Power resides in the Kampuchean People's Revolutionary Party (KPRP), formed from anti-Pol Pot remnants of the KCP. At first, the KPRP was quite small, and it reportedly numbered only about 700 in 1983. Membership in 1986 was estimated at 10,000. The leading body in the party is the Politburo, composed of nine members. Pro–Pol Pot members of the KCP continue to operate in the interior of the PRK. Popularly known as the Khmer Rouge, the movement has allied with two non-Communist factions, the Sihanoukists and Son Sann's KPNLF, into a so-called Coalition Government of Democratic Kampuchea (CGDC). The KCP formally dissolved itself in December 1981 in order to broaden its appeal to moderate elements in Kampuchea.

The Kampuchean People's Revolutionary Party (KPRP), the Communist Party originally installed by Viet-Nam in 1979 as the People's Republic of Kampuchea (PRK), was also known as the Heng Samrin Government in the late 1980s. On 31 October 1991 the KPRP dropped the word "Revolutionary" from the party name, becoming the Khmer People's Party or Cambodian People's Party (CPP). Hun Sen remained Chairman of the Council of Ministers of the government of the State of Cambodia a position he had held since 1985. At an extraordinary party congress, October 17–18 1991, Chea Sim was elected party president, replacing Heng Samrin, and Hun Sen was elected party vice-president; these events signaled a shift from hardline communist ideology to a reformist position prior to the UN-supervised elections. Chea Sim remained president of the national assembly. In February 1992 the National Assembly appointed two new deputy prime ministers, Sar Kheng (who is also Chea Sim's brother-in-law), and Prince Norodom Chakrapong, son of Sihanouk (lending credibility to the CPP by this link to the former royal family). The post-UN election secessionist movement, considered a CPP ploy to force power sharing, was led by Prince Chakrapong. The July 1994 coup attempt was also attributed to Prince Chakrapong and two other CPP stalwarts, Sin Sen and Sin Song, but suspicion was also cast on the CPP higher echelons, including Chea Sim and Sar Kheng, as at least having prior knowledge. Hun Sen was made Second Premier of the State of Cambodia in the post-election government of the State of Cambodia. The CPP's military force, Cambodian People's Armed Forces (CPAF) is the political army of the State of Cambodia regime.

The Coalition Government of Democratic Kampuchea (CGDK), the tripartite, anti-Vietnamese resistance group formed in June 1982, changed is name to the National Government of Cambodia (NGC) in 1990. Autonomous coalition members are FUNCINPEC, the KPNLF, and the Khmer Rouge. Prince Sihanouk's main political organization formed in 1981 was known as the National United Front for an Indpendent, Neutral, Peaceful, and Cooperative Cambodia, or its French acronym, FUNCINPEC; he resigned as its head in 1989. In 1992 the Front was registered as a political party for the 1993 elections and Prince Norodom Ranaridddh was elected president. FUNCINPEC's military force was the National Army of Independent Cambodia, formerly Sihanouk's Armee Nationale Sihanoukiste (ANS). In 1992 the Khmer People's National Liberation Front (KPNLF), headed by Son Sann, formed the Buddhist Liberal Democratic Party (BLDP), also headed by Son Sann. The military wing of the KPNLF was the KPNLAF, the Khmer People's National Liberation Army formed under Son Sann in 1979. Although it boycotted the elections and attempted to undermine the peace process, the Khmer Rouge had also formed a party to contest the elections, the Cambodian National Unity Party, headed by Kieu Samphan and Son Sen. The military force of the Khmer Rouge is the National Army of Democratic Kampuchea. The signing of the UN peace accords in 1991 triggered policy disagreements among the top echelon of the Khmer Rouge. In 1992 Ieng Sary, a member of the Khmer Rouge old guard, was stripped of power in a bitter break. Another member of the old guard, Son Sen, supported the peace accords, arguing for restoring international credibility to the Khmer Rouge, was also stripped of power in 1992. On 11 June 1994 the Khmer Rouge formed a parallel government with Khieu Samphan as president. In July 1994 the National Assembly outlawed the Khmer Rouge and seized its assets. Former government minister, Oung Phan and seven associates were arrested in May 1990 and imprisoned for circulating proposals for forming a new party, the Free Democratic Society Party (FDSP). FDSP advocated peace, freedom, democracy, and an end to poverty and corruption. All eight spent 17 months in prison. In January 1992 Oung Phan was shot, but survived. MOULINAKA, the Movement for the National Liberation of Kampuchea, a pro-Sihanouk group formed in 1979 by Kong Sileah, won one seat in the national assembly in the 1993 election. A number of other small political parties registered to contest the 1993 election.

15 LOCAL GOVERNMENT

Under the Lon Nol government, Cambodia was divided into 20 provinces (khet), 7 sub-provinces (anoukhet), 147 districts (srok), and more than 1,200 townships (sangkat or khum) and villages (phum). Under the Pol Pot regime, administration was essentially decentralized into several major regions. Regions were divided into 41 districts, and the population as a whole was organized in massive rural communes. Under the PRK regime, the pre-1975 system of administration has been restored. Based on the People's Republic of Kampuchea's new constitution of June 1981 Local Assemblies, popularly elected by the respective localities—province, district, sub-district, ward—were instituted with the number of representatives fixed by law, and People's Revolutionary Committee's chosen by the respective assemblies. This was an hierarchical system by each committees was responsible to its assembly and that assembly was responsible to the committee at the next higher level, and so on. In 1987 Cambodia was divided into 18 provinces, two special municipalities (krong), and Phnom Penh and Kampong Saom, which were under direct central government control. The provinces were subdivided into about 122 districts, 1,324 communes, and 9,386 villages. Municipalities were subdivided into wards (sangkat). The same system of assemblies and committees remains in place. The new constitution of the State of Cambodia was adopted on 21 September 1993. People's Committees established in all provinces, municipalities, districts, communes, and wards are responsible for local administration, public security, and local order. Within this system provincial officials and the governor effectively controlled the armed forces and security services, tax collection, civil service—and through them 80% of the Cambodian population. The country's provinces remained under the sway of the Cambodian People's Party (CPP) and responded to the old political loyalties rather than the central authority of the State of Cambodia. To alter this system the National Assembly passed laws to secure central control of the economy. Effective 1 January 1994 a national budget and financial laws were enacted to ensure that all revenues came totally and directly to the national treasury.

16 JUDICIAL SYSTEM

The 1993 constitution of the Kingdom of Cambodia provides due process protections such as presumption of innocence and also guarantees an independent judiciary. It is expected to take some time to train judicial personnel to implement these principles. The structure of the new judicial system will be defined by laws yet to be enacted. There is no known functioning judicial system in the PDK (Party of Democratic Kampuchea) zones.

The previous judicial system which was outlined in the constitution of 1989, provided for provincial court judges named by state officials. In practice, the judiciary was controlled by the government.

Prior to 1989, the constitution of 1976 provided for a supreme judicial tribunal whose members were to be appointed by a People's Assembly. Because of the civil and military turmoil, however, this system was never fully implemented.

17 ARMED FORCES

At the time of the Lon Nol coup in April 1970, the government's armed forces consisted of only 37,000 personnel. By September 1970, the army had been expanded to nearly 200,000. With the fall of the Lon Nol government in April 1975, the Khmer Republic's armed forces were disbanded. The GRUNK government's People's National Liberation Armed Forces of Kampuchea may have numbered 80,000 personnel in 1975.

As of mid-1986, the armed forces of the PRK were estimated at about 35,000 men. Khmer Rouge guerrillas reportedly numbered 40,000, and guerrillas loyal to Prince Sihanouk or the KPNLF totaled 25,000.

The restored Cambodian government has a regular army of 80,000, an air force of 1,000, and a navy of 4,000, armed with Russian and Chinese equipment, some left by the departed Vietnamese army. Another 270,000 Khmer and minorities constitute provincial and village militia. Three different opposition armies number perhaps 70,000. Russia provides 500 advisors while 29 nations support 10,200 UN peacekeepers. No reliable defense estimates exist.

18 INTERNATIONAL COOPERATION

Cambodia has been a member of the UN since 14 December 1955 and participates in ESCAP and all the nonregional specialized agencies except IFAD, IFC, UNIDO, and WIPO. The Cambodian seat at the UN had successively been occupied by the de facto government until the invasion by Viet-Nam and the establishment of the PRK. Since 1979, the UN General Assembly has repeatedly called for the withdrawal of all foreign forces from Cambodia. The Assembly has also annually accepted the credentials of the delegation representing Democratic Kampuchea (the Khmer Rouge) until 1982, and the CGDK thereafter. Kampuchea remains a member of the Asian Development Bank and G-77, and is a de facto adherent of GATT.

As of 1987, the PRK claimed diplomatic relations with 30 governments or liberation movements, most of them members of the Socialist bloc or otherwise allies of the former USSR, Vietnam's chief backer. China is the major supporter of the CGDK, although it also has ties with the ASEAN alliance. The PRK is intimately linked with Laos and Vietnam in a "special relationship" involving close political, economic, and military cooperation.

19 ECONOMY

Cambodia's economy has been based traditionally on agriculture. About 85% of the cultivated area is devoted to the production of rice, while rubber trees account for a major part of the remainder. Prior to the war years, Cambodia's rice crop was usually ample enough to permit exports. The Tonle Sap is one of the major fishing reservoirs in Asia, and its products have played a key role in the Cambodian economy and diet. Cattle breeding is another important source of income. During the 1970–75 period, Cambodia's economy came to rely critically on US assistance, as the expansion of the war caused widespread damage and limited economic activity. The Pol Pot regime which came to power in April 1975 was determined to emphasize the growth of agriculture and restore national self-sufficiency. The entire population was mobilized in a mass labor campaign to improve agricultural production through massive irrigation projects in the countryside. The cities were virtually emptied, and industrial production drastically declined. Private ownership of land was disallowed, and landholdings were transferred to the state or to state-organized cooperatives. All industrial enterprises were similarly transferred to state ownership. Sparse food supplies were distributed through a system of government food rationing and other forms of allotment. When the PRK government took over in 1979, it was faced with a major challenge in restoring the national economy. The first problem was to end the threat of famine. A massive international campaign to feed the population took place during 1979–82. In the meantime, similar efforts were undertaken to stimulate the industrial sector and expand exports in order to obtain needed foreign exchange. By the mid-1980s, the economy had essentially returned to the level of the pre-1975 period, although the regime was still vitally dependent on foreign aid, chiefly from Viet Nam and the former USSR. In July 1986, the PRK issued an emergency appeal to international organizations for rice. The World Food Program provided some food aid, but most international organizations adopted a wait-and-see posture.

Rule by the Khmer Rouge, 20 years of civil war, rule by the Khmer Rouge, economic isolation, and a centrally planned economy imposed heavy burdens on Cambodia. Serious damage to basic infrastructure, industrial and agricultural production, and human resources required massive rehabilitation and reconstruction. Reliable sources note that the infrastructure is so severely degraded that it has only 40–50% of prewar capacity. Market-oriented reforms have been introduced which dismantle the centrally-planned economy. Since 1989 Cambodia passed legislation to restore the right to own and inherit property, freed prices, passed a liberal foreign investment code, began to privatize state assets, and property, decontrolled the official exchange rate, and liberalized foreign trade. Reforms generated increased agricultural production and foreign investment. Phnom Penh and other urban areas received the greatest benefit from this economic activity. In the early 1990s Cambodia remained predominantly agricultural with more than 85% of workers employed in agriculture. Inflation rose steadily, the price of domestic commodities increased at least 140% in 1990. In 1991 Cambodia halted the free trade of gold as part of an effort to stabilize the value of the currency, the riel. Triple-digit inflation made currency worthless in 1992 and it was pulled from circulation. In 1994 the riel was stabilized at 2,400-2,600 Riel to the $1. In 1991–1993, the transition period from a command to a market-driven system, the presence of 22,000 UN personnel generously lubricated the Cambodian economy, although the growth was mainly urban, barely affecting rural areas. Western consumer goods such as motor vehicles, tinned food, alcohol, and cigarettes, were readily available in Phnom Penh and other cities. In 1990 GDP was negative, increasing to 13.5% in 1991 and estimated of 6—8% in 1992. On 4 January 1992 President Bush announced the lifting of the US trade embargo against Cambodia shortly after the signing of the Paris Peace Agreement on Cambodia in 1991. One outcome of the May 1993 elections was a division of government portfolios between the winning party, FUNCINPEC, and the surprised runner-up, the Cambodian People's Party (CPP). FUNCINPEC took over the financial and economic portfolios. An aggressive campaign was mounted to restructure tax, investment, banking and currency laws. As part of the battle against official corruption some contracts signed by the previous government were revised or abrogated. The International Monetary Fund promised to finance Cambodia's balance-of-payments needs for four years. The government moved to strengthen currency and provide new banking legislation. Effective 1 January 1994 were Cambodia's national budget and Financial Structure Laws aimed at establishing central control of the economy. Cambodian labor is inexpensive and unskilled, and labor is plentiful, however, there is a severe shortage of educated and trained personnel. In addition,

economic recovery still must overcome debilitating corruption and mismanagement, and the widening gap between the urban rich and the rural poor. Realization to take advantage of Cambodia's tourism potential awaits the maintenance of a sustained peace, as does development of Cambodia's significant natural resources– timber, rubber, gems, and oil and natural gas.

[20]INCOME

In 1992, Cambodia's GNP was $2 billion at current prices, or $280 per capita. For the period 1985–92 the average inflation rate was 250-300%.

[21]LABOR

In 1992, the economically active population was officially estimated at 3,964,011, of which 56% were female, due in large part to the holocaust of the Khmer Rouge. As before the war, the vast majority of Cambodia's population engages in farming, forestry, or fishing. From 1985–91, the labor force size grew by only about 0.9% per year. In August 1992, a new labor law was passed which allowed the right for workers to form unions, prohibited forced or compulsory labor, set a minimum wage, and set the legal working age at 16 (unless employment is within a family enterprise). By necessity, however, many youths under 16 engage in street trading, construction, and light manufacturing.

[22]AGRICULTURE

Because of the lack of natural resources and the primitive industrial base in Cambodia, agriculture is the key sector in the economy. Rice provides the staple diet and prior to 1970 was Cambodia's major export, along with rubber. Production peaked at 3,200,000 tons in 1968; it began falling because of the expansion of the war and by 1974 had declined to 635,000 tons, but had risen back to 2,155,000 tons in 1990. Arable land amounted to 3,066,000 hectares (7,576,000 acres) in 1991, or 17.4% of the total land area. In 1991, agriculture accounted for 44.3% of GDP.

Upon coming to power in April 1975, the Pol Pot regime embarked on a major rice production program, but the highest output achieved was only 1,800,000 tons in 1976 and in 1977; civil war, holocaust, and the Vietnamese invasion lowered the rice harvest in 1979 to 1 million tons. During the 1980s, rice production gradually increased, from about 1,564,000 tons in 1980/81 to an estimated 1,680,000 tons in 1985/86. During the mid–1980s the Khmer Rouge government attempted to stimulate production by delaying its plans for collectivization of the countryside. In 1989, the new government returned agricultural land to the tiller, which has significantly boosted food production. Rice production in 1992 totaled 2,2545,000 tons, two-thirds greater than in the years immediately following the Vietnamese invasion.

Rubber has traditionally been the second most important agricultural crop. However, rubber plantings, which covered 48,000 hectares (119,000 acres) in 1969, were almost completely destroyed by the end of 1971. Production, up to 51,100 tons in 1969, declined to virtually nil in 1971, recovering to about 16,000 tons in 1974. The Pol Pot and Khmer Rouge governments continued efforts to revive the rubber industry, the latter with aid from the former USSR and GDR. Recovery has been uneven and slow, however, and reached only 35,000 tons in 1992. Other crops, with 1992 production levels, are: corn (50,000 tons), cassava (64,000 tons), sweet potatoes (37,000 tons), dry beans (47,000 tons), tobacco (15,000 tons), and cotton (35,000 tons).

[23]ANIMAL HUSBANDRY

Livestock, raised primarily by private households, traditionally supplied an important supplement to the Cambodian diet. The Pol Pot regime placed heavy stress on cattle and poultry breeding, but thousands died during the chaotic years of the late 1970s. According to official sources, livestock levels in 1992 were cattle,

2.2 million (as compared with 700,000 in 1979), and pigs, 1.7 million (as compared with 100,000 in 1979). In 1992, Cambodia produced an estimated 97,000 tons of meat.

24FISHING

Production of freshwater fish, the main protein element in the Cambodia diet, traditionally ranked next to rice and rubber in the national economy. About half of Cambodia's freshwater catch came from the Tonle Sap. Offshore fishing grounds present a potential resource not yet fully exploited.

Marine fishing developed significantly developed during the 1980s; the saltwater catch totaled 3,015 tons in 1982 and 36,400 tons in 1991. In 1991, inland fishing amounted to 74,700 tons, up from 65,700 tons in 1982.

25FORESTRY

About 76% of the country is forested, but exploitation has been limited because of transportation difficulties and damage caused by war. The main products of the forest industry are timber, resins, wood oil, fuel, and charcoal. Production of roundwood, averaging about 4 million cu m in the late 1960s, fell off sharply during the 1970–75 war, but increased to 6.4 million cu m in 1991. Export of roundwood was 116,000 cu m in that year (up from only 35,000 cu m in 1990). Fuel wood production was 5.5 million cu m in 1991.

26MINING

Cambodia's known mineral resources are limited. Iron deposits and traces of gold, coal, copper, and manganese have been reported in the Kampong Thum area. Substantial deposits of bauxite, discovered in the early 1960s north of Battambang and southeast of Phnom Penh, have yet to be worked. Potter's clay is common, and deposits of phosphates, used for fertilizer, exist in southern Kampot province, as well as near Phnom Sampou. Precious gems are mined in Pallin, near the Thai border. High quality cornflower-blue sapphires have been the most value gemstone produced to date, and high quality rubies also have been found. It is unlikely that exploitation of the nation's limited mineral resources can be undertaken, however, until the myriad of explosive mines, which are planted throughout the country, can be safely removed..

27ENERGY AND POWER

Wood is the most widely used fuel for transportation, industrial, and domestic purposes. Most of the few existing electric power plants must use imported diesel oil and natural gas. Several new power-generating facilities were installed in the mid-1960s, but total capacity was reduced by about one-third in the course of the war, reaching 41,000 kw by 1973/74; in that period, production stood at 150 million kwh. Total generating capacity had increased to 126,000 kw by 1991, but production, at the approximate level of 20 kwh per capita, was still low. As of 1991, a 1,000 kw hydroelectric plant was under construction at O Chum with the assistance of Viet Nam.

Offshore oil was reportedly discovered by a French firm in August 1974 in the vicinity of the Wai Islands.

28INDUSTRY

Industrial activity has traditionally centered on the processing of agricultural and forestry products and on the small-scale manufacture of consumer goods. Rice milling has been the main food-processing industry. Industrial expansion came to a virtual halt in 1970 with the outbreak of war. A few sectors (such as textiles and beverages) enjoyed a short wartime boom due to military orders, but losses in territory and transport disruptions had caused a rapid decline in activity by 1973. The Pol Pot government placed all industries under state control in 1975. In the course of the

next four years, some 100 industries were abolished or destroyed. When the PRK took over in 1979, industrial plants began to reopen. By late 1985 there were a reported 60 factories in the state sector producing household goods, textiles, soft drinks, pharmaceutical products, and other light consumer goods. Most plants operate below capacity because of poor management and shortages of electricity, raw materials, and spare parts. There is little information on the small Cambodian private sector. The overall value of local and handicrafts industries in 1984 was estimated at about 50% of the output value in state industry.

Efforts at recovery continued in the early 1990s, but were hampered by dilapidated equipment and shortages which continued to affect industrial production, principally textiles and rubber production. For instance, following the cutback of assistance from the former Soviet Union in 1990, Cambodia's primitive industrial sector suffered from raw material shortages; three of six government-owned textile mills shut down because of shortages of cotton. When major Soviet oil supplies were depleted local companies imported oil, but the cash-strapped state companies suffered electricity brownouts daily. Major industries include rice milling, fishing, wood and timber products, rubber (largely abandoned since 1975), cement, and gem mining. Cambodia has significant mineral deposits of gold, silver, iron, copper, marble, limestone and phosphate, and a gem industry. Construction in urban areas boomed with the signing of the Paris peace accords in 1991. After Cambodia opened oil fields to foreign investors in February 1991, sixteen companies expressed interest in oil exploration. In January 1994 it was reported that five oil companies were conducting offshore oil and gas exploration.

29SCIENCE AND TECHNOLOGY

Since 1979, foreign technicians have been helping to revive the economy. Aside from a School of Medicine and Pharmacy, there is virtually no opportunity within Cambodia to pursue scientific training or research.

30DOMESTIC TRADE

Phnom Penh has traditionally been Cambodia's principal commercial center. Formerly, most wholesale and retail business was in the hands of French, Chinese, and Vietnamese. In April 1975, all private shops in the country were closed, and virtually all domestic trade fell under the control of the state. Official currency was abolished in favor of barter. Following the installation of the PRK, currency was reestablished, and some private trade resumed, with official encouragement. Since 1983, private shops have resumed operation in Phnom Penh. In 1986, the government began collecting license fees, rents, and utility fees from private businesses and substantially increased their taxes. In the early 1990s the Heng Samrin government fell behind in its payments to government troops and bureaucrats, printing more money to meet these obligations. Without revenue this vicious cycle peaked in triple-digit inflation by 1992, when the currency was rendered worthless and pulled from circulation. Market prices rose as the currency value dropped meaning poorer Cambodians, could not afford their staple food, rice. The United Nations Transitional Authority in Cambodia (UNTAC) introduced imported rice and sold it at a fixed price in an effort to halt the inflationary spiral. With the presence of the UN peacekeeping force Phnom Penh, and other urban areas experienced an economic boom. Consumer goods and products increased as did construction, and rents rose. In Cambodia depressed economic output is supplemented by goods smuggled in from Thailand and Singapore.

31FOREIGN TRADE

Cambodia has traditionally been an exporter of primary products and an importer of finished goods. The country's normal trade patterns virtually disintegrated during the war as exports declined, and Cambodia was largely sustained by US-subsidized imports. Under the Pol Pot regime, foreign trade virtually ceased. According to Western estimates, total trade (excluding trade with China) was $3 million in exports and $22 million in imports in 1977. With the installation of the PRK government, foreign trade began to rise in volume. The value of total exports rose from an estimated $3–4 million in 1982 to approximately $10 million in 1985; imports in that year came to about $120 million. Almost all foreign trade has been with the former USSR and its allies, and most imports are in the form of grants. In 1985 Cambodia imported R100.2 million of goods from the USSR, compared to R18.8 million in 1984. Cambodia exported R14.9 million worth to the USSR in 1985, up from R3.9 million in 1984. The main import categories are food, vehicles, fuels, and raw materials. Cereal imports dropped from 223,000 tons in 1974 to 60,000 tons in 1985. Foreign trade is legally restricted to licensed private-sector firms and government agencies, although there is considerable smuggling between Cambodia and Thailand. In 1985, Cambodia and Viet Nam signed an agreement to double their mutual trade in 1986.

In 1986 major export trading partners with Cambodia were Viet Nam, the former USSR, Eastern Europe, Japan, and India. For imports major trading partners were the same countries. Soviet Union and CMEA assistance to Cambodia ceased in 1991. The US trade embargo against Cambodia was lifted in January 1992 by President Bush. As of 1992 Cambodian exports were mostly agricultural, comprised of timber mainly and rubber. Logging is a ready source of badly needed export revenues for both the government and the other political factions. The United Nations Development Program (UNDP) estimated that the forest cover had fallen to as little as 40% of the land area by 1992. Cambodia's own forestry department figured that in 1969 forests covered 73% of the country's land area.

The UNDP concluded that deforestation was a major threat to Cambodia's development. In 1992 imports to Cambodia were capital goods, raw materials, and, in recent years vehicles, motorcycles and consumer products.

32BALANCE OF PAYMENTS

Cambodia's balance-of-payments position showed a deficit every year during the period 1954–74. Payments transactions with other countries virtually ceased under the Pol Pot regime, when China conducted Kampuchea's external financial dealings. Since 1979, Kampuchea continued to run a substantial trade deficit, much of which had been financed by grant aid and credits extended by the former USSR and Viet Nam. The country holds virtually no gold or foreign exchange reserves.

33BANKING AND SECURITIES

All banking institutions were nationalized by the Sihanouk government on 1 July 1964. The National Bank of Cambodia, a semi-autonomous government agency functioning as the sole currency authority, was charged with central banking responsibilities, including the control of credit. The decision by then Premier Lon Nol to permit foreign banks to do business in the country in early 1970 was a factor leading to his break with Prince Sihanouk and to the latter's overthrow in March 1970.

In April 1975, the Pol Pot government assumed control of the National Bank, and virtually all banking operations in Kampuchea were liquidated. The PRK government reintroduced a money economy, and by 1983 the National Bank of Cambodia and a Foreign Trade Bank had been established. In 1991 the government created a state commercial bank to take over the commercial banking operations of the national bank. Banks in Cambodia include the Cambodian Commercial Bank, Cambodian Farmers Bank, and the Cambodian Public Bank. There is no securities trading in Cambodia.

34INSURANCE

All insurance companies were "Cambodianized" in 1960; 16 companies were in operation prior to 1975. Under the Pol Pot government, normal insurance operations were suspended. No current information is available concerning insurance in the PRK.

35PUBLIC FINANCE

All government budgets of the two decades preceding 1975 were marked by an excess of expenditures over domestic revenues; foreign aid and treasury reserves made up the difference. There probably was no domestic public finance system during 1975–78; any public funds came from China. During the 1980s, public expenditures were financed by the former USSR, either directly or through Viet-Nam

From 1989–91, the public deficit nearly tripled as a result of falling revenue collection. As assistance from the Soviet bloc ceased after 1990, monetary expansion soared to cover the deficit. By the middle of 1992, with hyperinflation imminent, the government began a series of stabilization efforts to halt the fiscal deterioration. With only limited international aid, however, public expenditures for the necessary reconstruction and development of Cambodia have been limited.

36TAXATION

Until 1975, indirect taxes were the most profitable source of domestic revenue, especially such monopoly excises as the sales tax on salt. Other indirect taxes included those on alcohol, tobacco, sugar, radios, and livestock. Taxes ceased to exist with the abolition of currency during the Pol Pot regime and were replaced by payments in-kind. In 1984, the PRK introduced an agricultural tax to soak up profits earned by private farmers. The tax reportedly amounted to about 10% of total output. In 1986, taxes on private business were increased, which forced some shopkeepers out of business.

37CUSTOMS AND DUTIES

Since the 1960s and early 1970s, Cambodia has operated under a two-column tariff with minimum and general rates. Minimum rates apply to GATT contracting parties and other countries that have special agreements with Cambodia. Goods of other countries were subject to the general rates. Import duties range from 5–10% on essential goods, to 15–25% on consumer goods, and 35–100% on luxury items. Most duties are assessed ad valorem on c.i.f. value, and there are excise taxes of 50% for tobacco and 30% for alcohol.

38FOREIGN INVESTMENT

There was little private foreign capital in pre-1975 Cambodia. French capital in rubber plantations represented more than half of the total investment. Foreign investment was prohibited under the Pol Pot regime and was not resumed under its successor, the People's Republic of Kampuchea (PRK). As part of Cambodia's economic reforms the July 1989 Foreign Investment Law and the regulations implementing the law contained in the May 1991 sub-decree on foreign investment created a favorable foreign investment climate in Cambodia. From 1989 to 1991 there were over 200 investment applications, 20 being granted and 70 given tentative approval. Foreign investors from Thailand, Singapore, Taiwan, Hong Kong, France, and the US accounted for over half these applications; overseas Khmers accounted for 30%, and 10% were from local investors. By 1993 it was reported that final contracts had been signed for 45 of these 200 applications. The value of these proposals is small, $1–5 million, and the proposals are concentrated in services, tourism, and textiles. The most visible projects are the 380-room Cambodiana Hotel in Phnom Penh, a satellite earth station project which provides international direct dial service, and a cellular telephone system in Phnom Penh. As of mid-1994 a new foreign investment law was expected to be passed. Proposed were incentives for long-term projects and new industries: profits would be taxed at 20%, full exemptions would be granted for ventures that will increase non-traditional exports and increase value, and designated industrial zones would be set up. The primary hindrance to foreign investment is the lack of infrastructure—roads are in dismal condition, bandits roam, power outages are common, and phone service is inadequate.

39ECONOMIC DEVELOPMENT

Until 1975, Cambodian governments sought aid from public and private foreign sources and attempted to improve the climate for private foreign capital investment, although the volume of investment was small. Both Sihanouk and Lon Nol also increased local control of economic activities within the country. Aliens were prohibited from engaging in 18 professions or occupations, including those of rice merchant and shipping agent. The Sihanouk government promoted economic development through two five-year plans designed to improve the nation's light industrial sector and its educational and technological infrastructure. Progress was mixed. Strained economic conditions were a factor leading to the overthrow of Sihanouk in 1970. The outbreak of war following his fall brought almost all major production to a halt. The economic objectives of the 1975–79 Pol Pot regime were centered almost entirely on agriculture and the improvement of the irrigation network. Self-sufficiency was stressed, and foreign aid was almost nil except for an estimated $1 billion from China. When the PRK government took over, it inherited a shattered economy and a depleted population. The 1986–90 five-year plan stressed growth in the agricultural sector, the restoration of light industry (which faces shortages of raw materials and electrical supply), gradual socialist transformation of ownership, dependence upon the former USSR and its allies for foreign assistance, and an increase of economic cooperation with its Indochinese neighbors. The PRK signed a number of aid, trade, and cooperation agreements with the former USSR and other Eastern European countries and was receiving substantial technological aid from neighboring Viet Nam. Development assistance from the CMEA bloc totaled an estimated $700 million between 1980 and 1984. The PRK moved slowly on its plan to transform the Cambodian economy to full socialist ownership, in recognition of the relatively low socialist awareness of the population. A small private manufacturing and commercial sector was recognized by the constitution in 1981, and farmers were being introduced to collectivization through the formation of low-level "solidarity groups" which combined socialist and private ownership. PRK plans were to advance more rapidly toward socialist transformation during the 1990s. However, since the mid-1980sthe emphasis has been placed on private sector economic activities. Newly introduced market-oriented reforms dismantled the old central planning regime. However,the structural underpinnings of a capitalist systems–the legal, financial, and institutional–exist only in rudimentary form. Many of Cambodia's nationalized industries were allowed to operate with limited autonomy from the state planning system, but the lack of capital and management expertise, as well as institutionalized corruption and bureaucratic red tape have mired this recovery process. In 1991 at the Tokyo Conference on the Rehabilitation and Reconstruction of Cambodia, $880 million in assistance was pledged to Cambodia by donor countries and multilateral institutions. An additional $80 million in aid was pledged by the Asian Development Bank, and the World Bank planned a $75-million assistance program. Under Sam Rainsy, Minister of Finance and Economy, the national assembly passed a budget and new Financial Structure Laws effective 1 January 1994. The new government's aim is to establish central control of the economy and at the same time strike out at the corrupt practices of the current system. About 48% of the budget is made up of international assistance; there are no land or income taxes with tax revenues providing only 6% of GDP, and customs duties provide 54% of total revenue. Estimates are that underground trade is equal to official trade and thus a further drain on state revenue. The new law requires that all state revenues "be sent to the national treasury totally, directly, and immediately." Development in Cambodia inextricably linked to the government's ability to maintain peace. Prime Minister Norodom Ranariddh, leader of FUNCINPEC, has said, that Cambodia's weapon against them is development. Investment, job creation, infrastructure improvements, and vocational education are FUNCINPEC's approach both to economic development and undermining the Khmer Rouge.

40SOCIAL DEVELOPMENT

The Sihanouk and Lon Nol governments enacted limited social legislation regulating hours of work, wages, and workers' compensation. During the Pol Pot period, the social fabric of the country was severely damaged. Although installation of the PRK government brought an end to the wide-ranging trauma of 1975–79, overall social conditions in Cambodia remain among the worst in southeast Asia. While the Phnom Penh regime undoubtedly ended many of the human rights abuses practiced by its predecessor, the continuing civil war heightened the security consciousness of the government, and some Western observers believed that there were thousands of political prisoners in reeducation camps. Political violence crested in the period before the UN-sponsored elections of May 1993 and then fell sharply. Unstable conditions have also limited improvement in the standard of living, still one of the lowest in the region. Cambodia's new constitution provides equal rights for women in areas including work and marriage. Women have property rights equal to those of men, and have equal access to education and certain jobs.

41HEALTH

Life expectancy in Cambodia in 1992 was 51 years, and the infant mortality rate was 117 per 1,000 live births in the same year. The general mortality rate was 1.42 per 1,000 in 1993. Dysentery, malaria, tuberculosis (in 1990, 235 reported cases per 100,000 people) trachoma, and yaws are widespread. The 1970–75 war and the 1975–79 upheaval exacerbated many of these problems. Malnutrition became widespread among the millions driven to Phnom Penh in the wake of the fighting and who were driven out of that city when the Khmer Rouge took over. Tens of thousands died from food shortages, and medical facilities and supplies. In 1991, only 36% of the population had access to safe water and a mere 14% had adequate sanitation. Prior to 1975 there were 3 hospitals, with 7,500 beds (about 1 bed for every 893 persons). During 1979–81, 7 large hospitals and 3 pharmaceutical factories opened. In 1990, there were 2.2 hospital beds per 1,000 people. In 1992, there were 0.04 doctors per 1,000 people, with a nurse to doctor ratio of 8.0. In 1991, there were 262 pharmacists and 36 dentists. Cambodia's 1993 birth rate was 39.2 per 1,000 people. There were 349,000 births in 1992, and 53% of the population had access to health care services. The 1992 immunization rates for children up to 1 year old were: tuberculosis (50%); diphtheria, pertussis, and tetanus (32%); polio (32%); and measles (33%).

42HOUSING

Cambodia's housing traditionally compared favorably with that of other countries in Southeast Asia. The most common type of dwelling consists of one or more rooms raised on mangrove piles some 3 m (10 ft) above the ground; it is generally crowded. Many houses in the cities are larger and of better quality.

Mass emigration from the cities during 1975–76 resulted in many dwellings being left vacant, in contrast to the dire overcrowding that occurred in the last years of the war. In the countryside, meanwhile, the waves of new migrants placed inordinate pressures on existing facilities, with much of the transplanted population forced to reside in improvised shelters. By the early 1980s, this pattern had been reversed somewhat, and Phnom Penh was once again experiencing population growth. According to the latest available information for 1980–88, total dwellings numbered 1,474,000 with five people per dwelling.

43EDUCATION

Under the Pol Pot regime, education was virtually abolished, as all children were sent to work in the fields; education was limited to political instruction.

Most of the educated class had been killed by 1979. According to PRK sources, only 50 of 725 university instructors and 307 of 2,300 secondary-school teachers survived the Pol Pot era. Under the PRK, education was gradually recovering. Adult literacy was estimated to be 35.2% in 1990 (males: 48.2% and females: 22.4%). Total school enrollment increased from about 1 million in 1979 to more than 1.7 million in 1985, and the number of teachers more than doubled, from 21,000 to 46,500. All schooling is public, and six years of primary education (ages 6–12) is compulsory. Following this, children may go through seven years of secondary education. Most students continue their higher education at foreign universities.

44LIBRARIES AND MUSEUMS

Library facilities before the war were limited largely to the National Library (55,000 volumes, mostly French) in Phnom Penh. There were smaller libraries at the higher schools. The Khmer National Museum won repute as an excellent repository of national art. The Ècole Française de l'Extrême-Orient, which previously had charge of all archaeological research in the country, also had its own research library in Phnom Penh.

Cambodia, in effect, is a museum of the cultural achievements of the Khmer Empire. Surviving stone monuments, steles, temples, and statuary attest to a formidable and unique artistic heritage. Particularly imposing are the world-famous temple of Angkor Wat and the Bayon of Angkor Thom. After 1970, however, foreign access to historical sites in Cambodia has been almost totally cut off. The PRK government established museums in what it portrayed as GRUNK death camps, with exhibits on atrocities committed during 1975–79.

45MEDIA

Cambodia communications network was almost totally destroyed by the Khmer Rouge. There are two radio networks, the Voice of the Kampuchean People and the Voice of the Phnom Penh People. TV-Kampuchean began color transmissions in 1986. There were an estimated 955,000 radios and 70,000 television sets in 1991. There is one daily newspaper, *Pracheachun* (1991 circulation 25,000). In early 1994, over 40 Khmer-language newspapers were available. The English-language weeklies were launched in July 1992.

46ORGANIZATIONS

In 1975, cooperative organization became a central tenet of the GRUNK government's social and economic reorganization policy. By 1976, cooperative ownership had become a countrywide phenomenon, playing a major role in both agriculture and industry. Virtually all other social and commercial organizations, including chambers of commerce, were disbanded by mid-1975.

47TOURISM, TRAVEL, AND RECREATION

Until the encroachments of war in the late 1960s, Angkor Wat and other remains of the ancient Khmer Empire were the major attractions for visitors to Cambodia. Under the Pol Pot regime, tourism was nonexistent, and it was not substantially revived under the PRK. However, since the 1992 UN peace plan, tourism has rebounded, spurred by the opening of hundreds of new facilities and scores of new diplomatic missions. In 1993, 120,000 tourists visited Cambodia, and 50% increase was expected for 1994. Visas are available on arrival at Phnom Penh for US $20. There are two government-run tourist agencies and a number of new private tour groups. Dozens of hotels have opened in the capital, which only had 400 rooms in 1989.

48FAMOUS CAMBODIANS

Foremost among ancient heroes were Fan Shihman, greatest ruler of the Funan Empire (150–550), and Jayavarman II and Jayavarman VII, monarchs of the Khmer Empire who ruled between the 10th and 13th centuries. Prince Norodom Sihanouk (b.1922), who resigned the kingship and won Kampuchea's independence from France, is the best-known living Kampuchean. In exile in China during 1970–75, he founded the GRUNK government, from which he resigned in April 1976. In July 1982, he became president of the CGDK. Khieu Samphan (b.1931), a former Marxist publisher and leader of the insurgency in Kampuchea, was named chairman of the State Presidium in the GRUNK government in April 1976, replacing Sihanouk as chief of state. The de facto head of the GRUNK regime during 1975–79 was Pol Pot, the nom de guerre of Saloth Sar (b.1925), who presided over the drastic restructuring of Kampuchean society that left as many as 2–3 million dead in its wake. Heng Samrin (b.1934) became president of the Council of State of the PRK in 1979.

49DEPENDENCIES

Cambodia has no territories or colonies.

50BIBLIOGRAPHY

Briggs, Lawrence Palmer. *Ancient Khmer Empire.* Philadelphia: American Philosophical Society, 1951.

Cady, John Frank. *The Roots of French Imperialism in Eastern Asia.* Ithaca, N.Y.: Cornell University Press, 1954.

Cambodia, 1975–1978: Rendezvous with Death. Princeton, N.J.: Princeton University Press, 1989.

Carney, Timothy (ed.). *Communist Party Power in Kampuchea: Documents and Discussion.* Ithaca, N.Y.: Cornell University Press, 1977.

Chandler, David P. *The Land and People of Cambodia.* New York: HarperCollins, 1991.

———. *The Tragedy of Cambodian History: Politics, War, and Revolution since 1945.* New Haven: Yale University Press, 1991.

———. *A History of Cambodia.* 2d ed. Boulder, Colo.: Westview Press, 1992.

Cole, Allan Burnett (ed.). *Conflict in Indochina and International Repercussions: A Documentary History, 1945–1955.* Ithaca, N.Y.: Cornell University Press, 1956.

Ebihara, May M, Carol A. Mortland, and Judy Ledgerwood (eds.) *Cambodian Culture since 1975: Homeland and Exile.* Ithaca: Cornell University Press, 1994.

Etcheson, Craig. *The Rise and Demise of Democratic Kampuchea.* Boulder, Colo.: Westview, 1984.

Fifield, Russell H., and C. Hart Schaaf. *The Lower Mekong.* Princeton, N.J.: Van Nostrand, 1963.

Genocide and Democracy in Cambodia: New Haven, Conn.: Yale University Southeast Asia Studies, 1993.

Herz, Martin Florian. *A Short History of Cambodia.* New York: Praeger, 1958.

Kiernan, Ben. *How Pol Pot Came to Power.* London: Verso, 1985.

Picq, Laurence. *Beyond the Horizon: Five Years with the Khmer Rouge.* New York: St. Martin's, 1989.

Pradhan, Prakash C. *Foreign Policy of Kampuchea.* Atlantic Highlands, N.J.: Humanities, 1983.

Ross, Russell R. (ed.). *Cambodia: A Country Study.* 3rd ed. Washington, D.C.: Library of Congress, 1990.

Shawcross, William. *Sideshow: Kissinger, Nixon, and the Destruction of Cambodia.* New York: Simon & Schuster, 1987.

Sihanouk, Norodom. *War and Hope: The Case for Cambodia.* New York: Pantheon, 1980.

Sutter, Robert G. *The Cambodian Crisis and U.S. Policy Dilemmas.* Boulder, Colo.: Westview Press, 1991.

Welaratna, Usha. *Beyond the Killing Fields: Voices of Nine Cambodian Survivors in America.* Stanford, Calif.: Stanford University Press, 1993.

CHINA

People's Republic of China
Zhonghua Renmin Gongheguo

CAPITAL: Beijing (Peking).

FLAG: The flag is red with five gold stars in the upper left quadrant; one large star is near the hoist and four smaller ones are arranged in an arc to the right.

ANTHEM: *March of the Volunteers.*

MONETARY UNIT: The renminbi, or "people's money," denominated in yuan (Y), is equivalent to 10 jiao or 100 fen. There are coins of 1, 2, and 5 fen, 1, 2, and 5 jiao, and 1 yuan, and notes of 1, 2, and 5 fen, 1, 2, and 5 jiao, and 1, 2, 5, 10, 50, and 100 yuan. Y1 = $0.1148 (or $1 = Y8.7080).

WEIGHTS AND MEASURES: The metric system is the legal standard, but some Chinese units remain in common use.

HOLIDAYS: New Year's Day, 1 January; Spring Festival (Chinese New Year), from the 1st to the 3d day of the first moon of the lunar calendar, usually in February; International Women's Day, 8 March; May Day, 1 May; Army Day, 1 August; Teachers' Day, 9 September; and National Day, 1–2 October.

TIME: 8 pm = noon GMT.

¹LOCATION, SIZE, AND EXTENT

The People's Republic of China (PRC), the third-largest country in the world after the former USSR and Canada and the largest nation in Asia, claims an area of 9,596,960 sq km (3,705,406 sq mi), including Taiwan, which the PRC claims as a province; the major administrative divisions, excluding Taiwan and the off-shore islands, cover 9,444,292 sq km (3,646,448 sq mi). Comparatively, the area occupied by China is slightly larger than the United States. The mainland has an extension of 4,845 km (3,011 mi) ENE–WSW and 3,350 km (2,082 mi) SSE–NNW. The mainland's 5,774-km (3,588-mi) coastline, extending from the mouth of the Yalu River in the northeast to the Gulf of Tonkin in the south, forms a great arc, with the Liaodong and Shandong peninsulas in the north protruding into the Yellow Sea and the Leizhou Peninsula in the south protruding into the South China Sea. China's territory includes several large islands, the most important of which is Hainan, off the south coast. Other islands include the reefs and islands of the South China Sea, extending as far as 4°N. These reefs and islands include Dongsha (Pratas), to which Taiwan has also laid claim. China's claims to the Xisha (Paracel) and Nansha (Spratly) archipelagoes are also in dispute. In 1986, the UK agreed to transfer Hong Kong to the PRC in 1997.

China is bordered on the N by Mongolia (Mongolian People's Republic–MPR) and the former USSR; on the NE by the Democratic People's Republic of Korea (DPRK); on the E by the Yellow and the East China seas; on the S by Hong Kong, Macau, the South China Sea, the Gulf of Tonkin, Vietnam, and Laos; on the SW by Burma, India, Bhutan, and Nepal; on the W by India, Jammu and Kashmir (disputed areas), Pakistan (west of the Karakoram Pass), and Afghanistan; and on the NW by the USSR. China's total boundary length is 36,643.6 km (22,769 mi). China's capital city, Beijing, is located in the northeastern part of the country.

²TOPOGRAPHY

China may be divided roughly into a lowland portion in the east, constituting about 20% of the total territory, and a larger section consisting of mountains and plateaus in the west. The principal lowlands are the Manchurian (Dongbei) Plain, drained by the Songhua (Sungari) River, a tributary of the Amur (Heilongjiang), and by the Liao River, which flows to the Yellow Sea; the North China Plain, traversed by the lower course of the Yellow (Huang he) River; the valley and delta of the Yangtze (Chang jiang) River; and the delta of the Pearl (Zhu) River surrounding Guangzhou (Canton). West of these lowlands, the country's topography rises to plateaus of 1,200–1,500 m (about 4,000–5,000 ft): the Shanxi and Shaanxi loess plateaus, in central China, and the Mongolian Plateau, in the north.

Beyond lie the high plateaus of Tibet, with an average elevation of 4,600 m (15,000 ft), and the great mountain ranges. The highest mountains are the Kunluns and the Himalayas. North of Tibet are two plateau basins of Central Asia, the Tarim and the Junggar, which are separated from each other by the Tian Mountains. The Chinese portion of the Tian range, which also extends into the former USSR, rises above 7,000 m (23,000 ft).

The great rivers of China flow eastward toward the Pacific. In the northeast, the Amur drains a great part of the Manchurian Basin as it winds along its 4,000-km (2,500-mi) course. Other northeastern rivers include the Liao, the Tumen, and the Yalu, the last two both rising in Mt. Paaktu, flowing respectively northeast and southwest, and forming the boundary between China and the DPRK. The main river of north China, and the second largest in the country, is the Yellow River. From Gansu it winds about 4,800 km (3,000 mi) eastward to Shandong Province, where it empties into Bo Hai (Gulf of Zhili, or Chihli). The valley of the Yellow River covers an area of 1,554,000 sq km (600,000 mi).

Central China is drained mainly by the Yangtze and its tributaries. The largest river in China, the Yangtze travels 6,300 km (3,915 mi) and drains 1,808,500 sq km (698,300 sq mi) of land. As China's only long river with no natural outlet, the Huai River, flowing between the Yangtze and the Yellow and roughly parallel to them, is subject to frequent flooding. To the southwest are the upper courses of the Mekong (Lancang) and Brahmaputra (Yarlung Zangbo) rivers.

Northern China is in a major earthquake zone; on 28 July 1976, a tremor measuring 8.2 on the Richter scale struck the city of Tangshan (145 km/90 mi east of Beijing), causing widespread devastation and the deaths of over 650,000 people.

³CLIMATE

Although most of China lies within the temperate zone, climate varies greatly with topography. Minimum winter temperatures range from –27°c (–17°F) in northern Manchuria to –1°c (30°F) in the North China Plain and southern Manchuria, 4°c (39°F) along the middle and lower valleys of the Yangtze, and 16°c (61°F) farther south. Although summer temperatures are more nearly uniform in southern and central China, with a July mean of about 27°c (81°F), northern China has a shorter hot period and the nights are much cooler.

Rain falls mostly in summer. Precipitation is heaviest in the south and southeast, with Guangzhou receiving more than 200 cm (80 in), and diminishes to about 60 cm (25 in) in north and northeast China, and to less than 10 cm (4 in) in the northwest. Approximately 31% of the total land area is classified as arid, 22% as semiarid, 15% as subhumid, and 32% as humid.

⁴FLORA AND FAUNA

Much of China's natural vegetation has been replaced or altered by thousands of years of human settlement, but isolated areas still support one of the world's richest and most varied collections of plants and animals. Nearly every major plant found in the tropical and temperate zones of the northern hemisphere can be found there. In all, more than 7,000 species of woody plants have been recorded, of which 2,800 are timber trees, and over 300 species of gymnosperms. The rare gingko tree, cathaya tree, and metasequoia, long extinct elsewhere, can still be found growing in China. Among flowering plants, 650 of the 800 known varieties of azalea occur in China, while 390 of the 450 known varieties of primrose and about 230 of the 400 known varieties of gentian are also found there. The tree peony, which originated in Shandong Province, appears in 400 varieties.

The richest and most extensive needle-leaf forests occur in the Greater Hinggan ling (Khingan) Mountains of the northeast, where stands of larch, Asian white birch, and Scotch pine flourish, and in the Lesser Hinggan ling (Khingan) Mountains, with stands of Korean pine and Dahurian larch. In the Sichuan (Szechuan) Basin, vegetation changes with altitude to embrace a variety of conifers at high levels, deciduous trees and cypresses at middle elevations, and bamboo in lower elevations. Farther south, in subtropical Fujian and Zhejiang provinces, broadleaf evergreen forests predominate. Forests give way to natural grasslands and scrub in drier western and northwestern areas, especially in the semiarid regions of Shanxi and Shaanxi, in the steppes of Inner Mongolia, and along the desert margins of the Tarim and Junggar basins.

China's most celebrated wild animal is the giant panda, a rare mammal now found in the wild only in remote areas of Sichuan, Gansu, and Shanxi provinces; as of 1994, just over 500 wild pandas were still in their natural state. Other fauna unique to China include the golden-haired monkey, found in remote parts of Shaanxi, Gansu, Sichuan, Guizhou, and Yunnan; the northeast China tiger, found in the Lesser Hinggan ling and Changbai mountains, along the Korean border; the Chinese river dolphin and Chinese alligator, both found along the middle and lower Yangtze River; the rare David's deer and the white-lipped deer, the latter found mainly in Qinghai Province and Tibet; a rare kind of white bear found in Hubei Province; and the lancelet, an ancient species of fish representing a transitional stage between invertebrate and vertebrate development, now found only in Fujian Province. In addition, more than 1,000 species of birds have been recorded. Among the rarer kinds are the mandarin duck, the white-crowned long-tailed pheasant, golden pheasant, Derby's parakeet, yellow-backed sunbird, red-billed leiothrix, and red-crowned crane.

⁵ENVIRONMENT

Since 1973, China has taken significant steps to rectify some of the environmental damage caused by rampant use of wood for fuel, uncontrolled industrial pollution, and extensive conversion of forests, pastures, and grasslands to grain production during the Cultural Revolution. In 1979, the Standing Committee of the Fifth National People's Congress adopted an Environmental Protection Law and a Forestry Law. In 1989, China began a nationwide program called the Great Green Wall of China which began to accelerate the rate of reforestation. In 1994, China had 490,000 square miles of forest land.

Subsequent legislation provided for the protection of aquatic resources, including water quality standards for farmland irrigation and fisheries. In 1994, the World Health Organization reported that Chinese cities pollute water supplies more than any other country in the world. One-third of China's population does not have a pure water supply. By 1989, 436 of 532 rivers were polluted. Water supplies are limited—per capita consumption in China's cities is about 34 gallons a day, less than half that in many developing countries—and conservation, reclamation, and redistribution of water constitute major national priorities. To alleviate water shortages in the heavily populated Beijing-Tranjin region, a massive water transfer project from the Yangtze River to the north by means of a dam, first proposed in the 1930s, was being seriously investigated in the late 1980s. The project has aroused considerable controversy because hundreds of thousands of people would be uprooted, prime farmland flooded, many archaeological treasures submerged, and the ecology of the river area damaged.

Investment in pollution-reducing technology is required of all industrial enterprises. Penalties are imposed for noncompliance, and incentives, in the form of tax reductions and higher allowable profits, are available for those enterprises that meet environmental standards. By the end of 1980, according to official statistics, 143 of 267 principal pollution sources had been controlled. Reforestation, including construction of shelter belts, was also under way in many rural areas, with special emphasis directed toward reforestation of the erosion-prone loesslands in the middle reaches of the Yellow River. Among urban areas, Beijing has, since the late 1970s, implemented programs for controlling discharges of effluents, smoke and soot emissions, and noise pollution.

Of special interest to the PRC government has been the use of new technologies to reduce industrial pollution and conserve natural resources. The use of coal as a main energy source causes air pollution and contributes to acid rain. China's carbon dioxide emissions amount to 8.4% of the total for all nations of the world. Special success has been claimed for the recovery of oil from effluents of the Daqing oil field in Heilongjiang, refineries, and other oil-processing establishments; utilization of flare gases and elimination of nitric acid emissions in chemical plants; use of electrostatic precipitators and bag collectors by the cement and building industries; recovery of caustic soda and waste pulp from effluents of the pulp and paper industries; introduction of nonpolluting processes into the tanning and depilating of hides; recovery of mirabilite and waste hydrochloric acid by synthetic fatty-acid and detergent industries; popularization of nonmercuric batteries; recovery of fine ash from coal-burning power plants for use in the manufacture of bricks, tiles, cement, and road-surfacing materials; and development of new methodologies for recycling coal wastes and marine oil discharges.

To protect the nation's botanical and zoological resources, a program was adopted in 1980 to establish 300 new reserves, with

LOCATION: (not including islands south of Hainan): 18°9' to 53°34'N; 78°38' to 135°5'E. **BOUNDARY LENGTHS:** Afghanistan, 76 km (47 mi); Bhutan 470 km (292 mi); Myanmar 2,185 km (1,358 mi); Hong Kong, 30 km (19 mi); India 3,380 km (2,100 mi); Kazakhstan 1,533 km (953 mi); North Korea 1,416 km (880 mi); Kyrgyzstan 858 km (533 mi); Laos, 423 km (263 mi); Macau, 0.34 km (0.21 mi); Mongolia 4,673 km (2,904 mi); Nepal, 1,236 km (768 mi); Pakistan, 523 km (325 mi); Russia (NE) 3,605 km (2,240 mi); Russia (NW) 40 km (25 mi); Tajikistan 414 km (257 mi); Viet Nam, 1,281 km (796 mi); **TERRITORIAL SEA LIMIT:** 12 mi.

a total area of 9.6 million hectares (23.7 million acres). That goal was achieved by the end of 1985, one year ahead of schedule. The largest reserve, covering 800,000 hectares (1,980,000 acres), is the Changbai Mountain Nature Reserve, in the northeast. Others include the Wolong reserve in Sichuan Province, covering 200,000 hectares (494,000 acres) and famous for its research on the giant panda; the Dinghu Mountain reserve in Guangdong Province, where a subtropical evergreen broadleaf monsoon forest that has remained virtually untouched for four centuries provides opportunities for ecological studies; and the Nangun River area in Yunnan Province, where the principal focus of protection is the tropical rain forest.

As of 1987, endangered species in China included Elliot's pheasant, Cabot's tragopan, yarkand deer, Shansi sika deer, South China sika, North China sika, and the Chinese alligator. Extinct species in 1991 included the Amur leopard, Javan rhinoceros, Thailand brow-antlered deer, the white-lipped deer, Bactrian camel, the giant panda, and the Siberian white crane.

In total, 30 species of mammals out of 394 were endangered along with 83 species of birds and 350 plant species as of 1994.

6POPULATION

The 1990 census of population, reported a population of 1,130,510,638, up 12.6% from 1,003,913,927 reported in the 1982 census. The population as of July 1994 was estimated at 1,206,304,256. Not only is China the most populous country in the world, accounting for 22% of the estimated world population, but it is also the only one to have attained the status of demographic billionaire. Government policy calls for an extensive family planning program to limit population growth to no more than 1.7 billion by the year 2000; UN estimates for that year predict a population of more than 1.3 billion.

The birthrate in 1992 was 18.2 per 1,000 population, up from 17.8 in 1985; the death rate was 6.64, up from 6.57 in 1985 but down from 28.2 in 1932 and 18 in 1950. The net natural increase in 1992 was 11.6 From the standpoint of China's population policy, this was higher than the rate required if the population goal of 1.27 billion in 2000 is to be realized. Life expectancy was estimated to be 70 years in 1991. Estimates of the age structure of the population vary widely; according to the UN, 27.3% of the population in 1990 was 14 years of age or younger, 67% was between the ages of 15 and 64, and 5.7% was at or above 65 years. China is one of the few countries of the world where men outnumber women; as of 1990, China had an estimated 106 males for every 100 females.

The overall population density in 1990 was 120 per sq km (310 per sq mi), but the distribution of the population throughout China is extremely uneven. In 1986, 94% of the population was crowded onto 36% of the land, in eastern and southeastern China, while the remaining 6% was thinly distributed throughout the west and north. In 1990 about 795 million Chinese lived in the 12 most densely populated provinces—Anhui, Guangdong, Guangxi, Hebei, Henan, Hubei, Hunan, Jiangsu, Liaoning, Shandong, Sichuan, and Zhejiang—and the three municipalities of Beijing, Shanghai, and Tianjin (Tientsin). Population densities in 1992 ranged in these regions up to 671 per sq km (1,738 per sq mi) in Jiangsu Province and 2,242 per sq km (5,807 per sq mi) in Shanghai. By contrast, in the sparsely settled northern and western border regions, densities ranged as low as 2 per sq km (5.2 per sq mi) in Tibet (Xizang).

Only 26.2% of the population was urban in 1990. Government policy has sought to limit the growth of the large eastern cities, especially Beijing, Shanghai, and Tianjin, and to promote the growth of smaller cities away from the coast. In addition, a rustication campaign during the Cultural Revolution sent large numbers of urban youth to work in rural communes. By 1986, however, many of these young people had returned to their home cities. In 1992, the largest urban centers were Shanghai, 13,450,000; Beijing, 11,020,000; and Tianjin, 9,200,000. Within city limits the populations were (in 1991) 7,830,000; 7,000,000; and 5,770,000, respectively. Other large cities, all over 2,000,000 in 1990, included Wuhan, Guangzhou, Shenyang, Harbin, Chengdu, Xi'an, Zibo, Chongqinq, Nanjing, Changchun, Dalian, Jinan, and Qingdao.

7MIGRATION

The overseas migration of millions of Chinese reached its peak in the 1920s, when thousands of farmers and fishermen from the southeastern coastal provinces settled in other countries of Southeast Asia. Chinese constitute a majority in Singapore and Hong Kong, are an important ethnic group in Malaysia, and make up a significant minority in the Americas. In 1949, after the Communist victory, some 2 million civilians and 700,000 military personnel were evacuated to Taiwan.

Since in many places abroad the Chinese population has been growing at a rate faster than that of the local non-Chinese population, most countries have been trying to curtail the entrance of new Chinese immigrants. Emigration from China under the PRC government was once limited to refugees who reached Hong Kong, but is now denied only to a few political dissidents, if the state is reimbursed for postsecondary education costs. Immigration is for the most part limited to the return of overseas Chinese. At the end of 1992, the UNHCR reported 285,500 Vietnamese refugees in China. These people are of Chinese ancestry.

During the Cultural Revolution of the 1960s and 1970s, more than 60 million students, officials, peasant migrants, and unemployed were sent "down to the countryside" in a gigantic rustication movement. The goals of this program were to relocate industries and population away from vulnerable coastal areas, to provide human resources for agricultural production, to reclaim land in remote areas, to settle borderlands for economic and defense reasons, and, as has been the policy since the 1940s, to increase the proportion of Han Chinese in ethnic minority areas. Another purpose of this migration policy was to relieve urban shortages of food, housing, and services, and to reduce future urban population growth by removing large numbers of those between 16 and 30 years of age. Most relocated youths eventually returned to the cities, however.

Efforts to stimulate "decentralized urbanization" have characterized government policy since the late 1970s. Decentralized urbanization and the related relocation of industries away from established centers has also been promoted as a way for China to absorb the increasing surplus labor of rural areas, predicted at 100 million by the year 2000. The nation's minister of agriculture estimated that 50 million peasants migrated to the cities in 1993 to seek work.

8ETHNIC GROUPS

In the 1990 census, the largest ethnic group, accounting for 91.9% of the total population, was the Han. The Han form a majority in most of the settled east and south but remain a minority, despite continuing immigration (or Sinicization) in the west.

The nation's 55 recognized ethnic minorities had a total population of 91.2 million in 1990; because of their predominance in strategically sensitive border areas, they hold a political and economic importance disproportionate to their numbers. The largest minority, with a population in 1990 of 15,555,820, was the Zhuang, a Buddhist people, related to the Thai, who are primarily concentrated in Guangxi, Yunnan, and Guangdong. Other large minorities in 1990 were the Manchu (9,846,776), concentrated in Heilongjiang, Jilin, and Liaoning; the Hui (8,612,001), a Chinese-speaking Muslim people concentrated in Ningxia, Gansu, Henan, and Hebei; the Uygur (7,207,024), a Muslim Turkic people of Xinjiang; the Yi (6,578,524), formerly called Lolo, a Buddhist people related to the Tibetans and concentrated in Yunnan, Sichuan, and Guizhou; the Miao (7,383,622), in Guizhou, Hunan, Yunnan, and Guangxi; and the Tibetans (4,593,072), concentrated in Xizang (Tibet), Qinghai, and Sichuan. Other minority nationalities, with estimated populations in 1990 of more than 1 million, included the Mongolians 4,802,407;Tujia, 5,725,049; Buyi, 2,548,294; Koreans, 1,923,861; Dong, 2,508,624; Yao, 2,137,033; Bai, 1,598,052; Hani, 1,254,800; and Li, 1,112,498. The Kazaks, concentrated in Xinjiang, Gansu, and Qinghai, numbered 1,110,758.

The ethnic minorities have been exempt from nationally imposed birth limits; the 1990 census recorded an increase in the minority population of 24.7 million, or 37.1%, since 1982, compared with an increase of 10.9% among the majority Han during the same period. Two or more children per minority couple are generally allowed instead of the one-child norm promoted among the Han.

9LANGUAGES

Chinese, a branch of the Sino-Tibetan linguistic family, is a monosyllabic tone language written by means of characters representing complete words. The Chinese script is nonphonetic and remains constant throughout China, but the spoken language has regional phonetic differences. Spoken Chinese falls into two major groups, separated roughly by a northeast-southwest line running from the mouth of the Yangtze River to the border of Viet-Nam. North and west of this line are the so-called Mandarin dialects known as putonghua ("common language"). The most important dialect south of the linguistic divide is that of Shanghai, spoken in the Yangtze River Delta. Hakka and Hokkien are dialects of the southeastern coastal province. Cantonese, spoken in southern China, is the language of the majority of Chinese emigrants. Mandarin Chinese based on the Beijing dialect was adopted as the official language of China in 1955.

To communicate in written Chinese, thousands of Chinese characters must be memorized. Since the establishment of the PRC in 1949, reform of the written language has been a major priority. A simplified system of writing, reducing the number of strokes per character, has been adopted, and the language restructured so that anyone familiar with the basic 2,000–3,000 characters is functionally literate (defined as being able to read a newspaper).

A number of systems have been developed to transcribe Chinese characters into the Latin alphabet. The principal romanization scheme was the Wade-Giles system until 1979, when the PRC government adopted Pinyin, a system under development in China since the mid-1950s. Inside China, Pinyin is used in the schools to facilitate the learning of Chinese characters, in minority areas where other languages are spoken, and on commercial and street signs. Pinyin has replaced the Wade-Giles system in all of China's English-language publications and for the spelling of place names. In general, pronunciation of Pinyin follows standard American English, except that among initial sounds, the sound of *q* is like the sound of *ch* as in *chart*, the sound of *x* like the sound of *sh* as in *ship*, and the sound of *zh* like the sound of *j* as in *judge*, and among final sounds, the sound of *e* is like the sound of *oo* as in *look*, the sound of *eng* like the sound of *ung* as in *lung*, the sound of *ui* like the sound of *ay* as in *way*, and the sound of *uai* like the sound of *wi* as in *wide*.

Of the 55 recognized minority peoples in China, only Hui and Manchus use Chinese as an everyday language. More then 20 minority nationalities have their own forms of writing for their own languages. Minority languages are used in all state institutions in minority areas and in all newspapers and books published there.

10 RELIGIONS

Three faiths—Confucianism, Buddhism, and Taoism—have long been established in China. The religious practice of the average Chinese traditionally has been an eclectic mixture of all three. Confucianism has no religious organization but consists of a code of ethics and philosophy; filial piety, benevolence, fidelity, and justice are among its principal virtues. Taoism, a native Chinese religion that evolved from a philosophy probably founded in the 6th century BC by Lao-tzu (Laozi), and Buddhism, imported from India during the Han dynasty, both have elaborate rituals. Tradition-minded Chinese base their philosophy of life on Confucianism, but such old habits of thought came under strong attack during the Cultural Revolution.

Suppression of religion and the introduction of programs of antireligious indoctrination began in 1949 and intensified, with the closure of temples, shrines, mosques, and churches, from the mid-1960s through the mid-1970s. Overt antireligious activity eased in 1976, and the government reactivated its Bureau of Religious Affairs. The Constitution of 1982 provides for freedom of belief and worship. By 1980, by estimates still the only ones available, approximately 60% of the population was estimated to be nonreligious, although traditional Taoist practices and folk beliefs with religious origins were widely evident in such celebrations as weddings, births, the arrival of the Chinese New Year, and the tending of ancestors' graves. An estimated 6% of all Chinese were practicing Buddhists, mostly of the Mahayana type; in Tibet, Lamaism (a form of Mahayana Buddhism), whose institutions were decimated by Chinese armies in the 1950s, has been restored to much of its former importance. Many of its temples, however,

were destroyed by Red Guards during the Cultural Revolution, and ongoing tensions erupted anew in demonstrations and violence in late 1987. Islam claims an estimated 3–6% of the population, nearly all members of the ethnic minority nationalities; most belong to the Sunni branch, but the Tajiks are Shi'is. It is estimated that when the PRC was founded in 1949 there were up to 3 million Roman Catholics and 700,000 Protestants in China. As late as 1981, only small numbers of Christians were attending the approximately 80 Protestant and 40 Roman Catholic churches open in urban areas; by late 1983, however, when the Archbishop of Canterbury, Robert Runcie, visited China, the number of Protestants was put at 3 million and the number of churches at 1,600. These numbers were increasing rapidly by the mid-1980s. The tiny Jewish minority has virtually disappeared through emigration and assimilation.

11 TRANSPORTATION

Railways, roads, and inland waterways all play an important role in China's transportation system, which has undergone major growth since the 1940s. China's rail network forms the backbone of the transportation system. Chinese railways increased in length from 21,989 km (13,663 mi) in 1949 to 54,000 km (33,500 mi) in 1991, of which about 6,900 km (4,300 mi) were electrified. In the rush to expand rail facilities during the "Great Leap Forward," rails laid in 1958 totaled 3,500 km (2,175 mi); some 4,600 km (2,900 mi) were added in 1959. The construction pace slowed somewhat in the 1960s, but many major projects were completed in the 1970s, including double-tracking of major lines in the east; the electrification of lines in the west, including the 671-km (417-mi) Baoji-Chengdu link; and the addition of several new trunklines and spurs, many providing service to the country's more remote areas. While the total rail network is more than twice what it was in 1949, the movement of freight is more than 25 times that of 1949. Increased freight volumes have been achieved by loading freight cars up to 20% over their rated capacity and by containerization. Shortages of freight and tank cars continue to delay deliveries of coal and other industrial raw materials to their destinations. In 1991, China invested $8 billion for infrastructural improvements, including the building and/or upgrade of 309 km (192 mi) of double-track railway and the electrification of 849 km (528 mi) of track.

Road transportation has become increasingly important. Motor roads grew from about 400,000 km (249,000 mi) in 1958 to 550,000 km (342,000 mi) in 1964 and to 1,029,000 km (639,000 mi) by 1991. Major roads completed in the 1970s included the 2,413-km (1,499-mi) Sichuan-Tibet Highway, the 2,100-km (1,305-mi) Qinghai-Tibet Highway, and the 1,455-km (904-mi) Xinjiang-Tibet Highway. Between 1981 and 1985, 50,000 km (31,000 mi) of highways and more than 15,000 bridges were built. Public buses reached more than 90% of all communes in 1985. By 1992, an estimated 1,900,000 passenger automobiles used the highway system, up from 50,000 in 1949. In addition, there were some 4,500,000 commercial vehicles operating in 1992.

Navigable inland waterways reached a peak of 161,900 km (100,600 mi) in 1962 and decreased to 109,800 km (68,200 mi) in 1991. About 25% of the waterways are navigable by modern vessels; wooden junks are used on the remainder. The principal inland waterway is the Yangtze River; much work was done in the early 1980s to dredge and deepen the river, to improve navigational markers and channels, and to eliminate the treacherous rapids of the Three Gorges section east of Yibin. Steamboats can now travel inland throughout the year from Shanghai, at the river's mouth, upstream as far as Yibin; 10,000-ton oceangoing vessels can travel inland as far as Wuhan in the high-water season and Nanjing in the low-water season. Major ports on the river include Chongqing, the principal transportation hub for the southwest; Wuhan, its freight dominated by shipments of coal, iron, and steel; Wuhu, a rice-exporting center; Yuxikou, across the river from Wuhu and the chief outlet for the region's coal fields; Nanjing; and Shanghai. The Pearl River is navigable via a tributary as far as Nanning. The ancient Grand Canal, rendered impassable by deposits of silt for more than 100 years, has been dredged and rebuilt; it is navigable for about 1,100 km (680 mi) in season and 400 km (250 mi) year-round.

China's merchant fleet expanded from 402,000 GRT in 1960 to over 10,278,000 GRT in 1986, and to 13,407,000 GRT in 1991. China's 1,359 merchant ships can accommodate most of the country's foreign trade; the balance is divided among ships leased from Hong Kong owners and from other foreign sources. The principal ports are Tianjin, the port for Beijing, which consists of the three harbors of Neigang, Tanggu, and Xingang; Shanghai, with docks along the Huangpu River channel; Lüda, the chief outlet for the northeast and the Daqing oil field; and Huangpu, the port for Guangzhou, on the right bank of the Pearl River. Other important ports include Qinhuangdao; Qingdao; Ningbo, the port for Hangzhou; Fuzhou; Xiamen; and Zhanjiang.

The Civil Aviation Administration of China (CAAC) operates all domestic and international air services. Operations have grown significantly with the purchase, since the 1970s, of jet aircraft from the US, UK, and other Western sources. From Beijing there are scheduled daily flights to Shanghai, Guangzhou, Kunming, Chengdu, Shenyang, Changchun, Changsha, Wuhan, Zengzhou, and Harbin. The international airports at Beijing, Shanghai, Guangzhou, Tianjin, Ürümqi, Nanning, Kunming, and Hangzhou are equipped to handle large passenger jets. The total scheduled international and domestic service performed in 1992 included 40,605 million passenger-kilometers (25,232 million passenger-miles) and 1,319 million freight ton-kilometers (820 million freight ton-miles).

12 HISTORY

Fossils attest to hominid habitation in China more than 500,000 years ago, and Paleolithic cultures appeared in the southwest by 30,000 BC. Neolithic peoples appeared before 7000 BC; by 3000 BC there were millet-growing settlements along the Yellow River. The original home of the Chinese (Han) people is probably the area of the Wei, Luo (Lo), and middle Yellow rivers. According to tradition, the Xia (Hsia) dynasty (c.2200–c.1766 BC) constituted the first Chinese state. Its successor, the Shang, or Yin, dynasty (c.1766–c.1122 BC), which ruled over the valley of the Yellow River, left written records cast in bronze or inscribed on tortoiseshell and bone. The Shang was probably conquered by the Western Zhou (Chou) dynasty (c.1122–771 BC), which ruled a prosperous feudal agricultural society. Fleeing foreign attack in 771 BC, the Western Zhou abandoned its capital near the site of Xi'an and established a new capital farther east at Luoyang (Loyang). The new state, known as the Eastern Zhou dynasty (771–256 BC), produced the great Chinese philosophers including Confucius (K'ung Fu-tzu or Kong Fuzi) and the semi-historical figure, Lao Tzu (Lao Zi). Between 475 and 221 BC, the Qin (Ch'in) dynasty (221–207 BC) gradually emerged from among warring, regional states to unify China. Shi Huangdi (Shih Huang Ti, r.221–210 BC), the first Qin emperor (the outer edges of whose tomb, opened in the 1970s, were discovered to contain stunningly lifelike terra-cotta armies), ended the feudal states and organized China into a system of prefectures and counties under central control. For defense against nomadic proto-Mongolian tribes, Shi Huangdi connected walls of the feudal states to form what was later to become known as the Great Wall. By this time, the Yellow River had an irrigation system, and cultivation had begun in the

Yangtze Valley; at the end of Shi Huangdi's reign, China probably had close to 40 million people. During the period of the Han dynasties (206 BC–AD 8, AD 25–220), China expanded westward, nomadic tribes from the Mongolian plateau were repelled, and contacts were made with Central Asia, the West, and even Rome. The Han saw the invention of paper. Under the later Han, Buddhism was introduced into China. After the Han period, the Three Kingdoms (Wei, Shu, and Wu) contended for power, and nomadic tribes from the north and west raided northern China. From the 4th century AD on, a series of northern dynasties was set up by the invaders, while several southern dynasties succeeded one another in the Yangtze Valley, with their capital at Nanjing (Nanking). Buddhism flourished during this period, and the arts and sciences were developed. The empire was reunited by the Sui (589–618) dynasty, which built the Grand Canal, linking the militarily strategic north with the economic wealth of the south and laying the basis for the Tang (T'ang, 618–907) dynasty.

Under the early Tang, especially under Emperor Taizong (T'aitsung, r.627–49), China became powerful. The bureaucratic system, begun by the Han, was further developed, including the regular use of an examination system to recruit officials on the basis of merit. Handicrafts and commerce flourished, a system of roads radiated from the capital (at the site of Xi'an), successful wars were fought in Central Asia, and China became the cultural and economic center of Asia. Poetry and painting flourished, particularly under Emperor Xuan-Zong (Hsüan-tsung, r.712–56). Civil wars and rebellion in the late Tang led to a period of partition under the Five Dynasties (r.907–60) which was followed by the Northern and Southern Song (Sung) dynasties (960–1127, 1127–1279), distinguished for literature, philosophy, the invention of movable type, the use of gunpowder in weapons, and the improvement of the magnetic compass. However, Mongol and Tatar tribes in the north forced the Song to abandon its capital at Kaifeng in 1126 and move it to Hangzhou (Hangchow). In 1279, Kublai Khan (r.1279–94) led the Mongols to bring all of China under their control and became the first ruler of the Mongols' Yuan dynasty (1279–1368). The Mongols encouraged commerce and increased the use of paper money. The Grand Canal was reconstructed, and a system of relay stations ensured safe travel. Many European missionaries and merchants, notably Marco Polo, came to the Mongol court.

After a long period of peasant rebellion, Mongol rule was succeeded by the native Chinese Ming dynasty (1368–1644). The famous Ming admiral, Zheng He (Cheng Ho, 1371–1433) led seven naval expeditions into the South China Sea and the Indian Ocean between 1405 and 1433, reaching as far as the east coast of Africa. The Portuguese reached China in 1516, the Spanish in 1557, the Dutch in 1606, and the English in 1637. The Ming dynasty was overthrown by the Manchus, invaders from the northeast, who established the last imperial dynasty, the Qing (Ch'ing or Manchu, 1644–1911). The first century and a half of Manchu rule was a period of stability and expansion of power, with outstanding reigns by Kang xi (K'ang-hsi, 1662–1722) and Qian long (Ch'ien-lung, 1736–96). Although the Manchus ruled as conquerors, they adopted indigenous Chinese culture, administrative machinery, and laws. Under Manchu rule, Chinese territories included Manchuria, Mongolia, Tibet, Taiwan, and the Central Asian regions of Turkestan. The population of over 300 million by 1750 grew to over 400 million a century later.

By the close of the 18th century, only one port, Guangzhou (Canton), was open to merchants from abroad, and trade was greatly restricted. Demands by the British for increased trade, coupled with Chinese prohibition of opium imports from British India, led to the Opium War (1839–42), which China lost. By the Treaty of Nanjing (1842), the ports of Guangzhou, Xiamen (Amoy), Fuzhou (Foochow), Ningbo, and Shanghai were opened, and Hong Kong Island was ceded to Britain. The Taiping Rebellion (1850–64), nearly overthrew the Manchus and cost 30 million lives. A second war (1856–60) with Britain, joined by France, resulted in the opening of Tianjin (Tientsin) to foreign trade. The West's interest then turned from trade to territory. Russia acquired its Far Eastern territories from China in 1860. China's defeat in the Sino-French War (1884–85), in which it came to the defense of its tributary, Vietnam, resulted in the establishment of French Indo-China. In the First Sino-Japanese War (1894–95), Japan obtained Taiwan, the opening of additional ports, and the independence of Korea (which Japan subsequently annexed in 1910). This was a major turning point and led to the "scramble for concessions". In 1898, Britain leased Weihai in Shandong and the New Territories (for 99 years) of Hong Kong, Germany leased part of Shandong, Russia leased Port Arthur at the tip of Liaedong Peninsula, and France leased land around Guangzhou Bay in the south. The Boxer Rebellion, an uprising in 1899–1901 by a secret society seeking to expel all foreigners and supported by the Manchu court, was crushed by the intervention of British, French, German, American, Russian, and Japanese troops.

A revolution that finally overthrew Manchu rule began in 1911 in the context of a protest against a government scheme that would have handed Chinese-owned railways to foreign interests. City after city repudiated the Manchus, and in February 1912, the dowager empress, Ci Xi (Tz'u Hsi), signed an abdication document for the infant emperor, Puyi (P'u-yi). The Chinese republic, ruled briefly by Sun Zhongshan (Sun Yat-sen), followed by Yuan Shikai (Yuän Shih-kai), entered upon a period of internal strife. Following Yuan's death in 1916, the Beijing regime passed into the hands of warlords. The Beijing regime joined World War I on the Allied side in 1917. In 1919, the Versailles Peace Conference gave Germany's possessions in Shandong to Japan, sparking the May Fourth Movement as student protests grew into nationwide demonstrations supported by merchants and workers. This marked a new politicization of many social groups, especially those intellectuals who had been emphasizing iconoclastic cultural change.

Meanwhile, civil war grew more intense. In the south, at Guangzhou, the Nationalists (Guomindang, Kuomintang) led by Sun Zhongshan in alliance with the Communists (whose party was founded in Shanghai in 1921) and supported by Russia, built a strong, disciplined party. After Sun Zhongshan's death in 1925, his successor, Chiang Kai-shek (Jiang Jieshi), unified the country under Nationalist rule in 1928 with the capital in Nanjing. In 1927, the Nationalists began a bloody purge of the Communists, who sought refuge in southern Jiangxi Province. Their ranks severely depleted by Nationalist attacks, the Communists embarked on their arduous and now historic Long March during 1934–35. The Communists eventually reached Shaanxi Province in northwestern China, where, under the leadership of Mao Zedong (Tse-tung), they set up headquarters at Yan'an (Yenan). Japan, taking advantage of Chinese dissension, occupied Manchuria (Dongbei) in 1931.

Increasing Japanese pressure against northern China led, in July 1937, to the Second Sino-Japanese war, which continued into World War II and saw Japanese forces occupy most of China's major economic areas. Nationalist China, established in the southwestern hinterland with its capital at Chongqing, resisted with US and UK aid, while the Communists fought the Japanese in the northwest. Japan evacuated China in 1945, and both Communist and Nationalist forces moved into liberated areas. The rift between the two factions erupted into civil war. Although supported by the US, whose mediation efforts had failed, the Nationalists steadily lost ground through 1948 and 1949, were expelled from the mainland by early 1950, and took refuge on Taiwan.

The People's Republic

The Communists, under the leadership of Mao, as chairman of the Chinese Communist Party (CCP), proclaimed the People's Republic of China (PRC) on 1 October 1949, with the capital at Beijing. A year later, China entered the Korean War (1950–53) on the side of the Democratic People's Republic of Korea (DPRK). In the fall of 1950, China entered Tibet, which had asserted its independence after the overthrow of the Manchu dynasty, despite formal claims to it by all subsequent Chinese governments. In 1959, the Dalai Lama fled to India during a Tibetan revolt against Chinese rule. Tibet became an autonomous region in 1965. The Nationalists held, in addition to Taiwan, islands in the Taiwan (Formosa) Strait: the Pescadores, Quemoy (near Xiamen), and the Matsu Islands (near Fuzhou).

In domestic affairs, a rapid program of industrialization and socialization up to 1957 was followed in 1958–59 by the Great Leap Forward, a crash program for drastic increases in output and the development of completely collectivized agricultural communes. The program ended in the "three bad years" of famine and economic crisis (1959–61), which produced 20 million deaths above the normal death rate, followed by a period of restoration and retrenchment in economics and politics. In the early 1960s, Chinese troops intermittently fought with Indian border patrols over conflicting territorial claims in Ladakh and the northeastern Indian state of Assam. Mediation attempts failed, but in 1963, the Chinese withdrew from the contested areas that they had occupied, and war prisoners were repatriated. Meanwhile, growing discord between China and the former Soviet Union had become more open, and in 1960, the USSR withdrew its scientific and technical advisers from China. Public polemics sharpened in intensity in the succeeding years, as the two powers competed for support in the world Communist movement.

After the Chinese economy had recovered in 1965, Mao again steered the country onto the revolutionary path, and gradually he built up momentum for the Great Proletarian Cultural Revolution, one of the most dramatic and convulsive periods in modern Chinese history. It continued until Mao's death in 1976, but the most tumultuous years were from 1966 to 1969, during which the cities witnessed a chaotic and violent pattern of factional fighting, accompanied by attacks on bureaucrats, intellectuals, scientists and technicians, and anyone known to have overseas connections.

Increasing confrontation between Mao and the party establishment, beginning in the fall of 1965, culminated in August 1966 with the CCP Central Committee's "16-Point Decision" endorsing Mao's Cultural Revolution policy of criticizing revisionism. In response to Mao's initiative, high levels of urban protest demonstrated widespread dissatisfaction with bureaucracies and privilege. In the latter half of 1966, the Red Guard movement of radical students attacked educational and state authorities and split into competing factions. Amid the rising conflict, the party institution collapsed in major cities. Liu Shaoqi, second to Mao in the political hierarchy and Chairperson of the People's Republic, was ousted from power as the chief target of the Cultural revolution. In 1968, Liu was formally dismissed from all positions and expelled from the party. He died at the end of 1969. From January 1967 through mid-1968, the discredited political establishment was replaced by Revolutionary Committees, comprised of the new radical organizations, the officials who remained in power, and representatives of the army. Finally, the army was told to restore order. In 1968 and 1969, students were sent out of the cities into the countryside. Colleges did not reopen until 1970. At the Ninth Party Congress in April 1969, the military's role was confirmed when Lin Biao, the Minister of Defense, was named Mao's successor.

Estimates place the number of dead as a direct result of the Cultural Revolution from 1966 to 1969 at 400,000. Much of the countryside, however, was unaffected and the economy, despite a setback in 1968, suffered little. The remaining years of the Cultural Revolution decade, up to 1976, were marked by a legacy of struggles over policies and over political succession to the aging Mao (83 at his death in 1976). In September 1971, Lin Biao died in a plane crash, allegedly while fleeing to the former USSR following an abortive coup. The decade from 1966 to 1976 left persistent factionalism in Chinese politics and a crisis of confidence, particularly among the young.

These years of domestic upheaval also brought profound changes in international alignments. In 1969, Chinese and Soviet forces clashed briefly along the Amur River frontier of eastern Heilongjiang Province. Throughout the late 1960s and early 1970s, China played a major role in supporting the Democratic Republic of Vietnam (North Vietnam) in the Vietnamese conflict. In November 1971, the PRC government replaced Taiwan's Nationalist government as China's representative at the UN and on the Security Council, following a General Assembly vote of 76–35, with 17 abstentions, on 25 October. Following two preliminary visits by US Secretary of State, Henry Kissinger, President Richard M. Nixon journeyed to China on 21 February 1972 for an unprecedented state visit, and the two countries took major steps toward normalization of relations as the two nations sought common ground in their mutual distrust of Soviet intentions. In the period following the Nixon visit, US-China trade accelerated, cultural exchanges were arranged. In May 1973, the two countries established liaison offices in each other's capital and full diplomatic relations were established by 1979.

In 1975 at the Fourth National People's Congress, Zhou Enlai (Chou En-lai) announced a reordering of economic and social priorities to achieve the Four Modernizations (of agriculture, industry, national defense, and science and technology). Factional strife reminiscent of the late 1960s emerged between radical party elements led by Mao's wife, Jiang Qing (Chiang Ch'ing), and three associates (later collectively dubbed the Gang of Four), who opposed the modernization plans, and veteran party officials, such as Deng Xiaoping (previously associated with Liu Shaoqi and restored to power in 1973), who favored them. When Zhou died on 8 January 1976, the radicals moved to block the appointment of Deng (Zhou's heir apparent) as premier, with Mao resolving the impasse by appointing Hua Guofeng, a veteran party official and government administrator, as acting premier. Attacks on Deng continued until he was blamed for spontaneous disorders at a Beijing demonstration honoring Zhou on the Festival of the Dead, April 5, 1976 and, for the second time in his career, Deng was removed from all official positions.

After Mao

When Mao Zedong died on 9 September 1976, Hua Guofeng was quickly confirmed as party chairman and premier. A month later, the Gang of Four was arrested, and in early 1977, the banished Deng Xiaoping was again "reinstated." By 1978, Deng Xiaoping had consolidated his political dominance, and a new era of economic reforms began. The Third Party Plenum and the Fifth National People's Congress in 1978 adopted a new constitution and confirmed the goals of the Four Modernizations. Another new constitution in 1982 again confirmed policies of economic reform and emphasized legal procedure. The Cultural Revolution was officially condemned and Mao's historical role reevaluated. After a show trial from November 1980 to January 1981, the Gang of Four, together with Mao's former secretary and five others associated with Lin Biao, were convicted of crimes of the Cultural Revolution. Jiang Qing, whose death sentence was commuted to life imprisonment, committed suicide in 1991 after acquiring cancer.

In 1980, Zhao Ziyang, a protégé of Deng Xiaoping, replaced Hua Guofeng as Premier, and Hu Yaobang, another Deng pro-

tégé, became General Secretary of the CCP while Hua resigned as party Chairperson (a position which was abolished) in 1981. The 1980s saw a gradual process of economic reforms, beginning the countryside with the introduction of the household responsibility system in place of collective farming. As the rural standard of living rose, reforms of the more complex urban economy began in the mid-1980s in an attempt to use the economic levers of the market instead of a command system of central planning to guide the economy. These included, with varying degrees of success, reforms of the rationing and price system, wage reforms, devolution of controls of state enterprises, legalization of private enterprises, creation of a labor market and stock markets, the writing of a code of civil law, and banking and tax reforms. At the same time, the Chinese pursued a policy of opening toward the outside world, establishing Special Economic Zones, and encouraging joint ventures and foreign investment.

In the 1980s and 1990s, China attempted to settle its relations with neighboring states. After a border clash with Vietnam in 1979, there were agreements with Great Britain in 1984 for the return of Macao, a Portuguese colony since the 16th century, in 1999. In May 1989, Soviet President Mikhail Gorbachev visited Beijing in the first Sino-Soviet summit since 1959. Top Vietnamese leaders came to China in 1991, normalizing relations between the two countries after a gap of eleven years. In the early 1990s, China and South Korea established regular relations.

Until 1989, economic reforms were accompanied by relatively greater openness in intellectual spheres. A series of social and political movements spanning the decade from 1979 to 1989 were critical of the reforms and reacted to their effects. In the Democracy Wall movement in Beijing in the winter of 1978–79, figures like Wei Jingsheng (imprisoned from 1979 to 1994 and subsequently reimprisoned) called for democracy as a necessary "fifth modernization". A student demonstration in Beijing in the fall of 1985 was followed in the winter of 1986–87 be a larger student movement with demonstrations of up to 50,000 in Shanghai, Beijing, and Nanjing, in support of greater democracy and freedom. In June 1987, blamed for allowing the demonstrations, Hu Yaobang was dismissed as party General Secretary, and several important intellectuals, including the astrophysicist Fang Lizhi and the journalist Liu Binyan, were expelled from the party. At the 15th Party congress of November 1987, many hard-line radicals failed to retain their positions, but Zhao Ziyang, who was confirmed as General Secretary to replace Hu, had to give up his position as Premier to Li Peng. By the end of 1988, economic problems, including inflation of up to 35% in major cities. led to major disagreements within the government, resulting in a slowdown of reforms. In December 1988, student disaffection and nationalism were expressed in a demonstration against African students in Nanjing.

On 15 April, 1989, Hu Yaobang died of a heart attack. Students in Beijing, who had been planning to commemorate the 70th anniversary of the May Fourth Movement, responded with a demonstration, ostensibly in mourning for Hu, demanding a more democratic government and a freer press. Student marches continued and spread to other major cities. The urban population, unhappy with high inflation and the extent of corruption, largely supported the students and, by May 17th, Beijing demonstrations reached the size of one million people, including journalists, other salaried workers, private entrepreneurs and a tiny independent workers' organization, as well as students. On May 19th, martial law was imposed to no effect, and the government attempted to send troops to clear Beijing's Tiananmen Square, where demonstrators were camped, on May 19th and 20th, and June 3rd. Finally, in the early hours of June 4th, armed troops, armored personnel carriers, and tanks, firing on demonstrators and bystanders, managed to reach the Square. Firing continued in the city for several days, and estimates of the total number killed range from 200 to 3,000. The events of June Fourth sparked protests across the country, and thousands were arrested as the movement was suppressed. On June 24th, Zhao Ziyang was dismissed as General Secretary and Jiang Zemin, the mayor of Shanghai, was named in his place.

Parallel to, but separate from, the student movements were ongoing demonstrations by ethnic minorities. The most visible were those of the Tibetans, due to their international connections, but there have also been protests by other minorities, such as Muslims in Xinjiang province. Violent Tibetan demonstrations in the fall of 1987 and spring of 1988 were forcibly suppressed, and from March 1989 to April 1990, martial law was imposed in Lhasa, Tibet.

Following 4 June, 1989, economic reforms were curtailed and some private enterprises closed down. There was an anticorruption drive, ideological expression was greatly constricted, and higher education was more tightly controlled. The move toward a market-oriented economy began again, with increased speed, after Deng Xiaoping made a publicized visit in the spring of 1992 to the most developed areas in south China. China's economy became one of the most rapidly growing in the world but continued to be plagued by inflation and corruption. With a high rate of tax evasion, state revenues were shrinking and one-third went to subsidize state enterprises. Having been at the forefront of change in the early eighties, peasants in the early nineties were being left behind. In 1993 and 1994, there were peasant protests and riots over receiving IOUs for their produce and over local corruption. And there were workers' disputes and strikes (250,000 between 1988 and 1993) in response to low pay and poor working conditions.

13 GOVERNMENT

On 4 December 1982, China adopted its fourth constitution since 1949, succeeding those of 1954, 1975, and 1978. In theory, the highest organ of state power is the National People's Congress (NPC), in which legislative power is vested. The constitution stipulates, however, that the Congress is to function under the direction of the Chinese Communist Party. The NPC meets annually for about two weeks to review major new policy directions, to adopt new laws, and to approve the national budget submitted to it by the State Council. Each congress consists of more than 3,000 deputies elected indirectly for a term of five years. The NPC elects a Standing Committee as its permanent working organ between sessions. The State Council, the executive organ of the NPC, consists of a Premier (the head of government), 5 vice-premiers, ministers, and heads of other major government agencies. The State Council issues administrative regulations and both formulates and executes the economic plan and the state budget. The 1982 constitution restored the largely ceremonial post of State Chairman, or President, a position abolished by Mao Zedong in 1968. The Eighth National People's Congress, in March 1993, elected Jiang Zemin as President and reelected Li Peng, first elected in 1988, to a second five-year term as Premier. Since the 1980s, the NPC has slowly increased its function as a locus for discussion of issues instead of merely being a rubber stamp. The 1992 debate on the Yangtze River (Chang jiang) dam project is an example of this.

14 POLITICAL PARTIES

The Chinese Communist Party (CCP) has been the ruling political organization in China since 1949. Eight other minor parties have existed, since 1949, as members of a United Front, but their existence has been purely nominal. The party, with 50 million members (1990 estimate), plays a decisive role in formulating broad and detailed government policies and supervising their implementation at all levels of administration. Party supervision is maintained not only through placement of CCP members in key government posts, but also through specialized organs of the Central Committee of the CCP, which focus their attention on given subjects (e.g., propaganda or rural work). The CCP also forms branches within individual government units, as well as in factories, communes, schools, shops, neighborhoods, and military units.

Theoretically, the highest organ of party power is the National Party Congress, which usually meets once every five years. At each party congress a Central Committee is elected to oversee party affairs between sessions. The Central Committee (189 members elected in 1992) meets annually in plenary session to elect a Political Bureau, or Politburo (with 19 members as of 1992), and its Standing Committee, the party's most powerful organ (5 members in 1987). Directing day-to-day party affairs at the highest level is the Secretariat, headed by Jiang Zemin as General Secretary since June, 1989. In 1982, the post of party Chairman, formerly the most powerful in the nation, was abolished; the title had been held by Mao Zedong until his death in 1976, by Hua Guofeng from 1976 until his ouster in 1981, and by Hu Yaobang thereafter.

Deng Xiaoping, China's acknowledged political leader since 1977, retired from the Central Committee in 1987, retired as chairperson of the party's Central Military Commission in 1989, and retired as Chairperson of the state's Central Military Commission, his last formal position, in 1990. A new CCP charter, adopted at the 12th Communist Party Congress in September 1982, forbids "all forms of personality cult" and, in an implicit criticism of Mao, decrees that "no leaders are allowed to practice arbitrary individual rule or place themselves above the party organization." A major purge of party members in the early 1980s sought to exclude elements opposed to Deng's modernization policies. A reregistration program applicable to all party members, about half of whom were believed to have joined during the Cultural Revolution, was announced in 1983. The 13th Party Congress, convened in October 1987, affirmed Deng's reform policies and the drive for a younger leadership.

In the wake of the June Fourth massacre in 1989, Deng Xiaoping declared that Jiang Zemin, former mayor of Shanghai, should be the "core" of collective leadership after Deng's death. The Politburo announced prohibitions, largely ineffectual, against some forms of party privileges and nepotism, corruption which had sparked the 1989 protests. The 14th Party Congress, in October 1992, removed Yang Shangkun, State President (1988–1993), from the Politburo, weakening the power of his clique in the military. In 1993, the National People's Congress reelected Jiang Zemin, already party General Secretary, as Chairperson of the Central Military Commission and elected him as state President. This was the first time since the late 70s that top, formal positions in the party, government, and military were concentrated in one leader's hands.

15 LOCAL GOVERNMENT

The People's Republic of China (PRC) consists of 23 provinces (sheng) (the PRC claims Taiwan as its 23rd province), 5 autonomous regions (zizhiqu), and 3 centrally administered municipalities (zhixiashi). Provinces and autonomous regions, in turn, are divided into "special districts," counties (xian), and cities (shi) under provincial jurisdiction, as well as into autonomous minor regions (zhou) and autonomous counties (zizhixian), where non-Han Chinese minority groups reside. Counties, autonomous counties, and autonomous zhou are divided into townships (xiang), autonomous townships (for small minority groups), towns, and rural communes. From 1958 to 1982, local administrative authority formerly held by the xiang was transferred to the communes and their local people's councils. In 1988, Hainan Island, formerly part of Guangdong, was made China's newest province. The 1982 constitution returned local administrative control to the xiangs as the communes began to be disbanded. Local revolutionary committees, which replaced the local people's councils during the Cultural Revolution and under the 1975 constitution, were abolished in 1980. The 1980s brought an emphasis on placing younger and better educated officials in local party and government posts. In the 80s and 90s, there have been attempts to separate political and economic powers amid rising corruption.

16 JUDICIAL SYSTEM

China's legal system, instituted after the establishment of the PRC in 1949, is largely based on that of the former USSR. However, after 1957, Mao Zedong's government consistently circumvented the system in its campaign to purge the country of rightist elements and "counterrevolutionaries." The Ministry of Justice was closed down in 1959, not to reopen until 1979, and the excesses of the Cultural Revolution wrought havoc on legal institutions and procedures. Efforts to reestablish a credible legal system resumed in 1977 (when there were no lawyers in China), as party moderates came to power, and accelerated in the early 1980s, as China sought to provide the legal protection required by foreign investors.

The highest judicial organ is the Supreme People's Court, which, with the Supreme People's Procuratorates, supervises the administration of justice in the basic people's courts and people's tribunals (courts of first instance), intermediate people's courts, and higher people's courts. Defendants do not enjoy a presumption of innocence and, if convicted, may appeal their case to a higher level only once. The legal profession was still in an incipient stage of development in the mid-1980s. Over 25 law departments at universities and 4 special schools for training legal officials were in operation in 1987, when China had 26,000 lawyers. By 1993, there were 70,000 lawyers with plans to increase this number to 150,000.

A major anticrime campaign during the autumn of 1983 resulted in public executions at the rate of at least 200 a month; capital punishment may be meted out for more than two dozen offenses, including embezzlement and theft. Under the Chinese criminal codes, as revised in 1979, local committees may sentence "hoodlums" to terms in labor camps of up to four years, in proceedings that grant the suspect no apparent opportunity for defense or appeal. Government records for 1990 indicated that nearly 870,000 persons were assigned to such camps during the 1980s. Since 1990, sentences to labor camps may be judicially challenged under the Administrative Procedures Law. In practice the review of such a sentence is rarely sought.

Due process rights are afforded in the Constitution, but they have little practical import. Criminal defendants have no right to an attorney. The Criminal Procedural Law requires public trials, with an exception for cases involving state secrets, juveniles, or personal privacy. Cases are rapidly processed and conviction rates are about 99%. Appeal is possible but with little chance of success.

17 ARMED FORCES

Under the 1982 constitution, the military was removed from the command of the chairman of the CCP and placed under the supervision of a separate Central Military Commission, headed by Deng Xiaoping. Military service is voluntary. In a major reorganization in October 1985, the country was divided into 7 military regions, 28 military districts (based in the provinces), and 3 garrison commands. All armed forces and services, including naval and air units, are under the command of the People's Liberation Army (PLA). Army personnel in 1993 numbered 2.3 million (1 million conscripts). In addition, there are some 5 million men and women in the "basic militia" and up to 7 million in the "ordinary militia" who receive some training but are mostly

unarmed. Although most of the 100-plus division army is prepared for territorial defense, the PLA can display about twenty combined arms divisions beyoind its borders. Chinese ground combat weapons are locally produced from adaptations of Russian designs.

The Chinese navy in 1993 consisted of 260,000 personnel, including 6,000 marines, 25,000 naval air personnel, and 27,000 coastal defense forces, with 54 major combat ships, 44 attack submarines, and 1 nuclear-powered strategic missile submarine, armed with twelve missiles. The naval air force had 880 land-based combat aircraft, including 160 anti-ship bombers. The air force in 1993 was estimated to have 470,000 personnel, with about 5,000 combat aircraft, mostly jet fighters (4,000) but also including a bomber fleet of about 500. The conventional arms inventory is being modernized as part of a re-equipment program begun in 1978.

China has developed a sizable tactical nuclear capacity. China's first nuclear test occurred on 16 October 1964 and consisted of a 20-kiloton bomb exploded at the test site. A series of 25 tests followed, including a 3-megaton hydrogen bomb test in the atmosphere in October 1970. A multistage intercontinental ballistic missile with a range of 7,000 km was tested in 1976, and missiles with ranges of up to 15,000 km reached maturity in the 1980s. In 1993 the Strategic Rocket Forces (90,000 personnel) manned eight operational ICMBs (2 with 15,000 km range) with single 3–5 megaton warheads and 60 IRBMs of 2,700 km range with 2 megaton warheads.

Chinese defense spending for 1993 ranged between $12 and $20 billion, although the official budget is half this level. Arms exports in 1991 totaled $925 million, a decline from $1.9 billion in 1984, and arms imports $240 million. No Chinese forces are deployed in other countries except about 500 on UN and other peacekeeping teams.

18 INTERNATIONAL COOPERATION

China has held a seat in the UN since 24 October 1945. After the Communist victory in 1949, UN representation was exercised by the Republic of China (ROC) government on Taiwan until November 1971, when the PRC replaced the ROC in the world organization and its member agencies. As of January 1988, the PRC belonged to ESCAP and all the nonregional specialized agencies. The PRC displaced the ROC in the IBRD and IMF in 1980. China is a signatory to the Law of the Sea.

The US extended recognition to China on 15 December 1978 and resumed full diplomatic relations as of 1 January 1979. Continued US links with Taiwan in the 1980s, however, remained an irritant in US-PRC relations. The future of Hong Kong, for which part of the lease (the New Territories) expires in 1997, has dominated recent UK-Chinese discussions, and in 1986, an agreement to give Hong Kong back to China in 1997 was formally signed. Relations with the USSR, severed during the Sino-Soviet split in the 1960s, improved somewhat in the 1980s but remained strained over China's support of anti-Soviet forces in Kampuchea and Afghanistan. By the end of 1985, more than 130 nations had extended full diplomatic recognition to the PRC, with a parallel drop to about 10 in the number recognizing Taiwan's government. By the mid-1980s, the PRC had achieved normal relations with most of its Asian neighbors, including Japan, India, Pakistan, Malaysia, Thailand, and Singapore. Relations with Viet-Nam, Kampuchea, and Laos (all allies of the former USSR) were tense after the late 1970s, but among non-Communist nations, only the Republic of Korea (ROK) appeared firmly resistant to rapprochement.

19 ECONOMY

Traditional China was predominantly agricultural. Adhering to farming patterns developed over a score of centuries, China could sustain a harsh level of self-sufficiency, given surcease from natural calamities. For almost three decades prior to 1949, the incessant ravages of civil disorder, foreign (principally Japanese) invasion, and gross economic neglect virtually decimated China's frail abilities to sustain itself. The first task of the new PRC government thus was to restore the flow of natural resources to prewar levels. By the early 1950s, the government had succeeded in halting massive starvation. Almost all means of production and distribution were brought under state control, and vast parcels of land were redistributed to the peasantry. During 1953–57, China's first five-year plan stressed heavy industry. Economic development was aided by imports of machinery and other industrial equipment from the former USSR and East European countries. In return, China exported agricultural produce to them. A major geological prospecting drive resulted in the discovery of mineral deposits that provided a major thrust toward industrialization.

The Great Leap Forward of 1958–59 initially produced sharp gains in industry and agriculture, but the zeal for increased quotas quickly resulted in undue strain on resources and quality. The Great Leap was followed by "three bitter years" of economic crisis brought on by bad harvests and the economic dislocation of the previous period. By 1961, the GNP had fallen to an estimated $81 billion, roughly the level reached in 1955. By 1965, however, a readjustment of expectations, coupled with a careful program of industrial investment, helped the economy to recover. China's trade patterns, meanwhile, had shifted radically away from the USSR and toward Japan and Western Europe.

During the late 1960s, in the Cultural Revolution period, long-range central economic planning was abandoned in favor of policies promoting local self-reliance. Self-sufficiency in grain production was particularly stressed. The negative impact of this emphasis on agricultural development, together with the turmoil of the Cultural Revolution, resulted in a drop in industrial production of 10–20%, while agricultural output, aided by good weather, improved only marginally.

Centralized planning resumed in 1970 with Zhou Enlai's announcement of key goals for the fourth five-year plan (1971–75), including an increase in grain output. The fifth five-year plan (1976–80), disrupted during the political upheaval that followed the deaths of Mao and Zhou in 1976, was restructured in 1978 to embody the Four Modernizations, with the use of Western technology as necessary. At the same time, a 10-year plan (1975–85) calling for the traditional expansion of agriculture and heavy industry was revamped to emphasize the growth of light industries and the accelerated development of industrial raw materials. Trade with the US expanded after full diplomatic relations were restored in 1979, and four special economic zones were established as centers for foreign investment. The sixth five-year plan (1981–85), adopted in 1982, reflected this new pragmatic approach to economic development by emphasizing agriculture, light industry, energy, and improved transportation facilities. The seventh five-year plan (1986–90) made reform its paramount concern. Infrastructural development has been given special priority in the China's eighth plan covering 1991–1995. Long term targets for an annual GNP growth average of 7.2% through the year 2000 have recently been revised to 8–9%, while per capita GNP is expected to rise to $800 by the end of the century.

During the 1980s, the Chinese economy underwent a major restructuring under the leadership of Zhao Ziyang. Rural reforms launched in 1979, which linked remuneration to output and centered on household responsibility, had a profound and beneficial impact on the rural economy, and output and income rose to record levels for rural residents. The commune system was disbanded in 1983–84 and replaced by a system of townships, and the household or family became the main unit of rural production. In the wake of the success of these rural reforms, the CCP

Central Committee published "A Decision on the Reform of the Economic Structure" in October 1984, with the goal of totally overhauling the national economy and bringing urban industrial organization in line with rural practice. The main points of the decision were that all urban enterprises would be responsible for their own profits and losses, managers would have greater decision-making authority, and national and local governments would relinquish direct control over enterprises and assume a regulatory and supervisory position. Remuneration would be based on productivity, subsidies would be abolished, wages and prices would find their own level, and private and collective enterprises would be encouraged.

The reforms put forth in the 1984 decision and firmly anchored in the 1988 Enterprise Law proved remarkably successful, leading to much higher rates of industrial and general economic growth than previously expected. Real GNP grew by an average of 9.6% annually between 1979–1988, reaching 11% in 1988. By this time, however, indicators of a seriously overheated economy were also clearly emerging; inflation accelerated to 20.7% and shortages in raw material and energy supply as well as transportation capacity rapidly worsened. Austerity measures initiated by the government in late 1988 brought inflation to below 10% by the end of 1989, though at the cost of flagging economic expansion, as GNP growth declined to only 4% in 1989. A strong rebound was promoted by loosened credit controls in late 1990, bringing real GNP growth back up to 8% in 1991 and over 12% in 1992. Exports boomed as the country's trade balance totaled $41.3 billion in 1992. While China has thus emerged as the fastest growing economy in the world today, worrisome problems of rising inflation (accelerating from from 8.6% in 1992 to 14.5% in 1993) and infrastructural bottlenecks have re-surfaced, highlighting the need for further improvements in macroeconomic management. In 1992, the 14th National Party Congress provided important symbolic confirmation of the government's committment to transition from a fully centrally planned economy to a mixed or "socialist market" economy.

[20]INCOME

In 1992, China's GNP was $442,346 million at current prices, or $380 per capita. For the period 1985–92 the average inflation rate was 7.5%, resulting in a real growth rate in per capita GNP of 6.0%. In 1992 the GDP was $506,076 million in current US dollars.

[21]LABOR

In 1992, China's total civilian employment was estimated at 594,320,000. In 1990, the civilian labor force was 647,200,000, or twice as large as the populations of the US and Canada combined. About 43% of the labor force was female in 1992. About 59% of civilian employment was in agriculture, forestry, and fishing; 22% in industry; and 19% in services. Unemployment in urban areas for those age 16–25 was 2.3% in 1992.

China's labor policies have vacillated since 1949 between "to each according to his need," operative during the Great Leap Forward and the Cultural Revolution, and "to each according to his work." The first gave rise to job security—known as the "iron rice bowl" in China—but was generally associated with falling output. In 1978, a new economic formula, known as the "responsibility system," called for agricultural and industrial workers to sign a contract to produce a fixed amount of goods but provided for disposal on the free market for goods produced in excess of contractual levels.

On 27 December 1966, forces within the Cultural Revolution dissolved the All-China Federation of Trade Unions (ACFTU), previously the only nationwide labor organization. Some of its functions were then carried on by "revolutionary" organizations set up in factories, and by workers' congresses and trade unions organized on municipal and provincial levels. Strikes and lockouts became widespread during the Cultural Revolution. Other labor problems encountered during this period were "economism" among workers (i.e., emphasis on wages, bonuses, awards, and benefits, and appropriating factory funds and facilities under various pretexts); breakdowns in labor discipline (referred to as "anarchy"); disorders from fights between rival workers' factions (called "factionalism"); and slowness in developing sensitivity to nonmaterial incentives, as required by the prevailing ideology. Signs of labor unrest stemming from low wages and many of these same issues reemerged during 1974, bringing on notable disruptions among railway workers; in 1975, labor clashes in Hangzhou led to the calling in of the military. In October 1976, the ACFTU was restored to power. A new constitution of trade unions was adopted in 1978 and subsequently revised in 1982 to permit workers the right to strike when conditions are hazardous; strikes for purely economic advantages are forbidden, however.

Extreme reluctance on the part of the government to address any labor issues in 1989 and 1990 in the wake of Tiananmen gave way to caution in 1991. By 1992, the campaign to overcome policies of permanent employment guarantees, equal treatment of workers regardless of skill and performance, as well as barriers to prevent the demotion of cadres gained considerable momentum. Independent trade unions are illegal, although some allegedly exist in secrecy. In 1992, 92% of the state sector's labor was unionized. However, as the number of foreign-owned business ventures has increased, the union's ability to organize has diminished. In early 1993, Beijing enterprise unionization rates were at 40%, a drop of 20% since 1991.

22AGRICULTURE

With some 60% of the population engaged in farming, agriculture forms the foundation of China's economy. Limitations in topography, soil, and climate, however, have restricted cultivation to only about 10.3% of the total land area. Despite recent advances—record grain crops totaling an officially estimated 379 million tons were produced in 1985—the enormous pressures of feeding and clothing China's vast and growing population remain among the country's most compelling concerns. From 1980 to 1985, agricultural output grew at an average annual rate of 8.6%, far above the population growth rate and the first sustained expansion of agriculture since 1966; output increased at an average annual rate of 3.8% from 1985 to 1990, 2.4% in 1991, and 3.7% in 1992.

The PRC government expropriated large landholdings in a land reform carried out in 1951–52, redistributing the land among poor peasants. By the end of 1954, 11.5% of all peasant households had been collectivized; by 1955, 65%; and by 1965, 99%. The Chinese collective farms had virtually no mechanical equipment, but the peasants pooled their labor in various projects, such as water management, which were beyond the capacity of individual peasants. In 1958, the collective farms were merged into larger units as people's communes. The communes were concerned not only with agricultural output but also with subsidiary farm activities, such as light industry and handicrafts, usually produced for local consumption.

Far-reaching changes in the organization of communes took place during 1961–62. Formerly, the production brigade (the major division of a commune), of which there were about 719,438 in 1982, was regarded as the commune's "basic accounting unit." In 1962, however, the production team (the subdivision of a commune) became the commune's basic organizational element. The average production team consisted of 33 households and cultivated about 8 hectares (20 acres). Production teams functioned semiautonomously, making basic decisions on production and distribution of income, while the commune

mainly exercised the functions of a township government. Households, the final link in the system, were permitted the use of private plots, which made up about 5% of the arable land assigned to a team. In the early 1980s, these private holdings accounted for 19% of total agricultural output and the bulk of the country's production of vegetables, fruits, hogs, and poultry. Under the "responsibility system," which was introduced in 1978 and by 1983 was operating in 90% of rural China, all production in excess of assigned levels could be sold on the open market to yield a profit for individual production teams. In 1982, in addition to the rural communes, which provided most of China's agricultural output, there were 2,078 state farms working approximately 4.5% of all farmland. These farms, under the Ministry of State Farms and Reclamation, generally served as commodity production centers and as research units for the improvement of crop and livestock yields.

In 1983–84, a major reform of the agricultural system was launched. The 50,000 communes were disbanded and replaced by 92,000 townships, and the 6 million production brigades were broken up. Production decisions are now made by the household, which sets production targets in contracts with the government; households can sell their surpluses in the open market for cash. Crop diversification is encouraged. By the late 1980s, 60% of agricultural output was free of state controls, and most of China's peasants practiced the household responsibility system.

Grains are the chief crop, accounting for 70% of the total value of crop output and occupying 80% of all land under cultivation. While grain production surged from 305 million tons in 1978 to 407 million tons in 1984, the grain harvest stagnated in the 1985–87 period.

The main food crops are rice, wheat, and corn, followed by kaoliang (a type of sorghum), millet, potatoes, and soybeans. China is the world's leading producer of rice, with production increasing from 106.6 million tons in 1970 to 188 million tons (36% of the world's total) in 1992. Over 90% of all rice is produced in southern China, with two (and in the far south, three) crops being grown each year where irrigation facilities permit. The total wheat crop in 1992 (including Taiwan, which China considers a province) amounted to 101 million tons, more than double the 1970 output. Wheat is cultivated throughout the country, often as a dry-season crop in the rice-growing south, with specialized production centered in the Yangtze Valley and North China Plain. Output of other grains, including corn in the southwest and drought-tolerant millet and kaoliang in northern and northeastern China, exceeded 111 million tons in 1992. Production of roots and tubers, including sweet potatoes grown as a second crop in areas south of the Yellow River and white potatoes in cooler areas north of the Great Wall, totaled 147.8 million tons in 1992.

Industrial crops occupy only 8–9% of the cultivated areas. Among the most important are cotton (the chief raw material for the important textile industry), various oil-bearing crops, sugar, tobacco, silk, tea, and rubber. Cotton output totaled 4.5 million tons in 1992, up from 2 million tons in 1970, with production concentrated along the middle and lower reaches of the Yangtze River and on the plains of the Yellow and Huai rivers. Oilseed output in 1985 and was derived from a diverse assortment of widely grown industrial crops, including castor beans, 290,000 tons; sunflower seeds, 1,050,000 tons; rapeseed, 7,653,000 tons; sesame, 440,000 tons; and linseed, 520,000 tons. Sugar production reached 8.8 million tons in 1992, up from 1.8 million tons in 1974; an estimated 84% of all sugar is derived from sugarcane grown in the south, and the remaining 16% from sugar beets grown in the north and northeast. Production of tea, also an important traditional export, increased from 120,000 tons in 1956 to 580,000 tons in 1992 (23% of world production), with most of the tea grown in hilly regions of the south and southeast.

Most tobacco is produced as a sideline by commune householders working private plots; output rose to 3.1 million tons in 1992. Most natural rubber is produced on specialized state farms.

The irrigated area is estimated to have increased from about 15.3 million hectares (37.8 million acres) in 1950 to 47.9 million hectares (118 million acres) in 1992. The expansion of fertilizer production is viewed as a key to major growth in the agricultural sector. Toward this end, China during 1972–74 contracted for the purchase of 13 large urea plants from Japan, the US, and Western Europe. China's use of chemical fertilizers increased from only 300,000 tons in 1952 to 17,758,000 tons in 1985. In 1992, China imported $3.3 billion in fertilizers, and $320 million in pesticides.

23ANIMAL HUSBANDRY

Except in outlying areas, nearly all of China's arable land is devoted to crops. Most agricultural units, however, also support the raising of large quantities of hogs and poultry. Natural grasslands for the grazing of sheep and cattle occupy 3.53 million sq km (1.36 million sq mi), or 37% of China's total area; the four major pasture areas are Xinjiang, Gansu, Qinghai, and Inner Mongolia. In an effort to improve these pastures, 303 million hectares (749 million acres) were planted with improved forage seed strains from 1976 to 1980. Nonetheless, animal husbandry continues to be the weak link in the agricultural economy.

China leads the world in swine production, the total number of hogs reaching about 379 million in 1992, as compared with 89.8 million in 1952. Pig raising, often pursued as a private sideline by peasants, is the fastest-growing sector of the livestock industry, and hogs and pork products are becoming valuable export earners.

The number of sheep expanded from 36.9 million in 1952 to nearly 111 million in 1992. Most sheep are raised by pastoral herders, mostly the ethnic minorities, in the semiarid lands of Xinjiang, Inner Mongolia, Gansu, and Sichuan (Szechuan). Accelerated production of lambs and fine wool were government goals in the 1980s. Goats, also raised primarily in semiarid areas but increasingly promoted throughout China as a profitable household sideline for milk and dairy production, increased in number from 24.9 million in 1952 to 95 million in 1992. In that year there were also 82 million head of cattle and buffalo, up from 66.6 million in 1965; 10 million horses (792,000 in 1965); and 460,000 camels (448,000). Chickens and ducks are raised throughout China on private plots and constitute, together with fish and pork, China's chief sources of dietary protein. China produced nearly 192,000 tons of honey in 1992, more than any other nation. China also led the world in silk production in 1992, at some 64,000 tons.

24FISHING

With a coastline of some 6,500 km (4,000 mi) adjoining a broad continental shelf, China has excellent coastal fisheries. A vast number of inland lakes and ponds, covering a total area of about 300,000 sq km (116,000 sq mi), are also used for fish culture, and a 30-km (19-mi) section of the Yangtze below Gezhouba Dam at Yichang is a designated sturgeon preserve. The principal marine fisheries are located on the coast of southern and southeastern China, in the provinces of Guangdong, Fujian, and Zhejiang. China typically accounts for about 10% of the world's catch, but per capita Chinese consumption of fish amounts to only 9.3 kg (20.5 lb) per year (live weight equivalent), one of the lowest amounts in Asia.

Exports of fresh and frozen shellfish in 1990 accounted for 8% of the commodity's world exports, and were valued at over $831.6 million. Regulations for the protection of aquatic resources were enacted in 1979. In 1989 and 1990, production from fisheries grew by 7.2% and 10%, respectively.

25FORESTRY

China's forested area was estimated at 115 million hectares (284 million acres), or about 14% of the total territory. Most of the forests are in remote regions, however, and lack of transportation limits exploitation. Coniferous stands, which yield the most valuable commercial timber, are found mainly in the northeast and adjoining parts of Inner Mongolia. Deciduous trees are felled in Sichuan and Yunnan. While China is a major producer of softwood logs and lumber, virtually all of its production is domestically consumed. Paper production, which has benefited from the substitution of rice straw and other nonwood materials for wood pulp, nearly tripled from 1981 to 1991. Special forestry products originating in southwestern China include tung oil, cassia oil, and aniseed oil. Wood imports can vary widely from year to year. Production, consumption, import, and export amounts for 1991 (in 1,000 cu m) are shown in the following table:

	PRODUCTION	CONSUMPTION	IMPORTS	EXPORTS
Softwood logs	72,200	74,655	2,491	36
Softwood plywood	600	585	5	20
Temperate hardwood logs	40,000	39,955	30	75
Particle board	460	455	5	10
Woodchips*	790	620	0	170

*1,000 tons

Deforestation has been a persistent and serious problem in China, leading to massive erosion and desertification. The government has, from the start of its first five-year plan in 1953, given high priority to campaigns for afforestation. By 1980, 26 million hectares (64 million acres) of new forests had been planted, and during the 1980s, afforestation proceeded at the rate of 4.55 million hectares (11.24 million acres) per year. However, cutting of trees for fuel continued in rural areas, and many of the trees planted as part of afforestation efforts were lost because of neglect after planting. Production in the forestry sector expanded by 0.4% in 1989 and by 3.1% in 1990.

26MINING

Intensive geologic exploration has yielded greatly expanded mineral reserves. This increase in known subsurface resources is reflected in production rises for China's most important mineral products, including coal, petroleum, iron ore, copper, lead, zinc, tungsten, mercury, antimony, tin, and molybdenum.

Virtually all provinces contain coal deposits, and production rose from 66.5 million tons in 1952 to 1,090 million tons in 1991. The major coal-producing areas are Shanxi, Shandong, and Inner Mongolia. The top ten producing coal mines in China had proven reserves in 1990 of 12,996 million tons, and produced 167.3 million tons that eyar. China is the world's largest coal producer.

Iron ore reserves were estimated at 55 billion tons in 1991, with the largest resources in Liaoning, Hebei, and Sichuan. Iron ore production increased from 17.7 million tons in 1957 to 176 million tons in 1991. The metal content of the ore is relatively low (less than 35% on the average) and requires concentration; nevertheless, quantities have been sufficient to supply the country's sizable steel industry. Virtually all iron mining is presently carried out north of the Yangtze River. China is the world's largest producer of tin (43,000 tons estimated in 1991), mined chiefly in Yunnan, and a major producer of tungsten (25,000 tons), mainly from Jiangxi, and antimony (45,000 tons), from Hunan. Other important minerals, with their 1991 production, were bauxite, 2,600,000 tons; copper, 300,000; and lead, 380,000.

China is a world leader in the production of industrial minerals, metals, and fuels. It plans to increase the production of cement, copper, fertilizer, iron, lead, nickel, salt, soda ash, and zinc; but capital and technological constraints have caused the government to postpone plant construction and expansion. The interior was recently opened for foreign exploration, and China is expected to retain its dominance in the world market for antimony, barite, fluorespar, magnesite, rare earths, and tungsten.

27ENERGY AND POWER

China's petroleum resources are a key to its industrial development. Crude oil production increased from 102,000 barrels per day in 1960 to 2,850,000 per day in 1992, at which time China ranked as the world's fifth largest producer. In 1993, China had proven reserves of 24 billion barrels. The major producing centers are the Daqing field in Heilongjiang, which came into production in 1965 and had a capacity of 55 million tons in 1991; the Shengli field, developed in 1965 and located on the Bo Hai coast near the mouth of the Yellow River, with a 1991 capacity of 33.3 million tons; and the Liaohe field, located in Liaoning, with a 1991 capacity of 15 million tons. In addition to numerous other mainland finds, China has potential offshore reserves in the Bo Hai area and the South China Sea, especially in the vicinity of Hainan Island.

By the mid-1970s, China no longer had to rely on oil imports; petroleum exports had, in fact, emerged as a major source of foreign exchange earnings. More than 9,740 km (6,050 mi) of long-distance pipelines transport the oil from fields to refineries and other points of consumption and export.

After rising dramatically in the early 1980s, owing largely to the discovery and exploitation of vast deposits in Sichuan Province during the late 1950s and early 1960s, natural gas output has stagnated somewhat in the late 1980s, indicating only modest reserves. Proven reserves of natural gas in 1992 totaled 1.4 trillion cu m (49.4 trillion cu ft), or 1% of the world's total. By 1992, total national production had reached 15.3 billion cu m (540 billion cu ft). Some 10 billion cu m of gas production came from Sichuan, most of the remainder being oil-associated gas.

Although China's rivers provide a vast hydroelectric potential (an estimated 378 million kw), only a small part (9%) has been developed. According to the Ministry of Energy, 60 hydropower projects will be initiated between 1992 and 2000, with a total designed capacity of 70,000 Mw. As of 1991, 65 hydropower projects, with a total capacity of 16,000 Mw, were under construction. The main hydroelectric projects include Ertan in Sichuan Province, Yantan in Guangsxi Zhuang Autonomous Region, Manwan in Yunan Province, Geheyan in Hubei Province, Wuqiangxi in Hunan Province, Yamzho Yumco in Xizang Autonomous Region, and Lijia Xia in Qinghai Province. In April, 1992, the government approved the construction of the largest hydropower project in China—the Three Gorges Project on the middle reaches of the Chang Jiang. The Three Gorges Project has a designed capacity of 17,680 Mw and will require the relocation of millions of people just in Sichuan Province alone.

Traditionally, coal has been the major primary-energy source, with auxiliary biomass fuels provided by brushwood, rice husks, dung, and other noncommercial materials. China's recent emergence as a major oil producer is resulting in significant changes in primary-energy patterns, but severe power shortages limit further development of industry in the east and northeast, the situation being more critical for heavy than light manufacturing.

In 1991, China's net installed electrical generating capacity was 146 million kw, up from 115.5 million kw in 1988. The installed capacity of thermal power plants, fired by coal and oil, totaled 108 million kw in 1991, up from 82.7 million kw in 1988; the capacity of hydroelectric plants totaled 38 million kw in 1991 (32.7 million in 1988). Total output of electricity increased during the 1988–91 period from 545 billion to 677 billion kwh. In 1991, China imported less than 1% of its electrical consumption.

The abundance of coal continues to provide cheap thermal power for electric plants. Coal still dominates the energy sector, supplying 75% of China's energy needs. China was the world's largest coal producer in 1991, at 1,090 million tons. Coal comes from over two dozen sites in the north, northeast, and southwest; Shanxi Province is the leading producer. Known reserves as of 1991 were estimated at over 900 billion tons by Chinese authorities. As of 1992, China accounted for 11% of the world's proven reserves of coal. Large thermal power plants are situated in the northeast and along the east coast of China, where industry is concentrated, as well as in new inland industrial centers, such as Chongqing, Taiyuan, Xi'an, and Lanzhou.

The 288-Mw Qinshan nuclear power plant, near Shanghai, began trial operation on 18 December, 1991, initially running at 5% capacity during the first half of 1992. Nuclear generation is to play a secondary but important role, especially in areas that lack both hydropower potential and major coal resources.

China ranks as the world's third-largest producer and consumer of energy (after the US and the former Soviet Union), but utilization is estimated by the IMF to be five times more inefficient than that of the US and four times more wasteful than the world's average utilization.

28INDUSTRY

China has achieved a rapid increase in the gross value of industrial output (used before China switched to GNP accounting in 1986), which, according to official Chinese statistics, rose by 13.3% annually between 1950 and 1979. The greatest sustained surge in growth occurred during the first decade, with the rate averaging 22% annually during 1949–60. During 1961–74, the yearly growth rate fell to about 6%, partly as a result of the disruptions brought on by the collapse of the Great Leap Forward (which accompanied the withdrawal of Soviet technicians in mid-1960) and of work stoppages and transportation disruptions during the Cultural Revolution. Growth averaged 10% from 1970 to 1980 and 10.1% from 1979 to 1985. Major policy reforms of 1984 further accelerated the pace of industrial growth, which reached 20.8% by 1988. After a brief retrenchment period in 1989–90 as government policies prioritized inflation control over other concerns, expansion of the country's industrial sector resumed apace, exceeding 20% again by 1992.

While approximately 50% of total industrial output still derives from the state-owned factories, a notable feature of China's recent industrial history has been the dynamic growth of the collectively owned rural township and village enterprise as well as private and foreign joint-venture sectors. In 1991 output from collectives and privately owned operations expanded by 18% and 24%, respectively, as compared with only a 9% growth in output by state enterprises. Also apparent has been the spatial unevenness of recent industrial development, with growth concentrated mainly in Shanghai, the traditional hub of China's industrial activity, and, increasingly, a number of new economic centers along the southern coast. In 1992, the coastal provinces of Jiangsu, Guangdong, Shandong, Shanghai and Zhejiang provinces together accounted for close to 33% of the country's total industrial output and most of its merchandise exports. One key factor in this industrial geography has been the government's establishment of several Special Economic Zones in Guangdong, Fujian and Hainan provinces, and its designation of over 14 "open coastal cities" where foreign investment in export-oriented industries was actively encouraged during the 1980s.

Before the first five-year plan (1953–57), China had only one major steel center—Anshan, in the northeast—and several minor ones. All these produced 1.93 million tons of pig iron and 1.35 million tons of steel in 1952. By 1992, China was producing 80.9 million tons of steel 75.9 million tons of pig iron. Anshan continues to be the hub of the industry, but other huge steel complexes have been constructed at Baotou, Benxi (about 50 km/30 mi east of Anshan), Taiyuan, Wuhan, and Ma'anshan (near Nanjing).

China's cotton textile industry, the largest in the world, produced 5.0 million tons of yarn and 19.1 billion meters of cloth in 1992. In that year, 337.9 million m of woolen piece goods and 350,600 tons of knitting wool were also produced. Other products of the textile industry included 74,200 tons of silk, 617 million jute bags, and 1.9 million tons of synthetic fibers. Labor-intensive light industries in general have played a particularly prominent role in the recent industrial boom, presently accounting for 48.9% of total industrial output, as compared with 47.1% in 1985. In addition to garments and textiles, output from these industries in 1992 included 68.37 million electric fans (up from 31.75 million in 1985), 28.68 million television sets (up from 16.67 million in 1985), 5.26 million cameras (up from 1.79 million in 1985), 8.33 million sewing machines, 7.08 million household washing machines, 16.45 million radios, 32.32 million recorders, 19.82 million telephones, and 86.59 million watches. The electronics industry has also developed the capacity to produce high-speed computers, 600 types of semiconductors, and specialized electronic measuring instruments.

Since 1961, industry has been providing agriculture with farm machines, chemical fertilizers, insecticides, means of transportation, power, building materials, and other essential commodities. Handicraft cooperatives also have been busy making hand-operated or animal-drawn implements. In 1992, China produced an estimated 1.4 million 20+ horsepower tractors (up from 450,000 in 1985), 15,370 combines (up from 2,223 in 1985), and 555,100 motor thrashers. Chemical fertilizer production totaled 20.5 million tons nutrient equivalent, increasing from 13.2 million tons in 1985. Production of a variety of industrial goods has expanded, increasingly in order to supply the country's own expanding industrial base. Manufacture of power-generating equipment reached an equivalent of 12.97 million kw in 1992, up from 5.64 million in 1985. 4,047 large machine tools were produced in 1992, in addition to 1,266 high precision machine tools and 7,450 numerically controlled machine tools. In addition to fertilizers, the chemicals industry yielded calcium carbide, 2.42 million tons equivalent; ethylene, 2.00 million tons; and plastics, 3.31 million tons. Since 1963, great emphasis has been placed on the manufacture of transportation equipment, and China now produces varied lines of passenger cars, trucks, buses, and bicycles. In 1992, output included 1.07 million motor vehicles (more than double the 1985 figure), 40.8 million bicycles, 563 diesel and 200 electric locomotives, as well as 21,600 freight cars.

29 SCIENCE AND TECHNOLOGY

Modern China is the heir to a remarkably inventive civilization that pioneered in the development of the abacus (the first mechanical calculating device), paper (and paper money), printing by movable type, gunpowder, the magnetic compass, and the rocket. Contact with the West during the 19th century revealed how technologically backward China had become, and it is only in recent decades that the nation has begun to catch up.

China detonated its first fission device in 1964 and its first hydrogen bomb in 1967; the nation now possesses a variety of nuclear weapons mounted on missiles, bombers, submarines, and other delivery systems. Its first satellite was launched in 1970. By 1992, the PRC had launched an INTELSAT satellite on a Chinese launch vehicle. Other priorities have been the development of high-energy physics, laser research, powerful computer memory chips, color television broadcasting technology, and laser infrared devices, although the PRC still relies heavily on outside investment and technology transfer. Major advances have also been claimed in rice hybridization, insecticides, fertilizers, biogas digesters for rural electrification, and pollution control technology.

Two scientific exchange agreements between the US and China were signed in January 1984 during Premier Zhao Ziyang's visit to Washington, D.C. China has proposed to several Western nations that it provide long-term storage facilities in remote provinces for radioactive waste—a proposal that Western observers believed would provide China not only with hard currency but also with nuclear materials for possible reprocessing.

China's principal technological handicap is lack of skilled personnel. Currently, only 1% of the PRC's 127 million 22-year-olds receive a university degree. However, 37 percent of all Chinese degrees are in engineering, the highest ratio in Asia. Part of China's response to this shortage has been to send tens of thousands of students overseas for advanced study, especially in the US. By 1990, the number of trained scientists and technicians was 1.2 million. Scientific research is coordinated by the prestigious Chinese Academy of Sciences, the China Association for Science and Technology, institutes of higher learning, medical groups, and the military. International science and technology cooperation is also increasing. However, concerns over human rights issues has had the effect of cooling US-PRC science and technology exchanges.

30 DOMESTIC TRADE

Three types of retail trade outlets—the periodic market, the peddler, and the urban shop—constituted the basis of the traditional commercial structure. In the early 1950s, however, a number of state trading companies were established for dealing in commodities such as food grains, cotton, textiles, coal, building materials, metals, machinery, and medicines. These companies, under the control of the Ministry of Commerce, have established branch offices and retail stores throughout the country. In the 1960s, the establishment of state-owned department stores and cooperative retail outlets virtually replaced private trade. There was a resurgence of periodic open markets and private traders when domestic trading regulations were relaxed in 1978. By 1992 there were 79,188 fairs, or free markets, in China; only 18% of the retail work force worked in state shops (down from 63% in 1978). In addition, the government has progressively loosened or eliminated many of its former price controls; an estimated 90% of all retail sales are no longer controlled. Retail sales in 1992 exceeded ¥1,099 billion. Food accounted for 55% of retail sales, and clothing 16%.

The China Export Commodities Fair, usually held each spring and fall in Guangzhou, was for more than 20 years an important point of contact for Westerners doing business with China. Though still important as an initial introduction to the full range of China's potential suppliers, the decentralization of trading activities in recent years has greatly reduced the fair's role in mediating sustained contact between producers and buyers. As of 1993, local foreign trade commissions in various industrial centers of the country have taken on a much more active role in organizing many of the services associated with the commodities fair, while any domestic enterprise with foreign trading rights may now participate directly in all events related to trade promotion. Guangzhou still hosts two annual trade fairs, though on a reduced scale. In the major cities, Friendship Stores and other restaurants, hotels, service bureaux and taxis cater exclusively to foreign visitors; payment is made in foreign exchange certificates. By the mid-1980s, international credit cards could be used to obtain cash advances in selected outlets and for direct purchases in Friendship Stores.

31 FOREIGN TRADE

Though China has only recently become a major trading nation, its enormous trading potential is attracting great attention by both advanced and newly industrializing nations. Trade has performed important functions within the economy, providing needed capital goods and modern technology to abet development, as well as primary commodities (such as grains) to supplement local supply in slack years. Foreign trade is under the direction of a single Ministry of Foreign Economic Relations and Trade, created in 1982 through the merger of the former ministries of Foreign Trade and Foreign Economic Relations with the Export-Import and Foreign Investment commissions. A major albeit still incomplete trend since the early 1980s, however, has been the decentralization of trade management and greater reliance on currency devaluation (major devaluations were implemented in 1989 and 1991) and market incentives rather than direct export and import controls to promote desired trade patterns.

The total value of exports in 1992 was $85 billion, and that of imports $81 billion; this $4 billion surplus followed and almost $9 billion dollar surplus registered in 1990 and a $8 billion surplus in 1991—China's first positive trade balances since 1983. However, given burgeoning demand for industrial goods in the overheated economy of 1992, the newest indicators suggest that a large trade deficit (about $9 billion) re-occurred in 1993.

Prior to 1949, some three-fourths of China's exports were agricultural products. This proportion ebbed to a low of 13% during the agricultural crisis of 1961. Foodstuffs and other primary products including crude non-food raw materials, minerals and fuels averaged about 43–50% of exports through 1985, after which the proportion declined steadily to reach only 20% in 1992, as manufactured exports expanded rapidly. Textiles (excluding garments) accounted for 11% of all exports in 1992 and clothing for about 17.9% (up from 7.5% in 1985). However, China's efforts to emulate the success of Japan, Hong Kong, Taiwan, and the ROK in basing economic expansion on textile and clothing exports have encountered protectionist resistance from major potential markets in the US and EC. Food imports, which made up only about 2% of the import volume in the 1950s, averaged 20% of the total in 1973 and 1974 but, as total imports rose, fell to less than 4% by 1985 and remained at 3.9% in 1992. Annual grain imports (mainly wheat), which averaged 5–6 million tons during 1961–66, rose to 7.7 million tons in 1973 and over 11.7 million tons in 1992.

The principal exports in 1980, 1986 and 1992 (in millions of dollars) were estimated as follows:

EXPORTS	1980	1986	1992
Petroleum and petroleum products	4,280	3,683	4,692
Textiles	—	3,600	9,453
Food and live animals	2,985	4,448	8,354
Crude materials	1,711	2,908	3,144
Clothing	—	—	15,177
Chemicals	1,121	1,733	4,347
Machinery & transportation equipment	843	1,094	13,219
Other exports	7,179	13,476	26,612
TOTALS	18,119	30,942	84,998

The principal imports in 1980, 1986, and 1992 (in millions of dollars) were estimated as follows:

IMPORTS	1980	1986	1992
Machinery and transportation equipment	5,119	11,781	31,313
Light, textile & other manufactured goods	4,154	11,192	19,298
Chemicals	2,909	3,711	1,158
Crude materials	3,554	3,143	5,774
Food and live animals	2,927	1,625	3,146
Mineral fuels & lubricants	203	504	3,570
Other imports	1,151	10,296	16,351
TOTALS	20,017	42,252	80,610

The direction of China's trade has followed three major patterns since the 1930s. Prior to World War II, Japan, Hong Kong, the US, and the UK together made up about three-fourths of the total trade volume. With the founding of the PRC in 1949, trade shifted in favor of the former USSR and Eastern Europe. During 1952–55, more than 50% of China's trade was with the former USSR; during 1956–60, the proportion averaged about 40%. As Sino-Soviet relations deteriorated during the 1960s, trade exchanges steadily declined, reaching a bare 1% of China's total volume in 1970 (3.6% in 1986). By the early 1980s, most of China's leading trade partners were industrialized non-Communist countries, and China's trade pattern overall reflected a high degree of multilateralism. In recent years, as China has rapidly enlarged its role on the international market, the importance of Hong Kong as an entrepot and major source of foreign exchange has increased. In 1992, Hong Kong accounted for close to 35% of China's total trade (up from about 21% in 1986). Japan ranks as the second largest trading partner, importing oil and other raw material and claiming 15% of China's total trade. The most dramatic change in the mid-1980s was the emergence of the US as China's third largest trading partner, a rank it still maintains with 11% of total trade.

China's principal trade partners in 1992 (in millions of US dollars) were as follows:

	EXPORTS	IMPORTS	BALANCE
Hong Kong	37,512	20,538	16,974
Japan	11,699	13,681	–1,982
USA	8,594	8,900	–306
Taiwan	698	5,881	–5,183
FRG	2,448	4,023	–1,575
Russia	2,336	3,526	–1,190
Korea, Rep.	2,437	2,623	–186
Singapore	2,031	1,236	795
Other countries	17,243	20,202	–2,959
TOTAL	84,998	80,610	4,388

32 BALANCE OF PAYMENTS

Both foreign trade and international financing in China are state monopolies, with policies and transactions administered by the People's Bank of China (PBC). Among its various functions, the PBC sets exchange rates for foreign currencies. The PBC releases foreign exchange to the Bank of China, which plays a major payments role through its branches in Hong Kong, Singapore, and other overseas financial centers.

The government has, overall, maintained a record of financial stability, linked to a policy of stringent controls over its international transactions. Adhering generally to a principle of self-reliance, it has resorted to the use of commercial credit at certain junctures but until the 1970s avoided falling into long-term indebtedness as a means of financing major development goals. In the period 1958–60, the Great Leap Forward and the succeeding years of economic crisis caused a sharp deterioration in China's international payments position. In 1960, large negative clearing account balances with Communist countries (–$625 million) were $210 million more than the foreign exchange reserves of $415 million. By the end of 1964, however, the negative balance with Socialist nations had been reduced to $55 million, and China's net international financial resources stood at a surplus of $345 million, owing to monetary gold holdings of $215 million and foreign exchange balances from trade with non-Communist countries amounting to $185 million. By 1965, the Chinese had completely cleared their long-term debt to the former USSR, and by 1968, China had redeemed all national bonds and was free of all long-term external and internal debts.

Publication of official balance-of-payments statistics was discontinued during the Cultural Revolution and not resumed until September 1985. According to Western analyses, the period 1978–81 saw a continuing surplus in current accounts, as rising levels of imports were generally matched or exceeded by increases in exports over the same period. In addition, transfers of an estimated $1.1 billion in 1978 and $1 billion in 1980, derived from increased earnings in tourism, shipping, and remittances from Hong Kong and other sources, resulted in overall current accounts surpluses of $900 million and $1.2 billion in 1978 and 1980, respectively.

China's drive to industrialize under the Four Modernizations policy resulted in an unprecedented deficit on capital accounts of $1.1 billion in 1978. The subsequent unilateral decisions to cancel $2.6 billion in contracts with Japan (1979) and $2 billion with Japan and Western nations (1981) were interpreted by some observers as an indication of acute cash-flow problems and a reordering of investment priorities at the highest levels.

The trade account has also been helped by the slow but steady devaluation that has occurred since China went to a managed float exchange rate system in January 1991. Tourism receipts and visitor figures also have continued to grow, passing pre-Tiananmen levels. Foreign investment boomed in 1991, with a total of nearly $12 billion committed in new contracts, China's best year ever. Chine also maintains a comfortable reserve cushion which could provide an estimated nine months of import cover.

In 1992 merchandise exports totaled $69,568 million and imports $64,385 million. The merchandise trade balance was $5,183 million. The following table summarizes China's balance of payments for 1991 and 1992 (in millions of US dollars):

	1991	1992
CURRENT ACCOUNT		
Goods services and income	12,441	5,246
Unrequited transfers	831	1,155
TOTALS	13,272	6,401
CAPITAL ACCOUNT		
Direct investment	3,453	7,156
Portfolio investment	235	−57
Other long-term capital	3,982	−6,443
Other short-term capital	362	−906
Reserves	−14,537	2,060
TOTALS	−6,505	1,810
Errors and omissions	−6,767	−8,211
Total change in reserves	−14,557	—

33BANKING AND SECURITIES

Economic reforms under the Four Modernizations program adopted in 1978 have brought major changes in China's highly centralized and tightly controlled banking system. In 1982, the People's Bank of China (PBC) became the central bank and turned over its commercial operations to the new Industrial and Commercial Bank. Specialized agencies include the People's Construction Bank, the Agricultural Bank of China, the Bank of China, and the State General Administration of Exchange Control. The People's Construction Bank, reestablished in 1979 under the direction of the Ministry of Finance, makes payments for capital construction according to state plans and budgets. The Agricultural Bank of China, established on three separate occasions—1951, 1955, and 1965—and each time liquidated, was reestablished for a fourth time in 1979. Its main tasks are to finance agricultural expansion, grant rural loans, supervise agricultural credit cooperatives, and assist in the modernization of agriculture. By the end of 1992, the Agricultural Bank maintained 50,800 branches.

The Bank of China (BOC) handles foreign exchange and international settlements for the PBC. It has branches throughout China as well as in Singapore, Hong Kong, Paris, London, Luxembourg, New York, and Tokyo. The BOC is charged with financing China's foreign trade and also acquiring and channeling into appropriate areas the foreign capital needed for imports of industrial equipment and other items for modernization. In 1992, the BOC listed its total deposits at Y832,249 million, up from Y54.2 billion in 1979, and Y92.2 billion in 1981. A new investment bank, the China International Trust and Investment Corp. (CITIC), founded in 1979, has expanded dramatically and ended BOC's monopoly on dealing in foreign exchange. Another rival of BOC, the Shanghai Bank of Communications, was established in 1987 and had 44 branches by 1993.

Two foreign banks—the Standard Chartered Bank and the Hongkong and Shanghai Banking Corp.—maintain long-established offices in China. Over 90 foreign banks, representing Japan, the US, France, Italy, Pakistan, and the UK, received permission to establish offices in Beijing in the early 1980s. In 1985, for the first time, foreign banks were allowed to do business in the four special economic zones (established to attract foreign investment) in local as well as foreign currency. In 1987, stock exchanges opened in Shanghai and several other cities, and several stock and bond issues were floated domestically. Securities exchanges are controlled by the PBC, and trading in securities is very limited.

34INSURANCE

The People's Insurance Co. of China, formed in 1949 under the supervision of the PBC, is authorized to handle all kinds of insurance, including the insurance of China's foreign trade and foreign insurance operations in China. In 1993, it controlled 95% of China's insurance industry, with 4,200 branches and a workforce of 110,000. Two additional state enterprises, the China Insurance Co. and the Tai Ping Insurance Co., are in operation, and several foreign insurance companies have established representative offices in Beijing. Premiums totaled US$2.5 per capita in 1990, or 0.8% of the GDP.

35PUBLIC FINANCE

The annual state budget is prepared by the Ministry of Finance and approved by the National People's Congress. A major reform in public finance, introduced in 1980, was a new system of allocating revenues and expenditures between local and national levels of government. Previous revenue-sharing procedures allowed the central government to fix maximum spending levels for each province, autonomous region, and centrally administered municipality. The new system fixed for a five-year period the proportion of local income to be paid to the central government and (except for emergency appropriations for floods and other such disasters) the level of subsidies to be provided by the central government, as well as the proportion of local income to be retained by local governments. Autonomous regions receive proportionately greater state subsidies than the provinces and centrally administered municipalities, and they are entitled to keep all revenues from local industrial and commercial taxes.

During the early 1990s, the Chinese consolidated budget deficit was growing at a rapidly increasing rate. According to the IMF, the 1991 budget deficit amounted to Y66.6 billion, or 3.4% of GNP, due to rising expenditures and tax evasion. Deficits are largely financed by domestic debt issuance rather than by money creation.

36TAXATION

An overhaul of China's tax system began in 1979 as part of the Four Modernizations program. The principal domestic levies, as in the past, were commercial and industrial taxes imposed on all enterprises, but, after 1979, taxes were due only on assigned production quotas. In 1993, the Consolidated Industrial and Commercial Tax was levied (usually at 5–10%) on agricultural and industrial production, commercial retailing, and service, transportation, and communication earnings.

Under a tax law that took effect on 1 July, 1991, joint and foreign owned ventures pay a combined national and provincial tax levied at 33% of pre-tax income. A foreign-owned enterprise with income from sources in China but not established there pays a 20% withholding income tax, and royalties for certain types of technical knowledge are taxed at 10% of the revenue amount. Individuals are required to submit individual income tax returns to the Tax Bureau on a monthly basis.

37 CUSTOMS AND DUTIES

From 1960 to 1980, the General Customs Administration was under the control of the Ministry of Finance, but all customs work was handled at the provincial level. Central administration of the nation's 93 customhouses was restored in 1980 as part of the Four Modernizations program, and the General Customs Administration was returned to the direct control of the State Council. In 1985, China enacted a new set of regulations for import and export duties and tariffs.

China is in the process of aligning its trade system with international standards. It uses the Harmonized System for tariff classification. A minimum tariff rate is granted to countries that have special agreements with China, including the United States. Official PRC policy is that direct trade with Taiwan is interregional, rather than international, since Taiwan is considered a province of China, and therefore no customs duties are levied; however, Taiwanese products imported via Hong Kong or Macau are dutiable. There are free-trade zones in Shanghai, Tianjin, Dalian, Haikov, the Hainan Island Special Economic Zone, and within the Shenzhen Special Economic Zone. Smuggling, reportedly well organized along the coasts of Guangdong, Fujian, and Zhejiang provinces and in the frontier regions of Tibet and Yunnan, is a major governmental concern. In 1985, Chinese customs agents exposed over 10,000 smuggling cases, a sharp decline from 1984; nevertheless, the value of the smuggled goods far surpassed that of 1984.

38 FOREIGN INVESTMENT

China strongly emphasizes attracting foreign investment in projects that will enhance the nation's export capabilities. Beginning in the early 1970s, China contracted for the construction of a substantial number of complete plants, notably for iron and steel, automobile, and fertilizer manufacture and power generation, including nuclear power. Such agreements, often made with private firms from Japan, the FRG, Italy, France, the UK, and Canada, as well as with agencies of the Communist states, all called for direct purchase of materials and services, and residual ownership by foreigners or remittance of profits from production were expressly disallowed. In 1979, China established the Foreign Investment Control Commission to attract and coordinate the use of more foreign investment funds. The Japanese and Hong Kong financiers have been the most cooperative lenders. In 1992, Japanese loans totaled $2,432 million while Hong Kong provided a further $710.4 million in credit.

China attracts capital in four ways: (1) by soliciting loans and credits from foreign governments and international financial institutions; (2) by floating bonds and debentures on international capital markets; (3) by promoting direct foreign investment through joint ventures and other cooperative enterprises; and (4) by accumulating trade surpluses from export sales.

Under the Joint Ventures Law, enacted in 1979 and revised in 1982, direct nongovernmental investment by foreigners and

remittance of profits overseas became possible for the first time since 1950. The development of joint ventures for the production of exports has been particularly stressed as a means of securing for China the foreign exchange needed to pay for purchases of advanced technology. Foreign investment in products for the domestic market, other than those needed for modernization, is discouraged. Under the Joint Ventures Law, the foreign company is expected to invest between 35% and 100% of all registered capital for an enterprise, but there must be some Chinese participation in the venture, including a Chinese chairman of the board of directors. Joint ventures are coordinated by the China International Trust and Investment Corp., established in 1979. In a further move to attract foreign investment, a new patent law was enacted, effective 1 April 1985.

Most provinces, regions, and major municipalities have their own international and trust investment corporations, of which the one in Shanghai is the largest. Special corporations for the attraction of investment by overseas Chinese have been established in Fujian and Zhejiang provinces. The attraction of "spill-over" investment from Hong Kong was a major factor in the establishment of the Shenzhen special economic zone (which includes the Shekou special industrial zone and the city of Shenzhen) in southern Guangdong Province in 1979. The other four special economic zones, also designed to attract foreign investment, are located at Zhuhai, near Macau; Shantou, along the east coast of Guangdong; Xiamen, across the Taiwan Strait from Taiwan and on Hainan island. Further foreign investment incentives were developed through the designation of open coastal cities, where investment terms similar to those of SEZ's are offered to foreign companies. By the end of 1992, there were 18 open cities in China, mainly along the southern coast but also along the North Korean, Russian and Mongolian borders.

By the end of 1991, contracted foreign direct investment in China amounted to $50 billion. Investment inflows contracted sharply in wake of the open political conflicts in 1989, but rebounded strongly in 1991 and 1992, thanks especially to new investments from Hong Kong. Actual investment inflows in 1992 totaled $11.3 billion, more than double those of 1991. Of this total, $7.7 billion came from Hong Kong, $1.1 billion from Taiwan, $748 million from Japan, $519 million from the US, and $203 million from Macao. Guangdong province attracted about 27% of the year's foreign investment, followed by Jiangsu province (14%) and Fujian province (13%).

Until the early 1980s, the flow of Chinese funds abroad was confined to assistance to developing countries and to investment in Hong Kong real estate. In 1983, however, China began making direct investments overseas, in the US, Canada, the Solomon Islands, and Sri Lanka. By the mid-1980s, China had over 180 nontrade joint ventures abroad, scattered over 40 countries and regions.

39 ECONOMIC DEVELOPMENT

A profound restructuring of China's economy began in 1949 following the founding of the PRC. Adhering to orthodox models borrowed wholesale from the former USSR, the PRC brought all major industrial, infrastructural, and financial enterprises directly under state ownership. Agriculture was collectivized. Management of the economy was closely controlled by central authorities, whose powers extended to the allocation of basic commodities and the basic division of resources into investment, consumption, and defense channels. Centralized planning for economic development was introduced in the form of five-year economic plans.

The first five-year plan (1953–57), belatedly announced in 1957, pursued rapid industrialization along Soviet lines, with a special emphasis on increases in steel and other heavy industries. The plan reportedly achieved its goals of a 5% gain in gross value of agricultural output and a 4% gain in grain production, and exceeded the 19% growth target in gross value of industrial output. The second five-year plan (1958–62) was voided at its start by the social and economic upheavals of the Great Leap Forward. At the heart of the Great Leap was the establishment of the self-sufficient rural commune; decentralization of industry was stressed, and the rural unemployed put to work in "backyard steel furnaces" and other industrial enterprises of dubious efficiency. Incomes were determined by need, and coercion and revolutionary enthusiasm replaced profit as the motivation for work. Publication of economic data ceased at this time, but Western observers estimated a 1% decline in agriculture for the 1958–60 period, an increase in GNP of only 1%, and no more than a 6% increase in industrial output.

After the bad harvests of 1960 and 1961, an "agriculture first" policy was adopted under which large areas of semiarid steppe and other marginal lands in the north and west were converted to agricultural use. A third five-year plan (1966–70), formulated by governmental pragmatists and calling for rapid growth of all sectors, was aborted by the outbreak of the Cultural Revolution.

In 1969, the government published a report calling for a more open approach to foreign assistance and trade. Domestically, it confirmed the use of the "mass line"—the system of calling upon workers and peasants to take responsibility and initiative, and to work without material incentives. It favored the simultaneous use of modern and traditional employment methods (the "walking on two legs" policy), and recommended expansion of industry through investment of profits derived from the sale of agricultural and light industrial products. At the heart of the 1969 policy was a reversion to the commune system of 1958—a program to make the countryside self-sufficient, with every commune not only growing its own food but also producing its own fertilizer and tools, generating its own electricity, and managing its own small handicrafts factories, health schemes, and primary schools. In contrast to the hastily organized communes of 1958–60, however, the new units frequently adhered to the traditional—and more manageable—structure of Chinese rural life.

Long-range economic planning resumed in 1970 with the announcement of a fourth five-year plan, for 1971–75. In late 1975, Premier Zhou Enlai proclaimed the plan successful. Agricultural output was reported to have grown by 51% during the 1964–74 period, while gross industrial output was said to have increased by 190%. Specifically, the following growth rates (1964–74) for mining and industry were reported: petroleum, 660%; coal, 92%; steel, 120%; cotton yarn, 86%; tractors, 540%; chemical fertilizers, 350%; and electric power, 200%.

A fifth five-year plan (1976–80), announced in 1975, gave priority to modernization of the economy and, for the first time, emphasized the development of light rather than heavy industry. Implementation of this new departure was, however, delayed by the deaths of Mao and Zhou in 1976 and did not occur until 1978, by which time the economic pragmatists, led by Deng Xiaoping, had emerged victorious from the subsequent political and ideological struggles. The sixth five-year plan (1981–85), announced in November 1982, reemphasized China's commitment to the pragmatic line and to the Four Modernizations. Approximately $115 billion was allocated for capital construction, and another $65 billion for renovation of existing infrastructure. GNP increased by an annual average of 10%, industrial output by one of 12%, and agricultural output by one of 8.1%.

The seventh five-year plan (1986–90), announced in March 1986 and called by Deng Xiaoping "The New Long March," featured the following major goals: increasing industrial output 7.5% annually (to $357 billion), agricultural output 4% annually (to $95.4 billion), national income 6.7% annually (to $252.7 bil-

lion), and foreign trade 40% (to $83 billion); spending $54 billion on 925 major development projects in energy, raw materials, transportation, and postal and telecommunications; and investing $74.6 billion in technological transformation of state enterprises. Rural per capita income was to rise to $151 annually.

Concerns about the unevenness of China's economic development progess, both in geographic and sectoral terms, have shaped the country's eighth five-year plan. To ameliorate potentially crippling bottlenecks in the supply of raw materials, energy, transportation, and communications capacity, the government has prioritized the financing of infrastructural investments. Streamlining of inefficient state industrial enterprises has been targeted as well, with the setting up of an unemployment security fund planned in order to assist laid-off workers make the transition to employment in non-state industry and the services sector. Direct foreign investment in industry, services as well as infrastructure (especially energy and communications development) will continue to be promoted. Also emphasized in the plan is better distribution of the country's development momentum. Inland cities, especially along the Russian, Mongolian, and North Korean borders are being targeted for development as export-oriented special economic zones in addition to coastal areas.

In the course of the eighth plan's implementation, particular emphasis has been given to developing major infrastructure projects that will link Hong Kong, Macao and the Pearl River delta area of Guangdong province into an integrated economic area and major export base for the 21st century. This will be balanced by the strengthening of the existing communications and other finance and commerce-related infrastructure in Shanghai as well as major industrial and commercial development around the city, including the establishment of a large-scale special economic zone at Pudong, slated to be the country's first free trade zone. It is expected that Shanghai will thus become a major financial as well as industrial center in Asia during the next century.

Another critical measure slated for immediate implementation is the improvement of the central government's strained fiscal position, through enlargement of it share of revenue, an improved tax system, and strengthened tax collection strategies. Financial sector reform planned through 1995 will transform the the People's Bank of China into an independent bank, establish other policy-oriented financial institutions, develop a clearer legal framework for the banking sector, and expand the space for entry by foreign financial institutions.

China has been a significant supplier of development aid to other countries. Recipients of Chinese military and economic assistance have included the DPRK in the 1950s and Viet-Nam, Egypt, Pakistan, and Tanzania (notably the Tanzania-Zambia railway) in the 1970s. During the 1956–74 period, China is thought to have disbursed more than $5 billion in grants and economic credits; overseas development aid dropped sharply in the late 1970s but appeared to be increasing in the 1980s. In 1992, China signed $6.6 billion worth of contracts to build engineering projects and provide labor services overseas. Official development assistance flows to China from all sources between 1980 and 1990 totaled $12,289 million. A 40–60% increase in ADB loans to China was announced in 1992.

⁴⁰SOCIAL DEVELOPMENT

Social welfare programs cover workers in state-operated enterprises and institutions, which include virtually all employees of government agencies, mining, manufacturing, industry, railroad, shipping, and construction units. Welfare in rural areas is administered by the state and collective farms, which provide clothing, shelter, and food for sick and disabled people and place the aged in homes. Recreational and cultural services are also supported through welfare payments.

Although wage scales in China remain low, the range of benefits has been expanding. Male workers are eligible to retire between ages 55 and 60, female workers at 45–55. The state provides pensions at a rate of 60–90% of the last month's salary. Workers may receive six months' sick leave at 60–100% of salary. For work-related total disability, workers are entitled to lifetime compensation of 80% of the standard wage. Maternity leave at full pay is provided for 56 days. In addition, numerous health, day-care, and educational benefits are provided free of charge. In urban areas, housing rentals rarely exceed 5% of the monthly wage.

Population control and family planning have been given major stress at various junctures by the government, but with limited success. A 1971 program raised the minimum marriage age to 23 for all women and to 25 for men in rural areas and 28 for men in urban areas; a new marriage law, adopted in 1980, reduced these minimums to 20 for women and 22 for men. Abortion was legalized in 1953; sterilization, IUD insertions, and other contraceptive techniques are widely available and free of charge. Under a population policy announced in 1978, couples agreeing to have no more than one child enjoy special benefits in the form of cash payments, improved housing, and higher pensions; penalties are imposed on couples having more than two children, including reduced rations for each child over the limit. Many rural families, however, were found to be flouting the new rules, especially after the agricultural responsibility system introduced in 1979 restored the economic role of children in enhancing household income. There were reports of infanticide of females, as the traditional Chinese preference for males to continue the family line clashed with the new regulations. China's fertility rate was 2.4 in 1985–90. In 1988, 72% of couples of childbearing age used contraceptives. In 1991, 21.4 million persons received family planning services.

The economic status of women, formerly considered little more than chattels for their husband's family, improved considerably after 1950, aided by the introduction of a work-point system of payment on the communes and by legislation guaranteeing equal pay for equal work. A campaign to increase literacy among women, formerly denied education, also opened doors to increased employment opportunities. The 1950 Marriage Law abolished arranged marriages, outlawed polygamy, and further protected women's rights by granting widows the right to remarry without the consent of the dead husband's family and guaranteeing to women as well as to men the right of divorce. Nonetheless, it is still usual for a woman to move in with her husband's family after marriage, and women continue to be significantly underrepresented at the higher levels of government and the CCP. In 1993, the government continued to condemn and took steps to curb traditional abuse of women, including their abduction and sale for wives or prostitutes, abuse of female children, and female infanticide.

41HEALTH

National health practices, including the provision of both Western and traditional Chinese health services, are under the supervision of the Ministry of Health. The ministry has emphasized preventive medicine and general improvement of sanitary conditions. Since the early 1950s, mass campaigns have been mounted to deal with major public health problems. These have included nationwide cleanup campaigns and mass educational programs in the sanitary preparation of food, the treatment of drinking water, personal hygiene, and waste disposal. The entire population was mobilized to eradicate the four pests—rats, sparrows, flies, and mosquitoes—with mixed results. Epidemic prevention centers were established to carry out massive immunizations, while parasitic diseases, affecting hundreds of millions in China, were also attacked. As a result, schistosomiasis,

malaria, kala-azar, and hookworm are thought to have been largely brought under control. The country's five-year plan (1991–1995) was instituted to upgrade services yet again. Infectious diseases were to be 20% lower than in 1990; all provinces were to provide primary medical care to citizens; there were plans to add 450,000 hospital beds and 500,000 technical health workers; and the availability of health insurance was forecast to increase. From 1985 to 1992, 90% of inhabitants had access to health care services.

From 1988 to 1992 there were 1.37 doctors per 1,000 people, with a nurse to doctor ratio of 0.5. At the end of 1990, there were a total of 208,000 health care organizations (an increase of 7,000 since 1985). There were 62,000 hospitals (a rise of 3,000 over 1985), and total beds numbered 2.6 million (up by 370,000), a rate of 2.33 per 1,000. It has been the government's intention to increase the number of acute care beds to 4 per 1,000 and the number of doctors to 1.3 per 1,000. During the Cultural Revolution, in an effort to even out the disparity between rural and urban health services, medical personnel from hospitals (as much as 30–50% of a hospital's medical staff) were included in groups of people sent down to the countryside, and the number of locally trained paramedical personnel, called barefoot doctors, expanded. An increasingly important medical factor since the Cultural Revolution, these young peasants or middle-school graduates have been trained on the job by township doctors or in two-month courses at township health clinics. Barefoot doctors and production teams and brigade health stations are still the major deliverers of health care in the countryside.

There were 25,057,000 births in 1992 (a birth rate of 21 per 1,000). From 1980 to 1993, 83% of married women (ages 15 to 49) used contraception. The infant mortality rate was reduced from as high as 200 per 1,000 live births before 1949 to an estimated 35 per 1,000 in 1992, and it is continuing to decline. Between 1990 and 1992, China vaccinated a high percentage of its children up to one year of age: tuberculosis (94%); diphtheria, per- tussis, and tetanus (94%); polio (95%); and measles (94%). In 1990, there were 166 cases of tuberculosis per 100,000 people.

Average life expectancy in 1992 was 71 years, up from an average of 45 years in 1950. From 1985 to 1990, major causes of death were recorded as: communicable diseases and maternal/perinatal causes (117 per 100,000); noncommunicable diseases (696 per 100,000); and injuries (88 per 100,000). In an effort to prevent the spread of AIDS, the government in 1987 required the testing of all foreigners for the HIV virus. The 1993 death rate was 6.5 per 1,000 people.

42HOUSING

China has an acute shortage of housing, attributable not only to the large annual increases in population (over 10 million a year) that must be accommodated but also to the long-standing policy of directing investment funds into heavy industry rather than into housing and other social amenities. According to official Chinese sources, some 25 million peasant families, or 14% of all rural households, built new homes or rebuilt their existing homes between 1978 and 1980. Extensive rebuilding was reported in Tangshan, which had been virtually leveled during the 1976 earthquake. By the end of 1980, 7.69 million sq m (82.77 million sq ft) of housing had been rebuilt in the city, and more than 500,000 families relocated there. In 1985, housing construction in rural areas, reflecting the impact of rural reforms and the increasing capital accumulation of the peasantry, exceeded 700 million sq m (7,535 million sq ft) of dwelling space; in cities and towns, the 1985 total was 187.5 million sq m (2,018 million sq ft), of which 35 million sq m (377 million sq ft) was in Beijing. Of the new urban housing, about 6.3 million sq m (67.8 million sq ft) came in the form of private homes. In 1992, the total number of housing units in China stood at 276,502,000. In 1990, 400,000 new dwellings were completed. In 1991, 90.6% of all homes had piped water.

43EDUCATION

Prior to 1949, schools were available for less than 40% of school-age children; 85% of the people were illiterate. During 1949–59, school attendance increased nearly fourfold. In 1959, about 50 million children received preschool education; primary schooling was nearly universal, with some 92.6 million students (between 85% and 90% of all school-age children) in primary schools; 12 million were in secondary schools. By 1966, total school enrollment in China reached 116 million, with the average pupil receiving 5.5 years of formal schooling. In 1990, the rate of literacy (per UNESCO) was 77.8% (males: 87.0% and females: 68.1%).

The Cultural Revolution affected education more than any other sector of society. Schools were shut down in mid-1966 to give the student Red Guards the opportunity to "make revolution" on and off campus. The Cultural Revolution touched off purges within the educational establishment. Upper- and middle-level bureaucrats throughout the system were removed from office, and virtually entire university faculties and staffs dispersed. Although many lower schools had begun to reopen during 1969, several universities remained closed through the early 1970s, as an estimated 10 million urban students were removed to the countryside to take part in labor campaigns. During this period and its aftermath, revolutionary ideology and local conditions became the principal determinants of curriculum. A nine-year program of compulsory education (compressed from 12 years) was established for youths 7–15 years of age.

Education was reoriented in 1978 under the Four Modernizations policy, which restored the pre-1966 emphasis on competitive examinations and the development of special schools for the most promising students. The most striking changes were effected at the junior and senior high school levels, in which students were again streamed, according to ability, into an estimated 5,000 high-quality, well-equipped schools; into lower-quality high schools; or into the technical and vocational schools, which were perceived as the least prestigious. In addition, 96 universities, 200 technical schools, and 7,000 primary schools were designated as "key" institutions. Universities were reopened, with a renewed emphasis given to science and technology. During the 1980s, universal primary education by 1990 became a main target.

In 1991, there were 729,158 primary schools with 5,532,300 teachers and 121,641,500 students. At the secondary level, there were 3,557,000 teachers and 52,267,900 students. Of these, 46,835,000 were in general education; 661,400 were in teacher training; and 4,771,500 were in vocational courses.

In 1985 there were 1,016 colleges and universities in China. The number of regular college students increased by over 50% between 1983 and 1987. Among the largest and most prestigious institutions were Beijing University and Qinghua University, both in Beijing; Zhongshan University, in Guangzhou; Nanjing University and Nanjing Institute of Technology; Nankai University and Tianjin University, in Tianjin; and Fudan University, in Shanghai. Graduate education resumed in the late 1970s; the number of new graduate students increased from 3,600 in 1980 to over 20,000 by 1985. In 1992, all third-level institutions had a total of 2,270,800 students.

Tuition has traditionally been free in vocational secondary schools and in training schools for elementary teachers, as well as in colleges and universities; students in need of food, clothing, and textbooks receive state grants-in-aid. Primary and general secondary school students pay a nominal tuition fee. Part-time primary and secondary schools, evening universities, and correspondence schools exist for adult workers and peasants.

44LIBRARIES AND MUSEUMS

The National Library in Beijing (founded in 1909) is the largest in China, with almost 16 million volumes, including more than 200,000 rare ancient Chinese books and manuscripts. The Chinese Academy of Sciences Central Library, in Beijing, has a collection of 5.2 million volumes, with branches in Shanghai, Lanzhou, Wuhan, and Chengdu. The Capital Library in Beijing is the city's public library and operates lending, reference, and children's services.

By the end of 1989 there were 2,512 public libraries at and above the county level, with 283.7 million books; with 116.13 million readers. Small lending libraries and reading rooms can be found in factories, offices, and rural townships. The library of Beijing University, with over 4 million volumes, is the largest university library. Other important university collections are at Nanjing University in Nanjing, Fudan University in Shanghai, and Qinghua University in Beijing.

China had 711 museums in 1985, most of them cultural museums, and 93 new museums were being planned or built.

The Imperial Palace Museum in Beijing houses collections of art, sculpture, silk fabric, and furniture. The Museum of the Chinese Revolution, on Tiananmen Square, has exhibits of the revolutionary movement in China from the Opium War to the founding of the PRC. In Shanghai is the Museum of Art and History, with some of the country's outstanding archaeological and art collections. Many museums are memorials to Chinese artists and writers, and house collections of their work. China also has 500 historical sites with exhibitions.

45MEDIA

Postal service and telecommunications facilities fall under the authority of the Ministry of Posts and Telecommunications. The posts are responsible for the sale and distribution of newspapers and magazines, an important function in a country that relies heavily on these media for mass communication. Mail is delivered twice a day seven days a week. There were 53,600 post offices in 1990. In the same year, there were 6,850,300 telephones and 3,826 fax machines.

Radio and Television

China had 274 radio broadcasting stations at the end of 1989 (as compared with only 1 station after World War II). The most important station is Beijing's Central People's Broadcasting Station (CPBS); from there, programs are relayed by local stations. CPBS broadcasts daily on several channels using a variety of languages, including Mandarin (or standard Chinese), the Hokkien and Hakka dialects, Cantonese, Mongolian, Tibetan, Uygur, Kazakhi and Korean.

Television broadcasting began in 1958, and color transmissions in 1973. In 1989, China had 202 television stations, as compared with 12 in 1965 and 47 in 1982. Some 12,000 relay stations transmit programs originating from Beijing. In 1991, China had 213 million radios and 35.8 million television sets. Many of the sets are installed in public meeting places and in government and economic enterprises, although increasingly a television set has become a much-prized private acquisition. Since large segments of the rural population are as yet without radios and television sets, the government operates a massive wired broadcast network linked to 100 million loudspeakers.

The Press

The press is closely controlled by the government, the CCP, or the various political and mass organizations associated with the CCP. In 1990 there were 773 national and provincial newspapers and 5,751 magazines and other periodicals. Minority newspapers are published in Mongolian, Uygur, Tibetan, Korean, and other languages. The main news agencies are the official New China (Xinhua) News Agency; the China News Service, which supplies information to overseas Chinese newspapers and journals; and China Feature, which supplies articles to magazines and newspapers worldwide.

The Cultural Revolution caused substantial upheaval in the Chinese press establishment. Many publications closed down, and others underwent purges of editorial staffs. Publication of *Hongqi (Red Flag)*, the most authoritative of the CCP publications, resumed in 1968. The major newspapers, with their locations and circulations in 1992, are *Renmin Ribao (People's Daily;* Beijing, 4,000,000); *Jiefangjun Bao (Liberation Army Daily;* Beijing, 100,000), the army organ, which played a leading role in the Cultural Revolution; *Wenhui Bao (Wenhui Daily;* Shanghai, 1,300,000); *Jiefang Ribao (Liberation Daily;* Shanghai, 1,000,000); and *Beijing Ribao (Beijing Daily;* Beijing, 1,000,000). China's first English-language newspaper, the *China Daily,* founded in 1981, is published in Beijing and had a circulation of 70,000 in 1992. The most authoritative publication for foreigners is the weekly *Beijing Review,* distributed abroad in several languages.

46ORGANIZATIONS

Prior to 1966, the leading mass organizations, all closely tied to the regime, were the Communist Youth League, the Women's Federation, the Federation of Literary and Art Circles, the Federation of Scientific Societies, and the Federation of Industry and Commerce. These bodies were to some extent eclipsed by the Cultural Revolution, which spawned a host of new groups. After the Cultural Revolution passed its peak, many of the new organizations lost ground, while local Communist Youth League organizations, including the Young Pioneers, gained prestige. By the mid-1980s, the pre-Cultural Revolution groups were once again ascendant.

47TOURISM, TRAVEL, AND RECREATION

Chinese restrictions on tourism were eased to allow access by foreigners on group tours in 1976 and further relaxed in 1983, when the ban on individual travel was lifted. By 1985, 244 Chinese cities and scenic spots were open to foreign tourists, and a number of resorts specifically designed for foreigners were in operation. China was opened to tourists from Taiwan in 1987. Visa and travel arrangements are under the jurisdiction of the China Travel and Tourism Administration and the China International Travel Service. All visitors to China must have visas. In 1991, 2,710,103 foreign nationals visited China, of whom about 1,395,000 came from Southeast and Eastern Asia, 789,534 from Europe, and 418,498 from the Americas. Total foreign exchange from tourism in 1991 was estimated at us$2.84 billion. In the same year, there were 321,116 hotel rooms with 679,458 beds and a 61.35% occupancy rate. Beijing, Shanghai, and Guangzhou are the principal points of entry.

Tourist Attractions

The most famous tourist attraction in China is the Great Wall, the construction of which began in the 3d century BC as a barrier against northern invaders. Other leading tourist attractions include the Forbidden City, or Imperial Palace, in Beijing; the nearby tombs of the Ming emperors; historic Hangzhou, with its famous West Lake and gardens; busy Shanghai, with its well-stocked stores and superb cuisine; Xi'an, the site of monumental Qin dynasty excavations; and Guangzhou, the center of Cantonese cooking, with an extensive Cultural Park.

Sports

Sports activities in China are coordinated by the State Physical Culture and Sports Commission and the All-China Sports Federation. Active sports, represented by national associations, include gymnastics, diving, basketball, soccer, tennis, cycling, swimming,

tennis, volleyball, weight lifting, and mountain climbing. Chinese teams excelled in gymnastics, weight lifting, shooting, and volleyball at the 1984 Summer Olympics in Los Angeles; in these and other fields, the PRC won 15 gold medals, 8 silver, and 9 bronze.

Distinctively Chinese pastimes include wushu, a set of ancient exercises known abroad as gonfu (kung fu), or the "martial arts"; taijiquan, or shadow boxing, developed in the 17th century; and liangong shibafa, modern therapeutic exercises for easing neck, shoulder, back, and leg ailments. Qigong (literally "breathing exercises") is also widely practiced both as a sport and as physical therapy. A popular traditional spectator sport is Chinese wrestling. Traditional pastimes for the national minorities are horse racing, show jumping, and archery among the Mongolians; the sheep chase (in which the winner successfully locates and defends possession of a slaughtered sheep) among Uygurs and Kazaks; and yak and horse racing among Tibetans.

48FAMOUS CHINESE

Confucius (K'ung Fu-tzu or Kong Fuzi, 551–479 BC) is generally regarded as the most important historical figure, as well as the greatest scholar, of ancient China. His philosophy and social ideas include observance of filial piety, the sanctity of the family, and social responsibility. Other early philosophers were Lao-tzu (Laozi; Li Erh, 604?–531 BC), the traditional founder of Taoism; Mencius (Meng-tzu or Mengzi, 385–289 BC), who stressed the essential goodness of human nature and the right of subjects to revolt against unjust rulers; and Mo Ti (Di, 465?–390? BC), who stressed the theme of universal love. Among the principal early poets was Chu (Chü) Yuan, (340–278 BC), whose *Li Sao,* a melancholy rhapsody, is among the world's great poems. Sima Qian (Ssu-ma Ch'ien, 145–87 BC) produced the monumental *Shiji (Shih-chi; Historical Records),* the first general history of China. Ban Gu (Pan Ku, AD 32–92) wrote *Qian Hanshu (Ch'ien-Han shu; History of the Former Han Dynasty),* a continuation of Sima Qian's work. Zhang (Chang) Heng (78–139), an astronomer, is credited with having invented the first seismograph. Zhang Zhongjing (Chang Chung-ching, 152–219) was a celebrated physician, and Zu Zhongzhi (Tsu Chung-chih, 429–500) calculated the figure 3.14159265 as the exact value for π. Three brilliant poets of the Tang dynasty were Li Bo (Po, 701–62), Du (Tu) Fu (712–70), and Bo Juyi (Po Chü-yi, 772–846). Li Shizhen (Shichen, 1518–93), an outstanding pharmacologist, wrote a monumental *Materia Medica.* Great authors of the Qing dynasty were Wu Jingzi (Ching-tzu, 1701–54), who wrote *Rulin Waishi (Ju-lin wai-shih; Unofficial History of the Scholars),* a superb satire on the civil service system, and Cao Xueqin (Ts'ao Hsüeh-ch'in, 1715?–63), who produced a remarkable novel, *Honglou meng (Hung-lou meng; The Dream of the Red Chamber).* Lu Xun or Lu Hsun (Zhou Shuren or Chou Shu-jen, 1881–1936) is generally regarded as China's greatest writer of the modern period. Mao Dun (Shen Yanbing, 1896–1981) and Ba Jin (Li Feigan, b.1904) are leading novelists. Lin Yutang (Yu-t'ang, 1895–1976) popularized Chinese culture in the West.

Political Figures

Sun Yat-sen (Zhongshan or Chung-shan, 1866–1925) planned the revolution against the Manchus and became the first president (1911–12) of the republic. Mao Zedong (Tse-tung, 1893–1976), the foremost figure of postrevolutionary China, served as chairman of the Central Committee of the CCP from 1956 to 1976. Other prominent Chinese Communist leaders include Zhu De (Chu Teh, 1886–1976), who became commander in chief of the Red Army in 1931 and chairman of the Standing Committee of the NPC; Zhou Enlai (Chou En-lai, 1898–1976), first premier of China's State Council; Liu Shaoqi (Shao-ch'i, 1898–1969), who became China's head of state in 1959 and was purged during the Cultural Revolution but posthumously rehabilitated in 1985;

and Lin Biao (Piao, 1908–71), who became deputy premier and minister of defense in 1959 and who, prior to his death and subsequent political vilification, had been certified as Mao's successor in the constitution drawn up in 1969. Women in the political hierarchy have included Song Qingling (Soong Ch'ing-ling, 1892–1981), Sun Zhongshan's wife, and Jiang Qing (Chiang Ch'ing, 1913–1991), Mao's fourth wife, who emerged as a radical leader during the Cultural Revolution. Jiang, with other prominent radicals, was purged in the wake of the ascension of Hua Guofeng (b.1920) as CCP chairman in 1976. Deng Xiaoping (b.1904), twice disgraced (1966–73 and 1976) by radical administrations, reemerged in 1977 to become China's most powerful political figure, albeit without major office, and a major figure in its modernization drive; he officially retired in 1987. A protégé, Hu Yaobang (1915–1989), was party secretary until his ouster in 1987. Another protégé, who emerged in 1987 as the likely preeminent Chinese leader of the future, although still currently in the political shadow of Deng, was Zhao Ziyang (b.1919), who became general secretary of the CCP in 1987; Li Peng (b.1928) was named premier in the same year.

⁴⁹DEPENDENCIES

China has no territories or colonies.

⁵⁰BIBLIOGRAPHY

Bailey, Paul. *China in the Twentieth Century.* New York: B. Blackwell, 1988.

Bannister, Judith. *China's Changing Population.* Stanford, Calif.: Stanford University Press, 1983.

Bauer, E. E. *China Takes Off: Technology Transfer and Modernization.* Seattle: University of Washington Press, 1986.

Bianco, Lucien. *Origins of the Chinese Revolution, 1915–1949.* Stanford, Calif.: Stanford University Press, 1971.

China: from the Long March to Tiananmen Square. New York: H. Holt, 1990.

Clubb, O. Edmund. *Twentieth Century China.* 3d ed. New York: Columbia University Press, 1978.

Cotterell, Arthur. *China: a Cultural History.* New York: New American Library, 1988.

Creel, Herrlee Glessner. *Chinese Thought from Confucius to Mao Tse-tung.* Chicago: University of Chicago Press, 1953.

De Keijzer, Arne J. *China: Business Strategies for the '90s.* Berkeley, California: Pacific View Press, 1992.

Dryer, June Teufel. *China's Forty Millions: Minority Nationalities and National Integration in the People's Republic of China.* Cambridge, Mass.: Harvard University Press, 1976.

Evans, Richard. *Deng Xiaoping and the Making of Modern China.* New York: Viking, 1994.

Fairbank, John King. *The United States and China.* 4th ed., rev. Cambridge, Mass.: Harvard University Press, 1979.

——*The Great Chinese Revolution, 1800–1985.* New York: Harper & Row, 1986.

——*China: a New History.* Cambridge, Mass.: Harvard University Press, 1992.

Feinstein, Steve. *China in Pictures.* Minneapolis: Lerner Publications Co., 1989.

Garside, Roger. *Coming Alive!: China After Mao.* New York: McGraw-Hill, 1981.

Goldman, Merle. *China's Intellectuals: Advice and Dissent.* Cambridge, Mass.: Harvard University Press, 1981.

Gray, Jack. *Rebellions and Revolutions: China from the 1800s to the 1980s.* New York: Oxford University Press, 1990.

Howard, Pat. *Breaking the Iron Rice Bowl: Prospects for Socialism in China's Countryside.* Armonk, N.Y.: M.E. Sharpe, 1988.

Hsiung, James C., and Samuel S. Kim. *China in the Global Community.* New York: Praeger, 1980.

Hsu, Immanuel Chung-yueh. *The Rise of Modern China.* New York: Oxford University Press, 1990.

Hsu, Kai-yu. *Literature of the People's Republic of China.* Bloomington: Indiana University Press, 1980.

Hucker, Charles O. *China's Imperial Past: An Introduction to Chinese History and Culture.* Stanford, Calif.: Stanford University Press, 1975.

Kaplan, Fredric M. and Julian M. Sobin (ed.). *Encyclopedia of China Today.* 3d ed., rev. New York: Eurasia, 1982.

Lardy, Nicholas R. *Agriculture in China's Modern Economic Development.* New York: Cambridge University Press, 1983.

——*Foreign Trade and Economic Reform in China, 1978–1990 R. Lardy.* Cambridge; New York: Cambridge University Press, 1992.

Leung, Edwin Pak-wah. *Historical Dictionary of Revolutionary China, 1839–1976.* New York: Greenwood Press, 1992.

Leys, Simon. *The Burning Forest: Essays on Chinese Culture and Politics.* New York: Holt, Rinehart & Winston, 1986.

Lin, Bih-jaw (ed.). *The Aftermath of the 1989 Tiananmen Crisis in Mainland China.* Boulder, Colo.: Westview Press, 1992.

Link, Perry, Richard Madsen, Paul G. Pickowicz (eds.) *Unofficial China: Popular Culture and Thought in the People's Republic.* Boulder, Colo.: Westview Press, 1989.

Mackerras, Colin. *China Since 1978: Reform, Modernisation and Socialism with Chinese.* New York: St. Martin's Press, 1994.

Michael, Franz. *China Through the Ages: History of a Civilization.* Boulder, Colo.: Westview, 1986.

Nathan, Andrew J. *Chinese Democracy.* Berkeley: University of California Press, 1985.

Ogden, Suzanne. *China's Unresolved Issues: Politics, Development, and Culture.* 2nd ed. Englewood Cliffs, N.J.: Prentice Hall, 1991.

Oi, Jean Chun. *State and Peasant in Contemporary China: the Political Economy of Village Government.* Berkeley: University of California Press, 1989.

Orleans, Leo A. (ed.). *Science in Contemporary China.* Stanford, Calif.: Stanford University Press, 1980.

Pepper, Suzanne. *China's Universities: Post-Mao Enrollment Policies and their Impact on the Structure of Secondary Education.* Ann Arbor, Mich.: Center for Chinese Studies, 1984.

——*China's Education Reform in the 1980s: Policies, Issues, and Historical Perspectives.* Berkeley, Calif.: University of California at Berkeley, Center for Chinese Studies, 1990.

Perry, Elizabeth, and Christine Wong (eds.). *The Political Economy of Reform in Post-Mao China.* Cambridge, Mass.: Harvard University Press, 1985.

Rawski, Thomas G. and Lillian M. Li (eds.). *Chinese History in Economic Perspective.* Berkeley: University of California Press, 1992.

Rawski, Thomas G. *China's Transition to Industrialism.* Ann Arbor: University of Michigan Press, 1980.

Reynolds, Bruce L. (ed.). *Reform in China: Challenges and Choices.* Armonk, N.Y.: M.E. Sharpe, 1987.

Salisbury, Harrison E. *The Long March: The Untold Story.* New York: Harper & Row, 1985.

Scalapino, Robert, and George Yu. *Modern China and Its Revolutionary Process: Recurrent Challenges to the Traditional Order, 1850–1920.* Berkeley: University of California Press, 1986.

Schram, Stuart R. *The Thought of Mao Tse-Tung.* New York: Cambridge University Press, 1989.

Schrecker, John E. *The Chinese Revolution in Historical Perspective.* New York: Greenwood Press, 1991.

Snow, Edgar. *Red Star over China.* New York: Bantam, 1978 (orig. 1938).

Sullivan, Michael. *The Arts of China: A Short History.* Rev. ed. Berkeley: University of California Press, 1977.

Terrill, Ross. *Mao: A Biography.* New York: Harper & Row, 1981.

Wakeman, Frederick, Jr. *The Great Enterprise: The Manchu Reconstruction of Imperial Order in 17th Century China.* Berkeley: University of California Press, 1985.

Wittwer, Sylvan. *Feeding a Billion: Frontiers of Chinese Agriculture.* East Lansing: Michigan State University Press, 1987.

Worden, Robert L., Andrea Matles Savada, and Ronald E. Dolan (eds.) *China, a Country Study.* 4th ed. Washington, D.C.: Library of Congress, 1988.

World Bank. *China: Long-Term Development: Issues and Options.* Baltimore: Johns Hopkins University Press, 1985.

Wortzel, Larry M. *Class in China: Stratification in a Classless Society.* Westport, Conn.: Greenwood, 1987.

CYPRUS*

Republic of Cyprus
Kypriaki Dimokratia

CAPITAL: Nicosia.

FLAG: The national flag consists of the map of Cyprus in gold set above two olive branches in green on a white field.

ANTHEM: *Ethnikos Hymnos (National Hymn),* beginning "Se gnorizo apo tin kopsi" ("I recognize you by the keenness of your spade").

MONETARY UNIT: The Cyprus pound (c£) is a paper currency of 100 cents. There are coins of 1, 2, 5, 10, 20, and 50 cents and 1 pound, and notes of 50 cents, and 1, 5, 10, and 20 pounds. c£1 = $1.9833 (or $1 = c£0.5042). The Turkish lira (TL) of 100 kuruş is the currency in the Turkish Cypriot zone.

WEIGHTS AND MEASURES: The metric system is the legal standard. Imperial and local measures are also used.

HOLIDAYS: New Year's Day, 1 January; Epiphany, 6 January; Late President Makarios' Day, 19 January; Greek Independence Day, 25 March; Cyprus National Day, 1 April; Labor Day, 1 May; Cyprus Independence Day, 1 October; Greek Resistance Day, 28 October; Christmas, 25 December; Boxing Day, 26 December. Holidays observed by the Turkish Cypriot community include Founding of the Turkish Federated State of Cyprus, 13 February; Turkish National Sovereignty and Children's Day, 23 April; Turkish Youth and Sports Day, 19 May; Turkish Victory Day, 30 August; Turkish Independence Day, 29 October. Movable Christian religious holidays include Green Monday, Good Friday, Holy Saturday, and Easter Monday. Movable Muslim religious holidays are observed in the Turkish Cypriot zone.

TIME: 2 PM = noon GMT.

¹LOCATION, SIZE, AND EXTENT

Cyprus is the largest Mediterranean island after Sicily and Sardinia. Including small island outposts of Cape Andreas known as the Klidhes, its area is 9,250 sq km (3,571 sq mi). Comparatively, the area occupied by Cyprus is about three-fourths the size of the state of Connecticut. Since 1975, the northern third of the island, or 3,367 sq km (1,300 sq mi), has been under the de facto control of the Turkish Cypriot Federated State, which on 15 November 1983 proclaimed its independence as the Turkish Republic of Northern Cyprus; the southern two-thirds (5,884 sq km/2,272 sq mi) are controlled by the government of the Republic of Cyprus. A narrow zone called the "green line," patrolled by UN forces, separates the two regions and divides Nicosia, the national capital.

Cyprus is situated in the extreme northeast corner of the Mediterranean; it is 71 km (44 mi) s of Turkey, 105 km (65 mi) w of Syria, and some 800 km (500 mi) E of the Greek mainland. Cyprus extends 227 km (141 mi) ENE–WSW from Cape Andreas to Cape Drepanon and 97 km (60 mi) SSE–NNW. The average width is 56–72 km (35–45 mi); the narrow peninsula known as the Karpas, which is nowhere more than 16 km (10 mi) wide, extends 74 km (46 mi) northeastward to Cape Andreas. Cyprus has a total coastline of 648 km (403 mi).[1]

The capital city of Cyprus, Nicosia, is located in the north central part of the country.

---

1. *Unless otherwise noted, all statistical data refer to that part of the island controlled by the government of the Republic of Cyprus, i.e., the Greek Cypriot zone.

²TOPOGRAPHY

Two dissimilar mountain systems, flanking a central plain, occupy the greater part of the island. The Troodos Massif, in the southwest, attaining its highest point in Mt. Olympus (1,953 m/6,406 ft), sends out numerous spurs to the northwestern, northern, and southern coasts. In the north, a geologically older range, the Kyrenia Mountains, extend more than 160 km (100 mi) along the coast in a series of rocky peaks, capped often by medieval castles. Between these principal formations lies the Mesaoria, a low plain extending from Famagusta Bay on the east to Morphou Bay on the west. Once forested, this now treeless region, varying in width from 16 to 32 km (10–20 mi), contains the bulk of the island's cultivable and pastoral area. There are few lakes or rivers; rivers are little more than rocky channels that carry away torrents during the thaw of spring and early summer.

³CLIMATE

Cyprus is for the most part dry, sunny, and healthful. The warm currents of the Mediterranean ensure mild winters but bring humidity to the coastal area in the summer, when the central plain is hot and dry. On the hills, daily sunshine is interrupted only occasionally by a wet period rarely lasting more than a week. The mean annual temperature is about 20°C (68°F). A cool, rainy season lasts from November to March. In winter, snow covers the higher peaks of the Troodos; elsewhere the temperature seldom falls below freezing, and conditions are mild and bracing. Rainfall is erratic and varies greatly in different parts of the island. The annual average precipitation ranges from below 30 cm (12 in) in the west-central lowlands to more than 114 cm (45 in) in the higher parts of the southern massif. The main agricultural areas receive rainfall of from 30 to 40 cm (12–16 in) annually. Earthquakes are not uncommon.

⁴FLORA AND FAUNA

Except for some small lowland areas in which eucalyptus has been planted, the forests are natural growths of great antiquity, from which the Phoenician shipbuilders drew much of their timber. Forests consist principally of Aleppo pine; other important conifers, locally dominant, are the stone pine, cedar (which is becoming rare), Mediterranean cypress, and juniper, the last growing chiefly on the lower slopes of the Kyrenia Mountains. Oriental plane and alder are plentiful in the valleys, while on the hills, Olympus dwarf oak mingles with pines of various species. Wild flowers grow in profusion, and herbs are numerous.

Cyprus has few wild animals, but birdlife is varied and includes partridge, quail, snipe, plover, and woodcock. Eagles are commonly seen in the mountains.

⁵ENVIRONMENT

Under the Town and Country Planning Law of 1972, the government has the power to issue "reservation orders" in order to protect historic buildings, trees, or other specific points. Other conservation laws seek to preserve forests, restrict the hunting of wildlife, and maintain environmental health. The most significant environmental problems in Cyprus are water pollution, erosion, and wildlife preservation. The purity of the water supply is threatened by industrial pollutants, pesticides used in agricultural areas, and the lack of adequate sewage treatment. Cyprus has 0.2 cubic miles of water, of which 91% is used for farming activity. One hundred percent of Cyprus' urban and rural dwellers have access to safe water. The erosion of the land is accelerated by rainfall. It is particularly evident in the erosion of Cyprus' coastline. In accordance with the Foreshore Protection Law, several coastal areas have been zoned to prevent undesirable development. The Ministry of Agriculture and Natural Resources has primary responsibility for environmental matters. The expansion of urban centers threatens the habitat of Cyrpus' wildlife. As of 1994, one mammal species, 17 types of birds and 43 plant species in a total of 2,000 are threatened with extinction. About 20 species of flora are protected. The Cyprus mouflon or wild sheep is protected in the Paphos Forest game reserve.

⁶POPULATION

At the end of 1992, the population for the whole of Cyprus was estimated at 725,000, representing an increase of 13% over the 1982 census figure of 642,731. The population grew by an average of 1.1% a year in the 1980s. The population for the year 2000 was projected at 765,000, assuming a crude birthrate of 15.1 per 1,000 population, a death rate of 7.3, and a net natural increase of 7.8 for 1995–2000. The population density in 1992 was estimated at 78 per sq km (203 per sq mi). Nicosia, the capital, located near the center of the island in the Mesaoria plain, had an estimated population (in the Greek-controlled part) of 166,500 in 1992. Other chief towns—all seaports—are Limassol, Famagusta, Larnaca, Paphos, and Kyrenia.

⁷MIGRATION

Cyprus suffered massive population shifts following the Turkish military occupation of the northern third of the island in July 1974. Some 120,000 Greek Cypriots fled from the occupied area to the south, and about 60,000 Turkish Cypriots fled in the opposite direction. As of the 1989, some 611 Greek Cypriots lived in the north, mostly on the Karpas Peninsula, and about 100 Turkish Cypriots remained in the south.

External Greek Cypriot migration has dwindled sharply from 21,058 emigrants during 1974–79 to only 1,697 during 1980–88. There were 2,720 immigrants during 1984–90. Throughout the 1970s and 1980s, most Greek Cypriot emigrants went to Australia, the UK, the US, Canada, South Africa, or Greece. In the late 1980s, about 300,000 were living in seven foreign countries. After 1974, about 65,000 Turkish immigrants and Turkish Cypriots settled in northern Cyprus.

⁸ETHNIC GROUPS

Following the 16th-century Turkish conquest, Cyprus received a substantial permanent influx of Ottoman Turks. Many soldiers became owners of feudal estates, and there was immigration from Anatolia and Rumelia. There was virtually no intermarriage; each community preserved its own religion, language, dress, and other national characteristics, and major cities and towns had their Greek and Turkish quarters. The 1974 war had the effect of almost completely segregating the two communities.

Greek Cypriots outnumber Turks more than four to one. Estimates in 1989 put the proportion of Greek and Turkish Cypriots at 80% and 18.6%, respectively. The rest of the population included about 6,300 Lebanese Maronites and Armenians and 8,900 others (mainly British).

⁹LANGUAGES

After independence in 1960, Greek and Turkish became the official languages. Since 1974, Greek has been the language of the south and Turkish the language of the north. English is also used extensively.

¹⁰RELIGIONS

In 1990, 76.2% of the total population of Cyprus was Greek Orthodox, 18.7% Muslim, 2.7% members of various Christian churches, and 2.4% of other persuasions. Under the Cyprus ethnarch Archbishop Makarios III, who was president of Cyprus from 1960 until his death in 1977, the church was the chief instrument of Greek Cypriot nationalism. Makarios' successor as ethnarch, Archbishop Chrysostomos, elected for life, also has played an active role in Greek Cypriot political affairs.

The independence of the Church of Cyprus was recognized by the Council of Ephesus in AD 431 and confirmed by Emperor Zeno in 478. The Church of Cyprus is one of the oldest constituent bodies of the Holy Orthodox Eastern Church, being senior by centuries to the Orthodox Church of Greece, and junior only to the four original patriarchates of Constantinople, Alexandria, Antioch, and Jerusalem. Virtually all Turkish Cypriots are Sunni Muslims of the Hanafi sect. Religious minorities include Armenian, Anglican, and Maronite Christians and Roman Catholics.

¹¹TRANSPORTATION

Internal transport is exclusively by road. In 1991, 5,170 km (3,213 mi) of all-weather asphalted highways connected the island's principal towns and larger villages, and a 5,610 km (3,486 mi) system of subsidiary roads linked all but a few remote villages. In addition to numerous taxicabs, the chief towns are served by private buses, whose services are regulated by the Road Motor Transport Board. In 1991 there were 189,701 licensed private motor cars, and 11,180 commercial vehicles.

Although off the main world shipping routes, Cyprus is served by passenger and cargo shipping lines. Famagusta on the east coast was the main port, but it and the ports of Kyrenia and Karavostasi were closed to national shipping after the Turkish invasion in 1974. (The port of Famagusta was reopened by the Turkish Cypriots in 1978.) The Limassol and Larnaca ports have been modernized and are now considered good deepwater harbors. Other ports include Moni, Vasiliko-Ziyyi, and Paphos. In 1991, 1,210 ships totaling 20,036,000 GRT comprised the merchant fleet, which ranked fifth in the world in terms of deadweight tonnage, at 35,746,900. About two-thirds of the trade passed through Limassol. There are no inland waterways.

The civil airport at Nicosia was used by many international airlines until the 1974 war, after which nearly all flights were diverted to the new international airport built at Larnaca. In 1983, a new international airport opened in Paphos. In 1991, Larnaca international airport handled 2.5 million passengers and 26,600 tons of cargo. Cyprus Airways has services to Middle Eastern countries, but there is no regular internal air service.

12 HISTORY

Numerous Stone Age settlements excavated in Cyprus indicate that as early as 4000 BC a distinctive civilization existed on the island. Living in circular huts, this Neolithic people produced decorated pottery of great individuality, and used vessels and tools ground from the close-grained rocks of the Troodos Mountains. Cyprus was famous in the ancient world for its copper, which, from about 2200 BC, was used throughout the Aegean in the making of bronze. The island is believed either to have derived its name from or to have given it to this mineral through the Greek word *kypros*—copper. Although celebrated also for its cult of Aphrodite, Cyprus was at first only a far outpost of the Hellenic world. Greek colonizers came there in sizable numbers in 1400 BC, and were followed soon afterward by Phoenician settlers. About 560 BC, Cyprus was conquered by Egypt. Coveted by each rising civilization, it was taken in turn by Persia, Alexander the Great, Egypt again, Rome, and the Byzantine Empire. Its Christian history began with the visits of Paul, accompanied first (as described in the Acts of the Apostles) by Barnabas, and later by the apostle Mark. For several centuries after AD 632, Cyprus underwent a series of Arab invasions. The island was wrested from its Byzantine ruler Isaac Comnenus in 1191 by Richard I (the Lion-Hearted) during the Third Crusade. Sold by the English king to the Knights Templar, it was transferred by that order to Guy de Lusignan, under whose dynasty the island experienced a brilliant period in its history, lasting some 300 years. Conquered in 1489 by Venice, Cyprus fell to the Turks in 1571.

The administration of Cyprus by the UK began in 1878, under a convention with Turkey initiated by the British prime minister, Benjamin Disraeli, at the Congress of Berlin and designed to establish Cyprus as a defensive base against further Russian aggression in the Middle East. Upon the entry of Turkey into World War I, Cyprus was annexed to the British crown. It was declared a crown colony and placed under a governor in 1925.

For centuries, under Ottoman and British rule, Greek Cypriots had regarded Greece as their mother country and had sought union (enosis) with it as Greek nationals. In 1931, enosis agitation, long held in check, broke into violence. Government House was burned amid widespread disturbances, and the British colonial administration applied severe repressive measures, including the deportation of clerical leaders. Agitation was dormant until the close of World War II, when it recommenced, and demands that the UK cede the island to Greece were renewed. The National Organization of Cypriot Fighters, led by Col. George Grivas, a retired Greek army officer, began a campaign of terrorism in 1955; upward of 2,000 casualties were recorded. The unity of NATO was endangered by the opposing positions taken on the Cyprus question by Greece and Turkey, but efforts by NATO members to mediate the dispute proved unsuccessful.

Against this background, the prime ministers of Greece and Turkey met in Zürich, Switzerland, early in 1959 in a further attempt to reach a settlement. Unexpectedly, the Greek Cypriots set aside their demands for enosis and accepted instead proposals for an independent republic, with representation of both the Greek and Turkish Cypriot communities guaranteed. A formula for the island's future, approved by the governments of the UK, Greece, and Turkey, also received the blessing of the Cyprus ethn-

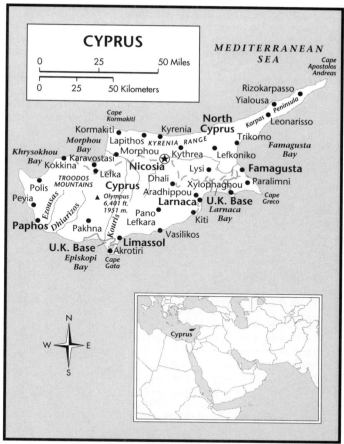

LOCATION: 34°33′ to 35°34′N; 32°16′ to 34°37′E.
TERRITORIAL SEA LIMIT: 12 mi.

arch, Archbishop Makarios III, who returned in triumph to the island from which he had been deported by the British government on charges of complicity with terrorism.

Besides determining Cyprus' legislative institutions, the Zürich settlement provided for a number of instruments defining the island's future international status. Enclaves on Cyprus were set aside for the continuation of British military installations in an effort to restore constitutional order. The UK, Greece, and Turkey, the guarantor powers, had the right to act together or singly to prevent either enosis or partition. In addition, provision was made for Greek, Turkish, and Cypriot forces to be stationed together at a tripartite headquarters. By 1 July 1960, agreement was reached on all outstanding differences, and independence was officially declared on 16 August.

From the outset, the two Cypriot communities differed on how the Zürich settlement would be implemented, and how much autonomy the Turkish minority would enjoy. In December 1963, Turkish Cypriots, protesting a proposed constitutional change that would have strengthened the political power of the Greek Cypriot majority, clashed with Greek Cypriots and police. When fighting continued, the Cyprus government appealed to the UN Security Council. On 4 March 1964, the Security Council voted to send in troops. Turkey and Cyprus agreed, on 10 August, to accept a UN Security Council call for a cease-fire, but on 22 December, fighting again erupted in Nicosia and spread to other parts of the island. The UN General Assembly passed a resolution, in December 1965, calling on all states to "respect the sovereignty, unity, independence, and territorial integrity of the Republic of Cyprus, and to refrain from any intervention directed against it." The General Assembly requested the Security Council to continue UN mediation.

Violent clashes between Greek and Turkish Cypriots nearly precipitated war between Greece and Turkey in 1967, but the situation was stabilized by mutual reduction of their armed contingents on Cyprus. By January 1970, the UN peacekeeping force numbered some 3,500 troops; both Greek Cypriot National Guard and Turkish Cypriot militia also maintained sizable national guards of their own. Although talks continued between the two communities, no agreement was reached on the two basic points of dispute. Politically, the Turks wanted full autonomy, while the Greeks demanded continued unitary majority rule. Territorially, the Turks wanted Cyprus divided into Greek- and Turkish-controlled zones, a position that was likewise at odds with the Greek Cypriot concept of a unitary state.

Meanwhile, tensions had developed between Makarios, who continued to oppose enosis, and the remnants of the military junta that had ruled Greece since 1967. On 2 July 1974, Makarios accused the Greek government of seeking his overthrow and called for the immediate withdrawal of 650 Greek officers in the Cypriot National Guard. Less than two weeks later, the National Guard toppled the Makarios government, forcing the Archbishop into exile and installing Nikos Sampson as president. To counter the threat of Greek control over Cyprus, Turkish Cypriot leaders asked Turkey to intervene militarily. Turkish troops landed on 20 July, but within two days the UN force had been augmented and a UN Security Council cease-fire resolution had taken effect. The coup failed, Sampson resigned on 23 July, and Glafcos Clerides became acting president in accordance with the Cyprus constitution. However, Turkey did not withdraw its forces, and while peace talks were conducted in Geneva, the Turkish military buildup continued. When talks broke down, a full-scale Turkish offensive began, and by mid-August, when a second cease-fire was accepted, Turkish forces controlled about 38% of the island. Makarios returned to Cyprus and resumed the presidency in December. On 13 February 1975, in an action considered illegal by the Cyprus government, the Turkish-held area proclaimed itself the Turkish Cypriot Federated State; Rauf Denktash, a former vice-president of Cyprus and the president of the interim Autonomous Turkish Cypriot Administration (formed after the 1967 crisis), became president. A Security Council resolution on 12 March regretted the proclamation of the new state and called for the resumption of intercommunal talks. The government of the Republic of Cyprus continued to be recognized as the legally constituted authority by the UN and by all countries except Turkey, although its effective power extended only to the area under Greek Cypriot control.

After the de facto partition, Greek and Turkish Cypriot leaders met several times under UN auspices to explore a possible solution to the Cyprus problem. President Makarios conferred with Denktash in Nicosia early in 1977. When Makarios died of a heart attack on 3 August, Spyros Kyprianou became president, and he also held talks with Denktash in May 1979. Further negotiations between leaders of the two communities were held in August 1980, but again no agreement was reached. In February 1982, Greek Premier Andreas Papandreou visited Nicosia, where he pledged to argue the Greek Cypriot cause before the UN, the EC, and the Council of Europe; three months later, in May, the Turkish prime minister paid an official visit to northern Cyprus, drawing protests from the governments of both Greece and the Republic of Cyprus. On 15 November 1983, the Turkish sector proclaimed itself an independent state, the Turkish Republic of Northern Cyprus (TRNC). Denktash was named president, but only Turkey recognizes the TRNC. The UN, which condemned the TRNC's declaration of independence, tried repeatedly to end the partition between north and south, but all proposals were rejected by both parts. The major stumbling block was the south's demand that the estimated 25,000 Turkish troops in the north be withdrawn before negotiations began and the north's refusal to remove the troops before a final solution was reached. In February 1988, George Vassiliou was elected president of Cyprus, and he stated that he would call for reunification talks with the Turkish Cypriots.

Talks between him and Turkish Cypriot President Denktash, who was reelected in 1990, have taken place at intervals since 1988. In 1991, the UN Security Council called on both sides to complete an overall framework agreement. There was speculation in 1994 that UN peacekeeping forces might be withdrawn if some progress is not registered. In February 1993 voting, Glafcos Clerides, a conservative, replaced right-wing George Vassiliou as president.

13 GOVERNMENT

The 1960 constitution of the Republic of Cyprus respects the two existing ethnic communities, Greek and Turkish, by providing specifically for representation from each community in the government. The president must be Greek and the vice-president Turkish. Under the constitution, these officers are elected for five years by universal suffrage by the Greek and Turkish communities, respectively; each has the right of veto over legislation and over certain decisions of the Council of Ministers, a body composed of seven Greek and three Turkish ministers, designated by the president and vice-president jointly. Legislative authority is vested in the 50-member House of Representatives, elected by the two chief communities in the proportion of 35 Greek and 15 Turkish. In January 1964, following the outbreak of fighting, Turkish representatives withdrew from the House, and temporary constitutional provisions for administering the country were put into effect.

Archbishop Makarios, who became president of Cyprus in 1960, was reelected in 1968 and 1973. Following his death in 1977, the leader of the House of Representatives, Spyros Kyprianou, became president; he was elected to two five-year terms in 1978 and 1983. (George Vassiliou, an independent, succeeded him in 1988 and Glafcos Clerides was elected in 1993.) Rauf Denktash was elected vice-president in 1973, but the post has remained effectively vacant since the 1974 war, in the absence of Turkish participation.

On 13 February 1975, subsequent to the Turkish invasion of Cyprus, the Turkish Cypriot Federated State (TCFS) was proclaimed in the northern part of the island, and Denktash became its president. A draft constitution, approved by the state's Constituent Assembly on 25 April, was ratified by the Turkish Cypriot community in a referendum on 8 June. Establishment of the TCFS was described by Denktash as "not a unilateral declaration of independence" but a preparation for the establishment of a federal system. Denktash was elected president of the TCFS in 1976 and again in 1981; elections to a unicameral legislature of 40 seats were held those same years. On 15 November 1983, the TCFS proclaimed itself the Turkish Republic of Northern Cyprus (TRNC), separate and independent from the Republic of Cyprus. In June 1985, TRNC voters approved a new constitution that embodied most of the old constitution's articles. The new constitution, however, increased the size of the Legislative Assembly to 50 seats. In elections held in June 1985, Rauf Denktash won reelection to a five-year term as president with more than 70% of the vote. Dervis Eroglu was made prime minister. Denktash was reelected in 1990.

14 POLITICAL PARTIES

The four principal political parties of the Greek community in 1992 were the center-right Democratic Party (Demokratiko Komma—DIKO), led by former president Spyros Kyprianou; the Progressive Party of the Working People (Anorthotikon Komma Ergazomenou Laou—AKEL), a pro-Communist group; the right-wing Democratic Rally (Demokratikos Synagermos—DISY); and the Socialist Party (Eniea Demokratiki Enosi Kyprou—EDEK). Party representation in the House and percentages of the popular vote won by the parties in the elections of May 1991 were DISY, 20 seats (35.8%); DIKO, 11 seats (19.5%); AKEL, 18 seats (30.6%); and EDEK, 7 seats (10.9%). The Orthodox Church of Cyprus also exercises substantial political influence.

The Turkish Republic of Northern Cyprus held elections for a 50-seat Legislative Assembly in 1985. The right-wing National Unity Party won 24 seats (37% of the vote); the Republican Turkish Party, 12 seats (21%); the Communal Liberation Party, 10 seats (16%); and the New Dawn Party, 4 seats (9%). Other minor parties, including the Turkish Settler Party, won the remaining 17% of the popular vote. In May 1990 elections, the Republican Turkish Party and Communal Liberation Party were losers and, subsequently, boycotted the assembly. Rauf Denktash was elected president one month earlier without party affiliation. The National Unity Party, which he founded, controlled all but five seats in the assembly in 1992.

15LOCAL GOVERNMENT
Elected municipal corporations function in the chief towns and larger villages. The smaller villages are managed by commissions comprising a headman (mukhtar) and elders (azas). Voluntary district committees are responsible for activities outside the scope of the major government development projects. There were six administrative districts for the island: Famagusta, Kyrenia, Larnaca, Limassol, Nicosia, and Paphos.

The 1960 constitution provided for two communal chambers, these bodies having wide authority within the two main ethnic groups, including the power to draft laws, impose taxes, and determine all religious, educational, and cultural questions. The Greek Communal Chamber, however, was abolished in 1965, and its functions reverted to the Ministry of Education. The Turkish Communal Chamber embraces municipalities that are exclusively Turkish. Originally the duties of the Turkish Communal Chamber were to supervise Turkish cooperatives, sports organizations, and charitable institutions. But since the late 1960s, the Turkish communities have maintained strict administrative control of their own areas and have insisted on civil autonomy.

16JUDICIAL SYSTEM
In the Greek Cypriot area, the Supreme Court is the final appellate court and has final authority in constitutional and administrative cases. It deals with appeals from assize and district courts, as well as from decisions by its own judges, acting singly in certain matters. There are six district courts and six assize courts, as well as seven Orthodox Church courts. The church courts have exclusive jurisdiction in matrimonial cases involving Greek Orthodox Church members. Appeals go from these courts to the appellate tribunal of the Church. The Supreme Council of Judicature appoints judges to the district and assize courts.

In the Turkish-held area, a Supreme Court acts as final appellate court, with powers similar to those of the Supreme Court in the Greek Cypriot area. In addition to district and assize courts, there are two Turkish communal courts as well as a communal appeals court.

The Cypriot legal system incorporates a number of elements of the British tradition including the presumption of innocence, due process protections, and the right to appeal. Both parts of Cyprus provide for fair public trials. Both in theory and in practice, the judiciary is independent of executive or military control.

17ARMED FORCES
Under the Zürich agreement, Cyprus was to have an army of 2,000 men, of whom 60% were to be Greek and 40% Turkish. Subsequently, the government passed a military conscription law,

enlisting men between the ages of 19 and 26 for 26 months' service. The Cypriot national guard, which is wholly Greek, comprised 8,000 men and 400 women in 1991, backed by 88,000 reservists. A paramilitary force of 3,700 men provides police services. About 1,000 troops and advisors from Greece were stationed in the south in 1986.

The Turkish community has its own police force and army of 4,000 regulars and 30,000 reserves. A sizable Turkish military presence on Cyprus (about 30,000 in a combined arms corps in 1993) has complemented these native forces since the 1974 intervention.

British forces, 4,200 ground troops and airmen in 1993, are stationed at two British bases, Akrotiri and Dhekelia. British economic aid, pledged in return for the bases, was suspended in 1965 following the outbreak of intercommunal conflict; the UK did, however, spend UK£2.5 million on refugee relief. The UN force (UNFICYP) is composed of a 2,300-man brigade from four nations.

The Cypriot government spends $284 million for defense or 5–6% of gross domestic product.

18INTERNATIONAL COOPERATION
Cyprus was admitted to UN membership on 20 September 1960 and is a member of ECE and all the nonregional specialized agencies. Cyprus is also a member of the Commonwealth of Nations, Council of Europe, and G-77, as well as a signatory to GATT and the Law of the Sea. A cooperation agreement between Cyprus and the EC became effective in June 1973, and an application for membership is pending as of 1994.

19ECONOMY
An agricultural country with few natural resources, Cyprus has been shifting from subsistence farming to light manufacturing. Farm mechanization has reached an advanced stage, and full use is ingeniously made of an erratic water supply. Large trade deficits have been partially offset by tourism and remittances from Cypriots working abroad.

The 1974 coup and the Turkish armed intervention badly disrupted the economy. Physical destruction and the displacement of about a third of the population reduced the output of the manufacturing, agricultural, and service sectors. The lands occupied by Turkish forces accounted for about 70% of the country's prewar economic output. In general, the Greek Cypriot zone recovered much more quickly and successfully than the Turkish-held region, which was burdened with the weaknesses of Turkey's economy as well as its own. Scarcity of capital and skilled labor, the lack of trade and diplomatic ties to the outside world, and the consequent shortage of development aid have aggravated the problems of northern Cyprus. In the south, on the other hand, tourism has exceeded prewar levels, foreign assistance has been readily available, and the business community has benefited from the transfer to Cyprus of the Middle Eastern operations of multinational firms driven from Beirut by the Lebanese civil war. The Republic of Cyprus fared well in 1992, increasing the GDP by 8.2%, compared to only 1.5% in 1991. Unemployment fell to 1.8%. In the north, however, GDP continued to grow slowly, and inflation and joblessness remained high.

20INCOME
In 1992, Cyprus' GNP was $7,070 million at current prices, or $9,820 per capita. For the period 1985–92 the average inflation rate was 4.2%, resulting in a real growth rate in per capita GNP of 5.1%.

21LABOR
In 1991, according to provisional data, the economically active population totaled 279,900, of whom 8,300 (2.9%) were unem-

ployed. Of total domestic employees, 57.7% were employed in services, 27.8% in industry, 13% in agriculture, and 1.5% in other sectors.

Trade unions, legalized in 1937, represent employees in agriculture, forestry, fishing, mining, quarrying, building construction, utilities, governmental services, trade, and general labor. Registration of trade unions is compulsory, but membership in a union is not. Most labor disputes are resolved by government mediation; in 1991, 10,300 man-days were lost as a result of work stoppages. Workers of the Turkish community have their own organizations: the Turkish Cypriot Trade Union Federation and the Revolutionary Trade Unions Federation.

22 AGRICULTURE

Agricultural methods are adapted to the island's hot and dry summers and generally limited water supply. Spring and early summer growth is dependent on moisture stored in the soil from the winter rains, but summer cultivation is dependent on irrigation. About 16.9% of the total land area is arable.

Most farmers raise a variety of subsistence crops, ranging from grains and vegetables to fruits. Since 1960 there has been increased production of citrus fruits and potatoes. Principal crops in 1992 (in tons) included barley, 170,000; potatoes, 170,000; grapes, 130,000; grapefruit, 67,000; oranges, 60,000; lemons, 35,000; and wheat, 12,000. Tomatoes, carrots, olives, and other fruits and vegetables are also grown. The areas that have been Turkish-held since 1974 include much of Cyprus' most fertile land; citrus fruits are a major export. Favorable weather in 1992 helped cereal farmers triple production over the previous year, pushing production of field crops up 90%.

The Agricultural Research Institute, through experiments with solar-heated greenhousing, soil fertility, and water usage optimization, and introduction of new varities of grain, attempts to improve the efficiency of Cypriot agriculture. Unprocessed agricultural products account for 25% of exports.

23 ANIMAL HUSBANDRY

Animal husbandry contributes about one-third of total agricultural production. Output of pork, poultry, and eggs meets domestic demand, but beef and mutton are imported. Sheep and goats, which feed upon rough grazing land unsuitable for cultivation, provide most of the milk products. In 1992, sheep numbered about 310,000, hogs 285,000, and goats 205,000.

Indigenous cattle, kept primarily as draft animals, are decreasing with the advance of farm mechanization. There is no indigenous breed of dairy cattle, but near main towns, dairy stock, mostly shorthorns, are kept under stall-fed conditions, and Friesian cattle have been imported from the Netherlands and the UK. Cattle numbered about 57,000 in 1992.

Livestock products in 1992 included 32,000 tons of pork, 20,000 tons of poultry meat, 113,000 tons of milk, and 8,000 tons of eggs.

24 FISHING

Year-round fishing is carried on mostly in coastal waters not more than 3.2 km (2 mi) from shore. The fish in Cyprus waters are small from the lack of nutrient salts, and the catches are meager. The 1991 catch was 2,690 tons. Fish exports in 1991 were valued at $4.4 million. There is no deep sea fishing. Sponges of good quality are taken, mostly by licensed fishermen from the Greek Dodecanese Islands.

25 FORESTRY

About 175,400 hectares (433,000 acres) are forested; 137,800 hectares (340,500 acres) are reserves managed by the Forest Department, the remainder being natural growths of poor scrub used by village communities as fuel and as grazing grounds.

Besides furnishing commercial timber, the forests provide protective cover for water catchment areas and prevent soil erosion. Their value is also scenic, numerous holiday resorts being situated in the forest reserves. Most numerous by far among forest trees is the Aleppo pine. The stone pine is found on the highest slopes of the Troodos Massif; the cedar, once a flourishing tree, has become a rarity. In the lowlands, eucalyptus and other exotic hardwoods have been introduced. Other important local species include cypress, plane, alder, and golden oak. The demand for timber during World War I resulted in some overcutting, and in 1956 large fires further reduced forests, particularly in Paphos, where 6 million cu ft of standing timber were destroyed. To offset these losses, all felling of fresh trees for timber was stopped and systematic reforestation begun. Most of Cyprus' timber requirements must be met by imports. The timber cut decreased from 152,415 cu m in 1977 to 56,000 cu m in 1991.

26 MINIING

Mineral production reached a peak in 1960, when minerals formed 58% of total exports, but by 1991, they represented only 0.5% of exports; the decline was attributed to depletion of minerals and unfavorable marketing conditions abroad. The place of mining in the GDP similarly declined from 16.7% in 1952 to 1.8% in 1991. In that year, 700 persons were employed in the mining industry. In 1991, the production of most mineral commodities other than sand and gravel, declined even though the value increased from the previous year. The higher value of mineral production was attributed to stable or higher commodity prices and to currency exchange rate variations.

Ownership and control of minerals and quarry materials are vested in the government, which may grant prospecting permits, mining leases, and quarrying licenses. Royalties on extracted mineral commodities ranged from 1% to 5%.

In 1991, the value of exported minerals was $3.7 million. Flotation pyrites and asbestos had been important export commodities, but production of both ceased in 1990. Production in 1991 included 58,500 tons of bentonite, 5,450,000 tons of sand and gravel, and 37,000 tons of crude gypsum. Other mine and quarry products included marl, umber, and lime.

27 ENERGY AND POWER

The principal source of power is steam-generated electricity, which is distributed by the Electricity Authority of Cyprus (EAC) from three generating stations at Dhekelia and Momi. These plants in 1992 had an installed capacity of 538,000 kw. The total number of consumers rose from 19,869 in 1952 to 302,792 in 1992; generation has risen from 12 million kwh in 1952 to 2,404 million kwh in 1992. The grid system included all towns and most villages. The south provides the Turkish sector with all of its electricity, although the EAC is prevented from collecting revenue from the Turkish sector. In 1992, the Turkish sector used 380 million kwh.

28 INDUSTRY

Industries are numerous and small in scale, most of them employing fewer than 10 workers. Working owners make up a large part of the industrial labor force. Manufacturing, encouraged by income tax concessions and protected by import tariffs, primarily involves the processing of local products for both export and the home market, or the production of consumer items such as canned fruits and vegetables; wine, beer and soft drinks; confectionery products, dairy products, and other foods; footwear, hosiery, and other wearing apparel; quilts, pottery, and earthenware; plastic products; vegetable and essential oils; chemical products; and cigarettes and tobacco. Wines, leather handbags and luggage, canned fruits and vegetables, lithographed crown corks, and nails are made principally for export. Major plants include modern flour mills, tire-treading factories, knitting mills, pre-processing facilities, and a petroleum refinery. Furniture and carts are also manufactured. Nine industrial estates have been established.

In 1992, 48,888 persons were employed in manufacturing. Gross output totaled c£1,129.1 million, an increase of 35.4% in real terms from 1985. In 1992, 1,131,604 tons of cement, 5,117 pairs of footwear, and 55.5 million liters of aerated soft drinks were produced.

29SCIENCE AND TECHNOLOGY

The Cyprus Research Center promotes research principally in the social sciences and in history, ethnography, and philology. In addition, Cyprus has four colleges and universities offering degrees in basic and applied sciences. In 1984, total expenditures for research and development amounted to c£1.2 million; 80 technicians and 51 scientists and engineers were engaged in research and development.

30DOMESTIC TRADE

A flourishing cooperative movement provides facilities for marketing agricultural products. There are more than 500 Greek cooperative societies, with some 100,000 members. Many towns and villages have cooperative stores; the towns also have small independent shops, general stores, and bazaars.

Business hours are from 8 AM to 1 PM, and 2:30 to 5:30 PM in winter and from 7:30AM to 1 PM and 4 to 6:30 PM in the summer. Shops are open only in the morning on Wednesday and Saturday. Normal banking hours are from 8:30 AM to noon, Monday–Saturday. Advertising is mainly through newspapers and television; limited use is made of advertising agencies.

31FOREIGN TRADE

With limited natural resources, Cyprus is dependent on other countries for many of its needs. Other than some agricultural commodities, it has few surpluses, and the balance of trade has steadily grown more unfavorable.

Principal export products are fruits and vegetables, beverages and tobacco, wines, and apparel. More than half of total output is exported. Imports reflect the heavy demand for fuels and lubricants, machinery, and other manufactured items, as well as for foods, chemicals, and textiles and fabrics.

Principal exports in 1992 (in thousands of Cyprus pounds), including reexports, were as follows:

Textiles, including clothings	105,551
Vegetable products	47,541
Machinery and electronic equipment	44,253
Mineral products	30,766
Chemical products	26,175
Prepared foodstuffs, beverages, and tobacco	113,983
Other exports	85,144
TOTAL	453,413

Principal imports in 1992 (in thousands of Cyprus pounds) were as follows:

Machinery and electronic equipment	276,231
Vehicles and transport equipment	210,042
Base metals and articles	121,566
Mineral products	132,574
Prepared foodstuffs, beverages and tobacco	161,745
Chemical products	88,059
Textiles	135,978
Other imports	364,560
TOTAL	1,490,755

In 1992, Arab countries took 32% of Cyprus' exports, EC countries received 41%. The UK is Cyprus' leading import supplier and export purchaser, accounting for 19.2% of exports and 11.3% of imports in 1992. There is believed to be a substantial illicit trade in luxury goods smuggled from the Greek Cypriot zone to northern Cyprus and thence to Turkey. Principal official trade partners in 1992 (in thousands of Cyprus pounds) were as follows:

	EXPORTS	IMPORTS	BALANCE
UK	87,033	168,598	−81,565
Italy	7,366	143,940	−136,574
France	8,466	117,673	−109,207
Greece	37,777	101,493	−63,716
Japan	1,250	156,815	−155,565
Germany	20,641	134,378	−113,737
Netherlands	7,881	35,193	−27,312
US	6,889	125,082	−118,193
Switzerland	3,524	29,966	−26,442
Former USSR	11,647	69,870	−58,223
Lebanon	54,818	5,123	49,695
Egypt	29,299	6,161	23,138
Spain	4,891	28,656	−23,765
Other countries	171,931	367,807	−195,876
TOTAL	453,413	1,490,755	−1,037,342

32BALANCE OF PAYMENTS

In 1990, the trade deficit amounted to $1.46 billion, up 8.5% from 1989. Cyprus' hugely increased trade deficits since 1976 have been largely offset by tourist revenues, spending by foreign military forces in Cyprus, remittances from Cypriot workers abroad, and foreign capital inflows.

In 1992, merchandise exports totaled $903.2 million and imports $2,989.9 million. The merchandise trade balance was $−2,086.8 million.

The following table summarizes Cyprus' balance of payments for 1991 and 1992 (in millions of US dollars):

	1991	1992
CURRENT ACCOUNT		
Goods services and income	−223.3	−272.7
Unrequited transfers	36.8	31.0
TOTALS	−186.4	−241.7
CAPITAL ACCOUNT		
Direct investment	66.7	92.5
Portfolio investment	124.3	54.0
Other long-term capital	0.1	51.7
Other short-term capital	54.5	111.1
Reserves	89.8	217.1
TOTALS	335.4	526.4
Errors and omissions	−148.9	−284.7
Total change in reserves	116.8	362.2

33BANKING AND SECURITIES

In 1963, the Ottoman Bank (since renamed the Central Bank of Cyprus) was designated as the government's banking and currency clearing agent. Central bank assets totaled c£578.1 million at the end of 1993. There were 21 commercial banks in Cyprus as of 1993: 8 were Turkish Cypriot banks, 7 were Greek Cypriot banks, and 6 were foreign. Since 1982, 18 offshore banks have been operating. There are no securities exchanges in Cyprus.

34INSURANCE

Insurance companies, mostly British, make available life, fire, marine, accident, burglary, and other types of insurance. Auto collision insurance is compulsory. In 1985, there were 4 life, 36 non-life, and 14 composite companies in operation.

35PUBLIC FINANCE

The fiscal year follows the calendar year. Import duties and income tax are the principal sources of government revenue. The principal ordinary expenditures are education, defense, and police and fire services. From 1989–92, the fiscal deficit averaged some 2.5% of GDP. Additional external borrowing was contracted by the government in 1991 as a result of the emergency situation caused by the Persian Gulf crisis.

Turkish Cypriots use the Turkish lira for currency, and the Turkish government reportedly provides a large part of the TRNC annual budget, most recently a $100 million loan in November 1992 for economic development projects.

The following table shows actual revenues and expenditures for 1990 and 1991 in millions of Cyprus pounds.

	1990	1991
REVENUE AND GRANTS		
Tax revenue	569.27	570.46
Non-tax revenue	136.81	150.13
Capital revenue	0.34	0.24
Grants	4.04	3.78
TOTAL	710.46	724.61
EXPENDITURES & LENDING MINUS REPAYMENTS		
General public service	60.29	67.38
Defense	24.22	26.50
Public order and safety	55.77	60.06
Education	79.39	91.03
Health	48.33	53.66
Social security and welfare	157.94	185.13
Housing and community amenities	31.10	32.92
Recreation, cultural, and religious affairs	6.39	9.18
Economic affairs and services	130.96	112.74
Other expenditures	106.96	120.46
Adjustments	57.92	65.59
Lending minus repayments	10.20	18.09
TOTAL	769.47	842.74
Deficit /Surplus	–59.01	–118.13

In 1991 Cyprus' total public debt stood at c£1,392.09 million, of which c£566.69 million was financed abroad. In 1993, budget expenditures exceeded revenues by $500 million.

36TAXATION

Taxes on expenditure (customs, excise, etc.) and taxes on income are the main sources of government revenue. Income tax was introduced in 1941. Individuals whose taxable income does not exceed c£2,000 are exempt; for others, the tax ranges from 20% on taxable income of c£2,001–4,000 to 40% on income over c£8,000. A withholding system, applying to both salaried employees and wage earners, has been in operation since 1953. On 1 January 1991, a unified tax rate for public and private companies was introduced. A 20% tax is levied on the first c£100,000 and 25% on the excess. Other taxes include a 20% capital gains tax, a value-added tax introduced in 1992, and "special contribution" and defense taxes. Cyprus is steadily conforming its tax code to that of the European Union in anticipation of eventual membership.

37CUSTOMS AND DUTIES

Import duty is payable on a wide variety of commodities; highest rates are imposed on jewelry, caviar, furs, and other items listed as luxuries, and may reach up to 180%. Taxable at lower rates are liquors, cigarettes, spirits, motor vehicles, cotton and cotton piece goods, medicines, undressed hides and skins, paints, and iron and milled-steel bars. Among some 175 items specifically exempt are most raw materials and components used in industry. Essential food items, mineral products, fertilizers, and computers are either duty-free or subject to very low tariffs. Imports from EC countries receive preferential rates of duty. In January 1988, a customs union with the EC went into effect, under which Cyprus exports products to EC countries under a special reduced tariff and quota system over a 10-year period This union will progressively abolish duties on most imports from the EC and adopt the Common Customs Tariff.

38FOREIGN INVESTMENT

The majority of factories are owned by domestic companies but, in most of the major industrial concerns, there has been considerable British and Greek capital. The central government encourages foreign investment that results in the import of new technology or new production methods and improves the quality of the goods produced, especially for export. Any purchase of shares in a domestic company by nonresidents requires approval by the Central Bank of Cyprus. Specific investment incentives include full repatriation of profits and capital gains, accelerated depreciation, and reduced tax rates for public companies during their first seven years of operation; additional incentives are offered to companies using Cyprus as a base for overseas operations. By 1993, there were some 8,000 offshore companies registered. In 1986, the government liberalized the investment code in order to encourage foreign investment. An industrial estate near Larnaca functions as a duty-free zone, and a free-trade zone with warehousing facilities is planned for the Limassol area.

39ECONOMIC DEVELOPMENT

The first development plan (1962–66), designed to broaden the base of the economy and to raise the standard of living, resulted in an average annual real growth rate of 5.4%. The second development plan (1967–71) called for an annual growth rate of 7% in the GDP; actual growth during this period was nearly 8% annually. The third development plan (1972–76) envisaged an annual economic growth rate of 7.2%, but a drought in 1973 and the war in 1974 badly disrupted development programs. Physical destruction, a massive refugee problem, and a collapse of production, services, and exports made it impossible for Cyprus to reach the targets.

Since 1975, multi-year emergency economic action plans inaugurated by the Republic of Cyprus have provided for increased employment, incentives to reactivate the economy, more capital investment, and measures to maintain economic stability. A 1994–98 plan was being drafted by the Planning Bureau.

The principal aid donor to the Republic of Cyprus is Germany, which contributed $268.2 million in 1991. Multilateral aid in 1991 totaled $47.2 million. Aid from all sources totaled $419.1 million. Turkey is the main supplier of development and relief aid to the Turkish Cypriots. Turkey promised TL200 billion Turkish lira in aid.

40SOCIAL DEVELOPMENT

A social insurance scheme that became effective in 1980 is compulsory for all employees and self-employed persons in the Greek Cypriot zone. It provides unemployment and sickness benefits; old age, widows', and orphans' pensions; maternity benefits; missing persons' allowances; injury and disablement benefits; and death and marriage grants. Benefits are financed through contributions of 6% of earnings, paid by employees (11% for self-employed), 6% of payroll, paid by employers, and of 3.5% of earnings, paid by the government on a maximum salary of US$420 or c£214 per week (in 1991).

Although women have the same legal status as men, women's

groups maintain that the divorce law discriminates in favor of men. A 1989 law requiring equal pay for both sexes in private sector employment was satisfactorily implemented by October 1992.

41HEALTH

In 1993, the birth rate was 16.9 per 1,000 people. In 1992, there were 12,300 births. There were 1,199 doctors, 96 pharmacists, and 428 dentists in 1990. In 1985, the number of beds in hospitals and clinics was about 4,450. There are both public and private medical facilities, including about 50 rural health centers. The island has a low incidence of infectious diseases, but hydatid disease (echinococcosis) is endemic. The infant mortality rate was estimated at 9 per 1,000 live births in 1992, and the average life expectancy was 77 years. The general mortality rate in 1993 was 7.6 per 1,000 inhabitants. Between 1991 and 1992, 74% of children were vaccinated against measles. In 1990, 95% of the population had access to health care services, and 100% had access to safe water.

42HOUSING

Village homes in Cyprus are generally constructed of stone, sundried mud bricks, and other locally available materials; in the more prosperous rural centers, there are houses of burnt brick or concrete. A growing population has resulted in a shortage of dwellings, especially in urban areas. This was further aggravated by the 1974 war, which resulted in the displacement of more than 200,000 people and the destruction of 36% of the housing stock. The government provided temporary accommodations for about 25,000 displaced people and embarked on a long-term plan to replace the lost housing units. Between 1974 and 1990, 50,227 families were housed in a total of 13,589 low-cost dwellings.

In 1982, the Cyprus Land Development Corporation was formed to address the housing needs of low- and middle-income families, including the replacement of old housing stock. By 1991, the corporation had disposed of 573 building plots and helped construct 391 housing units. Between 1975 and 1991, the private sector constructed 83,197 housing units. The total number of housing units grew from about 75,000 in 1976 to about 125,000 in 1988.

43EDUCATION

Adult literacy in Cyprus in 1985 was 92.4%. In 1959, the Greek and Turkish communities were made responsible for their own school systems. Education is compulsory for nine years with children attending six years of primary school and six years of secondary. In 1991, there were 390 primary schools with 3,524 teachers and 63,454 students attending them. At the secondary level, there were 3,848 teachers and 47,908 students attending. Of this number, 3,172 were in vocational schools.

Since Cyprus has no college, about 14,000 Cypriot students were studying abroad in 1983, including some 3,000 in the US. The Greek community made plans to open a university for both Greek and Turkish students. Unwilling to agree, the Turkish community instead upgraded the Higher Technological Institute, which is situated near Famagusta, to university level. It opened under the name of Eastern Mediterranean University in 1986.

44LIBRARIES AND MUSEUMS

Cyprus has numerous school, private, and public libraries, with combined holdings in excess of 1.3 million volumes. The Ministry of Education Library in Nicosia (60,000 volumes) serves as a central public library for the Republic of Cyprus. There are also municipal libraries in Famagusta, Limassol, Ktima, Larnaca, and Paphos, and bookmobile service in the Nicosia environs. Among the most important specialized libraries are those of the Cyprus Museum (14,500 volumes), the Phaneromeni Library of the Eastern Orthodox Church (50,000), and the Cyprus Turkish National Library (53,000), all in Nicosia.

The Department of Antiquities is responsible for a wide, continuing program of research at Neolithic and classical sites; on behalf of ecclesiastical authorities, it conserves the cathedrals, mosques, monasteries, and other monuments, and over a period of many years has cooperated with numerous scientific expeditions. The entire range of archaeological discoveries from prehistoric to medieval times is displayed in the Cyprus Museum at Nicosia. In addition to the Cyprus Historical Museum and Archives and the Folk Art Museum in Nicosia, there are important collections in museums at Paphos, Larnaca, and Limassol.

45MEDIA

The Cyprus Telecommunications Authority (CTA) operates the internal communications system. The telephone network is nearly wholly automatic, and the CTA connects Cyprus with 67 other countries; in 1980, its first telecommunications satellite, Makarios, was placed in earth orbit. In 1991 there were 303,822 telephones.

The Cyprus Broadcasting Corp. maintains regular service. Commercial spot announcements and a few sponsored programs are permitted on both radio and television. Radio programming in both AM and FM is transmitted by the CBC on three channels in Greek, Turkish, Arabic, and English. Private radio stations have been allowed since 1990, and there were 30 licenses issued by the end of 1992. The CBC has two channels, and licenses have been granted to four private stations (one of them cable) since April 1993. The main television transmitting station is located on Mt. Olympus. Since 1980, the television service has been linked via satellite with the Eurovision network for live transmission of major events in Europe. In 1991, 207,000 radios and 102,000 television sets were in use.

There were 16 daily newspapers and 8 weeklies published in English, Greek, or Turkish as of 1993. Nicosia has traditionally been the publishing center for the island and the editorial headquarters of nearly all the daily newspapers and weeklies. There is no censorship in the south, and newspapers are outspoken on political matters. The following are the major daily newspapers (with estimated 1991 circulations):

	ORIENTATION	CIRCULATION
Phileleftheros (Greek)	Independent moderate	20,000
Haravghi (Greek)	Communist	13,000
Simerini (Greek)	Conservative	13,000
Apogevmatini (Greek)	Independent moderate	10,000
Agon (Greek)	Independent right-wing	9,000
Halkin Sesi (Turkish)	Independent Turkish nationalist	6,000
Cyprus Mail (English)	Independent conservative	3,500

46ORGANIZATIONS

The government encourages cooperative societies in many ways, including exemption from certain forms of taxation. There are a great number of youth organizations, particularly athletic clubs. In 1962, the island's main commercial organizations, the Cyprus Chamber of Commerce, the Cyprus Federation of Trade and Industry, and the Union of Industrialists, combined to form the Cyprus Chamber of Commerce and Industry. There is also a Turkish Cypriot Chamber of Commerce in Nicosia.

47TOURISM, TRAVEL, AND RECREATION

Although Cyprus is located off the main routes of travel and has few luxury hotels, the island's salubrious climate, scenic beauties, extensive roads, and rich antiquarian sites have attracted numerous visitors. In 1991 there were 27,066 rooms with 56,859 beds available in licensed hotels, primarily located in the larger towns on the coasts, with a 49.7% occupancy rate. Tourism generated $1.02 billion in foreign exchange earnings in 1991. During the

1991 tourist season, Cyprus attracted 1.38 million foreign visitors, of whom an estimated 1.2 million came from Europe.

All visitors must have a valid passport. Tourists from certain countries, including the United States, Canada, and the UK, many stay for up to 3 months without a visa.

[48]FAMOUS CYPRIOTS

Most widely known of Cypriots in the pre-Christian world was the philosopher Zeno (335?–263? BC), who expounded his philosophy of Stoicism chiefly in the marketplace of Athens.

Makarios III (1913–77), archbishop and ethnarch from 1950 and a leader in the struggle for independence, was elected the first president of Cyprus in December 1959, and reelected in 1968 and 1973. His successor as president, Spyros Kyprianou (b. 1932), also was twice elected to the office, in 1978 and 1983. Rauf Denktash (Denktaş; b. 1924), the leader of the Turkish Cypriot community, was elected vice-president of Cyprus in 1973, became president of the TCFS in 1975, and of the TRNC in 1983; he was reelected in 1985.

[49]DEPENDENCIES

Cyprus has no territories or colonies.

[50]BIBLIOGRAPHY

Bahcheli, Tozun. *Greek-Turkish Relations Since 1955.* Boulder, Colo.: Westview Press, 1990.

Bolukbasi, Suha. *The Superpowers and the Third World: Turkish-American Relations and Cyprus.* Charlottesville: The University of Virginia, 1988.

Crawshaw, Nancy. *The Cyprus Revolt: The Origins, Development, and Aftermath of an International Dispute.* Winchester, Mass.: Allen & Unwin, 1978.

Cyprus—A Long-Term Development Perspective. Washington, D.C.: The World Bank, 1987.

Cyprus in Pictures. Minneapolis: Lerner, 1992.

Denktash, Rauf. *The Cyprus Triangle.* Winchester, Mass.: Allen & Unwin, 1982.

Foley, Charles, and W. I. Scobie. *The Struggle for Cyprus.* Stanford, Calif.: Hoover Institution Press, 1975.

Hart, Parker T. *Two NATO Allies at the Threshold of War: Cyprus, a Firsthand Account of Crisis Management, 1965–1968.* Durham, N.C.: Duke University Press, 1990.

Karageorghis, Vassos. *Ancient Civilization of Cyprus.* New York: Cowles, 1964.

Kitromilides, Paschalis and Marios Evriviades. *Cyprus.* Santa Barbara, Calif.: ABC-Clio, 1982.

Koumoulides, John T.A. (ed.). *Cyprus in Transition, 1960–1985.* London: Trigraph, 1986.

Necatigil, Zaim M. *The Cyprus Question and the Turkish Position in International Law,* 2nd ed. New York: Oxford University Press, 1993.

Polyviou, Polyvios G. *Cyprus: Conflict and Negotiation, 1960–1980.* New York: Holmes & Meier, 1981.

Salem, Norma (ed.). *Cyprus: a Regional Conflict and its Resolution.* New York: St. Martin's Press, 1992.

Solsten, Eric (ed.). *Cyprus, a Country Study.* 4th ed. Washington, D.C.: Government Printing Office, 1993.

Spyridakis, C. *Brief History of Cyprus.* Chicago: Argonaut, 1964.

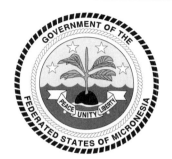

FEDERATED STATES
of MICRONESIA

Federated States of Micronesia

CAPITAL: Kolonia, Pohnpei Island.

FLAG: Adopted in 1978, the flag is light blue, bearing four five-pointed stars arranged in a diamond in the center.

ANTHEM: As of January 1988, the government had not yet adopted an anthem.

MONETARY UNIT: The US dollar is the official medium of exchange.

WEIGHTS AND MEASURES: British units are used, as modified by US usage.

HOLIDAYS: New Year's Day, 1 January; Federated States of Micronesia Day, 10 May; Independence Day, 3 November; Christmas Day, 25 December.

TIME: In Pohnpei and Kosrae, 10 PM = noon GMT; in Yap and Truk, 9 PM = noon GMT.

¹LOCATION, SIZE, AND EXTENT

The Federated States of Micronesia (FSM) is located in the western Pacific Ocean within the Carolinian archipelago. The four states consist of 607 islands with a total area of 7,866 sq km (3,037 sq mi), comprising 702 sq km (271 sq mi) of land, and 7,164 sq km (2,766 sq mi) of lagoons. Comparatively, the area occupied by the Federated States of Micronesia is slightly less than four times the size of Washington, D.C. Kosrae, the smallest and easternmost state, consists of five closely situated islands. Pohnpei consists of the single large island of Pohnpei and 25 smaller islands within a barrier reef, in addition to 137 outer islands, of which the major atolls are Mokil, Pingelap, Kapingamarangi, Nukjuoro, and Ngatik. Truk includes the large Truk lagoon, enclosing 98 islands, and major outer island groups, including the Mortlocks, Halls, Western, and Namwunweito islands. Yap, the westernmost state, consists of 4 large islands and 7 smaller islands surrounded by barrier reefs, in addition to 134 outer islands, of which the largest groups are Ulithi and Woleai. The cumulative coastline distance is 6,112 km (3,798 mi).

The capital city of the Federated States of Micronesia, Kolonia, is located on the island of Pohnpei.

²TOPOGRAPHY

The 607 islands constituting the four states include large, mountainous islands of volcanic origin and coral atolls. Kosrae is largely mountainous, with two peaks, Fenkol (634 m/2,080 ft) and Matanti (583 m/1,913 ft). Pohnpei contains a large volcanic island, with the highest elevation that of Mt. Totolom (791 m/ 2,595 ft). Truk contains 14 islands that are mountainous and of volcanic origin. Yap contains four large high islands, with the peak elevation that of Mt. Tabiwol (178 m/584 ft). The outer islands of all states are mostly coral atolls.

³CLIMATE

The climate is maritime tropical, with little seasonal or diurnal variation in temperature, which averages 27°C (80°F). The islands are subject to typhoons. In May 1986, the devastation caused by a typhoon resulted in Pohnpei being declared a disaster area. The short and torrential nature of the rainfall, which decreases from east to west, results in an annual average

of 508 cm (200 in) in Pohnpei and 305 cm (120 in) in Yap.

⁴FLORA AND FAUNA

There is moderately heavy tropical vegetation, with tree species including tropical hardwoods on the slopes of the higher volcanic islands and coconut palms on the coral atolls. The only native land mammal is the tropical bat. A rich marine fauna inhabits the open sea, reefs, lagoons, and shore areas.

⁵ENVIRONMENT

Solid waste disposal in urban areas is a continuous problem, and the land is threatened by toxic pollutants from mining operations. Micronesia's water supply is also threatened by industrial and agricultural pollutants. Population increases in the urban areas, untreated sewage, and contaminants from industrialized countries in the region add to the problem of water pollution.

United Nations research shows that global warming and the rise of sea levels are a threat to Micronesia's forests, agricultural areas, and fresh-water supply. Pollution from industrial and agricultural sources also threatens the nation's mangrove forests. The fish population is endangered by water-borne toxins and explosives used in commercial fishing. The country also has a problem with the degeneration of its reefs due to tourism. In 1984, the government established an FSM Environmental Protection Board.

⁶POPULATION

The population was estimated in 1992 at 110,000, with, in 1990, 7,200 in Kosrae, 33,100 in Pohnpei, 53,700 in Truk, and 13,900 in Yap. The crude birthrate in 1989 was 32.2 per 1,000 population. The majority of the population live in the coastal areas of the high islands, leaving the mountainous interiors largely uninhabited.

⁷MIGRATION

No significant permanent emigration has occurred; most emigration has been undertaken temporarily for higher education.

⁸ETHNIC GROUPS

The islanders are classified as Micronesians of Malayo-Mongoloid origins. The people of the Nukuoro and Kapingamarangi atolls in southwestern Pohnpei are of Polynesian descent.

9 LANGUAGES

English is the official language and is taught in the schools. The indigenous languages are of the Malayo-Polynesian family. Yapese, Ulithian, Woleaian, Trukese, Pohnpeian, and Kosraean are classed as Malaysian. Kapingamarangi and Nukuoro, spoken on two isolated atolls of the same names in Pohnpei, are Polynesian languages.

10 RELIGIONS

Roman Catholicism and Protestantism have been widely accepted throughout the country following their introduction by missionaries in the 1880s. Protestantism is predominant in Kosrae. In 1993, Roman Catholics comprised 42.4% of the population. Other churches represented are Assembly of God, Seventh-day Adventist, and United Church of Christ.

11 TRANSPORTATION

There were approximately 39 km (24 mi) of paved roads on the major islands, with another 187 km (116 mi) of stone, coral, or laterite-surfaced roads. Over 90% of all vehicles are located on the main islands of Pohnpei, Moen (in Truk), Kosrae, and Yap. The state of Yap provides public bus transportation, primarily used by students. International shipping services are provided by eight companies, some of them Japanese. There are commercial harbor facilities at Kolonia, Moen, Okat, and Colonia. An inter-island shipping service is provided by six government-owned vessels. International and interstate scheduled airline services are provided by Continental/Air Micronesia, Air Nauru, and Pacific Missionary Aviation.

12 HISTORY

The Carolinian archipelago was sighted by European navigators in the 16th century. In 1686, the Spanish captain Francisco Lezcano named Yap Island "La Carolina" after King Charles II of Spain; the name was later generalized to the islands as a whole. Until the end of the 19th century, the islands were under Spanish colonial administration. In 1899, following the Spanish-American War, Spain sold the islands to Germany. Japanese administration commenced at the end of World War I, and in 1947, following World War II, the four states of the FSM came under US administration as part of the UN Trust Territory of the Pacific Islands. The history of the FSM as a political entity began on 12 July 1978, when a constitution drafted by a popularly elected constitutional convention was adopted; it went into effect on 10 May 1979. The government of the FSM and the government of the US executed a Compact of Free Association in October 1982; in November 1986, that compact went into effect. The UN Security Council voted in December 1990 to terminate the FSM's status as a UN Trust Territory. A new capital was built about 10 km southwest of Kolonia in the Palikir Valley; it has served the FSM since 1990. The FSM became an independent state and joined the UN in September 1991. Its congress last met in March 1993.

13 GOVERNMENT

The national executive branch includes the president and vice-president, elected by the Congress from its membership, who serve a four-year term and may not be from the same state. The principal officers of the executive branch are appointed by the president, with the advice and consent of Congress. The judiciary consists of a Supreme Court that applies criminal and civil laws and procedures closely paralleling those of the US. The legislature consists of a unicameral Congress of 14 senators. Of the senators, 4 are elected at large on the basis of state equality and 10 on the basis of population apportionment, with 5 from Truk, 3 from Pohnpei, and 1 each from Yap and Kosrae. The 4 at-large senators serve four-year terms and the remaining senators serve two-

year terms. Congressional elections were last held in March 1991.

John R. Haglelgam of Yap was elected FSM's president in 1987. In May 1991 Bailey Otter of Pohnpei defeated Haglelgam and was elected president.

14 POLITICAL PARTIES

There are no formal political parties.

15 LOCAL GOVERNMENT

The state executive branch consists of state governors and lieutenant-governors, popularly elected for four-year terms. The state legislative branch consists of members popularly elected on the basis of proportional representation, numbering 20 in Pohnpei, 30 in Truk, 13 in Kosrae, and 9 in Yap. Municipalities are districts composed of a number of small communities (sections), some of which may be located in different islands.

16 JUDICIAL SYSTEM

The national judiciary consists of a Supreme Court, headed by a chief justice, and such subordinate courts as are established by statute. Justices are appointed by the president, with the advice and consent of Congress, and serve for life. The Supreme Court has both trial and appellate divisions. It may review cases heard in state or local courts if they require interpretation of the Constitution, national law, or treaties, and it may hear appeals from the highest state court where permitted by a state's constitution.

State and municipal court systems have been established in each of the states. State courts have jurisdiction over all matters not within the exclusive jurisdiction of the national courts. Municipal courts have jurisdiction over civil and criminal matters arising within their municipalities.

The Micronesian Constitution and judicial system are modeled after those of the United States. The civil and criminal laws also parallel those of the United States.

17 ARMED FORCES

The FSM maintains no armed forces. External security is the responsibility of the US.

18 INTERNATIONAL COOPERATION

The FSM participates in such regional organizations as the South Pacific Commission (SPC), South Pacific Bureau for Economic Cooperation (SPEC), and South Pacific Forum. In 1986, the FSM became an associate member of ESCAP. It also participates in the activities of other UN agencies, including FAO, ILO, IMF, UNDP, UNDTCD, UNESCO, UNFPA, UNICEF, and WHO. The government maintains overseas offices in Washington, D.C., Tokyo, Honolulu, and Guam.

19 ECONOMY

The gross national product (GNP) was US$1,500 per capita in 1988. In the same year, Micronesia received US$7.7 million from tuna-fisheries licensing agreements. Island governments employ around 60% of the work force. The private sector, except for wholesale and retail activities, is in an incipient stage of development. The economy faces severe development constraints, including small domestic markets, physical fragmentation, a limited fiscal base, shortages of technical and managerial skills, and large trade deficits.

20 INCOME

In 1989, Micronesia's GNP was estimated to be $150,000 and the per capital national product was estimated to be $1,500.

21 LABOR

The national labor force was estimated at about 50,000 in 1990. Chuuk and Pohnpei estimated their labor forces to be 23,000 and

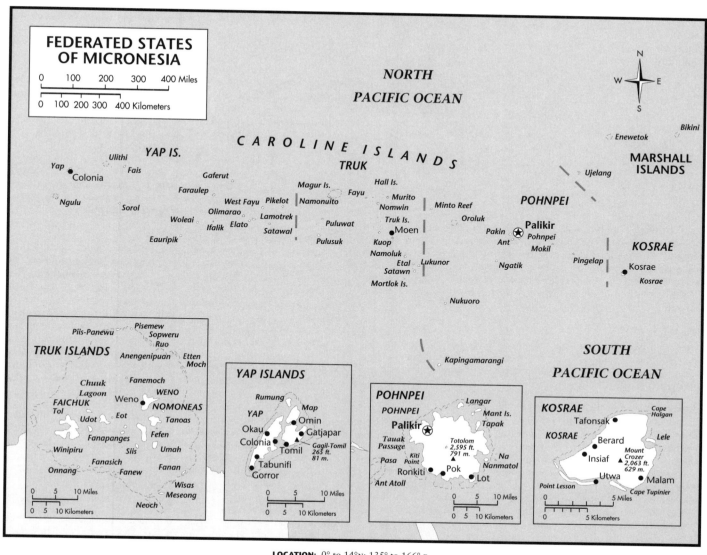

FEDERATED STATES OF MICRONESIA

0   100   200   300   400 Miles

0   100   200   300   400 Kilometers

NORTH PACIFIC OCEAN

CAROLINE ISLANDS

YAP IS.

Yap
Colonia
Ulithi
Fais
Ngulu
Gaferut
Faraulep
Sorol
West Fayu   Pikelot
Olimarao
Woleai   Lamotrek
Ifalik   Elato
Eauripik   Satawal
Magur Is.
Namonuito   Fayu
TRUK
Hall Is.
Murito
Nomwin
Nomwin
Puluwat
Pulusuk
Truk Is.
Moen
Kuop
Namoluk
Etal
Satawn
Mortlok Is.
Minto Reef
Oroluk
Lukunor
Ngatik
POHNPEI
Pakin   Palikir
Ant   Pohnpei
Mokil
Pingelap
Nukuoro
Ujelang
Enewetok
Bikini
MARSHALL ISLANDS
KOSRAE
Kosrae
Kosrae

Kapingamarangi

SOUTH PACIFIC OCEAN

TRUK ISLANDS

Piis-Panewu   Pisemew
Sopweru
Ruo
Anengenipuan   Etten
Moch
Chuuk   Fanemoch
Lagoon
FAICHUK   Weno   WENO
Tol   NOMONEAS
Udot   Eot   Tanoas
Fanapanges   Fefen
Winipiru   Siis   Umah
Fanasich   Fanan
Onnang   Fanew
Wisas
Meseong
Neoch

0   5   10 Miles
0   5   10 Kilometers

YAP ISLANDS

Rumung
YAP   Map
Okau   Omin
Colonia   Gatjapar
Tomil   Gagil-Tomil
265 ft.
81 m.
Tabunifi
Gorror

0   5   10 Miles
0   5   10 Kilometers

POHNPEI

POHNPEI
Palikir
Langar
Mant Is.
Tapak
Tauak
Passage
Kiti   Totolom
Point   2,595 ft.
Pasa   791 m.   Na
Ronkiti   Pok   Nanmatol
Lot
Ant Atoll

0   5   10 Miles
0   5   10 Kilometers

KOSRAE

Cape
Halgan
KOSRAE   Tafonsak
KOSRAE   Lele
Berard
Mount
Insiaf   Crozer
2,063 ft.
Utwa   629 m.
Point Lesson   Malam
Cape Tupinier

0   5   10 Miles
0   5 Kilometers

LOCATION: 0° to 14°N; 135° to 166° E.

17,400 respectively; Yap, 5,800; and Kosrae's, 3,600. Government employment accounted for two-thirds of the monetized-sector employment, and the private sector the remaining third. While unemployment remains high, the economy faces shortages of skilled personnel since over 50% of the population is under 16 years of age. In 1984, a training and trade-testing program was established by the ILO in cooperation with the government. While labor laws are applied mostly without variance in all four states, Pohnpei recently set a minimum wage of $1.35 per hour for private sector workers.

22AGRICULTURE

Agricultural production has traditionally been for subsistence and is based on a system of shifting cultivation in the high islands. Staple crops include taros, sweet potatoes, bananas, cassavas, and breadfruit. Yams are grown on Pohnpei, Kosrae, Yap, and Fais islands. Other vegetables, such as cucumbers, eggplant, head cabbage, Chinese cabbage, bell peppers, green onions, and tomatoes, are also produced. Other fruits include mangoes, papayas, pandanus, pineapples, lemons, and limes, with oranges and tangerines also produced on Kosrae. The ubiquitous coconut palm is used for a wide range of subsistence purposes, and copra is the main cash crop and the nation's leading export.

Black and white peppers were introduced to Micronesia in 1938, but pepper growing only began in Pohnpei (the FSM's most important pepper-producing island) in 1960. Rich volcanic soil and heavy rainfall make gourmet Pohnpei peppers highly regarded.

23ANIMAL HUSBANDRY

Livestock includes pigs, cattle, poultry, and goats. Pigs, traditionally kept by many households for ceremonial purposes, are being upgraded through the introduction of improved strains, two pig farms operate on Pohnpei. There are a small number of cattle, with the largest herd on Pohnpei Island. Eggs are produced commercially, and limited success has been achieved by commercial poultry chicken projects in the states of Pohnpei and Chuuk. Chickens are kept by many households. Goat projects are also operating in Kosrae and Chuuk. A few head of water buffalo are privately raised on Pohnpei and on Pata in Chuuk. As of 1993, the government was encouraging domestic feed production in order to decrease the reliance on imported feed meal.

24FISHING

Inshore marine resources of the reefs and lagoons are harvested mainly for subsistence. The FSM's exclusive economic zone covers some 2.6 million sq. km (1 million sq. mi) of ocean which contain the world's most productive tuna fishing grounds. Although the FSM now has sole ownership of tuna stocks capable of a sustained yield of well over 100,000 tons per year, there is virtually no national participation in its exploitation. The tuna catch is valued at about $200 million annually. The Micronesian Maritime Authority and the National Fisheries Corporation assist in the development and promotion of Commercial fisheries. Pohnpei and Kosroe have embarked on the construction of cold storage and tuna processing plants. The Yap Fishing Corporation plans to invest $20 million in its fleet by 1996. The total catch in 1991 was 1,411 tons.

25FORESTRY

The nation has abundant forestry resources, particularly on the high islands, consisting of approximately 45,200 ha (112,000 acres) of woodland, with some 26,700 ha (66,000 acres) suitable for harvesting. Two privately owned commercial sawmills are operated on Pohnpei; one in Kitti logging mangrove cedar, and one in Kolonia utilizing upland timber. Exploitation of the nation's forestry resources is limited, and virtually all lumber used in construction is imported. Mangrove timber is used for handicrafts and furniture making.

26MINING

There are deposits of phosphates on Fais Island in Yap and bauxite in Pohnpei, Truk, and Yap, but there is no commercial exploitation. Clays, coral, sand, rock aggregate, and quarry stone works supply construction materials.

27ENERGY AND POWER

The nation is dependent on imported petroleum, which supplies about 80% of the total energy requirements. Fuel wood for household use provides most of the remainder. Diesel fuel accounts for over two-thirds of petroleum imports, which. It is used primarily for electrical generation and ship services. Electricity is generated by government power stations located in each state center. About one-half of the electricity produced is used by the government. Little electricity is produced in outer island communities. In early 1993, the state governments of Yap and Kosrae placed priority on the expansion and upgrading of utilities to encourage economic growth.

28INDUSTRY

Manufacturing activity is limited and accounted for only 0.4% of GDP in 1983. Cottage industries involving handicrafts and small-scale processing are carried out in all states and constitute an important source of income for those not integrated into the monetary economy. To expand the industry sector, national and state governments have identified types of industrial activity, several of which were in operation in 1987. These include, in Truk, a small industries center, a garment factory, a coconut-processing plant, a boat-building plant, and a breadfruit flour plant; in Pohnpei, a coconut processing and soap and oil plant, a feedmill, an ice production plant, a brick-manufacturing plant; in Yap, a cottage industries program; and in Kosrae, a small industries center and a wood-processing plant.

29SCIENCE AND TECHNOLOGY

There are no institutions for advanced instruction or research and development in science and technology.

30DOMESTIC TRADE

Domestic commercial activity is dominated by wholesale and retail trade, which accounted for approximately 12% of GDP in 1983. Trade is highly localized in the four state centers of Kolonia, Tofol, Moen, and Colonia.

31FOREIGN TRADE

The FSM sustains a severe trade deficit. Visible imports amounted to $48.89 million in 1983, while exports amounted to only $1.63 million. Exports include copra, marine products, handicrafts, and a limited amount of farm produce sold to Guam and the Marshall Islands. Food, beverages, and tobacco accounted for 37% of imports in 1983; petroleum products, 23.5%; machinery and transportation equipment, 12.9%; manufactured goods, 11.2%; and other items, 15.4%. The US, Singapore, and Japan were the major trading partners, providing over 80% of total imports.

32BALANCE OF PAYMENTS

Foreign receipts totaled $86.1 million in 1983, of which $70.1 million (90.7%) were US government grants, including $31.3 million for capital investment projects. US government transfers provided adequate coverage of the large trade deficit.

33BANKING AND SECURITIES

Commercial banking operations are regulated by the FSM Banking Board. There are two foreign commercial banks: the Bank of Hawaii, with branches in Pohnpei, Yap and Kosrae; and the Bank of Guam, with branches in Pohnpei and Truk. The FSM Development Bank commenced operations in 1982. It provides loans for projects that meet criteria based on the government's development priorities and is authorized to provide loan guarantees to other financial institutions in the FSM. There are 18 credit unions in 1983. The FSM Employees Credit Union was chartered in 1986. Tradable securities are not issued by the FSM government, state governments, or enterprises residing in the FSM.

34INSURANCE

The Public Service System administers life insurance and worker's compensation programs. In 1984, a government-employee group health insurance program was instituted, and in 1987, a retirement pension program, for both state and national government employees, was initiated.

35PUBLIC FINANCE

State and national operational budgets are funded by US (85%) and by domestic revenues generated at the national and state levels (15%). In 1988, revenues totalled $165 million, and expenditures came to $115 million, including $20 million in capital expenditures. As of the beginning of 1988, the FSM government had no outstanding foreign debt.

36TAXATION

National taxes on wages and salaries are levied, as well as a business gross receipts tax. The states are constitutionally limited in the types of taxes they may impose; they may levy sales taxes on alcoholic beverages, soft drinks, and cigarettes. The municipal governments usually levy head taxes and boat license and business license fees.

37CUSTOMS AND DUTIES

As of 1988, specific duties were levied on cigarettes, beer and malt beverages, wine, distilled alcohol, and gasoline and diesel fuel. Ad valorem duties were levied as follows: tobacco, 50%; perfumes, cosmetics, and toiletries, 25%; soft drinks, 2% per 12 fl oz; foodstuffs for human consumption, 1%; and all other products, 3%. Micronesia's import taxes are among the lowest in the Pacific.

38FOREIGN INVESTMENT

There is little foreign private investment. The government has identified 11 priority areas and specific products for the encouragement of foreign investment, which include agricultural-, livestock-, and fish-processing products; real estate development; and cement, brick, and roofing tile production. In addition, joint venture operations involving large-scale manufacturing are welcomed.

³⁹ECONOMIC DEVELOPMENT

The first National Development Plan (1985–89) is the initial stage of the government's 15-year program designed to achieve national self-sufficiency. Funds accruing under the Compact of Free Association were required for implementing the plan, and rephasing of the plan was necessary. A multi-million dollar US-implemented capital improvement plan is nearing completion. It includes new airports, docks, water and sewage systems, paved roads, and hospitals.

⁴⁰SOCIAL DEVELOPMENT

The extended family and clan system, headed by traditional leaders or chiefs, is retained in varying degrees, especially in the outer islands. Rapid Westernization has resulted in an increasing incidence of juvenile delinquency, drug and alcohol abuse, and crime. A wide range of national and state social programs are ameliorating these trends. A social insurance system, instituted in 1983, includes old age, disability, and survivor benefits. Employees contribute 4% of their earnings; employers make a 4% payroll contribution. The basic retirement pension benefit in 1991 was 16.2% of the first $10,000 and marginal rates beyond that level. Survivor payments totaled 60% of the descendant's pension. A UNFPA family health and planning program was instituted in 1986. In spite of Constitutional safeguards, sex discrimination and violence against women are serious problems. Women's roles within the family remain essentially the traditional ones. In 1992, a National Women's Advisory Council was formed.

⁴¹HEALTH

In 1993, the country's population was 114,000, and in 1992, there were 3,700 births. The infant mortality rate in 1992 was 25 per 1,000 live births, and the life expectancy was 71 years. From 1991 to 1992, 88% of the Micronesia's children were vaccinated against measles.

There are hospitals in each state center, with approximately 500 beds. In 1989 there were 39 physicians in the country. In 1986, a community health center was established in Pohnpei, and in 1987, a medical school was started. In the outer islands, primary medical services are provided through dispensaries staffed by health assistants. In 1982, a superdispensary was initiated in the Lower Mortlock Islands to serve 3,769 people scattered on seven atolls. Tertiary medical treatment is provided through patient referral to hospitals in Guam and Hawaii.

⁴²HOUSING

In 1980, the total housing consisted of 11,562 units, of which 47% were in Truk, 32% in Pohnpei, 16% in Yap, and 5% in Kosrae. The average occupancy was seven persons per house. There has been a marked movement away from traditional construction materials toward imported lumber, plywood, and corrugated metal roofing.

⁴³EDUCATION

The state governments are responsible for the provision of education. Elementary education is compulsory up to the eighth grade or until age 15. In 1984 there were 142 primary schools, 9 of them private, with 968 teachers and 18,803 pupils. In 1986 the number of pupils rose to 23, 636. Secondary education was provided through 5 public high schools, 1 in each state center and one in Falalop on the Ulithi atoll, serving Yap's outer islands, and through 5 private secondary schools, 2 in Truk and 3 in Pohnpei. In 1986 there were 4,780 pupils in secondary schools. The only postsecondary institution is the Community College of Microne-

sia in Pohnpei, with 240 FSM students in 1984. FSM students are eligible for postsecondary education grants from the US government and attend institutions mainly in Guam, Hawaii, and the US mainland. In 1984 there were 1,200 students undertaking such education. Vocational education is provided by the Pohnpei Agriculture and Trade School and the Micronesian Occupational College in Palau.

⁴⁴LIBRARIES AND MUSEUMS

Most library materials are contained in the educational institutions; there are no public libraries. The Community College of Micronesia is the depository for documents from the trust territory government's archives in Saipan. There is a small museum in Kolonia, Pohnpei. The Nan Madol archaeological site was designated a historical landmark in 1986.

⁴⁵MEDIA

In 1983, the FSM Telecommunications Corp. provided interstate telecommunications via its satellite ground station in each state center and international connections through the Pohnpei and Truk stations. An interstate and international telex service has been available through the Pohnpei station since 1984. Telecommunications services to all inhabited outer islands are provided by radio links with the Pohnpei, Truk, and Yap stations. In 1986 there were 1,556 telephones.

There are no private newspapers. Newsletters are published by the national government, *The National Union* (twice monthly), and the four state governments, *Mogethin* (Yap), *Uss Me Auus*, (Truk), *Pohnpei Reports*, and *Kosrae State Newsletters*.

There is a state-owned radio station in each state capital that broadcasts in English and local languages; there are also private radio stations in Pohnpei and Truk. Yap has a government-owned television station, and Pohnpei has a private television station. In 1992, there were a total of 1 FM and 5 AM radio stations, 6 television stations, and 1 shortwave station. In the same year, there were 16,000 radios and 1,125 television sets.

⁴⁶ORGANIZATIONS

There are Community Action Agencies in Yap, Truk, and Pohnpei, which organize youth clubs and community self-help projects. Private institutions, most of them church-affiliated, play an active role in youth and community development. Many municipalities sponsor local women's organizations and community centers.

⁴⁷TOURISM, TRAVEL, AND RECREATION

There were 11,805 visitors in 1985. Tourist facilities have been developed in each state but are limited; in 1984 there were an estimated 260 rooms for tourist accommodation. Tourist attractions include the spectacular beauty of the high islands; the rich marine environment; World War II artifacts, including sunken Japanese ships in the Truk lagoon; and remains of an ancient culture on Yap Island, including stone platforms and large circular stones used as money.

⁴⁸FAMOUS MICRONESIANS

John Haglelgam, a former senator in the Congress, was elected president of the FSM from 1987 to 1991.

⁴⁹DEPENDENCIES

The FSM has no territories or colonies.

⁵⁰BIBLIOGRAPHY

Karolle, Bruce G. *Atlas of Micronesia*. 2d ed. Honolulu, Hawaii: Bess Press, 1993.

Kluge, P. F. *The Edge of Paradise: America in Micronesia*. New York: Random House, 1991.

Peattie, Mark R. *Nanyo: The Rise and Fall of the Japanese in Micronesia, 1885–1945*. Honolulu: University of Hawaii Press, 1988.

Poyer, Lin. *The Ngatik Massacre: History and Identity on a Micronesian Atoll*. Washington, D.C.: Smithsonian Institution Press, 1993.

FIJI

Republic of Fiji

CAPITAL: Suva.

FLAG: The national flag of Fiji consists of the red, white, and blue Union Jack at the upper left quadrant of a light blue field, with the Fiji shield in the fly.

ANTHEM: God Bless Fiji.

MONETARY UNIT: The Fiji dollar (F$) of 100 cents is the national currency. There are coins of 1, 2, 5, 10, 20, and 50 cents, and notes of 1, 2, 5, 10, and 20 Fiji dollars. F$1 = US$0.6642 (or US$1 = F$1.5056).

WEIGHTS AND MEASURES: The metric system is official, but some British weights and measures are still in use.

HOLIDAYS: New Year's Day, 1 January; Constitution Day, 24 July; Independence Day, 10 October; Christmas Day, 25 December; Boxing Day, 26 December. Movable religious holidays include Good Friday, Easter Monday, Dewali, and Milad an-Nabi.

TIME: 12 midnight = noon GMT.

¹LOCATION, SIZE, AND EXTENT

Fiji, situated in the South Pacific about 4,450 km (2,765 mi) SW of Hawaii and 1,770 km (1,100 mi) N of New Zealand, comprises some 850 islands, of which only about 100 are inhabited. The island of Rotuma, added to Fiji in 1881, is geographically separate from the main archipelago and has an area of 44 sq km (17 sq mi). The total area (including Rotuma) is 18,270 sq km (7,054 sq mi). Comparatively, the area occupied by Fiji is slightly smaller than the state of New Jersey. Fiji (not including Rotuma) extends 595 km (370 mi) SE–NW and 454 km (282 mi) NE–SW. The largest islands are Viti Levu, with an area of 10,386 sq km (4,010 sq mi), and Vanua Levu, with 5,535 sq km (2,137 sq mi). Fiji's total coastline is 1,129 km (702 mi).

Fiji's capital city, Suva, is located on the island of Viti Levu.

²TOPOGRAPHY

The larger Fiji islands are volcanic, with rugged peaks, and flatland where rivers have built deltas. Coral reefs surround the islands. Viti Levu's highest point, Mt. Victoria, is 1,323 m (4,341 ft); 28 other peaks are over 910 m (3,000 ft). Its main river, the Rewa, is navigable by small boats for 113 km (70 mi).

³CLIMATE

Temperatures at sea level range from 16° to 32°C (61–90°F); easterly trade winds blow during the greater part of the year. Annual rainfall is well distributed and averages 312 cm (123 in) in Suva. At sea level on the leeward sides of the islands there are well-defined wet and dry seasons, with a mean annual average of 178 cm (70 in) of rain.

Cyclone Meli devastated part of Fiji on 27 March 1979, killing 52 persons and leaving thousands homeless. Nearly four years later, on 1 March 1983, Cyclone Oscar claimed several lives and caused extensive property damage.

⁴FLORA AND FAUNA

The larger islands have forests on the windward side and grassland on the leeward slopes. Mangroves and coconut plantations fringe the coasts. Among indigenous fauna are bats, rats, snakes, frogs, lizards, and many species of birds.

⁵ENVIRONMENT

Fiji's natural environment is protected by the National Trust, which under the 1981–85 development plan began to establish national parks to conserve the island's unspoiled landscape, reefs, and waters, as well as indigenous flora and fauna. Endangered species in 1987 included the long-legged warbler and Fiji banded iguana. The main challenges to the environment in Fiji are deforestation, soil erosion and pollution. Over the last 20 years, 30% of Fiji's forests have been eliminated by commercial interests. The rainfall pattern, the location of agricultural areas, and inadequate agricultural methods contribute to the loss of valuable soils.

Pollution of the land and water supply continues from pesticides and chemicals used in the sugar and fish processing industries. The nation has 6.9 cu mi of water with 60% used for farming purposes, and 20% used for industrial activity. The nation's cities produce 0.1 million tons of solid waste per year.

As of 1994, 1 species of mammal, 5 types of birds, 4 species of reptiles and 1 type of amphibian are considered endangered, as well as 25 of Fiji's 1,500 plant species.

⁶POPULATION

Fiji's population at the end of 1992 was estimated at 758,275, an increase of 6% over the 1986 census figure of 715,375. The population was projected to be 800,000 in the year 2000, assuming a crude birthrate of 21.9 per 1,000 population, a crude death rate of 4.6, and a net natural increase of 17.3 during 1995–2000. In 1990, 38% of the population was under 15 years of age. The population density in 1992 was estimatd at 41.5 per sq km (107.5 per sq mi). Suva, the capital, had a population of 71,608 in 1986.

⁷MIGRATION

In the late 19th and early 20th centuries, about 50,000 Indian laborers arrived in the islands to work on sugar plantations. Most recent immigrants come from neighboring islands. There has been steady internal migration from rural to urban areas. There was a substantial increase in emigration by Indians in the immediate aftermath of the coup of May 1987. Most of the more than 35,000 people who left between 1987 and 1993 were Indian Fijians.

⁸ETHNIC GROUPS

The indigenous Fijian population is predominantly Melanesian, with a Polynesian admixture. In 1990, the population was estimated to be 46% of Indian origin, 49% indigenous Fijian, and 5% other Pacific races or European.

⁹LANGUAGES

English is the official language, but Fijian and Hindi are also used in Parliament. Fijian dialects belong to the Malayo-Polynesian language group; the Bau dialect is used throughout the archipelago except on Rotuma, where Rotuman is spoken. Hindustani (a local dialect of Hindi) is the lingua franca of the Indians of Fiji.

¹⁰RELIGIONS

About 53% of Fijians are Christians, primarily Methodist, with 9% Roman Catholic. Among Indian Fijians, 38% are Hindu, 8% Muslim, and 5% Sikh or other Christian.

¹¹TRANSPORTATION

During the late 1970s, Fiji completed a new highway between Suva and Nadi and constructed 885 km (550 mi) of rural roads. As of 1991, Fiji had 3,300 km (2,051 mi) of main roads, of which 12% were paved and 75% were improved earth; registered automobiles numbered about 32,000 at the end of 1991, and other vehicles, 28,000. A private rail system of about 644 km (400 mi) serves most of the sugar-producing areas. Major ports are Suva, Lautoka, and Levuka. In 1991, Fiji had 6 merchant ships in service, with a capacity of 38,000 GRT. Inland waterways consist of 203 km (126 mi), of which 122 km (76 mi) are navigable by motorized craft and 200-ton barges. An international airport at Nadi serves regularly scheduled flights to neighboring Pacific islands, Australia, and New Zealand via Air Pacific. Fiji Air provides domestic and charter service.

¹²HISTORY

Fiji was settled by Polynesian and Melanesian peoples at least 2,500 years ago. The first known European contact came when the Dutch navigator Abel Tasman sighted the Fiji group in 1643. English Captain James Cook visited it in 1774, and Charles Wilkes headed a US expedition there for three months in 1840.

European sandalwood traders, army deserters, and shipwreck survivors also landed on the islands during the first half of the 19th century, a period in which the chiefs of Bau rose to a dominant position. Protestant missionaries from Tonga arrived in 1835, and French Catholic priests in 1844; after a few chiefs had been converted, more and more Fijians embraced Christianity.

In the course of a civil war in the 1850s, Cakobau, the most powerful chief in Fiji, combined forces with the king of Tonga to become paramount chief of western Fiji. Following a period of administrative, economic, and financial difficulties, the 2,000 or so Europeans living in the islands formed an administration under Cakobau, and together they appealed to the UK for assistance. On 10 October 1874, Fiji was proclaimed a possession and dependency of the British crown.

From 1870 to 1916, nearly 50,000 indentured labourers from India arrived to work on European-owned sugar plantations, and by 1920 they had settled as free farmers. European settlers were granted elective representation in the Legislative Council in 1904, and Indians were admitted in 1929. Ethnic Fijian representation was based on traditional hierarchies until 1962, when the council

was reconstituted; the franchise was extended to women, and direct election of Fijian members was provided for. In 1966, the council was enlarged and again reconstituted, and Fiji attained virtual internal self-government. On 10 October 1970, Fiji became a sovereign and independent state within the Commonwealth of Nations, with Kamisese K. T. Mara, head of the Alliance Party, as prime minister. He and his majority party won elections in 1972, 1977, and 1982, but lost the April 1987 elections to an Indian-based coalition of the National Federation Party and the Labour Party, and Timoci Bavadra became prime minister. The new government was short-lived, however; within a month, it was toppled by a military coup led by Lt. Col. Sitivendi Rabuka and aimed at restoring political leadership to ethnic Fijians, and on 20 May thousands of rioting ethnic Fijians attacked Indians. Under a compromise reached the next day, the governor-general temporarily was to head the government, assisted by an 18-member advisory council, including the coup leader and former prime minister Mara and their followers; elections were to be held within six months, and the council was to propose constitutional revisions that would safeguard the political dominance of indigenous Fijians.

On 25 September 1987, however, Rabuka led a second coup. He subsequently suspended the constitution, dissolved the parliament, and declared Fiji a republic. The governor-general, Ratu Sir Penaia Ganilau, was appointed president of the republic, and Mara was reappointed prime minister. Full civilian rule returned in January 1990 when Rabuka gave up his position as Minister of Home Affairs and returned to barracks as head of the armed forces.

The second coup in 1987 and the adoption of the new Constitution in 1990, which favored rural Melanesian control of Fiji, led to heavy Indian emigration, especially among those Indians with sufficient capital to move. This emigration caused serious economic difficulties for Fiji, but it also ensured that Melanesians became the majority. In May of 1992 the Soqosoqo ni Vakavulewa ni Taukei (SVT) or the Fijian Political Party, led by Major-General Sitiveni Rabuka, won 30 of the 37 seats reserved for Melanesians. Rabuka formed a coalition government with the General Voters Party (GVP) and with the informal support of the Fijian Labour Party (FLP) and became Prime Minister. After President Ganilau's death in December 1993 the Council of Chiefs elected Ratu Sir Kamisese Mara as the new President in January 1994. Rabuka's government fell in November 1993 when the legislature defeated the government's budget. New elections were held in February 1994. The SVT won 31 seats, and Rabuka was able to form a coalition government with the GVP.

¹³GOVERNMENT

Before December 1987, the head of state was the British monarch, as represented by a governor-general. The cabinet, responsible to the Parliament of Fiji, consisted of a prime minister and ministers appointed by the governor-general on the former's advice. Parliament consisted of an elected House of Representatives and an appointive Senate. The 52-member House was apportioned as follows: 22 Fijian members (12 elected by voters on the Fijian communal roll, 10 by voters on the national roll); 22 Indian members (12 elected by voters on the Indian communal roll, 10 by voters on the national roll); and 8 general members, Chinese and European (3 elected by voters on the general communal roll, 5 by voters on the national roll). The Senate consisted of 22 members: 8 nominated by the Council of Chiefs (a traditional body that has veto power over bills passed by the House involving native Fijians' customs or land rights), 7 by the prime minister, 6 by the leader of the opposition, and 1 by the Rotuman Council.

The new post-coup Constitution went into effect in July 1990.

It established Fiji as a sovereign, democratic republic with a bicameral legislature. Fiji's president was to be appointed to a five-year term by the Great Council of Chiefs, which would also nominate 24 Melanesians to the 34-member Senate. Nine seats were guaranteed to Indians and other races, and one to Rotuma. The Senate would have veto power over legislation affecting Melanesians. The 70-member House of Representatives was to be elected every five years by universal suffrage under the communal system. In addition to stipulating that the Prime Minister must be held by a Melanesian, the Constitution also guaranteed 37 seats to the Melanesian community.. There would be 27 seats for the Indian community, 1 for Rotuman, and 5 for other races. The constitution provided for an independent judiciary.

14 POLITICAL PARTIES

The major political parties and leaders are Fijian Political Party (SVT—primarily Fijian), leader Maj. Gen. Sitivini Rabuka; National Federation Party (NFP—primarily Indian), Siddiq Koya; Christian Fijian Nationalist Party (CFNP), Sakeasi Butadroka; Fiji Labour Party (FLP), Jokapeci Koroi; All National Congress (ANC), Apisai Tora; General Voters Party (GVP), Max Olsson; Fiji Conservative Party (FCP), Isireli Vuibau; Conservative Party of Fiji (CPF), Jolale Uludole and Viliame Savu; Fiji Indian Liberal Party, Swami Maharaj; Fiji Indian Congress Party, Ishwari Bajpai; Fiji Independent Labour (Muslim); Four Corners Party, David Tulvanuavou.

15 LOCAL GOVERNMENT

Local government is organized under provincial and urban councils. Fiji is divided into 14 provinces, each with its own council. Some members are appointed, but each council has an elected majority. The councils have powers to make bylaws and to draw up their own budgets, subject to central government approval. Suva has a city council, Lautoka a town council, and certain other urban areas are administered by township boards. A few members of urban councils are appointed, but most members are elected on a common roll of taxpayers and residents.

16 JUDICIAL SYSTEM

The 1990 Constitution reorganized the judicial system, but it retains elements of the British system. The courts include the Magistrate Courts, a High Court, and the Court of Appeals. A Supreme Court established at the apex of the system by the 1990 Constitution is not yet functioning.

The magistrate courts are courts of first instance which try most cases. The High Court hears more serious cases in first instance and hears appeals from decisions in the magistrate courts. The appellate courts, including the High Court, may engage in constitutional review.

The 1990 Constitution makes the judiciary independent of the other branches of government. Due process rights are similar to those in English common law.

17 ARMED FORCES

Fiji's armed forces in 1993 consisted of 5,000 men, of whom 4,700 were in the army and 300 in the navy, which has 2 patrol aircraft. Of Fiji's 5 infantry battalions, 2 are deployed abroad in Egypt (MFO) and Lebanon (UNIFIL). Fiji spends about $25 million a year or 2% of GDP on defense.

18 INTERNATIONAL COOPERATION

Since joining the UN on 13 October 1970, Fiji has been a leading spokesman for Pacific island states and has contributed contingents to UN peacekeeping forces in Lebanon (1978) and the Sinai (1982). It belongs to ESCAP and all UN nonregional specialized agencies except IAEA and IMO. A de facto adherent of GATT, Fiji also is a member of the Asian Development Bank, G-77, and

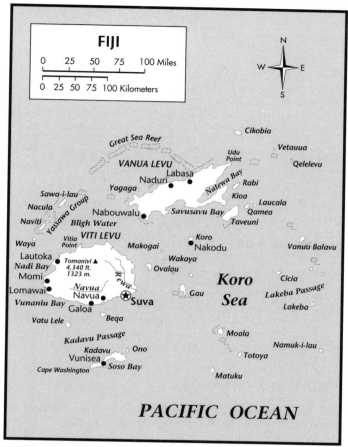

LOCATION: 15°43′ to 21°2′s; 176°54′E to 178°28′w (not including Rotuma, which is at 12°30′s; 177°5′E). TERRITORIAL SEA LIMIT: 12 mi.

the South Pacific Commission and Forum. Its membership in the Commonwealth of Nations was said to have "lapsed," according to a meeting of Commonwealth heads of government held shortly after the September 1987 coup.

On 10 December 1982, Fiji became the first nation to ratify the Law of the Sea. Fiji's delegates had taken a prominent role in framing the document.

19 ECONOMY

Fiji's economy is predominantly based on agriculture and tourism, and is heavily dependent on foreign trade. Since 1989, revenues from tourism have been the country's leading source of foreign exchange, reaching us$225 million in 1992 while exports of sugar and molasses earned us$158 million in the same year. Other chief exports include coconut oil, gold, ginger, molasses, timber, and vegetables. The coup of May 1987 had immediate negative effects on all major sectors of Fiji's economy, but government adjustments, including expenditure cuts, devaluations, and tightening of monetary policy, resulted in short-term stabilization.

20 INCOME

In 1992, FIJI GNP was $1,510 million at current prices, or $2,010 per capita. For the period 1985–92 the average inflation rate was 5.2%, resulting in a real growth rate in per capita GNP of 2.6%.

In 1992 the GDP was $1,558 million in current US dollars. It is estimated that in 1989 agriculture, hunting, forestry, and fishing contributed 18% to GDP; mining and quarrying, 3%; manufacturing, 9%; electricity, gas, and water, 3%; construction, 4%;

wholesale and retail trade, 20%; transport, storage, and communication, 9%; finance, insurance, real estate, and business services, 12%; community, social, and personal services, 10%; and other sources 13%.

21LABOR

In March 1992, Fiji had a wage labor force of 91,803 persons. Many more Fijians engage in subsistence agriculture. In 1992, the entire labor force was 265,200, or 35.2% of the population. Wages and conditions of employment are regulated by agreements between trade unions and employers. The normal workweek ranges from 40 to 48 hours. All unions must be registered, but they are not controlled by the government. The only central labor organization is the Fiji Trade Union Congress (FTUC). In November 1991, the interim government passed several decrees which established stricter conditions needed in order for strikes to be held. The unemployment rate was about 6% in 1992.

22AGRICULTURE

A total of 242,000 ha (598,000 acres), or over 13% of Fiji's area, was used for crop production in 1991. Sugarcane production was 3,500,000 tons in 1992. In 1992, sugar exports accounted for about 31% ($157 million) of total exports, and 90% of agricultural exports. Production of copra and coconuts in 1992 was 19,000 tons and 239,000 tons, respectively; paddy rice output was 33,000 tons. Corn, tobacco, cocoa, ginger, pineapples, bananas, watermelons, and other fruits and vegetables are also grown.

23ANIMAL HUSBANDRY

Beef production was some 5,000 tons in 1992, and the output of goat meat and pig meat was about 1,000 tons each. A breed of sheep highly adapted to the tropics was introduced in 1980. Fiji is self-sufficient in poultry and eggs.

24FISHING

The fishing industry has expanded in recent years, and a new cannery has increased tuna exports. The fish catch in 1991 totaled 31,089 tons, over 25% of which was tuna. Mackerel, snapper, grouper, and mullet are other principal species caught. In the early 1980s, several new fish farms began to produce carp, prawns, oysters, eels, and mussels. In 1990, prepared and preserved fish exports accounted for 6% of total exports, with a value of $26 million.

25FORESTRY

Some 65% of the land area is forested, and 253,000 ha (625,000 acres) are suitable for commercial use. Large-scale planting of pines under the 1986–90 development plan involved reforestation of 50,000 ha (120,000 acres). Output of logs in 1991 totaled 307,000 cu m. Exports of sawn timber and other wood products was valued at $47.5 million in 1992, or 6.5% of total exports. The first exports of pine logs started in 1980.

26MINING

The mining sector of Fiji contributes less than 1% to the GDP. Ownership of minerals is vested in the state, which grants mining and prospecting rights. Production of gold, the most important mineral, which declined during the late 1970s, surged in 1988, when 4,273 kg of the refined metal were produced. Preliminary gold production figures, however, indicate a decline in 1991—to only 2,827 kg. Large copper deposits have been found on Viti Levu, and prospecting continues for oil, manganese, bauxite, phosphates, and other minerals.

27ENERGY AND POWER

The Fiji Electricity Authority, set up in 1966, is responsible for the generation and distribution of electricity, which provides only about 10% of energy consumed. Sugar mills generate their own power, as do hotels and other establishments outside town limits. To lessen dependence on imported oil, the Monasavu hydroelectric project was completed in 1984, with a capacity of 80 Mw. Net installed capacity in 1991 was 200 Mw; output was 472 million kwh. In recent years, exploration for oil and natural gas has taken place, but has been unsuccessful. In December 1990, the government began creating a state-owned petroleum company, Finapeco, to act as the exclusive petroleum importer to Fiji. Finapeco also would be a supplier of petroleum to smaller countries in the region (e.g., Kiribati, Tonga, and Tuvalu). Although no transactions were recorded at the end of 1991, Finapeco is most likely the first step toward creating a Fijian-based petroleum product industry, which might also include a refinery, shipping terminals, and tanker farms in the future.

28INDUSTRY

Fiji's industry is based primarily on processing of agricultural products, mainly sugarcane and coconut, and on mining and processing of minerals. Other major product groups are processed foods, garments, lumber and paper products, chemicals, and cement. Estimated industrial production in 1993 included 415,000 cubic tons of sugar, 3,650 kg of gool, 9,750 tons of coconut oil, and 463,000 cu m of timber. Expensive power, lack of trained labor, and the limited local market have inhibited industrial production.

29SCIENCE AND TECHNOLOGY

Science education is provided by the University of the South Pacific at Suva, the Fiji College of Agriculture, Fiji Institute of Technology, Fiji School of Medicine, the Fiji Medical Association, and the Fiji Society. In 1986, total research and development expenditures amounted to F$3.8 million; 90 technicians and 36 scientists and engineers were engaged in scientific research.

30DOMESTIC TRADE

Fiji has several large trading corporations and hundreds of small traders. The corporations own retail stores, interisland ships, plantations, hotels, travel services, copra-crushing mills, and breweries. Small enterprises range from a single tailor or shopkeeper to larger family businesses, most of which are operated by Indians or Chinese. Businesses are normally open from 8:00 AM to 1 PM and from 2 to 4:30 PM on weekdays, and from 8 or 8:30 AM to 1 PM on Saturdays.

31FOREIGN TRADE

Fiji exports and reexports in 1993 were valued at an estimated F$772.5 million. Imports were valued at an estimated F$1,047.9 million. Australia remains Fiji's main trading partner, followed by New Zealand, Japan, the UK, the US, Singapore, the People's Republic of China, and Taiwan.

32BALANCE OF PAYMENTS

Fiji has an annual trade deficit and an annual deficit on current accounts. Long-term capital inflows, both public and private, generally cover the deficits, however in 1991, the trade deficit was $37 million, down from $84 million in 1990. By 1992, the current account balance registered a surplus (as in 1989), due to increased earnings from exported sugar cane and growing tourism.

In 1991 merchandise exports totaled $434.8 million and imports $553.2 million. The merchandise trade balance was $–118.4 million.

The following table summarizes Figi's balance of payments for 1990 and 1991 (in millions of US dollars):

	1990	1991
CURRENT ACCOUNT		
Goods services and income	−61.2	18.5
Unrequited transfers	1.7	0.4
TOTALS	−59.5	18.9
CAPITAL ACCOUNT		
Direct investment	100.2	33.8
Other long-term capital	−37.7	−32.1
Other short-term capital	20.3	0.8
Reserves	−35.8	−9.6
TOTALS	47.0	−7.1
Errors and omissions	12.6	−11.8
Total change in reserves	−48.1	−10.2

33BANKING AND SECURITIES

The Reserve Bank of Fiji is the central bank; the Fiji Development Bank is the main development finance agency. Commercial banking facilities consist of the National Bank of Fiji and branches of several foreign banks. Currency outside banks totaled F$90.9million in 1991. There is no securities exchange in Fiji.

34INSURANCE

In 1986 there were 11 insurance companies, of which 5 were life insurance firms. Premiums were divided almost equally between life (49%) and non-life (51%) insurance. Third-party motor liability coverage is compulsory.

35PUBLIC FINANCE

The following table shows actual revenues and expenditures for 1992 and 1993 in millions of Fiji dollars.

	1992	1993
REVENUE AND GRANTS		
Tax revenue	497.32	565.92
Non-tax revenue	77.05	96.24
Grants	10.78	13.52
TOTAL	585.15	675.68
EXPENDITURES & LENDING MINUS REPAYMENTS		
General public service	144.44	202.10
Defense	45.90	39.99
Education	133.95	141.22
Health	55.08	56.99
Social security and welfare	29.83	33.27
Housing and community amenities	12.92	14.25
Recreation, cultural, and religious affairs	1.15	8.20
Economic affairs and services	155.10	141.92
Other expenditures	67.86	81.17
Lending minus repayments	−37.74	5.95
TOTAL	608.49	725.06
Deficit/surplus	−23.34	−49.38

In 1992 Fiji's total public debt stood at F$775.57 million, of which F$203.66 million was financed abroad. From 1980 to 1988, total long-term debt outstanding increased by nearly 80%, to about 39% of GDP. From 1988 to 1992, however, public investment reductions enabled long-term outstanding debt to fall to 24% of GDP, with the public debt service equivalent to 7% of exports in 1992.

36TAXATION

Local councils levy taxes to meet their own expenses. National taxes include a nonresident dividend withholding tax (30%), an interest withholding tax (15%), and a dividend tax. On chargeable income the personal income tax is progressive to a maximum rate of 50%, with deductions for dependents. The normal corporate tax rate in 1993 was 35% on chargeable resident income and 45% on profits of branches of foreign companies.

37CUSTOMS AND DUTIES

About one-third of Fiji's revenues derives from customs duties. Tariffs range from 5% to 40%. Duties are levied on the c.i.f. value of the goods. The port and customs service tax, previously chargeable at a rate of 5%, has been abolished and incorporated within the tariff structure as a customs duty at the low rates of 7.5% on most items and 5% on selected items.

38FOREIGN INVESTMENT

The development of existing industries has been made possible largely by foreign investment. Fiji continues to promote overseas capital investment through the Fiji Trade and Investment Board because it requires foreign goods and services to meet many of its needs, including domestic employment. Tax and tariff concessions are offered to approved new industries, and special incentives apply to fuel-efficient or export-oriented enterprises.

39ECONOMIC DEVELOPMENT

Under the ninth development plan (1986–90), the government emphasized diversification of industries and expansion of tourism, and set the goal for real GDP growth at 5% annually. Four key areas that will be crucial for future economic prospects are domestic and foreign development in the sugar sector; trade liberalization in major export markets; the resolution of industrial disputes; and the replacement of middle-level skills lost to emigration caused by political turmoil.

In 1990, Fiji received US$43.5 million in bilateral aid and US$5.7 million in multilateral aid. UN Development Aid totaled US$3.76 million in 1991.

40SOCIAL DEVELOPMENT

General welfare work includes relief of destitution, maintenance of homes for the aged, free medical and legal aid to the needy, child care, and social casework to deal with delinquency. Employed workers are eligible for retirement, disability, and survivor benefits, to which they contribute 7% of their wages, while employers contribute an equal percentage. Employers also pay for workmen's compensation, covering both temporary and permanent disability benefits. A family planning program is included in the ninth development plan. In 1991, the fertility rate was 3.0. In spite of recent reforms, the government discriminates against women in the areas of spousal and offspring rights. Fijian women primarily fulfill traditional roles, although some do attain leadership roles in the public and private sectors.

41HEALTH

Fiji's health standards are relatively high. In 1986, there were 385 doctors, 67 dentists, and 1,572 nurses. Medical facilities included 3 main hospitals and 3 specialized hospitals; a total of 27 hospitals had 1,743 beds. The principal health problem is influenza; venereal diseases have increased in recent years, and infantile diarrhea persists. The total population in 1993 was 747,000, and in 1992, there were 17,600 births. The infant mortality rate was estimated at 24 per 1,000 live births in 1992, and estimated average life expectancy was 71 years. The overall death rate in 1993 was 4.6 per 1,000 people, and the birth rate was 23.6 per 1,000 that same year.

42HOUSING

According to government estimates in 1984, Fiji requires 4,282 new houses each year to maintain adequate housing standards. The Fiji Housing Authority provides accommodations for urban workers and extends credit for houses it builds and sells. In 1986, housing stock totaled 126,100 units, of which 30% were made of corrugated iron or tin, 30% were concrete, 26% were wood, and 9% were bure. The water supply was mostly either individually piped (53%), communally piped (20%), or obtained from wells (13%). Roughly 32% of all dwellings had private flush toilets, while 42% used latrines, and 49% had electricity.

43EDUCATION

Education from primary to university level is available in Fiji, and, though not compulsory, is free through the first 8 years. During 1984, some 98% of children aged 6–11 and about 75% of children aged 12–16 attended school. There are government schools as well as private schools operated by individual groups or by missions under government supervision. In 1991 there were 144,924 pupils and 4,664 teachers in primary schools. During this year, secondary school pupils numbered 61,614. Of these, 5,992 students were in technical and vocational schools. The University of the South Pacific, which opened in Suva in 1968, had more than 2,800 students in 1986. Its students are drawn from several Pacific island states. In 1991, all third-level institutions and universities had 7,908 students and a faculty staff of 277 personnel. The literacy rate in 1985 was 90% for males and 81% for females.

44LIBRARIES AND MUSEUMS

The Ministry of Education runs the Library Service of Fiji in Suva and provides public, special, and school services through 3 mobile libraries and 33 government libraries with a total collection of over 800,000 volumes. Suva maintains its own public library of 77,000 volumes, most of which is a children's collection. The library at the University of the South Pacific showcases 320,000 volumes. The Fiji Museum, established at Suva in 1906, has a collection of Fijian artifacts and Fijian oral traditions.

45MEDIA

Suva and its surrounding area are served by an automatic telephone exchange that had 62,373 telephones in 1991. Fiji is a link in the world Commonwealth cable system and has radiotelephone circuits to other Pacific territories. The Fiji Broadcasting Commission offers programs in Fijian, English, and Hindustani over Radio Fiji on three channels. There is no television broadcast service. In 1991, Fiji had 448,000 radios and 11,000 television sets. The leading daily newspapers, all published at Suva, are the English-language *Fiji Times* (with an estimated circulation of 31,600 in 1991) and *Daily Post* (10,000), the *Fijian Nai Lalakai* (10,500), and the Hindi *Shanti Dut* (9,187).

46ORGANIZATIONS

A few organizations represent specialized cultural, commercial, or professional interests, among them the Chamber of Commerce in Suva. In 1986 there were 1,203 registered cooperatives.

47TOURISM, TRAVEL, AND RECREATION

Tourism slowed following the 1987 coup but has began to recover. In 1991, there were 259,350 tourist arrivals, 33% from Australia, 12% from the United States, and 12% from New Zealand. Gross receipts from tourism amounted to us$211 million, and there were 4,466 rooms in hotels and other establishments, with 12,071 beds and a 52% occupancy rate.

Popular tourist attractions are the beach resorts and traditional Fijian villages. Visitors with valid passports are granted tourist visas renewable for up to six months. Spectator sports include soccer, cricket, rugby and basketball, and Fiji has excellent golf facilities.

48FAMOUS FIJIANS

The best-known Fijians are Ratu Sir Lala Sukuna (d.1958), the first speaker of the Legislative Council in 1954; Ratu Sir George Cakobau (b.1911), the first Fijian to be governor-general; and Ratu Sir Kamisese K. T. Mara (b.1922), the prime minister since 1970 and president as of 1994.

49DEPENDENCIES

Fiji has no territories or colonies.

50BIBLIOGRAPHY

Bayliss-Smith, Tim. *Islands, Islanders, and the World: The Colonial and Post-colonial Experience of Eastern Fiji.* New York: Cambridge University Press, 1988.

Brown, Stanley. *Men from under the Sky: The Arrival of Westerners in Fiji.* Rutland, Vt.: Tuttle, 1973.

Kelly, John Dunham. *A Politics of Virtue: Hinduism, Sexuality, and Countercolonial Discourse in Fiji.* Chicago: University of Chicago Press, 1991.

Lal, Brij V. *Broken Waves: A History of the Fiji Islands in the Twentieth Century.* Honolulu: University of Hawaii Press, 1992.

Roth, G. K. *Fijian Way of Life.* 2d ed. Melbourne: Oxford University Press, 1973.

Scarr, Deryck. *Fiji: Politics of Illusion, the Military Coups in Fiji Scarr.* Kensington, N.S.W., Australia: New South Wales University Press, 1988.

Siers, James. *Fiji: Celebration.* New York: St. Martin's, 1985.

FRENCH PACIFIC DEPENDENCIES

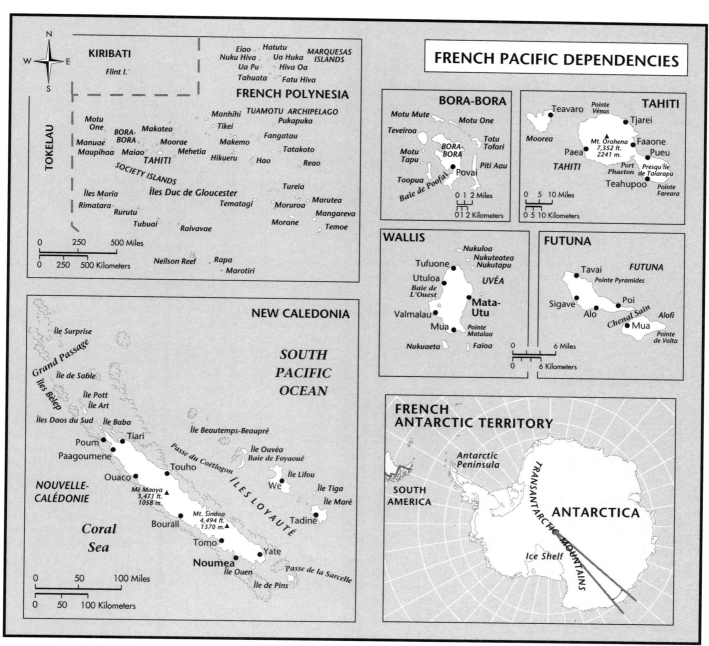

FRENCH PACIFIC DEPENDENCIES

FRENCH POLYNESIA

The overseas territory of French Polynesia (Polynésie Française) in the South Pacific Ocean includes five island groups: (1) The Society Islands (Îles de la Société), discovered by the British in 1767 and named after the Royal Society, are the most important. They include Tahiti (at 17°40′s and about 149°20′w), the largest French Polynesian island, with an area of 1,042 sq km (402 sq mi); Moorea; and Raiatea. The French established a protectorate in 1844 and made the islands a colony in 1880. (2) The Marque-

sas Islands (Îles Marquises, between 8° and 11°s and 138° and 141°w), about 1,500 km (930 mi) NE of Tahiti, were discovered by Spaniards in 1595 and annexed by France in 1842. (3) The Tuamotu Islands, about 480 km (300 mi) s and sw of the Marquesas and consisting of 78 islands scattered over an area of 800 sq km (310 sq mi), were discovered by Spaniards in 1606 and annexed by France in 1881. (4) The Gambier Islands, SE of the Tuamotus, were discovered by the British in 1797 and annexed by France in 1881. Three of the islands, Mangareva, Taravai, and

Akamaru, are inhabited. (5) The Tubuai or Austral Islands (Îles Australes), s of the Society Islands, were discovered in 1777 by James Cook and annexed by France in 1880. Clipperton Island (10°18′N and 109°12′W), an uninhabited atoll sw of Mexico and about 2,900 km (1,800 mi) w of Panama, was claimed by France in 1858 and given up by Mexico, which also had claimed it, in 1932. In 1979, it was placed under direct control of the French government. Total area of the territory is between 3,600 and 4,200 sq km (1,400 and 1,600 sq mi).

The estimated 1993 population was 210,333, of whom about 78% were Polynesian, 12% Chinese, and 10% European. About 55% of the population is Protestant and 30% is Roman Catholic; there are also small animist and Buddhist minorities. French is the official language; Tahitian (a Maori dialect) and English are also spoken. Marine life is abundant, both in the surrounding ocean and in rivers and streams; there are no indigenous mammals.

The territory is divided into five administrative areas (circonscriptions). A 48-member Territorial Assembly is elected every five years by universal suffrage. A Council of Ministers, headed by a president picked by the Assembly, chooses a vice-president and nine other ministers. He assists the French-appointed high commissioner, who is the administrator for the whole territory of French Polynesia. The Economic and Social Committee, composed of representatives of industry and professional groups, is a consultative body. Two deputies and a senator represent the territory in the French parliament.

Tourism earns two-thirds as much as the visible exports; in 1991, 121,000 persons vacationed in the territory. Seven international airlines operate to and from French Polynesia. Tropical fruit, vanilla, coffee, and coconuts are the principal agricultural products. Phosphate deposits, mined on Makatea in the Tuamotu Islands, were exhausted by 1966. The Pacific Nuclear Test Center, constructed on the atoll of Mururoa in the 1960s, employed some 9,000 persons in 1986, including 5,000 military personnel. The Office for Overseas Scientific and Technical Research and the Oceanological Center of the Pacific (which experiments with shrimp and oyster breeding) also operate in the region. A space telecommunications station is based at Tahiti.

Currency is the Communauté Française de Pacifique franc (cfp fr1=$.0100, or $1=cfp fr99.65). Exports in 1988 totaled us$88.9 million; imports, us$765 million.

There is 1 general hospital, 7 secondary hospitals, and 12 medical centers; the total number of hospital beds is 903. There are 161 public, 15 private primary schools, 4 public, 3 private secondary schools, and 18 colleges. Agricultural and technical schools offered postsecondary education.

French Polynesia in 1993 had 3 daily newspapers, 5 AM stations, 2 FM radio stations, and 6 TV stations.

FRENCH SOUTHERN AND ANTARCTIC TERRITORIES

The French Southern and Antarctic Territories (Terres Australes et Antarctiques Françaises), an overseas territory of France, have a total area of 7,781 sq km (3,004 sq mi), not including Adélie Land, and are administered by an appointed administrator and consultative council from Paris. Most of the population in the territories in 1993 were researchers.

The Kerguélen Archipelago, situated at 48° to 50°s and 68° to 70°E, about 5,300 km (3,300 mi) SE of the cape of good hope, consists of one large and about 300 small islands with a total area of 7,215 sq km (2,786 sq mi).

Crozet Archipelago, at 46°s and 50° to 52°E, consists of 5 main and 15 smaller uninhabited islands, with a total area of 505 sq km (195 sq mi).

St. Paul, at about 38°25′s and 77°32′E, is an uninhabited island with an area of about 7 sq km (2.7 sq mi). Some 80 km (50 mi) to the N, at about 37°50′s and with an area of about 54 sq km (21 sq mi), is Amsterdam Island.

Adélie Land (Terre Adélie), comprising some 432,000 sq km (167,000 sq mi) of Antarctica between 136° and 142°E, s of 67°s, was discovered in 1840 by Dumont d'Urville and claimed by him for France.

NEW CALEDONIA

New Caledonia (Nouvelle-Calédonie), a French overseas territory NE of Australia in the South Pacific Ocean, lies between 18° and 23°s and 162° and 169°E. the main island is about 400 km (250 mi) long and 50 km (30 mi) wide, with a surface area of 16,192 sq km (6,252 sq mi). mountainous and partly surrounded by coral reefs, the island is mostly forested or covered with low bush. with its dependencies and protectorates, it has an overall area of 18,576 sq km (7,172 sq mi). native fauna is sparse, but plant life is abundant; among the plants unique to the territory is niaouli, a tree of the eucalyptus family whose leaves are processed for the pharmaceutical industry.

Total population in 1993 was estimated to be 178,056, of whom 42.5% were native Melanesians and 37% were Europeans. French and various Melanesian and other local languages are spoken. Roman Catholicism is the majority religion.

New Caledonia was discovered in 1768 by Louis Antoine de Bougainville and was named by James Cook, who landed there in 1774. Local chiefs recognized France's title in 1844, and New Caledonia became a French possession in 1853. In 1946, it became a French overseas territory, and in 1958, its Assembly voted to maintain that status. Under 1976, 1984, and 1985 laws, New Caledonia is administered by an appointed high commissioner, an executive council, and a 46-seat Territorial Congress, consisting of the complete membership of the four regional councils. New Caledonia has two representatives in the French National Assembly and one in the Senate. The territory is divided into four administrative subdivisions, and there are 32 municipal communes.

The economy is based on agriculture and mining. Coffee, copra, potatoes, cassava, corn, wheat, and fruits are the main crops, but agricultural production does not meet the domestic demand. Nickel represents more than 75% of export value. Coffee, copra, and chromium make up most of the other exports. Trade is mainly with France, Australia, Japan, and the US. In 1989, exports totaled us$671 million, imports totaled us$764 million.

WALLIS AND FUTUNA

Wallis Island and the Futuna, or Hoorn, Islands in the Southwest Pacific constitute a French overseas territory, with the capital at Mata-Utu, on Wallis (also called Uvéa). Lying about 400 km (250 mi) w of Pago Pago, American Samoa, at 13°22′s and 176°12′w, Wallis, 154 sq km (59 sq mi) in area, is surrounded by a coral reef with a single channel. The Futuna Islands are about 190 km (120 mi) to the sw at 14°20′s and about 177°30′w. They comprise two volcanic islands, Futuna and Alofi, which, together with a group of small islands, have a total area of about 116 sq km (45 sq mi).

The Futuna group was discovered by Dutch sailors in 1616; Wallis (at first called Uvéa) was discovered by the English explorer Samuel Wallis in 1767. A French missionary established a Catholic mission on Wallis in 1837, and missions soon followed on the other islands. In 1842, the French established a protectorate, which was officially confirmed in 1887 for Wallis and in 1888 for Futuna. As of 1992, Wallis and Futuna had 17,095 inhabitants. Most of the population is Polynesian; only 2.5% are European. French and Uvean are the principal languages spoken; 99% of the population is Roman Catholic. A high administrator, representing the French government, is assisted by a Territorial Assembly. Principal commercial activities are the production of copra and fishing for trochus. The chief food crops are yams, taro, bananas, manioc, and arrowroot.

INDIA

Republic of India
Bharat Ganarajya

CAPITAL: New Delhi.

FLAG: The national flag, adopted in 1947, is a tricolor of deep saffron, white, and green horizontal stripes. In the center of the white stripe is a blue wheel representing the wheel (chakra) that appears on the abacus of Asoka's lion capital (c.250 BC) at Sarnath, Uttar Pradesh.

ANTHEM: *Jana gana mana (Thou Art the Ruler of the Minds of All People).* A national song of equal status is *Vande Mataram (I Bow to Thee, Mother).*

MONETARY UNIT: The rupee (R) is a paper currency of 100 paise. There are coins of 5, 10, 20, 25, and 50 paise, and 1, 2, and 5 rupees, and notes of 2, 5, 10, 20, 50, 100, and 500 rupees. R1 = 0.0319 (or $1 = R31.370).

WEIGHTS AND MEASURES: Metric weights and measures, introduced in 1958, replaced the British and local systems. Indian numerical units still in use include the lakh (equal to 100,000) and the crore (equal to 10 million).

HOLIDAYS: Republic Day, 26 January; Independence Day, 15 August; Gandhi Jayanti, 2 October. Annual events—some national, others purely local, and each associated with one or more religious communities—number in the hundreds. The more important include Shivarati in February; and Raksha Bandhan in August. Movable religious holidays include Holi, Ganesh Chaturthi, Durga Puja, Dussehra, 'Id al-Fitr, Dewali; and Christmas, 25 December.

TIME: 5:30 PM = noon GMT.

¹LOCATION, SIZE, AND EXTENT

The Republic of India, Asia's second-largest country after China, fills the major part of the South Asian subcontinent (which it shares with Pakistan, Nepal, Bhutan, and Bangladesh) and includes the Andaman and Nicobar Islands in the Bay of Bengal and Lakshadweep (formerly the Laccadive, Minicoy, and Amindivi Islands) in the Arabian Sea. According to 1986 figures, the total area is 3,287,590 sq km (1,269,345 sq mi), including 222,236 sq km (85,806 sq mi) belonging to Jammu and Kashmir; of this disputed region, 78,932 sq km (30,476 sq mi) are under the de facto control of Pakistan and 42,735 sq km (16,500 sq mi) are held by China. Comparatively, the area occupied by India is slightly more than one-third the size of the United States. China claims part of Arunachal Pradesh. Continental India extends 3,214 km (1,997 mi) N–S and 2,933 km (1,822 mi) E–W. India is bordered on the N by the disputed area of Jammu and Kashmir (west of the Karakoram Pass), China, Nepal, and Bhutan; on the E by Burma, Bangladesh, and the Bay of Bengal; on the S by the Indian Ocean; on the W by the Arabian Sea; and on the NW by Pakistan. The total boundary length is 21,103 km (13,113 mi).

India's capital city, New Delhi, is located in the northcentral part of the country.

²TOPOGRAPHY

Three major features fill the Indian landscape: (1) the Himalayas and associated ranges, a geologically young mountain belt, folded, faulted, and uplifted, that marks the nation's northern boundary and effectively seals India climatically from other Asian countries; (2) the Peninsula, a huge stable massif of ancient crystalline rock, severely weathered and eroded; and (3) the Ganges-Brahmaputra Lowland, a structural trough between the two rivers, now an alluvial plain carrying some of India's major rivers from the Peninsula and the Himalayas to the sea. These three features, plus a narrow coastal plain along the Arabian Sea and a wider one along the Bay of Bengal, effectively establish five major physical-economic zones in India.

Some of the world's highest peaks are found in the northern mountains: Kanchenjunga (8,598 m/28,208 ft), the third-highest mountain in the world, is on the border between Sikkim and Nepal; Nanda Devi (7,817 m/25,645 ft), Badrinath (7,138 m/23,420 ft), and Dunagiri (7,065 m/23,179 ft) are wholly in India; and Kamet (7,756 m/25,447 ft) is on the border between India and Tibet.

The Peninsula consists of an abrupt 2,400-km (1,500-mi) escarpment, the Western Ghats, facing the Arabian Sea; interior low, rolling hills seldom rising above 610 m (2,000 ft); an interior plateau, the Deccan, a vast lava bed; and peripheral hills on the north, east, and south, which rise to 2,440 m (8,000 ft) in the Nilgiris and Cardamoms of Kerala and Tamil Nadu. The Peninsula holds the bulk of India's mineral wealth, and many of its great rivers—the Narbada, Tapti, Mahanadi, Godavari, Krishna, and Kaveri—flow through it to the sea. The great trench between the Peninsula and the Himalayas is the largest alluvial plain on earth, covering 1,088,000 sq km (420,000 sq mi) and extending without noticeable interruption 3,200 km (2,000 mi) from the Indus Delta (in Pakistan) to the Ganges-Brahmaputra Delta (shared by India and Bangladesh), at an average width of about 320 km (200 mi). Along this plain flow the Ganges, Brahmaputra, Son, Jumna, Chambal, Gogra, and many other major rivers, which provide India with its richest agricultural land.

³CLIMATE

The lower east (Coromandel) and west (Malabar) coasts of the Peninsula and the Ganges Delta are humid tropical; most of the

Peninsula and the Ganges-Brahmaputra Lowland are moist subtropical to temperate; and the semiarid steppe and dry desert of the far west are subtropical to temperate. The northern mountains display a zonal stratification from moist subtropical to dry arctic, depending on altitude.

Extremes of weather are even more pronounced than the wide variety of climatic types would indicate. Thus, villages in western Rajasthan, in the Thar (Great Indian) Desert, may experience less than 13 cm (5 in) of rainfall yearly, while 2,400 km (1,500 mi) eastward, in the Khasi Hills of Assam, Cherrapunji averages about 1,140 cm (450 in) yearly. Sections of the Malabar Coast and hill stations in the Himalayas regularly receive 250–760 cm (100–300 in) yearly; many areas of the heavily populated Ganges-Brahmaputra Lowland and the Peninsula receive under 100 cm (40 in). Winter snowfall is normal for the northern mountains and Kashmir Valley, but for most of India, scorching spring dust storms and severe hailstorms are more common. The northern half of the country is subject to frost from November through February, but by May a temperature as high as 49°C (120°F) in the shade may be recorded. The daily temperature range in humid, tropical Kerala often averages only 2–3°C (4–5°F), while in dry Rajasthan the range may be 33–39°C (60–70°F). High relative humidity is general from April through September. Extratropical cyclones (similar to hurricanes) often strike the coastal areas between April and June and between September and December.

The monsoon is the predominant feature of India's climate and helps to divide the year into four seasons: rainy, the southwest monsoon, June–September; moist, the retreating monsoon, October–November; dry cool, the northeast monsoon, December–March; hot, April–May. The southwest monsoon brings from the Indian Ocean the moisture on which Indian agriculture relies. Unfortunately, neither the exact times of its annual arrival and departure nor its duration and intensity can be predicted, and variations are great. In 1987, the failure of the southwest monsoon resulted in one of India's worst droughts of the century.

[4]FLORA AND FAUNA

Almost one-fourth of the land is forested. Valuable commercial forests, some of luxuriant tropical growth, are mainly restricted to the eastern Himalayas, the Western Ghats, and the Andaman Islands. Pine, oak, bamboo, juniper, deodar, and sal are important species of the Himalayas; sandalwood, teak, rosewood, mango, and Indian mahogany are found in the southern Peninsula. Some 15,000 varieties of midlatitude, subtropical, and tropical flowers abound in their appropriate climatic zones.

India has over 500 species of mammals, 2,100 species of birds, 30,000 species of insects, and a great diversity of fish and reptiles. Wild mammals, including deer, Indian bison, monkeys, and bears, live in the Himalayan foothills and the hilly section of Assam and the plateau. In the populated areas, many dogs, cows, and monkeys wander as wild or semiwild scavengers.

[5]ENVIRONMENT

Among India's most pressing environmental problems are land damage, water shortages, and air and water pollution. During 1985, deforestation, which, especially in the Himalaya watershed areas, aggravates the danger of flooding, averaged 568 square miles per year. Despite three decades of flood-control programs that had already cost an estimated $10 billion, floods in 1980 alone claimed nearly 2,000 lives, killed tens of thousands of cattle, and affected 55 million people on 11.3 million hectares (28 million acres) of land. As of 1994, 60% of the land where crops could be grown had been damaged by the grazing of the nations 406 million head of livestock, deforestation, misuse of agricultural chemicals and salinization.

Due to uncontrolled dumping of chemical and industrial waste, fertilizers and pesticides, 70% of the surface water in India is polluted. The nation has 443.9 cubic miles of water, of which 93% is used for farming. Air pollution is most severe in urban centers, but even in rural areas, the burning of wood, charcoal, and dung for fuel, coupled with dust from wind erosion during the dry season, poses a significant problem. Industrial air pollution threatens some of India's architectural treasures, including the Taj Mahal in Agra, part of the exterior of which has been dulled and pitted by airborne acids. In what was probably the worst industrial disaster of all time, a noxious gas leak from a Union Carbide pesticide plant in Bhopal, the capital of Madhya Pradesh, killed more than 1,500 people and injured tens of thousands of others in December 1985. India contributes 3.5% of the world's gas emmissions.

The environmental effects of intensive urbanization are evident in all the major cities, although Calcutta—once a symbol of urban blight—has been freed of cholera, and most of the city now has water purification and sewer services. Analogous imporovements have been made in other leading cities under the Central Scheme for Environmental Improvement in Slum Areas, launched in 1972, which provided funds for sewers, community baths and latrines, road paving, and other services. However, as of 1994, only 21 of India's 3,245 cities had effective sewage treatment.

The National Committee on Environmental Planning and Coordination was established in 1972 to investigate and propose solutions to environmental problems resulting from continued population growth and consequent economic development; in 1980, the Department of the Environment was created. The sixth development plan (1979–84), which for the first time included a section on environmental planning and coordination, gave the Planning Commission veto power over development projects that might damage the environment; this policy was sustained in the seventh development plan (1985–90). The National Environmental Engineering Research Institute has field center areas throughout the country.

The Wildlife Act of 1972 prohibits killing of and commerce in threatened animals. In 1985 there were 20 national parks and more than 200 wildlife sanctuaries. In addition to 39 mammals 72 birds are endangered as well as 1,336 plant species. Endangered species in India include the lion-tailed macaque, five species of langur, the Indus dolphin, wolf, Asiatic wild dog, Malabar large-spotted civet, clouded leopard, Asiatic lion, Indian tiger, leopard, snow leopard, cheetah, Asian elephant, dugong, wild Asian ass, great Indian rhinoceros, Sumatran rhinoceros, pygmy hog, swamp deer, Himalayan musk deer, Kashmir stag or hangul, Asiatic buffalo, gaur, wild yak, white-winged wood duck, four species of pheasant, the crimson tragopan, Siberian white crane, great Indian bustard, river terrapin, marsh and estuarine crocodiles, gavial, and Indian python. On the Andaman Islands, the Narcondam hornbill is an endangered species. Although wardens are authorized to shoot poachers on game reserves, poaching continues, with the Indian rhinoceros (whose horn is renowned for its supposed aphrodisiac qualities) an especially valuable prize.

[6]POPULATION

India, the second most populous country in the world, had a population of 843,930,861 according to the census of 1 March 1991. The population increased 23.5% in the 10 years following the 1981 census, slightly lower than the rate in 1971–81. The July 1994 population estimate by the US Bureau of the Census was 919,923,712, with a UN projection of 1,018,673,000 for the year 2000, assuming a crude birthrate of 27 per 1,000 population, a crude death rate of 9 and a net natural increase of 18. The US Census Bureau expects India's population to surpass China's by 2035. The key to India's rapid population growth since the 1920s has been a sharp decline in the death rate because of improvements in health care, nutrition, and sanitation. In 1921, when India's population stood at 251,321,213, the birthrate was 48.1

INDIA

0 100 200 300 400 Miles

0 100 200 300 400 Kilometers

AFGHANISTAN

Srinagar

Jammu

Amritsar

Sutlej

Ludhiāna

Gangānagar

PAKISTAN

Indus

AKSAI CHIN

HIMALAYAS

CHINA

Kāthgodām

Delhi

Yamuna

New Delhi

Ganges

Great Indian Desert

Āgra

Jaipur

Jodhpur

Chambal

Indo-Gangetic Plain

Lucknow

NEPAL

Ghaghra

Kanchenjunga 28,208 ft. 8598 m.

HIMALAYAS

BHUTAN

Dafla Hills

Dibrugarh

Kānpur

Patna

Brahmaputra

Naga Hills

Hyderābād

Nimach

Kota

Allahābād

Benares

Ganges

Shillong

Imphāl

Lakhpat

Gulf of Kutch

Ahmadābād

Bhopāl

Indore

Narmada

VINDHYA RANGE

Son

BANGLADESH

Agartala

Mizo Hills

Jāmnagar

Vadodara

SĀTPURA

RANGE

Nāgpur

Jamshedpur

Hirakud Reservoir

Sambalpur

Calcutta

Mouths of the Ganges

MYANMAR

Surat

Gulf fo Khambhât

Deccan

Chandrapur

Mahānadi

Bhadrakh

Chilka Lake

Bombay

Plateau

Godāvari

Hyderābād

Pune

Bhima

WESTERN GHATS

EASTERN GHATS

Vishākhapatnam

Arabian Sea

Krishna

Bay of Bengal

Andaman Islands

False Divi Point

Ongole

North Andaman

Tungabhadra

Shriharikota I.

South Andaman

Lakshadweep

Kavaratti

Andrôth

Bangalore

Madras

Pondicherry

Cuddalore

Cauvery

Little Andaman

Ten Degree Channel

Kalpeni

Coimbatore

Madurai

Palk Strait

Car Nicobar

Cochin

Alleppey

Nicobar Islands

Minicoy

Cape Comorin

Gulf of Mannar

SRI LANKA

Great Nicobar

INDIAN OCEAN

N
W E
S

India

LOCATION: 8°4′ to 37°6′N; 68°7′ to 97°25′E. **BOUNDARY LENGTHS:** China (not including the 523-km/325-mi Pakistan-China boundary that is part of Jammu and Kashmir), 1,893 km (1,176 mi); Nepal, 1,508 km (937 mi); Bhutan, 573 km (356 mi); Myanmar, 1,403 km (872 mi); Bangladesh, 2,583 km (1,605 mi); total coastline, 5,110 km (3,175 mi); Pakistan, 2,028 km (1,260 mi). **TERRITORIAL SEA LIMIT:** 12 mi.

but the death rate was 47.2; by 1961, when the population reached 439,234,771, the birthrate was still high at 40.8, but the death rate had dropped by more than half to 22.8. A drop in the birthrate from 41.1 in 1971 to 30.2 in 1990/91, presumably attributable to an aggressive program of family planning, contraception, and sterilization, had little immediate impact on the compounded population growth rate, which averaged 1.97% in 1985–90.

The median age of the population was estimated at 22 years in 1990. At that time, 36% of the population was 14 years of age or younger; 57.5% was between the ages of 15 and 59; and the remaining 6.5% was age 60 or above. India is one of the very few countries of the world where men outnumber women (by 437,597,929 to 406,332,932 in the 1991 census). In 1991, the average population density (excluding areas of Jammu and Kashmir under Pakistani and Chinese control) was 267 per sq km (691 per sq mi); density varied from lows of 10 per sq km (26 per sq mi) in Arunachal Pradesh and 33 per sq km (85 per sq mi) in Mizoram to highs of 766 per sq km (1,984 per sq mi) in West Bengal and 747 per sq km (1,935 per sq mi) in Kerala.

In 1995, the population was estimated to be 26.8% urban and 73.2% rural; in 1991, most of India's inhabitants lived in 555,315 villages with fewer than 10,000 residents, of which 73.2% had populations under 1,000. In 1991 there were 98 cities with populations of 250,000 or more. Those containing more than 1.5 million inhabitants each at the 1991 census were Calcutta (4,399,819), Bombay (9,925,891), Delhi (7,206,704), Madras (3,841,396), Bangalore (3,302,296), Ahmadabad (2,954,526), Hyderabad (3,145,939), Pune (1,566,651), Kanpur (1,879,420), Nāgpur (1,624,752), Lucknow (1,619,115), and Surat 1,505,872. By 1995 Bombay had an estimated metropolitan area population of 15.1 million and Calcutta, 11.7 million.

[7]MIGRATION

The partitioning of the South Asian subcontinent to create India and Pakistan in 1947 produced one of the great mass migrations in human history, involving some 20 million people. Historically, major migratory movements have been to and from Sri Lanka, Malaysia, Burma, and Bangladesh. The influx of Muslim refugees (estimated at 280,000 in 1983) from Bangladesh to Assam state has sparked protests among Hindus since the late 1970s; the number of Bangladeshis illegally in India was estimated at anywhere from 2 to 15 million in 1993. Some 53,733 were apprehended at the border in 1991 and turned back. Persons of Indian origin domiciled abroad (excluding Pakistan) reside mainly in Sri Lanka, Malaysia, Nepal, Burma, South Africa, Mauritius, Trinidad and Tobago, Guyana, Fiji, the US, and the UK. Indian minority groups in foreign countries generally do not become assimilated with the local population but live as separate groups, intermarry, and retain their own distinctive culture even after a residence of several generations. An estimated 11,644,000 persons of Indian origin were living abroad in 1984 (excluding those in Pakistan and South Africa).

In 1993 India was harboring nearly 200,000 Tamils from Sri Lanka, including 88,000 in 131 government-run camps, and over 100,000 Tibetan refugees (of which 68,248 had been resettled). There were also smaller numbers of Afghans and of Chakma refugees from Bangladesh.

There has been a steady migration within India from rural to urban areas. Linguistic differences limit the degree of interstate migration, as do efforts by some states to limit job opportunities for migrants and to give preference in public employment to long-time local residents.

[8]ETHNIC GROUPS

India's ethnic history is extremely complex, and distinct racial divisions between peoples generally cannot be drawn clearly. However, Negroid, Australoid, Mongoloid, and Caucasoid stocks are discernible. The first three are represented mainly by tribal peoples in the southern hills, the plateau, Assam, the Himalayas, and the Andaman Islands. The main Caucasoid elements are the Mediterranean, including groups dominant in much of the north, and the Nordic or Indo-Aryan, a taller, fairer-skinned strain dominant in the northwest. The dark-complexioned Dravidians of the south have a mixture of Mediterranean and Australoid features.

[9]LANGUAGES

The 1961 census recorded 1,652 different languages and dialects in India; one state alone, Madhya Pradesh, had 377. There are officially 211 separate, distinct languages, of which Hindi, English, and 17 regional languages are officially recognized by the constitution.

The most important speech group, culturally and numerically, is the Indo-Aryan branch of the Indo-European family, consisting of languages that are derived from Sanskrit. Hindi, spoken as the mother tongue by about 240 million people (30% of the total population) in 1987, is the principal language in this family. Urdu differs from Hindi in being written in the Arabic-Farsi script and containing a large admixture of Arabic and Farsi words. Western Hindi, Eastern Hindi, Bihari, and Pahari are recognized separate Hindi dialects. Other Indo-Aryan languages include Assamese, Bengali, Gujarati, Kashmiri, Marathi, Oriya, Punjabi, Rajasthani, and Sindhi. Languages of Dravidian stock are dominant in southern India and include Telugu, Tamil, Kannada, and Malayalam. A few tribal languages of eastern India, such as Ho and Santali, fit into the aboriginal Munda family, which predates the Dravidian family on the subcontinent. Smaller groups in Assam and the Himalayas speak languages of Mon-Khmer and Tibeto-Chinese origin.

English is spoken as the native tongue by an estimated 10–15 million Indians and is widely employed in government, education, science, communications, and industry; it is often a second or third language of the educated classes. Although Hindi in Devanagari script is the official language, English is also recognized for official purposes. According to government policy, Hindi is eventually to become the national language; for that reason, Hindi instruction in non-Hindi areas is being rapidly increased, and large numbers of scientific and other modern words are being added to its vocabulary. However, there has been considerable resistance to the adoption of Hindi in the Dravidian-language areas of southern India, as well as in some of the Indo-Aryan-speaking areas, especially West Bengal.

The importance of regional languages was well demonstrated in 1956, when the states were reorganized along linguistic boundaries. Thus, multilingual Hyderabad state was abolished by giving its Marathi-speaking sections to Bombay (now in Maharashtra), its Telugu sections to Andhra Pradesh, and its Kannada sections to Mysore (now Karnataka). The Malayalam-speaking areas of Madras were united with Travancore-Cochin to form a single Malayalam state, Kerala. Madhya Bharat, Bhopal, and Vindhya Pradesh, three small Hindi-speaking states, were given to Madhya Pradesh, a large Hindi state, which, at the same time, lost its southern Marathi areas to Bombay state. Many other boundary changes occurred in this reorganization. Bombay state originally was to have been divided into Gujarati and Marathi linguistic sections but remained as one state largely because of disagreement over which group was to receive the city of Bombay. In 1960, however, it, too, was split into two states, Gujarat and Maharashtra, on the basis of linguistic boundaries. In 1966, the government of India accepted the demand of the Punjabi-speaking people, mainly Sikhs, to divide the bilingual state of Punjab into two unilingual areas, with the Hindi-speaking area to be known as Haryana and the Punjabi-speaking area to retain the name of Punjab.

India has almost as many forms of script as it has languages. Thus, all of the Dravidian and some of the Indo-Aryan languages have their own distinctive alphabets, which differ greatly in form and appearance. Some languages, such as Hindi, may be written in either of two different scripts. Konkani, a dialect of the west coast, is written in three different scripts in different geographic areas.

¹⁰RELIGIONS

India is the cradle of two of the world's great religions, Hinduism and Buddhism. The principal texts of Hinduism—the *Rig Veda* (Verses of Spiritual Knowledge), the *Upanishads* (Ways of Worship), and the *Bhagavad-Gita* (Song of the Lord)—were written between 1200 and 100 BC. The teachings of Buddha, who lived during the 6th–5th centuries BC, were first transmitted orally and then systematized for transmission throughout Asia. Jainism, a religion that developed contemporaneously with Buddhism, has largely been confined to India. The Sikh religion began in the 15th century as an attempt to reconcile Muslim and Hindu doctrine, but the Sikhs soon became a warrior sect bitterly opposed to Islam.

Freedom of worship is assured under the constitution. In 1986, an estimated 83.5% of the population adhered to Hinduism. Hindus have an absolute majority in all areas except Nagaland, Jammu and Kashmir, and the tribal areas of Assam. Sikhs (about 0.7% of the 1986 population) are concentrated in the state of Punjab, which since 1980 has been the site of violent acts by Sikh activists demanding greater autonomy from the Hindu-dominated central government. Other religious groups include Muslims (11% in 1986) and Christians (2.6%). The remaining 2.3% consisted of Buddhists, Jains, tribal religionists, and other groups. Muslims comprise more than 10% of the population in Maharashtra, Bihar, Karnataka, and West Bengal, and more than 30% of the total population in Assam and Kerala. Christians form the majority in Nagaland and are a sizable minority in Kerala. The Jains are an important minority in Rajasthan and Gujarat, and the Parsees (Zoroastrians) in Maharashtra.

The caste system is a distinct feature of Hinduism, wherein every person either is born into one of four groups—Brahmans (priests and scholars), Kshatriyas (warriors and rulers), Vaisyas (shopkeepers, artisans, and farmers), and Sudras (farm laborers and menial workers)—or is casteless and thus untouchable (now known as Harijan, from the term used by Gandhi). Within the four major castes there are 2,500 to 3,000 subcastes based upon occupation, geographic location, and other factors. Although the constitution outlaws caste distinctions and discrimination, especially those applying to untouchability, progress in changing customs has been slow.

¹¹TRANSPORTATION

The railway system is highly developed and is the major means of long-distance internal transport. In 1991, the railways spanned some 61,850 km (38,430 mi), forming the largest system in Asia and the fourth largest in the world. Indian railways operated about 11,000 trains per day, connecting 7,021 stations; 10,000 km (6,200 mi) of track were electrified by 1992. Virtually all railways are state owned. Passenger traffic increased from 2,653 million riders in 1972/73 to 3,700 million in 1991/92, and freight traffic from 201 million to 330 million tons. The state-owned railways are the nation's largest public enterprise. In October 1984, India's first subway began operation in Calcutta over 3 km (1.9 mi) of track; the line will eventually be extended to 16.4 km (10.2 mi).

The national and state road network in 1991 was about 1,120,000 km (695,970 mi), of which 515,000 km (320,020 mi) were hard-surfaced. In the seventh development plan (1985–90), R293.4 billion was earmarked for transportation and communi-

cations. In 1991 there were 4,667,749 motor vehicles, including 2,490,805 automobiles, and taxis; 1,845,377 trucks and jeeps; and 331,567 buses.

India has about 16,200 km (10,070 mi) of inland waterways, with 3,630 km (2,250 mi) navigable by large vessels. Most important are the Ganges, Brahmaputra, Godavari, and Krishna rivers and the coastal plain canals of Kerala, Madras, Andhra Pradesh, and Orissa. Canals span some 4,300 km (2,700 mi), but only 331 km (206 mi) are used by motorized vessels.

In 1991, India's merchant fleet totaled 293 vessels of 5.96 million GRT. The tonnage was sufficient to handle almost all of the country's coastal trade and about 37% of its trade with adjacent countries; the rest of India's trade is handled by foreign ships. Eleven major ports handle the bulk of the import-export traffic; the leading ports are Bombay and Mormugao. There are 140 smaller ports along the Indian coastline.

International airports are at Bombay (Santa Cruz), Calcutta (Dum Dum), Delhi (Indira Gandhi), Madras (Meenambakkam), and Trivandrum. A total of 202 airports have paved runways. The Indian Airlines Corp., a nationalized industry, operates all internal flights and services to neighboring countries with daily flights to 60 cities. Air-India, also government owned, operates long-distance services to foreign countries on five continents. During 1992, Indian Airlines and Air-India carried an estimated 10.9 million passengers and performed 429.4 million freight ton-kilometers of service. A new national airline, Vayudoot, was established in 1981 to provide service to otherwise inaccessible areas in the northeast; in 1992 it carried 150,700 domestic passengers to 55 different destinations. Private airlines are growing in importance also.

¹²HISTORY

India is one of the oldest continuously inhabited regions in the world. In Harappa, an area in the Indus Valley (now in Pakistan), between 3000 and 2000 BC, scores of thriving municipalities developed a distinct urban culture. This riverain civilization disappeared around 1500–1200 BC, probably owing to the arrival of Aryan (Indo-European-speaking) invaders, who began pouring through Afghanistan onto the lush plains of northern India. There followed over a thousand years of instability, of petty states and larger kingdoms, as one invading group after another contended for power. During this period, Indian village and family patterns, along with Brahmanism—the ancient form of Hinduism—and its caste system, became well established. Among the distinguished oral literature surviving from this period are two anonymous Sanskrit epics, the *Ramayana* (traditionally attributed to the legendary poet Valmiki) and the *Mahabharata* (the longest poem in the world, containing over 100,000 verses, including the *Bhagavad-Gita*).

The South Asian subcontinent already had a population of about 30 million, of whom approximately 20 million lived in the Ganges Basin, when Alexander the Great invaded the Indus Valley in 326 BC. His successors were absorbed by the new Maurya dynasty (c.321–c.184 BC); under Chandragupta (r. c.321–c.297 BC), from his capital at Pataliputra (now Patna), the Mauryans subdued most of northern India and what is now Bangladesh. His successor, Asoka (r.273–232 BC), put all of India under unified control for the first time; an early convert to Buddhism, his regime remembered for its sectarian tolerance, as well as for remarkable administrative, legal, and cultural achievements. Many of the Buddhist monuments and elaborately carved cave temples found at Sarnath, Ajanta, Bodhgaya, and other places in India date from the reigns of Asoka and his Buddhist successors.

In the years following Asoka, India divided again into a patchwork of kingdoms, as other invaders arrived from central and western Asia. In the process, Hinduism prevailed over Buddhism, which found wide acceptance in Asian lands other than India, its birthplace. Although predated by other states of Brahmanic origin, true Hindu kingdoms first appeared in the Peninsula after the 4th century AD. The era of the Gupta dynasty rule (AD 320–c.535) was a golden age of art, literature, and science in India. And Hindu princes of the Rajput sub-caste, ruling in the north, reached their peak of power from AD 700 to 1000, although their descendants retained much of their influence well into British days.

In the 8th century, the first of several waves of Islamic invaders appeared at the traditional northwest portals; between the years 1000 and 1030, Mahmud of Ghazni made 17 forays into the subcontinent. The first Muslim sultan of Delhi was Kutb-ud-din (r. c.1195–1210), and Islam gradually spread eastward and southward, reaching its greatest territorial and cultural extent under the Mughal (or Mogul) dynasty. "Mughal" comes from the Farsi word for Mongol, and the Mughals were descendants of the great 14th-century Mongol conqueror Timur (also known as "Timur the Lame" or Tamerlane), a descendant in turn of Genghis Khan.

One of the Timurid princes, the great Babur (r.1526–30), captured Kabul in 1504 and defeated the Sultan of Delhi in 1526, becoming the first of the Mughals to proclaim himself emperor of India. It was not until 1560 that Akbar (r.1556–1605), Babur's grandson, extended the dynasty's authority over all of northern India, and it was Akbar who was the first of the Muslim emperors to attempt the establishment of a national state in alliance with Hindu rajahs (kings). Though illiterate, he was a great patron of art and literature. Among his successors were Shah Jahan and his son Aurangzeb, who left their imprint in massive palaces and mosques, superb fortresses (like the Lahore fort), dazzling mausoleums (like the Taj Mahal at Agra), elaborate formal gardens (like those in Srinagar), and the abandoned city of Fatehpur Sikri (37 km/23 mi w of Agra). Under Aurangzeb (r.1658–1707), who seized his father's throne, the Mughal Empire reached its greatest extent and then began its decline, largely the result of his repressive policies. The Hindu Marathas fought the Mughals and established their own empire in western India.

Vasco da Gama reached India's southwest coast by sea in 1498, and for a century the Portuguese had a monopoly over Indian sea. Although it continued to hold bits of Indian territory until 1961, Portugal lost its dominant position as early as 1612, when forces controlled by the British East India Company defeated the Portuguese and won concessions from the declining Mughals. The Company, which had been established in 1600, had permanent trading settlements in Madras, Bombay, and Calcutta by 1690. Threatened by the French East India Company, which was founded in 1664, the two companies fought each other as part of their nations' struggle for supremacy in Europe and the western hemisphere in the 18th century. They both allied with rival Indian princes and recruited soldiers (sepoys) locally, but the French and their allies suffered disastrous defeats in 1756 and 1757, against the backdrop of the larger sweep of the Seven Years' War (1756–63), and by 1761, France was no longer a power in India. The architect of the British triumph, later known as the founder of British India, was Robert Clive, later Baron, who became governor of the Company's Bengal Presidency in 1764, to be followed by Warren Hastings and Lord Cornwallis in the years before 1800. The Company's rule spread up the Gangetic plain to Oudh and Delhi, and eventually, to western India where the Maratha Confederacy, the alliance of independent Indian states that had succeeded the Mughal Empire there, was reduced to a group of relatively weak principalities owing fealty to the British in 1818.

The British Government took direct control of the Company's Indian domain during the Sepoy Mutiny (1857–59), a widespread rebellion by Indian soldiers in the company's service, and in 1859,

Queen Victoria was proclaimed Empress of India. The succeeding decades were characterized by significant economic and political development, but also by a growing cultural and political gap between Indians and British. Indian troops were deployed elsewhere in the world by the Crown in defense of British interests but without any recourse of Indian views.

Nationalism and Independence

In this century, while the British moved gradually to expand local self-rule along federal lines, British power was increasingly challenged by the rise of indigenous movements advocating a faster pace. A modern Indian nationalism began to grow as a result of the influence of the influence of groups like the Arya Samaj, in the last century, of Western culture and education among the elite, and of the Indian National Congress (INC). Founded as an Anglophile debating society in 1885, the INC grew into a movement leading agitation for greater self-rule in the first 30 years of this century. Under the leadership of Mohandas Karamchand Gandhi (called the Mahatma, or Great Soul) and other nationalist leaders, such as Motilal and Jawaharlal Nehru, the INC began to attract mass support in the 1930s with the success of its non-cooperation campaigns and its advocacy of education, cottage industries, self-help, an end to the caste system, and non-violent struggle. But Muslims had also been politicized, beginning with the abortive partition of Bengal during the period 1905–1912. And despite the INC leadership's commitment to secularism, as the movement evolved under Gandhi, its leadership style appeared—to Muslims—uniquely Hindu, leading Indian Muslims to look to the protection of their interests in the formation of their own organization, the All-India Muslim League (ML).

National and provincial elections in the mid-1930s persuaded many Muslims that the power the majority Hindu population could exercise at the ballot box, however secular the INC's outlook, could leave them as a permanent electoral minority in any single democratic polity that would follow British rule. Sentiment in the Muslim League began to coalesce around the "two nation" theory propounded by the poet Iqbal, who argued that Muslims and Hindus were separate nations and that Muslims required creation of an independent Islamic state for their protection and fulfillment. A prominent Bombay attorney, Muhammad Ali Jinnah, who came to be known as "Quaid-i-Azam" (Great Leader), led the fight for a separate Muslim state to be known as Pakistan, a goal formally endorsed by the ML in Lahore in 1940.

Mahatma Gandhi, meanwhile, had broadened his demand in 1929 from self-rule to independence in 1929; in the 1930s, his campaigns of non-violent non-cooperation and civil disobedience electrified the countryside. In 1942, with British fortunes at a new low and the Japanese successful everywhere in Asia, Gandhi rejected a British appeal to postpone further talks on Indian self-rule until the end of World War II. Declining to support the British (and Allied) war effort and demanding immediate British withdrawal from India, he launched a "Quit India" campaign. In retaliation, Gandhi and most of India's nationalist leaders were jailed.

The end of World War II and the British Labor Party's victory at the polls in 1945 led to renewed negotiations on independence between Britain and the Hindu and Muslim leaders. Jawaharlal Nehru and the INC leadership pressed anew for a single, secular nation in which the rights of all would be guarded by constitutional guarantees and democratic practice. But Jinnah and the Muslim League persevered in their campaign for Pakistan. In mid-August 1947, with Hindu-Muslim tensions rising, British India was divided into the two self-governing dominions of India and Pakistan, the latter created by combining contiguous, Muslim-majority districts in British India, the former consisting of the remainder. Partition occasioned a mass movement of Hindus, Muslims, and Sikhs who found themselves on the "wrong" side of new international boundaries; as many as twenty million people moved, and up to three million of these were killed in bloodletting on both sides of the new international frontier. Gandhi, who opposed the partition and worked unceasingly for Hindu-Muslim amity, became himself a casualty of heightened communal feeling; he was assassinated by a Hindu extremist five months after Partition.

Among the unresolved legacies of Partition was that it did not address the more than 500 princely states with which the British Crown had treaty ties. Most princely rulers chose one or the other dominion on grounds of geography, but the state of Jammu and Kashmir, bordering both nations, had a real option. A Muslim-majority state with a Hindu maharaja, Kashmir opted first for neither but then chose to join the Indian Union when invaded in 1948 by tribesmen from Pakistan. Quickly, Indian and Pakistani armed forces were engaged in fighting that cut to the heart of the "two-nation" theory and brought the dispute to the fledgling United Nations. A UN cease-fire in 1949 left the state divided, one-third with Pakistan and the rest, including the prized Vale of Kashmir, under Indian control. An agreement to hold an impartial plebiscite broke down when the antagonists could not agree on the terms under which it would be held. While Pakistan administers its portion of the former princely state as Azad ("free") Kashmir and as the Northern Areas, under a legal fiction that they are separate from Pakistan, the Indian portion in governed as Jammu and Kashmir, a state in the Indian Union. Periodic state-wide elections were hled in Jammu and Kashmir through the 1980s, but no plebescite has been held on the state's future.

The issue has since defied all efforts at solution, including two spasms of warfare in 1965 and 1971. In the late 1980s, India's cancellation of election results and dismissal of the state government led to the start of an armed insurrection by Muslim militants. Indian repression and Pakistan's tacit support of the militants have threatened to spark renewed warfare and keeps the issue festering.

India and China have been at odds about their Himalayan border since the Chinese occupation of Tibet in 1959, leading to clashes between Indian and Chinese troops at a number of locations along the disputed Himalayan border, including remote areas of Ladakh. In 1962, Chinese troops invaded—then withdrew from—Chinese claimed areas along the border, defeating India's under-equipped and badly led forces. The border dispute with China remains unresolved, although tensions have been eased by a stand-still accord signed by the two countries in September 1993.

Nehru's Successors

After Nehru's death on 27 May 1964, his successor, Lal Bahadur Shastri, led India in dealing with an unprecedented round of Hindu-Muslim violence occasioned by the theft of a holy Islamic relic in Kashmir. In August and September 1965, his government successfully resisted a new effort by Pakistan to resolve the Kashmir dispute by force of arms. India was victorious on the battlefield, and an agreement both nations signed at Tashkent in January 1966, essentially restored the status quo ante. Shastri died of a heart attack at Tashkent, while at the height of his power, and his successor, Indira Gandhi (Nehru's daughter), pledged to honor the accords. India again went to war with Pakistan in December 1971, this time to support East Pakistan in its civil war with West Pakistan; Indian forces tipped the balance in favor of the separatists and led to the creation of Bangladesh from the former East Pakistan; in Kashmir, there were minor territorial adjustments.

Domestically, Indira Gandhi consolidated her power, first dividing, then converting the ruling Congress Party to her own political instrument. The party lost its accustomed majority in Parliament in the 1967 elections, but she continued to govern with the support of other parties and independents, winning again in 1972. In June 1975, after her conviction on minor election law violations in the 1972 polls, which required her to resign, she continued in power by proclaiming a state of emergency. By decree, she imposed press censorship, arrested opposition political leaders, and sponsored legislation that retroactively cleared her of the election law violations. These actions, although later upheld by the Supreme Court, resulted in widespread public disapproval.

Two years later, she held parliamentary elections in which she was defeated, forcing the CP into the parliamentary opposition for the first time. The state of emergency was lifted, and Morarji Desai, formerly Nehru's deputy prime minister and the compromise choice of the winning five-party Janata coalition, became prime minister. But Janata did not last. Formed solely to oppose Mrs. Gandhi, the Janata coalition had no unity or agreed program, and it soon collapsed. Mrs. Gandhi's newly reorganized Congress Party/I ("I" for Indira) courted Hindu votes to win a huge election victory in January 1980, and she regained office.

In February 1983, India was beset by communal violence, a residue of the police excesses during the alleged emergency. Hindu mobs in the state of Assam (where direct central government rule had been imposed after student-led protests toppled the government the year before) attacked Muslims from Bangladesh and West Bengal, killing at least 3,000 persons. In October, Sikh factionalism triggered by her partisan maneuvering led to widespread violence by Sikh separatist militants in Punjab and to the imposition of direct rule in that state. A year later, with the Sikh separatist violence unchecked, she became herself one of its victims—assassinated by Sikh members of her own guard.

Rajiv Gandhi immediately succeeded his mother as prime minister and, in parliamentary elections held in December 1984, led the CP/I to its largest victory. But during the next two years, Rajiv proved unequal to the task, and his popularity declined precipitously as the public reacted to government-imposed price increases in basic commodities, his inability to stem escalating sectarian violence, and charges of military kickbacks and other scandals. In October 1987, Rajiv Gandhi sent Indian troops to Sri Lanka to enforce an agreement he and the Sri Lankan president had signed in July, aimed at ending the conflict between the country's Sinhalese majority and Tamil minority.

After a rise in Indo-Pakistan tensions in 1986–87, Rajiv Gandhi and Prime Minister Benazir Bhutto of Pakistan signed a protocol in which both nations agreed not to attack the nuclear facilities of the other in 1988. And in September 1989, Rajiv agreed with Sri Lanka's request to pull his 100,000 troops out of their bloody stand-off with Tamil separatists by the end of the year. In elections later that fall, his Congress/I Party won only a plurality of seats in the Lok Sabha, and he resigned. Vishwanath Pratap Singh, formerly Rajiv's rival in the CP and leader of the second largest party (Janata Dal) in the house, formed a government with the support of two other parliamentary groups. Despite an encouraging start, V.P. Singh's government lost first its momentum, then its ability to command a majority in the parliament. He resigned on losing a confidence vote 11 months later and was succeeded, with Congress/I support, by longtime Janata and Congress leader Chandra Shekhar, who resigned after four months.

During the election campaign that followed in the spring of 1991, Rajiv Gandhi was assassinated by a disgruntled Sri Lankan Tamil while on the hustings in Tamil Nadu. Congress/I rallied around long-time party stalwart P.V. Narasimha Rao, a former minister under both Rajiv and Indira Gandhi, drawing on a sympathy vote, to finish close enough to a majority to form a minority government that as of fall 1994 continues in office. As prime minister, Rao—who is also Congress Party president—has dealt sensitively with widespread Hindu-Muslim violence focused on a dispute over the land on which "Babur's Mosque" sits at Ayodhya in the state of Uttar Pradesh. He and his finance minister have been dynamic and innovative on economic reform, opening India to foreign investors and market economics, including rupee convertibility. And, despite frail health and advancing years, he has brought new vigor to India's foreign policy in light of the end of the Cold War. He travelled abroad extensively during 1994, visiting European capital in the spring, Washington, D.C. in June, and southeast Asia (Vietnam and Malaysia) in September.

13 GOVERNMENT

India is a sovereign socialist secular democratic republic. Its constitution, which became effective 26 January 1950, provides for a parliamentary form of government, at the center and in the states. The constitution also contains an extensive set of directive principles akin to the US Bill of Rights. Legislative acts and amendments have weakened some of those guarantees, while a number of decisions by the Supreme Court have left some weakened and others—like the commitment to secularism and to representative government—strengthened. Suffrage is universal at age 21.

The parliament, or legislative branch, consists of the president, the Council of States (Rajya Sabha), and the House of the People (Lok Sabha). The Rajya Sabha has a membership of 244, of whom 12 are appointed by the president and 232, indirectly elected by the state legislatures and by the union territories for six-year terms, with one-third chosen every two years. The Lok Sabha had 542 directly elected members (525 from the states, 17 from the union territories) and 2 members appointed by the president to represent the Anglo-Indian community. More than 22 percent of the seats are reserved for so-called "backward classes," that is, Schedule Castes (formerly "Untouchables") and Scheduled Tribes. The Lok Sabha has a maximum life of five years but can be dissolved earlier by the president; under the state of emergency proclaimed in June 1975, elections scheduled for early 1976 were postponed until 1977.

The president and vice president are elected for five-year terms by an electoral college made up of the members of both parliamentary houses and the legislative assemblies of the states. Legally, all executive authority, including supreme command of the armed forces, is vested in the president, as head of state, who, in turn, appoints a Council of Ministers headed by a prime minister. In fact, power is exercised by the prime minister who, as head of government, is chosen by legislators of the political party, or coalition of parties, that commands the confidence of the parliament. The prime minister forms—and the president then appoints—the Council of Ministers, consisting of cabinet ministers, ministers of state, and deputy ministers to formulate and execute the government program. The vice president serves as President of the Rajya Sabha and usually succeeds the president at the end of the latter's term.

Shankar Dayal Sharma became president in July 1992; K.R.Narayanan became vice president in August 1992. By tradition, the presidency and vice presidency trade off between northern and southerner, although a Muslim and a Sikh—nonregional identifications—have also held these positions. P.V. Narasimha Rao from Andhra Pradesh became the first southerner to hold the office of prime minister in June 1991.

Elections at the state level are no longer timed to coincide with national elections, and their schedule has become erratic, as state governments have been more or less stable. The next general elections at the national level must be held by May–June 1996.

14 POLITICAL PARTIES

India began its independent existence with the Indian National Congress supreme at the center and in all state legislatures. In its various manifestations, it has controlled the government for most of the years since independence in 1947. Founded in 1885, the Indian National Congress, known after 1947 as the Congress Party (CP), was the most powerful mass movement fighting for independence in British India. It became the ruling party of a free India by reason of its national popularity and because most leaders of the independence movement were among its members, including Indian first prime minister, Jawaharlal Nehru. In its progression from independence movement to ruling party, the CP spawned many offshoots and continues to do so to this date, as often for personal reasons as for matters of party policy. The first to do so was the socialist wing that split off shortly after independence to form a party in its own right, dividing again several times thereafter.

Other major parties at the time of independence included the Communist Party of India (CPI), with its origins in the peasants and workers parties of the past, representing, like them, the communist left. The CPI began the independence period under a cloud because of its Moscow-directed cooperation with the British during World War II. On the right were parties like the Hindu Mahasabha (HMS), doomed to ignominy when one of its kind killed Mahatma Gandhi in 1948. Within the political system, the HMS, nonetheless, reflected a vital Hindu nationalist strain that has seen several party iterations in the years since and continues to be force in the Hindi-speaking belt of north India. Parties on the left, right, and center have continued to divide or split off over the years, and more recently, with the decline of the Congress Party as an All-India national party, there has been a rise in the number of single state linguistic, sectarian, and regional parties capable of governing only at the state level but available for coalition building at the center.

Over time, ideology, as traditionally defined, has come to mean less and less in Indian politics, even though use of the word socialism is widespread. The Congress Party platform supports a secular democratic state with planned economic and social development. In November 1969, as Indira Gandhi consolidated her political position as prime minister, she and her supporters split the party. Hew splinter group called itself the New Congress Party and advocated a stronger socialist line than the other CP group. In elections held in March 1971, the New Congress Party (which later resumed calling itself the Congress Party) won an overwhelming majority in the Lok Sabha. Prime Minister Gandhi's declaration of a state of emergency in 1975, followed by the arrest of thousands of her political foes, led several opposition parties of otherwise divergent viewpoints to form the Janata (People's) coalition, which, campaigning against her "dictatorship," scored a major election victory in March 1977. The Janata government began a judicial inquiry into Mrs. Gandhi's activities as prime minister (along with investigations of her son Sanjay and others), denied her a parliamentary seat that she had won in a by-election in late 1978, and briefly had her jailed.

Rather than disgracing the former prime minister, these measures revived her popular following as the Janata coalition leadership began to unravel. Mrs. Gandhi and her reorganized Congress/I Party—"I" for Indira—reemerged as the nation's dominant political force, winning a large majority of seats in elections to the Lok Sabha in January 1980. Congress–I subsequently won control of 17 of 22 state governments.

Janata reverted to its three principal constituents: the Lok Dal, with strong caste support in certain rural areas; the Bharatiya (Indian) Janata Party (BJP), a descendant of the Hindu nationalist Bharatiya Jana Sangh Party (and heir to the HMS tradition); and the rump Janata Dal (JD), Congress in all but name, reflecting various populist, socialist, business, personal, and regional interests. Other active parties include the traditional Congress/S—"S" for Socialist—Party; the once Maoist, now nationalist, Communist Party of India/Marxist (CPI/M), which has long controlled governments in the states of West Bengal and Kerala); the pro-

Moscow Communist Party of India (CPI); Telugu Desam, an Andhra Pradesh-based party; the All-India Dravida Munetra Kazagham (AIDMK) of Tamil Nadu, the Akali Dal factions representing Sikhs; the All-India Muslim League (AIML); and other ethnically or regionally based parties and groups.

In the 1990s, three changes took place in the government. In elections in the fall of 1989, the Congress/I lost its majority, and although it remained the largest single party, Rajiv Gandhi resigned as prime minister. and Vishwamath Pratap (V.P.) Singh, leader of the Janata Dal, formed a government and became prime minister, with the help of two other parliamentary groups in December 1989. Eleven months later, he lost a confidence vote and was replaced by Chandra Shekhar, a former Congress leader, who formed a government with Congress/I support, only to resign himself four months later. During the 1991 election campaign that followed, former prime minister Rajiv Gandhi was assassinated, but the Congress Party/I was swept back into power under P.V. Narasimha Rao, a former minister in both Gandhi governments and Rajiv Gandhi's successor as party leader. Rao became prime minister in June 1991.

The election results of June 1991, as modified by party shifts later that year, established the following party standings in the Lok Sabha: Congress (I), 245; the Bharatiya Janata Party (BJP), 119; the CPI/M, 35; the Janata Dal Party (JDP) of V.P.Singh, 31; the breakaway Janata Dal (JD) of Ajit Singh, 20; the CPI, 14; the Telegu Desam, 13, the AIDMK, 11; others 38 (including five parties with fewer than 5), and nine vacancies. Congress strength rose to 256 by July 1993 when Rao narrowly survived a confidence vote, but in December, Ajit Singh and nine JD members of parliament joined the Congress Party, giving Rao a slender majority of 266 members (with 16 other seats vacant). Flux continued in June 1994 when the former prime minister V.P. Singh and 13 others left the JDP and sought recognition from the Speaker of the House as a separate party.

15 LOCAL GOVERNMENT

The Republic of India is a union of states. The specific powers and spheres of influence of these states are set forth in the constitution, with all residual or non-specified powers in the hands of the central government (the reverse of the US Constitution). The central government has the power to set state boundaries and to create and abolish states. The state governments are similar to the central government in form, with a chief minister and a cabinet responsible to the state legislature, which may be unicameral or bicameral. State governors, usually retired civil servants or politicians, are appointed by the president for a five-year term and act only on the advice of the state cabinet.

The constitution gives the president the power—on the advice of the prime minister—to dissolve a state legislature and dismiss a state government if no party commands the support of a majority or if the state's constitutional machinery is incapable of maintaining order. The Lok Sahba, which must approve each six-month extension of direct rule, acts as the state legislature during its imposition, governing through the governor. Termed as "President's Rule" in the constitution, this power derives from a provision for "Governor's Rule" in the Government of India Act of 1935 and survives in the Pakistan constitution of 1973 in that form. It was invoked for the first time in 1959 by Prime Minister Nehru, and on the advice of Indira Gandhi, who was then Congress Party president; in power herself, she invoked the power repeatedly, often for partisan political purposes and, especially in the early 1980s, in the wake of ethnic/communal violence in Punjab, Assam, and Jammu and Kashmir. Limitations on its partisan use were imposed in a Supreme Court decision in spring 1994.

Under the States Reorganization Act of 1956, there were 14 states and 5 union territories, organized, where appropriate, on linguistic grounds. Through a gradual process of reorganization

and division, 2 former union territories have become states, while new ones have been created (there are now 7), and the number of states has grown to 25.

Administratively, the states and union territories are divided into districts,under the control of senior civil servants who are responsible for collecting revenues, maintaining law and order, and setting development priorities. Districts are further divided into subdivisions, and subdivisions into taluks or tehsils. State government and lower levels of representative councils vary in organization and function, but all are based on universal adult suffrage. Large towns are each governed by a corporation headed by a mayor; health, safety, education, and the maintenance of normal city facilities are under its jurisdiction. Smaller towns have municipal boards and committees similar to the corporations but with more limited powers. District boards in rural areas provide for road construction and maintenance, education, and public health. The constitution provides for the organization of village councils (panchayats), and nearly all the villages have been so organized. The panchayats are elected from among the villagers by all the adult population and have administrative functions and a judicial wing that enables them to handle minor offenses.

16 JUDICIAL SYSTEM

The laws and judicial system of British India were continued after independence with only slight modifications. The Supreme Court consists of a chief justice and up to 17 judges, appointed by the president, who hold office until age 65. The Court's duties include interpreting the constitution, handling all disputes between the central government and a state or between states themselves, and judging appeals from lower courts.

In 1986 there were 18 high courts, subordinate to but not under the control of the Supreme Court. Each state's judicial system is headed by a high court (two high courts have jurisdiction over more than one state), whose judges are appointed by the president and over whom state legislatures have no control. Each state is divided into districts; within each district, a hierarchy of civil courts is responsible to the principal civil courts, presided over by a district judge. The 1973 Code of Criminal Procedure, effective 1 April 1974, provides for the appointment of separate sets of magistrates for the performance of executive and judicial functions within the criminal court system. Executive magistrates are responsible to the state government; judicial magistrates are under the control of the high court in each state.

Different personal law are administered through the single civil court system. Islamic law (Shari'a) governs many noncriminal matters involving Muslims, including family law, inheritance and divorce.

There are strong constitutional safeguards assuring the independence of the judiciary. In 1993-94, the Supreme Court rendered important judgements imposing limits on the use of the constitutional device known as "President's Rule" by the central government and reaffirming India's secular commitment.

17 ARMED FORCES

The Indian Armed Forces have a proud tradition, having provided one million soldies during World War I and two million in World War II battles in Asia, Aftica, the Middle East, and Europe. The armed forces are entirely volunteer and consist of the regular army, navy, and air force; the territorial (reserve) army; and 13 different full-time or reserve special purpose paramilitary units for border, transportation, and internal defense. The home guard and provincial armed constabulary alone number 800,000 while the Ministry of Home Affairs controls 125,000 riot police and 171,000 in the Border Security Force (BSF).

In 1993 armed forces personnel totaled 1,265,000. The army had 1,100,000 personnel, organized into 2 armored divisions, 1 mechanized division, 22 infantry divisions, 10 mountain divisions, 5 independent armored brigades, 8 independent infantry brigades, 3 independent artillery brigades, 6 air defense brigades, 4 engineer brigades, and 1 parachute brigade. Armaments included 3,800 main battle tanks and 100 light tanks. The navy (including the naval air force) had 55,000 personnel; naval vessels included 15 submarines, 2 aircraft carriers, 5 destroyers, 21 frigates, 14 corvettes, 25 patrol boats, and 20 minewarfare ships. The naval air force had 5,000 personnel, with 46 combat aircraft and 75 armed helicopters. The air force had 110,000 personnel and 674 combat aircraft; there was 1 light bomber squadron, 28 fighter and ground attack squadrons, 17 interceptor squadrons, 3 reconnaissance squadrons, and 11 helicopter squadrons. There is a coast guard of 3,000 personnel, 20 aircraft, and 37 patrol craft.

Budgeted defense expenditures in 1991 were around $8 billion or less than 1% of gross domestic product. During 1985–1991, the nation imported armaments worth $18 billion, much of it Russian arms for rupee payment. India has also purchased submarines from the Federal Republic of Germany (FRG), Mirage jet fighters from France, and Jaguar jets from the UK. The US has not been a significant supplier of weapons to India since the 1965 war with Pakistan. India supplies an estimated 85% of its own arms needs.

India provides about 500 personnel to five peacekeeping operations. Although India has exploded a nuclear device, it has no operational, deployed nuclear forces.

[18] INTERNATIONAL COOPERATION

India is a member of the Commonwealth of Nations. Even before its independence in 1947, India became a charter member of the UN on 13 October 1945, and it belongs to ESCAP and all the nonregional specialized agencies. India also has joined the Asian Development Bank and G-77, and has signed GATT and the Law of the Sea.

India was a founder of the nonaligned movement and has pursued a formally neutralist foreign policy since independence. Relations between the US and India have ranged from correct to cordial; relations with China, hostile during the early 1960s, have been normalized since 1976. India's primary ally among the superpowers had been the former USSR, with which a 20-year treaty of peace, friendship, and cooperation was signed in 1971. Indian armed forces and political missions have assisted in implementing truce and cease-fire agreements in Korea, Viet-Nam, Laos, Cambodia (now Kampuchea), the Middle East, Congo (now Zaire), and Cyprus. India also negotiated a settlement in Sri Lanka's civil unrest in July 1987, sending in troops to enforce the agreement.

Since independence, India has fought three wars with neighboring Pakistan, in 1947–48, 1965, and 1971. Relations between the two countries improved in the early 1980s. On 10 March 1983, India and Pakistan signed a five-year agreement for improving economic and cultural ties, which was viewed as a major step in the normalization of their relations. Tension between India and Pakistan increased again in 1986–87, when both countries conducted military exercises near their common border in the sensitive Punjab region. Indo-Pakistan relations worsened again in 1990 and in the years immediately following as a consequence of Pakistan's support of Islamic insurgents in Indian Kashmir.

[19] ECONOMY

Agriculture is the largest sector of the Indian economy. It provides the livelihood for 67% of the population and (with forestry and fishing included) contributes about one-third of the GDP. The country is rich in mineral, forest, and power resources, and its ample reserves of iron ore and coal provide a substantial base for heavy industry. Coal is the principal source for generating electric power, although hydroelectric and nuclear installations supply a

rising proportion of India's power needs. The government also plans to promote considerable expansion in oil exploration and production in the coming decade.

Outside the agricultural sector, the Indian economy is a mixture of public and private enterprises. Under a planned development regime since independence, the public sector provided the impetus for industrialization and for absorption of sophisticated technology. Nevertheless, a large proportion of the total manufacturing output continued to be contributed by small, unorganized industries. In recent years, and especially so since 1991, the government has placed greater emphasis on private enterprise to stimulate growth and modernization. Reflecting this policy shift, public enterprises now account for only about 17% of the country's GDP, down from 23% in the mid-1980s.

Following the proclamation of a state of emergency in June 1975, a 20-point economic reform program was announced. Price regulations were toughened, and a moratorium on rural debts was declared. A new campaign was mounted against tax evaders, currency speculators, smugglers, and hoarders. This program, which lapsed when Indira Gandhi was out of power (1977–80), was revised and incorporated into the sixth and seventh five-year plans (1980–85 and 1985–90). Recurring episodes of severe weather and fluctuating oil prices contributed to variable GDP growth performance during the 1980s; nevertheless, annual growth in the GDP during the latter half of the decade averaged 6.2%. This expansion was, however, accompanied by numerous indicators of underlying structural weaknesses in the economy: meager growth in formal sector employment, persistent inefficiency and limited technological improvement in the public sector, accelerating fiscal and balance of payment deficits, as well as double-digit inflation by 1990. Given these already unfavorable conditions, political volatility in the late 1980s and oil price shocks resulting from the Gulf War catalysed an acute balance of payment crisis in early 1991. Swift stabilization measures taken by the newly elected government proved highly successful. Foreign exchange reserves recovered to a comfortable margin (equal to five months of imports) by mid-1992 and inflation declined from 13.1% in 1991/92 to 8.6% in 1993/94. Further reforms initiated as part of a wider structural adjustment program are credited with reviving GDP growth to 4.0% in 1992/93 and 3.8% in 1993/94 up from 1.2% in 1991/92.

[20] INCOME

In 1992, India's GNP was $271,638 million at current prices, or $310 per capita. For the period 1985–92 the average inflation rate was 9.5%, resulting in a real growth rate in per capita GNP of 3.3%.

In 1992 the GDP was $241,758 million in current US dollars. It is estimated that in 1991 agriculture, hunting, forestry, and fishing contributed 29% to GDP; mining and quarrying, 2%; manufacturing, 16%; electricity, gas, and water, 2%; construction, 5%; wholesale and retail trade, 11%; transport, storage, and communication, 7%; finance, insurance, real estate, and business services, 7%; community, social, and personal services, 5%; and other sources 16%.

[21] LABOR

In 1991, India's labor force totaled 345 million of whom 67% were employed in agriculture and 20% were unemployed. The labor force size grew by 2% annually during 1980–85, and by 1.9% per year during 1985–91. The female labor force comprised one-quarter of the total in 1992. Employment in the iron and steel industry in 1991 totaled 286,000, more than any other country except Japan.

Working hours are limited by law to 48 per week for adults, and factory employment of children under 14 years of age is prohibited, even though the government estimates the existence of 17 million child laborers, many of them working in the hand-knotted carpet industry. Bonded labor was abolished in 1976, but is still prevalent. The government estimates that there are 250,000 bonded laborers (although other estimates put that figure closer to 2,500,000), of whom 223,108 had been identified and freed by March 1992. By law, earned income also includes a cost-of-living allowance and an annual bonus (applicable to factories and all other establishments with 20 employees). Employers and employees contribute to the Employees State Insurance Scheme.

In 1992, an estimated 10 million workers belonged to unions. The leading trade union federations are the Indian National Trade Union Congress and the All-India Trade Union Congress. White collar strikes of doctors, lawyers, teachers, and bank workers occurred in 1992. Most public sector employment is aimed at providing temporary rural jobs.

22AGRICULTURE

In 1991, of the total land area of 297 million hectares (734 million acres), the net sown area was 169 million hectares (418 million acres), or about 57%. The irrigated area totaled 57.8 million hectares (142.8 million acres) in 1985/86, as compared with 48.1 million hectares (118.9 million acres) in 1978/79. At least 10 million hectares (24.7 million acres) were redistributed under land reform programs during 1951–79.

Agricultural production increased at an average annual rate of 2.9% during the 1970s, 3.2% during 1980–85, and 4.8% during 1985–1990, mainly as the result of the "green revolution," which has made India basically self-sufficient in grain output through the use of improved hybrid seeds, irrigation, and fertilizers. Cereal production averaged over 104 million tons per year from 1979 to 1981; in 1992, production totaled 101 million tons, down from 102 million tons in 1990. Rice leads all crops and, except in the northwest, is generally grown wherever the conditions are suitable. In 1992, 109.5 million tons of rice were produced on 42 million hectares (103.8 million acres). The combined acreage and production of other cereals, all to a large extent grown for human consumption, considerably exceed those of rice. These include jowar, a rich grain sorghum grown especially in the Deccan; wheat, grown in the northwest; and bajra, another grain sorghum grown in the drier areas of western India and the far south. A wheat crop of 55 million tons was harvested on 22.9 million hectares (56.5 million acres) in 1992. Vegetables, pulses, and oilseeds are the other main food crops. Oilseeds production in 1993 was a record 24.3 million tons. Nonfood crops are mainly linseed, cotton, jute, and tobacco. The cotton crop in 1993 totaled 10.3 million bales and was large enough to both supply the increasing demands of the domestic textile sector and provide export receipts. Since World War II, India has been the world's largest producer of black pepper (65,000 tons in 1985/86). It also handles about 70% of the world trade in cardamom, of which 4,400 tons were produced in 1985/86.

India was the world's second-leading producer (after Brazil) of sugarcane in 1992, with an output of 249.3 million tons. Tea, coffee, and rubber plantations contribute significantly to the economy, although they occupy less than 1% of the agricultural land (in hill areas generally unsuited to Indian indigenous agriculture), and are the largest agricultural enterprises in India. Tea, the most important plantation crop, is a large foreign exchange earner, with an export value of $554 million in 1992, based on production of 703,000 tons, the highest in the world. It is grown mostly in Assam and northern Bengal, but also in southern India. Coffee (200,000 tons in 1992) is produced in southern India, and rubber (350,000 tons) in Kerala. Leaf tobacco production totaled 538,000 tons.

Because of the ever-present danger of food shortages, the government tightly controls the grain trade, fixing minimum support and procurement prices and maintaining buffer stocks. The Food Corp. of India, a government enterprise, distributes 12 million tons of food grains annually and is increasing its storage capacity.

23ANIMAL HUSBANDRY

The livestock population of India is huge and animals as a whole play an important role in the agricultural economy, even though they often receive inadequate nourishment. Since Hindus believe that cows and other animals may contain reincarnated human souls, they do not eat beef and generally do not eat any kind of meat; however, many millions of Muslims, Christians, and Sikhs do.

In 1992 there were an estimated 192.6 million head of cattle—about 15% of the world's total and more than in any other country—117 million goats, 44.4 million sheep, 10.5 million hogs, 78.5 million water buffalo, 1.5 million camels, 1.5 million asses, 970,000 horses, and 410 million poultry. Bullocks and water buffalo are important for draft purposes. Dairy farming has made India self-sufficient in butter and powdered milk. To improve milk production, a dairy development program was begun in 1978 to build up the milch herd to 150 million crossbred cows. Milk output in 1992 was 29.4 million tons; estimated egg production was 1,434,000 tons. The production of cattle and buffalo hides and goat- and sheepskins is a major industry. About 54,500 tons of wool were produced in 1992. Animal dung is also used for fuel and fertilizer.

24FISHING

Fishing is an important secondary source of income to some farmers and a primary occupation in small fishing villages. Almost three-fifths of the catch consists of sea fish. The bulk is marketed fresh; of the remainder, more than half is sun dried. Fish and fish products account for about 2.5-3% of the total export value. Deep-sea fishing is not done on a large scale. Inland fishing is most developed in the deltaic channels of Bengal, an area where fish is an important ingredient of the diet. In recent years, the government has been encouraging ocean fishing through the establishment of processing plants and the introduction of deep-sea craft. Fishing harbors have been built along the coasts of the Bay of Bengal and the Arabian Sea. Under the fifth national plan (1974–79), fish farming was encouraged through the creation of Fish Farmers' Development Agencies. Fish production achieved a new high of about 3.7 million tons at the end of the seventh national plan (1986–91).

The total fish catch in 1991 was estimated at 4,036,931 tons, of which marine fish accounted for 2,336,101 tons and inland sources for 1,700,830 tons. Fish exports, still only a fraction of the potential, have shown a steady gain in recent years.

25FORESTRY

The major forestlands lie in the foothills of the Himalayas, the hills of Assam state, the northern highlands of the Deccan, the Western Ghats, and the Andaman Islands. Other forestlands are generally scrub and poor secondary growth of restricted commercial potential. India's forests are mostly broad-leaved; less than 10% are coniferous. In 1991 there were 66,950,000 hectares (165,433,000 acres) of forestland, about half of which was reserved for the production of timber and other forest products, such as firewood, charcoal, and lac. About 138,000 hectares (341,000 acres) were planted annually during the 1980s under afforestation programs. Most forests are owned by state governments and are reserved or protected for the maintenance of permanent timber and water supplies. Forest products in 1991 included about 279.8 million cu m of roundwood and 17.4 million cu m of sawn wood, as well as bamboos, canes, fibers, flosses, gums and resins, medicinal herbs, tanning barks, and lac.

²⁶MINING

India is well endowed with industrial minerals. Iron ore reserves, estimated at 11 billion tons of hematite ore containing at least 55% iron, are among the largest in the world. The best quality of mica comes from Bihar; India produced 3,607 tons of crude mica in 1991. Manganese deposits are estimated at 154 million tons. Bauxite deposits, estimated at 2.3 billion tons, slightly exceed those of Jamaica; however, India's output of 4,835,000 tons in 1991 was much less than Jamaica's. There are extensive workable reserves of fluorite, chromite, ilmenite (for titanium), monazite (for thorium), beach sands, magnesite, beryllium, copper, and a variety of other industrial and agricultural minerals. However, India lacks substantial reserves of some nonferrous metals and special steel ingredients. The exploration and processing of chrome, coper, diamonds, gold, iron ore, lead, manganese, molybdenum, nickel, platinum-group metals, sulfur, tungsten, and zinc were exclusively controlled by the Indian government.

Principal iron ore output comes from the rich fields along the Bihar-Orissa border, which are close to all major existing iron and steel works. Smaller amounts are mined in the Bababudan Hills of Karnataka and elsewhere. Iron content in mined ore output totaled 35.6 billion tons in 1991. Manganese is mined in Andhra Pradesh, Karnataka, the Nagpur section of Maharashtra, northward in Madhya Pradesh, along the Bihar-Orissa border adjoining the iron ore deposits, along the Maharashtra–Madhya Pradesh–Rajasthan border, and in central coastal Andhra Pradesh. Content of manganese in mined ore produced was 630,450 in 1991. Gold and silver come largely from the Kolar fields of southeastern Karnataka, where the gold mines have reached a depth of more than 3.2 km (2 mi) and contain reserves to produce about 55,000 kg of gold. Diamonds, emeralds, and fissionable materials also are mined. In 1991, 1,973 kg of gold and 19,000 carats of diamonds were produced.

Coal reserves, scattered through the central Peninsula and the northeast, are estimated at 191,857 million tons (97% bituminous, 3% lignite). Coal is among India's most important natural resources and has been the basis of the power, railway, and steel industries. The largest reserves are in the states of West Bengal and Bihar in the northeast. Almost the entire coal industry was nationalized by the government in 1972 and 1973. Coal output was about 239.8 million tons in 1991.

Estimated mineral production in 1991 also included 55,380 tons of mined copper ore, 994,674 tons of chromite, 163,474 tons of zinc concentrates, 1,563,056 tons of gypsum, and 25,000 tons of lead concentrates.

²⁷ENERGY AND POWER

Petroleum reserves were estimated at 600 million tons in 1992, or 0.6% of the world's reserves. From less than 100,000 tons in 1951, crude oil production rose to 34.2 million tons in 1989, before falling to 28.7 million tons in 1992. Oil exploration and production are undertaken in joint ventures between government and private foreign companies. As of 1992, 2,800 wells were in operation; the government also requested bids for the development of an additional 43 oil and gas fields from foreign and domestic companies that year. Extraction of natural gas increased from 920 million cu m in 1973 to 14,900 million cu m in 1992. Pipelines consisted of 3,497 km (2,173 mi) for crude oil, 1,703 km (1,058mi) for refined products, and 902 km (561 mi) for natural gas in 1991.

India supplied 82% of its own power requirements in 1992 and, in addition, has a large development potential. Total installed electric capacity, which was 18,500 Mw in 1974, rose to 65,000 Mw in 1991. An additional generating capacity of 10,000 Mw is a goal by 2000.

A 380-Mw nuclear power station, India's first, was completed with US assistance in 1969 at Tarapur, near Bombay. (The Tara-

pur plant has long been a center of controversy because of India's alleged failure to observe international safeguards to prevent the diversion of nuclear materials for military purposes.) Another nuclear station, in Rajasthan, began partial operations in the early 1970s, and two more plants were added by the end of the decade; six additional reactors of 235 Mw each were scheduled for construction under the 1980–85 development plan. As of 1991, nuclear power accounted for about 5.2 billion kwh of electricity, or less than 2% of India's total of 294.3 billion kwh; conventional thermal plants produced about three-quarters, and hydroelectric facilities about 23%.

Under the Commission on Additional Sources of Energy, within the Department of Science and Technology, research programs in biogas and biomass have been established. Demonstration projects in solar and wind energy were also undertaken in the early 1980s.

²⁸INDUSTRY

Modern industry has advanced fairly rapidly since independence, and the industrial sector now contributes close to a third of the GDP. Large modern steel mills and many fertilizer plants, heavy-machinery plants, oil refineries, and locomotive works have been constructed; the metallurgical, chemical, cement, and oil-refining industries have also expanded. Yet, though the total product is large, factories in these industries still absorb only a token fraction of the labor force. Nine states—Maharashtra, West Bengal, Tamil Nadu, Gujarat, Uttar Pradesh, Bihar, Andhra Pradesh, Karnataka, and Madhya Pradesh—together account for most of Indian industry.

Industrial production expanded at an average annual rate of 5–6% between 1970 and 1990. Forceful austerity and demand management measures taken to stabilize rapidly worsening macroeconomic imbalances in 1991/92 slowed growth in the industry sector to 0% for that year. This was followed by a modest rebound to 1.9% in 1992/93, though declining to an estimated 1.6% in 1993/94, due to lingering effects of the earlier stabilization measures as well as poorer than expected demand in key export markets.

Under the planned development regime of past decades, government directives channeled much of the country's resources into public enterprises. State-owned industrial enterprises increased from 113 in 1973 to 225 by 1986. Private investment was closely regulated for all industries, discouraging investors from formal entry into the sector. However, industrial policy changes of recent years have started to modify this pattern. Since 1991 government licensing requirements have been abolished for all but 15 industries and the credit and capital markets have been greatly liberalized. With these reforms, private investment in industry is now proceeding at a steady if still modest pace, fostering increased competition in most mining and manufacturing sectors previously monopolized by parastatals.

Textile production dominates the industrial field. Millions of cottage workers throughout the country handloom cotton, wool, silk, and rayon. Powerlooms accounted for an increasingly large share of production during the 1980s. Mill-based textile manufactures, by contrast, have stagnated over the last several decades, now accounting for barely 10% of total output due to equipment obsolesence, differential excise duties and curbs placed by the government on mill capacity expansion in the past. Recent changes in textile policy aim at lifting government controls on the industry to promote modernisation of the mill sector. Bombay, Ahmadabad, and the provincial cities in southern India lead in cotton milling. Total mill-based textile production in 1991/92 included 1,572 million meters of cotton fabrics and 1,448,000 tons of cotton yarn. Jute milling is localized at Calcutta, center of the jute agricultural area. Jute manufactures for 1990/91 amounted to 1,430,000 million tons. Wool, silk, coir, and a growing rayon textile industry are also important. Export-oriented garment production has expanded rapidly over the last several years.

In 1991/92, six integrated and 180 mini steel plants produced 14.3 million tons of finished steel. Other outputs from the metallurgical sector included 55 million tons of iron ore, 514,000 tons of aluminum ingots, and 1,205,000 tons of pipes and metal tubes. Mechanical engineering industries produced 192 thousand passenger vehicles. The electrical engineering industry produced 360 thousand radio receivers and electric motors totalling 6,116,000 horsepower unit equivalency. The production of computers and a wide range of consumer electronics (colour televisions, VCRs, electronic watches and watches) has been boosted by the recent liberalization of technology and component imports; total output in this sector grew from R8.1 billion in 1980/81 to about R106 billion in 1991/92. The oil-refining industry yielded 48 million tons of refined petroleum products. Nitrogen fertilizer production grew from 5,745,000 tons in 1985/86 to 7,564,000 in 1991/92, and cement production from 32 million tons to 52 million tons. Refined sugar production, a major agricultural processing industry, totaled 13.3 million tons in 1991/92.

²⁹SCIENCE AND TECHNOLOGY

India made remarkable advances in science and technology from the 1970s through the 1990s. Total expenditures on research and development increased from R3,240 million in 1974/75 to R43,582 million in 1992/93. Allocations are divided among government (87.4%) and industry (12.6%). There has been a marked growth in the training of engineers and technicians; around 1,600,000 qualified personnel emerge annually. Among the technological higher schools are the Indian Institute of Science at Bangalore, the Indian Institute of Technology at Kharagpur and Madras, and the Indian Statistical Institute at Calcutta. In 1947, there were 620 colleges and universities; by 1992, that number was over 7,150. One of the primary science and technology issues facing India is a "brain drain." Over 13,000 Indian students annually seek science and engineering degrees in the United States. Many contend this greatly reduces the quality of science and engineering education in India.

As of 1994 there are more than 2,500 national research and development institutions connected with science and technology in India. Principal government agencies engaged in scientific research and technical development are the Ministry of Science and Technology, the Council of Scientific and Industrial Research, the Ministry of Atomic Energy, and the Ministry of Electronics. The Council for Scientific and Industrial Research has 42 national laboratories under its umbrella. In March 1981, a cabinet committee, headed by the prime minister, was established to review science and technology programs and to decide future policy.

An importer of nuclear technology since the 1960s, India fully entered the atomic age at 8:05 AM on 18 May 1974 by testing its own underground nuclear device at Pokaran, in Rajasthan. The first Indian-built nuclear power plant, with two 235-Mw heavy-water reactors, began operating in July 1983, and an experimental fast-breeder reactor was under construction. The country's largest scientific establishment is the Bhabha Atomic Research Center at Trombay, near Bombay, which has four nuclear research reactors and trains 150 nuclear scientists each year. In the area of space technology, India's first communications satellite, *Aryabhata*, was launched into orbit by the former USSR on 19 April 1975, and two additional satellites were orbited by Soviet rockets in 1979 and 1981. The Indian Space Research Organization constructed and launched India's first satellite-launching vehicle, the SLV-3, from its Vikram Sarabhai Space Center at Sriharikota on 18 July 1980; the four-stage, solid-fuel rocket put a 35-kg (77-lb) Rohini satellite into near-earth orbit. Indian-built telecommunications satellites have been launched

into orbit from Cape Canaveral, Fla., by the US National Aeronautics and Space Administration, by the European Space Agency, and from French Guiana. India has established a satellite-tracking station at Kavalur, in Tamil Nadu. In 1984, the first Indo-Soviet manned mission was completed successfully; in 1985, two Indians were selected for an Indo-US joint shuttle flight. An important international sciences program is the United States-India Fund (USIF). The USIF has about 200 scientists and engineers participating in 65 Indo-US joint research projects at nearly 15 institutions in each country. Projects include earthquake, atmospheric, marine, energy, environment, medical, and life sciences.

³⁰DOMESTIC TRADE

Under a nationwide scheme launched in 1979 for the distribution of essential commodities, such goods as wheat, rice, sugar, cloth, kerosene, imported edible oils, and, in some cases, soft coke and cement are procured by the central government and then supplied through more than 270,000 outlets. Each state has its own consumer cooperative federation; all of these groups are under the aegis of the National Cooperative Consumers Federation. By the mid-1980s, more than 30,000 marketing societies, village service societies, and other cooperatives shared in the distribution of goods in rural areas.

With the government's new emphasis on growth in private enterprise since the late 1980s, the expansion of privately-owned retail outlets have outshadowed further development in the cooperative sector. Most private commercial enterprises are small establishments owned and operated by a single person or a single family; retail outlets are often highly specialized in product and usually very small in quarters and total stock. Often the Indian retail shop is large enough to hold only the proprietor and a small selection of stock; shutters fronting the store are opened to allow customers to negotiate from the street or sidewalk. Fixed prices are rare, and bargaining is the accepted means of purchase. In cities and larger towns, similar stores tend to agglomerate in specialized bazaar areas.

Government and business hours are generally from 10 AM to 5 PM, Monday through Friday, with a lunch break from 1 to 2 PM. Larger shops in Delhi are open from 9:30 AM to 1:30 PM and from 3:30 to 7:30 PM. Normal banking hours are from 10 AM to 4 PM on weekdays and from 10 AM to 12 noon on Saturdays.

³¹FOREIGN TRADE

Initially, India's foreign trade followed a pattern common to all underdeveloped countries: exporting raw materials and food in exchange for manufactured goods. The only difference in India's case was that it also exported processed textiles, yarn, and jute goods. Up until the late 1980s, the government's strongly import substitution-oriented industrial policy limited the importance of exports for the Indian economy, which even in 1991/92 accounted for only 8% of GDP. With imports exceeding exports almost continuously in the 1970s and 1980s, the country registered a chronic trade deficit that grew particularly large by the late 1980s, burgeoning to R106 billion in 1990/91 from R53,905 billion in 1984/85. Stabilization and structural adjustment measures taken in 1991, including a 50% currency devaluation, aimed at improving the country's balance of trade position both by depressing imports and promoting expanded exports. By 1991/92 the trade gap had narrowed to only R50,158 billion. Sustaining the recent surge in export growth, however, is being hampered by severe economic contraction in the countries of the former USSR, India's second largest trading partner during previous decades. Given the country's relatively well-developed manufacturing base, items like machine tools, industrial equipment, jewelry, chemicals, garments, and processed food (especially fish) now comprise the country's leading exported items, replacing jute, tea, and other food products that dominated its export base in the 1960s and early 1970s.

With a population size second only to China, and a per capita income of $1,250 measured in purchasing power terms, India potentially represents one of the world's important trading partners. The US remains India's largest partner, while Japan has replaced the former USSR in second place, followed by Germany and the UK. Leading purchasers of Indian exports in 1990/91 were the US and Japan. Leading import suppliers were the US, Japan, and the FRG. Principal trade partners in 1991/92 (in millions of dollars) were estimated as follows:

	EXPORTS	IMPORTS	BALANCE
US	2,931	1,999	932
Japan	1,644	1,378	266
FRG	1,269	1,553	−284
UK	1,144	1,203	− 59
USSR (former)	1,609	738	871
OPEC countries	1,555	3,823	−2,268
Other	7,718	8,716	−998
TOTALS	17,870	19,410	−1,540

32BALANCE OF PAYMENTS

India has a chronic deficit on current accounts. What bridges the gap between payments and receipts is mainly external aid (especially nonproject assistance), tourism earnings, and remittances from Indians working abroad. Heavy imports of food grains and armament purchases caused a decline in India's foreign exchange reserves in the mid-1960s. An economic recovery from 1968/69, however, eased the problem, and by 30 September 1970, foreign exchange reserves amounted to $616 million, as compared with $383 million on 31 December 1965. Reserves declined to $566 million by the end of 1972 but increased to $841 million as of 31 December 1975, despite massive deficits on current accounts, attributable to the quadrupling of oil import prices during 1973–74. Foreign exchange reserves declined from $6,739 million at the end of 1979 to $3,476 million as of 30 November 1982 but subsequently rose to $5,924 million by March 1987. The Gulf War crisis worsened the ratio of current account deficit to GDP. Foreign exchange reserves plummeted because of export losses in Kuwait, Iraq, and other nations. Remittances from Indian workers fell, and sudden price increases for oil imports caused an estimated loss to India of over $2.8 billion in earnings. By November 1993, however, India's foreign exchange reserves had risen to $8.1 billion, the highest level since 1951. A substantial reduction in the trade deficit, increased inflows from foreign institutional investors, a stable exchange rate, and imporved remittances all contributed in the recovery of reserves.

In 1989 merchandise exports totaled $16,144 million and imports $22,254 million. The merchandise trade balance was $−6,110 million. The following table summarizes India's balance of payments for 1988/89 (in millions of US dollars):

	1988	1989
CURRENT ACCOUNT		
Goods, services, and income	−9,900	−9,896
Unrequited transfers	2,781	3,083
TOTALS	−7,118	−6,813
CAPITAL ACCOUNT		
Other long-term capital	5,915	6,161
Other short-term capital	1,328	1,188
Reserves	−13	−251
TOTALS	7,230	7,098
Errors and omissions	−112	−285
Total change in reserves	1	−88

33BANKING AND SECURITIES

A well-established banking system exists in India. At the end of 1991 there were 60,519 branches of public sector and commercial banks. Scheduled banks maintained branches, mainly in the major commercial and industrial centers of Maharashtra, West Bengal, Uttar Pradesh, and Tamil Nadu states and the Delhi territory. Banks operating in the public sector account for almost all commercial banking. Most of these are regional banks that extend credit to small borrowers in rural areas. The largest public-sector bank is the State Bank of India, with 8,379 branches and deposits exceeding R601,920 million. Over 100 branches of Indian commercial banks operate overseas, primarily in the UK, US, Fiji, Mauritius, Hong Kong, and Singapore.

The Reserve Bank of India, founded in 1935 and nationalized in 1949, is the central banking and note-issuing authority. Currency in circulation on 31 December 1991 was R612,320 million. A new institution, the Export-Import Bank of India, was established in 1982 to finance medium- and long-term credit for the exporting of goods and services.

In an attempt to regulate lending practices and interest rates, the government has encouraged the formation of cooperative credit societies. Long-term credit is also provided by the cooperative land development banks. Nonagricultural credit societies and employees' credit societies supply urban credit.

The main stock exchanges are located in Calcutta, Bombay, and Madras, and there are secondary exchanges in Ahmadabad, Delhi, Kanpur, Nagpur, and other cities. Each exchange has its own regulations on membership and on security listings and transactions; outside Bombay and Ahmadabad these are not strict, and at times margin trading and other questionable practices have tended to produce wild speculation. Rules favor exchange members rather than public protection or benefit. Brokerage and jobbing are commonly combined. As of December 1992, India had 6,250 companies listed on the exchanges.

34INSURANCE

The life insurance business was formally nationalized on 1 September 1956 by the establishment of the Life Insurance Corp. of India (LIC), which absorbed the life insurance business of 245 Indian and foreign companies. LIC also transacts business in certain African and Asian countries where there are large Indian populations. As of 1991, life insurance in force within India had a value of R1.496 billion.

The general insurance business was nationalized as of 1 January 1973, and all nationalized general insurance companies were merged into the General Insurance Corp. of India.

35PUBLIC FINANCE

The government's financial year extends from 1 April to 31 March, and the budget is presented to the parliament on the last day of February. The executive branch has considerable control over public finance. Thus, while parliament can oversee and investigate public expenditures and may reduce the budget, it cannot expand the budget, and checks exist that prevent it from delaying passage.

Budgets in recent decades have reflected the needs of rapid economic development under rising expenditures of the five-year plans. Insufficient government receipts for financing this development have led to yearly deficits and a resulting increase of new tax measures and deficit financing. The Gulf crisis, increased interest payments, subsidies, and relief in 1991 caused the central government's fiscal deficit to reach 8.4% of GDP. The consolidated public sector deficit (including the states and public enterprises) fell from 13% of GDP in 1991 to 9% in 1993. Principal sources of government revenue are customs and excise duties and individual and corporate income taxes. Major items of expenditure are defense, grants to states and territories, interest payments on the national debt, and economic, social, and community services.

The following table shows actual revenues and expenditures for 1991 and 1992 in billions of rupees.

	1991	1992
REVENUE AND GRANTS		
Tax revenue	673.0	765.3
Non-tax revenue	191.1	225.4
Capital revenue	34.4	33.9
Grants	9.8	8.7
TOTAL	908.3	1,033.2
EXPENDITURES & LENDING MINUS REPAYMENTS		
General public service	73.5	81.4
Defense	162.6	174.1
Education	23.5	23.8
Health	16.7	18.5
Housing and community amenities	61.6	66.2
Economic affairs and services	224.3	215.4
Other expenditures	507.9	579.8
Lending minus repayments	197.9	214.1
TOTAL	1,267.8	1,373.2
DEFICIT/SURPLUS	−359.5	−340.0

In 1992 India's total public debt stood at ʀ3,685.5 billion, of which ʀ395.7 billion was financed abroad.

36TAXATION

Taxes are levied by the central government, the state governments, and the various municipal governments. The sources of central government tax revenue are union excise duties, customs duties, corporate and personal income (nonagricultural) taxes, wealth taxes, and gift taxes. State government sources, in general order of importance, are land taxes, sales taxes, excise duties, and registration and stamp duties. The states also share in central government income tax revenues and union excise duties, and they receive all revenues from the wealth tax on agricultural property. Municipal governments levy land and other property taxes and license fees. Many also impose duties on goods entering the municipal limits. There is no uniformity in types or rates of state and municipal taxes.

Because the lowest level of income subject to taxation (ʀ28,000 for individuals in 1993) is above the income of most Indians, the federal personal tax is paid by only a fraction of the total number of households. The tax rates in 1993 ranged from 20% on taxable income over ʀ28,000 but below ʀ50,000 per year to 40% on income exceeding ʀ100,000. Corporate tax in 1993 was 45% for publicly held companies, 65% for branches of foreign companies, and 50% for all other companies. There are also personal capital gains, wealth, and gift and inheritance taxes. Excise tax, however, is the chief source of revenue for the central government; sales tax is the chief source of revenue for state governments.

37CUSTOMS AND DUTIES

The majority of imports and some exports are subject to tariffs. There are both revenue and protective tariffs, although the former are more important and have long been a major source of central government income. Tariffs range from 40% to 60% for raw materials, 60% to 100% for semi-processed goods, and 100% and above on finished and consumer goods. Tariffs on luxury items can go as high as 110%. Tariffs may be waived on imports of capital goods for technological or export-oriented industries in designated free zones.

Excise duties are levied by both the central and, in a few cases, the state governments and, like import tariffs, are a major source

of central government income. Excise tax rates are normally revised each year.

38FOREIGN INVESTMENT

Until recently, foreign investment remained closely regulated. Rules and incentives directed the flow of foreign capital mainly toward consumer industries and light engineering, with major capital-intensive projects reserved for the public sector. Under the Foreign Exchange Regulation Act of 1973, which went into effect on 1 January 1974, all branches of foreign companies in which nonresident interest exceeded 40% were required to reapply for permission to carry on business; most companies had reduced their holdings to no more than 40% by 1 January 1976. Certain key export-oriented or technology-intensive industries were permitted to maintain up to 100% nonresident ownership. Tea plantations were also exempted from the 40% requirement. Although the government officially welcomed private foreign investment, collaboration and royalty arrangements were tightly controlled. Due to the restrictiveness of these policies, foreign investment remained remarkably low during the 1980s, ranging between $200 and $400 million a year, as compared with the $1 to $3 billion figure typical of other Asian countries at similar levels of development.

Government reform measures since 1991 are likely to change this picture greatly during the coming decade. Abolition of licensing requirements and other liberalization measures have improved the conditions for private investment overall. Majority foreign equity of up to 51% is now granted automatically for 34 priority industries, in addition to those where 100% foreign ownership is already allowed. Other regulatory changes have further facilitated the operation of foreign-owned firms. These changes have already had a sizeable impact on the inflow of foreign capital. Total foreign investments were estimated to have doubled by fiscal year 1993/94. The US response has been particularly strong, as US investment approvals jumped from $76 million in 1991 to $426 million in 1992. Other major investors now include Switzerland ($239 million approved in 1992), Japan ($211 million), the UK ($41 million), and Germany ($30 million).

39ECONOMIC DEVELOPMENT

Under a series of five-year plans through 1990, the government became a participant in many industrial fields and increased its regulation of existing private commerce and industry. Long the owner-operator of most railway facilities, all radio broadcasting, post, and telegraph facilities, arms and ammunition factories, and river development programs, the government reserved for itself the right to nationalize any industries it deemed necessary. Yet the government's socialist approach was pragmatic, not doctrinaire; agriculture and large segments of trade, finance, and industry remained in private hands. Planning is supervised by an eight-member Planning Commission, established in 1950 and chaired by the prime minister.

India's first four five-year plans entailed a total public sector outlay of ʀ314.1 billion. The first plan (1951–56) accorded top priority to agriculture, especially irrigation and power projects. The second plan (1956–61) was designed to implement the new industrial policy and to achieve a "socialist pattern of society." The plan stressed rapid industrialization, a 25% increase in national income (in fact, the achieved increase was only 20%), and reduction of inequalities in wealth and income. The third plan (1961–66) entailed total expenditures of ʀ85.8 billion (ʀ44.1 billion by the central government, ʀ41.7 billion by the states). Industrialization was again the focus, with 24.6% spent on transportation and communications and 20.1% on industry and minerals. Drought, inflation, and war with Pakistan made this plan a major disappointment; although considerable industrial diversification was achieved and national income rose, per capita income did not increase (because of population growth), and harvests were disastrously low.

Because of the unsettled domestic situation, the fourth five-year plan did not take effect until 1969. The 1969–74 plan sought to control fluctuations in agricultural output and to promote equality and social justice. Total outlays rose to R162 billion (R85.5 billion by the central government, R76.5 billion by the states). Agriculture and allied sectors received 16.9%, more than in any previous plan, while industry and minerals received 18.5%, transportation and communications 18.4%, and power development 17.8%, also more than in any previous plan.

The fifth plan (1974–79) aimed at the removal of poverty and the attainment of self-reliance. A total outlay of R393.2 billion was allocated (26% less than originally envisaged), and actual expenditures totaled R394.2 billion. Once again, the emphasis was on industry, with mining and manufacturing taking 22.5%, electric power 18.7%, transportation and communications 17.2%, and agriculture 12.1%. The fifth plan was cut short a year early, in 1978, and, with India enmeshed in recession and political turmoil, work began on the sixth development plan (1980–85). Its goal, like that of the fifth, was the removal of poverty, although the planners recognized that this gigantic task could not be accomplished within five years. The plan aimed to strengthen the agricultural and industrial infrastructure in order to accelerate the growth of investments and exports. Projected outlays totaled R975 billion, of which electric power received 27.1%, industry and mining 15.4%, transportation and communications 12.7%, and agriculture 12.2%. The main target was a GDP growth rate of 5.2% annually. The seventh development plan (1985–90) projected 5% overall GDP growth (which was largely achieved and even exceeded) based on increases of 4% and 8% in agricultural and industrial output, respectively. Outlays were to total R1,800 billion. The eighth development plan (for 1992–1997), drafted in response to the country's looming debt crisis in 1990–91, has laid the groundwork for long-term structural adjustment. The plan's overall thrust has been to stimulate industrial growth by the private sector, freeing government resources for greater investment in basic infrastructure and human resources development. In addition to liberalized conditions for private and foreign investment, the foreign exchange system has been reformed, the currency devalued, the maximum tariff reduced from 350% to 85%, import barriers generally loosened, and those for key intermediate goods removed altogether. Reform of the tax system, reduction of subsidies, which have been especially high in the agricultural sector, and restructuring of public enterprises have also been targeted, although less progress scored has been scored in these areas thus far. While the eighth plan generally supports expansion of private enterprise, unlike recent structural adjustment programs in other developing countries, it does not stipulate a large-scale privatization of the public sector. Actual GDP expansion has fallen 1–2 percentage points shy of the plan's 5.6% target, due principally to sluggish growth in manufacturing.

Economic expansion has depended heavily on foreign participation in the form of direct grants and loans, technical assistance, and private business investment. The governments and private agencies of the UK, US, former USSR, FRG, Canada, Australia, and other countries have contributed greatly, as have UN agencies and other international organizations. The IBRD has advanced large developmental loans to the government-owned railways, the Damodar Valley Corp., and two private steel corporations; IBRD funds have also been allocated for river projects, port expansion, expansion of Tata Iron & Steel and Indian Iron and Steel, colliery development, and the Industrial Credit and Investment Corp. From 1947 to 1986, authorized aid from the US cumulatively totaled $11.6 billion. In recent years, the principal donors have been the IBRD and IDA. All told, external assistance to India amounted to more than $37 billion from independence through 1986. From 1987 through 1990, the net flow of official development assistance from all sources totalled over $7.4 billion.

40SOCIAL DEVELOPMENT

India's governments have established an extensive social welfare system. Programs for children include supplementary nutrition for expectant mothers and for children under 7 years of age, immunization and health programs, vacation camps for low-income families, and prevocational training for adolescents. There are also services for the blind, deaf, mentally retarded, and orthopedically handicapped. Programs for women include welfare grants, women's adult education, and working women's hostels. Special measures are aimed at rehabilitating juvenile delinquents, prostitutes, and convicts. Begging in public places is forbidden by law in most states and localities. Other social welfare programs cover displaced persons; family planning and maternity care; rural community development; emergency relief programs for drought, flood, earthquake, and other disasters; untouchability (the Harijans); and underdeveloped tribal peoples.

There are welfare funds for providing medical, educational, and recreational facilities for workers in coal mines, mica mines, plantations, and certain government enterprises. A limited state health insurance scheme applies to workers in large factories, and many government employees and their families in Bombay and New Delhi are covered under a contributory health scheme. Other limited insurance extends to employees of factories, mines, and plantations.

During the administrations of Indira Gandhi legislation was passed in 1976 guaranteeing men and women equal pay for equal or similar work and raising the marriageable age for girls from 15 to 18 years. Below the highest political levels, however, and especially in rural India, the position of women remains subordinate to that of men. Laws aimed at preventing employment discrimination, female bondage and prostitution, and the Sati (widow-burning), are often not enforced. A National Commission for Women was established in 1992 to investigate abuses against women, including "dowry deaths," which still numbered 4,785 in 1992 according to government figures. Not only does the male population exceed that of females, but India is also one of the few countries where men, on the average, live longer than women. To explain this anomaly, it has been suggested that daughters are more likely to be malnourished and to be provided with fewer health care services. Virtually all women marry, the lone exception being victims of rape, who are often treated as outcasts. Despite the legal prohibition, child marriages are still arranged in many parts of India. For government employees, however, the giving and receiving of dowries have been declared unacceptable conduct, but the practice is widespread in all sectors of society.

In 1952, India became the first country in the world to launch a nationwide population control program. This program was greatly accelerated under Indira Gandhi, and allegations that the government had used coercive methods during the mid-1970s emergency period to increase the number of sterilizations played a major role in her 1977 electoral defeat. The family-planning program lagged during the Janata government's first year in office but revived thereafter, gaining added impetus from the 1981 census results, which showed an increase of more than 130 million people since 1971. Family planning remains a major social objective of the government. Between 1952 and 1986, 49.6 million sterilization operations (vasectomies and tubectomies) were performed, and insertions of an intrauterine device to prevent conception were made in 17.4 million women. From 1956 to 1986, a total of 76.2 million births were averted. A factory has been set up by the government for manufacturing contraceptive devices, and their commercial distribution is encouraged. Condoms are also distributed free of charge at family planning centers. In

1985–90, India's fertility rate was 4.2, down 11.2% from the previous 5-year period. In 1988–89, 43% of reproductive-age couples reported practicing contraception. Abortion is legal on medical, judicial, and socioeconomic grounds.

41HEALTH

Great improvements have taken place in public health since independence, but the general health picture remains far from satisfactory. The government is paying increasing attention to integrated health, maternity and child care in rural areas. An increasing number of community health workers and doctors are being sent to rural health centers. Primary health care is being provided to the rural population through a network of over 150,000 primary health centers and sub-centers by 586,000 trained midwives and 410,000 health guides (1992 data).

Total health care expenditures in 1990 were $17,740,000. Average life expectancy increased from 48 years in 1971 to 60 years in 1992. Infant mortality declined from 135 per 1,000 live births in 1973 to 83 in 1992. The high mortality rate among infants and children is directly linked to size of family, which is being reduced through the small family norm (National Family Planning Program). The overall mortality rate in 1993 was 10 per 1,000 people. The government's goal is to bring the mortality rate down to 9, and raise the life expectancy to 64 years.

The incidence of malaria was reduced by 98% between 1953 and 1965, but the number of reported cases increased from 14.8 million in 1966 to 64.7 million in 1976 because DDT-resistant strains of mosquitoes had developed. The death toll from smallpox was reduced to zero by 1977 through a massive vaccination program, and plague has not been reported since 1967. Between 1948 and 1980, 254 million people were tested for tuberculosis and 252 million received BCG, an antituberculosis vaccine. In 1990, there were 220 reported cases of tuberculosis per 100,000 people. And in 1994, there was a serious outbreak of pneumonic plague in western India which spread to others parts of the country, killing thousands. Many diseases remain, especially deficiency diseases such as goiter, kwashiorkor, rickets, and beriberi. However, India's immunization rates for children up to one year old are high. Data from 1992 shows vaccinations against tuberculosis (96%); diphtheria, pertussis, and tetanus (89%); polio (89%); and measles (85%). There is also a national system to distribute Vitamin A capsules to children because a lack of this vitamin contributes to blindness and malnutrition. As of 1993, 20–25% of the country's children had been reached.

The government is committed to a goal of "Health for All" by the year 2000 (implementing its eighth 5-year plan from 1990 to 1995). The plan includes eradication of malaria, and control of leprosy, tuberculosis, and cataracts. India also wants to achieve a goal of 1 hospital bed per 1,000 people. In 1991, there was a total of 39,026 hospitals and dispensaries. In addition, the rural population was served by 130,876 subcenters, 20,351 primary health centers, and 1,852 community health centers. There were 637,604 hospital beds (0.76 per 1,000 people). In that same year, India had 331,630 physicians (4 per 1,000 people) and 9,796 dentists. In 1988, there were 245,405 nurses and 132,923 midwives. There are also numerous herb compounders, along with some 278,000 registered practitioners following the Ayurvedic (ancient Hindu) and Unani systems.

India has 106 modern medical colleges, 19 dental colleges, 15 colleges of nursing, and 286 nursing schools. More than 100 colleges and schools teach the indigenous Ayurvedic and Unani systems of medicine, and 74 teach homeopathy. New drugs and pharmaceutical plants, some assisted by the UN and some established by European and American firms, manufacture antibiotics, vaccines, germicides, and fungicides. However, patent medicines and other reputed curatives of dubious value are still widely marketed; medical advisors of the indigenous systems and their curatives probably are more widely followed than Western doctors, drugs, and medical practices.

42HOUSING

Progress has been made toward improving the generally primitive housing in which most Indians live. According to the 1971 census, the usable housing stock consisted of 82.5 million units, of which 66.4 million units were in rural areas and 16.1 million in urban areas. By 1992, the total housing stock numbered 120,746,000. A number of subsidized, low-cost housing schemes have been launched by the government, but the goal of providing a house for every homeless family cannot be met because of the prohibitive cost. The sixth five-year plan envisaged an expenditure of R94 billion for rural housing and R35 billion for urban housing during 1980–85, including R11.9 billion to provide shelter for homeless people. The eighth five-year plan (1990–95) called for an investment of $40 billion in housing, with 90% of this sum earmarked for the private sector. The government's goal is to provide eight million new housing units between 1990 and 2000, two million to fill the existing backlog and six million to meet the needs that will be created by population growth.

43EDUCATION

According to the 1981 census, the population of India was 36.1% literate. In 1990, this figure rose to 48.2% (males: 61.8% and females: 33.7%). In 1986, the National Education Policy (NPE) was adopted in order to bring about major reforms in the system, primarily universalization of primary education. In 1988, a national literacy mission was launched, following which states like Kerala and Pondicherry achieved 100% literacy. In 1992, the second program of action on education was introduced to reaffirm the 1986 policy with plans to achieve total literacy and free education for all children up to grade eight by the year 2000.

Since 1947, public educational facilities have been expanded as rapidly as possible. The main goal has been primary education for children in the 6–11 age group. An emphasis on "basic education"—learning in the context of the physical and cultural environment, including domestic and commercial productive activities—has met with some success. In addition to expansion of primary education, there has been marked increase in educational facilities in secondary schools, colleges, universities, and technical institutes. An intensive development of adult education is under way in both urban and rural areas.

Free and compulsory elementary education is a directive principle of the constitution. The percentage of the school-age population actually enrolled in primary school increased from 62.4% in 1960/61 to an estimated 91.8% in 1984/85. In 1990, there were 558,392 primary level schools with 1,636,898 teachers and 99,118,320 pupils. In general secondary schools, there were 54,180,391 pupils the same year.

India's system of higher education is still basically British in structure and approach. The University system is second only to that of the United States in size with 150 universities and over 5,000 colleges and higher level institutions. Educational standards are constantly improving and especially in the area of science and mathematics are as high as those found anywhere in the world. The older universities are in Calcutta, Bombay, and Madras, all established in 1857; Allahabad, 1877; Banares Hindu (in Varanasi) and Mysore (now Karnataka), both in 1916; Hyderabad (Osmania University), in 1918; and Aligarh and Lucknow, both in 1921. Most universities have attached and affiliated undergraduate colleges, some of which are in distant towns. Christian missions in India have organized more than three dozen college-rank institutions and hundreds of primary, secondary, and vocational schools. In addition to universities there were some 3,500 arts and sciences colleges (excluding research institutes) and commercial colleges, as well as 1,500 other training schools and colleges, in 1984/85. The autonomous University Grants Commission promotes university education and maintains standards in teaching and research. Many college students receive scholarships and stipends.

44LIBRARIES AND MUSEUMS

The National Library in Calcutta, with over 2,000,000 volumes, is the largest in the country. Some of the other leading libraries are the Delhi Public Library in Delhi (970,391 volumes), the Central Secretariat Library in New Delhi (700,000 volumes), and the libraries of some of the larger universities. The Khuda Baksh Oriental Library in Patna, with a collection of rare manuscripts in Arabic, Urdu, and Farsi, is one of ten libraries declared "institutions of national importance" by an act of parliament. The National Archives of India, in New Delhi, is the largest repository of documents in Asia, with 25 km (16 mi) of shelf space.

Most of India's 462 museums specialize in one or several aspects of Indian or South Asian culture; these include 25 archaeological museums at ancient sites, such as Konarak, Amravati, and Sarnath. Some of the more important museums are the India Museum in Calcutta, the Prince of Wales Museum of Western India in Bombay, and the National Museum and the National Gallery of Modern Art, both in New Delhi. There also are thousands of architectural masterpieces of antiquity—the palaces, temples, mausoleums, fortresses, mosques, formal gardens, deserted cities, and rock-hewn monasteries—found in every section of the subcontinent.

Noted botanical gardens are located in Calcutta, Bombay, Lucknow, Ootacamund, Bangalore, Madras, and Darjeeling, and well-stocked zoological gardens are found in Calcutta, Bombay, Madras, Trivandrum, Hyderabad, Karnataka, and Jodhpur.

45MEDIA

All postal and telegraph and most telephone services are owned and operated by the government. At the end of March 1991 there were 148,719 post offices in operation. At the same time there were 39,906 telegraph offices. National telex service in English was inaugurated in 1963, and the first Devanagari script telex service began at New Delhi in 1969; there were 331 telex exchanges in 1990. As of 1991 there were 4,420,107 telephones. International telephone services, both radio and cable, are available between India and all major countries of the world through the Overseas Communications Service.

All-India Radio (AIR), government owned, operates short- and medium-wave transmission through 148 stations and broadcasts in all major languages and dialects for home consumption. AIR also operates external services in 24 foreign and 36 Indian languages. The number of radios totaled about 68.5 million in 1991. In 1959, India's first television station was inaugurated in Delhi, and color television broadcasting was inaugurated in 1982. By the end of 1985, the government's Doordarshan television network operated 22 broadcasting centers. In 1991, there were 30 million television sets in the country. The School Television Section broadcasts regular in-school instruction programs on selected subjects. India has a thriving film industry, centered at Bombay, Madras, Calcutta, and Bangalore. The output of feature films in 1991 totaled 910, and Indians are avid filmgoers and users of videocassettes.

The first newspaper in India, an English-language weekly issued in Calcutta in 1780, was followed by English-language papers in other cities. The first Indian-language newspaper (in Hindi) appeared in Varanasi (Benares) in 1845. In 1989 there were 30,153 newspapers published in some 85 languages, led by Hindi, English, Bengali, Urdu, and Marathi. The majority of Indian newspapers are under individual ownership and have small circulations.About 30% are published in Delhi, Bombay, Calcutta, and Madras.

The principal national English-language newspapers are the *Indian Express,* with editions published in Bombay and 10 other cities, and the *Times of India,* published in Ahmadabad, Bombay, Delhi, and 3 other cities. The largest Hindi daily is the *Navbharat Times,* published in Bombay. Principal dailies (with estimated 1992 circulation) are as follows:

	LANGUAGE	CIRCULATION
BOMBAY		
Indian Express	English	646,307
Times of India	English	538,132
Navbharat Times	Hindi	450,000
Lokasatta	Marathi	258,087
Maharashtra Times	Marathi	163,643
CALCUTTA		
Ananda Bazar Patrika	Bengali	414,600
DELHI		
Hindustan Times	English	273,628
Hindustan	Hindi	141,813
MADRAS		
The Hindu	English	421,000
Daily Thanthi	Tamil	313,624

In 1976, the four leading Indian news agencies—the Press Trust of India (English), United News of India (English), Hindustan Samachar (Hindi), and Samachar Bharati (Hindi)—merged to form Samachar, which means "news" in Hindi. The merger followed the cancellation by AIR of subscriptions to all four services. Samachar was dissolved in 1978, and as of 1991 there were three separate agencies: Indian News and Features Alliance, Press Trust of India and United News of India.

Freedom of the press has been nominally ensured by liberal court interpretations of the constitution, but the government has long held the right to impose "reasonable restrictions" in the interest of "public order, state security, decency, and morality." The government's censorship of newspapers imposed in June 1975 was declared illegal by the courts, and press restrictions proclaimed by Indira Gandhi's government in 1976 were relaxed by the Janata government in 1977. The independent Press Council, which had been abolished in 1975, was restored in 1979 with the function of upholding freedom of the press. On a day-to-day basis, the press is essentially unfettered, and news magazines abound in addition to the newspapers.

46ORGANIZATIONS

Cultural activities, especially traditional arts and crafts, are promoted throughout India by the National Academy of Fine Arts; the National Academy of Music, Dance, and Drama; and the National Academy of Letters. Other state organizations for the furthering of cultural activities include the Ministry of Information and Broadcasting, the Indian Council for Cultural Relations, and the National Book Trust. There are a great many private cultural and institutional organizations based on religion and philosophy, language (including Sanskrit and Pali), drama, music and dancing, modern writing, the classics, and painting and sculpture. There are many political, commercial, industrial, and labor organizations, and rural cooperatives and recreational organizations are of some importance. Almost all commercial and industrial centers have chambers of commerce.

47TOURISM, TRAVEL, AND RECREATION

The national Department of Tourism maintains tourist information offices at home and abroad. It has constructed many facilities for viewing wildlife in forest regions (by minibus, boat, or elephant) and operates tourist lodges in wildlife sanctuaries. All major cities have comfortable Western-style hotels that cater to tourists; in 1991 there were 44,495 hotel rooms with 88,990 beds and a 64.9 percent occupancy rate. Tourist arrivals numbered 1,677,508, of whom 591,210 came from Southern Asia and 562,731 from Europe. Foreign exchange earnings from tourism totaled $1.31 billion in 1991. The principal tourist attractions are India's distinctive music, dance, theater, festivals, and cuisines; the great cities of Calcutta, Bombay, and Madras; and such monuments as the Red Fort and Jama Masjid mosque in Delhi, the Taj Mahal at Agra, and the Amber Palace in Jaipur. Tourists and pilgrims also flock to the sacred Ganges River, the Ajanta temple caves, the temple at Bodhgaya where the Buddha is said to have achieved enlightenment, and many other ancient temples and tombs throughout the country. In general, all visitors must have a valid passport and an entry, transit, or tourist visa. Inoculation against cholera is recommended.

The big-game hunting for which India was once famous is now banned, but excellent fishing is available, and there are many golf courses. Cricket, field hockey, polo, football (soccer), volleyball, and basketball are all popular, as are pony-trekking in the hill stations and skiing in northern India.

48FAMOUS INDIANS

Unquestionably, one of the greatest Indians was Siddartha Gautama (624–544 BC according to Sinhalese tradition; 563?–483? BC according to most modern scholars), later known as the Buddha ("the enlightened one"). Born in what is now Nepal, he spent much of his life in eastern Uttar Pradesh and Bihar, propounding the philosophical doctrines that were later to become Buddhism. Contemporary with the Buddha was Vardhamana (599?–527 BC), also known as Mahavira ("great hero"), a saintly thinker of Bihar from whose teachings evolved Jainism. A great many later religious and political leaders left their indelible mark on the Indian scene. Some of the noteworthy were Chandragupta (r.321?–297? BC), founder of the Maurya Dynasty; Asoka (r.273–232 BC), who made Buddhism the religion of his empire; Chandragupta II (r. AD 375?–413), whose era marked a high point of Hindu art and literature; Shivaji (1627?–80), a hero of much Hindu folklore; Nanak (1469–1539), whose teachings are the basis of Sikhism; and Govind Singh (1666–1708), the guru who gave Sikhism its definitive form. Akbar (1542–1605) greatly expanded the Mughal Empire, which reached its height under Shah Jahan (1592–1666), builder of the Taj Mahal, and his son, the fanatical emperor Aurangzeb (1618–1707).

One of the greatest scholars of ancient times was the Sanskrit grammarian Panini (5th?–4th? cents. BC), who wrote the first book on scientific linguistics. The Bengali educator and reformer Rammohan Roy (1772–1833) has been called "the father of modern India." Swami Vivekananda (1863–1902), founder of the nonsectarian Ramakrishna Mission and a great traveler both in India and abroad, did much to explain the Hindu philosophy to the world and to India as well. Sarvepalli Radhakrishnan (1888–1975), a leading 20th-century Hindu scholar and philosopher, also served as president of India from 1962 to 1967. Another revered religious philosopher was Meher Baba (1894–1969). The rising position of India in science and industry is well exemplified by Jamshedji Nusserwanji Tata (1822–1904), founder of the nation's first modern iron and steel works as well as many other key industries; the physicist Jagadis Chandra Bose (1858–1937), noted for his research in plant life; Srinivasa Ramanujan (1887–1919), an amazingly original, although largely self-taught, mathematician; Chandrasekhara Venkata Raman (1888–1970), who was awarded the 1930 Nobel Prize for research in physics; and Vikram A. Sarabhai (1919–71), the founder of the Indian space program. Mother Teresa (Agnes Gonxha Bojaxhiu, b.1910, in what is now Yugoslavia) won the Nobel Peace Prize in 1979 for her 30 years of work among Calcutta's poor.

In modern times no Indian so completely captured the Indian masses and had such a deep spiritual effect on so many throughout the world as Mohandas Karamchand Gandhi (1869–1948). Reverently referred to by millions of Indians as the Mahatma ("the great-souled one"), Gandhi is considered the greatest Indian since the Buddha. His unifying ability and his unusual methods of nonviolent resistance contributed materially to the liberation of India in 1947. A leading disciple of the Mahatma, Vinayak ("Vinoba") Narahari Bhave (1895–1982), was an agrarian reformer who persuaded wealthy landowners to give about 600,000 hectares (1,500,000 acres) of tillable land to India's poor.

Gandhi's political heir, Jawaharlal Nehru (1889–1964), had a hold on the Indian people almost equal to that of the Mahatma. Affectionately known as Chacha (Uncle) Nehru, he steered India through its first 17 years of independence a played a key role in the independence struggle. Indira Gandhi (1917–84), the daughter of Nehru and prime minister from 1966 to 1977 and again from 1980 to 1984, continued her father's work in modernizing India and played an important role among the leaders of nonaligned nations. Her son Rajiv (1944–91) succeeded her as prime minister and, in the 1985 election, achieved for himself and his party the largest parliamentary victory since India became independent.

The greatest classical Sanskrit writer, and perhaps the greatest writer in Indian history, was the poet and playwright Kalidasa (fl. 5th cent. AD), whose best-known work is *Shakuntala*. In modern times, Rabindranath Tagore (1861–1941), the great Bengali humanist, profoundly influenced Indian thought in his many songs and poems. Tagore received the Nobel Prize in literature in 1913 and through his lifetime wrote more than 50 dramas and about 150 books of verse, fiction, and philosophy. Another Bengali writer highly esteemed was the novelist Bankim Chandra Chatterjee (1838–94). Tagore and Chatterjee are the authors, respectively, of India's national anthem and national song. The novel in English is a thriving genre; notable modern practitioners include Rasipuram Krishnaswamy Narayan (b.1906), Bhabani Bhattacharya (b.1906), and Raja Rao (b.1909) and Khushwaut Singh. Influential poets of the last two centuries include the Bengalis Iswar Chandra Gupta (1812–59) and Sarojini Naidu (1879–1949), known as "the nightingale of India," a close associate of Gandhi and a political leader in her own right.

Modern interpreters of the rich Indian musical tradition include the composer and performer Ravi Shankar (b.1920) and the performer and educator Ali Akbar Khan (b.1922). Zubin Mehta (b.1936) is an orchestral conductor of international renown. Uday Shankar (1900?–1977), a dancer and scholar, did much to stimulate Western interest in Indian dance. Tanjore Balasaraswati (1919?–84) won renown as a classical dancer and teacher. Preeminent in the Indian cinema is the director Satyajit Ray (1921–1992).

49DEPENDENCIES

Andaman and Nicobar Islands

The Andaman and Nicobar Islands are two groups of islands in the Indian Ocean, extending approximately 970 km (600 mi) N–S and lying about 640 km (400 mi) w of both the Tenasserim coast of Burma and peninsular Thailand. Their total area is 8,293 sq km (3,202 sq mi); their population was estimated at 188,254 in 1993. These islands together form a union territory with its capital at Port Blair. The legal system is under the jurisdiction of the high court of Calcutta.

The Andaman Islands extend more than 354 km (220 mi) between 10° and 14°N and 92°12′ and 94°17′E. Of the 204 islands in the group, the 3 largest are North, Middle, and South Andaman; since these are separated only by narrow inlets, they are often referred to together as Great Andaman. Little Andaman lies to the south.

The Nicobars extend south from the Andamans between 10° and 6°N and 92°43′ and 93°57′E. Of the 19 islands, Car Nicobar, 121 km (75 mi) s of Little Andaman, holds more than half the total population; the largest, Great Nicobar, 146 km (91 mi) NW of Sumatra, is sparsely populated.

The Andamans were occupied by the British in 1858, the Nicobars in 1869; sporadic settlements by British, Danish, and other groups were known previously. During World War II, the islands were occupied by Japanese forces. They became a union territory in 1956. That same year, the Andaman and Nicobar Islands (Protection of Aboriginal Tribes) Act came into force; this act, designed to protect the primitive tribes that live in the islands, prohibited outsiders from carrying on trade or industry in the islands without a special license. Six different tribes live in the Andaman and Nicobar Islands, the largest being the Nicobarese. There are lesser numbers of Andamanese, Onges, Jarawas, Sentinalese, and Shompens. in the dependency. Access to tribal areas is prohibited.

Agriculture is the mainstay of the economy. The principal crops are rice and coconuts; some sugarcane, fruits, and vegetables are also grown. There is little industry other than a sawmill and plywood and match factories, but the government is making plans to promote tourism in the islands. These plans include the construction of a 1,000-bed hotel, a casino, and duty-free shopping facilities in Port Blair.

Lakshadweep

The union territory of Lakshadweep consists of the Laccadive, Minicoy, and Amindivi Islands, a scattered group of small coral atolls and reefs in the Arabian Sea between 10° and 13°N and 71°43′ and 73°43′E and about 320 km (200 mi) w of Kerala state. Their total area is about 32 sq km (12 sq mi). Minicoy, southernmost of the islands, is the largest.

In 1993, the population of Lakshadweep was estimated to be 40,237. The inhabitants of the Laccadives and Amindivis are Malayalam-speaking Muslims; those on Minicoy are also Muslim, but speak a language similar to Sinhalese. The islanders are skilled fishermen and trade their marine products and island-processed coir in the Malabar ports of Kerala. The main cottage industry is coir spinning. Politically, these islands were under the control of the state of Madras until 1956. The present territorial capital is at Kavaratti. Judicial affairs are under the jurisdiction of the high court of Kerala.

50BIBLIOGRAPHY

Abbas, K. A. *Indira Gandhi: The Last Post.* Columbia, Mo.: South Asia Books, 1986.

Allchin, Bridget and Raymond. *The Rise of Civilization in India and Pakistan.* Cambridge: Cambridge University Press, 1982.

American University. *India: A Country Study.* Washington, D.C.: Government Printing Office, 1986.

Balasubramanyam, V. N. *The Economy of India.* Boulder, Colo.: Westview, 1985.

Banerjee, Anil Chandra. *Constitutional History of India.* 3 vols. Delhi: Macmillan, 1978.

Becker, Charles M. *Indian Urbanization and Economic Growth since 1960.* Baltimore: Johns Hopkins University Press, 1992.

Bhattacharya. Sabyasachi (ed.). *The South Indian Economy: Agrarian Change, Industrial Structure, and State Policy, c. 1914–1947.* New York: Oxford University Press, 1991.

Bradnock, Robert W. *India's Foreign Policy since 1971.* New York: Council on Foreign Relations Press, 1990.

Brown, Judith M. *Modern India: The Origins of an Asian Democracy.* 2d ed. New York: Oxford University Press, 1994.

Cassels, Jamie. *The Uncertain Promise of Law: Lessons from Bhopal.* Toronto: University of Toronto Press, 1993.

Choudhury, R. A., Shama Gamkhar, and Aurobindo Ghose (eds.). *The Indian Economy and its Performance since Independence.* Delhi: Oxford University Press, 1990.

Copley, A. R. H. *Gandhi: Against the Tide.* New York: Blackwell, 1987.

Dash, Narendra Kumar. *An Encyclopaedic Dictionary of Indian Culture.* Delhi: Agam Kala Prakashan, 1992.

Embree, Ainslie Thomas. *Imagining India: Essays on Indian History.* New York: Oxford University Press, 1989.

Embree, Ainslie Thomas and M. S. A. Rao (eds.). *Dominance and State Power in Modern India: Decline of a Social Order.* New York: Oxford University Press, 1989–1990.

Ghosh, Arun (ed.). *An Encyclopaedia of Indian Archaeology.* New York: E. J. Brill, 1990.

———. *Indian Industrialization: Structure and Policy Issues.* New York: Oxford University Press, 1992.

Hardgrave, Robert L., Jr. *India: Government and Politics in a Developing Nation.* 3d ed. New York: Harcourt Brace Jovanovich, 1980.

Heehs, Peter. *The Bomb in Bengal: The Rise of Revolutionary Terrorism in India, 1900–1910.* Oxford: Oxford University Press, 1993.

India in Pictures. Minneapolis: Lerner, 1989.

Jalan, Bimal. *India's Economic Crisis: The Way Ahead.* New York: Oxford University Press, 1991.

Jayaraman, R. *Caste and Class: Dynamics of Inequality in Indian Society.* New York: Apt, 1982.

Jha, Shiva C. *A History of Indian Economic Thought.* Columbia, Mo.: South Asia Books, 1981.

——— (ed.). *The New Cambridge History of India.* New York: Cambridge University Press, 1987–1993.

Kangas, Georgia. *Population Dilemma: India's Struggle for Survival.* Atlantic Highlands, N.J.: Humanities, 1985.

Khan, M. E., and C. V. S. Prasad. *Fertility Control in India.* New Delhi: Manohar, 1980.

Lal, Deepak. *Cultural Stability and Economic Stagnation: India, c. 1500 BC–AD 1980.* Oxford: Clarendon Press; New York: Oxford University Press, 1988.

Lu, Chih. *The Sino-Indian Border Dispute: A Legal Study.* Westport, Conn.: Greenwood, 1986.

Mahmud, S. F. *A Concise History of Indo-Pakistan.* 2d ed. New York: Oxford University Press, 1988.

Mehta, Ved. *A Family Affair: India under Three Prime Ministers.* New York: Oxford University Press, 1982.

Mitra, Sisirkumar. *India: Vision and Fulfillment.* New York: Apt, 1981.

Moorhouse, Geoffrey. *India Britannica.* New York: Harper & Row, 1983.

Pachauri, R. K. *Energy and Economic Development in India.* New York: Praeger, 1977.

Palmer, Norman. *The United States and India: The Dimensions of Influence.* Westport, Conn.: Praeger, 1984.

Rothermund, Dictmar. *India.* New York: St. Martin's, 1982.

Roy-Chaudhury, P. C. *Gandhi and His Contemporaries.* Livingston, N.J.: Orient, 1972.

Shepperdson, M. J., and C. P. Simmons. *The Indian National Congress Party and the Political Economy of India, 1885–1985.* Brookfield, Vt.: Gower, 1987.

Srinivas, M. N. *India: Social Structure.* Delhi: Hindustan, 1980.

Studdert-Kennedy, Gerald. *British Christians, Indian Nationalists, and the Raj Studdert-Kennedy.* New York: Oxford University Press, 1991.

Tomlinson, B. R. *The Economy of Modern India, 1860–1970.* New York: Cambridge University Press, 1993.

Wolpert, Stanley A. *India.* Berkeley: University of California Press, 1991.

———. *A New History of India.* 4th ed. New York: Oxford University Press, 1993.

INDONESIA

Republic of Indonesia
Republik Indonesia

CAPITAL: Jakarta.

FLAG: The national flag, adopted in 1949, consists of a red horizontal stripe above a white stripe.

ANTHEM: *Indonesia Raya (Great Indonesia).*

MONETARY UNIT: The rupiah (Rp) consists of 100 sen. There are coins of 1, 2, 5, 10, 25, 50, and 100 rupiahs, and notes of 100, 500, 1,000, 5,000, and 10,000 rupiahs. Rp1 = $0.0005 (or $1 = Rp2096).

WEIGHTS AND MEASURES: The metric system is standard.

HOLIDAYS: New Year's Day, 1 January; Independence Day, 17 August; Christmas, 25 December. Movable religious holidays include the Prophet's Birthday, Ascension of Muhammad, Good Friday, Ascension Day of Jesus Christ, the end of Ramadan, 'Id al-Fitr, 'Id al-'Adha', and the 1st of Muharram (Muslim New Year).

TIME: Western, 7 PM = noon GMT; Central, 8 PM = noon GMT; Eastern, 9 PM = noon GMT.

¹LOCATION, SIZE, AND EXTENT

The Republic of Indonesia consists of five large islands and 13,677 smaller islands (about 6,000 of which are inhabited) forming an arc between Asia and Australia. With a total area of 1,919,440 sq km (741,100 sq mi), Indonesia is the fourth-largest Asian country, after China, India, and Sa'udi Arabia. Comparatively, the area occupied by Indonesia is slightly less than three times the size of the state of Texas. It extends 5,271 km (3,275 mi) E–W and 2,210 km (1,373 mi) N–S. The five principal islands are Sumatra, 473,606 sq km (182,860 sq mi); Java, with an area of 132,600 sq km (51,200 sq mi); Borneo, of which the 72% belonging to Indonesia is known as Kalimantan, 539,460 sq km (208,286 sq mi); Sulawesi, formerly called Celebes, 189,216 sq km (73,056 sq mi); and Irian Jaya (West Irian), the western portion of the island of New Guinea, 421,981 sq km (162,927 sq mi). Indonesia claims East Timor (14,874 sq km/5,743 sq mi), a former Portuguese colony that was abandoned by Portugal in 1974 and declared an Indonesian province in 1976; as of 1994, the UN still declined to recognize the Indonesian claim. Indonesia has land boundaries with Malaysia (on Borneo) and Papua New Guinea (on New Guinea). It is bounded on the N by the South China Sea, on the N and E by the Pacific Ocean, and on the S and W by the Indian Ocean. Indonesia's total boundary length (including East Timor) is 57,318 km (35,616 mi).

Indonesia's capital city, Jakarta, is located on the island of Java.

²TOPOGRAPHY

The Indonesian archipelago consists of three main regions. One of the regions consists of Sumatra, Java, Kalimantan, and the islands that lie between them, which stand on the Sunda shelf, where the ocean depths are never more than 210 m (700 ft). Another region consists of Irian Jaya and the Aru Isles, which stand on the Sahul shelf, projecting northward from the north coast of Australia at similar depths. Between these two shelves is the remaining region, consisting of the Lesser Sunda Islands, the Maluku Islands (Moluccas), and Sulawesi, which are surrounded by seas with depths that reach 4,570 m (15,000 ft). The large islands have central mountain ranges rising from more or less extensive lowlands and coastal plains. Many inactive and scores of active volcanoes dot the islands, accounting for the predominantly rich volcanic soil that is carried down by the rivers to the plains and lowlands; there are 112 volcanoes, 15 of them active, on Java alone. Peaks rise to 3,650 m (12,000 ft) in Java and Sumatra. Java, Bali, and Lombok have extensive lowland plains and gently sloping cultivable mountainsides. Extensive swamp forests and not very fertile hill country are found in Kalimantan. Sumatra's eastern coastline is bordered by morasses, floodplains, and alluvial terraces suitable for cultivation farther inland. Mountainous areas predominate in Sulawesi.

³CLIMATE

Straddling the Equator, Indonesia has a tropical climate characterized by heavy rainfall, high humidity, high temperature, and low winds. The wet season is from November to March, the dry season from June to October. Rainfall in lowland areas averages 180–320 cm (70–125 in) annually, increasing with elevation to an average of 610 cm (240 in) in some mountain areas. In the lowlands of Sumatra and Kalimantan, the rainfall range is 305–370 cm (120–145 in); the amount diminishes southward, closer to the northwest Australian desert. Average humidity is 82%.

Altitude rather than season affects the temperature in Indonesia. At sea level, the mean annual temperature is about 25–27°C (77–81°F). There is slight daily variation in temperature, with the greatest variation at inland points and at higher levels. The mean annual temperature at Jakarta is 26°C (79°F); average annual rainfall is about 200 cm (80 in).

⁴FLORA AND FAUNA

The plant life of the archipelago reflects a mingling of Asiatic and Australian forms with endemic ones. Vegetation ranges from that of the tropical rain forest of the northern lowlands and the seasonal forests of the southern lowlands, through vegetation of the less luxuriant hill forests and mountain forests, to subalpine shrub vegetation. The bridge between Asia and Australia formed by the archipelago is reflected in the varieties of animal life. The fauna of Sumatra, Kalimantan, and Java is similar to that of Peninsular Malaysia, but each island has its peculiar types. The orangutan is found in Sumatra and Kalimantan but not in Java, the siamang only in Sumatra, the proboscis monkey only in Kalimantan, the elephant and tapir only in Sumatra, and the wild ox in Java and Kalimantan but not in Sumatra. In Sulawesi, the Maluku Islands, and Timor, Australian types begin to occur; the bandicoot, a marsupial, is found in Timor. All the islands, especially the Malukus, abound in great varieties of bird life, reptiles, and amphibians. The abundant marine life of Indonesia's extensive territorial waters includes a rich variety of corals.

5ENVIRONMENT

An extensive "regreening" and reforestation of barren land, initiated under the 1975–79 national economic development plan, was greatly expanded and integrated with flood control and irrigation programs under the national plans for 1979–84 and 1984–89. In 1993, estimates of deforestation rates in Indonesia over a 20-year period indicate an increase from 300,000 to 1 million hectares per year. Flood-control programs involve river dredging, dike strengthening, construction of new dams, and sandbagging of river banks at critical points. The burning of oil and coal along with the abuse of fertilizers and pesticides results in significant damage to the environment. In 1987, the nation used 3.1 million tons of fertilizer. The nation's cities produce 12.9 million tons of solid waste per year. Indonesia has 607.1 cubic miles of water with 76% used in farming activity and 11% used for industrial purposes. About 65% of all city dwellers and 67% of rural dwellers do not have pure water. Legislation introduced in 1982 endorsed, in principle, the establishment of penalties for environmental pollution.

Protection of indigenous wildlife is entrusted to the Directorate of Nature Conservation and Wildlife Management. As of 1986 there were 146 parks and nature reserves, with more in the planning stage; the government's goal was to allocate 10% of the nation's land area to reserves. In 1984/85, the government set up three new national parks, part of 19 included in the 1984–89 plan, and four new natural reserves. As of 1994, 49 of Indonesia's mammal species were endangered, and 135 bird species were threatened with extinction. As of 1987, endangered species in Indonesia included the pig-tailed langur, Javan gibbon, orangutan, tiger, Asian elephant, Malayan tapir, Javan rhinoceros, Sumatran rhinoceros, Sumatran serow, Rothschild's starling, lowland anoa, mountain anoa, Siamese crocodile, false gavial, river terrapin, and four species of turtle (green sea, hawksbill, olive ridley, and leatherback).

6POPULATION

Indonesia is the fourth most populous country in the world. As of the 1990 census, the population (including East Timor)was 179,378,946, as compared with the 1971 census figure of 119,232,499 and the 1980 total of 147,490,298. The estimated population in 1994 was 203,750,000 according to the US Bureau of the Cenusus; a population of 217,998,000 is projected by the UN for the year 2000, assuming a crude birthrate of 23.8 per 1,000 population, a crude death rate of 7.7, and a net natural increase of 16.1 during 1995–2000. The growth rate is high, estimated to be about 1.9% annually in the late 1980s. Of the 1990 population, 60% (107,513,798) was concentrated on Java and Madura in 1989. The estimated population of the other major regions in 1989 was Sumatra, 36,881,990 (including nearby islands); Sulawesi, 12,507,650; Kalimantan, 8,677,459; and Bali, 2,782,038. Overall density in 1990 was 94 persons per sq km (243 per sq mi). Java and Madura, with a density of 813 per sq km (2,106 per sq mi), is among the world's most densely populated areas of its size. In 1980, the Indonesian population was nearly 31% urban. Jakarta's population in 1990 was 8,254,000 Surabaya, 2,371,000; Medan, 1,840,000; Bandung, 2,522,000; and Semarang, 1,218,000.

7MIGRATION

Historically, there has been considerable migration from and to China. Following a decree banning foreigners from participating in retail trade in rural Indonesia, some 120,000 Chinese left Indonesia in 1960 and the first six months of 1961. After the attempted coup of 1965 and the resultant deterioration in relations with China, many more Chinese left Indonesia. Migration between the Netherlands and Indonesia has been greatly reduced since independence; nearly all the 250,000 Netherlands nationals in Indonesia in 1949 returned home. In 1990 there were 288,508 registered foreigners in Indonesia (91% Asian), and 251,389 Indonesian citizens were listed as being abroad.

Resettlement of people from crowded areas to the less populous outer islands is official government policy. The 1979–84 National Economic Plan had as a target the "transmigration" of 500,000 families from Java, Bali, and Madura to Sumatra, Kalimantan, Sulawesi, Maluku Province, and Irian Jaya. Participation was voluntary, and the actual number of families that resettled was about 366,000, containing about 1.5 million people. Since the annual population increase of Java is more than 2 million, the costly transmigration scheme did little to relieve that island's human congestion, but it had a considerable impact in developing sparsely settled areas. Each family was entitled to 2 hectares (5 acres) and was provided with housing, food, seedlings, fertilizers, pesticides, and other supplies that it could use to become productive. Under the 1987–91 plan, 338,433 families were resettled.

First asylum was granted to over 145,000 Indochinese refugees between 1975 and 1993. There is a refugee facility on Galang Island.

8ETHNIC GROUPS

The indigenous peoples, ethnologically referred to as Malays or Indonesians, also are found on the neighboring islands of the Philippines, in Peninsular Malaysia, and even as far away as Taiwan and Madagascar. Indonesians are characterized by smallness of stature, light- to dark-brown pigmentation, thick, sleek black hair, broad formation of the head, a wide nose, and thick lips. The inhabitants of eastern Indonesia have Negroid features, the result of intermarriage with the Papuans of New Guinea.

The population is officially classified into four main ethnic groups: Melanesians, who constitute the majority; Proto-Austronesians, including the Wajaks and the Irianese on Irian Jaya; Polynesians, including the Ambonese on the Maluku Islands; and Micronesians, found on the tiny islets of Indonesia's eastern borders. The Melanesians are subdivided into the Acehnese of north Sumatra; the Bataks of northeastern Sumatra; the Minangkabaus of west Sumatra; the Sundanese of west Java; the Javanese in central and east Java; the Madurese on the island of Madura; the Balinese on Bali; the Sasaks on the island of Lombok; the Timorese on Timor; the Dayaks in Kalimantan; and the Minahasa, Torajas, Makassarese, and Buginese on Sulawesi.

Ethnic Chinese, the principal minority, were the target of riots in 1974 and 1980. Active mainly in business in the major cities, they are relatively properous and widely resented by ethnic Indonesians. In 1992 all but about 300,000 of an estimated 5 million ethnic Chinese held Indonesian citizenship.

9LANGUAGES

Bahasa Indonesia, a product of the nationalist movement, is the official language, serving as a common vehicle of communication for the various language groups. Based primarily on Malay and similar to the official language of Malaysia, it also contains many words from other Indonesian languages and dialects, as well as from Dutch, English, Arabic, Sanskrit, and other languages. In 1973, Indonesia and Malaysia adopted similar systems of spelling. Outside of Jakarta, only 10–15% of the population speaks

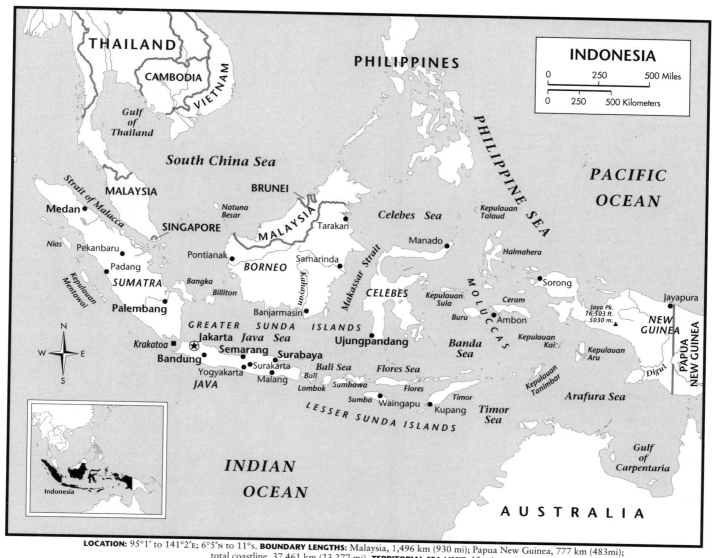

LOCATION: 95°1′ to 141°2′E; 6°5′N to 11°S. **BOUNDARY LENGTHS:** Malaysia, 1,496 km (930 mi); Papua New Guinea, 777 km (483mi); total coastline, 37,461 km (23,277 mi). **TERRITORIAL SEA LIMIT:** 12 mi.

the language in the home, but more than half the population uses it as a secondary language. Use of some 669 local languages persists, including Javanese, Sundanese, and Malay. English is widely used in industry and commerce.

10 RELIGIONS

An estimated 87% of the inhabitants are adherents of Islam, 10% are Christians, 2% are Hindus, 1% are Buddhists or Confucianists, and 1% follow tribal religions. Among Christians, an estimated 2.6% were Roman Catholics in 1993. Freedom of religion is guaranteed by the constitution, but the government actively supports Islamic religious schools and pays for a number of annual pilgrimages to Mecca. Hinduism was the religion of Java for several centuries, but when Islam swept over Indonesia in the 15th century, Hinduism retreated to Bali, and some 3 million Indonesians on Bali and elsewhere have remained Hindu in religion and culture. The religious faith of the Chinese in Indonesia may be characterized as Christian or Buddhist-Confucianist. The chief Christian communities are found on Ambon and adjacent islands, in northern Sulawesi, in north-central Sumatra, and on Timor and adjacent islands. In central Kalimantan and Irian Jaya, as well as a few other areas, substantial numbers of Indonesians follow animist tribal religions.

11 TRANSPORTATION

Indonesia is politically and economically dependent upon good communications and transportation among the islands. Transportation facilities suffered greatly from destruction and neglect during World War II and immediately thereafter. The revitalized and partially modernized system suffered an additional setback during 1957–58 as a result of the withdrawal of Dutch equipment and personnel.

Of the 119,500 km (74,257 mi) of public motor roads in 1991, mostly under local jurisdiction. In the same year, Indonesia had 1,416,157 passenger cars, 1,080,936 trucks, and 504,415 buses. Railways connect the main cities in Java and parts of Sumatra. The state owns all of the 6,964 km (4,327 mi) of railroad track in service. Air-conditioned cars and express service have been introduced in parts of Java, but no new lines have been built in recent years.

About 21,600 km (13,420 mi) of inland waterways form the most important means of transportation in Kalimantan and in parts of Sumatra. The principal ports of international trade are Tanjungpriok (for Jakarta) and Tanjungperak (for Surabaya) in Java, and Belawan (near Medan) and Padang in Sumatra. Ports with less traffic but capable of handling sizable ships are Cirebon and Semarang in Java; Palembang in Sumatra; Banjarmasin,

Balikpapan, and Pontianak in Kalimantan; Tanjungpinang in Bintan; and Ujung Padang in Sulawesi. In 1991, Indonesia's total fleet included 389 vessels of 1,000 gross tons or more, of which 267 were freighters and 96 oil tankers. Regulations were imposed in 1982 requiring that all government imports and exports be shipped in Indonesian vessels, and port charges were substantially altered to benefit Indonesia's national carriers. In 1984, a policy of scrapping old vessels was implemented.

The center of international air traffic is Jakarta's Sukarno-Hatta International Airport, which served some 7.5 million arriving and departing passengers in 1990. Garuda, Merpati Nusantara, and Sempati provide domestic and international services. As of 1992, the three airlines together carried 2,771,900 international and 7,553,100 domestic passengers.

12HISTORY

Evidence for the ancient habitation of Indonesia was discovered by the Dutch paleontologist Eugène Dubois in 1891; these fossil remains of so-called Java man (*Pithecanthropus erectus*) date from the Pleistocene period, when Indonesia was linked with the Asian mainland. Indonesia's characteristic racial mixture resulted from at least two waves of invasions from South China by way of the Malay Peninsula and from intermarriage of these Indonesians with later immigrants, especially from India. The important population groups of today trace their descent from the immigrants of the second wave, which occurred around the 2d or 3d century BC. They subjugated and absorbed most of the other inhabitants. Indian influences permeated Java and Sumatra from the 1st to the 7th century AD. During this period and extending into the 15th century, local Buddhist and Hindu rulers established a number of powerful kingdoms. Among the most powerful of these was the Buddhist kingdom of Srivijaya, established on Sumatra in the 7th century; it prospered by gaining control of trade through the Strait of Malacca. To the east, in central Java, the Sailendra dynasty established its Buddhist kingdom in the 8th century. Relics of Sailendra rule include the great temple of Borobudur, Asia's largest Buddhist monument, with hundreds of bas-reliefs depicting the life of Buddha. Succeeding the Sailendra dynasty in 856 were followers of the Hindu god Shiva; these Shivaites built the great temple at Prambanan, east of Yogyakarta. Other Hindu kingdoms subsequently extended Indian influence eastward into east Java and Bali. The last of these was the Hindu kingdom of Majapahit, which was at the height of its power during the 13th century, when Marco Polo visited Java and northern Sumatra. When Majapahit collapsed around 1520, many of its leaders, according to tradition, fled to Bali, the only island in Indonesia that retains Hinduism as the chief religion. Even before Majapahit disintegrated, Muslim missionaries, probably Persian merchants, had begun to win much of the archipelago for Islam. About this time, also, the first Europeans arrived, and the first Chinese settlements were made. The Portuguese captured Malacca (Melaka), on the west coast of the Malay Peninsula, in 1511 and established control over the archipelago.

Dutch ships visited Java in 1596. The Dutch came in increasing numbers and soon drove the Portuguese out of the archipelago (except for the eastern half of the island of Timor), beginning nearly 350 years of colonial rule. The States-General of the Dutch Republic in 1602 incorporated the East Indian spice traders as the United East India Company and granted it a monopoly on shipping and trade and the power to make alliances and contracts with the rulers of the East. By force and diplomacy, the company thus became the supreme ruler of what became known as the Dutch East Indies. However, maladministration and corruption weakened the company after its early years of prosperity, and the Dutch government nullified its charter in 1799 and took over its affairs in 1800. The British East India Company ruled the Indies during the Napoleonic wars, from 1811 to 1816. During this period, Sir Thomas Stamford Raffles became governor of Java. When Dutch rule was restored, the Netherlands government instituted the "culture system" on Java, under which the Javanese, instead of paying a certain proportion of their crops as tax, were required to put at the disposal of the government a share of their land and labor and to grow crops for export under government direction. From a fiscal point of view the system was very successful, yielding millions of guilders for the Netherlands treasury, but this "net profit" or "favorable balance" policy fell under increasing moral attack in the Netherlands and was brought to an end about 1877. Thereafter, private Dutch capital moved into the Indies, but the augmentation of Dutch prosperity at the expense of Indonesian living standards was increasingly resented. With the adoption of what colonial administrators called the "ethical policy" at the beginning of the 20th century, the first steps were taken to give Indonesians participation in government. A central representative body, the Volksraad, was instituted in 1918. At first it had only advisory powers, but in 1927 it was given colegislative powers. An Indonesian nationalist movement began to develop during those years and steadily gained strength. Although retarded in the 1930s by the world economic depression, which was strongly felt in Indonesia, the movement revived during the Japanese occupation (1942–45) in World War II. A nationalist group under the leadership of Sukarno and Mohammad Hatta proclaimed an independent republic on 17 August 1945, adopted a provisional constitution providing for a strong presidential form of government, formed a revolutionary government, and resisted Dutch reoccupation. After four years of intermittent negotiations and frequent hostilities, and after UN intervention, the Netherlands agreed to the Indonesian demands.

On 27 December 1949, the Dutch recognized the independence of all the former Dutch East Indies except West New Guinea as the Republic of the United States of Indonesia. A few months later, on 17 August 1950, the federal system was rejected and a unitary state, the Republic of Indonesia, was established under a new constitution. West New Guinea remained under Dutch control until October 1962, when the Netherlands transferred the territory to the United Nations Temporary Executive Administration (UNTEA). On 1 May 1963, Indonesia took complete possession of the disputed territory as the province of Irian Barat (West Irian); the province was renamed Irian Jaya in 1973. Indonesia, which aimed to acquire Sarawak and Sabah (which are on the island of Borneo with Kalimantan), opposed the formation of the Federation of Malaysia in September 1963 and announced a "crush Malaysia" policy. This policy was implemented by guerrilla raids into Malaysian territory that continued until August 1966, when a formal treaty was concluded between the two countries.

Sukarno became the first president of the new nation, and Hatta the vice-president. Internal difficulties, fostered by a multiplicity of political parties inherited from Dutch colonial days, soon developed, and regional rivalries also threatened the unity of the new nation. Then as now, Java had some two-thirds of the country's population, but the great sources of wealth were found on the other, much less densely settled islands. Those living in the so-called Outer Islands believed too much governmental revenue was being spent in Java and too little elsewhere. After Vice-President Hatta, a Sumatran, resigned in December 1956, many in the Outer Islands felt they had lost their chief and most effective spokesman in Jakarta. Territorial army commanders in Sumatra staged coups and defied the central government; other rebel movements developed in Sulawesi. The government took measures providing for greater fiscal and administrative decentralization, but discontent remained, and the rebellions were put down by force. Thereafter, Sukarno bypassed parliamentary procedures and pursued an increasingly authoritarian, anti-Western policy of "guided democracy." In 1959, he decreed a return to the 1945 constitution, providing for a centralized form of government, and consolidated his control.

Communist agitation within the country and secessionist uprisings in central and eastern Java came to a head in the 30th of September Movement under the direction of Lt. Col. Untung. Sukarno, whose foreign policy had turned increasingly toward the Communist Chinese, may have had advance knowledge of the Communist-led coup attempt on 30 September 1965, which was directed against Indonesia's top military men; the coup was crushed immediately by the army, however, and in the ensuing anti-Communist purges more than 100,000 persons (mostly Indonesian Chinese) lost their lives and another 700,000 were arrested. By mid-October, the army, under the command of Gen. Suharto, was in virtual control of the country. On 12 March 1966, following nearly three weeks of student riots, President Sukarno transferred to Suharto the authority to take, in the president's name, "all measures required for the safekeeping and stability of the government administration." In March 1967, the People's Consultative Assembly (Majetis Permusyawaratan Rakyat—MPR) voted unanimously to withdraw all Sukarno's governmental power and appointed Gen. Suharto acting president. One year later, it conferred full presidential powers on Suharto, and he was sworn in as president for a five-year term. The Congress also agreed to postpone the general elections due in 1968 until 1971. Sukarno died in June 1970. On 3 July 1971, national and regional elections were held for the majority of seats in all legislative bodies. The Joint Secretariat of Functional Groups (Sekber Golongan Karya—Golkar), a mass political front backed by Suharto, gained 60% of the popular vote and emerged in control of both the House of Representatives (DPR) and the MPR.

Suharto Gains Control

In March 1973, the MPR elected Suharto to a second five-year term. Thus Suharto, with key backing from the military, began a long period of dominance over Indonesian politics. Under Suharto's "New Order," Indonesia turned to the West and began following a conservative economic course stressing capital development and foreign investment. In foreign affairs, Suharto's government achieved vastly improved ties with the US, Japan, and Western Europe while maintaining links with the USSR.

On 7 December 1975, following Portugal's withdrawal from East Timor, a power struggle developed among various political groups, including the Revolutionary Front for an Independent East Timor (Frente Revolucionário de Este Timor Independente—Fretilin), a left-wing independence movement, which achieved military dominance. Indonesia sent troops into the former Portuguese colony and was shortly in full control of the territory. On 17 July 1976, the Suharto government incorporated the territory as an Indonesian Province. This action was neither recognized by the UN, which called on Indonesia to withdraw and allow the Timorese the right to self-determination, nor accepted by Fretilin. Discontent with the Suharto regime mounted after the elections of 1977, in which Suharto's Golkar Party gained an overwhelming majority. The government acknowledged holding 31,000 political prisoners; according to Amnesty International, the total was closer to 100,000. Student riots and criticism of government repression resulted in further government measures: political activity was suspended, and leading newspapers were temporarily closed. Suharto was elected by the MPR to a third five-year term in 1978; during late 1977 and 1978, some 16,000 political prisoners were released, and the remainder of those detained in 1965 were released by the end of 1979. To strengthen the government in the face of rising Muslim militancy, Suharto began to reestablish Sukarno as a national hero eight years after his death. Suharto called for greater loyalty by all political groups to the Pancasila ("five principles") framed by Sukarno in 1945, a credo encompassing belief in the one supreme God, a just and civilized

humanity, the unity of Indonesia, representative democracy, and social justice for the people of Indonesia. Golkar made further gains in the 1982 elections, and Suharto was elected for a fourth five-year term in March 1983. The war against Fretilin continued into the 1980s, with reports of massacres by government troops and severe economic hardship among the Timorese. Negotiations with Portugal, still considered responsible for decolonization by the UN, began in July 1983. In Irian Jaya, the Organization for a Free Papua (Organisasi Papua Merdeka—OPM), which desires unification with Papua New Guinea and has been active since the early 1960s, increased its militant activities in 1986. The Indonesian Army (ABRI) continued to play a dual military and socioeconomic function, and this role was supported by legislation in 1988. Golkar made further gains in the 1987 elections, and Suharto was again re-elected for a fifth five-year term in March 1988. During disagreements over nomination procedures for the vice-presidency ABRI's influence was eroded.

During Repelita I through IV and three years of V, FY 1969-92, the Transmigration Program, a policy aimed at overcoming uneven population distribution in Indonesia by moving families from the Inner Islands to the Outer Islands, almost 1,488,000 families had been moved in officially sponsored programs. Government projections were that over the 25-year period 1969-1994 over 1.7 million families would participate in the program. The Transmigration Program suffered from land disputes with local residents and environmental concerns over deforestation. Border incidents, which post-dated the 1970s Irian Jaya rebellion under the Free Papua Movement (OPM), were exacerbated by transmigration that was turning the indigenous Melanesian majority into a minority, thus stifling its opposition. Indonesian troops attempting to capture Melanesian separatists would cross the border into Papua New Guinea. The leader of OPM, Melkianus Salossa, arrested in Papua New Guinea and deported to Indonesia, was sentenced to life in prison in 1991. Indonesia and Papua New Guinea agreed to provide greater co-operation on security and trade issues. In 1989 tension from land disputes in Java and the Outer Islands produced social unrest that resulted in clashes between villagers and the armed forces. In 1990 armed rebellion in Aceh, in northern Sumatra, arose over hostility toward government policies regarding exploitation of Aceh's mineral resources and the transmigration program. The government squashed the rebellion with a massive display of force.

Political openness was increasingly espoused during 1990–91 by political and labor organizations. In 1990 a group of prominent Indonesians publicly demanded that Suharto retire from the presidency at the end of his current term; in 1991 labor unrest increased with a rash of strikes which the army was called in to quell. President Suharto made his first pilgrimage to Mecca in 1991. Government efforts to raise funds through a state lottery were opposed, and finally forbidden on religious grounds when the country's highest Islamic authority declared the lottery "haram" forbidden.

On 12 November 1991, during a funeral for a young Timorese killed in demonstrations against Indonesia's rule of East Timor, soldiers opened fire on the defenseless mourners. This massacre received worldwide attention. Although the government took unprecedented steps to punish those involved, western governments threatened to suspend aid, and demands were made linking aid to human rights issues. The Netherlands' demand, linking its aid to improvements in human rights, was rejected when Suharto refused Dutch economic aid on 25 March 1992, thus breaking all economic ties. In the aftermath of these events Suharto, in speeches to the Nonaligned Movement summit in Jakarta and to the UN General Assembly, suggested that developing nations needed to take a more prominent role in adjusting the inequalities in North-South relations. Suharto's challenge received a cool reception from Western nations, but it clearly signaled a reassessment of Indonesia's future international presence. By 1993 US policy toward Indonesia shifted toward criticism of Indonesia's rule in East Timor, and a threat to revoke trade privileges pursuant to Indonesia's treatment of the largest independent trade union, the SBSI (Indonesian Prosperous Labor Union). A UN resolution on Indonesia's human rights violations placed the country on a rights "watch" list in 1993. In late 1992 tensions between Muslims and Christians increased to the point of violence and vandalism of churches and mosques. Suharto requested that religious tolerance be practiced. A major scandal in November/December 1992 occurred when Bank Summa was suspended from clearing operations and slated for liquidation in April 1993. In early December 1992 government forces captured Jose Alexandre (Xanana) Gusmao, leader of the Fretilin, who was hiding in Dili, in Timor. On 21 May 1993 he was sentenced to life imprisonment. Also in December 1992 the island of Flores suffered Indonesia's worst earthquake in modern times. The quake, which registered 6.8 on the Richter scale, killed up to 2,500 people and destroyed 18,000 homes.

Although its total share of votes declined, Golkar won the 1992 elections, securing 282 of the 400 elective seats. In March 1993 Suharto was elected to a sixth term as president. The commander in chief of ABRI, Try Sutrisno, was chosen as vice president. Another major scandal occurred in March 1993 with the sale of $5 million in fake shares on the Jakarta Stock Exchange (JSE). In January 1994 President Suharto inaugurated 12 electric power plants with combined installed capacity of more than 2,000 Mw. Violent labor unrest broke out in Medan in April 1994 with the mysterious death of a union activitist. Ethnic Chinese who are only about 3% of the population of Indonesia were the target of demonstrators; one Chinese factory manager was killed. The success of the Chinese is widely envied and they are accused of exploiting the workers. On 21 June 1994 the government closed *Tempo* and two other publications by revoking publishing licenses. Tempo was accused of violating the journalistic code of ethics and pitting one person against another to the point where it affected national security, based on its coverage of a controversial purchase of 39 warships from the former East German navy. The other publications were accused of more technical infractions including the failure to comply with registration procedures and publishing political and general news in spite of license restrictions limiting a popular tabloid's coverage to detective stories and crime stories.

13 GOVERNMENT

The provisional constitution of 17 August 1950 provided for a unitary republic. The president and vice-president, "elected in accordance with rules to be laid down by law," were to be inviolable, but cabinet ministers were jointly and individually responsible. The House of Representatives was to be a unicameral parliament. Its members were elected by a system of proportional representation for a four-year term, but it might be dissolved earlier by presidential decree. Sukarno and Hatta, the first president and vice-president, were elected by parliament; no term of office was stipulated by the constitution. In practice, the government was not truly parliamentary, since President Sukarno played a role far greater than is usual for the head of state in a parliamentary system. He was the great national revolutionary hero, and his popularity with the masses enabled him to exert great influence on government policy. Parliament was not strong enough to hold the president to the role prescribed by the constitution. In 1957, Sukarno adopted a more authoritarian policy of "guided democracy." He further strengthened his powers in 1959 by decreeing a return to the provisional 1945 constitution, which called for a strong president and stressed the philosophy of Pancasila as a national ideology. On 5 March 1960, Sukarno suspended parliament and began to rule by decree. In June, he

appointed a new 283-member parliament drawn from 9 political parties and 14 "functional groups." In mid-August, Sukarno named another 326 legislators who, with the 283 members of parliament, were to constitute the Provisional People's Congress. This Congress was to meet at least once every five years and to be responsible for drawing up the outlines of national policy and electing the president and vice-president. In 1963, the Congress elected Sukarno president for life. Following the political upheavals of 1965–66, the army, led by Gen. Suharto, moved to establish a "New Order." In 1967, Sukarno formally relinquished power to Suharto, wh had become Indonesia's effective ruler in March 1966. Suharto reorganized the cabinet, making all of its 12 ministers responsible to him. In February 1968, he dismissed 123 members of the People's Consultative Assembly (MPR), an outgrowth of the Provisional People's Congress, and replaced them with his own nominees. In June of that year, following his appointment to a five-year term as president, Suharto formed a new cabinet, with himself as prime minister and defense minister.

On 3 July 1971, general elections—the first since 1955—were held for portions of two reconstituted national bodies, a 460-seat House of Representatives (often shortened to DPR) and a 920-seat MPR. In 1987, the memberships were increased to 500 and 1,000, respectively. Under the new system, legislative responsibility is vested in the DPR, which consists of 400 elected members and 100 members appointed by the president from the military (Armed Forces of people's republic of Indonesia, Angkatan Bersenjata Republik Indonesia or ABRI) and other groups. DPR members also sit as members of the MPR, forming one-half of the membership; two-thirds of the total membership consists of elected officials. As of 1992, 147 seats in the DPR were held by delegates elected by provincial-level legislative assemblies. The remainder of seats, 253 in 1992, were assigned on a provincial basis to representatives of the political parties, as determined in the 1987 DPR elections, depending on their respective membership in the DPR. In 1987 Golkar won 299 of the 400 elected DPR seats, the largest number of seats. (Golkar, or Golongan Karya, is the government formed de facto political parties organized around functioning groups in society.) As a result Gokar took a total of 540 seats in the MPR. Under the Suharto government, the MPR has acted as a consultative body, setting guidelines for national policy; its principal legislative task is to approve the Broad Outlines of State Policy. In March 1973, the MPR elected President Suharto to a second five-year term; he was reelected to a third term in 1978, a fourth in 1983, a fifth in 1988, and a six in 1993. Suffrage in Indonesia is universal at age 18 and for married citizens regardless of age.

14 POLITICAL PARTIES

Until the autumn of 1955, when the first national elections were held, members of the House of Representatives were appointed by the president in consultation with party leaders. Of the 37,785,299 votes cast in the 1955 general election, six parties received more than 1 million votes each: the Indonesian Nationalist Party (Partai Nasional Indonesia—PNI), 22.3% of the total; the Council of Muslim Organizations (Masjumi), 20.9%; the Orthodox Muslim Scholars (Nahdlatul Ulama—NU), 18.4%; the Indonesian Communist Party (Partai Komunis Indonesia—PKI), 16.4%; the United Muslim Party, 2.9%; and the Christian Party, 2.6%. In all, 28 parties won representation in the 273-member Parliament. Almost all the political parties had socialist aims or tendencies. The PNI, many of whose prominent members were leaders in the prewar nationalist movement, represented a combination of nationalism and socialism. Government officials and employees had originally constituted its backbone, but subsequently it grew powerful among labor and farmer groups as well. The Masjumi was more evenly distributed throughout Indonesia than any other party. Although it contained a large percentage of the small middle class, its principles were markedly socialist, owing to the influence in the party of a religious socialist group. The NU, which broke away from the Masjumi largely because of differences in religious outlook, represented the orthodox but not strictly conservative views of the rural people and religious teachers. The Christian Party was founded by Protestants; a smaller Roman Catholic Party was also formed. On 17 August 1960, Sukarno ordered the dissolution of the Masjumi and socialist parties on the grounds of disloyalty. A month later, on 13 September, political action by all parties was barred.

Early in 1961, notice was given that all political parties were required to apply for permission to function. On 15 April, parties certified to continue in existence included the PKI, PNI, NU, Catholic, Islamic Association, Indonesian, Indonesian Protestant Christian, Indonesian Islam Sarekat, and the League for Upholding Indonesian Independence. The PKI, which at the height of its power in 1965 had an estimated 3 million members and was especially strong on Java, was banned by Gen. Suharto in March 1966, by which time more than 100,000 PKI members were estimated to have been killed in riots, assassinations, and purges; many more PKI members were arrested. Since then, the party has operated underground. The Masjumi dissolved in 1960. Under the Suharto government, political opposition in Indonesia has become increasingly quiescent. Prior to the 1971 elections, the government formed a mass organization, known as Golkar (Golongan Karya), as the political vanguard for its "New Order" program. Golkar drew upon elements outside traditional party ranks—the civil service, labor, youth, cooperatives, and other groups—and succeeded in effectively circumventing the parties' ability to play a national role. Prior to the 1971 voting, a government-appointed election committee screened all prospective candidates, eliminating 735 from the initial list of 3,840; only 11 of those eliminated were from Golkar. Candidates were forbidden to criticize the government or to discuss religious issues. In the elections, held on 3 July 1971, Golkar candidates received 63% of the vote, while winning 227 of the 351 contested seats in the House of Representatives. Besides Golkar—which is not formally considered a political party—9 parties took part in the elections, as compared with 28 in 1955. The Orthodox Muslim NU placed second in the balloting, with 58 seats; the moderate Indonesian Muslim Party (Parmusi), an offshoot of the banned Masjumi Party, won 24 seats; and the PNI, Sukarno's former base, won only 20 seats. Four smaller groups—the Muslim Political Federation, the Protestant Christian Party, the Catholic Party, and the Islamic Party—divided the remaining 22 seats. The government subsequently announced that 57 million persons, or over 95% of the electorate, had taken part in the voting. An act of 1975 provided for the fusion of the major political organizations into two parties—the United Development Party (Partai Persuatan Pembangunan—PPP) and the Indonesian Democratic Party (Partai DemoKrasi Indonesia—PDI)—and Golkar. The PPP, Golkar's chief opposition, is a fusion of the NU, Parmusi and other Muslim groups, while the PDI represents the merger of the PNI, the Christian Party, the Roman Catholic Party, and smaller groups. In the third general election, held on 2 May 1977, Golkar won 232 seats in the House of Representatives, against 99 seats for the PPP and 29 seats for the PDI. Golkar made further gains in the elections of 4 May 1982, winning 246 of the 364 contested seats, against 94 for the PPP and 24 for the PDI. Both opposition parties charged that the government had falsified the vote totals. Rioting marred the campaign period, and 35,000 army troops were stationed in Jakarta on election day. In the election of 23 April 1987, Golkar won 292 of the 400 elected seats (73.2%), against 64 for the PPP (16%), and 44 for the PDI (10.8%).

For the 1992 election the campaign rules banned automobile rallies and picture posters of political leaders; large outdoor rallies were discouraged, radio and televised appeals had to be approved in advance by the elections commission, and no campaigning took place in the five days before the elections. In 1992 there were 17 million first-time voters in a population of 108 million registered voters. More than 97 million Indonesians voted, 90% of the registered voters. Golkar won 68% of the popular vote, down by 5% from 1987. The PPP took 17% of the vote. The PDI (a democratic opposition party) took 15% of the vote compared to 10.9% in 1987. These results in terms of DPR seats were: Golkar took 281 DPR seats (down 18 seats from 1987); PPP took 63 seats (down 2 seat from 1987); and the PDI took 56 seats (an increase of 16 seats).

15 LOCAL GOVERNMENT

The structure and organization of local governments follow the pattern of national government. Indonesia is divided into 27 provinces (including East Timor). Three of the provinces are special territories, namely the Capital City of Jakarta, the Special Territory of Yogyakarta, and the Special Territory of Aceh. Each province is administered by a governor chosen by the central government from candidates proposed by the provincial assembly. The provinces are divided into 241 districts (kabupatens), administered by Bupati appointed in the same manner as governors. Both provincial and district governments are granted autonomy. As of 1993 there were also 56 municipalities (kotamadyas) headed by a walikota (mayor), 3,625 subdistricts (kecamatan) headed by a camat, and 67,033 villages. Desa are rural villages and kelurahans are urban villages. The head of a desa is elected by the villages community. The head of a kelurahan, a lurah, is a civil servant appointed by a camat on behalf of the governor. A unique feature of village life is the Village Council of Elders, composed of 9 to 15 prominent village leaders.

16 JUDICIAL SYSTEM

Since 1951, the administration of justice has been unified. Government courts, each with a single judge, have jurisdiction in the first instance in civil and criminal cases. The High Court hears appeals in civil cases and reviews criminal cases. The Supreme Court is the highest court in the country; its primary function is judicial review. Judgement in civil cases involving Muslims is based on the principles of Muslim law. Judges are appointed by the central government. In the villages, customary law (adat) procedures continue unchanged.

Islamic law (Shari'a) governs many noncriminal matters involving Muslims, including family law, inheritance and divorce; a civil code based on Roman law is applied to Europeans; a combination of Codes is applied to other groups such as ethnic Chinese and Indians.

The Supreme Court since 1985 has had the power to review ministerial decrees and regulations for legality and conformity to the constitution, but it has not yet used this power. The Supreme Court does not have the power to review the constitutionality of laws passed by Parliament. Military and administrative courts exist below the Supreme Court level.

The judiciary is subordinate to the executive and the military and lacks independence.

17 ARMED FORCES

The Indonesian armed forces, established on 5 October 1945, consist of an army, a navy, and an air force, numbering 283,000 in 1993. The army of 215,000, some of whom are engaged in nonmilitary tasks, is divided into a combined arms "Strategic reserve" of 30 battalions and 10 territorial commands that control 90 battalions (mostly infantry). It is manned through a two-year conscription law, and it is armed with US and NATO equipment. There are four special forces battalions. The air force, with a total complement of 24,000, has 81 combat aircraft, largely of US origin. The navy, with 44,000 perosnnel (including naval aviators and marines), had two submarines, 17 frigates, and 48 large patrol craft. Naval forces include a naval air wing of aircraft and helos and a 12,000-man marine brigade. Paramilitary forces include a 180,000-man police force and three other armed security forces, including a trained People's Security force of 300,000.

Indonesia spent $1.7 billion for defense in 1991 or 2% of gross domestic product. Indonesia spent $11.7 billion on imported arms in 1985–90, but cut purchases to $70 million in 1991.

Indonesia has one infantry battalion in Cambodia (UNTAC). It faces three small guerrilla groups of 1,500 at home.

[18]INTERNATIONAL COOPERATION

Indonesia was admitted to UN membership on 28 September 1950 and is a member of ESCAP and all the nonregional specialized agencies. Following the seating of Malaysia in the Security Council, Indonesia withdrew from the UN on 7 January 1965; it resumed its seat on 28 September 1966. Indonesia is also a member of the Asian Development Bank, Colombo Plan, G-77, International Tin Council, OPEC, and other intergovernmental organizations. Indonesia became one of the founding members of ASEAN in 1967. In March 1970, a treaty of friendship was signed between Indonesia and Malaysia; the treaty also established the boundary between the two countries in the Strait of Malacca. Indonesia is a signatory to GATT and the Law of the Sea.

[19]ECONOMY

In colonial times Indonesia depended upon the export of a relatively small range of primary commodities. In the 17th and 18th centuries, the basis of the export-oriented economy was spices. In the 19th century, it shifted to sugar and coffee; in the 20th century, production of oil, tin, timber, and rubber has become fundamental. Despite export gains, however, subsistence agriculture, with rice as the chief crop, remains the principal occupation of the vast majority of Indonesians, and standards of living are low, but improving. Indonesia's record of economic growth, and diversification is among the most successful in the developing world. In equal measure it promotes stability, growth, and equitable distribution of development gains.

Indonesia is exceptionally rich in coal, oil, and other industrial raw materials, but industrial development has lagged in relation to the size of the population and the national income. In part, this was a consequence of expropriation policies carried out by Sukarno and of chronic inefficiency and corruption among government officials. After the 1964–66 political crisis, the government of President Suharto took steps to stabilize the economy. Exporters were allowed to keep a larger proportion of their foreign exchange earnings. The government also imposed strict controls on imports, encouraged foreign investment, returned many nationalized assets, ended nonproductive projects, and reduced government control of the economy. The inflation rate, which had been 635% in 1966 and 120% in 1967, fell to 85% in 1968 and further declined to 10% in 1971. National economic planning was used to guide economic growth. Under the 1969–74 plan, the government successfully introduced fiscal and credit restraints, rescheduled internal debts, returned expropriated properties, liberalized foreign investment laws, and actively sought assistance from overseas. Economic growth was set back by the near-collapse of Pertamina, the giant government-backed oil conglomerate, in 1975 and the financing of its $10.5 billion debt, but accelerated as rising oil prices increased revenues in the late 1970s. The economy was again severely strained in the early 1980s as falling oil prices forced the government to cut back on its spending plans. Legislation requiring majority participation of ethnic Indonesians (pribumi) in all enterprises formed since 1974 has also slowed foreign investment. Indonesia's obligation to reduce production of oil, its chief export, in line with OPEC

agreements, together with the decline in non-oil export earnings brought about by the worldwide recession, severely strained the government's resources. In an effort to meet the nation's developmental needs, Suharto was forced to make the unpopular move, long advocated by the IBRD and IMF, of ending subsidies on food and reducing subsidies on kerosene and other fuels. He also announced new trade policies to spur exports in an effort to reverse the nation's worsening economic condition.

In the 1980s policies were designed to reduce restrictions on imports and to encourage foreign investment. In areas of trade, debt, and currency management, Indonesia took a pro-active stance that was internationally acknowledged by increasing foreign investment and endorsement by multilateral organizations. Efforts focused on bureaucratic reform and efficiency, incentives to private investors, and diversification of sources of foreign exchange earnings resulted in steady growth in the manufacturing sector and in industrial exports. Specific structural reforms were deregulation of foreign investment allowing broader ownership rights in export oriented manufacturing sectors; and streamlining of the investment process, including the adjustment of procedural requirements; progressive reduction in tariffs and non-tariff barriers; major banking deregulation that opened the banking sector to foreign investment; privatization of the Jakarta Stock Exchange; the elimination of major subsidies and supports; and increasing participation of the private sector. The basis of recent Indonesian development still consists of smallholders (0.5 hectare on average) in a rural-based economy with pockets of industry and large-scale mining and forestry, and a sizeable range of state-owned enterprises.

From 1989 to 1993 real GDP growth averaged 6.7%. Through restrictive monetary policy and a conservative fiscal stance the inflation rate has been held under 10%. Export performance has remained strong, although in 1994 non-oil export growth showed signs of slowing down. Growth export industries as of 1993 were textile and apparel, plywood, footwear, electrical and electronic equipment, furniture, glass, paper, and leather products. An increasingly important component of national income and foreign exchange earnings is tourism with over 3 million visitors to Indonesia annually. While overall investment levels remain high the value of foreign investment projects outside the oil and gas and financial sectors has declined. The government continued deregulation in order to stimulate growth. Barriers to investment remain, such as inefficient procedures, overlapping jurisdictions, corruption, and inadequacies in the legal system and infrastructure. Indonesia has altered its development philosophy away from import-substitution and toward a market-oriented approach.

The labor force is estimated at about 84 million in 1993; women make up about 40% of the work force. Each year over 2 million new workers enter the Indonesian labor force; in 1993 the labor market grew by 2.5 million. Though 30% of the labor force is underemployed, shortages of skilled and managerial personnel exist.

[20]INCOME

In 1992, Indonesia's GNP was $122,825 million at current prices, or $670 per capita. For the period 1985–92 the average inflation rate was 8.8%, resulting in a real growth rate in per capita GNP of 4.7%.

In 1992 the GDP was $126,364 million in current US dollars. It is estimated that in 1991 agriculture, hunting, forestry, and fishing contributed 19% to GDP; mining and quarrying, 14%; manufacturing, 21%; electricity, gas, and water, 1%; construction, 6%; wholesale and retail trade, 17%; transport, storage, and communication, 6%; finance, insurance, real estate, and business services, 7%; community, social, and personal services, 3%; and other sources, 6%.

21LABOR

In 1992, the total employment including armed forces was 78,104,000. Of this total, 42.8 million (55%) were engaged in agriculture; 10.5 million (14%) in community and other services; 7.8 million (10%) in manufacturing; 11.1 million (14%) in commerce; and 5.9 million (7%) in other sectors. The present labor force was estimated at 84 million in 1993, with over 50% between the ages of 15–34. Women make up about 40% of the work force.

Skilled workers and trained management personnel are few, and labor productivity is low. Open unemployment was estimated at 3% in 1991, but actual unemployment likely is much higher, and about 44% of the present work force is underemployed. Problems faced by the government in creating jobs include a rate of population growth in excess of economic growth; a preponderance of workers under 25 years of age, with little working experience; the uneven distribution of labor, which makes for labor shortages in the resource-rich outer islands; and low levels of vocational training. Labor-intensive projects, including irrigation, terracing, and reforestation, are given high priority by the government; training centers instruct rural workers in the use of automotive and other equipment needed by an emerging industrial society. Some of the larger industrial enterprises offer training programs and courses.

Before 1965, the labor movement was linked with nationalist movements, and unions were regarded as important political and revolutionary groups. SOBSI, the largest federation, was Communist-oriented and wielded great influence, not only because its membership was large but also because Indonesians identified it with anticolonialism and the struggle for independence. Following the upheavals of 1965, SOBSI was banned. Unions were replaced by government-backed labor organizations that must belong to the All-Indonesian Labor Federation in order to receive official recognition. A 1963 presidential decree prohibiting strikes in vital industries was repealed. The number of strikes increased in 1990 to 61 involving 30,706 workers, up from only 20 strikes involving 4,245 employees the year before. Over 70% of the strikes took place in the industrial sector.

In 1991, the general minimum wage increased by 6.3% from the previous year. As of December 1990, there were 655 minimum wage rates in place—27 regional, 68 sectoral, and 560 subsectoral. The highest, at that time, was Rp4,250 in Bantam Island, and the lowest was Rp850 in Central and North Sulawesi.

The 40-hour workweek and a basic 7-hour day are standard throughout Indonesia. Under the labor accident law of 1951, in enterprises in which there are hazardous risks, an employer is liable for medical care and full or partial wages for workers injured on the job, as well as for burial expenses and compensation to dependents in the event of work-related death. In January 1978, a Government Social Insurance Program (ASTEK) providing accident insurance, life insurance, and retirement benefits was imposed on all large companies (those with more than ten employees as of 1991), although in practice foreign companies (those with more than ten employees as of 1991) are excluded.

22AGRICULTURE

About 55% of Indonesian workers are engaged in agriculture, which accounts for 19.5% of GDP. Some 22.2 million hectares (54.9 million acres) are under cultivation, with 35% to 40% of the cultivated land devoted to the production of export crops. Some 60% of the country's cultivated land is in Java.

There are three main types of farming: smallholder farming (mostly rice), smallholder cash cropping, and about 1,800 large foreign-owned or privately owned estates, the latter two producing export crops. Small-scale farming is usually carried out on modest plots—those in Java average about 0.8–1 hectare (2–2.5 acres)—often without benefit of modern tools and methods, good seed, or fertilizer. Although rice, vegetables, and fruit constitute the bulk of the small farmer's crops, about 20% of output is in cash crops for export, the chief of which is rubber. Of the estate-grown crops, rubber, tobacco, sugar, palm oil, hard fiber, coffee, tea, cocoa, and cinchona are the most important. Dutch, UK, US, French, and Belgian capital financed estate agriculture in colonial times, with the Dutch share being the largest. Management of Dutch interests was taken over by the Indonesian government in December 1957; in 1964, the 104 UK-operated plantations were confiscated without any compensation, and Indonesian managers were appointed. The following year, the US-operated plantations were expropriated, and all foreign plantations were placed under the control and supervision of the Indonesian government. In 1967, some of the estates seized in 1965, including the US-leased rubber plantations, were returned, but the majority were retained by the government.

Because the population is rapidly increasing, the government seeks to achieve food self-sufficiency through expansion of arable acreage, improved farm techniques (especially the use of fertilizers and improved seeds), extension of irrigation facilities, and expanded training for farmers. Production of rice, the staple food, has been gradually increasing (47.7 million tons in 1992, as compared with 12.6 million tons in 1964), and production comes close to meeting domestic requirements. This increase has resulted less from extension of cultivated area through the government's resettlement policy than from expanded use of irrigation, fertilizers, and pesticides and cultivation of high-yielding hybrid rice, especially insect-resistant hybrids. It also reflects the success of the government's "mass guidance" program, which provides technical assistance, easy credit terms, and marketing support through a system of village cooperatives. Additional support was provided by the National Logistics Board, which is responsible for price regulation and the national rice-rationing programs. Other important food crops are corn, which replaces wheat as a staple food on the drier islands; cassavas, which are widely used as a second crop in the dry season; and sweet potatoes, peanuts, and soybeans.

Rice is the primary staple crop; production in 1992 totaled 4,777,000 tons. Other staple crops in 1992 included cassava (1,333,000 tons), corn (7,987,000 tons), and sweet potato (2,172,000 tons). Sugar is the largest commercial crop, with production reaching 23,121,000 tons in 1992. About 1,300,000 tons of rubber were produced in 1991/92, as compared with about 648,400 in 1964. Faced with the prospect of declining yields, the government began an extensive replanting and rehabilitation program in 1981. In 1992, Indonesia was the world's third largest producer of coffee (after Brazil and Colombia); some 421,000 tons of coffee were grown that year, as compared with 188,900 tons in 1972 and an annual average of 120,400 tons during 1960–65. Indonesia is the world's second-largest producer of palm oil (after Malaysia); 3,162,228 tons were produced in 1992. Tobacco (84,000 tons in 1992) and copra (1,135,000 tons) are also important export crops.

23ANIMAL HUSBANDRY

In 1992, the livestock population was 11,000,000 head of cattle, 11,400,000 goats, 5,900,000 sheep, 7,000,00 hogs and 760,000 horses. There are also about 3,400,000 buffalo in the country. The production of meat (about 1,155,000 tons in 1992) and milk (330,000 tons) is secondary to the raising of draft animals for agricultural purposes and transportation. The government has established cattle-breeding stations and artificial-insemination centers to improve the stock and has been carrying on research to improve pastures. Technical and other assistance is also offered to chicken and duck farmers in an effort to increase protein supplies. There were an estimated 600 million chickens and 30 million ducks in 1992, when some 414,000 tons of eggs were produced.

Local demand for animal products is constrained by low purchasing power, but increases in consumer income will raise demand for animal protein.

[24] FISHING

As Indonesia is the world's largest archipelago (13,667 islands), fish is a readily-available source of animal protein for domestic consumption. In 1991, the total catch was 3.1 million tons; or 3.3% of the world catch. Fishing is more important than statistics indicate, because the catch of many part-time fishermen never enters trade channels. Commercial fishing is confined to a narrow band of inshore waters, especially off northern Java, but other fishing also takes place along the coast, as well as in the rivers, lakes, coastal swamps, artificial ponds, and flooded rice fields. The government has stocked the inland waters, encouraged cooperatives to provide credit facilities, introduced improved fishing methods, provided for the use of motorized fishing boats and improved tackle, and built or rehabilitated piers. Fish and fish product exports had a value of $1,192,082,000 in 1991.

[25] FORESTRY

Forests represent a potentially vast source of wealth in Indonesia. Of the 109.2 million hectares (269.8 million acres) of forests, nearly three-fourths are in Kalimantan and eastern Indonesia. The more accessible forest areas of Sumatra and Kalimantan furnish the commercially cut timber for domestic consumption and export. Practically all forestlands belong to the state. In Java, excessive cutting has caused soil erosion, aggravated floods, created water shortages, and damaged some irrigation facilities. Replanting and rehabilitation of the Javanese forests and reforestation in the Outer Islands are promoted as part of the nation's "regreening program." Teak and other tropical hardwoods are the most valuable species, but there is hope of obtaining wood pulp from pine and bamboo and commercial timber from new plantings of fir and pine.

Sawnwood production in 1991 totaled 9.1 million cu m. About two-thirds of the timber output is exported. Indonesia was the world's leading producer of plywood in 1991, at 9,227,000 cu m. In 1990, Indonesia accounted for over 29.6% of the world's exports of veneers and plywood (valued at over $2.5 billion), which comprised 10.8% of Indonesia's total exports that year. French, Japanese, US, and Philippine interests have large investments in the timber industry. Indonesia is the world's second largest producer of tropical hardwood logs and lumber, after Malaysia. Due to a hardwood log export ban enacted in 1985 to protect rapidly diminishing forests, Indonesia has exported no logs since then. Prohibitive export taxes imposed in 1990 have all but eliminated tropical hardwood exports, in order to conserve declining forest resources for production and export of higher value items such as plywood.

[26] MINING

In addition to oil, of which Indonesia is one of the world's leading suppliers, the economically important mineral industry produces large quantities of tin and bauxite. Indonesia is the world's second-largest producer of tin (after China). The output of tin ore reached 30,061 tons in 1986, down from 31,263 tons in 1989. The chief deposits of tin are in Bangka, Belitung, and Singkep, three islands off the east coast of Sumatra. The government is the principal shareholder in tin production, and Indonesia has 10.5% of the known world tin reserves. A tin-smelting plant began operations in Bangka in 1964, and by 1977, it was able to smelt all domestically produced tin ore. Indonesia possesses large deposits of high-grade bauxite; production, 648,000 tons in 1964, rose to 1,242,000 tons in 1991. The bauxite is produced at five mining localities on Sumatra. The output is exported primarily to Japan; the rest to the US.

The railroads use much of the low-grade coal mined in Indonesia. Coal production decreased from 828,000 tons in 1956 to 149,000 tons in 1973, but grew steadily under the 1975–79 and 1979–84 development plans to reach 13,600,000 tons in 1991. Most coal is produced on Sumatra, but in 1982, contracts were signed to develop the coal resources of Kalimantan. Iron ore is found in sizable quantities but is not commercially exploited except in central Java; nickel is produced on Sulawesi and in the Maluku islands, with some of the largest reserves in the world. Copper production began at Tembagapura on Irian Jaya in 1974 and amounted to 267,401 tons by 1991. There are fair to good reserves of manganese, small amounts of gold and silver, numerous minor metals in small quantities, iodine, diamonds, phosphates, and considerable supplies of limestone, asphalt, clay, and kaolin. The search for other minerals is being actively pursued.

[27] ENERGY AND POWER

Indonesia ranked twelfth among petroleum-producing countries in 1992, with an estimated output of 1.54 million barrels of oil daily, up from the 1.33 million barrels produced in 1988. Known reserves in 1993 were put at 5.8 billion barrels, and since most of the potential sources have not been surveyed, resources may be much larger. Sumatra, the richest oil area, produces about 70% of Indonesian oil. Kalimantan is the second-leading producer; Java and Madura have a scattering of smaller producing wells. Lesser amounts are also produced in Irian Jaya. Since Indonesia has the world's fourth highest population, domestic energy consumption is expected to grow 8% per year until 2000. Indonesia may become a net importer of energy early in the next decade.

Before 1965, nearly 90% of Indonesia's petroleum was extracted by foreign companies and slightly more than 10% by state-owned companies. In March 1965, the government took over all foreign-owned oil companies, at the same time offering to allow the companies to continue operations under Indonesian control and supervision. The petroleum law of 1960 provided for foreign private enterprise to develop oil and related resources subject to contract agreements on a production-share basis. A public-sector enterprise, Pertamina, was set up to represent the government in all matters relating to the petroleum industry, including the negotiation and conclusion of contracts with foreign companies for exploration and production. Contracts have been signed with Pertamina by UK, US, Japanese, Australian, and French concerns; more than 60% of all exports go to Japan. By the mid-1970s, Pertamina had assumed a dominant role in oil exploration and production and in such related fields as petrochemicals, fertilizers, and natural gas. In late 1974, Pertamina began to encounter serious financial difficulties and by 1975 was found to have debts of $10.5 billion. This led to charges of corruption and a severe curtailment of its autonomy; as a result, Bank Indonesia was made the direct recipient of the national share in Pertamina's oil-export earnings. During the 1980s, Pertamina spent $3 billion per year on high-risk oil development projects, which helped to maintain a 20-year reserve level of oil and a 40-year reserve level of natural gas. In 1992, there were 123 new exploratory wells drilled, with 207 projected for 1993. In May 1993, reserves estimated at 225 million barrels were discovered (the largest find in Asia in a decade) at the Widuri field.

Natural gas production increased rapidly in the 1970s and 1980s, with output totaling 54 billion cu m by 1992, as compared with 19.9 billion cu m in 1982. Part of production goes for industrial and domestic use, but large amounts are exported in the form of liquefied natural gas. About 25 million tons of LNG per year are exported to Japan, the ROK, and Taiwan. Indonesia is the world's largest producer of LNG, providing about 39% of the world's supply.

Power facilities are overtaxed, despite heavy government investment in electrical installations. Indonesia expected to increase total electrical output from 29,000,000 kw in 1991 to 42,700,000 kw by 1994. New power plants in Java and Bali were being expeditiously constructed; the first phase of the power plant in Cresik near Surabaya was scheduled to be finished by the end of 1992. Net installed capacity in 1991 was 11,800,000 kw, as compared with 10,830,000 kw in 1988. Production totaled 44,660 million kwh in 1991, up from 2,932 kwh in 1973. The nation's first geothermal electric power station was inaugurated in 1974 in West Java, and a 750-Mw hydroelectric plant was completed there in 1985. Indonesia's annual per capita consumption rate for electricity (238 kwh) has doubled since the mid-1980s, when most of the population was without access to supplies.

28INDUSTRY

Industrial expansion is given a high priority in development plans. Labor-intensive industries are stressed, together with industries producing consumer items for domestic consumption and export and products accelerating agricultural development. A large integrated industrialization project on Batam Island in the Malacca Strait was designed to attract trade and industries away from crowded Singapore, 20 km (12.5 mi) away. The Batam industrial park is a 485-hectare facility that began operation in 1991. Ownership is shared between a state-owned company from Singapore and two private Indonesian firms. Petroleum, wood, sugar, rubber, tea, coconuts, palm kernels, sisal, kapok, rice, and cassava are among Indonesia's primary products processed. Secondary industries produce consumer goods such as tires and tubes, rubber shoes, radios, batteries, soap, margarine, cigarettes, light bulbs, textiles, glass, paper, tractors, and trucks. Other industries established in recent decades include a modern steel plant at Cilegon (in northwest Java), plywood factories, cement works, spinning mills, knitting plants, iron works, copper and other foundries, a ceramics plant, a leather-goods plant, and a glass factory, as well as facilities for automobile assembly, shipbuilding, and the manufacture of petrochemicals and urea fertilizers. In 1985 Indonesia's eight oil refineries, all owned by Pertamina, produced 131.4 million barrels of refined petroleum. Steel production totaled 210,300 tons in 1985, and Indonesia also produced 5.1 million tons of fertilizer, 9.8 million tons of cement, 50,500 tons of pesticides, 515,200 tons of paper, 2.5 billion m of cloth, 1.9 million bales of yarn, and 4.7 million cu m of plywood.

Despite the new industries, overall industrial growth has been small since World War II with agriculture the dominant sector of the Indonesian economy. However, in 1991 manufacturing took over as the dominant sector. In that year textiles were the key industrial export, accounting for 47% of the total. In 1992 Indonesia's six oil refineries, all owned by Pertamina, produced 572.8 million barrels of refined petroleum. Steel billet production totaled 560,000 tons in 1992, and Indonesia also produced 6.5 million tons of fertilizer, 16.3 million tons of cement, 1.65 million tons of paper, 5.2 billion m of cloth, 4.1 million bales of yarn, and 8.5 million cu m of plywood. Indonesia is positioning itself to become a major chemical producer in Asia; the industry experienced an annual growth rate of 13% over the last several years prior to 1993. In the manufacturing sector involved in the production of consumer goods, activities are run primarily by private enterprise. All oil and natural gas processing are controlled by government enterprises, as are other major heavy industries, such as basic metals, cement, paper products, fertilizer, and transport equipment. As of 1990 the oil and mineral sector, while comprising only 15% of Indonesia's GDP, contributed about 40% to its foreign exchange earnings and 40% of government tax revenues. Prior to the fall in oil prices and a push to develop nonoil exports, these sectors accounted for nearly 80% of exports and 70% of revenues. Due to the rapid growth of domestic oil consumption Indonesia may become a net importer in about 2005. On the other hand, natural gas production has steadily increased, and

may take over as a major source of export revenue. Natural gas proven reserves will last 47 years at current production rates. In July 1992 non-tariff barriers were reduced and key industries were deregulated to allow free importation of essential manufacturing inputs. There is a shortage of skilled technical personnel to support high-tech industries; most technology has been imported through joint ventures. The agency for Strategic Industries (BPIS), a state-owned holding company including aircraft, telecommunications and high-technology industries, formed a joint venture with a major foreign multinational technology corporation to promote technology transfer to Indonesia.

29SCIENCE AND TECHNOLOGY

Like many developing nations, Indonesia has a shortage of scientific personnel and engineers. The chief research institute is the Indonesian Institute of Sciences, affiliates of which include the Centers for Research and Development in Biology, Oceanology, Geotechnology, Applied Physics and Chemistry, and Metallurgy. At a more basic level, Agricultural Training Center programs provide workshops throughout Indonesia to acquaint rural workers with the use of plumbing and automotive equipment, small engines, electric tools, and chain saws, and to familiarize farmers with the use of modern hybrid seeds, pesticides, and fertilizers. In 1988, total expenditures for research and development amounted to 259 billion rupiahs; 32,038 scientists and engineers were engaged in research and development.

30DOMESTIC TRADE

Jakarta, the capital and chief commercial city, is Indonesia's main distribution center. The principal business houses, shipping and transportation firms, and service agencies have their main offices there and branches in other cities. Since the end of World War II, the government has sought to channel trade and business activities into Indonesian hands by a policy of granting special privileges to Indonesian firms—including export license monopolies, sole agency rights, and exclusive licenses to import and sell specific goods—and of making government purchases through Indonesians. Indonesians have been moving into every sector of marketing operations, particularly in the import business. In an attempt to break the Chinese grip on the rural economy and develop indigenous trade, regulations were adopted late in 1959 barring alien traders from operating in rural areas after 1 January 1960 and calling for the evacuation of aliens from rural areas in western Java to larger cities; about 300,000 Chinese merchants were affected. Laws passed in 1974 require majority ethnic Indonesian participation in all economic ventures. Commercial business hours vary, but many are the same as those in government offices—usually 8 AM to 3 PM. Retail stores and some other businesses are open from 8 AM to 4 PM. Some shops are open from 9 AM to 8 PM. Offices and most businesses close at 11 AM on Fridays and 1 or 2 PM on Saturdays. Local banks transact business from 8 AM to 1 PM and 2 to 3 PM, Monday through Friday, and 8 to 11 AM on Saturdays. Newspapers, magazines, posters, and billboards are the advertising media directed toward the literate; movie slides, portable loudspeakers, pictorial advertising, and "medicine shows" are directed toward the masses. English is widely used in business and government. There is little advertising by mail, and none at all on radio or television.

31FOREIGN TRADE

Trade balances in the post World War II period have invariably been favorable, and as of 1992 yearly trade surpluses under the Fifth Five-Year Development Plan (1989–94) were expected to continue. Trade liberalization began in 1982 as an effort to increase non-oil exports. Exports in 1988 totaled $19,218 million; imports, $13,248 million. In that year, principal commodities exported were petroleum and products, rubber and coffee.

The non-oil sector gradually increased its contribution to total exports. In 1987 non-oil exports matched revenue from oil and gas exports for the first time. In 1991–92 non-oil exports accounted for 64% of Indonesia's total export revenue. The manufacturing sector accounted for 45% of export earnings in 1991–92. Imports, which are closely regulated in government efforts to restrain growth of merchandise imports, consisted mainly of machinery and raw materials, (65% in 1991–92), indicating a reliance on imports to support industrialization. Discrepancies in trade figures are common and reflect widespread smuggling and corruption of customs and government officials.

The principal exports (by SITC section) in 1984, 1986, and 1988 (in millions of US dollars) were as follows:

	1984	1986	1988
EXPORT			
Food & live animals	1,368	1,774	2,001
Beverages and tobacco	44	69	69
Crude materials except fuels	1,762	1,473	2,661
Mineral fuels, etc.	16,045	8,310	7,723
Animal, vegetable oils & fats	175	166	539
Chemicals	170	260	346
Basic manufactures	1,565	1,984	4,281
Machinery	223	63	126
TOTALS (inc. others)	21,888	14,805	19,218

The principal imports (by SITC section) in 1984, 1986 and 1988 (in millions of US dollars) were as follows:

	1984	1986	1988
IMPORT			
Food & live animals	676	610	642
Beverages and tobacco	29	28	34
Crude materials except fuels	883	830	1,205
Mineral fuels, etc.	2,705	1,107	959
Animal, vegetable oils & fats	52	18	177
Chemicals	2,137	1,910	2,541
Basic manufactures	1,885	1,668	2,062
Machinery	5,037	4,117	5,096
TOTALS (inc. others)	3,882	10,718	13,248

In the 1970s, Japan became Indonesia's dominant trade partner; it accounted for 41.7% of Indonesia's exports (mainly petroleum) in 1988 and supplied 25.4% of its imports. Although Japan remains the dominant trade partner, in 1992 its share of exports was reduced to 37.7%. Other leading trade partners are the US, Singapore, and the Federal Republic of Germany (FRG). Trade with the Netherlands, which was of primary importance in colonial times, has been decreasing since 1957. With the creation in 1992 of the ASEAN Free Trade Area (AFTA) intra-regional trade is expected to increase. The principal trade partners for non-oil/gas products in 1991–92 (in millions of US dollars) as follows:

	EXPORTS	IMPORTS	BALANCE
COUNTRY			
Australia	—	1,292.6	—
China	707	—	—
Germany	875	1,869.1	–994.1
Hong Kong	730	—	—
Japan	3,645	6,304.5	–2,659.5
The Netherlands	894	—	—
Singapore	2,343	792.8	1,550.2
South Korea	730	1,905.7	–1,175.7
Taiwan	—	1,222.9	—
US	2,960	4,472.8	–1,512.8
Other countries	6,282	6,674.3	–392.3
TOTALS	19,116	24,534.7	–5,368.7

32 BALANCE OF PAYMENTS

Indonesia has had persistent balance-of-payments difficulties since independence. Typically, surpluses on merchandise trade have been achieved by restricting imports, but these surpluses have not provided sufficient exchange for debt repayments or for other invisibles, such as profit remittances on foreign investment and interest payments on government loans from abroad. Indonesia's payments position brightened considerably in the late 1970s as a result of a rapid increase in oil prices mandated by OPEC. However, expansion of the non-oil export industries failed to keep pace with burgeoning import requirements for some consumer goods and machinery, equipment, and spare parts for development programs. The positive overall trade balance increased in 1992 and the negative balance on non-oil and gas trade shrank. While the ervices balance remained in deficit, lower global interest rates compensated for sharply higher private sector outstanding foreign commercial debt.

In 1992 merchandise exports totaled $32,502 million and imports $26,481 million. The merchandise trade balance was $6,021 million.

The following table summarizes Indonesia's balance of payments for 1991 and 1992 (in millions of US dollars):

	1991	1992
CURRENT ACCOUNT		
Goods services and income	–4,342	–3,976
Unrequited transfers	262	297
TOTALS	–4,080	–3,679
CAPITAL ACCOUNT		
Direct investment	1,482	1,774
Portfolio investment	–12	–88
Other Long-term capital	4,442	4,040
Other short-term capital	214	137
Reserves	–1,529	–2,069
TOTALS	4,597	3,794
Errors and omissions	–517	–115
Total change in reserves	–2,055	–1,335

33 BANKING AND SECURITIES

The government's Bank Negara Indonesia (BNI) was established in 1953 as the successor to the Java Bank. In 1965, all state banks with the exception of State Trading Bank were incorporated into the BNI as separate units. In 1969, this policy was reversed, and the state banks were again reorganized as individual banks.

Bank Indonesia, as the central bank, is responsible for the administration and regulation of the six state banks and other banking operations. Among the state banks, Bank Export Import Indonesia specializes in credits for the production, processing, and marketing of export products. Bank Rakjat Indonesia specializes in credits to agricultural cooperative societies but also provides fishing and rural credit in general. BNI specializes in credits to the industrial sector; Bank Bumi Daya, in credits to estates and forestry operations; Bank Dagang Negara, in credits to the mining sector; and Bank Tabungan Negara, in the promotion of savings among the general public. The Development Bank of Indonesia (Bank Pembangunan Indonesia—or BAPINDO) provides financial assistance to government enterprises and approved new industries. In addition, six finance corporations were established by the government in the 1970s to help fund development, and there are 68 private commercial banks.

In 1967, as part of the new regime's policy of encouraging foreign investment, foreign banks were again permitted to operate in Indonesia. By legislation enacted in December 1967, foreign banks were allowed to operate in Jakarta on condition that they invest at least $1 million, of which at least $500,000 had to be brought into the country. The law also provided that foreign banks were to appoint Indonesian banks as their correspondents for any dealings outside Jakarta. In 1985 there were 11 foreign banks operating in Jakarta, three of them from the US. In 1988 the country reform its banking system that year, the number of banking licenses granted to foreigners was increased in order to lessen the domination of the five state owned banks. In 1992 there were 128 local commercial banks and 29 foreign and joint venture banks in Indonesia.

As of 1993, foreign assets of Bank Indonesia stood at Rp34,751 billion; currency in circulation totaled Rp119,075 billion. As of 1993, deposit money banks held demand deposits totaling Rp16,997 billion compared with Rp5,850 billion in October 1985 and time and savings deposits of Rp67,560 billion (Rp10,870 billion in October 1986).

Indonesia's first stock exchange came into operation in 1952 but ceased to function six years later. It was replaced in 1977 by a new stock market. The market is regulated by the Capital Market Operations Board. A state investment company was established at the same time to sell low-cost units of shares purchased and thereby to accelerate public participation in the capital market. In 1987, the stock exchange established a secondary market, which was open to foreigners for the first time.

34INSURANCE

In 1986, 74 companies handled non-life and 19 handled life insurance. In 1992, Rp25,749 billion of life insurance was in force. Third-party motor liability insurance is compulsory. In 1990, per capita premium revenues totaled $5.3 or 0.9% of the GDP.

35PUBLIC FINANCE

Government expenditures (including capital expenditures) have outrun public income by a considerable margin each year since 1952, and this cash deficit has been met by foreign aid receipts. Since 1985, however, Indonesia has discouraged public sector and monetary growth, resulting in an overall budgetary surplus in 1991/92, despite a significant drop in oil revenues from falling prices.

The following table shows actual revenues and expenditures for 1990 and 1991 in billions of rupiah.

	1990	1991
REVENUE AND GRANTS		
Tax revenue	37,431	39,098
Non-tax revenue	2,134	3,317
TOTALS	39,566	42,415
EXPENDITURES & LENDING MINUS REPAYMENTS		
General public service	13,998	12,484
Defense	2,604	2,822
Public order and safety	554	635
Education	3,512	4,053
Health	938	1,145
Housing and community amenities	685	810
Recreation, cultural, and religious affairs	281	292
Economic affairs and services	10,505	12,219
Other expenditures	5,643	6,859
Lending minus repayments	48	114
TOTALS	38,768	41,433
Deficit/Surplus	798	982

In 1991, Indonesia's total public debt stood at Rp91,607 billion of which Rp87,435 billion was financed abroad. Indonesia's external public debt at the end of 1992 was equivalent to about $51 billion; most of the government's foreign debt is medium- to long-term, predominantly on concessional terms fro multilateral

and bilateral donors. Official debt service in 1993/94 was an estimated $7.5 billion. The government services its debt fully and has no plans to seek a rescheduling.

36TAXATION

Taxes on oil companies are the largest single source of central government income. The maximum corporation tax rate is 35%. Under the general corporation rate, corporate income up to Rp10 million is taxed at 15%, income between Rp10 million and Rp50 million is taxed at 25%, and income exceeding Rp50 million is taxed at 35%. Special corporation taxes, with generous depreciation and other deductions from taxable income, cover petroleum, mining, shipping, airline, and insurance companies. Individual incomes are taxed at the same rate as those of corporations: 15% on the first Rp10 million, 25% for incomes of Rp10–50 million, and 35% on incomes over that level. An 8-year carried-forward loss for investment in eastern Indonesia is allowed. Indirect taxes include a value-added tax, which replaces the former sales tax, and excise taxes on luxury goods.

37CUSTOMS AND DUTIES

Most tariffs are designed to stimulate exports and to protect infant domestic industries. However, the tariff system is burdensome and time-consuming, and evasion is widespread. Exempt from import duties are raw materials and manufactured items imported for use in government-backed or approved labor-intensive enterprises. Duties on imports from ASEAN member countries were lowered to 20% in 1978. Two years later, duties on 384 products—including cement, sarongs, engine pistons, cameras, and telecommunications equipment—were reduced or abandoned, regardless of origin. Many items may only be imported by government-approved importers, and there are quotas for certain non-durable goods. An import sales tax is imposed on imports at point of entry (except for those goods considered essential by the government) at rates of 10–30% for luxury consumer items. Duties usually range between 10–30%, except for inessential goods, which generally range between 50% and 60%. In 1984 there were reductions in import duties for materials needed in a project and for some personal necessities of foreign personnel. There is a free trade zone on Batam Island that is exempt from all import and export taxes.

38FOREIGN INVESTMENT

Foreign investments have played a key role in the Indonesian economy since the turn of the 20th century. The Dutch were for decades the principal foreign investors in Indonesia, involving themselves heavily in the production of sugar, cinchona, coffee, tobacco, rubber, and oil. UK investments were in oil, rubber, and manufacturing. Rubber estates, particularly those in northern Sumatra, were operated by Belgian, UK, Danish, French, Norwegian, Swiss, and US individuals and companies. In the dispute with the Netherlands over Irian Jaya, the Indonesian government took over Dutch enterprises in the country and seized Dutch assets. Although Indonesians recognized that foreign capital was needed to develop their economy, government policies were ambiguous and hesitant throughout the 1950s and early 1960s. The foreign investment law of 1958 attempted to provide certain guarantees to foreign investors and to establish safeguards for Indonesian interests. At the same time, the government guaranteed some foreign-owned industrial enterprises that they would not be expropriated by the state or nationalized for a maximum period of 20 or, in the case of large agricultural enterprises, 30 years. In November 1964, the government began to reverse this policy by nationalizing all British-owned commercial enterprises and placing them under direct Indonesian management and control. A decree of 25 February 1965 nationalized all US-owned rubber plantations in northern Sumatra, and another decree of 19

March placed three oil companies—two of them US companies—under the supervision and control of the government. Finally, on 24 April 1965, President Sukarno ordered the seizure of all remaining foreign property in Indonesia. This policy was again reversed after the ouster of Sukarno.

During 1967–70, the confiscated estates were gradually returned to their former owners (except in cases where the owner opted to accept compensation). The Foreign Capital Investment Law of 1967 governed foreign direct investment. The overall flow of private investments from overseas sources increased during the early 1970s, in response both to liberal terms offered under the Suharto government and to favorable world markets for Indonesian oil and other primary products. The annual flow of foreign investment funds approved by the government increased from $333 million in 1972 to $521 million in 1973 and to $1,050 million in 1974. Some 65 US firms invested more than $1 billion in petroleum enterprises during 1967–74, accounting for about 90% of the country's total production; in 1975 alone, an additional $1.2 billion was spent in the oil sector by US interests. During 1967–85, Japanese investments led all others in non-oil sectors, totaling $3.9 billion; US investors were second, supplying $1.4 billion. In all, between 1967 and 1980, a total of $8 billion was invested by foreign companies, of which $6.6 billion was in the petroleum sector. Between 1982 and 1985, direct foreign investment averaged $242.3 million annually. Since 1973, all foreign investment has been channeled through the Investment Coordinating Board (BKPM), and Indonesian partners have been mandated for all foreign concerns established since 1974. Among the incentives for investment approved in 1986 were regulations allowing foreign investment in more industries (arms production is still prohibited) and granting foreign partners in joint ventures the right to distribute the products themselves. The Negative Investment List, 1989 and as amended in July 1992, specifies the business areas that are closed to, or impose limitations on, foreign investors.

Between 1967 and 1992, more than 1,590 manufacturing projects involving $59 billion in foreign investment were approved by the BKPM. Japan was a major investor accounting for 21% of the total, along with Hong Kong (9%), and Taiwan (7%). Total new foreign investment for 1991, 1992, and 1993, estimated, respectively, at $8.8 million, $ 10.3 million, and $10.7 million. Foreign investment in manufacturing in Indonesia has been facilitated by the rising cost of labor and inputs in other Asian countries, incentives offered by Indonesia, easing of restrictions, and the streamlining of investment procedures. In 1993 new regulations on the requirements for share ownership in companies invested with foreign capital amended the 1967 Foreign Capital Investment Law, as well as streamlining the investment approval process, and reducing import tariffs on various goods. A new deregulation package approved in June 1994 further increased incentives for foreign investment by allowing 100% foreign ownership for locally based operations for the first 15 years, and requiring as little as 1% divestment afterwards.

39 ECONOMIC DEVELOPMENT

From the late 1960s through the mid-1980s, the Suharto government focused its efforts on financial stabilization, relying heavily on advice and assistance from multilateral aid donors. The results were mixed. The fiscal crisis threatened by the accumulated debts of the Sukarno years was averted through debt rescheduling and improved economic management; nevertheless, the depth of Indonesia's continuing reliance on foreign aid remained apparent through the mid-1980s. Efforts to develop capital-intensive import-substitution industries afforded only marginal benefits to the vast majority of Indonesians. Public expenditures on the first five-year plan (1956–60) included 25% for mining and manufacturing, 25% for transport and communications, 15.4% for power

projects, and 34.6% for all other categories. A new eight-year development plan was launched in January 1961. An estimated Rp240 billion was to be spent on 335 "A" projects, of which 25.1% was allocated for transport and communications, 21.7% for industry, 12.7% for special projects including the military, 12% for clothing, 10.5% for food, and 18% for all other categories. Eight "B" projects (petroleum, rubber, tin, and forestry) were to supply the financing for the "A" projects. Because of the lack of foreign financing, upon which most of the "B" projects depended, all "A" and some "B" projects were suspended in November 1964. For the period 1965–68, economic rehabilitation took precedence over development, and all official projects were evaluated on purely economic lines. A subsequent five-year plan (1969–74) placed emphasis on the development of agriculture. Aid to industries was encouraged for activities that support agricultural development, such as the production of fertilizers, cement, agricultural equipment, and machinery for processing agricultural products. Assistance was also given to such import-substitution industries as textiles, paper, rubber tires, and housing materials. Total expenditures over the five-year period were put at Rp1,420 billion, with financing from both domestic and foreign sources. The 1975–79 five-year plan represented a shift from stabilizing policies to stepped-up development. The plan placed considerable focus on the rural economy, stressing labor-intensive industries along with improved provision of housing and education. In the program to aid farmers in increasing their output and marketing their commodities, emphasis was placed on encouraging farmers' cooperatives and banks. Labor unions were encouraged to help improve the lot of plantation and industrial workers. Efforts to restructure the economy in the 1980s resulted in an expansion of real GDP 6% annually on average, and in 1993 Indonesia's per capita GNP passed $700. The 1979–84 development plan, called Repelita III, emphasized the "development trilogy" of economic growth, equity, and national stability. Out of a total planned outlay of Rp21,849 billion, the top priorities were tourism and communication (15%), agriculture and irrigation (14%), mining and energy (13%), education (10%), and regional and local development (10%); Rp34,129 million was actually spent. The 1984–89 five-year plan, called Repelita IV, with a planned outlay of Rp77,741 million, emphasized industry (9.5% growth rate), agriculture (3%), petroleum and mining (2.5%), transportation and communications (5.2%), and construction (5%). However, consistently low oil prices have affected the entire economy, causing the government to reduce its goals and to promote private and foreign investment. Repelita V, 1989–94, with a planned outlay of Rp239.1 trillion over the entire five-year period, emphasized industry (8.5% growth rate), agriculture (3.6%), petroleum and mining (4.2%), trade (6%), transportation and communications (6.4%), and construction (6%). The development of mining and energy were prioritized, as well as certain areas of manufacturing, forestry, agriculture, transportation, communications, and tourism.

The 1988 Guidelines of State Policy introduced Transmigration Development, a policy aimed at overcoming uneven population distribution in Indonesia. The policy had multiple objectives: to ease the burden of densely populated regions, to upgrade regional development, to expand job opportunities, to support national unity, and to strengthen national defense. Transmigration in densely populated areas such as Java, Bali and West Tenggara aimed to increase population productivity and decrease environmental hazards. Transmigration in sparsely populated regions such as Sumatra, Kalimantan, Sulawesi, Maluku, Irian Jaya, and East Timor, aimed to increase productivity of natural resources, as well as increase employment and job opportunities. Declining extent of land ownership by farmers was a major problem in both densely and sparsely populated areas. These activities are overseen by the Coordinating Body for the

Implementation of Transmigration (BAKOPTRANS). Forestry statistics from 1985 showed that some 30 million hectares of forest land in sparsely populated areas could be converted to agricultural uses. Agriculture was an important sector for development in the transmigration policy. As new areas opened more employment opportunities were predicted to be available. Productive land use included, fisheries, industry, services and industrial forest products. In Repelita V the transmigration target was to relocate 550,000 families into new settlement areas outside of Java and Bali. The third year of Repelita V (1991–92) targeted 70,000 families for transmigration, including 28,240 families of public transmigration and 41,760 families of self-initiated transmigration. In fact 64,211 families (91.7%) were resettled, consisting of 25,720 families of public transmigration and 38,491 families of self-initiated transmigration. Major obstacles to the implementation of the policy continued to be delay in the preparation of the settlements in the destination areas, and delays at the places of origin during assembly and departure of transmigrants. Agricultural productivity is an indicator of the program's success. In 1991/92 rice production was about the same as the previous year, but compared to the national production rate per hectare, production was considered low. The production rate of nuts, bean crops, and cassava declined during the same time periods, and while coconut plantations increased, coffee and clove estates decreased by about 30%. The increase of large and medium livestock was minor, while poultry numbers declined by 21%. (In order to stabilize the promotion of transmigration the government issues three certificates, for the plot of land where the house is located, and for production land I and II.) Land use certificates can then be converted to ownership certificates. The Sixth Five-Year Development Plan (1994–99), Repelita VI, forecasts an annual average GDP growth rate of 6.2%; estimated per capita income in 1992 $675 is targeted to reach $1000 by the end of the plan period.

Bilateral and multinational assistance has played a major role in Indonesia's development. Before 1965, Indonesia received substantial aid from the USSR and other Communist states; such funding included some $750 million in economic credits and more than $1 billion in military aid. Since 1966, the foreign-aid pattern has turned dramatically toward the West. A group of nations (including the US, Netherlands, Japan, Belgium, France, FRG, Italy, UK, Switzerland, Canada, and New Zealand) and organizations (including the IBRD and Asian Development Bank) have joined to form the Inter-Governmental Group on Indonesia (IGGI) as a major funnel for aid. Total IGGI assistance was estimated at $2.5 billion for 1985/86. During the 1970s and early 1980s, the IMF took a central part in reorganizing Indonesia's financial structure and planning methods. At the Indonesian government's invitation, the IMF has also evaluated the country's economic programs for the purpose of advising donor nations. More recently, the IMF expanded its role by advising the government on planning and foreign-aid allocation. In November 1991, in reaction to the Indonesian army's shootings of demonstrators in Dili, East Timor, the Netherlands, Denmark, and Canada suspended aid to Indonesia. In a blanket refusal to link foreign assistance to human rights issues, the government announced it would decline all future aid from the Netherlands. The Government also requested that the IGGI be disbanded and replaced by the Consultative Group of Indonesia (CGI) formed by the World Bank and comprised of 18 donor countries (Australia, Austria, Belgium, Canada, Denmark, Finland, France, Germany, Italy, Japan, New Zealand, Norway, South Korea, Spain, Sweden, Switzerland, the UK, and the US) and 12 multilateral agencies. International development assistance totaled $6,588 in 1989, $5,510 in 1990, $5,006 in 1991, and $5,600 in 1992. In 1993 the CGI was to reconvene to review the need for continued external funding assistance to Indonesia.

40SOCIAL DEVELOPMENT

In 1981, the nation's per capita income rose for the first time above the $500 level, leading the IBRD to reclassify Indonesia from a low- to a middle-income developing country. Much of this improvement, however, has not filtered down to the rural family, which typically maintains three or four children at a subsistence level on a small patch of farmland; most such families depend on remittances from family members working away from home. Millions of these jobholders or job-seeking migrants inhabit the large and fast-growing slums surrounding Jakarta and other large cities. A family-planning campaign was initiated in the 1970s; by 1985 there were 7,509 family-planning clinics. The fertility rate was 3.5 in 1985–90, down 14.1% from the previous 5-year period. In 1991, 50% of couples of childbearing age practiced contraception. Malnutrition is widespread, especially in rural areas.

Women in Indonesia enjoy a more favorable position than is customary in Muslim societies. This situation is largely the result of the work of Princess Raden Ajeng Kartini at the turn of the century in promoting the development of Javanese women. The movement for the emancipation of women preceded the nationalist movement by at least 10 years. Improvement of the status of women was specifically included in the guidelines for the 1979–84 national economic plan. Under the plan, a woman was appointed to the new cabinet post of associate minister for the role of women. In spite of women's official equality, in practice they often find it hard to exercise their legal rights. Although they constitute roughly one quarter of the civil service, they occupy very few of its top posts.

The constitution enjoins the government to protect the family and to provide for the needs of the "poor and the waifs," but implementation of these principles has proceeded slowly because of the cost and the lack of professional personnel to put into effect a broad welfare program. Various government departments are responsible for welfare activities: juvenile delinquents are under the care of the Ministry of Justice; child care and maternal health programs are part of the public health program; the Ministry of Labor has responsibility for enforcement of labor welfare legislation; and the Ministry of Social Affairs is concerned with narcotics traffic, exploitation of women and children, prostitution, and people unable to provide for themselves (particularly demobilized soldiers). There is nothing approximating a general public-assistance program in the Western sense, but the society is one in which family and clan relationships run strong. In addition, many orphanages, homes for the aged, youth activities, and private volunteer organizations meet special needs, in some cases receiving government subsidies. Firms with 10 or more employees or a payroll of 1 million rupiah or more a month paid 1.5% of their payroll (and employees paid 1% of earnings) for retirement, disability, and survivor benefits in 1991, and coverage was gradually being extended to smaller companies and casual workers.

41HEALTH

The Ministry of Health places emphasis on preventive work, while private initiative is encouraged in the curative field. National health programs, of which family planning is an important part, stress the building of small and healthy families. Eradication of contagious diseases focuses on malaria, rabies, elephantiasis, tuberculosis, cholera, and leprosy. Overcrowded cities, poor sanitation, impure water supplies, substandard urban housing, and dietary deficiencies are contributing factors to health problems. In 1991, only 51% of the population had access to safe water and 44% had adequate sanitation.

Average life expectancy in 1992 was 62 years for men and women. The 1992 infant mortality rate was 71 per 1,000 live births, and the overall death rate was 8.5 per 1,000 in 1993. In 1990, there were 220 reported cases of tuberculosis per 100,000 people and 14% of children under 5 years old were considered malnourished.

Indonesia has received much help from the UN, particularly through WHO and UNICEF, in solving health problems. The Ministry of Health is seeking to build up a health service, starting at the village level with a hygiene officer, who is an official of the village, and working up through groups of villages, with more facilities and better trained personnel, to the regional doctor, who directs the curative and preventive work.

In 1990, there were 25,752 doctors, 98,842 nurses, and 6,689 midwives. In 1992, there were 0.14 doctors per 1,000 people, and the nurse to doctor ratio was 2.8. In 1988, there were 1,777 pharmacists and 3,821 dentists. More than one- third of the country's doctors practice in Jakarta and other big cities. In 1992, 80% of the population had access to health care services.

In 1991, Indonesia had 1,552 hospitals, with about 120,711 beds (an average of 78 beds per institution and 0.7 beds per 1,000 people). In addition, there were 5,656 public health centers. Expenditures by the government on health care facilities accounted for just 1% of total development expenditures in 1990–91. Total health care expenditures were $2,148,000 for 1990.

Indonesia's population in 1993 was 194,617,000 and the birth rate that year was 38.4 per 1,000 people. There were 5,146,000 births in 1992, with about 48% of married women (ages 15 to 49) using contraception.

Immunization rates for 1992 for children up to 1 year of age were as follows: tuberculosis (95%); diphtheria, pertussis, and tetanus (91%); polio (91%); and measles (89%).

42HOUSING

Housing is an acute problem in both urban and rural areas. In the rural areas, housing falls below even the most modest standards. In the 1970s, about one-fifth of the country's housing consisted of one-room dwellings; in the countryside, most had no electricity. Overall, only 12% of all Indonesians had access to safe water in the early 1980s. In 1989, 55% of all households received their drinking water from wells, 13% from springs, 13% from pipes, 9% from air pumps, and 6% from rivers. Lighting was provided to 45% of all households by kerosene lamps, 44% by electricity, and 11% by pressure lamp. Roughly 43% of dwellings had private toilet facilities.

Under the 1970–75 plan, the government left construction of housing to private initiative and restricted itself to activities designed to stimulate house construction, such as town planning and the provision of water supplies and sanitation. The 1975–79 and 1979–84 plans included government construction of housing. The 1984–89 plan had a target of 300,000 units, of which 140,000 were to be provided by the government and 160,000 by private sources. In 1990 alone, 210,000 new housing units were completed and the total number of dwellings stood at 44,855,000 in 1992.

43EDUCATION

Vigorous efforts have been made to advance education and reduce illiteracy. In 1971, overall literacy was estimated to be about 58%, ranging from 77% in the cities to only 52% in rural areas; in 1990, the literacy rate was 81.6% with males rated at 88.3% and females a1 75.3%. Under the constitution, education must be nondiscriminatory, and six years of primary education are free and compulsory. In practice, however, the supply of schools and teachers is inadequate to meet the needs of the fast-growing under-15 age group. In 1985, an estimated 90% of school-age children were actually enrolled in primary schools. In 1989, 29,933,790 students were enrolled in the 168,625 schools. There were 1,286,286 teachers in primary schools. Secondary schools had 870,455 teachers and 11,243,323 students. Out of

this figure, 17,603 teachers and 137,099 students were in teacher training and 149,753 teachers and 1,349,050 students were in vocational programs. Schools are coeducational, except for certain vocational and religious schools. Private (mostly Islamic religious) schools receive government subsidies if they maintain government standards. Bahasa Indonesia is the medium of instruction, but local dialects may be used until the third level.

The school system includes a six-year primary or elementary school, a three-year junior secondary school, a three-year senior secondary school, and higher education in universities, faculties, teacher-training colleges, and academies. Junior and senior technical schools have been brought into line with junior and senior secondary schools. Patterned after Dutch practices, Indonesia's educational system divides secondary-school students into groups according to curriculum. In the third year of the junior secondary school, the students are separated into an A curriculum (languages) and a B curriculum (mathematics). In senior secondary school, the students normally continue in their previous curriculum, but B-curriculum students may shift to an economics curriculum (C). Teacher-training schools range from the basic teacher-training program of four years (postprimary education) up through teachers' colleges, academies, faculties, and universities. Upon entering institutions of higher learning, students must enter the division for which their curriculum has prepared them; thus, A-curriculum students enter the language and philosophical faculties.

There are 51 universities, the largest of which are the University of Indonesia (in Jakarta) and the University of Gajah Mada (in Yogyakarta). Most of the universities are new, having been established since the mid-1950s. In all universities and third-level institutions, there were 76,013 teachers and 1,758,260 students in 1991. Education received added stress in the 1975–79, 1979–84, and 1984–89 national development plans.

44LIBRARIES AND MUSEUMS

Indonesia's largest library was created in 1980 with the merger of 4 libraries into the National Library of Indonesia with a collection of over 750,000 volumes. This library includes the large National Museum collection which was established in 1778. Another well-established library is the Bibliotheca Bogoriensis, also called the Central Library for Biological Sciences and Agriculture; founded in 1814 as a library associated with the botanical gardens in Bogor, on Java, it holds more than 400,000 volumes. Another national library is the National Scientific and Technical Documentation Center, founded in 1965 in Jakarta, with a collection of more than 150,000 volumes. The Library of the Indonesian Parliament, also in Jakarta, has 200,000 volumes. At present there is little coordination of public libraries, but there are state libraries and local reading rooms in almost every province. University libraries tend to be autonomous faculty or departmental libraries lacking central coordination.

The two outstanding museums in Indonesia are the National Museum in Jakarta, which is a general museum of Indonesian history and culture, and the Zoological Museum in Bogor, on Java. There is also a Bali Museum at Denpassar, and there are several regional historical museums throughout the provinces.

45MEDIA

The government owns and operates postal services and telecommunications facilities through Perumtel, a state enterprise. In the ame year there were 1,015,275 telephones in Indonesia. In 1991 the total number of government-owned Radio Republik Indonesia local relay stations and private stations was 745. Programs originating in Jakarta are in Bahasa Indonesia; programs from regional stations are usually in local languages or dialects. In 1991 there were about 27,500,000 radios. The overseas service (Voice of Indonesia) broadcasts 11 hours daily in Arabic, Chinese, English, French, German, Japanese, Malay, and Thai. Television service was inaugurated in 1962. In 1991 there were three television networks, TV-Indonesia (TVRI), Rejawali Citra TV, and an educational network in Jakarta. In 1991 there were some 11,000,000 television sets. The Indonesian-owned telecommunications satellite Palapa B was launched in 1983.

The constitution declares that everyone has the "right to freedom of opinion and expression." Journalistic activities of foreigners, however, are limited in accordance with the policy that "freedom of expression" does not permit interference in domestic affairs or dissemination of "foreign ideologies" detrimental to the Indonesian system of government. The government censors foreign films and publications, and Indonesian newspapers have been temporarily closed down for violating news guidelines. In 1982, a new press law established a Press Council of government officials, journalists, and scholars empowered to decide what news may be printed.

Most newspapers are published in Bahasa Indonesia, with a small number appearing in local dialects, English, and Chinese. In a return to ,ore strigent censorship, the goernment banned three weekly newspapers in June 1994.

The leading dailies, with their estimated 1991 circulations, are as follows:

	LANGUAGE	CIRCULATION
JAKARTA		
Kompas	Bahasa Indonesia	500,000
Pos Kota	Bahasa Indonesia	250,000
Berita Buana	Bahasa Indonesia	150,000
Merdeka	Bahasa Indonesia	140,000
Indonesia Times	English	50,000
OTHER CITIES		
Pikiran Rakyat (Bandung)	Bahasa Indonesia	135,000
Suara Merdeka (Semarang)	Bahasa Indonesia	125,000
Surabaya Post (Surabaya)	Bahasa Indonesia	105,000
Analisa (Medan)	Bahasa Indonesia	80,000
Waspada (Medan)	Bahasa Indonesia	80,000

[46]ORGANIZATIONS

The most successful cooperatives in Indonesia have been village unit cooperatives, designed to meet the small farmer's need for credit and aid in marketing cash crops. The cooperatives have also been instrumental in distributing improved rice, fertilizers, pesticides, and superior cattle breeds and in instructing farmers in their handling. Village unit cooperatives also exist for such cottage industries as batik (a method of hand-painting textiles), textiles, and garment production, which are important forms of employment in rural areas.

Among social welfare and women's organizations are the Indonesian Women's Congress, a federation founded in 1928; the National Council on Social Welfare; the Indonesian Planned Parenthood Association; the Council of Muslim Women's Organizations; GOPTKI, a federation of organizations that run kindergartens; and the Indonesian National Commission on the Status of Women.

Many trade and business promotional organizations are concerned with individual sectors of the business world—exporters' organizations, sugar traders' associations, and so on. An Indonesian chamber of commerce and industries has connections with leading business organizations in the country. UK, Chinese, Indian, and Pakistani business people have national associations.

[47]TOURISM, TRAVEL, AND RECREATION

An estimated 2,569,870 foreign tourists visited Indonesia in 1991 of whom 1,926,663 came from Eastern Asia and 481,684 from Europe. There were 123,902 hotel rooms, and tourist expenditures amounted to $2.5 billion. Among the most popular tourist destinations are Bali, the restored Borobudur Buddhist temple in Java, and historic Yogyakarta. Cultural attractions include traditional Balinese dancing, the percussive sounds of the Indonesian orchestra (gamelan), the shadow puppet (wayang kulit) theater, and the famous Indonesian rijsttafel, a banquet of rice and savories. Tourism, as a means of affording wider employment, is strongly promoted by the government, which has supported the development of surfing, skindiving, and other marine sports in the reefs and tropical seas of the archipelago and the creation of resorts in Sumatra, Kalimantan, Nusa Tenggara, Maluku Province, and Irian Jaya. Gambling has been prohibited since 1981.

A valid passport and an entry visa are required of most foreigners entering Indonesia. Citizen of Israel and South America must obtain special travel affidavits from Indonesian officials in their own countries. For certain countries, including the US, a tourist visa does not need a visa for up to 60 days. For other countries, a tourist visa for visits up to 30 days is obtainable. Precautions against malaria, hepatitis, typhoid, and cholera are recommended.

[48]FAMOUS INDONESIANS

Gajah Mada, prime minister under King Hayam Wuruk (r.1350–89), brought many of the islands under one rule, the Majapahit Empire. Princess Raden Ajeng Kartini (1879–1904), founder of a school for girls, led the movement for the emancipation of women. Her posthumously published letters, *Door duisternis tot licht,* occasioned considerable interest in the Western world. Many creative and performing artists have attained local prominence, but Indonesia's only internationally known artist is the painter Affandi (b.1910). Contemporary novelists of considerable local importance include Mochtar Lubis (b.1922). H. B. Jassin (b.1917) is an influential literary critic. Sukarno (1901–70), a founder and leader of the nationalist movement, is the best-known figure of modern Indonesia; Mohammad Hatta (1902–80), one of the architects of Indonesian independence, served as Sukarno's vice-president and concurrently as prime minister. President Suharto (b.1921), leader of Indonesia since Sukarno's overthrow, has dominated Indonesia's political and economic life since 1968. Adam Malik (1917–84) established an international reputation as a negotiator in restoring and improving relations with Malaysia, the Philippines, the US, the UK, and the UN; formerly a foreign minister (1966–77), he became vice-president (1978–83). Umar Wirahadikusumah (b.1924), a retired army general, became vice-president in 1983.

[49]DEPENDENCIES

Indonesia has no territories or colonies.

[50]BIBLIOGRAPHY

Alisjahbana, S. Takdier. *Indonesia: Social and Cultural Revolution.* New York: Oxford University Press, 1968.

American University. *Indonesia: A Country Study.* Washington, D.C.: Government Printing Office, 1983.

Anderson, Benedict R. O'G. *Language and Power: Exploring Political Cultures in Indonesia.* Ithaca, N.Y.: Cornell University Press, 1990.

Booth, Anne, W. J. O'Malley, and Anna Weidemann (eds.). *Indonesian Economic History in the Dutch Colonial Era.* New Haven, Conn.: Yale Center for International and Area Studies, 1990.

———. *The Oil Boom and After: Indonesian Economic Policy and Performance in the Soeharto era.* New York: Oxford University Press, 1992.

Bresnan, John. *Managing Indonesia: The Modern Political Economy.* New York: Columbia University Press, 1993.

Caldwell, Malcolm. *Indonesia*. New York: Oxford University Press, 1968.

Comparative History of India and Indonesia. New York: E.J. Brill, 1987.

Cribb, R. B. *Historical Dictionary of Indonesia*. Metuchen, N.J.: Scarecrow Press, 1992.

Crouch, Harold. *The Army and Politics in Indonesia*. Ithaca, N.Y.: Cornell University Press, 1978.

Dahm, Bernhard. *Sukarno and the Struggle for Indonesian Independence*. Ithaca, N.Y.: Cornell University Press, 1969.

——. *History of Indonesia in the Twentieth Century*. New York: Praeger, 1971.

Drake, Christine. *National Integration in Indonesia: Patterns and Policies*. Honolulu: University of Hawaii Press, 1989.

Feith, Herbert, and Lance Castles (eds.). *Indonesian Political Thinking, 1945–1965*. Ithaca, N.Y.: Cornell University Press, 1970.

Frederick, William H. *Visions and Heat: the Making of the Indonesian Revolution*. Athens: Ohio University Press, 1989.

——. and Robert L. Worden (eds.). *Indonesia: A Country Study*. 5th ed. Washington, D.C.: Library of Congress, 1993.

Furnivall, John Sydenham. *Netherlands Indies: A Study of Plural Economy*. Cambridge: Cambridge University Press, 1967.

Hill, Hal (ed.). *Unity and Diversity: Regional Economic Development in Indonesia since 1970*. New York: Oxford University Press, 1989.

Holt, Claire, *et al.* (eds.). *Culture and Politics in Indonesia*. Ithaca, N.Y.: Cornell University Press, 1972.

Hugo, Graeme J. *Population Mobility and Wealth Transfers in Indonesia and Other Third World Societies*. Honolulu, Hawaii: East-West Center, 1983.

Lubis, Mochtar. *Indonesia: Land under the Rainbow*. New York: Oxford University Press, 1990.

MacIntyre, Andrew. *Business and Politics in Indonesia*. North Sydney, Australia: Asian Studies Association of Australia, 1991.

Mackie, J. A. C. *Konfrontasi: The Indonesia-Malaysia Dispute, 1963–1966*. New York: Oxford University Press, 1974.

Marshall, P. J.et al. *India and Indonesia during the Ancien Regime: Essays*. New York: E. J. Brill, 1989.

Neill, Wilfred T. *Twentieth-Century Indonesia*. New York: Columbia University Press, 1973.

Nitisastro, Widjojo. *Population Trends in Indonesia*. Ithaca, N.Y.: Cornell University Press, 1970.

Noer, Deliar. *The Modernist Muslim Movement in Indonesia, 1900–1942*. New York: Oxford University Press, 1973.

Palmier, Leslie (ed.). *Understanding Indonesia*. Brookfield, Vt.: Gower, 1985.

Reeve, David. *Golkar of Indonesia: An Alternative to the Party System*. New York: Oxford University Press, 1985.

Ricklefs, M. C. *A History of Modern Indonesia*. Bloomington: Indiana University Press, 1981.

——. *A History of Modern Indonesia since c. 1300*. 2d ed. Stanford, Calif.: Stanford University Press, 1993.

Roeder, O. G. *The Smiling General: President Soeharto of Indonesia*. Jakarta: Gunung Agung, 1969.

Rose, Mavis. *Indonesia Free: A Political Biography of Mohammad Hatta*. Ithaca, N.Y.: Cornell University, 1987.

Schiller, A. Arthur. *The Formation of Federal Indonesia, 1945–1949*. New York: Institute of Pacific Relations, 1955.

Stewart, Ian C. Indonesians: *Portraits from an Archipelago*. New York: Methuen, 1984.

Wilhelm, Donald. *Emerging Indonesia*. New York: Barnes & Noble, 1980.

IRAN

Islamic Republic of Iran
Jomhuri-ye Eslami-ye Iran

CAPITAL: Tehran.

FLAG: The national flag is a tricolor of green, white, and red horizontal stripes, the top and bottom stripes having the Arabic inscription *Allah Akbar* ("God Is Great") written along the edge nearest the white stripe. In the center, in red, is the coat of arms, consisting of a stylized representation of the word *Allah*.

MONETARY UNIT: The rial (R) is a paper currency of 100 dinars. There are coins of 1, 5, 10, 20, and 50 rials, and notes of 100, 200, 500, 1,000, 2,000, 5,000, and 10,000 rials. R1 = $0.0006 (or $1 = R1,745.47).

WEIGHTS AND MEASURES: The metric system is the legal standard, but local units are widely used.

HOLIDAYS: National Day, 11 February; Oil Nationalization Day, 20 March; No Ruz (New Year), 21–24 March; Islamic Republic Day, 1 April; 13th Day of No Ruz (Revolution Day), 2 April. Religious holidays (according to the lunar calendar) include Birthday of Imam Husayn; Birthday of the Twelfth Imam; Martyrdom of Imam 'Ali; Death of Imam Ja'afar Sadiq; 'Id al-Fitr; Birthday of Imam Reza; 'Id-i-Qurban; 'Id-i-Qadir; Shab-i-Miraj; Martyrdom of Imam Husayn; 40th Day after the Death of Imam Husayn; Birthday of the Prophet; Birthday of Imam 'Ali.

TIME: 3:30 PM = noon GMT.

¹LOCATION, SIZE, AND EXTENT

Situated in southwestern Asia, Iran covers an area of 1,648,000 sq km (636,296 sq mi) and extends about 2,250 km (1,400 mi) SE–NW and 1,400 km (870 mi) NE–SW. Comparatively, the area occupied by Iran is slightly larger than the state of Alaska. Iran is bounded on the N by Armenia, Azerbaijan, Turkmenistan, and the Caspian Sea, on the E by Afghanistan and Pakistan, on the S by the Gulf of Oman and the Persian Gulf, on the W by Iraq, and on the NW by Turkey, with a total boundary length of 7,880 km (4,896 mi). Iran's territory includes several islands in the Persian Gulf.

Iran's capital city, Tehran, is located in the northwestern part of the country.

²TOPOGRAPHY

Most of the land area consists of a plateau some 1,200 m (4,000 ft) above sea level and strewn with mountains. The Zagros and Elburz ranges stamp a "V" upon the plateau; the apex is in the northwest, and within the lower area between the arms are to be found salt flats and barren deserts. Most of the drainage is from these two great ranges into the interior deserts, with limited drainage into the Caspian Sea and the Persian Gulf. The ranges run in parallel files, enclosing long valleys that provide most of the agricultural land. Mt. Damavand, northeast of Tehran, rises to 5,671 m (18,606 ft), while the Caspian littoral is below sea level and has a semitropical climate. Only the Karun River, emptying into the Persian Gulf, is navigable for any distance, but the rivers that rush down from high altitudes offer fine sources of power.

Harbors of limited depth are found along the Persian Gulf, and the Caspian Sea has similar facilities for coastal fishing and trade. Iran is geologically unstable: an earthquake that struck eastern Iran, in Khorasan Province, on 16 September 1978, resulted in at least 25,000 deaths.

³CLIMATE

Iran has a continental type of climate, with cold winters and hot summers prevalent across the plateau. On the plateau, the annual rainfall does not exceed 30 cm (12 in), with the deserts and the Persian Gulf littoral receiving less than 13 cm (5 in). Snow falls heavily on the mountain peaks and is the principal source of water for irrigation in spring and early summer. The Caspian littoral is warm and humid throughout the year, and the annual rainfall is from about 100 to 150 cm (40–60 in). Clear days are the rule, for the skies are cloudless more than half the days of each year. The seasons change abruptly. By the Persian New Year, the first day of spring, orchards are in bloom and wild flowers abound. The Tehran temperature ranges from an average low of –3°C (27°F) to an average high of 7°C (45°F) in January, and from an average minimum of 22°C (72°F) to an average maximum of 37°C (99°F) in July.

⁴FLORA AND FAUNA

More than one-tenth of the country is forested. The most extensive growths are found on the mountain slopes rising from the Caspian Sea, with stands of oak, ash, elm, cypress, and other valuable trees. On the plateau proper, areas of scrub oak appear on the best-watered mountain slopes, and villagers cultivate orchards and grow the plane tree, poplar, willow, walnut, beech, maple, and mulberry. Wild plants and shrubs spring from the barren land in the spring and afford pasturage, but the summer sun burns them away. Bears in the mountains, wild sheep and goats, gazelles, wild asses, wild pigs, panthers, and foxes abound. Domestic animals include sheep, goats, cattle, horses, water buffalo, donkeys, and camels. The pheasant, partridge, stork, and falcon are native to Iran.

⁵ENVIRONMENT

Iran's high grasslands have been eroded for centuries by the encroachment of nomads and overgrazing by their livestock. Deforestation of the high plateau has been going on for centuries, as nomads and villagers devastate wide areas in the production of charcoal and herds of goats swarm over new shoots. The basic law controlling the use of forests dates from 1943. In 1962, the forests and pastures in Iran were nationalized to check trespassing deforestation. Desertification is also a problem due to soil erosion. UN sources estimate that 1 to 1.5 million hectares per year become desert land. In early 1983, blown-out oil wells in the Persian Gulf war zone between Iran and Iraq caused a huge oil slick that threatened ocean and shore life along the southwestern Iranian coast. Air and water pollution is a significant problem in Iran due to the aftermath of the Persian Gulf War in 1991. Iran contributes 0.6% of the world's total gas emissions. The water in the Gulf is polluted with oil and black rain. Significant air pollution resulted from the burning of Kuwaiti oil wells. Iran has 28.2 cubic miles of water with 87% used for farming activity and 9% used for industrial purposes. Twenty-five percent of the rural people do not have pure water. Iran's cities produce 6.2 million tons of solid waste per year. Iran's Department of Environment was established under the Environment Protection and Enhancement Act of 1974; no information is available on implementing legislation.

Thirty of Iran's mammal species and 20 bird species are endangered. More than 300 plant species are also threatened. As of 1987, endangered species in Iran included the Baluchistan bear, Asiatic cheetah, Persian fallow deer, Siberian white crane, hawksbill turtle, green turtle, Oxus cobra, Latifi's viper, dugong, dolphins, and whales.

6POPULATION

According to the 1991 census, the total population was 55,837,163. The UN projected a population of 77,929,000 for the year 2000, assuming a crude birthrate of 37.2 per 1,000 population and a death rate of 6.2 for 1995–2000. Population density increased from 25 per sq km (66 per sq mi) in 1983 to 34 per sq km (88 per sq mi) in 1991. In 1995, 60% of the population was urban; the rural population in 1987 included 1,152,099 nomads. Tehran, the capital, had a population of 6,042,584 in 1986. The populations of other major cities in 1986 were Mashad, 1,463,508; Esfahan, 986,753; Tabriz, 971,482; Shiraz, 848,289; Ahvaz, 579,826; and Bakhtaran, 560,514.

7MIGRATION

Traditionally, there has been little immigration to Iran, with the exception of Shi'i Muslims coming from Iraq. There has been some emigration to Europe and the US, particularly by Iranians who were studying overseas at the time of the revolution of 1979. About 100,000 Kurds were repatriated from Iran to Iraq during the mid-1970s after the suppression of a Kurdish rebellion in the latter country. Betwen 1980 and 1990, however, an increased number of Shi'i Muslims fled Iraq because of the Iran-Iraq and Gulf wars; at the end of 1992, 1,250,100 were refugees in Iran. Perhaps 2.8 million Afghan refugees moved to Iran after the Soviet invasion of Afghanistan in December 1979. About 200,000 returned in 1992, and about 2.1 million remained in mid 1993. At least 50,000 refugees from Azerbaijan had fled to Iran by late 1993 to escape Armenian occupation.

8ETHNIC GROUPS

Present-day Iranians, or Persians, are considered to be direct descendants of the Aryans who moved into the plateau in the second millennium BC. They speak Persian, or Farsi, and number nearly half the total population. In the Zagros range and its extensions are to be found the Kurds (about 9% of the population), Lurs, Bakhtiari, Qashqa'i, and Qajars; the first three are said to be of stock similar to the Iranian element, and they speak

languages that stem from ancient Indo-European languages. At various times after the 10th century AD, Turkish tribes settled in the region, and Turkish-speaking groups are still found in several parts of the country. One-eighth of the total population dwells in East and West Azerbaijan, and there are sizable groups of Azerbaijanis in major cities elsewhere, including Tehran. Arab groups arrived during and after the 7th century AD; their descendants live in the south and southwest and in scattered colonies elsewhere.

In general, non-Iranian elements are to be found along the perimeter of the country. Of these, certain nomadic groups move back and forth across the frontiers. Tribal groups have been a conspicuous element in Iran for many centuries, migrating vertically in spring and fall between high mountain valleys and hot, lowland plains. The important migratory groups include the Qashqai, Qajars, Bakhtiari, Baluchi, and Turkomans. A large proportion of these people are now settled, however. The nomadic way of life is on the decline, and official policy has sought to resettle these groups on farmlands.

9LANGUAGES

Farsi, commonly called Persian in the West, is the official language of Iran; it is taught in all schools and was spoken by 83% of the population in 1986. An estimated 50–60% spoke it as their native language. An Indo-European language of the Indo-Iranian group, Farsi derives from ancient Persian, with an admixture of many Arabic words. Arabic characters and script are used in writing modern Persian. Dialects of Turkish, or Turki—especially Azari, the language of the Azerbaijanis—are spoken throughout northwestern Iran, by the Qashqa'i tribe in the southwest, and in parts of the northeast by Turkoman tribes and others. The Lurs, Kurds, and Bakhtiari have languages and dialects of their own that descend from earlier Indo-European languages, and the Baluchi language spoken in southeastern Iran also is of Indo-European origin. A small number of Brahui in the southeast speak a Dravidian language.

10RELIGIONS

As of 1990, 93.8% of the people were Muslims, members of the Shi'i sect. Iran is the only Islamic country where Shi'i Muslims hold the reins of power. Shi'i Islam is the official religion of the country, and the president, prime minister, and cabinet ministers must be Muslims. Sunnis constitute only about 6%. The Christian population (about 333,000) includes Armenians and, in the northwest area, Nestorian Christians (Assyrians). Colonies of Parsis, or Zoroastrians, in Yazd, Kerman, and other large towns number about 30,000. The Baha'is number about 340,000; their faith, which sprang from the teachings of a 19th-century Muslim in Iran, has been denounced as heresy to Islam. The Baha'is have been severely persecuted by the Shi'i government since the 1979 revolution, and many of their religious leaders have been executed. The Jewish community, which numbered about 25,000 in 1984, had dwindled to no more than 14,000 by 1990 and may have declined still further since then under the impact of persecution.

11TRANSPORTATION

Iran had 140,072 km (87,041 mi) of roads in 1991. The 42,694 km (26,530 mi) of freeway, highway, by-roads, and access roads were asphalted; 96,306 km (59,845 mi) were dirt and gravel roads. A1, a major paved highway, runs from Bazargan on the Turkish border to the border with Afghanistan. Another major highway, A2, runs from the Iraqi border to the Pakistani border. Much of the revolutionary government's road-building activity has centered on improving roads in rural areas. In 1991 there were over 1.6 million passenger cars and 600,000 commercial vehicles.

The state-owned Iranian State Railway has 4,850 km (3,013

AZERBAIJAN

AZERBAIJAN

TURKEY

Orūmīyeh

Tabriz
Ardebil

Daryācheh-ye Orūmīyeh

Rasht

Aras

Caspian Sea

N
W E
S

IRAN

0   50   100   150   200 Miles

0   50   100 150   200 Kilometers

Saqqez

Qazvin

Qezel Owzan

Sanandaj

Hamadān

Kermānshāh

Baghdad

I R A Q

Dezfūl

Kārūn

R E S H T E H - Y E   A L B O R Z

Atrak

Sāri   Gorgān

Qūchān

K O P E T   M T S.

TURKMENISTAN

Tehrān ✪

▲ *Qolleh-ye Damāvand 18,605 ft. 5671 m.*

Qareh Chāy

Qom

Arāk

Sabezevār

Mashhad

Torbat-e Heydariyeh

Kāshmar

Herāt

Dasht-e Kavōr (Salt Desert)

Khorramābād

Esfahān

Qomsheh

Yazd

Birjand

Dasht-e Lūt

AFGHANISTAN

Ahvāz

K Ū H H Ā - Y E   Z Ā G R O S

Khorramshahr

Ābādān

KUWAIT

Kuwait ✪

SAUDI ARABIA

Behbehān

Khārk

Marv Dasht
Persepolis

Shirāz

Bandar-e Būshehr

Mand

Deyyer

Neyriz

Namakzār-e Shahdād

Zābol

Kermān

Halil

Bām

Zāhedān

PAKISTAN

Gazak

Hāmūn-e Jaz Mūriān

Kul

Bastak

Bandar-e 'Abbās

Kuhak

Iran

P e r s i a n   G u l f

QATAR

✪ Doha

UNITED ARAB EMIRATES

Qeshm I.

Strait of Hormuz

Jāsk

Hūmedān

Gulf of Oman

OMAN

LOCATION: 25° to 40°N; 44° to 63°E. **BOUNDARY LENGTHS:** Afghanistan, 936 km (582 mi); Armenia 35 km (22 mi); Azerbaijan (N) 432 km (268 mi); Azerbaijan (NW) 179 km (111 mi); Caspian Sea coastline, 740 km (460 mi); Gulf of Oman and Persian Gulf coastlines, 2,440 km (1,516 mi); Iraq, 1,458 km (906 mi); Pakistan, 909 km (565 mi); Turkey, 499 km (310 mi); Turkmenistan 992 km (616 mi). **TERRITORIAL SEA LIMIT:** 12 mi.

mi) of track. The main line runs south for 1,392 km (865 mi) from Bandar Turkoman on the Caspian Sea, through Tehran, to Bandar-e Khomeini on the Persian Gulf. As of 1991, some 480 km (298 mi) of railroad were under construction from Bafq to Bandar Abbas; rail construction from Bafq to Sirjan has been completed and is operational.

Iran's main port at Khorramshahr on the Persian Gulf, as well as the port at Abadan, were largely destroyed in fighting during the 1980–88 war with Iraq. Other ports on the Gulf are Bandar-e Khomeini, Bandar 'Abbas, and Bushehr. Both Bandar-e Khomeini and Bushehr were damaged because of the war. The government is continuing the previous regime's program to modernize the port at Bandar 'Abbas. On the Caspian Sea, there are the ports of Bandar Anzeli (formerly Bandar Pahlavi), and Naushahr. In addition, there are the oil shipment ports of Kharg Island (a principal target in the war with Iraq) and Abadan. The principal inland

waterways are Lake Orumieh and the Karun River. In 1991, the Iranian merchant marine included 126 vessels totaling over 100 GRT, with a total capacity of 4,449,000 GRT.

The state-owned Iran Air maintains frequent service to 15 cities in Iran and is an international carrier. There are international airports at Tehran, Bandar 'Abbas, and Abadan. In 1992, Iran Air carried 4,475,600 international and domestic passengers.

12 HISTORY

As early as 6000 BC, communities on the Iranian plateau were carrying on agriculture, raising domestic animals, and producing pottery and polished stone implements. Sites datable to later than 3000 BC are numerous and offer quantities of bronze instruments and painted pottery of the finest types. About 1500 BC, masses of Indo-Europeans, or Aryans, began to cross the plateau of Iran. The Iranian group included Medes, Persians, Parthians, Bactrians, and others. The Medes settled in western Iran (Media) about 900 BC and established their capital at Ecbatana (modern Hamadan); the Persians settled to the south of them (Parsis) around 700 BC. The Median king Cyaxares (625–585 BC), along with the Chaldeans, destroyed the power of neighboring Assyria. In the area of Parsis, the Achaemenid clan became overlords, and in 550 BC, their leader, Cyrus the Great, revolted against the Medes; forming a union of Medes and Persians, he then drove with armies both into Asia Minor and to the east of the Iranian plateau and established the Achaemenid Empire. Cambyses, Darius, Xerxes I, and Artaxerxes I were notable rulers of this line who penetrated Greece, Egypt, and beyond the Oxus. The Achaemenid power was centered at Susa and Persepolis; the ruined site of the latter is impressive even today. Zoroastrianism was the religion of the rulers.

In his eastward sweep (334–330 BC), Alexander the Great defeated vast Achaemenid forces and went on to capture Susa and to burn Persepolis. In the 3d century BC, the Parthians moved into the area east of the Caspian and then into the Achaemenid Empire, establishing the new Parthian kingdom; later rulers moved west to come in contact with and then to fight the Roman Empire. The Parthians considered themselves spiritual heirs of the Achaemenids and adopted Zoroastrianism as the official religion. Weakened by long wars with Rome, the Parthians were followed by a local dynasty, the Sassanian, which arose in the area of Fars in southwestern Iran. Wars with Rome continued and were followed by a struggle with the Byzantine Empire. The Sassanian period (AD 226–641) was one of cultural consolidation and was marked by economic prosperity and by a series of enlightened rulers.

During the first half of the 7th century AD, Arab warriors burst out of the Arabian Peninsula to overwhelm the Sassanian Empire and to spread the teachings of the prophet Muhammad, embodied in Islam. By the opening of the 9th century, Islamic doctrine and precepts had spread over the plateau, and local dynasties faithful to the Muslim creed emerged. Early in the 11th century, the Turkish Ghaznavid dynasty held power from western Iran to the Indus River. Their greatest ruler was Mahmud of Ghazni, a renowned conqueror and a patron of the arts. The Ghaznavids were replaced by the Seljuks, descended from Turkish nomad warriors enlisted in their service.

The Seljuk kingdom had its capital at Ray, just south of Tehran, and stretched from the Bosporus to Chinese Turkestan. Of rude origins, such rulers as Tughril Beg, Alp Arslan, and Malik Shah did much to promote cultural pursuits and enhance the character of Persian civilization.

In 1219, Mongol hordes under Genghis Khan (Temujin) began to move into Iran; successive waves subdued and devastated the country. Hulagu, a grandson of Genghis, settled in Maragheh in Azerbaijan and as Il-khan, or chief of the tribe, gave this title to the Il-khanid dynasty. His successors, such as Ghazan Khan and Oljaitu, ruled from Tabriz and Sultaniya, and once again untutored invaders became converts to Islam and patrons of Persian science, learning, and arts. Rivalries within the military leadership brought about the breakdown of Il-khanid power in the second half of the 14th century.

In 1380, Timur ("Timur the Lame" Nor, in the west Tamerland) began to move into the Iranian plateau from the east. Within a decade, the entire area was in his power, bringing a renaissance of culture at Herat (in modern Afghanistan) and other towns, but later rulers lacked the force and ability to hold the empire together. Early in the 16th century a number of smaller, local dynasties emerged throughout Iran. The most powerful was the Safavid dynasty, whose leaders, descendants of a spiritual head of the Shi'i sect, imposed this form of Islam on their subjects. The fourth and greatest of this line, Shah Abbas (r.1587–1628), moved the capital to Esfahan, where he had many splendid buildings constructed. The Safavid period, marked by the emergence of a truly native Iranian dynasty after the lapse of many centuries, was a period of military power and general prosperity. However, decline set in, and in 1722, Esfahan fell to invading forces from Afghanistan. Nadir Shah, an Afshar tribesman from the north, drove off the Afghans and in 1736 established the Afshar dynasty. By the end of the 18th century, Zand rulers, dominant in the south, were replaced by the Qajars, a Turkish tribe.

Qajar power began to fade at the turn of the 19th century. In the 1890s, Shia clerics led a national boycott that made the shah rescind a decree awarding a tobacco monopoly to a foreign agent. In 1906, a coalition of bazaar merchants, clerics, intellectuals, and tribal leaders forced the shah to accept a constitution. This liberal initiative was frustrated, however, by the power of the British and Russians who controlled spheres of influence in the south and north of Iran.

After a period of chaos, the British arranged for a Persian Cossack officer, Reza Rhan, to come to power, first as minister of war in 1921, then prime minister, finally in 1925 as Reza Shah, the first sovereign of the Pahlavi dynasty. With ruthless authority, he sought to modernize Iran along the lines of Ataturk in Turkey. In 1941, suspecting him of pro-German sympathies, the British forced Reza Shah to abdicate in favor of his 21-year-old son, Muhammad Reza. British and Russian forces set up a supply line across Iran to the USSR. In April 1946, the British left, but the USSR refused to withdraw its forces. Under pressure from the UN and the US, Soviet troops eventually withdrew in December 1946.

Oil, the source of nearly all Iran's national wealth, quickly came to dominate postwar politics. Muhammad Mossadeq, who as leader of the National Front in the National Assembly (Majlis) led the fight in 1947 to deny the USSR oil concessions in northern Iran, became chairman of the oil committee of the Majlis. On 15 March 1951, the Majlis voted to nationalize the oil industry, which was dominated by the Anglo-Iranian Oil Co. (AIOC), a prewar concession to the UK. When the government of Prime Minister Hosein Ala took no immediate action against the AIOC, the Majlis demanded his resignation and the appointment of Mossadeq, who became prime minister in April. The AIOC was nationalized, but its output rapidly declined when the UK imposed an embargo on Iranian oil, as well as other economic sanctions. As Iran's economic situation worsened, Mossadeq sought to rally the people through fervent nationalistic appeals. An attempt by the shah to replace him failed in the summer of 1952, but by August 1953, Mossadeq had lost his parliamentary majority, but not his popular support. With the backing of a referendum, Mossadeq dissolved the Majlis and then refused to resign when the shah again tried to oust him. The shah fled Iran for four days but returned on 22 August, with backing from the military, the US and the UK. A new conservative government issued an appeal for aid; in September, the US granted Iran $45 million. Mossadeq was convicted of treason in December.

After 1953, the shah began to consolidate his power. New arrangements between the National Iranian Oil Co. and a consortium of US, UK, and Dutch oil companies were negotiated during April–September 1954 and ratified by the Majlis in October. The left-wing Tudeh (Masses) Party, which had been banned in 1949 but had resurfaced during the Mossadeq regime, was suppressed after a Tudeh organization was exposed in the armed forces. In 1957, the government sponsored two new pseudo-parties, which contested parliamentary elections in 1960 and 1961. Meanwhile, Iran became affiliated with the Western alliance through the Baghdad Pact in 1955, later the Central Treaty Organization. (CENTO was dissolved after Iran pulled out in 1979.) Frontier demarcation agreements were signed with the USSR in April 1957.

US assistance and goodwill were plainly essential for the

shah. In 1961, President John F. Kennedy urged him to undertake a more liberal program. Under the "white revolution" of 1962–63, the shah initiated land reform, electoral changes (including, for the first time, the right of women to hold and vote for public office), and broad economic development. Opposition to the reform program, the dictatorial regime, and the growing American influence was suppressed. Political dissent was not tolerated.

The shah's autocratic methods, his repressive use of the secret police (known as SAVAK), his program of rapid Westernization (at the expense of Islamic tradition), his emphasis on lavish display and costly arms imports, and his perceived tolerance of corruption and of US domination fed opposition in the late 1970s. The economic boom of the previous 15 years also came to an end. Joining in the revolt were Islamic militants, radical students, the bazaar and middle classes, until virtually the entire population turned against the shah. Following nine months of demonstrations and violent army reactions, martial law was declared in Iran's major cities in September 1978, but antigovernment strikes and massive marches could not be stopped. On 16 January 1979, the shah left Iran, appointing an old-line nationalist, Shahpur Bakhtiar, as Prime Minister. However, the leader of the Islamic opposition, Ayatollah Ruhollah Khomeini (the term *ayatollah* is the highest rank of the Shia clergy), who had spent 15 years in exile, first in Iraq and briefly in France, refused to deal with the Bakhtiar regime. Demonstrations continued, and on 1 February the ayatollah returned to a tumultuous welcome in Tehran. He quickly asserted control and appointed a provisional government, which took power after a military rebellion and the final collapse of the shah's regime on 11 February.

After a referendum, Khomeini on 1 April declared Iran an Islamic Republic. The provisional government, led by Medhi Bazargan and other liberal civilians, could not exercise authority; revolutionary groups made indiscriminate arrests and summary executions of political opponents. Increasingly, radical clerics sought to take power for themselves. The crisis atmosphere was intensified by the seizure, on 4 November 1979, of 53 US hostages (50 of them in the US embassy compound in Tehran) by militant Iranian students who demanded the return of the shah from the US (where he was receiving medical treatment) to stand trial in Iran. Despite vigorous protests by the US government, which froze Iranian assets in the US, and by the UN over this violation of diplomatic immunity, the hostages were held for 444 days; in the intervening period, a US attempt to free the hostages by military force failed, and the shah died in Egypt on 27 July 1980. The crisis was finally resolved on 20 January 1981, in an agreement providing for release of the prisoners and the unfreezing of Iranian assets. A new constitution providing for an Islamic theocracy was ratified by popular referendum in December 1979. In presidential elections in January 1980, 'Abolhassan Bani-Sadr, a moderate, who supported the revolution, was elected president. Later elections to the Majlis resulted in victory for the hard-line clerical Islamic Republican Party (IRP).

In June 1981, President Bani-Sadr was ousted by Khomeini; later that month, a bomb explosion at IRP headquarters in Tehran killed Ayatollah Beheshti, who had been serving as chief justice, as well as 4 cabinet ministers, 20 paramilitary deputies, and dozens of others. Another bombing, on 30 August, killed the new president, Muhammad 'Ali Rajai, and his new prime minister, Muhammad Javad Bahonar. The bombings were ascribed by the government to leftist guerrillas. By 1982, at least 4,500 people had been killed in political violence, and some estimates placed the total much higher. In September 1982, Sadegh Ghotbzadeh, who had been foreign minister during the hostage crisis, was executed on charges of plotting to kill Khomeini and establish a secular government.

Iraq, meanwhile, had taken advantage of Iran's political chaos and economic disorder to revive a border dispute that had been settled in 1975 when Iranian and Iraqi representatives reached agreement on the demarcation of their frontiers and Iran ended its support for rebellious Kurds, who were then defeated by the Iraqi army. Full-scale war erupted in September 1980, when Iraq demanded sovereignty over the entire Shatt al-'Arab waterway. Iraqi forces invaded Khuzistan in the southwest, and captured the town of Khorramshahr and the oil refinery center of Abadan. The Iranian army, decimated by the revolution, was slow to mobilize, but by June 1982 it had driven Iraqi soldiers out of Abadan and Khorramshahr and from all undisputed Iranian territory. Iran then launched its own offensive, invading Iraq and thrusting toward Basra, but failed to make significant gains. At this point the land war became stalemated, with Iranian and Iraqi troops setting up an elaborate system of trenches. In 1983, Iraq broadened the war zone to include oil-tanker traffic in the northern Persian Gulf.

The Iraqis first attacked Iranian oil installations, disrupting, but not stopping, oil exports from the main oil terminal at Kharg Island. In mid-1983, Iraq took delivery of French jets bearing Exocet missiles. Iran responded that it would close the Strait of Hormuz if Iraq used the missiles. The US declared the strait a vital interest and said it would use military force to keep the strait open because of the large volume of oil that passed through it on the way to the West. During 1983, the Iraqis also began to attack civilian targets in Iran with long-range missiles. The attacks caused heavy casualties, and Iran responded by shelling Iraqi border cities. In 1984, Iran began to attack Arab shipping in the Persian Gulf.

Iranian forces staged a surprisingly effective attack on Iraqi forces in the Fao Peninsula in February 1986. The Iranians now controlled all of Iraq's border on the Persian Gulf and were in reach of the major Iraqi city of Basra. In April, Khomeini renewed his demands for ending the war: Iraqi President Saddam Hussein must step down, and Iraq must admit responsibility and pay war reparations. Iran rejected all demands for a cease-fire and negotiations until its demands were met.

In November 1986, it was revealed that US National Security Adviser Robert McFarlane had secretly traveled to Iran to meet with government leaders. The US supplied Iran with an estimated $30 million in spare parts and antiaircraft missiles in hopes that Iran would exert pressure on terrorist groups in Lebanon to release American hostages. In the wake of this affair, Iran in 1987 attacked Kuwaiti oil tankers reregistered as American tankers and laid mines in the Persian Gulf to disrupt oil tanker shipping. The US responded by stationing a naval task force in the region and attacking Iranian patrol boats and oil-loading platforms and accidently shot down a civilian passenger jet.

As the war continued to take its heavy toll of casualties and destruction and economic hardships persisted on the home front, the clerics maintained firm control through repression and Khomeini's charismatic hold over the people. In 1988, Iran finally yielded to terms for a cease-fire in the war. On 3 June 1989, a few months after calling for the death of novelist Salman Rushdie for blasphemy, Khomeini died of a heart attack. Over 3 million people attended his funeral. He was succeeded as spiritual guide by President Ali Khamenei. On 28 July 1989, Speaker of the Parliament Ali Akbar Rafsanjani was elected president with 95% of the vote. He was reelected in 1993.

Iran remained neutral during the Gulf War, receiving (and retaining) Iraqi planes that were flown across the border for safekeeping. Iran also accepted thousands of Kurdish refugees from Iraq to add to its heavy burden of Afghan refugees from the civil strife in that country. Inflation, shortages, and unemployment—the products of revolution, war, and mismanagement—continue to generate widespread popular discontent, fueled also by dissatisfaction with the closed and repressive political system.

13GOVERNMENT

Before the 1979 revolution, Iran was an absolute monarchy, with the constitution of 1906 modified by a supplement of 1907 and amendments of 1925, 1949, and 1957. The shah was the chief of state, with sweeping powers. He commanded the armed forces, named the prime minister and all senior officials, and was empowered to dissolve either or both legislative houses. The legislative branch comprised the National Assembly (Majlis) and the Senate. Members of the Majlis were elected for four-year terms from 268 constituencies by adults 20 years of age and older. Half of the 60 senators were named by the shah, and half were elected. Members of the Majlis ostensibly represented all classes of the nation, while the somewhat more conservative Senate consisted of former cabinet ministers, former high officials, and retired generals.

The constitution of December 1979, which was approved in a public referendum and revised in 1989, established an Islamic republic in conformity with the principles of the Shi'i faith. Guidance of the republic is entrusted to the country's spiritual leader (faqih) or to a council of religious leaders. An appointed Council of Guardians consists of six religious leaders, who consider all legislation for conformity to Islamic principles, and six Muslim lawyers appointed by the Supreme Judicial Council, who rule on limited questions of constitutionality. In accordance with the constitution, an Assembly of Experts was elected in December 1982 to choose a successor to Ayatollah Khomeini as Iran's spiritual leader in the event of his death. In November 1985, the council's choice was inadvertently made public when it became known that Ayatollah Hussein 'Ali Montazeri had been formally elected Ayatollah Khomeini's successor. He subsequently withdrew.

The executive branch consists of a president and Council of Ministers. The president is elected by popular vote to a four-year term and supervises government administration. Candidates for the presidency and parliament must have the approval of Iran's spiritual leaders. The Majlis consists of 270 members elected directly to four-year terms. Suffrage is universal for those over age 15.

14POLITICAL PARTIES

During the reign of Reza Shah (1925–41), political parties were not permitted to function. After 1941, parties sprang up, but most of them were of an ephemeral nature. The Communist-oriented Tudeh (Masses) Party was better organized than the others and benefited from the services of devoted followers and foreign funds. In 1949, an unsuccessful attempt to assassinate the shah was traced to the Tudeh, and it was banned. It continued to work through front groups, and its views were reflected in some periodicals, but the organization was extinguished in the Shah's post-1953 crackdown.

In 1957, the government created facade political parties, the Nationalist (Mellioun) Party, headed by Manochehr Eqbal, then prime minister and the People's (Mardom) Party, headed by former prime minister Asadullah Alam (the "loyal opposition"). None of these parties ever attracted any popular following. In 1975, the shah ordered the formation of a single political organization, the Iran Resurgence (Rastakhiz) Party, into which were merged all existing legal parties. Three cardinal principles were cited for membership in the party: faith in Iran's constitution, loyalty to the monarchical regime, and fidelity to the "white revolution." This party, like others before it, lacked a popular base.

After the overthrow of the shah's regime in February 1979, new political parties were formed. In elections to the Majlis in March and May 1980, the Islamic Republican Party (IRP), which was closely identified with Ayatollah Khomeini, emerged as the dominant group. A founder and the secretary general of the IRP, Hojatolislam 'Ali Khamenei, was elected president of the republic in November 1981 and was reelected in August 1985.

All parties determined not to have sufficient Islamic credentials have been banned. Some operate outside the country. These include the Mujahedeen al Khalq (a left-wing Shia group with a military arm supported by Iraq), royalist parties backing the son of the late shah and remnants of the Tudeh and National Front (dating from Mossadeq's period). Only the Liberation Movement of Mehdi Bazargan has been allowed limited participation in politics.

Since 1987, Iran has maintained an active political life strictly within the required Islamic framework. The IRP was abolished in 1987, but clerical groups maintain political power. A radical group, a pragmatic party headed by President Rafsanjani, and a conservative faction regularly contest for seats in the Parliament. A pragmatic/conservative coalition has been dominant under Rafsanjani's leadership since the mid-1980s.

15LOCAL GOVERNMENT

Iran is divided into 24 ostans (provinces), each headed by a governor-general; the governor-general and district officials of each province are appointed by the central government. The ostans are subdivided into 195 sharestans (counties), which are in turn divided into 500 bakhsh (districts). Each bakhsh consists of two or more dehistans, which are composed of groups of villages or hamlets. Each of the 475 municipalities (shahrdarys) is headed by a mayor. Some sharestan officials are elected; others are appointed by Tehran.

16JUDICIAL SYSTEM

The overthrow of the shah and the approval in 1980 of a constitution making Iran an Islamic state have radically changed Iran's judicial system. The 1980 constitution was revised in 1989.

In August 1982, the Supreme Court invalidated all previous laws that did not conform with the dictates of Islam, and all courts set up before the 1979 revolution were abolished in October 1982. An Islamic system of punishment, introduced in 1983, included flogging, stoning, and amputation for various crimes. There are two different court systems: civil courts and revolutionary courts.

The judicial system is under the authority of the religious leader (faqih). A Supreme Judicial Council responsible to the faqih oversees the Supreme Court, which has 16 branches. The Ministry of Justice oversees law courts in the provinces.

The revolutionary courts try cases involving political offenses, narcotics trafficking and "crimes against God." Although the constitution guarantees a fair trial, the revolutionary courts provide almost no procedural safeguards. The trials in revolutionary courts are rarely held in public and there is no guarantee of access to an attorney.

Elements of the prerevolutionary judicial system continue to be applied in common criminal and civil cases. In these cases the right to a public trial and the benefit of counsel are generally respected.

17ARMED FORCES

Two years' military service is compulsory for all males at age 18. The war with Iraq led to an almost fourfold increase in the size of the armed forces after 1980, but this force has demobilized. In 1993, the army had 305,000 soldiers (200,000 conscripts). Their equipment included 700 main battle tanks, 750 armored fighting vehicles, and 1,300 artillery pieces. The air force had 35,000 men and 262 combat aircraft. Only half of US-source aircraft are operational, which means that only 2 MiG and 1 Mirage squadron are fully ready. Iran also now holds 112 planes of the Iraqi air force. The navy of 18,000 men had 3 destroyers, 5 frigates, and 33 smaller patrol and coastal combatants. The Revolutionary Guards unit (Pasdaran) has an estimated 150,000-man army and 20,000 sailors and marines. Complementing the Pasdaran are the baseej, young volunteers who are fanatically devoted to an Islamic Iran. The baseej were the mainstay of Iran's human wave attacks, and membership has been as high as 500,000. The Party of God (Hezbollah), which acts as a domestic paramilitary force, has an estimated 2.5 million members and sends volunteers to Lebanon. The regular gendarmerie numbers 45,000. The official military budget in 1991 was $13 billion or 14% of gross domestic product. Fueled by oil revenues, Iran has imported $1–2 billion a year in arms for more than a decade, including advanced Chinese missiles and one Russian submarine.

18 INTERNATIONAL COOPERATION

Iran is a charter member of the UN, having joined on 24 October 1945, and belongs to ESCAP and all the nonregional specialized agencies except WIPO. Iran is also a member of G-77 and a signatory to the Law of the Sea. It is a founding member of OPEC and a leading supporter of higher petroleum prices. In 1979, Iran withdrew from CENTO, causing its demise.

Iran's revolutionary government has aligned itself with the radical Arab states of Libya and Syria, which were the only Arab countries to support Iran in its war with Iraq. Since before 1979, Iranian foreign policy has been to curtail superpower influence in the Persian Gulf area. It also encourages the Islamization of the governments throughout the Middle East, in such countries as Sudan and Algeria.

19 ECONOMY

A country with a substantial economic potential, Iran witnessed rapid economic growth during the reign of Shah Muhammad Reza Pahlavi. Development of its extensive agricultural, mineral, and power resources was financed through oil revenues. The traditional land tenure system, under which farmers were sharecroppers, was replaced through a land reform program inaugurated in 1962. In addition to carpets, Iran produces a variety of consumer goods and building materials. Oil, however, is still the lifeblood of the economy. With the astonishing growth of its oil revenues, Iran became a major world economic power, whose investments helped several industrialized countries pay for their oil needs during the 1970s.

The economy has changed drastically since 1979. The war with Iraq, which curtailed oil exports, coupled with the decrease in the price of oil, especially in 1986, sent oil revenues spiraling downward from $20.5 billion in 1979 to an estimated $5.3 billion in 1986. This forced annual GDP growth down from 15.2% in 1982 to 0.2% in 1984; GDP was estimated to have fallen by 8% in 1986. The war's drain on the state budget, the drop in oil prices, poor economic management, declining agricultural output, an estimated 1987 inflation rate of 30–50%, and large budget deficits combined to put enormous strains on the economy.

After Iran accepted a UN cease-fire resolution in 1988, it began reforming the economy. The reform measures emphasized revitalizing market mechanisms, deregulating the economy, and rebuilding basic infrastructure. These reforms led to economic growth and lowered budget deficits. GDP grew an average 7% a year in real terms over 1989–92. The general government deficit was reduced from 9% of GDP in 1988 to an estimated 2% in 1992. The inflation rate decreased from 29% in 1988 to around 10% in 1990. Since then, however, inflation edged up to an estimated 20% in 1991 and 1992.

20 INCOME

In 1992, Iran's GNP was $130,910 million at current prices, or $2,190 per capita. For the period 1985–92 the average inflation rate was 21.0%, resulting in a real growth rate in per capita GNP of -1.4%.

In 1992, the GDP was $113,274 million in current US dollars. It is estimated that in 1990 agriculture, hunting, forestry, and fishing contributed 23% to GDP; mining and quarrying, 11%; manufacturing, 12%; electricity, gas, and water, 1%; construction, 4%; wholesale and retail trade, 18%; transport, storage, and communication, 7%; finance, insurance, real estate, and business services, 12%; community, social, and personal services, 2%; and other sources, 10%.

21 LABOR

The total labor force was estimated at around 27.5 million in 1990, up from 15.4 million in 1988. According to official figures, 30% of the employed work force was in agriculture, 25% was in manufacturing, mining, construction, and utilities, and 45% was in the service industry. Experts believe that these distributions of the work force are misleading because they do not show the unemployment levels that exist within each area. Unemployment continues to be a problem; in 1982/83, unemployment was 19%, and by the end of the 1980s it was an estimated 30%. Unemployment has become pervasive because of the economy's poor performance and the large numbers of young people who have recently entered the work force.

Article 131 of the Labor Code grants workers and employees the right to form and join their own organizations. The government-controlled Workers' House, founded in 1982, is the only authorized national labor organization. There are however, many guild unions at the regional level, which operate with the support of the government.

As of 1992, no information was available on the right of workers to strike. Iranian labor law (which exempts agriculture, domestic service, family businesses, and some other small businesses) forbids employment of minors under 12 years. Women and minors are also prohibited from engaging in hard labor or night work.

22 AGRICULTURE

Of Iran's total area, 9.2% is cultivated, 26.9% consists of permanent pastures, and 11% is forest and woodland. The remaining 52.9% consists of wasteland, lakes, mountains, desert, and urban areas. About one-third of the labor force is employed in agriculture. In 1987, the total land area under cultivation was estimated at 19 million hectares (47 million acres).

Progress in Iranian agriculture was greatly stimulated by the land reform of 1962–63, under which 4,025,680 farmers and their family members had taken title to their land by 1975, after the old land tenure system was abolished. However, with a rapidly increasing population and a sharply rising standard of living, Iran is no longer self-sufficient in its agricultural production, and food imports have risen steadily in recent years.

In 1992, Iranian agricultural production (in thousands of tons) included wheat, 10,200; sugar beets, 6,000; barley, 3,700; rice, 2,500; grapes, 1,650; apples, 1,520; oranges, 1,300; dates, 635; cotton, 400; tea, 45; and tobacco, 22. Almonds and pistachios are grown primarily for export. In 1992, Iran was the largest producer of pistachios in the world (170,000 tons, or 59% of global production), and the third largest producer of almonds (after Spain and Italy), at 66,000 tons.

As of 1991, some 5.75 million hectares (14.2 million acres) were under irrigation. The fifth development plan (1973–78) envisaged an overall increase of 5.5% in agricultural production, but the revised plan raised the target to 8% annually, rescheduled allocations over six years instead of five, and slowed down the projects. Under the revolutionary government's first five-year plan (1983–88), agriculture was to receive 15.5% of total allocations, with food self-sufficiency the primary objective. However, because of the war with Iraq, planned expenditures were never attained. Moreover, food self-sufficiency remains only a goal: agricultural imports rose to $2.4 billion in 1992, up from $1.7 billion in 1987.

[23]ANIMAL HUSBANDRY

Not only is animal husbandry the major occupation of nomadic and seminomadic tribes scattered over Iran, but each farming village also keeps flocks that graze on the less productive areas. In 1992 there were 45,000,050 sheep, 23,500,000 goats, 6,900,000 head of cattle, 300,000 water buffalo, 130,000 camels, and 170,000,000 chickens. Cattle are raised as draft animals and for milk and are not fattened for beef. Sheep produce many staple items: milk and butter, animal fat for cooking, meat, wool for carpet making, and skins and hides. Poor weather during the 1970s sharply reduced the domestic flocks, and Iran became an importer of wool. The output of animal products has not kept pace with population growth.

[24]FISHING

The Caspian Sea provides a seemingly inexhaustible source of sturgeon, salmon, and other species of fish, some of which spawn in the chilly streams that flow into this sea from the high Elburz Mountains. In 1991, the total fish catch was 277,444 tons. Caviar of unrivaled quality is produced by the Iranian Fisheries Co., formerly a joint Russo-Iranian venture but now wholly owned by the government of Iran. About 200,000 kg of caviar are sold per year, most of which is exported, providing a substantial share of the world's supply. The fishing grounds of the Persian Gulf were long neglected, but during the 1970s new fishing fleets and packing and conserving facilities were established. The Iran-Iraq war and consequent environmental damage retarded the development of fisheries in this region. Total marine catch has more than doubled from 1982–84 levels.

[25]FORESTRY

About 18 million hectares (44.4 million acres) are covered by forest and woodland. An estimated 6.7 million cu m of roundwood were produced in 1991; about 36% was used for fuel. Along the northern slopes of the Elburz Mountains from near sea level to an altitude of about 2,100 m (7,000 ft) are dense stands of oak, ash, elm, beech, ironwood, cypress, walnut, and a number of other varieties. The high plateau forests of Fars, Kurdistan, Luristan, and Khorasan comprise sparse stands of scrub oak, ash, maple, cedar, wild almond, and pistachio. Date palms, acacias, and tamarisks grow in the Persian Gulf area. The deciduous forests on the Caspian littoral are among the best in the world. The timber industry is controlled by the government; its potential annual capacity is 3 million cu m.

A forest ranger school was started in 1957 as an extension of the government's forest service. In 1963, a forestry college was established at Karaj, west of Tehran, to train forestry engineers.

[26]MINING

Iran possesses extensive and varied mineral resources. Major iron and copper ore deposits are found in Kerman Province. Iran also has deposits of antimony, chromite, lead, zinc, manganese, sulfur, salt, mica, silica, limestone, and granite. The increase of metal production was high on the agenda of the government for postwar reconstruction and economic expansion. In 1991, the outputs of aluminum, cement, copper, lead, iron, and zinc were being expanded. Dimension stone also is adding to the value of mineral exports. Production of primary aluminum in 1991 was 80,000 tons; chromite, 44,000 tons; copper, 80,700 tons; lead, 16,000 tons; manganese, 16,000 tons; molybdenum, 400 tons; and zinc, 70,000 tons. Production of hard coal in 1991 was 1,480,000 metric tons; iron ore, 2,100,000 tons; sulfur, 700,000 tons; and unrefined salt, 900,965 tons. Mineral exports include chromite, refined sulfur, lead, zinc, copper, and decorative stone. More than 200,000 tons of chromite concentrates, 100,000 tons of zinc ore, and 25,000 tons of lead ore, worth a total of more than $50 million, were exported in 1991, mostly to Belgium, China, India, Japan, and North Korea. Export earnings from nonfuel minerals amounted to an estimated $300 million in 1991, and were expected to reach $1 billion by the mid-1990s.

[27]ENERGY AND POWER

Iran's oil reserves, estimated at 92.9 billion barrels (12.7 billion tons) at the end of 1992, constituted 9.2% of the world's known reserves and were exceeded only by those of Sa'udi Arabia, Iraq, UAE, and Kuwait. Iran was the second-largest oil producer among OPEC countries in 1992.

The first oil concessions were granted by the Iranian (Persian) government in 1872 and 1901, and the first recorded crude oil production began in 1913. Production was carried on by the Anglo-Iranian Oil Co. until the petroleum industry was nationalized in 1951, when the country's oil resources were placed under the management of the National Iranian Oil Co. (NIOC). Late in 1954, the active oil properties and facilities were awarded to a consortium of eight foreign companies, later joined by nine others, with US, British, Dutch, and French interests represented. In 1956, the Iranian Oil Co., another government enterprise, brought in a huge gusher at Qom, south of Tehran. The following year, the legislature ratified an agreement with an Italian company covering an exploited area of Iran, and a joint Italo-Iranian company (SIRIP) was formed to explore and produce. The Pan American Oil Co. acquired concession rights in the Persian Gulf in 1958, joining with the NIOC in a new mixed company, IPAC. By 1962, both SIRIP and IPAC were producing from wells in the Persian Gulf. Additional fields were explored, and production grew rapidly.

During the early 1970s, tremendous changes took place in the Iranian oil industry. The 1954 oil participation agreement was terminated, and on 31 July 1973 a new agreement was signed which replaced the concessionary arrangements with a buyer-seller relationship, the major Western oil companies agreeing to purchase crude petroleum under long-term contracts with the NIOC, which was given full control over the industry. In 1980, the revolutionary government ended joint-venture operations with Western oil companies and regrouped them under the Iranian Offshore Oil Co. of the Islamic Republic.

Meanwhile, largely through the concerted action of OPEC, world oil prices rose rapidly; the posted price of Iranian light crude oil increased from $1.36 a barrel in 1970 to $37 in 1981 before declining to $12.75 a barrel in 1989. The Gulf War caused prices to jump to $23.65 a barrel in 1991; by 1993, a barrel went for $16.70. In order to stabilize the price of oil, OPEC imposed quotas on its members. Iran consistently criticized the quota system and asked for a larger quota. Despite an OPEC-imposed production ceiling for Iran of 3,184,000 barrels per day (a 9% reduction agreed to in February 1992), petroleum production reached 3,455,000 barrels per day in 1992 and was scheduled to increase to about 4 million and 5 million barrels per day in 1993 and 1994, respectively. Iran accounted for 13% of OPEC production in 1991. Oil production fluctuated widely because of disruptions caused by the Iraqi attacks, especially the repeated bombing of Kharg Island. As of 1991, the export terminal on Kharg Island was to be expanded as reconstruction continues. In May 1993, Iran accused Iraqi rebels of dynamiting oil pipelines in the southwest. The lowest levels were recorded in 1986, when only 1.9 million barrels per day were produced. Production increased in 1987 to 2.3 million barrels per day and averaged 2.8 million during 1988–91. Oil revenues rose from $5.1 billion in 1986 to an estimated $16 billion in 1991.

In 1992, Iran's natural gas reserves were estimated at 19.8 trillion cu m (699.2 trillion cu ft); only Russia possesses larger natural gas reserves. Iran's output declined from 19,869 million cu m in 1973 to 7,300 million cu m in 1982 before climbing back to 26,600 million cu m in 1992. Exploitation of natural gas is controlled by the National Iranian Gas Co. Iran began supplying natural gas to the former USSR in 1970 for a 15-year period, at an initial rate of 6,000 million cu m a year, rising eventually to 20,000 million cu m. This agreement was abrogated by the new Islamic government in 1979. However, in December 1986, a new agreement was reached to resume natural gas deliveries. Inside Iran, a network of pipelines connects Tehran, Qazvin, Esfahan, Abadan, Shiraz, and Mashhad to Ahvaz and the gas fields. As of 1993, Iran agreed to a partnership with Azerbaijan and Ukraine to build gas pipelines from Iran to supply those countries as well as Eastern Europe.

Although Iran is one of the world's leading oil-producing countries, Iranian industry formerly depended on other energy sources, such as electricity, coal, and charcoal. Recently, however, oil and especially gas have been used increasingly in manufacturing. Work on a nuclear power plant with a 21,200-Mw capacity was halted in 1979. In 1991, hydroelectric power plants generated 6,600,000 Mwh, compared with 50,300,000 Mwh in conventional thermal facilities. In 1991, the total electricity output was 56,900,000 Mwh.

28INDUSTRY

Principal industries are oil refining, petrochemicals, steel, and copper. In 1987, there were six primary refineries—at Abadan, Bakhtaran, Tehran, Shiraz, Esfahan, and Tabriz—with a potential capacity of 950,000 barrels per day. In late 1980, Iraqi bombing forced the closure of the Abadan refinery, which had a total capacity of 600,000 barrels per day and was one of the world's largest refineries. Several other refineries suffered lesser damage during the war. The Kharg Island oil terminal also was severely damaged by bombing in 1985. Construction by a Japanese consortium of a $4-billion petrochemical complex at Bandar-e Khomeini, near the Iraqi border, was halted by the war; by mid-1983, the installation, which was 85% complete, had already been attacked six times. In September 1984, the Japanese withdrew their technicians from the site because of renewed Iraqi bombing. Iran has taken on much of the financial responsibility for the plant, and the ending of all payments of Japanese credits and loans in February 1986 most likely meant that the plant would never be completed according to the original plans. After the ceasefire in 1988, Iran began to rebuild its damaged oil export facilities, concentrating mainly on the rehabilitation of Kharg Island. A 500,000-barrel reservoir terminal at Uhang Island was put into operation in March 1993. The oil complex on the southern island of Lavan was reopened after reconstruction at the end of April 1993. The Abadan refinery became again operational at 200,000 barrels per day in May 1993. Isfaran's oil production unit became operational in 1992/93, while the construction of a new refinery at Bandar Abbas is underway. Major refinery products are motor fuel, distillate fuel oil, and residual fuel oil.

The Abadan plant for the production of plastics, detergents, and caustic soda was completed in the 1960s. Since then, the petrochemical industry has expanded considerably. It has been the main element of the post-war industrializion program. The heavy metals industry began in 1972 with the start of steel production at Esfahan National Steel Mill in Esfahan. It is also given priority by the Rafsanjani government. Manufactured goods include diesel engines, motor vehicles, television sets, refrigerators, washing machines, and other consumer items. The most important modern mining development was in San Cheshmeh, near Sirjan, where exploration evealed one of the world's largest deposits of copper. Although running on a smaller scale than originally envisaged, it produced 105,000 tons of copper in 1992.

The textile industry has prospered in recent years with increased production of cotton, woolen, and synthetic fabrics. The making of handwoven carpets is a traditional industry in Iran that flourishes despite acute competition from machine-made products. However, carpet exports declined throughout the war years. To promote self-sufficiency, Iran has encouraged development of the food-processing, shoemaking, paper and paper products, rubber, pharmaceutical, aircraft, and shipbuilding industries. Other industrial products include cement, nitrogenous fertilizer, phosphate fertilizers, and refined sugar.

Iran's industrialization program was set back by the political turmoil and labor disruptions of the late 1970s and by the revolutionary government's nationalization of industries in the summer of 1979, causing a flight of capital and trained managers. However, the sector recovered somewhat by 1983/84, when industrial production registered a 23% gain, according to the government.

A more recent development plan (1989/90–1993/94) has increased funding to develop heavy industry. A privatization decree in June 1991 led to the identification of 390 public manufacturing and trading firms for divestiture; of these, 185 have already been divested.

29SCIENCE AND TECHNOLOGY

The "white revolution" of the 1960s, which emphasized industrialization, involved the importation of petroleum technology and the training of Iranian technicians abroad, but it did not improve Iran's indigenous technology. Since 1979, the Khomeini regime has shown little interest in high technology, and there has been a "brain drain" of Western-trained personnel. The principal scientific institution in Tehran is the International Scientific Research Institute. Iran has 25 universities offering degrees in basic and applied sciences. In addition, Iran has about 50 colleges of higher education and about 40 technological institutes. In 1985, total expenditures for research and development amounted to R22 billion; 1,854 technicians and 3,194 scientists and engineers were engaged in research and development.

30DOMESTIC TRADE

In summer, offices open as early as 7 AM and close at about 1 PM; during the rest of the year the hours are 8 AM until 4 PM, with a rest period in the middle of the day. Since Friday is the official holiday, many establishments close early on Thursday afternoon. Outside the major cities, most goods are sold in small shops or open-air markets. Banking hours in summer are 7:30 AM to 1 PM and 5 to 7 PM, Saturday–Wednesday, and 7:30 to 11:30 AM on Thursday; winter opening times are 30 minutes to an hour later.

31FOREIGN TRADE

Iran enjoyed a surplus of trade throughout the 1960s, 1970s, and most of the early 1980s. But since 1984 the trade balance has shown wide fluctuations, mainly reflecting the volume of oil exports as well as inferential oil prices.

Principal exports and imports (in millions of US dollars) were as follows:

	1989	1990	1991[a]
Exports fob of which:	13,600	18,800	16,732
petroleum (crude oil & products)	10,809	17,300	15,280
non-petroleum	2,791	1,500	1,452
Imports cif	−14,500	−18,000	22,320
Balance	−900[a]	800	−5,588

[a] OPEC estimates

The revolution brought a major change in the type of imports. While the impact of capital goods and consumer goods declined, there was an import boom in 1991 and 1992 in consumption goods. Food imports rose rapidly throughout the early 1980s despite the government's emphasis on agricultural development.

Iran's principal trade partners in 1986 were West Germany and Japan. Barter arrangements with the former East bloc countries increased in importance during the 1980s but fell off by the early 1990s. The US was a leading customer for Iran's oil exports during the 1970s, but trade between the two countries has been curtailed since the US severed diplomatic relations in April 1980 during the hostage crisis. Turkey, which maintained a careful neutrality in the Iran-Iraq conflict, greatly expanded its trade with Iran during the early 1980s, signing a $1-billion-a-year export agreement with Iran in March 1982. In January 1985, Iran, Pakistan, and Turkey ratified a new regional trade group, the Economic Cooperation Organization; trade among the three countries was expected to total $3 billion a year. Trade with Japan is substantial: IMF figures indicate that in 1991, Iran exported 15.9% of its goods (mostly petroleum) to Japan, receiving $12.6% of its imports from Japan. That year, Italy bought 9.4% of Iran's exports and shipped Iran 8.9% of its imports. Germany sent Iran 20.6% of its imports.

The main trading partners with percentages of total import and export values were as follows (% of total by dollar value):

	1989	1990	1991
EXPORTS TO:			
Japan	14.3	20.6	15.9
Italy	6.5	9.4	9.4
France	8.3	8.1	7.5
Netherlands	8.2	6.0	6.7
Belgium/Luxembourg	8.6	5.8	6.3
Brazil	3.0	6.0	5.9
IMPORTS FROM:			
Germany	15.8	18.0	20.6
Japan	7.6	11.3	12.6
Italy	6.3	7.8	8.9
UAE	7.4	6.6	4.8
UK	4.4	4.9	4.6
France	2.1	4.2	4.5

Rising arms imports since 1991/1992 have caused concern among Iran's neighbors and in the US. These imports do not feature in official import data totals.

32BALANCE OF PAYMENTS

The remarkable rise in Iran's oil income has had measurable impact on the country's balance of payments. Throughout the 1960s and 1970s, Iran had a favorable trade balance, but substantial imports of services resulted in an annual deficit on current accounts. Long-term capital inflows from private sources reached a peak in 1965; between 1968 and 1973, capital from foreign governments played a prime role in Iranian development. Net long-term capital inflows from governmental sources reached $597 million in 1971 and $552 million in 1973, when, aided by rising oil prices, Iran registered its first surplus on current accounts and invested $343 million in foreign private enterprises. By 1974, with a net trade surplus of $17,718 million and a current accounts surplus of $10,893 million, Iran was one of the world's major exporters of capital. The current accounts balance remained in surplus annually through 1979/80. Between 1980/81 and 1983/84, the current accounts were in deficit except for 1982/83, when a $6.55 billion surplus was registered. The capital accounts were also in deficit, except for 1982/83, when a surplus of $1.3 billion was registered.

The reversal in Iran's payments position has been reflected in the country's accumulation of international reserves. Reserve holdings, which totaled $310 million at the end of 1969, reached $9,667 million in 1980, dropped to $1,605 million in 1981, and jumped to $5,701 million in 1982, the last year for which statistics were available. Foreign exchange reserves rose from $7,652 million in 1974 to $14,561 million in 1979 but then declined to

$5,287 million at the end of 1982. Gold holdings totaled $229 million at the end of 1982.

33BANKING AND SECURITIES

The Central Bank of Iran, established by the Monetary and Banking Law of 1960, issues notes, controls foreign exchange, and supervises the banking sector. Currency in circulation increased from r1,108 billion in December 1980 to r1,757 billion in December 1983. Currency outside banks totaled r3,517.9 billion in 1990. Demand deposits with banks totaled r7,850.9 billion in 1991.

The revolutionary government nationalized all commercial banks shortly after taking office in 1979 and announced that banking practices would be brought in line with Islamic principles, which include a ban on interest payments. By 1993 there were five Islamic banks, which had incorporated the previous banks. Instead of paying interest, the new banks give "guaranteed returns" or commissions on loans; the commissions, which equal 4% of the loan's total, were introduced in 1984.

The Tehran Stock Exchange, locally known as the Bourse, was created in 1971. Three years later, the National Bank of Iran and the Industrial and Mining Development Bank of Iran joined with the US firm of Merrill Lynch, Pierce, Fenner & Smith to begin international brokerage activities in Iran. The exchange has stayed open since the revolution but plays only a small role in the nation's business.

34INSURANCE

On 25 June 1979, the revolutionary government announced the nationalization of all insurance companies. According to official statistics, state-owned insurance companies received r41,335 million in direct premiums for fire, accident, car, and all other types of insurance in 1982; r14,467 million was paid out in damages that year. In 1985/86, there were 3 insurance companies operating. In 1990, per capita premium payments totaled US$29.0 or 0.3% of the GDP.

35PUBLIC FINANCE

Iran's fiscal year coincides with its calendar year, beginning on 21 March. The budget is prepared by the Finance Ministry and submitted to Parliament. Trade reforms implemented since 1991 have boosted economic growth and reduced budget deficits. The general government deficit fell from 9% of GDP in 1988 to 2% in 1992.

The following table shows actual revenues and expenditures for 1992 and 1993 in billions of rials.

	1992	1993
REVENUE AND GRANTS		
Tax revenue	5,203	6,860
Non-tax revenue	6,953	18,243
Capital revenue	256	81
TOTAL	12,412	25,184
EXPENDITURES & LENDING MINUS REPAYMENTS		
General public service	—	699
Defense	—	1,778
Public order and safety	—	807
Education	—	4,833
Health	—	1,847
Social security and welfare	—	2,844
Housing and community amenities	—	1,497
Recreation, cultural, and religious affairs	—	597
Economic affairs and services	—	7,499
Other expenditures	—	3,025
TOTAL	13,362	25,426
Deficit/Surplus	–950	–242

36TAXATION

Under new tax laws of March 1988 and May 1992, individual income is taxed at rates varying from 12–54%. Capital gains and investment income are also taxable, and employees pay a 7% social security contribution. Corporate income, which is also taxed at between 12% and 54%, varies among corporations, partnerships, and branches of foreign corporations. Also levied are real estate taxes, municipal tax, and a 23% levy on expatriate salaries.

37CUSTOMS AND DUTIES

Most goods entering Iran are subject to customs duties, the majority of which are on the c.i.f. value. A number of government organizations and charitable institutions have been permitted to import their requirements free of duty. As of 1993, the government was considering eliminating quantitative trade restrictions and reducing tariff levels, with a maximum rate of 30% for most goods.

38FOREIGN INVESTMENT

Until the early 1970s, Iran rarely participated in foreign businesses. The National Iranian Oil Company (NIOC) did invest in the construction of oil refineries in Madras, India, and other places, and it participated in several mixed ventures with foreign oil firms that held concessions for Iranian oil. But with the vast increase in oil revenues, Iran became one of the world's leading creditor nations; in 1974 alone, bilateral agreements worth hundreds of billions of rials were signed with France, West Germany, Italy, and the UK. In July 1974, Iran agreed to purchase a 25% interest in the German steel-making firm of Krupp Hüttenwerke, an investment believed to be the largest single stake purchased by any oil-producing nation in a major European firm up to that time. In 1975, Iran began negotiating investments through the UNDP in developing nations.

Prior to World War II, foreign companies had important investments in Iranian banks, insurance companies, transport, and the oil industry. In 1955, the legislature enacted a law providing for withdrawal of invested capital in the currency that was brought into Iran, for the export of annual profits, and for adequate compensation in the event of nationalization of the industry or business. In 1957, the US and Iran exchanged notes recognizing that the US would guarantee its private investments in Iran against loss through actions by Iran, and the following year the Majlis enacted a law protecting foreign capital investments. Foreign companies moved into Iran to exploit mineral resources, to establish banks in partnership with Iranian capital, to build factories, and to carry out segments of the shah's vast economic development program.

Since 1979, the instability of the revolutionary government and such actions as the holding of the US hostages have resulted in a virtual shutdown of Western investment in Iran. The lifting of the freeze on Iranian assets in the US when the hostages were finally released did not improve the situation, although some settlements were made with foreign creditors. Iranian assets reported by BIS banks were $5.8 billion in 1992 with liabilities at $9 billion.

39ECONOMIC DEVELOPMENT

Iran's first development plan (1949–56) foundered because of the lack of oil revenues during the nationalization dispute and also because the IBRD refused to lend the hoped-for one-third of the projected development expenditures. The second plan (1956–63) also ran into financial difficulties when the domestic budget consumed a larger proportion of the oil revenues than expected. An austerity program from 1960, however, facilitated economic recovery. The third plan (1963–68) was successful, and the period witnessed rapid economic growth. This plan placed emphasis not only on the building of an infrastructure but also on quick-payoff projects making use of local resources. The private sector exceeded the target planned for investment. Substantial foreign aid, varied in its sources, was also forthcoming, and foreign investment in Iran totaled more than $2.7 billion. The fourth plan (1968–73) was far more successful than the previous ones, with most of its objectives realized beyond expectation. The mean annual GNP growth was 11.2%, as compared with the projected figure of 9%. Similarly, per capita GNP rose to about $560 ($300 had been the goal).

In its revised form, the fifth plan (1973–78) provided for infrastructural development and other expenditures totaling R2,847 billion. However, a lag in oil revenues led to rescheduling of the plan for six years instead of five and the postponement or slowdown of individual projects. Because of political opposition and social unrest during the last year of the shah's reign, the plan was abandoned in 1978. The Islamic government that came to power in 1979 cut economic development funds because of a shortage of revenues, but in 1983 it proposed its own five-year development plan for 1983–88, with allocations totaling $166 billion and emphasis given to agriculture and service industries. However, the government's cutbacks on oil production (and, consequently, of the oil revenues that were to finance the plan), coupled with the diversion of resources to the war with Iraq, made it impossible to fulfill the plan's goals. The plan was revised twice after its introduction; in January 1986 the Parliament approved the outline of the revised plan, details of which were not available. The original plan called for 15.5% of development funds to be spent on agriculture, 5.3% on oil, 52.2% on industry and mines, and 27% on services.

The five-year plan (1989/90–1993/94) authorized up to $27 billion in foreign borrowing. It aimed to increase productivity in key industrial and economic sectors and to promote the non-oil export sector. A real GDP growth of 8% was projected.

The 1994/95–1998/99 plan under preparation aimed at investing money in transport, particularly in the railroad system and in the construction of a public underground for Tehran.

40SOCIAL DEVELOPMENT

Traditionally, the family and the tribe were supplemented by Islamic waqf (obligatory charity) institutions for the care of the infirm and the indigent. Iran's monarchical system was slow to awaken to the responsibility of the state in this respect. In 1974, the Ministry of Social Welfare was created with the object of coordinating and harmonizing the programs of social insurance organizations (previously affiliated with the Ministry of Labor) with those of the Social Security Organization, the Ministry of Health, and other government agencies engaged in social welfare. It was anticipated that by the end of the fifth plan (1973–78), some 50% of the urban population would enjoy insurance coverage, but coverage for the whole country was not envisaged until the end of the 1980s. Social welfare programs included workers' compensation, disability benefits, maternity allowances, retirement benefits, death benefits, and family and marriage allowances. In 1991, these programs covered only employed persons in specific occupations and geographical areas. There were also special pension systems in force for public employees. Old-age benefits were 2.9% of average earnings multiplied by the number of years of contributions. Survivor benefits were 50% of the descendant's pension. The 1979 constitution provided for health, unemployment, and old age insurance.

The human rights abuses that characterized the shah's regime were, if anything, intensified after his overthrow. The revolutionary government was accused of conducting arbitrary arrests and summary trials (resulting in at least 6,426 deaths as of October 1985, according to Amnesty International), of using torture in interrogating political prisoners, and of persecuting such religious minorities as Baha'is and Jews (at least 200 Baha'is had been executed and 767 imprisoned at the end of 1985). According to Amnesty International's 1981 annual report, the "guarantees necessary for a fair trial [were] effectively lacking in cases heard by the Islamic revolutionary tribunals," and executions occurred almost immediately after the guilty verdicts were pronounced, with little time to appeal the verdicts or to petition for clemency. The imposition of Islamic fundamentalism brought with it censorship of all media and a revocation, in large part, of the emancipation of women achieved during the previous regime. Wearing of the chador, the traditional cloak, was reimposed and vigorously enforced, and the liberalization of abortion and divorce laws in the mid-1970s was rescinded. Enforcement of Islamic restrictions on women has varied since the Ayatollah Khomeini's death in 1989. There was a pronounced surge in enforcement in 1993. Iranian groups that protest human rights abuses are severely harassed by the government. The UN Special Representative has been barred from Iran since 1991.

41HEALTH

Until the 1960s, Iran was plagued by many health problems: high infant mortality, smallpox outbreaks, venereal disease, trachoma, typhoid fever, amoebic dysentery, malaria, tuberculosis, and the debilitating effects of smoking opium. In 1990, there were 83 reported cases of tuberculosis per 1,000 people; in fact, one quarter of visits to health centers have been attributed to respiratory disease. National campaigns against such major diseases as malaria and smallpox were undertaken. The creation in 1964 of a health corps, consisting of physicians and high-school graduates who agreed to spend the period of their military service serving in semimobile medical units in rural areas, helped to reduce the death rate. Roving health corps teams, comprising a doctor, a dentist, a pathologist, and (when possible) a nurse, served the villages, offering medical services to 10,000–15,000 rural inhabitants annually. In 1993, the death rate was 7.1 per 1,000 population. In 1992, the infant mortality rate was 4 per 1,000 live births. The Islamic republic has continued to provide health care programs to the rural areas. In 1986, the Ministry of Health and Medical Education had 5,309 doctors (excluding those employed by universities), 4,188 specialists, and 2,359 independent pharmacists. In 1992, there were .about 3 physicians per 10,000 people. In 1991, there were 4,847 dentists in Iran. Many physicians left the country after the 1979 revolution, and health conditions were reportedly deteriorating; however, by the mid-1980s, many doctors who had been in exile during the shah's reign had returned. As of 1990, Iran had 1.5 hospital beds per 1,000 people and total health care expenditures of $3,024 million. Average life expectancy in 1992 was estimated at 67 years for both women and men. In 1991, 89% of the population had access to safe drinking water, and 71% had adequate sanitation. In 1992, 80% of the population had access to health care services. Iran's birth rate in 1993 was 39.9 per 1,000 people. In 1992, there were 2,473,000 births, with children up to 1 year old having been immunized against tuberculosis (92%); diphtheria, pertussis, and tetanus (87%); polio (87%); and measles (84%).

42HOUSING

Rapid urbanization has made housing one of the country's most acute social problems. Although housing has always been given top priority in development plans, the gap between supply and demand for dwellings has grown increasingly wide. During the fourth plan (1968–73), nearly 300,000 housing units were built, but because some 120,000 new families were added to the urban population during that period, the average density rose from 7.7 to 8.5 persons per dwelling. During the same period, the national urban housing deficit rose from 721,000 to 1,095,000 units. Under the fifth plan (1973–78), the housing target was increased

to 810,000 units, and the projected investment and credit for housing rose to more than R925 billion. However, housing starts fell sharply after the 1979 revolution, as construction declined precipitously because of lack of funding (construction of all buildings dropped by 21% in 1981/82 and 24% in 1982/83). In 1983/84, construction starts of buildings increased by 97%. In 1983/84, 15,468 new buildings were begun in Tehran (68,937 in other large cities). That same year, government figures showed that 104,698 residential units were completed in Tehran and other large cities throughout the country. In 1986, 43% of all housing units were constructed of brick with iron beams, 19% were adobe and wood, 16% were brick with wooden beams, 10% were adobe and mud, 5% were cement block, and 3% were iron with a cement skeleton. Electricity was available in 84% of all housing units, 95% had a water toilet, 75% had piped water, 54% had a kitchen, and 47% had a bath.

43EDUCATION

Literacy training has been a prime concern in Iran. In 1990, the literacy rate was estimated at 54.0%, 64.5% for males and 43.3% for females. A literacy corps was established in 1963 to send educated conscripts to villages. During its first 10 years, the corps helped 2.2 million urban children and 600,000 adults become literate. In 1991, there were 252,513 kindergarten pupils in 4,114 schools, 9,787,593 elementary-school pupils, and 5,619,057 total secondary-school students. Teacher training schools had 46,493 and vocational had 260,576 students out of the total.

Education is virtually free in Iran at all levels, from elementary school through university. At university level, however, every student is required to commit himself to serve the government for a number of years equivalent to those spent at the university. During the early 1970s, efforts were made to improve the educational system by updating school curricula, introducing modern textbooks, and training more efficient teachers.

The 1979 revolution continued the country's emphasis on education, but Khomeini's regime put its own stamp on the process. The most important change was the Islamization of the education system. All students were segregated by sex. In 1980, the Cultural Revolution Committee was formed to oversee the institution of Islamic values in education. An arm of the committee, the Center for Textbooks (composed mainly of clerics), produced 3,000 new college-level textbooks reflecting Islamic views by 1983. Teaching materials based on Islam were introduced into the primary grades within six months of the revolution.

The tradition of university education in Iran goes back to the early centuries of Islam. By the 20th century, however, the system had become antiquated and was remodeled along French lines. The country's 16 universities were closed after the 1979 revolution and were then reopened gradually between 1982 and 1983 under Islamic supervision.

While the universities were closed, the Cultural Revolution Committee investigated professors and teachers and dismissed those who were believers in Marxism, liberalism, and other "imperialistic" ideologies. The universities reopened with Islamic curriculums. In 1991, all higher level institutions had 25,208 teachers and 636,255 students. The University of Tehran (founded in 1934) has 10 faculties, including a department of Islamic theology. Other major universities are at Tabriz, Mashhad, Ahvaz, Shiraz, Esfahan, Kerman, Babol Sar, Rasht, and Orumiyeh. There are about 50 colleges and 40 technological institutes.

44LIBRARIES AND MUSEUMS

Public libraries and museums are fairly new in Iran. The National Library at Tehran has a good general collection of about 430,000 volumes. The Library of Parliament, with 155,000 volumes, has an extensive collection of manuscripts and an unrivaled collection of documentary material in Farsi, including files of all important newspapers since the inception of the press in Iran. The Central Library of the University of Tehran holds some 160,000 volumes. The public library system had 3,332,421 books in 1987.

Tehran has the Archaeological Museum, overflowing with fabulous treasures from the long cultural and artistic history of Iran, and the Ethnological Museum. The crown treasures of manuscripts, jeweled thrones, and a vast variety of other objects may be seen at the Golestan Palace. Museums at Esfahan, Mashhad, Qom, and Shiraz feature antique carpets, painted pottery, illuminated manuscripts, and fine craftsmanship in wood and metal; most of these objects date from the 12th to the 18th centuries. The Tehran Museum of Modern Art was founded in 1977.

45MEDIA

Telegraph, telephone, and radio broadcasting services are state-owned. In 1991 there were 2,103,830 telephones in service. Both radio and television were nationalized in 1980. Principal stations are located in Tehran, and other major stations broadcast from Ahvaz, Zahedan, Tabriz, Rasht, Kermanshah, and Bandar-e Lengeh. In 1991 there were over 13,860,000 radio receivers. Television of Iran, a privately owned station, began broadcasting in 1956 in Tehran and Abadan. The national radio organization and the government television network were merged in 1971 to form National Iranian Radio and Television (NIRT). After 1979, it became the Islamic Republic of Iran Broadcasting Company. In 1991, Iran had 585 television transmitters and relays; there were an estimated 3,750,000 television sets in 1991.

Until 1979, the local press operated under a law enacted by Parliament in 1955. To obtain licenses, newspaper owners had to have a B.A. degree, good character, and funds adequate for publishing for a stated period. Suspension of publication, fines, and imprisonment resulted from such violations of the law as printing false news or attacks on the royal family, revealing military secrets, and printing material injurious to Islam. At the time of the Khomeini revolution, Iran had 39 daily newspapers with a total circulation of about 750,000. The constitution of 1979 strictly limited freedom of the press; a new press law required publications to be licensed, and their editors were subject to imprisonment for printing reports the religious authorities deemed insulting. Newspapers that had favored the shah were closed down, and others considered unsympathetic to the ruling IRP were banned. In 1985, Khomeini stated "constructive" press criticism of the government would be allowed. In 1991 there were 11 "authorized" daily newspapers. The major Persian-language dailies were *Kayhan* (circulation 350,000) and *Ettal'at (250,000)*, both in Tehran.

46ORGANIZATIONS

Long renowned for their individualism, Iranians now actively associate with modern public and private organizations. Under the shah, the government greatly encouraged the growth of the cooperative movement; the first Workers' Consumers Society was established in 1948. Many villages have founded producers' cooperatives with official advice and support, and consumers' cooperatives exist among governmental employees and members of the larger industrial and service organizations. In 1984/85, there were 3,104 rural cooperative societies with some 3.9 million members. There were also more than 3,181 cooperative unions with 3,097 members.

Private charitable organizations date from as early as 1923, when the Iranian Red Lion and Sun Society (corresponding to the Red Cross) was established. Other charitable institutions include the Organization for Social Services and the Mother and Infant Protection Institute. The Society to Combat the Use of Opium has waged a campaign against use of the drug. The Boy Scout move-

ment in Iran began before World War II. The Chamber of Commerce, Industries, and Mines has its headquarters in Tehran.

47TOURISM, TRAVEL, AND RECREATION

Tourism, which had been stagnant since the 1979 revolution, has begun to grow since the death of Ayatollah Khomeini and the government's attempts to establish closer ties with the West. In 1991, 212,096 tourists visited Iran, 46% from southern Asia, 29% from Europe, and 17% from the Middle East. In 1989, there were 15,584 rooms in hotels and other facilities, with 31,167 beds and a 68% occupancy rate, and tourism receipts totaled US$62 million in 1990. Principal tourist attractions include historic and beautifully decorated mosques, mausoleums, and minarets. There are many sports and physical culture societies in Tehran and the provinces; emphasis is upon skiing and weight lifting.

48FAMOUS IRANIANS

The long history of Iran has witnessed a brilliant galaxy of conquerors, wise rulers and statesmen, artists, poets, historians, and philosophers. In religion, there have been diverse figures. Zoroaster (Zarathushtra), who probably lived in the 6th century BC, founded the religion known as Zoroastrianism or Mazdaism, with Ahura-Mazda as the god of good. In the 3d century AD, Mani attempted a fusion of the tenets of Mazdaism, Judaism, and Christianity. The Bab (Sayyid 'Ali Muhammad of Shiraz, 1819–50) was the precursor of Baha'ism, founded by Baha' Allah (Mirza Husayn 'Ali Nuri, 1817–92).

Great Persian rulers of the pre-Christian era include Cyrus ("the Great"; Kurush, r.550–529 BC), Cambyses II (Kambuiya, r.529–522 BC), Darius I ("the Great"; Darayavaush, r.521–486 BC), Xerxes I ("the Great"; Khshayarsha, r.486–465 BC), and Artaxerxes I (Artakhshathra, r.464–424 BC). Shah 'Abbas (r.1587–1628) expanded Persian territory and conquered Baghdad. Prominent political figures of modern times are Reza Shah Pahlavi (1877–1944), who reigned from 1925 to his abdication in 1941; and his son, Muhammad Reza Pahlavi (1919–80), who was shah from 1941 until his abdication in 1979. Until his death in 1989, Iran was under the leadership of Ayatollah Ruhollah Khomeini (1900–89).

The great epic poet Firdawsi (Abdul Qasim Hassan ibn-i-Ishaq ibn-i Sharafshah, 940–1020), writing about AD 1000, produced the *Shahnama (Book of Kings)*, dealing with four ancient dynasties and full of romantic and heroic tales that retain their popularity today. Omar Khayyam (d.1123?), astronomer and poet, is known in the Western world for his *Rubáiyât*, a collection of quatrains freely translated by Edward FitzGerald. Important figures of the Seljuk period (11th and 12th centuries) include Muhammad bin Muhammad al-Ghazali (1058–1111), philosopher and mystic theologian, who exerted an enormous influence upon all later speculative thought in Islam; Farid ad-Din 'Attar (Muhammad bin Ibrahim, 1119–1229?), one of the greatest of mystic poets; and Nizami (Nizam ad-Din Abu Muhammad, 1141–1202), noted for four romantic epic poems that were copied and recopied by hand and illuminated with splendid miniatures. In the 13th century, Jalal ad-Din Rumi (1207–73) compiled his celebrated long mystic poem, the *Mathnavi*, in rhyming couplets; and Sa'di (Muslih ud-Din, 1184?–1291), possibly the most renowned Iranian poet within or outside of Iran, composed his *Gulistan (Rose Garden)* and *Bustan (Orchard)*. About a hundred years later, in 1389, another poet of Shiraz died, Hafiz (Shams ud-Din Muhammad); his collected works comprise nearly 700 poems, all of them ghazals or lyrical odes.

Poets of the modern period include Iraj Mirza (1880–1926), Mirzadeh Eshqi (d.1924), Parveen Ettasami (d.1941), and the poet laureate Behar (Malik ash-Shuara Bahar, d.1951). Preeminent among prose writers was Sadeq Hedayat (1903–51), author of the novel *Buf i kur (The Blind Owl)* and numerous other works, including films.

Miniature painting came to full flower in the second half of the 15th century. The greatest figure in this field was Bihzad, whose limited surviving work is highly prized. The School of Herat was composed of his followers.

49DEPENDENCIES
Iran has no territories or colonies.

50BIBLIOGRAPHY
Abdulghani, Jasim M. *Iraq and Iran: The Years of Crisis.* Baltimore: Johns Hopkins University Press, 1984.

Abrahamian, Ervand. *Iran Between Two Revolutions.* Princeton, N.J.: Princeton University Press, 1982.

American University. *Area Handbook for Iran.* Washington, D.C.: Government Printing Office, 1978.

Amirahmadi, Hooshang. *Revolution and Economic Transition: The Iranian Experience.* Albany: State University of New York Press, 1990.

Amirahmadi, Hooshang and Manoucher Parvin (eds.) *Post-revolutionary.* Boulder, Colo.: Westview Press, 1988.

Amuzegar, Jahangir. *Iran's Economy under the Islamic Republic.* London and New York: St. Martin's, 1993.

Arjomand, Said Amir. *The Turban for the Crown: The Islamic Revolution in Iran.* New York: Oxford University Press, 1988.

Authority and Political Culture in Shi'ism Arjomand. Albany: State University of New York Press, 1988.

Bakhash, Shaul. *The Reign of the Ayatollahs: Iran and the Islamic Revolution.* New York: Basic Books, 1984.

Benard, Cheryl, and Zalmay Khalilzad. *The Government of God: Iran's Islamic Republic.* New York: Columbia University Press, 1984.

Bina, Cyrus and Hamid Zangeneh (eds.). *Modern Capitalism and Islamic Ideology in Iran Bina and Hamid Zangeneh.* New York: St. Martin's Press, 1992.

Bulloch, John. *The Gulf War: Its Origins, History and Consequences.* London: Methuen London, 1989.

Chehabi, H. E. *Iranian Politics and Religious Modernism: The Liberation Movement of Iran under the Shah and Khomeini.* Ithaca, N.Y.: Cornell University Press, 1990.

Chubin, Shahram. *Iran and Iraq at War.* Boulder, Colo.: Westview Press, 1988.

Cottam, Richard. *Iran and the United States.* Pittsburgh: University of Pittsburgh Press, 1988.

El-Azhary, M. S. *The Iran-Iraq War: Historical, Economic, and Political Analysis.* New York: St. Martin's, 1984.

Elm, Mostafa. *Oil, Power, and Principle: Iran's Oil Nationalization and its Aftermath.* Syracuse, N.Y.: Syracuse University Press, 1992.

Fischer, Michael M. J. *Iran: From Religious Dispute to Revolution.* Cambridge: Harvard University Press, 1980.

Gardner, J. Anthony. *The Iraq-Iran War: A Bibliography.* Boston, Mass.: G.K. Hall, 1989.

Gasiorowski, Mark J. *US Foreign Policy and the Shah: Building a Client State in Iran.* Ithaca, N.Y.: Cornell University Press, 1991.

Ghani, Sirus. *Iran and the West: A Critical Bibliography.* New York: K. Paul International, 1987.

Ghirshman, Roman. *Iran from the Earliest Times to the Islamic Conquest.* Harmondsworth: Penguin, 1954.

Hiro, Dilip. *Iran Under the Ayatollahs.* 2d ed. New York: Routledge and Kegan Paul, 1987.

Hunter, Shireen. *Iran after Khomeini.* New York: Praeger, 1992.

Iran in Pictures. Minneapolis: Lerner, 1988.

Kamrava, Mehran. *The Political History of Modern Iran: From Tribalism to Theocracy.* Westport, Conn.: Praeger, 1992.

Karshenas, Massoud. *Oil, State, and Industrialization in Iran.* New York: Cambridge University Press, 1990.

Keddie, Nikki. *Roots of Revolution: An Interpretive History of Modern Iran.* Berkeley: University of California Press, 1981.

Keddie, Nikki R., and Eric Hooglund (eds.). *The Iranian Revolution and the Islamic Republic.* 2d ed. Syracuse: Syracuse University Press, 1986.

Limbert, John W. *Iran, at War with History.* Boulder, Colo.: Westview Press, 1987.

Metz, Helen Chapin (ed.). *Iran, a Country Study.* 4th ed. Washington, D.C.: Library of Congress, 1989.

Mofid, Kamran. *The Economic Consequences of the Gulf War.* New York: Routledge, 1990.

Mottahedeh, Roy P. *Mantle of the Prophet.* New York: Pantheon, 1986.

Olmstead, Albert Ten Eyck. *The History of the Persian Empire.* Chicago: University of Chicago Press, 1960.

Ramazani, R. K. *Revolutionary Iran: Challenges and Responses in the Middle East.* Baltimore: Johns Hopkins University Press, 1987.

Sanchez, James. *Index to the Iran-Contra Hearings Summary Report.* Jefferson, N.C.: McFarland, 1988.

Schulz, Ann. *Buying Security: Iran under the Monarchy.* Boulder, Colo.: Westview Press, 1989.

Stempel, John D. *Inside the Iranian Revolution.* Bloomington: Indiana University Press, 1981.

Wilber, Donald Newton. *Iran, Past and Present: From Monarchy to Islamic Republic.* Princeton, N.J.: Princeton University Press, 1981.

Wright, Robin B. *In the name of God: The Khomeini Decade.* New York: Simon and Schuster, 1989.

Zonis, Marvin. *Majestic Failure: The Fall of the Shah.* Chicago: University of Chicago Press, 1991.

IRAQ

Republic of Iraq
Al-Jumhuriyah al-'Iraqiyah

CAPITAL: Baghdad.

FLAG: The national flag is a tricolor of red, white, and black horizontal stripes, with three five-pointed stars in green in the center of the white stripe.

ANTHEM: *Al-Salaam al-Jumhuri (Salute of the Republic).*

MONETARY UNIT: The Iraqi dinar (ID) is a paper currency of 1,000 fils. There are coins of 1, 5, 10, 25, 50, 100, and 250 fils, and notes of 250 and 500 fils and 1, 5, 10, 50, and 100 dinars. ID1 = $3.2169 (or $1 = ID0.3109).

WEIGHTS AND MEASURES: The metric system is the legal standard, but weights and measures in general use vary, especially in domestic transactions. The unit of land is the dunam, which is equivalent to approximately 0.25 hectare (0.62 acre).

HOLIDAYS: New Year's Day, 1 January; Army Day, 6 January; 14th Ramadan Revolution Day, 8 February; Declaration of the Republic, 14 July; and Peaceful Revolution Day, 17 July. Muslim religious holidays include 'Id al-Fitr, 'Id al-'Adha', Milad an-Nabi, and Islamic New Year.

TIME: 3 PM = noon GMT.

¹LOCATION, SIZE, AND EXTENT

Present-day Iraq, comprising an area of 437,072 sq km (168,754 sq mi), corresponds roughly to the former Turkish provinces of Baghdad, Mosul (Al-Mawsil), and Basra (Al-Basrah). Comparatively, the area occupied by Iraq is slightly more than twice the size of the state of Idaho. It extends 984 km (611 mi) SSE–NNW and 730 km (454 mi) ENE–WSW. Iraq is bordered on the N by Turkey, on the E by Iran, on the SE by the Persian Gulf and Kuwait, on the S by Sa'udi Arabia, on the W by Jordan, and on the NW by Syria, with a total boundary length of 3,689 km (2,292 mi). The Neutral Zone, administered jointly by Iraq and Sa'udi Arabia, was to be divided according to an agreement of 2 July 1975, which was confirmed by an agreement signed on 26 December 1981 in Baghdad. This pact was described by the Sa'udi signatory as defining and fixing the common border and dividing the Neutral Zone, but as of early 1988, no details of the agreement had been filed with the UN. A long-standing border dispute with Iran, seemingly resolved in 1975, led to a full-scale war in the 1980s. In August 1990, Iraq reasserted its claim, dating from the days of the monarchy (abolished in 1958), to Kuwait, invading and occupying it. In January 1991, Iraq was defeated by the US and its allies in an air war and withdrew.

Iraq's capital city, Baghdad, is located in the east central part of the country.

²TOPOGRAPHY

Iraq is divided into three distinct zones: the desert in the west and southwest; the plains; and the highlands in the northeast, which rise to 3,000 m (10,000 ft) or more. The desert is an upland region with altitudes of 600 to 900 m (2,000–3,000 ft) between Damascus in Syria and Ar-Rutbah in Iraq, but declines gently toward the Euphrates (Al-Furat) River. The water supply comes from wells and wadis that at times carry torrential floods and that retain the winter rains.

Dominated by the river systems of the Tigris (Dijlah) and Euphrates, the plains area is composed of two regions divided by a ridge, some 75 m (250 ft) above the flood plain, between Ar-Ramadi and a point south of Baghdad that marks the prehistoric coastline of the Persian Gulf. The lower valley, built up by the silt the two rivers carry, consists of marshland, crisscrossed by drainage channels. At Qarmat 'Ali, just above Basra, the two rivers combine and form the Shatt al-'Arab, a broad waterway separating Iraq and Iran. The sources of the Euphrates and Tigris are in the Armenian Plateau. The Euphrates receives its main tributaries before entering Iraq, while the Tigris receives several streams on the eastern bank within the country.

³CLIMATE

Under the influence of the monsoons, Iraq in summer has a constant northwesterly wind (shamal), while in winter a strong southeasterly air current (sharqi) develops. The intensely hot and dry summers last from May to October, and during the hottest time of the day—often reaching 49°C (120°F) in the shade—people take refuge in underground shelters. Winters, lasting from December to March, are damp and comparatively cold, with temperatures averaging about 10°C (50°F). Spring and autumn are brief transition periods. Normally, no rain falls from the end of May to the end of September. With annual rainfall of less than 38 cm (15 in), agriculture is dependent on irrigation.

⁴FLORA AND FAUNA

In the lower regions of the Euphrates and Tigris and in the alluvial plains, papyrus, lotus, and tall reeds form a thick underbrush; willow, poplar, and alder trees abound. On the upper and middle Euphrates, the licorice bush yields a juice that is extracted for commercial purposes; another bush growing wild in the semiarid steppe or desert yields gum tragacanth for pharmaceutical use. In the higher Zagros Mountains grows the valonia oak, the bark of which is used for tanning leather. About 30 million date palms produce one of Iraq's most important exports.

Wild animals include the hyena, jackal, fox, gazelle, antelope, jerboa, mole, porcupine, desert hare, and bat. Beaver, wild ass, and ostrich are rare. Wild ducks, geese, and partridge are the game birds. Vultures, owls, and ravens live near the Euphrates. Falcons are trained for hunting.

5ENVIRONMENT

UN reports in 1992 stated that Iraq's natural environment "underwent the worst destruction ever possible" during the 1991 Persian Gulf War. The major sources of environmental damage are effluents from oil refineries, factory and sewage discharges into rivers, fertilizer and chemical contamination of the soil, and industrial air pollution in urban areas. An estimated 1% of agricultural land is lost each year through soil erosion and salinization. The government has not developed a comprehensive environmental conservation policy, but it has initiated programs to prevent water pollution, to reclaim land by reducing soil salinity, and to protect wildlife by limiting hunting. As a result of war damage, water pollution has increased. Purification systems for water and sewage are inadequate. Toxic chemicals from damaged oil facilities contribute to water pollution. Iraq has 8.2 cubic miles of water with 92% used in farming activity. Fifty-nine percent of people living in rural areas do not have pure water. The nation's cities produce 6 million tons of solid waste per year. The Supreme Council for the Human Environment is the principal environmental agency; its implementing body, the Directorate General for the Human Environment, was established in 1975 and is attached to the Ministry of Health. As of 1994, 9 of Iraq's mammal species and 17 of its bird species are endangered. One plant species is threatened with extinction. Endangered species in 1987 were the northern bald Ibis, Persian fallow deer, and Sa'udi Arabian dorcas gazelle. The Asiatic cheetah and Syrian wild ass are probably extinct.

6POPULATION

According to the census of 1987, the population of Iraq was 16,335,199. In mid-1991, the population was officially estimated at 17,903,000; the population for the year 2000 was projected at 24,779,000, assuming a crude birthrate of 36.8 per 1,000 population, a crude death rate of 5.9, and a net natural increase of 30.9 during 1995–2000. The estimated average population density in 1991 was 41 per sq km (107 per sq mi). The annual growth rate in 1985–90 averaged about 3.3%. In 1995, about 75% of Iraq's population was urban. As of 1987, Baghdad, the capital, had 3,844,608 inhabitants; other major cities, with 1985 estimated populations, included Basra, the main port, 616,700, and Mosul, 570,926.

7MIGRATION

Immigration into Iraq was limited until the beginning of the 1970s. However, the rise in oil prices and the increase of oil exports, as well as extensive public and private spending in the mid-1970s, created a market for foreign labor. The result was a stream of foreign (mainly Egyptian) workers whose number may have risen as high as 1,600,000 before the Gulf War. During the Iran–Iraq war, many Egyptians worked in the public sector, filling a gap left by civil servants, farmers, and other workers who were fighting at the front. A number of Iraqis from the south, mainly Basra and its environs, influenced by family ties and higher wages, migrated to Sa'udi Arabia and Kuwait. To weaken local support in the north for Kurdish rebels, the government forced tens of thousands of Kurds to resettle in the south; in September 1987, a Western diplomat in Baghdad claimed that at least 500 Kurdish villages had been razed and 100,000 to 500,000 Kurds relocated.

In 1991 some 1.5 million Iraqis fled the country for Turkey or Iran to escape Saddam Hussein's increasingly repressive rule, but fewer than 100,000 remained abroad. Most of the refugees were Kurds who later resettled in areas in Iraq not controlled by the government.

8ETHNIC GROUPS

Arabs constitute about 76% of the total population. The Kurds, an Islamic non-Arab people, are the largest and most important minority group, constituting about 19%. A seminomadic pastoral people, the Kurds live in the northeastern Zagros Mountains, mostly in isolated villages in the mountain valleys near Turkey and Iran. Kurdish opposition to Iraqi political dominance has occasioned violent clashes with government forces. Other minorities include Turkomans (1.5–2%), living in the northeast; Yazidis, mostly in the Sinjar Mountains; Assyrians, mainly in the cities and northeastern rural areas; and Armenians.

9LANGUAGES

Arabic is the national language and is the mother tongue of an estimated 79% of the population. Kurdish (16%), or a dialect of it, is spoken by the Kurds and Yazidis. Aranaic, the ancient Syriac dialect, is retained by the Assyrians. Another Syriac dialect, Mandaean, is the liturgical language of the Sabaeans. The Turkomans speak a Turkic dialect.

10RELIGIONS

Islam is the national religion of Iraq, adhered to by over 95% of the population in 1993. A slight majority of Muslims belong to the Shi'i sect and a minority to the Sunni sect. Traditionally, the Shi'i majority has been governed and generally oppressed by members of the Sunni minority, which since the late 1970s has become increasingly concerned about the export of Shi'i militancy from Iran. There are also some heterodox Muslim groups, such as the Yazidis, who consider Satan a fallen angel who will one day be reconciled with God. They propitiate him in their rites and regard the Old and New Testaments, as well as the Koran (Qur'an), as sacred.

In 1991, Christianity claimed some 1 million adherents, of whom over 500,000 were Roman Catholic and nearly all the remainder belonged to various branches of Oriental Christianity. The Assyrians (who are not descended from the ancient Assyrians) are Nestorians. In the 19th century, under the influence of Roman Catholic missions, Christian Chaldaeans, originally also Nestorians, joined the Uniate churches, which are in communion with Rome; their patriarch has his seat in Mosul. The Sabaeans, or Mandaeans, are often called Christians of St. John, but their religious belief and their liturgy contain elements of many creeds, including some of pre-Christian Oriental origin. Since baptism is their main ritual, they always dwell near water and are concentrated on the riverbanks south of Baghdad. Iraq's Jewish community, which had its origins in Babylonian times and which produced outstanding scholars during the first millennium AD, dwindled from about 90,000 in 1948 to 200 in 1990, virtually all Iraqi Jewry having emigrated to Israel by the early 1950s.

11TRANSPORTATION

Major cities, towns, and villages are connected by a modern network of highways and roads which have made old caravan routes extinct. The city of Baghdad has been reshaped by the development of expressways through the city and by passes built since the 1970s. By 1991, Iraq had 34,700 km (21,563 mi) of roads; in 1991 there were some 650,000 cars and 350,000 commercial vehicles in use.

Railroads are owned and operated by the Iraqi State Railways Administration. A standard-gauge railroad connects Iraq with Jordan and Syria, and nearly all the old meter-gauge line connecting Irbil in the north with Basra, by way of Kirkuk and Baghdad, has been replaced. In 1991 there were about 2,457 km (1,527 mi) of railway lines.

Baghdad, Basra, and Mosul have international airports. Iraq Airways is the state-owned carrier; in the 1980s, its international flights landed only at night because of the Iraqi-Iranian war. The

IRAQ

0   50   100 Miles
0   50   100 Kilometers

TURKEY

Daryácheh-ye Orūmiyeh

Hakkâri
Orūmiyeh
Qezel Owzan
Zākhū
Dahūk
Az Zībār
Shanidar Cave
Al Ḥasakah
Tigris
Tall 'Afar
Al Mawşil
Calah
Arbil
Saqqez
Al Hadar
Zāb aṣ Ṣaḡōr
Dayr az Zawr
As Sulaymāniyah
Nuzi
Kirkūk
Sanandaj
Ba'iji
Al 'Uẓaym
Euphrates
'Anah
Buḥayrat al Qādisiyah
Tigris
Sāmarrā'
Khānaqin
Kermānshāh
IRAN
Tharthār Lake
Diyālá
Baqūbah
Mandali
Ar Ramādi
Al Fallūjah
Baghdād
Ctesiphon
Habbāniyah Lake
Ar Ruṭbah
Babylon
Al Kūt
Dīyīlah
Dezfūl
Trebil
Razzaza Lake
Karbalā
Al Ḥillah
An Najaf
Ad Diwānifsyah
Al 'Amārah
D E S E R T
Badanah
Ash Shaṭrah
As Samāwah
Al Furāt
An Nāṣiriyah
Kārūn
Ur
S a h a r á   a l   H i j a r a h
Al Baṣrah
Shatt al 'Arab
Ābādān
Az Zubayr

SYRIA
S Y R I A N
M E S O P O T A M I A

JORDAN

KUWAIT
Jūn al Kuwayt
Kuwait
Persian Gulf

SAUDI ARABIA

Iraq

LOCATION: 29° to 37°30′N; 39° to 48°E. **BOUNDARY LENGTHS:** Turkey, 305 km (190 mi); Iran, 1,458 km (906 mi); Persian Gulf coastline, 19 km (12 mi); Kuwait, 254 km (158 mi); Sa'udi Arabia, 895 km (556 mi); Jordan, 147 km (91 mi); Syria, 603 km (375 mi). **TERRITORIAL SEA LIMIT:** 12 mi.

war also virtually closed Iraq's main port of Basra and the new port of Umm Qasr on the Persian Gulf. Expansion of Iraq's merchant marine, which totaled 1,470,000 GRT in 1980, was halted by the war with Iran and again by the Persian Gulf War; by the beginning of 1992, the merchant marine totaled only 32 ships with 796,000 GRT.

12HISTORY

Some of the earliest known human settlements have been found in present-day Iraq. Habitations, shrines, implements, and pottery found on various sites can be dated as early as the 5th millennium BC. Some sites bear names that are familiar from the Bible, which describes the region of the Hiddekel (Tigris) and Euphrates rivers as the location of the Garden of Eden and the city of Ur as the birthplace of the patriarch Abraham. Scientific exploration and archaeological research have amplified the biblical accounts.

Recorded history in Mesopotamia (the ancient name of Iraq, particularly the area between the Tigris and Euphrates) begins with the Sumerians, who by the 4th millennium BC had established city-states. Records and accounts on clay tablets prove that they had a complex economic organization before 3200 BC. The reign of Sumer was challenged by King Sargon of Akkad (r.c.2350 BC); a Sumero-Akkadian culture continued in Erech (Tall al-Warka') and Ur (Tall al-Muqayyar) until it was superseded by the Amorites or Babylonians (about 1900 BC), with their capital at Babylon. The cultural height of Babylonian history is represented by Hammurabi (r.c.1792–c.1750 BC), who compiled a celebrated code of laws. After Babylon was destroyed by the Hittites about 1550 BC, the Hurrians established the Mitanni kingdom in the north for about 200 years, and the Kassites ruled for about 400 years in the south.

From Assur, their stronghold in the north, the Assyrians overran Mesopotamia about 1350 BC and established their capital at Nineveh (Ninawa). Assyrian supremacy was interrupted during the 11th and 10th centuries BC by the Aramaeans, whose language, Aramaic, became a common language in the eastern Mediterranean area in later times. Assyrian power was finally crushed by the Chaldeans or Neo-Babylonians, who, in alliance with the Medes in Persia, destroyed Nineveh in 612 BC. Nebuchadnezzar II (r.c.605–c.560 BC) rebuilt the city-state of Babylon, but it fell to the Persians, under Cyrus of the Achaemenid dynasty, in 539 BC. Under his son Cambyses II, the Persian Empire extended from the Oxus (Amu Darya) River to the Mediterranean, with its center in Mesopotamia. Its might, in turn, was challenged by the Greeks. Led by the Macedonian conqueror Alexander the Great, they defeated the Persians by 327 BC and penetrated deep into Persian lands. The Seleucids, Alexander's successors in Syria, Mesopotamia, and Persia, built their capital, Seleucia, on the Tigris, just south of Baghdad. They had to yield power to the Parthians, who conquered Mesopotamia in 138 BC.

The Arabs conquered Iraq in AD 637. For a century, under the "Orthodox" and the Umayyad caliphs, Iraq remained a province of the Islamic Empire, but the 'Abbasids (750–1258) made it the focus of their power. In their new capital, Baghdad, their most illustrious member, Harun al-Rashid (ar-Rashid, r.786–809), became, through the *Arabian Nights,* a legend for all time. Under Harun and his son Al-Ma'mun, Baghdad was the center of brilliant intellectual and cultural life. Two centuries later, the Seljuk vizier Nizam al-Mulk established the famous Nizamiyah University, one of whose professors was the philosopher Al-Ghazali (Ghazel, d.1111). A Mongol invasion in the early 13th century ended Iraq's flourishing economy and culture. In 1258, Genghis Khan's grandson Hulagu sacked Baghdad and destroyed the canal system on which the productivity of the region had depended. Timur, also known as Timur Lenk ("Timur the Lame") or Tamerlane, conquered Baghdad and Iraq in 1393. Meanwhile, the Ottoman Turks had established themselves in Asia Minor and, by capturing Cairo (1517), their sultans claimed legitimate succession to the caliphate. In 1534, Süleyman the Magnificent conquered Baghdad and, except for a short period of Persian control in the 17th century, Iraq remained an Ottoman province until World War I.

Late in 1914, the Ottoman Empire sided with the Central Powers, and a British expeditionary force landed in Iraq and occupied Basra. The long campaign that followed ended in 1918, when the whole of Iraq fell under British military occupation. The collapse of the Ottoman Empire stimulated Iraqi hopes for freedom and independence, but in 1920, Iraq was declared a League of Nations mandate under UK administration. Riots and revolts led to the establishment of an Iraqi provisional government in October 1920. On 23 August 1921, Faisal I (Faysal), the son of Sharif Hussein (Husayn ibn-'Ali) of Mecca, became king of Iraq. In successive stages, the last of which was a treaty of preferential alliance with the UK (June 1930), Iraq gained independence in 1932 and was admitted to membership in the League of Nations.

Faisal died in 1933, and his son and successor, Ghazi, was killed in an accident in 1939. Until the accession to the throne of Faisal II, on attaining his majority in 1953, his uncle 'Abdul Ilah, Ghazi's cousin, acted as regent. On 14 July 1958, the army rose under the leadership of Gen. 'Abd al-Karim al-Qasim (Kassim). Faisal II, Crown Prince 'Abdul Ilah, and Prime Minister Nuri al-Sa'id (as-Sa'id) were killed. The monarchy was abolished, and a republic established. Iraq left the anti-communist Baghdad Pact which the monarchy had joined in 1955. An agrarian reform law broke up the great landholdings of feudal leaders, and a new economic development program emphasized industrialization. In spite of some opposition from original supporters and political opponents, tribal uprisings, and several attempts at assassination, Qasim managed to remain the head of Iraq for four and a half years. On 9 February 1963, however, a military junta, led by Col. 'Abd as-Salam Muhammad 'Arif, overthrew his regime and executed Qasim.

The new regime followed a policy based on neutralism and aimed to cooperate with Syria and Egypt and to improve relations with Turkey and Iran. These policies were continued after 'Arif was killed in an airplane crash in 1966 and was succeeded by his brother, 'Abd ar-Rahman 'Arif. This regime, however, was overthrown in July 1968, when Gen. (later Marshal) Ahmad Hasan al-Bakr, heading a section of the Ba'th Party, staged a coup and established a new government with himself as president. In the 1970s, the Ba'th regime focused increasingly on economic problems, nationalizing the petroleum industry in 1972–73 and allocating large sums for capital development. Bakr resigned in July 1979 and was followed as president by his chosen successor, Saddam Hussein (Husayn) al-Takriti.

Since 1961, Iraq's Kurdish minority has frequently opposed with violence attempts by Baghdad to impose authority over its regions. In an attempt to cope with this opposition, the Bakr government passed a constitutional amendment in July 1970 granting limited political, economic, and cultural autonomy to the Kurdish regions. But in March 1974, Kurdish insurgents, known as the Pesh Merga, again mounted a revolt, with Iranian military support. The Iraqi army countered with a major offensive. On 6 March 1975, Iraq and Iran concluded an agreement by which Iran renounced support for the Kurds and Iraq agreed to share sovereignty over the Shatt al-'Arab estuary.

Tensions between Iraq and Iran rose after the Iranian revolution of 1979 and the accession to power of Saddam Hussein. In September 1980, Iraq sought to take advantage of the turmoil in Iran by suddenly canceling the 1975 agreement and mounting a full-scale invasion. Iraqi soldiers seized key points in the Khuzistan region of southwestern Iran, captured the major southern city of Khorramshahr, and besieged Abadan, destroying its large oil refinery. The Iraqi army then took up defensive positions, a tactic that gave the demoralized Iranian forces time to regroup and launch a slow but successful counterattack that retook Khuzistan by May 1982. Iraq then sought peace and in June withdrew from Iranian areas it had occupied. Iran's response was to launch major offensives aimed at the oil port of Basra. Entrenched in well-prepared positions on their own territory, Iraqi soldiers repelled the attacks, inflicting heavy losses, and the war ground to a stalemate, with tens of thousands of casualties on each side.

Attempts by the UN and by other Arab states to mediate the conflict were unsuccessful; in the latter stages of the war, Iraq accepted but Iran regularly rejected proposals for a compromise peace. Although most Arab states supported Iraq, and the Gulf oil states helped finance Iraqi military equipment, the war had a destabilizing effect both on the national economy and on the ruling Ba'th Party. France also aided Iraq with credits to buy advanced weapons (notably, Super Étendard fighters and Exocet missiles), and it provided the technology for Iraq to construct the Osirak nuclear reactor near Baghdad. (In June 1981, this installation was destroyed in a bombing raid by Israel, which claimed that the facility would be used to produce nuclear weapons, a charge Iraq denied.) Other Western countries provided supplies, financing, and intelligence to Iraq but denied the same to Iran.

In February 1986, the Iranians made their biggest gain in the war, crossing the Shatt al-'Arab and capturing Fao (Al-Faw) on the southernmost tip of land in Iraq. In early 1987, they seized several islands in the Shatt al-'Arab opposite Basra. The war soon spread to Persian Gulf shipping, as both sides attacked oil tankers and ships transporting oil, goods, and arms to the belligerents or their supporters.

The war ended on 20 August 1988 after Iran accepted a UN cease-fire proposal on 18 July. Having suffered enormous casualties and physical damage plus a massive debt burden, Baghdad began the postwar process of reconstruction. Before and after the war, there were scores to settle, primarily against the Kurds, some of whom had helped Iran and were the victims of Iraqi poison gas attacks. Many border villages were demolished and their Kurdish populations relocated.

When Iraq's wartime allies seemed unwilling to ease financial terms or keep oil prices high and questioned Iraq's rearmament efforts, Saddam Hussein turned bitterly against them. Kuwait was the principal target. After threats and troop movements, Iraq reasserted its claim (which dated from the days of the monarchy) to that country and on 2 August 1990, invaded and occupied it. Saddam Hussein was unflinching in the face of various peace proposals, economic sanctions, and the threatening buildup of coalition forces led by the US.

A devastating air war began on 17 January 1991 followed by ground attack on 24 February. Iraq was defeated, but not occupied. Despite vast destruction and several hundred thousand casualties, Saddam's regime remained firmly in control. It moved to crush uprisings from the Shia in the south and Kurds in the north. To protect those minorities, the US and its allies imposed no-fly zones which gave the Kurds virtually an independent state, but afforded much less defense for the rebellious Arabs in the south whose protecting marshes were being drained by Baghdad. There have been several clashes between allied and Iraq forces in both areas. The UN continued in 1994 to maintain tight economic sanctions and a ban on oil sales and to require that Iraq submit its non-conventional weapons centers to inspection and monitoring. Iraq has reluctantly complied. In October of 1994, Iraq again began to amass troops along the Kuwait border.

¹³GOVERNMENT

The coup d'état of 14 July 1958 established an autocratic regime headed by the military. Until his execution in February 1963, 'Abd al-Karim al-Qasim ruled Iraq, with a Council of State and a cabinet. On 27 July 1958, a fortnight after taking over, Qasim's regime issued a provisional constitution, which has been repeatedly amended to accommodate changes in the status of the Kurdish regions. Since the 1968 coup, the Ba'th Party has ruled Iraq by means of the Revolutionary Command Council, "the supreme governing body of the state," which selects the president and a cabinet composed of military and civilian leaders. The president (Saddam Hussein since 1979) serves as chairman of the Revolutionary Command Council, which exercises both executive and legislative powers by decree. He is also prime minister, commander-in-chief of the armed forces, and secretary-general of the Ba'th Party. A National Assembly of 250 members that was elected by universal suffrage in 1980, 1984, and 1989 has little

real power. Most senior officials are relatives or close associates of Saddam Hussein; nevertheless, their job security is not great.

¹⁴POLITICAL PARTIES

Under the monarchy, Prime Minister Nuri as-Sa'id dominated Iraq with the support of the upper-middle and upper classes. Tribal, religious, and local loyalties took precedence over any sense of Iraqi nationalism. Faisal I considered the existence of parties desirable for the political development of Iraq. During the decade 1935–45, however, they were ineffective as political factors. In 1946, five new parties were founded, including one that was Socialist (Al-Hizb al-Watani al-Dimuqrati, or the National Democratic Party), one avowedly close to communism (Ash-Sha'b, or the People's Party), and one purely reformist (Al-Ittihad al-Watani, or the National Union Party).

The response to these parties alarmed the conservative politicians. The Palestine War (1948) provided the pretext for suppression of the Sha'b and Ittihad parties. Only the National Democratic Party functioned uninterruptedly; in 1950, with the lifting of martial law, the others resumed work. In 1949, Nuri as-Sa'id founded the Constitutional Union Party (Al-Ittihad ad-Dusturi), with a pro-Western, liberal reform program to attract both the old and the young generations. In opposition, Salih Jabr, a former partisan of Nuri's turned rival, founded the Nation's Socialist Party (Al-Ummah al-Ishtiraki), which advocated a democratic and nationalistic, pro-Western and pan-Arab policy. In 1954, however, Sa'id dissolved all parties, including his own Constitutional Union Party, on the ground that they had resorted to violence during the elections of that year.

After the coup of 1958, parties "voluntarily" discontinued their activities. In January 1960, Premier Qasim issued a new law allowing political parties to operate again. Meanwhile, the Ba'thists, who first gained strength in Syria in the 1950s as a pan-Arab movement with strong nationalist and socialist leanings, had attracted a following among elements of the Syrian military. In February 1963, Qasim was overthrown and executed by officers affiliated with a conservative wing of Iraq's Ba'th movement. In November, a second coup was attempted by Ba'thist extremists from the left, who acted with complicity of the ruling Syrian wing of the party. 'Arif and the moderates survived the coup, and in the aftermath. Iraq's Ba'th organization receded from prominence. With the 1968 coup, rightist elements of the Ba'th Party were installed in prominent positions by Gen. Bakr. Since then, the Ba'thists, organized as the Arab Ba'th Socialist Party, have been the ruling political group in Iraq. In the National Assembly elections of 1980, the Ba'thists won more than 75% of the seats at stake; in the 1984 elections, they won 73% of the seats. Other parties are tolerated to give the appearance of pluralism. Outside of Iraq, ethnic, religious and political opposition groups have come together to organize a common front against Saddam Hussein, but they have achieved very little. The Shia al Dawa Party was brutally suppressed by Saddam before the Iran-Iraq war; its remnants are now based in Tehran.

¹⁵LOCAL GOVERNMENT

Iraq is divided into 18 provinces, three of which are Kurdish autonomous regions, each headed by a governor. Provinces are subdivided into districts, each under a deputy governor; a district consists of counties, the smallest units, each under a director. Towns and cities are administered by municipal councils led by mayors. Baghdad's municipality, the "governorate of the capital," under its mayor, or "guardian of the capital," serves as a model municipality. A settlement reached with the Kurds in 1970 provided for Kurdish autonomy on the local level. In 1974, the provisional constitution was further amended to provide the Kurdistan region with an elected 80-member legislative council; elections were held in 1980 and 1986, but, in fact, the Iraqi army controlled Kurdistan until the imposition of a UN-approved protected zone in the north at the end of the Gulf War. In May 1992, Kurds held elections there for a new 100-member parliament for the quasi-independent region.

16JUDICIAL SYSTEM

The court system is made up of two distinct branches: a security component and a more conventional court system to handle other charges. There is no independence in the operation of the judiciary; the President may override any court decision.

The security courts have jurisdiction in all cases involving espionage, treason, political dissent, smuggling and currency exchange violations, and drug trafficking. The ordinary civil courts have jurisdiction over civil, commercial, and criminal cases except for those that fall under the jurisdiction of the religious courts. Courts of general jurisdiction are established at governorate headquarters and in the principal districts.

Magistrates' courts try criminal cases in the first instance, but they cannot try cases involving punishment of more than seven years in prison. Such cases are tried in courts of sessions that are also appellate instances for magistrates' courts. Each judicial district has courts of sessions presided over by a bench of 3 judges. There are no jury trials. Special courts to try national security cases were set up in 1965; verdicts of these courts may be appealed to the military supreme court. In other cases, the highest court of appeal in the Court of Cassation in Baghdad, with civil and criminal divisions. It is composed of al least 15 judges, including a president and two vice-presidents.

Although there are no Shari'a (Islamic) courts, family courts may administer Shari'a law according to Iraqi custom.

17ARMED FORCES

Reeling from its defeat in the Gulf War of 1990–91, the Iraqi armed forces are estimated at 382,500 men, half its pre-war strength. The army had a strength of 350,000 men (100,000 recalled reservists) and 2,300 tanks; the navy had 1,000 men; and the air force had 30,000 men with perhaps 300 combat aircraft. Army figures include 4 Republican Guard divisions. Paramilitary forces include an armed militia, al-Jaish al-Sha'bi, of 650,000 men and 25,00 frontier and security guards.

During 1981–90, Iraq purchased some $45 billion in arms from the USSR, France, and China. It was the world's principal arms importer for this period. Much of the money for these arms imports was provided by Sa'udi Arabia, Kuwait, and other Persian Gulf oil states. During the war with Iran, Iraq's defense budget averaged more than $13 billion a year. Since the Gulf War, no reliable estimates are possible, but arms imports have shrunk to nothing because of a UN embargo.

18INTERNATIONAL COOPERATION

Iraq is a charter member of the UN, having joined on 21 December 1945, and participates in ESCWA and all the nonregional specialized agencies. A founding member of the League of Arab States, Iraq also participates in G-77 and OPEC, and has signed the Law of the Sea. Iraq has given both military and economic support to Arab parties in the conflict with Israel, which during the early and mid-1980s supplied Iran with military equipment. The war with Iran has preoccupied Iraq since 1980, and Iraq's relations with other countries in the Arab world has been varied. Egypt's material and diplomatic support for Iraq in the war with Iran resulted in warm relations between the two countries. In 1984, Iraq led efforts within the OIC to restore Egypt's membership. Iraq's relations with Jordan, Sa'udi Arabia, and Kuwait and other Arab states of the Persian gulf have also been warm. However, relations with Syria and Libya remained strained because of ideological conflicts between the two factions of the Ba'th Party, one ruling in Baghdad, the other in Damascus, and Syria's support for Iran in the war. Iraq also maintained friendly relations with some Western countries, notably France, a major arms supplier to Iraq. In November 1984, diplomatic relations between Iraq and the US were renewed after a break of 17 years, but were broken off again when Iraq invaded Kuwait in August of 1990. The US and its allies launched an air war against Iraq after diplomatic efforts and economic sanctions failed to convince Iraq to leave Kuwait. As of late 1994, Saddam Hussein's power was as strong as ever, and reports of Iraqi troop movements toward Kuwait were widely reported in the news media. A treaty of friendship with the former USSR, signed in 1972, was renewed in 1987.

19ECONOMY

Oil is the most important sector of the economy and provided about one-third of the GDP in 1986, down from about two-thirds in 1979 and 1980. Petroleum production was badly hurt by the war with Iran, however, and the economy was in serious trouble in 1987. The government allocated a major proportion of resources to the war effort in 1980, and after 1982 it stopped many development projects not essential to the war effort.

Agriculture, both commercial and subsistence, remains the principal occupation, involving somewhat less than one-third of the total population and contributing 5.1% to the GDP (1989). Industrial development was handicapped by the war with Iran, lack of raw materials other than oil, insufficient private capital for investment, traditional preference for investing in land, lack of credit for the small entrepreneur and investor, and lack of skilled labor. The greatest long-term obstacle to the development of a stable economy and general prosperity has been the traditional imbalance between a relatively small number of prosperous landholders and businessmen and the overwhelming majority of impoverished fellahin, with minute or no holdings of land, and small wage earners (government clerks or unskilled workers).

In response to the Iraqi invasion of Kuwait on 2 August 1990, the UN imposed comprehensive economic, financial, and military sanctions, placing the Iraqi economy under siege. UN Security Council resolutions authorized the export of Iraqi crude oil worth up to $1.6 billion over a limited time to finance humanitarian imports for the Iraqi people. After the food embargo took effect, Iraq recognized the strategic importance of agriculture. The effect of war in Kuwait and continuing economic sanctions reduced real GDP by at least 75% in 1991, on the basis of an 85% decline in oil production, and the destruction of the industrial and service sectors of the economy.

In order to overcome the demoralizing effects of the UN sanctions, Iraq reactivated in May 1991 the 565-km-long Third River project. This canal, renamed Saddam river, is designed to reclaim, for agricultural use, land affected by soil salinity. Fresh water from the canal is intended to flush the salts from the land.

20INCOME

In 1992, Iraq's GNP was US$35 billion at current prices, or $1,940 per capita. In 1992 the inflation rate of consumer prices was 200%.

It is estimated that in 1989 agriculture, hunting, forestry, and fishing contributed 16% to GDP; mining and quarrying, 19%; manufacturing, 13%; electricity, gas, and water, 1%; construction, 7%; wholesale and retail trade, 11%; transport, storage, and communication, 7%; finance, insurance, real estate, and business services, 11%; community, social, and personal services, 1%; and other sources, 14%.

21LABOR

Just before the Persian Gulf War in 1990, the total labor force was estimated at 4.4 million. Of the active labor force, agriculture employed 30%; services, 48%; and industry, 22%. In July 1990, the expatriate labor force totaled some 1.6 million.

Child labor is strictly controlled and in many cases prohibited. Historically, working women have been accepted in Iraq, but the number of women in the work force dramatically increased because of the prolonged war with Iran as well as the Persian Gulf War, as women replaced men in the labor market.

In many cases rural labor and farmers employed in government projects get reasonable salaries and good housing, but small, independent farmers receive fewer benefits. Since 1958, the Iraqi government has passed a number of agrarian reform laws. As a general rule, however, the quality of life differs greatly between rural areas and the cities, especially that in Baghdad. This differential has resulted in massive rural to urban migration.

The trade union organization law of 1987 established a centralized trade union structure of committees linked to trade unions, which in turn are part of provincial trade union federations under the control of the Iraqi General Federation of Trade Unions, and ultimately are controlled by the ruling Ba'th Party. Although workers are legally allowed to strike upon informing the Labor Ministry, no strike has been reported in over 20 years.

22AGRICULTURE

The rich alluvial soil of the lowlands and an elaborate system of irrigation canals made Iraq a granary in ancient times and in the Middle Ages. After the irrigation works were destroyed in the Mongol invasion, agriculture decayed. Today, about 12% of the land is considered arable.

Under various agrarian reform laws—including a 1970 law that limited permissible landholdings to 4–202 hectares (10–500 acres), depending on location, fertility, and available irrigation facilities—about 400,000 previously landless peasants have received land. Agrarian reform has been accompanied by irrigation and drainage works, and by the establishment of cooperative societies for the provision of implements and machinery, irrigation facilities, and other services.

Agricultural production in Iraq declined progressively because of the war with Iran and the Persian Gulf War. In 1992, wheat production was estimated at 600,000 tons compared with 965,000 tons in 1982. The comparable figures for barley were 400,000 tons and 902,000 tons; for cotton, 5,000 tons and 8,000 tons. Dates, Iraq's most important agricultural export, increased from 374,000 tons in 1982 to an estimated 580,000 in 1992. Crops grown for domestic consumption include millet, lentils, beans, cucumbers, melons, figs, potatoes, corn, sugarcane, tobacco (a government monopoly), and mulberries.

23ANIMAL HUSBANDRY

Animal husbandry is widespread. Sheep raising is most important, with wool used domestically for weaving carpets and cloaks. Wool was also exported before the Persian Gulf War (9,000 tons worth $6 million in 1990). In 1992, Iraq had an estimated 9 million sheep; 1.5 million goats; 1.4 million head of cattle, and numerous donkeys, camels, mules, buffaloes, and poultry. In 1992, of the 530,00 tons of milk produced by all livestock, 52% came from cows, 5% from buffaloes, 30% from sheep, and 13% from goats.

24FISHING

Centuries of overfishing without restocking reduced the formerly plentiful supply of river fish, but the fishing industry has rebounded since the early 1970s. The 1991 fish catch (including salmon and, especially in the Tigris, carp) was 12,000 tons. Since the war, and the closure of Iraq's ports because of fighting, the Iraqi fishing fleet has been dispersed around the world and does not operate in the Persian Gulf. In 1991, the total fish catch in the Indian Ocean was only 3,000 tons.

25FORESTRY

Forests of oak and Aleppo pine in the north cover less than 4% of Iraq's entire area and have been depleted by excessive cutting for fuel or by fires and overgrazing. Since 1954, indiscriminate cutting has been prohibited, and charcoal production from wood has ceased. The forestry research center at Irbil has established tree nurseries and conducted reforestation programs. Output of roundwood was estimated at 155,000 cu m in 1991.

26MINING

Iraq's mineral resources other than oil are limited. Exploitation is rendered uneconomical by inadequate transport facilities and lack of coal for processing the ores. Geological surveys have indicated usable deposits of iron ore, copper, gypsum, bitumen, dolomite, and marble; however, these resources have remained largely unexploited. The minerals industry was severely affected by the UN trade embargo and the ensuing Persian Gulf War in 1990/91. Production of all mineral commodities fell since international trade was halted by the embargo. Severe infrastructural damage from the war currently inhibits the mineral sector's expansion.

27ENERGY AND POWER

Iraq has the second-largest petroleum reserves in the Middle East (after Sa'udi Arabia), with proved deposits estimated at 100 billion barrels in 1992. Oil revenues ($13 billion in 1981) helped to balance the budget, stabilize the currency, establish a surplus balance of payments, and finance the development program. Because of the war with Iran and the Gulf War, however, crude oil production fell drastically, from 3,476,900 barrels per day in 1979 to 897,400 barrels daily in 1981 and from 2,897,000 barrels per day in 1989 to 305,000 barrels daily in 1991; in 1992 it was an estimated 450,000 barrels per day. In January, 1992, the Al-Bakr oil export terminal, the only outlet to the sea, was reopened at half capacity; by August, the full capacity of 1.6 million barrels per day was restored, even though UN sanctions prohibited Iraq from exporting its oil.

The most important fields are at Kirkuk, with lesser fields at Naft Khaneh, 'Ayn Zalah, and Butmah in the Mosul area, and at Az-Zubayr and Ar-Rumaylah near Basra. Oil for export was formerly piped to the Mediterranean through Syria and Lebanon, or to the Persian Gulf, but Syria closed the pipeline when Iraq invaded Iran, which Syria supported, and Iran closed Iraq's Gulf shipping. A new pipeline through Turkey transported more than half of Iraq's oil exports in the early 1980s; this was expanded by additions in 1985 and 1987, supplemented by a pipeline completed in 1985 running to Sa'udi Arabia's Red Sea port of Yanbu' al-Bahr; the pipeline was closed during the Persian Gulf War. Smaller amounts of crude oil are trucked to Jordan and Turkey.

Oil concessions were granted in 1925, and the first production began two years later. The three major oil companies operating in Iraq in the early 1970s were the Iraq Co. for Oil Operations (ICOO), the Basrah Petroleum Co. (BPC), and the Iraq National Oil Co. (INOC). By 1975, as a result of nationalizations carried out since 1972, state-owned operations controlled 100% of national oil production. In 1984, Iraq produced and marketed 28 billion cu ft of natural gas.

The development of both hydroelectric and thermal capacity proceeded rapidly during the 1970s. In Baghdad, electricity is supplied by the Baghdad Light and Power Co. This thermoelectric fuel-oil plant was installed by British-Belgian firms, but was later nationalized and supplemented by a second plant. Other cities generate power in small municipal power stations. Iraq's budding nuclear energy program was set back by the destruction of the Osirak nuclear reactor by Israeli bombers in June 1981. Total electricity production in 1991 was 20,810 million kwh. The country's generating capacity was about 9,000 Mw in 1991. Iraq's power installations were repeated targets of Iranian air attacks in the 1980s, and were badly damaged during the conflict in the Persian Gulf in 1990.

In September 1991, the UN proposed a plan to allow Iraq to raise revenue for humanitarian purchases and war reparations by exporting up to $1.6 billion worth of oil over six months. Iran repeatedly rejected the plan claiming that it would violate sovereignty. As of 1992, lost revenues and damage to oil installations had cost Iraq an estimated $35 billion since the 1990 invasion.

28INDUSTRY

Main industries are oil refining, food processing, textiles, leather goods, cement and other building materials, tobacco, paper, and sulfur extraction. Iraq has eight oil refineries, all managed by the government's Oil Refineries Administration. The Iraq-Iran and Gulf wars seriously affected Iraqi refining. Iraq has total refinery capacity of 656,000 barrels per day, with the largest refinery, Salaheddin, rated at 250,000 barrels per day. The second largest refinery, at Basra, has a capacity of 142,000 barrels per day, but due to the impact of the Iraq-Iran war, produces only 70,000 barrels per day. Refining capacity was restored to 460,000 barrels per day in 1991, and 550,00 barrels per day in 1992. The bulk of Iraq's refinery capacity—350,000 barrels per day—is concentrated in the Ba'iji complex

In 1964, the government took over all establishments producing asbestos, cement, cigarettes, textiles, paper, tanned leather, and flour. Public-sector industrial establishments include a sulfur plant at Kirkuk, a fertilizer plant at Basra, an antibiotics factory at Samarra', an agricultural implements factory at Iskandariyah, and an electrical equipment factory near Baghdad. Construction of a $1 billion chemical complex at Basra and other industrial plants has been delayed or suspended because of the war with Iran. In the 1970s, Iraq put strong emphasis on the development of heavy industry and diversification of its current industry, a policy aimed at decreasing dependence on oil. During the 1980s, the industrial sector showed a steady increase, reflecting the importance given to military industries during the Iran–Iraq war. By early 1992 it was officially claimed that industrial output had been restored to 60% of pre-Gulf War capacity.

29SCIENCE AND TECHNOLOGY

Iraq has imported Western technology for its petrochemical industry. The Scientific Research Council was established in 1963 and includes nine scientific research centers. The Nuclear Research Center (founded 1967) has conducted nuclear physics experiments and produced radioisotopes with equipment supplied by France. In 1982, the French government agreed to help rebuild the institute's Osirak reactor, knocked out by an Israeli air attack the previous year. Eight universities offer degrees in basic and applied sciences. In addition, the Ministry of Higher Education has 18 incorporated technical institutes.

30DOMESTIC TRADE

Modern shops and department stores are spreading throughout the country, replacing traditional bazaars. Baghdad, Mosul, and Basra, as well as other large and medium-size cities, all have modern supermarkets and branches of the official department store, "al-Makhazin al-Iraqiyyah."

Baghdad leads in wholesale trade and in the number of retail shops. Normal banking hours in summer are 8 AM to noon, Saturday–Wednesday, and 8 to 11 AM on Thursday; winter openings and closings are an hour later.

31FOREIGN TRADE

Iraq's most valuable export is oil, which has accounted for up to 99% of total export value. Rising oil prices during the 1970s created increases in export value. However, the drop in world oil prices and Iraq's exporting problems due to the war with Iran caused Iraq's exports to drop in value.

Iraq is traditionally the world's largest exporter of dates, with its better varieties going to Western Europe, Australia, and North America. Date exports were drastically reduced due to the war with Iran. Much fighting was centered in southern Iraq, where the highest concentration of Iraq's date-palm groves is located.

All trade is in the hands of the state and is controlled through state agencies and government purchasing boards. All imports and the domestic marketing of goods are strictly controlled by the state. Iraq's main imports included industrial machinery, vehicles and spare parts, iron and steel, and consumer goods such as tea, sugar, textiles, and dairy products. After the closing of Iraq's ports in 1980, imports arrived overland through Jordan, Turkey, and Kuwait.

The UN imposed trade restrictions on non-oil exports in August 1990. Non-oil exports (often illegal) were estimated at $2 billion for the 12 months following the March 1991 ceasefire. During 1992 Iraq exported 50,000 barrels per day of crude oil and products to Jordan and 20,000 barrels per day of products to Turkey. The Iraqi Kurds also began to export small quantities of crude oil from oil wells under their control.

Iraq's regular trading partners include Brazil, Turkey, and Romania. The US, Japan, and Germany topped the list of two-way trade, while the UK was an important importer to Iraq.

32BALANCE OF PAYMENTS

Although Iraq has not released national accounts data since 1977, it is estimated that the balance-of-payments deficit was $42.1 billion in 1981–83. Heavy borrowing has been required to finance war costs.

33BANKING AND SECURITIES

In 1964, banking was fully nationalized. The banking system comprises the Central Bank of Iraq, the Rafidain Bank, the main commercial bank, and three others: the Agricultural Cooperative Bank, the Industrial Bank, and the Estate Bank. In 1991 the government decided to end its monopoly on banking. As a result, there are three private banks: The Baghdad Bank (1992), Dula Bank (1992), and the Iraqi Commercial Bank (1991).

Preference for investing savings in rural or urban real estate is common. Major private investments in industrial enterprises can be secured only by assurance of financial assistance from the government. There is as yet no developed capital market, and only the beginnings of a small market in stocks and shares traded through the banks.

34INSURANCE

The insurance industry was nationalized in 1964. The State Insurance Organization supervises and maintains three companies: the National Insurance Co., the Iraqi Life Insurance Co., and the Iraqi Reinsurance Co. Third-party motor vehicle liability insurance is compulsory. In 1990, per capita premium payments totaled US$24.4, or 0.7% of the GDP.

35PUBLIC FINANCE

There are several budgets: the ordinary budget, under which the regular activities of the government are financed; separate budgets for the Iraqi State Railways, the Port of Basra Authority, the Al-Faw Dredging Scheme, and the tobacco monopoly; municipal budgets requiring government approval; and allocations for semi-independent government agencies. In addition, there is a separate development budget, as well as an undeclared budget for the military believed to have absorbed over half of state funds during the war with Iran.

Since 1980, the decline in oil exports and huge war expenditures have forced Iraq to borrow and to raise funds from abroad. Iraq's invasion of Kuwait in 1990, with the consequent infrastructural damage, UN sanctions, and oil embargo, have undoubtedly severely diminished revenues.

36TAXATION

Direct taxes are levied on income and on property. The rental value of dwellings, commercial buildings, and nonagricultural land is taxed, with a certain tax-free minimum. In 1939, graduated income tax rates were established on income from all sources except agriculture. Most agricultural income is not taxed.

Indirect taxation predominates. The land tax must be paid by all who farm government lands with or without a lease. Owners of freehold (lazimah) land pay no tax or rent. Much farm produce consumed on the farm or in the village is not taxed at all, but when marketed, farm products are taxed.

37CUSTOMS AND DUTIES

Since about 1950, tariffs have been used primarily to protect Iraqi industry or to stimulate industries that might eventually reduce the need for foreign imports. This tariff system levies duties on luxury items but has reduced rates on industrial equipment and on certain raw materials and foodstuffs. Iraq has a single-column tariff, with duties collected at Basra and Baghdad. In October 1992, Iraq banned the import of 157 "luxury items," including cheese, onions, shampoo, matches, shoes, and carpets. In 1989, Iraq joined the newly formed Arab Cooperation Council with Egypt, Jordan, and Yemen. The ACC's goals included formation of a common market and economic integration in other areas.

38FOREIGN INVESTMENT

UN sanctions have effectively frozen all of Iraq's foreign transactions for the near future. In October 1992, the UN Security Council permitted these frozen assets, including Iraqi oil in storage in Turkey and Sa'udi Arabia, to be sold without the permission of the Iraqi government. About $1 billion of frozen assets were to pay for compensation to Kuwaiti victims of the invasion and to cover UN operations inside Iraq.

39ECONOMIC DEVELOPMENT

The government both controls and participates in petroleum, agriculture, commerce, banking, and industry. In the late 1960s, it made efforts to diversify Iraq's economic relations and to conserve foreign exchange. As an example, it was announced in 1970 that contracts for all planned projects would be awarded to companies willing to receive compensation in crude oil or petroleum products. The government has also undertaken to build an Iraqi tanker fleet to break the monopoly of foreign oil-transport companies.

Iraq's series of five-year development plans failed by a wide margin to fulfill their targets, and in 1976 economic planning was changed to a yearly investment program. Development funding for 1981 was estimated at $22.8 billion, but the drain of the cost of the war with Iran in the 1980s resulted in a severe cutback of development expenditures. All development projects except those essential to the war were eliminated.

Iraq has an estimated foreign debt of more than $87 billion. The impositon of sanctions against Iraq has destroyed all attemps to stabilize Iraq's payments. Iraq also faces reparation claims. Iran is separately pursuing its claim for massive separation payments arising from the 1980–88 war. Iraq is also obligated by UN resolutions to pay for various UN agency activities.

40SOCIAL DEVELOPMENT

A social security law passed in 1971 provides benefits or payments for disability, maternity, old age, unemployment, sickness, and funerals. This law applies to all establishments employing five or more people. Roughly one-third of the social security contribution is paid by the insured person; the remaining two-thirds are paid by the employer. Men may retire at age 60 and women at

55 after they have worked for 20 years. Old-age and disability pensions equal 2.5% of average wages adjusted for the amount of contribution.

Although Iraq's constitution guarantees individual rights, the government sharply limits political freedoms and tolerates little public expression of dissent. Suspected political offenders are subject to arbitrary arrest and imprisonment, and torture is common in such cases. The war with Iran brought a tightening of political controls.

The government supports equality for women, who make up about 20% of the work force. Laws have been passed protecting women from sexual harassment, permitting them to join the police and armed forces, and equalizing their rights in divorce, land ownership, taxation, suffrage, and election to political office.

41HEALTH

There are many well-trained Iraqi physicians; however, their effectiveness is limited by a lack of trained nursing and paramedical staff. In 1992, 93% of the population had access to health care services. Private hospitals are allowed to operate in Baghdad and other major cities. Considerable effort has been made to expand medical facilities to small towns and more remote areas of the country, but these efforts have been hampered by a lack of transportation and a desire of medical personnel to live and work in Baghdad and the major cities. Dentists and other specialists are almost unknown in rural districts.

In 1991, Iraq had 10,900 physicians, 13,206 nurses, 1,719 pharmacists, and 1,628 dentists. In 1992, there were 58 doctors per 100,000 people. In 1990, there were 1.6 hospital beds per 1,000 inhabitants. Iraq's 1993 birth rate was 38.8 per 1,000 people. Of married women (ages 15 to 49), 18% used contraception. Life expectancy in 1992 averaged 66 years. Also in 1992, immunization rates for children up to one year old were: tuberculosis (79%); diphtheria, pertussis, and tetanus (63%); polio (64%); and measles (68%). In 1990, there were 111 reported cases of tuberculosis per 100,000 people. The infant mortality rate in 1992 was 64 per 1,000 live births. In 1993, the general mortality rate was 38.8 per 1,000 people.

42HOUSING

In the last 20 years, living conditions for the vast majority of the population have improved greatly. Electricity and running water are normal features of all Iraqi villages in rural areas. Mud huts in remote places are rapidly being replaced by brick dwellings. Major cities like Mosul, Basra, and especially Baghdad have most of the amenities of modern living. Traditionally, Iraqis have lived in single family dwellings, but in the last 15 years, the government has built a number of high-rise apartments, especially in Baghdad. It has done so to control urban sprawl and to cut down on suburban service expenditures. According to the latest available information for 1980–88, total housing units numbered 2,478,000 with 6.5 people per dwelling.

43EDUCATION

Six years of compulsory primary education has been in effect since 1978. An estimated 59.7% of adults were literate in 1990, 69.8% of men and 49.3% of women. In 1990, 3,328,212 students attended 8,917 primary schools and 1,166,859 attended secondary schools. Primary schools provide a six-year course, at the end of which the student must pass an examination to be admitted to secondary school. The curriculum is based on Western patterns but also includes religious teaching. The language of instruction is Arabic. Secondary schools have a three-year intermediate course, followed by a two-year course in preparation for entrance to college. A national examination must be passed at its end. Secondary education for girls dates from 1929. Traditional Quranic schools are nearly extinct.

Education at all levels from primary to higher education is free, and no private schools are permitted to operate. There are seven universities in Iraq, four of them in Baghdad. The University of Baghdad is the most important higher education institution in the country. Other universities include Mosul, al-Mustansiriya, Basra, and as-Sulaymaniyah. In addition to these universities, there are 19 technical institutes throughout Iraq. In 1988, all higher level institutions had 209,818 pupils and 11,072 instructors. Education in Iraq is under the control of the Ministry of Education and the Ministry of Higher Education and Research.

44LIBRARIES AND MUSEUMS

The National Library in Baghdad, founded in 1961, houses 417,000 volumes. Two noteworthy academic libraries are the Central Library of the University of Baghdad (319,000 volumes) and the Centeral Library of the University of Mosul (890,000 volumes). One of the country's outstanding libraries is the Iraqi Museum Library (founded 1934), with modern research facilities and more than 123,000 volumes, many of them rare editions.

With the exception of the National History Research Center and Museum and the National Museum of Modern Art, museums are under the control of the Department of the Directorate-General of Antiquities in Baghdad. Two of the most outstanding collections are at the Iraqi Museum in Baghdad, which contains artiquities dating from the early Stone Age and the Mosul Museum. The Abbasid Palace Museum and the Museum of Arab Antiquities, both located in Baghdad, are housed in restored buildings from the 13th and 14th centuries, respectively.

45MEDIA

All communications media are owned and controlled by the government, and criticism of government policies is not permitted. Newspapers that failed to observe strict government censorship have been suspended. The two leading Arabic newspapers in 1991 were *Al-Thawra* (circulation 200,000) and *Al-Jumhuriyah* (35,000); the only English-language daily was the state-sponsored *Baghdad Observer* (30,000).

The government's Radio Baghdad transmits in Arabic from 39 transmitters, and also has English, Kurdish, and some other foreign-language broadcasts. In 1991 there were two government-operated stations. In the same year, there were about 4,020,000 radios, 1,380,000 television sets, and 886,133 telephones in use in Iraq.

46ORGANIZATIONS

Chambers of commerce are active in Baghdad, Basra, and Mosul. Cooperatives, first established in 1944, have played an increasingly important social role, especially under the post-1968 Ba'th government. In 1986 there were 843 agricultural cooperatives in Iraqi with over 388,153 members. In 1985 there were 67 consumers cooperatives in the country with 256,522 members. Youth organizations have been stressed by the current regime; there are many youth centers and sports clubs. The General Federation of Iraqi Youth and the General Federation of Iraqi Women are government-sponsored mass organizations. Red Crescent societies provide social services in many cities and towns.

47TOURISM, TRAVEL, AND RECREATION

Tourism declined sharply during Iraq's occupation of Kuwait and the Gulf War. In 1991, 267,743 visitors arrived in Iraq, 73% from the Middle East. Many visitors from other Arab states are pilgrims to Islamic shrines. The other principal tourist attraction is visiting the varied archeological sites. Popular forms of recreation include tennis, cricket, swimming, and squash.

Tourism receipts totaled US$59 million in 1989. In 1991, there were 31,514 hotel rooms with 73,956 beds and a 29% occupancy rate.

48FAMOUS IRAQIS

The most famous kings in ancient times were Sargon (Sharrukin) of Akkad (fl.c.2350 BC), Hammurabi of Babylon (r.1792?–1750? BC), and Nebuchadnezzar II (Nabu-kadurri-utsur, r.605?–560? BC) of Babylon.

Under the caliphs Harun al-Rashid (ar-Rashid ibn Muhammad al-Mahdi ibn al-Mansur al-'Abbasi, r.786–809) and al-Mamun (abu al-'Abbas 'Abdullah al-Mamun, r.813–33), Baghdad was the center of the Arab scholarship that translated and modified Greek philosophy. A leading figure in this movement was Hunain ibn Ishaq (d.873), called Johannitius by Western scholastics. His contemporary was the great Arab philosopher Yaqub al-Kindi, whose catholicity assimilated both Greek philosophy and Indian mathematics. The founder of one of the four orthodox schools of Islamic law, which claims the largest number of adherents in the Muslim world, Abu Hanifa (d.767) was also a native Iraqi. Another celebrated figure in theology, 'Abd al-Hasan al-Ash'ari (c.913), who combated the rationalist Mu'tazila school, also lived in Baghdad; his influence still prevails in Islam. Al-Ghazali (Ghazel, d.1111), though Persian by birth, taught at the Nizamiyah University in Baghdad; he is one of the best-known Islamic philosopher-theologians. Iraq also produced famous mystics like Hasan al-Basri (642–728) and 'Abd al-Qadir al-Jilani (1077–1166); the latter's followers are numerous among Asian Muslims, and his tomb in Baghdad draws many pilgrims. Modern Iraq has produced no artist or writer famous outside the Arabic-speaking world.

The best-known contemporary Iraqi political leader is Gen. Saddam Hussein (Husayn) al-Takriti (b. 1937), who has served as chairman of the Revolutionary Command Council and president of the country since 1979.

49DEPENDENCIES

Iraq has no territories or colonies.

50BIBLIOGRAPHY

Alnasrawi, Abbas. *The Economy of Iraq: Oil, Wars, Destruction of Development and Prospects, 1950–2010*. Westport, Conn.: Greenwood Press, 1994.

Bulloch, John. *Saddam's War: The Origins of the Kuwait Conflict and the International Response*. Boston: Faber and Faber, 1991.

Gunter, Michael M. *The Kurds of Iraq: Tragedy and Hope*. New York: St. Martin's Press, 1992.

Haykal, Muhammad Hasanayn. *Illusions of Triumph: An Arab View of the Gulf War*. London: HarperCollins, 1992.

Nakash, Yitzhak. *The Shiis of Iraq*. Princeton, N.J.: Princeton University Press, 1994.

Simons, G. L. *Iraq: From Sumer to Saddam*. New York: St. Martin's Press, 1994.

ISRAEL

State of Israel
[Arabic:] *Dawlat Israel* [Hebrew:] *Medinat Yisrael*

CAPITAL: Jerusalem (Yerushalayim, Al-Quds).

FLAG: The flag, which was adopted at the First Zionist Congress in Basel in 1897, consists of a blue six-pointed Shield of David (Magen David) centered between two blue horizontal stripes on a white field.

ANTHEM: *Hatikvah (The Hope).*

MONETARY UNIT: The new Israeli shekel (NIS), a paper currency of 100 new agorot, replaced the shekel (IS) at a rate of 1,000 to 1 in 1985; the shekel replaced the Israeli pound (IL) in 1980 at the rate of 10 pounds per shekel. There are coins of 5, 10, and 50 agora, 1 and 5 shekels and notes of 10, 50, 100, and 200 shekels. NIS1 = $0.3368 (or $1 = NIS2.9690).

WEIGHTS AND MEASURES: The metric system is the legal standard, but some local units are used, notably the dunam (equivalent to 1,000 sq m, or about 0.25 acre).

HOLIDAYS: Israel officially uses both the Gregorian and the complex Jewish lunisolar calendars, but the latter determines the occurrence of national holidays: Rosh Hashanah (New Year), September or October; Yom Kippur (Day of Atonement), September or October; Sukkot (Tabernacles), September or October; Simhat Torah (Rejoicing in the Law), September or October; Pesach (Passover), March or April; Independence Day, April or May; and Shavuot (Pentecost), May or June. All Jewish holidays, as well as the Jewish Sabbath (Friday/Saturday), begin just before sundown and end at nightfall 24 hours later. Muslim, Christian, and Druze holidays are observed by the respective minorities.

TIME: 2 PM = noon GMT.

1 LOCATION, SIZE, AND EXTENT

Situated in southwestern Asia along the eastern end of the Mediterranean Sea, Israel claims an area of 20,770 sq km (8,019 sq mi), extending about 320 km (200 mi) N–S and 110 km (70 mi) E–W; at its narrowest, just north of Tel Aviv–Yafo, it is 19 km (12 mi) across. This total includes the Golan Heights area (1,176 sq km/ 454 sq mi), captured from Syria during the Six-Day War in 1967 and annexed on 14 December 1981; the annexation (technically described as the extension of Israeli "law, jurisdiction, and administration" to the region) was condemned by Syria and by unanimous resolution of the UN Security Council. The Labor Government in 1944 indicated that some (possibly all) of the Golan could be returned to Syria in a peace agreement. Other territories captured in 1967 and classified as administered territories were the West Bank (Judea and Samaria), 5,878 sq km (2,270 sq mi), and the Gaza Strip, 362 sq km (140 sq mi). (The Gaza Strip and Jericho area were transferred in 1994 to Palestinian administration). East Jerusalem, captured in 1967, was annexed shortly thereafter. The Sinai (53,242 sq km/20,557 sq mi), also taken in 1967, was fully restored to Egypt in 1982. Israel is bordered on the N by Lebanon, on the E by Syria and Jordan, on the S by the Gulf of Aqaba (Gulf of Elat), on the SW by Egypt, and on the W by the Mediterranean Sea. Comparatively, the area occupied by Israel is slightly larger than the state of New Jersey. The total boundary length was 1,279 km (795 mi) following the 1949 armistice and 1,102 km (684 mi) in 1988, including the administered areas.

Israel's capital city, Jerusalem, is located near the center of the country (including the West Bank).

2 TOPOGRAPHY

The country is divided into three major longitudinal strips: the coastal plain, which follows the Mediterranean shoreline in a southward widening band; the hill region, embracing the hills of Galilee in the north, Samaria and Judea in the center, and the Negev in the south; and the Jordan Valley. Except for the Bay of Acre, the sandy coastline is unindented for its entire length. The hill region, averaging 610 m (2,000 ft) in elevation, reaches its highest point at Mt. Meron (1,208 m/3,963 ft). South of the Judean hills, the Negev desert, marked by cliffs and craters and covering about half the total area of Israel proper, extends down to the Gulf of Aqaba on the Red Sea. The Jordan River, forming the border between Israel (including the West Bank) and Jordan, links the only bodies of water in the country: the Sea of Galilee (Yam Kinneret) and the heavily saline Dead Sea (Yam ha-Melah), which, at 393 m (1,290 ft) below sea level, is the lowest point on the earth's surface.

3 CLIMATE

Although climatic conditions are varied across the country, the climate is generally temperate. The coldest month is January; the hottest, August. In winter, snow occasionally falls in the hills, where January temperatures normally fluctuate between 4° and 10°C (40–50°F), and August temperatures between 18° and 29°C (65–85°F). On the coastal plain, sea breezes temper the weather all year round, temperature variations ranging from 8° to 18°C (47–65°F) in January and 21° to 29°C (70–85°F) in August. In the south, at Elat, January temperatures range between 10° and 21°C (50–70°F) and may reach 49°C (120°F) in August. The rainy season lasts from November until April, with rainfall averaging 108 cm (43 in) annually in the Upper Galilee and only 2 cm (0.8 in) at Elat, although dewfall gives the south another several inches of water every year.

4 FLORA AND FAUNA

The Bible (Deuteronomy 8:8) describes the country as "a land of wheat and barley, of vines and fig trees and pomegranates, a land of olive trees and honey." The original forests, evergreen and maquis, have largely been destroyed, but some 200 million new trees have been planted during this century, in a major reforestation program. Vegetation cover is thin except in the coastal plain, where conditions are favorable to the cultivation of citrus fruit, and in the Jordan Valley, with its plantations of tropical fruit. Among surviving animals, jackals and hyenas remain fairly numerous, and there are wild boar in the Lake Hula region. With the growth of vegetation and water supplies, bird life and deer have increased.

⁵ENVIRONMENT

In 1994, water pollution and adequate water supply were major environmental issues in Israel. Industrial and agricultural chemicals threaten the nation's already depleted water supply. Israel has only 0.4 cubic miles of water with 79% used for farming activity and 5% used for industrial purposes. Ninety-seven percent of the people living in rural areas have pure water. Air pollution is another significant environmental problem. Pollution comes from industrial sources, oil facilities, and vehicles. Israel contributes 0.2% of the world's total gas emissions.

Reforestation efforts, especially since 1948, have helped to conserve the country's water resources and prevent soil erosion. Israel has reclaimed much of the Negev for agricultural purposes by means of large irrigation projects, thereby stopping the desertification process that had been depleting the land for nearly 2,000 years. Principal environmental responsibility is vested in the Environmental Protection Service of the Ministry of the Interior.

As of 1994, 8 mammal species and 15 bird species are endangered. Three species of plants are threatened with extinction. Other endangered species include the northern bald ibis, South Arabian leopard, Sa'udi Arabian dorcas gazelle, three species of sea turtles, and Israel painted frog. The Mediterranean monk seal, cheetah, Barbary sheep, and Persian fallow deer became extinct in the 1980s.

⁶POPULATION

The population was estimated at 5,195,000 at the end of 1992, compared with the June 1983 census population of 4,037,620. The average annual population increase during the 1983–92 period was 2.6%; a population of 6,023,200 was projected for the year 2000. In 1992, the crude birthrate of the Jewish population was 18.7 per 1,000, and the death rate was 7. The non-Jewish minority's birthrate in 1992 was 33.8 per 1,000 population and the death rate, 3.4. The population density at the end of 1992 was 237 per sq km (614 per sq mi). Nearly 90% of Israelis lived in urban localities in 1992 (those of 2,000 or more people). Tel Aviv (founded 1908; now Tel Aviv–Yafo), had a metropolitan population of 356,900 in 1992. Other large cities and their 1992 metropolitan populations are Jerusalem (the capital), 556,500; Haifa (Hefa), 249,800; Holon, 162,800; Bat Yam, 145,300; Petah Tiqwa, 150,800; Beersheba (Be'er Sheva'), 134,700; Rishon LeZiyyon, 150,400; and Netanya, 141,800. Besides the population of Israel (including East Jerusalem), 1,051,500 persons, as of 1992, lived on the West Bank (also called Judea and Samaria), and 716,800 in the Gaza Strip.

⁷MIGRATION

In 1948, 65% of Israel's Jewish population consisted of immigrants; many of these 463,000 immigrant Jews had fled from persecution in Russia and, especially during the Nazi period, Central and Eastern Europe. Israel's declaration of independence publicly opened the state "to the immigration of Jews from all countries of their dispersion," and the 1950 Law of Return granted every returning Jew the right to automatic citizenship. The Nationality Law specifies other ways—including birth, residence, and naturalization—that Israeli citizenship may be acquired. In the years

1948–92, Israel took in 2,242,500 Jewish immigrants; during 1948–51, the flow was at its heaviest, averaging 171,685 per year, about evenly divided between East European Jews, who were war refugees, and Oriental Jews from ancient centers of the Arab world. In the years 1952–56, most immigrants came from French North Africa; in 1957–58 there was a renewed inflow from Eastern Europe. After a lull in 1959–60, the flow of immigrants was renewed, reaching substantial proportions by 1963, when 64,364 Jews arrived. Immigration fell to an annual average of 20,561 persons for 1965–68, rose to an average of 43,258 per year for 1969–74, then declined to an average of 24,965 for 1975–79. The number declined further to an average of 15,383 for 1980–89. Then the fall of communism in the USSR allowed a new exodux of Jews. Some 199,516 immigrants arrived in 1990; 176,100 in 1991; and 77,057 in 1992. The proportion of Jewish immigrants from Europe and North America (as opposed to those from Asia and Africa) varied during the 1960s, but it rose from 40.4% in 1968 to 97.3% in 1990. (For this purpose the Asiatic republics of the USSR were counted as part of Europe). In 1984–85, some 10,000 Ethiopian Jews, victims of famine, were airlifted to Israel via Sudan. In 1992, the Jewish immigrant population was 39.4% of all Israeli Jews and 31.8% of all Israelis. A certain amount of emigration has always taken place, but the pace increased after 1975. In a typical year after 1980, about 10,000 Israelis were added to the number who had been away continuously for more than four years. From 1967 to 1992, Israel established 142 settlements in the occupied territories; about 130,000 Jews were living there in 1994.

Considerable Arab migration has also taken place, including an apparent wave of Arab immigration into Palestine between World War I and World War II. During the 1948 war there was a massive flight of an estimated 800,000 Palestinians. As of March 1993 there were 476,236 Palestinian refugees in the West Bank who had registered with UNRWA. The registered number in the Gaza Strip was 528,684 in mid-1991. There are also Palestinians in Jordan, Syria, and Lebanon.

⁸ETHNIC GROUPS

Of the estimated population of 5,195,900 at the end of 1992, 4,242,500 (81.7%) were Jews, and 953,400 (18.3%) were non-Jews. Of the latter, 76.1% were Muslims, 14.8% were Christians, and 9.1% were Druzes or members of other ethnic groups. Of the Jewish population, 61.6% had been born in Israel, 25% in Europe or the Americas, and 14.4% in Asia or Africa.

The traditional division of the Jews into Ashkenazim (Central and East Europeans) and Sephardim (Iberian Jews and their descendants) is still given formal recognition in the choice of two chief rabbis, one for each community. A more meaningful division, however, would be that between Occidentals and Orientals (now also called Sephardim). Oriental Jews, who are in the majority, generally believe themselves to be educationally, economically, and socially disadvantaged by comparison with the Occidentals.

The minority non-Jewish population is overwhelmingly Arabic-speaking, but Israel's minorities are divided into a number of religious groups and include several small non-Arab national groups, such as Armenians and Circassians. The government of Israel has declared its intention to strive for equality between the Arab and Jewish sectors of the population. Israel's Arab citizens do not share fully in rights granted to, and levies imposed on, Jewish citizens. The rights of citizenship do not extend to Arabs in the administered territories. The living standards of Arabs in Israel compare favorably with those of Arabs in non-oil-producing Arab countries, but they are considerably below those of the Jewish majority, especially the Ashkenazim. As a consequence of repeated wars between Israel and its Arab neighbors and the development of Palestinian Arab nationalism and terrorism, tensions between Jews and Arabs are a fact of Israeli daily life, especially in the West Bank and Gaza Strip.

⁹LANGUAGES

The official languages are Hebrew and Arabic, the former being dominant. Hebrew is the language of most of the Old Testament; modern Hebrew is the biblical language as modified by absorption of elements from all historical forms of Hebrew and by development over the years. Arabic is used by Arabs in parliamentary deliberations, in pleadings before the courts, and in dealings with governmental departments, and is the language of instruction in schools for Arab children. English is taught in all secondary schools and, along with Hebrew, is commonly used in foreign business correspondence and in advertising and labeling. Coins, postage stamps, and bank notes bear inscriptions in Hebrew, Arabic, and Latin characters.

¹⁰RELIGIONS

The land that is now Israel (which the Romans called Judea and then Palestine) is the cradle of two of the world's great religions, Judaism and Christianity. In the Hebrew Scriptures, Jewish history begins with Abraham's journey from Mesopotamia to Canaan, to which the descendants of Abraham would later return after their deliverance by Moses from bondage in Egypt. Jerusalem is the historical site of the First Temple, built by Solomon in the 10th century BC and destroyed by the Babylonians in 586 BC, and the Second Temple, built about 70 years later and sacked by the Romans in AD 70. Belief in the life, teachings, crucifixion, and resurrection of Jesus of Nazareth (who, according to the Christian Scriptures, actually preached in the Second Temple) is the basis of the Christian religion. Spread by the immediate followers of Jesus and others, Christianity developed within three centuries from a messianic Jewish sect to the established religion of the Roman Empire. Jerusalem is also holy to Islam: the Dome of the Rock marks the site where, in Muslim tradition, Mohammed rose into heaven.

Present-day Israel is the only country where Judaism is the majority religion, professed by more than 82% of the population; over one-fourth of all the world's Jews live there. Freedom of religion is guaranteed. The Ministry of Religious Affairs assists institutions of every affiliation and contributes to the preservation and repair of their holy shrines, which are protected by the government and made accessible to pilgrims. Supreme religious authority in the Jewish community is vested in the chief rabbinate, with Ashkenazim and Sephardim each having a chief rabbi.

Most Arabs are Sunni Muslims (14%). Christians are largely Greek Catholic or Greek Orthodox, but there are also Roman Catholics, Armenians, and Protestants. The Druzes, who split away from Islam in the 11th century, have the status of a separate religious community. The Baha'i world faith is centered in Haifa.

¹¹TRANSPORTATION

In 1991, there were 4,750 mi (2,952 km) of highways, mostly paved. With the building in 1957 of a highway extension from Beersheba to Elat, the Red Sea was linked to the Mediterranean. Trackage of the state-owned railway totaled 594 km (369 mi) in 1991. Railways, buses, and taxis formerly constituted the principal means of passenger transportation; however, private car ownership nearly tripled during the 1970s. In 1991 there were 1,012,639 motor vehicles, including 848,554 private cars and 164,085 trucks, taxis, and buses.

At the end of 1991, Israel had 31 merchant vessels, with a capacity of 545,000 GRT. Haifa can berth large passenger liners and has a 10,000-ton floating dock, but Ashdod (south of Tel Aviv) has outstripped Haifa in cargo handled since the early 1980s. Elat is also a seaport.

Israel Airlines (El Al), which was founded shortly after Israel

LOCATION: 29°29′ to 33°17′N; 34°16′ to 35°41′E.
TERRITORIAL SEA LIMIT: 6 mi.

became a nation in 1948 and is almost entirely owned by the government, operates international flights from Ben-Gurion International airport near Tel Aviv. In 1991, the airport had 3.4 million passenger arrivals and departures. Israel Inland Airlines (Arkia) provides domestic service.

12 HISTORY

Archaeologists have established that the world's earliest known city was Jericho, on the present-day West Bank, built about 7000 BC. The formative period of Israel began in approximately 1800 BC, when the Hebrews entered Canaan, and resumed in approximately 1200 BC, when the Israelite tribes returned to Canaan after a period of residence in Egypt. At various times, the people were led by patriarchs, judges, kings, prophets, and scribes, and the land was conquered by Assyrians, Babylonians (or Chaldeans), Persians, Greeks, and Romans. The ancient period neared its end in AD 70, when the Roman legions conquered Jerusalem after an unsuccessful revolt and destroyed the Temple, and it ended in AD 135, when the Roman Empire exiled most Jews after another unsuccessful revolt, led by Simon Bar-Kokhba, and renamed the region Syria Palaestina, which eventually became Palestine. During the next two millennia there were successive waves of foreign conquerors—Byzantines, Persians, Arabs, Crusaders, Mongols, Turks, and Britons. Most Jews remained in dispersion, where many nourished messianic hopes for an eventual return to Zion; however, Jews in varying numbers continued to live in Palestine through the years. It is estimated that by 1900, only about 78,000 Jews were living in Palestine (less than 1% of the world Jewish population), compared with some 650,000 non-Jews, mostly Arabs.

Modern Zionism, the movement for the reestablishment of a Jewish nation, dates from the late 19th century, with small-scale settlements by Russian and Romanian Jews on lands purchased by funds from Western European and US donors. The movement received impetus from the founding of the World Zionist Organization in Basel, Switzerland, in 1897, under the leadership of Theodor Herzl. Zionist hopes for a Jewish national homeland in Palestine were greatly bolstered when the British government pledged its support for this goal in 1917, in the Balfour Declaration, which was subsequently incorporated into the mandate over Palestine (originally including Transjordan) awarded to the UK by the League of Nations in 1922. Under the mandate, the Jewish community grew from 85,000 to 650,000, largely through immigration, on lands purchased from Arab owners. This growth was attended by rising hostility from the Arab community, which felt its majority status threatened by the Jewish influx. In 1939, shortly before the outbreak of World War II, the British mandatory authorities issued a White Paper that decreed severe restrictions on Jewish immigration and a virtual freezing of land purchase and settlement. Armed Jewish resistance to this policy, as well as growing international backing for the establishment of a Jewish state as a haven for the survivors of the Nazi Holocaust, finally persuaded the British government to relinquish the mandate.

On 29 November 1947, the UN General Assembly adopted a plan for the partition of Palestine into two economically united but politically sovereign states, one Jewish and the other Arab, with Jerusalem as an international city. The Arabs of Palestine, aided by brethren across the frontiers, at once rose up in arms to thwart partition. The Jews accepted the plan; on 14 May 1948, the last day of the mandate, they proclaimed the formation of the State of Israel. The next day, the Arab League states—Egypt, Iraq, Jordan, Lebanon, Sa'udi Arabia, and Syria—launched a concerted armed attack. There followed a mass flight of hundreds of tens of thousands of Palestinian Arabs abroad. The war left Israel in possession of a much larger territory than that awarded the Jews under the UN partition plan; the planned Arab state failed to materialize, as Jordan annexed the West Bank. Meanwhile, the Palestinian refugees were resettled in camps on both banks of the Jordan River, in the Gaza Strip (then under Egyptian administration), in southern Lebanon, and in Syria.

Armistice agreements concluded in 1949 failed to provide the contemplated transition to peace, and sporadic Arab incursions along the borders were answered by Israeli reprisals. Tensions were exacerbated by Arab economic boycotts and by Egypt's nationalization of the Suez Canal on 26 July 1956. On 29 October 1956, Israel (with British and French support) invaded Egypt and soon gained control of the Gaza Strip and the Sinai Peninsula. Fighting ended on 4 November; Israel, under US pressure, withdrew from the occupied areas in March 1957 and recognized borders consistent with its military position at the end of the 1948 war. A UN Emergency Force (UNEF) patrolled the armistice line.

Violations by both sides of the armistice lines persisted, and in May 1967, Egypt, fearing an Israeli attack on Syria, moved armaments and troops into the Sinai, ordering withdrawal of UNEF personnel from the armistice line, and closed the Strait of Tiran to Israeli shipping. On 5 June, Israel attacked Egypt and its allies, Syria and Jordan. By 11 June, Israel had scored a decisive victory in the conflict, since termed the Six-Day War, and had taken control of the Sinai Peninsula, the Gaza Strip, the Golan Heights, and the West Bank (including Jordanian-ruled East Jerusalem). The Security Council on 22 November unanimously adopted UK-sponsored Resolution 242, calling for establishment of a just and lasting peace in the Middle East, withdrawal of Israeli armed forces from territories occupied during the war, and acknowledgment of the "sovereignty, territorial integrity, and political independence of every State in the area and their right to live in peace within secure and recognized boundaries free from threats or acts of force." Israel indicated that return of the captured territories would have to be part of a general settlement guaranteeing peace; in 1967, the Israeli government began Jewish settlement in these areas; due in good part to the later encouragement of the Likud governments, by 1994 there were some 120,000 settlers in the occupied territories.

Serious shooting incidents between Egypt and Israel resumed in June 1969, following Egypt's declaration of a war of attrition against Israel. In response to a US peace initiative, a cease-fire took effect in August 1970, but tensions continued, and Palestinian Arab guerrillas mounted an international campaign of terrorism, highlighted in September 1972 by the kidnap and murder of Israeli athletes at the Olympic Games in Munich.

On 6 October 1973, during Yom Kippur, Egypt and Syria simultaneously attacked Israeli-held territory in the Sinai Peninsula and the Golan Heights. The Arabs won initial victories, but by 24 October, when a UN cease-fire took effect, the Israelis had crossed the Suez Canal and were 101 km (63 mi) from Cairo and about 27 km (17 mi) from Damascus. Under the impetus of the "shuttle diplomacy" exercised by US Secretary of State Henry Kissinger, formal first-stage disengagement agreements were signed with Egypt on 18 January 1974 and with Syria on 31 May 1974. On 4 September 1975, a second-stage disengagement pact was signed in Geneva, under which Israel relinquished some territory in the Sinai (including two oil fields) in return for Egyptian declarations of peaceful intent, free passage of nonmilitary cargoes to and from Israel through the Suez Canal, and the stationing of US civilians to monitor an early-warning system.

The 30-year cycle of Egyptian-Israeli hostilities was broken in November 1977, when Egyptian President Anwar al-Sadat (as-Sadat) paid a visit to Jerusalem on 19–21 November 1977, during which, in an address to parliament, he affirmed Israel's right to exist as a nation, thereby laying the basis for a negotiated peace. In September 1978, at a summit conference mediated by US President Jimmy Carter at Camp David, Md., Israeli Prime Minister

Menachem Begin and Sadat agreed on the general framework for a peace treaty which, after further negotiations, they signed in Washington, D.C., on 26 March 1979. The treaty provided for the withdrawal of Israeli forces from the Sinai over a three-year period and for further negotiations concerning autonomy and future status of Arab residents of the West Bank and the Gaza Strip, territories still under Israeli occupation. Israel withdrew from the Sinai oil fields within a year, and from the remainder of Sinai by 25 April 1982. However, the two countries failed to reach agreement on Palestinian autonomy in the West Bank and Gaza, and Israel continued to establish Jewish settlements in the West Bank despite Egyptian protests.

Israel's relations remained tense with other Arab countries, which ostracized Egypt for signing the peace accord. In March 1978, Israel (which had long been supporting Lebanese Christian militias against the Palestine Liberation Organization—PLO—and its Muslim backers) sent troops into southern Lebanon to destroy PLO bases in retaliation for a Palestinian terrorist attack; Israel withdrew under US pressure. In April 1981, Israeli and Syrian forces directly confronted each other in Lebanon; Israeli jet aircraft shot down two Syrian helicopters in Lebanese territory, and Syria responded by deploying Soviet-made antiaircraft missiles in the Bekaa (Biqa') Valley, which Syria had been occupying since 1976. On 7 June 1981, Israeli warplanes struck at and disabled an Iraqi nuclear reactor under construction near Baghdad; the Israeli government claimed that the reactor could be employed to produce nuclear bombs for use against Israel.

Hostilities between Israel and the PLO and Syria reached a climax in early June 1982, when Israel launched a full-scale invasion of southern Lebanon, citing continued PLO shelling of the north and terrorist acts elsewhere. An estimated 90,000 troops rapidly destroyed PLO bases within a 40-km (25-mi) zone north of the Israeli border, captured the coastal towns of Tyre (Sur) and Sidon (Sayda), and then moved on to bomb and encircle Beirut by 14 June, trapping the main force of PLO fighters in the Lebanese capital causing massive casualties and destruction. Meanwhile, Israeli warplanes destroyed Syria's Soviet-built missile batteries in the Bekaa Valley—the announced objective of the invasion. A negotiated cease-fire was arranged by US envoy Philip Habib on 25 June, and more than 14,000 Palestinian and Syrian fighters were allowed to evacuate Beirut in late August. A multinational peacekeeping force of British, French, Italian, and US military personnel was stationed in the Beirut area.

Within Israel, the Lebanese war was divisive, and there were protest rallies against the Begin government. The protests mounted when, after Israeli troops moved into West Beirut in the wake of the assassination of Lebanese President Bashir Gemayel, Christian militiamen were allowed to "mop up" remaining resistance in the Palestinian camps. The ensuing massacres, for which an Israeli government investigating commission determined that some of Israel's civilian and military leaders were indirectly responsible, led to the resignation of Ariel Sharon as defense minister. Subsequent Israeli attempts to extricate its occupying forces from Lebanon by negotiating an agreement for the withdrawal of all foreign forces were rejected by Syria. In September, Israel pulled back its forces from the Shuf Mountains, east of Beirut, to south of the Litani River. In 1985, withdrawal from southern Lebanon took place in stages over six months, punctuated by terrorist acts of Shi'i Muslim militants against departing Israeli troops, resulting in retaliatory arrests and detention of hundreds of Lebanese. Negotiations over a Trans World Airlines (TWA) jetliner hijacked en route from Athens to Rome by Shi'i militants in June 1985 led to gradual release by Israel of its Shi'i prisoners. In 1986, troubles continued despite the establishment of a security zone by Israel in southern Lebanon, as Shi'i militants and infiltrating Palestinian guerrillas continued to launch attacks. The war was a drain on the economy, already suffering from hyperinflation and huge foreign-exchange deficits. Prime Minister Begin resigned because of failing health in the autumn of 1983 and was replaced by Yitzhak Shamir, who, after inconclusive elections in 1984, was replaced on a rotational basis by Labor Party leader Shimon Peres. In 1986, a ground-breaking summit meeting took place when Prime Minister Peres traveled to Morocco for two days of secret talks with King Hassan II. In that year, Israel also improved relations with Egypt when Prime Minister Peres conferred with Egypt's President Hosni Mubarek in the first meeting of the two nations since 1981. Shamir replaced Peres as prime minister in October 1986. Elections were again held with equally inconclusive results in November 1988, leading to a coalition government of the Labor and Likub parties. Four years later, Labor edged Likud in elections and was able to form a government supported by left-wing and religious parties. Yitzhak Rabin became Prime Minister with Shimon Peres as Foreign Minister; both were committed to reaching peace agreements with Arab antagonists.

In December 1987, unarmed Palestinians in Gaza began what became a multi-year series of stone-throwing riots against Israeli troops in the occupied territories. In this uprising (or intifada in Arabic), well over 1,000 Palestinians were killed and—by Palestinians—several hundred Israelis and Palestinian collaborators. Israeli use of lethal force, curfews, deportations, destruction of houses, and ten thousand detentions failed to stop the demonstrations while producing criticism abroad and anxiety at home. Waves of Jewish immigrants from the collapsing Soviet Union further provoked Palestinians.

During the Gulf War of 1991, Israel was hit by Iraqi missile attacks, demonstrating for some the state's vulnerability and need to move toward peace with the Arabs. Prime Minister Shamir, who opposed the return of occupied territory, reluctantly accepted a US and Russian invitation to direct peace talks in Madrid in October 1991. These and subsequent negotiations produced few results until, under a Labor Government, Israeli and Palestinian representatives met secretly in Oslo to work out a peace agreement involving mutual recognition and transfer of authority in Gaza and Jericho to interim Palestinian rule with the final status of a Palestinian entity to be resolved in five years. The agreement was signed at the White House in Washington on 13 September 1993. Promises of international aid for the new Palestinian units poured in but the agreement was opposed by extremists on both sides and further set back by a massacre of 30 Moslems at prayer in the Hebron mosque on 25 February 1994 by a militant Israeli settler. Finally, delayed by several months, the withdrawal of Israeli forces and establishment of Palestinian self-rule took place on 18 May 1994. Meanwhile, rumors persisted of progress in secret peace talks with Syria, while Jordan and Lebanon appeared ready to sign final agreements as part of a comprehensive settlement.

13 GOVERNMENT

Israel is a democratic republic, with no written constitution. Legislative power is vested in the unicameral Knesset (parliament), whose 120 members are elected for four-year terms by universal secret vote of all citizens 18 years of age and over, under a system of proportional representation. New elections may be called ahead of schedule, and must be held when the government loses the confidence of a majority of parliament.

The head of state is the president, elected by the Knesset for a five-year term. The president appoints the prime minister, after consultation with political party leaders, and performs ceremonial duties. The cabinet, headed by the prime minister, is collectively responsible to the Knesset, whose confidence it must enjoy.

14 POLITICAL PARTIES

Israel's multiparty system reflects the diverse origins of the people and their long practice of party politics in Zionist organizations.

The first five Knessets were controlled by coalitions led by the Mapai (Israel Workers Party), under Israel's first prime minister (1949–63), David Ben-Gurion, and then under Levi Eshkol (1963–69). The Mapai formed the nucleus of the present Israel Labor Party, a socialist party, which in coalition with other groups controlled Israel's governments under prime ministers Golda Meir (1969–74) and Yitzhak Rabin (1974–77).

In September 1973, four right-wing nationalist parties combined to form the Likud, which thus became the major opposition bloc in the Knesset. Unlike the Israel Labor Party, the core of support of which lies with the Ashkenazim and older Israelis generally, the Likud has drawn much of its strength from Oriental Jewry, as well as from among the young and the less well-educated. Besides the State List and the Free Center, the Likud consists of the Herut (Freedom) Movement, founded in 1948 to support territorial integrity within Israel's biblical boundaries and a greater economic role for private enterprise, and the Liberal Party, formed in 1961 to support private enterprise, a liberal welfare state, and electoral reform. The Likud originally advocated retention of all territories captured in the 1967 war, as a safeguard to national security. It won 39 seats in the 1973 elections and then became the largest party in the Knesset by winning 43 seats in the May 1977 elections, to 32 seats for the Israel Labor Party–United Workers (Mapam) alignment. Likud leader Menachem Begin became prime minister of a coalition government formed by Likud with the National Religious Party and the ultraorthodox Agudat Israel.

In elections on 30 June 1981, Likud again won a plurality, by taking 37.1% of the popular vote and 48 seats in the Knesset, compared with the Labor coalition's 36.6% and 47 seats. Begin succeeded in forming a new government with the support of smaller parties. The elections of July 1984 again left both Labor (with 44 seats) and Likud (with 41) short of a Knesset majority; under a power-sharing agreement, each party held an equal number of cabinet positions in a unity government, and each party leader served as premier for 25 months. Labor's Shimon Peres became prime minister in 1984, handing over the office to Likud's Yitzhak Shamir in late 1986. Elections in 1988 produced a similar power-sharing arrangement. In 1989, rotation was ended as Likud and Labor joined in a coalition. After a vote of no-confidence, Likud formed a coalition of religious and right-wing parties which held power for two years until 1992. Elections in June gave Labor 44 seats (32 for Likud) and enabled it to form a coalition with Meretz (a grouping of three left-wing parties) and Shas (a religious party) and the support of two Arab parties.

15LOCAL GOVERNMENT

Israel is divided into six administrative districts: Jerusalem, Tel Aviv, Haifa, Northern (Tiberias), Central (Ramle), and Southern (Beersheba). The occupied Golan Heights is a subdistrict of the Northern District. Each district is governed by a commissioner appointed by the central government. Most local governments are elected. Until 1994, Israel governed all of the occupied territories through the Civil Administration which is responsible to the Ministry of Defense. Palestinian towns have Israeli-appointed mayors. Israeli settlers in the territories are subject to Israeli law. In 1994, Israel withdrew its forces from Gaza and Jericho in favor of an interim Palestinian self-governing authority.

16JUDICIAL SYSTEM

The law of Israel contains some features of Ottoman law, English common law, and other foreign law, but it is shaped largely by the provisions of the Knesset. Judges are appointed by the president on recommendation of independent committees. Magistrates' courts in all towns deal with most cases in the first instance, petty property claims, and lesser criminal charges. Three district courts, serving mainly as courts of appeal, have jurisdiction over all other actions except marriage and divorce cases, which are adjudicated, along with other personal and religious matters, in the religious courts of the Jewish (rabbinical), Muslim (Shari'ah), Druze, and Christian communities. Aside from its function as the court of last appeal, the 11-member Supreme Court also hears cases in the first instance brought by citizens against arbitrary government actions. There is no jury system. Capital punishment applies only for crimes of wartime treason or for collaboration with the Nazis, and has been employed only once in Israel's modern history, in the case of Adolf Eichmann, who was executed in 1962. In the administered territories, security cases are tried in military courts; verdicts may not be appealed, and the rules of habeas corpus do not apply.

17ARMED FORCES

The defense forces of Israel began with the voluntary defense forces (principally the Haganah) created by the Jewish community in Palestine during the British mandate. Jewish and Druze men between the ages of 18 and 26 are conscripted for 36 and 24 months, respectively. Drafted Jewish women are trained for non-combat duties. Christians and Muslims may serve on a voluntary basis, but Muslims are rarely allowed to bear arms. All men and unmarried women serve in the reserves until the ages of 54 and 24, respectively. Men receive annual combat training until age 45.

In 1993, the Israeli army had 134,000 active duty soldiers (114,700 conscripts) and could mobilize as many as 600,000 more soldiers, about half as combat-ready units. There were 3 armored divisions, 4 mechanized infantry brigades, and 1 artillery brigade in the standing force. Armaments included 3,900 main battle tanks and 8,000 armored vehicles. The navy had 7,000 regulars, 3,300 conscripts, and 10,000 reservists; vessels included 3 submarines, 19 missile-equipped fast patrol boats, and 40 patrol craft. The air force had 11,000 regulars, 21,800 conscripts, and 5,000 reserves. There were 662 functional combat aircraft, with 102 aircraft in reserve, and 93 armed helicopters. The reserve force (430,000) can be effectively mobilized in 48–72 hours. There are 6,000 paramilitary border police.

The Ministry of Defense's expenditure was $7.5 billion in 1992 or 12% of gross domestic product, but this sum excludes reserve pay and some other expenses. Israeli arms purchases ($460 million in 1991) are principally from the US. In recent years, Israel has itself become an important exporter of arms ($380 million in 1991) to Latin American, South Korea, Africa, and other countries. The US made an outright grant of $1.4 billion for arms supplies in 1984/85 to ease Israel's difficulties in paying for previous weapons purchases. From 1946 through 1991, Israel received $29 billion in US military assistance.

Israel may have as many as 300 nuclear weapons, deliverable by aircraft or Jericho II (1500 km) missiles.

18INTERNATIONAL COOPERATION

Israel was admitted as the fifty-ninth UN member on 11 May 1949 and subsequently joined all the nonregional specialized agencies. It is also a member of the IDB, a permanent observer with the OAS, and a signatory of GATT. During the 1970s and early 1980s, Arab governments sought through the "oil weapon" to isolate Israel diplomatically and economically, but Israel's 1979 peace treaty with Egypt helped ease some of the pressure. The US is Israel's major political, economic, and military ally. A number of African countries reestablished diplomatic relations with Israel in the 1980s; these ties had been broken in 1973, following the Arab-Israeli war.

19ECONOMY

Since independence, Israel's economy has been faced with serious problems. Chief among these, especially during the first 10 years of statehood, has been the inflow of more than 1 million immigrants, most of them moneyless and unskilled, who had to be integrated into the country's economic life. The government makes large outlays for social welfare purposes, but is obliged to divert a considerable portion of its income to defense. In addition, traditional Middle Eastern sources of supply (e.g., of oil and wheat) and nearby markets for goods and services have been closed off. Israel must export on a large scale to maintain its relatively high standard of living; hence, it remains dependent on a continuing flow of investment capital and of private and public assistance from abroad.

The economy is a mixture of private, state, and cooperative ownership and holdings of the labor movement. In the first 35 years of Israel's existence, the number of industrial enterprises more than doubled; more than 700 agricultural settlements were established; and there were notable advances in housing, transportation, and exploitation of natural resources. From 1975 to 1980, GNP grew at an annual rate of 3.1% (at constant prices). Between 1980 and 1985, real GNP growth was 10%. In 1986, real GDP grew by 2.2%. In 1990 the Israeli economy grew by 5.3% and in 1992 by 5.8%. In 1993, real GDP growth was expected to slow down to 4.6%.

Inflation, a chronic problem, worsened drastically in the early 1980s: the consumer price index (1976 = 100) rose from 134.6 in 1977 to 834.9 in 1980; the new index (1980 = 100) stood at 477.7 at the end of 1982, 5,560 in 1984, and 22,498 in 1985. Israel's 1982 military action in Lebanon, which cost an estimated $2 billion, contributed to the inflationary increase of 131% in 1982. By early 1983, Israel's 130% rate of consumer price inflation was exceeded only by Argentina's. However, in 1985 and 1986, through a new austerity program that included strict wage and price controls as well as an 18.8% devaluation of the shekel, Israel's economy seemed to stabilize, and the triple-digit inflation had receded to 20.8% in 1989, 17.6% in 1990, 18.0% in 1991, and 9.4% in 1992.

The administered territories have expanded Israel's economic base, but living standards in these areas are much lower than in Israel proper. The territories' GNP in 1986 (at current prices) was NIS2,259 million for the West Bank and NIS836 million for Gaza. Since the outbreak of the *intifida* at the end of 1987, data collection regarding economic activity in the occupied territories has been severely disrupted. Agriculture dominates the economies of these regions. Total agricultural output for the West Bank rose by 47% in value terms in 1989–90 over 1986–87 and for Gaza by 29%.

20INCOME

In 1992, Israel's GNP was $68 billion at current prices, or $13,230 per capita. For the period 1985–92 the average inflation rate was 20.3%, resulting in a real growth rate in per capita GNP of 2.3%.

In 1992 the GDP was $57.4 billion in current US dollars. It is estimated that agriculture, hunting, forestry, and fishing contributed 2% to GDP; mining and quarrying, 22%; electricity, gas, and water, 2%; construction, 8%; wholesale and retail trade, 10%; transport, storage, and communication, 8%; finance, insurance, real estate, and business services, 24%; community, social, and personal services, 4%; and other sources 20%.

21LABOR

In 1992 there were 1,650,000 employed civilians in Israel, of whom 36.7% were employed in public services; 28.2% in industry, construction, and utilities; 13.9% in commerce; 10.4% in finance and business services; 6.3% in transportation; 3.5% in agriculture; and 1% in other sectors. The total represented an increase of nearly 11% over the 1990 figure. The unemployment rate in 1991 was 11.2%.

The majority of Israeli workers, including those in agriculture, are union members belonging to the General Federation of Labor (Histadrut, founded by Jewish farm workers in 1920), which claims a membership of 70–80% of the population (including self-employed, professionals, housewives, and young people). Histadrut also has an industrial corporation (Koor), which owns and operates many large factories, and a contracting corporation (Solel Boneh). Additionally, it manages an agricultural marketing society (Tnuva), a cooperative wholesale corporation (Hamashbir Hamerkazi), and a workers' bank. The nonresident workers, including the 90,000 Palestinians from the West Bank and Gaza, working in Israel are not permitted to join Histadrut, and are excluded from its activities and benefits. In 1991 there were 77 strikes involving 40,000 persons and 97,900 days lost (down from 406,000 in 1986); this decrease reflected concern over unemployment.

Wages and working conditions in the private sector are regulated by collective agreements between Histadrut and the Israel Manufacturers' Association. In 1985, rising inflation and economic instability led to a new pact that called for wage and government spending cuts, price controls, and layoffs in the public-sector area. The law provides for a maximum 8-hour day and 47-hour week, establishes a compulsory weekly rest period of 36 hours, and lays down minimum rates for overtime. The private sector set a maximum workweek of 45 hours in 1988, and the public sector established a 5-day, 42½ hour workweek in 1989.

22AGRICULTURE

Between 1948 and 1991, the cultivated area was expanded from 165,000 to 436,000 hectares (from 408,000 to 1,077,000 acres). Principal crops and 1992 production totals (in tons) were vegetables, 1,270,000; oranges, 513,000; grapefruit, 345,000; wheat, 260,000; potatoes, 215,000; cotton, 31,000; barley, 10,000; and almonds, 3,300. Owing to the uniquely favorable soil and climatic conditions, Israel's citrus fruit has qualities of flavor and appearance commanding high prices on the world market.

The main forms of agricultural settlement are the kibbutz, moshav, moshav shitufi, and moshava (pl. moshavot). In the kibbutz all property is owned jointly by the settlement on land leased from the Jewish National Fund, and work assignments, services, and social activities are determined by elected officers. Although predominantly agricultural, many kibbutzim have taken on a variety of industries, including food processing and the production of building materials. Devoted entirely to agriculture, the moshavim (workers' smallholder cooperatives) market produce and own heavy equipment, but their land is divided into separate units and worked by the members individually. This form of settlement has had special appeal to new immigrants. The moshavim shitufiyim are 47 collective villages that are similar in economic organization to the kibbutzim but whose living arrangements are more like those of the moshav. The moshavot are rural colonies, based on private enterprise. They were the principal form of 19th-century settlement, and many have grown into urban communities.

New immigrants settling on the land are given wide-ranging assistance. The Jewish Agency, the executive arm of the World Zionist Organization, absorbs many of the initial costs; agricultural credits are extended on a preferential basis, and equipment, seeds, livestock, and work animals are supplied at low cost.

Israeli agriculture emphasizes maximum utilization of irrigation and the use of modern techniques to increase yields. A national irrigation system distributed water to 178,000 hectares (439,800 acres) in 1991, down from 219,000 hectares (541,100 acres) in 1986 but still far exceeding the 30,000 hectares (74,000 acres) served in 1948. Water is transported via pipeline from the Sea of Galilee to the northern Negev. More than 90% of Israel's subterranean water supply is being exploited.

23ANIMAL HUSBANDRY

There is little natural pasturage in most areas, and livestock is fed mainly on imported feeds and farm-grown forage. Livestock farmers are aided by subsidies. In 1992 there were 349,000 head of cattle, 471,000 sheep and goats, 23,000,000 chickens, 4,000,000 turkeys, 11,000 equines, 10,000 camels, and 70,000 pigs. About 108,600 tons of eggs, 998,000 tons of milk, 198,000 tons of poultry meat, 37,000 tons of beef, and 2,200 tons of honey were produced.

24FISHING

Jewish settlers introduced the breeding of fish (mostly carp) into Palestine. The total fish catch was 20,723 tons in 1991. In addition to carp, important freshwater fish include catfish, barbel, and trout. The marine catch consists mainly of gray and red mullet, rainbow trout, grouper, sardines, and bogue.

25FORESTRY

Natural forests and woodlands cover about 120,000 hectares (297,000 acres), mostly in the north. Since 1986, timberland has increased by over 9%; about 180 million trees were planted between 1902 and 1986. Forestry products in 1991 included 109,000 cu m of plywood and 200,000 tons of paper, newsprint, and cardboard.

26MINING

Although Israel is not richly endowed with mineral resources, the Dead Sea is one of the world's richest sources of potassium chloride (potash), magnesium bromide, and other salts; more than 1% of the world's refractory-grade magnesia comes from the Dead Sea. The Negev Desert contains deposits of phosphate, copper (low grade), glass sand, ceramic clays, gypsum, and granite. Most of the phosphate deposits, located in the northeastern Negev, are at best medium grade; they are extracted by open-pit mining. Israel is the seventh largest producer of phosphate rock, accounting for 2% of world production; the third largest potash producer, with 5% of world production; and the second largest producer of bromine and bromine compounds, accounting for more than 31% of total world production in 1991.

Israel's mineral production in 1991 (in thousands of tons) included phosphate rock, 3,370; potash, 1,320; clays, 86; and glass sand, 60. The production of mineral products for the domestic building sector, especially cement, clay, crushed stone, and sand, increased in 1991 due to the surge in new home construction. Mineral exports, however, have stagnated due to low demand.

27ENERGY AND POWER

Israel's production of crude petroleum fell sharply after the return to Egypt in 1980 of the Sinai oil fields that Israel had held since the 1967 war. In 1991, Israel produced only 82,000 barrels of crude petroleum, compared with 131,000 barrels in 1988; domestic output of natural gas in 1991 totaled 32.2 million cu m. Crude petroleum and oil products were Israel's third-leading import in 1991, accounting for 7.7% of total import value. Oil has been produced in the Negev since 1955, and prospecting there continues.

Nearly all electricity is supplied by the government-owned Israel Electric Corp., which uses imported oil and coal. Electricity is generated principally by thermal power stations. Generating capacity has nearly quadrupled since 1970, reaching 4,135 Mw at the end of 1991; total production that year amounted to some 21,320 million kwh. In November 1993, the Israeli government announced that Israel and Egypt would connect their electricity grids and would construct a natural gas pipeline to Israel to supply 2 million tons per year of Egyptian natural gas.

28INDUSTRY

More than half of the industrial establishments are in the Tel Aviv–Yafo area, but a great deal of heavy industry is concentrated around Haifa. Most plants are privately owned. State enterprises are mainly devoted to exploitation of natural resources in the Negev; some other enterprises are controlled by the Histadrut.

Major expansion has taken place in textiles, machinery and transport equipment, metallurgy, mineral processing, electrical products, precision instruments, and chemicals. There were 10,500 industrial enterprises in 1985, employing a total of 301,000 workers. However, industry remains handicapped by reliance on imported raw materials, relatively high wage costs, low productivity, and inflation. Incentive schemes and productivity councils, representing workers and management, have been set up in an attempt to increase work output.

Whereas in the past Israel's industry concentrated on consumer goods, by the 1980s it was stressing the manufacture of capital goods. The chief branches of industry contributing to 1990 output included food, beverages, and tobacco, NIS11,543 million; metal products, NIS6,074 million; electrical and electronic equipment, NIS9,421 million; chemical and oil products, NIS7,140 million; and transportation equipment, NIS3,536 million. Israel also produced about 2.5 million tons of phosphate rock and 2.1 million tons of potash in 1990.

Israel is research and development-oriented. Currently, some 150 foreign companies are involved in high-technology projects in Israel in such fields as aviation, communications, computer-aided design and manufacturing (CAD/CAM), medical electronics, fine chemicals, pharmaceuticals, solar energy, and sophisticated irrigation.

29SCIENCE AND TECHNOLOGY

Israel manufactures and exports an expanding array of high-technology goods, especially for military purposes. In 1992, Israel spent nearly NIS3,600 million on research and development in science, engineering, agriculture, and medicine, 2.2% of national GDP, seventh among industrial nations. Of that total, national and local governments funded 37%, universities funded 34%, and industry, 29%. A privatization program, begun by the government, has resulted in the creation of many science and technology parks and high technology towns, like Migdal He'Emck. Israel has an advanced nuclear research program, and it is widely believed that Israel has the capacity to make nuclear weapons.

Among scientific research institutes are the Weizmann Institute; the Technion–Israel Institute of Technology; seven institutes and five experimental stations administered by the Agricultural Research Organization; the Rogoff–Wellcome Medical Research Institute; institutes for petroleum research, geophysics, and oceanographic and limnological research directed by the Earth Sciences Research Administration; institutes of fiber, metals, plastics, wine, and rubber research directed by the Office of the Chief Scientist, Ministry of Industry and Trade; the Institutes of Applied Research at the Ben-Gurion University of the Negev; the Israel Institute for Biological Research; the Israel Institute for Psychobiology; the National Research Laboratory; the Soreg and Negev nuclear research centers attached to the Israel Atomic Energy Commission; and the Israel Ceramic and Silicate Institute.

Immigration into Israel may be its best science and technology policy. In 1990, 3.5% of all Israeli residents were physicians, engineers, and scientists. The same year, a full 33% of all immigrants coming into Israel held these same positions. Some consider this a "brain drain" in reverse, and that it will help Israeli high technology competitiveness in the future.

30DOMESTIC TRADE

Banks, commercial institutions, and the Histadrut have their headquarters in Tel Aviv–Yafo, the business capital. Supermarkets and department stores are on the increase; installment sales are widespread. Packaged goods are becoming more common, but many sales are still made from bulk. Cooperative societies market the agricultural produce of their affiliated settlements and farms. Tnuva, the Histadrut agricultural marketing society, sells most of Israel's farm products. Advertising media include newspapers, periodicals, posters, billboards, radio broadcasts, and motion picture theaters.

Saturday closing is the custom for all shops, offices, banks, public institutions, and transport services, except in the Arab areas. Shopping and office hours are Sunday to Thursday, 8 AM to 1 PM and 4 to 7 PM. On Fridays and days preceding holidays, shops shut down about 2 PM, offices at 1 PM. Banks are open 8:30 AM to 12:30 PM and 4 to 5:30 PM; they close at noon on Fridays and days before holidays and have no afternoon hours on Wednesdays.

31 FOREIGN TRADE
Israel's export value in 1986 was equivalent to 74% of import value, and the trade imbalance increased from nearly $700 million in 1970 to more than $2.5 billion in 1986. Export revenue rose from $779 million in 1970 to $7.1 billion in 1986, but the value of imports in the same period rose from nearly $1.5 billion to $9.6 billion. The trade imbalances increased to about $6.1 billion in 1992 with export revenues of $12.43 billion and imports work $18.56 billion. US exports of non-military goods to Israel amounted to $3.34 billion in 1992. Israel must import nearly all of its petroleum and most of its raw materials for industry.

Polished diamonds, chemicals, machinery, transport equipment, and various other manufactures make up about 94% of Israel's exports; agricultural products, particularly fruits and vegetables, are also significant. Principal exports in 1991 (in millions of dollars) were as follows:

EXPORT	VALUE
Processed precious and precious stones and metals	3,720.1
Machinery and transportation equipment	2,584.6
Chemicals	1,435.0
Plants & vegetable products	633.8
Prepared foodstuffs*	416.2
Other exports	3,103.5
TOTAL	11,893.2

*including beverages and tobacco.

Machinery and precious stones and metals were Israel's leading imports in 1991, accounting for 39% of total import value. The value of these and other main imports in 1991 (in millions of dollars) was as follows:

IMPORT	VALUE
Machinery, include. electric	3,630.8
Precious stones and metals	2,965.0
Chemicals	1,168.5
Petroleum and oil products	1,443.6
Plants and vegetable products	622.3
Prepared foodstuffs*	412.4
Transportation equipment	1,698.8
Other imports	4,964.9
TOTAL	16,906.3

*including beverages and tobacco.

In 1991, Israel's chief trading partners were the US, Germany, Belgium, and Luxembourg. In that year, the US provided 19% of Israel's imports and took 30% of its exports. Principal trade partners in 1991 (in millions of dollars) were as follows:

	EXPORTS	IMPORTS	BALANCE
US	3,59.2	3,261.1	333.1
Germany	800.1	2,012.7	1,212.6
Belgium-Luxembourg	693.2	1,436.5	−743.3
UK	795.8	1,401.0	−605.2
Other countries	6,009.9	8,795	−2,785.1
TOTALS	11,893.2	16,906.3	5,013.1

Israel reported the trade of administered areas in 1986 as $378.3 million in exports and $890 million in imports. Most imports (90% by value) came from Israel; 73% of exports went to Israel and 27% to Jordan.

32 BALANCE OF PAYMENTS
Israel's foreign trade has consistently shown an extremely adverse balance, owing mainly to the rapid rise in population and the expansion of the industrialized economy, requiring heavy imports of machinery and raw materials. The imbalance on current accounts has been offset to a large extent by the inflow of funds from abroad. Deficits are often offset by massive US aid and American Jewish philanthropy. In 1992, exports (excluding capital) rose in volume by 15%, after falling 1% in 1991, the year of the Gulf War. The volume of industrial exports (excluding diamonds) grew by 11% in 1992. Service exports also rose; tourist arrivals increased from 1.1 million in 1991 to 1.8 milion in 1992, which generated an additional $60 million in earnings from tourism.

In 1992, merchandise exports totaled $13,282 million and imports $18,316 million. The merchandise trade balance was $-5,035 million. The following table summarizes Israel's balance of payments for 1991 and 1992 (in millions of US dollars):

	1991	1992
CURRENT ACCOUNT		
Goods, services, and income	−7,056	−6,854
Unrequited transfers	6,717	6,941
TOTALS	−339	86
CAPITAL ACCOUNT		
Direct investment	−161	−340
Portfolio investment	540	−606
Other long-term capital	−271	−10
Other short-term capital	−691	−1,810
Exceptional Financing	—	—
Other liabilities	—	—
Reserves	39	1,334
TOTALS	−544	−1,433
Errors and omissions	883	1,347
Total change in reserves	59	1,441

33 BANKING AND SECURITIES
The Bank of Israel, with headquarters in Jerusalem, began operations as the central state bank in December 1954 and had assets totaling $16 billion at the end of 1986. The bank issues currency, accepts deposits from banking institutions in Israel, extends temporary advances to the government, acts as the government's sole banking and fiscal agent, and manages the public debt. Among the largest commercial banks are the Bank Leumi, the Israel Discount Bank, and the Histadrut-controlled Bank Hapoalim. There are also numerous credit cooperatives and other financial institutions. Among the subsidiaries of commercial banks are mortgage banks (some of which were also directly established by the government). The largest of these specialized institutions, the Tefahot Israel Mortgage Bank, provides many loans to home builders.

Industrial development banks specialize in financing new manufacturing enterprises. The Industrial Bank of Israel, formed in

1957 by major commercial banks, the government, the Manufacturers' Association, and foreign investors, has received aid from the IBRD and has played a major role in the industrial development of the Negev area. The government-owned Bank of Agriculture is the largest lending institution in that sector. The Post Office Bank is concerned mainly with clearing operations, savings, sale of savings certificates, and postal orders.

The Bank of Israel's power to fix the liquidity ratio that banks must maintain against deposits has been an important instrument in governing both volume and types of loans. Legal interest rate ceilings formerly were 10% on loans to industry and agriculture and 11% for commercial loans, but in the early 1980s, rampant inflation caused the large commercial banks to raise the interest rate to 136%. As a consequence of hyperinflation, overdraft checking has become a way of life for many Israelis, who by 1985 were paying personal interest rates of up to 200% annually. The money supply was NIS109,891 million that same year. In 1993, the lending rate was 16.4% and the deposit rate was 10.4%.

Growing activity on the Israeli securities market made it necessary to convert the rather loosely organized Tel Aviv Securities Clearing House into the formally constituted Tel Aviv Stock Exchange in 1953. A further expansion took place in 1955, when debentures linked either to the US dollar or to the cost-of-living index—with special tax privileges—made their first appearance on the market. The market is largely devoted to loans of public and semipublic bodies, with provident funds and banks acquiring most of the securities placed. There is only one quotation daily for each security.

34INSURANCE

The State Insurance Controller's Office may grant or withhold insurance licenses and determine the valuation of assets, the form of balance sheets, computations of reserves, and investment composition. During 1992, life insurance premiums amounted to NIS109.4 billion, all Israeli. General insurance premiums totaled $619.5 per capita in 1990, or 5.7% of the gross domestic product. Automobile liability insurance is compulsory. War-damage insurance is compulsory on buildings and also on some personal property.

35PUBLIC FINANCE

In 1992/93, expenditures exceeded revenues by $2.9 billion. The following table shows actual revenues and expenditures for 1989 and 1990 in millions of new Israeli shekels.

	1991	1992
REVENUE AND GRANTS		
Tax revenue	33,988	53,853
Non-tax revenue	6,387	9,709
Capital revenue	29	405
Grants	6,458	9,074
TOTAL	46,862	73,086
EXPENDITURES & LENDING MINUS REPAYMENTS		
General public service	955	1,458
Defense	11,377	16,919
Public order and safety	1,265	1,964
Education	5,279	8,474
Health	1,888	3,359
Social security and welfare	11,358	17,329
Housing and community amenities	4,127	6,622
Recreation, cultural, and religious affairs	472	860
Economic affairs and services	5,154	7,150
Other expenditures	9,286	12,511
Lending minus repayments	4,558	2,845
TOTAL	55,376	79,318
Deficit/Surplus	–8,514	–6,232

In 1991 Israel's total public debt stood at NIS190,643 million, of which NIS42,782 million was financed abroad. At the end of 1992, the total external debt was $25 billion, of which government debt amounted to US$17 billion.

36TAXATION

Israel's population is heavily taxed. There are personal income taxes on gross income from employment, trade, business, dividends, and other sources, with limited deductions. Rates range from 20–48%, with the highest rate for amounts over $25,000 per year. Special tax concessions are granted to residents in border settlements, new settlements, and the Negev. Taxes of salaried persons are deducted at the source; self-employed persons make advance payments in 10 installments, subject to assessment. Also levied are a value-added tax (VAT) of 18%, a purchase tax, and various land taxes.

Municipalities and local and regional councils levy several taxes. There is an annual business tax on every enterprise, based on net worth, annual sales volume, number of employees, and other factors. General rates, a real estate tax (commonly based on the number of rooms and the location of the building), and water rates are paid by the tenants or occupants rather than the owners.

37CUSTOMS AND DUTIES

Israel has a single-column import tariff based on the Brussels nomenclature classification. Ad valorem rates predominate, although specific and compound rates are also used. Most basic food commodities, raw materials, and machinery for agricultural or industrial purposes are exempt from customs duties. The highest rates are applied to nonessential foodstuffs, luxury items, and manufactured goods that are of a type produced in Israel.

A free-trade agreement between Israel and the EC took effect on 1 July 1975. Under this agreement, EC tariffs on Israel's industrial exports were immediately reduced by 60% and were subsequently eliminated. Preferential treatment has also been extended to Israel's agricultural exports. In return, Israel has granted concessions to the EC on many categories of industrial and agricultural imports, and agreed to gradually abolish its customs duties on imports from the EC by 1989.

A free-trade agreement in 1985 between the US and Israel will gradually eliminate duties on all products traded between the two countries by 1995; most goods received immediate duty-free status.

38FOREIGN INVESTMENT

Apart from reparations, capital imports mainly consist of long-term loans and grants designed for investment by the government or the Jewish Agency.

A 1951 law was designed to encourage foreign investment in those industries and services most urgently required to reduce Israel's dependence on imports and to increase its export potential. Applying mainly to investments in industry and agriculture, the law offers such inducements as relief from property taxes during the first five years, special allowances for depreciation, exemption from customs and purchase tax on essential materials, and reductions in income tax rates. In a further effort to attract foreign investment, the government approved the "Nissim Plan" in 1990. This plan gives the investor the option of state loan guarantees for up to two-thirds of a project or the bundle of benefits offered under the "Encouragement of Capital Investments Law." A 1985 US–Israeli Free Trade Area (FTA) agreement reduces tariffs and most non-tariffs barriers for US firms. Israel also has an FTA agreement with the EC under which tariffs on industrial products and certain agricultural products fell to zero on 1 January 1989.

39ECONOMIC DEVELOPMENT

Economic policy is dictated by goals of national security, full utilization of resources, integration of immigrants, and institution of a broad welfare program. The urgency of these goals imposes responsibilities on the government for planning, financing, and directly participating in productive activities. About 3% of Israel's 1987/88 budget expenditure was allocated to development projects.

The government has influenced the setting in which private capital functions, through differential taxation, import and export licensing, subsidies, and high protective tariffs. The 1962 revaluation of the Israeli pound was accompanied by a new economic policy aimed at reduction of protective tariffs, continued support of development, planning and implementation of long-range development, and maximization of efficiency. Subsequently, the government has periodically decreed further monetary devaluations, new taxes, and other austerity measures designed to curb consumption and stimulate exports.

From 1946 through 1992, US economic assistance to Israel totaled $20.5 billion, of which 90.2% was in grants and 9.8% in loans. In 1992, US assistance amounted to $3 billion, $1.2 billion in economic assistance and $1.8 billion in military aid. At the end of 1990, total external debt was $24.4 billion, a $400 million increase over 1989. One-third of the proposed 1992 budget was dedicated to debt service.

The tourism sector was expected to bloom in 1994 with approximately 2 million arrivals.

40SOCIAL DEVELOPMENT

Aside from supervising a wide network of public and private social welfare agencies, the Ministry of Labor and Social Welfare maintains special enterprises employing blind and handicapped people, operates institutions for mentally and physically handicapped children, and administers a nationwide preventive service for problem children and youth.

Special legislation has established the legal right to assistance of persons incapacitated for work, of survivors of those who died in state service, and under certain conditions, of persons whose claims antedated their immigration to Israel. Pensions have thus been paid to persons disabled while fighting with the Allied forces in World War II and to those invalided as a result of Nazi persecution. A national insurance law, which came into force in April 1954, provides insurance for the disabled and for survivors, maternity benefits, and monthly allowances for large families. Workers' compensation provisions cover all employees, members of rural cooperatives, and since 1957, all of the self-employed. The National Insurance Institute is directly under the minister of labor and is governed by a 42-member council representing government, labor, and employers.

The Jewish Agency is primarily responsible for the initial phases of reception and absorption of immigrants. Hadassah provides vocational guidance and training to youth, and the Women's International Zionist Organization is active in family and child welfare. Mo'etzet Hapo'alot (Women's Workers Council), a Histadrut affiliate, is active in this area, along with Youth Aliyah, which operates a system of children's villages.

Family patterns differ among Israel's principal ethnic groups. As of 1986, the marriage rate among Jews was 6.7 per 1,000 population, the divorce rate 1.3, and the rate of natural increase 13.7. Among Muslims, the marriage rate was 9.1, the divorce rate 0.8, and the natural increase 30.4. Druzes and others had marriage and divorce rates of 8.2 and 1.1, respectively, and a natural increase (in 1985) of 28.2. Among Christians, the rates were 6.0, 0.2, and (in 1985) 13.1, respectively. Abortion is permissible for a variety of legal and medical reasons. Women's rights are protected by the Equal Rights for Women Law (1951) and the Employment of Women Law (1954), which requires equal pay for equal work. In 1993, common law spouses were permitted to take their partners' family names and a new law barred discrimination in unemployment compensation for elderly female citizens.

The subject of human rights in Israel and the administered territories has aroused much controversy, with international organizations citing police harassment of Arabs, especially on the West Bank and the Gaza Strip, and Israeli government officials pointing to the Arab terrorist threat. Within Israel, freedom of political expression is fully protected, and all shades of opinion are expressed; such guarantees do not extend to the administered territories, however, and the press, including foreign correspondents, is also monitored and censored for security reasons. Administrative detention is legal, but its use was legislatively restricted in Israel proper in 1979 and in the administered territories in 1980.

41HEALTH

The Ministry of Health supervises all health matters and functions directly in the field of medical care. National expenditure on health services totaled $2,301 million in 1990. The Arab Department of the Ministry of Health recruits public health personnel from among the Arab population, and its mobile clinics extend medical aid to Bedouin tribes in the Negev. In 1992, the infant mortality rate was 9 per 1,000 live births. Life expectancy was 76 years for both men and women. That same year, there were 2.9 doctors per 1,000 people, with a nurse to doctor ratio of 2.3. In 1988, there were 161 hospitals, 30 of which were government-operated. The Ministry of Health also operates infant welfare clinics, nursing schools, and laboratories. The largest medical organization in the country, the Workers' Sick Fund (Kupat Holim), the health insurance association of Histadrut, administers 14 hospitals, in addition to numerous clinics, convalescent homes, and mother-and-child welfare stations. The Sick Fund supplied 42% of national health care services (by value) in 1989, and government institutions distributed 34% for clinics and preventive medicine, 13% for dental, 5% for private physicians, 5% for consumer purchases of medications and medical equipment, and 1% for government administration. In 1990, there were 6.3 hospital beds per 1,000 people.

In 1993, Israel's birth rate was 21.1 per 1,000 people. In 1992, there were 110,000 births; in the same year, immunization rates for children up to one year old were: diphtheria, pertussis, and tetanus (85%); polio (89%); and measles (88%). The overall death rate in 1993 was 6.9 per 1,000 people, and major causes of death in 1990 were attributed to: communicable diseases and maternal/perinatal causes (64 per 100,000 people); noncommunicable diseases (444 per 100,000); and injuries (53 per 100,000). There were also 12 reported cases of tuberculosis per 100,000 inhabitants.

42HOUSING

Israel suffered from a severe housing shortage at its creation. Despite an extensive national building program and the initial allocation of some abandoned Arab dwellings to newcomers, in early 1958, nearly 100,000 immigrants were still housed in transit camps. By the mid-1960s, however, the extreme housing shortage had been overcome, and newcomers were immediately moved into permanent residences. From 1960 to 1985, a total of 943,350 housing units were constructed. In 1986, 94% of all housing units had piped water, 58.2% had flush toilets, and 99% had electric lighting. Between 1989 and 1991, a surge of immigration from the former Soviet Union and Ethiopia resulted in a dramatic increase in housing demand, and housing starts increased 28% in 1991 compared to 1990. By 1993, the immigration rate had dropped to 70,000 per year, generating a demand for 20,000 new apartments per year, which, added to the regular demand of 20,000, places the total demand at 40,000 annually. As of 1992, the total number of dwellings in Israel was 1,488,000.

43EDUCATION

Education is compulsory for 11 years and free for all children between 5 and 16 years of age. Primary education is for eight years followed by four years of secondary education. A state education law of 1953 put an end to the separate elementary school systems affiliated to labor and religious groupings and established a unified state-administered system, within which provision was made for state religious schools. Four types of schools exist: public religious (Jewish) and public secular schools (the largest group); schools of the orthodox Agudat Israel (which operated outside the public school system but were assisted with government funds); public schools for Arabs; and private schools, mainly operated by Catholic and Protestant organizations. The language of instruction in Jewish schools is Hebrew; in Arab schools it is Arabic. Arabic is taught as an optional language in Jewish schools, while Hebrew is taught in Arab schools from the fourth grade. In 1985, the estimated literacy rate among Israelis aged 14 and over was 97% for men and 93% for women.

In 1990, there were 1,514 primary schools with 724,502 students and 40,571 teachers. Secondary level schools had 309,098 students and 46,473 teachers. Vocational schools had 115,076 students.

Israel had seven institutions of higher learning in 1986/87. The two most outstanding are the Hebrew University (founded in 1918) in Jerusalem and the Israel Institute of Technology (Technion, founded in 1912) in Haifa, both of which receive government subsidies of about 50% of their total budgets; the remaining funds are largely collected abroad. The Tel Aviv University was formed in 1956. Other institutions include the Bar-Ilan University in Ramat-Gan, opened in 1955 under religious auspices; the Weizmann Institute of Science at Rehovot, notable for its research into specific technical, industrial, and scientific problems; Haifa University; and Ben-Gurion University of the Negev in Beersheba. In 1990, all higher level institutions of Israel had 119,124 students. Of these, 71,190 were in university and equivalent institutions.

44LIBRARIES AND MUSEUMS

Israel's largest library, founded in 1924, is the privately endowed Jewish National and University Library in Jerusalem, with 4 million volumes. Important collections are housed in the Central Zionist Archives and the Central Archives for the History of the Jewish People, both also in Jerusalem. There are more than 950 other libraries, and the Ministry of Education and Culture has provided basic libraries to 664 rural settlements.

Israel's 83 museums were visited by 8.08 million persons during 1984/85. The most important museum is the Israel Museum, opened in 1965 in Jerusalem. Included in the museum are the Bezalel Art Museum, with its large collection of Jewish folk art; a Jewish antiquities exhibit; the Billy Rose Art Garden of modern sculpture; the Samuel Bronfman Biblical and Archaeological Museum; and the Shrine of the Book, containing the Dead Sea Scrolls and other valuable manuscripts. The Rockefeller Archaeological Museum (formerly the Palestine Museum), built in 1938, contains a rich collection of archaeological material illustrating the prehistory and early history of Palestine and Transjordan. The Tel Aviv Museum of Art, founded in 1926, has more than 30,000 paintings, drawings, and sculpture. Among Israel's newest cultural institutions is the Museum of the Diaspora, in Tel Aviv–Yafo.

45MEDIA

The state owns and operates the major communications services. The state radio stations include the government's Israel Broad-casting Authority (Shidurei Israel), the army's Defense Forces Waves (Galei Zahal), and the Jewish Agency's Zion's Voice to the Diaspora (Kol Zion la-Gola), aimed mostly at Jewish communities in Europe and the US. The purchase of color television sets has become widespread since taxes on imported receivers were cut and the government stopped filtering out the color from imported television programs. In 1991, there were 2,285,000 telephones, 2,290,000 radios, and 1,310,000 television sets in use.

In 1991, 30 daily newspapers and numerous periodicals were published in Hebrew, English, and other languages. Most newspapers have 4–16 pages, but there are weekly supplements on subjects such as politics, economics, and the arts. Although there is no political censorship within Israel, restrictions are placed on coverage of national security matters. The largest national daily Hebrew newspapers (with their average 1991 circulations) are *Yediot Achronot* (280,000), *Ma'ariv* (220,000), *Hadashot* (100,000), and *Ha'aretz* (70,000), all published in Tel Aviv. The English-language *Jerusalem Post* (25,000) is published in Jerusalem.

46ORGANIZATIONS

The World Zionist Organization (WZO) was founded by Theodor Herzl in 1897 for the purpose of creating "for the Jewish people a home in Palestine, secured by public law." The organization is composed of various international groupings represented in its supreme organ, the World Zionist Congress. The Jewish Agency, originally founded under the League of Nations mandate to promote Jewish interests in Palestine, comprises the executive arm of the WZO; since 1948, it has been responsible for the organization, training, and transportation to Israel of all Jews who wish to settle there. The United Israel Appeal (Keren Hayesod) is the financial instrument of the Jewish Agency; it recruits donations from world Jewry. The Jewish National Fund (Keren Kayemet le'Israel) is devoted to land acquisition, soil reclamation, and afforestation. Hadassah, the Women's Zionist Organization of America, is also active in Israel; it sponsors the Hadassah Medical Organization, which provides hospital and medical training facilities.

The main labor organization is the General Federation of Labor (Histadrut), a large economic complex whose interests include some of the largest factories in the country, an agricultural marketing society (Tnuva), a cooperative wholesale association (Hamashbir Hamerkazi), and a workers' bank. An important youth organization is Youth Aliyah, founded in 1934, which has helped to rehabilitate and educate children from all countries of the world. First aid services in Israel are organized by the Red Shield of David (Magen David Adom), which cooperates with the International Red Cross.

There are numerous cultural, religious, business, and other societies and organizations.

47TOURISM, TRAVEL, AND RECREATION

A valid passport is required for tourists, with visas issued at time of entry. In 1991, 943,259 tourists visited Israel, 24% from the US, 12% from France, and 8% from Germany. Tourism receipts totaled $1.3 billion. There were 28,515 rooms in hotels and other establishments with 60,002 beds and a 49% occupancy rate. The Tourist Industry Development Corp. fosters tourism by granting loans for hotel expansion and improvement.

Principal tourist attractions are the many holy and historic places which include sites sacred to three religions: Judaism, Islam, and Christianity. In particular, the Old City of Jerusalem contains the Western ("Wailing") Wall, the Dome of the Rock, and the Church of the Holy Sepulchre; nearby are the Mount of Olives and Garden of Gethsemane. Another holy place is Bethlehem, the birthplace of both King David and Jesus. Also of great interest are the ruins of Jericho, the world's oldest city; the caves of Qumran, near the Dead Sea; and the rock fortress of Masada, on the edge of the Dead Sea Valley and the Judean Desert. Tourists are also drawn to Israel's rich variety of natural scenery, ranging from hills and greenery in the north to rugged deserts in the south, and including the Dead Sea, the lowest spot on Earth. The most popular team sports are football (soccer) and basketball; popular recreations include swimming, sailing, and fishing.

48FAMOUS ISRAELITES AND ISRAELIS

The State of Israel traces its ancestry to the settlement of the Hebrews in Canaan under Abraham (b. Babylonia, fl.18th cent. BC), the return of the Israelite tribes to Canaan under Moses (b. Egypt, fl.13th cent. BC) and Joshua (b. Egypt, fl.13th cent. BC), and the ancient kingdom of Israel, which was united by David (r.1000?–960? BC) and became a major Near Eastern power under Solomon (r.960?–922 BC). A prophetic tradition that includes such commanding figures as Isaiah (fl.8th cent. BC), Jeremiah (650?–585? BC), and Ezekiel (fl.6th cent. BC) spans the period of conquest by Assyria and Babylonia; the scribe Ezra (b. Babylonia, fl.5th cent. BC) and the governor Nehemiah (b. Babylonia, fl.5th cent. BC) spurred the reconstruction of the Judean state under Persian hegemony. Judas (Judah) Maccabaeus ("the Hammerer"; fl.165–160 BC) was the most prominent member of a family who instituted a period of political and religious independence from Greek rule. During the period of Roman rule, important roles in Jewish life and learning were played by the sages Hillel (b. Babylonia, fl.30 BC–AD 9), Johannan ben Zakkai (fl.1st cent.), Akiba ben Joseph (50?–135?), and Judah ha-Nasi (135?–220), the compiler of the Mishnah, a Jewish law code; by the military commander and historian Flavius Josephus (Joseph ben Mattathias, AD 37–100?); and Simon Bar-Kokhba (bar Kosiba, d.135), leader of an unsuccessful revolt against Roman rule. Unquestionably, the most famous Jew born in Roman Judea was Jesus (Jeshua) of Nazareth (4? BC–AD 29?), the Christ, or Messiah ("anointed one"), of Christian belief. Peter (Simon, d.AD 67?) was the first leader of the Christian Church and, in Roman Catholic tradition, the first pope. Paul (Saul, b. Asia Minor, d.AD 67?) was principally responsible for spreading Christianity and making it a religion distinct from Judaism.

The emergence of Israel as a modern Jewish state is attributed in large part to Chaim Weizmann (b. Russia, 1874–1952), the leader of the Zionist movement for 25 years, as well as a distinguished chemist who discovered methods for synthesizing acetone and rubber. Theodor Herzl (b. Budapest, 1860–1904), the founder of political Zionism, is buried in Jerusalem. Achad Ha'am (Asher Hirsch Ginsberg; b. Russia, 1856–1927) was an influential Zionist and social critic. Vladimir Jabotinsky (1880–1940) was a dedicated advocate of Jewish self-defense, both in his native Russia and in Palestine. David Ben-Gurion (Gruen; b. Poland, 1886–1973), also a leading Zionist and an eloquent spokesman on labor and national affairs, served as Israel's first prime minister. Golda Meir (Meyerson; b. Russia, 1898–1978), like Ben-Gurion a former secretary-general of Histadrut, became well known as Israel's prime minister from 1970 to 1974. Other prominent contemporary figures include Pinhas Sapir (b. Poland, 1907–75), labor leader and minister of finance; Abba Eban (Aubrey Eban; b. South Africa, 1915), former foreign affairs minister and representative to the UN; and Moshe Dayan (1915–81), military leader and cabinet minister. Menachem Begin (b. Russia, 1913), the former leader of guerrilla operations against the British, was prime minister from 1977 to 1983 and received the Nobel Peace Prize in 1978. He was succeeded by Yitzhak Shamir (b. Poland, 1915) in 1983, who gave way to Shimon Peres (b. Poland, 1923) in 1984. Shamir succeeded Peres in 1986.

Israel's foremost philosopher was Martin Buber (b. Vienna, 1878–1965), author of *I and Thou*. Outstanding scholars include the literary historian Joseph Klausner (1874–1958); the Bible researcher Yehezkel (Ezekiel) Kaufmann (b. Ukraine, 1889–1963); the philologists Eliezer Ben-Yehuda (b. Lithuania, 1858–1922) and Naphtali Hertz Tur-Sinai (Torczyner; b. Poland, 1886–1973); the archaeologist Eliezer Sukenik (1889–1953); and the Kabbalah authority Gershom Gerhard Scholem (b. Germany, 1897–1982).

The foremost poets are Haim Nahman Bialik (b. Russia, 1873–1934), Saul Tchernichowsky (b. Russia, 1875–1943), Uri Zvi Greenberg (b. Galicia, 1896–1981), Avraham Shlonsky (b. Russia, 1900–1973), Nathan Alterman (b. Warsaw, 1910–70), Yehuda Amichai (b. Germany, 1924), and Natan Zach (b. Berlin, 1930); and the leading novelists are Shmuel Yosef Halevi Agnon (b. Galicia, 1888–1970), a Nobel Prize winner in 1966, and Hayim Hazaz (b. Russia, 1898–1973). Painters of note include Reuven Rubin (b. Romania, 1893–1975) and Mane Katz (b. Russia, 1894–1962). Paul Ben-Haim (Frankenburger; b. Munich, 1897–1984) and Ödön Partos (b. Budapest, 1907–77) are well-known composers. Famous musicians include Daniel Barenboim (b. Argentina, 1942), Itzhak Perlman (b. 1945), and Pinchas Zukerman (b. 1948).

Significant contributions in other fields have been made by mathematician Abraham Halevi Fraenkel (b. Munich, 1891–1965); botanist Hugo Boyko (b. Vienna, 1892–1970); zoologist Shimon (Fritz) Bodenheimer (b. Cologne, 1897–1959); parasitologist Saul Aaron Adler (b. Russia, 1895–1966); physicist Giulio Raccah (b. Florence, 1909–65); rheologist Markus Reiner (b. Czernowitz, 1886–1976); gynecologist Bernard Zondek (b. Germany, 1891–1966); and psychoanalyst Heinrich Winnik (b. Austria-Hungary, 1902–82).

49DEPENDENCIES

Beginning at the end of the 1967 war and until recently, Israel administered the West Bank and the Gaza Strip. The Golan Heights, captured from Syria during the same war, was annexed in 1981; the Sinai Peninsula, taken from Egypt, was restored to Egyptian sovereignty in 1983, in accordance with a 1979 peace treaty. In 1994 Israel returned the lands it had captured in the war to Palestine. The move was in accord with a peace agreement it signed with the PLO (Palestine Liberation Organization). The West Bank, Gaza Strip, and Golan Heights will be under Palestine self-rule.

50BIBLIOGRAPHY

Aronson, Shlomo. *The Politics and Strategy of Nuclear Weapons in the Middle East*. Albany: State University of New York Press, 1992.

Bailey, Sydney Dawson. *Four Arab-Israeli Wars and the Peace Process*. New York: St. Martin's Press, 1990.

Begin, Menachem. *The Revolt*. New York: Nash, 1977.

Beilin, Yossi. *Israel: A Concise Political History*. New York: St. Martin's, 1993.

Ben-Gurion, David (ed.). *The Jews in Their Land*. Garden City, N.Y.: Doubleday, 1974.

Bickerton, Ian J. and Carla L. Klausner. *A Concise History of the Arab-Israeli Conflict*. Englewood Cliffs, N.J.: Prentice Hall, 1991.

Bright, John. *A History of Israel*. 3d ed. Philadelphia: Westminster, 1981.

Cohen, Michael Joseph. *Truman and Israel*. Berkeley: University of California Press, 1990.

Cohen, Mitchell. *Zion and State: Nation, Class, and the Shaping of Modern Israel*. New York: B. Blackwell, 1987.

Danzger, Murray Herbert. *Returning to Tradition: The Contemporary Revival of Orthodox Judaism*. New Haven: Yale University Press, 1989.

Eban, Abba. *My Country: The Story of Modern Israel.* New York: Random House, 1972.

Encyclopedia Judaica. 16 vols. Jerusalem: Keter, 1972.

Feinstein, Steve. *Israel in Pictures.* Minneapolis: Lerner, 1988.

Friedlander, Dov, and Calvin Goldscheider. *The Population of Israel: Growth, Policy, and Implications.* New York: Columbia University Press, 1979.

Gilbert, Martin. *Jewish History Atlas.* rev. ed. New York: Macmillan, 1976.

Hart, Alan. *Arafat, a Political Biography.* Bloomington: Indiana University Press, 1989.

Korn, David A. *Stalemate: The War of Attrition and Great Power Diplomacy in the Middle East, 1967–1970.* Boulder, Colo.: Westview Press, 1992.

Kretzmer, David. *The Legal Status of the Arabs in Israel.* Boulder, Colo.: Westview Press, 1990.

Mahler, Gergory S. (ed.). *Israel after Begin.* Albany: State University of New York Press, 1990.

Meir, Golda. *My Life.* New York: Putnam, 1975.

Metz, Helen Chapin (ed.). *Israel, a Country Study.* 3rd ed. Washington, D.C.: Library of Congress, 1990.

Morris, Benny. *Israel's Border Wars, 1949–1956.* New York: Oxford University Press, 1993.

———. *The Birth of the Palestinian Refugee Problem, 1947–1949.* New York: Cambridge University Press, 1987.

Parker, James. *A History of Palestine.* London: Gollancz, 1949.

Rabinovich, Itamar. *The Road Not Taken: Early Arab-Israeli Negotiations.* New York: Oxford University Press, 1991.

Razin, Assaf. *The Economy of Modern Israel: Malaise and Promise and Efraim Sadka.* Chicago: University of Chicago Press, 1993.

Reich, Bernard and Gershon R. Kieval. *Israel: Land of Tradition and Conflict.* 2d ed. Boulder, Colo.: Westview Press, 1993.

———. *Historical Dictionary of Israel.* Metuchen, N.J.: Scarecrow Press, 1992.

Rubin, Barry M. *Revolution Until Victory?: The Politics and History of the PLO.* Cambridge, Mass.: Harvard University Press, 1994.

Sachar, Howard Morley. *A History of Israel: From the Rise of Zionism to Our Time.* New York: Knopf, 1979.

Safran, Nadav. *Israel: The Embattled Ally.* Cambridge, Mass.: Belknap Press/Harvard University Press, 1978.

Sharkansky, Ira. *Ancient and Modern Israel: An Exploration of Political Parallels.* Albany: State University of New York Press, 1991.

Silberstein, Laurence J. *New Perspectives on Israeli History: The Early Years of the State.* New York: New York University Press, 1991.

Slater, Robert. *Rabin of Israel.* New York: St. Martin's Press, 1993.

———. *Warrior Statesman: The Life of Moshe Dayan.* New York: St. Martin's Press, 1991.

JAPAN

Nippon

CAPITAL: Tokyo.

FLAG: The Sun-flag (Hi-no-Maru) consists of a red circle on a white background.

ANTHEM: (de facto) *Kimigayo (The Reign of Our Emperor)*, with words dating back to the 9th century.

MONETARY UNIT: The yen (¥) of 100 sen is issued in coins of 1, 5, 10, 50, 100, and 500 yen, and notes of 500, 1,000, 5,000, and 10,000 yen. ¥ = 0.0097 (or $1 = ¥103.15).

WEIGHTS AND MEASURES: The metric system is the legal standard.

HOLIDAYS: New Year's Day, 1 January; Adults' Day, 15 January; Commemoration of the Founding of the Nation, 11 February; Vernal Equinox Day, 20 or 21 March; Emperor's Birthday, 29 April; Constitution Day, 3 May; Children's Day, 5 May; Respect for the Aged Day, 15 September; Autumnal Equinox Day, 23 or 24 September; Health-Sports Day, 10 October; Culture Day, 3 November; Labor-Thanksgiving Day, 23 November.

TIME: 9 PM = noon GMT.

¹LOCATION, SIZE, AND EXTENT

Situated off the eastern edge of the Asian continent, the Japanese archipelago is bounded on the N by the Sea of Okhotsk, on the E and S by the Pacific Ocean, on the SW by the East China Sea, and on the W by the Sea of Japan. The total area of Japan is 377,835 sq km (145,883 sq mi). Comparatively, the area occupied by Japan is slightly smaller than the state of California. It extends 3,008 km (1,869 mi) NE–SW and 1,645 km (1,022 mi) SE–NW and has a total coastline of 29,751 km (18,486 mi).

The five districts are Honshu, 231,058 sq km (89,212 sq mi); Hokkaido, 83,519 sq km (32,247 sq mi); Kyushu, 42,145 sq km (16,272 sq mi); Shikoku, 18,805 sq km (7,261 sq mi); and Okinawa, 2,254 sq km (870 sq mi). Each of the five districts consists of a main island of the same name and hundreds of surrounding islands.

Of the thousands of lesser islands, four are of significance: Tsushima, 698 sq km (269 sq mi), in the straits between Korea and Japan; Amami Oshima, 709 sq km (274 sq mi), of the northern Ryukyu Islands at the southern end of the Japanese archipelago; Sado Island, 857 sq km (331 sq mi), in the Sea of Japan off central Honshu; and Awaji Island, 593 sq km (229 sq mi), lying between Shikoku and Honshu. Two groups of islands returned to Japan by the US in 1968 are located some 1,300 km (800 mi) due east of the Ryukyus: the Ogasawara (Bonin) Islands, about 885 km (550 mi) south of Tokyo, and the Kazan (Volcano) Islands, directly south of the Ogasawara group.

Japan's principal island is Honshu, on which are located the capital city of Tokyo, the principal cities and plains, and the major industrial areas. This island is divided into five regions: Tohoku, from north of Kanto to Tsugaru Strait; Kanto, embracing seven prefectures in the Tokyo-Yokohama region; the Chubu, or central, region, from west of Tokyo to the Nagoya area; Kinki, including the important cities of Kyoto, Osaka, Kobe, and Nara; and Chugoku, a narrow peninsula thrusting westward from Kinki between the Sea of Japan and the Inland Sea, which lies between southern Honshu and the island of Shikoku.

The Japanese government maintains that the Habomai island group and Shikotan, lying just off Hokkaido and constituting fringe areas of the Kurils, belong to Japan and should be returned to Japanese administration. These islands and the Kuril Islands are currently occupied by the USSR, whose claims are not formally recognized by Japan.

Japan's capital city, Tokyo, is located on the east coast of the island of Honshu.

²TOPOGRAPHY

The Japanese islands are the upper portions of vast mountains belonging to what is sometimes called the Circum-Pacific Ring of Fire, which stretches from Southeast Asia to the Aleutian Islands. Mountains cover over 71% of the land's surface. Landforms are steep and rugged, indicating that, geologically speaking, Japan is still a young area. Through the central part of Honshu, running in a north–south direction, are the two principal mountain ranges: the Hida (or Japan Alps) and the Akaishi mountains. There are 25 mountains with peaks of over 3,000 m (9,800 ft). The highest is the beautiful Mt. Fuji (Fuji-san), at 3,776 m (12,388 ft). Japan has 196 volcanoes (including the dormant Mt. Fuji), of which 67 remain active. Earthquakes occur continually, with an average of 1,500 minor shocks per year. One of the world's greatest recorded natural disasters was the Kanto earthquake of 1923, when the Tokyo-Yokohama area was devastated and upward of 99,000 persons died.

The plains of Japan are few and small and cover only about 29% of the total land area. Most plains are located along the seacoast and are composed of alluvial lowlands, diluvial uplands, and low hills. The largest is the Kanto Plain (Tokyo Bay region), about 6,500 sq km (2,500 sq mi). Others include the Kinai Plain (Osaka-Kyoto), Nobi (Nagoya), Echigo (north-central Honshu), and Sendai (northeastern Honshu). There are four small plains in Hokkaido. The population is heavily concentrated in these limited flat areas.

Rivers tend to be short and swift. The longest is the Shinano (367 km/228 mi) in north-central Honshu, flowing into the Sea of Japan. The largest lake is Lake Biwa, near Kyoto, with an area of 672 sq km (259 sq mi). Lake Kussharo, in the Akan National Park of Hokkaido, is considered the clearest lake in the world, having a transparency of 41 m (135 ft). Good harbors are limited because in most areas the land rises steeply out of the sea. Yokohama, Nagoya, and Kobe are Japan's most prominent harbors.

The Ryukyu Islands, among which Okinawa predominates, are the peaks of submerged mountain ranges. They are generally hilly or mountainous, with small alluvial plains.

³CLIMATE

Japan is located at the northeastern edge of the Asian monsoon climate belt, which brings much rain to the country. The weather is under the dual influence of the Siberian weather system and the patterns of the southern Pacific; it is affected by the Japan Current (Kuroshio), a warm stream that flows from the southern Pacific along much of Japan's Pacific coast, producing a milder and more temperate climate than is found at comparable latitudes elsewhere. Northern Japan is affected by the Kuril Current (Oyashio), a cold stream flowing along the eastern coasts of Hokkaido and northern Honshu. The junction of the two currents is a bountiful fishing area. The Tsushima Current, an offshoot of the Japan Current, transports warm water northward into the Sea of Japan.

Throughout the year, there is fairly high humidity, with average rainfall ranging by area from 100 cm to over 300 cm (40–120 in). Autumn weather is usually clear and bright. Winters tend to be warmer than in similar latitudes except in the north and west, where snowfalls are frequent and heavy. Spring is usually pleasant, and the summer hot and humid. There is a rainy season that moves from south to north during June and July.

Average temperature ranges from 17°C (63°F) in the southern portions to 9°C (48°F) in the extreme north. Hokkaido has long and severe winters with extensive snow, while the remainder of the country enjoys milder weather down to the southern regions, which are almost subtropical. The Ryukyus, although located in the temperate zone, are warmed by the Japan Current, giving them a subtropical climate. The typhoon season runs from May through October, and each year several storms usually sweep through the islands, often accompanied by high winds and heavy rains.

⁴FLORA AND FAUNA

Hokkaido flora is characterized by montane conifers (fir, spruce, and larch) at high elevations and mixed northern hardwoods (oak, maple, linden, birch, ash, elm, and walnut) at lower altitudes. The ground flora includes plants common to Eurasia and North America. Honshu supports a panoply of temperate flora. Common conifers are cypress, umbrella pine, hemlock, yew, and white pine. On the lowlands, there are live oak and camphor trees and a great mixture of bamboo with the hardwoods. Black pine and red pine form the typical growth on the sandy lowlands and coastal areas. Shikoku and Kyushu are noted for their evergreen vegetation. Sugarcane and citrus fruits are found throughout the limited lowland areas, with broadleaf trees in the lower elevations and a mixture of evergreen and deciduous trees higher up. Throughout these islands are luxuriant growths of bamboo.

About 140 species of fauna have been identified. The only indigenous primate is the Japanese macaque, a small monkey found in the north. There are 32 carnivores, including the brown bear, ermine, mink, raccoon dog, fox, wolf, walrus, and seal. There are 450 species of birds and 30 species of reptiles. Japan's waters abound with crabs and shrimp; great migrations of fish are brought in by the Japan and Kuril currents. There are large numbers and varieties of insects. The Japanese beetle is not very destructive in its homeland because of its many natural enemies.

⁵ENVIRONMENT

Rapid industrialization has imposed severe pressures on the environment. Japan's Basic Law for Environmental Pollution Control was enacted in 1967, and the Environment Agency was established four years later.

Air pollution is a serious environmental problem in Japan, particularly in urban centers. The collection of toxic pollutants in the atmosphere has led to the appearance of acid rain throughout the country. As of 1994, Japan contributed 5.6% of the world's total gas emissions. Air quality is regulated under the Air Pollution Control Law of 1968; by 1984, on the "polluter pays" principle, compensation had been provided to 91,118 air-pollution victims suffering from bronchitis, bronchial asthma, and related conditions. The "polluter pays" principle was significantly weakened in 1987 as a result of years of business opposition. Nationwide smog alerts, issued when oxidant density levels reach or exceed 0.12 parts per million, peaked at 328 in 1973 but had declined to 85 (85% of which took place in the Tokyo and Osaka areas) by 1986, following imposition of stringent automobile emissions standards.

Water pollution is another area of concern in Japan. The nation has 131.3 cubic miles of water with 49.5% used in farming activity and 33.4% used for industrial purposes. Increase in acid levels due to industrial pollutants has affected lakes, rivers, and the waters surrounding Japan. Other sources of pollution include DDT, BMC, and mercury. Environmental damage by industrial effluents has slowed since the promulgation of the Water Pollution Control Law of 1971, but there is still widespread pollution of lakes and rivers from household sources, especially by untreated sewage and phosphate-rich detergents. Factory noise levels are regulated under a law of 1968. Airplanes may not take off or land after 10 PM, and the Shinkansen trains must reduce speed while traveling through large cities and their suburbs.

Most of the nation's forests, which play a critical role in retarding runoff and soil erosion in the many mountainous areas, are protected under the Nature Conservation Law of 1972, and large areas have been reforested. Parks and wildlife are covered by the National Parks Law of 1967. Japan, one of the world's chief whaling nations, vigorously opposed the 1982 resolution of the IWC calling for a phaseout of commercial whaling by 1986/87. However, since most of its trading partners, including the US, supported the measure and threatened retaliatory measures if whaling continued, Japan finally agreed to comply with the ban.

Of Japan's mammal species, 5 are endangered, as are 31 bird species, and 41 plants. As of 1994, endangered species in Japan included the Ryukyu sika, Ryukyu rabbit, Iriomote cat, Southern Ryukyu robin, Okinawa woodpecker, Oriental white stork, short-tailed albatross, Japanese sea lion, green sea turtle, and tailless blue butterfly.

⁶POPULATION

In 1990, Japan ranked seventh among the world's most populous nations, with a population of 123,612,000, an increase of 5.6% over the 1980 census figure of 117,057,485. The population for the year 2000 was projected to be 128,066,000, assuming a crude birthrate of 11.6 per 1,000 population, a crude death rate of 8.2, and a net natural increase of 3.4 during 1995–2000. In terms of density, Japan ranks among the world leaders, with 332 persons per sq km (860 per sq mi). In terms of density per unit of cultivated land, Japan has about 23 persons per hectare (9.5 per acre). The major concentrations are found in Honshu, where four out of five Japanese live; the least densely populated major island is Hokkaido, with less than 5% of the total population.

As of 1990 there were 11 cities with populations of more than 1 million: Tokyo, 8,163,127; Yokohama, 3,220,350; Osaka, 2,623,831; Nagoya, 2,154,664; Sapporo, 1,671,765; Kyoto, 1,461,140; Kobe, 1,477,423; Fukuoka, 1,237,107; Kawasaki, 1,173,606; Kitakyushu, 1,026,467; and Hiroshima, 1,085,677. The urban agglomeration centered on Tokyo had an estimated

JAPAN

0   100   200   300 Miles

0   100   200   300 Kilometers

CHINA

NORTH KOREA

SOUTH KOREA

Sea of Japan

East China Sea

Tsushima

Oki Guntō

Dōgo

Hinomi Saki

Matsue

Himeji

Okayama

Kobe

Hiroshima

Kitakyushu

Fukuoka

Nagasaki

Kumamoto

Miyazaki

Kagoshima

Sata Misaki

KYŪSHŪ

Tanega Shima

Yaku Shima

Ōsumi Shotō

NANSEI SHOTŌ (RYUKYU ISLANDS)

Kasari Saki

Amami ō Shima

Tokuno Shima

Okino Erabu Shima

Hedo Misaki

Naha   *Okinawa*

La Perouse Strait

Rebun Tō
Rishiri Tō

Haboro

Asahikawa

Kamui Misaki

Mombetsu

Shiretoko Misaki

Sea of Okhjotsk

Asahi Dake
7,513 ft.
2290 m.

Nemuro

Sapporo

Kushiro

HIDAKA SAMMYAKU

HOKKAIDŌ

Okushiri Tō

Hakodate

Erimo Misaki

Matsumae

Mutsu

Henashi Zaki

Aomori

Hachinhoe

Towada Ko

Akita

Morioka

Tsuruoka

Ishinomaki

Sado

Sendai

Ishinomaki Wan

Suzu Misaki

Niigata

Fukushima

HONSHŪ

Toyama Wan

Nagano

Kanazawa

Komatsu

Utsunomiya

Wakasa Wan

Gifu

Tokyo

Kyoto

Nagoya

Mt. Fuji
12,388 ft.
3776 m.

Kawasaki

Yokohama

Osaka

Shizuoka

Nojima Zaki

Wakayama

Hamamatsu

Ise Wan

Mikura Jima

Matsuyama

Kii Suidō

Izu Shichito

SHIKOKU

Shiono Misaki

Hachijō Jima

Bungo Suidō

PACIFIC OCEAN

N
W   E
S

Japan

LOCATION: 122°56′ to 153°59′E; 20°25′ to 45°33′N. **TERRITORIAL SEA LIMIT:** 12 mi.

population of about 26.8 million (highest in the world) in 1995 and Osaka, 10.6 million. The proportion of urban population was 78% in 1990. Since the 1965 census, however, the net population flow into the center cities has decreased, while the flow into the surrounding suburban areas has increased.

Japan's population pyramid shows that in 1992, 69.8% of the population was in the economically productive age group (15–64 years old), the largest subgroup consisting of those between 40 and 44 years old, a result of the postwar "baby boom." The number of births declined sharply thereafter, however. Japan is the only Asian country thus far with a birthrate that has declined to the level of industrial areas in other parts of the world. It was only 9.9 per 1,000 population in 1991, as compared with about 343 in 1947. The steep drop since 1950 has been attributed to legalization of abortion, increased availability of contraceptives, and the desire to raise living standards.

7MIGRATION

Japanese nationals living in other countries totaled 663,074 in 1991, including 257,845 in the US and 101,174 in Brazil. More than 1 million Japanese have emigrated since 1880; about 70% of them arrived on the US mainland and in Hawaii during the decades prior to World War II. Emigration continued after the war, encouraged by government policy as a way of relieving population pressure. By the mid-1960s, emigration had considerably decreased, as economic opportunities and living standards in Japan improved. Since the early 1970s, however, the number of emigrants has again risen sharply, reaching 82,619 in 1992 (compared to 12,445 in 1975 and 34,492 in 1985).

Immigration to Japan is generally small-scale, although in recent years the illegal entry of workers from neighboring countries has come to be regarded as a problem. In 1992 there were 1,281,644 registered aliens, of which 688,144 were Koreans. The number of illegal aliens may be even higher. Some 150,339 Chinese constituted the second-largest group. In 1992, 41,643 foreigners entered as permanent residents. Because citizenship is based on nationality of parent rather than place of birth, registered aliens may have spent their entire lives in Japan.

Internal migration, providing a steady exodus of people from farm and mountain communities to the cities and suburbs, has been accelerating since 1952. Most such migrants flocked to the three major population centers—the Tokyo, Osaka, and Nagoya metropolitan areas. As pollution and congestion in these areas increased, the government instituted programs to decentralize industry by directing new growth to smaller cities of the north and west, and also began efforts to improve rural living conditions and employment opportunities.

8ETHNIC GROUPS

Although it is known that the Japanese are descended from many varied peoples of Asia, there is no agreement as to origins or specific ethnic strains. In physical characteristics, the Japanese belong to the Mongoloid group, with faint admixtures of Malayan and Caucasoid strains. Waves of migration from the continental hinterland reached Japan during the end of the Paleolithic period, blending into a complicated and diverse ethnic, linguistic, and cultural system. It is believed that the Japanese have their roots in the Old Stone Age race of at least 30,000 BC. A major migration appears to have taken place in the 2d and 3d centuries AD, and by the 4th century this group, called the Yamato clan, had established a monarchy in the present Nara prefecture. Other ethnic strains may have come from Indonesia and China in the south, Korea in the west, and Siberia and Alaska in the north.

The one remaining distinct ethnic group in Japan is the Ainu. These people, living on the northern island of Hokkaido, are physically distinct from the contemporary Japanese, having Nordic-like features, including more pervasive facial and body hair. There is no agreement as to their origins; their current population is less than 20,000.

9LANGUAGES

Most linguists agree that Japanese is in a language class by itself, although there is some inconclusive evidence that traces it to the Malayo-Polynesian language family. In vocabulary, Japanese is rich in words denoting abstract ideas, natural phenomena, human emotions, ethics, and aesthetics, but poor in words for technical and scientific expression. For these latter purposes, foreign words are directly imported and written in a phonetic system (katakana). A distinct characteristic is the use of honorifics to show proper respect to the listener and his social station.

Written Japanese owes its origin almost entirely to Chinese forms. Having no indigenous script, the Japanese since the 5th century have used Chinese characters, giving them both an approximate Chinese pronunciation and a Japanese pronunciation. In addition, the Japanese invented phonetic symbols (kana) in the 9th century to represent grammatical devices unknown to the Chinese.

Attempts have been made to reduce the complexity of the written language by limiting the number of Chinese characters used. The government has published a list of 1,850 characters for use in official communications. Newspapers adhere to this list.

10RELIGIONS

The principal religions in Japan are Shintoism and Buddhism. Religious identities are not mutually exclusive, and many Japanese maintain affiliations with both a Buddhist temple and a Shinto shrine.

Shinto, originally concerned with the worship of spirits of nature, grew under the influence of Chinese Confucianism to include worship of family and imperial ancestors, and thus provided the foundation of Japanese social structure. Shinto became an instrument of nationalism after 1868, as the government officially sponsored and subsidized it, requiring that it be taught in the schools and that all Japanese belong to a state Shinto shrine. After World War II, Shinto was abolished as a state religion, and the emperor issued an imperial rescript denying divine origin. Today, Shinto exists as a private religious organization; its membership was 109 million in 1991.

Buddhism, considered by some the most important religion in Japan, had a following of 96,255,000 in 1991. Introduced through China and Korea around AD 552, Buddhism spread rapidly throughout Japan and has had considerable influence on the nation's arts and its social institutions. There are 13 sects (shu) and 56 denominations, the principal shu being Tendai, Shingon, Jodo, Zen, Soto, Obaku, and Nichiren. Japanese Buddhism was founded on the Mahayana school, which emphasizes the attainment of Buddhahood, whereas the Hinayana Buddhism of India emphasizes obedience to commandments and personal perfection. The great temples and gardens of Japan, the famous Japanese tea ceremony (chanoyu), and Japanese flower-arranging arts (ikebana) owe their development to the influence of Buddhism.

Christianity, introduced to Japan by the Jesuit St. Francis Xavier in 1549, was first encouraged by feudal lords but then banned in 1613. The prohibition was in force until 1873, following the reopening of Japan to international relations in 1854. Following World War II, when the emperor lost his claim to divinity, some Japanese gave up Shinto and converted to Christianity or Judaism. In 1991 there were 1,464,000 Christians in Japan and about 1,000 Jews.

After World War II, a considerable number of new religious groups sprouted up. One of these, the Soka-Gakkai, a Buddhist offshoot, controlled a political party (Komeito), the third-strongest political group in Japan, until politics and religion were officially separated in 1970. In addition to the established and new religions, Confucianism, an ethical system originating in China, has strongly influenced Japanese society since the earliest periods, providing underpinnings for some characteristically Japanese attitudes.

11TRANSPORTATION

Despite its rugged terrain, Japan has a highly developed transportation system. In 1991, Japan had 27,327 km (16,981 mi) of railways, of which 93% is 1.067-m narrow gauge. The government-owned Japan National Railways (JNR) was privatized in April 1987 and divided into six railway companies, which had a combined total of 27,327 km (16,981 mi) of lines; feeding into these six lines were 144 other private railroads. Like their counterparts elsewhere, Japan's rail lines face increasing competition from automotive, sea, and air transport, as well as rising operating costs. High-speed lines, however, have been successful in partially meeting these problems; the most famous of these is the Shinkansen, which opened to traffic in October 1964 between Tokyo and Osaka and was extended in March 1975 to Fukuoka in northern Kyushu; in 1984, the Shinkansen superexpress trains covered the 1,069 km (664 mi) between Tokyo and Fukuoka in less than seven hours, with maximum speeds of 210 km/hr (130 mph). In 1982, the first section of the northern Shinkansen line, between Tokyo and Omiya, began operations. This line was extended in 1983 to Niigata and to Morioka, in northern Honshu. By far the longest railway tunnel in the world, the 54.2-km (33.7-mi) Seikan tube linking Honshu with Hokkaido, was opened in 1983 and completed in 1985; the tunnel, lying beneath the Tsugaru Strait, cost well over $2 billion. A bridge linking Honshu and Shikoku was recently opened. Subway lines serve nine cities—Tokyo, Osaka, Nagoya, Kobe, Yokohama, Sapporo, Kyoto, Fukuoka, and Sendai. There are 410 km (255 mi) of track, with 196 km (122 mi) in Tokyo's 11 lines. Since 1964, downtown Tokyo has also been linked with that city's Haneda Airport by a monorail transport system, and several other monorails have been put into operation. In addition, a 7-km (4.3-mi) monorail serves the city of Yokohama.

Roads have become the most important means of domestic transport, carrying 65% of total passenger traffic and 90% of freight traffic in 1991. Motor vehicles in that year included 37,036,015 passenger cars and 22,838,608 commercial vehicles, up from 25,848,000 and 8,306,000, respectively, in 1985. To speed traffic flow, a total of 3,400 km (2,113 mi) of expressways were open to traffic in 1984. There are about 1,111,874 km (690,981 mi) of highways of which about 68% are paved.

Japan is one of the world's great maritime nations. The chief ports are Yokohama (for Tokyo), Nagoya, and Kobe. In 1986, Japan ranked fifth in the world in gross tonnage of its merchant fleet; its 944 merchant ships totaled 21,674,000 gross tons. In 1985, Japan's ships handled 15 million tons of exports and 243 million tons of imports. Since 1959, Japan has emerged as the world's leading shipbuilder, but output declined in the late 1970s and 1980s in the face of a worldwide recession and increased competition from the Republic of Korea (ROK).

Japan Air Lines (JAL), the nation's major domestic and international airline, began operations in 1952 and inaugurated international flights in 1954. All Nippon Airways, established in 1957, began as a domestic system serving smaller areas of the country and acting as a feeder line to JAL but now serves overseas routes; it began to carry freight in 1987. Principal domestic airports include Haneda in Tokyo, Itami in Osaka, Itazuke in Fukuoka, and Chitose on Hokkaido. In 1978, the new international airport at Narita (which is served by 40 international airlines), 72 km (45 mi) from downtown Tokyo, replaced Haneda as the chief international arrivals center. Vehement protests from environmentalists, local farmers, and others accompanied the construction of the Narita facility, which served 18,603,000 arriving and departing passengers in 1991. In 1992, Japan had a total of 2,349 registered commercial aircraft, accounting for 107,699 million passenger-km in domestic and international traffic.

From 1991–2000, the government plans to spend $8 trillion on infrastructural improvements, especially for the expansion of airports, bridges, roads, ports, heliports, and marinas.

12HISTORY

Recent archaeological discoveries have revealed the existence of paleolithic humans in Japan when the islands were still a part of the continental Asian land mass. Little is known about the origins of the earliest Japanese beyond the fact that they migrated from the continent. The first distinctive Neolithic culture, the Jōmon, inhabited Japan from 11,000 BC to 300 BC. The Jōmon was displaced by the Yayoi culture, which introduced new skills in agriculture and metallurgy from the continent. Tradition places the beginning of the Japanese nation in 660 BC with the ascendance to the throne of the legendary Emperor Jimmu. It is generally agreed, however, that as the Yayoi developed, a clan known as the Yamato attained hegemony over southern Japan during the first three or four centuries of the Christian era and established the imperial family line. Earlier contacts with Korea were expanded in the 5th century to mainland China, and the great period of cultural borrowing began: industrial arts were imported; Chinese script was introduced (thereby permitting the study of medical texts), as well as the Chinese calendar and eventually Buddhism also. Japanese leaders adopted Chinese governmental organization but based power upon hereditary position rather than merit. The first imperial capital was established at Nara in 710. In 794, the imperial capital was removed to Heian (Kyoto), where it remained until 1868, when Tokyo became the nation's capital.

Chinese influence waned as native institutions took on peculiarly Japanese forms. Outside court circles, local clans gained strength, giving rise to military clan influence over a weakening imperial system. The Minamoto clan gained national hegemony as it defeated the rival Taira clan in 1185, and its leader, the newly appointed shogun (Seii Taishōgun, Barbarian Suppressing General), Yoritomo, established a military form of government at Kamakura in 1192, a feudal system that lasted for nearly 700 years. Under this system, known as the shogunate, all political power was in the hands of the dominant military clan, with the emperors ruling in name only. The Kamakura period was followed by the Ashikaga shogunate (1336–1600) which saw economic growth and the development of high feudalism. For over 100 years, until the end of the 16th century, civil war was almost continuous between rival feudal lords (daimyos), and a class of professional warriors, the samurai, was developed. During this time, the first contact with the Western world took place with the arrival in 1543 of Portuguese traders, and the first guns, in southern Japan. Six years later, St. Francis Xavier arrived, introducing Christianity for the first time. Soon Spanish traders reached Japan.

By 1590, the country was pacified and unified by Hideyoshi Toyotomi, a peasant who had risen to a top military position. Hideyoshi also invaded Korea unsuccessfully, in 1592–93 and in 1598, dying during the second invasion. His work was consolidated by another great clan leader, Ieyasu Tokugawa. Appointed shogun in 1603, Tokugawa established the Tokugawa shogunate, which was to rule Japan until the imperial restoration in 1868. The Tokugawa made Edo (modern Tokyo) their capital, closed Japan to all foreigners except Chinese and Dutch traders (who were restricted to Nagasaki) and occasional Korean diplomats, and proscribed Christianity. For the next 250 years, Japan enjoyed peace, internal order, and a flowering of culture, although from the end of the 18th century onward, Japan came under increasing pressure from Western nations to end its isolationist policy.

The arrival of Commodore Matthew C. Perry from the US in 1853—with his famous "black ships"—started a process that soon ended Japanese feudalism. The following year, Perry obtained a treaty of peace and friendship between the US and Japan, and similar pacts were signed with Russia, Britain, and the Netherlands. A decade of turmoil and confusion followed over the question of opening Japan to foreigners. A coalition of southern clans led by ambitious young samurai forced the abdication of the Tokugawa shogun and reestablished the emperor as head of the nation. In 1868, Emperor Meiji took over full sovereignty. This Meiji Restoration, as it is known, signaled the entry of Japan into the modern era.

Intensive modernization and industrialization were initiated under the leadership of the restoration leaders. A modern navy and army were established with universal military conscription, and universal compulsory education was enforced. The government undertook the establishment of industry, with imported technological assistance. In 1889, a new constitution established a bicameral legislature (Diet), the upper house appointive, the lower house elective, with a civil cabinet headed by a prime minister responsible only to the emperor.

By the end of the 19th century, irreconcilable territorial ambitions brought Japan into open conflict with its much larger western neighbors. The First Sino-Japanese War (1894–95) was fought over the question of control of Korea, and the Russo-Japanese War (1904–5) over the question of Russian expansion in Manchuria and influence in Korean affairs. Japan emerged victorious from both conflicts, its victory over the Russians marking the first triumph of an Asian country over a Western power in modern times. Japan received the territories of Taiwan and the southern half of Sakhalin Island, as well as certain railway rights and concessions in Manchuria and recognition of paramount influence in Korea, which became a Japanese protectorate in 1905 and was annexed by Japan in 1910.

During the Taisho era (1912–26), Japan participated in a limited way in World War I, in line with the Anglo-Japanese Alliance of 1902. Japan was one of the Big Five powers at the Versailles Peace Conference and in 1922 was recognized as the world's third-leading naval power at the Washington Naval Conference. The domestic economy developed rapidly, and Japan was transformed from an agricultural to an industrial nation. Economic power tended to be held by the industrial combines (zaibatsu), controlled by descendants of those families that had instituted the modernization of the country decades earlier. In 1925, universal manhood suffrage was enacted, and political leaders found it necessary to take into consideration the growing influence of parties.

In 1926, Emperor Hirohito ascended the throne to begin the Showa era. By the 1930s, the power of political parties was undermined, and the military became dominant. In the context of severe social distress caused by the great depression, an ultra-nationalist ideology emerged, particularly among young army officers. Acting independently of the central government, the military launched an invasion of Manchuria in 1931, eventually establishing the puppet state of Manchukuo. In 1932, a patriotic society assassinated the prime minister, bringing an end to cabinets formed by the majority party in the Diet. Japan withdrew from the League of Nations (which had protested the Manchurian takeover) in 1933, started a full-scale invasion of China (the Second Sino-Japanese War, 1937–45), and signed the Anti-Comintern pact in with Germany in 1936 and a triple alliance with Germany and Italy in 1940. The military leadership, viewing the former USSR and the US as chief barriers to Japanese expansion, negotiated a nonaggression pact with the USSR in April 1941, thus setting the stage for the attack on Pearl Harbor and other Pacific targets on 7 December of that year. Thereafter, Japanese military actions merged into the more general conflict of World War II.

Japan's military fortunes proceeded apace during the war's early years. With its capture of the Philippines on 2 January 1942, Japan had gained control of most of East Asia, including major portions of China, Indochina, and the southwest Pacific. Japan's forces, however, could not long hold out against the full onslaught of Allied (mainly US) military power. A series of costly naval campaigns—including battles at Midway, Guadalcanal, and Leyte Gulf—brought an end to Japanese domination in the Pacific. By 1945, the Philippines had been recaptured, and the stage was set for a direct assault on Japan. US leadership, headed by President Harry S. Truman, argued that a full invasion of Japan would prove too costly and decided to seek to bomb Japan into surrender. Thus, after four months of intense bombardment with conventional weapons, the first atomic bomb ever used in warfare was dropped by the US on Hiroshima on 6 August 1945; a second bomb was dropped on Nagasaki on 9 August. An esti-mated 340,000 persons died from the two attacks and the subsequent effects of radiation disease.

On 14 August, Japan accepted the Potsdam Declaration for unconditional surrender. Formal surrender was signed aboard the USS *Missouri* on 2 September. The subsequent occupation, under the direction of Gen. Douglas MacArthur, Supreme Commander for the Allied Powers, began a series of ambitious reforms: a parliamentary system of government based on the sovereignty of the people, legal prohibition of any political role for the emperor other than as titular head of state, land reform, dissolution of the zaibatsu, greater local political autonomy, and establishment of a freer trade union movement. A new constitution was promulgated on 3 November 1946 and put into force on 3 May 1947.

The Postwar Period

Under the stimulus of heavy economic aid from the US and of the boom produced by the Korean War, in which Japan became a major matériel supplier, and with the determination of the Japanese people to rebuild their country, the Japanese economy rapidly recovered, and the standard of living quickly surpassed the prewar level by a substantial margin. The state of war between the Western powers and Japan was formally ended by the San Francisco Peace Treaty, signed in September 1951 by 56 nations. Allied occupation ended when the treaty went into effect in April 1952. Japan renounced claims to many of its former overseas territories, including such major areas as Taiwan and Korea. The Amami island group, comprising the northern portion of the Ryukyu Islands, nearest to Kyushu Island, was returned to direct Japanese control by the US in December 1953; the remainder of the group, including Okinawa, was returned to full Japanese sovereignty in May 1972. The Ogasawara (Bonin) Islands and Kazan (Volcano) Islands were returned to Japanese sovereignty in June 1968. The former USSR never signed the San Francisco Peace Treaty, and Japan and Russia continue to dispute sovereignty over the Kurile Islands, to the northeast of Hokkaido, which were occupied by the USSR in 1945. In 1956, Japan and the former USSR did agree to establish diplomatic relations.

In 1956 Japan was elected to UN membership. A revision of the 1952 defense treaty with the US, under which a limited number of troops were to remain in Japan for defense purposes, was signed amid growing controversy in 1960. On 22 June 1965, Japan signed a treaty with the ROK normalizing relations between the two countries. The US-Japanese security treaty was renewed in 1970, despite vigorous protest by the opposition parties and militant student organizations. In 1972, Japan moved to establish full diplomatic relations with the People's Republic of China. Formal diplomatic links with the Nationalist Chinese government on Taiwan were terminated by this move, but Japan's economic and cultural links with Taiwan nonetheless have survived virtually intact.

While Japan defined its new role in East Asian affairs, its remarkable economic expansion raised it to the level of a great trading power. From 1955 to 1965, Japan experienced a nominal growth rate of 10–20% annually and real growth rates (adjusted for inflation) of 5–12%. In 1968, it surpassed the Federal Republic of Germany (FRG) to stand second after the US among non-Communist nations in total value of GNP. The oil crisis of 1973—a combination of shortages and rising prices—revealed the crack in Japan's economic armor, the lack of domestic petroleum resources. A second oil crisis, in the form of a worldwide rise in oil prices during the late 1970s, was met by a reappraisal of Japan's dependence on foreign fuels and institution of long-range programs for energy conservation and diversification.

The yen declined in value in the early 1980s, causing Japanese exports to become cheaper in overseas markets and leading to huge trade surpluses with the US and other leading trading partners, who began to demand that Japan voluntarily limit certain exports and remove the barriers to Japan's domestic market. During 1985–87, the yen appreciated in value against the dollar and, by 1994, the dollar had hit a post-World War II low, but Japan continued to register substantial trade surpluses.

Political stability, maintained since the 1950s by the majority Liberal-Democratic Party (LDP), began to unravel in the 1970s, following the retirement from politics of Prime Minister Eisaku Sato in 1972. Sato's successor, Kakuei Tanaka, was forced to resign in December 1974 amid charges of improper use of his office for personal gain in the Lockheed Corporation bribery scandal. Tanaka was succeeded by Takeo Miki. Takeo Fukuda became prime minister when Miki resigned in December 1976, but was defeated in intraparty elections by Masayoshi Ohira in 1978. When Ohira died in June 1980, he was succeeded by Zenko Suzuki. Suzuki stepped down as prime minister in November 1982 and was replaced by Yasuhiro Nakasone. Noboru Takeshita became prime minister in November 1987.

Policy regarding military force has been a major political issue in the postwar years. In Article Nine of the 1947 constitution, Japan had renounced the use of war but soon developed a Self-Defense Force in the context of the cold war, with US encouragement. In 1986, breaking a long-standing policy, the government increased military spending to over 1% of the GNP. The Diet (parliament) approved a bill allowing the deployment of troops abroad for international peacekeeping in 1992 (with the United Nations in Cambodia). In January 1993, a ship bearing more than one ton of reprocessed plutonium arrived from France after a controversial two-month journey. The government planned for some 30 additional shipments over 20 years for use by the nuclear power industry, although opponents pointed out that plutonium can also be used to make nuclear weapons.

Emperor Hirohito died of cancer on 7 January 1989, at the age of 87. He was succeeded by the Crown Prince Akihito, who was enthroned in a formal ceremony in November 1990. The sense of entering a new era brought increased controversy over the assessment of Japan's role in the earlier part of the century, particularly during World War II. Some denied that Japan had committed atrocities during the war and there were attempts to further soften the wording of school textbooks. In March 1989, Prime Minister Takeshita apologized to North Korea (DPRK) for the suffering Japan caused over the 36 years of occupation of Korea (1910–45) and Emperor Akihito expressed similar regrets to President Roh Tae Woo of South Korea (ROK) in May 1990. In the same month, the government removed the requirement for fingerprinting of people of Korean descent living in Japan. In 1992, Prime Minister Miyazawa apologized for the forced prostitution of Korean, Chinese, and Japanese women in Japanese military brothels during World War II.

The 1980s ended with a major scandal involving illegal stock trading and influence peddling by the Recruit Cosmos Company. Between the summer of 1988 and the closing of the case in May 1989, the scandal led to the implication and resignations of prominent business people and politicians in top government positions, among them the finance minister Kiichi Miyazawa, and the former prime minister, Yashuhiro Nakasone. Scandals continued into the 1990s with stock dealings in the fall of 1991 and, in 1992, contributions to politicians from a trucking company linked to organized crime.

The economy entered a period of transition in the early 1990s. The stock market fell in 1990, more than 25% below its index at the start of the year by April. In the spring of 1992, the stock index fell rapidly again, until by the summer, the index was at its lowest point in six years at 62% below the record high of 1989. By the end of 1993, Japan was in the midst of its worst economic downturn in at least 20 years.

Against the background of scandals and economic recession, the political landscape began a major change. Taking responsi-

bility for political problems caused by the Recruit scandal, Noboru Takeshita resigned as prime minister in April 1989, to be succeeded in May by Sosuke Uno. In July, the LDP lost its majority in the upper house of the Diet, its worst defeat in 34 years, and Uno resigned. The next prime minister, Toshiki Kaifu, served his term from August 1989 to October 1991, but the LDP did not support him for a second term. Bringing with him into the government several politicians who, like himself, had been tied to the Recruit scandal, Kiichi Miyazawa was made prime minister in November 1991. When the lower house gave Miyazawa a vote of no confidence in June 1993 for abandoning electoral reform bills, Miyazawa dissolved the lower house and called for elections.

The dissolution of the House of Representatives and the ensuing election on 18 July 1993 marked a major turning point for Japanese politics as the LDP lost its political dominance and new parties formed. One new party, the Japan New Party (JNP), had been formed by Mirihiro Hosokawa, a former LDP member, in May 1992. On 21 June 1993, 10 more members of the LDP, led by Masayoshi Takemura, left to form the Sakigake (Harbinger Party) and another 44 LDP members quit two days later to create the Shinseito (Renewal Party) with Tsutomu Hata as its head. By 28 June, one-fifth of the LDP bloc of the dissolved lower house, 57 members, had left the party.

In the election for the 511 seats of the House of Representatives on 18 July 1993, the LDP, for the first time since its own formation in 1955, came up short, by 33 seats, of the 256 seats needed for a majority. Without a majority, the LDP was unable to form a government and the new prime minister, Mirihiro Hosokawa (JNP), was chosen on 29 July 1993, by a seven-party coalition of LDP defectors, Socialists, and conservatives. Hosokawa, too, was tainted by questions regarding personal finances and stepped down as prime minister to be replaced by Tsutomu Hata (Shinseito) in April 1994. Just as Hata took office, the Socialist Party quit the coalition which had chosen him, leaving a prime minister at the head of a minority government for the first time in four decades. Hata soon resigned and, in a surprise move, the LDP and the Socialist Party, traditionally opponents, allied to form a new coalition, which also included the Sakigake. The coalition selected as prime minister Tomiichi Murayama, the head of the Socialist Party and the first Socialist prime minister since 1948. Within the coalition, the LDP was the dominant factor, but the decades of LDP rule appeared to be over and the nature of the LDP itself changed.

13 GOVERNMENT

Japan follows the parliamentary system in accordance with the constitution of 1947. The most significant change from the previous constitution of 1889 was the transfer of sovereign power from the emperor to the people. The emperor is now defined as "the symbol of the state and of the unity of the people." The constitution provides for the supremacy of the National Diet as the legislative branch of the government, upholds the separation of legislative, executive, and judicial powers, and guarantees civil liberties.

The executive branch is headed by a prime minister selected from the Diet by its membership. The cabinet consists of the prime minister and 20 state ministers (as of January 1988), each heading a government ministry or agency. At least half the ministers must be selected from the Diet, to which the cabinet is collectively responsible. Upon a vote of no confidence by the House of Representatives, the cabinet must resign en masse.

The National Diet is bicameral. The House of Representatives (the lower house) has a membership of 512, with terms of office for four years, except that all terms end upon dissolution of the House. From 1947 through 1993, Representatives were elected from 130 "medium" (multiple-member) constituencies, apportioned on the basis of population. The House of Councillors (the upper house) has 252 members, 100 of whom are elected from a national constituency on the basis of proportional representation, the remainder from 47 prefectural constituencies. The term of office is six years, with one-half elected every three years. The lower house holds primary power. In case of disagreement between the two houses, or if the upper house fails to take action within 60 days of receipt of legislation from the lower house, a bill becomes law if passed again by a two-thirds majority of the lower house.

Suffrage is universal, the voting age being 20 years, with a three-month residence requirement. The 1947 constitution granted suffrage to women. In January 1994, the Diet passed an electoral reform bill. In addition to new laws on campaign financing, the legislation abolished the multiple-member districts and replaced them with 300 single-member districts. This would result, in the next general election, in a House of Representatives which more closely reflected the general population instead of giving disproportionate representation to rural constituencies, which have sparser and more conservative populations.

14POLITICAL PARTIES

The Liberal-Democratic Party (LDP) represents a wide spectrum of Japanese society, but most especially the conservative elements. Formed in 1955 by the merger of the two leading conservative parties, this party held the reins of government since its formation until July 1993.

The Japan Socialist Party (JSP), Japan's principal opposition party, draws its support mainly from the working class, but it suffers from personality as well as ideological problems within its ranks. The JSP split into right and left wings over the ratification of the US-Japan Security Treaty of 1952. In October 1955, however, the two factions reunited, preceding the unification of the conservative parties and actually forcing the conservative groups into a unified front, thus creating a formal two-party system in Japan.

Beginning in the late 1960s, a shift took place toward a multiple-party system, with the gradual increase of opposition parties other than the JSP. The Democratic Socialist Party (DSP) represents moderate elements of the working class. The Komeito (Clean Government Party), professing middle-of-the-road politics, was the political wing of the Soka-Gakkai, a Buddhist sect, until politics and religion were officially separated in 1970. The Japanese Communist Party, founded as an underground group in 1922 and legalized after World War II, has experienced major shifts in platform. In late 1987, it held 27 seats in the lower house. The party has traditionally sided with China in the Sino-Soviet ideological dispute, although in recent years the Japanese Communists have eschewed close identification with either side, focusing instead on social conditions at home.

The LDP continued to hold its majority in both houses through the late 1980s. Traditionally, the LDP has functioned as a coalition of several factions, each tightly organized and bound by personal loyalty to a factional leader. In the mid-1970s, policy differences among the factions and their leaders became acute, with the resignation under pressure of Prime Minister Tanaka in December 1974.

In the summer of 1993, after five years of scandals involving corruption, sex, organized crime, and in the midst of economic recession, the old political order disintegrated as dozens of younger LDP members defected to form new parties. Chief among these were the Japan New Party (JNP), formed in May 1992, and the Sakigake (Harbinger Party) and the Shinseito (Renewal Party), both formed in June 1993. A watershed election in July 1993 for the House of Representatives, the lower house of the parliament, resulted in the loss by the LDP, for the first time since 1955, of its majority. Of the 511 seats, the LDP won 223

seats (as compared with 275 in the 1990 election), the JSP won 70 seats (a loss of half of its previous seats), the Komeito won 51 seats, the Shinseito took 55 seats, the JNP 35 seats, and the Sakigake 13. A seven-party coalition, including new parties of LDP defectors, the JSP, and other conservative parties, formed the new cabinet, which governed for a year until the prime minister (Mirihiro Hosokawa, JNP) resigned over a financial scandal. The coalition formed a new government, led by Isutomi Hata of the Shinseito, in April 1993. However, the JSP, finding itself maneuvered out of any voice in the coalition, broke away and Hata, then with a minority in the House of Representatives, resigned after one month in office.

The next government was formed by a new, unorthodox coalition of the traditional opponents, the LDP and the JSP, as well as the Sakigake. Tomiichi Murayama, head of the JSP, was chosen prime minister in June 1994, the first Socialist to head a government since 1948, although the LDP appeared to be dominant in the coalition. This unusual partnership caused strains, leading to further defections, within the LDP and within the JSP. The Shinseito emerged as a serious focus of opposition, standing for an internationally more active Japan, including use of the military overseas, for a revision of the constitution, and for removing protective regulations to open the domestic economy to competition. The left wing of the JSP, unhappy with the alliance with the LDP, held that the Self-Defense Forces were unconstitutional, and that the North Korean government (DPRK) was the legitimate government of all of Korea, and advocated abolition of the security treaty with the United States.

15LOCAL GOVERNMENT

Local government throughout Japan was strengthened by the Local Autonomy Law of 1947. Administratively, Japan is divided into 47 prefectures. Within these prefectures there are 652 cities, 2,002 towns, and 596 villages. The local chief executives, mayors, and village heads, together with prefectural assembly members, are directly elected. The city of Tokyo comprises 23 wards.

Local public bodies have the right to administer their own affairs as well as to enact their own regulations within the law. The National Diet cannot enact legislation for a specific public entity without the consent of the voters of that district. Local governments control school affairs, levy taxes, and carry out administrative functions in the fields of land preservation and development, pollution control, disaster prevention, public health, and social welfare.

16JUDICIAL SYSTEM

The 1947 constitution provides for the complete independence of the judiciary. All judicial power is vested in the courts. The system consists of the Supreme Court, eight regional higher courts, district courts in each of the prefectures, and a number of summary courts. In addition, there are family courts, on the same level as the district courts, to adjudicate family conflicts and complaints such as partitions of estates, marriage annulments, and juvenile protection cases.

The Supreme Court consists of a chief justice and 14 other justices. The chief justice is appointed by the emperor on designation by the cabinet; the other justices, by cabinet appointment. All appointments are subject to popular review at the first general election following appointment and every 10 years thereafter in public referendum. Judges of the lesser courts also are appointed by the cabinet from lists of persons nominated by the Supreme Court. Their term of office is limited to 10 years, with the privilege of reappointment.

The Supreme Court is the court of last resort for determining the constitutionality of any law, order, regulation, or official act that is challenged during the regular hearing of a lawsuit. Abstract questioning of a law may not be instituted by the court.

The Constitution affords criminal defendants a right to a speedy and public trial by an impartial tribunal. There is no right to a trial by jury.

17 ARMED FORCES

The reestablishment of Japanese defense forces has been a subject of heated debate in the period since World War II. Article 9 of the constitution renounces war as a sovereign right and the maintenance of "land, sea and air forces, as well as other war potential." During the Korean War, Gen. MacArthur recommended the establishment of a national police reserve. Following the signing of the San Francisco Peace Treaty, the reserve force was reorganized into a National Safety Agency (1 August 1952). Laws establishing a Defense Agency and a Self-Defense Force became effective on 1 July 1954, both under firm civilian control.

The strength of Japan's armed forces in 1991 was 246,000. The Ground Self-Defense Force had 156,000 personnel, organized into 1 armored and 12 infantry divisions and 6 combined brigades; there were also 46,000 men in reserve components. The Maritime Self-Defense Force, consisting of 44,000 personnel, had 64 surface combatants, 13 combat submarines, and an air arm of 99 aircraft and 72 armed helicopters. Air Self-Defense Force personnel numbered 46,000; combat aircraft totaled 440, including US-supplied jet fighters and air defense missiles. Many units in the armed forces are understrength because military service is voluntary and arduous. As a result of the war-renunciation clause of the constitution, Japan has armed itself with weapons for strategic defense. It has no long-range bombers or missiles, and its aircraft and naval vessels are deployed for air defense and anti-submarine warfare. These platforms could use deep strike missiles if required.

Although Japan's defense budgets—about $34 billion in 1992—rank high by world standards, they are modest in relation to gross domestic product. Japanese defense spending hovers around 1% of GDP. In fact, Japan relies for its military security on US conventional and nuclear forces, and the US has repeatedly urged Japan to shoulder more of its own conventional defense burden. The US maintains extensive military facilities and 40,000 US troops in Japan. US military sales to Japan exceeded $3.8 billion between 1950 and 1986, and $5.2 billion in 1986–91.

18 INTERNATIONAL COOPERATION

Japan was admitted to UN membership on 18 December 1956, and it holds membership in ESCAP and all the nonregional specialized agencies. It is a signatory to GATT and the Law of the Sea, participates in the Colombo Plan, belongs to IDB, and has permanent observer status with the OAS. In 1963, Japan became a member of IMF and the OECD. It is also a charter member of the Asian Development Bank, which came into operation in 1966; Japan furnished $200 million, a share equal to that of the US. Japan has been actively developing peaceful uses for nuclear energy, and in 1970 it signed the Geneva Protocol, which prohibits the use of poisonous and bacteriological weapons. In June 1976, Japan—the only nation to have suffered a nuclear attack—became the 96th signatory to the international Nuclear Nonproliferation Treaty.

Japan has been extending technical and financial aid to many countries, and in 1974 it established the Japan International Cooperation Agency to provide technical assistance to developing nations. Japan also was instrumental in establishing the Asian Productivity Organization, the objective of which is to organize national productivity movements in various Asian countries into a more effective movement on a regional scale. Japan has entered into cultural agreements with many European and Asian nations and maintains an educational exchange program with the US. Through the Japan Overseas Cooperation Volunteers, Japan sends youths to work in developing countries.

19 ECONOMY

Japan's economy is the most advanced in Asia and the second largest in the world, behind that of the US; the size and wealth of its economic enterprises rival those of any nation. Japan was the first Asian country to develop a large urban middle-class industrial society. It was also the first Asian country where a sharp reduction in birthrate set the stage for notable further increases in per capita income.

Since 1952, the number of farmers has fallen sharply, while expansion has been concentrated in industry and trade. Domestic raw materials are far too limited to provide for the nation's needs, and imports are relied on for all the raw cotton, raw wool, bauxite, and crude rubber used, as well as for all oil supplies and varying proportions of other materials. To pay for these materials and for food and other import needs, Japan exports mainly manufactured products. Up until the mid-1980s, economic development depended on continued expansion in exports. With the steady appreciation of the yen in real terms since 1985, however, the country's economic structure has undergone some adjustment. Facilitated by growing wage rates, favorable credit conditions, cuts in personal and corporate income tax rates and other stimulative measures by the government, domestic demand as well as direct foreign investment have played an increasingly important role as a source of growth in recent years.

After two decades of rapid expansion following World War II, the Japanese economy, beginning with the world oil crisis in late 1973, suffered an extremely long and intense recession, one that weakened the world economy as well. In 1974, for the first time since World War II, the GNP fell (by 1.8%). The recession was cushioned, however, by the nation's ability to improve its trade balance (by $11 billion) by increasing exports while reducing imports. The recovery of the mid-1970s was slowed by a second oil crisis, and although the Japanese economy continued to outperform those of most other industrial countries, growth in GNP slowed to an estimated 4.1% yearly in real terms for 1979–82, compared with 8.9% for 1969–72. Meanwhile, the continued stimulation of exports, especially of automobiles and video equipment, combined with Japan's restrictive tariffs and other barriers against imports, led to increasingly strident criticism of the nation's trade practices in the US and Western Europe. As early as 1971, Japan agreed to limit textile exports to the US, and in the 1980s it also imposed limits on exports of steel, automobiles, and television sets. Similar limits were adopted for exports to Canada, France (where criticism focused on videocassette recorders), and the FRG. Nevertheless, Japan's trade surpluses with the US and other countries continued to swell through the mid-1980s, helped by a number of factors, most notably the misalignment of major currencies, particularly between the dollar and the yen.

During the late 1980s, a 70% appreciation of the yen's value against the US dollar helped narrow Japan's trade surplus by 19% for two consecutive years in 1988/89 and 1989/90. This was accompanied by low rates of unemployment as well as strong growth in consumer spending and private investment, in turn contributing to a healthy 5% annual growth rate in the GNP between 1987 and 1990. During the past several years, however, the trend has slowed considerably. The country's trade surplus rebounded to record high levels in 1993, while domestic demand has slackened and real GNP growth fell to 1.5% in 1992, its lowest level since the mid-1950s (aside from an episode of negative growth during the oil crisis-related recession of 1974). The recent downturn notwithstanding, it is likely that the country's educated and well-paid labor force, high rates of household savings and capital investment, and well managed government apparatus will facilitate a healthy pace of economic development in the long term.

²⁰INCOME

In 1992, Japan's GNP was $3,507,841 million at current prices, or $28,220 per capita. For the period 1985–92 the average inflation rate was 1.4%, resulting in a real growth rate in per capita GNP of 4.0%.

In 1992 the GDP was $3,670,980 million in current US dollars. It is estimated that in 1991 agriculture, hunting, forestry, and fishing contributed 2% to GDP; manufacturing, 32%; electricity, gas, and water, 3%; construction, 9%; wholesale and retail trade, 14%; transport, storage, and communication, 6%; finance, insurance, real estate, and business services, 16%; community, social, and personal services, 14%; and other sources, 3%.

²¹LABOR

The labor force in 1990 comprised 63,840,000 persons. The distribution of employed workers in 1992 was as follows: commerce and finance, 30.8%; manufacturing, 24.3%; services, 21.8%; construction, 9.6%; agriculture, forestry, fishing, aquaculture, 6.4%; transportation and communications, 6%; public utilities, 0.5%; mining, 0.1%; and unreported, 0.5%. Females comprised 41% of the work force in 1992. The number of unemployed reached 1,370,000, or 2.1% of the work force, in 1991—down from 2.8% in 1987, which is low by the standards of most industrial countries but high for Japan. Employers tend toward traditional paternalistic, often authoritarian, control over their workers, but in turn most regular workers enjoy permanent status. By 1983, much of the rote work on assembly lines was being done by more than 67,300 robots.

Union membership was always less than half a million before World War II, but jumped to 6.2 million in 1955 and to 12.4 million in 1991. However, the rate of union membership has been decreasing in the past three decades, with 24.5% of all eligible workers unionized in 1990, as against 39% in 1955. Union strength is greatest in local government employees, automobile workers, and electrical machinery workers. Most members are organized in units called enterprise unions, which comprise the employees of a single firm. About 12.4 million workers are affiliated with national organizations, of which the largest is the Japanese Trade Union Confederation (Shin-Rengo), established in 1987 following the dissolution of the Japanese Confederation of Labor (Domei), and incorporating the General Council of Trade Unions (Soyho) as of 1989. The Shin-Rengo comprised 13,262 unions and had 7,615,000 members as of June 1991.

²²AGRICULTURE

Crop production is vital to Japan despite limited arable land (12.1% of the total area) and the highest degree of industrialization in Asia. Steep land (more than 20°) has been terraced for rice and other crops, carrying cultivation in tiny patches far up mountainsides. With the aid of a temperate climate, adequate rainfall, soil fertility built up and maintained over centuries, and such a large farm population that the average farm has an area of only 1.2 hectares (3 acres), Japan has been able to develop intensive cultivation. In 1992, 6.2% of the labor force was engaged in agriculture. Since 1960, the number of farms has decreased by over 25%. Since World War II, modern methods, including commercial fertilizers, insecticides, hybrid seeds, and machinery, have been used so effectively that harvests increased substantially through the 1970s.

In 1990, Japanese production provided for much of domestic consumption: 91% for vegetables; 63% for fruit; 15% for wheat; and 8% for beans. Almost all soybeans and feedstuffs and most of the nation's wheat are imported. In 1992, Japan produced 13.2 million tons of rice, the chief crop. In that year, rice accounted for about 92% of all cereal production. About 46.4% of all arable land is devoted to rice cultivation. Overproduction of rice, as a result of overplanting and a shift to other foods by the Japanese

people, led the government in 1987 to adopt a policy of decreasing rice planting and increasing the acreage of other farm products. Other important crops and their annual production in 1992 (in thousands of tons) include potatoes, 3,650; sugar beets, 3,823; mandarin oranges, 1,400; cabbage, 2,500; wheat, 800; barley, 340; soybeans, 197; tobacco, 77; and tea, 85.

As a result of the US-occupation land reform, which began in late 1946, nearly two-thirds of all farmland was purchased by the Japanese government at low prewar prices and resold to cultivators on easy terms. By the 1980s, nearly all farms were owner-operated, as compared with 23% before reform. A more telling trend in recent years has been the sharp growth in part-time farm households. Most Japanese farm households have one or more persons earning income outside of agriculture.

²³ANIMAL HUSBANDRY

Livestock production has been the fastest-growing sector in Japanese agriculture, with meat production increasing from 1.7 million tons in 1970 to 3.4 million tons in 1992. Over the same time span, however, meat imports increased from 220,000 tons to 1,525,520 tons. In 1990, although Japan was 70% self-sufficient in meat production, it imported $5,013 million in meat and meat preparations; it also imported $571 million in dairy products and eggs, while producing 78% and 98% of domestic consumption of cow's milk and eggs, respectively. In 1992 there were 10,951,000 hogs, 5,025,000 head of beef and dairy cattle, and 335 million chickens. That year, pork production reached 1,446,000 tons (up from 147,318 tons in 1960); beef, 594,000 tons (142,450 tons in 1960); milk, 8,300,000 tons (1,886,997 tons in 1960); and eggs, 2,586,000 tons. Japan is the single largest recipient of US agricultural exports, importing about two-thirds of all US pork and beef exports in 1991.

²⁴FISHING

Japan is the world's foremost fishing nation (accounting on average for about 15% of the world's catch), with an average annual catch of 12 million tons (excluding whaling). The waters off Japan include cold and warm currents in which fish abound. In 1990, there were 416,000 registered fishing boats which sailed both on nearby waters and in other fishing grounds in the Pacific Ocean, the South China Sea, and the Indian and Atlantic oceans. In 1989, per capita daily consumption of fish and shellfish was about 198 gm, one of the world's highest such averages. Annual per capita fish and shellfish consumption from 1988 to 1990 averaged 72 kg (158.7 lb). In 1990, although Japan was 79% self-sufficient in fish production, about $10.5 billion in fish and shellfish was imported in order to satisfy domestic demand.

Whales have been prized in Japan as a source of both food and a variety of byproducts, and Japanese whalers caught 2,769 whales in 1986. Japan ended commercial whaling in 1987, following the imposition of a worldwide ban on the hunting of endangered species of whales by the International Whaling Commission, but announced that it would catch 875 whales for "research" purposes. The 1991 Japanese whale catch of over 20,000 toothed whales of various species included 327 minke, 54 beaked, 355 pilot, and 1 humpback.

Competition for overseas fishing privileges has at various times brought Japan into conflict with Canada over salmon, with the former USSR over fishing in the Sea of Okhotsk and other Soviet waters (between 1905 and 1945 Japan had special treaty privileges in these waters), with the ROK and China over their limitations on Japanese fishing operations, with Australia over pearl fishing in the Arafura Sea, with Indonesia over fishing in what Indonesia regards as inland waters, and with the US, especially over fishing in north Pacific and Alaskan waters. Japan has been adversely affected by the adoption of the 200-mi fishing zone by the US and more than 80 other world nations. Fishing in waters claimed by the US (where about 70% of the Japanese catch originates) or by many other nations now requires payment of fees and special intergovernmental or private agreements.

Fish culture in freshwater pools, as well as in rice paddies, has long been practiced in Japan. Aquaculture provides an additional 1.5 million tons of fish annually. Seaweed culture provides winter season activity for many fishermen. Pearl culture has for more than half a century been the foundation of a valuable export industry.

25FORESTRY

Forests cover nearly 67% of the total land area of Japan and in 1991 supplied about half the domestic demand for lumber and wood pulp. Of 25.1 million hectares (62 million acres) of forest, the Japanese government owns 30.3%, which it maintains under strict regulations limiting overcutting. On private forest lands, cutting is less controlled. About 6.6 million hectares (16.3 million acres) are reforested with trees less than 20 years old. Forest management and erosion control are urgent necessities in a land where gradients are very steep and flooding is frequent. Japan was the world's second leading producer of paper and paperboard in 1991, after the US.

The Japanese cedar (sugi), which grows in most of Japan, is the most exploited species, followed by Japanese cypress (hinoki) and Japanese red pine (akamatsu). In 1991, roundwood production totaled 28.3 million cu m, as compared with 49.1 million cu m in 1965. Throughout the 1980s and early 1990s, Japan has become more reliant on imported wood to satisfy domestic demand. Japan is the world's dominant importer of softwood and tropical hardwood logs, and has become one of the largest importers of softwood lumber.

26MINING

Japan is not rich in minerals, and mining is a relatively insignificant economic activity. For the last century, Japan has been compelled to import nearly all of its petroleum, iron ore, copper, aluminum, and nickel. Coal is the most important mineral product, accounting for slightly more than half of all mineral production by value. Like most other mineral production in Japan, coal production has been undergoing steady decline, falling from 38 million tons in 1970 to 8 million tons in 1991 (the lowest level since 1902). About 40% is produced on Hokkaido, and most of the remainder on Kyushu. Japan is the world's third largest cement producer, and is self sufficient in limestone production, in which it also ranks third highest globally. The following figures give production in thousands of tons in 1991: iron ore, 31; metallic zinc, 133; lead, 18; and copper, 12.

27ENERGY AND POWER

Japan's primary 1992 energy needs were supplied by oil (57%), coal (17%), liquefied natural gas (11%), nuclear power (13%), and hydroelectricity (2%). For many years, Japan has been second only to the US in oil imports, buying 5.3 million barrels of oil a day from overseas in 1992. In 1990, Japan imported some 1,404 million barrels of oil, primarily from the UAE, Saudi Arabia, and Indonesia; 107.5 million tons of coal , mostly from Australia and Canada; 326,751 tons of coke, mostly from China and Australia; and 35.5 million tons of liquefied natural gas, primarily from Malaysia. In 1990, 84.1% of Japan's energy needs were met by imports, the highest such percentage among industrial nations; in contrast, US dependency was 17.2%.

Japan produces less than 1% of its annual petroleum and natural gas requirements; exploration for petroleum continues in the East China Sea and the Sea of Japan. Japan also produced 8 million tons of coal in 1991 (the lowest level since 1902); imports that year totaled 109.4 million tons, more than any other nation. To meet the growing requirements for steam coal by power

plants, Japanese trading companies and energy firms are seeking long-term supply contracts with Australia, China, Colombia, New Zealand, South Africa, and the US In 1991, imports of fuels totaled $54.8 billion (55% of which was for crude and partially refined petroleum), accounting for 23.4% of total imports.

Japan ranked third in the world, behind the US and former USSR, in production of electricity in 1991, with an output of 837.7 billion kwh. Electricity is provided by nine private companies, with the public Electric Power Development Co. and the Japan Atomic Power Co. playing supplementary roles in distribution. As of January 1992, total electricity generating capacity stood at 200 million kw. Nuclear power plants accounted for 16.7% of the total; thermal (oil, natural gas, coal) plants, 63.6%; hydroelectric plants, 19.6%; and other plants (geothermal and other renewable resources), 0.1%. In 1992, Japan ranked fourth in conventional thermal electricity generation (after the US, China, and Russia), with 546.4 billion kwh, or 7.4% of the world's total. In 1990, Japan ranked fourth, behind the US, France, and the former USSR, in nuclear power production, with an installed capacity of 32.2 million kw in 41 reactors. An additional 14 reactors were under construction, with a combined capacity of 14.1 million kw. Japan's share of electricity consumed from nuclear plants is projected to increase by 4.3% each year between 1990 and 2010.

28INDUSTRY

Manufacturing has been a key element in Japan's economic expansion during three periods of phenomenal growth. First, during the 50-year rise of Japan from a feudal society in 1868 to a major world power in 1918, output in manufacturing rose more rapidly than that of other sectors. Second, during the 1930s, when Japan recovered from the world depression earlier and faster than any other country and embarked on an aggressive course in Asia, manufacturing, especially heavy industries, again had the highest rate of growth. Third, in the remarkable recovery since World War II, manufacturing, which had suffered severely during the latter stages of the war, was again a leader, although commerce and finance expanded even more rapidly.

During the 1970s and early 1980s, the rate of Japan's industrial growth surpassed that of any other non-Communist industrialized country. Of the 26 largest industrial companies in the world in the mid-1980s—those with sales of $20 billion or more—four were Japanese: Toyota Motor, Matsushita Electric, Hitachi, and Nissan Motor. In addition to spectacular expansion in the volume of output, Japanese industry has also achieved impressive diversity, with maximal application of efficiency standards and technological input. Manufacturing currently accounts for about 35% of GDP and 24% of the total labor force.

A brief recession forced production cutbacks in 1965; longer and deeper recessions, related to rising world oil costs and diminished supplies, slowed Japan's economy in 1973–75 and again in 1978–80. At the same time, wage rates rose substantially, thereby reducing Japan's competitive advantage vis-á-vis other industrialized nations and prompting a major government effort to promote high-technology industries capable of making the most efficient use of the high educational level and technical competence of the Japanese labor force. Japan's industrial strategy, which involves close cooperation between business, government, and labor, is coordinated by the Ministry of International Trade and Industry (MITI). Particular emphasis has been given by MITI and other government agencies to encouraging and assisting research and development of new products and technolgies.

Facing increasingly stiff competition from overseas trading partners in the 1980s, Japanese firms have responded with several strategies, including product diversification, increased investment in overseas plants, as well as a greater focus on production for the domestic market. Despite declining profits with the economic downturn of the early 1990s, Japanese companies have continued to make large investments in new plants and equipment; in 1992, these outlays amounted to over 20% of the GDP, well outstripping the level of private investment in the US

Manufacture of electrical machinery ranks first in value added, accounting for about 18% of the total in 1991. Nonelectrical machinery ranks second, accounting for 12% of total manufacturing value added, followed by transportation equipment (10% of MVA) and chemicals (9% of MVA). The electronics industry grew with extraordinary rapidity in the 1980s and now leads the world. Radio and television sets and household appliances have been exported in large quantities since World War II; in addition to generators, motors, transformers, and other heavy equipment, the industry now produces automatic devices, electronic computers, videocassette recorders, tape recorders, calculators, and communications and broadcasting equipment. Major electronic products in 1991 included 4.5 million facsimiles; 18.2 million telephones; 3.0 million computers; 28 billion transistors; and 17.7 billion semiconductor integrated circuits. Also produced that year were 11.2 million radios, 15.6 million television sets, and 30.7 million videocassette recorders. Japan plays an increasingly important role in the computer industry. The production value of Japanese personal and general purpose computers totaled ¥2.4 trillion in 1991. By 1987, Japan was fiercely competing with the US in developing high-tech products, such as superconducting materials.

Japan is the world's leading shipbuilder; more than half the ships built are exported, including some of the world's largest oil tankers. Rapid increases in shipbuilding capacity by Brazil and the ROK reduced demand for Japanese-built ships from a peak of 38 million gross tons of new orders in 1973 to 7.0 million gross tons in 1991. The decline prompted direct government intervention in the ailing industry and the closing of close to 37% of dockyard facilities in 1980.

Passenger car production expanded rapidly in the 1970s, as Japan moved to fill rising demand for fuel-efficient cars in the US and Europe. In the early 1980s, Japan emerged as the world's leading automobile producer, topping the US for the first time in the history of the industry. Dominant industry giants are Nissan and Toyota which together produced about three-fifths of all passenger cars in the mid- 1980s. In 1991, a total of 10,412,000 passenger cars and vans were manufactured (up from 7,860,000 in 1985). Restrictions imposed on Japanese automobile exports have promoted a marked increase in Japanese investment in automobile manufacturing facilities (engine manufacture, assembly as well as research and development) in the US, Western Europe, and other overseas markets. In recent years, Japanese manufactures have also sustained growth through greater focus on producing for the booming domestic motor vehicle market, currently the second largest in the world. Japan's superior technology in the design of bicycles, motorcycles, buses, and high-speed trains has been another major factor in the growth of the transport industry. In 1991, Japan produced 7.4 million bicycles and 5.0 million motorcycles, as well as 3.5 million trucks and buses.

The chemical and petrochemicals industry has been another of the economy's key growth sectors since the late 1960s, in part due to rising domestic demand. Products include industrial chemicals such as sulfuric acid (7,057,000 tons] in 1991), caustic soda (3,781,000 tons), and fertilizers, as well as plastics, dyestuffs, paints, and other items for domestic use. Polyethylene production increased by 10–15% annually during the late 1980s; output in 1991 was 2,982,000 tons. Japan must import much of the iron ore and coking coal used in its steel industry, which ranked second only to the former USSR's in the mid-1980s. Output of crude steel peaked at 119.3 million tons in 1973 but declined to 109.6 million tons in 1991.

Textiles and apparel, Japan's main exports during the years immediately following World War II, have steadily declined in importance and accounted for only 2.5% of total value added in 1991 (as compared with 3.5% in 1985). Output of cotton and woolen fabrics, yarns, and rayon and acetate remains substantially below 1965 levels. The Japanese textile industry has been especially hard hit by rising wage rates and competition from developing nations, especially the other industrializing countries of East Asia.

Other manufactures in 1991 included 389.8 million watches, 17.7 million 35-mm still cameras, and 4.3 million microwave ovens.

[29]SCIENCE AND TECHNOLOGY

The Japanese now rank second only to the United States in spending on scientific research and technology development, with a total of over one billion yen spent in 1993 (at 1993 exchange rates, this equals about $101 billion). By comparison, in 1993, the US government and industry funded nearly $180 billion in research and development. However, it is interesting to note that in Japan, 80% of all research and development is carried out by industry. In the United States, industry undertakes about 54% of all research and development (the US government supports the rest). This is important because industry is more likely to support the type of research that will result in new technologies and products. Therefore, the United States' lead over Japan may be much narrower than it appears: Japanese industry spent $80 billion, US industry spent $97 billion in 1993. For many people, this breakdown of research and development funding explains why Japan has become such an economic powerhouse: much more of the total research and development budget is focused on near-term and commercial science and technology. Some of the more successful applications of the fruits of Japanese research and development include high-speed trains, robotics, semiconductor chips, telecommunications, cancer research, and environmental technologies.

In 1990, slightly over 91,000 Japanese university students graduated with science and engineering degrees. Many joined the 2.3 million scientists and engineers already working in Japan. Despite Japan's economic downturn of the early 1990s, it is likely that investments in both equipment and personnel will grow.

In terms of the Japanese government's role in national science and technology, three ministries are important. The Ministry of Education, or *Monbusho*, provides most of the support and funding for scientific education and training at the university level in Japan. In the 1990s, *Monbusho* will lead a national effort to improve Japan's education of science and technology at universities, particularly in "basic" research (areas where research does not necessarily have to pay off in commercial products). Another organization, the Science and Technology Agency (STA) promotes science and technology policies, and acts as the Prime Minister's leading policy and budgetary agency. It performs this function through annual "white papers" which describe the current state—and future goals—of Japanese science and technology. The ministry of International Trade and Industry (MITI) is probably the ministry best known by Americans. MITI promotes and protects Japanese industry by sending them signals and giving guidance to those firms which undertake research and development. MITI has been instrumental in providing close government-industry cooperation in many high technology fields, including computers, electronics, and biotechnology.

Regional research institutions such as Tskuba Science City and Kansai Science Park also play a role in fostering Japanese research and development. Their growth since the 1970s has begun to shift some of the focus and power of the national government and industry in Tokyo to the regional prefectures. International cooperation with the United States in areas like global warming and space launches may create new opportunities for greater scientific research at local, regional, and national levels in Japan.

30DOMESTIC TRADE

Marketing services and channels are complex and varied. In 1991, 11,710,000 persons were engaged in domestic, wholesale, and retail trade. The number of wholesale and retail stores was 2,067,000; of these, 72% were small stores with fewer than four employees. Street hawkers and peddlers provide certain foods and small consumer items; street stalls offer food, clothing, and household and other goods. Specialty shops exist in great profusion, and about 100 associations of such shops represent common interests. Japan's first department store was opened in 1910. In 1957 there were 170 department stores; by 1991, the figure had risen to 2,004, accounting for 14% of total retail sales. There are chain stores owned and operated by a single management, and there are voluntary chains of independent stores operating in association. Japan also has numerous cooperatives, principally consumer, agricultural, and fishing. A key characteristic of the country's distribution system has been the long term and carefully cultivated nature of the supplier and wholesaler or retail store relationship, necessitating considerable committment of time and outreach effort by foreign companies wishing to enter the Japanese market. Recent revisions in the Large Scale Retail Store Law has loosened government regulation of the distribution system, allowing the establishment of large discounters and mega-stores such as Toys-R-Us, which are likely to offer growing competition to smaller retailers in the future.

In retail trade, cash transactions have been traditional, but various forms of installment selling are increasingly being used, especially in the sale of durable goods. The use of charge accounts is growing rapidly. Promotion by displays, advertising, and other methods used in Western countries is growing rapidly in Japan. Advertising appears in the daily press, in the numerous weekly and monthly magazines, and in special publications of many kinds. Radio and television also carry extensive advertising, excepting those channels run by the government's Japan Broadcasting Corporation. Normal shop hours are 10 AM to 8 PM, seven days a week, although department stores shut their doors at 7 PM and are closed one day a week; government offices are open 9 AM to 5 PM, Monday through Friday, and from 9 to 12:30 on the first and third Saturday of every month only. Banks are open from 9 AM to 3 PM Monday through Friday, and are closed on Saturdays and Sundays.

31FOREIGN TRADE

Foreign trade remains essential to the Japanese economy. Imports consist mostly of fuel, foodstuffs, industrial raw materials, and industrial machinery. Exports are varied, but manufactures now account for nearly all of the total. Cars represent a leading export product, with the US, Canada, Australia, Germany and the UK the main markets. The export of office machinery, scientific and optical equipment is also important. South Korea, China, and Taiwan are among the main buyers of Japan's iron and steel, while plastic materials and fertilisers are shipped primarily to South Korea and the Southeast Asian countries, and woven fabrics are supplied to China, the US, Hong Kong, and Saudi Arabia. Only a small fraction of Japan's total exports (around 0.5%) consists of food items, mainly fish.

In light of growing overseas concern about Japan's continuing large trade surplus, the US and Japanese governments collaborated on the Structural Impediments Initiative of 1989. Steps taken in wake of the Initiative's 1990 report have included a variety of import and direct foreign investment promotion measures, including deregulation, accelerated goverment spending on public infrastructure, and support services for foreign businesses.

Japan ranked third in the world in total trade, after the US and FRG, in 1992, with exports of ¥43.0 trillion and imports of ¥29.5 trillion. Exports that year were about 1.5% above those of 1991.

Principal Japanese exports in 1991 and 1992 (in billions of yen) were as follows:

	1991	1992
Transport equipment	10,485	11,030
Nonelectrical machinery	9,362	9,659
Electrical machinery	9,934	9,804
Chemicals	2,354	2,423
Iron and steel products	1,835	1,681
Precision instruments	2,087	2,028
Other exports	6,303	6,387
TOTALS	42,360	43,012

Principal imports in 1991 and 1992 (in billions of yen) were as follows:

	1991	1992
Petroleum & petrol. products	5,081	4,613
Electrical machinery	1,976	1,852
Nonelectrical machinery	1,936	1,844
Textile products	1,841	1,939
Fish and fish products	1,593	1,592
Gas	1,431	1,287
Metal ores and scrap	1,062	880
Coal and coke	862	770
Wood	965	968
Other imports	15,153	13,782
TOTALS	31,900	29,527

While the US retained its position as Japan's single most important trade partner through the early 1990s, its share of the export market has declined considerably since the mid-1980s. In 1992, the US accounted for only 28.1% of Japan's exports (down from 38.4% in 1986) and 22.4% of its imports (as compared with 22.8% in 1986). Other leading partners in 1992 included the FRG, the ROK, Taiwan, China, and Australia.

Distribution of trade by principal trade partners in 1991 (in billions of yen) was as follows:

	EXPORTS	IMPORTS	BALANCE
US	12,121	6,622	5,499
FRG	2,575	1,362	1,213
ROK	2,253	1,486	767
Taiwan	2,460	1,200	1,260
China	1,510	2,145	−635
Hong Kong	2,626	259	2,367
Australia	892	1,577	−685
Indonesia	706	1,550	−844
UK	1,558	620	938
Canada	898	973	−75
Thailand	1,312	753	559
Singapore	1,641	392	1,249
Sa'udi Arabia	614	1,290	−676
Malaysia	1,028	833	195
United Arab Emirates	345	1,233	−888
France	800	685	115
Netherlands	1,027	167	860
Iran	337	330	7
Other countries	8,309	6,050	2,259
TOTALS	43,012	29,527	13,485

32BALANCE OF PAYMENTS

Beginning in 1981, surpluses in Japan's current accounts increased rapidly, reaching $49 billion in 1985 and $86 billion in 1986, the latter being 18 times the level of 1981. These huge surpluses resulted largely from the high value of the dollar relative to the yen; price declines of primary goods, such as petroleum, also enhanced Japan's favorable trade position. Japan's mounting surpluses and the rising deficits of the US forced the US and other leading industrial nations to attempt to realign their currencies, especially the dollar and the yen, in September 1985. Within two years the yen rose 70% against the dollar. The yen's appreciation increased the competitiveness of American products and contributed to the reduction of Japan's external imbalances through 1990. Japan's current account balance surplus was less pronounced by 1989, partly due to an increasing services deficit from high foreign expenses. Rising transfer payments for the provision of foreign aid to developing nations have also reduced the current account surplus. In 1990, the current account surplus fell by 37.4%, due to higher expenses for imported oil and rising expenditures by Japanese traveling abroad. Whereas long-term capital outflows exceeded Japan's current account surplus from 1984 through 1990, in 1991 the outflow shifted predominantly to short-term capital, and overseas direct investment slowed.

In 1992 merchandise exports totaled $330.87 billion and imports $198.47 billion. The merchandise trade balance was $132.40 billion.

33BANKING AND SECURITIES

Japan's highly sophisticated banking system continues to play a dominant role in financing the country's economic development. Banks provide not only short-term but also long-term credit, which often in effect becomes fixed capital in industry. In terms of sheer size, Japanese banks occupy eight of the top ten spots in world-wide bank ratings.

The controlling national monetary institutions are the Bank of Japan (founded in 1882) and the Ministry of Finance. The Bank of Japan, as central bank, has power over note issue and audits financial institutions to provide guidance for improving banking and management practices. Ceilings for interest rates are set by the bank, while actual rates, commissions, and discounts are arranged by unofficial agreements among bankers and other financial institutions, including the National Bankers' Association. A new banking law, replacing the National Banking Law of 1928, was adopted in 1982. Its objectives are to increase competition in the financial world by enabling banks to sell bonds and by authorizing both banks and securities firms to sell commercial paper and certificates of deposit. At the end of 1993, the money supply, as measured by M2. totaled ¥518.2 trillion.

Twelve important city banks, with branches throughout the country, account for about two-thirds of all commercial bank assets, the rest accruing to 131 regional banks, 7 trust banks, and 83 foreign banks. In addition, 112 foreign banks have representative offices in Japan. Of special interest are the postal savings facilities, which are used by many Japanese families and have assumed many of the aspects of a huge state-owned banking business.

The Bank of Tokyo, a city bank and the only one that specializes in foreign exchange business under the provisions of the Foreign Exchange Bank Law, finances about one-fourth of all Japanese foreign transactions. Other foreign exchange banks include the city banks, long-term credit banks, trust banks, major local banks, major mutual loan and savings banks, and the Japanese branches of foreign banks. Such governmental financial institutions as the Japan Export-Import Bank, the Central Bank for Commercial and Industrial Associations, and the Central Bank for Agriculture and Forestry participate in foreign exchange markets by authorization of the Ministry of Finance.

Major securities exchanges are in Tokyo, Hiroshima, Fukuoka, Nagoya, and Osaka; small regional exchanges are in Kyoto, Niigata, and Sapporo. Although prior to World War II most stocks were held by large business firms (zaibatsu), stocks are now available for public subscription. The Tokyo Stock Exchange, one of the largest in the world, is the most important in Japan.

34INSURANCE

Firms may not engage in life and non-life insurance at the same time. In 1987 there were 47 Japanese insurance firms (24 life and 23 non-life) and 41 foreign companies transacting insurance business. Premiums totaled $241 billion, or 9.07% of the GDP. Per capita premiums totaled $678.6 for life and $989.6 for non-life insurance. Both joint-stock and mutual companies are permitted.

Life insurance is by far the most extensive of all classes of insurance; premium income is more than three times that of all non-life premium income. In 1985, life premium income totaled ¥15,480 billion. Life insurance firms had total assets of ¥53.9 trillion as of 1985. At the close of 1992, life insurance in force totaled ¥1,897 trillion. Japan is now the world's largest holder of life and health insurance.

In the non-life field, automobile insurance is the largest sector, accounting for 39.5% of the business in fiscal year 1989, when ¥2,234 billion of premiums were paid for voluntary and ¥1,160 billion for compulsory auto insurance. (Automobile liability insurance is compulsory.) Personal accident insurance was next in importance with 30.2%, followed by fire, marine cargo, and marine hull insurance.

35PUBLIC FINANCE

Plans for the national budget usually begin in August, when various agencies submit their budget requests to the Ministry of Finance. On the basis of such requests, the ministry, other government agencies, and the ruling party start negotiations. The government budget plan usually is approved by the Diet without difficulty, and the budget goes into effect in April. Deficits, financed by public bond sales, have steadily increased in size since the 1973 oil crisis. As a result, the ratio of gross debt to GNP has risen from 8% in 1970 to 60% by 1987. By 1990, debt servicing was absorbing over 20% of budgeted expenditures.

Since 1982, Japan has pursued tight fiscal policies and has attempted to constrain government debt. In June 1987, however, as a response to appeals from other nations to reduce international imbalances, Japan initiated a $35 billion public works spending package, followed up by $10 billion in tax cuts.

In 1990 Japan's total public debt stood at ¥239,932 billion, of which ¥1,186 billion was financed abroad. Public debt issued in 1992 amounted to ¥7.2 billion, with an outstanding amount of over ¥1.4 million per capita, or 35.9% of GNP.

36TAXATION

After World War II, Japan adopted a tax system relying mainly on direct taxes, like those in the US and the UK. The most important of these are the income tax and corporation tax.

The National Tax Administration Agency, a branch of the Ministry of Finance, administers income and corporation tax laws. In addition, the Tax System Council files recommendations for revision of the system every three years. Individuals are subject to a national income tax as well as local (prefectural and municipal) residence and business taxes. In 1993, income tax rates ranged from 20% on taxable income of ¥3 million or less to 65% on income over ¥20 million. In 1993, the national corporate income tax rate was 37.5%, with a local inhabitants tax of 7.76% and a local enterprise tax of 13.2%. These rates are exclusive of temporary surtaxes and a capital gains tax.

Additional national taxes include customs duties; a 3% value-added tax; a stamp tax; inheritance and gift taxes; a monopoly profits tax; a sugar excise tax; taxes on liquor, gasoline, and other commodities; and travel, admissions, and local road taxes.

37CUSTOMS AND DUTIES

The Japanese tariff system is administered by the Customs Bureau of the Ministry of Finance. Under pressure from trading partners alarmed over their trade deficits with Japan, the government in

1979 agreed to implement over an eight-year period (subsequently accelerated) a series of tariff cuts and associated market-opening measures known as the Tokyo Round Mutual Tariff Reductions. The Tokyo Round lowered the effective overall tariff rate from 3.7% to 3%, one of the world's lowest, with nearly half of all imports entering without levy. As of 1993, the tariff was 3.4%. In 1987, tariffs were removed from tobacco and liquor (except beer and sake), and the rates on aluminum products were lowered. Quantity quotas and tariff quotas are still applied to some goods. There is a free-trade zone at Naha, on Okinawa; no free-trade zones function on the main islands.

38FOREIGN INVESTMENT

Cumulative foreign investment in Japan totaled an estimated $22,770 million as of 1991 (up from $6,653 million in 1985), of which 44% was held by US firms; UK, Swiss, FRG, Netherlands, Canadian and Hong Kong holdings are also important. Most foreign direct investment in Japan has been directed towards the manufacturing sector (60%), followed by retail and wholesale trade (16%) and finance, insurance and business services (7%).

Japanese investments abroad have expanded steadily since the 1970s, the result both of liberalization on the outflow of capital and of the prosperity of the Japanese economy. It has also been due in part to increased investment in the US and EC as a conciliatory move to lessen the trade gap between Japan and the two industrial regions. Net annual direct investment outflows remained near $5 billion in the late 1970s but climbed steadily after between 1985 and 1991 when they reached $48,024 million, declining somewhat to $30,726 million in 1992. Of the total Japanese overseas investment of $352.4 billion outstanding in 1991, $148.6 billion was invested in the US (up from $25.3 billion in 1985), $23.2 billion in the UK, $18.6 billion in Australia, $14.8 billion in the Netherlands, $12.7 billion in Indonesia, and $10.8 billion in Hong Kong. Some 44% of Japanese investment was in North America (up from 32% in 1985), 15% in Asia (down from 23% in 1985), 12% in Latin America and the Caribbean (as compared with 19% in in 1985); 19% in Western Europe (as compared with 13% in 1985), 2% in Oceania and Africa and 1% in the Middle East and the Central and Eastern European countries. About 27% of the investment total was in manufacturing, 10% in retail and wholesale commerce, 35% in finance, insurance and business services and only 5% in mining.

39ECONOMIC DEVELOPMENT

Japan's phenomenal economic growth since the 1950s has been based on an efficient blend of two economic tendencies. First is government activism in national planning and implementation, with guidance of the largely free economy via sophisticated and powerful monetary and fiscal policies. Second is the distinctively Japanese way of coupling largely private ownership of assets with conservative, public-spirited management. Especially significant is the role of the Ministry of International Trade and Industry (MITI), which coordinates national industrial policies consistent with economic and social growth. In a unique government-industry collaboration sometimes referred to overseas as "Japan, Inc.," MITI selects and nurtures industries targeted as important to Japan's future economic growth. Industries so targeted have included chemicals, iron and steel, shipbuilding, and transistor radios in the 1960s; automobiles and electronics in the 1970s; and computers, computer chips, and other high-technology industries for the 1980s. In addition to stimulating new industries, MITI also smoothes the way for plant closings and worker retraining in industries targeted for de-emphasis, such as textiles in the 1970s and the ailing coal-mining and shipbuilding industries in the 1980s. Most recently, MITI has also assumed an active role in lessening Japan's positive trade imbalances through a variety of import promotion measures, in collaboration with both domestic companies and foreign firms.

The objectives of maintaining rapid GNP growth, controlling inflation, and developing Japan's social and industrial infrastructure have been the concern of the Economic Planning Agency, which produced the successful Ikeda plan (to double the national income between 1961 and 1970) and releases projections of key indicators at frequent intervals. In the main, the Ikeda plan consisted of a series of projections of growth in a free market economy, with the basic assumption—the continued growth of Japan's overseas trade—largely outside of government control. During the plan's 10-year span, an annual growth of 11% in GNP was realized, as against the forecast rate of 7.2%. An economic and social development plan (1967–75) accomplished a GNP growth rate of 10.6%, as against 8.2% projected.

A second economic and social plan (1970–75) projected a continued annual growth rate of 10.6%. The 1973 world oil crisis and its aftermath severely shook Japan's trade-dependent economy, however; in 1974, the GNP actually shrank by 1.8%, the first and only such negative growth in three decades. In 1975, the cabinet approved a new economic and social plan for 1979–85 calling for an average annual growth rate of 5.7%. However, the impact of the second oil crisis in 1978 necessitated downward revisions of projected growth targets. Plans to stimulate the economy by increasing public-works spending and cutting taxes were approved in October 1983 and in May 1987. Also enacted in 1989 was a Value-Added-Tax to strengthen the government's revenue base while allowing reductions in personal and corporate income tax.

In 1988, a five-year plan was adopted to sustain real GNP growth at 3.75% per year, maintain low unemployment (2.5% per year), contain inflation, reduce the country's trade surplus, and improve the quality of life through a shorter work week and stabilized property prices. Many these objectives were achieved or surpassed in the closing years of the decade. Since 1992, however, the economy's downturn has been likened by some some analysts to the 1974 recession in its severity and length. Economic indicators have included steep declines and sluggish recovery in the stock market index since 1989, falling real estate prices, as well as a shrunken rate of GNP growth, despite surging exports. To prompt a recovery, the Ministry of Finance approved large stimulus packages for 1992 and 1993, totaling $85.6 billion and $119 billion in expenditures, respectively. Under the Structural Impediments Initiative, the government has sought to sustain growth while also reducing the country's external trade imbalances. Among the main steps taken under the Initiative is a 10-year program targeting the expenditure of up to $8 trillion for the construction or renovation of airports, bridges, roads, ports, telecommunications systems, resorts, retirement communities, medical facilities, and other forms of public infrastructure development.

Japan's financial assistance to developing countries and international agencies has grown significantly in recent years, making it one of the world's leading donor countries and its largest net creditor. The government has committed itself to large increases in official development assistance to developing countries and multilateral agencies since the late 1980s. In 1991, ODA totaled $11.0 million, as compared with $3,797 million in 1985. Private outflows in 1991 totaled $11.1 million, as compared with $8,022 million in 1985. Current plans direct a further increase in the country's ODA budget to $20 billion by 1996. Among the top recipients of bilateral ODA from Japan are Indonesia, China, the Philippines, Thailand, Bangladesh, and Malaysia.

40SOCIAL DEVELOPMENT

Living standards reflect Japan's rapid economic development since the mid-1960s. Greatly contributing to the social stability of the nation is the strong sense of family solidarity among the Japanese; virtually every home has its butsudan, or altar of the ancestors, and most elderly people are cared for in the homes of their grown children. Further contributing to social stability is Japan's employment system, which is noted for its "lifetime employment" of workers from the time they enter the company after completing their education to the time they retire. Layoffs and dismissals of employees are rare, even during times of recession. Change is evident in the fact that women now make up 40% of Japan's employed workers; an increasing number of women pursue permanent careers, although very few have attained management positions. The Equal Employment Opportunity Law, passed in May 1987, makes it illegal to restrict women to low-paying or part-time jobs and prohibits segregated help-wanted advertisements. Between 1973 and 1988, the marriage rate declined from 9.9 per 1,000 population to 5.8, while the divorce rate increased from 1.04 to 1.3. Matches initiated by a go-between, or o-miai (half of all marriages in 1966), had declined dramatically by the mid-1980s. Roughly 58% of couples of childbearing age were using contraception in 1990. Abortion for health or economic reasons has been widely available since 1948.

The present social insurance system, considerably expanded in the 1970s, includes national health insurance, welfare annuity insurance, maternity coverage, unemployment insurance, workers' accident compensation insurance, seamen's insurance, a national government employees' mutual aid association, and day workers' health insurance. It also provides pension plans designed to maintain living standards for the elderly, based on years of employment, and for families of deceased workers. Per capita expenditure on social security programs remains low, however, in relation to expenditure in many other industrial nations.

Nearly the entire population receives benefits in one form or another from the health insurance system. Health insurance is compulsory for those employed at enterprises with five or more workers, and premiums are shared equally by the insured and their employers. Those not covered at work are insured through the National Health Insurance program. Other sickness and health insurance is in force among farmers, fishermen, and their dependents. Unemployment coverage is obligatory for all enterprises regardless of size; workers' compensation must also be provided by employers.

The Daily Life Security Law (1946) laid the groundwork for an ever-growing livelihood assistance (welfare) program. Out of this have come laws pertaining to child welfare, physically handicapped persons' welfare, social welfare service, welfare fund loans to mothers and children, aid to the war-wounded and ill, and aid to families of deceased soldiers. The system provides direct aid for livelihood; education; housing; medical, maternity, and occupational disability; and funerals. More than a thousand welfare offices throughout the nation are staffed by full-time, salaried welfare secretaries and assisted by voluntary help. Institutions have been established to care for the aged, those on relief, and those needing rehabilitation. Numerous private organizations assist government agencies.

In 1985, a two-tiered pension system was mandated by law. The first tier consists of "national pension insurance" paid to all residents at a flat rate; the second tier consists of employment- or earnings- related coverage. There are special pension programs for public employees, private school teachers and employees, and employees of agricultural, forestry, and fishery cooperatives.

41HEALTH

The Ministry of Health and Welfare has become the central administrative agency responsible for maintaining and promoting public health, welfare, and sanitation. All hospitals and clinics are subject to government control with respect to their standards and spheres of responsibility. In 1992, there were 16 hospital beds

and 1.64 doctors per 1,000 people. Every practitioner in the field of medicine or dentistry must receive a license from the Ministry of Health and Welfare. In addition, the ministry recognizes and authorizes certain quasi-medical practices, including massage, acupuncture, moxa-cautery, and judo-orthopedics, all based upon traditional Japanese health professions.

Expanded examination and treatment have brought about a dramatic decrease in the death rate from tuberculosis, the major cause of death in the 1940s. In 1990, there were 42 reported cases of tuberculosis per 100,000 people. At the same time, death rates from cancer and heart disease have risen considerably and now rank among the leading causes of death, trailing cerebrovas- cular diseases. In 1990, the number of cancer patients increased 60% (to 810,000) from 1985. Japanese medical researchers have been working on research for a new cure for breast cancer.

Infant mortality dropped to 4 per 1,000 live births in 1992, in contrast with the 1930 rate of 124. The overall mortality rate was 7.5 per 1,000 people in 1993. In 1990, major causes of death per 100,000 people were: noncommunicable diseases (306); communicable diseases and maternal/perinatal causes (51); and injuries (41). Average life expectancy was 80 years in 1992, among the highest rates in the world.

There were 1.22 million births in 1991 and 1.39 million in 1992. Immunization rates for children up to one year old in 1992 were: tuberculosis (85%); diphtheria, pertussis, and tetanus (87%); polio (90%); and measles (66%).

42HOUSING

A severe housing shortage plagued Japan after World War II. It is estimated that in 1947, two years after the war's end, the housing deficit amounted to more than 4 million units. A construction program resulted in 9.7 million new units by the end of 1965. The following year, the government undertook a five-year plan for the construction of 7.6 million houses by mid-1971; the plan was designed to fulfill the goal of "one house for each family."

Housing construction peaked at 1.9 million units in 1973; despite efforts to promote construction as a means of stimulating the domestic economy, construction lagged in later years, falling to between 1.1 million and 1.5 million units in the 1980s. The decline reflects not so much a saturation of demand—many Japanese regard their housing as inadequate—as a rapid rise in land and construction costs, especially in the Tokyo, Nagoya, and Osaka metropolitan areas, which has put new housing out of the reach of potential buyers. As of 1992, the average salaried worker in Tokyo could only afford a house 40km outside the Tokyo metropolitan area. Condominiums and prefabricated homes provided much of the nation's new housing in the 1980s. In fiscal 1987, low interest rates pushed new housing starts to 1.729 million units; they declined in 1988 to 1.6 million, and fell to 1.343 million in 1991 with the start of the recession. There were a total of 47,607,000 housing units in 1992.

43EDUCATION

Japan's entire educational system was reorganized along US lines after World War II, adhering to a 6-3-3-4 plan (6 years of primary school, 3 years of lower secondary school, 3 years of upper secondary school—full-time, part-time or correspondence—and 4 years of college). Education is compulsory and provided free of charge for the first 9 years, from age 6 through 14. Coeducation has become an accepted principle. Virtually the entire adult population is literate.

Entrance into high schools, the stage following the compulsory level, is by examination only, and most of these schools charge tuition. Would-be national and local public university students must pass entrance examinations in Japanese, English, mathematics, science, and social studies. There are three types of institutions for higher education—universities, junior colleges and technical colleges, all of which receive prefectural and national support or annual subsidies. There are 95 national universities, with each prefectural capital having one school; the remainder are in the principal cities. The largest religious bodies, both Christian and Buddhist, maintain important universities and other educational institutions. There are many special schools for the handicapped.

Enrollment at the compulsory elementary and junior high school levels is very high, approaching 100%, with some 95.1% continuing into more advanced levels as of 1990. In that year, 9,373,295 students were enrolled in the 24,827 elementary schools; 5,369,162 students in the 11,275 lower secondary schools; and 5,623,336 students in the 5,506 upper secondary schools. There were 947 special schools with 93,497 students enrolled. In the 62 technical colleges, 52,930 students were enrolled. The 593 junior colleges had 479,389 students and 507 universities had 2,133,362 students.

Educational activities for adults and youths are organized both by government and private bodies. There is a board of education in each of the 47 prefectures and 3,000 municipalities and these serve as the local education authority. The central education authority is the Ministry of Education, which provideS guidance and financial assistance to the local bodies.

44LIBRARIES AND MUSEUMS

In 1948, the National Diet Library Law established the National Diet Library to provide reference service to the Diet, other libraries, and the general public. In 1949, this library absorbed the Ueno Library (the former national library) as one of its branches. The National Diet Library acts as a legal depository for Japanese publications and is also a depository library for the UN. There are over 9.5 million volumes in the library's collection.

Public libraries are beginning to find their place in Japanese life. Prior to the enactment of the Library Law of 1950, 70% of those who utilized libraries were students and scholars. Today, libraries are information centers, and increasing numbers of citizens are patronizing them. In 1990 there were 1,475 public libraries with total holdings of almost 162 million volumes; in 1987 there were 1,398 public and private college and university libraries, with total holdings of over 200 million volumes.

Except in large cities, typical Japanese museums take the form of the treasure halls of shrines or temples. In 1987 there were 775 museums, zoos, botanical gardens, and aquariums. There were 61,862,000 museum visitors in 1987. Important museums include the National Science Museum, Museum of Modern Art, Calligraphy Museum, and the Tokyo Metropolitan Art Museum, all located in Toyko.

45MEDIA

Telephone and telegraph services are offered by Nippon Telephone and Telegraph, which was privatized in 1986, and by Japan Telecom and other companies that entered the market after Nippon Telegraph and Telephone's monopoly ended in 1985. In 1991, Japan had 66,636,000 telephones. Telex, fax, and international telegram services are provided by Kokusai Denshin–Denwa (KDD).

A semigovernmental enterprise, the Japan Broadcasting Corp. (Nihon Hoso Kyokai—NHK), plays a large role in Japan's radio and television communications. As of 1991, the total of NHK-operated and commercial radio stations reached 1,134 Many commercial stations are connected with large newspaper companies. Started in 1935, Radio Japan is also beamed by NHK throughout the world. NHK initiated television broadcasting in 1953. In 1992, Japan had 16,275 television stations, about half of them operated by NHK. Color television broadcasting began in 1960; multiplex broadcasting, for stereophonic or multiple-language programming, was made available in Tokyo and other metropolitan areas in 1978. In 1991, there were 112.5 million radios and 76 million television sets in Japan.

The Japanese press is among the world's largest in terms of newspaper circulation; in ratio of copies to population, roughly 570 per 1,000 in 1991, Japan leads the world. In 1991, daily newspapers numbered 158, with a total circulation of 71,228,000. The Japanese press is one of the most vigorous and outspoken in the world. It operates under the constitutional provision of an absolute prohibition of censorship.

The leading Japanese dailies, with their 1991 circulations, are as follows:

CIRCULATION	MORNING	EVENING
TOKYO		
Yomiuri Shimbun	9,722,000	4,705,700
Asahi Shimbun	8,197,600	4,740,700
Mainichi Shimbun	4,169,600	2,143,300
Nihon Keizai Shimbun	1,719,200	1,043,900
Tokyo Shimbun	800,300	533,100
Sankei Shimbun	773,600	220,200
OSAKA		
Yomiuri Shimbun	2,399,442	1,457,804
Asahi Shimbun	2,321,868	1,435,619
Mainichi Shimbun	1,437,610	939,986
Sankei Shimbun	1,188,255	717,466
OTHER CITIES		
Chunichi Shimbun (Nagoya)	2,160,100	845,100
Kyoto Shimbun (Kyoto)	498,000	364,600

There are two domestic news agencies: the Kyodo News Service, with 50 domestic bureaus and with foreign bureaus in every major overseas news center; and the Jiji Press, serving commercial and government circles.

46ORGANIZATIONS

There are an enormous number of organizations in Japan, including such standard bodies as the Japan Red Cross, Japan Chamber of Commerce (with regional and local branches), General Council of Trade Unions, Congress of Labor Unions, Federation of Employers Associations, Rotary Club, Japan Medical Association, Japan Actors' Society, Motion Picture Association of Japan, Japan Athletic Federation, All-Japan Boy Scouts League and Girl Scouts League, Japan YMCA and YWCA, and Japan Youth Association.

The Institute of Art Research and the National Institute of Japanese Literature are important in the cultural field. The Society for International Cultural Relations, established in 1934, is active in the publishing field and in cultural exchange.

47TOURISM, TRAVEL, AND RECREATION

Tourism in Japan is regarded as a major industry, since many foreign visitors as well as the Japanese themselves tour the country extensively. In 1991, Japan had an estimated 3.53 million foreign visitors. Roughly half a million were American and approximately the same number were European, while nearly 1.7 million came from Japan's neighbors in Northeast Asia. Almost one third (921,000) were business travelers. Tourist expenditures for 1991 totaled approximately $3.43 billion, and Japan's 217,016 hotel rooms had a 75% rate of occupancy.

Japan's chief sightseeing attractions are in the ancient former capital of Kyoto: Nijo Castle, Heian Shrine, the 13th-century Sanjusangendo temple and the Kinkaku-ji (Temple of the Golden Pavilion), the Ryoan-ji (Temple of the Peaceful Dragon), famed for its garden of stones and raked sand, and numerous other ancient Buddhist temples and Shinto shrines. Nearby sights in the vicinity of Nara include the Great Buddha, a huge bronze statue originally cast in the 8th century; the Kofuku-ji pagoda; and

Horyu-ji, the 7th-century temple from which Buddhism spread throughout Japan. There are few historic sites in the capital—Tokyo was devastated by an earthquake in 1923 and virtually destroyed in World War II—but nearby attractions include Mt. Fuji and the hot springs of Fuji-Hakkone-Izu National Park; Nikko National Park, site of the Toshogu Shrine, where the first Tokugawa shogun is entombed; and the summer and winter sports facilities in the mountains of central Japan—the so-called Japan Alps. The Hiroshima Peace Park and Peace Memorial Museum commemorate the destruction of the city by an atomic bomb in 1945.

Baseball is Japan's national pastime; there are two professional leagues, each with six teams. Sumo, a Japanese form of wrestling, is also popular, with tournaments held six times a year. Golf, an expensive sport because of the lack of open space, is used mainly as a means of entertaining business clients. Other pastimes include judo, karate, table tennis, fishing, and volleyball. Gardening is the most popular hobby among men and women alike.

48FAMOUS JAPANESE

Murasaki Shikibu (late 10th–early 11th cent.) was the author of *The Tale of Genji*, probably the best-known Japanese literary classic in English since it was first translated in the 1920s. Zeami (Motokiyo, 1363–1443) was an actor who established Noh theater and wrote a number of plays that have been part of the Noh repertoire ever since. Monzaemon Chikamatsu (1653–1724) wrote plays for the Bunraku theater, many of which later became part of the repertoire of Kabuki. Basho (Matsuo Munefusa, 1644–94) perfected the writing of the poetic form now known as haiku. In this genre, three other poets are also known: Buson Yosa (1716–83), Issa Kobayashi (1763–1827), and the modern reformer Shiki Masaoka (1867–1902). Ryunosuke Akutagawa (1892–1927) is best known for his story "Rashomon." Prominent modern novelists include Jun'ichiro Tanizaki (1886–1965); Yasunari Kawabata (1899–1972), winner of the 1968 Nobel Prize for literature; Kobo Abe (b.1924); and Yukio Mishima (1925–70). A leading modern writer and Zen Buddhist scholar was Daisetz Teitaro Suzuki (1870–1966).

In art, Sesshu (1420–1506) was the most famous landscape artist of his day. Ogata Korin (1658–1716) was a master painter of plants, animals, and people. The leader of the naturalist school was Maruyama Okyo (1733–95). The best-known painters and wood-block artists of the "ukiyo-e" style were Kitagawa Utamaro (1754–1806), Katsushika Hokusai (1760–1849), Saito Sharaku (fl.1794–95), and Ando Hiroshige (1797–1858). Four 20th-century Japanese architects whose work has had a marked influence on international style are Mayekawa Kunio (b.1905), Hideo Kosaka (b.1912), Kenzo Tange (b.1913), and Yoshinobu Ahihara (b.1918).

Noted Japanese film directors include Kenjii Mizoguchi (1898–1956), Yasujiro Ozu (1903–63), and Akira Kurosawa (b.1910). Toshiro Mifune (b.1920) is the best-known film star abroad. Contemporary composers include Toshiro Mayuzumi (b.1929) and Toru Takemitsu (b.1930). Seiji Ozawa (b.1935) is a conductor of world renown. The leading home-run hitter in baseball history is Sadaharu Oh (b.1940), manager of the Yomiuri Giants, who retired as a player for the same team in 1980 after hitting 868 home runs.

Hideyo Noguchi (1876–1928), noted bacteriologist, is credited with the discovery of the cause of yellow fever and is famed for his studies on viruses, snake poisons, and toxins. Hideki Yukawa (1907–81), Japan's most noted physicist, received the 1949 Nobel Prize for research on the meson. In 1965, Shinichiro Tomonaga (1906–79), a professor at Tokyo University of Education, became one of the year's three recipients of the Nobel Prize for physics for work in the field of quantum electrodynamics. Leon Esaki

(b.1925) won the Nobel Prize for physics in 1973; Kenichi Fukui (b.1918) shared the 1981 chemistry award; and Susumu Tonegawa (b.1939) won the 1987 medicine award.

Hirohito (1901–1989) became emperor of Japan in 1926. His eldest son, Crown Prince Akihito (b.1933), succeeded him in 1990. The leading statesman after World War II was Eisaku Sato (1901–75), prime minister from 1964 to 1972 and winner of the Nobel Peace Prize in 1974.

49DEPENDENCIES

Japan has no territories or colonies.

50BIBLIOGRAPHY

Beasley, W. G. (William G.). *Japanese Imperialism, 1894–1945.* New York: Oxford University Press, 1987.

Boger, Karl. *Postwar Industrial Policy in Japan: An Annotated Bibliography.* Metuchen, N.J.: Scarecrow Press, 1988.

Bowring, Richard and Peter Kornicki (eds.). *The Cambridge Encyclopedia of Japan.* New York: Cambridge University Press, 1993.

Burks, Ardath W. *Japan: A Postindustrial Power,* 3rd ed. Boulder, Colo.: Westview Press, 1991.

Cortazzi, Hugh. *Modern Japan: A Concise Survey.* New York: St. Martin', 1993.

Dolan, Ronald E. and Robert L. (eds.). *Japan, a Country,* 5th ed. Washington, D.C.: Library of Congress, 1992.

Encarnation, Dennis J. *Rivals Beyond Trade: America Versus Japan in Global Competition.* Ithaca: Cornell University Press, 1992.

Fukutake, Tadashi. *The Japanese Social Structure: Its Evolution in the Modern Century.* 2d ed. Tokyo: University of Tokyo Press, 1989.

Hane, Mikiso. *Modern Japan: A Historical Survey.* 2d ed. Boulder, Colo.: Westview Press, 1992.

Japanese Studies from Pre-History to 1990: A Bibliographical Guide. New York: St. Martin's, 1992.

Kodansha Encyclopedia of Japan. 9 vols. New York: Kodansha, 1983.

Mason, T. David and Abdul M. Turay (eds.). *US-Japan Trade Friction: Its Impact on Security Cooperation in the Pacific Basin.* New York: St. Martin's, 1991.

Mouer, Ross E. *Images of Japanese Society: A Study in the Social Construction of Reality.* New York: Kegan Paul International, 1990.

Packard, Jerrold M. *Sons of Heaven: A Portrait of the Japanese Monarchy.* New York: Scribner, 1987.

Perkins, Dorothy. *Encyclopedia of Japan: Japanese History and Culture, from Abacus to Zori.* New York: Facts on File, 1991.

Reischauer, Edwin O. *Japan: The Story of a Nation.* 4th ed. New York: Knopf, 1989.

Rowland, Diana. *Japanese Business Etiquette: A Practical Guide to Success with the Japanese.* 2d ed. New York: Warner Books, 1993.

Sansom, Sir George Bailey. *A History of Japan.* 3 vols. Stanford, Calif.: Stanford University Press, 1958–63.

Shulman, Frank Joseph. *Japan.* Santa Barbara, Calif.: Clio Press, 1989.

Stevenson, Michael I. *Education in Japan: A Bibliography of Materials in English since 1973.* Monticello, Ill.: Vance Bibliographies, 1987.

The Political Economy of Japan. Stanford, Calif.: Stanford University Press, 1987.

Tsuru, Shigeto. *Japan's Capitalism: Creative Defeat and Beyond.* New York: Cambridge University Press, 1993.

Woronoff, Jon. *The Japanese Economic Crisis.* New York: St. Martin's Press, 1993.

JORDAN

The Hashemite Kingdom of Jordan
Al-Mamlaka al-Urdunniyya al-Hashimiyya

CAPITAL: 'Amman.

FLAG: The national flag is a tricolor of black, white, and green horizontal stripes with a seven-pointed white star on a red triangle at the hoist.

ANTHEM: *As-Salam al-Maliki (Long Live the King).*

MONETARY UNIT: The Jordanian dinar (JD) is a paper currency of 1,000 fils. There are coins of 1, 5, 10, 20, 25, 50, 100, and 250 fils and notes of ½, 1, 5, 10, and 20 dinars. JD1 = $1.4286 (or $1 = JD0.7000).

WEIGHTS AND MEASURES: The metric system is the legal standard, but some local and Syrian units are still widely used, especially in the villages.

HOLIDAYS: Arbor Day, 15 January; Independence Day, 25 May; Accession of King Hussein, 11 August; King Hussein's Birthday, 14 November. Muslim religious holidays include the 1st of Muharram (Islamic New Year), 'Id al-Fitr, 'Id al-'Adha', and Milad an-Nabi. Christmas and Easter are observed by sizable Christian minorities.

TIME: 2 PM = noon GMT.

¹LOCATION, SIZE, AND EXTENT

Situated in southwest Asia, Jordan has an area of 83,335 sq km (32,175 sq mi). (Until 1967, Jordan's land area also included the West Bank, which, as of 1994, is part of the area including the Gaza Strip and Golan Heights now to be under Palistine home rule.) Jordan extends 562 km (349 mi) NE–SW and 349 km (217 mi) SE–NW. Comparatively, the area occupied by Jordan is slightly smaller than the state of Indiana. It is bounded on the N by Syria, on the NE by Iraq, on the E and S by Sa'udi Arabia, on the SW by the Gulf of Aqaba, and on the W by Israel, with a total boundary length of 1,804 km (1,121 mi) following the 1949 armistice with Israel and of 1,645 km (1,022 mi) following the 1967 cease-fire.

Jordan's capital city, 'Amman, is located in the northwestern part of the country.

²TOPOGRAPHY

The Jordan Valley has a maximum depression of 392 m (1,286 ft) below sea level at the Dead Sea; south of the Dead Sea the depression, called Wadi'Araba, slowly rises to reach sea level about halfway to the Gulf of Aqaba. To the east of the Jordan River, the Transjordanian plateaus have an average altitude of 910 m (3,000 ft), with hills rising to more than 1,650 m (5,400 ft) in the south. Farther eastward, the highlands slope down gently toward the desert, which constitutes 88% of the East Bank. The Jordan River enters the country from Israel to the north and flows into the Dead Sea; its main tributary is the Yarmuk, which near its juncture forms the border between Jordan and Syria. The Dead Sea, 89 km (55 mi) long and about 16 km (10 mi) wide, is the lowest point on the earth's surface, at 397 m (1,302 ft) below the level of the Mediterranean; the Dead Sea itself has a maximum depth of 792 m (2,598 ft) below sea level. The Dead Sea has a mineral content of about 30%.

³CLIMATE

The Jordan Valley has little rainfall, intense summer heat, and mild, pleasant winters. The hill country of the East Bank—ancient Moab, Edom, and Gilead—has a modified Mediterranean climate, with less rainfall and hot, dry summers. The desert regions are subject to great extremes of temperature and receive rainfall of less than 20 cm (8 in) annually, while the rest of the country has an average rainfall of up to 58 cm (23 in) a year. Temperatures at 'Amman range from about –4°C (25°F) in winter to more than 38°C (100°F) in summer.

⁴FLORA AND FAUNA

Plants and animals are those common to the eastern Mediterranean and the Syrian Desert. The vegetation ranges from semitropical flora in the Jordan Valley and other regions to shrubs and drought-resistant bushes in the desert. Less than 1% of the land is forested. The wild fauna includes the jackal, hyena, fox, wildcat, gazelle, ibex, antelope, and rabbit; the vulture, sand grouse, skylark, partridge, quail, woodcock, and goldfinch; and the viper, diced water snake, and Syrian black snake.

⁵ENVIRONMENT

Jordan's principal environmental problems are insufficient water resources, soil erosion caused by overgrazing of goats and sheep, and deforestation. Water pollution is an important issue in Jordan. Jordan has 0.2 cubic miles of water with 65% used for farming activity and 6% used for industrial purposes. One-hundred percent of all city dwellers and 97% of rural people have pure water. It is expected that the rate of population growth, amounting to 4–7 million by the year 2000, will place more demands on an already inadequate water supply. Current sources of pollution are sewage, herbicides, and pesticides. Jordan's cities produce 1.2 million tons of solid waste per year. Jordan's wildlife was reduced drastically by livestock overgrazing and uncontrolled hunting between 1930 and 1960; larger wild animals, such as the Arabian oryx, onager, and Asiatic lion, have completely disappeared. Under a law of 1973, the government has prohibited unlicensed hunting of birds or wild animals and unlicensed sport fishing, as well as the cutting of trees, shrubs, and plants. As of 1994, five of Jordan's mammal species and 11 bird species are endangered. Seven-hundred and fifty-two plant species are also endangered. As of 1987, endangered species in Jordan included the South Arabian leopard and the goitered gazelle.

⁶POPULATION

The 1992 estimated population was 4,291,000 including the West Bank's population of 1,051,500, which did not include East Jerusalem. A population of 5,624,000 was projected for the year 2000. The growth rate in 1985–90 was 3.25%, with the crude birthrate estimated at 38.9 per 1,000 population, the crude death rate at 6.4, and the net natural increase at 32.5. The estimated population density in 1992 (including the West Bank) was 43.9 per sq km (113.7 per sq mi). Over 80% of the East Bank population is concentrated in the northwestern 10% of area. In 1991, 'Amman, the capital, had an estimated population of 965,000; Az-Zarqa', 359,000; and Irbid, 216,000. The West Bank, held by Israel from 1967–1994, contains Arab Jerusalem (Al-Quds), Nabulus, Hebron (Al-Khalil), Jericho (Ar-Riha), and Bethlehem. In March 1993, 1,057,342 Palestinian refugees registered with the UNRWA were living on the East Bank, about 220,000 of them in the 13 refugee centers. Another 476,236 were on the West Bank. About 70% of Jordan's population is urban; 27–28% lives in small villages; and 2–3% is nomadic or seminomadic.

⁷MIGRATION

About one-half or more of the population consists of refugees from territory that became Israel. There is also considerable native-born migration by nomadic groups across the Syrian, Iraqi, and Sa'udi Arabian borders. Many Jordanians live abroad, attracted by job opportunities in the oil-rich Arab states. About 300,000 Jordanians returned from the Persian Gulf states after the 1991 war, mainly from Kuwait, and about 120,000 Iraqis fled to Jordan in 1991. By the end of 1993, no more than 30,000 of the latter remained in Jordan.

⁸ETHNIC GROUPS

Ethnically, the Jordanians represent a mixed stock. Most of the population is Arab, but, except for the Bedouin nomads and semi-nomads of the desert and steppe areas, this element is overlain by the numerous peoples that have been present in Jordan for millennia, including Greek, Egyptian, Persian, European, and Negroid strains. The Palestinian Arabs now resident in Jordan tend to be sedentary and urban. Perhaps 1% of the population is Armenian, and there are about 25,000 Circassians. There are also small Kurd, Druze, and Chechen minorities.

⁹LANGUAGES

Arabic is the language of the country and is spoken even by the ethnic minorities who maintain their own languages in their everyday lives. The spoken Arabic of the country is essentially a vernacular of literary Arabic; it is common to neighboring countries as well but is quite different from the spoken language in Egypt. There also are differences between the languages of the towns and of the countryside, and between those of the East and West banks. English is widely understood by the upper and middle classes.

¹⁰RELIGIONS

Islam is the state religion, although all are guaranteed religious freedom. Most Jordanians (about 92%) are Sunni Muslims. Christians constitute about 5% of the population and live mainly in 'Amman or the Jordan Valley; most are Greek Orthodox or Roman Catholic, and all are Arabic-speaking. Of the racial minorities, the Turkomans and Circassians are Sunni Muslims, but the Druzes are a heterodox Muslim sect. The Baha'is are mainly of Persian stock. A tiny community of Samaritans maintains the faith of its ancestors, a heterodox form of the ancient Jewish religion.

¹¹TRANSPORTATION

Jordan's transportation facilities are underdeveloped, but improvements have been made in recent years. The third development plan (1986–90) allotted JD445 million for transportation. A good road network links the principal towns and connects with Syria, Iraq, and Sa'udi Arabia. In 1991, of the 7,500 km (4,660 mi) of road, 5,500 km (3,418 mi) were paved. Passenger automobiles numbered 172,075; trucks, buses, and other commercial vehicles totaled 35,854.

The rail system, some 619 km (385 mi) of narrow-gauge single track, is a section of the old Hijaz railway (Damascus to Medina) for Muslim pilgrims. It runs from the Syrian border through 'Amman to Ma'an, where it connects with a spur line to the port of Al-'Aqabah. Reconstruction of the section from Ma'an to Medina in Sa'udi Arabia, which had been destroyed in World War I, was undertaken in the early 1970s as a joint venture by Jordan, Sa'udi Arabia, and Syria.

Al-'Aqabah, Jordan's only outlet to the sea, is situated at the head of the Gulf of Aqaba, an arm of the Red Sea. The port was initially developed after the 1948 Arab-Israeli war, which cut off Arab Palestine and Transjordan from Mediterranean ports; substantial development did not begin until the 1960s. The port has been enlarged for general use, including terminals for loading potash and fertilizers.

The government-owned Alia–Royal Jordanian Airline operates domestic and international flights. The major airport is the new Queen Alia International Airport, about 30 km (19 mi) south of the capital, which was opened in the early 1980s. Another international airport north of Jerusalem is in Israeli hands. In 1992, civil aviation on the East Bank amounted to 3,754 million passenger-km.

¹²HISTORY

As part of the Fertile Crescent connecting Africa and Asia, the area now known as Jordan has long been a major transit zone and often an object of contention among rival powers. It has a relatively well known prehistory and history. Neolithic remains from about 7000 BC have been found in Jericho, the oldest known city in the world. City-states were well developed in the Bronze Age (c.3200–2100 BC). In the 16th century BC, the Egyptians first conquered Palestine, and in the 13th century BC, Semitic-speaking peoples established kingdoms on both banks of the Jordan. In the 10th century BC, the western part of the area of Jordan (on both banks of the Jordan River) formed part of the domain of the Hebrew kings David and Solomon, while subsequently the West Bank became part of the Kingdom of Judah. A succession of outside conquerors held sway in the area until, in the 4th century BC, Palestine and Syria were conquered by Alexander the Great, beginning about 1,000 years of intermittent European rule. After the death of Alexander, the whole area was disputed among the Seleucids of Syria, the Ptolemies of Egypt, and native dynasties, such as the Hasmoneans (Maccabees); in the 1st century BC, it came under the domination of Rome. In Hellenistic and Roman times, a flourishing civilization developed on the East Bank; meanwhile, in southern Jordan, the Nabataean kingdom, a native Arab state in alliance with Rome, developed a distinctive culture, blending Arab and Greco-Roman elements, and built its capital at Petra, a city whose structures hewn from red sandstone cliffs survive today. With the annexation of Nabataea by Trajan in the 2d century AD, Palestine and areas east of the Jordan came under direct Roman rule. Christianity spread rapidly in Jordan and for 300 years was the dominant religion.

The Byzantine phase of Jordan's history, from the establishment of Constantinople as the capital of the empire to the Arab conquest, was one of gradual decline. When the Muslim invaders appeared, little resistance was offered, and in 636, Arab rule was firmly established. Soon thereafter, the area became thoroughly

LOCATION: (1949): 29°17′ to 33°20′N; 34°53′ to 39°12′E. **BOUNDARY LENGTHS:** Syria, 356 km (221 mi). Iraq, 146 km (91 mi). Sa'udi Arabia, 744 km (462 mi). Gulf of Aqaba, 27 km (17 mi). Israel: 1949 armistice line, 531 km (330 mi); 1967 cease-fire line, 480 km (298 mi). **TERRITORIAL SEA LIMIT:** 3 mi.

Arabized and Islamized, remaining so to this day despite a century-long domination by the Crusaders (12th century). Under the Ottoman Turks (1517–1917), the lands east of the Jordan were part of the Damascus vilayet (an administrative division of the empire), while the West Bank formed part of the sanjak (a further subdivision) of Jerusalem within the vilayet of Beirut.

During World War I, Sharif Hussein ibn-'Ali (Husayn bin 'Ali), the Hashemite (or Hashimite) ruler of Mecca and the Hijaz, aided and incited by the UK (which somewhat hazily promised him an independent Arab state), touched off an Arab revolt against the Turks. After the defeat of the Turks, Palestine and Transjordan were placed under British mandate; in 1921, Hussein's son 'Abdallah was installed by the British as emir of Transjordan. In 1923, the independence of Transjordan was proclaimed under British supervision, which was partially relaxed by a 1928 treaty,

and in 1939, a local cabinet government (Council of Ministers) was formed. In 1946, Transjordan attained full independence, and on 25 May, 'Abdallah was proclaimed king of the Hashemite Kingdom of Transjordan. After the Arab-Israeli war of 1948, King 'Abdallah annexed a butterfly-shaped area of Palestine bordering the Jordan (thereafter called the West Bank), which was controlled by his army and which he contended was included in the area that had been promised to Sharif Hussein. On 24 April 1950, after general elections had been held in the East and West banks, an act of union joined Jordanian-occupied Palestine and the Kingdom of Transjordan to form the Hashemite Kingdom of Jordan. This action was condemned by some Arab states as evidence of inordinate Hashemite ambitions. Meanwhile, Jordan, since the 1948 war, had absorbed about 500,000 of some 1,000,000 Palestinian Arab refugees, mostly sheltered in UN-administered camps, and another 500,000 nonrefugee Palestinians. Despite what was now a Palestinian majority, power remained with the Jordanian elite loyal to the throne. On 20 July 1951, 'Abdallah was assassinated in Jerusalem by a Palestinian Arab, and his eldest son, Talal, was proclaimed king. Because of mental illness, however, King Talal was declared unfit to rule, and succession passed to his son Hussein I (Husayn ibn-Talal), who, after a brief period of regency until he reached 18 years of age, was formally enthroned on 2 May 1953.

Between the accession of King Hussein and the war with Israel in 1967, Jordan was beset not only with problems of economic development, internal security, and Arab-Israeli tensions but also with difficulties stemming from its relations with the Western powers and the Arab world. Following the overthrow of Egypt's King Faruk in July 1952, the Arab countries were strongly influenced by "Arab socialism" and aspirations to Arab unity (both for its own sake and as a precondition for defeating Israel). Early in Hussein's reign, extreme nationalists stepped up their attempts to weaken the regime and its ties with the UK. Notwithstanding the opposition of most Arabs, including many Jordanians, Jordan maintained a close association with the UK in an effort to preserve the kingdom as a separate, sovereign entity. However, the invasion of Egypt by Israel in October 1956, and the subsequent Anglo-French intervention at Suez, made it politically impossible to maintain cordial relations with the UK. Negotiations were begun to end the treaty with Britain, and thus the large military subsidies for which it provided; the end of the treaty also meant the end of British bases and of British troops in Jordan. The Jordanian army remained loyal, and the king's position was bolstered when the US and Sa'udi Arabia indicated their intention to preserve Jordan against any attempt by Syria to occupy the country. After the formation of the United Arab Republic by Egypt and Syria and the assassination of his cousin, King Faisal II (Faysal) of Iraq, in a July 1958 coup, Hussein turned again to the West for support, and British troops were flown to Jordan from Cyprus.

When the crisis was over, a period of relative calm ensued. Hussein, while retaining Jordan's Western ties, gradually steadied his relations with other Arab states (except Syria), established relations with the USSR, and initiated several important economic development measures. But even in years of comparative peace, relations with Israel remained the focus of Jordanian and Arab attention. Terrorist raids launched from within Jordan drew strong Israeli reprisals, and the activities of the Palestine Liberation Organization (PLO) often impinged on Jordanian sovereignty, leading Hussein in July 1966, and again in early 1967, to suspend support for the PLO, thus drawing Arab enmity upon himself. On 5 June 1967, an outbreak of hostilities occurred between Israel and the combined forces of Jordan, Syria, and Egypt. These hostilities lasted only six days, during which Israel occupied the Golan Heights in Syria, Egypt's Sinai Peninsula, and the Jordanian West Bank, including all of Jerusalem. Jordan suffered heavy casualties, and a large-scale exodus of Palestinians (over 300,000) across the Jordan River to the East Bank swelled Jordan's refugee population (700,000 in 1966), adding to the war's severe economic disruption.

After Hussein's acceptance of a cease-fire with Israel in August 1970, he tried to suppress various Palestinian guerrilla organizations whose operations had brought retaliation upon Jordan. The imposition of military rule in September led to a 10-day civil war between the army and the Palestinian forces (supported briefly by Syria which was blocked by Israel), ended by the mediation of other Arab governments. Subsequently, however, Hussein launched an offensive against Palestinian guerrillas in Jordan, driving them out in July 1971. In the following September, Premier Wasfi al-Tal was assassinated by guerrilla commandos, and coup attempts, in which Libya was said to have been involved,

were thwarted in November 1972 and February 1973.

Jordan did not open a third front against Israel in the October 1973 war but sent an armored brigade of about 2,500 men to assist Syria. After the war, relations between Jordan and Syria improved. Hussein reluctantly endorsed the resolution passed by Arab nations on 28 October 1974 in Rabat, Morocco, recognizing the PLO as "sole legitimate representative of the Palestinian people on any liberated Palestinian territory," including, implicitly, the Israeli-held West Bank. After the Egyptian-Israeli Peace Treaty of 1979, Jordan joined other Arab states in trying to isolate Egypt diplomatically, and Hussein refused to join further Egyptian-Israeli talks on the future of the West Bank.

After the Israeli invasion of Lebanon in 1982 and the resulting expulsion of Palestinian guerrillas, Jordan began to coordinate peace initiatives with the PLO. These efforts culminated in a February 1985 accord between Jordan and the PLO, in which both parties agreed to work together toward "a peaceful and just settlement to the Palestinian question." In February 1986, however, Hussein announced that Jordan was unable to continue to coordinate politically with the PLO, which scrapped the agreement in April 1987. The following year the King renounced Jordan's claim to the West Bank and subsequently patched up relations with the PLO, Syria, and Egypt. In 1990, owing largely to popular support for Saddam Hussein, Jordan was critical of coalition efforts to use force to expel Iraqi forces from Kuwait. Relations with the US and the Gulf states were impaired; Jordan lost its subsidies from the latter while having to support hundreds of thousands of refugees from the war and the aftermath. Jordan's willingness to participate in peace talks with Israel in late 1991 helped repair relations with Western countries. In June 1994, Jordan and Israel began meetings to work out practical steps on water, borders, and energy which would lead to normal relations.

Internally in the 1980s, Hussein followed policies of gradual political liberalization which were given new impetus by serious rioting over high prices in 1989. In that year, for the first time since 1956, Jordan held relatively free parliamentary elections in which Islamists gained more than one-third of the 80 seats. Martial law was ended in 1991 and new parliamentary elections were held in 1993. The King's supporters won 54 seats with the Moslem Brotherhood and its allies taking only 18 places.

13GOVERNMENT

Jordan is a constitutional monarchy based on the constitution of 8 January 1952. The king has wide powers over all branches of government. The constitution vests legislative power in the bicameral National Assembly, composed of a 40-member Senate and a 80-member lower house, the Chamber of Deputies. Senators are appointed by the king for renewable eight-year terms; the Chamber of Deputies is elected by secret ballot for a four-year term, but the king may dissolve the chamber and order new elections. There is universal suffrage at age 18, women having received the right to vote in April 1973; general elections were held in 1989 and 1993.

The National Assembly is convened and may be prorogued by the king, who also has veto power over legislation. The executive power of the king is administered by a cabinet, or Council of Ministers. The king appoints the prime minister, who then selects the other ministers, subject to royal approval. The ministers need not be members of the Chamber of Deputies. In the prolonged emergency created by the wars with Israel and by internal disorders, especially since 1968, King Hussein exercised nearly absolute power. The National Assembly, adjourned by the king in 1974, met briefly in 1976 to amend the constitution; parliamentary elections were postponed indefinitely because of the West Bank situation, and the Assembly was then dissolved. In 1978, King Hussein established the National Consultative Council of 60 appointed members. The National Assembly was reconvened in

1984, as King Hussein sought to strengthen his hand in future maneuvering on the Palestinian problem. The freely elected parliaments of 1989 and 1993 have played an increasingly active and independent role in governance with open debate and criticism of government personalities and policies.

14POLITICAL PARTIES

Political parties were abolished on 25 April 1957, following an alleged attempted coup by pan-Arab militants. In the elections of 1962, 1963, and 1967, candidates qualified in a screening procedure by the Interior Ministry ran for office, in effect, as independents. The Jordanian National Union, formed in September 1971 as the official political organization of Jordan and renamed the Arab National Union in March 1972, became inactive by the mid-1970s. In 1992, political parties were again permitted and 20 were authorized to take part in elections. The principal opposition group has been the Islamic Action Front, the political arm of the Moslem Brotherhood. In 1990, the election law was amended to ban bloc voting or by party lists, substituting instead a "one person, one vote" system.

15LOCAL GOVERNMENT

Eastern Jordan is divided into eight governorates—'Amman, Irbid, Balga, Karak, Ma'an, Zarqa', Mafraq, and Tafilah—each under a governor appointed by the king on the recommendation of the interior minister. The towns and larger villages are administered by elected municipal councils; mayors and council presidents are appointed by the Council of Ministers. Smaller villages are headed by a headman (mukhtar), who in most cases is elected informally.

16JUDICIAL SYSTEM

There are six jurisdictions in the judiciary: four levels of civil and criminal jurisdiction, religious jurisdiction, and tribal courts. The New Civil Code of 1977 regulates civil legal procedures. The Supreme Court, acting as a court of cassation, deals with appeals from lower courts. In some instances, as in actions against the government, it sits as a High Court of Justice. The courts of appeals hear appeals from all lower courts. Courts of first instance hear major civil and criminal cases. Magistrates' courts deal with cases not coming within the jurisdiction of courts of first instance. Religious courts have jurisdiction in matters concerning personal status (marriage, divorce, wills and testaments, orphans, etc.), where the laws of the different religious sects vary. The Shari'ah courts deal with the Muslim community, following the procedure laid down by the Ottoman Law of 1913. The Council of Religious Communities has jurisdiction over analogous cases among non-Muslims. Tribal courts, which have jurisdiction in most matters concerning tribe members, are losing their importance as more people take their cases to the government courts instead.

In 1991, the State Security Court, which hears security cases in panels of at least three judges, replaced the Martial Law Court. Under 1993 amendments to the state security court law, all security court decisions may be appealed to the Court of Cassation on issues of law and weight of evidence. Prior to 1993, the Court of Cassation reviewed only cases involving death or imprisonment for over 10 years, and review was limited to errors of law.

17ARMED FORCES

In 1993, the Jordanian army had some 85,000 men. The air force had 14,000 men and 113 combat aircraft. The navy had only about 400 men and 3 patrol craft. Reserve manpower was estimated at 35,000. Defense expenditures for 1990 (excluding foreign military assistance) were $404 million or 9.5% of gross domestic product. Arms imports during 1981–91 totaled $5.4 billion. Jordan has 875 peacekeepers abroad.

18INTERNATIONAL COOPERATION

Jordan became a member of the UN on 14 December 1955 and belongs to ESCWA and all the nonregional specialized agencies. It is one of the founding members of the League of Arab States and also participates in G-77. Jordan has greatly benefited from the work of UNICEF and of UNRWA, which helps the Palestinian refugees. Jordan does not belong to GATT, nor does it adhere to the Law of the Sea.

19ECONOMY

Jordan's economy has been profoundly affected by the Arab-Israeli conflict. The incorporation of the West Bank after the war of 1948 and the first exodus of Palestinians from the territory that became Israel tripled the population, causing grave economic and social problems. The loss of the West Bank in 1967 resulted not only in a second exodus of Palestinians but also in the loss of most of Jordan's richest agricultural land and a decline in the growing tourist industry. The 1970–71 civil war and the October 1973 war also brought setbacks to development plans. The steadying influence has been foreign funds. An estimated 80% of annual national income in the early 1980s came from direct grants from and exports to oil-rich Arab countries and from remittances by Jordanians working there. Also important to the economy has been Western economic aid, notably from the US, the UK, and Germany. The economy expanded rapidly during 1975–80, growing in real terms by an average of 9% a year, but the growth rate slowed to 5% in 1985, primarily from reductions in aid from other Arab states because of their declining oil receipts. The onset of the recession in Jordan in the mid-1980s followed by the economic collapse of 1988–89 and the Gulf conflict in 1990 left the country with an unemployment rate of approximately 30–35%, high inflation, and about 25–30% of the population living below the poverty line. When in 1989 Jordan was unable to service its external debt due to 100 repayment commitments, the Jordanian government concluded an agreement with the IMF to reduce the budget deficit from 24% of GDP in 1988 to 10% of GDP by 1993, and to improve the current account balance from a deficit equivalent to 6% of GDP in 1988 to a balanced position in 1993. Export earnings were slated to grow from a projected $1.1 billion in 1989 to $1.7 billion in 1993. The rate of inflation was expected to drop from 14% in 1989 to 7% in 1993. However the effects of the Gulf crisis undermined the IMF readjustment package. The international economic embargo against Iraq meant that Jordan lost a lucrative export and re-export market. The loss of Iraq as the main source of the kingdom's oil supplies resulted in Jordan having to pay the market price for oil imports from Syria and Yemen. The balance of annual aid transfers, some $200 billion, promised by the Arab oil states in 1990, failed to take into consideration the influx of some 230,000 Jordanian nationals from Kuwait that resulted from the Iraqi invasion. They imposed a strain on government services, and added to the pool of unemployment.

20INCOME

In 1992, Jordan's GNP was $4,406 million at current prices, or $1,120 per capita. For the period 1985–92 the average inflation rate was 7.2%, resulting in a real growth rate in per capita GNP of -7.0%.

In 1992 the GDP was $4,788 million in current US dollars. It is estimated that agriculture, hunting, forestry, and fishing contributed 6% to GDP; mining and quarrying, 3%; manufacturing, 10%; electricity, gas, and water, 2%; construction, 6%; wholesale and retail trade, 13%; transport, storage, and communication, 11%; finance, insurance, real estate, and business services, 14%; community, social, and personal services, 2%; and other sources, 33%.

21LABOR

Jordan's labor shortage of the early 1980s changed to a serious labor surplus a decade later because of a high population growth rate (nearly 3%) combined with an influx of expatriate Jordanians from the Persian Gulf strained by the tight labor market. Ironically, in the 1980s, the government offered incentives to professionals to come to or to remain in Jordan, and integrated more women into the labor force. In 1991, with an unemployment rate of 18.9%, the government sought to limit unemployment by reducing the number of foreign workers, retraining Jordanians through vocational programs, and finding overseas outlets for skilled workers. In January 1992, a trade and labor agreement with Libya was signed, setting aside jobs for Jordanian doctors, engineers, and teachers in Libya. Yemen and Oman also agreed to accept Jordanian expatriates, as might Iran in the near future. Of the 237,060 non-agriculturally employed persons in Jordan at the start of 1991, services and government employed an estimated 62.7%, construction 1.3%, industry 21.4%, trade 5.5%, and transportation and communications 9.1%.

The General Federation of Jordanian Trade Unions, formed in 1954, was comprised of 17 trade unions in 1991. Independent unions include the Drivers' Union and the Union of Petroleum Workers and Employees. Labor disputes are mediated by the Ministry of Labor. The social security legislation of 1978 provides pensions, disability payments, and medical treatment for job-related illness or injury; employers pay 10% and workers 5% of wages to fund the system.

22AGRICULTURE

Agriculture still plays a role in the economy, although 40% of the usable land consists of the West Bank, lost to Jordan since 1967. As of 1991, only 4.5% of all land in Jordan was utilized for crop sown feed production. While the system of small owner-operated farms, peculiar to Jordan among the Arab countries and originating in the Land Settlement Law of 1933, limits the number of large landowners and share tenancy, the minuscule holdings have inhibited development. Agriculture accounted for 7.3% of GDP in 1992.

The main crops are wheat and barley, vegetables, fruits, and olives. In 1992, production (in tons) was as follows: tomatoes, 300,000; tangerines, 80,000; wheat, 80,000; barley, 65,000; olives, 60,000; lemons and limes, 50,000; grapes, 44,000; bananas, 27,000; and tobacco, 3,000. The output of fruits and vegetables has been encouraging, in part because of increased use of fertilizers, herbicides, and plastic greenhouses by the nation's farmers in the Jordan Valley.

Irrigation schemes and soil and water conservation programs have received emphasis in Jordan's economic development. The 77-km (48-mi) East Ghor Canal, substantially completed in 1966 and reconstructed in the early 1970s after heavy war damage, siphons water from the Yarmuk River and provides irrigation for about 13,000 hectares (32,000 acres). Water conservation in other areas has been undertaken with the rehabilitation of old water systems and the digging of wells. As of 1991, an estimated 63,000 hectares (155,600 acres) were irrigated.

The cooperative movement has made progress in the agricultural sector; the Central Cooperative Union, established in 1959, provides seasonal loans and advice to local cooperatives. The Agricultural Credit Corporation, founded in 1960, provides low-cost loans to finance agricultural investments.

23ANIMAL HUSBANDRY

Animal husbandry is usually on a small scale and is often of the nomadic or seminomadic type indigenous to the area. The large nomadic tribes take their camels into the desert every winter, returning nearer to the cultivated area in summer. The camels provide transportation, food (milk and meat), shelter, and cloth-ing (hair); the sale of surplus camels is a source of cash. Sheep and goat nomads make similar use of their animals. Imported milk and meat are sold at subsidized prices.

Animal products account for about one-third of agricultural output. In 1992, estimates of Jordan's livestock on the East Bank were 2,000,000 sheep, 600,000 goats, 32,000 head of cattle, and 18,000 camels. Jordan had an estimated 55,000,000 chickens in 1992; poultry is an important source of food.

24FISHING

Fishing is unimportant as a source of food. The rivers are relatively poor in fish; there are no fish in the Dead Sea, and the short Gulf of Aqaba shoreline has only recently been developed for fishing. The total fish catch was only 22 tons in 1992.

25FORESTRY

Jordan formerly supported fairly widespread forests of oak and Aleppo pine in the uplands of southern Jordan, both west and east of the Jordan River, but forestland now covers less than 1% of the total area. Scrub forests and maquis growths are the most common; the olive, characteristic of the Mediterranean basin, is widely cultivated. The important forests are around 'Ajlun in the north and near Ma'an. By 1976, some 3,800 hectares (9,400 acres) had been newly planted as part of a government afforestation program. From 1976 to 1991, an additional 10,000 hectares (24,700 acres) also was reforested. Roundwood production was 9,000 tons in 1991.

26MINING

Jordan's mineral resources consist chiefly of phosphate, potash, and limited manganese, copper, kaolin, and gypsum deposits. Phosphate deposits at Ruseifa, Wadi Al Abyad, Ash Shidiya, and Al-Hasa, are estimated at about 1 billion tons. Production of phosphates fell from 6,082,000 tons in 1990 to 4,433,000 tons in 1991, the lowest amount in nine years. However, Jordan still maintained its rank of fourth place globally in mined tonnage of phosphate rock. The Gulf War in 1990/91, with the UN trade embargo, helped exacerbate problems within the Jordanian mining sector by softening foreign demand. Development of potash was advanced by the completion in 1982 of the Arab Potash Co. plant near the Dead Sea, with a current annual productive capacity of 1.4 million tons. Production was a reported record 1,364,000 tons in 1991. Copper deposits between the Dead Sea and the Gulf of Aqaba remained undeveloped in the early 1980s. Other potential for progress lies in the availability of bromine, dolomite, gypsum, glass sands, iron, lead, oil shale, tin, travertine, and tripoli.

27ENERGY AND POWER

Although Jordan does not have petroleum deposits, its imports of oil from Sa'udi Arabia via the Trans-Arabian pipeline (Tapline) and its refinery at Az-Zarqa', with an annual productive capacity of 22 million barrels, supply virtually all the country's energy needs. In 1991, Jordan imported about 17,157,000 barrels of crude oil. Before the Gulf War, petroleum from Iraq was typically imported by tanker truck. With the UN embargo, however, only 200 trucks (out of 1,000) transported crude oil to the Zarga refinery in 1991. Large deposits of oil shale have been found, and exploratory drilling for oil and gas has begun in the eastern desert.

All electric power was thermal in the early 1980s, but hydroelectric development was planned for the Zarqa' River. The government electrification plan calls for establishment of a national grid, linking the major cities. At the end of 1991, net installed electrical capacity was 1,048 Mw, and electricity generated totaled 3,723 million kwh. A major new thermal station at Al'Aqabah had added 130 Mw of generating capacity by the mid-1980s.

28INDUSTRY

With government encouragement, industry plays an increasingly important part in Jordan's economy. In 1990, the manufacturing sector contributed 15% to GDP at factor cost. Manufacturing output fell by 2.9% in 1991 due to the adverse impact of the Gulf War. In 1992, the sector grew by 6.2%. Most industrial income comes from four industries: cement, oil refining, phosphates, and potash. Cement production rose from 553,000 tons in 1978 to 2,746,000 tons in 1992. Output of the oil refinery at Az-Zarqa' rose from 748,400 tons of petroleum products in 1974 to 2,839,000 tons in 1992 Phosphate production declined from 6,249,200 tons in 1986 to 4,295,900 that same year. Jordan's Dead Sea potash extraction plant began posting a profit in 1989. With an estimated 1.4 million tons capacity, the plant produced over 1.26 million tons in 1992.

Output of main manufactures for the period 1990–92 are as follows (1,000 tons unless otherwise indicated):

	1990	1991	1992
Cement	2,786.5	2,751.5	2,746.0
Petroleum products	2,593.8	2,307.2	2,839.6
Fertilizers	595.8	602.1	553.6
Iron	179.1	200.3	234.7
Textiles (1,000 yds)	1,436.7	1,084.1	1,100.8
Fodder (tons)	47.0	47.4	53.5
Cigarettes (m)	3,184.8	3,718.5	3,091.0
Paper & cardboard	22.6	21.2	17.0
Shoe sole leather & wool (tons)	87.9	34.2	49.0
Shoe upper leather (1,000 sq ft)	1,878.3	2,264.2	2,639.7
Spirits & alcoholic			
drinks (1,000 litres)	6,814.4	6,280.4	6,285.1
Liquid batteries (1,000)	59.5	85.1	86.7
Detergents	32.5	39.9	34.3

29SCIENCE AND TECHNOLOGY

Government allocations for science, technology, and statistics in the 1986–90 development plan totaled JD12.3 million. A dozen institutes offer scientific training. Five scientific learned societies and research institutes are located in Amman. In 1986, total expenditures for research and development amounted to 5.6 million dinars; 29 technicians and 418 scientists and engineers were engaged in research and development.

30DOMESTIC TRADE

Lack of proper storage facilities, inadequate transportation service, and a lack of quality controls and product grading are chronic handicaps to Jordanian trade. However, these deficiencies have been alleviated, directly and indirectly, under the 1976–80, 1981–85, and 1986–90 development plans. Traditional Arab forms of trade remain in evidence, particularly in villages, and farm products generally pass through a long chain of middlemen before reaching the consumer. In 'Amman, however, Westernized modes of distribution have developed, and there are supermarkets and department stores as well as small shops. Business hours are from 8 AM to 1 PM and from 3:30 to 6:30 PM, six days a week. Shops close either on Friday for Muslims or on Sunday for Christians. Banks stay open from 8:30 AM to 12:30 PM and from 3:30 to 5:30 PM, Saturday through Thursday.

31FOREIGN TRADE

Jordan exports mainly phosphates, manufactures, and fruits and vegetables; imports consist mainly of machinery, manufactured products, petroleum, and foodstuffs. Exports rose from JD60.2 million in 1977 to JD225 million in 1986 and to about JD634 million in 1992; imports increased from JD454.4 million to JD850.1 million in 1986 and about JD2.2 billion in 1992. The trade deficit in 1986 totaled JD624.5 million and soared to about JD1.6 billion in 1992.

Principal exports and imports (in thousands of dinars) were as follows:

DOMESTIC EXPORTS FOB	Jan–Dec 1991	Jan–Dec 1992
Foodstuffs	886,041	92,033
of which:		
dairy products	6,830	14,830
vegetables	43,531	39,563
fruit & nuts	10,929	10,453
Natural phosphates	123,092	122,464
Potash	96,764	86,220
Chemicals	177,045	196,932
Manufactured goods	63,411	66,990
of which:		
paper & manufactures	8,098	6,100
textile yarn, cloth & manufactures	11,852	15,286
cement	26,103	22,214
Machinery & transport equipment	7,442	11,838
Miscellaneous manufactured articles	26,627	41,009
of which:		
plastic products	5,796	9,515
TOTAL, INCLUDING OTHERS	598,627	633,755
IMPORTS CIF		
Foodstuffs	417,6687	416,023
Crude petroleum	193,663	228,845
Chemicals	218,764	245,544
Paper & manufactures	43,205	49,291
Textile yarn, cloth & manufactures	76,953	94,408
Iron & steel	84,520	133,580
Machinery include electric	149,177	273,727
Transport equipment	149,908	270,054
Clothing & footwear	25,238	42,107
Scientific instruments, etc	20,945	39,759
TOTAL, INCLUDING OTHERS	1,710,463	2,214,002

Until 1990 when the oil embargo against Iraq went into effect, Jordan bought the bulk of its crude oil from Iraq which was also been a key market for Jordanian goods. The next most important markets for Jordan were India, which purchased JD96.4 million worth of mainly mineral fertilizers in 1992 and Saudi Arabia, which topped the JD70.08 million mark. The US sold Jordan goods worth over JD246 million and Germany supplied goods worth JD186.8 million in 1992.

Principal trading partners (in millions of dinars) were as follows:

DOMESTIC EXPORTS FOB	Jan–Dec 1991	Jan–Dec 1992
Saudi Arabia	11.02	70.08
Iraq	55.82	48.82
India	109.65	96.37
Indonesia	24.21	28.97
UAE	26.07	25.92
China	32.57	14.01
Lebanon	10.04	9.73
Syria	9.11	12.93
Turkey	13.07	15.27
IMPORTS CIF		
Iraq	170.87	295.44
US	178.16	246.15
Germany	133.18	186.75
Italy	73.63	110.93
Japan	61.12	132.19
UK	77.57	108.41
France	73.60	78.09
South Korea	24.43	49.06
Belgium–Luxembourg	44.43	49.06

32 BALANCE OF PAYMENTS

Jordan's chronically adverse trade balance has long been offset by payments from foreign governments and agencies, especially from Jordan's oil-rich Arab allies, and by remittances from Jordanians working abroad, chiefly in Sa'udi Arabia. During the Gulf War, expatriate remittances and aid from Arab countries dropped sharply, causing the improvement of the trade deficit to halt. In 1992 merchandise exports totaled $1,218.9 million and imports $2,998.7 million. The merchandise trade balance was $-1,779.7 million.

The following table summarizes Jordan's balance of payments for 1991 and 1992 (in millions of US dollars):

	1991	1992
CURRENT ACCOUNT		
Goods, services, and income	1,277.4	1,932.7
Unrequited transfers	883.8	1,167.5
TOTALS	−393.5	−765.2
CAPITAL ACCOUNT		
Direct investment	−25.6	44.1
Portfolio investment	—	—
Other long-term capital	296.5	−54.1
Other short-term capital	1,826.4	1,006.3
Reserves	−2,025.2	−392.0
TOTALS	72.1	604.3
Errors and omissions	321.4	160.9
Total change in reserves	−1,403.3	−375.0

33 BANKING AND SECURITIES

The Central Bank of Jordan, founded in 1964 with a capital of JD2 million and reorganized in 1971, is in charge of note issue, foreign exchange control, and supervision of commercial banks, in cooperation with the Economic Security Council. Its total foreign assets in 1993 amounted to JD954.2. million. Money supply, as measured by M2, at that time totaled JD4,584.9 million

The banking system includes, besides the Central Bank, six specialized credit institutions. State banks include the Arab Bank PLC, The Bank of Jordan PLC, Cairo Amman Bank, Jordan-Kuwait Bank, and the Jordan National Bank. Commercial banks included those of Jordan, other Arab countries, the UK, and the US. Foreign commercial banks in Jordan include the British Bank of the Middle East, Citibank NA (US), the Arab Land Bank, and the Arab Banking Corporation (Jordan). Total assets of the commercial banks in Jordan totaled $2,131.6 million in 1993.

Loans outstanding by the Jordan Industrial Bank, Agricultural Credit Corp., Jordan Co-operative Organization, and other credit institutions totaled JD3,658.2 million at the end of 1993.

There is no securities exchange in Jordan.

34 INSURANCE

Jordan had 31 insurance companies at the end of 1986, when 17.6% of premiums were paid for life and 82.4% for non-life insurance. The Al Ahlia Insurance Co. and the Jordan Insurance Co. offer commercial insurance. Several US and British insurance companies have branches or agents in Jordan.

35 PUBLIC FINANCE

Jordan has had to rely on foreign assistance for support of its budget, which has increased rapidly since the 1967 war. During the late 1980s, Jordan incurred large fiscal deficits, which led to a heavy burden of external debt. Efforts at cutting public expenditures reduced the budget deficit from 21% of GDP in 1989 to 18% in 1991. The Persian Gulf crisis, however, forced Jordan to delay the IMF deficit reduction program begun in 1989. Economic recovery will depend on further foreign aid and debt relief

to finance reforms. In 1992, expenditures exceeded revenues by $600 million.

The following table shows actual revenues and expenditures for 1990 and 1991 in millions of dinars.

	1990	1991
REVENUE AND GRANTS		
Tax revenue	508.4	531.0
Non-tax revenue	200.4	229.2
Capital revenue	0.2	1.4
Grants	164.3	230.3
TOTAL	873.3	991.8
EXPENDITURES & LENDING MINUS REPAYMENTS		
General public service	47.7	55.7
Defense	205.0	282.2
Public order and safety	62.6	61.7
Education	142.2	135.7
Health	48.1	54.6
Social security and welfare	151.4	143.0
Housing and community amenities	19.2	16.1
Recreation, cultural, and religious affairs	14.7	12.5
Economic affairs and services	100.2	112.8
Other expenditures	177.7	194.5
Adjustments	−2.4	−13.2
Lending minus repayments	1.3	13.6
TOTAL	967.7	1,069.3
Deficit/Surplus	−94.4	−77.6

In 1991 Jordan's total public debt stood at JD3,845.4 million, of which JD2,824.0 million was financed abroad.

36 TAXATION

Corporations are taxed at a flat rate of 40% (50–55% for those involved in banking and finance). The personal income tax rate is 45%, less deductions and exemptions (25% for private sector employees and 50% for government workers). There are no capital gains or net worth taxes on individuals, and social security taxes are paid jointly by employers and employees.

37 CUSTOMS AND DUTIES

Customs and excise duties provide nearly two-thirds of all tax revenues. All imports and exports are subject to licenses. Import duties are levied by c.i.f. value, with a 13% customs surcharge. Jordan grants preferential treatment to imports from Arab League countries, under bilateral trade agreements that exempt certain items from duty and under multilateral trade and transit agreements with Arab League countries.

38 FOREIGN INVESTMENT

In the past there was little foreign investment in Jordan apart from the oil pipelines, but since the early 1970s, the government has offered liberal tax inducements, including a six-year corporate tax holiday established in 'Amman and a tax holiday of up to 10 years outside the capital, to encourage foreign investors; 100% foreign ownership of local enterprises is permitted in some cases. In 1980, the government formed the Jordanian Industrial Estates Corp., near 'Amman, to attract new industries to planned industrial complexes; investors were granted two-year income tax exemptions. Jordan also has established four free-trade zones, at Al-'Aqabah, Az-Zarqa', and the Queen Alia International Airport and along the Syrian frontier, near the Jordan-Syria rail link.

39 ECONOMIC DEVELOPMENT

Before the upheavals caused by the war of 1967, the government had begun to design its first comprehensive development plans. The Jordan Development Board, established in 1952, adopted a five-year program for 1961–65 and a seven-year program for 1964–70, which was interrupted by war. In 1971, a newly created National Planning Council, with wide responsibility for national planning, prepared the 1973–75 plan for the East Bank, with a planned total outlay of JD179 million. The main objectives were to reduce the trade deficit, increase the GNP, expand employment, and reduce dependence on foreign aid. At least 60% of the planned projects were completed, and a new five-year plan was instituted on 1 January 1976.

The 1976–80 plan entailed outlays of JD844 million (at 1975 constant prices) and achieved an annual GDP growth rate of 9.6%, below the goal of 11.9% Notable development projects included port expansion at al-'Aqabah and construction of Queen Alia International Airport. The 1981–85 development plan allocated funds totaling JD3,300 million and projected an economic growth rate of 10.4% annually (17% for industry and mining, 7% for agriculture). The plan envisaged completion of large potash and fertilizer installations, as well as the first stage of construction of the 150 m (492 ft) Maqarin Dam project on the Yarmuk River, which would store water for irrigation. This project also was to extend the East Ghor Canal 14 km (9 mi) from Karama to the Dead Sea. The Maqarin Dam project was shelved indefinitely, however.

The 1986–90 development plan allocated JD3,115.5 million, to be shared between the public sector (52%) and the private and mixed sector (48%). The goals of the plan were the following: realization of a 5.1% annual growth rate in the GDP; creation of 97,000 new employment opportunities; a decrease in imports and an increase in exports to achieve a more favorable balance of trade; expansion of investment opportunities to attract more Arab and foreign capital; development of technological expertise and qualified personnel; attainment of a balanced distribution of economic gains nationally through regional development; and expansion and upgrading of health, education, housing, and other social services.

Between 1953 and 1986, Jordan received development assistance from the IBRD and other international agencies, other Arab countries, the UK, Germany, and the US. The US provided nearly $1.7 billion in nonmilitary assistance and more than $1.4 billion in military aid. Aid from Arab oil-producing countries totaled $322 million in 1984. The April 1989 riots in Jordan led to a new surge of aid transfers. Arab grants to Jordan in 1989 fell between $360 million and $430 million. Political dissatisfaction in Kuwait and Saudi Arabia at Jordan's policy during the Gulf crisis resulted, however, in the Gulf states denying further direct grant assistance. Jordan received development loans worth JD57.5 million in 1990, down from JD70.3 million in 1989. Jordan's external debt rose from JD3,508 million in 1984 to JD7,418 million in 1989. In the 1989 budget 20% of total estimated expenditures were earmarked for servicing the civilian debt. Since repayment obligations had become an intolerable burden, the IMF was called in to reschedule these payments. During the Gulf conflict, Jordan suspended payments and to date has accumulated arrears of principal and interest estimated at around $750 million. Jordan and the IMF concluded a second agreement in October 1991. The Fund aims to see Jordan's budget deficit (excluding grants) decrease from 18% of GDP in 1991 to 5% in 1998. This will be accomplished partly by reducing public expenditures from 44.4% of GDP to 35%, while domestic revenues are to increase from 26.5% of GDP to 30%. Real GDP is expected to grow from 1% to 4%. Consumption is to be cut from 100.9% of GDP to 79.5%. Foreign and domestic borrowing will be cut from 10.6% of GDP to 3.5% in 1998.

40 SOCIAL DEVELOPMENT

The social insurance system provides old-age, disability, and survivor benefits, as well as workers' compensation. Workers con-

tribute 5% of their wages, employers pay 8% of payroll, and the government covers any deficit. The retirement age is 60 for men and 55 for women if coverage requirements are met. The UNRWA conducts an extensive welfare program for Palestinian refugees. Many Christian sects maintain hospitals, orphanages, and schools, financed mainly from foreign sources.

Since 1979, the government has sponsored a family planning program in an effort to improve maternal and child health. The fertility rate was 6.2 during 1985–90. Abortion is permissible on broad health grounds.

Women's rights are often dictated by Islam. Under Shari'a law, men may obtain a divorce more easily than women, a female heir's inheritance is half that of a male, and in court, a woman's testimony has only half the value of a man's. Jordan's chapter of the Business and Professional Women's Club gives seminars on women's rights and offers assistance in establishing small businesses.

41 HEALTH

In 1990, Jordan had 1.9 hospital beds per 1,000 people. In 1991, Jordan had 6,395 physicians, 2,220 pharmacists, 1,477 dentists, and 6,466 nurses. The UNRWA maintains its own hospitals and maternity centers. A medical faculty was added at the University of Jordan in 1972.

Medical services are concentrated in the main towns, but in recent decades the government has attempted to bring at least a minimum of modern medical care to rural areas. Village clinics are staffed by trained nurses, with regular visits by government physicians. As modern medicine has spread to the more remote areas, traditional methods have been dying out. The Ministry of Health, created in 1950, in cooperation with UNICEF, WHO, and the UNRWA, has greatly reduced the incidence of malaria and tuberculosis. In 1990, there were only 14 reported cases of tuberculosis per 100,000 people. Trachoma, hepatitis, typhoid fever, intestinal parasites, acute skin inflammations, and other endemic conditions remain common, however. In 1991, 99% of the population had access to safe water and 100% of the population had adequate sanitation. Total health care expenditures for 1990 were $149 million.

In 1992, average life expectancy was 68 years. In 1993, the birth rate was 39.5 per 1,000 people, with about 35% of married women (ages 15 to 49) using contraception. In 1992, there were 171,000 births.

The infant mortality rate was 25 per 1,000 live births in 1992, and the general mortality rate was 5.5 per 1,000 people in 1993. In 1992, 97% of the population had access to health care services.

42 HOUSING

A general housing shortage in the mid-1960s was aggravated by the influx of West Bank refugees after the 1967 war, and Jordan still lacked adequate housing in the early 1980s. During 1981–86, some 42,300 new residential building permits were issued. According to the latest available information for 1980–88, the total number of dwellings was 660,000 with 4.1 people per dwelling.

43 EDUCATION

The literacy rate rose from only 32% of the population in 1961 to 80% in 1990, with male literacy estimated at 89.3% and female at 70.3%. Education is compulsory for nine years: six years for the elementary and three years for the preparatory, or lower secondary, stage. A further three years prepares students for university education. In 1991, Jordan had 2,424 primary schools with 40,694 teachers and 981,255 pupils. Secondary schools had a total of 109,429 pupils the same year. Of these, 25,499 were in vocational schools.

Jordan has four universities: the University of Jordan (founded in 1962), at 'Amman; Yarmuk University at Irbid; Mut'ah University, in Karak governorate in southern Jordan; and the University of Jordan for Science and Technology. During the 1970s, several polytechnical and community colleges were established. UNRWA schools on the East Bank enroll Palestinian students. In 1991, 84,226 students were enrolled at all higher level institutions; higher education teaching staff numbered 3,753.

44 LIBRARIES AND MUSEUMS

The library at the University of Jordan has 516,800 volumes. The holdings of public libraries is 140,000 volumes compared to the 1,227,000 volumes held in academic libraries. In 1977, the department of Libraries, Documentation, and Archives was founded to establish the national library which has 40,000 volumes. 'Amman has four museums: the Jordan Archaeological Museum, Folklore Museum, Popular Life Museum, and the Mosaic Gallery.

45 MEDIA

Jordan's four daily newspapers (with 1991 estimated daily circulations) are *Al-Dustur* ("Constitution") (90,000), *Al-Rai* ("Opinion") (120,000), *Ash-Sha'ab* ("People") (30,000), and *Jordan Times* (13,000). All except the English-language *Jordan Times* are in Arabic, and all are published in 'Amman and are owned and operated by the private sector. *Al-Rai* is a government-controlled paper, founded after the 1970–71 civil war; *Al-Dustur* is 25% government owned. There are also weeklies and less frequent publications published in Arabic in 'Amman. One weekly, *The Star*, is published in English (estimated circulation 10,000). The press code, enacted in 1955, requires all newspapers to be licensed and prohibits the publishing of certain information, mainly relating to Jordan's national security, unless taken directly from material released by the government.

Public communications and broadcasting facilities are government controlled. Telephone and telegraph facilities were introduced soon after World War II. Telephone service, at first rudimentary, was expanded in the 1950s; in 1991 there were 280,092 telephones on the East Bank, mostly in 'Amman and the larger towns. Radio Jordan transmits AM and FM broadcasts in English, and the government–owned television station broadcasts programs in English, Arabic, French, and Hebrew on two channels. In 1991 there were more than 1,060,000 radios and about 330,000 television sets.

46 ORGANIZATIONS

Religious organizations still are of major importance, and membership in the hamula, the kinship group or lineage comprising several related families, also is of great significance as a framework for social organization. Literary and theatrical clubs have become popular, especially since World War II, but political organizations died out after the 1957 ban on political parties. There are chambers of commerce in 'Amman and other large towns.

47 TOURISM, TRAVEL, AND RECREATION

The Gulf War caused a decline in tourism; 2,227,688 visitors arrived in Jordan in 1991, compared with 2,633,262 the year before. Of these arrivals, 28% were from Egypt, 25% from Syria, and 13% from Iraq. There were 7,733 rooms in hotels and other establishments with 15,624 beds and a 40% occupancy rate, and tourism receipts totaled $317 million.

The East Bank is an area of immense historical interest, with some 800 archaeological sites, including 224 in the Jordan Valley. Jordan's notable tourist attractions include the Greco-Roman remains at Jerash (ancient Garasi), which was one of the major cities of the Decapolis (the capital, 'Amman, was another, under the name of Philadelphia) and is one of the best-preserved cities of its time in the Middle East. Petra (Batra), the ancient capital of Nabataea in southern Jordan, carved out of the red rock by the Nabataeans, is probably the East Bank's most famous historical site. Natural attractions include the Jordan Valley and the Dead Sea, which—at 392 m below sea level—is the lowest spot on Earth.

Eastern Jordan has modern hotel facilities in 'Amman and Al-'Aqabah, and there are government-built rest houses at some of the remote points of interest. Tourists are permitted to bring in unlimited foreign currency. Passport and visa are required for entry except for nationals of certain Middle Eastern countries.

The beaches on the Gulf of Aqaba offer holiday relaxation for Jordanians, as well as tourists. Sports facilities include swimming pools, tennis and squash courts, and bowling alleys.

48 FAMOUS JORDANIANS

The founder of Jordan's Hashemite dynasty—the term stems from the Hashemite (or Hashimite) branch of the tribe of the Prophet Muhammad—was Hussein ibn-'Ali (Husayn bin 'Ali, 1856–1931), sharif of Mecca and king of the Hijaz.

As a separate Arab country, Jordan has had a relatively short history, during which only two men have become internationally known. The first of these was the founder of the kingdom, 'Abdallah ibn-Husayn (1882–1951). Although he was born in Hijaz and was a son of the sharif of Mecca, he made 'Amman his headquarters. He was recognized as emir in 1921 and king in 1946. The second is his grandson, King Hussein I (Husayn ibn-Talal, b. 1935), who has ruled since 1953. In June 1978, 16 months after the death by helicopter crash of Queen Alia (1948–77), Hussein married his fourth wife, the reigning Queen Nur al-Hussein (Elizabeth Halaby, b. US, 1951).

49 DEPENDENCIES

Jordan has no territories or colonies.

50 BIBLIOGRAPHY

Badran, Adman, and Bichara Khader. *The Economic Development of Jordan*. Wolfeboro, N.H.: Longwood, 1986.

Garrard, Andrew N. and Hans Georg Gebel (eds.). *The Prehistory of Jordan: The State of Research in 1986*. Oxford, Eng.: B.A.R., 1988.

Hussein, King, of Jordan. *My War with Israel*. New York: Morrow, 1969.

Jordan in Pictures. Minneapolis: Lerner, 1988.

Lavy, Victor. *Foreign Aid and Economic Development in the Middle East: Egypt, Syria, and Jordan*. New York: Praeger, 1991.

Lawrence, T. E. *The Seven Pillars of Wisdom*. New York: Penguin, 1976 (orig. 1926).

Lewis, Norman N. *Nomads and Settlers in Syria and Jordan, 1800–1980*. New York: Cambridge University Press, 1987.

Lunt, James D. *Hussein of Jordan: A Political Biography*. London: Macmillan, 1989.

Metz, Helen Chapin (ed.). *Jordan, A Country Study*. 4th ed. Washington, D.C.: Library of Congress, 1991.

Mutawi, Samir A. *Jordan in the 1967 War*. New York: Cambridge University Press, 1987.

Pappe, Ilan. *Britain and the Arab-Israeli Conflict, 1948–51*. New York: St. Martin's, 1988.

Pundik, Ron. *The Struggle for Sovereignty: Relations Between Great Britain and Jordan, 1946–1951*. Cambridge, Mass: B. Blackwell, 1994.

Salibi, Kamal S. *The Modern History of Jordan*. New York: I.B. Tauris, 1993.

Seccombe, Ian J. *Jordan*. Santa Barbara, Calif.: ABC-Clio, 1984.

Wilson, Rodney (ed.). *Politics and the Economy in Jordan*. New York: Routledge, 1991.

KAZAKHSTAN

Republic of Kazakhstan
Kazakhstan Respublikasy

CAPITAL: Almaty (Alma Ata).

FLAG: Light blue with a yellow sun and soaring eagle in the center and a yellow vertical ornamentation in the hoist.

ANTHEM: National Anthem of Kazakhstan.

MONETARY UNIT: The tenge, issued in 15 November 1993, is the national currency. There is a coin, the tyin. One hundred tyin equal one tenge. As of fall 1994, 5o tenge = US$1, but exchange rates fluctuate widely.

WEIGHTS AND MEASURES: The metric system is in force.

HOLIDAYS: New Year, 31 December–1 January; International Women's Day, 8 March; Nauryz (Kazakh New Year), 28 March; Solidarity Day, 1 May; Victory Day, 9 May; Independence Day, 25 October.

TIME: 5 PM = noon GMT.

¹LOCATION, SIZE, AND EXTENT

Kazakhstan is located in southern Asia between Russia and Uzbekistan, bordering on the Caspian Sea and the Aral Sea, with a total area of 2,717,300 sq km (1,049,155 sq mi). Kazakhstan shares boundaries with Russia on the N and W, China on the E, Kyrgyzstan, Uzbekistan, and Turkmenistan on the S, and the Caspian Sea on the W. Kazakhstan's boundary length totals 12,012 km (7,464 mi). Its capital city, Almaty (Alma-Ata) is located in the southeastern part of the country. The process in underway to shift the capital to Aqmola, in the north central part of the state.

²TOPOGRAPHY

The topography of Kazakhstan is varied, as it extends from the Volga River to the Altai Mountains, and from plains in western Siberia to central Asian oasis and desert. Thirteen percent of Kazakhstan's land is arable with less than one percent under irrigation.

³CLIMATE

The country has an arid continental climate. In the capital the mean temperature in July is 27°C (81°F). In January, the mean temperature is −5°C (23°F). Rainfall averages between 25 cm (9.8 in) and 38 cm (15 in). Because of the wide ranges in elevation in the country, there are wide variations in temperature and rainfall.

⁴FLORA AND FAUNA

The sparse plant covering in the desert consists of saltworts, wormwoods, alhagi, and a haloxylon typical of the southern desert. Animals include the antelope, sand cat, and jerboa.

⁵ENVIRONMENT

Kazakhstan faces several important environmental issues. As the site of the former Soviet Union's nuclear testing programs, areas of the nation have been exposed to high levels of nuclear radiation, and there is significant radioactive pollution. The nation also has 30 uranium mines which add to the problem of uncontrolled release of radioactivity.

Mismanagement of irrigation projects has caused the level of the Aral Sea to drop by 13 m which has decreased its size by 50%. The change in size has changed the climate in the area and revealed 3 million hectares of land that is now subject to erosion.

Air pollution in Kazakhstan is another significant environmental problem due to the production of 5 million tons of airborne pollutants. One result is the formation of acid rain which damages the environment within the country and the surrounding countries. Pollution from industrial and agricultural sources has also damaged the nation's water supply. UN sources report that, in some cases, contamination of rivers with industrial metals was 160 to 800 times beyond acceptable levels.

As of 1994, Kazakhstan's wildlife is in danger of extinction due to the overall level of pollution. According to current estimates, some areas of the nation will not be able to sustain any form of wildlife by the year 2015. In the areas where pollution is the most severe, 11 species of mammals and 19 species of birds and insects are already extinct.

⁶POPULATION

The population of Kazakhstan was 16,536,511 in 1989. It was estimated at 17,035,000 at the end of 1992. The projection for 2000 was 18,332,000, based on a crude birth rate of 17 per 1,000 population and a death rate of 7.4, for a natural increase of 9.6 during 1995–2000. The estimated population density in 1992 was 6.3 per sq km (16.2 per sq mi). Alma–Ata, the capital, had an estimated population of 1,147,000 at the beginning of 1990. Karaganda had an estimated population of 613,000, and Chimkent, 401,000.

⁷MIGRATION

Kazakhs abroad (in China, Mongolia, and other newly independent republics of the former USSR) are encouraged to return. Those who fled in Stalin's time automatically received citizenship; others must apply. Emigration to other USSR republics exceeded immigration by 301,800 during 1979–90.

⁸ETHNIC GROUPS

Kazakhs constituted 40% of the population in 1989 and Russians, 38%. Germans accounted for 6%, Ukrainians for 5%, and Uzbeks and Tatars, 2% each.

⁹LANGUAGES

The constitution declares Kazakh to be the national language and requires the president to be a Kazakh speaker. Kazakh is a Turkic language written in Cyrillic script with many special letters (but in Roman script in China since 1960). No more than half of all Kazakhs can speak the language effectively. Almost everyone can speak Russian, which has special status as the "language of inter-ethnic communication."

¹⁰RELIGIONS

The Kazakhs, a distinct ethnic group originating with Turkic and Mongol settlers who arrived there in late antiquity (first century BC) are the dominant element in the population (40%) and are primarily Sunni Muslims of the Hanafi persuasion. The other ethnic groups are Christians, mostly Eastern Orthodox. In 1993 there was also a small but significant population of 500,000 Roman Catholics, and in 1990 some 17,000 Jews.

¹¹TRANSPORTATION

About 14,460 km (8,985 mi) of railroad tracks traverse Kazakhstan, all 1.52-m-gauge. Highways totaled 189,000 km (117,000 mi) in 1990, almost entirely hard-surfaced (paved or gravel). The primary port is Guryev, on the Caspian Sea. Much of the infrastructure connects Kazakhstan with Russia rather than points within Kazakhstan. Infrastructure will need to significantly improve before Kazakhstan's vast mineral resources can be effectively exploited.

¹²HISTORY

There is evidence of human habitation in present-day Kazakhstan from the earliest Stone Age, more than 300,000 years ago. The steppe characteristics of most of the region are best suited for nomadic pastoralism, which an ever-shifting pattern of peoples have pursued in this territory. Achaemenid documents give the name Sacae to the first such group to be historically recorded. In the 3rd and 2nd centuries BC they were displaced by the Usun in the east, the Kangiui in the south central region, and the Alani in the west.

The first well-established state was that of the Turkic Kaganate, in the 6th century AD, replaced in the early 8th century by the Turgesh state. In 766, the Karluks established dominance in what is now eastern Kazakhstan. Some of the southern portions of the region fell under Arab influence in the 8th-9th centuries, and Islam was introduced. Western Kazakhstan was under Oghuz control in 9th to the 11th centuries; at roughly the same time the Kimak and Kipchak tribes, of Turkic orgin, controlled the east. The large central desert of Kazakhstan is still called "Dashti-Kipchak," or the Kipchak Steppe.

The Karluk state was destroyed by invading Iagmas in the late 9th and early 10th centuries. They formed the Karakhanid state, which controlled extensive lands into what is now China. The Karakhanids were in a constant state of war with the Seljuks, to the south, and control of parts of what is now Kazakhstan passed back and forth between them. The Karakhanids collapsed in the 1130s when they were invaded by Khitans, who established the Karakitai state. In the mid-12th century, Khwarazm split off from the weakening Karakitais, but the bulk of the state survived until the invasion of Genghiz Khan, 1219–1221.

Kazakhstan was part of Batu's Golden Horde, which in the 14th century broke up into the White Horde and Mogulistan. By the early 15th century, the White Horde had split into several large khanates, including the Nogai Horde and the Uzbek Khanate.

The present-day Kazakhs formed in the mid-15th century when clan leaders Janibek and Girei broke away from Abul Khair, leader of the Uzbeks, to seek their own territory in Semirechie, between the Chu and Talas rivers. First to unite the Kazakhs into one people was Khan Kasym (1511–23). When the Nogai Horde and Siberian Khanates broke up in the mid 16th century, tribes from both joined the Kazakhs. The clans separated into three Hordes: the Great Horde, which controlled Semirechie; the Middle Horde, which had central Kazakhstan, and the Lesser Horde, which had western Kazakhstan.

Russian traders and soldiers began to appear on the northwestern edge of Kazakh territory in the 17th century, when Cossacks founded the forts which became the cities of Uralsk and Gurev. The Kazakh khanate was in disarray at the time, badly pressed by Kalmyk invaders who had begun to move in from the east. Pushed west in what the Kazakhs call their "Great Retreat," the Kazakh position deteriorated until, in 1726, Lesser Horde khan Abul'khair requested Russian assistance. From that point on the Lesser Horde was under Russian control. The Middle Horde was conquered by 1798. The Great Horde remained independent until the 1820s, when pressure from both the Kokand Khanate and Russia forced them to choose what they regarded as the lesser of evils, the Russians.

There was, however, considerable resistance, led by Khan Kenen (Kenisary Kasimov), of the Middle Horde, whose followers fought the Russians 1836–47. Khan Kene is now regarded as a Kazakh national hero. Russian attempts to quell this resistance led to establishment of a number of forts and settlements in Kazakh territory, which made Kazakh nomadism impossible and destroyed the Kazakh economy.

In 1863, Russia promulgated a policy in the Gorchakov Circular which asserted the right to annex "troublesome" border areas. It was on this basis that Russian troops began the conquest of Central Asia. Most of Kazakhstan was made part of the Steppe district of the Russian empire; the rest was in Turkestan.

Beginning in the 1890s Russian settlers were aggressively moved into fertile lands in northern and eastern Kazakhstan, further displacing the nomadic Kazakhs. Between 1906 and 1912 more than a half-million Russian farms were started as part of the Stolypin reforms. By the time of the 1916 uprising the Kazakhs were broken and starving. Despite a strong effort against the Russians, they were savagely repressed.

At the time of the revolution a group of secular nationalists called the Alash Orda attempted to create a Kazakh government, but it lasted less than two years (1918–20) before surrendering to the Bolsheviks.

The Kazakh Autonomous Soviet Socialist Republic was declared in 1920 and elevated to full republic status in 1936. In the period 1929–34, when Stalin was abolishing private agriculture and establishing huge collective farms, Kazakhstan suffered repeated famines which killed at least 1.5 million Kazakhs, as well as destroying 80% of the republic's livestock. Thousands more Kazakhs tried to escape to China, although most died on the road.

In World War II much Russian industry was evacuated to Kazakhstan; this was followed in 1953–65 by the so-called Virgin Lands campaign, which converted huge tracts of Kazakh grazing land to wheat and other cereal production. This campaign brought thousands more Russians and other non-Kazakhs to Kazakhstan; as a result Kazakhstan became the only Soviet republic in which the eponymous people were not a majority of the population. Because Russians and other Europeans nearly equal the number of Kazakhs in the republic, virtually every public act requires a delicate balancing of differing interests.

On 16 December 1986, Mikhail Gorbachev replaced Kazakhstan's long-time leader Dinmukhamed Kunaev, a Kazakh, with a Russian from outside the republic. This set off three days of rioting, the first public nationalist protest in the USSR. In June 1989, more civil disturbances hastened the appointment of Nursultan Nazarbaev as republic leader. A metallurgist and a Kazakh, Nazarbaev became prominent in the last Soviet years as a spokesman both for greater republic sovereignty and for continuation of the

KAZAKHSTAN

LOCATION: 48°N; 60°E. BOUNDARY LENGTHS: Total boundary lengths, 12,012 km (7,464 mi); China, 1,533 km (954 mi); Kyrgyzstan, 1,051 km (653 mi); Russia, 6,846 km (4,254 mi); Turkmenistan, 379 km (236 mi); Uzbekistan, 2,203 km (1,369 mi).

Soviet Union, on a renewed basis. He was elected president by the Kazakhstan parliament in 1990, and reaffirmed by public vote in an uncontested election in December 1991. Not a party to the original dissolution of the USSR, Nazarbaev prevailed in arguments that Kazakhstan must participate in formation of the Commonwealth of Independent States. Kazakhstan was the only Soviet republic to declare independence after dissolution of the USSR, on 16 December 1991.

13GOVERNMENT

The constitution of the Republic of Kazakhstan, adopted 28 January 1993, defines the nation as a "democratic, secular, and unitary state." It mandates three separate branches of government: a president and vice-president, to be elected every five years, and for no more than two terms; a parliament, called the Majlis or Supreme Soviet, of unspecified size and constituency, open to delegates elected for five-year terms; and a judiciary, appointed by the president. The president's executive powers also include appointment of a prime minister and his cabinet.

Of the new institutions, only the parliament has come into being, following President Nazarbaev's dissolution of the last Soviet parliament, whose 380 members were elected in April 1990 and dispersed in December 1993, before completion of the term mandated by the previous constitution. Elections to the new parliament were held 7 March 1994. This body has 177 seats, 42 of which are reserved for candidates selected by the president.

The constitution calls Kazakhstan a "strong presidential democracy;" most power indeed rests with the president, but parliament can and occasionally does interfere with implementation of some executive orders. President Nazarbaev, eligible to serve two more terms under the new constitution, is popular with all the republic's ethnic groups, and so is expected to be re-elected in the first presidential elections in 1996.

14POLITICAL PARTIES

The constitution permits the formation of registered political parties, but in practice it is difficult to get the necessary legal permissions. Three of the republic's parties were created at the initiative of President Nazarbaev, who as president is forbidden by the constitution from holding "posts in public associations." The Socialist Party is the successor to the Communist Party, outlawed after the August 1991 coup attempt. The current head is former legislative speaker S. Abdildin, but the membership is heavily Russian. It elected eight members to the new parliament. Related communist organizations, the Peasants' Union and the Trade Union, took 15 seats between them. A new Communist Party was allowed to register in 1994.

The People's Congress, or Social-Democratic Party, registered in October 1991, has both Kazakh and Russian members. The co-heads are two Kazakh poets, Mukhtar Shakhanov and Olzhas Suleimenov. Originally pro-Nazarbaev, the party became increasingly critical of the government in 1992–93. It has nine seats in the Majlis. A third party, the Party for National Unity (SNEK), was registered in October 1992. Now headed by Sultanov, a former deputy prime minister, SNEK is considered the presidential party. It has 33 seats in the new parliament.

There are at least four large Kazakh nationalist movements, three of which—Azat (Freedom), the Republican Party, and Zheltoksan (December)—speak of registering as one party, to be called Azat. The fourth, Alash, advocates a more actively nationalist and pro-Muslim line than do the other three parties. The Kazakh nationalists elected only two deputies to the Majlis.

There are at least four Russian nationalist political organizations: Edinstvo (Unity), Civic Contract, Democratic Progress, and Lad (Harmony). Despite considerable difficulty getting candidates on the ballot, Lad managed to elect four deputies.

In Uralsk (Western Kazakhstan) and Petropavlovsk (Northern Kazakhstan) there are also Cossack obshchinas, or communities, agitating for autonomous status. Denied registry by Kazakhstan, many are active in Cossack obshchinas across the border in Russia, where Cossacks have the right to maintain military organizations and carry weapons.

15 LOCAL GOVERNMENT

Kazakhstan is divided into 19 oblasts (provinces); the cities of Almaty and Leninsk (the site of the Baikonur space launching site) have special administrative status equivalent to that of oblasts. The 19 oblasts are in turn divided into rayons (regions). Each oblast, rayon, and even settlement has its own elective council, charged with drawing up a budget and supervising local taxation. Cities have local councils as well; if large enough, cities are also divided into rayons, each with its own council. These councils are also elected for five-year terms; the first elections under the new constitution were held in March 1994.

The local legislatures do not choose the local executive; the Heads of Administration of oblasts and rayons, known as Glavs or Hakims, are presidential appointments. The "Head" in turn appoints the members of his staff, who are the department heads of the oblast. There is some discussion of shifting to local election of the regional "heads."

16 JUDICIAL SYSTEM

The Parliament (Supreme Soviet) adopted a constitution in 1991 which guarantees basic political freedoms and individual rights. A Constitutional Court established in 1992 is responsible for interpreting the constitution, resolving conflicts between oblasts (provinces), and interethnic problems. The courts are arranged in three tiers: local level, oblast (province) level, and Supreme Court. Local level courts serve as courts of first instance for less serious crimes. Oblast level courts hear more serious criminal cases and also hear cases in rural areas where no local courts have been established. Judgment of local courts may be appealed to the oblast level. The Supreme Court hears appeals from the oblast courts. A special arbitration court hears disputes between state enterprises.

The president recommends and the Supreme Soviet approves nominees for the Supreme Court. Oblast judges are recommended by heads of oblasts and approved by the oblast soviet (council). Lower level judges are approved by regional or city councils. All judges serve 10-year terms.

17 ARMED FORCES

Without an independent national military establishment, Kazakhstan shares control of CIS forces within its borders: an army corps of six divisions and six special brigades, a tactical air force of 200 fighter-bombers, an air defense force of 60 interceptors and 150 missiles, and a strategic nuclear force of 104 SS–18s and 40 bombers, the latter controlled by agreement by the Russian Strategic Rocket Forces. There are no identifiable defense costs. The Committee for National Secutiry (KNB) focuses on issues of nuclear proliferation, counterterrorism, and combating oragnized crime and official corruption. It has the authority to deny citizens permission to travel in and out of the country, to requisition property, and to demand cooperation by citizens.

18 INTERNATIONAL COOPERATION

Kazakhstan was admitted to the UN on 2 March 1992. It is a member of the CSCE, EBRD, ECO, ESCO, IMF, NACC, UNCTAD, and the World Bank. It is applying for membership in other international organizations andis a member of the CIS. As of 1993, the country reported it had established formal diplomatic relations with 70 countries. It has established especially good relations with neighboring Central Asian states and China. The US established formal diplomatic relations with Kazakhstan in the early part of 1993.

19 ECONOMY

The Kazakhstan economy is extremely well-endowed with large tracts of arable land and rich reserves of coal, oil, and rare metals. The country's oil reserves alone are estimated to be equal to those of Kuwait; 470,000 barrels a day are currently produced. Animal herding was the mainstay of the nomadic Kazakh population before their incorporation into the Soviet Union; wool production remains an important agricultural product today, along with grains and meat. Currently, agriculture employs about 19% of the labor force and contributes over 36% of the NMP. Raw materials from the crop, livestock, and mining sectors help supply a sizeable industrial sector, which accounts for 20% of the labor force and 42% of NMP. With a 1991 per capita income of $2,470, an infant mortality rate of 26 per 1,000, and a relatively high adult literacy rate, welfare indicators have been among the best for Central and Western Asian standards, though still somewhat below average for those of the former Soviet Union.

Like other countries of the former USSR, Kazakhstan has faced serious economic dislocation since 1991, resulting from the disruption of trade with other post-Soviet republics, an end to the flow of official revenues from the Soviet central government, the decline in state production orders, and the need for sudden currency adjustments. Estimated GDP fell by 8.5% in 1991, 14% in 1992, and 15.3% in 1993; overall output is estimated to have shrunk by one-third between 1990–93. Inflation reached a staggering 2,000% in 1993, signifying a severe drop in real income for much of the population, 20% of whom are feared to be facing serious poverty.

The current crisis notwithstanding, given its rich resource endowments, the potential for strong growth in the near future is more apparent in Kazakhstan than many other Central Asian republics. Under President Nazarbayev the government has avoided much of the debilitating ethnic strife plaguing other parts of Central Asia and has targeted steady liberalization as its main strategy to revamp the national economy. Legislation adopted since 1992 has promoted the rapid transfer of small shops and services to the private sector, the spread of private ownership in housing, and the inflow of large foreign investments. The government has been among the strongest supporters of maintaining a ruble-based monetary union in the interest of facilitating inter-republic trade as well as ensuring transit routes for international exports and imports. However, by late 1993, failure to implement agreements made by post-Soviet republics on the ruble-zone prompted Kazakhstan to issue its own currency, the tenge.

20INCOME

In 1992, Kazakhstan's, GNP was $28,584 million at current prices, or $1,680 per capita. In 1992 the GDP was $28,580 million in current US dollars.

21LABOR

The labor force consists of some 8.2 million persons, with the service sector engaging 23%; agriculture, 19%; manufacturing and mining, 21%; construction, 12%; transportation and communications, 11%; trade, 8%; utilities, 4%; with finance, public administration, and defense accounting for the remaining 2%. The labor force grew about 0.8% annually from 1985 to 1991. The mining and quarrying industry is becoming a significant provider of employment opportunity.

All workers are entitled to join or form unions of their choosing. Union registration generally is a lengthy and difficult process. About 250,000 workers out of the total work force of 5,600,000 had joined independent unions as of 1992; some workers who have joined independent unions are subjected to various forms of harassment, indicating hostility by local authorities and state-sponsored trade unions.

The minimum age for employment is 16, and there is no minimum wage that covers all employment sectors. The legal maximum workweek is 48 hours, although most enterprises maintain a 40-hour work week.

22AGRICULTURE

Before the demise of the Soviet Union, Kazakhstan reportedly had 35,698,000 ha (88,209,000 acres) of arable land, representing 13% of the total land area, and comprising one-third of all agricultural land of the Soviet Union. Most cropland is found in the northern steppes, where the failed Virgin and Idle Land Project of the 1950s occurred. Small-scale privatization has created some 15,000 private farms.

Kazakhstan is the former Soviet Union's only grain exporter. Wheat makes up half of all sown grain acreage, which occupies two-thirds of seasonal cropland. A record wheat harvest in 1992 (32 million tons) provided 10 million tons for export. A smaller 1993 harvest (25 million tons), severely reduced exports, and was caused by poor weather, deteriorating equipment, and financial problems. Rice is produced in irrigated stretches along the Syrdar'ya near Qyzlorda and around Taldyqorghan in the east. Production amounted to 500,000 tons in 1992.

Potatoes, fruits, and vegetables are other significant food crops. Less than 2% of agricultural land is used to cultivate commercial crops such as cotton, sugar beets, sunflowers, and flax.

During the Soviet period, groundwater resources and chemical fertilizers were overused, resulting in depleted soils, decreasing yields, and environmental pollution.

23ANIMAL HUSBANDRY

About 60% of Kazakhstan's total land area is permanent pastureland. In 1992, the livestock population included 58 million chickens, 33.9 million sheep, 3 million pigs, 1.5 million horses, and about 0.7 million goats. Total meat production in 1992 amounted to 1,510,000 tons, of which 16% was mutton and lamb, 18% pork, 13% chicken, 48% beef, and 5% other meat.

Wool is an important animal product; in 1992, 168,000 tons

of greasy and scoured wool were produced. That year, fresh cow milk production totaled 4,948,000 tons, and 190,800 tons of hen eggs were laid.

24FISHING

Fisheries are concentrated around the Caspian Sea, and are of some importance to the local economy.

25FORESTRY

Only 3% of Kazakhstan is covered by forests and woodlands; forestry is of little commercial importance.

26MINING

The eastern region of Kazakhstan is rich in many metallic minerals, including: alumina, arsenic, bauxite, beryllium, bismuth, cadmium, chrome, copper, gold, iron ore, lead-zinc, manganese, molybdenum, rhenium, silver, titanium, and tungsten. Copper mining occurs at six facilities, most notably the Dzhezkazgan complex which in addition includes concentration, smelting, and refining facilities. Chromium is also an important mineral commodity; Kazakhstan had supplied more than 95% of chromite production for the former USSR through the Donskoy mining and beneficiation complex at Khromtau. Iron ore found near Rudnyy in the north supplies the iron and steel plants in the Russian Urals region as well as plants at Karaganda and Temirtau. Asbestos, barite, and phosphate are also mined.

27ENERGY AND POWER

Kazakhstan is richly endowed with energy reserves. Oil is the most promising energy source destined for exploitation in the post-Soviet era. Whereas current oil sources are located along the northeastern shore of the Caspian Sea near Aqtau, the enormous Tengiz oil field lies further north along the coast.

In May 1992, Chevron entered into a joint venture agreement with Kazakhstan to develop the Tengiz oil field which is estimated to contain 6–9 billion barrels of recoverable crude oil reserves. By April 1993, a 40-year agreement was signed, creating the Tengizchevroil joint venture. In May 1993, Kazakhstan announced plans to form an international consortium to develop oil reserves in the Kazakh portion of the Caspian Sea, which is estimated to contain up to 60 billion barrels; Kazakhstan also applied for observer status in OPEC at that time. Production of oil in 1992 totaled 26.7 million tons (540,000 barrels per day).

Some natural gas is also produced as a derivative from oil fields on the shores of the Caspian Sea. Production of natural gas in 1991 totaled 7.9 billion cu m, up 11% from 1990. Liquid natural gas production in 1992 amounted to 93,000 barrels per day. Hard coal is mined from the Qaranghandy and Ekibastuz basins, which produced 46.9 million and 82.8 million tons, respectively, in 1991. Total hard coal production in 1992 was 122.5 million tons; lignite and brown coal, 2.5 million tons.

Several hydroelectric projects also operate. The Qapshaghay Dam on the Ile River, north of Almaty, and the Shardara Dam, on the Syrdar'ya in the extreme south, produce electricity for various industries. In 1992, Kazakhstan's total installed electrical capacity was 17,900,000 kw, and production amounted to 79,100 million kwh.

28INDUSTRY

Overwhelmingly dominated by state-owned enterprises under the centrally planned economy of the USSR, Kazakhstan's industrial sector is slowly being privatized and re-oriented toward market-driven production. Through a combination of auctions, investment coupons issued to the public, and case-by-case deliberation (particularly for large enterprises), government plans have mandated the privatization of almost all industrial enterpises by the year 2000. However, the process of structural adjustment in

Kazakhstan's industrial sector has been fraught with difficulty. Industrial production declined by 1% in 1991 and over 15% in 1992. To stimulate recovery, foreign investment and joint ventures are being encouraged particularly in agro-processing, nonferrous metals, and light industry, as well as oil, gas, and energy. New joint ventures with foreign investors thus far involve photocopier, window frame, and mining, agricultural, and oilfield equipment manufactures. Among the largest enterprise sales has been the purchase of the Almaty Tobacco Factory by the Philip Morris Corporation in 1993.

Reflecting Kazakhstan's resource-based economy, agri-processing and metallurgy and mining accounted for 23.6% and 14.6% of industrial output in 1991, respectively. Food processing activities yielded 840,831 tons of meat; 302,900 tons of sugar (based mainly on imports of raw materials from Cuba); and 101,000 tons of vegetable oil. Output from the metal processing and mining sector in 1991 included crude steel, 6,377 thousand tons; finished rolled ferrous metals, 4,660 thousand tons; iron ore, 21,895 thousand tons; and pig iron, 4,952 thousand tons. Despite the country's large oil reserves, fuel production accounts for only about 11% of manufacturing value-added. Production yields included 130 million tons of coal in 1991, along with 26.6 million tons of oil, and 7.3 billion cu m of natural gas.

Textiles and leather manufacturing is relatively well-developed in Kazakhstan thanks to inputs of wool and other material from the country's own livestock sector as well as cotton imports from other areas of the former USSR. In 1991, textiles and leather accounted for 18.2% of total industrial output. Specific products manufactured in 1991 included knitted wear, 111,820 pieces; fabrics (wool, cotton and silk), 248,708 sq m; and shoes, 35,410 pairs. Other goods produced by light industry enterprises included 130,674 tape recorders, 86,300 radios, 535,000 electric irons, and 391,000 washing machines. Reflecting Kazakhstan's specialized role as a supplier of specific industrial goods within the USSR, machine-building is also among the largest of Kazakhstan's industries accounting for about 11% of total industrial output and over 23% of total manufacturing value. Production of the sector's main products in 1991 included bulldozers, 10,278 units; excavators, 577 units; and metal-cutting equipment, 2,414 units. Agricultural machinery manufactured in 1991 had a total value of R356 million. Other significant manufactures are construction materials, sawn wood, paper, and chemicals, including mineral fertilizers, sulfuric acid, caustic soda, and synthetic plastics.

29 SCIENCE AND TECHNOLOGY
The Kazakh Academy of Sciences has departments of physics and mathematics, earth sciences, chemistry, and biology. Many of Kazakhstan's 19 research institutes conduct agricultural research. Scientific training is available at three universities and 21 higher educational institutes.

30 DOMESTIC TRADE
The wholesale and retail sector, previously dominated by state-controlled distribution channels, has seen the dynamic growth of independent small shops and traders. Price controls have been lifted for 90% of consumer and 80% of wholesale prices, althugh basic goods and services such as bread, flour, baby food, medicines, fodder, housing rents, utilities, and public transportation have been excluded from liberalization. Total retail trade purchases equaled R24,039 million in 1990.

31 FOREIGN TRADE
In 1990, about 89% of Kazakhstan's exports and 88% of its imports represented trade with other former Soviet republics (at foreign trade prices). Most of its international trade was with other countries within the former CMEA block. A serious disrup-

tion in the country's trading patterns occurred as the input procurement system within the Soviet centrally planned economy disintegrated, the use of hard currency and world market-determined transaction prices was adopted by former USSR republics, and export demand from Eastern European countries shrank in the early 1990s. To facilitate adjustment to these hard new realities, the government decreed key trade liberalization measures in early 1992, ending export license requirements. With liberalization, exports and imports were expected to increase substantially by the mid-1990s, though the country's limited foreign exchange may make these goals difficult to reach.

Total inter-republic exports equaled about R13,208 million in 1991, up from R8,443 million in 1990 (foreign trade prices); the nominal value of imports rose as well, from R13,026 million to R17,363 million. Much of the apparent increase in inter-republic trade resulted from higher prices being charged for primary commodities rather than an increase in trading volume, which is estimated to have actually contracted in the early 1990s. Reflecting this contraction more clearly, the value of exports to countries beyond the former Soviet Union fell from $1.8 billion to $1.3 billion; imports dropped from $2.0 billion to $1.4 billion. In the past, budget transfers from Moscow covered Kazakhstan's chronic trade deficit with the rest of the USSR; presently, the country is coping with its current imbalance mainly through large credit extensions from Russia. Calculated on the basis of foreign trade prices, 1990 exports were dominated by petroleum products (26% of the total), followed by nonferrous and ferrous metals—a pattern likely to continue for some time to come. Kazakhstan's largest imports were machinery and oil and gas products. Principal exports and imports in 1990 were as follows (in millions of rubles, foreign trade prices):

EXPORTS	
Oil & gas	2,498.2
Nonferrous metals	1,291.5
Ferrous metals	1,170.7
Machinery	945.1
Agriculture	922.8
Chemicals & petrochemicals	879.2
Other exports	1,781.0
TOTAL	9,488.5

IMPORTS	
Machinery	5,955.9
Oil and gas	3,166.6
Chemicals & petrochemicals	1,448.3
Ferrous metals	1,160.1
Fabrics, knitted goods, sewn goods & footwear	942.8
Other imports	3,776.6
TOTAL	16,449.9

Russia dominated Kazakhstan's inter-republic trade, accounting for 63% of the total in 1990. Germany, Poland, Bulgaria, and former Czechoslovakia were the largest of its international trading partners that year. Metals (ferrous and nonferrous) comprised almost three-fourths of all exports beyond the former Soviet Union, while non-Union imports were mainly machinery, processed foods, and soft goods such as textiles and footwear.

32 BALANCE OF PAYMENTS
In 1992, the current account deficit totaled $2.1 billion, the majority of which was in rubles and was offset by net credits from Russia. A shortage of foreign currency has depressed imports and exports, thus continuing a weak balance of payments position as of early 1993. However, Kazakhstan has attracted significant private foreign investment, most notably for the development of the

Tengiz and Korolev oil fields, which are estimated to require $1.5 billion of development capital over the next several years.

33 BANKING AND SECURITIES

In December 1990, the Alma-Ata branch of Gosbank (the former Soviet State Bank) was made into the Independent Kazach (National Bank of Kazakhstan). In the next year the existence of private and public financial institutions were legalized. In 1993, the parliament approved a new banking law that separated the National Bank of Kazakhstan from the government, and gave the central bank the power to conduct monetary and credit policies and regulate the commercial banking sector. A new commercial banking law defined the broad principals of banking. Banks in 1991 included the Foreign Trade Bank and 72 commercial and cooperative banks. Five of the commercial banks are privately owned. Until November 1993, the currency unit in the country was the ruble. On 15 November 1993, Kazakhstan established its own currency, the tenge.

34 INSURANCE

No recent information is available.

35 PUBLIC FINANCE

The consolidated state budget ran a deficit of 6% of GDP in 1992, causing the government to maintain relatively restricted fiscal policies. But due to these tight fiscal conditions and lack of financing, however, 1992 government investment shrank to half its 1991 level. Kazakhstan had elected to join with Uzbekistan and Russia in establishing a single currency zone using the Russian ruble. However, Russian demands in connection with the ruble zone proved unacceptable, and on 15 November 1993, Kazakhstan introduced its own currency, the tenge.

36 TAXATION

Individual income is taxable at between 12% and 40%, and 1% of salaries is deducted for social security. As of 31 December 1992, the corporate tax rate was 25% for Kazakh firms, joint ventures, and wholly foreign-owned businesses operating locally. Foreign representative offices were taxed 30%. There was also a profits tax ranging from 10% for agricultural business to 70% for the entertainment and gaming industries. A value-added tax of 28% for most goods was introduced on 1 January 1992.

37 CUSTOMS AND DUTIES

In May 1992, the Republic of Kazakhstan and the US signed a most-favored nation agreement for reciprocal tariff treatment. Also in 1992, the turnover tax and sales tax were replaced by a combination of excise taxes and a 28% value-added tax.

38 FOREIGN INVESTMENT

In early 1991, the government adopted a new foreign investment code, allowing investment by foreign companies in any economic activity except the manufacture of military goods. The law specifies provisions for duty-free imports as well as tax breaks for firms with foreign investment, especially those involved in producing consumer goods, agricultural goods, and electronic and medical equipment. The code also established a number of free economic areas where imports of intermediate products and exports of finished goods are allowed without customs duties. Further revisions in legislation are now being formulated in order to provide stronger guarantees and greater clarity on investment requirements and credit facilities open to foreign investors.

In 1992 and 1993 extensive projects involving US, French, British, and Turkish corporations (including Chevron, Mobil, Agip, Elf-Aquitaine, and British Gas) were arranged to expand the exploitation of the country's immense oil and gas deposits and develop its energy sector. The expansion of gold production in partnership with foreign concerns is also being promoted as a means of quickly boosting the inflow of foreign exchange. By 1993, active joint ventures in Kazakhstan totalled 40; these are concentrated mainly in the energy sector where total foreign investment inflow for 1993 was about $400 million.

39 ECONOMIC DEVELOPMENT

Under the economic development regime of the USSR, the republic underwent rapid development of its agricultural as well as industrial sectors. Vast tracts of land were brought into cultivation with the expansion of irrigation under the USSR's "Virgin Lands" program, while within the industrial sector, development of its metallurgical, mining, and machinery industries were prioritized. Growth in these various economic sectors was fueled by a high labor force participation rate in the local population, especially among women, as well as the import of some skilled labor from Russia. Although achieving impressive expansion of production capacity in the span of just a few decades, by the 1980s growing problems of inefficiency and inadequate technological development in the overwhelmingly dominant state sector resulted in a flagging rate of output growth overall. Growth in the republic's NMP in 1986–89 averaged 1.9% per year, only slightly ahead of population growth. The region's industrial and agricultural development had, moreover, come at some high environmental costs. The structure of Kazakhstan's transportation and energy sectors today clearly highlight the overall orientation of the economic base fostered under the Soviet regime; railroads and paved roads are clustered mainly in the north and the south, serving more to link Kazakhstan with Russia, Uzbekistan, and Kyrgyzstan rather than to integrate the republic itself. Similarly, electricity transmission networks facilitate the exchange of energy with different republics in the former USSR rather than between different parts of Kazakhstan.

Since sovereignty was declared in 1990, Kazakhstan has embarked on a process of economic restructuring, aimed at establishing a market economy. Gradual privatization of most state enterprises has been the focal point of the restructuring program and the centralized state ordering system was abolished in 1992. Although far fewer large public enterprises had actually been transferred to the private sector than planned by 1993, the privatization process was still further advanced in Kazakhstan than in other Central Asian states and the Russian Federation.

In addition to price liberalization, government decrees since 1991 have mandated the gradual elimination of various subsidies to industry and other sectors, further reductions in state expenditures, and the development of a social safety net to assist households at high poverty risk. Under the Soviet system, the republic's budget was financed through profits from the public enterprises, turnover taxes, and transfers from the USSR central government. As part of its restructuring effort, the government has adopted a new revenue generating system, embodied in the comprehensive tax laws of July 1991. The legislation outlines a system of corporate, individual income, and value-added taxes as the basis for the government's future revenues. The government is also placing great emphasis on realizing the infusion of foreign capital both to the oil and gas industry as well as various other industrial subsectors, such as agro-processing, light industry and ferrous metals.

About 34% of budgeted expenditures in 1992 (totalling R190.3 billion) was directed at education, health, and social safety. A further 22% was allocated to the national economy, including subsidies to households and enterprises as well as transfers to public enterprises. Investment Fund expenditures for specific development projects were projected at about 13% of budget outlays. A special Public Investment Program (PIP) has been established under the control of the State Economic Committee within the executive branch, with the purpose of translating development objectives into investments for specific projects and of attracting needed external financing. The PIP will draw from the Investment Fund for the government's own contribution to project financing. Reflecting the legacy of centrally planned economic development, two-thirds of the investments proposed by the PIP in 1991 were targeted at the productive sectors; this orientation is expected to be gradually shifted toward social and physical infrastructure development, leaving investment in productive sectors to be financed from non-budgetary and private sources.

40SOCIAL DEVELOPMENT

Kazakh families averaged 4 members in 1989. The divorce rate was 7.8 per 1,000 women. There were 11.4 drug-related crimes and 3.1 alcohol-related deaths per 100,000 persons. The fertility rate in 1990 was 2.7.

Women generally have access to higher education but are still channeled into mostly low-level, low-paid jobs. There are several woman's organizations, including the Union of Women of Kazakhstan, the Union of Women Entrepreneurs, the League of Muslim Women, and the Union of Feminists. There are also mothers' groups organized around specific issues. Most women's groups work to obtain support for families during the nation's economic crisis and increase women's participation in public life.

The government has signed the UN Convention in children's rights. The constitution provides for the upkeep and education of orphans.

41HEALTH

The average life expectancy in 1992 was 69 years. The overall death rate in 1993 was 8 per 1,000 inhabitants. Major causes of death per 100,000 people in 1990 were: communicable diseases and maternal/perinatal causes, 86; noncommunicable diseases, 700; and injuries 103. There were 77 reported cases of tuberculosis per 100,000 people in 1990. In 1992, immunization rates for children up to one year old were: tuberculosis, 90%; diphtheria, pertussis, and tetanus, 85%; polio, 87%; and measles, 90%. In 1992, Kazakhstan had 4.12 doctors per 1,000 people, with a nurse to doctor ratio of 3.0. There were 13.6 hospital beds per 1,000 inhabitants. Total health care expenditures in 1990 were $2.6 million.

42HOUSING

In 1989, 23.3% of all privately owned urban housing had running water, 13.6% had sewer lines, 23.3% had central heating, and 0.9% had hot water. In 1990, Kazakhstan had 14.2 sq m of housing space per capita and, as of 1 January 1991, 520,000 households (or 18.8%) were on waiting lists for housing in urban areas.

43EDUCATION

In the early 1990s, the adult literacy rate was estimated at 97.5% with males at 99.1% and females at 96.1%). Both at the primary and secondary level, education is free and state funded. Although Russian is the most commonly taught language, Kazakh, which is the official state language, is now gaining popularity and is being extended to all areas. A small percentage are also taught Uzbek, Uigher, and Tajik. There are 8,064 secondary schools in which 3,021,070 students are enrolled. Included in the 55 institutions of higher education are three universities with 285,600 pupils. The University of Kazakh Al-Farabi State University was founded in 1934 and offers history, philosophy, economics, sociology, journalism, mathematics, physics, chemistry, biology, and geography. There are 1,530 teachers and 14,000 students enrolled. The Karaganda State University was founded in 1972 and teaches philosophy, economics, law, history, mathematics, physics, chemistry, and biology. It has 8,436 students enrolled. The Technical University at Karaganda Metallurgical Combine was founded in 1964 and has faculties of metallurgy, mechanics and technology, and chemical technology.

44LIBRARIES AND MUSEUMS

Three outstanding libraries are the State Public Library of Kazakhstan in Almaty (3,458 volumes), the Scientific and Technical Library of Kazakhstan also in Almaty (9.8 million), and the Central Library of the Kazakh Academy of Science (5.5 million). The Al-Farabi Kazakh State University Library in Almaty has 1,275,000 volumes.

The Central State Museum in of Kazakhstan in Almaty features 90,000 exhibits exploring the history and physical conditions of the region. The A. Kasteyer Kazakh State Art Museum (formerly the Kazakh T.G. Shevchenko State Art Gallery) in Almaty primarily contains works by modern Kazakh artists.

45MEDIA

There are only six phones per every 100 residents. Kazakhstan is connected to the other former Soviet republics by land line or microwave and to other countries through Moscow. Kazakh Radio broadcasts in Kazakh, Russian, Uighur, German, and Korean. Kazakh Television, established in 1959, broadcasts in the same languages except for Korean.

In 1989, there were 453 state-registered newspapers, 160 published in Kazakh, and 91 periodicals, with 31 in Kazakh. Major Kazakh newspapers were *Leninshil Zhas* and *Sotsialistik Kazakhstan*.

46ORGANIZATIONS

The two major economic organizations in Kazakhstan are the Chamber of Commerce and Industry of Kazakhstan and the Union of Cooperative Entrepreneurs.

47TOURISM, TRAVEL, AND RECREATION

Kazakhstan is open to both business travelers and tourists. Visas are required by all visitors and are obtainable upon arrival or through embassies abroad and companies that sell package tours of Central Asia. The principal accommodations are hotels that formerly belonged to the Soviet Intourist system. However, foreign chains are currently developing a number of projects in Central Asia.

Kazakhstan offers a wide variety of natural landscapes to the hardier traveler, ranging from forests and mountain ranges to the vast steppes where Kazakh nomads live in tents called yurts and race thoroughbred horses and camels. The capital, Alma-Ata, has no historic attractions but is an attractive city where tree-lined streets, parks, fountains, and canals give it a European flavor. In the winter, ice skating is popular on its waterways. Air service to Kazakhstan is good, with direct flights to Alma-Ata from Ankara, Frankfurt, Hamburg, and other cities, as well as frequent daily flights from Moscow.

48FAMOUS KAZAKHS

Nursultan A. Nazarbayev and Sergey Tereshchenko have been president and prime minister of Kazakhstan since December 1991 respectively. The novelist Kaltay Muhamedjanov is from Kazakhstan. In the 1990s, a popular poet is Mukhtar Auezov. Abay Ibragin Kunanbayev is an internationally known 19th century humanist and poet. Mukhtar Awezov wrote *Abay,* a novel about steppe life that was translated into English.

49DEPENDENCIES

Kazakhstan has no territories or colonies.

50BIBLIOGRAPHY

Edwards-Jones, Imogen. *The Taming of Eagles: Exploring the New Russia.* London: Weidenfeld & Nicolson, 1993.
Kazakhstan. Minneapolis: Lerner, 1993.
Kazakhstan. Washington, D.C.: International Monetary Fund, 1992.

KIRIBATI

Republic of Kiribati

CAPITAL: Tarawa.

FLAG: Above a blue and white heraldic representation of Pacific waters, a golden sun rises against a red background, with a golden frigate bird at the top.

ANTHEM: *Teiraki kain Kiribati (Stand Kiribati).*

MONETARY UNIT: The Australian dollar is the national currency. A$1 = US$0.7008 (or US$1 = A$1.4269).

WEIGHTS AND MEASURES: Kiribati is in transition from imperial to metric standards.

HOLIDAYS: New Year's Day, 1 January; Independence Day, 12 July; Youth Day, 4 August; Christmas Day, 25 December; Boxing Day, 26 December. Movable holidays include Good Friday, Easter Monday, Queen's Birthday (June), Bank Holiday (August), and Prince of Wales's Birthday (November).

TIME: Midnight = noon GMT.

¹LOCATION, SIZE, AND EXTENT

Kiribati (pronounced "Kiribass") consists of 33 islands in the central Pacific, situated around the point where the International Date Line intersects the Equator. Scattered over more than 5 million sq km (2 million sq mi) of ocean are the 17 islands of the Gilberts group (including Banaba, formerly Ocean Island); the 8 Line Islands (including Christmas Island); and the 8 Phoenix Islands. The distance between Christmas Island in the E and Banaba in the W is more than 3,200 km (2,000 mi). Kiribati's total land area is 717 sq km (277 sq mi), and its total coastline is 1,143 km (710 mi). Comparatively, the area occupied by Kiribati is slightly more than four times the size of Washington, D.C.

Kiribati's capital city, Tarawa, is located on the island of Tarawa.

²TOPOGRAPHY

With the exception of Banaba, an upthrust coral formation that reaches a high point of 265 m (868 ft), the islands are coral atolls built on a submerged volcanic chain and seldom rise more than 4 m (13 ft) above sea level. Christmas Island is the largest atoll in the world, with an area of 481 sq km (186 sq mi). In most of the atolls the reef encloses a lagoon, on the eastern side of which is a narrow stretch of land varying in length from about 45 m (150 ft) to 80 km (50 mi).

³CLIMATE

Tempered by prevailing easterly trade winds, the islands have a maritime equatorial climate, with high humidity during the November–April rainy season. Although the islands lie outside the tropical hurricane belt, there are occasional gales and even tornadoes. Rainfall varies from an average of 102 cm (40 in) near the Equator to 305 cm (120 in) in the extreme north and south. Severe droughts can also occur. On average, there is less than 1% variation between the cool and hot months, but daily temperatures range from 25°C (77°F) to 32°C (90°F), with an annual mean temperature of 27°C (81°F).

⁴FLORA AND FAUNA

The extreme poverty of the soil and the variability of the rainfall make cultivation of most crops impossible. Only babai (a kind of taro root), coconut palms, and pandanus trees grow easily on most islands. Pigs and poultry were probably introduced by Europeans. Sea life abounds.

⁵ENVIRONMENT

According the United Nations Report for Pacific Island Developing Countries (1992), the most significant environmental problems facing the nations in this area of the world are global warming and the rise of sea levels. Variations in the level of the sea may damage forests and agricultural areas and contaminate fresh water supplies with salt water. Kiribati, along with the other nations in the area, is vulnerable to earthquakes and volcanic activity. The nation also has inadequate facilities for handling solid waste, which has been a major environmental concern since 1992, particularly in the larger population centers. The environment in Kiribati has also been adversely affected by metals and chemicals from mining activities, and agricultural chemicals have polluted coastal waters. Like other Pacific islands, Kiribati is sensitive to the dangers of pollution and radiation from weapons tests and nuclear waste disposal. The UN Report describes the wildlife in these areas as "among the most critically threatened in the world." Endangered species in 1987 included the green sea turtle and mukojima bonin honeyeater.

⁶POPULATION

According to the census of November 1990, the population totaled 72,298; representing an average annual increase of 2.7% since the 1985 census. The population is unevenly distributed. In 1990, Tarawa had a population of 29,028, or 40% of the total, while some islands of the Phoenix and Line groups were uninhabited. Bairiki, the capital, on Tarawa, had an estimated population of 2,000 in the mid-1980s.

⁷MIGRATION

For the islanders, migration has been a perennial form of escape from drought and starvation. In the 19th century, recruiting ships forcibly took Gilbert Islanders for plantation work in Hawaii, Australia, Fiji, and Peru; some voluntarily reenlisted after the great drought of 1870. Although the majority eventually returned home, it is reckoned that between 1860 and 1890 some 10,000 islanders of a total population of 30,000 were overseas. In this century, Fiji and the Solomon Islands continued to be popular places for Gilbert Islanders in search of work. Internal migration was mainly to Banaba Island for work in the phosphate industry until 1979, and since then to Nauru or to copra plantations in the Line Islands. During 1988–93, 4,700 people were to be resettled on Teraira and Tabuaeran atolls of the Line Islands because of overcrowding on the main island group.

8ETHNIC GROUPS

About 99% of the people are Gilbertese of Micronesian extraction. Polynesians (mainly from Tuvalu) make up 0.5% of the total; Europeans and people of mixed races, 0.6%.

9LANGUAGES

The principal languages spoken are Kiribati and English. The official language is English, but it is seldom used on the outer islands. Kiribati is an Austronesian language related to many other Pacific tongues.

10RELIGIONS

Virtually the entire population is Christian, comprised in the 1990 census of some 39.1% Kiribati Protestant Church, and 53.5% Roman Catholics. Religious minorities include the Seventh-Day Adventists, the Church of God, Assemblies of God, Mormans, and Baha<ayn>is. Christian missionaries first arrived in 1857, when Dr. Hiram Bingham, of the American Board of Foreign Missionaries, began to spread Protestantism in the northern Gilberts with the help of Hawaiian pastors. In 1888, Catholicism was introduced to the islands by the Sacred Heart Mission. The American Board withdrew from the territory in 1917 and was succeeded by the London Missionary Society, which had placed Samoan pastors on the islands as early as 1870. The Kiribati Protestant Church identifies itself as Congregational.

11TRANSPORTATION

The remoteness of the scattered islands has severely hampered transport and communications. There are only about 640 km (400 mi) of roads, mostly on Tarawa. The Nippon Causeway, completed in 1987 with Japanese assistance, has replaced ferry service between Betio and Bonriki. There is no rail, river, or lake transport, although canoes travel freely on the lagoons. The main ports are Betio islet, near Tarawa, and on Tabuaeran and Christmas islands. Betio is equipped for handling containers, and Banaba has a cantilever for phosphate loading. A number of shipping lines call at the islands, and government boats provide interisland service. All the major islands have airstrips; the airports on Christmas Island and at Bonriki (Tarawa) are used for scheduled overseas flights. Bonriki International serviced 51,000 passengers in 1991, including 16,000 international passengers. Air Tungaru, the national airline, operates regularly scheduled flights to Honolulu and Tuvalu.

12HISTORY

The main wave of Micronesian settlement is thought to have come from Samoa in the 13th century, but Gilbertese tradition suggests that the Samoans were not the first settlers. European discovery dates from 1537, when Christmas Island was sighted by Spanish explorers. The English sea captain James Cook encountered the islands in 1777, and commercial activities in the region began early in the 19th century. The Gilbert Islands were a favorite whaling ground, and deserting crews began to settle in the islands in the 1830s. Trading ships were calling there regularly by the 1850s, and a flourishing copra and coconut trade was established by the 1860s, as well as an illicit human traffic. The Office of British High Commissioner to the Western Pacific was created in 1877 to help suppress abuses by recruiting ships

seeking Labour for overseas service. In 1888, Christmas, Fanning (now Tabuaeran), and Washington (now Teraina) islands were annexed by the British, and Phoenix Island was placed under their protection. A declaration of a British protectorate over the Gilbert and Ellice groups followed in 1892. A handful of administrators established local native governments, and a period of stability ensued.

Ocean Island was annexed by Britain in 1900, following Sir Albert Ellis's discovery of its valuable phosphate deposits. The Gilbert and Ellice groups (including Ocean, Fanning, and Washington islands) were declared a British colony in 1916. British control was extended to Christmas Island in 1919 and to the uninhabited Phoenix group in 1937, but after the US laid claim to Canton and Enderbury, a joint British-American administration over these islands was established. During World War II, the Gilberts were occupied by Japanese forces until 1943, when the invaders were driven out by US forces, after heavy casualties on both sides. Ocean Island was liberated by the Australians in 1945.

In a 1974 referendum, the Ellice Islands voted for separation, subsequently becoming the independent nation of Tuvalu. Internal self-government for the Gilberts was established as of 1 January 1977, and the islands became the independent Republic of Kiribati on 12 July 1979. In September, the new nation signed a treaty of friendship with the US (ratified by the US Senate in 1983), by which the US relinquished its claims to the Line and Phoenix groups (including Canton, Enderbury, and Malden).

Ieremia Tabai, chief minister at the time of independence, became president of the new republic in 1979 and was reelected in May 1982 and February 1983. Although the constitution limits a president to three terms, Tabai argued that he had not completed three full terms and was reelected in May 1987.

A special program was posed by the Banabans, who were resettled in 1946 on Rabi (Fiji)—bought for them by means of phosphate royalties—so that strip mining on their native island could continue unimpeded. In 1975, the Banabans sued, petitioning the British courts for damages. After a lengthy legal battle, representatives of the Banabans (most of whom still reside on Rabi) agreed in 1981 to the creation of a trust fund of nearly A$15 million for Banaban development. Recognition of Banaban minority rights is enshrined in Kiribati's constitution. Kiribati established diplomatic relations with the former Soviet Union in 1979 and with the People's Republic of China in 1980.

Kiribati opposes French nuclear testing in the Pacific and signed the 1985 Raratonga Agreement declaring the South Pacific a nuclear-weapons-free zone. In 1985, Kiribati signed a one-year fishing agreement with the former USSR that aroused controversy at home and abroad. The agreement was not renewed after talks for its renegotiation broke off in September 1986.

Kiribati began resettling more than 4,700 people on outlying atolls in August 1988 in an attempt to relieve overcrowded conditions on the Tarawa atolls. In September 1988 Kiribati ratified the South Pacific Regional Fisheries Treaty, which permits US tuna ships to operate within its 200-mile exclusive zone. In early 1992 the Parliament of Kiribati instructed the government (against its wishes) to seek compensation from the US for damage done to the country during the Pacific War, 1941–45.

13GOVERNMENT

Under the independence constitution of 1979, Kiribati is a democratic republic within the Commonwealth of Nations. It has a unicameral legislature, the House of Assembly (Maneaba ni Maungatabu), the members of which are elected every four years. The number of elected representatives was increased from 35 to 39 in 1987. One appointed seat is reserved for a representative of the Banaban community. The president (beretitenti), who is both head of state and head of government, is elected directly by popular vote, from among members of the Assembly, to a term of up to four years; candidates are selected by the House from among its own members. When the president no longer enjoys the confidence of the legislature, the House is dissolved and new parliamentary and presidential elections are held, with a Council of State (consisting of the head of the Civil Service Commission, the chief justice, and the speaker of the House) governing in the interim. The cabinet consists of the president, vice-president, attorney general, and up to eight other ministers.

Teatao Teannaki was elected the nation's seconnd President in July 1991. Ex-president Tabai continues to serve in the new government as Minister of Environment and Natural Resources Development.

¹⁴POLITICAL PARTIES

Kiribati had no formally constituted political parties until 1985, when opponents of the Soviet fishing agreement founded the Christian Democratic party, headed by Dr. Harry Tong. Its leader is now Teburoro Tito. Since 1991 the Liberal Party, led by Tewareka Tentoa, the Maneaba Party, led by Roniti Teiwaki, the New Movement Party, and the Health Peace and Honour Party have come into existence.

¹⁵LOCAL GOVERNMENT

There are fully elective local councils on all the islands, in accordance with a local government ordinance of 1966. For administrative purposes the islands are divided into six districts: Tarawa (including the Phoenix group); North, South, and Central Gilberts; Banaba; and the Line Islands. This structure has been further divided into 21 island councils, one for each of the inhabited islands. The geographic dispersion of the islands leaves considerable freedom for the districts; their councils have wide taxing powers, including land taxes, and draw up their own estimates of revenues and expenditures.

¹⁶JUDICIAL SYSTEM

The 1979 constitution provides for a High Court, with a chief justice and other judges, to act as the supreme court and court of appeal. Island courts were established in 1965 to deal with civil and criminal offenses. Native land courts have jurisdiction over property claims.

The judiciary is independent and free from government influence. Civil rights and civil liberties are guaranteed in the Constitution and respected in practice. Procedural due process safeguards are based on English common law.

¹⁷ARMED FORCES

Legislation providing for the establishment of a defense force of 170 men was repealed in 1978. There is a small police force.

¹⁸INTERNATIONAL COOPERATION

Kiribati participates in many Commonwealth activities and hosted the South Pacific Forum in 1981. Although as of early 1988 it did not belong to the UN, it was an associate member of ESCAP and a member of ICAO, IBRD, IMF, and ITU. Kiribati participates in the Asian Development Bank and G-77 and is a de facto adherent of GATT.

¹⁹ECONOMY

Kiribati's economy was supported by revenues from phosphate mining on Banaba until the deposits were exhausted in 1979. Since then, the nation has relied on fishing, subsistence agriculture, and exports of copra. The country is heavily dependent on aid from the UK and New Zealand and investment from Australia.

²⁰INCOME

In 1992, Kiribati's GNP was $52 million at current prices, or $700 per capita. For the period 1985–92 the average inflation

LOCATION: 4°N to 3°S; 168° to 176°E. TOTAL COASTLINE: 1,143 km (710 mi). TERRITORIAL SEA LIMIT: 12 mi.

rate was 5.1%, resulting in a real growth rate in per capita GNP of −1.1%.

²¹LABOR

Most of the population engages in subsistence agriculture or copra production, including the copra plantations on the Line Islands. As of 1990, nearly three-quarters of the labor force was engaged in agriculture or fishing. Overseas workers remitted most of their wages to Kiribati.

In urban areas there is a small but strong trade union movement. Affiliates of the Kiribati Trades Union Congress (KTUC), founded in 1982 with Australian assistance, include the Fishermen's Union, the Cooperative Workers' Union, the Seamen's Union, the Teacher's Union, and the Public Employees' Association; in 1992, the KTUC had about 2,500 members.

²²AGRICULTURE

Agriculture is limited chiefly to coconut and pandanus production. About 37,000 ha (91,400 acres) of land is considered arable, representing 5.1% of the total land area. Overseas technical aid has allowed some islands to cultivate bananas and papaws for the Tarawa market. About 8,000 tons of copra, 65,000 tons of coconuts, and 4,000 tons of bananas were produced in 1992.

²³ANIMAL HUSBANDRY

There were 9,000 pigs in Kiribati in 1992. The Agricultural Division has introduced improved breeds of livestock.

²⁴FISHING

Sea fishing is excellent, particularly for skipjack tuna around the

Phoenix Islands. Commercial fishing has expanded dramatically since 1979 as the result of projects funded by Japan, the UK, and the EC. The total sea catch in 1991 was 30,001 tons. Kiribati also receives revenue from the sales of licenses permitting foreign vessels to fish its offshore waters. Seaweed is also exported.

25FORESTRY
There is little useful timber on the islands.

26MINING
There has been no mining in Kiribati since the closing in 1979 of the Banaba phosphate industry. In its last year of operation, 445,700 tons of phosphates worth A$18 million were exported.

27ENERGY AND POWER
The government maintains electricity generating plants on Tarawa and Christmas Island, and there are private generators on Banaba and several other islands. In 1991, electric power generating capacity was 2,000 kw; production of electricity totaled 7 million kwh that year.

28INDUSTRY
Several small industries have been established, including a soft-drink plant, a biscuit factory, boat-building shops, construction companies, furniture plants, repair garages, bakeries, and laundries. The government also promotes local handicrafts. A pilot project on Kiritimati for producing solar-evaporated salt began operations in 1985. In 1987, a group of Japanese investors expressed interest in building a space center on Christmas Island, where a Japanese tracking station is already located, for launching geostationary satellites. In 1988, manufacturing accounted for only 1.8% of GDP.

29SCIENCE AND TECHNOLOGY
The Foundation for the Peoples of the South Pacific, founded in 1984, provides technical assistance for agriculture and nutrition programs. In 1980, one technician and two scientists and engineers were engaged in research and development.

30DOMESTIC TRADE
The village economy is on a subsistence and barter basis. Retail sales are handled by cooperative societies, which distribute the bulk of consumer goods and perform all merchandising functions not dealt with by the government. Although private trade is growing, cooperatives are preferred as a matter of public policy because they are closer to the local tradition than are individual enterprises.

31FOREIGN TRADE
The loss of the phosphate industry, copra price fluctuations, and the islands' remoteness have hindered overseas trade, but an upward trend in foreign trade was perceptible in the 1980s. Copra—the only commodity exported by Kiribati—accounted for 77% of total domestic exports in 1992. Fish and seaweed are also exported. Imports totaled A$34.4 million in 1990 (A$21.6 million in 1985), and exports were valued at A$3.7 million. Australia, New Zealand, and the UK are the major export destinations. Imports come chiefly from these countries, along with Fiji and Japan.

32BALANCE OF PAYMENTS
Continued deficits in the trade balance are often met by grants from the UK to the government's current and capital accounts.
In 1992 merchandise exports totaled $3.272 million and imports $-25.862 million. The merchandise trade balance was $-22.590 million.

The following table summarizes Kiribati's balance of payments for 1991 and 1992 (in millions of US dollars):

	1991	1992
CURRENT ACCOUNT		
Goods services and income	-16.354	-14.738
Unrequited transfers	22.661	26.882
TOTALS	6.307	12.144
CAPITAL ACCOUNT		
Other long-term capital	-2.263	-.389
Other short-term capital	-1.483	-.857
Reserves	-7.429	-9.971
TOTALS	-11.175	-11.217
Errors and omissions	4.869	-.927
Total change in reserves	-7.429	-9.971

33BANKING AND SECURITIES
The Bank of Kiribati in Tarawa is jointly owned by the Westpac Banking Corp. (Australia) and the government of Kiribati (49%). In 1992, it had total assets of A34.7 million. The Kiribati Development Bank, opened in 1987, was to take over the assets of the National Loans Board when it became fully operational.

34INSURANCE
Individual coverage is available in Tarawa through private and government agencies.

35PUBLIC FINANCE
Local revenues are derived mainly from import duties, philately, fishing fees, and investment income from the phosphate fund. In 1990, estimated government revenues were equivalent to US$29.9 million, and expenditures to US$16.3 million (including US$14 million in capital expenditures); external debt amounted to approximately US$2 million.

36TAXATION
The main source of tax revenue, the phosphate industry, ended in 1979. Other taxes have brought meager returns, except for a copra export tax, with producers protected by a government stabilization fund. An income tax, introduced in 1975, is levied on a sliding scale. Companies pay a flat rate on all chargeable income. Island councils levy local rates; a landowners' tax is based on land area and fertility.

37CUSTOMS AND DUTIES
Since a single line tariff was introduced on 1 January 1975, trade preferences are no longer granted to imports from Commonwealth countries. Tariffs, applying mostly to private imports, are imposed as a service of revenue. Most duties are levied ad valorem, with specific duties on alcoholic beverages, tobacco, certain chemicals, petroleum, cinematographic film, and some other goods.

38FOREIGN INVESTMENT
There is little private investment.

39ECONOMIC DEVELOPMENT
The economic development plans for 1979–82 and 1983–86 were financed chiefly by the UK and supplemented by Australia, New Zealand, and Japan, with loans from the Asian Development Bank and EC. Canada, the Federal Republic of Germany, and the Republic of Korea also have started small aid programs. The plan stressed infrastructural development, support for fisheries, and rural health programs. The goal of the 1987–91 plan was eco-

nomic self-reliance through gradual and sustainable development, with particular emphasis on the subsistence life-style of the outer islands. The UN Development Program is implementing an economic development plan for the northern Line Islands focusing on infrastructure, agriculture, and tourism. In 1991, Kiribati received US$17.7 in bilateral aid and US$2.8 million in multilateral aid. United Nations development assistance totaled US$1.36 million in 1991.

40 SOCIAL DEVELOPMENT

Migration and missionaries have proved to be the principal agents of social change. Mission lands are still used for social welfare purposes. The majority of the population still clings to traditional village life and the extended family system, which renders state welfare largely unnecessary. Problems exist mainly in the rapidly urbanized south Tarawa area, where some juvenile delinquency has developed. Women's clubs, organized by the women's section of the Ministry of Welfare, have raised funds for local projects. Rural training centers have also been established.

A provident fund system provides old age, disability, and survivor benefits in the form of lump sum payments only, with the worker contributing 5% of earnings and the employer paying an equal percentage of payroll. Workers' compensation is compulsory for employed persons earning A$4,000 a year (as of 1991) or less. The cost is covered by the employer.

Women are gradually breaking out of their traditional role and entering both skilled and unskilled occupations. There have also been signs of affirmative action in government hiring and promotions.

41 HEALTH

Tuberculosis remains the most serious public health problem (about 200 cases per 100,000 people in 1990); other endemic diseases are leprosy, filariasis, and dysentery. There was a cholera outbreak in 1977, after which projects to construct water and sewage pipes were speeded up. All health services are free. A nurses' training school is maintained at the 160-bed Central Hospital in Tarawa. There are four medical districts, each with its own medical officer and staff. Each inhabited island has a dispensary, and there is a medical radio network linking all the islands. In 1990, there were 14 doctors and 116 nurses. In 1992, there were 0.31 doctors per 1,000 people, with a nurse to doctor ratio of 3.0. In 1990, there were 1.8 hospital beds per 1,000 inhabitants.

Infant mortality was estimated at 60 per 1,000 live births in 1992, and average life expectancy was 56 years. The country's total population was 75,000 in 1993. In 1992, there were 2,400 births, with 77% of children having been vaccinated against measles. The general mortality rate in 1990 was estimated at 175 per 1,000 people.

42 HOUSING

Most Kiribatians live in small villages of from 10 to 150 houses and construct their own dwellings from local materials. The use of more permanent building materials, such as concrete with corrugated aluminum roofing, is becoming common in urban areas. Loans to prospective homeowners are provided by the National Loans Board. In 1978, 73% of all dwellings were traditional houses with thatched roofs, 21% were non-traditional houses with metal roofs, and 5% were non-traditional with thatched roofs. Only 16% had flush toilets and 63% used well water.

43 EDUCATION

The government has gradually taken over control of primary education from the missions. Education has been made compulsory by the government for children between the ages of 6 and 14 years. They go through seven years of primary education and five years of secondary education. In 1986 there were 13,440 children attending 112 registered primary schools. A resident government secondary school had 481 pupils in 1986; 1,086 students attended 5 church secondary schools. In 1990, there were 104 government primary schools with 500 teachers and 14,709 students. At the secondary level were 9 schools with 236 teachers and 2,903 students. In 1992, Kiribati had 95 primary schools with a teaching staff of 545 and 16,020 students enrolled. At the secondary level, there were 237 teachers and 3,357 students. Of these, 234 students were in vocational courses and 54 students were in teacher training programs. Kiribati has a teacher-training college, a technical institute, and a marine training school for personnel in merchant shipping. Higher education courses are available at the Kiribati Extension Centre of the University of the South Pacific (Fiji) in Tarawa. Other postsecondary education is provided by scholarships for study abroad.

44 LIBRARIES AND MUSEUMS

The National Library and Archives has a collection of 50,000 volumes, including those in small units throughout the islands. Items are being stored in the National Archives in anticipation of the formation of the national museum which is to be in Tarawa.

45 MEDIA

Radio Kiribati, operated by the Broadcasting and Publications Authority, transmits daily in I-Kiribati and English and broadcasts a few imported Australian programs. The authority also publishes a fortnightly bilingual newspaper, *Te Uekera*. There is no commercial press; all publications are government- or church-sponsored. Kiribati is on the Peacesat network, which provides educational transmissions from Suva. A satellite link with Australia was established in 1985. There were an estimated 12,000 telephones in use in 1991 on South Tarawa and Betio, and a direct link service for 7 other islands. In 1990 there were 4 cinemas.

46 ORGANIZATIONS

The most important organization is the mronron (a word meaning "sharing"), a cooperative society based on kinship or locality.

47 TOURISM, TRAVEL, AND RECREATION

Tourism is undeveloped because of a lack of regular transport. There is a visitors' bureau at Tarawa, and there are hotels in Betio and on Abemama and Christmas islands. The bureau makes available fishing, swimming, and boating facilities on Tarawa and arranges trips by sea or air to other islands.

Modern forms of recreation are developing, especially soccer. Traditional dancing and singing styles have survived. In 1991, 2,935 visitors arrived in Kiribati, 75% from Eastern Asia and the Pacific. There were 102 rooms in hotels and other establishments, with 161 beds, and tourism receipts totaled US$2 million.

48 FAMOUS KIRIBATIANS

Ieremia Tabai (b.1950) was president from independence until 1991.

49 DEPENDENCIES

Kiribati has no territories or colonies.

50 BIBLIOGRAPHY

American University. *Oceania: A Regional Study*. Washington, D.C.: Government Printing Office, 1984.
Geddes, W. H., et al. *Atoll Economy: Social Change in Kiribati and Tuvalu*. Canberra: Australian National University Press, 1982.
Graham, Michael B. *Mantle of Heroism: Tarawa and the Struggle*

for the Gilberts, November 1943. Novato, Calif.: Presidio, 1993.

Grimble, Arthur Francis. *Migrations, Myth, and Magic from the Gilbert Islands.* London: Toutledge & K. Paul, 1972.

———. *Return to the Islands: Life and Legend in the Gilberts.* New York: Morrow, 1957.

Mason, Leonard (ed.). *Kiribati: A Changing Atoll Culture.* Suva: University of the South Pacific, 1985.

KOREA, DEMOCRATIC PEOPLE'S REPUBLIC OF (DPRK)

Democratic People's Republic of Korea
Choson Minjujuui Inmin Konghwa-guk

CAPITAL: P'yongyang.

FLAG: A wide horizontal red stripe is bordered on top and bottom by narrow blue stripes, separated from the red by thin white stripes. The left half of the red stripe contains a red five-pointed star on a circular white field.

ANTHEM: *The Song of General Kim Il-sung.*

MONETARY UNIT: The won (w) of 100 ch'on (or jeon) is the national currency. There are coins of 1, 5, 10, and 50 ch'on, and 1 won, and notes of 1, 5, 10, 50, and 100 won. w1 = $1.06 (or $1 = w0.94).

WEIGHTS AND MEASURES: The metric system and native Korean units of measurement are used.

HOLIDAYS: New Year's Day, 1 January; Kim Jong Il's Birthday, 16 February; International Women's Day, 8 March; Kim Il-sung's Birthday, 15 April; May Day, 1 May; Liberation Day, 15 August; National Foundation Day, 9 September; Founding of the Korean Workers' Party, 10 October; Anniversary of the Constitution, 27 December.

TIME: 9 PM = noon GMT.

¹LOCATION, SIZE, AND EXTENT

The Democratic People's Republic of Korea (DPRK), often called North Korea, occupies the northern 55% of the Korean Peninsula in East Asia. It has an area of 120,540 sq km (46,541 sq mi), extending 719 km (447 mi) NNE–SSW and 371 km (231 mi) ESE–WNW. Comparatively, the area occupied by DPRK is slightly smaller than the state of Mississippi. It is bordered on the N by China, on the NE by the Russia, on the E by the Sea of Japan (including East Korea Bay), known in Korea as the East Sea, on the S by the Republic of Korea (ROK), and on the S and W by the Yellow Sea and Korea Bay, with a total boundary length of 2,309 km (1,435 mi). A demilitarized zone (DMZ), 4,000 m (13,100 ft) wide, covering 1,262 sq km (487 sq mi), and located north and south of the 38th parallel, separates the DPRK from the ROK, which occupies the southern part of the Korean Peninsula.

The DPRK's capital city, P'yongyang, is located in the southwestern part of the country.

²TOPOGRAPHY

The DPRK is mostly mountainous. Mt. Paektu (2,744 m/9,003 ft), an extinct volcano with a scenic crater lake, is the highest point; it is located on the border with China and forms part of the Mach'ol Range. Other peaks of note include Mt. Kwanmo (2,541 m/8,337 ft), in the Hamgyong Range; Mt. Myohyang (1,909 m/6,263 ft), in the Myohyang Range, north of P'yongyang; and Mt. Kumgang ("Diamond Mountain," 1,638 m/5,374 ft), in the Taebaek Range in the southeast. Only about 20% of the country consists of lowlands and plains, but it is in these areas that the population is concentrated. The principal lowlands are the Unjon, P'yongyang, Chaeryong, Anju, and Yonbaek plains, extending from north to south along the west coast; and the Susong, Yongchon, Kilchu, Hamhung, and Yonghung plains, along the eastern shore.

The principal rivers are the Tumen (521 km/324 mi) and Yalu (790 km/491 mi) along the northern border of the peninsula, both of which rise in Mt. Paektu, and the Taedong (397 km/247 mi), which flows past P'yongyang. The Imjin (254 km/158 mi) rises in the DPRK near the 38th parallel in the west and crosses into the ROK before entering the Yellow Sea. Yellow Sea tides on the west coast rise to over 9 m (30 ft) in some places; Sea of Japan tides on the east rise to only about 1 m (3 ft).

³CLIMATE

The climatic range is greater than the limited size of the peninsula would suggest. The average January temperature is −17°C (1°F) at Chunggang on the north-central border and −8°C (18°F) at P'yongyang. In the hottest part of the summer, however, the variation is not nearly so marked, average temperatures ranging from 24°C (75°F) in P'yongyang to 21°C (70°F) along the relatively cool northeast coast. Spring and fall are unusually pleasant, but winters are colder than average for the latitude, and summers are hot and humid. Precipitation is around 50 cm (20 in) along the upper reaches of the Tumen, but more than half of the peninsula receives 75–100 cm (30–40 in) per year. Nearly all the rainfall occurs in the April–September period, especially during the rainy season, from late June to early August. Typhoons occur occasionally in the early fall. Days without frost number about 180 in the northern part of the peninsula and increase toward the south.

⁴FLORA AND FAUNA

Cold temperate vegetation, including firs, spruces, and other needled evergreens, predominate in mountainous areas of the DPRK, with alpine varieties flourishing at the higher altitudes. The hilly terrain of Mt. Paektu is believed to be the peninsula's last remaining habitat for Siberian tigers and is also, along with other alpine areas, the home of bears, wild boar, deer, snow leopards, and lynx. Common at lower elevations are the roe deer, Amur goral, wolf, water shrew, and muskrat. Birds seen in the DPRK include the black Manchurian ring-necked pheasant, black grouse, and three-toed woodpecker; the hawk owl, lesser-spotted wood-pecker, and willow tit are indigenous to Mt. Paektu.

⁵ENVIRONMENT

The Democratic People's Republic of Korea has environmental problems in the area of water pollution from agricultural and industrial sources. The nation has 16.1 cubic miles of water with 73% used for farming activity and 16% used for industrial purposes. Korea's cities produce 2.6 million tons of solid waste per year. Of Korea's total land area, 20% can be used for agricultural purposes. The Korean government has established 220 facilities to regulate environmental conditions, industrial areas, protected land, and water reserves. The government has also created the Law of Environmental Protection. In 1994, 5 of Korea's mammal species and 25 of its bird species were endangered. As of 1994, endangered species in the DPRK included the tiger (particularly the Siberian tiger), Amur leopard, Japanese sea lion, Oriental white stork, Japanese crested ibis, and Tristram's woodpecker.

⁶POPULATION

The population of the DPRK in 1992 was estimated at 22,618,000, about half that of the ROK but more than double the post-Korean War low of 8,491,000 in 1953. The annual rate of population growth was estimated at 1.9% in 1990–95. The projected population for the year 2000 was 25,934,000, assuming a crude birthrate of 21.4 per 1,000 population, a crude death rate of 5.3, and a net natural increase of 16.1 during 1995–2000. The population density varies greatly from region to region, with an average of 184 per sq km (477 per sq mi) in 1992. Nearly 60% of the population was estimated to be urban in 1990 (as compared with 45% in 1965). The largest urban areas in 1986 were P'yongyang, which had an estimated population of 2 million; Hamhung, with 670,000 inhabitants; Ch'ongjin, 530,000; Kaesong, 310,000; and Sinuiju, 330,000.

⁷MIGRATION

During the generation of Japanese occupation (1910–45), some 3 million Koreans, mainly from the northern provinces, emigrated to Manchuria and parts of China, 700,000 to Siberia, some 3 million to Japan, and about 7,000 to the US (mostly to Hawaii). From the end of World War II in 1945 through 1950, at least 1.2 million Koreans crossed the 38th parallel into the ROK, refugees either from Communism or from the Korean War. Repatriation of overseas Koreans is actively encouraged in an attempt to ameliorate the nation's chronic labor shortages. Between 1945 and 1950, an estimated 300,000 Koreans were repatriated from Manchuria and Siberia; over 93,000 out of about 600,000 Koreans in Japan were repatriated to the DPRK between December 1959 and the end of 1974. The General Association of Korean Residents in Japan actively promotes the DPRK cause, and the P'yongyang government subsidizes some Korean schools on Japanese soil. Some 250,000 people of Korean origin in Japan have links to the DPRK, providing $600–$1,800 million in annual remittances to relatives.

⁸ETHNIC GROUPS

The Koreans are believed to be descended primarily from Tungusic peoples of the Mongoloid race, who originated in the cold northern regions of Central Asia. There is scant evidence of non-Mongoloid admixture. The DPRK has no sizable ethnic minority.

⁹LANGUAGES

The Korean language is usually acknowledged to be a member of the Altaic family and is clearly related to other agglutinative tongues like Turkish, Mongolian, and Japanese. Linguistic unification of the Korean Peninsula apparently followed political unification in the 7th century AD, and today the dialect differences are comparatively slight.

Korean is written with a largely phonetic alphabet called Han'gul. Created in 1443 under the great King Sejong, the Korean alphabet originally consisted of 14 consonants and 10 vowels; since then, 5 consonants and 11 vowels have been added. Han'gul letters are combined into syllables by clustering, in imitation of Chinese characters. Before the invention of Han'gul, Koreans wrote in Chinese, which continued to be both the official language and the language of most literature until the beginning of the 20th century. With the beginning of the Japanese colonial administration in 1910, Japanese became the official language, and the use of Korean was restricted.

Since 1949, the DPRK has used only Han'gul (calling it Choson Muntcha) for writing. North Korean linguists have studied Han'gul extensively, publishing comprehensive dictionaries in 1963 and 1969. In 1964, Kim Il-sung called for purification of Korean by replacing borrowings from English and Japanese with native Korean or familiar Chinese terms. The traditional honorifics of polite language remain in use, though in simplified forms, and have been sanctioned by the government.

Some Chinese (Mandarin dialect) and Russian are spoken in border areas.

¹⁰RELIGIONS

According to current estimates a majority of the population professes no religion or are avowed atheists. Indigenous shamanism, notable for its emphasis on exorcising evil spirits, is practiced by an estimated 16% of the population, mostly in rural areas. Followers of Ch'ondogyo (Religion of the Heavenly Way), an eclectic indigenous sect incorporating both Christian and Buddhist elements, originating in 1860, account for about another 14%; its organization went underground following the arrest of 10,000 Ch'ondogyo members in 1948. Almost 2% of the population continues to practice Buddhism despite the conversion of many Buddhist temples to secular uses. Up to the mid-1940s, P'yongyang was an important center of Korean Christianity. Most of the nation's Christians, predominantly Protestants, fled to the ROK to escape persecution between 1945 and 1953. Christians now make up less than 1% of the population.

¹¹TRANSPORTATION

The rail network, which has been rebuilt and extended following its almost complete destruction during the Korean War, is the principal means of transportation, carrying approximately 90% of the nation's freight and 70% of all passenger traffic. In 1986, railways in use comprised 8,533 km (5,302 mi) of track. The principal lines run along the west coast from P'yongyang to Sinuiju and across the peninsula from P'yongyang to Wonsan, Hamhung, and Ch'ongjin. A northern line, completed in the early 1980s, links P'yongyang to Hyesan and Musan. The major trunk routes are electrified. A subway system opened in P'yongyang in 1973 and was expanded under the 1978–84 development plan. There are also train services to Moscow and Beijing.

Road transportation is of secondary importance. In 1991, highways totaled some 30,000 km (18,600 mi), 99% of which are gravel, crushed stone, or earth surface. The exceptions are a superhighway connecting P'yongyang with Kaesong and two multilane highways, which link the national capital with the ports of Wonsan and Namp'o. About 180,000 automobiles were in use in 1982.

Most of the nation's 2,253 km (1,400 mi) of navigable waterways are suitable for small craft only. Rivers utilized for freight transportation are the Yalu, Taedong, and Chaeryong. The principal ports are Namp'o on the west coast, and Ch'ongjin and Hungnam on the east coast. In 1991, there were 71 ships in the merchant fleet with a capacity of 474,000 GRT. Limited air services connect P'yongyang with other cities within the DPRK and in China and the former USSR.

12HISTORY

The history of the Korean people begins with the migration into the Korean Peninsula of Tungusic tribes from northern China and Manchuria about 3,000 BC. The archaeological evidence indicates that these tribes possessed a Neolithic culture and that it was not until about the 8th century BC that the art of metalworking came to Korea from China. The recorded history of Korea begins around 194 BC, when the ancient kingdom of Choson ("Land of Morning Calm") in northwestern Korea was seized by Wiman, a military figure from China of either Chinese or Korean origin. He usurped the throne from a king who, according to legend, was a descendant of Kija, a historical Chinese nobleman who emigrated from China at the end of the Shang dynasty (c.1122 BC). A popular Korean legend of much later origin asserts that Kija was preceded in his rule over the Korean Peninsula by a dynasty started in 2333 BC by the semidivine figure Tan-gun, an offspring of the son of the divine creator and a "bear woman" (possibly a woman from a bear-totem tribe). Both Tan-gun and Kija are still widely revered.

The primitive state controlled by Wiman's successors fell victim to expanding Chinese power in 108 BC, and there followed more than four centuries of Chinese colonial rule. During this period, the advanced Chinese culture slowly spread into nearly every corner of Korea, giving impetus to the coalescence of the loosely knit Korean tribes into statelike formations. By AD 313, when the Chinese power was destroyed, three Korean kingdoms had emerged: Paekche, in the southwest; Silla, in the southeast; and Koguryo, in the northwest. The three kingdoms had advanced cultures for the time, each compiling a written history during the 4th–6th centuries. During the same period, Buddhism was introduced into Korea, from which it was later taken to Japan. Ultimately, the Silla kingdom crushed the other two and united all but the northernmost portion of the peninsula, ushering in the age of the Silla Unification (668–900). After rebellions broke out, Korea again suffered threefold division, until reunification was achieved in 936 under the leadership of Wang Kon, who had proclaimed a new dynasty in the kingdom of Koryo (founded in 918), which derived its name from Koguryo; the name Korea is derived from Koryo.

Chinese influence on political and social institutions and on Korean thought went on at an accelerated pace during the Koryo period, and there were some notable cultural achievements, including the traditional invention of the use of movable metal type in printing in the early 12th century. Beginning in 1231, however, the Mongols invaded Koryo, devastating the land and, from 1259 on, making puppets of the Korean kings. Following a revolt against the Mongol Empire in 1356 and a subsequent period of disorder, Gen. Yi Song-gye assumed the throne as King T'aejo in 1392, adopting the name Choson for Korea, moving the capital from Kaesong (the capital of Koryo since 918) to Seoul, and ushering in the long-lived Yi (or Li) Dynasty (1392–1910).

The first hundred years of Yi rule witnessed truly brilliant cultural achievements, especially during the reign of King Sejong (1418–50). The world's first authenticated casting of movable metal type was made in 1403. The Korean alphabet, Han'gul, was developed. A rain gauge was invented and put into use throughout the peninsula. A spate of basic texts—including histories, geographies, administrative codes, and works on music—were compiled and issued under state auspices. Scholars competed for government posts through the civil service examination

LOCATION: 37°38' to 43°1'N; 124°13' to 130°39'E. **BOUNDARY LENGTHS:** China, 1,025 km (637 mi); USSR, 16 km (10 mi); ROK, 240 km (149 mi); total coastline, 1,028 km (639 mi). **TERRITORIAL SEA LIMIT:** 12 mi.

system. By about 1500, however, factionalism divided the kingdom, and the Yi rulers were ill-prepared to meet foreign invasion. In 1592, in the course of an attempt to conquer China, the Japanese, under Hideyoshi Toyotomi, invaded Korea and were repulsed by an allied Chinese army and the Korean navy under Yi Sun-sin; in 1597 there was another invasion, which ended with Hideyoshi's death in 1598. After being invaded by the Manchus in 1636, Korea became a vassal state, eventually falling under the official but loose control of the Qing (Ch'ing), or Manchu, dynasty in China. During the 18th century, two energetic kings, Yongjo (r.1724–76) and Chongjo (r.1776–1800), were able to arrest somewhat the process of dynastic decline. The intellectual and cultural revival that they engendered, known as the Practical Learning Movement (Sirhak), was short-lived, however, and the Yi kingdom's bitterest century followed.

The first six decades of the 19th century were marked by a succession of natural disasters, by mounting peasant unrest and insurrection, and by administrative relapse into hopeless corruption and inefficiency. Eventually a Korean figure came forward to attempt to rescue the dynasty from impending collapse. This was Yi Ha-leng, known as the Taewon'gun (Prince Regent), who was the father of the king, Kojong, and held the actual power during the decade 1864–73. While his domestic reforms were generally enlightened and beneficial, he adopted an isolationist policy, including persecutions of the growing Roman Catholic community in Korea. Such a policy was doomed to failure. Soon after the Taewon'gun's downfall, the Kanghwa Treaty of 1876 with Japan opened Korea by force both to Japan and to the clamoring Western nations. During the last quarter of the 19th century, Korea was the prize in a complex rivalry for mastery of the peninsula among Japan, China, Western imperialist powers, and domestic political forces. During 1894–95, Japan seized upon the pretext of peasant uprisings in Korea's southern provinces (the Tonghak Rebellion, led by followers of what later came to be called the Ch'ondogyo religion) to destroy waning Chinese power in Korea in the First Sino-Japanese War. A decade later, Japan turned back the Russian bid for supremacy in the Russo-Japanese War (1904–5). In 1910, with the tacit approval of the US and the European powers, the Yi Dynasty came to an end with the formal annexation of Korea by Japan.

For 35 years, Korea (renamed Choson) remained under the Japanese yoke, until liberated by US and Soviet troops at the end of World War II. Although Japanese colonial rule brought to Korea considerable economic development along modern Western lines, the benefits went primarily to the Japanese, and the process was accompanied by ever harsher political and cultural oppression. The Korean people staged a nationwide passive resistance movement beginning on 1 March 1919 (the Samil or "March 1" Movement), only to have it swiftly and brutally crushed by their Japanese overlords. In the 1920s and 1930s, nationalist and Communist movements developed both within Korea and among Korean exiles in the former USSR, Manchuria (which was occupied by Japan in 1931), and the rest of China. After the onset of the Second Sino-Japanese War in 1937, the Japanese aimed to eradicate Korean national identity; even the use of the Korean language was banned.

The Democratic People's Republic

After Japan accepted the Potsdam Declaration for unconditional surrender on 14 August 1945, the 38th parallel was chosen, as a result of US initiative, as a line of demarcation between Soviet occupation forces (who had entered the north on 8 August) and US occupation forces (who were introduced on 8 September). While the Americans set up a full military government allied with conservative Korean political forces, the Soviets allied their government with leftist and Communist Korean forces led by Kim Il-sung, who had been an anti-Japanese guerrilla leader in Manchuria. After a joint commission set up by the US and the USSR failed to agree on plans for the reunification of Korea, the problem was placed on the UN agenda in September 1947. In accordance with a UN resolution, elections were held on 10 May 1948 in South Korea alone; North Korea did not recognize UN competency to sponsor the elections. The newly elected National Assembly formulated a democratic constitution and chose Syngman Rhee, who had been the leader of an independence movement in exile, to be the first president of the Republic of Korea, proclaimed on 15 August 1948. On 9 September, the Democratic People's Republic of Korea was established in the north, with Kim Il-sung at the helm. Like its southern counterpart, the DPRK claimed to be the legitimate government of all Korea. In December, however, the ROK was acknowledged by the UN General Assembly as the only government in Korea to have been formed according to the original UN mandate. The next year and a half brought sporadic border clashes between the two Koreas, coupled with increasing guerrilla activity in the south.

On 25 June 1950, the People's Army of the DPRK struck across the 38th parallel at dawn in a move to unify the peninsula under Communist control. The DPRK forces advanced rapidly; Seoul, the ROK capital, fell within three days, and the destruction of the ROK seemed imminent. At US urging, the UN Security Council branded the DPRK an aggressor and called for the withdrawal of the attacking forces. President Harry S. Truman ordered US air and naval forces into battle on 27 June and ground forces three days later. A multinational UN Command was then created to join with and lead the South Koreans. An amphibious landing at Inch'on (15 September) in the ROK under Gen. Douglas MacArthur brought about the complete disintegration of the DPRK's military position.

MacArthur then made a fateful decision to drive into the north. As the UN forces approached the Yalu River, China warned that it would not tolerate a unification of the peninsula under US/UN auspices. After several weeks of threats and feints, "volunteers" from the Chinese People's Liberation Army entered the fighting en masse, forcing MacArthur into a costly, pell-mell retreat back down the peninsula. The battle line stabilized nearly along the 38th parallel, where it remained for two years. On 27 July 1953, an armistice agreement finally was signed by the North Korean People's Army, the Chinese volunteers, and the UN Command at P'anmunjom in the DPRK, ending a conflict that cost the lives of an estimated 415,000 South Koreans, 23,300 Americans (combat dead), and 3,100 UN allies; casualties among Communist forces are officially estimated by the DPRK at 50,000 but may have been as high as 2 million. A military demarcation line, which neither side regarded as a permanent border, was established, surrounded by the DMZ. After the armistice agreement, all but a token force of UN Command troops withdrew, except those of the US, which in 1954 guaranteed the security of the ROK under a mutual defense treaty. A postwar international conference held in 1954 to resolve the problem of Korea's political division was unable to find a satisfactory formula for reunification. Meanwhile, the DPRK, with the aid of China and the former USSR, began to restore its war-damaged economy. A series of purges consolidated political power in the hands of Kim Il-sung and his supporters. By the end of the 1950s, Kim had emerged as the unchallenged leader of the DPRK and the focus of a personality cult that developed around him and his family.

In 1972, the government replaced the original 1948 constitution with a new document (which would be further revised in 1992), and reunification talks, stalled since 1954, resumed under Red Cross auspices, though without lasting effect. Throughout the 1970s and 1980s, as part of its "cold war" with the ROK, the DPRK extended its diplomatic relations to over 100 countries. The ROK continued to charge the DPRK with attempts at sabotage and subversion, including infiltration by tunnels under the DMZ. In the 1980s, Korea's basic divisions remained unresolved. Since 1980, President Kim has proposed that both the North and South be reunited as a confederal state, with each part retaining regional autonomy and its own ideological and social system, but the ROK has rejected the concept; the DPRK likewise has rejected the ROK's repeated proposals for the resumption of North-South talks on reunification unless the US is a third party in the negotiations, but neither the ROK nor the US has accepted that condition. Kim was unanimously reelected president in May 1990, and his son, Kim Jong-il (1942–), groomed since the 1960s as his designated successor, appeared to be running the nation's day-to-day affairs, though without benefit of any formal administrative post. Indications of an improvement in relations between the North and South included material relief provided by the DPRK to the ROK after a flood in 1984, talks under Red Cross auspices that led to a brief reunion of separated families in 1985, economic discussions, and interparliamentary contacts. The DPRK did not participate in the 1988 summer Olympic Games, officially hosted by the ROK, since it was not named as cohost.

During the 1990s, the DPRK was less able to rely on its allies, the large communist states of the former USSR and China. In

1990, the USSR and the ROK opened formal diplomatic relations and, by the 1990s, the collapse of the Soviet Union cut off an important source of economic and political support for the DPRK. After a break of twelve years since the DPRK sided with the former USSR in the Sino-Soviet clash of 1969, China and the DPRK had reestablished ties in 1982. Yet in 1990, China and the ROK began to encourage mutual trade and in 1992 established formal diplomatic relations. Beginning in 1993 China demanded that all its exports to the DPRK be paid for with cash instead of through barter. The DPRK found itself increasingly isolated and in severe economic difficulty. Reunification talks, and the DPRK's relations with the US, took on added urgency as the DPRK sought international recognition and economic aid.

In the first half of the 1990s, the DPRK's foreign relations revolved around issues of joint US-ROK military exercises and of nuclear capabilities. Repeatedly, since 1986, the DPRK canceled negotiations with the ROK during the annual "Team Spirit" exercises of US and ROK militaries. In 1991, the US withdrew its nuclear weapons from the ROK and the two Koreas signed a bilateral agreement to create a nuclear weapons-free peninsula. Yet it was suspected that the DPRK was developing the capability to reprocess nuclear fuels and build nuclear weapons. (Both the ROK and Japan had stockpiles of plutonium.) Conflicts over the access of an International Atomic Energy Agency inspection team, which the DPRK allowed into North Korea in May 1994, to a reprocessing plant led to new tensions. These tensions were defused with an agreement for high-level talks between the US and the DPRK, previously refused by the US, to be held on 8 July 1994, followed on 25 July by a summit in P'yongyang between the presidents of the two Koreas, the first such summit since Korea was divided in 1945.

On 8 July 1994, just as the US-DPRK talks were beginning, President Kim Il-sung died. The talks were suspended until after Kim's funeral on 17 July. It was anticipated that Kim Jong-il would replace his father as President in an election by the Supreme People's Assembly on 11 July 1994.

¹³GOVERNMENT

In theory, the highest organ of state power is the unicameral Supreme People's Assembly (SPA), with 687 members in 1993. In practice, however, governmental control rests with the leadership of the Korean Workers' (Communist) Party. SPA members are elected every four years and meet for only a few days each year to ratify decisions made by other governmental and party organs. To handle its functions between regular sessions, the SPA elects a Standing Committee of 19 members. Under the constitution (first adopted in 1948, completely revised in 1972, revisions in 1992), the SPA also elects the president of the DPRK; the Central People's Committee, headed by the president and containing 24 other members nominated by the president, which is the nation's top policymaking body, with executive, legal, and judicial power; and the Administrative Council (cabinet), headed by the premier under the leadership of the president. The state ideology is self-reliance (Chuch'e or Juch'e), the Korean version of Marxism-Leninism that was formulated in 1930 and adopted by the party in 1955. Under the new constitution (which created the post of president), Kim Il-sung, who had previously held state power as premier (1948–72), was elected to the presidency in 1972 and reelected in 1977, 1982, 1986, and 1990. Kim Il-sung died 8 July 1994, at which time it was anticipated that the SPA would elect his son, Kim Jong-il, to succeed him as president. Kang Song-san has been Premier since December 1992.

Suffrage extends to all men and women 17 years of age or older. Elections are on a single slate of Communist-approved candidates, on a yes or no basis. Following elections, it is usually asserted that nearly all those eligible voted and that their votes were unanimous in favor of the candidates.

¹⁴POLITICAL PARTIES

The Korean Workers' (Communist) Party, the ruling party of the DPRK, was formed on 10 October 1945 through a merger of the Communist Party and the New Democratic Party. Party membership in the mid-1980s was estimated to have risen to over 3 million, or about 16% of the population, the largest percentage of any Communist country. The principal party organ is the National Party Congress. The Congress adopts the party program and approves the political line set by its Central People's Committee. The party constitution states that a congress is to be convened every four years, but it has not always done so.

To guide the party between sessions of the National Party Congress, the Congress elects a Central People's Committee and a Central Auditing Commission, which looks after the party's financial affairs. The Central People's Committee (with 145 regular and 103 alternate members) elects the 9 members of the Secretariat, the executive arm of the party, and the 19 regular and 15 alternate members of the Politburo or Political Bureau. At the top of the party hierarchy are the three members of the Presidium of the Politburo. Kim Il-sung, the party's general secretary, ranks first among the Presidium members; the other two are Kim Jong-il, his son, and secretary of the Central Committee, O Chin-U, the minister of defense.

A "united front" policy confers nominal status on two ostensibly non-Communist political parties: the Korean Social Democratic Party, founded in 1945 and known as the Korean Democratic Party until 1981, and the Friends Party, founded in 1946 for adherents of the Ch'ondogyo faith.

¹⁵LOCAL GOVERNMENT

Of Korea's 13 historic provinces (do), 6 were wholly or partly within the DPRK after 1945. The Communist regime subsequently established 2 new provinces and divided another into two sections, thus raising the number of provinces to 9: North P'yongan, South P'yongan, Chagang, North Hwanghae, South Hwanghae, Kangwon, North Hamgyong, South Hamgyong, and Yanggang. In addition there are 3 provincial-level cities (jikhalsi) under the central government (P'yongyang, the capital, and Kaesong and Namp'o). The provinces were in turn divided into 20 cities (si) and 152 counties (kun, or gun) in the mid-1980s.

There are people's assemblies and people's committees at all levels of administration. Members of the people's assemblies are elected for four-year terms at the provincial level and for two-year terms at the county, township, and village levels. The assemblies supervise public, economic, and cultural activities. They also elect and recall people's committees, which are the permanent executive and administrative organs of the state at the local level.

¹⁶JUDICIAL SYSTEM

The DPRK's judicial system consists of the Central Court, formerly called the Supreme Court; the courts of provinces, cities, and counties; and special courts (courts-martial and transport courts). Most cases are tried in the first instance by people's courts at the city or county level. Provincial courts try important cases and examine appeals from lower court judgments. Members of the Central Court are named by the Standing Committee of the SPA to four-year terms concurrent with those of the SPA; lower courts are appointed by the people's assemblies at the corresponding level. A prosecutor-general, who is also appointed by the SPA, is the country's chief law-enforcement officer. He appoints prosecutors at the provincial, city, and county levels. Paralleling the court system is the Central Procurator's Office, a supervisory and investigative body.

Judges at the city and county levels serve two-year terms and are usually Korea Workers' Party members. Prosecution of alleged crimes against the state is conducted outside the judicial system and in secret. Reports from the DPRK in the early 1990s were that up to 150,000 political prisoners and family members were being detained in DPRK security camps in remote areas.

The Constitution declares that courts shall be independent and that judicial proceedings must be conducted according to elaborate procedural regulations. In practice, however, the principles of procedural due process as guaranteed by Western democratic systems are not respected.

[17]ARMED FORCES

The DPRK has one of the world's largest and best-equipped armed forces. Out of a total of 1.1 million personnel on active duty in 1993, one million were in the army, 40,000 in the navy, and 92,000 in the air force (with 732 combat aircraft). An additional 540,000 were in the reserves, and there was a civilian militia of 3–5 million. North Korea provides advisors to 12 African countries. The Ministry of Public Security controls 115,000 internal security forces. All males between the ages of 17 and 28 are required to serve 5–8 years in the army, 5–10 years in the navy or 3–4 years in the air force. Defense expenditures in 1993 totaled about $5 billion or 20 percent of gross domestic product. Arms imports were estimated to be worth $90 million in 1991; exports, $160 million. In the 1980s, the DPRK emerged as an important supplier of weapons and military training to the third world, but its foreign sales sunk from $130 million (1986) to $30 million (1991). The most worrisome development is the DPRK's growing capacity to produce weapons-grade nuclear material, improvement of its No-dong missile to reach regional targets beyond Korea, and its failure to submit to legal INEA inspections.

[18]INTERNATIONAL COOPERATION

During the mid-1970s, the DPRK came out of its relative isolation to pursue a vigorous international diplomacy. By 1986, it had diplomatic relations with 103 countries, including 67 that also had relations with the ROK. Although not a member of the UN, the DPRK maintains an observer group at UN headquarters and is a member of several nonregional specialized agencies, including FAO, IAEA, ICAO, ITU, UNESCO, UNIDO, UPU, WHO, WIPO, and WMO. The nation has signed the Law of the Sea and has been particularly active in third-world diplomacy; in August 1975, the DPRK entered the League of Non-Aligned Nations, and it has since joined G-77. In addition, the DPRK pursues a variety of exchanges with China, the former USSR, and East European nations. The DPRK retains treaties of friendship, cooperation, and mutual defense concluded with China and the former USSR in 1961. In 1986, a 20-year treaty of friendship and cooperation with Mongolia was signed. The DPRK has been the only Asian Communist country remaining neutral in the Sino-Soviet dispute.

[19]ECONOMY

By the end of the 1960s, the government's pursuit of a self-reliant economic policy had succeeded in transforming the DPRK into one of the most strictly regulated economies in the world. The Korean War devastated much of the DPRK's economy, but growth after postwar reconstruction was rapid. The Communist regime has used its rich mineral resources to promote industry, especially heavy industry. By 1965, industry accounted for 78% of the total output, and agriculture 22%; the two sectors had thus precisely reversed the proportions reported in 1946. A generally accepted figure put annual industrial growth during 1956–63 at about 25%. Since 1965, greater emphasis has been placed on agriculture and light industry, the latter stress owing to increasing demands for consumer goods. The industrial growth rate slowed in the late 1960s to around 14% and averaged about 16% during the 1970s. Efforts to accelerate the growth rate during the mid-1970s, requiring substantial imports of heavy industrial equipment from Japan and Western Europe, led to a payments crisis, and the DPRK was repeatedly compelled to reschedule its foreign debt. The seven-year plan for 1978–84 called for an annual increase in industrial output of 12%, and the plan for 1987–93 proposed an annual increase of about 10%.

Reliable data on recent economic developments in the DPRK are scant; however, available indicators suggest that since the early 1990s, the country has suffered serious economic dislocation. In particular, declining oil imports from Russia resulting from the latter country's recent insistence on hard currency transactions have constrained production in many key sectors of the economy. Reports by the Bank of Korea in Seoul suggest a decline in North Korea's GNP of 3.7% in 1990, followed by another 5.2% drop in 1991.

A State Planning Committee coordinates the economy, with corresponding committees at city, county, and province levels. Local and regional planning committees have been given greater latitude in planning since 1964. During 1981, management responsibilities were reportedly reassigned from central government ministries to new provincial economic guidance committees, which were controlled by provincial officials of the Korean Workers' Party. In order to foster some decentralization of the economic environment, since the mid-1980s various economic ministries have been consolidated into a smaller number of commissions and greater autonomy reportedly allowed in the management of state enterprises. Thus far, however, these measures have resulted in little further change in the overall structure of the North Korean economy.

[20]INCOME

The United States government estimated North Korea's GNP at $22 billion in 1992, with a declining growth rate of between –10 and –15 percent. The per capita GNP was estimated at $1,000.

[21]LABOR

Although figures on occupational distribution have not been published since 1963, it is known that the DPRK faces a chronic labor shortage. The civilian labor force is estimated at more than 6.1 million, about 43% of whom are engaged in agriculture, forestry, and fishing. Women are believed to constitute about 46% of the labor force. Girls are prepared for entering the labor force as early as nursery school.

There are no free trade unions in North Korea, but rather one single labor organization, the General Federation of Trade Unions of Korea, of which virtually all industrial and office workers are members. Salaries in the DPRK in 1986 averaged w100–200 per month. Labor conditions are governed by a national labor law of 1978. The eight-hour workday is standard but most laborers work 12-16 hours daily during production campaigns. Office and shop workers spend Fridays in public works and urban maintenance projects.

[22]AGRICULTURE

About 2 million hectares (4.9 million acres), or 16% of all land, can be classified as arable. Most of the agricultural land is concentrated in the west-coast provinces of North and South P'yongan and North and South Hwanghae. Irrigation, land reclamation, and flood-control projects have been carried out, especially in rice-growing areas; about one-half of the arable land is irrigated.

Rice is the principal crop, occupying about 30% of all farmland in 1992. Total rice production was put at 5 million tons in 1992, compared to 5.6 million tons in 1985 and 2.8 million tons in 1972. Improved rice yields have been achieved through the use of "miracle" rice strains, intensive application of fertilizer, and mechanization. In 1991 there were some 74,000 tractors in use, or about 1 for every 27 hectares (67 acres) of cultivated land. Double-cropping of rice is not possible because of the climate, but double-cropping of other grains has been maximized through the use of cold-bed seeding and new seed varieties, so that an estimated half of all cultivated land yields two harvests. The DPRK claims to be self-sufficient in grain products, with total production (including rice) increasing from 7 million tons in 1974 to 13.6 million tons in 1985, but falling to 9.8 million tons in 1992. According to other sources, heavy imports of wheat and flour are needed. The leading grains after rice are corn, wheat, millet, and barley. Other important crops include soybeans, potatoes, sweet potatoes, pulses, oats, sorghum, rye, tobacco, and cotton.

The country's farms were collectivized after the Korean War. The movement began late in 1953, and the process was completed by August 1958, when all of the DPRK's 1,055,000 farm families had become members of over 16,000 cooperatives. In order to establish larger and more efficient operating units, the cooperatives were merged in the autumn of 1958 into approximately 3,800 units with about 300 families each. Produce is delivered to the government, which controls distribution through state stores. Most farm workers retain small private plots (less than 100 sq m/1,100 sq ft) and can sell produce from them to the state or in peasant markets.

23 ANIMAL HUSBANDRY

Since the 1950s, a major effort has been made to increase corn and fodder supplies, to improve breeding practices, and to raise sharply the numbers of livestock in all categories. In 1992, livestock totals were estimated as follows: cattle, 1,300,000 head; hogs, 3,300,000; sheep, 390,000; goats, 300,000; and horses, 46,000. Livestock raising is generally associated with the state farms. Meat produced in 1992 totaled 258,000 tons; milk, 93,000; and eggs, 160,000. The DPRK was the world's third leading producer of silk in 1992 (after China and India), with 4,500 tons.

24 FISHING

The catch from the sea and from freshwater aquaculture includes mackerel, anchovy, tuna, mullet, rainbow trout, squid, kelp, sea urchin eggs, pollack eggs, and shrimp. The FAO estimated production for 1992 was 1.7 million tons. About 94% of fishing activity is marine, concentrated in the Sea of Japan. Much of the annual catch is now used for export.

The fishing industry is entirely socialized, with some 230 maritime cooperatives and more than 30 state-run fishery stations. The main fishing ports are on the east coast.

25 FORESTRY

Forests and woodland comprised about 8,970,000 hectares (22,165,000 acres) in the early 1990s. There are rich stands of coniferous forests in the northern provinces. Predominant trees include oak, alder, larch, pine, spruce, and fir. Timber production was estimated at 4.7 million cu m in 1991, an increase of more than 400,000 cu m over the 1980 figure. An estimated 4.1 million cu m were used for fuel, and only 875,000 cu m in industry. The Ministry of Forestry, created in 1980, was expected to spur development of forest industries.

26 MINING

Coal deposits include adequate supplies of anthracite and lignite, but bituminous coal must be imported for use as coke in the steel industry. Anthracite is mined chiefly along the middle course of the Taedong River (South P'yongan Province) and lignite in the Tumen River basin (North Hamgyong Province). The government reported a total coal production in 1991 of 90 million tons. Iron ore production was over 10 million tons in 1991. Other mineral products include gold, magnesite, tungsten, phosphate, sulfur, zinc, lead, silver, and copper. As of 1991, mineral trade between North Korea and the Republic of Korea had been increasing; that year, North Korea exported coal, gold, steel, and zinc to the south.

27 ENERGY AND POWER

Coal, oil, and natural gas provided 40% of the DPRK's electricity generation in 1991. Hydroelectricity accounted for the remainder. Coal is by far the most important component of energy production. Estimated coal production in 1991 was 90 million tons, 35 million tons more than domestic consumption that year. Installed electric capacity was 9.5 million kw by the end of 1991; production of electricity that year totaled 51.9 billion kwh, up from 9.1 billion kwh in 1960.

In 1986, the former USSR agreed to the construction of a nuclear power plant with an expected capacity of 1.8 million kw. In the same year, a hydroelectric power station at Taipingwan, jointly built by China and the DPRK, began operations. In February 1994, North Korea agreed to UN-supported demands that it open part of its nuclear program to international inspections. The International Atomic Energy Agency (IAEA) began inspections of North Korean nuclear facilities in March 1991 (almost one year after North Korea withdrew from the nuclear Non-Proliferation Treaty), in order to determine whether or not North Korea was reprocessing spent nuclear reactor fuel, which could be used to make a nuclear weapon. Tensions rose as the IAEA continued to pressure for inspections; on 25 March, 1994, North Korea urged its citizens to prepare for an all-out war.

28 INDUSTRY

Under Japanese rule, northern Korea was regarded mainly as a supplier of war materials, while manufacturing and processing branches were neglected. The Communist regime, however, emphasized the development of manufacturing. By 1963, the metal-fabricating, textile, and food-processing industries accounted for 33%, 18.6%, and 13.7% of industrial output, respectively. By the late 1980s, heavy industry (including metal fabricating and textile production) accounted for 50% of total industrial production. Private enterprise in industry declined from 27.6% of total output in 1946 to only 2% in 1956, and the private sector was said to have disappeared by 1959. About 90% of all industry is state-owned, and 10% is owned by cooperatives.

Under the 1978–84 economic plan, industrial output was scheduled to grow at an average annual rate of 12.2%; however, Western estimates put actual growth at less than 10%. An annual growth of 10% was targeted under the 1987–93 plan. Given the lack of official data released by the government in recent years, the actual growth rate achieved in the industrial sector during recent years is difficult to estimate.

Rough production estimates are available for a few key industries only. These include the iron and steel manufactures, which reportedly amounted to 3.7 million tons of pig and conversion pig iron and 7.7 million tons of steel (including rolled steel) in 1990. Major iron and steel works are located at Ch'ongjin, Kimch'aek, Kangso, Nampo, and Kaesong. Industrial plants produce sophisticated machinery, including generators, bulldozers, high-speed engines, and diesel locomotives. Other plants produce aluminum (21,000 tons in 1990), cement (7.6 million tons), magnesia clinker (1 million tons), lead (84,000 tons), zinc (170,000 tons), metal cutting lathes (28,000), tractors (23,000), and trucks (10,000). The chemical industry produced an estimated 3.9 million tons of chemical fertilizers and 92,000 tons of synthetic resins in 1990, and 74,000 tons of chemical fibres in 1989. The textile industry, based mainly on synthetic fibers, expanded rapidly in the 1970s; cloth production increased from 400 million m in 1970 to 600 million m in 1976. In 1986 it reached a reported high of 800 million m but is estimated to have declined to only 520 million m in 1990. The petrochemical industry is centered in the Hungnam area. About 2.3 million tons of oil products were produced in 1990.

In 1992, negotiations were conducted with South Korean business leaders over the establishment of a joint-venture factory complex for light industry in Nampo near P'yongyang; further progress on the plan, however, have since been stalled by the ongoing dispute over North Korea's nuclear policy. In 1987 an integrated circuit pilot project became operational with UNDP assistance and a handful of other plants have opened since, although electronics manufacture remains very limited in the country.

29 SCIENCE AND TECHNOLOGY

The Fifth Party Congress in 1970 called for the education of 1 million new technicians and specialists to aid economic modernization and development. By the mid-1990s, the government claimed that there were agricultural specialists on most rural cooperatives, although severe economic deprivation has curtailed DPRK agricultural output. Throughout this period, Russian and Chinese technicians helped train North Korean workers, and the DPRK actively sought to acquire advanced foreign technology through the importation of entire petrochemical and other manufacturing plants from Japan, France, Sweden, and other developed nations. In the 1990s, its nuclear energy program—with both peaceful and military applications—has gained international attention. By 1994, Kim Il-sung University in Pyongyang included faculties for information science and technology, biotechnology, mathematics, and physics.

30 DOMESTIC TRADE

Wholesale and retail trade is almost entirely in state and cooperative hands. In 1946, private trade accounted for 96.5% of total business volume. By 1960, private merchants had been entirely eliminated, and 78.8% of trade was conducted by the state, 20.4% by cooperatives, and 0.8% by farmers' markets.

Wholesale distribution is administered by the state ministries and enterprises, under the general jurisdiction of the Ministry of Material Supply. Most retail shops are run by the People's Service Committee, established in 1972. There are several state-run department stores in P'yongyang, and there is at least one in each provincial capital. All-purpose stores, cooperatives, factory outlets, and special stores for the military and for railroad workers also play an important part in retailing.

Normal business hours are from 9 AM to 12 noon and 1 to 6 PM, Monday–Friday. Saturday is a "study" day.

31 FOREIGN TRADE

The DPRK's principal exports include rice, pig iron, rolled steel, cement, machinery of various types, chemicals, magnesite, textiles, armaments, and gold. Imports included petroleum, coking coal, wheat, cotton, and machinery. No published trade figures are available from the North Korean government at present. However, Western estimates put the value of 1991 exports at $1,240 million and imports at $2,280 million. Exports in 1990, by contrast, totaled $1,857 as imports equalled $2,930. The steep drop in the DPRK's trade earnings between 1990 and 1991 was primarily a result of a policy shift by Russia and the CIS countries requiring trade to be denominated in hard currency at world prices, ending a previous goods exchange arrangement much more favorable to the North Korean situation. With this change in Russian-North Korean trade relations, China took the lead as the DPRK's largest trading partner in 1992, followed by Japan and Russia. Total trade with China amounted to almost $700 million, about 77% of which consisted of imports (mainly oil and related products). Inter-Korean trade has expanded particularly rapidly since 1988. By 1992, South Korea was the DPRK's fourth largest trading partner, behind China and Japan. Total trade between the two countries was reported to have reached $199 million, 90% of which consisting of exports from North to South.

32 BALANCE OF PAYMENTS

During the late 1970s, the DPRK enjoyed consistent trade surpluses, due in part to increasing shipments of agricultural products, gold and silver, and armaments in exchange for hard currencies. Despite the improving trade picture, the DPRK had still not emerged from the shadow of foreign debt left over from the mid-1970s. Declining prices for precious metals in the early 1980s made it difficult for the nation to meet its debt obligations, even after repeated rescheduling. In 1987, a new rescheduling agreement was worked out, after Western banks threatened to freeze the DPRK's bank assets if it failed to service bank loans.

33 BANKING AND SECURITIES

The Central Bank, established in 1946, is the sole recipient of national revenues and the repository for all precious metals. It supplies basic operating funds to various sectors of the economy and is subordinate to the Ministry of Finance. The Central Bank is also an administrative organ that executes the fiscal policies of the State Planning Commission. It supervises the Foreign Trade Bank, established in 1959, and the Industrial Bank, established in 1964. The latter provides loans and credits to farm and fishing cooperatives and has an extensive system of branches which help to manage the financial operations of all cooperatives.

There are savings facilities at all post offices, in industrial enterprises, and in the "trust" sections in the agricultural cooperatives. Through the latter, large farm and fishing cooperatives perform local banking functions, especially the raising and allocation of capital for local needs.

There are no securities exchanges in the DPRK.

34 INSURANCE

The State Insurance Bureau and the Korea Foreign Insurance Company carry fire and natural disaster insurance and, as appropriate, livestock, marine, and passenger insurance on a compulsory basis. Individuals may take out various types of property, life, and travel insurance, all provided by the government.

35 PUBLIC FINANCE

The annual state budget is approved at regular sessions of the SPA. In 1990, budget revenues came to $17.3 billion, while expenditures totaled $17.7 billion. Foreign aid, important after the Korean War, has not appeared as budgetary income since 1961. External debt in 1990 was about $7 billion.

36 TAXATION

All direct taxes were abolished in 1974; the DPRK thus became the first country in the world to abolish income tax. As a result, the socialist sector contributes 100% of total budget revenue. The government collects a percentage (turnover tax) on all transactions between producers and state marketing agencies. Fees are charged to farmers for seeds, fertilizer, irrigation water, and equipment, and consumers pay a tax for the use of water and certain other household amenities.

37 CUSTOMS AND DUTIES

No information is available.

38 FOREIGN INVESTMENT

In 1984, the Joint Venture Act permitted direct foreign investment for the first time. Relations have been established with Western companies in the areas of hotel construction, hydroelectricity, nonferrous metals, light industry, and services.

In 1991 plans were initiated for a multinational special economic zone in the Tumen River estuary region, involving investments from China and Russia as well as North Korea. New laws on foreign investment were passed in 1992, allowing 100% foreign ownership as well as loosened government control over employee layoffs. As yet, however, actual applications for investment by foreign companies remain very limited; most of the modest foreign investments which have been made in the country derive from Japan-based Korean investors.

39ECONOMIC DEVELOPMENT

The economy is operated on a planned basis, with priority given to the development of industry, particularly heavy industry. Planning began in 1947, when the economy operated first under two consecutive one-year plans (1947 and 1948), followed by a two-year plan (1949–50), which was interrupted by the Korean War in June 1950. After the war, economic reconstruction followed the terms of a three-year plan (1954–56) and a five-year plan (1957–61). The industrial goals of the five-year plan were fulfilled in just half the allotted time, so 1960 was set aside as a year of adjustment. An ambitious seven-year plan was then launched in 1961, with the general objectives of a 220% increase in industrial output and a 150% rise in grain production. This plan had to be extended until 1970, however, before its targets were fulfilled. In 1975, the DPRK announced completion of its six-year plan (1971–76) one year ahead of schedule, although certain outputs fell somewhat short of projected levels. Industrial growth slowed in 1976, and for the first time since the division of Korea, per capita GNP in the DPRK fell below that of the ROK.

A second seven-year plan (1978–84) called for a 12% annual industrial growth rate. Annual coal output was to increase to 70–80 million tons, steel to 7.4–8 million tons, fertilizers to 5 million tons, and electricity to 50–60 billion kwh. Although the government claimed that its goals had been met or exceeded, neither the actual results nor a new plan was announced during the following two years. The third seven-year plan (1987–93) had as its general aims increases of 90% in industrial output, 40% in agricultural production, and 70% in national income. Unofficial economic indicators of recent years suggest that actual performance has fallen far short of these targets (in some cases by as much as 50%) and that a drop in overall industrial output has occurred since the late 1980s, especially in wake of falling oil imports from the former USSR countries. Statement released by the Korean Workers' Party Central Committee in late 1993 confirmed the overall failure of the last seven-year plan and announced a two-to-three year period of economic adjustment during which investments in agriculture, light industry and foreign trade would be prioritized.

In the past, the DPRK's principal economic benefactors were the USSR and China. However, following a developing rapprochement between the former USSR and South Korea in 1990, with the latter now offering badly needed economic aid to the Soviet government, Soviet assistance to the North was curtailed in 1991. Credits extended by Japan reached $350 million by 1978; recent requests for more assistance from Japan have as yet not been filled, pending resolution of the current nuclear dispute and questions over the closed nature of the DPRK economy. For the 1983–86 period, the UNDP allocated $18.4 million, the largest such program since Korea was divided. The DPRK's external debt was estimated at more than $6.8 billion by the end of 1989.

40SOCIAL DEVELOPMENT

All citizens are entitled to free medical care, disability benefits, and retirement allowances. About 1% of workers' salaries is deducted for programs allowing paid vacations and paid maternity leaves, with the state making up the rest of the cost. The state runs about 400 rest centers and resorts providing free vacations to workers. Retirement pensions are roughly one-half of the annual average wage; those who continue working after retirement age receive both their salary and their pension.

The 1972 constitution guarantees equal rights for women. The state provides nurseries and day-care centers, and large families are encouraged. The fertility rate, estimated at 2.5 in 1985–90, has been held down by the tendency of women in the DPRK to marry late.

41HEALTH

The Ministry of Public Health is responsible for all national health services, including disease prevention and sanitation. In 1992, children up to one year old were immunized against tuberculosis (99%); diphtheria, pertussis, and tetanus (90%); polio (98%); and measles ((96%). In 1992, there were 2.72 doctors and 13.5 hospital beds per 1,000 people. Western medicine is used alongside traditional Eastern medicine (tonguihak). There were 162 reported cases of tuberculosis per 100,000 people in 1990. Cancer is now the leading cause of death, followed by heart disease and hypertension. Average life expectancy in 1992 was 71 years for both men and women. The infant mortality rate was 25 per 1,000 in 1992. The general mortality rate in 1993 was 5.3 per 1,000 people.

42HOUSING

A serious housing shortage was produced by the government's early stress on industrial rather than residential construction. The housing deficit was aggravated by the Korean War, which demolished about one-third of the country's housing. Since then, residential housing has received serious attention. About 886,000 new units were completed under the 1971–76 economic plan. Construction levels of 200,000–300,000 units a year were targeted for 1978–84, and 150,000–200,000 units a year were projected for 1987–93. Available figures for 1980–88 show a total housing stock of 4,566,000 with 4.5 people per dwelling.

43EDUCATION

Both primary and secondary education is free and compulsory for eleven years, beginning at age 6. Children aged 1 to 5 are cared for in nursery schools, followed by one year of kindergarten, four years of primary school, and six years of secondary school. The adult literacy rate was estimated to be 99% in 1991. In 1986, there were an estimated 4,792 primary institutions with 1,466,000 students enrolled. In the 4,738 secondary institutions, 2,842,000 students were enrolled. In August 1988, the government announced the establishment of new educational establishments, including a university, eight colleges, three factory colleges, two farmer colleges and five special schools.

Kim Il-sung University (founded in 1946) in P'yongyang is the only university, with about 12,000 full-time and part-time students and about 2,000 teachers. Admission to the university is by intensely competitive examination. Other institutions of higher learning include the Kimch'aek Polytechnic Institute, P'yongyang Agricultural College, and P'yongyang Medical School. In 1986 there were 473 colleges with 215,000 students enrolled; university-level institutions numbered 46 with 138,300 students enrolled. A system of adult schools, correspondence courses, and workplace schools makes higher education widely available.

44LIBRARIES AND MUSEUMS

The DPRK has more than 200 public libraries, the largest being the Central Library in P'yongyang. In addition, there are research libraries at the academies of sciences and social sciences and at Kim Il-sung University (2 million volumes).

Museums include the Central Historical Museum, the Memorial Museum of the War of Liberation, the Korean Art Gallery, the Ethnographic Museum, and the Korean Revolutionary Museum, all in P'yongyang. There is a large museum at Mangyongdae, Kim Il-sung's birthplace, near the capital.

45MEDIA

Postal, telephone, and telegraph services are operated by the government. The central broadcasting station in P'yongyang has a 1,500-kw transmitter. Broadcasts reach to every corner of the country through a system of more than 1 million loudspeakers, as well as through private radios. In addition, news is broadcast to other countries in English, Russian, French, and Spanish. There are two radio networks (Korean Central Radio and Radio P'yongyang) and two television networks, (Korean Central TV and Mansudae TV). In 1991 there were about 2.6 million radios and 338,000 television sets.

All newspapers and periodicals in the DPRK are published by government, party, or front organizations; each edition is subjected to prepublication review and censorship. The leading national newspapers and their publishers are: *Rodong Sinmun* (Central Committee of the Korean Workers' Party) (circulation 1,500,000); *Minju Choson* (Presidium of the Supreme People's Assembly and the cabinet) (circulation 200,000); *Pyongyang Shinmun*; and *Radong Changuyon*. Each province has a newspaper, and other mass organizations have their own organs. A state news service, the Korean Central News Agency, is the sole organ for the gathering and dissemination of news.

46ORGANIZATIONS

Mass organizations established for specialized political, economic, or cultural purposes include the powerful Democratic Front for the Reunification of the Fatherland, commonly known as the Fatherland Front. Among its constituent members are the Socialist Working Youth League, under the direct guidance of the Korean Workers' Party Central People's Committee; the Young Pioneer Corps, open to children aged 9–15; and the Korean Democratic Women's League. Also important are the Korean Red Cross Society and the Korean Agricultural Workers' Union.

47TOURISM, TRAVEL, AND RECREATION

Most sightseeing takes place in the capital city of P'yongyang. Travel outside P'yongyang is closed to individual tourists but available to groups. Nampe, the port city for P'yongyang, has a beach resort area. The two most outstanding tourist sites outside the capital are the Kumgang (Diamond) Mountains in the southwest and Packdu Mountain on the Chinese border. All visitors need visas secured in advance from DPRK diplomatic representatives. Increasingly anxious to obtain foreign exchange, the government has invited touring delegations from numerous nations, especially developing nations. All tourism from the US, Israel, the ROK, and South Africa, is banned without invitation.

Wrestling, tug-of-war, chess (with pieces different from the European form), and kite fighting are traditional sports.

48FAMOUS KOREANS

Among the many historical figures of united Korea are Ulchi Mundok, a Koguryo general of the early 7th century AD; Kim Yosin (595–673), a warrior and folk hero in Silla's struggle to unify the peninsula; Wang Kon (877–943), the founder and first ruler of the Koryo Dynasty; Yun Kwan (d.1111), a Koryo general who repulsed Chinese invaders; Kim Pu-sik (1075–1151), a scholar-official who wrote the great *History of the Three Kingdoms;* Yi Song-gye (1335–1408), a general and founder of the Yi (or Li) Dynasty; King Sejong (1397–1450), who called for the invention of Han'gul and was Korea's greatest monarch; Yi Hwang (1501–70) and Yi I (1536–84), Neo-Confucianist philosophers and officials; Yi Sun-sin (1545–98), an admiral who invented the "turtleboat," the first ironclad ship, and defeated the Japanese in every naval engagement of the Hideyoshi invasions, dying in the climactic battle; Chong Yag-yong (1762–1836), a pragmatic scholar-official and prolific writer; and Yi Ha-ung (1820–98), known as the Taewon'gun (Prince Regent), the regent for his son, Kojong, and the central political figure of the late 19th century.

The preeminent political figure of the DPRK is Kim Il-sung (1912–94), the leader of the nation from 1948 until his death. Other influential figures have included Kim Il (1910–84), a prominent officeholder since 1954; Kim Jong-il (b. 1941), the son of Kim Il-sung, who succeeded him; and Nam Il (1914–76), a chief of staff who became well known as an armistice negotiator at P'anmunjom (1951–53).

49DEPENDENCIES

The DPRK has no territories or colonies.

50BIBLIOGRAPHY

Chun Sin-yong (ed.). *Korean Society*. Seoul: International Cultural Foundation, 1976.
Cumings, Bruce. *The Origins of the Korean War*. Princeton, N.J.: Princeton University Press, 1981.
Eberstadt, Nick. *The Population of North Korea*. Berkeley: University of California, 1992.
Eckert, Carter J. *Korea, Old and New: A History*. Cambridge, Mass.: Harvard University Press, 1990.
Foot, Rosemary. *The Wrong War: American Policy and the Dimensions of the Korean Conflict, 1950–53*. Ithaca, N.Y.: Cornell University Press, 1985.
Grayson, James Huntley. *Korea: A Religious History*. New York: Oxford University Press, 1989.
Han, Woo-keun. *The History of Korea*. Honolulu: East-West Center Press, 1972.
Hoare, James. *Korea: An Introduction*. New York: Kegan Paul International, 1988.
Howe, Russell Warren. *The Koreans: Passion and Grace*. San Diego: Harcourt Brace Jovanovich, 1988.
Hwang, Eui-Gak. *The Korean Economies: A Comparison of North and South*. New York: Oxford University Press, 1993.
Kihl, Young Hwan. *Politics and Policies in Divided Korea*. Boulder, Colo.: Westview, 1984.
Kim Il-sung. *Selected Works*. 4 vols. P'yongyang: Foreign Languages Publishing House, 1972.
Koh, Byung Chul. *The Foreign Policy Systems of North and South Korea*. Berkeley: University of California Press, 1984.
Lee, Chong-sik. *Korean Workers' Party: A Short History*. Stanford, Calif.: Hoover Institution Press, 1978.
Lee, Peter (ed.). *Sourcebook of Korean Civilization*. New York: Columbia University Press, 1993—
Lone, Stewart. *Korea since 1850*. Melbourne, Australia: Longman Cheshire; New York: St. Martin's, 1993.
Macdonald, Donald Stone. *The Koreans: Contemporary Politics and Society*. Boulder, Colo.: Westview Press, 1990.
McNamara, Dennis L. *The Colonial Origins of Korean Enterprise, 1910–1945*. New York: Cambridge University Press, 1990.
Merrill, John. *Korea: The Peninsular Origins of the War*. Newark: University of Delaware Press, 1989.
Oliver, Robert Tarbell. *A History of the Korean People in Modern Times: 1800 to the Present*. Newark: Univ. of Delaware Press; London: Associated University Presses, 1993.
Olsen, Edward A. *US Policy and the two Koreas*. Boulder, Colo.: Westview Press, 1988.
Palais, James B. *Politics and Policy in Traditional Korea*. Cambridge: Harvard University Press, 1991.
Soh, Chung-Hee. *Women in Korean Politics*. 2d ed. Boulder, Colo.: Westview Press, 1993.
Song, Pyong-nak. *The Rise of the Korean Economy*. Hong Kong; New York: Oxford University Press, 1990.
Suh, Dae-Sook. *Kim Il Sung: The North Korean Leader*. New York: Columbia University Press, 1988.

KOREA, REPUBLIC OF (ROK)

Republic of Korea
Taehan Min-guk

CAPITAL: Seoul.

FLAG: The flag, called the T'aegukki, shows, on a white field, a central circle divided into two parts, red on top and deep blue below, in the shape of Chinese yin and yang symbols. Broken and unbroken black bars in each of the four corners are variously arranged in sets of three, representing divination diagrams.

ANTHEM: *Aegukka (The Song of Patriotism)*, officially adopted on 15 August 1948.

MONETARY UNIT: The won (w) is the national currency. There are notes of 500, 1,000, 5,000, and 10,000 won. w1 = $0.0012 (or $1 = w806.50).

WEIGHTS AND MEASURES: Both the metric system and ancient Korean units of measurement are used.

HOLIDAYS: New Year's Days, 1–3 January; Independence Movement Day, 1 March; Labor Day, 10 March; Arbor Day, 5 April; Children's Day, 5 May; Memorial Day, 6 June; Constitution Day, 17 July; Liberation Day, 15 August; Armed Forces Day, 1 October; National Foundation Day, 3 October; Han'gul (Korean Alphabet) Day, 9 October; Christmas, 25 December.

TIME: 9 PM = noon GMT.

¹LOCATION, SIZE, AND EXTENT

Occupying the southern 45% of the Korean Peninsula in East Asia, the Republic of Korea (ROK), also known as South Korea, has an area of 98,480 sq km (38,023 sq mi), extending 642 km (399 mi) NNE–SSW and 436 km (271 mi) ESE–WNW. Comparatively, the area occupied by South Korea is slightly larger than the state of Indiana. Bounded on the N by the Democratic People's Republic of Korea (DPRK), on the E by the Sea of Japan (known in Korea as the East Sea), on the S by the Korea Strait, and on the W by the Yellow Sea, the ROK has a total boundary length of 2,651 km (1,647 mi). A demilitarized zone (DMZ), 4,000 m (13,100 ft) wide, covering 1,262 sq km (487 sq mi) and located north and south of the 38th parallel, separates the ROK from the DPRK, which comprises the northern part of the Korean Peninsula.

Although the ROK's general (facing) coastline is estimated at 1,318 km (819 mi), a measurement taking account of its manifold indentations would be closer to 6,200 km (3,850 mi). Over 3,000 islands, most of them off the southern and western coasts and belonging to the ROK, add another 8,600 km (5,350 mi) of coastline.

The ROK's capital city, Seoul, is located in the northwestern part of the country.

²TOPOGRAPHY

Elevations in the southern part of the Korean Peninsula are generally lower than those in the north. Only about 30% of the ROK consists of lowlands and plains. The principal lowlands, all bordering the Yellow Sea along the west coast, include the Han River Plain, near Seoul; the Pyongtaek and Honam plains, south of the capital; and the Yongsan Plain in the southwest. Mt. Halla (1,950 m/6,398 ft), on volcanic Cheju Island, is the nation's highest point, while Mt. Chiri, or Chii (1,915 m/6,283 ft), is the highest point on the mainland.

Principal rivers of the ROK include the Han (514 km/319 mi), with Seoul near its mouth; the Kum (401 km/249 mi) and Yongsan (116 km/72 mi), which water the fertile plains areas of the southwest; and the Somjin (212 km/132 mi), in the south. The longest river in the ROK is the Naktong (521 km/324 mi), which waters the southeast. Yellow Sea tides on the west coast rise to over 9 m (30 ft) in some places, while Japan Sea tides on the east coast rise only about 1 m (3 ft).

³CLIMATE

The average January temperature ranges from –5°C (23°F) at Seoul to –2°C (28°F) at Pusan and 4°C (39°F) on Cheju Island. In the hottest part of the summer, however, the regional variation in temperature is not nearly so marked, with average temperatures ranging from 25°C to 27°C (77–81°F) in most lowland areas. Most of the nation receives between 75 and 100 cm (30 and 40 in) of rain a year, but more than 130 cm (50 in) of precipitation falls in the southeast. Nearly all the rainfall occurs in the April–September period, especially during the rainy season, late June to early August. From one to three mild typhoons normally strike the south in the early fall, with a severe one occurring every two or three years. Days free of frost number about 240 in the southern regions.

⁴FLORA AND FAUNA

The Korean Peninsula is rich in varieties of plant life typical of temperate regions. More than 3,000 species, some 500 of them unique to Korea, have been noted by botanists. Warm temperate vegetation, including camellias and other broad-leaved evergreens, predominate in the south and on Cheju Island. Zoologists have identified more than 130 freshwater fishes, 371 birds, 78 mammals, and 39 reptiles and amphibians on the peninsula. Bear, wild boar, deer, and lynx still are found in the highlands, but the shrinking of the forested area has reduced the animal population in recent years. Migratory water fowl, cranes, herons, and other birds are visible on the plains. Noxious insects and household pests infest the warmer regions, and aquatic life is generally infected with parasites.

⁵ENVIRONMENT

Efforts to control the detrimental effects of rapid industrialization, urbanization, and population growth focus on the Office of

Environment, established in 1980 to control air, water, and land pollution and manage solid wastes. The Environmental Preservation Law, revised in 1979, covers air, water, and noise pollution, soil preservation, and disposal of solid wastes.

The nation has 15.1 cubic miles of water with 75% used for agriculture and 14% used for industrial purposes; 24% of the people living in rural areas do not have pure water. The purity of the nation's water is threatened by agricultural chemicals. The country's cities produce 13.4 million tons of solid waste per year. In 1990, the nation dumped 10 million tons of sewage and 7 million tons of industrial chemicals into its water sources. Air pollution, associated mainly with the use of coal briquettes for home heating and the increase in automobile traffic, is also severe, with smog a common problem in Seoul. Korea contributes 0.8% of the world's total gas emissions.

The Naktong River delta, a marshland where thousands of birds spend the winter, is threatened by environmental pollution and by plans to dam the mouth of the river. The beginning of construction of the Kumgangsan hydroelectric dam by the DPRK near the DMZ in 1986 was protested by the ROK on the grounds that the central Korean Peninsula could be flooded. In response, the ROK began construction of its own Peace Dam near the DMZ in 1987.

Although 28 species of birds and 8 species of mammals—chipmunk, wild boar, squirrel, raccoon dog, badger, hare, river deer, and roe deer—are still classified as game species, hunting was banned by the government from August 1972 through December 1981, except in such game preserves as that of Cheju Island. In 1994, 6 of Korea's mammal species and 22 bird species were endangered, as were 33 plant species. Endangered species in the ROK include the Amur leopard, Japanese sea lion, Oriental white stork, Japanese crested ibis, and Tristram's woodpecker.

⁶POPULATION

The 1990 census for the ROK reported a total population of 43,520,199, or nearly twice the estimated population of the DPRK. A total of 46,897,000 was projected for the year 2000, assuming a crude birthrate of 15.7 per 1,000 population, a crude death rate of 6.3, and a net natural increase of 9.4 during 1995–2000. The annual rate of population growth in 1990–95 was estimated at 0.8%, and the population density in 1990 was 438 per sq km (1,134 per sq mi), making the ROK one of the world's most densely populated nations. An estimated 72% of the population was urban, up from 21% in 1950. Seoul, the largest city, had a population of 10,627,790 in 1990. The 1985 populations of other large cities were Pusan, 3,797,566; Taegu, 2,228,834; Inch'on,1,818,293; Kwangju, 1,144,695; and Taejon, 1,062,084.

⁷MIGRATION

During the Japanese occupation (1910–45), some 3 million Koreans emigrated to Manchuria and other parts of China, 700,000 to Siberia, perhaps 3 million to Japan, and about 7,000 to the US (mostly to Hawaii). The great majority of those who went to Japan were from the populous southern provinces, and large numbers (1.5–2 million) of them returned home following the end of hostilities in 1945. In addition, from 1945 through 1949, at least 1.2 million Koreans crossed the 38th parallel into the ROK, refugees from Communism or from the Korean War. Under the Emigration Law of 1962, the ROK government encouraged emigration to South America (especially Brazil), the Federal Republic of Germany (FRG), the Middle East, and elsewhere. Most of the emigrants are workers who remit earnings back home. A total of 409,922 Koreans emigrated during the 1962–80 period; emigration peaked at 48,270 in 1976 but had declined to 27,163 in 1990. In addition, Koreans have emigrated permanently to the US in large numbers since 1971; the population in the US of Korean origin was 798,849 as of 1990 (72.7%

foreign-born. In all, more than 2 million South Koreans were living abroad in 1988. Migration within South Korea, mainly from the rural areas to the cities, remains substantial, despite government efforts to improve village living conditions.

⁸ETHNIC GROUPS

The Koreans are believed to be descended primarily from Tungusic peoples of the Mongoloid race, who originated in the cold northern regions of Central Asia. There is scant evidence of non-Mongloid admixture. The ROK has no sizable ethnic minority.

⁹LANGUAGES

The Korean language is usually held to be a member of the Altaic family; there are only slight differences between the various dialects. Korean is written in a largely phonetic alphabet called Han'gul, created in 1443. The Korean alphabet originally consisted of 14 consonants and 10 vowels; since then, 5 consonants and 11 vowels have been added. Han'gul letters are combined into syllables by clustering, in imitation of Chinese characters. ROK governments have launched several "language beautification" drives designed to purge Korean of borrowings from Japanese and other languages, but more than half of the vocabulary consists of words derived from Chinese.

¹⁰RELIGIONS

Most South Koreans are quite eclectic in their religious beliefs, the majority subscribing to varying mixtures of Taoism, Confucianism, Buddhism, Christianity, Ch'ondogyo (Religion of the Heavenly Way, an indigenous sect originating in 1860), and local animism. Shamanism, especially its aspect of exorcism of evil spirits, survives in some rural areas of the ROK. Geomancy is also used in matters such as the selection of auspicious building and tomb sites.

In 1989, Mahayana Buddhism, with 8,059,000 followers, 25,205 clergy, and 9,231 houses of worship, was the principal religion. Traditional Protestant groups had 6,489,010 followers, 34,407 clergy, and 58,228 churches; Confucianism had 483,009 adherents, 17,477 clergy, and 231 temples; Roman Catholicism had 1,865,000 followers, 7,640 clergy, and 844 churches; Ch'ondogyo, the most widespread of more than 250 new religions, had 27,000 followers, and Wonbulgyo (Round Buddhism, founded in 1924 and based on the principles of propagation, education, and charity) had 92,000. Other religions with significant popular followings included Taejongyo, based on the worship of a trinity of ancient deities, and Soka Gakkai, a Buddhist sect of Japanese origin. There were also about 20,000 Muslims in 1986.

¹¹TRANSPORTATION

The bulk of ROK railroads, totaling 3,106 km (1,930 mi) of track in 1991, are government owned. In 1988, the railroads carried 556 million passengers. Rolling stock in 1991 included some 1,400 cargo and 15,000 passenger cars. The Seoul subway system, opened in 1991, had 123 km (76 mi) of track by 1985; construction of Pusan's first subway line was completed in 1985, a second line was scheduled to open in 1993.

The ROK had 62,936 km (39,108 mi) of roadway in 1991, of which 21% was national highway. There were 2,727,862 passenger automobiles, 1,092,304 trucks, and 427,650 buses. Bus transportation networks of varying quality serve most of the rural towns. Only 8% of all motor vehicles were for commercial use. In just three years, total registrations more than doubled from 2,035,448 in 1988 to 4,247,816 in 1991.

Maritime shipping expanded rapidly during the 1970s. By 1991, the ROK had a merchant fleet of 445 vessels, accounting for a total of 7,023,000 GRT. In that year, South Korea ranked fifteenth among the maritime nations of the world, with a total of 11,436,000 deadweight tons. Pusan is the chief port; other major ports include Inch'on (the port for Seoul), Kunsan, and Mokp'o.

Major airports are Kimpo International Airport at Seoul and Kimhae International Airport west of Pusan. In 1990, Kimpo International handled 113,200 flights and 16,821,000 passengers (up from 41,800 flights and 5,418,000 passengers in 1984). In 1992 civil aviation in the ROK amounted to 22,538 million passenger-km and 2,650 million freight ton-km of service. Korean Air Lines (KAL), privately owned since 1969, grew rapidly during the 1970s and now ranks as a major world carrier. On the morning of 1 September 1983, a KAL jetliner en route from New York to Seoul via Anchorage, Alaska, strayed over airspace of the former USSR and was shot down by Soviet interceptors, reportedly because they thought it was a military aircraft engaged in espionage; all 269 persons on board were killed, and worldwide protest followed. In November 1983, 115 people were killed when a bomb was apparently detonated aboard a KAL jet en route to Seoul.

12HISTORY

[For Korean history before 1948, see Korea, Democratic People's Republic of.]

The Republic of Korea, headed by President Syngman Rhee (Rhee Syngman), was proclaimed on 15 August 1948 in the southern portion of the Korean Peninsula, which had been under US military administration since 8 September 1945. Like the Democratic People's Republic of Korea (DPRK), established in the north on 9 September 1948 with Soviet backing, the ROK claimed to be the legitimate government of all Korea. The ROK was recognized as the legitimate government by the UN General Assembly.

At dawn on 25 June 1950, following a year and a half of sporadic fighting, the well-equipped People's Army of the DPRK struck south across the 38th parallel. Proclaiming that the war was for national liberation and unification of the peninsula, the DPRK forces advanced rapidly; Seoul fell within three days, and the destruction of the ROK seemed imminent. At US urging, the UN Security Council (with the Soviet delegate absent) branded the DPRK an aggressor and called for the withdrawal of the attacking forces. On 27 June, US President Harry S. Truman ordered US air and naval units into combat, and three days later, US ground forces were sent into battle. The UK took similar action, and a multinational UN Command was created to join with and lead the ROK in its struggle against the invasion. Meanwhile, DPRK troops had pushed into the southeast corner of the peninsula. At that juncture, however, UN lines held firm, and an amphibious landing at Inch'on (15 September 1950) in the ROK under Gen. Douglas MacArthur brought about the complete disintegration of the DPRK army.

MacArthur, commanding the UN forces, made a fateful decision to drive northward. As the UN forces approached the Yalu River, however, China warned that it would not tolerate a unification of the peninsula under US/UN auspices. After several weeks of threats and feints, "volunteers" from the Chinese People's Liberation Army entered the fighting en masse, forcing MacArthur into a costly, pell-mell retreat back down the peninsula. Seoul was lost again (4 January 1951) and then regained before the battle line became stabilized very nearly along the 38th parallel. There it remained for two weary years, with bitter fighting but little change, while a cease-fire agreement was negotiated.

On 27 July 1953, an armistice agreement finally was signed at P'anmunjom in the DPRK. The Korean War was ended, but it had brought incalculable destruction and human suffering to all of Korea (some 1,300,000 military casualties, including 415,000 combat deaths, for the ROK alone), and it left the peninsula still more implacably divided. A military demarcation line, which neither side regarded as a permanent border, was established, surrounded by the DMZ. An international conference envisioned in

LOCATION: 33°7′ to 38°38′N; 124°36′ to 130°56′E. **BOUNDARY LENGTHS:** DPRK, 240 km (149 mi); total coastline, 1,318 km (819 mi). **TERRITORIAL SEA LIMIT:** 12 mi.

the armistice agreement was not held until mid-1954. This conference and subsequent efforts failed to reach an agreement on unification of the north and south, and the armistice agreement, supervised by a token UN Command in Seoul and by the Military Armistice Commission and the Neutral Nations Supervisory Commission, both in P'anmunjom, remains in effect.

In 1954, the US and ROK signed a mutual defense treaty, under which US troops remained in the country. Financial assistance throughout the 1950s was provided by the US, averaging $270 million annually between 1953 and 1958, and by other nations under UN auspices. Syngman Rhee ran the government until 1960, when his authoritarian rule provoked the "April revolution," the culmination of a series of increasingly violent student demonstrations that finally brought about his ouster. The

Second Korean Republic, which followed Rhee, adopted a parliamentary system to replace the previous presidential system. The new government, however, was short-lived. Premier Chang Myon and his supporters were ousted after only 10 months by a military coup in May 1961, headed by Maj.-Gen. Park Chung-hee. The military junta dissolved the National Assembly, placed the nation under martial law, established the Korean Central Intelligence Agency (KCIA) as a means of detecting and suppressing potential enemies, and ruled by decree until late 1963 through the Supreme Council for National Reconstruction. Gen. Park created a well-organized political party—the Democratic-Republican Party (DRP)—designed to serve as a vehicle for the transition from military to civilian rule, and in October 1963, under a new constitution, he easily won election as president of the Third Republic.

During the summer of 1965, riots erupted all over the ROK in protest against the ROK-Japan Normalization Treaty, which established diplomatic relations and replaced Korean war-reparation claims with Japanese promises to extend economic aid. The riots were met with harsh countermeasures, including another period of martial law and widespread arrests of demonstrators. Further demonstrations erupted in 1966, when the ROK's decision to send 45,000 combat troops to Viet-Nam became known. Park was elected to a second term in May 1967, defeating his chief opponent, Yun Po-sun, and the DRP won a large majority in the National Assembly. In 1969, Park pushed through the National Assembly a constitutional amendment permitting him to run for a third term. He defeated Kim Dae Jung, leader of the opposition New Democratic Party (NDP), in the elections of April 1971, but Kim's NDP made significant gains in the National Assembly elections that May.

Student demonstrations against the government in the fall of 1971 prompted Park to declare a state of national emergency on 6 December. Three weeks later, in a predawn session held without the knowledge of the opposition, the Assembly granted Park extraordinary governmental powers. These failed to quell mounting opposition and unrest, and in October 1972 martial law was declared. A new constitution, promulgated at the end of the month and ratified by national referendum in November 1972, vastly increased the powers of the presidency in economic as well as political affairs. Under this new document, which inaugurated the Fourth Republic, Park was elected for a six-year term that December, with a decisive legislative majority for his DRP. Soon the economy began to expand at a rapid rate. But Park's regime became increasingly repressive. Typical of its heavy-handed rule was the abduction by KCIA agents of Kim Dae Jung from a Japanese hotel room back to Seoul, an incident that provoked considerable friction between Japanese and Korean officials. On 15 August 1974, a Korean gunman carrying a Japanese passport and sympathetic to the DPRK attempted to assassinate the president but killed Park's wife instead. Park responded by drafting a series of emergency measures; the harshest of these, Emergency Measure No. 9, issued in May 1975, provided for the arrest of anyone criticizing the constitution and banned all political activities by students.

Park was reelected for another six-year term in July 1978, but the NDP, now led by Kim Young Sam, made major gains in the National Assembly. In October 1979, Kim was expelled from the legislature after calling for governmental reform. Riots protesting Kim's ouster were reported in several major cities. On 26 October 1979, in what may have been an attempted coup, Park was assassinated by KCIA Director Kim Jae-gyu, who was later executed. Martial law was again imposed, and a period of relative calm followed as some of the more restrictive emergency decrees were lifted by Park's constitutional successor, the prime minister, Choi Kyu-hah, who promised a new constitution and presidential elections.

The Chun and Roh Regimes

In December 1979, Maj. Gen. Chun Doo Hwan led a coup in which he and his military colleagues removed the army chief of staff and took effective control of the government. Demonstrations, led by university students, spread through the spring of 1980 and, by mid-May, the government once more declared martial law (in effect until January 1981), banned demonstrations, and arrested political leaders. In the city of Kwangju, more than 200 civilians were killed in what became known as the Kwangju massacre. Choi Kyu-hah was pressured to resign and Chun Doo Hwan, now retired from the military, was named president in September 1990. Chun Doo Hwan came to power under a new constitution inaugurating the Fifth Republic. A total of 567 political leaders, including Kim Dae Jung and Kim Young Sam, were banned from political activity. Kim Dae Jung, arrested several times after his 1973 kidnapping, was originally sentenced to death but allowed to go to the United States in 1982. All existing political parties were dissolved, and all political activity banned until three months before the 1981 elections.

Twelve new parties (reduced to eight) were formed to enter the 1981 elections, in which Chun Doo Hwan was elected to a seven-year presidential term by a new electoral college and his Democratic Justice Party (DJP) secured a majority in the reconstituted National Assembly. Despite harsh controls, opposition to Chun continued. In 1982, 1,200 political prisoners were released, and in early 1983, the ban on political activity was lifted for 250 of the banned politicians. On 9 October 1983, Chun escaped an apparent assassination attempt in Rangoon, Burma, when an explosion took the lives of 17 in his entourage, including 4 ROK cabinet ministers. Chun subsequently blamed the DPRK for the bombing. In 1984, under increasing pressure for political reforms prior to the 1985 parliamentary elections, the government lifted its ban on all but 15 of the 567 politicians banned in 1980. In 1985, the ban was lifted on 14 of the remaining 15. Kim Dae Jung was allowed to return from exile in the United States in 1984 but rearrested. He remained banned from all political activity because of his conviction for sedition in 1980.

Opposition groups quickly formed the New Korea Democratic Party (NKDP) to challenge the DJP in the 1985 election; the new party became a strong minority voice in the National Assembly. The issue of constitutional reforms, particularly changes in the way in which presidents are elected and the way in which "bonus" seats in the legislature are distributed, became prominent, especially after Chun reaffirmed a commitment to step down in February 1988 and, in April 1986, dropped his long-standing opposition to any constitutional changes prior to that date. Demonstrations against Chun continued and became violent at Inch'on in May 1986 and at Konkuk University that fall. Opposition groups began collecting signatures on a petition demanding direct (instead of indirect, as at present) election of the president. In April 1987, as demonstrations became increasingly violent, Chun banned all further discussion of constitutional reform until after the 1988 Olympic Games in Seoul. The ban, which could have guaranteed the election of a hand-picked DJP successor, set off violent antigovernment demonstrations throughout the nation. In June 1987, the DJP nominated its chairman, Roh Tae Woo, a former general and a close friend of Chun, as its candidate for his successor. When Roh accepted opposition demands for political reforms, Chun announced in July that the upcoming election would be held by direct popular vote. On 8 July, 100,000 people demonstrated in Seoul in the largest protest since 1960 and, on the same day, the government restored political rights to 2,000 people, including the long-time opposition leader, Kim Dae Jung.

In the elections, held on 16 December 1987, Roh Tae Woo, as the DJP candidate, won a plurality of 37%, defeating the two major opposition candidates, Kim Young Sam and Kim Dae Jung, who had been unable to agree on a single opposition candidacy and split 55% of the total vote. Two minor candidates divided the remainder. A reported 89% of all eligible voters participated. The two leading opposition candidates charged massive fraud, and a series of demonstrations were held to protest the results. However, no evidence of extensive fraud was produced, and the demonstrations did not attract wide support. Roh Tae Woo was inaugurated as president in February 1988 when Chun Doo Hwan's term expired.

In the elections for the National Assembly, held on 26 April 1988, President Roh Tae Woo's party, the DJP, won only 34% of the vote. This gave the DJP 125 seats in the assembly, while Kim Dae Jung's Peace and Democracy Party (PDP) gained 70 seats, Kim Young Sam's Reunification Democratic Party (RDP) won 59 seats, 35 seats went to the new Democratic Republican Party (NDRP), and 10 to independent candidates. Thus, for the first time in 36 years, the government did not have a controlling vote in the National Assembly, which quickly challenged President Roh's choice for head of the Supreme Court and by year's end forced the president to work with the assembly to pass the budget.

In the fall of 1988, the National Assembly audited the government and held public hearings into former President Chun's abuses of power. In November, Chun apologized to the nation in a televised address, gave his personal wealth to the nation, and retired into a Buddhist temple. Following the revision of the constitution in 1987, South Koreans enjoyed greater freedoms of expression and assembly and freedom of the press and, in 1988, several hundred political dissidents were released from prison.

Unrest among students, workers, and farmers continued, however, and beginning in April 1989, the government repressed opposition. In October 1989, the government acknowledged making 1,315 political arrests so far that year. The National Assembly became less of a check on President Roh after two opposition parties (RDP, NDRP), including that of Kim Young Sam, merged with Roh's DJP, forming a new majority party, the Democratic Liberal Party (DLP) in January 1990. Kim Dae Jung was then left as the leader of the main opposition party (PDP).

There were continuing demonstrations into 1990 and 1991, calling for the resignation of President Roh and the withdrawal of United States troops. In May 1990, 50,000 demonstrators in Kwangju commemorated the tenth anniversary of the massacre, resulting in clashes with police which lasted several days. The US agreed to withdraw its nuclear weapons from the ROK in November 1991. And, on the last day of the year, the ROK and the DPRK signed an agreement to ban nuclear weapons from the entire peninsula.

In the presidential election on 19 December 1992, Kim Young Sam, now leader of the majority DLP, won with 41.9% of the vote, while Kim Dae Jung (DP) took 33.8%. Inaugurated in February 1993, Kim Young Sam began a new era as the first president in 30 years who was a civilian, without a power base in the military. President Kim granted amnesty to 41,000 prisoners and instituted a series of purges of high-ranking military officials, including four generals who had had roles in the 1979 coup. Among political and economic reforms was a broad anti-corruption campaign, resulting in arrests, dismissals, or reprimands for several thousands of government officials and business people. In March 1994, a former official of the National Security Planning Agency made public President Roh Tae Woo's authorization of a covert program to develop nuclear weapons at the Daeduk Science Town through 1991.

13GOVERNMENT

The Republic of Korea's (ROK) first constitution was adopted on 17 July 1948. Through repeated revisions, power remained concentrated in the hands of the president until the most recent revision, adopted by 93.1% of the vote in a popular referendum on 28 October 1987. Under the new constitution, which took effect in February 1988, the president is elected by direct popular vote, rather than indirectly as before, for a single term of five years. There are also a prime minister and two deputy prime ministers, who head the State Council (the cabinet). Kim Young Sam was elected president on 18 December 1992 for a five-year term beginning on 25 February 1993.

The ROK legislature is the unicameral National Assembly (Kuk Hoe). It has 299 seats, filled by a combination of direct and proportional election. During the first four decades of the ROK, the National Assembly had little authority. The 1987 constitution strengthened the National Assembly, giving it power to audit government activities and removing the president's power to dissolve the Assembly. Suffrage is universal at age 20.

14POLITICAL PARTIES

From 1948 to 1988, politics in the Republic of Korea were dominated by the executive arm of the government with military backing. Despite this, there were active opposition parties and, with the implementation of the revised 1987 constitution, political parties have had a greater governmental role. In the presidential election of December 1987, the governing Democratic Justice Party (DJP), with Roh Tae Woo as its candidate, won 37% of the vote; the Reunification Democratic Party (RDP), with Kim Young Sam, won 28%; the Peace and Democracy Party (PDP), with Kim Dae Jung, won 27%; and the New Democratic-Republic Party (NDRP), with Kim Jong Pil, won 10%. In a crucial election for the National Assembly in April 1988, the DJP gained only 34% of the popular vote, allowing the opposition parties to control the assembly. This was the first time since 1952 that the government party did not have a majority in and, hence control of, the National Assembly.

In a surprise move in January 1990, the DJP merged with two of the opposition parties, the RDP and the NDRP, to form a new majority party, the Democratic Liberal Party (DLP). In July of that year, two opposition parties, the PDP and the Democratic Party (DP) merged, retaining the name DP. In September 1991, the DP agreed to merge with another opposition party, the New Democratic Party (NDP), then led by the veteran oppositionist, Kim Dae Jung, forming a new DP.

The National Assembly election on 24 March 1992 saw 38.5% of the vote going to the DLP; 29.2% to the DP; 17.3% to the Unification National Party, which later changed its name to the United People's Party(UPP); and 15% to other parties. The actual distribution of seats in the National Assembly shifts as members frequently switch among parties. In the presidential election on 18 December 1992, 41.5% of the vote went to Kim Young Sam of the DLP; 33.8% to Kim Dae Jung of the DP; 16.3% to Chung Ju Yung of the UPP; and 8% to candidates of various smaller parties.

In 1994, the majority party was the DLP with Kim Young Sam as its president. The opposition parties were the DP and the UPP along with several smaller parties.

15LOCAL GOVERNMENT

The Republic of Korea (ROK) is divided into nine provinces (do), Cheju, North Cholla, South Cholla, North Ch'ungch'ong, South Ch'ungch'ong, Kangwan, Kyonggi, North Kyongsang, and South Kyongsang. There are six provincial-level cities (jikhalsi) directly under the central government: Seoul, the capital; Inch'on; Kwangju; Pusan, Taegu; and Taejon. Provinces are divided into cities (si), counties (kun or gun), townships (myon), and villages (i or ri). Between 1961 and March 1990, there were no local elections.

16JUDICIAL SYSTEM

The highest judicial court is the Supreme Court, under which are three intermediate appellate courts, located in Seoul, Taegu, and

Kwangju. Lower tribunals include district and family courts.

The President, with the consent of the National Assembly, appoints the Chief Justice, the other justices of the Supreme Court to six-year terms, and the Constitutional Committee. The Chief Justice in consultation with the other justices of the Court, appoints lower court justices.

The Constitution provides for a presumption of innocence, protection from self-incrimination, the rights to a speedy trial, protection from double jeopardy and other procedural due process safeguards.

[17]ARMED FORCES

The ROK has one of the world's largest and best-equipped armed forces, but it faces an even more impressive foe. Defense spending accounted for $12.6 billion in 1992 or 4.5% of gross domestic product. Of a total of 633,000 personnel on active duty, 520,000 were in the army, 60,000 in the navy and marines, and 53,000 in the air force (with 403 combat aircraft). An additional 4.5 million were in the reserves. Paramilitary forces included 4.5 million in the Civil Defense Corps and its student branches. Military service is compulsory for all males at age 19 and ranges from 26 to 30 months. Veterans retain reserve status until age 33.

South Korea's defense industry is capable of producing medium- and short-range missiles and other sophisticated armaments, but it also uses US and European armaments and equipment. The country imported arms worth $4.9 billion during the 1980s, of which 95% came from the US. Arms exports were valued at $29,570 million during the same period. In 1993, the US stationed 35,500 troops in the ROK under the 1954 Korea-US Mutual Defense Treaty. Since 1978, these troops have been integrated with Korean forces under the Korea-US Combined Force Command, headquartered in Seoul.

[18]INTERNATIONAL COOPERATION

Although not a UN member, the ROK maintains official observer status at UN sessions and participates in ESCAP and all the non-regional specialized agencies except the ILO. The UN Commission on the Unification and Rehabilitation of Korea was dissolved in 1973, but the UN Command originating from the Korean War continues to supervise implementation of the 1953 armistice agreement.

The ROK pursues a vigorous international diplomacy, and in recent years has modified both its militant anti-Communist stance and its close alliance with the US. By 1986, the ROK was recognized by 122 nations, 67 of which also had diplomatic relations with the DPRK. The ROK participates in the Asian Development Bank and G-77, is a permanent observer with the OAS, and is a signatory to GATT and the Law of the Sea.

[19]ECONOMY

Under a centralized planning system initiated in 1962, the ROK has been one of the fastest growing developing countries in the post-war period, shifting from an agrarian to an industrial economy in the course of only a few decades. By 1992 industry contributed 45.6% of the GDP, compared with 16.2% in 1965, while agriculture, forestry and fishing accounted for 8.1%, down from 46.5%. Much of this industrialization has been fueled by the government's stimulation of heavy industry, notably steel, construction, shipbuilding and technologically advanced goods such as electronics. To finance industrial expansion the ROK borrowed heavily up until the mid-1980s. By the end of 1986 its foreign debt reached $45 billion, equalling about 52% of GNP and making the country one of the world's four most deeply indebted developing economies. Steady current account surpluses scored during much of the 1980s allowed the ROK to slash this figure to only $3 billion by 1989. However, the years 1989 and 1990 also marked a turning point in the country's pattern of economic growth. The annual rate of GDP growth declined from an average of 9.6% between 1985–90 to 9.0% in 1990 and 8.4% in 1991, as a result of slow export growth due to rising labor costs and steady appreciation of the won against the US dollar. By contrast, the growth rate of the country's imports surged ahead of exports, with domestic demand now replacing the external sector as the primary growth factor. In 1990 the country ran a trade deficit for the first time since 1986. By 1991, this gap had almost doubled, threatening to seriously affect the current account balance. Also problematic was a sudden jump in inflation in 1990 and 1991. Government attempts to restrain domestic demand through tighter monetary policy and other measures helped curb inflationary tendencies by 1992 but slowed GDP growth to 4.8%. Current indicators suggest the onset of a recovery in 1993, assisted by the resurgence of demand in traditional export markets, new growth in non-traditional markets such as China, Southeast Asia and Eastern Europe, as well as marked appreciation in the currency of a major competitor, the Japanese yen.

[20]INCOME

In 1992, Korea's GNP was $296,349 million at current prices, or $6,790 per capita. For the period 1985–92 the average inflation rate was 6.8%, resulting in a real growth rate in per capita GNP of 8.5%.

In 1992 the GDP was $296,136 million in current US dollars. It is estimated that in 1991 agriculture, hunting, forestry, and fishing contributed 8% to GDP; mining and quarrying, 1%; manufacturing, 28%; electricity, gas, and water, 2%; construction, 15%; wholesale and retail trade, 11%; transport, storage, and communication, 7%; finance, insurance, real estate, and business services, 15%; community, social, and personal services, 4%; and other sources 9%.

[21]LABOR

The civilian labor force (over age 14) averaged 19,400,000 in 1992. Of the total of 18,921,000 employed, 3,025,000 (16%) were engaged in agriculture, forestry, and fishing; another 4,768,000 (25.2%) in manufacturing; and 11,128,000 (58.8%) in other occupations, mostly in the service sector. The unemployment rate in 1992 averaged 2.4%. The drop in employment between the summer peak and the winter off-season annually exceeds 1 million, virtually all of it in the agricultural sector.

Before 1987, the labor movement was heavily controlled by the government. By the end of 1991, however, with the expectations of democratic reform, there were 1,803,400 unionized workers, representing 12% of the work force (excluding farmers and soldiers), from 7,656 registered local unions. In 1992, there were 235 labor disputes (down from 3,749 in 1987). That year, average nominal wages increased 15.2%, while real wages rose 8.5%. The average monthly wage in 1992 was 869,000 won, with about one-third coming from overtime, bonuses, and allowances.

[22]AGRICULTURE

Some 21% of the ROK's land area is arable, with about 70% of it sown in grain, rice being the chief crop. In 1965, agriculture (including forestry and fishing) contributed nearly 50% to GNP, but by 1990 only accounted for 8%. Double-cropping is common in the southern provinces. The rice harvest in 1992 was 7,361,000 tons, down from 7,722,000 tons in 1990. Barley production in 1992 stood at 400,000 tons; potatoes, 416,000 tons; and soybeans, 180,000 tons. Despite increased yields due to mechanization, the use of hybrid seeds, and increased employment of fertilizers, the ROK runs a net deficit in food grains every year. In 1992, imports of grain, mostly from the US, totaled 10,488,500 tons, 97% of it wheat and corn. Virtual self-sufficiency has been attained in rice production.

Hemp, hops, and tobacco are the leading industrial crops. The ROK was the world's second leading producer (after China) of chestnuts in 1992. The orchards in the Taegu area are renowned for their apples, the prime fruit crop; output in 1992 was 555,000 tons. Pears, peaches, persimmons, and melons also are grown in abundance. About two-thirds of vegetable production is made up of the mu (a large white radish) and Chinese cabbage, the main ingredients of the year-round staple kimchi, or "Korean pickle."

Until the Korean War, tenant farming was widespread in the ROK. The Land Reform Act of June 1949, interrupted by the war, was implemented in 1953; it limited arable land ownership to 3 hectares (7.4 acres) per household, with all lands in excess of this limit to be purchased by the government for distribution among farmers who had little or no land. By the late 1980s, farms averaged 0.5–1 hectare (1.2–2.5 acres). The New Village (Saemaul) Movement, initiated in 1972, plays a major role in raising productivity and modernizing villages and farming practices.

[23] ANIMAL HUSBANDRY

The raising of livestock, traditionally a supplementary occupation among ROK farmers, expanded rapidly during the 1970s and 1980s. In 1992, 2,517,449 head of cattle were raised; pigs totaled 5,505,000, and chickens, 75 million. The silkworm industry has declined radically since the mid-1970s; the raw silk output of 8000 tons in 1992 was less than one-quarter of the 1979–81 annual average. The ROK is self-sufficient in the production of milk. Although the dairy industry has been protected by import restrictions, an incremental lifting of such trade constraints is underway, which will eventually include livestock imports.

[24] FISHING

Korean waters comprise some of the best fishing grounds in the world. Recent investments have led to rapid growth; the total catch in 1991 was 2,515,305 tons. Deep-sea fishing has shown remarkable growth since 1962, with marine output totaling 2,484,843 tons in 1992. Tuna provided much of the deep-sea catch. Korean fishing bases have been established in Western Samoa and Las Palmas, and cuttlefish caught in waters off the Falkland Islands are now available. Since the declaration of 200-mile economic sea zones by many nations in the 1970s, the ROK negotiated fishing agreements with several coastal nations to secure fishing rights in their waters. In 1990, ROK exports of fresh, chilled, and frozen fish accounted for 5.4% of the world's exports; fresh and frozen shellfish exports, 3.8%; and prepared and preserved fish exports, 5.5%.

[25] FORESTRY

Forests covered 6,480,000 hectares (16,012,000 acres) in 1991, or about two-thirds of the ROK's total area, but wood supplies are grossly inadequate to meet the needs of the fast-growing plywood and paper industries. Whereas plywood and wood pulp were once traditional export items, the role of forestry products in generating export earnings is now shrinking. About 20% of all forested land is nationally owned and is the focus of extensive reforestation efforts. Production of roundwood in 1991 totaled 6,485,000 cu m; sawnwood, 4,041,000 cu m; and plywood, 1,134,000 cu m.

[26] MINING

The ROK's limited supplies of iron ore, coal, copper, lead, and zinc must be supplemented by imports. Among mineral ores (metal content) produced in 1991, iron totaled 134,000 tons; zinc, 22,039 tons; lead, 12,633 tons; and tungsten ore, 780 tons. In addition, the ROK produced 20,809 kg of gold and 264,746 kg of silver.

[27] ENERGY AND POWER

Coal is the chief fuel mined, with reserves estimated at 1.45 billion tons and production totaling 14,850,000 tons in 1991. Most of the coal is low-quality anthracite, used mainly for home cooking and heating; imports of higher-grade coal (23 million tons in 1990) are required for industry.

In 1992, crude oil provided 62.4% of all primary energy consumed, up from 9.4% in 1962; coal, 20.4%; nuclear energy, 12.8%; natural gas, 4%; and hydroelectricity, about 0.4%. Plans for the future call for a de-emphasis on oil and promotion of atomic energy, coal, and hydroelectricity as energy sources, together with importation of liquefied natural gas from Indonesia and crude oil from the US.

In 1992, the ROK had an installed electrical generating capacity of 24.6 million kw, up from 9.8 million kw in 1981, of which about 10% was from hydroelectric plants and 31% from nuclear plants. The output of electricity in 1991 totaled 112.3 billion kwh. Industry accounted for two-thirds of the 115.2 billion kwh of electricity consumed in 1992. Electricity use has been growing at 1.5 times the rate of economic growth in recent years.

[28] INDUSTRY

Up until the 1960s, manufacturing was chiefly confined to production for domestic consumption, and a substantial proportion of the output was produced by handicraft methods in homes and small factories. While textiles, apparel and footwear were the first modern industries to be developed, heavy industry has grown rapidly over the last three decades, promoted by a series of five-year plans since 1962. The ROK now ranks as a major Asian producer of steel, chemicals, ships, machinery, nonferrous metals and electronic equipment. In the 1980s, the manufacture of metals, machinery, electronic and other equipment overtook textile production as the country's leading industries in terms of value, employment and export earnings. In recent years, ROK has supplied 20–30% of the world market in new ships; production of merchant vessels in 1991 totaled 3,674,000 gross tons.

Joint venture production with major US and Japanese car companies, growing domestic demand, and successful penetration of overseas markets by Korean-owned corporations has fuelled steady growth in automobile output. Production of electronics has recently shifted from assembly of imported parts to the manufacture of competitive high-technology products, such as office automation systems, for both the international and domestic markets. Producers of consumer durable goods have also succeeded in establishing their own brand names for international distribution. During the past decade, increasing domestic production costs has encouraged the relocation of production plants in some industries—particularly textiles and footwear but more recently also consumer electronics—to overseas locations in Southeast Asia, Eastern Europe, China, Mexico and Turkey.

In 1992, the government-owned P'ohang Iron and Steel Co. (POSCO) produced over 9 million tons of crude steel, or about 35% of the nation's total output capacity of 25.8 million tons. A second steel complex at Kwangyang, on the southern coast, began operations in late 1988. Output from major industries in 1991 included: pig iron, 18,546,000 tons; steel ingots, 1,059,000 tons; compound fertilizers, 1,823,000 tons; and cotton yarn, 569,000 tons. Large production increases were registered in the manufacture of a number of goods, including passenger cars (1,132,000 cars manufactured in 1991 as compared with 262,000 in 1985), motorcycles (334,113 in 1991, up from 126,516 in 1985), trucks (232,937 produced in 1991, compared with 71,217 in 1995), color television sets (13,353,000 units produced in 1991, up from 3,787,000 units in 1985), and video cassette recorders (9,221,000 produced in 1991, up from 1,329,000 in 1985).

[29] SCIENCE AND TECHNOLOGY

The ROK has often been compared to its powerful neighbor, Japan, but is said to be about ten years behind that nation in scientific and technological innovation. However, in areas such as semiconductor memory chips, cars, and steel, Korean industries provide innovation equal to that in the United States and Japan.

Two organizations will continue to provide most of the main support for Korean science and technology. The Korean Institute of Science and Technology (KIST), started in 1965 with the help of the United States, has begun to shift its emphasis on short-term, visible results in scientific research to longer-term basic scientific research in areas like robotics and molecular research. The other organization is the Korean Advanced Institute of Science and Technology (KAIST), the leading university in scientific research. KAIST attracts researchers from all over the world, including the United States, and is considered one of the top universities in the world for electrical and molecular engineering and computer science.

[30] DOMESTIC TRADE

The small family outlet, traditional in Korea, is giving way to chain stores and supermarkets. Large, modern department stores now operate in Seoul, Pusan and other major urban centers, although some trade in rural areas is still carried on by itinerant peddlers, mobile sidewalk stands, and periodic market fairs. Black markets offering all manner of foreign goods are much in use; haggling over prices is common. Seoul is the nation's wholesaling center. Banking hours are 9:30 AM to 4:30 PM, Monday through Friday and 9:30 AM to 1:30 PM Saturdays.

[31] FOREIGN TRADE

The ROK has the 11th largest volume of trade in the world. Ships, textiles, clothing, electronics equipment, electrical machinery, and iron and steel are its leading exports. Oil and related products, chemicals, and raw materials are major imports, as most raw inputs for the country's industrial sector are imported. Trade deficits were experienced in 1990 for the first time since the mid-1980s, though the country is expected to re-establish a surplus by the mid-1990s.

The US and Japan have continued to be the ROK's chief trading partners, although potential new markets in Eastern Europe and the rest of Asia are being explored. A trade deficit with the US occurred in 1991 for the first time since 1980, diffusing some of the mounting tensions between the two countries over trade liberalization. Saudi Arabia and Indonesia have been major providers of oil and liquefied natural gas. Australia is a leading supplier of iron ore, coal and grains. In 1991, leading trade partners were as follows (in millions of dollars):

	EXPORTS	IMPORTS	BALANCE
US	18,559	18,894	−335
Japan	12,356	21,120	−8,764
Germany	2,849	3,698	−849
Hong Kong	4,796	773	4,023
Singapore	2,702	1,030	1,672
UK	1,768	1,559	209
Canada	1,673	1,907	−234
Taiwan	1,609	1,515	94
Indonesia	1,349	2,052	−703
Saudi Arabia	777	3,269	−2,492
France	1,128	1,422	−294
Other	22,304	24,259	−1,955
TOTALS	71,870	81,525	−9,655

[32] BALANCE OF PAYMENTS

Robust export performance turned the ROK's overall balance of payments deficit into a $1.7 billion surplus in 1986, which grew to $12.1 billion in 1988. Since then, the balance of payments surplus has declined; in 1990, the balance of payments had a deficit of $274 million because of declining exports, rising imports, and a current account deficit. Over the long term, growth in exports will depend on industry's efforts to regain competitiveness lost through wage increases, labor unrest, and exchange rate changes over the past few years. The return to deficits raises the prospect of new external borrowing.

[33] BANKING AND SECURITIES

The Bank of Korea serves as the central bank, the bank of issue, and the depository for government funds. Other banking services are provided by the state-run Korea Development Bank, the Export-Import Bank of Korea, and 9 state-run specialized banks. Commercial banking operations in 1993 were handled by 8 nationwide commercial banks, 10 provincial banks, and 42 foreign banks. By 1986, as part of the government's economic stabilization program initiated in 1980, all of the 5 commercial banks previously under government control had been denationalized. Currency in circulation totaled w112,219 billion in December 1993. The Korean Stock Exchange, a share-issuing private corporation, functions as the country's only stock exchange.

[34] INSURANCE

In 1985/86, there were 6 life and 14 non-life insurance companies in operation. Per capita life insurance premiums totaled 8.34% of the GDP and non-life totaled 1.85% in 1989. In 1992, w587,598 billion of life insurance was in force.

[35] PUBLIC FINANCE

The following table shows actual revenues and expenditures for 1991 and 1992 in billions of won.

	1991	1992
REVENUE AND GRANTS		
Tax revenue	32,196	37,652
Non-tax revenue	3,752	4,159
Capital revenue	870	945
TOTAL	36,818	42,756
EXPENDITURES & LENDING MINUS REPAYMENTS		
General public service	3,471	4,271
Defense	7,892	8,924
Education	5,614	6,538
Health	716	969
Social security and welfare	3,381	3,958
Housing and community amenities	649	1,102
Recreation, cultural, and religious affairs	210	264
Economic affairs and services	6,851	6,675
Other expenditures	6,834	8,162
Lending minus repayments	4,693	4,400
TOTAL	40,312	44,764
Deficit/Surplus	−3,494	−2,008

[36] TAXATION

The principal sources of tax revenue are customs duties, corporate taxes, a defense tax surcharge imposed on corporations, a value-added tax of 10%, personal income taxes, and various excise taxes. As of 1993, the rates for corporate taxation ranged from 20% on taxable income up to w100 million to 34% on income over w100 million. Tax relief for up to five years, with a 50% exemption in the ensuing two years, is offered to new industries and corporations that are foreign exchange earners. The personal income tax is graduated from 5% to 50%, with a maximum marginal tax rate of 53.75% on incomes over w64 million.

37 CUSTOMS AND DUTIES

As of 1993, customs duties were levied on an ad valorem basis at up to 20% for industrial raw materials and equipment, 15–50% for industrial products, and 30–100% for agricultural products. The current phased reduction is geared toward bringing Korean duties on most industrial products into line with OECD levels in 1994.

38 FOREIGN INVESTMENT

The Foreign Capital Inducement Act (FCIA) and related regulations govern foreign investment in ROK. Japanese share of foreign investments fell from about 50% in 1987 to 16% in 1992, as Japanese investors have been increasingly attracted to new centers of economic growth in Southeast Asia. While foreign investment is prohibited or restricted in 204 industries, most manufacturing activities are open. Seeking to facilitate further technology transfer, the government offers particular incentives to foreign companies in 42 categories of advanced technology industries. Two free export zones geared towards highly technical business activities have been established at Masan (near Pusan) and Iri (near Kunsan) to provide additional incentives for investment in favored industries. Net foreign direct investment flow to the ROK was negative in 1990 ($–105.million), as compared to a high of $720 million in 1988, reflecting the trend towards growing overseas investment by private investors in the country.

39 ECONOMIC DEVELOPMENT

The ROK has a market economy in which both private enterprise and foreign investors play an important role. Overall economic development is guided, however, by the Economic Planning Board and, since 1962, by a series of five-year plans. The sixth plan for 1987–91, projected an annual GNP growth rate of 7.2%, liberalization of trade and foreign investment, and continuation of the "technology first" policy, designed to make the ROK a technology-intensive nation by the year 2000. While significant progress was scored in economic liberalization and technological development, the GNP growth rate was not as high as expected for some years. A revised Seventh Five-Year Economic and Social Development Plan for 1992–96 aims at establishing the ROK as an advanced industrialized economy by the year 2000. More specific goals include improving social and economic equity, continued liberalization, improving industrial and export competitiveness, as well as strengthening the role of the private sector while government intervention in economic management, especially in the financial sector, is reduced. The Plan targets an annual GNP growth rate of 7% and a decline of consumer price inflation to 3%. In 1995 the ROK is expected to graduate from its status as a recipient of World Bank loans, as outlined in a phase-out plan prepared by the government in 1991.

40 SOCIAL DEVELOPMENT

Few countries have faced health and social welfare problems as acute as those caused in the ROK by the devastation of the Korean War. The war left a residue of 348,000 war widows, most of them with dependent children, and 100,000 war orphans. Some 595,260 homes were destroyed, 5,000 villages wiped out, and many large cities badly damaged. Military relief payments consist mainly of financial support to veterans and their families; by 1985, the total number of people on the relief roll had diminished to 132,000. Other relief programs covered 2,273,000 destitute and needy in 1985. Plans to establish a national welfare pension plan were approved in 1973 but never implemented; however, the government passed legislation in 1988 that included old age, disability, and survivors' pensions, and it passed health insurance legislation in 1989. In 1991, workers and employers contributed 1.5% of earnings and payroll, respectively, and this figure was scheduled to rise to 2% in 1993 and 3% by 1998.

The ROK's nationwide family-planning program, inaugurated by the Park regime in 1962, succeeded in reducing the rate of population increase from 2.7% annually during 1960–66 to 1.5% during 1973–84; the fertility rate dropped to 1.7 in 1985–90, a 28% decrease from the previous 5-year period. According to the Korean Institute of Family Planning, the number of women using contraception increased from 9% in 1964 to 77% in 1985–90. Abortion was legalized in 1973 and is readily available. Most married women do not work outside the home. The wage of the average female worker is roughly half of that earned by a male counterpart. The Amended Family Law of 1991 recognizes women heads of households.

41 HEALTH

Health care has improved substantially and is directly related to improvement of diet, the rise in living standards, and the development of health and medical programs. Since the late 1970s, medical security, in the form of medical insurance and medical aid, has been expanded to cover a substantial portion of the population. The national medical insurance system was expanded in 1989, and now covers 94.1% of the population. As of 1992, the total number of people benefiting from medical insurance and medical aid was 41,690,000 and 2,370,000, respectively. In 1992, 100% of the population had access to health care services. Total health care expenditures in 1990 were $16.1 million.

In 1992, there were 236 general hospitals, 351 hospitals, 6 dental hospitals, 12,629 clinics, 6,708 dental clinics, 269 maternity clinics, 53 herb doctor hospitals, and 4,062 herb doctor clinics. In 1990, there were 3.0 hospital beds per 1,000 people. In 1992, there was one physician per 783 people, with a nurse to doctor ratio of 1.0.

In 1992, there were 723,000 births. In 1992, immunization rates for children up to one year of age were: tuberculosis, 76%; diphtheria, pertussis, and tetanus, 80%; polio, 79%; and measles, 96%. The 1992 infant mortality rate was 8 per 1,000 live births, and the general mortality rate in 1993 was 6.1 per 1,000 inhabitants. Major causes of death per 100,000 people were listed in 1990 as: noncommunicable diseases (454); injuries (194); and communicable diseases and maternal/perinatal causes (113);. In 1990 there were about 162 reported cases of tuberculosis per 100,000 people. Life expectancy is 71 years.

42 HOUSING

After the liberation in 1945, southern Korea faced a housing shortage greatly compounded by high population growth rates. A housing shortage continues to plague the nation, especially in Seoul, Pusan, and other large cities, where shantytowns house many recent rural arrivals. The 1985 census counted 9,588,723 households but only 6,274,462 housing units, for a deficit of 3,314,261. A total of 1,460,000 units were built under the 1981–86 economic plan. In 1988, the government inaugurated a plan to build two million new housing units in four years and exceeded its goal, reaching a total of 2,717,000 units by 1992. As of that year, the per capita housing space was 9.6 sq m (103 sq ft). The government, through the Korean Housing Corporation, plans to construct 500,000 to 600,000 housing units per year from 1993 to 1998, increasing the rate of home ownership to 90%. The program will continue to focus on small housing units. Through government efforts, the supply of piped water is projected to rise from 80% of dwellings in 1991 to 90% in 2001. The per capita water supply is slated to rise from 376 liters in 1991 to 440 liters in 2001.

43 EDUCATION

The Education Law of 1949 provided for a centralized system under the control of the Ministry of Education and made the six-year elementary schools free and compulsory for children between 6 and 12 years of age. Secondary education begins at 12 years of age and lasts for up to six years which are divided into two cycles of three years each. Nearly 87% of children in this age group were enrolled in the secondary schools in 1990 (male: 88% and female: 85%). In 1992 there were 4,560,128 students in primary schools, 2,336,284 in middle schools, 2,125,573 in high schools, 1,491,669 in colleges and universities, and 96,577 in graduate schools.

The leading government university is Seoul National University. The principal private institutions, all of them in Seoul, are Korea, Sung Kyun Kwan, Yonsei, Hanyang, Chungang, and Ewha universities; the last named is one of the largest women's universities in the world. The country had a total of 121 colleges and universities in 1992, along with 335 graduate schools with a combined 1,166,746 students enrolled. In 1990, UNESCO estimated the rate of adult literacy at 96.3% (males: 99.1% and females: 93.5%). In 1992, the government allocated 16.2% of its total expenditure to education.

44LIBRARIES AND MUSEUMS

In 1991 the Central National Library, founded in 1923, had 2,451,000 volumes. Most other sizable libraries in the ROK are found at universities. The largest academic collection is at the Seoul National University Library, (1.5 million volumes).

The National Museum, with centers in Seoul, Kyongju, Kwangju, Puyo, Chinju, Chunju, Chongju, and Kongju contains art objects reflecting more than 5,000 years of cultural history, including statuary pieces, ceramics, and painting. A major private museum is the Ho-Am Art Museum in Seoul. The National Museum of Modern Art in Seoul presents many special exhibits as well a permanent collection. The ROK also possesses collections of early printing, dynastic histories, and art in its palaces and Buddhist temples, and in university, college, and public libraries.

45MEDIA

In 1991, the number of telephone lines totaled 14,194,862. There were 79 AM radio stations and 46 FM stations in 1992. Television broadcasting began in 1956; in 1992 there were 57 commercial television stations, plus a US Armed Forces–Korea network broadcasting in English. Koreans owned 43,850,000 radios and 9.1 million television sets in 1991.

The ROK press has been severely muzzled since the early 1970s; press censorship remains in force, and reporters critical of the government have been harassed. In 1991, the number of daily newspapers published was 39; of these, about half were published in Seoul. The leading Korean-language newspapers, with their estimated daily circulations (in 1991), include *Joong-ang Ilbo*, 1,650,000; *Hankook Ilbo*, 2,000,000; *Dong-A Ilbo*, 1,095,000; *Seoul Shinmun*, 800,000; *Choson Ilbo*, 1,800,000; and *Kyunghyang Shinmun*, 700,000.

46ORGANIZATIONS

Clan and county associations are a conspicuous aspect of Korean social life. A traditional type of organization with a primarily economic function is the kye, a mutual loan association formed to provide funds for a specific and typically short-term purpose, such as to defray the expenses of a wedding or funeral. The National Agricultural Cooperative Federation comprises millions of farmers who work in cooperatives. There are also hundreds of religious, political, cultural, labor, business, and sports associations.

47TOURISM, TRAVEL, AND RECREATION

The tourist industry has grown rapidly, with 3,196,000 foreign visitors in 1991, of whom 2,088,000 came from Eastern or Southeast Asia. The number of hotel rooms increased to 42,318 in 1991, with 84,636 beds and a 64% occupancy rate. Major tourist attractions are Seoul, the former royal capital of the Yi (or Li) Dynasty, and Kyongju, with its treasures from the ancient kingdom of Silla.

Soccer and baseball are the most popular modern sports. Traditional sports for men are wrestling, archery, kite fighting, and t'aekwondo (a martial art). Popular games include paduk, the Korean name for Japan's board game go; changgi, or Korean chess, with pieces different from the European form; and yut, or Korean dice, played with four wooden sticks. In 1986, the Asian Games were held in Seoul, which also hosted the 1988 summer Olympic Games.

48FAMOUS KOREANS (ROK)

The dominant political figures of the contemporary period in the ROK have been Syngman Rhee (1875–1965), president from 1948 to 1960, and Park Chung-hee (1917–79), president from 1963 until his assassination in 1979. Chun Doo Hwan (Chon Duhwan, b.1931) became president in 1981. Other well-known modern figures include Kim Chong-p'il (b.1926), prime minister 1971–75; Bishop Daniel Chi (Chi Hak-sun, b.1921); and Kim Dae Jung (Kim Tae-jung, b.1925) and Kim Young Sam (Kim Yongsam, b.1927), prominent opposition leaders during the 1970s and 1980s. The Rev. Sun Myung Moon (Mun Son-myong, b.1920), a controversial evangelist and founder of the Tong-il (Unification) Church, and Kyung Wha Chung (Chung Kyung-wha, b.1943), a violinist, have both become internationally well known.

49DEPENDENCIES

The ROK has no territories or colonies.

50BIBLIOGRAPHY

Amsden, Alice H. *Asia's Next Giant: South Korea and Late Industrialization.* New York: Oxford University Press, 1989.

Grayson, James Huntley. *Korea: A Religious History.* New York: Oxford University Press, 1989.

Hoare, James. *Korea: An Introduction.* New York: Kegan Paul International, 1988.

Howe, Russell Warren. *The Koreans: Passion and Grace.* San Diego: Harcourt Brace Jovanovich, 1988.

Hwang, Eui-Gak. *The Korean Economies: A Comparison of North and South.* New York: Oxford University Press, 1993.

Lee, Peter H. (ed.). *Sourcebook of Korean Civilization.* New York: Columbia University Press, 1993—

Lone, Stewart. *Korea Since 1850.* New York: St. Martin's Press, 1993.

Macdonald, Donald Stone. *The Koreans: Contemporary Politics and Society.* Boulder, Colo.: Westview Press, 1990.

McNamara, Dennis L. *The Colonial Origins of Korean Enterprise, 1910–1945.* Cambridge [England]; New York: Cambridge University Press, 1990.

Merrill, John. *Korea: The Peninsular Origins of the War.* Newark: University of Delaware Press, 1989.

Nahm, Andrew C. *Historical Dictionary of the Republic of Korea.* Metuchen, N.J.: Scarecrow Press, 1993.

Oliver, Robert Tarbell. *A History of the Korean People in Modern Times: 1800 to the Present.* Newark: Univ. of Delaware Press, 1993.

Olsen, Edward A. *US Policy and the Two Koreas.* Boulder, Colo.: Westview Press, 1988.

Sanford, Dan C. *South Korea and the Socialist Countries: The Politics of Trade.* New York: St. Martin's Press, 1990.

Sohn, Hak-Kyu. *Authoritarianism and Opposition in South Korea.* London; New York: Routledge, 1989.

Song, Pyong-nak. *The Rise of the Korean Economy.* Hong Kong; New York: Oxford University Press, 1990.

South Korea, a Country Study, 4th ed. Washington, D.C.: Federal Research Division, Library of Congress, 1992.

KUWAIT

State of Kuwait
Dawlat al-Kuwayt

CAPITAL: Kuwait (Al-Kuwayt).

FLAG: The flag adopted in 1961 is a rectangle, twice as long as it is high, divided equally into green, white, and red horizontal stripes, with a black trapezoid whose longer base is against the staff and is equal to the breadth of the flag, and whose shorter base is equal to the breadth of the white stripe.

ANTHEM: National Anthem, melody only; no words.

MONETARY UNIT: The Kuwaiti dinar (KD) has 1,000 fils. There are coins of 1, 5, 10, 20, 50, and 100 fils, and notes of 250 and 500 fils and of 1, 5, 10, and 20 Kuwaiti dinars. KD1 = $3.3661 (or $1 = KD0.2971).

WEIGHTS AND MEASURES: The metric system is the legal standard, but imperial weights and measures also are in use, and some US measures are recognized.

HOLIDAYS: New Year's Day, 1 January; Emir's Accession Day, 25 February. Movable religious holidays include Muslim New Year (1st of Muharram); Laylat al-Miraj; Milad an-Nabi; 'Id al-Fitr; and 'Id al-'Adha'.

TIME: 3 PM = noon GMT.

¹LOCATION, SIZE, AND EXTENT

Kuwait is situated at the western head of the Persian (or Arabian) Gulf. Its undemarcated borders preclude any definite figure for its area, which is estimated at about 17,820 sq km (6,880 sq mi). Comparatively, the area occupied by Kuwait is slightly smaller than the state of New Jersey. Kuwait extends 205 km (127 mi) SE–NW and 176 km (109 mi) NE–SW. Islands that form part of Kuwait include Faylakah (an archaeological site that is the only inhabited island), Bubiyan, Maskan, 'Auha, Al-Warbah, Al-Kubr, Umm al-Maradim, Umm al-Nami, and Qaruh. Bounded on the E by the Persian Gulf, on the S and W by Sa'udi Arabia, and on the NW and N by Iraq, Kuwait has a total boundary length of 963 km (598 mi).

Kuwait's boundary with Sa'udi Arabia was settled by a treaty in 1922 that established a Neutral Zone, an area of approximately 6,500 sq km (2,500 sq mi) in which each country was to have an undemarcated half interest. In 1965, the two countries signed an agreement formally dividing the Neutral Zone and establishing a new international boundary; the agreements were ratified in 1969.

Kuwait's boundary with Iraq remains unsettled. Following Kuwait's declaration of independence in June 1961, the emir requested UK assistance to ward off an Iraqi invasion; the British forces were later replaced by troops from Arab League states. The UN upheld Kuwait's sovereignty, and in October 1963, Iraq formally recognized Kuwait's independence. In March 1973 there were armed clashes on the Iraq-Kuwait border, but a settlement was announced in June 1975; negotiations to demarcate the border have continued intermittently. Again in August 1990, Iraq invaded Kuwait, asserting their right to reclaim it as their territory. US-led international forces responded with a massive air attack in January 1991, and Iraq was defeated. Some Iraqi officials continued to assert their claim to Kuwait, and relations between the two countries remained tense. On 27 May 1993, the UN Security Council reaffirmed the established border between the two nations.

Kuwait's capital, Kuwait city, is located on the Persian Gulf coast.

²TOPOGRAPHY

Kuwait consists almost entirely of flat rolling desert and mud flats. There is a 120-m (400-ft) ridge at Mina' al-Ahmadi and a 275-m (900-ft) prominence in the southwest corner. There are no streams.

³CLIMATE

During the summer, which lasts roughly from May to October, the air generally is dry, but southeasterly winds often raise daytime humidity to 90% for a few weeks in August or September. Between November and April, the climate is pleasant, with cool nights and warm sunny days. In December and January, night temperatures occasionally touch the freezing point. Summer temperatures range from 29°C (84°F) in the morning to more than 49°C (120°F) in the shade at noon. Frost, almost unknown on the coast, is common in the interior. Annual rainfall, which averages less than 10 cm (4 in), comes in the form of showers or storms between October and April. Cloudbursts have amounted to as much as 6.4 cm (2.5 in) of rain in one day, and can heavily damage roads and houses. The prevailing northwest wind (shamal) is a cooling breeze in summer.

⁴FLORA AND FAUNA

Plants and animals are those common to the arid parts of Arabia. There is little vegetation except camel thorn in the desert and some shrubs along the coastal strip. Between October and March, however, when at intervals sufficient rain falls, the desert is transformed: grass and foliage are plentiful, flowers and plants appear in great variety, and in the spring truffles and mushrooms can be found. The fox and jackal have decreased in numbers. Fish are plentiful. Among the species of migratory birds are swallows, wagtails, chiffchaff, skylarks, and wrens.

⁵ENVIRONMENT

The Persian Gulf War of 1991 and its aftermath caused severe environmental problems for Kuwait. The nation's water supply has been threatened by large quantities of oil released into the environment. Kuwait has no reusable water supply and must rely on wells and desalinization of sea water. The nation's cities produce 0.9 million tons of solid waste per year. Kuwait contributed 0.1% of the world's total gas emission. In 1994, five of Kuwait's mammal species and seven of its bird species are endangered. One plant species is also endangered.

6POPULATION

According to the 1985 census, Kuwait had a total population of 1,697,301, but it was estimated at only 1,468,902 in mid-1994. The UN projection for the year 2000 was 1,718,000, assuming a crude birthrate of 25.9 per 1,000 population, a crude death rate of 2.2, and a net natural increase of 23.7 during 1995–2000. Metropolitan Kuwait, the national capital, had an estimated population of 1,090,000 in 1990. The average population density in 1994 was estimated at 82 per sq km (214 per sq mi). About 96% of the population was urban in 1990.

7MIGRATION

With the discovery of oil and the consequent rise in living standards, Kuwait acquired a large immigrant population, attracted by jobs, free education for their children, and free medical care. The number of foreign residents more than doubled during the 1970s, and in 1994 they accounted for an estimated 56.4% of the population. Of the estimated 400,000 Palestinians living in Kuwait before the 1990–91 Gulf War, reportedly only about one-sixth were allowed to remain. Only about 120,000 of the 220,000 prewar *bidoons* (mostly nomads from Syria, Jordan, and Iraq) were allowed to stay. These stateless Arabs had remained in Kuwait under Iraqi occupation and were suspected of collaboration. Most other foreign workers were able to return to their home countries. The citizenship law requires Arabs to have 8 years of continuous residence before applying for Kuwaiti citizenship; others need 15 years.

8ETHNIC GROUPS

Ethnic Kuwaitis are mostly descendants of the tribes of Najd (central Arabia) but some descend from Iraqi Arabs. Still others are of Iranian origin. The number of non-Kuwaitis was estimated at 812,000 in 1993 (about 55% of the total), divided roughly in half between Arabs and non-Arabs such as Iranians, Indians, and Pakistanis.

9LANGUAGES

Arabic is the official language. The Arabic spoken in Kuwait is closer to classical Arabic than to the colloquial Arabic spoken in many other parts of the Middle East. English is used generally by business people, employees of oil companies, foreign residents, and students, and it is the second language taught in the schools.

10RELIGIONS

In 1986, Muslims comprised 90% of the population. Of these, 63% were Sunni, with a substantial (27%) Shi'i minority. Other religious groups are present, primarily among foreign worker groups, and these include Roman Catholics and Anglicans. Islam is the official religion of the state.

11TRANSPORTATION

Kuwait has a modern network of roads, with all-weather highways running north to Iraq and south to Sa'udi Arabia. Main roads extended 3,900 km (2,400 mi) in 1991, with 77% of the road system bituminized. In 1991 there were some 500,000 passenger cars, and 150,000 commercial taxis, trucks, and buses in use. Land transport accounts for a significant share of Kuwait's imports and exports. There are no railways.

Kuwait has five ports, including a cargo port at Ash-Shuwaykh, on Kuwayt Bay, and an oil port at Mina' al-Ahmadi that is equipped with a huge pier at which eight large tankers can be loaded simultaneously. In 1991, Kuwait had 28 merchant ships in service with a capacity of 1,326,000 GRT. Kuwait has regular calls from ocean shipping, and local sailing craft carry goods between Kuwait and the neighboring sheikhdoms, Iraq, and Sa'udi Arabia. Sea transport accounts for most of Kuwait's foreign trade.

Air transportation is highly advanced, with Kuwait Airways providing service to and from the major Middle Eastern and European cities. There were an estimated 501,000 passenger arrivals and departures at Kuwait International Airport in 1991, only 35% of the 1990 total due to the airport's closing during the Persian Gulf War.

12HISTORY

The historical records of the Arab coast of the Persian Gulf are meager. Archaeological discoveries on Faylakah Island reveal an ancient civilization about 2800 BC that had trade links with the Sumerians. By the 6th century BC, this part of the Gulf was a principal supply route for trade with India. There is evidence of early migrations to the East African coast by the seafaring inhabitants. The historical turning point for the entire Arabian Peninsula was the conversion of the people to Islam in the 7th century AD, during the lifetime of Muhammad.

Kuwait's recent history starts in 1716, when several clans of the tribe of Aniza migrated from the interior of the Arabian Desert to a tiny Gulf coastal locality, later to be called Kuwait (a diminutive of the word *kut*, meaning "fort"). In 1756, the settled tribesmen rallied around the As-Sabah family and chose as their ruler Sheikh Sabah 'Abd ar-Rahim, founder of the present ruling dynasty. During the latter part of the century, raids by land and by sea resulted in the decline of Kuwait, but after the British suppression of piracy in the region, trading and shipbuilding prospered.

During the period in which Sheikh 'Abdallah as-Sabah ruled Kuwait (1866–92), a dynastic battle raged in Arabia between the rival houses of Ar-Rashid and As-Sa'ud. The Ottoman Turks, supporting Ibn Rashid, sought to extend their control over the coastal area to the south of Kuwait. Fearing that his territory would be lost to the Turks which considered it part of their province of Basra, Sheikh Mubarak as-Sabah (r.1896–1915) asked to be taken under British protection. The British were concerned not only because of the Turkish claims but also because the Russians were seeking to set up a coaling station in Kuwait, and both the Germans and the Turks had planned to make it a terminus of the Berlin–Baghdad railroad. In 1899, Sheikh Mubarak agreed not to alienate any of his territory or to receive representatives of any foreign power without British consent. In return, the British offered their services as well as an annual subsidy to support the sheikh and his heirs.

On 19 June 1961, the protective treaty relations with the UK were terminated by mutual consent, and Kuwait declared itself fully sovereign and independent. By this time, the sheikhdom had already become a major oil producer and had acquired a controlling interest in the petroleum industry. Iraq refused to recognize Kuwait's independence, asserting it had inherited the Ottoman claim to the territory. Baghdad's threat of an invasion was foiled by the dispatch of British troops and later the support for Kuwait of the Arab League. Iraq then appeared to acquiesce in Kuwait's sovereignty, although border issues were never definitely resolved. During the next two decades, Kuwait succeeded in establishing an open and prosperous economy, based in large part on foreign, especially Palestinian and Egyptian, labor.

During the Iran-Iraq War, Kuwait, albeit technically neutral, rendered important assistance to Baghdad, including the transshipment of goods and the provision of over $6 billion in loans.

As a response, members of Kuwait's large Shi'a minority and other radical dissidents waged a war of terrorism against the government. Throughout the 1980s, there were bombings, assassination attempts, hijackings, and sabotage against oil facilities.

In 1987, Iranian attacks on Persian Gulf shipping led Kuwait to request US protection for its supertankers. Washington agreed and when a "reflagged" Kuwaiti vessel was attacked, American forces retaliated against an Iranian offshore oil rig.

With the end of the war, Iraq-Kuwait relations were stable until 1990 when Saddam Hussein accused his neighbor of waging economic warfare against Iraq by illegally drilling oil from the shared Rumailia field, overproducing oil to drive down prices and unfairly demanding repayment of war-time loans. Tensions could not be defused by negotiations or mediation and on 2 August 1990, Iraqi forces invaded Kuwait, asserting that they were rightfully reclaiming their territory. Kuwaiti defense forces offered little resistance and most senior officials fled the country.

The US led an international coalition of Arab and other nations to demand the withdrawal of Iraqi forces. After a lengthy buildup of forces, Iraq was assaulted by massive air and land forces; after six weeks, its defenses collapsed and Kuwait was liberated in February 1991. Kuwait's leaders returned to find a disgruntled population that resented their abandonment and demanded greater political participation. Enormous physical damage had been inflicted on the country, including over 700 oil well fires that did serious ecological damage before being extinguished after almost nine months' effort.

The regime and many Kuwaitis turned harshly against those suspected of collaboration with Iraq. As a consequence, much of the large Palestinian community was ejected from the country.

Relations with Iraq naturally remained tense with some Baghdad officials continuing to assert their claim to Kuwait. On 27 May 1993, the UN Security Council reaffirmed the decision of a Boundary Demarcation Commission establishing the border between the two nations. Kuwait's vulnerability to possible attack from Iraq or Iran drew the nation closer to the US which has been willing to offer enhanced security collaboration. As of late 1994, Iraq was again moving troops toward the border of Kuwait.

13GOVERNMENT

According to the constitution of 16 November 1962, Kuwait is an independent sovereign Arab state, under a constitutional monarch. Executive power is vested in the emir, who exercises it through a Council of Ministers. Succession is restricted to descendants of Mubarak as-Sabah; an heir apparent must be appointed within one year of the accession of a new ruler. The emir appoints a prime minister after traditional consultations and appoints ministers on the prime minister's recommendation. Emir Sabah as-Salim as-Sabah died in December 1977 after a reign of 12 years and was succeeded by Emir Jabir al-Ahmad al-Jabir as-Sabah. The as-Sabah family, advised by wealthy merchants and other community leaders, dominates the government.

The National Assembly (Majlis) consists of 50 elected representatives and 25 appointed members. Elections are held every four years among adult literate males who resided in Kuwait before 1920 and their descendants; candidates must be Kuwaiti males at least 30 years of age. The assembly may be dissolved at any time by the emir. It was dissolved in 1976, as part of a political crackdown that followed the government's announced support of Syrian intervention in Lebanon. Elections were held in February 1981 and a new assembly was convened after elections in 1985; it was dissolved once again in 1986 as a result of national tensions over the Iran-Iraq war. It remained suspended until elections in October 1992. In 1993, the new Assembly actively produced new legislation, including a national budget.

LOCATION: 28°32′ to 30°6′N; 46°33′ to 48°27′E. **BOUNDARY LENGTHS:** Persian Gulf shoreline, 212 km (132 mi); Sa'udi Arabia, 163 km (101 mi); Iraq, 257 km (160 mi). **TERRITORIAL SEA LIMIT:** 12 mi.

14POLITICAL PARTIES

Political parties are prohibited, but opposition groups are active in the nation's political life. Thirty-one of the 50 members of the new Assembly ran as opposed to the regime. Nineteen of them professed Islamic political ideals. Political opinions are freely expressed in informal gatherings in the homes of government officials and leading citizens.

15LOCAL GOVERNMENT

There are five governorates, but political authority is highly centralized in the capital.

16JUDICIAL SYSTEM

The system of Muslim law (the Shari'ah) was augmented by 1959 legislation that established courts of law, regulated the judicial system, and adopted modern legal codes. A tribunal of first instance has jurisdiction over matters involving personal status, civil and commercial cases, and criminal cases, except those of a religious nature. The Court of Appeals, the highest in the land, is divided into two chambers, one with jurisdiction over appeals involving personal status and civil cases, the other over appeals involving commercial and criminal cases. Those charged with planning an attack on formerUS President George Bush were tried before a state security court. State security court decisions may be appealed to the court of Cassation. Ordinary criminal cases may be appealed to the High Court of Appeals. A military court handles offenses committed by members of the security forces. Religious courts, Sunni and Shi'a, decide family law matters.

While the 1962 constitution guarantees an independent judiciary, the executive branch retains control over its administration and budget. The Emir, after recommendation of the Justice Ministry, appoints judges in the regular courts. Kuwaiti nationals receive lifetime appointments; non-Kuwaiti judges receive renewable terms of one to three years.

[17]ARMED FORCES

Kuwait's rebuilt armed forces totaled 11,700 volunteers in 1993. The army had 8,000 men and 200 tanks; the air force, 2,500 men and 73 combat aircraft; and the navy, 1,200 men and 2 patrol craft. There is a 5,000-member National Guard. UN observors and advisors number 400. The US provides 1 air defense training battery. Estimated defense expenditures in 1992 were $9.7 million.

[18]INTERNATIONAL COOPERATION

Kuwait was admitted to UN membership on 14 May 1963 and is a member of ESCWA and all the nonregional specialized agencies except WIPO. It belongs to the Arab League, G-77, OPEC, and OAPEC; in 1981, it was a leader in forming the GCC with Sa'udi Arabia and four other Gulf states. Kuwait is a signatory of GATT and the Law of the Sea.

[19]ECONOMY

The discovery of oil in 1934 transformed the economy. Kuwait's enormous oil reserve of 94 billion barrels and huge quantities of natural gas have provided the base for an economic presence of worldwide significance. The Kuwaiti standard of living was among the highest in the Middle East and in the world by the early 1980s. Oil wealth has stimulated trade, fishery development, and service industries. The government has used its oil revenues to build ports, roads, an international airport, a seawater distillation plant, and modern government and office buildings. The public has also been served by the large-scale construction of public works, free public services, and highly subsidized public utilities, transforming Kuwait into a fully developed welfare state. Prudent management of budgetary allocations and development priorities, as well as substantial interest from overseas investment, helped cushion the adverse impact of the collapse of the Souk al–Manakh—an unregulated curbside securities market—in 1982, the collapse in world oil prices during the mid-1980s, and the 1980–88 Iran-Iraq war. In addition, acquisition in Western Europe of 5,000 retail outlets and expansion into the manufacture and sale of refined oil products bolster the Kuwaiti economy.

From 1984–89 oil extraction and processing accounted for about 45% of GDP, 90% of export earnings, and 50% of government revenues. Kuwait's economy suffered enormously from the effects of the Gulf War and the Iraqi occupation, which ended in February 1991 with the destruction of much of Kuwait's oil production capacity and other economic infrastructure. The damage inflicted on the economy is estimated at $20 billion. The cost of liberation and reconstruction were very high. Kuwait ran an estimated cumulative fiscal deficit of about $70 billion from 1990–92, reduced its foreign assets from about $100 billion to $65 billion, and increased its public debt from $5 billion to $40 billion. The fiscal deficit for 1992/93 was estimated at $7 billion, equivalent to 35% of GDP and 20% of the government's foreign assets.

By 1993, Kuwait had an estimated per capita income of about $17,234.

[20]INCOME

In 1992, the GDP was $15.3 billion in current US dollars or $11,100 per capita. It is estimated that in 1989 agriculture, hunting, forestry, and fishing contributed 1% to GDP; mining and quarrying, 41%; manufacturing, 14%; electricity, gas, and water, -1%; construction, 2%; wholesale and retail trade, 8%; transport, storage, and communication, 4%; finance, insurance, real estate, and business services, 12%; and unity, social, and personal services, 19%.

[21]LABOR

In 1992, the civilian labor force amounted to 600,000 and the government continued its post-war policy of reducing the number of expatriate workers, but with limited success. At the end of 1992, about 437,000 non-Kuwaitis were working in the private sector, and approximately 50,000 in the government sector. Also, over 100,000 non-Kuwaitis work as domestic servants. Egyptians make up 26% of the private sector expatriate work force; Indians, 18%; and non-Arabs, 56%.

The Kuwait Trade Union Federation (KTUF), made up of nine government sector and three oil sector unions, is the largest labor organization, and represents all but two unions in the nation.

The Ministry of Social Affairs and Labor controls manpower allocation, employment of foreign workers, vocational training, enforcement of labor regulations, and industrial relations. The General Confederation of Kuwaiti Workers is sponsored by the government. In general, all workers are entitled to a 48-hour workweek, compensation for overtime, sick leave, termination pay, and access to arbitration for settlement of disputes. However, many laborers from developing countries are willing to tolerate poor or unhealthy working conditions in order to earn a wage significantly higher than in their own countries.

[22]AGRICULTURE

Only 0.2% of the total land area is utilized for the cultivation of crops; permanent pasture land amounts to 7.6% of total land area. Despite the absence of rivers and streams, and the paucity of rain, the development of agriculture has been actively pursued. The government apportions arable land at nominal prices on a long-term basis among farmers to stimulate production of vegetables and other crops. It also provides farmers with long-term loans and low-cost irrigation. The state has supplied extension services and demonstration centers for new farming techniques in the attempt to increase agricultural production. Nevertheless, farming contributed less than 1% of the non-oil GDP before the Gulf War. Agricultural output in 1992 included 31,000 tons of vegetables and melons, and 1,000 tons of fruit.

[23]ANIMAL HUSBANDRY

A small number of Bedouins raise camels, goats, and sheep for meat and milk. When the desert is green (from the middle of March to the end of April), about one-fourth of Kuwait's meat supply is provided locally. The 1992 (and 1990 pre-Gulf War amounts in parentheses) livestock population included: cattle, 5,000 (25,000); sheep, 297,000 (200,000); goats, 1,000 (25,000); and chickens, 1,000,000 (21,000,000).

[24]FISHING

Small boats catch enough fish to satisfy local demand. Species caught include sardines, mackerel, tuna, shark (for the fins exported to China), barracuda, and mullet. Crabs, crayfish, and oysters are plentiful, and undik and zubaidi (butterfish) are both tasty and very popular. Shrimp are produced for a growing export market. The fish catch in 1991 totaled 1,979 tons, down from

4,500 in 1990 and 7,653 in 1989, because of the invasion.

25FORESTRY

There are no natural forests in Kuwait. The government's afforestation projects cover an area of about 2,000 hectares (4,900 acres).

26MINING

Aside from petroleum and natural gas, the only minerals and mineral products are cement and fertilizer. The production plants of both the cement and fertilizer industries were damaged by retreating Iraqi troops during the Gulf War.

27ENERGY AND POWER

The Persian Gulf is geologically unique: sedimentary deposits are combined with large, relatively unbroken folding that results in underground oil reservoirs 16 to 240 km (10–150 mi) long, containing billions of barrels of oil. Kuwait's known petroleum deposits outrank those of any other country except Sa'udi Arabia. With proved reserves of about 94 billion barrels (12.9 billion tons) in 1992, Kuwait possesses 9.3% of the known global resources of petroleum.

Since its liberation from Iraqi occupation in February 1991, Kuwait has focused on the quick rebuilding of its pre-invasion oil-based economy. During the occupation, oil production totally ceased following Iraqi sabotage and the havoc of Operation Desert Storm (the name of the allied military operation to free Kuwait). Iraqi troops had blown up 752 wells; 603 were ablaze while another 44 were gushing oil, creating oil lakes throughout the country. By November 1991, the fires were extinguished and the wells were under control. Crude oil production resumed in June 1991, exports in August 1991. The US firm, Bechtel Corp., was hired to oversee the reconstruction of Kuwait's oil, gas, and petrochemical facilities. Losses during the invasion had cost Kuwait $120 million per day.

In 1992, Kuwait had a crude oil output averaging 1,029,000 barrels per day. In 1993, Kuwait's average daily production was estimated at 2.1 million barrels, surpassing pre-invasion levels. The cost of production is perhaps the lowest in the world because Kuwait's vast pools of oil lie fairly close to the surface and conveniently near tidewater; the oil rises to the surface under its own pressure and, owing to a natural gradient, flows downhill to dockside without pumping. Reserves of natural gas in 1992 were estimated at 1.48 trillion cu m (52.4 trillion cu ft); 7,076 million cu m (250 billion cu ft) of natural gas were produced in 1992.

Oil was first discovered in commercial quantities in 1936, but only small amounts were produced before the end of World War II. In 1960, the Kuwait National Petroleum Co. (KNPC) was organized (60% government owned and 40% privately owned) to participate in all phases of the oil industry from prospecting to final sales. KNPC has a monopoly on all petroleum sold domestically and, since 1968, has operated a refinery complex at Sha'iba.

The Kuwait Oil Co. (KOC), originally owned in equal shares by British Petroleum Co. (BP) and Gulf Oil Corp., discovered commercial oil fields at Burgan, Magwa, Mina' al-Ahmadi, and Minagish in southern Kuwait, and at Rawdhatain, Sabriya, and Al-Bahrah in the north. Commercial production began in 1946, and from 1951 on, a 50–50 profit-sharing plan governed the split of revenue between the company and the emir. KOC's concession (which was to run to the year 2026) had covered all of Kuwait and its territorial waters, but in May 1962, it relinquished nearly half its area to the state. The Arabian Oil Co., owned by Japanese industrial interests, operates in the offshore region of the partitioned zone which is jointly administered by both Sa'udi Arabia and Kuwait. A London-based subsidiary, Kuwait Petroleum International (KPI), was organized in 1983 to manage newly acquired distribution outlets, mainly in Europe. KPI refines and markets its products in Europe under the brand name "Q8" with 5,000 filling stations in Italy, Sweden, the UK, and the Benelux nations. In 1991, KPC formed a new company, Kuwait Oil Thailand, to construct 100 new filling stations in Thailand.

The Kuwait government owns and controls all oil production within its boundaries through the Kuwait Petroleum Corp., the KNPC's parent company, and it has a 30% share in offshore operations in the partitioned zone. Kuwait's policy with regard to oil before the Iraqi invasion was to conserve its reserves as much as possible, primarily to stabilize prices. This policy, however, failed to prevent falling prices in the 1980s, and petroleum export revenues declined from $19.5 billion in 1980 to $6.3 billion in 1986. In 1993, oil exports brought in 92% of foreign revenues, or $9 billion.

All electric power is produced thermally from oil or natural gas. Installed capacity has grown dramatically during the past two decades, and electric power production increased from 2,661 million kwh in 1970 to 20,610 million kwh in 1990 before falling to only 9,100 million kwh in 1991, due to the Iraqi invasion. Most of the country is provided with electrical service; electric refrigeration and air conditioning are widely available. An extensive diesel power generating system serves outlying villages.

28INDUSTRY

Although oil extraction continues to be the economic mainstay, Kuwait has diversified its industry so that manufacturing—much of it based on petroleum—accounted for about 24% of the non-oil and gas GDP in 1989. Small-scale manufacturing plants produce ammonia, fertilizer, paper products, processed foods, and other consumer goods. Major refinery products were fuel oil, gas oil, naphtha, kerosene, and diesel fuel. Kuwait also produced soap, flour, cleansers, detergents, asbestos, and bricks. The construction industry was highly developed.

Manufacturing all but stopped during the Iraqi invasion due to shortages of inputs and looting of equipment. After liberation the sector was hard-hit by the departure of Palestinian skilled labor.

29SCIENCE AND TECHNOLOGY

High technology in Kuwait has been largely confined to the oil industry and has been imported, along with the scientists and technicians needed to install and operate oil refineries and related facilities. The Agriculture Affairs and Fish Resources Authority has an experimental research station in Safat. Kuwait University has colleges of science, medicine, engineering and petroleum, and allied health sciences and nursing.

The College of Technological Studies, in Shuwaikh, has 1,558 students. In 1984, total expenditures on research and development amounted to KD71 million; 561 technicians and 1,511 scientists and engineers were engaged in research and development.

30DOMESTIC TRADE

Until the early 1960s, the traditional small shop or market stall dominated retail trade. In recent decades, however, modern business centers with hundreds of new shops and offices have opened, and some smaller villages have developed retail stores with impressive stocks of foreign goods. The city of Kuwait is the distribution center for the sheikhdom and serves the transit trade of nearby states.

Usual business hours in summer (May to October) are from 6 AM to noon and from 4 to 6 PM; during the rest of the year, from 7 AM to noon and from 3 to 6 PM. Stores are closed Fridays.

31FOREIGN TRADE

Crude oil and oil products accounted for 91% of the total value of exports in 1989. Imports included chemicals, construction materials, petroleum equipment, iron and steel commodities, cement, timber, foodstuffs, electrical apparatus, power tools, household equipment, and motor vehicles. Since liberation, exports have been exclusively of oil and gas. To date, no data has been released regarding the composition of imports. Kuwait's foreign trade balance, in millions of Kuwaiti dinars, for 1987–89 was:

	1987	1988	1989
EXPORTS FOB OF WHICH	2,304	2,166	3,378
crude oil	667	525	—
IMPORTS CIF	–1,531	–1,714	1,849
Balance	773	452	1,529

Kuwait's major trading partners for the period 1989–91 as measured by percent total exports and imports by dollar value were:

	1989	1990	1991
EXPORTS			
France	1.4	1.1	16.1
Japan	19.2	19.1	12.3
UK	2.0	2.1	11.1
Egypt	—	0.1	10.0
US	6.0	4.9	7.6
IMPORTS			
US	13.0	10.9	34.8
Japan	12.7	11.4	12.4
UK	6.5	8.3	8.8
Canada	0.6	0.8	8.7
Germany	7.9	8.9	7.8
Yugoslavia	0.3	2.9	6.0

Kuwait had maintained a boycott of imports from Israel. However, after liberation, Kuwait relaxed regulations relating to this, so that Israeli companies previously subject to boycott were permitted to do business in Kuwait. Kuwait also announced a trade embargo against the countries which it regarded as having supported Iraq during the occupation—Jordan, Yemen, Tunisia, Sudan, Algeria, and Mauretania.

32BALANCE OF PAYMENTS

Kuwait enjoys a highly favorable payments position because of its huge trade surpluses. The Kuwaiti dinar is completely covered by the country's reserve fund, 50% of which must be in gold. As of March 1987, Kuwait's foreign exchange reserves totaled $4,406 million. Kuwait's balance of payments for 1984 and 1985 (in millions of US dollars) was as follows:

	1984	1985
CURRENT ACCOUNTS		
Trade, net	5,533	5,473
Other goods, services, and income, net	2,135	1,712
Transfers, net	–1,378	–1,569
TOTALS	6,290	5,616
CAPITAL ACCOUNTS		
Direct investment, net	–95	–57
Portfolio investment	209	–352
Other long-term capital	–1,189	–665
Other short-term capital	–6,188	–1,666
TOTALS	–7,263	–2,740
Errors and omissions	371	–1,995
Net change in reserves	–602	881

33BANKING AND SECURITIES

The Central Bank of Kuwait, established in 1969, formulates and implements the nation's monetary policy, regulates the currency, and controls the banking system. The Central Bank's foreign assets totaled KD1,151.4 million at the end of 1993. As of December 1993, the total money supply, as measured by M2, was KD5,614 million.

In 1993, Kuwait had 11 commercial banks, the largest of which were the National Bank and the Commercial Bank, and three specialized banks, including the government-owned Savings and Credit Bank. Foreign assets of commercial banks totaled KD2,105.5 million in December 1993. Private-sector claims (December 1993) amounted to KD930.3 million; claims on the government, KD3,037.3 million.

Kuwait's official securities exchange, founded in 1976, handles only government bonds and securities of Kuwaiti companies. An unofficial and unregulated securities exchange, the Souk al-Manakh, listing the stocks of 45 Gulf companies outside Kuwait and considered highly speculative, collapsed suddenly in August 1982. At the time of the crash, some 6,000 investors and $94 billion in postdated checks drawn in anticipation of future stock price increases were said to be involved. In order to limit the effect of the collapse on the Kuwaiti economy, the government created a special rescue fund to pay compensation to small investors for validated claims.

34INSURANCE

Both domestic and foreign insurance companies operate in Kuwait. In 1986 there were 19 insurance firms, most owned by joint-stock companies. Marine, fire, accident, and life insurance policies constitute the bulk of all policies issued. Third-party liability insurance for motor vehicles is compulsory. In 1984, life insurance premiums written totaled KD9.4 million; the total value of the policies was KD650 million.

35PUBLIC FINANCE

The following table shows actual revenues and expenditures for 1991 and 1992 in millions of dinars.

	1991	1992
REVENUE AND GRANTS		
Tax revenue	8	5
Capital revenue	—	1
EXPENDITURES & LENDING MINUS REPAYMENTS		
General public service	1,310	490
Defense	4,527	869
Public order and safety	89	323
Education	159	538
Health	63	235
Social security and welfare	319	582
Housing and community amenities	32	236
Recreation, cultural, and religious affairs	24	89
Economic affairs and services	74	381
Other expenditures	21	148

36TAXATION

Income from oil concessions is based on royalties, generally at the rate of 50% or higher. Individual or local company incomes are tax exempt. Profits of foreign corporations are taxed at rates ranging from 5-55% of the total Kuwait-source profit.

37CUSTOMS AND DUTIES

Customs duties are generally 4% ad valorem, but some goods are admitted duty-free and the tariff on cigarettes was raised to 30% as of August, 1992. Imports of liquor are prohibited by law.

38FOREIGN INVESTMENT

Through tax concessions, Kuwait welcomes foreign investment in heavy and light industries. While foreign investment is not permitted in certain sectors such as banking or insurance, it is restricted to less than 49% of ownership shares in permitted areas. The Kuwaiti government has successfully blocked any possibility of foreign investment in the oil industry. A sizable proportion of public and private savings in Kuwait is held in the form of foreign assets. The income from foreign investments exceeded $7 billion in 1986. In 1987, Kuwait purchased a 10% interest in the British Petroleum Co., the world's third-largest petroleum company.

39ECONOMIC DEVELOPMENT

Since the mid-1970s, Kuwait has restrained its spending on economic development and has fostered a policy of controlled growth. From 1977 to 1982, allocations for development projects remained steady at $1.7–2.5 billion annually, of which 76% was spent on public works, electric power plants, and desalination and irrigation projects. Development plans for the 1980s, stressing industrial diversification, include the expansion of local oil refineries and major projects in petrochemicals, electricity, water supply, highway construction, and telecommunications. Overseas, refining and marketing operations were stepped up. The 1985/86–1989/90 plan envisaged local investment of some $5 billion a year, 84% of which would be spent in the public sector. Post-war economic planning has been hampered by the expulsion of the mainly Palestinian middle-ranking civil servants in various government departments.

In December 1961, Kuwait established the Kuwait Fund for Arab Economic Development, patterned after Western and international lending agencies, to issue loans at low rates of interest for Arab economic development. By the end of 1985, Kuwait had extended loans to developing countries amounting to $4.3 billion. The Kuwait-based Arab Fund for Economic and Social Development also has contributed to various development institutions. However, in 1990 the AFESD transferred its operations to Bahrain. Since Iraq's invasion most of Kuwait's aid commitments have taken the form of government-to-government agreements. Within the Arab world, the overwhelming share of Kuwaiti aid goes to Egypt and Syria.

40SOCIAL DEVELOPMENT

Kuwait has a widespread system of social welfare on a paternalistic basis, financed by government oil revenues. It offers welfare services for the poor, provides free medical service and education to all residents, and spends heavily for waterworks, public gardens, and other public facilities. Social insurance legislation enacted in 1976 provides for old age, disability, and survivor pensions, for which the worker pays 5% of earnings and the employer pays 10% of payroll. Kuwait in 1982 became the first Gulf state to legalize abortion, on limited health grounds. In 1985–90, the fertility rate was 3.9, down 19.1% from the previous 5-year period.

Women have the same property rights as men, although they are not permitted to vote. Kuwaiti women married to foreign men suffer legal discrimination. Women (including foreign women) who wear Western clothing are subject to sexual harassment.

41HEALTH

Kuwait has a highly advanced public health service which is extended to all Kuwait residents, citizens and noncitizens alike. In 1992, 100% of the population had access to health care services. The incidence of typhoid fever and most infectious diseases is comparatively low; however, influenza is common, and measles has resulted in a high fatality rate among children up to age 5. In 1992, children up to 1 year of age were vaccinated against tuberculosis (93%); diphtheria, pertussis, and tetanus (92%); polio (92%); and measles (93%). In 1991, 100% of the urban population had access to safe water, and 100% of the urban population had adequate sanitation. In 1985, there were 16 public hospitals and sanatoriums, 157 dental clinics, 62 general clinics, 22 mater-

nity centers, 36 child care centers, and 25 health protection centers. Medical personnel included 2,818 doctors (290 of them private), 277 dentists, 392 pharmacists, 6,851 nurses, and 330 assistant nurses. That same year, there was 1 physician to every 602 persons and 1 hospital bed to every 314 persons. Life expectancy in 1992 was 75 years. That same year, infant mortality was estimated at 14 per 1,000 live births, and there were 54,000 births. The birth rate was 28.2 per 1,000 people according to 1993 statistics. The general mortality rate in 1993 was 2.2 per 1,000 people; however, in 1990 and 1991, there were approximately 200,000 deaths attributed to the war between Kuwait and Iraq.

42HOUSING

For centuries, housing in Kuwait consisted of small cottages, mud huts, and a few larger dwellings built of coral and plastered with cement and limestone. Improved housing for the general population has been a main government objective. The National Housing Authority built about 50,000 dwelling units in 1977–85, and a scarcity of low-income housing is particularly acute. According to the 1985 census, there were 227,288 private households with 1,469,557 persons and 9,441 collective households with 227,744 persons, for an average of 7.2 persons per household. About 50% of all housing units were apartments, 19% were villas, 15% were traditional dwellings, 10% were annexes, and 4% were shacks and other marginal dwellings.

43EDUCATION

Kuwait offers its students free education, including free food, clothing, books, stationery, and transportation, from kindergarten through the fourth year of college. In 1991, Kuwait had 218 primary schools with 114,641 students and 6,967 teachers. At the secondary level, there were 167,195 students. Schools below university level are segregated by sex. The children of foreign residents enjoy the same privileges as Kuwaiti children.

Kuwait University was opened in 1966 with 866 students, and in 1985/86 had a student enrollment of 16,359. Kuwaiti nationals composed 75% of the student body. Kuwaiti students who complete their secondary-school science courses in the upper 80% of their class and arts courses in the upper 70% are eligible to study abroad at government expense. All higher level institutions had 23,686 students in 1991.

The government has adopted a program to wipe out illiteracy by opening adult education centers. Estimated literacy rate in 1990 was 73%, 77.1% for men and 66.7% for women.

44LIBRARIES AND MUSEUMS

The Kuwait Central Library has over 150,000 volumes, 90% of them in Arabic; it has established 22 branches throughout the country. The Kuwait University library system has over 340,000 volumes. Other schools and the oil companies maintain special libraries. The Kuwait Museum displays ancient Kuwaiti artifacts (recovered from excavations on Faylakah Island), as well as exhibits concerning local plant, bird, and animal life. The Educational Science Museum was established in 1972 and features sections on natural history, space, oil, health and meteorology.

45MEDIA

The government administers telephone, television, radio, postal, and telegraph services. In 1991, 361,989 telephones were operated from a fully automatic exchange. Kuwait Television is government-controlled and has offered color broadcasts since 1974; it broadcasts over two channels. Radio Kuwait produces programs in English, Urdu, Persian, and Arabic. There are 20 radio and 6 television transmitters; some 590,000 television sets and 715,000 radios were in use in 1991. In that year, Kuwait had 8 daily newspapers. Major Arabic dailies (with estimated 1991 circulations), include *Al-Seyassa* (40,000), *Al-Qabas* (60,000), *Al-Rai al-'Amm* (50,000), and *Al-Anbaa* (60,000). English-language dailies include the *Arab Times* (40,000) and *Kuwait Times* (43,000). The popular monthly magazine *Al-'Arabi,* similar to the *Reader's Digest,* is widely read in Kuwait.

46ORGANIZATIONS

The Ministry of Social Affairs and Labor encourages and supports cultural and recreational organizations and sponsors theatrical activities for youth. Boy Scouts are active, and cultural and recreational centers encourage hobbies and sports. There is a chamber of commerce and industry in the capital.

47TOURISM, TRAVEL, AND RECREATION

Except for nationals of the other Gulf states, visitors must obtain visas in advance from Kuwaiti embassies or consulates. By the second anniversary of the Iraqi invasion, many of the physical scars of war and occupation had already been erased, and the government was well on its way to restoring the country's extensive prewar accommodations and amenities, although hotel prices have risen steeply since the war. In 1991 there were 42,318 hotel rooms and 84,636 beds with a 64% occupancy rate. In the same year, 3.19 million tourists (including same-day visitors) spent an estimated US$3.43 billion in Kuwait.

48FAMOUS KUWAITIS

During the reign of Emir Sir 'Abdallah as-Salim as-Sabah (1870–1965), Kuwait attained a prominent position among the great oil-producing nations of the world, and the state adopted a social welfare program founded on a unique patriarchal system; the emir was revered as a man of simplicity, devotion, and deep concern for his people. His successors as emir have been Sabah as-Salim as-Sabah (1913–77), from 1965 to 1977; and Jabir al-Ahmad al-Jabir as-Sabah (b. 1928), since 1977.

49DEPENDENCIES

Kuwait has no territories or colonies.

50BIBLIOGRAPHY

Al-Moosa, Abdulrasool, and Keith McLachlan. *Immigrant Labour in Kuwait.* Dover, N.H.: Longwood, 1985.

American University. *Area Handbook for the Persian Gulf States.* Washington, D.C.: Government Printing Office, 1984.

Assiri, Abdul-Reda. *Kuwait's Foreign Policy: City-state in World Politics.* Boulder, Colo.: Westview Press, 1990.

Crystal, Jill. *Kuwait: The Transformation of an Oil State.* Boulder, Colo.: Westview Press, 1992.

Crystal, Jill. *Oil and Politics in the Gulf: Rulers and Merchants in Kuwait and Qatar.* New York: Cambridge University Press, 1990.

Finnie, David H. *Shifting Lines in the Sand: Kuwait's Elusive Frontier with Iraq.* Cambridge, Mass.: Harvard University Press, 1992.

Ismael, J. S. *Kuwait: Social Change in Historical Perspective.* Syracuse, N.Y.: Syracuse University Press, 1982.

Kuwait in Pictures. Minneapolis: Lerner, 1989.

Sapsted, David. *Modern Kuwait.* London: Macmillan, 1980.

Slot, B. *The Origins of Kuwait.* New York: E.J. Brill, 1991.

KYRGYZSTAN

Kyrgyz Republic
Kyrgyzstan Respublikasy

CAPITAL: Bishkek.

FLAG: Red field with a yellow sun in the center; in the center of the sun is a red ring crossed by two sets of three lines, a stylized representation of the vent in a Kyrgyz yurt.

ANTHEM: *Kyrgyz National Anthem.*

MONETARY UNIT: The som, established in May 1993.

WEIGHTS AND MEASURES: The metric system is in force.

HOLIDAYS: Holidays not available.

TIME: 5 PM = noon GMT.

¹LOCATION, SIZE, AND EXTENT

Kyrgyzstan is located in southern Asia, between China and Kazakhstan. Comparatively, it is slightly smaller than the state of South Dakota with a total area of 198,500 sq km (76,641 sq mi). Kyrgyzstan shares boundaries with Kazakhstan on the N, China on the E, Tajikistan on the S, Uzbekistan on the W. The country's boundary length totals 3,878 km (2,410 mi), and its capital city, Bishkek is located in the north central part of the country.

²TOPOGRAPHY

The topography of Kyrgyzstan features the peaks of Tien Shan, which rise to 7,000 meters, and associated valleys and basins which encompass the entire nation. Slightly over 5% of Kyrgyzstan's land is under irrigation.

³CLIMATE

The country's climate is continental to polar in the Tien Shan Mountains. In the Fergana Valley the average temperature in July is 28°C (82°F). In January, the mean temperature is −21°C (−5°F). Rainfall data is unavailable.

⁴FLORA AND FAUNA

The country's flora and fauna is similar to Tajikistan, with wildflowers in the valleys of the mountains, and yak and snow leopards in the mountains.

⁵ENVIRONMENT

Among Kyrgyzstan's most significant environmental issues are water pollution and soil salinity. The pollution of the nation's water causes health problems for 25% of its people. Eighty percent of the nation's people living in rural areas do not have a publicly regulated water supply.

⁶POPULATION

The population of Kyrgyzstan was 4,290,442 in 1989. It was estimated at 4,769,877 for 1995. The projection for 2000 was 5,189,000, based on a crude birth rate of 23.7 per 1,000 population, a crude death rate of 6.3, and a net natural increase of 17.4 during 1995–2000. The estimated population density in 1995 was 24 per sq km (62.2 per sq mi). Bishkek (formerly Fronze), the capital, had an estimated population of 625,000 at the beginning of 1990.

⁷MIGRATION

Although internal and external migration are nominally free, administrative restrictions from the Soviet era persist. In 1993 about 24,000 people immigrated and 135,000 left the country. There has been a systematic out-migration of non-Kyrgyz, especially Russians, since independence.

⁸ETHNIC GROUPS

Kyrgyz constituted 52% of the population in 1989. Russians accounted for 21.5%, Uzbeks for 13%, Ukrainians, 2.5%, Germans, 2.4%, and Tatars, 1.6%. About 420,000 ethnic Kyrgyz reside elsewhere in the former Soviet Union and 170,000 in China. Kyrgyz speak a Turkic language and most are Sunni Moslems. There are major ethnic and clan-based cleavages, including north-south clan and regional tensions that threaten fragmentation. According to some reports, one-tenth or more of Russians left Kyrgyzstan during 1991 because of ethnic tensions. Ethnic Germans, deported to Kyrgyzstan by Stalin during World War II, are also leaving Kyrgyzstan. In June 1990, in the Osh region on the eastern edge of the fertile Fergana Valley, a major ethnic conflict broke out between Kyrgyz and Uzbek inhabitants over land distribution. Approximately 250 people died in what has been termed "the most explosive region of Central Asia," because of its mixed population of Uzbeks and Kyrgyz, poverty, and high unemployment. Periodic clashes also occur between Kyrgyz and Tajiks along the border with Tajikistan over water resources, Beefed-up Kyrgyz security forces were placed in Osh and Alais regions in early 1993 to prevent spillover from fighting going on between Tajik ex-communists and oppositionists in the mountains of northern Tajikistan and to halt the inflow of Tajik refugees.

⁹LANGUAGES

A Turkic tongue, Kyrgyz is the official language. It was written in the Arabic script until 1926, then in Roman letters until 1940, when the Cyrillic alphabet was adopted with three special characters.

¹⁰RELIGIONS

The population of Kyrgyzstan is primarily Sunni Muslims of the Hanafi persuasion. Data on other religious affiliations has not yet become available. Although it is not known how many Roman

Catholics live in Kyrgyzstan, diplomatic relations with the Vatican were opened in 1992.

11TRANSPORTATION

As of 1991, a single east-west rail line of 370 km (230 mi) went from Issyk-kul' across the Chuskaya region into Kazakhstan. There are some 30,300 km (18,800 mi) of highways, 75% of which are paved or graveled. As a landlocked nation, water transportation is of minor importance, although inland travel is possible on several east-west rivers.

12HISTORY

The area of present-day Kyrgyzstan contains evidence of human habitation from the time of the Lower Paleolithic on, approximately 300,000 years ago. Archeologists suggest that two types of economies developed on the territory—farming and pastoral nomadism. By the 7th century BC nomadism had become predominant, and the area was controlled by various tribal alliances. In the north the Saki (7th–3rd centuries BC) were succeeded by the Usuni (2nd century BC–5th century AD); in the south the Parkan state (2nd–1st centuries BC) was replaced by the Kushani kingdom (1st–4th century AD). The ethnic identity of those peoples is the subject of much debate, but they were not Turkic. From the 6th century on, various Turkic tribes began to push westward, eventually settling most of Central Asia, including Kyrgyzstan. Much of present Kyrgyzstan was united by the 7th century as part of the West Turkic Kaganate, and replaced in the 8th century by the Turgash, who in turn were conquered by the Karluk, who originated in the Altai region further north.

When the present-day Kyrgyz first came to this territory is the subject of much debate. References to tribes of that name living in the Altai occur in the 10th century, but another people with the same name who lived along the Enisei River, are first mentioned in records from 2nd century BC. The Enisei Kyrgyz formed the Kyrgyz Kaganate in about AD 650, which survived until defeat by Genghiz Khan in 1209. Kyrgyz tradition prefers to see its origin in that state, but ethnographers and archeologists view the claim with considerable skepticism.

Evidence suggests instead that the present-day Kyrgyz are an amalgamation of various peoples, as existing tribes incorporated themselves into fresh waves of conquerors. The territory was part of the Karakhanid state from about 950–1150, during which the urban population was actively involved in trade and manufacturing along the Silk Road. Conversion to Islam also began in this period.

Genghiz Khan's Mongols conquered the area in the 13th century, destroying most of the Karakhanid culture and introducing large numbers of new peoples into the area, of Turkic, Mongol, and Tibetan stock. The resulting mix of tribes was almost certainly the basis for the present-day Kyrgyz people, who retain much of the memory of those origins in the orally preserved geneologies of their 40 clans and tribes. The present Kyrgyzstan flag includes the depiction of a sun with one ray for each tribe. The Kyrgyz follow Mongol practice of dividing their people into left (*ong*) and right (*sol*) "wings," said to reflect either the deployment of troops in military formation, or the tribe's original place of habitation. There is also a third group, the *ichkilik*, which seems to include parts of the Kyrgyz identity.

From the 15th century until the 17th century the Kyrgyz tribes were part of the larger delineation of Central Asian history, which distinguished agricultural sedents from pastoral nomads. The appearance of the same tribal names among Kazakhs, Kyrgyz, and Uzbeks suggests how the people of this territory formed a series of tribal alliances, rather than a true state.

In the 18th century the Kyrgyz began to come under pressure from Mongol tribes farther east. This prompted some of the northern tribes to send delegations to the Russians, who had pushed into Siberia in the 17th century, and who were beginning to take what is now northern Kazakhstan under its control. The Russians made no distinction between the Kazakhs and Kyrgyz, calling both Kyrgyz. The southern Kyrgyz, however, were conquered by the Kokand Khanate, established in the late 18th century, separating them from the northern Kyrgyz. This split between south and north continues to the present day in Kyrgyz life.

Russian expansion into what it called the Steppe included Kyrgyzstan. Most of northern Kyrgyzstan was incorporated into the empire by 1863; the south followed in 1876, when Russia destroyed the Kokand Khanate. Administratively, present-day Kyrgyzstan was split among four *guberniias*. Beginning in the 1890s Russia settled Russian and other European farmers into the fertile river valleys of the north, forcing Kyrgyz nomads higher into the mountains.

By 1916, Russia's policies of livestock requisition and land use had left the Kyrgyz badly impoverished. When Russia attempted to issue a draft call-up for Central Asian males, including the Kyrgyz, wide-spread fighting broke out all across the territory. The uprisings were suppressed, with great loss of life; population in the northern part dropped as much as 40%. Since independence in 1991, the state has commemorated the 1916 uprising as a genocide.

Hostility to the tsars meant that there was some support for the Bolsheviks, at least until it became clear that Lenin was not going to encourage the development of national states. Resistance to the Russians continued sporadically until the mid-1920s, in what Russian historians have labeled the Basmachi Rebellion.

As Bolshevik power was consolidated, Kyrgyzstan was first made an autonomous oblast of the Russian Federation, in 1924, then upgraded in 1926 to be an autonomous republic, but still within Russia. It did not become a full Soviet Republic until 1936.

The republic was regarded as one of the least developed of the Soviet states, politically and economically, making it a great surprise when, in October 1990, the legislature refused to ratify Communist Party leader Masaliev's bid to become the republic's president, and elected instead Askar Akaev, president of the republic's Academy of Science. Thus Kyrgyzstan became the first Soviet republic to select its own leader. Akaev and his supporters began an ambitious program of uncoupling the republic from the Communist Party, which was interrupted by the attempted coup in Moscow of August 1991. In the aftermath, Kyrgyzstan declared its independence on 31 August.

On 12 October 1991, Akaev's presidency was confirmed by direct popular election. A constitution was adopted in May 1993. An economic and political crisis led to the resignation of the first government, in December 1993, but Akaev's presidency was reaffirmed by a popular referendum of support conducted in January 1994.

13GOVERNMENT

The 350 members of the current parliament were elected in October 1990, when Kyrgyzstan was still a Soviet republic. Although most were party members, many were from a reformist wing, and five were affiliates of the DDK, the Democratic Movement of Kyrgyzstan. It is this parliament which first elected Askar Akaev president, which declared independence, and which oversaw installation of a new constitution, ratified 5 May 1993.

That constitution specifies that Kyrgyzstan, or the Kyrgyz Republic, will be a secular, unitary state. It creates three branches of government: the *Zhogorku kenesh*, or Supreme Council, which has legislative responsibility; the ministries, appointed by the president to oversee executive responsibilities, but subject to ratification by the parliament; and a judiciary, appointed by the president. The president himself stands outside this system, as

KYRGYZSTAN

LOCATION: 41°30′N; 75°0′E. **BOUNDARY LENGTHS:** Total boundary lenths, 3,878 km (2, 410 mi); China, 858 km (533.2 mi); Kazakhstan, 1,051 km (653 mi); Tajikistan, 870 km (541 mi); Uzbekistan, 1,099 km (683 mi).

guarantor of the proper functioning of all three branches; he is also head of state.

The president is to be elected once every five years, for no more than two terms, from among those citizens who are between 35 and 65 years of age, who have lived at least 15 years in the republic, and who are fluent in the state language, which is Kyrgyz. The first presidential election is scheduled for 1996. There is no vice-president. The usual functions of vice-president, including the duty to replace the president in case of death or incapacity, are to be borne by the speaker of the parliament, or *Toraga*, who is elected from among the membership of the parliament.

The parliament is also to be elected every five years, with a membership of 105. The first legislative elections are set for 1995. The constitution makes no restriction on the number of terms a deputy may serve. All citizens who have lived in the republic for five years and who have reached the age of 25 are eligible to become deputies, without linguistic restriction.

Judges are to be chosen by the president, subject to parliamentary affirmation. Potential judges must be citizens between 35 and 65 years who have legal training and legal experience of at least ten years. The length of their service is unlimited, but can be terminated by the parliament.

In theory, the constitution provides a number of basic guarantees of human freedom, including freedom of religion, of the press and other forms of media, of movement about the republic and place of dwelling, of association, and unarmed assembly. It guarantees the privacy of post and other forms of communication, and guarantees private property. In terms of social benefits, the constitution guarantees pensions, unemployment compensation,

legal representation, medical treatment, and free basic education.

In practice, though, many features of the constitution have not been implemented or have been ignored. As of mid-1994 no date had been set for either parliamentary or presidential elections, meaning that the state has continued to be governed by a combination of decrees, presidential orders, and laws. Many of these, such as reimposition of press censorship and wiretapping in spring 1994, seem in direct contradiction to the constitution.

¹⁴POLITICAL PARTIES

The Communist Party of Kirgizia, which was the only legal political party during the Soviet years, was abolished at the time of independence. A successor, the Kyrgyz Communist Party, was allowed to register in September 1992. Another party with many former Communist officials is the Republican People's Party, founded by Sharshenaliev. Two other, smaller neo-Communist parties are the Social-Democrats of Kyrgyzstan, headed by Matus, and the People's Party of Kyrgyzstan, founded by Altymyshev. The other parties began as unsanctioned civic movements. The first was Ashar, begun in 1989 to take over unused land for housing. A fluctuating number of parties and groups are joined under the umbrella of the DDK (Democratic Movement of Kyrgyzstan); the most influential is *Erkin* (Freedom), which in late 1992 fissioned into two parties, one still called Erkin, headed by Turgunaliev, and the other called *Ata-meken* (Fatherland), founded by Tekebaev and chaired by Kenenbaev. Another democratically inclined party is *Asaba* (Banner), headed by Ormushev. An association, called "For National Values and Progress," headed by Egemberdiev, appears to have moved into commerce, rather than politics. Another group, the Freedom Party, was denied registration because it includes among its goals the creation of a Uighur autonomous district, which the Chinese government is against.

For all their proliferation, parties have not yet played a large part in independent Kyrgyzstan. Early enthusiasm for the democratic parties is fading as the republic's economy grows worse, and corruption proliferates. The Communist successor parties, on the other hand, appear to be gaining influence. In the absence of elections, and with President Akaev belonging to no party, it is difficult to predict the significance of any of these parties.

[15] LOCAL GOVERNMENT

The republic is divided into six oblasts, or administrative regions, plus the capital city of Bishkek. Each has a local legislature, but real power is wielded by the oblast supervisors, or *akims,* who are presidential appointees. Although in theory answering to the president, in practice some of the akims have become powerful spokesmen for regional interests, and have run their districts with considerable autonomy.

[16] JUDICIAL SYSTEM

The 1993 constitution instituted a Western concept of judicial review which did not exist under the former Soviet regime. A procurator remains responsible for preparation and presentation of criminal cases before a panel consisting of a judge and two people's assessors (pensioners or members of labor collectives). Appeal is possible to an appellate tribunal or to the procurator's office. There is a Supreme Court with a Constitutional Court of the Supreme Court. This Constitutional Court is authorized to engage in judicial review of legislation and administrative acts for consistency with the constitution. It also considers cases on appeal involving individual rights and liberties of citizens. Constitutional Court decisions are final and entitled to respect by the other branches.

Additional reforms of the judicial system are expected. The 1993 constitution declares the independence of the judiciary from the other branches of government. Thus far, however, the courts remain under the supervision of the Ministry of Justice.

The constitution allows the president to nominate judges for election to the Constitutional Court by the parliament (Jogorku Kenesh). Judges serve for 15 years and then are subject to renomination by the president. Judges can only be removed by a two-thirds vote of the parliament.

[17] ARMED FORCES

One Russian division garrisons Kyrgzstan, supported by 55 air defense missiles and around 200 combat aircraft, all under dual control of CIS military authorities. The new republic plans a national army of 20,000 (half active, half reserve) based on 18 months conscription. No financial data is available.

[18] INTERNATIONAL COOPERATION

Kyrgyzstan was admitted to the UN on 2 March 1992. The country is a member of the CSCE, ECO, IFC, IMF, UNCTAD, UNESCO, and the World Bank, and is applying for membership in other international organizations. As a member of the CIS, Kyrgyzstan is the only former union republic to establish formal diplomatic relations with all the union nations of the former Soviet Union.

The US and EC nations, along with many others, have diplomatic relations with the country. Kyrgyzstan has especially good relations with Germany, neighboring Central Asian states, and China.

[19] ECONOMY

Kyrgyzstan is among the poorest of the post-Soviet countries with a per capita income estimated to be roughly half that of Russia.

Although coal, gold, mercury, and uranium deposits are considerable, the country boasts few of the oil and gas reserves that promise a badly needed economic windfall to other Central Asian republics. Total GDP in 1990 was estimated at R8,320 million, making it one of the smaller economies in Central Asia. The country's post-Soviet economy remains dominated by agriculture; crop and livestock production accounts for about 36% of NMP, and about one-third of the labor force. The industrial sector was developed rapidly in the post-war period, yet highly specialized in line with the republic's position as constituent component of the centrally planned Soviet economy; presently, industry accounts for about 45% of NMP and 20% of the labor force.

Under the presidency of Askar Akaev, the process for economic restructuring toward a free market orientation has outpaced that of most other post-Soviet republics, yet the transition has been an extremely difficult one. Dissolution of the state ordering system in Kyrgyzstan and its reduction in other post-Soviet republics have disrupted the traditional supply channels and effective markets for the country's industries, severely affecting overall economic performance. The country's GDP is estimated to have declined by as much as 26% in 1992, following a 3.6% drop the year before. Price liberalization undertaken in early 1991 was accompanied by an immediate surge in inflation; by late 1991, retail prices were three times higher than those of late 1990. As inflation continued to acclerate in 1992, average wages were estimated to have declined by 35–40% by the end of the year.

A reform of the government structure in early 1992 consolidated 41 ministries into 13 ministries and 7 commissions. As part of this change, the Ministry of Economy and Finance was established to assume the fiscal and economic planning duties previously carried out separately by the Ministry of Finance and the State Planning Committee. In mid-1993, Kyrgyzstan was the first country of the CIS countries to announce the introduction of its own currency, the som. Although taken in order to stabilize the national economy in face of continuing turmoil in the ruble zone, this step posed a large setback to previous negotiations for a single monetary union with other post-Soviet republics.

[20] INCOME

In 1992, Kyrgyzstan's GNP was $3,667 million at current prices, or $810 per capita. For the period 1985–92 the average inflation rate was 11.3%, resulting in a real growth rate in per capita GNP of 2.3%. In 1992, the GDP was $3,665 million in current US dollars.

[21] LABOR

The labor force includes nearly 1.9 million persons, with agriculture engaging 33%; industry (including mining), 28%; personal services, 20%; trade, 7%; transportation and communication, 6%; finance and business services, 3%; and other sectors, 3%.

In February 1992, a comprehensive law was passed protecting the rights of all workers to form and belong to unions. The Federation of Independent Trade Unions of Kyrgyzstan (FITUK), successor to the former Soviet-era official unions, remains the single trade union umbrella organization. Nineteen of the 20 union organizations in Kyrgyzstan are affiliated with FITUK. The exception is the union of entrepreneurs and cooperative members, which essentially is an association of over 8,000 self-employed persons.

Strikes are legally permitted; strikes by FITUK taxi drivers, teachers, and air traffic controllers occurred in 1992. Collective bargaining was legally recognized as a right in April 1992. In most sectors of the economy, however, wage levels continue to be set by government decree. The standard workweek is 41 hours, and safety and health regulations in factories are often left unenforced.

[22]AGRICULTURE

Before the collapse of the Soviet Union, Kyrgyzstan's crop-producing land amounted to 1,360,000 ha (3,361,000 acres), or 6.9% of the total land area. About 50% of this area is used to cultivate fodder crops, 42% for winter wheat and barley, 5% for commercial crops (cotton, sugar beets, mulberry trees for silkworms, and tobacco), with the remaining 3% used for growing potatoes and other vegetables. Cultivation occurs primarily in the Shu, Talas, and Fergana valleys. About one-third of GDP is derived form agriculture.

Production levels (in 1,000 tons) for 1992 include: wheat, 550; barley, 550; potatoes, 325; tobacco, 56; and cotton, 18.

[23]ANIMAL HUSBANDRY

About 44% of the total land area is considered permanent pastureland. Because of the rugged topography, pasture-based stock breeding is the agricultural mainstay.

Livestock in 1992 included 13,000,000 chickens, 9,200,000 sheep, 1,200,000 dairy and beef cattle, 315,000 horses, and 300,000 goats. Yaks are also bred. Meat production in 1992 totaled 210,000 tons; cow's milk, 900,000 tons; wool, 59,200 tons; and eggs, 31,000 tons.

[24]FISHING

The Naryn River is the primary site of fishing activity; but fishing is of little commercial significance. The Yssk Kol Lake is slightly saline and not conducive to the development of fresh water species fishing.

[25]FORESTRY

Forests and woodlands account for about 3% of the total land area. With 85% of the country covered by high-altitude mountain ranges, and coupled with an underdeveloped transportation system, the forestry sector is not commercially significant.

[26]MINING

Southwestern Kyrgyzstan contains most of the nation's mineral wealth, which includes antimony (often found with lead-zinc) and mercury (often found with fluorspar). Principal deposits of these minerals are found in the Alay foothills, on the southern margin of the Fergana Valley. Uranium, from the center of the country, is processed in the Shu Valley. The mountains also contain deposits of tungsten, molybdenum, rare earth metals, indium, sulfur, and arsenic.

Gold is mined in the Issyk-Kul' region. A rich deposit of tin, a regionally scarce mineral commodity, is being developed in the eastern mountains.

[27]ENERGY AND POWER

Kyrgyzstan's principal energy resources are its deposits of coal; subbituminous coal deposits are found on the southern fringe of the Fergana Valley (at Suluktu and Kyzl-Kyya), while hard coal comes from the west and northwest fringes of the valley (at Tash-Komur, Jalal-Abad, and Osh) and in the Tien Shan foothills east of Ysyk Kol Lake. As of 1991, there were twelve coal mining enterprises operating, including six open pit mines.

About 50% of Kyrgyzstan's electricity comes from hydropower. Several large hydroelectric projects are spread along the Naryn River and its headwater tributaries, and a series of dams, built on irrigation canals, produce power for the manufacturing sector around Bishkek. In 1991, electrical production totaled 13,900 million kwh.

Production of oil and natural gas in small quantities comes from fields at the northeastern edge of the Fergana Valley; in 1991, Kyrgyzstan produced 100,000 tons of oil and 100,000,000 cu m of natural gas. Consumption of petroleum amounted to 1.7 million tons in 1992.

[28]INDUSTRY

In 1991, Kyrgyzstan's industrial sector was reported to be comprised of 7,500 operating units, 3,000 of which were classified as medium and large-scale enterprises. According to the government's "Privatization and Denationalization Act" of December 1991, the transfer of all small, medium, and large-scale industrial enterprises is to be completed in a three-phase process ending in 1996. The transition is also expected to involve the conversion of defense industries to civilian use under private ownership. One important conversion thus far involves the participation of a South Korean firm in establishing electronics manufacture at a plant previously geared toward military-related production. The government is encouraging the purchase of substantial shares of individual enterprises by worker collectives, although more widespread and non-collective ownership is also being promoted. Despite government targets, however, only a few medium and large-scale enterprises in the heavy, light, and food processing industry subsectors had been privatized by 1992.

Between 1985 and 1989, industrial output increased at a rate of over 5% annually. With the disruption of traditional supply and export arrangements within the former USSR, however, industrial output declined by 1% in 1990, remained flat in 1991, and was estimated to have dropped by 23% in the first nine months of 1992. Three-quarters of Kyrgyzstan's industrial output derives from the capital of Bishkek and surrounding areas. In 1991, mechanical and electrical engineering (vehicle assembly, washing machines, electrical appliances, electronics), light industry (mainly textiles and wool processing), and food processing made up close to 75% of the country's industrial production and 80% of its industrial exports. Other important industries include chemicals, leather goods, and construction materials.

[29]SCIENCE AND TECHNOLOGY

The Kyrgyz Academy of Sciences, founded in 1954, has departments of physics, engineering, mathematics, geology, chemistry, technology, and biology. Six scientific institutes conduct medical and agricultural research. Kyrgyz State University has faculties of geography, physics, mathematics, biology, and chemistry. Polytechnic, agricultural, and medical institutes are located in Bishkek.

[30]DOMESTIC TRADE

As in other post-Soviet republics, structural reform appears to be proceeding most rapidly in the domestic retail sector. By April 1992, about one-third of the government's target for privatization in the retail trade sector had been realized, more than in any other sector. Small shops and traders predominate among the country's private retailing entities at present. However, expansion in the number of private wholesale distributors has been much less marked, placing small retailers in a disadvantaged position compared with large-scale and potentially monopolistic producers within the country's industrial sector. Retail trade purchases totalled R5,031 million in 1990.

[31]FOREIGN TRADE

About 98% of Kyrgyzstan's total exports were sold within the former USSR in 1990, while almost three-quarters of total imports were derived from other post-Soviet republics. In 1991, the nominal value of Kyrgyzstan's exports to other Soviet republics jumped to R6,331 million from R2,446 million the year before (domestic trade prices); imports increased from R 2,863 million to R5,373 million. This change is thought to have resulted primarily from the effects of price liberalization implemented in 1991 which inflated the nominal value of inter-republic trade even as trade volume itself changed little or even declined, as was the case with imports. Thus, Kyrgyzstan's positive trade balance with other post-Soviet countries in 1991, coming in the wake of chronic deficits during the previous decade, at least partially reflects faltering import purchases accompanying the decline in its industrial sector. Principal inter-republic exports are dominated by agricultural equipment and other machinery (representing more than half the value of total exports in 1990), wool and textiles, refined sugar and tobacco, metals, electric power, and some electronic goods. Major imports include a wide range of engineering products (about 31% of total imports), chemicals and petrochemicals, oil and gas, light industry goods such as clothing, wood and paper products, as well as metals and various processed foods.

Exports and imports outside the former USSR contracted sharply in 1991, reflecting the economic dislocation faced both by Kyrgyzstan and its key East European trading partners. Total exports beyond the union equaled $20 million in 1991, down from $86 million in 1990, while imports declined to $443 million, down from $1,268 million in 1990.

International exports are dominated by non-ferrous metallurgy and machinery (60% of total exports in 1991), while imported goods include mainly processed foods (45% of total imports in 1991), machinery (25% of total), and clothing. The largest extra-republic trading partners in 1991 were Germany, the former Czechoslovakia, and Bulgaria.

32BALANCE OF PAYMENTS

Kyrgyzstan maintains a trade deficit, derived mostly from dependence on imports from other former Soviet republics; from 1989 to 1991, the trade deficit annually amounted to about 14% of GDP. Foreign exchange reserves are minimal, since imports directly from hard-currency countries are negligible.

33BANKING AND SECURITIES

The central bank of Kyrgyzstan is the National Bank of Kyrgyzstan. In 1992 there were 10 commercial banks in the country. Six of them were newly established commercial banks, one was a savings bank, and three were joint-stock banks formed from three state banks of the former Soviet Union. There were R2,883 million in circulation in 1991.The currency unit was initially the ruble following independence; however, with IMF support, the government introduced a new currency, the som, in May 1993 in order to stabilize the economy, avoid the inflation of the ruble, and attract foreign investment.

There are no security exchanges in Kyrgyzstan.

34INSURANCE

No recent information is available.

35PUBLIC FINANCE

Since 1991, economic output has been declining, while inflation has escalated. As a result, the proportion of public revenues in GDP has plummeted. Transfers from the former Soviet Union amounting to over 11% of GDP largely created an overall budget surplus equivalent to 4.1% of GDP in 1991.

In 1992, parliament agreed to a further tightening of fiscal policy (including decreased expenditures and the elimination of transfers to inefficient state enterprises) due to the virtual termination of in-flowing subsidies caused by the demise of the Soviet Union. The som, currency introduced by the government in May 1993, has proven fairly stable, and monthly inflation has slowed from 40% to about 10%.

36TAXATION

The personal income tax varies up to a maximum rate of 40%; the corporate rate ranges from 15–55% with a standard rate of 35%. Also levied are a 20% value-added tax; a withholding tax ranging from zero to 5%; and a social security contribution of 37% by employers and 1% by employees.

37CUSTOMS AND DUTIES

Kyrgyzstan and the US signed a most-favored nation agreement in 1992. Although Kyrgyzastan levies excise and value-added taxes, these are not applied to imports.

38FOREIGN INVESTMENT

In June 1991, the Kyrgyzstan parliament passed the Foreign Investment Law guiding the establishment of local enterprises with foreign shareholding as well as 100% foreign ownership. The law secures the right to repatriation of profits and allows foreign investment in all sectors of the economy except military production and certain forms of ownership in agriculture. Foreign buyers may acquire small enterprises being transferred from the state to the private sector directly on the open market; foreign participation in auctions or other forms of bidding for medium and large-scale enterprises requires special government permission. At present the government is attempting to attract overseas investors, particularly to the minerals, electronics, and agro-processing sectors of the economy. While a few contracts have been signed, they have been limited mainly to the hydroelectric sector. Actual foreign investment flows into the country were negligible in 1992. A weak institutional environment and lingering uncertainties around export licensing, foreign exchange surrender requirements, and state controls over inputs and outputs are cited as the main reasons for slow investment growth thus far.

39ECONOMIC DEVELOPMENT

Under the Soviet system, economic planning efforts in Kyrgyzstan focused on increasing agricultural production (particularly in the meat and dairy subsectors during the 1980s) and specialized development of industrial sectors in line with the wider Soviet economy. The ratio of fixed investment to GDP averaged 28% of GDP in the late 1980s, slightly higher than that in Russia. Consumption and investment growth outpaced GDP growth, with the difference financed largely by increased resource flow from the Soviet central government. Transfer payments from the central government as well as capital inflows into state enterprises covered the republic's modest balance of trade deficit with its Soviet trading partners and countries beyond. With this support, GDP growth was sustained at moderately high levels in the late 1980s, averaging 5.1% in 1985–89.

In the post-Soviet period, the Kyrgyzstan government faces the task of sustaining a viable national economy despite the sudden cessation of transfers from the central government, the country's critical dependence on oil and gas imports, and its landlocked geographic position that will hamper development of trading ties outside the economically troubled former Soviet Union. Since 1990, reforms aimed at structural transition to a market-oriented economy have been similar to those of other post-Soviet republics; in some areas they have been adopted much more rapidly, especially in the areas of privatizing state enterprises, ending the state ordering system, lifting price controls, and converting military enterprises to civilian uses. A value-added tax was introduced in 1992 to help strengthen the government revenue base. Expected state revenues however, have fallen short of expectation due to steeply declining consumption and collection difficulties within the new tax system. With seriously declining revenues since 1991, the government's ability to make new development investments in either the productive sectors or physical and social infrastructure has been severely constrained. Capital expenditures as a percentage of total budgetary expenditures declined from 15% in 1990 to only 7% in 1992. Even with sharply contracted expenditures, the government expected to run a fiscal deficit of R15.3 billion in 1992, amounting to over 12% of GDP. In face of these difficulties, it is expected that official and multilateral loans development assistance will play a major role in helping Kyrgyzstan to meet its financing requirements and develop its economic base during the next decade. Currently, a $400 million loan package from the European Bank for Reconstruction and Development is being negotiated to promote the development of sectors with the greatest potential for expanding the country's export capacity, including banking, mining, agribusiness, energy, transport, communications, leather, wool, and other textile production. In 1992, the government signed a formal agreement with Russia transferring its share of the former Soviet Union's external debt to the latter in return for relinquishing most claims to the financial and other assets of the former USSR.

40 SOCIAL DEVELOPMENT

In 1989, the average family size in Kyrgyzstan was 4.7 members. The divorce rate was 5.9 per 1,000 women. There were 11.8 drug-related crimes and 4.1 alcohol-related deaths per 100,000 persons.

Women have equal status under the law and are well represented in the work force in urban areas. A women's congress in Bishkek convenes periodically to consider women's issues. In 1990, the fertility rate was 3.7. The government is developing out a comprehensive program in the rights and welfare of youth.

41 HEALTH

In 1992, the country had 3.67 physicians per 1,000 people, with a nurse to doctor ratio of 2.8. There are approximately 12 hospital beds per 1,000 inhabitants.

The infant mortality rate in 1992 was 49 per 1,000 live births, and there were 8,000 deaths of children under 5 years old. The overall mortality rate in 1993 was 7 per 1,000 people, and major causes of death in 1990 (per 100,000 people) were: communicable diseases and maternal/perinatal causes, 124; noncommunicable diseases, 651; and injuries, 95. There were also 68 reported cases of tuberculosis per 100,000 inhabitants in 1990. In 1992, immunization rates for children up to one year old were: tuberculosis, 96%; diphtheria, pertussis, and tetanus, 88%; polio, 91%; and measles, 94%. Total health care expenditures in 1990 were $517 million. In 1992, the life expectancy was 66 years for both men and women.

42 HOUSING

In 1989, 42.7% of all privately owned urban housing had running water, 32.4% had sewer lines, 14% had central heating, and 1.4% had hot water. In 1990, Kyrgyzstan had 12.1 sq m of housing space per capita and, as of 1 January 1991, 85,000 households (or 18.6%) were on waiting lists for housing in urban areas.

43 EDUCATION

The adult literacy rate in 1990 was estimated at 97.0%, with 98.6% of men and 95.5% of women estimated as literate. The educational system was not developed until after the 1920s, when the country came under Soviet control. During the 1988/89 school year, there were over 1,800 secondary schools enrolling approximately one million students. During the same year, over 57,000 students were enrolled at 10 institutions of higher learning including 13,000 at the State University of Kyrgyzstan. In 1990, all higher level institutions had 58,800 pupils.

44 LIBRARIES AND MUSEUMS

Important libraries in Kyrgyzstan include the State Public Library of Kyrgyzstan, with over 3.5 million volumes, and the Scientific Technical Library of Kyrgyzstan, with over 5.8 million volumes. The Kyrgyzstan State University library contains over 930,000 volumes.

The State Historical Museum of Kyrgyzstan has 20,000 items on display depicting the history of Kyrgyzstan. The Kyrgyzstan Museum of Fine Arts collects primarily modern work.

45 MEDIA

Telephone links to other former Soviet republics are via land line or microwave, and to other countries through Moscow. Dom Radio in Bishkek broadcasts in Kyrgyz, German, Dungan, and Russian. Television programming is provided through Orbita and INTELSAT.

In 1990, daily newspaper circulation totaled 1.5 million, and over 40 periodicals were published.

The Supreme Soviet on 2 July 1992 passed a law on the press and mass media which supports freedom of the press but also provides guidelines proscribing publication of certain information. The law supports the right of journalists to work, obtain information, and publish without prior restraint. The law prohibits publication of state secrets, material which advocates the overthrow of, or changes to, the existing constitutional order in Kyrgyzstan or elsewhere, It also prohibits publication of material that advocates war, violence, or intolerance toward ethnic or religious groups. Desecration of national norms, ethics, and symbols like the national seal, anthem, or flag is prohibited. Publication of pornography is prohibited, as is propagation of untrue information.

During 1992 the press was free to publish material without prior government approval or restraint. Similarly, no prior restriction or censorship existed for the electronic media or cinemas. The Government owned all radio and television facilities. While a few fully independent newspapers and magazines existed, the Government continued to exert varying degrees of influence over most other publications.

Independent publishers said they were disadvantaged because they paid higher prices for materials and did not have some of the resources available to the government-owned media, such as office space. There were no reports of government pressure or threats against journalists, but government involvement in and ownership of the media did raise concerns among journalists about self-censorship.

46 ORGANIZATIONS

Important economic organizations in Kyrgyzstan include the Chamber of Commerce and Industry, and the Kyrgyzstan Federation of Trade Unions. Active political organizations include the Committee for the Defense of Human Rights, Slavic Fund, Free Kyrgyzstan, Agigat, and Ashar.

47 TOURISM, TRAVEL, AND RECREATION

Osh, Kyrgyzstan's second-largest city, is considered a holy city by Muslim pilgrims who visit it annually to pray at its Islamic shrines. The capital city of Bishkek is surrounded by some of the highest mountain ranges in the world.

Visas are required for entry to Kyrgyzstan and are obtainable upon arrival or through Kyrgyz embassies abroad and tour companies. The principal accommodations are hotels that formerly belonged to the Soviet Intourist system. However, foreign chains are currently developing a number of projects in Central Asia.

48 FAMOUS KYRGYZSTANIS

Askar A. Akayev has been president of Kyrgyzstan since October 1992 Apas Jumagulov has been prime minister since December 1993. Chingiz Aitmatov, winner of two Lenin Prizes for literature, is a native Kyrgyzstani.

49 DEPENDENCIES

Kyrgyzstan has no territories or colonies.

50 BIBLIOGRAPHY

Atkinson, Thomas Witlam, 1799–1861. *Oriental and Western Siberia: A Narrative of Seven Years' Explorations and Adventures in Siberia, Mongolia, the Kirghis Steppes, Chinese Tar-*

tary, and a Part of Central Asia. Philadelphia: J. W. Bradley, 1859.

Foreign Investment and Privatisation in Kyrgyzstan. London: Clifford Chance, 1993.

Kyrghyzstan. Washington, D.C.: International Monetary Fund, 1992.

Kyrgyzstan: The Transition to a Market Economy. Washington, D.C.: World Bank, 1993.

Pisarskoi, E. G. *Architecture of the Soviet Kirghizia.* Moskow: Stroiizdat, 1986.

LAO PEOPLES' DEMOCRATIC REPUBLIC (LAOS)

Lao People's Democratic Republic

Sathalanalat Paxathipatai Paxaxon Lao

CAPITAL: Vientiane (Viangchan).

FLAG: The national flag, officially adopted in 1975, is the former flag of the Pathet Lao, consisting of three horizontal stripes of red, dark blue, and red, with a white disk, representing the full moon, at the center.

ANTHEM: *Pheng Sat Lao (Hymn of the Lao People).*

MONETARY UNIT: The new kip (κ) is a paper currency of 100 at (cents). There are notes of 10, 20, 50, 200, and 500 new kip. κ1 = $0.0029 (or $1 = κ350).

WEIGHTS AND MEASURES: The metric system is the legal standard, but older local units are also used.

HOLIDAYS: Anniversary of the Founding of the Lao People's Democratic Republic, 2 December. To maintain production, the government generally reschedules on weekends such traditional festivals as the Lao New Year (April); Boun Bang-fai (Rocket Festival), the celebration of the birth, enlightenment, and death of the Buddha (May); Boun Khao Watsa, the beginning of a period of fasting and meditation lasting through the rainy season (July); Boun Ok Watsa (Water Holiday), a celebration of the end of the period of fasting and meditation (October); and That Luang, a pagoda pilgrimage holiday (November).

TIME: 7 PM = noon GMT.

¹LOCATION, SIZE, AND EXTENT

Laos is a landlocked country on the Indochinese Peninsula near the eastern extremity of mainland Southeast Asia. Laos occupies an area of 236,800 sq km (91,429 sq mi), extending 1,162 km (722 mi) SSE–NNW and 478 km (297 mi) ENE–WSW. Comparatively, the area occupied by Laos is slightly larger than the state of Utah. It is bordered on the N by China, on the E and SE by Viet Nam, on the S by Cambodia, on the W by Thailand, and on the NW by Myanmar, with a total boundary length of 5,083 km (3,158 mi).

The capital of Laos, Vientiane, is located along the country's western boundary.

²TOPOGRAPHY

The terrain is rugged and mountainous, especially in the north and in the Annam Cordillera, along the border with Vietnam. The mountains reach heights of more than 2,700 m (8,860 ft), with Pou Bia, the highest point in Laos, rising to 2,817 m (9,242 ft) in the north-central part of the country. Only three passes cross the mountains to link Laos with Viet Nam. The Tran Ninh Plateau, in the northeast, rises to between 1,020 m and 1,370 m (3,350–4,500 ft), and the fertile Bolovens Plateau, in the south, reaches a height of about 1,070 m (3,500 ft). Broad alluvial plains, where much of the rice crop is grown, are found only in the south and west along the Mekong River and its tributaries. Of these, the Vientiane plain is the most extensive.

Except for a relatively small area east of the main divide, Laos is drained by the Mekong and its tributaries. The Mekong flows in a broad valley along the border with Thailand and through Laos for 1,805 km (1,122 mi). In its low-water phase, it is almost dry, but it rises more than 6 m (20 ft) during the monsoon period. The river is wide, but except for a navigable stretch between Vientiane and Savannakhét, rapids are numerous. Below Savannakhét and at the extreme south there are large rapids and waterfalls. Floods are common in the rainy season.

³CLIMATE

Laos has a tropical monsoon climate with two main seasons, rainy and dry, each of five months' duration. From May through September, rainfall averages 28 to 30 cm (11–12 in) a month, but from November through March the monthly average is only about 1.3 cm (0.5 in). Humidity is high throughout the year, even during the season of drought. Average daily temperatures in Vientiane range from 14° to 28°C (57–82°F) in January, the coolest month, and from 23° to 34°C (73–93°F) in April, the hottest.

⁴FLORA AND FAUNA

Nearly two-thirds of Laos is covered by forest or thick jungle. The forests of southernmost Laos are an extension of the Kampuchean type of vegetation, while the highland forests of the north, consisting of prairies interspersed with thickets, resemble central Viet Nam. Bamboo, lianas, rattan, and palms are found throughout Laos.

Roaming the forests are panthers and a dwindling number of tigers, elephants, and leopards. The elephant, until 1975 depicted on the national flag as the traditional symbol of Lao royalty, has been used throughout history as a beast of burden. A local breed of water buffalo also is universally used as a draft animal. Reptiles include cobras, geckos, kraits, and Siamese crocodiles. There are many varieties of birds, fish, and insects.

⁵ENVIRONMENT

Soil erosion, deforestation, and flood control are the principal environmental concerns in Laos, there being only minimal industrial development. The government seeks to control erosion by discouraging the traditional slash-and-burn agriculture practiced by many mountain tribes, and by resettling the tribes in permanent villages. Reforestation projects have been promoted by the government as a means of increasing lumber exports and of restoring valuable hardwoods to logged-out forest areas. Each person was required to plant five trees in the course of the 1981–85 economic plan. In 1986, the government prohibited the cutting of 15 different varieties of trees. At that time, forests were reportedly being consumed at a rate of 300,000 hectares (741,000 acres) per year. Laos has 64.8 cubic miles of water with 82% used in farming activity and 10% used for industrial purposes. Seventy-five percent of the rural population and fifty-three percent of the city dwellers do not have pure water. The nation's water supply has begun to decrease due to a combination of factors, among them the loss of forest land, uncontrolled agricultural practices, flooding and drought. Pollution from fires, dust and cars is also becoming a national problem. Laos contributes .7% of the world's total gas emissions.

In 1994, 23 of Laos' mammal species and 18% of bird species are threatened. Three of the nations plant species are endangered. As of 1987, endangered species in Laos included the douc langur, three species of gibbon (pileated, crowned, and capped), tiger, Asian elephant, Sumatran rhinoceros, Javan rhinoceros, Thailand brow-antlered deer, kouprey, and Siamese crocodile.

6POPULATION

The first national census was taken, with the assistance of the UNFPA, in 1985, when the population was 3,584,803, up 21% from 1970 estimates. It was estimated at 4,469,000 in 1992. A population of 5,592,000 was projected for the year 2000, assuming a crude birthrate of 40.2 per 1,000 population, a crude death rate of 13.1, and a net natural increase of 27.1. An estimated 43.6% of the population was less than 15 years of age in 1990.

The overall density in 1992 was a sparse 19 per sq km (49 per sq mi), but the population is unevenly spread, with the greatest concentration in the Mekong Valley. More than 80% of the population was rural in 1990, living in some 9,000 villages. The capital, Vientiane, had a metropolitan population of about 442,000 in 1990. Other large towns, all on or near the Mekong and its tributaries, are Savannakhét, Pakxé, Luangphrabang (the former royal capital), Xaignabouri, and Ban Houayxay.

7MIGRATION

There has been only limited population movement into Laos in modern times. During the late 1960s and early 1970s, under pressure of combat operations, Black Tai tribesmen moved southward into the Mekong Valley. Since May 1975, thousands of Laotian refugees have fled to Thailand or elsewhere. All told, between 1975 and 1986, at least 300,000 Laotians—including Hmong, Yao, and other mountain tribesmen—crossed into Thailand. At the end of 1992, some 40,900 were living in UN-sponsored camps. In July 1985, Thailand began a screening process to distinguish between refugees and economic migrants, with the intention of forcibly repatriating the latter group. Laos has not cooperated with this policy. By the end of 1993, nearly 19,000 refugees had voluntarily returned under UN auspices, and some 30,000 others had returned on their own.

Urban migration accelerated in the three decades of war before 1975. Resettlement of these migrants, amounting to one-third of the population, began in 1975, with repopulation of abandoned areas an early priority.

8ETHNIC GROUPS

There are officially 68 ethnic groups in Laos. About 50–60% of all Laotians are Lao-lum, or lowland Lao, a people related to the people of Thailand; thought to have migrated to Laos from southwestern China in the 8th century, the Lao-lum are concentrated in the lowlands along the Mekong. On the hillsides live the Lao-theung, or slope dwellers, a diverse group dominated by the Lao-tai (with various subgroups, including the Black Tai), who are ethnically related to the Lao-lum. They form about one-third of the population. At higher altitudes are the Lao-soung, or mountain dwellers, a diverse group of ethnic minorities of mainly Malayo-Polynesian or proto-Malay backgrounds. They constitute about one-tenth of the population. Important among the Lao-soung, and more prosperous than most Lao because of the opium poppies they grow, are the Hmong (Meo), a people of Tibeto-Burman origin who supported the American presence until 1975 and, because of their continuing insurgency, became the targets of harassment by government and Vietnamese troops. Other important upland tribes, all with customs and religions considerably different from those of the lowland Lao, are the Ho, Kha, Kho, and Man (Yao).

9LANGUAGES

Lao, the official language and the language of the ethnic Lao, is closely related to the language of Thailand. It is monosyllabic and tonal and contains words borrowed from Sanskrit, Pali, and Farsi. Pali, a Sanskritic language, is used among the Buddhist priesthood.

Other groups speak the Tibeto–Burman, Non-Khmer, or Miao–Yao languages. French, formerly the principal language of government and higher education, has been largely replaced by Lao.

10RELIGIONS

Religious activity was discouraged by the state from 1976 to 1979, but freedom of religion has been legally guaranteed since the constitution of 1991. Almost two-thirds of all Laotians, including nearly all the Lao-lum, are adherents of Hinayana Buddhism, a large part of whose daily life is shaped by its rituals and precepts. Buddhist temples, found in every village, town, and city, serve as intellectual as well as religious centers. Vientiane and Luangprabang have been called cities of thousands of temples. More than 70 pagodas were built in Vientiane alone in the 16th century, including the famous Wat Phra Keo and That Luang. Despite the major role that Buddhism, its temples, and its priests have played in Laotian life, the average lowland Lao regulates a large part of daily activities in accordance with animistic concepts. Certain spirits (phi) are believed to have great power over human destiny and to be present throughout the material world, as well as within nonmaterial realms. Thus, each of the four universal elements (earth, sky, fire, and water) has its special phi; every road, stream, village, house, and person has a particular phi; forests and jungles are inhabited by phi. Evil phi can cause disease and must be propitiated by sacrifices.

About 34% of Laotians, including the upland tribes, are almost exclusively animists, although influenced by Buddhism to some extent. Christian missionaries have been active in Laos, but less than 2% of all Laotians profess the religion.

11TRANSPORTATION

Lack of adequate transportation facilities continues to be a major deterrent to economic progress. Of the approximately 27,530 km (17,107 mi) of roads, only 7% are bituminized; many are impassable in the rainy season. Only a single major road connects the northern and southern regions. Most of the roads were damaged by US bombing in the Viet Nam war, but the main links with Viet Nam (notably Highway 9, from Savannakhét to the Vietnamese port of Da Nang, and Highways 7 and 13, from Vientiane and Savannakhét to the Vietnamese port of Vinh and Ho Chi Minh City, respectively) are being rebuilt with Vietnamese aid. Under the 1981–85 economic plan, 844 km (524 mi) of roads were built or improved. The 1986–90 plan projected an additional 1,500 km

(932 mi), 50% of which was to be asphalted. As of 1992, there were only some 17,000 motor vehicles registered, including 8,500 passenger cars. There are no railroads in Laos, although construction of a railway parallel to Highway 9 was proposed in 1980.

Major cities in Laos are connected by air services operated by state-run Lao Aviation, founded with Soviet aid in 1976. There are 14 airfields of more than 1,220 m (4,000 ft) and another 43 airfields of lesser length, 10 of which are unused. Vientiane has the only international airport.

Landlocked Laos's only water-transport link with the outside world is via the Mekong, which forms a large part of the border with Thailand and flows through Cambodia and Viet Nam into the South China Sea. The Mekong is navigable for small transport craft and, with its tributaries in Laos, forms a 4,587-km (2,850-mi) inland waterway system, although rapids make necessary the transshipment of cargo. To lessen dependence on Thailand, Laos in 1977 signed an agreement with Viet Nam whereby the Vietnamese port of Da Nang would replace Bangkok as the chief outlet for Laos. Construction of a 395-km (245-mi) oil pipeline between Vientiane and Da Nang, intended to strengthen the economic bond with Viet Nam, was begun in 1981.

12HISTORY

Although archaeological evidence indicates that settlers along the Mekong had learned agriculture, metallurgy, and pottery making by 3000 BC; little is known about the early history of the land that today bears the name of Laos. The lowland Lao are believed to be the descendants of Thai tribes that were pushed southward in the 8th century. According to tradition, the kingdom called Lan Xang ("a million elephants") was established in 756 by King Thao Khoun Lo. In 1353, it was reunified by Fa-Ngoum, who had been raised at the court of Angkor in Kampuchea and returned with a force of Khmer troops. He is also credited with the introduction of Hinayana Buddhism into Laos. Lan Xang waged intermittent wars with the Khmers, Burmese, Vietnamese, and Thai and developed an effective administrative system, an elaborate military organization, and an active commerce with neighboring countries. In 1707, internal dissensions brought about a split of Lan Xang into two kingdoms, Luangphrabang in the north (present-day upper Laos) and Vientiane in the south (lower Laos). Strong neighboring states took advantage of this split to invade the region. Vientiane was overrun and annexed by Siam (Thailand) in 1828, while Luangprabang became a vassal of both the Chinese and the Vietnamese. In 1893, France, which had already established a protectorate over what is now central and northern Viet Nam, extended its control to both Vientiane and Luangprabang, and Laos was ruled by France as part of Indochina. Although French control over Luangprabang took the nominal form of a protectorate, the French colonial administration directly ruled the rest of Laos, legal justification being ultimately provided in the Lao-French convention of 1917.

During World War II, Laos was occupied by Japan. After the Japanese proclaimed on 10 March 1945 that "the colonial status of Indochina has ended," the king of Luangphrabang, Sisavang Vong, was compelled to issue a declaration of independence. The nationalist Free Lao (Lao Issarak) movement deposed the monarch soon after, but French forces reoccupied Laos, and on 27 August 1946, France concluded an agreement establishing him as king of Laos and reimposing French domination over the country. In May 1947, the king established a constitution providing for a democratic government. On 19 July 1949, Laos nominally became an independent sovereign state within the French Union. Additional conventions transferring full sovereignty to Laos were signed on 6 February 1950 and on 22 October 1953. All special economic ties with France and the other Indochinese states were abolished by the Paris pacts of 29 December 1954. In the meantime, Vietnamese Communist (Viet-Minh) forces had invaded

LOCATION: 100° to 107°E; 13°40′ to 22°40′N. **BOUNDARY LENGTHS:** China, 425 km (264 mi); Viet Nam, 1,555 km (966 mi); Cambodia, 541 km (336 mi); Thailand, 1,754 km (1,090 mi); Myanmar, 238 km (148 mi). **TERRITORIAL SEA LIMIT:** 12 mi.

Laos in the spring of 1953. A Laotian Communist movement, the Pathet Lao (Lao State), created on 13 August 1950 and led by Prince Souphanouvong, collaborated with the Viet-Minh during its Laotian offensive. Under the Geneva cease-fire of 21 July 1954, all Viet-Minh and most French troops were to withdraw, and the Pathet Lao was to pull back to two northern provinces, pending reunification talks with the national government under the leadership of Souvanna Phouma (Souphanouvong's half-brother). The negotiations were completed on 2 November 1957, and the Pathet Lao transformed itself into a legal political party called the National Political Front (Neo Lao Hak Xat). However, a political swing to the right that led to the ouster of Souvanna Phouma as prime minister, coupled with the refusal of the Pathet Lao forces to integrate into the Royal Lao Army, led to a renewal of fighting in May 1959.

A bloodless right-wing coup in January 1960 was answered in August by a coup led by paratroops, under the command of Capt. Kong Le; in the ensuing turmoil, Souvanna Phouma returned to power. After a three-day artillery battle that destroyed much of Vientiane, right-wing military elements under Gen. Phoumi Nosavan and Prince Boun Oum occupied the capital on 11 December. A new right-wing government under Prince Boun Oum was established, but further military reverses, despite a heavy influx of US aid and advisers, caused the government to ask for a cease-fire in May 1961. An international conference assembled in Geneva to guarantee the cease-fire. All three Laotian political factions agreed on 11 June 1962 to accept a coalition government, with Souvanna Phouma as prime minister. On 23 July, the powers assembled at Geneva signed an agreement on the independence and neutrality of Laos, which provided for the evacuation of all foreign forces by 7 October. The US announced full compliance, under supervision of the International Control Commission (ICC), set up in 1954. Communist forces were not withdrawn. Fighting resumed in the spring of 1963, and Laos was steadily drawn into the role of a main theater in the escalating Viet Nam war. The Laotian segment of the so-called Ho Chi Minh trail emerged as a vital route for troops and supplies moving south from the Democratic Republic of Viet Nam (DRV), also known as North Viet Nam, and was the target for heavy and persistent US bombing raids. While the Vientiane government was heavily bolstered by US military and economic support, the Pathet Lao received key support from the DRV, which was reported to have 20,000 troops stationed in Laos by 1974. Efforts to negotiate a settlement in Laos resumed with US backing in 1971, but a settlement was not concluded until February 1973, a month after a Viet Nam peace agreement was signed in Paris. On 5 April 1974, a new coalition government was set up, with equal representation for Pathet Lao and non-Communist elements. Souvanna Phouma, 73 years old and in failing health, stayed on as prime minister, while Prince Souphanouvong was brought closer to the center of political authority as head of the newly created Joint National Political Council.

The Pathet Lao had by this time asserted its control over three-fourths of the national territory. Following the fall of the US-backed regimes in Viet Nam and Cambodia in April 1975, the Laotian Communists embarked on a campaign to achieve complete military and political supremacy in Laos. On 23 August, Vientiane was declared "liberated" by the Pathet Lao, whose effective control of Laos was thereby secured. On 2 December 1975, the Lao People's Democratic Republic (LPDR) was established, with Prince Souphanouvong as president and Kaysone Phomvihan as prime minister. King Savang Vatthana abdicated his throne, ending the monarchy that had survived in Laos for 622 years. Elections for a new National Assembly were called for April 1976; however, voting was put off indefinitely, amid reports of civil unrest and sabotage. A Supreme People's Council was convened, meanwhile, with Prince Souphanouvong as chairman, and was charged with the task, still unfinished in 1987, of drafting a new constitution.

During the late 1970s, the Communists moved to consolidate their control and socialize the economy. Private trade was banned, factories were nationalized, and forcible collectivization of agriculture was initiated. "Reeducation" camps for an estimated 40,000 former royalists and military leaders were established in remote areas; as of 1986, the government maintained that almost all the inmates had been released, but Amnesty International claimed that about 5,000 remained. A 25-year friendship treaty with Viet Nam, signed in July 1977, led to closer relations with that country (already signaled by the continued presence in Laos of Vietnamese troops) and with the former USSR, and also to the subsequent dismissal from Laos of all Chinese technicians and advisers. China, for its part, began to give support and training to several small antigovernment guerrilla groups. With the economy in 1979 near collapse, in part because of severe drought in 1977 and flooding in 1978, the Laotian government slowed the process of socialization and announced a return to private enterprise and a readiness to accept aid from the non-Communist world. Throughout the 1980s armed opposition to the Government persisted, particularly from the Hmong (Meo) hill tribe rebels. At the Fourth Party Congress of the Lao People's Revolutionary Party (LPRP), in December 1986, a "new economic management mechanism" (NEM) was set up, aiming at granting increased autonomy in the management of formerly state-run enterprises to the private sector.

In 1988 the Lao national legislature, the Supreme People's Assembly (SPA), adopted new election laws and the first elections since the formation of the LPDR in 1975 were held. Local and provincial elections were held in 1988, and on 27 March 1989 national elections took place for an enlarged Supreme People's Assembly. In March 1991 the Fifth Party Congress of the LPRP changed Kaysone Phomvihan's title to President, elected a new 11-member politburo, pledged to continue economic reforms in line with free-market principles while denying the need for political pluralism, and changed the national motto by substituting the words "democracy and prosperity" for "socialism". The newly elected SPA drafted a constitution adopted on 14 August 1991. The constitution provided for a national assembly functioning on principles of "democratic centralism," established the LPRP as the political systems "leading organ", created a presidency with executive powers, and mandated a market-oriented economy with rights of private ownership. President Kaysone Phomvihan, longtime LPRP leader, died on 21 November 1992. A special session of parliament on 24 November 1992 elected hard-line Communist Nouhak Phoumsavan as the next president. Gen. Khamtai Suphandon, who had been prime minister since 15 August 1991, remained in that post. National Assembly elections were held in December 1992. One day before these elections, three former officials who called for a multiparty democracy and had been detained in 1990 were sentenced to 14 years imprisonment. The National Assembly convened in February 1993 and approved government reorganization designed to improve public administration. In April 1994 the first international bridge, the Mittaphap (Friendship) Bridge, linking Laos and Thailand across the Mekong River, was opened. The 1,174-m bridge built and paid for by Australia is part of a plan for an Asian super-highway to facilitate travel from Singapore to Shanghai by 1997. The most immediate benefits are anticipated by the tourism industry and as a spur to real estate investment.

Laos has actively improved its already "special relations" with Viet Nam and Cambodia, while seeking to improve relations with Thailand, the People's Republic of China (PRC), and the US. A joint communique providing for the co-operative development of the Mekong River was signed by Laos, Thailand, Viet Nam, and Cambodia in 1993. Laos and the People's Republic of China have restored full diplomatic relations (1989), resolved border disputes (1991–92), and reached agreement on the repatriation of Lao refugees in China (1993). Mutual suspicions, characterizing the relationship between Laos and Thailand, improved with agreements to withdraw troops and resolve border disputes, and by agreements between the United Nations High Commissioner for Refugees (UNHCR) to repatriate or resettle nearly 60,000 Lao refugees in Thailand by the end of 1994. During 1992–93 Laos cooperated with the US in recovering the remains of US soldiers missing in action in Laos since the Viet Nam war and reaffirmed its intent to cooperate in the suppression of drug-trafficking. The US Department of State *Country Reports on Human Rights Practices for 1993* notes that despite constitutional guarantees, freedom of speech, assembly and religion is restricted and that extrajudicial killings occur in the context of continuing insurgency, primarily among Hmong tribesmen.

¹³GOVERNMENT

Under the constitution of 1947 (as subsequently amended), Laos was a parliamentary democracy with a king as the nominal chief executive. The monarch was assisted by a prime minister (or president of the Council of Ministers), who was the executive and legislative leader in fact. The prime minister and cabinet were responsible to the National Assembly, the main repository of legislative authority, whose 59 members were elected every five years by universal adult suffrage. With the establishment of the Lao

People's Democratic Republic in December 1975, governmental authority passed to a national congress made up of 264 delegates elected by newly appointed local authorities. The congress in turn appointed a 45-member Supreme People's Council to draw up a new constitution. Pending the completion of this task effective power rested with Kaysone Phomvihan, a longtime Pathet Lao leader who headed the government as chairman of the Council of Ministers and was also secretary-general of the Lao People's Revolutionary (Communist) Party.

Prince Souphanouvong, the head of state and president of the Supreme People's Council since 1975, left office in October 1986 because of poor health. He was replaced first by Phoumi Vongvichit, a former vice-chairman of the Council of Ministers, and later by Sisomphon Lovansay, a former vice-president of the Supreme People's Council. The Lao national legislature, the Supreme People's Assembly (SPA), adopted new election laws in 1988, and the first national elections under the current government took place in March 1989 (local elections were held in 1988). Kaysone Phomvihan was elected President and Khamtai Siphandone was named Prime Minister. The newly elected SPA set out to draft a constitution, which was finished in mid-1990, and adopted on 14 August 1991 by the SPA. The executive branch consists of the president, prime minister and two deputy prime ministers, and the Council of Ministers (cabinet) which are appointed by the President with the approval of the National Assembly. The legislative branch is the National Assembly which is elected by universal suffrage for a period of five years. The judicial branch is the Supreme People's Court Leaders. The constitution calls for a strong legislature elected by secret ballot, but most political power continues to rest with the party-dominated council of ministers.

14POLITICAL PARTIES

Elections to the National Assembly were first held in 1947. In the elections of 4 May 1958, the Pathet Lao's newly organized National Political Front (Neo Lao Hak Xat) won 9 of the 21 seats in contention; 4 were won by the Santiphab faction, a neutralist group allied with them, and 8 were obtained by the Nationalist and Independent parties. After the elections, the Nationalists and Independents combined to establish a new political party, the Rally of the Lao People (Lao Luam Lao), which held 36 of the 59 Assembly seats. The remaining 23 seats were divided among the National Political Front (9), the Santiphab grouping (7), the Democrats (3), the National Union (2), and unaffiliated deputies (2). The leaders of the Rally, upon formation of that party, announced its purpose to be the defense of Laos against "an extremist ideology contrary to the customs and traditions of the Lao country" and the establishment of true unity and independence of the nation against "subversion from within and without." The Front then and later called for a reduction in the size of the armed forces and of US military aid. In December 1959, because of emergency conditions, election of new Assembly deputies was postponed until April 1960. When the balloting was finally held, the opposition Committee for the Defense of the National Interests won a landslide victory. The Committee leader, Phoumi Nosavan, then formed a new political party, the Social Democrats (Paxa Sangkhom).

In August 1960, a coup led by Kong Le brought down the government. After a period of struggle, Souvanna Phouma, who had earlier established the Neutralist Party (Lao Pen Kang) in order to build a broader popular following, became prime minister on 11 June 1962. In his 19-man cabinet, 4 posts were held by right-wing politicians, 11 by Neutralists, and 4 others by Pathet Lao adherents. The National Assembly came to the end of its five-year term in 1965. Political instability prevented the holding of national elections, and a provisional assembly was convened to amend the constitution so as to provide a means for maintaining

the legislature. The result was a general election held on 18 July, with the franchise limited to civil servants, teachers, merchants, and village headmen. The new National Assembly was convened on 16 August, with the Neutralists retaining 13 seats, the Social Democrats 11, the Rally 8, and various independents 27. The endorsement gained in the limited polling of 1965 was not sufficient to sustain Prime Minister Souvanna Phouma for long, and new voting—the first real and effective election in a decade—took place on 1 January 1967. About 60% of 800,000 eligible voters went to the polls in 1967, despite the Pathet Lao charge that the balloting was illegal. Souvanna Phouma's United Front took 32 of 59 seats in the National Assembly voting.

In the last years of the constitutional monarchy, the gulf between the Pathet Lao and the enclave of rightists and neutralists that held governmental power widened appreciably. The pressures of war—both the civil strife within Laos and the larger conflict pressed by the external forces of the US and the DRV—had thwarted the effectiveness of normal political processes. General elections held on 2 January 1972 were confined to government-controlled areas, with representatives for the Pathet Lao provinces elected by refugees from those regions. Despite the narrow range of political choices available to voters, only 20 of the 60 National Assembly deputies were reelected, reflecting a growing uneasiness both with the war and with the increasing evidence of corrupt practices among government officials. Despite right-wing pressures from within the National Assembly, Souvanna Phouma—whose neutralist policy was favored by both the US and the DRV—retained the position of prime minister. The withdrawal of US military support for the Thieu regime in the Republic of Viet Nam (South Viet Nam) was followed, in April 1974, by the creation of a new coalition in Vientiane that gave equal political footing to the Pathet Lao. The National Assembly, which had become little more than a forum for disputes among right-wing factions, was dissolved by King Savang Vatthana on 13 April 1975, an act that signaled the end of domestic political opposition to the inexorable progress of the Pathet Lao.

The formation of the Lao People's Democratic Republic in December 1975 effectively established the Communist Lao People's Revolutionary Party (Phak Pasason Pativat Lao—PPPL), the political incarnation of the Pathet Lao movement, as the sole political force in Laos. Kaysone Phomvihan, general secretary of the PPPL, was named head of government, and Prince Souphanouvong head of state. The PPPL plays the leading role in the Lao Front for National Reconstruction, which seeks to promote socialism and national solidarity. The Third Party Congress of the PPPL, and the first since the party assumed control, was held in Vientiane in April 1982. The congress, whose 228 delegates represented a party membership of 35,000, elected an enlarged Central Committee with 49 full and 6 alternate members. The Central Committee reelected Kaysone as general secretary. The Fourth Party Congress, held in Vientiane in December 1986, established the "new economic management mechanism." The most active dissident group is the Lao Socialist Party, reportedly based in China and drawing heavy support from the Hmong (Meo) hill tribes. Several governments-in-exile have been formed by former ministers of pre-1975 regimes.

In 1994 the only legal political party was the communist Lao People's Revolutionary Party (LPRP) which includes the Lao Front for National Construction (LFNC); other parties are moribund. Gen. Khamtai Siphandon was LPRP party president.

15LOCAL GOVERNMENT

Laos consists of 16 provinces (khoueng) and the municipality of Vientiane. The provinces are subdivided into districts (muong), townships (tasseng), and villages (ban). The president appoints provincial governors and mayors of municipalities. The prime minister appoints deputy provincial governors and deputy mayors and district chiefs. Since 1975, local administration has been restructured, with elected people's committees in the villages functioning as basic units. Both suffrage and candidacy are open to citizens 18 and over. Village heads administer at the village level.

16JUDICIAL SYSTEM

The 1991 Constitution provides for freedom of speech, assembly, and religion. The government is now in the process of developing a codified body of laws. Under the Constitution contains provisions designed to guarantee the independence of judges and prosecutors, but in practice the courts appear to be subject to influence of other government agencies. Some courts of first instance are still being established at the district level. There is a Central Supreme Court in Vientiane. In 1993 the government began publishing an official gazette in which all laws and regulations are disseminated.

17ARMED FORCES

In 1993 the armed forces in Laos numbered 37,000, with 18 months of military service compulsory for all males. A total of 33,000 Laotians served in the army. The navy, equipped with 50 patrol craft and boats, enlisted 500. The air force, with 3,500 men, was equipped with antiaircraft missiles and 31 combat aircraft. The village self-defense force numbers 100,000. Weapons are a mix of American and Russian arms. The armed forces face about 2,000 rebels. No reliable fiscal data are available.

18INTERNATIONAL COOPERATION

Laos, a UN member since 14 December 1955, belongs to ESCAP and all the nonregional specialized agencies except IAEA, IFC, IMO, and WIPO. The nation participates in the Asian Development Bank and G-77 and is a signatory to the Law of the Sea. Since 1961, it has been a member of the nonaligned movement. Laos's main diplomatic, economic, and military allies have been Viet Nam and the former USSR. In 1977, Laos signed a 20-year treaty of cooperation with Viet Nam. A four-year agreement with Viet Nam and Cambodia that pledged cooperation in regulating forestry, processing agricultural goods, producing consumer goods, and increasing trade was signed in 1986.

19ECONOMY

One of the world's poorest and least-developed nations, Laos is overwhelmingly agricultural, with some 70–80% of the population engaged in farming. Because industrialization is minimal, Laos imports nearly all the manufactured products it requires. Distribution of imports is limited almost entirely to Vientiane and a few other towns, and even there consumption is low. The hostilities of the 1960s and 1970s badly disrupted the economy, forcing the country to depend on imports from Thailand to supplement its daily rice requirements. With the curtailment of hostilities in 1975, the development of a unified political structure offered an immediate advantage. The government began in late 1975 to pursue in earnest a variety of projects to repair and improve the infrastructure and make use of the country's ample mineral, lumber, and hydroelectric resources. During 1978–80, the government gave priority to postwar reconstruction, collectivization of agriculture, and improvements in rice production. The first five-year plan (1981–85) had among its goals achievement of self-sufficiency in food and a doubling of industrial activity by 1985. The second five-year plan (1986–90) had similar overall objectives, but the specific strategies were designed to increase savings and reduce waste. Progress was hindered by shortages of capital and skilled workers, inefficient management, and inadequate equipment and spare parts. The third five-year plan (1991–95) continues to emphasize infrastructure improvement, promote export growth, and encourage import-substitution industries in order to redress the balance-of-payments deficit.

20INCOME

In 1992, Laos' GNP was $1,104 million at current prices, or $250 per capita. For the period 1985–92 the average inflation rate was 30.1%, resulting in a real growth rate in per capita GNP of 1.8%.

21LABOR

The estimated labor force is about 1.5 million. In the absence of additional data, it is estimated that 85% are subsistence farmers, with most of the remainder in the public sector. Since late 1975, labor has been organized into a single Federation of Lao Trade Unions (FLTU). In November 1990, the government permitted the formation of labor unions in private enterprises as long as they conform to the policies of the FLTU.

22AGRICULTURE

In 1991, Laos's sown-field area totaled 912,000 hectares (2,254,000 acres), or less than 4% of the country's total area. Agriculture accounts for 60% of production and 80% of employment. The main crop is rice, almost entirely of the glutinous variety. Except in northern Laos, where some farmers grow dry rice in forest clearings or on hillsides, most Lao are wet-rice farmers. The total area of rice plantings in 1992 was estimated at 593,000 hectares (1,465,000 acres), down from 739,000 hectares (1,826,000 acres) in 1981. Yields, which are relatively low, could be raised substantially through wider use of irrigation and fertilizers. Production, which averaged 609,000 tons annually during 1961–65, rose to 1,502,000 tons in 1992, so that self-sufficiency in rice was reportedly attained. Less important crops include corn (favored by some upland tribes and stressed by the government as a means of increasing livestock production), manioc, peanuts, and soybeans. The main commercial crops, emphasized by the government as part of its export drive, are coffee, cotton, and tobacco. Coffee exports in 1991 amounted to $2 million, or 2.6% of total exports. Also grown are cardamom, tea, ramie, hemp, sugar, bananas, and pineapples. The mountain peoples have been known to grow large quantities of opium poppies, sold to dealers in the plains. In 1986, the government invited the UN International Narcotics Control Board to visit Laos, reportedly to solicit assistance for a program to encourage the substitution of other cash crops.

23ANIMAL HUSBANDRY

Cattle raising is important, especially in the southern plains and in the valleys of the Noy, Banghiang, and Don rivers. Much of the livestock population was killed in the final stages of the civil war that ended in 1975. As of 1992, livestock included an estimated 1,131,000 buffalo, 993,000 head of cattle, 1,561,000 hogs, and 9,000,000 chickens. Livestock products in 1992 included 58,000 tons of pork, 25,000 tons of buffalo meat, 10,000 tons of beef and veal, and 35,000 tons of eggs.

24FISHING

Edible fish, found in the Mekong and other rivers, constitutes the main source of protein in the Laotian diet. The prize catch is the pa beuk, weighing 205 kg (450 lb) or more. Despite the abundance of fish and their important contribution to the Laotian subsistence economy, there has been no systematic commercial fishery development. The total catch in 1991 was 20,000 tons.

25FORESTRY

Timber is a major resource and one of Laos's most valuable exports. About 55% of the total area is forested, and about half of the forested area is commercially exploitable. The principal timber-producing areas are around Champasak, Savannakhét, Khammouan, and Vientiane. Muang Paklay, in western Laos, is noted for its teak. Exploitation is easiest in areas near the

Mekong River, which facilitates transportation. Elephants and oxen are used in most forestry operations. Aside from timber, firewood, and charcoal, forestry products include benzoin and benzoin bark, bamboo, copra, kapok, palm oil, rattan, various resins, and sticklac. Production of roundwood totaled an estimated 4.3 million cu m in 1991; over 90% of the annual output goes for fuel. Sawnwood output in 1991 was about 71,000 cu m.

26MINING

Although much of the country remains unprospected, the nature of the terrain has led to ardent speculation about the nation's mineral resources. Such hopes were in part borne out by the discovery, in 1974, of a potash-rich sylvite field in the middle of the Vientiane plain; the deposit, which covers at least 30 sq km (12 sq mi), was thought to hold sylvite in quantities of 10 million cu m per sq km. Sylvite can be used for the manufacture of fertilizers, soap, pharmaceuticals, and pesticides.

Tin production totaled 300 tons of tin concentrate in 1991, down from 450 tons in 1987. Important iron deposits, with reserves of 68% ore estimated at 11 billion tons, have been discovered on the Plain of Jars near Xiangkhoang. A substantial deposit of low-grade anthracite coal has been found at Saravan. Other mineral resources known to exist in Laos are magnesium, rock salt, antimony, copper, gold, gypsum, lead, manganese, pyrites, sulfur, and precious stones. Sapphire production went from 8,000 carats in 1987 to 35,000 carats in 1991. Tungsten and copper deposits and gold-bearing alluvials produce a limited income for the local population but have not been exploited by modern industrial methods.

27ENERGY AND POWER

In 1991, Laos had a net installed electrical generating capacity of 256,000 kw, up from 225,000 kw in 1988. Production of electricity in 1991 totaled 972 million kwh (up from 532 million in 1988), of which 95% was hydropower and 5% came from conventional thermal sources. The nation has an estimated hydroelectric potential of 12,500,000 kw, most of which is undeveloped. The largest power project is the Nam Ngum Dam, located on the Mekong 72 km (45 mi) from Vientiane. Construction began in 1969, with the first stage completed in 1971 and the second stage in 1978. Annual output at Nam Ngum is around 900 million kwh, with about 90% of the electricity produced being supplied to Thailand. In 1991, Laos exported two-thirds of its electrical production. An additional 3,000 kw of capacity comes from several smaller hydroelectric facilities, and about 14,000 kw is provided by diesel-powered generators throughout Laos.

28INDUSTRY

Industrial development is rudimentary. There are some small mining operations, charcoal ovens, a cement plant, a few brick works, carpenter shops, a tobacco factory, rice mills, some furniture factories, and more than two dozen sawmills. Industrialization plans center on cotton spinning, brewing, coffee and tea processing, and plywood milling. New resource developments, including the Nam Ngum hydroelectric project and the Vientiane sylvite field, should aid industrial growth. Handicrafts account for an important part of the income of many Laotians. Some villages or areas specialize in certain types of products: silk fabrics, baskets, lacquerware, and gold and silver jewelry and ornaments. Bricks, pottery, iron products, and distilled beverages are made in individual villages.

In 1992 the incipient industrial sector contributed to 17 % of GDP. Industrial activity in 1992 was based predominantly on hydroelectric production accounting for 15 % of GDP. Based on its water resources the potential for electricity generation has led to Laos' being dubbed the "battery" of Southeast Asia. Environmental degradation from mining and illegal logging has already

impacted decisions to construct dams for hydropower. Hydrocarbon exploration undertaken in Laos by three western oil companies has not yet led to commercially exploitable discoveries. Manufacturing is largely confined to the processing of agricultural and forestry products. Laos is not subject to EC quotas for garments, and over 29 factories were set up by 1992. In 1992 Laos' leading foreign exchange earner was garments, as opposed to forestry products, which were the leading export in 1991.

29SCIENCE AND TECHNOLOGY

Like many developing nations, Laos depends primarily on external expertise in science and technology. In the mid-1980s, an estimated 10,000 Laotians were receiving technical training overseas. Sisavangvong University has faculties of agriculture and medicine, and technical colleges in Luangphrabang, Savannakhét, and Champasak.

30DOMESTIC TRADE

Before the Pathet Lao came to power, there was a growing market in Laos for capital and consumer goods. Vientiane was the wholesale distributing point for much of the country. In late 1975, private trade was banned and many small traders and businessmen—including Chinese, Japanese, Pakistani, Thai, and Vietnamese—fled the country. The new government subsequently made it clear that the trend toward consumerism would be reversed in favor of a production-oriented society. The Pathet Lao entered directly into the distribution and sale of essential commodities, such as rice and sugar, and prices were brought under control. In 1979, however, the ban on private trade was lifted, and consumer items, which had all but disappeared from circulation, were once again available. In the countryside, barter replaces money as the principal method of exchange. Markets are held at regular intervals, generally one day a week, at central villages or smaller towns. Once or twice a year, lowland farmers barter cloth and handicraft products with the mountain peoples for cereals, deer and rhinoceros horns, and ivory. Certain items recognized as media of exchange include tea, opium, tobacco, salt, silver, and gold.

The New Economic Mechanism (NEM), a set of economic reforms instituted in 1986 across all sectors of the economy, has begun to demonstrate results in establishing a market-based economy. The government freed the market price of rice and other food staples in 1986, increasing agricultural output despite severe climatic conditions. Later reforms—floating the national currency, the kip, and freeing interest rates—stimulated a market-based economy and controlled inflation. Major land reforms in 1988 included the freedom to sell products at market-determined prices. Growth from these stimuli is demonstrated by the doubling of private shops in Vientian and abundant fairly-priced goods in the markets. The usual hours of business are from 8 AM until sunset. Banking hours are 8 to 10:30 AM and 2 to 3:30 PM, Monday–Friday. There are no advertising agencies.

31FOREIGN TRADE

The political reorganization of 1975 brought changes in Laos's foreign trade pattern, because regional alignments were shifting and because the aid needed to finance the nation's imports was no longer available from the US. In 1985 electricity, tin, and timber were the most important exports; oil, machinery, and food are the major imports. In 1985, the value of exports was estimated at $47.6 million, of which electricity represented $22.3 million and timber $5.1 million; the value of imports was $163.3 million. The resulting deficit was $115.7 million. The principal sources of imports changed dramatically after the withdrawal of US interests in 1975. In 1973, the US accounted for 69% of Laos's total trade with non-Communist countries, Thailand 11%, Singapore 5%, and Japan 5%; by 1979, the US contribution was nil, and Japan contributed 30%, Thailand 29%, and Singapore 11%.

In the 1980s, much of the nation's trade was subsidized by the former USSR. The export of electricity, the sale of overflight rights to foreign airlines, wood products, green coffee, and tin are sources of foreign earnings. In 1991 Laos' largest export earner, logging, was banned pending steps to prevent further destruction of the forests. There are 11 million ha of mature forests in Laos, and about 4.4 million are considered commercially exploitable. The ban on log exports was modified to allow the export of already cut logs and logs from stipulated cutting areas. Foreign aid grants exceeded export earnings in 1991. In that year export revenue decreased by 22%, compared with 1990, owing to the reduction of timber exports and a decline (caused by drought) in the production of electricity for export. At the same time the costs of imports increased by 62%, owing to the newly adopted free trade measures, which ended restrictions on imported goods. Total exports were estimated at $132 million in 1992, and imports at $266 million. Exports remained concentrated in wood (32%) and electricity (13%), while garment exports accounted for 20%.

32BALANCE OF PAYMENTS

Laos has experienced severe trade deficits since independence. From 1963 through mid-1975, substantial deficit financing was provided through the Foreign Exchange Operations Fund (FEOF), an agency backed largely by the US but also receiving funds from Japan, France, the UK, and Australia. In June 1975, the flight of gold and hard currencies from the country forced the government to ban exports of gold and silver bullion. A devaluation of the kip (to к1,200 per $1) had the effect of further inflating its price, with the black market exchange rate soaring to as high as к3,000 per $1. In the 1980s, financing came mainly from the former USSR, with smaller amounts from multilateral agencies.

In 1992 merchandise exports totaled $132.7 million and imports $244.4 million. The merchandise trade balance was $-111.7 million.

The following table summarizes Laos's balance of payments for 1991 and 1992 (in millions of US dollars):

	1991	1992
CURRENT ACCOUNT		
Goods, services, and income	–123.2	–110.6
Unrequited transfers	76.7	69.7
TOTALS	–46.5	–40.9
CAPITAL ACCOUNT		
Direct investment	8.0	9.0
Other long-term capital	36.6	36.6
Other short-term capital	29.5	–1.7
Reserves	–15.2	–4.4
TOTALS	58.9	66.0
Errors and omissions	–12.4	–25.1
Total change in reserves	–14.5	–5.3

33BANKING AND SECURITIES

The National Bank of Laos, which began operations in 1955 in Vientiane, has the exclusive right to issue currency and to control foreign exchange. It also has the authority to supervise the commercial banks and to control credit. The largest commercial bank, established in 1953, is the Bank of Indochina.

The large-scale flight of foreign currency that accompanied the Pathet Lao's ascendancy to power led the new government to shut down Vientiane's banks in September 1975. Officials subsequently announced the expropriation of most private accounts, claiming they were the property of former rightists and "traitors."

Banking reforms of the 1988–89 period opened Laos to foreign banks. There are six commercial banks n the country. Banks in Laos include: Banque Pour le Commerce Exterieur Lao, Joint Development Bank, Nakhonelouang Bank, and the Vientiane Commercial Bank. The Thai Military bank is the first foreign bank to be represented in Laos.

34INSURANCE

There are no private insurance firms.

35PUBLIC FINANCE

The civil war rendered normal budgetary procedures impossible, the budget being covered largely by US aid and monetary inflation. Deficit financing continued in the 1970s and 1980s, covered mostly by foreign aid from communist nations. In 1990, budgeted revenues came to an estimated $83 million, while expenditures amounted to $188.5 million (including $94 million in capital expenditures). The external debt in 1990 was $1.1 billion.

36TAXATION

In 1977, the government introduced a progressive agricultural tax on production. The tax revenues were to be used to develop forestry and mining without the need for outside aid, but the tax had the unwanted side effect of discouraging production by some of the largest landowners and slowing the achievement of self-sufficiency in food. In 1992, tax revenues totaled к73.51 billion, and revenues of к69.58 billion were projected for 1993. The 1992–93 budget included a new profits tax and a law requiring foreign firms engaged in construction projects to pay taxes. The agricultural tax was replaced by a land tax, and consumption taxes were raised on fuel oil, liquor, beer, and tobacco.

37CUSTOMS AND DUTIES

Import duties are determined on a specific and an ad valorem basis and range from 0–200%, mostly not exceeding 45%. Compensatory duties are imposed on imports of commodities in competition with local goods. A general internal tax is collected on the c.i.f.-plus-duties value of most imports. Certain commodities—including radios, alcoholic beverages, tobacco, and sugar—are subject to special excise taxes. A duty-free unloading zone for Laotian imports is located in the Vietnamese port of Da Nang.

38FOREIGN INVESTMENT

Before 1975, Laotian foreign economic relations were conducted under the FEOF and the US Commodity Import Program, under which dollar exchange was provided; Laos in turn allocated dollars to local importers, who then made kip payments to the government for the purchase of foreign goods. There was little direct foreign investment, however. From 1975 until the mid-1980s, all foreign capital has come in the form of development assistance.

Reforms, as part of the New Economic Mechanism (NEM) initiated in 1986, included the introduction of a the Laos Foreign Investment Code and Decree in 1988. The Foreign Investment Management Committee (FIMC) has the power to interpret the Code and to authorize and approve of investment. The Code and Decree focus on three types of transactions: contractual business, joint ventures, and wholly foreign-owned enterprises. Investment is now allowed in the areas of agriculture, forestry, industry, communications, transport, service, and tourism, for projects using the indigenous raw materials and natural resources of Laos. The Decree details the permitted sectors of foreign investment and outlines restrictions and prohibitions. For instance, environmentally damaging investment, investors with overwhelming debt, long-term projects making great use of imported materials, and enterprises that would compete with local entrepreneurs are prohibited and/or discouraged. Hindrances to foreign investment are poor legal and physical infrastructure and a lack of skilled labor and capital. Additional disadvantages in landlocked Laos are high transportation costs and limited domestic and foreign markets. In 1994 a new foreign investment law streamlined regulations and tax structures and included a flat corporate tax rate of 20%.

In 1992 the largest share of foreign investments by industry were hotels and tourism 25%, mining and petroleum 14%, and manufacturing 12%. Five foreign banks have been licensed since the end of 1992. The largest investor is Thailand (40%), followed by the US (19%) and France (7%). International donors—the International Monetary Fund (IMF), the World Bank, the Asian Development Bank (ADB) and the French, Swedish, Australian, and Japanese governments—still provide substantial donations for Laos' capital expenditures.

39 ECONOMIC DEVELOPMENT

The National Plan and Foreign Aid Council was established in June 1956 to prepare a general plan for the development of Laos and to set up a series of five-year plans. In view of its limited capital resources, the government sought increased private foreign investment, continued US governmental economic assistance, and help from international monetary bodies and the Colombo Plan organization. An economic plan drafted by the Laotian government in 1962 was never fully implemented, however, owing to internal instability. Little of the infrastructure for public works, industry, and mining that was abandoned in 1961 has been resumed. Although a major goal of the 1969–74 economic and social development plan, completion of the Nam Ngum Dam, was fulfilled, a host of other targets had to be abandoned because of disruption stemming from the war. Following the Pathet Lao takeover in 1975, efforts were made to restructure the Laotian economy along socialist lines. By 1979, with the economy reduced to a virtual standstill because of poor harvests, rapid inflation, and the absence of any private incentive, the government abandoned centralized planning as the sole route to economic development. Instead, a centrally coordinated amalgam of state-run enterprises, cooperatives, and private ventures was pursued. Laos's first five-year plan (1981–85) envisioned increases of 65–68% in the gross social product, 23–24% in agricultural production, and 100–120% in industrial production, as well as completion of repairs on major highways and waterways. These goals were not met because of managerial inefficiency and waste.

The second five-year plan (1986–90) emphasized exportation of food products, strengthening of economic management, rehabilitation of routes to seaports and rural feeder roads, reform of general education and training, and development of small- and medium-scale projects. US aid to Laos began in 1955 and continued until the US pullout in 1975. During this period, the Laotian economy became almost totally dependent on US aid, which amounted to over $900 million in nonmilitary loans and grants and $1.6 billion in military assistance. After the Pathet Lao took power, China supplied much of the needed assistance between 1975 and 1979. Since 1979, Laos has received direct aid mainly from the former USSR, Viet Nam, and their allies. Aid from Council for Mutual Economic Assistance (CMEA) countries totaled $90 million in 1985. Among non-Communist nations, Japan, Australia, Sweden, and the Netherlands have also furnished assistance. In 1985, the US ban on aid to Laos was lifted, largely because of Laotian cooperation in accounting for US military personnel missing in action in Laos during the Viet Nam war. Aid from international agencies totaled $183.1 million between 1946 and 1986. In the 1990s the US suspended aid and preferential treatment based on Laos' failure to assist the suppression of drug traffic, but reversed this decision fllowing renewed co-operation by Laos.

The New Economic Mechanism (NEM) approved in 1986 (based on *chin tanakan may,* "new thinking,") introduced free enterprise initiatives including decentralized decision making, deregulation of pricing and financial systems, and promotion of domestic and international trade and foreign investment Reforms have been introduced in phases. In 1988 land use reforms and market determined prices were introduced. In 1989 the tax system

was modified, a Foreign Investment Law was implemented, the banking system was restructured, and the privatization of state economic enterprises commenced. Creation of a national taxation system and a customs administration are aimed at increasing government revenue. The Ministry of Industry and Primary Resources, the Economic Planning Unit, which monitors existing and new businesses, and the Economic Development Board (EDB), which assists in the establishment of new industries, facilitate foreign investment in most sectors of the economy. Incentives offered to encourage the development of industrial and commercial enterprises include allowing 100% foreign ownership.

The third Five Year Plan (1991–95) continues previous policies of infrastructure improvement, export growth, and import substitution. Four sectors are considered as areas of future income for Laos: mining and energy; agriculture and forestry; tourism; and service, as a way-station and service center between China, Viet Nam, and Cambodia. Laos has untapped mineral resources and proven reserves of gold, gemstones and iron ore. Pulp and paper tree plantations would be substituted for the export of timber and agricultural products to serve the Thai market. Based on Thailand's experience, the LPDR recognizes that mass tourism involves environmental degradation, yet the opening of the Mittaphap (Friendship) Bridge over the Mekong between Laos and Thailand (1994) is an opportunity for both trade and tourism which is readily exploited. In 1993 three western oil companies, Enterprise Oil and Monument Oil, both from the UK, and Hunt Oil of Dallas, engaged in exploration for oil and gas in Laos. The potential for finding hydrocarbons in Laos is largely unknown and exploration risks are considerable, including inadequate geological maps, unexploded ordnance, tough terrain, encounters with the remnants of the anti-communist insurgency movement, tropical and dietary illness, and the expense of drilling and pipeline construction for transport to the Vietnamese coast. Two major hydroelectric projects, the Nam Thuen Dam on a tributary of the Mekong in Khammouan province,and the Xeset dam in southern Laos produce electricity sold to Thailand.

40 SOCIAL DEVELOPMENT

By almost any measure, Laos is one of the world's most impoverished nations. Food intake does not meet basic requirements; there are virtually no sanitary facilities; and contamination of drinking water is widespread. The fertility rate is high (6.7 in 1985–90), as is the birthrate. In 1980, the government indicated that it regarded the nation's population as too low and that previous family-planning programs had been disbanded and the use of contraceptives banned. Abortions are permitted only to save the mother's life. Almost no families own cars, and bicycles and radios are considered luxuries. In general, the lowland Lao have the highest living standards, with lower standards prevailing among the upland tribes.

Women in Laos have traditionally been subservient to men and have generally been discouraged from obtaining an education. However, the government claims that it has encouraged women to assume a larger role in national life, and that more girls are in school now than before 1975.

41 HEALTH

The use of Western medicine has improved health generally and reduced the incidence of malaria and smallpox specifically, but a high infant mortality and a variety of health problems remain. Most urban areas, including Vientiane, lack pure water and sanitary disposal systems. In 1991, only 36% of the population had access to safe water, and merely 21% had adequate sanitation. In parts of Laos, malaria—the most serious health threat—is known to affect the majority of children. Other health problems are acute upper respiratory infections (including pneumonia and influenza), diarrhea and dysentery, parasites, yaws, skin ailments, various childhood diseases, hepatitis, venereal disease, and tuberculosis. In 1990, there were 235 reported cases of tuberculosis per 100,000 inhabitants. Children up to 1 year of age were vaccinated in 1992 against tuberculosis (39%); diphtheria, pertussis, and tetanus (23%); polio (25%); and measles (55%).

Average life expectancy in 1992 was estimated at 51 years for men and women; infant mortality in 1992 was estimated at 98 per 1,000 live births. The overall mortality rate in 1993 was 15.2 per 1,000 people; the maternal mortality rate in 1991 was 300 per 100,000 live births; and, there were 30,000 deaths of children under 5 years of age in 1992.

In 1992, there were 0.23 doctors per 1,000 people, with a nurse to doctor ratio of 5.9, and 67% of the population had access to health care services. In 1990, total health care expenditures were $22 million.

42HOUSING

The typical house is rectangular, built entirely of wooden planks and bamboo, with a thatched roof, and is raised off the ground on wooden pilings 1–2 m (3–6 ft) high. There is a critical housing shortage in the towns, and many dwellings are substandard. As of 1990, 47% of urban and 25% of rural dwellers had access to a public water supply, while 30% of urban and 8% of rural dwellers had access to sanitation services.

43EDUCATION

Education in Laos is compulsory for eight years. Primary education lasts for five years. In 1991, there were 7,140 primary schools with 21,036 teachers and 580,792 students. In all secondary schools, there were 10,198 teachers and 125,702 students. Among these, 718 teachers and 4,495 students were in teacher training courses, and vocational programs had 544 teachers and 3,703 students. Attendance at Laotian primary and secondary schools increased from 300,000 in 1972 to 600,000 in 1979. Vocational schools reported an enrollment of 18,000. Sisavongvong University at Vientiane includes a school of education, a school of law and administration, a school of medicine, a school of vocational training, a school of agriculture, and a school of public works. There were also regional technical colleges and 63 teacher training colleges as of 1985. In 1989 there were 476 teaching faculty and 3,425 students enrolled at all higher level institutions.

44LIBRARIES AND MUSEUMS

The National Library (Vientiane), with 50,000 volumes in French, Lao, and English, is the nation's largest library. In addition, a Buddhist institute owns a number of classical manuscripts. Many excellent traditional works of art and architecture may be seen in Vientiane and Luangphrabang. Of particular interest in the latter city is the former royal palace and the Prabang (Golden Buddha), which was brought to Laos from Cambodia in the days of Fa-Ngoum.

45MEDIA

All communications, including the radio network, are operated by the government. Regular radio broadcasts were begun from Vientiane in 1968 and are now carried by Lao National Radio. Most broadcasts are in Lao, but government news broadcasts are also in English, French, and other languages. Domestic television service from Lao National TV began in 1983; in addition, programs are available by satellite from the former USSR, and it is possible to pick up Thai broadcasts. In 1991 there were over 8,136 telephones, about 540,000 radios, and about 25,000 television sets in use. In 1992 telephone owners were able to direct dial internationally, and private facsimile machines were permitted.

The press is government-controlled. The sole news agency is run by the Ministry of Information; the only foreign news bureaus are those of the former USSR and Viet Nam. The principal Vientiane newspapers are *Pasason* (*The People*), with a 1991 circulation of 10,000; *Viangchan May* (*New Vientiane*), with a circulation of 3,400; and *Khao San Pathet Lao* (*Laos Newsletter*), with a circulation of 1,500.

46ORGANIZATIONS

Before 1975 there were chambers of commerce in Vientiane and Pakxé. Boy Scout and Girl Scout organizations had long been active. Since 1975, the Lao People's Revolutionary Party and its allied social and political groups in the Lao Front for National Reconstruction have dominated Laotian life. The cooperative movement has been intensively developed. There is also a Lao Unified Buddhists' Association.

47TOURISM, TRAVEL, AND RECREATION

The Pathet Lao government has had little interest in tourism, and foreigners are rarely granted permits to travel outside Vientiane. Altough individual tourist visas are difficult to obtain, the government's official tourist organization, Inter-Lao Tourisme, has been issuing growing numbers of visas to tour groups. The main tourist destinations are Vientiane, with its Buddhist pagodas, and the city of Luangphrabang at the junction of the Nam Khan and Mekong Rivers in the North.

48FAMOUS LAOTIANS

One of the most cherished figures in Laotian history is Fa-Ngoum, who unified Lan Xang in the 14th century. Another dynastic personage still revered is the monarch Sethathirat, in whose reign (1534–71) the famous That Luang shrine was built. Chao Anou (r.1805–28) is remembered for having fought a war to recover Laotian independence from the Siamese (Thais) and for having restored Vientiane to a glory it had not known since the 16th century. Important 20th-century figures include Souvanna Phouma (1901–84), former prime minister; Prince Souphanouvong (b.1902), a half-brother of Souvanna Phouma, leader of the Pathet Lao and president of Laos from 1975 to 1986; and Kaysone Phomvihan (1920–1992), former chairman of the Council of Ministers.

49DEPENDENCIES

Laos has no territories or colonies.

50BIBLIOGRAPHY

Brown, MacAlister, and Joseph J. Zasloff. *Apprentice Revolutionaries: The Communist Movements in Laos, 1930–1985.* Stanford, Calif.: Stanford University Hoover Press, 1986.

Castle, Timothy N. *At War in the Shadow of Vietnam: U.S. Military Aid to the Royal Lao Government, 1955–1975.* New York: Columbia University Press, 1993.

Chan, Sucheng. *Hmong Means Free: Life in Laos and America.* Philadelphia: Temple University Press, 1994.

Cordell, Helen. *Laos.* Santa Barbara, Calif.: Clio, 1991.

Evans, Grant. *Lao Peasants under Socialism.* New Haven: Yale University Press, 1990.

Hamilton-Merritt, Jane. *Tragic Mountains: The Hmong, the Americans, and the Secret Wars for Laos, 1942–1992.* Bloomington: Indiana University Press, 1993.

Stuart-Fox, Martin (ed.). *Contemporary Laos: Studies in the Politics and Society of the Lao People's Democratic Republic.* New York: St. Martin's, 1982.

———. *Historical Dictionary of Laos.* Metuchen, N.J.: Scarecrow Press, 1992.

Zasloff, Joseph J. *The Pathet Lao: Leadership and Organization.* Lexington, Mass.: Heath, 1973.

———, and Leonard Unger (eds.). *Laos: Beyond the Revolution.* New York: St. Martin's Press, 1991.

LEBANON

Republic of Lebanon
Al-Jumhuriyah al-Lubnaniyah

CAPITAL: Beirut (Bayrut).

FLAG: The national flag, introduced in 1943, consists of two horizontal red stripes separated by a white stripe which is twice as wide; at the center, in green and brown, is a cedar tree.

ANTHEM: *Kulluna lil watan lil'ula lil'alam (All of Us for the Country, Glory, Flag).*

MONETARY UNIT: The Lebanese pound, or livre libanaise (LL), is a paper currency of 100 piasters. There are coins of 1, 2½, 5, 10, 25, and 50 piasters and 1 Lebanese pound, and notes of 1, 5, 10, 25, 50, 100, 250, 1,000 and 10,000 Lebanese pounds. LL1 = $0.0006 (or $1 = LL1,694.5).

WEIGHTS AND MEASURES: The metric system is the legal standard, but traditional weights and measures are still used.

HOLIDAYS: New Year's Day, 1 January; Arab League Day, 22 March; Independence Day, 22 November; Evacuation Day, 31 December. Christian religious holidays include Feast of St. Maron, 9 February; Good Friday; Easter Monday; Ascension; Assumption, 15 August; All Saints' Day, 1 November; and Christmas, 25 December. Muslim religious holidays include 'Id al-Fitr, 'Id al-'Adha', and Milad an-Nabi.

TIME: 2 PM = noon GMT.

¹LOCATION, SIZE, AND EXTENT

Situated on the eastern coast of the Mediterranean Sea, Lebanon has an area of 10,400 sq km (4,015 sq mi), extending 217 km (135 mi) NE–SW and 56 km (35 mi) SE–NW. It is bordered on the N and E by Syria, on the S by Israel, and on the W by the Mediterranean Sea, with a total boundary length of 679 km (422 mi). Comparatively, the area occupied by Lebanon is about three-fourths the size of the state of Connecticut.

The Lebanon of today is the Greater Lebanon (Grand Liban) created by France in September 1920, which includes the traditional area of Mount Lebanon—the hinterland of the coastal strip from Sidon (Sayda) to Tripoli (Tarabulus)—some coastal cities and districts such as Beirut and Tripoli, and the Bekaa (Biqa') Valley in the east. As of January 1988, more than two-thirds of the territory was under foreign military occupation. Syrian forces have held northern Lebanon and the Bekaa Valley since 1976; West Beirut and the Beirut-Sidon coastal strip fell into their hands in February 1987. In southern Lebanon, Israeli troops in conjunction with the South Lebanese Army, a local militia, control a 1,000-sq-km (400-sq-mi) strip along the Israeli border.

Lebanon's capital city, Beirut, is located on the Mediterranean coast.

²TOPOGRAPHY

The Mount Lebanon area is rugged; there is a rise from sea level to a parallel mountain range of about 2,000–3,000 m (6,600–9,800 ft) in less than 40 km (25 mi), and heavy downpour of winter rains has formed many deep clefts and valleys in the soft rock. The terrain has profoundly affected the country's history in that virtually the whole landscape is a series of superb natural fortresses from which guerrilla activities can render the maintenance of control by a centralized government an intermittent and costly affair. East of the Mount Lebanon Range is the Bekaa Valley, an

extremely fertile flatland about 16 km (10 mi) wide and 129 km (80 mi) long from north to south. At the eastern flank of the Bekaa rise the Anti-Lebanon Range and the Hermon extension, in which stands Mount Hermon straddling the border with Syria. Lebanon contains few rivers, and its harbors are mostly shallow and small. Abundant springs, found to a height of 1,500 m (4,900 ft) on the western slopes of the Lebanon Mountains, provide water for cultivation up to this height.

³CLIMATE

Lebanon's extraordinarily varied climate is due mainly to the wide range of elevation and the westerly winds that make the Mediterranean coast much wetter than the eastern hills, mountainsides, and valleys. Within a 16-km (10-mi) radius of many villages, apples, olives, and bananas are grown; within 45 minutes' drive in winter, spring, and fall, both skiing and swimming are possible. Rainfall is abundant by Middle Eastern standards, with about 90 cm (35 in) yearly along the coast, about 125 cm (50 in) on the western slopes of the mountains, and less than 38 cm (15 in) in the Bekaa. About 80% of the rain falls from November to March, mostly in December, January, and February. Summer is a dry season, but it is humid along the coast. The average annual temperature in Beirut is 21°C (70°F), with a range from 13°C (55°F) in winter to 28°C (82°F) in summer.

⁴FLORA AND FAUNA

Lebanon is rich in flora, with approximately 2,500 species. Olive and fig trees and grapevines are abundant on lower ground, while cedar, maple, juniper, fir, cypress, valonia oak, and Aleppo pine trees occupy higher altitudes. Vegetation types range from subtropical and desert to alpine. Although hunting has killed off most wild mammals, jackals are still found in the wilder rural regions, and gazelles and rabbits are numerous in the south. Many varieties of rodents, including mice, squirrels, and gerbils, and many types of reptiles, including lizards and snakes (some of them poisonous), may be found. Thrushes, nightingales, and other songbirds are native to Lebanon; there are also partridges, pigeons, vultures, and eagles.

[5]ENVIRONMENT

Lebanon's forests and water supplies suffered significant damage in the 1975–76 war and subsequent fighting. Explosive urbanization has also left its mark on the environment. Coastal waters show the effects of untreated sewage disposal, particularly near Beirut, and of tanker oil discharges and oil spills. The water pollution problem in Lebanon is in part due to the lack of an internal system to consistently regulate water purification. The nation has 1.2 cubic miles of water with 85% used for farming activity and 4% used for industrial purposes. Lebanon cities produce 0.5 million tons of solid waste per year. Air pollution is a serious problem in Beirut because of vehicular exhaust and the burning of industrial wastes. Control efforts have been ineffective or nonexistent because of political fragmentation and recurrent warfare since 1975, but in 1986 the National Preservation Park of Bte'nayel was created in the region of Byblos to preserve wooded areas and animals. The effects of the war and the growth of the nation's cities have combined to threaten the animal and plant life in Lebanon. Four of the nation's mammal species and 14 of its bird species are endangered. Five of its plant species are also threatened with extinction. In 1987, the Arabian gazelle and Anatolian leopard were extinct.

[6]POPULATION

In order not to upset the fragile political balance between the many ethnic and religious groups, no census has been taken since 1932. The Lebanese population was estimated by the UN as 2,668,000 in 1985 and 2,838,000 in 1992, but accurate counts have been rendered impossible by the heavy casualties and mass migrations during and after the war of 1975–76. The UN estimate for the year 2000 was 3,312,000, assuming a crude birthrate of 24.3 per 1,000 population, a crude death rate of 6.4, and a net natural increase of 17.9 during 1995–2000. Annual population growth, estimated before the war at 2.3%, fell to about 0.5% during 1985–90. Population density in 1992 was estimated at 272 persons per sq km (703 per sq mi). About 84% of the population was urban and 16% rural in 1990. Beirut, the capital, had an estimated population of 1,500,000 in 1988; Tripoli had approximately 160,000.

[7]MIGRATION

The economic roots of emigration may be traced to the increase of crop specialization during the 19th century and to the subsequent setbacks of the silk market toward the end of the century. Political incentives also existed, and many Lebanese left their country for Egypt (then under British rule) or the Americas at the turn of the century. After the mid-1960s, skilled Lebanese were attracted by economic opportunities in the Persian Gulf countries. Large numbers fled abroad, many of them to France, Syria. Jordan, Egypt, and the Gulf countries, during the civil war in 1975–76. In 1986, the Lebanese World Cultural Union estimated that some 13,300,000 persons of Lebanese extraction were living abroad, the largest numbers in Brazil, the US, and Argentina.

Since the outbreak of war in 1975, internal migration has largely followed the pattern of hostilities, peaking in 1975/76 and again after the Israeli invasion of 1982. In 1993, the number of refugees in various parts of the country was estimated at over 600,000. There were 310,585 Palestinians registered with the UNRWA in mid 1991, of which 157,977 were living in 13 camps.

[8]ETHNIC GROUPS

Ethnic mixtures dating back to various periods of immigration and invasion are represented, as are peoples of almost all Middle Eastern countries. A confusing factor is the religious basis of ethnic differentiation. Thus, while most Lebanese are Arabs, they are divided into Muslims and Christians, each in turn subdivided into a number of faiths or sects, most of them formed by historical development into separate ethnic groups. The Muslims are divided into Sunnis and Shi'is. The Druzes, whose religion derives from Islam, are a significant minority. The Christians are divided mainly among Maronites, Greek Orthodox, and Greek Catholics. All the major groups have their own political organizations, paramilitary units, and territorial strongholds. Other ethnic groups include Armenians (most of them Armenian Orthodox, with some Armenian Catholics) and small numbers of Jews, Syrians, Kurds, and others. The number of Palestinians is estimated at 450,000–500,000. In addition there are about 180,000 stateless undocumented persons. Some of these are inhabitants of disputed border areas.

[9]LANGUAGES

Arabic is the official language and is spoken throughout the country. Much of the population is bilingual, with French as the main second language. There are also significant numbers of English, Armenian, and Turkish speakers. The distinctive Lebanese Arabic dialect contains various relics of pre-Arabic languages and also shows considerable European influence in vocabulary.

[10]RELIGIONS

Religious communities in the Ottoman Empire were largely autonomous in matters of personal status law and were at times treated as corporations for tax and public security matters. Membership in a millet, as these groups were called in Ottoman law, gave the individual citizenship, and this position, although somewhat modified, has given Lebanese politics its confessional nature. Religion is closely connected with civic affairs, and the size and competing influence of the various religious groups are matters of overriding political importance. The imbalance of power between Christians and Muslims, aggravated by the presence of large numbers of Palestinians, was a major factor contributing to the bitter civil war in 1975–76. Christians, mostly Maronite, constituted about 43% of the population in the early 1980s, and Muslims and Druzes about 57%. Muslims have come to outnumber Christians as the result of long-term demographic trends and population displacements during and after the civil war.

Under an unwritten agreement made at the time of the National Covenant of 1943, the president of Lebanon must be a Maronite Christian and the prime minister a Sunni Muslim, with a ratio of six Christians to every five Muslims in the legislature. But this arrangement has subsequently ceased to reflect the strength of competing religious groups in the population and is widely criticized.

[11]TRANSPORTATION

As of 1991, Lebanon had about 7,300 km (4,500 mi) of roads, of which 85% were paved. Construction of new roads have been frequently delayed by recurrent hostilities. Many roads were badly in need of repair, and since 1982, fully one-third of the country's roads have been rehabilitated. Some new mileage has also been added.

The 378-km (235-mi) state-owned railway consists of a 1.435-m-gauge line running parallel to the coastal area where civil hostilities kept the railway virtually inoperable in 1991.

Beirut, a major Mediterranean port, was closed during the

1975–76 war and intermittently thereafter, reopening by March 1991. When Beirut port was closed, Sidon became the principal port for Muslims and Juniyah for Christians. Other ports include Tripoli and Tyre. As of 1 January 1992, Lebanon had a merchant fleet of 56 ships with a capacity of 234,000 GRT.

Beirut's airport remained generally open until bombing during the Israeli invasion forced its closure in June–October 1982. It had handled 1,660,000 passengers in 1980; by 1985, the number was down to 599,000. Lebanon's two airlines, Middle East Airlines (MEA) and Trans-Mediterranean Airways (TMA), suffered heavy losses during the 1975–76 war and the Israeli invasion.

12 HISTORY

The geographical features of Lebanon have had a major effect on its history. Its mountains enabled the minority communities to survive the despotisms that submerged the surrounding areas. The sea provided trade routes in ancient times for exports from Lebanese cedar and spruce forests, and for commerce in copper and iron during the time of the Ptolemies and the Romans. Both Lebanon and Syria were historically associated from early times as part of Phoenicia (c.1600–c.800 BC), and both were later swept up into the Roman Empire. In the 7th century AD, the Arabs conquered part of Lebanon. Maronite Christians had long been established there; Islam gradually spread by conversion and migration, although the country remained predominantly Christian. In the 11th century, the Druzes established themselves in the south of the Mount Lebanon area as well as in Syria. Parts of Lebanon fell temporarily to the Crusaders; invasions by Mongols and others followed, and trade declined until the reunification of the Middle East under the Ottoman Empire.

For the most part, Ottoman officials of the surrounding areas left the Mount Lebanon districts to their own emirs and sheikhs. Fakhr ad-Din (1586–1635) of the Ma'an family set out to create an autonomous Lebanon, opened the country to Western Europe through commercial and military pacts, and encouraged Christian missionary activity. In 1697, the Shihab family acquired dominance, and from 1788 to 1840, except for a few intervals, Mount Lebanon was ruled by Bashir II of the Shihab family, who extended his power and was partly successful in building a strong state. The Egyptian occupation of Syria (1832–40) opened the Levant to large-scale European penetration and tied Lebanese affairs to international politics. It also heightened the antipathy between Christians and Druzes, with the occupiers from time to time using armed groups of one against the other. The British invasion of 1840–41 served to deliver Lebanon from Egyptian rule and forced Bashir II into exile, but it also involved France and the UK in the problem of finding a modus vivendi for the religious factions. A partition of government did not work. Economic discontent was inflamed by religious antagonisms, and the Druzes, feeling their power dwindling, organized a major onslaught against the Christians in 1860. When the latter, fearing annihilation, requested European intervention, major powers sent fleets into Syrian waters and the French sent an army into Mount Lebanon. Under European pressure, the Ottoman government agreed to the establishment of an international commission to set up a new, pro-Christian government; an autonomous province of Mount Lebanon was created in 1864, with a Christian governor who, though the servant of the Ottoman state, relied upon European backing in disputes with his sovereign.

The entry of the Ottoman Empire into World War I led to an Allied blockade, widespread hunger, and the destruction of Lebanese prosperity. An Anglo-French force took the country in 1918, and in 1920, an Allied conference gave France a mandate over Syria, in which Mount Lebanon was included. The French separated from Syria the area they called Greater Lebanon (Grand Liban), which was four times as large as the traditional Mount

LOCATION: 35°6′ to 36°36′E; 33°4′ to 34°41′N. **BOUNDARY LENGTHS:** Syria, 359 km (223 mi); Israel, 102 km (63 mi); Mediterranean coastline, 195 km (121 mi). **TERRITORIAL SEA LIMIT:** 12 mi.

Lebanon and included a Muslim population almost as large as the Christian. The mandate years were a time of material growth and little political development.

Lebanon came under Vichy control in 1940, but in 1941, Lebanon and Syria were taken by a combined Anglo–Free French force. The Free French proclaimed Lebanese independence in November 1941, but when a strongly nationalistic government was created in 1943, the French intervened and arrested the new president, Bishara al-Khuri. An insurrection followed, prompting UK intervention and the restoration of the government. In 1945, agreement was achieved for the withdrawal of both UK and French forces, and in 1946, Lebanon assumed complete independence.

The 1950s and 1960s were generally characterized by economic and political stability. Beginning in 1952, Lebanon received increased US aid and also benefited from an influx of

Western commercial personnel and from growing oil royalties. It also seemed the calmest center of the Middle East, taking little part in the Arab-Israeli war of 1948 and no action in the wars of 1967 and 1973. In 1958, however, a reported attempt by President Camille Chamoun (Sha'mun) to seek a second term precipitated a civil war, and in July the US sent forces to help quell the insurrection; this move was in keeping with the Eisenhower Doctrine, which pledged US military and economic aid to any country requesting it in order to counter a Communist threat. The crisis was settled when Gen. Fu'ad Shihab (Chehab), who was supported by both government and opposition groups, was elected president in July. By October, US forces were withdrawn, and public security was reestablished.

In the late 1960s and early 1970s, Lebanon's economy was disrupted by conflict in the Middle East, vividly brought home by the presence, near the border with Israel, of thousands of well-armed Palestinian guerrillas, many of whom had come from Jordan following the "Black September" fighting there in 1970–71. Serious clashes between them and the Lebanese army occurred in 1969. Fearing civil war, the government that year signed the so-called Cairo Accord with the Palestinian Liberation Organization (PLO), which virtually made it a state within the state. The PLO gained the right to establish military bases and launch cross-border raids into Israel. This inevitably led to Israeli reprisals, and PLO interference in Lebanese affairs accelerated a slide toward anarchy. In April and May 1974, a series of Palestinian attacks on Lebanese villages killed scores of persons and injured hundreds. Government efforts to deal with the problem were denounced as insufficient by Christian rightists, while Muslim leftists defended the Palestinians, and both factions formed private militias.

During the early months of 1975, sporadic violence between the two factions gradually erupted into a full-scale civil war that pitted Maronite Christians against Muslims and against other Christian sects, and rightist militants against Palestinian guerrillas and other leftist Arab forces. At least 100,000 people on all sides were killed and some 600,000 persons displaced during the 18 months of fighting. In April 1976, Syrian forces entered Lebanon, in an apparent effort to prevent an all-out victory by left-wing Muslims and Palestinians; by the fall, some 20,000 Syrian troops controlled the Bekaa Valley. A cease-fire arranged through the mediation of Sa'udi Arabia and other Arab countries enabled a peacekeeping force (including Syrian troops) to separate the combatants and end the war in October. The conflict not only devastated Lebanon economically, but so weakened the central government that effective power lay with the Syrians, the Palestinians, and some 30 sectarian militias. In general, the Christian Phalangists held sway over east-central Lebanon; fighters loyal to Major Sa'ad Haddad, a right-wing Lebanese army officer, controlled the southern border area, in a security zone set up by Israel; and the PLO, other Muslim leftists, and Syrian forces occupied northern and eastern Lebanon.

Intermittent fighting between the armed factions continued, and raids by Palestinian guerrillas based in southern Lebanon drew Israel into the conflict. In March 1978, the Israeli army invaded southern Lebanon, destroyed PLO bases, and then withdrew when the UN Interim Force in Lebanon (UNIFIL) was established to keep the peace. Continuing PLO rocket attacks on northern Israel and Syria's installation of antiaircraft missiles in the Bekaa Valley prompted Israel to launch a full-scale invasion of Lebanon in June 1982. Israeli forces quickly destroyed PLO bases in the south and in Tyre and Sidon, penetrated to the outskirts of Beirut, and disabled the Syrian missile bases. Several cease-fires arranged by US envoy Philip Habib broke down, but following a two-month Israeli siege of West Beirut, where the Palestinians were encamped, a truce was agreed to by Israel, the PLO, and Syria; by 1 September, more than 14,000 Palestinian and Syrian fighters had been evacuated. The Lebanese estimated their war casualties at more than 19,000 dead and 30,000 wounded (figures disputed by Israel). A multinational peacekeeping force, comprising British, French, and Italian soldiers and US marines, was stationed in the Beirut area in early September.

Despite the truce, the violence continued. On 14 September, Bashir Gemayel, a Phalangist leader who in August had been elected president by the Lebanese parliament, was assassinated. Almost immediately, Israeli troops moved into west Beirut to wipe out pockets of Palestinian resistance causing tens of thousands of casualties. Phalangist forces were allowed into the Sabra and Shatila refugee camps, and at least 600 Palestinians, many of them civilians, were massacred; a subsequent Israeli government inquiry was critical of senior officials for indirect responsibility for the killings. In 1983, Israeli and Syrian troops still occupied large portions of Lebanon, and they became targets of attack by Muslim and Druze forces. In May 1983, Lebanon, Israel, and the US signed an agreement by which Lebanon and Israel agreed to end their state of war. Israel agreed to withdraw all its forces, and both countries agreed to establish a security zone in southern Lebanon patrolled by Lebanese forces and joint Israeli-Lebanese teams. However, Syria opposed it and the agreement, never implemented, was repudiated by Lebanon in 1984.

The American embassy in Beirut was bombed in April 1983, and US marines were harassed by sniper fire. On 23 October, 241 of them were killed by a truck-bomb explosion in their barracks at Beirut airport; on the same day, a similar bombing caused at least 58 deaths at a French paratroop barracks. Shortly before, Lebanon and Syria had agreed to a cease-fire pending a reconciliation conference, which began in Switzerland in November, with all major Lebanese political factions participating. Meanwhile, fighting broke out between a radical Syrian-supported PLO faction and guerrillas loyal to Yasser Arafat, chairman of the organization; defeated at Tripoli, Arafat withdrew from Lebanon in December.

As 1984 began, the position of the government headed by Amin Gemayel, who had been elected president to succeed his brother, was deteriorating. In February, the US, UK, and Italy pulled their ground troops and nonessential personnel out of the Beirut area. In March, the Lebanese reconciliation conference dissolved without reaching substantial agreement. The following month a "national unity" government was formed, bringing together the leaders of all the major warring factions. But it almost never met and could not pacify the country; intermittent clashes between factions continued. Israel's withdrawal of its troops from Lebanon (except the south) in early 1985 left in its wake renewed fighting for the evacuated territory. In December, a Syrian-sponsored cease-fire agreement that included constitutional reforms was signed by the Druze, Amal (Shi'i), and Christian factions, but its terms were never implemented. The general lawlessness encouraged terrorist groups of all kinds to promote their own ends by assassinations, kidnappings, and bombings. Among the most feared was the Hezbollah, or Party of God, which was aligned with fundamentalist Iranian Revolutionary Guards.

In 1985–86, there was sporadic fierce fighting between Palestinian and Shi'i Amal militia. Syria pushed for political reform and, when opposed by Gemayel and militant Christians, influenced Moslem ministers not to deal with the President, thus paralyzing the government. With the economy in serious decline, Prime Minister Rashid Karami was assassinated to be succeeded by Salim al-Huss. The badly divided factions could not agree on a successor to Gemayel when his term expired in September 1988. Christian Army Commander Michel Aoun asserted himself as prime minister, giving Lebanon two governments, a Moslem one in West Beirut and a Christian one in East Beirut. Aoun was opposed by the Syrians and Moslems and by rival Christian factions.

In January 1989, the Arab League appointed a committee on Lebanon which eventually, in September, arranged for a seven-point cease-fire and convened a meeting of Lebanese parliamentarians in Taif, Sa'udi Arabia. The Taif Accord that resulted in November led to the election of Elias Hrawi, a Maronite Christian, as president. He named al-Huss prime minister. When forces of General Aoun (who was technically deposed by Hrawi) attacked Christian and Syrian positions, they retaliated in strength and finally obliged him to take exile in France in 1991.

In 1991-92, the government gradually began to reassert its authority. Militias, except notably Hezbollah and the Israeli-backed army of South Lebanon, were dissolved in May 1991. Palestinian militants were repressed in Sidon in July. In May 1992, the last western hostages were released after years of confinement. Lebanon joined the Israeli-Arab peace talks in Madrid in October 1991. Internally, the poor economy aggravated political instability, but Rashid al Sulh, who became prime minister in May 1992, scheduled the first parliamentary elections in 20 years. Poor preparations, widespread irregularities, and Christian abstention produced results that did not prepare Lebanon for an assured future. Yet, the appointment of Prime Minister Rafiq al-Hariri in November 1992 promised a serious effort at reconstruction. In mid-1994, conditions were reasonably calm, although many opponents of Syria criticized it for failing to withdraw from Beirut in 1992 as stipulated in the Taif Accord.

13GOVERNMENT

As defined by the constitution of 1926 and subsequent amendments, Lebanon is an independent republic. Executive power is vested in a president (elected by the legislature for six years) and a prime minister and cabinet, chosen by the president but responsible to the legislature. Under an agreement dating back to the French mandate, the president must be a Maronite Christian, the prime minister a Sunni Muslim, and the president of the National Assembly a Shi'i Muslim. Decisions by the president must be counter-signed by the prime minister and concerned minister(s) after approval by the National Assembly. Legislative power is exercised by a 128-member National Assembly (formerly the Chamber of Deputies), elected for a four-year term by universal adult suffrage (compulsory for males of 21 or over, permitted for women over 21 with elementary education). The electoral reform law of 1960 determined the denominational composition of the legislature as follows: Maronites, 30; Sunni, 20; Shi'i, 19; Greek Orthodox, 11; Greek Catholics, 6; Druzes, 6; Armenian Orthodox, 4; Armenian Catholic, 1; Protestant, 1; and others, 1. Deputies were elected to the legislature in 1972, but elections scheduled for 1976 were postponed because of the war, and the legislature has extended its term every two years until 1992. The Taif Accord of 1989 set the Christian-Moslem balance in parliament at 50–50, but the failure of Christians to participate in the elections of 1992 gave Moslem groups the largest number of seats in the Chamber. There has been no official census in the country since 1932, but most observers believe Moslems now form the majority with the Shi'i as the largest single group.

14POLITICAL PARTIES

Political life in Lebanon is affected by the diversity of religious sects and the religious basis of social organization. The mainly Christian groups, especially the Maronites, favor an independent course for Lebanon, stressing its ties to Europe and opposing the appeals of Islam and pan-Arabism. The Muslim groups favor closer ties with Arab states and are opposed to confessionalism

(political division along religious lines). Principal political groups, with mainly Christian membership, are the National Liberal Party and the Phalangist Party. There are various parties of the left, including the Progressive Socialist Party (of mostly Druze membership), the Ba'th Party, and the Lebanese Communist Party. The various Palestinian groups, allied under the umbrella of the Palestine Liberation Organization, have played an important role in the political life of Lebanon since the late 1960s. Amal, a conservative grouping, and Hezbollah, more militant, represent the Shi'i community. The former gained 18 seats and the latter 12 seats in the elections of 1992. The Christian community, which was supposed to have half the seats, largely boycotted the elections and, as a result, won only 59 seats.

15LOCAL GOVERNMENT

Lebanon is divided into the five provinces (muhafazat) of Beirut, North Lebanon, South Lebanon, Bekaa, and Mount Lebanon, each with its district administration. The muhafazat are subdivided into districts (aqdiya), municipalities, and villages. Provincial governors and district chiefs are appointed by presidential decree. In most villages, councils of village elders or heads of families or clans still play a considerable role.

16JUDICIAL SYSTEM

Ultimate supervisory power rests with the minister of justice, who appoints the magistrates. Courts of first instance, of which there are 56, are presided over by a single judge and deal with both civil and criminal cases. Appeals may be taken to 11 courts of appeal, each made up of three judges. Of the 4 courts of cassation, 3 hear civil cases and 1 hears criminal cases. A six-person Council of State handles administrative cases. Matters of state security are dealt with by a special nine-member Court of Justice. Religious courts—Islamic, Christian, and Jewish—deal with marriages, deaths, inheritances, and other matters of personal status in their respective faiths. There is also a separate military court system. In the refugee camps, the Palestinian elements implement an autonomous system of justice in which rival factions try opponents without any semblance of due process.

The law provides for the right to a fair public trial and an independent and impartial judiciary. In practice, politically influential elements succeed in intervening to obtain desired results.

In domestic disputes, the legal system is skewed in favor of the male litigant. In so-called crimes of honor, men are typically acquitted of murder charges in cases involving the murder of allegedly adulterous wives. By law, a woman's testimony before a notary public carries half the weight of a man's.

17ARMED FORCES

The conflict of 1975–90 split the regular Lebanese army along Christian-Muslim lines. The force was later reformed, first by the US, then by Syria. In 1993 it numbered 35,700 men. There was a small navy of 450 and an air force of 800 personnel, neither well-armed.

Although much of the sectarian militia has disbanded, significant communal armies remain: the Christian Lebanese Forces (3,000), Moslem Amal (2,000 active, 15,000 reserves), Moslem Hezbollah (3,000 active, 12,000 reserves) and the Druze militia (4,000 active, 11 reserves), and 1,500 Iranian revolutionary guards. The South Lebanese Army, mostly Christian, numbers 2,500 and receives Israeli support for its border patrol duties. The official Lebanese army has US and European weapons, the Syrians and communal militias Warsaw Pact weapons. The government's defense budget is $271 million or 8% of gross domestic product (1989), including $2.4 million in US aid. Syrian, as well as 10,000 Palestinian, guerrillas, continued to occupy Lebanese soil. Also stationed in Lebanon were 5,900 UNIFIL troops.

[18]INTERNATIONAL COOPERATION

Lebanon has been a charter member of the UN since 24 October 1945 and belongs to ESCWA and all the nonregional specialized agencies except WIPO. It is the host to UNRWA and UNIFIL and is one of the founding members of the Arab League. Lebanon also is a member of G-77, and a signatory of the Law of the Sea.

[19]ECONOMY

Lebanon is traditionally a trading country, with a relatively large agricultural sector and small but well-developed industry. Until the civil war, it had always figured prominently as a center of tourist trade. The 1975–76 war caused an estimated $5 billion in property damage and reduced economic activities to about 70% of the prewar level. The cost of reconstruction after the Israeli-Palestinian-Syrian war of 1982 was estimated at $12–15 billion. Lebanon has been able to survive economically because of remittances from abroad by Lebanese workers and companies, external aid by the US, France, Germany, and Arab countries, and foreign subsidies to various political groups. A residual effect of the 1982 war was political uncertainty, which poisoned the economic climate in the following years. In 1984 and after, there was a pronounced deterioration in the economy. After the 1989 Taif Accord for National Reconciliation ended hostilities, the economy began to recover. Economic activity surged in 1991 and in 1993 the Hariri Government was able to stabilize the economy, and launch a program to reconstruct the economy's infrastructure. Real GDP grew 4.2% in 1992, after growing by about 40% in 1991.

[20]INCOME

In 1991 the GDP was $4.8 billion in current US dollars or $1,400 per capita. It is estimated that in 1982, the last year for which data are available, agriculture, hunting, forestry, and fishing contributed 9% to GDP; manufacturing, 13%; electricity, gas, and water, 5%; construction, 3%; wholesale and retail trade, 28%; transport, storage, and communication, 4%; finance, insurance, real estate, and business services, 17%; community, social, and personal services, 11%; and other sources, 10%.

[21]LABOR

The labor force in 1992, having been drastically reduced by the wages of war—death, injury, and emigration—was estimated to number 600,000 people, up from 452,900 in 1985, but still below the 748,000 in 1975. During the civil war, it was estimated that 50% of industrial workers, 30% of construction workers, and 25% of workers in service industries fled the country. In all, an estimated 600,000-900,000 persons fled the country during the 1975-76 civil strife. Some returned, but continued instability has resulted in more emigration; many work in Persian Gulf area nations. Both the consequent labor shortage and loss of jobs due to war damage has contributed to serious labor unrest and frequent strikes. Labor productivity is low compared with the US and Western Europe, but higher than in many developing countries. In 1992, unemployment averaged 35%.

There are some 160 labor unions and organizations. The General Confederation of Workers is composed of 23 unions with about 250,000 members. Organized labor has grown slowly, partly because of the small number of industrial workers, but also because of the availability of a large pool of unemployed. Agricultural and most trade workers are not organized. Palestinians in Lebanon are free to organize their own unions, but few do so because of their restrictions on the right to work in the country.

[22]AGRICULTURE

Before the civil war, 17% of the working population was engaged in agricultural activity, and agriculture accounted for about 10% of the national income. Less than one-fourth of Lebanon's total area is cultivated, and expansion of cultivated areas is limited by the arid and rugged nature of the land.

Agricultural production was severely disrupted by the 1975–76 war, and production of citrus fruits, the main crop, was reduced to low levels in the fertile Bekaa Valley by Israeli-Syrian fighting during 1982. Damaged irrigation systems still need repairing. Agriculture continues to contribute about 10% to GDP and makes up 20% of merchandise exports. Principal crops and estimated 1992 production (in thousand tons) were potatoes, 250; oranges, 245; apples, 190; lemons and limes, 80; wheat, 52; grapefruit, 50; bananas, 45; olives, 40; and sugar beets, 9. Two profitable, albeit illegal, crops produced are opium poppy and cannabis.

[23]ANIMAL HUSBANDRY

Much of Lebanon's livestock was lost during the protracted hostilities since the 1975–76 war and the Israeli invasion in 1982. In 1992 there were an estimated 465,000 goats, 230,000 sheep, 72,000 head of cattle, and 20,000,000 poultry. As Lebanon's own meat and milk production is below consumption needs, animal and milk products are imported.

[24]FISHING

The fishing industry has not progressed significantly, despite a government-sponsored effort to reduce fish imports and provide employment in the canned-fish industry. The catch in 1991 was 1,800 tons.

[25]FORESTRY

Forests comprised about 80,000 hectares (197,700 acres), or nearly 8% of the total area, in 1991. Most of the forests are in the central part of the country, with pine and oak predominant. Few of the ancient cedars have survived; small cedar forests have been planted at high altitudes.

[26]MINING

Mining activity is slight. According to 1991 estimates, cement production amounted to 900,000 tons; gypsum, 2,000 tons; lime, 10,000 tons; and salt, 3,000 tons.

[27]ENERGY AND POWER

While political instability and conflict have curtailed petroleum exploration for over a decade, early 1991 natural gas discoveries near El-Marq have encouraged further exploration.

In 1993, Kuwait promised to supply 25,000 barrels of crude oil per day to Lebanon at a reduced price for one year. The Islamic Development Bank approved a soft loan of $40 million to cover part of Lebanon's petroleum debt to Kuwait. The Tripoli refinery only satisfies about 15% of domestic demand; imports from Syria, Romania, Bulgaria, Greece, and Italy meet the remaining demand for petroleum products.

Lebanon's electricity rehabilitation will be financed by Kuwait, Italy, the Arab Fund for Economic and Social Development, and the European Investment Bank. Italian, French, and Korean firms have been contracted to rehabilitate power stations, install transmission networks, and distribute electricity outside greater Beirut. Another project seeking funding as of late 1993 would involve the construction of two new 415 Mw power stations. Lebanon's largest hydroelectric plants are on the Litani River. In 1991, net installed electrical capacity was about 870,000 kw and production totaled 4,750 million kwh.

[28]INDUSTRY

The civil war caused tremendous damage to the industrial sector. By 1993, it was estimated that the Lebanese industry suffered losses of $1.5 billion. Half of this damage is thought to have occurred in 1989 and 1990 alone. Inadequate infrastructure and shortage of skilled labor are major obstacles in the process of rehabilitation. In 1992, industrial exports amounted to $418 million. Major industrial products are clothing, metal, food, marble and sanitary equipment, cement, jewelry, furniture, paper, beverages, and plastic.

Lebanon's two main oil refineries, at Tripoli and Zahrani (near Sidon), have a combined capacity of more than 50,000 barrels per day. Both refineries suspended operations during the 1975–76 civil war; neither was fully active in 1987. In 1993, the Tripoli refinery operated at a capacity of 21,000 barrels per day (total capacity is 35,000 barrels per day). The Lebanese government estimates the cost of rehabilitating the Tripoli refinery at $50 million. The Zahrani refinery has an idle production capacity ranging up to 17,000 barrels per day. Its rehabilitation is estimated to cost $20 million.

29 SCIENCE AND TECHNOLOGY

Lebanon's advanced technology is limited to oil refining, the facilities for which were installed by international oil companies. The National Council for Scientific Research, established in Beirut in 1962, draws up national science policies and fosters research in fundamental and applied research. The council operates a marine research center at Al-Batrun. Five colleges and universities in Beirut offer degrees in basic and applied sciences. In 1980, total expenditures on research and development amounted to LL22 million; 6 technicians and 180 scientists and engineers were engaged in research and development.

30 DOMESTIC TRADE

Trade is by far the most important sector of the Lebanese economy. In normal times, Beirut is the commercial center of the Middle East, but its commercial losses have been enormous since the 1975–76 war. During the first year of civil violence alone, 3,600 commercial establishments were destroyed, burned, or looted. The main trading activity is related to the importation of goods and their distribution in the local market. Distribution is generally handled by traders who acquire sole right of import and sale of specific trademarks, and although competition is keen, the markup tends to be high. Distribution of local products is more widely spread among traders. The smallness and competitiveness of the market have discouraged the development of wholesale houses but have fostered the growth of small shops dealing directly with local and foreign suppliers.

There is no single price level for the same item; the actual price charged generally depends on the short-term condition of the market and on the result of bargaining. Retail credit is common, and advertising has developed rapidly in motion picture theaters and the press.

Government offices and the larger banks are generally open from 8 or 8:30 AM to 2 PM (to 1 PM in summer), and commercial offices from 8 or 8:30 AM to 1 PM (to 1 or 2 PM in summer) and from 3 to 6 or 7 PM, but shops stay open long hours.

31 FOREIGN TRADE

Foreign trade has been important in the economic life of Lebanon as a source of both income and employment. Information concerning Lebanon's foreign trade is rarely reliable, chiefly because currency conversions are made at different rates and unrecorded transactions are rife. It has been estimated that more than 40% of Lebanon's annual imports enter as contraband.

According to IMF data, Lebanese export value increased steadily to LL2,589 million in 1975, but then fell sharply as the result of the civil war to LL1,441 million in 1976; another steady climb of exports, from the 1976 figure to LL3,608 million in 1981, was temporarily halted by the 1982 conflict but reached LL7,755 million in 1985. In 1981, some 40% of total exports were actually reexports, principally machinery, metal products, foods, wood products, textiles, and chemicals. Lebanon's own exports were mainly cement, jewelry, nonmetallic minerals, clothing, and aluminum products. Lebanon's estimated import value dropped drastically from LL4,379 million in 1975 to LL1,646 million in 1976, and thereafter outpaced exports by a wide margin, rising from LL4,373 million in 1977 to LL33,521 million in 1985. In 1992, Lebanon registerd a trade deficit of over $3 billion (10.9% lower than in 1991). Total exports were $510 million and total imports about $3.6 billion. Industrial hardware, motor vehicles, oil, foodstuffs, and electrical equipment are leading imports.

Some 87% of Lebanon's exports, including reexports, go to other Middle Eastern countries. In 1993, Lebanon's principal trade partners included Sa'udi Arabia, the UAE, Jordan, and Syria. The major providers of 1993 imports were Italy, Syria, France, Germany, US, and Turkey.

32 BALANCE OF PAYMENTS

Lebanon has maintained a favorable balance of payments, with rising trade deficits more than offset by net earnings from services, transfers of foreign capital, and remittances from Lebanese workers abroad. Although the trade deficit increased substantially between 1977 and 1984, a balance-of-payments deficit was recorded only for the last two years of the period. By 1985, a surplus of $249 million was again achieved, with a modest trade recovery following in 1986–87. Hostilities in the industrial and prosperous areas of Lebanon in 1989–90 triggered a substantial outflow of capital, with order being restored by 1991. In the first quarter of 1993, a modest trade deficit was estimated at $1.8 million; a larger trade deficit was averted by capital inflows. Foreign exchange reserves were estimated at $1.2 billion at that time.

33 BANKING AND SECURITIES

The Bank of Lebanon, established on 1 April 1964, is now the sole bank of issue. Its powers to regulate and control commercial banks and other institutions and to implement monetary policy were expanded by amendments to the Code of Money and Credit promulgated in October 1973.

Total demand deposits in commercial banks in December 1993 were estimated at LL422.4 billion. Time, savings, and foreign currency deposits in 1993 totaled LL13,986.8 million. Financing foreign trade and discounting trade bills make up most banking transactions; exchange and transfer of capital in the international market are substantial. To encourage the movement and deposit of foreign capital in Lebanon, a bank secrecy law of 1956 forbids banks to disclose details of a client's business even to judicial authorities. Legislation to permit a banking free zone in Beirut to encourage foreign banks became effective in 1977.

In 1968, several banks were seized, liquidated, or merged; as a result, the number of commercial banks operating in Lebanon was reduced from 93 to 74. In 1993, there were 70 banks.

The Beirut Stock Exchange was officially opened in 1952 as a center in which the few available company shares could be traded. The exchange closed during the civil war but reopened in 1979; however, there was little trading in stock during 1980–81. In 1982, Beirut was chosen as the headquarters of the Arab Stock Exchange Union, reflecting Lebanon's continuing importance as financial center of the Middle East.

34 INSURANCE

Activities of insurance companies are regulated by the National Insurance Council. All insurance companies must deposit a specific amount of money or real investments in an approved bank and must retain in Lebanon reserves commensurate with their volume of business. In 1985, 62 Lebanese and 52 foreign insurance companies operated in the country. Non-life premiums written in 1985 were valued at LL121 million; life insurance premiums totaled LL152 million.

35PUBLIC FINANCE

The annual budget of the central government must be approved by the National Assembly. The Lebanese government annually faces the formidable problem of financing a massive deficit resulting from heavy financial obligations and huge shortfalls in revenues. To reduce the deficit, the government has tried to increase revenues by raising taxes and tightening the budget. In 1991, revenues amounted to $533 million, while expenditures totaled $1.3 billion. Lebanon's external debt was estimated in 1991 at $360 million (8% of GDP). The level of public debt is expected to increase to $1.8 billion by 1996 from the external financing of the recovery program.

36TAXATION

A graduated tax is imposed on individual salaries, real profits, and real estate income. Corporations and joint stock companies generally are taxed on net real profits derived in Lebanon at a flat rate of 26%. Also levied are inheritance and gift taxes, social security payroll taxes, flat and graduated property taxes, and a stamp duty.

37CUSTOMS AND DUTIES

Restrictions on some imports and exports were imposed in 1977, and licenses are needed for certain import items. Import duties ranging from 10–75% are levied on most goods. There is a stamp tax and surcharge on a number of luxury items, including cars, jewelry, garments, and alcoholic beverages.

Preferential duties are applicable to imports from Arab countries and from EC countries. A free zone in Beirut is widely used as a point of entrepôt trade.

38FOREIGN INVESTMENT

Foreign investment is principally from Kuwait, Sa'udi Arabia, the UAE, France, and the UK. Syrian investments were large until the Syrian army invaded Lebanon in 1976. US private investments, mainly in oil transportation, storage facilities, and a fertilizer plant, totaled about $40 million as of 1980. To encourage foreign investment, major new enterprises are exempt from income tax for six years after their establishment. There are no limitations on the entry and transfer of capital at the free rate of exchange, and no registration, taxes, or fees on such capital movement. The Kuwaiti government recently promised to supply 25,000 barrels per day of crude oil to Lebanon at a reduced price over a period of one year. The Islamic Development Bank (IDB) has approved a $40 million soft loan to cover part of Lebanon's petroleum bill to Kuwait.

39ECONOMIC DEVELOPMENT

Since World War II, Lebanon has followed free-enterprise and free-trade policies. The country's favorable geographical position as a transit point and the traditional importance of the trading and banking sectors of the economy helped make Lebanon prosperous by the early 1970s. Lebanon became a center of trade, finance, and tourism by means of a stable currency backed largely with gold, by a conservative fiscal policy, by various incentives for foreign investors, and by minimization of banking regulations.

Lebanon's development went awry in the mid-1970s, as factional conflict, always present in Lebanese society, erupted into open warfare. The loss to the economy was enormous, particu-

larly in Beirut. The reconstruction plan submitted in 1979 by the Council for Development and Reconstruction (CDR) envisaged total expenditures of LL22 billion for rebuilding, including LL10 billion in the public sector and LL12 billion in the private sector. The cost of new housing and repair of damaged homes was estimated at LL4.5 billion, and of major road construction at LL1.5 billion. Redevelopment of the port of Beirut and reconstruction of Beirut airport were begun under the program.

In November 1979, Sa'udi Arabia and six other oil-producing Arab countries promised to contribute $2 billion for Lebanon's reconstruction effort over a five-year period, but only $381 million had been provided by October 1987. (After Israel invaded Lebanon in June 1982, the Arab countries decided to withhold future funds until Israeli forces had withdrawn completely.) As a result of the additional war damage, the CDR revised the total cost of the reconstruction program to LL68 billion (at 1982 prices) over a period of eight years (1983–91). In February 1985, however, a CDR official suggested that a figure of $33 billion (LL495 billion at 1985 prices) would be more realistic.

Under the leadership of Prime Minister Rafiq al–Hariri, Lebanon has embarked on a National Emergency Rehabilitation Program (NERP), worth $2.3 billion, and a 10-year Regional Development Program worth $12 billion. Areas of major activity are the rehabilitation of telecommunications, electricity grids, highways, sewage, waste management, water networks, renovation of the Beirut International Airport, harbor, education, and housing.

Lebanon's external debt was estimated at about $700 million at the end of 1993, which is low by international standards.

40SOCIAL DEVELOPMENT

A government social security plan, not fully implemented, is intended to provide sickness and maternity insurance, accident and disability insurance, family allowances, and end-of-service indemnity payments. The employer contributes 8.5% of payroll, while the employee and government make no contribution. The system provides lump sum payments only for retirement, disability, and survivor benefits. Foreigners employed in Lebanon are entitled to benefits if similar rights are available for Lebanese in their home countries. Voluntary social work societies also conduct relief and welfare activities. In 1989, 45,300 persons received family planning services. The fertility rate in 1985-90 was 3.4. Abortion is permitted on narrow health grounds.

Women's activities outside the home are often undertaken at the mercy of male relatives. They must obtain permission from their husbands in order to engage in trade. Many of the religious laws governing family and personal status discriminate against women.

41HEALTH

Lebanon's hospitals and health centers in 1985 numbered 160, of which 15 were public and 145 private. In 1991, there were 6,638 physicians, 1,390 pharmacists, 1,248 nurses, and 153 midwives, and in 1990, there were 1,015 dentists. In 1993, the birth rate was 27.2 per 1,000 people; in 1992, there were 78,000 births, with about 55% of married women (ages 15 to 49) using contraception. Life expectancy in 1992 was 68 years, and the infant mortality rate was 35 per 1,000 live births. The general mortality rate in 1993 was 7.2 per 1,000 inhabitants, and between 1982 and 1990, there were approximately 144,000 war-related deaths due to the Israeli invasion. In 1991, 92% of the population had access to safe water and, in 1992, 95% had access to health care services. That same year, immunization rates for children up to one year old were: diphtheria, pertussis, and tetanus (85%); polio (85%); and measles (51%).

42HOUSING

Despite substantial construction activity since World War II and a boom in construction during the 1960s, which increased the number of housing units to 484,000 in 1970, there was a housing shortage, especially of low-cost residential units, in the early 1970s. The situation was aggravated by the civil war and subsequent factional strife in which half of the country's real estate was severely damaged or destroyed. Under the CDR 1983–91 plan, nearly 30% of total expenditures were allocated to build new dwellings and to restore war-damaged houses. According to the latest available information for 1980-88, total housing units numbered 820,000 with 3.3 people per dwelling. Housing needs until the year 2000 have been estimated at 400,000 units.

43EDUCATION

Lebanon's literacy rate is relatively high for the Middle East; by 1990, an estimated 87.8% of adult males and 73.1% of adult females could read and write. Free primary education was introduced in 1960, but about two-thirds of all students attend private schools. In 1988 there were 346,534 primary school pupils and 241,964 general secondary school students. In 1991, the total enrollment for all higher level institutions was 85,495 students with 5,400 instructors. Lebanon had 16 colleges and universities in 1986; the total enrollment for all postsecondary institutions was 78,500. Leading universities include the American University in Beirut; St. Joseph University; the Lebanese (State) University; the University of the Holy Spirit; and the Arab University of Beirut.

44LIBRARIES AND MUSEUMS

Lebanon has about a dozen sizable libraries with specialized collections of books, manuscripts, and documents. Most libraries are in Beirut, but there are also collections at Sidon and Harissa. The National Library of Lebanon, founded in 1921, had more than 100,000 volumes when it was destroyed at the beginning of the war in 1975. The Arab University Library has 200,000 volumes, but the largest library is that of the American University in Beirut, with 516,000 volumes. St. Joseph University has several specialized libraries, including the Bibliothèque Orientale, with 174,000 volumes. The library of the St. John Monastery in Khonchara, founded in 1696, contains the first known printing press in the Middle East.

The National Museum of Lebanon, in Beirut, has a collection of historical documents and many notable antiquities, including the sarcophagus of King Ahiram (13th century BC), with the first known alphabetical inscriptions. The American University Museum also has an extensive collection of ancient artifacts.

45MEDIA

Before the civil war, Beirut was an international communications center with an earth satellite station and two oceanic cables linking it to Marseille and Alexandria. Government-controlled Radio Lebanon broadcasts in Arabic, and Tele-Liban broadcasts on three channels in Arabic, French, and English. Some 2,320,000 radios and 905,000 television sets were estimated to be in use in 1986.

Historically, Lebanon has had the freest press in the Arab world, and even during the civil war some 25 newspapers and magazines were published without restriction. The government assumed censorship powers in 1977, but they have not been implemented. Newspapers freely criticize the government but refrain from criticizing political groups that have the power to retaliate forcibly. There were 10 daily newspapers in 1991. The largest Arabic dailies are *An-Nahar* (1991 circulation, 30,000) and *As-Safir* (20,000). Also influential are the French-language papers *L'Orient–Le Jour* (21,500) and *Le Réveil* (6,000).

46ORGANIZATIONS

There are chambers of commerce and industry in Beirut, Tripoli, Sidon, and Zahlah, and a Rotary Club in Beirut. Lebanon has an Automobile and Touring Club, a French Chamber of Commerce, an Association of Lebanese Industries, and several voluntary social welfare agencies.

47TOURISM, TRAVEL, AND RECREATION

Before the civil war, Lebanon's antiquities—notably at Sidon, Tyre, Byblos, and Ba'albek—combined with a pleasant climate and scenery to attract many tourists (more than 2 million in 1974), especially from other Arab countries. During the war, however, fighting and bombing destroyed or heavily damaged major hotels in Beirut and reduced the number of tourists to practically zero. Tourists who are not Arab nationals need visas to enter Lebanon.

48FAMOUS LEBANESE

Khalil Gibran (Jibran, 1883–1931), a native of Lebanon, achieved international renown through his paintings and literary works. He is best known for his long poem *The Prophet*. Charles Habib Malik (1906–87), for many years Lebanon's leading diplomat, was president of the 13th UN General Assembly in 1958/59.

49DEPENDENCIES

Lebanon has no territories or colonies.

50BIBLIOGRAPHY

Akarli, Engin Deniz. *The Long Peace: Ottoman Lebanon, 1861–1920*. Berkeley: University of California Press, 1993.

Binder, Leonard. *Politics in Lebanon*. New York: Wiley, 1966.

Bleaney, C. H. *Lebanon*. Santa Barbara, Calif.: Clio Press, 1991.

Bustros, Gabriel M. *Who's Who in Lebanon: 1990–1991*. 11th ed. Beirut: Publitec, 1990.

Collelo, Thomas. *Lebanon, a Country Study*. 3rd ed. Washington, D.C.: Library of Congress, 1989.

Cooke, Miriam. *War's Other Voices: Women Writers on the Lebanese Civil War*. New York: Cambridge University Press, 1988.

Deeb, Marius. *The Lebanese Civil War*. New York: Praeger, 1980.

Eshel, Isaac. *Lebanon in Pictures*. Minneapolis: Lerner, 1988.

Friedman, Thomas L. *From Beirut to Jerusalem*. New York: Farrar, Straus, Giroux, 1989.

Gabriel, Philip L. *In the Ashes: The Story of Lebanon*. Ardmore, Pa.: Whitmore, 1978.

Gordon, David C. *The Republic of Lebanon: A Nation in Jeopardy*. Boulder, Colo.: Westview, 1983.

Harik, Ilya F. *Politics and Change in a Traditional Society: Lebanon 1711–1845*. Princeton, N.J.: Princeton University Press, 1967.

Hiro, Dilip. *Lebanon: Fire and Embers: A History of the Lebanese Civil War*. New York: St. Martin's, 1993.

Hitti, Philip K. *Lebanon in History: From the Earliest Times to the Present*. London: Macmillan, 1967.

Hudson, Michael C. *Precarious Republic: Political Modernization in Lebanon*. New York: Random House, 1968.

Khalaf, Samir. *Lebanon's Predicament*. New York: Columbia University Press, 1987.

Khalidi, Walid. *Conflict and Violence in Lebanon: Confrontation in the Middle East*. Cambridge, Mass.: Harvard University Press, 1979.

Labaki, Georges T. *The Lebanon Crisis (1975–1985): A Bibliography*. College Park, Md.: Center for International Development and Conflict Management, 1987.

Makdisi, Samir A. *Financial Policy and Economic Growth: The Lebanese Experience*. New York: Columbia University Press, 1979.

Meo, Leila T. *Lebanon, Improbable Nation.* Bloomington: Indiana University Press, 1965.

Norton, Augustus Richard. *Amal and the Shia: Struggle for the Soul of Lebanon.* Austin: University of Texas Press, 1987.

Rabinovich, Itamar. *The War for Lebanon 1970–1985.* Ithaca, N.Y.: Cornell University Press, 1985.

Rubin, Barry M. *The May 1983 Agreement over Lebanon Blum.* Washington, D.C.: The Johns Hopkins University, 1987.

Salibi, K. S. *The Modern History of Lebanon.* New York: Praeger, 1965.

Salibi, Kamal S. *A House of Many Mansions: The History of Lebanon Reconsidered.* Berkeley: University of California Press, 1988.

Sirriyeh, Hussein. *Lebanon, Dimensions of Conflict.* London: Brassey's for the International Institute for Strategic Studies, 1989.

Toward a Viable Lebanon. Washington, D.C.: Center for Contemporary Arab Studies, Georgetown University, 1988.

Vocke, Harold. *The Lebanese Civil War.* New York: St. Martin's, 1978.

MALAYSIA

CAPITAL: Kuala Lumpur.

FLAG: The national flag consists of 14 alternating horizontal stripes, of which 7 are red and 7 white; a gold 14-pointed star and crescent appear on a blue field in the upper left corner.

ANTHEM: *Negara Ku (My Country).*

MONETARY UNIT: The Malaysian ringgit (M$), or dollar, is divided into 100 sen, or cents. There are coins of 1, 5, 10, 20, and 50 sens and 1 ringgit, and notes of 1, 5, 10, 20, 100, 500, and 1,000 ringgits. M$1 = US$0.3741 (or US$1 = M$2.6730).

WEIGHTS AND MEASURES: The metric system became the legal standard in 1982, but some British weights and measures and local units are also in use.

HOLIDAYS: National Day, 31 August; Christmas, 25 December. Movable holidays include Vesak Day, Birthday of His Majesty the Yang di-Pertuan Agong, Hari Raya Puasa, Hari Raya Haji, the 1st of Muharram (Muslim New Year), Milad an-Nabi, Dewali, Thaipusam, and the Chinese New Year. Individual states celebrate the birthdays of their rulers and other holidays observed by indigenous ethnic groups.

TIME: 7 PM = noon GMT.

¹LOCATION, SIZE, AND EXTENT

Situated in Southeast Asia, Malaysia, with an area of 329,750 sq km (127,581 sq mi), consists of two noncontiguous areas: Peninsular Malaysia (formerly West Malaysia), on the Asian mainland, and the states of Sarawak and Sabah, known together as East Malaysia, on the island of Borneo. Comparatively, the area occupied by Malaysia is slightly larger than the state of New Mexico. Peninsular Malaysia, protruding southward from the mainland of Asia, comprises an area of 131,587 sq km (50,806 sq mi), extending 748 km (465 mi) SSE-NNW and 322 km (200 mi) ENE-WSW. It is bordered on the N by Thailand, on the E by the South China Sea, on the S by the Strait of Johore, and on the W by the Strait of Malacca and the Andaman Sea, with a total boundary length of 2,068 km (1,285 mi). Sarawak, covering an area of 124,449 sq km (48,050 sq mi), on the northwest coast of Borneo, extends 679 km (422 mi) NNE-SSW and 254 km (158 mi) ESE-WNW. It is bounded by Brunei on the N, Sabah on the NE, Indonesia on the E and S, and the South China Sea on the W. Sarawak's total boundary length is 2,621 km (1,629 mi). Situated at the northern end of Borneo, Sabah has an area of 74,398 sq km (28,725 sq mi), with a length of 412 km (256 mi) E-W and a width of 328 km (204 mi) N–S. To the N is the Balabac Strait, to the NE the Sulu Sea, to the SE the Celebes Sea, to the S Indonesia, to the SW Sarawak, and to the W the South China Sea, with a total boundary length of 2,008 km (1,248 mi). The total boundary length of Malaysia is 7,344 km (4,563 mi).

Malaysia claims several atolls of the Spratly Island group in the South China Sea. The claim, in a region where oil is suspected, is disputed by China, the Philippines, Taiwan, and Viet Nam. Malaysia's capital city, Kuala Lumpar, is located in the western part of Peninsular Malaysia.

²TOPOGRAPHY

Four-fifths of Peninsular Malaysia is covered by rain forest, jungle, and swamp. The northern regions are divided by a series of mountain ranges that rise abruptly from the wide, flat coastal plains. The highest peaks, Gunong Tahan (2,190 m/7,185 ft) and Gunong Korbu (2,183 m/7,162 ft), are in the north central region. The main watershed follows a mountain range about 80 km (50 mi) inland, roughly parallel to the west coast. The rivers flowing to the east, south, and west of this range are swift and have cut some deep gorges, but on reaching the coastal plains they become sluggish. The western coastal plain contains most of the country's population and the main seaports, George Town (on the offshore Pulau Pinang) and Kelang (formerly Port Swettenham). The eastern coastal plain is mostly jungle and lightly settled. It is subject to heavy storms from the South China Sea and lacks natural harbors.

Sarawak consists of an alluvial and swampy coastal plain, an area of rolling country interspersed with mountain ranges, and a mountainous interior. Rain forests cover the greater part of Sarawak. Many of the rivers are navigable. Sabah is split in two by the Crocker Mountains, which extend north and south some 48 km (30 mi) inland from the west coast, rising to over 4,100 m (13,450 ft) at Mt. Kinabalu, the highest point in Malaysia. Most of the interior is covered with tropical forest, while the western coastal area consists of alluvial flats making up the main rubber and rice land.

³CLIMATE

The climate of Peninsular Malaysia is equatorial, characterized by fairly high but uniform temperatures (ranging from 23° to 31°C/73° to 88°F throughout the year), high humidity, and copious rainfall (averaging about 250 cm/100 in annually). There are seasonal variations in rainfall, with the heaviest rains from October to December or January; except for a few mountain areas, the most abundant rainfall is in the eastern coastal region, where it averages over 300 cm (120 in) per year. Elsewhere the annual average is 200–300 cm (80–120 in), the northwestern and southwestern regions having the least rainfall. The nights are usually cool because of the nearby seas. The climate of East Malaysia is relatively cool for an area so near the equator.

⁴FLORA AND FAUNA

About 70% of Malaysia consists of tropical rain forest. In Peninsular Malaysia, camphor, ebony, sandalwood, teak, and many varieties of palm trees abound. Jungle fauna includes seladang (Malayan bison), deer, wild pigs, tree shrews, honey bears, forest cats, civets, monkeys, crocodiles, huge lizards, and snakes. The seladang weighs about a ton and is the largest wild ox in the world. An immense variety of insects, particularly butterflies, and some 575 species of birds are found.

On Sabah and Sarawak, lowland forests contain some 400 species of tall dipterocarps (hardwoods) and semihardwoods; fig trees abound, attracting small mammals and birds; and groves are formed by the extensive aerial roots of warangen (a sacred tree to indigenous peoples). As altitude increases, herbaceous plants—buttercups, violets, and valerian—become more numerous, until moss-covered evergreen forests are reached from 1,520 to 1,830 m (5,000–6,000 ft). Large butterflies, brilliantly colored birds of paradise, and a great wealth of other insect and bird species inhabit the two states.

⁵ENVIRONMENT

The Environmental Quality Act of 1974 and other environmental laws are administered by the Division of Environment of the Ministry of Science, Technology, and Environment. Discharge of untreated sewage accounted for one-quarter of all water pollution in the mid-1980s, the most heavily polluted areas being along the west coast. Malaysia's water pollution problem is evident in the condition of its rivers, of which 40% are polluted. The coasts are affected by petroleum and sewage. The nation has 109.4 cubic miles of water with 47% used for farming and 30% used for industrial activity. Of the people in rural areas, 34% do not have pure water. Malaysia's cities product 1.5 million tons of solid waste per year. Clean-air legislation, limiting industrial and automobile emissions, was adopted in 1978. Discharge of oil by vessels in Malaysian waters is prohibited. Of Malaysia's total land area, 59% is tropical rainforest. The country's forests are threatened by commercial interests.

In 1994, 23 of the nation's mammal species and 35 bird species were endangered. As of 1987, endangered species in Malaysia included the orangutan, tiger, Asian elephant, Malayan tapir, Sumatran rhinoceros, Singapore roundleaf horseshoe bat, four species of turtle (green sea, hawksbill, olive ridley, and leatherback), and two species of crocodile (false gavial and Siamese).

⁶POPULATION

The population of Malaysia totaled 17,566,982 at the 1991 census, of whom 82.3% lived in Peninsular Malaysia, 9.4% in Salsrawak, and 8.3% in Sabah. The population for the year 2000 is projected at 22,263,000, assuming a crude birthrate of 25 per 1,000 population, a crude death rate of 4.8, and a net natural increase of 20.2 during 1995–2000. The overall population density in 1991 was 53 per sq km (138 per sq mi), and the annual rate of increase during 1985–90 was estimated at 2.64%. Approximately 38% of the total population was under 15 years of age in 1990.

The population of Peninsular Malaysia is concentrated along the west coast. Kuala Lumpur, the capital, with a population (1991 census) of 1,232,900, is the largest city.

⁷MIGRATION

Not until British economic enterprise first attracted foreign labor after 1800 did large-scale Chinese, Indian, and Malaysian migration (nonnative Indonesians and Borneans) take place. The early migrants were transients: in 1921, only 20.3% of the

Chinese and 11.9% of the Indians were Malayan-born. However, migration data for subsequent years show a general tendency toward permanent settlement by these nonindigenous portions of the population. The percentages of the total Chinese population reporting Peninsular Malaysia as their birthplace were 29.1%, 62.5%, and 74.4% for the years 1931, 1947, and 1957, respectively; the percentages of Indians reporting their birthplace as Peninsular Malaysia were 21.1%, 51.4%, and 64.6% for the same respective years. By 1953, the Malays were a minority in their own territory. The government enacted legislation restricting further immigration, and by 1968 the Malays formed slightly more than 50% of the population. Regulations which took effect in 1968 concerning passports and border crossings between Malaysia and Indonesia and between Malaysia and the Philippines were also intended to restrict immigration. By 1970, more than four-fifths of the Chinese and Indians were born in Peninsular Malaysia. Between 1975 and 1989, more than 250,000 Vietnamese refugees found asylum in Malaysia; the vast majority subsequently migrated to other countries. Between May 1989 and the end of 1993 all 10,495 arriving were denied entry. Nevertheless, an estimated 1 million illegal immigrants are believed to be in Malaysia.

⁸ETHNIC GROUPS

The population of Malaysia consists of three main ethnic groups—Malays, Chinese, and peoples of the South Asian subcontinent. Malays and other indigenous groups are known as Bumiputras ("sons of the soil"). Estimates for 1990 reported the following distribution: Malays and other indigenous groups (Bumiputras), 61.7%; Chinese, 29.7%; persons of Indian and Pakistani, and Bangladesh descent, 8.1%; and other groups, 0.5%. Malays predominate in the rural areas, while the Chinese are concentrated in urban and mining areas, where they control much of the nation's wealth; enmity between the two communities has occasionally erupted into violence. The non-Malay indigenous groups on the peninsula are collectively called the Orang Asli (aborigines) and number about 50,000.

Non-Malay indigenous tribes constitute about half of Sarawak's residents; the largest indigenous group consists of the Sea Dayaks, or Ibans, followed by the Land Dayaks, or Bidayuh. The majority of Sabah's population consists of indigenous peoples, principally Kadazans, Bajaus, and Muruts. The balance is dominated by Chinese (14%).

⁹LANGUAGES

Bahasa Malaysia, or Malay, is the national language and the lingua franca of all Malaysia. The traditional Bahasa Malaysia script is Jawi, which derives from Arabic script, but Rumi, based on the Roman alphabet, is officially used in government, education, and business. English is widely employed in government and commerce and is a compulsory subject in all schools. Chinese (notably the Mandarin, Cantonese, Hokkien, and Hakka dialects), Arabic, Tamil, Hindustani, Punjabi, Kadazan, and many other languages and dialects are spoken. Most Malaysians are bilingual or multilingual.

¹⁰RELIGIONS

Islam is the official religion, and about 53% of all Malaysians are Muslims. The head of state, the yang di-pertuan agong, is also the national leader of the Islamic faith. The constitution, however, guarantees freedom to profess, practice, and propagate other religions. Religious lines generally follow ethnic lines. Almost all Malays are Muslims; most Indians are Hindus, with a substantial minority of Muslims, Sikhs, and Parsees; and most Chinese are Confucian-Buddhists, with a minority Muslim representation. Christianity has won some adherents among the Chinese and Indians. The indigenous peoples of Sabah and Sarawak are still

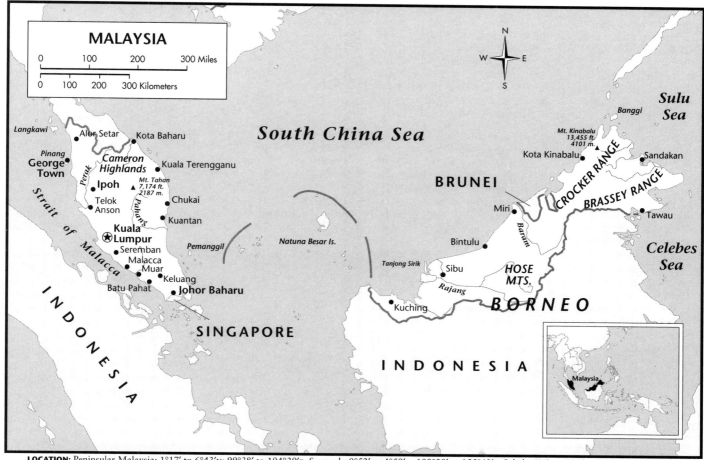

LOCATION: Peninsular Malaysia: 1°17′ to 6°43′N; 99°38′ to 104°39′E. Sarawak: 0°52′ to 4°59′N; 109°38′ to 155°43′E. Sabah: 4°6′ to 7°22′N; 115°7′ to 119°17′E
BOUNDARY LENGTHS: Peninsular Malaysia: Thailand, 576 km (358 mi); total coastline, 1,931 km (1,200 mi). Sarawak: Brunei, 418 km (260 mi); Sabah, 135 km (84 mi);
coastline, 888 km (552 mi). Sabah: Sarawak, 135 km (84 mi); total coastline, 1,558 km (968 mi). Total boundary length of Indonesia with
Sarawak and Sabah, 1,496 km (930 mi). TERRITORIAL SEA LIMIT: 12 mi.

largely animist, although many have become Christian. Roman Catholics were estimated at 3% of the population in (1993).

11TRANSPORTATION
In 1991, the highway system of Peninsular Malaysia consisted of 23,600 km (14,665 mi) of roads, of which 19,352 km (12,025 mi) were paved. The major highways run north–south along the east and west coasts; east–west links connect George Town and Kota Baharu in the north and Kuala Lumpur and Kuantan farther south. The sparser road network on Sabah totaled 3,782 km (2,350 mi) in 1991, the road network on Sarawak in 1991 totaled 1,644 km (1,022 mi). As of 1991, (according to the Malaysian Highway Authority) the East-West Highway (Federal Route 2) crossing Peninsular Malaysia, as well as the Klang Valley Expressway connecting Kuala Lumpur to Port Klang were completed. The 924 km (574 mi) North-South Highway along the west coast of Peninsular Malaysia connecting Thailand and Singapore was expected to be complete by early 1994. In 1991, registered vehicles included 2,000,000 automobiles and 400,000 commercial vehicles.

The national Malayan Railway Administration operates some 1,665 km (1,035 mi) of Peninsular Malaysia, which provides links to Thailand, Singapore, and eastern parts of the peninsula. Sabah State Railways provides diesel service along the west coast and in the interior for 136 km (85 mi). There are no railroads in Sarawak.

The three leading ports, all located on the busy Strait of Malacca, are Kelang (the port for Kuala Lumpur), Johor Baharu, and George Town. Kuching is the main port for Sarawak, and Kota Kinabalu the main port for Sabah. The Malaysian merchant fleet in 1991 consisted of 169 ships with a combined capacity of 1,676,000 GRT.

Most international flights enter or leave Malaysia through Kuala Lumpur Sabang International Airport; other international airports serve George Town and Kota Kinabalu. In 1991, Malaysia Airlines carried some 11,837,400 passengers, including 4,662,600 international passengers. The Malaysian Airline System (MAS) provides domestic service to most major cities of the peninsula and to Sarawak and Sabah.

12HISTORY
The ancestors of the Malays came down from South China and settled in the Malay Peninsula about 2000 BC. Sri Vijaya, a strong Indo-Malay empire with headquarters at Palembang in southern Sumatra, rose about AD 600 and came to dominate both sides of the Strait of Malacca, levying tribute and tolls on the ships faring between China and India. In the 14th century, however, Sri Vijaya fell, and Malaysia became part of the Majapahit Empire centered in Java. About 1400, a fugitive ruler from Temasik (now Singapore) founded a principality at Malacca (now Melaka) and embraced Islam. It was at Malacca that the West obtained its first foothold on the peninsula. At the height of glory and power, the Malacca principality fell to Portugal in 1511. In their turn, the Portuguese were driven out by the Dutch in 1641. The British East India Company laid the groundwork for British control of Malaya in 1786 by leasing from the sultan of Kedah the island of

Pinang, off the west coast of Malaya, about 800 km (500 mi) north of Singapore. Fourteen years later, it obtained from him a small area on the mainland opposite Pinang. In 1819, Sir Thomas Stamford Raffles obtained permission to establish a settlement at Singapore; in 1824, by agreement and financial settlement, the island was ceded to the British East India Company. In the following year, the Dutch settlement at Malacca was ceded to Great Britain. Pinang, Singapore, and Malacca were combined under British rule in 1829 to form the Straits Settlements. The states of Perak and Selangor in 1874 secured treaties of protection from the British. Similar treaties were subsequently made with the sultans of Negri Sembilan (1874–89) and Pahang (1888). In 1895, these four states became a federation (the Federated Malay States), with a British resident-general and a system of centralized government. In 1909, under the Bangkok Treaty, Siam (now Thailand) ceded to British control the four northern states of Kelantan, Trengganu, Perlis, and Kedah. These four, together with Johor, which in 1914 was made a British protectorate, became known as the Unfederated Malay States. Separate British control was extended to Sabah, then known as North Borneo, in 1882. Six years later, North Borneo and Sarawak each became separate British protectorates. Tin mining and rubber grew rapidly under British rule, and large numbers of Chinese and Indian laborers were imported, respectively, for these industries.

Japanese forces invaded Malaya and the Borneo territories in December 1941 and occupied them throughout World War II. Within a year after the Japanese surrender in September 1945, the British formed the Malayan Union, consisting of the nine peninsular states, together with Pinang and Malacca; also in 1946, Singapore and the two Borneo protectorates became separate British crown colonies. The Malayan Union was succeeded by the Federation of Malaya on 1 February 1948. Over the next decade, the British weathered a Communist insurgency, as Malaya progressed toward self-government. On 31 August 1957, the Federation of Malaya became an independent member of the Commonwealth of Nations. On 1 August 1962, Great Britain and Malaya agreed in principle on the formation of the new state of Malaysia—a political merger of Singapore and the British Borneo territories (Sarawak, Brunei, and North Borneo) with the Federation. On 1 September 1962, by a 70% plurality, Singapore voted in a referendum for incorporation in the proposed Malaysia, but an abortive revolt staged by Brunei's ultranationalist Brunei People's Party in December 1962 eliminated the sultanate from the proposed merger. On 16 September 1963, the Federation of Malaya, the State of Singapore, and the newly independent British colonies of Sarawak and Sabah merged to form the Federation of Malaysia ("Federation" was subsequently dropped from the official name). On 7 August 1965, Singapore seceded from the Federation and established an independent republic. From the outset, Indonesia's President Sukarno attempted by economic and military means to take over the young nation as part of Indonesia; cordial relations between the two countries were not established until after Sukarno's ouster in 1966. Internal disorders stemming from hostilities between Chinese and Malay communities in Kuala Lumpur disrupted the 1969 national elections and prompted the declaration of a state of emergency lasting from mid-1969 to February 1971. Successive governments managed to sustain political stability until 1987, when racial tensions between Chinese and Malay increased over a government plan to assign non-Mandarin-speaking administrators to Chinese-language schools.

In October 1987 the Malaysian government, under provisions of the Internal Security Act (ISA) which allows detention without trial on grounds of national security, arrested 79 political and civil leaders and closed four newspapers in an effort to stifle dissent. The government called its actions necessary to prevent racial violence, but many prominent Malaysians, including Tunku

Abdul Rahman, the country's first prime minister, condemned the actions. At the same time the government clamped down on all news sources disseminating what the government considered false news, and new legislation denied licensing to news sources not conforming to Malaysian values. In 1981 Dato' Hussein bin Onn was succeeded as prime minsiter by Sato' Sei Dr. Mahathir Mohamad, whose leadership came under criticism from within the UMNO and other political parties as racial tensions increased. Part of the challenge to Dr. Mahathir's party leadership came in the form of a legal suit claiming that some of the delegates to the UMNO elections of 1987 had not been legally registered, therefore, the election should be declared null and void. The High Court ruled that due to the irregularities UMNO was an unlawful society and that in effect the election was invalid. Dr. Mahathir held that the ruling did not affect the legal status of the government; he was supported by the ruling Head of State, Tunku Mahmood Iskandar. In 1988 Dr. Mahathir formed a New UMNO, Umno Baru, and declared that party members would have to re-register to join. (Umno Baru was thereafter referred to as UMNO.) Under provisions of the ISA four people linked to the Parti Bersatu Sabah (PBS) were detained over alleged involvement in a secessionist plot in Sabah in June 1990. In July 1990 elections the PBS won 36 of 48 seat in the Sabah State Legislative Assembly. Prior to the general election of 1990 the PBS aligned itself with the opposition, which had formed an informal electoral alliance, Gagasan Rakyat (People's Might). The National Front (BN) won 127 of the 180 seats, thus maintaining control of the House of Representatives with the two-thirds majority necessary to amend the Constitution. The opposition increased its seats from 37 to 53. In 1992 the People's Might registered as a political organization and Razaleigh was elected Chairman.

In 1990 the restructuring of the portfolio of the Ministry of Trade and Industry was rationalized into two new Ministries, the Ministry of International Trade and Industry (MITI) and the Ministry of Domestic Trade and Consumer Affairs (MDTCA). In an action that was widely regarded as politically motivated, Datuk Seri Joseph Pairin Kitingan, Chief Minister of Sabah and President of the PBS, was arrested in January 1991 and charged with corruption, then released on bail. After subsequent meetings with Dr. Mahathir it was announced that the PBS state Government had proposed power sharing with United Sabah National Organization (USNO). The head of USNO, Tun Mustapha Harun, resigned from USNO and joined UMNO. This switch necessitated a by-election and in May 1991 UMNO took its first seat in Sabah. The rise of Dayak nationalism in Sarawak was considered as less of a threat after the 1991 state elections. The Sarawak Native People's Party (PBDS, Parti Bansa Dayak Sarawak) retained only 7 of the 15 seats it had won in the 1987 election. A High Court ruling in 1991 upheld a ruling by the Ministry of Home Affairs banning the public sale of party newspapers. Speculation was that by targeting limited media outlets the government was muzzling the opposition press.

In 1991 UMNO raised the issue of the alleged abuse of privilege by Malaysia's nine hereditary rulers. A resolution tabled in 1990 had demanded the rulers be restrained from interfering in politics. In November 1992 the issue of the constitutional status of the Sultans again arose when it was proposed that the rulers' immunity from prosecution be removed. The cases in point were; the recent alleged assault on a hockey coach by the Sultan of Johore and the 1981 incident in which the Sultan of Johore (before he became Sultan) was convicted of homicide but pardoned by his father the pervious Sultan. In January 1993 these proposed amendments to the Constitution were passed. Immediately after passage of the bill royal privileges other than those sanctioned and allocations not expressly provided in the constitution were withdrawn. The nine hereditary rulers first rejected the constitutional changes; however, they agreed to a compromise formula on the bill that effectively removed the blanket legal immunity granted to them. The compromise upheld the constitutional stipulation of royal assent for laws affecting the monarchy. Criticism arose over Dr. Mahathir's handling of this situation as it emphasized the antipathy between his authoritarian style and the "Malay way." These constitutional changes also highlighted Dr. Mahathir's previous moves to strengthen executive power at cost of the the judiciary, to consolidate UMNO's control of the legislature, and to control the press. On 17 January 1994 Sabah's Chief Minister, Datuk Joseph Pairin Kitingan, was found guilty of corruption. The fine imposed on him fell short of the minimum required to disqualify him from office. Although PBS won the Sabah polls in February 1994, Pairin resigned as the PBS's leading members joined the National Front, and the Sabah wing of UMNO (with 18 of 48 seats) was about to be installed. In August 1994 the government moved to ban the radical Islamic sect, Al-Arqam.

Between 1978 and 1989 Malaysia provided asylum to about 230,000 Vietnamese refugees as they awaited resettlement in the West. In March 1989 Malaysia responded to the continuing influx of refugees and the Western nations' slow efforts to place them with a plan to screen refugees in order to separate economic migrants from political refugees. This policy was confirmed by the United Nations.

13GOVERNMENT

Malaysia is a constitutional monarchy consisting of 13 states, 9 of which were formerly sultanates under British protection and 4 of which (Melaka, Pulau Pinang, Sarawak, and Sabah) were former British settlements ruled by appointed governors.

The constitution, promulgated on 31 August 1957 and subsequently amended, derives from the former Federation of Malaya, with provisions for the special interests of Sabah and Sarawak. It provides for the election of a head of state, the yang di-pertuan agong, or paramount ruler, for a single term of five years by the Conference of Rulers. The constitution also provides for a deputy head of state, chosen in the same manner and for the same term.

The Conference of Rulers consists of the nine hereditary sultans. Its consent must be obtained for any law that alters state boundaries; affects the rulers' privileges, honors, or dignities; or extends any religious acts, observances, or ceremonies to the country as a whole. The conference must also be consulted on proposed changes of administrative policy affecting the special position of the Malays or the vital interests of other communities.

The yang di-pertuan agong, who must be one of the hereditary sultans, is commander-in-chief of the armed forces and has the power to designate judges for the Federal Court and the High Courts on the advice of the prime minister, whom he appoints. Until January 1984, the paramount ruler had the right to veto legislation by withholding his assent; this right was lost in a constitutional compromise that gave the paramount ruler the right to delay new laws for up to 60 days but also stipulated that, if passed by a two-thirds majority, a bill may become law after six months without his signature.

The yang di-pertuan agong from 1979 to 1984 was Ahmad Shah al-Musta'in Billah Ibni al-Marhum, the sultan of Pahang. The leading candidate to succeed him was Idris al-Mutawakil Allahi Shah Ibni al-Marhum, the sultan of Perak, but when Idris died of a heart attack on 31 January 1984, the Conference of Rulers selected Mahmud Iskandar Ibni al-Marhum Sultan Ismail, who as crown prince of Johor had been convicted of homicide in a shooting incident in 1977 but had been pardoned by his father and became sultan in 1981.

In 1989 the Sultan of Perak, Azian Muhibuddin Shah, became the yang di-pertuan agong. Executive power rests with the cabinet, chosen by the prime minister, who is the leader of the majority party or coalition of the House of Representatives (Dewan Rakyat), the lower house of Parliament. The 180 members of the House of Representatives must be at least 21 years old; they are elected by universal adult suffrage (at age 20). Their term is five years unless the House is dissolved earlier. (A constitutional amendment, approved in 1992, to increase the number of parliamentary constituencies from 180 to 192 would take effect at the next general election in August 1995.) Members comprise two representatives from each state elected by the respective state legislatures, three representatives from the federal territories, and other appointees. The 70-member Senate (Dewan Negara) consists of 26 elected members (2 from each state); 4 members (2 from each territory) appointed by the paramount ruler to represent the Federal Territories of Kuala Lumpur and the island of Labaun; and 40 members appointed by the paramount ruler on the basis of distinguished public service or their eligibility to represent the ethnic minorities. Senators must be at least 30 years old; they hold office for six-year terms.

14POLITICAL PARTIES

Before World War II, there was limited political activity in Malaya, but the Japanese occupation and its aftermath brought a new political awareness. Postwar political parties sought independence, and although the Malays feared domination by the populous minorities, particularly the economically stronger Chinese, the United Malays National Organization (UMNO), the leading Malay party, and the Malaysian Chinese Association (MCA) formed the Alliance Party in 1952. This party was later joined by the Malaysian Indian Congress (MIC) and became the nation's dominant political party. The Malayan Communist Party, a powerful and well-organized group after the war, penetrated and dominated the trade unions. In 1948, after the Communists had resorted to arms, they were outlawed.

In the elections of April 1964, the Alliance Party won a majority of 89 of the 154 House seats. The third general election since independence was held in Peninsular Malaysia on 10 May 1969; in the balloting, the Alliance Party suffered a setback, winning only 66 seats. The election was followed by communal rioting, mainly between Malays and Chinese, resulting in much loss of life and damage to property. The government suspended Parliament and declared a state of emergency; elections in Sarawak and Sabah were postponed until July 1970. By the time Parliament was reconvened on 22 February 1971, the Alliance had achieved a two-thirds majority (required for the passage of constitutional amendments) with the addition of 10 unopposed seats from Sabah and through a coalition with the Sarawak United People's Party, which controlled 12 seats.

The elections for state assemblies also resulted in a setback for the Alliance Party, which before the elections had controlled 10 of the 13 state assemblies, but after the elections only 7. In September 1970, Tunku Abdul Rahman retired as prime minister and was replaced by the deputy prime minister, Tun Abdul Razak. In 1973, the Alliance Party formed a broader coalition consisting of the UMNO, MCA, MIC, and eight minority parties. Known as the National Front and led by the UMNO, the ruling coalition was returned to power in the 1974, 1978, 1982, and 1986 elections with overwhelming majorities (148 of 177 seats in 1986). The principal opposition parties, which win few seats owing to a legislative apportionment scheme that heavily favors Malay voters, are the Chinese-based Democratic Action Party (DAP), founded in 1966, and the Pan-Malayan Islamic Party, dedicated to establishing an Islamic state.

In July 1981, Datuk Seri Mahathir bin Mohamad replaced Datuk Hussein bin Onn as prime minister. As of 1986, the National Front also had majorities in 11 of 13 state legislatures; the state assembly of Sabah, the lone exception, was under the control of the Sabah People's Union (Berjaya). In the 1986 elections, Chinese voters moved away from the MCA and toward the

DAP. In April 1987, Mahathir narrowly overcame a challenge to his leadership of the UMNO.

As of 1992 there were more than 30 registered parties, 13 of which are represented in the federal parliament. Some of the main parties are: the Barisan Nasional (National Front), a broad coalition comprising the United Malays National Organization (UMNO) and 12 other parties, most ethnically based; DAP; Parti Se-Islam Malaysia (PAS); Parti Bersatu Sabah (PBS); the Malaysian Chinese Association (MCA); and Semangat 46. In the election held 21 October 1990 of the 180 seats the results were: National Front (127 seats), DAP (20), PAS (7), independents (4), and other (22). Within the National Front UMNO took 71 seats and MCA 18 seats. The National Front lost control of two states: the Islamic opposition party (PAS) captured control of Kelantan and the PBS retained control of Sabah. The Semangat 46 (Spirit of 46) was a loose opposition front led by Tengku Razaleigh and composed of ideologically diverse parties which bolted from the Barisan coalition on the eve of the elections. The party registered in May 1989, its name being a reference to the year of UMNO formation.

15 LOCAL GOVERNMENT

Of the 11 Peninsular Malaysian states, 9 are headed by sultans, who act as titular rulers and as leaders of the Islamic faith in their respective states. The other two Peninsular states, Pinang and Melaka, are headed by federally appointed governors. State governments are parliamentary in form and share legislative powers with the federal parliament. Effective executive authority in each state is vested in a chief minister, selected by the majority party in the state legislature. The legislative assembly, composed of elected members, legislates in conformity with the Malaysian and state constitutions, subject to the sultan's assent. In Peninsular Malaysia the states are divided into districts, each of which consists of 5 to 10 subdistricts, called mukim (derah in Kelantan). Each mukim is responsible for varying numbers of kampongs (villages or compounds). The mukim may include villages, or consist of large, sparsely populated tracts of land. Each one is headed by a penghulu (penggawa in Kelantan), a part-time official locally elected for five years, who serves as the principal liaison between the district and the village. The village elects a chief (ketua).

Upon incorporation into the Federation of Malaysia in 1963, both Sabah and Sarawak adopted separate constitutions for their local self-government; each is headed by a chief minister, appointed by the majority party of the elective legislature. In Sarawak, divisions and districts are the main subdivisions; in Sabah their counterparts are residencies and districts. The district officer is the most important link between the governing and the governed. His responsibilities are administrative, fiscal and judicial. Kuala Lumpur, the national capital and former capital of Selangor State, was constituted as a separate federal territory, under the national government, on 1 February 1974. The mayor is appointed by the paramount ruler on the advice of the prime minister.

16 JUDICIAL SYSTEM

Malaysia has a unified judicial system, and all courts take cognizance of both federal and state laws. The legal system is founded on British common law. Most cases come before magistrates and sessions courts. Religious courts decide questions of Islamic law and custom. The Federal Court, the highest court in Malaysia, reviews decisions referred from the High Court of Peninsular Malaysia, the High Court of Sabah and Sarawak, and subordinate courts. The Federal Court, of which the yang di-pertuan agong is lord president, has original jurisdiction in disputes among states or between a state and the federal government. Administrative detention is permitted in security cases, in which certain other guarantees of due process are reportedly suspended.

The judiciary has traditionally functioned with a high degree of independence. Most civil and criminal cases are fair and open. The accused must be brought before a judge within 24 hours of arrest. Defendants have the right to counsel and to bail. Strict rules of evidence apply in court and appeal is available to higher courts. Criminal defendants may also appeal for clemency to the King or to the local state ruler. Severe penalties, including the death penalty, are imposed for drug-related offenses.

17 ARMED FORCES

In 1993, the all-volunteer armed forces numbered 127,500. The total strength of the army was 105,000, including 40 infantry and armored battalions, 5 artillery regiments, and supporting air defense, signal, engineer, special forces, and administrative units. Contingents of the Malaysian army patrol the Malaysia-Thailand border against Communist guerrillas and provide four UN observer teams. The navy had 10,500 personnel, 4 frigates, 8 missile-equipped fast-attack craft, and 29 large patrol craft. The air force had 12,000 personnel and 9 combat aircraft. Paramilitary forces numbered 30,000, and the People's Volunteer Corps had 200,000. There are 44,300 reserves. Malaysian arms and equipment are a mixture of domestic, UK, and US material. Australia provides a small training mission. Expenditures on defense amounted to $2.4 billion (1992) or 5% of the gross domestic product.

18 INTERNATIONAL COOPERATION

Malaysia is a member of the UN, having joined on 17 September 1957, and participates in ESCAP and all the nonregional specialized agencies except the IFAD and WIPO. It also belongs to the Asian Development Bank, ASEAN, the Commonwealth of Nations, and G-77. Malaysia is a signatory of GATT and the Law of the Sea.

Before the 1970s, Malaysia pursued a pro-Western policy, but in recent years it has promoted the neutralization of Southeast Asia while establishing ties with China, the Democratic People's Republic of Korea, and Cuba and strengthening relations with the USSR and other East European states. Links with its traditional allies, including the US, have remained strong in the course of this transition. Relations with the UK were strained in the early 1980s, after the British imposed surcharges on foreign students attending universities in the UK and issued new regulations reducing opportunities for foreign takeovers of British-owned companies. Malaysia agreed to drop its "buy British last" campaign in 1983 after the UK expanded scholarship opportunities for Malaysian students. In 1986 there was some friction with Singapore because of its improved relations with Israel. Malaysia shares the anti-Zionist ideology of the Arab League countries.

19 ECONOMY

Malaysia is one of the most prosperous nations in Southeast Asia, despite the periodic cyclical dislocations inherent in an export-oriented economy. In 1985, the GDP in current prices was estimated at US$31.2 billion, up from US$24.8 billion in 1981. Real growth rates were estimated at 6.9% in 1981, 7.6% in 1984, and –1.0% in 1985. Until the 1970s, Malaysia's economy was based chiefly on its plantation and mining activities, with rubber and tin the principal exports. Since then, however, Malaysia has added palm oil, tropical hardwoods, petroleum, natural gas, and manufactured items to its export list. This diversification has greatly reduced the nation's dependence on overseas commodity markets. By 1980, rubber accounted for about 7.5% of the value of all exports, down from 30% in the 1970s, and tin for about 4.3%, down from about 20% in the 1970s. The worldwide recession in 1981–82 hurt the Malaysian economy. Prices of Malaysia's traditional commodity exports were depressed, growth slowed, and investment fell. Government efforts to stimulate the economy through spending on heavy industry and infrastructure projects financed by borrowing pushed foreign debt from $4 billion in 1980 to $15 billion in 1984. In 1985–86 Malaysia's long period of high growth abruptly halted as oil and palm oil prices were halved. Recovery began in late 1986 and 1987; growth was spurred by foreign demand for exports. Growth rates continued on the average in the 8-9% range from 1987–92. In 1990 manufacturing was the economy's largest sector, accounting for about 27% of GDP. For the same year agriculture was the second largest sector for an estimated 19% GDP and 30% of employment.

In 1990 Malaysia had been the world's largest producer of natural rubber accounting for 25% of world production, however, by 1993 it was overtaken by both Thailand and Indonesia. In 1990 Malaysia was also the world's largest exporter of tropical hardwood, the world's fourth largest producer of cocoa, and of source 60% of the world's palm oil (1990). As of 1993 the manufacturing sector made up 69% of exports, and projections for 1995 were that manufacturing would make up one third of GDP, up 60% from the 1985 level. Into the 1990s Malaysia remains a major producer of commodities including rubber, tin, palm oil, tropical hardwoods, cocoa and pepper. It also produces and exports oil, petroleum products and liquified natural gas, amounting to 18% of total exports in 1990. The government or government-owned entities dominate a number of sectors (plantations and banking), and they may account for one-third of the economy. Since 1986 the government has moved toward corporatization and the eventual privatization of telecommunications, ports, a major highway, and the national electricity board. Tourism contributes significantly to the economy: in 1990 there were 7.5 million tourists. The estimated unemployment rate for 1992 was 4.1%. Malaysia's labor force is educated and disciplined but the labor market is tightening. Pressure is being exerted on wages and imported contract labor is used to relieve this bottleneck. The estimated inflation rate based on consumer prices for 1992 was 4.7%. Sarawak's basic economy is subsistence agriculture, supplemented by petroleum production and refining, the collection of forest produce, fishing, and the cultivation of cash crops, primarily rubber, timber and pepper. Sabah's economy rests on logging, petroleum production, rubber, pepper, and timber.

20INCOME

In 1992, Malaysia's GNP was $51,917 million at current prices, or $2,790 per capita. For the period 1985–92 the average inflation rate was 2.8%, resulting in a real growth rate in per capita GNP of 5.7%.

In 1992 the GDP was $57,568 million in current US dollars. It is estimated that in 1991 agriculture, hunting, forestry, and fishing contributed 17% to GDP; mining and quarrying, 9%; manufacturing, 28%; electricity, gas, and water, 2%; construction, 4%; wholesale and retail trade, 12%; transport, storage, and communication, 7%; finance, insurance, real estate, and business services, 10%; community, social, and personal services, 2%; and other sources, 9%.

21LABOR

In 1992, Malaysia's total civilian employment was estimated at 7,060,000. Of these, 1,870,000 (26%) were in agriculture and mining; 1,930,000 in industry; and the remaining 3,260,000 (46%) in services. Unemployment in 1992 was 4.1%, a rate that was due to the decline in major commodities. Malays constitute the bulk of the agriculturalists, cultivating most of the rice paddies or working on self-owned smallholdings in rubber. The Chinese, Indians, and Pakistanis live mainly in urban areas and are active in trade, manufacturing, and other nonagricultural pursuits.

Plantation workers and mining employees make up the two largest unions. The trade union movement is generally organized along ethnic lines. Indians have tended to dominate the central labor organization, the Malaysian Trade Unions Congress, and its 152 constituent unions, with more than 410,000 members. Negotiations between unions and employers are voluntary; strikes are permitted, but not if the dispute has already been referred to an industrial court for settlement.

Commerce and industry operate on a 48-hour week, although actual weekly hours tend to be closer to 44. Protective labor legislation in Malaysia is more extensive than in most Asian countries. New employment and labor legislation was enacted in 1955, ensuring fair contracts and safe working conditions; regulating the employment of children (the adult working age is 14) and women; and establishing rest days, as well as housing and medical care. The Employees' Social Security Act of 1969 comprises an Employment Injury Insurance Scheme and an Invalidity Pension Scheme. Coverage extends mostly to urban industrial workers and was expanded in March 1974 to include Sabah and Sarawak. As of mid-1992, the average daily wage rates for plantation and factory workers was about M$10-15 for unskilled labor and M$15-25 for semi-skilled labor.

22AGRICULTURE

Agriculture is no longer the most important sector of the Malaysian economy, contributing less than 20% of the GDP (down from almost one-third in 1970) and occupying about 26% of the employed work force in 1992. Diversification—including development of such newer crops as oil palm, cocoa, and pineapples—is promoted by the government. Much of Sabah and Sarawak is covered with dense jungle and is not conducive to farming. Peninsular Malaysia, however, is predominantly an agricultural region. Cultivation is carried out on the coastal plains, river valleys, and foothills.

Domestic rice furnishes Peninsular Malaysia with about 80% of its requirements; most of the rice supply for Sabah and Sarawak, however, must be imported. Rice production for 1992 totaled 1,860,000 tons, of which 70% came from Peninsular Malaysia. Rubber production totaled 1,250,000 tons in 1991. The government, through the Rubber Research Institute of Malaysia, has concentrated on improving production, but many estates have switched to production of the more profitable oil palm. Although Malaysia produced 23% (1,210,000 tons) of the world's rubber in 1992, and typically accounts for over one-third of the world's rubber exports, rubber is no longer the country's primary source of export income . Competition from Thailand and Indonesia has recently diminished the Malaysian market share for rubber.

Production of palm oil totaled 6,373,461 tons in 1992, more than any other country in the world. More than 90% of all rubber and palm oil is produced in Peninsular Malaysia. Black and white peppers are grown on Sarawak; 22,911 tons were exported in 1992, valued at $22.2 million. Output of lesser agricultural products in 1992 included coconuts, 1,087,000 tons, and copra, 90,000 tons. Cocoa production in 1992 was an estimated 217,000 tons, up from only 38,000 tons per year on average during 1979–81.

23ANIMAL HUSBANDRY

Peninsular Malaysia is free of most of the infectious and contagious diseases that plague livestock in the tropical zone, but the livestock industry is of minor importance. The livestock population in 1992 included 2,800,000 hogs, 720,000 head of cattle, 350,000 goats, and 200,000 buffalo. The swamp buffalo and indigenous breeds of cattle are used mainly as draft animals. Hog raising and export are handled mainly by non-Muslim Chinese.

The government prohibits the importation of chicken and chicken parts in order to protect domestic producers.

24FISHING

Fishing is being developed both as a means of reducing unemployment and as a primary source of protein in the country's diet. The total catch in 1991 was 620,000 tons, as compared with 296,300 tons in 1966; the increase has been largely the result of expanded and improved marketing facilities. A government training program in navigation and engine care is also accelerating the use of powered boats. Freshwater fishing in paddy fields and irrigation ditches is integrated with rice farming and hog production.

25FORESTRY

In 1991, Malaysia produced 49.3 million cu m of roundwood, the same year it exported over 19.4 million cu m of sawlogs and veneer logs, more than any other country. In keeping with the National Forestry Policy of 1978, exports of sawlogs are being progressively reduced in favor of domestic development of veneer, plywood, furniture, and other wood-using industries. In addition, to maintain the nation's forests as a resource, the government has offered incentives to the states to replant 188,000 hectares (465,000 acres) of logged-out timberland annually until 1995. Output of sawn timber totaled about 8.9 million cu m in 1981. Malaysian tropical hardwood exports increased by 86% from 1982 to 1991. Some Malaysian states maintain log export bans, while the state of Sarawak awarded quotas to individual logging companies for 1993, which limited output by 9% from 1992. In 1990, Malaysia accounted for 23.1% of the world's exports of rough, squared wood, valued at over $1.5 billion.

26MINING

Malaysia is the world's fourth largest tin producer, supplying about 14% of the world's output in 1991, but production and employment have declined significantly in recent decades. In 1991, Malaysia mined and processed some 20,710 tons of tin metal and concentrates, down from the 1985 total of 36,900 tons. The number of working mines also declined, from about 1,000 in 1974 to 92 at the end of 1990. Continued low prices and sluggish world demand for the metal are the main reasons for the slump.

Iron ore production increased markedly after World War II under the stimulus of Japanese demand, but production subsequently dwindled from a peak of 3,899,000 tons in 1965 to 181,600 tons in 1985, but rose back to 375,000 tons in 1991. The output of bauxite, all of which is exported, decreased from 703,561 tons in 1975 to 376,000 tons in 1991. Output of copper, of which there are large reserves on Sabah, increased from 21,190 tons in 1975 to 131,832 tons in 1985, before dropping to 98,313 tons in 1991. Other minerals extracted include gold, columbite, monazite, tungsten, manganese, kaolin, and ilmenite. Malaysia is a net exporter of all its coal, copper concentrate, ilmenite, rare earths, and zircon concentrate, and also exported about 85% of its smelted tin in 1991. Mining contributed 9.5% (about $3. billion) to Malaysia's GDP in 1991.

Subsoil resources are public property of the states, which grant prospecting licenses and mining leases. Royalties on coal and gold accrue to the states, and export duties are levied on other minerals by the government, which returns part to the states.

27ENERGY AND POWER

Malaysia's net installed electrical generating capacity in 1991 stood at 6,060 Mw. Electrical energy production increased from 1,622 million kwh in 1963 to 4,971 million kwh in 1974 and 23,905 million kwh in 1991. In that year, 4,457 million kwh was hydrogenerated, and 10,394 million kwh was of thermal origin. The National Electricity Board, a state-owned corporation, supplies the greater part of the nation's power.

Crude oil, developed in the 1970s, is now the chief mineral produced, with reserves estimated at 3.7 billion barrels in 1993. In 1992, output averaged 660,000 barrels per day. Of new and increasing importance are large offshore natural gas deposits, with reserves estimated at more than 1.9 trillion cu m. Production in 1992 totaled 26.6 billion cu m. The principal gas fields are the Trengganu, off the east coast of Peninsular Malaysia, and the Central Luconia, Bintulu, and Labuan fields, located off the coasts of Sabah and Sarawak. Malaysia currently exports about 11.3 million cu m of liquefied natural gas per year to Japan. Production of oil and natural gas is controlled by the National Petroleum Co. (PETRONAS).

Since reserves of oil are limited and local coal is of an inferior grade, the government has greatly expanded efforts to harness the country's hydroelectric potential and natural gas as alternative energy sources.

28INDUSTRY

In 1985, manufacturing contributed 19% of the GDP, as compared with 11.4% in 1968. Early industrialization efforts centered on the establishment of import-substitution industries and resulted in construction of sugar refineries and motor vehicle assembly plants. Industrialization has accelerated since the mid-1960s under the provisions of the Investment Incentives Act and the formation of the Malaysian Industrial Development Authority (MIDA). Special incentives are offered for industries that are labor intensive or export oriented or that utilize domestic rubber, wood, and other raw materials. In the mid-1980s the Malaysian economy changed from a commodity-based to a manufacturing-based economy. In 1986, the leading manufacturing industries included rubber processing, the manufacture of tires and other rubber products, palm oil processing, tin smelting, and the manufacture of chemicals, plywood, furniture, and steel. Other industries are textiles, food processing, and the manufacture of electronic and electrical components. Industrial products in 1985 included 3,128,000 tons of cement, 13,839 tons of cigarettes, 70,147 passenger cars, 568,387 television sets, 3,600,000 tires, and 180,746 m of cotton fabric. Most early industries were controlled by ethnic Chinese and foreigners, but current policies call for greater participation by ethnic Malays.

In 1993 the manufacturing sector accounted for 29% of GDP and 55% or 69% of exports, depending on sources. As of 1990, the leading manufacturing industries included rubber processing, the manufacture of tires and other rubber products, palm oil processing, and tin smelting. The value of other manufactured goods exported in 1990 was electrical/electronic machinery and appliances (M$10,164,000); textiles, clothing and footwear (M$2,032,000), chemicals and petroleum products (M$1,621,000); other machinery and transport equipment (M$1,308,000); and iron and steel products (M$782,000). Malaysia is the world's largest exporter of semiconductor devices. Industrial products in 1990 included 5,881,000 metric tons of cement, 17,331 metric tons of cigarettes, and an estimated 6,094,000 metric tons of crude palm oil. Oil production in 1990 averaged 626,400 barrels per day. Singapore, Japan, and South Korea were the major customers for Malaysian crude oil. All of Malaysia's LNG exports were shipped from Sarawak to Japan although LNG exports may expand to include Taiwan and South Korea. Malaysia's oil fields are split between the South China Sea off Borneo and those off Peninsular Malaysia. All exploration is conducted under production-sharing contracts between PETRONAS, the national oil company, and foreign companies. In 1990 the only foreign oil companies producing oil and gas were Exxon and Shell. Gas reserves were being developed to fuel power stations and to supply industries in Peninsular Malaysia and Singapore. In February 1992 Prime Minister Datuk Seri Mahathir Mohamad announced plans a possible automotive joint venture with Daihatsu Motor, an affiliate of Toyota Motor Corp. The Malaysian-built, Proton, had 60.8% of the local market for passenger cars in 1990. The proposed new national line of cars would have a smaller engine capacity and sell for about M$10,000 less than the least expensive Proton model.

29SCIENCE AND TECHNOLOGY

Training in science, technology, and related subjects was promoted at all levels during the 1970s and 1980s. Enrollment at technical and vocational secondary schools rose from 4,510 in 1970 to 20,720 in 1985. By 1993 there were six college-level institutions devoted to science and technology, with 67,295 students, including one school maintained by the Council of Trust for the People (Majlis Amanah Rakyat—MARA). In addition, the National University of Malaysia, the University of Malaya, Damansaura Utama College, and Tunku Abdul College offer degrees in basic and applied sciences. National science policy is administered by the Ministry of Science, Technology, and Environment. The Ministry of Agriculture undertakes all aspects of research for improvement of crops. The Institute of Medical Research is a branch of the Ministry of Health.

In 1989, total expenditures on research and development amounted to 97 million ringget. In 1988, 1,170 technicians and 5,537 scientists and engineers were engaged in research and development.

30DOMESTIC TRADE

Imported goods are channeled into the Malaysian market through local branches of large European mercantile firms; by local importers with buying agents abroad; through branch offices and representatives of foreign manufacturers; by local Chinese, Indian, and Arab merchants who import directly; and by commission agents. Chinese merchants occupy an important place in the marketing structure and control a large share of the direct import trade. For warehousing of imported goods, the facilities of the port of Singapore are used, while rubber for export is warehoused mainly on plantations.

The usual business hours of European firms are from 8:30 AM to 4:30 or 5 PM, Monday–Friday, with generally a half-day on Saturday. In some states, Thursday is a half-day and (in keeping with Islamic practice) Friday is the day of rest. Chinese and Indian firms are open longer hours, and seven days a week for family businesses. Normal banking hours are from 10 AM to 3 PM, Monday–Friday, and from 9:30 to 11:30 AM on Saturday. English is widely used in commerce and industry.

Newspaper and motion picture advertising is directed toward the higher-income consumer, while radio advertising, outdoor displays, and screen slides are used for the lower-income consumer, who is less likely to be literate. A code of practice and ethics governing advertising is in force. There are about 80 English, Malay, Chinese, and Tamil daily and weekly newspapers. Radio and television broadcasts are in Malay, Chinese, Tamil, and English. Trade fairs are supervised by the Ministry of Trade and Industry.

31FOREIGN TRADE

During the 1970s, petroleum and manufactures displaced rubber and tin as Malaysia's leading exports. The principal imports for domestic consumption are foodstuffs, machinery, and transport equipment.

Principal expots (by SITC section) in 1984, 1986 and 1989 (in millions of ringgits) were as follows:

	1984	1986	1989
Food & Live animals	1,480	1,964	3,130
Beverages and tobacco	28	37	80
Crude materials except fuels	8,121	7,868	12,666
Mineral fuels, etc.	11,435	8,006	11,003
Animal, vegetable oils & fats	5,868	3,610	6,197
Chemicals	427	604	1,233
Basic manufactures	2,555	2,587	5,721
Machinery and transport equipment	7,323	9,010	21,987
TOTAL (INC. OTHERS)	38,646	35,721	67,836

Principal imports (by SITC section) in 1984, 1986 and 1989 (in million of ringgits) were as follows:

	1984	1986	1989
Food & Live animals	3,227	2,914	4,609
Beverages and tobacco	213	210	237
Crude materials except fuels	1,158	1,017	2,495
Mineral fuels, etc.	3,332	2,388	2,908
Animal, vegetable oils and fats	120	68	270
Chemicals	2,636	2,686	5,419
Basic manufactures	5,086	4,038	9,990
Machinery and transport equipment	15,129	12,579	29,180
TOTAL (INC. OTHERS)	32,927	27,921	60,898

Malaysia sustained a favorable trade balance throughout the 1960s and 1970s, recording its first trade deficits in 1981 and 1982, as world prices for tin, crude oil, rubber, and palm oil, the major exports, weakened simultaneously. From 1983 to 1986, however, Malaysia registered trade surpluses. The substantial rise in imports, M$60.9 billion in 1989 against M$43.3 billion in 1988, resulted in the trade surplus declining by 42% over the period. Singapore was Malaysia's largest export market in 1988 and 1989. The US and Japan imported mainly primary commodities such as sawn logs and fuel respectively, as well as electronic goods and similar manufactures.

Malaysia's principal trading partners in 1989 (in millions of ringgits) were as follows:

	EXPORTS	IMPORTS	BALANCE
Australia	1,552	2,324	−772
China	1,302	1,650	−348
Germany	2,417	2,320	97
Hong Kong	2,085	1,254	831
Japan	10,989	14,723	−3,825
Netherlands	2,423	—	—
Singapore	13,397	8,281	5,116
South Korea	3,399	1,524	1,875
Taiwan	1,532	3,047	−1,515
Thailand	1,667	1,835	−168
UK	2,551	3,291	−740
US	12,678	10,290	2,388
Other countries	11,935	10,359	1,576

32BALANCE OF PAYMENTS

Malaysia's balance of payments, like that of many other producers of primary products, was adversely affected in 1981–82 by the prolonged recession in the world's industrial nations. In recent years, a significant growth in exports and a decrease in imports have led to trade surpluses (about $2.9 billion in 1992), along with a fairly large services deficit.

In 1992 merchandise exports totaled $39,745 million and imports $36,894 million. The merchandise trade balance was $2,851 million. The following table summarizes Malaysia's balance of payments for 1991 and 1992 (in millions of US dollars):

	1991	1992
CURRENT ACCOUNT		
Goods, services, and income	–4,641	–1,851
Unrequited transfers	111	124
TOTALS	–4,530	–1,727
CAPITAL ACCOUNT		
Direct investment	4,073	4,118
Portfolio investment	170	–1,108
Other long-term capital	642	243
Other short-term capital	616	3,076
Exceptional financing	—	—
Other liabilities	–1	3
Reserves	–1,238	–6,615
TOTALS	4,262	–285
Errors and omissions	270	2,012
Total change in reserves	–1,165	–6,894

33 BANKING AND SECURITIES

In 1958, the Bank Negara Tanah Melayu (renamed the Bank Negara Malaysia in 1963) was created as the central banking institution. During 1975–85, the bank's foreign assets grew from M$3,943 million to M$9,111 million. Malaysian currency in circulation amounted to M$12,070 million at the end of 1991, as compared with M$6,773 million at the close of 1985

At the end of 1990, Malaysia had 23 licensed commercial banks. A total of 16 foreign banks have offices in Malaysia, but their banking privileges are restricted. Other financial institutions include 12 merchant banks and a national savings bank. Specialized credit institutions include the Federal Land Development Authority (FELDA), the Agricultural Bank of Malaysia (Bank Pertanian Malaysia), and Bank Rakyat, serving rural credit cooperative societies. As of the end of 1992, demand deposits in commercial banks totaled M$18,931 million (M$7,950 million at the end of 1985), and time and savings deposits, M$80,172 million in 1992 (M$37,903 in 1985). In 1992, the commercial banks held M$47,223 million in foreign assets. International trade is financed mainly by the commercial banks.

The principal market for securities is the Kuala Lumpur Stock Exchange, which separated from the joint Stock Exchange of Malaysia and Singapore in 1973. A second, smaller exchange has operated since 1970 to serve indigenous Malay interests. In October 991 the Kuala Lumpur Stock Exchange completely severed its links with the Singapore Stock Exchange. In June of 1990 there were 292 Malaysian companies listed in the exchange. Industrials and government securities have attracted the bulk of activity on the exchange.

34 INSURANCE

Total assets of all insurance companies in Malaysia reached M$3,302.3 as of 1984, as compared with M$694.7 million in 1974. In 1986, there were 4 life, 44 non-life, and 14 composite insurance companies operating. Premiums paid in 1987 totaled $963 million, $29.1 per capita for life insurance alone. Life insurance in force in 1992 totaled M$129.5 billion. The law requires insurance firms to maintain a minimum of 80% of their assets in authorized Malaysian holdings, including (by an amendment passed in 1978) 24% in government securities. Third-party motor liability insurance is compulsory.

35 PUBLIC FINANCE

Although the federal deficit rose to M$6,091 million in 1991 (from M$5,516 million in 1990), the deficit as a proportion of GNP fell from 5% of GNP in 1990 to 4.9% in 1991. The total public sector deficit amounted to M$4,613 million in 1991 (3.7%

of GNP), up from M$2,018 million in 1990 (1.8% of GNP).

The following table shows actual revenues and expenditures for 1992 and 1993 in millions of ringgit.

	1992	1993
REVENUE AND GRANTS		
Tax revenue	30,790	30,863
Non-tax revenue	11,302	10,085
Capital revenue	63	106
TOTAL	42,155	41,054
EXPENDITURES & LENDING MINUS REPAYMENTS		
General public service	3,887	3,871
Defense	4,500	5,090
Public order and safety	2,469	2,479
Education	8,059	8,924
Health	2,414	2,519
Social security and welfare	2,303	2,266
Housing and community amenities	2,466	2,555
Economic affairs and services	7,996	8,179
Other expenditures	11,591	11,869
Adjustments	–260	—
Lending minus repayments	492	647
TOTAL	41,697	43,989
Deficit/Surplus	458	–2,935

In spite of increased capital expenditures and fiscal concessions, the overall budget deficit for 1994 was M$605 million, due to efforts to restrict current expenditure growth to 3%. In 1992 Malaysia's total public debt stood at M$96,830 million, of which M$20,922 million was financed abroad.

36 TAXATION

Income tax is levied on all individual and corporate income accrued in Malaysia during the previous year. The income of resident individuals is taxed (as of 1 January 1987) at rates ranging from 5% on the first M$2,500 to 34% on income exceeding M$100,000. Companies are charged a flat rate of 35% on taxable income; a 4% development tax is also assessed. Incentives are available for pioneer industries and for certain capital investments. Capital gains taxes are levied only on real estate. Indirect taxes include a 5% sales tax (10% for certain luxury items) and stamp taxes of up to 2% for property and stock transfers.

37 CUSTOMS AND DUTIES

Import tariffs on textiles and other items already produced in Malaysia are applied in order to protect domestic industries. Rates vary from 2% to 60%, and imports are also subject to a 10% sales tax and excise taxes. Items imported for industrial development, including machinery and raw materials imported for processing and reexport, are usually duty-free. Exports are generally free of control, except that licenses and strict governmental regulations apply to exports of unprocessed rubber, tin, palm oil, timber, and other raw materials.

38 FOREIGN INVESTMENT

The government encourages foreign investors with a tax holiday of up to 10 years for investments in new industries and assurance of convertibility and repatriation of capital and profits. In 1975, the Industrial Coordination Act established new equity participation guidelines that required a substantial majority of Malaysian ownership of new import-substitution industries catering to the domestic market and using local technology; 45–70% Malaysian ownership is now stipulated for export industries using "nondepleting" local raw materials, such as rubber and palm oil; and at least 70% Malaysian ownership is required for those using "depleting" raw materials, such as tin and timber. Export industries using imported raw materials may be as much as 100% foreign owned. Some of these regulations have been eased under the Fifth Malaysia Plan (1986–90). The Promotion of Investment Act of 1986 allows 100% foreign ownership if a company exports at least 50% of its product and does not compete with local industry, or if it exports at least 80% of its product regardless of competition.

In October 1990 the government established the Federal Territory of Labuan as an International Offshore Financial Center (IOFC) to provide offshore banking and insurance, trust fund management, offshore investment holding and licensing companies, and other offshore activities carried out by multinational companies. Free Zones (FZs) are specially designated geographic areas which create "climates of opportunity" for industry and trade. Areas specifically designed for manufacturing businesses producing or assembling products primarily for export are known as Free Trade Zones (FTZs) or Free Industrial Zones (FIZs). In Malaysia FIZ facilities provide export-oriented industries with minimum customs controls and formalities when importing raw materials, parts, machinery, and equipment. As of mid-1992 ten FIZs had been established in Bayan Lepas, Bukit Baru, Mukim Damansara, Mukim Pringgit, Mukim Plentong, Prai, Tanjong Kling, Telok Panglima Garang, Ulu Kinta, and Ulu Klang in the states of Johor, Melaka, Perak, Penang, and Selangor.

There are specially designated FCZs for businesses engaged in commercial activities including trading, breaking bulk, grading, repacking, relabeling, and transit. Within an FCZ goods are allowed to be imported without being subject to customs procedures, provided the goods are ultimately exported after processing. As of mid-1992 two FCZs had been established for trading purposes in Bukit Kayu Hitam, Kedah and Pengkalan Kubor, Kelantan. a third in Mukim of Plentong, Johor, was established for commercial activities other than trading.

Assets attracting foreign investors to Malaysia are location, cultural ties with Singapore and Taiwan and its economic and political stability, competent labor force, and good infrastructure. Liberalized tax and regulatory treatment attracted an average of $3.3 billion in direct foreign investment in each year from 1990–92. Total foreign direct investment 1981–92 was $ 29.5 billion. The largest investment sources are Japan, Taiwan, Korea, the US, and Indonesia. The US has emerged as an important investment source in recent years. Most foreign investment is concentrated in the production of electronic components, consumer electronics, and electrical goods (dominated by US and Japanese firms), petroleum production and distribution, textiles, vehicle assembly, steel, cement, rubber products, and electrical machinery.

[39]ECONOMIC DEVELOPMENT

The government remains generally committed to a policy of free enterprise, although it owns and operates the railway and communications systems and has become increasingly involved in certain key industries. In 1970, a government holding company, Perbadanan Nasional (PERNAS), was created to encourage Malay-controlled businesses; in 1975, the government attempted, through PERNAS, to strengthen Malaysian interests in the tin-mining sector. Also in 1975, the government established the National Oil Co. (PETRONAS), with the overall aim of acquiring majority control of the country's petroleum operations. The Industrial Coordination Act of 1975 attempted to accelerate indigenous Malay participation in the economy by setting limits on foreign participation in the processing, domestic distribution, and export of local raw materials. In 1971, the New Economic

Policy (NEP) was adopted, with the aim of channeling a greater share of future economic growth into Malay hands. It specifically called for raising the level of corporate ownership by Malays to 30% by 1990, reducing corporate ownership by other Malaysians (i.e., Chinese and Indians) to 40%, and restricting foreigners to ownership of no more than 30%. Short-term investment strategies are set forth in a series of economic plans. The Fourth Malaysia Plan (1981–85) proposed a level of development spending of M$42.8 billion and called for acceleration of the NEP goals for Bumiputra economic participation. Major industrial and infrastructural development projects included a M$900-million bridge between Pulau Pinang and the mainland and a M$600-million automobile-manufacturing plant, both of which opened in 1985. Recent economic planning has stressed a "look East" policy, with Malaysia attempting to emulate the economic successes of Japan and the Republic of Korea by importing technology from those countries. In response to deteriorating prices for oil and other exports, the Fifth Malaysia Plan (1986–90) has moved away from the goals of the NEP, aiming instead at promoting foreign investment, particularly in export industries.

The year 1990 marked the culmination of several economic development plans: the Fifth Malaysia Plan (FMP) 1986–90); the conclusion of the First Outline Perspective Plan (OPP1) 1971–1990; and the completion of the New Economic Policy (NEP) 1971–1990. The FMP emphasized industrialization. Specific targets were formulated to ensure that the distribution of ownership and participation in the commercial and industrial sector would be characterized by ethnic group participation, 30% bumiputra—Malays and other indigenous peoples of Malaysia, 40% other Malaysians (Chinese and Indian descent), and 30% foreign. The government provided funds to purchase foreign-owned shareholding on behalf of the Bumiputra population, increasing their equity to 20% by 1990. These policies are part of the new National Development Policy, although specific targets and time tables have been dropped. A post-1990 NEP defined Malaysian economic strategy for full development by 2020. Three ten-year Outline Perspective Plans which include a New Development Plan and six five-year plans make up the NEP. A Second Outline Perspective Plan (OPP2) 1991–2000 aims to sustain growth momentum and to achieve a more balanced development of the economy. The Sixth Malaysia Plan calls for an average annual growth rate of 7.5%, and expenditures on infrastructure are included to ensure prospects for further development. Development trends are toward privatization, encouraging the spread of industry throughout the country, increasing manufacturing in the free trade zones, and providing financing for industry through the establishment of specialized financing institutions.

From 1953 through 1986, Malaysia received more than US$3,295 million in multilateral development assistance, chiefly from the IBRD ($2,079 million) and ADB ($1,137 million). Economic aid also included US Export-Import (FY 1970–84) $170 million; and Western (non-US) countries, ODA and OOF bilateral commitments (1970–89), $4.7 million, and OPEC bilateral aid (1979–89), $42 million.

[40]SOCIAL DEVELOPMENT

Public financial assistance should be considered within the framework of Malaysian society, with its highly developed sense of family and clan responsibility. The government has generally encouraged volunteer social welfare activities and has subsidized programs of private groups. The Department of Social Welfare, under the Ministry of Welfare Services, administers and coordinates social assistance programs. The government's program of public assistance takes the form of cash, commodities, and institutional care. Children's services, begun in 1952, provide casework services and administer children's homes. A probation service provides care and assistance for juvenile delinquents and dependents, and a handicapped persons' service aids the deaf, mute, and blind. In addition, care is provided for the aged and chronically ill.

Since 1951, a provident fund has provided lump-sum benefits for old age, disability, and death. These benefits are funded by both employers and employees. The retirement age is 55. In 1969, legislation was enacted to provide injury insurance and disability pensions for low-income workers. Coverage is extended to all employees of firms with 5 or more workers, and the employer contributes 1.25% of payroll disbursements.

Women make up more than 40% of the nation's total labor force but, except in teaching and nursing, are underrepresented in professional occupations. In family and religious matters, Muslim women are subject to Islamic law, which allows polgyny and favors men in matters of inheritance. Some Malays practice a modified form of female genital mutilation. Non-Muslim women are subject to civil law. Although women do enter the professions, in 1990 they held fewer than 1% of administrative and managerial positions. In an effort to support mass-consumption industries, the government announced in 1984 that it would encourage early marriage and large families so as to increase the birthrate and achieve a population of 70 million by the year 2010. Contraception was reportedly practiced by 51% of all women in 1985–90; in the same period, the fertility rate was 4.0. Abortion is permitted on specified legal and medical grounds.

41HEALTH

Malaysia enjoys a comparatively high standard of health, the consequence of long-established health and medical services. The country has improved its health care and social conditions, and is considering a national health insurance plan. As of 1990, the government paid for three-fourths of health care expenses, with total expenditures that year of $1,259 million.

Total population in 1993 was 19.2 million, with a birth rate of 28.6 per 1,000 people, and 51% of married women (ages 15 to 49) using contraception. There were 545,000 births in 1992, and the population is expected to increase to 21 million by the end of the century. Life expectancy has risen over the last decade and was 71 years in 1992.

Under the tuberculosis control campaign, begun in 1961, the number of annual deaths from tuberculosis declined to 971 in 1970 and 672 in 1983. In 1990, there were only 67 reported cases of tuberculosis per 100,000 people. As a result of the yaws elimination campaign, begun in 1954, the disease was virtually eliminated in the late 1960s. A malaria eradication program, begun in 1967, resulted in a drop in the number of hospital admissions for malaria from 25,400 in 1970 to 8,274 in 1984. In 1991, 78% of the population had access to safe water and 81% had adequate sanitation. During 1970 to 1984, however, hospital admissions for mental illness, heart disease, and traffic and industrial accidents increased. In 1990, 24% of children under 5 years of age were still considered malnourished. Immunization rates for 1992 for children up to 1 year old were quite high: tuberculosis (99%); diphtheria, pertussis, and tetanus (90%); polio (90%); and measles (79%).

Infant mortality in 1992 was 14 per 1,000 live births, and the general mortality rate in 1993 was 5.1 per 1,000 people. The maternal mortality rate in 1991 was 59 per 100,000 live births.

In 1990, Malaysia had 16 general hospitals (with 13,680 beds), 79 district hospitals (with 12,589 beds), and 7 special medical institutes (7,116 beds). Hospital beds totaled 2.4 per 1,000 people that year. Smaller government facilities included 166 health centers, 318 health subcenters, and 1,150 rural clinics. In addition, there were 171 private hospitals with 4,618 beds.

In 1990, there were 7,012 physicians (1 for every 2,700 peo-

ple). In 1988, there were 1,084 pharmacists and 1,288 dentists.

42HOUSING

A total of 744,000 new housing units were built during 1970–80, and an estimated 923,300 units—43% public and 57% private—were planned under the 1981–85 development plan. As of 1980, 92% of all housing units were detached houses, 7% were apartments, and 1% were single rooms.

The need for urban housing is acute: an estimated 24% of Kuala Lumpur's population consists of recently arrived squatters living in overcrowded shantytowns with few urban amenities. A government plan for low-cost housing was expected to provide 80,000 units per year from 1986 to 1988. In 1992, the total number of housing units was 3,403,000.

43EDUCATION

The estimated expenditure on education in 1985 was M$3,768 million, as compared with M$556.8 million in 1970. Six years of free primary education is followed by three years of comprehensive general and prevocational education. Two further years of education at the postcomprehensive level, in either a vocational or an academic program, is offered. A two-year preuniversity course prepares students for admission to the universities. Malay is the medium of instruction in primary and secondary schools, with English a compulsory second language. Muslim religious instruction is compulsory for all Muslim children, while private Christian schools offer religious training to their students. In 1990, 21.6% were rated as illiterate. Of these, 13.5% were men and 29.6% were women.

School enrollment in Malaysia in 1991 was 2,540,623 pupils instructed by 126,139 teachers in 6,922 primary schools. In all secondary schools, there were 79,136 teachers and 1,482,530 pupils. Of these, 3,129 teachers and 32,219 pupils were from vocational schools. In 1990, 121,412 students were enrolled in institutions of higher education, which include the Universiti Kebangsaan Malaysia (the National University of Malaysia), the University of Malaya, and the Technological University of Malaysia, all in or near Kuala Lumpur, and the University of Science Malaysia (formerly the University of Pinang). The MARA Institute of Technology is considered the largest.

44LIBRARIES AND MUSEUMS

The National Library of Malaysia, with more than 678,000 volumes, was established in 1971 and has been charged with wide responsibilities under the National Library Act. Both the National Library and the National Archives are in Kuala Lumpur. The University of Malaya library has over 1 million volumes. Other important libraries are those at the universities; the Sabah (380,000) and Sarawak (500,000) state libraries; Tun Abdul Razak Library at the MARA Institute of Technology (272,850); and the library of the Rubber Research Institute of Malaysia (110,000). The largest public libraries are in Denang (225,000), Malacca (122,000), and Selangor (1,400,000).

The National Museum of Malaysia in Kuala Lumpur, constructed on the site of the former Selangor Museum (destroyed in World War II), houses extensive collections of Malayan archaeology, ethnography, and zoology. The Perak Museum, founded in 1883, has a varied collection exhibiting antiquities, ethnographic, and zoological materials. Sabah and Sarawak maintain anthropological and archaeological collections pertinent to East Malaysia.

45MEDIA

The government owns and operates a well-developed and well-equipped telecommunications system. In 1991, Malaysia had

1,645,698 telephones, including private wire and public coin stations. Automatic dialing for the majority of exchanges is provided by a VHF radio circuit. Telegraph and radiotelephone connections link Peninsular Malaysia with most foreign countries.

Radio-Television Malaysia (RTM) operates radio and television stations in Kuala Lampur, Sabah, and Kuching, and there is a commercial station, Sistem TV-3 Berhad, in Kuala Lumpur as well. Broadcasts are in English, Malay, five Chinese dialects, Tamil, and numerous local languages and dialects. In 1991, radios numbered 7,880,000 and televisions 2,724,000. Color television transmission began in 1978.

Malaysia generally has enjoyed a large measure of press freedom. In October 1987, however, the government closed four newspapers in an effort to end criticism of its policies. While the press is normally moderate and objective, it treads carefully when dealing with Malaysia's plural ethnic and cultural foundations. There are about 80 English, malay, Chinese, and Tamil daily and weekly newspapers. In 1991, Malaysia had 47 daily newspapers, with an estimated total daily circulation of 2,462,000. The Malay-language press is the largest segment, followed by English, Chinese, Tamil, Punjabi, and Kadazan. The leading Kuala Lumpur dailies (with their 1991 circulations) are as follows:

	LANGUAGE	CIRCULATION
Utusan Malaysia	Malay (Rumi)	300,000
Berita Harian	Malay	300,000
New Straits Times	English	260,000
New Life Post	Chinese	175,000
Star	English	152,000

46ORGANIZATIONS
The Malaysian government promotes thrift, credit, processing, marketing, farming, consumer, and housing cooperatives. The cooperative movement was introduced in Malaya in 1922. The Chinese are organized along clan, common dialect, or occupational lines into rural credit associations. These local associations set up and maintain schools, build temples, and provide burial, relief, and employment services. In the larger cities, chambers of commerce, organized along ethnic lines, promote the economic welfare of the group represented.

47TOURISM, TRAVEL, AND RECREATION
In 1991, Malaysia had 49,874 hotel rooms, with a 72.1 percent occupancy rate. Most large hotels are in Kuala Lumpur and George Town. The best-known hill resort areas are Cameron Highlands, Raub, and Pinang Hill. Island resorts off the coast of the peninsula are Langkawi and Pangkor. Tourists numbered 5,847,213 in 1991, with expenditures of $1.5 million, of the total numbers, 4,967,213 tourists came from Eastern Asia. Passports are required of all entrants, although Malaysia has visa abolition agreements with all Commonwealth countries, the US, and other countries. Yellow fever inoculations are necessary for those arriving from infected areas.

Horse racing, soccer, rugby, cricket, and sepak raga (a form of badminton) are popular spectator sports. Kite fighting and top spinning are traditional pastimes for children and adults, and silat (a Malay martial art) is popular in rural areas.

48FAMOUS MALAYSIANS
Among the foremost Malaysian leaders of the past was Sultan Mahmud, 16th-century ruler of Malacca. A great figure in Malay culture was 'Abdallah bin 'Abd al-Kabir (surnamed Munshi', 1796–1854), sometimes called the greatest innovator in Malay letters. The best-known figure in the political life of modern Malaysia is Tunku Abdul Rahman Putra bin Abdul Hamid Halimshah (b.1903), first prime minister of the Federation of Malaysia. Other political leaders are Tun Abdul Razak (1922–76), the nation's second prime minister (1970–76); Datuk Seri Mahathir bin Mohamed (b.1925), prime minister since 1981; Dato Onn bin Ja'afar (1895–1962), a founder of the United Malays National Organization; and Sir Cheng-lock Tan (1883–1960), leader of the Malaysian Chinese Association.

49DEPENDENCIES
Malaysia has no territories or colonies.

50BIBLIOGRAPHY
ABECOR. Malaysia and Brunei Darussalam. London: Barclays Bank, 1993.

Ahmad, Zakaria Haji (ed.). Government and Politics of Malaysia. New York: Oxford University Press, 1987.

American University. Malaysia: A Country Study. Washington, D.C.: Government Printing Office, 1984.

Andaya, Leonard and Barbara W. A History of Malaysia. New York: St. Martin's, 1982.

Bedlington, Stanley S. Malaysia and Singapore: The Building of New States. Ithaca, N.Y.: Cornell University Press, 1978.

Bowie, Alasdair. Crossing the Industrial Divide: State, Society, and the Politics of Economic Transformation in Malaysia. New York: Columbia University Press, 1991.

Clutterbuck, Richard. Conflict and Violence in Singapore and Malaysia, 1945–1983. Boulder, Colo.: Westview, 1984.

Esman, Milton J. Administration and Development in Malaysia. Ithaca, N.Y.: Cornell University Press, 1972.

Fisk, E. K., and H. Osman-Rani (eds.). The Political Economy of Malaysia. New York: Oxford University Press, 1982.

Kahin, George. Government and Politics of Southeast Asia. Ithaca, N.Y.: Cornell University Press, 1976.

Kaur, Amarjit. Historical Dictionary of Malaysia. Metuchen, N.J.: Scarecrow Press, 1993.

Kennedy, Joseph. A History of Malaysia, A.D. 1400–1959. London: Macmillan, 1970.

Mackie, J. A. C. Konfrontasi: The Indonesia–Malaysia Dispute, 1963–1966. New York: Oxford University Press, 1974.

Malaysia in Pictures. Minneapolis: Lerner Publications Co., 1988.

Mohamed Ariff. The Malaysian Economy: Pacific Connections. New York: Oxford University Press, 1991.

Nonini, Donald Macon. British Colonial Rule and the Resistance of the Malay Peasantry, 1900–1957. New Haven, Conn.: Yale University Southeast Asia Studies, 1992.

Ongkill, James. Nation Building in Malaysia, 1946 to 1974. New York: Oxford University Press, 1985.

Purcell, Victor. The Chinese in Malaya. New York: Oxford University Press, 1968.

Roff, William R. The Origins of Malay Nationalism. New Haven, Conn.: Yale University Press, 1967.

———. Kelantan: Religion, Society and Politics in a Malay State. Kuala Lumpur: Oxford University Press, 1974.

Runciman, Steven. The White Rajahs. Cambridge: Cambridge University Press, 1960.

Ryan, N.J. Malaya through Four Centuries: An Anthology, 1500–1900. London: Oxford University Press, 1959.

———. The Making of Modern Malaysia and Singapore. London: Oxford University Press, 1969.

Saw, Swee-Hock. The Population of Peninsular Malaysia. Singapore: Singapore University Press, 1988.

Stubbs, Richard. Hearts and Minds in Guerrilla Warfare: The

Malayan Emergency, 1948–1960. New York: Oxford University Press, 1989.

U.S. Department of Commerce, *Survery of Current Business* (August 1991): Vol. 71, No. 8.

Von Vorys, K. *Democracy without Consensus.* Princeton, N.J.: Princeton University Press, 1975.

Winstedt, Sir Richard Olof. *Malaya and Its History.* New York: Longmans, Green, 1966.

MALDIVES

Republic of Maldives

CAPITAL: Malé.

FLAG: The national flag consists of a white crescent at the center of a green field which, in turn, is at the center of a red field.

MONETARY UNIT: The Maldivian rupee, or rufiyaa (MR), is a paper currency of 100 laris. There are notes of 1/2, 1, 2, 5, 10, 50, and 100 rufiyaa. The dollar circulates freely and is the only currency accepted at some resorts. MR1 = $0.0891 (or $1 = MR11.225).

WEIGHTS AND MEASURES: The metric system has been adopted, but some local units remain in use.

HOLIDAYS: National Day, 7 January; Independence Day, 26 July; Republic Day, 11 November; Fishermen's Day, 10 December. 'Id al-Fitr, 'Id al-'Adha', and Milad an-Nabi are some of the Muslim religious holidays observed.

TIME: 5 PM = noon GMT.

¹LOCATION, SIZE, AND EXTENT

The smallest country in Asia, the Republic of Maldives consists of an archipelago of nearly 1,200 coral islands and sand banks in the Indian Ocean, some 200 of which are inhabited. The chain of islands sits astride the equator, south of India and west of Sri Lanka, extending 820 km (510 mi) but occupying an area of just 300 sq km (116 sq mi). The area occupied by Maldives is slightly more than 1.5 times the size of Washington, D.C. Grouped in 26 atolls, with a total coastline of 644 km (400 mi), the northernmost atoll lies some 110 km (70 mi) south of India's Minicoy Atoll, about 480 km (300 mi) southeast of India's Cape Comorin, and 649 km (400 mi) west of Sri Lanka.

Maldives' capital, Malé, is situated on a 2.5 sq km (1 sq mi) island, the largest in the entire chain, in the Malé Atoll.

²TOPOGRAPHY

The islands vary from tiny banks to real islets. Some of the islands are in process of formation and are constantly increasing in size; others are gradually washing away. The islands are level and extremely low-lying, with elevations rarely exceeding 1.8 m (6 ft) above sea level. Many contain freshwater lagoons.

³CLIMATE

The Maldives' equatorial climate is generally hot and humid, with a mean temperature of about 27°C (81°F). The weather during the northeast monsoon (November–March) is mild and pleasant; the southwest monsoon (June–August) is violent and very rainy. The northern atolls are subject to more violent storms than those in the south. Annual rainfall in the south averages about 380 cm (150 in); in the north, 250 cm (100 in).

⁴FLORA AND FAUNA

The islands are covered with a dense scrub. The northern and southern islands are more fertile than those in the central group, and the eastern islands generally are more fertile than the western. Coconut, breadfruit, plantain, papaya, mango, and banyan trees flourish. Shrubs and flowers are widespread. Rats, rabbits, and flying foxes are the only indigenous mammals. Birds include ducks, bitterns, crows, curlews, snipes, and various sea birds. Small scorpions, beetles, and land crabs are common. Inland lagoons and coastal reefs contain tropical ocean fish, crustaceans, and turtles; the surrounding waters contain sharks, swordfish, and porpoises.

⁵ENVIRONMENT

Environmental issues in the Maldives include dwindling freshwater supply and inadequate sewage treatment. Recent estimates indicate that the nation's water supply may be exhausted in the near future, and population increases have created a sanitation problem that threatens the waters surrounding this island nation. Another significant environmental problem is a rise in sea-levels due to global warming. The islands are particularly susceptible to flooding. Environmental preservation is complicated by the unique problems of a nation consisting of 1,190 islands spread over 510 miles of the Indian ocean. Preservation of the desert island ecology, protection of marine life, and coconut tree rehabilitation are additional environmental goals.

⁶POPULATION

In 1990, the population was 213,215, an increase of 17.5% over the 1985 census figure of 181,453. The population density in 1990 was 706 per sq km (1,828 per sq mi). Malé, the capital and sole urban settlement, had a population of 55,130 in 1990, concentrated on an island of only about 1.9 sq km (0.75 sq mi).

⁷MIGRATION

Interisland migration is limited to settlement in Malé; between 1967 and 1990, population in the capital rose from one-tenth to over one-quarter of the national total. In 1985 there were about 20,000 temporary residents, mainly Sri Lankan and Indian teachers, merchants, and other professionals.

⁸ETHNIC GROUPS

The original inhabitants of the Maldives are thought to have been of south Indian and Arab origin. The people of the northern atolls have to some extent intermarried with peoples from west-

315

ern India, Arabia, and North Africa. Inhabitants of the southern islands show stronger physical affinities with the Sinhalese of Sri Lanka. Black African slaves imported from Zanzibar and Arabia have intermarried with the Maldivians, and there are also some Caucasian and Malayan elements.

⁹LANGUAGES

The Maldivian language, called Divehi, is similar to the old Sinhala (Elu) of Ceylon. It has contributed the word *atoll* to international terminology. In recent years, the language has been influenced by Arabic and Urdu. Thaana, developed during the 17th century, is the corresponding script, written from right to left. Only a small number of Maldivians speak English.

¹⁰RELIGIONS

There is evidence that the early Maldivians were Buddhists. Their conversion to Islam dates from 1153. With few exceptions, the people are Sunni Muslims, and both land ownership and citizenship are limited to adherents to this faith. The government's Department of Religious Affairs regulates matters pertaining to religion.

¹¹TRANSPORTATION

Malé, the capital, and some other islands have fairly good streets. Most people travel by bicycle or on foot; in 1985, 135 trucks, 45 vans, 336 cars, and 941 motorcycles were registered in Malé. Interatoll transportation still depends mostly on local sailing boats, called batheli and odi. Although some mechanized boats carry cargo and, occasionally, passengers between Malé and other atolls, interisland transport is mainly by means of dhonis (small boats). Oceangoing shipping has been increasing. At the outset of 1992, the Maldives had a fleet of 15 vessels serving worldwide destinations, all controlled by Maldives Shipping Ltd., a public enterprise. Hulule, Malé's international airport, a mile away over water from the capital, was completed in 1966. Built with assistance by Sri Lanka under the Colombo Plan, it consists of two islands that were joined together to create a runway. It is served by Singapore Airlines, Air Lanka, various European tourist carriers, and Indian Airlines, the last also operating as Air Maldive on certain flights. In 1991, the airport served 486,000 passengers.

¹²HISTORY

The first inhabitants of the Maldives were probably Dravidian speakers from south India, who were followed by Indo-European speaking Sinhalese from Ceylon on the 4th and 5th centuries BC. The island chain first become known in the West through the writings of Ptolemy, during the second century AD. The island chain may have been ruled in ancient times by the Chinese; later, its rulers paid an annual tribute to principalities of western India. Maldivians were converted to Sunni Islam from Buddhism by Arab traders from east Africa and the Middle East in the middle of the 12th century, and from 1153, an unbroken line of 92 sultans served as local rulers for 800 years until 1953. In 1343, Ibn Battutah, the Arab traveler and historian, visited the islands and served for a time as a qadi.

After their discovery by the Portuguese traveler Dom Lourenço de Alameida in 1507, the Maldives were occupied by the Portuguese and forced to pay a tribute to Goa, the center of Portugal's South Asian holdings. But the Portuguese were driven out in 1573 by Muhammad Thakurufaani al-Azam, who, after becoming sultan, introduced a monetary system, a new script, and a standing militia. In the 17th century, the Dutch, who were controlled neighboring Ceylon (now Sri Lanka), concluded a treaty with the sultanate which thereafter paid tribute to the rulers of Ceylon and claimed their protection.

The British completed their occupation of Ceylon in 1815, and British responsibility for the protection of the Maldives was for-

mally recorded in 1887. By terms of the compact, the sultan recognized the suzerainty of the British sovereign and disclaimed all rights or intention to enter into any treaty or negotiations with any foreign state except through the (British) ruler of Ceylon. When Ceylon became a independent in 1948, a new agreement was signed with the British government, providing for the Maldives to remain under the protection of the British crown, for external affairs to be conducted by or in accordance with the advice of the British government, for Britain to refrain from interfering in the internal affairs of the islands, and for the sultan to afford such facilities for British forces as were necessary for the defense of the islands or the Commonwealth. No tribute was to be paid by Maldives. New agreements reaffirming these provisions were signed in 1953, 1956, and 1960.

The sultanate, dominated by the Didi family since 1759, was abolished in 1953, and the Maldives was declared a republic. The first president, Amin Didi, ordered the emancipation of women and other reforms that were resented by more conservative elements among the people, and nine months later he was overthrown. His cousins Muhammad Farid Didi and Ibrahim 'Ali Didi became co-presidents in September 1953, and a month later the National Assembly voted to restore the sultanate. The new sultan, Muhammad Didi, was installed at Malé on 7 March 1954, and Ibrahim 'Ali Didi, the prime minister, formed a new government.

The government's agreement in 1956 to permit Britain to maintain an air base on Gan Island in the southern Maldives produced a public reaction so strong that Prime Minister Ibrahim was forced to resign in December 1957. Ibrahim Nasir, who succeeded him, asserted that the British base would violate Maldivian neutrality, but when his government sent a representative to Gan to tell the islanders to stop working for the British, the islanders attacked him.

Early in 1959, the people of Addu Atoll, in which Gan Island is located, declared their independence. At the same time, a rebellion broke out in the three southernmost atolls (including Addu). The rebel headmen declared the formation of the United Suvadiva Republic (with a population of 20,000) and demanded recognition from London. The British refused to comply, but the Nasir government made public its suspicions that the coup had been engineered by the British. In the event, government forces crushed the rebels in two of the atolls but made no attempt to interfere on Gan or any of the other seven main islands in the Addu group. By March 1960, the Suvadiva Republic was declared dissolved, and a committee ruling under the sovereign control of the sultan was set up, including among its members 'Abdallah Afif, leader of the rebellion.

In February 1960, the Maldivian government made a free gift to the British government of the use of Gan Island and other facilities in Addu Atoll for 30 years, and a fresh agreement was drawn up between the governments. In return, the British agreed to assist in bringing about a reconciliation between the Maldivian government and the disaffected inhabitants of the southern islands. But by 1962, resentment had grown against the British owing to their lack of progress in implementing the agreement; in late 1962 a Royal Navy frigate was sent to the capital island of Malé to protect British citizens. 'Abdallah Afif was evacuated by the British to the Seychelles.

The Sultanate of the Maldive Islands achieved complete independence on 26 July 1965, with the British continuing to retain use of the facilities on Gan in return for the payment of $2,380,000, most to be spent over a period of years for economic development. In March 1968, a referendum resulted in an 81% vote to abolish the sultanate and to reestablish a republic. A new republican constitution came into force on 11 November 1968, establishing the Republic of Maldives, and Nasir—then prime minister—became president.

With the British secure in their control of facilities they share with the United States outside the Maldives in Diego Garcia, 400 miles east of Gan, Britain vacated the Gan air base on 31 December 1975, and the UK-Maldivian accord was formally terminated the following year.

Nasir declined renomination and was succeeded as president on 11 November 1978 by Maumoon Abdul Gayoom. who was chosen by the Citizens' Majlis (parliament) in June and was confirmed in a popular referendum by a majority of 90% on 28 July. Re-electd president by the Majlis in August 1983, Gayoom won confirmation in a national referendum on 30 September with a majority of 95.6%. Gayoom was re-elected to a third term in August 1988, and later that year. He successfully resisted a brief attempt to overthrow him by Sri Lankan Tamil mercenaries in November 1988 with the help of an Indian military contingent flown to the Maldives at his request. In addition to the presidency, Gayoom is also Minister of Defense and Minister for National Security.

Gayoom was re-elected for a fourth term as president in August 1993 and confirmed by popular referendum in September. Gayoom's only principal rival for the presidency, his brother-in-law Ilyas Ibrahim, subsequently was tried in absentia for violation of the constitution, found guilty of treason, and sentenced to more than 15 years banishment from the islands.

13GOVERNMENT

Under the 1968 constitution, the president is elected to a five-year term by the Citizens' Majlis (parliament) but must be confirmed in office thereafter by popular referendum. The president heads the executive branch and appoints the cabinet and is constitutionally permitted to have as many vice-presidents as he desires. Presidential elections must be held by September 1998.

The unicameral Majlis is a body of 48 members, 40 of whom are directly elected (2 from each of the 19 inhabited atolls and 2 from the capital island of Malé) by universal suffrage of citizens over 21. Eight members are appointed by the president. The Majlis drafts legislation that becomes law after ratification by the president.

Elections to the Majlis are held individually and do not necessarily coincide with its sessions. Elections were held in December 1989, and the next elections must be held not later than December 1994.

14POLITICAL PARTIES

Organized political parties, and they are officially discouraged, and there are none. Candidates for office stand for election as independents and campaign on their family and personal stature.

15LOCAL GOVERNMENT

The Maldives is divided administratively into 19 districts, each a discrete atoll headed by a government-appointed verin, or chief, who functions in the manner of a District Officer. On each inhabited island a khatib, or headman, also appointed by the government, supervises and carries out the orders of the government under the supervision of the atoll chief.

16JUDICIAL SYSTEM

Justice is meted out according to traditional Islamic law (Shari'ah) by the High Court and lower courts appointed for that purpose by the president and functioning under the Ministry of Justice. Civil law is also applied but remains subordinate to Shari'a.

On the capital island, Malé, there is a High Court and eight lower courts. The High Court hears a range of cases as a court of first instance and also serves as a court of appeal. The eight lower courts each deal with a specific area such as theft, property or family law issues.

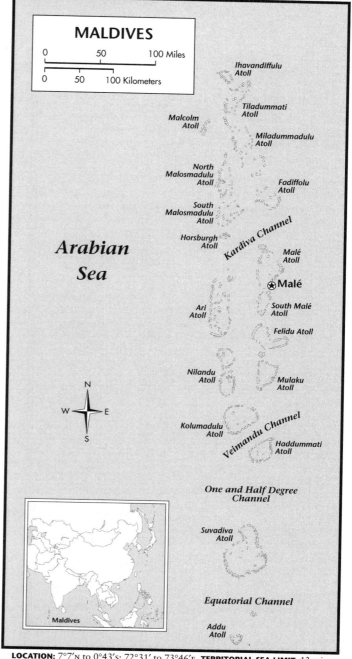

LOCATION: 7°7′N to 0°43′s; 72°31′ to 73°46′E. TERRITORIAL SEA LIMIT: 12 mi.

On the other islands, there is one all-purpose lower court in which cases are often adjudicated by traditional legal practitioners. Complex cases are referred to the appropriate specialized court in Malé.

In criminal cases there is no jury trial. The accused may call witness and may be assisted by a lawyer. There are, however, few professionally trained lawyers in Maldives, and the court does not provide a lawyer to an indigent defendant.

17ARMED FORCES

The armed forces of the Maldives consist of a paramilitary National Security Service and Militia of a few hundred. Armed boats patrol the territorial waters to protect the local fishing industry. Defense spending may reach $1.8 million a year.

[18] INTERNATIONAL COOPERATION

The Maldives, which joined the UN on 21 September 1965, is a member of ESCAP and all the nonregional specialized agencies except IAEA, ILO, UNIDO, and WIPO. Special membership status in the Commonwealth of Nations was granted 9 July 1982. Maldives is a de facto party to GATT, participates in G-77, and is a signatory to the Law of the Sea.

An active member of the nonaligned movement, Maldives has led efforts to declare an Indian Ocean Peace Zone, free of nuclear arms. In October 1977, the government rebuffed an offer from the former USSR to lease Gan as a base for its fishing fleet for $1 million annually. The Maldives participates in the Islamic Conference and has been a recipient of Arab financial and technical aid.

[19] ECONOMY

The Maldives is among the least developed countries in the world, yet economic progress over the past ten years has been steady. Per capita GNP has increased by about 10% annually over the last decade, reaching $600 in 1992. Fishing, tourism, and shipping are the mainstays of the economy. The tourism industry has become particularly important, presently accounting for about 18% of GDP and over 60% of the country's foreign exchange earnings. The staple foods are fish, caught locally, and rice, which must be imported. Fish alone still accounts for more than half of total merchandise exports, although apparel and clothing accessory exports have expanded greatly since the mid-1980s. Coconuts, copra, rope (made from dried coconut fibers), shells, tortoiseshell, bone dust, red stone, ambergris, and handicrafts are also produced locally as well as exported. The government is seeking to continue diversifying the economy through further promotion of tourism, processing industries, and garment production.

[20] INCOME

In 1992, Maldives's GNP was $117 million at current prices, or $600 per capita. For the period 1985–92 the average inflation rate was 6.7%, resulting in a real growth rate in per capita GNP of 8.5%.

It is estimated that in 1990 agriculture, hunting, forestry, and fishing contributed 22% to GDP; mining and quarrying, 1%; manufacturing, 4%; electricity, gas, and water, 0%; construction, 5%; wholesale and retail trade, 11%; transport, storage, and communication, 16%; finance, insurance, real estate, and business services, 3%; community, social, and personal services, 4%; and other sources 34%.

[21] LABOR

The fisheries sector (fishing, processing, and exporting) employed 40% of the labor force in 1992. The industrial sector employs only a few thousand individuals but accounts for 13% of GDP. The total employed work force in 1992 was 57,000. Unionization is not specifically prohibited, but the government does not legally recognize union formation or striking as rights.

There is no national minimum wage, but wage floors exist for certain kinds of work. Although no statutory provisions are in place, employers offer competitive pay and working conditions because of a skilled labor supply shortage.

[22] AGRICULTURE

Only 10% of the land is estimated to be cultivable. Millet, corn, pumpkins, sweet potatoes, pineapples, sugarcane, almonds, and many kinds of tropical vegetables and fruits are successfully grown, largely in homestead gardens. Coconut palms provide copra and coir, the most important exports after fish. Virtually all rice, a staple food for the population, must be imported. However, the FAO study team found that rice could be grown in swamps and low-lying areas, and that with improved crop management and diversification, the nation could achieve food-grain self-sufficiency. As of 1992, small amounts of corn, millet, and sorghum were cultivated. Production in 1992 included 13,000,000 coconuts.

[23] ANIMAL HUSBANDRY

Fodder is insufficient for more than a few head of cattle, but there are many goats and chickens.

[24] FISHING

Fishing is the chief industry, with the main catch being skipjack and yellowfin tuna. About half the annual harvest is frozen, canned, or dried and exported to Thailand, Europe, and Sri Lanka. The Maldivian fisheries sector underwent a major transformation during the 1980s and became increasingly productive through modernization of catch collection and processing methods. Expansion of the canning industry and investment in fisheries diversification is ongoing. The fish catch in 1991 totaled 80,713 tons, of which about 30,000 tons were exported. From 1988 to 1990, annual per capita consumption of fish and shellfish averaged 133.1 kg/293.4 lb (live-weight equivalent), greater than that of any other nation. Shell gathering is a relatively important activity in the Maldives, with large quantities of cowries exported for use as ornaments. Several rare shell species are also collected.

[25] FORESTRY

There are no forests as such. Coconut wood, however, is used in the building of boats and the construction of houses.

[26] MINING

There are no known mineral resources.

[27] ENERGY AND POWER

The power plant in Malé provided 28 million kwh of electricity for the island in 1991. More than half of this amount was distributed to residences, and one-quarter to government buildings. A smaller plant on Hulule supplies power for the airstrip on that island.

[28] INDUSTRY

The manufacturing sector is small but growing. After the fish industry, important traditional industries in the Maldives include the manufacture of coir, a rope made from dried coconut fibers, and lacemaking (handmade pillow lace), introduced by the Dutch in the 17th century. Maldivian lacquerwork and finely woven mats are famous for their quality and design. A fish-canning plant and several apparel factories built during the past decade have given a large boost to export-oriented manufactures.

[29] SCIENCE AND TECHNOLOGY

Mechanized fishing operations have been the focus of research and development efforts since the 1980s, with the help of UNDP.

[30] DOMESTIC TRADE

Malé Island is the chief commercial center. Sri Lankan and Indian merchants in Malé act as their own importers, exporters, and wholesalers. The importing of rice and exporting of ambergris are government monopolies. Most shops are open from 8 AM to 1:30 PM and from 2:30 to 5 PM, Sunday through Thursday. Banks and government offices are open from 9 AM to 1 PM on the same days.

[31] FOREIGN TRADE

The State Trading Organization enjoys a monopoly over fresh fish exports, and a favorable importing position resulting from preferential foreign exchange rates. Fish is the leading export product, in the past accounting for more than 90% of the total export value. With growth in garment manufactures, apparel and clothing accessories have rapidly become important export goods as well. Also exported are coconuts, copra, coir, cowrie shells, and some local handicraft products. Rice, wheat flour, and salt are imported, as are tobacco, beverages, manufactured goods, and petroleum products. Most trade is now with the US, UK, Japan, Sri Lanka, Germany, and Thailand, in contrast to the late 1970s, when Mauritius, Japan, and Pakistan comprised almost 90% of the country's export market. In 1991, exports were valued at $53,738,000; imports totaled $137,000,000; marine products accounted for about 60% of total exports, while apparel and accessories made up about 30%.

32BALANCE OF PAYMENTS

Balance of payments deficits during the first half of the 1980s were caused largely by the international shipping recession, the collapse of world tuna prices, and a brief downturn in tourism caused by the violence in nearby Sri Lanka. In 1992 merchandise exports totaled $51.1 million and imports $161.6 million. The merchandise trade balance was $–110.5 million.

33BANKING AND SECURITIES

The Maldives Monetary Authority, established 1 July 1981, issues currency, advises the government on banking and monetary matters, supervises commercial banks, and manages exchange rates and exchange assets. Other banking services are provided by the Bank of Maldives (created in 1982) and branches of the Bank of India, Habib Bank Ltd. of Pakistan, and the Bank of Ceylon. There is no securities exchange.

34INSURANCE

No information is available.

35PUBLIC FINANCE

Public enterprises, including the State Trading Organization, the state shipping line, and public utilities, account for nearly half of government revenues; customs and tourist receipts make up most of the rest. The following table shows actual revenues and expenditures for 1990 and 1991 in millions of rufiyaa.

	1990	1991
REVENUE AND GRANTS		
Tax revenue	286.8	366.1
Non-tax revenue	174.0	199.3
Capital revenue	5.5	3.8
Grants	85.0	226.2
TOTAL	551.3	795.4
EXPENDITURES & LENDING MINUS REPAYMENTS		
General public service	251.0	—
Education	78.8	—
Health	67.7	—
Social security and welfare	13.8	—
Housing and community amenities	83.3	—
Economic affairs and services	165.6	—
Other expenditures	39.3	—
Lending minus repayments	16.6	19.2
TOTAL	716.1	1,033.6
Deficit/surplus	–164.8	–238.2

In 1992 Maldives' total foreign debt stood at MR 432.2 million.

36TAXATION

Aside from customs duties, taxes on tourism constitute the main source of tax revenue. There is no income tax. License fees are charged for boats and motor vehicles. Uninhabited islands are leased for farming to individuals, who pay annual dues to the government; over 90% of these absentee landlords resided in Malé in 1985.

37CUSTOMS AND DUTIES

Customs duties are a primary source of government revenues and vary from 5-20% on essentials to 35-200% on luxury goods. Staple commodities and specified medicines and textbooks are duty-free. Import duties on consumer goods were reduced in May 1988.

38FOREIGN INVESTMENT

Assistance has been received from IBRD, WHO, UNDP, UNICEF, the EC, the Colombo Plan, CARE, and other international agencies, mostly in the form of grants and low-interest loans. Liberalized foreign investment policies have been adopted in recent years in order to attract needed development capital, especially for hotel and resort construction and other businesses related to the tourism industry. Net foreign direct investment inflow in 1989 totaled $51.7 million, up from $19.0 million in 1985.

39ECONOMIC DEVELOPMENT

The government has implemented a series of development programs to improve and expand fishing and related industries, textile manufacturing, food processing, tourism, communications, and health and education services. Part of the economic thrust has been to lessen the reliance on fishing and to diversify the economy. In 1986, Malé's new commercial harbor was opened, considerably speeding up cargo handling from 200–300 tons to 1,500 tons a day.

Malé's international airport was upgraded in the late 1980s, comprising a critical factor in the growth of the country's tourism sector. Given the growing wealth in the country in recent years, the government is considering bolstering government development revenues by instituting a personal income tax, though concerns remain that enforcement may prove difficult. Continued expansion of tourism has been particularly targeted in government development plans for the immediate future, along with facilitating a spread of economic activity to outlying island groups.

40SOCIAL DEVELOPMENT

There is no organized social welfare system. Assistance is traditionally provided through the extended family.

The average age at first marriage is low. Relationships are fluid and divorce rates high: according to the 1977 census, nearly half the women aged 30 and older had been married four times or more, and 80% had been married at least twice. The fertility rate in 1991 was 6.3. In spite of traditional Islamic restrictions on the role of women, they have increased their participation in public life. Women generally receive pay equal to men in similar positions. A Department of Women's Affairs and a National Women's Council protect women in traditional roles and help them enter nontraditional occupations. Approximately 10% of uniformed military personnel were women in 1993.

41HEALTH

In 1989, the Maldives had 15 physicians and 6 midwives. There is a relatively modern 86-bed hospital in Malé, backed by a 12-bed regional hospital and medical rescue services in the outlying atolls. Safe water is available to 53% of urban dwellers, but only 8% of those in rural areas. Under the 1985–87 three-year plan, priority was given to improvement of the water supply and sanitation. Life expectancy was 63 years in 1992, and the infant mortality rate 56 per 1,000 live births. In 1992, 98% of the country's children had been vaccinated against measles.

[42]HOUSING

Some of the houses on Malé are built in imitation of those in Colombo. Most, however, have coral or coconut-wood walls; the roofs are tiled or made of corrugated galvanized iron. The poorer houses are walled from the street with mats, called cadjan, or palm leaves. In 1985, 98% of all housing units were permanent dwellings, 1% were mobile homes, and the remainder were either improvised or collective housing. Roughly 80% were occupied rent free.

[43]EDUCATION

In 1985, 86.6% of the adult population was estimated to be literate. Primary level education is for five years and secondary education is in two stages: five years at the lower level and two years at the higher level. There are three streams of Maldivian education: traditional religious schools (makhtabs), which teach the Koran (Qur'an), basic arithmetic, and the ability to read and write Divehi; modern Divehi-language primary schools; and modern English-language schools. In 1992 there were 45,333 students in 134 primary schools. Secondary schools had 16,087 students with 154 in vocational schools. Maldivians must go abroad for higher education.

[44]LIBRARIES AND MUSEUMS

A National Library founded in 1945 contains 14,000 volumes and serves as a public library facility. A National Museum was founded in 1952 in Malé to conserve and display historical items.

[45]MEDIA

Interatoll communication is through a network of high-frequency transceivers; within atolls, communication between islands and with boats is by walkie-talkie. A satellite earth station was installed in 1977 to facilitate external communications. The Voice of Maldives has been transmitting radio broadcasts since 1962 in Dhivehi and English. Television Maldives is the country's only TV station. In 1991, 26,000 radio receivers and 5,000 television sets were counted; in addition, 2,485 telephones were in operation. There are two newspapers, *Aafathis* (1991 circulation 300) and *Haveeru* (1,500).

[46]ORGANIZATIONS

Several sport clubs and a Muslim religious organization operate in Malé.

[47]TOURISM, TRAVEL, AND RECREATION

Tourism is the pricipal industry and leading foreign exchange earner. It has developed rapidly with government support, climbing from 9,000 visitors in 1975 to 196,112 in 1991. Of these, 147,225 came from Europe, followed by 28,441 from East Asia. Income from tourism reached $87 million, and the hotel occupancy rate was 62.8%. Natural attractions are crystal-clear lagoons and white beaches that are ideal for swimming, fishing, and and both snorkeling and scuba diving. Modern, one- and two-story tourist facilities have been built on various otherwise uninhabited islands, mainly in the Malé atoll but also in neighboring atolls. Developed with European, Sri Lankan, and Indian assistance and part ownership, such resorts are confined to these individual islands, thus allowing the conservative Islamic government to profit from the presence of foreign tourists while shielding its citizens from the presence and consumption of alcoholic beverages and other un-Islamic holiday practices of these tourists. Maldivian resort workers maintain their homes and families on other islands, and non-Maldivians—often Sri Lankans—are hired to serve the alcohol. Passports are required of all visitors, as are yellow fever inoculation certificates for those arriving from infected areas.

[48]FAMOUS MALDIVIANS

Ibn Battutah (Muhammad bin 'Abdallah bin Battutah, b.Tangier, 1304–77), the remarkable Arab traveler and geographer, lived in the Maldives for several years, served as a quadi there, and married the daughter of a Maldivian vizier. Sultan Iskandar Ibrahim I, who reigned for nearly 40 years during the 17th century, built the Hukuru Miskit, the principal mosque on Malé Island, in 1674. Modern-day leaders include Amir Ibrahim Nasir (b.1926) and Maumoon Abdul Gayoom (b.1937).

[49]DEPENDENCIES

Maldives has no territories or colonies.

[50]BIBLIOGRAPHY

Bell, Harry Charles Purvis. *The Maldive Islands: Monograph on the History, Archaeology, Epigraphy.* Colombo: Ceylon Government Press, 1940.

Gardiner, J. Stanley (ed.). *The Fauna and Geography of the Maldive and Laccadive Archipelagoes.* 2 vols. Cambridge: Cambridge University Press, 1901–6.

Heyerdahl, Thor. *The Maldives Mystery.* Bethesda, Md.: Adler & Adler, 1986.

Hockley, T. W. *The Two Thousand Isles: A Short Account of the People, History and Customs of the Maldive Archipelago.* London: Witherby, 1935.

The Maldives: An Introductory Economic Report. IBRD. Washington, D.C., 1980.

Maloney, Clarence. *The People of the Maldive Islands.* Columbia, Mo.: South Asia Books, 1981.

Reynolds, C. H. B. *Maldives.* Santa Barbara, CA: Clio Press, 1993.

Stoddard, Theodore L. *Area Handbook for the Indian Ocean Territories.* Washington: Government Printing Office, 1971.

MARSHALL ISLANDS

Republic of the Marshall Islands

CAPITAL: Majuro, Majuro Atoll.

FLAG: The flag, adopted in 1979, is blue, with two diagonal strips of orange over white; in the canton is a white star with 4 large rays and 20 shorter ones.

ANTHEM: *Ij iokwe lok aelon eo ao ijo iaar lotak ie (I Love My Island, Where I Was Born).*

MONETARY UNIT: The US dollar is the official medium of exchange.

WEIGHTS AND MEASURES: British units are used, as modified by US usage.

HOLIDAYS: As of January 1988, the government had not legislated official holidays.

TIME: 11 PM = noon GMT.

¹LOCATION, SIZE, AND EXTENT

The Marshall Islands is located in the central Pacific Ocean, just north of the Equator. Isolated from major population centers, Majuro, the capital, lies 3,438 km (2,136 mi) W of Honolulu, 3,701 km (2,300 mi) SE of Tokyo, and 3,241 km (2,014 mi) SE of Saipan, the former trust territory capital. The country consists of 29 atolls and 5 islands extending over a sea area exceeding 1,942,500 sq km (750,000 sq mi), but a land area of only about 181 sq km (70 sq mi).

Comparatively, the area occupied by the Marshall Islands is slightly larger than Washington, D.C. The atolls and islands form two almost parallel chainlike formations: the Ratak ("Sunrise"), or Eastern, group and the Ralik ("Sunset"), or Western, group. The largest atolls in the Ratak group are Mili, Majuro, Maloelap, Wotje, Likiep, and Bikini; in the Ralik group, Jaluit, Kwajalein, Wotho, and Enewetak. The Marshall Islands have a coastline of 370.4 km (230 mi).

The capital city of the Marshall Islands, Majuro, is located on the island of Majuro. Majuro Atool is 3440 km (2,136 mi) from Honolulu, 3,700 km (2,300 mi) from Tokyo, and 3245 km (2,016 mi) from Saipan.

²TOPOGRAPHY

The majority of islands are in typical atoll formations, consisting of low-lying narrow strips of land enclosing a lagoon. Soils are porous, sandy, and of low fertility. There are five islands and 29 atolls scattered over 1.94 million sq km (750,000 sq mi) of the central Pacific Ocean. Kwajalein Atoll in the Ralik, or Western, atoll is the largest atoll in the world.

³CLIMATE

The maritime tropical climate is hot and humid, with little seasonal temperature change. Diurnal variations generally range between 21° and 34°C (70° and 93°F). Trade winds from the northeast cool the high temperatures from December through March.

Rainfall averages about 30–38 cm (12–15 in) per month, with October and November the wettest and December to April the driest. Average rainfall increases from the north to the south; the northern atolls average 178 cm (70 in) annually, compared with 432 cm (170 in) in the southern atolls.

⁴FLORA AND FAUNA

The flora and fauna of the atolls are limited in number and variety. The flora consists of species resilient to porous soils, salt spray, and relatively strong wind force. The dominant tree species include coconut palms, pandanus, breadfruit, and citrus trees. Fauna include rodents and indigenous strains of pig.

⁵ENVIRONMENT

Among the Marshall Islands' more significant environmental problems are water pollution due to lack of adequate sanitation facilities, and the rise of sea levels due to global warming. Any rise in the sea level is a constant and serious threat to an island nation whose land mass is 2–3 meters (6–10 ft) above sea level.

The Marshall Islands Environmental Protection Agency, established in 1984, is concerned with programs for water quality standards, solid waste disposal, earthworks, and use of pesticides. The environments of the Bikini, Enewetak, Rongelap, and Utirik atolls were contaminated by nuclear testing. Nuclear tests were carried out in the region from 1946–58. As of early 1988, the long-term environmental effects on these atolls and their populations remained undetermined.

⁶POPULATION

The 1988 census recorded a population of 43,380. About 60% of the total population resided on two atolls, Majuro and Ebeye. Almost 20,000 resided on Majuro atoll, and almost 9,000 on the island of Ebeye.

Government estimates in 1991, based on an annual population growth of 3.5%, indicated a total population of 48,000. The land density was estimated at 265 persons per sq km (686 per sq mi). Of the 34 atolls and major islands, 24 are inhabited. Over half the population in 1988 was under age 15.

⁷MIGRATION

Population has been steadily migrating from the outer atolls to the urban concentrations on Majuro and Ebeye. As a result, outer atolls have been left with unbalanced population structures of children, females, and the aged.

Provisions under the Compact of Free Association with the US permit unrestricted entry into the US and allow high-school graduates to join the US armed forces.

8ETHNIC GROUPS

The Marshallese people are Micronesians, who are physically similar to the Polynesian peoples. The largest non-Marshallese ethnic group is from Kosrae in the Federated States of Micronesia. There are also small numbers of Americans and Filipinos.

9LANGUAGES

Both English and Marshallese (Kajin Majol) are spoken. Marshallese is a Malayo-Polynesian language and the common source of each of the atolls' dialects. Both English and Marshallese are used in official communications and in commerce, while English is used to a lesser extent in the outer islands.

10RELIGIONS

The people are almost entirely Christian, primarily Protestant, as a result of the arrival of American and Hawaiian Protestant missionaries in the 1860s. The United Church of Christ is the principal denomination, representing some 90% of the population. The United Church of Christ is the successor of the Congregationalists from New England and Hawaii who converted the islanders in the latter half of the 19th century. In 1993 there were also 3,440 Roman Catholics. Other religious denominations represented include Assemblies of God, Seventh Day Adventists, Baptists, Baha'i, Mormons, and Jehovah's Witnesses.

11TRANSPORTATION

There are 56 km (35 mi) of paved road on the Majuro atoll and 3.7 km (2.3 mi) on the Kwajalein atoll. On the outer islands, roads consist primarily of cleared paths. There are few motor vehicles.

The many scattered atolls separated by long distances make sea and air transportation essential. Domestic sea transportation is provided by interisland ships, which service each of the outer islands about once every three months. Two commercial dock facilities in Majuro and one in Ebeye furnish port facilities for international shipping. The merchant fleet consists of 18 ships with a capacity totaling 1,436,000 GRT.

Majuro International Airport, completed in 1974, accommodates aircraft up to Boeing 707 size. There were 16 usable outer-island airstrips in 1991; all inhabited islands and atolls were equipped with airstrips, except for Ebon, Lib, and Ujelang. The government-owned Airline of the Marshall Islands (AMI), established in 1980, provides service to all outer islands with airstrips. International airline connections are provided to Tarawa in Kiribati, Funafuti in Tuvalu, and Nadi in Fiji. Air Micronesia/Continental Airlines links Majuro with major foreign destinations, including Hawaii, Guam, Manila, and Tokyo.

12HISTORY

Sighting of the islands was first recorded by the Spanish navigator Alvaro de Saavedra in 1529. The British captain John Marshall, after whom the islands are named, explored them in 1788. Throughout the late 1800s and early 1900s, foreign powers ruled the islands for such advantages as trade, religious propagation, exploitation of resources, strategic considerations, and maintenance of sea routes. Spain claimed the islands in 1874, but sold them to Germany in 1899. At the outbreak of World War I, Japanese naval squadrons took possession of the Marshalls and began formal administration under a League of Nations mandate in 1920.

In World War II, after bitter fighting between US and Japanese forces that included battles for Kwajalein and Eniwetok (now Enewetak), the islands came under US control. In 1947, the Marshalls became a district of a UN trusteeship, called the Trust Territory of the Pacific Islands, which was administered by the US. The US used Bikini and Enewetak atolls as nuclear testing sites from 1946 to 1958, exploding 66 atomic and

nuclear tests during this period. The nuclear testing program resulted in the displacement of the indigenous people.

The Marshallese people adopted a constitution in 1978, under which the Marshalls were designated the Republic of the Marshall Islands. In 1979, the constitution went into effect and the republic became a self-governing territory. Amata Kabua was elected the Republic's first president. In 1983, a Compact of Free Association with the US, providing for full self-government except for defense, was approved by plebiscite. In January 1986, the compact was ratified by the US, and on 21 October 1986 it went into effect.

The people of Bikini and Enewetak, along with those exposed to radioactive fallout in the 1954 Bravo Blast fought for compensation from the US, which in February 1990 agreed to pay $45,000,000 to the victims of the nuclear testing program. The UN Security Council voted in December 1990 to terminate the Marshall Islands' status as a UN Trust Territory. The Republic became an independent state and joined the UN in September 1991.

13GOVERNMENT

The Marshall Islands is an independent republic. The constitution effective on 1 May 1979 incorporates a blend of the British and American constitutional concepts. It provides for three main branches of government: the legislature, the executive, and the judiciary.

Legislative power is vested in the Parliament, known as the Nitijela, which consists of 33 members elected from 24 electoral districts, each corresponding roughly to an atoll. The Council of Iroij (Chiefs) has 12 members, whose main functions are to request reconsideration by the Nitijela of any bill affecting customary law, traditional practice, or land tenure, and to express on opinion to the cabinet on any matter of national concern.

Executive power is vested in the cabinet, headed by the president, who is also head of state. The president, a member of the Nitijela, is elected by a majority of that assembly. The constitution requires the president to nominate not more than 10 or fewer than 6 members of the Nitijela as ministers.

The last legislative elections were held in November 1991. Amata Kabua was reelected President in January 1992. All citizens who have attained the age of 18 are eligible to vote.

After the US trusteeship administration of the Marshall Islands came to an end on 21 October 1986, the governments of the US and the Marshall Islands entered into a Compact of Free Association which provides economic, technical, trade, and other benefits to the Marshall Islands for an initial period of 15 years.

14POLITICAL PARTIES

The Ralik Ratak Democratic Party, founded by Tony DeBrum in June 1991, acts as the opposition to the Kabua Government.

15LOCAL GOVERNMENT

There are 24 local governments for the inhabited atolls and islands. Typically, each is headed by a mayor, and consists of an elected council, appointed local officials, and a local police force.

16JUDICIAL SYSTEM

The judiciary consists of the Supreme Court, the High Court, the District Court, and 22 community courts. The Supreme Court has final appellate jurisdiction. The High Court has trial jurisdiction over almost all cases and appellate jurisdiction over all types of cases tried in subordinate courts. The District Court has limited civil and criminal jurisdiction nationwide.

Community courts in local government areas adjudicate civil and criminal cases within their communities. In 1984, a Traditional Rights Court was established to determine questions relating to titles or land rights and other legal interests involving customary law and traditional practice.

¹⁷ARMED FORCES

There are no armed forces. Under the Compact of Free Association, the US provides defense for a minimum 15-year period and operation of the Kwajalein Missile Range for 30 years.

¹⁸INTERNATIONAL COOPERATION

Until 21 October 1986, the Marshall Islands was administered by the US under a UN Trusteeship Agreement. As of January 1988, the Marshall Islands was not a UN member. Through UNDP's programs, however, it cooperates with a wide range of UN specialized agencies, including FAO, ILO, UNIDO, and the UN Department of Technical Cooperation for Development. In 1986, it became an associate member of ESCAP. The government continues to support and participate in the activities of regional bodies and has full membership in the SPC. The Marshall Islands has no diplomatic missions overseas, although an office of a resident representative to the US was established in 1986.

¹⁹ECONOMY

The economy consists of a monetary sector and a nonmonetary subsistence sector. The monetary sector is localized in Majuro and Ebeye and is sustained largely by expenditures of the government and Kwajalein Missile Range employees. Copra (dried coconut meat) production provides a source of cash income for outer-atoll families engaged in subsistence activities. The labor force numbered 10,156, of which 30% were employed in the services sector, 21.4% in agriculture, fisheries, and mining, 10.7% in construction, and 9.3% in manufacturing.

Of those in the labor force engagaed in agriculture and fishing, the main activities are copra (dried coconut meat) production, and the cultivation of breadfruit, taro, and pandanus.

The islands have few natural resources, and imports far exceed exports. In 1987, the US government provided grants of $40 million out of the Marshallese budget of $55 million.

²⁰INCOME

In 1989, the Marshall Island's GDP was an estimated $63 million, and per capita income was estimated at $1,500.

²¹LABOR

There is a considerable shifting of labor between the monetary and subsistence sectors of the economy, depending on opportunities for wage employment. As of 1992, over 50% of the population was under the age of 15, creating an acute labor shortage of trained and skilled workers. The labor force was 11,488 in 1988. Over 21% of employment is in agriculture, fishing and mining; 11% in construction, 14% in trade, 30% in personal services, 9% in manufacturing, 8% in business services and finance, and 7% in other sectors. The vast majority of monetary-sector employment is found in Majuro, Ebeye, and Kwajalein.

The government is the largest source of employment, followed by the service and construction sectors. Unemployment exceeded 12% in 1988; there is a high and rising number of unemployed youth.

There are no labor unions. A minimum wage of $1.50 per hour set by the government can be waived by new businesses or by employers who are training Marshallese employees. In order to create local jobs, the government is considering the creation of a duty-free transshipment zone.

²²AGRICULTURE

The traditional interplanting of root crops and other vegetables with coconuts, which maintained self-sufficiency in food and provided the Marshallese with dietetic variety before modern times,

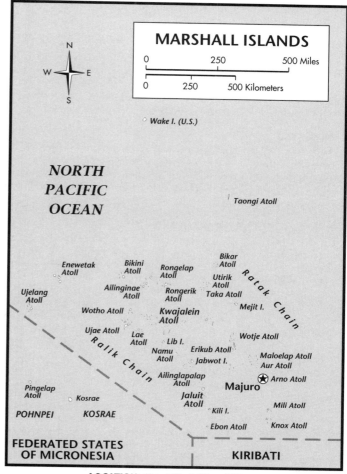

LOCATION: 4° to 14°N; 160° to 173°E.

is still widely practiced as a subsistence activity. Dried coconut meat, known as copra, is produced on almost all islands and atolls; some 6,500 ha (16,000 acres) of coconut palm were productive in the mid-1980s.

²³ANIMAL HUSBANDRY

Livestock on the islands consists of pigs and poultry. Most families raise pigs for subsistence and for family and community feasts. In 1981, pigs were imported from New Zealand to improve the strains of the local breed.

²⁴FISHING

While subsistence fishing for inshore species is carried out from all atolls, there is little domestic commercial fishing in the nation's 1,942,500 sq km (750,000 sq mi) of sea. The total catch in 1991 amounted to 200 tons. Principal marine resources include tuna, prawns, shrimp, seaweed, sponges, black pearls, giant clams, trochus, and green mussels. Colorful baby giant clams for ornamental aquariums are grown for export to the US.

A fisheries base with a freezer plant (200 tons capacity) and a chilling plant (50 tons capacity) was constructed in Majuro with Japanese government assistance. In 1986, the Marshall Islands Maritime Authority (MIMA) was reestablished to organize all marine resource activities, including protection, management, and development, under one agency. The Asian Development Bank had plans in mid-1993 to loan $7 million to a private fishing company on Ebeye, in order to build seven longliner fishing vessels. The boats are to be constructed in New Zealand with the assistance of Marshallese workers.

25FORESTRY
Some 8,900 ha (22,000 acres) are planted with coconut palm. Replanting has been undertaken on Arno, Lae, Maloelap, Rongelap, Ujae, Wotho, and Wotje. Pine species are under experimentation in a windbreak tree project on Ebeye. In 1984, a sawmill was purchased for processing coconut trunks and other tree species as lumber.

26MINING
There is no mining of mineral resources. However, preliminary surveys have revealed the presence of phosphate and manganese nodules in the seabed within the territorial waters. Lagoon dredging of sand and coral for construction purposes is undertaken in Majuro and Ebeye.

27ENERGY AND POWER
The Marshall Islands is dependent on imported fossil fuels for electric-power generation. The urban centers of Majuro and Ebeye have major generating facilities. The Majuro power plant, commissioned in 1982, has an installed power capacity of 14,000 kw. A new power plant was commissioned in Ebeye in 1987, with a capacity of 5,200 kw of electricity. The low power requirements in the outer islands are met by solar-powered systems. In 1988, fuel imports amounted to $3.6 million, or 10% of total imports.

28INDUSTRY
The economy's small manufacturing sector, localized largely in Majuro, accounts for less than 4% of the gross revenues generated in the private sector. The largest industrial operation is a copra-processing mill under a government and private-sector joint enterprise. (Copra is dried coconut meat.) The rest of the manufacturing sector consists of small-scale and domestic operations, such as coir making, furniture making, handicrafts, and boat making. A small fish-drying plant, preparing smoke-dried tuna for exportation to Japan, began operation after 1985. In 1986, a government-owned dairy factory was established in Majuro, producing liquid milk, ice cream, and yogurt from imported milk powder and butterfat. In 1987, a small tuna cannery began production in Majuro.

29SCIENCE AND TECHNOLOGY
While there are no institutions involved in scientific research or training, the College of Micronesia nursing facility and science center, located in the Majuro Hospital, provides instruction in nursing technology and science.

30DOMESTIC TRADE
Domestic trade accounts for the majority of the total gross trade revenue from urban private enterprises. Trade is concentrated in Majuro and Ebeye and consists mainly of imported goods, although increasing amounts of locally produced vegetables and fish are being marketed. Retailers ship imported goods to the outer islands where they are exchanged for copra, which is dried cocunut meat.

31FOREIGN TRADE
Heavy and increasing trade deficits result from limited exports and dependency on imports for consumer and capital goods. Over 90% of the value of exports is accounted for by coconut oil and copra cake, made of dried coconut meat. The total value of exports in 1989 was $2,253,000, of which $1,778,000 was derived from coconut oil and copra cake. The total value of imports was $33,764,000 in 1988, as compared with $17,155,000 in 1980. The US and Japan are the main sources of imports.

32BALANCE OF PAYMENTS
The economy suffers from a long-stnding imbalance of trade, with imports far exceeding exports. A comprehensive record of international transactions in the form of standardized balance-of-payments accounts was not maintained during the trusteeship period. The chronic trade deficit is offset by official unrequited transfers, predominantly from the US.

33BANKING AND SECURITIES
Financial services are provided by three commercial banks, the Bank of Guam, and the Bank of Marshalls, located in Majuro, and the Bank of Hawaii, located in Ebeye. The Marshall Islands Development Loan Office in Majuro was established as an independent government corporation in 1982. There are four credit unions, which are operated by over 2,000 members. The Marshall Islands has no stock issues or securities trading.

34INSURANCE
Two foreign insurance companies, located in Majuro, provide coverage. A US insurance company provides loan protection policies to credit unions.

35PUBLIC FINANCE
Government revenues are derived from domestic sources and US grants. Domestic revenues are from taxes and nontax sources (fishing rights, philatelic sales, and user charges). Budget revenues totaled $55 million in 1987, much of which consisted of US grants. Current expenditures, excluding debt service, remained relatively constant during 1980–85 at approximately $24.5 million. The leading areas of expenditure include health services, education, public works, and transportation and communication.

36TAXATION
Income tax is applied to wages and salaries at graduated rates. Business tax is applied to gross revenues of service-related enterprises generated anywhere in the Marshall Islands, the Federated States of Micronesia, and Palau, except on Kwajalein. A sales tax is applied only in Kwajalein. There is also a fuel tax.

37CUSTOMS AND DUTIES
Customs duties, which yielded $4.1 million in 1985, were roughly equal to the revenue yield from income taxes and close to one-third of the total domestically derived revenues in that year. Import taxes are generally ad valorem.

38FOREIGN INVESTMENT
The government favors joint ventures with foreign private investors. Foreigners may lease but not own land. The US department of defense operates a missile tesing range on behalf of the strategic defense command in Kwajalein.

39ECONOMIC DEVELOPMENT
The first five-year national development plan (1985–89), which was rephased to 1986/87–1990/91 to meet the requirements of the Compact of Free Association with the US, constituted the first phase of a 15-year development program. The plan focused on economic development, with emphasis on private-sector expansion, personnel development and employment creation, regional development, population planning and social development, and cultural and environmental preservation. Total funding requirements for implementation of the plan were $201 million, compared with identified funding sources of $155 million.

In 1991, the Marshall Islands received $154,000 in socio-economic development aid through the United Nations. Financial aid from the United States totals over US$65 million per year. Current development projects include a new capitol building, docks, and causeways.

40SOCIAL DEVELOPMENT

Private-sector provision of community and social services is mainly through the Marshalls Community Action Agency, a non-profit organization. Among government agencies, the Ministry of Social Services is involved in five major areas: housing, women's and youth development, feeding programs, aging, and other community development welfare programs. Funding of these services is provided almost entirely by the US. A social security system provides old age, disability, and survivor benefits, paid for by employers and employees.

The Marshallese society retains a traditional matrilineal structure. Each person belongs to the bwij, or clan, of his or her mother, and has the right to use the land and other proerty of the bwij. The head of the bwif is called an alap. The alap is the spokesperson between the clan members and the members of the iroij, or royal clan. Inheritance of traditional rank and of property is matrilineal, and women occupy important positions within the traditional social and economic system. No instances of sex discrimination have been reported.

The Marshallese have a casual attitude toward life, and informal dress is the norm in the Marshall Islands. American cultural influences can be observed there, especially in Majuro, Kwajalein, and on the island of Ebeye.

41HEALTH

During the period 1980–85, the leading causes of death after infancy were respiratory diseases, diarrhea and other intestinal diseases, diabetes, and heart disease. Infant mortality was 63 per 1,000 live births in 1992, a sharp increase from the 1980s. In 1992, there were 1,400 births and 86% of children were immunized against measles. Alcoholism and drug abuse are common, and there is a relatively high incidence of sexually transmitted diseases.

There are two hospitals: the Armer Ishoda Hospital in Majuro, with an 81-bed capacity, and a recently renovated hospital in Ebeye. Both hospitals provide dental services. In 1991, there were 20 doctors, 130 nurses, and 4 midwives.

Rudimentary health care on the outer atolls is provided through 69 dispensaries, staffed by health assistants. Emergency cases are sent to the Majuro or Ebeye hospital and, when necessary, to hospitals in Honolulu. Dental services to the outer atolls are provided by periodic visits by dental teams from Majuro and Ebeye.

42HOUSING

Houses in the urban centers are simple wooden or cement-block structures, with corrugated iron roofs; because of the limited land availability, houses are heavily crowded. In the outer atolls houses are constructed of local materials, with thatched sloping roofs and sides of plaited palm fronds.

The Ministry of Social Services provides housing grants, principally to low-income families, through a low-cost housing program and a grant-in-aid program. Government housing is administered by the Public Service Commission.

In 1988, there were 4,943 dwellings on the Marshall Islands, of which 43% received their water supply from rain catchment, while 30% had piped indoor water. About 44% had flush toilets, 56% had electricity, and 48% used kerosene for cooking.

43EDUCATION

The Ministry of Education provides for public education at the elementary, secondary, and higher education levels. In 1981, the literacy rate in Marshallese was 90% and in English 25%. The public elementary education provides eight years of basic education to those aged 7–14. In 1986/87 there were 71 elementary schools with 7,733 students enrolled and 347 teachers on the faculties. A comprehensive four-year program of secondary education provides instruction in general studies, college prepara-

tory courses, and vocational training. In 1986/87 there were two public secondary schools, enrolling 825 students.

Private elementary and secondary education is provided by two nondenominational schools and several religious-affiliated schools. Enrollment in 1986/87 was 2,432 at the elementary level and 607 at the secondary level.

Higher education is provided through formal programs of teacher training and the provision of grants for university training abroad. In 1986, approximately 160 students received financial assistance for foreign training. The Majuro campus of the College of Micronesia opened its School of Nursing and Science Center in 1986. In 1991, a University Center was to be opened at Majuro. The same year, Marshall Islands became a member of the University of the South Pacific.

44LIBRARIES AND MUSEUMS

In Majuro, the Alele Museum, which also houses a library, was completed in 1973. The library houses historical documents and photographs from the trust territory archives. More than 2,000 glass-plate negatives taken between 1890 and 1930 are on loan to the museum.

45MEDIA

The inter-island communications network consists of 53 short-wave outer-island radio stations, which link all major islands and atolls. The island of Ebeye is linked to Majuro by radio and also by satellite. There are three broadcast stations. The government radio station, which has advertising, relays world news from Voice of America and Radio Australia. There are two private-sector FM stations, one commercial and one church affiliated, and one television station. In 1988 there were 800 telephones on Majuro and Ebeye.

A weekly newspaper, *The Marshall Islands Journal* (1992 circulation 10,000), is published in Majuro in English and Marshallese. *The Marshall Island Government Gazette*, established in 1982, is a free four-page government newsletter, printed in English.

46ORGANIZATIONS

Marshallese society is matrilineal and organized on the basis of the clan (bwij). The head of the clan (alap) serves as spokesman between clan members and members of the royal clan.

At the community level there are youth organizations, including Boy Scouts and Girl Scouts, women's organizations, and various religiously affiliated social organizations. Preparatory work on the establishment of a national women's organization began in 1986. A number of consumers' cooperatives are in operation.

47TOURISM, TRAVEL, AND RECREATION

Tourist attractions include the sandy beaches on the atolls, protected lagoons, underwater coral reefs, and abundant marine life, including large gamefish. The outer atolls of Mili, Maloelap, Wotje, and Jaluit offer many Japanese and American relics from World War II. However, tourism remains undeveloped, and the outer atolls do not have any accommodations for visitors.

48FAMOUS MARSHALLESE

Amata Kabua (b.1928), president since 1979 and leader of the Ailin Kein ad Party, previously served as a member of the Congress of Micronesia and guided his country to self-governing status under the US-administered UN trusteeship.

49DEPENDENCIES

The Marshall Islands have no territories or colonies.

50BIBLIOGRAPHY

Dibblin, Jane. *Day of Two Suns: US Nuclear Testing and the Pacific Islanders.* New York: New Amsterdam, 1990.

Republic of the Marshall Islands First Five Year Development Plan 1985–1989. Majuro: Office of Planning and Statistics, 1984.

Trust Territory of the Pacific Islands, 1986. Washington, D.C.: US Department of State, 1986.

Weisgall, Jonathan M. *Operation Crossroads: The Atomic Tests at Bikini Atoll.* Annapolis, Md.: Naval Institute Press, 1994.

MONGOLIA

Mongolian People's Republic

Bügd Nayramdah Mongol Ard Uls

CAPITAL: Ulaanbaatar.

FLAG: The national flag, adopted in 1946, contains a light blue vertical stripe between two red stripes; in gold, on the stripe nearest the hoist, is a five-pointed star surmounting the soyombo, Mongolia's independence emblem.

ANTHEM: *Bügd Nayramdah mongol ard ulsyn töriin duulal (State Anthem of the Mongolian People's Republic).*

MONETARY UNIT: The tugrik (т) of 100 mongos. There are coins of 1, 2, 5, 10, 15, 20, and 50 mongos and notes of 1, 3, 5, 10, 20, 25, 50, and 100 tugriks. т1 = $0.298 (or $1 = т3.3555).

WEIGHTS AND MEASURES: The metric system is the legal standard.

HOLIDAYS: New Year's Day, 1 January; Women's Day, 8 March; Popular Revolution Day, 11 July. Movable holidays include Mongol New Year's Day, in February or March.

TIME: 8 PM = noon GMT.

¹LOCATION, SIZE, AND EXTENT

Situated in east-central Asia, the Mongolian People's Republic (MPR) has an area of 1,565,000 sq km (604,250 sq mi), extending 2,368 km (1,471 mi) E–W and 1,260 km (783 mi) N–S. Comparatively, the area occupied by Mongolia is slightly larger than the state of Alaska. The largest landlocked country in the world, Mongolia is bordered on the N by Russia and on the E, S, and W by China, with a total boundary length of 8,114 km (5,042 mi).

²TOPOGRAPHY

Mongolia is essentially a vast plateau with an average elevation of 1,580 m (5,184 ft). The MPR comprises a mountainous section in the extreme west, where the peak of the Khuiten (formerly Mönh Hayrhan) of the Mongolian Altay Mountains rises to a height of 4,374 m (14,350 ft). Other mountain ranges are the Hentiyn, along the Soviet border, and the Hangayn, in west-central Mongolia. The southern part of the country is occupied by the Gobi, a rocky desert with a thin veneer of shifting sand. Explorations have uncovered large reservoirs of water 2–3 m (7–10 ft) beneath the desert surface.

³CLIMATE

Mongolia has an arid continental climate with a wide seasonal range of temperature and low precipitation. In winter, it is the site of the great Siberian high, which governs the climate of a large part of Asia and gives Mongolia average January temperatures of −22° to −18°C (−8° to 0°F) and dry, virtually snowless winters. In summer, remnants of the southeasterly monsoon bring most of the year's precipitation. Annual precipitation ranges from 25 to 38 cm (10 to 15 in) in mountain areas to less than 13 cm (5 in) in the Gobi.

⁴FLORA AND FAUNA

Mongolia is divided into several natural regions, each with its characteristic plant and animal life. These regions are the mountain forests near the Soviet Siberian border; the mountain steppe and hilly forest farther south, followed by the lowland steppe grasslands; the semidesert; and finally the true desert. Larch and Siberian stone pine are characterisic trees of the northern forests, which are inhabited by bear, Manchurian red deer, snow panther, wild boar, and elk. The saiga antelope and the wild horse are typical steppe dwellers.

⁵ENVIRONMENT

As of 1994, the main environment problems facing Mongolia are desertification and inadequate water supply. The presence of the Gobi Desert in the southeastern part of the country and mountains in the northwest provide natural limits to the amount of agricultural land. Areas affected by deforestation and excessive grazing are eventually overtaken by the desert.

Water pollution is a particularly significant problem in Mongolia because the water supply is so limited. The country has only 5.9 cubic miles of water, 62% of which is used for farming. In 1994, 42% of the people living in rural areas did not have access to pure water.

The country's air pollution problems are due to increased industrial activity within the country and airborne industrial pollution from the former Soviet Union and the People's Republic of China.

As of 1991, Przewalski's horse, the Bactrian camel, the snow leopard, and the saiga are among 9 mammals and 13 birds which are considered endangered.

⁶POPULATION

As of January 1989, the population totaled 2,043,400; in 1993, it was estimated at 2,200,000. The projected population for the year 2000 is 2,830,000, assuming a crude birthrate of 31.8 (per 1,000 population) and a crude death rate of 6.8 for 1995–2000. In 1995, about 61% of the people lived in urban areas, in sharp contrast to the 19% urban total in 1950. In 1993, the population of Ulaanbaatar, the principal city, was 619,400. In 1991 Darhan had 90,000 and Erdenet, 58,200. Average density in 1989 was only 1.3 persons per sq km (3.4 per sq mi). The average rate of population increase in the late 1980s was about 2.7% per year. In 1990, Mongolians aged 15–60 made up an estimated 50% of the population, and those over 60 only 8.3%.

[7]MIGRATION

Few Mongolian nationals live outside the country, but 4,802,407 persons of Mongolian extraction lived in China in 1990—mainly in Inner Mongolia, but also in Manchuria, Qinghai, Kansu, and Xinjiang—and about 500,000 live in Russia—in the Buryat and Kalmyk republics. Between 1955 and 1962, some 20,000 Chinese laborers entered Mongolia to work on construction projects, but in 1964 the MPR expelled about 2,000 Chinese nationals who had refused to take part in an agricultural resettlement program, and another 1,700 in 1983. Since the independence of Kazakhstan, many Kazakhs have emigrated.

[8]ETHNIC GROUPS

In 1990, 87% of the population consisted of Mongols, approximately three-quarters of them Khalkha. The Kazakhs are the leading minority group, making up about 6%. Peoples of Soviet and Chinese origin are also present in substantial numbers (2% each).

[9]LANGUAGES

Khalkha Mongolian, the official language, is spoken by about 90% of the population. It is one of a large dialect group in the Mongolic branch of the Altaic language family. Early in the 13th century, the Mongols adopted an alphabet written in vertical columns from the Turkic Uighurs, and they retained that script until modern times. The literary language differed increasingly from the living spoken language, and in 1941 the Mongolian government decided to introduce a new phonetic alphabet that would accurately reflect modern spoken Mongolian. The new alphabet consisted of the Cyrillic letters used in Russian, except for two special characters needed to render the Mongolian vowels represented as ö and ü in Western European languages. After a period of preparation (1941–45), the new alphabet was introduced in 1946 in all publications and in 1950 in all business transactions, but, following independence, the traditional script was due to be restored in 1994. The differences between the Khalkha language spoken in the MPR, the Buryat language spoken in the Buryat Republic of Russia, the Chahar and Ordos languages of China's Inner Mongolian Autonomous Region, and other Mongolian dialects are comparatively small and chiefly phonetic. A characteristic phonetic feature of Mongolian is the law of vowel harmony, which requires that a word contain either the so-called back vowels, represented as a, o, and u in Western European languages, or the so-called front vowels, represented as e(ä), ö, and ü, but not an association of the two types of vowels. Kazakh, Russian, and Chinese are also spoken.

[10]RELIGIONS

About two-thirds of the people do not profess any religion or are avowed atheists. Of the remainder, most belong to Lamaist Buddhism, which has been strongly influenced by indigenous shamanism. Before the government's campaign against religion in the 1930s, there were about 700 monasteries, with about 100,000 lamas (theoretically celibate), in Mongolia. During 1936–39, the Communist regime closed virtually all monasteries, confiscated their livestock and landholdings, tried the higher lamas for counterrevolutionary activities, and induced thousands of lower lamas to adopt a secular mode of life. In the mid-1980s, only about 100 lamas remained. About 1% of the population is Muslim, and 0.2% Christian. The new constitution of 1992 established freedom of religion for all. Mahayana Buddhism, the primary religious following before the suppression of religion in the 1930s is making a surprising resurgence. Former monasteries are being restored, and there is a seminary at Gandantegchinlen Hiyd. In 1992, Roman Catholic missionaries were also encouraged to come to Mongolia to continue the presence they had initiated earlier in the century.

[11]TRANSPORTATION

The Trans-Mongolian Railway, about 1,500 km (930 mi) in length, connects Mongolia with both China and Russia. Ulaanbaatar has been connected to the Trans-Siberian Railway via Bayantümen since 1939 and via Sühbaatar since 1950, and to the Chinese Railways via Dzamïn üüd since the end of 1955. Choybalsan is also connected to the Trans-Siberian system via Ereenstav. Ulaanbaatar Railways has been linked to Nalayh since 1938 and to Darhan and Tamsagbulag since 1964. The Sharïn Gol Open-Pit Coal Mining Industry was connected to the Darhan industrial center during the third five-year plan (1961–65) by a 60-km (37-mi) rail line. A 200-km (124-mi) railroad line connects Erdenet, a copper-molybdenum mining and industrial center near the Russian border, with the Trans-Mongolian Railway. The total length of railroads in 1991 was 1,750 km (1,087 mi). In 1992, railroads in Mongolia carried some 2.6 million passengers, and performed 629.5 million passenger-km and 2,756 million freight ton-km of service.

Mongolia has about 1,000 km (620 mi) of asphalt or concrete roads and 45,700 km (28,400 mi) paved with crushed stone or gravel. Freight and passenger traffic are carried on the Selenge River and across Hövsgöl Lake. In 1992, Mongolian roads carried some 249.3 million passengers, and 6.7 million tons of freight.

Mongolia's first air service began operating between Ulaanbaatar and Verkhneudinsk in eastern Siberia in 1926. Miat-Air Mongol is the principal airline, carrying 615,700 passengers in 1991, including 40,300 international passengers. There were 31 airfields in operation in 1992.

[12]HISTORY

Archaeological investigations show that the land now known as Mongolia has been inhabited since the Lower Paleolithic period, more than 130,000 years ago. By about 1000 BC, animal husbandry of the nomadic type had developed, and by the 3d century BC, a clan style of organization based on horsemanship had emerged. The Huns, a Turkic-speaking people, driven westward during the Han dynasty in China (206 BC–AD 220), created a nomadic empire in central Asia that extended into Europe, beginning about AD 370. It reached almost to Rome under the leadership of Attila (r.433?–453) and declined after his death. Mongolia first played an important part in world history in AD 1206, when the Mongol tribes united under the leadership of the conqueror Temujin, or Genghis Khan. The Mongols set up their capital at Karakorum and established a vast empire extending from the northern Siberian forest to Tibet and from the Caspian Sea to the Pacific. After the death of Genghis in 1227, his empire was divided among his sons into Mongol states, or khanates: the Great Khanate of East Asia, which included the Yüan dynasty of China, and reached its peak under Kublai Khan (r.1260–94), who established his capital at Cambaluc (now Beijing); the Khanate of Chaghadai (Djakhatai) in Turkestan; the Hulagid Khanate, founded by Hulagu Khan in Persia; and the Golden Horde in southern Russia, founded by Batu Khan, who invaded Poland and Hungary in 1240. Having crossed the Danube River, Batu withdrew in 1241. The Mongols' century of dominance in Asia allowed for great trade and cultural interchange but also led to the spread of the bubonic plague to Europe.

During the 14th century, the great Mongol states disintegrated. The Yüan dynasty in China collapsed in 1368, to be replaced by the Ming dynasty; the western part of the Turkestan Khanate was incorporated into the empire of Timur in 1390; Hulagu's Persian empire disintegrated after 1335; and the Golden Horde was attacked and shaken by the forces of Prince Dmitry Donskoy in Russia in 1380 but ruled South Russia into the 15th century. In 1369, at the age of 33, Timur, also called Timur Lenk ("Timur the Lame") or Tamerlane, proclaimed himself ruler of all the land lying between the Tien Shan and the Hindu Kush mountain

MONGOLIA

LOCATION: 87°47' to 119°54'E 41°31' to 52°16'N. **BOUNDARY LENGTHS:** Russian Federation, 3,441 km (2,138 mi); China, 4,673 km (2,904 mi).

ranges. The Mongols retired to their original steppe homelands, splitting into three major groups: the northern Khalkha Mongols, north of the Gobi Desert; the southern Chahar Mongols, south of the Gobi; and the western Oirat Mongols. Babur, a descendant of Timur, founded the Mughal (or Mogul) Empire (so called from the Farsi word for "Mongol") in India in 1526; it lasted until the 18th century. Buddhism, which had been introduced by Tibetan monks in the 15th century, became widespread in the 16th and 17th centuries.

A cleavage developed between the northern (outer) Mongols and the southern (inner) Mongols, who had been more closely associated with Mongol rule in China. In the course of conquering China, the Manchus subdued the southern Mongols in 1636, placing them under the eventual rule of China's Qing (Ch'ing) or Manchu dynasty (1644–1911). The northern Mongols, who had been fighting with western Mongols for supremacy, sought Manchu aid against their foes and accepted Manchu suzerainty in 1691. Finally, the Manchus destroyed the western Mongols as a historical force in 1758. The Russian-Chinese border treaties of Nerchinsk (1689) and Kyakhta (1727) confirmed Chinese rule over both the southern and northern Mongols but assigned the Buryats to Russia.

Following the overthrow of the Manchu dynasty by the Chinese revolution in 1911, northern Mongol princes proclaimed an autonomous Outer Mongolia under the rule of Bogdo Khan, the Living Buddha (Jebtsun Damba Khutukhtu) of Urga, an earlier name of Ulaanbaatar. A treaty with the tsar's government pledged Russian assistance for the autonomous state. After the Bolshevik Revolution, the Chinese exploited Russia's weakness, reoccupying Outer Mongolia in 1919 and ending its autonomy. In early 1921, the Chinese were driven out by Russian counterrevolutionary forces under Baron von Ungern-Sternberg. He, in turn, was overcome in July 1921 by the Mongol revolutionary leaders Sukhe Baatar and Khorloin Choybalsan, assisted by the Soviet Red Army. Under Soviet influence, a nominally independent state, headed by the Living Buddha, was proclaimed on 11 July 1921 and lasted as a constitutional monarchy until his death in 1924.

The Mongolian People's Republic (MPR), the second Communist country in world history, was proclaimed on 26 November 1924. With the support of the former USSR, Communist rule was gradually consolidated. Large landholdings of feudal lords were confiscated, starting in 1929, and those of monasteries in 1938. A 10-year mutual assistance treaty, signed in 1936 and renewed for another 10 years in 1946, formalized the close relations between the former USSR and the MPR. In the summer of 1939, with Soviet support, the Mongolians fought invading Japanese along the border with Manchuria, ending with a solid defeat for the Japanese in September. After a virtually unanimous plebiscite by the Mongolians in favor of independence, the Nationalist government of the Republic of China formally recognized the MPR in 1945 (it withdrew its recognition in 1953) and the Nationalists on Taiwan still claim Mongolia as part of China. On 14 February 1950, the People's Republic of China and the former USSR signed a treaty that guaranteed the MPR's independence. In October 1961, the MPR became a member of the United Nations. Conflicting boundary claims between the MPR and China were settled by treaty on 26 December 1962, and on 30 June 1964 the MPR and the former USSR signed a 20-year treaty of friendship, cooperation, and mutual assistance. In June 1987, the MPR and the United States established diplomatic relations. With the growth of cities around the mining industry, Mongolian society shifted from being 78% rural in 1956 to being 58% urban in 1989.

With their close ties with the former USSR, Mongolians were well aware of Soviet policies of glasnost (openness) and perestroika (restructuring) and of the democratic movements in Eastern Europe after the mid-1980s. The MPR initiated its own policy of "openness" (il tod) and began economic reforms to serve as transitional steps away from a centrally planned, collective economy and toward a market economy. Following the first popular demonstrations calling for faster reforms, in Ulaanbaatar in December 1989, the ruling Mongolian People's Revolutionary Party (MPRP) opted for political as well as economic reforms. The MPRP's leadership resigned in March 1990 and in May the constitution (of 1960) was amended to allow for new, multiparty elections, which took place in July. The MPRP won a majority (85% of the seats) in the legislature, the People's Great Hural (PGH), which took office in September. The PGH elected as President a member of the MPRP, Punsalmaagiyn Ochirbat, but invited the opposition parties to join in forming the new government.

During 1991, the new government discussed Mongolia's economic and political transformation. It issued vouchers to all citizens for the purchase of state property as a step toward privatization. Economic reform was made more difficult by the economic collapse of the former Soviet Union. In 1991, Moscow insisted on trade based on cash rather than barter and dramatically cut aid. By 1992, Mongolia faced severe energy shortages. In 1991, the PGH also discussed the writing of a new constitution, which took effect in February of the next year. Based on that constitution, elections in June 1992 created a new legislature (with a MPRP majority), the State Great Hural (SGH) and, in June 1993, President Ochirbat was reelected (but with the support of a coalition of new parties, not the MPRP) in the first direct presidential elections. By September 1992, some 67,000 former Soviet troops (in the MPR since 1966 when Sino-Soviet tensions increased) completed a process of withdrawal begun in 1990.

¹³GOVERNMENT

The 1992 constitution went into effect February 12, replacing the 1960 constitution and completing Mongolia's transition from a single-party state to a multiparty, parliamentary form of government. Suffrage is universal at age 18. The unicameral legislature, the State Great Hural (SGH), has 76 members, who are elected by district to four-year terms. The SGH meets twice each year. It can enact and amend laws, set domestic and foreign policy, ratify international agreements, and declare a state of emergency.

A president, the head of state, is selected by direct, popular vote for a four-year term, with a limit of two terms. The president nominates the prime minister and can call for the dissolution of the government, initiate and veto legislation (subject to override by two-thirds vote of the SGH), and issue decrees which take effect with the signature of the prime minister.

A prime minister, the head of government, is nominated by the president and confirmed by the SGH to a four-year term. The prime minister selects a cabinet which must be confirmed by the SGH. The government dissolves when the prime minister resigns, when half the cabinet resigns simultaneously, or upon a vote for dissolution by the SGH.

¹⁴POLITICAL PARTIES

The Mongolian People's Revolutionary Party (MPRP), the single ruling party since 1924, legalized opposition parties in 1990. In addition to the MPRP, major parties include the Social Democratic Party (SDP), the Mongolian Democratic Party (MDP), the National Progress Party (NPP), the Mongolian Independence Party (MIP), the United Party of Mongolia (made up of the MDP, SDP, and NPP), and the Mongolian National Democratic Party (MNDP, a merger of the MDP, United Party, Renaissance Party, and NPP). Among other parties are the Mongolian Green Party, the Buddhist Believers Party, the Republican Party, the Mongolian People's Party, the United Herdsmen and Farmers Party, the Mongolian Bourgeois Party, the Mongolian Private Property Owners Party, and the Mongolian Workers Party.

In the first election for the State Great Hural (SGH), 28 June 1992, the MPRP won 56.9% of the vote and 71 of 76 seats in the SGH. In the first direct presidential election, 6 June 1993, President Punsalmaagiyn Ochirbat (first elected president 3 September 1990) was reelected with 58% of the vote. A former member of the MPRP, Ochirbat defeated that party's candidate, running as head of a coalition of the SDP and MNDP.

¹⁵LOCAL GOVERNMENT

Mongolia administratively consists of 18 provinces (aymag) divided into 299 counties (somon) and three autonomous cities (hot), Ulaanbaatar, Darhan, and Erdenet, which, in turn, are divided into districts. Each level of local administration has its own legislative body, or hural.

¹⁶JUDICIAL SYSTEM

Prior to the 1992 Constitution, justice was administered through a Supreme Court elected by the People's Great Hural; province and city courts, elected by the corresponding assemblies of people's deputies; and lower courts. Under the 1993 Constitution the Supreme Court remains the highest judicial body with a Constitutional Court vested with sole authority for constitutional review. While these two courts are now functioning, the new Constitution introduces a number of other structural changes in the court system await enactment of implementing legislation. In the interim, the existing three-level court system remains in operation. The local court's (people's courts) handle most routine civil and criminal cases. Provincial courts hear more serious cases and review local court decisions. The Supreme Court hears appeals from the local and provincial courts. The old specialized military justice and railway courts have been abolished. All courts are now organized under a single unified national system.

The new Constitution provides for a completely independent judiciary. It also promises procedural due process rights to a fair trial, legal assistance, right to appeal, and access to requests for pardons, among others.

¹⁷ARMED FORCES

The Mongolian People's Army is under the jurisdiction of the Ministry of Defense. Two years service is compulsory for all males. In 1993, the armed forces totaled 15,500. The army had 14,000 personnel (11,000 conscripts) in four divisions and a reserve strength of 200,000. The air force had 1,500 personnel and was equipped with 15 MiG-21s and 10 armed helicopters. Virtually all military equipment is of Soviet origin. Paramilitary forces consisting of about 10,000 frontier guards and security police, are under the jurisdiction of the Ministry of Public Security. Mongolia spent an estimated $22.8 million for defense in 1992.

[18]INTERNATIONAL COOPERATION

Admitted to the UN on 27 October 1961, the MPR participates in ESCAP, FAO, IAEA, ILO, ITU, UNESCO, UNIDO, UPU, WHO, WIPO, and WMO. It is a signatory to the Law of the Sea treaty. The MPR joined CMEA in June 1962.

The principal ally of the MPR is the former USSR, which has provided substantial economic and military assistance over the years. In 1986, the MPR made efforts toward normalizing relations with China, which had become strained after the expulsion of Chinese laborers in 1983, by establishing the first five-year trade agreement between the two countries, restoring air service and improving rail service between them, and exchanging consular delegations for the first time. In 1987, the US established diplomatic relations with the MPR.

[19]ECONOMY

After 70 years as a centrally planned economy, Mongolia has undergone a difficult transition towards a free market system since 1990. With the help of active government promotion, the country's industrial sector grew steadily for several decades, expanding from 7% of the national income in 1940 to 35% by 1985, as agriculture's share of total production declined from 79% to 20%. Despite these changes, animal husbandry has remained a dominant sector of the economy, with live animals and animal products accounting for a major share of current exports, and livestock providing much of the raw material processed in the country's industrial sector. A number of factors, including the sudden cessation of economic aid from the former Soviet Union and allied countries, the disruption of trade with traditional trading partners, as well as a severe winter in 1990/91, have caused a steep decline in the country's economic activity since the late 1980s. The annual growth rate of the GDP dropped steeply from 8.3% in 1986 to −9.9% in 1991 and −7.6% in 1992. Despite these difficulties, the government has continued its economic transformation program involving the privatization of most previously state-owned enterprises and other policy reforms. Development of the country's rich oil and mineral resources continues to be a high priority, and negotiations for the exploitation of oil, gold and rare earth elements with foreign companies are being actively pursued.

[20]INCOME

In 1992 the GDP was $1,292 million in current US dollars.

[21]LABOR

In 1991, the number of persons employed totaled 665,800, including 18% in industry, 27% in agriculture, 7% in construction, 7% in transportation, 1% in communications, 6% in trade and distribution, and 34% in government and other sectors. In 1991, about 7.7% of the economically active population (721,200 persons) was unemployed, with one-quarter of the unemployed residing in the Ulaanbaatar aymag. About 46% of the labor force is female. A shortage of skilled labor had required the procurement of a large supplementary work force from the former USSR and Eastern Europe. From 1985 to 1991, the labor force size has increased by about 2.8% per year.

The right to organize trade unions and professional organizations is granted by the 1990 Constitution. About 75% of the entire work force is unionized in Mongolia. In 1990, the Association of Free Trade Unions (AFTU) which includes about 70 unions, was chartered. In 1992, another organization, Blue Mongolia, was founded and had about 40,000 members. According to the labor code, the working week is fixed at 46 hours, and for those under 18, at 36 hours.

[22]AGRICULTURE

As of 1991, cropland amounted to 1,396,000 hectares (3,450,000 acres), up from only 1,212,000 hectares (2,995,000 acres) in 1981; the cultivated area represents only 1% of potentially arable land. The high altitude, temperature extremes, long winters, and low precipitation provide limited potential for agricultural development. Crop production in 1992 accounted for 3% of all employment.

The drop in fuel imports in 1990 caused a decreased grain harvest, which in turn lowered production of flour, rice, and fodder. Shortages of fuels and parts for agricultural equipment caused agricultural output to shrink by 7.4% in 1990/91, and by 6% in 1991/92. Principal crops produced in 1992 (in 1,000 tons) included: wheat, 460; barley, 20; oats, 10; potatoes, 76; and vegetables, 20. The gross value of agricultural output declined by 0.2% in 1992, when agricultural exports totaled $48.3 million.

[23]ANIMAL HUSBANDRY

Animal husbandry is the backbone of Mongolia's economy, employing 160,100 persons (24% total employment) in 1991. After Mongolia became the world's second communist country in 1924, many nomads settled down to raise livestock on state-owned collectives. Pastures constitute about 80% of the national territory. In 1992 there were 25,754,000 head of livestock, including 415,000 camels, 2,200,000 horses, 2,879,000 cattle, 14,657,000 sheep, 5,603,000 goats, and some 188,000 hogs. The meat produced in 1992 was 212,000 tons. Because of the harsh climate, Mongolians consume much fat and meat during winter, and dairy products in the summer.

Mongols claim that the Mongolian thoroughbred is the progenitor of many breeds of race horses worldwide; furthermore, its stamina and speed over long distances surpass Arabic and Akhaltec racers. The Mongolian Horse Association was founded in February 1989 in Zunmod to increase the population and preserve traditional horse-breeding techniques, which were largely being forgotten over the past three decades.

Hunting remains an important commercial activity, with furs and skins the chief products. In 1992, livestock production accounted for 81% of gross agricultural output.

[24]FISHING

Fishing is not a significant industry in Mongolia.

[25]FORESTRY

Forests cover about 9% of the total territory of Mongolia, mainly in the area around Hövsgöl Lake. It is estimated that the country's total timber resources represent at least 1.25 billion cu m. Birch, cedar, larch, and fir trees predominate. In 1991, the lumber industry yielded 470,600 cu m of sawn timber.

[26]MINING

Mongolia has many exploitable mineral resources, which accounted for 50% of export earnings in 1990. Coal, copper, fluorospar, and molybdenum are heavily mined, while clay, gold, gypsum, limestone, silver, precious stones, tin, and tungsten are mined by smaller operations. Most mining operations are in the northcentral and eastern regions. Production in 1991 included (in tons): copper, 90,300; fluorospar, 370; gypsum, 29,000; molybdenum, 1,130; tin, 250; and tungsten, 300. The Erdenet copper-molybdenum mine, completed in 1981, was developed by the state in cooperation with the former USSR; production at the mine declined sharply in 1991 because of shortages of parts and energy which had been supplied by the former USSR.

[27]ENERGY AND POWER

In 1991, the installed capacity of the electric power stations in the MPR amounted to 901,000 kw. About half the population is served with electricity. Three major power plants are in Ulaan-baatar, one is in Darhan, and smaller facilities are in Sühbaatar and Choybalsan. In 1991, the output was 3,500 million kwh. Declining diesel imports since August 1990 have significantly reduced harvests and internal distribution of food. As of 1991, imports of all petroleum products were still in short supply. Mongolia had been reliant on the former USSR to meet its refined petroleum requirements. As of 1991, Mongol Gazry Tos, a new state-owned petroleum company, was beginning to explore for new oil wells in the Dzuunbayan oil field near Saynshand in Dornogovi Aimag.

28INDUSTRY

Small-scale processing of livestock and agricultural products has historically been a mainstay of Mongolia's industrial sector. Economic reforms of the last several years have continued this general pattern; the manufacture of leather, fur, shoes and processed foods claimed 28.8% of industry's gross output value in 1992. With the establishment of the Erdenet copper plant in the late 1970s, metal processing also assumed an important place in the economy, accounting for 11.1% of industrial output by 1992. Textile and energy production contributed a further 8.0% and 12.5%, respectively. Much of the country's industrial activity is concentrated in four centers: Ulaanbaatar, Erdenet, Darhan, and Choybalsan.

During the past several years Mongolia's industrial development has been severely affected by dwindling imports of fuel, spare parts and equipment formerly obtained from the former USSR and allied trading partners. As a result, total output from the industrial sector has declined since 1990, shrinking by as much as 15% in 1992 alone. Recent production figures for individual industries reflect this decline. While increasing from 150,000 tons in 1985 to 264,600 tons in 1990, cement production was only 227,000 tons in 1991; output of processed meat decreased from 54 million tons in 1990 to 47 million in 1991; sawnwood production was only 270,000 cu m in 1991, down from 509,000 the year before.

29SCIENCE AND TECHNOLOGY

The Academy of Sciences, in Ulaanbaatar, was founded in 1921 and reorganized in 1961. It includes institutes for research in biology, botany, chemistry, geology, mathematics, medicine, and physics. The Mongolian State University has faculties of mathematics, natural sciences, and physics, and undertakes research with the State Construction Research Institute in pursuit of knowledge related to nuclear physics, biophysics, mineral resources, energy, and communications.

30DOMESTIC TRADE

Prior to economic reforms of the early 1990s, consumer goods produced at Ulaanbaatar or imported from abroad were distributed by state marketing agencies to retail outlets in local administrative centers. Prices for all items except consumer services and some luxury goods were set by the government. With steady price liberalization undertaken since 1990, prices are now closely regulated for only a few staples, such as fuel, rice, and flour. Because the rapid dismantling of the government's centrally planned distribution system proceeded without an effective alternative yet in place, severe supply shortages have been experienced especially in the country's urban centers. To reduce these shortages, a system of public markets has been developed where supplies in excess of targeted deliveries can be sold freely.

31FOREIGN TRADE

Although Mongolia continues to depend on the Commonwealth of Independent States (CIS, formerly USSR) as its dominant trading partner, the country's trading profile has changed greatly since the mid-1980s. In 1985, communist countries, excluding China

and North Korea, accounted for 95.5% of the MPR's exports and 98.1% of its imports. While diversification measures by the government in the 1980s reduced these proportions somewhat, poor industrial performance in many countries undergoing a transition from a centrally planned to free market economy catalyzed much more rapid change. By 1992, formerly communist countries accounted for only 65.3% of exports, while their share of imports fell to 61.3%. China and Japan presently follow the CIS as the country's 2nd and 3rd largest trading partners respectively.

Reflecting the cessation of traditional trading arrangements and the economic difficulties of formerly communist trading partners, total exports declined from US$689.1 million in 1985 to US$355.7 million in 1992, as imports also fell from US$1.1 billion to $400 million. Currently, minerals, mainly copper concentrates and molybdenum, are Mongolia's largest export accounting for nearly one half of the total in 1990. The second most important export category includes wool, hides, and skins, followed by consumer goods, mainly manufactured garments. It is expected that liberalization and expansion of free trade zones will help promote export of manfactured goods such as spun wool, carpets, leather goods, canned meat, and light consumer goods, although the production and export of minerals and oil will be promoted as well.

32BALANCE OF PAYMENTS

Mongolia consistently imports more than it exports. The sudden discontinuance of grants and debt cancellations by the former Soviet Union devastated the balance of payments position. However, in 1992, the trade deficit improved to $42.6 million, down from $158 million in 1991 and $607.8 million in 1990. In 1992, the current account (excluding grants) registered a deficit of $72.5 million, an improvement from $160.5 million in 1991 and $651.4 million in 1990. Gross reserves (excluding gold) stood at $53.9 million in 1992, having fallen from $125.6 million in 1990, while gross reserves including gold have risen from $270 million in 1990 to $1.084 million in 1992.

33BANKING AND SECURITIES

The State Bank of Mongolia remains the official bank of Mongolia but recent economic reforms have allowed the formation of a commercial banking sector. The economic reforms were brought about by the collapse of the Soviet Union.

Now Mongolia has a two-tier banking system where control of the money supply is invested in the Central Bank. The Bank of Mongolia has established lending rules the commercial banks must follow. Also, reserve requirements are set by the national bank. There are 11 state owned banks and development banks in Mongolia.

34INSURANCE

There is no private insurance system. However, the government was planning to introduce health insurance in 1993 as a cooperative effort between individuals, government agencies, and the private sector.

35PUBLIC FINANCE

The annual budget is submitted to the People's Great Hural for approval. In 1992, the budget of Mongolia called for current revenues in the amount of T11,801 million and current expenditures of T11,143 million. Capital expenditures amounted to T5,824 million in 1992; there were no capital revenues. Budget expenditures for 1991 were broken down as follows: 21% (T1,886 million) for development of the national economy; 55% (T4,909 million) for entitlements, services, social and cultural endeavors, 8% (T738 million) for defense; and 16% (T1,396 million) for administrative and other expenses. Deficit financing in 1992 came primarily from external borrowing (84% of the total T5,166 million).

[36]TAXATION

The turnover tax, accounting in 1986 for 66.3% of all state revenues, is an indirect sales tax levied at the production stage on all manufactured commodities. Personal taxes consist of income taxes, paid by salaried industrial workers and office employees, and livestock taxes on private herders, based on the number of livestock owned. In 1993, there was a ceiling of 40% on taxes levied on enterprises with foreign capital.

[37]CUSTOMS AND DUTIES

Customs duties are insignificant, yielding less than 1% of total state revenues.

[38]FOREIGN INVESTMENT

Prior to 1990, no private investments were possible in Mongolia; much of the country's investment capital was derived from government loans and grants provided by the former USSR and allied countries. New government policy and laws since the late 1980s, including the Foreign Investment Law of 1990, provide the legal basis and incentive for foreign investments. Thus far, however, private foreign capital remains a small source of investment in the country, due in part to contradictions between newly passed laws for foreign and private investment that have yet to be resolved.

[39]ECONOMIC DEVELOPMENT

In the past, MPR operated on the basis of a planned economy. The first annual economic plan, promulgated in 1941, was followed by six additional annual plans. The financing of these plans was assisted by loans totaling about T1.7 billion from the former USSR and about T300 million from China. In addition, Mongolia began to receive official development assistance from sources besides the former Soviet Union and China in the mid-1980s, totalling $37.5 million by 1990.

Planning on a multiyear basis began in 1947, after which the rate and value of capital investment increased rapidly. Investment amounted to T203.7 million during the first five-year plan (1947–51); T673.2 million during the second five-year plan (1952–57); T1,476.8 million during the subsequent three-year plan (1958–60); and T3,862.4 million during the third five-year plan (1961–65). The fourth five-year plan (1966–70), which called for capital investments of T5,290.2 million, envisioned the receipt of 550 million rubles in loans, 90% supplied by the former USSR. The fifth five-year plan (1971–75) stressed the development of permanently settled agricultural and livestock enterprises; industrial output increased 55% during this plan period. It increased another 150% during the sixth five-year plan (1976–80). The 1981–85 plan called for a 22–26% increase in agricultural production and a 52–58% increase in industrial production; the actual figures achieved were 18% and 55%, respectively.

The eighth five-year plan (1986–90) targeted energy development, expansion of mining, improved management, and increases of 30–34% in industrial production and 18–20% in agricultural producton. Development measures during this period also included important economic reforms aimed at simplifying the state's administrative apparatus, improving profitability of state enterprises and cooperatives, and a gradual reduction of the government's role in production and delivery targets. In 1990, with the establishment of a new consensus government, there followed a three-year plan that aimed for achieving greater efficiency in the allocation of resources and a diversified economic base by undertaking a sustained transition to a free market economy. Main components of the government's program have included privatization of state enterprises, price liberalization, changes in national law, devaluation of the tugrik, as well as drafting an action plan for environmental protection. Current plans specify development of the country's energy and mining sectors, and further action in environmental protection as well as continued

reforms in a number of areas including fiscal management, land tenure, and social benefit entitlements.

[40]SOCIAL DEVELOPMENT

The social insurance program provides for free medical services, benefits for temporary disability, and pensions for permanent disability and old age. Government policy is to encourage population growth, in part by taxing unmarried adults and childless couples; expectant mothers are granted paid maternity leaves, and state aid is provided for mothers with large families. Abortion is illegal. The fertility rate in 1985–90 was 4.7. Government funding for social programs was expected to increase by 22–26% under the 1986–90 economic plan. In 1992 the percentage of women in the work force was 51.3%. About half of all trade union members were women. Although women receive equal pay for equal work, they fill virtually no positions at the highest levels of government or the professions.

[41]HEALTH

Health care is administered under state auspices, and all medical and hospital services are free. The government gives special priority to increasing the number of physicians and other health personnel and expanding facilities in rural areas. Each province has at least two hospitals, and each agricultural cooperative and state farm has a medical station. In 1990, there were 5,625 physicians and 30 pharmacists. In 1991, there were 10,340 nurses. In 1992, 95% of the population had access to health care services.

Average life expectancy in 1992 was an estimated 63 years (45 years in 1950). Pulmonary and bronchial infections, including tuberculosis and brucellosis, are widespread but are being brought under control through the use of ayrag, an indigenous drink brewed from horse's milk and possessing demonstrated healing qualities. Cholera, smallpox, typhus, and other epidemic diseases have been virtually eliminated. In 1992, children up to one year of age were vaccinated against tuberculosis, 85%; diphtheria, pertussis, and tetanus, 84%; polio, 84%; and measles, 86%.

In 1992, there were 79,000 births. The general mortality rate in 1993 was 7.7 per 1,000 people, and the infant mortality rate was 61 per 1,000 live births in 1992. Maternal mortality in 1991 was 140 per 100,000 live births.

[42]HOUSING

Although there are many stone and wood buildings in Ulaanbaatar and some of the larger provincial centers, the standard housing of the nomadic herders, as well as of many city dwellers, is the yurt, a light, movable, dome-shaped tent consisting of skin or felt covering stretched over a lattice frame. However, more permanent housing facilities have been appearing in rural areas throughout the country. Large apartment-house complexes with stores, services, and cultural facilities are being built in Ulaanbaatar, as well as in various other cities and towns.

[43]EDUCATION

Ten years of schooling is compulsory, starting at age six, and free of charge under the new education law. Since the 1950s, the MPR has claimed that the entire adult population is literate; in 1985, however, UNESCO estimated the literacy rate at 93% for males and 86% for females. In 1992, there were 800 preschools, 679 primary and secondary schools and over 300 technical and professional training centers in the country. In 1991, there were 6,230 teachers and 154,600 pupils in primary schools. General secondary schools had 14,251 teachers and 257,100 pupils. In vocational schools, there were 1,142 teachers and 17,961 pupils. More than 70% of students from rural areas reside in dormitories adjoining the schools. The Mongolian State University, in Ulaanbaatar, was founded in 1942 and includes faculties in the social sciences, trade, and philology, as well as in science and technology. The 1991 Education Law introduced a number of changes in the system. The traditional Mongolian Script was introduced from the first grade and teaching of English in all schools was made compulsory. While higher and professional education is not free, tuition fees are subsidized by the government for needy students. Non-formal education offered by private institutions was also given due importance and recognition.

44LIBRARIES AND MUSEUMS
There were 983 libraries and reading rooms throughout Mongolia in 1985, with 13.4 million volumes. The Mongolian State University has a library of 350,000 volumes. The State Public Library, which is under the jurisdiction of the Academy of Sciences, contains 3 million volumes in Mongolian, Chinese, English, French, German, Manchu, Russian, Tibetan, and other languages. It also has a collection of valuable Buddhist manuscripts. The State Central Museum, containing art treasures and antiquities, the Museum of National History, the Ulaanbaatar Museum, the Fine Arts Museum, and the Museum of Religion, all in Ulaanbaatar, are under the jurisdiction of the Academy of Sciences.

45MEDIA
In 1989, 63,000 telephones were in use. Radio broadcasting began in the MPR in 1934. Radio Ulaanbaatar broadcasts programs in Mongolian, Russian, Chinese, English, French, and Kazakh. Mongel Telev 12, which transmits locally produced programs, and a satellite station are also located in Ulaanbaatar. In 1991 there were 297,000 radios and 90,000 television sets.

The 35 newspapers of the MPR include *Unen*, the organ of the Central Committee of the MPRP and the MPR Council of Ministers; *Novosti Mongoliy*, the organ of the Mongolian News Agency; *Hodolmor*, the organ of the trade unions; *Dzaluuchuudyn Unen*, the organ of the Central Committee of the Mongolian Revolutionary Youth League; *Shine Hodoo*, the organ of the Ministry of Agriculture and the Supreme Council of the Federation of Agricultural Cooperatives; *Utga Dzohiol Urlag*, the organ of the Union of Mongolian Writers and the Ministry of Culture; and *Ulaan Od*, the organ of the Ministry of Defense and the Ministry of Public Security. Also published are 41 periodicals, including *Namyn Am'dral*, a journal of the Central Committee of the MPRP , and *Shinjleh Uhaan Am'dral*, a bimonthly publication of the Mongolian Academy of Sciences.

46ORGANIZATIONS
Mongolia's mass organizations, all of which work closely with the MPRP, include the Mongolian Revolutionary Youth League (founded in 1922), Mongolian Pioneers' Organization, Committee of Mongolian Women (founded in 1933), and Mongolian-Soviet Friendship Society (founded in 1947). Professional and cultural organizations include the Union of Mongolian Artists, Union of Mongolian Composers, Mongolian Association for Lawyers, Union of Mongolian Journalists, Union of Mongolian Students, Union of Mongolian Writers, and Union of Mongolian Philatelists. Other organizations are the Mongolian Committee for Afro-Asian Solidarity, Mongolian Union for Peace and Friendship Organizations, and Mongolian Committee for the Defense of Peace.

47TOURISM, TRAVEL, AND RECREATION
In 1990, approximately 147,236 travelers visited the MPR from abroad, 123,996 from the former Soviet Union. Despite the birth of multipart democracy in the 1990's, Mongolia has not encouraged tourism. Tourist facilities are in short supply (there were 9,989 hotel beds in 1990), and prices are high.

Ulaanbaatar has two modern tourist hotels. Points of interest include the Gandan Lamasery in Ulaanbaatar and the ruined city of Karakorum, once the capital of the Mongol Empire. Mongolia offers abundant and varied scenery, including forests, steppes, lakes, and deserts, and a wide variety of wildlife. Traditional sports in Mongolia include wrestling, archery, and horse racing.

48FAMOUS MONGOLIANS
A long line of Mongol khans have left their mark on history ever since Temujin, or Genghis Khan (1162–1227), set up the first Mongol empire in 1206. Outstanding among them were Kublai Khan (1216–94), a grandson of Genghis, who conquered most of China; Hulagu Khan (1217–60), a brother of Kublai, who conquered Persia and Syria; Batu Khan (d.1255), Kublai's cousin, who overran Russia, Poland, and Hungary; Timur, also known as Timur Lenk ("Timur the Lame") or Tamerlane (1336?–1405), a descendant of Genghis, who extended his military power for short periods into southern Russia, India, and the Levant; and Babur (Zahir ad-Din Muhammad, 1483–1530), a descendant of Timur, who established an empire in India.

In recent times, two national leaders were Sukhe Baatar (1894–1923) and Khorloin Choybalsan (1895–1952). Yumjaagiin Tsedenbal (b.1916), intermittently general secretary of the Central Committee of the MPRP since 1940, became chairman of the Council of Ministers in 1952, was elected chairman of the Presidium of the People's Great Hural in 1974, and was named the MPRP general secretary in 1981. Jambyn Batmunkh (b.1926) became chairman of the Council of Ministers in 1974 and was elected chairman of the Presidium and general secretary of the MPRP in 1984.

The founder of modern Mongolian literature is D. Natsagdorj (1906–37). Tsendyn Damdinsuren (b.1908) is one of the most important writers. Leading playwrights are Ch. Oydov (1917–63) and E. Oyuun (b.1918). Other prominent writers are B. Rindhen (1905–78), D. Namdag (b.1911), U. Ulambayar (b.1911), and Ch. Lodoydamba (1917–70). B. Damdinsuren (b.1919) and L. Murdorzh are noted composers. Jugderdemidiyn Gurragcha (b.1947) became the first Mongolian in space in 1981, when he was carried into orbit aboard the former USSR's *Soyuz 39*.

49DEPENDENCIES
The MPR has no territories or colonies.

50BIBLIOGRAPHY
Bawden, Charles R. *The Modern History of Mongolia*. 2d ed. New York: Kegan Paul International, 1989.

Brown, William A., and Urgunge Onon. *History of the Mongolian People's Republic*. Cambridge, Mass.: Harvard University Press, 1976.

Cultural Policy in the Mongolian People's Republic. New York: Unipub, 1982.

Information Mongolia: The Comprehensive Reference Source of the People's Republic of Mongolia (MPR). New York: Pergamon Press, 1990.

Jagchid, Sechin, and Paul Hyer. *Mongolia's Culture and Society*. Boulder, Colo.: Westview, 1980.

———— *Essays in Mongolian studies*. Provo, UT: Brigham Young University, 1988.

Major, John S. *The Land and People of Mongolia*. New York: Lippincott, 1990.

Moses, Larry, and Stephen A. Halkovic, Jr. *Introduction to Mongolian History and Culture*. Bloomington: Indiana University Research Institute, 1985.

Nordby, Judith. *Mongolia*. Santa Barbara, Calif.: Clio Press, 1993.

Onon, Urgungge. *Asia's First Modern Revolution: Mongolia Proclaims Its Independence in 1911*. New York: E.J. Brill, 1989.

Worden, Robert L. *Mongolia: A Country Study*. Washington, D.C.: Library of Congress, 1990.

MYANMAR

Union of Myanmar
Pyidaungzu Myanma Naingngandaw

CAPITAL: Yangon (formerly Rangoon).

FLAG: The national flag is red with a blue canton, within which 14 white stars encircle a rice stalk and an industrial wheel.

ANTHEM: *Kaba Makye (Our Free Homeland)*.

MONETARY UNIT: The kyat (K) is a paper currency of 100 pyas. There are coins of 1, 5, 10, 25, and 50 pyas and 1 kyat, and notes of 1, 5, 10, 25, and 100 kyats. K1 = $0.1640 (or $1 = K6.0959).

WEIGHTS AND MEASURES: Both British and metric weights and measures are in general use, but local units are also employed.

HOLIDAYS: Independence Day, 4 January; Union Day, 12 February; Peasants' Day, 2 March; Defense Services Day, 27 March; Burmese New Year, 17 April; World Workers' Day, 1 May; Martyrs' Day, 19 July; Christmas, 25 December. Movable religious holidays include Full Moon of Tabaung, February or March; Thingyan (Water Festival), April; Full Moon of Kason, April or May; Waso (Beginning of Buddhist Lent), June or July; Thadingyut (End of Buddhist Lent), October; and Tazaungdaing, November.

TIME: 6:30 PM = noon GMT.

¹LOCATION, SIZE, AND EXTENT

Situated in Southeast Asia, Myanmar has an area of 678,500 sq km (261,970 sq mi), extending 1,931 km (1,200 mi) N–S and 925 km (575 mi) E–W. Comparatively, the area occupied by Myanmar is slightly smaller than the state of Texas. It is bounded on the N and E by China, on the E by Laos, on the SE by Thailand, on the S by the Andaman Sea, and on the W by the Bay of Bengal, Bangladesh, and India, with a total boundary length of 7,806 km (4,850 mi).

Myanmar's capital city, Yangon (formerly Rangoon), is located in the southern part of the country.

²TOPOGRAPHY

Myanmar is divided into four topographic regions: (1) a mountainous area in the north and west, ranging from about 1,830 to 6,100 m (6,000–20,000 ft) in altitude, and including the Arakan coastal strip between the Arakan Yoma mountain range and the Bay of Bengal; (2) the Shan Highlands in the east, a deeply dissected plateau averaging 910 m (2,990 ft) in height and extending southward into the Tenasserim Yoma, a narrow strip of land that projects some 800 km (500 mi) along the Malay Peninsula, in the southeast; (3) central Myanmar, a principal area of cultivation, bounded by the Salween River (2,419 km/1,503 mi) in the east and the Irrawaddy River (2,016 km/1,253 mi) and its tributary, the Chindwin, in the west; and (4) the fertile delta and lower valley regions of the Irrawaddy and Sittang rivers in the south, covering an area of about 25,900 sq km (10,000 sq mi) and forming one of the world's great rice granaries. Good harbors are located along the coastline.

³CLIMATE

Myanmar has a largely tropical climate with three seasons: the monsoon or rainy season, from June to mid-October; the hot season, generally from April through May and from October through November, immediately preceding and following the wet season; and the cool season, from December to March. Rainfall during the monsoon season totals more than 500 cm (200 in) in upper Myanmar and over 250 cm (100 in) in lower Myanmar and Yangon (formerly Rangoon). Central Burma, called the dry zone, and Mandalay, the chief city in the area, each receive about 76 cm (30 in). The mean annual temperature is 27°C (81°F); average daily temperatures in Yangon (Rangoon) range from 18° to 32°C (64–90°F) in January, during the cool season, and from 24° to 36°C (75–97°F) in April, during the hot season. The climate in upper Myanmar, particularly at altitudes ranging from about 300 to 1,220 m (1,000–4,000 ft), is the most temperate throughout the year, while lower Myanmar, especially in the delta and coastal regions, is the most humid.

⁴FLORA AND FAUNA

Myanmar has a wide variety of plant and animal life. Teak, representing about 25% of the total forested area, thrives mainly in the mountainous regions; evergreen, bamboo, and palm in the freshwater delta swamps and along the coastlands; mangrove in the salty coastal marshes; mixed temperate forests and rolling grasslands in the Shan Highlands; and scrub vegetation in the dry central area. There are about 12 species of monkeys, as well as tigers, leopards, elephants, and half-wild pariah dogs. Fish abound along the coastline, in the tidal waters of the delta, and in the rivers and streams.

⁵ENVIRONMENT

In Myanmar the principal environmental threat comes from cyclones and flooding during the monsoon season, and regular earthquakes. Deforestation for farming or illegal economic gain is the most persistent ecological effect of human encroachment. In 1985, 405 square miles were lost through deforestation. In 1994, two-thirds of Myanmar's tropical forests had been eliminated. Little information is available about the long-term effects of industrialization on the natural environment, although evidence of industrial pollutants has been found in the air, water, soil, and food. Myanmar has 259.6 cubic miles of water. About 21% of the city dwellers and 28% of the rural population do not have pure water. Inadequate sanitation and water treatment are leading contributors to disease. Environmental concerns have been given low priority by the government.

As of 1987, endangered species in Myanmar included the tiger, Asian elephant, Malayan tapir, Sumatran rhinoceros, Fea's muntjac, river terrapin, estuarine crocodile, and four species of turtle (green sea, hawksbill, olive ridley, and leatherback). The Javan rhinoceros is extinct. Out of a total of 300 species of mammals, 23 are endangered; of 1,000 bird species, 42 are endangered, and 10 reptiles in 360 indigenous species are threatened along with 2 types of freshwater fish. Myanmar also had 23 threatened species of plants in a total of 7,000 as of 1994.

6POPULATION

In 1992, Myanmar had an estimated population of 43,668,000. The population for the year 2000 was projected at 51,567,000, assuming a crude birthrate of 30.3 per 1,000 population, a crude death rate of 9.8, and a net natural increase of 20.5 during 1995–2000. The country's population increased at an average annual rate of about 2.2% during 1985–90. Average population density in 1992 was estimated at 64.5 persons per sq km (67.2 per sq mi). The rural population made up about 74% of the total in 1995, and the urban population 26%. Yangon (formerly Rangoon), the capital, had a population of 2,458,712 according to the 1983 census, and an estimated population of 3,852,000 in 1995. Other principal cities, with their 1983 census populations, are Mandalay, 532,985; Pathein (formerly Bassein), 144,092; Bago (formerly Pegu), 150,447; and Mawlamyine (formerly Moulmein), 219,991.

7MIGRATION

Indians were the most significant Asian minority in Myanmar until World War II, when hundreds of thousands fled the Japanese invasion; although many returned after the war, the Indian minority never regained its prewar proportions, because after independence in 1948 the government of Myanmar instituted rigid restrictions on Indian migration. The Indian population was substantially reduced between April 1963 and June 1965, when 100,000 were repatriated as part of a program to increase the wealth and holdings of Myanmar nationals. (Indians had dominated Myanmar's commerce.) The government has sought to curtail both immigration and emigration, although as many as 500,000 persons may have left Myanmar during 1962–71. About 187,000 Muslims who fled to Bangladesh in 1978 were repatriated with the help of UN agencies by the end of 1981; they had left Myanmar because of alleged atrocities by its soldiers in Arakan State. They lost their citizinship in 1982. In 1991–92 some 265,000 of these people fled to Bangladesh or were expelled. About 50,000 were repatriated in 1993. Besides the Arkanese refugees in Bangladesh estimates of the overall Myanma refugee populations in neighboring countries in 1992 were over 100,000 in Thailand, 10,000 in China's Yunan province, and thousands more in India's northeast.

About 500,000 poor urban residents were forcibly relocated to rural areas between 1989 and 1992. Rural residents are also subject to forced resettlement in connection with counterinsurgency operations.

8ETHNIC GROUPS

The Burmans, ethnically related to the Tibetans, constituted about 68% of Myanmar's total population in 1992. In remote times, the Burmans, migrants from the hills east of Tibet, descended the Irrawaddy Valley and intermarried with the previously settled Mon and Pyu peoples. Since then, however, many other migrant peoples from the northeast and northwest have settled in Myanmar: the Shans, Karens, Kachins, Kayahs, and Chins are among the more numerous. Although much ethnic fusion has taken place among these peoples and the Burmans, most of the later migrant groups remain distinct cultural entities, and have sought to preserve their autonomy, sometimes by violent means. As of 1992, Karens made up about 6% of the population, Shans 7%, Arikanese, 3.8%, and Chins, Kachins, and Mons, 2.3% each. Indians, Bangladeshis, and Pakistanis made up perhaps another 2% of the population, and Chinese 3%.

9LANGUAGES

Burmese, the official language, is spoken by at least 80% of the population. Pronunciation varies greatly from area to area. Although Burmese is monosyllabic and tonal like other Tibeto-Chinese languages, its alphabet of 10 vowels and 32 consonants is derived from the Pahlavi script of South India; loan words from other languages are common. Burmese is the language of government, but the ethnic minorities have their own languages; according to the 1974 constitution, "if necessary the language of the national race concerned may be used."

10RELIGIONS

The constitution guarantees freedom of religion. As of 1992, an estimated 89.2% of the people were Hinayana or Theravada Buddhists. Under the government of U Nu (overthrown in 1962), Buddhism was the state religion, but there is no longer any link between church and state. Many Buddhists, including most of the people of the hill areas, are also animists, believing in powerful spirits called nats.

The Chinese in Myanmar practice a traditional mixture of Mahayana Buddhism, Taoism, Confucianism, and ancestor worship; the Indians are Hindus, the Pakistanis are Muslims, and most of the Europeans are Christians. Although Christian missionaries had some success with peoples of the hill areas—the Karens, Kayahs, Kachins, and Chins—conversion among the Burmans and the Shans was negligible. In addition to the Buddhist population, 4% are Muslim, and the remainder of other religions, including 1% Hindu, and 1% Roman Catholic.

11TRANSPORTATION

Because of Myanmar's near encirclement by mountain ranges, international land transportation is virtually nonexistent. Historically, Myanmar has been dependent on sea and river transport externally and internally, supplemented in modern times by the airplane. The Myanmar Road, connecting Lashio with Kunming in southern China, and the Ledo Road between Myitkyina and Ledo in Assam, northeastern India, are the only land ties between Myanmar and adjacent nations. There were an estimated 20,900 km (13,000 mi) of roads in 1991, but only 15% were bituminized. In 1992, Myanmar had about 35,000 passenger cars and 35,000 commercial vehicles.

The Myanmar's railway system, a government monopoly, operates 3,990 km (2,480 mi) of track, of which 97% is metergauge. Only 362 km (225 mi) is double track. The main lines are from Yangon (Rangoon) to Prome (259 km/161 mi) and from Yangon to Mandalay (621 km/386 mi) and then to Myitkyina (1,164 km/723 mi from the capital).

Inland waterways, including some 12,899 km (8,015 mi) of navigable passages (25% of which are navigable by commercial vessels), are the key to internal transportation, partly compensating for limited railroad and highway development. Some 500,000 small river craft ply the Irrawaddy (navigable for about 640 km/ 400 mi), the Salween, the Sittang, and numerous tributaries. The Irrawaddy Delta, the focus of most water transportation, has some 2,700 km (1,700 mi) of rivers and streams, providing a seaboard for all types of craft. The state Inland Water Transport

Corp. operates a fleet of about 800 vessels; they carried 20 million passengers and 3 million tons of freight in 1984/85.

Ocean shipping, the traditional means of external transport, is controlled by the government, which operates coastal and ocean-going freight-passenger lines. Yangon, on the Rangoon River about 34 km (21 mi) inland from the Andaman Sea, is the chief port for ocean shipping, handling over 85% of the country's seaborne trade; it is also the principal terminus for the highways, railroad, inland waterways, and airways. Other ports include Sittwe (Akyab), serving western Myanmar; Pathein (Bassein), serving the delta area; and Mawlamgine (Moulmein), Dawei (Tavoy), and Mergui, which handle mineral and timber exports of the Tenasserim region.

As of 1992 there were 27 paved usable airfields; Mingaladon, outside of Yangon, is the principal airport. In 1990, the airport served some 580,000 passengers. In 1992 there were only 39 licensed airline transport and 6 commercial pilots in Myanmar.

12 HISTORY

The founding of a kingdom at Pagan in 1044 by Anawrahta marks the beginning of the history of Myanmar as a distinct political entity. The kingdom survived until 1287, when it was destroyed by the armies of Kublai Khan, and for the next five centuries disunity reigned. In 1754, however, Alaungpaya defeated the Shan kingdom in northern Myanmar and the Mon kingdom in southern Myanmar and founded the last ruling dynasty, which was in power until the British came in the early 19th century. The British conquest of Myanmar spanned 62 years: the first Anglo-Burmese War took place during 1824–26, when the British East India Company, acting for the crown, took possession of the Arakan and Tenasserim coastal regions. In 1852, at the end of the second war, the British acquired the remainder of lower Myanmar; and on 1 January 1886, following Myanmar's defeat in the third war, total annexation of Myanmar was proclaimed. Incorporated into the British Indian Empire, Myanmar was administered as a province of India until 1937, when it became a separate colony. At this time, Myanmar was permitted further steps toward responsible government; however, the British governor retained authority over foreign affairs, defense, currency, and the administration of frontier peoples. From 1886 to 1948, the inhabitants fought continually for independence. The nationalists who finally gained freedom for Myanmar were a group of socialist-minded intellectuals, called the Thakins, from the University of Rangoon. They included Aung San, one of the founders of modern Myanmar; U Nu, independent Myanmar's first premier; Shu Maung, also known as Ne Win, later U Nu's chief of staff; and Than Tun, a leader of the Communist revolt (1948–50) against the independent government. At the start of World War II, these anti-British nationalists collaborated with the Japanese, and with the aid of the Burma Independence Army, led by Aung San, Rangoon (now Yangon) fell to Japan on 8 March 1943. They were soon disappointed with the Japanese occupation, however, and under Ne Win's command the Burma Independence Army was converted into an anti-Japanese guerrilla force called the Anti-Fascist People's Freedom League, which later assisted the British liberation of Myanmar.

Having assumed leadership of the nationalist movement following the assassination of Aung San and six of his associates in 1947, U Nu signed an agreement with British Prime Minister Clement Attlee covering economic and defense relationships between the two countries. On 4 January 1948, the sovereign Union of Burma came into being outside the Commonwealth of Nations. After severe setbacks in 1948–49, the U Nu government was able to control the Communist insurgency and consolidate its own power, and in 1951 the nation held its first parliamentary elections. The decade of the 1950s also brought the implementation of an ambitious land reform program and an attempt to

LOCATION: 92°10′ to 101°11′E; 9°35′ to 28°28′N. **BOUNDARY LENGTHS:** China, 2,185 km (1,358 mi); Laos, 238 km (148 mi); Thailand, 1,799 km (1,118 mi); total coastline, 2,276 km (1,414 mi); Bangladesh, 233 km (145 mi); India, 1,403 km (872 mi). **TERRITORIAL SEA LIMIT:** 12 mi.

forge a neutralist foreign policy, in the face of sporadic Communist resistance and an intermittent border dispute with China. A coup d'etat of 2 March 1962 overthrew the U Nu government, and a military regime headed by a Revolutionary Council and led by Gen. Ne Win assumed control. Most major political figures in the democratic governments of the years 1948–62 were arrested but were released in 1966–68, including U Nu. Ne Win rejected a return to a multiparty parliamentary system and proclaimed the Socialist Republic of Burma on 3 January 1974. Under a new constitution, Ne Win became president, and the government continued to be dominated by the military. Ne Win retired as president in November 1981, with Gen. San Yu succeeding him in office; but Ne Win retained his influence, as chairman of the country's only legal political organization, the Burma Socialist Program Party (BSPP). Meanwhile, a guerrilla war in border areas of the north and east, fought by the underground Burmese Communist Party and insurgent ethnic groups, continued into the mid-1980s. The government issued an amnesty in May 1980 for about 5,000 political prisoners and for insurgents who surrendered within 90 days (including U Nu, who returned from exile), but secret peace talks between the military and Communist leaders broke down by May 1981. In mid-1983, Ne Win reportedly purged about 30 leading cabinet officials, army officers, and diplomats on charges of corruption and smuggling.

Despite President San Yu's reelection in 1985 to a four-year term and his appointment as vice-chairman of the BSPP, Ne Win continued to dominate the political scene and to make all major and many minor government policy decisions. One such decision, to withdraw large currency notes from circulation in September 1987, threw the economy and the country into turmoil. The move, possibly aimed against black marketeers who had accumulated large sums of money, made 80% of the country's currency valueless, touching off student demonstrations. As a result, on September 6, the government closed all schools indefinitely. Citing his personal responsibility for these economic conditions, Ne Win resigned as BSPP party chairman in July 1988. A protégé of Ne Win, Sein Lwin, was made BSPP chairman and president of the country. Sein Lwin's appointment triggered nationwide revolts. Army troops fired on peaceful demonstrations during the week of August 12 and killed substantial numbers of demonstrators. Sein Lwin resigned on 12 August and Dr. Maung Maung, a civilian lawyer and journalist, was appointed his successor on 19 August. Although Maung Maung proposed multiparty elections and decreed that government employees could not be members of any political party, his refusal to step down to allow an interim government resulted in the collapse of civil authority. On 18 September 1988 the army abolished the BSPP, took over the government and imposed military rule under the State Law and Order Restoration Council (SLORC) headed by the army Chief of Staff, General Saw Maung. He also named himself prime minister and retained the portfolios of the Defense Ministry and Ministry of Foreign Affairs. Several days of violence occurred countrywide with reports that over 1000 people, including children, students, and monks, had been killed. An amateur video of peaceful demonstrations outside the US Embassy (eventually broadcast worldwide) caught the scene of troops firing into a crowd of 1,000 students. Official accounts greatly underestimated the number of those killed with claims that most were looters. It is now generally accepted that over 10,000 deaths occurred in that year, but circumstances precluded accurately assessing the true number of losses. In announcing the takeover, General Saw Maung stated that the military rule would be temporary and that multiparty elections would be held once law and order were reestablished. In February 1989 Japan was the first nation to officially recognize SLORC as the legitimate government. Elections were set for 27 May 1990. On 18 June 1989 the Saw Maung regime renamed Burma "Myanmar," the historic ethnic Burman name for the country.

With the elections called, political parties formed. First to organize was U Nu's League for Democracy and Peace, later known as the League for Democracy. The BSPP was reformed as the pre-regime National Union Party (NUP). U Nu had declared

an interim government on 9 September 1988, but he garnered little support with his surprise move. In 1988 Aung San Suu Kyi, daughter of assassinated legendary hero General Aung San, had returned to Myanmar to visit her ailing mother. In the midst of the chaos of this period of demonstrations and protests Aung San Suu Kyi rose to prominence delivering speeches and establishing a coalition party opposing the military regime. On 24 September 1988 Suu Kyi with Tin Oo and Aung Gyi formed the National League for Democracy (NLD). In early 1989 Aung Gyi formed his own organization, the Union Nationals Democracy Party (UNDP). In speeches and interviews Suu Kyi challenged Ne Win's record, characterizing it as one of economic and sociopolitical degeneration. She also protested SLORC's repressive laws and actions. Aung San Suu Kyi was placed under house arrest in Yangon (Rangoon) by Ne Win on 20 July 1989. (As of July 1994 she was entering her sixth year of detention.) The top contenders in the elections were the NUP, the NLD, the UNDP, and the League for Democracy. Six other parties figured prominently: the Coalition League for Democratic Multi-Party Unity; the Democracy Party; the Union of Burma Main AFPFL Party led by the children of former Premier U Ba Swe; the Democratic National Front for national Reconstruction, a former leftist NUF group; the Graduates and Old Students Democratic Association; and the Original Anti-Fascist People's Freedom League. A total of 93 parties fielded 2,209 candidates who, along with 87 independent candidates, contested 485 seats out of a total of 492 constituencies designated for holding elections. Seven constituencies that were excluded from the election represented mostly the ethnic minority states of insurgency. Over 100 candidates each were fielded by only five parties: The National League for Democracy (NLD), 447 candidates; the National Unity Party backed by SLORC, 413 candidates; the League for Democracy and Peace (LDP), 309 candidates (another source indicates 325 candidates); the Union Nationals Democracy Party (UNDP), 247 candidates (another source indicates 270 candidates), and the Democracy Party, 105 candidates. The NLD won the elections by a landslide (392 candidates elected out of its field of 447, or 87.7% of the votes). The NUP took 2.4% of the votes for 10 seats out of 413 fielded. The UNDP, with 0.4% of the vote, took 1 seat in Shan State out of the 247(270) fielded. The Democracy Party with 0.95% of the vote took 1 seat out of 105 fielded. Of the candidates fielded by the LDP none won a seat. On 18 June 1989 Saw Maung indicated that the transfer of power to the winner of the election would not occur until a new constitution was drafted, one which met with SLORC's approval. However, on 13 July Khin Nyunt denied the initial promise of an immediate transfer of power made by General Saw Maung. SLORC's further response was to alter the purpose of the newly elected assembly from its original function as a legislative body, to that of a constituent assembly formed to draft the new constitution. SLORC would not transfer power until the resulting draft constitution had been approved both by a referendum and by SLORC.

1990–Present

In September 1990 SLORC revealed its intention to remain in power for a further five to ten years. After his mental collapse in December 1991, Senior General Saw Maung resigned due to ill health on 23 April 1992. On the same day he was replaced as Chairman of SLORC by General Than Shwe who was also named (and remains) Chief of State and Head of the Government. First Secretary is Major-General Khin Nyunt and Second Secretary is Major-General Tin Oo. Accompanying these leadership changes SLORC indicated that an effort was being made to appease and resolve criticism of its methods. Hundreds of political prisoners were released, and on 27 April SLORC announced that it had suspended operations against ethnic Karen rebels along the Thai border and reached an agreement between Dhaka and Yangon on the repatriation of 265,000 Rohingya refugees then living in camps in Bangladesh. In May, June, and July, Aung San Suu Kyi's family was allowed to visit her. On 24 August 1992 all universities were reopened, and curfews in effect since September 1988 were lifted on 11 September 1992. Two martial law decrees imposed in July 1989 also were lifted in September 1992, and a constitutional convention was promised. In early 1993 a National Convention of 700 mostly hand-picked members met to draft a new constitution. Meeting with resistance and presented with a proposal by Yo E La of the Lahu National Development Party suggesting a return to the basic principles of Myanmar's pre-1962 constitution, a bicameral parliament and the granting of basic freedoms, the convention was adjourned until 7 June 1993. Another impasse occurred with further resistance to certain clauses in the new constitution that the ruling military wanted implemented; the National Convention was adjourned until January 1994. On 18 January 1994 the convention met again to approve six objectives and 104 basic principles which would entrench and perpetuate the power of the military.

The plight of Aung San Suu Kyi garnered the attention of human rights groups internationally. In March 1991, based on a report released privately, the Geneva UN Human Rights Commission secretly passed a resolution to condemn and monitor the human rights abuses of SLORC. In 1991 Aung San Suu Kyi was awarded the 1990 Sakharov Prize for Freedom of Thought by the European Parliament, the 1990 Thorolf Rafto Human Rights Prize by Norway, and on 10 December 1991 Aung San Suu Kyi's son, Alexander, accepted the 1991 Nobel Peace Prize on her behalf. In 1992 SLORC allowed regular visits by her husband and her two sons. In December 1993 the UN General Assembly unanimously rebuked the military rulers of Myanmar for their refusal to hand over power to the Parliament democratically elected in May 1990, and called for the release of political prisoners, including Aung San Suu Kyi, in her fifth year of house arrest. Eight fellow Nobel prize-winners met in Thailand in February 1993 to speak on behalf of Aung San Suu Kyi, but were denied visas to visit Myanmar. US Congressman William Richardson visited with Aung San Suu Kyi, who was still under house arrest in Yangon, on 14-15 February 1994, her first non-family visit in four-and-a-half years. Richardson also met with Lieutenant-General Khin Nyunt of the State Law and Order Restoration Council (SLORC). The ninth family visit since her arrest occurred in July 1994. During talks in July 1994 Thai Prime Minister Chuan Leekpai urged Myanmar to release Aung San Suu Kyi. One other dissenting voice in Myanmar, that of the 74-year-old Aung Gyi, founder of the UNDP, was silenced when on 27 April 1993 he was sentenced to a six-month prison term. He had written a series of letters to Ne Win (much as he had paved the way for the pro-democracy movement in 1987-88 with a similar series of letters), and criticized the military regime in interviews with foreign journalists, but was convicted for failing to pay for eggs ordered as supplies for his tea and pastry shops. Another type of human rights violation in Myanmar which drew international attention was forced labor, which the government used on tourist projects such as the reconstruction of the gold palace in Mandalay. Of Mandalay's 500,000 residents each family had to contribute at least three days of free labor each month the work lasted from dawn until evening and was so strenuous that it took several days to recover from it. Prison inmates were required to work every day. Many military families could be exempted, as could any family that agreed to pay a monthly fine of about US$6, about a week's wages for some families. Forced labor was also used on many building projects including roads and railroads, and to carry supplies and munitions into malaria infested areas for the military. Muslim refugees who fled Myanmar said that Muslims had to pay two to three times as much as others to retain their rice ration card as a fine to escape labor. Forced labor is com-

monly referred to as "self reliance." Asia Watch also reported in 1994 that the government turned a "blind eye to traffic in women and girls from Myanmar to Thailand for forced-prostitution." Corrupt officials on both sides of the border were involved. It was estimated that there were about 20,000 Myanma women in Thai brothels.

A casualty of the China-Myanmar border agreement of 1988 was the Communist Party of Burma (CPB) which collapsed with the withdrawal of Chinese support and fragmented with the Wa mutiny of 1989. The CPB split into four different ethnic armies. SLORC's main objective was to neutralize the border rebel minorities and to prevent urban dissidents from getting access to arms and ammunition. SLORC's strategy was to divide and rule. Karen National Union President Bo Mya held that guerilla armies should hold joint talks with the government and not negotiate separately. The junta, however, would only negotiate separate agreements or treaties with each rebel group, increasing marginalization of Myanma pro-Democracy groups. Different philosophies prevailed: the minorities and allies advocated a modified version of the federal system that existed before first military coup in 1962, but SLORC wanted a system like that of China, which let minorities alone as long as they did not interfere in national politics. To achieve its objectives SLORC introduced the border development program into CPB areas. Infrastructure improvements of US$11.1 million in roads, bridges, schools, and hospitals were made. Necessities such as diesel, petrol, kerosene and rice were distributed. The Wa were the first to negotiate with the junta. In 1989 they were promised development assistance, were allowed to retain their arms, maintain control of their areas, and to engage in any kind of business. In exchange they promised not to attack government forces and to sever their ties with the other dissident groups and students. In 1993 the Wa complained that little of the promised aid had been delivered, and that their demand to create a separate state was never discussed. The next deal was made with the 2,000-member Shan State Army (SSA) on 2 Sept 1989 when it became the first ethnic rebel group to sign an agreement with SLORC. The SSA was followed in December 1990 by 800 men from the Kachin Independence Army (KIA). On 23 April 1991 the 600-member Palaung State Liberation Army made a truce with SLORC. The 500-member Pa-O National Army rebel group also signed a peace treaty with the military regime. These were the models for settlements with other rebels.

Since 1984 the Karen National Union (KNU) had had its camps near the Thai border; in 1992 it was estimated that 60,000 ethnic Karen refugees were on the Thai border. Manerplaw was an important Karen stronghold and also the seat of the "parallel government" set up by fugitive members of National League for Democracy. Government forces attacked the Karen rebels at Sleeping Dog Mountain, six miles from Manerplaw, and attacked the Karen across both the Thai and Indian borders from the rear. On 27 April 1992 SLORC declared a ceasefire on Karen rebels. Kachin and Shan minorities were also attacked by government forces. The Kachins which had been in rebellion since 1961, were the largest military group in the coalition of fighting forces. In 1992 approximately 30,000 people from Kachin state camped on the Sino-Myanma border. On 2 October 1993 a ceasefire was declared by the Kachin Independence Organization. China may have pressured the Kachin. Within an 18-month span 5 other rebel groups signed peace pacts with the junta. Karenni rebels, grown rich on the increase in the logging trade, attacked government forces with a surprise attack in September 1992. The government launched a major counter attack on the Karenni that spilled over the Thai border. The Karens, Mons, and Karenni along the Thai border began talks with the military regime in early 1994. The junta negotiated separate peace treaties with each rebel group. Along the Thai border the Mons made a deal in late December and the Karennis met with government representatives in January. On 24 February 1994 the Kachin Independence Army (KIA) signed a peace treaty with Yangon. They agreed to a ceasefire in exchange for permission to participate in commerce. The KIA's recapitulation was an enormous blow since it harbored some 700 pro-democracy activists including six MPs elected in 1990 who had been prevented from taking office. In addition in 1994 the government and Shan engagements increased. The government had 10,000 troops positioned across the Salween River shutting off almost all trade in Shan areas. In May 1994 alone over 17 battles occurred in Shan State. The Mong Tai Army (MTA) of Khun Sa was emerging as the only force of significance. Both the ethnic Karenni and the Wa signed treaties with the MTA. Khun Sa has altered his image from drug lord to politician. The Myanma government forces, while increasing in number, have also experienced increased factionalism amongst the leadership.

Added to this chaotic environment was the movement of large refugee populations. The junta carried out a pogrom against the Muslim community in Arakan. Once before in 1978 the government had launched Operation Naga Min (Dragon King) forcing over 200,000 Rohingyas Muslims to seek refuge in Bangladesh. This pattern was repeated in 1992 when the junta settled Myanma Buddhists with the support of troops in new towns in Muslim areas of northern Arakan. The Rohingyas whose history in the area went as far back as the 9–15th centuries when Moorish, Arab, and Persian traders arrived and married local women and settled in the area, were displaced from their land and homes by their failure to produce documents to prove that they were not "illegals." In early 1992 300,000 Rohingyas fled to Bangladesh when they were forced from their land, their belongings were confiscated and women were raped by government troops. Some co-religionists made statements of protest, but ASEAN offered a policy of "constructive engagement" thus resisting pressures by the US and EC to adopt a stand on human rights abuses. According to this regional attitude, taking a stand would amount to interference in the internal affairs of a neighboring country. Muslim refugees were also on the Thai border; estimates were that in 1990 they numbered 42,000, in 1991 at least 50,000 and in 1992 Muslim refugees on the Thai border numbered 65,000. In 1993 China, Thailand and India pressured both the Myanma government and rebels to negotiate and end to the civil war. In so doing these countries entered into "constructive engagement" with SLORC over trade and investment opportunities, thus altering the status of the Myanma exiles and refugees within their borders. India's change of heart affected 14,000 Myanma political exiles. Some 78,000 Mon and Karen refugees in Thailand were warned to return. SLORC continued to internally displace between 200–500,000 Karen on the Thai border with relocation programs forcing villagers to relocate to areas near military installations. As of mid-1994 the international community was still debating the most constructive approach to dealing with Myanmar. ASEAN countries argue that "engaging" Myanmar is more productive than "isolating" it. The European Union (EU) and Australia, Canada, Japan and New Zealand were reassessing their isolationist position. The US stuck to its hardline isolationist policy toward Myanmar to further the goals of the advancement of democracy and human rights. The merit of this varied, but coordinated approach remains to be tested.

13GOVERNMENT

Myanmar was officially proclaimed the Social Republic of the Union of Burma on 3 January 1974, after a new basic law had been approved by plebiscite. Under the 1974 constitution, the leading organ of state power is the 489-member unicameral People's Assembly (Pyithu Hluttaw). The head of state is the chairman of the Council of State (29 members in 1986), which is elected by the People's Assembly and theoretically responsible to it. The prime minister heads the Council of Ministers (24 mem-

bers in 1986) and also serves on the Council of State. Other main governmental organs are the Council of People's Justices (9 members), the Council of People's Attorneys (6), the Council of People's Inspectors (6), and the people's councils at the level of the state (or division), township, and ward or village tract. Nationwide legislative elections were held in 1974, 1978, 1981, and 1985; in each election, voters either accepted or rejected candidates from a single slate presented by the ruling BSPP. Suffrage is universal at age 18. A military coup in September 1988 brought the State Law and Order Restoration Council (SLORC) to power. SLORC abolished the previous government and the country was placed under martial law. On 18 September 1988 the official title of the state was changed to The Union of Myanmar. SLORC directs, supervises and co-ordinates the work of the central and local organs of state power.

In the multi-party election held 27 May 1990 the National League for Democracy (NLD) received 59.9% of the total vote and took 396 of the 485 contested seats, and the National Unity Party (NUP), the former BSPP re-registered as a new party, took only 10 seats with 21.2% of the votes.

SLORC refused to hand over power to the NLD, instead insisting that a new constitution need be drafted and approved by referendum, and by SLORC, prior to the transfer of power. Senior General Saw Maung resigned due to ill health on 23 April 1992 and General Than Shwe replaced him on the same day as Chairman of SLORC and as Chief of State and Head of the Government. First Secretary is Major-General Khin Nyunt and Second Secretary is Major-General Tin Oo.

14POLITICAL PARTIES

Between 1948 and 1962, Myanmar's parties were mostly socialist in economic orientation. The most important of these was the Anti-Fascist People's Freedom League (AFPFL), which gained independence for the country and which included within its ranks the distinct Burma Socialist Party. The AFPFL governed the country from 1948 to 1958, when a split between the Socialists and the more conservative independent members, led by U Nu, resulted in a temporary takeover by Gen. Ne Win. He voluntarily relinquished control of the government in 1960, when U Nu's new Union Party won a landslide victory. Other parties before 1962 included two Communist movements, the "White Flags" and the "Red Flags," both of which took up arms early after independence and were later defeated by the government (the White Flags, however, were not completely eradicated until 1975). An above-ground Communist Party existed after 1949 and became the nucleus of the National United Front (NUF) in 1952. Both the Communists and the NUF, like all other parties except the ruling Burma Socialist Program Party (BSPP), were banned in 1974. The BSPP, founded by Ne Win in 1962, is not, however, an autonomous institution, nor does it rule the state; although BSPP leaders have made efforts to develop it into a mass party (it had 2.3 million members in 1985), the organization is still dominated by the military. On 27 May 1975, five ethnic organizations—the Karen National Union, Karenni (Kayah) National Progressive Party, New Mon State Party, Shan State Progress Party, and Arakan Liberation Party—formed the Federal National Democratic Front (FNDF). They sought to overthrow the Ne Win government and establish a federal union based on national minorities. Their resistance, and that of Communists, continued into the 1980s, with the government mounting intermittent campaigns against them.

In 1987, army troops captured Communist Party headquarters at Panghsai, in northeast Myanmar. Chinese support for the Communist party of Burma (CPB) continued well after support for the Communist parties of Malaysia and Thailand was withdrawn, but from the mid-1980s aid did not compare with a decade earlier. China's priorities were shifting from politics to economics in the border zones. The capture of Panghsai by the "tatmadaw" reopened the Old Burma Road facilitating trade with China. ("Tatmadaw" refers to the Burmese Army as an embodiment of national identity and aspirations, "the life and soul of the country.") The democracy uprising of 1988 ended with the Saw Maung coup which installed the military officers of the State Law and Order Restoration Council (SLORC). SLORC charged the CPB with promoting the demonstrations and made inconsistent accusations of communist infiltration into participating organizations. In addition Ne Win loyalists accused the CPB of infiltrating the newly legalized political parties springing up after the coup. A series of mutinies within the CPB in 1989 displaced the aging Burman-dominated party leadership installing younger ethnic minority leaders. However, unresolved ethnic problems ultimately led to the collapse and fragmentation of the CPB. As the scale of the CPB's collapse became clear, China's neutral position toward the democracy uprising faded, and arms sales with the new regime began.

With the military takeover of September 1988, the Burma Socialist Program Party was formally abolished, and all governing authority was concentrated in the hands of the military. The earliest formation of the State Law and Order Restoration Council (SLORC) was made up of seventeen active military commanders of the Defense Services. On 18 September 1988 it was renamed the Organization for Building Law and Order in the State (OBLOS) and two more members were added. On 20 September 1988 the final version of the SLORC government was formed by maintaining the 19 members and adding two non-members to the Cabinet, increasing the number of Cabinet ministers from seven to nine. On 24 September 1988 the BSPP was reborn as the National Unity Party (NUP), inheriting the buildings and machinery of the old BSPP. Allied to the NUP were satellite parties, the former supporters of the BSPP.

On 24 September 1988 the National League for Democracy (NLD), a coalition party, was formed in opposition to the military regime. Leaders Aung San Suu Kyi, Tin Oo, and Aung Gyi soon parted ways over a personal feud over the issue of communist membership, based on vague accusations that the NLD was infiltrated by CPB supporters. The split occurred in December when Aung Gyi left to form the Union Nationals Democracy Party (UNDP) in early 1989. On 28 August 1988 U Nu at age 83, with his followers from the older generation of "Thakins," (British colonial administrators, or "Masters") formed Myanmar's first new political organization, called the League for Democracy and Peace (LDP), later known as the League for Democracy. The NLD won the 27 May 1990 elections by a landslide, electing 392 candidates; the NUP took 10 seats; the UNDP and the Democracy Party took 1 seat each; and the LDP did not win any seats. In April/May 1991 the Election Commission dropped the names of General Secretary Aung San Suu Kyi and President, U Tin Oo from a roster of NLD leaders, as well as the names of all other Central Executive Committee members who were jailed. NLD leader Aung San Suu Kyi had been placed under house arrest on 20 July 1989, and remained under house arrest as of July 1994.

Leader Dr. Sein Win of the party for National Democracy, winner of a seat in Pegu District, and seven NLD members legitimately elected to parliament but not recognized by SLORC, fled to border areas, joined with insurgents, the Democratic Alliance of Burma (DAB) on 18 December 1990 and formed a parallel government, the National Coalition Government Union of Burma (NCGUB). The DAB is a coalition of 21 ethnic minorities and political dissident groups formed in 1988. Sein Win was named prime minister of the eight-member cabinet of the NCGUB. The new political alliance was also called the Democratic Front of Burma (DFB). Following the formation of the DFB, the military regime stripped the eight opposition politicians of their seats. On 20 December 1990 Dr. Sein Win's Party for National Democracy

was declared illegal and deregistered. In February 1991 three more political parties were deregistered: U Nu's League for Democracy and Peace, the Anti-Fascist People's Freedom League and Mandalay's National Political Front for Youth.

On 29 January 1992 SLORC appointed additional ministers, mostly serving or ex-military, to the original nine-member cabinet, and three new military commanders were added to the original nineteen-member SLORC. Senior General Saw Maung resigned due to ill health on 23 April 1992. He was replaced as Chairman of SLORC by General Than Shwe on 23 April 1992. Than Shwe was named Chief of State and Head of the Government. First Secretary is Major-General Khin Nyunt and Second Secretary is Major-General Tin Oo. Formation of the Union Solidarity and Development Association (USDA), a new organization with the same aims as SLORC's, "non-disintegration of the union, non-disintegration of national unity, perpetual sovereignty and the promotion of national pride," was established on 15 September 1993. As a mass movement, the USDA, like the NUP before it, is a civilian counterpart through which control can still be maintained by SLORC. The USDA is an "association," and not registered as a political party, so the law preventing civil servants from joining political parties does not apply. By March 1993 all but seven political parties had been deregistered by SLORC. Other political or pressure groups are the Kachin Independence Army (KIA), the United Wa State Army (UWSA), the Karen National Union (KNU), and several Shan factions including the Mong Tai Army (MTA).

15LOCAL GOVERNMENT

Myanmar is a unitary Socialist Republic, ruled by a military junta, comprising seven states and seven divisions. The main distinction between the two kinds of units, which are functionally the same, is that the states represent an area where a national ethnic minority is the local majority, while the divisions have no such communal basis. The states are Arakan (Rakhine), Chin, Kachin, Karen (Kayin), Kayah, Mon, and Shan. The divisions are Irrawaddy, Magwe, Mandalay, Bago (Pegu), Sagaing, Yangon (Rangoon), and Tenasserim. States and divisions are segmented into 317 townships, which include 16,065 village tracts and towns. Village tracts consist of villages, and towns are divided into wards. There are people's councils at all levels of local government. Their members are elected, but only the Burma Socialist Program Party (BSPP) may nominate candidates. The local executive is the executive committee of the people's council. People's councils may refer questions to their counterparts at the next highest level of organization. The People's Councils replaced the former military Five-Man Security and Administrative Committees (SACs) of the Revolutionary Council (RCs) with Seven-Man People's Councils on the regional, district, township, and village tract levels. These councils became the most powerful arms of the State in the urban and rural communities. Under the new system it remained possible for the top positions to be filled by military and ex-military officials. As of September 1988, under the State Law and Order Restoration Council (SLORC), a Law and Order Restoration Council was formed for each State, Division, Township Sector and Ward/Village Sector. These councils are charged with maintaining law and order, providing secure and smooth transportation, striving for better supplies of food, clothing, and shelter for the populace, and rendering necessary assistance, both to the private sector and to co-operatives, as necessary. The councils were also charged with holding multi-party elections in May 1990.

16JUDICIAL SYSTEM

The British-style judicial organs with which Myanmar began its independence, including a Supreme Court, were disbanded by the Revolutionary Council. The 1974 constitution provides for a Council of People's Justices, state and divisional judges' committees, and township, ward, and village tract judges' committees. The Council of People's Justices is elected by the National Assembly from among its own members; nominations are made by the Council of State, which coordinates relations between central and local levels of government. People's courts function at all levels, with jurisdiction over both civil and criminal cases. Military tribunals which enforced orders issued by the State Law and Order Restoration Council (SLORC) were abolished in 1992. Ordinary courts now handle such cases. The Supreme Court appoints judges after approval of the SLORC.

17 ARMED FORCES

The armed forces play the major role in Myanmar's politics and administration; senior members of the government are officers who govern under martial law.

Myanmar's armed forces totaled an estimated 286,000 in 1993; military service for men and women is compulsory. The army, with 265,000 personnel, is organized in infantry battalions chiefly for internal security duties, mainly against the various insurgent groups that have challenged successive governments almost from the start of independence. The navy has 12,000–15,000 members, and the air force 9,000. The navy's responsibilities relate primarily to antismuggling and other coastal patrol duties; its ships include 30 gunboats and 36 river patrol craft. The air force is also concerned mainly with internal security; it has 37 combat aircraft, 10 transports, and 45 armed and general purpose helicopters. The armed forces use European and Chinese weapons, including 86 tanks of several makes and about 300 auxiliary pieces. Paramilitary forces total 85,000. Military expenditures were $1.25 billion in 1992. Various rebel groups and narcotics armies are estimated at perhaps 30,000 and operate inside and outside of northern Myanmar.

18 INTERNATIONAL COOPERATION

Myanmar was admitted to UN membership on 19 April 1948; it is a member of ESCAP and all the nonregional specialized agencies except IFAD and WIPO. Regional bodies to which Myanmar belongs include the Asian Development Bank and the Colombo Plan; it also is a member of G-77, a participant in GATT, and a signatory to the Law of the Sea. Myanmar's foreign policy is neutralist, and the country belongs to no alliances.

19 ECONOMY

Myanmar has an agricultural economy. As of 1992 nearly 70% of the economy was in the private sector comprised chiefly of agriculture (including fish and forestry), which is almost entirely private, contributing nearly 40% of GDP and employing close to 80% of the work force. Myanmar is self-sufficient in food. Principal crops are paddy rice, corn, oilseed, sugarcane, and pulses. Traditionally rice was the major product and the major foreign exchange earner, accounting for about 70% of the country's cultivated land. Myanmar has the world's largest stand of hardwood trees. In 1985 teak replaced rice as the largest export and maintains this position. Rice and teak account for 55% of export revenues. Industries include agricultural processing, textiles and footwear, wood and wood products, petroleum refining, mining production (mainly copper, tin, tungsten, and iron), construction materials, pharmaceuticals, and fertilizer. Industrial production accounts for 10% of GDP. In the past Myanmar was a net petroleum exporter, but production decreased steadily. In 1988 Myanmar could not fulfill its modest domestic energy needs without importing crude oil. Both oil and gas exploration is on-going with the participation of foreign companies, but exploration, repair, up-dating and construction will take several years to be productive. In addition, Myanmar's significant mineral resources have not been fully developed due to out-dated equipment and poor management.

Infrastructure is a major impediment to economic growth.

Water treatment and distribution, sewage disposal, and irrigation systems, as well as, power transmission and distribution, require up-grading. Industry faces chronic shortages of electricity. Roads are poor and many are not passable during parts of the year. Telephone facilities are lacking; in 1993 there were only 100,000 telephone lines for the entire country. Presently a telecommunications modernization program includes the installation of a cellular telephone system in Yangon. The financial sector is primitive and suffers from excessive bureaucratic red tape and footdragging by state economic enterprises fearing competition. The government drafted new laws on a central banking and financial institutions as steps toward improvement in the financial sector.

In 1977, the economic growth rate was about 6% annually, declining to 5.5% in 1986 because of dwindling export earnings and burdensome debt obligations. For the fiscal year ending 31 March 1992 official statistics show a GDP growth rate in real terms of only 1.3%. However, it is difficult to assess the true economic situation due to the existence of an enormous and all-pervasive informal market. Much of Myanmar's economic activity is illicit, notably the smuggling of gold and drugs. Myanmar, which forms part of the "Golden Triangle" (along with Laos and Thailand), is the world's largest supplier of illegal opiates. In the mid-1980s the annual opium crop was 500-600 tons; by 1994 annual production was more than 2,000 tons. In 1994 Myanmar's opium accounted for 60% of worldwide production and for 88% of Southeast Asia's heroin. The government's efforts to control poppy production and drug traffic to China and Hong Kong were ineffective. The US, which received perhaps 30% of the heroin originating as opium in the area, had provided more than $30 million in antinarcotics equipment (primarily helicopters) under a 1974 agreement with Myanmar. In 1986/87, 40,225 acres of poppy plantations were destroyed. Due to Myanmar's inability to stop the flow of drugs from its sector of the Golden Triangle, in February 1989 the US removed Myanmar from a list of countries eligible to receive aid for combating the drug trade. By 1993 Myanmar's opium cultivation was estimated to be 195,800 hectares. Large quantities of smuggled consumer goods are sold in Myanma cities, where the black market thrives.

The military regime, SLORC, which took over Myanmar in 1988, proclaimed a market oriented economic policy and invited foreign investment. A 1992 United Nations Development Programme report noted that Myanmar after a few years of recovery from the economic and political upheaval of 1988 was again slipping into recession and hyperinflation. Myanmar's main donors suspended aid. The country has not fully serviced its foreign debt since 1988. Two trends have been apparent in the government's economic policies: the capture of revenues from short term, quick turnover sources such as hardwoods, prospecting rights, and taxes on profits from illegal sources; and spending patterns which emphasize defense spending and acquisition of armaments. Myanmar receives no aid from US or EC programs and aid from Japan is run at a maintenance level. The International Monetary Fund (IMF), the World Bank, and the Asian Development Bank (ADB) extend no credit to Myanmar.

20 INCOME

In 1992 the GDP was $37,749 million in current US dollars. It is estimated that in 1991 agriculture, hunting, forestry, and fishing contributed 59% to GDP; mining and quarrying, 1%; manufacturing, 7%; construction, 2%; wholesale and retail trade, 23%; transport, storage, and communication, 2%; community, social, and personal services, 3%; and other sources 4%.

21 LABOR

In 1992, over two-thirds of Myanmar's civilian wage labor force of 15.7 million was engaged in agriculture, primarily rice cultivation. As of 1992, according to the government, 69% of the labor force worked in agriculture, 8.9% in trade, 10.6% in government and social services, 7.2% in manufacturing, 1.7% in construction, forestry, and mining, 2.5% in transport and communications, and 0.1% in other sectors.

No trade union or independent labor movement activity has occurred since 1988, when the government banned the workers' and peasants' organizations of the previous government, thereby eliminating any right to bargain collectively. Forced labor is frequently used by the military for building projects. Wage levels continue to be low and have been eroded by inflation.

There were some 502,550 officially unemployed in 1992, although the actual amount is likely to be much higher.

22AGRICULTURE

Myanmar is one of the few developing nations that is a net exporter of food, which accounted for 38% of its foreign exchange earnings in 1992. About 15% of the land is under cultivation. Rice, by far the most important agricultural product, in 1992 covered about 4.7 million hectares (11.6 million acres) of land in the fertile Irrawaddy delta region, the lower valleys of the Sittang and Salween rivers, and along the Arakan and Tenasserim coasts. Prior to World War II, Myanmar was the world's leading exporter of rice; annual production ranged between 13 million and 14 million tons, of which about 3 million tons were exported. However, the war caused extensive damage to the economy, and Myanmar did not achieve prewar levels of rice acreage and output until 1964. Rice production totaled 13.7 million tons in 1992, compared with 12.6 million annually during 1979–81. New high-yield varieties of rice contributed to the increase, as did favorable weather conditions and the completion of new irrigation systems and flood-control dams in the Irrawaddy delta during the early 1980s.

Other crops in 1992, grown mainly in central Myanmar and the state of Shan, included 2,400,000 tons of sugarcane, 466,000 tons of groundnuts, 241,000 tons of corn, and 183,000 tons of sesame. The use of high-yield varieties of seeds helped to more than triple the output of wheat, corn, and sunflower seeds and to double cotton production during 1976–86. Tobacco and jute are also produced, and rubber is grown on small plantations in the Tenasserim and Irrawaddy delta regions.

The total amount of land under cultivation declined in the 1970s, but the amount of paddy land increased. The Mu Valley irrigation project, implemented in north-central Myanmar with UNDP aid in the 1970s, irrigated 1.7 million hectares (4.2 million acres) of farmland. With the completion of the Nawin Dam in 1982, about 40,000 hectares (99,000 acres) of new irrigated land in the Prome region, north of Yangon (Rangoon), were added to the cultivated area. With IBRD and Asian Development Bank aid, new rice storage facilities, a system of drainage canals in the heavy-rainfall paddy land of lower Myanmar, and gravity irrigation systems in dry zones were constructed.

23ANIMAL HUSBANDRY

Despite Buddhist prohibitions against any kind of animal slaughter, the Myanma eat beef and other meats. Zebu cattle and water buffalo are mainly raised as draft animals; the output of such hides was 23,160 tons in 1992. Dairy farming is confined to the Shan and Kachin states; hogs and poultry are found in virtually every village.

In 1992, Myanmar had an estimated 9,470,000 head of cattle, 2,514,000 hogs, 2,099,000 water buffalo, 1,076,000 goats, 284,000 sheep, and 25,000,000 chickens, and 4,000,000 ducks. Milk production was 431,000 tons, and eggs 36,608 tons.

24FISHING

Fishing is the most significant nonagricultural pursuit in Myanmar. Fish, which supply the main protein element in the Myanma diet, generally are dried and salted before marketing or consumed fresh or as fish paste. Traditionally, the Myanma preferred fish from fresh or brackish water; but saltwater fishing in the shallow waters of the Bay of Bengal, Andaman Sea, and Gulf of Martaban has increased in recent years. To encourage a larger saltwater catch, the government embarked on expanded deep-sea fishing operations and erected a cold storage plant, a fish cannery, and a fish oil and meal factory. The total fish catch in 1991 was 769,236 tons (four-fifths saltwater, one-fifth freshwater), up from 686,515 tons in 1986.

25FORESTRY

Forests and woodland cover nearly half the country. Myanmar has a major share of the world's teak reserves, which constitute about one-third of the forested area. As the world's leading exporter of teak, Myanmar supplies about 75% of the world market. The lumbering of teak, a 10-year process from the first girdling of the tree to its arrival at the sawmill, was disrupted by World War II; production rebounded to about 136,000 tons in 1986. Increased output of teak in the 1980s was attributable to completion of four modern timber-extraction projects. Roundwood production in 1991 totaled 23,585,000 cu m. Other forest products include lac, catechu resin, and bamboo.

All foreign timber concessions have been nationalized, and all forests are government-owned; the State Timber Board (STB) lumbers, mills, and markets forest products. In 1990, exports of rough, squared wood, valued at $68.9 million, accounted for one-quarter of total exports. The export of forest products increased in value from $115.3 million in 1987 to $184 million in 1992.

26MINING

The government controls all mineral exploration, extraction, regulation, and planning through the two departments and six enterprises of the Ministry of Mines. Metallic ores are mined in small amounts; production in 1991 included (in tons): chromium (1,000), copper (5,670), lead (4,700), zinc (2,766), tin (606), and tungsten (277). Industrial mineral production in 1991 included (in tons): barite (9,000), fire clay (2,540), dolomite (2,000), limestone (1,860,000), graphite (36) and gypsum 930,000). Lead, zinc, silver, copper, nickel, and cobalt are produced at the Baldwin mine in Namtu. Jade, rubies, sapphires, and gold are also extracted, and deposits of iron ore, antimony, and coal have been found. Production of jade and refined silver totaled 101,600 kg and 4,791 kg, respectively.

27ENERGY AND POWER

The Myanmar's petroleum industry was completely nationalized in 1963–64, and the Petroleum and Mineral Development Corp. was formed by the amalgamation of the Mineral Resources Development Corp., the Mines and Explosives Department, and the Burma Geological Development Corp. Petroleum and natural gas deposits were found in 1963 in the Irrawaddy basin and delta. Myanmar has been self-sufficient in oil since 1977; petroleum reserves were estimated at 51.3 million barrels in 1991. Most natural gas comes from the field at Prome. Exploitation of the natural gas discovery in the Gulf of Martaban, Natmi, and Payagon will significantly raise Myanmar's energy reserves. Oil production reached 5.7 million barrels in 1991; in that year, natural gas production totaled 33,500 million cu ft (950 million cu m). Pipelines in Myanmar include 1,343 km (835 mi) for crude petroleum and 330 km (205 mi) for natural gas, although some of these lines are believed to be in disrepair. Coal resources in Myanmar are of relatively low thermal value. The two principal mines are an underground mine south of Kalewa and an opencast mine at Namma, south of Lashio. About 56,000 tons of coal came from the two mines in 1991.

Production of electricity totaled 2,400 million kwh in 1991, of which gas-fired plants provided 50% hydroelectric power 44%, and steam and diesel fuel 6%. Electric power capacity rose to 1,116 Mw in 1991.

28 INDUSTRY

Industry is geared largely to the processing of agricultural, mineral, and forest products. More than half of Myanmar industrial production is accounted for by the public sector. Large state-owned plants and workshops numbered 1,669 in 1986; there were 40,052 smaller private enterprises. Principal industrial products are cement, steel, bricks and tiles, fertilizers, and processed foods. Consumer goods which were imported before 1962 and are now manufactured domestically include blankets, paper, glass products, bicycles, and water pumps. Other major consumer manufactures are aluminum ware, jute and cotton cloth, pharmaceuticals, beverages, matches, and cigarettes. The assembly of television sets and motor vehicles is a recent development in Myanmar's industry. During the 1970s, the annual growth rate of industrial production was 5.4%; the rate increased to about 9% in both 1981 and 1982, but fell to 8.6% by 1986. A drop in productivity of plants dependent on imported raw materials was officially blamed for failure to reach the targeted 14.1% growth rate. However, a spurt in growth was expected with the inauguration in 1986 of new fertilizer, tire, and diesel-technology plants, financed by Japan, the Federal Republic of Germany (FRG), and Czechoslovakia. The main industrial area is Bago (formerly Pegu). In order to promote industrial expansion, the government established the Industrial Development Corp. in 1952. The Burma Economic Development Corp. (BEDC) was set up in 1961, and in 1963–64 the Ne Win government nationalized certain industries and took over control of the BEDC, together with its 39 subsidiary firms. Transfer of these firms to appropriate government offices began early in 1964. Some manufacturing industries are privately owned and operated under government supervision. Myanmar's oil refining capacity averaged 30,000 barrels per day in 1981, but rose to 55,000 with the opening of a new refinery in May 1982. In 1985/86, local refineries produced 76.7 million gallons of gasoline and 3.1 million gallons of kerosene.

Industrial products for 1989 included cement, 414,000 tons; bricks and tiles, 110.1 million units; cotton yarn, 10,900 tons; fertilizers, 401,400 tons; refined sugar, 25,300 tons; paper, 19,900 tons; and aluminum ware, 1.0 million lbs. For fiscal year 1990 the annual growth rate for industrial production was estimated to be 2.6%, accounting for 10% of GDP. The petroleum and petrochemical sector in Myanmar is entirely state-owned (excluding indigenous fuels such as charcoal). Existing fields are severely depleted due in part to outdated equipment and lack of modern techniques. Myanmar's hydrocarbon output is insufficient to support domestic consumption. No new oil fields have been opened since 1985. In 1988 Myanmar's crude petroleum production was 806,900 tons. In 1989 the government offered oil concessions to foreign companies. In 1992 Shell found gas. Declining gas and oil production has refineries and plants operating severely below capacity, three oil refineries at less than 25% of capacity, and the sole LPG plant at 63% of capacity. For the fiscal year ending 31 March 1992 Myanmar produced 15,600 barrels of oil per day, or 5.7 million barrels per year. In 1992 Myanmar purchased 500,000 tons of oil to supplement domestic production, having purchased a similar quantity the previous year.

29 SCIENCE AND TECHNOLOGY

Scientific research is conducted by the private Burma Research Society, founded in 1910, and by the government's Central Research Organization, consisting of various departments of the state ministries. Four institutes conduct research in applied sciences, medicine, and nuclear energy. In addition, the Research Division of the Institute of Economics investigates problems posed by modernization techniques and industrial development. The Universities of Mandalay, Mawlamyine, and Yangon offer degrees in basic sciences.

30 DOMESTIC TRADE

In 1964, the Ne Win government nationalized all wholesale businesses and the large private and cooperative shops; small retail shops, hotels, restaurants, and village cooperatives were exempted. The People's Stores Corp., established in 1964, was initially responsible for the importation and distribution of essential foreign goods, the distribution of consumer goods produced in Myanmar, and the sale of domestic products in foreign markets. The corporation was administered by a council headed by the Ministry of Supplies and Cooperatives. In 1970, the "people's stores," most of which had been unsuccessful, were replaced by consumer cooperatives. Beginning in 1966, the government set all commodity prices and controlled distribution systems; in September 1987, the Burmese people were told that they could buy, sell, and store rice and other grains free of government restrictions. Although significant marketing is done at Bago (Pegu), Mandalay, Mawlamyine (Moulmein), Pathein (Bassein), Henzada, Akyab (Sittwe), and Dawei (Tavoy), Yangon (Rangoon) is Myanmar's most important business center. Economic stagnation and the prolonged interruption to the economy during the unstable socio-political conditions of 1988–89, coupled with rapid inflation in 1989, affected all sectors of Myanmar's economy. In the early 1990s Myanmar's domestic economy was paralleled by a huge black market economy that coexists with the official one. A factor in the decline of Myanmar's domestic production is dependence on border trade, which undermines Myanmar's manufacturing sector with cheap foreign consumer goods. Normal business hours are 9:30 AM to 1 PM and 1:30 to 4 PM, Monday–Friday, and 9:30 AM to 12:30 PM on Saturday; small private shops keep longer hours than government offices and enterprises. Banks are usually open 10 AM to 2 PM, Monday–Friday, and 10 AM to noon on Saturday.

31 FOREIGN TRADE

During 1976–80, Myanmar's exports more than doubled, but imports tripled to create a trade deficit of κ1.2 billion. The trade picture worsened in the early 1980s, and by 1982/83 exports were stagnant at κ3.4 billion while imports had risen to κ6.9 billion, leaving a deficit of κ3.5 billion. In 1985/86, exports fell to κ2.7 billion and imports to κ4.8 billion, for a deficit of κ2.1 billion. A deficit of κ1.6 billion was projected for 1986/87. Myanmar's principal exports were rice and forest products; together these commodities accounted for 77.7% of export value in 1985/86.

For 1988/89 the Myanmar government reported that exports were distributed as follows: agricultural products 6%, forest products 32%, animal and marine products 3%, minerals and gems 8%, and other 51%. The "other" category "includes border trade not accounted by commodity." Imports for the same period were distributed as follows: consumer goods 5%, raw materials and spares for inter-industry use 24%, capital goods 41%, and commodity unspecified 30%. The "commodity unspecified" category again "includes border trade not accounted by commodity." The government's provisional figures for 1989/90 exports change substantially only in the increase in agricultural products to 19%, and the decrease in "others" to 37%. For this same period import of capital goods increased to 51% and unspecified commodities decreased to 21%. Although the Myanmar government's trade figures are suspect due to widespread underinvoicing and smuggling, in fiscal year 1990/91 the government reported exports of US$566.1 million, and imports of US$1153.9 million, the latter an increase of over 100% from the previous year. For fiscal year 1992 the major exports were agriculture and forestry products—teak and hardwood logs, beans and pulses. Exploration by foreign oil companies has been without success. Major export partners were China, India, Thailand, and Singapore. Major import partners were Japan, China, Singapore.

32BALANCE OF PAYMENTS

A decline in rice exports in the late 1960s and early 1970s produced a serious balance-of-payments problem, but a drastic cutback on imports and an infusion of long-term capital led to payments surpluses. By 1989, a small trade surplus was officially recorded, and the current account deficit had fallen from 2.4% of GDP to 0.2% of GDP.

In 1992 merchandise exports totaled $165.7 million and imports $370.2 million. The merchandise trade balance was $−204.5 million.

The following table summarizes Myanmar's balance of payments for 1987 and 1988 (in millions of US dollars):

	1987	1988
CURRENT ACCOUNT		
Goods, services, and income	−287.1	−268.4
Unrequited transfers	107.1	92.5
TOTALS	−180.0	−175.9
CAPITAL ACCOUNT		
Other long-term capital	188.6	151.1
Other short-term capital	14.3	−11.5
Reserves	−37.7	−80.5
TOTALS	165.2	59.1
Errors and omissions	14.7	116.7
Total change in reserves	−36.3	−80.5

33BANKING AND SECURITIES

Effective 23 February 1963, all 24 commercial banks in Myanmar—10 foreign and 14 indigenously owned—were nationalized and amalgamated into 4 state banks. In addition to the Union of Burma Bank, which serves as a central banks, the other state banks were the State Agricultural Bank, the State Commercial Bank, and the Industrial Bank. After subsequent reorganizations of the banking system, these became the Myanma Agriculture Bank, Myanma Economic Bank, and the Myanma Foreign Trade Bank. Bank demand and savings deposits totaled к1,376 million in 1990. Public savings increased sharply in 1977 after the banks raised interest rates. Myanmar's money supply in December 1990 totaled к42,376 million; currency in circulation amounted to к30,587 as of December 1990.

34INSURANCE

All 78 foreign insurance companies registered in Myanmar were nationalized on 1 March 1963. All forms of insurance, including life, fire, marine, automobile, workers' compensation, personal accident, and burglary, are handled by the Myanma Insurance Corp. Life insurance coverage is compulsory for government employees.

35PUBLIC FINANCE

The government presents its budget in March for the 1 April–31 March fiscal year. The public sector budget typically shows an overall deficit. Since the late 1980s, however, revenue collection methods have been improved, and several infrastructural projects have been funded by public donations rather than through the budget. With expenditures exceeding revenues in 1990 and 1991, increased deficits brought about another wave of monetary expansion and inflation. Military expenditures have accounted for up to one-third of annual current outlays.

The following table shows actual revenues and expenditures for 1990 and 1991 in millions of kyats.

	1990	1991
REVENUE AND GRANTS		
Tax revenue	9,417	10,480
Non-tax revenue	6,481	6,863
Capital revenue	150	696
Grants	140	300
TOTAL	16,188	18,339
EXPENDITURES & LENDING MINUS REPAYMENTS		
General public service	5,035	4,719
Defense	5,436	6,086
Education	3,875	4,810
Health	1,588	1,886
Social security and welfare	1,075	1,319
Housing and community amenities	2,031	2,020
Recreation, cultural, and religious affairs	378	782
Economic affairs and services	4,772	5,390
Other expenditures	150	611
Lending minus repayments	−372	−289
TOTALS	23,977	27,332
Deficit/Surplus	−7,789	−8,993

36TAXATION

Residents pay a progressive individual income tax of 3–30%. The corporate tax rate is 30% with a 10% capital gains tax (40% for non-residents). Indirect taxes include a commercial tax on sales and services, as well as social security taxes, customs duties, royalties on natural resources, stamp tax, and property tax.

37CUSTOMS AND DUTIES

Duties are primarily intended to raise revenue, although their financial importance is limited by the fact that the government itself—through its Myanma Export-Import Corp.—is by far the country's predominant importer. Import licenses are required for shipment of almost anything into the country. For most of the postindependence period, duties have been at the rate of 5% ad valorem. There is a sales tax of 0–25% on goods imported for sale.

38FOREIGN INVESTMENT

Foreign investment in Myanmar was heavy before World War II, but in the postwar period, and particularly after independence, a government policy of economic nationalism (and later socialism) strongly discouraged private foreign investment. After the nationalization of industry in 1963–64, private foreign investment in Myanmar was eliminated entirely. In 1976, the government indicated a willingness to establish "mutually beneficial economic cooperation" with foreign enterprises having the technology that Myanmar needed. In 1986, Japan, the FRG, Switzerland, IBRD, UNDP, and ADB provided investment credits for such projects as modernization of rice mills and irrigation systems and road development.The scope of state capitalism was expanded when the Saw Maung regime legalized internal and external trade without giving up control of major industries. Foreign investment in Myanmar has been permitted only since 1988 under the Union of Myanmar Foreign Investment Law, and the level and variety of investment is limited. Sectors eligible for foreign investment include manufacturing, oil and gas exploration and development, mining (except gold and precious stones), jewelry production, and agriculture. The Foreign Investment Commission (FIC) screens foreign investment proposals for export generation potential, technology transfer, and the size of the investment. Various investment incentives are provided, such as exemption from income tax, and relief or exemption from customs duties. Bureaucratic procedures hamper foreign and local investments alike. Foreign entities cannot own land in Myanmar. The government's maintenance of an official exchange rate for the domestic currency, the kyat, which is overvalued by some 20 times its unofficial value, is the major obstacle to foreign investment. As of September 1992 a total of 51 foreign investment agreements were approved, with the bulk of investment in 1989/90 from oil exploration. In 1994 US firms reported difficulty in obtaining economic and business information.

39ECONOMIC DEVELOPMENT

The major aim of Myanmar's government has been to rehabilitate, modernize, and diversify an economy that was extensively disrupted by World War II and that failed to develop from the 1940s through the 1960s. To this end, all foreign companies, all banks, the entire transport system, all foreign and much domestic trade, and all the main branches of industry have been nationalized. Some nationalized industries initially showed declines in output, while others were hard pressed to hold their own. By 1974, the government had no choice but to modify some of its more rigidly Socialist economic policies. A foreign investment ban imposed in the 1960s was relaxed, and foreign participation in mining was allowed for the first time in a dozen years. Privately owned businesses, to which the government had previously been unsympathetic, were allowed in specified fields. Economic development proceeded slowly under the four-year plan for 1974–78 and the 1978–82 development program, which was allocated 60% more funding than its predecessor and which achieved an annual growth rate exceeding 6%. The four-year plan for 1982–86, costing an estimated $5 billion, set an average annual growth target of 6.2%. The plan stressed infrastructural development, with particular emphasis on agriculture, construction, and energy production. The four-year plan for 1986–90 aims at real growth of 4.5% a year and the encouragement of foreign investment; total investment in the plan was estimated at $2.6 billion, with 20% coming from foreign aid. In recent years, Japanese firms have secured contracts for industrial projects in Myanmar, backed by financing from the IBRD and Asian Development Bank; bilateral assistance from Japan ranged from $144.2 million in 1980 to $114.5 million in 1984. US economic aid to Myanmar, which had ended in the late 1960s, resumed in 1980 with agreements to provide $35 million for rural health care and agricultural assistance projects; the US contributed $16.2 million in aid to Myanmar in 1986. Multilateral assistance during the 1949–86 period totaled $1,480.1 million, of which 49% came from the IDA and 37% from the Asian Development Bank.

In July 1988 the Burma Socialist Programme Party (BSPP) approved changes to existing economic policy that would, in theory, have permitted a dramatic liberalization of the economy, including private foreign investment and joint ventures. The BSPP government was paralyzed by an uprising that culminated in a military coup in September, and never had the opportunity to deliver on these promises. The new military regime, the State Law and Order Restoration Council (SLORC) pledged to follow through on these planned reforms.

However, in spite of the military government's commitment to the transformation of Myanmar's state-controlled economy to a market system, economic development has been limited by the government's failure to implement basic structural reforms. Such needed reforms include dismantling unproductive state-owned enterprises, establishing an independent state bank, making available private sector credit, controlling government spending, and adjustments to the official exchange rate. Basic infrastructure, transportation, telecommunications, and energy are inadequate.

After the disturbances of 1988, foreign aid was almost completely shut off. A new foreign investment law was promulgated in 1988 featuring tax breaks, guarantees against nationalization, and the right to remit hard currency. The Saw Maung regime announced in 1989 the legalization of trade, principally the border black market trade, and made trade concession agreements with Thailand and China. The economic purpose of legalizing border trade was to capture tax revenues from traders, but since these revenues also formed the economic base for the ethnic minority rebels it could also be considered a political policy aimed at pacifying the rebels. These border-trade agreements have also undermined Myanmar's manufacturing sector by flooding Myanmar with cheap Chinese consumer goods which contribute to a decline in domestic production. The government launched the Programme for the Development of the Border Areas and National Races with the objectives of "strengthening national solidarity, alleviating poverty and to bring remote areas into the mainstream of the economy." In 1990 several laws were introduced: the Financial Institutions Law, the Central Bank of Myanmar Law, and the Private Industrial Enterprise Law. In 1993 limited economic reforms were introduced: some privatization of state-owned enterprises (SEES) occurred through leasing to private businesses; private-public sector contracts increased; the government partly liberalized the foreign exchange system with the introduction of a parallel currency, the foreign exchange certificate; and the first private and joint-venture banks opened. As of December 1993 tourist visas were valid for 28 days instead of seven, encouraging joint ventures in the hotel and tourist industries.

40SOCIAL DEVELOPMENT

Although considerable advances have been made in health services, Myanmar's goal of establishing a welfare state has been limited by lack of public funds. In 1956, the government inaugurated a social security program that compensates workers for wage losses arising from sickness, injury, and maternity leave, provides free medical care, and establishes survivors' benefits. The program is funded by contributions from employers, employees, and the government. As yet, Myanmar does not have unemployment insurance, but workers are entitled to old age pensions.

Women have a high status in Myanmar's society and economic life. They may retain their maiden name after marriage, may obtain divorces without undue difficulty, and enjoy equal property and inheritance rights with men. In 1985, the fertility rate was 4.5. Abortion is permitted in order to save the woman's life.

41HEALTH

Until recent decades, few people in rural areas had the benefit of modern medicine. To correct this deficiency, the country's health services were reorganized by sending more doctors to rural areas and increasing the number of rural health centers. Doctors in private practice were inducted for two years of national service.

The progress of the health services is reflected in the reduction of the physician/ population ratio from 1 per 15,560 in 1960 to 1 per 3,578 by 1986. In 1986, Myanmar had 635 hospitals with 25,839 beds. To staff the new hospitals and dispensaries, medical schools have been expanded, nurse and midwife training courses increased, an institute of paramedical science established, and a new college of dentistry opened. There were 12,400 doctors in 1990, and 714 dentists, 7,895 nurses, and 8,372 midwives in 1986.

A team of nutritionists conducts research on the nation's diet (by 1982, Myanmar's population received 117% of minimum daily caloric requirements), and it disseminates its findings and recommendations through the press, radio, and demonstrations in offices and factories. One result of these efforts has been that the average height and weight of Myanmar's populace have increased.

Smallpox and plague have been virtually eliminated as health hazards, and programs are under way to eradicate malaria and tuberculosis. However, gastrointestinal diseases such as typhoid, dysentery, and cholera remain prevalent. One of the problems yet to be overcome is the lack of potable water for residents; in 1990, only 31% had access to safe water. Another serious health problem is drug addiction, exacerbated by the easy availability and low cost of opium. Under a drug abuse control program financed by the US and the UN, a new 300-bed hospital for addicts was opened in 1982 at Thayetmyo, along the Irrawaddy in central Myanmar; smaller facilities have been established in two dozen other towns.

The infant mortality rate dropped from 129.9 deaths per 1,000 live births in 1960 to about 65 in 1990, while average life expectancy rose to 61 years in 1990. In the same year, only 48% of the population had access to health care services.

42HOUSING
Prewar housing in Myanmar compared favorably with that in other Southeast Asian nations, but housing conditions have deteriorated. As of 1983, only 25% of the population had access to safe water. Urban dwellings are overcrowded and often unsafe. In the same year, 54% of all housing units were built of wood and bamboo, 26% were thatch and bamboo, 15% were wooden, 2% were made from pucca, and 1% from semi-pucca.

43EDUCATION
Education is free, and primary education is compulsory for five years. Generally, Burmese is the language of instruction, and English is taught in the secondary schools; as of 1982, however, English became the medium of instruction in the universities.

The system of education initiated by the Ne Win government in 1964 equates learning with livelihood. At that time, the government announced its intention of opening at least one agrarian high school and one technical high school in each district. By 1967 there were six agricultural high schools, seven industrial trade schools, and one technical high school in the country, and the government had taken over about 880 private schools. In 1989, Myanmar had 31,496 primary schools with 137,320 teachers and 4,848,158 students. Secondary schools had 62,856 teachers and 1,127,400 students. Primary education lasts for five years followed by four years of secondary education at the first stage and two years at the second stage. Postsecondary institutions, including 18 teacher-training colleges, 6 agricultural institutes, 8 technical institutes, and 35 universities and colleges, enrolled a total of 203,381 students with 9,028 teaching staff in 1987. The Arts and Science Universities at Yangon (Rangoon) and Mandalay together enrolled about 19,500 students in the mid-1980s.

The Mass Education Council has attempted to increase literacy through special programs. The 1990 adult literacy rate was estimated at 80.6% (males: 89.1% and females: 72.3%).

44LIBRARIES AND MUSEUMS
The National Library in Yangon (Rangoon), founded in 1952, contains over 49,000 volumes. Other large libraries are the Arts and Science University Library in Mandalay, with 110,000 volumes, and the Universities' Central Library (formerly the University Library of Rangoon), with 350,000 volumes. There are also several small college libraries, as well as state libraries and museums at Pathein (Bassein), Kyaukpyu, Mandalay, and Mawlamyine (Moulmein). The National Museum of Art and Archaeology in Yangon was founded in 1952 and includes among its collection a replica of King Mindon's Mandalay Palace. There are three other state museums. Sometimes called the "land of golden pagodas," Myanmar also has thousands of Buddhist temples, many of which have been repaired and restored.

45MEDIA
The director-general of posts and telegraphs controls the telephone, telegraph, radio, and postal communications systems. In 1991 there were an estimated 80,568 telephones in use; internal communication is mainly by wireless. A satellite communications station that began operating in 1979 links Myanmar with more than 100 countries. The government provides the only radio and television transmissions through Radio Myanmar and TV–Myanmar (which broadcasts in color). As of 1991, there were 3,500,000 radios and 80,000 TV sets.

The government professes to uphold freedom of the press, but there are no privately owned newspapers, and the print media are government-controlled. In 1963, the government established its own press agency, the News Agency of Burma, with a monopoly on internal news distribution. Chinese- and Indian-language newspapers are not allowed by the government, but two daily papers are still published in English. Leading newspapers in 1991 included the *Loketha Phithu Nayzin,* 330,000 circulation (published in English as *Working People's Daily,* 16,000). There are some privately published magazines, but none has a high circulation or major influence.

46ORGANIZATIONS
Although Myanmar has most common types of educational, religious, cultural, and social organizations, those associated with capitalist economic activity have all but disappeared. The Rotary Clubs were forced by the government to disband in late 1975, as were numerous other Western-style organizations before them. In 1988/89 there were 20,594 cooperative and producers' societies, as well as substantial numbers of consumer cooperatives.

47TOURISM, TRAVEL, AND RECREATION
Since the inception of military rule in 1988, tourism has declined sharply, from 41,904 visitors in 1987 to 8,061 in 1991. Principal attractions include the palaces and Buddhist temples and shrines in the two largest cities and in the ancient city of Pagan. A visitor to Myanmar must have a passport, visa, and certificate of yellow fever inoculation if arriving from an infected area.

48FAMOUS MYANMA
Anawrahta, who founded the early Burmese kingdom of Pagan in 1044 and established Hinayana Buddhism as the official religion, is a great figure in Burmese history, as are the Toungoo warrior-king Bayinnaung (r.1551–81) and Alaungpaya (r.1752–60), who established the dynasty that ruled Myanmar until 1886. Great writers of the Burmese past include Bhikkhu Ratthasara, author of the poem *Hatthipala Pyo,* on the life of Gautama Buddha; Nawedegyi and Natshinnaung, poets of the Toungoo dynasties; and Binnyadala, who wrote of the long struggles of the Burmese king of Ava. In more recent times, U Ba Nyan and U Ba Zaw, well-known painters of the 1920s, introduced Western-style art into Myanmar; both died in the 1940s.

U Nu (Thakin Nu, b.1907) was independent Myanmar's first premier (1948–62) and shares fame as founder of modern Myanmar with Aung San (1916–47), called the Father of the Burmese Revolution. Ne Win (Maung Shu Maung, b.1911) became premier in March 1962 and was president from 1974 to 1981. U Thant (1909–74) served as UN secretary-general from 1961 through 1971.

49DEPENDENCIES
Myanmar has no territories or colonies.

50BIBLIOGRAPHY
American University. *Burma: A Country Study.* Washington, D.C.: Government Printing Office, 1983.
Aung-Thwin, Michael. *Pagan: The Origins of Modern Burma.*

Athens: Ohio University Press, 1985.

Cady, John Frank. *The United States and Burma*. Cambridge, Mass.: Harvard University Press, 1976.

Harvey, Godfrey Eric. *History of Burma*. New York: Octagon, 1967.

Herbert, Patricia M. *Burma*. Santa Barbara, Calif.: Clio Press, 1991.

Lehman, F. K. (ed.). *Military Rule in Burma since 1962*. Singapore: Maruzen Asia, 1981.

Maung, Mya. *The Burma Road to Poverty*. New York: Praeger, 1991.

Nash, Manning. *The Golden Road to Modernity*. Chicago: University of Chicago Press, 1973.

Nu, U. *Burma under the Japanese*. New York: St. Martin's, 1954.

———. *Saturday's Son*. New Haven, Conn.: Yale University Press, 1975.

Orwell, George. *Burmese Days*. New York: Harcourt, Brace, 1935.

Silverstein, Josef. *Burmese Politics: The Dilemma of National Unity*. New Brunswick, N.J.: Rutgers University Press, 1980.

———. *The Political Legacy of Aung San*. Ithaca, N.Y.: Cornell University, 1993.

Steinberg, David J. *Burma's Road toward Development: Growth and Ideology under Military Rule*. Boulder, Colo.: Westview, 1981.

———. *The Future of Burma: Crisis and Choice in Myanmar*. New York: Asia Society, 1990.

Taylor, Robert (ed.). *Marxism and Resistance in Burma, 1942–1945*. Athens: Ohio University Press, 1984.

———. *The State in Burma*. London: Hurst, 1987.

Than Tun. *Essays on the History and Buddhism of Burma*. Whiting Bay, Isle of Arran, Scotland: Kiscadale Publications, 1988.

NAURU

Republic of Nauru

CAPITAL: There is no formal capital. The seat of government is in the district of Yaren.

FLAG: The flag has a blue background divided horizontally by a narrow gold band, symbolizing the equator. Below the band is a white 12-pointed star, representing the island's 12 traditional tribes.

ANTHEM: *Nauru Ubwema (Nauru, Our Homeland).*

MONETARY UNIT: The Australian dollar (A$) of 100 cents is the legal currency. A$1 = US$0.7008 (or US$1 = A$1.4269).

WEIGHTS AND MEASURES: Imperial weights and measures are used.

HOLIDAYS: New Year's Day, 1 January; Independence Day, 31 January; Angam Day, 26 October (a celebration of the day on which the population of Nauru reached the pre-World War II level); Christmas Day, 25 December; and Boxing Day, 26 December.

TIME: 11:30 PM = noon GMT.

¹LOCATION, SIZE, AND EXTENT

Situated in the western Pacific, Nauru is the world's smallest independent nation, with an area of 21.0 sq km (8.1 sq mi), extending 5.6 km (3.5 mi) NNE–SSW and 4 km (2.5 mi) ESE–WNW. Comparatively, the area occupied by Nauru is about one-tenth the size of Washington, D.C. It lies between two island groups, the Solomons and the Gilberts, 53 km (33 mi) S of the Equator and 3,930 km (2,442 mi) NNE of Sydney; its nearest neighbor is Banaba (formerly Ocean Island, now part of Kiribati), situated 305 km (190 mi) to the E. Nauru has a coastline of 30 km (18.6 mi).

²TOPOGRAPHY

Nauru, one of the largest phosphate-rock islands in the Pacific, is oval-shaped and fringed by a wide coral reef. It has no natural harbor or anchorage. A relatively fertile belt varying in width from 150 to 300 m (490–980 ft) encircles the island. From this belt a coral cliff rises to a central plateau about 60 m (200 ft) above sea level. Buada Lagoon, a permanent, often brackish lake, covers some 120 ha (300 acres) in the southeastern end of the plateau. Apart from some brackish ponds and an underground lake, the nation's water supply is provided by rainfall.

³CLIMATE

Nauru has a dry season, marked by easterly trade winds, and a wet season with westerly monsoons extending from November to February. The average annual rainfall is about 45 cm (18 in), but the amount varies greatly from year to year, and long droughts have been a recurrent problem. Temperatures remain steady, between 24° and 33°C (75–91°F) the year round, and relative humidity is also constant at about 80%.

⁴FLORA AND FAUNA

The plateau area contains large phosphate deposits that almost completely inhibit any natural growth useful for subsistence or commerce. Large areas of scrub and creeper, with occasional coconut and tamanu trees, grow in this region. On the coastal belt, coconut palms and pandanus (a type of screw pine) thrive. Some hibiscus, frangipani, and other tropical flowers grow, but they do not abound here as on other Pacific islands. Bird life is not plentiful, although noddies, terns, and frigate birds frequent the island. There are no indigenous land animals; however, hogs and poultry were introduced many years ago. Fish life is abundant in the seas encircling Nauru, and good catches of tuna and bonito are taken.

⁵ENVIRONMENT

Nauru's phosphate mining industry has done significant damage to the land. In 1987, the Nauruan government began to investigate the nation's mining operations with the goal of developing a plan to regenerate the land and replace lost vegetation. Land in the coastal region however, has not been affected by the development of the country's mining industry. Vegetation in the coastal areas such as pandanus and coconut palms is plentiful.

⁶POPULATION

The 1991 estimated population was 9,500. The annual population growth rate was estimated at 2.57% in 1985–90. Most Nauruans live around the coastal fringes, in their traditional districts. Most Chinese, as well as immigrants from Kiribati and Tuvalu, are settled in communities near the phosphate works. Nauru has no official capital city; government offices are located on the southwest coast, opposite the airport, in Yaren district.

⁷MIGRATION

Immigration to Nauru is now strictly controlled by the government. Nauruans are free to travel abroad.

⁸ETHNIC GROUPS

The Nauruan people (58% of the population in 1988) are the only indigenous ethnic group on the island. They are of mixed Micronesian, Melanesian, and Polynesian origin and resemble the last strain most closely. Nauruans are traditionally divided into 12 clans or tribes in which descent is matrilineal, although kinship and inheritance rules have some patrilineal features. The 12 clans are Eamwit, Eamwidumwit, Deboe, Eoaru, Emea, Eano, Emangum, Ranibok, Eamwidara, Iruwa, Irutsi (extinct), and Iwi (extinct). Admixtures of Caucasian and Negroid lineage in the

19th century and frequent intermarriage with other Pacific island-ers have changed the present-day features of Nauruans from those of their forebears.

The Caucasians on the island are almost all Australians and New Zealanders employed in administrative or teaching posts or in the phosphate industry. The Chinese and immigrants from Kiribati and Tuvalu originally came to the island as laborers in the phosphate industry, some being accompanied by their families. Filipino contract workers are also present but are not permitted to bring their families.

⁹LANGUAGES

Nauruan, which is distinct from all other Pacific tongues, is the official language. However, English is still commonly used in the schools, in government, and in business transactions. Most Nauruans are bilingual but use Nauruan in everyday life.

¹⁰RELIGIONS

The Nauruans have accepted Christianity since the end of the 19th century. In 1993, the majority of the population was Protestant, with 37.5% Roman Catholics.

¹¹TRANSPORTATION

Transport to and from Nauru has traditionally been by ships calling at the island to unload freight and pick up phosphates for delivery to Australia, New Zealand, and other countries. The public Nauru Pacific Line has a fleet of six ships. The government-owned Air Nauru flies regular air services to the Pacific islands, Taiwan, the Philippines, Hong Kong, Japan, Australia, and New Zealand. In 1985, in an effort to reduce public expenditure as a result of loss of income from phosphates, the government reduced the number of airplanes from seven to two and curtailed the number of routes.

A 19-km (12-mi) paved road encircles the island, accounting for 70% of the road system. Apart from a 3.9-km (2.4-mi) railway (used to carry phosphates), a school bus service, and fewer than 2,000 registered motor vehicles, there is no local transport.

¹²HISTORY

The original settlers are thought to have been castaways who drifted to Nauru from another Pacific island. The first recorded discovery of Nauru by a Westerner was made by Captain John Fearn of the whaling ship Hunter in November 1798. He named the island Pleasant Island. From the 1830s to the 1880s, the Nauruans had a succession of visitors—runaway convicts, deserters from whaling ships, and other men who can be classed as beachcombers. The beachcombers provided the Nauruans with their first real contact with Western civilization and introduced them to firearms and alcohol. They acted as a buffer between two cultures but were often a bad influence on the Nauruans. Several times beachcombers and Nauruans attempted to cut off and capture visiting ships, so that eventually Nauru came to be avoided as a watering place by ships whaling in the area. The advent of firearms also disturbed the balance of power between the tribes on the island; sporadic tribal warfare culminated in a 10-year civil war from 1878 to 1888 that reduced the native population to less than 1,000.

The British and German imperial governments agreed to the partition of the Western Pacific in 1886. Their purely arbitrary line of demarcation left Nauru in the German sphere of influence quite accidentally. It was not until 1888, on the petition of the beachcombers-turned-traders, that the German government annexed Nauru as a protectorate and disarmed the people. Christian missionaries arrived in 1899 and had a greater impact on the Nauruan culture than did the German administration.

In 1901, Sir Albert Ellis, a New Zealand geologist, discovered that there were large deposits of phosphate on both Nauru and Banaba (then called Ocean Island). Phosphate mining on Nauru began in 1907, after the German government had granted a concession to the British-owned Pacific Phosphate Co. Laborers from the German Caroline Islands were hired because the Nauruans had no interest in working in the mines.

Nauru was occupied by the Australian Expeditionary Force in 1914, and phosphate continued to be shipped all through World War I. In 1919, Nauru was made a League of Nations mandate of the British Empire, and the governments of Australia, New Zealand, and the UK agreed to administer the island jointly through an administrator to be appointed by Australia. At the same time the three governments obtained the mandate, they jointly purchased the Pacific Phosphate Co.'s rights to Nauruan phosphate for UK£3.5 million and began to work the deposits through a three-man board called the British Phosphate Commissioners (BPC).

The phosphate industry expanded greatly in the years between the wars. Australian and New Zealand farmers enjoyed substantial savings, for Nauru phosphate was sold at a much lower price than phosphate from other countries. As for the Nauruans, with their small royalty of eightpence a ton in 1939, they opted out of the industry completely and turned to their own culture for sustenance.

War came to Nauru in December 1940, when the island was shelled by a roving German raider, and four phosphate ships were sunk. Nauru was flattened by Japanese bombings beginning in December 1941, and all its industrial plant and housing facilities were destroyed. The Japanese occupied the island from August 1942 until the end of the war three years later. They deported 1,200 Nauruans to build an airstrip on Truk, a small atoll about 1,600 km (1,000 mi) northwest of Nauru, and many died there. Australian forces reoccupied Nauru in September 1945, and the surviving Truk Nauruans, who had been reduced in number to only 737, were repatriated in January 1946. Nauru's population thus fell from 1,848 in 1940 to 1,369 in 1946.

The three mandatory governments placed the mandate of Nauru before the UN. On 1 November 1947, the UN approved an agreement by which the island became a trust territory administered jointly by Australia, New Zealand, and the UK, who were to share the task of developing self-government on the island. The Nauruans had had a Council of Chiefs to represent them since 1927, but this body had advisory powers only. Dissatisfied Nauruans made a number of complaints to the administering authority and to the UN Trusteeship Council, with the result that a Nauruan local government council was established by the election of nine council members in December 1951. Since control of the council was exercised by the administrator, however, the Nauruans continued to press for further political power. They asked for positions of importance in the administration and an increase in royalty payments, and expressed concern about the future of the island because the increased rate of phosphate exportation would, it was feared, exhaust the deposits by the end of the century. By constant negotiations, the Nauruans forced the BPC to pay royalties on a rights rather than needs basis, and with the establishment of a world price in 1964, phosphate royalties were raised. The Nauruans achieved control of the industry in 1967 by purchasing the plant and machinery owned by the BPC, and in 1970 they took over the industry completely.

Meanwhile, in 1964, Australia had attempted to resettle the Nauruans on Curtis Island, off the coast of Queensland. The Nauruans, although in principle not averse to resettlement, refused it because of political considerations. They wanted to own their island and to maintain their identity by political independence. Australia would not agree to this, and the plan collapsed. This failure reinforced the Nauruans' desire for political independence. With the support of the Trusteeship Council, they established an elected Legislative Council in 1966. Although Australia wished to maintain control of defense and external affairs, the Nauruans insisted on complete self-determination. Thus, on 31 January 1968, the twenty-second anniversary of the return of the Nauruan survivors from Truk, Nauru became the smallest independent republic in the world. Since that time, Nauru has pursued a policy of isolation and nonalignment, although it does have a role in Commonwealth affairs. In October 1982, Queen Elizabeth II visited the island, the first British monarch to do so. Nauru established diplomatic ties with the former Soviet Union in 1988. Nauru filed a claim in 1989 for compensation from Australia at the International Court of Justice for the loss of nearly all its topsoil from phosphate mining during the League of Nations mandate and the UN trusteeship. In July 1992 Nauru hosted the 24th South Pacific Forum heads of government meeting, which focused on environmental issues, among other issues stating its opposition to nuclear testing in the area. Nauru's first president Hammer DeRoburt died on 15 July 1992 in Melbourne, Australia. Australia agreed to pay A$107,000,000 (about US$73,000,000) in August 1993 to settle the loss of topsoil case.

13GOVERNMENT

The constitution of the Republic of Nauru, adopted at the time of independence and subsequently amended, provides that the republic shall have a parliamentary type of government. It contains provisions for the protection of fundamental rights and freedoms—a subject of particular importance because many of the inhabitants are short-term migrants ineligible for citizenship (defined in the constitution as being restricted to those of Nauruan or of Nauruan and Pacific islander parentage). Legislative power is vested in the Parliament, composed of 18 members elected for a three-year term by Nauruan citizens who have attained the age of 20 years. Seven of the eight constituencies (representing 10 out of 14 districts) return two members each, and the constituency of Ubenide (representing 4 districts) returns four members. The first woman was elected in 1986.

Executive power is exercised by the president, who also fulfills the residual duties of head of state; he is elected by Parliament and is assisted by a cabinet, which he appoints. Hammer DeRoburt became president at independence in 1968 and was reelected in 1971 and 1973. He was defeated for reelection after the legislative voting in 1976, and Bernard Dowiyogo was chosen to succeed him as president. After DeRoburt's supporters forced Dowiyogo's resignation in 1978, DeRoburt again became president. He was reelected in 1980 and in 1983; after the 1983 victory, he persuaded his opponent Dowiyogo to become a cabinet member. In 1986, DeRoburt resigned in protest over opposition to his budget and was replaced by Kennan Adeang; however, DeRoburt's supporters quickly forced Adeang to resign, and DeRoburt was elected again. Because he did not have a clear majority, he called for a new election in 1987 and was reelected decisively. A vote of no confidence forced DeRoburt to resign in August 1989. He was replaced by Kenas Aroi, who then resigned in December 1989 for reasons of ill-health. The December 1989 general election resulted in Bernard Dowiyogo's election to the Presidency. He was re-elected President for a second three year term in November 1992. In June 1992 Nauru signed both the Climate Change and Biodiversity Conventions at the United Nations Conference on Environment and Development.

14POLITICAL PARTIES

After DeRoburt's reelection in 1987, Kennan Adeang formed the Democratic Party of Nauru, which aims to curb the power of the presidency. Eight members of Parliament joined the party. It remains the only political party in Nauru.

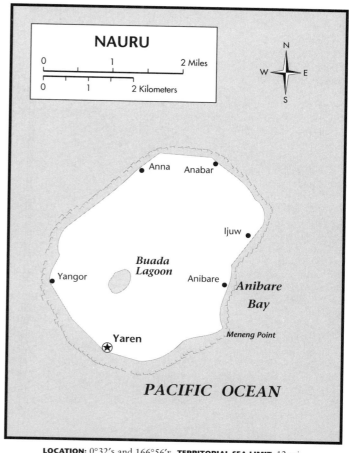

LOCATION: 0°32′s and 166°56′E. TERRITORIAL SEA LIMIT: 12 mi.

15LOCAL GOVERNMENT

The Nauru Island Council (NIC) is elected from the same constituencies as is the Parliament, except that seven of the eight constituencies return one member, and the constituency of Ubenide returns two members, making nine in all. The council elects a chairman, treasurer, and secretary. It holds its sessions in the Domaneab, a Nauruan meetinghouse. It acts as the local government and is responsible for public services. Many members of Parliament also serve as councilors.

16JUDICIAL SYSTEM

The constitution provides for a Supreme Court, with a chief justice presiding. Cases are also heard in the District Court or Family Court. The Supreme Court, which has original and appellate jurisdiction, is the supreme authority on the interpretation of the constitution. Cases may be appealed further to the High Court of Australia.

The judiciary is independent of the executive. The Constitution guarantees protection of fundamental human rights which in practice are generally respected.

17ARMED FORCES

Nauru has no armed forces. Although there is no formal agreement, Australia ensures its defense.

18INTERNATIONAL COOPERATION

Although Nauru does not belong to the UN, it does participate in ESCAP, ICAO, ITU, and UPU. The nation belongs to the South Pacific Commission and South Pacific Forum and is a special member of the Commonwealth of Nations, taking part in some

Commonwealth functions but not represented at heads-of-government conferences. Nauru has signed the Law of the Sea.

19ECONOMY

The economy of Nauru has long been dependent on phosphates. Almost three-fifths of the original deposits of over 96 tons have been extracted and exported, and estimates in the mid-1980s were that the deposits would be exhausted by about 1995. However, reduced demand from Australia in recent years has extended the projected date of depletion to the early 2000s. Revenue from phosphates has been used to diversify the island's economy, mainly through overseas investment and the development of a national airline and shipping line. Between 1983 and 1986, the gross revenue from the phosphate industry fell by 25%, causing great stress on the nation's economy. By 1987, an estimated us$450 million had been set aside to support the country after the phosphates run out.

Aside from phosphates, Nauru has few domestic resources, and many food products and virtually all consumer manufactures are imported. The government subsidizes imports so that food and other necessities are available at nominal cost. Nauru's economy is currently very weak and increasingly dependent on Australia. Offshore financial operations were begun in 1993, but the economy suffered in that year due to a major financial scandal.

20INCOME

The GNP of Nauru was estimated to be $90 million in 1989. The national product per capita was estimated to be $10,000. Revenues come from the export of phosphates, the reserves of which are expected to be exhausted by the year 2000. Phosphates have given Nauruans one of the highest per capita incomes in the Third World.

21LABOR

In the mid-1980s, about 1,200 workers were employed in the state-owned phosphate industry; about 1,000 others were employed by the government and the Nauru Cooperative Society. As of the early 1990s, about half of the over 9,000 inhabitants relied on the phosphate industry for their means of support. Only about 1% of employment is in the private sector. As of 1992, there were some 3,000 guest workers in Nauru, mostly from Vanuatu or Kiribati. The only trade unions are the Nauruan Workers' Organization and the Phosphate Workers' Organization.

22AGRICULTURE

Since the cultivated area is limited to about 200–240 ha (500–600 acres), there is little commercial agriculture. The main crop is coconuts; in 1992, production amounted to 2,000 tons. Some vegetables are grown, mainly by the Chinese population.

23ANIMAL HUSBANDRY

Pigs and chickens roam uncontrolled on the island; hence, there is no organized production. In 1992, there were an estimated 3,000 pigs.

24FISHING

There is as yet no organized fishing industry on Nauru, although the government plans to develop fishing facilities. The Nauru Fishing Corp., formed in 1979, is owned by the Local Government Council. Fish are plentiful and consumption is high, since almost all meat has to be imported from Australia. The total catch in 1991 was 190 tons.

25FORESTRY

There are no forests on Nauru, and all building timber has to be imported.

26MINING

Nauru's only natural resource is high-grade phosphate rock, which is exported to New Zealand, Australia, the Philippines, and South Korea. The government-owned Nauru Phosphate Corp. is the country's primary producer, employer, and exporter. Extraction is done mainly by mechanical shovels from between the coral pinnacles. Phosphate rock is trucked to a central storage pile and transported to storage hoppers by rail. After being crushed and dried, the rock is placed on conveyor belts to pass to the arm of two cantilevers, each about 60 m (200 ft) long, that project out over the reef to waiting ships. As of 1990, over 61 million tons of phosphate had been mined with about 926,000 tons exported in 1990. Phosphate rock reserves are expected to be depleted by the early 2000s, at which time the viability of the entire economy will be challenged.

27ENERGY AND POWER

Power requirements on the island are met by a diesel oil generator to which nearly all buildings are connected. In 1991, net installed electrical power capacity was 10,000 kw; production was 29 million kwh.

28INDUSTRY

The phosphate industry is the only industry on the island. It is under the control of the Nauru Phosphate Corp., a statutory corporation that is responsible to the president of the republic in his capacity as minister for island development and industry. About three-fourths of the profit from phosphate sales is invested in long-term trust funds that have been established to take care of the Nauruans after phosphate deposits are depleted.

29SCIENCE AND TECHNOLOGY

Nauru has little advanced technology, and Nauruans must travel abroad, usually to Australia, for scientific training.

30DOMESTIC TRADE

The Nauru Cooperative Society conducts most of the nation's retail trade. The island is completely dependent on imported goods; foodstuffs come mainly from Australia.

31FOREIGN TRADE

Nauru's only export is phosphate rock, with about three-quarters of it going to Australia, New Zealand, and Japan. The value of exports fluctuates as world phosphate prices rise or decline. Imports consist mostly of machinery and construction materials for the phosphate industry and food, water, fuel, and other necessities. About half of the imports come from Australia, and almost all the rest from New Zealand, the UK, and Japan. Virtually all manufactured goods must be imported.

32BALANCE OF PAYMENTS

Nauru has a strongly favorable balance of trade, and investments abroad are substantial.

33BANKING AND SECURITIES

The government-owned Bank of Nauru was founded in 1976. The Commonwealth Savings Bank of Australia and the Bank of New South Wales have branches in Nauru. The only commercial bank in the country is the Jefferson Bank and Trust Co. (1980). Most of the income from phosphates is invested in long-term funds overseas. There is no stock exchange.

34INSURANCE

The Nauru Insurance Corp., founded in 1974, is the only licensed insurer and reinsurer on the island. It underwrites all classes of insurance, including aviation and marine.

35 PUBLIC FINANCE

Administrative costs in Nauru are met from the proceeds of phosphate sales, which are in decline as reserves approach exhaustion. In 1993, the governments of Nauru and Australia reached a US$73 million out-of-court settlement as restitution for Nauruan lands ruined by Australian phosphate mining. This payment may assist the government (which relies almost entirely on phosphate receipts for revenue) in facilitating economic diversification. The fiscal year extends from 1 July to 30 June.

36 TAXATION

There is no income or other tax in Nauru, although Parliament has power to impose taxes.

37 CUSTOMS AND DUTIES

Duties are payable only on imported cigarettes, tobacco, and alcoholic beverages.

38 FOREIGN INVESTMENT

Apart from the investment in the phosphate industry, now owned by the government of Nauru, there has been little investment on the island. The government of Nauru has large investments overseas in long-term funds financed from phosphate royalties. Nauru also has invested in commercial property development, notably a 53-story office building in Melbourne.

In 1982, Nauru agreed to invest about US$80 million in a fertilizer plant in India. Plans were approved in 1985 to build an industrial, commercial, and residential complex in Honolulu and, with the help of Japanese companies, a 19-story, 450-room hotel on Guam.

39 ECONOMIC DEVELOPMENT

Government policy is to exploit the phosphate deposits to the fullest extent for the highest returns. The government has diversified into aviation and shipping and plans to develop fishing and tourism. It has acquired the Grand Pacific Hotel on the Fijian Island of Suva and, in 1993, began work on a F$18 million renovation of the facility. In 1993, Australia agreed to provide US$73 million in compensation for pre-independence mining of phosphate to aid in restoring the extensive areas damaged by it.

40 SOCIAL DEVELOPMENT

Medical, dental, and hospital treatment and education are free. Other benefits—old age and disability pensions, widows' and sickness benefits, and child endowment—are administered by the Local Government Council.

The Constitution guarantees women equal rights with men, although traditional social values still discourage many from pursuing careers. In particular, women face great social pressure to marry and raise families because Nauru's population was decimated in World War II due to massive removals by the Japanese.

41 HEALTH

Tuberculosis, leprosy, diabetes, and vitamin deficiencies have been the main health problems, but with modern facilities and treatments, all these diseases have been brought under control. Cardiovascular disease has also been a major cause of illness and death.

There are two modern hospitals, with a total of 207 beds, and 10 doctors. One hospital serves phosphate industry employees; the other provides free medical treatment for the rest of the population. Patients who need specialized care are flown to Australia. In 1990, the infant mortality rate was estimated at 25 per 1,000 live births. The country's 1993 population was 10,000.

42 HOUSING

Ownership of houses built for Nauruans under a housing scheme is vested in the Local Government Council, but some Nauruan homes are privately owned. Nearly all houses have electricity, and newer homes have a greater number of amenities.

43 EDUCATION

Attendance at school is compulsory for Nauruan children from 6 to 16 years old. Two types of schools are available, both coeducational: those run by the government and those conducted by the Roman Catholic Church. Education is provided free by the government. Education on Nauru is up to intermediate standard; higher education overseas, mainly in Australia, is assisted by the government in the form of competitive scholarships. There is also a university extension center affiliated to the University of the South Pacific. In 1985 there were 1,451 students in seven government primary schools and 465 students in two secondary schools, with 142 teachers in all.

44 LIBRARIES AND MUSEUMS

Nauru has one small lending library but no museums.

45 MEDIA

Most newspapers are imported, but the government publishes in Nauruan and English the weekly *Nauru Post* and fortnightly *Bulletin*, which report local news. Communication with the outside world is maintained by a ground satellite station established in 1975, providing 24-hour telephone, telegraph, and telex services worldwide. A small telephone exchange, handling 2,000 telephones in 1989, provides on-island communication. A satellite earth station was commissioned in 1990. Government-owned Radio Nauru broadcasts in English and Nauruan; there were some 5,500 radios on the island in 1984. In 1989 there were three cinemas.

46 ORGANIZATIONS

The Boy Scouts, Girl Guides, and similar organizations function on the island. One community group and several Nauruan district organizations are also active.

47 TOURISM, TRAVEL, AND RECREATION

With its sandy beach, coral reef, tropical climate, and sea breezes, Nauru has the potential for the development of tourism. Visas are required for entry, but inoculations are not mandatory.

48 FAMOUS NAURUANS

The best-known Nauruan is its first president, Hammer DeRoburt (b.1923), who led the Nauruan people to political independence; he was president from 1968 to 1976 and again from 1978 until his death in 1992 (except for a brief period in 1986).

49 DEPENDENCIES

Nauru has no territories or colonies.

50 BIBLIOGRAPHY

American University. *Area Handbook for Oceania*. Washington, D.C.: Government Printing Office, 1984.

Baker, Mark. "The Dying Island." Melbourne: The Age Saturday Extra, February 28, 1987.

Carter, John (ed.). Pacific Islands Year Book. (15th ed.) Sydney: Pacific Publications, 1984.

Ellis, A. F. *Ocean Island and Nauru*. Sydney: Angus & Robertson, 1935.

Oliver, Douglas. *The Pacific Islands*. Garden Dity, NY: Doubleday, 1961.

Osborne, Charles, ed. *Australia, New Zealand and the South Pacific: A Handbook*. New York: Praeger, 1970.

Petit-Skinner, Solange. *The Nauruans*. San Francisco: Macduff Press, 1981.

Skinner, Carlton. *Actualities in the Pacific: Micronesia: Nauru, the Remarkable Community.* Santa Cruz: Center for South Pacific Studies, University of California, 1977.

Trumbull, Robert. "World's Richest Little Isle." *New York Times Magazine,* March 7, 1982.

Viviane, Nancy. *Naura: Phosphate and Political Progress.* Canberra: Australian National University Press, 1970.

Weeramantry, C. G. *Nauru: Environmental Damage under International Trusteeship.* New York: Oxford University Press, 1992.

Williams, Maslyn. *Three Islands.* Melbourne: British Phosphate Commissioners, 1971.

Williams, Maslyn and Barrie Macdonald. *The Phosphateers.* Melbourne: Melbourne University Press, 1985.

NEPAL

Kingdom of Nepal
Nepal Adhirajya

CAPITAL: Kāthmāndu.

FLAG: The national flag consists of two red adjoining triangles, outlined in blue and merging at the center; the points are at the fly. On the upper triangle, in white, is a symbolic representation of the moon; on the lower triangle, that of the sun.

ANTHEM: The national anthem begins "May His Majesty, solemn and supremely valiant, be prosperous forever."

MONETARY UNIT: The Nepalese rupee (NR) is a paper currency of 100 paisa. There are coins of 1, 2, 5, 10, 20, 25, and 50 paisa and 1, 2, 5, 10, 20, 25, 50, and 100 rupees, and notes of 1, 2, 5, 10, 20, 50, 100, 500, and 1,000 Nepalese rupees. NR1 = $0.0203 (or $1 = NR49.240).

WEIGHTS AND MEASURES: The metric system is in use, but some traditional Indian standards are also employed.

HOLIDAYS: National Unity Day, 11 January; Martyrs' Day, 30 January; Rashtriya Prajatantra Divas—National Democracy Day, 18 February; Nepalese Women's Day, 8 March; Navabarsha—Nepalese New Year's Day, mid-April; UN Day, 24 October; Queen Aishworya's Birthday, 7 November; Constitution Day, 9 November; National Day (King Birendra's Birthday), 28 December. Hindu and Buddhist religious holidays are based on the lunisolar calendar. Saturday is the general day of rest.

TIME: 5:45 PM = noon GMT.

¹LOCATION, SIZE, AND EXTENT

A comparatively narrow strip of territory dividing India from China, landlocked Nepal has an area of about 140,800 sq km (54,363 sq mi), extending 885 km (550 mi) SE–NW and 201 km (125 mi) NE–SW. Comparatively, the area occupied by Nepal is slightly larger than the state of Arkansas. In its length lie some 800 km (500 mi) of the Himalayan mountain chain. Nepal is bounded on the N by China and on the E, S, and W by India, with a total boundary length of 2,926 km (1,818 mi). Nepal's capital city, Kāthmāndu, is located in the central part of the country.

²TOPOGRAPHY

Nepal is made up of three strikingly contrasted areas. Southern Nepal has much of the character of the great plains of India, from which it extends. Known as the Terai, this region comprises both cultivable land and dense jungle, the latter being for the most part a game preserve inhabited by the wild elephant, tiger, and other typically South Asian fauna. Besides being a hunting ground, the forests are worked for their valuable timber. The Terai contains about one-third of Nepal's population and makes up about one-fourth of the total area. The second and by far the largest part of Nepal is formed by the Mahabharat, Churia, and Himalayan mountain ranges, extending from east to west. Their altitude increases toward the north, culminating on the Tibetan border in Mt. Everest (Sagarmatha in Nepali), standing amid other noble peaks. Three principal rivers originate from glaciers and snow-fed lakes, break southward through deep Himalayan gorges, and enter, respectively, the Karnali, Gandak, and Kosi basins. Flowing toward India, they become tributaries (as are all Nepal's rivers) of the Ganges system. The third area is a high central region, some 890 km (344 sq mi) in extent between the main Himalayan and Mahabharat ranges; this region is known as the Kāthmāndu Valley, or the Valley of Nepal. Overlooked by mountains, the valley,

with its fertile soil and temperate climate, supports a thriving agriculture. Here Kāthmāndu, the capital, is situated, with the foothill towns of Bhaktapur and Patan nearby. This is the only region of Nepal that has any considerable population density.

Eight of the world's highest mountains are situated in the Himalaya range on the Tibetan border. Triangulated in 1850, Mt. Everest was officially given the status of the world's highest peak in 1859. The summit (29,028 ft; 8,848 m) was reached for the first time on 29 May 1953 by Sir Edmund Hillary, a New Zealander, and Tenzing Norgay, a Sherpa guide.

³CLIMATE

Below the Kāthmāndu Valley and throughout the Terai, the climate is subtropical and, in the swamps and forests, extremely humid. The valley itself enjoys the temperate conditions generally found between altitudes of 1,200 and 3,400 m (4,000–11,000 ft). At 1,300 m (4,300 ft) above sea level, the elevation of Kāthmāndu, the rainy season lasts from June to October; 80% of annual precipitation falls during this monsoon season. Colder weather follows, lasting until the middle of March, when the warm season begins. The warm season increases in intensity until broken by the rains, which account for precipitation of about 150 cm (60 in) annually. Temperatures in Kāthmāndu in January range from an average minimum of 2°C (36°F) to an average maximum of 18°C (64°F); the July range is 20–29°C (68–84°F). Northward of the Kāthmāndu Valley, a subalpine zone continues to altitudes of about 4,300 m (14,000 ft); above that elevation, the country is covered with snow during the long winter, and extreme cold is experienced in the upper Himalayas.

⁴FLORA AND FAUNA

The wide range of climate accounts for correspondingly marked contrasts in flora and fauna between different regions of the country. In the south, the sal (the wood of which is used for railroad ties), sisu, and other subtropical trees are abundant in forests; in the extreme north, junipers are seen even at the altitude of the glacial moraines. Many kinds of conifers also exist in the alpine zone, along with the yew, various hollies, birch, dwarf rhododendrons, and other alpine flora. At temperate altitudes are found the oak and maple.

Dominant in the Langtang Valley are the chir pine, willow, alder, and evergreen oak. Blue pine and silver fir are frequent in the subalpine zone, which also supports tree rhododendrons—magnificent plants often reaching a growth of 12 m (40 ft). Ground orchids, lilies, yellow and blue poppies, and crimson anemones are prevalent in central Nepal. The profusion of wild flowers extends to very high altitudes; at 5,200 m (17,000 ft), several varieties of primula, pink and white cotoneaster, and white erica have been gathered, along with many kinds of alpine mosses and ferns.

The tiger, hyena, and jackal still exist in southern Nepal, although in decreasing numbers. Rhesus monkeys and a variety of other small jungle mammals and rodents are common. At middle altitudes are found the black bear, several species of cats, squirrel, hare, deer, and antelope. Higher in the mountains, wild sheep and goats, marmots, and a species of tailless mouse-hare are numerous. Small black spiders were found at 6,900 m (22,500 ft) on rocky ledges traversed by the Mt. Everest expedition of 1953. Birds of Nepal include the green finch, dove, woodpecker, nuthatch, warbler, flycatcher, bulbul, and other familiar species. At about 2,700 m (9,000 ft) are found the hill partridge, pheasant, yellow-backed sunbird, minivet, and many of the flowerpeckers; the redstart, pipit, wagtail, snow pigeon, snowcock, and golden eagle thrive in both the alpine and subalpine zones.

⁵ENVIRONMENT

Nepal's environment has suffered the effects of agricultural encroachment, deforestation and consequent soil erosion, and contamination of the water supply. Between the mid-1960s and the late 1970s, forestland declined from 30% to 22% of the total area, mainly because of the felling of timber for firewood, which supplies over 90% of Nepal's fuel requirements. Moreover, it is estimated that erosion causes the loss of about 240 million cu m of topsoil each year. All of Nepal's forests were nationalized in 1957, but reforestation efforts have been minimal. A forest conservation program, begun in 1980, includes the establishment of village tree nurseries, free distribution of seedlings, and provision of wood-burning stoves of increased efficiency. By 1985, however, deforestation averaged 324 sq mi per year, while reforestation was only 4,000 hectares (9,900 acres) per year. The FAO estimates that at the present rate of depletion, the forests will be virtually wiped out by 2015.

Air and water pollution are significant environmental problems in Nepal. According to United Nations sources, the nation produces 18,000 tons of carbon monoxide and 3,300 tons of hydrocarbons per year and contributes 0.1% of the world's total gas emissions. Roughly one-third of the nation's city inhabitants and two-thirds of all rural dwellers do not have pure water. Untreated sewage is a major pollution factor: the nation's cities produce 0.4 million tons of solid waste per year.

In 1994, 22 of Nepal's mammal species and 20 of its bird species were endangered, as well as 33 plant species. Species classified as endangered in Nepal include the snow leopard, tiger, Asian elephant, pygmy hog, great Indian rhinoceros, Assam rabbit, swamp deer, wild yak, chir pheasant, and gavial.

⁶POPULATION

According to the 1991 census, Nepal had a population of 18,462,081, an increase of 22.9% from the 1981 census. The year 2000 population was projected at 24,858,000, assuming a crude birthrate of 34.6 per 1,000 population, a crude death rate of 11.3, and a net natural increase of 23.3 during 1995–2000. The average estimated density in 1991 was 125 persons per sq km (325 per sq mi). Population distribution is uneven, with about 45% of all Nepalese concentrated in the hilly central region, 47% in the fertile Terai plain, and only 8% in the mountains. Only 9.6% of the people lived in urban areas in 1991. Kāthmāndu, the capital, had a 1991 population of 419,073; Biratnāgar (130,129) and Patan (117,203) are the other chief towns.

⁷MIGRATION

Nearly 14,000 Tibetans settled in Nepal following the Chinese annexation of Tibet in 1959. Hundreds of thousands of Nepalese were believed to be working in India in the 1980s, and over 100,000 Indians were working in Nepal, particularly in the garment industry and on the building of highways. Some 86,000 ethnic Nepalese expelled from Bhutan were living in refugee camps at the end of 1993.

⁸ETHNIC GROUPS

Nepal consists of two primary ethnic elements: Mongoloids, who migrated to Nepal by way of Tibet, Sikkim, Assam, and northern Bengal; and Indo-Aryans, who came from the Indian plains and from the sub-Himalayan hill areas to the west of Nepal. There are also small remnants of Dravidian tribes. Bhotes, of Tibetan origin, are the principal occupants of northern Nepal. In the central valley, Newars and Murmis predominate, the former being responsible for most of the agriculture and trade. Less numerous groups include Gurungs and Magars in west-central Nepal and Kirantis and Rai in the east. Sherpas, a Himalayan people, have become well known as guides for mountain-climbing expeditions.

⁹LANGUAGES

Nepali is the official language, although some 16 different languages, of the Indo-Aryan and Tibeto-Burman groups, and 36 principal dialects are spoken. Nepali is the mother tongue of about 58% of the population and is the language for most intertribal communication; it is used in government publications and has been the language of most of the written literature since the Gurkha unification of Nepal. More than 11% of the people speak Maithili as their first language, 7.6% Bhojpuri, 4% Tharu, and about 3% Newari and Tamang each. Except in primary schools, where children are taught in their own language, Nepali is the medium of instruction. English is taught as a second language in secondary schools and colleges and is widely understood in business and government circles.

¹⁰RELIGIONS

Although the royal family is Hindu—as is, nominally, about 90% of the population—Hinduism and Buddhism, the latter practiced by about 5% of the population, exist side by side in Nepal and to some extent are intermingled. The importance of both in the national life is everywhere manifest; more than 2,700 temples and shrines have been counted in the Kāthmāndu Valley alone, while innumerable others are scattered along trails and roads extending to the most distant mountain passes. Bodhnath and Shambunath are famous Buddhist temples. The ancient temple of Chandrahigiri is dedicated to both religions. The Baghmati River, flowing through central Nepal, is considered sacred and is visited by pilgrims, as are certain mountains and lakes. Muslims constitute about 3% of the population. There are also small minorities of Christians, Baha'is, and Jains, amounting to less than 0.1% of the population. The constitution forbids proselytizing.

¹¹TRANSPORTATION

Nepal's ratios of road mileage to area and to population are among the lowest in the world, and the principal means of land

See continental map: **LOCATION:** 26°20′ to 30°16′N; 80°15′ to 88°15′E. **BOUNDARY LENGTHS:** China, 1,078 km (670 mi); India, 1,593 km (990 mi).

transport is by porters with pack animals. The main highways are the 190-km (118-mi) road that penetrates the Kāthmāndu Valley, connecting it with the Indian border; the 87-km (54-mi) road between Kāthmāndu and Kodari on the Tibetan (Chinese) border, which was severely damaged by flooding in late 1982 and was later rebuilt with Chinese assistance; the 862-km (536-mi) east–west Mahendra Highway; and the 200-km (124-mi) Kāthmāndu-Pokhara highway, which is being extended to Surkhet. In all, Nepal had 7,080 km (4,400 mi) of roadway in 1991, of which 37% was paved.

Nepal had a total of 62 km (38 mi) of railways in 1990. A narrow gauge railway, opened in 1927, runs from Jayanagar, in India, to Janakpur, a distance of 52 km (32 mi), of which 10 km (6 mi), running from Raxaul, India, to the frontier town of Birganj, is government owned. An electrically driven ropeway, inaugurated in 1925 and improved with US aid in 1962, carries 25 tons an hour a distance of 43 km (27 mi), to a height of nearly 1,400 m (4,500 ft) from Hetaura to Kāthmāndu.

Much of Nepal is easily accessible only by air. In 1992 there were 37 airfields, of which 5 had permanently surfaced runways. The leading air terminal is Tribhuwan airport at Kāthmāndu, which can handle medium-sized jets. Domestic flights are operated by the Royal Nepal Airlines Corp., which also schedules flights to Great Britain, Germany, India and eight other Asian countries.

12HISTORY

Fact, myth, and legend are intertwined in Nepal's historical literature, which, in the *Vamshavali*, traces the origins of the country in the distant past when Nepal was allegedly founded by Ne-

Muni and derived its name from this source. A reliable chronology can be established only after the conquest of Nepal by Harisinha-deva, rajah of Simraun in about AD 1324. Under the Malla dynasty, Nepal was administered in four separate states: Banepa, Bhadgaon (now Bhaktapur), Kantipur (modern Kāthmāndu), and Lalitpur (now Pātan).

Prithwi Narayan Shah, the ruler of Gorkha, a small principality west of Kāthmāndu, established the modern kingdom of Nepal in AD 1768 by incorporating the Kāthmāndu Valley into his domain and unifying with it many small independent principalities and states. Under his descendants, most of the present boundaries of Nepal were established and Hinduism was introduced from India as the official religion.

Nepal came in contact with the influence of larger powers outside South Asia in the late 18th century as a consequence of the British East India Company's conquest of India to its south and a trade dispute with Tibet that led to a Nepalese confrontation with China. Peace was imposed by China in 1792, after Chinese forces had invaded, then withdrawn from Nepal. In the same year, a commercial treaty was ratified between Britain and Nepal. Relations with British in India remained peaceful until 1814 when a border dispute led to inconclusive hostilities between Nepal and the British East India Company. When the fighting ended two years later, Nepal's independence was preserved in an agreement in which Nepal yielded a large piece of territory to the Company on its southern border and agreed to the establishment of a permanent British resident at Kāthmāndu.

The 1816 agreement (reaffirmed by a formal reaty of friendship between Nepal and Great Britain in 1923) also laid the groundwork for more than a century and a half of amicable relations between Britain and Nepal. Included under the agreement was Nepalese approval for British recruitment of Nepalese Gurkha mercenaries for the British-officered Indian army. During the Indian Mutiny of 1857, Nepal's Rana prime minister sent some 12,000 additional Nepalese troops in support of British garrisons; he also offered troops to US President Abraham Lincoln in 1866 during the US civil war. Over the years, the Gurkha regiments serving in the British Indian army (and after 1947 under both Indian and British flags) won renown for their bravery, skill, and endurance—in Afghanistan in 1879 and Tibet in 1904, in Europe, Asian, and Africa in the 20th century's two world wars, in the UN action in the Belgian Congo in the 1960s, in India's conflicts with China and Pakistan, and in 1982, in Britain's conflict with Argentina over the Falkland Islands.

In 1846, Shumshere Jung Bahadur (Rana) became Nepal's de facto ruler, banishing the king and ruling as regent for the king's minor heir. The prime ministership became a hereditary office in his Rana family, not unlike the Tokugawa Shogunate in Japan, ruling successively until 1951. Following the end of World War II, the termination of British rule on the South Asian subcontinent in 1947 caused deep stirrings of change in Nepal. Resentment grew against the autocratic despotism of the Ranas, who—as regents—had kept successive monarchs virtual prisoners. A political reform movement, begun in 1946 with the founding of the Nepali Congress Party on the model of the Indian Congress Party, won the support of King Tribhuvana Bir Bikram Shah, but in a power struggle in 1950, the king was forced to flee from the Ranas to India. With Indian support, insurgents began operations against the Rana government until, with the mediation of Indian Prime Minister Nehru, a political compromise was reached that returned the king to Kāthmāndu and ended a century of hereditary Rana family rule. By late 1951 a new government took office, headed by Matrika Prasad Koirala, with his brother, a co-founder of the Nepali Congress Party (NC).

1951 to 1994

Political life in Nepal in the years since the restoration of the monarchy in 1951 has been dominated by the struggle between the monarchy and the country's political elements to define the terms under which they will co-exist and bring the country into the modern world. Six different cabinets, each lacking popular support and riddled with dissension, held office in rapid succession between 1951 and 1957, and in 1957-58, King Mahendra Bir Bikram Shah, who had succeeded to the throne upon the death of his father in 1955, ruled directly for a period of months. In April 1959, he promulgated a democratic constitution, providing for a constitutional monarchy, two houses of parliament, and a cabinet and prime minister responsible to the lower house, in the Westminster model. Bisweswar Prasad (B.P.) Koirala of the NC assumed office on 24 July 1959 as first prime minister under this constitution.

Less than 18 months later, on 15 December 1960, the king suspended the constitution, dissolved parliament, dismissed the cabinet, and again established his own government, this time with an appointed council of ministers. He ruled directly until April 1962 when he promulgated a new constitution establishing an indirect, non-party system of rule through a tiered system of panchayats (council) culminating in a National Panchayat. Five years later, after growing agitations and hit-and-run attacks by NC elements based in India, the king—again under Indian pressure—promulgated a series of amendments introducing gradual liberalization.

In January 1972, Mahendra died suddenly and was succeeded by his 27-year-old son, Birendra Bir Bikram Shah Dev. The young monarch, who had attended Harvard University in the United States, was committed to maintaining the authority of the monarchy while keeping Nepal on the course of gradual political and social reform set by his father. Student demonstrations in early 1979 led him to call for a national referendum on whether to continue the panchayat system or create a more conventional multi-party system. With the king promising further liberalization, the existing panchayat system was endorsed by 55% of the voters in May 1980, and later that year, the king's subsequent constitutional amendments established direct elections and permitted the Panchayat, not the king, to choose the prime minister. The king's failure to lift the ban on political parties led party members—ineffectively—to boycott the elections of 1981 in which Surya Bahadur Thapa, a former civil servant who had become prime minister in 1979, was reaffirmed in June 1981 and continued in office until 1983 when he was replaced by Lokendra Bahadur Chand following the government's loss of its majority on an opposition "no confidence" motion.

In non-party elections to the National Panchayat in May 1986, again in the face of a major party boycott, a majority of the incumbents were defeated, and Marich Man Singh Shrestha became prime minister. Most new members were opponents of the panchayat system. foreshadowing a new struggle between the king and his legislators. By early 1990, the NC and the United Leftist Front (ULF), a Communist alliance of seven parties, again went to the streets, organizing agitations that forced the king to make further constitutional changes in April; included were an end to the ban on political parties and their activities. The king dissolved the National Panchayat and appointed NC president Krishna Prasad Bhattarai interim prime minister, who was assisted by a cabinet made up of members of the NC, the ULF, independents, and royal appointees. A Constitutional Reforms Commission produced a new constitution in November 1990 that ended the panchayat era and restored multi-party democracy in a constitutional monarchy. In May 1991, the first openly partisan elections in 32 years were held, resulting in an NC majority in the new House of Representatives which chose Girija Prasad Koirala as prime minister.

Factionalism within the NC and agitation on economic issues by the Communist Party of Nepal (CPN), now called the United Marxist-Leninists (UML), forced a reshuffle of the cabinet in May 1992. But local elections, also in May, reaffirmed the NC hold on the electorate despite rivalries among top party leaders and the absence of progress on reform. The UML continued agitational politics sporadically until reaching an agreement with the NC in August 1993, in the face of several natural disasters, on the handling of several contentious issues.

The Koirala government resigned suddenly on 10 July 1994 when a new outbreak of infighting within the NC led to the defection of 36 MPs. The defection cost the government its majority on a confidence motion of thanks to the king for his annual throne speech outlining government policies. After consulting parliamentary experts, the king dissolved parliament and scheduled national elections for 13 November 1994. The king named Koirala caretaker prime minister on 12 July, but the situation continued tense amid concerns by Koirala's inner-party rivals that Koirala would exploit his position for his own partisan advantage during the run-up to elections.

Nepal's foreign policies have remained generally nonaligned through this 43-year period of political ferment, maintaining friendly relations with China and with India, despite efforts to minimize traditional Indian influence inside its smaller norther neighbor and the occasional clash of policies on matters of relating to trade. Nepal also has pursued friendly relations with the great powers and has been the recipient of economic aid from India, the US, the former USSR, and the World Bank. In 1961, Nepal signed an agreement with China (which had earlier absorbed Tibet) defining the boundary between the two countries along the traditional watershed and Nepal was uninvolved in the 1962 hostilities between India and China on portions of the border to the east and west of Nepal.

13GOVERNMENT

The 1990 constitution, Nepal's third (with variations) since 1951, established a constitutional monarchy in which the legislature consists of the king and two houses of parliament, the lower house called the House of Representatives and the upper house, the National Council. The House of Representatives has 205 members elected to terms of five years; at least 5% of the contestants from every party must be women. The National Council has 60 members, 35 of whom—including 3 women—are elected by the House of Representatives. Suffrage is universal at 18 years of age.

The National Council is a permanent body, retiring one-third of its members every two years in elections that take place in May of even-numbered years. The king appoints 10 of the 60 members in the National Council.

For development purposes, the country is also divided into 5 development regions by geography, i.e. Eastern, Central, Western, Mid-Western, and Far-Western, each of which serve also as a parliamentary constituency, electing three members of the lower house. In 1992, the government undertook a reform of the civil service, lowering the age of retirement from 60 to 58, committing itself to reducing its overall size by 25% by 1993, and engaging in wholesale dismissals of those with 20 or more years of service.

The King is Birendra Bir Bikram Shah Dev, the descendent of an unbroken Rajput line going back to more than 200 years. The prime minister since 29 May 1991 is Girija Prasad Koirala, who continues in office as head of a caretaker government following his loss of a vote of confidence in the parliament in July 1994. Elections were scheduled for 13 November 1994. Had the government not fallen, the constitution would have required the next election to be scheduled not later than May 1996.

14POLITICAL PARTIES

The 1962 constitution originally prohibited the formation of political parties and associations, even though political groups continued to exist and operate underground, at times on a quasi-legal basis. Parties were legalized in 1990 and now operate freely in Nepal's multi-party constitutional monarchy. The main party through Nepal's modern history—providing nearly all of the country's prime ministers even when the ban on parties prohibited party activity—is the Nepali Congress Party (NC). Inspired by the socialist wing of the Indian National Congress and founded by the Koirala brothers, M.P. and B.P., in 1946, the party led Nepal's first democratic government in 1959. Most of its leaders were imprisoned during the 1960s, but with Indian help, the party operated from India, mounting hit-and-run attacks and maintaining an underground presence in Nepal.

The NC leadership led the opposition to King Mahendra's tiered panchayat system of indirect government. Although NC leaders called for a boycott of the May 1986 elections to the National Panchayat, 1,547 candidates ran for office, and only 40 of the previously elected members retained their seats. After these elections, a Democratic Panchayat Forum (DPF) was formed by NC members to mobilize voters on a non-party basis to counter the influence in local elections of the Communist Party of Nepal (CPN), whose members had won 16 seats in the National Panchayat.

In 1991, the NC won 113 seats in the House of Representatives and 18 in the National Council, as well as mayoralty contests in 22 of 36 municipalities and two-thirds of the 1,074 seats at stake in district development committees. Political in-fighting within the NC has been endemic; it was responsible in July 1994 for bringing down the NC government of G.P. Koirala and continued unabated in the anticipation of elections in November 1994.

The communist movement in Nepal has been severely fragmented for years by personal and ideological schisms, some of them occasioned by splits and the loss of orthodoxy in the communist movement worldwide in the 1960s and 1980s. Operating for electoral and agitational purposes in the 1980s as the United Leftist Front (ULF), the Communist Party (CPN) and its several communist allies have since split, fragmenting the movement into a number of splinter parties but leaving the CPN, now reassembled as the United Marxist-Leninists (UML) as the leading opposition party in the parliament, with 69 seats in the House of Representatives and 11 in the National Council. Most of the remaining seats in the lower house are in the hands of minor left/communist parties, including the United People's Front–Nepal (UPF/N), with 9; the Nepal Sadbhavana Party (NSP), with 6; the National Democratic Party (DDP), with 4; and the CPN (Democratic) and the Nepal Peasants and Workers Party, each with 2. The UML won 6 mayoralty contests in 1991.

The government in 1992 lowered the civil service retirement age from 60 to 58 and committed itself to reducing the size of the civil service, dismissing thousands with 20 or more years of service and promising a reduction of 25% overall by 1993.

15LOCAL GOVERNMENT

For centuries, the heads of petty principalities within Nepal exercised local judicial, police, and other powers. Under the panchayat reforms introduced in 1962, the country was divided into 14 zones, which in turn were divided into 75 districts. The zones were directly administered by commissioners appointed by the central government, and the zonal panchayats were executive bodies elected from the 11-member panchayats at the district level, the members of which were in turn selected from village and town panchayats. Each of the 3,600 villages with populations of more than 2,000 and each of the 33 towns with populations over 10,000 also had an 11-member panchayat, as well as its own local assembly.

The country now remains divided into 14 zones (headed by appointed commissioners) and 75 districts (under the charge of district officers responsible for law and order, collecting revenues, and setting development priorities); municipal councils and district development committees are directly elected.

16JUDICIAL SYSTEM

Each district has a court of first instance, civil and criminal, as well as a court of appeals and 14 zonal courts. There are five regional courts—at Kāthmāndu, Dhankuta, Pokhara, Surkhet, and Dipayal—to which further appeals may be taken. At the apex is the Supreme Court in Kāthmāndu, which is empowered to issue writs of habeas corpus and decide on the constitutionality of laws. The Court is composed of a chief justice, assisted usually by six other judges, with seven additional judges in reserve; all are appointed by the king. The Supreme Court is the court of last resort, but the King may grant pardons and suspend, commute or remit sentences of any court. There are separate military courts which generally deal only with military personnel. In 1992, the Supreme Court ruled that civilians may not be tried in the military courts.

The 1990 Constitution declared the independence of the judiciary. The Supreme Court has exercised considerable independence in practice, declaring provisions of the Citizenship Act of 1991 and parts of the Labor Act of 1992 unconstitutional.

The 1990 Constitution affords a number of procedural safeguards for criminal defendants including the right to counsel and protection from double jeopardy and from retroactive application of laws.

17ARMED FORCES

Nepal maintains a small standing army which is adequate to its main role of backing civil authority within the country and providing occasional contingents for international peacekeeping units, like UNIFIL in Lebanon in the 1980s and the UNEF in Sinai in the 1970s. The force is predominantly made up of hardy hill people, generally known as gurkhas, who account for most of the 35,000 regulars organized in 8 brigades; they also predominate in the police force of 28,000. The army maintains 11 air transports and helicopters. In 1992, Nepal spent an estimated $34 million on defense or 2 percent of gross domestic product.

Under separate treaty arrangements going back to 1816, gurkhas of the same mountain stock (especially Magars, Gurungs, Rais, and Limpus) are recruited in Nepal by Great Britain and, since 1947, by the Republic of India. Under British and Indian flags, and with arms, training, and officers provided by their foreign recruiters, gurkhas are among the world's most renowned fighting men with extensive service in all parts of the globe in both world wars and several UN actions of this century.

[18]INTERNATIONAL COOPERATION

Nepal was admitted to UN membership on 14 December 1955 and is a member of ESCAP and all the UN nonregional specialized agencies except IAEA and WIPO. It also belongs to the Asian Development Bank and G-77, and is a signatory to the Law of the Sea. Nepal joined the Colombo Plan group in 1952. In 1985, Nepal joined with six other Asian nations to form the South Asian Association for Regional Cooperation (SAARC); the secretariat is in Kāthmāndu.

[19]ECONOMY

Despite social and economic reforms begun in the 1950s, Nepal's per capita income was only $180 in 1991, and general living standards are low. The economy is based on subsistence agriculture, which engages about 90% of the labor force but is inefficiently organized and limited by a shortage of arable land in relation to population. Seven development plans, extending from 1955 to 1990, have slowly built up the nation's infrastructure. Nevertheless, the industrial sector is still small and dominated by traditional handicrafts, spinning and weaving, and similar occupations. Growth in medium-scale and cottage industry-based production of carpets and garments for export, expanding tourism, and some government-promoted development of heavy industry sustained an average GDP growth rate of over 5% from 1980–88. In 1989/90, Nepal weathered a major trade and transit dispute with India, maintaining a GDP growth rate of 2%, despite the potentially debilitating tariffs suddenly placed on trade with its largest import supplier and external market.

Nepal's economic potential is by no means insignificant. Kāthmāndu Valley and the Terai zone are fertile areas; there is great forest wealth, including valuable medicinal plants such as pyrethrum, belladonna, and ipecac; deposits of several minerals are known to exist; and swift Himalayan rivers offer great possibilities for hydroelectric development. The Khulekhani Hydroelectric Project provides 40% of the country's power, but still harnesses less than 1% of its total megawatt production potential.

The principal challenge for the Nepalese is to provide for a rising and unequally distributed population and to achieve material progress without irrevocably depleting the environmental resource base. Structural adjustment measures initiated in 1989 have reduced the regulation of industry and imports, and are supported by similar liberalization in India, to which Nepal's economy is closely tied. However, aggregate economic growth remained sluggish during the early 1990s. GDP growth declined from 4.6% in 1990/91 to only 2.1% in 1991/92, due in large part to declining agricultural output following poor weather.

[20]INCOME

In 1992, Nepal's GNP was $3,285 million, or $180 per capita. For the period 1985–92 the average inflation rate was 10.0%, resulting in a real growth rate in per capita GNP of 2.1%.

In 1992 the GDP was $2,956 million in current US dollars. It is estimated that in 1990 agriculture, hunting, forestry, and fishing contributed 56% to GDP; mining and quarrying, less than 1%; manufacturing, 5%; electricity, gas, and water, 1%; construction, 7%; wholesale and retail trade, 4%; transport, storage, and communication, 4%; finance, insurance, real estate, and business services, 8%; community, social, and personal services, 1%; and other sources 14%.

[21]LABOR

As of 1992, over 90% of the 19.4 million population were subsistence farmers while handicrafts, porterage, trade, military service, industry, and government work engaged the remainder. Most agriculturists are peasant farmers, and there are many wage laborers, but only in the peak seasons. Among some tribes, women do most of the farm work, while in others, especially among strict Hindus, they do no farming at all. Many occupations are effectively restricted to certain castes, although the practice has been declared illegal.

Minimum wage rates and working conditions in the small industrial sector are set by the Nepal Factories and Factory Workers' Act of 1959, as amended. The 1990 Constitution grants the freedom to form and join unions and associations, and permits strikes except against public utilities.

[22]AGRICULTURE

In 1992, agriculture provided about 54% of national income. Only about 19% of the land can actually be cultivated. Regional imbalance and lack of integration also hamper Nepal's agriculture. Although the country produces an overall exportable surplus of food grains, some areas of the country, particularly Kāthmāndu Valley and the hill areas, have a food deficit. Lack of transportation and storage facilities prevents the movement of food grains from the Terai to the hills, with the result that Nepal both exports and imports the same food items.

Agriculture has been hampered by the lack of irrigated land, by the small size of farms (an average of 4 hectares/10 acres), and by inefficient farming methods. Some of the arable land is still held free of taxation by a few large landowners and farmed by tenants, whose productivity is low. The government has officially abolished tax-free estates (birta), eliminated the feudal form of land tenure (jagira), set a limit on landholdings, and redistributed the extra land to farm tenants. Its economic plans also include the use of fertilizers, insecticides, improved seeds, and better implements; the extension of irrigation; and the construction of transportation and storage facilities.

Rice, Nepal's most important cereal, is grown on more than half the cultivated land, mainly in the Terai but also on every available piece of ground in the Kāthmāndu Valley during the monsoon season. In 1992, rice production totaled 2,509,000 tons. Production of maize, grown on the carefully terraced hillsides, was 1,164,000 tons in 1992; land under cultivation with maize was 28% of the area allotted to food grains. The output of wheat in 1992 was 779,000 tons; millet, 230,000 tons; and barley, 28,000 tons. Cash crops (with 1992 output) included sugarcane, 1,291,000 tons; potatoes, 733,000 tons; linseed, 31,000 tons; jute, 10,000 tons; and tobacco, 6,000 tons. Sugarcane, jute, and tobacco are the major raw materials for Nepal's own industries. Potatoes are grown in Ilam and fruit mainly in Dharan, Dhankuta, and Pokhara. Tea is also grown in Ilam and elsewhere. In 1990 and 1992, food exports totaled $19 million, representing 10.6% and 6.1% of total exports, respectively.

[23]ANIMAL HUSBANDRY

Livestock, adapted to many uses, forms an essential part of the economy. Livestock accounts for about 30% of gross agricultural output. In farm work, bullocks and asses are largely employed.

Herds of yaks, cows, and their hybrids, zobos, are grazed in the central valley and to some extent along the borders of the foothill jungles. A few hogs usually are kept on the larger farms. Sheep and goats are used for food and also as pack animals, particularly in the distribution of salt over the trade routes; the sheep also supply a valuable type of wool.

In 1992, Nepal had an estimated 6,246,000 head of cattle, 3,058,000 water buffalo, 912,000 sheep, 5,406,000 goats, and 599,000 hogs. Modern poultry farms are operated principally by the Newaris, who carry on most of the agriculture in the Kāthmāndu Valley. There were about 7 million chickens in 1992, when 9,000 tons of poultry meat were produced. Traditionally, butter and cheese are among the leading exports of Nepal. Livestock products in 1992 included an estimated 612,000 tons of buffalo milk, 259,000 tons of cow's milk, 15,600 tons of butter and ghee, and 620 tons of wool (greasy basis).

24FISHING

The commercial fish catch amounted to 15,595 tons in 1991 (up from 9,443 tons in 1986). In the Terai are many small fish ponds and several government fish farms. Common fish species are carp, gar, and murrel.

25FORESTRY

In the early 1990s, forests covered about 18% of Nepal's total area. The proportion has been declining at a rapid rate because of overcutting and clearing for farmland. Timber cutting has been contracted out to private firms. About 97% of the roundwood removals in the 1991s were for fuel; approximately 4,000 cu m of roundwood were exported in 1991.

In 1961, the government established a department of medicinal plants to encourage Nepal's commercially important herb exports. There are regional herbal farms at Kāthmāndu and Nepalgānj. There is also a royal research laboratory for drug analysis.

26MINING

Although mining in Nepal is an ancient occupation, the country's mineral resources have been little exploited. There are known deposits of iron, copper, zinc, lignite, graphite, cobalt, mica, limestone, marble, talc, quartz, ceramic clays, and slate. A lead and zinc deposit near Lari supposedly has reserves of 2 million tons. Development plans include the encouragement of small-scale mining and provide for continuing mineral surveys. In 1963, the Bureau of Mines was established at Kāthmāndu to coordinate prospecting efforts. Copper mining activity has increased in recent years; production in 1991 amounted to 22 tons, up from 6 tons in 1987. Salt production rose sharply from 6 tons in 1988 to 7,300 tons in 1991.

27ENERGY AND POWER

Although Nepal's hydroelectric potential is great and development has been rapid in recent years, the kingdom still lacks an adequate power supply. In 1991, total installed capacity was 280,000 kw; production (not including losses) was 981 million kwh, 91% of which was hydropower. The remainder was either imported from India or produced by diesel generators. India has joined with Nepal in the construction of hydroelectric and irrigation projects on the Kosi and Gandak rivers. China has helped build a 10-Mw plant on the Kosi as well. India has also constructed a 14-Mw hydroelectric station at Devighat, in central Nepal. A 60-Mw hydroelectric project on the Kulekhani, funded by the IBRD, Kuwait, and Japan, has been completed. There is an integrated grid system in central Nepal. Several small-scale hydroelectric power stations, as well as a high-power transmission line were under construction in 1991. Exploration for oil and natural gas deposits began in the mid-1980s.

28INDUSTRY

Until recently, modern industry was almost nonexistent; only 0.66% of Nepal's GDP was derived from industry in 1964/65. Since then, industrial development has been given emphasis in economic planning. The industrial share of the GDP increased to 12% by 1985/86 and reached 18% by 1991/92.

Aside from small-scale food processing (rice, wheat and oil mills), light industry, largely concentrated in southeastern Nepal, includes the production of jute goods, refined sugar, cigarettes, matches, spun cotton and synthetic fabrics, wool, footwear, tanned leather, and tea. Despite import restrictions by the US and the closing of many firms by the government in 1985, the garments and carpets presently account for 80% of manufactured exports, as compared with 60% in the mid-80s. The carpet, garment and spinning industries are the three largest industrial employers, followed by structural clay products, sugar and jute processing. Sugar production was 41,400 tons in 1990/91, jute goods, 15,000 tons; and soap, 21.4 thousand tons. In 1988/89 11,848 thousand meters of synthetic textiles and 7,057 thousand meters of cotton textiles were produced.

Heavy industry includes a steel-rolling mill, established in 1965, which uses imported materials to produce stainless steel. During the 1980s, the government gave priority to industries such as lumber, plywood, paper, cement, and bricks and tiles, which make use of domestic raw materials and reduce the need for imports. Production by heavy industries in 1990/91 included cement, 182 thousand tons; iron goods, 42,500 tons; and stainless steel utensils, 237 tons. Output of bricks and tiles was 33,440 thousand pieces.

29SCIENCE AND TECHNOLOGY

The only advanced technology is that brought in under the various foreign aid programs. Foreign technicians provide training in cottage industries, and local workers are trained at the Cottage Industry Center in Kāthmāndu. In 1982, the Royal Nepal Academy of Science and Technology was established to aid in socioeconomic development. The National Council for Science and Technology aims to formulate science and technology policy, promote scientific and technological research, coordinate research among ministries and Mehendra Sanskrit University, and disseminate information to the public. Tribhuvan University has faculties of science and technology, medicine, agriculture and animal science, engineering, and forestry.

30DOMESTIC TRADE

For many Nepalese, local trade is a part-time activity, limited to such products as cigarettes, salt, kerosene, and cloth. Marketing centers are along the main trails and are supplemented by small local markets. Poor communications facilities make extensive domestic trade impractical.

Most shops are open from 10 AM to 8 PM, and government offices and banks from 10 AM to 5 PM. Saturdays are holidays.

31FOREIGN TRADE

Traditionally, Nepal's foreign trade was limited to Tibet and India. After 1956, Nepalese trading agencies were confined in Tibet to Xigaze, Gyirong, and Nyalam, with Lhasa, Xigaze, Gyangze, and Yadong specified as markets for trade. In 1980, however, Nepal and China agreed to open 21 new trade routes across the Tibetan frontier. Treaty arrangements with China strictly regulate the passage of both traders and pilgrims in either direction across the border. Up until 1989, treaty agreements between India and Nepal allowed for unrestricted commerce across 21 customs posts along the border, and duty-free transit of Nepalese goods intended for third countries through India. India remitted levies on most goods intended for Nepal, subject to the possibility of export controls being tightened by the Nepalese government to prevent such imports from leaking back into India for sale at lower than market rates. In 1989, a breakdown in the treaty renewal negotiations resulted in retaliatory actions and the replacement of previous arrangements with far less favorable relations for both sides. India's share of Nepali exports plummeted from 38% in 1986/87 to 9% in 1989/90. India's share of the country's imports declined by about one-half to 25%. Total exports dropped from NR5,249 million to NR4,843 million. Despite the sudden shock sustained by the Nepali economy overall, the signing of a new interim agreement in 1990 prevented a prolonged crisis, helping to fuel a robust recovery in export growth as exports increased by 28% in 1990/91 over 1989/90, and again by 35% in 1991/92. A slower rate of growth in imports helped narrow Nepal's trade deficit to NR17.2 billion by 1992/93, from a peak of NR17.6 billion in the previous year. (Nepal's recorded trade statistics must be interpreted cautiously, however, in view of the porous border with India.)

Carpets and garments presently account for 70% of all merchandise exports, far surpassing timber, rice, and jute; major imports are heavy machinery, transport equipment, textiles, chemicals, fertilizers, metal manufactures, and petroleum products.

As the export of manufactured goods has expanded since the mid-1980s Nepal has diversified its trading partners somewhat. The US absorbs over 90% of garment exports, while Germany and Belgium have become the main buyers of Nepali carpets. Still, India remains Nepal's largest export market and supplier of imported goods.

32BALANCE OF PAYMENTS

Despite large annual trade deficits, Nepal usually maintains a fairly consistent surplus in its balance of payments. Unrecorded, informal exports to India lessen the significance of the trade deficit. A principal source of foreign exchange consists of remittances from Nepalese civilians and Gurkha soldiers abroad in British and Indian employ and from pensions paid to Nepalese veterans of service in the British and Indian armies. Increasingly, tourism has become a significant source of revenue, and foreign aid remains so. In 1992 merchandise exports totaled $376.3 million and imports $752.1 million. The merchandise trade balance was $-375.8 million.

33BANKING AND SECURITIES

Nepal's domestic banking system consists of the Nepal Rastra (National) Bank, the central bank, with its commercial subsidiary, the Rastriya Banijya (National Commercial) Bank; the Nepal Bank, three commercial banks; and state-owned banks for industrial and agricultural development. In 1984, Nabil, or Nepal Arab Bank, a joint venture with the UAE, was established. The French Indosuez Bank followed in 1986. The Rastra Bank was inaugurated by King Mahendra in 1956 as the central banking institution, with a capital of NR10 million. Besides regulating the national currency, it issues notes of various denominations and assists in preparation of the government budget. The Rastra Bank may advance loans to industry if both the government and the bank consider the loan sound.

In December 1993, net foreign assets of government monetary authorities totaled NR21,320 million; claims on the government were NR17.907 million. As of that date, the money supply, as measured by M2, totaled NR49,316 million. A vast expansion of paper currency resulted from the progressive monetization of the Nepalese economy and from the decree making Nepalese currency the only legal tender, thus abolishing the old dual currency system under which both Indian and Nepalese rupees circulated freely. In May 1986, the 30-year direct link between the Nepalese and Indian rupees was ended. Since then, the Nepalese rupee has floated against a group of international currencies, including the Indian rupee.

The Nepal Bank was established in 1938 as a joint venture of the government and private shareholders, with an authorized capital of NR10 million, to be the chief source of credit for financing trade. The Nepalese Industrial Development Corp., founded in 1958, partly finances most new ventures in manufacturing; the Department of Cottage Industries also gives industrial loans. The Agricultural Development Bank is the principal institution granting financial assistance to farmers. In December 1993, the net foreign assets of Nepal's commercial banks totaled NR6,525 million; demand and savings deposits totaled NR28,888 million.

A stock exchange was established in 1984 in Kāthmāndu. Since 1964, the government has issued several series of 6% and 7% development bonds.

34INSURANCE
The National Insurance Corp. is Nepal's sole insurer.

35PUBLIC FINANCE
For many years, government revenue was derived chiefly from privately owned land (amounting to about 30% of the country's area), customs duties, and forest and mining royalties. In 1955, however, because of increasing costs of development projects and administration, the government discarded the practice of adjusting the budgetary deficit by drawing on reserves and adopted a policy of raising additional revenue through taxation. Subsequently, a progressive income tax was introduced. Nepal has an operating budget and a development budget, the latter accounting for over two-thirds of total public expenditures each year.

Budget deficits grew steadily during the 1970s and 1980s, but were offset by foreign grants, domestic loans, foreign exchange borrowings, and transfers. The government's spending on development projects is funded mainly by aid from India, China, and the US. Expenditures in the 1990/91 budget increased by 6%, in order to accommodate an increase of nearly 30% in public employee wages, demands for price relief, and costs for national elections.

The following table shows actual revenues and expenditures for 1990 and 1991 in millions of Nepalese rupees.

	1990	1991
REVENUE AND GRANTS		
Tax revenue	7,236	8,130
Non-tax revenue	1,498	1,672
Capital revenue	34	45
Grants	1,829	2,509
TOTAL	10,596	12,357
EXPENDITURES & LENDING MINUS REPAYMENTS		
General public service	1,487	1,525
Defense	1,077	1,114
Education	1,950	2,079
Health	855	885
Housing and communityamenities	1,489	1,284
Economic affairs and services	7,341	8,161
Other expenditures	3,612	3,942
Lending minus repayments	−202	−205
TOTAL	17,609	18,784
Deficit/surplus	−7,013	−6,427

In 1991 Nepal's total public debt stood at NR60,846 million, of which NR43,926 million was financed abroad.

36TAXATION
The principal sources of public revenues are customs tariffs, sales tax, and excise duties. A progressive income tax is levied, as well as a tax on income from industrial undertakings. Rent-free land is

taxed on a modest scale. Registration taxes levied on houses and land totaled about NR170 million in 1984/85. Sales tax rates on locally manufactured goods vary, depending on the commodity traded.

37CUSTOMS AND DUTIES

Exports and imports are subject to tariffs and surcharges, which combine to form the second most important source of revenue. Much potential revenue is lost, however, because of the open borders and untrained customs officers at the customs checkpoints. Indian imports receive preferential tariff treatment. In 1986, the government began to auction licenses for importing luxury goods. Critics of this policy complained that it led to increased smuggling and placed an economic burden on the Nepalese by raising the rates on such goods from 25% to 81%. Duties are on an ad valorem basis. There is also a sales tax on imports of 8–12% and customs surcharges of 5–10%.

38FOREIGN INVESTMENT

Foreign investment remains low and overwhelmingly dominated by Indian investors benefiting from the preferential trade regime. Liberalization measures undertaken with structural reform, including a review of the Industrial Policy Act, are expected to attract more foreign investment in the future. For the immediate future, however, the response is likely to be muted by lingering concerns about prolonged flood-induced power shortages which threatened to constrain industrial production in 1993.

39ECONOMIC DEVELOPMENT

Planned economic development began in 1953 with construction of roads and airfields and of irrigation projects to bring more acreage under cultivation. In 1956, these projects were integrated into a five-year plan (1956–61) to assist existing industries, revive and expand cottage industries, encourage private investment, and foster technological training. After a plan for three years (1962–65), declared successful by the government, had run its course, a new plan (1965–70) was drawn up. This five-year program, which aimed at a 19% increase in national income, was the first to be framed within the context of the panchayat system, which was to serve as an important medium of project administration. The fourth plan (1970–75) and the fifth (1975–80) continued to emphasize infrastructural development, primarily in transportation, communications, electricity, irrigation, and personnel. The sixth development plan (1980–85) allocated nearly one-third of its total expenditure to agriculture and irrigation. However, money targeted for development projects was used for other purposes.

The objectives of the seventh plan (1986–90) were to increase production, create opportunities for employment, and fulfill basic needs. Of the total expenditure of NR54.1 billion, 65% was to be used for investment, allocated as follows: agriculture, irrigation, and forestry, 30.6%; industry, mining, and electricity, 26%; transportation and communications, 17.7%; social services, 25.2%; and other sectors, 0.5%. Foreign aid was expected to fund about 70% of these projects.

In 1988 a structural adjustment program was initiated in response to accelerating inflation and burgeoning negative fiscal and balance of payment imbalances. Following further deterioration of macroeconomic indicators, especially in wake of the trade dispute with India and slippage in reform policy due to internal political tensions, the newly elected government in 1991 re-emphasized its commitment to structural adjustment through a series of reforms affecting virtually all sectors of the economy. Immediate stress was placed on tax reform, easing import restrictions, lowering tariffs, and reunifying the exchange rate market to effect a currency devaluation of 35% in 1992 and a further 17% in 1993. To streamline government investments in economic development, a list of priority development projects has been drafted. While four public enterprises were transferred to private ownership by mid-1993, 14 more have been targeted for privatization during the following year, freeing government revenues for other budgetary items, including the social sector, drinking water, and rural infrastructure development. The government plans a rolling three-year development program to be in place by late 1994.

40SOCIAL DEVELOPMENT

The government maintains a countrywide village development service, which endeavors to meet the villagers' needs for food, clothing, shelter, health services, and education. Village development workers demonstrate improved methods of sanitation and health and teach the villagers to read and write. The Employee Provident Fund administers a program of old age, disability, and death benefits for government and corporate employees. Miners and employees of factories with 10 or more workers are protected by a workers' compensation program run by the Labor Department.

Women are subject to gender discrimination, especially in traditional rural areas. According to the 1991 census, the female literacy rate was 26%, compared to 57% for males. The new Constitution has strengthened provisions for women, including equal pay for equal work, but few women work in the money economy.

41HEALTH

Although protected by mountain barriers, Nepal is in frequent danger from epidemics, notably cholera. Common afflictions are black fever (kala-azar), amoebic dysentery, eye diseases, typhoid, and venereal diseases. Malnutrition, contaminated water, and inadequate sanitation cause widespread health problems. Improved health programs in rural areas have helped control malaria, leprosy, and tuberculosis. There were an estimated 167 cases of tuberculosis per 100,000 people in 1990. In 1992, immunization rates for children up to one year old were as follows: tuberculosis (82%); diphtheria, pertussis, and tetanus (72%); polio (72%); and measles (64%).

Nepal has an estimated 22,000 drug addicts. Stringent amendments to the Narcotic Drug Control Act were adopted in 1986 in response to pressures from the US and UK.

The infant mortality rate in 1992 was 90 per 1,000 live births; the general mortality rate in 1993 was 13 per 1,000 people. Maternal mortality was 83 women per 1000 live births in 1991. Average life expectancy in 1992 was 53 years for both women and men.

In 1990, there were 3 hospital beds per 100,000 inhabitants. Medical personnel in 1990 included 1,124 physicians, 19 pharmacists (in urban areas), 24 dentists (in urban areas), 601 nurses, and 2,380 midwives. In 1990, the population per physician was 16,830, and per nursing professional was 2,760. Most of the medical personnel work in the Kāthmāndu Valley, and health services elsewhere are in short supply. Traditional medicine and faith healing are still used frequently, especially in the hill districts. Health care expenditures in 1990 were $141 million.

42HOUSING

In the Kāthmāndu Valley, village houses are made of stone or mud bricks, with thatched roofs and raised eaves. Elsewhere, houses are often made of bamboo and reeds. Most houses have two stories, but some contain only two rooms, a sleeping room and a room for cooking. The well-constructed houses of the Sherpas are generally built of stone and timber, roofed with wooden slats. About four out of five urban dwellings in Nepal are owner occupied. The latest available figures for 1980–88 show a total housing stock of 3,056,000 units with 5.6 people per dwelling.

43EDUCATION

The proportion of literate persons, although small, is rising and was estimated in 1990 at 25.6% of adults (males: 37.6% and females: 13.2%). After free primary education was introduced in 1975, school enrollment for children aged 6–11 increased from about one-fourth of the total to over one-half by the mid-1980s. In 1988, there were 13,514 primary schools with 2,108,739 pupils and 57,204 teachers. Secondary students numbered 612,943 with 21,132 teachers teaching.

Traditional schools (pathshalas) provide a classical education emphasizing languages. Gompas along the northern border train boys and men to become Buddhist religious leaders. English schools are modeled after those in India. Under a 1954 plan, a national school system with a single curriculum has been replacing the traditional schools, although English schools have increased.

In 1991, 110,239 students were enrolled in all higher level institutions with 4,925 teachers.

44LIBRARIES AND MUSEUMS

Kāthmāndu, the repository of the country's historical literature, has the National Library (70,000 volumes) and National Museums. The Bir Library, founded in the 14th century, contains 15,000 manuscripts. Other important collections are maintained by the library of Tribhuvan University (162,923 volumes) and the Singh Darbar, Nepal-Bharat (43,000), and the British Council libraries, all in Kāthmāndu.

45MEDIA

Postal, telephone, and telegraph services are operated by the government. Telephone service connects Kāthmāndu with Bīrganj on the Indian frontier, and another line links the capital with foothill towns in the eastern Terai. The telecommunications network includes a 5,000-telephone automatic exchange of over 90 radio relay stations, and an earth satellite station established with help from the UK in 1982. In 1991 there were some 67,000 telephones in use, up from 18,000 in 1985 with the completion of a $56-million IDA project to consolidate the Nepal Telecommunications Corp. Radio Nepal, a commercial, semi-governmental network, broadcasts in Nepali and English on both short and medium wavelengths. Television was introduced into the Kāthmāndu Valley in 1986, and the Nepalese Television Corporation broadcasts about 23 hours a week. In 1991, there were 670,000 radios and 40,000 television sets.

Freedom of the press is guaranteed by the constitution. However, the press is licensed by the government, and licenses have been suspended and individuals arrested for criticism of the monarchy or support of a political party. Dailies, weeklies, and monthlies in Nepali, Newari, Hindi, and English are published mainly in Kāthmāndu. In 1991, the country had 28 dailies, with a total circulation of about 122,000. The largest daily newspapers (with 1991 circulations) are the Nepali *Gorkha Patra* (40,000) and the English-language *Rising Nepal* (25,000).

46ORGANIZATIONS

The leading commercial organization is the Nepal Chamber of Commerce. Professional organizations include the Nepal Medical Association and the Nepal Drivers' Association. Social organizations include the Nepal Women's Organization, the Nepal Youth Organization, the Nepal Peasants' Organization, the Nepal Children's Organization, and an organization for ex-servicemen.

47TOURISM, TRAVEL, AND RECREATION

In 1951, the government of Nepal reversed its long-standing policy and began to encourage visitors; before then, mountaineering expeditions had been permitted into the country only under severe official scrutiny and restraining regulations. For the first time in 1956, tourism was officially included among the country's major potential assets. There were 292,995 foreign tourists in 1991; 118,065 came from Europe and 100,077 from Southern Asia. There were 5,206 hotel rooms with 11,207 beds. Foreign exchange earnings from tourism totaled $126 million.

For mountain trekkers, travel agencies in Kāthmāndu provide transportation to mountain sites, as well as Sherpa guides and porters. Tents, sleeping bags, and other mountain-climbing gear are available in Kāthmāndu. Travel is difficult; roads are generally poor.

48FAMOUS NEPALESE

Buddhism, one of the world's great religions, is based on the teachings of Siddhartha Gautama, who became known as the Buddha ("Enlightened One"). He was born (traditionally about 624 BC but according to most modern scholars about 563 BC) in Lumbini, near Kapilavastu in the Terai, then part of India, and died at Kushinagara (traditionally about 544 BC but according to the modern view about 483 BC).

Amar Singh Thapa, Nepalese military leader of the 19th century and rival of Gen. David Ochterlony in the war between British India and Nepal, is a national hero. The two best-known Rana prime ministers were Sir Jung Bahadur Rana (1817–77) and Sir Chandra Shamsher Jang Rana (1863–1929). The most highly regarded writers are Bhanubhakta, a great poet of the 19th century, and the dramatist Bala Krishna Sama (Shamsher, b.1903).

King Mahendra Bir Bikram-Shah (1920–72), who introduced the partyless political system, based on the Nepalese tradition of the village panchayat (council), was succeeded on the throne by his son, King Birendra Bir Bikram Shah Dev (b.1945), who democratized the panchayat system. Well-known political leaders include the brothers Matrika Prasad Koirala (b.1912), head of the Nepali Congress Party and the first post-Rana prime minister of Nepal (1951–52 and 1953–55), and Bisweswar Prasad Koirala (1915–82), head of the Nepali Congress Party and the first elected prime minister of Nepal (1959–60).

World renown was gained for Nepal by a Sherpa porter and mountaineer, Tenzing Norgay (Namgyal Wangdi, 1914–86), who, with Sir Edmund Hillary, a New Zealander, ascended to the summit of Mt. Everest in 1953.

49DEPENDENCIES

Nepal has no territories or colonies.

50BIBLIOGRAPHY

Fisher, James F. *Sherpas: Reflections on Change in Himalayan Nepal*. Berkeley: University of California Press, 1990.

Fraser, Mary Ann. *On Top of the World: The Conquest of Mount Everest*. New York: H. Holt, 1991.

Landon, Perceval. *Nepal*. New Delhi: Asian Educational Services, 1993.

Pradhan, Kumar. *The Gorkha Conquests: The Process and Consequences of the Unification of Nepal, with Particular Reference to Eastern Nepal*. Calcutta: Oxford University Press, 1991.

Regmi, Mahesh C. *Landownership in Nepal*. Berkeley: University of California Press, 1976.

Savada, Andrea Matles (ed.). *Nepal and Bhutan: Country Studies*. 3rd ed. Washington, D.C.: Library of Congress, 1993.

Shaha, Rishikesh. *Modern Nepal: A Political History, 1769–1955*. Riverdale, Md.: Riverdale Co., 1990.

Thapa, N. B. and D. P. *Geography of Nepal*. Columbia, Mo.: South Asia Books, 1981.

Whelpton, John. *Nepal*. Santa Barbara, Calif.: Clio, 1990.

Zivetz, Laurie. *Private Enterprise and the State in Modern Nepal*. Oxford: Oxford University Press, 1992.

NEW ZEALAND

CAPITAL: Wellington.

FLAG: The flag has two main features: the red, white, and blue Union Jack in the upper left quarter and the four-star Southern Cross in the right half. On the blue state flag the stars are red outlined in white; on the red national flag, used by individuals or commercial institutions at sea, the stars are white.

ANTHEM: *God Save the Queen* and *God Defend New Zealand* have, since 1977, enjoyed equal status.

MONETARY UNIT: The New Zealand dollar (NZ$) is a paper currency of 100 cents; it replaced the New Zealand pound on 10 July 1967. There are coins of 5, 10, 20, and 50 cents and 1 and 2 dollars, and notes of 5, 10, 20, 50, and 100 dollars. NZ$1 = US$0.3982 (or US$1 = NZ$2.5113).

WEIGHTS AND MEASURES: Metric weights and measures are used.

HOLIDAYS: New Year's Day, 1 January; Waitangi Day, 6 February; Anzac Day, 25 April; Queen's Birthday, 1st Monday in June; Labor Day, 4th Monday in October; Christmas Day, 25 December; Boxing Day, 26 December. Movable holidays are Good Friday and Easter Monday. Each province has a holiday on its own anniversary day.

TIME: 12 midnight = noon GMT.

¹LOCATION, SIZE, AND EXTENT

Situated in the southwest Pacific Ocean, New Zealand proper, with a total area of 268,680 sq km (103,738 sq mi), consists of the North Island, covering 114,669 sq km (44,274 sq mi) including small islands nearby; the South Island, 149,883 sq km (57,870 sq mi); Stewart Island, 1,746 sq km (674 sq mi); and various minor, outlying islands. Comparatively, the area occupied by New Zealand is about the size of the state of Colorado. The Chatham Islands, lying 850 km (528 mi) E of Lyttelton, on South Island, have a land area of 963 sq km (372 sq mi). Other outlying islands have a combined area of 778 sq km (about 300 sq mi). New Zealand extends 1,600 km (994 mi) NNE–SSW and 450 km (280 mi) ESE–WNW. It has a total coastline of 15,134 km (9,404 mi).

New Zealand's capital city, Wellington, is located on the southern tip of North Island.

²TOPOGRAPHY

Less than one-fourth of the land surface of New Zealand lies below the 200-m (650-ft) contour. The mountain ranges in the North Island do not exceed 1,800 m (6,000 ft) in height, with the exception of the volcanic peaks of Egmont, or Taranaki (2,518 m/ 8,261 ft), Ruapehu (2,797 m/9,176 ft), Ngauruhoe (2,290 m/ 7,513 ft), and Tongariro (1,968 m/6,457 ft), the last three of which are still active. This volcanic system gives rise to many hot springs and geysers.

The South Island is significantly more mountainous than the North Island, but is without recent volcanic activity. The Southern Alps, running almost the entire length of the South Island from north to south, contain 19 peaks of 3,000 m (9,800 ft) or above, of which the highest is Mt. Cook or Aorangi, 3,764 m (12,349 ft). There are also several glaciers in the Southern Alps, the largest being the Tasman Glacier, 29 km (18 mi) long and 1 km (0.6 mi) wide. The rivers are mostly swift-flowing and shallow, few of them navigable. There are many lakes, those in the South Island being particularly noted for their magnificent mountain scenery.

³CLIMATE

New Zealand has a temperate, moist ocean climate without marked seasonal variations in temperature or rainfall. The prevailing winds are westerly, with a concentration of strong winds in the Cook Strait area. The generally mountainous nature of the country, however, causes considerable variation in rainfall (e.g., between the eastern and western sides of the Southern Alps), and, by preventing stratification of air into layers of different density, results in an absence of extensive cloud sheets and a consequent high percentage of sunshine. Mean annual temperatures at sea level range from about 15°C (59°F) in the northern part of the North Island to 12°C (54°F) in the southern part of the South Island. Mean annual rainfall ranges from around 300 cm (120 in) near Dunedin to more than 800 cm (315 in) in the Southern Alps.

⁴FLORA AND FAUNA

Like other regions separated from the rest of the world for a long period, New Zealand has developed a distinct flora. About 75% of the native flora is unique, and it includes some of the world's oldest plant forms. However, the flowering plants, conifers, ferns, lycopods, and other vascular tracheophytes that constitute much of the land vegetation do show affinities with plants of the Malayan region, supporting the theory of an ancient land bridge between the two regions. More than 250 species are common to both Australia and New Zealand. The Antarctic element, comprising more than 70 species related to forms in the flora of South America and the Southern Ocean islands, is of great interest to botanists. The kauri pine, now found only in parts of the North Island, for more than a century has been world famous for its timber. The rimu and the totara also are timber trees. Other handsome trees include the pohutukawa and other species of rata and kowhai. New Zealand flax, formerly of great importance in the Maori economy, is found in swampy places. Undergrowth in the damp forests consists largely of ferns, of which there are 145 species; they clothe most of the tree trunks and branches, and tree ferns form part of the foliage. Tussock grass occurs on all mountains above the scrub line and over large areas in the South Island.

Apart from seals and two species of bats, New Zealand has no indigenous land mammals. Some of the land mammals introduced to New Zealand have become pests, such as the rabbit, the deer, the pig (now wild), and the North American opossum. Sea mammals include whales and dolphins.

There is a great diversity of birds, some 250 species in all. Among the flightless birds the most interesting is the kiwi, New Zealand's national symbol and the only known bird with nostrils at the tip of the bill instead of at the base. Other characteristic birds are the kea, a bird of prey, and the tui, a beautiful songbird. All but one of the genera of penguins are represented in New Zealand. Several species of birds, the most famous being the Pacific godwit, migrate from breeding grounds in the Arctic Circle to spend spring and summer in New Zealand. There are many flightless insects and a diversity of small life forms.

⁵ENVIRONMENT

Because of its relatively small population, New Zealand's natural resources have so far suffered less from the pressures of development than have those of many other industrialized nations. Air pollution from cars and other vehicles is an environmental concern in New Zealand. The use of fossil fuels also contributes to the problem. New Zealand's concern about the effects of air pollution on the atmosphere is, in part, due to the fact that the nation is among the world leaders in skin cancer frequency. New Zealand contributes 0.1% of the world's total gas emissions. Water pollution is also a problem due to industrial pollutants and sewage. The nation has 95.3 cu mi of water, of which 44% is used for farming activity and 10% for industrial purposes. The nation's cities produce 2.3 million tons of solid waste per year. Another environmental issue in New Zealand is how to pursue the development of resources—forests, gas and coal fields, farmlands—without serious cost to natural beauty and ecological balance. Principal governmental agencies with environmental responsibilities are the Commission for the Environment (established in 1972), an investigatory and advisory agency that audits environmental impact reports; the Environmental Council (1970), an advisory body that publishes information on environmental issues; and the Nature Conservation Council (1962), an advisory body that may inquire into the environmental effects of proposed public or private works projects and is free to make its reports and recommendations public. In 1981, according to the latter, 531 endangered species were threatened with extinction; more than three-quarters of New Zealand soils showed signs of erosion; and more than 30 out of 300 estuarine systems supporting fisheries were polluted. Two-thirds of the nation's forests have been eliminated.

In 1994, 1 of New Zealand's mammal species and 26 types of birds were endangered, as well as 232 plant species. Endangered animal species in New Zealand in 1987 included the takahe, two species of petrel (black and New Zealand Cook's), the black stilt, orange-fronted parakeet, kakapo, and Codfish Island fernbird. Extinct are the bush wren, South Island kokako, and New Zealand grayling. Endangered species on the Chatham Islands were the Chatham Island petrel, magenta petrel, Chatham Island oystercatcher, New Zealand plover, Chatham Island pigeon, Forbes's parakeet, and Chatham Island black robin.

⁶POPULATION

The population as of the census of 5 March 1991 was 3,434,950, a 3.9% increase over the March 1981 census total of 3,307,084. The minimal rate of increase (less than 1% per year) was largely attributed to low birthrates. The intercensal rate of increase was still greater than in 1976–81, when the population grew only

1.5% over five years, or 0.3% a year. In 1990, the crude birthrate was 17.8 per 1,000 population (up from 15.8 in 1985), the death rate was 8.3, and the net natural increase 9.5 (up from 7.4 in 1985). A population of 3,710,000 was forecast for 2000, assuming a crude birthrate of 16.8, a death rate of 8.1, and a net natural increase of 8.5 during the 1995–2000 period.

The population density in 1991 was 12 per sq km (32.9 per sq mi), with nearly 75% of the population living on the North Island. Some 85% of New Zealand's inhabitants live in urban areas. The largest of the urban areas are Auckland (855,571 in 1991); Wellington, the capital (325,682); Christchurch (307,179); Dunedin (109,503); Hamilton (148,625); Palmerston North (70,951); and Tauranga (70,803). Within city limits, Auckland had 315,668 people; Christchurch, 292,858; and Wellington, 150,301.

⁷MIGRATION

Between 1946 and 1975, New Zealand experienced a net gain from migration of 312,588; from 1975 to 1990, however, there was a net outflow of 110,877. Under new immigration policy guidelines issued by the government in May 1974, immigrants are selected according to specific criteria, such as job skills, health, character, age, and family size. The same restrictions now apply to British subjects as to others who wish to take up permanent residence. Citizens of Fiji, Tonga, and Western Samoa may be admitted under special work permits for up to 11 months. There were a total of 57,088 permanent and long-term arrivals in 1990/ 91. Of the 25,437 people granted permanent residence in 1991, 5,322 came from Hong Kong and 3,875 from the UK. About 7,000 Indochinese refugees settled in New Zealand between 1975 and 1990. During 1990/91, New Zealanders departing permanently or long-term numbered 45,472. Australia is the preferred destination.

⁸ETHNIC GROUPS

About 80% of the population is classified as European; the overwhelming majority is of British descent. There are small groups of Dutch, Chinese, Indians, Arabs, Yugoslavs, Greeks, and Poles. The most significant minority group is the indigenous Maori people, a Polynesian group with a distinctive culture and a well-ordered social system.

Although the Treaty of Waitangi (1840) guaranteed to the Maori people all the rights and privileges of British subjects and full and undisturbed possession of their lands, these guarantees were often overlooked. As a result of war and disease, the Maori population declined to fewer than 42,000 by 1896. At the turn of the century, however, a group calling itself the Young Maori Party began to devote itself to the promotion of Maori welfare and status. In the 20th century, and especially after World War II, a more enlightened government policy prevailed.

In March 1991 there were 321,396 Maoris or part-Maoris (those reporting a Maori ancestry of 50% or more). In all, there were 511,947 people with Maori ancestry, representing 14.9% of the census population. About 90% live on North Island. Although Maori acquisition and development of land have been promoted, there is not enough land to afford a livelihood to more than about 25% of the Maori population. Thus, many Maoris leave their tribal villages to seek job opportunities in the towns and cities. By 1981, four-fifths of all Maoris lived in urban areas.

During recent years, increasing numbers of migrants from New Zealand's former colonies and from other Pacific islands have come to New Zealand. Many of these, especially the Cook Islanders, are Polynesians having ethnic and linguistic ties with the Maoris. The non-Maori Polynesian population in 1991 was 121,935, or 3.6% of the population. Chinese and Indians totaled 31,632 in 1986, or almost 1% of the population.

LOCATION: 33° to 53°s; 162°E to 173°w. **TERRITORIAL SEA LIMIT:** 12 mi.

⁹LANGUAGES

English is the universal language, although Maori, a language of the Polynesian group, still is spoken among the Maori population and is taught in Maori schools. It is the first language of about 50,000 Maori New Zealanders and became an official language in 1987, with the right of use in courts of law and before a num-

ber of tribunals. There are Maori-language preschools, immersion primary schools, and many radio stations.

¹⁰RELIGIONS

New Zealand has no state church. The bulk of the population in 1991 belonged to one of four main churches: the Church of

England, 21.4%; the Presbyterian Church, 16.0%; the Roman Catholic Church, 14.8%; and the Methodist Church, 4.1%. There are numerous other Protestant denominations, two Christian sects (Ratana and Ringatu) that are indigenous to New Zealand, and a small Hindu community. In 1990 there were an estimated 4,500 Jews.

11TRANSPORTATION

The mountainous nature of New Zealand has made the development of rail and road communications difficult and expensive, particularly on the South Island. In 1991, 4,716 km (2,931 mi) of state-owned railways were operative. New Zealand has electrified some 113 km (70 mi) of its rail lines in order to reduce dependence on imported fuel.

Capital investment in roads exceeds that for all other forms of transport service. Total length of maintained roadways as of 1991 was 92,648 km (57,571 mi); almost all roads were hard surfaced. As of 1992, registered motor vehicles included 1,557,951 passenger cars and 324,852 commercial vehicles.

With a registered merchant marine of only 180,000 gross tons in 1991, New Zealand is largely dependent on the shipping of other nations for its overseas trade. In 1974, a government-owned firm, the Shipping Corp. of New Zealand, was set up to operate shipping services; its trade name, the New Zealand Line, was adopted in 1985. Auckland and Wellington, the two main ports, have good natural harbors with deepwater facilities and modern port equipment. Other ports capable of efficiently handling overseas shipping are Whangarei, Tauranga, Lyttelton (serving Christchurch), Bluff, Napier, Nelson, Dunedin, and Timaru.

The government-owned Air New Zealand Ltd. operates air services throughout the Pacific region to Australia, Singapore, Hong Kong, Tokyo, Honolulu, and Los Angeles, among other destinations. Of the 33 airports with permanent-surface runways, 13 are major airports, of which those at Auckland, Christchurch, and Wellington are international airports. In 1992, Air New Zealand carried 3,865,500 passengers on domestic and international flights.

12HISTORY

The first European to discover New Zealand was Abel Tasman, a navigator of the Dutch East India Co., who sighted the west coast of the South Island in 1642. He did not land, because of the hostility of the Maori inhabitants. Owing to the absence of written records, it is impossible to give any accurate date for the settlement of the Maoris in New Zealand. According to their oral traditions, they migrated from other Pacific islands to New Zealand several centuries before Tasman's discovery, the chief migration having taken place about 1350; it seems likely, however, that ancestors of the Maoris had come to New Zealand from Southeast Asia by the end of the 10th century AD. No other Europeans are known to have visited New Zealand after Tasman until Capt. James Cook of the British Royal Navy made his four voyages in 1769, 1773, 1774, and 1777. In this period, he circumnavigated both islands and mapped the coastline.

In the 1790s, small European whaling settlements sprang up around the coast, and in 1814 the first mission station was set up in the Bay of Islands by Samuel Marsden, chaplain to the governor of New South Wales. In 1840, the Maori chieftains entered into a compact, the Treaty of Waitangi, whereby they ceded sovereignty to Queen Victoria while retaining territorial rights. In the same year, the first organized attempt at colonization from Britain was made by the New Zealand Co. The first group of British migrants arrived at Port Nicholson and founded the city of Wellington. Further settlements were made in the South Island by the New Zealand Co. in Nelson in 1842, in Dunedin in 1848 (with the cooperation of the Presbyterian Church of Scotland), and in Canterbury in 1850 (with the cooperation of the Church of

England). After the Maori Wars (1860-70), resulting largely from discontent with the official land policy, the colony of New Zealand rapidly increased in wealth and population. Discovery of gold in 1861 resulted in a large influx of settlers. The introduction of refrigerated shipping in 1882 enabled New Zealand to become one of the world's greatest exporters of dairy produce and meat. The depression of the early 1930s revealed to New Zealand the extent of its dependence on this export trade and led to the establishment of more local light industry. New Zealand entered World Wars I and II at the side of the UK, New Zealand troops serving in Europe in both wars and in the Pacific in World War II.

Representative institutions were granted to the colony by the British Parliament in 1852. In 1907, New Zealand was made a dominion; and in 1947, the New Zealand government formally claimed the complete autonomy that had been available to self-governing members of the British Commonwealth under the Statute of Westminster, enacted by the British Parliament in 1931.

After World War II, New Zealand and US foreign policies were increasingly intertwined. New Zealand signed the ANZUS Pact in 1951 and was a founding member of the Southeast Asia Treaty Organization (SEATO) in 1954. New Zealand troops fought with UN forces in the Korea conflict and with US forces in South Viet-Nam. The involvement in Viet-Nam touched off a national debate on foreign policy, however, and all New Zealand troops were withdrawn from Viet-Nam by the end of 1971; New Zealand's military participation in SEATO was later terminated.

In 1984, a Labour government led by Prime Minister David Lange took office under a pledge to ban nuclear-armed vessels from New Zealand harbors; a US request for a port visit by one of its warships was denied because of uncertainty as to whether the ship was nuclear-armed. The continuing ban put a strain on New Zealand's relations within ANZUS, and in 1986 the US suspended its military obligations to New Zealand under that defense agreement. The US also banned high-level contacts with the New Zealand government.

Extensive Maori land claims (all the country's coastline, 70% of the land, and half of the fishing rights) led, in December 1989, to the formation of a new Cabinet committee designed to develop a government policy towards these claims. The committee, including former Prime Minister Lange, aimed to work with the 17-member Waitangi Tribunal, established in 1975 to consider complaints from Maoris.

The US ended its ban on high-level contacts in March 1990.

13GOVERNMENT

New Zealand is an independent member of the Commonwealth of Nations. Like the UK, it is a constitutional monarchy, the head of state being the representative of the crown, the governor-general, who is appointed for a five-year term.

Government is democratic and modeled on that of the UK. The single-chamber legislature, the House of Representatives, has 97 members (1987), elected by universal adult suffrage for a term of three years. Adult male suffrage dates from 1879; adult women received the right to vote in 1893. The voting age was lowered to 18 in November 1974. Since 1867, the House has included four representatives of the Maoris, and in 1985, the Most Reverend Paul Reeves, Anglican archbishop of New Zealand, became the first person of Maori descent to be appointed governor-general. Persons of at least half Maori ancestry may register in either a Maori electoral district or a European district. Members are elected by simple majority. Although there have been coalition governments, the two-party system usually operates. The party with a majority of members elected to the House of Representatives forms the government, the other party becoming the Opposition.

On his appointment, the prime minister, leader of the governing party, chooses some 20 other ministers to form the cabinet.

Each minister usually controls several government departments, for which he is responsible to the House of Representatives. Although the cabinet is the de facto governing body, it has no legal status. Members of the cabinet and the governor-general form the Executive Council, the highest executive body.

An act of 1962 established the post of ombudsman, whose principal function is to inquire into complaints from the public relating to administrative decisions of government departments and related organizations. In 1975, provision was made for the appointment of additional ombudsmen under the chief ombudsman.

Nearly 85% of voters, in a September 1992 referendum, rejected the established electoral system of simple plurality (first-past-the-post) in favor of a system based upon a mixed member proportional system as used in Germany. Final approval came in a second referendum held as part of the 1993 general election.

14POLITICAL PARTIES

Although the New Zealand legislature began to function in 1854 under an act of 1852, it was not until near the end of the century that political parties with a national outlook began to be formed. This development was hastened by abolition of the provincial parliaments in 1876.

From 1890 to 1912, the Liberal Party was in power. It drew its strength from small farmers and from the rapidly increasing working class in the towns. It enacted advanced legislation on minimum wages, working conditions, and old age pensions, and established the world's first compulsory system of state arbitration. The Liberals were replaced as the government by the Reform Party in 1912; the main items in the Reform platform were the "freehold" for certain types of farmers (i.e., the right to purchase on favorable terms the land they leased from the crown) and the eradication of patronage in the public service. During part of World War I, there was a coalition of Reform and Liberal parties. In the meantime, the Labour Party had been formed in 1916, when several rival Labour groups finally came together. This party derived partly from old Liberal tradition, but its platform on socialization and social welfare was more radical.

The Reform Party continued in office until 1928 and was then succeeded by the United Party, a revival of the old Liberal Party. In 1931, these two parties came together, governing as a coalition until 1935. In that year, after a severe economic depression, a Labour government came to power. Labour remained the government until 1949, although for periods during World War II a coalition war cabinet and later a war administration were created in addition to the Labour cabinet. During its term of office, Labour inaugurated an extensive system of social security and a limited degree of nationalization.

After their defeat in 1935, the old coalition parties joined to form the National Party. Coming to power in 1949, this party held office until 1957, when it was replaced by Labour. The National Party was returned to power at the 1960 election, and maintained its majority in the elections of 1963, 1966, and 1969. A Labour government was elected in 1972, but in 1975 the National Party reversed the tide, winning 55 seats and 47.4% of the total vote; a National Party cabinet was formed, with Robert Muldoon as prime minister. Led by Muldoon, the National Party was returned again in the 1978 and 1981 elections, but by much lower margins.

On 14 July 1984, the National Party was defeated at the polls, winning only 37 seats (36% of the vote), to 56 seats (43%) for Labour. The Social Credit Political League won 2 seats (8%), and the new New Zealand Party, a conservative group formed in 1983, won most of the remaining popular vote but no seats. David Lange formed a Labour government, which took office on 26 July. Lange was reelected in August 1987, when Labour won 56 seats and 47.6% of the vote, and the National Party won 41 seats and 45% of the vote. No other parties won seats.

David Lange resigned as Prime Minister on 7 August 1989 after Roger Douglas, a political foe in the Labour Party, was reelected to the Cabinet on August 3. Labour's MPs selected Geoffrey Palmer as Prime Minister and party leader. Palmer resigned as Prime Minister in September 1990 and was replaced by Michael Moore, also of the Labour Party. In October 1990 the National Party, led by Jim Bolger, won a general election victory. Bolger's government instituted major cuts in New Zealand's welfare programs. The National Party won reelection in the November 1993 general election, capturing 50 of 99 seats. The Labour Party won 45, and both the New Zealand First Party, led by Winston Peters, and The Alliance, led by Jim Anderton, won 2 seats. In December 1993 Helen Clark replaced Michael Moore as leader of the Labour Party, becoming the first woman to lead a major party in New Zealand.

15LOCAL GOVERNMENT

The Local Government Act (1974), with subsequent modifications, substantially changed the structure of local government in New Zealand. The previous system was based on territorial local authorities: boroughs, which served concentrated populations of at least 1,500; counties, which were predominantly rural; and town districts, an intermediate form. In addition, there were special-purpose authorities to administer harbors, hospitals, electricity and water distribution, and other public services. The 1974 legislation added two tiers to this structure. Regional bodies—including united councils, which are appointed by the constituent territorial authorities in a region, and regional councils, which are directly elected—are charged with two mandatory functions, regional planning and self-defense, and may undertake other regional functions. Moreover, within territorial local authorities, communities may be established. Each community may have either a district community council (if the population is 1,500 or more), which exercises nearly all the powers of its parent territorial authority, or a community council, to which the parent authority may delegate powers. The purpose of these community bodies is to increase residents' participation in local government. The Local Government Act also introduced a new form of territorial local authority, the district council, established to serve areas of mixed rural and urban character.

The Local Government Commission was charged with the task of constituting the regional bodies, of which there were 22 (2 regional councils and 20 united councils) by 1983. As of 1986 there were also 90 county councils, 128 borough councils, 10 district councils, 15 district community councils, and 118 community councils. Most units of local government are elected at three-year intervals. In boroughs the mayor is elected directly by the voters. The chairman of a county council is elected by the council itself.

16JUDICIAL SYSTEM

In most civil and criminal cases, heard first in district courts (known until 1980 as magistrates' courts), there is the right of appeal to the High Court (formerly Supreme Court), which is usually the court of first hearing for cases where a major crime or an important civil action is involved. Family courts were established in 1980 to hear cases involving domestic issues. The highest court, the Court of Appeal, exercises an appellate jurisdiction only. Its decisions are final unless leave is granted to appeal to the Privy Council in London. There are also several special courts, such as the Arbitration Court, the Maori Land Court, and the Children and Young Persons Court. The judicial system is based on British common law. The judiciary is independent and impartial.

17ARMED FORCES

Service in the New Zealand regular armed forces is voluntary, but some white males (18–21) may be required to have military training for service in the territorial force (5,650).

In 1993, the army had a full-time regular force of 4,800 and 1,650 reserves; the navy had 2,400 regulars (300 women) and 1,050 reserves; and the air force had 3,700 regulars (600 women) and 1,050 reserves. The army has one active brigade, the navy 8 small surface combatants and 7 ASW helos, and the air force 41 combat aircraft. Weapons are US and European. New Zealand has 35 personnel working abroad in 6 different nations. The defense budget in 1992 was $792 million or 2% of GDP.

18INTERNATIONAL COOPERATION

A charter member of the UN, New Zealand joined the world organization on 24 October 1945. It participates in ESCAP and all the nonregional specialized agencies. In addition, New Zealand belongs to the Asian Development Bank, Colombo Plan, Commonwealth of Nations, OECD, South Pacific Commission, and South Pacific Forum, among other intergovernmental organizations. A signatory to GATT, the Law of the Sea, and the South Pacific Regional Trade and Cooperation Agreement, New Zealand also forms part of the ANZUS alliance with Australia and the US; in 1986, however, following New Zealand's decision to ban US nuclear-armed or nuclear-powered ships from its ports, the US renounced its ANZUS treaty commitments to New Zealand.

19ECONOMY

New Zealand's economy has traditionally been based on pastoral farming. The last decades, however, have seen the beginnings of heavy industry, and there has been a large expansion in light industries such as plastics, textiles, and footwear, mostly to supply the home market. In recent years there has been a trend toward the development of resource-based industries, and the forest industry has greatly expanded. Pulp, log, and paper products are now a major earner of overseas exchange. As of 1985, 11% of the work force was employed in agriculture, hunting, forestry, and fishing, and 32.4% in manufacturing. For 1988/89, agricultural production amounted to 8.9% of GDP, and manufacturing 18.5%. The economy has been subjected to two major crises in 20 years: first, the loss of a large part of the British market for New Zealand's agricultural products when the UK joined the EC in 1973, and, secondly, the curtailment of overspending by the government in the early 1980's, which enforced a 10-year austerity program. Real GDP grew about 7% in 1984/85, then fell off markedly to 0.8% in 1986. Tight economic policies have slowed growth into the early 1990's. Real GDP growth was −0.7% in 1990 and 0.2% in both 1991 and 1992. Unemployment from 1990 to June of 1992 ranged from 8.7% to 11%.

For financing imports both of raw materials and of a high proportion of manufactured goods, New Zealand has traditionally relied on the receipts from the export of its restricted range of primary products (mainly wool, meat, and dairy products). This dependence on the income from so few commodities makes the economy vulnerable to fluctuations in their world prices, and sharp drops in these prices, as have occurred periodically, inevitably result in the restriction of imports or a substantial trade deficit.

20INCOME

In 1992, New Zealand's GNP was $41,186 million at current prices, or $12,060 per capita. For the period 1985–92 the average inflation rate was 6.6%, resulting in a real growth rate in per capita GNP of −0.4%.

It is estimated that agriculture, hunting, forestry, and fishing contributes 9% to GDP; mining and quarrying, 1%; manufacturing, 18%; electricity, gas, and water, 3%; construction, 5%; wholesale and retail trade, 15%; transport, storage, and communication, 8%; finance, insurance, real estate, and business services, 22%; community, social, and personal services, 3%; and other sources 16%.

21LABOR

In 1992, total civilian employment amounted to 1,467,000, including 159,000 in agriculture, 240,000 in manufacturing, 308,000 in wholesale or retail trade, and 416,000 in community or personal services. Before 1978, New Zealand had maintained virtually full employment, but the oil crisis had a major impact, and since 1978 unemployment has climbed from about 3% to 10.6% in 1991.

Compulsory unionization during the 1936–61 period resulted in the creation of many small unions; the law was modified in 1962, and abolished in 1991 with the Employment Contracts Act, which radically deregulated the labor market and put the employer-employee relationship on a civil contract basis. In 1987, the private sector Federation of Labor and the public sector Combined State Unions merged to form the New Zealand Council of Trade Unions (NZCTU), which had 49 affiliated unions with a total membership of 430,000.

The Industrial Relations Act of 1973 restructured New Zealand's industrial legislation and institutions, setting up three bodies to aid in the settlement of disputes: the Industrial Mediation Service, the Industrial Conciliation Service, and the Industrial Commission. The Commission is involved only if conciliation fails, and its arbitration is binding. The 1973 act also provides for the right to strike, although there are restrictions once a dispute is before conciliation. Higher unemployment and lower welfare benefits created a decreased willingness for workers to strike. In 1984, there were 364 work stoppages; by 1990 that number had fallen to 137, and in 1991 to 71. Legislation enacted in 1991 prohibits strikes designed to force an employer to become a party to a multicompany contract. In 1992, there were 160 registered trade unions, representing about 37% of the total labor force.

In 1991, the minimum wage rate was NZ$6.125 per hour; minimum wages for men and women were equalized in 1977. These wage rates are set lower than the standard rate for unskilled labor; the average hourly earnings for non-agricultural activities in 1992 were NZ$14.98. By law, employees in most occupations have a 40-hour workweek, 8 hours a day, 5 days a week. The average number of hours worked per week in 1991 was 38.6, up from only 36.2 the previous year. Excess hours are generally paid at overtime rates. Legislation or industrial contracts secure sick leave, paid holidays, and accident compensation for all workers. The safety, health and welfare benefits, holiday provisions, hours of work, and overtime of all workers are closely regulated.

22AGRICULTURE

Over 50% of the total area of New Zealand is devoted to agriculture and animal husbandry. Capital investment in land improvement and mechanization has contributed greatly to the steady growth in agricultural production without an increase in the farm labor force. About 75,000 tractors and 2,950 harvesters were in use in 1991. Agriculture contributes about 9% to GDP.

Cereal cultivation, more than 90% of which takes place on the South Island plains and downlands, fluctuates in terms of both acreage and size of crop. In 1992, areas harvested to wheat totaled an estimated 42,000 ha (103,780 acres), with a yield of 168,000 tons; 17,000 ha (42,000 acres) yielded 65,000 tons of oats; and 79,000 ha (195,210 acres) yielded 420,000 tons of barley.

New Zealand is largely self-sufficient in horticultural products and exports some of these, such as apples and honey. In 1992, 848,000 tons of fresh fruit, (excluding melons) were produced. The kiwi, a fruit that has become popular in the US, Japan, and elsewhere, represented 90% of horticultural exports. In 1985, New Zealand accounted for more than half the world's supply of kiwi fruit. New Zealand is beginning to lose some of its market share in the production of kiwi, as other countries have started or expanded their own domestic kiwi production. In 1992, New Zealand produced 407,000 tons of apples, 16,000 tons of pears,

60,000 tons of peas, 160,000 tons of corn, and 300,000 tons of potatoes.

The Department of Agriculture and the Department of Scientific and Industrial Research provide farmers and horticulturalists with advice and encouragement on new farming methods, elimination of plant diseases, and improvement of unproductive land. Government subsidies have assisted in improving and bringing under cultivation marginal and hitherto unused scrub land. However, in the mid-1980s there was a shift in government policy, and many subsidies to agriculture were removed or phased out.

23ANIMAL HUSBANDRY

Relatively warm temperatures, combined with ample rainfall, make New Zealand one of the world's richest pastoral areas. Even in the south, where winters may be quite severe, animals need not be housed. In 1992, there were 5,250,000 head of beef cattle, 3,200,000 head of dairy cattle, 53,500,000 sheep, and 409,000 pigs. Dairying and beef production are concentrated in the North Island, and sheep farming is more evenly distributed between the North and South islands. The natural tussock land in the mountainous areas of the South Island and the surface-sown grassland in the less steep parts of the North Island are used to raise sheep for wool. The extensive use of aircraft for the spread of top dressing has greatly improved hill pasture, most of which is not readily accessible to normal top dressing with fertilizers. Some 24,000 farms stock mainly sheep, occupying over 11 million ha (27.1 million acres), with an average flock of 1,800 head. Although fine-woolen Merino sheep have grazed in New Zealand since the 1830s, most of the clip nowadays comes from Romney sheep, whose coarser, thicker wool is ideal for carpet-making and knitting yarns.

Products of animal origin account for more than half the total value of New Zealand's exports. New Zealand is the world's largest exporter of mutton and lamb, second largest exporter of wool, and a leading exporter of cheese. The wool clip, which, having increased steadily since 1948, had fallen during the early 1970s, later rose to 380,700 tons in 1980/81; in 1992, 296,000 tons were produced. Meat production in that year reached 1,226,000 tons. Mutton and wool accounted for 17% of gross agricultural output in 1991/92, when exports of pastoral products totaled $4.3 billion. Butter production totaled about 286,750 tons; cheese output was 139,500 tons. In 1992, 47,600 tons of eggs were produced.

With many more cows than people to milk them, New Zealand pioneered and relies on mechanical milking. Whole milk is pumped through coolers to vats where it is transferred to tanker trucks. In 1992, 8,140,000 tons of fresh milk was produced. Milkfat production averages about 330,000 tons annually, of which 13% is consumed as milk or fed to stock. The balance is used for dairy products.

Although wild goats and deer were once regarded as vermin, over the last decade, the profitability of venison and mohair exports led to the domestication of both animals. About 780,000 deer and 1.3 million goats are being farmed. Alpacas, llamas, and water buffalo have recently been imported to improve the breeding potential as well as wool and meat production.

24FISHING

Although many kinds of edible fish are readily obtainable in New Zealand waters, the fishing and fish-processing industry has remained relatively small. Since the 1960s, however, the government has taken a number of measures to expand the industry and increase fishery exports. In 1978, the government began implementing a 322-km (200-mi) exclusive economic zone. During the next four years, it approved nearly 40 joint ventures with foreign companies in order to exploit the zone, which, with an area of about 1.2 million sq mi (nautical), is one of the world's largest.

The volume of fish landed in New Zealand increased from 6,488 tons in 1936 to 609,031 tons in 1991. With the rapid growth of fishing in the 1980s, about 75% of the catch is exported (with a value of $460.7 million in 1991), mostly to the US, Japan, and Australia. The principal finfish species caught included blue grenadier, mackerel, whiting, snoek, and orange roughy. In addition, New Zealand fishermen in 1991 landed 2,997 tons of rock lobster, 4,497 tons of oysters, 43,600 tons of mussels, and 1,032 tons of scallops. The most valuable part of the catch is made of orange roughy, hoki, squid, and rock lobster. Aquaculture is also developing; oyster and mussel farming are well established, with scallop, salmon, and abalone farming under consideration.

25FORESTRY

At the time Europeans began coming to New Zealand, about 70% of the land was forest. This proportion has been reduced by settlement, farming, and exploitation to about 28%. Much of the remaining natural forest is reserved in national parks, or as protection forest on mountain land. In 1986, about 75% of the total forest area was crown owned and administered by government departments. In 1986, about 20,000 ha (50,000 acres) of new forest were planted by the government and about 30,600 ha (76,000 acres) by the private sector. The Kaingaroa State Forest in the Rotorua district covers 149,735 ha (370,001 acres) and is claimed to be the largest planted forest in the world.

For wood production, New Zealand now relies heavily on its planted forests of quick-growing exotic species, mainly radiata pine, which can be harvested every 25–30 years. These provide over 90% of the wood for production of sawn timber, wood panel products, pulp, paper, and paperboard. Due to these replanting efforts and privatization of forest lands, exports of softwood logs have skyrocketed since the early 1980s. Most of New Zealand's softwood logs and lumber go to Japan and Australia.

Total sawn wood production in 1991 was 2,198,000 cu m. Total paper and paperboard production amounted to 815,000 tons, including 321,000 tons of newsprint, 35,000 tons of other printing and writing paper, and 459,000 tons of other paper and paperboard. Wood-pulp production reached 1,350,000 tons in 1991; wood-based paneling amounted to 687,000 cu m. In 1992, exports of forest products accounted for over 10% of total exports.

26MINING

Many different minerals are found in New Zealand, but few have been extensively exploited. In 1991, the extractive mineral industry constituted only about 1.5% of the GDP. Coal production is sufficient for domestic consumption, and a small amount is exported; 1991 coal output was 2,550,000 tons. Estimated recoverable coal reserves amount to over 8.6 billion tons. The once-important gold deposits of the South Island, discovered in 1861, were believed to have been exhausted; however, production for 1991 (6,611 kg) increased by more than 40% over that of 1990, reaching the highest production level since 1920. Silver production has also sharply risen from 1,845 kg in 1988 to a reported 11,000 kg in 1991.

Large quantities of iron-bearing sands are present, especially on North Island beaches; 2,300,000 tons of iron sands were extracted in 1991. Titanomagnetite concentrates are produced for Japanese use from iron-sand deposits on the North Island's west coast. Uranium-bearing minerals have been located on the South Island. Output of building materials in 1991 included 5,000,000 tons of sand and gravel for building aggregate, and 1,400,000 tons of limestone for roads.

27ENERGY AND POWER

New Zealand's per capita consumption of electricity is among the highest in the world. A network of transmission lines links all major power stations, bringing electricity to 99% of the population. Of the 29,556 million kwh generated for public supply in 1991, 74% was produced from hydroelectric resources, and 26% from steam. Future hydroelectric potential is limited, however, and thermal power based primarily on coal and natural gas is becoming increasingly important. Net installed generating capacity was 7,504,000 kw in 1991. Hydroelectricity's net installed capacity from 30 stations was 4,294,000 kw in 1991. The geothermal power station at Wairakei has been operating since 1958, while a second at Ohaaki was commissioned in 1989.

New Zealand now meets some 75% of its total energy requirements from indigenous resources, the balance coming from imports of crude oil and refined petroleum products. The Kapuni natural gas field, discovered in 1959, began production in 1970; the Maui offshore natural gas and condensate field, one of the largest in the world, began production in 1979. Oil and gas exploration and development of indigenous resources continue to be stressed, in efforts to reduce dependence on imports. Crude oil and natural gas liquid production levels in 1991 were estimated at 10 million and 1.6 million barrels, respectively. Proven reserves of natural gas totaled 100 billion cu m in 1992; oil reserves were 200 million barrels. Over the last 40 years, coal's contribution to the energy supply has fallen from 50% to about 11%. Within the next ten years, however, coal mining will likely increase to meet increased demands for electricity and steel production; in 1991, coal production was estimated at 2,550,000 tons. Coal reserves are estimated at 6.3 billion tons, of which 85% is located in the untapped lignite fields in Southland.

28INDUSTRY

Industrial production has increased rapidly since the end of World War II, stimulated by intermittent import controls that often enabled domestic industry to increase output without competition. A most significant feature of New Zealand industry in recent decades has been the establishment of heavy industry with Commonwealth and US capital. Plants include metal and petroleum processing, motor vehicle assembly, textiles and footwear, and a wide range of consumer appliances. The New Zealand Steel company manufactures billet slabs and ingots using domestically produced iron sands; Pacific Steel, which processes scrap metal, uses billets from New Zealand Steel. The Tiwai Point aluminum smelter, operated by an Australian-Japanese consortium, has an annual capacity of 244,000 tons. The small but growing electronics industry produce, consumer goods as well as commercial products such as digital gasoline pumps. Wool-based industries have traditionally been an important part of the economy, notably wool milling, the oldest sector of the textile industry. Other significant industrial areas include a diverse food-processing sector, tanneries, sheet glass, rubber, and plastics.

Progressive withdrawal of government support beginning in 1985 led manufacturing to decline from 1987–89 due to a more competitive environment. However, after cutting overcapacity, many firms increased productivity and were ultimately in a stronger financial position. Manufacturing output recovered slightly in the year ending March 1990.

29SCIENCE AND TECHNOLOGY

Most scientific research in New Zealand is funded by the government, principally by the Department of Scientific and Industrial Research (DSIR) and the Ministry of Agriculture and Fisheries. The Cawthron Institute at Nelson, established in 1920, conducts research in chemistry, biology, and environmental and marine studies. New Zealand has 14 other institutes conducting research in agriculture, veterinary science, medicine, and general sciences and 16 universities and colleges offering degrees in basic and applied sciences.

In 1984/85, the DSIR awarded NZ$9,331,000 in research

grants to New Zealand universities and other institutions, three of them overseas. The DSIR and other government departments spent NZ$199,335,000 for scientific and industrial research in 1984/85.

30DOMESTIC TRADE

In 1992, total retail sales income was NZ$29,086 million. Many smaller retailers are being supplanted by small supermarkets and shopping centers; others have converted to self-service operations. There is very little retail mail-order trade. Automobiles and large appliances are increasingly being sold on the installment (hire-purchase) plan. General and trade papers, regional publications, and television and radio are used extensively as advertising media.

Business hours vary, especially since the introduction of staggered work hours, known as glide time. Offices open as early as 7:30 AM and remain open until about 6 PM. Stores may be open at any time between 7 AM and 9 PM, Monday through Saturday. Saturday trading is becoming more prevalent at popular beach resorts near the larger urban areas. Sunday trading is confined to "dairy shops," permitted by law to sell a restricted range of foodstuffs. All offices and banks are closed on Saturdays, Sundays, and statutory holidays.

31FOREIGN TRADE

New Zealand's trade per capita and as a percentage of GNP is among the highest in the world. In 1974/75, more than 70% of export receipts derived from meat, dairy products, and wool; but this figure was down to 56% by 1984/85, as manufactured goods and forest products took an increasing share of the total. Imports consist mainly of manufactured goods, petroleum and petroleum products, and raw materials for industry. Foreign trade more than doubled in value between 1976 and 1981 and again from 1981 to 1985. In 1990/91, exports reached a total of NZ$15,147 million.

Principal exports in 1990/91 (in millions of NZ dollars) were as follows:

Manufactured goods	3,643
Meat	2,588
Dairy products	2,015
Wool	963
Forest products	1,560
Fruit and vegetables	1,069
Iron and steel	429
Aluminum and alloys	778
Fish and crustaceans	625
Hides and skins	559
Casein	513
Other exports and reexports	405
TOTAL	15,147

Principal imports in 1990/91 (in millions of NZ dollars, value for duty) were:

Machinery and electrical equipment	3,773
Transport	2,059
Mineral fuels, lubricants	1,169
Chemicals	3,863
Textiles, clothing, footwear	832
Iron, steel, metals	905
Food and live animals	993
Other imports	457
TOTAL	14,051

Especially since the UK entered the EC, New Zealand has diversified its trade relations. The proportion of total trade with the UK fell from 45% in 1958/59 to 6.6% in 1990/91, at which point Australia was the biggest market for New Zealand's exports (18.9%), while Japan was its biggest source of imports (15%). The US also now ranks ahead of the UK as a trading partner.

Principal trade partners in 1989/90 (in millions of NZ dollars) were:

	EXPORTS	IMPORTS
Australia	2,985.2	2,999.0
Japan	2,483.4	2,371.7
US	2,029.7	2,615.4
UK	1,094.0	1,303.2
South Korea	502.0	267.8
USSR	354.2	
FRG	353.2	634.1
Canada	274.9	265.1
Italy	268.2	291.4
Fiji	249.1	
Sa'udi Arabia	—	440.8
Other countries	4,633.9	2,830.7
TOTALS	15,227.8	14,420.1

³²BALANCE OF PAYMENTS

Since New Zealand's foreign trade depends on agricultural and livestock products, and since prices for these commodities are volatile, New Zealand's balance of payments may swing sharply from one year to the next. Generally, deficits outweighed surpluses during the 1950s and 1960s. Consistent surpluses were recorded between 1969 and 1973, when international reserves nearly quadrupled. However, a poor trade performance in 1974, largely attributable to increased oil import costs, contributed to a large current accounts deficit. Since then, New Zealand has continued to register payments deficits, which have been partially offset by compensatory financing, including overseas loans. The current account deficit improved markedly in 1991/92 to $174 million from $1,243 million in 1990/91, and was driven by a strong increase in the merchandise trade surplus from $859 million in 1990/91 to $1,990 million in 1991/92. The trade surplus was expected to narrow, as investments started boosting imports of capital goods.

In 1992 merchandise exports totaled $9,772 million and imports $8,108 million. The merchandise trade balance was $1,644 million.

The following table summarizes New Zealand's balance of payments for 1991 and 1992 (in millions of US dollars):

	1991	1992
CURRENT ACCOUNT		
Goods services and income	−1,218	−1,448
Unrequited transfers	683	685
TOTALS	−535	−763
CAPITAL ACCOUNT		
Direct investment	726	91
Portfolio investment	54	—
Other long-term capital	−1,373	−2,356
Other short-term capital	509	5
Exceptional Financing	192	1,608
Reserves	1,319	−131
TOTALS	1,427	−783
Errors and omissions	−893	1,546
Total change in reserves	1,179	—

³³BANKING AND SECURITIES

The Reserve Bank of New Zealand, established in 1933, exercises control over monetary circulation and credit. It is the bank of issue, handles all central government banking transactions, manages the public debt, and administers exchange control regula-

tions. The Reserve Bank of New Zealand Amendment Act (1973) empowers the Bank to regulate credit from all sources and requires it to make loans (as the minister of finance may determine) in order to ensure continued full employment. Notes and coins in circulation at the end of 1990 amounted to NZ$1,032.8 million, up from NZ$868.6 million in March 1987 and NZ$717.6 million in 1985.

There are 18 registered banks in New Zealand, one of which, the Bank of New Zealand, is state owned. Total demand deposits in the commercial banks for 1993 totaled NZ$23,284 million, up from NZ$11,639 million in 1985.

There are numerous trustee savings banks. The Post Office Savings Bank (established in 1865) has about 1,270 offices and agencies throughout New Zealand.

The stock exchanges in Auckland, Wellington, Christchurch, Dunedin, and Invercargill are members of the Stock Exchange Association of New Zealand, with headquarters in Wellington. Official listing is granted to companies that comply with the Association's requirements. These do not impose qualifications as to share capital but do provide that the company must be of sufficient magnitude and its shareholding sufficiently well distributed to ensure a free market for its shares. Subject to the recommendation and approval of the stock exchange nearest to the registered offices, companies may secure unofficial listing for their shares. All transactions in shares quoted in the unofficial list are subject to special brokerage rates. In 1978, a five-member Securities Commission was established to oversee law and practice relating to securities.

³⁴INSURANCE

There were 41 life insurance offices conducting business in New Zealand in 1989, 169 non-life insurance companies, and no composite companies. The government provides insurance through the Government Life Insurance Office and the State Insurance Office, which undertakes accident, fire, and marine insurance.

Growth in life insurance assets has averaged more than NZ$100 million annually in recent years, totaling NZ$6,846 million at the end of the 1985/86 fiscal year. New Zealand has one of the world's highest ratios of value of life insurance policies to national income.

³⁵PUBLIC FINANCE

The following table shows actual revenues and expenditures for 1993 and 1994 in millions of dollars.

	1993	1994
REVENUE AND GRANTS		
Tax revenue	24,224	25,220
Non-tax revenue	2,356	2,281
Capital revenue	160	107
TOTAL	26,740	27,608
EXPENDITURES & LENDING MINUS REPAYMENTS		
General public service	1,364	1,603
Defense	1,068	1,136
Public order and safety	1,303	1,365
Education	4,001	4,190
Health	3,495	3,681
Social security and welfare	11,265	11,341
Housing and community amenities	131	68
Recreation, cultural, and religious affairs	277	299
Economic affairs and services	1,529	1,576
Other expenditures	4,000	3,769
Lending minus repayments	−1,782	239
TOTAL	26,651	29,267
Deficit /surplus	83	−1,659

In 1991/92, the financial deficit narrowed marginally to 13.4% of GDP from 3.5% in 1990/91. Total government expenditure declined from nearly 43% of GDP in 1991/92 to 39% in 1992/93, as measures introduced by the National Party government in December 1990 and July 1991 to contain social welfare expenditures began to have an impact. Such fiscal restraint is expected to reduce expenditure to 37% of GDP by 1995/96, but revenues are expected to remain at 34–35% of GDP until that time. Many companies have tax losses to carry forward and personal income is expected to grow slowly.

In 1991 New Zealand's total public debt stood at NZ$43,931 million, of which NZ$22,950 million was financed abroad.

36TAXATION

Earnings are taxed in one combined general income and social security tax, which for wage and salary earners is deducted by the employer on a pay-as-you-earn basis (called PAYE), with annual adjustments. Effective in 1993, the rates were 24% on income up to NZ$30,875, and 33% an additional income. The system of special tax rebates (credits) includes a standard rebate for the taxpayer and other rebates for dependent relatives, housekeeping or child-care expenses, and tuition. There are also deductions for certain dividend and interest income, life insurance premiums, and contributions to retirement funds. The income tax rate for corporations, including subsidiaries of overseas corporations, was 33%, applied to net income after certain deductions. There are tax incentives for exporters.

On 1 October 1986, a new 10% value-added tax on goods and services (GST) was introduced, replacing the previous sales tax except in a few instances. As of 1993, this tax was 12.5%. Excise taxes are imposed on motor vehicles, gasoline, tobacco products, and alcoholic beverages.

Local authorities are largely dependent on property taxes. There are three main systems of rating: (1) capital (land improvements) value; (2) annual value; (3) unimproved value. The actual amount of the rate is fixed by each local authority.

37CUSTOMS AND DUTIES

Customs taxation is based principally on an ad valorem scale, but specific duties are applied to some goods. Rates of duty payable depend on the country of origin. With the exception of some automotive products, preferential rate scales for the UK were phased out by 1 July 1977, as a result of that nation's entry into the EC. In 1978, preferential rates for Commonwealth countries were also discontinued. Two years earlier, New Zealand had introduced a revised Generalized System of Preferences favoring the developing countries. As of 1993, the government was planning to reduce most tariffs about one-third by 1996.

38FOREIGN INVESTMENT

Investment in New Zealand's economy by overseas companies through New Zealand subsidiaries has increased steadily, with the largest contribution from Australian sources, which have outstripped UK sources in recent years. Total overseas investment reached US$11,000 million at the end of 1991. Of this total, US$1,900 million was from the UK, US$4,800 million from Australia, US$2,809 from the US, and US$950 from Japan.

39ECONOMIC DEVELOPMENT

Economic policy is established and directed by the government through taxation, Reserve Bank interest rates, price and monopoly controls, and import and export licensing. Import controls, introduced early in 1958, were further tightened in 1961 and 1973 to correct deficits in the balance of payments. Since then, the government has gradually liberalized import controls; in 1981, about 79% of private imports to New Zealand were exempt from licensing. An industrial restructuring program, begun in the mid-1970s, focuses on certain industries (e.g., textiles, footwear, automobiles, and electronics) whose domestic prices are much higher than those of foreign substitutes, with the aim of reducing the protection granted such products.

To help maintain economic stability, the government assists, and in some cases controls, various economic enterprises (agricultural distribution and marketing, commercial banking, and some insurance). In June 1982, in an effort to reduce inflation, the government announced a freeze on wages, prices, rents, and dividends. The freeze was lifted in March 1984, temporarily reimposed by a new Labour government, then terminated late in 1984. Its termination, combined with a devaluation of the dollar, led to a resumption of high inflation. The government implemented severe monetary policies to reduce inflation in order to enhance a market- and export-led recovery from the October 1987 financial markets crash. The cost was a large increase in unemployment (from 7% to 10.4% of the labor force), but by 1991 inflation had been practically eliminated (2.2% for the year ending September 1991).

Since 1977, the New Zealand Planning Council has been charged with advising the government on economic, social, and cultural planning and in the coordination of planning. Working independently of the Planning Council, the Economic Monitoring Group, established in 1978, produces reports on economic trends.

In 1984/85, New Zealand contributed a total of NZ$61.4 million in technical and capital assistance and direct aid or loans to developing nations. An additional NZ$12.5 million was given in multilateral aid through the UN, the South Pacific Commission, ADB, and other organizations. The major recipients of development assistance are the nations of the South Pacific, who receive about 70% of New Zealand's bilateral aid and about 62% of its total overseas aid.

40SOCIAL DEVELOPMENT

The Social Security Act of 1964 consolidated and advanced existing social legislation. By a system of monetary benefits on a compulsory contributory basis and a system of medical and hospital benefits, all persons in New Zealand are now protected economically in the event of sickness, unemployment, and widowhood, and when they age. The former separate social security tax was combined, as of 1 April 1969, with the graduated general income tax applicable to all wage earners. Monetary benefits under the Social Security Act are paid for retirement, unemployment, sickness, and emergencies; and to widows, orphans, families, invalids, and miners. National superannuation (retirement) benefits, for persons aged 60 or over, replaced separate retirement and old age benefits in 1977. Benefits are funded by ordinary government revenues and provide a percentage of the average weekly wage after tax. Benefits are taxable, but are not subject to an income test. Medical benefits include medical, hospital, and pharmaceutical payments.

A revised accident compensation plan enacted in 1982 provides continuous coverage for all persons in regular employment whether injured at work or not. The plan is financed by a levy on employers (1.71% of payroll in 1991) and by a contribution from general revenue; compensation is 80% of average earnings. Levies on motor vehicle owners, fund coverage for injury or death by motor vehicle accident, regardless of blame. A special Accident Compensation Corporation was established in 1983 to administer the program.

The marriage rate in New Zealand declined between 1976 and 1979, but rose slightly for the next three years, reaching 8.02 per 1,000 population in 1982. It declined to 7.5 by 1988. The minimum age for marriage is 16, and the consent of a parent or guardian is required for a person under 20 to marry. In 1988, the average age at first marriage was 23 for women and 24 for men. The Family Proceedings Act of 1980, which took effect on

1 October 1981, provides only one ground for divorce—that the marriage has broken down irreconcilably. To establish this, the parties must have been living apart for two years. In 1988, there were 2.5 divorces per 1,000 inhabitants. The fertility rate in 1985–90 was 2.0. New Zealand law forbids spousal rape, and there is effective coordination between police and agencies providing support services for rape victims. New Zealand was the first country to grant full suffrage to women, and it celebrated the 100th anniversary of that event in 1993 with conferences and other activities.

41HEALTH

New Zealand's health care system has been undergoing a restructuring since the mid-1980s. Area health boards, formed to combine primary and hospital care facilities for each region under a single administrative unit, were established in 1985. In 1991, more changes were announced by the government announced plans to expand health care resources for those in financial need. The number of purchases of private health insurance has risen steadily in recent years and, by 1991, covered about half the population. At that time, there were six main companies in the private health insurance market.

In 1993, there were 8,100 doctors (1.74 per 1,000 people in 1992, with a nurse to doctor ratio of 0.1), and over 1,000 dentists. New Zealand had more than 39,000 nurses and midwives in 1985. Most physicians practice under the National Health Service, established by the Social Security Act of 1938, but private practice outside the scheme is permitted.

For over 50 years, comprehensive health services, most of them supported by the State, have been available to all New Zealanders. About 80% of all health care costs are met by the public sector. There are about 1,000 voluntary health service groups, often state subsidized. Treatment at public hospitals is free for people ordinarily resident in New Zealand. In private hospitals, medical care is subsidized; a full range of maternity services is paid for by the Department of Health. The Health Service provides hospital treatment, maternity services from a general practitioner, most prescribed drugs, laboratory diagnostic services, dental care, routine immunizations for children under 16, and some health appliances free of charge. Partial benefits are paid for private hospitalization, X-ray services, physiotherapy, and hearing aids. Care is free for infants and preschool children. Most children are immunized free by their family doctors, but the Department of Health also has immunization clinics. In 1992, children up to one year old were vaccinated against tuberculosis (20%); diphtheria, pertussis, and tetanus (81%); polio (68%); and measles (82%).

In 1990, there were 344 hospitals with 30,000 beds (6.6 per 1,000 inhabitants). Public hospitals are managed under the supervision of the Minister of Health by local hospital boards, whose members are elected; all costs are borne by the state. Private hospital costs are partly paid for by the state; additional fees may be claimed from patients. Voluntary welfare organizations make valuable contributions to public health, and are assisted by grants from public funds. Total health care expenditures in 1990 were $3,150 million.

New Zealand's population in 1993 was 3.5 million, with a birth rate of 17.4 per 1,000 inhabitants. About 70% of married women (ages 15 to 49) were using contraceptives. There were 60,000 births in 1992. Infant mortality in 1992 was 8 per 1,000 live births for the total population. The rate for the Maori population in 1984 was 18.4 per 1,000 live births, a significant improvement over the 1967 rate of 29.7. The overall death rate in 1993 was 8.2 per 1,000 inhabitants. Life expectancy at birth was 76 years in 1992. The principal causes of death are heart disease, cancer, and cerebrovascular diseases. There were about 10 reported cases of tuberculosis per 100,000 people in 1990. Alco-

holism is a significant public health problem in New Zealand. Estimates of the number of chronic alcoholics range upward from 53,000, and another 250,000 New Zealanders may be classified as excessive drinkers.

42HOUSING

The number of houses and apartments built in New Zealand fell steadily from 1974/75, when 34,000 new houses and flats were built, to 1981, when only 14,300 were constructed; since then, numbers have generally risen, reaching 18,000 in 1992, when New Zealand's housing stock totaled 1,220,000. More than half the total housing stock has been constructed since 1957. In recent decades, the government has introduced measures designed to assist the financing of housing by contractors and private owners. These include increases in the maximum housing loans advanced by the State Advances Corporation, low-interest loans for families with low incomes, and the establishment of a home savings scheme through the Post Office Savings Bank. Since 1937, the government Housing Corp. has built houses and flats for rental, with preference given to low-income families; by March 1985, 90,469 of these had been completed. Since 1951, the government has generously subsidized local authorities to provide pensioners' housing.

The average cost of a house was about NZ$75,630 in 1985. The average bank loan to homeowners was about two-thirds to three-fourths of the sale price. Most families own their own homes. The average private dwelling has three bedrooms, a living room, dining room, kitchen, laundry, bathroom, toilet, and garage. Most units are built of wood and have sheet-iron or tiled roofs.

43EDUCATION

Education in New Zealand is compulsory for 10 years for children between 6 and 15, although most children attend school from the age of 5; the adult literacy rate is 99%. Public primary and secondary schools are administered by district education boards (or boards of governors) and school committees (the latter elected by householders), under the authority of the Department of Education. Kindergartens are run either by private persons or by voluntary organizations with partial state subsidies. Primary education is given at primary and intermediate schools (the latter giving the last two years of primary education), and postprimary education at secondary schools, technical high schools, or consolidated schools for pupils who live in rural areas. Evening classes are given by technical and secondary schools, and adult education classes are offered by the universities. Most state schools are coeducational, but some private schools not. New Zealand has 2,300 state primary schools and 60 privately owned schools. At the secondary level, there are 315 state-run schools and 15 private schools.

In 1990 there were 72,025 students in preschool institutions; 314,487 students in primary schools and 335,456 students in secondary schools. Out of this number of secondary students, 5,690 were in vocational courses. For children in isolated areas, there is a public Correspondence School. In some regions there are special state primary and secondary schools for Maori children, but most Maori children attend public schools. Private primary and secondary schools are operated by individuals and religious bodies. Since 1975, under new legislation, many private schools have been voluntarily integrated into the public system.

There are six universities, all operating under the aegis of the University Grants Committee and the Universities Entrance Board: the University of Auckland, University of Waikato (at Hamilton), Massey University (at Palmerston North), Victoria University of Wellington, University of Canterbury (at Christchurch), and University of Otago (at Dunedin). All universities offer courses in the arts, social sciences, commerce, and science. An agricultural institution, Lincoln College, is associated with the University of Canterbury. Law is offered at Auckland, Waikato, Victoria, Canterbury, and Otago, and medicine at Auckland and Otago. The Central Institute of Technology, near Wellington, is the leading institution in a network of 24 polytechnic institutions. There are evening classes for adults interested in continuing their education at secondary schools, institutes and community centers. University tuition fees are low, and financial assistance is given to applicants who have passed special qualifying examinations.

44LIBRARIES AND MUSEUMS

The National Library of New Zealand was founded in 1966 by the amalgamation of three state libraries and service divisions. It contains 715,000 volumes, 12,000 periodical titles, and 1,685,000 microfiches, not including material in certain special collections. Its Extension Division provides services to public and school libraries throughout the country, and the Library School offers courses for the training and certification of librarians. The two largest libraries are at the University of Auckland (1.4 million volumes) and the University of Otago (1.3 million). The largest public libraries are in Auckland, Christchurch, Dunedin, and Wellington. Free local libraries have a book stock of 6.5 million volumes.

Outstanding art galleries and museums are the Auckland City Art Gallery (European and New Zealand paintings); the Canterbury Museum, Christchurch (ornithology, anthropology, and history); the Dunedin Public Art Gallery (paintings, period furniture, and china); the Otago Museum, Dunedin (ethnography, classical antiquities, ceramics); the National Museum, Wellington (botany, ethnology, history); and the National Art Gallery, Wellington (paintings, sculpture, etchings, engravings). The nation's largest collection of Maori and Polynesian artifacts is found in the War Memorial Museum in Auckland.

45MEDIA

The government is in the process of privatizing and deregulating the telecommunications sector. In 1990, Telecom Corp., which runs the country's telephone services, was sold to a consortium led by American Information Technologies Corp. and Bell Atlantic. The number of telephones in 1991 was 2,402,619.

After undergoing decentralization in the early 1970s, the national broadcasting system was again reorganized in the latter half of the decade, and united under one central board, the Broadcasting Corp. of New Zealand. Under its authority are the Radio New Zealand network, a unified television service operating the two formerly competing national networks, TV1 and TV2, and one privately owned channel. The Corporation also (as of 1991) operated 37 commercial community radio stations, 4 popular music stations, 26 non-commercial national stations, and 4 classical music stations. Color television was introduced in October 1973, and most households now have color sets. There were 1,515,000 television sets and 3,180,000 radios in 1991.

Aside from the usual British legal limits for libel, there is complete freedom of the press in New Zealand. The *Taranaki Herald*, founded in 1852, is New Zealand's oldest surviving newspaper. In 1991 there were 35 daily newspapers in New Zealand. The largest daily newspapers and their estimated 1991 circulation figures are:

New Zealand Herald (m)	Auckland	252,000
The Press (m)	Christchurch	95,900
Auckland Star (e)	Auckland	86,200
The Dominion (m)	Wellington	74,900

46ORGANIZATIONS

Almost all aspects of New Zealand life have their appropriate organizations. A few of the more important ones are the Federated Farmers of New Zealand, the New Zealand Fruitgrowers' Association, the New Zealand Employers' Federation, the Chamber of Commerce (represented in almost every large town), the Returned Servicemen's Association, the New Zealand Federation of Labour, the Plunket Society (which deals with child welfare), the Royal Society of New Zealand, "Heritage" (devoted to the assistance of children deprived of one parent), the New Zealand Red Cross Society, the New Zealand Press Association, the New Zealand Institute of Public Administration, and the New Zealand Public Service Association. Important cultural organizations are the New Zealand Symphony Orchestra, the New Zealand Opera Company, the New Zealand Ballet, the Queen Elizabeth II Arts Council, and the New Zealand Music Federation.

47TOURISM, TRAVEL, AND RECREATION

New Zealand draws many thousands of tourists to its shores because of the beauty, diversity, and compactness of its natural attractions and its varied sporting facilities. There are 10 national parks and 3 maritime parks. Of these, Fiordland is the largest, with some portions still unexplored. Urewera, noted for its forests and bird life, is the park in which early Maori culture is most strongly preserved; Tongariro includes two active volcanoes and is an important ski resort; and Mount Cook National Park includes Tasman Glacier, the largest glacier outside the polar regions. New Zealand has numerous thermal spas, particularly in the Rotorua area, which also offers Maori villages where traditional arts and crafts may be observed. The Waitomo Cave, on the North Island, is lit by millions of glowworms and may be toured all year. Lake Taupo and its streams form one of the world's richest trout fishing areas; Christchurch is home to one of the world's finest botanical gardens. Skiing is available on both the North and South Islands, and good deep-sea fishing along the North Island coast. New Zealand has first-class golf courses. Spectator sports include horse racing, soccer, cricket, and rugby.

All overseas visitors (except Australian nationals) need passports valid for at least six months beyond their intended stay in New Zealand. No visas are required for persons who are traveling on valid British passports; for citizens of Belgium, Canada, Denmark, Finland, France, Germany, Ireland, Liechtenstein, Luxembourg, Monaco, the Netherlands, Norway, Sweden, or Switzerland; or for US or Japanese nationals not planning to stay in New Zealand more than 30 days. There are no vaccination requirements.

Tourism has slowed since 1989 due to the strengthening of the New Zealand dollar, rising costs, and international factors, including the 1991 Persian Gulf War. In 1991, there were 963,470 visitor arrivals, 35% from Australia, 14% from the United States, 12% from Japan, and 9% from the United Kingdom. In the same year, tourism receipts totaled US$1.02 billion. As of 1988, there were 39,327 rooms in hotels and motels.

48FAMOUS NEW ZEALANDERS

Among New Zealand's best-known statesmen are Sir George Grey (1812–98), governor and later prime minister; Richard John Seddon (1845–1906), prime minister responsible for much social legislation; William Ferguson Massey (1856–1925); and Peter Fraser (1884–1950), World War II prime minister. Robert David Muldoon (b.1921) was prime minister from 1975 to 1984, when David Lange (b.1942) became the youngest man to hold that office in the 20th century. Sir John Salmond (1862–1924) was an eminent jurist. William Pember Reeves (1857–1932), outstanding journalist, politician, and political economist, was the director of the London School of Economics. Frances Hodgkins (1869–1947) was a highly regarded painter. Katherine Mansfield (Kathleen Beauchamp Murry, 1888–1923), author of many evocative stories, was a master of the short-story form. Other well-known authors include Sylvia Ashton-Warner (1908–84) and Maurice

Shadbolt (b.1932). Two outstanding leaders of the Maori people were Sir Apirana Ngata (1874–1950) and Sir Peter Buck (1880–1951). Sir Truby King (1858–1938) pioneered in the field of child care.

Lord Ernest Rutherford (1871–1937), pioneer in atomic research and 1908 Nobel Prize winner for chemistry, was born in New Zealand. Other scientists include Sir Harold Gillies (1882–1960) and Sir Archibald McIndoe (1900–62), whose plastic surgery methods did much to rehabilitate war victims; Sir Brian G. Barratt-Boyes (b.1924), a researcher in cardiac-thoracic surgery; and Albert W. Liley (b.1929), a researcher in perinatal psychology. Prominent in the arts have been ballet dancers Alexander Grant (b.1925) and Rowena Jackson (b.1926); the singer and actor Inia Watene Te Wiata (1915–71); and the soprano Kiri Te Kanawa (b.1944). Sir Edmund Percival Hillary (b.1919) was the conqueror of Mt. Everest. The celebrated political cartoonist David Low (1891–1963) was born in New Zealand.

49DEPENDENCIES

Cook Islands

Part of New Zealand since 1901, the Cook Islands became internally self-governing on 4 August 1965. The Cook Islands Constitution Act of 1964 established the island group as wholly self-ruling but possessed of common citizenship with New Zealand as well as of a common head of state (the Queen). New Zealand exercises certain responsibilities for the defense and external affairs of the islands, in consultation with the Cook Islands government.

A parliamentary type of government, like New Zealand's, characterizes the new political relationship, with a cabinet composed of a prime minister and six other ministers. The 24-member Legislative Assembly—to which the prime minister and other cabinet members are responsible—is elected by the adult population of the islands every four years and can void the applicability of New Zealand laws to the territory under its jurisdiction. The constitution of the autonomous islands also allows a declaration of independence, if ever this should be the wish of the political leadership. The office of New Zealand high commissioner was abolished in 1975 and replaced by the office of Queen's representative. Cook Islands products continue to enter New Zealand freely, and the level of subsidies to the islands from the New Zealand government has persisted.

The Cook Islands, 15 islands lying between 8° and 23°s and 156° and 167°w, more than 3,220 km (2,000 mi) northeast of New Zealand, were discovered by James Cook in 1773. They became a British protectorate in 1888 and were annexed to New Zealand in 1901. They consist of the Southern Group, 8 islands the largest of which are Rarotonga (6,666 ha/16,472 acres) and Mangaia (5,191 ha/12,827 acres), and the Northern Group, 7 islands varying in size from Penrhyn (984 ha/2,432 acres) to Nassau (121 ha/299 acres). The total area is 241 sq km (93 sq mi). The northern islands are low-lying coral atolls, while the southern islands, including Rarotonga, the administrative seat, are elevated and fertile, and have the greater population. Except for Rarotonga, the islands suffer from lack of streams and wells, and water must be conserved. The islands lie within the hurricane area and sometimes experience destructive storms.

The population (estimated in 1993 at 18,903) is Polynesian and close in language and tradition to the New Zealand Maori. They are converts to Christianity. The islands are visited by government and freight vessels, and interisland shipping services are provided by commercially owned boats. An international airport opened for full services in 1973. Each inhabited island has a radio station.

The economy is based on agriculture, with the main exports being citrus fruits and juices, tomatoes, bananas, and pineapples. Other exports are copra, pearl shell, and clothing. In 1988,

exports amounted to us$4.0 million. The main imports are foodstuffs, piece goods, oils, gasoline, tobacco, vehicles and parts, timber, and cement. In 1988, imports amounted to us$39.7 million.

Revenue for public finances is derived mainly from import duties and income tax. The 1990–91 budget envisioned expenditures of us$34.5 million. The New Zealand government provided grants and subsidies for capital development in health, education, other social services, economic development, and other purposes, covering one-third of the budget.

Free compulsory education is provided by the government at primary and secondary levels for all children between the ages of 6 and 15. All Cook Islanders receive free medical and surgical treatment, and schoolchildren receive free dental care.

Niue

An isolated coral island, Niue is 966 km (600 mi) northwest of the southern Cook Islands, and located at 19°02′s and 169°52′w. Nieue became a British protectorate in 1900 and was annexed to New Zealand in 1901. Although Niue forms part of the Cook Islands, because of its remoteness and cultural and linguistic differences it has been separately administered. Niue has an area of 258 sq km (100 sq mi). Its population (of Polynesian stock) was 1,997 in 1993, down from a peak of 5,194 in 1966, and is continuing to decline, principally because of emigration to New Zealand, where Niueans outnumber those remaining on the island by two to one.

Niue became self-governing on 19 October 1974, in free association with New Zealand. Under the constitution, the former leader of government became the premier. An assembly of 20 members is elected by universal suffrage; 14 members represent village constituencies, and 6 are elected at large. The constitution provides for New Zealand to exercise various responsibilities for the external affairs and defense of Niue and to furnish economic and administrative assistance.

Niue's soil, although fertile, is not plentiful; arable land is confined to small pockets of soil among the coral rocks, making agriculture difficult. Since there are no running streams, the island is dependent on rainwater. The economy is based mainly on agriculture. Passionfruit products, coconut cream, lime juice and lime oil, and honey are exported, along with leather footballs and handicrafts. There are 124 km (77 mi) of all-weather roads. A steamship company maintains monthly service to New Zealand. A telephone system connects the villages, and an airport became fully operational in 1971.

Budget deficits are met by the New Zealand government, which also makes grants for capital development. Between 1970 and 1989 Western (non-US) and ODA and OOF bilateral commitments total us$62. Health services and education are free. Education is compulsory for children 5 to 14 years of age.

Tokelau Islands

The Tokelau Islands, situated between 8° and 10°s and 171° and 173°w, about 483 km (300 mi) north of Western Samoa, consist of three atolls, Fakaofo, Nukunonu, and Atafu. Total area is about 10 sq km (4 sq mi). Each atoll has a lagoon encircled by a number of reef-bound islets varying in length from about 90 m to 6.4 km (100 yards to 4 mi), in width from 90 m to 360 m (100–400 yards), and extending more than 3 m (10 ft) above sea level. All villages are on the leeward side, close to passages through the reefs. Lying in the hurricane belt, the islands have a mean annual rainfall of 305 cm (120 in). The inhabitants, of Polynesian origin, are British subjects and New Zealand citizens. Total population in 1992 was estimated at 1,760. Formerly part of the Gilbert and Ellice Islands group, the Tokelaus were transferred to New Zealand at the beginning of 1949. There is no resident European staff; executive functions are carried out on each atoll by appointed Tokelau mayors, magistrates, clerks, and other officials. An administrative officer based in Western Samoa coordinates administrative services for the islands. Samoan is the official language.

Subsistence farming and the production of copra for export are the main occupations. Visits are made regularly by New Zealand Air Force planes, and a chartered vessel makes regular trading visits. Sources of revenue are an export duty on copra, customs dues, postage stamps, and trading profits.

Government expenditure is devoted mainly to agriculture, the provision of social services, and administrative costs. Annual deficits are met by New Zealand government subsidies. New Zealand's budgetary aid for 1991/1992 totaled US$2.4 million. Nutrition and health are reasonably good.

Ross Dependency

The Ross Dependency (between 160°E and 150°W and south of 60°s) is a section of the Antarctic continent that was brought under the jurisdiction of New Zealand in 1923. Its area is estimated at 414,400 sq km (160,000 sq mi). It is almost entirely covered by ice and is largely uninhabited. New Zealand activities in the dependency are coordinated and supervised by the Ross Dependency Research Committee (a government agency) and implemented by the Antarctic division of the Department of Scientific and Industrial Research. Exploitation of the region, apart from scientific expeditions, has been confined to whaling. A joint US-New Zealand scientific station established at Cape Hallett in 1957 for participation in the International Geophysical Year continues to operate for purposes of scientific research.

50BIBLIOGRAPHY

Alley, Roderick (ed.). *New Zealand and the Pacific*. Boulder, Colo.: Westview, 1984.

Bloomfield, G. T. *New Zealand: A Handbook of Historical Studies*. Boston: G. K. Hall, 1984.

Buck, Sir Peter Henry. *The Coming of the Maori*. 2d ed. Wellington: Whitcombe and Tombs, 1974.

Camilleri, Joseph A. *The Australia, New Zealand, US Alliance: Regional Security in the Nuclear Age*. Boulder, Colo.: Westview Press, 1987.

Duncan, Ian. *Corporatization and Privatization: Lessons from New Zealand*. Auckland; New York: Oxford University Press, 1992.

Hawke, G. R. *The Making of New Zealand*. Cambridge: Cambridge University Press, 1985.

Henderson, John, Keith Jackson, and Richard Kennaway. *Beyond New Zealand: The Foreign Policy of a Small State*. Auckland: Methuen, 1980.

Hoadley, Steve. *The New Zealand Foreign Affairs Handbook*. Auckland: Oxford University Press, 1989.

Johnston, Carol Morton. *The Farthest Corner: New Zealand, a Twice Discovered Land*. Honolulu, Hawaii: University of Hawaii Press, 1988.

Lane, P. A. *Economy in the Balance: An Introduction to the New Zealand Economy*. Wellington: Methuen, 1976.

Lealand, Geoffrey. *A Foreign Egg in Our Nest?: American Popular Culture in New Zealand*. Wellington: Victoria University Press, 1988.

Levine, Stephen. *The New Zealand Political System*. Auckland: Allen & Unwin, 1979.

McClymont, William Graham. *Exploration of New Zealand*. London: Oxford University Press, 1959.

McKinnon, Malcolm. *Independence and Foreign Policy: New Zealand in the World since 1935*. Auckland: Oxford University Press, 1993.

McLauchlan, Gordon (ed.). *The Illustrated Encyclopedia of New Zealand*. Auckland: D. Bateman, 1992.

Metge, Joan. *The Maoris of New Zealand*. London: Routledge & Kegan Paul, 1976.

Miller, Harold Gladstone. *New Zealand*. Westport, Conn.: Greenwood, 1983.

Mulgan, R. G. *Democracy and Power in New Zealand: A Study of New Zealand Politics*. 2d ed. New York: Oxford University Press, 1989.

Oddie, Graham and Roy W. Perrett (eds.). *Justice, Ethics, and New Zealand Society*. New York: Oxford University Press, 1992.

Rice, Geoffrey W. (ed.) *The Oxford History of New Zealand*. 2nd ed. Auckland; New York: Oxford University Press, 1992.

Sharp, A. *Justice and the Maori: Maori Claims in New Zealand Political Argument in the 1980s*. New York: Oxford University Press, 1990.

Sinclair, Keith. *Origins of the Maori Wars*. 2d ed. Auckland: Auckland University Press, 1974.

The Oxford Illustrated History of New Zealand. New York: Oxford University Press, 1990.

OMAN

Sultanate of Oman
Saltanat 'Uman

CAPITAL: Muscat (Masqat).

FLAG: The flag is red with a broad stripe of white at the upper fly and green at the lower fly; in the canton, white crossed swords overlay a ceremonial dagger.

ANTHEM: *Nashid as-Salaam as-Sutani (Sultan's National Anthem).*

MONETARY UNIT: The Omani riyal (RO), established in November 1972, is a paper currency of 1,000 baizas. There are coins of 2, 5, 10, 25, 50, 100, 250, and 500 baizas, and notes of 100, 250, and 500 baizas (the last two being replaced by coins) and 1, 5, 10, 20, and 50 riyals. RO1 = $2.6008 (or $1 = RO0.3845).

WEIGHTS AND MEASURES: The metric system was adopted on 15 November 1974; the imperial and local system are also used.

HOLIDAYS: Accession of the Sultan, 23 July; National Day, 18 November; Sultan's Birthday, 19 November. Movable Muslim religious holidays include 'Id al-Fitr, 'Id al-'Adha', and Milad an-Nabi.

TIME: 4 PM = noon GMT. Solar time is also observed.

¹LOCATION, SIZE, AND EXTENT

The Sultanate of Oman is the second-largest country after Sa'udi Arabia on the Arabian Peninsula, with an area officially estimated at 212,460 sq km (82,031 sq mi). Comparatively, the area occupied by Oman is slightly smaller than the state of Kansas. Oman's territory includes the tip of the strategically important Ra's Musandam, which juts into the Strait of Hormuz. Oman's part of the peninsula is separated from the rest of the country by the territory of the United Arab Emirates (UAE). Oman proper extends 972 km (604 mi) NE–SW and 513 km (319 mi) SE–NW. It is bordered on the N by the Strait of Hormuz, on the NE by the Gulf of Oman, on the E and S by the Arabian Sea, on the SW by the People's Democratic Republic of Yemen (PDRY), on the W by the Ar-Rub' al-Khali (Empty Quarter) and Sa'udi Arabia, and on the NW by the UAE. The total estimated boundary length is 3,466 km (2,154 mi).

²TOPOGRAPHY

Physically, Oman, except for the Dhofar (Zufar) region, consists of three divisions: a coastal plain, a mountain range, and a plateau. The coastal plain varies in width from 16 km (10 mi) to practically nothing near Muscat, where the hills descend abruptly to the sea. The mountain range reaches its greatest height in the Jabal al-Akhdar, about 3,075 m (10,090 ft). The plateau has an average height of about 300 m (1,000 ft) and is mostly stony and waterless, extending to the sands of the Ar-Rub' al-Khali. The coastline southward to Dhofar is barren and forbidding. From Salalah, a semicircular fertile plain extends to the foot of a steep line of hills, some 1,500 m (4,920 ft) high, and forms the edge of a stony plateau also extending to the sands of the Empty Quarter.

³CLIMATE

Annual rainfall in Muscat averages 10 cm (4 in), falling mostly in January. Dhofar is subject to the southwest monsoon, and rainfall up to 64 cm (25 in) has been recorded in the rainy season from late June to October. While the mountain areas receive more plentiful rainfall, some parts of the coast, particularly near the island of Masirah, sometimes receive no rain at all within the course of a year. The climate generally is very hot, with temperatures reaching 54°C (129°F) in the hot season, from May to October.

⁴FLORA AND FAUNA

Desert shrub and desert grass, common to southern Arabia, are found. Vegetation is sparse in the interior plateau, which is largely gravel desert. The greater rainfall in Dhofar and the mountains makes the growth there more luxuriant. Coconut palms grow plentifully in Dhofar, and frankincense grows in the hills. Oleander and varieties of acacia abound.

Indigenous mammals include the cheetah, hyena, fox, wolf, and hare. Birds include the Arabian see-see partridge, redleg chukor partridge, and Muscat bee eater.

⁵ENVIRONMENT

Maintaining an adequate supply of water for agricultural and domestic use is Oman's most pressing environmental problem. The nation has only 0.5 cubic miles of water. Ninety-four percent is used in farming and 3% for industrial activity. Thirteen percent of people living in the cities and 58% of rural dwellers do not have pure water. Drought and limited rainfall are contributing factors to shortages in the nation's water supply. The water may also be contaminated by sea water. Salinization of the soil can occur when exposed to water with a high salt content. Pollution from oil tanker traffic through the Strait of Hormuz and Gulf of Oman is also a persistent problem. In 1994, the nation had six endangered species of mammals and one endangered type of bird. Two plant species are threatened with extinction. Decrees have been passed to protect endangered species, which included the South Arabian leopard, Arabian oryx, mountain gazelle, goitered gazelle, Arabian tahr, green turtle, hawksbill turtle, and olive turtle.

⁶POPULATION

In 1990, the total population was officially estimated at 2,000,000, with a density of 6.6 per sq km (17.2 per sq mi). The

UN, which estimated the population at 1,637,000 in mid 1992, projected a population of 2,168,000 for the year 2000, assuming a crude birthrate of 39.1 per 1,000 population, a crude death rate of 4.4, and a net natural increase of 34.7 during 1995–2000. The greatest concentrations are around Muscat and on the Batinah coast; together, they have more than half the population. Salalah is the principal town of the south. About 90% of the population remains rural, including some 100,000 nomads and seminomads. Muscat had an estimated population of 53,000 in 1990.

7MIGRATION

There is frequent movement of workers between Oman and neighboring states. In 1992, about 350,000 foreigners were working in Oman, most of them Indians, Pakistanis, or Bangladeshi.

8ETHNIC GROUPS

The indigenous population is predominantly Arab except on the Batinah coast, where there is significant Baluchi, Iranian, and African representation, and in Muscat and Matrah, where there are Khojas and other Indians, Baluchis, and Pakistanis. Tribal groups are estimated to number over 200.

9LANGUAGES

The official language is Arabic. Urdu, Farsi, and several Indian dialects are also spoken, especially in the cities of Muscat and Matrah. English is taught as a second language.

10RELIGIONS

The state religion is Islam. Three-quarters of the population belongs to the Ibadhi sect. Tribes in the north are mainly Sunni Muslims of the Hanbali, Shafai, and Wahhabi rites. The remainder of the population is Hindu. Anglican communities are entirely composed of visitors and foreign workers. In 1993 there were some 75,000 Roman Catholics.

11TRANSPORTATION

At the end of 1991 there were 22,800 km (14,170 mi) of graded roads, of which only 18% were bituminous surfaced. A major 800-km (500-mi) highway links Nazwa in the north to Thamarit and Salalah in the Dhofar region. A main coastal road has been laid from Muscat to Suhar, a distance of 240 km (150 mi), and the road from Muscat to Buraymi on the UAE border has been completed. In 1991, vehicle registrations totaled 220,000.

Seeb International airport, 30 km (19 mi) northwest of Muscat, is served by numerous international carriers, including Gulf Air, in which Oman holds a 20% interest. In 1992, Gulf Air performed 11,372 million passenger-km of service. A second modern airport, at Salalah in the south, serves domestic flights.

Mina's Qabus, near Muscat, is the main port in the north, serving international and regional shipping. Mina's Raysut, adjacent to Salalah, is the main port for the south. All Omani crude oil is exported from Mina's al-Fahl, west of Matrah.

12HISTORY

Oman's history can be traced to very early times. In Genesis 10:26–30, the descendants of Joktan are said to have migrated as far as Sephar (now Dhofar). The area was already a commercial and seafaring center in Sumerian times, and Phoenicians probably visited the coastal region. Other groups that probably came to the area in ancient times include the Baida and Ariba, Semitic tribes from northern Arabia, now extinct; the first Himyar dynasty from Yemen, which fell to the Persians in the time of Cyrus, about 550 BC; ancient Greek navigators; and the Parthians (174–136 BC).

The entire population was converted to Islam during the lifetime of Muhammad, but Oman soon became—and remains today— the center of the Ibadhi sect, which maintained that any pious Muslim could become caliph or imam and that the imam should be elected. Omani tribes have elected their imams since the second half of the 8th century.

The first prolonged contact with Europe came in 1507–08, when the Portuguese overran Muscat. They maintained control until they were driven out with Persian aid in 1649. During the next 75 years, Oman conquered Mombasa, Mogadishu, the island of Zanzibar, and the Portuguese possessions in East Africa. Later it held parts of what are now Iran and Pakistan.

The first sultanate was established in Muscat about 1775. In 1798, Britain concluded its first treaty with Muscat. Sa'id bin Sultan (r.1804–56) became dependent on British support, and after his death his sons quarreled over his succession (the basic Ibadhi tenet having been rejected). Thus weakened by political division, Muscat lost control of the interior. In 1920, the Treaty of Seeb was signed between the sultan of Muscat and the imam of Oman, acknowledging the autonomy of the imamate of Oman under the sovereignty of the Sultan. From 1920 to 1954 there was comparative peace. On the death of the imam in 1954, Sultan Sa'id bin Taymur moved to succeed him.

That year, Sa'id concluded a new agreement with Petroleum Development (Oman) Ltd., a British-managed oil company that had the oil concession for Oman. By this agreement, the company maintained a small army, the Muscat and Oman Field Force (MOFF), raised and led by the British. In early 1955, it subdued the area up to and including the town of 'Ibri. When British troops took Buraymi, MOFF occupied the rest of Oman and expelled the rebellious new imam. By 1959 when the last of the insurgents supporting the imam were defeated, the sultan voided the office and declared the Treaty of Seeb terminated. The imam, exiled in Sa'udi Arabia, tried in vain to muster Arab support for his return.

Under the terms of the Anglo-French Declaration of 10 March 1962, the sultanate of Muscat was proclaimed an independent and sovereign state. Certain Arab states charged, however, that the UK was maintaining a colonial presence in the former imamate of Oman. In 1965 and repeatedly thereafter, the UN called unsuccessfully for the elimination of the British presence. Oman joined the UN late in 1971.

Meanwhile, as early as 1964, a tribal rebellion had been brewing in the Dhofar region. The rebel tribes, organized as the Dhofar Liberation Front and aided by South Yemen, later joined forces with the Marxist Popular Front for the Liberation of Oman and the Arab Gulf. The insurgency was suppressed in 1975 with direct military assistance from Jordan and Iran. A treaty with Yemen defining the border was ratified in 1992.

Qabus bin Sa'id ousted his father, Sa'id bin Taymur, on 23 July 1970 and has ruled as sultan since that time. He immediately changed the name of the country from Muscat and Oman to the Sultanate of Oman and has presided over an extensive modernization program, easing his father's harsh restrictions and opening the country to the outside world, while preserving political and military ties with the British. Oman has been a proponent of cooperation among the Gulf states. A member of the GCC, it has also sought to keep good relations with Iran. Because Oman dominates the Strait of Hormuz, which links the Gulf of Oman with the Persian Gulf, its strategic importance drew it and the US closer together with the start of the Iran–Iraq war in 1979. Under the terms of a pact signed in 1980, US military personnel and ships have been given access to Omani military and naval base and are permitted to preposition military material for use in contingencies.

Oman pursues a moderate, independent foreign policy. Unlike most Arab states, it supported the Camp David accords and did not break relations with Egypt following its peace treaty with Israel. Similarly, during the Gulf War, Oman sent forces to Sa'udi

Arabia and granted strategic facilities to the US, but did not sever diplomatic relations with Iraq during the conflict.

13GOVERNMENT
Oman's sultan is an absolute monarch. The sultanate has no constitution, legislature, or suffrage. In 1970, Sultan Qabus appointed a cabinet of ministers responsible for various government departments and functions.

A State Consultative Council, established in 1981, consisted of 55 appointed representatives of government, the private sector, and regional interests.

This body was replaced in 1991 by a Majlis Ash-Shura, or Consultative Council, which is seen as a first step toward popular participation in government. The new Council has no legislative function, but reviews measures affecting economic development and social services and can question cabinet members on their policies and plans.

14POLITICAL PARTIES
There are no legal political parties nor, at present, any active opposition movement. As more and more young Omanis return from education abroad, it seems likely that the traditional, tribal-based political system will have to be adjusted.

15LOCAL GOVERNMENT
The nation is divided into three governates (Muscat, Musandam, Dhofar) and 41 wilayats (districts), governed by walis, who are responsible to the Ministry of the Interior. The Governorate of the Capital is responsible for the administration of Muscat.

16JUDICIAL SYSTEM
Shari'ah courts based on Islamic law administer justice, with the Chief Court at Muscat. Qadis, or religious judges, appointed by the sultan, function within each wilayat. Appeals from the Chief Court are made to the sultan, who exercises powers of clemency. The Shari'a courts, adhering to Islamic law, equate the testimony of one man with that of two women. The magistrate court, a criminal court, adjudicates violations of the criminal code. There is also a security court, rarely used, which handles internal security cases.

17ARMED FORCES
Oman's armed forces, including some 3,700 foreign personnel and British advisors numbered 35,700 in 1993. The army had 20,000 personnel, the air force 3,500, and the navy 3,000. Another 3,500 men (Jebalis, or mountain dwellers) are organized into paid Home Guard units (Firqats) in their tribal areas. The elite Royal Household brigade, naval unit, and air unit number 6,000, including 2 special forces battalions. All military service is voluntary. Of Oman's $955 million worth of arms imports during 1981–85, $550 million came from the UK. Arms imports dropped to $360 million during 1986–91. In 1992 Oman spent $1.7 billion on defense or 16% of gross domestic product.

18INTERNATIONAL COOPERATION
On 7 October 1971, Oman gained membership in the UN; the nation belongs to ESCWA and all the nonregional specialized agencies except IAEA, ILO, and WIPO. Oman also participates in G-77, GCC, and the League of Arab States, as well as the Islamic Conference.

19ECONOMY
Oman's location at the entrance to the Persian Gulf for centuries made it an entrepôt for trade, including a substantial traffic in arms and slaves. Its prosperity declined in the 19th century, when, as a result of Western dominance in Asia, traditional trade patterns and communications routes were radically changed. Oman's

LOCATION: 51°50′ to 59°40′E; 16°40′ to 26°20′N. **BOUNDARY LENGTHS:** Total coastline, 2,092 km (1,301 mi); Yemen, 288 km (179 mi); Sa'udi Arabia, 676 km (420 mi); UAE, 410 km (255 mi). **TERRITORIAL SEA LIMIT:** 12 mi.

economy then became predominantly dependent on agriculture and fishing.

The situation changed with the discovery of oil in 1964. Production began in August 1967, and by the mid-1970s most of the economy revolved around oil. The hydrocarbons sector accounted for 90% of government revenue and over 80% of total export earnings, which amounted to $556 billion in 1992. Based on current oil production of about 800,000 barrels per day, oil reserves should last some 16 years. In recent years, the production of natural gas has become a significant factor of the economy. Gas reserves increased from 9.8 trillion cubic feet in 1990 to 17 trillion cubic feet at the end of 1992 and are further increasing. A project has been launched to build an underwater gas pipeline to India for the export of gas.

20INCOME

In 1992, Oman's GNP was $10,683 million at current prices, or $6,490 per capita. For the period 1985–92 the average inflation rate was 1.1%, resulting in a real growth rate in per capita GNP of 1.0%.

In 1992 the GDP was $11,520 million in current US dollars. It is estimated that agriculture, hunting, forestry, and fishing contributed 4% to GDP; mining and quarrying, 42%; manufacturing, 4%; electricity, gas, and water, 2%; construction, 4%; wholesale and retail trade, 14%; transport, storage, and communication, 4%; finance, insurance, real estate, and business services, 9%; community, social, and personal services, 2%; and other sources, 15%.

21LABOR

Of an estimated Omani work force of 430,000 in 1992, approximately 258,000 were still engaged in subsistence agriculture or fishing. The skilled local labor force is small, and many of the larger industries depend on foreign workers from India, Pakistan, the Philippines, Bangladesh, and Sri Lanka—foreign laborers constituted 58% of the work force in 1992.

Omani law does not address the right of union formation. Any employee, though, may file a grievance with the Labor Welfare Board. Lower-paid workers, such as clerks, mechanics, and salesmen, use the board frequently; about 80% of all cases involved foreign workers in 1992.

22AGRICULTURE

Agriculture contributes only about 3% to GDP, but engages 70% of the economically active population, mostly at a subsistence level. The potential for expanding agriculture in Oman is good. Land use is determined primarily by the availability of water. There is extensive cultivation along the Batinah and Shumailiyah coasts; in the interior, however, cultivation is confined to areas near wadis, where water is taken off by a system of water channels (fallaj). The total area under cultivation is estimated to be about 61,000 hectares (150,700 acres).

The principal agricultural product is the date. On the Baunah coast, date groves form a strip 240 km (150 mi) long and 40 km (25 mi) wide. Fruits grown in Dhofar include bananas, mangoes, and coconuts. Citrus fruits (notably limes), nuts, melons, bananas, coconuts, alfalfa, and tobacco are also grown. Tomatoes, cabbages, eggplant, okra, and cucumbers are important winter crops. Along the Batinah coast, a wide variety of produce is grown, including fruits, wheat, rice, and durra. Agricultural exports were valued at $71.7 million in 1992.

23ANIMAL HUSBANDRY

Goats, sheep, donkeys, and camels are widely raised. There is a relatively large-scale cattle-raising industry in Dhofar. The camels of Oman are famous for their fine riding qualities.

24FISHING

The waters of the Gulf of Oman are rich in sardines, mackerel, shrimp, lobsters, crayfish, tuna, barracudas, groupers, and sharks. The annual catch in 1991 was 117,780 tons, mainly sardines. Fishing and fisheries employ about 10% of the labor force. Recent investment in onshore processing and refrigeration plants, harbors, and repair yards has facilitated commercial fishing development. The government subsidizes the cost of boats and engines to promote employment in fishing. Fish stocks and breed-

ing patterns are studied at a research center south of Muscat.

25FORESTRY

The use of wood as the sole fuel and overgrazing by goats have depleted the forests of Oman, but the interior of the country is fairly well wooded.

26MINING

Large copper deposits have been discovered northwest of Muscat; the Sohar mining and smelting complex was built by the government-owned Oman Mining Co. in the early 1980s. As of 1991, the Sahar copper deposits were nearly exhausted; however, other deposits were discovered at Hajl al-Safi and at Raka in Ibri. More than half of Oman's copper production wsa taken from the Lasail Mine, with much of the remaining output from the Aarja surface mine. Oman also has large deposits of limestone, gypsum, asbestos, and marble, along with chromite and manganese.

27ENERGY AND POWER

Oil, discovered in 1964 in western Oman, has transformed the nation's economic life. As of 1990, the crude petroleum sector accounted for 43% of GDP. When production began in 1967, several foreign interests combined to form a majority backing in Petroleum Development Oman (PDO). In July 1974, foreign participation dropped to 40%, with the remaining 60% held by the government. PDO was the lone oil producer in the country until the Elf-Sumitomo-Wintershall group was granted a concession in 1980. Annual output during 1992 averaged 720,000 barrels per day. Petroleum reserves are estimated at 4.5 billion barrels (600 million tons). Proved reserves of natural gas are estimated to be 16.9 trillion cu ft (475 million cu m), and it is anticipated that Oman will increasingly replace oil with gas as fuel. Although Oman currently does not export natural gas, it plans to construct both a natural gas pipeline to the UAE and a large liquified natural gas project.

With limited oil reserves, Oman is currently trying to reduce its reliance on oil as the chief source of revenue. Oman is trying to establish itself as a consultant to other independent oil and natural gas producing nations, like Kazakhstan and India.

In 1991, net installed electric capacity was 1,564,000 kw and production totaled 5,548 million kwh.

28INDUSTRY

Besides oil, industry in Oman still consists largely of small-scale food-processing enterprises. Many new industries were set up in the 1980s, including a cement plant with an annual capacity of 609,000 tons. From 1981 to 1987, 2,587 new industrial establishments were registered, bringing the total to 2,990. The majority of these manufacture non-metallic mineral products followed by wood and wood products, and fabricated metal products. The Rusail industrial estate had 43 working factories by mid–1989. Another four such industrial sites are planned in Salalah, Sohar, Sur, and Nizwa.

29SCIENCE AND TECHNOLOGY

Most research conducted in Oman has been done at the behest of the government; agriculture, minerals, water resources, and marine sciences have drawn the most attention. Sultan Qaboos University has colleges of science, medicine, engineering, and agriculture. The Institute of Health Sciences, under the Ministry of Health, has 275 students. Oman Technical Industrial College has departments of mathematics and mechanical engineering.

30DOMESTIC TRADE

In Muscat and Matrah, much of the business is carried on by long-established and settled Khoja and Hindu merchants. Normal business hours are 8:30 AM to 1:30 PM and 4 to 7 PM, Saturday–

Wednesday; banking hours are generally 8 AM to noon, though some banks reopen from 4 to 6 PM. Banks and businesses close at 11:30 AM on Thursday and remain closed Friday. Business hours are reduced during the Ramadan fast.

31 FOREIGN TRADE

Since 1967, oil has been the chief export. The main imports are food, live animals, machinery, textiles, chemicals, petroleum products, and motor vehicles; exports, aside from oil, consist chiefly of copper, dates, dried limes, dried fish, tobacco, and hides. In 1992, exports totaled $5.56 billion, over 80% of which was from oil; imports were worth $3.51 billion. Most of the non-oil exports go to the UAE. Since 1972, the UAE has replaced the UK as Oman's principal source of imports, mostly transshipments. Japan is now the principal source of direct imports, followed by the UK, Germany, US, and France.

32 BALANCE OF PAYMENTS

Oman's balance of payments account is dominated by crude oil export earnings, consumer and capital goods and services, imports payments, and by large outgoing remittances by foreign workers.

In 1992 merchandise exports totaled $5,555 million and imports $3,508 million. The merchandise trade balance was $2,047 million.

The following table summarizes Oman's balance of payments for 1991 and 1992 (in millions of US dollars):

	1991	1992
CURRENT ACCOUNT		
Goods services and income	737	763
Unrequited transfers	−874	−1,128
TOTALS	−137	−365
CAPITAL ACCOUNT		
Direct investment	149	59
Other long-term capital	211	94
Other short-term capital	146	120
Reserves	−507	−163
TOTALS	−1	110
Errors and omissions	139	256
Total change in reserves	−137	−160

33 BANKING AND SECURITIES

The Central Bank of Oman, set up in April 1975, has powers to regulate credit and is authorized to make temporary advances to the government; its assets in 1993 stood at $720.1 billion. Oman has 24 licensed banks with 249 branches. A stock exchange was established in 1989.

34 INSURANCE

As of 1985, one national insurance firm and 17 foreign-owned firms were operating in Oman.

35 PUBLIC FINANCE

Deficits have been typical since 1982, and are financed by withdrawals from the State General Reserve Fund and external borrowing. Oman's oil resources and low foreign debt enable the government to easily borrow from abroad. Revenues expand largely on the vicissitudes of the world's oil market. When oil prices fell in 1986, the government responded with a 14% currency devaluation and postponement of development expenditures. The Persian Gulf crisis did not severely affect revenues in 1991.

The following table shows actual revenues and expenditures for 1991 and 1992 in millions of rials.

	1991	1992
REVENUE AND GRANTS		
Tax revenue	327.4	334.8
Non-tax revenue	926.8	995.6
Capital revenue	7.2	7.7
Grants	23.0	0.9
TOTAL	1,284.4	1,339.0
EXPENDITURES & LENDING MINUS REPAYMENTS		
General public service	170.6	174.0
Defense	557.4	679.5
Public order and safety	106.8	120.5
Education	180.1	209.4
Health	85.3	108.5
Social security and welfare	53.0	91.2
Housing and community amenities	153.7	156.3
Recreation, cultural, and religious affairs	36.8	51.5
Economic affairs and services	162.0	210.9
Other expenditures	69.4	98.5
Lending minus repayments	−6.4	23.2
TOTAL	1,568.7	1,923.5
DEFICIT/SURPLUS	−284.3	−584.5

In 1992 Oman's total public debt stood at RO1,446.5 million, of which RO1,036.3 million was financed abroad.

36 TAXATION

Introduced in 1971, a corporate income tax on commercial enterprises other than individual traders remains the only tax in the country. Rates range from 5% to 50%. Legislation in 1981 reduced the maximum tax rate to 15% for companies in which Omanis hold at least a 51% equity, and to 20% for companies in which the Omani equity is between 35% and 50%.

37 CUSTOMS AND DUTIES

General import duties are 5% ad valorem on the c.i.f. value of the good. There are a number of exempt goods, including many imports from GCC member states. Protective tariffs are levied seasonally on a number of fruits and vegetables.

38 FOREIGN INVESTMENT

The principal foreign investment is in the oil sector. Foreign private investment is officially encouraged in certain areas—such as industry, agriculture, and fishing—through an initial five-year tax exemption, which may be renewed for another five years. Foreign participation in a local company cannot exceed 65% (this also applies to the sharing of profits). Companies holding commercial agencies must also have at least 51% Omani participation.

39 ECONOMIC DEVELOPMENT

Oman's second five-year plan (1981–85) suffered to some extent from the impact of declining oil prices in the early 1980s. The objectives of the third development plan (1986–90) were to encourage the private sector to play a larger role in the economy and to expand such areas as agriculture, fishing, manufacturing, and mining. The fourth five-year development plan (1991–1995), aimed to achieve average annual GDP growth rates of just over 6% and the diversification of the sources of national income in order to reduce the dependence on the oil sector. Oman spends at least 35% of its $4.6 billion budget on defense.

Oman's sovereign debt of about $2.4 billion is easily manageable and is owed to commercial banks. Oman does not divulge the amounts and distinctions of its foreign aid with the exception of the building of an airport in Zanzibar.

40SOCIAL DEVELOPMENT

Oman maintains a welfare program that, in 1985, gave direct monetary aid of RO7.8 million to 27,973 families. Support is provided for maternity and child-care centers, and the fertility rate remains high (7.2 in 1985-90).

Women have begun to enter professional areas such as medicine and communications in greater numbers in recent years. Almost 14% of all civil servants are women. Women comprise roughly half of the 3,000 students at Sultan Qaboos University, and in 1993 more than 50% of the medical school's first graduating class were women. Islamic precepts result in de facto discrimination against women in a number of areas, such as inheritance.

41HEALTH

In 1985 there were 40 hospitals and 75 health centers, with 2,861 beds; in addition, there were 4 maternity centers. Personnel included 1,033 medical and public health officers and 2,420 nurses. In 1990, the population per physician was 1,060, and per nursing professional was 400.

Average life expectancy in 1992 was 69 years. Infant mortality was 24 per 1,000 live births, and the general mortality rate was 4.9 per 1,000 in 1993. The 1993 birth rate was 40.5 per 1,000 people. About 9% of married women (ages 15 to 49) were using contraception. There were 67,000 births in 1992.

In 1991, 84% of the population had access to safe water and 71% had adequate sanitation. In 1992, 97% of the population had access to health care services. In the same year, children up to one year old were vaccinated against tuberculosis (97%); diphtheria, pertussis, and tetanus (97%); polio (97%); and measles (97%).

42HOUSING

In May 1973, Sultan Qabus approved the Law of People's Housing to make housing loans to needy Omanis. By 1985, 5,300 low-income units had been built. In 1989, 34% of all housing units were traditional Arabic houses, 30% were flats, and 27% were villas. Owners occupied 70% of all dwellings, 20% were rented, and 9% were provided by employers.

43EDUCATION

The adult literacy rate was estimated to be below 50% in 1985. In 1991, there were 436 primary schools with 277,370 students and 10,184 teachers, of whom 48% were women. In secondary schools, there were 7,264 teachers and 119,497 students. Three teachers' colleges were functioning as of 1986. The Institute of Agriculture at Nazwa had become a full college by 1985. Sultan Qabus University opened in 1986. In 1991, all higher level institutions had 7,322 students.

44LIBRARIES AND MUSEUMS

The library at Sultan Qaboos University has 25,000 volumes. A British Council Library of almost 9,000 volumes was founded in 1973 in Matrah. The Ministry of National Heritage and Culture administers the National Museum of Ruwi, the Qurm Museum, and the Oman Natural History Museum, which includes the National Herbarium of Oman and the National Shell Collection.

45MEDIA

Postal, telephone, and telex systems are supervised by the Ministry of Posts, Telegraphs, and Telephones. By the end of 1991, the entire country was connected to a 79,000-line telephone network. Oman now has international direct dialing to most major countries. Radio and television facilities are government owned; color television was introduced in 1974. There were 1,150,000 television sets and 1,006,000 radios in use in 1991.

Newspapers and journals in Arabic include the daily *Al-Wattan* (1991 circulation 23,500) and *Oman*(20,000) and weekly periodicals such as *Al-Aquida* and *Al-Usra*. Two English-language newspapers are also published. Criticism of the sultan is illegal.

46ORGANIZATIONS

There is a Chamber of Commerce and Industry in Muscat. Among the social and cultural organizations are the Oman Women's Association, the Oman Cultural Club (for university graduates), and the Omani Historical Association (open to non-Omanis).

47TOURISM, TRAVEL, AND RECREATION

Oman is cautiously developing tourism, which was discouraged by previous rulers. All travelers except citizens of other Gulf states, must obtain a visa and a No Objection Certificate. Most large hotels have clubs that offer various recreational activities; water sports are popular, but spear fishing has been prohibited as a conservation measure. In 1991, 161,000 foreign tourists visited Oman, spending an estimated $63 million. There were 2,204 hotel rooms with 3,065 beds and a 45.2% occupancy rate.

48FAMOUS OMANIS

Oman's great Islamic religious leader, whose followers are called Ibadhis, was 'Abdallah bin Ibad (fl.8th century); many of his teachings are still followed in Oman. Ahmad ibn Sa'id (r.1741–83), founder of the present dynasty, freed Muscat from Persian rule. Sultan Qabus bin Sa'id (b.1940) has ruled Oman since his removal of Sa'id bin Taymur (1910–72), his father, in 1970.

49DEPENDENCIES

Oman has no territories or colonies.

50BIBLIOGRAPHY

Allen, Calvin H. *Oman: the Modernization of the Sultanate.* Boulder, Colo.: Westview Press; London: Croom Helm, 1987.

American University. *Area Handbook for the Persian Gulf States.* Washington, D.C.: Government Printing Office, 1984.

Clements, F. A. *Oman: The Reborn Land.* New York: Longman, 1980.

Pridham, B.R. (ed.). *Oman: Economic, Social, and Strategic Developments.* Wolfeboro, N.H.: Croom Helm, 1987.

Skeet, Ian. *Oman: Politics and Development.* New York: St. Martin's, 1992.

Townsend, John. *Oman: The Making of the Modern State.* London: Croom Helm, 1977.

Wilkinson, John Craven. *The Imamate Tradition of Oman.* New York: Cambridge University Press, 1987.

PAKISTAN

Islamic Republic of Pakistan
Islami Jamhooria Pakistan

CAPITAL: Islāmābād.

FLAG: The national flag is dark green, with a white vertical stripe at the hoist and a white crescent and five-pointed star in the center.

ANTHEM: The opening lines of the national anthem, sung in Urdu, are "Blessed be the sacred land, Happy be the bounteous realm, Symbol of high resolve, land of Pakistan, Blessed be thou citadel of faith."

MONETARY UNIT: The rupee (R) is a paper currency of 100 paisa. There are coins of 1, 2, 5, 10, 25, and 50 paisa and of 1 rupee, and notes of 1, 2, 5, 10, 50, 100, 500, and 1,000 rupees. R1 = $0.0328 (or $1 = R30.500).

WEIGHTS AND MEASURES: The metric system was introduced in 1966 and made mandatory as of 1 January 1979.

HOLIDAYS: Pakistan Day, 23 March; May Day, 1 May; Independence Day, 14 August; Defense of Pakistan Day, 6 September; Anniversary of Death of the Quaid-e-Azam, Mohammad Ali Jinnah, 11 September; Christmas and Birthday of the Quaid-e-Azam, 25 December. Religious holidays include 'Id al-Fitr, Id al-'Adha', 1st of Muharram, and Milad an-Nabi.

TIME: 5 PM = noon GMT.

¹LOCATION, SIZE, AND EXTENT

Situated in southern Asia, Pakistan has an area of 803,940 sq km (310,403 sq mi), extending 1,875 km (1,165 mi) NE–SW from the ranges of the Hindu Kush and the Himalaya to the Arabian Sea and 1,006 km (625 mi) SE–NW. Comparatively, the area occupied by Pakistan is slightly less than twice the size of the state of California. The enclave of Junagadh, claimed by Pakistan, and Jammu and Kashmir, divided between Pakistan and India by the 1971 "line of control," are not included in the area. Pakistan is bordered on the NE by China, on the E by Jammu and Kashmir to the Karakoram Pass, on the E and SE by India, on the S by the Arabian Sea, on the SW by Iran, and on the W and NW by Afghanistan. The total boundary length is 7,790 km (4,840 mi). Pakistan's capital city, Islāmābād, is located in the northern part of the country.

²TOPOGRAPHY

More than two-thirds of Pakistan is arid or semiarid. The west is dominated by the Baluchistan plateau, consisting of arid plains and ridges. Rivers, streams, and lakes exist only seasonally. The arid south ends at the rugged Makran coast and rises to the east into a series of rock-strewn ranges, the Kirthar, and to the north, the Sulaiman, which extends to the Indus plains. A semiwatered plateau surrounds Rawalpindi, bounded to the south by the salt range. Southward, the extensive Punjab plains support about 60% of the country's population.

In the northern areas of Pakistan, the forest-clad hills give way to lofty ranges, including 60 peaks over 6,700 m (22,000 ft) high. K-2 (Godwin Austen), at 8,611 m (28,250 ft), is the second-highest mountain in the world.

The principal ranges, trending NW–SE, include several Himalayan ranges—notably the Pir Panjal and Zaskar—leading into the Karakoram Mountains. The Indus is the principal river of Pakistan. Its major tributaries are the Jhelum, Chenab, Ravi, and Sutlej.

³CLIMATE

Pakistan's climate is dry and hot near the coast, becoming progressively cooler toward the northeastern uplands. The winter season is generally cold and dry. The hot season begins in April, and by the end of June the temperature may reach 49°C (120°F). Between July and September, the monsoon provides an average rainfall of about 38 cm (15 in) in the river basins and up to about 150 cm (60 in) in the northern areas. Rainfall can vary radically from year to year, and successive patterns of flooding and drought are not uncommon.

⁴FLORA AND FAUNA

The mangrove forests of the coastal region give way to the mulberry, acacia, and date palms of the sparsely vegetated south; the foothills support phulai, kao, chinar, and wild olive, and the northern forests have stands of oak, chestnut, walnut, pine, ash, spruce, yew, and fir. Above 3,000 m (10,000 ft), birch, dwarf willow, and juniper are also found.

Pakistan's wide range of animal life includes the Siberian ibex, wild sheep, buffalo, bear, wolf, jackal, fox, wildcat, musk cat, hyena, porcupine, gazelle, peacock, python, and boar.

⁵ENVIRONMENT

Relatively high population growth contributed to the depletion of forestland from 9.8% of Pakistan's total area in 1947 to 4.5% by 1986, despite the forest conservation measures mandated by the Forest Act of 1927. The nation's forest lands are eliminated at a rate of 1% of the total 13,707 square miles per year. Deforestation has contributed to increased soil erosion, declining soil fertility, and severe flooding.

Primary responsibility for environmental matters belongs to the Environmental and Urban Affairs Division of the Ministry for Housing and Works. Laws to set air and water quality standards and regulate coastal zones to prevent pollution were under consideration in the 1980s. The nation's water supply is at risk due to untreated sewage along with agricultural and industrial pollutants. Some 18% of the people living in cities and 58% of rural dwellers do not have pure water. In addition, 80% of the nation's diseases are related to impure water.

In 1994, 15 mammal species were endangered, as well as 25 bird species and 14 plant species. Endangered species include the Indus dolphin, Baluchistan bear, tiger, Pakistan sand cat, snow leopard, Indian wild ass, green sea turtle, olive ridley turtle, gavial, Central Asian cobra, Kabul markhor, chi pheasant, western tragopan, great Indian bustard, and Siberian white crane. The Asiatic cheetah is probably extinct in Pakistan. Hunting or capturing wild animals was banned in 1981.

⁶POPULATION

The estimated population in 1993 was 125,213,732. Population growth averaged 3.2% annually between 1985 and 1990, but was estimated at 2.9% in 1993. Nearly 44% of the population was under 15 years of age in 1990. The population density was estimated at 149.6 per sq km (387.5 per sq mi) in 1992. Urban areas accounted for 32% of the population in 1991, compared with 25.5% in 1972.

The following cities had more than 1 million inhabitants, according to 1990 estimates: Karachi (the former national capital), 7,943,000; Lahore, 4,179,000; Faisalabad (formerly Lyallpur), 1,540,000; Rāwalpindi, 1,069,000; Peshāwar, 1,215,000; Multān, 1,029,000; and Gujrānwāla, 1,249,000. The national capital, Islāmābād, had about 558,000.

⁷MIGRATION

Some 6,000,000 Muslims migrated to Pakistan from India at the time of independence in 1947, and Muslims have continued to arrive from India in much lesser numbers since then. The Soviet military intervention in Afghanistan in December 1979 led to an influx of Afghan refugees. As of the end of 1991, Pakistan was harboring 3,098,000 Afghan refugees. One year later, this refugee population had dropped to 1,627,000 as many Afghans returned home. Pakistan was paying less than half of the direct costs of maintaining more than 300 refugee camps; the Office of the UN High Commissioner for Refugees and other public and private agencies paid the remainder. But many Afghan refugees were uncounted, having gone to Karachi, Lahore, and other cities in search of work.

As of 1986, at least 2,500,000 Pakistanis were working abroad, chiefly in Middle Eastern countries and the UK.

⁸ETHNIC GROUPS

The majority of the population is Punjabi (an estimated two-thirds). Other major ethnolinguistic groups include the Sindhi (13%), Pathan (8.5%), and Urdu speakers (or Muhajirs), (7.6%). The Baluchi (2.5%) live in the vast western section of Pakistan and are divided into 12 major tribes, some of them purportedly of Dravidian origin. In the area of the delta and the lower course of the Indus River are Sindhi peasant tribesmen. The Rajputs and the Jats are the most numerous of the Punjabi castes. In the north and northwest are the hardy, warlike nomadic and seminomadic Pathans. Native speakers of Urdu, the Muhajirs are refugees, or descendants of refugees, from pre-partition India. They are well represented in the cities.

⁹LANGUAGES

During the Mughal (or Mogul) period, a fusion of local dialects and Persian produced Urdu, a "language of the camp" (*zaban-i-urdu*). Although regional languages and dialects persist, Urdu is the official language of Pakistan; while it is spoken by only about half the population, it is understood everywhere except in the rural or mountainous areas on the western frontier and is becoming the lingua franca of higher education. Punjabi, Pushtu, Balu-

chi, Gujarati, and Sindhi are important regional languages. Many other languages, including representatives of the Austroasiatic, Dravidian, Indo-European, Central Asian, and Tibeto-Chinese families, are spoken by small groups. English, which formerly had official status, is still used extensively in business, government, and higher education.

¹⁰RELIGIONS

Pakistan is an Islamic state. In 1993, some 118,952,000 people, or 95% of the population, were Muslim, giving Pakistan one of the largest Islamic communities in the world. Most of the Muslims are of the Sunni sect, although there is a substantial number of Shi'is and a few members of the Isma'ili sect, concentrated at Karachi. Ahmadis, who consider themselves Muslims but who are not accepted as orthodox by other Muslim groups and were officially declared non-Muslims by the government in 1974, numbered perhaps 2,500,000 by 1985. Christians constituted an estimated 2% of the population in 1993, and Hindus about 1.8%. About 5,000 Parsis, believers in Zoroastrianism, live in Karachi.

¹¹TRANSPORTATION

Railways are a major carrier of passenger and freight traffic. In 1991, Pakistan Railways operated 8,775 route km (5,453 mi) of track and owned 714 locomotives, more than 3,000 coaching vehicles, and about 36,000 freight cars.

In 1991, Pakistan's road system included 120,000 km (74,600 mi) of all-weather roads; road traffic drives on the left. The 800-km (500-mi) Karakoram highway, built jointly by Pakistan and China to connect Islāmābād with western China, was opened in 1979. There were 690,850 passenger cars, 84,814 buses, 30,300 taxis, and 115, 346 trucks in use in 1991. The road network carries 85% of all goods and passengers moving within the country. The harbor of Karachi, which provides Pakistan with its major port, covers an area of 6.5 sq km (2.5 sq mi) and handles over 10.5 million tons annually. Port Qasim, 22 km (14 mi) south of Karachi, was developed during the 1970s to help handle the increased shipping traffic. As of January 1992, Pakistan's nationalized shipping industry operated 26 oceangoing vessels, totaling 315,000 GRT.

The government-run Pakistan International Airlines (PIA) maintains all domestic services as well as flights to Europe, the US, and the Far East. In 1992, PIA carried 5,680,600 passengers. Karachi Airport is the main international terminus.

¹²HISTORY

The ruins of ancient civilizations at Mohenjodaro and at Harappa in the southern Indus Valley testify to the existence of an advanced urban civilization that flourished in what is now Pakistan in the second half of the third millennium BC during the same period as the major riverain civilizations in Mesopotamia and Persia. Although overwhelmed from 1500 BC onward by large migrations of nomadic Indo-European-speaking Aryans from the Caucasus region, vestiges of this civilization continue to exist in the traditional Indic culture that evolved from interaction of the Aryans and successive invaders in the years following. Among the latter were Persians in 500 BC, Greeks under Alexander the Great in 326 BC, and—after AD 800—Arabs, Afghans, Turks, Persians, Mongols (Mughals), and Europeans, the last of whom first arrived, uniquely, by sea beginning in AD 1601.

Islam, the dominant cultural influence in Pakistan, arrived with Arab traders in the 8th century AD. Successive overland waves of Muslims followed, culminating in the ascendancy of the Mughals in most of the subcontinent. Led initially by Babur, a grandson of Genghis Khan, the Mughal empire flourished in the 16th and 17th centuries and remained in nominal control until well after the British East India Company came to dominate the region in the early 18th century. Effective British governance of

LOCATION: 23°41' to 37°5'N; 60°52' to 77°49'E. **BOUNDARY LENGTHS:** China, 523 km (325 mi), including boundary of Jammu and Kashmir to the Karakoram Pass; India, 2,028 km (1,260 mi); Arabian Sea coastline, 814 km (506 mi); Iran, 830 km (516 mi); Afghanistan, 2,466 km (1,532 mi). **TERRITORIAL SEA LIMIT:** 12 mi.

the areas that now make up Pakistan was not consolidated until well into the second half of the 19th century.

In 1909 and 1919, while the British moved gradually and successfully to expand local self-rule, British power was increasingly challenged by the rise of indigenous mass movements advocating a faster pace. The Indian National Congress, founded in 1885 as little more than an Anglophile society, began to attract wide support in this century—especially after 1920—with its advocacy of non-violent struggle. But because its leadership style appeared, to many Muslims, to be uniquely Hindu, Muslims formed the All-India Muslim League to look after their interests. National and provincial elections held under the Government of India Act of 1935 confirmed many Muslims in this view by showing the

power the majority Hindu population could wield at the ballot box.

Sentiment among Muslims began to coalesce around the "two-nation" theory propounded by the poet Iqbal, which declared that Muslims and Hindus were separate nations and that Muslims required creation of an independent Islamic state for their protection and fulfillment. A prominent Bombay attorney, Muhammad Ali Jinnah, who came to be known "Quaid-i-Azam" (Great Leader), led the fight—formally endorsed by the Muslim League at Lahore in 1940—for a separate Muslim state to be known as Pakistan.

Despite arrests and setbacks during the Second World War, Jinnah's quest succeeded on 14 August 1947 when British India was divided into the two self-governing dominions of India and Pakistan, the latter created by combining contiguous, Muslim-majority districts in British India, the former consisting of the remainder. Partition occasioned a mass movement of Hindus, Muslims, and Sikhs who found themselves on the "wrong" side of new international boundaries; more than 20 million people moved, and up to 3 million of these were killed.

The new Pakistan was a state divided into two wings, East Pakistan (with 42 million people crowded mainly into what had been the eastern half of Bengal province) and West Pakistan (with 34 million in a much larger territory that included the provinces of Baluchistan, Sind, the Northwest Frontier, and western Punjab). In between, the wings were separated by 1600 km (1000 miles) of an independent, mainly Hindu, India professing secularism for its large Muslim, Christian, and Sikh minorities.

From the capital in Karāchi, in West Pakistan, the leaders of the new state labored mightily to overcome the economic dislocations of Partition, which cut across all previous former economic linkages, while attempting to establish a viable parliamentary government with broad acceptance in both wings. Jinnah's death in 1948 and the assassination in 1951 of Liaquat Ali Khan, its first prime minister, were major setbacks, and political stability proved elusive, with frequent recourse to proclamations of martial law and states of emergency in the years following 1954.

Complicating their task were the security concerns that Pakistan's new leaders had regarding India in the aftermath of the bitterness of partition and the dispute over Jammu and Kashmir. In the early 1950s, they sought security in relationships external to the subcontinent, with the Islamic world and with the United States, joining in such American-sponsored alliances as the Baghdad Pact (later—without Baghdad—the Central Treaty Organization or CENTO) and the Southeast Asia Treaty Organization (SEATO). They received extensive American economic and security assistance.

In the years leading up to 1971, the domestic political process in Pakistan was dominated by efforts to bridge the profound political and ethnic gap that—more than geography—separated the east and west wings despite their anxiety about India and shared commitment to Islam. Economically more important, the Bengali east wing, governed as a single province, chafed under national policies laid down in a west wing dominated by Punjabis and recent refugees from northern and western India. Seeking greater autonomy, voters in East Pakistan voted the Muslim League (ML) out of office as early as 1954, resulting in a period of direct rule from Karachi.

In 1958, the Army chief, Gen. Muhammad Ayub Khan, seized control of Pakistan, imposing martial law and banning all political activity for several years. Ayub later dissolved provincial boundaries in the west wing, converting it to "one unit," to balance East Pakistan. Each "unit" had a single provincial government and equal strength in an indirectly elected national legislature; the effect was to deny East Pakistan its population advantage, as well as its ability, as the largest province, to play provincial politics in the west wing.

Ayub's efforts failed to establish stability or satisfy the demands for restoration of parliamentary democracy. Weakened by his abortive military adventure against India in September 1965 and amid rising political strife in both wings in 1968, Ayub was eventually forced from office. Gen. Muhammad Yayha Khan, also opposed to greater autonomy for the east wing, assumed the presidency in 1969. Again martial law was imposed and political activity, suspended.

Yahya's attempt to restore popular government in the general elections of 1970 failed when the popular verdict supported those calling for greater autonomy for East Pakistan, even in the national assembly. The results were set aside, and civil unrest in the east wing rapidly spread to become civil war. India, with more than a million refugees pouring into its West Bengal state, joined in the conflict in support of the rebellion in November 1971, tipping the balance in Bengali favor and facilitating the creation of Bangladesh from the ruins in early 1972.

Bhutto and his successors

The defeat led to the resignation on 20 December 1971 of Yahya Khan and brought to the presidency Zulfikar Ali Bhutto, whose populist Pakistan Peoples Party (PPP) had won a majority of seats in the west wing. A long-time minister under Ayub Khan, the experienced Bhutto quickly charted an independent course for West Pakistan, which became the Islamic Republic of Pakistan. He distanced Pakistan from former close ties with the United States and the west, seeking security from India by a much more active role in the Third World and especially in the growing international Islamic movement fueled by petrodollars.

His political base broadened by his promises of "clothing, food, and housing" to the rural and urban poor, Bhutto launched limited land reform, nationalized banks and industries, and obtained support among all parties for a new constitution promulgated in 1973, restoring a strong prime ministership, which position he then stepped down to fill. In the years following, Bhutto grew more powerful, more capricious, and autocratic. His regime became increasingly dependent on harassment and imprisonment of foes and his popular support seriously eroded by the time he called for elections in March 1977. His PPP had lost many of its supporters, and he came to rely increasingly on discredited former PML members for support.

At the polls, the PPP was opposed by the Pakistan National Alliance (PNA), a nine-party coalition of all other major parties including the Jamaat-i-Islami (JI) on the Islamic right, the National Democratic Party on the secular left, the Pakistan Muslim League (PML/Pagaro) in the center, Asghar Khan's Tehrik Istiqlal (TI) on the secular right, and others. Although the results gave the PPP a two-thirds majority in parliament, allegations of widespread fraud and rigging undercut its credibility. PNA leaders demanded new elections, and Bhutto's exercise of emergency powers to arrest them led to widespread civil strife. On 5 July 1977, the army intervened, with the support of the civil and uniformed services and tacit acceptance of the PNA leaders. In ousting Bhutto, army chief Gen. Muhammad Zia-ul-Haq partially suspended the 1973 constitution, imposed martial law, and assumed the post of Chief Martial Law Administrator (CMLA). As calm returned to Pakistan, Zia promised elections for October 1977, but for the first of many times to come, he reversed himself before the event, arguing that he needed more time to set matters aright. And as the months passed, he began to assume more of the trappings of power, creating a cabinet-like Council of Advisers of made up of serving military officers and senior civil servants, chief among whom was long-time Defense Secretary, Ghulam Ishaq Khan, who became Finance Advisor and Zia's strong right arm.

In mid-1978, Zia brought Bhutto to trial for conspiracy to murder a political rival in which the rival's father was killed. He also expanded his "cabinet" with the addition of several PNA leaders as advisors, and, when the incumbent resigned, he assumed the added responsibilities (and title) of president. He allowed a return of limited political activity but put off elections scheduled for fall when he was unable to get agreement among the PNA parties on ground rules that would keep the PPP from returning to power.

Bhutto's conspiracy conviction was upheld by the Supreme Court in March 1979, and he was hanged on 4 April. In the fall, and with the PNA now in disarray, Zia again scheduled, then postponed elections and restricted political activity. But he did hold "non-party" polling for district and municipal councils, only to find at year's end confirmation of his concerns about PPP strength when PPP members, identifying themselves as "Friends of the People," showed continuing appeal among the electorate.

Opposition to martial law began slowly to coalesce in 1980 when most of the PNA leadership joined with PPP leaders Ghulam Mustafa Jatoi and Nusrat Bhutto, Zulfikar's widow, to form the Movement for the Restoration of Democracy (MRD) and to demand Zia's resignation and the restoration of the 1973 constitution. But Zia, benefiting from excellent monsoons and from Ishaq Khan's sound economic policies, proceeded by a series measures to expand the role of Islamic values and institutions in society. The public mood stayed quiescent, encouraged by Zia's regular reminders of the turmoil his predecessors had created.

Meanwhile, in neighboring Afghanistan, following a communist coup in 1978 and a Soviet invasion in 1979, Zia assumed a strong anti-communist leadership role, rallying the Islamic world and the UN. He resurrected close ties with the United States to enhance Pakistan's security and in the 1980s signed $3.2 and $4.02 billion economic and security assistance agreements with the US. He also improved relations—normally parlous—with India with normalization in trade, transport, and other non-sensitive areas. Nonetheless, Pakistan's anxiety about the much more powerful India on its borders remained high in the absence of a solution of the dispute with India over the status of the former princely state of Jammu and Kashmir.

The Kashmir dispute cuts to the heart of the "two-nation" theory and as such is part of the unresolved legacy of the 1947 partition of British India which did not address the future of the over 500 princely states with which the British Crown had treaty ties. Most chose one or the other dominion on grounds of geography, but Kashmir bordered both new nations and thus had a real option. A Muslim-majority state, with a Hindu ruler, Kashmir opted first for neither but then chose to join the Indian Union when invaded by tribesmen from Pakistan. Open warfare ensued in Kashmir between Indian and Pakistani troops in 1948–49 and brought the dispute to the fledgling United Nations.

A UN cease-fire left a third of Kashmir under Pakistani control and the remainder, including the Vale of Kashmir, under Indian control. A 1949 agreement to hold an impartial plebescite broke down when the protagonists could not agree on the conditions under which it would be held. Pakistan today administers its part—Azad (free) Kashmir—legally separate from the rest of Pakistan; Indian Kashmir is a state in the Indian Union, which has held state-wide elections but no plebescite.

The Kashmir issue has defied all efforts at resolution, including two additional spasms of warfare in 1965 and 1971, and subsequent Indo-Pakistan summits at Tashkent (1966) and Simla (1972). In the late 1980s, India's cancellation of election results and the dismissal of the state government led to the beginning of an armed insurrection against Indian rule by Kashmiri Muslim militants. Indian repression and Pakistan's support of the militants has threatened to spark new Indo-Pakistan conflict and keeps the issue festering.

In Pakistan in 1984, President Zia held a referendum on his Islamization policies in December and promised that he would serve a specified term of five years as president if the voters endorsed his policies. The MRD opposed him but did not prevent what Zia claimed was a 63% turnout, with 90% in his favor. On the strength of this disputed showing, Zia announced national and provincial elections, on a non-party basis, for February 1985. The MRD again boycotted, but the JI and part of the Pakistan Muslim League (PML) supported Zia. Deemed reasonably fair by most observers, the elections gave him a majority in the reconstituted National Assembly and left the opposition in further disarray.

Ten months later, on 30 December 1985, Zia ended martial law, as well as the state of emergency he had inherited from Zulfikar Bhutto, turning over day-to-day administration to the PML's Mohammad Khan Junejo, whom he had appointed prime minister in March. He also restored the 1973 constitution but not before amending it to strengthen presidential powers vis-a-vis the prime minister. As the Eighth Amendment to the constitution, these changes were approved by the National Assembly in October 1985. They remain a contentious issue today, having subsequently played a key role in institutional tension between incumbents of the presidency and the prime ministership. In the first such instance, frictions developed slowly through 1987, but on 29 May 1988, Zia suddenly fired Junejo, alleging corruption and a lack of support for his policies on Islamization and on Afghanistan. He called for new elections in November, and in June he proclaimed the Shari'a (Islamic law) supreme in Pakistan.

However, Zia was among 18 officials (including the American Ambassador) killed in the crash of a Pakistan Air Force plane two months later, leading to the succession to power of the Chairman of the Senate, Ghulam Ishaq Khan. As acting president, Ghulam Ishaq scheduled elections for November 1988 in which the PPP emerged with a strong plurality in the National Assembly. Benazir Bhutto, Zulfikar's daughter, who had returned from exile abroad in April 1986, became prime minister with a thin majority made up of her party members and independents. With her support Pakistan's electoral college chose Ghulam Ishaq President of Pakistan in his own right on 12 December 1988.

On 20 August 1990, with Bhutto and Ghulam Ishaq in a growing constitutional struggle over their respective powers, the president, with the support of the army chief, used his Eighth Amendment powers to oust her, alleging corruption, illegal acts, and nepotism. Declaring a state of emergency, he dissolved the National Assembly, named Ghulam Mustafa Jatoi (then leader of the opposition) prime minister, and called for new elections on 24 October. The Punjab High Court upheld the constitutionality of his actions, and on 24 October, the voters gave a near-majority to the Islamic Jamhoori Ittehad (IJI), a multi-party coalition resting mainly on a partnership of the PML and the JI. Mian Muhammad Nawaz Sharif, PML leader and former Chief Minister of Punjab, became prime minister on 6 November and quickly ended the state of emergency.

During late 1992 and early 1993, the president and the new prime minister moved toward a new confrontation over the exercise of their respective powers. Challenged by Nawaz Sharif on the president's choice of a new army chief, Ghulam Ishaq again used his Eighth Amendment powers to dismiss the government and dissolve the Assembly on 18 April, alleging mismanagement and corruption. But public reaction to the president's actions was strong, and on 26 May, a Supreme Court ruling restored Nawaz Sharif to power, creating a period of constitutional gridlock until 18 July when the army chief brokered a deal in which both Ghulam Ishaq and Nawaz Sharif left office. Sharif resigned and was replaced by Ishaq Khan as interim prime minister by Moeen Qureshi, a former World Bank Vice President; the president was then replaced by Wasim Sajjad, Chairman of the Senate.

Under Qureshi, Pakistan entered an period of fast-paced non-partisan rule and reform in which widespread corruption was exposed, corrupt officials dismissed, and political reforms undertaken. In his actions, Qureshi was strengthened by public support and his disavowal of interest in remaining in power. He held elections as promised on 19 October, and the PPP, leading a coalition called the People's Democratic Alliance (PDA), was returned to power, with Benazir Bhutto again Prime Minister, this time with a thin majority. On 13 November, with her support, long-time PPP stalwart Farooq Leghari was elected president.

13GOVERNMENT

Pakistan came into being as a self-governing dominion in the British Commonwealth in 1947 and declared itself a republic in 1956. Under a constitution framed by Zulfikar Bhutto and effective as of 14 August 1973, it is federal in nature, and Westminster-style cabinet systems operate at the federal and provincial levels. All powers not otherwise specified are reserved for the federal government, which is armed also with extensive emergency powers in the event of a breakdown in constitutional government.

Pakistan is governed under the constitution of 14 August 1973 (as amended) which declared Islam the state religion and provided for a president as a nominal head of state and a prime minister as executive head of government. The president and prime minister were chosen by members of parliament, and the prime minister was responsible to that body, which was elected under universal suffrage at 18 (since changed to 21) years of age. In 1973, the parliament consisted of a National Assembly of 200 elected members plus 10 seats reserved (until 1982) for women and 6 for tribal areas, these reserved seats filled by vote of the elected members. A Senate of 63 members included 14 legislators from each of the four provincial legislatures, plus 5 seats reserved for tribal areas and 2 for the federal capital area.

This constitution was suspended in part by the martial law administration that seized power in 1977, army chief Gen. Zia-ul Haq retaining his military position while exercising executive powers as Chief Martial Law Administrator (CMLA). He took on the position of president in 1978 when the incumbent stepped down, In an interim document of 24 March 1981, Zia revived much of the 1973 constitution, although its Fundamental Principles and its electoral provisions remained suspended until martial law was lifted in 1985. The CMLA was initially assisted by an appointive council of advisors, then by an advisory Federal Council (Majlis-e-Shoora) of 277 appointed members that was formed in 1982 to assist and advise the martial law government.

The 1973 constitution was fully restored with the lifting of martial law in December 1985, although amended in a number of ways. It redressed—in favor of the presidency—the balance of powers between the positions of prime minister and president, who also remained commander-in-chief of the armed forces. It established term limits of five years for the incumbents, and provided that their successors in 1990 would be elected, the president by an electoral college composed of members of the National Assembly, the Senate, and the provincial assemblies, and the prime minister, by the National Assembly.

The National Assembly now has 217 members (including 10 reserved for non-Muslims) elected for five-year terms, plus 20 seats to be filled by vote of the elected members for women and others deserving of representation. The Senate has 84 members elected for six-year terms by the provincial assemblies and tribal councils, plus 3 seats reserved for the federal capital area.

In May 1994, after what appeared to be an encouraging start, Benazir Bhutto's government again appeared haunted by ineffectiveness when she failed to get her candidate elected president of the senate—effectively vice president. Instead, she was forced to acquiesce in the reelection, one more time, of the PML's Wasim Sajjad.

¹⁴POLITICAL PARTIES

Political parties have existed in Pakistan during all of its turbulent political history but have been regulated by legislation to ensure that they support the concept of Pakistan—a vestige of an early effort to repress the activities of the National Democratic Party (NDP) and the Jamaat-i-Islami (JI), which had opposed Partition in 1947. Parties have been frequently banned or restricted by the government, beginning with the 1952 ban on—and suppression of—the Communist Party of Pakistan (CPP). In most instances, banning of political activity has simply limited overt, outdoor rallies and demonstrations, while banning of parties has left the parties essentially intact, merely forcing them underground, as in the most recent ban in 1979.

In February 1981, leaders of nine political parties opposing the martial law regime, and led by the Pakistan Peoples Party (PPP), formed the Movement for the Restoration of Democracy (MRD) and by declaration called for an immediate end to martial law and restoration of the parliamentary system of 1973. Following the end of martial law in 1985, political parties were legalized, although regulated by the Political Parties Act that required all parties to register to be eligible for election. The elections that followed President Zia's sacking of Prime Minister Junejo in 1986, coupled with national elections called after Zia's subsequent death in an airplane crash in 1988, have resulted in a rebirth of full and open political activity.

The populist Pakistan Peoples Party (PPP) now led by Benazir Bhutto, daughter of the late Prime Minister Zulfikar Bhutto, won a plurality in the National Assembly and formed a government with the support of appointed members and independents. The opposition coalesced around other parties, especially the Pakistan Muslim League (PML), and the Jamaat-i-Islami (JI), as well as disaffected PPP members who had been displaced when Benazir Bhutto claimed the party leadership on her return from exile overseas in 1986. One of these, Ghulam Mustafa Jatoi, joined with Nawaz Sharif, the PML chief minister of Punjab, to become leader of the opposition in the Assembly. In 1990, Jatoi became interim prime minister when Benazir Bhutto was dismissed by the president.

In the elections of fall 1990, Nawaz Sharif emerged as prime minister and leader of the Islamic Jamhoori Ittehad (IJI), a multi-party coalition based on Sharif's PML and the JI. But in elections in the fall of 1993, following the resignations of both the president and the prime minister, Bhutto's PPP, the lead party in the PDA, commanded a thin majority in the National Assembly, guaranteeing her return to power. The IJI came in a close second even though and the Islamic parties suffered severe reverses nationally.

In the 1990s, party politics in Pakistan became increasingly regional, and party lines relatively porous, with much shifting of supporters into and out of the PPP and the PML. Each of these parties drew nearly 40% of the popular vote, and they have emerged as the only parties with national scope; both improved their positions in provincial assemblies.

In 1994, the PPP government depended on the support of former PML members and non-elected assembly members, plus leaders like Jatoi, a charter PPP member who had been in and out of the party in recent years. Similarly, during its period in power from 1990 to 1993, the PML formed a government only with the support of other parties, most of which have strength only in regional terms, mainly the JI, the Jamhoori Watan Party (JWP), the Jamiat Ulema-i-Pakistan (JUP), and the Jamiat-ul-Ulema-Islam (JUI). And both the PPP and the PML have competed successfully in forming governments in provincial assemblies only when they have recruited (or neutralized) strong regional parties, like the Awami National Party (ANP) in the Northwest Frontier Province (NWFP) and the Muhajir Quami Movement (MQM) in Sindh.

¹⁵LOCAL GOVERNMENT

Pakistan is divided into four provinces, each with deep historic roots and both linguistic and cultural associations, since 1972. Outside the provinces, there are 11 federally administered tribal areas and the Federal Capital of Islāmābād. In addition, provincial governments directly administer 11 tribal areas within their territories.

The provinces, in order of population size, are Punjab (with its capital at Lahore), Sindh (Karāchi), Northwest Frontier Province (Peshāwar), and Baluchistan (Quetta), the largest in area. Under the 1973 constitution, provinces have popularly elected provincial assemblies, a governor appointed by the president, and a chief minister in whom executive power is vested. The governor acts on the advice of a chief minister who is elected from the party commanding the support of the assembly.

The senior administrative officer of each province is the chief secretary. Each province is divided administratively into divisions headed by commissioners who, like the chief secretary and the secretaries of provincial ministries, are senior members of the Pakistan Civil Service (CSP). Divisions are further subdivided into districts headed (depending on local usage) by deputy commissioners, district officers, or collectors, also members of the CSP, who manage development funds, collect the revenues, supervise the police, abjudicate disputes, administer justice, and interface with the elected councils at the local level which have limited taxing authority, decide on priorities for local development programs, and try certain local legal cases.

The Pakistan-controlled third of the original state of Jammu and Kashmir is divided into two areas. The southern portion, referred to as Azad Kashmir, is administered from Muzaffarabad by an appointed president and council of ministers. The larger portion to the north is known as the Northern Areas and is administered by a Commissioner and an elected council.

16JUDICIAL SYSTEM

Pakistan's judicial system stems directly from the system that was used in British India. The Supreme Court has original, appellate, and advisory jurisdictions. The president of Pakistan appoints the justices. Each province has a high court, the judges of which are also named by the president. Below the high courts are district and session courts, and below these are subordinate courts and village courts on the civil side and magistrates on the criminal side.

The British tradition of an independent judiciary in Pakistan was undermined by the imposition of martial law in 1977. Military courts had jurisdiction over trial and punishment of civilians found guilty of violating martial law regulations; the verdict may not be appealed to a higher civilian court. Moreover, a provision of the 1973 constitution that judges could be removed only by the Supreme Judicial Council, consisting of the chief justice and two ranking judges from the Supreme Court and the high courts, was revoked by the military government in June 1979. Other legal changes were designed to emphasize the primacy of Islamic law (the Shari'a). The Federal Shari'at Court was given the power to nullify any law it finds repugnant to Islam. Under the 1981 interim constitution, a new oath was imposed on all Supreme Court, high court, and Shari'at Court judges, and all laws promulgated by the martial law regime were exempted from judicial review. The Supreme Court chief justice and several other judges were replaced after refusing to take the oath. Although the military courts were abolished in December 1985, their decisions still cannot be appealed to civilian courts.

Courts are subject to pressure from the executive branch in part because of presidential power over transfer and tenure of High Court justices and lower court judges. Judges in the special courts are retired jurists hired on renewable contracts so that their decisions may be influenced by a desire for contract renewal. Nonetheless, the provincial High Courts and the Supreme Court have exercised some degree of independence in recently handing down a number of cases against the government.

A 1990 Shari'a court decision read into the Penal Code the Islamic concepts of Qisas (roughly "an eye for an eye") and Diyat ("blood money").

17ARMED FORCES

In 1993, Pakistan's armed forces totaled 580,600. Its army of 515,000 men was the world's ninth largest, comprising 2 armored division, 19 infantry divisions, and 40 brigades of specialized troops and supporting arms. The navy, (20,000) had 6 submarines, 3 destroyers, and 25 patrol and coastal combatants with a small naval air arm. The air force, with a total strength of 45,000 men, had 352 combat aircraft. Paramilitary forces, including the Pakistan rangers, the frontier corps, a maritime security agency, a national guard and local defense units, totaled 260,000. Military service is voluntary. Defense expenditures in 1992 were estimated at $2.9 billion or 6% of gross domestic product. Security assistance programs from the US averaged $400 million a year through the 1980s, but were suspended in 1990 because of differences over Pakistan's nuclear program.

18INTERNATIONAL COOPERATION

Pakistan became a member of the UN on 30 September 1947 and is a member of its specialized agencies, including ESCAP.

As an Islamic state, Pakistan is an active member of the Organization of the Islamic Conference (OIC) and participates in various Muslim Afro-Asian organizations. Pakistan also belongs to the Asian Development Bank, the Colombo Plan, and G-77 and participates in GATT and the Law of the Sea. Following the establishment of Bangladesh, Pakistan withdrew from the Commonwealth of Nations in 1972.

In 1960, Pakistan and India signed an Indus water basin treaty opening the way to the peaceful use and development of water resources. Pakistan, Turkey, and Iran established a tripartite arrangement, called Regional Cooperation for Development (RCD), in 1964. In 1985, Pakistan and six other South Asian countries, including India and Bangladesh, formed the South Asian Association for Regional Cooperation (SAARC).

19ECONOMY

Despite steady expansion of the industrial sector during the 1980s, Pakistan's economy remains dominated by agriculture. In 1990/91, agriculture engaged 50% of the labor force, and accounted for 26% of the GDP as well as close to 70% of export revenues, including agriculture-based manufactures. Exports of primary agricultural products are concentrated in cotton and rice. At $420, per capita income has improved marginally since the mid-1980s when it was $400. One-fourth of the land is farmed or used for grazing, and much of this is planted to food crops for domestic consumption. Pakistan is generally poor in natural resources, although extensive reserves of natural gas and petroleum are being exploited. Iron ore, chromite, and low-quality coal are mined.

When the country was created in 1947, there were few industries, banks, or mercantile firms. Since that time, industrial production has risen significantly. In 1990/91, industry accounted for about 26% of the GDP, compared with only 7% in 1950. Thanks in part to significant expansion of power facilities, largely in the Indus basin, the pace of economic development was particularly rapid during the 1980s. For most of the decade, the annual GDP growth rate averaged 6.5%, reflecting an expansion of over 4% annually in the agricultural sector and over 7% in value added in the industrial sector.

This strong performance notwithstanding, a growing debt-servicing burden, large government expenditures on public enterprises, low tax revenues, high levels of defense spending, and a rapid rise in imports with burgeoning domestic demand contributed to serious fiscal and current account deficits during the late 1980s. In response, in 1988 the government initiated a major structural reform program with World Bank and IMF support. Overall growth indicators remained promising with the reform measures, as GDP increased by 5.5% in 1990/91 and 7.8% in 1991/92, and export growth averaged a robust 14% between 1989 and 1992. These improvements notwithstanding, reform efforts secured less than expected reductions in the country's balance of payment deficits, due in part to deteriorating terms of trade in the wake of rising oil prices during the 1991 Gulf War. Reflecting these difficulties, rising inflation became a serious problem in the early 1990s, reaching 11.8% in 1990/91 and declining only somewhat to 9.2% in 1991/92. Severe floods in the Sindh and Punjab provinces in late 1992 and a contraction in international commodity markets weakened Pakistan's export sector during 1992/93, further exacerbating the country's trade and current account deficits and helping to reduce GDP growth to only 3% for that year. Peformance is expected to improve again with continued policy reform, although the country's dependence on a narrow range of exports with uncertain price prospects on the international market may prove a serious constraint.

20INCOME

In 1992, Pakistan's GNP was $49,477 million at current prices, or $420 per capita. For the period 1985–92 the average inflation rate was 8.6%, resulting in a real growth rate in per capita GNP of 1.7%.

In 1992 the GDP was $47,287 million in current US dollars. It is estimated that agriculture, hunting, forestry, and fishing contributed 22% to GDP; mining and quarrying, 1%; manufacturing, 15%; electricity, gas, and water, 3%; construction, 4%; wholesale and retail trade, 15%; transport, storage, and communication, 8%; finance, insurance, real estate, and business services, 6%; community, social, and personal services, 7%; and other sources 19%.

21LABOR

In 1991–92, the total labor force was estimated at 33,800,000 compared with 20,500,000 in 1975. The low proportion of the population included in the labor force (about 29% in 1991–92) is in part attributable to the limited participation of women, and each year, over 1 million new workers are added to the labor force. In 1991–92, agriculture accounted for 51% of the total work force, and industry for 19%. Some 70% of rural residents engage in agricultural pursuits. Unemployment and underemployment are major problems; while unemployment is officially 3.1%, underemployment has frequently gone as high as 25%, and ranged from 10–15% in 1991–92. The Ministry of Labor operates employment exchanges.

There are more than one million Pakistani workers in the Middle East and Gulf countries, most of them from the poor regions of Pakistan's NWFP. There are also several million refugees from Afghanistan that have, in part, become part of the Pakistan labor force in those regions and in Karachi.

The trade union movement is of recent origin. In 1992, the principal federations included the National Labor Federation and the All Pakistan National Federation of Trade Unions. Labor-management differences are handled by the central conciliation machinery, established under the provisions of the Industrial Disputes Act of 1947. Benefits such as bonuses, paid holidays, and job security regulations are set forth in the basic West Pakistan Industrial and Commercial Employment Ordinance of 1968. Workers' compensation (the basic law passed in 1923) and child labor provisions (1991) are also in force, even though the practice of child labor is widespread, with some 2–8 million persons under 14 years of age working, usually in agriculture. There may also be some 20 million bonded laborers in Pakistan.

Employment abroad is an important source of domestic income, with some 1.6 to 2 million Pakistanis working abroad, mostly in thirteen European and Persian Gulf countries.

22AGRICULTURE

Whereas agriculture engages 44.5% of the economically active population, it contributes only about 25% (the same as industry) to GDP. The development of a huge irrigation network covering two-thirds of the total cultivated area—together with massive land reclamation projects—has made possible the farming of vast tracts of previously barren and unusable land. The Indus Valley of Punjab is Pakistan's agricultural heartland. Grains constitute the most important food crops, with wheat, rice, corn, and citrus the major products. Cotton, the most important cash crop, generates more

foreign trade income than any other export item. Rice, sugarcane, tobacco, rapeseed, and mustard are also large export earners.

Improved government policies over the past decade have made Pakistan a net exporter of guar products, tobacco, cotton, and rice. Cotton, rice, and wheat make up 70% of the value-added in crop output, with the former two accounting for 7% ($412 million) and 5.9% ($346 million) of total exports, respectively, in 1992. Principal crops with 1992 output (in thousands of tons) were wheat, 15,684; sugarcane, 1,291; and rice, 2,509. Seed cotton production for the year totaled 4,782,000 (9% of the world's total). Other crops include millet, barley, sesame, flax, groundnuts, mangoes, citrus fruits, and vegetables. Opium poppies are grown in the North-West Frontier Province, despite sporadic government efforts to stamp out the opium and heroin trade, which grew rapidly during the 1980s.

Farming production remains limited by primitive methods, and mechanization is uncommon. The introduction of improved wheat and rice varieties has met with some success, although the greatest impact on agriculture has derived from the Indus basin irrigation schemes, which by the 1970s had provided Pakistan with the largest irrigated network in the world. The availability of water has made possible increased use of chemical fertilizers, with the most intensive consumption occurring in cotton production. The government has instituted soil conservation, farm mechanization, land reclamation, and plant protection programs.

To increase smallholders' equity and provide further incentives for agricultural improvement, the government decreed in 1959 that the maximum holding for any person should be 200 hectares (500 acres) of irrigated land or 400 hectares (1,000 acres) unirrigated. Land in excess of these amounts was acquired by the government and paid for in interest-bearing 30-year bonds. In March 1972, the maximum permissible size of a holding, measured in terms of production index units, was reduced by two-thirds, with the government empowered to confiscate without payment all excess land for free redistribution to landless peasants and small tenants. To help the new landowners, the government provided loans for purchase of seed, feed, and bullocks. In accordance with a statement of national agricultural policy issued in 1980, the Agricultural Price Commission was established to provide incentives to Pakistani farmers through higher prices for farm products. Agriculture absorbed some 30% of total investment as of 1992.

23ANIMAL HUSBANDRY

Some 30 to 35 million people are engaged in the livestock industry. Camels are used for transport throughout the more barren south and west, and bullocks and donkeys elsewhere. Sheep range widely over the grazing lands of middle and northern Pakistan; the bulk of their wool is exported. Among local breeds of cattle, the Red Sindhi, the Tharparker, the Sahiwal are renowned for milk, and the Bhagnari and Dhanni for draft purposes. The production of powdered milk, cheese, butter, and ice cream is carried out by several large dairy plants. From 1984 to 1990, milk production increased by 41%, and meat production rose 48%. Even so, domestic milk production still falls short of demand. Poultry production has recently became prominent, especially through scientific research in breeding, feeding, and disease control. With the assistance of the Asian Development Bank, several livestock development projects are currently underway.

In 1992 there were 17.7 million head of cattle, 26.9 million sheep, 18.2 million buffalo, 38.5 million goats, 1 million camels, and 164 million poultry. The livestock industry contributed 8% of GDP. In 1991/92, leather exports represented 3.5% of total export value. Cattle dung is an important cooking fuel and fertilizer.

24FISHING

With a coastline of 814 km (506 mi), Pakistan is rich in fishery resources that remain to be fully developed. Almost the entire population of the coastal areas of Sindh and Balochistan depends on fisheries for its livelihood. In all, fishing engages some 220,000 persons. The fish catch in 1991 was estimated at 515,497 tons, 78% of it landed off coastal waters. Species include salmon, mullet, pomfret, mackerel, shrimp, and local varieties. About 10% of the annual catch is exported.

To exploit potential fishery resources, the government has undertaken such projects as construction of a modern harbor for fishing vessels at Karachi, procurement of diesel-powered vessels, establishment of cold storage and marketing facilities, export of frozen shrimp, and encouragement of cooperative fish-marketing societies. An aquaculture project financed by the AsDB and EC aimed to increase the annual fish catch and to promote prawn farming.

25FORESTRY

Of Pakistan's depleted forest resources, amounting to about 4.8% of the total area, only about 1,120,000 hectares (2,767,500 acres) are classified as commercial or productive forests. Privately-owned forests cover some 3,783,000 hectares (9,348,000 acres), located primarily in the North Western Frontier Province (NWFP) and Punjab. Hill forests predominate in the north and northwest temperate and subtropical regions. Fir, spruce, *deodar*, bluepine, chirpine, *Chalghoza*, and juniper, as well as broadleaved species like oak, maple, walnut, poplar, and chestnut are found in the hill forests. These forests are the main source for constructional timber and supply great quantities of fuelwood, while providing groundcover to the fragile mountain ecosystems (thereby lessening floods and droughts in the plains). Forests in the foothills consist of broadleaved evergreens, with main species of olive and *phulai*. Irrigated plantation forests grow such species as *sheesham*, mulberry, *bakain*, and *semal*, mostly for timber, furniture, and sporting goods production.

About 500,000 cu m of timber is produced annually by state forests, which are under the authority of the Pakistan Forest Institute. One-half of annual wood production is consumed as fuelwood. Since forest resources are limited, Pakistan must import wood and wood products in increasing volumes to satisfy rising demand.

26MINING

The prospecting and exploitation of mineral resources are subject to government planning and regulation. The Mineral Development Corp. and the Resource Development Corp. (RDC), both established in 1974, direct development of the mining sector and manage government-owned mining enterprises.

Except for petroleum and natural gas, mineral reserves are meager and of poor quality. Local coal is of inferior grade, and the demand requires massive imports; coal production stood at 3,040,000 tons in 1991. Chromite is one of the few valuable minerals available; chromium content in mined ore rose from 1,090 tons in 1988 to 10,380 tons in 1991. Small quantities of antimony, fire clays, iron ore, uranium, gold, and silver are also produced. The Mineral Development Corp. operates three coal mines in Baluchistan, and one each in Punjab and Sind.

27ENERGY AND POWER

Pakistan is about 64% self-sufficient in energy, owing largely to crude oil reserves of an estimated 118 million barrels (chiefly at the Meyal oil field, near Rawalpindi) and large natural gas reserves of 736 billion cu m (mainly at Sui, Baluchistan). In the early and mid-1980s, accelerated exploitation of these resources reduced the nation's oil imports and improved its trade balance. In 1992, 37 new wells were drilled; crude oil production rose from 62,000 barrels per day in 1991 to 76,000 barrels per day in 1992. The seventh five-year plan (1988–93) saw the energy sector receive 36% of total government expenditures.

Oil, about two-thirds of which is imported, meets about 40% of Pakistan's energy needs. Natural gas satisfies 35% of energy needs, while the remainder is met by hydroelectricity (18%) and coal (7%). Energy production in 1991 included petroleum, 23,027,000 barrels; natural gas, 14,680 million cu m; and electricity, 43,700 million kwh. Installed electrical generating capacity totaled 10,100,000 kw in 1992, of which 7,100 million kw came from thermal plants, 2,900 million kw from hydroelectric sources, and 100 million kw from nuclear reactors.

Two factors have contributed to the growth of the electric power sector: the initial harnessing of the vast hydroelectric potential of the Indus basin (estimated at 25,000 Mw) and the increased availability of natural gas as a fuel for thermal generators. About 40% of Pakistan's electrical output in 1991 came from hydroelectric sources. The Tarbela Dam, the world's largest earth- and rock-filled dam, completed in 1976 at a cost of $1.1 billion, generates 2.1 million kw of hydroelectric power. Pakistan's 137-Mw nuclear plant at Karáchi is to be augmented by construction of a 900-Mw nuclear installation at Chashma. In August, 1992, the government entered into an agreement with a consortium of western nations to build a $1.7 billion oil-fired 1,292 Mw power station at Hub Chowki, which will raise Pakistan's installed capacity by 15%. The project is one-third funded by the World Bank and will be Pakistan's first private sector power project.

28INDUSTRY

Since 1947, the government has given the highest priority to development of the industrial sector. Perhaps one of the most promising signs of the country's industrial development during recent years has been continued growth in manufacturing value-added, which reached 8.3% in 1992 and is estimated to be 5.6% in 1993, despite overall constraints on industrial production due to flooding and poor cotton crops. Manufacturing currently employs about 12% of the work force.

During the 1960s and 1970s, light industry expanded rapidly—especially textiles, sugar refining, fertilizers, and other manufactures derived from local raw materials. Large government investments in the 1970s established the country's first large-scale ship-bulding and steel milling operations; the production of chemical fertilizers was also given special government support. The Pakistan Industrial Development Corp., established in the early 1980s with IDA credit, developed industrial estates for small- and medium-scale industries, assisting their occupants in obtaining credit, raw materials, technical and managerial assistance, access to production facilities, as well as marketing support. Despite steady overall industrial growth during the 1980s, the sector remains concentrated in cotton processing, textiles, food processing and petroleum refining. Small-scale and cottage industries employ about three-fourths of Pakistan's industrial workers and account for about one-fourth of its industrial production as well as 6% of the GDP.

The 1973 nationalization program, which placed 10 basic industries wholly within the public sector, was reversed in 1991 with the enactment of an ambitious privatization program. In 1992, the government began auctioning off majority control in nearly all public sector industrial enterprises, including those manufacturing chemicals, fertilizers, engineering products, petroleum products, cement, automobiles, and other industrial products requiring a high level of capital investment, to private investors. Remaining shares are now being offered to the public at large.

Cotton textile production is the most important of Pakistan's industries, accounting for 20% of both manufacturing value-added and total exports. Pakistan has become self-sufficient in cotton fabrics (307 million sq m produced in 1991/92) and exports substantial quantities. Factories also produce synthetic fabrics, worsted yarn and jute textiles. Cotton yarn production equalled 1,171,000 tons in 1991/92; jute textile output amounted to over 100,000 tons. The textile industry as a whole employs about 40% of the industrial work force.

Other important industries include food processing, accounting for 14% of the industrial workforce and about 20% of MVA; chemicals manufacture, employing 9% of the labor force and contributing 16% of total MVA; and the iron and steel industries which together account for a further 8% of all industrial workers and 7% of MVA. Production output from major industries in 1991/92 included 2,322,000 tons of sugar, 642,000 tons of vegetable ghee, 1,048,000 tons of pig iron, 1,898,000 tons of urea, 185,875 tons of soda ash, 5,757,000 rubber tubes, 8,321,000 tons of cement, 33,056 electric motors and 85,112 sewing machines.

29 SCIENCE AND TECHNOLOGY

Pakistan made notable advances in nuclear technology since the 1980s, when its Atomic Energy Commission (AEC) developed a nuclear plant for electric power generation and research programs. The AEC's three nuclear centers for agricultural research have employed nuclear techniques to improve crop varieties. Six nuclear medical centers provide diagnosis and treatment of patients with radioisotopes produced from Pakistan's own uranium resources. The government denies Western intelligence reports that Pakistan is developing nuclear weapons.

The Karachi Export Processing Zone (EPZ), established in 1980, has attracted foreign capital investment in advanced technologies. Another EPZ has been proposed for Lahore. EPZ now include those for computer assembly and parts manufacture, television assembly, other electrical and electronic products, and engineering.

The Pakistan Academy of Science is located in Islāmābād. Scientific learned societies include the Pakistan Association for the Advancement of Science (Lahore) and the Scientific Society of Pakistan (Karachi). Scientific research bodies include the Cancer Research Institute (Karachi), Irrigation Research Institute (Lahore), National Science Council of Pakistan (Islāmābād), Pakistan Council of Scientific and Industrial Research (Karachi), Pakistan Medical Research Council (Karachi), and Research Society of Pakistan (Lahore).By the late 1980s, Pakistan spent over 5 million rupoes per year on national research and development.

30 DOMESTIC TRADE

The government supervises the supply and pricing of essential commodities, including fruits, vegetables, livestock, and dairy products, and has established several cooperative marketing and distribution organizations. Foreign goods are brought in by large importing concerns, centered at Karachi, and distributed to retailers through many intermediaries. There are several produce exchanges at Karachi, and the trade organizations are represented by the Federation of Chambers of Commerce and Industry. Steps have been taken to improve marketing and distribution facilities throughout the country.

Banks are customarily open from 9 AM to 1 PM. Advertising remains small in scope, in part because of the high rate of illiteracy. Outlets include television, newspapers, posters, handbills, and color slides shown in the motion-picture houses.

31 FOREIGN TRADE

Pakistan has suffered a weak trade position since the early 1970s, as the cost of oil imports have risen while prices for the country's main exports have declined on the international market. Between 1973 and 1980, export value rose by 16% in constant dollars, but import value increased by 28%, resulting in a 1979/80 trade deficit of nearly $3 billion. The trade deficit remained substantial during the 1980s despite continued strength in the country's export performance, due in part to expansionary domestic demand policies by the government as well as worsening terms of trade resulting from the Gulf War and worldwide economic reces-

sion. In 1991/1992, the trade deficit was still $2.2 billion. The country's flexible exchange rate system, in place since 1982, has been an important factor in boosting exports. A variety of other trade liberalisation measures enacted since 1991 should have a positive impact on Pakistan's export-oriented industries by reducing the cost of imported intermediate goods. However, tariffs and other levies remain stiff for many items. Manufactures now dominate Pakisan's exports, though these are concentrated in textile and leather goods.

During the 1980s, the UK, traditionally Pakistan's most important trading partner, slipped behind the US, Japan, and the Federal Republic of Germany (FRG). In 1991/92, the US was the leading purchaser of Pakistan's export goods, and Hong Kong had emerged as its third largest market, behind Japan. Leading import suppliers were Japan, the US and Germany, with both China and Malaysia comprising important new sources as well. Principal trade partners in 1991/92 (in millions of rupees) were as follows:

	EXPORTS	IMPORTS	BALANCE
US	22,006	24,124	− 2,118
Japan	14,226	32,934	−18,708
FRG	12,174	18,275	− 6,101
UK	11,375	12,533	− 1,178
Saudi Arabia	7,339	12,048	− 4,709
France	6,667	10,883	− 4,216
Hong Kong	12,503	1,058	11,445
China	1,378	9,932	− 8,554
Malaysia	1,547	9,663	− 8,116
Other countries	82,508	98,439	−15,931
TOTAL	171,723	229,889	−58,166

32 BALANCE OF PAYMENTS

Pakistan's payments problems have been chronic since the 1970s, with the cost of oil imports primarily responsible for the trade imbalance. The growth of exports and of remittances from Pakistanis working abroad (mostly in the Middle East) helped Pakistan to keep the payments deficit in check. Since the oil sector boom began subsiding in the early 1980s, however, remittances have been declining. This trend especially accelerated during the Gulf War, when nearly 80,000 Pakistanis in Kuwait and Iraq lost their jobs. Only about 25% of these jobs had been regained a year after the end of the conflict. Increased imports and softer demand for Pakistan's textiles and apparel in major markets in 1992 also caused the current account deficit to further increase.

In 1992 merchandise exports totaled $6,352 million and imports $8,599 million. The merchandise trade balance was $-2,247 million. The following table summarizes Pakistan's balance of payments for 1990 and 1991 (in millions of US dollars):

	1990	1991
CURRENT ACCOUNT		
Goods, services, and income	−4,434	−4,213
Unrequited transfers	2,779	2,284
TOTALS	1,655	−1,929
CAPITAL ACCOUNT		
Direct investment	242	261
Portfolio investment	87	92
Other long-term capital	1,054	1,132
Other short-term capital	−212	−586
Exceptional Financing	782	1,059
Reserves	304	16
TOTALS	1,757	1,958
Errors and omissions	−103	−46
Total change in reserves	114	3

33BANKING AND SECURITIES

The central banking institution is the State Bank of Pakistan, established in 1948 at Karachi and with branches in the larger cities. The government holds 51% of the bank's paid-up capital; 49% is held by corporations, societies, and individuals. The State Bank has exclusive responsibility for the issuance of currency; it is the financial agent of the central and provincial governments, and is responsible for the flotation and management of the public debt. In December 1993, the money supply, as measured by M2, amounted to R608,626 million; bank time deposits totaled R230,515, and demand deposits R191,163 million.

The nation's largest commercial banks were nationalized in 1974 and regrouped under five state banking institutions: the National Bank of Pakistan, Habib Bank, United Bank, Muslim Commercial Bank, and Allied Bank of Pakistan. The government-controlled banking system thus comprised all but a few of the nation's banks and accounted for a large share of total bank deposits and outstanding domestic credit. In 1981, in accordance with the Islamic condemnation of usury, virtually all banks opened special accounts for depositors who preferred, in lieu of interest, to share in the profits or losses from investments made with their money. In 1985, all savings accounts stopped yielding interest and converted to sharing in profit and loss. Pakistan instituted banking reform in 1991. The Muslim Commercial Bank and the Allied Bank of Pakistan Ltd. reverted to private ownership shortly thereafter. In 1991 banking licenses were granted to private commercial banks that wanted to establish foreign bank branches in the country.

The state provides credit through the Agricultural Development Bank of Pakistan and the House Building Finance Corp. Industrial loans are made available through the Pakistan Industrial Credit and Investment Corp. (established in 1957), the Industrial Development Bank of Pakistan (1961), and the National Development Finance Corp. (1973).

There are stock exchanges at Lahore and Karachi, with the latter accounting for a major share of the business.

34INSURANCE

Pakistan's life insurance sector, nationalized in 1972, operated under the aegis of the State Life Insurance Corp. and Postal Life Insurance until 1992, when the government opened it to private sector participation. As of May 1992, three Pakistani companies were authorized to sell life insurance. Foreign companies are no longer barred from the life insurance business, but they are restricted to minority ownership. Private companies function in non-life insurance areas, but the government insurance business is controlled by the National Insurance Corp. One of the state's first steps was to standardize and reduce premium rates and to encourage coverage among a wider segment of the population. In 1990, premiums totaled $3.1 per capita, or 0.9% of GDP. During 1992, life insurance in force amounted to R169.801 million.

35PUBLIC FINANCE

The fiscal year extends from 1 July to 30 June. The federal government frames two separate budgets: revenue (current account) and capital. Deficits have appeared since 1971/72, a combined result of the loss of revenues from East Pakistan, stepped-up defense expenditures, lax expenditure controls, and a low and inelastic tax base. Current expenditures (debt service, defense, administration) now consume over 70% of the budget; development needs (education, health, energy, and rural development) receive the remainder. In 1990/91, defense spending amounted to 43% of current expenditures, while debt service took another 23%. Tax revenues have not kept pace with expenditure growth due to widespread evasion, corruption among tax officials, over-reliance on foreign trade taxes, and a tax exemption for agricultural income, which comprises 20% of GDP. In 1991/92, the government sought to limit public expenditures and enlarge the tax base.

In 1989 Pakistan's total public debt stood at R581,192 million, of which R253,658 million was financed abroad. As a proportion of GNP, the outstanding debt of Pakistan stood at 36.2% in 1989/90 (as compared to 42.3% in 1974/75) and has grown annually by about 6.5% since 1977/78.

36TAXATION

Pakistan lives predominantly by foreign trade, and its import tariff is essentially revenue-producing. The national government does not levy income tax on agricultural income, and personal and noncorporate business incomes below R40,000 a year are also exempt from income tax. Rates are progressive, rising from 10% in the lowest category to 35% in the highest, with a net wealth tax of up to 2.5%.

The basic corporation tax is levied on total taxable income at a flat rate equivalent to 30%. In addition, there is a 10% supertax (30% for banks), on which rebates are available for nonbank public companies (5%) and life insurance companies (12.5%), among other categories. There is a capital gains tax of 25%, and a tax ranging from 15–20% applied to stock dividends of nonpublic companies.

Special taxes include the zakat, a religious levy to provide aid for the poor, which imposes a 2.5% tax on bank deposits and invested wealth, and the ushr, a 5% tax on farm products, collected from landowners.

Established proportions of the various taxes levied by the federal government are distributed to the provincial governments. In addition, the provinces collect, for their exclusive use, taxes on land revenue, immovable property, vehicles, professions and services, and mineral rights, as well as excise taxes. Municipalities and other local governments also levy taxes.

37CUSTOMS AND DUTIES

Pakistan's customs tariff brings in the largest single share of national revenue. Most dutiable items are subject to ad valorem duties that range from 2% to 100% (as on certain luxury items), with the average about 30%. There is also a 10% import surcharge, a 5% education tax, and, in many cases, a 12.5% sales tax on imported goods. (Food, raw materials, and capital goods are exempt from this tax.) The use of a tariff for protection covers specific developing local industries. Tariffs are levied on major items of export, but these rates are subject to change as measures are taken to encourage or discourage the export of raw materials. Exports of certain foods, used copper and brass utensils, and some hides and skins are banned. Trade with Israel, South Africa, and Taiwan is prohibited.

38FOREIGN INVESTMENT

Foreign aid and investment have played a critical role in Pakistan's economic development since the first years of independence. Since 1954, the government has tried to attract foreign investment to maintain economic development, provide specialized technical knowledge, and bring in much-needed foreign exchange. Incentives for private investment include guarantees for the repatriation of capital invested in approved industries, facilities for remittance of profits, and guarantees for equitable compensation in the event of nationalization of an industry. In addition, special tax concessions available to certain local industries are also available to foreign investors. In 1980, the government established the Karāchi Export Processing Zone (EPZ) to attract foreign investment into Pakistan on very favorable terms: no customs duties or other restrictions on imports and exports, a five-year tax holiday, and full repatriation of capital and profits. The objectives of the EPZ were to develop modern technologies, create employment and training opportunities for Pakistanis, and enlarge the international market for Pakistan's raw materials and manufactures. Since the late 1980s, a series of regulatory reforms related to exchange controls, repatriation of profits, credit for foreign-owned firms, issuing of equity shares, foreign currency accounts, and transactions on the stock exchange have significantly reduced the restrictions on general foreign investor activity in the wider Pakistani economy. The effects of these measures on foreign investor interest in Pakistan have already been tangible. Net foreign direct investment flow in 1990/91 equalled $242 million, up from only $167 million in 1989/90 and $173 million in 1988/89. The US presently accounts for roughly one-half of yearly FDI, followed by the United Arab Emirates and the UK.

³⁹ECONOMIC DEVELOPMENT

After the founding of the Pakistani state in 1947, the government's economic policy concentrated attention on developing an economic infrastructure, achieving self-sufficiency in food, and developing export industries. A major new land reform program introduced in March 1972 had resulted by March 1975 in the confiscation (for eventual redistribution) of 45.3% of all privately cultivated farmland. By November 1973, the government had nationalized industries in 10 major categories of production. In a third major step, most of the commercial banks were nationalized on 1 January 1974, resulting in control of more than 90% of all banking business by the State Bank and the five newly created units.

By the late 1970s, however, Pakistan's martial law government, claiming the nationalization program had stifled production and discouraged private investment, moved to restore private sector confidence by fostering economic stability and by redressing the balance-of-payments deficit, which was causing large overseas debt obligations. A new five-year plan (1978–83), Pakistan's fifth, reserved 48% of industrial investment for the private sector and set goals for an annual economic growth rate of 7.2%, a 4.2% rise in per capita income, and increases of 6% in agricultural output and 10% in industrial production. The plan was allocated a budget of $21 billion, of which 25% was to come from external sources. Indications were that the agricultural sector would meet its target, but that rising oil costs and the burden of providing for the Afghan refugees had impeded progress in other sectors.

The sixth five-year plan (1983–88), with a proposed outlay of R210 billion, envisioned further investments in water and power development, deregulation to increase private sector activity, and a new emphasis on provision of social services and infrastructural improvements for rural areas. Prime Minister Junejo announced a program for 1986–90, with an outlay of R70 billion, focusing on rural development, particularly in the areas of education, village electrification, potable water supply, roads, health care, and employment.

By the late 1980s, a number of structural factors resulted in increasingly critical fiscal and balance of payment deficits. With less than 30% of the budget devoted to infrastructural development and other needs in health and education, the prognosis for long-term social and economic development remained poor. In response, a medium-term structural reform program was developed under the government of Prime Minister Benazir Bhutto for implementation in 1989–91. Aimed at correcting fiscal and external imbalances, the program targeted a reform of the tax collection system, tighter government spending controls and monetary management, the privatization of state-owned industrial enterprises, banks and utilities, the phasing out of state monopolies in the transportation, insurance, telecommunications and energy sectors, and liberalization of investment and foreign exchange regulations. Implementation of the ambitious program proceeded under the government of Nawaz Sharif who assumed the prime minister's office in 1991. Results have been somewhat uneven thus far, with little effective improvements scored in the country's

tax system or its fiscal and balance of payments deficits. While the rapid change of government in 1993 and ongoing political tensions appear to be dampening private investment somewhat, official assurances have been given that structural reform and privatization will continue.

Since the early 1950s through 1993, Pakistan is estimated to have received about $37 billion in aid disbursements, including both long-term and medium-term loans and grants, making it one of the largest recipients in the developing world. For the Indus Valley project, Pakistan received funding of more than $1.3 billion from the IBRD, IDA, ADB, US, UK, and other countries. In addition to US aid (a six-year commitment of $4.02 billion made in 1988 with $2.1 billion disbursed by 1990), Pakistan has also received aid from Iran and the Arab states. New economic aid from the US was halted in 1990, under the terms of a Congressional amendment requiring certification of Pakistan's status as a nuclear weapons-free country.

⁴⁰SOCIAL DEVELOPMENT

Although traditionally described by its leaders and politicians as an Islamic social welfare state, Pakistan has been slow in taking over major responsibility for such welfare problems as unemployment, sickness, handicaps, and old age. Until the 1970s, the full scope of social welfare programs remained to be implemented. Some modest improvements were effected by setting up service units in rural communities, instituting pilot projects to overcome extreme poverty, opening centers for vocational training of the handicapped, and providing instruction in local welfare in the schools. A social security scheme enacted in 1972 covers employees of firms with 10 or more workers. Family and self-employed labor is excluded, and there are separate systems for the armed forces, police, and other public employees. Social security coverage includes old age, disability, and survivor benefits, as well as sickness and maternity payments, workers' compensation, and unemployment benefits. Since 1973, cost-of-living allowances have been paid to workers earning less than minimum wages. The ILO has assisted the government in completing a pension and disability scheme.

The government has taken steps to meet the threats of overpopulation. In 1991, 1,749,300 persons availed themselves of family planning services. Pakistan's fertility rate was 6.8 in 1985–90. In 1990–91, 12% of reproductive-age couples practiced contraception. A population planning council, assisted by provincial planning boards, supplies contraceptives.

The martial law government's Islamization program to promote social welfare in accordance with Islamic precepts was introduced in 1977. Islamic welfare taxes, the zakat and ushr, were levied to redistribute wealth. The ushr tax on landowners took effect in 1983. Islamic beliefs are inculcated in the public schools and disseminated widely by the mass media. Laws against drinking alcoholic beverages, adultery, and bearing false witness have been strictly enforced.

The Women's Ministry, established in 1979, has sponsored some 7,000 centers in rural areas and urban slums to provide women with a basic education and to teach them such skills as livestock farming, midwifery, and secretarial work. Employment for college-educated women has traditionally been limited to teaching, medical services, and the law. However, a growing number of women are entering the commercial and public sectors. In 1993, there were about 30 female judges in civil courts. The government's 1991 Shari'a Bill, aimed at bringing Pakistani society more fully into conformity with Islamic tenets, included provisions to protect women's constitutional and property rights.

⁴¹HEALTH

Health facilities in Pakistan are inadequate, mainly due to a lack of resources and a high population growth rate. Despite notable advances in health care provision, 45% of the population was still without modern medical care in 1992. Total health care expenditures in 1990 were $1,394 million.

The country needs food availability, a proper water supply, and adequate sanitation. Its goal, under the direction of the Federal Ministry of Health, is to be able to provide health care services to every Pakistani by the year 2000. Pakistan is also working towards universal immunization, disease prevention, health promotion, and curative and rehabilitative services, and, as of 1990, there were several programs underway to improve health care coverage and control tuberculosis, leprosy, and cancer. One such program is a Child Survival/Primary Health Care program to reduce mortality, malnutrition, and deaths due to diarrheal diseases. In 1990, 57% of children under 5 years old were considered malnourished. In 1992, 91% of children up to one year of age were immunized against tuberculosis; 78% against diphtheria, pertussis, and tetanus; 78% against polio; and 76% against measles. In 1991, there were 150 reported cases of tuberculosis per 100,000 people and 40,000 people suffered from leprosy.

In 1991/92, there were 60,250 physicians, 2,410 dentists, and 33,740 nurses, and 20,000 registered homeopathic medical practitioners. Many medical students have been sent abroad under an advanced medical training program. Special attention has been given to the training of nurses, and several training centers are in operation. However, medical personnel ratios, though much improved, remain inadequate: 1 doctor per 2,940 persons and 1 nurse per 5,040 in 1990. The country's 652 hospitals had 55,000 beds in 1986, the vast majority located in urban areas. In 1992, there were 0.7 hospital beds per 1,000 inhabitants. There were 302 health centers with 2,462 beds serving the rural population. In 1991, centers for the disabled included 11 physical therapy centers, 12 mental retardation centers, 11 centers for the visually impaired, and 12 centers for the hearing impaired.

Malaria, tuberculosis, intestinal diseases, venereal diseases, and skin diseases remain Pakistan's main public health problems. Drug addiction, especially among university students, is an increasing concern; government detoxification centers helped about 30,000 addicts recover during 1981–85. In 1991, the infant mortality rate was 103.6 per 1,000 live births. Major causes of infant mortality were immunizable diseases, diarrhea, malnutrition, and poor environmental sanitation. The overall mortality rate was 10.5 per 1,000 people in 1993. The leading causes of death were diarrhea, pneumonia, tuberculosis, cardiovascular diseases, and cancer. Average life expectancy in 1992 was estimated at 57 years.

42HOUSING

The rapid increase in urbanization, coupled with the rising population, has added to the housing shortage in urban areas. About 25% of the people in large cities live in katchi abadis (shantytowns). The Public Works Department has built more than 8,000 units in Islāmābād, Lahore, Peshāwar, and Quetta at a cost of R1,588 million. Under the 1986–90 program, the residents in the katchi abadis were to be given proprietary rights. In 1987, the National Housing Authority was created to coordinate the upgrading of the existing katchi abadis and prevent the growth of new ones. As of 1991, 171 abadis had been renovated at a cost of R454 million, and 522 more were under development. Overall, 53% of Pakistanis have adequate sanitation facilities.

43EDUCATION

The education system is poor, notwithstanding a massive educational reform announced in 1972 and aimed at providing free and universal education through the 10th year of formal schooling for both boys (by 1983) and girls (by 1987). In addition, the study of Islam was to be compulsory at all levels. In 1990, the literacy rate

was 34.8% (male 47.3% and female 21.1%). As an initial step, private educational institutions at all levels were nationalized. Additional steps included a reform of the curriculum away from general education and in favor of agricultural and technical subjects, equality of access to formal schooling for low-income groups and females, financial aid programs for poor students, and broad expansion and improvement of higher-level facilities. Curriculum bureaus were set up at federal and provincial levels, and the National Council of Education was established to formulate and evaluate educational development policy.

As of 1989–90, there were 107,210 primary schools with some 9,236,000 pupils and 13,911 secondary schools with 3,647,000 students. Girls attend separate schools at both primary and secondary levels.

During the same year, 483,000 students were enrolled at 619 arts and sciences colleges, and an additional 83,482 attended 22 universities. Arts and sciences colleges are affiliated with the universities of the Punjab (at Lahore, established 1882), Sind (at Hyderābād, 1947; at Karāchi, 1951), Peshāwar (1950), Baluchistan (1970), and Multān (1975). An agricultural university was established in 1961 at Lyallpur (now Faisalābād). Two engineering and technological universities have been founded at Lahore (1961) and Islāmābād (1966). Research institutions include the Institute of Islamic Studies at Lahore, the Iqbal Academy at Lahore, and the Pakistan Institute of International Affairs at Karāchi. Urdu and English are the languages of instruction.

Many adult literacy centers have been established in recent years, the majority in Sind. In addition, the People's Open University was established at Islāmābād (1974) to provide mass adult education via correspondence and the communications media.

44LIBRARIES AND MUSEUMS

The largest library in Pakistan is that of the Punjab University at Lahore, with a collection of about 335,000 volumes, including some 20,000 manuscripts. Sizable collections are also at the University of Karachi (306,000 volumes) and the University of Sind (208,000 volumes). Other important libraries are the Punjab Public Library in Lahore (232,000 volumes), the Liaquat Memorial Library (130,000 volumes), the Central Secretariat Library (27,000 volumes), and the National Archives (16,000 volumes), all in Karāchi. The National Library of Pakistan at Islāmābād has more than 80,000 volumes.

Museums are widely dispersed. The National Museum of Pakistan (Karāchi) contains prehistoric material from the Indus Valley civilization, Buddhist statues and carvings, and material from the Islamic centuries, including the renowned Mughal period. The Peshāwar Museum has a splendid collection of Buddhist sculpture of the Gandhara style. The Lahore Museum has an outstanding collection of Greco-Buddhist sculpture. Fine mosques, shrines, and mausoleums of the Islamic centuries are scattered throughout the country. Among the best of the surviving gardens of the Mughal period are those at Lahore, including the Shalimar gardens.

45MEDIA

Postal, telegraph, and telephone services are owned and operated by the state. As of 1991 there were 11,985 post offices. The number of telephones then in use totaled 740,340, or about 6 per 1,000 population. Automatic telephone service has been installed in most cities and large towns. Radiotelephone and radiotelegraph services are available within the country and to foreign countries.

Through Azad Kashmir Radio and the Pakistan Broadcasting Corporation, the government operates 16 medium-wave radio stations. Karāchi is the broadcasting center, and there are important transmitters at Hyderābād, Quetta, Lahore, Rawalpindi, Peshāwar, Multān, Bahāwalpur, and Islāmābād. Government-run

Pakistan-TV broadcasts at least 10 hours a day through 28 transmitters. In 1991 there were 945,000 licensed radios and 1,558,000 licensed television receivers; the latter figure represented nearly a tenfold increase since 1974. Pakistan's Indian Ocean INTELSAT communications stations began service in 1971 near Karachi.

In 1991 there were 183 daily newspapers–most of them with very small circulations—printed in Urdu, English, and a few other languages. English-language newspapers are read by less than 1% of the population but are very influential, especially *Dawn* (1991 estimated circulation, 70,000), published in Karāchi, and *Pakistan Times* (75,000), published in Lahore and Rāwalpindi. Leading Urdu-language dailies (with 1991 circulations) are *Jang* (215,000) and *Jasarat Karāchi* (50,000), both in Karāchi, and *Mashriq* (4,100,000) and, *Nawa-i-Waqt* (450,000), both in Lahore.

While freedom of the press has always been provided for constitutionally, censorship was imposed on the press by the martial law governments. Between 1979 and 1982, local censors reviewed items prior to publication, and some books and periodicals were confiscated. Even after the lifting of censorship, the government continued to influence press coverage by controlling the availability of newsprint, which must be imported, and the placement of government advertising, which is a source of newspapers' revenue. There are no longer restrictions on the importation of newsprint.

46ORGANIZATIONS

Most major cities contain chambers of commerce, and there are numerous employers' associations, such as the All-Pakistan Textile Mills Association, the Pakistan Carpet Manufacturers' and Exporters' Association, and the Pakistan Shipowners' Association. The Islamic community is represented by several flourishing organizations, and other religious communities, such as the Zoroastrians, have their own groups.

47TOURISM, TRAVEL, AND RECREATION

The government actively promotes tourism to boost its foreign-exchange earnings. Pakistan Tours, a government subsidiary, provides daily tours of Karāchi, Rāwalpindi, and other main cities. In Karāchi are the National Museum and the Mausoleum of the Quaid-e-Azam. In Lahore, the "city of gardens" and Pakistan's foremost cultural and educational center, remnants of the Mughal Empire are resplendently preserved. Islāmābād, the wholly planned capital, offers notable examples of architecture in the modern style. Popular recreations include mountain climbing in the Himalaya foothills, sailing, and deep-sea fishing off the Arabian Sea coast. Hockey and cricket are the leading sports, but golf is also popular, with courses in Lahore, Rāwalpindi, Islāmābād and other cities.

Most visitors to Pakistan are required to have a visa and a valid passport. Tourists planning to stay more than 30 days must register with the government. Road permits are available for land crossings into India at Wagah (between Lahore and Amritsar in India). There are no health restrictions on visitors entering Pakistan except in regard to cholera and yellow fever immunizations for those who have been in infected areas. In 1991, 438,088 tourists visited the country, 212,887 from Eastern Asia and 127,934 from Europe. There were 26,329 hotel rooms and 39,493 beds with a 60.5% occupancy rate, and tourist receipts were valued at $163 million.

48FAMOUS PAKISTANIS

Several figures of monumental stature are associated with the creation and establishment of Pakistan. The poet and philosopher of a revitalized Islam, Mohammad Iqbal (1873–1938), who wrote in Urdu, Farsi and English, first called for the establishment of a Muslim state on the subcontinent in a statement made in 1930. Mohammad Ali Jinnah (1876–1948), the Quaid-e-Azam, or "Great Leader," rallied the Muslims to this cause and became the first governor-general of the Commonwealth of Pakistan. His "right hand," Liaquat Ali Khan (1896–1951), was the first prime minister of the nation until his assassination. Chaudhury Mohammad Ali (1905–80), a former prime minister, played a key role in the organization of the new government in 1947. Field Marshal Mohammad Ayub Khan (1908–74) served as commander-in-chief of the Pakistani army, as minister of defense in 1954–55, and as president of Pakistan from October 1958 to March 1969. Sir Mohammad Zafrulla Khan (1893–1985), a distinguished jurist, was several times minister of foreign affairs and later a member of the World Court at The Hague; in 1962, he served as president of the 17th UN General Assembly. Zulfikar Ali Bhutto (1928–79), who rose to prominence as founder and leader of the socialist-leaning Pakistan People's Party, was prime minister during 1973–77 and guided the country's political and economic transformation following the loss of East Pakistan. After Bhutto's execution in 1979, his elder daughter, Benazir (b.1953), became titular head of the Pakistan People's Party. Gen. Mohammad Zia-ul-Haq (1924–1987) came to power in 1977 and assumed the presidency in 1978. The Pakistani-born scientist Abdus Salam (b.1926) shared the 1979 Nobel Prize for Physics for his work in electromagnetism and the interaction of elementary particles.

In literature, the paramount position is still held by the great Urdu writers who lived before the establishment of Pakistan. Ghalib (1796–1869) and Iqbal are recognized as the two greatest Urdu poets. Contemporary writers who have won fame include the Urdu poet Faiz Ahmad Faiz (1911–84), imbued with a strongly socialist spirit, and the Urdu short story writer Saadat Hasan Manto (1912–55). Foremost among Pakistan's artists is Abdur Rahman Chughtai (1899–1975).

49DEPENDENCIES

Pakistan has no territories or colonies.

50BIBLIOGRAPHY

Ahmed, Akbar S. (ed.). *Pakistan: the Social Sciences' Perspective.* Karāchi: Oxford University Press, 1990.

American University. *Pakistan: A Country Study.* Washington, D.C.: Government Printing Office, 1984.

Burki, Shahid Javed. *Historical Dictionary of Pakistan.* Metuchen, N.J.: Scarecrow Press, 1991.

Donnan, Hastings and Pnina Werbner (eds.). *Economy and Culture in Pakistan: Migrants and Cities in a Muslim Society.* New York: St. Martin's Press, 1991.

Hasan, Mushirul (ed.). *India's Partition: Process, Strategy and Mobilization.* Delhi: Oxford University Press, 1993.

Khan, Riaz M. *Untying the Afghan Knot: Negotiating Soviet Withdrawal.* Durham, N.C.: Duke University Press, 1991.

Korson, J. Henry (ed.). *Contemporary Problems of Pakistan.* Boulder, Colo.: Westview Press, 1993.

Mahmud, S. F. *A Concise History of Indo-Pakistan.* 2d ed. New York: Oxford University Press, 1988.

Noman, Omar. *Pakistan: A Political and Economic History since 1947.* New York: Kegan Paul International, 1990.

Qasir, Nadeem. *Pakistan Studies: an Investigation into the Political Economy, 1948–1988.* Oxford: Oxford University Press, 1991.

Taylor, David D. *Pakistan.* Santa Barbara, Calif.: Clio Press, 1990.

Weinbaum, Marvin G. *Pakistan and Afghanistan: Resistance and Reconstruction.* Boulder, Colo.: Westview Press, 1994.

PALAU

Republic of Palau
Belau

CAPITAL: Koror, Koror Island.

FLAG: The flag, adopted 1 January 1981, is light blue, with a yellow disc set slightly off center toward the hoist.

ANTHEM: *Belau er Kid.*

MONETARY UNIT: The US dollar is the official medium of exchange.

WEIGHTS AND MEASURES: British units are used, as modified by US usage.

HOLIDAYS: New Year's Day, 1 January; Youth Day, 15 March; Senior Citizens Day, 5 May; Constitution Day, 9 July; Labor Day, 1st Monday in September; United Nations Day, 24 October; Thanksgiving Day, 4th Thursday in November; Christmas, 25 December.

TIME: 8 PM = noon GMT.

¹LOCATION, SIZE, AND EXTENT

Palau (also known as Belau) is located in the western extremities of the Pacific Ocean. It consists of the Palau group of islands, in the western Caroline Islands, and four remote islands to the sw. Palau is isolated from larger land masses, with Papua New Guinea/Irian Jaya (Indonesia) 660 km (410 mi) to the s, the Philippines 885 km (550 mi) to the w, and Japan 3,042 km (1,890 mi) to the N. Yap Island in the Federated States of Micronesia lies 579 km (360 mi) to the NE. The country consists of more than 200 islands, with a total land area of 441 sq km (170.4 sq mi). Babeldaob is the largest island, with an area of 397 sq km (153.2 sq mi); Koror Island, containing the capital, has an area of 18 sq km (7.1 sq mi). The islands of Peleliu and Angaur are about 50 km (30 mi) s of Koror. Sonsorol and Hatohobei, the two smallest island states, lie 560–640 km (350–400 mi) sw of Koror. Kayangel is a coral atoll 45 km (28 mi) N of Babeldaob.

²TOPOGRAPHY

The islands include four types of topographical formation: volcanic, high limestone, low platform, and coral atoll. The Palau barrier reef encircles the Palau group, except Angaur Island and the Kayangel atoll. The reef encloses a lagoon (1,267 sq km/489 sq mi) on the western side, containing a large number of small elevated limestone islets known as the Rock Islands. Babeldaob and Koror, with peak elevations of 217 m (713 ft) and 628 m (2,061 ft), respectively, contain elevated limestone and volcanic formations. Arakabesan, Malakal, and several small northern islands are volcanic formations. Peleliu and Angaur are low-platform reef islands.

³CLIMATE

Located near the Equator, Palau's climate is maritime tropical, characterized by little seasonal and diurnal variation. The annual mean temperature is 28°C (82°F) in the coolest months. There is high precipitation throughout the year and a relatively high humidity of 82%. Heavy rainfall occurs from May to January. The short torrential nature of the rainfall produces up to 381 cm (150 in) of precipitation annually. Typhoons and tropical storms occur from July through November.

⁴FLORA AND FAUNA

Plant life, abundant throughout most of the islands, includes mangrove swamps, savanna land, and rain forest in upland areas. Food crops, such as taros, cassavas, sweet potatoes, coconuts, bananas, papayas, and citrus fruits, are mostly wild. Marine life is also abundant, with more than 1,500 species of tropical fish and 700 species of coral and anemones in the lagoons and reefs. Fauna includes the sea turtle, which is consumed as a delicacy, and the dugong, or sea cow, a marine mammal that is close to extinction.

⁵ENVIRONMENT

While much of Palau's fragile natural environment remains free of environmental degradation, there are several areas of concern, including illegal fishing with the use of dynamite, inadequate facilities for disposal of solid waste in Koror, and extensive sand and coral dredging in the Palau lagoon. Like the other Pacific island nations, a major environmental problem is global warming and the related rising of sea level. Water coverage of low-lying areas is a threat to coastal vegetation, agriculture, and the purity of the nation's water supply. Palau also has a problem with inadequate water supply and limited agricultural areas to support the size of the population. The nation is also vulnerable to earthquakes, volcanic activity, and tropical storms. Sewage treatment is a problem, along with the handling of toxic waste from fertilizers and biocides.

⁶POPULATION

The 1990 census recorded a total population of 15,122, of whom 12,321 were Palauans by birth. Koror, with 10,501, and Airai, with 1,234, were the most populous states, together containing over 77% of the total population. As a result of a family planning program, the crude birthrate declined from 31 per 1,000 population in 1974 to 17.4 in 1988; in that year, the crude death rate was 7, and the net natural increase was 10.4. The density of population varies significantly in the different states; the overall density in 1990 was 34.3 per sq km (88.8 per sq mi). The population is youthful, with 49% below the age of 25 years in 1990. Population increased at an estimated annual rate 1.9% between 1985 and 1990.

[7]MIGRATION

In 1990, persons not Palau-born numbered 2,801, or 18.5% of the total population. Some 1,459 were born in the Philippines, followed numerically by the Federated States of Micronesia (307), the US (266), and Japan (180). The vast majority of these foreigners (89%) were located in Koror. There is continuous migration to Koror; in 1990, 21% of Koror's population five years of age and over had been living outside Palau in 1985. About one-fifth of all Paluans live abroad, many on Guam.

[8]ETHNIC GROUPS

Most Palauans are Micronesians with a Melanesian genetic admixture. In 1990, the largest non-Palauan ethnic groups included Filipinos (9.8%), other Micronesians (1.8%), Chinese (1.3%), and people of European descent (0.8%).

[9]LANGUAGES

Palauan, a Malayo-Polynesian language related to Indonesian, is the most commonly spoken language; it is used, in addition to English, as an official language. It was the language spoken at home by 81% of the people five years of age or over in 1990, in contrast to 3% who spoke only English at home.

[10]RELIGIONS

Most Palauans are Roman Catholic Christians, but indigenous beliefs are common.

[11]TRANSPORTATION

The nation's roads in 1991 totaled 171.1 km (106.3 mi), of which 22.3 km (13.9 mi) were paved. Asphalt roads are found only in Koror, Airai, and Melekeok. A two-lane concrete bridge, constructed in 1976, links Koror with Airai. The Koror state government provides a public bus service. Palau's deepwater harbor at Malakal in Koror offers international port facilities. Heavy reliance is placed on small private watercraft throughout the country. There is one international airport, located in Airai, 10 km (6 mi) from Koror. Three airlines provide international service: Air Micronesia/Continental, Air Nauru, and South Pacific Island Airways. There are three domestic airlines: Palau Paradise Air, Aero Belau, and Freedom Air.

[12]HISTORY

As part of the Carolinian archipelago, the islands were sighted by European navigators as early as the 16th century. In 1686, the Spanish explorer Francisco Lezcano named Yap Island (now in the Federated States of Micronesia) "La Carolina" after King Charles II of Spain. The name was later generalized to include all the islands. Spanish sovereignty was established in 1885. In 1899, after Spain's defeat in the Spanish-American War of 1898, Palau, with the rest of the Carolines, was sold to Germany. At the outbreak of World War I in 1914, the islands were taken by the Japanese. As a member of the League of Nations, Japan was given a mandate over Palau in 1920, and Koror was developed as an administrative center of Japanese possessions in the north Pacific.

In 1947, following occupation by US forces in World War II, Palau became part of the UN Trust Territory of the Pacific Islands, which was administered by the US. After the adoption of a constitution in 1980, Palau became a self-governing republic in 1981. Since 1982, the republic has been involved in negotiating a Compact of Free Association (CPA) with the US. Negotiations have stalled because the 1980 constitution prohibits any placement of nuclear weapons, and the US has wanted to use the islands as a military site. In June 1985, President Haruo Remeliik was assassinated; Vice-President Alfonso Oiterang served as acting president until August 1985, when he was defeated in an election by Lazarus E. Salii. President Salii committed suicide in

August 1988. In November 1988 Ngiratkel Etpison, a strong advocate of the proposed CPA, was elected President. A referendum to reduce the requirement for the approval of constitutional amendments to a simple majority passed in November 1992. In November 1993 the eighth referendum on the CPA finally won approval of 68% of voters.

A new capital is under construction in eastern Babelthuap, about 20 km northeast of Koror.

[13]GOVERNMENT

The government comprises three branches: the executive, the legislative, and the judicial. The executive branch is headed by the president, who is elected by popular vote for not more than two terms of four years each. The president is assisted by a cabinet of ministers, one of whom is the vice president and is also elected by popular vote. A council of chiefs, based on Palau's clan system, advises the president on traditional and customary matters.

The legislative branch, known as the Olbiil Era Kelulau, or National Congress, is a bicameral form of legislature, comprising 14 senators and 16 delegates. The senators, elected for four-year terms, are apportioned throughout Palau on the basis of population and traditional regional political groupings. The delegates are elected from each of the 16 states and have the same four-year term as the senators.

In November 1992 Kuniwo Nakamura was elected Palau's new President. Legislative elections were last held at the same time.

[14]LOCAL GOVERNMENT

Each of Palau's 16 states has a government headed by a governor, who is popularly elected, in most cases, for a four-year term. The members of the state legislatures are popularly elected for a four-year term, although in a few states, the term of office is limited to two years. The states are empowered to make their own laws, which must not be in conflict with the national constitution or any existing laws.

[15]POLITICAL PARTIES

While Palau does not have formal political parties, two loose coalitions have developed in response to the continued debate over the CPA: the Coalition for Open Honest and Just Government opposes the CPA, while the Ta Belau Party supports it.

[16]JUDICIAL SYSTEM

The Supreme Court is the highest court in the land. Other courts include the National Court, which, although constitutionally mandated, was not operational as of 1987, and the lower court system, consisting of the Court of Common Pleas. In October, 1990 US Interior Secretary Manuel Lujan issued an order granting the Interior Department in Washington the power to veto laws and reverse decisions by Palau's courts. This reassertion of legal authority by the United States was partially in response to the decade of unsuccessful negotiations concerning a plan for eventual self-government.

[17]ARMED FORCES

The US is responsible for defense. Palau has no armed forces and does not have US armed forces within its borders except for a small contingent of US Navy Seabees who undertake civil action projects.

[18]INTERNATIONAL COOPERATION

Although not a UN member, Palau has worked closely with the UN and its agencies, including FAO, ICAO, ILO, IMO, UNDP, and UNFPA. Palau is a full member of the SPC and other regional agencies and an associate member of ESCAP. The government maintains liaison offices in Guam, Hawaii, and Washington, D.C.

[19]ECONOMY

The economy has a narrow production base as a result of limited natural resources and few skilled personnel. The services sector, consisting largely of government administration and trade. Large gaps exist between government revenues and expenditures and between imports and exports. These gaps are financed largely by grant assistance from the US. Unemployment is a major problem.

[20]INCOME

The GDP of Palau was estimated to be $36.1 million in 1986. The per capita national product was estimated to be $2,260.

[21]LABOR

The economically active population was 6,250 persons in 1986, of whom 4,467 (71.5%) were in the monetary sector, 603 (9.6%) were in the nonmonetary or subsistence sector, and 1,180 (18.9%) were unemployed. National government workers accounted for 40% of monetary-sector employment in 1986, private wage earners 52.8%, and other workers, 7.2%.

[22]AGRICULTURE

Agricultural production belongs almost entirely to the nonmonetary, or subsistence, sector. Most households outside Koror are fully or partially engaged in subsistence agriculture. Staple subsistence crops include taros, cassavas, sweet potatoes, bananas, and papayas. Commercial produce is marketed mainly in Koror, consisting mostly of copra and coconut oil, vegetables, and a wide variety of tropical fruits.

[23]ANIMAL HUSBANDRY

Livestock is limited to pigs, chickens, ducks, cattle, and goats. Pigs and chickens are raised by most households. Several small commercial egg-producing operations supply eggs to the Koror market. The Livestock Branch of the Division of Agriculture maintains breeding herds of pigs, cattle, and goats.

[24]FISHING

Palau's marine resources are rich and diverse. Subsistence fishing within the reef is a major activity and dominates market production. The total catch was 4,068 tons in 1991. Deep-sea fishing for pelagic species, resulted in a tuna catch of 2,706 tons in 1991. Seasonal trochus harvesting for shell button manufacture is an important source of income for most fishermen. Other marine resources include pearls, shrimp, ornamental fish, seaweed (agar agar), and mollusks. Palau is known for having some of the best diving, snorkeling, and sport fishing areas in the world.

[25]FORESTRY

Forestry resources consist of coastal mangrove, coconut and pandanus palms, and rain forest species in upland areas. Palau is heavily dependent on imported forestry products, including furniture and lumber for house construction. The government's forestry station at Nekken on Babeldaob Island, of which more than half of the 1,257 ha (3,105 acres) consists of natural forest, provides primarily mahogany seedlings to farmers.

[26]MINING

Crystalline calcite from glistening limestone caves was first quarried as long as 1,500–2,000 years ago. The doughnut-shaped finished carved products would be transported by canoe some 250 miles to Yap (now part of the Federated States of Micronesia), and used as currency.

The Koror state government engages in commercial production of dredged coral from the Palau lagoon, with a production capacity of 800 cu m per day. Other states are also involved in coral dredging. A private company supplies aggregates for concrete from crushed basalt rock and beach sand.

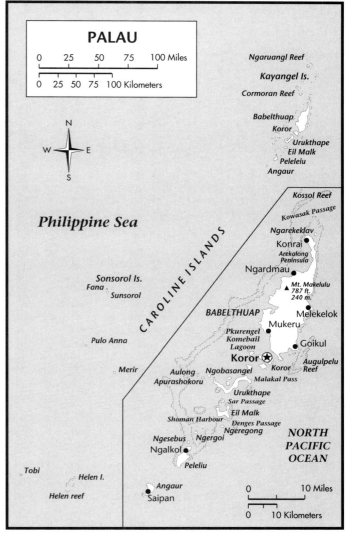

LOCATION: 131° to 135°E; 3° to 8°N.

[27]ENERGY AND POWER

The economy is almost totally dependent on imported petroleum for energy. Electricity is supplied from the Malakal power plant, located in the state of Koror, with an installed capacity of approximately 8,000 kw. There are state-owned power plants with capacities ranging from 30 kw to 120 kw in Peleliu, Angur, Ngiwal, Ngeremlengui, Airai, Ngaraard, and Ngerchelong.

[28]INDUSTRY

Manufacturing plays a limited role in the economy. A copra-processing plant is located in Malakal. Concrete blocks are manufactured, utilizing imported cement, and there is a small-scale sawmill industry.

[29]SCIENCE AND TECHNOLOGY

Palau's Micronesian Mariculture Demonstration Center, established in 1973, promotes the cultivation of commercially valuable and ecologically threatened marine species. The center attracts visiting marine scientists; its giant clam hatchery was the first and remains the largest of its kind.

[30]DOMESTIC TRADE

Domestic trade is centered in Koror. Private-sector activities in tourism, restaurants and hotels, small workshops, banking, wholesale and retail outlets, transportation, and freight handling are located in Koror and, to a limited extent, the adjacent state of Airai.

31FOREIGN TRADE

The economy sustains a large trade deficit. Food, beverages, and tobacco accounted for 27.8% of imports; manufactured goods, 26.4%; machinery and transportation equipment, 22.8%; mineral fuel and lubricants, 9.2%; and other imports, 13.8%. The country's low volume and limited range of exports include trochus shell, 37.3%; fresh, frozen, and smoked fish, 31.6%; wooden handicrafts, 29.8%; and other exports, 1.3%.

32BALANCE OF PAYMENTS

Standardized balance-of-payments accounts have not yet been prepared by the government. The chronic trade deficit is largely offset by US grant assistance.

33BANKING AND SECURITIES

There are five commercial banks. Two are branches of foreign banks, the Bank of Hawaii and the Bank of Guam; the other, a local bank which started in 1985, is the Bank of Palau.

34INSURANCE

Social security and pension fund contributions are made by the government on behalf of its employees.

35PUBLIC FINANCE

Revenues include grants from the US and domestic revenues from taxes and other fees.

36TAXATION

Graduated income taxes are levied on wages and salaries. Business gross revenue tax is imposed at a flat rate minus employees' remuneration. There is also a profits tax on financial institutions.

37CUSTOMS AND DUTIES

There are no import duties on raw materials if they are processed for sale outside Palau. There is also an import duty rebate offered by Palau as an investment incentive.

38FOREIGN INVESTMENT

There is a Foreign Investment Board for processing applications from foreign investors; the Division of International Trade of the Bureau of Foreign Affairs is responsible for establishing contacts with foreign companies to promote Palau's trade interests.

39ECONOMIC DEVELOPMENT

The government's first 5-year national development plan (1987–91) is considered the first phase of its 15-year development program. The plan focuses on the development of a private-sector production-based economy, efficient public-sector management, development of natural resources to earn foreign exchange, personnel development, regional development, and environmental preservation. In 1990, Palau received us$320 million in bilateral foreign aid, us$56.4 million in multilateral aid, and us$2.37 million in development aid from the United Nations (us$1.35 million of it from UNICEF).

40SOCIAL DEVELOPMENT

Social organization is based on the maternal kin group, or clan. Villages ideally consist of ten clans, with the leader of the highest ranking clan serving as village chief. Rapid socioeconomic change has given rise to a range of social problems for communities and social groups, particularly youth. Most social development activities in the areas of health and education are funded by US government programs.

41HEALTH

Hospital services are provided by the MacDonald Memorial Hospital in Koror, which has 60 beds. Medical services in Koror are also provided by the Belau Medical Clinic and the Seventh-Day Adventist Eye Clinic.

42HOUSING

There were 2,501 occupied houses in 1986, of which 72% were located in Koror and the adjacent state of Airai. Most house walls are constructed from metal sheets, wood, or concrete blocks, and roofs are of corrugated material. About 80% of all houses have water and electricity. The majority of homeowners finance their house construction under the traditional "ocheraol" system, whereby clan members contribute to construction costs.

43EDUCATION

Elementary education is free and compulsory for all Palauan children aged 6–14. In 1990, there were 369 students in private schools and 1,756 in public schools. The Palau High School in Koror, the only public high school, enrolls 64% of the total secondary-school enrollment. In 1990, 445 secondary students attended private schools and 165 were in public schools. Postsecondary education is provided by the College of Micronesia's Micronesian Occupational College (MOC) in Koror.

44LIBRARIES AND MUSEUMS

There is a small public library in Koror, with a collection comprising about 5,000 books. The Belau National Museum, established in 1973, is also located in Koror.

45MEDIA

The Palau National Communications Corp., established in 1982, provides domestic and international telephone connections, radio broadcasting, telex and telegram communications, and navigational and weather services. A radio station in Koror broadcasts to listeners in the outer islands. Television is limited to one channel in the Koror area, provided by a local private company.

46ORGANIZATIONS

The clan system forms the basic unit of social organization. Youth, women's, and community development organizations provide economic self-help, community involvement and leadership training, skills training, and sports and recreation.

47TOURISM, TRAVEL, AND RECREATION

Palau's scenic areas include the Rock Islands, a large number of small, mushroom-shaped islands that are unique in the region. The marine environment is rich in live coral formations and tropical fish, making the country a prime destination for snorkeling and scuba diving. Many tourists visit the World War II battlefields, war memorials, and shrines.

48FAMOUS PALAUANS

Lazarus E. Salii (b.1937) became the third president of Palau in September 1985.

49DEPENDENCIES

Palau has no territories or colonies.

50BIBLIOGRAPHY

Parmentier, Richard J. *The Sacred Remains: Myth, History, and Polity in Belau.* Chicago: University of Chicago Press, 1987.
Roff, Sue Rabbitt. *Overreaching in Paradise: United States Policy in Palau Since 1945.* Juneau, Alaska: Denali Press, 1991.
Trust Territory of the Pacific Islands, 1986, 39th Annual Report to the United Nations. Washington, D.C.: Department of State, 1986.

PAPUA NEW GUINEA

Independent State of Papua New Guinea

CAPITAL: Port Moresby.

FLAG: The flag is a rectangle, divided diagonally. The upper segment is scarlet with a yellow bird of paradise imposed; the lower segment is black with five white stars representing the Southern Cross.

ANTHEM: *O, Arise All You Sons.*

MONETARY UNIT: The kina (K) of 100 toea is linked with the Australian dollar. There are coins of 1, 2, 5, 10, 20, and 50 toea and 1 kina, and notes of 2, 5, 10, 20, and 50 kina. K1=US$1.0391 or US$1=K 0.9624.

WEIGHTS AND MEASURES: The metric system is the legal standard.

HOLIDAYS: New Year's Day, 1 January; Queen's Birthday, 1st Monday in June; Remembrance Day, 23 July; Independence Day, 16 September; Christmas, 25 December; Boxing Day, 26 December. Movable religious holidays include Good Friday and Easter Monday.

TIME: 10 PM=noon GMT.

¹LOCATION, SIZE, AND EXTENT

Situated to the north of Australia, Papua New Guinea has a total land area of 461,690 sq km (178,259 sq mi), including the large islands of New Britain, New Ireland, and Bougainville and hundreds of smaller islands. Comparatively, the area occupied by PNG is slightly larger than the state of California. The country extends 2,082 km (1,294 mi) NNE–SSW and 1,156 km (718 mi) ESE–WNW. Mainland Papua New Guinea shares the island of New Guinea, the second-largest island in the world, with Irian Jaya, a province of Indonesia. To the N is the US Trust Territory of the Pacific Islands; to the E, the Solomon Islands; to the W, Irian Jaya; and about 160 km (100 mi) to the S, the nearest neighbor, Australia. Papua New Guinea has a total boundary length of 5,972 km (3,711 mi).

PNG's capital city, Port Moresby, is located on the country's southern coast.

²TOPOGRAPHY

Papua New Guinea is situated between the stable continental mass of Australia and the deep ocean basin of the Pacific. The largest section is the eastern half of the island of New Guinea, which is dominated by a massive central cordillera, or system of mountain ranges, extending from Indonesia's Irian Jaya to East Cape in Papua New Guinea at the termination of the Owen Stanley Range, and including the nation's highest peak, Mt. Wilhelm (4,705 m/15,436 ft). A second mountain chain fringes the north coast and runs parallel to the central cordillera. Active and recently active volcanoes are prominent features of New Guinea landscapes; there are no glaciers or snowfields. In the lowlands are many swamps and floodplains. Important rivers are the Sepik, flowing about 1,130 km (700 mi) to the north coast, and the Fly, which is navigable for 800 km (500 mi) in the southwest.

The smaller islands of Papua New Guinea are also areas of extreme topographic contrast and generally feature mountain ranges rising directly from the sea or from narrow coastal plains. Volcanic landforms dominate the northern part of New Britain and Bougainville, and some of the smaller islands are extremely volcanic. The Bougainville–New Ireland area comprises Bougainville and Buka islands, the Gazelle Peninsula of New Britain, New Ireland, New Hanover, the St. Matthias group, and the Admiralty Islands.

³CLIMATE

The climate of Papua New Guinea is chiefly influenced by altitude and by the monsoons. The northwest or wet monsoon prevails from December to March, and the southeast or dry trade winds from May to October. Annual rainfall varies widely with the monsoon pattern, ranging from as little as 100 cm (40 in) at Port Moresby to as much as 750 cm (300 in) in other coastal regions. Most of the lowland and island areas have daily mean temperatures of about 27°C (81°F), while in the highlands temperatures may fall to 4°C (39°F) at night and rise to 32°C (90°F) in the daytime. Relative humidity is uniformly high in the lowlands at about 80%.

⁴FLORA AND FAUNA

The flora of Papua New Guinea is rich and varied, with habitats ranging from tidal swamps at sea level to alpine conditions. In low-lying coastal areas, various species of mangroves form the main vegetation, together with the beautiful casuarina, sago, and palm. Most of the country is covered by tropical and savanna rain forest, in which valuable trees such as kwila and cedar are found. Orchids, lilies, ferns, and creepers abound in the rain forests. There are large stands of pine at elevations of 910 to 1,220 m (3,000–4,000 ft). At the highest altitudes, mosses, lichens, and other alpine flora prevail.

Papua New Guinea supports a great diversity of bird life. About 850 species have been recognized, as compared with about 650 known in Australia and 500 in North America. Papua New Guinea is the major center for a number of bird families, particularly the bird of paradise, bower bird, cassowary, kingfisher, and parrot. There are about 200 species of mammals, many nocturnal, of which rodent and marsupial orders predominate. Butterflies of Papua New Guinea are world famous for their size and vivid coloring.

⁵ENVIRONMENT

Papua New Guinea's environmental concerns includes pollution, global warming, and the loss of the nation's forests. Coastal waters are polluted with sewage and residue from oil spills. The nation has 192.2 cu mi of water, of which 49% is used to support farming and 22% for industrial activity. Some 6% of the nation's city dwellers and 30% of rural people do not have pure water. Another significant source of pollution is open-pit mining. The country's cities produce 0.1 million tons of solid waste per year. Global warming and the resulting rise in sea level are a threat to Papua New Guinea's coastal vegetation and water supply. The Department of Physical Planning and Environment is responsible for integrating environmental planning and conserving natural resources. In 1994, 5 of the nation's mammal species and 25 of its bird species were endangered, as well as 88 types of plants. As of 1987, endangered species in Papua New Guinea included four species of turtle (green sea, hawksbill, olive ridley, and leatherback) and Queen Alexandra's birdwing butterfly.

⁶POPULATION
The census population in 1990 was 3,689,038, compared with 3,010,727 at the 1980 census. The UN projection for the year 2000 was 4,867,000, assuming a crude birthrate of 32.4 per 1,000 population, a crude death rate of 9.7, and a net natural increase of 22.7 during 1995–2000. Estimated population density in 1990 was 8 persons per sq km (20.6 per sq mi).

The population was about 82% rural and 18% urban in 1995. The major areas of population are in the highlands and eastern coastal areas of the island of New Guinea. The largest cities and their 1990 populations were Port Moresby, the capital, 193,242; Lae, 80,665; Goroka, 17,855; Madang, 27,057; Wewak, 23,224; and Rabaul, on New Britain, 17,855.

⁷MIGRATION
The numbers of emigrants and immigrants have been roughly equal in recent years. In 1982–86, an average of 4,079 residents left the country each year, while 5,109 persons entered intending residency. Many more came as refugees from Irian Jaya. In 1993, some 3,750 such immigrants were living in a camp in Western Province, while another 6,000 or so had land or kinship ties with Papuan New Guineans and were living near the border. The emigration in earlier years of nonindigenous residents may have been influenced by constitutional provisions that restricted eligibility for naturalization to those with eight years' residency, but limited their tax and business rights to the same status as those of aliens. Many rural dwellers migrated to Port Moresby and other urban centers during the 1970s and 1980s.

⁸ETHNIC GROUPS
Indigenous Papua New Guineans vary considerably in ethnic origins, physical appearance, and spoken languages. The indigenous people are Melanesians. They are usually classified by language group, with Papuans representing the descendants of the original Australoid migration and Austronesian speakers descended from later migrants. The former are generally found in the highlands and the latter in coastal areas and on the islands other than New Guinea. Of the nonindigenous population, the largest group is Australian, followed by others of European origin and Chinese. The noncitizen population in 1993 was estimated at 30,000.

⁹LANGUAGES
Under the Australian administration of the former Territory of Papua and New Guinea, English became the official language and was spoken by about 364,000 people; however, it was the mother tongue of only some 72,000. There are now two other official languages: Pidgin, a Melanesian lingua franca with roots primarily in English and German, and Hiri Motu, another lingua franca of Papuan derivation. In all, there are more than 700 indigenous languages, most of them spoken by a few hundred to a few thousand people.

¹⁰RELIGIONS
Indigenous religions, varying widely in ritual and belief, remain important in tribal societies in Papua New Guinea. More than 90% of the population are nominally Christian; of these, an estimated two-thirds are Protestants and about one-third Catholics. There are European missionaries of the Anglican, Roman Catholic, Lutheran, Methodist, and Seventh-day Adventist churches. Baha'ism is the only other nonindigenous faith that has gained a foothold.

¹¹TRANSPORTATION
Transportation is a major problem in Papua New Guinea because of the difficult terrain. Major population centers are linked chiefly by air and sea, although road construction has increased to supplement these expensive means of transport. Of some 19,200 km (11,900 mi) of roads, only 640 km (400 mi) are paved. In 1992 there were 41,300 motor vehicles, of which about one-third were cars and station wagons and the rest commercial vehicles. Papua New Guinea has no railroads.

The government operates a fleet of coastal work boats, none more than 9 m (30 ft) long. The principal harbors are Madang, Port Moresby, Lae, and Rabaul. There are international shipping services by refrigerated container ships, other cargo vessels, and some passenger service to Australia, Southeast Asian and Pacific island countries, the US west coast, and Europe. The main shipping lines are government owned.

Papua New Guinea's national air carrier, Air Niugini, established in 1973, has undertaken most of the services previously provided by Australian lines. In 1992, it carried 764,600 international and domestic passengers. There are 19 principal airports with permanent-surface runways out of a total of 567 airports.

¹²HISTORY
Papua New Guinea appears to have been settled by 14,000 BC, with migrations first of hunters and later of agriculturists probably coming from the Asian mainland by way of Indonesia. Early communities had little contact with each other because of rough terrain and so maintained their independence, as well as their individual languages and customs.

New Guinea was first sighted by Spanish and Portuguese sailors in the early 16th century and was known prophetically as Isla del Oro (Island of Gold). The western part of the island was claimed by Spain in 1545 and named New Guinea for a fancied resemblance of the people to those on the West African coast. ("Papua" is a Malay word for the typically frizzled quality of Melanesian hair.) Traders began to appear in the islands in the 1850s, and the Germans sought the coconut oil trade in northern New Guinea about that time. The Dutch and the British had earlier agreed on a division of their interests in the island, and from 1828, the Dutch began to colonize the western portion.

Although the British flag was hoisted on various parts of eastern New Guinea, annexation was not ratified by the British government. Some Australian colonists were eager to see New Guinea become a British possession, for trade, Labor, gold mining, and missionary reasons; however, it was not until 1884, after an abortive Australian annexation attempt and under fear of German ambitions in the area, that Britain established a protectorate over the southern coast of New Guinea and adjacent islands. The Germans followed by laying claim to three different parts of northern New Guinea. British and German spheres of influence were delineated by the Anglo-German Agreement of 1885. Germany took control of the northeastern portion of the island, as well as New Britain, New Ireland, and Bougainville, while Britain took possession of the southern portion and the adjacent islands.

British New Guinea passed to Australian control in 1902 and was renamed the Territory of Papua in 1906. German New Guinea remained intact until the outbreak of war in 1914, when

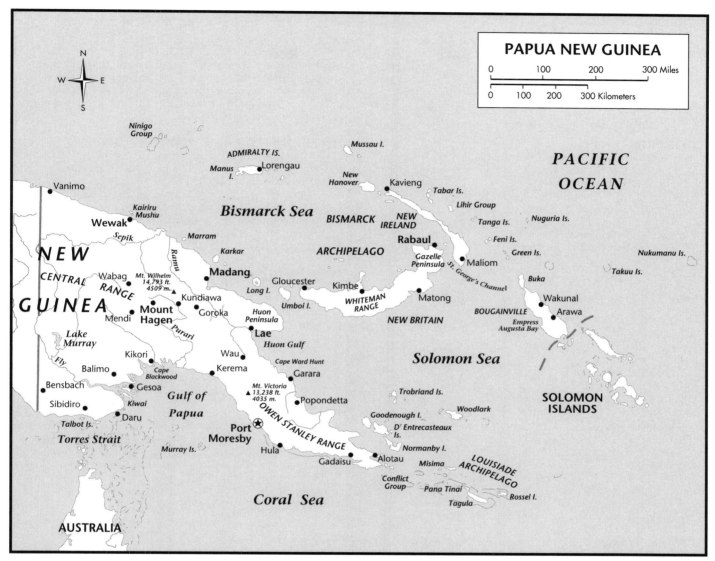

LOCATION: 140°51′ to 160°E; 0° to 12°S. **BOUNDARY LENGTHS:** Total coastline, 3,795 km (2,358 mi); Indonesia, 777 km (483 mi). **TERRITORIAL SEA LIMIT:** 12 mi.

it was seized by Australian forces. Although the territories retained their separate identities and status, they were administered jointly by Australia from headquarters at Port Moresby. In 1921, the former German New Guinea was placed under a League of Nations mandate administered by Australia; in 1947, it became the Trust Territory of New Guinea, still administered by Australia but now subject to the surveillance of the UN Trusteeship Council.

Both territories were merged into the Territory of Papua and New Guinea in 1949. A Legislative Council, established in 1953, was replaced by the House of Assembly in 1964. Eight years later, the territory was renamed Papua New Guinea, and on 1 December 1973, it was granted self-government. Separatist movements in Papua in 1973 and secessionist activities on the island of Bougainville in 1975 flared briefly and then died out, though debates over citizenship and land-reform provisions were vigorous until the passage of a constitution in 1975. Papua New Guinea achieved complete independence on 16 September 1975, with Michael Somare as prime minister of a coalition government.

Somare was voted out of office in 1980 but reelected in 1982; subsequently, he put through a constitutional change giving the central government increased authority over the provincial governments. Soon after, he suspended three provincial administrations for financial mismanagement. Somare also had to contend with social unrest, which culminated in June 1985 in a state of emergency after a prolonged wave of violent crime in Port Moresby. At the same time, his Pangu Pati was split by his deputy, Paias Wingti, who then founded a new party, the People's Democratic Movement (PDM). In November 1985, Somare was again voted out of office on a no confidence motion, and Wingti formed a cabinet. Though unrest continued, with serious riots in the Highlands in 1986, elections in mid-1987 returned Wingti to office at the head of a shaky five-party coalition.

Wingti's government was defeated in a no confidence vote in July 1988; a coalition government led by Rabbie Namaliu replaced the PDM government. A secessionist crisis on Bougainville dominated domestic politics during 1990–91. The Bougainville Revolutionary Army (BRA) declared the island of Bougainville to be independent from Papua New Guinea in May 1990, and in response government forces landed on the north of Bougainville in April 1991. Namaliu adjourned parliament early in 1991 to avoid a vote of no-confidence over the Bougainville crisis. Paias Wingti, the leader of the People's Democratic Movement (PDM), was reelected Prime Minister in July 1992 as the leader of a new coalition government with the support of the People's Progress Party, and the League for National Advancement.

During 1993 the Government continued to extend its control over Bougainville, partly because of popular revulsion against human rights violations by members of the BRA. A dispute with the Solomon Islands over its support of the BRA led to an incursion by troops of the Papua New Guinea army into the Solomon Islands in April 1993.

[13]GOVERNMENT

Papua New Guinea is an independent, parliamentary democracy in the Commonwealth of Nations, with a governor-general representing the British crown.

Under the 1975 constitution, legislative power is vested in the National Parliament (formerly the House of Assembly) of 109 members, including 20 representing provincial electorates and 89 from open electorates, serving a term of up to five years. Suffrage is universal and voting compulsory for adults at age 18. The government is formed by the party, or coalition of parties, that has a majority in the National Parliament, and executive power is undertaken by the National Executive Council, selected from the government parties and chaired by the prime minister.

[14]POLITICAL PARTIES

Several parties have emerged in Papua New Guinean politics. In the House of Assembly elected in 1973, the Pangu Pati, headed by Michael Somare, formed a coalition government with the People's Progress Party, and Somare became prime minister. Opposition parties at the time were the United Party, which maintains a strong following in the Highlands, and the Papua Besena Party, which stands for the secession of Papua from Papua New Guinea and has had fluctuating support even on its home ground.

Generally, party allegiances have been fluid, and regional and tribal politics have had an important impact on political events. No fewer than eight parties have been founded since 1978. One of them, the People's Democratic Movement, formed in 1985 by dissident members of the Pangu Pati, won 18 seats in the 1987 elections, while the Pangu Pati captured 25. Other parties that participated in the 1992 elections were the People's Action Party, the People's Progress Party, the League for National Advancement, the United Party, the Papua Party, the National Party, and the Melanesian Alliance.

[15]LOCAL GOVERNMENT

Papua New Guinea is divided into 20 provinces, including the National Capital District. Each province has its own government, headed by a premier. In addition, there are more than 160 locally elected government councils.

[16]JUDICIAL SYSTEM

The Supreme Court is the nation's highest judicial authority and final court of appeal. Other courts are the National Court; district courts, which deal with summary and nonindictable offenses; and local courts, established to deal with minor offenses, including matters regulated by local customs.

The Papua New Guinea government has undertaken a process of legal reform under which village courts have been established to conserve and reactivate traditional legal methods. Special tribunals deal with land titles and with cases involving minors. An Ombudsman Commission has been established to investigate and refer to the public prosecutor cases involving abuse of official authority.

The Constitution declares the judiciary independent of executive, political or military authority. It also provides a number of procedural due process protections including the right to legal counsel for criminal defendants.

[17]ARMED FORCES

The main armed force is the Papua New Guinea Defense Force, which in 1993 had 3,800 men, 5 large patrol boats, 1 landing craft, and 9 aircraft (3 armed). The Papua New Guinea Police Force is an armed constabulary with a strength of about 4,600. Australia provides 100 advisors and engineers to contribute to the upkeep of the military forces. Defense costs $42 million a year (1989) or 1.3 percent of gross domestic product. The Bougainville rebels number perhaps 2,000.

[18]INTERNATIONAL COOPERATION

Papua New Guinea became a member of the UN on 10 October 1975 and participates in ESCAP and all the UN nonregional specialized agencies except WIPO and UNIDO. It also belongs to the Asian Development Bank, Commonwealth of Nations, G-77, South Pacific Forum, and South Pacific Commission. Papua New Guinea has signed the Lomé Convention, the Law of the Sea, and the Antarctic Treaty, and it has observer status at ASEAN. It is also a de facto adherent of GATT.

[19]ECONOMY

Economic activity is concentrated in two sectors, agriculture and mining. The subsistence sector, which occupies more than two-thirds of the working population, produces livestock, fruit, and vegetables for local consumption; agricultural products for export include copra, palm oil, coffee, cocoa, and tea. Rubber production has declined in recent years, and in the mid-1980s, coffee crops were threatened by the spread of coffee rust fungus through Western Highlands Province. New mining operations have compensated for the 1989 closure of the Bougainville mine, which had been a chief foreign exchange earner since the early 1970s. Currently, the main gold and silver mines are located at Ok Tedi in the Star Mountains, on Misima Island, and at Porgera. Oil and natural gas have been discovered in Southern Highlands Province. Forestry and fishing hold increasing importance.

Economic growth, which averaged 3.7% between 1985 and 1988, rose to about 9% in 1991 and 1992. Papua New Guinea's economy relies heavily on the inflow of Australian aid, which was to be reduced by 5% per year between 1985 and 1990 by mutual agreement.

[20]INCOME

In 1992, Papua New Guinea's GNP was $3,846 million at current prices, or $950 per capita. For the period 1985–92 the average inflation rate was 4.1%, resulting in a real growth rate in per capita GNP of −0.1%.

In 1992 the GDP was $4,228 million in current US dollars. It is estimated that in 1991 agriculture, hunting, forestry, and fishing contributed 26% to GDP; mining and quarrying, 17%; manufacturing, 10%; electricity, gas, and water, 2%; construction, 6%; wholesale and retail trade, 10%; transport, storage, and communication, 7%; finance, insurance, real estate, and business services, 4%; community, social, and personal services, 16%; and other sources 3%.

[21]LABOR

Although most of the adult population engages in productive activity, only 7% (270,000 persons) of the population were wage earners in 1992. While official information is incomplete, government indices show that employment in the country has not kept pace with the increase in population. An overwhelming majority of indigenous wage earners are male, and significantly more of them work in rural areas than in urban areas. Wage and salary earners are concentrated in agriculture, including fishing and forestry; commerce; and government and public authority employment. Legislation covers working conditions and wages, and provides for collective bargaining. The minimum weekly wage in urban areas was κ47.70 as of November 1991; in rural areas, the minimum was κ21.08 per week. The Papua New Guinea Trade Union Congress is the main union federation.

22AGRICULTURE

Agriculture in Papua New Guinea is divided into a large subsistence sector and a smaller monetary sector for export. Agriculture's importance has steadily declined since 1985, when it made up 33.8% of GDP—in 1992, agriculture only contributed 24.7% to GDP. About 85% of the population engages in subsistence agriculture. Subsistence crops include yams, taro, and other staple vegetables. Cash crops are increasing in rural areas, stimulated by government-financed development programs. Production by small farmers of coffee, copra, cocoa, tea, rubber, and oil palm is important for export, although production on plantations, which are usually foreign owned, is also significant. Such plantations are gradually being sold back to nationals. Principal crops and 1985 output (in tons) included sweet potatoes , 475,000; sugar cane, 450,000; copra, 110,000; coffee, 47,000; cocoa, 34,000; and rubber, 4,000.

23ANIMAL HUSBANDRY

Livestock in 1992 included an estimated 1,010,000 hogs, 4,000 sheep, and 3 million chickens. That same year there were 105,000 head of cattle, and production was being encouraged with the aim of achieving self-sufficiency in meat supplies. Local poultry and beef production is sufficient to almost meet domestic demand. Beef imports are subject to quota controls. The farming of crocodiles, whose hides are exported, has also been expanded.

24FISHING

In many coastal parts of Papua New Guinea, fishing is of great economic importance. The government is involved in the development of fishing through supply of freezers and of transport and research facilities. Fish exports in 1992 were up 5.4% over 1991, and were valued at κ7.8 million. In 1991, fish and fish product exports were valued at $12.4 million.

25FORESTRY

Exploitable forests account for roughly 40% of the total land area and include a great variety of hardwood and softwood species. The total roundwood production in 1991 was 8,188,000 cu m, as compared with about 7,058,000 cu m in 1981. Production of sawn timber in 1991 was estimated at 117,000 cu m. Plywood, hardwoods, and logs are regularly exported to Japan, New Zealand, Australia, and Europe.

26MINING

In 1888, gold was discovered on Misima Island, marking the start of the history of mining on Papua New Guinea. As of 1991, the country was the 11th largest copper and 6th largest gold producer in the world. Prior to World War II, gold mining contributed 75% of Papua New Guinea's export earnings. This proportion declined greatly in subsequent years, but gold exports still accounted for 35% of the total export value in 1985. Gold production in 1986 was estimated at about 60,780 kg.

In 1971/72, the Bougainville copper mine, one of the richest in the world, began to export copper ores and concentrates, which amounted to almost 220,000 tons in 1988 when the mine was still in full operation. The mine remained closed in 1991 because of civil unrest caused by Bougainville Revolutionary Army militants. All copper production now comes from the Ok Tedi mine in the Star Mountains near the Indonesian border. In 1991, production at this mine amounted to 204,459 tons. In the same year, production of silver totaled 124,880 kg.

Mineral exploration is being expanded. Bauxite is known to exist on Manus Island, in the Admiralty Islands, and on New Ireland Island. Additionally, lead, manganese, molybdenum, zinc,

limestone, and phosphate guano and rock deposits are present. Major deposits of chromite, cobalt, and nickel are believed to be recoverable at a site on the Ramu River northeast of Ok Tedi. Reserves on Lihir Island in New Ireland Province have been estimated to contain some 613 tons of recoverable gold, and deposits at Porgera, near Ok Tedi, are considered to hold another 470 tons. A newer gold mine on Misima Island produced 10,050 kg of gold in 1991.

27ENERGY AND POWER

As of 1986, Papua New Guinea had a net installed electrical capacity of 490 Mw; electricity generated was 1,790 million kwh. Of the total production, about one-quarter comes from hydroelectric facilities and three-quarters from thermal plants. Several new hydro projects are at different stages of study and planning. In 1992, fuel and energy imports totaled $152 million, or 9% of total imports.

Exploration for oil and gas has been conducted in the Gulf of Papua, on the Turama River, and off Bougainville. The Kutubu oil project (the nation's first oil production project) in the Southern Highlands began exporting in June 1992. In 1992, Kutubu produced 14,547,900 barrels of oil; recoverable reserves were estimated at 236 million barrels in 1991.

28INDUSTRY

The industrial sector, constrained by the small domestic market and the population's low purchasing power, is largely undeveloped. Industries are concentrated in industrial metals, timber processing, machinery, food, drinks, and tobacco. Manufacturing accounted for only 9% of GDP in 1992.

Handicraft and cottage industries have expanded. A government-sponsored program assists Papua New Guineans in setting up businesses and purchases equity in existing firms. It has also encouraged small-scale import-substitution operations.

29SCIENCE AND TECHNOLOGY

The major learned society is the Papua New Guinea Scientific Society. The University of Papua New Guinea and the Papua New Guinea University of Technology provide scientific and technical training. The Lowlands Agricultural Experiment Station is in Kerevat. The Papua New Guinea Institute of Medical Research was founded in 1968.

30DOMESTIC TRADE

Trade in rural areas is mostly informal, and cash is used in transactions. The local market, particularly in fruit and vegetables, is an important feature of economic and social life. Domestic trade in urban centers is dominated by large Australian-owned stores with multiple outlets.

Most stores are open weekdays from 8 AM to 5 PM and until noon on Saturdays; banks are open from 9 AM to 2 PM Monday to Thursday and from 9 AM to 5 PM on Fridays.

31FOREIGN TRADE

In 1992, Papua New Guinea's exports totaled US$1,756 million. Imports amounted to US$1,686 million. Principal exports in 1988 (in millions of kina) were the following:

Copper ore and concentrates	702.8
Gold	112.0
Coffee	113.6
Cocoa	46.1
Forest products	98.3
Copra and copra oil	38.1
Tea	6.4
Fish and shellfish	7.3
Rubber	4.4
TOTAL	1,129.0

Through most of the period when Papua New Guinea was a territory administered by Australia, the two were also major trading partners. In the 1970s, Papua New Guinea's trade with other countries, especially Japan and West Germany, increased. Leading trade partners are the FRG, Japan, Australia, Singapore, the US, and the UK.

32BALANCE OF PAYMENTS

Because of the trade imbalance, Papua New Guinea registered deficits on current accounts during the early 1980s, after recording annual surpluses in the late 1970s. In 1992, the overall deficit in the balance of payments was κ68 million compared to κ81 million in 1991. The trade account surplus in 1991 was κ476 million (up from κ32 million in 1991). The trade account surplus in 1992 was κ476 million (up from κ32 million in 1991), reflecting the increased value of merchandise exports coupled with lower imports. The increased value of exports was the result of the start of crude oil exports from the Kutubu oil project combined with higher mineral, agricultural, forestry, and fisheries exports.

In 1989 merchandise exports totaled $–1,318.5 million and imports $1,341.3 million. The merchandise trade balance was $–22.8 million.

The following table summarizes Papua New Guinea's balance of payments for 1988 and 1989 (in millions of US dollars):

	1988	1989
CURRENT ACCOUNT		
Goods services and income	–429.6	–441.9
Unrequited transfers	93.1	86.6
TOTALS	–336.5	355.3
CAPITAL ACCOUNT		
Direct investment	119.7	221.3
Other long-term capital	90.8	30.7
Other short-term capital	34.6	13.0
Reserves	53.5	58.7
TOTALS	298.5	323.7
Errors and omissions	–3.2	–92.8
Total change in reserves	–41.0	–12.1

33BANKING AND SECURITIES

The Bank of Papua New Guinea, the country's central bank, was established in 1973, and the currency, the kina, was first issued in April 1975. The kina is backed by a standby arrangement with Australia, and the value of the kina is tied to the Australian dollar. The money supply, as measured by M2, was κ120.0 million at the end of 1992. The central bank's assets totaled κ242.31 million at that time.

The Papua New Guinea Banking Corp. was set up in 1973 to take over the savings and trading business of the former Australian-government-owned bank operating in Papua New Guinea. It competes with seven other private commercial banks, three of which are subsidiaries of Australian banks. Commercial bank deposits totaled κ293.1 million at the end of 1992.

There is no securities exchange in Papua New Guinea.

34INSURANCE

In 1986, there were 1 life and 12 non-life insurance companies in operation.

35PUBLIC FINANCE

Despite the government's efforts to hold down public expenditures, there was a budgetary deficit all through the 1980s. Shortfalls are covered by the Mineral Resources Stabilization Fund and by supplementary foreign grants and loans. The deficit as a proportion of GDP rose from 0.9% in 1988 to 3.3% in 1990 to 5.4% in 1992.

The following table shows actual revenues and expenditures for 1992 and 1993 in millions of kina.

	1992	1993
REVENUE AND GRANTS		
Tax revenue	771.27	669.18
Non-tax revenue	158.46	455.21
Capital revenue	0.90	0.79
Grants	196.32	197.51
TOTAL	1,126.95	1,322.69
EXPENDITURES & LENDING MINUS REPAYMENTS		
General public service	136.18	110.65
Defense	56.50	54.40
Public order and safety	114.80	129.91
Education	200.39	251.14
Health	106.35	128.13
Social security and welfare	10.02	10.99
Housing and community amenities	8.32	12.22
Recreation, cultural, and religious affairs	21.42	21.74
Economic affairs and services	288.52	346.47
Other expenditures	395.32	416.38
Lending minus repayments	7.66	3.63
TOTAL	1,345.48	1,485.66
DEFICIT/SURPLUS	–218.53	–162.97

The deficit of approximately κ160 million (3.2% of GDP) budgeted in 1993 was above the budgeted deficits of 1990 and 1991. Revenue increases in 1993 were due primarily to an advance tax payment system for mining and petroleum companies, changes in personal income taxes, and a restructuring of indirect taxes. In 1992, Papua New Guinea's total public debt stood at κ1,894.62 million, of which κ1,218.21 million was financed abroad.

36TAXATION

Company incomes are taxed at a rate of 30%, except for mining and petroleum companies, which are taxed at 35%. In addition, progressive tax rates are applied to individuals' wages and salaries, with taxes automatically withheld from paychecks. Tax rates range from 15% to 28%. Land and property taxes, estate and death taxes, gift taxes, stamp taxes, excise taxes, and sales taxes are also imposed.

37CUSTOMS AND DUTIES

A general levy of 8.5% is charged on all imports, except on supplies for the government, the missions, and the Bougainville copper project. There is a 30% tariff on imports of products that compete with domestically-produced goods. An export tax is levied on numerous items, such as agricultural products, logs, and minerals.

38FOREIGN INVESTMENT

In past years, most foreign investment came from Australia, but since the completion in the 1970s of the bulk of the investment in the Bougainville copper mine, Australian investment in Papua New Guinea has declined. However, direct investment from Japan, China, Malaysia, Singapore, the US, and other countries has been increasing in the oil, minerals, timber, fishing, and livestock sectors. In the 1980s, major foreign investment (close to κ1 billion) was in the Ok Tedi copper, silver, and gold mine, in which the US, Australia, the FRG, and the Papua New Guinea government all held shares. Planned US investments in 1986 included us$117 million in a hydroelectric power project. In 1974, Papua New Guinea established the National Investment and Development Authority to coordinate, register, and establish priorities for foreign investment. Tax and tariff concessions are offered. In 1991, an investor group led by Chevron finalized plans for a US$850 million oilfield in the southern highlands.

39ECONOMIC DEVELOPMENT

The fundamental purposes of Papua New Guinea's economic strategy have been distilled into the nation's eight aims: a rapid increase in the proportion of the economy under the control of Papua New Guineans; a more equal distribution of economic benefits; decentralization of economic activity; an emphasis on small-scale artisan, service, and business activity; a more self-reliant economy; an increasing capacity for meeting government spending from locally raised revenue; a rapid increase in the equal and active participation of women in the economy; and governmental control and involvement in those sectors where control is necessary to achieve the desired kind of development.

These aims were incorporated in the government's national public expenditure plan for 1983–86, which allocated K152.3 million for development projects in 1983 and a total of K486.4 million for the four-year period. The emphasis was on increased production, rural welfare projects, and more effective administration. In 1991, Rio Tinto Zinc was planning to develop the largest gold deposit discovered in this century at Lihir Island.

A central policy aim of the government is to increase its self-reliance by reducing dependence on Australian aid, although Papua New Guinea will continue to rely on large amounts of Australian aid pending further development of natural resources. Under a five-year agreement in 1985, Australia was to reduce its budgetary aid by 5% annually. In 1990, Papua New Guinea received $320 million in bilateral aid and $56.4 in multilateral aid. UN development aid totaled $10.27 million in 1991.

40SOCIAL DEVELOPMENT

A social security system, called the National Provident Fund, was formed in 1981 and covers persons employed by firms with 25 or more workers, providing old age, disability, and survivor benefits. Workers' compensation is provided by employers through direct provision of benefits or insurance premiums. Rural communities traditionally assume communal obligations to those in need. The government supports the goal of family planning in an effort to lower the fertility rate, which was 5.3 in 1985–90. Abortion is permitted on broad health grounds.

Despite a Constitution guaranteeing them equal rights, women remain second-class citizens due to traditional patterns of discrimination. Village courts tend to enforce these patterns, and intertribal warfare often involves attacks on women.

41HEALTH

Government policy is to distribute health services widely and to provide comprehensive medical care, both preventive and curative. In 1985, there were 19 hospitals and 482 rural health centers, with more than 16,000 beds; in 1990, there were 3.4 hospital beds per 1,000 people. Medical personnel in 1990 included 301 doctors and 2,447 nurses. In the same year, the population per physician was 12,870, and the population per nursing professional was 1,180. In 1992, there were 0.08 doctors per 1,000 people, with a nurse to doctor ratio of 8.1. In the same year, 96% of the population had access to health care services.

The main health problems are malaria, tuberculosis, leprosy, and venereal disease. Significant malnutrition occurs in some areas, and pneumonia and related respiratory infections are major risks. In 1990, there were about 275 reported cases of tuberculosis per 100,000 inhabitants. In 1991 only 33% of the population had access to safe water. Immunization rates for children up to one year old were fairly high in 1992: tuberculosis

(67%); diphtheria, pertussis, and tetanus (61%); polio (61%); and measles (66%).

The country's population in 1993 was 4.2 million, with a birth rate of 33.5 per 1,000 people, and only 4% of married women (ages 15 to 49) using contraception. There were 136,000 births in 1992.

The infant mortality rate decreased from 110 deaths per 1,000 live births in 1974 to 54 in 1992. The general mortality rate was 10.7 per 1,000 people in 1993, and the maternal mortality rate was 900 per 100,000 live births in 1991. Life expectancy was still only 56 years in 1992. Total health care expenditures in 1990 were $142 million.

42HOUSING

Traditional housing in rural areas appears to be adequate, but in urban areas there are acute shortages because of migration. In most urban areas, squatter settlements have been established. New housing (923 dwellings in 1984) has fallen far short of meeting the demand, especially for medium- and low-cost units. As of 1988, the housing stock totaled 555,000, and the number of people per dwelling averaged 5.8.

43EDUCATION

Education in Papua New Guinea is not compulsory, and in the mid-1980s only one-third of the population was literate. The present government aims at upgrading and improving the system and quality of education. Children attend state-run community schools for primary education and provincial and national high schools for secondary education. After grade 6, they are tested and screened for continuing their studies in provincial high school. After grade 10, students have to qualify through an examination to enter one of the four national senior high schools, where they attend grades 11 and 12. After grade 10, students may enter one of the many technical or vocational schools which train them in various careers and skills, depending on their interests.

In addition to the National Government System, there is an international School System which ends at high school. Fees are considerably higher than the government run schools and the curriculum is based on the British system. There are also privately run preschools and primary schools.

The University of Papua New Guinea in Port Moresby offers degrees in law, science, medicine and arts. The University of Technology in Lae offers degrees in technical subjects such as engineering, business, architecture, and forestry. The Pacific Adventist College, a privately run university outside Port Moresby, offers courses in education, business, accounting, secretarial studies, and theology.

44LIBRARIES AND MUSEUMS

The largest libraries are at the University of Papua New Guinea (407,000 volumes) and at the Papua New Guinea University of Technology (130,000). Local libraries are well established in urban centers. The Papua New Guinea National Museum and Art Gallery, in Boroko, has a good collection of art and general ethnography. The museum is working to implement the National Cultural Property Act to protect the country's cultural heritage and to further establish appropriate museums.

45MEDIA

Telephone, telegraph, and telex services are available; there were 72,223 telephones in 1991. A coastal radio service provides communications between land-based stations and ships at sea. The National Broadcasting Commission operates three radio networks and one national television station. It broadcasts in English, Pidgin, Hiri Motu, and a dozen other vernaculars. In 1991 there were an estimated 288,000 radios and 9,000 television sets.

The major newspaper is the *Papua New Guinea Post-Courier*, which is published daily in English with a 1991 circulation of about 33,900. Other local news sheets are published, many in Pidgin. The twice-weekly *Times of Papua Guinea* is an English-language paper published in Boroko. It had a circulation of some 15,000 in 1992. *Niugini Nius*, also in Boroko, is published Tuesday–Friday (circulation 15,000) and also has a weekend edition(16,000).

46ORGANIZATIONS

Chambers of commerce and industry, service clubs, farmers' associations, and various trade unions form the nucleus of formal organizations in Papua New Guinea. Various youth and church groups also operate.

47TOURISM, TRAVEL, AND RECREATION

In 1991, 37,346 tourists visited Papua New Guinea, 46% from Australia, 16% from Europe, and 16% from the Americas. There were 2,631 rooms in hotels and other establishments in 1991, with 5,262 beds, and tourism receipts totaled US$47 million.

Water sports, golf, tennis, and rock climbing are popular pastimes. Tourists must have a valid passport, obtain an entry visa to Papua New Guinea, and hold an onward ticket; malaria suppressants are advisable, although Port Moresby is considered a low-risk area.

48FAMOUS PAPUA NEW GUINEANS

The best known Papua New Guineans are Michael Thomas Somare (b.1936), chief minister during colonial rule and the nation's first prime minister; Sir Albert Maori Kiki (b.1931), author of *Kiki: Ten Thousands Years in a Lifetime*; and Vincent Eri, author of *The Crocodile*.

49DEPENDENCIES

Papua New Guinea has no territories or colonies.

50BIBLIOGRAPHY

Ballard, J. A. (ed.). *Policy Making in a New State: Papua New Guinea 1972–77*. Brisbane: University of Queensland Press, 1981.

Bulbeck, Chilla. *Australian Women in Papua New Guinea: Colonial Passages, 1920–1960*. New York: Cambridge University Press, 1992.

Feil, D. K. *The Evolution of Highland Papua New Guinea Societies*. New York: Cambridge University Press, 1987.

Fitzpatrick, Peter. *Law and State in Papua, New Guinea*. New York: Academic Press, 1981.

Gillison, Gillian. *Between Culture and Fantasy: A New Guinea Highlands Mythology*. Chicago: University of Chicago Press, 1993.

Griffin, James. *Papua New Guinea: A Political History*. Portsmouth, N.H.: Heinemann, 1980.

Leahy, Michael J., 1901–1979. *Explorations into Highland New Guinea, 1930–1935*. Tuscaloosa: University of Alabama Press, 1991.

McConnell, Fraiser. *Papua New Guinea*. Santa Barbara, Calif.: Clio Press, 1988.

Mead, Margaret. *Growing Up in New Guinea*. Middlesex: Penguin, 1973 (orig. 1930).

Meigs, Anna S. *Food, Sex and Pollution: A New Guinea Religion*. New Brunswick, N.J.: Rutgers University Press, 1984.

Siers, James. *Papua New Guinea*. New York: St. Martin's, 1984.

Strathern, A. *A Line of Power*. New York: Methuen, 1984.

PHILIPPINES

Republic of the Philippines
Republika ng Pilipinas

CAPITAL: Manila.

FLAG: The national flag consists of a white equilateral triangle at the hoist, with a blue stripe extending from its upper side and a red stripe extending from its lower side. Inside each angle of the triangle is a yellow five-pointed star, and in its center is a yellow sun with eight rays.

ANTHEM: *Bayang Magiliw (Nation Beloved)*.

MONETARY UNIT: The peso (P) is divided into 100 centavos. There are coins of 1, 5, 10, 25, and 50 centavos and 1, and 2 pesos, and notes of 5, 10, 20, 50, 100, and 500 pesos. P1 = $0.0363 (or $1 = P27.565).

WEIGHTS AND MEASURES: The metric system is the legal standard, but some local measures are also used.

HOLIDAYS: New Year's Day, 1 January; Freedom Day, 25 February; Labor Day, 1 May; Heroes' Day, 6 May; Independence Day (from Spain), 12 June; Thanksgiving, 21 September; All Saints' Day, 1 November; Bonifacio Day, 30 November; Christmas, 25 December; Rizal Day, 30 December; Last Day of the Year, 31 December. Movable religious holidays include Holy Thursday and Good Friday.

TIME: 8 PM = noon GMT.

¹LOCATION, SIZE, AND EXTENT

The Republic of the Philippines consists of an archipelago of 7,107 islands situated SE of mainland Asia and separated from it by the South China Sea. The total land area is approximately 300,000 sq km (115,831 sq mi), 67% of which is contained within the two largest islands: Luzon, 105,708 sq km (40,814 sq mi) and Mindanao, 95,586 sq km (36,906 sq mi). Other large islands include Samar, 13,079 sq km (5,050 sq mi); Negros, 12,704 sq km (4,905 sq mi); Palawan, 11,784 sq km (4,550 sq mi); Panay, 11,515 sq km (4,446 sq mi); Mindoro, 9,736 sq km (3,759 sq mi); Leyte, 7,213 sq km (2,785 sq mi); Cebu, 4,411 sq km (1,703 sq mi); Bohol, 3,864 sq km (1,492 sq mi); and Masbate, 3,269 sq km (1,262 sq mi). Comparatively, the area occupied by the Philippines is slightly larger than the state of Arizona. The Philippines' length is 1,851 km (1,150 mi)SSE-NNW, and its width is 1,062 km (660 mi) ENE-WSW.

The Philippines is separated from Taiwan on the N by the Bashi Channel (forming part of the Luzon Strait) and from Sabah, Malaysia (northern Borneo), on the sw by the Balabac Strait (off Palawan) and the Sibutu Passage (off the Sulu Archipelago). Bordering seas include the Philippine Sea and the Pacific Ocean on the E, the Celebes Sea on the S, the Sulu Sea on the sw, and the South China Sea on the w. The Philippines has a total coastline of 36,289 km (22,549 mi).

The Philippines claims the Spratly Islands, in the South China Sea, as do China, Malaysia, Taiwan, and Viet-Nam. About 1,000 Philippine marines were stationed in the Spratlys in 1983. The Philippines also has a claim on Sabah, dating back to 1670.

The Philippines' capital city, Manila, is located on the island of Luzon.

²TOPOGRAPHY

The topography is extremely varied, with volcanic mountain masses forming the cores of most of the larger islands. The range culminates in Mt. Pulog (elevation 2,928 m/9,606 ft) in northern Luzon and in Mt. Apo, the highest point in the Philippines (eleva-tion 2,954 m/9,692 ft), in Mindanao. A number of volcanoes are active, and the islands have been subject to destructive earthquakes. Lowlands are generally narrow coastal strips except for larger plains in Luzon (Cagayan Valley and Central Plains), Mindanao (Cotabato and Davao-Agusan valleys), and others in Negros and Panay. Rivers are short and generally seasonal in flow. Important ones are the Cagayan, Agno, Abra, Bicol, and Pampanga in Luzon and the Cotabato and Agusan in Mindanao. Flooding is a frequent hazard. The shores of many of the islands are embayed (Manila Bay is one of the finest harbors in East Asia); however, several islands lack adequate harbors and require offshore lightering for sea transport. The only two inland water bodies of significant size are Laguna de Bay in Luzon and Lake Sultan Alonto in Mindanao.

³CLIMATE

The Philippine Islands, in general, have a maritime tropical climate and, except in the higher mountains, temperatures remain warm, the annual average ranging from about 26° to 28°c (79 to 82°F) throughout the archipelago. Daily average temperatures in Manila range from a minimum of 21°c (70°F) to a maximum of 30°c (86°F) in January and from 24°c (75°F) to 33°c (91°F) in June. Annual normal relative humidity averages 80%. Rainfall and seasonality differ markedly throughout the islands, owing to varying exposures to the two major wind belts, northeast trades or monsoon (winter) and southwest monsoon (summer). Generally, the east coasts receive heavy winter maximum rainfall (about 200–300 cm/80–120 in), the west coasts heavy summer maximum (200–360 cm/80–140 in); intermediate and southern locales receive lesser amounts more equally distributed (100–200 cm/40–80 in). Violent tropical storms (baguios), or typhoons, are frequent. Typhoons hit the Philippines 2-3 September 1984. Thirteen hundred people were killed during Typhoon Ike. On 5 November 1991 a typhoon hit central Philippines, killing 3,000 people. The average annual rainfall in the Philippines exceeds 250 cm (100 in).

[4]FLORA AND FAUNA

The Philippines supports a rich and varied flora with close botanical connections to Indonesia and mainland Southeast Asia. Forests cover almost one-half of the land area and are typically tropical, mixed in composition, with the dominant family, Dipterocarpaceae, representing 75% of the stands. The forest also has vines, epiphytes, and climbers. Open grasslands, ranging up to 2.4 m (8 ft) in height, occupy one-fourth of the land area; they are man-made, the aftermath of the slash-and-burn agricultural system, and most contain tropical savanna grasses that are nonnutritious and difficult to eradicate. The diverse flora includes 8,500 species of flowering plants, 1,000 kinds of ferns, and 800 species of orchids.

Common mammals include the wild hog, deer, wild carabao, monkey, civet cat, and various rodents. There are about 500 species of birds, among the more numerous being the megapodes (turkeylike wildfowl), button quail, jungle fowl, peacock pheasant, dove, pigeon, parrot, and hornbill. Reptilian life is represented by 100 species; there are crocodiles, and the larger snakes include the python and several varieties of cobra.

[5]ENVIRONMENT

Primary responsibility for environmental protection rests with the National Pollution Control Commission (NPCC), under whose jurisdiction the National Environmental Protection Council (NEPC) serves to develop national environmental policies and the Environmental Center of the Philippines implements such policies at the regional and local levels. Uncontrolled deforestation in watershed areas, with consequent soil erosion and silting of dams and rivers, constituted a major environmental problem in the 1980s, together with rising levels of air and water pollution in Manila and other urban areas. The NPCC has established standards limiting automobile emissions but has lagged in regulating industrial air and water pollution. Pollution from industrial sources and mining operations is a significant environmental problem in the Philippines. Domestic waste also contributes to the problem. The nation's cities create 5.4 million tons of solid waste per year, and 38 of the country's rivers contain high levels of toxic contaminants. The nation has 77.5 cubic miles of water, with 61% is used to support farming and 21% is used for industrial activity. About 28% of the nation's rural dwellers do not have pure water, while 93% of the city dwellers have pure water. Similarly unprotected are the increasingly polluted coastal mangrove swamps, which serve as important fish breeding grounds, and offshore corals, about 50% of which are rated dead or dying as a result of pollution and dynamiting by fishermen. The nation is also vulnerable to typhoons, earthquakes, floods, and volcanic activity which can present devastating environmental problems.

In 1994, 12 of the nation's mammal species and 39 bird species were endangered, and 159 plant species are threatened with extinction. As of 1987, endangered species in the Philippines included the monkey-eating eagle, Philippine tarsier, tamarau, four species of turtle (green sea, hawksbill, olive ridley, and leatherback), Philippines crocodile, sinarapan, and two species of butterfly.

[6]POPULATION

The 1990 census reported the population at 60,559,116, an increase of 25.9% over the 1980 census count. As of 1990, 40% of the people were under 15 years of age. The projected population for the year 2000 was 76,091,000, assuming a crude birthrate of 27.6 per 1,000 population, a crude death rate of 6.3, and a net natural increase of 21.3 during 1995–2000. The population remains predominantly rural (about 57% in 1990), with one major urban concentration—metropolitan Manila—containing 7,929,000 inhabitants. Created in 1975, metropolitan Manila includes four cities—Manila proper (1,601,234 at the 1990 cen-

sus), Quezon City (1,669,776), Caloocan City (763,415), and Pasay City (368,366)—and 13 surrounding municipalities. Other major cities (with 1990 populations) include Davao (849,947), Cebu (610,417), Zamboanga (442,345), Bacolod (364,180), Cagayan de Oro (339,598), and Iloilo (309,505).

Average population density in 1990 was 202 per sq km (524 per sq mi). The population is unevenly distributed, being most densely concentrated in Luzon and the Visayan Sea islands.

[7]MIGRATION

The rapid growth of the Philippine population has led to considerable internal migration. On Luzon, frontierlike settlements have pushed into the more remote areas. Mindoro and Palawan islands also have attracted numerous settlers, and hundreds of thousands of land-hungry Filipinos have relocated to less densely populated Mindanao. There also has been a massive movement to metropolitan Manila, especially from central Luzon. Emigration abroad is substantial. In 1989 it came to 55,703. Emigration to the US particularly has been considerable: as of the 1990 US census, 1,406,770 Americans (chiefly in California and Hawaii) claimed Filipino ancestry. To reduce domestic unemployment, over 500,000 Philippine citizens were working abroad in the late 1980s and early 1990s, mainly in the Middle East, but also in Hong Kong and Singapore.

[8]ETHNIC GROUPS

Filipinos of Malay (Malayan and Indonesian) stock constitute about 90% of the total population. They are divided into nine main ethnic groups: the Tagalog, Ilocanos, Pampanguenos, Pangasinans, and Bicolanos, all concentrated in Luzon; the Cebuanos, Boholanos, and Ilongos of the Visayas; and the Waray-Waray of the Visayas, Leyte, and Samar. The Chinese minority numbered about 600,000 in 1990. In addition, ten Muslim groups, mainly of Mindanao and the Sulu Archipelago, comprised about 5% of the population. Numerous smaller ethnic groups inhabit the interior of the islands, including the Igorot of Luzon and the Bukidnon, Manobo, and Tiruray of Mindanao. The 73 hill tribes had a combined population of 5,756,018 in 1986, nearly 10% of the Filipino population.

[9]LANGUAGES

There are two official languages: Pilipino (based on Tagalog), the national language adopted in 1946 and understood by a majority of Filipinos; and English, which is also widely spoken and understood. Spanish, introduced in the 16th century and an official language until 1973, is now spoken by only a small minority of the population. More than 80 indigenous languages and dialects (basically of Malay-Indonesian origin) are spoken. Besides Tagalog, which is spoken around Manila, the principal languages include Cebuano (spoken in the Visayas), Ilocano (spoken in northern Luzon), and Panay-Hiligaynon. The teaching of Pilipino is mandatory in public and private primary schools, and its use is encouraged by the government.

[10]RELIGIONS

The Philippines is the only predominantly Christian country in Asia. Most of the population (about 83%) belongs to the Roman Catholic Church. Members of the Filipino Independent Church (Aglipayan), founded in 1890 in protest against the dominance of foreign clergy in the Roman Catholic Church, and over 300 other indigenous churches, constitute about 3.9% of the population. Muslims (representing about 5%), commonly called Moros by non-Muslims, are concentrated in Mindanao and the Sulus. Various Protestant churches represent about 4%. Tribal religionists, mainly in the more inaccessible mountainous areas of Luzon and Mindanao, constitute about 0.7%, Buddhists about 0.2%, Baha'i is about 0.1%, and Chinese folk religionists about 0.1%. There are also small communities of Hindus and Jews. Freedom of religion is guaranteed by the constitution. In an effort to reduce tensions between Christians and Muslims in the southern islands and to answer Muslim autonomist demands, the government established a Ministry of Muslim Affairs in 1981 and allocated funds for Islamic legal training and for Muslim schools and cultural centers.

11TRANSPORTATION

The total length of roadways in 1991 was 156,000 km (96,938 mi), of which about 19% was paved. Luzon contains about one-half of the total road system, and the Visayas about one-third. There were 456,606 passenger cars (including jeepneys, or mini-buses) in 1991, nearly half of them registered in Manila; there were also 158,828 commercial vehicles, 138,138 trucks, and 20,690 buses. In 1991 there were 378 km (235 mi) of common-carrier railroad track on Luzon and Panay, which only plays a minor role in transportation.

Water transportation is of paramount importance for interisland and intraisland transportation. A small offshore fleet registered under the Philippine flag is engaged in international commerce, but most ocean freight is carried to and from the Philippines by ships of foreign registry. In 1991, the merchant fleet totaled 536 ships with 7.9 million GRT, eleventh in the world. Manila is the busiest Philippine port in international shipping, followed by Cebu and Iloilo. In 1991 there were 452 seaports.

Philippine Air Lines (PAL), the national airline, provides domestic and international flights. Under the Aquino government there were plans to sell PAL stock to the private sector. The Benigno S. Aquino International Airport, formerly Manila International Airport, is the principal international air terminal. As of 1991 there were 235 usable airports, of which 71 had permanent-surface runways. Five airports serve international flights.

12HISTORY

Evidence of human habitation dates back some 250,000 years. In more recent times, the Philippine Islands are thought to have been settled by Negritos, who crossed then existing land bridges from Borneo and Sumatra some 30,000 years ago. These peoples were later outnumbered by successive waves of Malays, who arrived from the south, at first by land and later on boats called barangays, a name also applied to their communities. By the 14th century, Arab traders made contact with the southern islands and introduced Islam to the local populace. Commercial and political ties also linked various enclaves in the archipelago with Indonesia, Southeast Asia, India, China, and Japan. Ferdinand Magellan, a Portuguese-born navigator sailing for Spain, made the European discovery of the Philippines on 15 March 1521 and landed on Cebu on 7 April, claiming the islands for Spain; he was killed in battle by the Filipino chieftain Lapulapu. The Spanish later named the islands in honor of King Philip II, and an invasion, under Miguel López de Legaspi, began in 1565. The Spanish conquest was facilitated by the almost complete conversion of the natives to Christianity; by 1571, it was concluded, except for the Moros (Moro is the Spanish word for Moor; the Spanish gave this name to Muslim Filipinos, mostly inhabitants of southern and eastern Mindanao, the Sulu Archipelago, and Palawan. The Philippines, as a province of New Spain, was administered from Mexico. Trade became a monopoly of the Spanish government; galleons shipped Oriental goods to Manila, from there to Acapulco in Mexico, and from there to the mother country.

Although Spain governed the islands until the end of the 19th century, its rule was constantly threatened by the Portuguese, the Dutch, the English (who captured Manila in 1762, occupying it for the next two years), the Chinese, and the Filipinos themselves. After the 1820s, which brought the successful revolts of the Spanish colonies in the Americas, the Filipinos openly agitated against

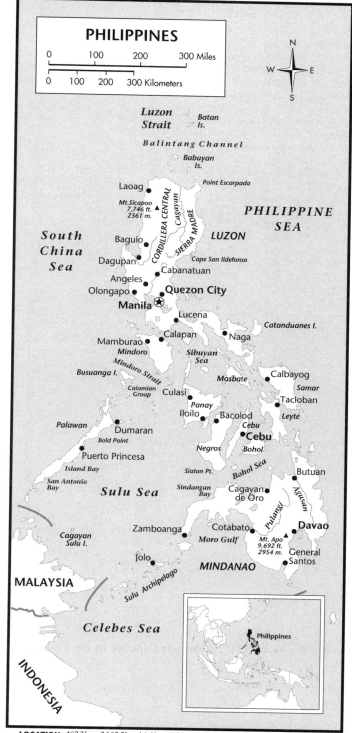

LOCATION: 4°23′ to 21°25′N; 116° to 127°E. TERRITORIAL SEA LIMIT: 12 mi.

the government trade monopoly, the exactions of the clergy, and the imposition of forced labor. This agitation brought a relaxation of government controls: ports were opened to world shipping, and the production of such typical Philippine exports as sugar, coconuts, and hemp began. Filipino aspirations for independence, suppressed by conservative Spanish rule, climaxed in the unsuccessful rebellion of 1896–98. José Rizal, the most revered Filipino patriot, was executed, but Gen. Emilio Aguinaldo and his forces continued the war. During the Spanish-American War (1898), Aguinaldo declared independence from Spain on 12 June. When the war ended, the US acquired the Philippines from Spain for $20,000,000. US rule replaced that of the Spanish, but Philippine nationalists continued to fight for independence. In 1899, Gen. Aguinaldo became president of the revolutionary First Philippine Republic and continued guerrilla resistance in the mountains of northern Luzon until his capture in 1901, when he swore allegiance to the US. Over the long term, the effect of US administration was to make the Philippines an appendage of the US economy, as a supplier of raw materials to and a buyer of finished goods from the American mainland. Politically, US governance of the Philippines was a divisive issue among Americans, and the degree of US control varied with the party in power and the US perception of its own security and economic interests in the Pacific. In the face of continued nationalist agitation for independence, the US Congress passed a series of bills that ensured a degree of Philippine autonomy. The Tydings-McDuffie Independence Law of 1934 instituted commonwealth government and further stipulated complete independence in 1944. In 1935, under a new constitution, Manuel Luis Quezon y Molina was elected first president of the Commonwealth of the Philippines.

On 8 December 1941, Japan invaded the Philippines, which then became the focal point of the most bitter and decisive battles fought in the Pacific during World War II. By May 1942, the Japanese had achieved full possession of the islands. US forces, led by Gen. Douglas MacArthur, recaptured the Philippines in early 1945, following the Battle of Leyte Gulf, the largest naval engagement in history. In September 1945, Japan surrendered. On 4 July 1946, the Republic of the Philippines was inaugurated, with Manuel A. Roxas y Acuña as its first president. Both casualties and war damage wreaked on the Philippines were extensive, and rehabilitation was the major problem of the new state. Communist guerrillas, called Hukbalahaps, were threatening the republic. Their revolutionary demands were countered by land reforms and military action by Ramón Magsaysay, the minister of national defense. He was elected to the presidency in 1953 but died in an airplane crash in 1957. Magsaysay was succeeded by Carlos P. García, who was confirmed in office by elections in 1958. Diosdado Macapagal was elected president in November 1961. He was succeeded by Ferdinand Edralin Marcos, following the 1965 elections. Marcos was reelected in 1969 by a record majority of 62%. Renewed Hukbalahap insurgency, begun in 1969, was brutally suppressed by the Marcos government, but armed opposition by Muslim elements, organized as the Moro National Liberation Front (MNLF), by the Maoist-oriented New People's Army (NPA), and by other groups gathered force in the early 1970s.

Unable under the 1935 constitution to run for a third term in 1973, President Marcos on 23 September 1972 placed the entire country under martial law, charging that the nation was threatened by a "full-scale armed insurrection and rebellion." Marcos arrested many of his more vehement political opponents, some of whom remained in detention for several years. In January 1973, a new constitution was promulgated, but many of its provisions remained in abeyance until 17 January 1981, when martial law was lifted. During the intervening period, Marcos consolidated his control of the government through purges of opponents, promotion of favorites, and delegation of leadership of several key programs—including the governorship of metropolitan Manila and the Ministry of Human Settlements—to his wife, Imelda Romualdez Marcos. Although Marcos made headway against the southern guerrillas, his human-rights abuses cost him the support of the powerful Roman Catholic Church, led by Jaime Cardinal Sin. Elections were held in April 1978 for an interim National Assembly to serve as the legislature until 1984, but local elections

held in 1980 were widely boycotted. Pope John Paul II came to Manila in February 1981, and even though martial law was no longer in effect, he protested the violation of basic human rights. In June 1981, Marcos was elected for a new six-year term as president under an amended constitution preserving most of the powers he had exercised under martial rule. New threats to the stability of the regime came in 1983 with the rising foreign debt, a stagnant economy, and the public uproar over the assassination on 21 August of Benigno S. Aquino, Jr. Aquino, a long-time critic of Marcos, was shot at the Manila airport as he returned from self-exile to lead the opposition in the 1984 legislative elections. The gunman was immediately killed, and 26 others suspected of conspiracy in the assassination were acquitted in December 1985 for lack of evidence. Public sympathy gave opposition parties 59 out of 183 elective seats in 1984.

In 1985, political pressures were mounting on Marcos. He was forced to call for an election in February 1986 in view of a widespread loss of confidence in the government. Marcos was proclaimed the winner by the Commission on Elections and the National Assembly, which was controlled by his own political party. His opponent, Maria Corazon Cojuangco Aquino, the widow of Benigno S. Aquino, claimed victory, however, and charged the ruling party with massive election fraud. This charge was supported by the National Movement for Free Elections, the Bishops' Conference, and the US and other international observers. Accordingly, other countries withheld recognition of Marcos. On 21 February 1986, a military revolt grew into a popular rebellion, urged on by Jaime Cardinal Sin. US President Reagan gave Marcos only an offer of asylum, which would be guaranteed only if he left the Philippines without resistance. Marcos went into exile in Hawaii.

After Marcos

On 25 February 1986, Corazon Aquino assumed the presidency. Civil liberties were restored, political prisoners were released, and the NPA was offered a six-month cease-fire, with negotiations on grievances, in exchange for giving up violence. Because Aquino came to power through the forced departure of an officially proclaimed president, the legality of her regime was suspect. Consequently, she operated under a transitional "freedom constitution" until 11 February 1987, when a new constitution was ratified by the electorate. On 11 May 1987 the first free elections in nearly two decades were held under the new constitution. More than 83% of eligible voters cast their ballots, 84 candidates ran for the 24 senate seats, and 1,899 candidates ran for the 200 house seats. There were 63 election-related killings. Old-line political families were still amply represented as 169 House members out of the 200 elected either belonged to or were related to these families. On 20 December 1987 one of the worst disasters in maritime history occurred when an overcrowded passenger ship collided with an oil tanker off Mindoro Island and at least 1,500 people perished. Local elections were delayed until 18 January 1988. Nationwide 150,000 candidates ran for 16,000 positions as governor, vice governor, provincial board member, mayor, vice mayor, and town council member. In 1988 more than 100 people were killed in election-related violence. Members of the pro-government parties, a faction of the PDP-Laban and Lakas ng Bansa, formed a new organization, Laban ng Demokratikong Pilipino (LDP) in June 1988. In March 1989 the thrice-postponed election for barangay officials was held, electing some 42,000 barangay captains. In August 1989 President Aquino signed a law giving limited autonomy to provinces where most Philippine Muslims lived—Mindinao, Palawan, Sulu, and Tawi-Tawi islands.

There were five coup attempts between the time Aquino took office and the end of 1987. This continuing succession of coup plots culminated in a large, bloody, well-financed attempt in December 1989. Led by Colonel Gregorio Honasan (who participated in the 1987 coup attempt, and was a close associate of Enrile) and involving more than 3,000 troops that targeted several bases, it was quelled with US air support. The Senate granted Aquino emergency powers for six months. President Aquino's administration lost international credibility with the appeal for US military support to quell this coup attempt. Arrests were made but the Supreme Court ruled that Senator Juan Ponce Enrile could not be charged with murder, nullifying the criminal case against him. He was charged in a lower court with rebellion. In September 1990 16 military members were convicted of the assassination of Senator Benigno Aquino in 1983 and sentenced to life in prison.

Former President Ferdinand Marcos had appealed to Aquino to allow him to attend the funeral of his mother, as he had appealed several times to visit his mother while she was ill; he was denied every time. The Philippine government had traced at least $5 billion in deposits to Swiss bank accounts made by Marcos. Marcos attempted to negotiate his return to the Philippines, promising his support for Aquino and the return of $5 billion to the Philippines. Aquino also rejected his wife Imelda's plea for her husband's return. An anti-graft civil suit for $22.6 billion against Marcos had been filed by the Philippine government in 1987. Marcos and his wife, Imelda, were indicted in the US, charged with the illegal transfer of $100 million in October 1988. On 28 September 1989 former President Ferdinand Marcos died in Honolulu. Aquino refused to allow him to be buried in the Philippines.

Under pressure from Communist rebels Aquino removed the US military bases from the Philippines in 1989. Three US servicemen were murdered outside Clark Air Force Base and the Communists took responsibility for the murders. A Communist guerrilla who admitted participating in the 21 April 1989 assassination of US Army Colonel James Row was arrested. In September 1989 US Vice President Dan Quayle met with Aquino to discuss the renewal of the lease on US military bases. Prior to his arrival two American civilians working on the bases were killed and this was officially attributed to Communist guerrillas. The Communists continued to threaten US servicemen and local politicians. Anti-American demonstrations at Clark Air Base and in Manila led to clashes with the police and injuries. The Communists continued their threats and 2 more US servicemen were killed near the Clark Air Base. In June of 1990 the Peace Corps removed 261 volunteers from the Philippines after Communist threats against them. In September 1990 Aquino said it was time to consider an "orderly withdrawal" of US forces from the Philippines.

Within a year the Philippines was pummeled with three major natural disasters. In July 1990 an earthquake measuring 7.7 on the Richter scale struck. The epicenter was 55 miles north of Manila and more than 1,600 people were killed. A super-typhoon devastated the central Visayas in November 1990. An even more destructive natural disaster occurred on 12 June 1991 when Mount Pinatubo in Zambales province, a volcano dormant for more than 500 years, violently erupted. Clark Air Base in Angeles City was abandoned due to the damaging effects of the eruption; 20,000 US military, their dependents, and civilian employees were evacuated to the US from Clark and the Subic Bay Naval Station. The Philippine-American Cooperation Talks (PACT) reached agreement on military base and non-base issues, but the proposed treaty failed to be approved by the Philippine Senate. On 6 January 1992 the Philippines government served notice of the termination of the US stay at Subic Naval Base in Zambales. After almost a century of US military presence, on 30 September 1992 the US handed over Subic Naval Base to the Philippines. As of 1994, future plans for the area were to turn it into a free port. Amnesty International (AI), the human rights organization, published a report in 1992 critical of the Aquino administration's assent to human rights violations perpetrated by the military; AI

alleged that 550 extrajudicial killings occurred during 1988–91. The military refuted the AI report citing its oversight of rebel activities.

In March 1991 President Aquino stated that Imelda Marcos could return to the Philippines, but that she faced charges that her husband stole $10 billion during his 20 years as president. By November she returned, after five years in Hawaii, to face civil and criminal charges including tax fraud. In January 1992 Imelda Marcos announced that she would run for election in 1992; in the same month she was arrested and then released for failing to post bail on charges that she unlawfully maintained accounts in Switzerland. In September 1993 the embalmed body of Ferdinand Marcos was returned to the Philippines for burial near his home in northern Luzon. On 24 September 1993 Imelda Marcos was found guilty of participating in a deal that was "disadvantageous to the government" under the Anti-Graft and Corruption Practices Act. She faced a maximum prison sentence of 24 years, but she was free on bail while her appeal was considered.

National and local elections were held 11 May 1992. Fidel V. Ramos and Joseph E. Estrada were elected president and vice president, respectively. On 30 June 1992 Fidel Ramos succeeded Corazon Aquino as president of the Philippines with a plurality of 23.6%. Nearly 85% of eligible voters turned out to elect 17,205 officials at national, regional, and local levels. The election was relatively peaceful with only 52 election-related deaths reported. Voters were required to write the names of the candidate they wanted for office. This combined with the number of candidates meant it was several weeks before the votes were completely tallied. Ramos, a Methodist and the Philippine's first non-Catholic president, considers the country's population growth rate as an obstacle to development. A rally of 300,000 Catholics led by Cardinal Sin took place in Manila in 1993 to protest the Ramos administration's birth control policies and the public health promotion of prophylactics to limit the spread of AIDS.

Domestic insurgency by the Muslim population continued throughout the 1980s. By the 1990s this threat was greatly reduced by internal divisions, reduced external support, military pressure, and government accommodations, including the creation of the Autonomous Region in Muslim Mindanao in 1990. In January 1994 the government signed a cease-fire agreement with the Moro National Liberation Front ending 20 years of guerrilla war. The last remaining communist insurgency in Asia was reduced by the Ramos government's peaceful signal, the 1992 Anti-Subversion Law, and the 1993 split in the ranks of the NPA that created a lull until issues related to the weakened leadership are resolved. In January 1994 a law was passed restoring the death penalty for 13 crimes including treason, murder, kidnapping and corruption. Police reform was a particular goal of the legislation. This legislation was partly in response to a series of abductions of wealthy ethnic Chinese Filipinos abducted for ransom, in which the Philippine National Police were found to be involved.

Conflicting claims to the Spratly Islands in the South China Sea are a source of tension between the Philippines and the People's Republic of China. In 1989 Chinese and Philippine warships exchanged gunfire in the vicinity of the Spratly Islands. The incident was resolved by diplomatic means. In June 1994 an oil exploration permit was granted to Vaalco Energy of the US, and to Alcorn Petroleum and Minerals, its Philippine subsidiary. China protested. The Philippine response was to refer to a principle of "common exploration" and development of the Spratlys. China had employed this same principle when the Philippines had protested China's granting the US permission to explore in the Spratlys in 1993. China, Viet-Nam, Taiwan, the Philippines, Malaysia, and Brunei all lay claim to all, or a portion, of the Spratly Islands. In June 1994 a 5-day conference on East Timor held in Manila, ended with an agreement to establish a coalition for East Timor in the Philippines and proposed a peace plan based on the gradual withdrawal of Indonesian troops.

13GOVERNMENT

Between 1972 and 1981, the government operated under martial law. A new constitution that took effect on 17 January 1973, replacing a 1935 document, was not fully implemented until 1981, by which time it had been significantly amended to provide for a presidential form of government. The head of state was the president, elected for an unlimited number of six-year terms by direct popular vote. Under the new constitution, the president had the power to initiate most legislation. Legislative power was vested in a unicameral National Assembly (Batasang Pambansa), a body whose membership (of up to 200) was to be elected for six-year terms by universal suffrage beginning at age 18. An interim National Assembly, with 165 members elected from 13 regions, plus 25 appointees, was convened in June 1978. The 1981 constitutional amendment set 14 May 1984 for the first National Assembly elections following the end of martial law. Under the constitution of 11 February 1987 the Philippines is a democratic republican state. Executive power is vested in a president elected by popular vote for a six-year term, with no eligibility for reelection. The president is assisted by a vice-president, elected for a six-year term, with eligibility for one immediate reelection, and a cabinet, which can include the vice-president. Legislative power is vested in a bicameral legislature. Congress consists of a Senate, with 24 members elected for six-year terms (limited to two consecutive terms). Senators are chosen at large. The 24 highest vote-getters nationwide are elected. Senators must be native-born Filipinos and at least 35 years old. A House of Representatives is elected from single-member districts for three-year terms (limited to three consecutive terms). Districts are reapportioned within three years of each census. In 1991 200 members were elected and up to 50 more may be appointed by the president from "party lists" and "sectoral lists." Representatives must be native-born Filipinos and at least 25 years of age.

14POLITICAL PARTIES

The first Philippine political party, established in 1900, was the Federal Party, which advocated peace and eventual statehood. Later, the Nationalist Party (NP) and the Democratic Party were established. They did not produce an actual two-party system, since the Nationalists retained exclusive control and the Democrats functioned as a "loyal opposition." However, following Japanese occupation and the granting of independence, an effective two-party system was instituted by the Liberal Party (LP) and the NP. The Progressive Party, formed in 1957 by adherents of Ramón Magsaysay, polled more than 1 million votes in the presidential election of 1958. In the elections of November 1965, Senator Ferdinand Marcos, the NP candidate, received 55% of the vote. In the 1969 election, he was elected to an unprecedented second term. All political activity was banned in 1972 following the imposition of martial law, and was not allowed to resume until a few months before the April 1978 elections for an interim National Assembly. That election and the 1980 and 1982 balloting for local officials were won overwhelmingly by the Marcos government's New Society Movement (Kilusan Bagong Lipunan—KBL), amid charges of electoral fraud and attempts by opposition groups to boycott the voting. The principal opposition party was the People's Power Movement–Fight (Lakas Ng Bayan–Laban), led by Benigno S. Aquino, Jr., until his assassination in 1983. This party joined with 11 other opposition parties in 1982 to form a coalition known as the United Nationalist Democratic Organization (UNIDO). Following Aquino's murder, some 50 opposition groups, including the members of the UNIDO coalition, agreed to coordinate their anti-Marcos efforts. This coalition of opposition parties enabled Corazon Aquino to campaign

against Marcos in 1986. In September 1986 the revolutionary left formed a legal political party to contest congressional elections. The Partido ng Bayan (Party of the Nation) allied with other left-leaning groups in an Alliance for New Politics. This unsuccessful attempt for electoral representation resulted in a return to guerilla warfare on the part of the Communists.

After assuming the presidency, Aquino formally organized the People's Power Movement (Lakas Ng Bayan), the successor to her late husband's party. In the congressional elections of May 1987, Aquino's popularity gave her party a sweep in the polls, making it the major party in the country. Marcos's KBL was reduced to a minor party. Some of its members formed their own splinter groups, such as the Grand Alliance for Democracy (GAD), a coalition of parties seeking distance from Marcos. Others revived the LP and the NP, seeking renewed leadership. The left-wing People's Party (Partido Ng Bayan), which supports the political objectives of the NPA, was a minor party in the elections. In May 1989 the Nacionalista Party was reestablished by Juan Ponce Enrile. A new opposition party, the Filipino Party (Partido Pilipino), was organized in 1991 as a vehicle for Aquino's estranged cousin Eduardo "Danding" Cojuangco's presidential campaign. He ran third in the election taking 18.1% of the vote, behind Miriam Defensor Santiago with 19.8% of the vote. On 30 June 1992 Fidel Ramos succeeded Corazon Aquino as president of the Philippines with a plurality of 23.6%. In September 1992 Ramos signed the Anti-Subversion Law signaling a peaceful resolution to more than 20 years of Communist insurgency, with the repeal of the anti-subversion legislation in place since 1957. On 26 August 1994 Ramos announced a new political coalition that would produce the most powerful political group in the Philippines. Ramos' Lakas-National Union of Christian Democrats (Lakas/NUCD) teamed with the Democratic Filipino Struggle (Laban ng Demokratikong Pilipino, Laban). The LDP controls the Senate with 17 of the 23 members.

In 1993 recognized political organizations and their leaders were: Bayan, Bagong Alyansang Makabyan, James Tadeo; Communist Party of the Philippines, Partido Kommunista ng Pilipinas (PKP), Felicisimo Macapagal; Democratic Filipino Struggle (Laban ng Demokratikong Pilipino, Laban), Edgardo Espiritu, reorganized in 1988 as an alliance of Kakas ng Bansa and a conservative faction of the PDP-Laban Party; Laban is comprised of defectors from the LDP who joined Ramos's "rainbow coalition"; Liberal Party, Jovito Salonga, represents the center-liberal position of the former Nationalista Party which split in 1946; Nacionalista Party (NP), Salvador H. Laurel; Nationalist People's Coalition (NPC), Eduardo Cojuangco; New People's Alliance, Partido ng Bayan, organized by the former head of the CPP (is a militant left-wing), nationalist, Fidel Agcaoli; New Society Movement (Kilusan Bagong Lipunan, KBL), organized by President Marcos and former members of the Nationalista Party, Imelda Marcos/Vincent Mellora; Partido ng Masang (PMP), Joseph Estrada; PDP-Laban Party was led by Benigno S. Aquino, Jr. until his assassination in August 1983 (centrist party), Aquilino Pimentel; People Power-national Union of Christian Democrats (Lakas ng Edsa, NUCD and Partido Lakas Tao, Lakas/NUCD), alliance to support the presidency of Gen. Fidel Ramos, Jose de Veneccia; People's Reform Party (PRP), Miriam Defensor-Santiago; Philippine Democratic Socialist Party, Partido Demokratiko Sosyalista ng Pilipinas (PDSP), Norberto Gonzales; Philippine Nationalist Party, Partido Nationalista ng Pilipinas (PNP), Blas F. Ople; Pusyon Visaya Party of the Visayas region of the central Philippines, Valentino Legsapi; Strength of the Nation (Lakas ng Bansa), was organized as a pro-Aquino party, Neptali Gonzales; and, Women for the Mother Country, Kababaihan Para Sa Inang Bayan, a militant group and the first all-women's political party in the Philippines and Asia, Tarhata Lucman.

Parties organized in opposition to the Government are: Mindanao Independence Movement, Reuben Canoy; Moro Islamic Liberation Front (MILF), is based mainly in Lanao del Sur (receives support from Egypt), Hashim Salamat; Moro National Liberation Front (MNLF), Nur Misuari, Bangsa Moro National Liberation Front (BMNLF), supported by Saudi Arabia, Dimas Pundato; National Democratic Front, is a left-wing alliance of 14 groups, spokesperson Saturnino Ocampo; Communist Party of the Philippines (CPP), Jose Maria Sison; New People's Army (NPA), the military wing of the CPP, Romulo Kintanar.

[15]LOCAL GOVERNMENT

Under the constitutions of 1935, 1973, and 1987, the country has been divided into provinces, municipalities, and chartered cities, each enjoying a certain degree of local autonomy. Each of the 73 provinces (in 1991) and subprovinces elects a governor, a vice-governor, and two provincial board members for terms of six years. As of 1991, there were 61 chartered cities headed by a mayor and a vice-mayor. Chartered cities stand on their own, are not part of a province, do not elect provincial officials, and are not subject to provincial taxation, but have the power to levy their own taxes. Municipalities, of which each province is composed, are public corporations governed by municipal law. In 1991 there were approximately 1,500 municipalities. Within each municipality are communities (barangays), each with a citizens' assembly. In 1991 there were about 42,000 barangays. Metropolitan Manila is a separate political unit, created in 1975, with Imelda Romualdez Marcos as the first governor. The 1987 constitution provides for special forms of government in the autonomous regions created in the Cordilleras in Luzon and the Muslim areas of Mindanao. Any region can become autonomous by a referendum. The Local Government Code of 1991 provides for a mores responsive and accountable local-government structure. Local governments are to be given more powers, authoriity, responsibilities and resources through a system of decentralization.

[16]JUDICIAL SYSTEM

Under the 1973 constitution, the Supreme Court, composed of a chief justice and 14 associate justices, was the highest judicial body of the state, with supervisory authority over the lower courts. The entire court system was revamped in 1981, with the creation of new regional courts of trials and of appeals. Justices at all levels were appointed by the president. Philippine courts functioned without juries. Delays in criminal cases were common, and detention periods in national security cases were long. Security cases arising during the period of martial law (1972–81) were tried in military courts. The 1987 constitution restored the system to what it had been in 1973. Despite the reinstitution of many procedural safeguards and guarantees, the slow pace of justice continues to be a major problem.

The Constitution calls for an independent judiciary and defendants in criminal cases are afforded the right to counsel.

[17]ARMED FORCES

The all-volunteer active armed forces numbered 106,500 in mid-1993, and reserves 131,000. The army, with 68,000 personnel, had 8 infantry divisions and 6 specialized brigades. The navy had a total of 23,000 personnel (including 8,500 marines and 2,000 in the coast guard), with 1 frigate, and 42 patrol and coastal combatants. The air force had a strength of 15,500, with 49 combat aircraft and 94 armed helicopters. The Philippine national police totaled 90,000, and the Citizen Armed Forces had 45,000 personnel. Estimated defense expenditures in 1991 were $1 billion or more, 2% of gross domestic product.

The US has abandoned Clark Air Base and Subic Naval Base, southwest of Manila, because of volcano damage and excessive rent charges.

The rebel New People's Army in Luzon numbers 15,000, and Moslem guerrillas, as many as 20,000.

The PAF has 92 observors in Cambodia.

[18]INTERNATIONAL COOPERATION

The Philippines is a charter member of the UN, having joined on 24 October 1945, and belongs to ESCAP and all the nonregional specialized agencies. It participates in the International Sugar Agreement and the International Wheat Agreement. The Philippines is a member of ASEAN and led in the formation of the Asian Development Bank, which opened its headquarters in Manila in 1966. The International Rice Research Institute and the Southeast Asia Research Center for Agriculture are both located in Los Banos, south of Manila. In 1973, the Philippines acceded to GATT as a provisional member. The nation is also a member of G-77 and a signatory to the Law of the Sea.

[19]ECONOMY

The Philippines is primarily an agricultural nation, raising crops for subsistence and export. About 50% of the total labor force is engaged in agriculture, fisheries, and forestry. It is the world's largest producer of coconuts and manila hemp (abacá). Manufacturing, which has expanded and diversified since political independence, depends on imported raw materials and cannot supply internal needs. Mining, once centered on gold, is now diversified, with chromite, copper, and iron providing important earnings. The economy is heavily dependent on foreign trade. Traditionally, exports of primary products have failed to balance imports, leading the government to restrict imports. Structural change accelerated in the 1970s, as the contribution of industry (including construction) to GDP rose from 29.5% in 1970 to 36.5% by 1980, primarily as a result of export-oriented industrialization promoted by the Marcos government. The Aquino assassination in August 1983 had immediate economic as well as political consequences for the Marcos government. Hundreds of millions of dollars in private capital fled the Philippines, leaving the country with insufficient foreign exchange reserves to meet its payments obligations. The government turned to the IMF and its creditor banks for assistance in rescheduling the nation's foreign debt. In addition, imports and exports were tightly controlled, and an austerity program was set up during 1984–85.

The government of Corazon Aquino launched a privatization program in December 1986 with the establishment of the Assets Privatization Trust (APT). Aquino's agrarian reform program, the Comprehensive Agrarian Reform Programme, was only partially accomplished by the end of her term. The land distribution process is scheduled for completion in 1998. The monopolies established under the Marcos administration in coconuts, sugar, meat, grains, and fertilizer were dismantled. The copra export ban was lifted, and all export taxes were abolished; in addition, the government allowed free access to lower-cost or higher-quality imports in order to improve the cost-competitiveness of domestic producers. Many difficulties remained, however. The prices of commodity exports, such as sugar, copper, and coconut products, were still weak, while demand for nontraditional manufactured products, such as clothing and electronic components, failed to rise. Despite the structural reforms and an initial recovery between 1986 and 1989, sustainable growth eluded the Philippines.

Throughout 1990–92 stagnant economic growth plagued the Philippines; inadequate infrastructure and prolonged drought curtailed industrial and agricultural expansion. In 1991 the labor force was estimated to be 25.7 million workers, of which 22.9 million were employed. Official unemployment rates are believed to be understated. Widespread unemployment and underemployment characterize the Philippine labor market. High rates of labor migration abroad (686,137 in 1992) provide some relief and accounts for a substantial portion of the country's foreign exchange earnings. In periods of no growth, or modest growth, reducing unemployment continues to be a difficult problem. A total of 5,232 active labor union with a membership of 3.1 million were registered in 1991.

The Philippines has great potential as a tourist destination. However, since the early 1990 the tourist industry has been affected by the worldwide economic recession, political difficulties, natural disasters and the energy shortage. Since 1990 the most visible constraint on the economy has been the shortage of electric power. In 1992, water level of Lake Lanao fell, causing a 50% reduction in the power supply to Mindanao. Full power did not resume until the end of 1992. The power shortage in Luzon was chronic. In Manila, the industrial hub, power outages would last from four to six hours per day. In 1992 exports rose by 11%, led by earnings from the Philippines' two leading manufactures, electronics and garments. Consumer protection was provided by the Price Act of 1992 through the stabilization of the price of basic necessities and prime commodities and by measures against undue price increases during emergency situations. In 1993 the inflation rate continued to decline and the return to economic growth was expected to accelerate through 1994. Further positive signs for sustained growth were the following government actions: opening the telecommunications market, liberalizing the foreign exchange market, an increase in the supply and reliability of electric power, and provision of a better investment climate. The country's program with IMF expired in April 1993, and the necessity for new arrangements delayed pending agreement on growth plans. In turn, absence of new IMF arrangements delayed plans for a fifth Paris Club Debt rescheduling accord.

In February 1994 as part of continuing moves to attack the budget deficit President Ramos announced a 15% to 25% increase in petroleum prices. Facing nationwide strikes and demonstrations he backed down. With the same goal of decreasing the deficit he then announced a crackdown on an alleged tax evasion scheme by banks. In May 1994 Ramos pushed a law through the Senate amending the Philippines' 10% value-added tax (VAT) system. The amendment extended it to cover most service industries and closed loopholes in the 1988 version. The law became tied up in court as the Supreme Court blocked implementation in order to rule on suits that claimed the law violated the constitution.

20INCOME

In 1992, Philippines' GNP was $49,462 million at current prices, or $770 per capita. For the period 1985–92 the average inflation rate was 10.1%, resulting in a real growth rate in per capita GNP of 1.9%.

In 1992 the GDP was $52,463 million in current US dollars. It is estimated that in 1991 agriculture, hunting, forestry, and fishing contributed 21% to GDP; mining and quarrying, 1%; manufacturing, 25%; electricity, gas, and water, 2%; construction, 5%; wholesale and retail trade, 15%; transport, storage, and communication, 6%; finance, insurance, real estate, and business services, 11%; community, social, and personal services, 5%; and other sources, 7%.

21LABOR

The Philippines had an employed labor force estimated at 21.9 million in 1992, of whom 45% were engaged in agriculture, forestry, and fishing (compared with 58% in 1968). Unemployment fluctuates seasonally. In 1992, the unemployment rate was estimated at 8.6% overall, with a much higher rate (about 26%) in metropolitan Manila, where manufacturing is concentrated; annual underemployment was put at 36%.

In May 1974, the government passed a new labor code that restructured the trade union movement on a one-industry, one-union basis. Most of the more than 3,700 trade unions are small; industrial unions have been united in the Philippines Trade Union Congress, and agricultural workers in the Federation of Free Farmers. Strikes are prohibited in such essential services as transportation, communications, and health care. In 1990, 12.1% of the labor force was unionized.

In 1990, the average legal daily minimum wage for an eight-hour day ranged from P118 for nonagricultural workers in metropolitan Manila to P74-77 for plantation agricultural workers and P74 for nonplantation agricultural workers. In the same year, the legal minimum wage was increased by 32%; the resulting wage increases, however, coupled with fuel price increases, caused 400 metropolitan Manila companies to either close down or decrease shifts.

Overseas employment is a very important part of the Philippines' income. Remittances from overseas workers in 1990 were the second largest source of foreign exchange, and the number of overseas workers annually deployed is equivalent to 40% of each year's entrants into the labor market.

22AGRICULTURE

About one-third of the total land area is classified as arable. Three-fourths of the cultivated area is devoted to subsistence crops and one-fourth to commercial crops, mainly for export. Farms tend to be small, and many areas are double-cropped. Soils are generally fertile, but 30% of the agricultural land is suffering erosion.

In 1973, the Marcos government began a land-reform program that undertook to transfer landownership to about half of the country's 900,000 tenant farmers. By February 1986, over one-half of the area—about 600,000 hectares (1,482,600 acres)—had not been distributed. The Aquino administration proposed a program in two stages: the first, covering 1.5 million hectares (3.7 million acres) in 1987–89, involved previously undistributed land and other land held by the state; the second, covering 3.9 million hectares (9.6 million acres) in 1990–92, involved land cultivating sugar, coconuts, and fruits. A more detailed 1990–1995 plan proposes to increase productivity of small farms, maintain self-sufficiency in rice and corn production, and to increase the agricultural sector's role in the trade balance.

Roughly half the cultivated land is devoted to the two principal subsistence crops, palay (unhusked rice) and corn. Production of palay decreased in 1992 to 9,129,000 tons from 9,670,000 tons in 1991, but long-term production has increased, mainly through the use of high-yielding hybrid seeds under a government development program begun in 1973. The lower harvests were caused primarily by drought, typhoons, and the Mount Pinatubo eruption. The Philippines attained self-sufficiency in rice in 1974 and became a net exporter of rice for the first time in 1977. A similar development plan was aimed at raising yields of corn, which is the chief food crop in areas unsuitable for rice-growing and is increasingly important as feed for use in the developing livestock and poultry industries. The Philippines has been self-sufficient in corn for human consumption since the late 1970s, but since production of animal feed lags behind the demand, imports are still necessary. Corn output in 1992 was 4,570,000 tons. Lesser food crops include sweet potatoes, beans, cassava, peanuts, and various fruits and vegetables.

Commercial agriculture, dominated by large plantations, centers on coconuts and copra, sugarcane, tobacco, bananas, and pineapples. Coconuts are the most important export crop, accounting for 20% of world production; in 1992, 8,465,000 tons were produced. Copra production, in which the Philippines leads the world, rose from 1,470,000 tons in 1965 to an estimated 1,670,000 tons in 1992. As oil milling capacity rose, the domestic market for copra expanded, accounting for almost all of the output and leaving only marginal amounts for exportation. The government put a ban on copra exports in March 1983, but it was lifted in March 1986. Sugarcane production provided the country's single largest export item until 1978, when output and prices fell. Production was forecast at only 27.3 million tons in 1992 (compared with an annual average of 31.5 million tons during 1979–81); exports of sugar cane were valued at $111 million, or 1% of total exports in 1992. Pineapple production rose to 1.17 million tons in 1992; production of coffee was 110,000 tons, and 3,900,000 tons of bananas were produced that year.

23 ANIMAL HUSBANDRY

Animal husbandry never has been important, meat consumption being very low. The carabao, or water buffalo, are the principal draft animals, particularly in the rice paddies; hogs are the chief meat animals (except in Muslim sections). The Philippines is self-sufficient in pork and poultry, but imports of beef and dairy products are still necessary. In 1992 there were 1.6 million head of cattle, 2.5 million buffaloes, and 8 million hogs. Dairying is insignificant, a prolonged drought in 1992 caused dairy production to decline. In 1992 there were 63 million chickens.

24 FISHING

Fish is the primary source of protein in the Filipino diet. Some 2,000 species abound in Philippine waters. Despite more than a doubling in output since the 1960s, the fishing industry remains relatively undeveloped, and large quantities of fish are imported. In 1991, the catch totaled 2,311,797 tons, of which 1,699,437 tons were from commercial fishing and 612,360 tons were from aquaculture.

Anchovy, mackerel, sea bass, red snapper, sardines, herring, mullet, barracuda, pompano, tuna, bonito, and shark are the most plentiful. Principal commercial fishing grounds are off Palawan, north of Panay and Negros, and to the south and west of Mindanao. Subsistence fishing is conducted throughout the archipelago. Fish ponds, chiefly for cultivation of bangos or milkfish, are principally in the swampy coastal areas of western Panay and around Manila Bay.

Pearl shells (including cultured pearls), sponges, sea cucumbers (trepang), shark fins, and sea turtles are exported.

25 FORESTRY

Forests are an important economic resource in the Philippines. As of 1991, 34% of the land area was forest and woodland. Major commercial forest reserves are located in Mindanao, Luzon, Samar, Negros, and Palawan. In the early 1980s, the Philippines was a significant exporter of tropical hardwood logs and lumber, but production fell by over 50% over the decade, leaving the country a net importer of tropical hardwood logs by 1990. In 1991, the production of roundwood totaled 38.7 million cu m.

Among other forest products are bamboo, rattan, resins, tannin, and firewood. Rubber output totaled 82,000 tons in 1985.

26 MINING

Mining and related processing activities are promoted by the government as part of the Philippines' industrialization effort. Since the government controls mineral resources, mining can be undertaken in the Philippines as a public sector activity, which can enter into coproduction, joint-venture, or production-sharing agreements with the domestic private sector or with corporations and associations whose capital is 60% owned by Filipinos. Mining and quarrying contribute about 2% to the GDP. Copper (150,000 tons produced in 1991, from northern Luzon, Cebu, Negros, Marinduque, and Mindanao) is the leading mineral, followed by gold (24,938 kg in 1991 from northern Luzon, Mindanao, and Masbate Island), manganese ore (14,000 tons in 1991 from the Islands of Busuanga, Marinduque, Masbate, and Siquijor, and also from the Provinces of Zamboanga del Sur and Agusan del Norte on Mindanao), and nickel (18,400 tons of metal content in 1991 from Palawan Island and Surigao del

Norte). The Philippines reportedly has the world's largest source of refractory chromite (from Masinloc) and produces sizable quantities of metallurgic chromite (from western Luzon); chromite ore production in 1991 totaled 184,010 tons. Silver, lead, and zinc also are produced for export. Clays, limestone, pyrites, guano, silica sands, and salt are produced for local consumption. Coal deposits are found in Antique Province, Cebu, and Mindanao; production rose from 331,000 tons in 1981 to 1,267,102 tons in 1991.

27 ENERGY AND POWER

Commercial oil deposits were found in 1978, with production beginning the following year. Oil drilling centers on the Matinloc, Nido, and Cadlao fields off Palawan. Domestic production increased from 1.4 million barrels in 1981 to 3.3 million barrels in 1982 but decreased to 1.5 million barrels in 1991. In addition, the Philippine government has developed an alternative energy program, including, for example, the use of "alcogas" (gasohol) and "cocodiesel" (coconut oil in diesel fuels).

Net installed electrical capacity at the end of 1991 amounted to 6,789,000 kw, of which hydroelectric plants contributed 32%, coal-fired thermal plants 55%, and geothermal energy 13%. Large hydroelectric plants have been installed on the Agno and Angat rivers on Luzon and at María Cristina Falls on the Agusan River in Mindanao. Brownouts and power outages were common in 1993. The Philippine National Power Plan for 1993–2005 calls for spending $35 billion to correct current electrical shortfalls and meet expected demand growth. Geothermal energy is produced on Luzon, Leyte, and Negros. Several nuclear power plants have been initiated, but they were all abandoned because of ceilings on foreign borrowing and, in the case of the completed plant at Bataan, the location of the site near a seismic fault line. Total electrical output in 1991 was 22,484 million kwh, of which 51% was conventional thermal, 23% was hydropower, and 26% was geothermal. With the recent discovery of oil off the shores of Palawan, more drilling and deep-sea exploration is expected. In 1991, about 1.5 million barrels of crude oil were produced.

28 INDUSTRY

Industry is concentrated in the Manila area. The leading manufactured goods (by value) are foods, tobacco products, chemicals and pharmaceuticals, beverages, wood products, and wearing apparel. There was growth in the number of plants that assemble imported components into finished products (such as transistors, radios, televisions, refrigerators, and stoves) during the 1970s, as there was in the production of intermediate goods (such as chemicals, textiles, timber products, structural steel, and cement). The industrialization strategy proposed by the government in 1981 stressed development of exports and the accelerated implementation of 11 major industrial projects—a copper smelter, a phosphatic fertilizer plant, an aluminum smelter, a diesel-engine manufacturing plant, an expansion of the cement industry, a "cocochemical" complex (based on coconuts), an integrated pulp and paper mill, a petrochemical complex, heavy engineering industries, an integrated steel mill, and the production of "alcogas." The copper smelter, the phosphatic fertilizer plant, and the "cocochemical" complex went into operation in 1985. By the 1990s manufacturing production was geographically concentrated in the Metro Manila area (50%) and the adjoining regions of Southern Tagalog and Central Luzon (20%). In 1990 the industrial sector was characterized by its inefficiency and oligopolistic structure. Most industrial output was concentrated in a few large firms. A government inquiry into the cement industry exposed that eight of 17 cement-manufacturing firms were under the control of a single firm. In this environment although small- and medium-sized businesses accounted for 80% of manufacturing employment, they accounted for only 25% of the value added in manufacturing.

The agricultural sector accounted for 22% of GDP and 15% of export earnings in 1992 and employed nearly 40% of the labor force. In 1992 the manufacturing sector accounted for about 25% of the country's GDP and employed 10% of the working population. Food manufacturing has remained the primary industry, accounting for some 37% of total manufacturing output in 1992. Petroleum and coal products (17.9%), chemicals and chemical products (6.6%), and apparel and footwear (6%) were next in importance. Industrial production decling in 1992 was the output of beverages, wood furniture and textiles. New emphasis has been placed on developing industries with good export potential that process primary products of the agriculture and mining sectors. Total mineral production for 1992 was valued at P20.7 billion, with metallic minerals accounting for nearly 72% and non-metallic minerals 28%. Copper and gold are the most significant metals produced. The Philippines has extensive onshore and offshore mineral resources; however, only 14 million out of an estimated 20 million hectares have been geologically surveyed.

29SCIENCE AND TECHNOLOGY

Leadership in formulating and implementing national science policy is exercised by the National Science and Technology Authority (NSTA). Special training in science is offered by the Philippine Science High School, whose graduates are eligible for further training through the NSTA's scholarship program. The International Rice Research Institute, founded by the Rockefeller and Ford foundations and US AID in 1960, conducts training programs in the cultivation, fertilization, and irrigation of hybrid rice seeds. The Southeast Asian Regional Center for Graduate Study and Research in Agriculture maintains genotype and information banks for agricultural research. The French Institute of Scientific Research for Development and Cooperation has an institute in Manila conducting research in molecular biology.

30DOMESTIC TRADE

The archipelagic structure of Philippine marketing requires the establishment of regional centers and adds considerably to distribution costs, alien domination of much of marketing, direct government participation, and the proliferation of small firms. Warehousing facilities are available at most ports. Small stores typify retail trade. Manila has major shopping centers and malls. Generally, sales are for cash or on open account. Retailing is conducted on a high markup, low-turnover basis. A law provides for price-tagging on retail items. Shops are usually open from 10 AM to noon and from 2 to 7:30 PM, Monday through Saturday; banking hours are weekdays from 9 AM to 3 PM. Staggered hours, with up to three shifts, are common in the metropolitan Manila area. English is the general language of commercial correspondence. Most advertising is local; the chief media are newspapers, radio, television, posters, billboards, and sound trucks.

31FOREIGN TRADE

The Philippines' exports are largely primary commodities and raw materials (agricultural and forest products and minerals) and labor-intensive manufactured goods, the leading one in the 1992 being garments (valued at 53,560 million pesos in 1992); imports are generally fuels, machinery, and metals. In 1992 the top major export products were garments, semiconductors and electronic microcircuits, crude coconut oil, bars and copper rods, and bananas and plantains. In 1992 the top major import products were mineral fuels/lubricants and related materials, non-electrical machinery, electrical machinery, base metals and metal products, and transport equipment.

The nation's trade balance has not shown a surplus since 1973, chiefly because of the rise in mineral fuel imports. The US and Japan continued through 1992 to be the Philippines' primary trading partners. The appreciation of the peso, weak local pro-

duction, and sluggish demand world-wide were factors in the meager growth in exports in 1992. In 1992 Germany, Hong Kong, and the UK were important trade partners.

Major trading partners with the Philippines for 1992 in millions of pesos:

	EXPORTS	IMPORTS	BALANCE
Australia	—	10,959	—
France	4,655	—	—
Germany	13,287	17,979	−4,692
Hong Kong	11,928	19,383	−7,455
Japan	44,666	82,719	−38,053
Malaysia	—	7,800	—
The Netherlands	9,336	—	—
Saudi Arabia	—	23,517	—
Singapore	6,316	14,742	−8,426
South Korea	5,008	19,422	−14,414
Taiwan	7,147	25,155	−18,008
UK	11,752	—	—
US	92,856	70,278	22,578
Other countries	44,690	98,044	−53,354
TOTALS	251,641	389,998	−138,357

32BALANCE OF PAYMENTS

Since World War II, the Philippines has experienced frequent trade deficits, aggravated by inflationary pressures. Deficits have been counterbalanced by US government expenditures, domestic gold production, transfer of payments from abroad, official loans (US Export-Import Bank, IBRD, and private US banks), net inflow of private investment, tourist receipts, remittances from Filipino workers overseas, and contributions from the IMF. In 1992, stronger service export receipts, led by overseas remittances and tourism-related earnings, helped offset a record-high merchandise trade deficit. During the first half of 1993, however, the Philippines posted a $739 million surplus, over nine times the $80 million level of the same period in 1992. An improvement in the capital account more than offset a wider current account deficit.

In 1992 merchandise exports totaled $9,824 million and imports $14,519 million. The merchandise trade balance was $−4,695 million. The following table summarizes Philippines balance of payments for 1991 and 1992 (in millions of US dollars):

	1991	1992
CURRENT ACCOUNT		
Goods, services, and income	−1,861	−1,734
Unrequited transfers	827	817
TOTALS	−1,034	−917
CAPITAL ACCOUNT		
Direct investment	544	228
Portfolio investment	110	40
Other long-term capital	1,234	1,362
Other short-term capital	1,039	1,486
Exceptional financing	—	—
Other liabilities	—	—
Reserves	−1,755	−1,689
TOTALS	1,172	1,427
Errors and omissions	−138	−510
Total change in reserves	−322	49

33BANKING AND SECURITIES

The Philippine banking structure consists of the government-owned Central Bank of the Philippines (created in 1949), which acts as the government's fiscal agent and administers the monetary and banking system, and (as of March 1991) of some 32 commercial banks, of which 26 are private domestic banks, 2 government-affiliated, and 4 foreign. Other institutions include 802 rural banks, 38 private development banks, 7 savings banks, and 17 investment houses, and 2 specialized government banks. The largest commercial bank, the Philippine National Bank (PNB), is a government institution with over 194 local offices and 12 overseas branches. It supplies about half the commercial credit, basically as agricultural loans. In 1985, the authorized capital of the PNB was increased from ₱5 billion to ₱25 billion. The government operates about 1,145 postal savings banks and the Development Bank of the Philippines, the Land Bank of the Philippines, and the Philippine Amanah Bank (for Mindanao). The money supply as 1992, as measured by M2, stood at ₱489.0 billion.

Philippine stock exchanges are self-governing, although the Philippine Securities and Exchange Commission, established in 1936, has supervisory power over registrants. There are three stock exchanges: the Manila Stock Exchange, the Makati Stock Exchange, and the Metropolitan Stock Exchange.

34INSURANCE

As of 1986, some 124 private insurance companies operated in the Philippines. In that year, 20 firms were engaged in life insurance, 102 in non-life coverage, and 2 in both. In 1990 premiums totaled $12.4 or 2% of the GDP. Life insurance in force in 1992 totaled ₱327 billion.

The Government Service Insurance System, a government organization set up in 1936, provides life, permanent disability, accident, old age pension, and burial insurance and salary and real estate loan benefits. Compulsory third-party motor liability insurance went into effect on 1 January 1976.

35PUBLIC FINANCE

Despite an improved tax structure and fiscal restraints, deficits continue to be a feature of the Philippine national budget because of the nation's rising external indebtedness, continuing need for development funds, and falling revenues (as world commodity prices decline). Infrastructural improvements, defense expenditures, and debt service continue to lead among the categories of outlays. The principal sources of revenue are income taxes, taxes on sales and business operations, and excise duties.

The following table shows actual revenues and expenditures for 1991 and 1992 in millions of pesos.

	1991	1992
REVENUE AND GRANTS		
Tax revenue	182,275	208,705
Non-tax revenue	31,148	29,987
Capital revenue	4,175	1,878
Grants	3,189	2,144
TOTALS	220,787	242,714
EXPENDITURES & LENDING MINUS REPAYMENTS		
General public service	21,221	25,868
Defense	26,010	26,321
Public order and safety	4,567	5,066
Education	38,643	39,917
Health	10,158	10,971
Social security and welfare	5,885	7,022
Housing and community amenities	3,035	4,535
Recreation, cultural, and religious affairs	1,514	2,707
Economic affairs and services	59,158	7,249
Other expenditures	81,628	95,427
Adjustments	−4,683	−30,403
Lending minus repayments	7,666	−6,949
TOTALS	247,136	258,680
Deficit/Surplus	−26,349	−15,966

The national budget deficit fell from 2.1% of GDP in 1991 to 1.2% in 1992. In 1991, Philippines' total public debt stood at ₱620,258 million, of which ₱289,858 million was financed abroad. The consolidated public sector deficit increased from 1.6% of GDP in 1991 to 1.9% in 1992, and was expected to have risen to over 3% in 1993. This deterioration discouraged the IMF from granting a new $800 million loan as of late 1993.

36TAXATION

The individual income tax consists of taxes on compensation income (from employment), business income, and passive income (interests, dividends, royalties, and prizes). As of 1987, compensation income tax rates varied from 1% to 35% and business rates varied from 3% to 30%. Corporate taxes are at a uniform rate of 35%. For resident foreign corporations, after-tax profits remitted abroad are subject to a 15% tax, except for corporations registered with the Export Processing Zone Authority. New and necessary industries, including those authorized as investment priorities, may be wholly tax-exempt, subject to reduced taxation, or granted tax holidays.

Excise taxes are imposed on selected commodities such as alcoholic beverages, tobacco products, and petroleum products. In addition, the government levies a variety of other taxes, including mining and petroleum taxes, stamp taxes, residence taxes, estate and gift taxes, a head tax on immigrants above a certain age and staying beyond a certain period, and a valued-added tax on goods and services. Some cities, such as Manila, levy their own wholesale and retail sales taxes.

37CUSTOMS AND DUTIES

All imported goods are subject to ad valorem duties of 5–50%, based on the home consumption value plus 10%, unless they are imported by the government or are relief items. Under the Aquino administration, as of the end of 1987, import taxes were cut on 437 items; in addition, export duties, previously applied to shipments of mineral, vegetable, and animal products, including wood, were eliminated. The government plans to lower tariffs to no more than 30% on all but 200 items by the end of 1995.

38FOREIGN INVESTMENT

In 1986, new foreign investments registered with the government's Board of Investment (BOI, established in 1967) reached ₱1,593 million, 35% below the 1985 level. New foreign investments increased by 20.8% in 1986, while additional investments (expansions) decreased by 43%. Investments have been concentrated in trade, utilities, mining, petroleum refining, and export-oriented agriculture, with accelerating interest in labor-intensive textiles, footwear, electronics, and other nontraditional export industries. Investment is affected by import controls, exchange controls, and equity controls that favor Filipino participation in foreign ventures. The Omnibus Investments Code of 1987 generally limited foreign equity ownership to 40%, but allowed 100% foreign ownership in a "pioneer" priority industry identified in the annual Investment Priorities Plan (IPP). Special encouragement is given to pioneer manufacturing endeavors, export-oriented and labor-intensive industries, projects outside metropolitan Manila, and to joint ventures with a minimum of 60% Filipino capitalization. Attempts to liberalize the economy of the Philippines are fighting three centuries of entrenched interests. Filipino political science research points out the influence and effects of Spanish colonialism which delivered the control of politics and economics into the hands of a small number of families. In support of nationalism these families legislated against foreign competition in the 1950s. The Foreign Investment Act of 1991 (FIA) liberalizes the investment climate of the Philippines. The FIA permits 100% foreign ownership, without prior BOI approval, of companies engaged in any activity not included in the foreign investment negative list. The foreign investment negative list is comprised of three categories where foreign investment is fully or partially restricted by the constitution or by specific laws. In all three categories foreign ownership is restricted to between zero and 40%. Restriction on setting up export processing zones has also been considerably relaxed. Since 1948 foreign banks have not been allowed to open branches; four existing banks were allowed to continue. Under a 1994 law, 10 foreign banks will be allowed to enter the Philippines, with three branches each. Japan was the largest source of foreign investment in the Philippines until 1991 when the Pilipinas Shell Petroleum Corporation (UK) invested ₱17 billion in a refinery project. Foreign direct investment for 1991 totalled $415.3 million compared to $197.6 million for 1990. Major investors are Taiwan, Hong Kong, South Korea, the US, and China, as well as the UK and Japan. In 1992 Asian investors dominated foreign investment. Filipino capital investment in foreign countries is negligible.

[39]ECONOMIC DEVELOPMENT

Beginning in 1972, the main tenets of the Marcos government's economic policies, as articulated through the National Economic Development Authority, included substantial development of infrastructure, particularly through the use of labor-intensive rather than capital-intensive (i.e., mechanized) methods, and a shift in export emphasis from raw materials to finished and semi-finished commodities. The policies of the Aquino administration have stressed labor-intensive, small- and medium-scale agricultural projects and extensive land reform. In addition, wealth believed to have been amassed by President Marcos was actively being pursued all over the world. Long-range planning has followed a series of economic plans, most of them covering five-year periods. The development program for 1967–70 aimed to increase the growth rate of per capita income from the 0.9% level in 1961–65 to 2.4%; to increase national income by 5.7% per year during the plan period, and to reduce the unemployment rate from 13% (1965) to 7.2% (1970). The government invested $3.5 billion in integrating the traditional and modern sectors of the economy. Marcos's first long-range plan following the 1972 declaration of martial law was a four-year (1974–77) infrastructural development program calling for a total outlay of ₱21,500 million; of the total, 35% was to be expended on transportation, 33% on energy and power, 20% on water resources, 10% on education, health, and welfare, and 2% on telecommunications. A 1974–78 plan, announced in late 1975, envisioned a total outlay of ₱38,000 million (after inflation, a lower figure than the previous plan's). Energy was to be the major focus of the new plan, with 34% of expenditures, followed by transportation, 30%; water resources, 23%; social programs, 7%; and other sectors, 6%. The goals of the 1978–82 plan included an 8% annual growth in GNP, rural development, tax incentives for export-oriented industries, continued self-sufficiency in grain crops despite rapid population growth, and accelerated development of highways, irrigation, and other infrastructure. The 1983–87 plan called for an annual expansion of 6.2% in GNP, improvement of the rural economy and living standards, and amelioration of hunger.

Under the Aquino administration the goals of the 1987–92 plan were self-sufficiency in food production, decentralization of power and decision making, job creation, and rural development. Economic performance for real growth fell far short of plan targets by 25% or more. Structural changes to provide a better investment climate were carried out. The Foreign Investment Act of 1991 liberalized the environment for foreign investment. An Executive Order issued in July 1991 reduced the number of tariff levels over five years and reduced the maximum duty rate from 50% to 30%. Quantitative restrictions were removed from all but a few products. The foreign exchange market was fully deregulated in 1992. A new six-year medium-term development plan

for 1993–98 was presented by the government in May 1993. The plan aimed for 6.5% GNP growth in 1994 and 10% by 1998. Fort Banifacio, the garrison that protected the Marcos dictatorship, situated between two crowded financial districts in Manila, was the subject of a fierce business competition between developers in 1994. The site is slated for development as a commercial center. In May 1994 three laws intended to jump-start the economy were passed by Congress: the expansion of the value-added system (VAT), an increase in stock transaction taxes, and liberalized regulations to encourage more foreign participation in infrastructure needs. Export Processing Zones (EPZs) are industrial estates within which export-oriented firms can operate free of trade barriers and enjoy certain tax advantages. The Export Processing Zone Authority (EPZA) operates four EPZs in the country: in Bataan (the largest), Baguio City(the smallest), Mactan Island, and Cavite (the newest). New growth areas exist in these industrial estates such as the Gateway Industrial Park, Cavite Industrial Estate outside Manila, and rural industrial sites in Laguna and Batangas. The success of the Mactan Export Processing Zone created a boom in Cebu City. Davao City and General Santos City became part of the East Asian Growth Area (EAGA) along with nearby areas of Indonesia, Malaysia, and Brunei. Both former US military facilities, Subic Bay and Clark Air Force Base, were being redeveloped as a free port and an industrial and tourism estate, respectively. During 1946–86, total aid commitments by the US were $3,053.1 million in nonmilitary loans and grants and $1,405.9 million in military loans and grants. Multilateral development aid over the same period totaled $7,173.5 million, of which $4,459.8 million came from the IBRD and $2,220.2 million from the Asian Development Bank. Economic aid to the Philippines as reported by CIA sources (1993) were: US commitments, including Ex-Im (FY70–89), $3.6 billion; Western (non-US) countries, ODA and OOF bilateral commitments (1970–88), $7.9 billion; OPEC bilateral aid (1979–89), $5 million; Communist countries (1975–89), $123 million.

[40]SOCIAL DEVELOPMENT

The government social program includes the purchase and subdivision of big estates for resale on installment plans, the settlement of landless families in new areas, building of rural roads, schools, and medical clinics, and the distribution of relief supplies to the needy. Other programs directly geared to social change fall under the Ministry of Human Settlements and Community Development. Among these are nutrition programs for infants, the Bagong Lipunan Improvement of Sites and Services (BLISS) program for depressed areas, and the Livelihood Improvement Program (Kilusang Kabuhayan at Kaunlaran—KKK) designed to channel economic growth into projects—notably in agriculture, fishing, and cottage and light industries—capable of enhancing self-sufficiency at the village level.

The Social Security System (SSS) covers employees of private firms in industrial and agricultural production. Membership for employers is compulsory. Government employees are covered under the Government Service Insurance System (GSIS). The system's benefits include compensation for confinement due to injury or illness, pensions for temporary incapacity, indemnities to families in case of death, old age pensions, and benefits to widows and orphans. Charges to cover the system are paid jointly by employers and employees. A medical care plan (Medicare), consisting of two programs, one now compulsory for social security participants and another for those not under any insurance system, provides hospital, surgical, medicinal, and medical-expense benefits to members and their dependents. Children below 15 years old cannot be employed except in special circumstances, and there are restrictions on nighttime work by women. Women are eligible for paid maternity leaves of six weeks for the first four births. The maximum maternity benefit in 1991 was ₱4,500.

The government has actively promoted family planning, and despite opposition from Roman Catholic traditionalists (including Pope John Paul II in his February 1981 visit), the program has met with significant success. The fertility rate in the late 1980s was 3.9, down from 5 in the late 1970s. Abortion is illegal.

A handful of women enjoy high prestige and visibility, but most women occupy traditional social roles and occupations. Most, but not all, of the legal rights enjoyed by men are extended to women. Restrictions on property ownership were removed by a 1992 law. In the past, however, anti-discrimination laws have not always been implemented.

41 HEALTH

In 1991, there were 1,663 hospitals; 562 operated by the government, and 1,101 in the private sector. Government hospitals had 46,388 beds, and private hospitals had 35,309. In addition, there were 2,299 rural health units.

In 1991, there were 31,375 physicians, 1,523 dentists, 10,117 nurses, and 12,408 midwives. In 1988, there were 730 pharmacists. There were 0.12 doctors per 1,000 people in 1992, with a nurse to doctor ratio of 3.1. The 1990 population per physician was 8,120.

Pulmonary infections (tuberculosis, pneumonia, bronchitis) are prevalent, but malaria is virtually unknown in larger cities and is being eradicated in the countryside. Malnutrition remains a health problem, despite government assistance in the form of Nutripaks, consisting of indigenous foods such as mung beans and powdered shrimp, made available for infants, children, and pregnant women. In 1990, 19% of children under 5 years old were considered malnourished, and there were 280 reported cases of tuberculosis per 100,000 people.

During the 1980s, a nationwide primary health care program was implemented. As a result, community involvement in health services increased, the prevalence of communicable diseases decreased, and the nutritional state of the population improved. In 1991, 82% of the population had access to safe water and 69% had adequate sanitation. Children up to 1 year of age were immunized in 1992 against tuberculosis (94%); diphtheria, pertussis, and tetanus (92%); polio (92%); and measles (90%).

The infant mortality rate declined from 78.4 per 1,000 live births in 1972 to 46 in 1992. The general mortality rate in 1993 was 6.8 per 1,000 people and maternal mortality was 100 per 100,000 live births in 1991. Average life expectancy was 65 years.

The population of the Phillines was 66.5 million in 1993, with a birth rate of 30.3 per 1,000 people, and 36% of married women (ages 15 to 49) using contraception. There were 2 million births in 1992. Health care expenditures were $883 million in 1990, and 75% of the population had access to health care services in 1992.

42 HOUSING

As of 1980, 93% of all housing units were detached houses, 4% were apartments, 2% were duplexes, and 1% were improvised housing. Owners occupied 80% of all dwellings, 12% were rented, and 7% were occupied rent free. In 1981, government officials placed the need for new housing at over 1.1 million units. Tens of thousands of barrios are scattered throughout the Philippines, each consisting of a double row of small cottages strung out along a single road. Each cottage is generally built on stilts and has a thatched roof, veranda, and small yard. Construction is largely undertaken by the private sector, with the support of government agencies. The Ministry of Human Settlements (MHS), created in 1978, sets housing programs in motion. Its first major program was the Bagong Lipunon Improvement of Sites and Services (BLISS), which undertook 445 projects involving 6,712 units housing 40,272 people. As with many programs begun during the Marcos administration, the projects became rid-den with scandal. More creditable was the Pag-IBIG fund, which was set up to promote savings for housing and provide easy-term housing loans, with contributions from individuals, banks, industries, and the government. By the end of 1985, ₱98 million in loans had been provided to 171,585 members. In 1985, membership contributions totaled ₱1.34 billion, and 1,451 housing loans were approved. The Aquino administration offered tax exemptions to domestic corporations and partnerships with at least 300 employees that invest funds in housing. From 1984 to 1987, an annual average of about 103,150 units were built by the private sector with minimal assistance from the government. The total number of dwellings in 1992 was 10,550,000.

43 EDUCATION

Education is free and compulsory in the primary schools and is coeducational. In 1987, a bill to provide free public secondary education for all students was due for approval in Congress. English is the main medium of instruction, although Pilipino or the local vernacular is used for instruction in the lower primary grades. In 1990, 89.7% of adults were literate (men: 90.0% and women: 89.5%).

In 1991, 34,081 primary schools had an enrollment of 10,558,105 students and secondary schools had 4,208,151 students. The same year, there were 316,182 primary school teachers and 129,700 secondary school teachers. The University of the Philippines, in Quezon City, with branches in major islands, is the leading institution of higher learning. In addition, there are some 50 other universities, including the University of Santo Tomás, founded in 1611 and run by the Dominican friars. In 1991, universities and all higher level institutions had 1,656,815 students.

44 LIBRARIES AND MUSEUMS

The National Library in Manila has an estimated 1.3 million volumes. The Filipiniana, and Asia Division contains over 100,000 Filipiniana books. Large libraries are in the universities, notably the University of the Philippines (878,000 volumes), the University of Santo Tomás (306,000), the University of the East (278,000), and the University of San Carlos (215,000).

The National Museum in Manila collects and exhibits materials and conducts research in anthropology, ethnography, archaeology, botany, geology, history, and maps. The Santo Tomás Museum contains an art gallery and archaeology and anthropology collections. Three relatively new museums in Manila exhibit primarily art: Lopez Memorial Museum (1960) exhibits Filipino painters; Metropolitan Museum (1976) exhibits a variety of art forms; and the Philippines Presidential Museum (1986) exhibits fine and decorative arts.

45 MEDIA

There are four nationwide telephone networks, including the Philippine Long Distance Telephone Company, run mainly by the private sector, with services concentrated in urban areas. Overseas communications operate via satellites and undersea cables. In 1991 there were 986,117 telephones. A 20-year national telecommunications development plan is designed to modernize and improve the services in the country by the year 2000. Radio and television are operated by both government agencies and private concerns. Radio transmitting stations numbered 322 (267 AM and 55 FM) in 1989, and there were 5 major television networks and 33 broadcasting stations. In 1991, there were 8,810,000 radios and 2,800,000 television sets.

Under martial law, censorship of the press, radio, and television was imposed by the Marcos government. Many reporters, editors, and publishers were arrested during this period. Censorship was revoked under the Aquino administration. In 1991 there were some 38 daily newspapers, as compared with 6 during the Marcos era. The following were among the leading dailies published in metropolitan Manila (with estimated 1991 circulations):

	LANGUAGE	CIRCULATION
People's Journal	English/Pilipino	345,000
Manila Times	English	275,000
Manila Bulletin	English	275,000
Philippine Daily Inquirer	English	165,000
Balita	Pilipino	150,900

46ORGANIZATIONS

Between 1939 and 1949, some 1,370 cooperative associations with 260,134 members were organized. In general, however, consumer cooperatives were ineffectual before 1952. In that year, the first effective cooperative movement, the Agricultural Credit Cooperative Finance Administration, was established with an authorized capital of ₱100 million; its general aims were to promote organization of small farmers, assist in obtaining credit, establish orderly and systematic marketing, and upgrade agriculture. However, because of graft and corruption within the agency and other parts of the cooperative movement, the cooperative associations slowly died out.

The Philippine Chamber of Commerce and Industry has branches in metropolitan Manila and other important cities, and there are associations of producers and industrial firms in many areas. The Philippine Academy is the oldest and best-known scholarly organization. There are many associations of persons active in such fields as agriculture, architecture, art, biology, chemistry, economics, library service, literature, engineering, medicine, nutrition, veterinary service, and the press.

47TOURISM, TRAVEL, AND RECREATION

The increase in tourism that followed the ouster of Ferdinand Marcos was dampened by the national disasters of the early 1990's. In 1991 visitor arrivals dropped 7.1% between 1990 and 1991. That year, 849,000 tourists arrived, 452,000 from Southeast Asia and 216,000 from the Americas. The Japanese were the top visitors (20.8%) and US visitors were the next largest group. Hong Kong, Taiwan, an Australians were other important sources of visitors. Revenues from tourism totaled $1.28 billion.

Hotels in Manila meet international standards. A convention center and several major new hotels were added in Manila in the mid-1970s. In recent years, hotels with good accommodations have been constructed in some provincial cities. In 1991, there were 13,262 hotel rooms with 26,524 beds and a 64.7% occupancy rate. Manila remains the chief tourist attraction. Other points of interest are the 2,000-year-old rice terraces north of Baguio; Vigan, the old Spanish capital; Cebu, the oldest city; numerous beaches and mountain wilderness areas; and homes formerly owned by the Marcoses. Each tourist must have a valid passport and an onward or return ticket; no visa is required for a stay of less than 21 days.

Basketball is the national sport, followed in popularity by baseball and soccer. Jai-alai is popular in Manila and Cebu. Cockfighting is legal and often televised.

48FAMOUS FILIPINOS

Filipinos have made their most important marks in the political arena. Foremost are José Rizal (1861–96), a distinguished novelist, poet, physician, linguist, statesman, and national hero; Andrés Bonifacio (1863–97), the leader of the secret Katipunan movement against Spain; and Emilio Aguinaldo y Famy (1869–1964), the commander of the revolutionary forces and president of the revolutionary First Philippine Republic (1899). Notable Filipinos of this century include Manuel Luis Quezon y Molina (1878–1944), the first Commonwealth president; Ramón Magsaysay (1907–57), a distinguished leader in the struggle with the Hukbalahaps; and Carlos Peña Rómulo (1899–1985), a Pulitzer Prize-winning author and diplomat and the president of the

fourth UN General Assembly. Ferdinand Edralin Marcos (b.1917–89), who won distinction as a guerrilla fighter during the Japanese occupation, was the dominant political figure in the Philippines from his first election to the presidency in November 1965 to his ouster in February 1986. His wife, Imelda Romualdez Marcos (b.1930), emerged as a powerful force within her husband's government during the 1970s. Leading critics of the Marcos government during the late 1970s and early 1980s were Benigno S. Aquino, Jr. (1933–83) and Jaime Sin (b.1928), who became the archbishop of Manila in 1974 and a cardinal in 1976. Maria Corazon Cojuangco Aquino (b.1933), the widow of Benigno, opposed Marcos for the presidency in February 1986 and took office when he went into exile in the same month.

Lorenzo Ruiz (fl.17th cent.) was canonized, along with 15 companion martyrs, as the first Filipino saint. Fernando M. Guerrero (1873–1929) was the greatest Philippine poet in Spanish. Two painters of note were Juan Luna y Novicio (1857–99) and Félix Resurrección Hidalgo y Padilla (1853–1913). Contemporary writers who have won recognition include Claro M. Recto (1890–1960), José García Villa (b.1914), and Carlos Bulosan (1914–56). José A. Estella (1870–1945) is the best-known Filipino composer. Filipino prizefighters have included two world champions, Pancho Villa (Francisco Guilledo, 1901–25) and Ceferino García (1910–81).

49DEPENDENCIES

The Philippines has no territories or colonies.

50BIBLIOGRAPHY

Brands, H. W. *Bound to Empire: The United States and the Philippines.* New York: Oxford University Press, 1992.

Bresnan, John (ed.). *Crisis in the Philippines: The Marcos Era and Beyond.* Princeton, N.J.: Princeton University Press, 1986.

Carlson, Sevinc, and Robert A. Kilmarx (eds.). *U.S.–Philippines Economic Relations.* Washington, D.C.: Georgetown University Center for Strategic and International Studies, 1971.

Davis, Leonard. *The Philippines: People, Poverty, and Politics.* New York: St. Martin's, 1987.

Dolan, Ronald E. (ed.). *Philippines: A Country Study.* 4th ed. Washington, D.C.: Library of Congress, 1993.

Doronila, Amando. *The State, Economic Transformation, and Political Change in the Philippines, 1946–1972.* New York: Oxford University Press, 1992.

Karnow, Stanley. *In our Image: America's Empire in the Philippines.* New York: Random House, 1989.

Kessler, Richard J. *Rebellion and Repression in the Philippines.* New Haven: Yale University Press, 1989.

Marcos, Ferdinand E. *The Democratic Revolution in the Philippines.* New York: Prentice-Hall International, 1974.

Miller, Stuart Creighton. *"Benevolent Assimilation": The American Conquest of the Philippines, 1899–1903.* New Haven, Conn.: Yale University Press, 1982.

O'Brien, Niall. *Revolution from the Heart.* New York: Oxford University Press, 1987.

Pedrosa, Carmen Navarro. *Imelda Marcos.* New York: St. Martin's, 1987.

Rómulo, Carlos Peña. *Crusade in Asia: Philippine Victory.* New York: Day, 1955.

Richardson, Jim. *Philippines.* Santa Barbara, Calif.: Clio Press, 1989.

Steinberg, David Joel. *The Philippines, a Singular and a Plural Place.* 3rd ed. Boulder, Colo.: Westview Press, 1994.

Thompson, W. Scott. *The Philippines in Crisis: Development and Security in the Aquino Era 1986–92.* New York: St. Martin's, 1992.

Wurfel, David. *Filipino Politics: Development and Decay.* Ithaca: Cornell University Press, 1988.

PORTUGUESE ASIAN DEPENDENCY

MACAU

Macau (Macao) is situated on the south coast of China, at the mouth of the Pearl (Zhu) River, almost directly opposite Hong Kong, which is about 65 km (40 mi) away. Located at 22°6' to 22°13'N and 113°33' to 113°37'E, Macau consists of a peninsula, about 5 km (3 mi) long and 1.6 km (1 mi) wide, and two small islands, Taipa and Coloane. The total area is about 16 sq km (6 sq mi), and the total coastline is 41 km (25 mi). The climate is subtropical, with high humidity from April to October, when Macau receives most of its rainfall. Daily maximum temperatures average 29°C (84°F) during the summer; normal daily temperatures are less than 20°C (68°F) during the winter months.

The 1993 population was 477,850, representing an increase of 83% over the 1981 census figure of 261,680. The population density of 29,866 per sq km (79,642 per sq mi) was among the highest in the world. Chinese, many of them refugees from the People's Republic of China (PRC), constitute 97% of the total; the remaining 3% are Portuguese or of mixed Chinese-Portuguese ancestry. Large-scale movement of Chinese in and out of Macau has inevitably affected the economic and social life of the territory. The common language is Chinese, usually spoken in the Cantonese or Mandarin dialect. Portuguese is spoken by government officials, and some English, French, and Spanish are also understood. Buddhism and Roman Catholicism are the dominant religions.

In 1993 there were about 42 km (26 mi) of highways. A causeway links Taipa and Coloane islands, and a 2.7-km (1.7-mi) bridge connects Macau and Taipa. Macau's main asset is its harbor; in 1985, 4,699,992 ship passengers and 2,677,900 tons of cargo entered the port. Ferries, hydrofoils, and jetfoils offer shuttle service between Macau and Hong Kong; in 1994, a 240-km (149-mi) road between Macau and Hong Kong, runs through Guangdong Province in the PRC.

Macau is the oldest European settlement in the Far East. The first Portuguese attempts to establish relations with China were made in the early 16th century. In 1557, the Chinese authorities agreed to Portuguese settlement of Macau, with leasehold rights. The Portuguese, however, treated Macau as their possession and established a municipal government in the form of a senate of the local inhabitants. Disputes concerning jurisdiction and administration developed. In 1833, Macau together with Timor became an overseas province of Portugal under the control of the governor-general of Goa, and in 1849, Portugal succeeded in having Macau declared a free port. On 26 March 1887, China confirmed perpetual occupation and governance of Macau and its dependencies by Portugal, but the question of the delimitation of the boundaries was left unsettled.

The former overseas province of Portuguese Timor, now known as East Timor, is under the de facto control of Indonesia, having been incorporated as an Indonesian province on 3 May 1976. Neither the UN nor Portugal has formally recognized the annexation.

As the only neutral port on the South China Sea during World War II, Macau enjoyed a modicum of prosperity. In 1949, the government of the PRC renounced the "unequal treaty" granting Portuguese suzerainty over Macau. Civil disturbances in late 1966 between Macau police and Chinese leftist groups resulted in

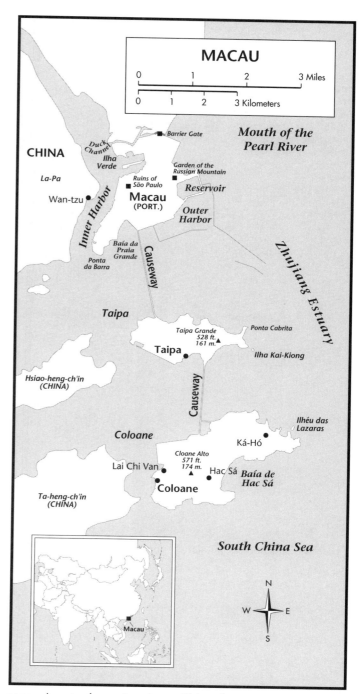

concessions to the territory's pro-China elements. The 1974 military coup in Portugal led to a constitutional change in Macau's status from a Portuguese province to a "special territory." In January 1976, Portugal's remaining few hundred troops were withdrawn from Macau. China and Portugal established diplomatic ties in 1980. In March 1987, the PRC and Portugal reached an agreement for the return of Macau to the PRC on 20 December 1999. The PRC guaranteed not to interfere in Macau's capitalist economy and way of life for a period of 50 years.

In the interim, Macau continues to be ruled by a Portugal-appointed governor, although it is now empowered to make its own laws, appoint and control its own civil service, and contract directly for foreign loans. A 17-member Legislative Assembly has 6 members elected directly, 6 members nominated by cultural, economic, and religious groups, and 5 appointed by the governor. One delegate is elected from Macau to Portugal's National Assembly.

The unit of currency is the Macau pataca (P) of 100 avos; Hong Kong dollars also circulate freely. There are coins of 10, 20, and 50 avos and 1 and 5 patacas, and notes of 5, 10, 50, 100, and 500 patacas. As of January 1991, P1 = US$0.1248 (or US$1 = P8.0134). In 1985, the government budget was balanced at P2,268.8 million. Corporate taxes and import duties are important sources of revenue; major expenditures are for finance, security, education, and health and welfare. The territory has its own currency-issuing bank, 12 commercial banks, and 10 foreign banks.

Macau's economy is consumer-oriented. There is little agriculture, and the territory is heavily dependent on imports from China for food, fresh water, and electricity. Important economic sectors are commerce, tourism, gambling, fishing, and light industry. There are small- or medium-scale enterprises concerned especially with the finishing of imported semimanufactured goods, in particular the manufacture of clothing, ceramics, electronic equipment, toys, and fireworks, and the printing and dyeing of cloth and yarn.

Macau's historic role has been that of a gateway for southern China. It has close trade relations with neighboring Hong Kong, another free port, which serves as a point of transshipment for Macau's exports and imports. Gold trading, formerly a major facet in Macau's economy, virtually came to a halt in 1974–75 following Hong Kong's decision to lift its own restrictions on gold trading. Total exports in 1990 were valued at $1.5 billion. The principal exports are textiles, clothing, artificial flowers, ceramics, optical equipment, electronic goods, leatherwork, toys, and fish. Of total 1990 exports, Hong Kong took 13%, the US 36%, Germany 12%, and France 8%. The principal imports for domestic use are food, fuel, machinery, iron and steel, and automobiles. Total imports in 1990 were valued at $1.8 billion, of which Hong Kong provided 35%, China 22%, Japan 17%. Transit trade still dominates the flow in and out of Macau.

Government schools are operated mainly for the children of civil servants and wealthier families, while poor Chinese students are educated in schools indirectly supported by China. Macau's University of East Asia, opened in 1981. The Medical and Health Department, although critically understaffed, operates a 400-bed hospital. The 800-bed Kiang Vu Hospital has a largely China-trained staff.

Macau has six postal stations and two telephone and two telegraph stations. The number of telephones in Macau was 52,000 in 1993. Macau has 4 AM and 3 FM stations. A government and a private radio station each broadcast in Portuguese and Chinese; there were 11 newspapers in 1985, 6 in Chinese and 5 in Portuguese. Macau receives television broadcasts from Hong Kong.

With its picturesque seaport and varied gambling facilities, Macau looks to tourism as its chief source of revenue. In 1991 there were 1,695,453 visitors, over 80% from Hong Kong. Of those classed as tourists, 88,331 came from Japan, 7,209 from the UK, and 9,800 from the US and Canada. Travelers must have a valid passport and a visa, which is generally purchased at the point of disembarkation.

QATAR

State of Qatar
Dawlat Qatar

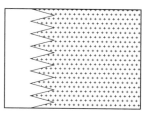

CAPITAL: Doha (Ad-Dawhah).

FLAG: Maroon with white serrated border at the hoist.

ANTHEM: *Qatar National Anthem.*

MONETARY UNIT: The Qatar riyal (QR) of 100 dirhams was introduced on 13 May 1973. There are coins of 1, 5, 10, 25, and 50 dirhams, and notes of 1, 5, 10, 50, 100, and 500 riyals. QR1 = $0.2747 (or $1 = QR3.64).

WEIGHTS AND MEASURES: The metric system is the legal standard, although some British measures are still in use.

HOLIDAYS: Emir's Succession Day, 22 February; Independence Day, 3 September. Muslim religious holidays include 'Id al-Fitr, 'Id al-'Adha', and Milad an-Nabi.

TIME: 3 PM = noon GMT.

¹LOCATION, SIZE, AND EXTENT

Comprising an area of 11,000 sq km (4,247 sq mi), the State of Qatar consists of a peninsula projecting northward into the Persian Gulf, extending about 160 km (100 mi) N-S and 90 km (55 mi) E-W. Comparatively, the area occupied by Qatar is slightly smaller than the state of Connecticut. It is bordered on the S by the United Arab Emirates (UAE) and Sa'udi Arabia and has a total boundary length of 623 km (387 mi). In the late 1970s, Sa'udi Arabia and the UAE reportedly reached a border agreement making Sa'udi Arabia Qatar's only land neighbor, but as of 1987, no documentation had been filed with the UN. Qatar also includes a number of islands, of which the most important is Halul. Qatar's boundary disputes with Bahrain disrupted relations between the two countries in the mid-1980s. In 1991, they agreed to refer their dispute over the Hawar Islands to the International Court of Justice at The Hague. In 1992, there was a minor clash between Qatari and Sa'udi troops over a disputed border. That quarrel was resolved with a boundary agreement signed in Cairo in December 1992.

Qatar's capital city, Doha, is located on the Persian Gulf coast.

²TOPOGRAPHY

The terrain is generally flat and sandy, rising gradually from the east to a central limestone plateau. About 56 km (35 mi) long, the Dukhan anticline rises from the west coast as a chain of hills of up to 100 m (325 ft) in height. Some low cliffs mark the northern end of the east coast. The presence of extensive salt flats at the base of the peninsula supports the theory that Qatar was once an island.

³CLIMATE

Qatar's summer, from May to October, is extremely hot. Mean temperatures in June are 42°C (108°F), dropping to 15°C (59°F) in winter. Humidity is high along the coast. Rainfall is minimal.

⁴FLORA AND FAUNA

Vegetation is generally sparse and typical of Gulf desert regions. The gazelle, once common in Qatar, is now rarely seen. Jerboas (desert rats) and an occasional fox are found. Birds include flamingo, cormorant, osprey, kestrel, plover, lark, and other

migrants. Reptiles include monitors, other lizards, and land snakes. Life in the seas around Qatar is considerable and varied, including prawn, king mackerel, shark, grouper, and swordfish.

⁵ENVIRONMENT

Environmental responsibility is vested in the Ministry of Industry and Agriculture. An Environmental Protection Committee was created in 1984 to monitor environmental problems. Conservation of oil supplies, preservation of the natural wildlife heritage, and increasing the water supply through desalination are high on Qatar's environmental priority list. Air, water, and land pollution are also significant environmental issues in Qatar. In addition to smog and acid rain, the nation was affected by the air pollution generated during the Persian Gulf War. Pollution from the oil industry, along with heavy metals from other industrial facilities, are a threat to the nation's water. Salinization of the water supply is also a problem. The nation's soils have been damaged by pesticides and fertilizers, and its agricultural land is in danger of desertification. As of 1987, the hawksbill and green sea turtle were considered endangered species, and protection was afforded to a group of rare white oryx.

⁶POPULATION

The 1986 population was 369,079, with some 80% residing on the eastern coast in the vicinity of Doha. It was estimated at 486,000 in 1990. Two other towns have grown up around the oil industry; Dukhan, on the west coast, and the port of Umm Sa'id, south of Doha. Average density in 1990 was 42.5 per sq km (110 per sq mi). A population of 542,000 was projected for the year 2000, assuming a crude birthrate of 20.4 per 1,000 population and a death rate of 4.1 during 1995–2000.

⁷MIGRATION

In 1993, the number of immigrant workers was about 85,000, including Pakistanis, Indians, and Iranians.

⁸ETHNIC GROUPS

The indigenous population (about 100,000) descends from Bedouin tribes which migrated to Qatar during the 1700s. Pakistanis, Indians, Iranians, and Gulf and Palestinian Arabs are among the leading immigrant groups.

9LANGUAGES

Arabic is the national language, but English is widely spoken, and Farsi is used by smaller groups in Doha.

10RELIGIONS

Islam is the official religion of Qatar and is practiced by the great majority of the people. The Qataris are mainly Sunni of the Wahhabi sect. There are also small populations of Christians, Hindus, and Bahais.

11TRANSPORTATION

The modern road system dates from 1967. As of 1991 there were an estimated 1,500 km (932 mi) of highways, about 67% bituminized. Qatar has overland truck routes from Europe through Sa'udi Arabia via the Trans-Arabian Highway and road links with the UAE and Oman. In 1991, there were 115,149 passenger cars and 47,228 commercial vehicles registered. Doha International Airport, served by more than a dozen international airlines, serviced an estimated 1.1 million passengers in 1990. Qatar maintains modern deepwater ports at Doha and Umm Sa'id, where a tanker terminal is located. Qatar's National Navigation and Transport Co. enjoys a monopoly on arriving shipments. In 1991, the merchant fleet consisted of 23 vessels with 474,000 GRT.

12HISTORY

Archaeological evidence shows that human habitation existed in Qatar for many centuries prior to the modern age; however, little is known of Qatar's history until the 18th century. The ath-Thani family, forebears of the present rulers, arrived in Qatar then from what is now Sa'udi Arabia. During the same century, the al-Khalifah family, who currently rule Bahrain, arrived from Kuwait.

In 1868, Britain intervened on behalf of the Qatari nobles and negotiated the Perpetual Maritime Truce, signed by Muhammad bin Thani, an accord that terminated the Bahraini claim to Qatar in exchange for a tribute payment. In 1872, however, Qatar fell under Ottoman occupation, and Jasim bin Muhammad bin Thani became Turkish deputy-governor of Qatar. Turkish dominion prevailed until the outbreak of World War I and the subsequent withdrawal of the Turks from the Arabian Peninsula. Qatar thereupon established its independence and, in 1916, Sheikh 'Abdallah bin Jasim ath-Thani signed a treaty with the UK granting British protection in exchange for a central role for the UK in Qatar's foreign affairs. A 1934 treaty further strengthened this relationship. Commercial quantities of high-quality oil were discovered at Dukhan in 1940, but full-scale exploitation did not begin until 1949.

In 1960, Sheikh Ahmad bin 'Ali ath-Thani succeeded his father, who had become too old to rule effectively. Social and economic development during the subsequent decade was disappointing, especially in view of the increasing availability of oil revenues. In January 1968, the UK announced its intention to withdraw its forces from the Persian Gulf States by the end of 1971. Discussions took place among the Trucial States, Bahrain, and Qatar, with a view to forming a federation. The Trucial States formed the UAE, but Qatar could not agree to the terms of the union. On 3 September 1971, the independent State of Qatar was declared. A new treaty of friendship and cooperation was signed with the UK, and Qatar was soon admitted to membership in the Arab League and the UN.

On 22 February 1972, Sheikh Khalifa bin Hamad ath-Thani, the deputy emir and prime minister, seized power in a peaceful coup, deposing his cousin, Sheikh Ahmad. Since his accession, Sheikh Khalifa has pursued a vigorous program of economic and social reforms, including the transfer of royal income to the state. On 31 May 1977, Sheikh Khalifa appointed Sheikh Hamad bin Khalifa ath-Thani as heir apparent and minister of defense.

In 1981, Qatar, along with the other Persian Gulf states of Bahrain, Kuwait, Oman, Sa'udi Arabia, and the UAE, established the Gulf Cooperation Council (GCC). The GCC attempted to mediate the war between Iran and Iraq, which had erupted in September 1980, but at the same time gave support to Iraq. Qatar's boundary disputes with Bahrain disrupted relations between the two countries in the mid-1980s. In 1991, they agreed to refer their dispute over the Hawar Islands to the International Court of Justice at The Hague. In 1992, there was a minor clash between Qatari and Sa'udi troops over a disputed border. That quarrel was resolved with a boundary agreement signed in Cairo in December 1992.

Qatari forces, although small in size, are active in the collective defense of the GCC and played a helpful role on the allied side in the Gulf War against Iraq.

13GOVERNMENT

Qatar is a monarchy ruled by an emir. In 1970, in anticipation of independence, Qatar promulgated a Basic Law, including a bill of rights, that provides for a 9-member executive Council of Ministers (cabinet) and a 30-member legislative Advisory Council, whose members serve three-year terms. The Council of Ministers, appointed by the emir and led by a prime minister (the head of government), formulates public policy and directs the ministries. Sheikh Khalifa has served as acting prime minister since the 1972 coup, and the Advisory Council has had little effective power. The ruling ath Thani family holds a majority of cabinet positions and most of the key posts. All government posts have remained appointive; no electoral system has been instituted, and no provisions for suffrage have been established.

14POLITICAL PARTIES

There are no organized political parties. Security measures against dissidents are firm and efficient. There is no serious opposition movement. Citizens with grievances may appeal directly to the emir.

15LOCAL GOVERNMENT

Municipal councils have been established in Doha, Khor, Ash-Shamal, and several other towns. The councils manage their own planning and development programs, but they remain directly accountable to the Ministry of Municipal Affairs.

16JUDICIAL SYSTEM

The legal system is based on the Shari'ah (canonical Muslim law). The Basic Law of 1970, however, provided for the creation of an independent judiciary, including the Court of Appeal, which has final jurisdiction in civil and criminal matters; the Higher Criminal Court, which judges major criminal cases; the Lower Criminal Court; the Civil Court; and the Labor Court, which judges claims involving employees and their employers. The Shari'ah Court has jurisdiction in family and criminal cases, and may also assume jurisdiction in commercial or civil cases if requested by a Muslim litigant. Non-Muslims may not bring suits as plaintiffs in the Shari'ah Court. As a result, non-Muslim residents have difficulty obtaining full legal recourse in disputes with Qatari nationals.

The losing party in all types of courts may submit their cases to an appeals court. In cases tried by the Shari'ah Court, however, it is possible that the same judge will hear both the original case and the appeal.

17 ARMED FORCES

The Qatar security force consists of 6,000 army, 700 naval, and

800 air force personnel. Military equipment includes 18 combat aircraft, 20 armed helicopters, and 9 missile-equipped coastal patrol boats; most of the weaponry has been purchased from France. During the 1980–84 period, Qatar's arms imports totaled more than $6.5 billion, then dropped to $170 million (1985–1991). A police force, numbering around 6,000, has responsibility for internal security, criminal investigations, traffic, and marine patrols. Defense spending may be as high as $934 million (1991).

[18]INTERNATIONAL COOPERATION

Following independence, Qatar joined both the UN (21 September 1971) and the Arab League. Qatar participates in ESCWA and all the nonregional specialized agencies except IDA and IFC; it is also a de facto participant in GATT. Qatar belongs to OPEC and OAPEC, as well as to G-77 and the GCC.

[19]ECONOMY

Until recent decades, the Qatar peninsula was an undeveloped, impoverished area, with a scant living provided by the traditional occupations of pearl diving, fishing, and nomadic herding. In 1940, a major oil discovery was made at Dukhan and, in the ensuing decades, oil has been the dominant factor in the Qatari economy. Oil exports in 1985 earned an estimated QR10.3 billion, or 91% of the total, down from 95% in 1980. The collapse of international oil prices in 1986 reduced export earnings by half and cut nominal GDP by 18%. In 1990, crude oil and petroleum-related manufacturing accounted for more than 50% of GDP. The discovery of a vast field of natural gas unassociated with Qatar's oil fields promises to add a new dimension to the economy. In 1987, work on the first phase of the North Gas Field project Phase I, with a production capacity of 800 million cubic feet per day, began and was inaugurated in 1991. While Phase I production is meant for domestic consumption, the Phase II development envisages the production of at least an additional 800 million cubic feet per day for export to Japan as liquefied natural gas. The first shipment is scheduled for early 1997.

Other economic activities remain limited. Agriculture has received considerable attention in recent years, but most food is still imported. The state encourages free enterprise, provided it does not conflict with the public interest. Real property, however, may be acquired only by Qatari nationals.

[20]INCOME

In 1992, Qatar's GNP was $8,511 million at current prices, or $16,240 per capita, with a real growth rate in per capita GNP of –6.9%.

In 1991 the GDP was $8.1 billion in current US dollars. It is estimated that in 1988 agriculture, hunting, forestry, and fishing contributed 1% to GDP; mining and quarrying, 27%; manufacturing, 12%; electricity, gas, and water, 2%; construction, 5%; wholesale and retail trade, 7%; transport, storage, and communication, 2%; finance, insurance, real estate, and business services, 11%; community, social, and personal services, 1%; and other sources, 32%.

[21]LABOR

About 70% of the economically active population is engaged in industry (largely oil-related), commerce, and services. Of the remainder, about 10% work in the agricultural sector and 20% in government. No labor may be recruited without the approval of the Department of Labor, and vacancies must be offered first to Qataris, second to Arabs, and only then to foreigners, who comprised 85% of the work force in 1992. Working conditions are governed by the labor laws of 1972, which provide for a 48-hour workweek, annual leave, severance notice, and holiday and sick-

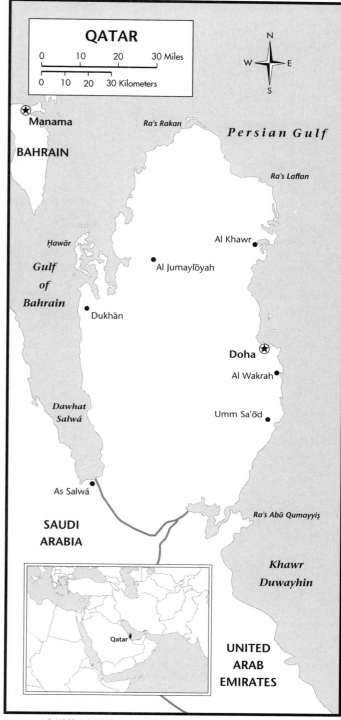

LOCATION: 26°23′ to 24°31′N; 50°43′ to 51°41′E. **BOUNDARY LENGTHS:** Persian Gulf coastline, 378 km (235 mi); UAE, 45 km (28 mi); Sa'udi Arabia, 67 km (42 mi). **TERRITORIAL SEA LIMIT:** 3 mi.

ness allowances. The minimum working age is 18. There are no trade unions, and strikes are permitted only after the case has been presented to the Labor Conciliation Board and an agreement cannot be reached. Government employees, security forces employees, domestic workers, and members of an employer's family are not permitted to strike, nor are workers in public health or security if such a strike would harm the public or lead to property damage.

22AGRICULTURE

Agriculture is constrained by lack of adequate fertile soil, rainfall, and underground water sources; the aquifers which supply the crops are expected to soon run dry. Recently, treated waste water has been used for irrigation. In 1992, only 0.5% (6,000 hectares/14,800 acres) of the total land area was under cultivation. That year, 6,000 tons of dates were produced, mostly for local consumption. Rice is also grown for the domestic market.

23ANIMAL HUSBANDRY

According to 1992 estimates, Qatar had 11,000 head of cattle, 132,000 sheep, 103,000 goats, and 29,000 camels. Output in 1992 included about 5,000 tons of beef and mutton, and 4,000 chickens. Dairy and poultry production meets about 25% of domestic needs. Public, private, and foreign financing have all been used recently to establish or expand dairy and poultry farming.

24FISHING

The Qatar National Fishing Co., formed as a Qatar-UK partnership in 1966, was wholly taken over by Qatar in 1980 and has its own shrimp fishing fleet and processing facilities. Fish and shellfish production in 1991 totaled 8,136 tons (up from 5,702 tons in 1990), more than 80% of local requirements.

Pearl fishing, once important in Qatar, has virtually disappeared. The principal fishing facilities at Doha and Al Khor have been improved. Overfishing and pollution have adversely affected catches, and there is further concern that oil pollution from the Gulf War may worsen conditions even further.

25FORESTRY

There are no forests in Qatar.

26MINING

Aside from petroleum and natural gas, Qatar has few exploitable minerals. In 1991, estimated production of cement was 336,000 tons; limestone, 850,000 tons; and sulfur, 53,000 tons.

27ENERGY AND POWER

Qatar's substantial oil reserves, estimated at 3.7 billion barrels in 1993, dominate the country's economy. For reasons of financial stability and resource conservation, the decision was made in the mid-1970s to limit oil production to no more than 500,000 barrels a day. Production has fluctuated but steadily risen from 310,000 barrels per day in 1983 to 410,000 by 1989 to 485,000 in 1992. Offshore production accounts for about 40% of the total, mainly from three fields about 50 miles from the coast. Petroleum extraction and refining accounts for 50% of GDP; oil revenues for 1990 totaled $3.6 billion.

Total control over oil production and marketing was assumed by the government in early 1977. The Qatar General Petroleum Corp. (QGPC) controls all oil and gas extraction and refining and also acts as an umbrella organization for a number of joint ventures. Qatar's gas reserves are estimated at 227 trillion cu ft (6.4 trillion cu m), representing 4.6% of the world's known reserves; output was estimated at 330,000 million cu ft (9,340 million cu m) in 1992. Nearly all of Qatar's natural gas reserves are in the North Dome Field, considered to be the largest natural gas field (unassociated with oil) in the world. The first of three development phases was completed in 1991, resulting in the production of 800 million cu ft per day of natural gas.

Qatar's electrical capacity was 1,410 Mw in 1991, as compared with 70 Mw in 1970. Power production in 1991 reached 4.7 billion kwh. There are three main electrical power stations, at Ra's Abu Aboud, Al-'Arish, and Ra's Abu Fantas.

28INDUSTRY

Industry in Qatar is restricted by the small size of the population and the paucity of resources other than petroleum and natural gas. Qatar has nevertheless launched an ambitious industrialization plan aimed at diversifying the sources of national income and creating an economy which is not totally dependent on oil revenues. State enterprises in the late 1980s included the Qatar Iron and Steel Co., which produced 550,000 tons in 1989, the Qatar Fertilizer Co., responsible for 714,000 tons of ammonia and 780,000 tons of urea in 1989; the Qatar National Cement Co., with an output of 275,200 tons of portland and cement in 1988; and the Qatar Petrochemical Company, with an output of 295,000 tons of ethylene, 181,000 tons of polyethylene, and 52,00 tons of sulphur in 1989.

29SCIENCE AND TECHNOLOGY

The Scientific and Applied Research Center, within the University of Qatar, coordinates the nation's technological development and seeks to develop ways to utilize the country's natural resources. A soil research station is located at Rodet al-Farassa. In 1986, total expenditures on research and development amounted to 6.7 million riyals; 61 technicians and 229 scientists and engineers were engaged in research and development.

30DOMESTIC TRADE

As elsewhere in the Gulf, wholesale and retail operations in Qatar are frequently combined in the same enterprise. Local laws require that commercial agents be of Qatari nationality.

Normal business hours are from 7:30 AM to 12 noon and from 3:30 to 6 PM. Government offices are open from 7 AM to 1 PM, and banks from 7:30 to 11:30 AM. Consumer advertising can be displayed in motion picture theaters, in the press, and on billboards. Radio and television services do not accept advertising.

31FOREIGN TRADE

By 1985, crude oil supplied 91% of Qatar's annual export earnings. Exports fell from $5.82 billion in 1981 to $3.74 billion in 1992. Principal non-oil products are fertilizers and basic metals. The main destinations of crude oil exports are Japan, Singapore, Brazil, and Taiwan.

Imports, traditionally less than exports, amounted to $2 billion in 1992. Main imports are food, industrial supplies, processed goods, machinery, capital equipment, transport equipment, and consumer items. The most important suppliers are Japan, UK, US, Germany, Italy, and France.

32BALANCE OF PAYMENTS

In recent years, Qatar has had a persistent trade surplus, while maintaining an overall balance of payments deficit. The gap in the balance of payments is largely due to massive imports in services and person transfers, and somewhat to outflowing capital transfers.

33BANKING AND SECURITIES

Qatar's monetary and banking system comprises the Qatar Monetary Agency, established in 1973, and 13 commercial banks, 5 of which are Qatari owned. The Qatar National Bank handles most government business and some central bank functions. The Qatar Monetary Agency, a quasi-central bank, plays a large role in controlling and supervising the monetary sector. In 1993, foreign assets of the commercial banks stood at QR8,224.0 million.

There is no stock exchange. Shares in Qatari public companies are traded through banks.

34INSURANCE

The Qatar National Insurance Co. was among the seven insurance companies represented in Qatar in 1984. Gross premiums paid to insurance companies in 1984 totaled QR219.7 million.

35 PUBLIC FINANCE

Revenues from oil and gas constitute about 90% of total government income. From 1986 to 1990, the government ran a deficit due to the drop in oil revenues from fallen prices. These deficits often have resulted in the procrastination of payments by the government, which creates a financial difficulty for many private companies.

36 TAXATION

The major tax is an income tax levied on companies producing oil. The first QR70,000 of corporate income is not taxed, and the maximum rate is 50%. There is no personal tax liability in Qatar for either foreigners or nationals.

37 CUSTOMS AND DUTIES

Import licenses are not required except for liquor (consumption of which is limited to non-Muslims). Customs duties are 4% on all commodities except for alcoholic beverages (50%), tobacco and cigarettes (50%), and records and phonographs (15%). A 20% tariff is imposed on cement, steel bars, and other products that compete with goods produced in Qatar. The importing of pork and any goods from Israel or South Africa is forbidden.

38 FOREIGN INVESTMENT

The Qatar government encourages overseas investment in Qatar conditioned on a majority Qatari interest. Norway's Norsk Hydro owns 25% of the Qatar Fertilizer Co.; Kobe Steel and Tokyo Boeki owns 20% and 10%, respectively, of the Qatar Steel Co.; and Orkem of France holds 16% of the Qatar Petrochemical Company. The Qatar Investment Board, established in February 1972, develops both incoming and outgoing investments.

39 ECONOMIC DEVELOPMENT

Qatar follows a policy of diversifying and extending its industrial and commercial activities to reduce the current dependence on oil. Infrastructure, heavy and light industry, agriculture, and fishing have all been development targets. The Industrial Development Committee encourages investment and supervises industrial growth. The government also uses surplus oil revenues on the international money market to protect the purchasing power of those revenues. Qatar is currently preparing to launch some major/minor projects worth about $7 billion: LNG plant expansion of the present fertilizer and petrochemical plants, aluminum smelter, Al-Wusail power/water desalination plant, new Doha international airport, and upgrading and expansion of the offshore oil fields.

Qatar has extended economic assistance to other Arab states, to other developing nations, and to Palestinian organizations.

40 SOCIAL DEVELOPMENT

Public health services and education are provided free by the state through the Ministry of Labor and Social Affairs, which also provides help to orphans, widows, and other Qatari nationals in need of assistance. The government seeks to encourage population growth by reducing mortality rates and improving maternal and child health. The fertility rate in 1991 was 4.5

Both law and Islamic customs closely restrict the activities of Qatari women, who are largely limited to roles within the home. However, growing numbers of woman are receiving government scholarships to study abroad, and some women work in education, medicine, and the media.

41 HEALTH

Free public health services are extended to all residents of Qatar, regardless of nationality. The Ministry of Health has tried with some success to keep pace with an expanding population. The birth rate in 1993 was 22.7 per 1,000 people and there were 10,400 births in 1992.

As of 1985 there were 3 hospitals with a total of 885 beds, and 20 health centers. Qatar's 1985/86 budget had allocated funds for a 288-bed women's hospital. In 1990 there were 2.9 hospital beds per 1,000 inhabitants. In 1985, Qatar had 473 physicians, 52 dentists, 115 pharmacists and pharmacists' assistants, and 1,260 nurses and nurses' assistants. In 1992 there were 1.04 doctors per 1,000 people, with a nurse to doctor ratio of 1.5.

Life expectancy in 1992 was 70 years. That same year, infant mortality was 27 per 1,000 live births. The overall death rate was 3.9 per 1,000 in 1993. Estimated cases of tuberculosis in 1990 were 99 per 100,000 people.

In 1991, 95% of the population had access to safe water and 100% of the population had access to health care services. In 1992, 79% of the country's children were immunized against measles.

42 HOUSING

A "popular housing" scheme provides dwellings through interest-free loans and installment repayments on easy terms. Occupants are required to pay only 60% of the cost of their houses during a period of 20–35 years. To qualify for ownership, an applicant must be a married Qatari national with a limited income, between the ages of 20 and 50 years, and unable to build a house on his own. Qataris facing extreme hardship can receive a free house; in 1985, 559 free houses were distributed and another 635 were under construction. Between 1988 and 1990, 100% of the urban and 48% of the rural population had access to a water supply, while 100% of urban and 85% of rural dwellers had sanitation facilities.

43 EDUCATION

Literacy in 1982 stood at about 51% and was increasing rapidly. Education is compulsory and free for all residents 6–16 years of age; a 100% attendance rate for primary levels is the immediate target. As of 1991, there were 157 schools with 4,598 teachers and 48,785 pupils at the primary level. Secondary level schools had 3,724 teachers and 31,120 pupils. Over 840 students attended vocational schools. All children receive free books, meals, transport, clothing, and boarding facilities if required. Scholarships for higher education abroad are given to all who qualify. In 1985, 1,155 Qataris, 283 of them women, were studying abroad.

The leading higher educational institution is the University of Qatar, founded at Doha in 1973. In addition to faculties of education, science, humanities, social sciences, Islamic studies, and engineering, the university comprised a Language Teaching Institute (founded in 1972) and a Regional Training Center, established in 1979 with UNDP technical assistance. Enrollment in all higher level institutions in 1989 was 6,469 pupils with 451 teaching staff.

44 LIBRARIES AND MUSEUMS

The Qatar National Library in Doha (founded in 1962) has 157,346 volumes in Arabic and 27,553 in English. The University of Qatar library has 130,000 volumes. The Qatar National Museum in Doha has five major sections: the old Amiri Palace (11 buildings), new palace, aquarium, lagoon, and botanical gardens.

45 MEDIA

Qatar enjoys excellent external telephone, telex, and cable facilities. Direct-dial telephone service is available for most parts of Europe, the Middle East, and the US. A second earth satellite station was completed in 1985, and domestic service and capacity are undergoing constant expansion. There were an estimated 134,823 telephones in 1991, up from 29,000 in 1982.

Radio transmissions, broadcast over FM and two AM stations, include 12 hours per day of English-language service. A French-language service was instituted in 1985. Two television channels transmit mostly in Arabic. In 1991 there were 195,000 radios and 198,000 television sets.

Commercial publications available in Qatar (with 1991 circulation figures) include the daily newspapers *Al-'Arab*(45,000), *Ar-Rayah*(70,000), *Al-Sharq*(25,000), *Al-Usbun*(15,000), and *Gulf Times*(30,000); and the political weeklies *Al-Orouba*(50,000) and *Al-Ahad*(11,000).

46ORGANIZATIONS

The Qatar Chamber of Commerce was founded in Doha in 1963. In 1993, there were numerous family, social, and sporting clubs, including the Beacon Club and the Doha Sailing Association.

47TOURISM, TRAVEL, AND RECREATION

Most visitors to Qatar are business travelers; a convention center managed by the Sheraton Hotel Group opened in 1982. The country officially opened its doors to tourists in 1989, but its remoteness and a ban on alcohol have kept tourism weak. All visitors except nationals of Gulf states and of the UK need a visa. In 1991, there were 143,000 tourist arrivals at hotels. Rooms numbered 1,729, with 2,384 beds and a 29.3% occupancy rate.

48FAMOUS QATARIS

Sheikh Khalifa bin Hamad ath-Thani (b.1932) became emir of Qatar in 1972. His heir-apparent and minister of defense is Sheikh Hamad bin Khalifa ath-Thani (b.1948).

49DEPENDENCIES

The State of Qatar has no territories or colonies.

50BIBLIOGRAPHY

Abu Saud, Abeer. *Qatari Women, Past and Present*. New York: Longman, 1984.

American University. *Area Handbook for the Persian Gulf States*. Washington, D.C.: Government Printing Office, 1984.

Anthony, John Duke. *Arab States of the Lower Gulf*. Washington, D.C.: Middle East Institute, 1975.

Crystal, Jill. *Oil and Politics in the Gulf: Rulers and Merchants in Kuwait and Qatar*. New York: Cambridge University Press, 1990.

El Mallakh, Ragaei. *Qatar, Energy & Development*. Dover, N.H.: Croom Helm, 1985.

Graham, Helga. *Arabian Time Machine*. London: Heinemann, 1978.

Kelly, John B. *Britain and the Persian Gulf, 1795–1880*. Oxford: Oxford University Press, 1968.

Long, David. *The Persian Gulf*. Boulder, Colo.: Westview, 1976.

Nafi, Zuhair Ahmed. *Economic and Social Development in Qatar*. Dover, NH: F. Pinter, 1983.

Unwin, P. T. (ed.). *Qatar*. World Bibliographic Series. Santa Barbara, Calif.: ABC-Clio, 1982.

Zahlan, Rosemarie Said. *The Creation of Qatar*. London: Croom Helm, 1979.

SA'UDI ARABIA

Kingdom of Sa'udi Arabia
Al-Mamlakah al-'Arabiyah as-Sa'udiyah

CAPITAL: Riyadh (Ar-Riyad).

FLAG: The national flag bears in white on a green field the inscription, in Arabic, "There is no god but Allah, and Muhammad is the messenger of Allah." There is a long white sword beneath the inscription; the sword handle is toward the fly.

ANTHEM: The National Anthem is a short instrumental selection.

MONETARY UNIT: The Sa'udi riyal (SR) is divided into 20 qursh (piasters), in turn divided into 5 halalah. There are coins of 1, 5, 10, 25, 50, and 100 halalah and notes of 1, 5, 10, 50, 100, and 500 riyals. SR1 = $0.2670 (or $1 = SR3.7450).

WEIGHTS AND MEASURES: The metric system has been officially adopted.

HOLIDAYS: Muslim religious holidays include 1st of Muharram (Muslim New Year), 'Id al-Fitr, and 'Id al-'Adha'.

TIME: 3 PM = noon GMT.

¹LOCATION, SIZE, AND EXTENT

Sa'udi Arabia constitutes about four-fifths of the Arabian Peninsula in Southwest Asia. Although Sa'udi Arabia is known to be the third-largest country in Asia, after China and India, its precise area is difficult to specify because several of its borders are incompletely demarcated. According to the UN, the nation has an area of 1,960,582 sq km (756,985 sq mi); it extends 2,295 km (1,426 mi) ESE–WNW and 1,423 km (884 mi) NNE–SSW. Comparatively, the area occupied by Sa'udi Arabia is slightly less than one-fourth the size of the US. Sa'udi Arabia is bounded on the N by Jordan and Iraq, on the NE by Kuwait, on the E by the Persian Gulf, Qatar, and the United Arab Emirates (UAE), on the SE by Oman, on the S and SW by Yemen and on the W by the Red Sea and the Gulf of Aqaba, with a total estimated boundary length of 7,055 km (4,384 mi).

An agreement was reached in 1965 whereby the Neutral Zone separating Sa'udi Arabia from Kuwait was divided administratively between the two countries. A dispute between Sa'udi Arabia and the newly formed UAE over control of the Buraymi oasis was settled in 1974, when they reached an accord fixing their common border. An agreement dividing the Neutral Zone between Sa'udi Arabia and Iraq was reportedly reached in 1975 and confirmed in 1981, but as of early 1988, no details of the agreement had been filed with the UN. In the Ar-Rub' al-Khali ("Empty Quarter") of the southeast, Sa'udi Arabia's borders with Oman and the PDRY are not yet fully defined.

Sa'udi Arabia's capital city, Riyadh, is located in the east central part of the country.

²TOPOGRAPHY

A narrow plain, the Tihamat ash-Sham, parallels the Red Sea coast, as do, farther north, the Hijaz Mountains (with elevations of 910–2,740 m/3,000–9,000 ft), which rise sharply from the sea. The highest mountains (over 2,740 m/9,000 ft) are in 'Asir in the south. 'Asir is a region extending about 370 km (230 mi) along the Red Sea and perhaps 290–320 km (180–200 mi) inland. East of the Hijaz, the slope is more gentle, and the mountains give way to the central uplands (Najd), a large plateau ranging in elevation

from about 1,520 m (5,000 ft) in the west to about 610 m (2,000 ft) in the east. The Dahna, a desert with an average width of 56 km (35 mi) and an average altitude of 460 m (1,500 ft), separates Najd from the low plateau (Hasa) to the east (average width, 160 km/100 mi; average altitude, 240 m/800 ft). This, in turn, gives way to the low-lying Gulf region.

At least one-third of the total area is sandy desert. The largest of the deserts is the famed Ar-Rub' al-Khali in the south, with an area of roughly 647,500 sq km (250,000 sq mi). An-Nafud, its northern counterpart, has an area of about 57,000 sq km (22,000 sq mi). There are no lakes, and except for artesian wells in the eastern oases, there is no perennially flowing water.

³CLIMATE

The climate is generally very dry and very hot; dust storms and sandstorms are frequent. Day and night temperatures vary greatly. From May to September, the hottest period, daytime temperatures reach 54°C (129°F) in the interior and are among the highest recorded anywhere in the world. Temperatures are slightly lower along the coasts, but humidity reaches 90%, especially in the east, which is noted for heavy fogs. From October through April, the climate is more moderate, with evening temperatures between 16° and 21°C (61° and 70°F). Average annual rainfall is 9 cm (3.5 in), with most rain falling from November to May. Between 25 and 50 cm (10 and 20 in) of rain falls in the mountainous 'Asir area, where there is a summer monsoon.

⁴FLORA AND FAUNA

Vegetation is sparse, owing to aridity and soil salinity. The date palm, mangrove, tamarisk, and acacia are prevalent. Wild mammals include the oryx, jerboa, fox, lynx, wildcat, monkey, panther, and jackal. The favorite game bird is the bustard. The camel and Arab stallion are renowned, as is the white donkey of Al-Ahsa. Fish abound in the coastal waters, and insects, scorpions, lizards, and snakes are numerous.

⁵ENVIRONMENT

The Sa'udi government has not given priority to environmental protection, but in recent years it has become concerned about the continuing encroachment of sand dunes on agricultural land, the preservation and development of water resources, and pollution and sanitation problems. Legislation enacted in May 1978 forbids the felling of trees and regulates the protection of forestland. Sa'udi Arabia's natural environment was threatened by the Persian Gulf War. The dumping of up to six million barrels of oil in the surrounding waters and the destruction of Kuwait's oil wells by fire polluted the nation's air and water. Sa'udi Arabia contributes 0.6% of the world's total gas emissions. Sa'udi Arabia has 0.5 cubic miles of water with 47% used for farming and 8% used for industrial purposes. Twenty-six percent of the nation's rural people do not have pure water. At current rates of consumption, the nation's water supply may be exhausted in 10–20 years. Sa'udi Arabia's cities produce 4.8 million tons of solid waste per year. Pollution of the sea by oil is prohibited, and Sa'udi Arabia has signed the 1954 Convention for the Prevention of Pollution of the Sea by Oil. Under the 1976–80 and 1980–85 development plans, new desalination facilities were built, and urban sewage, waste, and storm drainage facilities were constructed.

The Directorate General for Environmental Protection is responsible for environmental protection measures and preservation of natural resources. In the late 1970s, the 'Asir Kingdom Park, in the southwest, was created to preserve the landforms, flora, and fauna of the 'Asir region, which forms part of the Great Rift Valley. In 1994, nine of the nation's mammal species and 12 types of birds are endangered. Two type of plants are threatened with extinction. Endangered species in Sa'udi Arabia included the Asiatic cheetah (possibly extinct), South Arabian leopard, two species of gazelle (Sa'udi Arabian dorcas and goitered), northern bald ibis, and two species of turtle (green sea and hawksbill). The Syrian wild ass is extinct.

6 POPULATION

A preliminary results of a 1992 census recorded the population as 16,929,294. A population of 20,667,000 was projected for the year 2000, assuming a crude birthrate of 34.9 per 1,000 population, a crude death rate of 4.5, and a net natural increase of 30.4 during 1995–2000. In 1974, the last previous census year, the population stood at 7,012,642, of whom 4.9 million (73%) were settled and 1.8 million (27%) were nomads; it is estimated that the proportion of nomads had fallen to about 5% in 1987. There is considerable debate as to the reliability of official census figures, and it is possible that the actual Sa'udi population in 1990 was no more than 6 million persons.

Urbanization has proceeded swiftly. In 1960, about 30% of the population lived in urban areas; by 1995 it had risen to 80%. The estimated population density in 1992 was 7.9 persons per sq km (20.4 per sq mi). Estimates of the population of major cities in 1990–91 were: Riyadh, the capital, 1,975,000; Jiddah, the principal port, 1,216,000; Mecca (Makkah), containing Islam's holiest shrine, 618,006; At-Ta'if, 204,857; Medina (Al-Madinah), the second-holiest city of Islam, 500,000; Ad-Dammam, 127,884; and Al-Hufuf, 101,271.

7 MIGRATION

Emigration is limited. Immigration of professionals, technicians, and others from the surrounding Arab states and growing numbers from outside the region has been spurred by the development of the oil industry and by the lack of adequately trained and educated Sa'udi personnel. Palestinian Arabs, displaced by the establishment of the state of Israel, are the chief immigrant group. In the early 1990s there were significant numbers of expatriate workers from the US, European countries, Turkey, Jordan, Syria, Jordan, Kuwait, Yemen, the Republic of Korea (ROK), Pakistan, India, Sri Lanka, and the Philippines. In 1990 when Iraq invaded Kuwait, Sa'udi Arabia reacted by expelling workers from Jordan,

Yemen, and Palestinians, for their countries' support of Iraq. The foreign population was 4,624,459 in 1992 (27% of the total population). There were some 25,000 Iraqi refugees in Sa'udi Arabia at the end of 1993.

8 ETHNIC GROUPS

The great majority of the Sa'udis have a common Arabian ancestry, and the population is homogeneous in religion and language. Divisions are based mainly on tribal affiliation or descent, the primary distinction being between groups with a tradition of being sedentary agriculturalists or traders, and the Bedouins, who have a tradition of nomadic pastoralism. The two groups traditionally have been antagonistic. There has been some loosening of tribal ties, however, caused by rapid economic development. Admixtures of Turks, Iranians, Indonesians, Pakistanis, Indians, various African groups, and other non-Arab Muslim peoples appear in the Hijaz, mostly descendants of pilgrims to Mecca.

9 LANGUAGES

Arabic, the native language of the indigenous population, is a Semitic language related to Hebrew and Aramaic. Local variations in pronunciation do not prevent oral communication between people from opposite sections of the Arabian Peninsula. The language is written in a cursive script from right to left. The 28 letters of the alphabet have initial, medial, and terminal forms; short vowels are seldom indicated. Most business people and merchants in oil-producing areas and commercial centers understand English. Government correspondence must be written in Arabic.

10 RELIGIONS

About 85% of the people of Sa'udi Arabia are Sunni Muslims. The dominant form of Islam is Wahhabism, a fundamentalist Muslim reform movement first preached by the 18th-century religious leader Muhammad bin 'Abd al-Wahhab. Most other Sa'udis up to 15% are Shi'i Muslims. The holy city of Mecca is the center of Islam and the site of the sacred Ka'bah sanctuary, toward which all Muslims face at prayer. A pilgrimage to Mecca is one of the five basic obligations of Islam and is incumbent on every Muslim who is physically and financially able to perform it; in the Islamic year 1409 (1988/89), foreign pilgrims totaled 244,560.

There are several thousand foreign Christian employees—Arab, US, and European. Jews have not been allowed to enter the country since the establishment of the state of Israel in 1948 except under special circumstances.

11 TRANSPORTATION

Until recent decades, the camel was the chief means of transportation in Sa'udi Arabia, but enormous strides have been made since the early 1970s. By 1991 there were 74,000 km (45,880 mi) of highways, of which 47% were bituminous surfaced. Modern roads link Jiddah, Mecca, Medina, At-Ta'if, and Riyadh; a new highway connects Sa'udi Arabia with Jordan, and a causeway completed in 1986 offers a direct connection with Bahrain. In 1991, motor vehicle registrations totaled 4.5 million. The Sa'udi Government Railroad, which operates between Ad-Dammam and Riyadh over a length of 575 km (357 mi), was built by the Arabian American Oil Co. (ARAMCO) during the 1950s. Railroad lines totaled 886 km (551 mi) of standard-gauge track in 1991.

The government-owned Sa'udi Arabian Airlines (Saudia) operates regular domestic and foreign flights to major cities. There are major airports at Dhahran, Jiddah, Riyadh, and 20 other cities; a new international airport located north of Jiddah was completed in 1986.

Jiddah, on the Red Sea, is the chief port of entry for Muslim pilgrims going to Mecca; other ports include Ad-Dammam,

SAUDI ARABIA

LOCATION: 16°23' to 32°14'N; 34°30' to 56°22'w. **BOUNDARY LENGTHS:** Jordan, 744 km (462 mi); Iraq, 895 km (556 mi); Kuwait, 163 km (101 mi); Persian Gulf coastline, 549 km (341 mi); Qatar, 67 km (42 mi); UAE, 586 km (364 mi); Oman, 676 km (420 mi); Yemen 1,458 km (906 mi); Red Sea and Gulf of Aqaba coastlines, 1,889 km (1,174 mi). **TERRITORIAL SEA LIMIT:** 12 mi.

Yanbu' al-Bahr, Jizan, and Jubail (Al-Jubayl). In 1991 there were 81 ships with a capacity of 992,000 GRT in the merchant fleet. The traditional dhow is still used for coastal trade.

12 HISTORY

For several thousand years, Arabia has been inhabited by nomadic Semitic tribes. Towns were established at various oases and along caravan routes. During the seventh century AD, followers of Muhammad, imbued with religious zeal, expanded beyond the Mecca-Medina region and within a century conquered most

of the Mediterranean region between Persia in the east and Spain in the west. Although Arabs were dominant in many parts of the Muslim world and there was a great medieval flowering of Arab civilization, the Peninsula itself (except for the holy cities of Mecca and Medina) declined in importance and remained virtually isolated for almost a thousand years. Throughout this period, Arabia was barely more than a province of successive Islamic caliphates that established their capitals in Damascus, Baghdad, Cairo, and Constantinople (now Istanbul).

The foundations of the kingdom of Sa'udi Arabia were laid in the 18th century by the fusion of the military power of the Sa'ud family and Wahhabism, an Islamic puritan doctrine preached by Muhammad bin 'Abd al-Wahhab. Muhammad ibn-Sa'ud (r.1744–65) and his son 'Abd al-'Aziz (r.1765–1803) gave the religious reformer refuge at Ad-Dar'iyah, in central Arabia, and together they embarked on a program of religious reform and territorial expansion. By 1801, Najd and Al-Ahsa were occupied. 'Abd al-'Aziz's son and successor, Sa'ud (r.1803–14), brought the Hijaz under Sa'udi control and took the holy city of Mecca. The Ottoman Turks called on their governor of Egypt, Muhammad 'Ali, to put down the Sa'udis. A long struggle (1811–18) finally resulted in Sa'udi defeat. During that time, Sa'ud died, and his son 'Abdallah (r.1814–18) was captured and beheaded.

When international conditions forced Muhammad 'Ali to withdraw his occupation forces in 1840, the Sa'udis embarked upon a policy of reconquest. Under Faisal (Faysal, r.1843–67), Wahhabi control was reasserted over Najd, Al-Ahsa, and Oman, with Riyadh as the new capital. (Hijaz remained under the control of the sharifs of Mecca until 1925.) After Faisal's death, conflict between his sons led to a decline in the family's fortunes. Taking advantage of these quarrels, the Ibn-Rashids, a former Sa'udi vassal family, gained control of Najd and conquered Riyadh. The Sa'udi family fled to Kuwait in 1891.

In January 1902, 'Abd al-'Aziz, a grandson of Faisal, who was to gain fame under the name Ibn-Sa'ud, succeeded in driving the Ibn-Rashid garrison out of Riyadh. At a decisive battle in 1906, the Rashidi power was broken. In 1913, the Sa'udis again brought Al-Ahsa under their control, and in December 1915, Ibn-Sa'ud signed a treaty with the British that placed Sa'udi foreign relations under British control in return for a sizable subsidy.

Warfare broke out again in Arabia in 1919, when Hussein ibn-'Ali (Husayn ibn-'Ali), the sharif of Mecca, who had become an independent king, attacked the Sa'udis. Hussein was defeated, and Ibn-Sa'ud annexed 'Asir. In 1921, he finally rid Arabia of the Rashids, and by 1923, he had consolidated his kingdom by occupying the districts west and north of Ha'il. Hussein of Mecca provoked another conflict with Ibn-Sa'ud in March 1924 by proclaiming himself caliph. War broke out, and the Sa'udis captured At-Ta'if, Mecca, and Medina (December 1925). 'Ali ibn-Hussein ('Ali ibn-Husayn), who had replaced his father as king of Hijaz, then abdicated, and in November 1925, Ibn-Sa'ud entered Jiddah. This increase in Ibn-Sa'ud's territory was acknowledged by the British in a treaty of 20 May 1927 that annulled the 1915 agreement and recognized his independence. On 22 September 1932, the various parts of the realm were amalgamated into the Kingdom of Sa'udi Arabia, with much the same boundaries as exist today.

With the discovery of oil in the 1930s, the history of Sa'udi Arabia was irrevocably altered. Reserves have proved vast—about one-fourth of the world's total—and production, begun in earnest after World War II, has provided a huge income, much of it expended on infrastructure and social services. Sa'udi Arabia's petroleum-derived wealth has considerably enhanced the country's influence in world economic and political forums. Following the 1967 Arab-Israeli war, the Sa'udi government undertook a vast aid program in support of Egypt, Syria and Jordan. Sa'udi Arabia joined the 1973 Arab boycott against the US and the Netherlands and, as a key member of OPEC, lent its support to the huge rise in oil prices during the 1970s. This move had stunning consequences for the world economy and also caused a dramatic upsurge in Sa'udi Arabia's wealth and power. Since the 1980s, the government has regulated its petroleum production to stabilize the international oil market and has used its influence as the most powerful moderate member of OPEC to restrain the more radical members.

Political life in Sa'udi Arabia has remained basically stable in recent decades, despite several abrupt changes of leadership. In November 1964, Crown Prince Faisal (Faysal ibn 'Abd al-'Aziz as-Sa'ud), a son of Ibn-Sa'ud, became king and prime minister following the forced abdication of his brother King Sa'ud. His first act as prime minister was to announce a sweeping reorganization of the government, and his major social reform was the abolition of slavery. In March 1975, King Faisal was assassinated by a nephew in an apparently isolated act of revenge. Faisal was succeeded by Crown Prince Khaled (Khalid ibn-'Abd al-'Aziz as-Sa'ud), who embarked on an expanded development program. King Khaled died of a heart attack in June 1982, and his half-brother, Crown Prince Fahd ibn-'Abd al-'Aziz as-Sa'ud, ascended the throne. King Fahd has encouraged continuing modernization while seeking to preserve the nation's social stability and Islamic heritage. As the custodian of the holy Moslem shrines at Mecca and Medina, the monarchy has been deeply embarrassed by several incidents in recent years; e.g., seizure of the Grand Mosque in Mecca by about 500 Islamic militants in 1979, which led to the deaths of more than 160; a riot by Iranian pilgrims during the 1987 pilgrimage, which cost 400 lives; and the suffocation of over 1,000 pilgrims in a tunnel at the Grand Mosque in 1990.

Sa'udi Arabia's wealth and selective generosity has given it great political influence throughout the world and especially in the Middle East. It suspended aid to Egypt after that country's peace talks with Israel at Camp David, Md., but renewed relations in 1987. It made substantial funds secretly available to US President Ronald Reagan's administration for combating Marxist regimes in Central America. The kingdom played a key role in creating the GCC and in working for an end to the civil strife in Lebanon. It actively supported Iraq during the war with Iran and tried, in vain, to prevent the conflict with Kuwait.

When Iraq invaded Kuwait in 1990, Sa'udi Arabia, fearing Iraqi aggression, radically altered its traditional policy to permit the stationing of foreign troops on its soil. (The government was criticized by senior Saudi religious scholars for taking this step.) Riyadh made substantial contributions of arms, oil, and funds to the allied victory. It reacted sharply, cutting off subsidies and expelling workers from Jordan, Yemen, and the PLO, for giving support to Iraq in the period after the invasion.

Sa'udi Arabia and the US consult closely on political, economic, commercial, and security matters. The U.S, with the UK, is a major supplier of arms and offers training and other support to the kingdom's defenses.

[13]GOVERNMENT

Sa'udi Arabia is a religiously based monarchy in which the sovereign's dominant powers are regulated according to Muslim law (Shari'ah), tribal law, and custom.

There is no written constitution; laws must be compatible with Islamic law. In a decree of March 1992, the King was granted exclusive power to name the crown prince, his successor. The Council of Ministers, first set up in 1953, is appointed by the king to advise on policy, originate legislation, and supervise the growing bureaucracy. The post of prime minister has been reserved for the king, and the crown prince has been appointed first deputy prime minister. Most other important posts in the cabinet are reserved for members of the royal family.

In 1992, King Fahd announced the creation of the Majlis al Shura, an advisory body that would provide a forum for public debate. The King appointed 60 male citizens not belonging to the royal family to four-year terms on this body, which held its first meeting on 29 December 1992.

[14]POLITICAL PARTIES

Although there are no political parties in Sa'udi Arabia, various groups do function as blocs, contending for influence. Important among these groups are the conservative 'ulama (religious scholars) and the members of the royal family. Other alliances—by merchants, businessmen, professionals, and leading families—are concerned with economic matters. There is also a small but growing, middle class that seems to want greater political participation and a less restrictive social environment. Each group brings its weight to bear on the policymaking bodies of the government and the king, whose leadership is upheld so long as he adheres to Islamic law, tradition, and the collective decisions of the 'ulama.

15 LOCAL GOVERNMENT

The kingdom is divided into 14 emirates, each headed by a crown-appointed governor, often a prince or other member of the royal household or from an allied family. Tribal and village leaders (sheikhs) report directly to provincial governors, giving the central government some control over outlying regions. Each sheikh traditionally rules in consultation with a council. A large segment of the population remains tribally organized: tribes, headed by paramount sheikhs, are divided into subtribes, headed by local sheikhs. Decisions are made by tribal sheikhs, emirs, or other chiefs and their councils (majlis).

16 JUDICIAL SYSTEM

The king acts as the highest court of appeal and has the power of pardon; access to the king and the right to petition him are well-established traditions. The judiciary consists of lower courts that handle misdemeanors and minor civil cases; high courts of Islamic law (Shari'ah), and courts of appeal. Islamic law of the Hanbali school prevails in Sa'udi Arabia, but justice is also based on tribal and customary law. Capital and corporal punishment are permitted; an 11-member Supreme Council of Justice reviews all sentences of execution, cutting, or stoning. A separate military justice system exercises jurisdiction over uniformed personnel and civilian government authorities.

There is no written constitution. The Justice Ministry is responsible for appointment and promotion of judges. Judges may be removed only by the Supreme Council of Justice or by royal decree. Although independence of the judiciary is guaranteed by law, courts are subject to the influence of royal family members. At the provincial level, governors also reportedly exercise influence over local judges.

17 ARMED FORCES

Sa'udi Arabia's armed forces totaled 102,500 personnel in 1993, having doubled in size to meet the Iraqi threat. The army had 73,000 personnel, 700 main battle tanks, 700 armored fighting vehicles, and 33 batteries of surface-to-air missiles, manned by 4,000 special air defense troops. The navy's strength was about 11,000 personnel (1,500 marines) and manned 8 frigates and 12 other combatants. The air force had 18,000 personnel and 273 combat aircraft. The national guard, numbering 75,000, is used chiefly for internal security and is an elite strategic reserve loyal to the Royal family. Sa'udi Arabia also had an 10,500-member frontier force and coast guard, a helicopter-equipped countert-errorist unit, and 5,000 foreign military personnel under contract from members of the GCC. The armed forces are equipped with the most advanced weaponry, including 5 Airborne Warning and Control Systems (AWACS) aircraft, which were sold to Sa'udi Arabia by the US in 1981, over Israel's strenuous objections, as part of an $8.5 billion arms deal. From 1981 through 1985, the Sa'udis imported arms worth $14.7 billion, of which 43% came from the US, 29% from France, 9% from the UK, and 19% from other countries. Arms imports then jumped to $34 billion for 1986–1991 with offset agreements for infrastructure investment. In 1992 Sa'udi Arabia spent $14.5 billion (13% of gross domestic product) on its own forces, plus paid a total (1991–92) of $17 billion for US Gulf War costs.The US maintains air defense misiles and interceptors on a rotational basis.

18 INTERNATIONAL COOPERATION

Sa'udi Arabia is a charter member of the UN, having joined on 24 October 1945, and participates in ESCWA and all the nonregional specialized agencies. It is a founding member of the Arab League and of OPEC (as well as OAPEC), belongs to G-77 and GCC, and has permanent observer status with the OAS. It is also signatory to the Law of the Sea. Although supporting the Palestinian cause and the Arab League's boycott of Israel, the Sa'udi government in 1981 proposed that the Arab nations show willingness to extend diplomatic recognition to Israel in return for its withdrawal from lands occupied in the 1967 war (including the West Bank and East Jerusalem). Relations with Iran have long been tense and have worsened since that nation's Islamic revolution in 1979. In 1987, Iranian pilgrims rioted in Mecca in an attempt to destabilize the royal family. Although Sa'udi Arabia was not a combatant in the Iran-Iraq war, it actively supported Iraq against Iran.

19 ECONOMY

The economy is heavily dependent on oil production, which provided over 99% of export value and 77% of government revenues in 1985/86. Rapidly increasing oil income during the 1970s was used to increase disposable income, economic development, and defense expenditures. However, the contribution of the oil sector to GDP has fluctuated. In 1969/70, petroleum-sector output amounted to 54.5% of GDP, of which crude oil output accounted for 47.3% and refining for 7.2%. In 1974/75, at the end of the first development plan, it generated 59.1% of GDP. Because of the diversification effort during the second and third development plans and the precipitous decline of oil prices, the contribution of the oil sector (crude oil and refined products) to GDP declined from 70% in 1980/81 to 33.6% in 1985/86 and 21.5% in 1989. The increase in the oil price in 1990 as well as higher oil production levels—partly compensating for the loss of Iraqi and Kuwaiti oil exports—was largely responsible for the increase in the contribution of the oil sector to the 1990 GDP (37%). The $16 billion increase in oil export revenues boosted the Saudi economy by 22% in 1990 compared with 1985 levels. Additional growth of 5% occurred in 1991.

The government has tried to diversify the economy by development of industries utilizing petroleum, including steel and petrochemical manufacture, in the massive Jubail and Yanbu' al-Bahr industrial complexes, which were largely completed by 1989. It was estimated that by the end of 1987 Sa'udi Arabia was producing between 4% and 5% of world output of methanol, urea, and high- and low-density polyethylene. The government continues to stress diversification of the economy as part of its 1990–95 development plan. The agricultural sector is targeted to grow by an average of 7% a year over the period 1990–95. The government encourages growth in agriculture as a means to reduce Sa'udi Arabia's net reliance on food imports. Nonetheless, defense accounts now for 31% of the budget.

20 INCOME

In 1992, Sa'udi Arabia's GNP was $126,355 million at current prices, or $7,940 per capita. For the period 1985–92 the average inflation rate was 1.5%, resulting in a real growth rate in per capita GNP of 1.3%.

In 1992 the GDP was $111,343 million in current US dollars. It is estimated that in 1988 agriculture, hunting, forestry, and fishing contributed 7% to GDP; mining and quarrying, 23%; manufacturing, 9%; electricity, gas, and water, and construction, 11%; wholesale and retail trade, 9%; transport, storage, and communication, 8%; finance, insurance, real estate, and business services, 8%; community, social, and personal services, 4%; and other sources, 21%.

21LABOR

The concept of a hired labor force came to Sa'udi Arabia with the arrival of ARAMCO and other industrial ventures connected with the exploitation of oil. By 1991, about 3 million foreigners worked in Sa'udi Arabia, mostly in the oil and construction sector; the total labor force stood at 5 million, with 34% in government, 28% in industry and oil, 22% in services, and 16% in agriculture.

No labor unions exist, but there are professional and trade guilds. Labor-industry relations are prescribed by law. The Ministry of Labor and Social Affairs supervises both labor and industry, arbitrates labor disputes, and supervises vocational and trade schools. Traditional values, embodied in government decrees, continue to hinder the entry of women into the industrial work force. There has been a slight change, however. The fourth development plan (1986–90) called for an effort to find more employment for women "in a manner that would not be contrary to the Muslim faith."

A 1969 royal decree instituted a series of social insurance provisions that provide compensation for work-related disability, old age, and death. Working hours are set at a maximum of 11 per day, although an 8-hour day and 48-hour week are the norms. Paid holidays and vacations (15–21 days per year) are provided. Labor regulations require protection from hazard and disease for employees (except farmers, herdsmen, domestic servants, and family-operated business employees). Labor outdoors is prohibited when the temperature exceeds 122°F.

22AGRICULTURE

Agriculture employed 569,000 persons in 1990. Only about 1.1% of Sa'udi Arabia's land area is cultivated, although 40% is suitable for grazing. Small owner-operated farms characterize Sa'udi Arabia's land-tenure system. About 96% of the farm area is owned, and only 4% rented. Less than 3% of the agricultural holdings are of 8 hectares (20 acres) or more, and 45% are 0.4 hectare (1 acre) or less in size. About two-thirds of the cropped land is used for cereals and the remainder for vegetables and fruit. Although Sa'udi Arabia has more than 7 million date palms and provides about 15% of the world's supply of dates (an estimated 545,000 tons in 1992), the growing of dates has declined in recent decades in favor of wheat, corn, sorghum, tomatoes, onions, grapes, and a variety of other fruits and vegetables. Nevertheless, dates remain the only major staple food crop with production sufficient to meet local demand. Wheat output increased from an estimated 150,000 tons in the late 1970s to 1,700,000 tons in 1985, and the government claimed that it met total domestic demand by 1986/87. In fact, production of wheat totaled 4,100,000 tons in 1992, and government subsidies have led to a recurring overproduction of wheat. In 1989, the government attempted to discourage production by cutting price supports, but production is still several times higher than domestic demand, which necessitated the export of 2 million tons in 1990.

Aquifers supply 80% of agriculture's water requirements, but are not renewable. Agricultural irrigation accounts for 90% of total water needs, with wheat production alone using about one-third of the country's annual water supply. Under the government's fifth development plan, agriculture is expected to increase to 9% of GDP by 1995 (up from 3.4% in 1985 and 8% in 1990) through the budgeting of SR14.4 billion during 1990–95 for agricultural development.

23ANIMAL HUSBANDRY

As of 1992, Sa'udi Arabia had an estimated 6,008,000 sheep, 3,350,000 goats, 419,000 camels, 216,000 head of cattle, and 102,000 donkeys. As imports of animal foodstuffs have increased and as greater varieties of agricultural products have been produced locally, camels have declined steadily in importance as a source of food. Arabia has long been famed for its horses, but the importance of the Arabian horse as an export item is now virtually nil. Donkeys and mules are still valued as pack animals, and the white donkeys of Al-Ahsa are well known. Sheep are found in all parts of Sa'udi Arabia where pasturage is available; they are raised for milk, as well as meat and wool or hair. Goats are kept for milk; their hair is used in rugs and tents, and the skins serve as water bags. As of 1990 there were 75 sheep farms, 4 cattle farms, and 40 dairy farms. In 1992, the kingdom was 68% self-sufficient in mutton consumption, 36% in beef, and 94% in fresh milk. The output of poultry and eggs doubled during 1975–80, and in 1992, Sa'udi Arabia had an estimated 83 million poultry. In 1992, domestic production of chickens met 54% of domestic consumption and egg production met 98%. There is no hog raising, and importation of pork products is banned as contrary to Islamic law.

24FISHING

Fishing provides employment and self-sufficiency to some communities on both Sa'udi coasts, although cash earnings are negligible. With rare exceptions, traditional fishing techniques are used. One of the few growth areas in this sector has been the export of Gulf shrimp. The fish catch was estimated at 43,251 tons in 1991.

25FORESTRY

The only forest growth is found in the mountainous area that extends from southern Hijaz to 'Asir, accounting for no more than 0.6% of the total area. The principal varieties—acacia, date, juniper, wild olive, sidr, tamarind, and tamarisk—are generally not useful for timber, but some wood from date palms is used for construction.

26MINING

A modern mining firm, the Sa'udi Arabian Mining Syndicate, was founded in 1934 to exploit the mineral resources of Hijaz. Only one mine has been worked—the ancient gold and silver mine of Mahd adh-Dhahab (literally, "cradle of gold"), which is located southeast of Medina and probably dates from the time of King Solomon (10th century BC). In 1991, a second gold mine, Sukhaybirat, was opened. Substantial national reserves of gold, iron ore (up to 4 million tons), silver, copper, zinc, lead, pyrites, phosphate, magnesite, barite, marble, and gypsum have been suspected, and an intensive search is still being carried on by Sa'udi and foreign companies. As of 1991, about 3,000 showings for at least 50 metallic and nonmetallic minerals had been located. Production of metal concentrate and bullion in 1991 included copper, 900 tons; gold, 6,400 kg (crude bullion); and silver, 16,400 kg. A modern mining code encourages foreign participation, although majority holdings by national interests have increasingly been stressed. All minerals, including the vast petroleum and natural gas reserves, are owned by the government.

27ENERGY AND POWER

Oil was first discovered in Sa'udi Arabia in 1938, and exploitation of the world's largest oil field, Ghawar (west of Al-Hufuf), began 10 years later. By 1975, Sa'udi Arabia had become the world's third-leading producer (after the US and USSR) and largest exporter of crude oil. With the continued developed of Sa'udia Arabia's production capabilities and the dissolution of the Soviet Union in December 1991, Sa'udi Arabia became the world's largest oil producer. Most oil exports are transported by tanker from the Persian Gulf port of Jubail, and the rest moves by pipeline to the Red Sea port of Yanbu' al-Bahr. In 1991, oil exports contributed $47 billion and accounted for 94% of the total export revenue. Proven reserves of crude oil, found along the Gulf in a quadrangular area northeast of Riyadh, were estimated at 257.8

billion barrels (35.1 billion tons), or about one-fourth of the world's known deposits, in 1992. ARAMCO, a US-controlled firm that held the original oil concession, divested 60% of its interests to the Sa'udi government in 1974 and the remainder in 1980, but it continues to produce 96% of Sa'udi oil under a management contract with the Sa'udi government.

After the Iranian revolution of 1979 and the outbreak of war between Iran and Iraq in 1980, the Sa'udi government made up for the diminished oil exports of both countries by increasing its average oil output to a record 9.9 million barrels per day in 1980. Production remained high at 9.8 million barrels a day in 1981 but was cut to 6.5 million barrels daily in 1982. Because of the continued oversupply of oil, Sa'udi Arabia cut its production from 1983 to 1985, when it averaged about 3.3 million barrels per day. In 1986, in an attempt to increase its market share, Sa'udi Arabia temporarily abandoned its role as OPEC's swing producer and flooded the market, producing about 5 million barrels a day, forcing the price to less than $10 per barrel. Since 1987, when production amounted to 4.2 million barrels per day, Sa'udi Arabia has dramatically intensified production, especially since the end of the Persian Gulf War. In 1992, an estimated 8.4 million barrels of crude oil were produced per day, up from 8.1 million in 1991 and 6.4 million in 1990.

In recent years, Sa'udi Arabia had been receiving oil by pipeline from Iraq to Yanbu' al-Bahr. The IPSA 1 pipeline, carrying 500,000 barrels per day, began operations in 1985. Sa'udi Arabia is also planning a network of pipelines that will connect the smaller fields with the larger pipeline running from Hawtah (south of Riyadh) to the East-West Pipeline, the capacity of which will be expanded from 3.2 to 4.7 million barrels per day.

Natural gas production was 34,600 million cu m (1,211 billion cu ft) in 1992. Reserves of natural gas were estimated at 5.2 trillion cu m (182.6 trillion cu ft) in 1992, or 3.7% of the world's total.

Sa'udi Arabia has limited waterpower resources, and oil-powered diesel engines generate most of its electric power. Electrical service, which reached 2.2 million people in 1975, was extended to 4.2 million in 1979 and, by 1990, reached 92% of the population. Total installed generating capacity is expected to increase from 15,700 Mw in 1990 to 19,500 Mw by 1995. Production in 1991 amounted to 47,710 million kwh. Solar energy is becoming increasingly important as an alternative to diesel power, particularly for use in the desalination of seawater.

28INDUSTRY

Although the Sa'udi economy has been virtually synonymous with crude oil, the country is attempting to diversify its manufacturing. In 1985, some 1,800 operating factories turned out cement, steel, glass, metal manufactures, automotive parts, building materials, and other industrial products, along with petroleum refinery products and petrochemicals. Total refinery capacity in 1985 was 1,548,000 barrels per day. Production of refined products totaled 415,255,000 barrels in 1985. Jubail is to have a 171-sq-km (66-sq-mi) industrial park encompassing a $1 billion oil refinery, a $4 billion industrial chemicals installation, a $300 million petrochemical plant, a $2 billion polyethylene project, a $600 million iron and steel facility, and a $360 million fertilizer complex. By the end of 1991, there were over 1880 industrial units of all types, with capitalization of $30.6 billion. These firms employed 156,000 workers. The goal of the fifth development plan is to open 60–80 new factories per annum. However, the refining and petrochemical industries accounted for 55% of the value of total industrial investment between 1985 and 1990.

Industries producing consumer goods for the local market rely for the most part on imported raw materials. The most notable growth has occurred in food processing and includes meat-packing plants, flour mills, ice cream, yogurt, other dairy processing plants, and vegetable canneries. Other companies produce canvas cloth, surgical supplies, paper products, plastic pipes, electric appliances, paints, detergents, and pharmaceuticals.

29SCIENCE AND TECHNOLOGY

The government encourages importation of high technology, especially in the oil industry, but its own commitment to national technological development has been limited, although the 1976–80 development plan outlined proposals for developing an indigenous technological capacity. The Industrial Studies and Development Center is located in Riyadh, and the University of Petroleum and Minerals is in Dhahran. The King Abdul Aziz City for Science and Technology was founded in 1977 to formulate the national policy for science and technology development, and to draw up the strategy and plans for its implementation.

30DOMESTIC TRADE

Barter is the traditional means by which nomads and farmers have obtained each other's products, and weekly markets are held in villages and small towns. However, the economy is being progressively monetized, and is now completely so in the towns and cities. Newspapers, magazines, and billboards are the principal means of advertising.

Normal business hours vary in different provinces but are usually from 7:30 AM to 1:30 PM and 2:30 to 8 PM, Saturday through Wednesday. The normal workday is eight hours; during the month of Ramadan, however, the workday is limited to six hours. Banks are generally open from 8:30 AM to 12 noon and 5 to 7 PM, Saturday through Wednesday, and 8:30 to 11:30 AM, Thursday. Friday is the day of rest in Sa'udi Arabia.

31FOREIGN TRADE

Total exports were valued at $43.9 billion in 1990, and at $47.8 billion in 1991. Oil export revenues those years averaged $41.5 billion annually, compared with $24 billion in 1989. Non-oil exports included dates, pearls, jewelry, mineral products, and hides and skins. Total imports in 1990 were valued at $21.1 billion. The major categories of imports were machinery and electrical appliances, food grains and other comestibles, transportation equipment, and basic metals. Oil earnings have generally produced vast trade surpluses, with the value of exports running at more than three times the cost of imports through 1981. After that year, however, the trade surplus dwindled year by year.

In 1989, Western European countries accounted for 21.3% of Sa'udi Arabia's exports and supplied 39.8% of imports. Japan took 17.5% of exports and supplied 14.2% of imports. The US accounted for 25.8% of exports and 18.2% of imports.

Sa'udi Arabia's main trading partners measured as a percent of total exports or imports are as follows:

	1989	1990	1991
EXPORTS TO			
US	25.8	24.0	22.9
Japan	17.5	19.0	16.0
Singapore	6.0	5.4	5.1
France	5.2	4.8	4.6
Netherlands	4.5	4.7	6.0
Bahrain	4.5	3.9	3.3
IMPORTS FROM			
US	18.2	16.7	20.2
Japan	14.2	15.3	13.7
UK	10.2	11.3	11.3
Germany	6.3	7.4	7.8
Switzerland	5.0	6.6	4.9
Italy	5.7	4.6	4.6

32BALANCE OF PAYMENTS

Before the 1970s, government development spending, special payments to other Arab countries, and import costs combined to offset Sa'udi Arabia's oil income. The payments situation altered radically in the mid-1970s, however, owing to the dramatic jump in world oil prices and, hence, in Sa'udi Arabia's oil income. Even though merchandise trade has shown a surplus for several years, the current account, including invisibles, was negative throughout the 1980s. However, from 1985 to 1989, the trade deficit fell from 19% of GDP to 10% of GDP. Lower demand for imports (especially for building materials) has caused the trade imbalance to stabilize.

In 1992 merchandise exports totaled $42,769 million and imports $-29,778 million. The merchandise trade balance was $12,991 million. The following table summarizes Sa'udi Arabia's balance of payments for 1991 and 1992 (in millions of US dollars):

	1991	1992
CURRENT ACCOUNT		
Goods services and income	–7,1124	–5,231
Unrequited transfers	–20,606	–14,201
TOTALS	–27,730	19,432
CAPITAL ACCOUNT		
Direct investment	160	—
Portfolio investment	470	—
Other short-term capital	27,150	13,767
Reserves	–49	5,664
TOTALS	27,731	19,431
Errors and omissions		
Total change in reserves	–6	5,738

33BANKING AND SECURITIES

Although lending at interest is prohibited by Islamic law, banking has flourished in Sa'udi Arabia as a conduit for the investment of oil money. The Sa'udi Arabian Monetary Agency was established by royal decree in 1952 to maintain the internal and external value of currency. The agency issues notes and coins with 100% cover in gold and convertible foreign exchange and regulates all banks and exchange dealers. Its foreign assets were once larger than those held by any other single banking institution, totaling an estimated SR213,924 million in 1990.

In 1993 there were 12 commercial banking houses, of which three were wholly owned Sa'udi banks including the Riyadh Bank and the National Commercial Bank; the remainder were owned partly by foreign banks. Credit and development agencies include the Agricultural Credit Bank, Sa'udi Credit Bank (which extends interest-free loans to needy Sa'udis), and the Sa'udi Investment Banking Corp.

As of 1990 total currency in circulation was SR39,985.8 million; commercial bank demand deposits reached SR62,940.2 million. Much gold and silver are privately hoarded. Bank advances and loans to the private sector stood at SR67 billion in 1991. There is a stock exchange in Sa'udi Arabia. The value of traded shares was SR2.4 billion in 1989. Between 1985 and 1989 stock transactions increased from 7,842 a year to 110,030 a year. There are 60 companies listed on the exchange.

34INSURANCE

There are at least nine insurance firms operating in Sa'udi Arabia. The National Company for Cooperative Insurance, founded by royal decree in 1985 and owned by three government agencies, had capital of SR250 million in 1986. There is no regulatory body for insurance or reinsurance.

35PUBLIC FINANCE

Public expenditures typically have acted as the vanguard for economic growth and development since the early 1970s. Budgeted expenditures amounting to SR143 billion (over 50% of GDP) were allocated in 1990, but were actually much higher due to the Gulf crisis. Deficits have been common since 1983, as oil revenues have declined. Whereas expenditures in 1990 were one-half those of 1982, revenues were less than one-third of the 1982 amount. Defense and police account for approximately 35% of annual public expenditures.

36TAXATION

The taxing authority in Sa'udi Arabia is the Department of Zakat and Income Tax. During the early 1970s, a progressive income tax was levied on all personal income of foreign residents in excess of SR6,000, at the rate of 5–30%; there was also a progressive tax of 25–45% on the profits of foreign companies. These taxes were abolished in 1975; in January 1988, an attempt was made to revive them, but it was rescinded almost immediately after widespread complaint. However, foreign companies that have not obtained exemption under the Foreign Investment Code and foreigners who are self-employed professionals or general partners in Sa'udi partnerships are subject to these taxes.

Corporate taxes range from 25-45% of net income. The zakat is an Islamic tax derived from the Shari'ah and applied directly to the income and property of Sa'udis (and resident Gulf state nationals); half of the zakat rate of 2.5% is paid to the government, and the other half is distributed by citizens to the poor. The income of members of the royal family is tax-exempt.

37CUSTOMS AND DUTIES

Most imports enter duty free. Customs duties vary from 0–30%. ARAMCO does not pay duty on items imported for use in its operations. Importation of liquor, firearms, ammunition, and narcotics, and certain other items is strictly forbidden, as are all imports from Israel and South Africa.

38FOREIGN INVESTMENT

A small group of upper-class Sa'udis have traditionally held substantial investments overseas. These Sa'udis hold large demand deposits in US and Western European banks and considerable investments in commercial ventures, especially real estate, in Egypt and other Middle Eastern countries. Since the early 1970s, the Sa'udi government has vastly increased its overseas investments in the US, Western Europe, and Japan. Foreign assets managed by the central banking authority, SAMA, have fallen from the 1981 level of (current) $127.7 billion to the 1991 figure of (current) $55 billion. US capital invested in Sa'udi Arabia, especially ARAMCO money, has increased despite the Sa'udi government's nationalization of the oil industry. A tax holiday of 5–10 years is offered to qualifying new foreign firms with a minimum 25% Sa'udi ownership.

39ECONOMIC DEVELOPMENT

Sa'udi Arabia's first two development plans (1971–75 and 1976–80) stressed improvement of the country's economic infrastructure by expanding the highway system, port capacity, electric power output, water supply, and irrigated land. The third plan (1981–85), continuing the Sa'udi program of modernization without Westernization, aimed at diversifying and expanding the productive economic sectors of industry, mining, and agriculture. The government's long-term goal was to reduce the nation's dependence on oil exports and foreign labor. Expenditures for the 1981–85 plan were initially estimated (at current prices) at $235.8 billion, compared with $140 billion for the 1975–80 plan. At the end of the third development plan, most of the infrastructure had been put in place. The fourth development plan (1985–90) emphasized consolidation of the gains of the previous 15 years and rational planning of economic activity. From the plan's emphasis on cost reduction and improvement of economic performance, it was clear that it had been drawn up under the assumption that the days of huge surpluses in the oil sector were over. Planned expenditures for the fourth plan were reduced several times. The fifth plan (1990–95) follows the goals of the fourth plan closely. Stressing economic diversification, this plan supports industry, agriculture, finance, and business services. Where possible, public sector industries will be privatized and private investment rather than government expenditure will become the main impetus for growth.

The most spectacular projects have been the development of two giant petrochemical complexes at Jubail, on the salt flats of the Persian Gulf, and at Yanbu' al-Bahr, on the Red Sea. The new industrial city of Jubail, on which construction was begun in 1977 by the US-owned Bechtel Corp., is to have 16 primary industrial plants and a population of about 290,000 people by 2010; Yanbu' will house 150,000. These projects had been largely completed by 1987, but the government estimated an investment of more than $100 billion more before the cities are completed in the 1990s. Construction projects completed in 1986 included a new airport at Riyadh and a 1,154-km (717-mi) natural gas pipeline.

Sa'udi Arabia is a major supplier of economic aid to developing countries. It has provided two-thirds of OPEC assistance to some 60 nations since 1972; the cumulative aid total exceeds $30 billion. In 1985, Sa'udi Arabia contributed $2.6 billion, or 2.9% of GNP, to developing countries, chiefly Arab states. During the Iran-Iraq war, substantial foreign aid was given to Iraq to prevent a victory by Iran and possible exportation of the Ayatollah Khomeini's Shi'i revolution. During the Gulf conflict, considerable costs were incurred by Sa'udi Arabia as a result of providing local services to the allied forces, in addition to pledging financial compensation to various countries that were either directly involved in the conflict or suffered as a result of abiding by the UN embargo placed on Iraq.

40SOCIAL DEVELOPMENT

Social welfare in Sa'udi Arabia is traditionally provided through the family or tribe. Those with no family or tribal ties have recourse to the traditional Islamic religious foundations or may request government relief, which is supported by the collection of the zakat. Social insurance provides health care, disability, death, old age pension, and survivor benefits for workers and their families. ARAMCO has a welfare plan for its employees that includes pension funds, accident compensation, and free medical care. Sa'udi Arabia's fertility rate was 6.8 in 1985–90, and abortion was legal on broad medical grounds.

The customs and regulations governing the behavior of women are strict even by the standards of the Islamic world. Despite the shortage of Sa'udi labor, the government is unsympathetic to the role of women in the workplace; in the 1993, only 5% of the labor force was female. Extreme modesty of dress is required, and women are not permitted to drive motor vehicles.

41HEALTH

The country has made important advances, after a slow start, in the provision of health care services. From 1990 through 1995, the government intended to spend SR63.9 billion on health and social services (of a total budget of SR497.6 billion). Targets include improved immunization coverage and achieving better regional coverage of health care provision (which remains inadequate). The government wants to have 1 doctor per 500 people, as well as 150 new health centers. Development of the private sector (and links between public and private) is to be encouraged; it also plans to have a local manufacturer of pharmaceuticals and medical equipment and supplies. In 1990, hospital beds per 1,000 people equaled 3.35. Health personnel in 1990 included 21,110

physicians (about 1.82 per 1,000), 1,967 dentists, and 48,066 nurses (about 3.8 per 1,000). In 1991, there were 1,811 pharmacists. It is the government's intention to provide integrated health services free of charge, or at a nominal fee, to all citizens. The public health care system is supplemented by a small but generally excellent private health sector. Despite these advances, Sa'udi Arabia still suffers from severe health problems. A major cause of disease is malnutrition, leading to widespread scurvy, rickets, night blindness, and anemia, as well as low resistance to tuberculosis. In 1990, there were 22 reported cases of tuberculosis per 100,000 people. Immunization rates for 1992 for children up to one year old were: tuberculosis (97%); diphtheria, pertussis, and tetanus (96%); polio (96%); and measles (90%). Dysentery attacks all ages and classes, and trachoma is common. A government campaign was successful in eradicating malaria; typhoid is endemic, but acquired immunity prevents serious outbreaks of this disease. Sewage disposal and other health and sanitation facilities have been improved, but much still needs to be done. In 1991, 95% of the population had access to safe water and 86% had adequate sanitation.

In 1960, life expectancy at birth was 43 years, but it averaged 69 years in 1992. During the same time period, infant mortality fell from 185 to 35 per 1,000 live births. The infant mortality rate stands considerably above those of middle-income countries. This fact may reflect the high infant death rate among the Bedouin, which has been estimated to account for about one-third of all infant deaths. The maternal mortality rate was 41 per 100,000 live births in 1991, and the general mortality rate was 4.9 per 1,000 people in 1993. The country's 1993 birth rate was 35.9 per 1,000 inhabitants. There were 574,000 births in 1992. In 1992 97% of the population had access to health care services. Total health care expenditures in 1990 were $4,784 million.

42HOUSING

The continuing influx of rural people to towns and cities, coupled with the rise in levels of expectation among the urban population, has created a serious housing problem; improvement in urban housing is one of Sa'udi Arabia's foremost economic needs. Some 506,800 dwelling units were built during 1974–85, 389,000 by the private sector, with the help of the Real Estate Development Fund, and 117,800 by the Deputy Ministry of Housing and other government agencies. In 1984, 78,884 building permits were issued, 84% of these for concrete dwellings and 8% for housing units of blocks and bricks. In the oil districts, ARAMCO, through loans and other assistance, has encouraged construction of private homes and has built accommodations for its unmarried Sa'udi staff members.

43EDUCATION

Until the mid-1950s, Sa'udi Arabia's educational system was primarily oriented toward religious schooling that stressed knowledge of the Qur'an (Koran) and Hadith (sayings of Muhammed and his companions). Except for basic arithmetic, reading, and writing, secular subjects were not taught in the schools. There was a highly developed oral culture, however. Nearly all of the students were boys; education of girls was virtually nonexistent and took place in the home, if at all. In 1960/61, 143,000 students attended public and private schools. Of those attending public schools, 96.2% were boys. The literacy rate in the 1960s was 3%. In the mid-1980s, about 43% of students were female. The literacy rate was more than 51%; in 1990, it was 62.4%. As of 1985, attendance in primary school was required by law. Education is free at all levels, including college and postgraduate study. In 1990 there were 9,097 primary schools, with 1,876,916 pupils and 119,881 teachers. Secondary schools had 892,585 students and 71,149 teachers. Higher education was pursued in 99 institutions, with 84,740 students and 9,512 instructors. The principal universities are King Sa'ud University (formerly Riyadh University), founded in 1957, and King 'Abd al-'Aziz University of Jiddah, founded in 1967. All higher level institutions had 153,967 pupils and 13,260 teachers in 1990.

44LIBRARIES AND MUSEUMS

The National Library, founded in Riyadh in 1968, has 37,000 volumes. The largest library system is that of King Sa'ud University established in 1957, with 14 branches and a collection of more than 1.1 million volumes; the library at King 'Abd al-'Aziz University has 434,592 volumes. The library of the University of Petroleum and Minerals in Dhahran, with almost 300,000 volumes, is the nation's largest specialized collection. The largest public library, at Riyadh, contains almost 150,000 volumes.

The Museum of Archaeology and Ethnography was opened at Riyadh in 1978. Six museums located at archaeological sites are to be opened shortly. There are plans to establish a national museum and five regional museums.

45MEDIA

Postal, telephone, cable, and wireless services are regulated by the Ministry of Communications. Sa'udi Arabia is directly connected by radiotelephone with the US, other Arab countries, and Western Europe, and automatic internal lines connect most of the major cities. The telephone system was greatly expanded in the late 1970s, and in 1991 some 1,752,204 telephones were in use. Broadcasting emanates from the government-owned Sa'udi Arabian Broadcasting Service, Saudi ARAMCO FM stations, Saudi-Arabian TV, and an ARAMCO channel in Dhahran. The number of radios was estimated at 4.7 million, and the number of television sets at 4.1 million in 1991.

The first newspaper in what is now Sa'udi Arabia was *Al-Qiblah*, the official publication of King Hussein of Hijaz, founded in 1915. With the end of the short-lived Hijaz kingdom in 1925, a Sa'udi-sponsored paper, called *Umm al-Qura (The Mother of Towns*, Mecca), was established. Newspapers are privately owned; criticism of the fundamental principles of Islam and of basic national institutions, including the royal family, is not permitted. The largest Arabic daily papers (with 1991 circulations) are *Asharq Al-Arusat* (175,000); *Al-Jazirah* (90,000); and *Al-Bilad* (90,000). Leading English-language dailies are the *Arab News* (50,000) and *Saudi Gazette* (50,000).

46ORGANIZATIONS

Sa'udi social tradition, which emphasizes the exclusiveness of family, clan, and tribe, militates against the formation of other social organizations. The absence of political and economic organizations also is a result of the prevalence of tradition. There are chambers of commerce in Ad-Dammam, Jiddah, Mecca, Medina, and Riyadh.

47TOURISM, TRAVEL, AND RECREATION

Sa'udi Arabia is one of the hardest places in the world to visit. Tourist visas are not issued, and foreign visitors must show letters of invitation from Sa'udi employers or sponsors to enter the country. Every year, however, there is a great influx of pilgrims to Mecca and Medina, cities that non-Muslims are forbidden to enter. In 1991 the number of pilgrims totaled 720,000. Total visitor arrivals totaled 2.3 million. Evidence of a previous or planned trip to Israel is grounds for denial of admission to Sa'udi Arabia.

Traditional sports include hunting with salukis, falconry, and horse and camel racing. Modern sports facilities include the Riyadh Stadium, complete with Olympic-standard running tracks and soccer fields.

The 445,000-hectare (1,100,000-acre) 'Asir National Park was opened to the public in 1982. A second national park is planned in the Al-Ahsa region.

48FAMOUS SA'UDIS

Although Sa'udi Arabia has a relatively short history as a nation-state, it is heir to an Islamic civilization that developed from the teachings of Muhammad (570–632), born of the tribe of Quraysh in Mecca. The branch of Islam which claims most contemporary Sa'udis is that preached by Muhammad bin 'Abd al-Wahhab (1703?–91), a fundamentalist reformer.

The Sa'udi who has gained greatest renown outside the modern kingdom of Sa'udi Arabia is 'Abd al-'Aziz ibn 'Abd ar-Rahman al-Faysal as-Sa'ud, better known as Ibn-Sa'ud (1880–1953), the father of his country. Forced into exile with his family at a young age, he reconquered his patrimony and left behind him the state of Sa'udi Arabia. In 1964, Faisal (Faysal ibn-'Abd al-'Aziz as-Sa'ud, 1906–75) was proclaimed king. In his role as prime minister, Faisal instituted many economic and social reforms, including the abolition of slavery. Upon his assassination in March 1975, he was succeeded as king and prime minister by Khaled (Khalid ibn-'Abd al-'Aziz, 1913–82). Together with Crown Prince Fahd ibn-'Abd al-'Aziz (b.1920), King Khaled broadened the country's development policies. After Khaled's death, Fahd became king; he has pursued the same cautious program of modernization as his two predecessors. Ahmad Zaki Yamani (b.1930), a former minister of petroleum and mineral resources, gained an international reputation as a spokesman for the oil-exporting countries.

49DEPENDENCIES

Sa'udi Arabia has no territories or colonies.

50BIBLIOGRAPHY

Abir, Mordechai. *Sa'udi Arabia: Government, Society, and the Gulf Crisis*. New York: Routledge, 1993.

Beling, Willard A. (ed.). *King Faisal and the Modernization of Sa'udi Arabia*. Boulder, Colo.: Westview, 1980.

Farsy, Fouad. *Modernity and Tradition: The Saudi Equation*. New York: Kegan Paul International, 1990.

Gause, F. Gregory. *Saudi-Yemeni Relations: Domestic Structures and Foreign Influence*. New York: Columbia University Press, 1990.

Holden, David, and Richard Johns. *The House of Saud*. New York: Holt, Rinehart & Winston, 1981.

Katz, Mark N. *Russia and Arabia: Soviet Foreign Policy Toward the Arabian Peninsula*. Baltimore, Md.: Johns Hopkins University Press, 1986.

Kostiner, Joseph. *The Making of Sa'udi Arabia, 1916–1936: from Chieftancy to Monarchical State*. New York: Oxford University Press, 1993.

Lawrence, T. E. *Seven Pillars of Wisdom*. New York: Penguin, 1976 (orig. 1926).

Looney, Robert E. *Economic Development in Sa'udi Arabia: Consequences of the Oil Price Decline*. Greenwich, Conn.: JAI Press, 1990.

Metz, Helen Chapin (ed.). *SA'UDI ARABIA: A Country Study*. 5th ed. Washington, D.C.: Library of Congress, 1993.

Nicholson, Reynold Alleyne. *A Library History of the Arabs*. Cambridge: Cambridge University Press, 1956.

Philipp, Hans-Jurgen. *Sa'udi Arabia: Bibliography on Society, Politics, Economics*. New York: Saur, 1984–1989.

Presley, John R. *A Guide to the Sa'udi Arabian Economy*. 2d ed. Basingstoke: Macmillan, 1989.

Riley, Carroll L. *Historical and Cultural Dictionary of SA'UDI ARABIA*. Metuchen, N.J.: Scarecrow, 1972.

Winder, R. Bayly. *Sa'udi Arabia in the Nineteenth Century*. New York: St. Martin's, 1965.

Zwemer, Samuel M. *Arabia, The Cradle of Islam: Studies in the Geography, People and Politics of the Peninsula*. New York: Gordon, 1980.

SINGAPORE

Republic of Singapore

CAPITAL: Singapore.

FLAG: The flag consists of a red stripe at the top and a white stripe on the bottom. On the red stripe, at the hoist, are a white crescent opening to the fly and five white stars.

ANTHEM: *Long Live Singapore.*

MONETARY UNIT: The Singapore dollar (s$) of 100 cents is a freely convertible currency. There are coins of 1, 5, 10, 20, and 50 cents and 1 dollar and notes of 2, 5, 10, 20, 50, 100, 500, 1,000, and 10,000 dollars. s$1 = us$0.6373 (or us$1 = s$1.5692).

WEIGHTS AND MEASURES: The metric system is in force, but some local measures are used.

HOLIDAYS: Major Western, Chinese, Malay, and Muslim holidays are celebrated, some of which fall on annually variable dates because of the calendars used. Major holidays include New Year's Day, 1 January; Chinese New Year; Good Friday; Vesak Day (Buddhist festival); Labor Day, 1 May; Hari Raya Puasa (Muslim festival); National Day, 9 August; Hari Raya Haji (Malay Muslim festival); Dewali; Christmas, 25 December.

TIME: 8 PM = noon GMT.

¹LOCATION, SIZE, AND EXTENT

The Republic of Singapore, the second smallest country in Asia, consists of Singapore Island and several smaller adjacent islets. Situated in the Indian Ocean off the southern tip of the Malay Peninsula, Singapore has an area of 632.6 sq km (244.2 sq mi), of which Singapore Island comprises 570.4 sq km (220.2 sq mi) and the islets 50.1 sq km (19.3 sq mi). Comparatively, the area occupied by Singapore is slightly less than 3.5 times the size of Washington, D.C. Singapore Island extends 41.8 km (26 mi) ENE–WSW and 22.5 km (14 mi) SSE–NNW and has a coastline of 193 km (120 mi), including about 84 km (52 mi) along the water channel between the island and the Malay Peninsula. Singapore is connected to the nearby western portion of Malaysia by a causeway 1,056 m (3,465 ft) in length across the narrow Johore Strait. Singapore's position at the eastern end of the Strait of Malacca, which separates western Malaysia and the Indonesian island of Sumatra, has given it economic and strategic importance out of proportion to its small size. Singapore's capital city, Singapore, is located on the country's southern coast.

²TOPOGRAPHY

Singapore Island is mostly low-lying, green, undulating country with a small range of hills at the center. The highest point of the island is Bukit Timah (177 m/581 ft). There are sections of rain forest in the center and large mangrove swamps along the coast, which has many inlets, particularly in the north and west. Singapore's harbor is wide, deep, and well protected.

³CLIMATE

The climate is tropical, with heavy rainfall and high humidity. The range of temperature is slight; the average annual maximum is 31°C (88°F), and the average minimum 24°C (75°F). The annual rainfall of 237 cm (93 in) is distributed fairly evenly throughout the year, ranging from 39 cm (15 in) in December to 28 cm (11 in) in May. It rains about one day in two.

⁴FLORA AND FAUNA

Singapore Island is in the main denuded, the dense tropical forest that originally covered it being mostly cleared. There is some rain forest in the central area of the island, however, as well as extensive mangrove swamps along the coast. Urban development has limited animal life.

⁵ENVIRONMENT

Environmental responsibility for Singapore is vested in the Ministry of the Environment and its Anti-Pollution Unit. Air quality is protected by the Clean Air Act, as adopted in 1971 and amended in 1975 and 1980, and by the Clean Air (Standards) Regulations of 1975. Regulations limiting the lead content of gasoline were imposed in 1981, and emissions standards for motor vehicles were tightened in 1986. Air pollution from transportation vehicles is a problem in the nation's growing urban areas. In 1985, the ministry took over the control of hazardous substances. Water quality is regulated through the Water Pollution Control and Drainage Act of 1975 and the Trade Effluent Regulations of 1976. Singapore does not have enough water to support the needs of its people. In total, the nation has .1 cubic miles of water. Four percent is used for farming and 51% for industrial purposes. Pollution from the nation's oil industry is also a significant problem. It contributes 0.1% of the world's total gas emissions. The nation's cities produce 0.9 million tons of solid waste per year. Waste water is treated and recycled to conserve water supplies. In 1985, the ministry spent s$47.2 million to construct new drains and s$86.4 million to improve sewage infrastructure. The Environmental Public Health Regulations of 1988 include environmental legislation concerning the control of the nation's pollution problem.

In 1994, 19 plant species were considered to be in danger of extinction. As of 1987, endangered species in Singapore included the Ridley's leaf-nosed bat and the Singapore roundleaf horseshoe bat.

⁶POPULATION

Singapore's mid-1993 estimated population was projected at 2,874,000; it had been 2,705,115 at the time of the 1990 census. The population for the year 2000 was projected at 2,976,000, based on an estimated birthrate of 14.2 per 1,000 population and a death rate of 5.8, for a net natural increase of 8.4 in the 1995–2000 period. As of mid-1992, nearly 40% of the population was under 20 years of age. The government has in the past pressed a vigorous birth-control campaign; as of 1991, the rate of population increase was 2.1% annually, having been as high as 4.9% in 1950–55.

Singapore is virtually a city-state, and the entire population is considered urban. The population density, estimated at 4,632 persons per sq km (11,995 per sq mi) in 1993, is the highest of any nation in the world (excluding Monaco).

⁷MIGRATION

Singapore had only a few Malay fishermen as inhabitants at the time of its founding as a British trading post in 1819. It was subsequently, and quite rapidly, populated by immigrant peoples, primarily Chinese but also Malays (from Sumatra as well as adjacent Malaya) and Indians (who took advantage of common British governance to migrate to Singapore in search of better employment). Thus immigration, rather than natural increase, was the major factor in Singapore's fast population growth through the mid-20th century.

In November 1965, following separation from Malaysia, Singapore's newly independent government introduced measures to restrict the flow of Malaysians entering the country in search of work. These immigrants, who averaged 10,000 a year up to 1964, had to establish residence for several years to qualify for citizenship. In addition, all non-citizens were required to apply for a work permit or employment pass. Immigration is now generally restricted to those with capital or with special skills.

⁸ETHNIC GROUPS

The people of Singapore are predominantly of Chinese origin. Of an estimated 1992 population of 2,818,200, about 2,187,200 (77.6%) were ethnic Chinese (most of them, however, born in Singapore or in neighboring Malaysia). Some 399,400 (14.2%) were Malays; 199,600 (7.1%) were Indians (including Pakistanis, Bangladeshis, and Sri Lankans).

⁹LANGUAGES

There are four official languages: Chinese (Mandarin dialect), Malay, English, and Tamil. English is the principal medium of government and is widely used in commerce. By 1987, under a government mandate, English was made the primary language of the school system. Malay is the national language. In 1990 Chinese dialects were the first language of 36.7% of the population and Mandarin of 26%. English was used by nearly 20%.

¹⁰RELIGIONS

There is complete separation of state and religion in Singapore. Freedom of religion is both constitutionally guaranteed and honored in practice. The Chinese for the most part (54% in 1991) adhere in varying degrees to Buddhism, Taoism, and Confucianism. Malays and persons with origins in the Pakistani and Bangladeshi portions of the Indian subcontinent—about 16% of the population—are almost exclusively Muslims. Most of the Indian minority are Hindus. The Christian population was estimated in 1991 at 13%.

¹¹TRANSPORTATION

Singapore's history is partly the history of the island-country's important regional role as a transportation link between East and West and between the mainland and insular portions of Southeast Asia. As long ago as 1822—only three years after the establishment of a British colonial presence on the island—1,575 ships called at the new port of Singapore from nearby islands, Europe, India, and China. With a natural deepwater harbor that is open the year round, Singapore now ranks as the largest container port in the world, with anchorage facilities that can accommodate supertankers. Ships of some 600 shipping lines, flying the flags of nearly all the maritime nations of the world, regularly call at Singapore. In 1991, Singapore itself had the 14th largest merchant fleet, at 478 ships totaling 8,684,350 GRT.

Commercial air service was inaugurated in Singapore in 1930. There are two major airports: Singapore Changi International Airport and Seletar Airport. Singapore's own flag carrier is Singapore Airlines, which carried 8,477,300 passengers in 1992, including about 50% of all visitors who came by air.

In 1991 there were 415,442 motor vehicles, of which 285,298 were automobiles. They traveled on 2,644 km (1,643 mi) of roads, of which 2,507 km (1,558 mi) were paved. Singapore's sole rail facility is a 26-km (16-mi) section of the Malayan Railways, which links Singapore to Kuala Lumpur. The first stage of a 66.8-km (41.5-mi) rapid-transit system opened to the public in November 1987.

¹²HISTORY

The early history of Singapore is obscure. There appears to have been a reference to an island at the tip of the Malay Peninsula by a Chinese explorer as early as AD 231. Some historians believe a city was founded on the island as early as the 7th century, while other sources claim that "Singapura" (Lion City) was established by an Indian prince in 1299. It is thought to have been a thriving trading center in the 13th and 14th centuries, until it was devastated by a Javanese attack in 1377. Singapore, however, was an almost uninhabited island when Sir Stamford Raffles, in 1819, established a trading station of the British East India Company on the island. In 1824, the island was ceded outright to the company by the Sultan of Johore, the Malay state at the extreme southern end of the Peninsula, and in 1826 it was incorporated with Malacca (Melaka, Malaysia) and Penang (Pinang, Malaysia) to form the Straits Settlements, which was the form of its legal status and administration up to World War II. The trading center grew into the city of Singapore and attracted large numbers of Chinese, many of whom became merchants, until it became a largely Chinese-populated community.

With its excellent harbor, Singapore also became a flourishing commercial center and the leading seaport of Southeast Asia, handling the vast export trade in tin and rubber from British-ruled Malaya. In 1938, the British completed construction of a large naval base on the island, which the Japanese captured in February 1942 during World War II, following a land-based attack from the Malay Peninsula to the north.

Recaptured by the UK in 1945, Singapore was detached from the Straits Settlements to become a separate crown colony in 1946. Under a new constitution, on 3 June 1959, Singapore became a self-governing state, and on 16 September 1963, it joined the new Federation of Malaysia (formed by bringing together the previously independent Malaya and Singapore and the formerly British-ruled northern Borneo territories of Sarawak and Sabah). However, Singapore, with its predominantly urban Chinese population and highly commercial economy, began to find itself at odds with the Malay-dominated central government of Malaysia. Frictions mounted, and on 9 August 1965, Singapore separated from Malaysia to become wholly independent in its own right as the Republic of Singapore. Singapore, Indonesia, Malaysia, the Philippines and Thailand formed the Association of South-East Asian Nations (ASEAN) in 1967. Brunei became a member of ASEAN in 1984. Harry Lee Kuan Yew, a major figure in the move toward independence, served as the country's prime minister from 1959, the achievement of state-hood.

The People's Action Party (PAP) founded in 1954 has been the dominant political party winning every general election since 1959. The PAP's popular support rested on economic growth and improved standards of living along with unrelenting repression of opposition leaders. Although the PAP regularly carried 60% to 75% of the popular vote, it has stayed in power with a declining percentage of the popular vote. The PAP won all Parliamentary seats in the general elections from 1968 to 1980. In the 1981 by election J. B. Jeyaretnam, Secretary-General of the Workers' Party, won a seat; he maintained it in the 1984 general election. Chiam See Tong leader of the Singapore Democratic Party (SDP) won another seat for the opposition in the same election. (See Political Parties and Government) In March 1985 the third state President, Devan Nair, former trade unionist and member of Singapore's "old guard" resigned from office under clouded allegations having to do with alcoholism. The new President, Wee Kim Wee, took office in August. In May and June 1987 the Government detained 22 persons under the Internal Security Act (ISA) for alleged involvement in a "Marxist conspiracy." These detentions triggered an international response on human rights critical of the detentions without trial and allegations of torture of the detainees. Most of the alleged conspirators were released by December, but eight were rearrested in April 1988 after issuing a joint press statement regarding the circumstances of their detention. Francis Seow represented two of the detainees, Teo Soh Lung and Patrick Seong. Patrick Seong was first arrested when the detainees were rearrested in April 1988, and Teo Soh Lung was amongst the original group arrested. Both Teo and Seong are lawyers. In May 1988 Seow was arrested under the ISA while visiting Teo at the Whitley Detention Centre, and released in July. Seow (Workers' Party) contested a seat in the 1988 general election. Based on his narrow defeat he was offered one of the two non-constituency seats. In December 1988 Seow sought medical treatment in the United States. During his absence he was tried for tax evasion, convicted, and fined S$19,000. The amount of the fine precluded his taking the seat in parliament. Seow has remained in exile in the US. Teo Soh Lung and Vincent Cheng remained in detention until their release in June 1990.

For the September 1988 general election the electoral system was altered by increasing the 79 existing constituencies to 81. These 81 were structured by the creation of 42 single-member constituencies and the reorganization of the other 39 seats into 13 group representation constituencies (GRCs). The GRCs were contested by teams of three representatives for each party, at least one of which must be a from an ethnic minority, i.e., non-Chinese. Ostensibly these changes were to ensure minority participation, but at the same time small and/or resourceless opposition parties were handicapped by a requirement to field three candidates. In November 1992 it was announced that Deputy Prime Minister, Lee Hsien Loong (son of Lee Kuan Yew), and Ong Teng Cheong had been diagnosed with cancer. On 28 November 1990 Lee Kuan Yew, Prime Minister of Singapore for over thirty-one years, transferred the prime ministership to Goh Chock Tong, the former First Deputy Prime Minister. Lee remained in the Cabinet as Senior Minister to the Prime Minister's Office and retained the position of Secretary-General of the PAP. Singapore's first direct presidential elections were held on 28 August 1993. Ong Teng Cheong is the first elected President.

An incident that garnered worldwide attention was the Singapore Government's arrest in October 1993 of nine foreign youths charged with vandalism of some 70 cars which were spray painted. Michael Fay an American student and the oldest in the group, 18 years, was suspected to be the leader. Under police interrogation Fay admitted his guilt, pleaded guilty in court to two counts of vandalism and one count of receiving stolen prop-

LOCATION: 1°9′ to 1°29′N; 103°38′ to 104°6′E. **TERRITORIAL SEA LIMIT:** 3 mi.

erty. In March 1994 Fay was sentenced to four months' in prison, a fine of US$2,230 and six strokes of the cane. On 7 March 1994 President Clinton urged Singapore to reconsider the flogging of Fay. Fay's appeal was dismissed. A plea to the president for clemency was rejected, but as a "goodwill gesture towards President Clinton," the sentence of caning was reduced from six strokes to four. The sentence was carried out on 5 May 1994.

13GOVERNMENT

The constitution of the Republic of Singapore, as amended in 1965, provides for a unicameral parliamentary form of government, with a president who prior to 1991 served as titular head of state. Singapore practices universal suffrage, and voting has been compulsory for all citizens over 21 since 1959.

In 1993 the unicameral legislature consisted of an 81 elected-member parliament and six nominated members (NMPs) appointed by the president. The maximum term for parliamentary sessions is five years, although elections may be called at any time within that period. A general election is held within three months of a dissolution. The number of parliamentary seats has increased with each general election, since the general election seating Singapore's First Parliament, 58 seats (1968), 60 seats (1972), 69 seats (1976), 75 seats (1980), 79 seats (1984), and 81 seats (1988).

Until the 1988 election all constituencies were single-member constituencies. In 1988, sixty of the original 81 constituencies (out of the increased number for 1988 i.e. from 79 in 1984 to 81 in 1988) were reorganized into 15 group representation constituencies (GRCs). In each GRC teams of three candidates must be fielded, one of whom must be from a minority community, i.e., of an ethnic minority group, Malay, Indian, or an Other (all persons other than Chinese, Malay, or Indian). A 1984 constitutional amendment allowed for the presence of at least three opposition representatives as non-constituency (nominated) Members of Parliament (NMPs), and in 1990 a law increasing their number was passed. Accordingly, up to six NMPs can be appointed from among opposition candidates who were unsuccessful in an election; these NMPs are given limited voting rights.

In the 1991 General Election 60 members were elected from the 15 four-member GRCs, 21 from single-member constituencies, and the President appointed 6 Nominated Members of Parliament. In this election a change was made to the election procedures, i.e., in each team contesting a GRC the number of candidates fielded was increased to four, and the minority qualification of one person from a minority community was still maintained.

The prime minister, who commands the confidence of a majority of Parliament, acts as effective head of government. The prime minister appoints a cabinet which, in 1993, consisted of a senior minister, two deputy prime ministers, and 11 other ministers. Prior to 29 November 1991 the president of the republic was elected by Parliament for a term of four years. Since 1991, under an amendment to the constitution passed by parliament, the president is no longer elected by parliament but by the electorate, and has custodial powers over the country's reserves, as well as playing a major role in deciding key appointments to the judiciary, civil service and statutory boards. The president is elected for a term of six years. The first direct presidential elections were held on 28 August 1993. Singapore's first elected president is Ong Teng Cheong.

¹⁴POLITICAL PARTIES

Singapore in the late 1980s was effectively a single-party state. The ruling People's Action Party (PAP) of former Prime Minister Lee Kuan Yew has dominated the country since 1959. In 1961, the radical wing of the PAP split from Lee's majority faction to form a new party, the Socialist Front (SF), also known as the Barisan Socialis. In 1966, 11 SF members resigned their seats in Parliament, and 2 others joined the underground opposition to the Lee government, leaving the PAP as the sole party represented in Parliament. In the general elections of 1972, 1976, and 1980, the PAP won all seats in Parliament, but carried a declining percentage of the total votes; 65 seats (84.4%); 69 seats (72.4%); and 75 seats (75.5%)[Far Eastern Economic Review (FEER) 77.7%], respectively. The Workers' Party (WP), the strongest opposition party, had won its first parliamentary seat in a 1981 by-election; under its leader, Joshua B. Jeyaretnam, the WP has been critical of undemocratic practices within the PAP government. In the 1984 general elections, the PAP won 77 of the 79 seats, even though it captured only 62.9% of the popular vote, compared with 75.5% in 1980.

The two other seats went to J. B. Jeyaretnam (WP) and to Chiam See Tong of the Singapore Democratic Party (SDP). In 1984, Jeyaretnam was accused of making false statements involving irregularities in the collection of WP's funds; he was acquitted of two of three charges and fined. In 1986 the government appealed the case and the higher court set aside the initial judgment; Jeyaretnam was again fined and jailed for one month, enough to disqualify him from parliament and ban him from contesting elections for five years. On the basis of his criminal convictions he was disbarred, and denied a pardon. He was refused permission to appeal against the conviction and sentence that resulted in his disqualification as an MP. But on appeal to the Privy Council against the decision to disbar him, he was vindicated and allowed to practice law again. In October 1991 Jeyaret-

nam avoided bankruptcy by paying legal costs in a defamation suit he lost, filed by Lee Kuan Yew over remarks made by Jeyaretnam in a 1988 election rally. On 10 November 1991, the ban on Jeyaretnam standing election expired. By avoiding bankruptcy he would be able to contest the by-elections that Prime Minister Goh promised to hold in the next 12–18 months. However, the WP failed to field the four required candidates for a GRC.

In the 1984, 1988, and 1991 general elections Opposition parties gained small ground, and the PAP continued to garner a declining percentage of the total votes: 77 seats (62.9%) PAP [FEER 64.8%], 1 seat Workers Party (WP), 1 seat Singapore Democratic Party (SDP); 80 seats (61.7%) PAP [FEER 63.2%], 1 seat SDP; 77 (61%) PAP [FEER 61.%], 1 seat WP, 3 seats SDP, respectively. In the 1991 elections Chiam See Tong was again the winner for the SDP, along with Ling How Doong and Cheo Chai Chen. The Workers' Party MP was Low Thai Khiang.

In March 1993 Dr. Chee Soon Juan, an opposition politician from the Singapore Democratic Party (SDP) who ran against Prime Minister Goh Chok Tong in the 1992 by-election, was expelled from his post as lecturer in the Department of Social Work and Psychology at the National University of Singapore (NUS) based on claims of "dishonest conduct." Chee was charged with using US$138 out of his research grant to courier his wife's doctoral thesis to a US university. Chee claimed that his wife's work was relevant to his own work, and that he had been open about what was done. Chiam See Tong defended Chee in Parliament claiming that Chee's dismissal was political. After he made an unsuccessful appeal against his dismissal, Chee began a hunger strike on 5 April 1993, calling it off ten days later. The government denied that Chee's dismissal was politically motivated. Chiam See Tong reversed his position on Chee's dismissal and criticized his hunger strike as detrimental to the credibility of the SDP. Dr. Chee was sued for defamation by three individuals associated with NUS. He lost all three case and was fined a total of S$315,000 plus interest and costs in 1994.

In May 1993 Chiam See Tong was re-elected as secretary-general of the SDP, but quit the post due to internal party strife over lack of party support for his motion to censure Dr. Chee. After many serious attempts to encourage Chiam to stay with the SDP, which he refused, Chiam was expelled from the party. On 20 August 1993 Chiam got a court order preventing the SDP's Central Executive Committee (CEC) from expelling him from the party, an action which would cause him to lose his seat in parliament. On 10 December 1993 Singapore's High Court ruled that Chiam was sacked illegally from the SDP, and he was reinstated. He continued serving as MP.

The main opposition parties are the SDP and the WP. Smaller minority parties are the United People's Front, which is also critical of antidemocratic aspects of Lee's rule and is pro-Malaysian; the Singapore Malays' National Organization; and the Singapore Solidarity Party, formed in 1986 by three former leaders of the SDP. There were 22 registered political parties at the beginning of 1993: Singapore Chinese Party; Persatuan Melayu Singapura; Partai Rakyat, Singapore State Division; Angkatan Islam; The Workers' Party; Pertubohan Kebangsaan Melayu Singapura; People's Action Party (PAP); United People's Party; Barisan Socialis (BS), Socialist Front (SF); Parti Kesatuan Ra'ayat (United Democratic Party); Singapore Indian Congress; Alliance Party Singapura; United National Front; National Party of Singapore; The People's Front; Justice Party, Singapore; Democratic Progressive Party; People's Republican Party; United People's Front; Singapore Democratic Party (SDP); National Solidarity Party (NSP); Singapore National Front. The Malay Communist Party and the underground Malayan National Liberation Front are illegal.

¹⁵LOCAL GOVERNMENT

Singapore, veritably a city-state, has no local government divisions. When the People's Action Party (PAP) came to power in 1959, the post-colonial City Council was abolished. The former city council and rural board were integrated into departments of the central government. The Town Councils Act enacted in June 1988 reintroduced a local organizational structure. Town councils were formed to take over the management and maintenance of the common properties of housing estates within towns. As of 1 March 1991, 27 town councils had been formed. After the general elections of August 1991, five town councils were dissolved and three new town councils were established, bringing the number of town councils to 25. Suggestions have been introduced to create the position of mayor for each council.

[16]JUDICIAL SYSTEM

Singapore's legal system is based on British common law. The judiciary includes the Supreme Court as well as district, magistrate's, and special courts. Minor cases are heard in the country's ten magistrate's courts and in district courts (two civil and four criminal), each presided over by a district judge. The Supreme Court is headed by a chief justice and is divided into the High Court, the Court of Appeal, and the Court of Criminal Appeal. The High Court has unlimited original jurisdiction in both criminal and civil cases but ordinarily chooses to exercise such jurisdictional authority only in major cases. In its appellate jurisdiction, the High Court hears criminal and civil appeals from the magistrates' and district courts. Appeal in a civil case heard by the High Court in its original jurisdiction is to the Court of Appeal, and in a criminal case, to the Court of Criminal Appeal.

In 1993 the former Court of Appeal (for civil cases) and the Court of Criminal Appeal were combined to form a single Court of Appeal. This reform is part of an overall plan to the eventual elimination of referrals to the Privy Council in London. The Privy Council continues to hear appeals from very serious cases involving convictions for life imprisonment or the death penalty.

The President appoints judges of the Supreme Court to renewable two-year terms. A Legal Service Commission supervises and assigns the placement of the subordinate court judges and magistrates who have the status of civil servants.

[17]ARMED FORCES

Singapore has made major efforts since 1965 to develop its own armed forces. Compulsory national service has been in effect since 1967. Male citizens are called up for 24 months' full-time military service at age 18. The active forces number 55,500 (84,800 conscripts).

Singapore's armed forces are small, but they are well trained and equipped, and their reserve strength (250,000 in 1993) is substantial. In 1993, the army had an estimated 45,000 personnel, including one combined arms division; the navy had 4,500 personnel and a fleet of 30 ships, including 6 corvettes and 6 missile gunboats. The air force, established in 1969, had 6,000 personnel and more than 192 combat and transport aircraft. Paramilitary forces included 11,600 police and a home guard of 100,000. The 1990 defense budget was $1.7 billion or 4 percent of gross domestic product.

[18]INTERNATIONAL COOPERATION

Singapore follows a policy of cooperation with international bodies and the community of nations. Having joined the UN on 21 September 1965, Singapore participates in ESCAP and all the nonregional specialized agencies except FAO, IDA, IFAD, UNESCO, UNIDO, and WIPO. It is a participant in the Asian Development Bank, the Colombo Plan, the Commonwealth of Nations, and G-77 and has acceded to GATT and to the Law of the Sea. Probably its most important international association is its membership—along with Indonesia, Malaysia, Thailand, the Philippines, and Brunei—in ASEAN. Singapore has played a lead-

ing part in this important regional grouping, which has sought to maximize economic cooperation among its member states, to regularize political consultation on the part of the constituent governments, and to limit foreign political and military interference in the area. Under Premier Lee Kuan Yew, Singapore has had particularly close relations with the US, although relations with the USSR have also been cordial. Because of its large ethnic Chinese majority, however, Singapore has been reluctant to seek out full diplomatic ties with China, although there have been a variety of economic and other exchanges.

[19]ECONOMY

Historically, Singapore's economy was based primarily on its role as an entrepöt for neighboring countries due to its strategic geographic location. It did not have minerals or other primary products of its own to export, but it served a major economic function by processing and transshipping the goods of nearby lands. Its most significant natural resource is a deep water harbor. As a result of these circumstances, Singapore became highly active in shipbuilding and repair, tin smelting, and rubber and copra milling. Until about 1960, however, its economy was frequently shaken by major fluctuations in its export earnings (particularly from rubber and tin) as a consequence of often adverse commodity and price trends. Since the early 1960s, Singapore has attempted to break away from this economic pattern. Its government embarked on an ambitious and largely successful program of promoting industrial investment (both from abroad and locally), developing industrial estates, and providing industrial financing and technical services.

By the early 1980s, Singapore had built a much stronger and diversified economy, which gave it an economic importance in Southeast Asia out of proportion to its small size. Government plans during the first half of the 1980s called for realigning industrial activities from traditional labor-intensive, low-wage activities to capital-intensive, high-wage and high-technology activities, notably the electrical and electronic industries and oil refining. In 1985, however, Singapore's economy declined for the first time in 20 years. One of the reasons for the decline was high wages, which made Singaporean products less competitive on the world market. Other reasons for the economic downturn included a slumping demand for oil and electronic products and the economic woes of Malaysia, Indonesia, and other important trading partners.

By the late 1980s, Singapore had begun to further diversify its economy, making it capable of providing manufacturing, financial, and communications facilities for multinational firms. Real GDP expanded by 1.8% in 1986. In the late 1980s one of the fastest growing sectors of Singapore's economy was international banking and finance, accounting for some 25% of GDP. It ranked behind Tokyo and Hong Kong amongst financial service centers in the Southeast Asia region. In 1989 earnings from manufacturing accounted for 30% of GDP; Singapore was world's largest producer of disk drive parts.

In the 1990s Singapore planned to develop the economy through privatization of its highly profitable utilities and major investments abroad. In 1990 as a percent of GDP industry accounted for 35.8%, services for 67.8%, and agriculture for 0.3%. For 1991 the main sectors contributing to GDP were: manufacturing (27.3%), financial and business services (26%), and commerce (15.7%). The inflation rate based on consumer prices in 1992 was 2.3%. The unemployment rate as of June 1992 was 2.7%. Major export commodities were computer equipment, rubber and rubber products, petroleum products and telecommunications equipment. Major export partners were the US 21%, Malaysia 13%, Hong Kong 8%, Japan 7%, and Thailand 6%. Major import commodities were aircraft, petroleum, chemicals and foodstuffs. Major import partners were Japan 21%, US 16%,

Malaysia 14%, and Taiwan 4%. Tourism was a major foreign exchange earner. Total revenue from tourism in 1992 increased by 9.1% over 1991. In 1992 the employment rate grew by 2.1%; 27.5% were employed in manufacturing, 22.6% in commerce, 10.9% in financial and business services, 10% in transport and communications, 6.6% in construction, and the remainder in other services, agriculture, and utilities. The unemployment rate remained below 2.7%. The exodus of professional and skilled personnel remained a problem; in 1992 the number of Singaporeans recruited for oversees work grew by an estimated 10-15%. A 3% Goods and Services Tax (GST), essentially a form of value-added tax (VAT), was effected on 1 April 1994. As of mid-1994 Singapore experienced a boom with an annual GDP growth for 1993 of 9.9%, and a 1994 first quarter growth rate of 11%. Productivity increased as did labor costs. Export growth in high-technology manufactured goods signaled Singapore's success in shifting to higher value-added production. The electronics industry accounted for the largest share of value-added in manufacturing. Manufacturing was dominated by the production of computer peripherals and oil processing. Since 1992 property prices have doubled and residential property prices were still climbing in mid-1994. The main constraints on Singapore's economic performance are labor shortages, rising labor costs, and erosion of productivity. The Government encouraged local companies to invest in the region in order to internationalize the economy.

20INCOME

In 1992, Singapore's GNP was $44,315 million at current prices, or $15,750 per capita. For the period 1985–92 the average inflation rate was 2.7%, resulting in a real growth rate in per capita GNP of 5.9%.

In 1991, manufacturing contributed an estimated 29% to GDP; electricity, gas, and water, 2%; construction, 7%; wholesale and retail trade, 17%; transport, storage, and communication, 13%; finance, insurance, real estate, and business services, 28%; community, social, and personal services, 4%.

21LABOR

In 1992, Singapore's employed work force totaled 1,576,200. Of this number, 27.5% were employed in manufacturing; 22.6% in commerce; 21.5% in community, social, and personal services; 10% in transportation, storage, and communications; 6.5% in construction; 10.9% in finance, insurance, real estate, and business services; and 1% in other sectors. The unemployment rate, was 4.5% in April 1987 and 1.9% in mid-1991. Continued growth of the work force from the mid-1960s through the 1980s was largely the result of the government's successful industrialization program.

There is no minimum wage legislation. At the end of 1991, the average real weekly earnings for a semi-skilled factory worker was $146.20. Employees generally work 46.7 hours a week and are entitled to 11 paid holidays and a vacation of 7–14 days, depending on length of service. An annual bonus equal to at least one month's salary is customarily paid. The Industrial Relations Act of 1968 controls relations between management (public and private) and labor.

In 1992, there were 83 registered trade unions in Singapore, all but nine of which were affiliated with Singapore's National Trade Unions Congress (which represents, as a result, about 98.5% of the country's organized workers). The government generally asserts a strong influence over trade policies.

22AGRICULTURE

Urbanization and industrialization have taken ever larger amounts of land away from agricultural activity in post-World War II Singapore. Many of the rubber and coconut plantations that dominated Singapore's landscape before the war have disappeared altogether. Housing for a growing population—and factories for its employment—stand where rubber and coconut trees used to grow. Nonetheless, agriculture remains part of Singapore's total economic activity. Growing methods on the island are the most intensive in all of Southeast Asia.

About 1.6% of the land area is used for farming, and vegetables remain a significant source of income. Remarkably, through the decades of the 1960s and 1970s and into the 1980s, Singapore was able to increase its primary produce annually through intensification. In 1992, production of fresh vegetables totaled 5,000 tons, resulting in a decreased need to rely on foreign produce imports. Despite this improvement, Singapore still imported 40% more by value in agricultural products than it exported in 1992. Orchids are grown for export.

23ANIMAL HUSBANDRY

Singapore has been self-sufficient (or nearly so) in the production of pork, poultry, and eggs since 1964, a notable achievement considering the modest amount of land available and the demands of growing urbanization and industrialization. Hog and poultry farming together constitute Singapore's largest primary products industry. However, hog farming is being phased out because of environmental pollution; domestic pork requirements are increasingly being met by imports. In 1992, the livestock population included 3 million chickens, 280,000 pigs, and 1,000 goats. That year also, about 15,000 tons of eggs, 69 tons of sheepskins, and 42 tons of cattle hides were produced.

The Pig and Poultry Research and Training Institute and Lim Chu Kang Veterinary Experimental Station conduct research on feeding, housing, breeding, management, and disease control.

24FISHING

Local fishermen operate chiefly in inshore waters, but some venture into the South China Sea and the Indian Ocean. Traditional fishing methods are in use along coastal waters, but there is a trend toward mechanization in both offshore and deep-sea fishing. In 1991, Singapore's fishermen caught 13,054 tons of fish.

All fresh fish are auctioned at the Jurong Central Fish Market and at the Punggol Fishing Port and Wholesale Fish Market. The Jurong facility provides modern shore-support assistance and processing plants. Aquaculture concentrates on the breeding of grouper, sea bass, mussels, and prawns; a marine fish-farming scheme to encourage aquaculture in designated coastal waters was implemented in 1981; by the end of 1985, 60 marine fish farms were in operation. By 1990, Singapore was contributing 1.5% to the world's total exports of fresh, chilled, and frozen fish, valued at $198.1 million. In 1991, Singapore exported $499 million worth of fish and fish products.

25FORESTRY

There is little productive forestry left on the island, but Singapore continues to have a fairly sizable sawmilling industry, processing timber imported largely from Malaysia (with some additional imports from Indonesia). Both Malaysia and Indonesia are expanding their processing capacities, however, and the industry is declining in Singapore in the face of the government's policy shift to high-technology industries.

26MINING

There is no mining in Singapore.

27ENERGY AND POWER

Net installed electrical capacity in 1991 was 3.5 million kw; all power was generated thermally, largely from imported mineral fuels. Electricity generated in 1991 totaled 16.5 billion kwh, more than four times the 1974 total of 3.9 billion kwh. To meet increasing demand for electricity, a new power station was built on the island of Pulau Seraya off the southwest coast of Singapore. The first stage of this station became operational in 1987. Singapore, a major petroleum-refining center, produced gasoline in 1991 at a rate of 86,000 barrels per day; distillate fuel oil, 239,000; residual fuel oil, 232,000; jet fuel, 168,000; and kerosene, 55,000. The total output of 945,000 barrels per day ranked Singapore fifth in the Far East in 1991, after Japan, China, South Korea, and India.

28INDUSTRY

Singapore's major industries were once rubber milling and tin smelting. Political and economic factors combined to change this situation, however. Economically, the rubber-milling industry steadily declined as a result of a drop in demand, supply problems, and other factors. Singapore's separation from Malaysia in 1965 prompted the latter country to develop its own tin-smelting facilities.

The modern industrialization of Singapore began in 1961 with the creation of the Economic Development Board to formulate and implement an ambitious manufacturing scheme. Most of the first factories set up under this program were of an import-substitute nature requiring tariff protection, but many such protective tariffs were subsequently withdrawn. Large-scale foreign manufacturing operations in Singapore commenced in 1967 with the establishment of plants by several major multinational electronics corporations. The Jurong Town Corporation was established under the Jurong Town Corporation Act of 1968 to develop and manage industrial estates and sites in Singapore. In 1985, the corporation managed 25 industrial estates. Emphasis was on upgrading of facilities to attract high-technology and skill-intensive industries. The manufacturing sector grew by an average annual rate of about 20% during the 1962–74 period, and it registered an average annual increase of over 10% from 1975 to 1981.

Reflecting the nation's rapid industrialization, industry's share of the GDP rose from 12% in 1960 to 29% in 1981. Such dramatic achievements were in large measure made possible by the existence in Singapore even before the 1960s of one of the most developed economic infrastructures in Southeast Asia, as well as by government efforts to provide a skilled, disciplined, and highly motivated work force. However, during 1980–85, the manufacturing sector underwent major structural changes due to weakened global demand and accounted for only 23% of GDP in 1985. In 1985, Singapore's main industrial activity centered on electronics. Machinery and appliances accounted for 38% of all value added in manufacturing. Next in value-added manufacturing was chemical products at 10%. Other leading manufacturing sectors in 1985 were transport equipment, paper products and printing, fabricated metal products, and food and beverages. Foreign investment in manufacturing totaled us$4.2 billion; the aggregate value of all industrial production was s$38,735.1 million, of which machinery and appliances contributed 32.4% and petroleum refining 27.5%.

Manufacturing accounted for 28% of GDP in 1992 and employed some 27.5% of the work force. About 80% of the investment in manufacturing is from foreign sources. Petroleum refining is a well-established industry in Singapore. After Rotterdam and Houston, Singapore is the world's third largest refining center. Production capacity is one million barrels a day. A major petrochemical complex is planned to be built on a site created by joining five offshore islands through reclamation. Labor-intensive operations are encouraged to move offshore by the government, and service and high-technology industries are encouraged. Major industries are petroleum refining, electronics, oil drilling equipment, rubber processing and rubber products, processed food and beverages, ship repair, entrepôt trade, financial services, and biotechnology.

29SCIENCE AND TECHNOLOGY

The Science Council, established in 1967, advises the government on scientific and technological matters relating to research and development and to the training and utilization of manpower. The Singapore National Academy of Science includes institutes of physics, biology, chemistry, and statistics, as well as the Singapore Association for the Advancement of Science. Scientific education is stressed at the university level and supported by training programs for more than 20,000 students (1990) in the nation's technical and vocational institutes. Special centers have been established for research on cancer, human reproduction, viruses, and immunology. In industry, electronics research and development expanded by over 20% in 1993. Two new research institutions were established in 1985: the Institute of Systems Science, which does research in the area of information technology, and the Institute of Molecular and Cell Biology, a center for biotechnological research. The Singapore Science Park, located near the National University of Singapore, was developed in 1987. In 1993, the National Computer Board announced an effort to create an "intelligent island" through an information infrastructure linking all of Singapore. In the 1980s, Singapore had over 60,000 scientists and engineers working in industry, the universities, and government.

In 1991, the government announced a s$250 million spending program to create science and high technology parks. Expenditures totaled s$1,400 million in 1993, about 2% of GDP, funded by both the private sector and government incentives.

30DOMESTIC TRADE

Marketing has always been an activity in which Singapore's Chinese, Indian and Arab merchants have played a major role, and their participation has increased in recent years as local branches of European firms have become less important. Warehousing, packaging, freight forwarding, and related services are of a high standard. Usual business hours for Western firms are 8:30 AM to 4:30 or 5 PM, with many businesses closed from 1 to 2 PM. Most major enterprises and foreign firms operate Monday through Friday and are open a half day on Saturday. A number of Chinese and Indian businesses maintain longer hours, with some open seven days a week. Bank hours are 9:30 AM to 3 PM Monday through Friday, and Saturday from 9:30 AM to 11:30 AM. Government offices are open from 8 AM to 5 PM Monday through Friday, and 8 AM to 1 PM on Saturday. Retail stores are open from 10 AM to 9:30 PM Monday through Saturday, with most shops also open on Sunday.

A wide range of consumer goods, such as luxury, electronic, handicraft, and food items, are available in Singapore from international department stores, brand name specialty stores, local department store chains, and neighborhood shops and markets. Singapore has four official languages, Malay, Chinese (Mandarin), Tamil, and English. English is the language of administration and the predominant language of commerce; the local version of Singapore English, i.e., Singlish, predominates in less formal settings. There are English, Chinese, Malay, Tamil and Malayalam daily newspapers. Foreign publications reporting on Southeast Asian political and social affairs must obtain an annual permit to distribute more than 300 copies of each edition in Singapore. Advertising is done by radio and television, outdoor displays, slides in motion picture theaters, and newspapers. Singapore Broadcasting Corporation airs three television channels and transmits nine radio services. There are several advertising agencies. Consumers are highly brand-conscious, and advertising concentrates considerably on product trademarks.

31FOREIGN TRADE

Since World War II, Singapore has changed from an entrepôt center for the incoming and outgoing traffic of its neighbors in

Southeast Asia to an exporting country in its own right. The leading exports of the mid-1960s—rubber, coffee, pepper, and palm oil—were replaced in the early 1980s by a variety of capital-intensive manufactures. Exports in 1992 stood at s$103,351.0 million, a 1.4% increase from the previous year. Imports increased by 2.9%, to s$117,530 million. Machinery and transport equipment constituted the leading import and also headed the export list, followed by mineral fuels. The principal exports by product in 1992 (in millions of Singapore dollars) were as follows:

Machinery and equipment	56,939.3
Mineral fuels	13,509.8
Miscellaneous manufactured goods	9,593.0
Manufactured goods	7,114.5
Chemicals	6,731.8
Beverages and tobacco	1,969.0
Crude materials	2,278.3
Food	2,986.7
Animal and vegetable oils	746.7
Other exports	1,481.9
TOTAL	103,351.0

The principal imports by product in 1992 (in millions of Singapore dollars) were as follows:

Machinery and equipment	56,330.5
Manufactured goods	15,045.8
Mineral fuels	14,987.2
Miscellaneous manufactured goods	11,718.4
Chemicals	8,854.7
Food	4,837.1
Crude materials	1,867.4
Beverages and tobacco	1,651.5
Animal and vegetable oils	877.5
Other imports	1,359.4
TOTAL	117,529.7

Singapore's main trading partners are the ASEAN group—principally Malaysia—the US, and Japan. Export and import activities with principal trade partners in 1992 (in millions of Singapore dollars) were as follows:

	EXPORTS	IMPORTS	BALANCE
US	21,778.9	19,340.5	2,438.4
Malaysia	12,925.4	17,287.2	-4,361.8
Hong Kong	8,080.8	3,587.0	4,493.8
Japan	7,856.7	24,753.1	-16,896.4
China	3,667.6	—	—
Thailand	6,441.8	4,365.3	2,076.5
Germany	4,388.6	3,839.3	549.3
Taiwan	4,187.8	4,721.3	-533.5
Netherlands	3,217.1	—	—
UK	3,003.3	—	—
Australia	2,456.8	—	—
Sa'udi Arabia	—	6,018.3	—
Other countries	29,013.8	26,081.4	2,932.4
TOTALS	103,351.0	117,529.7	14178.7

32BALANCE OF PAYMENTS

Singapore's foreign trade is characterized by a near-continuous deficit, although there were individual years in the 1960s and 1970s when Singapore exported more than it imported. Trade deficits, which have expanded since 1990 to about $5 billion annually, are more than offset by income from services in connection with transshipments, tourism, insurance, financing, and capital investments from abroad.

In 1992 merchandise exports totaled us$61,570 million and imports us$66,470 million. The merchandise trade balance was us$–4,900 million. The following table summarizes Singapore's balance of payments for 1991 and 1992 (in millions of US dollars):

	1991	1992
CURRENT ACCOUNT		
Goods, services, and income	3,844	3,574
Unrequited transfers	-539	-646
TOTALS	3,305	2,928
CAPITAL ACCOUNT		
Direct investment	3,235	4,288
Portfolio investment	-1,245	-1,190
Other long-term capital	-121	-194
Other short-term capital	1,085	1,313
Exceptional financing	—	—
Other liabilities	—	—
Reserves	-4,198	-6,100
TOTALS	-1,244	-1,883
Errors and omissions	-2,063	-1,047
Total change in reserves	-6,385	-5,752

Current account surpluses have led to a significant rise in reserves, from us$20.3 billion in 1989 to us$39.9 billion in 1992.

33BANKING AND SECURITIES

As of 1993, Singapore had 128 commercial banks. Some 13 of the 35 banks with full banking licenses were locally incorporated; the remainder were branches of various overseas banks. Since 1971, the government has sought to attract representation by a variety of foreign banks in terms of countries and geographical regions. Most of the new foreign banks allowed into Singapore have been offshore banks that have concentrated on foreign-exchange transactions. As of 1993, reserves of deposit money banks stood at s$5,770 million; demand deposits totaled s$13,940 million; and time and savings deposits, s$58,248.

Currency is issued by the Singapore Board of Commissioners of Currency. As of the end of 1993 the money supply, as measured by M2, amounted to s$82,130 million.

The Singapore Stock Exchange has 11 members. In October 1992, the Kuala Lumpur Stock Exchange severed all links with the Singapore Stock Exchange. All the Singapore stocks moved to the Singapore exchange and the Malaysian companies moved to the Kuala Lumpur Stock Exchange.

The Singapore International Monetary Exchange (SIMEX) opened in 1984. SIMEX traded, as of the end of 1985, futures contracts in gold, Eurodollar time deposit interest rates, and US/Deutschemark and US/yen currency exchanges. Trading in Japanese stock index and sterling futures began in 1986.

34INSURANCE

In 1985, there were 84 insurance companies; 71 provided non-life, 6 life, and 7 both life and non-life coverage. Most insurance firms are branches or agencies of UK (or other Commonwealth), European, and US companies, although local participation in insurance—particularly business insurance—is increasing. Marine and warehouse insurance constitutes most of the business insurance, but almost all types of commercial insurance are available.

Premiums collected totaled us$1.04 billion in 1992, and total assets were us$3.9 billion. In 1991 estimated per capita life insurance coverage was estimated at us$16,000.

35PUBLIC FINANCE

Budget surpluses have been registered since 1987; the 1993/94 budget planned to stimulate domestic consumption through a

15% rise in development expenditures for infrastructure and housing subsidies. The budget surplus was therefore projected to fall to s$1.7 billion in 1993/94 from s$3.7 billion in 1992/93.

The following table shows actual revenues and expenditures for 1990 and 1991 in millions of Singapore dollars.

	1990	1991
REVENUE AND GRANTS		
Tax revenue	10,254	13,244
Non-tax revenue	7,618	6,675
Capital revenue	3,764	3,315
Grants	—	—
TOTAL	21,636	23,234
EXPENDITURES & LENDING MINUS REPAYMENTS		
General public service	897	1,478
Defense	3,409	3,523
Public order and safety	506	568
Education	2,828	3,655
Health	652	994
Social security and welfare	300	344
Housing and community amenities	870	808
Recreation, cultural, and religious affairs	174	58
Economic affairs and services	2,389	1,714
Other expenditures	2,198	2,824
Adjustments	—	—
Lending minus repayments	221	813
TOTAL	14,444	16,779
Deficit/Surplus	7,192	6,455

In 1991 Singapore's total public debt stood at s$62,031 million, of which s$38 million was financed abroad.

36TAXATION

Individual and commercial incomes are taxed whether derived in Singapore or from outside sources. Types of direct taxation include income, property, estate duty, and payroll taxes; the Inland Revenue Department is responsible for the assessment and collection of all such levies. In 1994. individuals paid income taxes on a sliding scale that ranged from 2.5% on the first s$5,000 to 30% on income exceeding s$400,000, less a s$700 rebate on the first s$10,000 of income. In 1986, in an effort to stimulate the economy, the rates were reduced to between 3.5% and 33%, and taxpayers were given an across-the-board rebate of 25%. Companies are charged at a fixed rate of 27% on taxable income. Industrial establishments, companies, and various other businesses are eligible to deduct from their gross profits varying and usually generous depreciation allowances for building, plants, and machinery. There are tax holidays of 5 to 10 years for investing in robotics and other approved "pioneer" industries; other tax incentives for investing in export industries and for expansion of established enterprises; and special incentives for research and development companies to locate in Singapore.

37CUSTOMS AND DUTIES

Prior to the 1960s, Singapore was essentially a free port, with import duties levied only on alcoholic beverages, tobacco and tobacco products, petroleum products, and certain soaps. In 1959, however, a law was passed empowering the government to levy import duties on other products to protect local industries. In the 1960s, many new tariffs were established with the primary aim of helping to support development of local manufacturing firms. In the early 1970s, many items were withdrawn from the tariff list, and by 1982 there were only 176 items on the list, compared with 349 in 1972. In 1985, excise duties on sugar and sugar substitutes and import and excise duties on fuel oil were lifted. By 1993, there were almost no import tariffs except for duties on alcoholic beverages, tobacco products, petroleum products, and a few other items. Duties ranged from 5%–45%. There are no export duties.

Singapore has six free-trade zones, five for seaborne cargo (in the five gateways of the port) and one for air cargo.

38FOREIGN INVESTMENT

Legislation to attract new foreign investments, the Economic Incentives Act, was passed in 1967; it granted exemption from taxation for a five-year period to investors for export development and provided inducements and guarantees with respect to repatriation of profits and capital. Overseas offices to promote such foreign investment were set up in New York, Chicago, San Francisco, London, Paris, Frankfurt, Zürich, Tokyo, Hong Kong, Stockholm, and Melbourne. The Capital Participation Scheme, adopted in 1973, permitted high-technology industries to set up branches in Singapore with 50% equity participation by the government. With changes in Singapore's industrial development, there have also been alterations in incentives. In the early 1980s, the main criteria for granting tax incentives were capital investment ratios (including training costs) per worker, value added per worker, and the ratio of technical personnel and skilled workers to the total work force. Major investment activity focused on petroleum refining, general manufacturing, electronics, and hotel construction, as well as on traditional endeavors. However, in 1985, with decreasing world demand and rising costs of doing business, Singapore experienced a reduction in foreign investment to s$1,141.2 million, as compared to s$1,833.4 million in 1984. During the first half of 1986, foreign investment commitments fell another 6%. As of 1986, almost half of all foreign investment in Singapore came from the US.

Since the mid-1980s the government's incentive policies have broadened to include Singapore's development as a total international business center, an international air-sea cargo center, a location for the regional operational headquarters of multinational corporations, and a major exporter of services. Investment in the manufacturing sector is encouraged in areas of medium-range or higher technology, or the design and production of higher value-added products. Singapore does not require that foreign investors take on private sector or government joint venture partners. In 1992, s$2.8 billion investment commitments were from foreign sources. About 80% of the investment in manufacturing was from foreign sources. The US was responsible for one-third of the total investment commitments in 1992, Japan 24%, Europe (petroleum and petrochemical industries), 17.5%. New foreign direct investment in 1991 was us$1,423 million and in 1992 it was us$1,710 million.

39ECONOMIC DEVELOPMENT

Technological change and political considerations in the post-World War II period—not least of all the nationalism that accompanied the quest for independence among the region's European colonies—have combined to alter dramatically the economic self-perception and public policies of this diminutive island-state. By the late 1950s, it was obvious that prospects for economic growth would be severely limited if Singapore remained bound by its old economic role as entrepôt. The decision to industrialize—and to do so rapidly—was deliberate policy. Initial emphasis in the government's economic development program was upon employment. The increasing trend toward economic self-sufficiency in neighboring Indonesia and Malaysia—and the steady retreat of the UK from defense responsibilities in the region as a whole (centered on its large Singapore naval and air facilities)—prompted the government to focus completely on finding alternative employment for the island's highly skilled and disciplined workforce. By the end of the 1960s, this problem was effectively solved, with Singapore boasting one of the lowest unemployment rates in all of Asia.

Emphasis in the mid-1970s was on labor skills and technology, especially as these were identified with such modern industries as machine tools, petrochemicals, electronics, and other precision work. A high level of participation by private foreign capital provided an important cornerstone to this development. In 1979, the government abandoned its earlier policy of stimulating low-wage industries and adopted a policy of encouraging capital-intensive and technologically sophisticated industries. Especially targeted for investment promotion in the 1980s were computers, computer peripherals, electronic medical instruments, automotive components, specialty chemicals and pharmaceuticals, and optical and photocopying equipment. Following the recession of 1985–86, the government concentrated on developing new markets and on turning Singapore into a manufacturing, financial, and communications center for multinational corporations.

In the 1990s the economic development strategy emphasized both the manufacturing and service sectors. The Economic Development Board (EDB), formed in 1961, has guided Singapore's industrialization. Early emphasis was placed on promoting investment in manufacturing. The Strategic Economic Plan (SEP) announced in 1991 focused on education and human resources to enhance export competitiveness. Emphasis on developing the service sector has been supported and enhanced by the Operational Headquarters (OHQ) program, encouraging companies to use Singapore as regional headquarters or as a central distribution center. The Creative Business Program promotes investment in the film, media, and publishing, arts and entertainment, textile, fashion and design sectors. Currently the EDB works toward Singapore's vision of its future as a developed country through the promotion of business. Singapore's globalization strategy hinges on making a transformation from a production-driven economy to an innovation-driven one. Other key elements of this strategy are the reversal of downward trends in productivity, and sustaining foreign investment in Singapore's capital investment. Singapore initiated the formation of a growth-triangle, linking Johor, Malaysia, Singapore and Indonesia's Riau province focusing on Batam Island. Singapore benefits by tapping a supply of low-wage workers and offshore land to sustain its more labor-intensive industries. Within the first nine months of 1994, nine trade shows or events were planned.

40 SOCIAL DEVELOPMENT

Government-provided social welfare services are directed by the Ministry of Community Development, which is often assisted by various voluntary organizations, most of them affiliated with the Singapore Council of Social Service. Besides institutionalized care, the Ministry of Community Development administers foster and homemaker service schemes for needy young persons. In January 1986, the government operated 88 child care centers and three welfare homes for aged and destitute persons. Social welfare assistance is also provided by mutual-benefit organizations and voluntary services. All employers and employees must contribute to the Central Provident Fund, a public pension and retirement program which provides lump-sum benefits for old age, disability, death, sickness, and maternity. Employers fund workers' compensation benefits for job-related injuries.

The Family Planning and Population Board, created in 1965, had responsibility for implementation of the government's family planning and population program. The family planning program was so successful that by 1976, the fertility rate was down to replacement level. As a result, in early 1984, the government mounted a campaign to encourage the well-educated to bear more children. This campaign was later extended to less-educated groups. In 1986, the Family Planning and Population Board was disbanded. In 1985–90, the fertility rate was 1.7. Women's legal

rights are equal to those of men in most areas, including civil liberties, employment, business, and education. Women comprise over half the labor force and are well represented in the professions. However, they still fill most low-paying clerical positions, and their average salary is only 70% that of men.

41 HEALTH

Singapore's population enjoys one of the highest health levels in all of Southeast Asia. This achievement is largely attributed to good housing, sanitation, and water supply, as well as the best hospitals and other medical facilities in the region. Fully 100% of the population has access to safe drinking water, and 99% has adequate sanitation. Nutritional standards are among the highest in Asia. In 1984, Singapore initiated a Medisave scheme, a compulsory savings plan for medical expenses. About half the population pays hospital bills through this plan, although as of 1990 the plan did not cover outpatient expenses. In 1990, there were 19 hospitals, 5 of which were administered by the government, and 5 were "government restructured" (as of 1989, given a large degree of administrative autonomy). The remaining nine hospitals were privately run. The main multidisciplinary hospitals are: Alexandra Hospital, Changi Hospital, Tan Tock Hospital (all government run); and National University Hospital, Singapore General Hospital, and Toa Payoh Hospital (all government restructured). In 1989, there were 9,801 hospital beds in Singapore (3.5 per 1,000 people). In 1991, there were 3,779 doctors, 600 dentists, and 10,240 nurses; in addition, there were almost 600 pharmacists (80% of whom operated privately).

In 1992, there were 1.09 doctors per 1,000 people, with a nurse to doctor ratio of 3.8; in 1990, the population per physician was 820. The 1993 birth rate was 15.9 per 1,000 people and an estimated 74% of married women (ages 15 to 49) used contraception. There were 44,000 births in 1992. Life expectancy in 1992 was 74 years, and infant mortality was 6 per 1,000 live births. In the same year, 100% of the population had access to health care services. According to a national health survey by the Ministry of Health, high cholesterol had fallen from 27% in 1984 to 19% in 1992; hypertension levels were also down from 15.3% to 13.6% in the same period. However, smoking had increased among 18–19 year olds, from 12% in 1984 to 15.2% in 1992; for 20–39 year olds, the increase was 15.8% to 19.4%. The occurrence of diabetes increased from 4.7% in 1984 to 8.6% in 1992 among people 18–69 years; cancer increased as well. Fourteen percent of Singaporeans exercise regularly. The general mortality rate in 1993 was 5.6 per 1,000 inhabitants. Leading causes of death per 100,000 people in 1990 were: communicable diseases and maternal/perinatal causes, 114; noncommunicable diseases, 498; and 3 injuries (39). There were also 82 cases of tuberculosis per 100,000 people reported in the same year. The principal causes of death in 1985 were heart disease and cancer. In 1992, vaccination rates for children up to one year old were as follows: tuberculosis (99%); diphtheria, pertussis, and tetanus (85%); polio (85%); and measles (90%). Overall health care expenditures for 1990 were s$658 million.

42 HOUSING

Sustained rapid population growth in the years preceding and following World War II provided Singapore with an acute housing shortage. In 1947, a housing committee determined that, with a squatter problem worsening each year, 250,000 persons required immediate housing, while another 250,000 people would need new housing by the late 1950s. In 1960, the Housing and Development Board was established by the new PAP government. During its first five-year building program (1960–65), the board spent s$230 million to construct 53,000 dwelling units for more than 250,000 people. It was in this period that Queens Town, Singapore's first satellite community, was developed; by the mid-

1970s, Queens Town had a total of 27,000 living units in seven neighborhood complexes, housing upward of 150,000 people.

In the second five-year building program (1966–70), 67,000 additional units, accommodating 350,000 persons and costing s$305 million, were built. About 113,000 more units were erected by the board in the third building program (1971–75), and over 130,000 in the fourth building program (1976–80). Another 100,000 units were constructed in the fifth building program (1981–85), and 160,000 were planned for the sixth building program (1986–90). In 1985, as a result of these government-sponsored efforts, 2,148,720 persons—or 84% of the total population of Singapore—lived in 551,767 apartments under the management of the Housing and Development Board. Some 397,180 units had been sold to the public. In 1990, 84% of all housing units were apartments, 7% were bungalows and terrace houses, 5% were condominiums, and 1% were dwellings with attap or zinc roofs. The total number of housing units in 1992 was 758,000.

43EDUCATION

Approximately 93% of men and 79% of women were literate in 1985. All children who are citizens are entitled to free primary education. Primary schooling is available in all four official languages. Under the education system implemented in stages after 1980, the first three years of primary schooling emphasize the learning of English and any other official language, after which students are streamed, on the basis of performance, into an additional three or five years of primary school. Upon completion of primary school, they can join the Vocational and Industrial Training Board for vocational training, or if they qualify, they can take four or five years of secondary schooling leading to two-year courses in junior colleges or three-year courses in school centers at the preuniversity level.

In 1989, there were 203 primary schools in Singapore (including government and government-aided schools), 145 secondary schools and junior colleges, and 4 secondary full schools (primary and secondary combined). The total school population was 257,833 primary and 199,076 secondary and preuniversity students. Fifteen vocational institutes offered training courses in the metal, woodworking, electrical, electronic, and building trades. There were 9,998 teachers in primary schools, and 9,236 at secondary and pre-university levels.

The National University of Singapore was established on 8 August 1980 through the merger of the University of Singapore and Nanyang University. In addition, there are the Singapore Technical Institute, Ngee Ann Polytechnic, Singapore Polytechnic, and Nanyang Technological Institute.

44LIBRARIES AND MUSEUMS

The National Library of Singapore (founded in 1844 and known, until 1960, as Raffles National Library) contains almost 2.5 million volumes, including books in the four official languages. The National Library houses the government archives and serves as a repository for official publications printed in Singapore since 1946. The library has eight full-time branches, and a mobile library service for rural portions of the island. The National University of Singapore Library contains 1.7 million volumes, including extensive medical and science/technology collections. The National University of Singapore was formed in 1980 with the merger of the former University of Singapore and Nanyang University.

The National Museum (formerly Raffles Museum), established in 1849, has collections of natural history, ethnology, and archaeology. Since 1965, it has also specialized in the art, culture, and way of life of Singapore's multiracial communities. The National Art Gallery, established in 1976, features works by the peoples of Southeast Asia, and is a part of the National Museum. The Art

Museum and Exhibition Gallery of the National University of Singapore includes in its collections Asian art objects and contemporary Singaporean and Malaysian painting and textiles.

45MEDIA

Postal, telephone, and telegraph services in Singapore are among the most efficient in Southeast Asia. In 1985, there were 77 post offices and 48 postal agencies. National and international telecommunications services are administered by the Telecommunication Authority of Singapore. Service is available on a 24-hour basis for worldwide telegraph, telephone, and telex communication. There were 1,219,604 telephones in 1991; the ratio of 45.59 telephones per 100 population was among the highest in East Asia.

The Singapore Broadcasting Corp., created in 1980, operates radio and television services. Radio Singapore broadcasts in Chinese, Malay, English, and Tamil. Television Singapore, inaugurated in 1963, operates daily on three channels. There were 1,770,000 radios and 1,035,000 television sets in 1991.

Singapore has eight daily newspapers, with at least one printed in each of the four official languages. The total circulation of daily papers in 1991 was 858,000. The oldest and most widely circulated daily is the English-language *Straits Times,* founded in 1845.

Although freedom of the press is guaranteed by law, the International Press Institute has on various occasions cited Singapore for interference with press freedom. Magazines, motion pictures, and plays are censored for sexual content and presentation of ethnically sensitive matters. In August 1986, parliament passed a bill enabling the government to restrict sales and distribution of foreign publications "engaging in domestic politics." Two months later, the government announced that the distribution of *Time* magazine would be reduced because the magazine had refused to print the entire text of a letter from a government official. In 1987, similar distribution restrictions were placed on the *Asian Wall Street Journal.*

In 1991 Singapore's largest newspapers, with their estimated daily circulations, were as follows:

	LANGUAGE	CIRCULATION
Straits Times (m)	English	300,000
Lian He Zao Bao (m)	Chinese	191,000
Lian He Wan Bao (e)	Chinese	107,000
Shin Min Daily News (e)	Chinese	102,000
Berita Harian (m)	Malay	47,000
Business Times (m)	English	24,000
Tamil Murasu (m)	Tamil	9,000

46ORGANIZATIONS

Singapore has a wide variety of organizations, some private in their origin and direction and others essentially government controlled. There are service clubs belonging to international associations; YMCAs and YWCAs; Chinese, Indian, and Malay chambers of commerce; and a multicommunal Singapore chamber of commerce. In addition to such largely private organizations, the government established in 1960 the People's Association, to organize and promote mass participation in social, cultural, educational, and recreational activities. In Singapore, there is a comprehensive network of 133 community centers throughout the country set up by the People's Association. Management, women's, youth, and senior-citizen subcommittees exist as active units of the association.

47TOURISM, TRAVEL, AND RECREATION

Tourists wishing to enter or visit Singapore must have a valid passport or other internationally recognized travel document. Visas are required by nationals of Afghanistan, India, Cambodia, Laos, China, Russia, Viet Nam and holders of Palestinian refugee papers and Hong Kong certificates of identity. Vaccinations are required against yellow fever for travelers from an infected country.

Singapore's tourist volume has increased steadily. In 1991, 5,414,651 tourists visited Singapore, 3,326,331 from East Asia and 1,157,562 from Europe. That year Singapore earned a record US$5.02 billion from tourism, and there were a total of 25,592 hotel beds, filled to 76.8% of capacity.

Shopping, with bargaining the usual practice, is a major tourist attraction. Points of interest include the Van Kleef Aquarium at Fort Canning Park, the Singapore Zoological and Botanical Gardens, and the resort island of Sentosa. Singapore has a number of tourist attractions, including an amusement park at Haw Pav Village, site of historic Chinese statues, and the restoration of the Alkaff Mansion.

Singapore has many sports clubs and associations, notably in the areas of badminton (in which Singaporeans have distinguished themselves internationally), basketball, boxing, cricket, cycling, golf, hockey, horse racing, motoring, polo, swimming, tennis, and yachting. The Singapore Sports Council, designed to develop and promote competitive and recreational sports in the country, was created in 1973.

[48] FAMOUS SINGAPOREANS

Sir Thomas Stamford Bingley Raffles (1781–1826) played the major role in the establishment of a British presence on Singapore Island in 1819; he introduced policies that greatly enhanced Singapore's wealth, and he suppressed the slave trade. Raffles also distinguished himself as a collector of historical and scientific information. The English writer and educator Cyril Northcote Parkinson (b.1909), formerly a professor at the University of Singapore, became internationally known as the originator of Parkinson's Law. Singapore's dominant contemporary figure is Lee Kuan Yew (b.1923), prime minister of the Republic of Singapore since 1965.

[49] DEPENDENCIES

Singapore has no territories or colonies.

[50] BIBLIOGRAPHY

Bedlington, Stanley S. *Malaysia and Singapore: The Building of New States.* Ithaca, N.Y.: Cornell University Press, 1978.

Chan, Heng Chee. *The Dynamics of One Party Dominance: The PAP at the Grass Roots.* Singapore: University of Singapore Press, 1976.

Chew, Ernest and Edwin Chew (eds.). *A History of Singapore.* New York: Oxford University Press, 1991.

Darusman, Suryono. *Singapore and the Indonesian Revolution, 1945–50 of Suryono Darusman.* Singapore: Institute of Southeast Asian Studies, 1992.

Fletcher, Nancy McHenry. *The Separation of Singapore from Malaysia.* Ithaca, N.Y.: Southeast Asia Program, Cornell University, 1969.

Flower, Raymond. *Raffles: The Story of Singapore.* Singapore: Eastern Universities Press, 1984.

Gamer, Robert E. *The Politics of Urban Development in Singapore.* Ithaca, N.Y.: Cornell University Press, 1972.

Hassan, Riaz (ed.). *Singapore: Society in Transition.* Kuala Lumpur: Oxford University Press, 1976.

Jayapal, Maya. *Old Singapore.* New York: Oxford University Press, 1992.

Kennedy, Joseph. *When Singapore Fell: Evacuations and Escapes, 1941–42.* New York: St. Martin's, 1989.

Lee, W. O. *Social Change and Educational Problems in Japan, Singapore, and Hong Kong.* New York: St. Martin's, 1991.

LePoer, Barbara Leitch (ed.). *Singapore: A Country Study.* 2d ed. Washington, D.C.: Library of Congress, 1991.

Makepeace, Walter (ed.). *One Hundred Years of Singapore.* New York: Oxford University Press, 1986.

Minchin, James. *No Man is an Island: A Portrait of Sinapore's Lee Kuan Yew.* 2d ed. Sydney: Allen & Unwin, 1990.

Mulliner, K. *Historical Dictionary of Singapore.* Metuchen, N.J.: Scarecrow Press, 1991.

Quah, Jon S., *et al.* (eds.). *Government and Politics of Singapore.* New York: Oxford University Press, 1985.

Quah, Stella R. *Singapore.* Oxford: Clio, 1988.

Regnier, Philippe. *Singapore: City-state in South-East Asia.* Honolulu: University of Hawaii Press, 1991.

Trocki, Carl A. *Opium and Empire: Chinese Society in Colonial Singapore, 1800–1910.* Ithaca, N.Y.: Cornell University Press, 1990.

Turnbull, C. M. *A History of Singapore, 1819–1988.* 2d ed. New York: Oxford University Press, 1989.

SOLOMON ISLANDS

CAPITAL: Honiara.

FLAG: The flag consists of two triangles, the upper one blue, the lower one green, separated by a diagonal gold stripe; on the blue triangle are five white five-pointed stars.

ANTHEM: *God Save the Queen.*

MONETARY UNIT: The Solomon Islands dollar (SI$), a paper currency of 100 cents, was introduced in 1977, replacing the Australian dollar, and became the sole legal tender in 1978. There are coins of 1, 2, 5, 10, 20, and 50 cents and 1 dollar, and notes of 2, 5, 10, 20, and 50 dollars. SI$1 = US$0.3064 (or US$1 = SI$3.2637).

WEIGHTS AND MEASURES: The metric system is in force.

HOLIDAYS: New Year's Day, 1 January; Queen's Birthday, June; Independence Day, 7 July; Christmas, 25 December; Boxing Day, 26 December. Movable religious holidays include Good Friday, Easter Monday, and Whitmonday.

TIME: 11 PM = noon GMT.

¹LOCATION, SIZE, AND EXTENT
The Solomon Islands consists of a chain of six large and numerous small islands situated in the South Pacific, some 1,900 km (1,200 mi) NE of Australia and about 485 km (300 mi) E of Papua New Guinea. Extending 1,688 km (1,049 mi) ESE–WNW and 468 km (291 mi) NNE–SSW, the Solomon Islands has an area of 28,450 sq km (10,985 sq mi). Comparatively, the area occupied by the Solomon Islands is slightly larger than the state of Maryland. The largest island is Guadalcanal, covering 5,302 sq km (2,047 sq mi); other major islands are Makira (formerly Malaita), San Cristobal, Vella Lavella, Choiseul, Rennell, New Georgia, and the Santa Cruz group. The total coastline of the Solomon Islands is 5,313 km (3,301 mi).

The capital city of the Solomon Islands, Honiara, is located on the island of Guadalcanal.

²TOPOGRAPHY
The topography varies from the volcanic peaks of Guadalcanal to low-lying coral atolls. Densely forested mountain ranges are intersected by precipitous, narrow valleys. The highest peak is Mt. Popomanasiu, at 2,447 m (8,127 ft), on Guadalcanal, an island that also contains the country's most extensive alluvial grass plains. Rivers are narrow and impassable except by canoe. Extensive coral reefs and lagoons surround the island coasts.

³CLIMATE
The climate is tropical. From December to March, northwest equatorial winds bring hot weather and heavy rainfall; from April to November, the islands are cooled by drier southeast trade winds. Damaging cyclones occasionally strike during the rainy season. The annual mean temperature is 27°C (81°F); annual rainfall averages 305 cm (120 in), and humidity is about 80%.

⁴FLORA AND FAUNA
Dense rain forest covers about 90% of the islands, with extensive mangrove swamps and coconut palms along the coasts. The islands abound in small reptiles (over 70 species), birds (150 species), and mammals, as well as insect life. There are over 230 varieties of orchids and other tropical flowers.

⁵ENVIRONMENT
Most of the coral reefs surrounding the islands are dead or dying. As an island nation, the Solomon Islands are concerned with the effects of global warming and rising sea levels. Deforestation is another significant environmental problem. United Nations sources estimate that the nation's forests will be exhausted in 10–15 years. The related problem of soil erosion threatens the country's agricultural productivity. The nation has 10.7 cu mi of water, of which 40% is used for farming and 20% for industrial activity. Some 42% of the nation's rural people do not have pure water. Sources of pollution include sewage, pesticides, and mining by-products. In 1994, two mammal species and 20 bird species were endangered, as well as 28 types of plants. Endangered species in 1987 included the gizo white-eye and the hawksbill, green sea, and leatherback turtles.

⁶POPULATION
The population at the 1986 census was 285,796, an increase of 45% over the 1976 figure of 196,823. It was estimated at 342,000 in 1992 and was projected by the UN at 444,000 in 2000, assuming a crude birth rate of 36.1 per 1,000 population and a crude death rate of 4.1 in 1995–2000. The population growth rate was 3.4% annually in 1985–90. The estimated overall population density in 1992 was only 12.4 per sq km (32.1 per sq mi), but there are significant variations from island to island; moreover, most mountainous and heavily wooded areas are inaccessible (except to tribal groups of the interior), and most of the population is concentrated in the coastal regions. Malaita, the most populous island, had an estimated 85,900 inhabitants in 1990; Guadalcanal had 85,300. Honiara, on Guadalcanal, is the largest town and chief port, with an estimated 1989 population of 33,749.

[7] MIGRATION

Since 1955, immigrants from the Gilbert Islands (now Kiribati) have settled in underpopulated areas. Movements from the countryside to Honiara and north Guadalcanal have created problems of overcrowding.

[8] ETHNIC GROUPS

According to the 1986 census, Melanesians numbered 268,536, or 94% of the total population. Also enumerated were 10,661 Polynesians, 3,929 Micronesians, 1,107 Europeans, 379 Chinese, and 564 others. Melanesians live mainly on the larger islands; Polynesians tend to inhabit the smaller islands and atolls.

[9] LANGUAGES

Pidgin English is the lingua franca, but English is the official language. Some 87 local languages and dialects are spoken, each within a very restricted geographical area. Melanesian languages are spoken by about 85% of the population, Papuan languages by 9%, and Polynesian languages by 4%.

[10] RELIGIONS

Christianity, introduced by missionaries, is the principal organized religion. As of the 1986 census, 33.9% of the islanders were Anglicans, 23.5% were Evangelical Protestants, and 19.2% were Roman Catholics. Indigenous religions are practiced by up to 5% of the population, and there is a small Baha'i community.

[11] TRANSPORTATION

In 1991 there were about 2,100 km (1,300 mi) of roads in the Solomons, of which 38% were private logging and plantation roads. Shipping services link the Solomons with other Pacific islands, Australia, Japan, and Europe. Honiara is the principal port, followed by Ringi Cove. A fleet of government vessels provides interisland connections and handles about one-third of total tonnage carried; vessels in operation numbered 150 in 1986. There are 2 permanent-surface runways, out of 30 total in the country. Henderson's Field, on the northern coast of Guadalcanal, is the site of Honiara's civil airport. Solomon Airlines provides regular flights between islands and to nearby Papua New Guinea and Vanuatu. In 1992, Solomon Airlines performed 5.4 million and 183 million passenger-km of domestic and international service, respectively.

[12] HISTORY

The islands now known as the Solomons are thought to have been inhabited originally by Melanesians, whose language has affinities with Malay but whose precise origin has not been determined. The first European contact with the Solomons, in 1567, was the sighting of Santa Isabel Island by the Spanish explorer Alvaro de Mendaña; the following year, Mendaña and another Spaniard, Pedro de Queirós, explored some of the islands. Mendaña named the islands Islas de Salomon, thinking that the gold source for King Solomon's riches was located there.

European contact with the Solomons was cut off for nearly two centuries until they were visited by the English navigator Philip Carteret in 1767. Following Carteret's visit, the British navy began to make periodic calls at the islands. During the period 1845–93, the Solomons were frequently visited by missionaries and traders. Indigenous peoples were also subjected to exploitation by "blackbirders," who impressed their captives into forced Labour, often on colonial sugar plantations in Fiji, Hawaii, Tahiti, or Queensland. The brutality of the kidnappers provoked reprisals by the islanders, resulting in mass slayings of both Europeans and local peoples.

In 1893, the British government stepped in and established a protectorate over certain islands in the southern Solomons, including Guadalcanal, Malaita (now Makira), San Cristobal,

and the New Georgia group. The remainder of the Solomons had by this time fallen under German dominion; some of these, including Choiseul and Santa Isabel, were transferred by treaty to the UK in 1900. The British Solomon Islands Protectorate, as the entire group came to be known, initially was under the jurisdiction of the Office of the British High Commissioner for the Western Pacific.

During World War II, the Solomons provided the theater for some of the most bitter fighting of the Pacific war after Japanese troops invaded and occupied Guadalcanal in 1942. A Japanese airfield on the island's northern coast—later known as Henderson's Field—was captured by US marines on 7 August 1942, the opening foray in the Battle of Guadalcanal, which cost the lives of about 1,500 US soldiers and 20,000 Japanese. Guadalcanal was evacuated by Japan in February 1943, although Japanese forces remained elsewhere in the Solomons until 1945. Widespread destruction and loss of life were visited on the local peoples during the war, and the legacy of social dislocation gave impetus to the development of a pro-independence nationalist movement in Malaita known as the Marching Rule.

In 1953, local advisory councils were set up in Malaita, eventually spreading to other islands of the protectorate. In 1960, the territorial government appointed executive and legislative councils, which were granted their first elected minority in 1964. A new constitution promulgated in April 1970 provided for replacement of the two councils by a unitary Governing Council, the majority of whose members were to be elected. During May and June, the Solomon Islands' first general election was held, with voters selecting 17 of the council's 26 members. On 21 August 1974, a new constitution introduced a ministerial system of government headed by a Council of Ministers. A Legislative Assembly subsequently chose Solomon Mamaloni as the Solomons' first chief minister. In May 1975, a delegation from the Solomon Islands, led by Mamaloni, met with UK officials in London and set up a timetable for internal self-government and for full independence. On 22 June 1975, the territory's name was officially changed from the British Solomon Islands Protectorate to the Solomon Islands.

The islands achieved internal self-government in 1976 and became an independent member of the Commonwealth of Nations on 7 July 1978. Peter Kenilorea was prime minister until his coalition government collapsed in August 1981, after which Mamaloni returned to power. In October 1984, Sir Peter Kenilorea (as he had become) was reelected prime minister, but he resigned in November 1986, following allegations of mismanagement of funds; Ezekiel Alebua, deputy prime minister, succeeded him. In the general elections of February 1989 the People's Alliance Party (PAP), led by Solomon Mamaloni, defeated the Alebua government. Mamaloni became the new Prime Minister in March 1989. Mamaloni resigned as PAP leader in October 1990 and formed a coalition government with several members of the opposition. Francis Billy Hilly, an independent supported by members of the National Coalition Partners (a loose six-party coalition), became the Solomon Islands new Prime Minister in June 1993. Hilly has worked with the Melanesian Spearhead Conference to ease tension between the Solomon Islands and Papua New Guinea.

[13] GOVERNMENT

Under the independence constitution of 1978, the Solomon Islands is a parliamentary democracy with a ministerial system and a unicameral National Parliament, consisting of 47 (38 until the 1993 election) members elected to four-year terms; suffrage is universal for citizens over the age of 18. The prime minister, who must command a parliamentary majority, selects the 14-member cabinet. The head of state is the British monarch, represented by the governor-general, Sir George Lepping (since July 1989). There is a constitutionally provided Ombudsman to provide protection against improper administrative treatment.

14 POLITICAL PARTIES

The members of the first Parliament formed after independence in 1978 had no party affiliations. However, political parties emerged shortly before the elections of August 1980, in which the Solomon Islands United Party, headed by Peter Kenilorea, won 14 seats; the People's Alliance Party (PAP), led by Solomon Mamaloni, received 8 seats; the National Democratic Party (NDP), 2 seats; and independents, 14 seats. Parliamentary realignment in August 1981 forced Kenilorea from office and led to Mamaloni's installation as prime minister, heading a coalition of the PAP, NDP, and the independent bloc. In the elections of November 1984, the United Party won 13 seats, the PAP 12; the others were split among smaller parties and independents. Sir Peter Kenilorea formed a coalition government; forced from office in 1986, he was succeeded by Deputy Prime Minister Ezekiel Alebua. A new political party, the Nationalist Front for Progress, was formed in 1985 with the goal of reforming local government. The Group for National Unity and Reconciliation (GNUR), led by Solomon Mamaloni gained the most seats in the 1993 election. Other parties receiving seats were the National Action Party, the Labour Party, and the Christian Fellowship Group.

15 LOCAL GOVERNMENT

The islands are divided into eight administrative districts, of which seven are provinces with elected assemblies; the eighth is the town of Honiara, governed by an elected council. In outlying areas, village headmen exercise administrative responsibilities.

16 JUDICIAL SYSTEM

The judicial system is based on a blend of British and traditional systems and consists of the High Court, magistrate's courts, and local courts. Appeals from magistrate's courts go to the High Court; customary land appeals courts hear appeals from the local courts.

Defendants in criminal cases are entitled to counsel and to the writ of habeas corpus. Violations of civil liberties are punishable by fines and jail sentences.

17 ARMED FORCES

The Solomon Islands has no military forces. A police force of about 500 officers is deployed among 19 stations in 5 police districts.

18 INTERNATIONAL COOPERATION

The Solomon Islands joined the UN on 19 September 1978 and belongs to ESCAP, IBRD, IDA, IFAD, IFC, ILO, IMF, UPU, and WHO. It participates in the Asian Development Bank, Commonwealth of Nations, G-77, and South Pacific Commission and Forum. The nation is a de facto adherent of GATT and a signatory of the Law of the Sea. The Solomon Islands has resident diplomatic representation only at the UN; the UN ambassador is also accredited to the US. The minister for foreign affairs serves as a roving envoy. The UK, Australia, New Zealand, Japan, China, and Papua New Guinea maintain diplomatic missions in Honiara; US interests are handled by its ambassador to Papua New Guinea.

19 ECONOMY

At least 80% of the population is tied to subsistence agriculture. Agriculture (including forestry and fishing) accounted for about 48% of GDP in the 1991. The capital sector is dependent on the production of copra, timber, and fish for export, but outputs of other cash commodities—particularly cocoa, spices, and palm oil—have grown in recent years. The development of large-scale

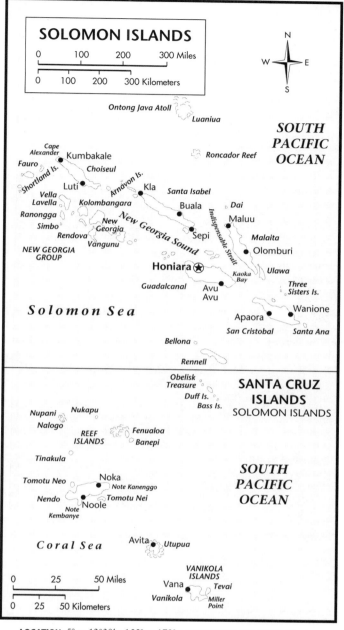

LOCATION: 5° to 12°30's; 155° to 170°E. **TERRITORIAL SEA LIMIT:** 12 mi.

lumbering operations has increased timber production considerably (log production nearly doubled in 1992), and concern about the preservation of forest resources led to government restriction of log exports in 1993. Cyclone Namu, which struck three of the six main islands in May 1986, caused serious damage both to crops and the economic infrastructure.

20 INCOME

In 1992, Solomon Islands' GNP was $237 million at current prices, or $710 per capita. For the period 1985–92 the average inflation rate was 11.2%, resulting in a real growth rate in per capita GNP of 2.7%.

In 1992 the GDP was $241 million in current US dollars. It is estimated that in 1986 agriculture, hunting, forestry, and fishing contributed 43% to GDP; mining and quarrying, −1%; manufacturing, 4%; electricity, gas, and water, 1%; construction, 5%;

wholesale and retail trade, 8%; transport, storage, and communication, 5%; finance, insurance, real estate, and business services, 6%; community, social, and personal services, 19%; and other sources 10%.

21LABOR
About 90% of Solomon Islanders engage in subsistence farming. The wage labor force in 1990 totaled 26,122, of whom 28.9% worked in agriculture; 20.3% had jobs in manufacturing, construction, transportation, and utilities; and the remaining 49.2% were in services. The country suffers from an acute shortage of skilled workers, and an estimated 80% of professional and technical employees are recruited from overseas.

The Solomon Islands has 14 trade unions, the largest one being the Solomon Islands National Union of Workers. Most employed persons have a standard workday of between 5 and 6 hours, six days a week, with overtime bringing the average workweek to 45 hours. Government regulations require employers to provide housing for workers whose jobs do not permit them to travel to and from home each day. The law requires provision of medical attention in the case of illness; the payment of wages during sickness is customary rather than mandatory.

22AGRICULTURE
About 2% of the total land area is utilized for temporary or permanent crops. Agriculture accounted for about 8% of real GDP in 1992. Exports of palm, copra, and cocoa accounted respectively for 11.4%, 6.6%, and 4.4% of total exports in 1992. Copra is typically the dominant export and the economic lifeline of the Solomons; world copra prices strongly affect the economy, so that a decline in copra prices in 1985 inaugurated an economic slump, exacerbated by the effects of Cyclone Namu. In 1992, production of copra increased by over 30% from 1992, for a total of 38,500 tons. The rebound in 1992 came from a near doubling of world prices and better coordination of domestic shipping. About 75% of the copra is produced by small holders, principally on Guadalcanal, Choiseul, the Russell Islands, San Cristobal, Santa Isabel, and Vella Lavella. Development plans called for crop diversification and the construction of a copra mill on the islands. The overseas marketing of copra is a monopoly of the government's Solomon Islands Copra Board. Other agricultural products in 1992 included cocoa, 4,453 tons, palm oil, 31,000 tons, and palm kernels, 6,900 tons. Palm oil and kernel production in 1992 set a new record, each 40% above the average levels for 1989–91.

The major food crops are coconuts, yams, taro, sweet potatoes, cassava, and green vegetables. The government has encouraged the cultivation of rice, rotated with soybeans, in the Guadalcanal plains; however, cyclone losses resulted in increased dependence on imported rice.

23ANIMAL HUSBANDRY
Cattle were traditionally kept on coconut plantations as a means of controlling the growth of grass, and many large copra plantations raised cattle for slaughter. There were 13,000 head of cattle and 54,000 pigs on the islands in 1992. Over 40% of the cattle are raised by small holders. The government's Livestock Development Authority (LDA) maintains about 3,200 head on Guadalcanal and Western Province. The LDA is now mostly a producer of trader pigs and poultry, raising 25,000 chicks and 120 piglets per month for sale. Production of pork has doubled since the early 1980s, yet still has not kept up with domestic demand. About 3,000 tons of meat were produced in 1992. In the same year, the Solomon Islands imported about $2.4 million in meat, dairy, and egg products, accounting for almost 2.2% of all 1992 imports (by value).

24FISHING
Fish are an essential part of the local diet, and fishing has become an important commercial activity. In 1991, the total catch reached a record high of 69,292 tons; fish exports represented 48.7% of export earnings. In 1992, the annual catch of skipjack and yellowfin tuna declined by 20% from 1991's record levels, to just over 39,000 tons. Heavy worldwide catches in 1991 depressed tuna prices in 1992, making deep-sea pelagic fishing less profitable.

25FORESTRY
Forests cover about 90% of the total area, with about 2,560 sq km (990 sq mi) of timber stands providing an estimated timber yield in 1992 of 640,000 cu m, of which about 580,000 cu m was exported as logs; about 8,500 cu m of sawn timber was also exported. Important forest timbers are kuari, balsa, teak, Honduras and African mahoganies, Queensland maple, silky oak, and black bean. Several hundred chainsaw operators and about 40 portable sawmills produce over one-fifth of all sawn timber. Logging at current rates (15–16,000 ha/37–39,000 acres per year) exceeds the estimated maximum sustainable annual cut by three times, which means that logging at current rates will presumably exhaust commercially loggable forests in less than ten years. As of 1992, there was no long-term silvicultural plan, and little effort has been made to minimize damage to young trees, topsoil, streams, lagoons, or the water table.

26MINING
Although the archipelago was named in the 16th century for the fabled gold mines of King Solomon and has long-term mining potential, there have been insufficient high-quality mineral deposits to justify extensive mining investment. The Gold Ridge mine at Mavu on Guadalcanal is expected, however, to effect a significant increase in export earnings, possibly raising the mining sector's contribution to the GDP from 1% to 15%. Deposits of bauxite, nickel, copper, chromite, and manganese ores have also been found.

27ENERGY AND POWER
Most electric power is supplied by the government-controlled Solomon Islands Electricity Authority, although some private undertakings produce their own electricity. Electric generating capacity was 21,000 kw in 1991, and electrical output was 30 million kwh. Honiara accounts for 90% of electricity consumption.

The Komarindi hydropower project, planned to produce up to 8,000 kw of power on the upper Lungga River, advanced from engineering design to provisional funding in 1992. The total cost for the project is estimated at $31 million, funded primarily by grant aid from Norway, the EC, and the ADB.

Oil and natural gas exploration continues, especially in Iron Bottom Sound, north of Guadalcanal. The government regulates petroleum exploration and production.

28INDUSTRY
Industrial activity in the Solomons is rudimentary, lacking in both the capital and the skilled labor necessary for significant development. The leading industries are fish processing and timber milling; soaps are made from palm oil and coconut oil. Small firms produce a limited array of goods for the local market: biscuits, tobacco products, rattan furniture, baskets and mats, concrete blocks, boats, and fiberglass products.

29SCIENCE AND TECHNOLOGY
The Solomon Islands College of Higher Education has schools of nursing, natural resources, and marine studies.

30DOMESTIC TRADE
Honiara is the commercial center. Most commercial enterprises have been controlled by Chinese or Europeans; a large segment of

the population still relies on bartering. Normal banking hours are 9 to 11:30 AM and 1:30 to 3 PM, Monday–Thursday, and 9 AM to 3 PM on Friday.

31FOREIGN TRADE

Overseas trade volume has expanded rapidly in recent years. World market conditions and the devastating Cyclone Namu in 1986 combined to cause wide fluctuations in the composition of exports. Copra, which accounted for 27.6% of the export value in 1984, accounted for only 5% in 1986; in that year, wood and lumber made up 31% of the total, and fish 46% (up from 24.7% in 1984). In 1992, timber accounted for 37% of exports. Total exports in 1991 were valued at si$222.1 million; total imports in 1990 came to si$233.2 million.

The distribution of the Solomon Islands' trade continues to be limited by the huge distances to potential export markets. In 1991, Japan, the Solomons' most important trade partner, received close to 50% of exports. Other important trade partners are Australia, the UK, the Netherlands, Thailand, Singapore, New Zealand, and the US.

32BALANCE OF PAYMENTS

In 1992 merchandise exports totaled $83.43 million and imports $91.72 million. The merchandise trade balance was $8.29 million.

The following table summarizes Solomon Islands' balance of payments for 1990 and 1991 (in millions of US dollars):

	1990	1991
CURRENT ACCOUNT		
Goods, services, and income	−58.76	−70.69
Unrequited transfers	34.87	83.3
TOTALS	−23.89	−37.39
CAPITAL ACCOUNT		
Direct investment	12.85	18.71
Other long-term capital	4.08	5.3
Other short-term capital	−2.10	0.37
Exceptional Financing	5.93	4.94
Reserves	7.73	7.71
TOTALS	28.49	37.03
Errors and omissions	−4.61	0.36
Total change in reserves	8.19	7.97

In 1992, export earnings were exceptionally high, due to a massive income windfall from the steep rise in the volume of log exports at a time when prices in Asian markets were being driven up by a supply shortage. Net foreign assets, reflecting both current and capital accounts, rose steadily form $16 million at the end of 1991 to $70 million in November 1992. By April 1993, however, net foreign assets had dropped back to $60 million, reflecting a slackening of export receipts and a rise in import payments.

33BANKING AND SECURITIES

The Solomon Islands Monetary Authority became the Central Bank of the Solomon Islands in January 1983; the bank's assets totaled si$44.9 million at the end of 1990. Three commercial banks also operate on the islands. There are 80 credit unions with 9,300 members on the islands. There is no securities market.

34INSURANCE

Insurance is sold through representatives of foreign firms. In 1986 there were 6 non-life insurance companies operating in the Solomon Islands.

35PUBLIC FINANCE

Recurrent outlays of si$203 million were close to the budgeted level for 1992, reflecting the efforts of the Ministry of Finance to keep a lid on expenditure pressures. Although the deficit reflected in domestic borrowing was si$7 million above budget, a revenue shortfall arose, mainly in the form of non-tax revenue. Even though the fiscal deficit rose sharply from si$5 million in 1988 to si$70 million in 1991, the amount of foreign borrowing vis-à-vis domestic borrowing plummeted.

The following table shows actual revenues and expenditures for 1990 and 1991 in millions of dollars.

	1990	1991
REVENUE AND GRANTS		
Tax revenue	108.40	120.73
Non-tax revenue	14.41	13.95
Capital revenue	4.45	1.67
TOTAL	124.26	136.35
EXPENDITURES & LENDING MINUS REPAYMENTS		
Capital expenditures	20.88	47.05
Current expenditures	146.69	184.62
Lending minus repayments	4.89	6.46
TOTAL	172.46	238.13
Deficit/surplus	48.20	−101.78

36TAXATION

Individual incomes are taxed on a graduated scale ranging for single taxpayers from 14% on the first si$2,100 of taxable income to 42% on taxable income exceeding si$14,700. Companies incorporated in the Solomon Islands are taxed at a fixed rate of 35%; a rate of 50% applies to those incorporated elsewhere. A value-added tax on telephone services, restaurant food, and overseas travel tickets went into effect in August 1990. Employers contribute 7.5% of employee wages for social security; employees contribute 5% minimum. On 1 July 1990, a resident withholding tax went into effect for royalties, fishing operations, sales of copra and cocoa, and certain other sources of income.

37CUSTOMS AND DUTIES

All products imported into the Solomons are subject to customs duties, and a 20% surcharge is levied on all ad valorem goods. Concessionary rates have been granted to imports of industrial machinery and equipment, raw materials, chemicals, and building materials. Licenses are required for the importation of firearms, ammunition, animals, seeds, soil, and plant material.

38FOREIGN INVESTMENT

The government encourages direct foreign investment through tax concessions, remission of customs duties, and other forms of assistance. Foreigners may repatriate profits (after taxes) and, under most conditions, capital investments. A primary role in the development of resources is reserved to the government. Japanese interests have been the major new source of private foreign capital; investment in 1986 totaled si$17 million for 47 projects. In 1990, Lever Brothers opened a coconut oil plant at Yandina.

39ECONOMIC DEVELOPMENT

The government has attempted to diversify agricultural production in order to make the economy less vulnerable to world price fluctuations of such key cash crops as copra. Important development projects during the 1980s included new sawmills, a fish cannery, a spice industry, and the Lungga hydroelectric plant.

Fisheries receive significant portions of development funds. A rubber industry is being developed, and plans are under way to export the indigenous ngali nut as an upscale confectionery product under the name "Solomons nut." In 1991, plans were announced for a si$60 million hydroelectric plant on Guadalcanal, financed by the Asian Development Bank.

Foreign assistance plays an essential role in the nation's development strategy, with Australia and Japan the largest donors. In 1990, the Solomon Islands received us$31.1 million in bilateral, and us$13.1 million in multilateral aid, as well as us$1.5 million in UN development aid. Aid is also received from the IBRD, ADB, and EC.

[40]SOCIAL DEVELOPMENT

A National Provident Fund covering certain categories of wage workers provides old age, disability, and survivor benefits in lump-sum payments, and employers cover the cost of workers' compensation. The 1981 Employment Act mandates that employers pay dismissal indemnity of 2 weeks' wages for each year of employment. The bulk of organized welfare services are provided by church missions. In small villages and outlying areas, assistance is traditionally provided through the extended family. The government, seeking to reduce the population growth rate to 2% annually (it was 3.5% in 1986), has mounted a modest family-planning effort. Although women are accorded equal rights by law, their role is limited by customary family roles in most Solomon Islands societies. Only 1 of 47 members of Parliament in 1993 was female, and there is a general shortage of employment opportunities for women.

[41]HEALTH

Poor standards of general hygiene and inadequate sanitation continue to make malaria and tuberculosis endemic. In 1985 there were 6 government hospitals, a mission hospital, and 124 clinics, providing a total of 1,398 beds. There were 38 doctors and 420 nurses in 1985. Infant mortality was estimated at 46 deaths per 1,000 live births in the 1980s; average life expectancy was 54 years for both men and women.

[42]HOUSING

The government has built low-cost housing projects in Honiara to help ease congestion. Outside Honiara, housing is primitive, with overcrowding a problem even in the smaller villages. As of 1990, 82% of urban and 58% of rural dwellers had access to a public water supply, while 73% of the urban population had access to sanitation services.

[43]EDUCATION

About 60% of the adult population is estimated to be literate. Education is not compulsory, and many schools charge fees. In 1976, the government began substantial aid to primary as well as secondary schools. Christian missions (mainly Anglican), supported by government grants, continue to provide some primary schooling. In 1991 there were 520 primary schools, with 60,259 pupils and 2,388 teachers. Secondary schools (general) had 5,607 pupils and 298 teachers in 1987. Higher education is provided by the Solomon Islands Teachers College (Honiara), the Honiara Technical Institute, and the University of the South Pacific Solomon Islands Center, also in Honiara.

[44]LIBRARIES AND MUSEUMS

The National Library (founded in 1974) in Honiara has two branches, and has a collection of over 100,000 volumes. The Solomon Islands National Museum and Cultural Center began collecting in the 1950s and opened a permanent site in 1969. The Center promotes and provides research into all aspects of Solomons culture.

[45]MEDIA

The main post office is at Honiara. There were some 7,000 telephones on the islands; a radiotelephone service provides overseas links. A government-owned radio service has 5 transmitters; there were an estimated 40,000 radios in 1991. There are no daily newspapers. The two weeklies are the *Solomon Star* (1992 circulation 3,000) and the *Solomon Toktok* (3,000).

[46]ORGANIZATIONS

Cooperative societies are important in rural areas for the distribution of locally produced goods. In 1986 there were 156 cooperatives. Honiara has a chamber of commerce.

[47]TOURISM, TRAVEL, AND RECREATION

Tourism, although encouraged by the government's Tourist Authority, is not seen as a major growth area, owing to lack of investment. In 1991, 11,105 tourists visited the Solomon Islands, 36% from Australia, 14% from New Zealand, and 9% from the United States. There were 293 rooms in hotels and other establishments, with 673 beds, and tourism receipts totaled us$5 million. Popular pastimes include rugby football, soccer, basketball, and water sports. A passport and an onward ticket are required for entry.

[48]FAMOUS SOLOMON ISLANDERS

Sir Peter Kenilorea (b.1943), Solomon Mamaloni (b.1943), and Ezekiel Alebua (b.1947) were the Solomons' political and government leaders from independence to the 1990s.

[49]DEPENDENCIES

The Solomon Islands have no territories or colonies.

[50]BIBLIOGRAPHY

Bennett, Judith A. *Wealth of the Solomons: A History of a Pacific Archipelago*. Honolulu: University of Hawaii Press, 1986.

Feinberg, Richard. *Polynesian Seafaring and Navigation: Ocean Travel in Anutan Culture and Society*. Kent, Ohio: Kent State University Press, 1988.

Keesing, Roger M. *Custom and Confrontation: The Kwaio Struggle for Cultural Autonomy*. Chicago: University of Chicago Press, 1992.

Oliver, D. L. *A Solomon Island Society*. Cambridge, Mass.: Harvard University Press, 1955.

Scott, Jonathan (ed.). *The Solomon Islands Project: A Long-term Study of Health, Human Biology, and Culture Change*. New York: Oxford University Press, 1987.

Trumbull, Robert. *Tin Roofs and Palm Trees*. Seattle: University of Washington Press, 1978.

White, Geoffrey M. *Identity through History: Living Stories in a Solomon Islands Society*. New York: Cambridge University Press, 1991.

SRI LANKA

Democratic Socialist Republic of Sri Lanka
Sri Lanka Prajathanthrika Samajavadi Janarajaya

CAPITAL: Colombo.

FLAG: The national flag contains, at the hoist, vertical stripes of green and saffron and, to the right, a maroon rectangle with yellow bo leaves in the corners and a yellow lion symbol in the center. The entire flag is bordered in yellow, and a yellow narrow vertical area separates the saffron stripe from the dark maroon rectangle.

ANTHEM: *Sri Lanka Matha (Mother Sri Lanka).*

MONETARY UNIT: The Sri Lanka rupee (R) of 100 cents is a paper currency with one official rate. There are coins of 1, 2, 5, 10, 25, and 50 cents and 1 and 2 rupees, and notes of 10, 20, 50, 100, 500, and 1,000 rupees. R1 = $0.0204 (or $1 = R49.065).

WEIGHTS AND MEASURES: The metric system is the national standard, but British weights and measures and some local units are also used.

HOLIDAYS: Independence Commemoration Day, 4 February; May Day, 1 May; National Heroes Day, 22 May; Bank Holiday, 30 June; Christmas Day, 25 December; Bank Holiday, 31 December. Movable holidays include Maha Sivarathri Day, Milad-an-Nabi, Good Friday, 'Id al-Fitr, Dewali, and 'Id al-'Adha'; in addition, the day of the rise of the full moon of every month of the Buddhist calendar, called a Poya day, is a public holiday.

TIME: 5:30 PM = noon GMT.

¹LOCATION, SIZE, AND EXTENT

Sri Lanka (formerly Ceylon) is an island in the Indian Ocean situated S and slightly E of the southernmost point of India, separated from that country by the 23 km- (14 mi-) wide Palk Strait. Including 958 sq km (370 sq mi) of inland water, Sri Lanka has a total area of 65,610 sq km (25,332 sq mi), extending 435 km (270 mi) N–S and 225 km (140 mi) E–W. Sri Lanka's total coastline is 1,340 km (833 mi). Comparatively, the area occupied by Sri Lanka is slightly larger than the state of West Virginia. Sri Lanka's capital city, Colombo, is located on the Gulf of Mannar coast.

²TOPOGRAPHY

The south-central part of Sri Lanka is a rough plateau cut by a range of mountains whose highest peak is Pidurutalagala, 2,524 m (8,281 ft). Narrow coastal plains skirt the mountainous section on the east, south, and west, but in the north the extensive coastal plain fans out, reaching from the eastern to the western shores of the island. Five-sixths of the land is less than 300 m (1,000 ft) in elevation. Numerous rivers and streams flow seaward in all directions from the central mountain area; the longest river, flowing northeastward, is the Mahaweli Ganga (335 km/208 mi).

³CLIMATE

The climate, although tropical and monsoonal, varies from warm in the coastal plains and lowlands to temperate in the hill and mountain regions. The lowlands in the northeast receive an average rainfall of about 130 cm (50 in), and the hill country in the southwest has an average of 510 cm (200 in), most of the rain coming during the monsoon season. Elsewhere, average rainfall varies from 63 cm (25 in) to 190 cm (75 in). Located only 879 km (546 mi) north of the equator, Sri Lanka has neither summer nor winter but only rainy and dry seasons. Average temperature is 27°C (80°F).

⁴FLORA AND FAUNA

Most plants and animals are those common to southern India, but there are additional varieties. The plant life ranges from that of the equatorial rain forest to that of the dry zone and the more temperate climate of the highlands. Tree ferns, bamboo, palm, satinwood, ebony, and jak trees abound. The wide range of mammals, birds, and reptiles once found in Sri Lanka has been reduced by the conversion of forests into rice fields, but water buffalo, deer, bear, elephants, monkeys, and leopards are among the larger animals still present. The Ceylon elk (sambhur) and the polonga snake are unique to Sri Lanka. Birds are numerous, many varieties from colder countries wintering on the island. Sri Lanka has well-organized game and bird sanctuaries. Insects abound, and numerous fish are found in the shallow offshore waters.

⁵ENVIRONMENT

Sri Lanka's principal environmental problem has been rapid deforestation, leading to soil erosion, destruction of wildlife habitats, and reduction of water flow. In 1985, the total amount of land affected by deforestation was 224 sq mi. The government began a reforestation program in 1970, and since 1977, it has banned the export of timber and the felling of forests at elevations over 1,500 m (5,000 ft) and the export of timber. Nevertheless, between 1981 and 1985, some 58,000 hectares (143,000 acres) of forestland were lost each year. The nation's water has been polluted by industrial and agricultural by-products along with untreated sewage. As a result, 20% of the nation's city dwellers and 45% of the people living in rural areas do not have pure water. Air pollution from industry and transportation vehicles is another significant environmental concern. The nation contributes 0.1% of the world's total gas emissions. The main environmental agency is the Central Environmental Authority within the Ministry of Industry and Scientific Affairs. Although legislation to protect flora and fauna and to conserve forests has been enacted, there has been inadequate enforcement of the laws.

Wildlife has been protected since 1937; by 1985 there were 37 protected areas, which together covered about 10% of the country's total land area. As of 1994, seven of Sri Lanka's mammal species and eight of its bird species were endangered. Endangered species include the Asian elephant, green labeo, spotted loach, and four species of turtle (green sea, hawksbill, olive ridley, and leatherback). In addition, 220 types of plants are threatened with extinction.

6POPULATION

The 1992 population totaled an estimated 17,405,000, as compared with 14,846,750 at the time of the 1981 census. For many years the population grew at an annual average rate of 2.4%, but the birthrate has declined significantly, and the annual growth rate in 1985–90 was estimated at 1.33%. Of the 1990 population, 33.6% was under 15 years of age. The annual birthrate declined from 28.4 per 1,000 population in 1980 to 20.6 per 1,000 in 1991. During the same period, the death rate fell from 6.2 per 1,000 to 5.5, for a net annual natural increase of 15.1 in 1991, representing a decline from 22.2 in 1980. A population of 19,438,000 was forecast for the year 2000, assuming a crude birthrate of 19 and a death rate of 5.8 for 1995–2000. The average population density in 1985 was 265 per sq km (687 per sq mi), one of the highest among nonindustrial countries. About 50% of the population is concentrated in the southwestern quarter of the island.

About 22% of the population was urban in 1985, only fractionally changed from 1970. Colombo, the commercial capital and chief city, had an estimated population of 615,000 in 1990. Other urban centers (with their estimated 1990 populations) are Dehiwala-Mt. Lavinia, 96,000; Moratuwa, 70,000; Jaffna, 129,000; Kotic, 109,000; and Kandy, 104,000.

7MIGRATION

Under an agreement signed in 1964, India pledged to repatriate 525,000 of the 975,000 persons of Indian origin (Tamils) then on the island, while Ceylon agreed to absorb 300,000 and grant them Ceylonese citizenship. Of the remaining 150,000, 75,000 were repatriated by a separate agreement concluded in 1974, and an equal number became citizens of Sri Lanka. With the intensification of communal fighting in the 1980s, about 230,000 Tamils had fled to India by 1992, but more than 30,000 returned in that year. About 620,000 Sri Lankans remained internally displaced in 1993.

In recent years, many Sri Lankan workers have migrated to work in Middle Eastern countries. Others—over 200,000 in all—have emigrated to Western Europe, Australia, and North America, in part as a result of the Tamil insurgency.

8ETHNIC GROUPS

According to official 1985 data, the Sinhalese constitute the largest population group, numbering 11,719,390 (74% of the total population). Sri Lankan Tamils (descendants of medieval invaders from India) totaled 1,900,440 (12%); Sri Lankan Moors, 1,140,265 (7.2%); Indian Tamils, 950,220 (6%); Malays (mostly of Arab extraction), 47,511 (0.3%); and Burghers (descended from the Dutch) and Eurasians, 47,511 (0.3%). A small group of Veddas, an aboriginal tribe, in the most inaccessible forest regions of southeastern Sri Lanka, together with other scattered groups, made up the remaining 0.2%.

9LANGUAGES

English was the official language under the British and remained so until 1956, when Sinhala became the nation's one official lan-

guage. This measure was bitterly opposed by the Tamil minority. Riots, disorders, and dissension grew, leading to a Tamil civil disobedience campaign and a temporary state of emergency. The 1978 constitution recognized Sinhala as the official language but also recognized Tamil as a national language. Sinhala is a member of the Indo-Aryan subgroup of the Indo-European language family, related to Pali. Tamil is a Dravidian language spoken in northern and eastern Sri Lanka and in southern India. It became an official language in December 1988.

10RELIGIONS

Of the total population, Buddhists constitute nearly 70% and are almost without exception ethnic Sinhalese; Hindus amount to 15% of the total population and are almost exclusively ethnic Tamils; Muslims account for 8% (and may or may not be Tamil speakers) and include the Moor and Malay communities; and Christians, accounting for 8%, are to be found in the Sinhalese, Burgher/Eurasian, and Sri Lankan Tamil communities (not to be confused with the so-called Indian Tamils, who were imported as plantation workers in the last century and are exclusively Hindu.) A majority of Christians are Roman Catholic, with Anglicans and Baptists also significant, the latter the result of American missionary activity in the north in the 19th century. The religious atmosphere is traditionally tolerant, and the issues involved in the Tamil insurgency are communal and ethnic rather than religious in origin. The 1978 constitution established Sri Lanka as a secular state and guarantees freedom of religion, while stipulating that Buddhism enjoys the foremost place in the republic.

11TRANSPORTATION

In 1991, the country had about 75,263 km (46,768 mi) of highways, of which 37% were paved surface, 44% were gravel or crushed stone surface, and 19% were packed-earth surface, (29,748 mi) of roads, and registered motor vehicles numbered 326,934, including 180,135 passenger cars, and 146,799 commercial vehicles.

In 1991, there were 1,948 km (1,210 mi) of broad-gauge (1.868 m) railroad, state-owned and state operated.

Colombo, one of the great commercial seaports of Asia, formerly was an open roadstead, but the construction of breakwaters has made it one of the world's greatest artificial harbors. In 1991, the merchant fleet consisted of 31 ships with a capacity of 321,000 GRT. In 1985, shipping freight cleared by all ports totaled 12,579,000 tons. Ports of the open roadstead type are Trincomalee, Galle, Batticaloa, Kankesanturai, Kayts, and Jaffna. A car ferry service links Mannar Island with the Indian mainland.

The country has 12 airports with permanent runways. The principal international airport is Katunayaka, 39 km (24 mi) north of Colombo. Air Lanka (formerly Air Ceylon), the national airline company, serves international routes only. In 1992, Air Lanka handled all of Sri Lanka's international passenger air traffic, with 1,045,600 passengers arriving and departing. Upali Travels, a private carrier, provides domestic service.

12HISTORY

The earliest Indo-European speaking settlers, the Sinhalese, came late in the 6th century BC, probably from northern India. Later arrivals from India brought Buddhism beginning about 240 BC, and at such cities as Anuradhapura and Polonnaruwa, the Sinhalese developed a great civilization, much of which was later destroyed by civil wars and by the incursions of Hindu Dravidian-speakers from across the Palk Strait, who established a Tamil kingdom in the northern part of the island.

The Portuguese East India Company brought the first of Ceylon's European rulers in the early 16th century, and in time, the Portuguese conquered the entire island with the exception of the Sinhalese kingdom in Kandy in the central plateau. By the middle of the 17th century, the Portuguese were driven out of Ceylon (and southern India) by the Dutch East India Company, which governed for more than 100 years, introduced plantation agriculture, developed trade, and left a legacy that includes Roman-Dutch law. But they too found themselves displaced.

Having won their struggle with France for mastery in India (and in North America), the British laid claim to Ceylon at the end of the 18th century after the Netherlands fell under French control. After a brief period as part of the British East India Company's Indian domain, Ceylon was designated a crown colony in 1802, and by 1815, the entire island was united under British rule. The British introduced coffee, tea, coconut, and rubber plantations, and efficient and enlightened administration.

With the development of a nationalist movement across the Palk Strait in India in the 20th century, nationalists in Ceylon also pressured for greater self-rule, leading to further democratic political reforms in constitutions enacted in 1910, 1920, 1924, 1931, and 1947; included in the 1931 enactment was limited self-rule under universal suffrage. In 1948, with little actual struggle, and a year after Indian independence, Ceylon became a self-governing dominion within the British Commonwealth.

The period from 1948 through 1970 saw the evolution of Ceylon's multiparty parliamentary system in which orderly and constitutional elections and changes of government took place. Beginning in 1970, executive power began to be highly centralized under Prime Minister Sirimavo Bandaranaike, who from 1971–77 ruled with the use of unpopular emergency powers in support of her socialist, pro-Sinhalese policies. She introduced a new constitution in 1972, converting the dominion of Ceylon to the republic of Sri Lanka, reaffirming a parliamentary system under a weak, ceremonial presidency, and making the protection of Buddhism a constitutional principle.

The SLFP defeat in the July 1977 elections brought Junius Richard Jayewardene of the more moderate United National Party (UNP) to power. He became Sri Lanka's first elected executive president in February 1978, under a constitutional amendment of fall 1977 establishing a presidential form of government. Seven months later, a new, more liberal constitution came into effect, rejecting many of the authoritarian features of the 1972 constitution, introducing proportional representation, and defining the presidential executive system. As his prime minister, he chose Ranadive Premadasa, a long-time follower with lower caste support. In October 1982, Jayewardene was popularly elected to a new six-year term, and two months later, in a successful effort to avoid general elections, the life of the sitting parliament was extended through July 1989 by means of a constitutional amendment endorsed by popular referendum.

Since 1978, rising tensions and violence between the majority (mostly Buddhist) Sinhalese and minority (mostly Hindu) Sri Lankan Tamil communities that have long shared the island have dominated political life. Going back to 1956, when the Sinhalese-dominated government had declared Sinhala the official language and replaced English with separate language tracks in education for Sinhala and Tamil speakers, a chasm had been developing between the communities. In the late 1970s, moderate Sri Lankan Tamils looked to the leadership in the Tamil United Liberation Front (TULF) and to negotiations with the new UNP government in 1978 to pursue changes aimed at protecting their cultural heritage by giving greater control to elected officials at the local level in Sri Lankan Tamil majority areas of the island.

By the early 1980s, their efforts had failed. Participation in Parliament as a responsible opposition had brought no changes, despite government promises; and many rounds of talks with Jayewardene and the majority Sinhalese community had netted no progress in redressing Tamil grievances. Violence was on the rise, and a spasm of communal bloodletting in summer 1983 had

LOCATION: 5°55' to 9°50'N; 79°42' to 81°53'E. TERRITORIAL SEA LIMIT: 12 mi.

left hundreds, if not thousands, dead in Colombo and elsewhere. By 1984–85, Sri Lankan Tamil leadership had fallen into the hands of extremists advocating violence, dooming to failure before it began the government's eleventh-hour convening of an All-Party conference in 1984 to seek a political solution to the ethnic conflict.

Fighting between the Sinhalese-dominated army and well-armed Sri Lankan Tamil separatists escalated in 1986 and 1987, with no solution in sight. It should be noted that the insurgency is limited to the larger group of Sri Lankan Tamils; the so-called Indian Tamils who were imported in the last century and continue to work the plantations in the highlands at the center of the island, and whose partial repatriation to India has been at times a subject for separate negotiations with India, have played no role in the insurgency.

In the spring of 1987, the government began a military offensive against Tamil forces in the Jaffna Peninsula in the Northern Province. India, sensitive to its own large Tamil population just across the strait, served as a base for rebels. Earlier, the Indian government had attempted to negotiate a settlement between the Sri Lankan government and the rebels, but in 1987 India reacted to the offensive by airlifting food and supplies to the rebels, creating considerable tension between the two countries. On 29 July, Jayewardene and Prime Minister Rajiv Gandhi of India signed an agreement by which the Sri Lankan government reluctantly accepted the need for devolution of power to the provinces, agreed that Tamil would have official status, and conceded that a semiautonomous administrative unit would be created for the Tamils in the Northern and Eastern provinces, subject to a vote by the Eastern Province on joining such a unit. An Indian peacekeeping force which grew eventually to more than 100,000 troops was sent to Sri Lanka to implement the agreement and enforce a cease-fire. But it was already too late. In the fall of 1987, Tamil separatists—notably and most prominently, the extremist Liberation Tigers of Tamil Ealam (LTTE)—resumed their attacks, killing about 300 people. When they refused the protection of the Indian Peacekeeping Force (IPKF), the IPKF launched an offensive against the rebel stronghold in Jaffna. Fighting continued, inconclusively, between the IPKF and (mainly) the LTTE for 18 months thereafter, with heavy casualties on both sides.

Meanwhile, through 1988 and 1989, the government was under attack from the militant Sinhalese nationalist JVP, which sought its overthrow for agreeing to the presence of Indian forces in Sri Lanka. The rebellion was put down firmly and brutally by President Premadasa, who succeeded Jayewardene in 1988 in a close race against Sirimavo Bandaranaike.

In 1990, V.P. Singh, who had replaced Rajiv Gandhi as Indian Prime Minister, agreed to Sri Lanka's request that India pull its forces out of the country; the Indian effort to crush the rebellion had failed at the cost of an estimated 1200 Indian lives alone. With the JVP eliminated and the Indians gone, Premadasa turned his attention to the possibility of expanding the new situaion, including a de facto ceasefire with LTTE, into a negotiated settlement. But a new spasm of LTTE violence in the eastern province led him to order an all-out army and air force campaign against the north in the second half of 1990, and guerrilla warfare resumed. Through 1991 and 1992, Premadasa's government continued to pursue the possibility of a negotiated settlement with the LTTE, denying it sought a military solution. But the LTTE's Velupillai Prabakaran, dominating the separatist side, rejected most government terms.

Under President Wijetunga, who replaced Premadasa when the latter was assassinated by Tamil rebels on May Day 1993, the warfare, and the search for a solution, continued inconclusively, with frequently announced cease-fires and resumptions. The death toll and the cost, reportedly $1 million per day, continued to mount.

Chandrika Bandaranaike Kumaratunga, 49-year-old daughter of former prime minister Sirimavo Bandaranaike and widow of a Communist Party leader assassinated nearly a decade earlier, became prime minister when her seven-party alliance of left parties won a plurality in snap elections to parliament in August 1994. With President Wijetunga's approval, she made resolution of the conflict her first priority on taking office by arranging for the economic blockade of the insurgent-held Jaffna peninsula to be partially lifted and offering to restore electric power to the area. She also offered unconditional talks for a resolution of the dispute, actions welcomed by the LTTE's Prabhakaran, who responded by releasing ten police constables held prisoner by the LTTE since mid-1990. Talks were scheduled for mid-October 1994.

13GOVERNMENT

The constitution of September 1978 established the Democratic Socialist Republic of Sri Lanka as a free, sovereign, independent state based on universal suffrage at 18 years of age. The president of the republic is directly elected for a six-year term and serves as head of state and as executive head of government, appointing and heading the cabinet of ministers whom he chooses and who are (or must quickly become) members of parliament. A prime minister, similarly selected, serves mainly as parliamentary leader.

Legislation approved by parliament cannot be vetoed by the president, and the president may be removed by parliament upon a two-thirds majority vote, following a finding by the Supreme Court of incapacity, treason, corruption, or intentional constitutional violation. The constitution can be amended by two-thirds' majority vote in the parliament, subject to ratification (for certain provisions) by popular referendum. The constitution provides that popular referenda also may be held on issues of national importance, but the normal business of legislation is in the hands of a unicameral parliament consisting first of 168—now 225—members elected for six-year terms under a proportional representation system. The sitting parliament elected in July 1977 took the unusual step of extending its own life for another six years by a national referendum in 1982, thus avoiding elections in which the competition for places on the ballot might have weakened the UNP's constitution-amending 2/3 majority.

In June 1994, the Wijetunga government scheduled "snap" elections for parliament on 16 August 1994, six months earlier than would have been required; elections to the presidency will follow parliamentary polling. Paced by the electoral appeal of SLFP deputy leader Chandrika Bandaranaike Kumaratunga, the People's Alliance of seven leftist parties won a clear plurality in the elections, ousting the UNP after 17 years in power. To the 91 parliamentary seats the Alliance won directly were added an additional 14 under the proportional system, and with the further support of 9 members of the Sri Lanka Muslim Congress, the new Peoples' Alliance government was able to command a majority of 114 seats in the 225-member house and to elect Kumaratunga as leader of the house, facilitating her prompt appointment as prime minister—an office previously held by both her ailing 80-year old mother and her late father, S.W.R.D. Bandaranaike.

Because the presidential system incorporated in the 1978 constitution vests the substantial powers of head of state and head of government in the hands of the president, Kumaratunga's capacity for independent action remains limited. As prime minister, she is actually little more than leader of the house, but she is committed to reviewing the free enterprise policies of the previous UNP government and to revising the constitution to restore the executive prime ministership of the Westminster system. Much depends, therefore, on the result of the presidential election scheduled for November 1994 when, under the existing constitution, effective control of government—whether divided between parties or unified under one—will be in the balance.

In the meantime, with the president's reportedly reluctant approval, Kumaratunga made—and the Tamil Tiger insurgents welcomed—a new opening by offering unconditional talks and lifting the embargo on 28 of the 70 items proscribed from being sent to the northern areas under Tiger control.

14POLITICAL PARTIES

Political life in Sri Lanka is open and vigorous, with a wide range of views represented among the political parties, many of which have their roots deep in the pre-independence era. In the time since independence, considerations of religion, language, and culture have largely displaced ideology as the issues around which multi-ethnic Sri Lanka's political life evolves. In the last decade, ethnic struggle—and violence—between the government, dominated by majority Sinhalese, and militant minority

Tamil separatists has dominated the political process.

The United National Party (UNP) was the main party of the independence movement, and its widely respected leader, D. S. Senanayake, as head of a coalition of which the UNP was the chief unit, became Ceylon's first prime minister after independence. He won a major victory in 1952 and continued in power until he died in 1956. The divided opposition failed to agree on a leader until 1951, when Solomon Bandaranaike left the UNP to form the Sri Lanka Freedom Party (SLFP). Over the years, the SLFP became the island's other major political party, advocating—like the UNP—a non-aligned foreign policy, with the UNP friendlier to the West, the SFLP, to the former Eastern bloc. Both find their support from within the majority Sinhalese community, and like most other parties, both are led mostly by high caste Sinhalese.

Shortly before the 1956 elections, Bandaranaike formed the People's United Front (Mahajana Eksath Peramuna—MEP), composed of his own SLFP, the Trotskyite Lanka Sama Samaja (LSSP), and a group of independents. The MEP called for the extension of state control, termination of British base rights, nationalization of tea and rubber plantations, and a foreign policy of strict nonalignment. In the elections, the MEP won 51 seats, and Bandaranaike became prime minister, holding power until September 1959 when he was assassinated by a Buddhist monk.

In elections March 1960, the UNP won 50 of the 151 seats at stake, the SLFP, 46 seats, and other parties, the remaining 55. UNP leader Dudley Senanayake failed to muster a majority, and new elections were called for July. In this second round of polling, the UNP won a majority of the popular vote but only 30 seats. The SLFP, led by its slain leader's widow, Sirimavo Bandaranaike, won 75, and with her supporters on the left, she was able to form a government, becoming the first woman in the world to hold office as prime minister. She committed her government to pursuing continuation of her husband's agenda, including nationalization of enterprises.

In the 15 years that followed, the UNP and the SLFP alternated in power for periods no longer than seven years. In 1965, Dudley Senanayake became prime minister after the UNP won 66 of the 151 legislative seats, but the SLFP's Sirimavo Bandaranaike was returned to power in the 1970 elections as the head of a coalition that included the Trotskyite LSSP and the pro-Soviet Ceylon Communist Party (CCP). In response to an insurrection fomented in 1971 by the Janatha Vimukhti Peramuna (JVP), a militant Sinhalese party in the south, Bandaranaike imposed a state of emergency on the island that lasted for 6 years. She pushed through a new constitution in 1972.

By 1977, Banderanaike's public image had declined. No longer supported by her former coalition partners, she was humiliated at the polls by J. R. Jayewardene's UNP which was returned to power with 51% of the popular vote and 142 of (the then) 168 seats in parliament. The moderate Tamil United Liberation Front (TULF), which had swept Tamil areas of the north and east, became the major opposition party in parliament with 16 seats and the SLFP representation in the house fell to a bare eight seats.

Jayewardene's sweeping victory enabled him to fulfill the UNP's campaign pledge to introduce a French-style presidential system of government. Forsaking the now-eclipsed office of prime minister, he set out as president to use his new powers to open the economy and to make a new effort to reconcile with the increasingly disaffected Tamil minority. In the local elections and parliamentary by-elections of May 1983, the UNP strengthened its commanding position by gaining control of a majority of municipal and urban councils and winning 14 of 18 parliamentary seats contested.

The CCP and two other leftist groups, the People's Liberation Front and the New Socialist Party, were banned in 1983 on charges of playing a role in the ethnic riots which swept the island

in July; leaders of the Communist Party were subsequently arrested. In August 1983, TULF members of parliament, after several fruitless years of negotiations with Jayewardene aimed at devolving power to local levels, were confronted with a constitutional amendment aimed at them by the UNP's two-thirds majority that required all MP's to pledge their allegiance to a unitary state. They abandoned parliament, and by now most have been killed, as the leadership of the Tamil movement fell into the hands of those advocating violence and complete independence as the only sure ways to protect Tamil ethnicity. The TULF was decimated in parliamentary elections in February 1989, which saw the emergence of several small Tamil parties with reputed ties to the rebels.

In presidential elections held in December 1988, Prime Minister Premadasa beat the SLFP's Sirimavo Bandaranaike in a close race marred by ethnic violence. He was sworn in as Jayewardene's successor on 2 January 1989. In February, he led the UNP to a strong victory in parliamentary polling, capturing 125 of the 225 seats under a new proportional voting system; he then named Dingiri Wijetunga as prime minister. These elections also saw the debut of the United Socialist Alliance (USA), a new political grouping set up in 1987 and composed of the SLFP's former coalition partners on the far left, including the CCP, the LSSP, and the Sri Lanka Mahajana Party (SLMP); the USA took 4 seats, while the SLFP won 67.

In the summer of 1991, Premadasa beat back a sudden challenge to his position by leading members of his party in parliament, suspending the parliament for a month to delay debate on a motion they had filed to impeach him for abuse of his authority. But in a rising tide of violence and assassinations of governmental officials across the island, President Premadasa himself became a victim of a Tamil bomber on 1 May 1993. The Parliament unanimously elected Prime Minister Wijetunga as his successor on 7 May 1993.

A "snap" election called six months early by President Wijetunga as part of his campaign for re-election himself in November 1994 backfired on 16 August 1994 when the voters rejected the UNP by a small margin. In its place, they elected to office a seven-party, leftist coalition—now dubbed the People's Alliance—led by the SLFP's Sirimavo Bandaranaike and Chandrika Bandaranaike Kumaratunga—mother and daughter, 80 and 49 years of age, respectively. More vigorous but less experienced, the younger Kumaratunga promptly became prime minister.

15 LOCAL GOVERNMENT

Although Sri Lanka is a unitary state, it is nonetheless divided into nine provinces whose borders follow historic and traditional lines. The key administrative unit has traditionally been the district, into which the provinces are further divided. A total of 24 districts under the control of senior civil servants who are District Officers responsible to the government in Colombo for ensuring justice, maintaining law and order, collecting revenues, and allocating development funds. There is, in addition a system of district ministers that was created after 1978 to assist the District Officers and to provide a political input at the district level. Appointed by the President, District Ministers are members of parliament but from a constituency other than one in the district for whom they bear district responsibility. Not full members of the cabinet, they nonetheless sit with the President in the Council of Ministers and otherwise enjoy ministerial perquisites.

Districts are also served in rural areas by popularly elected District Councils which have limited powers but which assist the District Officer and the District Minister in assessing public views and mood and in setting development priorities. Municipal and urban councils perform a similar function in urban areas.

In conformity with Indo-Lankan agreement in 1987 to devolve power to the provinces, the Parliament voted to establish, at the provincial level, elected councils headed by chief ministers. In presence of the IPKF in 1988, elections were held to these Provincial Councils (PC), and the UNP took control of 7 in non-Tamil areas; the ERPLF, a new, anti-LTTE Tamil party supported at the time by the IPKF, took control of the two in the Tamil north and east. While unsettled conditions have slowed progress on devolution, elections to the seven PC's in non-Tamil areas in 1993 reportedly produced more mixed results, with gains and losses for all parties, including the UNP, the SLFP, and the ERPLF.

[16]JUDICIAL SYSTEM

Civil law is based on Roman-Dutch law introduced during the period of Dutch rule, but in the area around Kandy, an indigenous type of law prevails. Criminal law is British. Tamils and Muslims have their own laws governing property disposition and certain observances. Sri Lanka's judicial system includes district courts, magistrates' courts, courts of request (restricted to civil cases), and rural courts.

In criminal cases, the Supreme Court (composed of a chief justice and from 6 to 10 associate justices, all appointed by the president) has appellate jurisdiction. Under the 1978 constitution, the other high-level courts are the Court of Appeal, High Court, and courts of first instance. Sinhala is the official language of the courts.

The Constitution declares the independence of the judiciary and the courts appear to be independent in practice.

Defendants are guaranteed a number of procedural due process protections but trials under the Emergency Regulations (ER) and the Prevention of Terrorism Act (PTA) lack significant procedural safeguards.

[17]ARMED FORCES

Budgeted defense expenditures have increased dramatically since 1984 as a consequence of the Sri Lankan Tamil insurgency in the northern half of the island. In 1991, they amounted to $416 million (6% of gross domestic product).Between 1983 and 1993 the army expanded from less than 15,000 to 39,000, with reserves adding another 2,500. In 1993, the navy 8,900 in uniform (with another 1,000 reserves). The air force had 8,000, with another 8,500 reserves. Although primarily involved in combating the insurgency, the military's traditional duties also include backing up civilian authority, curbing illegal immigration, and providing air surveys and search and rescue services. The armed forces, traditionally lightly armed, have been re-equipped with US and European weaponry purchased abroad, at a cost of $160 million since 1986 alone.

Sri Lanka has a police force of 30,000, backed up by a volunteer auxiliary force of 20,000 and a home guard of 15,200—also the product of expansion in the since 1985.

[18]INTERNATIONAL COOPERATION

The government of Sri Lanka is opposed to all military defense alliances but actively participates in other forms of international cooperation. On 14 December 1955, Ceylon was admitted to membership in the UN. Sri Lanka is a member of ESCAP and all the nonregional specialized agencies, the Asian Development Bank, the Commonwealth of Nations, the Colombo Plan, and G-77, among other intergovernmental organizations. It also signed GATT and the Law of the Sea treaty.

[19]ECONOMY

While Sri Lanka remains a primarily agricultural country, since 1980 expansion of the economy has been fueled by strong growth in its industrial and services sectors. In 1992, Sri Lanka's GDP totaled $9.7 billion. Agriculture employed 40% of the workforce and accounted for over 20% of the GDP. Annual growth in agricultural output however, averaged only 0.4% between 1985 and

1990, as compared with 5.1% in industry and 3.1% in services. Expansion of manufacturing, international trade-related services and tourism accounted for much of the strong performance in industry and the services sectors, which in 1992 made up 25% and 49% of the country's GDP, respectively.

From 1973 to 1977, the channeling of resources into social welfare programs, combined with frequent droughts and inflated world oil prices, helped to depress the economy and discourage business initiative. In 1977, the new UNP government accelerated economic growth by lifting most price controls, shifting government spending into capital investment, liberalizing foreign exchange and import restrictions, and eliminating some government monopolies to permit more business competition. The result of these policies was an annual increase in real GNP of 6% during 1978–81, compared with only 3% in 1971–77. However, the economic boom also catalyzed several years of high inflation through the mid-1980s.

In the latter half of the 1980s, the national economy faced several grave problems: escalating defense expenditures as a result of the civil insurgency, recurrent drought, stagnant government revenues and sharply depressed prices for the country's major export crops, tea and coconut-based goods. These conditions led to a resurgence of inflation, increasing unemployment, critical current account and balance of payment imbalances and stagnating economic growth. By 1989, unemployment stood at 18% while total growth in the GDP fell to 2% from 2.8% in 1988 and an average of 4.7% in 1980–85. Exports registered an increase of only 5% as compared with an average of 20% from 1984–88. Declining economic indicators spurred renewed stabilization and structural adjustment efforts by the government, which emphasized tightened monetary and fiscal policies and stimulating private sector investment through privatization.

In 1990 the economy experienced a strong rebound. Between 1990 and 1992, average GDP growth rose to 5%, average inflation declined to 11.4% from 20%, and the budget deficit was reduced by over 3 percentage points to 7.4% of GDP. These improvements occurred despite an extreme drought in 1991/92 —the worst in 50 years—which caused a decline of 1.5% in agricultural output from the previous year. Though per capita income in Sri Lanka remains low at $540, other social welfare indicators such as adult literacy, school enrollment, infant mortality and life expectancy compare very favorably with those of countries at much higher income levels.

[20]INCOME

In 1992, Sri Lanka's GNP was $9,459 million at current prices, or $540 per capita. For the period 1985–92 the average inflation rate was 11.3%, resulting in a real growth rate in per capita GNP of 2.2%.

In 1992 the GDP was $9,799 million in current US dollars. It is estimated that agriculture, hunting, forestry, and fishing contributed 22% to GDP; mining and quarrying, 1%; manufacturing, 17%; electricity, gas, and water, 2%; construction, 7%; wholesale and retail trade, 20%; transport, storage, and communication, 10%; finance, insurance, real estate, and business services, 6%; community, social, and personal services, 3%; and other sources 13%.

[21]LABOR

In 1992, the economically active population totaled about 5,948,226. That year, the agricultural sector accounted for 40%; 19.6% worked in industry and commerce; and 14.4% were sales and service workers. The number of unemployed persons in 1992 was estimated at 789,256, or about 13.3% of the economically active population.

An employer is liable for compensation to workers hurt, disabled, or incurring occupational diseases while on the job but is not obligated to carry insurance. Sri Lanka has minimum wage, safety, health, and welfare laws and legislation dealing with women, young persons, and children in industry, but adequate staff to enforce the labor laws is lacking. About 250,000 children younger than the minimum age of 14 are estimated to be employed, and they each contribute 30–40% of household income.

In 1991, 1,083 registered labor unions had a total membership of 1.75 million. During that year there were 103 strikes of 5 or more employees involving 50,013 workers, compared with 52 strikes involving 42,843 workers in 1989. The largest trade union federations are the Ceylon Workers' Congress, the National Workers' Union, the Democratic Workers' Congress, and the Ceylon Federation of Labor.

The Bureau of Foreign Employment reported 300,000 Sri Lankan workers abroad in 1991, mostly in Saudi Arabia, Kuwait, UAE, Singapore, Hong Kong, Bahrain, Qatar, and Oman, and many of them housemaids and nannies valued for their literacy and English language skills.

22AGRICULTURE
Agriculture, the mainstay of the economy, employs about 40% of the working population: three-fourths of those working in agriculture are engaged in the production of tea, rubber, and coconuts, the three crops that comprise nearly three-fifths of Sri Lanka's agricultural land. Tea production in 1992 was 179 million kg, down from 250 million kg in 1991 (due to poor weather, resulting in the lowest harvest since 1956); plantings were 210,000 hectares (518,900 acres). Rubber production was 105 million kg, and coconut production totaled 1,750,000 tons. In 1992, tea exports ($340 million) and rubber exports ($67 million) accounted for 13.5% and 2.7% of total exports, respectively.

In 1990, total agricultural production (including forestry and fishing) contributed 26.9% to GNP. Production of paddy (rice), the staple food crop, totaled 2,250,000 tons in 1992, as compared with 2,538,000 tons in 1990; the average yield per hectare on the 790,000 hectares (1,952,000 acres) harvested was 2,848 kg, a decrease of 7% over that of 1990. Lesser crops include sugar, pepper, cinnamon, chilies, sesame, cardamom, tobacco, cashew nuts, betel leaves, coffee, and cocoa.

Under the Land Reform Law of 1972, all property holdings exceeding 20 hectares (50 acres), except for property controlled by publicly owned companies, were vested in the Land Reform Commission for redistribution; a total of 226,373 hectares (559,377 acres) were redistributed, including one-fifth of the land under tea. Under the Land Reform Amendment Bill of 11 October 1975, all publicly owned estates (including the major British-owned tea and rubber plantations) were nationalized. As of 1990, the Janatha Estate Development Boards and the Sri Lanka Plantation Corporations accounted for 60% of total tea production and 30% of the total area under rubber cultivation.

23ANIMAL HUSBANDRY
Sri Lanka's livestock population is comparatively small; in 1992 there were 1,568,000 head of cattle, 896,000 water buffalo, 91,000 hogs, 502,000 goats, 17,000 sheep, and 9,000,000 chickens. Animals are not of high quality, partly as a consequence of religious considerations and primitive agricultural conditions. The natural pasturage lacks both nutritional value and palatability, and prospects for new pastures are not promising. In 1992, milk output was 194,000 tons, and 45,800 tons of eggs were produced.

24FISHING
Fishing produces less than the country's needs and yields a meager income to fishermen, most of whom use primitive boats and gear in the shallow waters surrounding the island. In 1991, the total fish catch was estimated at 198,063 tons, down from 205,286 tons in 1989.

25FORESTRY
About one-third of the total land area consists of woodland. In 1991, 9,096,000 cu m of roundwood were cut. Forestry products included 5,000 cu m of sawn timber and 8,453,000 cu m of firewood for domestic use.

26MINING
Gemstone and graphite extraction are the primary operations of the mining industry in Sri Lanka. Graphite production amounted to 6,381 tons in 1991, and is controlled by the government. The island's gem industry is world famous. In the Ratnapura district there are considerable deposits of sapphire, ruby, chrysoberyl, beryl, topaz, spinel, garnet, zircon, tourmaline, quartz, and moonstone. A lapidary industry has been established for the international marketing of cut and polished precious and semi-precious gemstones. Rare earth minerals of the cerium, yttrium, zirconium, niobium, tantalum, thorium, and uranium groups have been found; thorianite appears to be widely distributed. Large quantities of kaolin and apatite have also been found. There are large surface deposits of quartz sand. Miocene limestone from the Jaffna peninsula is used in the manufacture of cement. The beach sands contain large quantities of ilmenite, rutile, monazite, and zircon. In the dry-zone coastal areas, salt is manufactured by solar evaporation of seawater.

27ENERGY AND POWER
The Sri Lanka Electricity Board, a state enterprise, supervises the generation and transmission of electric power in Sri Lanka. Installed capacity in 1991 was 1,300,000 kw, of which almost three-fourths was hydroelectric; power generation totaled 4,200 million kwh, or about 250 kwh per capita per year.

The Mahaweli hydroelectric project, originally begun in 1970, included the construction of four reservoirs and hydroelectric plants at Victoria, Kotmale, Randenigala, and Maduru Oya, all of which are now in place. The four hydroelectric stations have a combined capacity of 580,000 kw (with the Victoria station contributing 210,000 kw), which accounted for 46% of the total energy generated domestically in 1990.

28INDUSTRY
Since 1977, the government's market-oriented economic policies have encouraged industrial growth in the private sector, particularly in textiles, wood products, rubber and plastics, food and beverages, and other consumer goods. While most small- and medium-owned enterprises are now privately owned, state ownership continues to predominate among the country's large corporations in basic industries such as as oil refining, cement, chemicals, paper and plywood, fertilizers, and ceramics. In 1992, manufacturing accounted for 15% of the GDP. Between 1990 and 1992 output increased by an average of 8.4% per year, with virtually all of this improvement derived from the private sector. Textiles production exhibited particularly strong growth with a 30% increase in 1992.

Output from major industries in 1992 (or previous years where indicated) include cement, 649,900 tons; paper and paperboard, 25,899 tons; tea, 340,000 tons; cotton fabric, 49 million sq. meters; cotton yarn, 8,400 tons; plywood, 7,000 cubic meters; rubber tires, 228,000. In 1988, the state-run Sri Lanka Petroleum Corp. produced 1,141,000 tons of distillate and residual fuel oil, 169,000 tons of gasoline, and 159,000 tons of kerosene.

29SCIENCE AND TECHNOLOGY
With the launching in 1978 of a free-trade zone north of Colombo, Sri Lanka was able to establish such high-technology

enterprises as the manufacture of integrated circuits and of control and relay panels. In 1982, two US electronics manufacturers contracted to build semiconductor assembly plants in the zone. The textile industry, located there, ranked nineteenth in 1985 as a supplier to the US. In 1984, total expenditures on research and development amounted to 257 million rupees. In 1985, 693 technicians and 2,790 scientists and engineers were engaged in research and development.

The Sri Lanka Association for the Advancement of Science is located in Colombo. Research institutions include the Ceylon Institute of Scientific and Industrial Research; Natural Resources, Energy, and Science Authority of Sri Lanka (formerly the National Science Council); and Colombo Observatory, all in Colombo. The National Academy of Sciences of Sri Lanka was founded in 1976.

30 DOMESTIC TRADE

Most retail stores are small and unspecialized. Marketing and distribution are dominated by the strong and well-developed cooperative movement, which the government assists with loans, price guarantees, and supervision. Although government monopolies played a major role in the wholesale distribution of imported goods, as well as many domestic commodities during the 1970s and 1980s, liberalization policies since the late 1980s are decreasing direct state involvement in domestic trade. Prices are administered for a few staple commodities such as diesel, kerosene, electricity and flour.

The usual business hours are from 8:30 AM to 1 PM and 2 to 5 PM, Monday through Friday. Banks open from 9 AM to 1 PM on Monday and to 1:30 PM, Tuesday through Friday. Products are advertised in newspapers, trade journals, motion picture theaters, and on commercial radio. There are several advertising firms in Colombo, some of which have connections abroad.

31 FOREIGN TRADE

The principal exports in 1990 and 1992 in millions of rupees were as follows:

	1990	1992
Tea	18,587	16,181
Textiles and apparel	18,420	51,537
Rubber	3,079	2,918
Coconut products	1,825	2,473
Other exports	34,713	34,261
TOTALS	76,624	107,369

The principal imports in 1990 and 1991 (in millions of rupees) were as follows:

	1990	1991
Machines & transport equipment	21,459	26,728
Basic manufactures	19,435	24,204
Food and live animals	17,677	20,486
Misc. manufactured goods	10,456	14,829
Mineral fuels, etc.	13,307	14,007
Crude materials excl. fuel	9,037	12,978
Other imports	14,188	14,137
TOTALS	105,559	127,369

Sri Lanka's principal exports traditionally have been tea, natural rubber, and coconut products, especially desiccated coconut and coconut oil. However, the share of total export earnings accounted for by these three commodities declined steadily from 87% in 1972 to 48% in 1985 and 20% in 1992; tea decreased from its 58% share of total export value in 1972 to only 14% in 1992. Declining export shares for the country's agriculturally-

based exports are due to adverse weather conditions in recent years as well as rapid growth in the export earnings of industrial products. 1992 proved a boom year, particularly for the textile and garment sector, which registered an increase of 49% in export earnings over 1991 and accounted for 48% of total exports. Textiles, apparel and petroleum refinery products are now the country's leading foreign exchange earners.

Sri Lanka's trade balance has been chronically negative since 1974 with the exception of 1977. In 1990, the US, the Federal Republic of Germany (FRG), the UK, and Japan were Sri Lanka's chief export markets; Japan, Iran, the United States, and India were the principal import suppliers.

The chief trade partners in 1990 (in millions of dollars) were as follows:

	EXPORTS	IMPORTS	BALANCE
US	490.4	207.3	283.1
Japan	102.3	325.2	−222.9
Iran	38.9	222.2	−183.3
UK	107.9	145.9	− 38.0
FRG	126.5	86.7	39.9
Other	1029.3	1,649.1	−619.8
TOTAL	1,895.3	2,636.4	−741.1

32 BALANCE OF PAYMENTS

Sri Lanka's balance-of-payments position is highly sensitive to price changes in the world market because it depends in large part upon a few export crops to pay for its imports. Since 1977, the country's rapid economic growth and the government's import liberalization have resulted in a large rise in the current-accounts deficit. Since 1983, sharply rising defense expenditures, a decline in tourism caused by continuing civil violence, and slumping world tea and coconut prices have combined to exert pressure on the balance of payments. The deficit has also been partially offset by substantial foreign exchange earnings from tourism and from remittances by Sri Lankans working abroad. In 1992, total merchandise exports increased 23%, while imports grew by 14%. Tea export earnings fell 21% (due to drought), while rubber and coconut exports grew by 6% and 33% respectively. The 1992 $1.2 billion in earnings from textile and garment imports were partially offset by textile import costs of $611 million.

In 1992 merchandise exports totaled $2,301.4 million and imports $3,012.3 million. The merchandise trade balance was $-710.9 million. The following table summarizes Sri Lanka's balance of payments for 1991 /92 (in millions of US dollars):

	1991	1992
CURRENT ACCOUNT		
Goods, services, and income	−1,196.8	−1,095.9
Unrequited transfers	603.7	644.3
TOTALS	−593.1	−451.6
CAPITAL ACCOUNT		
Direct investment	63.0	121.1
Portfolio investment	32.1	25.7
Other long-term capital	508.1	259.3
Other short-term capital	105.2	109.4
Other liabilities	3.8	−22.2
Reserves	−323.7	−201.7
TOTALS	388.5	291.6
Errors and omissions	204.6	160.2
Total change in reserves	−271.3	−177.7

33 BANKING AND SECURITIES

The Central Bank of Sri Lanka, established in 1949, began operations in 1950 with a capital of R15 million contributed by the government. The sole bank of issue, it administers and regulates the country's monetary and banking systems. At the end of 1993 foreign assets of the Central Bank amounted to R78,290 million.

Other statutory banks include the Development Finance Corp. of Ceylon, the National Savings Bank, the National Development Bank of Sri Lanka, and the State Mortgage and Investment Bank (established in 1931 to provide long-term credit primarily for agriculture). Total loans outstanding from all state banking institutions were R2,945 million by the end of 1985.

By the end of 1990 the commercial banking system consisted to 24 commercial banks including 118 foreign banks such as the Hong Kong and Shanghai Banking Corporations Ltd. According to central bank policy, foreign banks must be capitalized at R50 million. A percentage of the capital fund is set aside to finance the country's development programs. The commercial bank demand deposits totaled R27,169 million in 1993, time and savings deposits R100,780 million, and total foreign assets totaled R25,567 million. In 1979, the government began to promote Colombo as an international financial center for South Asia by permitting commercial banks to exercise "offshore" banking functions free of strict foreign currency controls.

The Colombo's Brokers Association operates an organized stock market, whose transactions have grown significantly sine the 1984 tea export boom increased liquidity in the economy. The Colombo Stock Exchange was established by the Association of Stock Brokers in 1987. Turnover in the market for the 1990 calendar year was R1.5 billion compared with R225 million in 1989.

34INSURANCE

Insurance was almost wholly a foreign enterprise until 1 January 1962, when the life insurance business was nationalized. The stateowned Insurance Corp. of Sri Lanka now has a monopoly on life insurance and all other insurance. In 1984, the premium income for life insurance was estimated at R171.89 million; and for fire, motor, accident, and marine insurance, R159.98 million. In 1986, 8.4% of premium payments were for life and 91.6% for non-life insurance.

35PUBLIC FINANCE

Budget deficits are financed largely through domestic and foreign borrowing. Budgetary performance improved in 1992 as the deficit (before grants) decreased to 7.4% of GPD. Current expenditures accounted for 75% of total expenditures.

The following table shows actual revenues and expenditures for 1991 and 1992 in millions of rupees.

	1991	1992
REVENUE AND GRANTS		
Tax revenue	68,157	76,575
Non-tax revenue	7,989	8,365
Capital revenue	33	60
Grants	7,870	8,720
TOTAL	84,049	93,720
EXPENDITURES & LENDING MINUS REPAYMENTS		
General public service	7,292	9,761
Defense	10,317	10,148
Public order and safety	4,624	4,432
Education	9,129	12,050
Health	5,230	5,644
Social security and welfare	19,281	16,833
Housing and community amenities	919	2,294
Economic affairs and services	26,967	28,486
Other expenditures	25,965	29,154
Lending minus repayments	9,803	5,208
TOTAL	119,527	124,010
DEFICIT/SURPLUS	−35,478	−30,290

In 1992 Sri Lanka's total public debt stood at R866,697 million, of which R214,579 million was financed abroad. In 1992, Sri Lanka received over $800 million in foreign assistance, equivalent to about 8% of GDP.

36TAXATION

Individual income taxes are graduated, increasing from 10–35% of taxable income. At the beginning of 1993, the rate of corporate tax on resident and foreign companies was 45%, but substantial tax benefits, such as depreciation allowances and incentive deductions, were permitted. Tax holidays on profits were available for certain approved companies and for small or medium-sized companies and corporate bodies. A business with an annual turnover of R100,000 or more was subject to a business turnover tax ranging from 5% to 20%. The corporate tax rate was scheduled to drop to 35% on 1 April 1993.

Also levied are license and property transfer taxes, estate duty, and a wealth tax.

37CUSTOMS AND DUTIES

After the substantial relaxation of customs and import controls in 1977, the number of items requiring import licenses fell to less than 150; firearms, automobiles, jewelry, precious metals, and certain chemicals are still under license. In 1991, Sri Lanka adopted a 4-band import tariff schedule with rates of 10, 20, 35, and 50 percent. Within Sri Lanka's free-trade zone, imports of industrial and construction equipment, base metals, and coal and coke are duty-free. Export duties are levied on tea, rubber, and coconut products.

38FOREIGN INVESTMENT

The great agricultural enterprises, insurance companies, and banks were developed originally by foreign capital. In 1959, foreigners owned almost 36% of the country's rubber acreage and 6% of the tea plantations; 80% of the insurance business was written by foreign companies, and the banking business was largely a monopoly of British and Indian firms. After 1961, when nationalization became widespread, private investors were reluctant to place new funds in Sri Lanka. Consequently, during the 1960s, the country had to depend almost entirely on loans and short-term credits. During the 1970–77 period, foreign companies, principally Japanese, were more willing to collaborate with public sector enterprises.

With the change of direction in the government's economic policy since 1977, foreign investment flowed more freely into the private sector. The Greater Colombo Economic Commission (GCEC) and Foreign Investment Advisory Committee promoted outside investment in export-oriented and high-technology industries, largely through joint ventures in which majority equity is held by Sri Lankan companies. Exceptions to this policy were large luxury hotels and construction projects for the Mahaweli development program, in which foreign partners hold the major share. The GCEC's Investment Promotion Zone, the country's first free trade zone (established in 1978), had attracted 116 foreign companies by 1985; 96 firms operating in the zone, chiefly clothing manufacturers, employed 35,786 workers and made capital investments with a total value of R286 million during that year. Continued liberalization and deceleration of insurgency since 1989 have attracted greater foreign investment. The entire country is now an open investment zone, where 100% equity by foreign investors is possible. A national Board of Investment is responsible for assisting entrepreneurs in meeting their basic business needs such as dealing with the appropriate government agencies and labor recruitment. In 1992, foreign investment in Sri Lanka almost doubled to $120 million from $64 million in 1991.

³⁹ECONOMIC DEVELOPMENT

Since independence, successive governments have attempted ambitious economic development programs with mixed results. The nationalization in 1962 of three Western oil companies and in 1975 of large rubber and tea plantations was intended to end the nation's economic dependence and neocolonialism, and to create an egalitarian socialist society. The goals of the last five-year plan for 1972–76—to achieve an economic growth rate of 6% annually, to create new jobs, and thereby to ameliorate unemployment—were not met, in part because of drought and unexpected increases in the costs of crude oil, fertilizer, and other imports.

The UNP government elected in 1977 chose as the centerpiece of its development strategy the Mahaweli hydroelectric-irrigation-resettlement program, the largest development project ever undertaken in Sri Lanka. The project involved diverting the Mahaweli Ganga in order to irrigate 364,000 hectares (900,000 acres) and generate 2,037 million kwh of hydroelectricity annually from an installed capacity of 507 Mw. Launched in 1978, construction was largely completed by 1987, at a cost of about $2 billion. Even as the UNP government launched this massive capital program, it sought to encourage private investors, limit the scope of government monopolies, and reduce subsidies on consumer products. Foreign trade, investment, and tourism were all encouraged by the government authorities. In 1986, foreign aid rose 23% in real terms over 1985, largely to finance further massive hydroelectric projects.

While government development policies resulted in moderate growth during the late 1970s and early 1980s, the outbreak of civil war in 1983 led to a rapid rise in defense spending (from 1% of GDP in 1980 to over 3% in 1989), exacerbating structural weaknesses in the Sri Lankan economy. By 1989, rapidly declining economic growth and worsening fiscal and balance of payment problems reached crisis proportions, prompting renewed stabilization and adjustment efforts. Corrective policies involved stimulating savings through new banking regulations and other monetary-tightening measures, reduction of subsidies on wheat and fertilizers, government expenditure reductions, currency devaluation, privatization of many state enterprises, and other incentives for private investment. These measures resulted in greatly improved economic performance in the early 1990s, despite unfavorable weather and lingering insurgency. Current government plans target further structural reform, an increase in GDP growth to 6.5%, a reduction of the fiscal deficit to 6.5% of GDP, and a narrowing in the current account deficit to 4.5%, all by 1995.

US economic assistance loans and grants to Sri Lanka for 1953–86 totaled $926 million. During that same period, Sri Lanka received $1,656 million in aid from international organizations, including $870 million from the IDA and $450 million from the Asian Development Bank. Between 1986 and 1990, net flow of official development assistance from all sources to Sri Lanka equaled $2.3 billion.

⁴⁰SOCIAL DEVELOPMENT

Despite low per capita income, Sri Lankans have enjoyed a relatively high standard of living because of generous social welfare programs. In 1978, the government began to pursue a vigorous population control program, combining an emphasis on family planning and voluntary sterilization with tax disincentives for larger families. The fertility rate was 2.7 in 1985–90, down 17.8% from the previous 5-year period. In 1987, 62% of reproductive-age couples practiced contraception, and family planning services were provided to 144,900 people in 1990. Abortion is only allowed to save the mother's life.

Through a provident fund system, the government pays monthly allotments to the aged, sick, and disabled, to destitute widows, and to wives of imprisoned or disabled men. To stimulate private efforts, the government makes grants to supplement the funds of volunteer agencies engaged in various welfare activities, particularly orphanages, homes for the aged, and institutions for the mentally and physically handicapped. Although women have equal rights under law, their rights in family matters, including marriage, divorce, child custody, and inheritance, are often dictated by their ethnic or religious group.

⁴¹HEALTH

The government provides medical service free or at a nominal cost to almost everyone, but its health program is hampered by a worsening shortage of trained personnel and hospital beds. Medical standards, traditionally British, are considered excellent, but in recent years many Sri Lankan physicians and surgeons have moved their practices abroad—particularly to the US and UK, where remuneration is much higher. In 1989, the Department of Health Services had 2,456 physicians (1 for every 7,363 persons), 520 pharmacists, 333 dentists, 9,632 nurses, and 5,030 midwives. In 1990, there were 2.8 hospital beds per 1,000 people. There are a limited number of private hospitals and medical practitioners. About 93% of the population has access to health care services. Total health care expenditures in 1990 were $305 million.

Malaria, smallpox, cholera, and plague have been virtually eliminated. Malnutrition, tuberculosis (167 cases per 100,000 people in 1990), and the gastrointestinal group of infectious diseases are the chief medical problems. In 1990, 45% of children under 5 years of age were considered malnourished. In 1992, immunization rates for children up to one year old were: tuberculosis (89%); diphtheria, pertussis, and tetanus (86%); polio (86%); and measles (79%).

The infant mortality rate in 1992 was 15 per 1,000 live births, while the maternal mortality rate was 80 per 100,000 live births. The general mortality rate was 5.8 per 1,000 inhabitants in 1993. Between 1984 and 1992, there were 32,000 civil war-related deaths. Other leading causes of death from 1990 statistics were: (1) communicable diseases and maternal/perinatal causes (232 per 100,000 people); (2) noncommunicable diseases (459 per 100,000); and (3) injuries (194 per 100,000). Average life expectancy is 71 years.

⁴²HOUSING

Rapid population increase, coupled with a lag in construction during and immediately following World War II, led to an acute housing shortage, high rents, high building costs, and many unsanitary and unfit houses in Sri Lanka's first decades after independence. According to estimates by the Ministry of Housing, 28,000–30,000 houses a year were built between 1970 and 1975, compared with 18,000–19,000 annually during the previous five-year period. Under the UNP government's urban development program, 184,860 public-sector housing units were built during the 1978–86 period.

The 1981 census showed a total of 2,813,844 housing units, of which 2,084,841 were rural, 511,810 urban, and 217,193 situated on agricultural estates. The average housing unit had 2.5 rooms and was occupied by 5.2 persons, or 2.1 persons per room. Although about 46% of urban units had electricity and 49% had running water, only 8.3% of rural houses were equipped with electricity and 5.1% supplied with piped-in water. About 51% of all housing units were semi-permanent, 42% were permanent, and 7% were improvised. Owners occupied 70%, 12% were occupied rent free, and 10% were rented.

⁴³EDUCATION

In 1990, 88.4% of the adult population was estimated as literate with men estimated at 93.4% and women at 83.5%. All education from kindergarten up to and including university training is free. Education is compulsory for 10 years, except when schools are not within walking distance of the pupil's home.

The public educational system was consolidated in 1970 into five years of elementary, six years of secondary, and two years of higher levels. In 1991, there were 9,590 primary schools, with 2,112,723 students and 173,811 teachers. General secondary schools had 2,106,050 students the same year. The estimated government expenditure on education in 1985 was R3,356.2 million. Since 1986, the educational system has been separated into two systems based on language, one in which Sinhalese is the medium of instruction and the other in which the medium is Tamil.

Beginning in 1978, Sri Lanka reorganized its higher education system; in 1986 there were nine universities: Colombo, Peradeniya, Moratuwa, Sri Jayawardhanapura, Kelaniya, Jaffna, Ruhuna, Open University, and Batticaloa. These universities operate as independent units under the University Grants Commission, which is funded by the Ministry of Education. Included in the consolidated university system are the former Vidyalankara University (established 1959), previously known as the Vidyalankara Pirivena (established 1875), a celebrated seat of learning for Oriental studies and Buddhist culture; the former Vidyadaya University (established 1959); and the former University of Ceylon (founded 1942). In 1990, all universities and equivalent institutions had 2,013 teaching staff and 38,424 students.

44LIBRARIES AND MUSEUMS

The Public Library in Colombo, with 567,828 volumes and 14 branches, is the largest public library in the country. Apart from the libraries in Anuradhapura, Jaffna, Kandy, and a few other towns, most public libraries have only small collections of books. The University of Peradeniya has holdings of 540,000 volumes, while the Colombo campus has 190,000. There are several special libraries in Colombo, including the National Museum Library, which contains 600,000 items (147,000 which are monographs) and has been a depository for Ceylonese and Sri Lankan publications since 1885.

The five national museums, at Colombo, Kandy, Ratnapura, and Galle, contain collections pertaining to paleontology, zoology, prehistory, archaeology, and ancient art. One of Asia's finest zoological collections, as well as the largest known collection of Sinhala palm-leaf manuscripts, is in the Colombo museum. Three national botanical gardens, located at three different elevations above sea level, represent Sri Lanka's three distinct zones of vegetation.

45MEDIA

The central government owns and operates all telephone, telegraph, cable, and radio facilities, except in a few rural districts, which are served by private exchanges. In 1991 there were about 166,057 telephones, more than half of which were in Colombo. The government operates both commercial and noncommercial radio broadcasting services in Sinhala, Tamil, and English and began television service in 1982. There were 3,460,000 radios in 1991, and 17,100,000 television sets in 1991. The Sri Lanka broadcasting Corporation airs broadcasts on AM, FM, and shortwave. In 1992, two television broadcasting stations served Sri Lanka.

In 1972, a five-member national Press Council with extensive powers over the press was established; since then varying degrees of censorship have been imposed with changing political conditions. In 1991, Sri Lanka had 21 daily newspapers. The principal morning and evening dailies (with their 1991 daily circulations) were the following:

COLOMBO	LANGUAGE	CIRCULATION
Dinamina (m)	Sinhala	116,000
Daily News (m)	English	65,000
Lankadipa (m)	Sinhala	75,000
Virakesari (m)	Tamil	45,000
Dinapathi (m)	Tamil	41,200
Aththa (m)	Sinhala	40,000

Sri Lanka also has more than 100 weekly and monthly publications.

46ORGANIZATIONS

Chambers of commerce include the National Chamber of Commerce of Sri Lanka, the Ceylon Chamber of Commerce, the Indian Chamber of Commerce, and the Moor Chamber of Commerce. There are numerous trade and industrial organizations.

47TOURISM, TRAVEL, AND RECREATION

In the 1980s tourism suffered due to prolonged civil unrest, but it has since recovered. In 1991, 317,703 tourists visited Sri Lanka; 198,413 came from Europe. The country had 10,870 hotel rooms with 21,347 beds and a 48.4% occupancy rate. Gross earnings from tourism were estimated at $156 million.

With the exception of areas of conflict between government and insurgent forces—mainly in the north and northeast, all parts of the island are easily accessible by train, bus, or rented car. The principal tourist attraction is the sacred city of Anuradhapura, home of the Seated Buddha, Buddhist temples, palaces, and the sacred bo tree, grown from a sapling of the tree under which the Buddha is said to have attained enlightenment. Other popular sites include the ancient cities of Polonnaruwa and Kandy, with its Dalada Maligawa temple, where a sacred tooth relic of the Buddha is preserved. The botanical gardens near Kandy and the Dehiwela Zoo at Colombo are also popular.

Sri Lanka's recreational facilities include the beach resorts of Bentota and Negombo, which, like Colombo, have modern hotels. Popular water sports are swimming, fishing, sailing, surfing, water skiing, and skin diving. The island has excellent facilities for golf, tennis, squash, soccer, rugby, and cricket.

Visitors need a valid passport and a visa, except for nationals of most Western European, ASEAN, and ANZUS countries, as well as Japan, who may stay for up to a month without a visa. Passengers traveling through infected areas must also possess valid certificates of vaccination against yellow fever.

48FAMOUS SRI LANKANS

One of the great rulers of the Anuradhapura period was Dutugemunu (fl.100 BC), who is famous for having saved Ceylon and its religion from conquest by Indian invaders. Mahasen, a king in the 3d century AD, built many fine dagobas and other monuments that delight and amaze visiting art lovers. The classic period of Ceylonese art flourished under Kassapa, a king of the 5th century. The great figure of the Polonnaruwa period was Parakramabahu I (the Great, r.1153–86), who unified the government of Ceylon, built many magnificent structures, and organized the economy. The most famous political figure in modern Ceylon was Don Stephen Senanayake (1884–1952), leader of the independence movement and first prime minister of independent Ceylon. Solomon West Ridgway Dias Bandaranaike (1899–1959), prime minister from 1956 to 1959, is regarded as the founder of Ceylon as a socialist state. His widow, Sirimavo Bandaranaike (b.1916), was twice prime minister (1960–65, 1970–77). Junius Richard Jayewardene (b.1906) became Sri Lanka's first president in 1978 and served until 1982.

49DEPENDENCIES

Sri Lanka has no territories or colonies.

50BIBLIOGRAPHY

Bruton, Henry J. *Sri Lanka and Malaysia*. New York: Oxford University Press, 1992.

De Silva, Chandra Richard. *Sri Lanka, a History*. New Delhi: Vikas, 1987.

Fernando, Tissa, and Robert N. Kearney. *Sri Lanka: Profile of an Island Republic*. Boulder, Colo.: Westview, 1986.

Juppe, James. *Sri Lanka: Third World Democracy*. London: Cass, 1978.

Kemper, Steven. *The Presence of the Past: Chronicles, Politics, and Culture in Sinhala Life*. Ithaca: Cornell University Press, 1991.

Manor, James (ed.). *Sri Lanka in Change and Crisis*. New York: St. Martin's, 1984.

Peebles, Patrick. *Sri Lanka: A Handbook of Historical Statistics*. Boston: G. K. Hall, 1982.

Ross, Russell R. and Andrea Matles Savada (eds.). *Sri Lanka, a Country Study*. 2d ed. Washington, D.C.: Library of Congress, 1990.

Samaraweera, Vijaya. *Sri Lanka*. Santa Barbara, Calif.: Clio Press, 1987.

Spencer, Jonathan (ed.). *Sri Lanka: History and the Roots of Conflict*. New York: Routledge, 1990.

Sri Lanka in Pictures. Minneapolis: Lerner Publications Co., 1988.

Wilson, A. Jeyaratnam. *The Break-up of Sri Lanka: The Sinhalese-Tamil Conflict*. Honolulu: University of Hawaii Press, 1988.

SYRIA

Syrian Arab Republic

Al-Jumhuriyah al-'Arabiyah as-Suriyah

CAPITAL: Damascus (Dimashq).

FLAG: The national flag is a horizontal tricolor of red, white, and black stripes; in the white center stripe are two green five-pointed stars.

ANTHEM: *An-Nashid as-Suri (The Syrian National Anthem)* begins "Protectors of the nation, peace be upon you."

MONETARY UNIT: The Syrian pound (s£) is a paper currency of 100 piasters. There are coins of 25 and 50 piasters and 1 Syrian pound and notes of 1, 5, 10, 25, 50, 100, and 500 Syrian pounds. s£1 = $0.0891 (or $1 = s£11.225).

WEIGHTS AND MEASURES: The metric system is the legal standard, but local units are widely used.

HOLIDAYS: New Year's Day, 1 January; Revolution Day, 8 March; Egypt's Revolution Day, 23 July; Union of Arab Republics Day, 1 September; National Day, 16 November. Muslim religious holidays include 'Id al-Fitr, 'Id al-'Adha', Milad an-Nabi, and Laylat al-Miraj. Christian religious holidays include Easter (Catholic); Easter (Orthodox); and Christmas, 25 December.

TIME: 2 PM = noon GMT.

¹LOCATION, SIZE, AND EXTENT

Situated in southwest Asia, at the eastern end of the Mediterranean Sea, Syria has an area of 185,180 sq km (71,498 sq mi). Comparatively, the area occupied by Syria is slightly larger than the state of North Dakota. Included in this total is the Golan Heights region (1,176 sq km/454 sq mi), which Israel captured in 1967 and annexed on 14 December 1981; the annexation was denounced by Syria and unanimously condemned by the UN Security Council. Syria extends 793 km (493 mi) ENE–WSW and 431 km (268 mi) SSE–NNW. It is bounded on the N by Turkey, on the E and SE by Iraq, on the s by Jordan, on the sw by Israel, and on the w by Lebanon and the Mediterranean Sea, with a total boundary length of 2,415 km (1,500 mi) following the 1949 armistice with Israel and of 2,446 km (1,520 mi) as of January 1988.

²TOPOGRAPHY

There are five main geographic zones: (1) the narrow coastal plain along the Mediterranean shore; (2) the hill and mountain regions, including the Ansariyah ('Alawite) Mountains in the northwest paralleling the coast, the eastern slopes of the Anti-Lebanon Mountains, and the Jabal Ad-Duruz in the southeast; (3) the cultivated area east of the Ansariyah and Anti-Lebanon ranges, which is widest in the north, discontinuous between Homs and Damascus; (4) the steppe and desert region, traversed by the Euphrates (Al-Furat) River; and (5) the Jazirah in the northeast, steppe country with low rolling hills.

The Anti-Lebanon Mountains, extending southward along the Lebanese border, serve as a catchment for the rainfall of central Syria. To the north of this range, the Ansariyah Mountains, which reach heights of over 1,500 m (5,000 ft), slope westward to the Mediterranean. The Orontes (Asi) River irrigates areas on the eastern side of the Ansariyah Mountains.

³CLIMATE

The climate varies from the Mediterranean type in the west to extremely arid desert conditions in the east. The coastal regions have hot summers and mild winters; in the mountains, summer heat is moderated according to elevation and the winters are much more severe.

The steppe and desert areas have extremely hot, arid summers and greatly varying winter temperatures ranging from 21°C (70°F) to below freezing. Average temperatures for Damascus range from about 21° to 43°C (70–109°F) in August and from about –4° to 16°C (25–61°F) in January. Rainfall averages about 75 cm (30 in) on the coast, around 125 cm (50 in) in some mountain areas, and less than 25 cm (10 in) in the eastern three-fifths of the country. In dry years, rainfall may be reduced by half.

⁴FLORA AND FAUNA

The coastal plain is highly cultivated, and the little wild growth found is mainly of the brushwood type, such as tamarisk. On the northern slopes of the Ansariyah range are remnants of pine forests, while oak and scrub oak grow in the less well-watered central portion. Terebinth is indigenous to the low hill country of the steppes, and wormwood grows on the plains. Some sections of the Jabal Ad-Duruz are covered with a dense maquis.

The wildlife of Syria includes types common to the eastern Mediterranean region, together with typical desert species. There is a diminishing number of bears in the mountains; antelope are found wherever grazing is available and human competition not too severe; there are also deer in some sections. Smaller animals include squirrel, wildcat, otter, and hare. In the desert, the viper, lizard, and chameleon are found in relatively large numbers. Native birds include flamingo and pelican, as well as various ducks, snipe, and other game birds.

⁵ENVIRONMENT

Much of Syria's natural vegetation has been depleted by farming, livestock grazing, and cutting of trees for firewood and construction. The thick forests that once covered western Syria have been drastically reduced; as a result, soil erosion and desertification are extensive. The salinity of the soil is also a problem. Syria loses

473

more than $300 million worth of agricultural products per year due to soil salinity. Other environmental problems include pollution of coastal waters from oil spills and human wastes, and contamination of inland waterways by industrial wastes and sewage. Syria has 1.8 cubic miles of water. Eighty-three percent is used for farming and 10% for industrial activity. Thirty-two percent of the people living in rural areas do not have pure water. The pollution of the nation's water supply also leads to the spread of diseases. The nation's cities produce 1.3 million tons of solid waste per year. Environmental awareness has been a growing concern in the Arab world. The UN and Middle Eastern environmental organizations have sponsored Arab Environment Day to bring the focus of the nation's attention on environmental problems. The quantity of native wildlife has been so seriously depleted that in 1979 the government banned hunting for five years. In 1994, two of Syria's mammal species and 15 of its bird species are endangered. Eleven types of plants are also endangered. The Syrian wild ass is one of the endangered species, and the Anatolian leopard, cheetah, Asiatic wild ass, and Persian fallow deer are extinct.

6POPULATION

According to the 1981 census, Syria's population was 9,046,144, representing an annual growth rate since 1970 of 4%, one of the highest in the world. The population was estimated at 12,958,000 in mid-1992, and 17,546,000 was projected for the year 2000, assuming a crude birthrate of 39.7 per 1,000 population, a crude death rate of 5, and a net natural increase of 34.7 during 1995–2000. In 1990, 48% of the population was under 15 years of age. In 1992, the population density was estimated at 70 per sq km (181 per sq mi), but most of it was concentrated in a small area; 70% of Syria's people live in Damascus and the six western provinces. About half of the population was urban in 1990. Damascus, the capital, had an estimated population of 1,378,000 in 1990. The population of Aleppo (Halab), a northern trading and agricultural center, was an estimated 1,355,000. Other main cities are Homs (Hims), 481,000; Hamath (Hama); and Latakia (Al-Ladhiqqiyah).

7MIGRATION

In the past there was sizable emigration by Syrians to Europe, Africa, and the Western Hemisphere, but emigration had virtually ceased by the late 1940s. Since World War I there has been substantial internal migration from the coastal mountains to the central plains and, in general, from rural areas to the towns. There is considerable migration across the borders with Lebanon and Jordan. About 150,000 Syrians working in Kuwait returned during 1990–91. In mid-1991, 289,923 Palestinian refugees were registered with the UNRWA, of which 84,972 were living in 10 camps.

8ETHNIC GROUPS

Racially, the Syrians are varied, and except where ethnic distinctions have found religious expression, racial types are generally intermixed. It is estimated that Arabs make up about 90% of the population. Other ethnic groups include Kurds (about 9%), Armenians, Turkomans, Circassians, Assyrians, and Jews.

9LANGUAGES

The language of the majority is Arabic (about 89%), but dialect variations are distinct from region to region and even from town to town. The written language, classical Arabic, based on the Koran (Qur'an), is the basis of the standard spoken form. Kurdish (6%) and Armenian (3%) are the principal minority languages. Aramaic, the language of Jesus, is still spoken in some villages.

10RELIGIONS

Islam is the religion of the vast majority. Most of the Muslims are Sunnis; some are Isma'ili Shi'is. The 'Alawis constitute an important minority in Syria and hold a disproportionate share of political power; although they consider themselves Muslims, they combine their avowed creed with Christian rituals and esoteric cults. Also important are the Druzes (most of whom live in the Jabal Ad-Duruz), whose religion is an offshoot of Shi'i Islam. Orthodox Muslims, Alawis, and Druzes together constituted about 90% of the population in 1993. The Christian population—including Greek Orthodox, Armenian Catholic, Armenian Orthodox (Gregorian), Syrian Catholic, Syrian Orthodox, Maronite Christian, Protestant, and Nestorian—make up an estimated 9%. The small Jewish population (4,000 in 1984) is urban, living primarily in Damascus and Aleppo.

Under the 1973 constitution, Islam is no longer declared to be the religion of the state, but the president of Syria must still be a Muslim, and Islamic law is a major source of legislation. Freedom of worship is guaranteed by the constitution. Armed opposition to the government by Muslim fundamentalists grouped in an Islamic Front took many lives during 1976–82. The movement collapsed following the government's suppression of a major uprising in Hamath in February 1982, an action in which upwards of 5,000 died.

11TRANSPORTATION

The Syrian national railway system consists of 2,035 km (1,265 mi) of standard gauge line: three sections are the Syrian section of the old Baghdad Railway; the main line from Damascus to Aleppo, with connections to Tartus, points in Lebanon, and the phosphate mines; and the railway linking Latakia, Aleppo, and Al-Qamishli, built with Soviet help and completed in 1981. There is also 315 km (196 mi) of narrow-gauge line—part of which is the pre–World War I Hejaz Railway—linking Damascus to Jordan and Lebanon. Syria is also connected by rail with Turkey (hence, with Europe) and Iraq.

The road system, though growing, remains inadequate in view of the demands imposed by increased economic activity. In 1985, Syria had 28,960 km (17,995 mi) of roads, 74% asphalted; there were 254,456 motor vehicles in 1991. There are road connections between the major towns and with Iraq, Jordan, Lebanon, and Turkey.

Tartus and Latakia are the main ports. Jablah and Baniyas are minor ports. In 1991, the merchant fleet comprised 31 vessels with a capacity of 87,000 GRT. Damascus is a connecting point for a number of major airlines; the main passenger terminal of its international airport was completed in 1982. A total of 1,293 million passenger-km were performed by Syrian airports in 1992. Syrian Arab Airlines provides service to Aleppo, Al-Qamishli, Latakia, and other airports; it also flies to other Arab countries and to Europe and Africa, carrying 551,900 passengers in 1992.

12HISTORY

Archaeological excavations at Ebla, in northern Syria, have revealed that Syria was the center of a great Semitic empire extending from the Red Sea north to Turkey and east to Mesopotamia around 2500 BC. At that time, Damascus, traditionally the world's oldest continuously occupied city and certainly one of the world's oldest cities, was settled. Later, an advanced civilization was developed along the Syrian and Lebanese coastlands under the Phoenicians (c.1600–c.800 BC), among whom trade, industry, and seafaring flourished. The wealth of the land attracted many conquerors, and Syria was invaded successively by Hittites, Egyptians, Assyrians, Persians, and others. In the 4th century BC, Syria fell to Alexander the Great, first in a long line of European conquerors. After the breakup of his empire, dominion over Syria was disputed by the Seleucid and Ptolemaic successor states, and Persians invaded when the opportunity arose; eventually the Seleucids gained control. In the 1st century BC, all of Syria, Lebanon, Palestine, and Transjordan was conquered by the Romans

SYRIA

0   40   80 Miles

0   40   80 Kilometers

LOCATION: (1949): 32°30′ to 37°30′N; 35°50′ to 42°E. **BOUNDARY LENGTHS:** Turkey, 845 km (525 mi). Iraq, 596 km (370 mi). Jordan, 356 km (221 mi). Israel: 1949 armistice line, 76 km (47 mi); 1988 line, 80 km (50 mi). Lebanon, 359 km (223 mi). Mediterranean coastline, 183 km (114 mi). **TERRITORIAL SEA LIMIT:** 35 mi.

and organized as the province of Syria; these areas are termed "geographic" Syria. Christianity, particularly after its official recognition in the early 4th century AD by Constantine the Great, spread throughout the region.

In 637, Damascus fell to the Arabs. Most Syrians were converted to Islam, and Arabic gradually became the language of the area. Under the Umayyad caliphs, Damascus became the capital of the Islamic world and a base for Arab conquests. Under the 'Abbasids, the caliphate was centered at Baghdad, and Syria was reduced to provincial status. Thereafter, geographic Syria fell prey to a succession of invaders, including Byzantines and Crusaders from Western Europe. Some parts of Syria came under the sway of Seljuks and Ayyubids, a Kurdish dynasty. The latter was most prominent under its leader Saladin (Salah ad-Din). During the

13th century, Mongols frequently invaded Syria, and for 200 years parts of Syria were controlled by Mamluks, who ruled it from Egypt through local governors. In 1516, the Ottoman forces of Sultan Selim I defeated the Mamluks, and for the next four centuries, Syria was a province of the Ottoman Empire.

During World War I, Sharif Hussein (Husayn Ibn-'Ali) of Mecca threw in his lot with the Allies and revolted against Ottoman rule. After the war, with British forces in control, the formal entry of Allied troops into Damascus was made by Arab forces under Faisal (Faysal), Hussein's son, on 30 October 1918. Faisal and the Arab nationalists, whose number had been growing since 1912, opposed French aspirations to Syria and claimed independence under the terms of agreements between the British government and Hussein. In March 1920, Faisal was proclaimed king by a congress representing Syria, Lebanon, and Palestine. However, geographic Syria was divided into British and French mandates. In June, the French, who had been allotted a mandate for Syria and Lebanon by the Agreement of San Remo (April 1920), ejected Faisal and installed local administrations of their own choosing. Arab nationalists resented French rule; there was a major revolt from 1925 to 1927, and unrest persisted until the outbreak of World War II. In 1941, Free French and British forces wrested control of Syria from Vichy France. Two years later, under pressure from the UK and the US, the French permitted elections and the formation of a nationalist government. The UK and the US recognized Syria's independence in 1944, and the last French troops departed on 17 April 1946.

Two parties that had led the struggle for independence, the Nationalist Party and the People's Party, dominated Syrian political life in the immediate postwar period. However, the Palestine War of 1948–49, which resulted in the defeat of the Arab armies and the establishment of Israeli statehood, discredited the Syrian leadership. In December 1948, riots against the government were put down by the army, and several army factions struggled for more than a year to gain control of the Syrian state. Col. Adib Shishakli ruled Syria for most of the period from December 1949 to March 1954, when he was ousted by another army coup.

The years from 1954 to 1958 were marked by the growth of pan-Arab and left-of-center political forces at the expense of the traditional merchant-landowner class, which dominated the Nationalist and People's parties. Foremost among these forces was the Arab Socialist Ba'th Party, which saw in Gamal Abdel Nasser (Nasir), the president of Egypt, a kindred pan-Arabist. Military officers remained active in political affairs but were split into competing factions. Some elements of the Nationalist and People's parties sought to counter the left by seeking help from Iraq and other countries. In late 1957, influential military officers decided to seek unity with Egypt as a means of suppressing factionalism. Enthusiastically supported by the Ba'th and other pan-Arabists, they appealed to Cairo. Nasser agreed, and on 1 February 1958, Egypt and Syria proclaimed the union of Syria and Egypt as the United Arab Republic (UAR).

A monolithic single-party structure replaced the lively Syrian political tradition; decisions were made in Cairo; land reforms were introduced. Syrians chafed under Egyptian rule, and in September 1961, after a military coup, Syria seceded from the UAR. A period of political instability followed until, on 8 March 1963, power was seized by a group of leftist army officers calling themselves the National Council of the Revolutionary Command, and a radical socialist government dominated by the Ba'th Party was formed.

The period that followed was marked by internal struggles between the founders of the Ba'th Party and a younger generation of party militants, many in the military. That generation came to power in 1966 but split in succeeding years. In the June 1967 war between Israel, on one side, and Syria, Egypt, and Jordan on the other, Israel gained control of the Golan Heights. Gen. Hafez al-Assad (Hafiz al-Asad), a former chief of the Air Force and Defense Minister, became chief of state on 16 November 1970; he assumed the presidency, a reinstituted office, for the first of four seven-year terms beginning in March 1971, and a permanent constitution was ratified by popular referendum on 12 March 1973. On 6 October of that year, Syrian troops launched a full-scale attack against Israeli forces in the Golan Heights, as the Egyptians attacked in the Suez Canal area. After the UN cease-fire of 24 October, Israel remained in control of the Golan Heights, and Syria boycotted peace negotiations in Geneva. However, on 31 May 1974, Syria signed a US-mediated disengagement accord with Israel, restoring part of the Golan Heights to Syria and creating a buffer zone, manned by a UN peacekeeping force. The occupied sector of the Golan Heights was annexed by Israel in 1981; outside powers criticized and did not recognize the annexation.

In recent years, Syria has intervened militarily in neighboring Arab states to secure political ends. In September 1970, Syrian armored forces crossed the border into Jordan to support the Palestinians during the Jordanian civil war, but the Syrians were driven back by troops loyal to Jordan's King Hussein (Husayn) and by the threat of Israeli intervention. In 1976, Syrian troops entered Lebanon, nominally to enforce a cease-fire between Christian and Muslim forces but actually to help the Christian forces prevent a victory by leftist Muslims and Palestinians. Syria strongly opposed the Egyptian-Israeli peace treaty of 1979 and was one of the few Arab states to support Iran in its war against Iraq, with which Syria earlier had hoped to merge. Another merger plan, this one with Libya, was announced in September 1980, but the effort was stillborn. In October, Syria signed a 20-year friendship treaty with the USSR; subsequently Syria received large quantities of Soviet arms, including antiaircraft missiles, which it deployed in the Bekaa (Biqa') Valley in Lebanon. After Israel invaded southern Lebanon in June 1982, the Israelis knocked out the missile batteries, crippled Syria's Soviet-equipped air force, and trapped Syrian as well as Palestinian fighters in Beirut before allowing their evacuation. Having reequipped its army with Soviet weapons, Syria has maintained 25,000-30,000 troops in Lebanon ever since. In the continuing Lebanese civil war, Syria has supported the Druze and Muslim militias against the Maronite Lebanese Forces.

Syria has made repeated attempts to establish a cease-fire among Lebanon's factions. In 1989, it endorsed the Taif Accord for ending the conflict and, later, when Christian militia General Michel Aoun declared himself president of Lebanon and sought to expel the Syrian forces, assaulted his enclave with artillery and drove him out of the country. In 1991, Syria backed moves to disarm and disband the militias and signed a treaty with Beirut to put relations on a stable and peaceful basis. Under the Taif Accord, Syria was to have withdrawn its forces from Beirut and coastal areas by September 1992. The move was still pending in mid-1994.

The authoritarian Assad regime has been condemned by outsiders for assisting terrorist and drug smuggling groups. Both charges have been played down since Syria joined the coalition of forces against Iraq in 1990 and agreed to participate in direct peace talks with Israel in 1991. The collapse of the Soviet Union removed Syria's most important external support, nullifying Assad's proclaimed strategy of refusing to negotiate with Israel until Syria had gained military parity.

Internally, the regime is resented for its denial of democracy and the concentration of power with members of Assad's minority religious sect, the Alawis. The most serious internal threat came from Islamic militants in the late 1970s and early 1980s. In 1982, Assad sent the army against their stronghold in Hama, devastating a section of the city and causing tens of thousands of casualties. There has been no serious threat to the regime since then and the Ba'th Party has continued to be used as a means of control throughout the country. In the 1990s, Assad took steps to liberalize economic controls and to permit some political freedoms. About 300 political prisoners were released in 1992 and Syrian Jews were again allowed to travel.

¹³GOVERNMENT

After independence, Syria made several attempts at establishing a constitution. The constitution of 1950 was revived in amended form in 1962 and then abrogated. A provisional constitution adopted in April 1964 was suspended in 1966 and replaced to some extent by a continuing series of edicts. The fundamental law that thus emerged considered Syria a socialist republic forming part of the Arab homeland, required that the head of state be a

Muslim, recognized Islamic law as a main source of legislation, ordained collective ownership of the means of production, but permitted some private ownership.

The constitution of 12 March 1973, embodying these principles and ratified by popular referendum, vests strong executive power in the president, who is nominated by the Ba'th Party and elected by popular vote to a seven-year term. The president, who appoints the cabinet (headed by a prime minister), also serves as commander-in-chief of the armed forces and as secretary-general of the Ba'th Party; three vice-presidents (including President Assad's younger brother Rifaat) were named in March 1984. The unicameral People's Council has 250 members who are elected every four years, but who have no real power. Suffrage is universal, beginning at age 18. Syria has been under a state of emergency since 1963 (except for 1973-74).

14POLITICAL PARTIES

The Arab Socialist Ba'th Party is Syria's dominant political institution. It has a countrywide organization and controls mass organizations for youth, students, women, and the like. Only the Ba'th may carry on political activity in the armed forces. It is far larger and more influential than the combined strength of its four partners in the National Progressive Front (NPF). This official political alignment, formed by President Assad in 1972, groups the Communist Party of Syria (SCP) and small leftist parties—the Syrian Arab Socialist Union (ASU), the Socialist Unionist Party (ASUM), the Democratic Socialist Union Party (DSUP), and the Arab Socialist Party (ASP)—with the Ba'th. The Ba'th Party was founded in 1947 with goals of Arab liberation, Arab unity, and socialism. Ba'thists attained control of the government in 1963, but the party became divided into two factions, a wing of doctrinaire socialists and a more pragmatic wing. Assad, then minister of defense and a strong nationalist, seized power in a bloodless coup in November 1970 and purged the doctrinaire Ba'thists from the government. The Ba'thists have relied for public support on the minority Alawi sect, of which Assad is a member, and on the rural sector of the population generally. Assad has appointed Ba'thist Alawis to influential positions in the government and in the military and security services.

Assad, the sole presidential candidate, won national plebiscites by 99% majorities on 12 March 1971, 8 February 1978, 13 March 1985, and 2 December 1991. In elections in May 1990, the Ba'th won 134 seats; the ASU, 8; SCP, 8; ASUM, 7; ASP, 5; DSUP, 4; and independents, 84.

15LOCAL GOVERNMENT

Syria is divided into 13 provinces (muhafazat) and Damascus; every province has a governor (muhafiz) and council. Each province is in turn divided into districts (mantiqat), each headed by a qaimmaqam. Each district is further subdivided into subdistricts, each in the charge of a mudir. Governors are appointed by and are directly responsible to the authorities in Damascus.

16JUDICIAL SYSTEM

The Syrian legal system is based partly on French law and partly on Syrian statutes. Investigating magistrates determine whether a case should be sent to trial. Minor infringements are handled by Peace Courts, more serious cases go to courts of first instance. There are civil and criminal appeals courts, the highest being the Court of Cassation. Separate State Security Courts have jurisdiction over activities affecting the security of the government. In addition, Shari'ah courts apply Islamic law in cases involving personal status. The Druzes and non-Muslim communities have their own religious courts.

A High Constitutional Court investigates and rules on petitions submitted by the president or one-fourth of the members of the People's Assembly challenging the constitutionality of laws or legislative decrees. This court has no jurisdiction to hear appeals form cases from the civil or criminal courts.

17ARMED FORCES

In 1993, the army had an estimated 300,000 regular troops (130,000 conscripts) and 300,000 reserves of whom 50,000 were recalled. There were 6 armored divisions, 3 mechanized infantry divisions, a Republican Guard division, 3 mechanized brigades, 3 SCUD missile brigades, 2 artillery brigades, 8 special forces battalions, and 4 special supporting arms brigades. The army had more than 4,600 heavy and medium tanks, 2,500 artillery pieces, and sophisticated antitank and antiaircraft weapons. The navy had 8,000 men and 8,000 reserves; naval vessels included 3 submarines, 2 frigates, 30 missile-equipped fast patrol boats, and 2 amphibious landing vessels. Naval aviation includes 17 armed helos. The air force had 40,000 men, 639 combat aircraft, and 100 armed helicopters. The air defense command numbered 60,000 with 24 SAM brigades or regiments. Paramilitary forces included 8,000 gendarmes companies, 4,500 members of 3 Palestinian Liberation Army brigades, and an 1,800-man desert frontier force. In 1989, budgeted military expenditures totaled $2.5 billion or about 8% of the gross domestic product. The USSR, formerly Syria's principal weapons supplier, imported $2 billion-plus a year in armed forces supplies the 1980s. Syria has 30,000 troops in Lebanon and employs 500 Russian advisors. Some 1,300 UN observors of UNDOF work out of Damascus.

18INTERNATIONAL COOPERATION

Syria is a founding member of the UN, having joined on 24 October 1945, and belongs to ESCWA and all the nonregional specialized agencies except WIPO. It is a charter member of the League of Arab States, set up in 1945 to foster cooperation in foreign and domestic affairs. Syria also belongs to G-77 and OAPEC.

Between February 1958 and September 1961, Syria and Egypt were joined in the United Arab Republic. During that period, the UAR was technically joined with Yemen in the United Arab States, though with little practical effect. Another federation, established formally in April 1963 between Syria, Egypt, and Iraq, was never implemented; it was officially terminated in July 1963 after Nasserite loyalists attempted unsuccessfully to overthrow Syria's Ba'thist regime. On 1 January 1972, Syria formally became part of the Federation of Arab Republics, with Egypt and Libya; the federation also had little practical effect because of a deterioration in Egypt's relations with Syria and especially with Libya. In June 1974, Syria and Jordan established a joint commission to coordinate foreign and military policy. Subsequent efforts to establish unions with Iraq and Libya bore little fruit. Diplomatic relations between Syria and the US, which had been suspended after the 1967 Arab-Israeli war, were resumed on 16 June 1974, after US Secretary of State Henry Kissinger successfully mediated a Golan Heights disengagement agreement.

19ECONOMY

Syria is traditionally an agricultural country; agriculture provided the livelihood of 25% of the work force and 31.0% of the GDP in 1988. Subsistence agriculture has given way in recent years to modern production and marketing methods. Wheat and barley constitute two-thirds of the cultivated area, but cotton is the main cash crop. The socialist government has set a limitation on landholdings and has undertaken projects to extend land cultivation. In 1988, 92% of cultivable area was cultivated. Since 1961, seven successive five-year plans have invested heavily in irrigation and land reclamation schemes and in industrial projects.

The economy grew rapidly through the 1970s until 1981, a year that saw a 10% growth in GDP. Since then the economy has done poorly, burdened by heavy military expenditures and hurt by drought especially in 1985, leaving Syria with a heavy debt burden. Annual GDP growth during 1981–85 was about 2.5% and in 1989 about 3.2%. Nonetheless, development of the state-owned oil industry and exploitation of other mineral resources, notably phosphates, have helped to diversify Syrian industry, which was formerly concentrated in light manufacturing and textiles. Although Syria's oil production is small by Middle Eastern standards, oil was by far the leading export in the 1980s.

Syria's economy improved since 1990 due to substantial increase in oil production, the recovery of the agricultural sector from drought, aid from the Gulf states, and economic reforms which boosted Syria's private sector. During 1990–92, the economy registered average annual private rates of 7–8%. Oil production increased from 150,000 barrels per day in the mid–1980s to 580,000 barrels per day in 1992. Syria may face a serious water shortage by the end of the decade given current water policies.

Foreign aid is important to Syrian economic development. Syria's attempts to expand its economy and living standards have depended heavily on technical aid from Socialist countries, especially the former USSR, and financial assistance from Arab oil states. Syria has received billions of dollars in foreign aid as a "reward" for its participation in the coalition against Iraq, but aid commitments are insufficient to pay for the more than $4 billion in new projects currently planned.

20 INCOME
In 1992, Syria's GNP was $14,607 million at current prices, or $1,170 per capita. For the period 1985–92 the average inflation rate was 19.4%, resulting in a real growth rate in per capita GNP of 0%.

In 1991 the GDP was $30 billion in current US dollars. It is estimated that in 1991 agriculture, hunting, forestry, and fishing contributed 31% to GDP; mining and quarrying, 13%; manufacturing, 5%; construction, 4%; wholesale and retail trade, 23%; transport, storage, and communication, 9%; finance, insurance, real estate, and business services, 4%; community, social, and personal services, 2%; and other sources 9%.

21 LABOR
The Syrian labor force is well educated and well trained in comparison with those of other Arab countries, but its size is small because about half the population is under 15 years of age and because many skilled workers are employed abroad in OPEC member nations. It has been estimated that 3,485,368 persons were employed in 1991, of whom 26.3% worked in agriculture, 27.3% in social and personal services, 13.1% in manufacturing, 9.8% in building and construction, 10.9% in commerce, 4.8% in transportation and communication, and 7.8% in other sectors. The majority of employed women engage in agriculture, but small numbers of women have found employment in industry and in technical professions. There is a high level of underemployment, and unemployment was officially reported at 6.8% in 1991. Many unskilled persons in agriculture and industry work only seasonally. The government is attempting to meet the demand for trained workers by establishing vocational schools.

The Labor Law of 1959 established the right of workers to form unions and empowered the government to regulate hours of work, vacations, sick leave, health and safety measures, and workers' compensation. The government also is authorized to arbitrate labor disputes. About one-third of nonagricultural wage and salary earners belong to trade unions affiliated with the General Federation of Labor Unions. The statutory workweek is 36 hours.

22 AGRICULTURE
About 6.1 million hectares (15.1 million acres) are arable, but the area actually cultivated is about 5.6 million hectares (13.8 million acres), or 30% of the total area. Since only one-third of cultivated land is irrigated, agriculture depends on rainfall, which is uncertain, and in lean years Syria becomes a net importer of wheat and barley; this strains the whole economy and hampers development. The government has two approaches to this problem: to increase the use of fertilizers in low rainfall areas and to add substantially to irrigated cultivation. The irrigated area was expected to be doubled through the Euphrates Dam project, which was completed in 1978. Lake Assad, formed by the dam, was planned eventually to provide irrigation for some 640,000 hectares (1,581,000 acres). Costs of land reclamation, technical difficulties due to gypsum in the soil, and low water, in part caused by Turkish damming upstream, have slowed progress. Total irrigated area had reached an estimated 700,000 hectares (1,730,000 acres) in 1991. The government has allocated an increasing share of its investments to irrigation, but full development of irrigation schemes is expected to take at least another 20 years. However, given the current water management policies, Syria could face a serious water shortage by the end of the 1990s.

Traditionally, much of Syria's agricultural land was held by landowners in tracts of more than 100 hectares (250 acres); sharecropping was customary. This picture was greatly altered by the government's agrarian reform program, begun in 1958. The law, as modified in 1963, fixed the maximum holding of irrigated land at 15–50 hectares (37–124 acres) per person and that of nonirrigated land at 80 hectares (198 acres) per person. All expropriated land available for cultivation has been allotted to farmers.

The principal cash crop is cotton, but cotton's share of total export value declined from 33% in 1974 to 7% in 1992. Other cash crops are cereals, vegetables, fruit, and tobacco. Principal crops and 1992 output (in 1,000 tons) were wheat, 3,046; sugar beets, 1,272; barley, 1,092; olives, 491; tomatoes, 448; and cotton, 215. Fruits include grapes, apples, apricots, and figs. Since the government suspended convertibility of the Syrian pound, grain and other agricultural products have been smuggled to Lebanon in exchange for goods not available through the state importing agencies.

23 ANIMAL HUSBANDRY
Grazing land occupies 7.7 million hectares (19.1 million acres), or about 42% of Syria's total area. Stock raising contributes significantly to the Syrian economy. Between 1963 and 1981, livestock herds more than doubled in number, and since 1975 the number of model farms, veterinary units, and livestock artificial insemination centers has increased considerably. From 1985 to 1990, livestock production rose by 63%, milk by 17%, and wool by 26%. In 1992 there were 15,782,000 sheep, 986,000 goats, 762,000 head of cattle, and 16,000,000 poultry. Animals and animal products account for 40% of total agricultural output by value. Production of milk in 1992 totaled 775,000 tons; cheese, 67,550 tons; butter and ghee, 13,357 tons; and eggs, 65,250 tons.

24 FISHING
There is some fishing off the Mediterranean coast and from rivers and fish farms. The commercial catch is small (5,500 tons in 1991).

25 FORESTRY
Syria is almost entirely denuded of forests. Although 730,000 hectares (1,804,000 acres) were officially listed as forestland in 1991, only about 58,000 cu m of roundwood was produced that year. Most of the designated forestland consists either of wholly barren land or of rangeland with arboreous shrubs. The substantial forests are mainly on the northern slopes of the Ansariyah range, on the windward side of the Anti-Lebanon Mountains, and in the Latakia region.

26MINING

Syria's mineral resources are not extensive, but deposits of phosphate, iron, and petroleum have been exploited in recent years. The first phosphate plant began operating near Homs in 1971, and production of phosphate rock was 1,359,000 tons in 1991. Other mineral deposits include asphalt, salt, chromite, and marble, but only marble and salt are mined in commercial quantities. In 1991, output of salt totaled 127,000 tons; of marble, 18,000 cubic meters.

27ENERGY AND POWER

Oil in commercial quantities was first discovered in the late 1950s. Production reached a record 10 million tons in 1976 and then declined to 9 million tons in 1984; since then, production has steadily increased to 14.5 million tons in 1988 and 25.2 million tons in 1992. In 1986, production of 2.5 million tons a year of low-sulphur crude from a new field, near Deir ez-Zor in eastern Syria, began, lessening Syrian dependence on external sources. By 1992, Syria was exporting 60% of its oil output. The proven reserves of Syria's five oil fields, all located in the northeastern part of the country, amounted to an estimated 1.7 billion barrels (200 million tons) of crude petroleum at the end of 1992. A 663-km (412-mi) pipeline linking the oil fields, the coast at Tartus, and the refinery at Homs was completed in 1968. The pipeline, carrying Iraqi oil across Syria to Lebanon, was closed by Syria in April 1982, showing Syrian support for Iran in the Iraqi-Iranian war. Syria also refused to support Iraq during the Persian Gulf War, for which it was "rewarded" with billions of dollars in foreign aid.

All oil concessions were granted exclusively in 1964 to the General Petroleum Authority, a government agency that owns the Homs refinery. In 1972, the pipelines and facilities in Syria of the Iraq Petroleum Co. were nationalized; the same year, Syria joined OAPEC. During the early 1980s, the government-owned Syrian Petroleum Co. and three Syrian subsidiaries of US oil companies—Marathon, Shell, and Coastal States—were engaged in further oil exploration. Proven natural gas reserves were officially estimated at 7 trillion cu ft in 1992.

Prior to 1983, more than half and as much as 70% of the production of electricity was hydroelectric. In 1983, however, as a result of increased demand and lower production from the Euphrates River plant, thermal production, primarily oil-fueled plants, supplied 56% of electricity production; this percentage increased to 58% in 1984 and 87% in 1991. Total electricity production in 1991 was 12,179,000 kwh net; installed capacity was 3,717,000 kw, up from 3,230,000 kw in 1988.

28INDUSTRY

A series of nationalization measures after 1963 resulted in public control of most industry, but recent efforts have been made to stimulate the expansion of the private sector. Industrial growth of 15% annually was provided for under the 1981–85 development plan but fell far short of the goal, with industrial production declining by 2.4% between 1983 and 1985. Industry's share of investment in the 1986–90 plan was expected to rise from 12.2% to 13.7%.

Syria has been renowned since ancient times for such handicrafts as Damascus brocade and Syrian soap. Some of these traditions endured even after 1933, when the first mechanized plant for spinning and weaving was set up in Aleppo. In 1965, the textile industry was nationalized and reorganized into 13 large state corporations. Syria's production in 1988 included 24,000 tons of cotton and silk textiles and 642 tons of woolen fabrics, down from 1,673 tons in 1985.

Also important are the chemical and engineering industries, the food industry, and oil refining. The largest component of the chemical and engineering sector is the cement industry, which produced 3.33 million tons in 1988. Syria has three fertilizer plants, an iron-rolling mill at Homs, and factories producing furniture, refrigerators, paper, glass and plastic products, and television sets. Production declined in many areas. In 1988, Syria produced 20,000 tons of sugar, down from 199,000 tons in 1984. Vegetable and olive oils are traditional Syrian products; 109 tons were produced in 1988. Some 15,455 tons of iron bars were produced in 1988, compared with 102,363 tons in 1981, and 21,821 refrigerators were produced, compared with 146,451 in 1981. In 1990 the petroleum refinery at Homs, with a capacity of 5.4 million tons per year and drawing crude from the Iraqi pipeline, was converted to run on gas, thus releasing 292,000 tons per year of fuel oil for export. The country's second refinery, with a capacity of 120,000 barrels per day, began operations in 1981.

29SCIENCE AND TECHNOLOGY

Except for university faculties of sciences and engineering, Syria's principal scientific research institution is the International Center for Agricultural Research in the Dry Areas (ICARDA), in Aleppo Province. The country's advanced petrochemical technologies have been installed by foreign oil companies. In early 1987, an estimated 2,500 Soviet military technicians were stationed in Syria; civilian personnel also provided assistance in various fields.

30DOMESTIC TRADE

Damascus and Aleppo are the principal commercial centers. Virtually all importers, exporters, and wholesalers have offices in one or both cities. The chief retail centers have general and specialized stores as well as large bazaars. Smaller bazaars and open markets are found in many Syrian towns and villages. Usual business hours are from 9 AM to 1 PM and from 3:30 PM to 7 PM. Friday is the weekly day of rest. Banking hours are Saturday–Thursday, 8 AM to 2 PM. An international fair is held every summer in Damascus. Advertising agencies use newspapers, magazines, moving picture theaters, signs on buses, and other media.

Because of active commodity smuggling from Lebanon, a substantial "unofficial market" exists in Syria for all imported products at the free market exchange rate reflective of world price levels.

31FOREIGN TRADE

Syria's trade balance has been negative through the 1980s. Exports reached a record s£8,273 million in 1980, nearly double the 1977 total, before declining to s£7,275 million in 1984 and s£5,199 million in 1986. In 1990, exports soared to s£ 47,282 million. Imports reached s£20,302 million in 1981 and s£26,936 million in 1990. In 1987 and 1988 Syria's merchandise trade deficit narrowed significantly, largely due to import compression. Thus, in 1989, the trade surplus amounted to s£ 10.2 billion, the first in more than two decades and rose to s£ 20.35 billion in 1990. Syria's principal exports since 1974 have been crude petroleum and oil products.

During the 1980s, Syria increased its trade with the Socialist nations. Between 1980 and 1988, Syria's exports to Socialist countries increased from 16.1% of total exports to 41.4%; the Socialist countries supplied 19.0% of Syria's imports in 1988. The EEC countries took 33.8% of exports and supplied 36.1% of imports, while Arab countries took 13.1% of exports and supplied 5.2% of imports.

32BALANCE OF PAYMENTS

Syria has had serious deficits in its trade balance since 1976, but import restrictions, foreign aid (especially from other Arab governments), and drawdown of foreign exchange holdings have enabled the government to cover the losses. Since the late 1980s, the government has been encouraging private sector trade. Private sector exports consequently skyrocketed from $79 million in 1987 to $517 million in 1990, thus reducing the trade deficit.

In 1992 merchandise exports totaled $3,100 million and imports $2,941 million. The merchandise trade balance was $-159 million. The following table summarizes Syria's balance of payments for 1991 and 1992 (in millions of US dollars):

	1991	1992
CURRENT ACCOUNT		
Goods services and income	115	−808
Unrequited transfers	584	863
TOTALS	699	55
CAPITAL ACCOUNT		
Other long-term capital	−35	173
Other short-term capital	−480	−222
Reserves	−72	−76
TOTALS	−587	−125
Errors and omissions	−112	70
Total change in reserves	−72	−76

33BANKING AND SECURITIES

Syria has five government banks. The Central Bank, founded in 1956, is the bank of issue for currency, the financial agent of the government, and the cashier for the treasury. The Agricultural Bank makes loans to farmers at low interest; the Industrial Bank (nationalized in 1961), the Popular Credit Bank and the Real Estate Bank (both founded in 1966), and the Commercial Bank of Syria (formed in 1967 by a merger of five nationalized commercial banks) make loans in their defined sectors. At the end of 1992, commercial bank demand deposits totaled s£53,341million; Syria has no securities exchange.

34INSURANCE

All insurance in Syria was nationalized in 1963 and is controlled by the government-owned General Insurance Organization of Syria (formerly the Syrian Insurance Co.). Motor vehicle insurance is compulsory. In 1985, non-life insurance accounted for 95.6% of all premiums.

35PUBLIC FINANCE

In 1991, budget revenues amounted to $5.4 billion, while expenditures amounted to $7.5 billion, including capital expenditures of $2.9 billion. Total external debt amounted to $5.3 billion in 1990. Support payments from Arab countries declined during the 1980s.

36TAXATION

Relatively low salaries have kept the tax base narrow, and price controls have restricted the taxable profits from industry. There are taxes on income, production, expenditure, and consumption.

37CUSTOMS AND DUTIES

Syria is a member of the Arab Common Market, with Iraq, Jordan, Libya, Mauritania, and Yemen. Trade among these countries is free of customs duties (except for tobacco). There is a single-column tariff modified by trade and transit agreements with other Arab League states, under which member countries are granted preferential duties on some products and duty-free entry for others. Duties on imports from non-Arab countries vary widely with the product. Most items are dutiable on an ad valorem basis.

38FOREIGN INVESTMENT

Although a government decree prohibits confiscation of foreign investments, there are no safeguards against nationalization of property, and there are few opportunities for foreign investment in Syria. Large companies are required to offer a majority of their shares to the public and to their employees. A foreign firm may take 50% of its profits out of the country each year and may repatriate its invested capital after five years.

In May 1991, the government announced a new investment law ("Law No. 10") which grants qualifying investors tax holidays and duty-free privileges for the import of capital goods and inputs. However, due to Syria's poor infrastructure, power outages, lack of financial services, and complex foreign exchange regulations, foreign investors have been slow to respond.

39ECONOMIC DEVELOPMENT

The transformation of Syria's economy began with the Agrarian Reform Law in 1958, which called for the expropriation of large tracts of land. During the union with Egypt, laws were passed for the nationalization of banks, insurance companies, and large industrial firms. After the Ba'th Party came to power in 1963, the socialist trend reasserted itself with greater force. A series of laws created a new banking system and instituted public ownership of all large industries. By the early 1970s, however, the government had relaxed many restrictions on trade, foreign investment, and private-sector activity, in an effort to attract private and foreign, especially Arab, contributions to Syria's economic growth.

Since 1961, a series of five-year plans has concentrated on developing the nation's infrastructure and increasing agricultural and industrial production. Investments reached 60% of the target under the first plan (1961–65); the second plan (1966–70) aimed to expand real GDP by 7.2% annually but achieved a yearly growth rate of only 4.7%. The third plan (1971–75) was disrupted by the 1973 Arab-Israeli war, but thanks to aid from other Arab states and large oil price increases, Syria experienced an economic boom with a high annual growth rate of 13%. The fourth plan (1976–80) was hampered by the high cost of Syria's military intervention in Lebanon and a cutoff of aid from Gulf states; economic growth varied widely, from −2.8% in 1977 to 9.2% in 1980.

Under the fifth plan (1981–85), development projects begun during the previous plan were to be continued or completed. Total investment was estimated at s£101 billion, of which 23% was to be provided by the private sector. Real GDP was to grow by 7.7% annually; actual growth rates ranged from 10.2% in 1981 to −3.6% in 1984, averaging 2.3% for the period.

Syria's sixth development plan (1986–90) emphasized increased productivity rather than new projects, with special emphasis on agriculture and agro-industries. Actual investment in agriculture accounted for 18.7% of total spending. The share of the industry and energy sector ws at 19.7%, far below the planned 30.9%. Services received the highest share, with 53% of the total.

The seventh five-year plan (1991–95) proposed total investments of s£259 billion, more than double the amount spent under the previous plan. It aims at spending 81.7% of the total on the public sector and 18.3% on the mixed sector/private-sector cooperatives. Officials at the Supreme Planning Commission have stated that agriculture and irrigation continue to receive top priority, with self-sufficiency in cereal production a policy objective. Output in agriculture and manufacturing is planned to expand by 5.6% per annum.

During 1949–86, multilateral assistance to Syria totaled $822.7 million, of which 77% came through the IBRD. US loans and grants during the same period amounted to $581.9 million. Financial aid to Syria from Arab oil-producing states is not made public. Since 1982, Syria has received a million tons of oil annually from Iran, free of charge. Since Syria is in arrears on payments to the World Bank, disbursements were halted in 1988 and projects canceled. Syria has been in violation of the Brooke Amendment since 1985. The improvement in Syria's external payment position in 1989 as well as the resumption of aid flows to Syria in 1990 due to its participation in the coalition against Iraq helped to restore its ability to repay its debt.

⁴⁰SOCIAL DEVELOPMENT

The Ministry for Social and Labor Affairs was formed in 1956 to protect the interests of the working population, provide hygienic housing conditions for workers, and support philanthropic endeavors. A system of social insurance, introduced in 1959, provides old age pensions and disability and death benefits. Employers contribute 1–3% of payroll, according to risk, to fund workers' compensation providing temporary and permanent disability benefits, as well as medical and survivor benefits. Although the government considers the rate of population growth satisfactory, modest efforts have been made to support a family-planning program. The fertility rate was 6.7 in 1985–90. Abortion is permitted only to save the woman's life.

Although the government supports equal pay for equal work and encourages education for women, Islamic precepts govern many areas of women's lives, including marriage, divorce, child custody, and inheritance. In recent years, President Assad's regime has been accused of widespread human rights violations. Amnesty International has repeatedly charged that Syrian security forces detain thousands of political suspects without trial and subject prisoners to torture and in some cases to arbitrary execution. Public criticism of the Ba'th Party or of government officials is not permitted.

⁴¹HEALTH

Since World War II, malaria has been virtually eliminated with the aid of WHO, but intestinal and respiratory diseases associated with poor living conditions are still common, particularly in rural areas. In 1990, there were an estimated 58 cases of tuberculosis per 100,000 reported. In 1991, 74% of the population had access to safe water, with 83% having adequate sanitation. The 1993 birth rate was 42.4 per 1,000 people, and about 52% of married women (ages 15 to 49) used contraception. There were 569,000 births in 1992. The same year, the infant mortality rate was 34 per 1,000 live births. In 1991, maternal mortality was 140 per 100,000 live births. The overall death rate was 5.8 per 1,000 people in 1993. Average life expectancy in 1992 was 67 years for both men and women. In 1947, Syria had only 37 hospitals, with a total of 1,834 beds, but by 1985, the number of hospitals had increased to 195, with 11,891 beds. In 1990, there were 1.1 hospital beds per 1,000 people. The government also maintains mobile hospital units, modern laboratories, X-ray centers, sanatoriums, and dispensaries. In 1991, there were 10,114 physicians, 3,362 dentists, 3,634 pharmacists, and 11,957 nurses. In 1992, there were 85 doctors per 100,000 people, with a nurse to doctor ratio of 1.2. The population per physician in 1990 was 1,160 and per nursing professional was 870. Immunization rates for children up to one year old in 1992 were: tuberculosis (93%); diphtheria, pertussis, and tetanus (89%); polio (89%); and measles (84%). In the same year, about 83% of the population had access to health care services. Total health care expenditures for 1990 were $283 million.

⁴²HOUSING

The 1981–85 development plan allocated s£2.6 billion to construction projects, including housing. According to the latest available information for 1980-88, total housing units numbered 1,670,000 with 6.4 people per dwelling.

⁴³EDUCATION

Elementary schooling is free and compulsory for six years. The estimated literacy rates in 1990 were 78.3% for men and 50.8% for women. The school program starts with a primary course, after which the student may obtain an elementary-school certifi-

cate. In 1991 there were 2,539,081 primary-school pupils with 102,617 teachers in 9,934 schools. At the secondary level, there were 902,819 students and 55,029 teachers in 1991. Syria has four universities: the University of Damascus (founded in 1923); the University of Aleppo (1960); Tishrin University (Latakia, 1971); and Al-Ba'th University in Homs (1979). In 1991, all higher level institutions had a total of 183,079 students enrolled.

⁴⁴LIBRARIES AND MUSEUMS

Az-Zahiriyah, the national library founded in 1984 in Damascus and an adjunct of the Arab Academy, has almost 150,000 volumes and is well known for rare books and manuscripts. There are three other national libraries, located in Aleppo, Homs, and Latakia. The library of the University of Damascus has 150,000 volumes.

The most important museum is the National Museum in Damascus, founded in 1919. It contains ancient Oriental, Greek, Roman, Byzantine, and Islamic collections and houses the Directorate-General of Antiquities, established in 1947, which supervises excavations and conserves antiquities under the Antiquities Law. There are small museums in Aleppo, Hama, Homs, Palmyra, Tartos, and other cities.

⁴⁵MEDIA

All communications facilities are owned and operated by the government, including postal service, telegraph, telephone, radio, and television. There were 685,000 telephones in use in 1991. The Syrian Broadcasting Service transmits on medium wave and shortwave, and broadcasts in Arabic and 10 foreign languages. Syrian Arab TV has two stations. There were about 3,270,000 radios and 770,000 television sets in use in 1991.

Syrian newspapers are published by government ministries and popular organizations, and are subject to censorship. Principal dailies in Arabic (with 1991 circulations) include *Al-Ba'th*, the party organ (75,000), *Tishrin* (75,000), and *Al-Thawrah* (75,000) in Damascus and *Al-Jamahir* (10,000) in Aleppo.

⁴⁶ORGANIZATIONS

Syria has chambers of commerce, industry, and agriculture. The most prominent organizations are the Arab Academy and the Arab Club, both in Damascus. The General Women's Federation was established in 1967 as one of several organizations through which the Ba'th Party has tried to mobilize popular energies and consolidate its control. Analogous groups include the General Union of Peasants, the General Federation of Trade Unions, the General Union of Students, and the Revolutionary Youth Organization. The cooperative movement is well developed.

⁴⁷TOURISM, TRAVEL, AND RECREATION

Passports, visas, and smallpox vaccinations are required of visitors. In 1991 there were 622,000 tourists, mostly from neighboring Middle Eastern countries, and tourist expenditures totaled us$300 million. As of that year, Syria had 13,960 hotel rooms with 30,117 beds, and the hotel occupancy rate was 34%.

Syria has many famous tourist attractions, such as the Krak des Chevaliers, a Crusaders' castle; Ra's Shamrah, site of the ancient city of Ugarit; Ar-Rusafah, with its early Christian monuments and a Muslim palace; and the ancient town of Dura Europus (now As-Salihiyah). Palmyra, the capital of Queen Zenobia, is a fairly well preserved ruin of an Arabo-Hellenic city. The Umayyad Mosque, which incorporates parts of the Byzantine Cathedral of St. John the Baptist, in Damascus, is popular. Syria's mountains and Mediterranean beaches also attract visitors.

⁴⁸FAMOUS SYRIANS

Among famous Syrians of an earlier period are the philosopher Al-Farabi (Muhammad bin Muhammad bin Tarkhan abu Nasr al-Farabi, 872–950), considered by the Arab world as second only to Aristotle; the poet Al-Mutanabbi (Abu at-Tayyib Ahmad bin al-Husayn al-Mutanabbi, 915–65); the mystic-philosopher Shihab ad-Din as-Suhrawardi (d.1191); and the theologian-philosopher Taqi ad-Din Ahmad bin Taymiyah (1263–1328).

Of the Umayyad caliphs, Umar bin 'Abd-al-'Aziz (r.717–20) is still revered as a restorer of true Islam. In a later era, Nureddin (Nur ad-Din, 1118–74), ruler of Aleppo, annexed Damascus and brought Egypt under his control. By unifying Muslim forces against the Crusaders, he made possible the victories of the renowned Saladin (Salah ad-Din, 1138–93), sultan of both Syria and Egypt, whose tomb is in Damascus. Hafez al-Assad (Hafiz al-Asad, b.1928) has ruled Syria since 1970.

49 DEPENDENCIES
Syria has no territories or colonies.

50 BIBLIOGRAPHY

Castle, Wilfred Thomas Frogatt. *Syrian Pageant: The History of Syria and Palestine, 1000 B.C. to A.D. 1945.* New York: Gordon, 1977.

Choueiri, Youssef M. (ed.). *State and Society in Syria and Lebanon.* Exeter: University of Exeter Press, 1993.

Collelo, Thomas (ed.). *Syria: A Country Study.* 3rd ed. Washington, D.C.: Library of Congress, 1988.

Copeland, Paul W. *The Land and the People of Syria.* Philadelphia: Lippincott, 1964.

Devlin, John F. *Syria: Modern State in an Ancient Land.* Boulder, Colo.: Westview, 1983.

Fedden, Robin. *Syria and Lebanon.* London: Murray, 1965.

Fisher, William Bayne. *The Middle East: A Physical, Social and Regional Geography.* London: Methuen, 1950.

Gaunson, A. B. *The Anglo-French Clash in Lebanon and Syria, 1940–45.* New York: St. Martin's, 1987.

Haddad, Robert M. *Syrian Christians in a Muslim Society.* Princeton, N.J.: Princeton University Press, 1970.

Hinnebusch, Raymond A. *Authoritarian Power and State Formation in Ba'thist Syria: Army, Party, and Peasant.* Boulder, Colo.: Westview Press, 1990.

Hitti, Philip Khuri. *History of Syria, Including Lebanon and Palestine.* London: Macmillan, 1957.

Hopwood, Derek. *Syria 1945–1986: Politics and Society.* London: Unwin Hyman, 1988.

Khoury, Philip S. *Syria and the French Mandate: the Politics of Arab Nationalism 1920–1945.* Princeton University Press, 1987.

Lesch, David W. *Syria and the United States: Eisenhower's Cold War in the Middle East.* Boulder, Colo.: Westview Press, 1992.

Longrigg, Stephen Hemsley. *Syria and Lebanon under French Mandate.* New York: Oxford University Press, 1958.

Maoz, Moshe. *Assad: The Sphinx of Damascus: A Political Biography.* New York: Weidenfeld & Nicholson, 1988.

Petran, Tabitha. *Syria.* New York: Praeger, 1972.

Pipes, Daniel. *Greater Syria: The History of an Ambition.* New York: Oxford University Press, 1990.

Roberts, David. *The Ba'th and the Creation of Modern Syria.* New York: St. Martin's, 1987.

Salibi, Kamal S. *Syria Under Islam: Empire on Trial.* New York: Caravan Books, 1977.

Seale, Patrick. *Assad of Syria: The Struggle for the Middle East.* Berkeley: University of California Press, 1989, 1988.

Seale, Patrick. *Struggle for Syria: A Study of Post-War Arab Politics, 1945–1958.* 2nd ed. New Haven, Conn.: Yale University Press, 1987.

Seccombe, Ian J. *Syria.* Santa Barbara, Calif.: Clio, 1987.

Tibawi, A. L. *A Modern History of Syria: Including Lebanon and Palestine.* New York: St. Martin's, 1970.

Torrey, Gordon H. *Syrian Politics and the Military, 1945–1958.* Columbus: Ohio State University Press, 1964.

TAIWAN

Republic of China
Chung Hwa Min Kuo

CAPITAL: T'aipei.

FLAG: The flag is red with a 12-pointed white sun on the blue upper left quadrant. The 12 points of the sun represent the 12 two-hour periods of the day in traditional Chinese horology and symbolize progress. The colors red, white, and blue represent the Three Principles of the people (San Min Chu I) of Sun Yat-sen, father of the Republic of China, and symbolize the spirit of liberty, fraternity, and equality.

ANTHEM: *Chung Hwa Min Kuo Kuo Ke (Chinese National Anthem).*

MONETARY UNIT: The new Taiwan dollar (NT$) is a paper currency of 100 cents. There are coins of 50 cents and 1, 5, and 10 dollars, and notes of 50, 100, 500, and 1,000 new Taiwan dollars. NT$1 = US$0.0350 (or US$1 = NT$28.54).

WEIGHTS AND MEASURES: The metric system is employed in government and industrial statistics. Commonly used standards of weights and measures are the catty (1.1 lb or 0.4989 kg), the li (0.5 km or 0.31 mi), the ch'ih (0.33 m or 1.09 ft), and the chia (0.97 hectare or 2.39 acres).

HOLIDAYS: New Year's Day and the Founding of the Republic of China (1912), 1 January; Youth Day (formerly known as Martyrs' Day), 29 March; Tomb-Sweeping Day and Anniversary of the Death of Chiang Kai-shek, 5 April; Birthday of Confucius and Teachers' Day, 28 September; National Day (Double Tenth Day), 10 October; Taiwan Retrocession Day, 25 October; Chiang Kai-shek's Birthday, 31 October; Sun Yat-sen's Birthday, 12 November; Constitution Day, 25 December.

TIME: 8 PM = noon GMT.

¹LOCATION, SIZE, AND EXTENT

Taiwan, the seat of the Republic of China, lies in the western Pacific Ocean astride the Tropic of Cancer, less than 161 km (100 mi) from the southeast coast of mainland China, from which it is separated by the Taiwan (Formosa) Strait. To the NE, less than 129 km (80 mi) away, is the W end of the Japanese Ryukyu Islands; to the E is the Pacific Ocean; the Philippine island of Luzon lies 370 km (230 mi) to the S.

Besides the island proper, Taiwan comprises 21 small islands in the Taiwan group and 64 islands in the Penghu (Pescadores) group; the total area is 35,980 sq km (13,892 sq mi). Comparatively, the area occupied by Taiwan is slightly larger than the states of Maryland and Delaware combined. Leaf-shaped Taiwan island extends 394 km (245 mi) NNE–SSW and 144 km (89 mi) ESE–WNW; it has a coastline of 1,448 km (903 mi) and, with adjacent islands, an area of 35,873 sq km (13,851 sq mi). The Penghu group, lying 40 km (25 mi) west of Taiwan island, has a total area of 127 sq km (49 sq mi).

Also under the control of the Taiwan government are Quemoy (Chinmen) and Matsu, two island groups located strategically close to the mainland Chinese province of Fujian (Fukien). Quemoy is the biggest of a group of six islands, two of which are occupied by the People's Republic of China; it is situated in Xiamen (Amoy) Bay at 118°23′E and 24°27′N and has a total area of 176 sq km (68 sq mi). The Matsu group, consisting of Nankan (the largest), Peikan, Tungyin, and about 10 small islets, is located at 119°56′E and 26°9′N, 30.6 km (19 mi) off the mainland port city of Fuzhou; it has a total area of 28.8 sq km (11.1 sq mi).

²TOPOGRAPHY

Taiwan perches on the margin of the continental shelf. Along the west coast the sea is rather shallow, averaging 90 m (300 ft) and not exceeding 210 m (690 ft) at the deepest point; however, it deepens abruptly along the east coast, dropping to a depth of 4,000 m (13,000 ft) only 50 km (31 mi) offshore. The terrain is precipitous on the east coast, with practically no natural harbor except Suao Bay in the north. The west coast is marked by wide tidal flats. Kaohsiung, the southern port, is situated in a long lagoon called Haochiung Bay. The north coast with its many inlets provides Taiwan with its best harbor, Chilung (Keelung).

The eastern two-thirds of the island is composed of rugged foothill ranges and massive mountain chains. A low, flat coastal plain, extending from north to south, occupies the western third. Hsinkao Shan, with an elevation of 3,997 m (13,113 ft), is the highest peak on the island. Mild earthquake tremors are common.

All the rivers originate in the mountains in the central part of the island. They have short courses and rapid streams. The longest river, Choshui, draining westward, is only 183 km (114 mi) long. Only the Tanshui, which flows past T'aipei in the north, is navigable.

³CLIMATE

Taiwan enjoys an oceanic, subtropical monsoon climate. The warm and humid summer lasts from May until September, the mild winter from December until February. The average lowland temperature in January is 16°C (61°F) in the north and 20°C (68°F) in the south; the average July temperature is 28°C (82°F) in both the north and south. The growing season lasts throughout the year, except at elevations above 1,200 m (4,000 ft), where frost and snow occasionally occur.

The average rainfall is 257 cm (101 in), ranging from 127 cm (50 in) at the middle of the western coast to 635 cm (250 in) and more on exposed mountain slopes. Southwest monsoon winds blow from May through September and northeast monsoon winds from October to March. Only the extreme southwest has a distinct dry season. As a result of the tropical cyclonic storms that sweep out of the western Pacific, typhoons occur between June and October.

⁴FLORA AND FAUNA

The flora is closely related to that of southern China and the Philippines. Taiwan has almost 190 plant families, about 1,180 genera, and more than 3,800 species, of which indigenous members constitute about one-third of the total flora. Mangrove forest is found in tidal flats and coastal bays. From sea level to a height of 2,000 m (6,600 ft) is the zone of broad-leaved evergreen tropical and subtropical forest, where ficua, pandanus, palms, teak, bamboos, and camphors are commonly found. The mixed forest of broad-leaved deciduous trees and conifers occupies the next zone, extending from a height of 2,000 to 3,000 m (6,600–9,800 ft). Pines, cypresses, firs, and rhododendrons are grown in this region. Above this level is the zone of coniferous forests, composed mainly of firs, spruce, juniper, and hemlock.

The mammals so far discovered number more than 60 species, 45 of which appear to be indigenous to the island. The largest beast of prey is the Formosan black bear. Foxes, flying foxes, deer, wild boar, bats, squirrels, macaques, and pangolins are some of the mammals seen on the island. There are more than 330 species and subspecies of birds, of which 33 are common to the island, China, and the Philippines, and about 87 are peculiar forms. More than 65 species of reptiles and amphibians inhabit the island. There is an abundance of snakes, of which 13 species are poisonous. The insect life is rich and varied.

⁵ENVIRONMENT

The Environmental Protection Agency (EPA) has the main responsibility for environmental policy. Water pollution is a significant problem in Taiwan. Outside of the larger hotels and urban centers, the water is likely to be impure. Health problems, like hepatitis, result from waterborne contaminants. Water quality is regulated under provisions of the sanitary drinking water legislation of 1972 and the 1974 Water Pollution Control Act. Air pollution is another significant problem, complicated by a high pollen count. Solid waste disposal regulations and air quality standards were adopted in 1975. All factories are required to comply with established standards, the cost of installing antipollution devices being written off as a depreciable item over two years. Taiwan in 1978 adopted the safety procedures for nuclear facilities issued by the IAEA. In the mid-1980s, the government began tightening emission standards for automobiles and ordered many factories and power plants to install filters and dust collectors. The EPA announced plans in 1987 to install an island-wide pollution-monitoring system.

Wildlife management is the responsibility of the National Wildlife Protection Association of the Republic of China. The nation's marine life is threatened by the use of driftnets. Endangered species as of 1987 included the Formosan sika, Oriental white stork, and Lan Yü scops owl.

⁶POPULATION

According to the 1990 census, Taiwan had a population of 20,352,900, an increase of 5.7% since 1985. Taiwan had an estimated population of 20,992,000 in 1994; a population of 22,065,000 was forecast for the year 2000. The population density, among the world's highest, was 566 per sq km (1,466 per sq mi) in 1990. The average annual rate of growth declined from 3.3% in 1952 to 2.9% in 1966 and 1% in 1992; 73.7% of the population was aged 15 or over in 1991. T'aipei, the capital and principal city, had a population of 2,696,073 at the end of 1992. Other large cities are Kaohsiung (1,405,909), T'aichung

(794,960), T'ainan (694,930), and Panch'iao (543,982).

⁷MIGRATION

In 1963, the Nationalist government stated that since the completion of the Communist conquest of the mainland in 1949/50, a total of 146,772 Chinese refugees had come to Taiwan for resettlement. The number of refugees has varied from year to year. There may be as many as 100,000 illegal immigrants.

In 1986, the Taiwan government reported that there were 28,714,000 overseas Chinese (25,799,000 in Asia, 2,044,000 in the Americas, 584,000 in Europe, 214,000 in Oceania, and 73,000 in Africa), including those with dual nationality.

⁸ETHNIC GROUPS

The term "Taiwanese" is often used when referring to those Chinese who are natives of the island as distinct from the 2 million "mainlanders" who migrated from China after the end of World War II. Most of the more than 20 million inhabitants of Taiwan are descendants of earlier immigrants from Fujian and Guangdong (Kwangtung) provinces in South China. They form several distinct groups. The Hakka are descendants of refugees and exiles from Guangdong who came to Taiwan before the 19th century; they are farmers and woodsmen who occupy the frontiers of settlement. The more numerous Fujians are descendants of peasants from Fujian who migrated to Taiwan in the 18th and 19th centuries; they form the bulk of the agricultural population.

In 1991 there were 345,523 aborigines, primarily of Indonesian origin. They live mainly in central and eastern Taiwan. They are mainly divided into nine major tribes, with the Ami, Atayal, Paiwan, and Bunun accounting for about 88%; the balance is mainly distributed among the Puyuma, Rukai, Saisiyat, Tsou, and Yami. The language and customs of the aborigines suggest a close resemblance to the Malays.

⁹LANGUAGES

Most people on Taiwan now speak Mandarin (Peking dialect). It is the official language and is used in administration, jurisprudence, education, and, to a large extent, in commerce; it has come into increasingly common use during the last three decades. The Wade-Giles system of romanization, which has been replaced on the mainland by the pinyin system, is still used in Taiwan.

Native Taiwanese speak a variety of southern Chinese dialects, but mainly Southern FuKienese. This is the native tongue of about 70% of the population. It has also influenced the vocabulary of Mandarin spoken on Taiwan. There is also a sizable populaiton of Hakka speakers. This dialect is mainly spoken in Kwantung Province on the mainland. As a result of 50 years of Japanese rule, most Taiwanese and aborigines over the age of 60 speak or understand Japanese. Tribal peoples speak dialects of the Malay-Polynesian family which have no written script.

¹⁰RELIGIONS

The Chinese are traditionally eclectic in their religious beliefs. The Taiwan folk religion is a fluid mixture of ancestor worship, animism, Buddhism, and Taoism. Natural phenomena have been deified, and ancestors, sages, virtuous women, and historical personalities have been given the status of gods. As of 1985, Taiwan had an estimated 10 million folk-religionists and 4.86 million Buddhists in 1991.

The first Westerners to bring Christianity to Taiwan were the Dutch (1624). However, a great persecution of Christians took place when the island was lost to Cheng Ch'eng-kung in 1662. Christianity made another beginning in 1860, when a missionary from Scotland came to the island. The English Presbyterian Mission started its work in the southern part of Taiwan about 100 years ago. Since the end of World War II, more than 80 Protestant denominations have been established on the island, and the activities of Christian missions, many coming over from the mainland, have become widespread. As of 1991, the Christian population was estimated at 720,000, about 300,000 of whom were Roman Catholics. Muslims numbered about 52,000.

11 TRANSPORTATION

As of 1991, Taiwan had about 4,600 km (2,900 mi) of railroad track. The main trunk line, now electrified, links the main cities of the populous west coast between Chilung and Kaohsiung. A second trunk line, the North Link between T'aipei and Hualien on the east coast, was completed in 1979. It connects with an eastern line between Hualien and T'aitung, which was modernized in the early 1980s. Construction of the 98-km (61 mi) South Link (between T'aitung and P'ingtung) has been completed. Forming the last link in the round-the-island rail system, the South Link opened on 6 December 1991, taking over 11 years and $770 million to complete. Construction of a US$6.5-billion rapid-transit system was just starting in T'aipei in 1989.

As of 1991, Taiwan had 20,041 km (12,453 mi) of highways, of which 85% were paved. By the end of 1992 there were 2,781,000 registered motor vehicles, three-fourths of which are passenger cars.

Taiwan has five international seaports, all of them extensively modernized in the 1970s. Kaohsiung in the southwest is by far the largest, handling about two-thirds of all imports and exports. Other major ports are Chilung, on the north coast; Hualien and Suao, both on the east coast; and T'aichung, on the west coast. At the end of 1991, Taiwan's merchant marine consisted of 211 vessels totaling 5.8 million GRT.

There are two international airports. The main one, opened in 1979, is Chiang Kai-shek International Airport, at T'aoyüan, southwest of T'aipei; the other serves Kaohsiung. T'aipei Airport handles only domestic flights. Regular domestic flights also reach Hualien, T'aitung, Chiai, T'ainan, and several other cities. Principal air service is provided by China Air Lines, Taiwan's international airline, and other international carriers, and by Taiwan's leading domestic airline, Far Eastern Air Transport.

12 HISTORY

Although Taiwan can be seen on a clear day from the China mainland, ancient Chinese chronicles contain few references to the island. The earliest inhabitants were Malayo-Polynesian aborigines. Historians have surmised from the brief information available in the early dynastic histories that Chinese emigration to Taiwan began as early as the T'ang dynasty (618–907). During the reign of Kublai Khan (1263–94), the first civil administration was established in the neighboring Pescadores. Taiwan itself, however, remained outside the jurisdiction of the Mongol Empire. During the Ming dynasty (1368–1644), Japanese pirates and Chinese outlaws and refugees wrested the coastal areas from the native aborigines. The Chinese settled in the southwest region, while the Japanese occupied the northern tip of the island. Significant Chinese settlement, by immigrants from Fujian and Guangdong, began in the 17th century.

In 1517, the Portuguese sighted the island and named it Ilha Formosa (Beautiful Island). The Dutch, who were disputing the monopoly of Far Eastern trade held by the Portuguese, captured the Pescadores in 1622 and used them as a base for harassing commerce between China, Japan, and the Philippines. Two years later, the Chinese offered the Dutch a treaty that gave them certain commercial privileges if they withdrew from the Pescadores and occupied instead a trading post on Taiwan. The Dutch complied by building Fort Zeelandia and Fort Providentia in the southwestern part of the island. The Spaniards, wishing to compete, seized the northern part of Chilung in 1626 and later extended their domain to nearby Tanshui. The Japanese, con-

LOCATION: 21°45′25″ to 25°56′39″N; 119°18′3″ to 124°34′30″E.
TERRITORIAL SEA LIMIT: 12 mi.

strained by the policy of national seclusion adopted by the Tokugawa Shogunate, withdrew voluntarily in 1628. The Dutch captured the Spanish settlement in 1642 and, after putting down a Chinese uprising in 1656 with the aid of the aborigines, gained complete control of the island.

While the Dutch were consolidating their hold on Taiwan, the Ming dynasty on the China mainland was overthrown by the Manchus, who established the Qing (Ch'ing) dynasty (1644–1912). Remnants of the Ming forces, led by Zheng Chenggong (Cheng Ch'eng-kung Koxinga, 1624–62), son of a Chinese pirate and a Japanese mother, decided to establish an overseas base in Taiwan. They landed on the island in 1661 and ousted the Dutch in the following year. It was not until 1683 that the Manchus succeeded in wresting Taiwan from Zheng Chenggong's successors.

From 1683 to 1885, Taiwan was administered as a part of Fujian Province. During this period, Chinese colonization proceeded steadily, as the aborigines were either assimilated into the Chinese population or pushed back into the mountains. The imperial government, however, paid scant attention to the island administration. As a result, official corruption and inefficiency often provoked armed rebellions. In the latter part of the 19th century, the strategic importance of Taiwan for the defense of the South China coast was recognized by the authorities, particularly after the French bombardment and blockade of the island in 1884 during the Sino-French War over Annam. The local administration was reorganized, and the island was made into a separate province in 1885.

Upon the conclusion of the First Sino-Japanese War in 1895, Taiwan was ceded to Japan. Refusing to submit to Japanese rule, the islanders declared their independence and established a republic, although organized resistance against the Japanese lasted only a few months. Ineffective armed resistance, chiefly by aborigines, continued. Under the Japanese, the island's agricultural resources were developed rapidly to supply the needs of the home islands. Transportation was modernized. A policy of Japanization of the Taiwan population was adopted and, by 1944, 71% of children attended primary school. During World War II, a beginning was made for the industrialization of the island in support of the Japanese southward expansion.

In accordance with the Cairo Declaration of 1943 and the Potsdam Proclamation of 1945, Taiwan was restored to China in September 1945. The carpetbagging malpractices of the mainland Chinese officials, however, aroused the resentment of the local population. In February 1947, a police incident touched off a popular revolt, which was suppressed with bloodshed. In May, more troops were brought from the mainland and the Taiwanese leadership systematically killed. Estimates of the dead range from 5,000 to 50,000. On 8 December 1949, as the Chinese Communists were sweeping the Nationalist armies off the mainland, the government of the Republic of China (ROC), led by Gen. Chiang Kai-shek (Jiang Jieshi), was officially transferred to Taiwan.

The Republic of China

With the removal of the ROC government to Taiwan, two million mainland Chinese came to the island where they instituted an authoritarian rule under martial law. Strong government policies contributed to steady economic progress, first in agriculture and then in industry. In the 1950s, with US aid and advice, the ROC undertook a successful program of land redistribution. Japan had built an infrastructure; the Nationalists from the mainland brought skills and capital, to which were added two billion dollars in US aid in 1968. Japanese investment and the Vietnamese War in the 1960s further stimulated economic growth.

In 1951, Japan, in signing the San Francisco Peace Treaty, formally renounced its claim to the island of Taiwan. A Sino-Japanese Peace Treaty was concluded in T'aipei the following year. In 1954, the ROC and the United States concluded a Mutual Defense Treaty. The question of which China—the People's Republic of China (PRC), on the Chinese mainland, or the ROC in Taiwan—should occupy China's seat at the UN was debated by the UN General Assembly for more than two decades, beginning in 1950. Support for Taiwan's representation gradually eroded over the years, and on 25 November 1971 the General Assembly voted 75–36 (with 17 abstentions) to remove recognition from the ROC and recognize the PRC. In a significant policy reversal, the United States voted with the majority to seat the mainland government. Although maintaining full diplomatic ties with Taiwan, the US took the occasion of President Nixon's visit to China to acknowledge, in what became known as the Shanghai communiqué of February 1972, that "all Chinese on either side of the Taiwan Strait maintain there is but one China and that Taiwan is part of China. The United States government does not challenge that position."

By 1975, most nations had shifted recognition from the ROC to the PRC. On 1 January 1979, the US formally recognized the PRC as the sole legal government of China and severed diplomatic ties with Taiwan. It also announced the unilateral termination of the 1954 US-ROC Mutual Defense Treaty, effective 1 January 1980, and withdrew its remaining military personnel. Nonetheless, the US continued to sell arms to Taiwan, and commercial and cultural contacts were unofficially maintained through the American Institute in Taiwan and the Coordination Council for North American Affairs. Taiwan successfully warded off worldwide political and economic isolation by maintaining a host of similar contacts with other countries.

When President Chiang Kai-shek died at age 87 on 5 April 1975, he was succeeded in office by former Vice-President Yen Chia-kan (Yan Jiagan). Leadership of the Nationalist Party (Kuomintang, Guomindang) and, hence, of the government passed to Chiang's elder son, Chiang Ching-kuo (Jiang Jingguo). The younger Chiang was elected to a six-year term as president in March 1978 and reelected in 1984. While control of the central government had remained in the hands of mainlanders in the first decades of the Nationalists' rule on Taiwan, Taiwanese Chinese increasingly won elections at local levels, and Chiang Ching-kuo instituted a policy of bringing more Taiwanese into the Nationalist Party. By the 1980s, economic development had produced a new middle class, and the passage of time, together with intermarriage between mainlanders and Taiwanese, had brought a new generation for which the distinction between mainlander and Taiwanese held diminished importance. These factors contributed to popular pressure for a more democratic government. In November 1986, 5,000–10,000 demonstrated in support of an exiled dissident, Hsu Hsin-liang (Xu Xinliang), when he was not allowed to return to Taiwan. Thousands protested the 38th anniversary of martial law in May 1987. And, in March 1990, more than 10,000 demonstrators demanded greater democracy and direct presidential elections. This was followed in the same month by a demonstration involving some 6,000 students.

In 1987 martial law was revoked. Press restrictions were eased, citizens were allowed to visit relatives on the mainland, and it became legal to form political parties. In January 1988, Chiang Ching-kuo died and was succeeded as president by the Vice-President, Lee Teng-hui (Li Denghui, 1923–). Lee, a protégé of Chiang Ching-kuo, is a native Taiwanese. In March 1990, Lee was reelected by the National Assembly as president in his own right for a six-year term. In July, he was also named Chairman of the Nationalist Party by the Party Congress.

13 GOVERNMENT

The government of the Republic of China in T'aipei claims to be the central government of all of China. Its constitution was drafted by a constitutional convention at Nanjing (Nanking) on 15 November 1946; it was adopted on 25 December 1946 and promulgated by the national government on 1 January 1947. The government derives its powers from the National Assembly, which, according to the constitution, exercises political powers on behalf of the people. The first National Assembly, which was elected in November 1947, had 2,961 delegates, selected on the basis of regional and occupational representation. The Assembly has the power to elect and recall the president and the vice-president, amend the constitution, and approve constitutional amendments proposed by the legislative council (Legislative Yuan). The original delegates held their seats "indefinitely," until control of the mainland can be reestablished. Since 1969, the number of seats gradually increased with the addition of new seats for Taiwan. In April 1990, President Lee Teng-hui revoked the emergency decree of 1948 which had allowed the 1,947 deputies to remain in office and the "indefinite" deputies had to retire by December 1991. (In November 1990, there were 651 members.)

The president is the head of state. His tenure of office is six years, with eligibility for a second term. The constitutional prohibition against third terms was suspended in March 1960 to permit President Chiang Kai-shek to continue in office; he was reelected in 1972 for a fifth six-year term. Chiang was granted special emergency powers in 1948, which were extended in 1954. He was empowered to govern by virtual decree and, under martial law, civil liberties provided in the constitution were suspended in the interest of national security. In July 1987, President Chiang Ching-kuo lifted martial law, the basis for which was finally removed by President Lee's 1990 revocation of the 1948 emergency decree.

Under the president, there are five government branches known as yuans (councils or departments): Legislative, Executive, Control, Examination, and Judicial. The Legislative Yuan, elected by popular vote, is the highest lawmaking body. As in the National Assembly, many members of the 1948 Legislative Yuan held their seats until 1991. (In August 1990, there were 257 members.) Since 1972, elections have been held every three years and members are appointed to represent overseas Chinese.

The Executive Yuan, comparable to the cabinet in other countries, is the highest administrative organ in the government. There are eight ministries, two commissions, and a number of subordinate organs under the Executive Yuan. The Premier—the President of the Executive Yuan—is appointed by the President of the republic, with the consent of the Legislative Yuan. The president is empowered to compel the premier to resign by refusing to sign decrees or orders presented by the latter for promulgation.

The Control Yuan, the highest supervisory organ, exercises censorial and audit powers over the government and may impeach public functionaries. It also supervises the execution of the government budget. In December 1991, the remaining "indefinite" term members retired. Members are elected to six-year terms by the Taiwan Provincial Assembly and by the T'aipei and Kaohsiung city councils. The president appoints additional members to represent overseas constituencies.

The Examination Yuan is the equivalent of a civil service commission. It consists of two ministries. The Ministry of Examination appoints government personnel through competitive examination. The Ministry of Personnel registers, classifies, promotes, transfers, retires, and pensions. Its president, vice-president, and 19 commissioners are appointed by the president of the republic with the consent of the Control Yuan.

14POLITICAL PARTIES

The Chinese Nationalist Party, better known as the Kuomintang—KMT (Guomindang—GMD), is the dominant political party in Taiwan. The teachings of Sun Yat-sen (Sun Zhongshan), which stress nationalism, democracy, and people's livelihood, form the ideology of the party. After the fall of the mainland to the Communists in 1949, a reform committee was organized to chart a new program for the party. The paramount aim of the KMT has been the overthrow of Communist rule on the mainland; opposition to this doctrine is proscribed by the government.

The KMT is led by a party Chairman and a Central Standing Committee, which is elected annually by the Central Committee from among candidates nominated by the Chairman. Party committees are organized at the lower levels of province, county, and district, as well as on the basis of vocational groupings. The KMT organization parallels the state administrative structure, with members of the cabinet (Executive Yuan) and the Governor of Taiwan Province generally holding membership in the party Central Standing Committee. The President of the ROC has also been the Chairman of the KMT. In 1975, chairmanship of the KMT passed from Chiang Kai-shek to his son, Chiang Ching-kuo.

Upon Chiang Ching-kuo's death in 1988, it passed to Lee Teng-hui. While the KMT was initially an organization of primarily mainland Chinese, Chiang Chinq-kuo and after him Lee Teng-hui, himself Taiwanese, followed a policy of broadening Taiwanese Chinese membership in the party. In the KMT's 14th Party Congress in 1993, Lee Teng-hui's Taiwanese faction won 80% of the seats on the Central Committee and the Central Standing Committee.

Under martial law, from 1949 through 1986, the formation of new political parties was illegal, although there were two nominal, previously formed parties. Non-KMT candidates ran as independents or "Nonpartisans," with increasing success by the end of the 1970s. In September 1986, a group of "nonpartisans" formed a new opposition party, the Democratic Progressive Party (DPP), which had an orientation toward the Taiwanese population and advocated "self-determination." Although technically illegal, the DPP's candidates took 22% of the vote in the December 1986 elections, winning 12 out of 73 contested seats in the Legislative Yuan; the KMT won 59. The lifting of martial law in 1987 made the formation of new parties legal, although a new security law continued to restrict political activity. In addition to the DPP, new parties include the Labor Party, the Workers Party, and other minor parties. In the first fully competitive, democratic national elections, in December 1992, the KMT won 53% and the DPP 31% of the votes for the Legislative Yuan.

15LOCAL GOVERNMENT

The Taiwan provincial government holds jurisdiction over the main island of Taiwan, 21 smaller islands in adjacent waters, and the 64 islands of the Penghu (Pescadores) group. The provincial capital is located at T'aichung. The province is divided into 16 county (hsien) administrative areas and 3 municipalities under the direct jurisdiction of the provincial government. In addition, T'aipei (since 1967) and Kaohsiung (since 1979) are self-governing "special" municipalities. Subdivisions of the county are the township (chen), the rural district or group of villages (hsiang), and the precinct. Quemoy and Matsu are administered by the military.

The province is headed by a governor who is nominated by the President of the Executive Yuan and appointed by the President of the republic. Department heads and members of the Provincial Council are recommended by the governor for appointment by the Executive Yuan. The governor is the ex officio chairman of the appointed 21-member Provincial Council, the policymaking body, and holds veto power over its resolutions. The provincial government can issue ordinances and regulations for the administration of the province as long as they do not conflict with laws of the central government. The mayors of T'aipei and Kaohsiung are appointed in the manner of the provincial governor. Their city councils are elected.

The Provincial Assembly, an elected body, meets for two yearly sessions of two months each. Nominally it possesses broad legislative powers; however, its prerogatives are circumscribed by a provision in its organic law that in the event of a disagreement between the provincial executive and the Assembly, the former may request a reconsideration. Should the Assembly uphold its original resolution, the provincial executive may submit the dispute to the Executive Yuan for final judgment. The Executive Yuan may dissolve the Provincial Assembly and order a new election if it holds that the Assembly is acting contrary to national policy.

At the lower level, the county government is headed by a magistrate (hsien-chang) and the municipal government by a mayor (shih-chang). Each county or municipality has a representative body called the hsien, or municipal assembly. Further down are the councils and assemblies of townships and rural districts, each headed by a chief officer. These officials are elected by universal suffrage of citizens over age 20.

16JUDICIAL SYSTEM

The Judicial Yuan is Taiwan's highest judicial organ. It interprets the constitution and other laws and decrees, adjudicates administrative suits, and disciplines public functionaries. The president and vice-president of the Judicial Yuan are nominated and appointed by the president of the republic, with the consent of the Control Yuan. They, together with a number of grand justices, form the Council of Grand Justices, which is charged with the power and responsibility of interpreting the constitution, laws, and ordinances. The tenure of office of a grand justice is nine years. The judicial system is based on the principle of three trials in three grades of courts: district court, high court, and supreme court. The Supreme Court, the highest tribunal of the land, consists of a number of civil and criminal divisions, each of which is formed by a presiding judge and four associate judges. The judges are appointed for life.

In 1993 a separate Constitution Court was established. Staffed by the 15 grand justices of the Judicial Yuan, but with the Judicial Yuan excluded from the court, the new court is charged with resolving constitutional disputes and regulating the activities of political parties and accelerate the democratization process.

There is no right to trial by jury, but the right to a fair public trial is protected by law and respected in practice. Defendants are afforded a right to counsel and to a right to appeal to the High Court and the Supreme Court in cases in which the sentence exceeds three years. Those sentenced to three years or less may appeal only to the High Court. The Supreme Court automatically reviews all sentences to life imprisonment or death.

17ARMED FORCES

Two years' military service is compulsory for all male citizens. The armed forces totaled 360,000 in 1993, a decrease of 80,000 from 1986. The army had 260,000 members, the navy 30,000, the marines 30,000, and the air force 70,000. In addition, reserves totaled 1.6 million. The navy had 24 destroyers, 4 submarines, 10 frigates, and 93 patrol and coastal combatants; the air force had 486 combat aircraft. For the period 1985–91, US military sales to Taiwan totaled US$3 billion of $3.5 billion in imports. Taiwan uses US weapons of all kinds. It spends $9.17 billion (1992) on defense or 4.5% of gross domestic product.

18INTERNATIONAL COOPERATION

The ROC, a charter member of the UN, became the first government to lose its recognition from that body following a General Assembly vote on 25 November 1971 to recognize the PRC as the sole legitimate representative of China. The ROC subsequently lost its membership in most UN bodies, as well as in several other international organizations—usually with its place taken by the PRC. As of 1987, the Asian Development Bank was one of the few major intergovernmental groups to which Taiwan still belonged.

As of September 1985, Taiwan had formal diplomatic ties with only 24 countries. The government claimed to have "substantive" trade relations with more than 140 countries and territories, however. Although trade with mainland China is officially forbidden, unofficial trade is substantial, and was estimated as at least US$1 billion in 1986.

19ECONOMY

In contrast to Taiwan's industry-led economic growth of previous decades, since the late 1980s the country has undergone a shift towards a services-dominated economy. As of 1992, services made up 55% of the GDP, compared to less than 50% in the mid-1980s and 44% in the early 1960s. Though still expanding in absolute terms, industry's share of the GDP declined from 52% in 1986 to 42% in 1992. Agriculture has continued to claim only a small share of the economy, making up 4% of the GDP in 1992.

Under the Japanese, the island was developed as a major source of foodstuffs for Japan. Production of rice and sugar increased rapidly, but little effort was directed toward industrialization until after 1937. Immediately after World War II, a number of factors—including repatriation of Japanese technicians, dismantling of industrial plants, and lack of fertilizer for agriculture—caused a rapid deterioration of the economy, which was aggravated by the influx of refugees from the mainland. The situation improved after 1949 with the removal of the ROC government to Taiwan. The arrival of technical and experienced personnel and capital equipment from the mainland facilitated the island's economic rehabilitation. Currency and tax reforms stabilized the monetary situation. The supply of fertilizer from the US and a land reform program aided the revival of agricultural production.

Energetic government measures in the form of successive four-year plans, at first supplemented by US aid, resulted in substantial economic progress. In the first decade (1951–60), the stress was on agricultural development and the establishment of textile and other labor-intensive industries. From 1961 to 1970, the promotion of industrial products for export was emphasized. In 1963, Taiwan registered its first favorable trade balance. By 1965, the economy appeared stable enough to warrant the cessation of US economic aid programs. Medium and light industry led the expansion, with striking gains registered in electronics, household goods, and chemicals. The decade 1971–80 saw the development of such capital-intensive industries as steel, machinery, machine tools, and motor vehicle assembly. Such industries, based on imports of raw materials, were encouraged through massive government support for major infrastructural improvements in roads, railroads, ports, and electricity. During the 1980s, emphasis was placed on the development of high-technology industries. As a result, between 1981 and 1991, the share of high-technology industries in total manufactures increased from 20% to 29%, making Taiwan the 7th largest producer of computer hardware on the global market.

Taiwan's GNP advanced at an average annual rate of 9% in real terms between 1952 and 1980. The growth rate declined to 4.5% in 1981/82 in the face of worldwide recession, recovering quickly though unevenly in subsequent years. For the 1981–89 period as a whole, the growth rate averaged 8.2% a year. During 1990–92, however, the GNP increased only 6% annually due to declining export growth and sluggish performances in the mining and agricultural sectors.

20INCOME

In 1992, Taiwan's GNP was $209 billion at current prices, or $10,000 per capita. In 1992 the inflation rate for consumer prices was 4.4% and the national product real growth rate was estimated at 6.7%.

21LABOR

In 1992, the civilian labor force in Taiwan numbered 8,770,000. The share of persons employed in farming, forestry, and fishing has been declining steadily, while the share of the work force employed in mining, manufacturing, construction, and utilities has increased. About 20% of the labor force is engaged in agriculture, 32% in services, 41% in industry and commerce, and the remainder in other activities. Only about 1.5% of the labor force was unemployed in 1992, a figure kept low by growth in the service sector in spite of continued departure of labor-intensive industries.

Productivity has been improving. The law provides for an 8-hour day (which may be extended to 11 hours for men and 10 for women) and a six-day workweek; overtime is paid at 40–100%

above the regular wage. Most large firms give allowances for transportation, meals, housing, and other benefits, which can increase base pay by 60–80%. A minimum of one week's vacation is provided after a year's employment, and there are 14 or 15 other paid holidays. Women are entitled to eight weeks of maternity leave at full pay and an extra paid holiday on Woman's Day (8 March). Average monthly earnings in the industrial sector in 1992 were NT$29,736. In 1992, the monthly minimum wage was NT$12,365.

Trade unions are weak and cannot be called unions in the real sense of the term, for the law does not provide for effective collective bargaining and also prohibits strikes, shutdowns, and walkouts in vital industries. The trade unions, organized under government supervision, tend to be used for carrying out government policies, but they carry on a considerable amount of welfare work. In 1992, there were 3,657 unions in Taiwan, with membership totaling 3.06 million, or 34.9% of all employed persons.

22AGRICULTURE

Although still important as both an export earner and a domestic food source, agriculture has fallen far from the preeminent position it long held in the Taiwan economy. From 1973 to 1987, the crop production growth rate increased on average only 0.1% per year. In 1993, agriculture accounted for only 3.5% of GNP, down from 28% in 1964. Nearly 1,100,000 persons (12.3% of the labor force) were employed in agriculture. High production costs and low return have driven much of the agricultural work force away to industry.

Rice, the principal food crop, is grown along the western plain and in the south. Other food crops include sweet potatoes, bananas, peanuts, soybeans, and wheat. Sugar, pineapples, citrus fruits, crude tea, and asparagus are plantation-grown and are the principal cash and export crops. Small amounts of Taiwan's world-famous oolong tea, cotton, tobacco, jute, and sisal are also produced. A fast-rising industry, mushroom canning, led to the development of mushroom cultivation, a specialty crop well suited to Taiwan since it is labor-intensive and requires little space and small investment.

Generally, Taiwanese agriculture is characterized by high yields, irrigation, terracing, multiple cropping, intertillage, and extensive use of fertilizers. Farms are small, averaging 1.1 hectares (2.7 acres) of cultivable land per farm family. Mechanization, once confined largely to sugarcane and rice production, is increasing rapidly as a result of government subsidies and other incentives. Since there is an oversupply of rice, the government has encouraged farmers to grow soybeans, wheat, and corn, which are more profitable.

23ANIMAL HUSBANDRY

Hog raising is surpassed in importance only by rice and sugarcane in Taiwan's rural economy. By 1990, there were some 11 million pigs. Chickens and ducks are raised by most households. In the 1980s, slaughtering of cattle and goats decreased, due to religious and economic reasons. However, the amount of imported beef quadrupled.

24FISHING

In 1990, Taiwan accounted for 5.6% of the world's fresh, chilled and frozen fish exports, valued at $742.3 million, and 4.7% of the world's prepared and preserved fish exports, valued at $257.8 million. Bonito, shark, sturgeon, tuna, red snapper, lobster, and shrimp are the main items of the inshore and coastal catch. Deep-sea fishing, which was practically wiped out by World War II, has shown strong gains following heavy investments in vessels and harbors. Fish culture in ponds increased at a rate of 10% annually from 1972 to 1981 and has continued to expand, although more slowly.

25FORESTRY

Approximately 55% of Taiwan is forested. Production declined from a peak of 1,219,118 cu m in 1971 to 474,584 cu m in 1985. The decline of timber processing during the 1980s was largely the result of policies which favored conservation. Principal timbers are oak, cedar, and hemlock. Taiwan is a major furniture exporter that relies heavily on imported wood products to support the industry.

26MINING

Coal, oil, and natural gas are the country's most valuable mine products. Dolomite, limestone, and marble are the most important nonfuel mineral commodities. Other minerals produced are small amounts of sulfur, pyrite, gold, silver, copper, manganese, mercury, petroleum, and natural gas. The western third of the island has adequate amounts of sand, gravel, and limestone for building purposes.

27ENERGY AND POWER

The island's installed power capacity reached 17,000,000 kw in 1991, more than triple the 1975 total. Total electric power output reached 76,900 million kwh in 1991 (more than 39 times the 1,966 million kwh generated in 1955). As of 1991, about 38% of Taiwan's electricity came from three nuclear plants with a combined installed capacity of 5,144 Mw. Total energy requirements have increased from about 82 million barrels of oil (equivalent) in 1971 to about 365 million barrels in 1991, representing an annual average increase of 7.8%. Power is controlled by the Taiwan Power Co., a government-owned corporation, but some enterprises generate power for their own consumption. The principal sources for consumption in 1992 were oil (51%), coal (29%), nuclear energy (15%), natural gas (3.5%); and hydroelectricity (1.5%). Oil is imported from the Middle East, Indonesia, Brunei, and Venezuela. River basin development is being vigorously pushed for irrigation, flood control, and power generation. In addition, experiments during the late 1970s and 1980s concentrated on developing Taiwan's geothermal potential.

Energy reserves at the end of 1991 included 170 million tons of coal and 20,000 million cu m of natural gas.

28INDUSTRY

Under the Japanese, about 90% of the industrial enterprises were owned by the government or by Japanese corporations with government assistance. After the restoration of Taiwan to China, the ROC government took over these enterprises. Some were sold to private owners, and the rest were grouped under the management of 18 public corporations, operated either by the national government or by the provincial government, or by both. Added to the confiscated enemy properties were public enterprises evacuated from the mainland. As a result, government-operated enterprises came to dominate Taiwanese industry. Although the proportion accounted for by these enterprises in the production value of manufacturing industries has been falling in recent years in contrast to the private sector, it still accounts for about one-sixth of value added. The average annual growth rate in manufacturing was 12.5% during 1953–62, 19.8% during 1963–72, 9.6% during 1973–85 and 5.9% for 1986–92; the private sector outpaced the public sector during each of these periods. The number of workers in manufacturing rose from 362,000 in 1952 to 736,000 in 1967 and to almost 2.8 million in 1987. By 1992, however, this number declined to about 2.6 million as the rapidly expanding service sector absorbed more of the workforce. Industrial production for export has been encouraged by the establishment of free-trade export-processing zones (EPZs) in the Kaohsiung harbor area, at Nantze (near Kaohsiung), and at T'aichung. Since the late 1980s rising production costs and a 40% appreciation of the New Taiwan dollar have prompted many export-oriented companies to relocate their manufacturing plants to mainland China and Southeast Asia.

Production rose spectacularly after the end of World War II, especially between 1952 and the early 1980s. Slower economic growth since the mid-1980s and greater investment emphasis on heavy and high-technology industries as well as services resulted in declining production figures for some traditional manufactures during the past decade. Rising from 13,576 tons in 1952 to 224,000 tons in 1985, cotton yarn production totaled only 197,133 tons in 1992. Production of cotton fabrics peaked at 840 million m in 1977, declining to 568,639 m in 1992. Similarly, fertilizer production rose from 148,000 in 1952 to 2.1 million tons in 1980, but declined 1.9 million tons in 1992. Television set production declined from 5,748,000 in 1986 to 2,623,000 units in 1992; caustic soda from 386,505 to 290,348 tons. Nevertheless, reflecting continued development of heavy and electronic industries, production increases continued to be registered for a number of key products. Cement production grew from 446,000 tons in 1952 to 14.8 million tons in 1986 and 21.5 million tons in 1992; paper from 29,512 in 1952 to 530,224 in 1986 and 1.0 million tons in 1992. Production of integrated circuits increased from 1,651 million pieces in 1986 to 3,694 million pieces in 1992; motor vehicle production from 170,923 passenger cars in 1986 to 429,208 units in 1992; steel bars from 6,164,000 to 14,556,298 tons; synthetic fibers from 1,371,000 to 2,163,662 tons; polyvinyl chloride from 795,000 tons to 1,042,564; ship building from 552,294 d.w.t. to 1,342,018; sewing machines from 2,675,000 in 1986 to 3,208,430 sets in 1992.

29SCIENCE AND TECHNOLOGY

In the 1970s, Taiwan instituted its Science and Technology Development Program. Coordinated by the National Science Council, the program seeks to encourage the development of "knowledge-intensive" industries through grants for the training of scientific personnel, subsidies for recruitment of distinguished scientists from abroad, and grants to universities to promote scientific research. Specific goals of the program are to integrate and promote research in geothermal energy, battery-powered vehicles, electronics, cancer treatment, pharmaceuticals, nuclear safety, and the development of high-precision instrumentation and computers.

The Industrial Technology Research Institute is charged with the transfer of pertinent technologies developed to manufacturing and other industries. College students are encouraged to build careers in engineering and science. In 1979, the Science-Based Industrial Park was established at Hsinchu, near the National Tsinghua University, with the objective of encouraging computer manufacturing and other high-technology industries by offering loans, tax incentives, and low-cost housing and factory buildings. By 1990, over 60 companies had established R&D and joint production facilities there. These include computer, semiconductor, precision electronics and instrumentation, telecommunications, and biotechnology firms.

The highest institution for scientific research on Taiwan is the Academia Sinica. Its nine associated institutes carry on research in mathematics, history and philology, economics, modern history, physics, botany, zoology, ethnology, and chemistry. An atomic energy committee promotes atomic research.

30DOMESTIC TRADE

The marketing system is partly free and partly controlled. Salt, tobacco, alcoholic beverages, and certain commodities are produced and distributed by the government. Prices of basic living commodities are controlled. Retail sales in cities are handled by department stores, specialty shops, general stores, convenience stores, roadside stands, and peddlers. Since roadside stands and peddlers have little overhead and are satisfied with a small profit, their prices are generally lower than those of the large stores and shops, if the customer bargains. In recent years, wholesale discounters, hyper markets and franchises have become significant distribution channels for consumer goods, increasing the efficiency of the marketing system overall.

Chilung and T'aipei are the distribution centers for the northern end of the island, while Kaohsiung and T'ainan are the principal distribution centers for the southern area. Most registered import and export trading firms are located in T'aipei. Accounts are usually settled during festival periods, according to Chinese custom.

Local markets open about 7 AM and close at 6 PM or later. Business firms and stores are usually open from 9 AM to 5:30 PM, and some stores close as late as 10 PM. Most stores are open seven days a week. Banks are open six days a week: Monday–Friday, 9 AM to 3:30 PM, and Saturday, 9 AM to noon.

Advertising is becoming increasingly evident and is mainly carried by newspapers and on radio and television stations.

31FOREIGN TRADE

Foreign trade is of great importance to the economy. To fulfill both production and consumer needs, Taiwan must import large quantities of industrial raw materials and manufactured goods. The export pattern has changed significantly since the end of World War II. In 1952, industrial products represented only 10% of Taiwan's total exports and agricultural exports made up the rest; but by 1992, industrial exports (excluding processed agricultural products) had jumped to an overwhelming 95.7% share of the total. Exports increased from us$8,166.3 million in 1976 to us$39,789.1 million in 1986 and US$81,480 million in 1992. However, the export growth rate has declined steeply in recent years, from 23% in 1986 to 13% in 1991 and 0.4% in 1992, due to recession in Taiwan's major markets and the movement of export-oriented manufacturing plants to China and Southeast Asia. With rising consumer wealth within Taiwan as well as recent tariff reductions and other liberalisation measures by the government, imports have risen rapidly from us$24,165 million in 1986 to us$71,977 million in 1992.

Principal exports in 1986 and 1992 (in millions of US dollars) were as follows:

	1986	1992
Electric machinery	8,892	22,222
Textiles	7,305	11,842
Metal manufactures and machinery	3,957	10,035
Electronic products	3,907	8,862
Plastics and plastic products	1,747	4,815
Transportation equipment	1,690	4,200
Toys, games, & sports accessories	2,408	3,318
Other exports	12,291	16,176
TOTALS	39,789	81,470

Principal imports in 1986 and 1992 (in millions of US dollars) were as follows:

	1986	1992
Electrical machinery and apparatus	4,304	9,308
Electronic products	3,811	9,051
Chemicals	2,764	7,148
Basic metals	2,668	8,625
Nonelectrical machinery	2,625	6,988
Crude oil	2,043	3,052
Food, beverages, and tobacco	1,075	2,436
Transportation equipment	877	6,015
Other imports	3,998	19,354
TOTALS	24,165	71,977

The US remains Taiwan's single most important trade partner, although Japan has made major gains, becoming Taiwan's major supplier in the 1970s and 1980s. Trade with mainland China via Hong Kong has expanded rapidly over the past decade, resulting in a sharp increase in Taiwan's trade surplus with the latter country. Principal trade partners in 1992 (in millions of US dollars) were as follows:

	EXPORTS	IMPORTS	BALANCE
US	23,572	15,772	7,800
Japan	8,894	21,767	–12,873
Hong Kong	15,415	1,781	13,634
FRG	1,428	3,919	–2,491
Australia	563	2,056	–1,493
UK	2,205	1,338	867
Singapore	2,505	1,695	810
Canada	1,643	1,178	465
Malaysia	1,600	1,829	–229
Thailand	1,810	825	985
Other countries	21,835	19,817	2,018
TOTALS	81,470	71,977	9,493

Although Taiwan has not been a signatory to international copyright conventions in the past, in response to US pressure a government crack-down on companies infringing coprights and trademarks has been in effect since the mid-1980s. A revised copyright bill was adopted in 1992 meeting most of the Berne Convention standards at least formally, with additional legislation currently under both legislative and ministerial review. A major case involving Encyclopaedia Brittanica was decided against a local publishing firm in early 1991, setting an important precedent for future litigation. Continued pressure by the US is aimed at full enforcement of recent legislation and further improvements in protecting copyrights, patents and trademarks.

32BALANCE OF PAYMENTS

There has been a consistent trade surplus since the mid-1970s, which has annually exceeded $10 billion since the mid-1980s. A decline in the current account surplus is expected to continue over the next few years, as a result of increased imports of capital goods, coupled with the lifting of import restrictions and relaxed foreign exchange controls. In 1992, the trade and current account surpluses amounted to $12.8 billion and $8.1 billion, respectively; reserves (excluding gold) totaled $82.3 billion that year. Private remittances from overseas Chinese and other foreign investors constitute another important source of payments inflow.

33BANKING AND SECURITIES

Almost all banking institutions are either owned or controlled by the government. The Bank of Taiwan (with 75 branches) issued currency notes, handled foreign exchange, acted as the government's bank, and performed central banking functions in addition to its commercial banking activities before reactivating of the Central Bank of China in T'aipei in 1961. The functions of the Central Bank include regulation of the money market, management of foreign exchange, issuance of currency, and service as fiscal agent for the government. The Bank of China is a foreign exchange bank with branch offices in major world capitals. The Bank of Communications is an industrial bank specializing in industrial, mining, and transportation financing. The Export-Import Bank of China, inaugurated 1 February 1979, assists in the financing of Taiwan's export trade. The Central Trust of China acts as a government trading agency and handles most of the procurements of government organizations. The Postal Savings System accepts savings deposits and makes domestic transfers at post offices.

At the end of 1992 there were 41 domestic commercial banks and 40 branches of foreign banks. Total deposits of domestic banks at the end of 1991 were NT1,775,780 million. The money supply reached NT2,163 billion as of 1991, as compared with NT1,138.17 billion at the end of 1986 and NT305.4 billion at the end of 1980.

The law stipulates that transactions in stocks and securities can be made only in the registered business places of stock dealers; the first private corporate bond issue was floated in 1958. The first stock exchange in Taiwan opened on 4 February 1962. It is not, as yet, a major source for the supply of capital to local or foreign investors, and the volume of transactions remains relatively small and fluctuates widely.

34INSURANCE

Insurance in Taiwan is supervised by the Ministry of Finance and may be written only by a limited liability company or a cooperative association.

Aside from group insurance operated by the government, life and annuity insurance are comparatively undeveloped in Taiwan. The Chinese tradition that the family should take care of its members in sickness and old age lowered demand in the past, but social change and rapid economic growth have modified this situation, especially in industrial areas. In 1986 there were 20 insurance companies in Taiwan; in that year, the Taiwanese government agreed to allow US companies to compete equally for insurance business. Life insurance premiums totaled US$6,258 million in 1991. In 1992, all insurance premiums totaled US$569.8 billion.

35PUBLIC FINANCE

Central government revenues come mostly from taxation, customs and duties, and income from government monopolies on tobacco and wines; other revenues are derived from profits realized by government enterprises. Government accounts continued to show surpluses through the early 1980s, despite the worldwide recession.

Local governments derive the bulk of their revenues from local taxes on real estate, slaughtering, vehicles, boats, and entertainment. Most revenues are spent on education and police administration.

Taiwan suffered a fiscal deficit of NT$136 billion ($5 billion) in 1990/91, when the island experienced an economic slowdown. Public authorities are anticipating a growing fiscal deficit throughout the late 1990s as Taiwan's six-year development plan requires over $300 billion of investment in public infrastructural construction projects and in upgrading industries. To finance these upcoming fiscal deficits, the government plans to issue increasing amounts of public bonds. In 1992, a surplus of NT$82.5 billion was recorded.

36TAXATION

All taxes are collected by the local government and transferred to the relevant provincial or central government agency. Tax revenues reserved for the central government include the income tax, estate (inheritance) tax, gift tax, customs duty, stamp tax, commodity tax, securities transaction tax, and mine tax. The rates for income tax payment for individuals in 1993 ranged from 6% for up to NT$300,000 to a top rate of 40% for income above NT$3.0 million. Corporate income taxes rose to a maximum of 25% for taxable income over NT$100,000. A value-added tax was applied in April 1986, amounting in most cases to 5%.

37CUSTOMS AND DUTIES

Customs duties are important revenue earners and consist principally of import duties and tonnage dues; the former are levied on dutiable commodities, the latter on ships that call at Taiwan ports. Office equipment, movie projectors, phonographs, and bicycles are typical dutiable items. Duties range from 0-10% for raw materials to 35% for consumer goods. In 1987, Taiwan reduced tariffs on some 3,100 agricultural, industrial, and marine products. Articles imported for military use, for relief, or for educational or research purposes are exempted from import duty. Duties on imported raw materials for business can be rebated.

Exports to mainland China are prohibited, and an export licensing system, designed to prevent diversion of Taiwan shipments to Communist-controlled areas, is in effect on many commodities.

38FOREIGN INVESTMENT

In 1992 approved foreign investment in Taiwan from private sources since 1952 totaled US$16.4 billion. About $2,485 million of this amount was derived from overseas Chinese investors; $4,626 million from Japan; and $4,063 million from US sources. Of the new investments approved in 1992, overseas Chinese contributed 21%; Japan investors contributed 29%; and US investors only 13%. Some 24% of all foreign investments during 1952–92 were directed at the electronic and electrical appliance industries; 18% went to chemicals, 12% to services, and 8% to machinery, equipment, and instruments.

39ECONOMIC DEVELOPMENT

Since 1950, the government has adopted a series of economic plans to help guide and promote economic growth and industrialization. The first four-year economic development plan (1953–56) emphasized reconstruction and increased production of rice, fertilizers, and hydroelectric power; it resulted in an increase of 36.6% in GNP and 17.4% in income per capita. In the second four-year plan (1957–60), import substitution industries were encouraged. Industry and agriculture both registered significant gains; GNP increased by 31.1%, and national income per capita by 13.3%. The third four-year plan (1961–64) emphasized labor-intensive export industries, basic services, energy development, industries contributing to agricultural growth, and exploration and development of the island's limited natural resources. The results were a 41.5% increase in GNP and a 30.7% increase in per capita income. US loans and grants, totaling US$2.2 billion, and foreign (mostly overseas Chinese) investment financed these early stages of development.

Following the curtailment of AID assistance in 1965, the fourth four-year plan (1965–68) was introduced, followed by the fifth four-year plan (1969–72); increases in GNP for these periods were 45.9% and 55.2%, respectively. By 1971, exports of manufactured goods had registered spectacular increases, and Taiwan's foreign trade pattern changed from one of chronic deficit to consistent trade surpluses. At this point, the government began to redirect its priorities from labor-intensive industries to the development of such capital-intensive sectors as shipbuilding, chemicals, and petrochemicals. The sixth four-year plan (1973–76), adversely affected by the worldwide recession, was terminated in 1975 after producing only an 18.9% increase in GNP. It was replaced by a six-year plan (1976–81) that focused on expansion of basic industries and completion of 10 major infrastructural projects, including rail electrification, construction of the North Link railroad, development of nuclear energy, and construction of the steel mill at Kaohsiung and of the new port of T'aichung.

In 1978, the six-year plan was revised, and 12 new infrastructural projects were added, including completion of the round-the-island railroad, construction of three cross-island highways, expansion of T'aichung Port's harbor, and expansion of steel and nuclear energy facilities. A subsequent four-year plan (1986–89), designed to supplement a longer-range 10-year plan (1980–89), had as a target average annual GNP increase of 6.5%. Among its goals were price stability, annual growth of 7.5% in the service sector, trade liberalization, encouragement of balanced regional development, and redirection of new industrial growth into such high-technology industries as computers, robotics, and bioengineering. In response to flagging export growth and a slowdown in private investment following a stock market collapse in 1990, the government devised a Six-Year Plan for 1991–97 aimed at economic revitalisation. The final plan has targeted up to NT$5 trillion for investment mainly in transportation, telecommunications, power generation and pollution control. A "Statute for Upgrading Industries" enacted in early 1991 continues the government's efforts to provide incentives for private investment in research and development and high-technology sectors of the economy.

40SOCIAL DEVELOPMENT

Living standards have improved considerably since 1952, and improvements in diet and medical care have pushed the average life expectancy at birth from 58.6 years in 1952 to 73.3 years in 1985. That year, the marriage rate was 8.03 per 1,000 population and the live birthrate 18.03, down, respectively, from 9.3 and 22.97 in 1981. Since 1985, abortion has been permitted on social, medical, and juridical grounds. The husbands' consent is required for married women seeking abortions on socioeconomic grounds.

A social insurance system provides medical, disability, old age, survivor, and other benefits, with employers paying 5.6% of payroll and workers contributing 1.4% of earnings. All enterprises and labor organizations must also furnish welfare funds for workers and "welfare units," such as cafeterias, nurseries, clinics, and low-rent housing. Fishermen, farmers, and salt workers have their own welfare funds. Government programs include relief for mainland refugees, calamity-relief assistance, and direct assistance to children in needy families.

Most laws discriminating against women in regard to property, divorce, and child custody have been eliminated. The law now provides for equitable distribution of conjugal property in divorce cases. In the workplace, women tend to receive lower salaries and less frequent promotion, and are often denied federally mandated maternity leave.

In 1992, 131,000 persons received family planning services. Abortions are permitted for medical reasons.

41HEALTH

As a result of improved living conditions and mass vaccinations, significant progress has been made in controlling malaria, tuberculosis, venereal disease, leprosy, trachoma, typhoid, diphtheria, and encephalitis. In 1992, the death rate was estimated at 7 per 1,000 population. The infant mortality rate in 1990 was 6 per 1,000 live births, and life expectancy was 74 years. At the end of 1985, Taiwan's public health facilities included 55 general hospitals and 888 health stations. In 1990, there were 22,300 doctors.

42HOUSING

The evacuation of more than 2 million persons from the mainland to an already densely populated island in 1949 made the provision of low-cost housing an early priority. By 1979, more than 150,000 units of public housing had been built. Since the 1970s, government housing programs have focused on the cities, with slum clearance and the construction of high-rise apartment dwellings for low-income groups the major priorities. Two new towns were constructed in the early 1980s, and a third was planned. The government set a target of 600,000 new housing units for the 1979–89 decade, but only 236,106 units were completed as of 1986. The total housing stock stood at 4,740,000 units in 1992. The number of people per dwelling was 4.3 as of 1988.

⁴³EDUCATION

Taiwan enjoys one of the world's highest literacy rates because of its emphasis on education. About 91% of the people aged six or older are literate. All children receive nine years of free and compulsory education provided at government expense, including six years in public primary school and three years in junior high. Salaries of the teaching staff are paid by local governments. While textbooks and tuition are free, children must buy their own notebooks and pencils. In 1968 the curriculum was revised with more emphasis on science, while maintaining the Chinese cultural tradition. In order to attend high school, students must pass an examination after junior high. In 1985, 234,674 children attended 2,210 preschools; 2,321,700 were in 2,486 primary schools, and 1,062,226 attended junior high. After completing nine years of compulsory schooling, 194,757 students chose to attend senior high school, and 421,784 sought vocational training. Agriculture, engineering, commerce, maritime navigation, home economics, and nursing are some of the skills taught in vocational schools, which offer three-year programs.

In the 1980s, enrollment showed a decided shift to the natural sciences and engineering, a trend that was expected to accelerate in the future as educational curricula were restructured to conform with economic planning policies. The government relaxed many restrictions which prevented students from studying abroad. Many students attend college in Japan, Europe and the United States. In 1985, 428,576 students attended 105 institutions of higher education. In addition, 5,979 Taiwanese students were approved for advanced education overseas.

Taiwan has a highly developed college curriculm. Taiwanese college and graduate students are particularly interested in engineering, computer science, natural science, and business management. In 1989–90, there were 116 universities, junior colleges, and independent colleges in Taiwan.

⁴⁴LIBRARIES AND MUSEUMS

The National Central Library in T'aipei holds more than 1,615,000 items, including a collection of rare Chinese books (180,000 volumes). The National Taiwan University in T'aipei has more than 1,500,000 volumes in collected holdings.

The major museums, all in T'aipei, are the National Palace Museum, National Museum of History, and the Taiwan Museum. The National Palace Museum houses one of the world's largest collections of Chinese art—the collection consists primarily of treasures brought from the mainland. The National Museum of History, founded in 1955, has more than 30,000 items in its collections of oracle bones and ritual vessels of the Shang and Chou dynasties, earthenware of the Sui and T'ang dynasties, stone engravings of the Han dynasty, and jade articles of the Chou dynasty. The Taiwan Museum has the most complete collection of natural history specimens in the country. The National Taiwan Science Education Center in T'aipei houses a planetarium and scientific exhibits.

⁴⁵MEDIA

Telecommunications services are owned by the government. By 1992 there were 7,800,000 telephone subscribers in Taiwan, as compared with 598,504 in 1974. Nearly all telephone service is automatic. The postal service is managed by the Directorate General of Posts under the Ministry of Communications. There were 13,224 post offices in 1991.

Radio broadcasting stations in Taiwan are under the supervision of the Ministry of Communications. By 1988 there were about 186 broadcasting stations. The largest network is the Broadcasting Corp. of China, which operates three systems: an overseas service, known as the Voice of Free China; the mainland service, known as the Central Broadcasting Station, aimed at the Chinese mainland; and the domestic service. These stations broadcast in 14 languages and dialects. Television was introduced in 1962; the number of television sets in 1992 was estimated at 6,386,000 and the number of radios at 8,620,000.

In 1991 there were 232 daily newspapers. The leading papers, their orientation, and estimated 1992 daily circulations are as follows:

	ORIENTATION	CIRCULATION
United Daily News (T'aipei)	Independent	1,200,000
China Daily News (T'aipei)	NA	724,915
China Times (T'aipei)	Independent	623,500
Central Daily News (T'aipei)	Official KMT	530,000
Independence Evening Post (T'aipei)	NA	192,000

The Central News Agency was established on the mainland by the KMT in 1924. In 1985 there were 44 news agencies, serving newspapers and radio and TV stations. As of 1985 there were 2,952 magazines.

The press law of 1954 stipulates that a publisher is liable to punishment should his paper be found to incite treason, disturb the public order, or commit acts of moral turpitude. There is no prior censorship, but all printed matter is checked by security officers after publication and may be seized or banned if found objectionable. Viewpoints diverging from KMT positions are rarely seen, and those expressing public support for Communism or the PRC run the risk of trial for sedition by military tribunal. In 1986, nearly all issues of opposition magazines were banned.

⁴⁶ORGANIZATIONS

The most influential private organizations are the occupational or trade associations. These include associations of farmers, fishermen, trade unions, business leaders, and professional persons. Organizations devoted to social welfare and relief work are sponsored by the government, by religious groups, and by civic clubs. The Taiwan Federation of Chambers of Commerce has branches in all the principal cities.

Cooperatives are an important adjunct to economic life, especially in the urban centers. In rural areas, agricultural cooperatives help the farmers transport and market special farm products such as fruits, tea, citronella oil, and handicrafts. Consumer cooperatives numbered 4,428 at the end of 1990, with 3,584,433 members. Cooperative farms, organized with the help of the government, operate either on a community basis, with the products distributed among the members, or on an individual basis, with the cooperative functioning as a purchasing, processing, and marketing agency.

Agricultural services and 4-H clubs in various parts of Taiwan provide training and social activities for boys and girls. Both the YMCA and YWCA are active in Taiwan, as is Little League baseball.

⁴⁷TOURISM, TRAVEL, AND RECREATION

In 1991, tourist arrivals totaled an estimated 1,855,000 of whom 1,233,000 were from Eastern and Southeast Asia. Hotel construction has boomed as a result of government investment. In 1991 there were 19,786 rooms with a 54.3% occupancy rate. Visitors need a valid passport and tourist visa good for two weeks to 60 days. The Tourism Bureau, under the Ministry of Communications, oversees tourist development.

T'aipei is the chief tourist attraction, with such popular sites as the seat of government in Presidential Square, Lungshan Temple, and the nearby National Palace Museum and famous Yangmingshan Park. Attractions outside the capital include Shihmen Dam recreation area, Lake Tzuhu, and the mausoleum of Chiang Kaishek. The many temples and Dutch relics of T'ainan, Taiwan's oldest city, and Sun Moon Lake near T'aichung also attract numerous visitors. The national sports are baseball, soccer, and basketball.

[48]FAMOUS TAIWANESE

Among the many Chinese scholars who have lived in Taiwan since 1949 are Hu Shih (1891–1962), philosopher and president of the Academia Sinica; Chiang Monlin (1886–1964), educator and chairman of the Joint Commission on Rural Reconstruction; Li Chi (1896–1979) and Tung Tso-pin (1895–1963), archaeologists, whose discoveries at the Anyang site laid the foundation for modern Chinese archaeology; and Tsiang Ting-fu (Ting-fu Fuller Tsiang, 1895–1965), historian and long-time delegate to the UN. Chang Ta-chien (1899–1983) is known for his painting of landscapes and figures and his copies of the famous Buddhist mural paintings of Tunhwang caves in Gansu Province. Lin Yutang (1895–1976), poet, philosopher, lexicographer, and historian, was one of China's foremost interpreters for Western cultures.

The outstanding political and military figure of Nationalist China and postwar Taiwan was Chiang Kai-shek (Chiang Chung-cheng, 1887–1975), who was responsible for sustaining the spirit of anticommunism in Taiwan. His son, Chiang Ching-kuo (1910–88), assumed leadership of the Taiwan government from Chiang Kai-shek's death to his own.

[49]DEPENDENCIES

Taiwan has no territories or colonies.

[50]BIBLIOGRAPHY

Ahern, Emily. *The Anthropology of Taiwanese Society.* Stanford, Calif.: Stanford University Press, 1981.

Fairbank, John King. *The United States and China.* Rev. ed. Cambridge, Mass.: Harvard University Press, 1974.

Galenson, Walter (ed.). *Economic Growth and Structural Change in Taiwan: The Postwar Experience of the Republic of China.* Ithaca, N.Y.: Cornell University Press, 1979.

Goddard, William G. *Formosa: A Study in Chinese History.* East Lansing: Michigan State University Press, 1966.

Hsueh, Chi. *The Foreign Factor: The Multinational Corporation's Contribution to the Economic Modernization of the Republic of China.* Stanford, CA: Hoover Institution Press, 1990.

Li, Kuo-ting. *The Evolution of Policy Behind Taiwan's Development Success.* New Haven: Yale University Press, 1988.

Lin, Zhiling and Thomas W. Robinson (eds.). *The Chinese and their Future: Beijing, Taipei, and Hong Kong.* Washington, D.C.: AEI Press, 1994.

Long, Simon. *Taiwan: China's Last Frontier.* New York: St. Martin's, 1991.

Metraux, Daniel Alfred. *Taiwan's Political and Economic Growth in the Late Twentieth Century.* Lewiston: E. Mellen Press, 1991.

Shepherd, John Robert. *Statecraft and Political Economy on the Taiwan Frontier, 1600–1800.* Stanford, Calif.: Stanford University Press, 1992.

Tien, Hung-mao. *The Great Transition: Political and Social Change in the Republic of China.* Stanford, Calif.: Hoover Institution Press, Stanford University, 1989.

TAJIKISTAN

Republic of Tajikistan
Respublica i Tojikistan

CAPITAL: Dushanbe.

FLAG: Red field divided at the center by a white stripe and narrow green stripe, a yellow hammer and sickle and red star outlined in yellow in the canton.

MONETARY UNIT: Ruble. (As of the end of 1993, Tajikistan was the only former Soviet republic still using Soviet rubles as the single currency.)

WEIGHTS AND MEASURES: The metric system is used.

HOLIDAYS: New Year's Day, 1 January; Navruz ("New Day"), 21 March; Independence Day, 9 September.

TIME: 6 PM = noon GMT.

1LOCATION, SIZE, AND EXTENT

Tajikistan is located in southern Asia, between Uzbekistan and China. Comparatively, it is slightly smaller than the state of Wisconsin with a total area of 143,100 sq km (55,251 sq mi). Tajikistan's boundary length totals 3,651 km (2,269 mi).

Its capital city, Dushanbe, is located in the western part of the country.

2TOPOGRAPHY

The topography of Tajikistan features the Pamir and Altay mountains which dominate the landscape. The western Fergana Valley lies in the north with the Kafirnigan and Vakhsh valleys in the southwest. Six percent of Tajikistan's land is arable with approximately 5% under irrigation.

3CLIMATE

The climate is semiarid to polar in the Pamirs and Tien Sham mountains. The mean temperature in July is 30°C (86°F). The mean temperature in January is 0°C (32°F). Rainfall in the country averages 12.2 cm (4.8 in).

4FLORA AND FAUNA

Wildflowers can be found in the valleys of the mountains, Marco Polo sheep, yak, and snow leopards can be found in the mountains.

5ENVIRONMENT

The condition of Tajikistan's soil is a significant environmental problem. Over the last 30 years, the nation has increased its irrigation practices to support agricultural activity. The result has been increasing levels of soil salinity, which damage the soil and threaten its productivity.

The nation's water supply is threatened by pollution. Eighty-five percent of Tajikistan's farm population does not have an indoor water supply.

6POPULATION

The population of Tajikistan was 5,108,576 in 1989. It was estimated at 6,155,474 in 1995. The projection for 2000 was 6,871,000, based on a crude birth rate of 30.8 per 1,000 population, a crude death rate of 5.1, and a net natural increase of 25.7 during 1995–2000. The estimated population density in 1995 was 43 per sq km (111.4 per sq mi). Dushanbe, the capital, had an estimated population of 602,000 at the beginning of 1990. Khojand (formerly Leninabad) had a population of about 163,000.

7MIGRATION

The number of Russians dropped from about 400,000 to 250,000 during 1992–93 because of political turmoil, which also left about 30,000 people internally displaced. About 90,000 minority peoples in the Pamirs fled to Afghanistan in 1992, but some 50,000 returned in 1993 under an amnesty. About 50,000 displaced people in Dushanbe were forcibly expelled to their home regions in the south during 1993.

8ETHNIC GROUPS

In 1989, Tajiks constituted 62% of the population and Uzbeks (who live in the northwest) 23.5%. Russians comprised 7.6% and Tatars 1.4%.

9LANGUAGES

Tajik, an Iranian language, was scheduled to become the sole official language by 1996. All government officers were mandated to conduct business in Tajik by 1994. The language has no genders or cases. Its vocabulary borrow from Arabiz, Uzbek, and Russian. Russian is the language for "interethnic communication."

10RELIGIONS

Most Tajiks are Sunni Muslims of the Hanafi sect, although the people of the Pamirs are Ismaili. The Russian Orthodox Church is also present, and in 1990 the Jewish population numbered some 11,500.

11TRANSPORTATION

Some 480 km (298 mi) of railroads are utilized in Tajikistan. A 258-km (160 mi) line connects Dushanbe with Termez, Uzbekistan, and ultimately with the other rail systems of the former Soviet Union.

In 1990, there were some 29,900 km (18,600 mi) of highways, of which 24,400 km (15,200 mi) were hard-surfaced. The major roads connect Khudzhand in the north to Kulyab in the south via Dushanbe. Only one main road services the eastern Gorno-Bada-khshanskaya region, meandering from Khrough to Kyrgyzstan.

Air service is underdeveloped; freight often must be transported by charter plane.

12HISTORY

The territory of Tajikistan has been continuously inhabited since the early Stone Age. The first Central Asian states of Sogdia and Bactria in the first millenium BC, included portions of Tajikistan. The territory was Persian-controlled from the 6th century BC, until conquered by Alexander the Great in 329 BC. Much of Tajikistan was included in the Greco-Bactrian kingdom in 3rd century BC, and after displaced by the Tochari tribes who invaded Sogdia a century later. The Kushana kingdom was established in the first centuries of the Christian era, when a number of cities were established, and agriculture and commerce grew. In the 5th and 6th centuries, parts of Tajikistan were conquered by nomadic tribes, the Chionites and, later, the Ephthalites.

At the end of the 6th century the large Ephthalite empire was displaced by the Eastern Turkic Kaganate. Arabs conquered the area in the 8th century, introducing Islam. Later in the 9th century they were displaced by the Samanides, who encouraged the development of trade and of material culture. From the 10th to the 13th centuries a number of kingdoms succeeded one another in Central Asia; among the ones which included parts of Tajikistan were the Ghaznavids, the Karakhanids, the Ghorids, the Karakitai, and the Khwarazmites.

In 1219–1221 Genghiz Khan's troops conquered the entire area, destroying many cities. Tajikistan became part of the lands given to Genghiz Khan's son, Chagatai. In the 14th century Timur (Tamerlane) created a large empire, with its capital in Samarkand. In the 16th century Tajikistan was conquered by the Sheibanids, who had their capital in Bukhara. Portions of territory were included later in the Ashtarkhanid state and then in the Kokand Khanate, which emerged in the Fergana Valley in the mid 18th century Present-day Tajikistan was split between the Khanates of Bukhara and Kokand in the 18th and 19th centuries.

In 1863, Russia asserted a right to exercise dominance in Central Asia, and began the military conquest of the khanates. Bukhara and Samarkand were incorporated into Russia in 1868. Kokand was eliminated in 1876, and the border with Afghanistan was set by accord with England in 1895. At that point, part of Tajikistan was in the Emirate of Bukhara, part was in Turkestan. When the Tsar's draft call-up of 1916 was announced, rebellions broke out all over Central Asia, including in Tajikistan. These were surpressed, at great loss of life.

Northern Tajikistan was conquered by the Bolsheviks in 1918, who extended control to the rest of the country when Bukhara was captured, in 1920. The so-called Basmachi Rebellion continued until 1924–1925, when Tajikistan was established as an autonomous republic within the Uzbek Soviet Socialist Republic. The republic became a full Soviet republic in 1929.

Border delineations were very arbitrary. For several hundred years educated Central Asians had used Persian and Turkic languages essentially equally, so that separation into Turkic-speaking Uzbeks and Persian-speaking Tajiks, as if to create separate nationalities, was primarily administrative. Bukhara and Samarkand, the major Tajik cities, were included in Uzbekistan, while Tajikistan was left only with smaller cities, and little arable land. People were forced to assume one nationality or another.

In the late Soviet period Tajikistan was the poorest and least developed of the republics. It comprised four separate areas, the elites of which competed for power. Traditionally power was held by people from Khojent, which is geographically and culturally closest to Uzbekistan's Fergana valley. They were contested by families and clans from Kuliab. Poorest were people from Badakhshan, most of which is in the unfarmable Pamir Mountains. The final area was Kurgan-Tiube, where the influence of Islam was strong; public calls for establishing an Islamic state were heard here as early as 1976.

In 1985, Mikhail Gorbachev replaced long-time republic leader Rahmon Nabiev with Makhkamov, whose control never penetrated to the most local levels. Riots in February 1990 exposed his weaknesses, and encouraged a proliferation of political parties and groups. When the August 1991 attempted coup came, Makhkamov was the only republic leader to welcome it. When the coup failed, Makhkamov was forced to resign, and Nabiev returned to power.

The republic declared independence on 9 September 1991, and hotly contested presidential elections were conducted 27 October 1991. Nabiev took 57 percent of the vote; his principal opponent was Davlot Khudonazarov, former head of the USSR Union of Cinematographers. However, power struggles continued. Parliamentary speaker Aslonov was killed soon after the election by the Kuliab militia; he was replaced by Kendzhaev, who set about rooting out anti-Nabiev opposition. By April 1992, demonstrators for and against Nabiev took over two public squares in Dushanbe, about a mile apart. Clashes between the two caused several deaths, and tensions mounted. Nabiev, responding to popular demands, named Iskandarov to replace Kendzhaev, and also brought token democrats and Islamic activists into the government, including Kazi-kolon Khojiakbar Turajonzoda, the senior Muslim cleric in the republic.

Civil disorder grew throughout summer 1992. In September 1992, Nabiev was forced from office at gunpoint by a disgruntled democratic faction, and Iskandarov assumed control of the government. By this time full civil war had erupted, with casualties perhaps as high as 50,000. By October, Uzbekistan and Russia had joined in the effort to help drive the Iskandarov government and its supporters out of the country, mostly into neighboring Afghanistan. In November 1992, the post of president was abolished, and Speaker I. Rakhmonov, of Kuliab, took power, brutally rooting out all opposition. Although recognized as a legitimate leader by the outside world, Rakhmonov's control of the republic remains spotty. Important opposition leaders have set up bases in Afghanistan, vowing to return to fight. The parts of the republic Rakhmonov controls have become essentially Russian protectorates, relying upon Russian soldiers to keep order and using Russian subsidies to prop up the economy. Tajikistan is the only ex-Soviet republic (other than Russia) which continues to use the ruble as its currency; however, its specially marked rubles are not negotiable outside the republic.

13GOVERNMENT

The formal structure of government in Dushanbe rests in an 80-member Majlis, or Assembly, which replaced the Soviet-era Parliament in May 1992. The office of president has been abolished, and chairman of the Majlis Imomali Rakhmonov has been declared head of state. He appoints the Prime Minister and his cabinet, who hold executive power. He also appoints the judiciary and security organs. Work had begun on a new constitution, but none had been adopted as of late 1994. The republic is essentially a Russian client state, so most important governmental decisions are made administratively, many of them in Moscow or by the Russian military.

14POLITICAL PARTIES

The principal party is the Communist Party, which was renamed the Socialist Party in September 1991, but reverted to its old name in December 1991. It was likely to rename itself again in preparation for elections anticipated in 1994 or 1995. However, in the period preceding the Rakhmonov government, there were several political parties, now in exile. The most important were: the Democratic Party, founded by Shodmon Iusuf, with a program of Western-style liberal democracy; Rastokhez (Renais-

LOCATION: 15°0'N; 39°0'E. BOUNDARY LENGTHS: Total boundary lengths, 3,651 km (2,269 mi); Afghanistan, 1,206 km (749.4 mi); China, 414 km (257.3 mi); Kyrgyzstan, 870 km (541 mi); Uzbekistan, 1,161 km (721.4 mi).

sance), a nationalist party primarily of artists and intellectuals; and the Islamic Renaissance Party, founded by Dovlat Usmon, which wanted to return Islam to a central place in the republic's life. However, political life in the republic is based much more upon regional and clan connections than upon considerations of party or platform.

15 LOCAL GOVERNMENT

In the Soviet era the republic was divided into two oblasts, or provinces, and one autonomous oblast. The region surrounding the capital, Dushanbe, was separately administered by the republic's government. At present the Rakhmonov government controls Dushanbe and Kuliab, but Gorno-Badakhshan, the very mountainous eastern half of the country, has a number of rebel and opposition groups. Opposition is also said to control much of the Kurgan-Tiube and Zeravshan regions. Uzbekistan maintains a

strong governing influence in the northern Khojent region, while Russian troops control the capital region and patrol the borders with Afghanistan and China.

16 JUDICIAL SYSTEM

The judicial system from the Soviet period remains in place. There are courts at the city, district, regional, and republic levels with a separate but parallel system of military courts. Regional and republic level courts function in an appellate capacity to the lower courts.

The system suffers from a lack of trained judges and lawyers and from pressures applied by local political factions and armed paramilitary groups.

The law requires public trials except in cases involving national security or protection of minors. There is a right to appointed counsel in criminal cases. Although the Soviet system presumed the guilt of persons brought to trial, procuracy officials now declare that defendants are presumed innocent until proven guilty.

17 ARMED FORCES
There are Uzbek, Kyrgyz, and Kazakh forces in Tajikistan, as well as two resident Russian division.

18 INTERNATIONAL COOPERATION
Tajikistan became a member of the UN on 2 March 1992. It also is a member of the CSCE, IMF, NACC, and the World Bank, and is applying for membership in other international organizations. A member of the CIS, the country is recognized by the US and EC countries. Western nations are especially concerned with the security of the country's uranium reserves. Tajikistan has especially close ties with Iran.

19 ECONOMY
Tajikistan is the poorest of the post-Soviet republics; per capita NMP is only 55% of the former USSR average. Agriculture, dominated by cotton production, is the largest of the country's economic sectors, providing 38% of NMP and 43% of total employment. Industry is poorly developed, making up just 29% of total production and 13% of employment, and involving mainly electric power generation, aluminum production, and some labor intensive processing of local and imported raw materials. Imports provide virtually all of the country's manufactured consumer needs. Deposits of nonferrous metals are significant but underdeveloped.

Wracked by conflict between rival groups vying for control of the central government, Tajikistan has also been among the economies hardest hit by sociopolitical and economic instability following the dissolution of the USSR. Already in decline by the late 1980s, NMP shrunk by 0.6% in 1990 and 8.7% in 1991. Legislation adopted in 1992 aimed at laying the groundwork for the transition to a market economy and creating conditions favorable to badly needed foreign investment. Implementation of restructuring plans, however, has been stunted by the outbreak of violent civil strife during the summer of 1992. Partial price liberalization undertaken in the former Soviet Union in 1990 and more sweeping decontrol initiated by the Tajikistan government in early 1992 have resulted in surging consumer prices. By the end of January 1992, prices were 551% higher than those of January the year before. Average monthly wages, by contrast, rose only 40% in 1991. The outbreak of open civil war in 1992 dashed most hopes for swift economic revitalization in the country.

20 INCOME
In 1992, Tajikistan's GNP was $2,723 million at current prices, or $480 per capita.

21 LABOR
Over two-thirds of the population relied on agriculture or personal services as a means of support in 1992. Violence in the Kurgan Tyube region has created serious internal displacement problems (an estimated 300,000 persons by the end of 1992).

With the demise of the Soviet Union, there is no longer the mandate for a single labor union structure. As of 1992, the Confederation of Trade Unions remained the dominant labor organization (1.6 million members), even though it no longer is subordinate to the Communist Party. In April 1990, the independent Labor Union of Private Sector Enterprises and Organizations was formed, and claims 40,000 members.

Employment in Tajikistan may legally begin at age 16, or at age 15 with local trade union permission. Children from the age of 7 often help with harvests, but their work is considered "family assistance." The 40-hour work week is standard. A minimum wage is in place, although it does not provide a decent standard of living for the worker and family. In 1991, an estimated 20% of industrial laborers worked in unhealthy or otherwise hazardous conditions.

22 AGRICULTURE
Tajik agriculture relies extensively on irrigation. About 6% of the total area is cropland, although 23% is used for permanent pastures. A network of canals expands agriculture into semidesert areas. Cotton is the major commercial crop; three irrigated valleys (Vakhsh, Kofarnihon, and Zeravshan) are the sites of most production. In 1992, about 109,000 tons of cotton were produced, down from 247,000 tons in 1991. Wheat and barley occupy over one-quarter of all cropland. Wheat production in 1992 totaled 200,000 tons; and barley, 40,000 tons. Potatoes, vegetables, and various fruits and melons are widely grown for domestic consumption.

Horticulture has been important since antiquity. Most orchards and vineyards are located in the northern valleys, where apricots, pears, plums, apples, cherries, pomegranates, figs, and nuts are grown.

23 ANIMAL HUSBANDRY
Livestock herding is a major part of Tajikistan's economy. As of 1992, the livestock included 6,000,000 chickens, 2,600,00 sheep, 1,400,000 cattle, 780,000 goats, and 100,000 pigs. Meat production in 1992 included 43,000 tons of beef, 20,000 tons of mutton, 8,000 tons of poultry, and 5,000 tons of pork. Livestock products in 1992 included milk, 475,000 tons; eggs, 18,000 tons; wool (greasy), 4,000 tons; and butter and cheese, 4,000 tons.

24 FISHING
Some fishing occurs in the upper Amu Darya River; the Kayrakkum Reservoir, and the Syrdar'ya River.

25 FORESTRY
Tajikistan's forests and woodlands occupy about 5% of the total land area. Forestry is of little commercial importance.

26 MINING
Tajikistan's mineral wealth lies in the northwestern region. Mercury and antimony are mined at the Dzhidzhikrutskiy complex north of Dushanbe; fluorospar at the Takob complex northeast of Dushanbe; arsenic, cadmium, tungsten, and lead-zinc north of the Zeravshan River; and uranium and graphite northeast of Khudzhand. Gold is mined southeast of Garm and in the Pamir Mountains. Other nonmetals mined throughout Tajikistan include salt, carbonates, quartz, dolomite, limestone, asbestos, and precious and semiprecious stones.

27 ENERGY AND POWER
More than 90% of Tajikistan's electricity production is hydropower, provided by a series of dams and reservoirs on mountain rivers. Two major hydroelectric facilities on the Vakhsh River have attracted aluminum, chemical, and other energy-intensive industries oriented toward inexpensive energy. The Qayroqqum Dam on the Syrdar'ya River in the north (which forms a reservoir known as the "Tajik Sea") has a hydroelectric station which provides energy for the Fergana Valley in Uzbekistan. Further expansion of hydroelectric power was planned, especially around Khojand, with the potential of exporting energy to Pakistan. In 1991, total installed electrical capacity was 4,575,000 kw; production of electricity that year amounted to 17,500 million kwh.

Brown coal, though declining in production, is mined in the northeast and shipped by rail to Dushanbe. Natural gas is extracted from fields in the lower Kakhsh and elsewhere. Tajikistan also has small deposits of petroleum.

28INDUSTRY

A small number of state-owned enterprises dominate Tajikistan's industrial sector although the state's role in the sector is visibly declining with privatization. By early 1992, the state accounted for only 84% of asset ownership in the industrial sector, as compared to a high of 98% in the late 1980s. One of the largest enterprises in the country is an aluminum plant at Regar, near the capital of Dushanabe, with a production potential of 500,000 tons annually, making up almost 15% of the total aluminum production capacity of the former USSR. Non-ferrous metal processing accounted for about 11% of gross industrial output in 1990. Hydroelectric installations on the Vakhsh River in central Tajikistan supply three-fourths of the country's power needs. Light industry generates the largest share of gross industrial output (roughly 45% in 1990); this subsector includes mainly cotton cleaning, silk processing, textiles production, knitted goods, footwear, sewing, tanning, and carpet making. The food industry is the second-largest contributor to gross industrial output (18% of the total), processing domestically harvested fruit, wheat, tobacco, and other agricultural products. Aside from aluminum and other processed metals, the country's small intermediate and heavy industry subsectors produce engineering goods, power transformers, cables, and agricultural equipment.

29SCIENCE AND TECHNOLOGY

The Tajik Academy of Sciences, founded in 1951, has departments of physical-mathematics and chemical sciences, earth sciences, and biology. Tajik State University has faculties of mathematics, physics, chemistry, geology, and biology. Tajik Abu-Ali Ibc-Lina State Medical Institute was founded in 1939. Tajik Agricultural Institute has 6,960 students. Tajik Polytechnic Institute is in Dushanbe.

30DOMESTIC TRADE

Although trade is still dominated by the state sector, transfer of much of the retail and wholesale trade sector into private ownership is targeted by the government. Two rounds of price liberalization lifted controls on most consumer and wholesale trade by early 1992, although subsidies and lowered ceilings have been applied to staple goods like flour, sugar, oil, bread, meat, and children's footwear. Trade on the black market has expanded significantly in the growing economic disarray since independence. Recent surveys show that black market turnover may be equivalent to about one-fourth of total official retail turnover.

31FOREIGN TRADE

International trade is dominated by transactions with former USSR republics, which account for 80–90% of all imports and exports. To diversify both the country's trade and production structure, development plans of the newly independent government placed high priority on expanding trade with neighboring countries not within the former USSR bloc, including Pakistan, China, Iran, and Afghanistan. Active trade negotiations with the latter countries and a review of transportation infrastructure needs were initiated shortly after independence. Limited trade liberalization undertaken in 1991 loosened export license requirements and increased the share of foreign currency earnings that may be reclaimed by exporting enterprises.

Until 1991, Tajikistan's trade balance with the former USSR and the rest of the world registered a chronic deficit that had been largely covered by transfer payments from Moscow. In 1991, the country registered a sudden trade surplus of R512 million, (current domestic prices) due largely to the sharp compression of imports in the wake of falling domestic demand and the disruption of traditional state-directed trading arrangements within the former USSR. Aluminum, raw cotton, and textile products presently account for about 60% of Tajikistan's exports. Energy,

intermediate industrial goods and equipment, manufactured consumer goods, and food are its principal import items. Trade with foreign countries beyond the former USSR in 1990 was dominated by Germany, the former Czechoslovakian republics, and Bulgaria. Close to 80% of foreign (non-interrepublic) exports were nonferrous metals; foreign imports were more diversified, including machinery, chemicals, light industry, food, and unprocessed agricultural products. Open civil war during 1992 disrupted many of the country's trade routes, causing severe shortages of basic items in many areas of the country.

32BALANCE OF PAYMENTS

Foreign income earnings depend highly upon cotton exports; since independence, the centrally planned economy has suffered from the effects of civil war, the severing of trade relations with other former Soviet republics, and a series of natural disasters. By the end of 1993, Tajikistan had, however, attracted investment and trade relations with Israel, Turkey, Germany, and several other countries, which could potentially boost hard currency earnings in the future.

33BANKING AND SECURITIES

The National Bank of Tajikistan is the country's bank charged with implementing a monetary policy and issuing currency. Commercial and state banks include the Bank for Foreign Investment, three large banks formed from the former Soviet state bank, and three branches from the Russian Commercial Bank.

34INSURANCE

No recent information is available.

35PUBLIC FINANCE

Revenues from domestic taxes and resources are limited; Tajikistan had the lowest per capita income of all the former Soviet republics. The external debt at the end of 1991 was an estimated $650 million.

36TAXATION

Tajikistan's maximum personal income tax rate is 40%; corporate taxes range from 25–60% with a standard rate of 30%. Also levied are a 20% value-added tax; a 10–90% excise tax; and a social security combination of 37% by employers and 1% by employees.

37CUSTOMS AND DUTIES

The government maintains a list of commodities and services subject to import licensing and quotas. There is a 28% value-added tax, and excise taxes are levied on some products.

38FOREIGN INVESTMENT

After independence, Tajikistan's government emphasized the promotion of foreign investment particularly to develop labor-intensive manufacturing industries. With ongoing civil unrest, however, few investments have flowed into the country and most foreign aid except that of Russia has been stalled.

39ECONOMIC DEVELOPMENT

Soviet development policy in Tajikistan prioritized the development of the country's agricultural and other primary resources, while capital goods and manufactured consumer goods were imported from elsewhere within the former USSR. Since the late 1970s, greater development of small food processing and consumer plants had been urged by local government officials in order to absorb more of the republic's rural labor force; however, these proposals found little favor with Soviet central planners. After independence, the government targeted the development of hydroelectric power production and a number of other industries (silk, fertilizer, fruit and vegetables, coal, nonferrous metals, and marble production), seen as particularly important for improving the country's export base.

In 1991, a "Program of Economic Stabilization and Transition to a Market Economy" was adopted by the newly independent government. In accordance with the program's principles, price liberalization, privatization measures, and fiscal reform were initiated in 1991 and 1992. The privatization program was placed under the directorship of the Committee on State Property established in 1991. Over the long term, the program aimed for the transfer of 840 enterprises into private ownership; as of early 1992, 29 had in fact been sold, mainly to employees. With some of the early privatization aims met in the industrial and service sectors by 1992, the possibility of privatizing the housing and agricultural sector came under review as well. Excise taxes and a newly instituted value-added tax were expected to become the most important sources of government revenue, supplemented by enterprise profits taxes. A new Employment Fund providing unemployment benefits, the national Pension Fund, and the Social Insurance Fund were to be financed mainly by employer contributions in order to provide a social safety net for persons at high poverty risk during the restructuring process. A monetary and credit policy program submitted for approval of the Supreme Soviet in 1992 proposed to promote the functioning of the financial sector on the basis of a market economy, increasing credit availability to the non-government sector.

The government's overthrow in the course of civil war in 1992 brought economic development to a virtual standstill in the country. With its economy in shambles, Tajikistan remains highly dependent on Russia for military aid and economic assistance. Accordingly, Tajikistan has been the only one of the Central Asian nations that has opted to stay within the ruble zone.

40 SOCIAL DEVELOPMENT

The average family size in 1989 was 6.1, and there were 5.1 divorces for 1,000 women. There were 2.8 drug-related crimes and one alcohol-related deaths per 100,000 inhabitants.

There is no formal discrimination against women in employment, education, or housing. However, women in rural areas are less likely to receive a higher education or work outside the home, and were likely to marry early.

The government's comprehensive security note for children has been threatened by civil war and economic turmoil. Children returning from Afghanistan after the war suffered from malnutrition and had high mortality rates in resettlement camps. Women are provided with 3 years' maternity leave and monthly subsidies for each child. In 1990, the fertility rate was 5.08. Approximately 28% of the budget is spent on social welfare programs.

41 HEALTH

In 1992 there were 229,000 births and an infant mortality of 65 per 1,000 live births. The general mortality rate was 7 per 1,000 inhabitants in 1993. Life expectancy was 65 years in 1992. That same year, there was 1 doctor for every 350 people, and 10.6 hospital beds per 1,000 people. Leading causes of death per 100,000 population in 1990 were: communicable diseases and maternal/perinatal causes, 182; noncommunicable diseases, 558; and injuries, 53. In 1992, there were approximately 20,000 war-related deaths. In 1990, there were 133 cases of tuberculosis per 100,000 people and, in 1992, 92% of children up to one year old had been vaccinated against diphtheria, pertussis, and tetanus. Total health care expenditures in 1990 were $532 million.

42 HOUSING

In 1989, 13.8% of all privately owned urban housing had running water, 1.6% had sewer lines, 2.5% had central heating, and 82.5% had gas available. In 1990, Tajikistan had 9.3 sq m of housing space per capita and, as of 1 January 1991, 90,000 households (or 24.6%)were on waiting lists for urban housing.

43 EDUCATION

The adult literacy rate was estimated at 97.7% (98.8% for males and 96.6% for females) in 1990. Before the country came under Soviet control in 1920, there were no state-supported schools, only Islamic ones. Since then, many schools have been built. Education is free and compulsory between the ages of 7 and 17 (for 10 years). Since 1989, there has been an increased emphasis on Tajik language, literature, and culture. In the 1989–90 school year, 65,586 students were enrolled at 10 schools of higher education including the Universities of Dushanbe and Khudzhand. In 1990, all higher level institutions had a total of 68,800 pupils.

44 LIBRARIES AND MUSEUMS

No recent information is available.

45 MEDIA

Telephone links to other former Soviet republics is by land line or microwave and to other countries through Moscow. Tajik Radio broadcasts in Russian, Tajik, Persian, and Uzbek; Tajik Television, with four channels, broadcasts in Tajik, Russian, and Uzbek. Satellite earth stations receive Orbita and INTELSAT broadcasts. According to 1990 statistics, 90% of Tajikistan's 74 newspapers were published in Tajik, and there were 48 periodicals. There are several publishing houses in Dushanbe, including educational, literary, and reference publishers.

46 ORGANIZATIONS

The Tajikistan Chamber of Commerce and the Tajikistan Industrial Association are important economic organizations. The most important mass movement in the country is the People's Front. The members of the Writers Union and intellectuals in the country formed the "Rascokbez" (Rebirth) Popular Front, an opposition movement opposed to the government of Tajikistan.

Tajikistan's Academy of Science coordinates and finances the scientific research of 19 affiliated natural sciences, social sciences, and humanity research institutions The country has one state-sponsored academic institution, the Tajik State University.

47 TOURISM, TRAVEL, AND RECREATION

Civil strife has dampened Tajikistan's potential as a tourist site, already limited by the destruction of most ancient monuments and buildings by numerous earthquakes (500 in this century alone). Visas are required for entry into Tajikistan and are obtainable upon arrival or through Russian embassies abroad. There are daily flights from Moscow to the capital city of Dushanbe.

48 FAMOUS TAJIKISTANIS

Outstanding representatives of culture and literature in Tajikistan are the Tadzhik poet Rudaki (d. 941) and the scientist and poet Avicenna (Hussayn ibn 'Abd' Addallah ibn Sine, 980?-1037), born near Bukhara. Avicenna wrote an encyclopedia of science. Pre-Soviet Tajik cultural figures include the author Abdalrauf Fitrat, who wrote *Last Judgement*, and Sadridalin Aymi, author of the novels *Slaves* and *Dokhunala*.

49 DEPENDENCIES

Tajikistan has no territories or colonies.

50 BIBLIOGRAPHY

Atkin, Muriel. *The Subtlest Battle: Islam in Soviet Tajikistan.* Philadelphia: Foreign Policy Research Institute, 1989.
Rakowska-Harmstone, Teresa. *Russia and Nationalism in Central Asia: The Case of Tadzhikstan.* Baltimore: Johns Hopkins Press, 1970.

THAILAND

Kingdom of Thailand
Prates Thai

CAPITAL: Bangkok (Krung Thep).

FLAG: The national flag, adopted in 1917, consists of five horizontal stripes. The outermost are red; those adjacent are white; the blue center stripe is twice as high as each of the other four.

ANTHEM: There are three national anthems: *Pleng Sansen Phra Barami (Anthem Eulogizing His Majesty); Pleng Chard Thai (Thai National Anthem);* and *Pleng Maha Chati (Anthem of Great Victory),* an instrumental composition.

MONETARY UNIT: The baht (B) is divided into 100 satang. There are coins of 1, 5, 10, 25, and 50 stangs and 1, 5, and 10 baht, and notes of 50 satang and 1, 5, 10, 20, 50, 60, 100, and 500 baht. B1 = $0.0396 (or $1 = B25.13).

WEIGHTS AND MEASURES: The metric system is the legal standard, but some traditional units are also used.

HOLIDAYS: New Year's Day, 1 January; Chakkri Day, 6 April; Songkran Day, mid-April; Coronation Day, 5 May; Queen's Birthday, 12 August; Chulalongkorn Day, 23 October; King's Birthday, 5 December; Constitution Day, 10 December. Movable holidays include Makabuja Day, Plowing Festival, and Visakabuja Day.

TIME: 7 PM = noon GMT.

¹LOCATION, SIZE, AND EXTENT

Comprising an area of 514,000 sq km (198,456 sq mi) in Southeast Asia, Thailand (formerly known as Siam) extends almost two-thirds down the Malay Peninsula, with a length of 1,555 km (966 mi) N–S and a width of 790 km (491 mi) E–W. Comparatively, the area occupied by Thailand is slightly more than twice the size of the state of Wyoming. It is bordered on the NE and E by Laos, on the SE by Cambodia and the Gulf of Thailand (formerly the Gulf of Siam), on the S by Malaysia, on the SW by the Andaman Sea, and on the W and NW by Myanmar, with a total boundary length of 8,082 km (5,022 mi).

Thailand's capital city, Bangkok, is located on the Gulf of Thailand coast.

²TOPOGRAPHY

Thailand may be divided into five major physical regions: the central valley, the continental highlands of the north and northwest, the northeast, the southeast coast, and the peninsula. The heartland of the nation is the central valley, fronting the Gulf of Thailand and enclosed on three sides by hills and mountains. This valley, the alluvial plain of the Chao Phraya River and of its many tributaries and distributaries, is 365 km (227 mi) from north to south and has an average width of 160–240 km (100–150 mi). On this plain, and most especially on its flat deltaland bordering the Gulf, are found Thailand's main agricultural wealth and population centers.

The continental highlands lie north and west of the central valley. They include North Thailand, surrounded on three sides by Myanmar (Burma until June 1989) and Laos, which is a region of roughly parallel mountain ranges between which the Nan, Yom, Wang, Ping, and other rivers flow southward to join and create the Chao Phraya in the central valley. In the northernmost tip, drainage is northward to the Mekong River; on the western side, drainage runs westward to the Salween in Myanmar. Most of the people of North Thailand live in small intermontane plains and

basins that are generally widenings in the major river valleys. Doi Inthanon (2,576 m/8,451 ft) is the highest point in Thailand. Along the Myanmar border from North Thailand to the peninsula is a sparsely inhabited strip of rugged mountains, deep canyons, and restricted valleys. One of the few natural gaps through this wild mountain country is Three Pagodas Pass along the Thailand-Myanmar boundary, used by the Japanese during World War II for their "death railway" (now dismantled) between Thailand and Myanmar.

The northeast, much of it often called the Khorat, is a low, undulating platform roughly 120 to 210 m (400–700 ft) above sea level in the north and west, gradually declining to about 60 m (200 ft) in the southeast. Hill and mountain ranges and scarps separate the northeast from the central valley on the west and from Cambodia on the south; its northern and much of its eastern boundaries are marked by the Mekong River. Most of the northeast is drained by the Mun River and its major tributary, the Chi, which flow eastward into the Mekong. The northeast, in the rain shadow of the Indochina Cordillera, suffers from shortage of water and from generally thin and poor soils.

The small southeast coast region faces the Gulf of Thailand and is separated from the central valley and Cambodia by hills and mountains that rise in places to over 1,500 m (5,000 ft). This is a well-watered area, and the vegetation is, for the most part, lush and tropical. Most of the people live along the narrow coastal plain and the restricted river valleys that drain southward to the Gulf.

Peninsular Thailand extends almost 960 km (600 mi) from the central valley in the north to the boundary of Malaysia in the south and is anywhere from 16 to 217 km (10–135 mi) wide between the Gulf of Thailand on the east and the Andaman Sea (Indian Ocean) and Myanmar (Burma prior to June 1989) on the west. At the Isthmus of Kra, the Peninsula itself is only 24 km (15 mi) wide. A series of north-south ridges, roughly parallel, divide the Peninsula into distinct west and east coast sections. The west coastal plain is narrow—nonexistent in many places—and the coast itself is much indented and often very swampy. The east coastal plain is much wider, up to 32 km (20 mi) in sections, and the coast is smooth, with long beach stretches and few bays. Well-watered (especially the west coast), hot, and densely forested, the Peninsula, unlike most of Thailand, lies within the humid tropical forest zone.

³CLIMATE

Thailand has a tropical climate. For much of the country there are three distinct seasons: the hot season, from March through May; the rainy or wet monsoon, June to October; and the cool season, November through February. While continental Thailand receives most of its precipitation from June through October, rain occurs at all seasons in peninsular Thailand, the largest amount along the west coast from May to October, and along the east coast from October to January. For most of Thailand the temperature rarely falls below 13°C (55°F) or rises above 35°C (95°F), with most places averaging between 24°C and 30°C (75°F and 86°F). The annual rainfall ranges from 102 cm (40 in) in the northeast to over 380 cm (150 in) in the peninsula. Bangkok has an average annual temperature of 28°C (82°F); monthly mean temperatures range from a low of around 25°C (77°F) in December to a high of around 30°C (86°F) in May, and annual rainfall is about 150 cm (59 in).

⁴FLORA AND FAUNA

Many distinctive forms of plant and animal life are found. Forestlands support hardwoods (notably teak), pine, bamboos, and betel and coconut palms; in the coastal lowlands, mangroves and rattan abound. Among the larger mammals are the bear, otter, and civet cat. Climbing animals include the gibbon and many species of monkeys. There are also sheep, goats, oxen, single-horned rhinoceroses, deer, tapirs, wild cattle, wild hogs, and snakes. About 1,000 varieties of birds are indigenous, and crocodiles, lizards, and turtles are numerous. Fish abound in the rivers and coastal waters.

⁵ENVIRONMENT

The Promotion and Enhancement of Environmental Quality Act of 1975 charges the National Environment Board with coordination of environmental protection programs in Thailand. The nation's water supply is at risk due to contamination by industry, farming activity, sewage, and salt water, especially in the Bangkok area. Thailand has 26.3 cu mi of water. Ninety percent is used for farming activities and 6% for industrial purposes. Thirty-three percent of the nation's city dwellers and 15% of the rural dwellers do not have pure water. Thailand's cities produce 2.5 million tons of solid waste per year. Industry is responsible for producing 2 million tons of toxic pollutants annually. Watershed regions, undergoing rapid deforestation as a result of increased cultivation of upland areas, have been targeted for protection in the fourth and fifth national plans; overexploitation and pollution of freshwater and marine fisheries have yet to be remedied. Land use in urban areas is regulated by the City Planning Act of 1975, the Control of Construction of Buildings Act of 1936, and the 1960 Act for Cleanliness and Orderliness of the Country. Parts of Bangkok were reportedly sinking at a rate of 10 cm (4 in) a year because of depletion of the water table. Urban air and noise pollution was also severe, largely as a result of increasing automobile traffic. Thailand contributes 1.4% of the world's total gas emissions.

Wildlife is partially protected under the Wild Animals Preservation and Protection Act of 1960, but species have been depleted through illegal hunting and trapping. In 1994, 26 of the nation's mammal species and 34 bird species are endangered. Sixty-eight types of plants are also endangered. As of 1987, endangered species in Thailand included the pileated gibbon, tiger, Asian ele-

phant, Malayan tapir, Sumatran rhinoceros, Fea's muntjac, Thailand brow-antlered deer, kouprey, green turtle, hawksbill turtle, olive ridley, leatherback, river terrapin, estuarine crocodile, Siamese crocodile, and false gavial. The Javan rhinoceros is extinct.

⁶POPULATION

The 1990 census recorded a population of 56,303,273. A population of 61,202,000 was projected for the year 2000, assuming a crude birthrate of 17.4 per 1,000 population and a death rate of 5.6 for the period of 1995–2000. Average density in 1990 was 100 per sq km of land (284 per sq mi), but there are great regional variations in density.

Most Thais (about 75% in 1995) live in rural areas. Bangkok is the single major urban area. Metropolitan Bangkok (including suburbs and satellite towns) had a population of 546,937 in 1990. Outside of Bangkok, most major cities are provincial capitals, each generally centered in a changwat (province or county) with the same name as the city.

⁷MIGRATION

Immigration to Thailand, except for the Chinese, has traditionally been comparatively small. The decade of the 1920s was a period of large-scale Chinese immigration of 70,000 to 140,000 a year. Strict immigration regulations have all but stopped the legal flow of Chinese into the country, but during the Franco-Indochinese war some 45,000 Vietnamese refugees settled in Thailand. An immigration quota, introduced in 1947, now limits migration from any one country to 100 persons annually. In 1990, there were only 287,105 registered aliens, of whom 250,043 were Chinese.

As of December 1992, the UN estimated that 63,600 refugees were living in Thailand; these represented part of the flood of over 4 million refugees who had left Laos, Cambodia, and Viet-Nam since the 1970s. All of the 370,000 Cambodians on the Thai–Cambodian border were repatriated during 1992–93. In 1986, the Thai government began forcibly repatriating many refugees from Laos. The Lao refugee camps were to be closed by the end of 1995.

⁸ETHNIC GROUPS

Thailand contains more than 30 ethnic groups varying in history, language, religion, appearance, and patterns of livelihood. However, the Thai, akin to the Lao of Laos, the Shan of Myanmar (Burma prior to June 1989), and the Thai groupings of southern China, comprise about 84% of the total population of Thailand. The Thai may be divided into three major groups and three minor groups. Major groups are the Central Thai (Siamese) of the Central Valley; the Eastern Thai (Lao) of the Northeast (Khorat); the Northern Thai (Lao) of North Thailand; and the Southern Thain (Chao Pak Thai) of peninsular Thailand. Minor groups are the Phuthai of northeastern Khorat, the Shan of the far northwestern corner of northern Thailand, and the Lue in the northeastern section of northern Thailand. The several branches of Thai are united by a common language.

Major ethnic minorities are the Chinese (about 11%), engaged in business and commerce throughout the country; Malays (3–4%), in the southern peninsula near the border and, to a lesser extent, along the southeast coast; Khmers (1%), all along the Cambodian border from the Mekong to the Gulf of Thailand; and Vietnamese or Annamese, in the southern Khorat and on the southeast coast. Small numbers of residents from India, Europe, and the US live mainly in urban areas. Principal tribal groups, mainly hill peoples, include the Kui and Kaleung, in the northeast; the Mons, living mainly on the peninsula along the Burmese border; and the Karens, living along the northern Burmese border. There are, in addition, some 20 other minority groups, including the Akha, Musso, Meo, Kamuk, Tin, Lawa, and So; most of these peoples, primitive and small in number, live by shifting cultivation in rugged, isolated mountain or dense forest terrain.

9LANGUAGES

The Thai language, with northern, eastern, central (Bangkok or official Thai), and southern dialects, all distantly related to Chinese, prevails throughout the country. Thai, written in a distinctive alphabet, is thought to be part of the Sino-Tibetan language family, although links to Indian languages are also evident. The Thai dialects for the most part are mutually intelligible only with difficulty. Although the ethnic minorities (including the Malays) generally speak their own languages, Thai is widely understood. The Chinese population is largely bilingual. All official documents are in the central Thai language and script, although English, taught in many secondary schools and colleges, is also used in official and commercial circles.

10RELIGIONS

Hinayana Buddhism is the state religion of Thailand; only Buddhists are employed by the government, and the Thai monarch is legally required to be a Buddhist. Buddhism was the religion of an estimated 95% of the population in 1993. Although virtually all Thai are nominally Buddhists, the dominant form of religion in Thailand might be described as a spirit worship overlaid or mixed in varying degrees with Buddhist and Brahman beliefs imported from India. About 4% of the population, including the Malay ethnic minority, are Muslim. Among the other ethnic minorities, the Chinese practice a traditional mixture of Mahayana Buddhism, Taoism, Confucianism, and ancestor worship. Most Vietnamese are Mahayana Buddhists, and most Indians are Hindus. Christians have been active in Thailand since the 17th century, and there were an estimated 305,000 in 1993. There are also small Muslim and Bahai communities.

11TRANSPORTATION

Thailand's transportation system is not fully developed, but it is growing rapidly. Owned and operated by the government, the railways, consisting in 1991 of 3,940 km (2,448 mi) of primarily meter-gauge track, radiate from Bangkok to Malaysia in the south, to the Cambodian border in the east, to Ubon Ratchathani and Nong Khai in the northeast, and to Chiang Mai in the north.

The highway system, significantly expanded during the 1960s and 1970s, serves many areas inaccessible to railway. In 1991 there were 44,534 km (27,673 mi) of highway, including 28,016 km (17,409 mi) of paved, 5,132 km (3,189 mi) of earth surface, and 11,386 km (7,075 mi) of road under development. Modern two-lane highways now connect Bangkok with the rest of the country. In 1991, registered motor vehicles totaled 2,727,509, including 825,072 passenger cars.

Waterways, both river and canal, are Thailand's most important means of inland transport; they carry much of the nation's bulk freight over a network of some 4,000 km (2,500 mi). The Chao Phraya River with its tributaries is the main traffic artery, and Bangkok is its focal point. The modern port of Bangkok at Klong Toey is the chief port for international shipping. Lying some 40 km (25 mi) inland from the sea, its harbor is navigable for vessels up to 10,000 tons, but constant dredging of the Chao Phraya is necessary. To relieve the congestion at Klong Toey, a new modern port was being developed at Sattahip, a former US naval base, and new seaports at Laem Chabang and Hap Ta Phut. Phuket Harbor in southern Thailand has been improved to accommodate 15,000-ton cargo ships. An extensive shipping service also exists along the Gulf of Thailand, and a small Thai merchant fleet plies between local and neighboring ports. In 1991 there were 154 oceangoing vessels of more than 1,000 gross tons in the Thai merchant fleet (up from only 80 in 1986), including 106 freighters and 43 tankers.

LOCATION: 97° to 106°E; 6° to 21°N. **BOUNDARY LENGTHS:** Laos, 1,754 km (1,090 mi); Cambodia, 803 km (499 mi); Gulf of Thailand coastline, 1,875 km (1,165 mi); Malaysia, 576 km (358 mi); Andaman Sea coastline, 740 km (460 mi); Myanmar, 1,799 km (1,118 mi). **TERRITORIAL SEA LIMIT:** 12 mi.

Since the end of World War II, Bangkok has become an important center of international aviation; Don Muang, a modern airfield outside Bangkok, and Chiang Mai Airport are Thailand's two international air terminals. There is a total of 129 airfields, 56 airports with permanent-surface runways. The government-owned Thai Airways International and Thai Airways Co. handle international and domestic air traffic, respectively. Scheduled airline traffic performed in 1992 included 20,508 million passenger-km and 926 million ton-km of freight.

12HISTORY

Archaeological excavations in the 1970s in Ban Chiang in northeastern Thailand have yielded traces of a Bronze Age people, dating as far back as 3600 BC and thus predating Bronze cultures in China and the Middle East. The technical achievements of the Ban Chiang society, as surmised from archaeological evidence, indicate the existence of a settled agrarian people with an advanced knowledge of bronze and iron metallurgy. Moreover, the skills indicated in their pottery, housing, and printing of silk textiles are thought to be the product of at least 2,000 years of prior development—a finding that challenges previous concepts of incipient civilization and technology, and Southeast Asia's role in it.

The Thai, descendants of ancient Pamir plateau stock, are racially related to the Chinese and were one of the major peoples that migrated from southern China to mainland Southeast Asia. While in southern China, the Thai had created the powerful Nan-Chao kingdom, but continued pressure from the Chinese and the Tibetans and final destruction by Kublai Khan in 1253 forced the Thai southward across the mountain passes into Southeast Asia. After entering the valley of the Chao Phraya River, they defeated and dispersed the Khmer settlers, ancestors of the Cambodians, and established the kingdom of Thailand.

By the mid-14th century, the Thai had expanded and centralized their kingdom at the expense of the Lao, Burmese, and Cambodians. Although Thailand had had trading contacts with the Dutch and Portuguese in the 16th century and with the French and British in the 17th, it remained a feudal state with a powerful court of nobles. During the reigns of Mongkut (1851–68) and his son Chulalongkorn (1868–1910), however, Thailand emerged from feudalism and entered the modern world. A cabinet of foreign advisers was formed; commercial treaties of friendship were signed with the British (1855) and with the US and France (1856); the power of nobles was curtailed, slavery abolished, and many court practices, such as prostration in the royal presence, were ended. Despite the progressive policies of Mongkut and Chulalongkorn, the Thai government continued as an absolute monarchy. In 1932, however, a bloodless revolution of Westernized intellectuals led to a constitutional monarchy. Since that time, Thailand has had several constitutions, changes of government, and palace and barracks revolutions. With the government in a state of flux, political parties have tended to cluster around strong personalities rather than political programs.

From 1932 through the 1940s, political life in Thailand centered around Pridi Banomyong and Marshal Phibul Songgram and thereafter around Marshal Sarit Thanarat, until his death in 1963. Sarit's handpicked heir, Marshal Thanom Kittikachorn, subsequently emerged as the country's political leader.

At the start of World War II, Thailand, after annexing Burmese and Malayan territories, signed an alliance with Japan and declared war on the US and the UK. After the war, however, Thailand became an ally of the US through their common membership in the Southeast Asia Treaty Organization (SEATO), as well as through various bilateral treaties and agreements. In January 1965, China announced the formation of the Thailand Patriotic Front, whose purpose was "to strive for the national independence" of Thailand. A limited insurgency subsequently developed

in the North and Northeast, growing in intensity in the late 1960s and early 1970s as the Southeast Asian conflict raged on Thailand's northern and northeastern borders.

As a SEATO member, Thailand took a direct role in the Viet Nam war by supplying a small number of troops in support of the Republic of Viet-Nam (RVN) government and, more important, by granting US forces the use of air bases in Thailand for massive bombing sorties against the Democratic Republic of Viet-Nam and the Vietcong. US forces stationed in Thailand increased to as many as 25,000 by the end of 1972. With the termination of the direct US combat role in Viet-Nam in early 1973, the US began a gradual withdrawal of military personnel from Thailand. In March 1976, the Thai government ordered the US to close its remaining military installations in the country and to remove all but a few military aid personnel by July. Communist insurgency continued, with sporadic armed attacks on the government in remote northeastern border provinces.

Internally, Thailand weathered a series of political upheavals in the 1970s. In November 1971, Marshal Thanom, who had been reconfirmed as prime minister in the 1969 general elections, led a bloodless military coup that abrogated the constitution and imposed a state of martial law. An interim constitution that worked to preserve rule by the military was promulgated in December 1972. During 1973, student and labor groups began agitating for a more representational base in Thai government. By early October, demonstrations erupted into riots, and on 14 October, Marshal Thanom resigned and quit the country. King Bhumibol Adulyadej stepped into the vacuum and named a national legislative assembly to draft a new constitution. On 7 October 1974, the new constitution—the tenth such document to be promulgated in Thailand since 1932—came into effect. On 26 January 1975, Thailand held its first truly open parliamentary elections since 1957. Some 42 parties competed in the balloting, which produced a coalition government under Seni Pramoj. In March 1975, Seni's government was forced to resign on a no-confidence vote; a right-wing coalition government led by Kukrit Pramoj (Seni's brother) then assumed control, but it was forced to resign in January 1976. Elections held in April restored Seni Pramoj to power at the head of a four-party coalition, but when civil disorder again erupted among students in Bangkok, he was overthrown by the military. Martial law was declared, strikes and political parties banned, and yet another constitution put into effect. Promulgation of a subsequent constitution in December 1978 paved the way for elections in 1979, 1983, and 1986. On 9 September 1985, an abortive military coup was put down within several hours. It was the 16th coup or attempt at a coup since 1932. Gen. Prem Tinsulanonda was appointed for a third term as prime minister following the 1986 elections.

Contributing to the nation's political instability was the activity of Communist insurgents in border areas and the presence of large numbers of refugees from Laos and Kampuchea (known as Cambodia until 1976 and again after 1989). In 1979, the government estimated the number of insurgents at 10,000. The insurgents were organized by the Communist Party of Thailand, whose active military arm was the Thai People's Liberation Army. Insurgents operating during the mid-1970s from safe havens in Laos and Kampuchea (known as Cambodia until 1976 and again from 1989). However, following the Vietnamese victory in Kampuchea in January 1979, thousands of insurgents took advantage of a government offer of amnesty and surrendered to Thai security forces. Others were apprehended. By the beginning of 1986, there were fewer than 1,000 active Communist insurgents, according to government estimates.

During 1985 and 1986 the replacement of cabinet ministers effected a transition to the Progress Party. A parliamentary defeat over proposed vehicle tax legislation resulted in the dissolution of the House of Representatives. In July 1986 a general election for an enlarged house was held. A coalition government was formed and Gen. Prem accepted the position of prime minister. Opposition parties accused his government of corruption and mismanagement. Additional dissent arose over proposed copyright legislation aimed at controlling counterfeiting of Western products and intellectual property. Gen. Prem dissolved the House of Representatives and announced a general election. This tactic avoided a motion of "no confidence" against the government.

In the July 1988 election, the Chart Thai gained the largest number of seats. Although its leader, Gen. Chatichai Choonhavan, declared his unsuitability for prime minister, he was appointed nonetheless. Gen. Chatichai took an active role in foreign affairs and made bold initiatives to improve relations with Laos, Viet Nam, and Cambodia. His support declined as his preoccupation with foreign affairs was considered a detriment to his handling of domestic issues, especially regarding government response in the aftermath of a devastating typhoon in November 1989. In a move to allay military dissatisfaction and retain loyalty Gen. Chatichai permitted Gen. Chaovalit unrestricted responsibility for military appointments. Leaders of the powerful Class 5 group (Chulachomklao Military Academy 1958) were promoted, and the most influential member of Class 5, Gen. Suchinda Kraprayoon, was appointed commander-in-chief, subsequent to Gen. Chaovalit's resignation.

Accusations of corruption were again raised, but a motion of "no confidence" in the government was rejected by the House of Representatives in July 1990. Gen. Chaovalit resigned as deputy director of the internal security operations command and formed the New Aspiration Party to contest the next election. In December 1990, Gen. Chatichai resigned as prime minister, only to be reappointed the next day, enabling him to form a new coalition government. In a bloodless military coup the National Peace Keeping Council (NPKC) ousted Gen. Chatichai's government on 23 February 1991 on the grounds of corruption. Martial law was declared by the NPKC, the constitution was abrogated, and the Government was dissolved. An interim constitution approved by the king was published in March 1991. A former diplomat and business executive, Anand Panyarachun, was appointed prime minister. A draft constitution presented in November, still a subject of public protest, was approved on 7 December 1991. The general election of 22 March 1992 and the failure of Narong Wongwan, head of Samakkhi Tham, to qualify for premiership due to drug trafficking charges, paved the way for the appointment of Gen. Suchinda as prime minister, despite the threat of public unrest.

In May 1992, a call for the resignation of Gen. Suchinda and amendment of the constitution was made by Maj. Gen. Chamlong at a rally attended by 100,000 demonstrators. Maj. Gen. Chamlong pledged that he would fast until death, but gave the government a one-week grace period to respond by amending the constitution to prevent the appointment of an unelected prime minister. When it appeared that the government might renege on this agreement, the peaceful demonstrations resumed. On 17 May 1992, about 150,000 demonstrators met at Sanam Luang parade ground in central Bangkok. Leaders called for the demonstrators to walk toward Government House down Ratchadamnoen Avenue. The conditions were thus set for confrontation, since the demonstrator's plan was considered threatening by the police, and in fact, some of the demonstrators were looking for a confrontation. Demonstrators broke through roadblocks were set up by the police, and set fire to vehicles and a nearby police station. At 4 AM on 18 May the demonstrators were counterattacked with armored vehicles and machine guns. Chamlong was arrested, over 100 demonstrators were killed, and several thousands were detained. Four days of violence ended with intervention by the king. On 24 May, Gen. Suchinda resigned after amnesty was guaranteed to the military who had participated in quelling the

demonstrations. On 10 June, the National Assembly approved the constitutional amendments. The general election took place on 13 September 1992, and Chuan Leekpai, leader of the winning Democratic Party was approved as prime minister.

Chuan's policies have been based on four goals: to eradicate corrupt practices, to reduce the powers of the appointed Senate, to decentralize government from Bangkok to the provinces, and to enhance rural development. In 1993 and 1994, Chuan's government faced "no confidence" motions in parliament, and in both instances emerged stronger. In 1994, Chamlong and Palang Dharma became more assertive in demands for constitutional reform, decentralization of state power, and progress in solving Bangkok's traffic problems.

Once-sacred religious institutions have come under increasing censure in Thailand. In 1993, (Monk) Phra Chamroon Panchan, abbot of Tham Krabok monastery north of Bangkok was accused by Ventiane of giving sanctuary to ethnic Lao and others who support rebel groups in Laos. Although not a qualified medical practitioner or a mainstream member of Thai Buddhist sangha, Chamroon's monastery is dedicated to the work of curing drug addicts—he claims a 70% cure rate from opium addiction. There are 13,000 Hmong at the monastery. In 1993 the government's Religious Affairs Department assembled a special 200-member monk police force to monitor behavior.

Unresolved scandals involve the murders of four Saudi diplomats and a Saudi businessman occurring in 1989–90, and the theft of jewels by a Thai worker from a palace in Saudi Arabia. The Saudis suspect police culpability in these cases, and have reduced the embassy staff from fourteen to four.

Refugees and "displaced people" remain a problem for Thailand. In 1994, there were 43,939 immigrants remaining in Thailand from Indochina: 32,221 Lao (of whom 28,000 are hill tribe people); 11,603 Vietnamese; and 115 Cambodians. Vietnamese are at large in the northeast. Illegal Myanmar (Burmese) immigrants number 343,235. Prior to 1976, 47,735 came for political reasons; after 1976, 33,000 immigrated for economic reasons; since 1984, 60,000 arrived fleeing border fighting, and another 200,000 illegal workers and 2,500 students seeking political sanctuary.

13GOVERNMENT

Thailand has been a constitutional monarchy since 1932. The present king is Bhumibol Adulyadej, who succeeded to the monarchy in 1946 and was formally invested as Rama IX on 5 May 1950. Until 1958, Thailand was governed under a constitution that was originally promulgated in December 1932. In October 1958, however, the constitution was suspended, and three months later the king proclaimed an interim basic law providing for a constituent assembly to draft a new constitution. Nine years in the making, a new constitution was promulgated in June 1968, and the first elections under it were held in 1969. The document was overturned in November 1971, however, by the man who was elected under it, Marshal Thanom Kittikachorn.

A period of martial law under a National Executive Council ensued, with the military continuing in power by virtue of an interim constitution of December 1972. A new constitution was promulgated in 1974, but in the face of civil disorder, it was suspended and replaced by martial law in 1976. The 1976 constitution was abrogated after an October 1977 coup; under an interim constitution, the king empowered a legislative assembly to draft a new governing document. This constitution, approved by the legislature on 18 December 1978, lifted the ban on political parties and eased some of the martial law provisions imposed in 1976. It provided for a parliamentary form of government, headed by the king as head of state, chief of the armed forces, and upholder of Buddhism and of all religions; he has the power to declare a state of emergency and rule by decree. The 1978 constitution also provided for a bicameral legislature consisting of a Senate appointed by the king and a House of Representatives elected by universal suffrage. In 1986, the House had 347 members and the Senate, 261. The head of government is the prime minister, nominated by the legislature and formally appointed by the king. The prime minister personally selects the cabinet.

On 23 February 1991, the National Peacekeeping Council (NPKC), led by the supreme commander of the Royal Thai Armed Forces, Gen. Sundhara Kongsompong, took over the administration of the country. On 9 December 1991, the NPKC promulgated a new constitution. It provided for a National Assembly comprised of elected representatives and an appointed Senate, and a cabinet headed by an appointed prime minister. This charter was sympathetic to the needs of the military and gave the junta power over the Senate. Protests that resulted in the deaths of pro-democracy demonstrators between 17–20 May 1992 quickly led to a constitutional amendment to provide for an elected prime minister and to curb some of the appointed Senate's power. This constitutional amendment was approved by the National Assembly on 10 June 1992 and required the prime minister to be a member of the House of Representatives. In addition, the revised constitution significantly cut back the powers of the Senate by ruling that the speaker of the lower House will be president of the Parliament (previously it was the speaker of the Senate). The Senate is also barred from initiating, or taking part in, "no-confidence" motions. New elections were held on 13 September 1992.

Efforts to amend the constitution again came before Parliament in April 1994, and the seven government-sponsored amendments were defeated. These amendments were designed to reform Thailand's political structure by expanding the lower House membership so that each MP represented 150,000 people; reducing the voting age from 20 to 18; appointing the leader of an opposition party with at least one fifth of the lower House membership as the opposition leader; reducing the number of candidates each party is required to field in a general election; requiring cabinet ministers to answer questions in parliament; giving wider powers to House committees; and establishing an administrative court to hear public complaints about abuse by government officials. These amendments have been thrown out and, as of late 1994, an opposition draft of amendments was still on table. Pro-democracy circles are concerned that this opposition draft is based on an earlier constitution which allowed a non-elected politician to become prime minister. In defiance of their coalition partners, the Palang Dharma (PD) group of legislators in July 1994 set up a parliamentary committee to draft a new constitution. Democrats and three other government parties declined to support the PD measure. The PD continues to demand decentralization of state power, constitutional reform, and progress.

14 POLITICAL PARTIES

Constitutional government in Thailand has been hindered by traditional public apathy, and political parties generally have been formed by military personalities rather than around political issues and programs. Military leader Phibul Songgram, who became prime minister in 1938, did not favor political parties. The pro-Japanese Phibul's immediate postwar successor, Pridi Banomyong, encouraged the growth of parties, but these were generally ineffective, primarily because of Thai inexperience with such institutions. The return of Phibul and the other military leaders to power in 1947 by means of a coup was followed by the banning of parties. In a move designed to undercut a growing threat from other soldiers, Phibul reinstated political parties in 1955, and such parties participated in the elections of 1957. A new coup, led by Marshal Sarit Thanarat, deposed Phibul in 1957, and political parties were again banned. Following the promulgation of a new constitution in June 1968, parties were again

legalized and hotly contested the 1969 parliamentary elections. Prime Minister Thanom Kittikachorn's United Thai People's Party won a plurality (76) of the 219 seats in the House of Representatives, giving it a majority in partnership with 72 "independents" supported by Deputy Premier (and army chief) Praphas Charusathien. The Democrat Party, led by civilian politician Seni Pramoj, won 56 seats, becoming the chief opposition party. Following Marshal Thanom's 1971 coup, political activity again subsided in favor of the military. The collapse of military rule in October 1973 led to a resurgence of civilian political groups. In the parliamentary elections of 26 January 1975, 269 seats in the House of Representatives were contested by 2,193 candidates from 42 political parties. Voter apathy remained a problem, however, as only 47% of the electorate (33% in Bangkok) took part. The conservative Bangkok-based Democrat Party emerged with a meager plurality of 72 seats, thereby failing to secure a majority coalition. On 13 March, Kukrit Pramoj, leader of the Social Action Party (SAP), which held 18 seats, was elected prime minister in a controversial vote; he formed a ruling right-wing coalition with the Social Justice Party (45 seats), the Chat Thai (28 seats), and four smaller groups. The coalition collapsed in January 1975, and in new elections held on 4 April, Seni Pramoj gained the premiership.

In the wake of the 1976 coup, massive arrests were made of liberal and leftist political elements; political parties were banned, and martial law instituted. Political activity was restored and martial rule partially relaxed under the 1978 constitution. Elections held on 22 April 1979 gave no party a clear majority. The SAP won a plurality of 82 seats, and the Thai Nation Party finished second with 38. Gen. Prem Tinsulanonda, who became prime minister in March 1980, formed a new coalition government after the April 1983 elections, in which the SAP emerged with a plurality of 92 seats. Several days after the elections, the Thai Nation Party, which had won 73 seats, subsumed the Siam Democratic Party, which controlled 18. In subsequent elections on 27 July 1986, the Bangkok-based Democrat Party improved its position greatly, winning 100 seats. The Thai Nation Party won 63, and the SAP, 51. These three parties, along with the small Rassadorn—or People's—Party which won 18 seats, formed a new coalition, but with Gen. Prem again as prime minister. The election campaign and balloting were marred by scattered incidents of violence.

In the bloodless military coup of 23 February 1991 by the National Peacekeeping Council (NPKC), Gen. Chatichai's government was turned out. The NPKC promulgated a provisional constitution, and after a brief period paved the way for a civilian interim government headed by Anand Panyarachun. A general election was held 22 March 1992, with 15 parties contesting 360 seats with 2,185 candidates. Persistent vote-buying marred an election in which 59.2% of the electorate voted. Results were: Samakkhi Tham (79), Chart Thai (74), New Aspiration Party (72), DP (44), and Palang Dharma (41). A coalition government controlling 195 seats in the House of Representatives was comprised of Samakkhi Tham, Chart Thai, Pracjakorn Thai, the SAP and Rassadorn parties. Narong Wongman was proposed as prime minister until the US made allegations of Narong's involvement in illegal drug trafficking. In April 1992 Gen. Suchinda was named prime minister. His appointment as an unelected prime minister met with immediate protest. Agreement was reached to amend the Constitution to prevent an unelected prime minister, but an apparent change of mind by the government resulted in violent rioting. Suchinda resigned and constitutional amendments were approved by parliament on 10 June. The National Democratic Front, four parties that had opposed the military government, the DP, New Aspiration Party, Palanf Dharma, and Ekkaparb, formed an alliance to contest the elections called for in September 1992.

In the 13 September 1992 general election 12 parties contesting 360 seats in the House of Representatives. Voter turnout was 62.1%. Election results were: the DP (79), Chart Thai (77), Chart Pattana (60), New Aspiration Party (51), SAP (22). The DP formed a coalition party with Palang Dharma (47 seats) and Ekkaparb for control of 185 of the 360 seats. The SAP was invited to join the coalition. The leader of the DP, Chuan Leekpai, was named prime minister.

As of 1994, Thai political parties and leaders were: Democrat Party (DP), Chuan Leekpai; Thai National Party (TNP or Chart Thai Party), Praman Adireksan; National Development Party, (NDP or Chart Phattan), Chatichai Coonhavan; New Aspiration Party, Gen. Chavalit Yongchaiyut; Phalang Tham (Palang Dharma), Bunchu Rotchanasatien (formed by Chamlong Srimuang); Social Action Party (SAP), Montri Phongphanit; Liberal Democratic Party (LDP or Seri Tham), Athit Uraurat; Solidarity Party (SP), Uthai Phimchaichon; Mass Party (Muanchon), Pol. Cpt. Choem Yubamrung; Thai Citizen's Party (Prachakon Thai), Samak Sunthonwet; People's Party (Ratsadon), Chaiphak Siriwat; People's Force Party (Phalang Prachachon), Col. Sophon Hanchareon. Opposition parties were Chart Thai, Chart Pattana, Palang Dharma, Ekkaparb (Ruam Thai, Community Action Party, Prachachon Party, and the Progressive Party), the New Aspiration Party, and the DP. The National Democratic Front is a colaition made up of the DP, the New Aspiration Party, Palang Dharma, and Ekkaparb.

15 LOCAL GOVERNMENT

Thailand is divided into 72 administrative provinces (changwats), each under the control of an appointed governor responsible to the Ministry of the Interior. The Bangkok Metropolitan Administration has an elected governor and is divided into 24 districts. Provincial governors are appointed by the Interior Ministry and have the power to coordinate local administration. Provincial councils, comprising 24 elected members, have limited authority in local affairs. Provinces are subdivided into districts (amphoes), communes (tambons), and villages (mubans). Districts are administered by state-appointed district officers (nai amphoes). Municipality and district councils are elected, but have little authority. Villages have locally elected headmen (puyaibans), directly responsible to their governor and district officer. Governments exist for cities (nakhorns), towns (muangs), and hamlets (tambols). In 1994, the election of provincial governors became a political issue championed by the Palang Dharma party in a general pro-democracy effort to decentralize authority away from Bangkok.

16 JUDICIAL SYSTEM

The 1978 constitution provided for an independent judiciary. Courts of the first instance, juvenile courts, and magistrate's courts exist in Bangkok and in each of the provincial capitals. A court of appeal, sitting in Bangkok, hears cases for the entire kingdom. The Supreme Court, also in Bangkok, consists of at least three judges and decides only on points of law. Judges in Thailand are appointed (and removed) by the king. All appointments are subject to initial approval by a judicial commission. There is no trial by jury in Thailand.

The constitution also provided for establishment of a constitutional tribunal to adjudicate disputes among the courts. Military courts deal primarily with military justice, but have broader jurisdiction when martial law is in force. There is no appeal of decisions by military courts. Defendants in ordinary criminal courts are afforded a wide range of procedural due process protections. Although there is no right to counsel during the investigative phase of cases, detainees are afforded access to counsel during trial.

Islamic courts hear civil cases concerning members of the Muslim minority.

17 ARMED FORCES

The armed forces are organized as 283,000 active duty personnel (80,000 conscripts) and 500,000 reservists. Males between the ages of 21 and 30 are liable for two years of active military duty and 23 years of various kinds of reserve status. The army, organized into 14 divisions and 33 smaller units, numbered 190,000 personnel in 1993. The air force, reorganized with US assistance, consisted of 43,000 personnel with 166 combat aircraft, plus transport, training, and helicopter rescue units. The navy had 50,000 personnel (including 20,000 marines) and was equipped with 8 frigates, 65 patrol and coastal combatants, and 30 other vessels. In addition, a paramilitary volunteer defense corps of 61,000 was available for the maintenance of national security, along with other paramilitary police forces that number 90,000. Foreign military assistance in 1986–91 amounted to $1.8 billion, more than half from the US. In 1992, Thailand spent $2.7 billion on defense, or 3% of gross domestic product.

18 INTERNATIONAL COOPERATION

Thailand, a member of the UN since 16 December 1946, is the headquarters for ESCAP and belongs to all the nonregional specialized agencies except WIPO. Bangkok has served as regional headquarters for several other UN agencies, and for the former Southeast Asia Treaty Organization (SEATO). Thailand is identified more closely than most Asian countries with the Western nations largely because of its alliances with the US. The country is a member of the Asian Development Bank, Asian and Pacific Council, ASEAN, the Association of Natural Rubber Producing Countries, G-77, and the International Tin Council. In November 1982, Thailand became a member of GATT, and is a signatory of the Law of the Sea.

Thailand is a participant in the Colombo Plan, and it receives economic aid from UN agencies for agricultural, industrial, and health projects. US assistance has been a vital factor in Thailand's economic development since World War II. Although never engaged in direct combat on Thai soil, the US has been Thailand's paramount military ally in recent decades, supplying funds, equipment, advisers, and large-scale training programs for personnel. On order of the Seni government, the US military presence in Thailand was almost completely withdrawn by mid-1976, although some US assistance, including military aid, continued.

Prior to the military and political upheavals of the 1970s, Kampuchea (known as Cambodia until 1976 and again in 1989), Laos, Thailand, and the RVN had been cooperating on the development of the lower Mekong Basin in terms of hydroelectric power, irrigation, navigation improvement, and flood control. As of the mid-1980s, however, the prospect for continued cooperation in the area appeared in doubt.

19 ECONOMY

Traditionally agriculture and allied sectors dominated the Thai economy, employing some 75% of the work force and producing about 25% of the GNP. In 1986 agricultural activity accounted for 16.7% of GDP and 65% of the labour force. By 1992 agriculture accounted for 12% of GDP and 60% of the labor force. Although rice remains the major crop, other cash crops have become increasingly important. In addition to new crops introduced—corn and cassava (tapioca)—strong gains have been recorded in recent decades by rubber, cotton, sugarcane, and fruits and vegetables. The manufacturing sector is increasingly diversified. In 1992 the manufacturing sector accounted for 27% of GDP surpassing the agricultural sector (11%) as the leading sector of the economy. High growth in the construction sector slowed from 22.7% in 1990 to about 16% in 1991. Industrial production of computers and electronics, garments and footwear, furniture and wood products, canned foods, gems and jewelry, toys and plastic products, is increasing rapidly.

Significant air and water pollution accompanied Thailand's rapid industrialization. Exports have continued to increase rapidly, particularly for manufactured items. The new deep-water port of Laem Chabang, part of the Eastern Seaboard Development Plan, opened in the 1990s. In 1992, merchandise exports grew by over 14%. The progressive diversification of Thai exports is underscored by the reduction in the share of exports of four traditional commodities—rice, rubber, tin, and teak—from some 90% prior to 1950 to around 25% in 1985. Many light industries flourish, such as textiles, rice milling, sugar refining, and native handicrafts. Economic growth is still hampered by shortages of skilled personnel and infrastructure bottlenecks. Efforts to promote industrial decentralization to areas outside of Bangkok are underway as overtaxed public works and diminishing water supplies cause concern. Thailand's competitiveness relative to other countries in Southeast Asia diminishes as wage rates rise.

From 1988–90, tourism was one of the country's largest foreign exchange earners. In 1992, tourism, at US$4.4 billion, topped the list of the country's total exports. As hotels increased rates by 41% in 1989, Bangkok, Pattaya, and Phuket became the most expensive destinations in Southeast Asia. In 1992, Thailand had 190,000 hotel rooms with another 12,700 rooms expected to be added by the end of 1994. In 1992, the combination of the military coup and Gulf War, high incidence of AIDS (600,000 Thais are HIV-positive), horrendous traffic jams and pollution of Bangkok, and unfair treatment of foreign visitors (foreigners charged double the rates) combined to yield a drop in tourist arrivals. Tourism from China is increasing, however.

The GDP grew at an average annual rate of 8.4% in 1960–70, but slowed to 7.2% in the following decade and to an average of 6.6% under the 1982–86 five-year plan. Thailand experienced a five year economic boom from 1987 to 1992, with GDP growth at 7.8%. Since then trouble has loomed on several fronts. The military coup of February 1991 and the political clashes of May 1992 have affected Thailand's investment and general economic environment. With international reductions in commodity prices, rice and tapioca prices tumbled sharply (Thailand is the world's largest exporter), and prices for rubber and sugar, the country's other two leading raw-material exports, dropped as well.

In 1992, the military junta dissolved powerful state-enterprise unions, one of its few popular acts. Pledges were made to return union rights to the 250,000 state enterprise employees. Trouble with the organized labor movement also occurred in small textile and garment factories as companies retrenched unskilled and semi-skilled workers in order to introduce modern machinery. Coupled with this was neglect of industrial safety. In 1993, a strike was called at the Thai Durable Textile Co. (TDT) after 376 workers were laid off by the management which claimed the move was necessary if the company was to remain competitive and solvent. Workers suspected—and management later confirmed—that layoffs were made to pave the way for new machinery that required less labor. Thailand now faces keen export competition from countries such as China, Indonesia, Viet Nam, Pakistan and Bangladesh, where labor is cheaper. About 85% of the estimated 800,000 workers in the textile and garment industry are women. Trade union membership increased from 90,000 in 1987 to 150,000 in 1993.

Thailand's economic boom is centered in Bangkok. As a result there is an increasing income gap between urban rich and rural poor, with 60% of population still working on farms cultivating mainly rice. On the other hand, manufacturing in Bangkok, employing only 15% of the population, accounted for 51% GNP in 1991. Labor migration has become a key fixture of the Thai economy. A shift in emphasis from export growth to domestic consumption is occurring. The uneven development between urban and rural areas leads to social problems that are the source of political instability. In 1994, drought conditions affected rice production and forested areas. Forest in Thailand have declined by about 50% over the last 30 years. Water had been supplied free to users, but in 1994 three draft water laws are being developed which will impose fees for water usage.

20 INCOME

In 1992, GNP was $106,559 million at current prices, or $1,840 per capita. For the period 1985–92 the average inflation rate was 5.8%, resulting in a real growth rate in per capita GNP of 8.3%.

In 1992 the GDP was $110,337 million in current US dollars. It is estimated that in 1991 manufacturing contributed 28% to GDP agriculture, hunting, forestry, and fishing, 13%; construction, 7%; mining and quarrying, 2%; electricity, gas, and water, 2%; wholesale and retail trade, 23%; transport, storage, and communication, 7%; finance, insurance, real estate, and business services, 9%; community, social, and personal services, 5%; and other sources, 5%.

21 LABOR

The labor force in 1992 totaled some 32.4 million (compared with 21.7 million in 1981 and 15.1 million in 1967). Of the 31 million employed in 1992, about 7.65 million (25%) were engaged in agriculture and related occupations, 4.7 million (15%) in industry, and 18.65 million (60%) in services. In 1990, unemployment amounted to 2.2% of the economically active population.

Because of persisting government opposition to unions, organized labor was not a major factor in Thai life prior to the 1970s. Labor legislation in 1969 delineated certain basic workers' rights, and unions were granted greater freedom to organize under the Labor Relations Act of 1975. In 1992, the Thai Trade Union Congress was the largest labor federation, with 42,748 members from 152 unions. As of 1 January 1992, the total number of unions was 749 with 194,681 members. Only 1.6% of the labor force was unionized. Minimum daily wage rates during 1991/92 ranged from B100 in Bangkok and the central valley provinces to B82–93 in the other regions. Legislation regulating hours and conditions of labor, workers' compensation, and welfare also exists.

22 AGRICULTURE

With some 20 million hectares (49 million acres) of arable land, of which about 13.5 million hectares (33.5 million acres) are under cultivation, Thailand continues to rely heavily on agriculture, although the country has suffered from declining export prices in recent years. Rice is the major crop grown; Thailand is the world's biggest rice exporter, with over 5.1 million tons sent abroad in 1992, for a value of $1,425 million. (4% of total exports). Total rice production amounted to 18,500,000 tons in 1992. Rice is grown on over half of the Thai farmland. The government has embarked on large-scale irrigation projects and introduced higher-yielding varieties of rice in an effort to increase production.

Rubber, also a major export, is grown on the peninsula and, to a lesser extent, on the southeast coast. Total production in 1992 was 1,400,000 tons, the highest in the world and accounting for 26% of all production in 1992. Demand for natural rubber is growing along with the international concern about AIDS. Sugarcane production reached 46.8 million tons, while output of cassava (tapioca), traditionally important in Thailand, totaled 21.1 million tons. As of 1991, Thailand provided 95% of the world's cassava exports. Much of the harvest is processed into chips and pellets and exported to the EC for fodder. Higher EC tariffs, however, have caused the Thai government to promote dairy, fruit, rubber, and cashew farming instead. Corn production, which has increased significantly in recent decades, reached 3.6 million tons in 1992. One third of annual corn production is consumed annually as fodder, with the remainder being exported to Europe and

Japan. Kenaf, tobacco, cotton, and kapok are cultivated mainly for domestic use, but quantities of jute, cocoa, peanuts, soybeans, and medical plants are exported. Canned pineapple and fresh flowers, especially orchids, are important exports. The Thai government's official policy of encouraging mountain villagers to grow coffee, apples, strawberries, kidney beans, and other temperate crops instead of the lucrative opium poppy and marijuana has had some success; another aim of the project is to discourage deforestation through slash-and-burn cultivation. In 1987, King Bhumibol Adulyedej received a Magsaysay Award for International Understanding for his 20 years of effort in this area.

In the mid-1970s, farmers began to organize to express their discontent over the disparity between farm and nonfarm incomes. To improve farm conditions, the government legitimized squatters' rights to nearly 500,000 hectares (1,236,000 acres) of land classified as forest reserve and established credit and crop insurance programs for farmers. The government Marketing Organization for Farmers, founded in 1975, allows farmers to buy fertilizers, machinery, and equipment at the lowest possible prices and assists in crop marketing. It is also government policy to channel revenues from agricultural export taxes to a welfare fund called the Farmers Assistance Fund.

23 ANIMAL HUSBANDRY

Cattle, used for plowing and harrowing, are important to rice farming, and most rural households have some cattle as well as hogs, chickens, and ducks. In 1992, Thailand had 136 million chickens, 17 million ducks, 6.8 million head of cattle, 4.7 million head of buffalo, and 5.1 million swine. Overall meat production from livestock increased 5% in 1991 and again in 1992. Elephants, important as draft animals in rural areas, are used to haul teak. Crocodiles, raised for their skins, are a specialty livestock product.

24 FISHING

Fish is a major protein element in the Thai diet. Freshwater fish, abundantly found in rivers and canals, and marine fish (from the waters along the lengthy coastline) produced a catch of 3,065,170 tons in 1991 (as compared with 846,600 tons in 1967). Plat-thu (rastrelliger species) is the most common fish in Thailand's diet. Thailand exports cured fish to neighboring countries, and frozen shrimp and prawns mainly to Japan. In 1990, Thailand accounted for 16.8% of the world's exports of prepared and preserved fish, valued at over $920 million.

25 FORESTRY

Thailand's forested area declined from 57% of the nation's land area in 1961 to only 27% by 1991, mainly as a result of the continued use of slash-and-burn practices by farmers. Teak, once a major export, has declined in importance, largely because of government restrictions on cutting and past depletion of the forests through excessive harvesting and inadequate replanting. In 1991, production of roundwood totaled 37.9 million cu m, up from 33.6 million cu m in 1980. Production of veneer sheets (including teak) in 1991 amounted to 136,000 cu m, up from 23,000 cu m in 1981.

Lac, a resinous insect substance found on trees, has always had value for the Thai, but its derivatives—seedlac, sticklac, and shellac—have also found a ready international market. Other important forestry products include charcoal, gums and resins, and kapok fiber and seed.

26 MINING

Thailand is relatively poor in mineral reserves, except for tin and natural gas. In 1991, Thailand was the sixth-largest tin-producing country in the world. Tin ore is mined mainly on the southern peninsula; production in 1991 totaled 14,937 tons, most of it exported. Tin production has been steadily declining in the face of falling world prices and output curbs. Deposits of lignite were developed with US aid in the 1960s and have begun to show a good yield; 14,689,000 tons were produced in 1991. Iron ore is mined at Lop Buri for use in a small smelting plant; in 1991, total iron ore output was 240,075 tons, up from 97,026 tons in 1987. Other minerals exploited on a small scale include tungsten, lead, manganese, gold, silver, and many kinds of building stones. Rubies, sapphires, topaz, and zircon are also mined. The first commercial gypsum mine began operations in 1957; production in 1991 totaled 7,196,390 tons. Cement production in 1991 was 18,054,000 tons, up from 9,850,000 in 1987.

27 ENERGY AND POWER

From 1975 to 1992, total installed generating capacity nearly quadrupled, from 2,755,000 kw to 10,800,000 kw. In 1992, 65% of primary energy consumed was derived from oil, 20% from natural gas; 13% from coal; and 2% from other sources. Distribution, however, is far from adequate, with only about 20% of the population having access to the system. The Metropolitan Electrical Authority serves Bangkok; the Provincial Electricity Authority provides service to the rest of the kingdom. Total national output in 1991 was 52,486 million kwh, up from 15,948 million kwh in 1981 and only 1,092 million kwh in 1964.

Thailand is heavily dependent on imports of foreign oil. Proven and potential domestic deposits have been estimated at 231 million barrels, but exploitation and development have been inhibited by declining oil prices. In 1991, the Sirikit oil field accounted for more than 90% of the total production of 8,938,000 barrels. Natural gas reserves were estimated at more than 8 trillion cu ft (225 billion cu m) in 1993, and production has been aided by the exploitation of new fields in the Gulf of Thailand. Production in 1992 was put at 260 billion cu ft (7.3 billion cu m), double the 1987 amount.

28 INDUSTRY

Seven government agencies supervise the Thai industrial sector. The Industrial Restructuring Committee was created in 1982 to coordinate the various agencies and to formulate policy proposals in line with economic development plans. The most important protective measure for the industrial sector were import tariffs. In the 1960s tariffs were low. During the 1970s tariffs increased, but at an uneven rate, some increased to above 90 percent. In conjunction with the Fifth Economic Development Plan the government in the 1980s attempted to form a more even tariff structure and to lower protectionism. Price control was another protective measure pervasive in the 1970s which was relaxed in the 1980s. In the 1990s trade liberalization continued. As of 1 January 1993 an Association of Southeast Nations Free Trade Area was established. Since 1988 the Thai customs tariff has been based on the Harmonized System. Most duties are ad valorem. In Thailand arbitrary customs valuation act as an import barrier.

Manufacturing grew at an average rate of 12% annually in the 1960s and 10% in the 1970s. Subsequently, falling commodity prices, rising interest rates, and reduced demand adversely affected manufacturing, which grew 6.7% in 1984 and only 3.8% in 1985. Most industries still functioned at a modest scale, and Thailand continued to import most manufactured goods. However, growth in some areas has been impressive. From 1971 to 1985, production of food products nearly tripled, textiles grew over 500%, and transportation equipment showed even greater growth. Production of sugar reached 2,678,180 tons in 1982, though it fell off to 2,293,600 tons by 1985. In 1984, production of gunny bags totaled 153,153,655; also, 904,860 tons of synthetic fabrics and 937,758 tons of cotton fabrics were produced. A total of 320,538 motorcycles and 3,547,540 auto, truck, bus, and motorcycle tires were manufactured in the same year. Among chemical products, 6,136,430 cu m of nitrogen and 23,799,106 cu m of oxygen were produced. Other manufactured goods included 533,346 television sets, 29,407,076 incandescent and fluorescent lamps, and 130,074 tons of galvanized iron plate.

Since 1979, Thailand's manufacturing sector has increasingly diversified and made the largest contribution to the economy. The export-oriented component of the sector is dynamic and growing. Production for the domestic market also increased temporarily, only to slow in 1992. As reported in 1993, high-growth industries targeting domestic consumption were construction materials, foods and beverages, and electrical appliances.

29 SCIENCE AND TECHNOLOGY
The lack of skilled workers remains a drag on industrial development. Many students seek technical training overseas, and some receive postgraduate education in specialized technical subjects at the Asian Institute of Technology in Bangkok, which offers advanced degrees in agricultural engineering, human settlements, and computer applications. The institute also operates receiving equipment for LANDSAT transmissions that provide Southeast Asian countries with the aerial surveys vital to agricultural development, forest inventories, and city planning.

Scientific organizations include the Medical Association of Thailand (founded 1921), the Applied Scientific Research Corp. of Thailand (1963), and the Science Society of Thailand (1948). National science policy is the responsibility of the Ministry of Science, Technology and Energy. Government appropriations for science, technology, energy, and environment totaled B2,664 million, or nearly 1% of the budget total, in 1987.

30 DOMESTIC TRADE
Bangkok, the port of entry and distribution point for the whole country, is the commercial center of Thailand; all foreign firms have their main offices there. Other commercially important cities are Chiang Mai (teak, rice, and textiles), Ubon Ratchathani (rice, jute, and leather), Phuket (tin), and Songkhla (rubber). Many essential commodities are grown and consumed by the producer, or distributed at the local level. Production for the domestic market has continued to increase led by high growth industries such as construction materials, foods and beverages, and electronic appliances. In the greater Bangkok metropolitan area, almost every kind of retail outlet is represented, including speciality shops and over 40 department stores. A large segment of retailing is Chinese controlled. In metropolitan areas, professional, personal, and technological services are available. Usual business hours are from 8:30 AM to 4:30 PM, Monday through Friday. Shops are open from 9 AM to 8 or 9 PM, and banks from 8:30 AM to 3:30 PM. Newspaper, radio, television, and motion picture advertising is available. The annual Bangkok fair in December, originally conceived for entertainment, has developed into a trade fair.

31 FOREIGN TRADE
Thailand is primarily an importer of petroleum of petroleum and manufactured goods and an exporter of agricultural products and raw materials. During 1981–85, the value of Thailand's exports increased by about one-third, although trade deficits continued. Rice, traditionally the dominant export item, accounted for 45% or more of total export value in 1948; during the 1960s, however, it dropped to between 33% and 36%, and accounted for only 11.6% by 1985. Rubber, fluctuating between 10% and 30% in the 1960s, accounted for 7% of total exports in 1985; more important were textile products and tapioca (cassava) products. Principal exports in 1988 (in millions of baht) were: rice, 34,676; rubber, 27,189; and tapioca products, 21,844. The US, Japan, Singapore, the Netherlands, and Germany are principal purchasers of Thailand's exports.

Principal imports in (in millions of baht) were: machinery and transport equipment, 251,001; basic manufactures, 152,105; chemicals, 74,204; mineral fuels, 59,819; crude materials except fuels, 45,143; and food and live animals, 30,001.

Principal trade partners in 1989 (in millions of baht) were as follows:

	EXPORTS	IMPORTS	BALANCE
China	13,900	19,175	−5,275
France	11,359	33,992	−12,952
FRG	21,040	33,992	−12,952
Hong Kong	20,395	8,836	11,559
Japan	87,933	200,937	−113,004
Malaysia	15,062	17,194	−2,132
Singapore	36,840	50,867	−14,027
Sa'udi Arabia	9,267	9,235	32
UK	19,175	16,912	2,263
US	111,788	74,637	37,151
Other countries	41,253	74,336	−33,083
TOTALS	388,012	516,820	−128,808

32 BALANCE OF PAYMENTS
Several factors account for Thailand's balance-of-payments problem since the mid-1950s. Probably the most important has been the fluctuation in the international market for its traditional primary exports. The value of rice and rubber exports dropped significantly between 1964 and 1968, and that of rice, sugar, and tin during the 1970s. The needs of a modernizing economy are difficult to support by agricultural exports alone. In addition, prior to the development of its own industries, Thailand imported large quantities of automobiles and machinery, fuel to run them, and many luxury and convenience manufactures. Another cause for these deficits is high imports of capital goods, raw materials, and other inputs to manufacturing and export. In recent years, the trade imbalance has been offset by foreign assistance, loans, and income from tourism. In 1992, the current account deficit was about 6.4% of GDP, substantially below the almost 9% of 1990.

In 1992 merchandise exports totaled $32,106 million and imports $36,261 million. The merchandise trade balance was $−4,155 million.

The following table summarizes Thailand's balance of payments for 1991 and 1992 (in millions of US dollars):

	1991	1992
CURRENT ACCOUNT		
Goods, services, and income	−7,832	−7,006
Unrequited transfers	267	325
TOTALS	−7,565	−6,681
CAPITAL ACCOUNT		
Direct investment	1,847	1,979
Portfolio investment	−81	750
Other long-term capital	3,327	1,515
Other short-term capital	6,666	5,385
Exceptional financing	—	—
Other liabilities	—	—
Reserves	−4,618	−2,925
TOTALS	7,141	6,704
Errors and omissions	425	−23
Total change in reserves	−4,698	−2,737

33 BANKING AND SECURITIES
The central bank in the Bank of Thailand, established in 1942. It operates as an independent body under government supervision; its entire capital is owned by the government. The Bank issues notes, a function previously handled by the Ministry of Finance.

As of December 1993, Thailand had 15 commercial banks. In addition there were 14 foreign banks. As of 1992, demand deposits of the commercial banks totaled B66.1 billion; time and savings deposits, B1,898.1 billion. Currency in circulation rose from B63.85 billion at the end of 1986 to B180.2 billion as of 1992.

Thailand's first public stock exchange was opened in Bangkok on 30 April 1975. All of its 30 members were Thai-owned securities firms. The Ministry of Finance encourages companies to go public by reducing income tax for listed companies and also by according favorable tax treatment of dividends.

34INSURANCE

In 1986, there were 7 life, 62 non-life, and 5 composite insurance companies, and life insurance accounted for 53.9% of all premiums. In 1992, life insurance in force, was valued at B561,763 million. Per capita premium expenditures totaled us$25.5, or 1.8% of the GDP, in 1990.

35PUBLIC FINANCE

A surplus equivalent to 3.2% of GDP was recorded in fiscal 1992. The lower 1992 surplus resulted from revenue losses by tax restructuring measures, uncertainties regarding the impact of the value-added tax, and political unrest in May which adversely affected tourism. Expenditures for land, construction, and related hardware also rose considerably.

The following table shows actual revenues and expenditures for 1991 and 1992 in millions of baht.

	1991	1992
REVENUE AND GRANTS		
Tax revenue	443,267	450,077
Non-tax revenue	36,741	49,341
Capital revenue	−115	8,818
Grants	5,006	3,472
TOTAL	485,129	511,708
EXPENDITURES & LENDING MINUS REPAYMENTS		
General public service	22,409	24,400
Defense	62,214	73,200
Public order and safety	15,884	18,716
Education	73,503	89,600
Health	26,794	34,673
Social security and welfare	12,919	16,815
Housing and community amenities	8,732	11,500
Recreation, cultural, and religious affairs	1,865	2,500
Economic affairs and services	88,344	111,570
Other expenditures	47,575	40,652
Adjustments	948	−2,678
Lending minus repayments	2,696	3,657
TOTAL	366,715	429,169
Deficit/Surplus	118,414	82,539

In 1992, Thailand's total public debt stood at B307,975 million, of which B97,410 million baht was financed abroad.

36TAXATION

Personal income tax rates are graduated, rising from 5% on income below B500,000 to 37% on income of B4 million and over. Business and individual citizens are also subject to a host of indirect taxes, including customs duties, sales tax, and excise taxes. Corporate income taxes on net profit in 1992 were levied at the flat rate of 30%. Stock dividends and capital gains are taxed as regular income.

All companies and individuals engaged in industry, commerce, or services are subject to sales tax; remittances out of Thailand in the form of profits, income, or dividends are taxed at 20%.

Reductions are available under the Investment Promotion Act. Import surcharges, designed to deter imports, were imposed in 1981 at rates between 5% and 30% on certain fibers, piston rings, palm oil, and telephones.

There are excise taxes on tobacco, petroleum products, alcoholic beverages and soft drinks, and other products. Automobiles are subject to a special tax based on engine size.

37CUSTOMS AND DUTIES

Thailand's customs tariff is primarily for revenue, although in a limited fashion it protects local industry. No preferential treatment is afforded any country, and all goods are subject to the general rate. Only a few goods require import licenses, including some foods, materials, and industrial products. Most duties are ad valorem, ranging from 5%–15% for raw materials to 30%–150% for finished goods.

38FOREIGN INVESTMENT

Growth of the Thai economy has been directly related to the flow of investments from abroad. In order to stimulate such investment, the government passed the Industrial Promotion Act (1962), which established the Board of Investment for Industry, renamed the Board of Investment (BOI) in 1972. The Alien Business Law of 1972 restricts the participation of non-Thai nationals in certain types of business activities. The BOI, the powers and responsibilities of which were broadened in 1977, grants the following benefits to promoted industries: guarantees against nationalization and competition from government industries; exemption from import duties and business tax on plant, machinery, spare parts, and raw materials; exemption from duty on exports; exemption from tax on corporate income for a specified period; and repatriation of capital and remittance of profits abroad. The BOI considers applications for promotional benefits to both Thai and foreign investors. Projects meeting any or all of the following criteria are eligible for investment incentives: significantly strengthen Thailand's balance-of-payments position, especially through production for export; support of the development of the country's resources; substantially increase employment; locate operations in the provinces; conserve energy or replace imported energy supplies; establish or develop industries which form the base for further stages of industrial development; or, projects considered necessary or important to the government.

By the end of 1980, foreign investments in BOI-promoted firms amounted to B4.6 billion, of which B1.5 billion was derived from Japan, B644 million from Taiwan, and B577 million from the US. Between 1982 and 1985, foreign direct investment averaged $143.4 million per year. Applications to the BOI increased from $2.5 billion in 1985 to $20 billion in 1988; three-fourths of these projects were foreign investment. Japan, Taiwan, the US, and Hong Kong were the major investors. By 1991 applications to BOI had declined by 50% as a result of reductions in new investment from Japan, Hong Kong, and Taiwan, and from competition by the new markets in Mexico based on the North American Free Trade Agreement and in China.

The May–June 1992 political instability added a new negative factor for investors who regarded Thailand as a "calm" culture—especially the Japanese who had provided the largest flow of direct investment between 1986 and 1991. In April 1993, BOI offered import duty exemptions and extended the tax holiday for investors willing to locate factories outside greater Bangkok. The single largest foreign investment in Thailand's economy is an estimated us$3 billion investment by Unocal (Union Oil of California) in the development of natural gas fields in the Gulf of Thailand.

39ECONOMIC DEVELOPMENT

The Thai government, vulnerable in its financial dependence on a few primary commodities (rice, rubber, tin, and teak), has pursued a policy of economic diversification through industrial development and increased agricultural production. With the beginning of the first development plan in 1961, the government committed itself to the primacy of private enterprise and to a policy of fostering and assisting it. Thailand has also followed a policy of foreign trade and exchange liberalization. Foreign exchange control is nominal.

Thailand's first five-year plan, covering the period 1961–66, aimed to raise the standard of living by means of greater agricultural, industrial, and power production. In the second development plan (1967–71), emphasis was placed on agricultural development, highways, irrigation, education, and industrial development in the private sector. The third development plan (1972–76) placed special emphasis on improvements in the rural infrastructure, growth in the financial and commercial sectors, and further assistance to crop diversification and to import-substitution industries. The government also committed itself to a reduction in the role of state-owned enterprises. The first three plans did much to increase the standard of living and to bring new roads, irrigation schemes, and land reform to the prosperous Bangkok region. But these changes also increased the income gap between rural and urban Thailand and drew increasing numbers of migrants to the city in search of work. Accordingly, the fourth economic plan, covering the years 1977–81, emphasized decentralization of industry and economic growth from the capital region to the provinces. It also ended the policy of encouraging import-substitution industries and began the promotion of export-oriented industries able to benefit from the nation's low wage rates. Plans were made for the establishment of industrial estates under the direction of the Industrial Estate Authority of Thailand. The first estate, at Bangchan, 30 km (19 mi) from Bangkok, was fully occupied in 1980 by 51 companies, producing a range of industrial products, including automotive and electrical equipment, chemicals, and processed food. Another industrial estate, established in 1979 at Lard Krabang, also in the Bangkok vicinity, includes, in addition to a general industrial area, a duty-free export-processing zone open to manufacturers willing to establish high value-added and labor-intensive industries for export.

The fifth development plan, covering the years 1982–86, stressed reduction of rural poverty and social tensions and expansion of employment opportunities in the poorer regions. To this end, four investment promotion zones were established. After completion in 1981 of the natural gas pipeline from the Gulf of Thailand, investment priority was reassigned to the Eastern Seaboard Development Program. This ambitious program called for the creation of a new urban-industrial complex in the Rayong-Sattahip region that was expected to draw industries from the congested Bangkok area. Heavy industries were to be emphasized, with early construction of a natural gas separator and plants for the manufacture of soda ash, fertilizers, and petrochemicals. The sixth National Economic and Social Development Plan (1986–91) stressed continuing export promotion, streamlining of the public sector, and strict monetary and fiscal policies, with growth targeted at only about 5% yearly. Emphasis was placed on the less capital-intensive industries, and more emphasis was given to improved utilization of resources. The plan targeted private sector investment and initiatives. Privatization of state enterprises would proceed in clear-cut phases, and enterprises were required to seek their own revenue. Agricultural production was forecast to grow at 2.9% per year. The development of small-scale industry, particularly in rural areas, was emphasized. In 1993, the Eastern Seaboard Development Plan southeast of Bangkok—begun 10 years before as a US$4 billion investment—demonstrated results with the new port, Laem Chabang. This plan extends greater Bangkok, and the next phases include extending all main national arteries into four-lane highways and double-tracking the railway.

Themes for each region guided development. In the north, Chiang-mai, Lamphrun and Lampang, light and clean industries are encouraged, such as clothing, high-value electronics, and agro-industry. In the south, transport links and natural gas networks developed between the Andaman Sea and the Gulf of Thailand would attract heavy industry such as petrochemicals, and cross-border development with Malaysia would link with Penang's industrial sector. Development plans for the impoverished northeast included linking with Laos, Cambodia, and Viet Nam for processing raw materials from those countries, and for provding services involved with investment and manufacturing in those countries. The Board of Investment (BOI) encourages development with varying incentives for investors depending on zoned areas of the country. For instance, minimum wage rates in Zone 3 (73 provinces) are 20% below Zone 1 (greater Bangkok) and Zone 2 (provinces closest to Bangkok and eastern seaboard). Zone 3 investors would have eight-year tax holidays, with no requirement (such as in Zones 1 & 2) for export of all of their production. Cheap credit—6%–7%—is available for rural areas, compared to 16% or more elsewhere. The T-BIRD—Thai Business Initiative Rural Development—is run by the Population and Community Development Association (PDA), one of Thailand's largest nongovernmental organizations. Schemes assisting villagers to remain on the land have been developed. Farmers are encouraged to raise more lucrative vegetable crops rather than drought-prone rice, pigs, dairy cows or chickens, and to form vegetable banks and/or rice pools. The dwindling of forest cover in Thailand impacts negatively on economic, as well as ecological, development, especially in rural areas. In the northeast, tourism and textile production is replacing the agriculture that had earlier replaced opium cultivation.

Between 1946 and 1986, Thailand received nonmilitary loans and grants totaling $956.1 million; military assistance during the same period amounted to $2,187.5 million. Development aid from multilateral sources totaled $6,220.5 million, of which $3,675 million came from the IBRD and $1,730.9 million from the Asian Development Bank. In 1990, 1991, and 1992, respectively, total economic assistance to Thailand was (in millions of US dollars) $258.4, $270.2, and $279.4. Japan was the greatest contributor.

⁴⁰SOCIAL DEVELOPMENT

Since 1940, social welfare has been the responsibility of the government and it is only in recent years that private organizations have actively engaged in social welfare programs. A 1990 law established a social security system which began paying disability and death benefits in 1991, and will pay old age benefits effective 1996. The same law provides for sickness and maternity benefits. Employers are required to provide workers' compensation coverage, including temporary and permanent disability benefits, and medical and survivor benefits.

The government has sought to promote family planning and reduce population growth. In 1992, a total of 1,807,300 persons became new acceptors of family planning devices or procedures. The fertility rate for 1985–90 was 2.6, and in 1987, 66% of couples of childbearing age practiced contraception. Women have equal legal rights in most areas, but inequities remain in domestic areas, including divorce and child support. In 1991, a Commission on Women's Affairs was established.

⁴¹HEALTH

In the 1960s, the government, with UN and US assistance, extended free medical treatment, expanded health education activities in schools and rural areas, and built many hospitals. In the private sector, two thirds of health care funding comes from employers and private households. A national social security scheme is underway, but private insurers are few. Owing largely to success in eradicating malaria and other tropical diseases, as well as to better sanitation and medical care, health conditions have steadily improved in Thailand. By 1991, 77% of the population had access to safe water and 74% had adequate sanitation. In 1990, there were 173 cases per 100,000 people of tuberculosis reported. The same year, 26% of children under five years of age were considered malnourished. In 1992, about 90% of the population had access to health care services. Health care facilities are concentrated in the Bangkok metropolitan area, where about 15% of the population is located. In 1987, there were over 900 general hospitals in the public sector; in addition, there were 95 specialist hospitals and 7,675 health centers. In 1989, there were 180 private hospitals with 9,377 beds. Private clinics also expanded and, in 1989, there were 11,443. In the same year, there was a total of 85,000 beds (1.6 per 1,000 people). Thai hospitals tend to be small in size.

In 1988, Thailand had 11,260 physicians, 3,681 pharmacists, and 1,670 dentists. In 1991, there were 51,091 nurses and 10,606 midwives. In 1992, there were 20 doctors per 100,000 inhabitants, with a nurse to doctor ratio of 5.5. Thailand's 1993 population was 56.9 million, with a birth rate of 20.5 per 1,000 people, and 66% of married women (ages 15 to 49) using contraception. There were 1.2 million births in 1992, and life expectancy was 69 years. Infant mortality in 1992 was 27 per 1,000 live births, and maternal mortality was 50 per 100,000 live births in 1991. The general mortality rate was 5.8 per 1,000 people in 1993. Regional inequities in the distribution of health facilities and personnel persist, with Bangkok and other urban centers being much better supplied than rural areas. Total health care expenditures in 1990 were $4,061 million.

42HOUSING

Most families in Thailand live in dwellings that compare favorably with living facilities anywhere in Southeast Asia. The Thai government has stimulated housing and community development by means of a housing plan that provides government mortgages for building, renovation, or purchase of government land and houses. Under a self-help settlement scheme, the government sets up whole new communities, surveys sites, constructs roads and irrigation systems, and provides public utilities and medical care.

In 1973, to house Bangkok residents who had been living in makeshift shelters, the government formed the National Housing Authority (NHA), which undertook overall responsibility for coordination of public and private housing programs. By 1979, the NHA had completed 54,780 housing units. From 1979 to 1984, a total of 1,442,250 housing units were built in Thailand. In 1986, 86% of all living quarters were detached houses, 11% were row-houses, and 2% were single rooms. Owners occupied 84% of all dwellings, 8% were rented, 3% were occupied rent free, and 3% were occupied in exchange for a service. The total number of housing units in 1992 was 11,151,000.

43EDUCATION

Literacy, estimated at 44% in 1947, rose to 93% in 1990; 96.1% for men and 89.9% for women. Compulsory education provisions, first introduced in 1921, call for universal school attendance starting at age seven through the fourth year of primary school or through age 15. Both teacher training and technical and vocational training (especially in agriculture) have been stressed in recent development plans.

In 1989, about 952,012 students were enrolled in higher education programs. In Bangkok, Chulalongkorn University (founded 1917) is Thailand's most eminent university. Also in Bangkok are the University of Thammasart (founded 1933), spe-

cializing in social and political sciences, and Kasetsart University (founded 1943) specializing in agriculture. Newer universities established in provincial areas include Chiang Mai University (founded in 1964), Khon Kaen University (founded in the northeast in 1966), and Prince of Songkhla University (founded in 1968). King Mongkut's Institute of Technology was formed in 1971 through the amalgamation of three institutes, and eight colleges of education were combined into Sri Nakharinwirot University in Bangkok in 1974. A correspondence school, the University of Ramkhamhaeng, opened in Bangkok in 1974 and the Sukhothai Thammathirat Open University began operations in 1978.

44LIBRARIES AND MUSEUMS

The National Library (founded in 1905) contains about 900,000 books and over 180,000 manuscripts. Other important libraries in Bangkok include the Asian Institute of Technology (200,000 volumes), Chulalongkorn University (297,000), the University of Thammasart (525,000), Kasetsart University (259,000), and Sri Nakharinwirot University (196,000). The Library of the Department of Science Services maintains a special collection of 350,000 volumes. Outside Bangkok, sizable collections are maintained at the University of Chiang Mai and Khon Kaen University (340,000).

The National Museum in Bangkok (founded in 1926) has an extensive collection of Thai artifacts, including sculptures, textiles, ceramics, jewels, coins, weapons, and masks. Many of Bangkok's temples and palaces contain excellent examples of Thai frescoes and sculptures. The Temple of the Emerald Buddha has a famous mural of the Ramayana, the Sanskrit epic, and the Marble Temple contains a fine collection of bronze and stone Buddhas.

45MEDIA

The Ministry of Communications is responsible for Thailand's public postal, telegraph, and telephone services. The postal service, employing both railway and air mail, operates from the central post office in Bangkok and covers the entire country. Telephone service now reaches the principal towns, with 999,678 telephones in use in 1991 (compared with 98,000 in 1968), of which over 70% were in metropolitan areas. Despite recent expansions, service remains highly erratic. Thailand is a member of INTELSAT and maintains trans-Pacific and Indian Ocean satellite communications stations.

Ownership of broadcasting is both public and private. There are six government and military radio networks and Bangkok alone has five television stations. The first mainland Asian television station was established in Bangkok in 1955. In 1991, there were 6,300,000 television sets and 10,550,000 radios.

The first daily newspaper, the *Siam Daily Advertiser*, appeared more than a century ago. In 1991 there were 40 daily newspapers published in Bangkok, including eight in Chinese and four in English. The provinces have weekly and semiweekly publications, all in Thai, but no daily papers. Bangkok also has a variety of weekly and monthly periodicals, most appearing in Thai. Among Bangkok's leading daily newspapers (with language medium and estimated 1991 daily circulation) were:

	LANGUAGE	CIRCULATION
Thai Rath (m)	Thai	800,000
Daily News (m)	Thai	400,000
Ban Muang (m)	Thai	150,000
Matichon (m)	Thai	100,000
Dao Siam	Thai	100,000
Tawan Siam (m)	Thai	97,000
Sing Sian Yit Pao (m)	Chinese	40,000
Bangkok Post (m)	English	37,000
Srinakorn Daily News (m)	Chinese	30,000

46ORGANIZATIONS

Thailand has an extensive cooperative movement. Credit societies are the dominant type of cooperative; consumer cooperatives are the next largest, followed by agricultural marketing and processing cooperatives. Other kinds of cooperatives, mostly formed during and since the 1930s, include colonization and land improvement cooperatives.

Trade organizations under the Ministry of Economic Affairs include the Thai Chamber of Commerce, the Board of Trade, and several foreign trade associations. Cultural organizations include the Royal Institute (founded 1933); the Thai-Bhara Cultural Lodge (founded 1940), which sponsors studies in the fields of linguistics, philosophy, and religion; and the Siam Society (founded 1904), which issues studies on Thai art, literature, and science.

47TOURISM, TRAVEL, AND RECREATION

Tourism has become a vital industry in Thailand, constituting the greatest single source of foreign exchange. In the late 1960s and early 1970s, the large US troop presence in Southeast Asia produced a surge in Thailand's tourism largely from US military personnel. Since then, the boom has continued, although the large number of hotels has led to heavy competition and fairly low occupancy rates. In 1991, a total of US$3.92 billion was spent in the country by 5,086,899 foreign visitors, 3,116,983 from East Asia and 1,207,670 from Europe. There were 190,453 hotel rooms. Most tourists visit Bangkok and its Buddhist temples (wats). All visitors must have passports; visitors from most countries may stay up to 15 days without a visa. Typhoid, tetanus, and gamma globulin immunizations are recommended, especially for travel in rural areas. Yellow fever inoculation is required of tourists arriving from an infected area.

Major sports include soccer and baseball. Thai bull, cock, and fish fighting are also popular (though illegal), along with Thai boxing, golf, badminton, and kite fighting.

48FAMOUS THAI

Many ancient Thai kings enjoy legendary reputations. Rama Khamheng (the Great), a 13th-century monarch, is traditionally regarded as the inventor of the Thai alphabet; Rama Tibodi I in the 14th century promulgated the first-known Thai laws; Trailok instituted lasting governmental reforms in the 15th century; and Phya Tak in the 18th century rebuilt a war-defeated Thailand. Two great monarchs, Mongkut (r.1851–68) and his son Chulalongkorn (r.1868–1910), became famous for introducing Thailand to the modern world. They are, respectively, the king and his young successor in Margaret Landon's *Anna and the King of Siam*. Further progress toward modernization was accomplished in more recent times by three outstanding premiers: Phibul Songgram (1897–1964), Pridi Banomyong (1900–83), and Sarit Thanarat (1900–63). Prince Wan Waithayakon (1891–1976), foreign minister and Thailand's representative to the UN, played a major role in diplomacy for many years following World War II. Marshal Thanom Kittikachorn (b.1911) was leader of Thailand from 1963 until October 1973, when political protests compelled his resignation as prime minister. King Bhumibol Adulyadej (b.US, 1927) ascended the throne in 1946.

Prince Akat Damkoeng was the author in 1940 of the first modern novel written in Thailand, *Yellow Race, White Race*. Modern styles in painting and sculpture are reflected in the work of Chitr Buabusaya and Paitun Muangsomboon, and the traditional manner in the art of Apai Saratani and Vichitr Chaosanket.

49DEPENDENCIES

Thailand has no territories or colonies.

50BIBLIOGRAPHY

Benedict, Ruth. *Thai Culture and Behavior.* Ithaca, N.Y.: Cornell University Press, 1952.

Bowring, Sir John. *The Kingdom and People of Siam.* London: Parker, 1857.

Ingram, James C. *Economic Change in Thailand, 1850–1970.* Stanford, Calif.: Stanford University Press, 1971.

Keyes, Charles F. *Thailand; Buddhist Kingdom as Modern Nation-State.* Boulder, Colo.: Westview Press, 1987.

Kulick, Elliott. *Thailand's Turn: Profile of a New Dragon.* New York: St. Martin's, 1992.

Leonowens, Anna Harriette. *The English Governess at the Siamese Court.* New York: Oxford University Press, 1988.

LePoer, Barbara Leitch (ed.). *Thailand, A Country Study.* 6th ed. Washington, D.C.: Library of Congress, 1989.

Mungkandi, Wiwat, and William Warren. *A Century and a Half of Thai-American Relations.* Bangkok: Chulalongkorn University Press, 1982.

Muscat, Robert J. *Thailand and the United States: Development, Security, and Foreign Aid.* New York: Columbia University Press, 1990.

———. *The Fifth Tiger: A Study of Thai Development Policy.* Helsinki: United Nations University Press, 1994.

Silcock, Thomas Henry. *Thailand: Social and Economic Studies in Development.* Durham, N.C.: Duke University Press, 1968.

Skinner, George William. *Chinese Society in Thailand: Analytical History.* Ithaca, N.Y.: Cornell University Press, 1957.

Stowe, Judith A. *Siam becomes Thailand: A Story of Intrigue.* Honolulu: University of Hawaii Press, 1991.

Trerwiel, B. J. *A History of Modern Thailand, 1767–1942.* St. Lucia: Queensland University Press, 1983.

Wyatt, D. K. *Thailand.* New Haven, Conn.: Yale University Press, 1984.

Xuto, Somsakdi (ed.). *Government and Politics of Thailand.* New York: Oxford University Press, 1987.

TONGA

Kingdom of Tonga
Pule'anga Tonga

CAPITAL: Nuku'alofa, Tongatapu.

FLAG: The flag, adopted in 1862, is crimson with a cross of the same color mounted in a white canton.

ANTHEM: *Koe Fasi Oe Tu'i Oe Otu Tonga (Tongan National Anthem)* begins "'E 'Otua Mafimafi Ko homau 'Eiki Koe" ("O Almighty God above, Thou art our Lord and sure defense").

MONETARY UNIT: The Tongan pa'anga (T$) of 100 seniti is a paper currency at par with the Australian dollar. There are coins of 1, 2, 5, 10, 20, and 50 seniti, and 1 and 2 Tongan pa'angas, and notes of ½, 1, 2, 5, 10, 20, and 50 pa'angas. T$1 = US$0.7390 (or US$1 = T$1.3532).

WEIGHTS AND MEASURES: The metric system is the legal standard, but some imperial and local weights and measures are also employed.

HOLIDAYS: New Year's Day, 1 January; ANZAC Day, 25 April; Crown Prince's Birthday, 4 May; Independence Day, 4 June; King's Birthday, 4 July; Constitution Day, 4 November; Tupou I Day, 4 December; Christmas, 25–26 December. Movable religious holidays include Good Friday and Easter Monday.

TIME: 1 AM (the following day) = noon GMT.

¹LOCATION, SIZE, AND EXTENT

The Tonga archipelago, also known as the Friendly Islands, lies scattered east of Fiji in the South Pacific Ocean. Nuku'alofa, the capital, is about 690 km (430 mi) from Suva, Fiji, and about 1,770 km (1,100 mi) from Auckland, New Zealand. Consisting of 172 islands of various sizes, only 45 of which are inhabited, Tonga has a total area of 748 sq km (289 sq mi), including inland waters as well as Teleki Tokelau and Teleki Tonga (formerly the Minerva Reefs). Comparatively, the area occupied by Tonga is slightly more than four times the size of Washington, D.C. It extends 631 km (392 mi) NNE–SSW and 209 km (130 mi) ESE–WNW. Areas of the major islands are Tongatapu and 'Eua, 350 sq km (135 sq mi); Ha'apai, 119 sq km (46 sq mi); Vava'u, 143 sq km (55 sq mi); Niuatoputapu and Tafahi, 18 sq km (7 sq mi); and Niuafo'ou, 52 sq km (20 sq mi). The remaining islands have a combined area of 67 sq km (26 sq mi). Tonga's total coastline is about 419 km (260 mi).

²TOPOGRAPHY

The islands run roughly north–south in two parallel chains; the western islands are volcanic, and the eastern are coralline encircled by reefs. At 10,800 m (35,400 ft) deep, the Tonga Trench is one of the lowest parts of the ocean floor. The soil on the low-lying coral islands is porous, being a shallow layer of red volcanic ash, devoid of quartz, but containing broken-down limestone particles.

The volcanic islands range in height to a maximum of 1,033 m (3,389 ft) on Kao. Fonuafo'ou (formerly Falcon Island), about 65 km (40 mi) northwest of Nuku'alofa, is famous for its periodic submergences and reappearances, as a result of earthquakes and volcanic action. There are few lakes or streams. Tofua, Vava'u, Nomuka, and Niuafo'ou each have a lake, and there are creeks on 'Eua and one stream on Niuatoputapu. Other islands rely on wells and the storage of rainwater to maintain a water supply.

³CLIMATE

The climate of Tonga is basically subtropical. Because the islands are in the southeast trade wind area, the climate is cooler from May to November, when the temperature seldom rises above 27°C (81°F). The mean annual temperature is 23°C (73°F), ranging from an average daily minimum of 10°C (50°F) in winter to an average maximum of 32°C (90°F) in summer. Mean annual rainfall, most of which occurs from December to March during the hot season, is 178 cm (70 in) on Tongatapu, 188 cm (74 in) on Niuatoputapu, and 279 cm (110 in) on Vava'u. The mean relative humidity is 80%.

⁴FLORA AND FAUNA

Coconut palms, hibiscus, and other tropical trees, bushes, and flowers are abundant. Tonga is famous for its flying foxes.

⁵ENVIRONMENT

Agricultural activities in Tonga are in the process of exhausting the fertility of the soil. Attempts at reforestation have had limited success. The forest area is declining because of land clearing. Water pollution is also a significant problem due to salinization, sewage, and toxic chemicals from farming activities. The impurity of the water supply contributes to the spread of disease. The nation is also vulnerable to cyclones, flooding, earthquakes, and drought. As of 1992, Tonga participated in several environmental plans to protect the nation's heritage. The government has established a Water Master Plan to manage the nation's water resources for two decades. The more general National Development Plan is a more comprehensive attempt to address the nation's environmental concerns. The Fiji banded iguana and the loggerhead, green sea, and hawksbill turtles were classified as endangered species in 1987.

⁶POPULATION

The 1986 census recorded a population of 94,649, of which the Tongatapu group had 67%. The 1995 population was estimated by the UN at 99,000 and the US Bureau of the Census at 105,600. Based on the former, the estimated population density in 1995 was 132 inhabitants per sq km (343 per sq mi). The average annual rate of population increase between 1980 and 1990 was about 0.5%. Nuku'alofa, the capital and chief port, had a population of 21,383 in the 1986 census and an estimated 34,000 in 1990.

7 MIGRATION

There is considerable movement toward the larger towns as population pressure on agricultural land increases. Some ethnic non-Tongans born on the islands migrate mainly to Fiji and New Zealand. Emigration by Tongan workers, both skilled and unskilled, has long been of concern to the government. In 1989 approximately 39,400 Tongans lived in the US, Australia, and New Zealand. Persons wishing to reside in Tonga must obtain a government permit; permission is granted only to those taking up approved employment. Immigrant settlement is not encouraged because of the land shortage.

8 ETHNIC GROUPS

The Tongans are a racially homogeneous Polynesian people. Less than 2% of the population is of European, part-European, Chinese, or non-Tongan Pacific island origin.

9 LANGUAGES

Tongan, a Polynesian language not written down until the 19th century, is the language of the kingdom, but government publications are issued in both Tongan and English, and English is taught as a second language in the schools.

10 RELIGIONS

Over 98% of Tongans are Christian. About 64% belong to the Free Wesleyan Church of Tonga, which is headed by the Tongan monarch. There are also Roman Catholics (14%), Anglicans, Seventh-Day Adventists, members of the Church of Jesus Christ of Latter-day Saints (Mormon), and Polynesian Christian denominations.

11 TRANSPORTATION

In 1991, Tonga had 272 km (169 mi) of surfaced roads (73% on Tongatapu, 27% on Vava'u) and 94 km (58 mi) of motor roads usable only in dry weather. There are no bridges in Tonga, but three islands in the Vava'u group are connected by two causeways. In 1992 there were 3,757 commercial vehicles and 3,297 automobiles. Tonga has no railways.

Nuku'alofa and Neiafu are the ports of entry for overseas vessels. In 1991, the merchant fleet consisted of three cargo ships and one liquefied gas tanker, for a total of 11,511 GRT. Work on extending the port at Nuku'alofa began in 1985. The Pacific Forum Line and the Warner Pacific Line maintain scheduled service from Australia and New Zealand to Tonga via the Samoas and other islands, and cargo ships visit the group from time to time for shipments of copra. Internal sea connections are maintained by the Polynesia Triangle and by the Shipping Corp. of Polynesia.

Tonga's main airfield is 21 km (13 mi) by road from Nuku'alofa. Air Pacific, Air New Zealand, Polynesian Airlines, and Hawaiian Air operate scheduled international flights from Fuaamotu International Airport at Tongatapu. In 1991, the airport serviced 98,000 passengers, including 34,000 international passengers. The government-owned Friendly Island Airways has scheduled flights between Tongatapu, Ha'apai, 'Eua, Vava'u, and Niuatoputapu.

12 HISTORY

Since the Tongan language was not written down until the 19th century, the early history of Tonga (which means "south") is

based on oral tradition. Hereditary absolute kings (Tu'i Tonga) date back to Ahoeitu in the 10th century. Around the 14th century, the twenty-third king, Kau'ulufonua, while retaining his sacred powers, divested himself of much of his executive authority, transferring it to his brother Ma'ungamotu'a, whom he thereafter called the Tu'i Ha'atakalaua. About the middle of the 17th century, the seventh temporal king, Fotofili, transferred the executive power to his brother Ngala, called the Tu'i Kanokupolu, and thereafter the powers gradually passed into the hands of the latter and his descendants. According to tradition, in the mid-19th century, upon the death of the then Tu'i Tonga, those powers were conferred upon the nineteenth Tu'i Kanokupolu, Taufa'ahu Tupou, founder of the present dynasty.

European chronicles disclose that the island of Niuatoputapu was discovered by the Dutch navigators Jan Schouten and Jacob le Maire in 1616. In 1643, Abel Tasman discovered Tongatapu, and from then until 1767, when Samuel Wallis anchored at Niuatoputapu, there was no contact with the outside world. Capt. James Cook visited the Tongatapu and Ha'apai groups in 1773 and again in 1777, and called Lifuka in the Ha'apai group the "friendly island" because of the gentle nature of its people—hence the archipelago received its nickname, the Friendly Islands. It was in the waters of the Ha'apai group that the famous mutiny on the British ship Bounty occurred in 1789. The first Wesleyan missionaries landed in Tonga in 1826.

The first half of the 19th century was a period of civil conflict in Tonga, as three lines of kings all sought dominance. They were finally checked during the reign of Taufa'ahu Tupou, who in 1831 took the name George. By conquest, George Tupou I (r.1845–93) gathered all power in his own hands and united the islands; he abolished the feudal system of land tenure and became a constitutional monarch in 1875. Meanwhile, by the middle of the century, most Tongans had become Christians, the great majority being Wesleyans, and the king himself was strongly influenced by the missionaries.

In the latter part of the century, there were religious and civil conflicts between the Wesleyan Mission Church and the newly established Free Wesleyan Church of Tonga. After the dismissal of the prime minister, the Rev. Shirley Waldemar Baker, in 1890, the new government allowed full freedom of worship. Ten years later, during the reign (1893–1918) of George II, a treaty of friendship was concluded between the UK and Tonga, and a protectorate was proclaimed. During World War II, Tongan soldiers under Allied command fought the Japanese in the Solomon Islands, and New Zealand and US forces were stationed on Tongatapu, which served as an important shipping point.

Two more treaties of friendship between the UK and Tonga were signed in 1958 and 1968, according to which Tonga remained under British protection, but with full freedom in internal affairs. On 4 June 1970, Tonga ceased being a British protectorate and became an independent member of the Commonwealth of Nations, with King Taufa'ahau Tupou IV—who had succeeded to the throne upon the death of his mother, Queen Salote Tupou (r.1918–65)—as head of state. The new status brought few immediate changes, apart from the fact that it added Tongan control of foreign affairs to self-rule in domestic matters.

In 1972, Tonga claimed the uninhabited Minerva Reefs (now Teleki Tokelau and Teleki Tonga), situated about 480 km (300 mi) southwest of Nuku'alofa, in order to prevent an Anglo-American corporation from founding an independent Republic of Minerva on the reefs in order to gain certain tax advantages. The nation in 1973 celebrated the bicentennial of Cook's first visit by inaugurating the new runway for jet aircraft at the main airport, near Nuku'alofa. The worst tropical storm in Tonga's history, Cyclone Isaac, devastated the islands in March 1982.

Many of the government's strongest critics gained seats in the 1987 legislative elections; the unprecedented turnover was thought to reflect changing attitudes toward traditional authority. However, the traditional leaders continued in charge of the government, with Prince Fatafehi Tu'ipelehake elected as Prime Minister. The island's dissident pro-democracy movement, led by Akilisi Pohive, won the February 1990 general election, but it remained a minority within the legislature. A government scandal over selling Tongan passports to Hong Kong Chinese led to popular support for the opposition. Baron Vaea replaced Prince Fatafehi Tu'ipelehake as Prime Ministers August 1991. King Taufa'ahau Tupou IV organized the Christian Democratic Party in time for the 1993 election to provide greater coordination for his supporters, and to weaken the democracy movement. However, pressure from the pro-democracy forces continued in the February 1993 general election when Pohiva's People's Democratic Movement won six of the nine seats open.

13GOVERNMENT

Tonga is an independent kingdom. According to the constitution of 1875, as amended, the government is divided into three main branches: the sovereign, Privy Council, and cabinet; the Legislative Assembly; and the judiciary. The King-in-Council is the chief executive body, and the cabinet, presided over by the appointed prime minister, makes executive decisions of lesser importance. Lawmaking power is vested in the Legislative Assembly, which consists of a speaker (appointed by the sovereign), the members of the Privy Council, 9 nobles elected by the 33 hereditary nobles of Tonga, and 9 representatives popularly elected every three years. Sessions must be held at least once in every calendar year. Legislation passed by the Privy Council is subject to approval at the next meeting of the Legislative Assembly. Women voted for the first time in 1960, and the first woman was elected to the legislature in 1975. All literate citizens 21 years of age or older are eligible to vote.

14POLITICAL PARTIES

There were two political parties as of 1993: the Democratic Reform Movement, led by 'Akilisi Pohiva, and the Christian Democratic Party.

15LOCAL GOVERNMENT

The islands are divided administratively into three districts: Vava'u in the north, Ha'apai in the center, and Tongatapu in the south. Ha'apai, Vava'u, and the outlying islands are administered by governors who are members of the Privy Council and are responsible to the prime minister. Minor officials perform statutory duties in the villages. Town and district officials have been popularly elected since 1965. They represent the central government in the villages; the district official has authority only over a group of villages.

Titles of nobility were first bestowed in 1875, and later in 1882, 1887, 1903, and 1923. With the hereditary titles were granted villages and lands.

16JUDICIAL SYSTEM

The Supreme Court exercises jurisdiction in major civil and criminal cases. Other cases, heard in the Magistrate's Court or the Land Court, may be appealed to the Supreme Court and then to the Court of Appeal, the appellate court of last resort. With the ratification of the 1968 friendship treaty, UK extraterritorial jurisdiction lapsed, and British and other foreign nations became fully subject to the jurisdiction of the Tongan courts. The judiciary is independent of the King and the executive branch. Criminal defendants are afforded the right to counsel and the right to a fair public trial is protected by law and honored in practice.

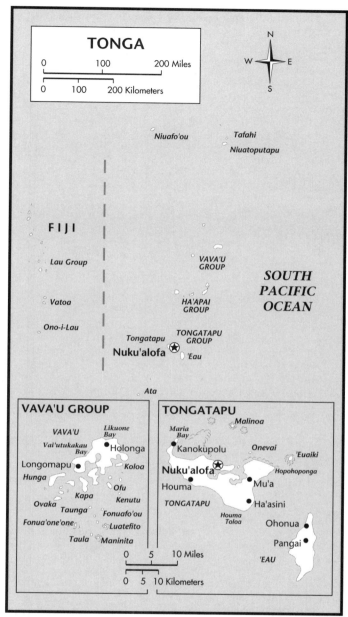

LOCATION: 15° to 23°30's; 173° to 177°w. TERRITORIAL SEA LIMIT: 12 mi.

17ARMED FORCES

The Tonga Defense Force was organized during World War II, became defunct in 1946, and was reactivated in 1952. It consists of a regular cadre and volunteers serving an initial training period, followed by attendance at annual training camps. The minister of police heads a department of more than 200. A naval squadron consisting of several fast patrol boats polices territorial waters.

18INTERNATIONAL COOPERATION

Although not a UN member, Tonga participates in ESCAP, FAO, ICAO, IFAD, IMF, ITU, UNESCO, UPU, and WHO. Tonga is also a member of the Asian Development Bank, Commonwealth of Nations, G-77, IBRD, and South Pacific Forum. It is also a de facto member of GATT. Tongan representatives have attended and taken a leading part at South Pacific conferences. Since 1965, Tonga has received aid under the Australian South Pacific Technical Assistance Program. Tonga has only one diplomatic mission overseas, in the UK.

¹⁹ECONOMY

The economy is largely agricultural, depending principally on the export of copra and coconut products, bananas, and vanilla bean extract. In recent years, pumpkins have become a major export crop, providing 60% of total export earnings in 1991. Fishing (particularly snapper) has also grown in importance. There has been no development of mines, commercially exploitable forests, or large factories. The manufacturing sector remains small but is expanding. Tourism has become a major source of revenue. Arrivals numbered 38,823 in 1990, 23% higher than the previous year. The sale of postage stamps and remittances from overseas workers are additional sources of revenue. Unemployment and inflation are major problems.

²⁰INCOME

In 1992, Tonga's GNP was $136 million at current prices, or $1,350 per capita. For the period 1985–92 the average inflation rate was 10.4%, resulting in a real growth rate in per capita GNP of −0.1%.

²¹LABOR

The total wage labor force in 1990 was about 32,000, of whom 36.5% were employed in agriculture, 14.4% in manufacturing, 22% in public administration and services, 8.1% in commerce, 5.7% in transportation and communication, 3.9% in construction, and 9.4% in other sectors. The unemployment rate was 4.2%. Many Tongans cultivate their own statutory holdings. The government has issued a labor code establishing a wage structure, a system of job classification, and provisions for workers' compensation. Holidays are prescribed by law. According to the constitution, it is not lawful to work, to play games, or to engage in trade on Sunday. Workers have the right to form unions under the 1964 Trade Union Act, but as of 1992, none had been formed. Various government agencies and public enterprises offer vocational training.

²²AGRICULTURE

About 69% of Tonga is agricultural land, including small amounts of permanent pasture. With increasing population pressure on the land, more land is being intensively cultivated and less is available for fallow. The use of fertilizers, high-protein strains of corn, and similar methods to improve the efficiency of land use has become increasingly necessary.

According to the constitution of 1875, all the land in the kingdom belongs to the crown and cannot be alienated. Much of it, however, consists of hereditary estates that were bestowed upon various chiefs, who lease the lands to farmers at a nominal annual rent. Since 1890, the crown has been responsible for the collection of rents and the granting of allotments.

On reaching the age of 16, every Tongan male taxpayer is entitled under the constitution to a tax allotment of 1 'api (3.34 ha/ 8.25 acres). These allotments are hereditary, pass from generation to generation in accordance with the law of succession, and may not be sold. A tenant may be ejected for nonpayment of rent or for failing to comply with the planting regulations, under which every Tongan holder of a tax allotment is legally required to plant 200 coconut trees, which he must keep free from weeds. In recent years, however, population increases have made it impossible to guarantee the 'api to all those entitled to one.

Principal subsistence crops are yams, taro, sweet potatoes, and manioc. Agricultural exports in 1984/85 included 4,262 tons of coconut oil and 463 tons of desiccated coconut. Estimated production in 1992 included coconuts, 25,000 tons; sweet potatoes, 14,000 tons; cassava, 15,000 tons; oranges, 3,000 tons; and bananas, 1,000 tons. Vanilla beans have become an important cash crop, especially on Vava'u.

²³ANIMAL HUSBANDRY

Beef cattle are generally kept for grazing in coconut plantations to keep the undergrowth in check and to provide additional income. Every householder has several hogs, which generally are not sold but are used for feasts. Sheep were brought into Tonga in 1954 but did not thrive, and in 1956 the entire flock was slaughtered. Livestock in 1992 included 97,000 hogs, 16,000 goats, 12,000 horses, and 10,000 head of cattle.

²⁴FISHING

Fish are abundant in the coastal waters, but the fishing industry is relatively undeveloped, and the supply of fish is insufficient to meet local demand; thus, canned fish has been imported in recent years. Principal species caught are tuna and marlin; the fish catch was 1,889 tons in 1991.

²⁵FORESTRY

Forestland covers about 11% of Tonga's total area, mainly on 'Eua and Vava'u, but this diminishing resource has not been efficiently exploited, and much wood for construction must be imported. There is a government sawmill on 'Eua. Charcoal is manufactured from logs and coconut shells.

²⁶MINING

Tonga has few known mineral resources. A limited amount of crushed stone is produced at local quarries.

²⁷ENERGY AND POWER

All power is derived from thermal sources. Installed capacity in 1991 was about 7,000 kw; electricity production totaled 22 million kwh. Oil has been discovered through seepage into water wells, but test wells have been unproductive.

²⁸INDUSTRY

Encouragement of new industries has been a goal of Tonga's five five-year plans (1966–90). Recent industries include the manufacture of concrete blocks, metal products, woolen knitwear, leather goods, furniture, soft drinks, soap, sports equipment, yachts, and paint. At the government-backed Small Industry Centre, refrigerators, jewelry, bicycles, toys, furniture, wheelbarrows, mini-excavators, and other consumer goods are assembled for use locally and in neighboring countries. In 1992, about 500 Tongans, working for 30 different companies, were employed through this program. Long-established industries are coconut processing, sawmilling, and local handicrafts.

²⁹SCIENCE AND TECHNOLOGY

Hango Agricultural College, part of the Free Wesleyan Church Education System, offers diploma and certificate courses. Tonga Maritime Polytechnical Institute is located in Nuku'alofa. In 1980, total research and development expenditures amounted to 426,000 pa'anga; four technicians and eleven scientists and engineers were engaged in research and development.

³⁰DOMESTIC TRADE

Village stores carry a stock of flour, sugar, canned meats, textiles, hardware, soap, kerosene, tobacco, and matches; in the larger towns, these shops are managed by Tongans for European trading firms. Storekeepers act as agents for the Commodities Board and often extend credit to their customers until the end of the harvest. The board's produce division helps market bananas, melons, and pineapples. Development of cooperatives, which serve as savings-and-loan, produce-marketing, and handicraft-manufacturing organizations, has been actively pursued.

Usual banking hours are weekdays from 9:30 AM to 3:30 PM.

31 FOREIGN TRADE

Tonga suffers from chronic trade deficits. In 1992, total exports were valued at P17.4 million, and imports at P84.3 million. Tonga's chief exports are pumpkins, vanilla, woolen knitwear, tuna, leather jackets, coconut oil, taro, and other manufactured goods.

Tonga's trade is chiefly with other Commonwealth countries. The major trading partners are New Zealand, Australia, Japan, Fiji, and the UK.

32 BALANCE OF PAYMENTS

Since 1960, Tonga has had a growing trade deficit, offset by funds from the UK, New Zealand, Australia, and the Asian Development Bank.

In 1992 merchandise exports totaled $14.28 million and imports $50.72 million. The merchandise trade balance was $-36.44 million.

The following table summarizes Tonga's balance of payments for 1991 and 1992 (in millions of US dollars):

	1991	1992
CURRENT ACCOUNT		
Goods services and income	−39.31	−39.02
Unrequited transfers	37.3	37.6
TOTALS	−2.01	−1.42
CAPITAL ACCOUNT		
Direct investment	0.20	1.24
Portfolio investment	−3.73	−.45
Other long-term capital	1.04	1.13
Other short-term capital	4.41	4.29
Reserves	1.00	−3.62
TOTALS	2.92	2.59
Errors and omissions	−0.91	−1.18
Total change in reserves	0.92	−3.52

33 BANKING AND SECURITIES

The Bank of Tonga was formed in 1971, with the government holding 40% of the shares and 20% each held by the Bank of Hawaii, the Bank of New Zealand, and the Bank of New South Wales. The overseas banks provided staff and supervision for the Bank of Tonga, which offers all commercial services and has assumed responsibility for government savings, traders' current accounts, and foreign exchange dealings. At the end of 1993, the bank's assets totaled us$37.1 million, including foreign assets of P50,356 thousand. The Tongan Development Bank was founded in 1977. Tonga has no stock issues or securities trading.

34 INSURANCE

No recent information is available.

35 PUBLIC FINANCE

About half of all public revenues accrued from customs duties on imported goods; the remainder came mainly from export duties, port fees, income taxes, and stamp revenues. Principal items of expenditure were public health, medical services, education, and agriculture.

36 TAXATION

Income tax is levied at progressive rates. Businesses pay a flat rate. All male Tongans 16 years of age and older, except the aged and infirm, pay an annual head tax, the receipts of which are used to finance free education and medical benefits.

37 CUSTOMS AND DUTIES

Tonga has a single column tariff levied primarily for revenue purposes, with protective tariffs applied to certain items, including paint and wire fencing. Exemptions from customs duty are granted for capital goods, raw materials, and semi-finished products under certain conditions. There is a "Port and Service Tax" of 10% ad valorem on all imports.

38 FOREIGN INVESTMENT

Although some non-Tongans have leased large plantations and residential and business sites, there is little private foreign investment. Government policy is that foreign investment is welcome, and that the government will arrange conditions for leasing of land, tax liberalization, and the issuance of import and export licenses. The bulk of Tonga's foreign reserves is invested in Australia.

39 ECONOMIC DEVELOPMENT

Tonga's third five-year plan (1976–80) emphasized development of the islands' economic infrastructure and productive capacity. The fourth five-year plan (1981–85) aimed at increasing agricultural production by revitalizing the copra and banana industries, a task made particularly urgent by the damage done these crops by the March 1982 cyclone; the plan also stressed improvements in telecommunications and transport. The fifth five-year plan (1986–90) emphasized the diversification of the economy through the expansion of tourism, industry, and exports. Through the nonprofit Commodities Board, the government has a trading monopoly in copra, bananas, melons, and other produce. In the early 1990s, tourism revenues helped offset Tonga's large merchandise trade deficits, but substantial amounts of foreign aid continued to be required. In 1990 Tonga received us$24.2 million in bilateral and us$7 million in multilateral aid. The following year, us$1.26 million in UN development aid was granted.

40 SOCIAL DEVELOPMENT

Every family is provided by law with sufficient land to support itself. There is no social welfare department; the medical and education departments and the missions provide what welfare services are available. The only pension scheme is one for civil servants.

Tonga has a family planning program which is integrated with maternal and child health services. Popular acceptance of family planning services has increased notably in recent years. Polynesian cultural traditions have kept most women in subservient roles, although some have risen to positions of leadership. Domestic violence is infrequent and is dealt with according to tribal law and custom.

41 HEALTH

Tonga is free of malaria and most tropical diseases, but tuberculosis, filariasis, typhoid fever, dysentery, and various eye and skin diseases remain common health problems. Nevertheless, in comparison with many other Pacific islands, Tonga is a healthy country. Approximately 90% of children were vaccinated against measles in 1992. By 1969, a joint WHO-UNICEF project had considerably reduced the incidence of yaws. Other health projects deal with school sanitation, community water supplies, maternal and child health, and nursing education.

Life expectancy in 1992 was 68 years. Infant mortality was 21 per 1,000 live births in 1992, with 100 deaths of children under 5 years old that year (25 per 1,000 live births). Tongans receive free medical and dental treatment, but must pay for dentures. Non-Tongans are charged on a fixed scale. Each of the three main islands has a public hospital, but medical personnel are in short supply. In 1985, there were 4 hospitals and 14 health care centers, with a total of 307 beds on the islands. In 1991, Tonga had 49 physicians; in 1989, 138 nurses and 30 mid-wives; and in 1988, 27 dentists.

42HOUSING

Village houses usually have reed sides and a sloping roof thatched with sugarcane or coconut leaves; the posts are of ironwood, and braided cord takes the place of nails. More modern houses, especially in the towns, are built of wood, with roofs of corrugated iron. Unlike the village houses, they often contain more than one room and have verandas. In 1986, the housing stock totaled 15,091 units, of which 60% were European-style wooden houses, 17% were European houses of bricks or cement, 8% were Tongan houses of wood with iron roofs, 7% were Tongan thatch houses, and 4% had wooden walls with thatch roofs.

Rainwater is stored in concrete cisterns. With the help of WHO, underground fresh water has been tapped to improve the water supply. The success of the plan has led to the extension of fresh water supplies to villages on all major islands.

Each urban Tongan taxpayer receives an annual rent subsidy in lieu of the land allotment to which each is entitled.

43EDUCATION

The first schools in Tonga were started by the Wesleyan Mission in 1828, even before the conversion to Christianity of the Tongans, and practically all primary education was controlled by the Mission until 1882, when the government took over the educational system. In 1906, various missionary organizations again were allowed to establish schools.

Primary education is compulsory for all Tongans. Adult literacy is estimated at higher than 90%. Mission schools, which follow a government syllabus, enrolled about 8% of all primary pupils in 1985, and 89% of students at postprimary level. Education is free in government schools (except the high school), but small fees are charged at mission schools. In 1990 there were 16,522 pupils in Tonga's 115 primary schools and 14,749 in secondary schools. The same year, there were 689 primary school teachers and 832 secondary school teachers. Elementary instruction is given in the Tongan language; English is also taught. Selected Tongan students prepare for the New Zealand school certificate examination.

A teacher-training college, established in 1944, provides a two-year course. A government scholarship program provides the opportunity for Tongan students to pursue higher education abroad.

44LIBRARIES AND MUSEUMS

Since 1983, the Ministry of Education has operated a joint library service with the University of the South Pacific. The Tonga College Museum's collection includes artifacts of Tonga's history. Notable monuments include the great trilithon known as the Ha'amanga and some 45 langis, great rectangular platforms of recessed tiers of coral limestone blocks that were erected as the tombs of medieval kings.

45MEDIA

The government's radiotelegraph station at Nuku'alofa has substations at Neiafu (Vava'u), Pangai, Ha'afeva and Nomuka (in the Ha'apai group), 'Eua, and Niuatoputapu. There is also a direct overseas telegraph service linking Nuku'alofa with Wellington, Suva, Apia, and Pago Pago. An internal radiotelephone service connects Nuku'alofa, 'Eua, Nomuka, Ha'afeva, and Vava'u, and a direct overseas radiotelephone service links Nuku'alofa to other Pacific island capitals. The Tonga Broadcasting Commission's Radio Tonga was established in 1961. It has two medium-wave transmitters of 10 kw each, and broadcasts about 75 hours a week in Tongan, English, Fijian, and Samoan; commercial advertising is accepted. In 1991 there were about 75,000 radio sets on the islands. There is no television.

The government publishes a weekly newspaper, the *Tonga Chronicle,* which has an average circulation of 6,000 copies in Tongan and 1,200 in English. There are also church newspapers issued by missions at regular intervals.

46ORGANIZATIONS

Every Tongan village has a community house where ceremonial cloth (tapa) is made by groups of women. The Tongan Women's Progressive Association, formed in 1956, conducts programs for the betterment of village conditions and holds classes in a variety of subjects. There are Boy Scout and Girl Guide groups, and meetings of Christian Endeavor societies and Bible classes are well attended. Extension of consumer cooperatives has been actively encouraged by the government.

47TOURISM, TRAVEL, AND RECREATION

The tourist industry is a small but growing source of foreign exchange revenues. In 1991 there were 22,006 tourist arrivals, 25% from New Zealand, 24% from Canada, and 16% from Australia. There were 564 rooms in hotels and other facilities, with 1,274 beds, and tourism receipts totaled US$10 million. The government-owned International Dateline Hotel and several other modern hotels provide good accommodations. In addition to air and boat services between the islands, taxis and rental cars with drivers are available in the larger towns. Popular tourist sites with visitors are the royal palace and terraced tombs in Nuku'alofa. Most visitors enjoy a traditional evening feast of suckling pig, crayfish, chicken, and assorted accompaniments. Fishing, swimming, and sailing are popular, and rugby football is a favorite spectator sport.

The minister of police grants prior-arrival visitors' permits up to a maximum of six months. Permits are not required from persons in direct transit, holders of Tongan passports, or foreign government officials traveling on official business. Vaccination against yellow fever is required.

48FAMOUS TONGANS

King George Tupou I (Taufa'ahu Tupou, 1797–1893) ruled for 48 years; during his reign, Tonga became a Christian nation and acquired a constitution. His prime minister, Shirley Waldemar Baker (1831–1903), was a Wesleyan clergyman who, after being deposed in 1890, became an Episcopal minister and then returned to Tonga. The most famous Tongan of this century was Queen Salote Tupou (1900–1965), whose rule began in 1918. Her dynasty, the Tupou, is the third branch of the royal family and traces its descent back to Ahoeitu, the first Tu'i Tonga of whom there is record. Queen Salote's son, King Taufa'ahau Tupou IV (b.1918), succeeded to the throne in 1965 and was formally crowned in 1967.

49DEPENDENCIES

Tonga has no territories or colonies.

50BIBLIOGRAPHY

Bain, Kenneth. *The New Friendly Islanders: The Tonga of King Taufa'ahau Tupou IV.* London: Hodder & Stoughton, 1993.

Bott, Elizabeth. *Tongan Society at the Time of Captain Cook's Visit: Discussions with Her Majesty Queen Salote Tupou.* Honolulu: University of Hawaii Press, 1983.

Cook, James. *The Explorations of Captain James Cook in the Pacific, as Told by Selections of His Own Journals, 1768–1779.* Magnolia, Mass.: Peter Smith, n.d.

Ferdon, Edwin N. *Early Tonga: As the Explorers Saw It, 1616–1810.* Tucson: University of Arizona Press, 1987.

Gailey, Christine Ward. *Kinship to Kingship: Gender Hierarchy and State Formation in the Tongan Islands.* Austin, Tex.: University of Texas Press, 1987.

Marcus, George E. *The Nobility and the Chiefly Tradition in the Modern Kingdom of Tonga.* Honolulu: University of Hawaii Press, 1980.

TURKEY

Republic of Turkey
Türkiye Cumhuriyeti

CAPITAL: Ankara.

FLAG: The national flag consists of a white crescent (open toward the fly) and a white star on a red field.

ANTHEM: *Istiklâl Marşi (March of Independence).*

MONETARY UNIT: The Turkish lira (TL) is a paper currency of 100 kuruş. There are coins of 1, 5, 10, 20, 25, 50, and 100 liras, and notes of 5,000, 10,000, 20,000, 50,000, 100,000, 250,000, and 500,000 liras. TL1 = $0.000045 (or $1 = TL22,159.8).

WEIGHTS AND MEASURES: The metric system is the legal standard.

HOLIDAYS: New Year's Day, 1 January; National Sovereignty and Children's Day, 23 April; Spring Day, 1 May; Youth and Sports Day, 19 May; Victory Day, 30 August; Independence Day (Anniversary of the Republic), 29 October. Movable religious holidays include Şeker Bayrami (three days) and Kurban Bayrami (four days).

TIME: 3 PM = noon GMT.

¹LOCATION, SIZE, AND EXTENT

The Republic of Turkey consists of Asia Minor, or Anatolia (Anadolu); the small area of eastern Thrace (Trakya), or Turkey in Europe; and a few offshore islands in the Aegean Sea, with a total area of 780,580 sq km (301,384 sq mi), extending about 1,600 km (1,000 mi) SE–NW and 650 km (400 mi) NE–SW. Comparatively, the area occupied by Turkey is slightly larger than the state of Texas. Of the overall area, 97% is in Asia, and 3% in Europe. Turkey lies athwart the important Black Sea straits system—the Dardanelles, the Sea of Marmara, and the Bosporus. It is bordered on the N by the Black Sea, on the NE by Georgia and Armenia, on the E by Iran, on the SE by Iraq, on the S by Syria and the Mediterranean Sea, on the W by the Aegean Sea, and on the NW by Greece and Bulgaria, with a total boundary length of 9,827 km (6,106 mi). Turkey's capital city, Ankara, is located in the northwest part of the country.

²TOPOGRAPHY

Other than the low, rolling hills of Turkish Thrace, the fertile river valleys that open to the Aegean Sea, the warm plains of Antalya and Adana on the Mediterranean, and the narrow littoral along the Black Sea, the country is wrinkled by rugged mountain ranges that surround and intersect the high, semiarid Anatolian plateau. Average elevations range from 600 m (2,000 ft) above sea level in the west to over 1,800 m (6,000 ft) amid the wild eastern highlands. The highest point is Mount Ararat (Büyük Ağri Daği, 5,137 m/16,854 ft), which rises just within Turkey at the intersection of the Turkish, Armenian, and Iranian frontiers. There are over 100 peaks with elevations of 3,000 m (10,000 ft) or more. Other than the Tigris and Euphrates, which have their sources in eastern Anatolia, rivers are relatively small. Because the watersheds of these streams are semibarren slopes, the seasonal variations in flow are very great. The largest lake is Lake Van (3,713 sq km/1,434 sq mi); the other major lake is Lake Tuz (1,500 sq km/580 sq mi), whose water has a salinity level so high that it serves as a commercial source of salt. Turkey's 8,333 km (5,178 mi) of coastline provide few good natural harbors.

Most of Turkey lies within an earthquake zone, and recurrent tremors are recorded. On 29–30 March 1970, more than 1,000 earthquakes were felt in the Gediz region of western Turkey, killing 1,086 persons. A quake on 6 September 1975, 120 km (75 mi) west of Lake Van, resulted in at least 2,300 deaths, and another, on 24 November 1976, in the Van region, left an estimated 4,000 persons dead. On 30 October 1983, over 1,200 people were killed when a quake struck the Erzurum region, in the northeast. The record destructive earthquake, however, was that of 29 December 1939—near Erzincan—which killed 30,000 persons.

³CLIMATE

Turkey's southern coast enjoys a Mediterranean climate, and the Aegean coastal climate as far north as Izmir is much the same. The mean temperature range in these regions is 17–20°C (63–68°F), and the annual rainfall ranges from 71 to 109 cm (28–43 in). The northern Aegean-Marmara area is somewhat cooler, but also quite moist, the mean temperature range being 14–17°C (57–63°F) and annual rainfall between 56 and 71 cm (22 and 28 in). The Black Sea coast is also relatively mild (14–15°C/57–59°F) and very moist, with 71–249 cm (28–98 in) of rainfall. The central Anatolian plateau is noted for its hot, dry summers and cold winters: the average annual temperature is 8–12°C (46–54°F), and annual precipitation is 30–75 cm (12–30 in). With the exception of some warmer pockets in the valleys, the eastern third of Turkey is colder (4–9°C /39–48°F), and rainfall averages 41–51 cm (16–20 in). The little precipitation there is on the central plateau tends to be concentrated during the late fall and winter months.

⁴FLORA AND FAUNA

A wide variation of flora is found, semitropical to temperate, desert to alpine. In the mountains of southern, southwestern, and northern Turkey are extensive coniferous stands of commercial importance and some deciduous forest. Licorice, valonia oaks, and wild olive trees grow in the southwest. Principal varieties of wild animals are the fallow deer, red deer, roe deer, eastern mouflon, wild boar, hare, Turkish leopard, brown bear, red fox, gazelle, beech marten, pine marten, wildcat, lynx, otter, and badger. There is a large variety of birds, including the snow partridge, quail, great bustard, little bustard, widgeon, woodcock, snipe, and a variety of geese, ducks, pigeons, and rails. About 30 species of snakes are indigenous. Bees and silkworms are grown commercially.

⁵ENVIRONMENT

Environmental responsibilities are vested in the Under Secretariat for Environment and in the Ministry of Energy and Natural Resources. Among Turkey's principal environmental problems is air pollution in Ankara and other cities. The smog in Ankara grew worse after 1979, when the government banned oil heating systems in new buildings in order to reduce costly oil imports; the resultant increased burning of Turkish lignite, which is high in sulfur content, greatly increased the levels of sulfur dioxide and dust in the air. In 1983, the government reversed itself and banned the conversion of heating systems to coal. At the same time, it introduced an antipollution program designed to reduce air pollution levels by more than 50% within a year. In addition to heating restrictions, the plan called for strict traffic controls, the closing of the worst industrial polluters, a prohibition on the import of high-sulfur fuel oil, special emergency hospital wards for smog victims, and the building of green areas and parks in and around cities. By 1993, the nation produced 771.4 tons of hydrocarbon emissions. Turkey contributes 0.4% of the world's total gas emissions. A $220-million project to clean up the polluted water in the Golden Horn, an inlet of the Bosporus forming a harbor in Istanbul, was begun in 1984. The nation's rivers are polluted with industrial chemicals. Among them, mercury has created a serious threat to the nation's water. Soil erosion affects both coastal and internal areas. The combination of water and wind eliminates 500 metric tons of soil each year.

In 1994, five of Turkey's mammal species and 18 of its bird species were endangered. Eighteen types of plants were threatened with extinction. Endangered species included the Anatolian leopard, Mediterranean monk seal, and hawksbill and green sea turtles.

⁶POPULATION

According to the 1990 census, Turkey's population was 56,473,035 an average annual increase of close to 2.3% over the 1985 census figure of 50,664,458. A population of 68,165,000 was projected for the year 2000, assuming a crude birthrate of 25.6 per 1,000 population, a crude death rate of 6.5, and a net natural increase of 19.1 during 1995–2000. Population density was 73 per sq km (189 per sq mi) in 1990. About 41% of the population lived in rural communities; the urban population was 59%. Istanbul (formerly Constantinople), the largest city, had a 1990 population of 6,620,241. The largest cities after Istanbul were Ankara, the capital, 2,559,471; Izmir (formerly Smyrna), 1,757,414; and Adana, 916,150.

⁷MIGRATION

Much Turkish emigration has consisted of workers under contract for employment in EC countries. Germany alone had 1,779,600 Turks at the end of 1991. There are also large numbers of Turks in prosperous Muslim countries such as Sa'udi Arabia, the Gulf states, and Libya. In 1985, 2,282,000 Turkish nationals were living abroad, and the number has grown since then.

⁸ETHNIC GROUPS

About 85% of the population is Turkish. The major ethnic minority (by mother tongue), the Kurds, is estimated at 12% of the population. Arabs, Turkmen, Circassians, Greeks, and others make up about 3% of the population. Hundreds of thousands of Armenians were either killed or forced to flee during and immediately following World War I; bitterness between Armenians and

Turks continues to this day, and during the late 1970s and early 1980s, Armenian terrorists took the lives of more than two dozen Turkish diplomats. The Greek component in Turkey was reduced as a result of the 1919–22 hostilities with Greece, the 1923 Treaty of Lausanne (which provided for an exchange of population with Greece), and the post–World War II Cyprus controversy. The Kurds, some of whom were forcibly dispersed after an uprising in 1935, still tend to be concentrated in the southeastern provinces. The Arabs live in the south along the Syrian and Iraqi frontiers, and the Greeks, Armenians, and Jews live in Istanbul and, to a lesser extent, in Izmir. Separatist Kurdish groups are outlawed, and there is a heavy military presence in the nine provinces where a state of emergency has been in effect since 1987.

⁹LANGUAGES

Turkish, which belongs to the Ural-Altaic group, is the official language. In addition to the Roman alphabet, modern Turkish uses the letters ç, ğ, ı (undotted), ö, ş, and ü, but no q, w, or x. With only minor exceptions, words are spelled phonetically. The language is agglutinative.

A 1928 language reform substituted the Roman alphabet for the Arabic script, which had been used by the Turks since their conversion to Islam. During the 1930s there was a state-sponsored effort to rid the language of Arabic and Persian words and grammatical constructions. Turkish grammatical rules are now applied for all words, regardless of origin, though many Persian and Arabic expressions persist. Traditionally, there was a great difference between vernacular Turkish and written Ottoman Turkish, the latter being heavily influenced by Arabic and Persian and almost unintelligible to the mass of Turks. This difference has been almost obliterated, though some regional differences in dialect, particularly in the villages, still make effective communication difficult.

Kurdish is a language of the Iranian group and is written in Arabic script in Turkey. Two of the three major dialects are spoken in Turkey.

¹⁰RELIGIONS

Religious freedom is provided for by the constitution. Although about 99% of the population is Muslim, there is no official state religion. Nonetheless, the state maintains urban mosques and other Muslim religious properties, licenses Muslim religious leaders, and provides Muslim religious education in the public schools. Proselytizing by either Muslim or non-Muslim is proscribed by law. Laws against the use of religion for political purposes are rigorously enforced. The vast majority of Turkish Muslims are Sunni, but there is a substantial Shi'i minority. Although at times suppressed by law, secret dervish orders have remained active in some areas.

In 1986, religious minorities included an estimated 100,000 Christians and 20,000 Jews. The Greek Orthodox patriarch at Istanbul is considered first among equals of the seven patriarchs in the Eastern Orthodox churches. Turkey was a haven for Jewish refugees from Spain and Portugal in the late 15th and 16th centuries, and Jews have lived there in relative peace until recent years. On 6 September 1986, two armed men fired on worshippers in a synagogue in Istanbul, killing 22; various Arab groups claimed responsibility. On 8 July 1993, thirty-seven people died in connection with an attack by militant Muslim fundamentalists on a meeting of writers and intellectuals including supporters of the novelist Salman Rushdie.

¹¹TRANSPORTATION

Turkey's size and difficult terrain, together with limited economic resources, have proved great obstacles to the construction of transportation facilities. When the republic was founded in 1923 there were about 4,000 km (2,500 mi) of railway track and 7,400

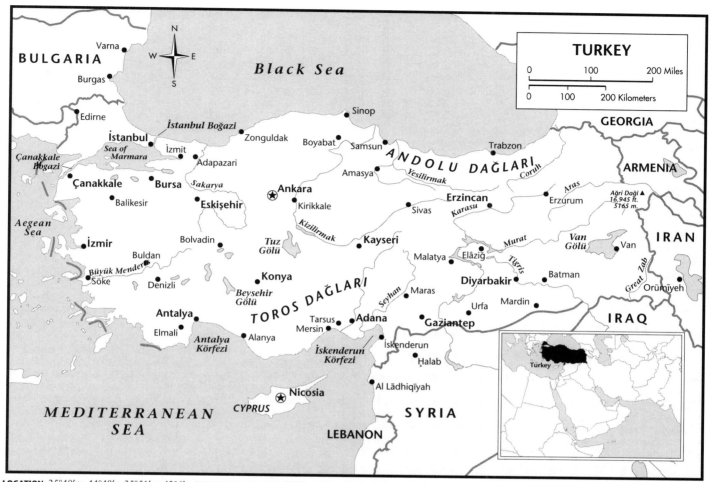

LOCATION: 25°40′ to 44°48′E; 35°51′ to 42°6′N. **BOUNDARY LENGTHS:** USSR, 610 km (379 mi); Iran, 454 km (282 mi); Iraq, 331 km (206 mi); Syria, 877 km (545 mi); Greece, 212 km (132 mi); Bulgaria, 269 km (167 mi); total coastline, 8,333 km (5,178 mi). **TERRITORIAL SEA LIMIT:** 6 mi, Aegean Sea; 12 mi, Mediterranean and Black seas.

km (4,600 mi) of motor roads in Anatolia and Thrace, all in disrepair. By 1991, 8,401 km (5,220 mi) of track connected most of the important points in the country with Ankara, Istanbul, and the Black Sea and Mediterranean ports. The railways are owned and operated by the Turkish State Railways, a public corporation. Railways carried 129.4 million passengers and 14.85 million tons of freight in 1991.

Animal transportation in most of the country has gradually given way to trucks and buses that use roads provided by extensive construction programs since World War II. In October 1973, the Bosporus Bridge in Istanbul was opened, facilitating the crossing of the Straits of the Bosporus by motorists; this six-lane steel suspension bridge had a main span of 1,074 m (3,524 ft). As of 1991, 1,864,344 automobiles, 202,605 buses and minibuses, and 554,300 trucks, were registered.

The Turkish merchant fleet in 1991 consisted of 347 vessels of all types totaling 4.08 million GRT. The leading ports were Mersin, Istanbul, Izmir, Iskenderun, and Izmit.

With minor exceptions, domestic air transportation is the monopoly of the semipublic Turkish Airways Corp. (Türk Hava Yollari), which connects most major centers within the country on a regular schedule and operates some international flights. Two international airports—Atatürk (Istanbul) and Esenboğa (Ankara)—are served by some 20 international air carriers. Other international airports are located at Antalya, Dalaman, and Izmir. In 1992, scheduled airline traffic amounted to 5,239 million passenger-km and 102 million freight ton-km performed.

[12]HISTORY

In ancient times, Turkey was known as Asia Minor or Anatolia. Among the many inhabitants were the Hittites (c.1800–c.1200 BC), the first people to use iron; the Greeks, who, according to legend, destroyed Troy (or Ilium) about 1200 BC and who colonized the Aegean coast from about 1000 BC on; the Phrygians (c.1200–c.600 BC); the Lydians (c.700–546 BC), the first people to mint coins; the Persians (546–333 BC); and the Romans, beginning in the 2d century BC. Roman Emperor Constantine I (the Great) changed the name of the city of Byzantium to Constantinople (now Istanbul) and made it his capital in AD 330; a division between the Western and Eastern Roman Empires, with their respective capitals at Rome and Constantinople, became official in 395. Constantinople, seat of the Byzantine Empire, became the center of Eastern Orthodox Christianity, which officially separated from Roman Catholicism in 1054, when the pope and the patriarch of Constantinople excommunicated each other.

The Turks are a Ural-Altaic people who emerged from the plains between the Ural Mountains in Europe and the Altay Mountains in Asia. The forerunners of the inhabitants of present-day Turkey, known as the Seljuk Turks (named after the Turkish conqueror Seljuk, fl.10th century), defeated the Byzantines in the battle of Malazgirt (1071) and established themselves in Anatolia. They attained a highly developed Muslim culture in their great capital at Konya, in central Turkey. The Turkish conquest of Syria, including Palestine, led to the Crusades (1096–1270), a series of intermittent and inconclusive wars. Various Latin (Roman Catholic) and Greek (Eastern Orthodox) states were formed in parts of the Turkish Empire, but none lasted. The sack of the Christian city of Constantinople by Crusaders in 1204, followed by the establishment of the Latin Empire there (1204–61), shocked Europe and tended to discredit the Crusading movement.

Seljuk power was shattered when the Mongols, another Ural-Altaic people, swept across Asia Minor in 1243. As the Mongols withdrew, Turkish power revived and expanded under the Ottoman Turks, a group of frontier warriors whose first chief was Osman I (called Ottoman in the West, r.1300?–1326). In 1453, the Ottomans under Mehmet II (the Conqueror) occupied Constantinople and made it their capital. In 1516, they conquered Syria; in 1517, Egypt. In 1529, they were at the gates of Vienna, at which point the European expansion of Turkish power was stopped. The Turkish fleet was decisively defeated in a battle near Lepanto (now Navpaktos) in Greece in 1571. At its peak, generally identified with the reign of Sultan Süleyman I (the Magnificent, r.1520–66), the Ottoman Empire encompassed an estimated 28 million inhabitants of Asia Minor, much of the Arabian Peninsula, North Africa as far west as modern Algeria, the islands of the eastern Mediterranean, the Balkans, the Caucasus, and the Crimea. During the 17th, 18th, and 19th centuries, as a result of the rise of nationalism and encroachment by the European powers, it gradually shrank in size, the independence of the remainder being maintained only by shrewd balance-of-power diplomacy.

The process of modernization began with the Imperial Rescript of 1839, promulgated by Sultan Abdul Mejid (r.1839–61), and by a body of reforms known as the Tanzimat, which to some extent curbed the absolute powers of the sultan-caliph. (The Turkish sultans had added the title "caliph" following the conquest of Egypt in 1517.) The Illustrious Rescript of 1856 was largely dictated by Britain, France, and Austria as part of the negotiations leading to the settlement of the Crimean War (1853–56), a clash between the Russian and Ottoman Empires; it ensured equal rights for non-Muslims, provided for prison reform and the codification of Turkish law, and opened Turkey to European skills and capital. A constitution was introduced in 1876 by Sultan Abdul Hamid II (r.1876–1909) but was suspended in the following year. Thereafter, an absolute monarchy prevailed until the Young Turk revolution of 1908, at which time the constitution of 1876 was reinstated. In 1913, leaders of the Committee for Union and Progress (the organizational vehicle of the Young Turks) took effective control of the government under Sultan Mehmet V (r.1909–18). The principal leaders were Talat and Enver Paşa, who, at the outbreak of World War I, threw what little remained of Ottoman strength behind the Central Powers, which had sided with Turkey in its fruitless attempt to retain its last major European possessions in the Balkan Wars of 1912–13. Although the Turks were unable to make any headway against British forces defending the Suez Canal, they did offer a heroic defense at Gallipoli (the Gelibolu Peninsula) and the Dardanelles, in a prolonged battle between Turkish and British-French forces that lasted from February 1915 to January 1916 and took the lives of about 100,000 soldiers on each side. In 1917, however, Turkish resistance collapsed, and the British pushed Turkey out of Syria, Palestine, Iraq, and Arabia. An armistice was concluded on 30 October 1918, and Enver Paşa and his colleagues fled the country.

Before and during the war, Armenians sought to establish their independence and were brutally repressed by the Turks. Over a million people are said to have died being driven from their homes; many survived in exile.

On the basis of a series of earlier Allied agreements, the Ottoman Empire was to be stripped of all non-Turkish areas, and much of what remained—Asia Minor—was to be divided among the UK, France, Greece, and Italy. A substantial portion was actually occupied. In 1919, with Allied assistance, the Greeks invaded Anatolia through Izmir, but a Turkish nationalist resistance move-

ment under the leadership of Mustafa Kemal (later called Atatürk), who had commanded a division at Gallipoli, finally defeated them in 1922. The sultan, being virtually captive in Istanbul, was disgraced in Turkish eyes by his identification with Allied policy. After much maneuvering, a rival nationalist government under Mustafa Kemal was established in Ankara and gained national and international recognition. On 1 November 1922, the sultanate was abolished by Mustafa Kemal's provisional government. The following year, the Ankara government negotiated the Treaty of Lausanne with the Allies, which recognized Turkish sovereignty over Asia Minor and a small area in Thrace. There was a massive exchange of Greek and Turkish populations. On 29 October 1923, a republic was proclaimed, with Ankara as its capital, and on 3 March 1924, the caliphate was abolished and all members of the dynasty banished.

During the next few years, a series of social, legal, and political reforms were accomplished that, taken collectively, became known as the Atatürk Reforms. They included the substitution of secular law for religious law, the writing of a republican constitution based on popular sovereignty, suppression of religious education in Turkish schools, introduction of a Roman alphabet to replace the Arabic script, and the legal upgrading of the position of women. With minor exceptions, political power resided in a single party, the Republican People's Party, and to a very substantial extent in Mustafa Kemal personally until his death in 1938. His chief of staff, Ismet Inönü (Paşa), became president and established a two-party system of government with the formation of the opposition Democrat Party (DP) in 1946.

Although pro-Allied, Turkey remained neutral during most of World War II, but early in 1945 it declared war on the Axis and became a charter member of the UN. In 1947, the Truman Doctrine pledged US support to Turkey in the face of mounting Soviet pressure. This move was followed by large-scale military and economic assistance from the US. Turkey thus became firmly committed to the Western alliances—NATO and the Central Treaty Organization, or CENTO (Baghdad Pact).

The DP came to power in 1950. Under Prime Minister Adnan Menderes, the government stressed rapid industrialization and economic expansion at the cost of individual liberties. Restrictive press laws were passed in 1954 and 1956, and by 1960 the Menderes government had curtailed judicial independence, university autonomy, and the rights of opposition parties. On 27 May 1960, after student demonstrations (joined by War College cadets and some army officers) were harshly suppressed, Prime Minister Menderes, President Celâl Bayar, and other government leaders were arrested by a newly formed Committee of National Unity. Gen. Cemal Gürsel became acting president and prime minister. Menderes was found guilty of violating the constitution and was hanged in 1961. A new constitution was popularly ratified in 1961, and elections were held in October. Gen. Gürsel was elected president by the New Grand National Assembly, and Inönü became prime minister of a coalition government.

The opposition Justice Party (JP) won 52.3% of the vote in the 1965 elections and formed a new government under Süleyman Demirel. Four years later, the JP was returned to power, and Prime Minister Demirel began a new four-year term. But Turkey's four top military commanders forced the resignation of Demirel's government in 1971 and called for a "strong and credible government" that would restore economic and political stability and suppress student disorders, which had steadily grown more frequent and more violent since 1968. Martial law had been imposed from June to September 1970, and a new "above party" government under Nihat Erim reimposed martial law in 11 provinces (including Ankara and Istanbul) from 1971 to 1973.

Political stability proved no easier to achieve: a succession of weak coalition governments, headed alternately by Demirel and Republican leader Bülent Ecevit, held office between 1973 and

1980. Ecevit's government was in power during the Greco-Turkish war on Cyprus in July–August 1974. Relations with Greece, strained by a dispute over mineral rights on the Aegean continental shelf, reached the breaking point on 15 July, when Cypriot President Makarios was overthrown in a Greek-led military coup. Fearing the island would be united with Greece, Turkish forces invaded on 20 July. A UN cease-fire came into effect two days later, but after peace talks at Geneva broke down, Turkish troops consolidated their hold over the northern third of the island by 16 August. As the result of this action, the US embargoed shipments of arms to Turkey until 1978; as of 1994, an estimated 25,000 or more Turkish troops remained on Cyprus to support the Turkish Republic of Northern Cyprus which only Turkey recognizes.

During the late 1970s, escalating acts of violence by political groups of the extreme left and right, coupled with economic decline, threatened the stability of Turkey's fragile democracy. By April 1980, 47,000 people had been arrested, and martial law had spread to 20 of Turkey's 67 provinces; at midyear, more than 5,000 persons had been killed (including former Prime Minister Nihat Erim), and the factional strife was claiming an average of 20 victims each day. With the legislature deadlocked, the military intervened in the political process for the third time in 20 years. A five-man military National Security Council (NSC), headed by Gen. Kenan Evren, took power in a bloodless coup on 12 September 1980. The NSC suspended the 1961 constitution, banned all political parties and activities, and arrested thousands of suspected terrorists. With the entire country under martial law, factional violence was drastically reduced. By April 1982, 40,000 alleged "political extremists" had been arrested; 23,000 had been tried and convicted in martial law courts, some 6,000 of them for "ideological offenses." Under an NSC edict forbidding Turkey's former political leaders from speaking out on political matters, former Prime Minister Ecevit was twice arrested and imprisoned during 1981–82. In protest against the treatment of Ecevit, the EEC froze payment of $650 million in loans and grants previously pledged to Turkey.

In a national referendum on 7 November 1982, Turkish voters overwhelmingly approved a new constitution (prepared by a constituent assembly chosen by the NSC) under which Gen. Evren became president of the republic for a seven-year term; campaigning against ratification had been illegal under martial law. Parliamentary elections were held in November 1983, although martial law remained in effect. Following the elections, Jurgut Özal, leader of the victorious Motherland Party, was installed as prime minister. Martial law was lifted in most provinces over the next two years, but emergency rule remained in effect; legislation was passed to broaden police powers, freedom of expression remained limited, and trials of alleged extremists continued. Human-rights groups complained of torture, suspicious deaths, overcrowding, and substandard conditions in Turkish jails; the government denied any improprieties. Özal's Motherland Party retained its parliamentary majority in November 1987 elections, and he was reelected for a second five-year term. In 1989, Özal was elected president. His Motherland Party continued in power but with declining popularity as shown in 1989 municipal elections. Özal's ambition was to tie Turkey closely to Europe but, despite improvements in Turkey's human rights record, its application for full membership in the European Union was deferred indefinitely. Özal also sought to give Turkey a leading role with the Turkic republics of former Soviet Central Asia. He continued Turkey's long-standing policy of quiet contacts with Israel while seeking better ties with the Arab states. During the Gulf War, he joined the embargo against Iraq, closed Iraq's oil pipelines, provided facilities for allied air raids and later supported protective measures for Iraqi Kurds. In compensation, Turkey received increased aid worth $300 million.

In October 1991 elections, the Motherland Party lost its parliamentary majority to the True Path and Social Democratic Party in coalition. True Path leader Demeril was named Prime Minister. He succeeded to the presidency in May 1993 following the death of Özal. Tansu Ciller, True Path chairperson, became Turkey's first female Prime Minister in July. In 1994, Ciller faced three major tasks: dealing with the problems of high inflation (about 70%) and unemployment as she continued Özal's free market policies of export-led growth (7–8%), reducing government regulations and privatization; pacifying the rebellious Kurdish areas of eastern Turkey where large numbers of troops have been tied down in a conflict that has taken thousands of lives and millions in treasure; and responding to the rising challenge to Turkey's secular nationalism from politically militant Islamic groups.

13GOVERNMENT

The 1961 constitution vested legislative power in the Grand National Assembly, consisting of the House of Representatives, with a membership of 450 (elected for four-year terms), and the Senate of 165 members, of whom 150 were elected and 15 appointed by the president. The president of the republic—the head of state—was elected for a single seven-year term by a joint session of the National Assembly. The president was empowered to designate the prime minister from among the Assembly members; the prime minister in turn chose other cabinet ministers, who were responsible for general government policy.

The constitution ratified in November 1982, which replaced the 1961 document, declares Turkey to be a democratic and secular republic that respects the human rights of its citizens and remains loyal to the nationalistic principles of Atatürk. It vests executive powers in the president of the republic and the Council of Ministers. Legislative functions are delegated to the unicameral National Assembly, consisting of 400 members elected for five-year terms (the Senate was abolished). Under the constitution's "temporary articles," the five-person National Security Council (NSC) remained in power until the new parliament convened, at which time the NSC became a Presidential Council, to function for a period of six years before dissolving. These "temporary" provisions expressly forbade all former leaders of either the Justice or the Republican People's Party from participating in politics for 10 years; all former members of the previous parliament were forbidden to found political parties or to hold public office for five years. Proposals to change the voting age from 21 to 20 years and expand the National Assembly from 400 to 450 members were approved in May 1987. A referendum in September 1987 approved a proposal to lift the 10-year ban on political participation by leaders of the Justice and Republican People's Parties and numerous other politicians.

Although the constitution guarantees individual freedoms, exceptions may be made in order to protect the republic and the public interest, or in times of war or other national emergency. The provision holding that an arrested person cannot be held for more than 48 hours without a court order may likewise be suspended in the case of martial law, war, or other emergency.

14POLITICAL PARTIES

The first significant nationwide party, the Republican People's Party (Cumhuriyet Halk Partisi—CHP), was organized by Mustafa Kemal in 1923. Strong, centralized authority and state economic planning marked its 27 years of power (1923–50). It deemphasized everything religious to the point of subordinating religious activity and organization to state control.

Not until 1946 did a second popular party, the Democrat Party (Demokrat Parti—DP), come into being. Initially formed by a small group of dissident CHP members of parliament, the DP demanded greater political and economic liberalism and specifically a relaxation of central controls. When they came to power in 1950, the Democrats put into effect their policies of economic expansion through rapid mechanization and free enterprise; they also emphasized rural development through liberal credit terms to farmers. These policies, aimed at broadening the base of the economy, helped to return the Democrats to power three times in succession. After 1954, however, the Democrat regime reinstituted many of the former controls and instituted others, notably over the press. The CHP condemned these moves as well as what it regarded as lack of economic planning and of adequate fiscal and commercial controls. Both the Democrats and the CHP supported a firmly pro-Western, anti-Communist foreign policy.

In the first elections of the Second Republic (October 1961), none of the four competing parties won a controlling majority in either chamber, and a coalition government was formed for the first time in 1962. The coalition, however, was short-lived, for the newly formed Justice Party (Adalet Partisi—AP) withdrew from the governing group of parties and became the chief political opposition. The AP, which became the main political force in the country after the 1965 elections, favored private enterprise (in this respect it can be considered the successor of the DP, which was banned in 1960). Organized originally by local Democrat leaders, the AP came to reflect the views of modernization-minded professionals as well as workers and villagers. In the 1965 elections, the AP won 53.8% of the seats in the House of Representatives and 61% of the Senate seats. The elections of October 1969 confirmed its legislative predominance.

In December 1970, dissident members of the AP created the Democratic Party (Demokratik Parti). Another new organization, the Republican Reliance Party (Cumhuriyetçi Güven Partisi—CGP), formed by dissident members of the CHP, put up its first candidates in the 1969 elections. The National Salvation Party (Milli Selâmet Partisi—MSP) was created in March 1973 for the purpose of preserving Islamic traditions and bringing about economic and social reforms. In the general elections of 14 October 1973, the CHP replaced the AP as the most popular party in Turkey, although it did not achieve a parliamentary majority, and the CHP and MSP formed a coalition government under Bülent Ecevit. After the Ecevit government fell in September 1974, more than six months passed before a new permanent government was formed by Süleyman Demirel. His minority Government of the Nationalist Front, which included representatives of the AP, CGP, MSP, and National Action Party (Milliyetçi Hareket Partisi), commanded 214 out of 450 National Assembly seats. After the CHP won 213 Assembly seats in the 1977 elections, Ecevit, having formed a minority cabinet, lost a parliamentary vote of confidence and had to resign. But his rival, Demirel, fared little better as prime minister, and his coalition government soon dissolved. Each served another brief stint as head of government prior to the 1980 military coup.

The new military government banned all political parties and, under the 1982 constitution, forbade the leaders of the AP and CHP from active participation in politics for 10 years. After the new constitution was approved, however, the government allowed the formation of new political groups. The first new party, the Nationalist Democracy Party, was formed in May 1983 by certain retired military officers, former government officials, and business leaders; it received support from the military but fared poorly in local and national elections and was disbanded three years later. Another new group, the rightist Great Turkey Party, was abolished by the government soon after its founding because of alleged close resemblances to the banned AP; the True Path Party (Dogru Yol Partisi—DYP) was established in its place but was not allowed to participate in the elections to the National Assembly on 6 November 1983. Also barred were the newly formed Welfare Party and the Social Democratic Party, and Demirel and other politicians were temporarily placed under military detention. The Populist Party, which the military was said to regard as a loyal opposition, and the Motherland Party (Anata-van Partisi—ANAP), formed by conservative business leaders and technocrats, did win approval to run. In the balloting, the ANAP won a majority in the National Assembly, with 212 out of 400 seats, and its leader, Turgut Özal, became prime minister on 13 December.

Subsequently, all parties were allowed to participate in local elections. In 1985, the Populist Party merged with the Social Democratic Party to form the Social Democratic Populist Party (Sosyal Demokrasi Halkçi Partisi—SDHP). The Free Democrat Party was formed in 1986 as a successor to the Nationalist Democracy Party. In September 1987, the 10-year ban on political participation by over 200 leaders of the AP and CHP was lifted after a referendum indicated approval by a bare majority of just over 50%. At the same time, Özal announced elections in November of that year and had a law passed requiring nomination of candidates by party leaders rather than by popular choice. After challenges from opposition groups, the Constitutional Court declared the new procedure illegal. In the November 1987 elections, Özal was reelected as prime minister, with 36.3% of the vote; the ANAP won 292 of the 450 seats in the National Assembly (although polling only 36% of the vote), the SDHP 99 seats, and the DYP 59 seats. A coalition of True Path and Social Democrats defeated the Motherland Party in 1991. Outside the established political system are the Kurdistan Workers Party (PKK) and other smaller separatist parties which have been banned.

15LOCAL GOVERNMENT

The chief administrative official in each of Turkey's 73 provinces (vilayets or ils) is the provincial governor (vali), an appointee of the central government who is responsible to the Ministry of Internal Affairs. During the military takeover in 1980s, governors were made responsible to the military authorities, and provincial assemblies were suspended. In 10 southeastern provinces, a regional governor exercises authority under a state of emergency declared in 1987. For administrative purposes, provinces are subdivided into districts (kazas or ilces), which in turn are divided into communes (nahiyes or bucaks), comprising kasabas and villages. In municipalities and villages, locally elected mayors and councils perform government functions. Both levels of government have specified sources of income and prepare budgets for the allocation of such income, which are then subject to approval by the central government. Most public revenue, however, is collected by the Ministry of Finance in Ankara.

16JUDICIAL SYSTEM

The judicial system was left substantially intact by the 1982 constitution, except for the addition of special state security courts to handle cases involving terrorism and state security. There are four branches of courts: civil, administrative, military, and constitutional.

Civil courts are specialized into five sections: civil, enforcement, criminal, commercial, and labor. The same judges may serve in various sections. Decisions of civil courts of original jurisdiction are appealable to a High Court of Appeals in Ankara. The High Court of Appeals also hears cases involving charges against members of the Cabinet and other high functionaries.

Administrative courts include courts of first instance, regional appellate courts, and a Council of State at the apex. The Council of State also renders advisory opinions on draft legislation.

The Military Courts have jurisdiction over military personnel and include courts of first instance and a Military Court of Appeals.

The Constitutional Court reviews the constitutionality of legislation at the time of passage both when requested by the required percentage of members of Parliament and in the context of review of constitutional issues which emerge during litigation.

The constitution guarantees the independence of the judiciary from the executive and provides for life tenure for judges. It also explicitly prohibits state authorities from issuing orders or recommendations concerning the exercise of judicial power. The High Council of Judges and Prosecutors selects judges and prosecutors for the higher courts and oversees those in lower courts. In practice, the courts act independently of the executive.

The constitution guarantees defendants the right to a public trial. The bar association is responsible for providing free counsel to indigent defendants. There is no jury system. All cases are decided by a judge or a panel of judges.

[17]ARMED FORCES

The total armed forces strength in 1993 was 560,300 (including 481,000 conscripts), plus 1.1 million reserves. The army had 450,000 men (410,000 conscripts) in 5 infantry divisions (1 mechanized), 7 armored brigades, and 18 infantry divisions (1 mechanized), 7 armored brigades, and 18 independent specialized brigades. An estimated 30,000 Turkish soldiers were stationed on Cyprus. The navy had 52,300 personnel; naval strength included 2 submarines, 12 destroyers, 8 frigates, 47 patrol and coastal combatants, 37 mine warfare vessels, and about 35 auxiliary ships. Naval aviation provides 37 ASW aircraft and helicopters. The air force had 58,000 personnel and 573 combat aircraft. Paramilitary forces totaled 125,000. The defense budget for 1992 was $5.2 billion or 3–4% of gross domestic product. Since 1947, US military aid to Turkey has totaled about $12 billion and is probably higher.

The principal challenge to Turkey is the guerrilla war run by the PPK party, the Kurdish resistance movement.

[18]INTERNATIONAL COOPERATION

Turkey is a charter member of the UN, having joined on 24 October 1945, and belongs to ECE and all the nonregional specialized agencies. In December 1964, Turkey became an associate member of the EEC; Turkey applied in 1987 for membership in the EC, including full membership in the EEC, but the application was opposed by Greece (unanimous consent of all EEC members is required for admission). Turkey is also a signatory to GATT and a member of the Council of Europe, NATO, and OECD. Because of the imposition of martial law in Turkey, the Council of Europe decided in 1981 not to seat Turkish delegates at its parliamentary sessions.

Relations with the US, Turkey's principal aid benefactor, were strained during the 1970s over the Cyprus issue. After the Turkish military forces, using US-supplied equipment, had occupied the northern third of the island, the US Congress in 1975 embargoed military shipments to Turkey in accordance with US law. In response, Turkey abrogated its 1969 defense cooperation agreement with the US and declared that it would take over US military installations in Turkey (except the NATO base at Adana). The US government then relaxed the arms embargo and finally ended it in 1978, after which Turkey lifted its ban on US military activities. Turkish-US relations improved markedly thereafter, and a new defense and economic cooperation agreement between the two countries was signed in 1980. In 1986, the 1980 agreement was renewed, allowing the US to use some 15 Turkish military bases in exchange for continuing military and economic subsidies.

[19]ECONOMY

During the late 1960s and early 1970s, Turkey enjoyed a high economic growth rate, averaging about 7% annually. This growth was financed largely by foreign borrowing, increased exports, and remittances from Turkish workers in Western Europe. As a result of the large increases in oil import costs during 1973-74, however, Turkey's economic growth declined in real terms during 1974–80, and the country suffered a severe financial crisis. Stabilization programs implemented in 1978 and 1979

under a standby agreement with the IMF proved inadequate, but in January 1980, as a condition of further IMF aid, Turkey imposed a more stringent economic reform program, involving currency devaluation, labor productivity improvements, and restructuring of the nation's inefficient state enterprises. As a result, the GNP rose by 5.3% in 1981 as exports expanded, fuel costs declines, domestic demand weakened, and investments increased. Except for 1990, however, there was only low growth from 1980 through 1991. In 1992, the GDP grew by 5.8% and in 1993 by 7.3%. However, continued high population growth and income disparities left much of the population unaffected by these gains.

The government achieved limited success in controlling inflation, reducing the annual rate from more than 100% in 1980 to a range of around 30-50% during the next seven years. But between 1988 and 1993, the rate was always in the 60-70% range. In early 1994, the lira was devalued, leading to even higher inflation.In 1992, about 17% of Turkey's GDP was derived directly from agriculture. Since the end of World War II, the agricultural share has declined, while that of the industrial sector (including construction) expanded to 33% of the 1992 GDP; sservices accounted for 51%. This shift in economic activity is in part the result of deliberate government policy. Mechanization of agriculture has produced a significant shift in population from farms to cities, necessitating substantial urban and industrial development and, hence, a high rate of investment. However, this heavy investment, plus an explosion of consumer demand, has also led to severe inflation and balance-of-payments problems. Using 1987 prices as a base 100, the cost of living index in Istanbul rose to 276 in 1989 and to 1,220 in 1992; and in Ankara, in the same period, it rose to 281 and then to 1,362. Growth also increased the need for foreign borrowing; in mid-1993, foreign debt exceeded $59 billion.

[20]INCOME

In 1992, Turkey's GNP was $114,234 million at current prices, or $1,950 per capita. For the period 1985–92 the average inflation rate was 54.7%, resulting in a real growth rate in per capita GNP of 2.7%.

In 1992 the GDP was $112,971 million in current US dollars. It is estimated that in 1991 agriculture, hunting, forestry, and fishing contributed 17% to GDP; mining and quarrying, 2%; manufacturing, 22%; electricity, gas, and water, 2%; construction, 6%; wholesale and retail trade, 18%; transport, storage, and communication, 14%; finance, insurance, real estate, and business services, 8%; community, social, and personal services, 2%; and other sources, 9%.

[21]LABOR

Of the total civilian labor force of 20,319,000 in 1992, 18,700,000 persons were employed. Of these, 44% worked in agriculture (including forestry and fishing); the industrial labor force amounted to 18% of the working population. The unemployment rate was 7.8% in 1992, down from 8.2% in 1991.

A detailed labor code administered by the Ministry of Labor controls many aspects of labor-management relations. Turkey has a basic 45-hour workweek, with a maximum of 7.5 hours per day and Saturday a partial holiday. Overtime is limited, and must be paid for at a 50% premium. No overtime is permitted in night work, underground work, or in industries considered dangerous to health. Workers usually are entitled to one paid day off per week. Compulsory accident and occupational disease insurance has been in effect since 1946, and workers enjoy a variety of other social security coverages.

A 1946 law authorized the formation of labor unions and enabled them to engage in collective bargaining, and the right to strike was legally permitted in 1963, although general, solidarity, and wildcat strikes are explicitly prohibited. Employers' unions also exist, but members of one kind of union are prohibited from joining the other. In 1991 there were 7,485 public and 5,684 private enterprises (with 630,844 and 458,705 workers, respectively) which were covered by collective bargaining agreements. The major labor confederation was the Turkish Trade Confederation. Union membership was largest in the textile industry, tobacco manufacturing, public utilities, transport and communications, and coal mining. After the 1960 overthrow of the Menderes government, trade unions pressed the government to act upon their demands for the right to strike, for collective labor contracts, and for various social benefits, which were provided for in law but had not been fully implemented. A new labor law enacted in 1967 broadened existing protection and coverage of nonagricultural workers.

The military government that took power in September 1980 immediately banned strikes and lockouts, suspended union activities, and prohibited employers from laying off workers without military authorization. After the prohibition was repealed in 1983, strikes in the subsequent years escalated (especially after 1987). In 1991, there were 398 strikes involving 62,189 workers and 3,809,354 workdays lost. In 1992, the number of strikes dropped to 98, with 62,189 workers involved and 1,53,578 workdays lost. The Turkish Confederation of Revolutionary Workers Unions (DISK), was closed down in 1980, and its leaders were arrested. In 1991, however, DISK was relegalized, and its $300 million in assets and property were returned in March 1992.

22AGRICULTURE

About 27.6 million hectares (68.1 million acres), or 36% of Turkey's total land area, are considered arable; in any given year, about two-thirds of arable land is under crops, and one-third is fallow. Little uncultivated arable land remains. The average holding is not more than 4 or 5 hectares (10–12 acres). Dry grain farming—in which half the land must lie fallow each year—offers little more than a subsistence standard of living. Almost half of the labor force is engaged in agriculture, which provides about 16% of GNP. Large farms are concentrated mainly in the Konya, Adana, and Izmir regions. Agricultural methods still tend to be primitive, but modern machinery has been introduced. Much new land has been brought under cultivation since World War II, and the increased use of chemical fertilizers and expansion of irrigated lands have increased yields per acre overall. In 1991, about 9% of all arable land was irrigated. Nevertheless, crop yields are still extremely sensitive to variations in rainfall. In good crop years, Turkey exports cereals, but in drought years, it must import them.

About 90% of the cultivated area is devoted to cereals. Wheat is the principal crop, accounting for 66% of total grain production in 1992; 19,318,000 tons of wheat were grown in that year, followed by barley with 6,900,000 tons. Turkey also produced 14,800,000 tons of sugar beets and about 3,460,000 tons of grapes. Other agricultural products were grown in lesser but still important quantities in 1992: maize, 2,100,000 tons; sunflower seeds, 950,000 tons; cotton, 605,000 tons; and oranges, 420,000 tons.

Turkish tobacco is world famous for its lightness and mildness. Most of the crop is grown in the Aegean region, but the finest tobacco is grown around Samsun, on the Black Sea coast. Tobacco represented 9% of total agricultural exports in 1992 and 2% of all Turkish exports that same year (6% in 1982). Some 320,000 tons of tobacco were produced in 1992. Most of the cotton crop is grown around Adana and Izmir. Other crops of commercial importance include olives (950,000 tons in 1992), tea (142,000 tons), fruits, nuts, and vegetable oil. Turkey usually leads the world in the production and export of hazelnuts (about 520,000 tons produced in 1992) and pistachio nuts, and as of

1991 also ranks first (ahead of the US) in the production of raisins.

The government stimulates production through crop subsidies, low taxation, price supports, easy farm credit, research and education programs, and the establishment of model farms. The government also controls the conditions under which farm products can move into world markets. For some products, such as grain, the government is the sole exporter. Turkey has recently begun exporting vegetables and fruits abroad, which has affected domestic market prices. Cotton and tobacco production levels are increaseing as demands by the textile and cigarette industries have risen.

Turkey is one of seven countries authorized under the 1961 UN Convention on Narcotic Drugs to grow opium poppies for legitimate pharmaceutical purposes. In June 1971, after persistent US complaints that up to 80% of all opiates smuggled into the US were derived from Turkish poppies, the Turkish government banned poppy growing; however, after efforts to find substitute crops failed, the government decided to rescind the ban on 1 July 1974. Areas authorized for poppy cultivation were estimated at 37,500 hectares (92,700 acres) in 1983; 5,000 hectares (12,350 acres) of opium capsule were sown in 1985. Government steps to curtail illegal cultivation, refining, and export of opiates were reportedly successful; in fact, Turkey has been one of the few opium-growing countries to crack down hard on drug smuggling.

23ANIMAL HUSBANDRY

Turkey is heavily overgrazed. Many animals are used for transport and draft purposes as well as to supply meat and dairy products. The principal animals of commercial importance are mohair goats and sheep. The sheep wool is used mainly for blankets and carpets, and Turkey is a leading producer of mohair. Nevertheless, animal husbandry is generally poorly developed despite the great number of animals. In 1992 there were 51.1 million sheep and goats, 11.9 million head of cattle, and 139 million hens and roosters. Production of wool was estimated at 42,000 tons in 1992. Other livestock products included milk, 6.1 million tons; meat, 1,009,000 tons; and hen eggs, 390,000 tons. Turkish apiculture produced some 55,000 tons of honey in 1992, fourth in the world after China, the US, and Mexico.

24FISHING

The total marine catch by Turkey's deep-sea fishermen was 317,424 tons in 1991, most of it tuna and sardines caught as they migrate seasonally through the Bosporus. In addition, 47,216 tons of freshwater fish were caught. Fishing equipment and methods have been substantially upgraded in recent years. For most of the population, however, the sea is not an important source of food.

25FORESTRY

Forests, occupying 20,199,000 hectares (49,913,000 acres), or 26% of Turkey's total area, are classified into three types according to ownership. State forests include almost all the forestland. Community or municipal forests and private forests are small. Care of state forests and all cutting therein are the responsibility of the Directorate-General of Forestry within the Ministry of Agriculture. Roundwood production in 1991 included 26,000 cu m of sawnwood, and 781,000 cu m of wood-based panels. Other forestry products were firewood, 9,796,000 cu m; wood pulp, 96,000 tons; and paper and paperboard, 833,000 tons.

26MINING

Turkey has a wide variety of known minerals, but its resources are only partially developed. Much of total mineral output is carried out by government-controlled organizations, principally the Coal Board and the Etibank, founded in 1935. In recent years, the government has been encouraging mineral exports as well as domestic and foreign private mining investment. Among the minerals actively exploited and marketed are copper, chromite, iron ore, sulfur, pyrite, manganese, mercury, lead, zinc, barite, and meerschaum. Production of chrome ores and concentrates in 1991 were almost entirely by the private sector and fell to about 652,000 tons. Iron ore output increased from 2,645,367 tons in 1987 to a reported 3,942,254 tons in 1991. Other minerals produced in 1991 (in thousands of tons) were lignite, 46,029; boron minerals, 1,815; sulfur, 135.2; and strontium, 65. Eskişehir, in northwestern Anatolia, is the world center of meerschaum, and Turkey is famous for its meerschaum pipes. Production has fallen in recent years from the 1989 level of 10,350 kg to 2,800 kg in 1991. Ongoing privatization costs will likely result in layoffs and the closure of inefficient operations in the near future.

27ENERGY AND POWER

Turkey provides about 60% of its energy needs overall; but in recent years, it has had to import several times as much petroleum as it produced. The bituminous coal field at Zonguldak on the Black Sea coast produces excellent coking coal. In 1992, output of coal totaled 50.6 million tons (89% soft coal). In 1991, production of crude oil came to a reported 4.3 million tons, while consumption totaled 22.1 million tons that year. Fuel imports in 1990 accounted for 20.8% of total imports, down from 33.4% in 1985 and 48.4% in 1980. Botas, a joint Turkish-Iraqi venture with its headquarters in Ankara, has created a system of oil pipelines running from Iraq to Turkey, thus bypassing the Persian Gulf; in 1991, Turkey had 2,092 km (1,300 mi) of crude oil and 2,321 km (1,442 mi) of petroleum products pipelines).

Hydroelectric and thermal power plants in 1991 produced 60,338 million kwh of electricity (38% hydro) and had a net installed capacity of 17.2 million kw. In the 1960s, lignite and water increased in importance as sources of energy, while coal and diesel oil dropped, but from the 1970s into the early 1980s, the importance of oil increased relative to other sources. In the 1980s, lignite again came to play an increasing role. Of the total electrical output in 1991, lignite-burning plants accounted for 34%; natural gas, 21%; fuel oil, 5.5%; and hard coal, 2%. Turkey is currently expanding its electrical generating capacity through the construction of the Southeast Anatolian Project, which involves 21 dams and 17 hydroelectric plants. The project will add another 8 million kw of capacity when finished.

28INDUSTRY

Overall industrial production, which had increased by annual rates of close to or over 10% from 1973 to 1977, fell sharply because of Turkey's financial crisis in 1978-79 and actually declined by 5% in 1979 and 1980. After the government's economic reform program slowed inflation and stabilized the lira, industrial production improved. Production rose 28% during 1985-87. State enterprises were restructured to reduce their government subsidies and to make them more productive and competitive with private firms. However, industry has continued to suffer from structural weaknesses and, in many firms, production facilities are obsolete. Production rose by an annual average of 4.5% during 1988-92.

The textile industry, the largest industrial unit in Turkey next to petroleum refineries, is centered in Izmir, Istanbul, Adana, and Kayseri. Major industrial complexes include the government-owned iron and steel mill at Karabuk and the Eregli iron and steel works. Other important Turkish enterprises are brick and tile, glass, leather, chemicals and pharmaceuticals, metalworking, cordage, flour milling, vegetable-oil extraction, fats and oils, paper products, printing and publishing, plastic products, and rubber processing. The sugar-beet industry ranks first among food-processing industries and produces more than domestic consumption requires. The automobile industry expanded rapidly in the 1970s. Much of the production of machines, consumer goods, and tools takes place in hundreds of small machine shops and foundries, where little special-purpose machinery is used. Industrial output totaled TL119,546 billion in 1989, of which the private sector accounted for 71%.

Textile enterprises in 1992 produced 180 million m of cotton and woolen fabrics. Other industrial commodities in 1992 (in thousands of tons) included coke, 3,252; steel castings, 10,343; crude iron, 4,508; cement, 28,560; sugar, 1,572; and newsprint, 119. Selected consumer items produced in 1992 were home refrigerators, 1,093,776; washing machines, 870,888; sewing machines, 197,100; television receivers, 2,320,464; and passenger cars, 265,092. Output of petroleum products (in thousands of tons) included gasoline, 2,946; kerosene, 150; fuel oil, 8,441; and motor oil, 6,565.

29SCIENCE AND TECHNOLOGY

Turkey's industrial economy has just begun to apply advanced technology to basic industries. The government body that coordinates scientific research is the Scientific and Technical Research Council of Turkey (founded 1963), in Ankara. The Mavmara Scientific and Industrial Research Institute (1972), in Istanbul, has a staff of 631; the Ankara Nuclear Research and Training Center (1967), attached to the Turkish Atomic Energy Authority, studies nuclear physics and radioisotope applications for industry. In 1985, total expenditures on research and development amounted to TL192 billion; 7,367 technicians and 11,276 scientists and engineers were engaged in research and development.

30DOMESTIC TRADE

Individual firms tend to be small and specialized. There is virtually no commercial activity in villages; the villager comes into the market town to buy and sell. Government-operated exchanges for cereals are located in municipalities. If the price of grain in the free market falls below the supermarket price, the government-operated exchanges purchase the grain and market it. In this manner, the government controls the price range of cereals.

Because of the scarcity of some commodities, the government controls the distribution of various essential goods, notably cement, coal, lignite, and steel. Under a 1954 law, municipal authorities enforce specified profit margins on designated commodities. These margins are established at four levels: importer or manufacturer, distributor, wholesaler, and retailer. Customarily, a Turkish wholesaler supplies credit to retailers who, in turn, often extend credit beyond their own means to consumers. Wholesalers' margins tend to be small because of low overhead and keen competition. In 1991, 17,942 new enterprises began operations; there were 262 consumer cooperatives.

Most commercial firms belong to chambers of commerce, which exist in all cities. Chambers of industry are increasingly important in larger manufacturing centers. The government sponsors an international trade fair every year at Izmir. Shops are normally open from 9 AM to 1 PM and from 2 to 7 PM, Monday through Saturday; smaller establishments tend to stay open later and not close for lunch. Banking hours are from 8:30 AM to noon and 1:30 to 5 PM Monday through Friday.

31FOREIGN TRADE

Turkey's trade balance has long been negative, but the deficit reached crisis proportions in 1974–75 and again in 1980-81, when import value was nearly double that of exports and the annual trade deficit approached $5 billion. A new emphasis on exports, abetted by the currency reforms of the early 1980s, helped narrow the trade gap to around $3 billion in 1982. By 1990, the deficit had risen to over $9 billion and the ratio of exports to imports fell to 58%, compared to 81% in 1988. The gap narrowed slightly in 1991 and 1992, but widened alarmingly in 1993. In 1985, the government mandated the creation of four free trade and export processing zones aimed at expansion and diversification of exports.

The principal exports in 1991 and 1992 (in millions of dollars) were as follows:

	1991	1992
Textiles	1,429	1,619
Iron and steel	1,309	1,379
Apparel and clothing accessories	3,478	4,179
Chemicals and related products	605	632
Machinery and transport equipment	1,017	1,291
Fruits and vegetables	1,749	1,570
Tobacco products	572	333
Other exports	3,434	3,712
TOTAL	13,593	14,715

The principal imports in 1991 and 1992 (in millions of dollars) were as follows:

	1991	1992
Machinery, including appliances	5,726	5,848
Mineral fuels	2,749	3,550
Chemicals and related products	2,874	3,112
Iron and steel	1,201	1,283
Textiles	538	705
Transportation vehicles	1,403	2,126
Metalliferous ores and metal scrap	686	646
Food and live animals	467	594
Other exports	5,403	5,007
TOTAL	21,047	22,871

In 1992, EEC countries supplied about 44% of Turkey's imports and received about 52% of its exports. Islamic countries of the Middle East and North Africa accounted for approximately 15% of Turkey's total imports and 19% of its exports. The principal trade partners in 1992 (in millions of dollars) were as follows:

	EXPORTS	IMPORTS	BALANCE
Germany	3,660	3,754	−94
US	865	2,600	−1,735
Italy	943	1,919	−976
Netherlands	500	698	−198
UK	796	1,187	−391
France	809	1,351	−542
Iran	455	365	90
Japan	162	1,113	−951
Sa'udi Arabia	486	1,665	−1,179
Russia	442	1,041	−599
Belgium-Luxembourg	290	551	−261
Other countries	5,307	6,627	−1,320
TOTAL	14,715	22,871	−8,156

32BALANCE OF PAYMENTS

Between 1961 and 1991, Turkey typically registered a balance of payments deficit. In 1990, because of the Gulf War and decreases in remittances by Turks working abroad, the current accounts deficit soared to $2.6 billion. Most of the shortfall was financed through borrowing abroad.

In 1992, merchandise exports totaled $14,891 million and imports $23,082 million. The merchandise trade balance was $-8,191 million. The following table summarizes Turkey's balance of payments for 1991 and 1992 (in millions of US dollars):

	1991	1992
CURRENT ACCOUNT		
Goods, services, and income	−4,827	−5,002
Unrequited transfers	5,099	4,059
TOTALS	272	−943
CAPITAL ACCOUNT		
Direct investment	783	779
Portfolio investment	648	2,411
Other long-term capital	−808	−938
Other short-term capital	−3,020	1,396
Reserves	1,199	−1,484
TOTALS	−1,198	2,164
Errors and omissions	926	−1,221
Total change in reserves	880	−1,015

33BANKING AND SECURITIES

The Central Bank of the Republic of Turkey was founded in 1930 as a privileged joint-stock company. It possesses the sole right of note issue and has the obligation of providing for the monetary requirements of the state agricultural and commercial enterprises by discounting the treasury-guaranteed bonds they issue. All foreign exchange transfers are handled exclusively by the Central Bank, which operates the clearing accounts under separate agreements with foreign countries. The bank has 25 domestic branches, plus a banknote printing plant and foreign branch offices in New York, London, Frankfurt, and Zürich.

As of 1992 there were 9 state banks, 30 domestic commercial banks, 23 foreign banks, and 7 investment and development banks. Two of Turkey's most important banks, the Sümerbank and Etibank, are also state investment-holding companies. Another important state financial institution is the Agricultural Bank, which supplies credit to the farm population. The largest private commercial bank is the Business Bank. Another private bank, the Industrial Development Bank of Turkey, stimulates the growth of private industrial development and channels the flow of long-term debt capital into the private industrial sector for both short- and long-range development programs.

Bank deposits increased from TL1,630.4 billion in 1985 to TL5,069.0 billion at the end of 1992. In 1991 the discount rate was 45%. The government's monetary policy resulted in the devaluation of the lira from TL47.1 to the US dollar in June 1979 to over 1,000 per dollar by early 1988. Credits issued by deposit money banks reached TL297,767 million at the end of 1992.

Turkey's only securities exchange is located in Istanbul. Because of the shortage of foreign exchange, there are no transactions in foreign bonds and stocks. With few exceptions, trading is in government bonds. Virtually all securities issued by private enterprises are sold privately through personal arrangements between buyers and sellers.

34INSURANCE

Government regulations effective 1929 and subsequently amended require all insurance companies to reinsure 30% of each policy with the National Reinsurance Corp., a state organization; in 1954, life policies were exempted from this requirement. It is possible to secure insurance policies for flood damage, third-party liability, earthquake, commercial shipments, theft, fire, and accident, as well as life. In 1989 there were 46 insurance companies, including foreign companies (mainly of Germany, UK, and France); 21 companies handled life insurance. Varied social security schemes are administered directly by the state.

In 1990, premiums totaled US$12.9 per capita, or 0.8% of the GDP.

35PUBLIC FINANCE

Beginning in 1983, the fiscal year was changed to start on 1 January instead of 1 March. The consolidated budget includes the general budget of the government (by ministry) and a number of annexed budgets, which pertain to semiautonomous state activities, such as universities. Additionally, each section is divided into operating and investment expenditures. The budget is invariably in deficit. As part of its economic reform program of 1980, the Turkish government cut budget expenditures, principally in subsidies to state economic enterprises.

In 1990, 12.7% of budgetary expenditures were attributed to the Defense Ministry and 13.9% to the Ministry of Education. The following table shows actual revenues and expenditures for 1991 and 1992 in billions of liras.

	1991	1992
REVENUE AND GRANTS		
Tax revenue	78,734	141,797
Non-tax revenue	11,369	33,770
Capital revenue	547	803
Grants	8,434	1,700
TOTAL	99,084	178,070
EXPENDITURES & LENDING MINUS REPAYMENTS		
General public service	34,192	65,563
Defense	13,783	25,558
Education	23,294	45,114
Health	3,934	7,870
Social security and welfare	2,661	4,782
Housing and community amenities	1,716	3,900
Recreation, cultural, and religious affairs	787	1,554
Economic affairs and services	33,386	43,909
Other expenditures	18,598	27,006
Lending minus repayments	51	142
TOTAL	132,401	225,398
Deficit/surplus	–33,317	–47,328

In 1991 Turkey's total external debt stood at US$48,661 million.

36TAXATION

All persons domiciled in Turkey, whether of Turkish citizenship or otherwise, are subject to taxation on income. Certain categories of foreigners are taxed only on income earned in Turkey—specifically, foreign business representatives, consultants, scientists, government officials, press correspondents, and others who have come to Turkey with no intention of becoming permanent residents, regardless of their length of residence. Income tax rates are progressive, ranging up to 50%. The basic tax for corporations is 46%; together with various surcharges, the total effective rate is 49.22%. The previous dividend withholding tax was abolished. A tax law of 1961 required farmers, not previously subject to income tax, to file a return.

Land and buildings are taxed on the basis of assessed value. Other levies include stamp taxes on documents, vouchers, shares, and securities; fees on legal, bank, and insurance transactions; output taxes; a petroleum production tax; a sales tax; service taxes; and inheritance and gift taxes. A value-added tax was introduced in 1985 and stood at 12% as of 1992. Business establishments are subject to an old age insurance tax and an illness and disability tax, shared by employers and employees.

37CUSTOMS AND DUTIES

Turkish customs duties are assessed on an ad valorem basis only. Present customs classification conforms with standardized international nomenclature. Duty-free entry is provided for many types of imports; in 1993, surcharges were levied on 5,000 out of 18,000 products. Other charges include a value added tax (VAT) ranging from 1–20%, a 15% municipal tax, and a 10% stamp tax.

38FOREIGN INVESTMENT

Although Turkey has been the recipient of considerable foreign aid, its leaders have also recognized the need for private foreign investment. By 1970, foreign capital could operate in any field of economic activity open to Turkish private capital, and there was no limit on the percentage of foreign participation in equity capital. However, direct capital investment by foreign companies from 1960 to 1979 averaged no more than $20 million annually, very low by OECD standards. This changed dramatically in 1980 with new foreign investment policies that cut red tape to gain more rapid approval for investment applications; inflows of private capital increased to $97 million in 1980, $337 million in 1981, and $913 million in 1992. In 1992, direct cumulative foreign investment totaled $6.5 billion, of which the US accounted for $715 million.

39ECONOMIC DEVELOPMENT

Economic policy is formulated by the State Planning Organization. In June 1961, an integrated 15-year plan was announced, consisting of three five-year plans designed to achieve a 7% yearly increase in national income. In March 1963, the first five-year plan was inaugurated; this 1963–68 program to some extent fell short of its goals, but its average annual increase of 6.7% in GNP was still impressive. Two objectives of the second five-year plan (1968–72) were economic viability and social justice. The role of the public sector under this program was twofold: creation and expansion of the economic and social infrastructure and development of modern manufacturing industries. Economic policy, however, still sought the largest possible active role for private enterprise in the development of industries, and the government sought with limited success to encourage private activity through fiscal concessions, financial assistance, and state participation in mixed enterprises. The third five-year plan was inaugurated in 1973 with the objective of helping Turkey prepare for its future membership in the EC. The long-term goals were to increase the per capita GNP from $400 in 1972 to $1,500 by 1995, to reduce agriculture's share of the GDP to 12%, and to increase industry's share to 37%. One of the main aims of the third five-year plan, still largely unmet, was to increase the efficiency of the tax-collection service. In agriculture, the objectives were to increase food supplies for export and to feed a growing population through improved irrigation, technical advice to farmers, and the establishment of more cooperative farms.

All these efforts required large new investments and massive foreign loans which, coupled with the huge increases in the cost of oil imports after 1973, led to the financial crisis of 1977–78. Since 1980, Turkey has deliberately pursued a deflationary policy, allowing the international exchange rate of the lira to fluctuate on a daily basis from 1 May 1981. The government also delayed several ambitious development proposals, mainly because new foreign credits were not available. However, a number of smaller projects financed by the IBRD went forward. Meanwhile, the fourth (1979–83) and fifth (1985–90) five-year plans continued to stress industrial development, deflationary monetary policy, and export promotion. The creation of free trade zones, in the mid-1980s, was a major step in line with these policies.

A long-term economic program adopted in November 1991, planned to reduce inflation, implement tax reforms, and restructure state enterprises, transferring certain inefficient ones to the private sector. Foreign aid from all sources totaled $2,720.2 million in 1991. Germany and Japan were the chief donors.

40 SOCIAL DEVELOPMENT

Since 1936, various forms of social security have been introduced, all of which are administered by the Social Insurance Institution and include industrial accident and disease, old age, sickness, disability, and maternity insurance. The first is financed entirely by the employer's contribution. To qualify for an old age pension, a worker must be at least 60 years old and must have worked at least 25 years in a qualified work place and made contributions on at least 5,000 days' wages. In some localities, the social insurance organization operates its own hospitals and other facilities.

The social organization, Bağ-kur, pays monthly benefits to artisans, craftsmen, and other self-employed workers. Government workers are covered by the Government Employees Retirement Fund.

The Turkish government has supported family-planning services within the context of an integrated maternal and child health program. As of 1985–90, the fertility rate was 3.8. In 1988, 63% of reproductive-age couples practiced contraception, and family planning services were provided to 720,200 persons in 1991. In 1992, abortion was available on request.

41 HEALTH

Free medical treatment, given at state hospitals or health centers, is provided by the state to any Turkish citizen who obtains a certificate of financial need from a local administrator. Total health care expenditures for 1990 were $4,281 million.

In 1992, there were 941 hospitals with 139,606 beds (2.4 per 1,000 people). Of this number, 616 were public with 72,513 beds. In 1990, the Ministry of Health employed 23,254 doctors (0.9 per 1,000 people) with a further 17,750 in other public institutions, including universities, and 9,635 private practitioners. There were 44,984 nurses (675 in the private sector) and 30,415 midwives (1,362 private). In 1989 there were 15,201 pharmacists and 10,132 dentists.

Malaria, cholera, and trachoma have been effectively controlled by large-scale public preventive measures. In 1990 there were 57 cases of tuberculosis per 100,000 people. In 1991, 78% of the population had access to safe water and 83% had adequate sanitation. Immunization rates for children up to one year old in 1992 were: tuberculosis (65%); diphtheria, pertussis, and tetanus (76%); polio (76%); and measles (72%).

Turkey's 1993 birth rate was 28.1 per 1,000 people, and about 63% of married women (ages 15 to 49) used contraception. There were 1.7 million births in 1992, with an average life expectancy of 67 years.

Infant mortality was estimated at 70 per 1,000 live births in 1992; maternal mortality was 150 per 100,000 live births in 1991; and general mortality was 7.1 per 1,000 people in 1993. Between 1984 and 1992, there were approximately 5,000 war-related deaths in the Kurd rebellion.

42 HOUSING

A traditional village house consists of sun-dried brick (adobe) or rough-hewn stone walls across which are laid timbers piled with brush and then topped with packed earth. The flat roof is often used for storage of feed grain. Floors are often bare earth covered with matting or lightweight carpets. Little furniture is used. Urban housing varies from houses similar to those in villages to modern, centrally heated apartment buildings. From 1981 through 1985, 305,890 new residential buildings containing 929,104 apartments were completed; virtually all these apartments had electricity, piped water, kitchens, and baths. As of 1985, 71% of all housing units were detached houses, 23% were apartments, 6% were squatters' houses, and under 1% were marginal dwellings. About 93% of all households were heated by stoves and 6% had central heating; 47% used coal for heating fuel and 43% used wood.

43 EDUCATION

In 1990, the literacy rate was 89.7% for males and 71.1% for females. Primary, secondary, and much of higher education is free. Education is compulsory for children aged 6 to 14 or until graduation from primary school (grade 5). However, owing to the inadequate number and distribution of schools and teachers, only about two-thirds of the children of primary-school age attend school. Secondary schooling is for six years.

The regular school system consists of five-year primary schools, three-year junior high schools, and three-year high schools. Parallel to this system is a variety of technical, trade, and commercial schools. Among private schools in operation are a number of foreign schools, and those maintained by ethnic or religious minorities. Among Turkey's 28 universities are the universities of Istanbul (founded 1453) and Ankara (founded 1946), the Technical University of Istanbul (founded 1773), and the Middle East Technical University at Ankara (founded 1957).

In 1991 there were 50,669 primary schools, with 234,961 teachers and 6,878,923 students. In 1991, enrollment in all secondary-level schools was 3,987,423 students, with 170,611 teachers. Of these, 12,607 students and 1,116 teachers were were enrolled or teaching at teacher training schools, and 976,916 students and 54,999 teachers were from vocational schools. The universities and other public higher institutions had 810,781 students and 35,123 faculty members that same year.

44 LIBRARIES AND MUSEUMS

In 1985 there were 638 public libraries with total collections of 6,260,000 volumes, and 113 children's libraries with holdings of 449,000 volumes. The principal collections are at the National Library (1,016,000 volumes), the combined libraries of the University of Ankara (750,000), the University of Istanbul (293,000), and the Middle East Technical University (378,000). The new Atatürk Library in Istanbul was founded in 1980 and contains 174,000 volumes.

The most famous museums and ancient buildings are located in Istanbul. The old seraglio, now Topkapi Museum, is perhaps the most famous; it houses a large collection of paintings, manuscripts, and historically important items. Nearby is the Ayasofya (Saint Sophia) Museum, the world-renowned Byzantine church. Next to it is the Blue Mosque, famous for the beauty of its interior and the grace of its dome. Also in Istanbul are the museums of Archaeology and of the Ancient Orient, housing some of the world's finest collections of Greek art, including the sarcophagus of Alexander the Great. The Museum of Archaeology in Ankara contains the world's outstanding collection of Hittite works. In Konya are located museums of Islamic art, one of which is housed in the mausoleum of Mevlana. Along Turkey's Aegean coast are situated the ruins of Ephesus, Pergamum, Troy (Ilium), Halicarnassus, and other famous ancient cities. A zoological garden is located in Ankara.

45 MEDIA

Postal, telephone, and telegraph service is owned and operated by a semi-independent government enterprise under the jurisdiction of the Ministry of Transport and Communications. Telephones in 1991 numbered about 7,467,151. The state operates AM and FM radio stations and television broadcasting. The number of radio sets in 1991 was 9,200,000; of registered television sets, 10,000,000.

Although the 1982 constitution guarantees freedom of expression, it also authorizes newspaper confiscations and closures in the cases of crimes against the unity, security, or republican principles of the state. After the 1980 coup, the military government, which had vested control of the press in the provincial martial law administrators, repeatedly closed down newspapers it claimed had published material damaging to the national interest. The independent leftist Istanbul daily *Cumhuriyet* (1991 circulation 76,300) has been closed a number of times. Other leading Istanbul dailies (with 1991 circulation figures) are *Sabah* (737,000); *Hurriyet* (588,200); *Milliyet* (396,400); *Bugun* (228,000); and *Turkiye* (160,200).

46 ORGANIZATIONS

Professional organizations, charitable associations, student organizations, and athletic clubs are active in the major cities. There are several Masonic lodges and branches of the Rotary and Lions clubs. Women are active in a number of their own charitable organizations. Since World War II, international cultural associations have appeared, chief among them being Turkish-American, Turkish-French, Turkish-German, and Turkish-English.

Chambers of commerce and chambers of industry are semiofficial agencies for the control of import license and foreign exchange allocations.

47 TOURISM, TRAVEL, AND RECREATION

Citizens of the US, Canada, Japan, and most Western European countries need a valid passport but no visa for stays of up to three months. Foreigners entering without a visa and remaining longer than three months must secure a residence permit from the police. No vaccinations or inoculations are required of visitors arriving directly from Europe or the US.

In 1991, 5,517,897 visitors (including same-day visitors) arrived in Turkey, including 14% from Germany, 13% from the former Soviet Union, and 9% from Romania. Tourism receipts totaled us$2.6 billion. There were 94,383 hotel rooms and 192,386 beds with a 37% occupancy rate.

In addition to the museums and monuments of Istanbul, places of interest include the Aegean ports of Izmir and Bodrun; the ancient cities of Troy (Ilium), Ephesus, Tarsus, Konya, Samsun, Erzurum, and Trabzon; Mt. Ararat, traditionally considered the landing place of Noah's Ark, the remains of which some expeditions have tried to find; the ski resort of Uludağ, 36 km (22 mi) south of Bursa; and the sea resort of Antalya, on the Mediterranean coast. Water sports, mountaineering, and football (soccer) are popular forms of recreation, as are such traditional Turkish sports as grease wrestling (yağli güreş), camel fighting (deve güreşi), and a horseback javelin competition (cirit oyunu) played mainly in eastern Turkey.

48 FAMOUS TURKS

The most famous rulers before the coming of the Turks were Croesus (r.560–546 BC), a king of Lydia noted for his wealth and for the loss of his kingdom to the Persians; Constantine I (the Great; Flavius Valerius Aurelius Constantinus, b.Moesia, AD 280?–337), the first Roman emperor to accept Christianity and to use Constantinople as a capital; and Justinian I (the Great; Flavius Petrus Sabbatius Justinianus, b.Illyricum, 483–565), a Byzantine emperor whose collection of laws and legal principles has been the model for European law down to modern times. Outstanding political figures since the arrival of the Turks include Sultan Mehmet II (1429–81), conqueror of Constantinople in 1453; Sultan Süleyman I (the Magnificent, 1495–1566); the Barbarossa brothers, Aruj (1473?–1518) and Hayreddin Paşa (Khayr ad-Din, 1466?–1546), naval commanders, born in Mytilene, who established Turkish supremacy in the Mediterranean; Mehmet Köprülü Paşa (1583–1661), Mehmet IV's grand vizier and founder of a family line of outstanding grand viziers; Sultan

Abdul Hamid II (1842–1918), a despotic ruler whose tyranny led to the formation of the Young Turk movement; Enver Paşa (1881–1922), Young Turk leader who was the ruler of Turkey during World War I; Mustafa Kemal Atatürk (1881–1938), World War I military commander, nationalist leader, and first president of the republic; Ismet Inönü (Paşa, 1884–1973), Atatürk's chief of staff and prime minister, who succeeded him as president (1938–50) and was the first prime minister of the Second Republic (1961–65); Celâl Bayar (1883–1986), who helped found the Democrat Party and was president (1950–60) until ousted by the military; and Adnan Menderes (1899–1961), prime minister (1950–60) until he was forced to resign and then executed.

Outstanding religious figures include Haci Bektaş Veli (1242–1337), founder of the Bektashi dervishes, and Mevlana (Celâleddin-i Rumi or Jalal al-Din Rumi, 1207–73), author of the epic *Mesnevi* (or *Mathnavi*) and founder of the Mevlevi dervishes.

Revered literary figures include the mystical poets Yunus Emre (1238?–1320?) and Süleyman Çelebi (d.1422), author of *Mevlidi Sherif (Birth Song of the Prophet)*. Other significant poets of the imperial epoch are Ahmedi (1334–1413), Şeyhi (d.1429?); Fuzulî (1494–1555), renowned for his lyrical verses about platonic love; Ali Şir Nevâî (1441–1501); Nef'î (1582?–1636); Nabî (1642?–1712); Ahmet Nedim (1681–1730), perhaps Ottoman Turkey's greatest love poet; and Şeyh Galib (1757–98), the last great poet of the mystical and classical tradition. Renowned for his geographical and historical writings is Kâtip Çelebi (known in Europe as Haji Khalifa, 1609–57); the great traveler Evliya Çelebi (1611–82) is noted for his books on travel and history. The greatest folk poet was the 17th-century minstrel Karacaoğlan.

Sinasi (1826–71), a dramatist, journalist, and essayist, was the first Turkish writer in the Western tradition. Other significant playwrights are Musaipzade Celal (1870–1959), Haldun Taner (1916–86), and Necati Cumali (b.1921). The poet Ziya Paşa (1825–80) was the outstanding literary figure of the reform period. Namik Kemal (Ahmed Kemal, 1840–88) and Mehmet Emin Yurdakul (1869–1944) dedicated their poetry to the achievement of political ideals. Four widely read novelists are Huseyin Rahmi Gurpinar (1864–1944), Ahmet Rasim (1864–1932), Halit Ziya Usakligil (1865–1945), and Mehmet Rauf (1871–1931). Omer Seyfettin (1884–1920) was a major short-story writer. Ziya Gökalp (1875–1924) was a noted poet and sociologist. Significant contemporary novelists include Halide Edib Adivar (1884–1966), Yakup Kadri Karaosmanoglu (1888–1974), Refik Halit Karay (1888–1974), Reşat Nuri Güntekin (1892–1957), Kemal Tahir Demir (1910–74), Orhan Kemal (1914–70), and Yasar Kemal Gokceli (b.1922). Two fine modern poets were Yahya Kemal Beyatli (1884–1958) and Nazim Hikmet Ran (1901–60). Two prominent journalists and political writers were Hüseyin Çahit Yalçin (1875–1957) and Ahmet Emin Yalman (1889–1973). Outstanding historians were Naima (1752–1815), Mehmet Fuat Köprülü (1890–1966), and Ahmet Zekî Velidî Toğan (1890–1970).

Other famous Turks include the architect Sinan (1490–1588), the miniaturist Abducelil Celebi Levni (d.1732), and the modern painter Bedri Rahmi Eyuboglu (1913–75). Famous contemporary composers include Ulvi Cemal Erkin (1906–72) and Ahmet Adnan Saygun (b.1907). The operatic soprano Suna Korad (b.1934) and bass-baritone Ayhan Baran (b.1929) have won renown in European musical circles.

49 DEPENDENCIES

Turkey has no territories or colonies.

50 BIBLIOGRAPHY

Ahmad, Feroz. *The Making of Modern Turkey*. New York: Routledge, 1993.

Ahmad, Feroz. *The Turkish Experiment in Democracy, 1950–1975.* London: Hurst, 1977.

Berberoglu, B. *Turkey in Crisis: From State Capitalism to Neocolonialism.* Westport, Conn.: Hill, Lawrence, 1982.

Bianchi, Robert. *Interest Groups and Political Development in Turkey.* Princeton, N.J.: Princeton University Press, 1984.

Davison, Roderic H. *Essays in Ottoman and Turkish history, 1774–1923: The Impact of the West.* Austin: University of Texas Press, 1990.

Dodd, C. H. *Democracy and Development in Turkey.* Atlantic Highlands, N.J.: Humanities Press, 1980.

Finkel, Andrew and Nukhet Sirman (eds.) *Turkish State, Turkish Society.* New York: Routledge, 1990.

Hale, William. *The Political and Economic Development of Modern Turkey.* New York: St. Martin's, 1981.

Heper, Metin and Ahmet Evin (eds.). *State, Democracy, and the Military: Turkey in the 1980s.* New York: W. de Gruyter, 1988.

Heper, Metin and Jacob M. Landau (eds.). *Political Parties and Democracy in Turkey.* New York: I.B. Tauris, 1991.

Kasaba, Resat. *The Ottoman Empire and the World-economy: The Nineteenth Century.* Albany: State University of New York Press, 1988.

Palmer, Alan Warwick. *The Decline and Fall of the Ottoman Empire.* New York: M. Evans, 1993.

Persner, L. W. *Turkey's Political Crisis.* New York: Praeger, 1984.

Pitman, Paul M. (ed.). *Turkey: A Country Study.* 4th ed. Washington, D.C.: Library of Congress, 1988.

Robinson, Richard D. *The First Turkish Republic.* Cambridge, Mass.: Harvard University Press, 1963.

Schick, Irvin C. and Ertugrul Ahmet Tonak (eds.). *Turkey in Transition: New Perspectives.* New York: Oxford University Press, 1987.

Shaw, Stanford J., and Ezel Kural. *History of the Ottoman Empire and Modern Turkey.* 2 vols. Cambridge, England: Cambridge University Press, 1977.

Toprak, Binnez. *Islam and Political Development in Turkey.* Leiden: Brill, 1981.

Weiker, Walter F. *The Modernization of Turkey from Atatürk to the Present Day.* New York: Holmes & Meier, 1981.

Zurcher, Erik Jan. *Turkey: A Modern History.* New York: I.B. Tauris, 1993.

TURKMENISTAN

Туркменистан
Turkmenistan

CAPITAL: Ashgabat (Ashkhabad).

FLAG: Green field with claret stripe of five carpet patterns; white crescent and five white stars symbolizing five major conditions of life on earth—light, sound, sense of smell, sense of touch, and sense of balance—to the right of the stripe.

ANTHEM: *Independence Turkmenistan.*

MONETARY UNIT: Manat, the unit of currency, was introduced by the government in November 1993. As of fall 1994, 60 manat = $1, but exchange rates are likely to fluctuate widely.

WEIGHTS AND MEASURES: The metric system is used.

HOLIDAYS: Independence Day, 27 October.

TIME: 5 PM = noon GMT.

¹LOCATION, SIZE, AND EXTENT

Turkmenistan is located in southern Asia, bordering the Caspian Sea, between Iran and Uzbekistan. Comparatively, Turkmenistan is slightly larger than the state of California, with a total area of 488,100 sq km (188,456 sq mi). Turkmenistan shares boundaries with Kazakhstan and Uzbekistan on the N, Afghanistan on the SE, Iran on the SW, and the Caspian Sea on the W. Turkmenistan's boundary length totals 5,504 km (3,420 mi). Turkmenistan's capital city, Ashgabat, is located in the southwestern part of the country.

²TOPOGRAPHY

The topography features flat to rolling sandy desert with dunes to the Caspian Sea, which lies in the west. Three percent of Turkmenistan's land is arable with approximately 2.5% under irrigation.

³CLIMATE

The climate is arid continental. In July the mean temperature is 28°C (82°F). The mean temperature in January is –4°C (25°F). It can become very hot in the Kara Kum desert, with daytime temperatures of 122°F not unusual. It does not rain much in Turkmenistan. Rainfall averages 25 cm (9.7 in) a year).

⁴FLORA AND FAUNA

The Kara Kum (Black Sea) desert covers 90% of the country, and there is little plant or animal life. Herders raise goats, camels, and sheep in the desert. Farmers use reservoirs for irrigation to grow crops not indigenous to the area.

⁵ENVIRONMENT

The most significant environmental problems in Turkmenistan include salinization of the soil and water pollution. The nation's water supply is threatened by chemical contaminants from farming activity. The problem is complicated by the lack of adequate sewage treatment facilities.

⁶POPULATION

The population of Turkmenistan was 3,533,925 in 1989. It was estimated at 4,075,316 in 1995. A population of 4,479,000 was projected for 2000, assuming a crude birth rate of 25.5 per 1,000 population during 1995–2000, a crude death rate of 6.2, and a net natural increase of 19.3. The estimated population density in 1995 was 8.3 per sq km (21.6 per sq mi). Ashgabat, the capital, had an estimated population of 517,200 at the end of 1992.

⁷MIGRATION

Emigration to other former USSR republics exceeded immigration by 20,600 during 1979–90. More than 40,000 people fled from Tajikstan to Turkmenistan in 1992 to escape civil war.

⁸ETHNIC GROUPS

In 1989, 72% of the population consisted of Turkmens (or Turkomans). Some 9.5% were Russians, 9% Uzbeks, and 2.5% Kazakhs. Like the Turkmens, the Uzbeks and Kazakhs are Turkic-speaking peoples.

⁹LANGUAGES

Turkmen is mandatory in the schools. It is a Turkic language of the Oghez group. Russian remains in common use in government and business.

¹⁰RELIGIONS

Formerly the Turkmen Soviet Socialist Republic, the Turkmen Republic declared independence in August 1990 and became a member of the Commonwealth of Independent States in December 1991. The population is primarily Sunni Muslim, with strong elements of local Shamanism and Sufi mysticism in included in its practices. Under legislation enacted in 1991, there is freedom of religion and practices.

¹¹TRANSPORTATION

Nebit-Dag, Ashkhabad, Mary, and Chardzhou are connected by railroad to the nation's main port of Krasnovodsk on the Caspian Sea. Other lines include a railroad from Mary along the Murgab and Kushka rivers to Afghanistan and a line from Chardzhou along the Amu Dar'ya which nearly parallels Uzbekistan's border. Smaller rail spurs are located at Tashauz and Kerki.

In 1990, there were some 23,000 km (14,300 mi) of highways, of which 80% were hard-surfaced.

[12]HISTORY

The territory of present-day Turkmenistan has been inhabited since the Stone Age, with evidence of agricultural communities as early as 6000 BC and of planned irrigation works from 3500 BC. The first states were Margiana and Parthia, from about 1000 BC. In 7th–6th centuries BC, Margiana was part of Bactria, while Parthia was part of the Median state. In the 6th–4th centuries BC the region was ruled by the Achaemenids, who were conquered by Alexander the Great at the end of the 4th century In his wake there emerged a Parthian Empire which lasted until AD 224, when Persians of the Sassanid dynasty seized the territory. In the 5th century much of Turkmenistan was conquered by Ephthalites, who in turn were conquered in the 6th century by the Tiu-chue nomads, of Turkic origin. The Arab caliphate conquered Turkmenistan in 716, and began to introduce Islam. In the 10th century part of Turkmenistan was under Samanid control.

Oghuz Turks began to migrate into Turkmenistan in the 9th century In 1040 the Seljuk clan took control of the territory, and held sway until the 13th century, when Turkmenistan was part of the Khwarazm-Shah state. The entire region was conquered by Mongols in 1219–1221, and Turkmenistan was split between the Golden Horde and the Chagatai Khanate, as well as the Hulaguid Khanate of Persia.

In the 1380s Turkmenistan became part of the empire of Timur (Tamerlane). By the 16th century part of the territory was ruled by the Khiva Khanate, part by Bukhara, and part by Persia. The course of the Amu Dar'ya river changed, and the Kara Kum desert claimed a great deal of once arable land.

Russia began to make commercial contacts with the Turkmens as early as the 16th century; by the 18th century almost all trade between Europe and Central Asia passed through Turkmenistan. Local tribes were used diplomatically by the Persians, Russians, and British as part of the Great Game of the 18th and 19th centuries Beginning in 1865, Russia undertook direct annexation, which because of heavy resistance by the Turkmen tribesmen was not complete until the 1885, making Turkmenistan the last portion of the Russian Empire to be conquered. The territory then was called the Transcaspian District.

Turkmen joined the uprising of 1916, when the Tsar attempted to draft Central Asians into work battalions, and remained in general rebellion throughout the period of the revolution and civil war. Muslim and nationalist opposition, whom the Russians called "basmachi," resisted the Bolsheviks until 1924, when the area was made part of the Trans-Caspian Republic. In 1925, the present-day territory became a Soviet Socialist Republic.

Throughout the Soviet period, Turkmenistan was the poorest and least assimilated of the republics. In 1985, longtime Communist Party boss M. Gapurov was fired by Mikhail Gorbachev, who picked Sapamurat Niyazov as new republic head. Niyazov has remained in power ever since. In October 1990, when Turkmenistan became independent, Niyazov was elected president by the republic's Supreme Soviet. The decision was reaffirmed by direct popular election in June 1992, and he later was named president for life. Turkmenistan declared independence on 27 October 1991. An elaborate cult of personality has grown up around Niyazov, who now prefers the title "Turkmenbashi," or Head Turkmen.

[13]GOVERNMENT

Although the new constitution adopted 18 May 1992 stipulates that Turkmenistan is a secular, democratic republic, in fact the republic is a presidential autocracy, under the control of President Niyazov. The executive branch of government is the responsibility of a Prime Minister and his cabinet, all of whom are appointed by the president. The republic's economy is still centrally planned and controlled, as in Soviet times, giving the government wide powers. The legislative branch stipulates two bodies, a 50-member Majlis, or Assembly, which is elective for five-year terms, and the Halk Maslahaty, or People's Council, which includes all deputies of the Majlis, all senior government officials, and the administrative heads of all the local administrative sub-divisions. The People's Counci also has 50 elected positions. Term of office is five years, but the council is convened as the president desires, to function as a nationwide "council of elders" in considering the most serious issues of statehood, such as constitutional changes or declarations of war. The entire judiciary is appointed by the president.

[14]POLITICAL PARTIES

The only legally registered party in the republic is the Democratic Party of Turkmenistan, which is what the Communist Party renamed itself in September 1991. There have been attempts to create two opposition parties, Agzybirlik (Unity) and another, which also calls itself the Democratic Party of Turkmenistan. However, political control in the republic is sufficiently tight that Agzybirlik's organizational meetings drew only about two dozen people, while the opposition Democratic Party was able to meet only in Moscow. Although there have been isolated jailings and one disappearance which seem to be politically motivated, there in fact seems to be little political opposition in the republic, in large part because Niyazov has used the country's natural gas wealth to keep prices near Soviet levels, and had provided many public services free of charge.

[15]LOCAL GOVERNMENT

There are five large regional subdivisions, called velayets. Beneath these are shekhers, then etraps, then ovs. Velayets, shekhers, and etraps have presidentially appointed executives called vekils. In addition each administrative sub-unit has an elected council called a gengeshchi, the chairman of which is an archyn.

The clan system is said still to be very strong in Turkmenistan, and the velayets reflect distribution of the five major clans, whose totems are represented in the state flag.

[16]JUDICIAL SYSTEM

The court system is a holdover from that which existed under the Soviet regime. There are 61 district and city courts of first instance, 6 provincial courts, and a Supreme Court at the apex. There are also military courts and a Supreme Economic Court which hears cases involving disputes between business enterprises and ministries. Decision of lower courts are appealable to higher courts.

The constitution declares the establishment of an independent judiciary. In practice, the President's role in selecting and dismissing judges may compromise judicial independence.

Defendants in criminal cases are afforded a number of procedural due process rights, including the right to a public trial and the right to defense counsel. In death penalty cases, defendants may petition the President for clemency.

[17]ARMED FORCES

A Russian air-ground force of 34,000 is under joint control. The government has organized a Republic Security Forces and National Guard for law enforcement.

[18]INTERNATIONAL COOPERATION

Turkmenistan was admitted to the UN on 2 March 1992, and is a member of the CSCE, ECO, IMF, and the World Bank. It is a member of the CIS, and is recognized by the US, EC countries, and many other nations of the world. The US established formal diplomatic relations with Turkmenistan in February 1992.

[19]ECONOMY

Turkmenistan boasts rich deposits of oil, gas, potassium, sulfur, and salts, which offer important potential sources of raw indus-

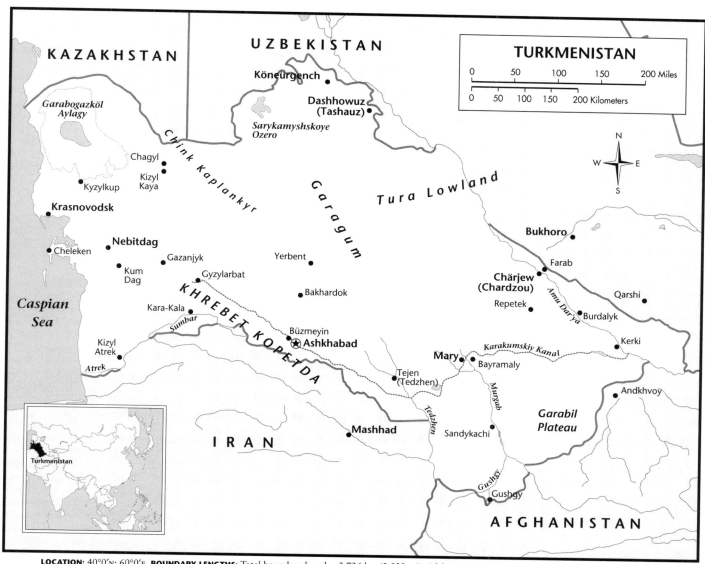

LOCATION: 40°0′N; 60°0′E. **BOUNDARY LENGTHS:** Total boundary lengths, 3,736 km (2,322 mi); Afghanistan, 744 km (462.3 mi); Iran, 992 km (616.4 mi); Kazakhstan, 379 km (236 mi); Uzbekistan, 1,621 km (1007.3 mi).

trial inputs and high-value exports. Proven gas reserves in the country amount to 10 trillion cu m; proven oil reserves are 213 million tons. Despite this natural wealth, per capita NMP (net material product) was only 60% of the average Soviet republic in the late 1980s, and Turkmenistan's social welfare indicators are among the lowest in the former USSR. The economy is dominated by agriculture which generates 46% of NMP, accounts for 42% of employment (together with forestry), and supplies cotton both to other former Union republics and to the country's own industry.

Although the instability and trade disruptions following dissolution of the USSR have posed serious difficulties for Turkmenistan since 1990, its economy has been less severely affected than many of its post-Soviet counterparts. Contraction in output occurred mainly in industrial output while growth in the agricultural and transportation sectors—the latter particularly due to increased government investment—lessened the rate of decline in the overall economy. Dropping 6.9% in real terms in 1989, NMP increased by 1.5% in 1990 and decreased again in 1991, but only by 0.6%.

Ultimate responsibility for economic policy setting lies with the Economic Committee in the Presidential Council. Turkmenistan has been among the more conservative of the post-Soviet republics in instituting a transition to a free market economy.

Government plans envision a gradual reform over a 10 year period, in which the state will continue to play a directing role in the economy, *albeit* within a liberalized market environment. Currently, the country's farms and industrial enterprises produce largely on the basis of state orders, and the state-owned sector continues to employ 80% of the labor force. Initial moves toward price decontrol have been accompanied by a steady rise in retail and wholesale prices. After a 90% increase in 1991, retail prices surged by 800% in 1992 and have continued to increase since. Enlarged subsidies, increased wages and family allowances, and reinstatement of some price controls have been instituted by the government to cushion the effect of rising prices and offset the potential for social unrest, especially in light of developments in neighboring Tajikistan and other former Soviet republics. In November 1993, Turkmenistan dropped out of the ruble-based monetary union with other post-Soviet states and introduced its own currency, the manat.

[20]INCOME

In 1992, Turkmenistan's GNP was $4,895 million at current prices, or $1,270 per capita. For the period 1985–92 the average inflation rate was 13.2%.

21LABOR

From 1985 to 1991, the size of the labor force grew by 2.7% per year. Of an estimated 2.2 million inhabitants of working age in 1991, agriculture engaged 43%; personal services, 26%; manufacturing, mining, and utilities, 11%; construction, 10%; trade, 6%; and other sectors, 4%.

As of 1992, there were no independent unions or attempts to register an independent trade union. The Federation of Trade Unions, the government-associated organization of the Soviet era, is still present but divided along sectoral and regional differences.

Although Turkmen law does not protect the right to bargain collectively, strikes are allowed, although none occurred in 1992. State economic control is still prevalent, and little progress toward privatization has occurred. The standard legal workweek is 40 hours. Many industrial workers often labor in unsafe conditions, and agricultural workers especially are subjected to ecological health hazards.

22AGRICULTURE

About 30–35% of Turkmenistan is considered arable, but less than 10% is under cultivation. Almost all the sown agricultural land is under irrigation. Yields are relatively low because of poor water usage, salinization, inefficient irrigation, and overdevelopment of cotton cultivation. From 1989 to 1992, agriculture accounted on average for 42% of employment and 46% of NMP.

Cotton is the main crop, with production on the Mary and Tejen oases and along the Amu Dar'ya. Reported cotton production in 1992 ranges from 395,000 to 1.4 million tons. Wheat also is cultivated to avoid dependency on unstable cotton export earnings. In 1992, reports of production ranged from 400,000 to 470,000 tons, up from 206,000 tons in 1991. Citrus fruit, dates, figs, grapes, pomegranates, olives, and sugarcane are grown in irrigated groves and fields in the southwest. Sesame, pistachios, and oilseeds are other important export crops.

23ANIMAL HUSBANDRY

The inability to raise sufficient fodder impedes livestock development. The livestock population in 1992 included sheep, 5,380,000; chickens, 8,000,000; pigs, 300,000; and goats, 220,000. Karakul sheep are raised for wool export; in 1992, 17,000 tons of greasy wool and 860,000 karakul skins were produced. As of 1993, a private tannery in Mary processed 100,000 sheepskins per year, selling its product to the state-run leathery factory.

Akhaltekin horses, raised at the Akhaltekin oasis, are a breed which dates date to the 3rd century. Bucephalus, the favorite horse of Alexander the Great, was Akhaltekin. In 1986, an Akhaltekin horse, Dancing Brave, was sold for $50 million. Akhalteking have a large share of the racehorse breeding market worldwide, and are depicted on Turkmenistan's national emblem.

24FISHING

The Caspian Sea provides fishing resources; fishing is an important export activity.

25FORESTRY

About 5% of the land is forested. Arid conditions and the expansive Kara Kum Desert inhibit the development of commercial forestry.

26MINING

Sulfur is mined at the Gaurdak complex in the east; Turkmenistan has the world's third-largest reserves of sulfur. An extensive mirabilite (sodium sulfate) site exists on the Garabogazkol; ozocerite, iodine, and bromine are found on the Cheleken Peninsula; salt is mined north of Nebitdag. Other mineral deposits include potassium and polymetallic ores.

27ENERGY AND POWER

Turkmenistan is essentially self-sufficient in energy resources, with natural gas by far the most plentiful resource. Proven reserves of natural gas in 1992 amounted to 88.1 trillion cu ft (2.5 trillion cu m), or 1.8% of the world's total. Production in 1992 (excluding gas-flared or recycled) totaled 1,995 billion cu ft (56.5 billion cu m), fifth in the world after Russia, the US, Canada, and Iran. Natural gas is found primarily near Mary; these fields in south-central Turkmenistan account for 80% of annual production. Turkmenistan is a major exporter of natural gas to the former USSR, and is the only republic, besides Russia, to export to Europe. Production in 1992 fell by 28.9% from 1991, because its chief competitor, Russia, was able to market its gas at a lower price and because of several pricing and payment disputes between the former Soviet republics. About 70% of electricity generation is powered by natural gas. In 1990, Turkmenistan's total installed electrical capacity was 3,170,000 kw, and 14,900 million kwh were generated.

Oil is produced in small quantities in the west, on the Cheleken Peninsula, near Nebitdag and Kum Dag, and along the Caspian lowlands. Enough oil is extracted to satisfy domestic demand and to export, but refining capabilities are limited and antiquated.

28INDUSTRY

In 1991, industry accounted for 19% of total net product in Turkmenistan, and employed about 11% of the country's labor force. After growing at an average rate of 2.3% during the 1980s, the industrial sector has been most severely affected by the recent economic instability in the former Soviet republics. In 1992, total output declined by 15%.

Sixty-one large state-owned textile enterprises together generate over one-third of total output in Turkmenistan's industrial sector. Goods produced in 1991 included 28.2 million sq m of cotton fabrics, 21 million sq m of wool, silk and other fabrics, 10.5 million knitted pieces, and 12.7 million pairs of stocking hosiery. In addition, Turkmen carpets are known worldwide for their quality, and represent a source of national pride for the people of Turkmenistan. Turkmen carpets have been known erroneously on Western markets by the label Bukhara, which actually represented the Uzbekistan city where the carpets were sold. Turkmen carpets feature deep red wool, with stylized geometric patterns. Ornaments of Turkmen carpets are a component of the flag and national emblem of Turkmenistan. In 1991, 1.38 million sq m of carpets and tapestry were produced.

Fuel-related production (mainly gas and oil) is the second-largest component of the industrial sector, accounting for about 22% of total sector output in value terms. Eighty-four billion cu m of natural gas were produced in 1991, 89% of which was exported, making Turkmenistan the second-largest natural gas producer in the former USSR region. The country's gas processing capacity is underdeveloped, although construction of a polyethane plant by an Italian firm is slated to begin soon. In 1991, Turkmenistan produced 5.4 million tons of oil. The Krasnovodsk refinery has been the country's main oil processing center, with an annual capacity of 5.5 million tons; this is expected to soon be rivaled by the new Chardzou refinery, completed in 1991, which boasts a production capacity of 6 million tons, and uses oil imported from Siberia. Food processing (especially meat and dairy processing), construction materials, and electricity generation accounted for 14%, 6%, and 5% of total industrial output value in 1991, respectively. Principal goods include meat, 36,000 tons; whole milk products, 128,000 tons; vegetable oil, 104,000 tons; asbestos-cement shingles, 67 million standard units; and construction bricks, 698 million units. Chemicals and machinery are also among the country's most important manufacturing subsectors, producing 190,000 tons of mineral fertilizer, 788,000 tons of sulfuric acid, 343,000 tones of sulphur, 135,000 tons of phosphorus, 95,000 tons of pesticides, and 15,900 tons synthetic detergent in 1991. Sixteen thousand km of electrical and radio wires and 870 turbine pumps were manufactured in 1989.

29 SCIENCE AND TECHNOLOGY

The Turkmen Academy of Sciences has 17 attached institutes. In addition, six independent institutes conduct medical research. In 1991, the Academy of Agricultural Sciences was established, and in 1992, the Academy of Medical Sciences was created, both in Ashkhabad.

30 DOMESTIC TRADE

Like the rest of the Turkmenistan economy, much of the country's retail and wholesale sector remain under the control of the central government. However, informal markets also operate in the country, at which a wide variety of consumer goods, including food, clothing and household wares, may be purchased. Officially recorded retail trade purchases totalled about R3,977 million (current rubles) in 1990.

31 FOREIGN TRADE

Like other Central Asian countries, Turkmenistan is highly trade dependent; 26% of domestic consumption derives directly from imports while exports are equivalent to about 22% of its annual production. While natural gas and processed cotton fiber are the country's most important export items, Turkmenistan is heavily dependent on imports for industrial equipment, industrial raw materials, and a number of basic food items such as grain, milk and dairy products, potatoes, and sugar. The Turkemenistan government reported in 1994 that export activity had doubled since 1989, to include exports of about 60,000 tonnes of ginned cotton; 220,000 tonnes of oil products; 25,000 metres of handmade carpets, 1,300 tonnes of licorice and licorice extract, and more than 20,000 astrakhan pelts. Exports and imports are heavily dominated by inter-republic trade, which accounted for 86% of the country's total trade in 1990 (in domestic prices). By bargaining steep increases in the prices Turkmenistan receives for its oil exports to its post-Soviet counterparts, the country has been able to strengthen its external trading position considerably. In 1990, the country registered a drop in its formerly chronic trade deficit with the rest of the former USSR, due in part to a probable reduction in trading volume, but in part also to more favorable terms of trade with rising world petroleum prices.

Russia is Turkmenistan's dominant inter-republic trade partner, claiming 44% of its exports and supplying over half of its imports in 1990. Beyond the former Soviet Union, principal foreign markets for the country's goods (mainly cotton fibers and some fuel) were other member countries of the former CMEA, led by Germany, Bulgaria, and the former Czechoslovakia. Germany, Poland and the former Czechoslovakia were the three largest international import sources, mainly for machinery, foodstuffs, and consumer goods.

32 BALANCE OF PAYMENTS

Since the demise of the Soviet Union, Turkmenistan has concentrated on exporting ginned cotton, oil and natural gas, and sulphur, along with hand-made carpets at world market prices to generate foreign earnings. This practice, however, has caused some trade difficulties, especially among the other former Soviet republics.

33 BANKING AND SECURITIES

The State Bank of Turkmenistan is charged with issuing currency and executing a monetary policy, and represents the top tier of a two-tiered banking system. Commerical banks are responsible for collection, settlement, and handling of assets for clients and other banks. The State Bank for Foreign Economic Activities has been established to provide hard currency credits for foreign economic activities.

34 INSURANCE

No recent information is available.

35 PUBLIC FINANCE

Although still a centrally planned economy, Turkmenistan has slowly begun to decrease the size of the public sector's influence; in October 1993, public expenditures for most price subsidies were eliminated. The estimated 1991 external debt was $650 million.

36 TAXATION

Personal income taxes in Turkmenistan range from 10–40%; the maximum corporate rate is 45%, with a standard rate of 25%. Also levied are a value-added tax ranging from 16.67% to a standard rate of 20%, and a 6–15% withholding tax.

37 CUSTOMS AND DUTIES

Turkmenistan ha a procedure for levying customs duties , export and timport taxes and tariffs, and for the trasit of goods, defined by the Customs Code of Turkmenistan. Certain imports from countries outside the rural area are prohibited or require a license.

38 FOREIGN INVESTMENT

A law on foreign investment and other legislation regarding private entrepeneurship passed since 1991 now provide most of the conventional guarantees to foreign investors in Turkmenistan. However, the purchase of property by foreign parties remains highly restricted. Reflecting some of this ambiguity, by 1992, only 23 joint ventures had been established, most of a relatively small scale and with negligible impact on foreign trade. Nevertheless, the country's political stability and rich natural resources are likely to make it a favored target for foreign investors in the near future. Significant inflows of foreign assistance have already allowed expansion of the petroleum industry to begin. Negotiations with foreign firms and several countries are underway for establishing a liquified natural gas plant and the joint construction of a new gas pipeline to Europe that would bypass the need to transverse potentially unstable states of the former USSR.

39 ECONOMIC DEVELOPMENT

Athough still a largely agricultural and poorly developed economy, Turkemenistan's relatively well educated population and natural resources provide a promising basis for the growth of a diverse set of industries. In 1990, the government began efforts to reduce the country's dependence on the export of raw materials and the import of finished and intermediate goods as well as basic foodstuffs. Initiated in time to help avoid some of the most severe economic dislocation being experienced in other post-Soviet republics, these efforts have included increasing wheat production and developing the country's oil and gas processing capacity, as well as investing in internal transportation facilities.

In addition to these changes, the government has also expressed commitment to a cautious reform agenda aimed at economic liberalization. The guiding principles of this program were detailed in a formal document in early 1991 calling for a series of legislative, fiscal, and monetary measures related to price controls, privatization, and industrial infrastructure development. More specific legislation and policies have followed, including new laws on privatization and foreign investment adopted in 1992, price decontrol measures taken the same year, adoption of a value-added tax and other tax reform, and measures taken to control the growth of money supply. Under the liberalized property regime, leasing arrangements have expanded in both the agricultural and industrial sectors. The leasing or purchase of individual enterprises by workers is favored by the current legislation, although land, water, and the oil and gas industries are excluded from the possibility of outright purchase by private individuals or companies. Despite liberalization only a handful of enterprises had been privatized by 1992 and four-fifths of the labor force remained employed in the state-owned sector. Most industrial enterprises continue to run on the basis of centrally planned state orders and resource allocations.

Following the government's expressed committment to minimizing the negative impact of post-Soviet economic restructuring on the population, the terms for Turkmenistan's social safety net are more generous than many other former Soviet countries; allowances for large families, social security payments, as well as pensions have all been increased substantially since 1992, and as of 1993 all citizens receive free electricty and water. Potential fiscal imbalances resulting both from these increased expenditures and the end of transfers from the Soviet government have thus far been avoided by increased profit transfers from key enterprises, export duties, and a variety of smaller revenue sources. Twenty-nine percent of the 1992 budget expenditures was allocated to price-differential subsidies paid to retail agencies required to sell food and medicines below wholesale prices. Capital expenditures claimed a further 12% of total expenditures while combined social and cultural expenditures allocated to education, health care, and social security totalled about 30%. A five-year production and investment plan set out in 1992 proposes large investments in the development of infrastructure and the energy sector financed by the budget and large inflows of foreign investment. In line with the plan's long of food self-sufficiency and increased cotton processing, the budget for 1993 included financing for projects to expand grain production and cotton processing.

40 SOCIAL DEVELOPMENT

Under the constitution, women are protected from discrimination in employment, inheritance, marriage rights, and other areas. However, they are barred from working in some jobs deemed dangerous or ecologically unsafe. Practicing Muslims often follow religious practices giving men precedence over women in property and inheritance matters.

41 HEALTH

Health care expenditures for 1990 were $459 million. Average life expectancy is 66 years. In 1992, there was 1 doctor for every 290 people, and 11.3 hospital beds per 1,000 inhabitants. Immunization rates for children up to one year old in 1992 were: tuberculosis, 97%; diphtheria, pertussis, and tetanus, 84%; polio, 91%; and measles, 76%. The infant mortality rate in 1992 was 72 per 1,000 live births; the maternal mortality rate in 1991 was 150 per 100,000 live births; and the general mortality rate was 8 per 1,000 people in 1993. Leading causes of death per 100,000 people in 1990 were: communicable diseases and maternal/perinatal causes 216; noncommunicable diseases, 737; and injuries, 68. There were 72 reported cases of tuberculosis per 100,000 people in 1990.

42 HOUSING

In 1989, 27.3% of all privately owned urban housing had running water, 7.2% had sewer lines, 16% had central heating, and 1% had hot water. In 1990, Turkmenistan had 11.1 sq ft of housing space per capita and, as of 1 January 1991, 108,000 households (or 30.9%) were on waiting lists for urban housing.

43 EDUCATION

The adult literacy rate was estimated at 97.7% in 1990, with men estimated at 98.8% and women at 96.6%. Before the Soviet Union established control over the region in the 1920s, few schools, mainly Muslim, existed. Education is now state funded and compulsory from the age of 7 to 17 (10 years). The government reports 1,764 schools with enrollment of 850,000. In 1,400 of the schools, instruction is in the Turkmen language; in the remaining 364, Uzbek, Russian, Kazakh, and Karakalpak languages are used.

In 1990, all higher level institutions had 41,800 pupils enrolled. There are several institutions of higher learning, including one university at Ashgabat, the Turkmen State University (founded in 1950) with an enrollment of over 11,000 pupils.

44 LIBRARIES AND MUSEUMS

The capital city of Ashgabat is the center for cultural activities, with four theatres, a philharmonic society, and museums. Major libraries include the Science and Technology Library of the Academy of Sciences and the Central State Public Library. Museums of note are the Exhibition Hall of Turkmen Painter's Union, State Museum of Fine Art, State Museum of Turkmen Carpets, Zoological Museum of Turkmenistan, and the Museum of History.

45 MEDIA

Telephone links to other former Soviet republics and Iran are provided by land link or microwave and to other countries through Moscow. Turkmen Radio in Ashgabat broadcasts transmissions from Moscow, as does Turkmen Television, which also receives Turkish television broadcasts. Orbita and INTELSAT are received by satellite earth stations. Turkmenistan also has its own movie studio, Tukmenfilm.

In 1989, 66 newspapers and 34 periodicals were published, mostly in Ashgabat.

46 ORGANIZATIONS

The economic affairs and other concerns of workers are handled by the Chamber of Committee and Industry and the Federation of Trade Unions of Turkmenistan, respectively. The most important mass movement in the country is the Communist Party. It controls all aspects of Turkmenistan's politics, society and culture. Its organizations of control are the Committee on National Security, Ministry of Internal Affairs, and various trade unions. The trade unions, all controlled by the state, serve to promote government production plans and policies.

47 TOURISM, TRAVEL, AND RECREATION

Turkmenistan is open to both business travelers and tourists. Visas are required by all visitors and are obtainable upon arrival or through Russian embassies abroad and companies that sell package tours of Central Asia. The principal accommodations are hotels that formerly belonged to the Soviet Intourist system. There are daily flights from Moscow to the capital city of Ashgabat.

48 FAMOUS TURKMENISTANIS

Saparmuryad A. Niyazov has been president of Turkmenistan since December 1991. Outstanding representatives of culture and literature of Turkmenistan include Abdulhekin Qulmukam Medoghli, a writer, researcher and political activist who was killed in 1937 during one of Stalin's purges, and the poet and thinker, Maktum Kuli, who first envisioned an independent Turkmenistan. The country has established the Makhtumkuli International Prize in his name, and awarded it to President Niyazov.

49 DEPENDENCIES

Turkmenistan has no territories or colonies.

50 BIBLIOGRAPHY

Maslow, Jonathan Evan. *Sacred Horses: The Memoirs of a Turkmen Cowboy*. New York: Random House, 1994.

TUVALU

CAPITAL: Funafuti.

FLAG: The national flag has the Union Jack in the upper quarter nearest the hoist; nine yellow stars on a light blue field are arranged in the same pattern as Tuvalu's nine islands.

ANTHEM: Begins "Tuvalu for the Almighty"

MONETARY UNIT: Both the Australian dollar (A$) and the Tuvaluan dollar (T$) of 100 cents are legal tender at par. There are coins of 1, 2, 5, 10, 20, and 50 Tuvaluan cents; 1 and 5 Tuvaluan dollars; and notes of 5, 10, 20, 50, and 100 Australian dollars. T$1 = US$0.7008 (or US$1 = T$1.4269).

WEIGHTS AND MEASURES: The metric system is being introduced, but imperial measures are still commonly employed.

HOLIDAYS: New Year's Day, 1 January; National Children's Day, first Monday in August; Tuvalu Day, 1 October; Christmas Day, 25 December; Boxing Day, 26 December. Movable holidays include Commonwealth Day (March), Queen's Official Birthday (June), and Prince of Wales's Birthday (November); movable religious holidays include Good Friday and Easter Monday.

TIME: Midnight = noon GMT.

¹LOCATION, SIZE, AND EXTENT

Tuvalu (formerly the Ellice Islands) comprises a cluster of nine islands, plus islets, located in the southwestern Pacific Ocean just south of the Equator. These remote atolls are situated about 1,050 km (650 mi) N of Suva, Fiji, and 4,000 km (2,500 mi) NE of Sydney, Australia. They lie in a 595-km-long (370-mi) chain extending over some 1,300,000 sq km (500,000 sq mi) of ocean and have a total land area of 26 sq km (10 sq mi). Comparatively, the area occupied by Tuvalu is about 0.1 times the size of Washington, D.C. Tuvalu has a coastline of 24 km (15 mi).

Tuvalu's capital city, Funafuti is located on the island of Funafuti.

²TOPOGRAPHY

Tuvalu consists entirely of low-lying coral atolls, none of which is more than 5 m (16 ft) above sea level; few of the atolls are more than 0.8 km (0.5 mi) wide. The islands are coral reefs on the outer arc of ridges formed by pressure from the Central Pacific against the ancient Australian landmass. On five islands, the reefs enclose sizable lagoons; the others are mere pinnacles rising abruptly from the ocean floor. Only two of the islands, Funafuti and Nukufetau, have natural harbors for oceangoing ships. There are no rivers on the islands.

³CLIMATE

Tuvalu has a tropical climate with little seasonal variation. The annual mean temperature of 30°C (86°F) is moderated by trade winds from the east. Rainfall averages over 355 cm (140 in). Although the islands lie north of the main hurricane belt, Funafuti was devastated by hurricane Bebe in 1972.

⁴FLORA AND FAUNA

The surrounding sea is rich in flora and fauna, but land vegetation is limited to coconut palm, pandanus, and imported fruit trees. Pigs, fowl, and dogs, all of which were imported in the 19th century, flourish on the islands. The only indigenous mammal is

the Polynesian rat. There are 22 known species of butterfly and moth.

⁵ENVIRONMENT

Environmental dangers include uncontrolled spread of the crown of thorns starfish, which flourishes in deepened channels and which is destructive to coral; erosion of beachheads because of use of sand for building materials; and excessive clearance of forest undergrowth for firewood. Global warming and the related rise of sea level are also a significant environmental concern for the island nation of Ruvalu. The nation is vulnerable to the loss of coastal forests and damage to farmlands. The invasion of sea water would also contaminate the limited water supply. The purity of the water supply is already at risk due to untreated sewage and the by-products of the mining industry and farming. The nation is also threatened by earthquakes, cyclones, and volcanic activity. In 1986, the government approved the first phase of an EC-financed sea-wall system to protect the coast. According to a 1992 report from the United Nations, the wildlife on Tuvalu and the Pacific island countries in general is seriously endangered. Current fishing methods threaten the survival of fish that are the basis for the nation's fish industry. The green sea turtle and the leatherback turtle were endangered species in 1987.

⁶POPULATION

According to the mini-census of June 1985, the resident population was 8,229, with another 1,500 citizens working or studying abroad. The 1995 population was estimated at 9,995 by the US Bureau of the Census but 13,000 by the UN. Population density is high, with 500 residents per sq km (1,300 per sq mi) in 1995, based on the UN estimate. The most populated island is Funafuti, the capital, with a 1985 mini-census population of 2,810. Vaitupu ranked second with 1,231, followed by Niutao, 904; Nanumea, 879; Nukufetau, 694; Nanumanga, 672; Nui, 604; Nukulaelae, 315; and Niulakita (formerly uninhabited), 74.

[7]MIGRATION

During the 19th century, recruitment of Tuvaluans to work on plantations in other Pacific islands, Australia, and South America reduced the resident population from about 20,000 to 3,000; the islands have only recently recovered from the population loss.

[8]ETHNIC GROUPS

Apart from a few Europeans, the islanders are almost entirely Polynesian and have strong ties with the Samoans and Tokelauans. There is no evidence of pre-Polynesian settlement. Language and tradition indicate that the Tuvaluans were part of a Samoan-Tongan migration from the 14th through the 17th century.

[9]LANGUAGES

English and Tuvaluan, a Polynesian tongue related closely to Samoan, are the principal languages. A Gilbertese dialect is spoken on Nui.

[10]RELIGIONS

In 1865, a member of the London Missionary Society reached Tuvalu from Samoa, and Samoan pastors were sent to the islands. The Tuvaluans rapidly embraced the Christian faith, and today 98% of them are Protestants, members of the Church of Tuvalu, a congregationalist group. There are small Roman Catholic, Seventh-Day Adventist, and Baha'i communities.

[11]TRANSPORTATION

Transportation is inadequate. Most roads are little more than tracks, although Funafuti has about 8 km (5 mi) of coral-impacted roads for use by the island's few cars and trucks. Funafuti and Nukufetau are the only seaports, used chiefly by freighters in the copra trade. Ships drawing up to 9 m (30 ft) can dock in Funafuti harbor at a deepwater wharf completed in 1980. All the islands are served by Tuvalu's one interisland ferry. Funafuti has the lone airport, a grass strip that cannot be used for jet aircraft.

[12]HISTORY

The islands were probably settled between the 14th and 17th centuries by Polynesians drifting west with prevailing winds from Samoa and other large islands. The first European to discover Tuvalu is thought to have been the Spanish navigator Álvaro de Mendaña de Neyra, who sighted Nui in 1568 and Niulakita in 1595. Further European contact was not made until the end of the 18th century. Between 1850 and 1875, the islands were raided by ships forcibly recruiting plantation workers for South America, Fiji, Hawaii, Tahiti, and Queensland. To help suppress such abuses, the Office of British High Commissioner for the Western Pacific was created in 1877.

In 1892, after ascertaining the inhabitants' wishes, the UK proclaimed the Ellice Islands (as Tuvalu was then known), together with the Gilberts, as a British protectorate. After further consultation, the protectorate became the Gilbert and Ellice Islands Colony in 1916. After the Gilberts were occupied by the Japanese in 1942, US forces occupied the Ellice group in 1943 and drove the Japanese out of the Gilberts. After the war, the ethnic differences between the Micronesians of the Gilberts and the Polynesians of the Ellice Islands led the Ellice Islanders to demand separation. In 1973, a British commissioner appointed to examine the situation recommended administrative separation of the two island groups. The British government agreed, provided that the Ellice Islanders declared their wishes by referendum. The vote, held during August-September 1974 with UN observers in attendance, produced an overwhelming majority of 3,799—293 for separation. Accordingly, on 1 October 1975, the Ellice Islands were established as the separate British colony of Tuvalu, and a ministerial system was instituted. Pursuant to a constitutional conference held at London in February 1978, Tuvalu became an independent member of the Commonwealth of Nations on 1 October 1979. Sir Fiatau Penitala Teo became Tuvalu's first governor-general, and Toaripi Lauti, chief minister at the time of independence, took office as Tuvalu's first prime minister. Following new elections in September 1981, Lauti was succeeded in office by Tomasi Puapua, who was reelected in September 1985. In March 1986, Tupua Leupena replaced Sir Fiatau Penitala Teo as governor-general. In a poll held that same year, Tuvaluans rejected the idea that Tuvalu should become a republic. As a result of the 1989 general election the Parliament elected Bikenibeu Paeniu as Prime Minister in September 1989. In the same election, Naama Latasi became the first woman to serve in Tuvalu's Parliament. Since 1992, Toaripi Lauti has served as Governor-General.

[13]GOVERNMENT

Tuvalu is an independent constitutional monarchy. The head of state is the British monarch, whose representative on the islands is the governor-general, a Tuvaluan who has the power to convene and dissolve parliament. There is a unicameral legislature, the House of Assembly, with 12 members elected to four-year terms by universal adult suffrage. Four islands—Funafuti, Nanumea, Niutao), and Vaitupu—elect two members each; the other islands elect one each. The cabinet is headed by the prime minister and has four ministers (all House members), plus the attorney-general.

[14]POLITICAL PARTIES

There are no political parties, and political life and elections are dominated by personalities. Small island constituencies with a few hundred kin-related electors judge the leaders by their service to the community. Bikenibeu Paeniu's Cabinet in 1989 was composed primarily of those who had opposed the outgoing government of Tomasi Puapua.

[15]LOCAL GOVERNMENT

Local administration by elected island councils was established following the creation of the protectorate in 1892. Local governments were established on the eight inhabited islands by a 1966 ordinance that provided the framework for a policy aimed at financing local services at the island level. Funafuti's town council and the other seven island councils (Niulakita has none) each consist of six elected members, including a president.

[16]JUDICIAL SYSTEM

District magistrates were established with the protectorate in 1892, and a simple code of law based on mission legislation and traditional councils has been observed by native courts. Eight island courts were constituted in 1965 to deal with land disputes, among other local matters. In 1975, a High Court of Justice was set up to hear appeals from district courts. Appeals from the High Court may go to the Court of Appeals in Fiji and ultimately to the UK Privy Council in London.

[17]ARMED FORCES

Tuvalu has no armed forces except for the local police. For defense the islands rely on Australian-trained volunteers from Fiji and Papua New Guinea.

[18]INTERNATIONAL COOPERATION

As a special member of the Commonwealth of Nations, Tuvalu is not represented at heads-of-government conferences. However, Tuvalu does cooperate with several Commonwealth regional bodies, particularly the South Pacific Forum, which it hosted in 1982. The country also belongs to UPU and is associated with the EC under the Lomé Convention. It is an associate member of ESCAP, a de facto adherent of GATT, and a signatory of the Law of the Sea. In 1979, Tuvalu signed a treaty of friendship with the US, which in 1983 formally dropped its prior claim to four of the nine islands. Tuvalu opposes French nuclear testing in the South Pacific and signed the 1985 Rarotonga Agreement declaring the region a nuclear-weapons-free zone.

¹⁹ECONOMY

Prime Minister Lauti noted at the time of independence that all Tuvalu has is sun and a portion of the Pacific. Economic life is simple, but there is no extreme poverty. Subsistence is based on intensive use of limited resources, namely coconuts and fish; copra is the only cash crop. The islands are too small and too remote for development of a tourist industry.

²⁰INCOME

Tuvalu's GDP (A$11.5 million in 1990) is the smallest of any independent state. Wholesale and retail trade account for about one-third of the GDP; government and other services, 9%; agriculture and fishing, 20%; and other sectors for the balance. Major sources of income are British aid and remittances from Tuvaluan workers abroad, which bring in around A$1.6 million a year.

²¹LABOR

Most of the active labor force is engaged in subsistence agriculture, outside the cash economy. In Funafuti, the government-controlled philately bureau is the largest single employer, with a staff of several dozen workers. The nation's only trade union, the Tuvalu Seamen's Union, has about 600 members who work abroad on foreign merchant vessels.

²²AGRICULTURE

Although agriculture is the principal occupation, it contributes less than 10% of the GDP because of poor soil quality (sand and rock fragments), uncertain rains, and primitive catchment. Coconuts form the basis of both subsistence and cash cropping; the coconut yield in 1992 was about 3,000 tons. Other food crops are pulaka (taro), pandanus fruit, bananas, and pawpaws.

²³ANIMAL HUSBANDRY

The Agricultural Division, based on Vaitupu, has attempted to improve the quality and quantity of livestock to lessen the islands' dependency on imports. Pigs and fowl, which were imported in the 19th century, have been supplanted by goats and rabbits. In 1992, there were some 13,000 pigs on the islands.

²⁴FISHING

Sea fishing, especially for tuna and turtle, is excellent. Although fishing is mainly a subsistence occupation, fish is sold in the capital, and bêche-de-mer is exported. The fish catch in 1991 was 526 tons, down from 1,409 tons in 1988. Japanese aid in 1982 provided a commercial fishing vessel for the islands. The Republic of Korea and Taiwan are both licensed to fish within the territorial waters of Tuvalu. In October 1986, Tuvalu, along with several other Pacific island nations, signed an agreement with the US giving US tuna boats the right to fish its offshore waters.

²⁵FORESTRY

There is little useful timber on the islands.

²⁶MINING

There is no commercial mining.

²⁷ENERGY AND POWER

International aid by UNDP and the European Development Fund is helping to develop electrical power. Funafuti has a limited

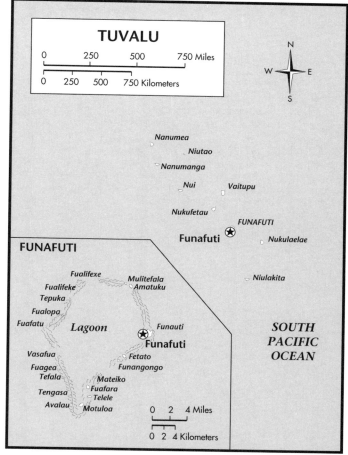

LOCATION: 5° to 11°s; 176° to 180°E.
TOTAL COASTLINE: 24 km (15 mi). TERRITORIAL SEA LIMIT: 12 mi.

amount of electricity to operate its meteorological and broadcasting stations and for use by the hospital and hotel; very few private households have electrical service. Installed electrical capacity totaled 2,600 kw in 1990; electricity production that year amounted to 3 million kwh, or 330 kwh per capita. The Tuvalu Solar Electric Cooperative Society, formed in 1984, provides a limited supply of photovoltaic electricity.

²⁸INDUSTRY

There is no industry apart from handicrafts, baking, and small-scale construction; the islands lack the population, capital, and resources to make commercial enterprises cost effective.

²⁹SCIENCE AND TECHNOLOGY

There is no advanced science and technology except for that imported under foreign aid programs.

³⁰DOMESTIC TRADE

Cooperative societies dominate commercial life, controlling almost all retail outlets, the marketing of local handicrafts, and the supply of fish to the capital. Barter remains an important part of the subsistence economy.

³¹FOREIGN TRADE

Copra, the main cash crop, took many years to recover from the 1972 hurricane and has been affected by fluctuating market prices (although there is a subsidy to producers). Most food, fuel, and manufactured goods are imported. Total imports and exports of Tuvalu and Kiribati were valued at US$27 million in 1990. About 48% of total trade in 1982 was with Fiji, 40% with Australia, and 5% with New Zealand.

32BALANCE OF PAYMENTS

Continuing deficits in the trade balance have been offset by payments from the UK to both current and capital accounts and by remittances from Tuvaluans abroad. Philatelic sales, a government-controlled enterprise which had sometimes exceeded copra as a source of income, suffered a serious decline in the 1980s.

33BANKING AND SECURITIES

The Bank of Tuvalu was founded in Funafuti in 1980 and has branches on all the islands. The bank is jointly owned by the Tuvalu government (75%) and by Barclays Bank, which was responsible for its operation until mid-1985.

34INSURANCE

Insurance plays a minimal role in Tuvaluan life.

35PUBLIC FINANCE

The chief sources of domestic revenue are customs duties and personal taxes.

36TAXATION

Revenue is obtained principally by means of indirect taxation: stamp sales, the copra export tax, and fishing licenses. Income tax was levied on chargeable income on a sliding scale of 9–50% until 1983, when the rate was changed to a flat 30% of all individual income above A$1,800. A year later, the corporate rate was changed to 40%. Island councils also levy a head tax and a land tax based on territorial extent and soil fertility.

37CUSTOMS AND DUTIES

Since a single line tariff was implemented on 1 January 1975, trade preferences are no longer granted to imports from Commonwealth countries. Tariffs, applying mostly to private imports, are levied as a source of revenue. Most duties are ad valorem, with specific duties on alcoholic beverages, tobacco, certain chemicals, petroleum, cinematographic film, and some other goods.

38FOREIGN INVESTMENT

The cash economy is not sufficiently developed to attract substantial foreign investment. As of 1993, a new hotel was slated for construction on Funafuti by Taiwanese interests, and its airstrip was to be paved with aid from the EC.

39ECONOMIC DEVELOPMENT

Development aid, which rose rapidly during the 1960s, peaked at independence in 1979, when the UK undertook to provide £6 million. Supported by other donors, the UK still underwrites basic development projects, including fisheries development and agricultural diversification. Foreign aid is also provided by New Zealand, Taiwan, and the UN, and the UK is phasing out its role as that of Taiwan grows. In 1990, Tuvalu received a total of US$4.8 million in bilateral, and US$0.2 million in multilateral aid.

40SOCIAL DEVELOPMENT

Tuvaluans cling strongly to their traditional way of life. Villages are organized on a communal rather than a clan basis and have a customary system of social welfare. Young men's clubs and women's committees are standard features of social life, concerning themselves with sailing, fishing, crafts, and child welfare.

41HEALTH

There are no serious tropical diseases on the islands except for a dwindling number of leprosy and dysentery cases. In 1990, there were 1.8 hospital beds per 1,000 people. In 1992, there were 31 doctors per 100,000 people. The infant mortality rate was 40 per 1,000 live births in 1992.).

42HOUSING

Most islanders live in small villages and provide their own housing from local materials. After the 1972 hurricane, Funafuti was rebuilt with imported permanent materials, but there is still a critical housing shortage on Funafuti and Vaitupu. Government-built housing is largely limited to that provided for civil servants. In 1979, 46% of all dwellings had no sanitation facilities and only 10% had flush toilets; 44% received water from a communal tap and 30% drank well water.

43EDUCATION

All children receive free primary education from the age of 6. Education is compulsory for nine years. The Tuvalu school system has seven years of primary and six years of secondary education. Secondary education is provided at Motufoua, a former church school on Vaitupu now jointly administered by the government. In 1990, 1,485 students were enrolled in primary school while secondary schools had 345 students. Tuvalu Marine School was opened in 1979 with Australian aid. In the same year, the University of the South Pacific (Fiji) established an extension center at Funafuti.

44LIBRARIES AND MUSEUMS

The first book published in Tuvaluan was the Bible, in 1977. Apart from school facilities, the only library is in Funafuti and it also houses the Archives.

45MEDIA

The Tuvalu Broadcasting Service, on Funafuti, transmits daily in Tuvaluan and also broadcasts news in English. There is efficient interisland radio communication. In 1985 there were 2,500 radio receivers in use. There is no commercial press, but *Tuvalu Echoes* is published biweekly by the government. Other local publications are produced by the churches or the government.

46ORGANIZATIONS

Apart from cooperative societies and local traditional bodies connected with island councils, there are few organizations. Organized youth groups include the Tuvalu Youth Fellowship and Pathfinder, and there are Girl Guide and Boy Scout troops on most islands. The Tuvalu Amateur Sports Association and the Pacific Red Cross are also notable.

47TOURISM, TRAVEL, AND RECREATION

Tuvalu's remoteness has discouraged tourism; the few visitors are on commercial or official business. In 1991, 976 tourists visited Tuvalu, 82% of them from Eastern Asia and the Pacific. There were 26 rooms in hotels and other facilities, with 51 beds, and tourism receipts totaled US$300,000.

48FAMOUS TUVALUANS

Tuvalu's first prime minister was Toaripi Lauti (b. Papua New Guinea, 1928).

49DEPENDENCIES

Tuvalu has no territories or colonies.

50BIBLIOGRAPHY

Geddes, W. H., et al. *Atoll Economy: Social Change in Kiribati and Tuvalu.* Canberra: Australian National University Press, 1982.

MacDonald, Barrie. *Cinderellas of the Empire.* Canberra: Australian National University Press, 1982.

UNITED ARAB EMIRATES

United Arab Emirates
Al-Imarat al-'Arabiyah al-Muttahidah

CAPITAL: Abu Dhabi (Abu Zaby).

FLAG: The flag consists of a red vertical stripe at the hoist and three equal horizontal stripes of green, white, and black.

ANTHEM: The National Anthem is an instrumental piece without words.

MONETARY UNIT: The United Arab Emirates dirham (UD), introduced as the currency in May 1973, is divided into 100 fils. There are coins of 1, 5, 10, 25, and 50 fils and 1 and 5 dirham and notes of 5, 10, 50, 100, 200, 500, and 1,000 dirhams. UD1 = $0.2724 (or $1 = UD3.6710).

WEIGHTS AND MEASURES: The metric system and imperial and local measures are used.

HOLIDAYS: New Year's Day, 1 January; Accession of the Ruler of Abu Dhabi (Abu Dhabi only), 6 August; National Day, 2 December; Christmas, 25 December. Muslim religious holidays include Lailat al-Miraj, 'Id al-Fitr, 'Id al-'Adha', Hijra New Year, and Milad an-Nabi.

TIME: 4 PM = noon GMT.

¹LOCATION, SIZE, AND EXTENT

Comprising a total area of approximately 75,581 sq km (29,182 sq mi), including some 6,000 sq km (2,300 sq mi) of islands, the United Arab Emirates (UAE), in the eastern Arabian Peninsula, consists of seven states: Abu Dhabi, or Abu Zaby, with an approximate area of 67,350 sq km (26,000 sq mi); Dubai, or Dubayy, 3,900 sq km (1,500 sq mi); Sharjah, 2,600 sq km (1,000 sq mi); Ra's al-Khaimah, or Ra's al-Khaymah, 1,700 sq km (650 sq mi); Fujairah, or Al-Fujayrah, 1,150 sq km (450 sq mi); Umm al-Qaiwain, or Umm al-Qaywayn, 750 sq km (300 sq mi); and 'Ajman, 250 sq km (100 sq mi). Comparatively, the area occupied by UAE is slightly smaller than the state of Maine. Extending 544 km (338 mi) NE–SW and 361 km (224 mi) SE–NW, the UAE is bordered on the N by the Persian (or Arabian) Gulf, on the E by Oman, on the S and W by Sa'udi Arabia, and on the NW by Qatar, with a total boundary length of 2,185 km (1,358 mi). In the late 1970s, Sa'udi Arabia and Qatar reportedly reached a boundary agreement according to which a narrow corridor of land was ceded by Abu Dhabi, thus allowing Sa'udi Arabia access to the Gulf near the Khawr Duwayhin and eradicating the former Qatar-UAE frontier. However, through 1987, no documents attesting to the accord had been submitted to the UN. The remainder of the boundary with Sa'udi Arabia is not yet fully demarcated.

The UAE's capital city, Abu Dhabi, is located on the Persian Gulf.

²TOPOGRAPHY

The UAE consists mainly of sandy desert. It is bounded on the west by an immense sebkha, or salt flat, extending southward for nearly 112 km (70 mi). The eastern boundary runs northward over gravel plains and high dunes until it almost reaches the Hajar Mountains in the Ra's Musandam near Al-'Ayn. The flat coastal strip that makes up most of the UAE has an extensive area of sebkha subject to flooding. Some sand spits and mud flats tend to enlarge, and others enclose lagoons. A sandy desert with limestone outcroppings lies behind the coastal plain in a triangle between the gravel plain and the mountains of the east and the

sands of Sa'udi Arabia to the south. Far to the south, the oases of Al-Liwa' are aligned in an arc along the edge of dunes, which rise above 90 m (300 ft).

The main gravel plain extends inland and southward from the coast of Ra's al-Khaimah to Al-'Ayn and beyond. Behind Ra's al-Khaimah and separating Fujairah from the Persian Gulf is an area of mountains that rise over 900 m (3,000 ft) in height, with isolated cultivation. Finally, alluvial flats on the Gulf of Oman fill the bays between rocky spurs. South of Khor Fakkan (Sharjah), a continuous, well-watered fertile littoral strip known as the Batinah Coast runs between the mountains and the sea and continues into Oman. There are, in addition, many islands, most of which are owned by Abu Dhabi. These include Das, the site of oil operations, and Abu Musa, exploited for oil and red oxide.

³CLIMATE

The months between May and October are extremely hot, with shade temperatures of between 38° and 49°C (100–120°F) and high humidity near the coast. Winter temperatures can fall as low as 2°C (36°F) but average between 17° and 20°C (63–68°F). Normal annual rainfall is from 5 to 10 cm (2–4 in), with considerably more in the mountains; most rainfall occurs between November and February.

⁴FLORA AND FAUNA

Apart from cultivated plants, there are two categories of plant life in the UAE: the restricted salt-loving vegetation of the marshes and swamps, including the dwarf mangrove, and the desert plant community, which includes a wide range of flora that is most abundant after the fall of rain.

Animal and reptile life is similar to that of Bahrain, with the addition of the fox, wolf, jackal, wildcat, and lynx. Hedgehogs have been seen. More than 250 species of small birds have been reported in the UAE, along with many of the larger birds—kites, buzzards, eagles, falcons, owls, and harriers. Sea birds include a variety of gulls, terns, ospreys, waders, and flamingos. Popular game birds include the houbara (ruffed bustard), as well as species of ducks and geese.

[5]ENVIRONMENT

The clearing of natural vegetation, livestock overgrazing on rangelands, and extensive deforestation (in ancient times) have led to desertification. Overpumping of groundwater has brought a rise in soil salinity levels, and effluents from the oil industry have contributed to air pollution. The nation has 0.1 cubic miles of water. Eighty percent is used for farming activity and 9% is used for industrial purposes. Ninety-five percent of the city dwellers and 100% of the people living in rural areas have pure water.

The nation's cities produce 0.5 million tons of solid waste per year. As of 1993, the nation does not have any of its land area protected by environmental legislation, but the government has begun to establish national parks to protect threatened flora and fauna. The Al-'Ayn zoological gardens contain some 280 species of wildlife, including the gazelle, which had been on the verge of extinction in the region. In 1994, four of the country's mammal species were endangered. Seven bird species are threatened with extinction. Endangered species in the UAE are the peregrine falcon, gray wolf, Arabian oryx, Arabian tahr, green sea turtle, and desert monitor.

[6]POPULATION

The population totaled 1,622,464 at the December 1985 census, representing an increase of 64% over the 1980 census figure of 1,042,099. It was estimated at 1,909,000 in 1991. The UN projected population for the year 2000 is 1,970,000, assuming a crude birthrate of 21.3 per 1,000 population, a crude death rate of 4.2, and a net natural increase of 17.1 for 1995–2000. The estimated populations in 1991 of the individual emirates were Abu Dhabi, 798,000; Dubai, 501,000; Sharjah, 314,000; Ra's al-Khaimah, 130,000; 'Ajman, 76,000; Fujairah, 63,000; and Umm al-Qaiwain, 27,000. The population of each emirate is concentrated largely in its capital. The towns of Dubai and Abu Dhabi are the most important urban centers; Abu Dhabi grew rapidly into a city of 670,125 people in 1985 by attracting large numbers of internal and external migrants to its booming oil industry. The estimated population density was 22.8 per sq km (59.1 per sq mi) in 1991.

[7]MIGRATION

About 80% of the UAE's population originates from outside its borders. In the early 1980s, the government took steps to reduce the immigration rate by limiting the number of visas issued to foreign workers.

[8]ETHNIC GROUPS

South Asians account for about 45% of the population, followed by Arabs (about 33%, 13% of whom are from outside the UAE) and Iranians (17%). Westerners account for about 5%. Jordanians, Palestinians, Egyptians, Iraqis, and Bahrainis are employed throughout the bureaucracy, including the educational system.

[9]LANGUAGES

Arabic is the universal language. Farsi is spoken in Dubai, and English is widely used in business.

[10]RELIGIONS

Virtually all UAE nationals and many immigrants are Muslims. Most are Sunnis, with the exception of a comparatively large Shi'i community in Dubai. The non-Muslims are principally Christians and Hindus.

[11]TRANSPORTATION

With most of the population concentrated in coastal towns and the Al-'Ayn oasis, road links between these centers have been given priority. There is now a paved coastal road linking Abu Dhabi, Dubai, Sharjah, 'Ajman, Umm al-Qaiwain, and R'as al-Khaimah. Roads linking the interior to the main towns have been constructed; of particular importance is the transpeninsular road from Fujairah through the Hajar Mountains. A six-lane, 209-km (130-mi) highway has been built between Abu Dhabi and Al-'Ayn, and two bridges connect Abu Dhabi island with the mainland. Another highway links the UAE coastal network with the Trans-Arabian Highway at As-Silah on the Qatar border. In 1991 there were 1,800 km (1,118 mi) of bituminized highways. In 1992 there were 5.4 million registered vehicles.

The UAE is well provided with port facilities. Dubai's Port Rashid, with its deep-water berths and warehouses, is one of the largest artificial harbors in the Middle East. Other ports are the Jabal 'Ali complex, also in Dubai, completed in 1980; Abu Dhabi's Port Zayid; Sharjah's Port Khalid; and the deepwater port at Ra's al-Khaimah. Sharjah constructed a new port at Khor Fakkan in the early 1980s; the Fujairah port became fully operational in 1983. In 1991, the merchant fleet consisted of 51 ships with a capacity totaling 766,000 GRT.

A new international airport in Abu Dhabi, on the mainland across from the island, opened in 1982 and serviced 1,075,000 embarking and disembarking passengers in 1991. The other international airports in the UAE are in Dubai, Sharjah, and Ra's al-Khaimah. The Dubai Airport was planning to begin a $1.5 billion, six year expansion in 1994. In July 1991, a "cargo village" opened at the airport, designed to handle 250,000 tons of cargo per year by 1997. The village operations can transfer cargo received at the port into air containers ready for airlift in three hours, and have the facilities to handle frozen and hazardous goods.

[12]HISTORY

Although the Trucial Coast has for centuries been situated on one of the main trade routes between Asia and Europe, very little is known about the early history of the states that now make up the UAE. The northern states of the UAE, and in particular Ra's al-Khaimah, first came into historic prominence during the period of Portuguese occupation in the 16th and early 17th centuries, when Portugal used the territories as a base to fight a rear guard action against Persia. At that time and down to the mid-18th century, neighboring Oman played an integral role in the history of the maritime states.

Abu Dhabi island was settled by its present ruling family, Al-Nahyan, toward the end of the 18th century, and Dubai was founded by an offshoot of the same family in 1833. The late 18th and 19th centuries brought the division of the area between the Nahyan and the Qawasim, who ruled Ra's al-Khaimah and neighboring territories and whose clashes with British and Indian shipping led to British naval expeditions against what came to be known as the Pirate Coast. Treaties concluded in 1820 and 1835 established a formal relationship between the states of the southern Gulf and Britain that was to last until 1971. In 1853, the sheikhs agreed to a "perpetual maritime truce" to be enforced by the British navy. Under a treaty signed in 1892, the UK promised to protect the Trucial Coast from all aggression by sea and to lend its good offices in case of land attack. In 1955, the UK effectively intervened on the side of Abu Dhabi in the latter's dispute with Sa'udi Arabia over the Buraymi oasis, control of which is now shared by Abu Dhabi and Oman.

When, in 1968, the UK announced its intention to withdraw its forces from the area, a decision to establish a federation of Arab emirates—embracing the seven Trucial States, Bahrain, and Qatar—was agreed on in principle. However, it proved impossible to reconcile the differences among all the members, and in 1971, six Trucial States (excluding Ra's al-Khaimah) agreed on the establishment of the United Arab Emirates. The UAE was officially proclaimed a sovereign, independent nation on 2 December 1971, with Ra's al-Khaimah joining in early 1972.

Externally, the move to independence in 1971 placed the UAE in difficult straits with its two powerful neighbors, Sa'udi Arabia and Iran. Sa'udi Arabia asserted a territorial claim on a group of oases in the south of the UAE, and Iran laid claim to its offshore islands. In 1974, a border agreement on the Liwa' oases was signed with Sa'udi Arabia, but apparently has not been fully recognized by the rulers of either country. The dispute with Iran over the Abu Musa and Tumb Islands became tense when Iranian forces unilaterally asserted control over the UAE section of Abu Musa in 1992. Tehran backed down and relations between the two countries returned to a cautious normality.

The UAE became a founding member in 1981 of the Gulf Cooperation Council (GCC), a political and economic alliance directed, at least implicitly, against Iran. During the Iran-Iraq war, the UAE gave aid to Iraq but also maintained diplomatic relations with Iran and sought to mediate the conflict.

In the Gulf War, forces from the UAE participated with allied troops and the government gave some $4.5 billion to the coalition war effort. Subsequently, the UAE has increasingly looked to the GCC, the US, and friendly Arab states for its security protection. The UAE's generosity with foreign aid to Arab states (over $15 billion through 1991) makes it a significant player in the affairs of the region.

In 1991, the Bank of Commerce and Credit International (BCCI), which was based in the UAE and largely owned by the ruling family of Abu Dhabi, was accused of fraudulent dealings and closed down, causing repercussions all around the world.

13GOVERNMENT

According to the provisional constitution of the UAE, promulgated on 2 December 1971, the executive branch of the UAE government consists of the Supreme Council of Rulers, headed by the president, and the Council of Ministers. The Council of Rulers, composed of the hereditary rulers of the seven emirates, has responsibility for formulation and supervision of all UAE policies, ratification of federal laws, and oversight of the union's budget. Sheikh Zayed bin Sultan al-Nahayyan, emir of Abu Dhabi, was elected president upon independence and was reelected to five-year terms from 1976 to 1991. The president is assisted by the Council of Ministers, or cabinet, headed by the prime minister. Sheikh Rashid bin Sa'id al-Maktoum, ruler of Dubai, has served as vice-president since 1971 and as prime minister from 1979. The member states are represented in the cabinet in numbers relative to their size and importance.

The Federal National Council, consisting of 40 delegates from the member emirates, appointed by their respective rulers for two-year terms, can question cabinet ministers and make recommendations to the Supreme National Council. The latter meets only occasionally and the Federal National Council, which has no legislative powers, was inactive from 1991 to 1993. The constitution stipulates the distribution of the 40 seats as follows: Abu Dhabi and Dubai, 8 each; Sharjah and Ra's al-Khaimah, 6 each; and 'Ajman, Umm al-Qaiwain, and Fujairah, 4 each.

Most of the emirates are governed according to tribal traditions, including open meetings in which citizens express themselves directly to their rulers.

14POLITICAL PARTIES

No political parties exist in the UAE. Arab nationalist feeling has developed, however, and there is growing sentiment, particularly among urban youth, in favor of political liberalization and accelerated economic development. Several small clandestine groups with ties to radical Arab organizations or militant Islamic groups are believed to be active and are watched closely by the federation's security services.

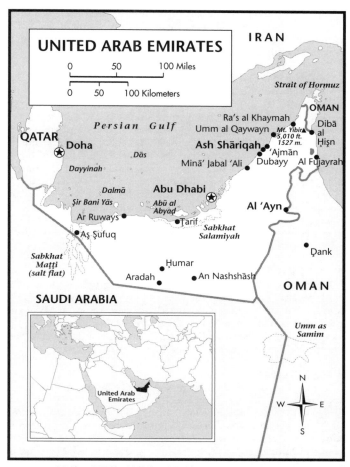

LOCATION: 51°3' to 56°23'E; 22°30' to 26°17'N. **BOUNDARY LENGTHS:** Persian Gulf coastline, 777 km (483 mi); Oman, 513 km (319 mi); Sa'udi Arabia, 586 km (364 mi); Qatar, 64 km (40 mi). **TERRITORIAL SEA LIMIT:** 3 mi, except Sharjah (12 mi).

15LOCAL GOVERNMENT

The major institutions of local government are the municipalities of Abu Dhabi town, Al-'Ayn, Dubai, Sharjah, Ra's al-Khaimah, Fujairah, 'Ajman, and Umm al-Qaiwain and a handful of traditional councils known as majalis and amiri diwans.

16JUDICIAL SYSTEM

Abu Dhabi, Dubai, and Sharjah have developed relatively sophisticated judicial systems based, as in other Gulf states, on a combination of Shari'ah law for civil matters, and contemporary legal codes. The 1971 constitution established a Supreme Court and an indeterminate number of courts of first instance. The Supreme Court consists of a president and a maximum of five judges, all of whom are appointed by presidential decree upon approval of the Supreme Council of Rulers. The Supreme Court president and member judges are deemed independent of the executive and legislative branches; once appointed, they cannot be removed. The lower courts were incorporated into a unified federal judiciary as of 1978.

Shari'a courts in each emirate are subject to review in the Federal Supreme Court. There is no separate national security court system. Military tribunals try only military personnel and apply a system based on Western military judicial procedure.

Court systems in the Emirates of Dubai and Ra's-al-Khaimah function independently of the federal system. Each system has multiple levels of appeal and verdicts in capital cases are appealable to the President.

There are no jury trials. Under the new Criminal Procedural

Code, the accused has a right to counsel in capital cases and in those involving a possible penalty of life imprisonment. Due process rights are uniform under both the civil court and the Shari'a court procedure.

17 ARMED FORCES

The armed forces of the UAE were placed under a unified command in 1976, and the forces of Abu Dhabi, Dubai, Ra's al-Khaimah, and Sharjah were merged. In 1993, the combined forces totaled 54,000 men, all volunteers. One-third are Asian contract soldiers. The army had 50,000 men, organized into 6 brigades. The navy comprised 2,000 men and 19 patrol and coastal combatants. The air force had 2,500 men, 105 combat aircraft, and 19 armed helicopters.

Many military personnel are expatriates from Oman, Jordan, and other countries. The UAE's military equipment is largely supplied by France, Germany, and the UK. Defense spending in 1989 was about $1.47 billion or 5.3% of gross domestic product. Morocco provides some 5,000 soldiers and police to the UAE.

18 INTERNATIONAL COOPERATION

On 9 December 1971, shortly after achieving independence, the UAE became a member of the UN, and it now belongs to ESCWA and all the nonregional specialized agencies except WMO. The country is a member of G-77, GCC, the Islamic Conference, the League of Arab States, and OPEC. The UAE is a de facto adherent of GATT and signatory to the Law of the Sea.

19 ECONOMY

The economy of the UAE centers primarily on oil and oil-based industries, but the share of this contribution to the GDP fell from 70% in 1980 to 33% in 1986 and has remained at around 36–38% for several years. (The oil revenue in 1990 was significantly higher as a result of the Gulf conflict.) This is principally the result of falling oil prices, but also of growth in other sectors of the economy, such as manufacturing, finance and insurance, real estate, and government services. In Abu Dhabi, by far the wealthiest of the seven emirates, oil revenues are supplemented by income from a huge investment fund. Dubai joined the ranks of the oil producers only in 1971, and entrepôt trade continues to play a major role in its economy. Although 'Ajman has a small shipbuilding and ship repair yard and a recently established cement company, and Umm al-Qaiwain has a fish hatchery, a cement plant, and some small handicraft operations, these poorer emirates depend on federal aid—in effect, on revenue sharing by Abu Dhabi and Dubai. Oil production in Sharjah began in July 1974, and manufacturing and tourism there have been expanded. Ra's al-Khaimah has three large cement plants, pharmaceutical factory, a lime kiln, and the gulf's first explosives plant. Fujairah remains predominantly agricultural, but the emirate's government has also been developing an industrialization program, with emphasis on establishing mining-based industries.

With its strategic location, modern communications facilities, seaports and international airports, its own international airline, and strong banking system, the UAE has become the major entrepôt in the Gulf region.

The economy, which provides the UAE with one of the highest per capita incomes—$20,143 in 1990, is heavily dependent on foreign labor, which constitutes 80% of the population.

20 INCOME

In 1992, United Arab Emirates' GNP was $37,068 million at current prices, or $22,220 per capita. For the period 1985–92 the average inflation rate was 2.4%.

In 1992 the GDP was $34.9 billion in current US dollars. It is estimated that agriculture, hunting, forestry, and fishing contributed 2% to GDP; mining and quarrying, 47%; manufacturing, 7%; electricity, gas, and water, 2%; construction, 8%; wholesale and retail trade, 9%; transport, storage, and communication, 5%; finance, insurance, real estate, and business services, 11%; community, social, and personal services, 2%; and other sources, 7%.

21 LABOR

In 1992, the total work force was estimated at 700,000, but only 10% were UAE nationals, of which women comprised 6.5%.

The UAE leans heavily on skilled labor, technology, and management abilities provided by foreigners. Non-UAE Arabs are employed at all economic levels, including the government bureaucracy and civil service. Manual labor is largely performed by Pakistanis and Iranians, while many Indians are to be found in clerical positions. Most domestic servants are women from Sri Lanka or the Philippines. There is a high proportion of Europeans at management levels. Until recently, the large influx of immigrants was insufficient to cope with labor needs. But with declining oil revenues in the mid-1980s, well-paying, skilled jobs were becoming harder to find in both the private and public sectors. The federal government and other state organizations began cutting back on employees. Many foreign workers were laid off and repatriated. A 1984 decree guarantees UAE nationals priority in hiring, in order to reduce dependence on expatriates.

In 1991, major industries employing workers were construction, 17.2%; government service, 16.5%; sales and hotels, 14.7%; finance, 11.3%; transportation and communication, 10.4%; domestic work, 3%; and agriculture, 1.7%. Labor legislation guarantees a minimum wage, certain basic conditions of work, and some degree of social insurance. Collective bargaining provisions do not exist, and strikes are strictly prohibited in the public sector.

22 AGRICULTURE

Only about 39,000 hectares (96,300 acres) of land are cultivated. About 24% of cultivated land is used to grow vegetables, 30% fruit, 10% feed crops, and 36% for other uses. The most productive region is Ra's al-Khaimah, which receives underground water supplies from the nearby mountains of Oman and which enjoys the most plentiful rainfall. The main crops are tomatoes, melons, and dates.

The Digdagga Agricultural Trials Station in Ra's al-Khaimah is central to all agricultural research and training efforts in the UAE. Abu Dhabi has two large wheat farms at Al-'Ayn, and experimental farms at Rawaya and Mazaid (near Al-'Ayn) are designed to encourage local Bedouins to take up settled farming. The Abu Dhabi Arid Land Research Center on Sadiyat Island produces vegetables through special irrigation and hydroponic techniques. In 1992, UAE agriculture produced 361,000 tons of vegetables and 235,000 tons of fruit.

The Ministry of Agriculture and Fisheries reported a 44% increase in agricultural production between 1987 and 1991. Dates, traditionally grown on oases by nomads, are becoming less important because of vegetable and fruit production. The UAE currently satisfies about 60% of its domestic fruit and vegetable demand; bans on imports of certain vegetables and government incentives and subsidies are used to encourage domestic production.

23 ANIMAL HUSBANDRY

Livestock production has risen sharply in recent years. In 1992, the UAE had 720,000 goats, 275,000 sheep, 132,000 camels, and 55,000 head of cattle. Dairy farming is centered in Ra's al-Khaimah, with other dairy farms in Al Ain, Umm Al Quwain, Sharjah, and Dubai. The UAE produces about 40% of its dairy needs. Local poultry and egg production satisfy 65% and 80% of domestic demand, respectively. The poultry farm at Fujairah has the capacity to supply over 15% of domestic demand for broilers and eggs. Ra's al-Khaimah and Al Ain are other centers of poultry production.

24FISHING

Fishing is an important source of domestic food and fodder. From 1988 to 1990, per capita annual consumption of fish and shellfish in the UAE was 26.3 kg (58 lb) live weight equivalent, more than any other country in the Middle East. UAE coastal waters abound in fish and shellfish, and the country borders two high-potential fishing regions, the Persian Gulf and the Gulf of Oman. Many varieties of fish are caught, including rock cod, tuna, mackerel, sardines, anchovies, jack, marlin, red mullet, bream, and snapper. Over 70% of the catch typically is dried and processed into animal feed. The fish catch in 1991 was 92,300 tons, which supplied about 97% of local demand. Modern fishing techniques have been introduced with government assistance, and two new ports permitting the use of larger fishing boats were opened in 1981. The government also provides facilities for ship maintenance pro bono, as well as interest-free loans for the purchase of fishing boats and equipment. Umm Al Quwain is the site of a new 1,300 sq m marine farm which will research fish breeding. A fishmeal plant is in operation in Ra's al-Khaimah.

25FORESTRY

Natural woodland is scarce, apart from palm groves along the northern and eastern coasts. Wooded areas covered only 3,000 hectares (7,400 acres), or about 0.04% of the total land area in 1991. The Forestry Department planted 1.6 million trees during the 1970s, and its main nursery grows more than 300,000 seedlings each year.

26MINING

Apart from oil and natural gas, mining is limited to the production of construction materials, marble, and stone quarried from the Hajar Mountains. Copper and chromium have been found in Fujairah and Ra's al-Khaimah; in 1992, an estimated 20,000 tons of chromite ore were exported.

27ENERGY AND POWER

The UAE, with crude oil production of 2.3 million barrels per day in 1992 (up from 1.8 million barrels per day in 1989), ranked as the third-largest OPEC producer; total reserves of crude oil were estimated at 98.1 billion barrels. Production is confined to Abu Dhabi, Dubai, Sharjah, and Ra's al-Khaimah, which together have an estimated maximum daily capacity of 2.7 million barrels. Abu Dhabi accounted for 85% of the total output in 1992, Dubai and Sharjah 15%. Abu Dhabi's oil output comes almost exclusively from the onshore drilling activities of the Abu Dhabi Co. for Onshore Oil Operations (ADCO) and the offshore activities of Abu Dhabi Marine Operating Co. (ADMA-OPCO). Abu Dhabi has a 60% participation in the operations of both companies, which are managed by the government-owned Abu Dhabi National Oil Co. (ADNOC). The remaining 40% of ADCO's ownership is divided mainly among UK, US, and Dutch interests; the balance of ADMA-OPCO is owned by UK, French, and Japanese firms. Japan imports about 20% of its crude oil from the UAE, which represents about 45% of annual production.

Offshore oil exploration by foreign companies has produced major new finds in recent years. Discovery of the offshore Butainah field in 1979 added about 1 billion barrels of oil to the UAE's proved reserves. That year, a US company, Amerada Hess, began producing crude oil at a rate of 15,000 barrels a day from the Arzanah offshore field. The Japan Oil Development Co. (JODCO), in partnership with ADNOC, began production at the offshore Umm ad-Dalkh field near Abu Dhabi in 1982. The two

companies also agreed to develop three other small offshore areas, and both joined a French firm, CFP, to produce a projected 50,000 barrels of oil per day from the Upper Zakum field. The offshore Saleh field was found in 1983.

In 1981, Abu Dhabi and Dubai began to transfer up to half of their annual revenues from oil operations to the federation. The UAE's oil export receipts were $13.4 billion in 1992, up from $12.3 billion in 1985, but down from $19.4 billion in 1980. The UAE's production of oil in 1992 exceeded its OPEC production quota of 2,161,000 barrels per day.

The UAE increased to three the number of oil refineries with the dedication in March 1982 of its new Ar-Ruwais installation, with production capacity of 120,000 barrels a day, and the completion in 1983 of the Umm an-Nar complex, with capacity of 60,000 barrels daily. Refined capacity was 195,000 barrels a day in 1992, while the UAE's proven natural gas reserves totaled about 5.8 trillion cu m (205 trillion cu ft); net production amounted to 23.6 billion cu m.

All electricity is thermally generated from oil or natural gas. Electric power production was 13,790 million kwh in 1991.

28INDUSTRY

To diversify the economy, the UAE has been introducing a wide spectrum of new industries: aluminum, cement, pharmaceuticals, fabricated metals, processed foods, fertilizer, and explosives.

The Ar-Ruwais industrial complex in Abu Dhabi includes an oil refinery with a processing capacity of 120,000 barrels per day; a fertilizer factory, with a production capacity of 1,000 tons of ammonia and 1,500 tons of urea per day; and a gas liquefaction installation. A master plan for Ar-Ruwais, which called for construction of a port, a petrochemical plant, a steel mill, and other projects, has been scaled down due to declining oil revenues. Near Umm An-Nar, a large plant belonging to National Chlorine Industries produces salt, chlorine, caustic soda, and hydrochloric acid.

In Dubai, the industrial port complex at Jabal 'Ali includes an aluminum smelter, which produced over 150,000 tons in 1985; the largest dry dock in the world, with a capacity of 1 million tons; and a free trade zone. A $90 million phosphoric acid plant, which will utilize Gabal Ali's port facilities, is planned. Dubai's older industrial zone of Rashidiya is the site of some 40% of the emirate's processing industries. The other emirates have developed industries that produce construction-related materials such as cement, asphalt, and concrete blocks. Umm al-Qaiwain is planning to build a 120,000-ton-per-year aluminum smelter.

29SCIENCE AND TECHNOLOGY

Advanced technology in the UAE has been imported mostly by foreign oil companies and is limited largely to heavy industry; nearly all of its technological specialists are foreigners. In the 1980s, the UAE took major steps to decrease its reliance on foreign scientists and technicians. The Ministry of Agriculture and Fisheries has a research center in Ra's al-Khaimah. United Arab Emirates University has faculties of sciences, engineering, agriculture, and medicine. Ajman University College of Science and Technology was founded in 1988. The Higher Colleges of Technology have 1,150 students.

30DOMESTIC TRADE

Dubai remains the most important center of trade and commerce, although the commercial facilities of Abu Dhabi grew rapidly during the 1970s. Barter methods still prevail outside the coastal towns, where specialized shops stocked with imported goods are common. Business hours tend to vary, although general hours of 8 AM to 1 PM and 4 to 7 PM are observed; most offices are closed Thursday afternoon, and Friday is the weekly holiday. Banks are open from 8 AM to noon, Saturday–Thursday.

31 FOREIGN TRADE

Virtually all export earnings derive from oil. In 1985, the UAE's petroleum exports amounted to $12.4 billion, down from $19.4 billion in 1980. All other exports combined amounted to only $1.5 billion in 1985. Petroleum products accounted for approximately 75% of total exports in 1992, which amounted to $23.4 billion. As of the early 1980s, the UAE remained basically a one-commodity state and was thus dependent on imports to satisfy consumer needs and demands. The value of imports in 1992 was $17.4 billion compared to $6.7 billion in 1985. Consumer goods, especially foodstuffs, accounted for about half of all imports, followed by capital goods such as transportation equipment, oil-field equipment, and building materials.

Japan, Singapore, India, South Korea, the EEC countries, and the US are the leading purchasers of petroleum from the UAE. Of the UAE's total 1992 imports, Japan supplied 15.3%, China 8.0%, the US 7.9%, and Germany 7.4.

32 BALANCE OF PAYMENTS

Oil and natural gas exports have allowed the UAE to sustain a trade surplus for many years, but changes in oil prices cause the surplus to fluctuate widely from year to year. In 1990, exports exceeded imports by $9 billion; in 1989 the trade surplus was only $5.6 billion. International reserves totaled $5.1 billion in October 1991.

33 BANKING AND SECURITIES

The UAE Currency Board came into existence with its issuance of the UAE dirham in May 1973. In 1975–76, statutes came into force providing for the board's gradual transformation into a central bank, including powers to impose minimum liquidity ratios and other credit regulations. The board was duly replaced in 1980 by the UAE Central Bank, with enhanced authority to regulate the banking system. Capitalized at $81.7 million, the bank was granted additional capital of $2 billion from the government in 1982, which was to increase by 20% per year until a total deposit of $4 billion had been reached. The money supply, as measured by M2, was UD68,414 million in 1993.

In 1993, 51 banks were operating in the UAE, including 51 foreign banks with 287 branches. In recent years, banking assets have increased considerably, and deposits have also shown an overall upward trend; commercial bank foreign assets reached UD66,070 million in 1993, and demand, time, and savings deposits advanced to UD50,240 million. In 1991, the Bank of Commerce and Credit International (BCCI), based in the UAI and owned in large part by the ruling family of Abu Dhabi, was accused of fraudulent dealings, and closed. Securities are bought and sold through the banks.

34 INSURANCE

Because of tightening federal regulations, the number of insurance companies declined from 126 in 1980 to 56 in 1987. The Federal Insurance Companies and Agents Law of 1984 requires all insurance companies established in the UAE to be public joint-stock companies, with equity wholly owned by UAE nationals. Companies already established in the country can obtain a concession from the local equity provision. Minimum capital must be UD10 million. Non-life insurance accounted for 90.3% of all premiums in 1985.

35 PUBLIC FINANCE

A federal budget is prepared according to the UAE's development policy, while each emirate is responsible for municipal budgets and local projects. Conservative public expenditure policies have become more necessary as oil revenues have declined since 1983. Nevertheless, deficit spending is now typical— UD1.2 billion in 1991, up from UD660 million in 1990. Abu Dhabi's oil income

accounts for the bulk of federal revenues; under the constitution, each emirate contributes 50% of its net oil income to the federal budget.

The following table shows actual revenues and expenditures for 1988 and 1989 in millions of dirhams.

	1988	1989
REVENUE AND GRANTS		
Tax revenue	479	573
Non-tax revenue	1,438	766
Capital revenue	4	9
Grants	10,950	11,298
TOTAL	12,871	12,646

EXPENDITURES & LENDING MINUS REPAYMENTS

	1988	1989
General public service	739	613
Defense	5,827	5,827
Public order and safety	1,697	1,789
Education	1,882	1,985
Health	919	916
Social security and welfare	420	420
Housing and community amenities	58	54
Recreation, cultural, and religious affairs	353	357
Economic affairs and services	582	572
Other expenditures	708	731
Adjustments	—	—
Lending minus repayments	—	—
TOTAL	13,185	13,264
DEFICIT/SURPLUS	–315	–618

36 TAXATION

Corporate taxes are paid only by oil companies (at rates that vary among emirates) and branches of foreign banks (at 20%). Municipal taxes are 5% on residential and 10% on commercial rents. A 5% tax is imposed on hotel services and entertainment. There is no personal income tax.

37 CUSTOMS AND DUTIES

Dubai, the major area for foreign trade, is a free-trade zone and free port with no restrictions on imports or exports. The individual governments exert no control over imports, except for licensing. Customs duties are levied ad valorem; the rates differ among the emirates but are generally nominal, except for a duty of up to 30% on alcoholic beverages (importation of which requires special permission). Duty-free imports include machinery, construction materials, foodstuffs, medicine, and printed matter.

38 FOREIGN INVESTMENT

All the emirates are eager to attract foreign investment. One obstacle to foreign investment may be the federal requirement that investments must be on a joint venture basis with the local partner owning at least 51% of the venture. The exception to this requirement is investment in the free trade zones where 100% foreign ownership is allowed.

39 ECONOMIC DEVELOPMENT

The federation used its vast oil wealth during the 1970s to transform the national economy through expansion of roads, ports, airports, communications facilities, electric power plants, and water desalination facilities, as well as construction of huge oil-processing complexes. With the completion of major infrastructural projects by the early 1980s, the focus of development shifted to diversifying the economy by establishing capital-intensive industries based on oil and gas resources.

The country's major industrial projects are the Jabal'Ali industrial zone in Dubai and the refinery complex at Ar-Ruwais in Abu

Dhabi. Jabal 'Ali includes the Dubai Aluminum Co. smelter, a natural gas liquefaction plant, a cable factory, and a desalination plant that is one of the world's largest, with an output of about 25 million gallons of water daily. The construction of Dubai's first refinery at Jabal 'Ali is still in the planning stage. In 1993, approximately 600 companies were operating in the Jabal 'Ali Free Zone with capital investment of about $1.1 billion. Abu Dhabi plans to increase the production of liquefied natural gas (LNG) as part of its 1991–95 development plan, with major gas development centering on the Das Island complex.

In relation to GNP, the UAE is one of the world's major aid donors; disbursements of official development assistance in 1975, for example, amounted to more than $1 billion, or nearly 12% of the GNP for that year. Official loans and grants amounted to $35.2 billion in 1981; in 1985, they fell to $7 billion. The principal vehicle for bilateral aid has been the Abu Dhabi Fund for Arab Economic Development, which by the end of 1985 had extended 86 loans to 41 developing countries, Arab and non-Arab. The UAE makes regular annual payments totaling hundreds of millions of dollars to Syria, Jordan, Lebanon, and the PLO. In 1989, the UAE granted Jordan $70 million. Responding to Iraq's invasion of Kuwait in 1990, the UAE made significant financial contributions to assist the frontline states and to share the cost of the foreign military forces. The UAE's commitments amount to $3.87 billion in cash in addition to $197 million of payments in kind totaling $4.07 billion.

40SOCIAL DEVELOPMENT

There is no social security law in the UAE, but many welfare benefits are available to citizens, among them free hospital treatment and medical care and subsidies for education. Relief for any domestic catastrophe is provided from a disaster fund. If the father of a family is unable to work because of illness, disability, or old age, he receives help under the National Assistance Law; should he die or divorce his wife, the woman's future is secured.

Female employment is growing in government service and in occupations such as education and health. Women are also accepted for military service. Women account for 70% of the student body at the UAE University. Islamic precepts apply to family law, although some, such as polygamy for men, are not usually practiced. The UAE fertility rate in 1985–90 was 4.8.

41HEALTH

Health facilities have been expanded rapidly since independence. Modern hospitals have been built in Abu Dhabi, Dubai, and other towns. The number of hospital beds totaled 6,025 in 1985. In 1991, there were 1,526 doctors and 2,800 nurses; in 1989, there were 285 dentists. Typhoid fever and tuberculosis are rare; malaria remains a problem, however. In 1991, 95% of the population had access to safe water and 77% had adequate sanitation. In 1992, 99% of the population had access to health care services.

Average life expectancy in 1992 was 71 years, and the infant mortality rate was 18 per 1,000 live births. General mortality was 3.9 per 1,000 people. The country's 1993 birth rate was 21.2 per 1,000 people; there were 35,000 births in 1992. Children up to one year old were immunized in 1992 against tuberculosis (98%); diphtheria, pertussis, and tetanus (86%); polio (86%); and measles (85%).

42HOUSING

The federal government is attempting to make modern low-cost homes available to poorer families, supplying them with amenities such as piped water, sewerage systems, and electricity. The Ministry of Housing constructed about 4,000 houses for free distribution to poor families between 1978 and 1981. In 1980, 33% of all housing units were flats, 30% were traditional Arabic dwellings, 9% were low-cost housing, 8% were shacks, and the remainder were sheds, caravans, single rooms, tents, and other facilities. About 85% had water closets and 26% had electricity, piped-in water, and access to a sewage system.

43EDUCATION

The educational system of the UAE has burgeoned since 1971. Education in the six northern emirates, formerly financed and administered by Kuwait, has been managed by the UAE Ministry of Education since 1972. Education is compulsory for six years at the primary level, from age 6, and is free to all UAE citizens, as are school uniforms, books, equipment, and transportation. The system remains concentrated at the primary level. At the secondary level, children go through six years of education in two stages. In 1991, there were 231,674 pupils and 13,139 teachers at the primary level and 118,011 pupils and 9,430 teachers in secondary schools. In 1980, the government issued new regulations concerning private schools, which enrolled nearly 90,000 students in 1985; Arabic was made a compulsory subject, and segregation of classes by sex was required. United Arab Emirates University is at Al-'Ayn. In 1991, all higher level institutions had 10,405 students and 1,082 instructors.

44LIBRARIES AND MUSEUMS

There are excellent museums in Abu Dhabi town and Al-'Ayn The National Library located in Abu Dhabi established in 1981 contains over 800,000 volumes.

45MEDIA

The communications system has been dramatically improved and expanded in recent years. Telecommunications operations in the emirates are all handled by ETISALAT. The Jabal 'Ali earth satellite station in Dubai maintains telephone and telegraph traffic, telex data transmission, and color television broadcasting; computer-controlled automatic telex systems have been installed in both Dubai and Abu Dhabi. In 1991, the UAE had 463,398 telephones and 7,000 telex lines. A color television network connects Abu Dhabi with Dubai and Sharjah. UAE Radio has broadcasting stations in four emirates; the first commercial station was opened in Abu Dhabi in 1980. There were an estimated 530,000 radios and 175,000 television sets in 1991.

Five Arabic-language dailies were published in 1991 in the UAE: *Al-Ittihad* (Federation, 1991 circulation 75,000), *Al-Fajr* (The Dawn, 20,000), and *Al-Wahdah* (Unity, 30,000), in Abu Dhabi; *Al-Bayan* (45,000) in Dubai; and *Al-Khalij* (57,000) in Sharjah. There were three English-language dailies: the *Gulf News* (54,100) and *Khaleej Times* (56,000), published in Dubai, and the *Emirates News* (15,000), published in Abu Dhabi.

46ORGANIZATIONS

There are chambers of commerce in the larger states. Various social and sporting clubs provide outlets for philanthropic work and recreation.

47TOURISM, TRAVEL, AND RECREATION

Except for Gulf nationals and citizens of the UK, most visitors must secure a visa in advance. Tourism is encouraged by all the emirates, whose varied scenery includes mountains, beaches, deserts and oases. Activities include visits to Bedouin markets, museums, zoos, and aquariums. Many large world-class hotels have opened in recent years. The emirates attract tourists from Western Europe during the winter, when the main attractions are the beaches and sunny climate.

48FAMOUS EMIRIANS

Sheikh Zayed bin Sultan an-Nahyan (b.1918) has been ruler of Abu Dhabi since 1966 and president of the UAE since 1971.

[49]DEPENDENCIES
The UAE has no territories or colonies.

[50]BIBLIOGRAPHY

Abdullah, Muhammad Morsy. *The United Arab Emirates: A Modern History.* New York: Barnes & Noble, 1978.

Alkim, Hassan Hamdan. *The Foreign Policy of the United Arab Emirates.* London: Saqi, 1989.

American University. *Persian Gulf States: Country Studies.* Washington, D.C.: Government Printing Office, 1984.

Anthony, John Duke. *Arab States of the Lower Gulf: People, Politics, Petroleum.* Washington, D.C.: Middle East Institute, 1975.

El Mallakh, Ragaei. *The Economic Development of the United Arab Emirates.* New York: St. Martin's, 1981.

Ghanem, Shihab M. A. *Industrialization in the United Arab Emirates.* Brookfield: Avebury, 1992.

Heard-Bey, Frauke. *From Trucial States to United Arab Emirates: A Society in Transition.* New York: Longman, 1982.

Peck, Malcolm C. *The United Arab Emirates: A Venture in Unity.* Boulder, Colo.: Westview, 1986.

Taryam, Abdullah Omran. *The Establishment of the United Arab Emirates, 1950–85.* New York: Croom Helm, 1987.

Vine, Peter. *United Arab Emirates: Profile of a Country's Heritage and Modern Development.* London: Immel, 1992.

Zahlan, Rosemarie Said. *The Origins of the United Arab Emirates: A Political and Social History of the Trucial States.* New York: St. Martin's, 1978.

UNITED KINGDOM ASIAN AND PACIFIC DEPENDENCIES

HONG KONG

Hong Kong is a UK crown colony consisting of 237 small islands off the southeast coast of China and a small peninsula adjoining Guangdong Province on the mainland between 22°29' and 22°37'N and 113°52' and 114°30'E. With a total area, including recent reclamation, of 1,068 sq km (412 sq mi), it comprises the island of Hong Kong and adjacent islands, 79 sq km (30 sq mi); the Kowloon Peninsula, 11 sq km (4 sq mi); and the New Territories (a leased section of the Chinese mainland) and the remaining islands, 978 sq km (377 sq mi). Most of Hong Kong territory is rocky, hilly and deeply eroded. The climate is subtropical, with hot and humid summers. Rainfall is heavy, and there are occasional typhoons.

Total population, which was under 600,000 in 1945, was approximately 5,900,000 at the end of 1992, making Hong Kong the world's most populous non-self-governing territory. The annual rate of growth is .6%. The phenomenal increase since World War II resulted primarily from a large influx of mainland Chinese. During the late 1970s and early 1980s, hundreds of thousands of "boat people" arrived from Viet-Nam. Most have been resettled in other countries, and by mid-1987 only 8,500 remained in camps. In the summer of that year, however, Hong Kong faced another influx of Vietnamese, most of them ethnic Chinese. These people—more than 6,000 of them—had fled to China after the Viet-Nam war but found it difficult to assimilate there.

The birthrate fell from 13 per 1,000 in 1986 to 11 per 1,000 in 1992, while the death rate remained at about 6 per 1,000. About 98% of the inhabitants are Chinese, and about 95% of the people live in metropolitan areas. The overall population density in 1992 was 5,524 per sq km (14,320 per sq mi). Chinese (Cantonese dialect) is the principal spoken language; both Chinese and English are official languages. Taoists, Confucianists, and Buddhists constitute a majority of the population. The Christian population (10%) is split about evenly between Roman Catholics and Protestants. There are also Muslim and Hindu communities (1%). The capital is Victoria, commonly known as Hong Kong.

Hong Kong has regular shipping, air, cable, and wireless services to every part of the world. Government-maintained roads spanned more than 1,450 km (901 mi) in 1992, and there were 370,000 registered vehicles. The mile-long Cross Harbour Road Tunnel connecting Hong Kong Island to Kowloon was opened in 1972, and the Lion Rock Tunnels link Kowloon with Sha Tin; the Aberdeen Tunnel beneath Hong Kong Island entered service in 1982. The government-owned Mass Transit Railway, a 38.6-km (24-mi) subway system, was begun in November 1975 and started operations in October 1979. The government also owns and operates a 56-km (35-mi) rail line, known as the Kowloon-Canton Railway. The railroad links up with the rail system of Guangdong Province and constitutes a major land-entry route to China; passenger service, suspended in 1949, was resumed in 1979. The Kowloo-Canton Railway operates a 34-km (21-mi) light rail system for the New Territories. Hong Kong has one of the finest natural harbors. There are deepwater berths in Kowloon Peninsula and in Hong Kong; a new container terminal at Kwaichung in Kowloon handles some 60% of Hong Kong's exports. An extensive ferry service connects Hong Kong's islands; hydrofoils provide service to Macau. A cross-harbor tunnel has

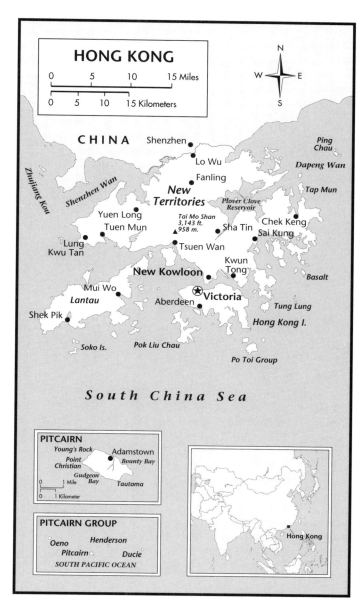

been constructed between Hong Kong and Kowloon, and another was under construction in the mid-1990s. The Hong Kong airport, Kai Tak, is suitable for both land and sea aircraft. The airport can handle upwards of 27 million passengers a year.

A bleak fisherman's island for most of its early history, Hong Kong was occupied in 1841 by the British. Formal cession by China was made in 1842 by the Treaty of Nanking. The Kowloon Peninsula and adjacent islands were added in 1860, and in 1898, the New Territories were leased from China for 99 years. Hong Kong fell under Japanese occupation from 25 December 1941 to 30 August 1945. Negotiations between the UK and China culminated in an agreement on 26 September 1984 under which sovereignty over the entire colony would be transferred to China as of 1 July 1997. For a 50-year period, Hong Kong would be a Special Administrative Region and would retain its capitalist economy, its political rights, and its general way of life. A Basic Law, forming a constitution for this period, took effect in 1990.

In the interim, the colony was ruled by a UK-appointed governor, with an advisory Executive Council headed by the local commander of UK forces, and an appointed Legislative Council presided over by the governor. The Urban Council of 30 members (15 elected and 15 appointed by the governor) dealt primarily with municipal affairs, and the government secretariat was responsible for the work of some 40 executive departments. The public sector's share of GDP decreased from 11% in 1973 to 7% in 1986. That year, the UK maintained a garrison of 8,945 troops (including four Gurkha battalions) in Hong Kong. Under a 1981 defense agreement, about three-fourths of the cost of the maintenance was borne by the Hong Kong government. The currency unit is the Hong Kong dollar (HK$1 = US$7.7855; US$1 = HK$0.1284).

Located at a major crossroads of world trade, Hong Kong has become a center of commerce, shipping, industry and banking. Rapid industrialization, accelerated by the influx of new labor, skills, and capital, has changed the pattern of the economy since the end of World War II. The value of industrial exports wholly or principally of Hong Kong origin rose from 42% of the total value of exports in 1958 to about 75% as the 1980s began but decreased bellow 55% in the mid-1990s. While heavy industries, such as shipbuilding and ship repairing, iron, and steel, remain important, light industries—especially watches, clocks, toys, and electronics—have developed more rapidly in recent years. Clothing and textile manufacturers, constituting the largest industrial sector. In 1990, the GDP stood at US$80.9 billion.

Although less than 10% of the total land area is used for farming, agriculture has been expanding and has changed from subsistence rice farming to intensive vegetable cultivation. However, most of Hong Kong's agricultural produce still has to be imported (mainly from China). Hong Kong produces 37% of its live poultry requirements and 18% of all hogs slaughtered. Fishponds have been built to supplement the ocean catch.

Electricity is supplied by two franchise companies; total installed capacity in 1992 was 9,566 Mw. Water resources, for long a serious deficiency, have been increased by converting Plover Cove into a lake. About one-quarter of the water supply is purchased annually from China.

Imports in 1990 were valued at HK$642,531 million, and exports and reexports at HK$639,875 million. Principal exports listed in a decreasing order is as follows: manufactured articles, clothing, textiles, electorial machinery, apparatus and appliances, telecommunications, sound recording and reproducing equipment, photographic equipment and supplies, optical goods, watches and clocks. Major import sources in 1992 were China (37%) and Japan (16); primary export destinations were the US, China, Germany, the UK , Japan, and Canada.

As the world's third-largest banking center, Hong Kong receives a continuous flow of outside capital; in 1992, 166 licensed banks, including 138 banks incorporated in foreign countries, were in operation. The Hong Kong Association of Banks was created in January 1981 to regulate charges and deposit interest rates and oversee banking standards. There is no central bank; currency is issued by two commercial banks. In addition to the licensed banks, many Chinese firms handle Chinese remittances from overseas. In 1992, bank deposits totaled HK$5.2 trillion. Hong Kong reportedly supplies about one-third of China's foreign exchange.

Hong Kong is self-supportive except for external defense. Revenues in 1986/87 were estimated at HK$43,409 million, derived mainly from internal taxation and import duties. Expenditures amounted to HK$43,002 million.

Tourism has become an important industry. In 1992, more than 5.9 million tourists visited Hong Kong, giving the colony more than HK $40 billion in earnings. About 23.5% of the tourist earnings came from the US, Canada and Western Europe and twenty-three percent came from Japan

Telephones numbered about 3.1 million in 1992. Broadcasting services are provided by a government station, Radio Television Hong Kong, and by commercial operators. By 1986, two commercial television stations with two channels each were in operation. Broadcasting services are in both Chinese and English. An estimated 90% of all households have one or more television sets. The Hong Kong press comprises 66 newspapers and 520 other periodicals. Almost all the newspapers are in Chinese; five are English-language dailies.

The infant mortality rate was 7 per 1,000 live births. The average life expectancy was 78.5 years for females and 73 for males in 1992. Despite law enforcement efforts, drug addiction afflicts an estimated 38,000 persons; more than 15,000 receive daily treatment through government-owned or -aided health centers.

The Hong Kong Housing Authority plans, builds, and manages public housing developments. Despite recent initiatives in housing construction, an estimated 100,000 "squatter" families resided in urban centers in 1986. Ambitious housing and business development projects undertaken in the late 1970s were linked to steeply rising property values; uncertainty over the future of the New Territories has since contributed to a real estate market decline.

In September 1980, education until the age of 15 was made compulsory; 6 years of primary and 3 years of secondary schooling are provided by the government free of charge. Schools are of three types: Chinese, English, and Anglo-Chinese. Prevocational training was offered in more than a dozen government-run institutions. Student enrollment in primary and secondary school is about a quarter of the population. Higher education is provided primarily by the University of Hong Kong and the Chinese University of Hong Kong. Hong Kong Polytechnic and the City Polytechnic of Hong Kong also provides post-secondary education for the colony's residents.

PITCAIRN ISLAND

Pitcairn is a mountainous island of volcanic origin about 4.5 sq km (1.75 sq mi) in area, in the South Pacific at 25°4's and 130°6'w. Three smaller islands (Henderson, Ducie, and Oeno) associated with Pitcairn are uninhabited. Pitcairn Island was discovered in 1767 by the British and settled in 1790 by H.M.S. *Bounty* mutineers and the Polynesian women who accompanied them from Tahiti. The population, mainly descendants of the *Bounty* mutineers, after reaching a peak of 233 in 1937, decreased to 120 in 1962 and to about 52 in 1992. Most of the younger members of the community have migrated to New Zealand. The climate is warm, with very little change throughout the year.

There is one village, Adamstown. Pitcairn is administered, together with the three other small islands, as a UK colony by the UK high commissioner in New Zealand. The local government consists of an island magistrate and a 10-member Island Council. Four of the Council's members are elected. New Zealand dollars (NZ$) are used locally; NZ$1 = US$0.5132 (or US$1 = NZ$1.9486). There is no port or harbor; goods from ships are conveyed ashore in longboats. Cargo ships plying the route between Panama and New Zealand call periodically.

The main occupation is subsistence agriculture. A small surplus of fresh fruit and vegetables is sold to passing ships. Fish are abundant, and the annual catch averages 2,000 lb. Imports, mainly food, come from New Zealand. Fruit, woven baskets, carved curios, and stamps are sold to ships' passengers. Government revenues in 1989 were US$430,440; expenditures, US$429,983.

UNITED STATES PACIFIC DEPENDENCIES

AMERICAN SAMOA

American Samoa, an unincorporated and unorganized insular US territory in the South Pacific Ocean, comprises that portion of the Samoan archipelago lying E of longitude 171°w. (The rest of the Samoan islands comprise the independent state of Western Samoa.) While the Samoan group as a whole has an area of 3,121 sq km (1,205 sq mi), American Samoa consists of only seven small islands (between 14° and 15°s and 168° and 171°w) with a total area (land and water) of 197 sq km (76 sq mi). Five of the islands are volcanic, with rugged peaks rising sharply, and two are coral atolls.

The climate is hot and rainy; normal temperatures range from 24°C (75°F) in August to 32°C (90°F) during December–February; mean annual rainfall is 330 cm (130 in), the rainy season lasting from December through March. Hurricanes are common. The native flora includes flourishing tree ferns, coconut, hardwoods, and rubber trees. There are few wild animals.

As of 1992, the estimated population was 51,115, an increase of 37% over the 1986 population estimate of 37,500. However, the total population has remained relatively constant for many years, however, because of the substantial number of Samoans who migrate to the United States. The inhabitants, who are concentrated on the island of Tutuila, are almost pure Polynesian. English is the official language, but Samoan is also widely spoken. Most Samoans are Christians.

The capital of the territory, Pago Pago, on Tutuila, has one of the finest natural harbors in the South Pacific and is a duty-free port. Passenger liners call there on South Pacific tours, and passenger and cargo ships arrive regularly from Japan, New Zealand, Australia, and the US west coast. There are regular air and sea services between American Samoa and Western Samoa, and scheduled flights between Pago Pago and Honolulu.

American Samoa was settled by Melanesian migrants in the 1st millennium BC. The Samoan islands were visited in 1768 by the French explorer Louis-Antoine de Bougainville, who named them the Îles des Navigateurs as a tribute to the skill of their native boatmen. In 1889, the US, the UK, and Germany agreed to share control of the islands. The UK later withdrew its claim, and under the 1899 Treaty of Berlin, the US was internationally acknowledged to have rights extending over all the islands of the Samoan group lying east of 171°w, while Germany was acknowledged to have similar rights to the islands west of that meridian. The islands of American Samoa were officially ceded to the US by the various ruling chiefs in 1900 and 1904, and on 20 February 1929 the US Congress formally accepted sovereignty over the entire group. From 1900 to 1951, the territory was administered by the US Department of the Navy, and thereafter by the Department of the Interior. The basic law is the Constitution of 1966.

The executive branch of the government is headed by a governor who, along with the lieutenant governor, is elected by popular vote; before 1977, the two posts were appointed by the US government. Village, county, and district councils have full authority to regulate local affairs.

The legislature (Fono) is composed of the House of Representatives and the Senate. The 15 counties elect 18 matais (chiefs) to four-year terms in the senate, while the 20 house members are elected for two-year terms by popular vote within the counties.

The secretary for Samoan affairs, who heads the Department of Local Government, is appointed by the governor. Under his administration are three district governors, the county chiefs, village mayors, and police officials. The judiciary, an independent branch of the government, functions through the high court and five district courts. Samoans living in the islands as of 17 April 1900 or born there since that date are nationals of the US.

The economy is primarily agricultural. Small plantations occupy about one-third of the land area; 70% of the land is communally owned. The principal crops are bananas, breadfruit, taro, papayas, pineapples, sweet potatoes, tapioca, coffee, cocoa, and yams. Hogs and poultry are the principal livestock raised; dairy cattle are few. The principal cash crop is copra. More than half of the total labor force is employed by the federal and territorial government. The largest employers in the private sector, with more than 15% of the labor force, are two modern tuna canneries supplied with fish caught by Japanese, US, and Taiwanese fishing fleets.

Samoans are entitled to free medical treatment, including hospital care. Besides district dispensaries, the government maintains a central hospital, a tuberculosis unit, and a leprosarium. US-trained staff physicians work with Samoan medical practitioners and nurses. In 1983 there were 27 physicians and 7 dentists. The 170 bed LBJ Tropical Medical Center opened in 1986.

Education is a joint undertaking between the territorial government and the villages. School attendance is compulsory for all children from 6 through 18, and about 99% of the population 10 years of age and over is literate. The villages furnish the elementary-school buildings and living quarters for the teachers; the territorial government pays teachers' salaries and provides buildings and supplies for all but primary schools. Since 1964, educational television has served as the basic teaching tool in the school system. In the early 1990s total enrollment in elementary and secondary schools was 12,258. American Samoa Community College enrolled 582 in the early 1990s.

Radiotelegraph circuits connect the territory with Hawaii, Fiji, and Western Samoa. Every village in American Samoa has telephone service.

GUAM

The largest and most populous of the Mariana Islands in the Western Pacific, Guam (13°28'N and 144°44'E) has an area, including land and water, of 540 sq km (208 sq mi) and is about 48 km (30 mi) long and from 6 to 12 km (4–7 mi) wide. The island is of volcanic origin; in the south, the terrain is mountainous, while the northern part is a plateau with shallow fertile soil. The central part of the island (where the capital, Agana, is located) is undulating country.

Guam lies in the typhoon belt of the Western Pacific, and is occasionally subject to widespread storm damage. In May 1976, a typhoon with winds of 306 km/hr (190 mph) struck Guam, causing an estimated $300 million in damage and leaving 80% of the island's buildings in ruins. Guam has a tropical climate with little seasonal variation. Average temperature is 26°C (79°F); rainfall is substantial, reaching an annual average of more than 200 cm (80 in). Endangered species in 1987 included the giant Micronesian kingfisher and Marianas crow.

The 1992 population, excluding transient US military and civilian personnel and their families, was estimated at 142,271, a growth of 21% over the 1986 estimate of 117,500. The increase was attributed largely to the higher birthrate and low mortality rate. The present-day Chamorro, who comprise about 47% of the permanent resident population, descend from the intermingling of the few surviving original Chamorro with the Spanish, Filipino, and Mexican settlers, plus later arrivals from the US, UK, Korea, China, and Japan. Filipinos (25%) are the largest ethnic minority. English is the official language, although Chamorro is taught in the primary schools. The predominant religion is Roman Catholicism.

The earliest known settlers on Guam were the original Chamorro, who migrated from the Malay Peninsula to the Pacific around 1500 BC. When Ferdinand Magellan landed on Guam in 1521, it is believed that as many as 100,000 Chamorro lived on the island; by 1741, their numbers had been reduced to 5,000—most of the population either had fled the island or been killed through disease or war with the Spanish. A Spanish fort was established in 1565, and from 1696 until 1898, Guam was under Spanish rule.

Under the Treaty of Paris that ended the Spanish-American War in 1898, the island was ceded to the US and placed under the jurisdiction of the Department of the Navy. During World War II, Guam was occupied by Japanese forces; the US recaptured the island in 1944 after 54 days of fighting. In 1950, the island's administration was transferred from the Navy to the US Department of the Interior. Under the 1950 Organic Act of Guam, passed by the US Congress, the island was established as an unincorporated territory of the US; Guamanians were granted US citizenship, and internal self-government was introduced.

The governor and lieutenant governor have been elected directly since 1970. A 21-member unicameral legislature elected for two years by adult suffrage is empowered to legislate on all local matters, including taxation and appropriations. The US Congress reserves the right to annul any law passed by the Guam legislature, but must do so within a year of the date it receives the text of any such law.

Judicial authority is vested in the district court of Guam, and appeals may be taken to the regular US courts of appeal and ultimately to the US Supreme Court. An island superior court and other specialized courts have jurisdiction over certain cases arising under the laws of Guam. The judge of the district court is appointed by the US president; the judges of the other courts are appointed by the governor. Guam's laws were codified in 1953.

Guam is one of the most important US military bases in the Pacific, and the island's economy has been profoundly affected by the large sums of money spent by the US defense establishment. During the late 1960s and early 1970s, when the US took the role of a major combatant in the Viet-Nam conflict, Guam served as a base for long-range US bombers on sorties over Indochina.

Prior to World War II, agriculture and animal husbandry were the primary activities. By 1947, most adults were wage earners employed by the US armed forces, although many continued to cultivate small plots to supplement their earnings. Since World War II, agriculture has generally contributed less than 1% of the GNP, partly because a considerable amount of arable land is taken up by military installations. Fruits and vegetables are grown and pigs and poultry are raised for local consumption, but most food is imported. Current fish catches are insufficient to meet local demand.

Tourism has become a major industry and sparked a boom in the construction industry in the mid-1980s. The number of visitors grew rapidly from 6,600 in 1967 to over 900,000 in 1992 and provided $600 million in revenues to the economy.

The Guam Rehabilitation Act of 1963 has funded the territory's capital improvement program. Further allocations in 1969 and 1977 provided over $120 million for additional capital improvements and development of the island's power installations. More than $200 million of federal funds were authorized for typhoon relief in 1977–78. Total expenditures by the government of Guam were $395 million in 1991; revenues were $525 million.

Guam's trade usually shows large deficits. In 1984, exports totaled $34 million, while imports amounted to $493 million. The bulk of Guam's trade is with the US, Micronesia, and Japan.

US income tax laws are applicable in Guam; all internal revenue taxes derived by the US from Guam are paid into the territory's treasury. US customs duties, however, are not levied. Guam is a duty-free port. In its trade with the US mainland, Guam is required to use US shipping.

Typical tropical diseases are practically unknown today in Guam. Tuberculosis, long the principal killer, was brought under control by the mid-1950s. The Guam Memorial Hospital has a capacity of 147 beds. Village dispensaries serve both as public health units and first-aid stations. In addition, there are a number of physicians in private practice. Specialists from the US Naval Hospital in Guam, assisting on a part-time basis, have made possible a complete program of curative medicine.

School attendance is compulsory from the age of 6 through 16. The yearly graduates from the islands' schools is 1,161 pupils. The University of Guam and Guam Community College graduates a total of 920 students. Telephones numbered 45,081 in 1991.

HOWLAND, BAKER, AND JARVIS ISLANDS

Howland Island (0°48′N and 176°38′W), Baker Island (0°14′N and 176°28′W), and Jarvis Island (0°23′S and 160°1′W) are three small coral islands, each about 2.6 sq km (1 sq mi) in area, belonging to the Line Islands group of the Central Pacific Ocean. All are administered directly from Washington as US unincorporated territories. Howland was discovered in 1842 by US sailors, claimed by the US in 1857, and formally proclaimed a US territory in 1935–36. It was worked for guano by US and British companies until about 1890.

Baker, 64 km (40 mi) S of Howland, and Jarvis, 1,770 km (1,100 mi) E of Howland, also were claimed by the US in 1857, and their guano deposits were similarly worked by US and British enterprises. The UK annexed Jarvis in 1889. In 1935, the US sent colonists from Hawaii to all three islands, which were placed under the US Department of the Interior in 1936 and are administered as part of the National Wildlife Refuge system. Baker was captured by the Japanese in 1942 and recaptured by the US in 1944. The three islands lack fresh water and have no permanent inhabitants. They are visited annually by the US Coast Guard. A lighthouse on Howland Island is named in honor of the US aviatrix Amelia Earhart, who vanished en route to the island on a round-the-world flight in 1937.

JOHNSTON ATOLL

Johnston Atoll, located in the North Pacific 1,151 km (715 mi) sw of Honolulu, consists of two islands, Johnston (16°44′N and 169°31′W) and Sand (16°45′N and 169°30′W), with a total land and water area of about 2.6 sq km (1 sq mi). The islands are enclosed by a semicircular reef. It was discovered by English sailors in 1807 and claimed by the US in 1858. For many years, it was worked for guano and was a bird reservation. Commissioned as a naval station in 1941, it remains an unincorporated US territory under the control of the US Department of the Air Force. In recent years, it has been used primarily for the testing of nuclear weapons. Plans to build a chemical disposal facility on the atoll were announced in 1983.

As of 1991 there were 1,337 people living on the atoll. The atoll's population was composed entirely of government personnel and contractors.

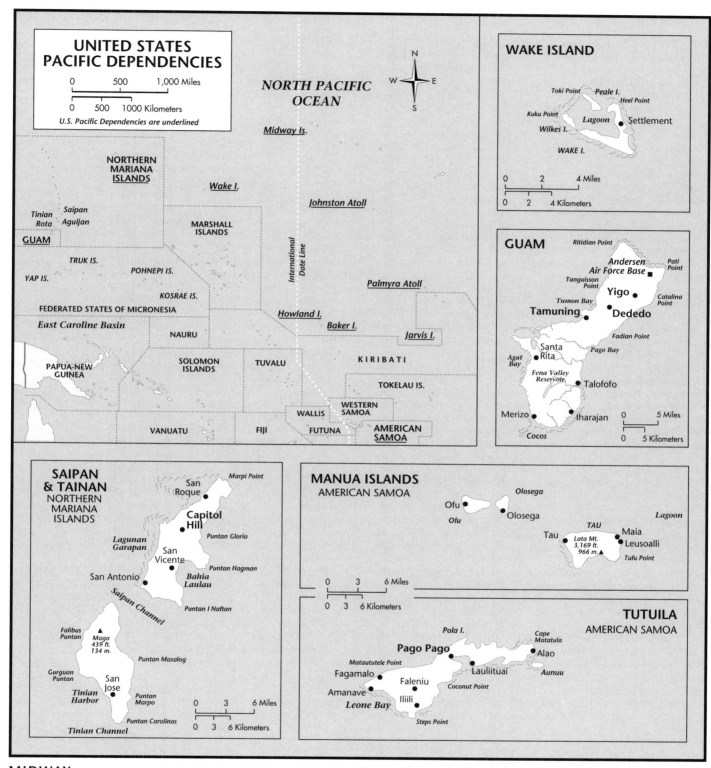

UNITED STATES PACIFIC DEPENDENCIES

0 500 1,000 Miles
0 500 1000 Kilometers
U.S. Pacific Dependencies are underlined

NORTH PACIFIC OCEAN

N
W E
S

Midway Is.

NORTHERN MARIANA ISLANDS

Wake I.

Johnston Atoll

Tinian
Rota   *Saipan*
        Aguijan
GUAM

MARSHALL ISLANDS

International Date Line

TRUK IS.
YAP IS.   POHNEPI IS.

KOSRAE IS.

FEDERATED STATES OF MICRONESIA

East Caroline Basin

NAURU

Palmyra Atoll

Howland I.
Baker I.

Jarvis I.

KIRIBATI

PAPUA-NEW GUINEA

SOLOMON ISLANDS   TUVALU

TOKELAU IS.

VANUATU   FIJI   WALLIS   WESTERN SAMOA
FUTUNA   AMERICAN SAMOA

WAKE ISLAND

Toki Point   Peale I.
Kuku Point   Heel Point
Wilkes I.   Lagoon   Settlement
WAKE I.

0 2 4 Miles
0 2 4 Kilometers

GUAM

Ritidian Point
Andersen Air Force Base   Pati Point
Tanguisson Point
Tumon Bay   Yigo   Catalina Point
Tamuning   Dededo
Fadian Point
Santa Rita   Pago Bay
Agat Bay
Fena Valley Reservoir   Talofofo
Merizo   Iharajan   0 5 Miles
Cocos   0 5 Kilometers

SAIPAN & TAINAN
NORTHERN MARIANA ISLANDS

Marpi Point
San Roque
Capitol Hill
Lagunan Garapan   Puntan Gloria
San Vicente
San Antonio   Puntan Hagman
Bahia Laulau
Puntan I Naftan
Saipan Channel

Falibus Puntan   Maga 439 ft. 134 m.
Gurguan Puntan   Puntan Masalog
Tinian Harbor   San Jose
Puntan Marpo
Puntan Carolinas
Tinian Channel   0 3 6 Miles
0 3 6 Kilometers

MANUA ISLANDS
AMERICAN SAMOA

Ofu   Olosega
Ofu   Olosega
TAU   Lagoon
Tau   Lata Mt. 3,169 ft. 966 m.   Maia
Leusoalli
Tufu Point

0 3 6 Miles
0 3 6 Kilometers

TUTUILA
AMERICAN SAMOA

Pola I.   Cape Matatula
Pago Pago   Alao
Matautele Point   Lauliituai   Aunuu
Fagamalo   Faleniu   Coconut Point
Amanave   Ilili
Leone Bay
Steps Point

MIDWAY

The Midway Islands (28°12′–17′N and 177°19′–26′W) consist of an atoll and two small islets, Eastern Island (177°20′W) and Sand Island (177°22′–24′W), 2,100 km (1,300 mi) WNW of Honolulu. Total land and water area is 5 sq km (2 sq mi). Their population was 468 at the 1980 census, a decline from 2,220 in 1970 because of the cessation of US military involvement in Indochina. As of 1991, 453 military personnel lived on the base.

Discovered and claimed by the US in 1859 and formally annexed in 1867, Midway became a submarine cable station early in the 20th century and an airlines station in 1935. Made a US naval base in 1941, Midway was attacked by the Japanese in December 1941 and January 1942. In one of the great battles of World War II, a Japanese naval attack on 3–6 June 1942 was repelled by US warplanes. There is a naval station at Midway, and the islands are important nesting places for seabirds. Midway is a US unincorporated territory under the administrative control of the US Department of the Navy.

NORTHERN MARIANAS

The Northern Marianas, a US commonwealth in the Western Pacific Ocean, is comprised of the Mariana Islands excluding Guam (a separate political entity). Located between 12° and 21°N and 144° and 146°E, it consists of 16 volcanic islands with a total land area of about 475 sq km (183.5 sq mi). Only six of the islands are inhabited, and most of the people live on the three largest islands—Rota, 85 sq km (33 sq mi); Saipan, 122 sq km (47 sq mi); and Tinian, 101 sq km (39 sq mi).

The climate is tropical, with relatively little seasonal change; temperatures average 21–29°C (70–85°F), and relative humidity is generally high. Rainfall averages 216 cm (85 in) per year. The southern islands, which include Rota, Saipan, and Tinian, are generally lower and covered with moderately heavy tropical vegetation. The northern islands are more rugged, reaching a high point of 959 m (3,146 ft) on Agrihan, and are generally barren due to erosion and insufficient rainfall. Insects are numerous and ocean birds and fauna are abundant. As of 1987, endangered species included the Marianas mallard.

The Northern Marianas had an estimated population of 47,168 in 1992. Three-fourths of the population is descended from the original Micronesian inhabitants, known as Chamorros. There are also many descendants of migrants from the Caroline Islands and smaller numbers of Filipino and Korean laborers and settlers from the US mainland. English is the official language and Chamorro and Carolinian are taught in school. About 90% of the people are Roman Catholic.

It is believed that the Marianas were settled by migrants from the Philippines and Indonesia. Excavations on Saipan have yielded evidence of settlement around 1500 BC. The first European to reach the Marianas, in 1521, was Ferdinand Magellan. The islands were ruled by Spain until the Spanish defeat by the US in the Spanish-American War (1898). Guam was then ceded to the US and the rest of the Marianas were sold to Germany. When World War I broke out, Japan took over the Northern Marianas and other German-held islands in the Western Pacific. These islands (the Northern Marianas, Carolines, and Marshalls) were placed under Japanese administration as a League of Nations mandate on 17 December 1920. Upon its withdrawal from the League in 1935, Japan began to fortify the islands, and in World War II they served as important military bases. Several of the islands were the scene of heavy fighting during the war. In the battle for control of Saipan in June 1944, some 23,000 Japanese and 3,500 US troops lost their lives in one day's fighting. As each island was occupied by US troops, it became subject to US authority in accordance with the international law of belligerent occupation. The US planes that dropped atomic bombs on Hiroshima and Nagasaki, bringing an end to the war, took off from Tinian.

On 18 July 1947, the Northern Mariana, Caroline, and Marshall islands formally became a UN trust territory under US administration. This Trust Territory of the Pacific Islands was administered by the US Department of the Navy until 1 July 1951, when administration was transferred to the Department of the Interior. From 1953 to 1962, the Northern Marianas, with the exception of Rota, were administered by the Department of the Navy.

The people of the Northern Marianas voted to become a US commonwealth by a majority of 78.8% in a plebescite held on 17 June 1975. A covenant approved by the US Congress in March 1976 provided for the separation of the Northern Marianas from the Caroline and Marshall island groups, and for the Marianas' transition to a commonwealth status similar to that of Puerto Rico. The islands became internally self-governing in January 1978. On 3 November 1986, US President Ronald Reagan proclaimed the Northern Marianas a self-governing commonwealth; its people became US citizens. The termination of the trusteeship had been approved by the UN Trusteeship Council in May 1986

but technically required approval from the UN Security Council. Approval from the council was latter obtained.

A governor and a lieutenant governor are popularly elected for four-year terms. The legislature consists of 9 senators elected for four-year terms and 14 representatives elected for two-year terms. A district court handles matters involving federal law and a commonwealth court has jurisdiction over local matters.

The traditional economic activities were subsistence agriculture, livestock raising, and fishing, but much agricultural land was destroyed or damaged during World War II and agriculture has never resumed its prewar importance. Today, government employment and tourism are the mainstays of the economy. Tourism has increased 7.5% over the last decade. The construction industry is also expanding, and there is some small-scale industry, chiefly handicrafts and food processing.

The Northern Marianas is heavily dependent on federal funds; the US government provided $228 million for capital developments, government operations, and special programs between 1986 and 1992. The US also pays to lease property on Saipan, Tinian, and Farallon de Medinilla islands for defense purposes. The principal exports are milk and meat; imports include foods, petroleum, construction materials, and vehicles. US currency is the official medium of exchange.

Health care is primarily the responsibility of the commonwealth government and has improved substantially since 1978. Tuberculosis, once the major health problem, has been controlled. There is a hospital on Saipan and health centers on Tinian and Rota. The largest hospital in the commonwealth is a 74 bed, 110,000 square foot facility.

Education is free and compulsory for children between the ages of 8 and 14, and literacy is high. Enrollment in primary and secondary schools in 1987/88 totaled 6,600.

PALMYRA ATOLL

Palmyra, an atoll in the Central Pacific Ocean, containing some 50 islets with a total area of some 10 sq km (4 sq mi), is situated about 1,600 km (1,000 mi) ssw of Honolulu at 5°52′N and 162°5′W. It was discovered in 1802 by the USS *Palmyra* and formally annexed by the US in 1912, and was under the jurisdiction of the city of Honolulu until 1959, when Hawaii became the 50th state of the US. It is now the responsibility of the US Department of the Interior. The atoll is privately owned by the Fullard-Leo family of Hawaii.

Kingman Reef, NW of Palmyra Atoll at 6°25′N and 162°23′N, was discovered by the US in 1874, annexed by the US in 1922, and became a naval reservation in 1934. Now abandoned, it is under the control of the US Department of the Navy.

WAKE ISLAND

Wake Island, actually a coral atoll and three islets (Wake, Peale, and Wilkes) about 8 km (5 mi) long by 3.6 km (2.25 mi) wide, lies in the North Pacific 3,380 km (2,100 mi) W of Honolulu at 19°17′N and 166°35′E. The total land and water area is about 8 sq km (3 sq mi). Discovered by the British in 1796, Wake was long uninhabited.

In 1898, a US expeditionary force en route to Manila landed on the island. The US formally claimed Wake in 1899. It was made a US naval reservation in 1934, and became a civil aviation station in 1935. Captured by the Japanese on 23 December 1941, Wake was subsequently the target of several US air raids. It was surrendered by the Japanese in September 1945 and has thereafter remained a US unincorporated territory under the jurisdiction, since 1972, of the Department of the Air Force.

In 1991, 156 US Air Force personnel and 224 Thai contractors inhabited Wake Island. It is a stopover and fueling station for civilian and military aircraft flying between Honolulu, Guam, and Japan.

UZBEKISTAN

Republic of Uzbekistan
Uzbekiston Respublikasi

CAPITAL: Tashkent (Toshkent).

FLAG: Horizontal bands of blue (top), white, and green separated by narrow red bands; white crescent moon and twelve stars on the blue band.

MONETARY UNIT: The som is the official currency, introduced when Uzbekistan left the ruble zone in November 1993.

WEIGHTS AND MEASURES: The metric system is used.

HOLIDAYS: Independence Day, 1 September.

TIME: 5 PM = noon GMT.

¹LOCATION, SIZE, AND EXTENT

Uzbekistan is located in central Asia bordering the Aral Sea, between Kazakhstan and Turkmenistan. Comparatively, it is slightly larger than the state of California, with a total area of 447,400 sq km (172,742 sq mi). Uzbekistan shares boundaries with Kazakhstan on the N, Kyrgyzstan and Tajikistan on the E, Afghanistan on the S, and Turkmenistan on the SW. Uzbekistan's boundary length totals 6,221 km (3,866 mi). Its capital city, Tashkent, is located in the eastern part of the country.

²TOPOGRAPHY

Uzbekistan consists of mostly flat to rolling sandy desert with dunes. The Fergana Valley lies in the east surrounded by mountainous Tajikistan and Kyrgyzstan. The Aral Sea lies in the northwest. There is semiarid grassland in the east. Ten percent of Uzbekistan's land is arable, most of which is under irrigation.

³CLIMATE

The climate is mid-latitude climatic desert. Temperatures in the desert can reach upwards of 32°C (90°F). In the capital city of Tashkent the mean temperature is 32°C (90°F) in the summer. In January the mean temperature is 3°C (37°F). Winter temperatures can fall bellow −23°C (−10°F) in some areas. There is very little rainfall in the country.

⁴FLORA AND FAUNA

Ecological damage has left much of the country devoid of animal life. The country, a member of the former Soviet Union, was part of Nikita Krushchev's 1954 "Virgin-Lands" plan. Khrushchev wanted Soviet farmers to grow cotton and grain on the steppes of Uzbekistan. At one point the country grew 70% of the Soviet Union's cotton. Unfortunately the farmers had to irrigate the crops to obtain meaningful results. Now the Amu Darya and Syr Darya rivers run dry in certain places. Half of the Aral Sea is now a dry lake bed, and the land is poisoned from the overuse of fertilizer.

⁵ENVIRONMENT

Uzbekistan's main environmental problems are soil salinity, land pollution, and water pollution. Chemicals used in farming, such as DDT, contribute to the pollution of the soil. Desertification is a continuing concern. The nation's forestlands are also threatened and continue to dwindle.

The country's water supply also suffers from toxic chemical pollutants from industrial activity. Uzbekistan has 1,051.9 cu mi of water. Sixty-five percent is used for farming and 29% is used for industrial purposes. The nation's cities produce 45.8 million tons of solid waste per year.

In 1994, 20 of Uzbekistan's mammal species were endangered and 38 of its bird species were threatened with extinction.

⁶POPULATION

The population of Uzbekistan was 19,905,158 in 1989. It was estimated at 23,089,261 in 1995. A population of 25,224,000 was projected for 2000, assuming a crude birth rate of 25.7 per 1,000 population during 1995–2000, a crude death rate of 5.2, and a net natural increase of 20.5. The estimated population density in 1995 was 51.6 per sq km (133.7 per sq mi). Tashkent, the capital, had an estimated population of 2,094,000 at the beginning of 1990, and Samarkand, about 370,000.

⁷MIGRATION

Emigration to other former USSR republics exceeded immigration by 328,200 during 1979–90. About 30,000 people fled to Uzbekistan in 1993 to escape the civil war in Tajikistan, but only some of them were allowed to stay.

⁸ETHNIC GROUPS

In 1989, 71.4% of the population was Uzbek. Russians constituted 8.4%; Tajiks, 4.7%; Kazakhs, 4.1%; Tatars, 2.4%; Karakapaks, 2.1%; and Crimean Tatars, 1%.

⁹LANGUAGES

Uzbek, the state language, was the most widely spoken non-Slavic tongue in the USSR. It is a Turkic language with six vowels—virtually identical to those of Tajik, which has surely influenced it—rather than the original eight or nine. In 1993, it was decided that the language would be written in the Roman alphabet rather than in the Cyrillic alphabet.

¹⁰RELIGIONS

Freedom of religion is guaranteed under the constitution of 1992, adopted after independence, and there is a specific provision prohibiting the establishment of any state religion. Ethnic Uzbeks are primarily adherents of the Hanafi School of Sunni Islam, but the

Wahhabi sect has flourished as well in recent years. Uzbekistan also had a significant Jewish population of some 93,000 in the early 1990s.

11TRANSPORTATION

Uzbekistan has some 3,460 km (2,150 mi) of railroad; separate lines serve eastern and western regions. There are also 78,400 km (48,700 mi) of highways, of which 85% are hard-surfaced. As a landlocked nation, there is no direct connection to the open sea; the Zeravshan River is the largest inland waterway.

12HISTORY

Some parts of present-day Uzbekistan have been inhabited since the Paleolithic era. The first states in the region were Khwarazm, Bactria, Sogdiana, and the Parthian Empire, in the first millenium BC. The territory was consolidated under the Achaemenids in the 6th century BC, until it was conquered by Alexander the Great, 329–327 BC. The Greeks were displaced by the Tochari in the 3rd century BC. From the 1st century BC to the 4th century AD Uzbekistan was part of the Kushana Kingdom. This in turn was replaced by the Ephthalite state.

In the 6th century the area was part of the West Turkic Kaganate, a loose confederation of largely nomadic tribes. By the 8th century the region was conquered by the Arabs, who introduced Islam. The Ummayid dynasty was displaced by the Abbasids in 747–750. In the 9th century the Samanids took control of most of Central Asia, including Uzbekistan. Turkic tribes again began to push into the area from the east in the 10th century, eventually forming the Karakhanid state. A lesser part of that state, Khwarazm, grew more powerful in the 12th century and came to dominate most of Central Asia.

Genghiz Khan's Mongols invaded in 1219, conquering all of Central Asia by 1221. In 1224 Genghiz Khan's son Chagatai was made ruler of this area. As Chingisid influence waned, Timur (Tamerlane, 1336–1405) established an empire in Samarkand. Upon his death it split into Khorasan, ruled by his son Shah Rukh, and Maweranahr, ruled by his grandson, Ulgh Beg. Although Timur is now claimed as the father of the modern Uzbeks, more likely candidates are the Sheibanid nomadic Uzbeks who fought to take the area in the early 16th century. They settled among the other populations and became farmers, making Bukhara their capital.

In the 16th century Khwarazm, Balkh, and Khiva separated from Bukhara, becoming separate principalities. Bukhara was conquered by Persia in 1740, but sovereignty was retaken soon after by the Mangyt dynasty, which ruled until 1920. In the early 19th century the Kokand Khanate grew powerful in the eastern part of present-day Uzbekistan.

Russia had begun trading with Bukhara, Khiva, and Kokand in the 18th century. Concern about British expansion in India and Afghanistan led eventually to Russian conquest, which began in the 1860s and ended in the 1880s, when Uzbekistan became part of Turkestan guberniia, with Bukhara and Khiva administered as separate emirates under Russian protection.

In 1916 Tsar Nicholas II issued a call for Central Asian males to be drafted into labor battalions. This sparked resistance throughout the region, including in Uzbekistan, which was bloodily repressed. During the conflict from 1917–1920, Uzbekistan was the site of competing attempts to create governments; the Bolsheviks announced a short-lived Turkestan Autonomous Republic, while a Muslim Congress also attempted an Autonomous Government of Turkestan. Red Army forces intervened savagely, but armed resistance continued as late as 1924, in the so-called Basmachi Rebellion.

The Uzbek Soviet Socialist Republic was created in 1925. In 1929, Tajikistan, which had been an administrative sub-unit, was elevated to full republic status, changing the boundaries. They were changed once again in 1936.

Under the leadership of long-time leader S. Rashidov, Uzbekistan was politically conservative during the 1970s and early 1980s. The republic was targeted for big anti-corruption purges in the mid-1980s, when considerable fraud in the cotton industry was discovered. The present leader, Islam Karimov, was appointed by Moscow in 1989.

In March 1990, he was elected to the newly-created post of President by the Uzbek Supreme Soviet. Uzbekistan declared independence on 1 September 1991, in the aftermath of the abortive Moscow coup of 19–21 August. Karimov's presidency was reaffirmed in a popular, contested election in December 1991.

13GOVERNMENT

The state constitution adopted on 8 December 1992, mandates a civil democratic society. The executive branch consists of the president and his appointed prime minister and Cabinet of Ministers. The legislative branch consists of a unicameral Supreme Soviet of 150 seats. The judicial branch is appointed by the president, subject to legislative confirmation, for 5- and 10-year terms. Elections were expected in late 1994 or early 1995. The legislature elected in February 1990, while Uzbekistan was part of the USSR, has 500 seats, but exercised little power independent of the president's directives and wishes. The president is the head of state and has responsibility for the function of the other branches of government as well as for making sure the constitution is observed.

14POLITICAL PARTIES

In the Soviet period, the only legal political party was the Communist Party. As Soviet control began to disintegrate in 1989–90, a number of mass-based "informal organizations" appeared which grew to be the equivalents of parties, although not all were legally registered. The largest, claiming as many as 100,000 members, was Birlik (Unity), founded by Abdurakhim Pulatov in 1989. Erk (Freedom) was founded in 1990 by M. Solih, who split away from Birlik; in 1991, Solih was a candidate for president, drawing approximately 12% of the vote. Another group, never legally registered, was the Islamic Renaissance Party.

After independence President Karimov began to establish strong authoritarian control. Political opposition was forbidden. Opposition leaders have been beaten, jailed, and exiled. There are four registered parties, but their platforms are essentially identical. The National Democratic Party is the renamed Communist Party. In 1992 Vatan Tarrakiyeti (Fatherland Progress) and the Party of Social Progress were registered. Erk repudiated its founder, M. Solih, who was forced into political exile, and has reformed as a pro-Karimov party. Birlik, which was never formally a party, was banned in mid-1993.

15LOCAL GOVERNMENT

The republic is divided into 12 oblasts, or provinces. There is also the autonomous Republic of Karakalpakstan, which has the right of legal secession, though is unlikely to exercise it. Administration is performed by locally elected councils, overseen by presidential appointees.

16JUDICIAL SYSTEM

The Soviet judiciary system, featuring trials by panels of three judges, still prevails. There are three levels of courts: district courts (people's courts) at the lowest level, regional courts, and the Supreme Court. District court decisions may be appealed through the higher levels. Under the constitution, the president appoints judges for 10-year terms.

Defendants have the right to an attorney and most trials are open to the public. In political cases, the judiciary may experience pressure from the government.

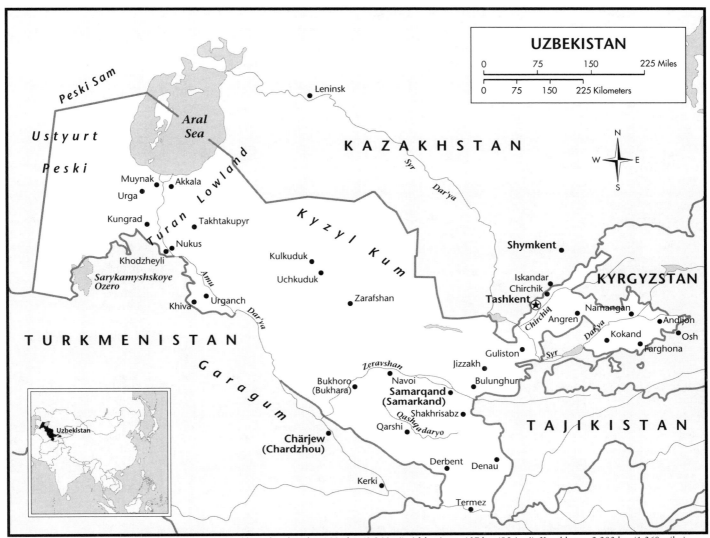

LOCATION: 41°0′N; 64°0′E. **BOUNDARY LENGTHS:** Total boundary lengths, 6,221 km (3,866 mi); Afghanistan, 137 km (85.1 mi); Kazakhstan, 2,203 km (1,369 miles); Kyrgyzstan, 1,099 km (683 mi); Tajikistan, 1,161 km (721.4 mi); Turkmenistan, 1,621 km (1,007.3 mi).

¹⁷ARMED FORCES

Uzbekistan has a significant army in place; in addition, it has about 1,000 internal security forces and exercises joint control over 15,000 ground and air troops within its borders. The nation plans a small army.

¹⁸INTERNATIONAL COOPERATION

Uzbekistan was admitted to the UN on 2 March 1992. It is also a member of the CSCE, EBRD, FAO, IAEA, IMF, UNCTAD, and the World Bank. The country has signed the Nuclear Non-proliferation Treaty and is a member of the CIS. It has close ties with the US, Austria, South Korea, Malaysia, Indonesia, and Turkey. The US established formal ties with Uzbekistan in February 1992.

¹⁹ECONOMY

Although characterized by one of the lowest per capita incomes in the Central Asian and other post-Soviet republics, Uzbekistan's rich reserves of gold, oil, natural gas, coal, silver, and copper provide a promising endowment for future development. As a major source of cotton for the textile industry in the former USSR and the world's third largest cotton producer, Uzbekistan has a predominantly agricultural economy. Agriculture and forestry provided 39% of employment and 44% of the country's NMP in

1990. Industry, oriented mainly toward the processing of primary goods, contributed 24% of NMP; about 24% of the labor force is employed in the industry and construction sectors combined. Only 12% of Uzbekistan's total cotton production and 60% of its silk cocoons were processed locally in the early 1990s, reflecting the country's principal role as supplier of raw material goods for downstream manufacturing elsewhere in the former USSR.

Uzbekistan has a centrally planned economic structure in which most production and employment is in the state sector, and all health, education, social security, and welfare services are provided by the government. Under the present leadership, measures taken toward establishing a greater market orientation within the economy have been more cautious than in many other post-Soviet countries. A differentiated process of price control liberalization was applied to the wholesale and retail sectors in 1991 in an attempt to avoid socially destabilizing surges in consumer prices. Nevertheless, inflation ran 790% in retail prices and 2,700% in wholesale prices in 1992; by the end of the year, real wage earnings had declined by 56%. The disruption of trading arrangements with former Soviet republics and the cessation of transfers from the Union's central government is evident in the erosion of other major economic indicators since 1990. In addition to a seriously deteriorating fiscal balance, estimated GDP shrank by 4.3%

in 1991 and a further 12.8% in 1992 in real value terms. Following a breakdown in agreements over the conditions of a new ruble zone with Russia and other CIS countries, Uzbekistan adopted its own currency, the som, in late 1993.

²⁰INCOME
In 1992, Uzbekistan's GNP was $18,377 million at current prices, or $860 per capita. For the period 1985–92 the average inflation rate was 61.7%. In 1992 the GDP was $18,251 million in current US dollars.

²¹LABOR
The labor force was estimated at over 7.9 million. Agriculture engaged 29% of the labor force in 1991; personal services, 30%; mining, utilities, and manufacturing, 18%; construction, 11%; trade, 7%; and other sectors, 5%.

The new labor code, adopted on 2 June 1992, recognizes the right for all workers to voluntarily create and join unions, which may in turn voluntarily associate territorially or sectorally and may choose their own international affiliations. Unions also were granted independence from government administrative and economic bodies (except where provided by law), and were encourage to develop their own charters, structure, and executive bodies.

The standard work week is 41 hours, and minimum wages are set by the Ministry of Finance in consultation with the Federation of Trade Unions. Some factories have reduced work hours to avoid layoffs, and overtime pay is rarely given.

²²AGRICULTURE
Uzbekistan was the former Soviet Union's largest producer of fruits and vegetables. About 10% of the total area is crop land. In 1992, about 36% of GDP came from agriculture.

Cotton is grown on almost half of all sown land, although recent efforts to diversify crops have been successful. Almost 40% of the gross value of agricultural production is derived from cotton; Uzbekistan is the world's third-largest producer of cotton, accounting for 25% of world supply in 1992.

Rice, wheat, barley, and corn are important grain crops. Half of the former Soviet Union's rice production typically came from Uzbekistan. In 1992, over 2.1 million tons of cereals were produced. Sesame, tobacco, onions, flax, and various fruits are also grown. Mulberry trees have been grown for silkworm breeding since the 4th century.

²³ANIMAL HUSBANDRY
Sheep are the main livestock product, with Karakyl sheep (noted for their black wool) raised in the Bukhara region. The livestock population in 1992 included 9,200,000 sheep, 5,100,000 cattle, 34,000,000 chickens, 900,000 goats, and 700,000 pigs. Meat production that year totaled 510,000 tons, of which 67% was beef, 11% was mutton, 10% was pork, and 12% was poultry. Wool (greasy) production in 1992 was estimated at 26,000 tons.

²⁴FISHING
Fishing occurs mainly in the Fergana Valley. The Aral Sea in the north (the world's fourth-largest lake) is too saline and becoming more so, especially since its water surface area has decreased by 33% since 1960.

²⁵FORESTRY
Forests and woodlands make up 18% of the total land area, mostly in the Fergana Valley and Zeravshan regions. Commercial forestry is not a significant part of the economy.

²⁶MINING
Besides natural gas, Uzbekistan possesses several mineral commodities. Copper, lead-zinc, and molybdenum are mined at the Almalyk complex northeast of Tasken; gold at the Muruntau complex near Zarafshan; and fluorospar at the Toytepa complex, south of Tashkent. Production of fertilizers is an important part of the domestic chemical industry; the fertilizers are used for the production of cotton.

²⁷ENERGY AND POWER
Uzbekistan is the third-largest producer of natural gas in the CIS behind Russia and Turkmenistan. In 1992, production totaled 40.3 billion cu m (1,425 billion cu ft); proven reserves amounted to 1.1 trillion cu m (38.5 trillion cu ft) that year, located mainly in the western Qizilkum Desert.

About 50,000 barrels of oil per day are drilled from wells in the Fergana Valley. With consumption at about 189,000 barrels per day in 1992, however, Uzbekistan must import oil to satisfy domestic demand. Hydroelectric stations on the Syrdar'ya, Chirchiq, and Naryn rivers depend largely on Kyrgyzstan and Tajikistan for their power. In 1992, total installed electrical capacity was 11,400,000 kw, and production came to 54,100 million kwh. Brown coal deposits at the head of the Angren Valley, southeast of Tashkent, are used for local electricity generation. About 6.3 million tons of coal were produced in 1990.

²⁸INDUSTRY
Growth of Uzbekistan's industrial production averaged 3.2% in the 1980s, although on a per capita basis, the republic's industrial output remained less than half that of the USSR average by the end of the decade. Most industry is based on the processing of local agricultural products. Soft goods (mainly cotton, wool, and silk fiber) and processed foods (including cottonseed oil, meat, dried fruit, wines, and tobacco) accounted for about 39% and 13% of industrial production respectively in 1990; their manufacture is concentrated in Tashkent and the Farghona Valley. Production figures for 1991 reflect the impact of economic dislocation in the post-Soviet period. Total fabric production in 1991 was 519 million sq m, down from 614 million in 1990. The output of vegetable oil dropped to 461,000 tons in 1991 from 514,000 the previous year. Meat production totaled 224,800 tons, down from 261,000 in 1990.

Heavy industry contributes about 41% of the country's industrial production. Though modest in size, Uzbekistan's machinery industry is the primary producer of machines and heavy equipment in central Asia. Around 21,100 tractors were produced in 1991, down somewhat from 23,300 in 1990. Metal processing industries are clustered in the Olmaliq-Oharangan (Almalyk-Akhangaran) complex, southeast of Tashkent. Metal alloys, wire, rods and sheet and gas-based nitrogen are manufactured in Chirchiq, close to the Kazakhstan border in the northeast. The country's total steel production equaled 0.9 million tons in 1991; rolled ferrous metal manufactures totalled 0.8 million tons. Chemical fertilizers used mainly in cotton production are also produced in the Chirchiq; total mineral fertilizer production in 1991 was 1.7 million tons. Gold is mined and processed in the Kyzylkum Desert and the Chadak area of the Farghona Valley in the Qurama mountains, producing about 65 tons a year, or one-third of total annual production in the former Soviet Union.

²⁹SCIENCE AND TECHNOLOGY
The Uzbek Academy of Sciences has departments of physical-mathematical sciences, chemical-technological and earth sciences, and biological sciences. Uzbekistan has 17 institutes conducting research in veterinary science, technology, and medicine. Nineteen colleges and universities offer scientific training.

³⁰DOMESTIC TRADE
Although dominated by state-owned stores and distribution channels under the Soviet economy, retailing has seen a marked

shift toward private business. About 350 small shops have been privatized since 1991, and 27% of all retail trade and dining is accounted for by enterprises leased by cooperatives or private individuals. Urban markets provide an important outlet for the sale of vegetables and other foodstuffs. Retail purchases totaled R17,837 million in 1990.

31 FOREIGN TRADE

While supplying the former USSR with light industry goods (mainly cotton fiber), basic equipment related to agriculture and agricultural processing, and some oil, Uzbekistan has been highly dependent on the other Soviet republics for critically needed grain, food, machinery, and other industrial inputs. In the late 1980s, Uzbekistan imported about 22% of its total domestic consumption and exported 18% of its domestic production.

Trade with other post-Soviet republics accounted for 89% each of total exports and imports in 1990 (expressed in world prices). Among Uzbekistan's Soviet trading partners, Russia was dominant, supplying about one-half of its inter-republic imports and purchasing close to 60% of its exports; a pattern that has remained largely unchanged since dissolution of the USSR in 1990. Trade beyond the former Soviet Union involves mainly the export of light industry products (particularly cotton and other fibers) and machinery along with the import of food items, light industry products, and chemicals. The largest foreign trading partners in 1990 were Germany, Bulgaria, former Czechoslovakia, and Japan. With severe economic dislocation in the former Czechoslovaki, however, the UK, Belgium, and Germany emerged as the country's leading extra-republic export markets in 1992; Switzerland, China, and Turkey were its largest suppliers.

32 BALANCE OF PAYMENTS

Uzbekistan was extremely reliant on cotton exports as a means of trade throughout its association with the former USSR, but earnings fluctuated widely from year to year depending on the performance of the agricultural sector. Exports of natural gas and petroleum are expected to generate much needed hard currency reserves within the next several years.

33 BANKING AND SECURITIES

The Central Bank of the Republic of Uzbekistan was created in the late 1980s when the State Soviet Bank (Gosbank) transferred its duties as the Soviet Union's central bank to the members of its union. The bank is in charge of the country's two-tier banking system, and has the responsibility of issuing rubles, the country's currency unit, and regulating the commercial banks by setting reserve requirements and the discount rate. The other important state bank is the Uzbek National Bank of Foreign Economic Activities, which deals exclusively with the foreign exchange rate.

Commercial banks in the country include the Uzbek Commercial Bank and the Uzbek Joint-Stock Innovation Bank. The country does not have a security market, but the trading of commodities is widely practiced in the country.

34 INSURANCE

No recent information is available.

35 PUBLIC FINANCE

Uzbekistan's spiraling inflation as a member of the ruble zone necessitated the introduction of a transition currency after it left the ruble zone in November 1993. Subsidies for basic consumer goods (except some food staples and energy products) were ended in 1993. Most enterprises, including those in the energy sector, remain in state hands; natural gas and petroleum exports are an important source of revenues.

The external debt of the end of 1991 was estimated at $2 billion.

36 TAXATION

The maximum personal income tax rate in Uzbekistan is 50%; corporate rates range from 10–60%, with a standard rate of 18%. Also levied is a 25% value-added tax.

37 CUSTOMS AND DUTIES

On 1 August 1992, a presidential decree lifted import taxes on all goods until 1 January 1994. Uzbekistan is a member of the Economic Cooperation Organization, together with Azerbaijan, Turkmenistan, Iran, Pakistan, and Turkey.

38 FOREIGN INVESTMENT

While Uzbekistan's store of valuable natural resources is likely to provide a strong basis for covering the costs of long-term economic development, significant amounts of external funding will be needed to support its short-term development plans over the next decade. To stimulate foreign direct investment, legislation adopted in mid-1991 provides tax incentives and guarantees against expropriation, though falling short of securing the right to repatriate profits and third-party dispute arbitration. By the end of 1992, 450 joint ventures were registered in the country but only 135 were actually operating. The largest of these is with the US-based Newmont Mining Corp. Negotiations over further Western participation in the exploitation of a major oil field discovered in the Fergana Valley in early 1992 are currently underway. Fourteen bilateral agreements with China were signed in 1992. Though still minimal at present, the inflow of direct foreign investment is projected to reach $200–250 million by 1997.

39 ECONOMIC DEVELOPMENT

Under centralized Soviet economic planning, Uzbekistan's economic growth was fueled by expanded agricultural production, as extensive stretches of land were brought under irrigation particularly for cultivation of cotton. While highly critical of the former Soviet's government emphasis on promoting cotton monoculture in the republic, the country's new government has found that at least for the immediate future, extensive cotton production will continue to play an indispensable role as a central source of foreign exchange earnings. A little over 26% of state investment allocations were directed at the agricultural sector in 1990. Industry received about 22%, with the largest allocations directed toward energy development, non-ferrous metallurgy (another important export product), as well as chemicals and machinery industries associated with supplying needed equipment and inputs for cotton production. Housing and trades and services were other large state investment targets.

Since independence the government has aimed at facilitating a greater market orientation in the economy, though the steps taken toward this goal have been smaller and slower-paced than in other parts of the former USSR. A series of basic laws and new policies have been adopted regarding property ownership, land, privatization, foreign investment, price controls, trade, taxes, and banking. Progress made in implementing new mandates has been halting. Government plans aimed for the privatization of 10–15% of state assets by end of 1993. However, despite the emergence of some small producer cooperatives and joint ventures, industrial production remained largely state-controlled by the end of 1992. In the agricultural sector, the number of peasant farmers reached 5,800 in April 1993, up from 1,358 at the beginning of January. Although representing only a small fraction of total cultivated land, the potential role of these private farmers in the country's food supply is significant. Most import tariffs have been removed; however, export licenses are required for strategic exports (such as cotton), leaving 85% to 90% of the all exports under government control. Riots which erupted in Tashkent in 1992 over rising consumer prices prompted the government to reduce some price ceilings, and raise student stipends as well as salaries for some categories of employees.

For the immediate future, developing the country's oil and natural gas fields, bolstering cotton exports through productivity enhancement, and sustaining gold exports are likely to be key strategies for procuring some of the necessary financing to support economic development. Some $250 million in bilateral loans and export credits were pledged in 1992, of which about one-half actually have been paid out. During the same year, Uzbekistan signed an agreement with Russia transferring its share of the former Soviet Union's debt to the latter in exchange for relinquishing all claims on Soviet assets. One area of serious concern for the government will be the increasing threat to public health and economic productivity posed by the environmental damage resulting from past development strategies. Addressing growing water shortages, severe river and lake pollution caused the heavy use of chemical inputs in agriculture, the dessication of the Aral Sea due to massive irrigation, and high levels of both air and water pollution in the country's industrial centers will be among the country's most pressing environmental management problems in the coming decade.

40 SOCIAL DEVELOPMENT

In 1989, the average family size was 4.7 members, and the divorce rate was 5.0 per 1,000 women. There were 7.2 drug-related crimes and 0.7 alcohol-related deaths per 100,000 persons.

Although nominally equal under the law, women hold few high-level positions. Traditional customs decree that women generally marry young and confine their activities to the home. Uzbekistan has one of the highest birthrates in the former Soviet Union. The fertility rate in 1990 was 4.09. In 1993, over half the public's population was under the age of 15. The state cares for and educates orphans and other children deprived of parental guardianship.

41 HEALTH

The infant mortality rate was 56 per 1,000 live births in 1992, and the general mortality rate was 7 per 1,000 people in 1993. The average life expectancy is 69 years. In 1992, 97% of children up to one year old were immunized in against tuberculosis; 63% against diphtheria, pertussis, and tetanus; 8.5% against polio; and 84% against measles. Leading causes of death per 100,000 people in 1990 were: communicable diseases and maternal/perinatal causes, 137; noncommunicable diseases, 601; and injuries, 65. There were 55 reported cases of tuberculosis per 100,000 people in 1990. In 1992, Uzbekistan had 3.58 doctors per 1,000 people, with a nurse to doctor ratio of 2.9. There were 12.4 hospital beds per 1,000 people. Total health care expenditures in 1990 were $2,388 million.

42 HOUSING

In 1989, 31.9% of all privately owned urban housing had running water, 11.3% had sewer lines, 21.1% had central heating, and 1.5% had hot water. In 1990, Uzbekistan had 12.1 sq m of housing space per capita and, as of 1 January 1991, 204,000 households (or 11.5%) were on waiting lists for urban housing.

43 EDUCATION

The estimated adult literacy rate in 1990 was 97.2% with men estimated at 98.5% and women at 96.0%. For centuries, Uzbekistan was a noted Muslim educational center. Muslim schools in the cities of Bukhara, Samarkland, Tashkent, and Khiva attracted students from other Muslim countries. In 1920, after the Soviet Union took control of the region, schools and mosques were closed down and a secular state-funded educational system was established. The educational system is now being modified. In recent years, there has been an increased emphasis on Uzbek literature, culture, and history. Over 75% of the students are taught in the Uzbek language. There are three universities in Uzbekistan: Tashkent State University; Nukus State University; and Samarkland Alisher Naroi State University. There are several other institutions offering specialized training. In 1990, all higher level institutions had 340,900 students enrolled.

44 LIBRARIES AND MUSEUMS

Tashkent is the cultural center of Uzbekistan.

45 MEDIA

Telephone links to other former Soviet Republics are provided by land link or microwave and to other countries through Moscow. Radio Tashkent, established in 1947, broadcasts in Uzbek, English, Urdu, Hindi, Farsi, Arabic, and Uighur. There is also a television station in Tashkent, and satellite earth stations receive Orbita and INTELSAT. In 1990 there were 279 newspapers and 93 periodicals, published in a variety of languages. Several different kinds of publishing houses are located in Tashkent.

46 ORGANIZATIONS

The Uzbekistan Chamber of Commerce and Industry promotes the country's exports in world markets. An umbrella organization, the Federation of Trade Unions of Uzbekistan, coordinates the activities of the country's trade unions. The Society for Human Rights is an important political association.

47 TOURISM, TRAVEL, AND RECREATION

Uzbekistan tourist attraction's include the Islamic cities of Samarkand, Bukhara, Khiva, and Kokand. Muslims from Pakistan, Iran, and the Middle East have been drawn to these sites with their palaces, mosques, madrasses (religious colleges), and pre-Islamic remains.

Uzbekistan is open to both business travelers and tourists. Visas are required and are obtainable upon arrival or through Russian embassies abroad and companies that sell package tours of Central Asia. The principal accommodations are hotels that formerly belonged to the Soviet Intourist system. International air service includes direct flights once or twice a week to the capital city of Tashkent from New Delhi, Islamabad, Teheran, Jeddah, Ankara, and other cities. There are also daily flights to Tashkent from Moscow.

48 FAMOUS UZBEKISTANIS

Islam A. Karimov and Leonid Kuchma have been president and prime minister of Uzbekistan since October 1992, respectively. A famous 20th century writer is Abdullah Quaisi, who wrote the historical novels *Days Gone By* and the *Scorpion from the Pulpit*, published in the 1920s. Quaisi was killed in the 1930s during Stalin's purges.

49 DEPENDENCIES

Uzbekistan has no territories or colonies.

50 BIBLIOGRAPHY

Critchlow, James. *Nationalism in Uzbekistan: A Soviet Republic's Road to Sovereignty.* Boulder, Colo.: Westview Press, 1991.

Gippenreiter, Vadim Evgenevich. *Fabled Cities of Central Asia: Samarkand, Bukhara, Khiva.* New York: Abbeville Press, 1989.

Malcomson, Scott L. *Borderlands--Nation and Empire.* Boston: Faber and Faber, 1994.

Nazarov, Bakhtiyar A. and Denis Sinor (eds.). *Essays on Uzbek History, Culture, and Language.* Bloomington, Ind.: Indiana University, 1993.

Uzbekistan. Minneapolis: Lerner, 1993.

Uzbekistan. Washington, D.C.: International Monetary Fund, 1992.

VANUATU

Republic of Vanuatu
[French:] *République de Vanuatu* [Bislama:] *Ripablik blong Vanuatu*

CAPITAL: Port-Vila.

FLAG: Red and green sections are divided horizontally by a gold stripe running within a black border and widening at the hoist into a black triangle on which is a pig's tusk enclosing two crossed yellow mele leaves.

ANTHEM: *Yumi, Yumi, Yumi (We, We, We).*

MONETARY UNIT: As of 1 January 1981, the vatu (VT) replaced at par value the New Hebridean franc as the national currency. There are coins of 100 vatu and notes of 100, 500, 1,000, and 5,000 vatu. VT1 = $0.0084 (or $1 = VT119.29).

WEIGHTS AND MEASURES: The metric standard is used.

HOLIDAYS: New Year's Day, 1 January; May Day, 1 May; Independence Day, 30 July; Assumption, 15 August; Constitution Day, 5 October; National Unity Day, 29 November; Christmas Day, 25 December; Family Day, 26 December. Movable religious holidays include Good Friday, Easter Monday, and Ascension.

TIME: 11 PM = noon GMT.

¹LOCATION, SIZE, AND EXTENT

Vanuatu, formerly the Anglo-French Condominium of the New Hebrides, is an irregular Y-shaped chain of some 80 islands, with a total land area of about 14,760 sq km (5,699 sq mi) and a total coastline of 2,528 km (1,571 mi). Comparatively, the area occupied by Vanuatu is slightly larger than the state of Connecticut. Of the 70 inhabited islands, the largest is Espiritu Santo (3,947 sq km/1,524 sq mi); the island of Efate is the administrative center. The island chain is about 800 km (500 mi) long and lies about 1,000 km (600 mi) W of Fiji and 400 km (250 mi) NE of New Caledonia. Vanuatu and France both claim Matthew and Hunter islands, which lie between Vanuatu and New Caledonia; one of the islands has been occupied by French forces.

Vanuatu's capital city, Port-Vila, is located on the island of Efate.

²TOPOGRAPHY

The islands are of coral and volcanic origin; there are active volcanoes on several islands, including Ambrym, Lopevi, and Tanna. Most of the islands are forested and mountainous, with narrow coastal strips. The highest peak, Tabwemasana, on Espiritu Santo, rises 1,878 m (6,161 ft) above sea level. The islands are generally well watered.

³CLIMATE

The tropical oceanic climate is moderated by southeastern trade winds, which blow between the months of May and October. Winds are variable during the remainder of the year, and cyclones may occur. Average midday temperatures in Port-Vila range from 25°C (77°F) in winter to 29°C (84°F) in summer. Humidity averages about 74%, and rainfall on Efate is about 230 cm (90 in) a year.

⁴FLORA AND FAUNA

Despite its tropical forests, Vanuatu has a limited number of plant and animal species. There are no indigenous large mammals, poisonous snakes, or spiders. The 19 species of native reptiles include the flowerpot snake, found only on Efate. There are 11 species of bat (3 unique to Vanuatu) and 61 species of land and water birds. While the small Polynesian rat is thought to be indigenous, the large species arrived with Europeans, as did domesticated hogs, dogs, and cattle. (The wild pig and fowl appear to be indigenous.)

The region is rich in sea life, with more than 4,000 species of marine mollusks. Coneshell and stonefish carry poison fatal to humans. The giant East African snail arrived only in the 1970s but already has spread from the Port-Vila region to Luganville.

⁵ENVIRONMENT

Vanuatu's population growth has caused concern for the environment in several areas. Water pollution in the urban areas is a problem due to inadequate sanitation systems. The nation's logging industry threatens the forests and contributes to the problem of soil erosion. Forests currently cover 75% of the land area. The reefs on Vanuatu's coasts which are the home of the country's marine life, are threatened by inappropriate fishing methods and siltation. In 1987, the government formed the National Advisory Committee on the Environment (NACE) to address the nation's developing environmental concerns. The green sea and hawksbill turtles were endangered species in 1987.

⁶POPULATION

The population is unevenly distributed, with the vast majority of Vanuatuans living in some 2,000 small villages. The census of May 1989 established a total population of 142,419; estimated population in 1995 was 169,000. The most populous islands in 1989 were Efate, 30,868; Espiritu Santo, 25,581; and Malekula, 19,298. The average 1985–95 annual rate of population increase was 2.45%. As of May 1989, the population of the capital, Port-Vila, on Efate, was 19,311; Luganville (Espiritu Santo), the only other large town, had a population of 6,983.

⁷MIGRATION

Vanuatu's earliest known settlers probably migrated from the northwestern Pacific about 3,000 years ago. They were followed a thousand years later by migrants from the Solomon Islands. Tradition describes a series of subsequent incursions. In the 19th century, thousands of New Hebrides islanders were recruited as indentured laborers for plantation work in Australia, Fiji, New Caledonia, and Samoa. This migration gradually died down after the establishment of the Anglo-French Condominium, although voluntary emigration to New Caledonia continued until independence. In recent years, adverse economic conditions have encouraged emigration to Fiji, New Zealand, and the US.

⁸ETHNIC GROUPS

Nearly 95% of the total population is of Melanesian origin. Minority groups include (about 3%), Europeans, mostly French (about 2%), and other Pacific Islanders (about 1%).

⁹LANGUAGES

More than 100 languages and dialects are spoken in Vanuatu. Melanesian, the principal language, is related to Fijian and New Caledonian speech. Pidgin English, known as Bislama or Bichelama, is recognized by the constitution as the lingua franca, although English and French are also official languages. The national anthem is in Bislama, which is also used in parliamentary debate, with the proceedings reported in English and French as well. Children often speak as many as four languages, and every aspect of public life—including education, law, and the media—is complicated by language problems.

¹⁰RELIGIONS

About 80% of the population is considered to be Christian; other Vanuatuans follow indigenous traditional religions. The Anglican, Presbyterian, and Roman Catholic churches began missionary work in the New Hebrides during the 19th century. More recently, the Seventh-Day Adventists and other nontraditional Protestant groups have been active in mission work. Most mission schools have been handed over to the government, but the missions have continued to make important contributions to education and health. Since 1940, the John Frum cargo cult (a rejection of the white Christian's beliefs but not his goods) has flourished, mainly on Tanna and provides a remarkable example of religious development in a situation of cultural challenge and transition.

¹¹TRANSPORTATION

During World War II, Vanuatu became an important Allied base, and many roads and airstrips were built by the US forces. In 1991 there were 1,027 km (638 mi) of roads, of which 240 km (149 mi) were paved, and 7,000 registered motor vehicles, including 4,200 passenger cars.

The 31 small usable airfields serve all the main islands. The chief airports are Bauerfield, on Efate, and Pekoa, on Espiritu Santo; both have been upgraded to handle jet aircraft. Air Vanuatu, the national airline operated by Ansett Airlines of Australia, maintains regular service to Australia; an internal airline, Air Melanesiae, links 22 airfields on various islands. Other external service is provided by Air Pacific, UTA, Polynesian Airlines, Solair, and Air Nauru. Port-Vila and Luganville are the chief seaports. Small ships provide frequent interisland service. Vanuatu maintains a policy of open registry for merchant ships, allowing foreign shipowners to avoid the higher costs and regulations of registration under their own flags. As of 1 January 1992, there were 109 ships in the Vanuatuan merchant fleet, with a total capacity of 1.8 million GRT.

¹²HISTORY

Although the Portuguese navigator Pedro Fernandes de Queir—

established a short-lived settlement on Espiritu Santo in 1606, little more is known about the history of the New Hebrides until French and British explorers arrived in the late 18th century. Captain James Cook discovered, named, and charted most of the southern islands in 1774. The next century brought British and French missionaries, planters, and traders, and for many years the islanders suffered from the depredations of the recruiting ships and from other lawless acts by Europeans in the region.

By the Anglo-French Convention of 1887, a joint naval commission was established, with a resident commissioner to protect the lives and interests of the islanders. In 1906, following a London conference, the Anglo-French Condominium was established, largely to settle land claims and to end difficulties caused by lack of clear local jurisdiction. Indigenous political activity developed after World War II, with increasing native concern over land alienation and European dominance.

In 1975, a representative assembly replaced the nominated advisory council under which the New Hebrides had been governed; 29 assembly members were elected by universal suffrage, 9 members represented economic interests, and 4 members represented the traditional chiefs. In 1977, the National Party (Vanuaaku Pati), which held 21 of 42 assembly seats, demanded independence and staged a boycott of the legislature; in response, at a conference in Paris, self-government was agreed on for 1978, to be followed by a 1980 referendum on independence. After considerable difficulty, a constitutional conference in 1979 finally agreed on an independence constitution. In the November 1979 elections for a newly constituted, fully elective assembly, the National Party, led by Father Walter Lini, obtained 26 of the 39 seats.

In May 1980, however, a dissident francophone group, based on Espiritu Santo, attempted to break away and declared an independent government of Vemarana, under Jimmy Stevens and the Nagriamal Party. Attempts made during June to resolve the differences between the new central government and the rebels failed, and UK and French troops were sent to Luganville on 24 July. No shots were fired, but the soldiers remained until Vanuatu's formal declaration of independence on 30 July 1980. They were then replaced at the new government's request by forces from Papua New Guinea, who were assisted by the local police in putting down the rebellion.

Since independence, Vanuatu has followed a nonaligned foreign policy. As of late 1987, it was the only South Pacific nation to have joined the nonaligned movement, and in January 1987 it signed a controversial fishing agreement with the USSR. In May 1987 Vanuatu announced a ban on all military ships and aircraft in a dispute over a proposed Libyan diplomatic mission. The dispute ended with the expulsion of two Libyan diplomats. Relations with the French government remained strained throughout much of the Lini government's rule, though they improved at the end of 1989 with the signing of the Matignon Accord relating to New Caledonia..

In December 1988 President George Ati Sokomanu attempted to dismiss the Lini government by ordering the dissolution of the country's Parliament. Sokomanu appointed Barak Sope as Prime Minister. Lini refused to surrender office and reconvened Parliament. Sope and several supporters were arrested and charged with inciting mutiny. Sope was sentence to six years' imprisonment.

Fr. Lini lost a parliamentary vote of confidence in September 1991 and stood down as Prime Minister. Donald Kalpokas replaced Lini. In December of 1991 the francophone Union of Moderate Parties (UMP), led by Maxime Carlot won the largest bloc of seats and formed a coalition government with the National United Party (NUP), led by Walter Lini. Strains between the coalition members led to Lini joining the opposition in August of 1993. Carlot's government has survived the defection.

13GOVERNMENT

Under the independence constitution adopted in 1979 and effective in 1980, Vanuatu is an independent republic within the Commonwealth of Nations. The head of state is the president (Ati George Sokomanu since 1980); the head of government is the prime minister (Father Walter Lini since 1979). The unicameral legislature consists of 46 members (39 before 1987) elected by universal adult suffrage to four-year terms. The cabinet is responsible to parliament, and the president is chosen by an electoral college for a five-year term. The electoral system includes a degree of proportional representation. A Council of Chiefs chosen by their peers in the chiefs' district councils advises the government on the protection of Vanuatuan languages and culture.

The People's Republic of China signed an accord with Vanuatu in December 1993 to finance 75% of a 3.6 million dollar hydroelectric dam on the northern island of Mallicolo. The Japanese government will help build a similar hydroelectric dam on the Sarakata River on the northern Vanuatu island of Santo.

14POLITICAL PARTIES

The country has at least six established political parties. The Union of Moderate Parties (UMP, Maxime Carlot) is the largest single party in the legislature. Its coalition partner in governing is the National United Party (NUP) pro-government faction (John Sethy Regenvanu). In opposition are the Vanua'aku Pati (VPNOur Land Party, Donald Kalpokas), Melanesian Progressive Party (MPP, Barak Sope), National United Party (NUP) opposition faction, (Fr. Walter Lini), and Fren Melanesian Party (FMP), a splinter group established when the UMP was formed from the New Hebrides Federal Party in 1982.

15LOCAL GOVERNMENT

Vanuatu is divided into four administrative districts. There are municipal councils in Port-Vila and Luganville, and community councils elsewhere. Espiritu Santo and Tanna have special regional councils.

16JUDICIAL SYSTEM

Despite the great difficulty in unifying laws based on the very different English and French traditions, Vanuatu has sought to establish a single system based on British criminal procedure and the French penal code. The constitution establishes a Supreme Court, with a chief justice and three other judges, as well as an appeals court. Village and island courts have jurisdiction over customary and other matters.

The judiciary is independent of the executive and free from military influence. The Constitution guarantees a range of procedural due process protections including the presumption of innocence, fair public trial, habeas corpus, and the prohibition against double jeopardy.

17ARMED FORCES

The nation maintains close links with Papua New Guinea, where Vanuatuan cadets train for a mobile defense force under the auspices of the Australian Ministry of Defense, which also helps to train skilled manpower for national development tasks.

18INTERNATIONAL COOPERATION

A member of the Commonwealth of Nations, Vanuatu joined the UN on 15 September 1981 and participates in FAO, IBRD, ICAO, IDA, IFC, IMF, UPU, and WHO. It also belongs to the Asian Development Bank (which opened a regional office in Port-Vila in 1984), the French Community, G-77, and various regional Pacific bodies. Vanuatu has taken an active role in Pacific affairs, campaigning for a nuclear-free zone and advocating independence for New Caledonia. Vanuatu has established diplomatic

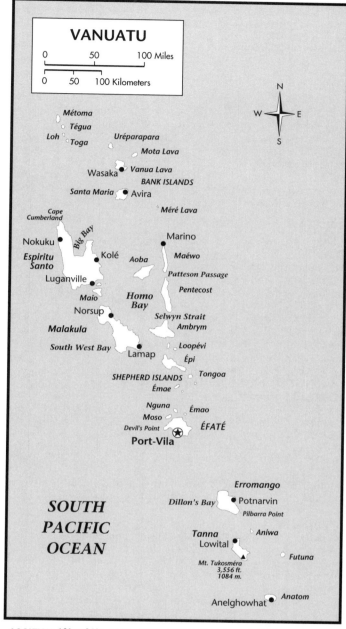

LOCATION: 13° to 21°s; 166° to 171°E. **TOTAL COASTLINE:** 2,528 km (1,571 mi). **TERRITORIAL SEA LIMIT:** 12 mi.

relations with a number of OECD countries, as well as China, Cuba, Viet-Nam, Libya, and the former USSR.

19ECONOMY

Vanuatu has a mixed traditional and modern economy. Agriculture supports about 75% of the population, but the service industry is playing an increasingly important role in the economy. Services account for 65% of the GDP, while agriculture provides 21% and industry 14%. Tourism has been developed since the 1980s; in 1992 there were 42,673 tourist arrivals, and it is hoped that that number will rise to 100,000 by the end of the decade. The absence of personal and corporate income taxes have made Vanuatu an offshore financial center, and the government also earns fees from a "flag of convenience" shipping registry.

20INCOME
In 1992, Vanuatu's GNP was $189 million at current prices, or $1,220 per capita. For the period 1985–92 the average inflation rate was 6.3%, resulting in a real growth rate in per capita GNP of 0.5%.

21LABOR
About 80% of the people are engaged in peasant labor either for subsistence or producing such cash crops as copra. The employed wage-labor force is concentrated in Port-Vila and Luganville. For persons engaged in government enterprises, port work, construction, and certain other jobs, the terms of employment, wages, and union membership are set by legislation. The nation's first trade unions were formed in 1984. By 1992, there were seven trade unions; the largest two were the Oil and Gas Workers' Union and the Vanuatu Airline Workers' Union.

22AGRICULTURE
About 14% of the land is cultivated or used as pasture land. While most crops, including yams, taro, manioc, sweet potato, and breadfruit, are raised for local consumption, cash crops like copra, cocoa, and coffee have been increasingly important. Production of copra totaled 27,000 tons in 1992. Copra production was adversely affected by cyclones in 1985 and 1987.

In 1983, Vanuatu's first agricultural census was taken, with British assistance. A land alienation act passed in 1982 limits land ownership to indigenous owners and their descendants, but expatriates can lease land for up to 75 years.

23ANIMAL HUSBANDRY
Hogs and fowl form part of the village economy. Vanuatu is ideal for cattle, and large numbers are raised on plantations; in 1992 there were 131,000 head of cattle, up nearly 44% from the early 1980s. The growing meat-packing industry produces frozen, chilled, and tinned beef; production of beef totaled about 3,000 tons (dressed carcass weight) in 1992, coming from 17,000 slaughtered head. The beef industry is centered on the island of Espiritu Santo, where the country's main abattoir is located. Beef is exported primarily to Japan, with a lesser amount going to New Caledonia.

24FISHING
Although the South Pacific Fishing Co., a joint Vanuatuan government and Japanese venture, has facilities at Luganville that freeze and export both tuna and bonito to Japan and the US, the full fishery potential has not been realized. Fishing is currently focused on domestic consumption; exporting fish requires a government permit. Vanuatu's fish exports totaled only $19,000 in 1990.

25FORESTRY
About 75% of the total land area is forest or bushland. Sawlog and veneer log exports were 39,000 cu m in 1991. The government approved the establishment of a large commercial forestry plantation on Espirito Santo in 1987.

26MINING
Vanuatu has few known minerals, although gold deposits have recently been discovered. A small manganese mine on Efate ceased exports in 1980.

27ENERGY AND POWER
Temporary generators established throughout the islands by the US during World War II have mostly deteriorated. Net installed capacity was about 11,000 kw in 1991, all of it conventional thermal; electricity production totaled 26 million kwh.

28INDUSTRY
The manufacturing sector is small: in 1989, it contributed less than 15% of the GDP. Industries include fish freezing, meat canning, sawmilling, and the production of furniture, soft drinks, and fabricated aluminum goods. Indigenous crafts include basketry, canoe building, and pottery. In 1990, National Breweries, a joint venture with Sweden, began producing Tusker beer and Pripps Lager.

29SCIENCE AND TECHNOLOGY
There is no advanced technology apart from overseas aid programs.

30DOMESTIC TRADE
A large part of the population still relies on barter. In Port-Vila, European businesses dominate commercial life; there are hotels, supermarkets, fashion shops, and patisseries, as well as recently established Australian steak houses and small Chinese restaurants. Some Vanuatuans have entered the cash economy in urban areas. The nation's numerous cooperative societies handle most of the distribution of goods on the islands. As part of a program to create regional trade centers, Japan donated $2.8 million in 1987 to build a wharf and commercial center on Malekula. Normal business hours in the capital are 7:30 to 11:30 AM and 1:30 to 5 PM, Monday–Friday. Banks in Vanuatu are open on weekdays from 8 to 11:30 AM and 1:30 to 3 PM.

31FOREIGN TRADE
Service receipts have helped offset the traditionally adverse trade balances. Copra accounted for 37% of total exports in 1990, although efforts to diversify the product base had some success, with beef constituting 23% of the total that year, cocoa 15%, and timber 6%. A commodities marketing board exports copra and cocoa, and cooperatives play a major role in foreign trade. Exports totaled vt2,202 million in 1990, and imports totaled vt11,288. Vanuatu's main trade partners are Australia, France, the Netherlands, and New Zealand.

32BALANCE OF PAYMENTS
Continuing trade deficits have been offset by aid from the UK and France, but this assistance is being steadily reduced.

In 1992 merchandise exports totaled $14.86 million and imports $74.01 million. The merchandise trade balance was $−59.15 million.

The following table summarizes Vanuatu's balance of payments for 1990 and 1992 (in millions of US dollars):

	1990	1992
CURRENT ACCOUNT		
Goods services and income	−28.04	−30.04
Unrequited transfers	36.05	12.98
TOTALS	8.01	−17.06
CAPITAL ACCOUNT		
Direct investment	13.19	18.45
Other long-term capital	2.86	2.21
Other short-term capital	6.06	−79.85
Exceptional Financing		3.45
Reserves	4.07	1.94
TOTALS	−26.18	−53.8
Errors and omissions	−32.20	70.86
Total change in reserves	4.07	1.94

33BANKING AND SECURITIES
Vanuatu's banking system includes a Central Bank, local retail banks, and a Development Bank that provides loans for agricultural projects, housing, and industrial development. The country's Financial Centre, a tax haven created by the British in 1971, is the

third-largest source of government revenue. Favorable regulatory and tax structures have stimulated foreign interest in Vanuatu as an international financial center; more than 600 offshore companies and banks were registered in Port-Vila in 1985. There is no stock exchange.

34INSURANCE

Insurance coverage is available through agents of overseas companies, mainly British and French.

35PUBLIC FINANCE

The following table shows actual revenues and expenditures for 1988 and 1989 in millions of vatus.

	1988	1989
REVENUE AND GRANTS		
Tax revenue	3,149.1	3,379.9
Non-tax revenue	597.3	699.4
Capital revenue	103.8	75.3
Grants	1,806.0	1,798.0
TOTAL	5,656.2	5,952.6
EXPENDITURES & LENDING MINUS REPAYMENTS		
General public service	1,110.4	999.3
Public order and safety	312.4	331.4
Education	1,206.7	919.7
Health	542.3	478.8
Housing and community amenities	13.7	2.5
Recreation, cultural, and religious affairs	13.8	9.8
Economic affairs and services	2,659.2	4,349.3
Other expenditures	377.7	196.4
Lending minus repayments	49.5	−10.9
TOTAL	6,285.7	7,276.4
DEFICIT/SURPLUS	−629.5	−1,323.8

In 1989 Vanuatu's total public debt stood at VT3,559.7 million, of which VT1,714.8 million was financed abroad.

36TAXATION

Vanuatu has no income, corporation, or sales tax. Government revenues are derived from indirect taxes, which include stamp taxes, an excise tax on locally produced alcoholic beverages, a 10% hotel tax, and a rent tax.

37CUSTOMS AND DUTIES

A single tariff is imposed on an ad valorem basis and ranges from exemption to 85%. A 5% service tax is also charged on all imported goods. Export duties are levied on the country's primary products.

38FOREIGN INVESTMENT

The government encourages all forms of foreign investment, especially if there is joint local participation. There are no major foreign ownership restrictions, and duty exemptions are available on application to the Ministry of Finance.

39ECONOMIC DEVELOPMENT

The British independence settlement provided grants of £23.4 million to Vanuatu, including £6.4 million in budgetary aid (with additional grants provided annually), £4 million for technical aid, and £13 million for development projects aimed at promoting national economic self-sufficiency. Projects under the five-year development plan for 1982–86 included harbor development, agricultural training, and road improvements. Aid for other infrastructural development is provided by Australia, New Zealand, the UN, and the EC. Government development projects emphasize local participation and preservation of Vanuatu's cultural

heritage. In 1987, foreign donors pledged an estimated $20 million to repair damage caused by the 1987 cyclone. In 1990, Vanuatu received US$42.1 million in bilateral aid, and US$6.8 million in multilateral aid. In 1991, US$2.2 million in UN development assistance was granted to Vanuatu. The objectives of the 1987–91 five-year development plan include increasing economic self-reliance, using natural resources to generate economic growth, and expanding the private sector's contribution to development.

40SOCIAL DEVELOPMENT

The majority of the people cling to traditional village life. The extended family system ensures that no islanders starve, while church missions and the social development section of the Education Ministry concentrate on rural development and youth activities. The government incorporates family planning into its overall maternal and child health program. A provident fund system provides lump-sum benefits for old age, disability, and death. Workers contribute 3% of earnings, and employers contribute 3% of payroll.

Women are just beginning to emerge from traditional cultural roles. Village chiefs are viewed as a primary obstacle to female advancement. There are no women leaders in Vanuatu's civic, business or religious institutions.

41HEALTH

Malaria is the most serious of the country's endemic diseases, which also include leprosy, tuberculosis, filariasis, and venereal diseases. In 1981, about 1 in 10 residents of Espiritu Santo suffered from malaria and, in 1983, a new malaria epidemic was reported. In 1990, there were an estimated 200 cases of tuberculosis per 100,000 people reported.

Medical care is provided by 94 hospitals, health centers, and clinics administered by the Ministry of Health, assisted by WHO and a number of voluntary agencies. Local training schemes in basic community nursing are provided by Port-Vila hospitals, and local clinics train health and sanitation orderlies.

The country had 15 physicians in 1991. In 1992, the infant mortality rate was 65 per 1,000 live births; there were 500 deaths of children under 5 years old that year. Life expectancy was an average of 65 years in 1992, and 74% of children were immunized against measles in that year. Vanuatu's population was 161,000 in 1993, with 6,000 births in 1992.

42HOUSING

In urban areas only the emerging middle class can afford government-built housing. Other migrants to the towns buy plots of land and build cheap shacks of corrugated iron and waste materials, principally near Port-Vila and Luganville. The vast majority of villagers still build their own homes from local materials. As of 1979, 62% of all dwellings were traditional Melanesian houses with earth or coral floors, no glass windows, and palm, bamboo, or cane walls and roofing. The most widely used exterior construction material was bush, found in 61% of all housing units. In February 1987, a cyclone damaged 95% of the buildings in Port-Vila.

43EDUCATION

The overall literacy rate is low (probably 10–20% of the population), but literacy is relatively widespread among persons under 35 years of age. Primary education is available for almost all children except in a few remote tribal areas. In 1992, there were 272 primary schools with 852 teachers and 26,267 students. General secondary schools had 220 teachers and 4,269 students. There were also 124 students in teacher training schools and 444 in vocational schools. Full secondary education is provided by the anglophone Malapoa College and the French Lycée at Port-Vila; limited secondary education is also available in five English postprimary schools and three French mission schools. For post-secondary education, especially medical and technical training, selected students go principally to Fiji, Australia, and New Zealand.

44LIBRARIES AND MUSEUMS

There is practically no secular reading matter in the many vernaculars. A cultural center at Port-Vila has a well stocked library of both French and English books and periodicals and houses fine collections of Melanesian art and artifacts, as well as a valuable stamp collection. The secondary schools also have libraries. Efate has a small museum displaying South Pacific artifacts and current works of art.

45MEDIA

The weekly government newspaper, *The Vanuatu Weekly,* appears in English, French, and Bislama. In 1991, it had a circulation of 2,000. Radio Vanuatu (founded 1966) broadcasts daily in English, French, and Bislama. Vanuatu is linked by telegraph and telex to Hong Kong; Paris; Noumea, New Caledonia; and Sydney, Australia. An earth satellite tracking station came into service in 1979. In 1991 there were 3,240 telephones, 45,000 radios, and 1,000 television sets.

46ORGANIZATIONS

There are a great number of European organizations, but the cooperative movement has had the greatest local impact. Cooperative units have organized a training center in Port-Vila for such skills as accounting, management, law, and marketing. Cooperatives receive British aid and government support but remain firmly independent.

47TOURISM, TRAVEL, AND RECREATION

Although tourism is officially regarded as a quick means to earn foreign exchange revenue, it is supported only as an aid to national development. In recent years, tourism has recovered from the decline it experienced in the mid-1980s due to a drop in tourist arrivals from Australia and cyclone damage to tourist facilities. The number of tourist arrivals reached 39,784 in 1991; of these, 53% were from Australia and 18% from New Zealand. There were 536 rooms in hotels and other establishments, with 1,150 beds and a 63% occupancy rate, and tourist receipts totaled US$30 million. Popular recreations include marine sightseeing, deep-sea fishing, sailing, and beachcombing for shells.

48FAMOUS VANUATUANS

Father Walter Hayde Lini (b.1943), ordained as an Anglican priest in 1970, has been the major political force in Vanuatu since independence.

49DEPENDENCIES

Vanuatu has no territories or colonies.

50BIBLIOGRAPHY

Douglas, Norman. *Vanuatu: A Guide.* Sydney: Pacific Publications, 1987.

Lini, Walter. *Beyond Pandemonium: From the New Hebrides to Vanuatu.* Wellington: Asia Pacific Books, 1981.

MacClancy, Jeremy. *To Kill a Bird with Two Stones: A Short History of Vanuatu.* Port-Vila: Vanuatu Cultural Center, 1981.

Geology and Offshore Resources of Pacific Island Arcs—Vanuatu Region. Houston, Tex.: Circum-Pacific Council for Energy and Mineral Resources, 1988.

Harrisson, Tom. *Living Among Cannibals.* New York: AMS Press, 1979.

Lindstrom, Lamont. *Knowledge and Power in a South Pacific Society.* Washington, D.C.: Smithsonian Institution Press, 1990.

Rodman, Margaret. *Masters of Tradition: Consequences of Customary Land Tenure in Longana, Vanuatu.* Vancouver: University of British Columbia Press, 1987.

Sturton, Mark. *Policy Modeling in the Small Island Economies of the South Pacific: The Case of Vanuatu.* Honolulu: East-West Center, 1989.

VIET NAM

Socialist Republic of Viet Nam
Cong Hoa Xa Hoi Chu Nghia VietNam

CAPITAL: Hanoi.

FLAG: The flag is red with a five-pointed gold star in the center.

ANTHEM: *Tien Quan Ça (Forward, Soldiers!).*

MONETARY UNIT: The dong (D) is a paper currency of 10 hao and 100 xu. There are coins of 1, 2, and 5 xu, and notes of 5 xu, 1, 2, and 5 hao, and 1, 2, 5, and 10 dong. D1 = $0.0027 (or $1 = D368).

WEIGHTS AND MEASURES: The metric system is the legal standard, but some traditional measures are still used.

HOLIDAYS: Liberation of Saigon, 30 April; May Day, 1 May; Independence Day, 2 September. Movable holidays include the Vietnamese New Year (Tet).

TIME: 7 PM = noon GMT.

¹LOCATION, SIZE, AND EXTENT

Situated on the eastern coast of mainland Southeast Asia, the Socialist Republic of Viet Nam (SRV) has an area of 329,560 sq km (127,244 sq mi), extending 1,650 km (1,025 mi) N–S and 600 km (373 mi) E–W. Comparatively, the area occupied by Viet Nam is slightly larger than the state of New Mexico. At its narrowest, Viet Nam is only 50 km (31 mi) across. The nation is bordered on the N by China, on the E by the Gulf of Tonkin, on the E and S by the South China Sea, on the SW by the Gulf of Thailand, and on the W by Cambodia and Laos, with a total boundary length of 7,262 km (4,512 mi). Before unification, which was proclaimed on 3 July 1976, Viet Nam was divided in two by the 17th parallel. To the south was the Republic of Viet Nam (RVN), also known as South Viet Nam; to the north, the Democratic Republic of Viet Nam (DRV), also known as North Viet Nam.

Viet Nam, China, the Philippines, Brunei, Taiwan, and Malaysia claim all or part of the Spratly Islands and Paracel Islands, located in the South China Sea roughly 600 km (350 mi) east of Ho Chi Minh City and 400 km (250 mi) east of Da Nang, respectively. The Paracel Islands are known in Vietnamese as the Hoang Sa archipelago, and the Spratlys as the Truong Sa. Both archipelagoes are reportedly surrounded by rich undersea oil reserves, and are productive fishing grounds. China has occupied the Paracel Islands since 1974, when Chinese troops drove a South Vietnamese garrison from the western islands. Viet Nam occupies six of the Spratlys, and has unsuccessfully engaged in negotiations with Malaysia and the Philippines over the remainder. Periodic clashes between Chinese and Vietnamese naval forces have taken place in the vicinity of both island groups.

Viet Nam's capital city, Hanoi, is located in the northern part of the country.

²TOPOGRAPHY

Viet Nam has been described as a carrying pole with a rice basket hanging from each end. The description is a fitting one, for a single mountain chain, the Annam Cordillera (in Vietnamese, Truong Son), extends along Viet Nam's western border from north to south, connecting two "rice baskets," which are formed by the densely populated Red River Delta of the Tonkin region in the north and the rich Mekong River Delta in the south. Over two-thirds of the entire population of the country lives in the two low-lying delta regions, both of which are composed of rich alluvial soils brought down from the mountainous regions of southern China and mainland Southeast Asia. The remainder of the population lives along the narrow central coast, in the hilly regions of the Central Highlands north of Ho Chi Minh City (formerly Saigon), or in the mountains north and west of the Red River Delta. The highest mountain peak is Fan Si Pan (3,143 m/ 10,312 ft), near the northern border.

³CLIMATE

Viet Nam is entirely located in the tropical belt lying between the equator and the Tropic of Cancer. While there are slight variations in temperature, depending on the season and the altitude, the primary seasonal changes are marked by variations in rainfall.

In the north, the rainy season extends from mid-April to mid-October; the city of Hanoi has a mean annual rainfall of 172 cm (68 in), and in the mountains, annual rainfall sometimes exceeds 406 cm (160 in). Daily temperatures fluctuate considerably in the Red River Delta region, particularly in the dry season, when the thermometer may drop as low as 5°C (41°F) in the region of Hanoi. During the rainy season, the average temperature in Hanoi is about 30°C (86°F).

The south is more tropical; temperatures in Ho Chi Minh City vary only between 18° and 33°C (64–91°F) throughout the year. Temperatures in the Central Highlands are somewhat cooler, ranging from a mean of about 17°C (63°F) in winter to 20°C (68°F) in summer. The rainy season extends from early May to November, with annual rainfall averaging about 200 cm (79 in) in lowland regions. The typhoon season lasts from July through November, with the most severe storms occurring along the central coast. Typhoons in this region frequently lead to serious crop damage and loss of life.

⁴FLORA AND FAUNA

The mountainous regions of Tonkin, as well as the Annam Cordillera, are characterized by tropical rain forest broken by large areas of monsoon forest. In the higher altitudes of the far northwest there are pine forests. Shifting cultivation has resulted in many sections of secondary forest. Tropical grasses are widespread, and there are mangrove forests fringing parts of the Red River Delta and in the Ca Mau peninsula, which juts into the Gulf of Thailand. Tropical evergreen forests predominate in the south, with extensive savanna in the southwest.

Deer and wild oxen are found in the more mountainous areas. There are many species of tropical birds and insects.

5ENVIRONMENT

During the Viet Nam war, massive bombing raids and defoliation campaigns caused severe destruction of the natural foliage, especially in the Central Highlands in the south. Scientists touring Viet Nam in January 1983 found that the damaged forests have recovered much faster than had been predicted. Over 50% of the nation's forests have been eliminated. UN sources estimate that Viet Nam loses 160,000 to 200,000 hectares of forest land annually. However, dioxin, a toxic residue of the herbicide known as Agent Orange, had leached into water supplies. Air and water pollution result from the uncontrolled dumping of industrial and domestic contaminants. The nation has 90.2 cu mi of water; 78% is used for farming activity and 9% is used for industrial purposes. Salinization and alkalinization are a threat to the quality of the soil. Excessive use of pesticides and fertilizers have also damaged the nation's soils.

Environmental damage has also been caused by slash-and-burn agriculture, practiced by nomadic tribal peoples in the Central Highlands and in the mountainous regions in the north. The government is engaged in a program to introduce to such peoples the practice of settled agriculture.

In 1994, 28 of Viet Nam's mammal species and 34 bird species were endangered. Three-hundred and thirty-eight types of plants are also endangered. As of 1987, endangered species included the tiger, elephant, Sumatran rhinoceros, Thailand brow-antlered deer, kouprey, river terrapin, Siamese crocodile (probably extinct), and estuarine crocodile. The Javan rhinoceros and the pileated, crowned, and caped gibbons are extinct.

6POPULATION

Rapid population growth is a serious problem in Viet Nam. According to the 1989 census, the total population was 64,411,668. In 1995, the population was estimated at 73,811,000, making Viet Nam the thirteenth most populous nation in the world. Population density was estimated at 191 per sq km (495 per sq mi) in 1987. The annual growth rate averaged almost 2.2% during 1980–85 and 2.15% during 1985–90; the government is attempting to reduce it to 1.7% through family planning measures, including late marriages and small families, in order to stabilize the population at 75 to 80 million by the end of the twentieth century. The UN projection for the year 2000 was 81,516,000, based on an estimated birthrate of 27.7 per 1,000, a death rate of 7.6 per 1,000, and a net natural increase of 20.1 per 1,000 during 1995–2000.

Approximately 20% of the population lives in urban areas. The three largest cities in 1989 were Ho Chi Minh City (3,924,435), Hanoi (3,056,146), and Haiphong (1,447,523).

7MIGRATION

The 1954 partition of Viet Nam resulted in the exodus of over 820,000 refugees, the majority of them Catholics, from the northern part of the country. Most eventually settled with government assistance in the Central Highlands or on the outskirts of the capital city of Saigon (now Ho Chi Minh City). During the same period, about 80,000 Viet-Minh troops and their dependents moved from the south to the north.

The Viet Nam war caused severe disruption of living patterns in both the north and the south. In the north, intensive US bombing of major industrial cities led to a dispersal of the population from urban areas, while a government-sponsored program resulted in the resettlement of nearly 1 million Vietnamese from crowded areas in the Delta to less densely populated regions in upland areas of the country. In the south, migration was primarily from the countryside to the cities, as millions of peasants fled their villages to escape the effects of the war or to seek employment in the affluent cities of Saigon and Da Nang. At the end of the war in 1975, nearly one-half of the population lived in urban areas, many in refugee camps on the edges of the major cities.

After seizing control of the south in 1975, the Hanoi regime announced a new program that called for the resettlement of over 10 million Vietnamese into uncrowded areas of the country by the end of the century. Many were to be moved from refugee camps in the south to New Economic Zones established in the Central Highlands or along the Cambodian border. Although the zones were unpopular because of poor living conditions, between the end of the war and 1981, nearly 1.5 million Vietnamese were resettled into new areas. The overall aim was to disperse the entire population into several hundred "agroindustrial districts" that would provide the basis for development of an advanced Socialist economy. Since 1981 another 2.1 million have been resettled.

In addition to this migration within the country, since the war there has been a substantial outflow of Vietnamese fleeing to other countries. About 150,000 were evacuated from the south in the final weeks of the war, many of them eventually settling in the United States. There were 593,213 people of Vietnamese ancestry in the US in 1990. In 1978, a new exodus began after the government nationalized all private trade and manufacturing in the country. During 1978–87, an estimated 1 million Vietnamese fled by sea to other countries in Southeast Asia, or overland to China. Many later resettled in Australia, France, the US, and other countries. From 1979 to 1984, 59,730 persons emigrated legally through the US Orderly Departure Program; this program was suspended by the Vietnamese government in 1986 but later resumed, with 57,000 emigrating to the US in 1993 alone. In 1984, the US started a program that offered asylum to Vietnamese political prisoners and all Asian-American children. This program was restarted in September 1987. Between 1975 and 1984, about 554,000 persons, known as the "boat people," emigrated illegally. In 1992, Viet Nam signed agreements with the UK providing for the forcible repatriation of almost all the 55,700 "boat people" remaining in Hong Kong. The major refugee community was in China, which was harboring 285,500 Vietnamese of Chinese ancestry at the end of 1992.

8ETHNIC GROUPS

About 87% of the population of the SRV is composed of ethnic Vietnamese. The racial origins of the Vietnamese are obscure, although many scholars believe they represent a mixture of Australoid peoples who lived in mainland Southeast Asia during the Stone Age with Mongoloid peoples who migrated into the area from southern China.

In addition to the ethnic Vietnamese, there are 53 other ethnic groups living in the SRV. Many, like the Tay, the Thai, the Nung, the Rhadé, and the Jarai, are nomadic tribal peoples living in the mountainous areas of the Central Highlands and along the Sino-Vietnamese border. The overseas Chinese (Hoa) are descendants of peoples who migrated into the area in recent centuries. The Cham and the Khmer are remnants of past civilizations that controlled the southern parts of the country.

Until recently, the largest ethnic minority in the country was the overseas Chinese, numbering more than 2 million. Many have fled the country for economic or political reasons in recent years, however, and the total number remaining in the mid-1980s was estimated at just over 1 million. Other sizable minority groups, with approximate populations, are the Tay (2 million), Montagnards (1 million), Khmer (600,000), Muong (750,000), Thai (650,000), and Nung (450,000).

9 LANGUAGES

The national language of the SRV is Vietnamese (Quoc ngu). A tonal language, it bears similarities to Khmer, Thai, and Chinese, and at least one-third of the vocabulary is derived from Chinese. Formerly, Vietnamese was written in Chinese characters, but under French rule a romanized alphabet originally developed by Roman Catholic missionaries in the 17th century was adopted as the standard written form of the language. Most of the minority groups have their own spoken languages, and some have their own writing systems, but all children in the SRV today receive instruction in the national language.

10 RELIGIONS

The religion of the ethnic Vietnamese was traditionally derived from China. It was under Chinese rule that the three major religions and philosophical systems of traditional Viet Nam—Mahayana Buddhism, Taoism, and Confucianism—all entered the country. Like many Asian peoples, the Vietnamese also practiced spirit worship, a form of religious belief that was particularly prevalent among the tribal peoples.

Christianity was first brought to Viet Nam in the 17th century by Roman Catholic missionaries sponsored by the French, the Spanish, the Portuguese, or the papacy. Eventually, however, propagation of the Christian faith was forbidden by the imperial court, and Catholicism could only be practiced in secret. French priests were especially active in provoking the French decision to conquer Viet Nam in the 19th century.

Under French rule, Christianity prospered, and when Viet Nam restored its independence in 1954 there were more than 2 million Catholics in the country, a population that increased to 4.6 million in 1989. Most of the remainder of the population were at least nominally Buddhist, although two millenarian religious sects, the Cao Dai and the Hoa Hao, had become popular among peasants and townspeople in the Mekong Delta. In 1976, the Hoa Hao sect claimed 1.5 million adherents, but no later statistics are available.

Since reunification in 1975, religious activities have been restricted, although freedom of religion is formally guaranteed in the 1980 constitution. The government granted permission in 1983 for church organizations to carry on activities that correspond to official policies, but it has cracked down on dissident elements that resist state control. In 1989, approximately 56% of the population was Buddhist.

11 TRANSPORTATION

The war wreaked massive damage on Viet Nam's transportation network, especially its railways, roads, and bridges. Further damage occurred during the Chinese invasion in 1979, after which direct rail and air connections with China were severed. The nation's truck fleet is ancient and seriously lacking in spare parts. Most goods move by small barges or sampans along the countless waterways. The length of inland navigable waterways totals about 17,702 km (11,000 mi), of which 29% is navigable year-round by vessels with less than a 1.8 m draft. Major ports such as Haiphong in the north and Da Nang in the south, are frequently clogged with goods because many of the stevedores—often overseas Chinese—have fled abroad. In 1991, Viet Nam had 73 oceangoing freighters totaling 444,000 GRT, and another 8 carriers and tankers, totaling 33,000 GRT.

LOCATION: 102°10′ to 109°30′E; 8°30′ to 23°22′N. **BOUNDARY LENGTHS:** China, 1,281 km (796 mi); Cambodia, 982 km (610 mi); Laos, 1,555 km (966 mi). **COASTLINE:** 2,309 km (1,435 mi). **TERRITORIAL SEA LIMIT:** 12 mi.

Recognizing its importance to economic growth, the government is making a major effort to improve the transportation network. The railroads, with 3,059 km (1,900 mi) of track in 1991, are to be expanded. There are 50 airports with permanent-surface runways. The nation's air fleet remains primitive, as the national airline (Hang Khong Viet Nam) uses Soviet passenger liners built in the 1950s. There are 85,000 km (52,800 mi) of roads in the country, but less than 10,000 km (6,200 mi) are bituminized. The main route from Hanoi to Ho Chi Minh City badly needs improvement.

12HISTORY

During the 1st millennium BC, the Lac peoples, the ancestors of the modern-day Vietnamese, formed a Bronze Age civilization in the vicinity of the Red River Delta in northern Viet Nam. The Lac were primarily rice farmers, although those living in mountain valleys occasionally practiced the slash-and-burn agriculture now prevalent among nomadic tribes in the Central Highlands and the mountainous regions in the north. In the 3d century BC, the Vietnamese kingdom of Van Lang was conquered by a Chinese military adventurer who incorporated the Red River Delta area into his own kingdom in southern China. A century later, Viet Nam was integrated into the expanding Chinese empire. During 1,000 years of Chinese rule, Vietnamese society changed significantly as it was introduced to Chinese political and social institutions; Chinese architecture, art, and literature; and the Chinese written language. In AD 939, during a period of anarchy in China, Vietnamese rebels restored national independence.

During the next several hundred years, the Vietnamese Empire, then known as Dai Viet (Great Viet), gradually developed its own institutions and expanded steadily to the south. Under two great dynasties, the Ly (1009–1225) and the Tran (1225–1400), the Vietnamese fended off periodic attempts by China to resubjugate Viet Nam, while gradually expanding southward at the expense of their southern neighbor, Champa. In the early 15th century, Chinese rule was briefly restored, but a national uprising led by Le Loi led to the expulsion of the Chinese and the formation of an independent Le Dynasty (1428–1788). Under the Le, expansion to the south continued, and the entire Mekong River Delta came under Vietnamese rule during the 17th century. But expansion brought problems, as a weakened Le court slipped into civil war between two princely families, the Trinh in the north and the Nguyen in the south.

The division of Viet Nam into two separate political entities came at a time when European adventurers were beginning to expand their commercial and missionary activities into East and Southeast Asia. In 1771, a major peasant revolt led by the Tay Son brothers destroyed the Nguyen and the Trinh and briefly united the entire country under Emperor Nguyen Hue, ablest of the Tay Son. But a prince of the defeated Nguyen house enlisted the aid of a French Roman Catholic bishop and raised a military force that conquered the Tay Son and reunited the country under a new Nguyen Dynasty (1802–1945). When the founding emperor, Gia Long, died in 1820, his son Minh Mang refused to continue the commercial and missionary privileges granted by his predecessor to the French. In 1858, French forces attacked near Saigon and forced the defeated Vietnamese Empire to cede territory in the area to the French, which became the colony of Cochin China. In 1884, France completed its conquest of the country, establishing a protectorate over central and northern Viet Nam (now renamed Annam and Tonkin). In 1895, the three sections of Viet Nam were included with the protectorates of Laos and Cambodia into a French-ruled Indochinese Union.

The first Vietnamese attempts to resist French rule were ineffectual. Western-style nationalist movements began to form after World War I, and an Indochinese Communist Party, under the leadership of the veteran revolutionary Ho Chi Minh, was formed in 1930. After the collapse of France in World War II, Japan forced the French administration to accept a Japanese military occupation of Indochina. During the joint French-Japanese rule, Communist forces under the umbrella of the Viet-Minh Front began to organize for a national uprising at the end of the war. In March 1945, the Japanese, nearing defeat, disarmed the French and seized full administrative control over French Indochina. At the same time, the Japanese set up a puppet government, with Bao Dai, the figurehead emperor of Viet Nam, as nominal ruler. Shortly after Japan surrendered to Allied

forces in August 1945, Viet-Minh forces, led by the Indochinese Communist Party, launched the nationwide August Revolution to restore Vietnamese independence. On 2 September, President Ho Chi Minh declared the formation of an independent Democratic Republic of Viet Nam (DRV) in Hanoi. Under the Potsdam agreements, Nationalist Chinese troops occupied all of Indochina north of the 16th parallel, while British troops occupied the remainder of the old Indochinese Union. Chinese commanders permitted the Viet-Minh to remain in political control of the north, but the British assisted the French to restore their authority in the south.

In March 1946, the French and the DRV signed a preliminary agreement (the Ho-Sainteny Agreement) recognizing Viet Nam as a "free state" in the new French Union. The agreement also called for a plebiscite in Cochin China to permit the local population in that colony to determine their own future. During the summer of 1946, French and Vietnamese negotiators attempted without success to complete an agreement on the future of Viet Nam. In September, Ho Chi Minh signed a *modus vivendi* calling for renewed talks early in 1947, but military clashes between Vietnamese and French troops in the DRV led to the outbreak of war in December 1946. The Franco–Viet-Minh war lasted nearly eight years, ending in July 1954 after a successful siege of the French garrison at Dien Bien Phu by Viet-Minh forces. According to the Geneva agreement signed on 21 July, Viet Nam was temporarily partitioned along the 17th parallel, pending general elections to bring about national reunification. North of the parallel, the DRV began to build a Socialist society, while in the south, an anti-Communist government under the Roman Catholic politician Ngo Dinh Diem attempted with US aid to build a viable and independent state. In the summer of 1955, Prime Minister Diem refused to hold consultations with the DRV on elections called for by the Geneva accords. On 26 October, Diem proclaimed the Republic of Viet Nam (RVN), with its capital at Saigon. In a referendum held three days earlier, Diem had defeated ex-Emperor Bao Dai, and in 1956, Diem became president of the RVN under a new constitution written with US support. With the Geneva accords thus abrogated, Vietnamese guerrillas, supported by the DRV, initiated low-level political and military activities to destabilize the Saigon regime. Their efforts were assisted by Diem's own shortcomings, as he brutally suppressed all political opposition and failed to take effective measures to bring to an end the unequal division of landholding in South Viet Nam.

In December 1960, revolutionary forces in the south formed a National Liberation Front (NLF) to coordinate political activities against the Diem regime. Guerrilla activities by the People's Liberation Armed Forces (known in the US as the Viet-Cong) were stepped up, and Hanoi began to infiltrate trained cadres from the north to provide leadership to the revolutionary movement. Despite increasing economic and military assistance from the US, the Diem regime continued to decline, and in November 1963, Diem was overthrown by a military coup waged with the complicity of US President John F. Kennedy's administration, which had watched in dismay as Diem had alienated Buddhist elements by his open favoritism to fellow Roman Catholics. A Military Revolutionary Council, led by the popular southern general Duong Van (Big) Minh, was formed in Saigon. General Minh promised to continue efforts to defeat the insurgency movement in the south but was unable to reverse the growing political anarchy in Saigon. Early in 1964, he was replaced by another military junta. During the next 15 months, a number of governments succeeded each other, while the influence of the NLF, assisted by growing numbers of regular troops that were infiltrating from the north, steadily increased in the countryside. By early 1965, US intelligence was warning that without US intervention, South Viet Nam could collapse within six months.

Beginning in February 1965, US President Lyndon Johnson took two major steps to reverse the situation in South Viet Nam. American combat troops were introduced in growing numbers into the south, while a campaign of heavy bombing raids was launched on military and industrial targets in the north. In Saigon, the political situation stabilized with the seizure of power by a group of army officers led by Nguyen Van Thieu and Nguyen Cao Ky. Encouraged by the US, the new military regime drafted a constitution, and in elections held in September 1967, Gen. Thieu was elected president of the country. By 1967, US troop strength in South Viet Nam had reached over 500,000, while US air strikes over DRV territory were averaging about 100 sorties a day. The Hanoi regime attempted to match the US escalation by increasing infiltration of North Vietnamese military units into the south, but under the sheer weight of US firepower, the revolution began to lose momentum, and morale was ebbing.

On 30 January 1968, in an effort to reverse the military decline on the battlefield and encourage the growing popular discontent with the war in the US, Hanoi launched the Tet Offensive, a massive effort to seize towns and villages throughout the south. The attempt to seize Saigon or force the collapse of the Saigon regime failed to achieve its objective, but the secondary aim of undermining support for the war in the US succeeded. President Johnson canceled plans to increase the US military commitment and agreed to pursue a political settlement. To bring about negotiations with Hanoi, a complete bombing halt was ordered on 1 November, just before the US presidential election that brought Richard M. Nixon to office as the new Republican president. President Nixon announced a policy of "Vietnamization," according to which US forces would be gradually withdrawn and the bulk of the fighting in the south would be taken over by RVN forces. On 30 April 1970, in order to destroy enemy sanctuaries beyond the South Vietnamese border, US and South Vietnamese forces invaded neutral Cambodia. The invasion backfired, however, stimulating the rise of revolutionary activities by the Hanoi-supported Cambodian Communist movement and arousing protests in the US that the war was being expanded. The withdrawal of US military forces continued, and in March 1972, the DRV attempted to test the capability of the South Vietnamese forces by launching a direct offensive across the 17th parallel. The "Easter Offensive" succeeded in capturing the provincial capital of Quang Tri, but further gains were prevented by the resumption of US bombing raids.

By this time, both sides were willing to compromise to bring the war to an end; on 26 October 1972, the DRV announced that the secret talks between US Secretary of State Henry Kissinger and its representative, Le Duc Tho, had produced a tentative agreement. Hanoi agreed to recognize the political authority of President Nguyen Van Thieu in Saigon, while the US agreed to complete the withdrawal of US forces without demanding the removal of existing North Vietnamese troops in the south. The negotiations briefly ran aground in late autumn, leading President Nixon to order an intensive bombing assault on the DRV, but the talks resumed in early January, and the Paris Agreement was formally signed on 27 January 1973.

The Paris Agreement and the withdrawal of US forces by no means signaled the end of the conflict. Clashes between revolutionary forces and South Vietnamese units continued in the south, while provisions for a political settlement quickly collapsed. In January 1975, North Vietnamese forces in the south launched a major military offensive in the Central Highlands. When South Vietnamese resistance in the area disintegrated, further attacks were launched farther to the north, and by late March the entire northern half of the country was in North Vietnamese hands. President Thieu resigned on 21 April, but his

successor, Gen. Duong Van Minh, was unable to achieve a negotiated settlement. The capital of the RVN, Saigon, was occupied by North Vietnamese troops on 30 April. Thus ended a war in which some 2,000,000 Vietnamese and more than 56,000 Americans were killed and an estimated 4,000,000 people were injured. In the DRV, US bombing was estimated to have destroyed 70% of the industrial plant; in the RVN, more than 4 million were homeless. During the 1950–74 period, total US economic and military aid to Viet Nam was $23.9 billion (including $16.1 billion in direct military aid), representing the largest bilateral assistance program in modern history. Chinese aid to the DRV (according to intelligence estimates) probably averaged over $200 million a year. No complete figures are available on the extent of Soviet assistance to the DRV, but some scholars estimate it at about $1 billion annually.

During the next 15 months, the DRV moved to complete national reunification of north and south. Nationwide elections for a new National Assembly were held on 25 April 1976. On 24 June, the first Assembly of the unified country met and proclaimed the establishment on 2 July of the Socialist Republic of Viet Nam (SRV), with its capital remaining at Hanoi. In December, the Communist Party, known as the Vietnamese Workers' Party since 1951, was renamed the Vietnamese Communist Party. The NLF was dissolved into a nationwide Fatherland Front for the entire country. The nation's Communist leadership, with Le Duan the general secretary of the Communist Party and Pham Van Dong the prime minister, remained unchanged, while loyal members of the revolutionary movement in the south were given positions of prominence at the national level. Ton Duc Thang, figurehead president of the DRV after the death of Ho Chi Minh in 1969, remained in that position until his death in 1980.

Economic reconstruction and the building of a fully Socialist society proved more difficult than reunification. Nationalization of industry and collectivization of agriculture had been achieved in the north in the late 1950s, but the south proved more resistant to official efforts to end private enterprise after 1975. When the regime attempted to destroy the remnants of capitalism and private farming in the south in 1978, thousands fled, and the economy entered a period of severe crisis. Its problems were magnified by the outbreak of war with China. In December 1978, Vietnamese forces had invaded neighboring Kampuchea (known as Cambodia until 1976 and again from 1989) to overthrow the anti-Vietnamese government of the revolutionary Pol Pot. A pro-Vietnamese government was installed in early January 1979. China, which had been supporting Pol Pot to retain its own influence in Southeast Asia, mounted a punitive invasion of North Viet Nam in February 1979. After a short but bitter battle that caused severe casualties on both sides, the Chinese forces withdrew across the border. China, however, continued to support guerrilla operations led by Pol Pot against the current government in Kampuchea (known as Cambodia until 1976 and again from 1989).

During the 1980s, the SRV attempted to recover from its economic crisis. Party leaders worked out a compromise permitting the survival of a small private sector while maintaining a program of gradual Socialist transformation. With the death of Le Duan in June 1986, a new leadership emerged under General Secretary Nguyen Van Linh at the Sixth National Party Congress. This leadership promised a new "openness" in political affairs and a policy of economic renovation (doi moi) to improve the livelihood of the population. A strong conservative coalition of party leaders seriously reduced Linh's effectiveness as they stressed the dangers of political liberalization and slowed the pace of economic reform. In March 1988 Prime Minister Pham Hung died, and Linh's choice of a conservative replacement, Do Muoi, was a clear concession to these groups.

Economic recovery continued to be difficult due to a serious lack of investment capital, resources, and technical skills. The SRV's internal problems were compounded by the continuing dispute with China. To protect itself from Chinese intimidation, Hanoi had formed a military alliance with the USSR and was deeply dependent upon Soviet economic assistance. The continuing civil war in Kampuchea (known as Cambodia until 1976 and again from 1989) also represented a steady drain on the SRV's slender resources and prevented foreign economic assistance, particularly from the US. In December 1988 the constitution was amended to remove derogatory references to the US, China, France and Japan, as an attempt to improve international relations. In August 1991 Do Muoi resigned as prime minister. His successor Vo Van Kiet favored free-market reforms. A new constitution was adopted by the National Assembly in April 1992. A general election took place in July 1992 and, for the first time, independent candidates were allowed to present themselves, but neither of the two deemed qualified were elected. On 23 September 1992, the National Assembly elected Lu Duc Anh as president and reelected Vo Van Kiet as prime minister. In 1994, it was rumored that Do Muoi, Communist Party leader, probably would retire in 1996. The aging Party leadership wants political change and a free economy without ending their rule—that is, communist rule combined with capitalist development.

Since the sixth party congress in December 1986, Viet Nam attempted to open and run its economy in a more rational and less political manner, and to adjust its international relations to reflect the evolving international economic and political situation in Southeast Asia. In January 1989 the first direct talks between Viet Nam and China since 1979 resulted in Viet Nam's agreement to withdraw its troops from Cambodia by the end of September 1989 and China's agreement to end aid to the Khmer Rouge guerrillas once the Vietnamese withdrawal has been achieved. Later, Viet Nam insisted that the withdrawal was contingent on the end of all foreign military aid to factions opposing Cambodian Prime Minister Hun Sen. Hanoi hoped to use the September 1989 withdrawal of its troops from Cambodia as leverage for improved relations with Association for Southeast Asian Nations (ASEAN), Japan, and the West. On 23 October 1991 a Cambodian peace agreement was signed, paving the way for Viet Nam's eventual entry into ASEAN.

Viet Nam has also stepped up its efforts to attract foreign capital from the West and regularize relations with the world financial system. Issues that affect these processes are the status and repatriation of Vietnamese refugees; border and troop withdrawal disputes with Cambodia, Thailand, and the People's Republic of China; conflicts over the Spratly and Paracel island groups in the South China Sea; conflicts with the US over the recovery of the remains of US soldiers missing-in-action (MIA); and Vietnamese cooperation in a diplomatic settlement in Cambodia. In October 1991 Viet Nam agreed to accept the forced repatriation of Vietnamese refugees—known as boat people—who have been designated economic migrants, not seekers of political asylum. These Indochinese boat people were in camps around Asia from 1975–1994. The "comprehensive plan of action" adopted by the UN High Commission for Refugees in 1989 reduced the number of boat people fleeing Viet Nam and Laos. In 1994, the Commission reached a final solution regarding the fate of those still living in camps: all were to be repatriated. The refugees in the camps outside Viet Nam and Laos were judged to be economic migrants and not political refugees; repatriation could be voluntary, or would be forcible. A new category, "non-objectors," was also established for those refugees who neither voluntarily returned to Viet Nam, nor actively refused to be repatriated. The result was the same—repatriation—after up to 19 years as refugees. The last 60,000 Vietnamese and 26,000

Laotians were scheduled to be resettled or back home by the end of 1995.

In June 1992, Viet Nam announced that all South Vietnamese officials had been released from reeducation camps, a US-mandated prerequisite for lifting its embargo against Viet Nam. As a result, on 3 February 1994 President Bill Clinton lifted the US trade embargo against Viet Nam. Before the embargo was lifted, US policy had permitted businesses to establish offices and investments in Viet Nam, but not to profit from them. At the time Clinton lifted the embargo, there were still 2,238 US servicemen listed as missing. Viet Nam agreed to cooperate with their recovery to the "fullest possible extent."

The US State Department *Country Report on Human Rights: Practices for 1993* notes that Viet Nam continues arbitrary arrest and detention of citizens. In contradiction to assertions of commitment to the cause of human rights, authorities continue to severely limit freedom of speech, press, assemblage and association, workers' rights, and rights of citizens to change their government. With the decline of the USSR in 1990 and 1991, its economic assistance to Viet Nam declined. After the dissolution of the USSR, the government of the newly independent Russia assured the Vietnamese government that close economic relations would be maintained. In January 1993, Viet Nam agreed to allow Russian vessels continued use of the former Soviet naval base at Cam Rahn.

The controversy between the People's Republic of China and the SRV over the control of the Spratly and Paracel archipelagoes in the South China Sea dates to the early part of this century. After the Viet Nam War, when oil supplies became an issue, the dispute intensified, leading to numerous armed clashes between China and Viet Nam. Viet Nam, China, the Philippines, Brunei, Taiwan, and Malaysia claim all or part of the Spratly and Paracel archipelagoes. These competing claims have broad geopolitical implications regarding oil reserves, fishing rights, rights of passage for ships, prevention of nuclear dumping, and security in the region. A law on territorial waters passed by China in February 1992 claimed all the islets in the South China Sea. In July 1992 Chinese soldiers landed on Da Lac in the Spratly archipelago and placed a territorial marker. In 1994, a possible solution to these contested claims was proposed. It would create a Spratly Development Authority with China and Taiwan sharing 51% of shares and the remainder divided amongst Brunei (which has the smallest claim), Viet Nam, Malaysia and the Philippines. To pave the way for this arrangement, China and Taiwan would need to set aside their "historic" claims, and China and Viet Nam to settle disputes over the Gulf of Tonkin and the Vanguard Bank area.

13 GOVERNMENT

The Communist Party-controlled government of Viet Nam has ruled under four state constitutions. The first was promulgated in 1946, the second in 1959, the third in 1980, and the fourth in 1992.

The 1946 constitution of the Democratic Republic of Viet Nam (DRV), adopted shortly before the war with the French, was never fully implemented because of wartime conditions. On 1 January 1960, a new constitution was promulgated, instituting a largely presidential system to capitalize on Ho Chi Minh's considerable prestige. In the Republic of Viet Nam (RVN), formerly South Viet Nam, two constitutions were promulgated. The first, by the regime of Ngo Dinh Diem was introduced in 1956. The second was put forth when Nguyen Van Thieu was elected president in 1967. Like the DRV constitution, it created a modified presidential system, with a cabinet responsible to the legislative branch. Following the fall of the RVN in 1975, the north moved quickly toward national reunification. A nationwide National Assembly was elected in April 1976, and the

Socialist Republic of Viet Nam was proclaimed in early July. In December 1980, the SRV adopted a new constitution for the entire country. The new charter, more doctrinaire than its predecessors, described Viet Nam as a "proletarian dictatorship" led by the Communist Party, and called for an early transition to full Socialist ownership. The highest state authority was the National Assembly. Members were elected for five-year terms by universal adult suffrage at age 18. The Assembly appointed the Council of Ministers (a cabinet of 33 ministers), the chairman of which ranked as premier. The Council of State (12 members in 1987) served as the collective presidency of Viet Nam, elected by the National Assembly from among its own members and accountable to it.

In 1992 a new constitution was adopted by the National Assembly. Like the 1980 constitution it affirmed the central role of the Communist Party, stipulating that the party must be subject to the law. In support of a free-market economy, constitutional protection of foreign investment was guaranteed. However, land remained the property of the state, with individuals or enterprises entitled to the right to long-term leases that can be inherited or sold. The newly created position of president replaced the Council of State; the president has the right to appoint a prime minister subject to the approval of the National Assembly. The National Assembly, with a maximum of 400 members, retained legislative power. Members are elected to five-year terms by universal adult suffrage.

14POLITICAL PARTIES

The government of the SRV is a de facto one-party state ruled by the Vietnamese Communist Party (VCP). In theory, two other political parties, the Democratic Party and the Socialist Party, are granted legal existence. The Vietnamese Communist Party is the political successor to the Indochinese Communist Party, created in 1930 and formally dissolved in 1945. From 1945 until 1951, the party operated in clandestine fashion, until it emerged once more as the Vietnamese Workers' Party at the Second National Congress in 1951. The party assumed its current name in 1976, shortly after the unification of the country into the Socialist Republic of Viet Nam.

The Communist Party is administered through an assembly of national delegates. National party conventions elect a Central Committee to guide party affairs between sessions of the national convention. The Central Committee in turn elects the Politburo, the highest policymaking body, and a secretariat to direct day-to-day party operations. In 1987, there were 13 members and 1 alternate in the Politburo, headed by Secretary-General Nguyen Van Linh, who replaced Truong Chinh in the post at the Sixth Congress held in December 1986. In 1987, party membership was approximately 1.85 million.

The Democratic Party, founded in 1944, is composed chiefly of intellectuals, small entrepreneurs, and merchants. The Socialist Party, formed in 1946, represents the progressive intelligentsia. The programs of these two parties are generally indistinguishable from that of the Communist Party. An additional form of quasi-political organization in Viet Nam is the United Front, composed of various functional, ethnic, and religious organizations under the umbrella of the Fatherland Front. The Fatherland Front is the linear successor of the Viet-Minh Front, formed in 1941 to provide the Communist Party with a broad organization to unify all elements in Viet Nam against the French colonial regime. The Fatherland Front was formed in North Viet-Nam in 1955 as a device to mobilize the population to support the regime's goals. A similar organization, the National Liberation Front (NLF), was established in South Viet-Nam in 1960 by Nguyen Huu Tho to provide a political force in favor of national reunification. After the fall of the RVN in 1975, the NLF was merged into the Fatherland Front.

Under the RVN government, development of a political party system in the Western sense never passed the rudimentary stage. President Thieu, who headed the People's Alliance for Social Revolution, tried to consolidate anti-Communist political organizations in the RVN through a multiparty National Social Democratic Front, but formal political organizations were weak and plagued with religious and regional sectarianism. Wartime conditions and the lack of a national tradition of political pluralism were additional factors preventing the rise of a multiparty system. All such parties were abolished after the fall of Saigon in 1975.

In the SRV, elections for national and local office are controlled by the Communist Party and the state. In the National Assembly elections in April 1981, 614 candidates—all nominated by the Fatherland Front—contested 496 seats in 93 constituencies. Those elected included 121 political cadres, 110 Socialist intellectuals, 100 workers, 92 peasants, 49 soldiers, and 24 other members. In elections held in April 1987, the regime offered more choice, with 829 candidates for 496 seats in 167 constituencies. The new Assembly included 88 women, 70 members of national minorities, 123 intellectuals, 105 farmers, 100 political cadres, 91 workers, and 49 members of the armed forces.

In the July 1992 general elections 601 candidates contested 395 National Assembly seats. For the first time independent candidates—not Communist Party members or endorsed by organizations affiliated with the Party—were permitted to contest seats. Independent candidates required Party approval in order to present themselves. Two candidates qualified, but neither was elected. A special mid-term party congress was called for January 1994 to deal with the transition of leadership to the next generation: Viet Nam Communist Party (VCP) General Secretary Du Muoi is 77, President Le Duc Anh is 73, and Prime Minister Vo Van Kiet is 71. At the congress, the Politburo was expanded to 17, the Central Committee to 161.

15LOCAL GOVERNMENT

Viet Nam is divided into 36 provinces, 1 special zone (Vung Tau–Con Dao), and 3 municipalities (Hanoi, Haiphong, and Ho Chi Minh City), all administered by the national government. Districts, towns, and villages are governed by locally elected people's councils. Council candidates are screened by the party. Council members' responsibilities include upholding the Constitution and laws and overseeing local armed forces units. The councils in turn elect and oversee executive organs, called people's committees, to provide day-to-day administration. The entire system functions in a unitary fashion, with local organs of authority directly accountable to those at higher levels.

16JUDICIAL SYSTEM

The judicial system of the SRV, as defined by the 1980 constitution, parallels that of the former DRV. The highest court in Viet Nam is the Supreme People's Court, whose members are appointed for five-year terms by the National Assembly. In addition, there are local people's courts at each administrative level; military courts; and "special courts" established by the National Assembly in certain cases. Law enforcement is handled by the People's Organs of Control; the president, or procurator-general, of this body is appointed by the National Assembly.

Although the Constitution provides for the independence of judges and jurors, there is close control of the entire governmental system by the Vietnamese Communist Party (VCP) and a judicial selection process which favors appointment of jurists supportive of the VCP. Prison sentences are frequently imposed through administrative procedures without the protections of procedural due process or judicial review.

17ARMED FORCES

Since reunification in 1975, Viet Nam has emerged as one of the world's leading military powers. As of mid-1993, the People's Army of Viet Nam was estimated at 857,000 with 65 divisions and 25–40 brigades. Of that figure, the regular army had about 700,000 personnel, the air force 15,000, the air defense force 100,000, and the navy 42,000. Reserves numbered between 500,000 and 2 million. Military service is compulsory for two or three years; members of non-Vietnamese minority groups may have to serve two years.

Military expenditures may take $2.3 million of a national income of $15 billion (1990). Military assistance from the then-Soviet Union reached $6 billion, 1987–91. Viet Nam also has substantial quantities of US military hardware, including combat aircraft, captured during the 1975 collapse of the RVN government. The naval base at Cam Ranh Bay, built by the US during the war, is now an air and naval base for Russia.

18 INTERNATIONAL COOPERATION

The SRV was admitted to UN membership on 20 September 1977. The nation belongs to ESCAP and all the nonregional specialized agencies; in mid-1983, however, Viet Nam announced that it was indefinitely suspending its participation in the ILO. Viet Nam is also a member of the Asian Development Bank, CMEA, and G-77 and is a signatory to the Law of the Sea.

By 1982, the SRV had diplomatic relations with 112 countries. Its principal ally and supporter is the Russia. Relations with China have deteriorated since 1975, as Viet Nam has moved to assert its political dominance over the remainder of Indochina. As of late 1994, the SRV does not have diplomatic relations with the US, although progress is being made toward normalization. President Bill Clinton has taken steps to normalize relations in the areas of economic development and trade.

19 ECONOMY

Wet-rice agriculture is the most important segment of the Vietnamese economy, and approximately 73% of the population was engaged in agriculture in 1986. The most diversified area in Southeast Asia in terms of mineral resources, Viet Nam is well endowed with coal, tin, tungsten, gold, iron, manganese, chromium, and antimony. Cement, textiles, silk, matches, and paper are the main industrial products. Most of the nation's mineral resources are located in the north, while the south is a major producer of rice and tropical agricultural products, such as rubber, coffee, and tea. The war took its heaviest economic toll on Viet Nam's infrastructure, which even in the best of times was far from adequate to afford access to and mobilization of the country's agricultural and industrial resources. Further setbacks came in the late 1970s. According to official sources, in 1978 floods destroyed 3 million tons of rice, submerged over 1 million hectares (2.5 million acres) of cultivated land, and killed 20% of all cattle in the affected areas along the central coast. The termination of all Chinese aid in the same year, followed by the Chinese attack on the north in February–March 1979, dealt the economy further blows. Viet Nam's economy had already been weakened by the military effort in Kampuchea (known as Cambodia until 1976 and again after 1989) and by the suspension of food aid from the EC, the UK, Australia, and New Zealand because of objections to Viet Nam's refugee policies. Reportedly, the country came close to general famine in 1979, and industrial production grew at a rate of only 0.6% from 1976 to 1980.

In 1976, the regime announced a five-year plan, calling for rapid industrialization and Socialist transformation by the end of the decade. In 1979, faced with serious shortages of food and consumer goods, Vietnamese leaders approved a new program granting incentives for increased productivity and delaying the construction of farm collectives in the southern provinces. During the 1981–85 five-year plan, emphasis was placed on agriculture

and the production of consumer goods. As a result, economic performance improved in the early 1980s, with the growth rate estimated at about 10% annually. Price inflation, however, became a major problem, averaging 700% in 1986–87. The SRV remains heavily dependent upon imports from Russia and carries an enormous debt to the former USSR and other Socialist countries. The economic decline of the USSR phased down this aid and trade to the SRV, the full impact occurring in 1991. The Sixth National Party Congress (1986) and the appointment of Nguyen Van Linh, with his campaign for political and economic renewal (doi moi), to party leadership marked changes in the SRV's domestic and foreign policy.

The SRV's efforts at a transition from a state-controlled economy to a free-market-oriented economy has occurred in a political environment that rejects political pluralism. Motivated by a fear of being left behind economically, the government of Viet Nam simultaneously fears the consequences of rapid development and accompanying social deterioration. It also does not want to abandon its socialist base, and fears any forces that promote increased democratization. Policy changes have been introduced incrementally. In 1992, per capita GNP was estimated at US$230, which is low by world standards. Nevertheless, in 1994 Viet Nam enjoys benefits from its sustained economic policies: decontrolled prices, currency control, and increased private sector activity. The results are growth, low inflation, and increased foreign investment.

The tourism industry is growing: there were 170,000 visitors in 1990, 250,000 in 1991; 325,000 in 1992; and doubled in 1993 to 650,000. The Viet Nam Post and Telecommunications Company announced the completion of a national communications network linking all 53 provinces of the country in 1994. In Hanoi, the increased presence of a foreign community is spurring the availability of western-style restaurants and bars, hotel and airport renovation and upgrading, accessible public telephones, and advertising of consumer goods. On 3 February 1994 US President Bill Clinton lifted the thirty-year-old US trade embargo against Viet Nam.

If Viet Nam's economy is to experience sustained growth, massive improvements to transport and communications infrastructure, combined with industrial development and expansion of the export sector, are needed. Party leadership, moreover, is concerned about growing unemployment (estimated to be over 25%), the widening gap between rich and poor, bankruptcy, prostitution, and corruption. Several factors contributed to Viet Nam's growing unemployment in the early 1990s: natural increases in the population; monetary and other adjustments for hyperinflation, which intensified the unemployment problem by limiting growth in some sectors of the economy; the return of demobilized troops from Cambodia; repatriation of refugees; workers laid off from state enterprises; and returning guest workers. However, with capital investment, this labor force is a resource for growth in labor-intensive manufacturing, considering the low wage base in Viet Nam, the good skill levels, and high motivation.

20 INCOME

In 1992 the GDP was $16 billion in current US dollars. It is estimated that agriculture, hunting, forestry, and fishing contributed 41% to GDP; manufacturing, 20%; construction, 3%; wholesale and retail trade, 12%; transport, storage, and communication, 4%; finance, insurance, real estate, and business services, 11%; community, social, and personal services, 9%; and other sources, 1%.

21 LABOR

The total employed labor force in the SRV was estimated at about 28.7 million persons by 1990. Of this total, 71% worked in agriculture, about 13% in industry and construction, 9% in trade, transportation, and communications, and 7% in services. Open unemployment has recently become a problem and is further exacerbated by the army's planned demobilization of over 500,000 troops in the near future. However, a more prominent role given to private enterprise has the potential to leading to substantial job opportunity increases. Unemployment estimates as of 1991 ranged from 5 to 20%, with the number of unemployed rising.

The Tong Cong Doan Viet Nam trade union, founded in 1946 and merged with the South Viet-Nam Trade Union Federation for Liberation, is the largest labor organization. As of 1992, Vietnamese workers were not free to form or join unions. The government-controlled Confederation of Vietnamese Workers is the sole labor organization, and all workers automatically become members of the union of their workplace. Strikes and collective bargaining are prohibited, and citizens allegedly are required by law to give 15 days of work per year to the state or pay a fee.

22AGRICULTURE

Nearly 70% of the total population of the SRV derives its livelihood from agriculture; arable land in 1992 was 6,380,000 hectares (15,770,000 acres), of which 1,100,000 hectares (2,718,000 acres) were in permanent crops.

Only about 15% of the land in the north is arable, and 14% of it is already under intensive cultivation. Agriculture in the north is concentrated in the lowland areas of the Red River Delta and along the central coast to the south. The Mekong Delta, among the great rice-producing regions of the world, is the dominant agricultural region of the south. Excess grain from the area is shipped to the northern parts of the country. Annual food-grain production averaged 20 million tons in the early 1990s, reaching 22.1 million tons in 1992.

Rice, the main staple of the Vietnamese diet, accounted for 44% of agricultural exports and 17% of total exports in 1992. In the north, two and in some cases three crops a year are made possible through an extensive system of irrigation, utilizing upward of 4,000 km (2,500 mi) of dikes. Single-cropping remains the rule in the south, where heavy rains fall for six months of the year and virtually no rain at all during the other six months. The southern region's extensive network of canals is used mainly for transport and drainage, although some irrigational use was attempted under the RVN government. Rice production between 1975 and 1980 was adversely affected by bad weather and the regime's attempt to promote collectivization, but it began to rebound during the early 1980s. In 1980, 11.7 million tons of paddy rice were produced; output rose to 16.2 million tons in 1985 and to 19.2 million tons in 1990.

Other crops include corn, sorghum, cassava, sweet potatoes, beans, fruits, and vegetables. In 1992, estimated production (in thousands of tons) was sugarcane, 5,900; corn, 660; groundnuts in shell, 215; and soybeans, 87. Rubber, formerly a major crop and a leading source of foreign exchange, was grown mostly on large plantations organized under the French colonial regime. As a result of the Viet Nam war, practically all of the large plantations in the "redlands" area in the south were shut down, and damage to the trees was severe. In 1975, the SRV announced that rubber workers had resumed the extraction of latex from hundreds of thousands of rubber trees on plantations north and northwest of Ho Chi Minh City, most of which had lain fallow for years. Rubber production was given high priority by the Hanoi regime and increased from 40,000 tons in 1975 to 65,000 tons in 1992. Other industrial and export crops produced in Viet Nam include coffee, tea, tobacco, pepper, and jute. In 1992, 65,000 tons of coffee, 35,000 tons of tea, 30,000 tons of jute, 28,000 tons of tobacco, and 11,200 tons of pepper were harvested.

Agriculture in the north has reached an advanced stage of collectivization. A land-reform program completed in 1956 distributed 810,000 hectares (2,002,000 acres) to 2,104,000 peasant families. The share of the Socialist sector in agricultural land increased from 1% in 1955 to 95% in 1975. By 1977, the north had 15,200 agricultural cooperatives and 105 state farms.

In the south, rapid collectivization began in 1978, when the regime announced a program to place the majority of southern farmers in low-level cooperative organizations by the end of the 1976–80 five-year plan. Popular resistance was extensive, however, and by 1981, less than 10% of the rural population was enrolled in full-scale collectives and a roughly equal number in low-level, semi-Socialist production solidarity teams and production collectives.

In an effort to make collectivization more palatable, the regime announced a "household contract" system, permitting members of cooperatives to lease collective land in return for an agreed proportion of total output. This system apparently encouraged many peasants to join cooperative organizations, and the regime announced in mid-1986 that collectivization at the low level had been "basically completed" in the south, with 86.4% of the rural population enrolled in some form of collective organization. As of 1985, there were more than 15,600 agricultural cooperatives nationwide.

23ANIMAL HUSBANDRY

The most important aspect of animal husbandry in the SRV remains the raising of draft animals, mainly water buffalo. Lack of feed, shelter, and technical guidance and an inability to control disease combine with the legacy of war damage to hinder the growth of this sector. Increasing the livestock is now a major priority of the Hanoi regime. The sizes of herds in 1992 (with 1975 figures in parentheses) was as follows: hogs, 12,140,000 (8,800,700); buffalo, 3,135,000 (2,193,000); and cattle 2,867,000 (1,485,000).

24FISHING

Fresh and dried fish and fish sauce (known as nuoc mam) are major ingredients of the Vietnamese diet, and fishing is an important occupation. Shrimp, lobster, and more than 50 commercial species of fish are found in Vietnamese waters. Ha Long Bay, the major fishing area of the north, is particularly rich in shrimp and crayfish. Fish also abound in Viet Nam's rivers and canals.

The fishing industry was severely depleted after the Viet Nam war, when many fishermen (often overseas Chinese) fled the country. The government has recently ordered a serious effort to increase marine production into a major export industry. In 1991, ocean production was estimated at 610,000 tons, and inland production was estimated at 267,000 tons.

25FORESTRY

In 1991, forests covered 29% of the total land area of Viet Nam. Important forestry products include bamboo, resins, lacquer, quinine, turpentine, and pitch. Depletion of forests, however, has been serious, not only through US defoliation campaigns in the south during the war, but also because of the slash-and-burn techniques used by nomadic tribal groups in mountainous areas.

According to Western scientists who have visited the SRV in recent years, the damaged areas are recovering faster than anticipated, although reforestation has been slow and some regions are faced with sterility and erosion. Official policy currently emphasizes the replacement of natural forests with export crops such as cinnamon, aniseed, rubber, coffee, and bamboo. Roundwood production was estimated at 29,525,000 cu m in 1991.

26MINING

Viet Nam has some important mineral resources. The principal reserves, located mainly in the north, are anthracite coal, antimony, tin, chrome, apatite, phosphate, manganese, titanium, bauxite, copper, zinc, lead, nickel, graphite, mica, and some gold. Iron reserves are estimated at 250 million tons and apatite reserves at more than 1.7 billion tons. Coal production dominates the mining sector. In 1991, estimated exports amounted to 783,000 tons of coal, or 25% of domestic production. The coal mines at Hong Gai, near Haiphong, are the most important in Southeast Asia. There is also a small coal-producing region in central Viet Nam. Coal output has been seriously hindered by technical difficulties and the exodus of trained workers; according to official sources, coal production declined from 5.2 million tons in 1975 to 4 million tons in 1991. Output of chromium ore declined from 10,400 to 3,500 tons during the same period.

27ENERGY AND POWER

Lack of energy is one of Viet Nam's major obstacles to economic development. While coal output is substantial, most of it has been reserved for export. Until the late 1970s, the nation had no proved oil reserves, and hydroelectric power, while showing considerable potential, was poorly developed.

Since the end of the war, the regime has announced a number of major projects to provide the nation with sufficient energy resources. Several hydroelectric power stations are currently under construction, and some are already in operation. Hydropower accounts for about one-sixth of the annual electrical output. Net electric generating capacity in 1991 was 1,645,000 kw; in 1991, 8,550 million kwh was generated.

In February 1975, the Mobil Oil Company, a US firm, struck oil off the southern coast, producing an initial outflow of 2,400 barrels per day. By mid-April, however, US oil firms—which had invested some $100 million in oil exploration in the RVN—had left the country. The SRV granted permission for several foreign companies to resume the search for oil, and in 1976 private concerns from the US, Japan, France, Canada, and the UK were quietly involved in negotiations to resume exploration. Offshore oil was also discovered by Soviet geologists working the Gulf of Tonkin. In the late 1970s, Western firms abandoned their explorations because of unpromising results, but the USSR continued its efforts and began to achieve promising results in late 1984. In September 1992, Viet Nam demanded that China immediately withdraw all oil exploration ships from disputed waters in the Gulf of Tonkin. In April 1994, Mobil Corporation signed a production-sharing contract to explore for oil off the southern coast of Viet Nam, becoming the first American company to drill in Vietnamese waters since 1975. Proven oil reserves as of 1 January 1993 totaled 500 million barrels; production in 1992 amounted to 110,000 barrels per day. In 1992, exports of petroleum accounted for $2.5 billion, or 33% of total exports. Natural gas is believed to exist throughout much of northern Viet Nam; reserves are estimated at 14 billion cu m (500 billion cu ft).

28INDUSTRY

Like most countries in Southeast Asia, the SRV has a small and relatively primitive industrial sector. Most heavy and medium industry is concentrated in the north, including the state-owned coal, tin, chrome, and other mining enterprises; an engineering works at Hanoi; power stations; and modern tobacco, tea, and canning factories. The industrial sector in the south is characterized by light industry and consumer goods industry, including pharmaceuticals, textiles, and food processing, although there are some large utilities and cement works. Much of the industrial sector in the north was badly damaged by US bombing raids during the war, including the Thai Nguyen steel complex

(the target of over 120 bombing raids); chemical, sugar-refining, and pulping mills at the Viet Tri light industry complex; and the cement works in Haiphong. Lack of resources and inadequate technology have hindered official efforts to promote industrial growth in the north. In the south, the private sector was permitted to continue in operation after 1975, but all industry and commerce above the family level was nationalized in March 1978. The results were disastrous, and the regime now permits the existence of a small private sector, mainly in the area of consumer goods and other light industry. The results have been generally favorable; industrial production in the 1980s has increased at an average annual rate of 9.5%, as compared with a rate of 0.6% between 1976 and 1980. The rate for 1984/85 was reported to be 14.4%. According to official sources, industrial production in 1986 provided 38% of the GNP. Lack of capital, shortage of power, and managerial inefficiency continue to be serious obstacles to future growth, however.

This situation continues into the 1990s with industrial production burdened by uncompetitive state-owned enterprises the government is unwilling or unable to privatize. The industrial sector is still marked by inefficiency and low productivity. This is due the low level of development, characterized by obsolete plants and machinery, shortages of capital, raw materials, energy and transport, and a command-style economic system. In 1992, the growth rate for industrial production was 15% and accounted for 30% of GNP, largely due to increases in the output of oil. Viet Nam's assets include low wages, good skill levels, and a motivated work force.

Output of selected major industries during the period from 1975–1991 are given in the following table, in metric tons.

PRODUCT	1975	1984	1991
Cement	536,600	1,296,500	3,127,100
Paper	41,700	69,500	108,800
Beer	76,800,000	91,500,000	—
Finished cloth	146,400,00	364,300,000	280,400,000
Chemical fertilizer	447,000	422,000	450,300
Bricks (million)	3,135,000	2,907,000	3,769,500
Steel production	36,000	53,000 [1985]	141,000

Industrial production for 1975, 1984, and 1991 reflected the changing structure of the SRV's economy and outputs, which added to the perception in the mid- to late-1980s that "renovation" was essential.

29SCIENCE AND TECHNOLOGY

Science and technology have been one of the key weak spots in the Vietnamese economy and were targeted for significant growth during the second five-year plan (1976–80). As of 1994, there are few signs of improvement. Viet Nam's leading learned societies are the Union of Scientific and Technical Associations and the General Association of Medicine. The State Commission for Science and Technology supervises research at the universities and institutes attached to the Ministry of Higher Education; the Institute of Science organizes research at other institutions. All research institutes are attached to government ministries.

In 1985, total expenditures on research and development amounted to D498 million; 20,000 scientists and engineers were engaged in research and development.

30DOMESTIC TRADE

Since 1975, the SRV has been attempting to abolish the private commercial sector and transform it along Socialist lines. In the south, private merchants were initially encouraged to form either cooperative enterprises or joint private-state enterprises in which a substantial proportion of the capital and management was provided by the state. The results were somewhat disappointing, and in March 1978, 30,000 shops above the family level were nationalized in the southern cities. The results were disastrous, and since 1979, the regime has permitted the existence of a private commercial sector, mainly in southern cities as Ho Chi Minh City and Da Nang. Official policy, however, continues to encourage gradual Socialist transformation of the private commercial sector throughout the country. The policy of gradual transformation has had only modest success. There is a serious shortage of consumer goods throughout the country, particularly in the north.

By 1984, the state was forced to concede that it lacked the ability to handle the circulation of goods and began to ease restrictions on private trade and to provide tax breaks and bank loans, but official policy alternated between restrictive and liberal approaches. To encourage the flow of goods from the relatively affluent south into the north, checkpoints set up along the major highways to collect commercial taxes were abolished in 1987.

Two macroeconomic problems were severe between 1985 and 1988: hyperinflation and shortages of the major food crop, rice. The ambitious program of "renovation" launched in 1989 had immediate results. Reforms included decentralizing economic decision-making and liberalizing prices. From shortages and hoarding of rice, Viet Nam became the third largest rice exporter in 1989. Runaway inflation, 700% in 1986, was reduced to feasible levels by mid-1989. With increasing wealth and foreign demand the property market, construction throughout the country (but especially in Hanoi), and real estate sales and rentals in Hanoi and Ho Chi Minh City (formerly Saigon), experienced a boom in 1991–92. In 1991, private-enterprise and company laws were adopted by the National Assembly. In late 1991, only 76 private enterprises had registered, but by January 1993 some 4,403 private concerns made application. It is estimated that private entrepreneurs account for 70% of domestic trade. Consumer items, durable, and non-durable goods, are available in greater abundance. The government has banned the use of foreign imagery in advertising by placing restrictions on foreign language, landscapes, models for outdoor advertising.

31FOREIGN TRADE

As separate entities in the post-World War II period, neither the DRV nor the RVN succeeded in establishing a viable foreign-trade balance. Profound disruptions in production and transportation brought about by the Viet Nam War accompanied an intrinsic liability imposed by each side's inaccessibility to the other's resources and capacities. The north had never produced enough rice to support its population and, until 1954, had relied heavily on supplies from the Mekong Delta. The south, while traditionally a net exporter of rice and rubber, lacked both the raw materials and the industrial plant to sustain industrial growth. During the war, both the DRV and the RVN were heavily dependent on their allies for assistance in sustaining their economies and maintaining the standard of living of the population. Neither was able to pay for such assistance through exports. In consequence, both countries suffered chronic balance-of-payments difficulties with their trading partners, the DRV with the Socialist community (which represented an estimated 85% to 90% of total DRV trade) and the RVN with the US and other countries in the West or in non-Communist Asia.

In the RVN, exports never exceeded about 20% of the annual value of imports. In 1968, they represented only about 2.5% of the total value of imports, recovering to only 8.2% by 1973. Formerly a rice exporter, the RVN had to import rice after the mid-1960s. The postcolonial low in exports—due to war—was reached in 1968; exports in that year were limited to 25,600 tons of rubber and small quantities of fish, tea, duck feathers, and cin-

namon. In 1972, RVN exports totaled $13,313,000, while imports reached $706,904,000—leaving a deficit of $693,591,000. The shortfall was covered by large-scale US economic assistance, principally in the form of grants.

Since reunification, the SRV has attempted with little success to address this chronic problem. Hopes for large-scale assistance were quickly disappointed as the Western nations and China cut their aid programs to Viet Nam because of political differences with the regime. Soviet aid continued at a high level, but not enough to take up the slack. In order to reduce its chronic trade deficit, mainly with Socialist countries, the SRV has attempted to increase exports and to expand its trade relations with other countries in Asia. Beginning in 1980, emphasis was placed on the development of potential export commodities such as cash crops, marine products, and handicrafts, while imports were severely limited. To promote trade expansion with such countries as Japan, Singapore, and Hong Kong, several export-import firms were set up in Ho Chi Minh City under loose official supervision. The results were favorable, resulting in record exports of $595 million in 1981, but the experiment aroused distrust among conservative party leaders, and the freewheeling enterprises were integrated into a single firm strictly supervised by the government.

Today, the SRV's foreign trade difficulties continue. According to official sources, exports in 1986 totaled about $800 million, while imports were nearly $1 billion. Three-quarters of that trade was with the USSR and other Council for Mutual Economic Assistance (CMEA) countries. Thousands of Vietnamese worked in the USSR and Eastern Europe. Part of their salaries (according to unofficial sources, usually about 50%) was remitted to the Vietnamese government.

The economic reforms of the late-1980s in Viet Nam, including currency devaluation, adoption of a flexible exchange rate system, and lifting restrictions on foreign trade contributed to the rapid growth in exports in the early 1990s. Investments in Viet Nam are contributing to the development and/or expansion of tourism, telecommunications, and international shipping connections.

Export commodities in 1992 were agricultural and handicraft products, coal, minerals, crude oil, ores, and seafood. Major exports were rice and crude oil, accounting for about half of 1992 exports. In 1992, Singapore was Viet Nam's largest trading partner. Other major trading partners were Japan, Thailand, Hong Kong, and Taiwan. Import commodities in 1992 were petroleum and steel products, railroad equipment, chemicals, medicines, raw cotton, fertilizer, and grain. Major trading partners were Japan, Singapore, and Thailand. After December 1994, the International Civil Aviation Organization decided to restore Viet Nam's air control over two-thirds of the South China Sea.

32BALANCE OF PAYMENTS

Major increases in rice and crude oil exports in the late 1980s have helped improve the balance of trade. In 1991, imports exceeded exports by $2.2 billion, up from a trade deficit of $1.9 billion in 1990. The current account deficit remained relatively unchanged from 1990 to 1991, at $1.7 billion.

Viet Nam's foreign trade balance had been dominated by transactions with non-convertible currency countries, several of which, however, now require hard-currency payment. Foreign investment is constricted by infrastructural problems. A more uniform and flexible exchange rate policy is expected to help increase exports.

33BANKING AND SECURITIES

The State Bank of Viet Nam, created in 1951, was the central bank of issue for the DRV, with numerous branches throughout the territory and an extensive agricultural and industrial loan service; in 1976, it became the central bank of the SRV. Foreign exchange is regulated by the Foreign Trade Bank. The Bank for Agricultural Development provides loans to the agricultural and fishing sectors.

Financial chaos became a constant threat during the final years of the RVN. The National Bank of Viet Nam (NBV), established in 1954, was the sole authority for issuing notes, controlling credit, and supervising the formation of new banks and changes in banking establishments.

In early May 1975, shortly after the fall of Saigon, the new revolutionary regime announced the temporary closure of all banks in the south, although the RVN piaster continued to circulate as the only legal tender. Two months later, the National Bank of Viet Nam was reopened under new management. Stringent regulations were announced to control inflation and limit currency accumulation. All private Vietnamese and foreign banks were closed in 1976. By then, the Hanoi regime had ordered a complete withdrawal from circulation of the RVN currency and its replacement by the dong, in use in the north.

34INSURANCE

Before May 1975, life and property insurance coverage was available in the RVN from three small Vietnamese insurance companies and through local representatives of about 70 French, UK, and US insurance firms. By the end of 1975, all private insurance facilities had ceased to operate, and the Viet Nam Insurance Co., established in the DRV in 1965, had become the nation's lone insurance firm. In 1981, the main types of insurance offered were motor vehicle, personal accident, hull and cargo, offshore exploration, aviation, and third-party risk. In 1986, 71.1% of all premiums were for transport insurance, and 8.8% were for automotive coverage.

35PUBLIC FINANCE

The main sources of monetary revenue are the sale of taxes paid in kind, the sale of products of the Socialist sector, and taxes levied on the free market. Annual deficits are financed by foreign aid, and by expansion of the money supply. Despite efforts in the late 1980s to increase revenues and reduce expenditures, the fiscal deficit was estimated at about 40% of total expenditures in 1989. Monetary policy reforms enacted since 1988 helped end the hyperinflationary spiral of the 1980s. Aid from the former Soviet Union, formerly Viet Nam's most prominent donor, was greatly reduced after the dissolution of the USSR in 1991.

36TAXATION

Individual income is subject to a progressive tax ranging from 10% to 50%, with an additional 30% tax on amounts over US$583.33 per month. In the industrial and commercial sector, taxes ranged from about 15% to 25% of actual profits. Indirect taxes include a turnover tax ranging from 1–40% of gross receipts; a special sales tax on tobacco products, spirits, beer, and other items; royalty taxes from 1–20% in most cases, and customs duties.

37CUSTOMS AND DUTIES

Since 1980, however, provinces, cities, and individual enterprises have been permitted to sign contracts with foreign traders. All imports must be authorized by one of the state trading corporations. Customs duty is generally charged on imports and exports, with many exemptions and duty reductions available (including imports related to an aid program, and goods to be used for security, national defense, scientific, educational, training, or research purposes).

38FOREIGN INVESTMENT

France was the dominant foreign investor in Indochina before World War II. Resident Chinese, however, played a major role in rice milling, retailing, and other activities (and continued to do so in the south through the early 1970s). Following the 1954 partition agreement, the French economic position in the DRV was completely liquidated, and the participation of private foreign investors in the DRV economy was prohibited. The RVN government encouraged the introduction of private capital. In March 1957, a presidential declaration provided guarantees against nationalization and expropriation without due compensation, temporary exemption from various taxes, and remittance of profits within existing regulations. Despite these efforts, because of wartime conditions, relatively little new private foreign investment was attracted to the country, apart from a few ventures by US and Japanese interests. In 1977, the SRV issued a new investment code in an effort to attract private foreign capital to help develop the country. However, because of stringent regulations and a climate of government suspicion of private enterprise, the 1977 code attracted little enthusiasm among potential investors. Only the USSR and France made sizable investments, although in recent years Japan has laid the foundation for future investment by bank loans. Beginning in 1984, the regime began to encourage the formation of joint ventures and announced that preparations were under way for a new foreign investment code.

According to reports, the new code would provide a guarantee against nationalization of assets and set up an export-processing zone, perhaps in Haiphong or Ho Chi Minh City. Both joint ventures (of which foreigners were to be permitted to own up to 99%, as compared with 49% under the 1977 code) and wholly foreign-owned companies would be permitted to operate under the new code.

In 1987 the National Assembly passed a liberalized investment law seeking to improve the overall investment climate and emphasize the development of export industries and services. The Vietnamese investment laws are much more liberal than those of other countries in Southeast Asia. The code permitted wholly owned foreign enterprises in Viet Nam, levied low taxes on profits, allowed full repatriation of profits after taxes, and guaranteed foreign enterprises against government appropriation. The law also encouraged oil exploration. Factors hindering performance of foreign investors are bureaucracy, lack of management expertise, smuggling and corruption, and an underlying distrust and uncertainty on the part of officialdom. Foreign investment is likely to remain in extractive industries, such as oil, and at the low end of the technological scale.

Infrastructure improvements are necessary to sustain increased foreign investment. Approved foreign investment proposals amounted to $2.86 billion in 1993, a 47% increase over 1992. In early 1994 the government announced three proposals intended to improve the investment environment and increase foreign trade: to expedite decisions for licensing on small investment projects; to eliminate the requirements for import-export licenses for certain unspecified commodities; and to prepare a list of industries that would be off limits to foreign investors. Another recent decision is to allow insurance companies and brokerages, and reinsurance between companies.

39ECONOMIC DEVELOPMENT

With the defeat of the RVN forces in April 1975, Viet Nam faced the task of restoring its infrastructure, damaged by the war, while working toward the goal of a technologically advanced society. Long-range planning centered on the second five-year plan (1976–80), which called for major emphasis on heavy industry and rapid agricultural growth. Due to factors including unfavorable weather, decreased foreign aid, and high military expenditures—combined with managerial inefficiency—the plan was a disaster. Industrial production grew by only 0.6% and agriculture by 1.9%. The third five-year plan (1981–85) was more modest in its objectives. Emphasis was placed on agricultural development and the promotion of consumer goods, with industrial development in the background. Socialist transformation remained a high priority, although a less rapid rate of change was expected than during the previous five years. Although the goals of the new plan were more realistic than those set for its predecessor, its success was limited. Growth figures in industry (9.5%) and agriculture (4.9%) improved significantly over the previous five years. Production remained spotty in key areas, however, and problems of mismanagement—primarily by the state sector—proliferated.

The fourth five-year plan (1986–90) continued the previous plan's emphasis on agricultural growth and expansion of exports and light industry. Efforts to promote Socialist transformation were to continue, but at a gradual pace and "by appropriate forms." Development aid continued to come primarily from the USSR and other CMEA countries. Since 1978, the SRV has become fully integrated into the CMEA planning and development structure, and its five-year plans are coordinated with those of its CMEA partners. Planned Soviet outlays for the 1986–90 period total some $11–13 billion. This aid and trade waned with the decline of the USSR, with the full cut-off occurring in 1991. The SRV's new economic emphasis, doi moi (renovation) was instituted by Nguyen Van Linh following the Sixth National Party Congress (1986). His plan included policy and structural reforms for a market-based economic system: price decontrol (liberalized prices), currency devaluation, private sector expansion through decollectivization of agriculture (food production), legal recognition of private business, new foreign investment laws, autonomy of state enterprises, business accounting methods, devolution of government decision-making in industry to enterprise level, and limiting government participation to macroeconomic issues. Implementation of these policies was achieved with varied success.

Inflation policy and agricultural reform resulted in immediate increases in rice production. Viet Nam changed from a net importer of rice to the third major rice exporter after Thailand and the US. Agriculture remains the most important economic sector, accounting for half of GNP and almost 70% of the labor force. A 1992 initiative aimed at privatizing state enterprises met with less positive results. There were 12,000 government-owned companies employing 30% of Viet Nam's labor force that held 75% of the country's assets, and monopolized 86% of bank credit. The privatization program met with resistance from conservative politicians, the companies, and from foreign investors. Conservatives feared that privatization undermined the economic basis of socialism, and foreign investors were wary of poor investments with meager legal underpinnings. Opposition from managers who would lose a "free hand," and employees whose jobs might be replaced by new equipment also arose. In 1994 the director and deputy director of the textile company that was the flagship for this privatization program were dismissed for alleged corruption. US President Bill Clinton's lifting of the 30-year-old trade embargo in 1994 opened the way for waiting American companies to do business in Viet Nam. Anticipated international assistance during the mid-1990s is from the World Bank for education and agricultural reforms, the Japan Overseas Economic Cooperation Fund for infrastructure programs, the UK for soft loans, technical training and refugee resettlement, and from the Asian Development Bank.

40SOCIAL DEVELOPMENT

The war hindered systematic provision of social services in both the DRV and the RVN. Social security legislation under the RVN included the workers' compensation provisions of the labor code of 1952, which required that some degree of medical care be given employees under contract. Also established by law in 1953 was an employer-financed family-allowance system, which covered about 15% of the population. In the DRV, social services had been provided to the extent that scarce resources permitted.

Since the end of the war in 1975, the SRV has been attempting to lay the foundations of an advanced Socialist society. However, attempts to improve social services have been hampered by the poor performance of the economy. During the late 1970s, severe food shortages put per capita caloric intake below the subsistence level. Housing and health services were seriously inadequate, and individual freedom was severely restricted. By 1987, equality for women had been substantially achieved, but religious freedom was severely restricted, and potential dissidents were jailed without trial. Censorship was routinely practiced.

According to the US state department, Viet Nam had not completely improved its human rights situation in 1992, and restrictions on freedom of the press, speech, and assembly continued. The crackdown on dissent begun in 1990 was maintained, and the government forcibly resettled thousands of people into "new economic zones." However, travel restrictions were eased, artistic and literary expression were tolerated, and there was an increasing separation between the Communist Party and the State.

41HEALTH

Wars in Viet Nam since 1946 have undermined much of the progress made by the DRV, RVN, and SRV in the health field. Especially severe was the damage to urban hospitals in the north. A 1976 WHO report indicated the dimensions of that destruction: 24 research institutes and specialized hospitals, 28 provincial hospitals, 94 district hospitals, and 533 community health centers all destroyed, mainly as the result of U.S. bombing. The three decades of intermittent war also had a devastating effect on health conditions in the south. At the war's end in 1975, many endemic diseases were observed to be on the increase, in alarming contrast with trends among other affected countries in Southeast Asia. WHO reported in 1976 that malaria had been both widespread and increasing in the south in 1975. During 1965–74, 5,000 cases of bubonic plague were occurring annually, with a mortality rate of 5%. Saigon was said to have had a tuberculosis rate two to three times that of neighboring countries, while leprosy (involving an estimated 80,000–160,000 cases) was increasing. Venereal and paravenereal diseases were said to have afflicted 1 million persons in the south (about 5% of the total population) and, WHO claimed, 80% of RVN soldiers. Opiate addiction, it was said, affected about 500,000 persons.

Since reunification in 1975, some progress in health care has been made. Tuberculosis has been largely controlled (166 cases per 100,000 people reported in 1990), and the incidence of many contagious diseases has been reduced. In 1991, 24% of the population had access to safe water, and 17% had adequate sanitation. Immunization rates for children up to one year old in 1992 were: tuberculosis (91%); diphtheria, pertussis, and tetanus (88%); polio (89%); and measles (90%).

The SRV reported life expectancy in 1992 to be 64 years, and infant mortality to be 37 per 1,000 live births. Maternal mortality was 120 per 100,000 live births in 1991, and overall mortality was 8.5 per 1,000 people in 1993.

In 1993 the birth rate was 29.2 per 1,000 people. An estimated 53% of married women (ages 15 to 49) using contraception, and family planning services were provided to 2,157,000 people in 1992. Abortion is available on request. There were 2,039,000 births in 1992. Viet Nam's fertility rate in 1985–90 was 4.2, down 10% from the previous 5-year period.

In 1991, the country had 275,560 physicians, 58,912 nurses, and 14,813 midwives. In 1989, there were 160 pharmacists. In 1992, there were 35 physicians per 100,000 people, with a nurse to doctor ratio of 4.9. In 1990, there were 3.3 hospital beds per 1,000 inhabitants. About 91% of the population had access to health care services in 1992, and the country spent $157 million on health care in 1990.

During the early 1980s, foreign visitors routinely reported observing severe cases of malnutrition and shortages of medical equipment and supplies. While conditions have probably improved as agricultural production has increased, most Vietnamese continue to live at the minimum level of subsistence.

42HOUSING

Housing is a serious problem in the SRV, particularly in urban areas of the north where war damage caused problems of overcrowding, and lack of resources has hampered efforts to resolve the problem. By 1986, housing had become a critical problem in Hanoi, particularly in the central sections of the city, where per capita living space was reduced to four sq m. Large flats are gradually being erected in the suburbs to ease the problem. In the meantime, many families live in temporary quarters built directly on the sidewalk or attached to other buildings. Housing is less a problem in the countryside, where many farm families have begun to take advantage of a rising standard of living to build new houses of brick and stone. Similarly, in the south, housing is available to meet the requirements of the population because building construction had continued at a relatively high level during the war years. In 1989, the majority of housing units were semi-permanent (structures with brick walls and tile roofs lasting about 20 years).

43EDUCATION

In the mid-1970s, literacy in the south was estimated at about 65%, while in the north a rate of 85% was claimed in 1975. By 1990, the adult literacy rate for the reunified country was 87.6% (males, 92.0% and females, 83.6%). After 1975, the educational system in the south was restructured to conform to the Socialist guidelines that had been used in the DRV. The 12-year school cycle was reduced to 10 years, and the more than 20,000 teachers in the south were among those subjected to "reeducation." By 1976, some 1,400 tons of textbooks printed in the DRV had been shipped to the south, and the books used previously under the RVN were destroyed. In addition, more than 1,000 formerly private schools in the south were brought under state control. Today, education is free at all levels, and five years of primary education is compulsory.

In the mid-1980s, the educational system was rapidly expanding to cope with the nation's rising population. In 1990, primary schools had 252,413 teachers and 8,862,292 students. The same year, general secondary schools had 179,493 teachers and 3,235,992 students. In addition, second-level vocational schools had 15,814 teachers and 188,989 students. There are 90 colleges and three universities in the SRV. The major university is in Hanoi.

44LIBRARIES AND MUSEUMS

The École Française d'Extrême-Orient maintained an extensive research library in Hanoi, which was transferred intact to the DRV. Now the National Library, it has about 1,200,000 volumes; the bulk of the present collection has been added since 1954 and includes a substantial number of Russian titles. The General Scientific Library in Ho Chi Minh City (formerly the National Library) maintains a collection of over 600,000 volumes. Many books in the south's library system were burned following the reunification, especially in the larger libraries at Ho Chi Minh City, Hué, and Da Nang. According to official

sources, the number of libraries in the country has increased since 1975.

The collections of the Musée Louis-Finot, an archaeological and cultural museum established by the French in Hanoi, were also transferred intact to the DRV. These collections, now part of the Historical Museum, contain artifacts and related material from archaeological discoveries in Thanh Hoa and Yen Bay, including a 2,500-year-old burial boat and an excellent array of bronze implements. Hanoi's National Art Gallery includes a folk-art collection and Vietnamese Bronze Age artifacts. Notable also is the Museum of the Revolution, grouping memorabilia of Viet Nam's struggle for independence from the French since the early 1900s. The Army Museum, housed in the Hanoi Citadel, contains a collection of weapons and documents concerning the Indochina war. The Vietnamese Fine Arts Museum houses exhibits on the decorative and applied arts, and folk and modern art. The architecture of religious edifices and former Vietnamese imperial structures reflect the country's cultural heritage. The Ho Chi Minh City Museum, founded in 1977, has a section devoted to the revolution and another to ancient arts. The Ho Chi Minh Museum, also founded in 1977, studies his life and work.

45MEDIA

Viet Nam's postal, telegraph, and telephone services are under the Ministry of Communications. There were 115,000 telephones in 1991. Hanoi has a strong central broadcasting station, the Voice of Viet Nam, boosted by local relay transmitters. Since 1975, almost the entire country has been blanketed by a wired loudspeaker system. Radio programs beamed abroad include broadcasts in Chinese, English, French, Japanese, Spanish, Thai, Bahasa Indonesia, Russian, Khmer, and Lao, and there are special broadcasts to mountain tribes. Television was introduced into the RVN in 1966, and an extensive service, reaching some 80% of the population, was in operation by the early 1970s. A pilot television station was inaugurated in the DRV in 1971. Many of the major cities now have television stations, all under the guidance of the Ministry of Information which replaced the State Committee for Radio and Television in 1987. In 1991, there were 7,050,000 radios and 2,800,000 television sets.

The DRV press was controlled by the government, either directly or through various party organs and agencies. Officially, censorship existed in the RVN only for the foreign-language newspapers, but in fact, all papers practiced a policy of self-censorship in order to avoid trouble—newspapers were closed down on occasion because of the government's objection to news policies or editorial line. Most newspapers in the south were shut down by the PRG in 1975, but some papers that had been sympathetic to the NLF/DRV cause were allowed to continue publication.

All press is strictly controlled by the Ministry of Culture and Information. Principal Vietnamese dailies (with their estimated 1991 circulations) are shown in the following table:

	AFFILIATION	CIRCULATION
HANOI		
Nhan Dan	Communist Party	160,000
Quan Doi Nhan Dan	Army	55,000
Hanoi Moi	Communist Party	32,000
HO CHI MINH CITY		
Giai Phong	Communist Party	100,000

46ORGANIZATIONS

The principal mass organization is the Fatherland Front, which merged in January 1977 with the National Liberation Front and with the Viet Nam Alliance of National, Democratic, and Peace

Forces. The Fatherland Front draws up single slates of candidates in all elections and seeks to implement the political, economic, and social policies of the Communist Party. Other organizations that form part of the Fatherland Front are the Peasant Union, with some 5 million members; the Ho Chi Minh Communist Youth Union, with 4 million members; and the Vietnamese Women's Union, with 11.4 million members. Industrial and commercial enterprises are represented by the Chamber of Commerce of the SRV in Hanoi.

Many of the various types of organizations found in Western countries had existed in the RVN since the 1950s. Among them were the Boy Scouts and Girl Scouts, cooperatives, sports organizations, and various cultural, professional, and youth associations. Most of these bodies were disbanded after 1975.

47 TOURISM, TRAVEL, AND RECREATION

Viet Nam possesses a number of historic and scenic areas of interest to tourists. In the north, the beauty of Ha Long Bay, with its countless grottoes and rock spits jutting vertically into the sea, is well known. Hanoi itself, with its historical monuments, its lakes and pagodas, and its extensive French colonial architecture, is extremely picturesque, but hotel facilities are both inadequate and expensive.

In 1986 and 1987, the government made plans to expand international and domestic airline service, double hotel capacity in the major cities, simplify the complicated visa restrictions, and grant shore leave passes to passengers on cruise ships stopping at Vietnamese ports. As a result of these measures, tourism grew rapidly. By 1992, an estimated 450,000 tourists were arriving in Viet Nam each year, up from 20,000 in 1986. All visitors need visas and must register with the government within 48 hours of arrival.

48 FAMOUS VIETNAMESE

Important figures in Vietnamese history include the sisters Trung Trac and Trung Nhi, national heroines who led a revolt (AD 40–43) against China when that nation was imperial master of Tonkin and North Annam; Ngo Quyen, who regained Vietnamese independence from China in 938; Tran Hung Dao, who defeated the forces of Kublai Khan in 1288; Emperor Le Loi, national hero and brilliant administrator, in whose reign the Vietnamese legal code was promulgated in 1407; Emperor Gia Long (d.1820), who reunified Viet Nam in the early 19th century; and Le Van Duyet (1763–1832), a military leader who helped the emperor to unify the country.

Phan Boi Chau (1875–1940) was Viet Nam's first modern nationalist and, like China's Sun Yat-sen, is claimed by Vietnamese Communists and nationalists alike as their spiritual leader. Ho Chi Minh ("The Enlightener"), born Nguyen That Thanh (1890–1969), was a man of many other pseudonyms. Ho Chi Ming was a founding member of the French Communist Party in 1920 and founded the Vietnamese Communist Party in 1930. Often referred to as "Uncle Ho," he was president of the DRV from 1945 until his death. Gen. Vo Nguyen Giap (b.1912), a professor of history turned strategist, organized the first anti-French guerrilla groups in 1944, led the Viet-Minh in its eight-year struggle against France, and defeated the French at Dien Bien Phu; subsequently he served as minister of defense, commander in chief of the army, and vice-premier of the DRV. Truong Chinh ("Long March," b.1906), the DRV's foremost Communist thinker, was secretary-general of the Vietnamese Communist Party from 1940 until 1956, when he was purged from his post for having mismanaged the land reform; exonerated shortly thereafter, he was president of the Council of State (1981–87). Pham Von Dong (b.1906), a member of the nobility, joined the Vietnamese revolutionary movement at its inception and became minister of foreign affairs in 1954, premier of the DRV in 1955, and premier of the SRV in 1976; he resigned in 1987. Le Duan (1907–86), first secre-

tary of the Communist Party, presided over Viet Nam's reunification and the formation of the SRV. Le Duc Tho (b.1911), a member of the Communist Party Politburo but with no post in the government, was the DRV's chief negotiator in talks that led to the 1973 Paris Peace Agreement; for his role, Le shared with US Secretary of State Henry Kissinger the 1973 Nobel Peace Prize.

Prominent political figures in the formation of the RVN included Bao Dai (Nguyen Vinh Thuy; b.France, 1913), who had served as nominal emperor of Annam under the Japanese and had attempted to form a unified national government after the war, and Ngo Dinh Diem (1901–63), who served as president of the RVN from its founding on 26 October 1955 until his overthrow and death in November 1963. Nguyen Cao Ky (b.1930), an RVN air force commander, took control of the government in the coup of June 1965. Gen. Nguyen Van Thieu (b.1923) was elected president of the RVN in the elections of September 1967 (with Ky as his vice-presidential running mate), an office he retained until the RVN's defeat in 1975. Both Thieu and Ky left the country in 1975, Thieu taking up residence in Taiwan and Ky in the US. The new leadership in the south, following the 1975 NLF victory, was headed by Pham Hung (1912–1988), chairman of the southern wing of the Communist Party since 1967; Huynh Thanh Phat (b.1913), the PRG premier, who later became a member of the Council of State; and Nguyen Thi Binh (b.1927), the PRG's foreign affairs minister who had headed the NLF delegation at the Paris talks and who also became a Council of State Member. Pham Hung became premier of the SRV in 1987, and Vo Chi Cong (b.1913?) became president of the Council of State. Nguyen Van Linh (b.1913) became general secretary of the Communist Party in December 1986.

The 13th-century writer Nguyen Si Co is regarded as one of the first truly Vietnamese authors; he is best known for his collection titled *Chieu Quan Cong Ho*. Other leading literary figures are two 15th-century poets, Ho Huyen Qui and Nguyen Binh Khien; the latter's collection, *Bach Van Thi Tap*, is a classic of Vietnamese literature. Nguyen Du (1765–1820) wrote a famous novel in verse, *Kim Van Kieu*. Hoang Ngoc Phach, who wrote the romantic novel *To Tam* (1925), is credited with the introduction of Western literary standards into Vietnamese literature.

49 DEPENDENCIES

Viet Nam has no territories or colonies.

50 BIBLIOGRAPHY

Beresford, Melanie. *National Unification and Economic Development in Vietnam*. New York: St. Martin's, 1989.

Buttinger, Joseph. *A Dragon Defiant: A Short History of Vietnam*. New York: Praeger, 1972.

Chanda, Nayan. *Brother Enemy: The War After the War*. San Diego: Harcourt Brace Jovanovich, 1986.

Cima, Ronald J. (ed.). *Vietnam: A Country*. Washington, D.C.: Library of Congress, 1989.

Duiker, William J. *Historical Dictionary of Vietnam*. Metuchen, N.J.: Scarecrow Press, 1989.

Fall, Bernard B. *The Two Viet-Nams: A Political and Military Analysis*. New York: Praeger, 1967.

Fforde, Adam. *The Limits of National Liberation*. New York: Methuen, 1987.

Gardner, Lloyd C. *Approaching Vietnam: from World War II through Dienbienphu, 1941–1954*. New York: W.W. Norton, 1988.

Fall, Bernard B. (ed.) *Ho Chi Minh on Revolution: Selected Writings, 1920–66*. New York: Praeger, 1967.

Hoang, Van Chi. *From Colonialism to Communism: A Case His-

tory of North Vietnam. New York: Praeger, 1964.

Hodgkin, Thomas L. *Vietnam: The Revolutionary Path.* New York: St. Martin's, 1980.

Karnow, Stanley. *Vietnam: A History.* New York: Viking, 1983.

Kolko, Gabriel. *Anatomy of a War: Vietnam, the United States, and the Modern Historical Experience.* New York: Pantheon, 1985.

Lewy, Guenter. *America in Vietnam.* New York: Oxford University Press, 1978.

Marr, David G. and Kristine Alilunas-Rodgers *Vietnam.* Santa Barbara, Calif.: Clio Press, 1992.

Nguyen Khac Vien. *Contemporary Vietnam (1858–1980).* Hanoi: Red River, 1981.

Oberdorfer, Don. *Tet!* New York: Doubleday, 1971.

Olson, James Stuart. *Where the Domino Fell: America and Vietnam, 1945 to 1990.* New York: St. Martin's, 1991.

Pimlott, John. *Vietnam, the Decisive Battles.* New York: Macmillan, 1990.

Porter, Gareth. *Vietnam: the Politics of Bureaucratic Socialism.* Ithaca, N.Y.: Cornell University Press, 1993.

Shaplen, Robert. *Bitter Victory.* New York: Harper & Row, 1986.

Short, Anthony. *The Origins of the Vietnam War.* New York: Longman, 1989.

Terzani, Tiziano. *Giai Phong! The Fall and Liberation of Saigon.* New York: St. Martin's, 1976.

Truong Nhu Tang. *Vietcong Memoir.* San Diego: Harcourt Brace Jovanovich, 1986.

Williams, Michael C. *Vietnam at the Crossroads.* New York: Council on Foreign Relations Press, 1992.

Woodside, Alexander. *Community and Revolution in Modern Vietnam.* Boston: Houghton-Mifflin, 1976.

WESTERN SAMOA

Independent State of Western Samoa
Malo Sa'oloto Tuto'atasi o Samoa i Sisifo

CAPITAL: Apia.

FLAG: The upper left quarter of the flag is blue and bears five white, five-rayed stars representing the Southern Cross; the remainder of the flag is red.

ANTHEM: *The Flag of Freedom.*

MONETARY UNIT: The Western Samoa tala (ws$) is a paper currency of 100 sene. There are coins of 1, 2, 5, 10, 20, and 50 sene and 1 tala, and notes of 2, 5, 10, 20, and 100 talas. ws$1 = us$0.3858 (or us$1 = ws$2.5920).

WEIGHTS AND MEASURES: British weights and measures are used.

HOLIDAYS: New Year's, 1–2 January; Independence Holidays (first three workdays of June), Anzac Day, 25 April; Christmas Day, 25 December; Boxing Day, 26 December. Movable religious holidays are Good Friday, Easter Monday, and Whitmonday.

TIME: 1 AM = noon GMT.

¹LOCATION, SIZE, AND EXTENT

Western Samoa consists of the islands of Savai'i and Upolu and several smaller islands, of which only Manono and Apolima are inhabited. The group, situated almost centrally both in the Pacific Ocean and among the South Sea islands, has a total land area of 2,860 sq km (1,104 sq mi), extending 150 km (93 mi) ESE–WNW and 39 km (24 mi) NNE–SSW. Savai'i and Upolu, separated by the Apolima Strait at a distance of nearly 18 km (11 mi), have a combined coastline of 403 km (250 mi). Comparatively, the area occupied by Western Samoa is slightly smaller than the state of Rhode Island.

²TOPOGRAPHY

The islands are volcanic, with coral reefs surrounding most of them. Rugged ranges rise to 1,100 m (3,608 ft) on Upolu and 1,857 m (6,094 ft) on Savai'i. Apolima is a volcanic crater whose wall is pierced by a passage that connects its harbor with the sea. Manono, about 70 m (230 ft) high, consists chiefly of coral sand. The islands are in an area of active volcanism. Severe eruptions occurred in Savai'i during 1905–11.

³CLIMATE

The climate is tropical, but because of the oceanic surroundings, temperature ranges are not considerable. The hottest month is December, and the coldest is July; the mean daily temperature is about 27°C (81°F). The year is divided into a dry season (May to October) and a wet season (November to April). Rainfall averages 287 cm (113 in) annually, and the average yearly relative humidity is 83%. Although the islands lie outside the normal track of hurricanes, severe storms occurred in 1889, 1966, and 1968. Trade winds from the southeast are fairly constant throughout the dry season.

⁴FLORA AND FAUNA

Lush vegetation covers much of the land. Along the coast there are mangrove forests, pandanus, Barringtonia, hibiscus, and strand vegetation, commonly found throughout the Pacific. The adjacent lowland forest, which originally stretched inland over

the lower slopes of the mountains, has been cut down extensively on Upolu and in more limited areas on Savai'i. Inland and at higher elevations, the rain forests contain trees and lianas of many genera and species. The higher elevations of Savai'i contain moss forest and mountain scrub.

Fifty species of birds are found; 16 of these are seabirds, many of which visit Samoa only during the breeding season. Sixteen of the 34 species of land birds are indigenous. Among the latter are small doves, parrots, pigeons, and wild ducks. The most interesting bird, scientifically, is the tooth-billed pigeon (*Didunculus strigirostris Peale*), which some ornithologists regard as the connecting link between bird life of the present and the tooth-billed birds of zoological antiquity.

The only indigenous mammals in Western Samoa are the rat (*Mus exulans Peale*) and the flying fox (*Pteropus samoensis Peale*). Numerous species of birds and mammals, chiefly domesticated, have been introduced by the Samoans and Europeans. Two species of snakes, several different lizards, and the gecko are found. Insect life includes many species of moths, beetles, spiders, and ants. The mosquito (*Stegomyia pseudoscutellaris*) is a carrier of human filaria.

⁵ENVIRONMENT

Western Samoa's environmental problems include damage to the nation's forests and the need for protection of its wildlife. According to United Nation's sources, the forests are eliminated at a rate of 4–8,000 ha per year due to the expansion of farming activity. The country's reefs are the home of its fish population. A lack of adequate sewage disposal facilities and other forms of pollution, such as siltation and industrial by-products, are a threat to both the reefs and the marine life which inhabit them. Western Samas's water supply is too small to support its current population.

⁶POPULATION

The population of Western Samoa in 1991 was 159,862. The average annual rate of population increase between 1955 and 1965 was about 3% but had fallen to 0.1% in 1985–90. The population density in 1991 was 56 per sq km (146 per sq mi).

Upolu, including the islands of Manono and Apolima, had a population of 112,228 in 1986; the population of Savai'i was 44,930. Apia is the only major town; it is the administrative and commercial center, with a 1986 population of 32,196.

[7]MIGRATION

Under German colonial rule, many Chinese laborers were imported to work on plantations. More recently, there has generally been a net annual loss of population through migration. Emigration (estimated at 5,278 in 1988) consists mainly of students going to New Zealand to continue their education and Samoans seeking work there. In addition, several thousand Western Samoans live in American Samoa and other parts of the US. the total abroad in these countries and Australia was estimated at 76,200 in 1989.

[8]ETHNIC GROUPS

Samoans comprise more than 90% of the total population. The Samoans are the second-largest branch of the Polynesians, a people occupying the scattered islands of the Pacific from Hawaii to New Zealand and from eastern Fiji to Easter Island. Most of the remaining Western Samoans are of mixed Samoan and European or Asian descent. Europeans, other Pacific islanders, and Asians make up less than 1% of the total.

For many years, all inhabitants of Western Samoa were accorded a domestic status as Samoan or European. Residents are now officially classed as either citizens or foreigners. Among Western Samoan citizens, however, the distinction between persons of Samoan or European status is still recognized. Most Samoans live in foreshore villages, while non-Samoans predominate in Apia and its environs.

[9]LANGUAGES

Samoan is the universal language, but both Samoan and English are official. Some Chinese is also spoken. Most of the part-Samoans and many others speak English, and it is taught in the schools.

[10]RELIGIONS

Over 99% of Samoans profess some form of Christianity, and religious observance is strong among all groups. The Congregational Christian Church of Western Samoa, a successor to the London Missionary Society, is self-supporting and is the largest religious body in the country, comprising some 47% of the population in 1986. The Roman Catholic (36,700) and Methodist (36,000) churches also had large followings in 1993. The Mormon and Seventh-Day Adventist churches, the Baha'is, and a number of other denominations have smaller congregations located in various parts of the country.

[11]TRANSPORTATION

The road system in 1991, including plantation roads, totaled 2,042 km (1,269 mi), of which 375 km (233 mi) were paved; most are on the northern coast of Upolu. Buses and taxis provide public transport. In 1992 there were 10,830 passenger cars and 1,204 commercial vehicles.

Diesel-powered launches carry passengers and freight around the islands, and small motor vessels maintain services between Apia and Pago Pago in American Samoa. Fortnightly cargo and passenger connections are maintained with New Zealand, and scheduled transpacific services connect Western Samoa with Australian, Japanese, UK, and North American ports. Apia is the principal port; Asau, on Savai'i, was opened as a second deep-sea port in 1972. Polynesian Airlines provides daily air connections with Pago Pago and regularly scheduled flights to other Pacific destinations; through Pago Pago there are connecting flights to New Zealand, Australia, and the US. Faleolo Airport, 35 km (22 mi) west of Apia, is the principal air terminal. Air Samoa and Samoa Aviation provide internal air services between Upolu and Savai'i, and Hawaiian Airlines provides direct service between Honolulu and Faleolo and commuter service between Faleolo and Pago Pago.

[12]HISTORY

Archaeological evidence on Upolu indicates that Samoa was colonized by maritime traders of the Lapita culture at least as early as the 1st millennium BC. From the mid-13th century AD, genealogies, important titles, traditions, and legends give considerable information on the main political events. The first Europeans to sight the islands were the Dutch explorer Jacob Roggeveen in 1722 and the French navigator Louis de Bougainville in 1768. But the world knew little about Samoa until after the arrival of the missionary John Williams in 1830 and the establishment of the London Missionary Society.

Williams' arrival coincided with the victory of one group of chiefs over another, ending a series of violent internecine wars. Runaway sailors and other Europeans had already settled among the Samoans and had assisted the chiefs in their campaigns. Whalers also visited the islands, and from time to time the warships of great powers visited Apia to oversee the activities of whaling crews and settlers. Naval officers and missionaries both began to consult with the dominant group of chiefs as if it represented a national government and to treat its leader as a king. In time, semiofficial representatives of Great Britain and the US were stationed in Apia. Between 1847 and 1861, the US appointed a commercial agent, and Britain and the city of Hamburg appointed consuls.

Factional rivalries took a new turn as British, US, and German consular agents, aided sometimes by their countries' warships, aligned themselves with various paramount chiefs. Intrigues among the chiefs and jealousies among the representatives of the great powers culminated in civil war in 1889. In the Berlin Treaty, which followed, Britain, the US, and Germany set up a neutral and independent government under King Malietoa Laupepea, and their consuls were authorized to constitute Apia as a separate municipality. The death of King Malietoa in 1898 led to a dispute over the succession, and the three powers intervened once again. In 1899, they abolished the kingship, and in 1900, they signed a series of conventions that made Western Samoa a German protectorate. The German administration continued to experience difficulties, leading to the exile of several Samoan leaders and the suspension of others from office. With the outbreak of World War I in 1914, New Zealand military forces occupied Western Samoa, and from 1919 to 1946, New Zealand administered the islands as a mandate of the League of Nations.

In 1927, local opposition to the New Zealand administration among both the Samoan and the European communities resulted in the formation of a nationalistic organization known as the Mau, which embarked on a program of civil disobedience. Its members withdrew from political life, from schools, and from all contact with the government. The protests lasted in one form or another until 1936, when the leaders of the Mau reached an agreement with the administration and reentered the political life of the territory.

In 1946, a trusteeship agreement was approved by the UN General Assembly, and New Zealand formally committed itself to promote the development of Western Samoa toward ultimate self-government. The passage of the Samoa Amendment Act of 1947 and a series of further amendments governed Western Samoa's subsequent evolution toward independence. An Executive Council was reconstituted in 1957, and the New Zealand high commissioner withdrew from the Legislative Assembly, which thenceforth was presided over by an elected speaker. In 1959, an executive cabinet was introduced, and in 1960, the constitution of the Independent State of Western Samoa was adopted. This was followed by a plebiscite under UN supervision in 1961 in which an overwhelming majority of voters approved the adoption of the constitution and supported independence.

On 1 January 1962, Western Samoa became an independent nation. Tupua Tamasese Meaoli and Malietoa Tanumafili II became joint heads of state. When the former died on 5 April 1963, the latter became the sole head of state. Fiame Faumuina Mataafa was independent Western Samoa's first prime minister (1962–70) and served again in that post from 1973 until his death in 1975.

During the late 1970s and early 1980s, Western Samoa suffered from a worsening economy and growing political and social unrest. A divisive public-sector strike from 6 April to 2 July 1981 cut many essential services to a critical level. The leadership of Tupuola Taisi Efi, who later became head of the Christian Democratic Party and was prime minister from 1976, was successfully challenged by the Human Rights Protection Party (HRPP), which won the February 1982 general election. Judicial rulings subsequently nullified some of the election results, and Tupuola returned to power from September to December. On 30 December 1982, however, a second HRPP government was formed, with Tofilau Eti as prime minister. Controversy erupted in 1982 over the signing by the HRPP government in August of a protocol with New Zealand that reduced substantially the right of Western Samoans to New Zealand citizenship. Tofilau resigned in December 1985, and Va'ai Kolone became prime minister in January 1986 as head of a new coalition government comprised of 15 CDP members and 12 former HRPP members. Tupuola was named deputy prime minister of the new government. Since independence, there have been sporadic calls for electoral reforms.

13 GOVERNMENT

Executive power is vested in the head of state. Although Malietoa Tanumafili II has lifetime tenure, the constitution, which took effect 1 January 1962, provides for his successors to be elected for a term of five years by the Fono, or Legislative Assembly. The powers and functions of the head of state are far-reaching. All legislation must have his assent before it becomes law. He also has power to grant pardons and reprieves and to suspend or commute any sentence by any court. Executive authority is administered by a cabinet consisting of a prime minister and eight other ministers appointed by him. The head of state and the cabinet members comprise the Executive Council.

The parliament consists of the head of state and the Fono, which comprises 1 elected member from each of 45 Samoan constituencies and 2 members elected by persons whose names appear on the individual voters' roll. The election of the 45 Samoan members is by universal adult suffrage, but candidates for office are confined to some 20,000 matai, or chiefs. Citizens of non-Samoan origin who qualify for registration on the individual voters' roll elect the two other members by universal suffrage. The next elections are scheduled for 1996.

14 LOCAL GOVERNMENT

With the exception of the Apia area, local government is carried out by the village fono, or council of matai and orators, and where and when necessary, through meetings of matai and orators of a district. The main administrative link between the central government and the outside districts is provided by the part-time officials in each village who act as government agents in such matters as the registration of vital statistics; local inspectors represent the various government departments.

15 POLITICAL PARTIES

Technically, candidates for public office campaign as individuals, but political parties are becoming increasingly important. The

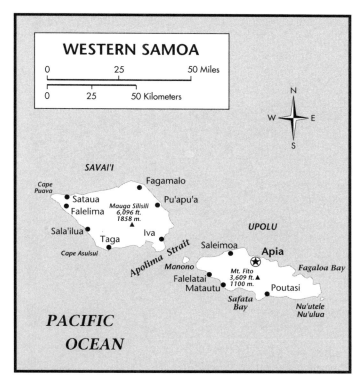

LOCATION: 13° to 15°s; 171° to 173°w. **BOUNDARY LENGTHS:** Savai<ayni coastline, 188 km (117 mi); Upolu coastline, 183 km (114 mi). **TERRITORIAL SEA LIMIT:** 12 mi.

Human Rights Protection Party (HRPP) was founded in 1979 as an opposition party to the government of Prime Minister Tupuola Efi. Tupuola's followers, although not yet formally organized, had, in effect, constituted the ruling party. Following the elections of 27 February 1982, the HRPP was able to command 23 votes in the Fono, as compared with 22 for Tupuola's party. The HRPP leader, Va'ai Kolone, was chosen as prime minister, but in September the Supreme Court, upholding charges of electoral fraud, voided the election of two HRPP candidates, including the prime minister himself. Tupuola was then named prime minister, but by-election victories soon restored the HRPP majority in the Fono, and in December his government fell. On 30 December 1982, Tofilau Eti, the new HRPP leader, was chosen prime minister. He remained prime minister following the February 1985 elections, in which the HRPP captured 31 of the 47 seats, but resigned that December after his budget failed to win approval and the head of state refused to call new elections. In January 1986, a new coalition government led by Va'ai Kolone was formed.

Tofilau Eti Alesana, leader of the HRPP, was reelected Prime Minister in April 1988 as the result of a contested election that was settled by a judge flown in from New Zealand. A gradual deterioration in the bilateral relationship between Western Samoa and New Zealand continued with a dispute concerning the special immigration quota applied to Western Samoans. In October 1990 a referendum on the issue of universal suffrage narrowly passed. A proposal to establish an upper legislative chamber composed of traditional chiefs failed. In a general election held in April 1991 the ruling HRPP won 28 of 47 seats in the Fono. Alesana was reelected Prime Minister in May 1991. Among the new ministers appointed was Fiame Naomi, the first female Cabinet member, as Minister of Education, Youth, Sports and Culture, and Labour.

16 JUDICIAL SYSTEM

Court procedure is patterned after practices in British courts. Samoan custom is taken into consideration in certain cases.

English is the official language of the court, but Samoan is also used. The Supreme Court has full civil and criminal jurisdiction for the administration of justice in Western Samoa. It is under the jurisdiction of the chief judge, who is appointed by the head of state, acting on the advice of the prime minister. The Court of Appeal consists of three judges who may be judges of the Supreme Court or other persons with appropriate qualifications.

Magistrates' courts are subordinate courts with varying degrees of authority. The highest, presided over by the senior magistrate, may hear criminal cases involving imprisonment of up to three years or cases involving only fines. The Land and Titles Court has jurisdiction in disputes over Samoan land and succession to Samoan titles. Samoan assessors and associate judges possessing a good knowledge of Samoan custom must be present at all sittings of the court. Lawyers are not permitted to appear in the Land and Titles Court; each party appoints its own leader, usually a chief or an orator. Court decisions are based largely on Samoan custom.

Some civil and criminal matters are handled by village "fonos" (traditional courts) which apply a considerably different procedure than that used in the official western-style courts. The Village Fono Law of 1990 affords legal status to the decision of the village fono and allows appeal from fono decisions to the Lands and Titles Court and to the Supreme Court.

[17] ARMED FORCES

Western Samoa had no armed forces. The government foresees no military development because of financial considerations and no threats from abroad.

[18] INTERNATIONAL COOPERATION

Western Samoa became a member of the UN on 15 December 1976 and belongs to ESCAP, FAO, IBRD, IDA, IFAD, IFC, IMF, UNESCO, and WHO. The nation also participates in the Asian Development Bank, Commonwealth of Nations, G-77, South Pacific Commission, and South Pacific Forum, and is a signatory of the Law of the Sea. An Inter-Samoa Consultative Committee, made up of representatives from Western Samoa and American Samoa, holds meetings alternately in both countries to discuss matters of mutual interest. By treaty, New Zealand is the exclusive representative of Western Samoa in the conduct of its foreign affairs outside the Pacific region.

[19] ECONOMY

The economy is based largely on agriculture, which, including fisheries, provides over one-third of the GDP and employees two-thirds of the work force, mostly in subsistence farming of food crops. In addition to agricultural exports, tourist revenues and remittances from overseas workers are also important sources of foreign exchange. Economic performance has suffered since 1990 due to the devastation to crops, tourism, and infrastructure caused by cyclones Ofa and Val. Western Samoa has the highest unemployment rate and the lowest wages in Oceania. The 1987, per capita GDP was A$939.

[20] INCOME

In 1992, Western Samoa's GNP was $153 million at current prices, or $940 per capita. For the period 1985–92 the average inflation rate was 10.6%, resulting in a real growth rate in per capita GNP of –0.1%.

[21] LABOR

Cash crops are raised as supplements to subsistence crops. No Samoan is entirely dependent on wages for sustenance; all share in the products of their family lands and can always return to them. The government and WSTEC were by far the next-largest sources of employment, followed by construction, tourism, transportation and communications, and services.

Although small, a trade union movement has been established. Public employees are represented by the Public Service Association. Labor is generally restricted to a 40-hour week. Payment is in cash, and in many cases rations are also supplied to workers either as part of their wages or in addition to them. In most cases, living quarters are provided for plantation workers.

Over the years, thousands of skilled and semiskilled Samoans have left the islands, mainly drawn away by better economic opportunities in New Zealand, Australia, and the United States. Agriculture, forestry and fishing account for half of wage employment; agriculture engaged the vast majority of the population of 161,000 in 1991.

[22] AGRICULTURE

Tropical agriculture employs about 60% of the labor force, and makes up about 40% of GDP. Most Samoans grow food crops for home consumption and cash crops for export. Village agriculture, in which the family is the productive unit, involves the largest areas of land, occupies the preponderance of the labor force, and produces the major portion of food and cash crops. Coconut products, cocoa, taro, and bananas are produced for export, and bananas, taro, and ta'amu are grown for local sale. Village plantings are invariably mixed, containing some or all of the following crops: coconuts, cocoa, bananas, taro, ta'amu, breadfruit, sugarcane, yams, manioc, and various fruits. Plantation agriculture has been controlled mainly by non-indigenous residents.

Exports of unprocessed copra have been largely replaced by coconut oil, coconut cream, and copra cake. Due to a decline in world prices, coconut production has fallen to 95,000 tons in 1992 from 138,000 tons in 1990 and from an annual average of 169,000 tons during 1979–81. Taro (coco yam) production in 1992 amounted to 32,000 tons. Exports of cocoa have fallen in recent years, thereby discouraging production. In 1992, no production over 1,000 tons was reported. Banana exports fluctuate greatly from year to year. Exports of food products in 1990 amounted to $5 million, or about 46% of total exports.

[23] ANIMAL HUSBANDRY

Pigs and cattle form the bulk of the livestock. In 1992, pigs, which are common in the villages, were estimated to number 270,000 and cattle 31,000. A small number of cattle are kept for milk; the remainder are raised for beef. Nearly one-half of the cattle population is owned by WSTEC, the most progressive cattle breeder. Other livestock in 1992 included an estimated 3,000 horses and 1,000 goats.

[24] FISHING

The government has sought to expand the fishing industry, but most fishing is still conducted along the reefs and coasts; deep-sea fishing, save for bonito and shark, is not developed. A $3-million fish market and wharf, built with Japanese aid, was completed in Apia in 1982. The local fish catch, however, has steadily fallen from 4,020 tons in 1982 to 565 tons in 1991.

[25] FORESTRY

The nation's forest area is estimated at 134,600 ha (331,000 acres). Reforestation projects are concentrated on Savai'i, which accounts for 80% of the nation's forest area. A large-scale timber-milling enterprise, established on Savai'i in 1970, began to produce kiln-dried sawn timber and veneer sheets for export. Timber exports were estimated at $11,000 in 1992.

[26] MINING

No minerals of commercial value are known to exist in Western Samoa.

[27]ENERGY AND POWER

Western Samoa has depended heavily on imported energy, but hydroelectric power, first available in 1985, accounted for 43% of electrical generation in 1991. Net electricity generating capacity in 1991 was 19,000 kw, and production totaled 47 million kwh.

[28]INDUSTRY

The government has encouraged industrial growth, and manufacturing, geared mainly to processing primary products, is increasing steadily. Industries include food- and timber-processing facilities, a brewery, cigarette and match factories, and small individual enterprises for processing coffee and for manufacturing curios, soap, carbonated drinks, light metal products, garments, footwear, and other consumer products. A coconut oil mill, an additional coconut cream factory, a veneer mill, and a meat cannery began operations in the 1980s. In 1991, the Japanese Yazaki Samsa Company began manufacturing automotive seat belts. The firm also produces electrical wiring systems.

[29]SCIENCE AND TECHNOLOGY

New Zealand provides extensive scientific and technical aid to Western Samoa. Other donors include Japan, the Federal Republic of Germany (FRG), Australia, the US, the UK, and the UNDP. UNESCO has an integrated field office in Apia to promote science in the Pacific States. The National University of Samoa has a faculty of science. The University of the South Pacific has a school of agriculture in Apia.

[30]DOMESTIC TRADE

Apia, the capital, is the center of commercial life. Many firms act as agents for shipping and airlines and for overseas commercial organizations generally. Outside Apia, trading stations, linked with the capital by launch and road transport, collect produce and distribute consumer goods. Several major firms operate about 200 stations in the outer districts and secure a large share of the total commercial business. There are also a number of smaller firms and independent traders. In Apia, various firms and small shops sell imported commodities and domestic products.

[31]FOREIGN TRADE

The fact that Western Samoa has a limited number of exports—principally agricultural and timber products—renders its economy extremely vulnerable to weather conditions and market fluctuations. Imports consist chiefly of food, fuels and chemicals, machinery, transportation equipment, and other manufactured articles. The principal exports are taro, coconut cream, and automotive seat belts. Also exported are coconut oil, coconuts, copra, cocoa, timber, and clothing. Shipments of copra have lagged due to low prices and adverse growing conditions. Despite a continued decline in exports of traditional tradeables, total exports of goods and services grew in 1992, mainly due to orders for Yazaki Company seat belts. Imports totaled us$112 million, while exports amounted to us$6 million. Western Samoa's leading trade partners are Australia, New Zealand, the FRG, the US, Japan, and other Pacific islands.

[32]BALANCE OF PAYMENTS

In the early 1970s, Western Samoa's heavy trade deficits were largely offset by tourist revenues, remittances from Western Samoans working abroad, and long-term investment capital. By the early 1980s, however, rising import costs and declining export earnings led to a critical balance-of-payments situation. By 1992, the external account deficit (excluding grants) had increased to about 28% of GDP. Remittances also declined (due to mediocre growth in Australia, New Zealand, and the US), amounting to $39 million in 1992.

[33]BANKING AND SECURITIES

Legislation in 1974 set up the Monetary Board to act as the central bank. The activities of the Monetary Board were taken over in 1984 by the new Central Bank of Samoa, which had foreign assets of ws$112.4 million in 1993. The Bank of Western Samoa, owned jointly by the government and by the Bank of New Zealand (50% each), offers all normal commercial banking services and operates a savings division.

[34]INSURANCE

There is a private life insurance company in Apia.

[35]PUBLIC FINANCE

Western Samoa's financial year ends on 31 December. Government budgets have commonly shown deficits in recent years. In 1991/92, budget revenues amounted to us$95.3 million, while expenditures came to us$95.4 million (including us$41 million in capital expenditures). Whereas the budget balance represented 8.3% of GDP in 1980, the 1992 budget balance was equivalent to 16.9% of GDP. Debt outstanding and disbursed grew from 62% of GDP in 1990 to an estimated 80% in 1992. The debt service is equivalent to about 10% of annual exports.

[36]TAXATION

Individuals and companies are liable for the payment of income tax. The basic nonresident corporate tax rate is 48%, and the resident corporate tax rate is 39%; rates for both domestic and foreign insurance companies are lower. Personal income tax rates range from 5% to 50%. There are also gift, inheritance, and stamp taxes.

[37]CUSTOMS AND DUTIES

Customs duties provide almost half of current government revenue and are levied on all imports except those specifically exempted. Preferential rates for imports from Commonwealth countries were abolished in 1975.

[38]FOREIGN INVESTMENT

The government actively promotes the establishment of industries financed by overseas companies. These include milling and logging operations by a US company on Savai'i and by a joint Japanese-Samoan enterprise on Upolu, and a US hotel resort center near Apia.

[39]ECONOMIC DEVELOPMENT

The government has consistently stressed diversification of agriculture. It has also sought through a series of plans to promote growth in manufacturing, forestry, fishing, hydroelectric power, and tourism which received a boost when the Falento Airport got a new terminal and runway extension in 1985. In 1989, an offshore banking center was launched. New Zealand, Australia, the US, the Asian Development Bank, and the EC are major sources of development aid, and recently, Japan and the FRG have provided technical and financial aid. Assistance from the UN family of organizations totaled us$2.6 million in 1991. The country's fifth development plan (1985–87) called for an investment of ws$146.9 million, ws$114.2 million of it from external sources. Investment increased significantly in 1990 and 1992, mainly due to increased public capital expenditure. External aid has been a major source of public investment financing, providing approximately 68% of capital expenditure in 1991 and 47% in 1992.

[40]SOCIAL DEVELOPMENT

A social security system was established in 1972 under the Western Samoan National Provident Fund. It provides for employee retirement pensions, disability benefits, and death benefits. Workers' compensation is funded by employers and is compulsory.

In Western Samoan society, obligations to the aiga, or extended family, are often given precedence over individual rights. While there is some discrimination against women, they can play an important role in society, especially female matai, or heads of families. Universal suffrage was enacted in 1990, and the following year a Women's Affairs Ministry was established.

41HEALTH

The Department of Health oversees health care on the islands. The country is divided into 14 health districts, each under a medical officer. In 1982, there were 16 hospital centers with 735 beds. In 1990, there were 50 physicians in Western Samoa.

District nurses are stationed at strategic points throughout the islands. Child health clinics, and particularly clinics for young children and infants, are a regular feature of their work. In 1991, 91% of children were vaccinated against measles. A mobile dental clinic operates in the villages, while all schools in Apia are visited at regular intervals by a team of dental practitioners. Life expectancy at birth was 66 years.

42HOUSING

Most Samoans live in villages in traditional Samoan houses called fales. A fale is usually round or oval, with pebble floors and a thatch roof. It has no walls, being supported on the sides by posts. Coconut-leaf blinds can be lowered to exclude wind and rain. In areas more affected by contact with Europeans, the fale may have a concrete floor, corrugated iron roof, and lattice-work walls. Another fused Samoan-European type, much used by chiefs and pastors, is an oblong concrete house with some walls, often with separate rooms in each corner; like the fale it is open at the sides. Fales are grouped around an open area in the center of the village and have separate cookhouses behind them.

43EDUCATION

The adult literacy rate is estimated to be over 97%. Formal education is provided by the Department of Education and five religious missions. Government and mission schools have a uniform syllabus and common examinations. The government school system is the more comprehensive, with almost all its teachers holding Samoan teachers' certificates. Village schools provide four years of primary schooling. District schools draw the brighter pupils from village schools and educate them through the upper primary level. In the Apia area, urban schools provide a lower-through upper-primary curriculum. A major educational goal has been to make Samoans bilingual, with English as their second tongue. In the senior classes of the primary schools, all instruction is in English. In 1991 there were 30 primary level schools with 7,884 pupils and 524 teachers. At the secondary level, there were 3,643 pupils and 266 teachers.

The government maintains secondary schools, in which the medium of instruction is English. Samoa College is patterned after a New Zealand secondary school; each year, 100 pupils from government and mission schools are selected for admission by competitive examination. Vaipouli High School, in Savai'i, provides a general secondary curriculum, and Avele College, in Apia, offers training in modern agricultural methods. In addition, the University of the South Pacific School of Agriculture maintains a campus at Alafua, on the outskirts of Apia. The medium of instruction in mission secondary schools is English, with curriculum and textbooks similar to those used in New Zealand.

Enrollment at all higher level institutions was 909 in 1988. The University of Samoa, which was founded in 1988, offers courses in both arts and sciences.

44LIBRARIES AND MUSEUMS

The Nelson Memorial Public Library in Apia has 76,000 volumes. The library of the University of the South Pacific has around 20,000 volumes, and Avele College has a library of around 5,000 volumes. A bookmobile service operates on Upolu and Savai<ayni. The National Museum and Culture Center was established in 1984.

45MEDIA

In 1992 there were 7,500 telephones in use; internal and overseas wireless telegraph services are available. The government-controlled Western Samoan Broadcasting Service, in Apia, transmits radio programs on two stations in Samoan and English and provides direct broadcasts from the Fono. In 1991 there were an estimated 75,000 radios in use. There is no domestic television service, but broadcasts may be received from American Samoa.

There are several bilingual weeklies, including the *Samoa Weekly* (1991 circulation 4,500), *Samoa Observer* (3,500), *Samoa Times* (3,000), and *South Sea Star* (3,000).

46ORGANIZATIONS

Among the numerous clubs, societies, and organizations in Western Samoa are the Chamber of Commerce, Red Cross, Catholic Club, Returned Servicemen's Association, Mothers' Club, Calliope Lodge of Freemasons, Federation of Women's Committees, and the South-East Asia and Pan-Pacific Women's Association.

47TOURISM, TRAVEL, AND RECREATION

Until 1965, official policy in Western Samoa was opposed to tourism, but during 1966–67 there was a complete reversal of policy. The government hired international tourist consultants to advise it on long-term means of developing a tourist industry. Western Samoa joined the Pacific Area Travel Association, extended tax holidays and import-duty concessions to hotel building, and appropriated money for the building of new hotels.

The major tourist attractions are the beaches and traditional villages. In Apia is Vailima, the residence of the head of state and once the home of Robert Louis Stevenson; Stevenson's grave is nearby. Pastimes include swimming, water skiing, and fishing. Soccer and cricket are popular local sports.

48FAMOUS WESTERN SAMOANS

The Scottish author Robert Louis Stevenson (1850–94) lived principally on Upolu from 1889 until his death. Western Samoans famous since independence include Malietoa Tanumafili II (b.1913), who was named head of state in 1962, and Fiame Faumuina Mataafa (d.1975), who served as prime minister from 1962 to 1970 and again from 1973 until his death. Tupuola Taisi Efi (b.1938), was prime minister from 1976 to 1982. Tofilau Eti (b. American Samoa, 1925?) was prime minister from December 1982 to December 1985, when he resigned and was succeeded by Va'ai Kolone.

49DEPENDENCIES

Western Samoa has no territories or colonies.

50BIBLIOGRAPHY

Freeman, Derek. *Margaret Mead and Samoa: The Making and Unmaking of an Anthropological Myth*. Cambridge, Mass.: Harvard University Press, 1983.

Gilson, R. P. *Samoa 1830 to 1900: The Politics of a Multi-Cultural Community*. New York: Oxford University Press, 1970.

Henderson, Faye. *Western Samoa*, a country profile. 2d ed. Washington, D.C.: Library of Congress, 1980.

Lockwood, Brian. *Samoan Village Economy*. New York: Oxford University Press, 1971.

Mead, Margaret. *Coming of Age in Samoa*. London: Penguin, 1961 (orig. 1928).

Turner, George. *Samoa a Hundred Years Ago and Long Before*. London: Macmillan, 1884.

YEMEN

Republic of Yemen
Al-Jumhuriyah al-Yamaniyah

CAPITAL: Sana (Ṣanʿā).

FLAG: The national flag is a tricolor of red, white, and black horizontal stripes, with a green star on the white stripe.

ANTHEM: *Al-Watani (Peace to the Land).*

MONETARY UNIT: The Yemeni riyal (YR) is a paper currency of 100 fils. There are coins of 1, 5, 10, 25, and 50 fils and notes of 1, 5, 10, 20, 50, and 100 riyals. YR1 = $0.1013 (or $1 = YR9.875).

WEIGHTS AND MEASURES: The metric system is being introduced, but local measures remain in common use.

HOLIDAYS: International Women's Day, 8 March; Corrective Movement Day, 13 June; National Day, 14 October. Movable Muslim holidays include Laylat al-Miraj, 'Id al-Fitr, 'Id al-'Adha', Milad an-Nabi, and 1st of Muharram.

TIME: 3 PM = noon GMT.

¹LOCATION, SIZE, AND EXTENT

Yemen is located in the southern part of the Arabian Peninsula. It is slightly larger than twice the size of the state of Wyoming with a total area of 527,970 sq km (203,850 sq mi). Yemen shares boundaries with Saʿudi Arabia on the N, Oman on the E, Gulf of Aden on the S, and the Red Sea on the W, and has a total boundary length of 3,652 km (2,269 mi).

²TOPOGRAPHY

The topography of Yemen features a narrow coastal plain backed by flat-topped hills and rugged mountains. Dissected upland desert plains in the center of the country slope into the desert interior of the Arabian Peninsula. The highest known point is the summit of Jabal Hadhur, rising 3,760 m (12,336 ft) above the Red Sea coast. The western part of the country contains fertile soil in its highland plateaus which rise from about 1,200 to 3,000 m (4,000 to 10,000 ft). Approximately 6 percent of Yemen's land is arable. A system of wadis drain mountain slopes into the desert and into the Gulf of Aden.

³CLIMATE

Extreme humidity combines with high temperatures—as high as 54°C (129°F) in the shade—to produce a stiflingly hot climate. Winds blowing northwest in summer and southwest in winter bring little rain but cause severe sandstorms. During January and February, however, the temperature averages about 20°C (68°F). The climate of the highlands is generally considered the best in Arabia. Summers are temperate and winters are cool, with some frost. Temperatures vary from 22°C (72°F) in June, the hottest month, to 14°C (57°F) in January. Rainfall in the highlands ranges from 41 cm (16 in) at Sana to 81 cm (32 in) in the monsoon area of the extreme southwest. The average year-round temperature at Sana is 18°C (64°F).

⁴FLORA AND FAUNA

Vegetation is sparse along the coast, but in the highlands and wadis, it is plentiful. Acacia, date palm, and many fruit trees are common. Many varieties of grapes are cultivated. Custard apple, euphorbia, and spurge grow in abundance. Alpine roses, balsam, basil, wild elder, and Judas tree are among the flowers and herbs. Wild mammals include the baboon, gazelle, leopard, and mountain hare. Scorpions and millipedes are everywhere, but snakes are less common. Many varieties of birds are found, including the bustard, hawk, vulture, raven, parrot, hornbill, honeysucker, and weaver finch. More than 27,000 varieties of insects and over 600 specimens of flowering plants have been collected in Yemen.

⁵ENVIRONMENT

Yemen's main environmental problems have long been scarcity of water, soil erosion, and desertification. Water pollution is a problem due to contaminates from the oil industry, untreated sewage, and salinization The nation has 0.6 cubic miles of water with 93.4% used for farming activity and 2% for industrial purposes. Damage to the nation's soils can occur due to desertification, erosion, flooding, and salinization. Natural forests in mountainous areas have been destroyed by agricultural clearing and livestock overgrazing. There is no national environmental policy, although the National Environmental Council, established in 1976, has begun to disseminate information on conservation. In response to the nation's environmental needs, the government of Yemen has created laws governing the use of the country's water supply. Law Number 42 (1991) protects water and marine life.

As of 1987, endangered species included the northern bald ibis, the South Arabian leopard, and two species of turtle (green sea and hawksbill).

⁶POPULATION

The population of Yemen was officially estimatd at 11,279,470 in 1990. In 1986 it had been 9,371,462 for the Yemen Arab Republic (YAR, or North Yemen) and 2,076,339 for the People's Democratic Republic of Yemen (PDRY, or South Yemen). The US Census Bureau estimated the 1995 population to be 11,482,366, but the UN estimate was 13,897,00 for the same year. The UN projection for 2000 was 16,424,00, assuming a crude birth rate of 45 per 1,000 population, a crude death rate of 11.7, and a net natural increase of 33.3 during 1995–2000.

Based on the official 1990 population estimate, the population density was 21.2 per sq km (54.9 per sq mi). Most of the population is concentrated in the Tihama foothills and central highlands of the former YAR. Most of southern Yemen is very sparsely populated. About one-third of the population was urban in 1990. Sana, the capital, had about 500,000 people in 1990. Aden, the chief port and former capital of the PDRY, had a population of 417,366 in 1987.

7MIGRATION

There were 1,168,199 citizens of Yemen working abroad in 1986. Most were working in Sa'udi Arabia and other Gulf states. When Yemen took Iraq's side in the war that followed its 1990 annexation of Kuwait, Sa'udi Arabia effectively expelled an estimated 800,000–1,000,000 Yemeni workers by revoking their work privileges. These workers had been sending home some $3 billion a year in remittances.

Many people from the Wadi Hadramawt in southern Yemen have worked abroad in East Africa, India, and Indonesia for centuries. Following independence and the establishment of a leftist regime in the PDRY, more than 300,000 people fled to the north, including about 80,000 Yemenis from the YAR, and virtually all minority groups left the country. Subsequent political upheavals resulted in further emigraiton.

In 1992 more than 60,000 Yemenis returned from the Horn of Africa, chiefly because of turmoil in Somalia. Yemen was harboring 56,200 Somali refugees at the end of 1992.

8ETHNIC GROUPS

Since independence, the population has been almost entirely Arab. Many ethnologists contend that the purest "Arab" stock is to be found in the YAR. Classified as Joktanic Semites, the Yemenis claim descent from Himyar, great-grandson of Joktan, who, according to Genesis, was descended from Shem, the son of Noah. Yemenis were prominent in the early armies of Islam and thus helped to Arabize much of the Middle East. The Tihama has been subjected to occupation and infiltration by many conquerors, and its people show significant admixtures of other racial types, including Negroid peoples. A small minority of Akhdam perform menial tasks throughout the country. The history of the Yemenite Jews predates by centuries the Islamic Hijra (AD 622). How they came to settle in the region has not been determined.

9LANGUAGES

Arabic, the national language, is spoken in a variety of dialects. In vocabulary and other features there is a considerable difference between the classical language used for writing and formal speaking and the spoken dialect used for ordinary discourse. Traces of the ancient South Arabian languages spoken prior to the coming of Muhammad appear in the dialects of the more remote districts of southern Yemen. Mahri, a rare and relatively unstudied language of unknown origins, is spoken in the east. English is widely understood in the former PDRY.

10RELIGIONS

The Republic of Yemen is a Muslim country. Almost all of the inhabitants are Sunnis of the Shafi'i school, one of the four major schools of Islamic law. They reside chiefly in the coastal plains and the southwestern part of the country. Most of those remaining are Shi'is of the Zaydi sect, who live in the highlands. This sect, originating in the 9th century, takes its name from Zayd bin 'Ali (d.740), a descendant of Muhammad, and doctrinally is very close to Sunni Islam. In addition, there is a small minority of Isma'ilis, members of another Shi'i sect. Of the 45,000 Jews who lived in the country in 1949, some 44,000 left for Israel; about 1,100 Jews remained in 1990. In remote areas there is still evidence of shamanism, animism, and other indigenous forms of religion.

11TRANSPORTATION

Through the 1950s, the YAR's transportation system consisted of a few primitive mud tracks connecting the larger towns. Then, in 1961, technicians from China completed a 224-km (139-mi) road between Sana and Al-Hudaydah, the YAR's first asphalt highway. Seven years later, the US finished the 386-km (240-mi) highway linking Sana, Ta'izz, and Al-Mukha; the USSR completed a road from Ta'izz to Al-Hudaydah in 1969. Other paved roads extend from Sana to Ma'rib, from Sana to Sa'idah, from Ta'izz to At-Turba, from the Sana-Ta'izz highway to Al-Bayda, and from Ta'izz to Aden ('Adan) in the PDRY. By 1991, Yemen had about 15,000 km (9,630 mi) of roadway, of which 26% was bituminized. Passenger cars numbered only 165,438 in 1991, and there were 237,957 commercial vehicles.

Improvements to the main port of Al-Hudaydah were expected to expand berthing, storage, and handling facilities and increase cargo capacity to 1,750,000 tons annually. Other ports are Al-Mukha, Aden, and Salif, which have sheltered harbors and deepwater berths capable of taking 10,000-ton ships.

Progress in air transportation has been rapid in recent years. Yemen Airways (Yemenia), the national airline, operates services between Sana, Ta'izz, Al-Hudaydah, and Al-Bayda and also schedules flights to Egypt, Ethiopia, Kuwait, Sa'udi Arabia, and the UAE. The airline carried 99,500 passengers in during six months of operation in 1991. The principal airfield, capable of handling modern jet aircraft, is Ar-Rahba International Airport, north of Sana. There are smaller international airports at Al-Hudaydah, Ta'izz, and Aden.

12HISTORY

In mid-1994, the future of the Republic of Yemen was in doubt. North (the Yemen Arab Republic, or YAR) and South Yemen (the People's Democratic Republic of Yemen, or PDRY) had united in 1990 but, four years later, they fought a bitter civil war and it was not clear the union would survive.

Classical geographers divided Arabia into three regions: Arabia Petraea ("rocky"), Arabia Deserta ("deserted"), and Arabia Felix ("fortunate"). The last, the southwestern corner, included the territory now occupied by Yemen. The region was the site of a series of rich kingdoms that dominated world trade. The wealthy kingdom of Sheba (or Saba), with its capital at Ma'rib, is the best known of the South Arabian kingdoms. The prosperity of this kingdom (10th to 2d centuries BC) was based on the spice and incense trade. Competition from new trade routes undermined Sabaean prosperity and caused the kingdom to decline. From the 2d century BC to the 6th century AD, the Himyarite dynasty, of ethnic stock similar to that of the Sabaeans, ruled in Arabia Felix, and paganism gradually gave way to Christianity and Judaism.

The Himyarite hegemony was ended in 525 by invading Christian Ethiopians, whose rule lasted until 575, when they were driven out by Persian invaders. Islam was accepted in the next century, and Yemen became the battleground of Muslim religious factions. The coastline (Tihama) was held by the Sunnis of the Shafi'i School, while the highlands were controlled by the Zaydis, a Shi'i sect.

In the 9th century, a Zaydi ruler, Yahya al-Hadi ila'l Haqq, founded a line of imams that survived until the second half of the 20th century. Nevertheless, Yemen's medieval history is a tangled chronicle of contesting local imams. The Fatimids of Egypt helped the Isma'ilis maintain dominance in the 11th century. Saladin (Salah ad-Din) annexed Yemen in 1173. The Rasulid dynasty (Kurdish and Turkish in origin) ruled Yemen, with Zabid as its capital, from about 1230 to the 15th century. In 1516, the Mamluks of Egypt annexed Yemen; but in the following year, the Mamluk governor surrendered to the Ottoman Turks, and Turkish armies subsequently overran the country. They were challenged by the Zaydi imam Qasim the Great (r.1597–1620) and

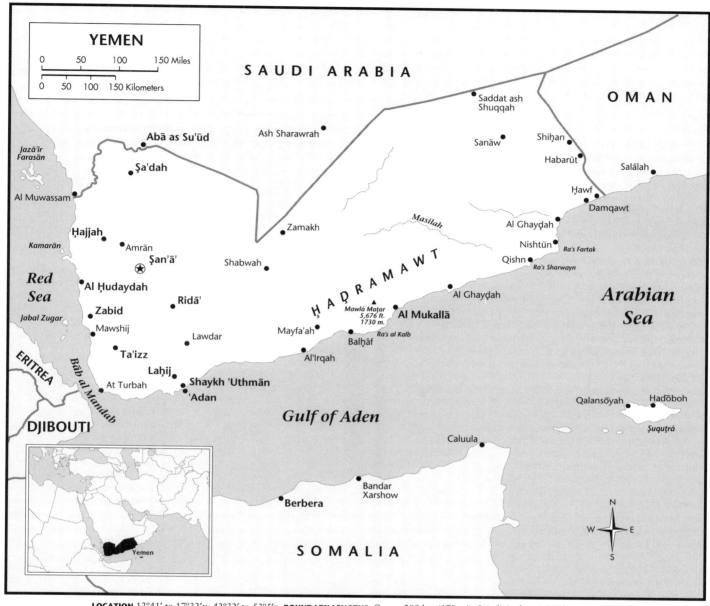

LOCATION 12°41′ to 17°32′N; 42°32′ to 53°5′E. **BOUNDARY LENGTHS:** Oman, 288 km (179 mi); Sa'udi Arabia, 1,458 km (907 mi).

expelled from the interior around 1630. From then until the 19th century, the Ottomans retained control only of the coastal area, while the highlands generally were ruled by the Zaydi imams.

Early in the 19th century, Yemen was overrun by Wahhabis, but in 1818, Ibrahim Pasha, the son of Muhammad 'Ali of Egypt, drove them out of Yemen and reestablished Zaydi control. Egyptian troops occupied the main ports of Yemen until 1840, when they were withdrawn. The Zaydi imams recognized Ottoman suzerainty and paid a large annual subsidy to the Ottoman sultan. After 1840, the situation was anarchic, and law and order in any form was not reestablished until 1872, when the Ottomans again occupied Sana and consolidated their control. The northern mountains remained under the control of Zaydi imams from the Hamid ad-Din family. The Ottomans kept a large force in Yemen during World War I, but under the armistice terms evacuated it in 1918 and Yemen became independent.

In 1834, the British had occupied Aden as a coaling station on the route to India; the importance of the territory was substantially increased with the opening of the Suez Canal in 1869.

To protect its foothold in Aden, the UK had signed a treaties of "protection and advice" with rulers of the tribes and states in the hinterland, leading to the adoption of the names Western Aden Protectorate (WAP) and Eastern Aden Protectorate (EAP). As long as northern Yemen remained at least nominally a part of the Ottoman Empire, relations on the frontier between the UK (in the WAP and EAP) and the Turks (in Yemen) were relatively peaceful.

During World War I, the British supported the Idrisi tribe's attempt to establish itself in Yemen. In 1919, the UK occupied Al-Hudaydah, which came into Idrisi hands when the British withdrew in 1921. The Zaydis, now led by Imam Yahya ibn Muhammad Hamid ad-Din, who had become imam in 1891, waged an armed struggle against the Idrisis that ended when Imam Yahya seized Al-Hudaydah in 1925. The imam also sought to move into the states of the Western Aden Protectorate in an attempt to reestablish his suzerainty in these territories formerly held by the Yemenis. The Idrisis came under the protection of King Ibn Sa'ud, and in 1934, a war broke out between the Sa'udis and Yemenis. By the Treaty of Ta'if (May 1934), Yemen lost 'Asir to Sa'udi Arabia but won British and Sa'udi recognition of its independence. However, incursions by the imams against the UK protectorate in Aden continued until 1962.

In 1959, the UK formed the six WAP states into the Federation of Arab Emirates of the South, with others joining later. The inhabitants of Aden, who were more politically and economically advanced than those of the protectorates, opposed adherence to the federation. Nevertheless, Aden in 1963 was merged into the federation, which then became known as the Federation of South Arabia.

The dispute over the future form and direction of this new political entity, as well as over which other states would join it, resulted in several years of factional violence, as various political parties, labor organizations, and other groups struggled for political ascendancy. Finally, in 1967, the National Liberation Front (NLF) emerged as the strongest political group, and the UK agreed to negotiate with it concerning future independence. On 30 November 1967, all the states of the WAP and EAP were amalgamated, the last British soldiers withdrew, and the NLF declared the independence of the People's Republic of South Yemen. On 22 June 1969, the head of the NLF, Qahtan ash-Sha'bi, was deposed by a group of young leftists of the NLF. The new regime, headed by a five-man council, renamed the country the People's Democratic Republic of Yemen, developed close ties with the USSR, and secured economic aid from it and China. A further political alignment occurred in 1971, when Salim Rubaya 'Ali became head of state and 'Abd al-Fattah Isma'il was named head of the party, in an uneasy rivalry. In 1978, Isma'il, the head of the Yemen Socialist Party (YSP), formerly the NLF, overthrew and executed President 'Ali and assumed the presidency. Isma'il resigned his position in 1980, ostensibly for reasons of health, and went into exile. 'Ali Nasir Muhammad al-Hasani, the prime minister, assumed the presidency.

Meanwhile, Yemen joined the League of Arab States in 1945, and in 1958, it formed a federation, the United Arab States, with the newly established United Arab Republic (UAR). In December 1961, however, the pro forma federal connection with Egypt was severed, and in September 1962, the government of Imam Muhammad al-Badr, only a few days old, was overthrown by revolutionary forces led by Brig. (later Marshal) 'Abdallah as-Sallal. He proclaimed himself president and commander-in-chief of the army and declared the establishment of the Yemen Arab Republic. Badr escaped to the northern regions of the YAR, where he organized a counterrevolutionary force.

A civil war between the royalists (defenders of the imamate) and the republican government broke out, and appeals by both sides for support brought about the active intervention of other Arab states. Sa'udi Arabia supported the royalist cause, and the UAR came to the assistance of the republic, dispatching up to 70,000 troops to the YAR; fighting was particularly bitter during the winter of 1963/64. Eventually the conflict subsided, as the Sa'udis curtailed their aid to the royalists and the Egyptians to the republicans. Sallal was deposed in November 1967 and replaced by a Republican Council. Talks between republican leaders and Sa'udi Arabia in March 1970 at Jiddah concluded with an agreement that ended the civil war and left the republicans in control.

In June 1974, 'Abd ar-Rahman al-Iryani (who had been president since 1967) resigned, thrusting the country into a state of political confusion. By the end of the year, Lt. Col. Ibrahim Muhammad al-Hamdi had emerged as president, heading a government with powers of centralized control that were progressively strengthened. Hamdi was assassinated by unknown assailants in October 1977. His successor, Col. Ahmad ibn Hussein al-Ghashmi, who formed a civilian government and established the Constituent People's Assembly, met a similar fate in June 1978, in a bomb blast in which PDRY involvement was suspected. Lt. Col. 'Ali 'Abdallah Saleh thereupon became president.

In 1982, he inaugurated the General People's Congress as an instrument for popular political mobilization.

On 13 January 1986, PDRY President Muhammad attempted to eliminate his rivals within the YSP. A number of officials were killed, including Isma'il, and Muhammad was forced into exile, along with thousands of his followers. A civil war ensued during the following two weeks, in which about 4,200 died and the supporters of Muhammad were defeated. Haydar Abn Bakr al-'Attas, the prime minister, took over as acting president; Dr. Yasin Sa'id Nu'man was appointed prime minister, and 'Ali Salim al-Bayd was chosen as the new head of the YSP. President al-'Attas was officially elected in November 1986.

Since independence, the PDRY was embroiled in conflicts with all three of its neighbors. A separatist movement was supported in Oman; there were border skirmishes with Sa'udi forces in 1969 and 1973; and the PDRY fought a brief war with the YAR in February–March 1979. The war ended with a truce, mediated by the Arab League, and with an agreement in principle to seek unification of the two Yemens.

In late 1981, a constitution for the two Yemens was drafted. However, implementation was hampered by the continuing insurgency against President Saleh by the leftist National Democratic Front (NDF), which was based in, and reportedly aided by, the PDRY. Saleh was able to defeat the NDF militarily in 1982. Movement toward unification was maintained in repeated declarations and meetings through 1985, but no real progress was achieved. The January 1986 civil war in the PDRY set back relations between the two countries, particularly since 50,000 refugees fled the YAR, but both governments subsequently reaffirmed their commitment to unity.

In 1989, the leaders of the YAR and PDRY approved the 1981 draft constitution and their legislatures ratified it on 21 May 1990. The unified Republic of Yemen was proclaimed the following day. A 30-month transition period was set for unifying the different political and economic systems. The army, police, and civil service were never integrated as planned, however. Meanwhile, the economy was hard hit by the consequences of Yemen's support for Iraq after the Kuwait invasion. It is estimated that Sa'udi Arabia expelled between 800,000 and 1 million Yemeni workers, thus depriving Yemen of some $3 billion in foreign exchange. In addition, the Sa'udis and Gulf states ended $2 billion in foreign aid. Unemployment in Yemen reached 30%.

Free and fair parliamentary elections were held in April 1992 with President Saleh's General People's Congress barely missing a majority victory. A three-party coalition was formed but foundered in late 1993 when Vice President Ali al-Beidh of the Yemen Socialist Party boycotted meetings. Although the quarrel appeared to be patched up with an agreement in February 1994, fighting broke out in May of that year. In a few months, thousands of casualties had been suffered; tribes, clans, and militias were engaged in seeking their own selfish goals and the city of Aden was under siege. Some observers attributed the civil conflict to the recent discovery of massive oil reserves in the south and to Sa'udi Arabia's interest in weakening Yemen by promoting the breakup of the union. The future was bleak, despite efforts of the UN and some Arab states to promote peace.

13GOVERNMENT

The 1970 YAR constitution affirmed Islamic law as the basis of all legislation and established the unicameral Consultative Assembly as the supreme legislative body. The assembly was authorized to name the president and to appoint the ruling Executive Council. In the first national elections, held in 1971, voters selected 119 members of the Consultative Assembly; the 40 remaining members were appointed by the president. This body was dissolved in 1974, and in 1978, it was replaced by the Constituent People's Assembly, with (as of 1987) 99 members elected and 60 members appointed by the president for a two-year term.

In the General People's Congress (GPC), created in 1982, 700 of the 1,000 members were elected, with the other 300 appointed by the government. Between meetings (held every two years), the GPC's affairs were to be handled by a 75-member standing committee. The president, elected by the Constituent People's Assembly for a five-year term, served as secretary-general of the GPC and commander-in-chief of the armed forces and appointed the prime minister and a ministerial council.

The 1970 constitution of the PDRY was ratified by the general command of the United Political Organization–National Front, which later became the Yemen Socialist Party (YSP). The Supreme People's Council, which had 111 members elected by universal suffrage at age 18, enacted laws; elected a Presidium and its chairman, who served as head of state; and chose the prime minister and the Council of Ministers. The YSP apparatus and the organs of government were closely intertwined.

The 1990 unity constitution established a political system based on free, multiparty elections. During the transitional period a presidential council was created with five members, three from the North and two from the South, to oversee executive operations. The council appointed a prime minister who picked a 38-member cabinet. A 301-member parliament was also formed, with 159 members chosen from the North, 111 from the South, and 31 at large. In the May 1990 election, 121 seats were won by the northern General People's Congress, 62 by Islaah (an Islamist and tribalist party), 56 by the southern Yemeni Socialist Party, 47 by independents, and 15 by five other parties.

14POLITICAL PARTIES

The National Liberation Front, which emerged in 1967 as the strongest faction in the disputes before South Yemen's independence, became the United Political Organization–National Front in 1970 and changed its name to the Yemen Social Party (YSP) in 1978, when two smaller leftist parties were merged with it. This Marxist-Leninist organization, the PDRY's lone political party, was the only group to offer candidates in the 1986 legislative elections and survived to represent southern interests in the unified Yemen.

In pre-unification north Yemen, political parties in the Western sense played no role. Tribal allegiances were more important political factors. After unity, the northern leader, General Saleh, formed the General People's Congress which became the country's largest party. The second largest bloc in the parliament is held by the Islaah Party, a fusion of tribal and Islamic interests which opposed the unity constitution because it did not sufficiently adhere to Islamic principles. At least five smaller parties have been active in the politics of unified Yemen.

15LOCAL GOVERNMENT

The YAR was divided into 11 governorates (muhatazat), each headed by a governor. Each governorate contained a varying number of sectors (nawahi). Traditional divisions still extant included the uzlah, a group of villages (qura) of people who belong to the same tribe, headed by a sheikh; and the mahall, a group of houses administratively subordinate to a village. The central government retained ultimate authority over local officials, although certain administrative sanctions were granted to traditional local rulers. In 1982, local people's congresses were established. At elections in 1985, these congresses totaled about 17,500 seats.

In an effort to de-emphasize older loyalties and associations, the PDRY government created a highly centralized state and divided the country into six governorates, all closely controlled by the central authorities. Each had an appointed governor, and each was divided into districts, which were also administered by appointed officials.

The unified government established 17 governorates, subdivided into districts. In the countryside, especially in the north and east, tribal authority is often stronger than formal government institutions.

16JUDICIAL SYSTEM

Under a 1991 decree, the separate judicial systems of the former YAR and the former PDRY have been unified at the Supreme Court level. The separate lower courts systems continue to function in their respective halves of the country. The judiciary, at the lower levels, is susceptible to pressure and influence from the executive branch.

The former YAR judicial system consisted of Shari'a law and courts for criminal and family law areas administered in each district by a hakim and commercial law and courts for business matters. In remote areas, tribal law was applied in tribal courts. The Shari'a courts applied Islamic law and litigants could appeal the decision of a hakim to another hakim, and from him take a final appeal to the Istinaf, the highest court of appeal, in Sana. Both sets of courts were considered generally fair and impartial. Former YAR state security courts were abolished with unification.

The former PDRY court system was organized in three tiers: magistrate or divisional courts, provincial courts, and military courts. Magistrate courts handled most criminal, juvenile, family, housing, agrarian and other minor civil matters. Provincial courts handled more serious criminal cases as well as inheritance cases, major civil claims and appeals form magistrates' courts. Shari'a courts applying Islamic law and tribal courts applying traditional law also existed alongside the modern court system.

17ARMED FORCES

In 1990, the consolidated armed forces numbered 63,500, based on two years obligated service. The army of 60,000 has all 45,000 conscripts. Its 50 brigades have Russian weapons, including 1,300 tanks and 700 artillery pieces and missile launchers. The navy of 1,500 mans 16 patrol and coast combatants and 17 other ships. The air force, with 2,000 members, has 101 combat aircraft. Reserve forces number 40,000 police and militia. There are 300 Russian advisors. Yemen spends $1 billion for defense or 20% of gross domestic product.

18INTERNATIONAL COOPERATION

Yemen joined the Arab League in 1945 and was admitted to UN membership on 30 September 1947; the republican government became Yemen's UN representative in December 1962. Yemen participates in the ESCWA and all the nonregional specialized UN agencies except IAEA. The country is also a member of G-77 and signatory to the Law of the Sea.

Yemen is on good terms with both conservative and radical Arab states. Several thousand PLO fighters from Beirut were accepted in 1982. Military aid and advisers are accepted from both the US and the former USSR. In 1984, the YAR became the fourth Arab state to sign a friendship treaty with the USSR.

19ECONOMY

Traditionally an agricultural country, north Yemen was self-sufficient in food and a net exporter of agricultural product until the Civil War in the 1960s and a prolonged drought in the early 1970s which drastically reduced the output of coffee and cotton. In the late 1970s and early 1980s many farmers switched from labor intensive food crops to the more profitable cultivation of qat, a mild stimulant chewed by many Yemenis. The Yemeni economy depends today on imports of wheat, flour and rice, and other foodstuffs. Food imports in 1987 accounted for 26.5% of total official imports. Trade deficits were offset by remittances from Yemenis working abroad and by foreign aid. Despite recent investments, industrial development is still in its early stages. About half of the industry has been based on food processing. Building materials were the second most productive sector, followed by textiles, leather wear, basketry, jewelry, and glass making. Oil exports started in 1988.

The economy of South Yemen, although planned along "scientific socialist" lines, developed similarly to North Yemen's economy. Most of the country's development was made possible by foreign assistance (especially from the former USSR). Until the commercial discovery of oil in 1987, most economic potential seemed to lie in the fishing industry. Modern industry was very limited, apart from the oil refinery in Aden.

Crude oil is now a significant sector of the economy, with exports accounting for the majority of total exports. Following the unification of the country in 1990, responsibility for development of the oil sector fell to the state-owned general corporation for oil and mineral resources. Yemen has also large reserves of natural gas.

While the unification of the struggling economies of North and South Yemen might have improved long term prospects, it posed the immediate challenge of merging two different economies. When Yemen aligned with Iraq during the Gulf War, Sa'udi Arabia and the Gulf states, Yemen's main aid donors and hosts to large numbers of Yemeni workers and their families, ended the Yemenis' privileged status. The economic impact of lost remittances is estimated at about $1 billion per annum. After the Gulf crisis, Yemen was confronted with high unemployment (perhaps as high as 25–30%), lost remittances, halving of US military aid, a sharp cutback in US AID programs, other canceled foreign assistance, and the cost of food imports and social services for the returnees totaling about $500 million. In addition, the civil conflict in 1994 between the North and South has exacerbated the need for external aid.

20INCOME

In 1990, GDP stood at YR77.2 billion (US$6.5 billion). Preliminary estimates put GDP in 1991 at YR97.1 billion (US$9.8 billion), up 25.9%. The government predicted 14.7% growth in GDP to YR111.4 billion in 1992. However, in 1992, Yemen's GNP was reported to be US$6.7 billion at current prices or US$520 per capita. In 1992 the inflation rate for consumer prices was 100%.

21LABOR

In 1992, Yemen's work force was estimated at 2.8 million. According to 1992 estimates, 64% of the labor force is employed in agriculture and fishing, 25% in services, and 11% in commerce and industry.

Since the united Yemen had not enacted a new labor code as of 1992, the labor codes of the former YAR and PDRY remained in effect for their respective parts of the country. The labor federations of the two countries merged in 1990, creating the Yemeni Confederation of Labor Unions.

There were no legal minimum age or minimum wage requirements in the YAR; in the PDRY, children under 12 were prohibited from working, and a minimum wage provided a minimal standard of living. Throughout Yemen, child labor is common, especially in rural regions. Old YAR legal codes called for a maximum 8-hour workday (6 hours during Ramadan); the PDRY code stipulated a 42-hour workweek. Health and safety standards have been widely ignored in both parts of Yemen.

22AGRICULTURE

The united Yemen, with its wide range of arable climatic zones, has the greatest potential for agricultural development of any nation on the Arabian Peninsula. Agriculture is an important part of the economy (accounting for 22% of GDP in 1991), despite the lack of arable land, scarcity of water, periodic droughts, and difficult terrain. Employment in the agricultural sector accounts for more than 60% of the workforce, but with only 15% of its land area arable, Yemen's potential for agricultural self-sufficiency is very remote. As of July 1993, Yemen imported 70% of its food requirements, including 1.8 million tons of wheat annually.

Traditionally, Yemen was famous for its coffee, shipped from the port of Al-Mukha, from which the English word *mocha* derives. The main cash crop is qat, a mild stimulant chewed by many Yemenis on a daily basis, but not exported significantly. Industrial farming of fruits and vegetables, using modern irrigation techniques, provides a level of production to nearly satisfy domestic demand. As a high-cost producer, Yemen is not yet able to internationally compete in marketing its produce, especially since such exports are often blocked at the borders.

Agriculture output in 1992 (in 1,000 tons) included sorghum, 459; tomatoes, 172; wheat, 152; grapes, 145; bananas, 55; seed cotton, 21; sesame seed, 12; coffee, 8; and cotton, 7.

23ANIMAL HUSBANDRY

Animal husbandry is a key sector of the economy, and the export of hides and skins has long been an important source of foreign exchange. In 1992, the livestock population was estimated at 3,850,000 sheep, 3,470,000 goats, 1,190,000 head of cattle, 690,000 donkeys, and 185,000 camels. The poultry population has quadrupled since the early 1980s; there were approximately 24 million chickens in 1992. Yemen is self-sufficient in poultry production. Producers, however, are decreasing output to one-third of capacity due to import restrictions, high feed costs, and stiff competition from French and Brazilian frozen imports.

24FISHING

Fishermen work along the Arabian Sea, Gulf of Aden, and Red Sea coasts. The annual fish catch in 1991 was about 85,261 tons. Principal species of that catch included Indian and Spanish mackerel, cuttlefish, lobster, and scavengers. Fish-processing plants are located at Al-Hudaydah and Al-Mukalla. Exports of fish and fish products were valued at $13.6 million in 1991. Pearl and coral diving have been practiced for centuries.

25FORESTRY

Forests once covered Yemen, but overgrazing by goats and the systematic cutting of timber for fuel and construction have almost completely eliminated the forest cover, especially in the south. Roundwood production totaled 324,000 cu m in 1991; much lumber is imported.

26MINING

Until the recent discovery of petroleum, the mineral industry had been limited to the production of cement, dimension stone, gypsum, and salt. In 1991, production of cement amounted to 850,000 tons; dimension stone, 410,000 cubic meters; gypsum, 75,000 tons; and salt, 225,000 tons. The government of the new republic is focusing on creating conditions favorable to foreign investment, which could help develop the nation's mineral resources. The government has exclusive domain over the precious stone and hydrocarbon industries; mining legislation guarantees the rights of private property for all other commodities.

27ENERGY AND POWER

A number of companies have held oil concessions, but commercial deposits were not discovered until July 1984, when the US-based Hunt Oil Company struck oil in the eastern governorate of Ma'rib. As of 1993, Yemen had two operating refineries. The Aden facility had a capacity of 104,500 barrels per day and the newer Ma'rib plant had a capacity of 10,000 barrels daily. The Aden facility, which was built in 1954, is scheduled for renovation. In December 1992, Canadian Occidental (which had been operating in North Yemen since 1987) announced the discovery of six new oil fields in the Masillah block, which were expected to increase Yemen's oil production to 320,000 barrels per day. In April 1993, oil production amounted to 200,000 barrels per day. Proven oil reserves as of 1 January 1993 were 4 billion barrels. In 1992, revenues from oil exports totaled $1.2 billion.

Before the onset of civil war in 1994, Yemeni officials sought to expand production of oil by increasing exploration in the Masillah block, improving the infrastructure, and by intensifying the export marketing efforts. In 1993, oil company employees in the Masillah area experienced kidnappings and hijackings, severely limiting any further development.

Total electricity production was 1,750 million kwh in 1991, over 90% of which was produced by public utilities. Net installed capacity in 1991 was 810,000 kw, entirely based on conventional thermal sources.

28INDUSTRY

The governments of both North and South Yemen had invested extensively in manufacturing, but these investments have been money-losers, requiring continued subsidies.

In North Yemen about 50% of the industry has been based on food processing, but this sub-sector has suffered from poor productivity of agriculture—around 80% of the raw materials were imported. Building materials, textiles, leather wear, jewelry, and glass making are other industries. Manufacturing accounted for 6.1% of GDP in 1981 and 11.1% in 1987.

The largest industry in South Yemen was the British Petroleum refinery at Little Aden (capacity 176,000 barrels per day), which was sold to Yemen National Oil Company in May 1977. In 1982 Iran reached an agreement with South Yemen to send crude oil to Aden for processing and further supplies came from Sa'udi Arabia, Libya, Kuwait, Algeria, the UAE, India and the USSR. Local manufactures included clothing, processed food, metal products, soap, and perfumes.

Planning for industrial development using Yemen's oil and natural gas as feedstock is underway. Fertilizer plants, another refinery, and a lubricant plant are projects under consideration. The top priority project, however, is the modernization of the Aden refinery which is expected to cost several hundred million dollars.

29SCIENCE AND TECHNOLOGY

The University of Aden has schools of scientific research, agriculture, engineering, and medicine. Sana University has faculties of science, medicine, engineering, and agriculture.

30DOMESTIC TRADE

At the center of most towns is a market place (sug), the lanes of which are lined with open-front booths where food and implements are displayed and sold. Some goods are bartered. Others sold for cash, usually after bargaining. The production of qat, a mild stimulant which many Yemenis chew, plays an important role in domestic trade. Relying on a highly sufficient internal distribution system, the production of qat would increase per capita GDP an estimated 15–20% were it included in the national income statistics. Customary business hours are from 8AM–1PM and from 4–7PM, Saturday–Thursday. Banks are open from 8AM–12PM(11:30AM on Thursdays).

Some cooperative societies still exist in the south—primarily in the fishing industry, but they are being phased out.

31FOREIGN TRADE

South Yemen, the former People's Democratic Republic of Yemen, imported vastly more than it exported. At least three-quarters of the country's exports can be attributed to the Aden refinery. Other exports in recent years have included foodstuffs,

machinery, and light consumer goods; these have been directed to the UK, North Yemen, East Africa and Japan. South Yemen imported mainly from Japan, Sa'udi Arabia, and other Gulf states. Imports reached nearly US$600 million in 1988 and consisted mostly of food and live animals, machinery and transport equipment, mineral fuels and lubricants, and manufactured goods. Official figures put total export earnings in 1987 at YR24.3 million (US$2.5 million); of this total, 11.8% is accounted for by mineral fuel and lubricants, 4.8% by fish, and 3.8% by honey.

In North Yemen, the former Yemen Arab Republic, foreign trade was controlled by the government. Trade deficits were huge, mainly because of the decline in the export value of coffee, a half in cotton exports, and increased import costs for petroleum, food, and machinery. In 1987, 32% of the import total consisted of foodstuffs, followed by manufactured goods (29%) and machinery and equipment (22%). Food and live animals accounted for over 55% of total non-oil exports, followed by raw materials (22%) and beverages and tobacco (17%). In 1987, a small amount of oil was exported for the first time. In 1988, oil exports helped to narrow the trade deficit to below $900 million compared to above, or close to, the $1 billion level in the mid–1980s. In that year, the trade pattern was changed radically by oil exports. While in 1987 the main destination was Sa'udi Arabia, taking nearly 40% of North Yemen's total exports, West Germany took the lead the following year with over 21% followed by South Korea (20%), the US (19%), Japan (14%), and Italy (10%).

In 1990, over half of the unified Yemen's oil exports went to the US, which is one of Yemen's main suppliers of agricultural commodities. In 1991, oil accounted for over 70% (454.3 million) of Yemen's total export earnings. Other than oil, Yemen exports little. In 1990, fisheries products, the second largest export, earned only $15.6 million, or 2.5% of the total for exports, far behind oil's $515 million.

32BALANCE OF PAYMENTS

No recent information is available.

33BANKING AND SECURITIES

The republican government set up the Yemen Currency Board in 1964 with a capital of YR2 million; in 1971, the Currency Board was replaced by the Central Bank of Yemen. The state-owned Yemen Bank for Reconstruction and Development (YBRD), founded in 1962, finances development activities, and the International Bank of Yemen, organized in 1980, operates as a commercial bank. In the 1970s, the YBRD dominated the banking business, controlling some 70% of the loans outstanding in the YAR; during the same decade, a number of foreign commercial banks, including ones from Hong Kong, Iraq, Pakistan, the US, and the UK, opened offices in Sana. Commercial bank reserves totaled YR4,849 million at the end of 1986, when currency in circulation reached YR18,415 million. There is no stock exchange.

34INSURANCE

There are three insurance firms in the Yemen. Much of the Yemen's insurance business is transacted abroad.

35PUBLIC FINANCE

Since unification, Yemen has run a budget deficit equivalent to 15–20% of GDP, financed primarily by bank credit. The 1992 budget, however, restricted current expenditures, especially for defense. Yemen's decision to back Iraq in the Gulf War caused it to lose some $2 billion in development aid. The recent civil conflict between the north and south has also exacerbated the need for external assistance and debt restructuring.

The following table shows actual revenues and expenditures for 1990 and 1991 in millions of riyals:

	1990	1991
REVENUE AND GRANTS		
Tax revenue	13,733	20,077
Non-tax revenue	10,173	17,672
Capital revenue	35	233
Grants	1,397	300
TOTAL	25,338	38,282
EXPENDITURES & LENDING MINUS REPAYMENTS		
General public service	4,913	4,644
Defense	10,382	13,227
Public order and safety	3,248	4,110
Education	6,120	8,461
Health	1,439	1,954
Housing and community amenities	427	1,116
Recreation, cultural, and religious affairs	730	1,242
Economic affairs and services	3,643	2,579
Other expenditures	2,957	4,279
Adjustments	2,957	4,279
Lending minus repayments	1,312	1,335
TOTAL	40,929	45,387
DEFICIT/SURPLUS	–11,167	–7,120

At the beginning of 1990, Yemen's external debt stood at US$5.75 billion.

36TAXATION

Personal income taxes are levied on wage workers and the self-employed. Taxes on business profits are graduated. Zakat (the religious charity tax) is state enforced. Taxes were increased substantially in the 1970s, with taxes on imports providing about 70% of total tax revenues. There are excise duties, road and vehicle taxes, port fees, a tax on rents, and telegraph fees. The state also derives income from the confiscated property of the imamate. The chronic budget deficits of the 1980s forced the government to place considerably more emphasis on the traditionally lax collection of taxes.

37CUSTOMS AND DUTIES

Import duties are generally levied at rates varying from 5% on essential goods to 50% on luxury items; medical and agricultural items are duty free, while tobacco is dutiable at 145%. Surcharges are added to these basic rates to cover defense expenditures, to finance schools and orphanages, and to assist the poor. Export duties are levied on a variety of products.

38FOREIGN INVESTMENT

Foreign investment is encouraged by the Yemeni government as is prospecting for more oil. Parliament has enacted a new investment law, but it has not yet been implemented. The law seeks to encourage joint ventures and especially to attract investments by expatriate Yemenis. Another new law authorizes free trade zones, the first planned for Aden. Oil companies, eager for a stake in one of the least explored tracts on the Arabian Peninsula, signed exploration and production agreements bringing signature bonuses and payments to the government of $436 million in 1991.

39ECONOMIC DEVELOPMENT

Hampered by the civil war and by a lack of statistical information that crippled economic planning, North Yemen (YAR) in the 1960s could do little more than establish the bare rudiments of a modern economy in the form of a national budget, paper currency, and administrative machinery. In 1973, the newly established Central Planning Organization, aided by the IBRD, issued the country's first three-year development plan (1973–76) to improve the economic infrastructure. The first five-year plan

(1976–81) continued modernization and achieved a GDP growth rate of 5.9% annually. Under the second five-year plan (1982–86), the target GDP growth rate was 7%, and investment was estimated at $6.5 billion. Of total allocations, transportation and communications accounted for 16%, government services 16%, agriculture 15%, housing 13%, manufacturing 12%, and other sectors 28%. About half the total investment was expected to come from foreign sources. However, economic development was severely set back by a 1982 earthquake. Also, severe decreases in assistance from the Gulf states, beginning in 1983, forced reductions in the plan's projections. The third five-year plan (1986–90) aimed to boost self-sufficiency in food, a major component of imports. The lack of government resources has spurred establishment of a number of local development cooperatives, to carry out local projects with minimal government assistance.

During 1946–67, North Yemen received $42.8 million in grants from the US, but during the Arab-Israeli war in 1967, it announced that it would no longer accept US aid. US aid resumed in the 1970s, and the US provided military assistance during the 1979 war with South Yemen. Between 1962 and 1982, North Yemen borrowed an estimated $2,325 million. Of this amount, the USSR lent some $819 million and Arab states $744 million. Only $110 million had been repaid by 1983. Since 1971, Sa'udi Arabia has been the single largest contributor (with $250 million of aid in 1978 but only $100 million in the late 1980s), followed by Kuwait, China, and Germany. Assistance from multilateral agencies totaled $541.1 million from 1946 through 1986, of which $463.9 million was supplied through the IDA. In 1983, Sa'udi Arabia, the Netherlands, the IMF, and other countries and agencies supplied emergency earthquake relief. Overall, total foreign debt at the end of 1987 stood at $2.4 billion. In 1987, China committed itself to a $42 million interest-free loan to finance the construction of a 127 km road between Jihang and Sirwa. Abu Dhabi has granted $22.4 million for the Marib Dam scheme. The Netherlands pledged $32.4 million in 1988 and France agreed to a $25 million loan. Substantial aid from the Arab regional development has also continued. In 1986, North Yemen obtained a $200 million euroloan.

In 1971, South Yemen inaugurated a series of development plans designed to satisfy the basic needs of the people, strengthen the economic infrastructure, and develop productive capacity. A three-year plan (1971–74) concentrated on developing the transportation system and extending the irrigated land area; the total expenditure was YD25.1 million. The first five-year plan (1974–78), which was extended through 1980 to complete projects in progress, spent a total of YD195 million and emphasized capital-intensive projects. The second five-year plan (1981–85) aimed to increase real GDP by 11% annually; it allocated expenditures of YD508 million, of which socioeconomic services accounted for 31%, industry for 29%, transportation and communications 23%, and agriculture and fisheries 17%. The third five-year plan (1986–91) was delayed by the 1986 civil war, and a $1.7 billion plan was approved in April 1987, emphasizing fisheries and agriculture. Most of the funding for development in the 1980s was provided by foreign grants and aid from Kuwait, Algeria, Libya, Sa'udi Arabia, the United Arab Emirates, the Soviet bloc, the World Bank, and the OPEC Fund for International Development. The civil war in 1986 caused a significant drop in aid disbursement.

Despite the important contributions made by expatriate workers' remittances, South Yemen ran an account deficit. The import restrictions of 1986 helped cut the deficit that year by about $176 million, with a further fall to $130 million in 1987. In 1988, however, this trend was reversed as growth in imports of goods and services, combined with an 18% drop in remittances, led to a record deficit of $383 million

At unification, the new government assumed all debts incurred by former governments. Yemen's external debt is now estimated at between $5–7 billion, roughly equal to the combined GDP. Between 40% and 60% of the debt originated in South Yemen. Over half is owed to Eastern European countries and the former USSR. The government suspended service on its debt to the former Soviet Union. Although current on its US obligations, Yemen is in arrears to other Western countries. The 1992 scheduled debt service ratio was estimated at about 29%, but since Yemen did not service half of its debt to the former Socialist Eastern European countries, the actual debt service ratio is much lower.

A major objective of the new government is to diversify the economy and create new jobs. The establishment of a free trade zone t the port of Aden, estimated to cost $5.6 billion over a period of 25 years, is central to Yemen's industrial planning. Considerable resources are also being spent on enhancing the agricultural sector in order to increase food production for a fast rising population. In this regard, the World Food Program approved the allocation of $13.4 million in food aid in 1992 to support the development of rural areas. The World Bank also approved a loan of $33 million to help finance agricultural development and improve water resources management.

40SOCIAL DEVELOPMENT

Families and tribes care for their sick, handicapped, unemployed, and widows and orphans. Those without family or tribal ties beg or have recourse to Islamic pious foundations (waqfs). The state operates orphanages and finances other welfare measures. Effective in 1988 a provident fund system provides old age, disability, survivor, and workers' compensation benefits. A health insurance program was scheduled to go into effect in 1992. While the government has expanded its role in providing assistance, traditional means still predominate. The fertility rate in 1985 was estimated at 7.7. The Yemen Family Planning Association provides contraceptives and advisory services through local clinics and health centers. Abortion is permitted if the woman's life is at stake. Until recently, the relatively progressive family law of the south was still applied in Aden. In 1993, however, a presidential decree mandated implementation of more restrictive measures. Payment of large dowries is widespread. Conservative estimates place the illiteracy rate for women at 80%, compared with 40–50% for men.

41HEALTH

Conservative North Yemen and socialist South Yemen merged in May 1990. As of 20 May 1994, the South declared its independence again and became the Democratic Republic of Yemen; however, it was not recognized internationally. Fighting ensued and, as of 6 July 1994, the southern city of Aden was increasingly short of water, food, and medical supplies. Relief officials feared that the city was on the verge of catastrophic health problems. On 7 July 1994, the North took over the city of Aden and the war was apparently over.

Malnutrition and the diseases associated with it are major health problems. Malaria, typhus, tuberculosis, dysentery, whooping cough, measles, hepatitis, schistosomiasis, and typhoid fever are also widespread, and sewage disposal of the most rudimentary type constitutes a general health hazard. In 1990, there were 96 cases of tuberculosis per 100,000 reported. In 1991, only 36% of the population had access to safe water, while 65% had adequate sanitation. In 1992, children up to one year old were immunized against tuberculosis (77%); diphtheria, pertussis, and tetanus (62%); polio (62%); and measles (64%).

Life expectancy in 1992 was estimated at 52 years; the infant mortality rate in 1992 was 107 per 1,000 live births. General mortality was 13.7 per 1,000 people in 1993.

Since the 1970s, many new hospitals and dispensaries have been established. In 1990, there were 0.9 hospital beds per 1,000 people. Medical personnel that year included 2,640 doctors, 120 dentists, and 6,480 nurses. In 1992, there were 18 doctors per 100,000 people, with a nurse to doctor ratio of 2.9.

The 1993 birth rate was 48.3 per 1,000 people, and about 7% of married women (ages 15 to 49) use contraception. There were 611,000 births in 1992.

Only about 38% of the population had access to health care services as of 1992; in 1990, total health care expenditures totaled $217 million.

42HOUSING

Housing is inadequate; about one-fourth of urban housing units are huts, tents, or other makeshift structures. In the hot coastal region, most dwellings, except those of the ruling classes, are straw huts. In the highlands, the poorer people live in huts of stone or baked brick. Wealthier Yemenis live in large houses whose style is unique to southwestern Arabia: the lower part is generally built of sandstone, basalt, or granite, while the upper part, which may rise from two to eight stories, is usually of baked brick with windows outlined in decorative designs. Often a loggia topped with brass and open on all sides rises from the roof.

43EDUCATION

Early Yemeni education, with regard to medieval disciplines of law, religion, history and poetry, was sophisticated and, for a country of its type, remarkably widespread. Its people contributed nobly to medieval Islamic civilization. The Al-Azhar University of Cairo was well known for its education during the 10th and 11th centuries and it attracted students from nearby countries such as Ethiopia, Arabia, and Somalia. However, in the 19th and 20th centuries, there was slow progress in the field of education.

Prior to the 1962 revolution, no proper educational system was in place. Civil war and internal political upheaval only worsened the situation. Also, highly skilled and educated Yemenis are scarce.

In the unified Republic of Yemen, the literacy rate was estimated to be over 40% (In 1990, the literacy rate for the People's Democratic Republic of Yemen was 39.1%; males, 52.8% and females, 26.1%. The rate for the Yemen Arab Republic was 38.5%; males, 53.3% and females, 26.3%).

The country has over 5,000 schools including over 100 secondary schools. In 1990, the PDRY had 13,240 primary level teachers and 379,905 pupils. The YAR had 35,350 teachers and 1,291,372 pupils the same year. At the secondary level in 1990, PDRY had 34,179 pupils in general secondary schools; 6,351 in vocational schools; and 2,752 enrolled in teacher training schools. YAR had 394,578 pupils in general secondary schools; 5,068 were in vocational schools; and 21,051 in teacher training and the same year.

There are two universities: Sana University (founded in 1970) and the University of Aden (established in 1975). Total university enrollment now exceeds 27,800. In addition, over 2,000 Yemenis are being educated at foreign universities.

44LIBRARIES AND MUSEUMS

Both the National and Miswal libraries are located in Aden. Each has a collection of 30,000 volumes. The Miswal Library also maintains another 9,000 volumes as a traveling library to serve citizens. The Library of the Great Mosque of Sana maintains a collection of 10,000 manuscripts.

The two National Museums are located in Midan at Tahrir and in Sana (which has just recently been opened to the public). There is also a Military Museum with exhibits dealing primarily with the Civil War and the current Yemeni army.

45 MEDIA

Since unification, efforts have been underway to upgrade the country's telecommunications infrastructure. Two-way radio links Yemen directly with Cairo, Rome, and the PDRY. Telephone and telegraph facilities are available in major cities, and a modern dial telephone system has been installed in Sana, Ta'izz, and Al-Hudaydah. There were about 65,000 telephones in 1991. The government operates several radio stations and two television networks, one of them partly commercial. There were about 325,000 radios and 330,000 television sets in 1991. In the same year there were four daily newspapers: *Al-Thawrah,*(circulation 40,000) published in Sana; *Al-Jumhuriyah,*(30,000) in Ta'izz; and *Al-Shararah* (6,000) and *Ar-Rabi Ashar Min Uktubar* (20,000), both published in Aden.

46 ORGANIZATIONS

The government has encouraged the formation of cooperatives, but private associations with political overtones are suspect. There are chambers of commerce in the major cities.

47 TOURISM, TRAVEL, AND RECREATION

Tourism is expected to grow as a reunified Yemen undergoes modernization but seeks to retain its cultural heritage. Tourists can visit historic and religious sites (such as the Ghumdau Palace and the Great Mosque in Sana) and exotic markets, and enjoy scenic areas including the Red Sea coast. Passports and visas are required by foreign visitors. Vaccination against yellow fever and cholera is recommended. In 1991, there were 43,656 tourist arrivals in hotels and other establishments, 49% from Europe and 24% from the Middle East. There were 4,040 hotel rooms with 8,523 beds, and tourism receipts totaled US$21 million.

48 FAMOUS YEMENIS

Imam Yahya ibn Muhammad Hamid ad-Din (1869?–1948) ruled during the period when Yemen established its independence; he was assassinated during an uprising. 'Ali 'Abdallah Salih (b.1942) became president of the YAR in 1978, ending a period of upheaval in which his two immediate predecessors were assassinated. 'Ali Nasir Muhammad al-Hasani (b.1940?) was prime minister of the PDYR in 1980 and president from 1980 to 1986. Haydar Abu Bakr al-'Attas (b.1939) was prime minister of the PDYR during 1985–86.

49 DEPENDENCIES

Yemen has no territories or colonies.

50 BIBLIOGRAPHY

American University. *The Yemens: Country Studies.* Washington, D.C.: Government Printing Office, 1986.

Bidwell, Robin. *The Two Yemens.* Boulder, Colo.: Westview, 1983.

Crouch, Michael. *An Element of Luck: To South Arabia and Beyond.* New York: Radcliffe Press, 1993.

Dresch, Paul. *Tribes, Government, and History in Yemen.* New York: Oxford University Press, 1989.

Halliday, Fred. *Revolution and Foreign Policy: The Case of South Yemen, 1967–1987.* New York: Cambridge University Press, 1990.

Ismael, Tareq Y. and Jacqueline S. Ismael. *The People's Democratic Republic of Yemen: Politics, Economics and Society.* Boulder, Colo.: Lynne Rienner, 1986.

Lackner, Helen. *P.D.R. Yemen: Outpost of Socialist Development in Arabia.* London: Ithaca Press, 1985.

Madaj, Abd al-Muhsin Madaj M. *The Yemen in Early Islam.* Atlantic Highlands, NJ: Ithaca Press, 1988.

Page, Stephen. *The Soviet Union and the Yemens: Influence in Asymmetrical Relationships.* New York: Praeger, 1985.

Pridham, B. R. (ed.). *Contemporary Yemen: Politics and Historical Background.* London: Croom Helm, 1984.

———. (ed.) *Economy, Society and Culture in Contemporary Yemen.* London: Croom Helm, 1985.

Stookey, Robert W. *South Yemen: A Marxist Republic in Arabia.* Boulder, Colo.: Westview, 1982.

Wenner, Manfred W. *The Yemen Arab Republic: Development and Change in an Ancient Land.* Boulder, Colo.: Westview Press, 1991.

INDEX TO COUNTRIES AND TERRITORIES

This alphabetical list includes countries and dependencies (colonies, protectorates, and other territories) described in the encyclopedia. Countries and territories described in their own articles are followed by the continental volume (printed in *italics*) in which each appears, along with the volume number and first page of the article. For example, Argentina, which begins on page 7 of *Americas* (Volume 3), is listed this way: Argentina—*Americas* 3:7. Dependencies are listed here with the title of the volume in which they are treated, followed by the name of the article in which they are dealt with. In a few cases, an alternative name for the same place is given in parentheses at the end of the entry. The name of the volume *Asia and Oceania* is abbreviated in this list to *Asia*.

ISBN 0-8103-9882-6

EAST & SOUTH ASIA

0   250   500   750   1,000 Miles

0   250 500 750 1000 Kilometers

MIDDLE EAST

0   250   500 Miles

0   250   500 Kilometers